Thrash Metal

Garry Sharpe–Young

Zonda Books Limited, New Plymouth

Thrash Metal
By Garry Sharpe-Young

ISBN 978-0-9582684-3-1

Copyright © Garry Sharpe-Young, 2007.

First published in 2007 by Zonda Books Limited, New Plymouth, New Zealand.

Find us on the World Wide Web at www.zondabooks.com

First Edition, October 2007.

All rights reserved. No part of this publication may be reproduced, stored in a retrieval system, or transmitted in any form or by any means, electronic, mechanical, photocopying, recording or otherwise, without the prior permission of the copyright owner.

While every precaution has been taken in the preparation of this book, the publisher and author assumes no responsibility for errors or omissions, or for damages resulting from the use of the information contained herein.

National Library of New Zealand Cataloguing-in-Publication Data

Sharpe-Young, Garry.
Thrash metal / Garry Sharpe-Young. 1st ed.
Updated version of: Rockdetector : A to Z of thrash metal.
London : Cherry Red, 2002.
ISBN 978-0-9582684-3-1
1. Extreme metal (Music) 2. Rock groups.
I. Sharpe-Young, Garry. Rockdetector. II. Title.
781.66—dc 22

Contents

2 TON PREDATOR 1	ANCESTOR 21
21 LUCIFERS 1	ANCHOR 22
32ND CHAMBER 1	ANESTHESY 22
5 BE HATED 1	ANGEL DUST 22
8 FOOT SATIVA 2	ANGEL WITCH 23
A COLD REALITY 2	ANGELUS APATRIDA 24
A LIFE ONCE LOST 2	ANGER 25
A.N.I.M.A.L. 3	ANGKOR WAT 25
A.R.G. 4	ANGOR 25
AARDVARKS 4	ANIHILATED 25
ABANDONED 4	ANIMAL ALPHA 26
ABATTOIR 5	ANNIHILATOR 26
ABHORRENT 5	ANNIHILATUS 29
ABOMINATION 5	ANONYMUS 29
ABSURDUS 6	ANTHRAX 30
ACCELERATOR 6	ANTIDOTE 35
ACCU§ER 6	ANVIL 36
ACERO 7	ANVIL CHORUS 37
ACID 7	ANYONE 38
ACID DRINKERS 7	APOCALYPTICA 38
ACID REIGN 8	APOCRYPHA 39
ACID STORM 8	APOKALYPTIC RAIDS 40
ACRIDITY 9	APOSTASY 40
ACROPHET 9	AQUAMORTA 41
ACT OF FATE 9	ARA'KUS 41
ADDICTIVE 9	ARAKAIN 41
ADRENALIN O.D. 9	ARBITRATER 42
ADVERSITY 10	ARBITRATOR 42
ADX 10	ARCADIA 42
AECRON 10	ARCH ENEMY 42
AETURNUS DOMINION 10	ARISE 45
AEVUM 10	ARMAGEDDON 45
AFTER ALL 11	ARMAGEDOM 46
AFTER FOREVER 11	ARMED FORCE 46
AFTERDEATH 11	ARMED FORCES 46
AFTERMATH 12	ARMORED SAINT 46
AFTERMATH 12	ARMOURED ANGEL 49
AGENT STEEL 12	ARROW 49
AGGRESSION 14	ARS MORIENDI 49
AGGRESSION CORE 14	ARTILLERY 50
AGGRESSIVE 14	AS IT BURNS 50
AGGRESSOR 15	AS SAHAR 51
AGNOSTIC FRONT 15	ASMODEUS 51
AGONY 16	ASSALANT 51
AGRESSOR 16	ASSASSIN 52
AGRO 17	AT WAR 52
AIRDASH 17	ATHANATOR 52
ALASTOR 18	ATHEIST 53
ALISTER 18	ATOMICA 54
ALLFATHER 18	ATOMIZER 54
ALLIGATOR 18	ATOMKRAFT 54
ALTAIR 19	ATROPHY 55
ALTERED AEON 19	ATTOMICA 56
AMEBIX 19	AUDIOPAIN 56
AMNESIA 19	AURA 57
AMOK 20	AURA NOIR 57
AMULANCE 20	AUTOPSIA 57
ANACRUSIS 20	AVENGER OF BLOOD 58
ANARION 21	AVENGING ANGELS 58
ANATA 21	AZOTIC REIGN 58

BABYLON WHORES	59
BAL SAGOTH	59
BATHORY	60
BATTALION	62
BATTLEFIELD	62
BEAST PETRIFY	63
BEDIMMED	63
BELIEVER	63
BELLADONNA	63
BENEATH	64
BENEDICTION	64
BESTIAL DESECRATION	66
BETRAYAL	66
BETRAYER	66
BEYOND THE EMBRACE	66
BIOHAZARD	67
BIOMECHANICAL	69
BITTERNESS	69
BK 49	70
BLACKEND	70
BLACKSTAR	70
BLAKK MARKET	70
BLASTER	70
BLESSED DEATH	71
BLIND FURY	71
BLIND ILLUSION	71
BLIND JUSTICE	71
BLINDED COLONY	71
BLITZKRIEG	72
BLIZZARD	73
BLO.TORCH	73
BLOOD FEAST	74
BLOOD MONEY	74
BLOOD RED ANGEL	75
BLOOD TSUNAMI	75
BLOODCUM	75
BLOODWRITTEN	75
BLUDGEON	75
BOLT THROWER	76
BOMBSTRIKE	78
BOMBTHREAT	78
BRAIN IMPLOSION	78
BRAINDAMAGE	78
BRAN BARR	79
BREATHSTEALER	79
BREJN DEDD	79
BRICK BATH	79
BRIDE	79
BROKEN DAGGER	80
BULLDOZER	80
BURIED GOD	81
BY NIGHT	81
ČACHTICE	82
CACOPHONY	82
CADAVERES DE TORTUGAS	82
CALHOUN CONQUER	82
CANCER	82
CANTARA	83
CAPELLAN	84
CAPRICORN	84
CAPTOR	84
CARNAL FORGE	84
CARNIVORE	85
CARRION CARNAGE	86
CASBAH	86
CATALEPSY	86
CELLADOR	87
CELTIC FROST	87
CENTINEX	89
CEREBRAL FIX	91
CESSATION OF LIFE	92
CESSATION OF LIFE	92
CHAIN OF HATE	92
CHAINSAW	93
CHAKAL	93
CHANNEL ZERO	93
CHAOSYS	94
CHECKER PATROL	94
CHILDREN OF BODOM	94
CHRIS POLAND	96
CIRITH UNGOL	97
CLAUSTROPHOBIA	97
CLUSTER BOMB UNIT	98
COCKROACH	98
CODEON	98
COMMANDER	99
CONCRETE SOX	99
CONSPIRACY	99
CONVICTION	99
CORAM LETHE	100
CORONER	100
CORPORAL PUNISHMENT	101
CORPORATION 187	101
CORPSECANDLE	101
CORROSION OF CONFORMITY	101
CORRUPT	103
CORRUPTED	103
COURAGEOUS	103
COURAGOUS	103
COVEN	104
CREATION OF DEATH	104
CREATURE	104
CRO-MAGS	105
CRONOS	105
CROSSFIRE	106
CROSSFIRE	106
CRUCIFIER	106
CRUMBSUCKERS	107
CRUSTACEAN	107
CRYOGENIC	108
CRYPTIC SLAUGHTER	108
CRYSTAL LAKE	109
CULPRIT	109
CYCLES	109
CYCLONE	109
CYCLONE TEMPLE	110
CYNIC	110
CYST	110
D.A.M.	110
D.R.I.	111
DARCANE	112
DARK ANGEL	112
DARKANE	113
DAVE LOMBARDO	114
DE LIRIUM'S ORDER	115
DEAD HEAD	115
DEAD SAMARITAN	115
DEAD TO FALL	116
DEAD TO THIS WORLD	116
DEAD TROOPER	116
DEADSOIL	117
DEAFENING SILENCE	117
DEARLY BEHEADED	117
DEATH ANGEL	118
DEATH SS	119
DEATHCHAIN	120
DEATHGUY	120
DEATHRASH	121

Entry	Page
DEATHROW	121
DEATHWISH	121
DECADENCE	121
DECAY LUST	122
DECEASED	122
DECEIVER	123
DEFENDER KFS	123
DEFIANCE	124
DEFLESHED	124
DEFORME	125
DEHUMANIZED	125
DEKAPITATOR	125
DELIRIOUS	126
DELIRIUM TREMENS	126
DELIVERANCE	126
DELLAMORTE	127
DEMIRICOUS	128
DEMISE	128
DEMOLITION	128
DEMONIZER	128
DEMONSPEED	129
DENATA	129
DENIAL FIEND	129
DEPRESSIVE AGE	129
DESCAMISADOS	130
DESECRATED DREAMS	130
DESERT STORM	130
DESEXULT	130
DESPAIR	130
DESTINITY	131
DESTINY'S END	131
DESTROYERS	132
DESTRUCTION	132
DETENTE	134
DETONATION	135
DETRITUS	135
DEUCE	135
DEVASTATION	136
DEVIATE	136
DEVILISH	136
DEVOURED	136
DEW-SCENTED	136
DIE KREUZEN	138
DIECELL	138
DIOS HASTIO	138
DISCIPLES OF AGGRESSION	139
DISCIPLES OF POWER	139
DISINCARNATE	139
DIVINE SIN	140
DIZORDERZ	140
DOFKA	140
DOG FACED GODS	140
DOMAIN	141
DOMINATION BLACK	141
DOOM	141
DORSAL ATLANTICA	142
DOWNWARD SPIRAL	142
DRAGONFORCE	142
DREAM DEATH	144
DREAM DEVOID	144
DREAMS OF DAMNATION	144
DRUNKEN STATE	144
DRY ROT	145
DYOXEN	145
EDENBEAST	145
EKTOMORF	145
ELEKTRASH	146
ELVARON	146
ENCRYPTION	146
ENDERS GAME	146
ENDLESS TORMENT	146
ENEMYNSIDE	147
ENERTIA	147
ENGLISH DOGS	147
ENTERA	148
EROSION	148
ESCABIOS	148
ETERNAL AUTUMN	148
ETERNAL DIRGE	149
EULOGY	149
EUTHANAUSEA	149
EVIL DEAD	150
EVILDOER	150
EVILE	150
EXCEL	150
EXCESSUM	151
EXCITER	151
EXECUTIONER	152
EXHORDER	153
EXOCET	153
EXODUS	153
EXTERMINATOR	156
EXTREMA	156
EXUMER	156
F.K.Ü.	157
F.T.G.	157
FACE DOWN	157
FAITH OR FEAR	158
FATAL EMBRACE	158
FEAR OF GOD	158
FIERCE CONVICTION	159
FIGHT	159
FLAGELADÖR	160
FLASHOVER	160
FLEGMA	161
FLESH MADE SIN	161
FLOTSAM AND JETSAM	161
FORBIDDEN	163
FORCED ENTRY	164
FORCEFIELD	164
FORM	164
FORTE	164
FRANKENBOK	165
FREEDOM CALL	165
FROZEN SUN	166
FUELBLOODED	166
FURIOUS TRAUMA	166
FURY	167
FUTURE TENSE	167
G.O.R.E.	167
GAMMACIDE	168
GANG GREEN	168
GARGANTUA SOUL	169
GEHENNAH	169
GENETIC WISDOM	169
GENOCIDE	170
GLACIAL FEAR	170
GLADIATOR	170
GOATSODOMIZER	171
GOD FORBID	171
GODSEND	172
GOOSEFLESH	172
GRAVE DIGGER	172
GRIFFIN	175
GRIM FORCE	175
GRINDER	175
GRINDNECKS	176
GRIP INC.	176

Entry	Page
GROPE	176
GUARDIANS OF STEEL	177
GUILLOTINE	177
GURD	177
GWAR	178
HADES	180
HALLOWS EVE	181
HAMMER	181
HANGÖVER	181
HARTER ATTACK	182
HATE SQUAD	182
HATEFRAME	182
HATESPHERE	182
HATEWORK	183
HAVE MERCY	184
HAVOC MASS	184
HAVOCHATE	184
HAWAII	184
HAZARD	185
HAZY AZURE	185
HEADHUNTER	185
HEATHEN	185
HEAVEN SHALL BURN	186
HELLFIRE B.C.	187
HELLHAMMER	187
HELLION	188
HELLOWEEN	189
HELLRAISER	193
HELLRAPER	193
HELLSTORM	193
HELLWITCH	193
HELSTAR	194
HEMATOMA	195
HERESY	195
HERETIC	195
HEVEIN	195
HEXENHAUS	196
HEXX	196
HIMSA	197
HIRAX	197
HITTMAN	198
HOBBS' ANGEL OF DEATH	199
HOLOCHAUST	199
HOLOSADE	199
HOLY MOSES	200
HOLY TERROR	201
HOMICIDE HAGRIDDEN	202
HORFIXION	202
HORRORSCOPE	202
HOSTIL	202
HURTLOCKER	203
HYDRA VEIN	203
HYPNOSIA	203
HYSTE´RIAH G.B.C.	204
ICE AGE	204
IGNORANCE	204
IKINAE	204
IMAGIKA	204
IMPERIAL	205
IMPULSE MANSLAUGHTER	205
IN AETERNUM	206
IN VAIN	206
INCARNATE	207
INCRIMINATED	207
INCUBUS	207
INDESTROY	208
INDUNGEON	208
INEARTHED	208
INFECTION CODE	209
INFERNAL	209
INFERNAL MAJESTY	209
INGER INDOLIA	210
INHIBITION	210
INNER THRESHOLD	210
INRAGE	211
INSANITY	211
INSENSE	211
INTERZONE	211
INTO THE DEMENTIA	212
INTRINSIC	212
INVOCATOR	212
IRON ANGEL	213
IRREVERENCE	213
ISOLATED FIELDS	213
IZEGRIM	213
JERSEY DOGS	214
JESUS CHRYSLER SUPERSKUNK	214
JOE STUMP'S REIGN OF TERROR	214
JUMALATION	214
JUST ONE FIX	214
KAOTEON	215
KARKADAN	215
KAT	215
KATAFALK	216
KAYSER	216
KAZJUROL	216
KILL FOR SATAN	216
KILLER	217
KINETIC	217
KISS OF DEATH	217
KORROSIA METALLA	218
KORZUS	218
KREATOR	218
KREMATE	221
KRISIUN	221
KRYPTOR	222
KRYZALID	222
KRÄMATORIUM	222
KUBLAI KHAN	222
LAMENT	223
LAST RITES	223
LATVALA BROS	223
LAWNMOWER DETH	223
LEAD WEIGHT	224
LEGACY	224
LEGEN BELTZA	224
LEPROSY	225
LESS THAN HUMAN	225
LETHAL AGGRESSION	225
LEVIATHAN	226
LIGHT THIS CITY	226
LIVING DEATH	226
LORDES WERRE	227
LORDS OF DARKNESS	227
LOS SIN NOMBRE	227
LOST CENTURY	227
LOW TWELVE	228
LUDICHRIST	228
LUNGSPIT	228
LYZANXIA	228
LÄÄZ ROCKIT	229
MACE	230
MACHINE HEAD	230
MACHINERY	232
MAD DRAGZTER	233
MAGOG	233
MAKINA	233
MALEDICTION	234

MALEVOLENCE	234
MALISHA	234
MANIC MOVEMENT	234
MANIFEST	235
MANIPULATED SLAVES	235
MANNGARD	235
MANTAS	235
MAPLE CROSS	236
MARTYR	236
MARTYR	237
MASTER	237
MASTIFAL	238
MEANSTREAK	238
MEGACE	238
MEGADETH	239
MEKONG DELTA	245
MELANCHOLIC SEASONS	246
MELIAH RAGE	246
MEMORAIN	246
MENDEED	247
MERCENARY	247
MERCILESS	248
MERENDINE ATOMICHE	248
MESHUGGAH	248
MESSIAH	250
METAL CHURCH	250
METAL DUCK	252
METAL MESSIAH	252
METALLICA	253
METALLICA: TRIBUTE	267
METHEDRAS	267
MEVÂDIO	267
MEZZROW	268
MICTLAN	268
MIDAS TOUCH	268
MILITIA	268
MINDLOCK	268
MINOTAUR	269
MNEMIC	269
MOBY DICK	270
MOKOMA	270
MONONOFU	270
MONSTERWORKS	271
MONUMENT	271
MORBID ANGEL	271
MORBUS INFERNO	274
MORDRED	274
MORIGAN	275
MORS SUBITA	275
MORTAL FORM	275
MORTAL SIN	275
MORTUARY I.O.D.	276
MOX NIX	276
MUNICIPAL WASTE	276
MX	277
NAGLFAR	277
NAILGUNNER	278
NAPALM	278
NARCOTIC GREED	279
NASTY SAVAGE	279
NATASTOR	279
NATIONAL NAPALM SYNDICATE	280
NATTAS	280
NECRODEATH	280
NECROMANCIA	281
NECROSADISTIC GOAT TORTURE	281
NECROSIS	281
NEON GOD	281
NEVERMORE	282
NICTA	284
NME	284
NME WITHIN	284
NO MERCY	285
NO RETURN	285
NOCTURNAL	285
NODE	286
NOKTURNEL	286
NOMICON	287
NORTHWORLD	287
NOSTRADAMEUS	287
NOSTROMO	288
NUCLEAR ASSAULT	288
NUCLEAR DEATH	289
NUCLEAR WARFARE	290
NUMSKULL	290
OBLIVEON	290
OCCULT	291
ODIN	291
OGRESS	292
OIL	292
OMEN	292
ONSLAUGHT	293
OPPRESSION	294
ORIGIN BLOOD	295
ORIGINAL SIN	295
OSAMENTA	295
OUTBURST	295
OUTCAST	296
OVERDOSE	296
OVERKILL	296
P.C.P.	298
P.I.T.T.	299
PAGANIZER	299
PAINSTORM	299
PAINSTRUCK	300
PANDEMONIC	300
PANTERA	300
PANZER	304
PARABELLUM	304
PARADOX	304
PARALEX	305
PARALYSIS	305
PARIAH	305
PARKWAY DRIVE	305
PATRIARCH	306
PENTAGRAM	306
PENTAGRAM	306
PERSECUTION	306
PERSONAL WAR	307
PERSUADER	307
PERZONAL WAR	307
PILEDRIVER	308
PITCH BLACK	308
PLANAR EVIL	309
POLLUTED INHERITANCE	309
POLTERGEIST	309
POSSESSED	310
POSSESSED: TRIBUTE	311
POWERMAD	311
PRECIPICE	311
PRESTIGE	311
PRO-PAIN	312
PROFANE OMEN	313
PROFECIA	313
PROJECT: FAILING FLESH	313
PROTECTOR	314
PROTOTYPE	314
PSI.KORE	314

PSYCHONAUT	315
PSYCHOTRON	315
PULMONARY ABSCESS	315
PURITY	315
PYOVELI	316
PYURIA	316
QUICK CHANGE	316
QUO VADIS	317
RAGE	317
RAGEDATE	320
RAGING FURY	320
RAISE HELL	320
RAISING FEAR	320
RAMP	321
RAVAGE	321
RAVEN	321
RAWPOWER	323
RAZOR	323
RE-ANIMATOR	324
REAPERS	325
REATOR	325
RECKLESS TIDE	325
RECLUSION	325
RECON	325
REQUIEM	326
RESPONSE NEGATIVE	326
RETRIBUTION	326
REVEREND	326
RIGOR MORTIS	327
ROOTWATER	328
ROSTOCK VAMPIRES	328
RUINS OF TIME	328
RULES OF ENGAGEMENT	328
RUMORS OF GEHENNA	328
RUNNING WILD	329
RYKER'S	330
S.N.I.F.F.	331
S.O.D.	331
SABBAT	332
SABBAT	334
SACRAMENT A.D.	335
SACRED REICH	335
SACRED WARRIOR	336
SACRIFICIAL	337
SACRILEGE	337
SACRILEGE B.C.	338
SADUS	338
SALAMANDRA	339
SAMMOHAN	339
SANCTUARY	339
SARCOFAGO	339
SATAN	340
SATANIC SLAUGHTER	341
SATORIUM	342
SAVAGE	342
SAVAGE GRACE	343
SCAAR	343
SCAR CULTURE	343
SCARIOT	343
SCARVE	344
SCAVENGER	345
SCAVENGOURS	345
SCEPTRE	345
SCORCH	345
SCORNAGE	346
SCORNGRAIN	346
SECTARIAN	346
SENTENCED	346
SENTINEL BEAST	348
SEPULTURA	348
SERAPH	352
SERMON	352
SERPENT MOVES	353
SERPENT OBSCENE	353
SERPENTOR	353
SEVENTH ANGEL	353
SHADOW OF SADNESS	354
SHAH	354
SHARKRAGE	354
SHEER TERROR	354
SHUBEND	355
SIEGES EVEN	355
SILENCER	355
SILENT SCYTHE	356
SINDROME	356
SIREN	356
SIROCCO	356
SITHLORD	357
SKANNERS	357
SKITZO	357
SKLEROTIKZ	357
SKULLKRUSHER	358
SKYCLAD	358
SLAMMER	360
SLAPDASH	361
SLAUGHTER	361
SLAVE ZERO	362
SLAYER	362
SODOM	367
SOILWORK	369
SOLITAIRE	370
SOLITARY	371
SOLSTICE	371
SOMBER	371
SORG	372
SOUL DEMISE	372
SOULS ON FIRE	372
SOULSCAR	372
SOULSCARRED	373
SPEARHEAD	373
SPECTRAL	373
SPEEDICA	373
SPEED\KILL/HATE	373
SPERMBIRDS	374
SQUEALER	374
STEEL TORMENTOR	375
STEELER	375
STONE	376
STORMWARRIOR	376
STRESSFEST	377
SUBLIMINAL CRUSHER	377
SUICIDAL ANGELS	377
SUICIDAL TENDENCIES	377
SUN DESCENDS	379
SUNRISE	379
SWARM	380
SWEDISH MASSACRE	380
TALION	380
TALIÖN	381
TANK	381
TANKARD	382
TANKWART	383
TEARABYTE	383
TENEBRAE	384
TERROR 2000	384
TERROR SQUAD	384
TESTAMENT	385
THANATOS	387

THE ACCURSED	388
THE ACCUSED	388
THE BLAMED	389
THE BRAINWASH	389
THE COUP DE GRACE	390
THE CROWN	390
THE CRUCIFIED	391
THE EMBODIMENT	391
THE ENCHANTED	391
THE FALLEN	392
THE GREAT KAT	392
THE HAUNTED	393
THE MACHETE	394
THE MIST	395
THE SCOURGER	395
THORNCLAD	395
THRASHER	395
THRAWN	396
THREINODY	396
TIMELESS MIRACLE	396
TORANAGA	396
TORCHBEARER	397
TORMENT	397
TOURNIQUET	398
TOXIC HOLOCAUST	398
TOXIC SHOCK	398
TOXIK	399
TRAGEDIAN	399
TRANSFIXION	399
TRANSMETAL	399
TRANSPARENT	401
TRAUMA	401
TRIBULATION	401
TRIBULATION	401
TRIVIUM	402
TYRANT'S REIGN	403
TYSONDOG	403
UNCLE SLAM	404
UNDER THREAT	404
UNDER THY GUN	405
UNGOD	405
UNITED	405
UNKNOWN	406
UPPERCUT	406
URKRAFT	406
V.A.R.	407
VADER	407
VENGEANCE RISING	409
VENIA	410
VENOM	410
VEXED	413
VICIOUS	413
VICIOUS ART	413
VICIOUS RUMORS	414
VICTIMIZER	416
VII ARCANO	416
VIKING	416
VIO-LENCE	417
VIOLENT HEADACHE	417
VIPER	418
VIRGIN SIN	418
VIRUS	418
VITUPERATION	419
VIU DRAKH	419
VOIVOD	419
VOLKANA	422
VULCANO	422
VÖRGUS	422
WARFARE INCORPORATED	423
WARGASM	423
WARHEAD	423
WARLORD UK	423
WARPATH	424
WASTELAND	424
WATCH MY DYING	424
WATCHTOWER	425
WAYNE	425
WEB	426
WENGELE	426
WHIP	426
WHIPLASH	426
WITCHBURNER	427
WITCHHAMMER	428
WITCHHAMMER	428
WITCHMASTER	428
WITCHTRAP	429
WIZZARD	429
WOUNDS	430
WRATH	430
X-COPS	431
XENTRIX	431
YEAR OF DESOLATION	432
ZADKIEL	432
ZARATHUSTRA	432
ZEENON	433
ZEUS	433
ZNOWHITE	433

2 TON PREDATOR

ÖREBRO, SWEDEN — *Mogge (vocals), Petter Freed (guitar), Tobbe (bass), Mathias Borg (drums).*

Örebro's 2 TON PREDATOR started life during 1993 billed as WEDGE. Founded by vocalist Mogge and bass player Tobbe, WEDGE was soon brought up to strength the addition of two erstwhile MANIFREST musicians, guitarist Petter 'Mazza' Freed and drummer Mathias Borg. The same year the band cut an opening demo with DAN SWANÖ of EDGE OF SANITY at the production helm.

WEDGE's career would be interrupted by the imprisonment of Mogge. However, the remaining band members stayed loyal and upon his release Mogge resumed his position. Changes would be afoot though as the group opted for a new title of 2 TON PREDATOR. A 1998 demo 'Burned '98' secured a deal with the Danish Diehard label resulting in the 1999 Tue Madsen produced 'In The Shallow Waters'. A second album 'Boogie' arrived in August of 2001 and 2 TON PREDATOR duly promoted its release with a European tour as guests to ENTOMBED and CATHEDRAL during September.

Borg, as "Matt Von Superstars", also plies his trade with a side band, the Punk Rock act GENOCIDE SUPERSTARS. Tobbe started side act ALL HELL in January 2004.

2 TON PREDATOR marked a return in 2005 with an untitled download album, recorded at Antfarm Studios in Århus, Denmark with producer Tue Madsen and featuring a cover version of CROWBAR's 'You Know I'll Live Again'.

Burned '98, 2 Ton Predator (1998) (Cassette demo).

IN THE SHALLOW WATERS, Diehard Music PCD-39 (1999). Still Remains / Hole In My Mind / Burned / The Bitteraftertaste / From Her Eyes / Rage Out Of Silence / Backstabbed / Get Out / Some Way / Lynch Mob / How.

Checkpoint #3, Diehard Music (2001) (Split promotion release with AURORA BOREALIS, DAEMON, ILLDISPOSED & NECROSPHERE). Pumpjack Pleasures.

BOOGIE, Diehard Music PCD-61 (2001). Boogie / Duct Tape Story / Broken Bond / Pumpjack Pleasure / Hail From Sweden / Freak 2000 / Downright Evil / 4 Tongues Strong / Turning Point / September Flu / Last Boost / Empty Chambers.

Checkpoint # 4, Diehard Music (2003) (Split promotion release with GURD, AURORA BOREALIS, KOLDBORN & THORIUM). Slowly Slaughtered.

DEMON DEALER, Diehard Music PCD-63 (2003). Slowly Slaughtered / Bone Brigade / Pipeyard Killings / Demon Dealer / A Funeral Romance / Hell Is Where You're Headed / Transparent Venom Addiction / Henchmen / Hammered / Ready To Die / Killing Flames.

UNTITLED, www.2tonpredator.net (2005) (Downloadable until 26. August 2005). A Big Bastard Of A Bad Day / Butcher's Bill / Closet Guy / Diabolic / Creature Of The Middle East / You Know I'll Live Again / Golddigger / Nightmares / No. 1 Crematorium / Reckoning Day / Two Bullets / White Knuckles.

21 LUCIFERS

FALUN, SWEDEN — *Erik Skoglund (vocals), Tobias Ols (guitar), Nicklas Lindh (guitar), Pär Eriksson (bass), Olle Ferner (drums).*

A Falun based Death / Thrash unit 21 LUCIFERS was formulated in 2002 by former FIVE MORE VICTIMS vocalist / guitarist Erik Skoglund, ex-WITHOUT GRIEF bassist Ola Berg and BLUDGE drummer Björn Åström. Two Grindcore orientated tracks would be recorded after which the trio settled on a band name of GRIDLOCK. Subsequently another WITHOUT GRIEF member, guitarist Nicklas Lindh, enrolled and steered the band into Thrashier territory. With Skoglund opting to concentrate purely on vocals a third WITHOUT GRIEF man was enlisted as second guitarist in the form of Tobias Ols.

21 LUCIFERS issued the 2002 demo 'Retaliation', recorded at Black Lounge Studios and produced by Jonas Kjellgren. Changes in the 21 LUCIFERS line-up during 2003 saw the incorporation of bassist Pär "Sodomizer" Eriksson and drummer Olle Ferner, both having credits with AVSMAK. The demo 'Hope Fades' emerged in 2004, prompting a label deal with the Dutch record company Karmageddon Media. Recording at Black Lounge Studios the band wrapped up their debut album 'In The Name Of . . .' in October.

21 LUCIFERS signed to JMT Music in December 2005.

Retaliation, 21 Lucifers (2002) (Demo). Hate Will Prevail / Kill Or Blood / Self Pollution / Five Infernal Years / Retaliation.

Hope Fades, 21 Lucifers (2004) (Demo). Hope Fades / Man Made Misery / Killing At Will / Addicted To Chaos.

IN THE NAME OF . . . , Karmageddon Media (2005). In The Name Of . . . / . . . Violence / Art Of Chaos / Greed Spreader / Die Dead Gone / Hate Will Prevail / Hope Fades / Perfect Hell / Broken / Kill Or Blood / Manmade Misery / Surprise! You're Dead! / Killing At Will / Where Apathy Dwells / Self Pollution / Quid Pro Quo / 5 Infernal Years / Retaliation.

IN THE NAME OF . . . , JMT Music JMT30303 (2006). In The Name Of . . . / . . . Violence / Art Of Chaos / Greed Spreader / Die Dead Gone / Hate Will Prevail / Hope Fades / Perfect Hell / Broken / Kill Or Blood / Manmade Misery / Surprise! You're Dead! / Killing At Will / Where Apathy Dwells / Self Pollution / Quid Pro Quo / 5 Infernal Years / Retaliation.

32ND CHAMBER

HERNING, DENMARK — *Shaun T (vocals), Chris Kaad (guitar), Nicolaj (guitar), Michael (bass), Anders Kyxi (drums).*

Herning neo-Thrash band 32ND CHAMBER was forged in October 2002 under an early billing of ZERO DIVIDE. Featuring ANTHENASIA man Shaun T on guitar, the first formation also included singer Kasper, bassist Mikkel and drummer Anders Kyxi. With Kasper's exit Shaun took on lead vocal responsibilities. Briefly, the band employed Kenneth as second guitarist. Drafting Nicolaj into the vacancy the band switched title to MOPE. This version of the band cut a two track demo in February of 2004, after which Chris Kaad boosted the guitar contingent.

Ex-ANTHENASIA man Michael took over from Mikkel on bass. First product would be the June 2004 EP 'A Drop Of Sin', recorded at Jailhouse Studios in Horsens. Upon completing these tracks the group evolved into 32ND CHAMBER. Second session, 'Falling Angels, Rising Demons' crafted at Empire Recordings in Herning, arrived in 2005.

A Drop Of Sin, Mope (2004). Self Portrait / A Drop Of Sin / Hero's Never Tell / Forget What You Know / Shout.

Falling Angels, Rising Demons, (2005). Injected / Crossing The Fire / Hell In Your Eyes / Cast In Life.

5 BE HATED

HOLLAND — *Mario van der Heyden (vocals), Berry de Klein (guitar), Roel van Hees (guitar), Ron van Kuringen (bass), Thijs Brouwers (drums).*

Founded in 1997 by the guitar pairing of Berry de Klein and Roel van Hees alongside drummer Thijs Brouwers 5 BE HATED incorporated the former SACRAMENTAL SACHEM duo of singer Mario van der Heyden and bass player Ron van Kuringen that same year. Van der Heyden had also spent a term with STIJF LIJF. Initially the band, pursuing a Thrash Metal direction, cut the 1998 conceptual demo 'Somewhere In Nowhere'. However, in October of that year de Klein exited, his position swiftly filled by erstwhile LAST DAYS OF HUMANITY man Mark Snijders. At this juncture the band, inspired by medieval themes and endeavouring to capture the spirit of "True Metal", adopted the BATTLEHEART title. A second recording session, originally billed 'The Skydiving Heroes' but subsequently changed to 'Return Of The Ancient Knight', was laid down in January of 1999 and released as an EP. BATTLEHEART folded in 2002.

Somewhere In Nowhere, 5 Be Hated (1998). Scattered Sand / Somewhere In Nowhere / Thor—Man—Thor / Sword Of Justice.

8 FOOT SATIVA (pic: Jonathan Pilkington)

8 FOOT SATIVA

NEW ZEALAND — *Ben Read (vocals), Gary Smith (guitar), Christian Humphreys (guitar), Romilly Smith (bass), Jamie Saint Merat (drums).*

West Auckland modern Metal band 8 FOOT SATIVA, comprising lead vocalist Justin Niessen, guitarist Gary Smith, bass player Brent Fox and Sam Sheppard on the drums, established themselves during 1998. Rapidly building a large local following the band broke through into national radio and TV rotation, so much so that the band was scoring more viewer support than many international Pop artists. Prior to the issue of debut album 'Hate Made Me' the group played a number of gigs around the country, including opening for PANTERA and CORROSION OF CONFORMITY at the Auckland Town Hall early 2001. A line-up change shortly after release of 'Hate Made Me' saw Sam Sheppard of SINATE and O.C.D. ('Obsessive Compulsive Disorder') taking over from original drummer Speed.

The December 2002 headline trek across New Zealand, dubbed 'The Hate Made Us All' tour, was capitalised on by gaining valuable supports to visiting artists such as DISTURBED in February 2003. The group would also attract attention in the USA with an appearance at the Austin, Texas SXSW event. Spreading their international reach even further 8 FOOT SATIVA would be one of the very few Kiwi acts to accomplish a full world tour, taking in shows in London, Toronto, Hong Kong, Sydney and New York.

8 FOOT SATIVA's second album 'Season For Assault' arrived in October of 2003. The group performed at the Auckland METALLICA headlined 'Big Day Out' festival in January of 2004. August and September shows throughout New Zealand saw the band allied with FRANKENBOK with SUBTRACT handling opening honours in the North Island and SYNDIKAT in the South Island. 'Season For Assaults impact spread further when renowned Swedish label Black Mark records picked the album up for European license. The band worked their way across Australia in May and June forming up the 'Army Of Darkness' trek in union with FRANKENBOK, FULL SCALE and SUNK LOTO.

With 8 FOOT SATIVA making waves internationally, it came as a shock for fans to see both Matt and Sam Sheppard breaking away to re-forge SINATE mid 2005. From this point on the band's experienced numerous changes starting with the recruitment of new drummer Corey Friedlander and a short-lived return of vocalist Justin Niessen. Vocalist Ben Read replaced Niessen in late 2005 with additional guitarist William Cleverdon joining around the same time.

HATE MADE ME, Intergalactic IR007 (2002) (New Zealand release). Before Your Suffering / Hate Made Me / Fuel Set / Cocktease / Believer / It's All So Real / Grown Aggression / Stolen Life / Kick It All Away / 8 Foot Sativa / Engine / Invention. Chart position: 43 NEW ZEALAND.
HATE MADE ME, Roadrunner (2003) (Australian release). Before Your Suffering / Hate Made Me / Fuel Set / Cocktease / Believer / It's All So Real / Grown Aggression / Stolen Life / Kick It All Away / 8 Foot Sativa / Engine / Invention.
SEASON FOR ASSAULT, Intergalactic IR666 (2003) (New Zealand release). What's Lost Tomorrow / For Religions To Suffer / Hatred Forever / Chelsea Smile / Disorder / Escape From Reality / Destined To Be Dead / Season For Assault / The Abused / Gutless. Chart position: 6 NEW ZEALAND.
SEASON FOR ASSAULT, Roadrunner (2004) (Australian release). What's Lost Is Tomorrow / Escape From Reality / For Religions To Suffer / Destined To Be Dead / Hatred Forever / Season For Assault / Chelsea Smile / The Abused / The Abused / Disorder / Gutless.
SEASON FOR ASSAULT, Black Mark BMCD177 (2004) (European release). What's Lost Is Tomorrow / Escape From Reality / For Religions To Suffer / Destined To Be Dead / Hatred Forever / Season For Assault / Chelsea Smile / The Abused / Disorder / Gutless.
BREED THE PAIN, Intergalactic IR011 (2005) (New Zealand release). Perpetual Torment / Breed The Pain / I Live My Death / Mentally Castrated / Altar Of Obscenity / Human Abattoir / Brutal Revenge / The Punishment Within / Genetic Treason.
BREED THE PAIN, Roadrunner (2005) (Australian release). Perpetual Torment / Breed The Pain / I Live My Death / Mentally Castrated / Altar Of Obscenity / Human Abattoir / Brutal Revenge / The Punishment Within / Genetic Treason.
BREED THE PAIN, Black Mark BMCD182 (2005) (European release). Perpetual Torment / Breed The Pain / I Live My Death / Mentally Castrated / Altar Of Obscenity / Human Abattoir / Brutal Revenge / Punishment Within / Genetic Treason.
POISON OF AGES, Black Mark (2007). For The Birds / Crosses For Eyes / Napalm Existence / Exeunt / The Great Western Cliff-Hanger / Emancipate / Ashes Of The Arsonist / We, The Termites / Pirates And Capitalists / Thumbs, Eye-Sockets, Love.

A COLD REALITY

WALTHAM, MA, USA — *Jimmy Campbell (vocals), Justin Joseph (guitar), Brian Higgins (guitar), Neil Souza (bass), Josh Hamwey (drums).*

Waltham, Massachusetts Death / Thrash Metal band COLD REALITY, featuring ex-SLAUGHTERED AT DAWN guitarist Justin Joseph, debuted with a June 2001 demo 'The Silence Remains No Longer', actually taken from a live radio broadcast on WBRS 100.1 FM, with second promotion session 'Remnants Of A Shattered Dream' following in August 2002. COLD REALITY's first, self-financed album, 'As Fading Moments Elapse Into Memories', was delivered in January 2003. However, throughout much of the following year the group remained in stasis, eventually splitting with singer John Reid in October. Guitarist Justin Joseph, previously active with THE INTRICATE SLAUGHTER PROCESS, initiated side projects ABREACTION and AS A DEAD ROSE WITHERS. Returning to the studio, A COLD REALITY cut an October 2003 pre-production demo with Joseph taking lead vocals.

The band re-introduced former singer Jimmy Campbell in August 2004 and added new guitarist Brian Higgins in October.

The Silence Remains No Longer, A Cold Reality (2001). Frozen In Time (Intro) / Staring At The Sky / Strong / Passion Within / Forsaken Soul.
Remnants Of A Shattered Dream, (2002). My Flesh, My Blood / Staring At The Sky / Passion Within.
AS FADING MOMENTS ELAPSE INTO MEMORIES, (2003). The Fallen Angel / My Flesh, My Blood / Your Voice Remains / Remnants Of A Shattered Dream / Staring At The Sky / Prayer For The Living / Passion Within / Forsaken Soul / Deliverance.
My Flesh, My Blood, (2003). Your Voice Remains / My Flesh, My Blood / Prayer For The Living / Remnants Of A Shattered Dream.
A Cold Reality, (2003). Children Of Babylon / Seventh Seal / Empty / Cleanse / Ignorance, I Slay / Of The Everlasting.

A LIFE ONCE LOST

PHILADELPHIA, PA, USA — *Bob Meadows (vocals), Bob Carpenter (guitar), Doug Sabolick (guitar), Alin Ashraf (bass), Justin Graves (drums).*

Langhorne, Philadelphia's A LIFE ONCE LOST debuted in 2003 with the album 'A Great Artist' for Jake Bannon of CONVERGE's Deathwish Inc. The group dated its formation to 1998, undergoing many formative line-up changes. Loudnet Records took A LIFE ONCE LOST on for the album 'Open Your Mouth For The Speechless ... In Case Of Those Appointed To Die', the membership at this juncture featuring singer Bob Meadows, guitarists Doug Sabolick and Vadim Taver, bassist Rich and drummer TJ. However, Taver subsequently opted out to join THIS DAY FORWARD and A LIFE ONCE LOST inducted Robert Carpenter of AS WE GROW as replacement during 2001. The group then switched to Robotic Empire for 'The Fourth Plague: Flies', recorded at Skylight Studios in 2002. Drummer Justin Graves was installed just prior to recording their debut for Deathwish Inc. Further line-up changes then saw bassist Nick Frasca replaced by Alin Ashraf of THE JUNE SPIRIT.

The band signed with Ferret Records in October 2004, entering Trax East Studios in South River, New Jersey with producer Eric Rachel in January 2005 to record their sophomore album 'Hunter'. Closing out 2004 the group acted as support to FEAR FACTORY and LAMB OF GOD. US touring in April had the band announcing a touring partnership with BURY YOUR DEAD, THE RED CHORD and IF HOPE DIES.

The Summer of 2005 found the group participating in the US 'Sounds of the Underground' touring extravaganza, a collaboration between independent labels Ferret Music, Prosthetic Records, Trustkill Records and Metal Blade Records. The mammoth billing for these shows saw the band sharing stages with CLUTCH, OPETH, POISON THE WELL, FROM AUTUMN TO ASHES, CHIMAIRA, NORMA JEAN, EVERY TIME I DIE, STRAPPING YOUNG LAD, THROWDOWN, HIGH ON FIRE, DEVILDRIVER, ALL THAT REMAINS, UNEARTH and GWAR. Regional additions included MADBALL and TERROR, splitting the East and West portions of the tour respectively, THE RED CHORD on the East Coast, FEAR BEFORE THE MARCH OF FLAMES in the Midwest and Southeast and HIMSA for Western gigs before the band joined EVERY TIME I DIE and TWELVE TRIBES for the UK 'Under The Gun' tour in August. In September the band maintained the road ethic, hooking up with THE DILLINGER ESCAPE PLAN, UNEARTH and ZAO. A run of November Canadian dates would be backed by THE END and THE BLACK DAHLIA MURDER. The group closed the year on a Winter run alongside AS I LAY DYING, NORMA JEAN and MADBALL.

The band engaged in US dates throughout February 2006 backed by HIMSA, DARKEST HOUR, THE ACACIA STRAIN and DEAD TO FALL. In April the group hit the US campaign trail once again, this time with CEPHALIC CARNAGE, SCARLET and THROUGH THE EYES OF THE DEAD in tow.

'Ozzfest' loomed for the 2006 summer touring season, the group hitting Canada as a warm up in June, flanking ALL THAT REMAINS, THE RED CHORD, UNEARTH, WALLS OF JERICHO and IF HOPE DIES, before sharing the festival stages with OZZY OSBOURNE, SYSTEM OF A DOWN, HATEBREED, LACUNA COIL, DISTURBED, BLACK LABEL SOCIETY, UNEARTH, BLEEDING THROUGH, NORMA JEAN, ATREYU, STRAPPING YOUNG LAD, THE RED CHORD, FULL BLOWN CHAOS, WALLS OF JERICHO, ALL THAT REMAINS and BETWEEN THE BURIED AND ME.

The group hit the road with NAPALM DEATH, DEAD TO FALL, IMPALED, ARSIS and ANIMOSITY throughout November and December as part of the 'Death By Decibels' US tour. The band forged a road union with THE HANDSHAKE MURDERS, NORMA JEAN and NORMA JEAN for the 'Great American Noise' tour commencing March 2007 lasting into mid-April.

A Life Once Lost, (1999). Disease / Summer Sky, Winter Air / A Falls River Farewell / This Kiss Dead Of Compassion / Why Do You Make Me Bleed?

OPEN YOUR MOUTH FOR THE SPEECHLESS ... IN CASE OF THOSE APPOINTED TO DIE, Loudnet (2000). Joan Said Please /

A LIFE ONCE LOST

This Is What She Call's Home / Prelude / Almost Perfect But I Failed / A Fall's River Fairwell / Gentle And Elegant / Everything Becomes Still / Just Before His Crucifixtion / Why Do You Make Me Bleed?

2 Song Promo, (2001). Prepare Yourself For What Is About To Come / The Tide.

The Fourth Plague: Flies, Robotic Empire (2002). Chileab / Our Second Home / The Dead Sea / Prepare Yourself For What Is About To Come / The Tide.

A GREAT ARTIST, Deathwish Inc. (2003). Surreal Atrocities / Cavil / The Change Came Suddenly / Nevermore Will I Have An Understanding ... / ... In Anything Under The Sun / Maudlin / Pious / The Wicked Will Rot / Overwhelming.

HUNTER, Ferret Music (2005). Rehashed / Needleman / Vulture / Pain & Panic / Hunter / Grotesque / Salai / A Rush & Siege / I Give In / Ghosting / With Pitiless Blows.

A GREAT ARTIST, (2007). Surreal Atrocities / Cavil / Change Came Suddenly / Nevermore Will I Have An Understanding ... / ... In Anything Under The Sun / Maudlin / Pious / Wicked Will Rot / Overwhelming.

A.N.I.M.A.L.

ARGENTINA — *Andrés Giménez (vocals / guitar), Marcelo Corbata Corbalán (bass), Andrés Vilanova (drums).*

Power trio A.N.I.M.A.L. ('Acosados Nuestros Indios Murieron Al Luchar') formed in 1991 with a founding line up of vocalist / guitarist Andrés Giménez, Marcelo Corbata Corbalán and drummer Martín Carrizo. During 1998 BOTAFOGO's Andrés Vilanova took the drum position in time for recording of that years 'Poder Latino' album, produced by none other than SOULFLY mainman Max Cavalera. The band underwent further changes in 2000, Giménez being joined by a new rhythm section of bassist Christian "Titi" Lapolla and drummer Marcelo Castro.

In 2005 Andrés Giménez guested on the DIA DE LOS MUERTOS project album 'Day Of The Dead' assembled by BODY COUNT bassist Vincent Price, and guitarist Andres Jaramillo and drummer Alfonso Pinzon from the Colombian Metal act AGONY.

A.N.I.M.A.L., Tommy Gun (1993). No Despertaremos / Criminales De Raíces / Paz Artificial / Esclavo De Ilusión / Dueña De La Sombra / Sentimientos Primitivos / Juega Con Tu Suerte / Preso Del Olvido / Cruel Adicción / Cerebro Incendiado / Mal Camino / Desde La Trinchera.

FIN DE UN MUNDO ENFERMO, Tommy Gun (1994). Sólo Por Ser Indios / Más Cabezas Para Tu Pare / Fin De Un Mundo Enfermo / Esperando El Final / Hijos Del Sol / Hambre! / Sobrevivencia / Mi Barrio / Vacíos De Fe / El Balz / Muriendo En Su Interior.

EL NUEVO CAMINO DEL HOMBRE, Warner Music (1996). Guerra De Razas / El Nuevo Camino Del Hombre / Guerreros Urbanos / Lo Mejor De Lo Peor / Pueblos Erguidos / Lejos De Casa / Sol / Antes De Morir / Amigos / Alas / Sabia Naturaleza / Chalito.

PODER LATINO, Warner Music (1998). Milagro / Familia (Es La Oportunidad) / Los Que Marcan El Camino / Poder Latino / Loco Pro / Dejar De Ser / Latinoamérica / Gracias Doy / Esclavo De Ilusión / Aliento Inocente / Camouflage / Cop Killer / Fuerza Para Aguantar / Cinco Siglos Igual.

USA TODA TU FUERZA, Warner Music (1999). Revolución / Cuida Tu Fe / Usa Toda Tu Fuerza / Barrio Patrón / Ganar O Perder / Dios / Choli Rancho / Vamos Por Mas / Solo / Atropello / Aura / Highway To Hell.

A.N.I.M.A.L. 6, Warner Music Argentina (2001). Gritemos Para No Olvidar / Raza Castigada / Vamos De Pie / Discriminación / Marcado A Fuego / A.N.I.M.A.L. / Por Que? / Límites / Nuestra Elección / Buscando Llegar Hasta El Sol / Represión / Mañana En El Abasto.

A.R.G.

KUUSAMO, FINLAND — *Tepa Karjalainen (vocals / bass), Vesa Säkkinen (guitar), Jari Kelloniemi (guitar), Pasi Takkula (drums).*

A.R.G., (standing for "Anarchy Rules Games" and subsequently "Ancient Rotten Graveyards"), respectable Thrashers from Kuusamo, Finland, had a keen enough humour to label themselves as "Reindeer Metal". An early line-up included Aku Raaska of NATIONAL NAPALM SYNDICATE as vocalist. Guitarist Vesa Säkkinen, bass player Jari Kelloniemi and drummer Pasi Takkula would be known for parallel membership of LYCANTROPHY.

Oddly the B side to their debut 1988 single 'Aggressive Confessor' featured a song about a tractor, 'Massey Ferguson'. A demo, 'Heathenism In Penitentiary', followed that same year. The first album, 1989's 'Entrance', was produced by Mara Mäntyniemi and Ilari Niemelä. A second album, 'One World Without The End', was delivered through Megamania in 1991. A.R.G. returned in 1993, brandishing the eleven track demo 'Purged To Blaze Again', which notably included a cover version of CELTIC FROST's seminal 'Dethroned Emperor'. The 'Electro-Orgasm' promotional session followed up in 1994.

A.R.G. vocalist / bassist Tepa Karjalainen was also known on the Finnish Metal scene for running the 'Epitaph' fanzine. Guitarist Vesa Säkkinen, re-billed as 'Wesleyer', founded PAIN CONFESSOR.

Heathenism In Penitentiary, A.R.G. (1988) (Demo). Intro (Fuck You) / Aggressive Confessor / Rip / Perforation / Inter Arma / Massey Ferguson.
Aggressive Confessor, Megamania MGS 139 (1988). Aggressive Confessor / Massey Ferguson / Heathenism In Penitentiary.
Prevailing Sickness, Megamania MGS 151 (1989). Prevailing Sickness / Mosher.
ENTRANCE, Megamania MGM 2024 (1989). Intro: The Ultimate Entrance / Pesticide / Something In The Dark / Perforation / Chemical Snot / Prevailing Sickness / R.I.P. / Heathenism In Penitentiary / Window To Unknown / Foul Vigour / Inter Arma.
Back To Life, Megamania MGX 170 (1990). Back To Life / Hey Hey My My / In The Depths Of Sanity / Skateboarding Death.
ONE WORLD WITHOUT THE END, Megamania MGM 2036 (1991). Intro: Last Dawn Of Humanity / Died For What / In The Depths Of Sanity / Adoration Of The Kings / Happy Times / Misfortune Along My Side (R.I.P. II) / Hey Hey My My / Back For Life / One World Without The End / Descent From The Heaven / Straybullet.
Purged To Blaze Again, A.R.G. (1993) (Demo). Intro / The Dice Is Cast / Dark Clouds (It's Snowing Again) / No Sorrow, No Pain / One Who Failed / A Grotesque Stranger / Infinite Euphoria / Picture / Dethroned Emperor / Whatever / Perunannustulaulu / Huora.
Electro-Orgasm, A.R.G. (1994) (Demo). Far / Swimming In A Digital Stream / Take You Down / It's Not Over Yet / Stronger Than Fear.

AARDVARKS

BONN, GERMANY — *Guido Meyer De Voltaire (vocals / guitar), Hernan Andres Martinez Riveros (guitar), Sven Krautkrämer (bass), Nick Holmfeldt (drums).*

A Bonn based Thrash Metal unit forged in 1993 by the Meyer De Voltaire siblings of vocalist Guido of AUGERY and guitarist Andreas along with ex-DERB man Sven Krautkrämer on bass and Nick Holmfeldt of HEATRASH and ARTIFICIAL TEETH on drums. The band debuted with the 'Eyes' demo in 1994, following this with a second session 'Farka's Lemma' two years

ABANDONED

later. Andreas Meyer De Voltaire would decamp in February of 1998 being replaced by Daniel Hauenstein.

Hauenstein would make his exit during 2001, duly supplanted by DAKRIA man Nardi Ramirez. Further ructions saw Krautkrämer too opting out in May, this last loss putting AARDVARKS on hold as a suitable replacement could not be found. During the interim Holmfeldt deputised for Death Metal act SYRE and Meyer De Voltaire cut session lead vocals for the high profile avant-garde Black Metal act BETHLEHEM.

Much to AARDVARKS relief Krautkrämer was persuaded to rejoin and the new face of Colombian guitarist Hernan Andres Martinez Riveros also entered the fold. However, Krautkrämer bailed out in 2003 to join PERZONAL WAR.

Profundo Rosso EP, (2001). Conglomerate / Profundo Rosso / Grey / Meat / Farkas' Lemma / Homeless / Late Onus / Merry-Go-Round / For God & The Nation.

ABANDONED

DARMSTADT, GERMANY — *Eric Kaldschmidt (vocals / guitar), Holger Ziegler (guitar), Günter Auschrat (bass), Konrad Cartini (drums).*

ABANDONED are Thrashers hailing from the Darmstadt / Frankfurt area of Northern Germany. The group was assembled in the Autumn of 1999 by guitarist Holger Ziegler, a local scene veteran of such outfits as SINUS, OBSTSALAT, LUNATIC DICTATOR, KALÖGENA, GOOD VIBRATIONS, ELYSIAN FIELDS, RECKONING, COURAGEOUS, RAWBONED and BÖSE DEATH, together with lead vocalist / guitarist Eric 'Kally' Kaldschmidt. Ex-SLAM and MINDLESS DRONE man Konrad Cartini enrolled as drummer in 2000 and the Summer the four song 'Forcefed' demo was recorded. Over the following two years ABANDONED's work ethic would result in no less than 300 gigs to their credit. In late 2000 Günter Auschrat, a former member of OUT OF ORDER, GRACE and REVENANT, assumed the bass position.

ABANDONED signed to Dockyard 1 Records to issued the 'Thrash Notes' album.

ABANDONED entered Kohlekeller Studios in late January 2007 to curt new album tracks. The group contributed their cover version of TANKARD's 'Face Of The Enemy' to the tribute album 'A Tribute To Tankard' included as a bonus disc on the AFM Records TANKARD release 'Best Case Scenario: 25 Years In Beers'.

Forcefed EP, Independent (2002). Forcefed / Demonic Invocation / Haunted House / At The Gates Of Hell.
MISANTHROPE, Independent (2003). Misanthrope / Private Little Hell / Meat / I Am The Sun / Thousand Sorrows / Forcefed 240 / I Am The Sun (Zipped version).
THRASH NOTES, Dockyard 1 (2006).

ABATTOIR

LOS ANGELES, CA, USA — *Steve Gaines (vocals), Mark Caro (guitar), Danny Oliverio (guitar), Mel Sanchez (bass), Danny Anaya (drums).*

Cut throat metal act ABATTOIR surfaced in Los Angeles during 1978. The band bowed in with a two track demo in 1983 with an inaugural line up of vocalist Raul Preston, guitarists Mark Caro and Juan Garcia, bassist Mel Sanchez and drummer Danger Wayne. The band debuted live at the notorious Troubadour but by ABATTOIR's studio session for the track 'Screams From The Grave' included on the now illustrious 'Metal Massacre IV' compilation Preston was ousted in favour of erstwhile SCEPTRE frontman John Cyriis. This valuable exposure led to support slots to W.A.S.P. and METALLICA.

Line up ructions beset the band though, with both Cyriis and Garcia quitting to form AGENT STEEL and Danny Amaya coming in as a new face on the drum stool. ABATTOIR was brought up to strength with the addition of vocalist Steve Gaines (brother of STRYPER bassist Tim Gaines) and guitarist Danny Oliverio. ABBATOIR's debut album, released on Combat Records in America and Roadrunner in Europe, featured a cover of the MOTÖRHEAD classic 'Ace Of Spades'.

Gaines departed to form BLOODLUST releasing the 'Terminal Velocity' single in 1988. His replacement was ex-HERETIC singer Mike Towers (nee Torres) who appears on the slightly tamer 'Only Safe Place' album, which was released on Noise Records in Europe, although they retained a deal with Combat in America. Sanchez quit in 1988 to create EVIL DEAD.

Eventually scuttled by continuous line up hassles ABATTOIR finally split. However, more than a decade later the band came out of retirement debuting with cover versions for tribute albums.

ABATTOIR lent their touch to Dwell Records IRON MAIDEN tribute 'Call To Irons', W.A.S.P.'s 'School Daze' and SAXON's 'Motorcycle Man'. With interest resurging in mainland Europe German label Century Media re-released both albums as ABATTOIR, now comprising of Gaines, Sanchez, Caro and drummer Kevin McShane prepared for a full blown return. ABATTOIR would bounce back in October of 2001 with the live album 'No Sleep 'Til Kalamazoo'. Not only did the band give a nod to MOTÖRHEAD's infamous live album but confirmed their appreciation with a cover version of 'Ace Of Spades'. The album, a strict limited edition, was made only available through the band's website.

ABATTOIR were busying themselves with recording of a fresh studio album provisionally entitled 'Evil Incarnate' during the latter half of 2001. Mid 2002 found frontman Steve Gaines in league with DARK ANGEL and DREAMS OF DAMNATION guitarist Jim Durkin, MASTABA six stringer guitarist Marcelo Lima and drummer Al Mendez in the project band PAGAN WAR MACHINE. Steve Gaines signalled his intention to issue a solo album, billed 'Anger As Art', in August of 2004.

As ABATTOIR readied a new album for 2005 release through Artillery Music a special concert, being filmed for DVD to mark the 20th anniversary of the 'Vicious Attack' album, was set to include appearances from original members bassist Mel Sanchez, guitarist Mark Caro, drummer Robert Wayne, and guitarist Juan Garcia. German Heavy Metal band POWERGOD cut a cover version of 'Screams From The Grave' for inclusion on their 'Long Live The Loud–That's Metal Lesson II' released through Massacre Records in July 2005.

Gaines' ANGER AS ART concept flourished into a whole new band entity, the singer being joined by HANGAR 18 and RAVEN MAD guitarist William Rustrum, NEW EDEN bassist Javier Marrufo with Mars Castro of COFFINTEXTS and DREAMS OF DAMNATION on drums.

VICIOUS ATTACK, Roadrunner RR 9788 (1985). Screams From The Grave / Vicious Attack (Maniac) / The Enemy / Ace Of Spades / The Living And The Dead / Don't Walk Alone / Stronger Than Evil / Game Of Death.
THE ONLY SAFE PLACE, Noise N0045 (1986). Beyond The Altar / Bring On The Damned / The Only Safe Place / Hammer Of The Godz / Back To Hell / Temptations Of The Flesh / Under My Skin / S.B.D. (Feel The Fire) / Night Of The Knife / Piano Outro.
Abattoir, (1993). Screams From The Grave / Vicious Attack.
NO SLEEP 'TIL KALAMAZOO, (2001). Vicious Return / The Enemy / Under My Skin / Vicious Attack / Everybody Dies / Stronger Than Evil / Off / Screams From The Grave / Ace Of Spades.

ABHORRENT

BRASÍLIA, DF, BRAZIL — *Robson Aldeoli (vocals), Ricardo Thomaz (guitar), Leandro Soares (guitar), Caio Duarte (bass), Gabriel Teykal (drums).*

Brasília Thrash infused Death Metal act ABHORRENT was forged during January of 1988. However, this original inception of the band would collapse after issuing the 'Horrible Slaughter' demo. ABHORRENT was reconvened in 1991 for a further session 'Blood On Your Lips'. Inclusion on a compilation album entitled 'Brazil Alternativo 6' the following year spread the bands sound into international realms. With guitarist Marcus Vireoli handling bass the band cut album tracks in 1994. Bass player Leandro Soares would be inducted shortly after but these songs would take a full three years to be issued as the 'Rage' album. ABHORRENT did manage to put in a set of European dates, oddly kicking off in the small town of Rugely in England, to promote the album.

Another tape 'Live In Rage' arrived which included a version of SLAYER's 'Reign In Blood'. During 1998 the band enlisted guitarist Hudson Andre and supplanted drummer Fabricio with the 18 year old Carlos Fibrian.

ABHORRENT's progress would be stalled though following a horrific auto accident. The band was travelling to Sao Paulo to attend a METALLICA gig when their vehicle overturned severely injuring Andre, Fibrian and Vireoli. The band's new guitarist would lose his left ear, Vireoli suffered numerous cuts and a fractured jaw whilst Fibrian damaged his arms badly.

Recuperated, ABHORRENT donated cover versions to a set of Dwell Records tribute albums namely SEPULTURA's 'Clenched Fist' and MEGADETH's 'She-Wolf'. The ABHORRENT line up of 2004, vocalist Robson Aldeoli, guitarist Fabrício Moraes, bassist Leandro Soares and drummer Gabriel Teykal, prepared a new album entitled 'Blasting' for Zenor Records. However, line-up changes in January 2005 resulted in a re-shaped group as guitarist Fabricio Moraes departed and former guitar player Ricardo Thomaz rejoined the fold. Bassist Leandro Soares duly took over the lead guitar role.

RAGE, Abhorrent (1996). Intro / Let Me Live / Eternal Doubt / Blood On Your Lips / No Chance / Prelude Of The End / The Witch / One Step / Face Of Terror.
CAUTION: STRONG IRRITANT, (2000). Answer / Nailpoint / Grief / Growing Coward / God Little Man / Rejected / Malpractice / Beg For Mercy / Family / Another Chance / Tarantula´s Curse.

ABOMINATION

CHICAGO, IL, USA — *Paul Speckmann (vocals / bass / guitar), Dean Chioles (guitar), Aaron Nickeas (drums).*

ABOMINATION is another weapon in MASTER vocalist Paul Speckmann's arsenal of Thrash and Death Metal projects. Speckmann, initially just handling bass guitar duties, had begun his journey into the world of Metal with the 1983 act WARCRY. This unit issued the 'Trilogy Of Terror' demo and also scored a track on Metal Blade's 'Metal Massacre IV' compilation. Speckmann then forged a union with Chris Middlebrunt to create DEATHSTRIKE. After a solitary demo DEATHSTRIKE would evolve into MASTER by 1984. A deal was struck for a proposed album with the Combat label but in the midst of negotiations MASTER splintered. 1985 saw the manifestation of another project band FUNERAL BITCH, Speckmann founding this act together with ASSAULT's Alex Olvera.

In 1987 Speckmann resolved to start afresh enlisting drummer Aaron Nickeas and erstwhile IMPULSE MANSLAUGHTER guitarist Mike Schaffer, and subsequently guitarist Dean Chioles, for the formation of ABOMINATION. A brace of demos, commencing with 'The Slaughter Cult Begins', then ensued. ABOMINATION would sign to the German Nuclear Blast concern to release the eponymous debut.

1993 would see ABOMINATION members guitarist Dean Chioles and drummer Aaron Nickeas founding another extreme Metal unit entitled BODY BAG. However, sadly Chioles would soon after be diagnosed with Amyotrophic Lateral Sclerosis and was forced to give up the guitar.

In February of 2000 Speckmann joined Czech Deathsters KRABATHOR.

ABOMINATION, Nuclear Blast (1989). The Choice / Murder, Rape, Pillage And Burn / Reformation / Redeem Deny / Possession / Suicidal Dreams / Life And Death / Victim Of The Future / Tunnel Of Damnation.
TRAGEDY STRIKES, Nuclear Blast NB050 (1991). Blood For Oil / They're Dead / Pull The Plug / Will They Bleed / Industrial Sickness / Soldier / Kill Or Be Killed / Oppression.

ABSURDUS

VEIKKOLA, FINLAND — *Aki Martin Kauppi (vocals / guitar), Juha Moilanen (guitar), Taneli Nyholm (bass), Matti Roiha (drums).*

Black Thrash act founded in Veikkola by school friends vocalist / guitarist Aki Martin Kauppi, guitarist Juha Moilanen, bass player Taneli Nyholm and drummer Matti Roiha. Formative sessions commenced with December 1993's 'Under The Never Setting Sun' with the 'Flames' demo surfacing in 1995 followed by 'Demon III' during 1996. During 1996 both Taneli and Roiha would deputize for RAVENSFALL (later CRYHAVOC) but would return to ABSURDUS for recording of the 'No Heaven In Sight' album. Released on the British Candlelight label in December 1998, 'No Heaven In Sight' included a version of MOTÖRHEAD's seminal 'Bomber'.

A second album was planned but ABSURDUS opted for a more basic Rock n' Roll approach and were dropped by their label. ABSURDUS would later evolve into PANDEMONIUM OUTCASTS with all members adopting the revised names of guitarist J. 'Aki' Boa (also 'Snake'), bassist Daniel Rock (also 'Daniel Stuka' and 'Serpent') and drummer Matt C. (also 'Dragon').

Bassist Taneli Nyholm (as 'Daniel Stuka') would join BABYLON WHORES in late 1999.

Under The Never Setting Sun, Absurdus (1993) (Demo). Intro / Son Of The Winterfire / Nocturnal / The Ending Of The Path / Outro: Poetry.
Flames, Absurdus (1994) (Demo). A Short Introduction To Absurdity / Aurora / The Eternal One / Flaming Lake Of Fire.
Demon 3, Absurdus (1996) (Demo). Blood Drive / My Kingdom / Life Of Agony.
NO HEAVEN IN SIGHT, Candlelight CANDLE024CD (1998). Ad Absurdum (One Hell Of An Introduction) / On The Way To Hell / Devil's Ride / My Kingdom / You're Below Everything / Concord In Diablo / Joyreaper / Pure Pleasure / Blood Drive / Life Is Agony / Bomber.

ACCELERATOR

SWITZERLAND — *Fredi Zaugg (vocals / guitar), Sascha Von Arx (guitar / keyboards), Roger Friedrich (bass), Adi Krebs (drums).*

ACCELERATOR's 1997 debut album 'The Prophecy' saw guest vocals from Patrick Schaad with female vocals from Esther Hofer. The band, created in late 1993 as a trio of vocalist / guitarist Fredi Zaugg, ex-GOMORRHA bassist Roger Friedrich and drummer Adi Krebs, had previously gone under the titles of DEAD END and APOPLEXY. As ACCELERATOR they had made their mark with the 1995 demo session 'The Dark Side'.

Following the release of 'The Prophecy' Von Arx departed and Esther Hofer took over the role of guitarist / keyboard player. ACCELERATOR's 2003 line-up comprised vocalist Stefan Gehri, vocalist / guitarist Fredi Zaugg, guitarist / keyboard player Esthi Hofer, bass player Sascha von Arx and drummer Adi Krebs.

ACCU§ER

SIEGEN, GERMANY — *Eberhard Weyel (vocals / bass), Rene Schutz (guitar), Frank Thoms (guitar), Volker Borchet (drums).*

A Siegen Speed Metal band that specialised in long drawn out 'Techno-Thrash' material, ACCU§ER was formed in 1986 by ex BREAKER men vocalist / bassist Eberhard Weyel and drummer Volker Borchert together with ex-EXPECT NO MERCY guitarist Frank Thoms. Original bassist Thomas Kircher, who featured on a 1986 demo cassette billed 'Speed Metal', departed before the first album. Following the release of debut album 'The Conviction' in 1987 for Atom H Records, ACCU§ER, having drafted second guitarist René Schütz, toured Europe with MUCKY PUP and then released a mini-album 'Experimental Errors'. Limited editions of this 1988 release were pressed on collectable clear vinyl.

For the tour to promote the 'Who Dominates Who?' album of 1989 vintage ACCU§ER toured on a bill with GRINDER and DESPAIR. However, by the time the ensuing 'Double Talk' was released in 1991, guitarist René Schütz had been replaced with Milan Peschel.

Frontman Weyel departed in 1991 leaving Thoms to take over lead vocals for 1992's 'Repent', issued via Our Choice Records.

Members of ACCU§ER would then hook up with noted German Industrial Metal act DIE KRUPPS in a union resulting in the 1992 album 'Metal Machine Music'. Borchert would actually be enrolled as live drummer for DIE KRUPPS and both Thoms and Schütz would session on the album '1'. ACCU§ER promptly went through a series of bassists prior to settling on Guido Venzlaff in 1993. In this format the group cut the EP 'Confusion/Romance' for Koch International Records.

Two of ACCU§ER's more recent albums, 1994's 'Reflections' and 'Taken By The Throat' were produced by the noted American recording engineer Alex Perialis. This union in the studio signified a change of direction into more groove orientated material.

The band, still signed to Koch International, put out 1995's 'Taken By The Throat' album but were unable to achieve as high sales figures as they had anticipated the switch would give them. The band remained hiatus for many years but resurfaced in January of 2003 touting a four track demo.

Speed Metal, Accu§er (1986) (Demo). Evil Liar / Down By Law / Screaming For Guilty / Law Of War.
THE CONVICTION, Atom H 003 (1987). Evil Liar / Sadistic Terror / Down By Law / Law Of War / Accu§er / The Conviction / Screaming For Guilt.
Experimental Errors, Atom H 006 (1988). The Persuasion / Black Suicide / Terroristic Violence / Technical Excess / F.H.W.C. / Ratouli.
WHO DOMINATES WHO?, Atom H 008 (1989). Master Of Disaster / Who Pulls The Wire? / Elected To Suffer / Symbol Of Hate / Who Dominates Who? / Bastard / Called To The Bench.
DOUBLE TALK, Atom H AH014 (1991). Double Talk / The Freeze / Money / Flag Waver / Why Me / Indistinct Articulation / Revolution / Alcowhore.
REPENT, Our Choice RTD 195 1178 3 (1992). Rotting From Within / Repent / Get Saved / Sacrifice Machine / The Living Dead / The Drones / Judgement Gone Blind / Nosferatu / Metal Machine Music.
CONFUSION ROMANCE, C&C 025052-2 (1994). Head Like A Hole / Confusion Romance / Cowboy On A String / Driver's Seat / Misery / Repent.
REFLECTIONS, Major LC6249 (1994). The Wreckage / Misery / Cowboy On A String / The Jack Of All Trades / Reflections / Unite-divide / Into The Void / Burn / Manic Ride.

TAKEN BY THE THROAT, Koch International 341 682 (1995). Healium / Taken By The Throat / Fatal Vision / Fire Ignites / Obey! / Condemnation / Blasting In Progress / The Slug / Stonefaced / Amnesia.

ACERO

COSTA RICA — *Adrián Moya (vocals), Jorge Molina (guitar), Carlos Aguilar (guitar), Francisco Pujol (bass), Eric Nassar (keyboards), Fernando Alvarado (drums).*

The Speed Metal inclined ACERO was forged in 1985, the direct result of the disbanding of a prior act entitled CICLOS D. The band's inaugural formation numbered vocalist / guitarist Jorge Molina, bass player Francisco Pujol and drummer Francisco Paz. The following year another CICLOS D man, Marcelo Galli, usurped Paz. However, Johnny Soto then took the drum stool and ACERO also welcomed onboard singer Franklin Umaña.1989 witnessed further changes with the defection of Umaña and the incorporation of keyboard player Adrián Ortiz and drummer Juan Carlos Araya. The drum position would not stay stable until 1990 though, when Fernando Alvarado made it his own.

Franklin Umaña would make a return to front the band but in 1999 Adrián Moya became the new ACERO vocalist. The following year Carlos Aguilar brought his skills as both guitarist and keyboard player.

PASADO Y PRESENTE, Independent (2002). Pasa La Raya / Libertad / El Rey Del Rock & Roll / Dos Lunas Negras / Péndulo / Reencarnación / Reina De La Noche / Luces En El Cielo.

ACID

BRUGES, BELGIUM — *Kate (vocals), Demon (guitar), Dizzy Lizzy (guitar), T-Bone (bass), Anvill (drums).*

Bruges based Thrash Metal band. The female fronted ACID formed in 1980 with the trio of Demon, Kate and T-Bone splintering from PRECIOUS PAGE and recruiting drummer Anvill. Second guitarist Dizzy Lizzy was added in 1981 in time to record their debut single 'Hooked On Metal', of which 2'000 copies were pressed and its success led to a deal with the independent Giant label resulting in three albums between 1983 and 1985.

The group played throughout France, Belgium and Holland with the likes of VENOM, BLACK SABBATH, MANOWAR, LOUDNESS, PICTURE, BODINE and MOTÖRHEAD, but split up after the third album 'Engine Beast'.

Having been off the scene for nearly a decade ACID surprisingly announced a reformation for a one off show in Germany during 1994 sponsored by 'Heavy Oder Was!?' magazine, but realism dawned however and the reunion failed to materialise.

1988's 'Acidify' and 1989's 'Don't Lose Your Dreams' are from a German ACID although many publications have mistaken them for their Belgian predecessors.

Hooked On Metal, Acid ACID001 (1981). Hooked On Metal / Hell On Wheels.

Lucifera, Giant GS 501 (1983). Lucifera / Ghostriders.

Black Car, Hartdog (1983). Black Car / Drop Dead / The Day You Die / Exterminator.

ACID, Giant 6711 (1983). Acid / Ghostriders / Hell On Wheels / Anvil / Demon / Hooked On Metal / Woman At Last / Five Days Hell / Heaven's Devils / Satan.

MANIAC, Bullet Megaton 007 (1983). Max Overload / Maniac / Black Car / America / Lucifera / No Time / Prince Of Hell And Fire / Bottoms Up.

ENGINE BEAST, Giant G713 (1985). STC / Lost In Hell / Halloween Queen / Big Ben / Lady Death / Warriors Of The Dark / Let Me Die / She Loves You / Engine Beast / Satan's Delivery.

ACID DRINKERS

POLAND — *Titus (vocals / bass), Litza (guitar), Popcorn (guitar), Mangood (drums).*

A Thrash Heavy Metal act with strong Crossover influences, ACID DRINKERS began as a three piece in 1985 comprising guitarist Dariusz "Popcorn" Popowicz, vocalist / bassist Tomasz "Titus" Pukacki and drummer Chomik. Initial progress was halted when Titus was drafted for his national military service in 1987. Upon his return the band pulled in TURBO guitarist Robert "Litza" Friedrich and drummer Maciej "Slimak" Staorsta to cut the debut album 'Are You A Rebel?' ACID DRINKERS garnered an international profile courtesy of the Music For Nations Thrash offshoot label Under One Flag who would license their initial three albums, released domestically by Metal Mind, for Western consumption. Friedrich later forged CREATION OF DEATH.

The oddly titled 1994 'Fishdick' album witnessed the band delving deep into covers territory offering forth their renditions of PINK FLOYD's 'Another Brick In The Wall', KISS' 'Deuce', MOTÖRHEAD's 'Ace Of Spades', AC/DC's 'Whole Lotta Rosie', BLACK SABBATH's 'N.I.B.' and DEEP PURPLE's 'Highway Star'.

ACID DRINKERS attempted a Black Metal pastiche with the less than serious 'Infernal Connection' album. Whilst still a high grade Thrash Metal album the record, lyrically the album took on the whole question of implied satanic messages in Metal music. The band would have a crack at covering the hoary anthem 'Wild Thing' by THE TROGGS on their 1996 effort 'The State Of Mind Report'. 'High Proof Cosmic Milk' issued in March 1998, included a cover of CREEDANCE CLEARWATER REVIVAL's staple 'Proud Mary'.

Litza departed following issue of the live album 'Varran Strikes Back', his position being taken by Perla, previously a member of GUESS WHY. ACID DRINKERS 1999 album 'Amazing Atomic Activity' featured a spin off single, a cover of the ROLLING STONES '(I Can't Get No) Satisfaction'. The record also saw a digipack version featuring extra bonus tracks 'Cigarettes', 'The Last Lap' and 'Human Bazooka'. The following year's 'Broken Head' album would also be issued in a limited digipack format including exclusive tracks and a video clip.

Perla's last contribution to the band would be the 2002 'Acidofilia' album. He left the ranks in 2003 and was replaced by ex-ILLUSION player Tomka 'Lipy' Lipnickiego . This latest recruit decamped in 2004 and ACID DRINKERS drew in Olass from the band NONE as their new rhythm guitarist. However, the 2004 album 'Rock Is Not Enough' album still featured Lipa's guitar work.

The entire ACID DRINKERS catalogue would be re-issued as double packaged metal box CDs by Metal Mind Productions. Besides their activities with ACID DRINKERS various members also operate numerous side project acts such as ARMIA, ALBERT ROSENFIELD, KAZIK, FLAPJACK and the PARA WINO BAND. Titus, billed as "Tomasz Titus Vaginus Rex Pukacki", also holds membership of HOMO TWIST.

ARE YOU A REBEL?, Under One Flag FLAG45 (1990). Del Rocca / Barmy Army / I Mean Acid (Do Ya Like It?) / Waitin' For The Hair / Lammin', Obtrusive, Vulgar, Emasculatin' Machine / Fuck The Violence (I'm Sure I'm Right) / I Am The Mystic / Woman With Dirty Feet / Megalopolis / Nagasaki Baby / Moshin' In The Night / Mike Cwel.

DIRTY MONEY, DIRTY TRICKS, Under One Flag FLAG 59 (1991). Are You A Rebel? / Too Many Cops / Acid Drinker / Smoke On The Water / Yahoo / Max-He Was Here Again / Ziomas / Traditional Birthday / Dirty Money, Dirty Tricks / Angry And Bloody / Street Rockin' / WGFS Power / Don't Touch Me / Zorba / Flooded With Wine.

STRIP TEASE, Under One Flag FLAG76 (1992). Striptease / King Kong Bless You / Seek And Destroy / Rock n' Roll Beast / Rats / Feeling Naughty / Poplin' Twist / Masterhood Of Hearts Devouring / You Are Lost My Dear / Menel Song / Always Look On The Bright Side Of Life / Blood Is Boiling / My Caddish Promise / Mentally Deficient / Hell It Is A Place On Earth / Ronnie And The Brotherspider / I'm A Rocker.

VILE VICIOUS VISION, Loud Out Records LOR 050 (1993). Zero / (Voluntary) Kamikaze Club / Vile Vicious Vision / Pizza Driver / Under

The Gun / Marian Is A Metal Guru / Murzyn Mariusz / Balbilator Edzy / Then She Kissed Me / Hats Off (2 This Lady) / Polish Blood / Freeze Me / Midnight Visitor.

INFERNAL CONNECTION, Mega Czad CSO 777 (1994). Hiperenigmatic Stuff Of Mr. Nothing / Anybody Home??!! / The Joker / Track Time 66.6 Sec. / Drug Dealer / Slow And Stoned (Method Of Yonash) / Dancing In The Slaughterhouse / IQ Cyco / Backyard Bandit / Infernal Connections / Consument.

FISHDICK, Loud Out Records LOR 100 (1994). Ace Of Spades / Oh No! Bruno / Deuce / N.I.B. / Another Brick In The Wall / Whole Lotta Rosie / Run Run Away / Fuckin' The Tiger / Highway Star / Balada.

Pump The Plastic Heart, (1995). Pump The Plastic Heart / 24 Radical Questions.

ACID DRINKERS 1985: ACIDS ON THE DANCE FLOOR, Stage Diving Club Records SDC001 (1995). Bonarowski Mix Gitarowy / Hrohomyloh Mix / Versya Spoko / Running With The Devil / Konsument / OK! I Fell Alright / Ill Wojna.

THE STATE OF MIND REPORT, Polton Warner Music Poland PC176 (1996). Private Ego / Two Be One / 24 Radical Questions / Solid Rock / United Suicidal Legion / Pump The Plastic Heart / Maximum Overload / Solid Rock Part II / Wild Thing / Walkway To Heaven.

Walkway To Heaven, (1996). Walkway To Heaven / Private Eco.

AMAZING ATOMIC ACTIVITY, (1997). Amazing Atomic Activity / You Better Shoot Me / Satisfaction / Cops Broke My Beer / Wake Up! Here Come The Acids / My Pick / She's Gonna Be A Porno Star / Justify Me (I Was So Hungry) / Home Submarine / House Full Of Reptiles / What A Day / Cigarettes / The Last Lap.

VARRAN STRIKES BACK - ALIVE!, (1998). Zero / The Joker / High Proof Cosmic Milk / Popilin Twist / United Suicide Legion / Street Rockin' / Slow And Stoned (Method Of Yonash) / Barmy Army / Flooded With Wine / Pizza Driver / I Fuck The Violence (Im Sure, Im Right) / Always Look On The Bright Side Of Life / Wild Thing / Proud Mary.

HIGH PROOF COSMIC MILK, Metal Mind MMP050 (1998). Rattlesnake Blues / Human Bazooka / High Proof Cosmic Milk / What's Happenin' In The Heart Of A Pacifist / More Life / Be My Godzilla / Dementia Blvd. / Blind Leadin' The Blind / Gain On Shit / Proud Mary.

(I Cant Get No) Satisfaction, (1999). (I Cant Get No) Satisfaction / Cops Broke My Beer / (I Cant Get No) Satisfaction (Acid remix).

BROKEN HEAD, Metal Mind (2001). Superstitious Motherfucker / Dog Rock / El Pecado / Calista / Don't Go To Where I Sleep / A Rubber Hammer And A Broken Head / There's So Much Hatred In The Air / The Wildest Planet In Space / Youth / Red And Grey.

ACIDOFILIA, Sony (2002). Intro / Disease Foundation / Drunk Eyes / Pig To Rent / Be Careful With This Gun Daughter! / Hydrogen / Stick Around / Edmund's Hypocrisy / Damned Diamonds / Propaganda / Acidofilia.

ROCK IS NOT ENOUGH, Sony (2004). E.E.G.O.O. / Life Hurts More Than Death / The Ball And The Line / Fill Me / Black Blood Canyon / When You Say To Me 'Fuck You' (Say It Louder) / Stray Bullets / Jennifer & Ben / Primal Nature / Hate Unlimited.

ACID REIGN

HARROGATE, YORKSHIRE, UK — *H (vocals), Kev (guitar), Gaz Jennings (guitar), Ian Gangwer (bass), Mark Ramsey Wharton (drums).*

A Yorkshire Thrash Metal band blessed with a rather over the top sense of humour. ACID REIGN, pitching in with the British Thrash wave, was created in Harrogate during 1985 by frontman H (Howard Smith) and guitarist Gaz Jennings who recruited drummer Mark Ramsey Wharton and bassist Ian Gangwer. Their first recording was the 'Moshkinstein' demo, which was laid down before the group had taken the decision on bringing in Kev on second guitar. This demo secured them management with LITTLE ANGELS guiding force Kev Nixon and a record deal with Under One Flag, a subsidiary of Music For Nations.

After releasing the 1988 'Moshkinstein' mini-album ACID REIGN supported FLOTSAM AND JETSAM at London's Astoria, although a subsequent European tour was put in jeopardy when Gangwer was unable to travel due to insufficient documentation. Macc, a scene veteran of EXXPLODER, PHANTOM and HOLOSADE, filled in on bass in the interim.

In late 1988, after issue of 'The Fear' album, the band underwent a line-up change, with both Jennings and Gangwer leaving. Gangwer's departure enabled temporary bassist Macc to join the band on a permanent basis whilst Jennings place was taken by former LORD CRUCIFER guitarist Adam Lehan. Another prominent release, the 10" 'Humanoia' EP, sporting three live tracks, mimicked the ANTHRAX "Apple-core" humour.

With the Trash scene faltering in the UK, ACID REIGN, like so many of their ilk, resorted to a cover version and issued a December 1989 single of 'Hangin' On The Telephone', made famous by BLONDIE. A live version of 'Blind Aggression', recorded at the London Astoria, featured on the 'Kerrang!' magazine 'Plastic Explosive' flexi disc cover mount. Second album 'Obnoxious', alarmingly eschewing traditional Metal visuals in favour of a shocking charise pink sleeve, ensued but this was not enough to save them and, sadly, ACID REIGN split in mid 1991 citing the flagging fortunes of the British Thrash scene as the main reason. Vocalist H formed short-lived outfits STRANGE THING then DULLABYE prior to setting himself up in a new career as a stand up comedian.

Lehan formed BITTER AND TWISTED with ex-DEADLINE and SLAMMER bass player Russell Bertram. Jennings, Lehan and Ramsey Wharton all joined Doom outfit CATHEDRAL. Unsurprisingly, Kev teamed up with Nottingham Spoof Thrashers LAWNMOWER DETH, re-billed "Baron Kev Von Thresh Meister Silo Stench Chisel Marbles".

Moshkinstein, (1987). Intro / Goddess / Suspended Sentence / Bullyboy / Lucifer's Hammer / Motherly Love / Two Minded Takeover / R.F.Y.S. / The Burial.

Moshkinstein EP, Under One Flag FLAG20 (1988). Goddess / Suspended Sentence / Freedom Of Speech / Motherly Love / Respect The Dead / Chaos (Lambs To The Slaughter).

THE FEAR, Under One Flag FLAG31 (1989). You Never Know (W.T.N.W.S.) / Reflection Of Truths / Insane Ecstasy / Humanoia / The Fear / Blind Aggression / Life In Forms / All I See / Lost In Solitude.

Humanoia, Under One Flag 10FLAG106 (1989) (10" single). Humanoia / All I See (Live) / Goddess (Live) / Bully Boy / Chaos (Live).

Hangin' On The Telephone, Under One Flag FLAG 109 (1989). Hangin' On The Telephone / Bad News (Live) / Warriors Of Genghis Khan (Live) / Motherly Love (Live).

Kerrang! Plastic Explosive, BANG! 2 (1990) ('Kerrang!' magazine cover mount flexi disc split with TESTAMENT). Blind Aggression.

OBNOXIOUS, Under One Flag FLAG39 (1990). Creative Restraint / Joke Chain / Thoughtful Sleep / You Are Your Enemy / Phantasm / My Open Mind / Codes Of Conformity / This Is Serious.

THE WORST OF, Under One Flag FLAG 60 (1991). Billy Boy / Lucifer's Hammer / Motherly Love / Two Minded Takeover / R.F.Y.S. / Amnesiac / Magic Roundabout / The Argument / Sabbath Medley / Reflections Of Truths / Hangin' On The Telephone / Warriors Of Genghis Khan / Three Year War / The Joke's On Us / Big White Teeth.

ACID STORM

SÃO PAULO, SP, BRAZIL — *Robson Goulart (vocals), Eric Weber (guitar), Marcos V. (guitar), Chico Comelli (bass), Alessandro J. (drums).*

São Paulo Thrashers originally formulated under the banner EXTERMINIATOR in 1986. ACID STORM lead singer Robson Goulart was previously with the renowned HARPPIA whilst bass player Chico Comelli held credits with MX. For the band's sophomore release, 1990's 'Last Day Of Paradise', ACID STORM enrolled new frontman Mario Astorg Pastore. However, in 1992 Pastore decamped, subsequently heading up REVENGE, TAILGUNNERS, DELPHT and SACRED SINNER, and ACID STORM welcomed back Goulart to the vocal role. Surreally Goulart then backed out again during 1995 and Pastore resumed his position. The 'Twilight Zone' demo emerged in 1997.

ACID STORM credited drummer Fábio Buitvidas also worked with ENGRAVE and JUDAS PRIEST covers band HELL PATROL.

WHY? DIRTY WAR, RSL (1989). Choose Live Or Die / Scourge Of The Gods / Terminator / The Madness / Why?... Dirty War / Never Renounce.

LAST DAY OF PARADISE, (1990).
BIOTRONIC GENESIS, Heavy Metal Maniac (1991). Intro (The Beginning) / Metal Beasts / Hungry For War / Symbiotic Love / Last Days Of Paradise / Galactic Holocaust / Biologic Mechanization / Star Host.

ACRIDITY

TX, USA — *Darrin Carroll (vocals), Mel Langenberg (guitar), Anthony Pedone (guitar), Mark Cox (bass), Mark Soto (drums).*

Progressive styled Thrash Metal band ACRIDITY heralded their arrival with the 1987 demo 'Countdown To Terror'. At the time of their inaugural effort ACRIDITY could boast two 17 year old guitarists in Mel Langenberg and Anthony Pedone as well as a 14 year old drummer Mark Soto. A further demo, 'For Freedom I Cry', surfaced in 1989.

A solitary album, also titled 'For Freedom I Cry', arrived the same year courtesy of Prophecy Records. ACRIDITY would also donate the track 'Whisper Of Reality' to a Texas scene compilation album issued by Saturn Records 'Voices Of A Red God'. A later variant of ACRIDITY would witness the introduction of a keyboard player Coby Cardosa.

FOR FREEDOM I CRY, Prophecy (1989). Beyond / The Verdict / Exist In Misery / For Freedom I Cry / Countdown To Terror / Denied Right / Lethal Idol / Nothing Held Sacred / Vigilante.

ACROPHET

BROOKFIELD, WI, USA — *Dave Baumann (vocals / bass), Todd Saike (guitar), Dave Pelino (guitar), Jason Mooney (drums).*

Wisconsin's ACROPHET were judged 'Intelligent Speedcore'. The second album was released on the Triple X label in America. Following the issue of 1990's 'Faded Glory' album the band inducted guitarist Rob Anthony. Touring then ensued across America and Mexico but although plans for a third album were laid ACROPHET in fact folded in 1993.

Anthony and vocalist / bassist Dave Baumann forged a fresh non Metal act titled SOUL CITY. This unit, together with the addition of erstwhile VIOGRESSION drummer Barry Jaeger, would develop into the ROB ANTHONY BAND. As such a much lauded acoustic Rock album 'Hard To Believe' surfaced in the late 90s.

CORRUPT MINDS, Roadrunner RR 9523 (1988). Intro To Corruption / Lifeless Image / Crime For Loving / Holy Spirit / Ceremonial Slaughter / Forgotten Faith / Corrupt Minds / Slaves Of Sin / From The Depths / Living In Today / Warped Illusions / Victims Of The Holocaust.
FADED GLORY, Roadracer RO9404 (1990). When Time Stands Still / Dependency / Silent Insanity / Legend Has It / Dead Cell Day / The American Zone 1990 / Independence At It's Finest / Return To Me Life / Innocent Blood / Forever The Fall / Haunting Once Again.

ACT OF FATE

AURICH, GERMANY — *Karsten Schöning (vocals), Thorsten Nieland (vocals / bass), Carsten Schmidt (guitar), Benjamin Hakbilir (guitar),.*

Thrash outfit ACT OF FATE was formulated during the Autumn of 1997, first quoting a line-up of vocalist / bassist Torsten Nieland, lead guitarist Benjamin Hakbilir, rhythm guitarist Stefan Pupkes and drummer Alexander Oberdick. However, in early 1998 the group folded, with both Nieland and Hakbilir joining DAMNATION in March. Oberdick subsequently resurfaced with EBOLA BEACH PARTY.

The founding duo of Nieland and Hakbilir would resurrect ACT OF FATE though, pulling in new members vocalist / guitarist Michael Meyer and drummer Swen Ludwigs. In August the group entered Friesensound Studios in Aurich to record the demo 'Soul Puzzlement'. From these sessions the tracks 'Paingod' would be included on the 'Eternity Underground' fanzine compilation and 'Nighthunter' was donated to the 'Death'O´Phobia #6' album.

Live work throughout 1999 generated of 350 sales of 'Soul Puzzlement'. The momentum was maintained by using Audio Check Studios in Emden to craft a full length album 'Despise The Light'. Following this release ACT OF FATE underwent line-up changes. In side activity, Hakbilir joined ANASARCA whilst Nieland teamed up with GALLERY OF DARKNESS. Meantime, ACT OF FATE was re-built by drafting singer Christian Sap and drummer Gerd-Peter Mumme of KING CARRION. Second guitarist Carsten Schmidt, a veteran of Danish act MALTESE FALCON and of WOUNDED, completed the roster in September 2000.

Soul Puzzlement, Act Of Fate (1998). Autumn Dawn (Intro) / Paingod / Soul Puzzlement / Perpetual Hate / Nighthunter / Act Of Fate.
DESPISE THE LIGHT, (1999). Bleeding Again / Final Destination / Euphoria / Conscience Demand / Cold Emotions / Blinded By . . . / Starvation / The Gate / XXX / Dream Destroyer.

ADDICTIVE

SYDNEY, NSW, AUSTRALIA — *Greg Smith (vocals / bass), Joe Buttigieg (guitar), Mick Sultana (guitar), Matt Coffey (drums).*

Heavy Metal act from Sydney evolving in 1988 with a line up of vocalist / bassist Greg Smith, guitarists Joe Buttigieg and Mick Sultana with drummer Matt Coffey. ADDICTIVE debuted with the 1988 demo 'Ward 74'. After the issue of debut album 'Pity Of Man' in 1989 Coffey lost his place to former ENTICER drummer Steve Moore.

The veteran English bassist Bob Daisley, a man who lists OZZY OSBOURNE, RAINBOW and MOTHERS ARMY to his credit, produced the band's second album 'Kick 'Em Hard'. Apparently the master tapes of these recordings went astray and it was to be 1993 before the album was finally issued. Both guitarists, Joe Buttigieg and Mick Sultana, went on to join the ranks of veteran Thrash Metal band MORTAL SIN.

Ward 74, (1988). Addictive Friend / Sonder Commando / What Ward Are You In? / Pity Of Man / Come Before The Storm.
PITY OF MAN, Survival (1989). Get Out Of My Life / Come Before The Storm / Boiling Point / Sonder Kommando / The Forge / What Ward R.U. In? / Echoes Of The Mind / Addictive Friend / My Foe / Pity Of Man.
KICK 'EM HARD, Survival (1993). Distemper / Waiting For Yesterday / Kick 'Em Hard / You're Perfect / Towards Extinction / Wacked / You Never Know / Man Made Act Of God / Serves You Right / Bitch.

ADRENALIN O.D.

USA — *Paul Ricard (vocals / guitar), Bruce Wingate (guitar), Jack Steeples (bass), Dave Scott (drums).*

Bassist Jack Steeples was replaced by Keith Hartel for 1988's 'Cruising with Elvis in Bigfoot's UFO' album. The EP 'Theme From An Imaginary Midget Western' features a B side containing covers of the KISS classic 'Detroit Rock City' and the SKULLS song 'Coffincruiser'.

Ex ADRENALIN O.D. founder and guitarist Jim Foster later founded Punk band ELECTRIC FRANKENSTEIN.

HUMONGOUS FUNGUS AMONGUS, Buy Our Records (1987). AOD Vs Godzilla / Office Building / Yuppie / Answer / Pope On A Rope / Fishin' Musician / Pizza n' Beer / Bugs / Youth Blimp / Commercial Cuts / Survive / Masterpiece / Crowd Control / Velvet Elvis / Fuck The Neighbours / Surfin' Jew / Bruce's Lament / The Nice Song.
THE WACKY HI-JINKS OF ADRENALIN OD,, Buy Our Records (1987). AOD Vs Godzilla / White Hassle / New Years Eve / Small Talk / Going To A Funeral / Corporate Disneyland / Trans Am (The Saga Continues) / Sightseeing / Middle Aged Whore / World War IV / Clean And Jerk / Sleep / Rah-Jah! / Rock n' Roll Gas Station / Paul's Not Home.
Theme From An Imaginary Midget Western, Buy Our Records BOR12016 (1988). Theme From An Imaginary Midget Western / Detroit Rock City / Coffin Cruiser.

A Nice Song In The Key Of D, Buy Our Records (1988). A Nice Song In The Key Of D.
CRUISING WITH ELVIS IN BIGFOOT'S UFO,, Buy Our Records (1988). It's Tuesday . . . It Must Be Walla-Walla / Bulimec Food Fight / Swindel / Slow / Second To None / My Mother Can't Drive / Theme From An Imaginary Midget Western / Something About . . . Amy Carter / Flipside Unclassified / Baby Elephant Walk.

ADVERSITY

CANADA — *Kyle (vocals), Phillipe (guitar), Franz (guitar), Brendan (drums).*

Hardcore band ADVERISTY were found in 1986 releasing the demo 'You Can Run But You Can't Hide' demo the following year.
LOST IT ALL, Manic Ears ACHE 13 (1988). Wasted Life / Jester / Destinized / Religions For Sale / No More Wars / Smash The Odds / Lost It All / Total Extremes / Metaphysics / Fight Back / Angel To Bread.

ADX

FRANCE — *Phil (vocals), Herve Marquis (guitar), Yves Louis XV (guitar), Deuch (bass), Didier Dog (drums.).*

ADX came to being in 1982 and have surprisingly managed to retain a stable line-up until relatively recently. All their albums until 'Weird Visions' are sung in their native tongue. 'Le Terrieur' was produced by Laurent Thibault. In 1999 ex-guitarist Pascal Betov featured as a studio guest on CARNIVAL IN COAL's irreverent cover of OZZY OSBOURNE's 'Bark At The Moon' on their 'French Cancan' album.
EXECUTION, Madrigal MAD2009 (1984). Dresse Du Crime / Prisonnier De La Nuit / L'Etranger / Execution / Le Fleau De Dieu / Piere De Satan / Vampire / Caligula.
CHAPIRE II—LE TERREUR, Sydney Music 11027 (1986). Les Enfants De L'Ombre / Marquis Du Mal / Alesia / Le Terreur / Memoire De L'Eternal / Le Blason De La Monte / Tourmente Et Paseion.
SUPREMATIE, Sydney Music 11052 (1987). Nostromo / Suprematie / Le Judgement De Salem / Notre Dame De Paris / Victime / Les Secrets De L'Olympe / Broceliende / La Peur Et L'Oubli / L'Order Sacre.
EXECUTION PUBLIQUE, Sydney / Musidisc 191101 (1989). Memoire De L'Eternal / Le Judgement De Salem / Broceliande / Caligula / Les Enfants De L'Ombre / L'Etranger / L'Ordre Sacre / Tourmente Et Passion.
WEIRD VISIONS, Noise N0161 (1991). Weird Visions / King Of Pain / Lost Generation / Sacrifice In The Ice / Mystical Warfare / Fortune Telling / Behind The Mirror / Sign Of The Time / Trouble / Invasion / Kill The King.
IN MEMORIUM, XIII Bis (1997). Le Fleau De Dieu / Notre Dame De Paris / Fortune Telling / L'Etrangeur / Memoire De L'Eternel (Live) / L'Ordre Sacré / Deesse Du Crime / Sign Of The Time / Suprematie / Les Enfants De L'Ombre (Live) / Marquis Du Mal ('98 version) / King Of Pain / Broceliande (Live) / Caligula / Lost Generation / Tourmente Et Passion.
RESURRECTION, Execution Productions (1998). Intro: VII / Resistance / L'Ombre Du Desespoir / Le Maudit / L'Esprit Malade / De L'Autre Cote / La Dame En Noire / Jeux De Chair / Resurrection / Marquis Du Mal.
VIII SENTENCE—LIVE, AxeKiller (2000). Nostromo / Resurrection / Notre Dame De Paris / Desse Du Crime / La Dame Noire / Marquis Du Mal / L'ordre Sacre / De L'autre Ca'te / Broceliande / Caligula / XII / Resistance / Medley / Suprematie.

AECRON

ASIKKALA, FINLAND — *E. Hereticius (vocals / guitar / drums), Krim Reaper (guitar), J. Karjalainen (bass).*

Asikkala Thrash Metal band AECRON comprises vocalist / guitarist / drummer E. Hereticius (a.k.a. E. Paavola), of ARGANATH, AZAROK, FUNERIUM and TYR repute, alongside guitarist Krim Reaper (K. Höök) and bassist J. Karjalainen. The outfit, initiated in 2005, at first traded under the THÖ ROJEKTI banner, this antecedent unit featuring formative personnel guitarist J. Niemeläinen and drummer V. Härkönen. THÖ ROJEKTI issued a 2004 EP 'Kalman Kaunis Tyttö', the demo 'Thö Rojekti', another 2004 EP 'White Man', the video 'Songs That We Destroyed' and an EP 'Aecron' in 2005.

As AECRON, Stay Brutal distributed the May 2005 demo 'Old Scars'. The 'Rehearsal Scheisse' set followed in July.
Old Scars, Aecron (2005) (Demo). War / Fallen / No Sign Of (Fucking) Life / White Man / Kalmankaunis / Veljeni / New God / Aecron / The Unknown Harmony.
Rehearsal Scheisse, Aecron (2005) (Demo). Fallen / War / Veljeni / No Sign Of (Fucking) Life / (Untitled).

AETURNUS DOMINION

CENTRAL COAST, NSW, AUSTRALIA — *Jester (vocals), Demented (vocals /. guitar), Thrax (guitar / vocals), Spud (bass), Ozi (drums).*

New South Wales Death Metal band forged in 2003, issuing the 'Terrorize' demo that same year. Upfront of September 2004 recordings AETURNUS DOMINION parted ways with singer Jester. Guitarist Demented duly took over the role of vocalist as the band persevered as a quartet. The 'Semper Tyrannis' album was originally released in June of 2004 as a self financed effort, being subsequently re-issued by Statue Records. AETURNUS DOMINION line-up changes in 2005 saw the exit of guitarist Spud and bassist Rat, replaced by the TRITURA duo of Thrax and Lex. However, Spud returned, ousting Lex.

AETURNUS DOMINION paid tribute to late PANTERA and DAMAGEPLAN guitarist "Dimebag" Darrell Abbott with their rendition of 'Mouth For war' being donated to 'The Art Of Shredding—A Tribute To Dime' assembled by DarkStar Records.

The band teamed up with fellow Australian act THE FUROR and Dubai, United Arab Emirates band NERVECELL for the "Metalstock Road Rage" Tour, commencing at Australia's Arthouse in Melbourne on Friday, March 30th 2007, followed by five more shows including Adelaide, Wagga Wagga, Wollongong, Canberra and Sydney.
Terrorize, (2003). Aeternus Dominion / Unsanitized / Traumatic Amputation / Solitude Of My Soul / Global Cremation Suicide / Meathook / Terrorize.
SEMPER TYRANIS, Statue (2004). Holocaust / God Has Failed / Aeternus Dominion / They Wait / Unsanitized / Global Cremation Suicide / Meathook / Unholy / Cyanide.

AEVUM

LIMA, PERU — *Christopher Bryson (vocals / guitar), Jarot Mansilla (guitar), José A.Gazzo (bass), Kenneth Nava (keyboards), Alejandro Benavides (drums).*

Lima Power Metal band AEVUM began life billed as ABSOLOTU in 2000, prior to adopting ETERNA. The opening Thrash influenced ABSOLOTU formation counted guitarists Carlos Galiano and Christopher Bryson, bassist Rodolfo Cáceres, keyboard player Kenneth Nava and drummer Alejandro Benavides. The group evolved into ETERNA in 2001 as they struck out into a Power Metal direction, adding vocalist Gustavo F. Zaferson to the ranks. Under their revised name they debuted with the demo 'Pandaemonium' in July of 2003, this session featuring a cover of HELLOWEEN's 'Phantoms Of Death'. Changes in the line-up saw Ian Halfin assuming vocals, then Rodrigo Prado and bass delegated to Ricardo B. Praelli then José A.Gazzo. On the guitar front Galiano would be superseded by Jarot Mansilla.

As AEVUM the band re-debuted with the demo 'Wisdom Of Light'. The EP 'Heaven Burns', recorded in October of 2004, would be scheduled for 2005 release. With Prado's exit, Bryson took over vocal duties.
Heaven Burns, (2004). Angeluz (In Nomine Patris) / Prince Of The Dawn / Ragnarok / Genesis / Wisdom Of Light / White Menace.
Pandaemonium, (2004). Wisdom Of Light / Pandaemonium / Phantoms Of Death.

AFTER ALL (pic: Cindy Frey)

AFTER ALL

BRUGES, BELGIUM — *Piet Focroul (vocals), Dries Van Damme (guitar), Christophe Depree (guitar), Erwin Casier (bass), Chris De Neve (drums).*

Bruges Heavy Metal band AFTER ALL, although undergoing some radical shifts in musical approach over various releases, has maintained a stable band line up since 1992. By 2002 AFTER ALL had rediscovered their roots and issued and out and out retro Heavy Metal album. The band debuted with a self financed four track EP 'Dusk', of which only 500 copies were pressed. Signing to the Donor label the band recorded the first album 'Wonder', produced by LA MUERTE guitarist Dee J., in 1995.

The 1999 album 'Dead Loss' would find the band exploiting melancholy, almost Gothic themes. Nevertheless, the bands roots were still on display as former CYCLONE vocalist by Guido Gevels aided on guest vocals for the opening track. A 2001 split 12" EP 'Armageddon Come', in alliance with DOUBLE DIAMOND, surfaced on the collectable Steelhunter label. AFTER ALL signed the Belgian Mausoleum label for recording of their sophomore Harris Johns produced album 'Mercury Rising'. The record also came in a lavish gatefold white vinyl variant through TPL Records. Released in Russia and the Baltic States through CD Maximum Records 'Mercury Rising' would be clad in a different sleeve art for those territories. AFTER ALL would support ANTHRAX on their March 2003 dates and again in June. Further high profile gigs came in October as the group landed supports to AGENT STEEL and the November OVERKILL and SEVEN WITCHES European tour.

The band entered Spiderhouse Studio in Berlin to cut the 2004 opus 'The Vermin Breed' opus, recorded and mixed by veteran producer Harris Johns. AFTER ALL drummer Kevin Strubbe would act as stand in for SEVEN WITCHES for European tour dates. AFTER ALL would open Low Countries gigs for RAGE in January 2005. That same month the band negotiated a new recording deal with newly established German label Dockyards 1, a concern co-owned by IRON SAVIOR's Piet Sielck. Another German label, Killer Metal Records, released 'The Vermin Breed' as a limited edition pressing of 500 LPs on blue vinyl clad in exclusive artwork. March found the band acting as support to AGENT STEEL's European tour. The band also put in a brace of guest slots to METAL CHURCH in June then supported HEATHEN in July. AFTER ALL provided support to the DESTRUCTION, CANDLEMASS and DEATHCHAIN touring package in November.

AFTER ALL's Dockyard 1 debut 'This Violent Decline', recorded by Dee J. at Hype Studio in Mechelen, emerged in July 2006. The band teamed up with VICIOUS RUMORS and AGENT STEEL for the 'Alienigma' European Tour 2007 beginning in early September.

Dusk EP, All (1992). Soulcrise / A Utopic Thought / Blind Euphoria / Rivalry To Whom.
WONDER, Donor (1995). Pleading For Heart / Wonder / Victim Of Your Television / Witchcraft / I Don't Care / The Blood And The Mission / Ride The Snake (Breaking Down The Doors) / Afraid / Distress / Sense Of Hate / Seven Hyades.
TRANSCENDENT, Watt's'On (1997). Sixteen, Black Sunday / Behind The Mask (Part I) / The Force Within / Darkest Rage / Burn A Hole / Damaged Trust / The Last Sigh / Selfdestruct / On Forbidden Grounds / The Avenger / Visionary Thoughts / June / Behind The Mask (Part II).
No Recollection, CanniBaelus (2000) (Split single with PATRIARCH). No Recollection.
DEAD LOSS, Rokorola (2000). Erase Your Past / Self-Inflicted / A Sweet Departure / Fragments Of Time / Condemned Heritage / Into The Sun / Reflection Of The Light / Lost—Insane / The Rapture / A Sweet Departure (Edit).
Armageddon Come EP, Steelhunter (2001) (Split EP with DOUBLE DIAMOND). Candle Of Burning Red / Taste The Bitterness.
The Bereaved EP, Near Dark (2001). Exhale (Including A Sweet Departure) / Turn The Tide.
MERCURY RISING, Mausoleum (2002). Mercury Rising / Beneath The Flesh / Rectify / Whispering Words / Crave For More / Descending Pain / The Shadow Wall / For Us Immortals / Immortals—The Aftermath / Last Day Of Winter / Twist Of Fate / Black God, White Devil / Beneath The Flesh (Video) / For Us Immortals (Video).
THE VERMIN BREED, Dockyard 1 (2005). Forgotten / Maze Of Being / The Insufferable / Unnamed Sorrow / The Great Divide / Reasonable Doubt / Cascade / Deny The Dream / Downward / Descending Pain (video) / The Vermin Breed (video).
THE VERMIN BREED, Killer Metal (2005) (Limited edition 500 copies blue vinyl). Forgotten / Maze Of Being / The Insufferable / Unnamed Sorrow / The Great Divide / Reasonable Doubt / Cascade / Deny The Dream / Downward.
THIS VIOLENT DECLINE, Dockyard 1 (2006).

AFTER FOREVER

ST. JOHN'S, NF, CANADA — *Dan Moore (vocals / guitar), Keith Bradbury (guitar), Dwayne Pike (bass), Kevin Dominic (drums).*

Newfoundland Thrashers AFTER FOREVER featured ex-SACRAMENT A.D. guitarist Danny Moore and drummer Kevin Dominic. The band's 1992 cassette release 'Visions Of Darkness' featured a line-up of Dan Moore on lead vocals and guitar, second guitarist Rick Hollett, bassist Dwayne Pike with Kevin Dominic on the drums. A two song follow up entitled 'Breathe' had Keith Bradbury replacing Hollett. AFTER FOREVER issued the 'Death Of One' album in 1994.

Post AFTER FOREVER Moore became a member of highly respected Stoners SHEAVY as well as HARDLINER. Rick Hollett joined Alt-Rockers TIMBER. Dwayne Pike opted out of Rock n' Roll and became a police officer.

Visions Of Darkness, Afterforever (1992).
DEATH OF ONE, (1994).
Breathe, (1996). Breathe / Brother's Keeper.

AFTERDEATH

LISBON, PORTUGAL — *Sergio Paulo (vocals), Nuno Maciel (guitar), José Ramos (bass), Mário Rui (drums).*

Lisbon Death Metal act AFTERDEATH, founded in 1990 mix a blend of Thrash Metal and Hardcore on their 1995 album 'Backwords'. The band comprised singer Sergio Paulo, guitarist Nuno Maciel, bassist José Ramos and drummer Mário Rui. AFTERDEATH tested the water with a brace of demos 'Unreal Sight' and 'Behind Life', the first of these seeing a recording line-up including erstwhile THORNADO personnel guitarist Virgílio Neto, bass player Roberto Monteiro and drummer Filipe Martins.

This new formation recorded the track 'Dark Atmosphere' for inclusion on the compilation 'Sometimes Death Is Better' released by the Belgian Shiver Records label. In February of 1994, AFTERDEATH recorded a further demo 'Unreal Sight' but then once again went through line-up changes, at first re-installing Nuno Maciel both soon substituting him for Vítor Silva. In addition, José Ramos assumed bass duties. In July of 1995 AFTERDEATH recorded the album 'Backwards' at Rec n' Roll Studios with producer Luís Barros of TARANTULA fame. However, the band had once again undergone a membership overhaul. AFTERDEATH's final performance would be the song "World Deformed By Man' included on the 'Guardians of Metal Vol. IV' compilation released through Guardians of Metal.

Behind Life, (1992). Intro / Digital Horizons / Afterdeath / Heart Of Fire / Fortune.
Unreal Sight, (1994). Justice Manipulation / Live For Today / Speaks On Your Thoughts / Hunger Calling / Deep In Natural Art.
BACKWORDS, Guardians Of Metal (1995). Caught In The Web / Swallowed / Drowning / Within My Self / Eye For War / Undertow / Digital Horizons / Without Words / Confidence Betrayed / View (From Behind) / Dye In Agony.

AFTERMATH

BELFAST, NORTHERN IRELAND, UK — *Kev McVeigh (guitar), Jon Hope (guitar), Chris Brady (bass), Charles Canning (drums).*

Belfast's AFTERMATH was assembled as a secondary school act during 1999, initially formed up as a quartet of guitarists Jon Hope and Kev McVeigh, bass player Chris Brady and drummer Eoin Devenney. Despite the musicians only being sixteen years old at the time this combo cut the 2000 demo 'S.S. Deity', scoring valuable praise from such mainstream media as 'Terrorizer' magazine. Gigs to support this session included supports to WAYLANDER and appearances at a Chuck Schuldiner tribute gig and the 'Fastfude' mini-festival.

The band entered Doghouse Studios in 2002 to craft the follow up demo 'To Die Or To Seize'. Released in early 2003 this set of recordings once again elicited positive feedback. AFTERMATH also featured on the compilation album 'Staring Back At The Present', also being chosen to appear at the launch gig for this record alongside STAND UP GUY, CONDEMNED and Scotland's MADMAN IS ABSOLUTE. Charles Canning would subsequently assume the drum role. The band supported GOD DETHRONED at the Dublin Temple venue in September of 2003.

For gigs in early 2005 supporting NAILED and SKYFORGER the band pulled in CONDEMNED drummer Willy Taylor. AFTERMATH issued the 7" single 'The Meeting Of Blood With Blood' that same year.

S.S. Deity, Aftermath demo (2000). Self Serving Deity / Prepared For War / Seventh Seal.
To Die Or To Seize, (2002). Gates Of Valhalla / Sands Of Time / Wartorn / The Enemy Within.
The Meeting Of Blood With Blood, (2005). Dies Irae, Dies Illa / War Of Attrition.

AFTERMATH

CHICAGO, IL, USA — *Charlie Tsiolis (vocals), Steve Sacco (guitar), John Lazerty (guitar), Pat Delagarza (bass), Ray Schmidt (drums).*

Chicago based AFTERMATH, fronted by the Greek born Kyriakas "Charlie" Tsiolis, formed in October 1985 issuing the five track demo 'Killing The Future' featuring the tracks 'When Will You Die', 'Going No Place', 'Chaos', 'Meltdown' and 'War For Freedom'. The band pursued a technical minded brand of Thrash that soon set them apart from the pack. Adding bassist John Lazerty, AFTERMATH followed the demo release but then switched Lazerty to second guitar recruiting Pat Delagarza on bass. Featured on the British 'Metal Forces' magazine compilation 'Demolition' in 1988.

A further demo 'Words That Echo Fear' featuring new guitarist John Lovette was released prior to the band demoing for Roadracer Records. Negotiations broke down however and AFTERMATH signed to New York's Big Chief Records. However, this label collapsed forcing AFTERMATH to issue the album under their own steam on the private Thermometer imprint.

AFTERMATH added bassist Chris Waldron in 1990 and released alive four track demo featuring the songs 'Eyes of Tomorrow', 'Afraid Of Time', 'The Act Of Unspoken Wisdom' and 'Reflecting Pictures'.

In January of 1997 the group, retaining a stable line up but augmenting their sound with the addition of DJ Delta 9 and female vocalist Roxanne, retitled themselves MOTHER GOD MOVIESTAR opting to pursue an alternative Rock direction.

Quite famously as AFTERMATH the act lost a notable court case with high profile millionaire rapper DR. DRE over the ownership of the name. The Rapper reportedly made a conciliatory offer of some $50,000 for rights to use the name but would go ahead and use it regardless. Fortunately for the band this period of turmoil had built bridges with Interscope Records. After the name change to MOTHER GOD MOVIESTAR signed to Interscope for the eponymous Electro-Metal debut of March 1998

THE EYES OF TOMORROW, Black Lotus BLRCD 006 (1992). Words That Echo Fear / Eyes Of Tomorrow / Being / Experience / Afraid Of Time / Reflecting Pictures / Change Of Mood / The Act Of Unspoken Wisdom / Whisper Of A Dream / Proud Reflex / Snuff.

AGENT STEEL

LOS ANGELES, CA, USA — *Bruce Hall (vocals), Juan Garcia (guitar), Bernie Versailles (guitar), Karlos Medina (bass), Rigo Amezcua (drums).*

Created by ex-SCEPTRE and ABATTOIR frontman John Cyriis, Los Angeles based AGENT STEEL soon forged a reputation for surgically precise intense metal honed by Cyriis' distinct high altitude vocal range. AGENT STEEL's distinction in the Metal world is also undoubtedly enhanced by the band's Sci-Fi apocalyptic lyrical stance.

Created by frontman John Camps, the roots of AGENT STEEL lay in SANCTUARY, an act which dated back to 1980, when John Cyriis and drummer Chuck Profus co-founded a band under that name in November of that year, which folded during December 1981. Cyriis then forged a short-lived outfit dubbed TOKIX SHOK, initiated by ex-DECEIVER guitarist Kurt "Kilfelt" Colfelt. When this project faltered, Camps was next to be found on the track 'Taken By Force' contributed by SCEPTRE to the Metal Blade Records 1983 compilation album 'Metal Massacre IV'. As guitarist for SCEPTRE, the São Paulo born, Guitar Institute of Technology trained John Camps (a.k.a. João Campos), also featured as lead vocalist on the ABATTOIR track 'Screams From The Grave'. Camps, renaming himself 'John Syriis', later 'Cyriis', had auditioned for the position of lead vocalist with ABATTOIR, and, demonstrating an impressive multi-octave range, secured the position easily. However, within six months Cyriis was ousted and along with Chuck Profus engineered a new proposition billed as AGENT STEEL. During the interim, Profus was in a band called ABUSER with bass player George Robb between October 1983 and July 1984.

Subsequently, the pair hooked up with George Robb in August to form AGENT STEEL, rounded out by guitarists Bill Simmons and Mark Marshall. Strangely, John Cyriis issued a statement on September 17th, 1984 claiming that AGENT STEEL had officially changed their name to SANCTUARY—the line-up of the band at this time credited Cyriis, Mark Marshall, John Gott, George Robb and Chuck Profus. This was followed soon afterward, on September 25th, with another statement asking people to disregard the previous letter and stating that "the band is and always will be called Agent Steel"! This inaugural line-up cut the four song '144'000 Gone' demo in 1984.

AGENT STEEL had a complete switch of guitarists when Marshall and Simmons were ejected. Marshall would later make his mark with SAVAGE GRACE. John Gott briefly occupied the six string position before ex-ABATTOIR man Juan Garcia and Kurt "Kilfelt" Colfelt were inducted as permanent members for the groundbreaking, Jay Jones produced 'Skeptics Apocalypse' album. This Jay Jones produced album, released in August 1985, by Combat in the USA and Roadrunner Records in the UK, would make an immediate impact globally. The leading Thrash Metal journal of the time, Britain's 'Metal Forces' magazine, would see editor Bernard Doe citing 'Skeptics Apocalypse' as one of his favourite albums of the year whilst readers voted Cyriis fourth best Metal vocalist. Predictably, this band roster was also to prove fragile. Colfelt would bow out, later gaining recognition with the 'Terror And Submission' album for his new act HOLY TERROR, and in his stead would come the teen protégé of Bernie 'Versailles' Versye.

The band made their first live appearance opening for SLAYER in September 1984 at the Los Angeles Country Club. A brace of headliners later and AGENT STEEL were invited to open dates for British metallers RAVEN. Robb too made his exit in favour of bassist Michael Zaputil. The band released a highly praised EP in September 1985 titled 'Mad Locust Rising', cut at Indigo Ranch Studios in Malibu, California, which featured an extreme cover version of JUDAS PRIEST's 'The Ripper'.

With Thrash Metal riding a high AGENT STEEL put in a notable show at the infamous Dutch 'Aardschok Dag' festival and toured Europe as support to OVERKILL and ANTHRAX, billed the "Speed Metal attack" tour, during May of 1986. The band's media profile would be raised during this period with stories that Cyriis, convinced that a Mayan end times theory was set to signal the end of the world, started to sign his autograph as "2011" - the supposed date of the impending apocalypse.

The 'Unstoppable Force' album, produced by Dan Johnson at Morrisound Studios, only served to heighten the band's reputation although critics did note a mellowing of Cyriis' vocal delivery. AGENT STEEL were by now the subject of numerous major label inquiries and in November 1986 reports leaked out that Capitol Records were showing a serious desire to sign the band. AGENT STEEL showcased successfully for the label but as negotiations dragged on the proposed deal withered. 'Unstoppable Force' emerged in March 1987.

Garcia quit to form EVIL DEAD with his ex-ABATTOIR colleague bassist Mel Sanchez. Garcia, alongside future TESTAMENT and SLAYER drummer John Dette, would also found the Spanish language Metal band TERROR cutting the Mexican release album 'Hijos De Los Cometas'.

Cyriis and Profus, now relocated to Florida, conducted a European tour by drafting in hired hands. Guitarists JAMES MURPHY and Jay Weslord figuring among their number. Another musician to be included in the AGENT STEEL ranks would be ex-PURGATORY bassist Richard Bateman.

This variant of AGENT STEEL, strangely decked in bright orange boiler suits, put in a London Hammersmith Odeon gig on June 20th supported by NUCLEAR ASSAULT, ATOMKRAFT and ONSLAUGHT.

In December 1987 members of AGENT STEEL were arrested in Arizona on charges of aggravated assault on a youth. The bizarre allegations centred upon a 17 year old male (actually a band roadie) the band had allegedly tied to a bed whilst they subsequently urinated on him and exploded firecrackers on his chest. Charges were dropped, but the group folded shortly after following another strange incident in which Cyriis allegedly tried to force band members to get AGENT STEEL tattoos. Whether the rumours of forced tattooing are true or not are unclear but the fact remains that many of Cyriis' former associates sport AGENT STEEL tattoos.

In 1988 AGENT STEEL officially disbanded. Whilst Cyriis, Garcia, Hill and Profus assembled the short-lived PONTIUS PROPHET, issuing a two-track demo 'Rites Of Hatred' that same year, guitarist JAMES MURPHY later joined HALLOWS EVE, DEATH, OBITUARY and CANCER. He would also figure in the ever fluid TESTAMENT line-up, record with Danes KONKHRA and release solo product.

Cyriis would declare his intention to retire in 1988. Profus would put his efforts into a new venture billed as MALFEITOR in union with ex-PONTIUS PROPHET guitarist Michael Hill. Intriguingly it was soon revealed that MALFEITOR's vocalist 'Max Kobol' was in truth none other than John Cyriis. Cyriis / Kobol would next be spotted as frontman for Tampa, Florida band LEMEGETON appearing on their 'Evil Against Evil' demo. Cyriis re-emerged in 1990 fronting New York's BLACK REIGN.

Ex-member Richard Bateman was added to the NASTY SAVAGE ranks in 1989. A decade later Bateman founded AFTER DEATH with ex-MORBID ANGEL, NOCTURNUS and INCUBUS man Mike Browning. Bateman would later tragically be killed in a car accident.

AGENT STEEL reformed in 1999 prompted by an offer to perform at the annual German 'Wacken Open Air' festival. German label Century Media would aid their cause by re-issuing their entire back catalogue. AGENT STEEL's reformation line-up now comprised ex-SYBIL singer Bruce Hall, guitarists Juan Garcia and Bernie Versailles, erstwhile EVIL DEAD bassist Karl Medina and drummer Chuck Profus.

Versailles also contributed the ENGINE project album assembled by ARMOURED SAINT's Joey Vera and FATES WARNING's Ray Alder. He would also act as live guitarist for FATES WARNING too.

The band cut another JUDAS PRIEST track 'Beyond The Realms Of Death' for the Dwell Records tribute album 'Hell Bent For Metal'. This track would also be included as a bonus track on American release versions, on the Metal Blade label, of the band's uncompromisingly intense comeback album 'Omega Conspiracy'.

The band toured Germany in early 2000 on a package bill with RIOT, ANVIL and DOMINE. Cyriis, apparently now going under the title of 'Max Havlock', resurfaced again in 2000 with a fresh act titled OUTER GATEWAYS.

AGENT STEEL would re-title themselves ORDER OF THE ILLUMINATI for new recording projects in 2001. As such the band laid down a cover of BLACK SABBATH's 'Hole In The Sky' for donation to a tribute album 'Evil Lives: A True Metal Tribute To Black Sabbath'. The same year would witness the retirement of Profus with Rigo Amezcua taking over the drum stool for the band's appearance at the 'Kalamazoo Metal' festival. Versailles would also find time to act as producer for Death Metal band SADISTIC INTENT.

As 2002 dawned it appeared that the relationship between Cyriis and the ongoing band had had defrosted somewhat with a possibility that the next studio album may emerge under the AGENT STEEL banner after all. In March the band performed the second annual 'Hellfest' event in Whittier, California ranked alongside fellow vets EXODUS. In December former frontman John Cyriis resurfaced in a new band unit STELLAR SEED.

AGENT STEEL signed to the Italian based Scarlet label to issue the 'Order Of The Illuminati' album, under the AGENT STEEL banner, in May 2003. UK and European dates projected into October 2003, dubbed the 'Bonded By Metal' trek, found AGENT STEEL co-headlining a billing comprising EXODUS, NUCLEAR ASSAULT, GOD DETHRONED, MORTICIAN, OCCULT and CALLENISH CIRCLE. However, the band dropped off this billing half way through the trek due to disagreements with the booking agency.

AGENT STEEL announced a high profile return to the live circuit with an appearance at the 'Keep It True IV' festival held in April 2005 at the Tauberfrankenhalle in Lauda-Koenigshofen, Germany. They would use this opportunity to celebrate the 20th anniversary of the 'Skeptics Apocalypse' by performing the Thrash classic in its entirety. Regular European gigs saw Belgian Thrashers AFTER ALL as support. That same month Bruce Hall was announced as new frontman for STEEL PROPHET.

On 9th July 2005 AGENT STEEL lined up at The Pound outdoor amphitheatre in San Francisco alongside TESTAMENT, VICIOUS RUMORS, LÄÄZ ROCKIT, HIRAX, DREAMS OF DAMNATION, DEKAPITATOR, MUDFACE, NEIL TURBIN, BROCAS HELM and IMAGIKA for the 'Thrash Against Cancer' benefit. Working with producer Bill Metoyer the band entered the studio on 17th October to craft a new album. AGENT STEEL announced signature with Dutch label Mascot Records in July 2006.

Former AGENT STEEL players bass player George Robb and drummer Chuck Profus returned to the scene in 2006 with OBSCENE GESTURE, a union with frontman Guy Green and the STEEL PROPHET and BODY COUNT credited Vincent Dennis on guitar.

AGENT STEEL teamed up with VICIOUS RUMORS and AFTER ALL for the 'Alienigma' European Tour 2007 beginning in early September.

144,000 Gone, (1984). 144,000 Gone / Evil Eye, Evil Minds / Agents Of Steel / Bleed For The Gods.
Agent Steel, (1984). Evil Eye, Evil Minds / Agents Of Steel / Bleed For The Gods / 144,000 Gone / Guilty As Charged.
SKEPTICS APOCALYPSE, Roadrunner RR 9759 (1985). The Calling / Taken By Force / Bleed For The Godz / 144'000 Gone / Back To Reign / Agents Of Steel / Evil Eye / Children Of The Sun / Guilty As Charged.
MAD LOCUST RISING, Music For Nations KUT124 (1985). The Swarm Is Upon Us / Mad Locust Rising / The Ripper / Let It Be Done / The Day At Guyana.
THE UNSTOPPABLE FORCE, Music For Nations MFN 66 (1987). Unstoppable Force / Never Surrender / Indestructive / Chosen To Stay / Still Searchin' / Rager / The Day At Guyana / Nothing Left / Traveller.
OMEGA CONSPIRACY, Metal Blade 39841438-2 (1999). Destroy The Hush / Illuminati Is Machine / Fighting Backwards / New Godz / Know Your Master / Infinity / Awaken The Swarm / Into The Nowhere / Bleed Forever / It's Not What You Think.
Earth Under Lucifer, Scarlet SC 075-2 (2003). Earth Under Lucifer / Mad Locust Rising (Live) / Unstoppable Force (Live) / Agents Of Steel (Live).
ORDER OF THE ILLUMINATI, Scarlet SCCD0632 (2003). Avenger / Ten Fists Of Nations / Earth Under Lucifer / Enslaved / Insurrection / Apocalypse / Forever Black / Dance Of St. Vitus / Dead Eyes / Kontrol / Human Bullet Brainwashed.

AGGRESSION

MONTREAL, QC, CANADA — *Butcher (vocals), Sasquatch Barth (guitar), Burn (guitar), Dug Bugger (bass), Gate (drums).*

Originally formed as ASYLUM in late 1985, this Québec five piece were based in Montreal. After a four track demo in 1986, counting a band line up of vocalist Butcher, guitarists Death and Burn, bass player Dug Bugger and drummer Gate, and another 5 track demo later that year the band managed to get a track on the Greenworld Records, 'Speed Metal Hell II' compilation and another 2 tracks on the New Renaissance compilation 'Thrash Metal Attack'. By this juncture Death had exited, being superseded by Sasquatch Barth. A proposed debut album entitled 'Forgotten Skeleton' was recorded for the Facemelt label during 1986 but disagreements between the two parties led to these tapes being shelved.

In 1987 Cactus Pete replaced Butcher on vocals and Stephan Prudhomme replaced Gate on drums shortly after. The band recorded a couple of solid albums but disbanded shortly after. News arrived in mid 2002 that guitarist Denis 'Sasquatch' Barth, now involved with CRADLE TO GRAVE, had plans to revitalise the band and issue the 1986 shelved album 'Forgotten Skeleton' re-billed as AGGRESSION A.D.

AGGRESSION announced they were to play their first show in over sixteen years at the Le Saphir venue in Montreal on 27th May 2005. The event was planned to comprise the original line-up of singer Botcher, guitarists Sasquatch and Burn, bassist Dug Bugger and drummer Gate, the latter "If released from jail in time". Sasquatch's current band CRADLE TO GRAVE would also be on the bill. As it transpired, Gate was substituted by Jeremy for the proceedings, apparently due to illness on the original drummer's part.

FORGOTTEN SKELETON, Facemelt (1986).
THE FULL TREATMENT, Banzai (1988). Forsaken Survival / Frozen Aggressor / Green Goblin / One For The Woods / Dripping Flesh / By The Reaping Hook / Demolition / Rotten By Torture / The Final Massacre.

AGGRESSION CORE

USA — *James King (vocals), Curran Murphy (guitar), John Winters (guitar), Eric Close (bass), Henry Rice (drums).*

Seattle Thrashers dating back to 1994, debuting with the self financed 'Dead God' the following year. AGGRESSION CORE guitarist Curran Murphy would tour with the esteemed Seattle Metal band NEVERMORE and later join renowned Canadian Thrashers ANNIHILATOR. Completing a full eight years service with the band drummer and founder member Dale Puckett was ousted in 2002, joining Seattle's AGONY OF DECEIT. He would also unite with former AGGRESSION CORE members Jeff Bloomfield and Joe Jauregui in the Seattle based FURY 161.

AGGRESSION CORE were reported to have folded in August of 2003 but news then emerged a new album was in the works. Intriguingly the band's headline on their official website would state "Curran Murphy is no longer associated in any way, shape or form with the band Aggression Core, its name, music or likeness of any sort".

DEAD GOD, Independent (1995).
AGGRESSION CORE, Peak (2000). Invisible Empire / Pure / So What If I Murder / Loser / Drown In Your Pain / Face Down / Hypervoid / Strung / Let It Be Dead / Visionary / Disillusion.
VICTIM OR ENEMY, (2002). Victim Or Enemy / Talk To Me / Forgive / What Your Life Has Become / Dethroned / Dreaming Of Murder / My Hate, My Pain / Shine / I Hate You / Broken Back / (Fuck You) Nazi Boy / Drunk.

AGGRESSIVE

GOTHENBURG, SWEDEN — *Eerie (vocals), Christer Van Der Rock (guitar), Jones (bass), Johan The Grindmaster (drums).*

Gothenburg Thrash Metal act. AGGRESSIVE's debut demo, 'Aggressive Behaviour' released in December 2000, comprised entirely of cover versions numbering BLACK SABBATH's 'Symptom Of The Universe', MOTÖRHEAD's 'I Am The Sword', DRAIN's 'Klotera' and SEPULTURA's 'Slave New World'. Indeed, the band had started life in Gothenburg as a covers band dubbed ACILLATEM of vocalist / guitarist Fredrik, bassist Andreas and drummer Eerie. A line-up change saw the exit of Andreas but the introduction of Axl on lead guitar. Tragically, this newest member would commit suicide. ACILLATEM persevered, drafting Jonas on bass. Chris of Oi! Band PERKELE was pulled in on guitar as Eerie and Jonas activated Punk side endeavour LOWLIFE. With Eerie handling both lead vocals and drums the newly billed AGGRESSIVE recorded the first demo. After these sessions André took over on drums but his tenure would be brief.

The 'Aggressive Behaviour #2' session, this time four originals, followed in 2001 with Johan the Grindmaster on drums. AGGRESSIVE's next move would be to enter Rivertoon Studios to craft the nine track 'World Of Hate' release. Ructions resulted in the exit, then return of Eerie. A permanent casualty though would be Fredrik, replaced by Peter Stranne. However, this latest candidate would also leave. The 'Death/Degenerate' demo was recorded in February 2004.

Aggressive Behaviour, Aggressive (2000) (Demo). Symptom Of The Universe / I Am The Sword / Klotera / Slave New World.
Aggressive Behaviour #2, Aggressive (2001) (Demo). Rock 'n' Roll Bitch / The Chosen One / Aggressive Behaviour / Time.

AGGRESSOR

World Of Hate, Aggressive (2002) (Demo). No Reason / Insomnia / World Of Hate / Dead Forever / Long Gone Love / Rot In Hell / Upon The Cross / Lord Of Destruction / Same Old Shit.
Death/Degenerate, Aggressive (2004) (Demo). Time Will Tell / Bright Shining White / World Down Fall / Death/Degenerate / Slow Fade / Bodies.

AGGRESSOR

TALLINN, ESTONIA — *Villem Tarvas (vocals / guitar), Kristo Kotkas (guitar), Marek Piliste (bass), Marko Atso (drums).*

Tallinn Thrash / Death outfit AGGRESSOR date to 1989, first making their mark on the Estonian Metal scene with the 1990 demo session 'Indestructible' and debuting live on 17th April that year. Band line-up comprised vocalist / guitarist Villem Tarvas, guitarist Kristo Kotkas, bassist Marek 'Cram' Piliste with Marko Atso on the drums. A 1991 demo preceded the cassette album 'Procreate The Petrifications', this recorded at the Townhall Studios in May of 1992, released on the Theka label and promoted with gigs in Moscow. 'Of Long Duration Anguish' followed in 1994 for Fugata Records. During 1999 a change in style prompted a name change to NO BIG SILENCE.

'Procreate The Petrifications' was re-issued in 2004 with bonus demo tracks. Drummer Marko Atso subsequently figured as a member of LOITS, HUMAN GROUND and SOLWAIG.

Aggressor, (1991). Meaningless Life / Don't Be So Stupid / Lifestyle / Legal Requirement.
PROCREATE THE PETRIFACTIONS, Theka EHL 001 (1993). Legal Requirement / Wrong Faith / Meaningless Life / Fire Below The Ash / Procreate The Petrifactions / Fear The Future / Never End The Odds / Lifestyle / Widow's Mourning / Don't Be So Stupid.
OF LONG DURATION ANGUISH, Fugata FUGCD 1001 (1994). Path Of The Lost God / Unholy Trinity / The Dark Tower / Sanctimonious / Fled Into Immunity / Enchantress Of Desires / Immaculate Conception / Those Who Leave In The End / Of Long Duration Anguish / Russian Vodka.

AGNOSTIC FRONT

NEW YORK, NY, USA — *Roger Miret (vocals), Vinnie Stigma (guitar), Lenny DiSclafani (guitar), Mike Gallo (bass), Steve Gallo (drums).*

New York's AGNOSTIC FRONT date back to 1982 and debuted with the heavily Hardcore influenced 'Victim Of Pain' album. Strangely a lot of the lyrical content of this album was the work of CARNIVORE's Pete Steele. The initial recording line-up comprised the heavily tattooed front man Roger Miret, guitarists Vinnie Stigma and Alex Kinon, bassist Rob Kabula and drummer Louie 'Raybeez' Beatto.

Guitarist Alex Kinon departed after the release of 1986's 'Cause For Alarm' to have his position filled by ex-NYC MAYHEM guitarist Gordon Ancis. AGNOSTIC FRONT added drummer Joe 'Fish' Montanero at this juncture. Ancis having left to form ZERO HOUR, a short-lived act that also involved singer Joe Haggerty, ex-WHIPLASH drummer T.J. Scaglione, former MASSACRE guitarist Robbie Goodwin and DEATHRASH bassist Pat Burns.

Vinnie Stigma also quit shortly after but returned to record 'Liberty And Justice' as the band completely re-evolved itself. AGNOSTIC FRONT drafted Alan Peterson bass guitar, drummer Will Sheplar and ex-STRAW DOGS guitarist Steve Martin. However, the album, produced by Norman Dunn and Alex Perialas, was overshadowed by Miret's imprisonment on drug charges.

AGNOSTIC FRONT added ex-SMEGMA, MAYHEM, YOUTH OF TODAY and REST IN PIECES bassist Craig Setari, coming into the fold after recording of the album on which Alan Peters performs drum duties. Montanero had joined British Punks GBH for their 1992 record 'Church Of The Truly Warped'.

The 1992 Don Fury produced album 'One Voice', recorded with guitarist Matt Henderson, has a central theme based on Miret's two year sojourn in prison. Reaction to the album was muted and by late 1992 AGNOSTIC FRONT had splintered yet again. Stigma, Sheplar and Matt soon had MADBALL up and running whilst Miret opted for a day job as a motorbike mechanic. In a surreal twist of fate Miret broke his back within month's stage diving at a show by his younger brother's band. Eventually Stigma opted out of MADBALL to concentrate on family life.

AGNOSTIC FRONT was drawn together in 1997 quite by coincidence when Miret and Stigma were invited onstage to jam at a MADBALL show. With MADBALL guitarist Hoya handing his guitar over to Miret AGNOSTIC FRONT were reunited. Kabula was drawn away from his act AGAINST THE GRAIN for the reunion.

Miret guested on RANCID's 1998 album 'Life Won't Wait' guesting on two tracks. RANCID returned the favour when Tim Armstrong and Lars Fredericksen showed up on AGNOSTIC FRONT's 'Something's Gotta Give' album. That same year leading Industrial Metal band FEAR FACTORY covered 'Your Mistake' for inclusion on their limited edition 'Revolution' album.

1999 found Miret guesting on the track 'Faster Than The World' on fellow New York Hardcore mongers H20's 'FTTW' album. The singer also produced the debut album from UNDER THE GUN. Meanwhile, AGNOSTIC FRONT released a three track single 'Puro De Madre' all sung in Spanish and their first album for Epitaph 'Something's Gotta Give'.

By 2000 Sheplar had created AMONG THIEVES with erstwhile LIFE OF AGONY bassist Alan Robert and SPUDMONSTERS man Scott Roberts. Roger Miret turns up with his kin Denise Miret on the 2000 album by LADY LUCK 'Life In Between'. By 2002 drummer Jimmy Colletti, acting as lead vocalist, was touting his new side project LOVED AND HATED, a union with SON OF SKAM guitarist Larry Nieroda and MINOR DISTURBANCE drummer Mike Reese.

AGNOSTIC FRONT, supported by ASSERT, would tour Britain in July of 2002. The band revealed an impressive package tour of Europe, dubbed the 'Eastpack Resistance' dates, during November and December. Co-headlined with BIOHAZARD the pair topped a billing of HATEBREED, DISCIPLINE, ALL BORO KINGS, DEATH THREAT, and BORN FROM PAIN. The band announced touring plans for 2003, participating in THE MISFITS led 'Misfits Fiend Fest' US dates in June alongside THE DAMNED, THE DICKIES, BALZAC and D.I. Yet more gigs that same month had the band forming up part of the 'Jailhouse Rock' trek alongside BIOHAZARD, HATEBREED, THROWDOWN and FULL BLOWN CHAOS.

In the Spring of 2004 a new album with the working title 'Another Voice' was recorded at Planet Z studio in Massachusetts with HATEBREED's Jamey Jasta acting as producer. The studio line-up comprised vocalist Roger Miret, guitarists Vinnie Stigma and Lenny DiSclafani, bass player Mike Gallo and Steve Gallo on drums. In August the band signed to Nuclear Blast Records. A promotional video for the song 'Peace', directed

AGNOSTIC FRONT

by director Dale "Rage" Resteghini, would see a guest inclusion from former AGNOSTIC FRONT guitarist Matt Henderson with Scott Vogel of TERROR and Karl Buechner from EARTH CRISIS and FREYA also making their presence felt. On 7th November AGNOSTIC FRONT filmed their performance at New York's at the legendary CBGBs club for their first DVD collection. The group scheduled US gigs in alliance with HATEBREED, DIECAST, LOVE IS RED and THE AUTUMN OFFERING for the second leg of the 'Heavyweights Of Hardcore' tour in January 2005 prior to European dates. Back on the road in April, AGNOSTIC FRONT headed up a billing combining MARTYR A.D., LOVE IS RED and ALL SHALL PERISH before forming up with HATEBREED for South American gigs in the Summer. The band, having parted ways with guitarist Lenny Disclafani and pulled in Joseph James of INHUMAN in his stead, then undertook a European package tour billed 'Persistence' co-billed with HATEBREED, NAPALM DEATH, BORN FROM PAIN, THE RED CHORD and BLEED THE SKY. Roger Miret made studio time to guest session on German Hardcore band MAROON's 'When Worlds Collide' album.

AGNOSTIC FRONT announced their 2006 season of live campaigning with US dates in March sharing stages SHADOWS FALL, STILL REMAINS, and BYZANTINE.

CAUSE FOR ALARM, Rough Justice JUST 3 (1986). The Eliminator / Existence Of Hate / Time Will Come / Growing Concern / Your Mistake / Out For Blood / Toxic Shock / Bomber Zee / Public Assistance / Shoot His Load / Liberty And Justice / Crucial Moment / Strength / Genesis / Anthem / Another Side / It Happened Yesterday / Lost Land / Hypocrisy / Crucified / Censored.
VICTIM IN PAIN, Combat Core 88561-8181-1 (1986). Victim In Pain / Remind Them / Blind Justice / Last Warning / United And Strong / Hiding Inside / Power / Fascist Attitude / Society Sucker / Your Mistake / With Time.
LIBERTY AND JUSTICE, Rough Justice JUST 8 (1987). Liberty And Justice / Crucial Moment / Strength / Genesis / Anthem / Another Side / Happened Yesterday / Lost / Hypocrisy / Crucified / Censored.
LIVE AT CBGB'S, Combat 3001 (1988). Victim In Pain / Public Assistance / United Blood / Friend Or Foe / Strength / Blind Justice / Last Warning / Toxic Shock / United And Strong / Crucified / Liberty And Justice / Discriminate Me / Your Mistake / Anthem / With Time / Genesis / Pain Song / Fascist Attitudes / Eliminator.
ONE VOICE, Relativity RO 9222 (1992). New Jack / One Voice / Infiltrate / The Tombs / The Fall / My Faith / Undertow / Now And Then / Todd's Song / Retaliate / Forcefeed / Bastard.
TO BE CONTINUED ... THE VERY BEST OF AGNOSTIC FRONT, Rough Justice JUST 20 (1992). Victim In Pain / Your Mistake / Hypocrisy / New Jack / Liberty And Justice / Time Will Come / Power / Society Sucker / Toxic Shock / Public Assistance / Blind Justice / The Eliminator / One Voice / Crucified / United And Strong / Your Mistake / Fascist Attitudes (Live) / Anthem (Live) / Last Warning (Live).
LAST WARNING—LIVE, Roadrunner RR 90782 (1993). Undertow / Your Mistake / Victim In Pain / One Voice / Infiltrate / Strength / United Blood / Public Assistance / Over The Edge / Blind Justice / Last Warning / Crucified / Toxic Shock / United And Strong / Fascist

Attitudes / Anthem / The Eliminator / No One Rules / Final War / Last Warning / Traitor / Friend Or Foe / United Blood / Fight / Discriminate / In Control / Crucial Changes.
RAW UNRELEASED, Grand Theft Auto GTA 002R051 (1995).
Puro De Madre, Epitaph 0414-7 (1998). Puro De Madre.
SOMETHING'S GOTTA GIVE, Epitaph 65362 (1998). Something's Gotta Give / Believe / Gotta Go / Before My Eyes / No Fear / Blinded / Voices / Do Or Die / My War / Bloodsucker / Blame / Today, Tomorrow, Forever / Rage / Pauly The Dog / Crucified.
RIOT RIOT UPSTART, Epitaph (1999).
ANOTHER VOICE, (2004). Still Here / All Is Not Forgotten / Fall Of The Parasite / Pride, Faith, Respect / So Pure To Me / Dedication / Peace / Take Me Back / Hardcore (The Definition) / Casualty Of The Times / No One Hears You / I Live It / It's For Life / Another Voice.

AGONY

STOCKHOLM, SWEDEN — *Peter Lündstrom (vocals), Magnus Sjölin (guitar), Conny Wigström (guitar), Pele Ström (guitar), Nappe Benschemsi (bass), Tommy Moberg (drums).*

A Stockholm Thrash act originating in August 1984 when their Punk influences prevailed, the group was originally titled AGONI and found themselves going in a more Metal oriented direction following the addition of drummer Tommy Moberg and guitarist Magnus Sjölin. The group, still spelling the name AGONI, toured in Britain with Swedish Punk outfit ANTI CIMEX in June and July 1986 having released the 'The Future Is Ours' demo the previous March. With a second demo, 'Execution Of Mankind' released in August 1986, AGONY obtained a deal with Music For Nations in 1987.

Although the 1988 debut album, 'The First Defiance', released through Combat Records in North America, was recorded with two guitarists, Pelle Ström was fired before Christmas 1987. He was to later join KRIXJÄLTERS, OMNITRON and COMECON. After AGONY broke up Tommy Moberg joined RUBBERMEN. Moberg and Sjölin made a return with TRICKBAG in 1995.

Execution Of Mankind, Agony (1986) (Demo). Deadly Legacy / Stealing Your Life / Execution Of Mankind / Bribed / Night Of The Emperor (Live).
THE FIRST DEFIANCE, Under One Flag FLAG 19 (1988). Storm Of The Apocalypse / The First Defiance / Execution Of Mankind / Mass Manipulation / Night Of The Emperor / Shadows Of Fear / Madness Reigns / Deadly Legacy.

AGRESSOR

ANTIBES, FRANCE — *Alex Colin-Tocquaine (vocals / guitar), Adramelech (guitar), Joel Guigou (bass), Gorgor (drums).*

Antibes Black-Thrash Metal trio that recorded their first demo in November 1986, AGRESSOR released a couple more demos and played dates with APOCALYPSE and LIVING DEATH. The band signed to Swedish label Black Mark Production for the 1987 album, subtly titled 'Satan's Sodomy', graced with an album cover showing the immediate after effects of buggery with the devil!

The line-up at this juncture was as a trio of vocalist / guitarist Alex Colin-Tocquaine, bassist J.M. Libeer and drummer Jean Luc Falsini. This incarnation recorded the first two demos 'Merciless Onslaught' and 1987's 'Satan's Sodomy'. Things swiftly changed for the group when AGRESSOR added new drummer Thierry and ex-HELLRAISER bassist Laurent in 1988. The group then signed to Noise, recording 'Neverending Destiny', after which both new men split leaving Alex Colin-Tocquaine to soldier on alone. Thierry joined LOUDBLAST.

Undaunted, Alex put together a brand new line-up of his band, thus the 1992 version of AGRESSOR, which recorded the 'Towards Beyond' album, consisted of Colin-Tocquaine, ex-OUTBURST guitarist Patrick Gibelin, ex-OUTBURST bassist Joel Guigon and ex-DEATH POWER drummer Stéphane Guegan.

Gibelin had quit by the time AGRESSOR returned to the studio to cut the ensuing 'Symposium Of Rebirth' album, his place being taken by new guitarist Manu Ragot. The TERRORISER cover track 'After World Obliteration', incidentally, features a guest vocal performance from NAPALM DEATH's Barney Greenaway. AGRESSOR toured as guests to CRADLE OF FILTH on their British tour of June 1996.

The band returned to the studio for the 'Medieval Rites' album. Employing a vast array of traditional instrumentation the multi-faceted release would see both Krell and Christina from Norwegians BLOODTHORN guesting. Also donating their services would be former MERCYFUL FATE drummer Morten Nielsen, ROTTEN SOUND and ENOCHIAN CRESCENT drummer Kai Hahto and the journeyman Death Metal guitarist JAMES MURPHY.

November of 1999 found AGRESSOR on the road in Europe on a package billing in collusion with BLOODTHORN and Finns AND OCEANS. The line up for these shows would see Colin-Tocquaine and Guigo joined by WITCHES guitarist Bernard Queral and Kai Hahto on drums.

Colin-Tocquaine would also session for touring purposes with American occult ancestral Metal act ABSU and renew the relationship with BLOODTHORN by sessioning on their 2000 album 'Under The Reign Of Terror'. As if this activity was not enough, the guitarist would also announce that he had joined another veteran French Metal combo LOUDBLAST. Meantime, Guigou had re-activated his former outfit OUTBURST.

The January 2001 incarnation of AGRESSOR cited a roster of Colin-Tocquaine, guitarist Adramelech, bassist Joel Guigou and drummer Gorgor. Both Adramelech and Gorgor were previously with Black Metal band BELEF. Gorgor also drummed for Grindcore band IMPERIAL SODOMY. Season Of Mist issued an album 'The Spirit Of Evil' during March 2002 comprising rarities plus three live tracks.

Season Of Mist issued the 'Deaththreat' album in November 2006.

SATAN'S SODOMY, Black Mark Production BMCD 36 (1987). Satan's Sodomy / Brainstorm / Blood Feast / Uncontrolled Desire / Black Church / It's Pandemonium.
LICENSED TO THRASH, New Wave 024 (1987). Satan's Sodomy / Brainstorm / Bloodfeast / Uncontrolled Desire / Black Church / It's Pandemonium.
NEVERENDING DESTINY, Black Mark N 0154-2 (1990). Paralytic Disease / The Unknown Spell / Element Decay / Voices From Below / Blood Feast / Neverending Destiny / Prince Of Fire / Dark Power / The Arrival / Brainstorm / Bloody Corps.
TOWARDS BEYOND, Black Mark BMCD 23 (1992). Intro / Primeval Transubtantion / The Fortress / Positionic Showering / Antediluvian / Epileptic Alra / Hyaldid / The Crypt / Future Past - Eldest Things / Turkish March.
SYMPOSIUM OF REBIRTH, Black Mark Production BMCD 55 (1994). Barabas / Rebirth / Negative Zone / Apocalyptic Prophecies / Erga Meam Salutem / Overloaded / Theology / Civilisation / Wheel Of Pain / Abhuman Dreadnought / Torture / Dor Fin-I-Guinar / After World Obliteration.
MEDIEVAL RITES, Season Of Mist (1999). Medieval Rites / Bloodshed / The Woodguy vs. The Black Beast / The Sorcerer / Spirit Of Evil / Wandering Soul / Tye-Melane Melda / God From The Sky / Welcome Home / Ondolinde / Burial Desecration / Tribal Dance / At Night.
THE SPIRIT OF EVIL, Season Of Mist (2002) (Limited edition. 1000 copies). The Spirit Of Evil (Extended version) / God From The Sky / The Sorceror / Wandering Soul / Brainstorm (Live) / Bloodshed (Live) / God From The Sky (Live).
DEATHTHREAT, Season Of Mist (2006).

AGRO

GUATENG, SOUTH AFRICA — *Clifford Crabb (vocals), Daniel Lambinon (guitar), Shane Pennicott (guitar), Robbie Riebler (bass), Enoque Carrancho (keyboards), Grant Merricks (drums).*

AGRO, a melodic Thrash act hailing from Guateng and dating to 1992, cut their 'From Within' 1995 debut at B# Studios in Johannesburg. Recording line up for the band comprised lead vocalist Clifford Crabb, the guitar pairing of Shane Pennicott and David 'Mountain' Kietzmann, bassist Phil du Tiot and drummer Grant Merricks. The band's second effort, 'Eyes' recorded at Tech Studios Welkom, arrived in 1998. Tragically, Kietzmann died in a car accident shortly after completion of these sessions. AGRO would return to B# Studios in early 2000 for their third album 'The Tree', the title song and the album cover depicting the exact same tree that their late colleague passed away at. The group underwent a line-up change upfront of these sessions with Daniel Lambinon taking over second guitar, Robbie Riebler now on bass and the introduction of keyboard player Enoque Carrancho.

AGRO maintained this membership roster for their fourth album, 2003's 'Forthcoming'. This record, which included a cover of TWISTED SISTER's 'The Price', saw guesting vocalists Glynn Albery of GORELOCK, Prince Vince of MANIFEST and even Jonny Lindkvist of NOCTURNAL RITES. Armageddon Music issued the 'Ritual 6' album in October 2006. Guest vocals in the studio came courtesy of Jo Day and CHOKEHOLD's Alessandro Forgilai.

FROM WITHIN, (1995). From Within / Destroyed / Agro / Yo Baby Yo / Life You Made / Lean On Me / Afrika / Power Of The Brave / Sandstorms / Dawrapup.
EYES, (1998). Eyes / Reason For War / What Is Wrong / Glass God / Slave To Your Greed / Time To Review / Agrolesse / Big Women / Forced Entry / Tears.
THE TREE, (2000). Darkened Skies / Life? / Unite As One / Taken By Misery / The Path Of The Fallen / Hotel Albertonia / If At First / Take A Step Forward / Away From Fear / A New Beginning (Another Murder) / The Tree.
FORTHCOMING, (2003). Forthcoming / Woken By Silence / Chalk Outline / The Price / Ein Prosit / Til Death / Culling The Meek / Through The Chaos / My Scars Are Real / At Liberty / A Rule So Deformed / The Tree II.
RITUAL 6, Armageddon Music (2006). Thukutela / Carpe Diem / 10 x Over / Time Heals Old Wounds / B.D.F.P. / C7511 / Whizzdel / TR333 / The Crimson Sea / Willowmore / A Place Of Healing.

AIRDASH

HELSINKI, FINLAND — *Juha Laine (vocals), Roope Sirén (guitar), Tommy Dolivo (guitar), Kirka Sainio (bass), Ykä (drums).*

Helsinki Speed Metal act AIRDASH, founded in 1986, has supported both SUICIDAL TENDENCIES and ANTHRAX in their home country. AIDRASH debuted with the 'Without Lies' single for the Kerberos label during 1988, the same label subsequently releasing the first album 'Thank god It's Monday'. Major label BMG would pick up the album for Japanese release the following year.

AIRDASH switch to the Diablo label for follow up 'Hospital Hallucinations Take One'. Prior to the release of third album 'Both Ends Of The Path', licensed to Black Mark for European release, original guitarist Markku 'Nirri' Niiranen was replaced by Tommy Dolivo. Both Nirri and guitarist Roope Sirén subsequently joined STONE.

In later years Roope Sirén would make his mark alongside STONE bassist Janne Joutsenniemi in SUBURBAN TRIBE. Bassist Kirka Sainio would team up with GANDALF for their 1995 demo session 'The Cradle'. Drummer Ykä (a.k.a. Agathon Frosteus) united with GLOOMY GRIM, WALHALLA, SOULGRIND, THY SERPENT, NOMICON and BARATRUM and Thrashers CORPORAL PUNISHMENT.

Airdash, Airdash (1987) (Cassette demo). Enjoyment (Eat Shit) / A Hell Of A Noise / Without It / Blow Under Belt / Knowing Means To Die / No Vacance / Big Ben.
Without It, Kerberos KES 186 (1988). Without It / White Lies.
Thank God It's Monday, Kerberos PROMO 100 (1988) (Promotional release). Thank God It's Monday / Helluva Noise.
THANK GOD IT'S MONDAY, Kerberos KEL 677 (1988). Give Up / Helluva Noise / Another Day / White Lies / Spit Your Guts / Without It / Reaper / Thank God It's Monday / Eat Shit.

Vengeance Through Violence EP, Diablo NADAX 1 (1989). Vengeance Through Violence / Blow Under The Belt / Cable Terror.
HOSPITAL HALLUCINATIONS TAKE ONE, Diablo NADALP 1 (1990). If . . . / Youth Hostel (Burial Side) / Jungle Jim / Decent Citizen / Vengeance Through Violence (No Bullshit) / Trigger Happy / Forbidden Thoughts / Sleepwalk.
Liquid Bliss, Diablo NADAX 3 (1991) (12" vinyl single). Liquid Bliss / Take A Look At Me / Got No Blues.
BOTH ENDS OF THE PATH, Black Mark Production BMLP 14 (1991) (Vinyl version). Liquid Bliss / Hollow Men / Savage Ritual / So It Goes / Soul Of A Renegade / Silent Wall / Deeper Shades / Letter Of Indulgence / Choking Child / View.
BOTH ENDS OF THE PATH, Black Mark BMCD 14 (1991). Liquid Bliss / Hollow Men / Savage Ritual / So It Goes / Soul Of A Renegade / Silent Wall / Deeper Shades / Letter Of Indulgence / Choking Child / View / Take A Look At Me / Got No Blues / Eat Shit (New version).
Soul Of A Renegade, Diablo NADAS 5 (1991) (7" vinyl single). Soul Of A Renegade / View.
BOTH ENDS OF THE PATH, Diablo NADACD 3 (1991) (Finnish CD release). Liquid Bliss / Hollow Men / Savage Ritual / So It Goes / Soul Of A Renegade / Silent Wall / Deeper Shades / Letter Of Indulgence / Choking Child / View / Take A Look At Me / Got No Blues.

ALASTOR

PORTUGAL — *Tormentor (vocals / bass), Desecrator (guitar).*

Not to be confused with the Polish Death Metal and both Austrian and Costa Rican Black Metal outfits sharing the same name. These Lusitanians, signed to the German Barbarian Wrath label, deliver retro Thrash inspired music with Black lyrical overtones. ALASTOR made their entrance with the 'Gates Of Darkness' album, a split affair with DECAYED, featuring cover versions of BLACK SABBATH's anthem 'Children Of The Grave' and even BOB DYLAN's 'Knockin' On Heaven's Door'. A deal was scored with the Swedish label Iron Fist Productions for the 'Crushing Christendom' opus but never concluded. The album subsequently arrived courtesy of Barbarian Wrath.

The December 2001 album 'Hellward' was not only notable for including a cover version IRON ANGEL's 'Sinner' but for reputedly being the very first Black Metal record with Portuguese lyrics.

GATES OF DARKNESS, (1996) (Split album with DECAYED). Through The Gates / Sacrifice To Satan / Hell On Earth / No Exorcism / Bestial Wrath Of The Antichrist / Possessed By Darkness / Children Of The Grave.
CRUSHING CHRISTENDOM, Barbarian Wrath WRATH666-004 (2000). The Return Of Alastor / Spawn Of Evil / Infernal Power / Witch Hammer / Necronomicunt / The Fall Of God / Total Devastation / Black Mass / Power Thrashing Death.
HELLWARD, Barbarian Wrath WRATH666-014 (2001). Para O Mundo Inferior / Ataque Final Do Inferno / Rainha Dos Mortos / Demonios Antigos / Sacrificio Em Golgota / Serva De Satanas / (Metal) Blasfemia Eterna / Sinner.

ALISTER

JAGODINA, SERBIA — *Igor Miladinovic Raven (vocals), Marko Ognjanovic Boldie (guitar), Marko Vuckovic Wolfy (guitar), Ivan Petrovic (bass), Milos Simic (keyboards), Marko Stosic Goofie (drums).*

Jagodina Death-Thrashers forged in 1998 under the previous title of POLTERGEIST. Their first demo, 'The Snakepit', was recorded in Cesnjak Studios, Kragujevac during September of 1999. Cutting four more tracks that Winter at ZIP Studios in Jagodina, including the song 'Alone' featuring Huanita Matic Hana as guest female vocalist, the group collated these recordings as the 'Powerbeat' demo release.

ALISTER's debut album 'Obscurity', laid down at Paradox Studios in Smederevo, would include guest appearances from the PSYCHOPARADOX and ALOGIA triumvirate of Miroslav Brankovic, Branislav Dabic and Ana Useinovic. Live work across Serbia was prolific, including a support slot to PAUL DIANNO, before the band entered the same studios as previous to cut second record 'Memories And Dreams' for One Records during August of 2002. ALOGIA's Srdjan Brankovic would guest.

MEMORIES AND DREAMS, One Records (2002). Flames / See You On The Other Side / Awake / Fiction / Living Hell / The Abyss / In My Memories / Dreams / Raven's Chant / Dark Depth / Life Is Just A Dream . . . / If / Light The Darkness / Cicatrice.

ALLFATHER

BC, CANADA — *Justin Hagberg (guitar), Jasper van der Veen (guitar), Adam Angus (bass), Paul Jacobsen (drums).*

ALLFATHER was initially assembled as a trio of vocalist Paul Jacobsen, guitarist Justin Hagberg and drummer Craig Stewart during 1996. As such the band created the opening demo 'Render To The Unlight' that same year'. Subsequently the band would morph with Jacobsen taking over the drumming role and Cam Pipes being inducted to handle bass. In this formation ALLFATHER recorded the 1998 six track mini album 'Wrath Of The Bloodthirsty'. For live work the band introduced lead vocalist Chad Klassen.

A further recording, a five track promotion issue, was distributed in 1999 after which Adam Angus took command of the bass role. ALLFATHER's next move was to participate in a four way split album release. Released by Realms of Darkness Productions this unique outing billed as 'Lead Us To War And Final Glory' allied ALLFATHER with Hungarian act NEBRON and American bands GNOSTIC and HORDES OF THE LUNAR ECLIPSE.

In September of 2004 Justin Hagberg joined 3 INCHES OF BLOOD. A full length album, 'Weapon Of Ascension', would be readied for January 2005 issue as the band acquired Jasper van der Veen on guitar, a former member of Dutch act FLUISTERWOUD. Chad Klassen resigned from the band following this release.

Wrath Of The Bloodthirsty, (1998). Thy Quest Of Abyssal Plight / Flesh Of The Ancient Bode / Prince Of Many Faces / Wrath Of The Bloodthirsty / Ageless Eternity / Choose Who My Destiny.
Promo 2000, (2000). Bringer Of The Tides Of Disorder / Unbonding Of Thine Forgotten Hymn / And With God Bereft / Dog Lords Resurgence / Hoch Und Steil Leben.
LEAD US TO INTO FINAL GLORY AND WAR, Realms Of Darkness Productions DHR012 (2002) (Split album with GNOSTIC, HORDES OF THE LUNAR ECLIPSE and NEBRON). Warlust / With Glory Unbound / Artifice / Tyranny, Revenge! / Ancestral Resurrection.
Allfather, Invictus Productions (2003). Bringer Of The Tides Of Disorder / Unbonding Of Thine Forgotten Hymn / And With God Bereft / Dog Lords Resurgence / Hoch Und Steil Leben / Sealed In Blood (Live).
WEAPON OF ASCENSION, Invictus Productions IP005 (2005). Evolution To Supremacy / Forever Unconquerable / Flight Into Exile / Hail! Tyrants Of War / Storm Assault / Through Ages Wrought / Invictus / Of Man And Valour / Blood And Soil / In The Face Of Nobility / Progency Of Vengeance / Path Of Glory.

ALLIGATOR

ITALY — *Gianluca Melino (vocals), Francesco Capasso (guitar), Tiziano Colombi (guitar), Dario Zanaboni (bass), Andrea Bellazzi (drums).*

Northern Italian Thrash Metal act founded in 1988. The band, heavily influenced by Bay Area Thrash, debuted with a 1990 demo 'Bog Of Horrors'.

CEREBRAL IMPLOSION, Scream SCREAM003CD (1994). Cerebral Implosion / Beyond The Reach Of Fate / The Cage / Decimation / Help / Lullaby For The Unborn / Skeleton's Beach / Tarantula / Drinking Milk From My Knees / Fetching Fear / Natural Dreams.
RULES, Last Scream (1996).

ALTAIR

STOCKHOLM, SWEDEN — *Henrik Andersson (vocals), Kalle Stenberg (guitar), Martin Forssman (bass), Daniel Hållams (drums).*

Stockholm Thrash Metal band ALTAIR date back to December of 1997, being initiated by a rhythm section of drummer Daniel Hållams and bassist Martin Forssman. Guitarist Mathias Brinley joined the duo in early 1998, but was soon discarded in favour of Kalle Stenberg, an erstwhile school friend of Hållams and Forssman. This formative version of ALTAIR spent its first year of operations performing cover versions whilst building up a catalogue of original material. Subsequently, P.Henrik Andersson enrolled as lead vocalist. The repertoire at this juncture included tracks by RUNNING WILD, POWERMAD and a super-speed version of JUDAS PRIEST's 'Breaking The Law' clocking in at less than 90 seconds.

In 2000 ALTAIR adopted a more aggressive musical stance. The band first performed live in October of 2001 at a Stockholm outdoor festival alongside four non-Metal bands. A Spring 2002 demo duly secured a label deal with Metal Inquisition Records in the USA. A further demo, recorded in Stockholm Sound Recording, followed in late 2004.

Altair, Altair (2004) (Demo). Icecream Man / Scorch And Burn / Manicfesto.

ALTERED AEON

UPPSALA, SWEDEN — *K. Andersson (vocals), Per Nilsson (guitar), Niklas Rehn (guitar), Anders Hedlund (bass), Henrik Ohlsson (drums).*

Founded as the "Occult Thrash" Metal outfit THRAWN, first postulated during 2001 as the result of creative discussions between Henrik Ohlsson, able to boast a wealth of associations to acts such as ADVERSARY, LEGIA, MUTANT, SCAR SYMMETRY, DIABOLICAL and THEORY IN PRACTICE, together with AZOTIC REIGN's Kjell Andersson. Due to the pair's schedules with their priority bands THRAWN, based in Uppsala, took some time to formulate but by 2002 guitarist Niklas had augmented the band roster. In February of 2003 the trio entered the studio to cut a EP 'Light Creates Shadows'. For these sessions, produced by CENTINEX and CARNAL FORGE member Jonas Kjellgren, Andersson took on lead vocals, Niclas rhythm guitar whilst Ohlsson handled guitar, bass and drums. Per Nilsson donated additional lead solos.

The band, adding the THEORY IN PRACTICE credited Anders Hedlund on bass and second guitarist Per Nilsson, subsequently evolved into ALTERED AEON. Signing to Black Lotus Records the band cut the album 'Dispiritism' for 2004 issue. That same year both Nilsson and Ohlsson hooked up with Jonas Kjellgren's new combo SCAR SYMMETRY for an album 'Symmetric In Design'. In January 2005 Per Nilsson was announced as having joined WORLD BELOW.

Light Creates Shadows, Altered Aeon (2003) (Demo). Dispirited Chambers / Patriots Of Sin (Aeturnum Essentia) / Dreamscape Domain / Transcendence Duology.
DISPIRITISM, Black Lotus BLRCD 069 (2004). Dispirited Chambers / The Resonance Of Form In Transition / Descensitizer / Behind The Lodge Door / Patriots Of Sin (Aeturnum Essentia) / Carpe Noctem / Dreamscape Domain / Oath To Endure / Light Creates Shadows / Transcendence Duology / Cellular Disorganization / Welcome Home.

AMEBIX

UK — *The Baron (vocals / bass), Stig Da Pig (guitar), A. Droid (keyboards), Spider Arachno Blaster (drums).*

AMEBIX offered up Thrash Metal with heavy doses of caustic Punk rawness. The band, led by vocalist / bassist The Baron and guitarist Stig Da Pig, formed at the tail end of 1978 originally dubbed THE BAND WITH NO NAME. One of these formative tracks, 'University Challenged', turned up on the renowned compilation album 'Bullshit Detector 1'.

A series of line up fluxes eventually saw keyboard player Norman being enrolled in 1981 as the group relocated to Bristol. Another inductee would be drummer Virus from local act DISORDER and in this incarnation AMEBIX signed to Spiderleg Records issuing three EPs. More line up changes saw AMEBIX making do as a trio for a tour of Italy before the quick fire changes in the keyboard department settled when George came in during November of 1984 for dates in Holland.

Spider Arachno Blaster took the drum mantle from Virus as AMEBIX signed to Alternative Tentacles for the 1985 album 'Arise'. Sophomore effort 'Monolith' arrived on the Wolverhampton Heavy Metal label but the band folded in late 1987. Spider, George and Stig stuck together to forge ZYGOTE with new bass man Tim Crow to cut the album 'A Wind Of Knives' in 1991. In later years Spider would be found in MUCKSPREADER. According to reports The Baron lives on the Isle of Skye manufacturing swords.

In 2002 Canadian Black Metal band MEGIDDO delivered tribute by covering 'Last Will And Testament' on a split 7 single on the German Iron Bonehead label. A live AMEBIX album, 'Make Some Fucking Noise!' recorded during 1986 in Ljubljana, Slovenia, surfaced in 2003. In 2004 Californian gore Metal band EXHUMED revealed they had included a rendition of the AMEBIX song 'The Power Remains' on their covers album entitled 'Regurgitated Requiems: Garbage Daze Re-Regurgitated'.

Who's The Enemy?, Spiderleg SDL 6 (1982). Who's The Enemy? / Carnage.
NO SANCTUARY, Spiderleg SDL14 (1983). Battery Humans / Control / Progress? / Sanctuary / The Church Is For Sinners / Sunshine Ward / Moscow Madness (No Gods Part 2).
Winter, Spiderleg SDL 10 (1983). Winter / Beginning Of The End.
ARISE, Alternative Tentacles VIRUS 46 (1984). The Moor / Axeman / Fear Of God / Largactyl / Drink And Be Merry / Spoils Of Victory / Arise! / Slave / The Darkest Hour.
NO GODS, (1985). The Moor—Largactyl / Axeman / Spoils Of Victory / Fear Of God / Slave / Arise / Drink And Be Merry / The Darkest Hour / Largactyl.
NO MASTERS, (1986). Intro / Arise / Largactyl / Drink And Be Merry / Chain Reaction / Axeman / Spoils Of Victory / Fallen From Grace / The Fear Of God / The Darkest Hour / The Power Remains.
MONOLITH, Heavy Metal HMR99 (1987). Monolith / Nobody's Driving / The Power Remains / Time Bomb / Last Will And Testament / ICBM / Chain Reaction / Fallen From Grace / Coming Home.
THE POWER REMAINS, (1994). I.C.B.M. / The Power Remains / Chain Reaction / Last Will And Testament / Nobody's Driving / Fallen From Grace / Arise / Drink And Be Merry.
MAKE SOME FUCKING NOISE!, Alternative Tentacles (2003). Arise / Largactyl / Drink And Be Merry / Fallen From Grace / Axeman / Spoils Of Victory / I.C.B.M. / The Darkest Hour.

AMNESIA

BARNSLEY, YORKSHIRE, UK — *Simon Rose (vocals), Clive Heeley (guitar), Simon Fairhurst (guitar), Matt Foster (bass), Michael Vincent (drums).*

A Melodic Thrash band formed in Barnsley during 1988 with ex-SACRAMENT vocalist Simon Rose joining in 1990. Prior to the release of the debut album, 1991's 'Unknown Entity' recorded at Academy Studios, West Yorkshire, AMNESIA supported TORANAGA, SLAMMER and XENTRIX. The 'Unknown Entity' album was recorded in a mere nine days and produced by TORANAGA guitarist Andy Mitchell. In 1991 the band supported both METAL CHURCH and SABBAT.

In late 2006 guitarist Simon Fairhurst emerged with a new band entitled KABEN, fronted by Dame (Damian Walsh), previously of Birmingham bands GRAVEL and HOOKJAW.

UNKNOWN ENTITY, Major WADES 3 (1991). Solution / Memories Of Me / Final Revelation / Epitaph / Unknown Entity / No More Tomorrow / One Below Zero / Perish.

AMOK

BERGEN, NORWAY — *Necrocum (vocals), Lava (guitar / drum programming), Iscariah (bass).*

AMOK, conceived in Bergen during 2001, is a Grind imbued retro-Thrash venture of Norwegian underground elite. Featured musicians would be AETERNUS and TAAKE vocalist / guitarist Radomir Michael Nemec (a.k.a. 'Larva'), bass player Stanley and CULT OF CATHARSIS drummer Tormod Haraldson (a.k.a. 'Mord'). Subsequently Lava re-invented the group to incorporate MYSTICUM's Necrocum on lead vocals and the NECROPHAGIA, WURDULAK and IMMORTAL credited Iscariah on bass guitar.

AMOK delivered the demos 'Sadistic Attack', seeing AUDIOPAIN's Sverre Dæhli adding a guest guitar solo to the track 'Toxic Slayer', in 2001 and 'Lava Dictatorship' the following year. This latter session featured a cover of the SEX PISTOLS 'Bodies' with a guesting Tore Bratseth of OLD FUNERAL, DESEKRATOR and BÖMBERS as guest vocalist. A further demo, 'Effective Mass-Torture', arrived in 2003. That same year Witchhammer Productions re-issued the 'Lava Dictatorship' sessions as a split cassette, limited to 500 copies, shared with AUDIOPAIN's 'Revel In Desecration' demo. The following year Perverted Taste re-published 'Sadistic Attack' with a bonus track on a 10" grey vinyl split in alliance with TAAKE.

Iscariah would found GRIMFIST and also be an active member of the British based Pagan collective THE CLAN DESTINED, led by ex-SKYCLAD frontman Martin Walkyier. Both Mord and Stanley would feature on DEATHCON's 2004 'Zerohuman' EP. Stanley joined AETERNUS in the Autumn of 2004.

AMOK crafted a new album during November 2004, at first branded 'Urinal Graveyard' then switched to 'Necrospiritual Deathcore', being signed to the newly established label Planet Satan Revolution. Iscariah and Mord's next band project would be DEAD TO THIS WORLD. In mid 2006 Mord joined the live line-up of BLACK HOLE GENERATOR.

'Necrospiritual Deathcore' arrived in September 2006, these sessions seeing guests including Kybermensch, Taipan of ORCUSTUS, U. Höst of TAAKE and Fabban Malfeitor from ABORYM.

Sadistic Attack, Amok (2001) (Demo). Ebola To The People / Flamethrower / Chemical Dissection / Nuclear Warbeast / Toxic Slayer.

Lava Dictatorship, Amok (2002) (Demo). Ebola To The People / Nuclear Warbeast / Necro-Guerrilla / Atomic Warfare Fetish / Flamethrower / Project A.I.D.S. / Organized Hate / Chemical Dissection / Skullfucked / Toxic Slayer / Bodies.

Effective Mass-Torture, Amok (2003) (Demo CD single). Effective Mass-Torture / Project A.I.D.S. / Nuclear Warbeast / Skullfucked.

Lava Dictatorship, Witchhammer Productions WHP-025D (2003) (Split demo with AUDIOPAIN. Limited edition 500 copies). Ebola To The People / Nuclear Warbeast / Necro-Guerrilla / Atomic Warfare Fetish / Flamethrower / Project A.I.D.S. / Organized Hate / Chemical Dissection / Skullfucked / Toxic Slayer / Bodies.

SADISTIC ATTACK, Perverted Taste PT 666674 (2004) (Split album with TAAKE. Limited edition 1000 copies. 10" grey vinyl). Ebola To The People / Flamethrower / Chemical Dissection / Nuclear Warbeast / Toxic Slayer / Ranch Apocalypse.

A Norwegian Tribute To VON, Holycaust S810-11 (2006) (Split gatefold double red vinyl 7" with TAAKE, URGEHAL and NORWEGIAN EVIL). Von.

NECROSPIRITUAL DEATHCORE, Planet Satan Revolution PSR 002 (2006). Necropsy Cunt / Geitehelvete / Channelling Black Horns / Effective Mass-Torture / Organ Ejaculator / Providentialism / Postapokalyptisk Korstog / Goatflesh Removal (Corpus Christi) / Goatflesh Removal (Memento Mori) / Goatflesh Removal (Gloria In Excelsis Deo).

AMULANCE

AURORA, IL, USA — *Rik Baez (vocals), Vince Varriale (guitar), Bob Luman (guitar), Tom Braddish (bass), Kent Wagner (drums).*

A self styled "Bash Metal" outfit out of Aurora, Illinois. The band was convened during the early 80's citing a line up of founder and guitarist Bob Luman, vocalist Rik Baez, bassist Tom Braddish and drummer Eric Wedow. Adding second guitar player Vince Varriale in January of 1986 AMULANCE issued a six track demo 'The Rage Within' to positive response. An album, 'Feel The Pain' on New Renaissance Records, followed before Wedow departed. His place would be taken by Tony 'T-Bone' DiVozzo. However, AMULANCE had folded by 1989.

DiVozzo would later join DARKLIN REACH for the 'Where Evil Dwells' album and later BLACK CUNTRY ROCK. Guitarist Bob Luman and drummer Eric Wedow founded BLACKLYST. A 1991 demo entitled 'Liars, Killers & Master Thieves' would be pressed up on CD format in 2004 by Germany's Iron Glory label.

In March 2007 San Jose based Stormspell Records announced the release of 'The Rage Within And The Aftermath', this set comprising the band's original 1987 'The Rage Within' six song demo plus previously unreleased demo recordings taken from the 'The Aftermath Sessions', recorded in 1988-1989.

The Rage Within, (1987). Black Moon Rising / Living On The Run / 7th Son / Deathwish / Witch's Sin / Rage Within.

FEEL THE PAIN, New Renaissance NRR56 (1989). Holocaust / Schizophrenia / Violent Victory / Witch's Sin / Feel The Pain / Black Moon Rising / Shark Attack / Death Wish / 7th Son.

Holocaust, New Renaissance (1989) (Promotion). Holocaust.

ANACRUSIS

ST. CHARLES, MO, USA — *Ken Nardi (vocals / guitar), Kevin Heidbreder (guitar), John Emery (bass), Mike Owen (drums).*

Highly rated ANACRUSIS, a technically minded Thrash unit with a Progressive edge, date from 1984 and are based in St. Louis, Missouri. Frontman Ken Nardi had previously operated with HEAVEN'S FLAME. ANACRUSIS debuted with the 1987 'Annihilation Complete' demo. The band featured a track on the UK 'Metal Forces' magazine compilation 'Demolition' in 1988. The band would record the inaugural 'Suffering Hour' album self financing it to the tune of $1200. The European Axis label, headed by 'Metal Forces' magazine editor Bernard Doe, would be quick to snap the band up.

1989's 'Reason' would be issued on the Active imprint, actually an evolvement of the Axis concern. However, an American issue licensed to Metal Blade witnessed completely different artwork. Touring in the States found ANACRUSIS as openers to D.R.I..

As the band signed to the Metal Blade concern on a global basis for the 'Manic Impressions' outing drummer Mike Owen was superseded by Chad Smith for the 1991 'Manic Impressions' album. Promotion included a 38 date American tour in the Autumn of 1991 third on the bill to GALACTIC COWBOYS and OVERKILL. The group would then secure further supports stepping up to larger venues with MEGADETH.

The fourth and final ANACRUSIS effort, 1993's 'Screams And Whispers', would herald another change on the drum stool with Paul Miles taking on duties. Chad Smith went on to TOBY REDD before finding a stable and high profile base with the RED HOT CHILI PEPPERS.

SUFFERING HOUR, Axis LP4 (1988). Present Tense / Imprisoned / ROT / Butcher's Block / A World To Gain / Frigid Bitch / Fighting Evil / Twisted Cross / Annihilation Complete / Disemboweled.

REASONS, Active ATV9 (1989). Stop Me / Terrified / Not Forgotten / Wrong / Silent Crime / Misshapen Intent / Afraid To Feel / Child Inside / Vital / Quick To Doubt / Killing My Mind / Injustice.

MANIC IMPRESSIONS, Metal Blade ZORRO23 (1991). Paint A Picture / I Love The World / Something Real / Dream Again / Explained Away / Still Black / What You Became / Our Reunion / Idle Hours / Far Too Long.

SCREAMS AND WHISPERS, Metal Blade ZORRO59 (1993). Sound The Alarm / Sense Of Will / Too Many Prophets / Release / Division / Tools Of Separation / Grateful / A Screaming Breath / My Soul's Affliction / Driven / Brotherhood? / Release.

ANARION

MELBOURNE, VIC, AUSTRALIA — *Riccardo Mecchi (vocals / guitar), Steve Stergiadis (guitar), Joe Fresina (bass), Luke Burnham (drums).*

Melbourne Power Metal band ANARION is known internationally as being the post PEGAZUS port of call for vocalist Dany Cecati. The group had been first assembled in 1999 with guitarist Riccardo Mecchi handling lead vocals, the inaugural line-up comprising second guitarist Michael Vrljic, bassist Simon D'Alfonso with drummer Luke Burnham swelling the ranks in October of that year.

In January of 2000 Cecati suggested a union. Having rehearsed previously with the PEGAZUS frontman Mecchi agreed to concentrate his energies on guitar. With Cecati now enrolled it would be only a short time before he was fired from his position in PEGAZUS. In June both Vrljic and D'Alfonso bailed out. Steve Stergiadis filled the vacant second guitar position in November and the four string position was subsequently occupied by Chris Binding. A further switch had another erstwhile member of THE EMBER TIDE, the Iranian born Erf, as the next bassist in line.

Although Cecati left for Progressive Metal act EYEFEAR, necessitating Mecchi resuming his prior responsibilities as lead vocalist, ANARION recorded a self financed debut album 'The Journey Begins' for December 2001 release. The band toured Australia as support to EDGUY in May of 2002.

ANARION added bassist Joe Frisina in June 2003. In December of 2005 the band signed to UK label Majestic Rock for the February 2006 album 'Unbroken'. Citing "irreconcilable musical and personal differences", ANARION parted ways with guitarist Steve Stergiadis in May. Scott Griffith was announced as replacement in October.

THE JOURNEY BEGINS, (2001). Space-Time / My Own / The Battle Of Old / Kingdom Of Stone / Earth Reborn / Life Of Descent / Hidden Mind / Principles Of Uncertainty / The Journey Begins . . . .
UNBROKEN, Majestic MAJCD074 (2006). New Eyes, Old Lies / Blind Mortality / Greed Of Man / Live In Me / Broken Truths / Below / Conflicting Self / Buried / Another Level.

ANATA

VARBERG, SWEDEN — *Fredrik Schälin (vocals / guitar), Andreas Allenmark (guitar), Henrik Drake (bass), Conny Petersson (drums).*

Varberg act ANATA began life as a Thrash / Crossover quartet boon soon evolved into a fully fledged lethal Death Metal machine. The band started life in 1993 comprising of vocalist / guitarist Fredrik Schälin, guitarist Matthias Svensson, bass player Martin Sjöstrand and drummer Robert Petersson. ANATA released the June 1995 demo session 'Bury Forever The Garden Of Lie'.

During 1996 both Svensson and Sjöstrand bade their farewell and new recruits guitarist Andreas Allenmark and bass player Henrik Drake were welcomed into the fold for the 1997 demo 'Vast Lands Of My Infernal Dominion'. ANATA signed with French label Season Of Mist for the debut album 'The Infernal Depths Of Hatred'.

ANATA's second effort formed part of the Seasons Of Mist 'War' series pitching the band up against BETHZAIDA. The band covered BETHZAIDA's 'The Tranquility Of Your Last Breath' and MORBID ANGEL's 'Day Of Suffering' whilst BETHZAIDA reciprocated with their take on ANATA's 'Under Azure Skies'.

During 2000, ANATA members vocalist and guitarist Fredrik Schälin, guitarist Andreas Alllenmark and bassist Henrik Drake

ANATA

in league with ETERNAL LIES members guitarist Björn Johansson and drummer Conny Pettersson forged the side project ROT INJECTED.

ANATA pulled in ETERNAL LIES drummer Conny Pettersson during early 2001. ANATA signed to Earache/Wicked World in August 2002. Promoting the album 'Under A Stone With No Inscription' a short spurt of UK dates in February of 2004 saw the band ranked alongside DECAPITATED, ROTTING CHRIST and THUS DEFILED. Further shows had the band allied with DISMEMBER, PSYCROPTIC and SANATORIUM for a full European tour commencing 3rd November in Nürnberg, Germany.

ANATA entered StudioMega in Varberg during July 2005 to craft a new album with a title of 'The Conductor's Departure'.

Bury Forever The Garden Of Lie, Anata (1995) (Demo). River / Infectious Souls Of Mine / Lashes Upon His Face / Livid / In My Eyes.
Vast Lands Of My Infernal Dominion, Anata (1997) (Demo). Let The Heavens Hate / Vast Lands / Infernal Gates / Those Who Lick The Wounds Of Christ (One Is The Remedy) / Under Azure Skies.
THE INFERNAL DEPTHS OF HATRED, Season Of Mist SOM 012 (1998). Released When You Are Dead / Let The Heavens Hate / Under Azure Skies / Vast Lands Infernal Gates / Slain Upon His Altar / Those Who Lick The Wounds Of Christ / Dethroned The Hypocrites / Aim Not At The Kingdom High.
WAR VOLUME II: VS. BETHZAIDA, Season Of Mist SOM 022 (1999) (Split album with BETHZAIDA). Let Me Become Your Fallen Messiah / With Me You Shall Fall / Day Of Suffering / The Tranquility Of Your Last Breath.
DREAMS OF DEATH AND DISMAY, Season Of Mist SOM 035 (2001). Die Laughing / Faith, Hope, Self Deception / God Of Death / Metamorphosis By The Well Of Truth / Dreamon / Can't Kill What's Already Dead / Insurrection / The Enigma Of Number Three / Drain Of Blood / The Temple—Erratic.
UNDER A STONE WITH NO INSCRIPTION, Wicked World WICK15CD (2004). Shackled To Guilt / A Problem Yet To Be Solved / Entropy Within / Dance To The Song Of Apathy / Sewerages Of The Mind / Built On Sand / Under The Debris / The Drowning / Leaving The Spirit Behind / Any Kind Of Magic Or Miracle.
THE CONDUCTOR'S DEPARTURE, Wicked World WICK22CD (2006). Downward Spiral Into Madness / Complete Demise / Better Grieved Than Fooled / The Great Juggler / Cold Heart Forged In Hell / I Would Dream Of Blood / Disobedience Pays / Children's Laughter / Renunciation / The Conductor's Departure.

ANCESTOR

PUDASJÄRVI, FINLAND — Pudasjärvi based ANCESTOR released the 1992 'Ethereal Devotion', following this with the 'Come Back Towards The Light' session' in 1993. The band was borne out of a musical union in 1993 by vocalist Pekka Kokko and ETERNAL TEARS OF SORROW drummer Petri Sankala. In this incarnation the duo cut a series of demos later enlisting guitarist Antti Kokko and keyboard player Antti Matti Talala.

ANCESTOR would bow out with their fifth session 'Under The Burbot's Nest' and evolve into KALMAH during August of 1998. This transition not only saw a name change but a shift in musical direction from Death Metal to a more melodically inclined path. KALMAH heralded their arrival with the 'Svieri Obraza' promotional tape in late 1999.

Ethereal Devotion, Ancestor (1993) (Demo). Over The Threshold / The Last Excursion / Sceneries Of Life / Mortal Storms Of Eternity.
With No Strings Attached, Ancestor (1993) (Demo). Intro—Depressed / Until You Suffer / Punishment / The Thread Of Life / Come Back Towards The Light.
Material World God, Ancestor (1996) (Demo). Black Paradise / The Black Waltz / Medical Transfusion / Demons.
Tomorrow, Ancestor (1998) (Demo). Seeking The Truth / The Black Waltz / Tomorrow / Demons.
Under The Burbot's Nest, Ancestor (1998) (Demo). Tune Of Death / The Hellfire / Darkness That Lights Ahead.

ANCHOR

JÄRVENPÄÄ, FINLAND — *Saku Korosuo (vocals / guitar), Miika Rynkänen (bass), Jani Aalto (drums).*

Järvenpää based Nu-Thrash trio ANCHOR came into being during 1995. A demo, 'No More Lies', arrived in 1999, followed by the 2001 EP 'Pain Inside'. ANCHOR's third session resulted in the EP 'Anccd-004' in 2002. Line-up changes along the way saw the loss of bass player Jarkko Laine and keyboard player Osku Louhelainen.

No More Lies, Anchor (1999) (Demo). No More Lies / Prisoner Of Life / I Don't Care / Thief In The Night / Fear Not / Strange Afternoon / Cosmic Rage.
Pain Inside EP, (2001). Angry Thoughts / Disease / Pain Inside / Blinded Eyes / Search / Broken Day.
Anccd-004, (2002). Set Me Free / It Takes Me / Chains.

ANESTHESY

BELGIUM — *Frank Libeert (vocals / guitar), Werner Vanlaere (guitar), Chris Decaesteker (bass), Diego Denorme (drums).*

A Thrash Metal act with distinct Death overtones dating to 1986 and formed by ex-VENDETTA guitarist Frank "Liberty" Libeert, ANESTHESY debuted with their 'Seasons Of The Witch' demo. A further demo tape 'Overdose', released in 1989, led to a deal with English label C.M.F.T. Unfortunately, after recording their debut album the record label went bust and the tracks seemed destined to remain unreleased.

Undeterred, ANESTHESY re-recorded some of these songs, releasing them as the self financed 'Just Married' EP in 1991. The band would lose their original drummer Ringo around this juncture pulling in Diego Denorme as replacement. Soon after the release of 'Just Married' ANESTHESY would also induct bassist Chris Decaessteker then second guitarist Werner Vanlaere into the fold.

Further recordings were submitted to the Tessa Records compilation 'Demolition' which led in turn to an album deal with the Black Mark label. Recording of the 1994 'Exaltation Of The Eclipse' record would take its toll on the band though witnessing the departure of Decaesteker. A substitute was duly located in Stefaan Vanijzere.

Tragedy would strike the band on the 15th July 1994. A horrific car crash would injure Vanijzere and kill Libeert. The remaining members vowed to continue and built the band back up to strength with the addition of singer Sven Houfflijn and guitarist David Vandewalle.

This unit prepared the way for their next release 'The Fifth Season' but would be disappointed to find Black Mark failing to renew their option. Vanlaere broke ranks to be replaced by Guy Commeene. Shortly after Vandewalle bade farewell too. His position would be taken by Jason Masschelein and this variant of ANESTHESY eventually committed 'The Fifth Season' to tape for new label Midas Productions.

The group would capitalise on this release by self financing a third effort 1999's 'Let The Mayhem Begin'. Wouter Nottebaert would now assume bass duties and with the recordings completed Reiner Schenk usurped Masschelein.

ANESTHESY supported the likes of NAPALM DEATH, KREATOR, GOREFEST and MORGOTH but would enter a period of inactivity in 2000. Putting closure to this hiatus, the band was resurrected for a July 2004 live show at the Wevelgem 'Metal Assault fest'. Sven Houfflijn joined FLESHMOULD in August of 2004.

JUST MARRIED, Anesthesy (1991). Ace Of Death / Inflammation Of The Bowels / The Ballad Of Jimmy F. / Rerisin' Humanist / Disbelieve / Just Married.
EXALTATION OF THE ECLIPSE, Black Mark BMCD 54 (1994). Primal Exaltation / Beyond Sadness / The Defector / Guardian / Survival Of The Fittest / Intestinal Haemorrahage / The Change / The Ultimate Reincarnatior / Enstrangled Minds / The Sun, The Red, The Blood / Eclipticus Finale Exclinatum.
THE FIFTH SEASON, Midas Productions (1998). Black Soul / Tears Of A Mortal / Cruelty / Brutal Expressions / Forgotten Epitaph / Across The Burning Fields / Retribution / Those Left Behind / Perishable Considerations.
LET THE MAYHEM BEGIN, Anesthesy (1999). Introduction / The Pain I Hide / Darknight Slaughter / The Chaos Path / The Final Sleep / Forever Silent / A Walk Through Infinity / The Last Straw.

ANGEL DUST

DORTMUND, GERMANY — *Dirk Thurisch (vocals), Bernd Aufermann (guitar), Frank Banx (bass), Steven Banx (keyboards), Dirk Asmuth (drums).*

Dortmund's ANGEL DUST have proven to be stoic Thrash flagbearers since their inception in 1984. The band has made no less than three reunion attempts, all more successful than the last. Enduring numerous line up changes ANGEL DUST have stuck to their guns watching musical trends come and go. With the close of the millennium ANGEL DUST are still reaching out to an ever appreciative and growing international fan base.

ANGEL DUST, founded by bass player Frank Banx and drummer Dirk Assmuth, created ripples outside of Germany with their uncompromising Speed Metal debut 1987 album 'Into The Dark Past'. The record would sell over 30'000 copies in Germany alone. However, the band was never totally capable of promoting the product other than a few European gigs as guitarists Andreas Lohrum and Romme Keymer were committed to their homeland's military service.

ANGEL DUST folded, only to be resurrected by Coe, Banx and Assmuth with two new guitarists Vinni Lynn and Stefan K. Nauer. The ensuing 'To Dust You Will Decay' album being produced by the highly regarded veteran Kit Woolven. The band toured Germany in alliance with RUNNING WILD during January of 1989 but that November the band folded.

Vocalist S.L. Coe later joined SCANNER and REACTOR. He was later to issue a creditable solo album in 2000 titled 'Metal'. Banx meantime joined Speed Metal band CROWS in 1991 alongside the future SODOM duo of guitarist Bernd Kost and drummer Bobby Schottkowski together with SCANNER's Leczek Szpigiel. The CROWS issued the Century Media album 'The Dying Race' but folded in 1993.

1998 saw the reformation of ANGEL DUST with the 'Border Of Reality' album for new label Century Media. Joining Banx was his sibling Steven on keyboards, vocalist / guitarist Dirk Thurisch and guitarist Bernd Aufermann.

ANGEL DUST toured Europe in the Spring of 1998 on a package bill with OVERKILL, NOCTURNAL RITES and NEVERMORE. A later jaunt found the band sharing European stages with JAGPANZER and the comeback was completed with appearances at the 'Wacken Open Air' and 'Rock Hard' festivals. The 'Bleed' album, produced by Siggi Bemm and crafted in less than three weeks, would spread word of ANGEL DUST's resurrection globally. American variants of the album would come complete with differing artwork and no less than three bonus tracks.

ANGEL DUST, marking their growing maturity, issued the 2000 album 'Enlighten The Darkness'. Touring in September to promote the release had the band as part of a package billing in Europe alongside STEEL PROPHET, LEFAY and STORMHAMMER. The following month founder member Dirk Assmuth announced his departure as the band inducted former HOUSE OF SPIRITS man Michael Sticken for live work.

In November ANGEL DUST retired to the recording studio to commit to tape tracks for tribute albums, namely 'Believe' by SAVATAGE and URIAH HEEP's seminal 'Easy Livin'. Thurisch would also find time to guest on the GB ARTS album 'The Lake'.

Aufermann would find his services requested by DEMONS & WIZARDS for live work but turned this offer down. In June of 2001 as the guitarist busied himself with a solo side project dubbed THE SHINING he would find himself ejected from the band. Ironically his quickfire replacement would be none other than DEMONS & WIZARDS touring guitarist and member of Indianapolis outfit 12FLUIDOUNCES Ritchie Wilkinson. Assmuth would also be welcomed back into the fold as ANGEL DUST got to grips with their debut American shows billed alongside NEVERMORE, OPETH and GOD FORBID.

ANGEL DUST would perform at the 2001 'ProgPower' festival utilising drummer Nick Seelinger of Colorado act SILENCER, Ritchie Wilkison's present act, as stand in. The 2002 album 'Of Human Bondage' would surprisingly include a cover of the SEAL tune 'Killer'. Touring in Europe during April found ANGEL DUST on a package billing with RHAPSODY and AT VANCE. However, just as ANGEL DUST seemed to be on the verge of an international breakthrough the band suddenly splintered, pulling out of both the 'Wacken Open Air' and 'Metal Dayz' festivals at short notice. An aggrieved Steven Banx, together with Wilkison, vowed to carry on.

With ANGEL DUST seemingly on ice, vocalist Dirk Thurisch set to work on a proposed solo venture, recording tracks with band mate Bernd Aufermann on guitar alongside TIAMAT bass player Anders Iwer and drummer Stefan Gemballa of FLOWING TEARS. By October of 2004 an all new ANGEL DUST line-up had been unveiled, counting vocalist Dirk Thurisch, guitarist Bernd Aufermann, keyboard player Steven Banx and drummer Dirk Assmuth. The group drafted a new singer in October 2005, former EVERFLOW frontman Carsten Kaiser. New album recordings, with new bassist Christian Pohlmann, would be scheduled for March 2006.

INTO THE DARK PAST, Disaster 10004 (1987). Into The Dark Past / I'll Come Back / Legions Of Destruction / Gambler / Fighters Return / Atomic Roar / Victims Of Madness / Marching For Revenge.

TO DUST YOU WILL DECAY, Disaster 10008 (1988). Third Challenge / Mr. Inferno / Wings Of An Angel / Into The Dark Past (Chapter II) / The King / To Dust You Will Decay / Stranger / The Duel / Hold On.

BORDER OF REALITY, Century Media CD 77220-2 (1998). Of Reality / No More Faith / Nightmare / Centuries / When I Die / Where The Wind Blows / Spotlight Kid / Behind The Mirror / Coming Home.

BLEED, Century Media (1999). Bleed / Black Rain / Never / Follow Me (Part I) / Follow Me (Part II) / Addicted To Serenity / Surrender / Sanity / Liquid Angel.

ENLIGHTEN THE DARKNESS, Century Media (2000). Let Me Live / The One You Are / Enjoy! / Fly Away / Come Into Resistance / Beneath The Silence / Still I'm Bleeding / I Need You / First In Line / Cross Of Hatred / Oceans Of Tomorrow.

OF HUMAN BONDAGE, Century Media (2002). The Human Bondage / Inhuman / Unreal Soul / Disbeliever / Forever / Unite / Got This Evil / The Cultman / Freedom Awaits / Killer.

ANGEL WITCH

LONDON, UK — *Kevin Heybourne (vocals / guitar), Kevin Riddles (bass), Dave Dufort (drums).*

A NWoBHM era London band that generated a cult following among the Metalheads of the American West coast based upon the occult overtones and contrasting speed and heaviness of their original 1980 album. Latterly the band has found appreciation amongst the Doom crowd for the acknowledged Sabbathian sounds delivered on their debut album.

ANGEL WITCH was founded in 1977 by guitarist Kevin Heybourne. Originally titled LUCIFER Heybourne switched to ANGEL WITCH when he heard of another LUCIFER doing the rounds. The band went through numerous line-ups, which would include guitarist Rob Downing and drummer Steve Jones, before the classic power trio comprising Heybourne, bassist Kevin Riddles and drummer Dave Hogg. The band's official debut on record was the cut 'Baphomet' on the now legendary EMI Records 'Metal For Muthas' compilation in February 1980. ANGEL WITCH also submitted a track 'Extermination Day' to the 1980 BBC compilation album 'Metal Explosion'.

EMI released a solitary single, 'Sweet Danger', which scored a minor impact on the national charts, peaking at number 75. The label did not take up an option to release an album though and ANGEL WITCH switched over to the Bronze concern to craft their full-length opus, succinctly self-titled and produced by Martin Smith from the ELECTRIC LIGHT ORCHESTRA. However, at this critical juncture, Hogg was found to be suffering from leukemia necessitating, ex-E.F. BAND drummer Dave Dufort stepping in as replacement after the album release.

Dufort actually has a lengthy history in rock n' roll being an ex-member of 1965's THE VOICE, THE SCENERY and PAPER BLITZ ISSUE. All of these mid 60's acts featured latter day SAVOY BROWN, DOG SOLDIER and CHICKEN SHACK guitarist MILLER ANDERSON. Dufort then moved on to EAST OF EDEN in the late 60's, he appears on the 1968 album 'Mercator Projected', as well as being a member of KEVIN AYERS band.

At the height of their popularity ANGEL WITCH ranked alongside IRON MAIDEN and SAXON at the forefront of the NWoBHM. The band's success was relatively short lived though, as gigs became few and far between. British shows were limited to London Marquee appearances and one off events, whilst the only date abroad was at the East German Erfurt Festival. A band issued rarity, the 'Give It Some Tickle' live cassette, saw limited issue in 1981. This tape, released to fan cub members of the ANGEL WITCH 'coven', was recorded at The Norbeck Castle, Blackpool on January 29th 1981 and closed out with a cover version of BLACK SABBATH's 'Paranoid'.

At one point Polydor were due to release a live album culled from a 1982 show, but this never surfaced. The original band split after the debut with Riddles and Dufort going on to form TYTAN. Riddles was last spotted in a covers band with ex-ONSLAUGHT, TORINO and HIGHWIRE vocalist Tony O'Hora.

The beginning of 1982 saw Heybourne flirting briefly with DEEP MACHINE before persevering by playing the odd club gig as ANGEL WITCH featuring new members, namely REMUS DOWN BOULEVARD bassist Gerry Cunningham and DEEP MACHINE drummer Ricky Bruce. ANGEL WITCH became Heybourne's full time act once more in early 1982 as Cunningham and Bruce were enticed away from DEEP MACHINE along with vocalist Roger Marsden. The line-up was merely a brief tenure, however as in May 1983 Heybourne announced he was fronting BLIND FURY in alliance with singer Lou Taylor, MARQUIS DE SADE bassist Peter Gordelier and drummer Steve Coleman. Marsden joined the Swedish band E.F. BAND then in 1984 forged a union with another ex-ANGEL WITCH and E.F. BAND man drummer Dave Dufort to create NEVADDA FOXX.

ANGEL WITCH surfaced again in 1985 with Heybourne and Gordelier splitting from BLIND FURY and enrolling original drummer Dave Hogg together with vocalist Dave Tattum. With this incarnation of the band they laid down the quite commercial edged 'Screamin And Bleedin'' album. Hogg left the band once more after its release and was replaced by former DEXYS MIDNIGHT RUNNERS drummer Spencer Hollman. Gigs were still few and far between.

Third album 'Frontal Assault' saw ANGEL WITCH return to their former heaviness but Tattum left upon its completion to join melodic Rock outfit NIGHTWING leaving Heybourne to assume vocal duties. In 1989 the band added a second guitarist Grant Dennison. A short tour of Holland followed with support act SATAN, but Heybourne eventually relocated to California where nostalgia for early ANGEL WITCH reaped the reward of a live set of 'classics'. The band recorded a demo, at Prairie Sun Studios in San Francisco, with EXODUS drummer Tom Hunting, LÄÄZ ROCKIT bassist Jon Torres and guitarist Lee Altus of HEATHEN but failed to secure a new deal. Ex-bassist Peter Gordelier went on to join DRIVESHAFT.

Although ANGEL WITCH failed to live up to the legend that was created around the band early on the band remained an influence with groups that arrived on the scene in later years with both ONSLAUGHT and TROUBLE covering the ANGEL WITCH classic 'Confused'.

Interest was renewed in 1996 by the release of a live album on High Vaultage Records. ANGEL WITCH themselves were far from dormant issuing a CD compilation of various demos including the 1987 'Psychopathic' tapes and 1999's set 'Twist Of The Knife'. The resulting album 'Resurrection' was at first only available via the internet, then in 2000 released through Crook'd Records in the US and by Zoom Records in the UK.

ANGEL WITCH was back in 2000 for live gigs and a projected new album. Alongside Heybourne the fresh look band comprised guitarist Keith Herzberg, bass player Richie Wicks, a former lead vocalist of SONS OF EDEN and VIOLENTLY FUNKY, and drummer Scott Higham. The band bounced back in quite spectacular style with a performance at the prestigious 'Wacken' Metal festival in Germany before setting to work on fresh studio material.

The list of bands to have covered 'Confused' increased in 2001 as Americans SIX FEET UNDER cut a grindingly heavy take for their latest album. In August 2001 it was announced that Higham had decamped to join the highly regarded SHADOWKEEP. Ace Finchum, a former member of Glam band TIGERTAILZ, took his place.

In November the ANGEL WITCH ranks splintered further with Wicks opting to resume his former role as a lead singer and opting to join fellow NWoBHM resurrectees TYGERS OF PAN TANG. Statements issued by band members in January 2002 would confirm the fact that ANGEL WITCH had folded once again, Wicks resuming action with SONS OF EDEN. However, in August a surprise official statement confirmed that Kevin Heybourne, Keith Herzberg, Richie Wicks and Scott Higham had resolved their differences and were back in action yet again. During October Richie Weeks, maintaining his position with both ANGEL WITCH and TYGERS OF PAN TANG, enrolled as lead vocalist for Power Metal band SHADOWKEEP.

By January of 2003 ANGEL WITCH had been re-built once more, Heybourne now being joined by former colleagues Jon Torres and Tom Hunting with Lee Altus of HEATHEN repute plus Doug Piercy, also from HEATHEN. This version of the group appeared at the German 'Bang Your Head' festival that same year. However, the trio of guitarist Keith Herzberg, bassist/vocalist Richie Wicks and drummer Scott Higham claimed that the band was, in fact, over. The US Heybourne version of the band soon encountered line-up problems though as Hunting decamped in order to concentrate on his priority act EXODUS. Erstwhile HEATHEN and current DECONSTRUCT Darren Minter filled in.

Sadly guitarist Myk Taylor, who appeared three tracks featured on the 'Resurrection' album, died from leukemia on 21st August 2003. He was just 41 years old.

Sweet Danger, EMI 5064 (1980). Sweet Danger / Flight Nineteen. Chart position: 75 UK.
Angel witch, Bronze BRO 108 (1980). Angel witch / Gorgon.
Sweet Danger, EMI 12 EMI 5064 (1980). Sweet Danger / Flight Nineteen / Hades Paradise.
ANGEL WITCH, Bronze BRON532 (1980). Angel Witch / Atlantis / White Witch / Confused / Sorcerers / Gorgon / Sweet Danger / Free Man / Angel Of Death / Devil's Tower.
Give It Some Tickle, (1981) (Live demo cassette). Sweet Danger / They Wouldn't Dare / Angel Of Death / The Sorcerers / Confused / Evil Games / Gorgon / White Witch / Baphomet / Angel Witch / Devils Tower / Paranoid.
Loser, Bronze BRO 121 (1981). Loser / Suffer / Dr Phibes.
SCREAMIN' N' BLEEDIN', Killerwatt KILP4001 (1985). Who's To Blame / Child Of The Night / Evil Games / Afraid Of The Dark / Screamin' And Bleedin' / Reawakening / Waltz The Night / Goodbye / Fatal Kiss / UXB.
Goodbye, Killerwatt KIL 3001 (1985). Goodbye / Reawakening.
FRONTAL ASSAULT, Killerwatt KILP4003 (1986). Frontal Assault / Dreamworld / Rendezvous With The Blade / Religion (Born Again) / Straight From Hell / She Don't Lie / Take To The Wing / Something Wrong / Undergods.
LIVE, Metal Blade ZORRO 1 (1990). Angel Of Death / Sweet Danger / Confused / Sorceress / Gorgon / Baphomet / Extermination Day / Atlantis / Flight 19 / Angel Witch / White Witch.
'82 REVISITED (LIVE), High Vaultage HV-1005 (1996). Gorgon / Nowhere To Run / They Wouldn't Dare / Sorceress / Evil Games / White Witch / Angel Of Death / Angel Witch / Evil Games (Studio Version) / They Wouldn't Dare (Studio Version) / Nowhere To Run (Studio Version).
RESURRECTION, Angel witch (1998). Psychopathic I / Time To Die / Violence / Silent But Deadly / Twist Of The Knife / Psychopathic II / Slowly Sever / Worm / Scrape The Well / Inertia.
2000: LIVE AT THE LA2, (2000). Atlantis / Confused / Twist Of The Knife / Gorgon / White Witch / Sorceress / Extermination Day / Psychopathic / Baphomet / Angel Of Death / Guitar solo / Angel Witch.
They Wouldn't Dare, Archaic Temple Productions TREASURE002 (2003) (Limited edition 666 copies). They Wouldnt Dare / Nowhere To Run / Evil Games / They Wouldnt Dare (Live).
ANGEL WITCH: 25TH ANNIVERSARY EXPANDED EDITION, Sanctuary (2005). Angel Witch / Atlantis / White Witch / Confused / Sorcerers / Gorgon / Sweet Danger / Free Man / Angel Of Death / Devil's Tower / Loser / Suffer / Dr Phibes / Flight Nineteen / Baphomet / Hades Paradise / Sweet Danger / Angel Of Death / Extermination Day / Angel Witch.
ANGEL OF DEATH, Mausoleum (2006). Gorgon / Nowhere To Run / They Wouldn't Dare / The Sorceress / Evil Games / White Witch / Angel Of Death / Angel Witch / Evil Games (Studio) / They Wouldn't Dare (Studio) / Nowhere To Run (Studio).

ANGELUS APATRIDA

SPAIN — *Guillermo Izquierdo (vocals / guitar), David G. Álvarez (guitar), Jose J. Izquierdo (bass), Víctor Valera (drums).*

Thrash Metal act ANGELUS APATRIDA debuted with the demo 'Lost In The Realms Of Orchinodaemon', issued in July 2001. They followed up with the demo 'Unknown Human Being' in September 2003. The band recorded the 2004 album 'Evil Unleashed' at Korsakov Studios in Madrid with producer Kosta Vázquez. Set to be released by Red Dragon Records, it would originally include a cover version of METALLICA's 'Master Of Puppets'. The track 'Supremacy In Chaos' would be featured on the Lithuanian compilation album 'Atlantida Metal Vol. 23'.

The band committed their take on 'Danza De La Muerte' for the Red Dragon album 'Despertando Al Innombrable' in honour of veteran Spanish act PANZER.

'Evil Unleashed' was issued in March 2006 through Producciones Malditas, now closing with a cover version of PANTERA's 'Domination'. The group also included the track 'Negotiating The Clowns' on the compilation album 'Viñarock 2006' in April.

Lost In The Realms Of Orchinodaemon, (2001). The Realms Of Orchinodaemon / Metal Flesh / Behind The Fog Of War / Libris Arcana / Magonia.

Unknown Human Being, (2003). Backbone Crasher / Supremacy In Chaos / Sons Of Revolution / Unknown Human Being.

EVIL UNLEASHED, Producciones Malditas PM CD 210 (2006). Overture: The Dictate / Versus The World / Fuck You / Backbone Crusher / Gone Away / Time To Rise Hell / Negotiating The Clowns / The Thornmaker / Sons Of Revolution / Hereditary Genius / Killers And Killed / Domination.

ANGER

AVEIRO, PORTUGAL — *Pedro Pereira (vocals / guitar), Lino Vinagre (guitar), Ricardo Melo (bass), Luís Silva (keyboards), Afonso Corte-Real (drums).*

Thrash / Crossover outfit ANGER was formulated in the city of Aveiro during late 1994, counting a membership of vocalist / guitarist Pedro Pereira, guitarist Lino Vinagre, bassist Tó Viegas and Afonso Corte-Real on the drums. ANGER's first commercial showing would be with the inclusion of the song 'Revolution' on the compilation album 'Hypermetal' in 1995. It would be their second live performance, at the Johnny Guitar venue in Lisbon in October 1995, that scored a deal with the NorteSul record company. Their first album, an eponymous 1997 outing, would be released through NorteSul subsidiary Valentim de Carvalho, preceded by the single 'Low Life'.

Ricardo Melo substituted Viegas for the bass position in July 1997. Subsequent live dates included an appearance at the SCORPIONS and MEGADETH headlined 'Imperial ao Vivo' festival plus other outdoor events such as the 'Sudoeste', 'Paredes de Coura' and 'Rock in Ria' festivals, the latter once again with MEGADETH. Support shows included dates with ONE MINUTE SILENCE, CLAWFINGER, BREED 77 and D.R.I. on shows in 1998 throughout the Netherlands, Belgium, France, Switzerland, Germany, Austria, Hungary, Slovenia, Italy and Spain.

N November of 1998 the band, adding keyboard player Luís Silva, set to work on follow up 'Y2K', undertaking a nationwide guest slot to TARANTULA and European headline shows supported by Dutch act VANITY FAIR before the album release. A single, 'Look Sharp', emerged before 'Y2K' issue in May 1999. The live campaign to push the album found ANGER appearing at the 'Super Bock Super Rock', 'T99' with METALLICA and MONSTER MAGNET, 'Hard Fest' and 'Sudoeste' festivals and performed as the opening act for MEGADETH in Coliseu do Porto. Other dates into 2000 saw stage alliances with BREED 77 and LEADFOOT.

ANGER and NorteSul parted company in February 2001 due to the label's business problems. That April ANGER contributed their rendition of 'If You Close Your Eyes' to a TARANTULA tribute album. They also managed to support SOULFLY at Praça Sony in Lisbon that year.

Cobra Records picked the band up for their third album, recording in May and July of 2003 at Area 51 Studios in Hannover, Germany, with VICTORY guitarist Tommy Newton acting as producer. 'The Bliss' would see the light of day in September 2003, anticipated by the single 'Say (What You Wanna)'.

ANGER, Valentim de Carvalho (1997). Low Life / Liar / Bring In The Pain / Man With A Vision / Awakened Unconsciousness / War Way! / I (dentity) / Survive / Dont Blame Me / Save Us / Lost Soul / Careless Toys.

Y2K, Nortesul (1999). Pinky In Vitro / Obsession / Nightliner / Torn Mind / Mobill / I Am A Lone / Misfit / Religion Of Fear / Warchild / Call It Revolution / Look Sharp.

THE BLISS, Cobra (2003). Feel My Anger / Another Game / Iced / Devil In My Mind / Say (What You Wanna) / Instants / Upside Down / Innersight / Xenemy / God In Me / Gonna Drown / Lost Soul.

ANGKOR WAT

CORPUS CHRISTI, TX, USA — *David Brinkman (vocals), Adam Grossman (guitar), Danny Lohner (guitar), Mike Titsworth (bass), Dave Nuss (drums).*

Highly rated experimental Thrash Metal act, named after the Cambodian Buddhist Khmer temple complex, out of Corpus Christi, Texas. The band was created during the late eighties by formed by guitarists Adam Grossman and Danny Lohner. A demo, 'Demonstration Under Duress', surfaced in 1987. Signing with Metal Blade Records the debut album, the Kerry Crafton produced 'When Obscenity Becomes The Norm ... Awake!', surfaced in April 1989. Recording line-up comprised Grossman and Lohner alongside singer David Brinkman ("Dee"), bassist Mike Titsworth ("Titty") and drummer Dave Nuss ("Bambi"). Both Corpus Christi and Brinkman were out of the picture for the 1990 'Corpus Christi' follow up.

Having operating under pseudonyms for ANGKOR WAT, "Edith Bunker" and "King Bunnie" respectively, Danny Lohner and Adam Grossman went on to Industrialists SKREW upon ANGKOR WAT's demise during 1991, the latter under yet another nom de guerre of 'Opposum'. Metal Blade combined both ANGKOR WAT albums as a posthumous release in 1995.

Lohner joined NINE INCH NAILS in 1996. In 2005 Lohner formed up BLACK LIGHT BURNS with former LIMP BIZKIT guitarist Wes Borland.

WHEN OBSCENITY BECOMES THE NORM—AWAKE, Metal Blade 72408 (1989). Innocence '89 / Something To Cry About / Seat Of Power / Prolonged Agony / Ricky / The Search / Awake! / Under Lock And Key / Emotional Blackmail / Warsaw / Died Young / Circus Of Horrors / Civilized.

CORPUS CHRISTI, Metal Blade ZORRO 5 (1990). Indestructible: Innocence '90 / Corpus Christi / Turn Of The Screw / Golden / Anne Marie / Birdsong (Earth) / Ordinary Madness / Sinking / Schizophrenic / Barracuda / Sour Born.

ANGOR

CHILE — *Felipe Roa (vocals / guitar), Jose Ign. Solari (guitar), Felipe Cordova (bass), Luis Castillo (drums).*

ANGOR was founded in 1995 by vocalist / guitarist Felipe Roa and drummer Cristian Espinoza, subsequently introducing bass player Pedro Barrera. Later recruits would be singer Cristian Espinoza and new drummer Cristian Herrera with second guitarist José Solari enrolled in 1997. Line up changes then saw the bass position being handed over to Carlos Briones. However, both Briones and Herrera exited in 1999. Espinoza took over the lead vocal role whilst Felipe Córdova was installed on bass as the group opened with a 1999 EP 'Sin Fin De Tormento'.

Luis Castillo came onboard as new drummer in 2000. Frontman Cristian Espinoza took his leave in 2001 as the band trimmed to a quartet. ANGOR band supported CANNIBAL CORPSE in Santiago during September of 2002.

Sin Fin De Tormento EP, Independent (1999). Muerto Humano / Once / Fracaso / Rapto.

ANIHILATED

UK — *Simon Cobb (vocals / guitar), Mark Beuchet (guitar), Lee Hittman (bass), Paul Rodwell (drums).*

ANIHILATED began life as the early 80s Punk act PROSPEX, citing a line-up of vocalist Andy, guitarist Si (Simon Cobb), bassist Lee Hittman and drummer Bod (Paul Rodwell). A spate of local gigs led up to the recording of a demo, during which Andy parted ways with the band. Si duly took on the lead vocal role. The band would be further augmented with the addition of second guitarist Mark Beuchet, previously with fellow Punks POISON. A shift in musical direction was prompted by the first wave of American Thrash Metal. Retaining their Punk ethos, exemplified by socially conscious lyrics, the band evolved into ANIHILATED. In 1986 the EP 'Path To Destruction' emerged on the Brew label, recorded by Simon Cobb, Mark Beuchet, Lee Hittman and Paul Rodwell.

The group signed to the Endangered Musik label for debut album 'Created In Hate'. Although declared by the influential

'Metal Forces' magazine as "The most important UK thrash release to date" it was acknowledged the album was let down by a below par production. Live work to promote the record was sporadic. ANIHILATED shifted label to the Metalworks concern for 1989's follow up 'The Ultimate Desecration'.

Unfortunately the release date was continually pushed back and projected tours of Europe never materialised. The band was put in an unenviable position of having a record advertised that was unavailable in stores. When the album finally did emerge all momentum was lost and the group managed just a handful of gigs to support it. Disillusioned both Lee and Mark Beuchet decamped, the latter founding LOVE LIES BLEEDING. ANIHILATED soldiered on by drafting new members for a third album projected as 'Carnival Of Souls'. The recordings never reached conclusion and the group unsurprisingly splintered.

Bod subsequently joined Beuchet in LOVE LIES BLEEDING prior to creating CROWROAD. Si forged NIGHTBREED, a short-lived band that at one juncture included future CRADLE OF FILTH bassist Rob Eaglestone in the ranks. Rodwell joined KERBSLIDER.

The 'Ultimate Desecration' album was re-issued on the Real Metal label during 2002. A live album surfaced in 2005.

Path Of Destruction, Brew BREW 001 (1986). Innocent Victims / Anihilated / Thunderflash / Shadows Of Fear.

CREATED IN HATE, Metalworks VOV668 (1988). Chase The Dragon / Slaughter / Power Is The Path / Anihilated (Part Two) / Final Dawn / Nightmare / Aftermath / Seventh Veil.

THE ULTIMATE DESECRATION, Metalworks (1989). Desolation / Into The Flames Of Armageddon / Skinned Alive / Lost Souls / Lethal Dose / No Rest For The Wicked / Internal Darkness / Legacy Of Hate / Enter The Realm / Exeunt.

LIVE, Brew (2005). Desolation / Into The Flames Of Armageddon / Skinned Alive / Lost Souls / Lethal Dose / No Rest For The Wicked / Internal Darkness / Legacy Of Hate / Enter The Realm / Exeunt.

ANIMAL ALPHA

OSLO, NORWAY — *Agnethe Skjølsrud (vocals), Christer Andre Cederberg (guitar), Christian (guitar), Lars Imre Bidtnes (bass), Christian (drums).*

ANIMAL ALPHA was formed in 2002 when lead singer Agnethe Skjølsrud located guitarist and songwriter Christian Wibe through a musicians-wanted ad placed at the men's room at a local club in Oslo. This founding duo would soon be joined by bass player Lars Imre Bidtnes, guitarist Christer Andre Cederberg and drummer Thomas Jacobsen. The band rapidly fostered a strong live following built on club gigs and a performance at the 'Øya' festival in 2004. With a reported eleven labels after their signature, ANIMAL ALPHA signed to the independent Racing Junior imprint to issue an eponymous EP.

ANIMAL ALPHA's 2005 album 'Pheromones' was produced by the high profile industry figure Sylvia Massy Shivy at her Radiostar Studios in California. The lead in single, 'Bundy', featured on soundtrack to two Playstation 2 games 'Burnout Revenge' and 'NHL 06', made it to number 4 on the national Norwegian charts. Other exposure would be less desirable though, when the sinister promotional video was mistakenly aired on children's television much to the anger of the daytime public. 'Pheromones' reached number 11 on the charts with a second single 'Most Wanted Cowboy' also scoring significant airplay.

On the live front, ANIMAL ALPHA appeared on the summer 2005 festival front at 'Rock Am Ring' and 'Rock Im Park' in Germany, 'Download' in the UK and the 'Hultsfred Festival' in Sweden.

Animal Alpha, Animal Alpha (2004). Bundy / I Really Want You To Dance / Billy Bob Jackson / Catch Me.

Animal Alpha, Racing Junior RJCDS030 (2005). Bundy / Big Surprise / Trobbel / Waltz.

PHEROMONES, Racing Junior RJCD032 (2005). Billy Bob Jackson / I. R. W. Y. T. D. / Bundy / Most Wanted Cowboy / Catch Me / 101 Ways / Deep In / My Droogies / Bend Over / Remember The Day. Chart position: 11 NORWAY.

ANNIHILATOR

VANCOUVER, BC, CANADA — *Dave Padden (vocals), Jeff Waters (guitar), Curran Murphy (guitar), Sandor de Bretan (bass), Rob Falzano (drums).*

Vancouver based, speed orientated, Heavy Metal band ANNIHILATOR first came to attention with their opening 1985 'Welcome To Your Death' six song demo cassette, also known as the 'Psycho Metal Kids' tape. Guitarist and band mentor Jeff Waters is known for infusing his band with a creative edge personified by his inventive riffing style. Prior to founding ANNIHILATOR guitarist Jeff Waters had been a member of Ottawa's TROJAN HAMMER. Featuring a line-up of Waters, vocalist John Perinbam, bass player Kevin Jung and drummer Mike Lane TROJAN HAMMER only managed two gigs, at the Churchill Arms. Waters and Perinbam also assembled a recording project, along with drummer Mike Farmer, dubbed THE JEFF WATERS PROJECT prior to assembling the first ANNIHILATOR line-up.

At its earliest stage ANNIHILATOR was basically a duo of vocalist / guitarist Jeff Waters and vocalist John Bates. This pair would demo up the song 'Annihilator', with Waters handling all instrumentation, including the drums. Once this song had been put down onto tape, bass player David Scott was then enrolled but the trio's keenness to present the act as a full-blown band unit meant that friend Rob Lange, who had just rendered the demo artwork, stood in as a pseudo-drummer for the first ANNIHILATOR "band" photograph.

The outfit located a real drummer, Paul Malek, then expanded their sound by employing second guitarists Myles Rourke and Joe Bongiorno in quick, and equally fleeting, succession. Malek offered the basement of his mother's clothing store as rehearsal space and it was here that the 'Welcome To Your Death' sessions were conducted. However, Malek was to opt out and Québec native Richard Death manned the drums for a short period.

Reinstating Paul Malek, this line-up produced a further demo, billed 'Phantasmagoria' with Waters assuming lead vocals, after which ANNIHILATOR once again re-formulated. Interest had been gained from a business manager in Vancouver, prompting a relocation from Ottawa for the guitarist in August 1987. Once in British Columbia Waters set about constructing an entirely fresh band unit, being joined by second guitarist Casey Taeves and drummer Ray Hartmann. Taeves tenure would only last as long as a photo shoot. Singer Dennis Dubeau had been auditioned but Waters chose the peroxide maned hard drinking ex-D.O.A. and IRON GYPSY bassist RANDY RAMPAGE. D.O.A. had been a renowned act which also provided the launch platform for BLACK FLAG and DANZIG drummer Chuck Biscuits. Pre-ANNIHILATOR, Rampage had even issued a solo 12" EP in 1982. The new look ANNIHILATOR cut a two song 'Alison Hell' demo in 1988, this effort landing the band a deal with Roadrunner Records. Two further tracks, 'Wicked Mystic' and 'Word Salad', were also worked up during this period. Casey Taeves tenure was to last a matter of days, enough to appear in one official photograph. Bassist Wayne Darley enrolled in 1989. Meantime, erstwhile ANNIHILATOR drummer Paul Malek created IVORY KNIGHT alongside former Waters compatriot singer John Perinbam, for the demo 'Voices In Your Nightmare'.

ANNIHILATOR's traditional approach to Metal gave them prominence toward the end of the Thrash boom and their debut September 1989 album 'Alice In Hell' won them many converts. Acknowledged as one of the very finest works of the genre, 'Alice In Hell', assembled at Fiasco Bros. Studios during the latter half of 1988, was financed courtesy of a national

Canadian government grant. Although guitarist Anthony Greenham, bassist Wayne Darley and former ASSAULT drummer Ray Hartmann are credited on the debut ANNIHILATOR album they did not take part in recording as Waters himself laid down all the instrumentation except drums.

Despite rapid progress, ructions within the band found Rampage out much to fans chagrin. Second guitarist Anthony Greenham, who had featured in the promotional video for the song 'Alison Hell', also made way for Dave Scott Davis. Although ANNIHILATOR had come late in the day in relation to the opening Thrash wave, the sheer quality and ferocity of the debut soon had many earmarking the group as a force to be reckoned with. Title track 'Alison Hell' made great inroads on the international Metal scene, generating solid album sales.

Taking 'Alison Hell' onto the road ultimately led to the dismissal of Rampage. Towards the close of a US / Canadian trek allied with TESTAMENT the singer apparently voiced concerns over commitments to his day job. Fearing this would jeopardise touring plans, Rampage was let go.

For 1990's 'Never Neverland' album the PANTHER and PRISONER credited singer Coburn Pharr took the vocal position, as ANNIHILATOR seemed poised on the edge of becoming a major act. Sections of the fan base bemoaned the absence of Rampage's high powered roar, despite Pharr's greater range, and many were bemused by the oddball 'Kraf Dinner', an ode to macaroni and cheese. The bulk of 'Never, Neverland' stood up well though, capitalising on the debut. The band set out on a world tour as a single guitar combo, Scott Davis having lost his place, these shows including the prestigious European support slot to JUDAS PRIEST's 'Painkiller' tour. 'Never Neverland' doubled the sales of its illustrious predecessor but Waters still had his eye on potential recognition outside of the band though, as he auditioned for MEGADETH in 1990. According to Dave Mustaine Waters came close to securing the position but it was not to be. Once live work for 'Never Neverland' had been fulfilled, Pharr took his leave, only to return to the ranks shortly afterward as ANNIHILATOR also pulled in second guitar player Neil Goldberg. However, once again Pharr decamped, subsequently re-fronting OMEN. The band fractured yet further still as Ray Hartmann relinquished his post.

Further line-up changes though slowed progress with August 1993's 'Set The World On Fire' seeing another singer in Aaron Randall. Whilst Hartmann had contributed percussive work to three tracks, drum work on the song 'Phoenix Rising' was supplied by both and Mike Mangini and Rick Fedyk of DOUBLE DEALER and later of KING KARMA and BILLY BUTCHER repute. 'Set The World On Fire' mellowed the trademark sound somewhat, a factor picked up by both fans and critics alike. The single from the album featured a nod to their former touring colleagues by way of a rework of JUDAS PRIEST's 'Hell Bent For Leather'. The ANNIHILATOR formula of Waters, Randall, Goldberg, bassist Wayne Darley and drummer Mike Mangini took to the European stages, after which the drummer bailed out to join EXTREME in time for their 1994 Castle Donington festival appearance. Goldberg too exited, and was replaced by former guitarist Dave Scott Davis for a headlining Canadian tour and US dates supporting LILLIAN AXE. The beleaguered band stoically committed themselves to Japanese shows. Despite Darley being unable to participate on the Japanese dates, ANNIHILATOR soldiered on with former guitar player Dave Scott Davis covering the bass position. New man Randy Black took on drum duties. This quartet also embarked on a short run of US shows.

Further line-up shuffles continued and ANNIHILATOR in 1994, now minus their deal with Roadrunner Records, had Waters, now also tackling lead vocals, alongside drummer Randy Black. This duo delivered the 1994 album 'King Of The Kill' for the Music For Nations label. Subsequently Dave Scott Davis was reinstated and Cam Dixon was drafted on bass. Roadrunner too delivered a parting shot with the 'Bag Of Tricks' compilation in October, this valuable collection pooling demos, live material and previously unreleased songs 'Back To The Crypt', 'Gallery' and 'Fantastic Things'.

By 1996 ANNIHILATOR had effectively trimmed down to Waters, Scott Davis and Black. Drafted to promote the groove orientated 'Refresh The Demon' album, arriving in March 1996, would be bassist Lou Bujdoso. Label distribution for 'Refresh The Demon' included CMC International for the USA, Music For Nations in the UK and FEMS in Japan. Just prior to European gigs the band was dealt a heavy blow as Randy Black backed out. Drafting new drummer Dave Machander the shows still went ahead. Waters also took time out from his main act to guest on rather more mellow outings including POKERFACE's 1996 album 'Life's A Gamble' and the following year's self titled effort from THE DISTANCE. Roadrunner raided their archives further to issue the live album 'In Command' that November, comprising concerts fronted by both Rampage and Pharr line-ups and closing with a cover version of AC/DC's 'Live Wire'.

By the December 1996 effort, the suitably titled 'Remains' recorded at the guitarist's own Watersound Studios in Maple Ridge, ANNIHILATOR had effectively become Waters solo project. Having progressively retreated farther from their Thrash roots with each and every release, 'Remains', to the abject horror of their devoted following, took an even greater leap into the realms of Electro and even Dancecore. Contributing musicians included guitarist John Bates and singer Dave Steele. The following year the group's first label Roadrunner re-issued the band's early albums in re-mastered form adding additional demo tracks.

1999 had the band bowing to fan pressure and reinstating both Rampage and Hartmann for the much lauded 'Criteria For A Black Widow' album, a welcome return to the band's former spirit and heaviness that unashamedly utilised visual, lyrical and musical themes from 'Alice In Hell'. Evolving yet again, the band pulled in new bass man Russell Bergquist. Randall and Hartmann meantime had founded SPEEED with SEVEN WITCHES and FROSTBITE guitarist Jack Frost for their 1999 album 'Powertrip Pigs'.

Ex-LIEGE LORD and OVERKILL man Joe Comeau joined the band in 2000 for 'Carnival Diablos', cementing the Thrash revival. With riffs once more in abundance, the group offered up a latter day Metal classic in the gargantuan 'Hunter Killer' but their quirky Canadian humour, and penchant for food, failed them at the last post with the unaccredited 'Chicken & Corn'. Comeau would divert himself in late 2000 for a one off reunion with his erstwhile LIEGE LORD guitar partner Paul Nelson to cut a version of 'Too Scared To Run' for a URIAH HEEP tribute album.

February 2001 found ANNIHILATOR on a headlining tour of Germany supported by a strong billing of NEVERMORE, SOILWORK and RAWHEAD REXX. Drummer Ray Hartman would bow out in favour of a returning Randy Black. In his time away from the fold the drummer had also been busying himself with an ambitious German based conceptual project band entitled REBELLION. Fronted by erstwhile XIRON and BLACK DESTINY vocalist Michael Seifert REBELLION had been established by ex-GRAVE DIGGER men guitarist Uwe Lulis and bassist Tommi Göttlich, Black as drummer and with WARHEAD's Bjorn Eilen on second guitar. This unit issued the Shakespeare inspired 'A Tragedy In Steel' debut in March of 2002.

Throughout the latter half of 2001 ANNIHILATOR would be in preparation for a new studio album billed 'Waking The Fury' and slated for a March 2002 release through the German Steamhammer label. The European version came complete with a bonus live recording of 'Shallow Grave' whilst Japanese variants added a live 'Refresh The Demon', recorded in Rumania. During November guitarist Curran Murphy of AGGRESSION CORE and NEVERMORE joined the ranks. However, bassist

David Scott would be forced out of the band due to injury. ANNIHILATOR announced European tour dates for April / May 2002, commencing in Vienna, Austria, backed up with strong support from SEVEN WITCHES and DEBASE.

In an odd twist of events Waters would end up joining the veteran epic Power Metal band SAVATAGE for their summer European 2002 dates. Al Pitrelli, SAVATAGE's regular and then only recently re-inducted six-stringer, was unable to make the tour due to prior commitments. ANNIHILATOR revealed during October they had signed to the German AFM label for a double live album suitably entitled 'Double Live Annihilation' set for early 2003 release. That same month it emerged that former ANNIHILATOR guitarist Neil Goldberg had assembled a Rap flavoured Nu-Metal project dubbed REDLIST, working in league with TALISMAN and YNGWIE MALMSTEEN veteran singer JEFF SCOTT SOTO, keyboard player and programmer Dave Fraser with a rapper named Eric.

Guitarist Curran Murphy garnered production credits with San Francisco Metal band VENGINCE, crafting their debut album at Smiley Studios in Seattle. ANNIHILATOR drummer Randy Black would deputise for German Power Metal band PRIMAL FEAR's summer 2003 US dates. He would also work with another German Metal act, REBELLION, and subsequently joined PRIMAL FEAR on a full term basis during August. In May vocalist Joe Comeau backed out and ANNIHILATOR duly replaced him with the Vancouver native Dave Padden. The band's European tour schedule throughout June and July saw appearances at the German 'Rock Harz' and 'Wacken Open Air' festivals, the Italian 'Summer Day In Hell' event, the Swiss 'Metal Dayz' gig and the 'Waldrock' Netherlands show.

With Randy Black firmly in position with PRIMAL FEAR the band welcomed back former drummer Mike Mangini in October for recording of a new studio album entitled 'All For You', released through The End Records in the USA and by the German AFM label. Bassist Russell Bergquist, pursuing a solo venture, exited the band in January of 2004. A new rhythm section of bassist Sandor de Bretan, previously with SUDDEN THUNDER, and drummer Rob Falzano would be installed during March. 'All For You' certainly presented a new sound for the band, fans and critics picking up on Padden's vocal similarities to Simon Le Bon and the music containing a good deal more diversity than before. Of these sessions, one track, 'Weapon X', did not make the final running order but would be subsequently issued as an internet download.

In other activity, Jeff Waters and Curran Murphy would have their composition 'Forever Ends' included on the April 2004 CANS 'Beyond The Gates' album, a solo effort from HAMMERFALL vocalist Joacim Cans. Also keeping himself active, Joe Comeau stepped in as temporary bassist for PAINMUSEUM's performance at the New Jersey 'March Metal Meltdown VI' festival. ANNIHILATOR gained a valuable round of support dates to JUDAS PRIEST's European dates in June.

In August it would be revealed that Jeff Waters had been holding talks with MEGADETH's Dave Mustaine. Waters, a man already holding a placing in MEGADETH's history, would be in consideration for the live line up of the band, but this union did not transpire. Waters would though be engaged as engineer on a remix project for fellow Canadian veterans EXCITER, remixing the band's first six albums, 'Heavy Metal Maniac' (1983), 'Violence and Force' (1984), 'Long Live the Loud' (1985), 'Better Live Than Dead' (1990), 'Unveiling the Wicked' (1986) and 'O.T.T.' (1988) for re-issue by Megaforce Records. Another project under proposal would be an all new band unit also featuring ANNIHILATOR singer Dave Padden.

In October Jeff Waters created some media waves by brazenly claiming he was "the fastest/tightest-picking guitarist in the world." Pointedly, not too many people came forward to refute his claims. 2005 opened with the guitarist contributing guitar work for Spanish Thrash Metal band LEGEN BELTZA's

ANNIHILATOR

conceptual track dubbed 'War of Wars' included on their album 'Dimension Of Pain'. Waters and Curran also guested on the 2005 album 'Repent Or Seal Your Fate' by Hannover Thrashers RECKLESS TIDE. Waters The also guested on 2005 solo album recordings by Greek keyboard player BOB KATSIONIS.

In March 2005 the former ANNIHILATOR pairing of lead vocalist Randy Rampage and drummer Ray Hartmann teamed up with bassist Stu Carruthers of GRIP INC. and JUST CAUSE, guitarist Ash Blue, ex-STRAPPING YOUNG LAD, and guitarist/vocalist Kick from VERTICAL AFTER to forge the "Urban Punk / Metal" band STRESS FACTOR 9. Meantime, Curran Murphy announced his new project, SHATTER MESSIAH. Fronting the band would be BREAKER and ex-ARCHETYPE singer Greg Wagner with ANNIHILATOR's Rob Falzano on drums. ANNIHILATOR returned in September 2005 with the 'Schizo Deluxe' album, the band's eleventh studio opus having Waters and Padden joined by Ottawa native Tony Chappelle on drums. 'Schizo Deluxe' closed the circle in the group's steady musical journey back towards 'Alice In Hell'. Reaction to the new records unbridled retro-thrash, particularly in Europe, was ecstatic. ANNIHILATOR would be rejoined by bassist Russ Bergquist for European touring.

In early January 2006 Dave Padden announced the formation of Heavy Metal concept SILENT STRAIN, a unit hailing from Canada, Denmark and Russia, comprising MNEMIC guitar player Mircea Eftemie Gabriel, second guitarist Cory McBain of CYANOTIC, bassist Rick Struve from GOD AWAKENS and CIVIL RUIN and Igor Chiefot on the drums. The following month ex-ANNIHILATOR man Joe Comeau joined Swedish Metal band TAD MOROSE as their new frontman.

European gigs were announced for July but then postponed in order to complete album recordings. However, ANNIHILATOR did still play the Spanish 'Metalway' festivals, in Guernika and Jerez, as a quartet with Waters, Dave Padden handling both vocals and rhythm guitar, a returning bassist Russ Bergquist and drummer Ryan Ahoff.

To promote the succinctly titled 'Metal' album, a mammoth European tour kicked off with a two night stand at the Ambassador in Dublin, Ireland on April 8th 2007 supporting TRIVIUM. The band acted as guests for the entire trek, which covered the UK, France, Belgium, Holland, Germany, Poland, Denmark, Sweden, Finland, Norway, Austria, Italy, Spain and Switzerland.

Welcome To Your Death, (1985). Crystal Ann / Welcome To Your Death / Lust Of Death / Burns Like A Buzzsaw Blade / Back To The Crypt / I Am In Command.

Phantasmagoria, (1986). Gallery / Alison Hell / Phantasmagoria / Ligeia.

Alison Hell, (1988). Alison Hell / Crystal Ann.

ALICE IN HELL, Roadrunner RR 9488 2 (1989). Crystal Ann / Alison Hell / W.T.Y.D. (Welcome To Your Death) / Wicked Mystic / Burns Like

A Buzzsaw Blade / Word Salad / Schizos (Are Never Alone) (Parts 1 & 2) / Ligeia / Human Insecticide.
The Fun Palace, Roadrunner (1990) (European 12" promotion release). The Fun Palace / Sixes And Sevens.
NEVER, NEVERLAND, Roadrunner RR 93742 (1990). The Fun Palace / Road To Ruin / Sixes And Sevens / Stonewall / Never, Neverland / Imperiled Eyes / Kraf Dinner / Phantasmagoria / Reduced To Ash / I Am In Command. Chart position: 48 UK.
Stonewall, Roadrunner RR 24256 (1991). Stonewall / W.T.Y.D. (Live) / Word Salad (Live).
Phoenix Rising, (1993) (Japanese release). Phoenix Rising / The Edge / Phoenix Rising (Live acoustic).
Set The World On Fire, Roadrunner RR 23856 (1993). Set The World On Fire / Hell Bent For Leather.
SET THE WORLD ON FIRE, Roadrunner RR 92002 (1993). Set The World On Fire / No Zone / Bats In The Belfry / Snake In The Grass / Phoenix Rising / Knight Jumps Queen / Sounds Good To Me / The Edge / Don't Bother Me / Brain Dance. Chart position: 79 GERMANY.
I'll Show You My Gun, Mokum (1994) (Promotion release). I'll Show You My Gun.
KING OF THE KILL, Music For Nations MFN 171 (1994). The Box / King Of The Kill / Hell Is A War / Bliss / Second To None / Annihilator / 21 / In The Blood / Fiasco (Slate) / Fiasco / Catch The Wind / Speed / Bad Child.
BAG OF TRICKS, Roadrunner RR 8997-2 (1994). Alison Hell (Remastered) / Phantasmagoria (Demo) / Back To The Crypt / Gallery / Human Insecticide (Live) / The Fun Palace (Extended mix) / W.T.Y.D. (Live) / Word Salad (Live) / Live Wire (Live) / Knight Jumps Queen (Demo) / Fantastic Things / Bats In The Belfry (Demo) / Evil Appetite / Gallery '86 / Alison Hell '86 / Phantasmagoria '86.
REFRESH THE DEMON, Music For Nations MFN 197 (1996). Refresh The Demon / Syn. Kill 1 / Awaken / The Pastor Of Disaster / A Man Called Nothing / Ultraparanoia / City Of Ice / Anything For Money / Hunger / Voices And Victims / Innocent Eyes.
IN COMMAND LIVE 1989, Roadrunner RR 8852-2 (1996). W.T.Y.D. / Wicked Mystic / Ligeia / Alison Hell / Word Salad / W.T.Y.D. / The Fun Palace / Never, Neverland / I Am In Command / Stonewall / Road To Ruin / Sixes And Sevens / Alison Hell / Live Wire.
REMAINS, Music For Nations MFN 228 (1996). Murder / Sexecution / No Love / Never / Human Remains / Dead Wrong / Wind / Tricks And Traps / I Want / Reaction / Bastiage.
CRITERIA FOR A BLACK WIDOW, Roadrunner RR 8640 (1999). Bloodbath / Back To The Palace / Punctured / Criteria For A Black Widow / Schitzo / Nothing Left / Loving The Sinner / Double Dare / Sonic / Mending. Chart position: 79 GERMANY.
CARNIVAL DIABLOS, Steamhammer SPV 088-72140 (2000). Bomb / Battered / The Perfect Virus / Carnival Diablo / Shallow Grave / Denied / The Rush / Insomniac / Liquid Oval / Epic Of War / Hunter Killer / Chicken And Corn. Chart position: 71 GERMANY.
WAKING THE FURY, Locomotive Music 700778 (2002). My Precious Lunatic Asylum / Nothing To Me / Ritual / Striker / The Blackest Day / Cold Blooded / Torn / Fire Power / Ultra-Motion / Prime-Time Killing.
DOUBLE LIVE ANNIHILATION, AFM DCD064 (2003). Murder / Ultra Motion / The Box / Denied / The Blackest Day / King Of The Kill / Torn Lunatic Asylum / Set The World On Fire / I Am In Command / Refresh The Demon / Syn. Kill 1 / Never, Neverland / Striker / Bliss / Phantasmagoria / Crystal Ann / Alison Hell / Shallow Grave.
The One, AFM (2004). All For You / Weapon X / The One / All For You (Album version) / Never, Neverland (Live video) / Refresh The Demon (Live video) / Alison Hell (Live video).
ALL FOR YOU, AFM 4081-2 (2004). All For You / Weapon X / The Nightmare Factory / The One / Demon Dance / Rage Absolute / Both Of Me / Bled / Dr. Psycho / Holding On / The Sound Of Horror.
SCHIZO DELUXE, AFM 1009-2 (2005). Maximum Satan / Drive / Warbird / Plasma Zombies / Invite It / Like Father, Like Gun / Pride / Too Far Gone / Clare / Something Witchy.
METAL, Steamhammer (2007) (Limited edition double CD). Clown Parade / Couple Suicide / Army Of One / Downright Dominate / Smothered / Operation Annihilation / Haunted / Kicked / Detonation / Chasing The High / Carnival Diablos / Time Bomb / Blackest Day / My Precious Lunatic Asylum / Shallow Grave (Live) / Murder / Tricks And Traps / Refresh The Demon / Ultra Paranoia / King Of The Kill / Second To None.
METAL, Steamhammer (2007). Clown Parade / Couple Suicide / Army Of One / Downright Dominate / Smothered / Operation Annihilation / Haunted / Kicked / Detonation / Chasing The High.

ANNIHILATUS

TURKU, FINLAND — *Centurion (vocals), Commander Serpentor The Annihilator (guitar), 9mm (guitar), Warmachine Rasputin (bass).*

'War' Black Metal formation forged in Turku during 1999 by Commander Serpent The Annihilator on guitar, also then a member of NIGHTSIDE, and guitarist T '9mm' H of UNHOLA. The latter also uses the stage names T 'Howitzer' H and T 'AK47' H. Demo recordings surfaced billed as 'Unholy Mass Destruction' prior to the recruitment of bass player Warmachine Rasputin of SEPTENTRION in March of 2000. The band's debut gig, in Turku during April of the same year, saw Beleth of NIGHTSIDE deputizing on drums.

Northern Heritage released the debut ANNIHILATUS product, a 7 track 10" vinyl album limited to just 400 copies, entitled suitably 'Annihilation'. ANNIHILATUS drafted frontman Centurion (a.k.a. Matti Liuke), delivering "Death yells & war-kries", in 2001. The new singer made his mark on the 2002 album 'Blood And War'. This album witnessed drummer B-50 credited with "Artillery & bombardments" whilst Commander Serpent The Annihilator, "Assault & terror kommands", adopted a subtle name change to that of War Inquisitor Serpent.

Both Centurion and Warmachine made their exit after the issue of 'Blood And War', Centurion fronting TORTURE KILLER and also joining FUNERAL FEAST as bass player. Former ANNIHILATUS drummer Taneli 'Korpse' Hatakka would join TORTURE KILLER as guitarist and also forge AN, issuing a 2003 7" single 'Pure Northern Hell' with Centurion aiding on session vocals. ANNIHILATUS included a track on the Northern Heritage 10", six way split EP 'Primitive Finland' of 2003 alongside BAPTISM, INCRIMINATED, CLANDESTINE BLAZE, BLOODHAMMER and BLASPHEMOUS EVIL.

Unholy Mass Destruction, Annihilatus (2000) (Cassette demo). Unholy Mass Destruction / Crush The Kingdom Of Holiness / Storm Of Steel / Interlude Of Darkness / Winter.
ANNIHILATION, Northern Heritage NHR013LP (2001) (10" vinyl. Limited edition of 400). Global Destruction / March Of Death / 9mm Solution / Crush / Warmageddon / Kill The Priest / Cut Your Flesh.
BLOOD AND WAR, Northern Heritage NH019CD (2002). Intro (Prelude To War) / Retaliation / Death To Our Enemies / Day Of Execution / Christian Slut / Fanatics Of Battle / Unholy Mass Destruction / Storm Of Steel / March Of Death (Live) / Warmageddon (Live) / Apokalypse.
Primitive Finland, Northern Heritage NH033 (2003) (Split single with BAPTISM, INCRIMINATED, CLANDESTINE BLAZE, BLOODHAMMER and BLASPHEMOUS EVIL). One Eight Seven.

ANONYMUS

MONTRÉAL, QC, CANADA — *Marco Calliari (guitar / vocals), Daniel Souto (guitar), Oscar Souto (bass / vocals), Carlos Araya (drums).*

ANONYMUS is a Thrash band that does not deserve to be anonymous, having been around for many years and are a strong part of the Quebec Metal scene. The band has a cosmopolitan feel with lyrics being written and sung by two vocalists in English, French and Spanish. The band has a strong do-it-yourself ethic and has produced a number of videos. Formed in Montréal in January 1989, ANONYMUS unleashed an independent debut called 'Ni Connu, Ni Vu'. After paying their dues for two years gigging, practicing and touring around Quebec they caught the attention of the small label MPV Records. MPV re-issued their debut in 1996 and quickly followed it up with their second CD simply called 'Stress'. What followed was another two years of touring, practicing always growing in strength and popularity. The band can easily draw 1000 fans in their hometown of Montreal and has appeared on a number of Quebec Metal compilations.

The first two CD's caught some big name attention because the producer on their third album, 'Instinct', was none other than Colin Richardson. Again following a pattern that had brought them success the band hit the road across Canada and into the US building show by show on their loyal following. Performing at small festivals and opening for such luminaries as ANTHRAX and BIOHAZARD has given this band experience and raw edge necessary to compete in a tough genre. The band has a chemistry that is flawless giving them the enviable stability of never having had a line-up change as of early 2002. The band had the good fortune to be handpicked by BLIND GUARDIAN to open for a few select dates in Mexico, where they were reportedly well received.

ANONYMOUS parted ways with founder Marco Calliari in March 2006. During October the band contracted with Galy Records for a new album 'Chapter Chaos Begins', produced by KATAKLYSM guitarist Jean-François Dagenais.

NI VU, NI CONNU, Anonymus (1994). Cyclope / Cremoecremoepas / Choisor ou Mosisor / Mer Noire / X / Ni Vu, Ni Connu / Amen Tote / Prosternez-vous / Balle D'or / Obstinato / Demonamane.

STRESS, MPV (1997). Sous Pression / Un Poing C'est Tout / Questo E'L Destin / La Verite Choc / This Life / Ad Vitam Aeternam / Un Pied Dans La Tombe / Sans Dessein / Maquinas / Casse-Tete / F.L.Y. / In Extremis.

INSTINCT, MPV MPVCD 1376 (2000). Virtually Insane / Out Of Breath / Feed The Dragon / Impact Is Imminent / Hi-Tech Resurrection / Garde-Fou / Evil Blood / Stuck / Goal / Tierra / Be The Other / Que Le Diable M'Emporte.

DAEMONIUM, MPV MPVCD 1398 (2002). Invisible Man / Demons Are Forever / Twice / Burning The Candle Both Ends / Loto-Destruction / In Your Face / Mephisto / Why Be The Judge? / La Mano Criminal / Mean World Symptom / Fou Moi La Paix / Cane Di Vita.

CHAPTER CHAOS BEGINS, Galy 49 (2007).

ANTHRAX

NEW YORK, NY, USA — *Joey Belladonna (vocals), Dan Spitz (guitar), Scott Ian (guitar), Frank Bello (bass), Charlie Benante (drums).*

Major status New York Thrash act ANTHRAX was without the most adventurous in terms of crossing musical boundaries and experimentation. The band formed part of the mid 80's Thrash 'Big Four' alongside METALLICA, MEGADETH and SLAYER. Formed by FOUR X guitarist Scott Ian Rosenfeld and WHITE HEAT guitar player Dan Lilker, ANTHRAX featured vocalist Jason Ian, Scott's then 14 year old brother in the original line-up with Ken Kushner on bass. This latter candidate soon lost his post to Paul Kahn, (Kushner subsequently forged WORLD BANG), who in turn was replaced on four-string duties by Dan Lilker as Greg Walls joined as second guitarist. Further singers trying out would be band roadie John Connolly during 1981-82 and HITTMAN vocalist Dirk Kennedy. Eventually the role of frontman was stabilised in August 1982, with the acquisition of ex-AMRA singer Neil Turbin. Ian, Lilker and Turbin had all attended Bayside High School in Queens.

Before enrolling Turbin, the budding ANTHRAX had performed "pay to play" shows at the North Stage Dinner Theatre in Glen Cove and Great Gildersleeves. Drummer Greg D'Angelo, having replaced original sticksman Dave Weiss, also formed part of the fledgling line-up. Weiss had been forced out due to being severely injured in a hit n' run auto accident. A further switch in personnel saw Walls briefly replaced by Bob Berry, the Blues styled player recommended by RIOT's Rhett Forrester. Berry's tenure would prove fleeting though and Dan Spitz, an employee on Rudi's Music on 48th Street, and ex-member of OVERKILL, was drawn into the fold. Already ANTHRAX's dedication was paying dividends. Their refusal to perform only original material an impressive onstage array of equipment, including road cases purchased from KISS, gave the band a high profile in New York.

The band's first tracks committed to tape, at Sonic Recording Studios in Fremont, Long Island, would be a three song demo comprising of 'Sin', 'Antichrist' and 'Hunting Dog'. Other tracks put onto tape would be 'Pestilence' and 'Satan's Wheels'. During a second round of recording D'Angelo decided to quit. D'Angelo opted to join CITIES and subsequently enjoying a high profile with WHITE LION. He was duly replaced by Charlie Benante in September 1983. Ex-frontman Jason Ian would in later years turn up as drummer for REVEREND.

The band captured the interest of Megaforce Records guru Johnny Zazula with the track 'Soldiers Of Metal' from a further demo. Zazula, and wife Marsha, ran the infamous import shop 'Rock n' Roll Heaven' on the New Jersey turnpike and was already integrally involved in the career of another budding Speed Metal band—METALLICA. In fact, ANTHRAX had first met Zazula at one of his live promotions featuring RAVEN, RIOT and ANVIL. ANTHRAX registered their first single, again cut at Sonic Studios and produced by none other than MANOWAR guitarist Ross Friedman; a.k.a. Ross 'The Boss' Funicello, 'Soldiers of Metal' backed by 'Howling Furies'. Three thousand copies of the single were sold in a mere two weeks during November 1983.

Playing a variety of shows locally and as far a field as Boston, where they opened for KROKUS, earned the band an ever increasing following and contributed to the initial success of their 'Fistful Of Metal' debut album, produced by Carl Canedy of THE RODS. Initially Ross the Boss was projected to record the record but delays caused by having the intended studios in Rochester being out of commission saw this plan scotched. Before a new location could be found, the band spent three nights sleeping in a hotel basement before travelling on to finally craft their record at Pyramid Recording in Ithaca. Notably, 'Fistful Of Metal' included a cover version of ALICE COOPER's 'I'm Eighteen'. Although the album cover, a fist punching out of a mouth, forced many critics to baulk the music gave fans of the burgeoning Thrash scene reason to celebrate.

ANTHRAX toured the American heartland for the first time on a 40-date trek with RAVEN. Following the release of 'Fistful Of Metal' Dan Lilker left ANTHRAX and was replaced in the bass slot by Charlie Benante's cousin and Scott Ian's roadie, Frank Bello. Lilker went on to form the Thrash-Hardcore act NUCLEAR ASSAULT.

Neil Turbin quickly parted company with ANTHRAX due to differences both musical and personal with his new band mates. The singer would raise ready cash, employed as a New York cab driver for a short spell, to finance a relocation to Los Angeles. There he turned up on Japanese guitar God KUNI's 1986 album 'Masque' and in 1988 was fronting the KURT JAMES BAND.

In late 1984 ANTHRAX debuted their new vocalist, ex-BIBLE BLACK and MEGAFORCE man Joey Belladonna (real name Joseph Bellardini), first putting down vocals on the February 1985 'Armed And Dangerous' mini-album. This stop gap release featured re-worked songs from 'Fistful Of Metal' plus a version of the SEX PISTOLS 'God Save The Queen'. Road work in Europe during May of 1985 saw the band billed on the 'Metal Hammer Road Shows' alongside OVERKILL and AGENT STEEL.

Ian and Benante's side project with M.O.D.'s vocalist Billy Milano and erstwhile ANTHRAX member Dan Lilker S.O.D. (STORMTROOPERS OF DEATH) released their debut album 'Speak English Or Die' two months prior to the second ANTHRAX album 'Spreading The Disease'.

The sophomore effort, issued in February 1986, carved out a distinctive niche for the band as ANTHRAX, while firmly in the Thrash Metal camp, set themselves apart from other contenders with a unique edge.

Meantime, ANTHRAX's ascendancy had been duly noted by the major labels and Island Records took the band on for future product. The 'Among The Living' album proved the band's popularity was on the way up achieving sales figures of 400'000 plus. Lyrically ANTHRAX delved into the imaginative realms of horror writer Stephen King for the title track, 'Efilnikufesin (N.F.L.)'

concerning actor John Belushi's drug tragedy, the plight of native Americans for 'Indians' and even Judge Dredd comics for 'I Am The Law'. The latter two of these tracks would be issued as singles and make valuable impressions on the charts. 'I Am The Law' soon became a crowd favourite as did 'Indians', often performed onstage by Belladonna in full chieftain feathered head-dress.

February of 1987 saw the band traversing mainland Europe with support acts CELTIC FROST and CRIMSON GLORY. ANTHRAX toured North America supporting KISS during 1987 and also appeared at the British Castle Donington 'Monsters Of Rock' festival. ANTHRAX would guest to METALLICA on European dates too, these shows being curtailed with the tragic death of METALLICA bassist Cliff Burton.

That same year, the band's increasing popularity in Japan led to the re-issue of the 'Fistful Of Metal' album in new packaging with the addition of a couple of live tracks featuring Joey Belladonna singing 'Panic' and 'Raise Hell'. Further British shows saw TESTAMENT supporting whilst a nationwide tour of America, supported by EXODUS and CELTIC FROST, rounded off the year.

Anthrax activated huge crossover appeal with their rap metal single 'I'm The Man', was swiftly certified gold in America with 500'000 sales. Truly a cross-culture piece of work, 'I'm The Man', co-produced by Eddie Kramer and Paul Hammingson with a guitar run inspired by traditional Jewish folk song Hava Nagila, reached number 53 on the singles charts but importantly remained lodged on radio for a steadfast run and bridged the divide between the two genres, enabling other acts in their wake to take up the same opportunity. The EP also included two live cuts and a rendition of BLACK SABBATH's 'Sabbath Bloody Sabbath'. 'I'm The Man's tenacity on radio rewarded Anthrax with their first platinum award.

The September 1988 album 'State Of Euphoria', produced by Alex Perialis, included a version of TRUST's 'Antisocial'. 'State Of Euphoria' continued the upward trend in sales, peaking at number 30 on the US charts and 12 in the UK, their career highest.

Touring was once again intensive as ANTHRAX opened arena shows for OZZY OSBOURNE in late 1988. Dates in Britain with guests LIVING COLOR followed prior to a lengthy headlining jaunt sponsored by MTV and supported by EXODUS once more and Germans HELLOWEEN. Live work did not end there though and ANTHRAX returned to Britain with guests KING'S X. ANTHRAX also featured as guest musicians on the rap single by New Yorkers U.F.T.O. in 1988.

Anthrax had recorded various cover versions during the 'State Of Euphoria' sessions as intended B sides, including TRUST's 'Le Sects', SEX PISTOLS 'Friggin' In The Riggin', KISS' 'Parasite' and the Ventures 'Pipeline'. These tracks emerged in August of 1989 as the 'Penikufesin' EP (Nice Fuckin' EP backwards). This set, also bolstered by a French language versions of 'Antisocial', gave Anthrax another gold sales certification in the USA.

The band opened for IRON MAIDEN on a European tour at the close of 1990 but returned to America to find a radical reshaping of their label Island Records as a consequence of it's buy out by Polygram had effectively severed the ties between label and band. In spite of this upward struggle, the Mark Dodson produced 'Persistence Of Time' album went on to gold status shifting more than 600'000 copies as Island and ANTHRAX parted company. Undoubtedly stung by criticism aimed at the group's light hearted manner, questionable apparel and a glut of gimmickry, Persistence Of Time showed a darker side to ANTHRAX, bordering on the progressive with tracks not only longer but deadly serious in nature. An offbeat cover version came with a take on JOE JACKSON's 'Got The Time', another hit for the band.

ANTHRAX toured as part of the 'Clash of the Titans' package during 1991 sharing a co-headlining bill with MEGADETH, SLAYER and ALICE IN CHAINS. The original intention of this touring project was to have been an awesome combination of Thrash's 'big four' (inc. METALLICA) but nevertheless the assembled bill drew in sizeable crowds. For the European leg ALICE IN CHAINS were replaced by SUICIDAL TENDENCIES but attendances remained almost sell out status throughout.

In June 1991 the band compiled the album 'Attack Of The Killer B's', a novel approach that garnered ANTHRAX yet another gold record. The album comprised 'Bring The Noise', B sides, live tracks and previously unreleased material. A brace of live numbers, 'Keep It In The Family' and 'Belly Of The Beast' had been recorded live in 1990 of the 'Persistence Of Time' tour.

ANTHRAX's next move was a brave endeavour following their recent full on metal tour. The 'Bring The Noise' track, recorded originally by rappers PUBLIC ENEMY, and originally part of the 'Attack Of The Killer B's' album, had found it's way onto mainstream radio giving ANTHRAX an airing to fans outside of the hard rock sphere. With such exposure, ANTHRAX and PUBLIC ENEMY teamed up to tour America as a unique pairing with support act YOUNG BLACK TEENAGERS, a band that Benante had given his drumming services on their debut album.

The groundbreaking tour encountered problems from reluctant promoters but in the end over twenty highly successful shows were performed in America. British dates saw PRONG as third band on the bill. Despite riding on an undoubted high, Belladonna shocked fans by leaving. For many years the rumour machine had suggested differences between the singer and the core of the band regarding musical tastes. ANTHRAX drafted John Bush, a man who had carved his reputation with Californian Metal act ARMORED SAINT and had famously rejected METALLICA overtures in 1982.

Replacing Joey Belladonna, ANTHRAX drafted new frontman John Bush, a man who had carved his reputation with Californian Metal act ARMORED SAINT. Bush's debut with ANTHRAX, May 1993's Dave Jerden produced 'Sound Of White Noise', entered the Billboard top ten and broke the million sales mark in America. Limited edition variants hosted cover versions of CHEAP TRICK's 'Auf Wiedersehen', THIN LIZZY's 'Cowboy Song', THE SMITH's 'London', BEASTIE BOYS' 'Looking Down The Barrel Of A Gun' and KISS' 'Love Her All I Can' and a Strings Mix of 'Black Lodge'. The Japanese version of the album also had an Al Jourgensen remix of 'Potters Field'.

In April 1994 ANTHRAX's former partner Island Records issued a live album simply dubbed 'The Island Years', mixed by Michael Barbiero and Steve Thompson and taped at Irvine Meadows, California on October 19th, 1991 and the Electric Lady Studios, on January 28th, 1992.

Although 'Sound Of White Noise' performed beyond expectation, the band's fall from grace came remarkably swiftly when, in 1995, ANTHRAX hit an all-time low. The band had switched to work with the Butcher Brothers production team on the 'Stomp 442' album. Spitz left the band before recording and although it was a fine album, 'Stomp 442' proved to be the nadir for the band sales wise, only scoring a Number 47 position on Billboard that October. Elektra and ANTHRAX duly severed relations: undaunted, a determined Anthrax teamed up with horror punks the MISFITS for yet another successful tour of America.

Scott Ian and Charlie Benante resurrected the original line-up of S.O.D. for a 1997 American tour culminating in a slot at the Milwaukee Metalfest. Other offbeat endeavours included the convening of DOOM SQUAD, being one of the more interesting interpretations lent to a JUDAS PRIEST tribute album 'Legends Of Metal'. DOOM SQUAD, a one off band convened for a very much tongue in cheek rendition of 'Burnin' Up'. Those involved included ANTHRAX men Scott Ian and John Bush, ARMORED SAINT bassist Joey Vera and drummer Gonzo with ACCEPT's Jörg Fischer on guitar.

Strangely, a full two years after Danny Spitz had quit ANTHRAX his guitar tech Paul Crook was still temping on a live basis. Lead guitar duties on the 'Volume 8: The Threat Is Real' album were shared by Ian, Benante and Crook.

PANTERA's Dimebag Darrell guested on 'Inside Out' and 'Born Again Idiot' whilst his band mate, vocalist Phil Anselmo, guested on 'Killing Box'. Frank Bello sang lead vocals on the 'hidden' bonus track 'Pieces' that closed the record. Outside of the Metal sphere of operations, Scott Ian sessioned on TRICKY's 'Angels With Dirty Faces' album.

ANTHRAX returned to Britain for a one off show in London during October 1998 and by the following year had bounced back with a best of album 'Return Of The Killer A's'. The CD had both Belladonna and Bush uniting to record 'Ball Of Confusion' and remixes by Al Jourgenson of MINISTRY. Former bassist Dan Lilker also puts in an appearance.

John Bush returned temporarily to ARMORED SAINT during 1999 for their much lauded 'Revelation' album but maintained his position with ANTHRAX. Bush also guested on a version of the SCORPIONS 'Blackout' on SIX FEET UNDER's 'Graveyard Classics' album.

The band's 2000 American tour found SKID ROW guitarist Snake filling in. ANTHRAX went out as guests to MÖTLEY CRÜE but, due to less than anticipated attendances across the board, were unable to fulfill all of the shows and bailed out before the tour's completion. In the summer of 2001 a TWISTED SISTER tribute album 'Twisted And Strange' would witness ANTHRAX offering up their take on the Glamsters 'Destroyer'.

Bush's focus in mid 2001 would be concentrated on promoting an ARMORED SAINT archive album upfront of recording a new album with ANTHRAX. Later in the year ANTHRAX, complete with new guitarist Rob Caggiano, of New York's BOILER ROOM and well known for his production credits with acts such as PRIMER 55, DRY KILL LOGIC and 36 CRAZYFISTS, would jump on the high profile 2001 American tour of Metal legends JUDAS PRIEST for the late summer. The act also announced the inking of a new deal with Beyond Records, a subsidiary of BMG. First fruits of this liaison was the re-issue of 'Stomp 442' and 'Sound Of White Noise', both complete with a glut of rare foreign B side tracks.

However, just upfront of the JUDAS PRIEST tour the terrorist attacks on America on September 11th forced the cancellation of all shows. The terrorist actions would not only disrupt tour plans but put the very nature of ANTHRAX's existence into jeopardy. With America assailed by fears of biological and chemical warfare an Anthrax virus scare in October put the spotlight firmly on the band. In a Washington Post article Scott Ian confessed to having stocked up on supplies of the Anthrax virus antidote Cipro vowing "I will not die an ironic death." Meantime fans were asked to consider if the band should change its name.

As the Anthrax terror campaign worsened paradoxically the group found themselves afforded the kind of heavyweight press exposure on TV, radio and newsprint it had been lacking for so long. Indeed, the band's official website scored a massive three million hits in just under two weeks.

ANTHRAX, billed alongside ACE FREHLEY, ANTHRAX, OVERKILL, SEBASTIAN BACH and a reunited TWISTED SISTER, put in a live appearance on the 28th of November at New York's Hammerstein Ballroom 'New York Steel' event as a benefit event aimed to raise funds for families of the New York Police and Fire Departments who lost their lives at the World Trade Center disaster. The whole event was organised by Eddie Trunk, the esteemed host of WNEW FM's 'Saturday Night Rocks!'. Pointedly the band wore matching boiler suits, bearing the legend 'We're Not Changing Our Name'.

Amidst all this publicity former vocalist Neil Turbin announced his comeback with the 'Threat Con Delta' album. Involved in the studio sessions for a forthcoming album from Turbin's crew would be AMSTERDAM's Ronnie Borchert, erstwhile MICHAEL SCHENKER GROUP, HEAVEN and TALAS guitarist MITCH PERRY and Kurt James of STEELER and DR. MASTERMIND.

ANTHRAX finally got to tour with JUDAS PRIEST in January of 2002 as the re-scheduled dates got back under way., An early untoward incident on the sold out tour being when Caggiano was arrested and jailed for throwing a hot dog at a taxi driver in Denver!

Amongst the traditional cover versions laid down by the band for the new album would be takes on 'Next To You' by THE POLICE, the RAMONES 'We're A Happy Family' and U2's 'Exit'. PANTERA guitarist Dimebag Darrell put in a by now traditional guest appearance making his make on the tracks 'Cadillac Rock Box' and 'Strap It On'. Quite incredibly the band also managed to draft ROGER DALTREY of THE WHO into the studio to lay down vocals on the song 'Taking The Music Back'.

ANTHRAX would head up a Thrash billing of MACHINE HEAD, TESTAMENT and EXODUS in Sao Paolo, Brazil on April 20th. Former ANTHRAX guitarist Paul Crook, firmly ensconced as a member of SEBASTIAN BACH's live band, debuted his new group GOTHAM whilst rumours surfaced that ex-ANTHRAX guitarist Dan Spitz had recently united with IRON MAIDEN drummer Nicko McBrain for an undisclosed band project. This revelation would come as unexpectedly as Spitz had been out of the Rock n' Roll limelight for many years, becoming a vocal Christian since his departure from the band and devoting himself to gaining qualifications in the art of watchmaking. By late December MEGADETH bassist David Ellefson was also seemingly involved in this venture. Subsequently it would be revealed that Spitz was working up new material with his bassist brother, erstwhile BLACK SABBATH, GREAT WHITE and NUCLEAR ASSAULT man Dave 'The Beast' Spitz and having none other than eighties white Rap artist VANILLA ICE contributing vocals.

The much anticipated new ANTHRAX studio album 'We've Come For You All', originally slated for September issue through Sanctuary, was postponed, first pushed back to a February 2003 release then extended further back until April. This disappointing news would be tempered by word that the band would hook up with MOTÖRHEAD for European tour dates throughout October. That same month a new ANTHRAX track 'Love Siege' was made available through internet download. The song had been cut for the soundtrack for director John Carpenter's 'Ghost Of Mars' movie and included none other than GUNS N' ROSES guitarist Buckethead on guest lead solos.

Former guitarist Paul Crook joined MEAT LOAF's touring band in early 2003. Although the group had originally opted to sign with another label for the North American release of 'We've Come For You All' this relationship dissolved and ANTHRAX signed on with Sanctuary for this territory too. US versions of the album came with exclusive live video footage of 'Got The Time' in addition to the rare 'Among The Living / I'm The Man / Caught In A Mosh' medley. A promotional video for the album track "Safe Home" scored a coup by not only including a cameo appearance from Nu-Punks SUM 41 but also 'The Matrix' movie star Keanu Reeves. European headline dates in March saw Belgian's AFTER ALL as support after which ANTHRAX reprised the union with MOTÖRHEAD for US gigs in May.

To coincide with European shows in June ANTHRAX released a special two disc variant of 'We've Come For You All', the second disc comprising eight rare tracks. The band would be back out on the road in the US commencing 29th July in San Diego for their ambitious 'Taking The Music Back 2003' trek. Support for the first leg of shows was lent by LAMB OF GOD and E.TOWN CONCRETE whilst dates from mid August onward had LACUNA COIL and E.TOWN CONCRETE as guests.

The band projected a retrospective project as their next al-

ANTHRAX (pic: Andy Buchanan)

bum release, the 'Metallum Maximus Aeternus' being a collection of archive Turbin and Belladonna era classics re-recorded with John Bush. ANTHRAX entered the DVD age too in December, capturing their show at a sold out Chicago Metro on film for a 'Music Of Mass Destruction' release. Meantime the 2004 New Year opened on a happy note for Scott Ian, the guitarist announcing his engagement to longtime girlfriend Pearl Aday, none other than eldest daughter of MEAT LOAF. Fortune continued to smile on Crook as he was subsequently hand picked as lead guitarist for the QUEEN stage musical 'We Will Rock You'. Present day guitarist Rob Caggiano would be kept busy outside of ANTHRAX activities by acting as producer for renowned British Black Metal band CRADLE OF FILTH.

In a surprise move bassist Frank Bello, after two decades of service to ANTHRAX, quit in February, relocating to Los Angeles in order to work with a new band being assembled by Page Hamilton of HELMET. The HELMET connection would be strengthened as Scott Ian forged a temporary union with Hamilton to cut a version of 'Motorbreath' for a METALLICA tribute album through Big Deal Records entitled 'Metallic Assault'.

The band reacted to Bello's defection by pulling in ARMORED SAINT and FATES WARNING man Joey Vera as a temporary substitute. Getting back to road work ANTHRAX toured Japan and Australia, with support coming from KILLSWITCH ENGAGE and SOILWORK, in April of 2004 upfront of European festival performances. Unfortunately their promotional video for the track 'What Doesn't Die' was rejected by MTV, after it had originally been accepted by the 'Headbangers Ball' programme. Apparently MTV's watchdogs deemed scenes depicting zombies on fire and guitarist Scott Ian knocking the head off a zombie too graphic.

Maintaining momentum, a collection of Joey Belladonna/Neil Turbin-era songs performed by the band's present line up, initially dubbed 'Metallum Maximum Aeturnum' but then switched to 'The Greater Of Two Evils', arrived in November. The songs had been recorded "live" in the Avatar studios in New York City over the course of two days and the track list voted on by fans through the band's website. Upfront of this release ANTHRAX launched their own range of limited edition, vintage shaped skateboards. The record was promoted by a promotional video for the track 'Deathrider', filmed at the Snitch nightclub in New York City. A US tour, allied with DIO and FIREBALL MINISTRY, commenced in September.

In December a slip from SHADOWS FALL frontman Brian Fair ignited rumours of a full blown "Classic" ANTHRAX reunion of Joey Belladonna, Dan Spitz, Scott Ian, Frank Bello and Charlie Benante. The conjecture gathered pace when this proposed reformation was alleged to be in discussion for a position at the 'Ozzfest' event. By February these rumours would be confirmed, the "classic" ANTHRAX apparently set to take up position on 'Ozzfest' alongside IRON MAIDEN and BLACK SABBATH. Strangely, as it transpired this union did not take place.

In January of 2005 ANTHRAX's appearance at Holland's 'Dynamo Open Air' festival in May and the French Fury Fest', 'Sweden Rock' and Italian 'Gods Of Metal' events in June would be confirmed as planning to feature both Joey Belladonna and Dan Spitz, reuniting the pre-1987 line-up. The band's South American shows of February would be affected by the Argentine club fire tragedy of the previous year as new government restrictions forced cancellations in Buenos Aires, Argentina and Bogata, Colombia.

An all Brazilian tribute album would be unveiled with 'Indians ... NOT!', released by São Paulo's Collision Records and featuring such artists as ARENA AGE, RHESTUS, STILL LIFE, HELL TRUCKER, BLAKK MARKET and DYNAHEAD.

On the 23rd February, a special show at Chicago's Aragon Ballroom, featuring ANTHRAX, DISTURBED, DROWNING POOL and SOIL, was organised to cover bereavement costs for the family of DAMAGEPLAN security guard Jeffrey "Mayhem" Thompson and medical expenses for injured DAMAGEPLAN crew members John "Kat" Brooks and Chris Paluska. ANTHRAX opened their show with PANTERA's 'Fucking Hostile' before delivering a take of 'A New Level' with Vinnie Paul and Pat Lachman. Guesting for lead guitar solos in the ANTHRAX set would be GRIM REAPER's Nick Bowcott.

ANTHRAX made the "Classic" reunion official on 1st April with a global press conference and luncheon held at Sirius Satellite Radio in New York City. The band also used the occasion to announce their participation in the 'Slave to the Metal Foundation', created to "bring public awareness to the dangers of the Anthrax Vaccine".

Australian gigs in May found fellow veteran Thrashers MORTAL SIN as support. The band stopped in London in June to perform a short set at the 'Metal Hammer' magazine awards, delivering 'Got The Time', 'Caught In Mosh' and 'Indians' then, with a guesting Brian Fall of SHADOWS FALL, a set closing rendition of PANTERA's 'A New Level'. US and Canadian shows in September had ANTHRAX replacing DREAM THEATER as co-headliners of the MEGADETH led 'Gigantour' dates. On the release front, a two disc compilation, entitled 'Anthrology: No Hit Wonders (1985-1991)', was accompanied by a live album culled from the reunion shows dubbed simply 'Alive 2'. Maintaining the pace on the road, ANTHRAX opened for JUDAS PRIEST in September and October.

In December 2004 a slip from SHADOWS FALL frontman Brian Fair ignited rumours of a full blown "Classic" ANTHRAX reunion of Joey Belladonna, Dan Spitz, Scott Ian, Frank Bello and Charlie Benante. The conjecture gathered pace when this proposed reformation was alleged to be in discussion for a position at the 'Ozzfest' event. By February these rumours would be confirmed, the "classic" ANTHRAX apparently set to take up position on 'Ozzfest' alongside IRON MAIDEN and BLACK SABBATH. Strangely, as it transpired this union did not take place.

In January of 2005 ANTHRAX's appearance at Holland's 'Dynamo Open Air' festival in May and the French Fury Fest', 'Sweden Rock' and Italian 'Gods Of Metal' events in June would be confirmed as planning to feature both Joey Belladonna and Dan Spitz, reuniting the pre-1987 line-up. The band's South American shows of February would be affected by the Argentine club fire tragedy of the previous year as new government restrictions forced cancellations in Buenos Aires, Argentina and Bogata, Colombia.

An all Brazilian tribute album would be unveiled with 'Indians ... NOT!', released by São Paulo's Collision Records and featuring such artists as ARENA AGE, RHESTUS, STILL LIFE, HELL TRUCKER, BLAKK MARKET and DYNAHEAD.

On the February 23rd, a special show at Chicago's Aragon Ballroom, featuring ANTHRAX, DISTURBED, DROWNING POOL and SOIL, was organised to cover bereavement costs for the family of DAMAGEPLAN security guard Jeffrey "Mayhem" Thompson and medical expenses for injured DAMAGEPLAN crew members John "Kat" Brooks and Chris Paluska. ANTHRAX opened their show with PANTERA's 'Fucking Hostile' before delivering a take of 'A New Level' with Vinnie Paul and Pat Lachman. Guesting for lead guitar solos in the ANTHRAX set would be GRIM REAPER's Nick Bowcott.

ANTHRAX made the "Classic" reunion official on 1st April with a global press conference and luncheon held at Sirius Satellite Radio in New York City. The band also used the occasion to announce their participation in the 'Slave to the Metal Foundation', created to "bring public awareness to the dangers of the Anthrax Vaccine".

Australian gigs in May found fellow veteran Thrashers MORTAL SIN as support. The band stopped in London in June to perform a short set at the 'Metal Hammer' magazine awards, delivering 'Got The Time', 'Caught In Mosh' and 'Indians' then, with a guesting Brian Fall of SHADOWS FALL, a set closing rendition of PANTERA's 'A New Level'. US and Canadian shows in September had ANTHRAX replacing DREAM THEATER as co-headliners of the MEGADETH led 'Gigantour' dates. On the release front, a two disc compilation, entitled 'Anthology: No Hit Wonders (1985-1991)', was accompanied by a live album culled from the reunion shows dubbed simply 'Alive 2'. Maintaining the pace on the road, ANTHRAX opened for JUDAS PRIEST in September and October. On 15th December Scott Ian notably joined the ROADRUNNER UNITED conglomerate at the New York Nokia Theater for an all star Metal evening.

Maintaining the classic line-up, ANTHRAX kicked off 2006 US headline tour dates with support acts GOD FORBID, MANNTIS and SWORN ENEMY throughout January. However, SHADOWS FALL drummer Jason Bittner filled in for Charlie Benante for the last batch of dates while Charlie Benante and his wife awaited the birth of their first child. The band's gig in Boulder, Colorado would be cancelled whilst Bittner temped in San Francisco and Los Angeles.

Scott Ian took a break from the band to film a VH1 television series entitled 'Supergroup', a reality show also starring TED NUGENT, Evan Seinfeld of BIOHAZARD on bass, vocalist SEBASTIAN BACH and Jason Bonham of BONHAM, UFO and FOREIGNER on drums. In further side activity, Scott Ian guested on comedian Brian Posehn's debut stand-up album 'Live In: Nerd Rage'.

European touring in 2006 saw support from BEYOND FEAR. In January 2007 Universal Music issued the double live retrospective album 'Caught In A Mosh—BBC Live in Concert' comprising the band's performance at the Hammersmith Odeon in London on February 15th 1987 plus the band's Monsters Of

ANTHRAX (pic: Andy Buchanan)

Rock Festival set at Castle Donington on August 22nd 1987.

The ANTHRAX reunion was over as 2007 dawned. In January Scott Ian issued a statement claiming Joey Belladonna had declined participation in a proposed US tour support to a major act. At the same juncture former singer John Bush, active with ARMORED SAINT spot dates and also generating revenue by vocalising on Burger King adverts, revealed that he was still legally a member of the band.

Soldiers Of Metal, Megaforce (1983). Soldiers Of Metal / Howling Furies.

FISTFUL OF METAL, Megaforce 469 (1984). Deathrider / I'm Eighteen / Subjagator / Howling Furies / Death From Above / Across The River / Metal Thrashing Mad / Panic / Soldiers Of Metal / Anthrax.

ARMED AND DANGEROUS, Megaforce MRS 05 (1985). Armed And Dangerous / Raise Hell / God Save The Queen / Metal Thrashing Mad / Panic.

SPREADING THE DISEASE, Music For Nations MFN62 (1986). A.I.R. / Lone Justice / Madhouse / S.S.C. / Stand Or Fall / The Enemy / Aftershock / Armed And Dangerous / Medusa / Gung-Ho. Chart position: 113 USA.

Madhouse, Island 12IS 285 (1986). Madhouse / A.I.R. / God Save The Queen.

Madhouse, Island (1986). Madhouse / A.I.R.

I Am The Law, Island 12IS316 (1987) (USA release. 12" single). I Am The Law / I'm The Man / Bud E Luvbomb And Satan's Lounge Band.

I Am The Law, Island 12IS316 (1987). I Am The Law / I'm The Man / Bud E Luvbomb And Satan's Lounge Band / Madhouse (Live).

I Am The Law, Island IS LAW1 (1987). I Am The Law / Bud E. Luvbomb & Satan's Lounge Band. Chart position: 32 UK.

AMONG THE LIVING, Island ILPS 9865 (1987). Among The Living / Caught in A Mosh / I Am The Law / Efinkufsin (N.F.L.) / Skeleton In The Closet / Indians / One World / ADI Horror Of It All / Imitation Of Life. Chart positions: 18 UK, 43 SWEDEN, 62 USA.

Indians, Island IS325 (1987). Indians / Sabbath Bloody Sabbath / Taint. Chart position: 44 UK.
I'm The Man, Island (1987). I'm The Man / Caught In A Mosh. Chart position: 20 UK.
I'm The Man, Megaforce Island 90685-1 (1987). I'm The Man (Censored Version) / I'm The Man (Def uncensored version) / Sabbath Bloody Sabbath / I'm The Man (Live & Extremely Def II uncensored version) / Caught In A Mosh (Live) / I Am The Law (Live). Chart positions: 42 SWEDEN, 53 USA.
I'm The Man, Island IS338 (1987). I'm The Man / Caught In A Mosh / I Am The Law (Live).
Make Me Laugh, Island (1988) (Red vinyl). Make Me Laugh / Anti-Social (Live). Chart position: 26 UK.
Make Me Laugh, Island IS379 (1988). Make Me Laugh / Anti-Social (Live) / Friggin' In The Riggin'.
STATE OF EUPHORIA, Island ILKPS 9916 (1988). All, End All / Out Of Sight, Out Of Mind / Make Me Laugh / Antisocial / Who Cares Wins / Now it's Dark / Schism / Misery Loves Company / 13 / Finale. Chart positions: 12 UK, 21 SWEDEN, 30 USA.
Anti-Social, Island 1S409 (1989). Anti-Social / Parasite. Chart position: 44 UK.
Anti-Social, Island IS409 (1989). Anti-Social / Parasite / Le Sects.
Penikufesin, Island 209 950 (1989). Now It's Dark / Antisocial (French version) / Friggin' In The Riggin' / Parasite / Le Sects / Pipeline.
In My World, Island (1990). In My World / Keep It In The Family / In My World (Extended version) / Keep It In The Family (Extended version).
In My World, Island IS470 (1990). In My World / Keep It In The Family. Chart position: 29 UK.
PERSISTENCE OF TIME, Island ILPS 9967 (1990). Time / Blood / Keep It In The Family / In My World / Gridlock / Intro To Reality / Belly Of The Beast / Got The Time / H8 Red / One Man Stands / Discharge. Chart positions: 4 NEW ZEALAND, 13 UK, 24 USA, 46 SWEDEN.
Got The Time, Island (1990). Got The Time / Who Put This Together. Chart position: 16 UK.
Got The Time, Island IS 475 (1990). Got The Time / Who Put This Together / I'm The Man (Live).
ATTACK OF THE KILLER B'S, Island ILPS9980 (1991). Milk (Ode To Billy) / Bring The Noise / Keep It In The Family (Live) / Startin' Up A Posse / Protest And Survive / Chromatic Death / I'm The Man '91 / Parasite / Pipeline / Sects / Belly Of The Beast (Live) / NFB (Dallabnikufesin). Chart positions: 13 UK, 20 AUSTRIA, 27 USA, 27 NEW ZEALAND, 38 SWEDEN.
Bring The Noise, Island (1991) (With CHUCK D). Bring The Noise / I Am The Law '91. Chart position: 14 UK.
Bring The Noise, Island (1991) (With CHUCK D). Bring The Noise / I Am The Law '91 / Keep It In The Family (Live).
Only, Elektra EKR 166CD1 (1993). Only / Cowboy Song / Sodium Pentaghol.
Only, Elektra EKR 166 (1993). Only / Only (Mix). Chart position: 36 UK.
Only, Elektra EKR 166CD2 (1993). Only / Auf Wiedersehn / Noisegate.
Black Lodge, Elektra 7559662772 (1993) (Australian release). Black Lodge (Black strings mix) / Black Lodge (Tremelo mix) / Black Lodge (Mellow to mad mix) / Love Her All I Can / Cowboy Song.
Only, Elektra EKR166CD1/2 (1993) (Double CD single). Only (Radio Edit) / Cowboy Song / Sodium Pentathol / Only (LP Mix) / Auf Wiedersehen / Noisegate.
Black Lodge, Elektra EKR171TE (1993) (Limited edition 10" single). Black Lodge (Black Strings Mix) / Black Lodge (Tremelo Mix) / Potters Field (HypoLuxa / Hermes Pan Remix) / Potters Field (Extended Mutated Version by HypoLuxa And Hermes Pan).
SOUND OF WHITE NOISE, Elektra 755961430-2 (1993). Potters Field / Only / Room For One More / Packaged Rebellion / Hy Pro Glo / Invisible / 1000 Points Of Hate / Black Lodge / C11 H17 / Burst / This Is Not An Exit. Chart positions: 7 USA, 14 UK, 21 SWEDEN, 35 GERMANY, 46 NEW ZEALAND.
Black Lodge, Elektra EKR 171TP (1993) (Picture disc). Black Lodge (Black strings mix) / Black Lodge (Tremelo mix) / Black Lodge (Mellow to Mad mix) / Black Lodge (LP version).
Black Lodge, Elektra (1993). Black Lodge / Black Lodge (Black Strings mix). Chart position: 53 UK.
Black Lodge, Elektra EKR 171CD (1993). Black Lodge / Potters Field / Love Her All I Can.
Hy Pro Glo, Elektra EKR 171T (1993). Hy Pro Glo / London / Room For One More (Live).
Hy Pro Glo, Elektra EKR 178 (1993). Hy Pro Glo / London.
STOMP 442, Elektra 7559-61856-2 (1995). Acts Of Senseless Violence / Fueled / King Size / Riding Shotgun / Perpetual Motion / In A Zone / Nothing / American Pompeii / Drop The Ball / Tester / Bare. Chart position: 47 USA.
Nothing EP, Elektra 755960392 (1996) (Australian release). Nothing / Fueled (Remix) / Remember Tomorrow / Grunt And Click / No Time This Time.
Nothing, Elektra EKR 216CD1 (1996). Nothing / Fuelled (Remix) / Remember Tomorrow / Grunt And Click.
Nothing, Elektra EKR 216CD2 (1996). Nothing / Dethroned Emperor / No Time This Time.
VOLUME 8: THE THREAT IS REAL, Ignition IGNPRO74036-2 (1998). Crush / Catharsis / Inside Out / Piss & Vinegar / 604 / Toast / Born Again Idiot / Killing Box / Harm's Way / Hog Tied / Big Fat / Cupajoe / Alpha Male / Stealing From A Thief / Pieces. Chart positions: 43 GERMANY, 73 UK, 118 USA.
Safe Home, Nuclear Blast NB1093 (2003). Safe Home / Taking The Music Back / Safe Home (Radio edit).
WE'VE COME FOR YOU ALL, Nuclear Blast NB0699 (2003). Contact / What Doesn't Die / Superhero / Refuse To Be Denied / Safe Home / Anyplace But Here / Nobody Knows Anything / Strap It On / Black Dahlia / Cadillac Rock Box / Taking The Music Back / Crash / Think About An End / W.C.F.Y.A. / We're A Happy Family. Chart positions: 22 GERMANY, 95 FRANCE, 101 CANADA, 102 UK, 122 USA.
Taking The Music Back, Nuclear Blast (2003) (German release). Taking The Music Back / Ghost / Exit / Next To You / Safe Home (Video) / Taking The Music Back (Video).
Taking The Music Back, Irond CD 03-665 (2003) (Russian release). Taking The Music Back / Ghost / Exit / Next To You / Safe Home (Video) / Taking The Music Back (Video).
MUSIC OF MASS DESTRUCTION, Nuclear Blast 126488 (2004). What Doesn't Die / Got The Time / Caught In A Mosh / Safe Home / Room For One More / Antisocial / Nobody Knows Anything / Fuelled / Inside Out / Refuse To Be Denied / I Am The Law / Only. Chart position: 88 GERMANY.
THE GREATER OF TWO EVILS, Sanctuary 06076-84709-2 (2004). Deathrider / Metal Thrashing Mad / Caught In A Mosh / A.I.R. / Among The Living / Keep It In The Family / Indians / Madhouse / Panic / I Am The Law / Belly Of The Beast / N.F.L. / Be All End All / Gung-Ho.
ALIVE 2, Sanctuary SNTU84764 (2005). Among The Living / Caught In A Mosh / A.I.R. / Antisocial / N.F.L. / Deathrider / Medusa / In My World / Indians / Time / Be All End All / I Am The Law / Metal Thrashing Mad / I'm The Man / I Am The Law.
CAUGHT IN A MOSH—BBC LIVE IN CONCERT, Universal (2007). A.I.R. / Metal Thrashing Mad / Panic / The Enemy / I Am The Law / Madhouse / Howling Furies / Medusa / Armed And Dangerous / Sabbath Bloody Sabbath / God Save The Queen / Gung-Ho / Among The Living / Caught In A Mosh / Madhouse / I Am The Law / Medusa / Indians / God Save The Queen / A.I.R. / I'm The Man.

ANTIDOTE

FINLAND — *Nino Laurenne (vocals / guitar), Tuomo Louhio (guitar), Pete Peltonen (bass), Mika Arnkil (drums).*

Finnish Thrashers dating back to 1986. Various demo sessions led up to the 1990 tape 'Epoch Of Insanity' followed up by the following year's 'Spaced Out'. Following the release of their debut album ANTIDOTE toured with ACCUSER and HEADHUNTER. The second album, mixed by Timmo Tolkki of STRATOVARIOUS, was recorded utilising Pete Eloranta as the main songwriter in place of Tuomo Louhio. In 1996 ANTIDOTE pulled in erstwhile INCREDIBLE BRAINSHELLS man Titus Hjelm on bass.

In later years Laurenne and Hjelm would with members of Progressive metal band TUNNELVISION to create the Symphonic Metal band THUNDERSTONE. Drummer Mikael 'Arkki' Arnkil, an ex-ABHORRENCE man, would join the notorious IMPALED NAZARENE, switching instruments to bass guitar. During 2003 ANTIDOTE guitarist Tuomo Louhio would join IMPALED NAZARENE for recording of the album 'All That You Fear'.

Epoch Of Insanity, Antidote (1990) (Demo). Careless World / Melancholia / Epoch Of Insanity / One Crime.

THE TRUTH, Shark 026 (1992). Symphony Of Death / Within His Power / Act Of Violence / Melancolia / 3rd Time In Greenland / RoseMachine / Grandiloguent Passaway / Subordinated People / Spaced Out.

TOTAL, Shark 100 (1994). Cold / Woe Betide Them / Life For A Lie / Rain / Multiverse / My Million Years / You Medicate / Slow Motion / Life Recall / Into The Dreamside.

TOTAL, Teichiku TECX-25870 (1995) (Japanese release). Cold / Woe Betide Them / Life For A Lie / Rain / Multiverse / My Million Years / You Medicate / Slow Motion / Life Recall / Into The Dreamside / Mirror Images / New Winds.

MIND ALIVE, Bluelight BLR 3334-0 (1996). The Mind Alive / Fall From Disgrace / The Agressor Within / Icon Of Hate / Dying To Be Dead / Wallow In Vice / Bridges / In The Land Of Nod / Masked Dance / Attitude / Books Of The Moon.

ANVIL

TORONTO, ON, CANADA — *Lips (vocals / guitar), Dave Allison (guitar), Ian Dickson (bass), Robb Reiner (drums).*

Originally known as LIPS upon their formation, this no frills metal combo out of Toronto even pre-dated Canadian rock institution RUSH. The main protagonists, frontman Steve Kudlow (a.k.a. 'Lips') and drummer Robb Reiner, had been operational even before with the band GRAVESTONE. Active on the live scene throughout the decade from April 1973 onwards, being solidified in 1978 with the acquisition of rhythm guitarist Dave Allison and bassist Ian Dickson, the first ANVIL product was originally issued under the LIPS handle. The debut 1981 album, 'Hard 'N' Heavy' released in 1981, was in fact intended to be purely demo material but as an enterprising unit and eager to recoup their recording costs the band issued 1,000 vinyl copies on their own Splash label. Gradually LIPS graduated from an S&M bondage themed shock Rock show into raw heavy metal. However, many of the early onstage appendages, such as Lips' notorious dildo holster, made the transition into later years. Still as LIPS the outfit's initiative came to the attention of Attic Records, who quickly re-released the album although now under the band name of ANVIL due to protestations from disco act LIPPS INC.

'Hard 'N' Heavy' still retained a large degree of the LIPS Rock n' Roll routine but, along with their lyrical obsession with sex, did hint at much, much heavier things to come. Tracks such as 'Bondage' and 'School Love' would prove harbingers of familiar output throughout the band's future catalogue. 'Hard 'N' Heavy' also boasted a beefed up take on the ROLLING STONES classic 'Paint It Black'.

Onstage Lips would famously cultivate press coverage too by performing lead guitar solos with the aid of a vibrator. Anvil made their first foray onto the live scene in Canada with a bunch of club shows leading to the nationwide support to GIRLSCHOOL although Lips did take time out to produce a demo for KRAKEN.

1982's 'Metal On Metal', produced by Chris Tsangarides, boasted the unique honour of having the track 'Mothra' being recorded by Lips using a vibrator on his guitar rather than the more usual plectrum. An uncompromising slab of heaviness, 'Metal On Metal' was the first in line not only to demonstrate the band's adherence to full on metal, powered by the frenetic double bass drumming from the engine room of Robb Reiner. Taking the songs to the people, ANVIL conducted a world tour that took in a high profile gig at Castle Donington's August 1982 'Monsters Of Rock' festival in the UK sharing the stage with STATUS QUO, GILLAN, SAXON and HAWKWIND.

The follow up, 1983's 'Forged In Fire', an equally heavyweight offering again with Tsangarides in charge of the faders, strangely became the focus of a media backlash in previously robust bastions of support such as the UK and Europe. ANVIL's road work spanned the entire globe to promote the record, including a slot at the BLACK SABBATH headlined UK Reading festival in August, supports to WHITESNAKE in Europe and Japanese dates in September 1983.

Many major name acts took direct inspiration from 'Forged In Fire', indeed it is today recognised as the band's creative high point, but reeling from savage reviews, album sales plateaued and Anvil found themselves without a record deal. Nevertheless, Attic Records capitalised on the group's standing with the 1985 'Backwaxed' collection, this semi-compilation comprising five previously unreleased outtake tracks, B side 'Steamin' and songs taken from the previous three records. Lips surprised many by revealing that the title track, recorded during the 'Forged In Fire' sessions, was originally deemed too offensive for public consumption.

ANVIL got to perform in Japan again, playing the 'Super Rock' festival at Seibu Stadium in Tokyo during August 1985. ANVIL went into the studio that same year to cut demos with producer Ric Browde, a somewhat strange choice for Anvil as Browde's credits included notably lighter acts such as POISON. Songs recorded were 'Rockin', 'Mad Dog', World's Apart' and 'Straight Between The Eyes'. Finding a new stable with Metal Blade Records, ANVIL bowed back in with 1987's 'Strength Of Steel', featuring a cover version of THE STAMPEDERS 'Wild Eyes'.

Following completion of the 'Pound For Pound' and live 'Past And Present' albums, both co-produced by the band and Paul LaChapelle, Dave Allison quit in 1989, ditching the music business entirely to find a new vocation in stereotypical Canadian tradition as a lumberjack. This defection prompted a period of inactivity for the band broken finally by press statements indicating a forthcoming album title of 'Tools Of Torture', then 'Evoke The Evil'. They finally bounced back signed to the Belgian label Mausoleum and Canadian label Maximum, a newly founded concern of HELIX manager William Seip, for the 1992, re-branded yet again, 'Worth The Weight' album with new guitarist Sebastian Marino, being a New Yorker Anvil's only non-Canadian, in tow. Following the album release, Anvil pulled in bassist Mike Duncan. Meantime, English Metal crew BENEDICTION had covered 'Forged In Fire' for their 1992 album 'Dark Is The Season'. TUNGSTEN would also pay tribute to the same song on their 1996 album '183.85'.

Guitarist Sebastian Marino made himself busy with RAMROD cutting two demos in 1994 with LIEGE LORD singer Joseph Comeau and drummer Bill Mount prior to teaming up with cult New York Speed Metal merchants OVERKILL for their 1997 effort 'From The Underground And Below'. Marino had also found time to produce the 1996 album by DEVASTATOR.

ANVIL had been away from the public eye for their lengthiest hiatus yet, but got back into action with an all new cast, involving bassist Michael Duncan and guitarist Ivan Hurd, for 1996's de-tuned 'Plugged In Permanent', released by Hypnotic in Canada and Massacre Records in Germany. Japanese versions added an exclusive track 'Stolen'. ANVIL at this juncture in their career included the lynchpin of Lips, mainstay drummer Robb Reiner and new faces guitarist Ivan Hurd and former EDGE UNKNOWN bassist Glenn Five (real name Gyorffy).

Quickly back into the fray, ANVIL followed up with 'Absolutely No Alternative' in 1997, boasting a completely re-recorded take on 'March Of The Crabs'. Song titles such as 'Piss Test', 'Hair Pie' and 'Show Me Your Tits' gave ample evidence that the Canucks humour had remained intact. They were back again 1998 with 'Speed Of Sound', issued across the globe by way of Massacre for Europe, Rock Brigade in Brazil, Avalon Marquee in Japan and Hypnotic in their homeland. 'Speed Of Sound' observed an ANVIL aware of the present Metal climate, Robb Reiner even introducing blast beats. A curious distinction in the artwork, depicting an anvil-plane, saw only the German version firing a missile. Japanese variants hosted two extra studio tracks, 'Kick Some Ass' and 'Vengeance To Kill'.

With Germany's fascination in the late 90s for early 80s

cult metal acts ANVIL made a return to the touring circuit undertaking dates with FLOTSAM AND JETSAM and fellow Canucks EXCITER. The band rounded off 1998 by performing at the long established 'Wacken Open Air' festival in Germany.

ANVIL toured Germany in early 2000 sharing a package bill with RIOT, AGENT STEEL and DOMINE. The year 2000 also saw an 'Anthology Of Anvil' compilation released with an unreleased track and extensive liner notes by the esteemed Canadian Metal journalist, Martin Popoff.

German Massacre label variants of the 2001 Pierre Rémillard produced album 'Plenty Of Power' differed to Canadian distributed CDs in having the final exclusive track as 'Dirty Dorothy'. The Hypnotic Canadian imprint replaced this song with 'Left Behind', actually a tune dating back to the Lips / Reiner GRAVESTONE days. Sebastian Marino and his colleagues in the RAMROD rhythm section took to the stage at the German 'Wacken Open Air' festival the same year as part of a reunion line-up of LIEGE LORD.

Anvil would be scheduling a new album, 'Still Going Strong', for release through Massacre Records in June 2002. The band headlined the Montreal 'Powerpack' festival on November 8th, topping a bill over HANKER, HEAVEN'S CRY and SOULFORGE.

ANVIL's March 2004 album, 'Back To Basics', was recorded with producer Pierre Rémillard in Quebec. As a bonus, digipacks of 'Back To Basics' included a second DVD disc of the band's August 1998 'Wacken Open Air' festival performance. The band's profile was momentarily heightened in the USA when Screaming Ferret Wreckords undertook a campaign to release no less than seven back catalogue albums. Although announced, the albums failed to appear in stores.

Unfortunately Ivan Hurd fell from a ladder in May, breaking four ribs, his left wrist and also suffered a cracked tailbone. As a result, he would not be able to perform with the band at the July 24th festival dubbed 'The Gates of Hell' at the FunHaus in Toronto, Ontario. His replacement would be George Vee.

German Heavy Metal band, POWERGOD, cut a cover version of 'Motormount' for inclusion on their Long Live The Loud– That's Metal Lesson II released through Massacre Records in July 2005. Lips guested on this version, as did ROUGH SILK's Ferdy Doernberg on pedal steel guitar. ANVIL scheduled European dates, in a road alliance with PHANTOM-X, for November. In early 2006 it was learned that ANVIL had re-forged links with producer Chris Tsangarides for a new album.

HARD 'N' HEAVY, Attic LAT 1100 (1981). School Love / AC/DC / At The Apartment / I Want You Both (With Me) / Bedroom Game / Ooh Baby / Paint It Black / Paint It Black / Hot Child / Bondage.

School Love, Polydor (1981) (Japanese Release). School Love / Paint It Black.

METAL ON METAL, Attic LAT 1130 (1982). Metal On Metal / Mothra / Stop Me / March Of The Crabs / Jackhammer / Heat Sink / Tag Team / Scenery / Tease Me, Please Me / 666.

Anvil EP, Noir MET 12 001 (1982). Steamin' / Tease Me, Please Me / Jackhammer / Stop Me.

Make It Up To You, Attic (1983). Make It Up To You / Metal On Metal / School Love.

FORGED IN FIRE, Attic LAT 1170 (1983). Forged In Fire / Shadow Zone / Free As The Wind / Never Deceive Me / Butter Bust Jerky / Future Wars / Hard Times—Fast Ladies / Make It Up To You / Motormount / Winged Assassins.

Forged In Fire, Attic ANVIL 1 (1983) (Free flexidisc 7" single with 'Kerrang!' magazine). Forged In Fire.

Make It Up To You, Attic (1983) (Canadian release). Make It Up To You / Hard Times—Fast Ladies.

Make It Up To You, Noir MET12 002 (1983). Make It Up To You (Remix) / Metal On Metal.

BACKWAXED, Roadrunner RR 9776 (1985). Backwaxed / Steamin' / Pussy Poison / You're A Liar / Fryin' Cryin' / Metal On Metal / Butter Bust Jerky / Scenery / Jackhammer / School Love.

Anvil, (1985) (Demo). Rockin' / Mad Dog / Worlds Apart / Straight Between The Eyes.

STRENGTH OF STEEL, Roadrunner RR 9618 (1987). Strength Of Steel / Concrete Jungle / 9-2-5 / I Dreamed It Was The End Of The World / Flight Of The Bumble Beast / Cut Loose / Mad Dog / Straight Between The Eyes / Wild Eyes / Kiss Of Death / Paper General.

Blood On The Ice, Metal Blade (1988) (USA promotion release). Blood On The Ice / Blood On The Ice.

POUND FOR POUND, Metal Blade 73336 (1988). Blood On The Ice / Corporate Preacher / Toe Jam / Safe Sex / Where Does All The Money Go? / Brain Burn / Senile King / Machine King / Fire In The Night / Cramps.

PAST AND PRESENT LIVE, Roadrunner RO 94532 (1989). Concrete Jungle / Toe Jam / Motornaut / Forged In Fire / Blood On The Ice / March Of The Crabs / Jack Hammer / Metal On Metal / Winged Assassins / 666 / Mothra.

WORTH THE WEIGHT, Mausoleum 904 004-2 (1991). Infanticide / On The Way To Hell / Bushpig / Embalmer / Pow Wow / Sins Of The Flesh / AZ 85 / Sadness / Love Me When I'm Dead.

PLUGGED IN PERMANENT, Massacre MASSCD 098 (1996). Racial Hostility / Doctor Kevorkian / Smokin' Green / Destined For Doom / Killer Hill / Face Pull / I'm Trying To Sleep / Five Knuckle Shuffle / Truth Or Consequence / Guilty.

ABSOLUTELY NO ALTERNATIVE, Massacre MASCD 0134 (1997). Old School / Green Jesus / Show Me Your Tits / No One To Follow / Hair Pie / Rubber Neck / Piss Test / Red Light / Black Or White / Hero By Death.

SPEED OF SOUND, Massacre MASCD 0173 (1998). Speed Of Sound / Blood In The Playground / Deadbeat Dad / Man Over Board / No Evil / Bullshit / Mattress Mambo / Secret Agent / Life To Lead / Park That Truck.

Massacre's Classix Shape Edition, Massacre (1999) (Cut to shape CD single. German release). Blood On The Ice / Doctor Kevorkian / Old School / Speed Of Sound / Metal On Metal (Live).

PLENTY OF POWER, Massacre MASSCD 256 (2001). Plenty Of Power / Groove Science / Ball Of Fire / The Creep / Computer Drone / Beat The Law Pro Wrestling / Siren Of The Sea / Disgruntled / Real Metal / Left Behind.

STILL GOING STRONG, Massacre MASCD 302 (2002). Race Against Time / In Hell / Holy Wood / Still Going Strong / Don't Ask Me / Waiting / White Rhino / What I'm About / Sativa / Defiant.

BACK TO BASICS, Massacre MASSCD 410 (2004). Fuel For The Fire / Keep It Up / Song Of Pain / You Get What You Pay For / The Chainsaw / Can't Catch Me (When My Pants Are Down) / Go Away / Bottom Feeder / Cruel World / Fast Driver.

THIS IS THIRTEEN, (2006).

ANVIL CHORUS

SAN FRANCISCO, CA, USA — *Aaron Zimpel (vocals), Thaen Rassmussen (guitar), Douglas Piercy (guitar), Bill Skinner (bass), Gere Fennelly (keyboards), Joe Bennett (drums).*

Formed from the ashes of the Progressive Rock band LEVIATHAN and other Bay Area groups, assorted members of the defunct San Franciscan bands began jamming with another local act HEAD ON to eventually forge ANVIL CHORUS. The story has it that HEAD ON's manager was impressed enough to offer the guys a support slot to his band in 1982.

Adopting the name ANVIL CHORUS, the new group not only played the HEAD ON show but also opened up for MÖTLEY CRÜE's earliest forays into Northern California. Other ANVIL CHORUS gigs had METALLICA as the opening act. Early rehearsals were held with guitarists Thaen Rasmussen, previously with VY-KING, and Douglas Piercy, ex-COBRA and DELTA, bassist Grant Williams, drummer Michael Hegos and vocalist Tim Montana.

By early 1982 ANVIL CHORUS comprised ex-LEVIATHAN vocalist Aaron Zimpel, guitarists Thaen Rasmussen and Doug Piercy, bassist Bill Skinner and drummer Ken Farragen, both previously with LEVIATHAN. The latter was eventually replaced by Joe Bennett, Farragen seemingly having ideas to become a policeman. Gere Fennelly, Rasmussen's girlfriend and a member of BLEU FOOD, was brought in on keyboards.

There were strong links between ANVIL CHORUS and the Seattle Metal band METAL CHURCH, Aaron Zimple (a.k.a. Aaron Whymer) having played drums on some early demos.

Both bands would also play the old LEVIATHAN track 'Red Skies' in their live sets.

METAL CHURCH mainman Kurdt Vanderhoof had once been in the San Franciscan Punk band THE LEWD and had formed METAL CHURCH with ex-LEVIATHAN guitarist Rick Condran, Aaron Whymer and bassist Steve Haat. For the group's first demo the act was titled ANVIL CHORUS—THE CHURCH OF METAL. When this early incarnation of METAL CHURCH folded Whymer took the name ANVIL CHORUS. The links between the two acts remained though as ANVIL CHORUS paid homage with their track 'Bow To The Church Of Metal'.

Despite strong sales of the ANVIL CHORUS single 'Blondes In Black', especially in Europe as an import, ANVIL CHORUS never released further product and drifted into a more keyboard orientated direction. Although Warner Brothers expressed some form of interest in the band, the Bay Area band faded into oblivion.

Fennelly and Zimpel quit in 1985. Piercy, having produced demos for LEGACY (later to be retitled TESTAMENT) and EXODUS wished to pursue harder material and joined CONTROL. After CONTROL's second guitarist Dino Carvosia bailed out Rasmussen joined the ranks of CONTROL too in a line-up comprising of the two ex-ANVIL CHORUS guitarists with vocalist Ed Bull, bassist Michael Thinger and drummer Eric Rasmussen (no relation). When the latter departed another ANVIL CHORUS refugee Joe Bennett joined.

Doug Piercy would appear with HEATHEN. For HEATHEN's second album the band recut the ANVIL CHORUS track 'Guitarmony' with a guesting Rasmussen. Percy quit HEATHEN in 1991 for ANGEL WITCH and the German based THE COMPANY. Gere Fennelli toured with RED KROSS circa the band's 'PhaseShifter' tour.

ANVIL CHORUS reformed for a one off San Francisco gig in 1987 opening for EXODUS and MEGADETH at the Kabuki venue. Rasmussen founded an ANVIL CHORUS II in the 90's with ex-RELEASE man Steve Kilgore, bassist Ryan Connor and the now jailed Dan Brian. Later work included Pop act PORCELAIN.

Rasmussen and Piercy formed part of the HEATHEN reformation in 2000. In early 2006 Thaen Rasmussen joined VICIOUS RUMORS for a series of European concerts. Reforming once again, ANVIL CHORUS performed a one-off gig at Ron Quintana's KUSF Rampage Radio 24th anniversary show on April 21st at Annie's Social Club in San Francisco. Band line-up comprised Aaron Zimpel on vocals and bass, guitarists Thaen Rasmussen and BLACK SUN's Carlos Hernandez, keyboard player Phil Bennett, replacing Gere Fennelly, and Joe Bennett on drums.

ANVIL CHORUS reunited to perform alongside fellow Bay Area veterans MORDRED and MERCENARY to perform on April 12th 2007 at Bottom of the Hill in San Francisco for a benefit concert for the family of late San Francisco rock musician Curtis Grant, of BLACK CHERRY, AMERICAN HEARTBREAK and TOUCH ME HOOKER, who lost his battle with Non-Hodgkin's Lymphoma on March 20th. This show marked the first ANVIL CHORUS appearance following the return of guitarist Doug Piercy.

Blondes In Black, Leviathan (1982). Blondes In Black / Once Again.

ANYONE

ORANGE COUNTY, CA, USA — *Riz Story (vocals / guitar), Static (bass), Ransom (drums).*

Acid fuelled Alt-Rockers ANYONE made a significant impact upon the European festival scene during 2001. ANYONE frontman Riz Story had formerly been an integral part of the short-lived yet influential SYLVIA, a trio that had also included latter day FOO FIGHTERS man Taylor Hawkins and Juano of SKY CRIES MARY on bass guitar. ANYONE was the subject of a high profile label bidding war with Social Distortion, KORN's Elementary imprint and Roadrunner all pitching in. The latter label would secure the deal with reports suggesting Roadrunner had placed its largest bid to date for a band signing. The group, having since drafted bassist Static, relocated to Seattle to lay down a debut album but returned after three months dissatisfied with the end results. Reconvening in Los Angeles with producer Mudrock ANYONE re-recorded the entire set of songs.

LIVE ACID, Orchard (2000). Giving Thrills / Hitches / Daddy Skypig / Pass the Reality / Whole World's Insane / Fly / Magic Dust / Don't Swallow Tomorrow / Running Dry / Real / Baby Blue.

ANYONE, Roadrunner (2001). Giving Thrills / Don't Wake Me / Lazy Hazy / Whole World's Insane / Hitches / Slaves (Part 12) / Real / Fly / Turnaround / Running Dry / Drops Of Miracle / She / Peace Love And Toxic / Dear Sylvia / Kissing God / Wait Until Morning.

APOCALYPTICA

HELSINKI, FINLAND — *Antero Manninen (cello), Max Lilja (cello), Paavo Lötjönen (cello), Eicca Toppinen (cello).*

An unexpected hit from an unlikely source. Four Helsinki based Sibelius Academy tutored cellists, Max Lilja, Antero Manninen, Paavo Lötjönen and Eicca Toppinen, reinterpreted METALLICA tunes in a sparse classical format. APOCALYPTICA's non-conformist juxtaposition of Classical and Metal inspired many in their wake, opening up the marketplace for a greater range of traditional expression of Heavy Metal such as RONDELLUS, a glut of string instrument tributes and even pre-empting METALLICA's own orchestral experimentation. The 1996 Pekka Ritaluoto produced debut album, 'Apocalyptica Plays Metallica By Four Cellos' originally issued through Zen Garden Records before being picked up on the Polygram Finland Oy label, was such a success APOCALYPTICA undertook live dates. Seasonal non-album tracks, 'Oh Holy Night' and 'Little Drummer Boy' placed the group into the Finnish charts that December.

A second album, 'Inquisition Symphony', emerged in 1998, which alongside more METALLICA renditions included reworks by contemporaries SEPULTURA, FAITH NO MORE and PANTERA. That year the group performed at the Dutch 'Headbanger's Heaven' festival, the show including the 'Mandatory Suicide' / 'South Of Heaven' medley with SLAYER drummer DAVE LOMBARDO guesting.

Perttu Kivilaakso replaced Antero Manninen in 1999 as the latter took up an offer from the Tahu Symphony Orchestra. APOCALYPTICA's third outing, 'Cult' emerging in September 2000, was recorded at Petrax Studios, Hollola in Finland and for the first time saw the inclusion of original material alongside a rendition of Edward Grieg 'Hall Of The Mountain King' and METALLICA's 'Until It Sleeps' and 'Fight Fire With Fire'.

The band issued a single 'Path Vol. 2' in March of 2001 from the 'Cult' record featuring guest vocals from Sandra Nasic of GUANO APES. Other tracks on the album included Matthias Sayer of FARMER BOYS as well as live tracks. The band would also guest on the 2001 SEPULTURA album 'Nation'.

Touring in the UK found the Finns guesting on MEGADETH's summer dates. Max Lilja would decamp in January 2002 to join the ranks of HEVEIN, being substituted by Antero Manninen for live performances as Mikko Sirén took up the percussion role. Recordings taking place in 2002 for a new studio album 'Reflections' would witness the inclusion of the esteemed DAVE LOMBARDO of SLAYER infamy on drums. The band undertook a further interesting collaboration in 2003 when they united with German Punk Rock diva NINA HAGEN to record a cover version of RAMMSTEIN's 'Seemann'.

Eicca Toppinen guests on the track 'Juoksevan Veden Aika' featured on the 2004 TIMO RAUTIAINEN & TRIO NISKALAUKAUS album 'Kylmä Tila'. APOCALYPTICA's 2004 album, seeing SLAYER drummer DAVE LOMBARDO featured on the album track 'Betrayal', would be preceded by the single 'Bittersweet', this featuring guest appearances by H.I.M.'s Ville Valo and THE RASMUS' Lauri Ylönen. Both singers also put in showings in the accompanying Antti Jokinen directed video for 'Bittersweet', the single finding success by entering the national Finnish singles charts at no. 3. The song, featuring both Valo and Ylönen, was premiered live on 17th January at a benefit concert for the victims of the Indian Ocean tsunami disaster at Helsinki's 12,000 seat Hartwall Arena. That week, 'Bittersweet' rose to no.1 on the Finnish charts.

APOCALYPTICA lent support to leading German industrial metallers RAMMSTEIN throughout Europe in February 2005. The band then announced their debut North American shows for March. A second single picked from the album, 'Wie Weit', added three different language versions of Quutamo'. The French version featured Manu of DOLLY whilst both English and German versions included Marta Jandová of Germany's DIE HAPPY. Touring the USA in September saw support from Orange County's EYES OF FIRE.

APOCALYPTICA's career retrospective CD and DVD package for 2006, 'Amplified—A Decade Of Reinventing The Cello', included new tracks recorded with Max Cavalera of SOULFLY and Matt Tuck from BULLET FOR MY VALENTINE. The group also collaborated with German Electro-Metal outfit OOMPH! On their single 'Die Schlinge', inspired by the famous harmonica melody from composer Ennio Morricone's film soundtrack 'Once Upon A Time In The West'.

PLAYS METALLICA BY FOUR CELLOS, Zen Garden 532 707-2 (1996). Enter Sandman / Master Of Puppets / Harvester Of Sorrow / The Unforgiven / Sad But True / Creeping Death / Wherever I May Roam / Welcome Home (Sanitorium).
Apocalyptica, Mercury 172139-2 (1996). Oh Holy Night / Little Drummer Boy. Chart position: 11 FINLAND.
Nothing Else Matters, Mercury 566 256-2 (1998) (Finnish release). Nothing Else Matters (Radio edit) / Nothing Else Matters (Album version).
INQUISITION SYMPHONY, Mercury 558 300-2 (1998). Harmageddon / From Out Of Nowhere / For Whom The Bell Tolls / Nothing Else Matters / Refuse—Resist / M.B. / Inquisition Symphony / Fade To Black / Domination / Toreador / One. Chart position: 69 GERMANY.
Harmageddon, Mercury 568 766-2 (1998). Harmageddon / Enter Sandman (Live).
Harmageddon, Mercury 568 745-2 (1998). Harmageddon / From Out Of Nowhere / Enter Sandman / The Unforgiven.
Path, Universal CDP634-2 (2000) (Mexican promotion). Path / Until It Sleeps / For Whom The Bell Tolls / Nothing Else Matters / Master Of Puppets / Nothing Else Matters (Video) / Harmageddon (Video) / Electronic Press Kit For 'Cult'.
CULT, Island 542 984-2 (2000). Path / Struggle / Romance / Pray! / In Memoriam / Hyperventilation / Beyond Time / Hope / Kaamos / Coma (Live) / Hall Of The Mountain King / Until It Sleeps / Fight Fire With Fire. Chart positions: 31 GERMANY, 58 AUSTRIA, 80 SWITZERLAND.
Path Vol. 1 & 2, Island 572 798-2 (2001) (feat. SANDRA NASIC). Path Vol. 2 / Path / Pray (Live in Munich) / Romance (Live in Munich). Chart positions: 85 AUSTRIA, 100 SWITZERLAND.
CULT—SPECIAL EDITION, Island 548 801 2 1 (2001). Path / Struggle / Romance / Pray! / In Memoriam / Hyperventilation / Beyond Time / Hope / Kaamos / Coma (Live) / Hall Of The Mountain King / Until It Sleeps / Fight Fire With Fire / Path Vol. 2 / Hope Vol. 2 / Nothing Else Matters (Live in Munich) / Harmageddon (Live in Munich) / Inquisition Symphony (Live in Munich).
Hope Vol. 2, Island 588 763-2 (2001) (feat. MATTHIAS SAYER of FARMER BOYS). Hope Vol. 2 (Radio edit) / My Friend Of Misery / South Of Heaven—Mandatory Suicide / Hope (Album version).
REFLECTIONS, Island 0440 077015-2 (2003). Prologue (Apprehension) / No Education / Faraway / Somewhere Around Nothing / Drive / Cohkka / Conclusion / Resurrection / Heat / Cortège / Pandemonium / Toreador II / Epilogue (Relief). Chart position: 15 GERMANY.
Faraway Vol. 2, Motor 077889-2 (2003) (feat. LINDA SUNDBLAD from LAMBRETTA). Faraway Vol. 2 / Faraway Vol. 2 (Extended version) / Perdition. Chart position: 43 GERMANY.
Seemann, Motor 981288-2 (2003) (feat. NINA HAGEN). Seemann (Radio edit) / Seemann (Album version) / Heat (Album version) / Seemann (Video).

REFLECTIONS REVISED, Universal 9865964 (2003). Prologue (Apprehension) / No Education / Faraway / Somewhere Around Nothing / Drive / Cohkka / Conclusion / Resurrection / Heat / Cortège / Pandemonium / Toreador II / Epilogue (Relief) / Seemann (Album version) / Faraway Vol. 2 (Extended version) / Delusion / Perdition / Leave Me Alone / Faraway Live (Live 2003) / Enter Sandman Live (Live 2003) / Inquisition Symphony (Live 2003) / Nothing Else Matters (Live 2003) / Somewhere Around Nothing (Live 2003) / Somewhere Around Nothing (Video) / Faraway Vol. 2 (Video) / Seemann (Video) / Faraway Vol. 2 (EPK) / Reflections (EPK) / Seemann (EPK).
REFLECTIONS, Universal UICO-1061 (2004) (Japanese release). Prologue (Apprehension) / No Education / Faraway / Somewhere Around Nothing / Drive / Cohkka / Conclusion / Resurrection / Heat / Cortège / Pandemonium / Toreador II / Epilogue (Relief) / Seemann (Album version) / Faraway Vol. 2 (Extended version) / Delusion / Perdition / Leave Me Alone.
Bittersweet, Universal 0602498692431 (2004). Bittersweet / Bittersweet (Acoustic version) / Bittersweet (Instrumental version) / Misconstruction / Monitor. Chart positions: 1 FINLAND, 55 SWEDEN.
APOCALYPTICA, Universal 0602498698310 (2005). Life Burns! / Quutamo / Distraction / Bittersweet / Misconstruction / Fisheye / Farewell / Fatal Error / Betrayal / Forgiveness / Ruska / Deathzone. Chart positions: 4 GREECE, 5 FINLAND, 5 GERMANY, 6 SWITZERLAND, 6 AUSTRIA, 61 FRANCE.
Wie Weit, Universal 0602498703502 (2005) (feat. MARTA JANDOVÁ of DIE HAPPY). Wie Weit / Quutamo / How Far / En Vie / Multimedia Track: Apocalyptica-Software Player. Chart positions: 23 GERMANY, 43 AUSTRIA, 60 SWITZERLAND.
How Far, Universal 06024 9870580 (2005) (feat. MARTA JANDOVÁ of DIE HAPPY). How Far / Quutamo / En Vie / Wie Weit.
Life Burns, Universal 0602498711965 (2005). Life Burns (feat. Lauri Ylönen) / Life Burns (instrumental) / Deep Down Ascend (demo version) / Kellot (demo version). Chart position: 17 FINLAND.
Repressed, Vertigo 06024 987852 25 (2006). Repressed (Single version) / Path Vol. 2 / Betrayal / Repressed (Video).
AMPLIFIED—A DECADE OF REINVENTING THE CELLO, Vertigo 06024 984033 58 (2006). Enter Sandman / Harmageddon / Nothing Else Matters / Refuse/Resist / Somewhere Around Nothing / Betrayal / Farewell / Master Of Puppets / Hall Of The Mountain King / One / Heat / Cohkka / Kaamos / Deathzone / Angel Of Death / Repressed / Path Vol. 2 / Bittersweet / Hope Vol. 2 / En Vie / Faraway Vol. 2 / Life Burns / Seemann. Chart positions: 19 GREECE, 23 SWITZERLAND, 24 GERMANY, 28 AUSTRIA, 33 FINLAND, 41 CZECH REPUBLIC, 158 FRANCE.

APOCRYPHA

LAS VEGAS, NV, USA — *Steve Plocica (vocals), Tony Friedanelli (guitar), Al Rumley (bass), Mike Poe (drums).*

Las Vegas outfit APOCRYPHA was viewed by many as the vehicle to promote guitarist Tony Friedanelli. The band's debut album line-up comprised Friedianelli, vocalist Steve Plocica, bassist Al Rumley and drummer Mike Poe. Of note is that 'The Forgotten Scroll' is produced by MARTY FRIEDMAN, then a member of CACOPHONY.

APOCRYPHA added second guitarist Chip Chrovian for 1988's 'The Eyes Of Time' album. Third album 'Area 54' saw the recruitment of a new rhythm section of bassist Breck Smith and drummer Dave Schiller.

Friedianelli issued a solo album 'Breakneck Speed'. He also performed with covers band LOVESHACK before a stint in MAJIK ALEX. By 2000 he was guitarist with multi platinum Pop Rockers artists THIRD EYE BLIND.

THE FORGOTTEN SCROLL, Roadrunner RR9568 (1987). Penance (Keep The Faith) / Lost Children Of Hope / Holy Wars (Only Lock The Doors) / Fall Of The Crest / Tablet Of Destiny / Look To The Sun / Riding In The Night / Distorted Reflections / Broken Dream.
THE EYES OF TIME, Roadrunner RR 9507-2 (1988). Father Time / West World / Twilight Of Modern Man / Alexander The King / The Day Time Stood Still / The Hour Glass / H.G. Wells / The Man Who Saw Tomorrow / Mystic.
AREA 54, Roadrunner RR 9345 (1990). Terrors Holding On To You / Catch 22 / A Night In Fog / The Power Elite / Instrubation No 3 / Area 54 / Tiananmen Square / The Detriment Of Man / Refuse The Offer That You Can't Refuse / Born To This World.

APOKALYPTIC RAIDS (pic: Victor "Whipstriker")

APOKALYPTIC RAIDS

RIO DE JANEIRO, RJ, BRAZIL — *Nekromaniac (vocals / guitar), Sub Umbra (bass), Skullcrusher (drums).*

Rio De Janeiro trio founded in 1997 and massively influenced by the genre defining HELLHAMMER right down to the band name and album cover artwork. The group would operate as 'APOCALYPTIC RAIDS' until 2001, when the subtle incorporation of a 'K' was made. Following the self issued 1999 EP APOKALYPTIC RAIDS signed to the Demise label for 2000's full length 'Only Death Is Real ...'

The band—Gustavo Belo—'Adrameleck' (Witch Hunts & Machine Guns), Leon Manssur—'Nekromaniac' (6-String Damnation & Vokills) and A. Aguinaga—'Sub Umbra' (Low Frequency Armageddon). Manssur also has affiliations with NIGHTBREED and EXPLICIT HATE whilst Aguinaga is operational with POETICUS SEVERUS. Belo had usurped 'Hofgodhar' on bass, this former candidate in actuality being Eduardo of NOCTURNAL WORSHIPPER and SONGE D'ENFER.

During 2001 APOKALYPTIC RAIDS shared a split 7" single, 'Maximum Metal Mayhem' released by the underground German label Iron Bonehead Productions, with the American act GRAVEWURM. The 2003 album 'The Return Of The Satanic Rites' saw Skullcrusher (a.k.a. Pedro Rocha of FARSCAPE) installed on the drums. The band returned in 2005 with third outing 'The Third Storm—World War III', this seeing a version of HELLHAMMER's 'Revelations Of Doom'.

Apocalyptic Raids EP, (1999). Evil / The Impaler / Tyrant, Emperor / Apocalyptic Raids.
ONLY DEATH IS REAL ..., Demise DMS CD019 (2000). The Enemy (Intro) / Evil / Forgotten Tales / Into The Twilight Zone / Eternal Gloom / Angels Of Hell / Humankind Dies / Tyrant, Emperor / Apocalyptic Raids / Tales Of Horror (Outro).
Maximum Metal Mayhem, Iron Bonehead Productions (2001) (Split single with GRAVEWURM). Maximum Metal Mayhem.
THE RETURN OF THE SATANIC RITES, Dark Sun SUN 006 (2003). Apokalyptic Raids / Ready To Go (To Hell) / The Atheist / The Way Of The Warrior / Satanic Slaughter / Impaler / Emperor's Return / Skullkrusher / Voyeur.
THE THIRD STORM—WORLD WAR III, Dark Sun (2005). I'm A Metal Head / Fallen Beyond Hope / Vision Shadows / Manifesto Politicamente Incorreto / Never Forget What You Are / Humankind Dies / Mankind Defeated (Humankind Dies pt. II) / The Power in My Mind / When The World Ends In Fire (Metal Returns) / I'm A Metal Head (Reprise).

APOSTASY

NORTH HAVEN, CT, USA — *Ryan Early (vocals), Danielle Gambardella (guitar), Joe Tursi (guitar / vocals), Zach Green (bass / vocals), Gus Griffen (drums).*

APOSTASY was formulated under the formative banner of HOLLOW POINT in the Summer of 2002 by vocalist / guitarist Ryan Early and drummer Nicole Sestito. Subsequently, guitarist John DeAngelo was enrolled as initial writing sessions led to a name switch to DRESSED IN BLACK. Early the next year second guitarist Danielle Gambardella was inducted, freeing Ryan Early up to prioritise lead vocals. Further material was penned, prompting another title switch to CORPORAL DOWNFALL, under which brand the demo 'Black Winter' was crafted.

Yet another name change, to NECROSIS, saw the introduction of keyboard player Jaime Pompilli and bassist Madison Roseberry. The band inaugurated itself on the live front on 16th August 2003 performing a rain shortened set alongside ALL UNDONE. The group then went into a lengthy period of stasis, broken with the acquisition of Dave Guckian on bass. The revised formation first performed live on 1st November, at the Polish National Alliance in Wallingford.

NECROSIS then unravelled as both Sestito and Guckian exited. Shortly after this defection Pompilli too opted out. The beginning of 2004 marked a new beginning as the remaining band members took on another title change to become APOSTASY. Bassist Zach Green was adopted in February and APOSTASY's stage debut, complete with drum machine, came on 13th March at a gig dubbed 'Rebfest', held in John DeAngelo's basement. The band put in two more gigs with the drum machine before being offered an album deal through Statue Records of California. Brett Pieper was installed on the drum stool and Rob Spalding for 'Shadows Of The Apocalypse' album recordings commencing in August. However, progress in the studio was minimal and Spalding was let go. The existing tapes would be scrapped and work began afresh, this time billing the album 'Invocation'.

Following a support gig to STRAPPING YOUNG LAD in Hartford in April of 2005 APOSTASY dispensed with Pieper's services. Drummer Mike Formanski would then be replaced by Gus Griffen. January of 2006 ushered in further changes with the recruitment of guitarist Joe Tursi.

Live At Rebfest, EarlCore Productions (2004). The New Millennium Holocaust / Damian / Anything To Belong / Dressed In Black / Society Is The Enemy / Pledge Your Allegiance / Sin America / Cataclysm Theory / Happy Song / Bloodlust.
Thornton Wilder Hall (Live), EarlCore Productions (2004). Bloodlust / Cataclysm Theory / Pledge Your Allegiance / Society Is The Enemy / Interstate Hate Song / The New Millennium Holocaust.
Black Summer Tour Demo, EarlCore Records (2004). Twilight Sonata / Bloodlust / Cataclysm Theory / Interstate Hate Song (Demo) / Malefaction (Demo) / The New Millennium Holocaust (Live) / Interstate Hate Song (Remix) / The New Millennium Holocaust (Live Video).
Shadows Of Autumn Tour Sampler, EarlCore Productions (2004). Exordium / No Tomorrow / 44 Minutes / Interstate Hate Song / Cataclysm Theory (Demo) / Nuclear Sunrise (Live) / Sin America (Live) / Bloodlust (Live) / Prelude To The Endtimes.
Spring Sampler, EarlCore Productions (2005). Intro / In God We Trust / Interstate Hate Song / No Tomorrow / 44 Minutes / Bloodlust 2003 / Society Is The Enemy (Live) / Pledge Your Allegiance (Live) / Nuclear Sunrise (Techno version) / Abortion 0235.
Shadows Over Stony Creek (Live), EarlCore Productions (2005). Intro / In God We Trust / No Tomorrow / The New Millennium Holocaust / Bloodlust / Nuclear Sunrise / Pledge Your Allegiance / Interstate Hate Song / Abortion 0235.
DISSECTION OF THEOCRACY, EarlCore Productions (2005). Invocation / Nuclear Sunrise / Vatican In Flames / In God We Trust / The New Millennium Holocaust / Eye Of The Storm / No Tomorrow / Pledge Your Allegiance / Interstate Hate Song / U.S.S.R. / Aftermath.
Summer Campaign Sampler, EarlCore Productions (2005). In God We Trust (Demo) / Interstate Hate Song (Video Edit) / No Tomorrow (2005 Demo) / Cataclysm Theory (2004 Demo) / 44 Minutes.
THE END OF PARADISE, (2006). Revelation 12 / Humanitarian Genocide / Building Bridges To Burn / Oracle Of Desolation / Tunguska / A Thousand Ways To Destroy A Man / My Declaration / Tsavo / Disaster Holiday / The End Of Paradise / Where The River Flows.
TRANSCENSION, Sonic Overload (2006). Invocation / Tunguska 1908 / Building Bridges To Burn / A Thousand Ways To Destroy A Man / Nuclear Sunrise / Transcension / Aftermath.

AQUAMORTA

MINSK, BELARUS — *Jermak (vocals / bass), Astron (guitar), Zhen (guitar), Denis Galitskiy (drums).*

Minsk Thrashers founded during 1997 by the erstwhile DEVIL'S EMPIRE pairing of guitarist Astron and bassist Jermak. The opening line up also included second guitarist Vadim Kaltigi and the WOLAND credited drummer Sergey Timoshik, this unit debuting live the following year at a youth music festival. Subsequently, VICIOUS CRUSADE's Alexey Gladysh took over the drum position. At this juncture their classic Thrash style began to develop with the introduction of Death Metal elements and Jermak switched from English language lyrics to Belarussian.

In the Autumn of 1998 AQUAMORTA enrolled ex-SEPTIC SCHIZO man Vadim Yasnogorodskiy as their new drummer. However, he in turn would be usurped by Denis Galitskiy of HOSPICE and ZNICH during 1999. For live work that year Kaltigin was superseded by OUT OF REACH, PARTYZONE and PATHOLOGIST DEPARTMENT man Eugene Tsilikov.

AQUAMORTA released the 2001 cassette 'Zaklik Kryvi'. This outing witnessed the inclusion of traditional pipe player Todar Kashkurevich and a DESTRUCTION cover version. In 2003 the band contributed the track 'Ružy Albo Dym' to the compilation album 'Hard Life—Heavy Music, Part II'.

ZAKLIK KRYVI, Aquamorte (2001). Zaklik Kryvi / Moj Cas / Slach / Krocym Poelec / Cyrvan / In The Mood / The Ritual / Krocym Poelec (unplugged).

ARA'KUS

SILVERDALE, WA, USA — *Jeremiah Johnson (guitar / vocals), Scott Helms (guitar), Jesse Halton (bass), Tony Ellison (keyboards / black vocals), Jeremy Veleber (drums).*

Silverdale, Washington Progressive Black Metal forged in 2002 following the dissolution of PLAGUE WITCH. Ex-member Ryan Kelly united with ex-DECRY guitarist Jeremiah Johnson, the duo composing the album 'Aeterno Elementum'. Later recruits would be bassist John Blackwell and drummer Davy Slyter. Working with producer and engineer Joel Martin ARA'KUS entered Pigboat Recording Studios, drafting erstwhile PERFECT NIGHT, GRAVITY FLUX and DECRY keyboard player Tony Ellison.

In March of 2004 founder member Ryan Kelly exited with Davy Slyter opting out soon after as Jeremy Veleber stepped into the drum vacancy. The erstwhile duo duly forged AS LONG AS I BREATHE in union with former CONSEQUENTIAL VALOR frontman Ron Adkins and bassist Dan Krogman.

ARA'KUS underwent line-up changes, with long-standing bassist John Blackwell being replaced by Jesse Halton in April of 2005.

AETERNO ELEMENTUM, PRS Records (2005). Stain The Dove / Lure Of The Flames / Syren's Embrace / Falling / Abyss / Shadows Of Twilight / Lord Of The Night / The Conquered / Aeterno Elementum.

ARAKAIN

CZECH REPUBLIC — *Ales Brichta (vocals), Daniel Krob (guitar), Kiri Urban (guitar), Zdenek Kub (bass), Robert Vondrovic (drums).*

Since their inception ARAKAIN have been considered one of the leading lights of the Thrash and Speed Metal scene in the Czech Republic. The band came together in 1982 with an initial line up of singer ALES BRICHTA, guitarist Kiri Urban and drummer Miroslav Nedved. Shortly after formation two more guitarists were added in Rudolfa Rozdalovského and Ivana Cifrince with Oldricha Maršíka handling bass. Line up changes during the first half of the eighties witnessed the introduction of guitarist Milon Šterner supplanting Rozdalovského in 1984, Marek Podskalský then taking the position the following year and bass guitarist Václav Jezek enrolled in 1984.

In 1986 ARAKAIN underwent a major overhaul of its members, incorporating bassist Zdenek Kub, guitarist Miroslav Mach whilst the drumming role was handed over to Karel Jencík. ARAKAIN released their first official product in 1988 with the single 'Gladiator' / 'Excalibur'. Yet more changes found Robert Vondrovic behind the drum kit in 1989, who in turn was superseded by Štepán Smetácek. Two more singles surfaced that year on the Supraphon label 'Amadeus' / 'Proc?" and 'Ku Klux Klan' / 'Orion'. These releases paved the way for the 1990 debut album 'Thrash The Trash'.

ARAKAIN underwent several line up changes following 1991's 'Schizofrenie'. Guitarist Daniel Krob founded ZEUS to issue the 1993 album 'The Little Hero'. Frontman ALES BRICHTA helped forge the tribute band ZEMEETRESENI with members of TÖRR and VITACIT in the same year as a homage to Czech musician Jiri Schelinger.

The band took the unusual step of issuing a live album 'Live History' made up of tracks from their early demo days and not previously released commercially. ARAKAIN's 1994 album 'Thrash!' is in fact the debut re-recorded with English lyrics. The band followed it with 'Legendy', an album comprising cover versions of bands such as BLACK SABBATH, DEEP PURPLE, URIAH HEEP, THE BEATLES, JUDAS PRIEST, GRAND FUNK RAILROAD, SLADE and LED ZEPPELIN sung in Czech. Following the 1998 release 'Apage Satanas' Kiri Urban and Zdenek Kub forged the extracurricular band project KAIN.

Brichta has issued solo albums and would re-emerge in 2003 fronting a new band GRIZZLY. That same year ARAKAIN made a return with new vocalist PETR KOLAR, previously with SARAH and PRECEDENS, for the album 'Metalmorfóza'. Kolár has also issued the solo album 'Mackie Messer'.

For a 21st April 2005 concert at Prague's Sazka Arena, to unveil new album 'The warning', ARAKAIN announced they were to be joined onstage not only by former band members but also DORO and ex-IRON MAIDEN singer Blaze Bayley.

THRASH THE TRASH, Supraphon (1990). Thrash The Trash / Šakal / Šeherezád / Ne! / Pán Boure / Štvanice / 311. Perut / Noc / Amadeus.

SCHIZOFRENIE, Supraphon (1991). Strázci Casu / Teror / Rekni A Máš Me / Kamennej Andel / Antikrist / Gilotina / Sedmá Pecet / Zlá Krídla Osamení / Hibernatus / Iluzorium / Schizofrenie.

LIVE HISTORY, Monitor (1992). Metalománie / Ruce Zla / Jáma A Kyvadlo / Ztráty A Nálezy / Symfonie Pro El. Kreslo / Myšlenky / Pulnocní Hollywood / Motýl Noci / Snaz Se / Dáblovi Soustruzníci / Gladiátor / Dotyky.

SALTO MORTALE, Popron Music (1993). Brána Iluzí / Ultraparoháč / Rám Krivejch Zrcadel / Zase Spíš V Noci Sama / Kleptoman / Gambler / Jen Jednou / Salto Mortale / Marilyn / Stárnem.

THRASH!, Popron Music (1994). Stormmaster / Jackal / Prostitute / Ku Klux Klan / Manhunt / R.A.F. Squadron 311 / Thrash The Trash.

LEGENDY, Popron Music (1995). Karambol / Eleanor Rigby / Hymna Zoufalcu / Slecna Závist / Snezná Slepota / Dál Dál Se Ptej / Chameleon / Derniera (Zbývá Uz Jen Mávnout).

S.O.S., Popron Music 54108-2 (1997). To Jsme My / S.O.S. / Pátecní Flám / Trináctá Komnata / Loutky / Adrian / Schody Nikam / Hladit Vlasy Tvý / Hanibal / Hlas Krve / Blázni Víry / Tuším Zradu.

APAGE SATANAS, Popron Music 54250-2 (1998). A Zvony Zvoní / Mý Jméno Je Plamen / Karavana Slibu / Kyborg / Princess / Špatný Dny / Návrat Bohu / Šer Chán / Hey Kritik / Pul Století / Trip / Promine Slecno / Apage Satanas.

FARAO, Popron Music 54368-2 (1999). Uz Ho Vezou / Mám To Za Pár / Global Street Debil / Uhonenej / Já Nejsem Já / Madam Tasemnice / Šeherezád II / Do Zdi / Millenium / Rajské Zahrady / Zkouším Se Zvednout / Rízená Strela / Farao / God Save The Araqueen.

GAMBRINUS LIVE!, Popron Music 54407-2 (2000). A Zvony Zvoní / Antikrist / Kyborg / Zapomen / Kolonie Termitu / Princess / Jsem Trochu Jako / Já Nejsem Já / Promine Slecno / Trip / Hlas Krve / S.O.S. / Amadeus / Gladiátor / Slecna Závist / Proc? / Apage Satanas / Markétka / Víc Uz Nehledám.

FORREST GUMP, Popron Music 54470-2 (2000). Major / Zmizím Pryc / Forrest Gump / Dezo / Hvezdár / Bulldog / Fcelka Mája / Nech Me / Vzdávám Se / 1,000,000 / Cernej Švihák / Televize / Peníze / Na Dne.
ARCHEOLOGY, Popron Music 54520-2 (2001). Nikotin / Kostlivec / Le Mans / Otec Z Rozhodnutí Komise / Zádnej Metal / My Si Zijem / Quasimodo / Slecna Heavy / Holka Ty Jsi Jak Vlkodlak / Prodavac Barev / May Day / Wendy / Cornouto / Zimní Královna / Nechceš / Kat / Poseidon / Automat Svet.
METALMORFOZA, Popron Music 54589-2 (2003). Ptáci Z Ráje / Prázdnej Kout / Padej / Jsou Tady / Aut / Muzeum Zla / Slávou Opilí / Bláhová Víra / Mládí V Hajzlu / Výlet (Trip II) / Barbari / Zpátky Jít / Tah Jezdcem / Znamení Doby / SpiDr.man.
WARNING!, Sony (2005). Chart position: 20 CZECH REPUBLIC.

ARBITRATER

WARWICKSHIRE, UK — *Tony Martin (vocals), Tony Ingrams (guitar), Dominic Jeaves (guitar), Neil Henderson (bass), Dave Barrows (drums).*

A Warwickshire based Thrash outfit dating from 1987 that included the SACRILIGE and CEREBRAL FIX credited drummer Andy Barker in an earlier incarnation, playing in a line-up also featuring vocalist Tony Martin, of THE VARUKERS, guitarist Dominic Jeaves, bassist Gavin Ward and guitarist P.M., before he quit in late 1988. Taking over on drums would be Dave Barrows. ARBITRATER submitted the track 'Memories Of Yesterday' to the 'Taste of Armageddon' compilation in 1989 and released a three track demo featuring 'Deadly Assassin', 'Evil Emperor' and 'Time For Destiny' in 1990.

The quintet finally released product in 1991 with the 'Balance Of Power' album. However, the following year a major split in the ranks saw Ingrams, Henderson and Barrows all exiting. ARBITRATER regrouped, enlisting New Zealand drummer Lawrence Paterson, previously with DESTROYER, TALON and THE WARNING, and followed up three years later with the 'Darkened Reality' album. Upon completion of these sessions the band inducted bassist Grant Edwards.

ARBITRATOR disbanded with both Martin and Paterson forging CHIMERA. In 2003 Paterson founded Northampton's METALHEAD. Paterson joined SHADOWKEEP in early 2005.

BALANCE OF POWER, Cyclone 101 (1991). Allegiance / The Treaty / Evil Emperor / Conquest / Life Line / Graveyard Of Fools / Time For Destiny / Deadly Assassin.
DARKENED REALITY, Cyclone 2 (1994). Judge And Jury / Suicide Commerciality / Guilty Of No Crime / No Second Chance / Racist Nation / Deadline / Nightmare Vision / Choose Your Weapons / Darkened Reality.

ARBITRATOR

KIROV, RUSSIA — *Lonewolf (vocals / guitar), Johann (bass), Igor Bechterev (drums).*

Kirov based Thrash Metal act ARBITRATOR was forged as a creative alliance between vocalist / guitarist Lonewolf, former XWZ bassist Axel and drummer Tormentor during January of 1994. Both Lonewolf and Tormentor were ex-HYSTERIA members, the drummer also holding credits with SATAN CHURCH and BURGLAR. That March, Lice of GANGRENA was added as lead vocalist and the band first performed live in December. After recording of an opening demo, 'Exception Allegory', Tormentor exited in 1995, being superseded by ABSCESS and FAYTREMOR veteran Blacksmith.

ARBITRATOR's line-up evolved further in 1996, Lice, Blacksmith and Axel opting out and Nick from RESSENTIMENT being drafted on bass. The following year Andrew of KILL'S BAND, and THE ABC & THE DEVILS was introduced on drums. Blacksmith Productions issued the cassette album 'Kill Their Religion' in 1998. 1999 brought yet more changes, the band acquiring FASHION SHIT and BRAIN O'POWER bass player Den and PROPAGANDA and BRAIN O'POWER drummer Alex. This rhythm section lasted until 2002, Den joining METAREASON as ARBITRATOR pulling in Johann and Igor Bechterev on bass and drums respectively. Metalism Records released 'Voice Of The Dead' in March 2004. Bechterev left the ranks in October 2004, but had returned by December.

KILL THEIR RELIGION, Blacksmith Productions (1998). Inhumanity / Hard Hearted / In A Nunnery / Sansara's Wheel / Icefire / Anchorite / The Rain And The Pain (The Song Of Hate) / E.S.T (Envy Strangles Them) / Kill Their Religion.
VOICE OF THE DEAD, Metalism (2004). Against The World (Intro) / Voice Of The Dead / Peacemaker's Mission / Under Fire / The Arabian Dance / Gorgons Burn / Recreation / No Fate! / The Cloven Hoof / The Powderkeg.

ARCADIA

ITALY — *Michele Nocentini (vocals), Demetrio Scopelliti (guitar), Alberto Rudoni (guitar), Marco Mastrobuono (bass), Eduardo Nicodemo (drums).*

Formed in 1996 ARCADIA weighed in with the March 1998 demo 'War Of Silence'. Follow ups comprised the 1999 'Trust' demo and the 2001 full-length 'Synth' album for NoBrain Records. ARCADIA's line-up at this juncture comprised vocalist / guitarist Tomas Tassistro, guitarist Demetrio Scopelliti, bass player Fabio Dacovich and Eduardo Nicodemo on drums. Further product came with a 2002 single entitled 'Net Realm'. In March of 2004 the group broke new ground by performing in Florida, USA. ARCADIA's second album offering 'Fracture Concrete', recorded at Nadir Studios in Genoa, arrived in 2005. This recording saw the addition of new members vocalist Michele Nocentini, guitarist Alberto Rudoni and bassist Marco Mastrobuono.

The War Of Silence, (1998). Time's End / War Of Silence / Bloody Rain / Thunderbolt.
Trust, (1999). Behind / H.I.R.A. / Senseless-Inane.
SYNTH, No Brain Records (2001). Mind Control / Belief Machine / Future Shock / Behind / Shiver Vision / Human Assault / Terminal Breath / Inner Hate / Termin@tion / H.I.R.A. / System Failure.
FRACTURE CONCRETE, (2005). Angelbitch / Prozac Generation / Seven7een B3low / Fragile / Net Realm / Deviated / Mi Sangre / Sick Sick Sick / Join A New Pain / Zero And Less / ... Et In Arcadia Ego.

ARCH ENEMY

HALMSTAD, SWEDEN — *Angela Gossow (vocals), Mike Amott (guitar), Christopher Amott (guitar), Sharlee D'Angelo (bass), Daniel Erlandsson (drums).*

Old style extreme Metal band ARCH ENEMY, based in Halmstad, feature ex-members of CARNAGE, CARCASS and EUCHARIST. Despite ploughing a niche market ARCH ENEMY have managed to attain a degree of commercial success, particularly in Japan. A switch in singers and a quite awesome live campaign would transfer their European and Asian support to the USA, ARCH ENEMY breaking onto the Billboard charts in 2003 with 'Anthems Of Rebellion'.

Frontman Johan Liiva previously played with CARNAGE and FURBOWL whilst guitarist Mike Amott, best known for his role in CARCASS, was also once a CARNAGE member early on and, in addition to ARCH ENEMY, performed in parallel in SPIRITUAL BEGGARS. Christopher Amott, Mike's younger brother, would appear to be following in his brother's footsteps by not laying all his eggs in one basket by also contributing to his side band ARMAGEDDON, whilst drummer Daniel Erlandsson occasionally sat in with IN FLAMES and was previously with EUCHARIST.

The opening ARCH ENEMY album, 1996's 'Black Earth' produced by Fredrik Nordström at Studio Fredman and originally released through Wrong Again Records, a mix of Thrash and Death elements but delivered in a quite unique style, would prove to be a genuine groundbreaking release, the resulting word of mouth amongst the Metal cognoscenti prompting huge world wide sales and respect. 'Black Earth' found ARCH ENEMY more of a solo effort conducted by Mike Amott rather than a full band release, the guitarist composing all of the material and, in spite of sleeve credits to the contrary giving Johan Liiva bass credits, both guitar and bass. The record scored considerable success in Japan and a video clip for the song 'Bury Me An Angel' provided valuable global awareness. The band contributed a cover of 'Aces High' to the Toy's Factory Records tribute to IRON MAIDEN, namely the cheesily titled compilation album 'Made In Tribute'.

Christopher Amott, working in collaboration with along with IN THY DREAMS vocalist Jonas Nyrén and drummer Daniel Erlandsson, launched his side band entitled ARMAGEDDON shortly afterward, the album 'Crossing The Rubicon' arriving in 1997.

For their next record, ARCH ENEMY pulled in ARMAGEDDON bass player Martin Bengtsson to allow Liiva to prioritise his vocals whilst Peter Wildoer, of ARMAGEDDON, Helsingborg's AGRETATOR and earlier ZANINEZ, was recruited onto the drum stool for the next recording sessions. Fredrik Nordström once again manned the desk as ARCH ENEMY's second outing, April 1998's 'Stigmata', benefited from an upward label shift over to Germany's Century Media Records. Japanese editions boasted three extra tracks, 'Damnation's Way', 'Vox Stellarum' and 'Bridge Of Destiny'.

The band shifted shape again in 1999, Sharlee D'Angelo, also an active member of WITCHERY and MERCYFUL FATE as well as citing credits with SINERGY and DISMEMBER, assumed the role of permanent bassist, whilst Daniel Erlandsson was again invited to handle drum duties once again. That March the group undertook their first dates in South America co-headlining with fellow Swedes HAMMERFALL and also performed at the famed 'Dynamo' festival in the Netherlands. In the Autumn the band hit Europe for a full-scale tour, sharing stages on a package bill with DARK TRANQUILLITY, IN FLAMES and CHILDREN OF BODOM. However, US touring would see Dick Lövgren, a seasoned campaigner quoting credentials with ARMAGEDDON, CROMLECH, IN FLAMES and EUCHARIST amongst many others, installed in the four-string position.

ARCH ENEMY built up quite a global reputation with tours of Japan and Europe. The band also opened for CRADLE OF FILTH in 1999, a support slot gained by admitted nepotism as Daniel Erlandsson's older brother Adrian had favourably gained the CRADLE OF FILTH drummer's job. Japanese versions of the Fredrik Nordström produced 'Burning Bridges' album, issued in July 1999, hosted extra tracks including a cover version of EUROPE's 'Scream Of Anger' plus a newly re-recorded version of 'Fields Of Desolation'. A live album, 'Burning Bridges In Japan', saw issue in Japan but fan pressure prompted a wider international release. Again the band recruited a temporary bassist for live action in 2000, Roger Nilson of SPIRITUAL BEGGARS, THE QUILL and FIREBIRD taking on the obligation this time around.

ARCH ENEMY would transform into a completely new beast for the next studio outing. The Amott siblings would be joined by German singer and journalist Angela Nathalie Gossow, previously with Cologne based acts ASMODINA and MISTRESS. Gossow had been prolific on the local scene, heading up ASMODINA for a November 1991 six song demo 'Your Hidden Fear' followed in February 1994 by 'The Story Of The True Human Personality' session. A further three track promotion outing was delivered in 1996 and the 'Inferno' album arrived in January of 1997 before a move was made to Death Rockers MISTRESS, featuring on two demos, May 1999's 'Worship The Temptress' and 2000's 'Party In Hell'. This band briefly operated as DEVIL IN THE DETAILS during which time Gossow opted out.

Ensconcing themselves in the familiar surrounds of Studio Fredman, the new unit worked with co-producer Fredrik Nordström, mixing the final tracks in league with erstwhile SABBAT guitarist Andy Sneap, to craft their comeback opus 'Wages Of Sin'. Any concerns over the incorporation of a female into the formula were blown away within seconds of Gossow's aural introduction, her bile, spit and venom easily outstripping her predecessor whilst the schizophrenic, twisted tongues approach, ranging from seductive whispers to trollish rumbles, gave ARCH ENEMY an entirely new character. 'Wages Of Sin' also marked a further turning point, often overlooked in the magnitude of Gossow's arrival, in that the Amotts shifted gear down to precision intimidation rather than the chaotic crunch that had previously driven all before them.

The ARCH ENEMY 'Wages Of Sin' album, arriving in April 2001, would see a belated North American release but did come complete with not only a bonus track 'Lament Of A Mortal Soul' and a video clip for 'Ravenous' but a whole separate CD of rarities. Included on the latter would be an unreleased version of JUDAS PRIEST's 'Starbreaker' plus covers of IRON MAIDEN's 'Aces High', EUROPE's 'Scream Of Anger' and a glut of bonus tracks originally only to be found on Japanese albums. The band would perform at the prestigious 2001 Japanese 'Beast Feast' Festival during August at the 30'000 capacity Yokohama Arena alongside SLAYER, V.O.D., STATIC X and SEPULTURA among others.

The ousted Johan Liiva announced the formation of a new endeavour in late 2001 billed as NONEXIST in union with Matte Modin of DEFLESHED and ANDROMEDA's Johan Reinholdz issuing the 'Deus Deceptor' album. However, by early 2002 the man had made a reappearance in HEARSE alongside former FURBOWL members drummer Max Thornell and guitarist Mattias Ljung for a debut 'Dominion Reptilian' album.

ARCH ENEMY toured Japan once again during March 2002 and put in debut British shows, as support to OPETH, in May. The band would be confirmed as one of the headline attractions at the mammoth 'Beast Fest' event in Japan during December of 2002, preceded by UK headliners with support coming from CORPORATION 187 and Hungarians WITHOUT FACE.

ARCH ENEMY guitarist Michael Amott laid down a guest solo on recording sessions by THE HAUNTED in November. As 2003 broke ARCH ENEMY put in January headline dates in Sweden, once again supported by CORPORATION 187. In April the band recorded new versions of 'Beneath The Skin', 'Young Man, Old Soul', 'Mantra' as well as a cover version of BACHMAN TURNER OVERDRIVE's 'Not Fragile' for a BBC radio session.

Sharlee D'Angelo was embroiled in a brand new side venture in early 2003 dubbed FIREGOD. This union saw the bassist uniting with an esteemed cast of MERCYFUL FATE and KING DIAMOND guitarist Mike Wead, the KING DIAMOND, DREAM EVIL and NOTRE DAME credited guitarist Snowy Shaw and drummer Simon Johansson of MEMORY GARDEN and ABSTRAKT ALGEBRA.

ARCH ENEMY, promoting new studio album 'Anthems Of Rebellion', would land a first by headlining the Busan International Rock Festival at Daedepo Beach in Korea on 8th August. The group then allied with HATE ETERNAL, EVERGREY and THE BLACK DAHLIA MURDER for a short but intensive run of US dates coming in mid August before pairing up with NEVERMORE for co-headline European gigs throughout September and October. The closing shows of this trek would be pulled though as ARCH ENEMY were dealt the quite unique blow of suffering from a bug infestation on their tour bus. Maintaining their road presence a lengthy string of US Jägermeister sponsored dates commencing 9th October and running through until mid December saw the band hooked up with SLAYER and HATEBREED. 'Anthems Of Rebellion', breaking the charts across Europe would prove to be Century Media's fastest ever selling record to date. In the USA the record took just three months to sell over 25,000 copies. UK dates in December allied the band with AKERCOCKE.

The band's profile rose higher into 2004 as ARCH ENEMY lent

support to IRON MAIDEN's Canadian January dates and the British veterans four show run at New York City's Hammerstein Ballroom then Japanese gigs. European headline dates in February and March saw ZYKLON and STAMPIN' GROUND as support. However, gigs in Osnabruck, Essen and Antwerp would be pulled when Angela Gossow lost her voice. US gigs in April had the band scheduled as heavyweight support to MACHINE HEAD, although the band missed the first show, in Philadelphia on the 25th, due to an apparent delay in processing Angela Gossow's work visa. As it transpired the group then pulled out of the entire tour, headliners MACHINE HEAD issuing a sarcastic press statement claiming the band had withdrawn "because singer Angela 'Gossard' broke a fingernail which had recently been through a vigorous French manicure".

Returning to Japan as headliners, ARCH ENEMY put in a short burst of June dates. Meantime Daniel Erlandsson debuted his new act in mid 2004, REVENGIA issuing the opus 'A Decade In The Dark'. Michael Amott took time out to record a guest guitar solo for the song 'Murder Fantasies' on the latest KREATOR album. Amott's parallel act SPIRITUAL BEGGARS entered Studio Fredman in Gothenburg, Sweden in July with producer Fredrik Nordström to cut a new album. ARCH ENEMY's Sharlee D'Angelo would cut the bass guitar for these tracks.

November 'Headbanger's Ball III' US touring partners would be CRADLE OF FILTH, BLEEDING THROUGH and HIMSA. That same month a US issue of 'Dead Eyes See No Future' saw release whilst December saw the band on the road in Europe, forming up the 'Hammered at Xmas' tour in alliance with THE HAUNTED and DARK TRANQUILLITY. A London show would be filmed for DVD use. A 2005 compilation inclusion of note would be the track 'We Will Rise' featured on the 'Code Red' album, an exclusive collection given to US Marine Corps soldiers active duty in the Middle East.

In mid 2005 Greek guitarist Gus G. (a.k.a. Kostas Karamitroudis) of NIGHTRAGE, MYSTIC PROPHECY, DREAM EVIL and FIREWIND joined ARCH ENEMY as the group's touring guitarist for the US 'Ozzfest' festival dates after Christopher Amott bowed out of that band in order to "fully concentrate on his studies". The 'Doomsday Machine' arrived in stores worldwide during July. Japanese variants on the Toys Factory label added the traditional bonus tracks, live versions of 'Heart Of Darkness' and 'Bridge Of Destiny'. In the USA, the album sold just under 12,000 copies in its first week of release to debut at no. 87 on the Billboard charts.

Building the band back up to strength, new guitarist Fredrik Åkesson was inducted, a scene veteran of such acts as ONE CENT, TAURUS, TALISMAN, the JOHN NORUM band, KRUX, TIAMAT and SOUTHPAW. ARCH ENEMY's September and October European headline dates, taking in the UK, France, Belgium, Holland, Germany, Norway, Sweden and Denmark, saw strong support from TRIVIUM. The two bands stuck together for Japanese gigs in October. However, the UK dates were re-scheduled for December when co-headliner DARK TRANQUILLITY withdrew. STRAPPING YOUNG LAD duly joined forces for the tour. Meantime, the band engaged in touring throughout November in the USA sharing stages with ALL THAT REMAINS, MNEMIC and A PERFECT MURDER.

ARCH ENEMY, CHIMAIRA, NEVERMORE and HATE ETERNAL announced US shows for April 2006. That same month it was learned Gossow was set to feature as guest singer on the all female Greek Black Metal band ASTARTE's 'Demonized' album. ARCH ENEMY's Mexican debut came in May with shows in Monterrey and Mexico City. The band put in a significant appearance at the METALLICA and KORN headlined 'Download' festival in Castle Donington, UK on June 10th. ARCH ENEMY joined up with the MEGADETH headlined 'Gigantour' North American festivals in early September, sharing billing with OPETH, LAMB OF GOD, OVERKILL, INTO ETERNITY, SANCTITY and THE SMASHUP. The group returned to Scandinavia in November, heading up the 'Close Up made me do it' tour alongside COLDWORKER and PATH OF NO RETURN. December continental concerts were supported by Dutch act TEXTURES.

In January 2007 it was learned that Angela Gossow had contributed guest vocals to the AMASEFFER "Holy" project fronted by VANDEN PLAS vocalist Andy Kuntz in union with Israeli musicians guitarists Yuval Kramer, Hanan Abramovitch and drummer Erez Yohanan. South American concerts in February witnessed large crowds in Chile, Argentina and Brazil.

Guitarist Christopher Amott rejoined the ranks of ARCH ENEMY in March.

Arch Enemy, Arch Enemy (1996) (Demo). Bury Me An Angel / Dark Insanity / Eureka / Idolatress.

BLACK EARTH, Wrong Again WAR011CD (1996). Bury Me An Angel / Dark Insanity / Eureka / Idolatress / Cosmic Retribution / Demoniality / Transmigration Macabre / Time Capsule / Fields Of Desolation.

BLACK EARTH, Toy's Factory TFCK-88792 (1996) (Japanese release). Bury Me An Angel / Dark Insanity / Eureka / Idolatress / Cosmic Retribution / Demoniality / Transmigration Macabre / Time Capsule / Fields Of Desolation / Losing Faith / The Ides Of March.

STIGMATA, Toy's Factory TFCK-87149 (1998) (Japanese release). Beast Of Man / Stigmata / Sinister Mephisto / Dark Of The Sun / Let The Killing Begin / Black Earth / Hydra / Tears Of The Dead / Diva Satanica / Damnations Way / Vox Stellarum / Bridge Of Destiny.

STIGMATA, Century Media 77212-2 (1998). Beast Of Man / Stigmata / Sinister Mephisto / Dark Of The Sun / Let The Killing Begin / Black Earth / Tears Of The Dead / Vox Stellarum / Bridge Of Destiny.

BURNING BRIDGES, Toy's Factory TFCK-87184 (1999) (Japanese release). The Immortal / Dead Inside / Pilgrim / Silverwing / Demonic Science / Seed Of Hate / Angelclaw / Burning Bridges / Scream Of Anger / Fields Of Desolation.

BURNING BRIDGES (LIMITED EDITION), Century Media 77276 (1999). The Immortal / Dead Inside / Pilgrim / Silverwing / Demonic Science / Seed Of Hate / Angelclaw / Burning Bridges / Diva Satanica / Hydra.

BURNING BRIDGES, Century Media 77276-2 (1999). The Immortal / Dead Inside / Pilgrim / Silverwing / Demonic Science / Seed Of Hate / Angelclaw / Burning Bridges.

BURNING JAPAN LIVE 1999, Toy's Factory TFCK-87217 (2000). The Immortal / Dark Insanity / Dead Inside / Diva Satanica / Pilgrim / Silverwing / Beast Of Man / Bass Intro / Tears Of The Dead / Bridge Of Destiny / Transmigration Macabre / Angelclaw.

WAGES OF SIN, Toy's Factory TFCK-87245 (2001) (Japanese release). Enemy Within / Burning Angel / Heart Of Darkness / Ravenous / Savage Messiah / Dead Bury Their Dead / Web Of Lies / The First Deadly Sin / Behind The Smile / Snow Bound / Shadows And Dust.

Burning Angel, Toy's Factory TFCK-87281 (2002) (Japanese release). Burning Angel / Lament Of A Mortal Soul / Starbreaker.

WAGES OF SIN, Century Media 77383-2 (2002) (2 CD). Enemy Within / Burning Angel / Heart Of Darkness / Ravenous / Savage Messiah / Dead Bury Their Dead / Web Of Lies / The First Deadly Sin / Behind The Smile / Snow Bound / Shadows And Dust / Lament Of A Mortal Soul / Ravenous (Video) / Starbreaker / Aces High / Scream Of Anger / Diva Satanica / Fields Of Desolation '99 / Damnation's Way / Hydra (Instrumental) / The Immortal (Video).

BLACK EARTH, Regain 002AS (2002). Bury Me An Angel / Dark Insanity / Eureka / Idolatress / Cosmic Retribution / Demoniality / Transmigration Macabre / Time Capsule / Fields Of Desolation / Losing Faith / The Ides Of March / Aces High.

STIGMATA, Dream On PARK-9023 (2003) (South Korean release). Beast Of Man / Stigmata / Sinister Mephisto / Dark Of The Sun / Let The Killing Begin / Black Earth / Hydra / Tears Of The Dead / Diva Satanica / Damnation's Way / Vox Stellarum / Bridge Of Destiny.

BURNING BRIDGES, Dream On PARK9024 (2003) (South Korean release). The Immortal / Dead Inside / Pilgrim / Silverwing / Demonic Science / Seed Of Hate / Angelclaw / Burning Bridges / Scream Of Anger / Fields Of Desolation.

ANTHEMS OF REBELLION, Toy's Factory TFCK-87322 (2003) (Japanese release). Tear Down The Walls / Silent Wars / We Will Rise / Dead Eyes See No Future / Instinct / Leader Of The Rats / Exist To Exit / Marching On A Dead End Road / Despicable Heroes / End Of The Line / Dehumanization / Anthem / Saints And Sinners.

ANTHEMS OF REBELLION (LIMITED EDITION), Century Media 77483-2 (2003) (European release). Tear Down The Walls (Intro) / Silent Wars / We Will Rise / Dead Eyes See No Future / Instinct / Leader Of The Rats / Exist To Exit / Marching On A Dead End Road / Despicable Heroes / End Of The Line / Dehumanization / Anthem / Saints And Sinners / Lament Of A Mortal Soul (Live) / Behind The Smile (Live) / Diva Satanica (Live) / Leader Of The Rats (Remix) / Dead Eyes See No Future (Remix).

ANTHEMS OF REBELLION, Century Media 77483-2 (2003). Tear Down The Walls / Silent Wars / We Will Rise / Dead Eyes See No Future / Leader Of The Rats / Exist To Exit / Marching On A Dead End Road / Despicable Heroes / End Of The Line / Dehumanization / Anthem / Saints And Sinners. Chart positions: 42 FINLAND, 60 SWEDEN, 69 USA, 69 GERMANY, 97 HOLLAND.

ANTHEMS OF REBELLION (LIMITED EDITION), Century Media 77483-2 (2003) (USA release). Tear Down The Walls (Intro) / Silent Wars / We Will Rise / Dead Eyes See No Future / Instinct / Leader Of The Rats / Exist To Exit / Marching On A Dead End Road / Despicable Heroes / End Of The Line / Dehumanization / Anthem / Saints And Sinners / Lament Of A Mortal Soul (Live) / Behind The Smile (Live) / Diva Satanica (Live) / Exist To Exit (Remix) / Leader Of The Rats (Remix) / Dead Eyes See No Future (Remix).

Dead Eyes See No Future, Toy's Factory TFCK-87358 (2004) (Japanese release). Dead Eyes See No Future / Burning Angel (Live) / We Will Rise (Live) / Symphony Of Destruction / Kill With Power / Incarnated Solvent Abuse.

Dead Eyes See No Future, Century Media 82762-9 (2004) (European release). Dead Eyes See No Future / Burning Angel (Live in Paris 2004) / We Will Rise (Live in Paris 2004) / Heart Of Darkness (Live in Paris 2004) / Symphony Of Destruction / Kill With Power / Incarnated Solvent Abuse / We Will Rise (Enhanced video clip).

Arch Enemy, Century Media 8234-2 (2005) (Split promotion release with NEVERMORE). Nemesis / I Am Legend—Out For Blood.

Doomsday Machine Two-Song Sampler, Century Media 41270-6 (2005) (Promotion release). Nemesis / I Am Legend—Out For Blood.

DOOMSDAY MACHINE, Toy's Factory TFCK-87388 (2005) (Japanese release). Enter The Machine / Taking Back My Soul / Nemesis / My Apocalypse / Carry The Cross / I Am Legend / Out For Blood / Skeleton Dance / Hybrids Of Steel / Mechanic God Creation / Machtkampf / Slaves Of Yesterday / Heart Of Darkness (Live) / Bridge Of Destiny (Live).

DOOMSDAY MACHINE (LIMITED EDITION), Century Media 77583 (2005) (CD + DVD). Enter The Machine / Taking Back My Soul / Nemesis / My Apocalypse / Carry The Cross / I Am Legend / Out For Blood / Skeleton Dance / Hybrids Of Steel / Mechanic God Creation / Machtkampf / Slaves Of Yesterday / Intro / Dead Eyes See No Future / Ravenous / Nemesis (Video).

DOOMSDAY MACHINE, Century Media 77583-2 (2005). Enter The Machine / Taking Back My Soul / Nemesis / My Apocalypse / Carry The Cross / I Am Legend/Out For Blood / Skeleton Dance / Hybrids Of Steel / Mechanic God Creation / Machtkampf / Slaves Of Yesterday. Chart positions: 23 SWEDEN, 34 GERMANY, 74 AUSTRIA, 81 UK, 87 USA.

ARISE

ALINGSAS, SWEDEN — *Erik Ljungqvist (vocals / guitar), L.G. Jonasson (guitar), Patrick Skoglow (bass), Daniel Bugno (drums).*

ARISE, founded in Alingsas during 1994 and titled in honour of the SEPULTURA album of the same name, blend traditional Swedish style Death Metal with retro Thrash influences. The group was assembled by a triumvirate of erstwhile HOLOCAUST members guitarist Erik Ljungqvist, bassist Patrick Skoglow and drummer Daniel Bugno. Second guitars were on hand from L.G. Jonasson, an ex-member of FUTURE DEVELOPMENT.

Initially the band was fronted by vocalist Jorgen Sjolander who was in turn replaced by Bjorn Andvik. When Andvik decamped Ljungvist took over the lead vocal role as ARISE switched from playing covers to writing original material. They then proceeded to issue a rush of demos including 'Hell's Retribution', 'Resurrection' and 1999's 'Statues'.

ARISE cut an April 2000 session 'Abducted Intelligence' with KING DIAMOND man Andy LaRocque at the production helm. This last tape duly securing a deal with the Finnish Spinefarm label.

ARISE would also contribute a version of 'Communication Breakdown' to the Dwell Records LED ZEPPELIN Death Metal tribute album 'Dead Zeppelin'. Japanese issues of the debut album 'A Godly Work Of Art' include an extra track, namely of cover of METALLICA's 'Motorbreath'. ARISE cut a new album, 'The Beautiful New World', at StudioMega in Bollebygd during 2004.

ARISE lent support to MORBID ANGEL's March 2005 Swedish dates. That December the band parted ways with guitarist/vocalist Erik Ljungqvist and bassist Patrik Skoglow due to "differences in opinion."

Arise, Arise (1998) (Cassette demo). The Last Of Centuries / Forsaken / Crucified Within.

Statues, Arise (1999) (Demo). Purgatory Unleashed / Statues / New Omen.

Resurrection, Arise (1999) (Demo). Intro / Abducted Intelligence / Black Souls / Cellbound / Infinite Sorrow (Outro).

Hell's Retribution, Arise (2000) (Demo). Black Souls / Delusion Of Life.

Abducted Intelligence, Arise (2000) (Demo). Abducted Intelligence / Cellbound / Black Souls / Delusion Of Life.

THE GODLY WORK OF ART, Spinefarm SPI 121CD (2001). A Godly Work Of Art / Generations For Sale / Within / Delusion Of Life / Haterush / Cellbound / Wounds / Abducted Intelligence / . . . And The Truth Is Lies / Motorbreath.

KINGS OF THE CLONED GENERATION, Spinefarm SPI 179CD (2003). Strangled Love / Stains Of Blood / Another World To Consume / Kings Of A Cloned Generation / Corroded / Way Above Life / Nuclear Ray Infected / Stick To The Line / Master Of Gravity / Wasted Life.

THE BEAUTIFUL NEW WORLD, Spinefarm SPI 235CD (2005). How Long Can You Pretend? / A New World / Profit Trom The Weak / Dreams Worthy Gods / King Of Yesterday, Slave Of Today / Of Life And Death / Expendable Heroes / Inject The Machine / Misery / Broken Trust / Tribute To The Flesh.

THE BEAUTIFUL NEW WORLD, Woodbell WBEX-25008 (2005) (Japanese release). How Long Can You Pretend? / A New World / Profit Trom The Weak / Dreams Worthy Gods / King Of Yesterday, Slave Of Today / Of Life And Death / Expendable Heroes / Inject The Machine / Misery / Broken Trust / Tribute To The Flesh / A Godly Work Of Art / Generations for Sale / Within / Haterush / Wounds / Abducted Intelligence / Motorbreath.

ARMAGEDDON

HALMSTAD, SWEDEN — *Christopher Amott (vocals / guitar), Tobias Gustafsson (bass), Daniel Erlandsson (drums).*

An uncompromising, brutal Metal band, Halmstad's ARMAGEDDON, created by Christopher Amott of ARCH ENEMY along with IN THY DREAMS vocalist Jonas Nyrén, spread the word initially with their inclusion on a Japanese released IRON MAIDEN tribute album with their version of 'Die With Your Boots On'.

Founder member and drummer Daniel Erlandsson, an IN FLAMES veteran, left to form EUCHARIST prior to recording of the 1997 'Crossing The Rubicon' album. This album, released by Toy's Factory in Japan, was recorded by a quartet comprising singer Jonas Nyrén, guitarist Christopher Amott, bassist Martin Bengtsson and the ZANINEZ, AGRETATOR and DARKANE credited drummer Peter Wildoer. The band went into stasis after this album but Amott, Bengtsson and Wildoer all featured on ARCH ENEMY's 1998 album 'Stigmata'.

Under Amott's guidance, ARMAGEDDON would resurface to issue a brace of albums for the Japanese and South Korean markets. First up would be 2000's 'Embrace The Mystery', seeing Amott joined by a returning Daniel Erlandsson, TRISTITIA and LAST TRIBE singer Rickard Bengtsson and bass player Dick Lowgren, also of LAST TRIBE.

A later recruit would be bassist Tobias Gustafsson, a scene veteran of EUCHARIST, THE END, CROAM, TIMEMACHINE and ETERNAL LIES, featuring on 2002's 'Three' album.

CROSSING THE RUBICON, Toy's Factory TFCK-87103 (1997) (Japanese release). 2022 (Intro) / Godforsaken / The Juggernaut Divine / Astral Adventure / Funeral In Space / Asteroid Dominion / Galaxies Away / Faithless / Children Of The New Sun / Into The Sun.
CROSSING THE RUBICON, War Music 970304-1 (1997). 2022 (Intro) / Godforsaken / The Juggernaut Divine / Astral Adventure / Funeral In Space / Asteroid Dominion / Galaxies Away / Faithless / Children Of The New Sun / Into The Sun.
EMBRACE THE MYSTERY, Toy's Factory TFCK-87234 (2000) (Japanese release). Awakening / The Broken Spell / Blind Fury / Worlds Apart / Cry Of Fate / Illusions Tale / Moongate Climber / Embrace The Mystery / Sleep Of Innocence / Grain Of Sand.
EMBRACE THE MYSTERY, Dream On PARK-9007 (2001) (South Korean release). Awakening / The Broken Spell / Blind Fury / Worlds Apart / Cry Of Fate / Illusions Tale / Moongate Climber / Embrace The Mystery / Sleep Of Innocence / Grain Of Sand.
THREE, Toy's Factory TFCK-87286 (2002) (Japanese release). Gathering Of The Storm / Burn The Sun / Stranglehold / Heart Of Ice / Well Of Sadness / Rainbow Serpent / Winter Skies / Final Destination / Spirit Kiss / The Contract.
THREE, Dream On PARK-9016 (2002) (South Korean release). Gathering Of The Storm / Burn The Sun / Stranglehold / Heart Of Ice / Well Of Sadness / Rainbow Serpent / Winter Skies / Final Destination / Spirit Kiss / The Contract.
CROSSING THE RUBICON, Dream On PARK-9027 (2003) (South Korean release). 2022 (Intro) / Godforsaken / The Juggernaut Divine / Astral Adventure / Funeral In Space / Asteroid Dominion / Galaxies Away / Faithless / Children Of The New Sun / Into The Sun / Die With Your Boots On.

ARMAGEDOM

SÃO PAULO, SP, BRAZIL — *Eduardo (vocals), Javier (guitar), Claudinei (bass), Barrigo (drums).*

A Sao Paulo Thrashcore act heavy on the Punk influences. ARMAGEDOM date back as far as 1982 under their formation as ULTIMA CHANCE with a line up of Javier on vocals, Barriga on guitar, Zero on bass and Ricardo on drums. The act, adding bassist Eduardo, evolved into ARMAGEDOM during 1983.

ARMAGEDOM debuted with a track inclusion on the 1985 compilation 'Ataque Sonoro', following this with a 1986 full length album 'Silencio Funebre'. The band would then undergo a radical shift with band members swapping instruments. Javier took to guitar, Eduardo became lead vocalist whilst Barrigo became drummer. New face Beto took the bass mantle.

ARMAGEDOM welcomed in another bassist, Claudinei, in 1999. The same year a split album emerged in league with FORCA MACABRE.

SILENCIO FUNEBRE, Rainbow (1986). Sofrer Demais / Cegos Por Ódio / Gritos De Dor / Mentes Insanas / Políticos, Militares, Religiosos / Torturam Os Pobres / Super Projetos / Sobreviver / Asilo Na Existência / Pessoas Caem, Pessoas Morrem / Dívida Externa / Mutilações / Total Alienação / Mortos De Fome.
ARMAGEDOM, Six Weeks (1999) (Split album with FORCA MACABRE).
DAS CINZAS AO INFERNO, Mothra (2001).

ARMED FORCE

NEW YORK, NY, USA — *Kevin Burns (vocals), Billy Blakk (guitar), Michael Manne (guitar), Torch Tetro (bass), Dante Renzi (drums).*

Essentially the Glam Metal new line-up of New York Thrashers ARMED FORCES. Only guitarist Michael Manne and bassist Torch Tetro remaining from the band that recorded the previous mini-album 'Let There Be Metal'. Joining the revamped line-up came vocalist Kevin 'Blazin' Burns, guitarist Billy 'Flash' Blakk and drummer Dante 'Madman' Renzi. The band originally recorded this album under the impression it would spark off a fierce bidding war amongst the labels before deciding to drop the 's' in their name and let the Iron Works label have the 'Heavy Artillery' album.

By 1988 Dante Renzi had linked up with N.R.G. vocalist Les Brown and ex BLACK LACE members Carl and Anthony Fragnito to form DAMN CHEETAH. Renzi's later bands included GREEN DEVIL INDUSTRY and by 2000 the Nu-Metal crew REACH.

HEAVY ARTILLERY, Iron Works (1986). Take No More / Machine Gun Alley / Another Day's Gone / Outraged / Soldier Of Fortune / Land Of Destiny / Ninth Day Be Damned / Heavy Artillery.

ARMED FORCES

NEW YORK, NY, USA — *Scotty Knight (vocals), Michael Manne (guitar), Tommy Bolan (guitar), Steve A. Tetro (bass), Joey Cussamano (drums).*

NWoBHM influenced quintet from Brooklyn, New York, ARMED FORCES were originally formed in 1980 and went through the usual phase of having to play covers, in this instance songs by JUDAS PRIEST and IRON MAIDEN, in order to get the gigs and pay the bills.

By the time the band recorded their debut offering, the mini LP 'Let There Be Metal', lead guitarist Michael Manne was the only original member of the band. Whilst the band's demos had publications such as Britain's 'Metal Forces' magazine proclaiming the band to be the future of Metal, the actual record once released turned out to be a rather disappointing, muted affair.

By 1985 the band had undergone severe line-of changes and, almost overnight, turned themselves into a Glam band, much to the horror of some of their strongest supporters, with only Manne and Tetro remaining from the band that recorded the mini album. Joining the revamped line up came vocalist Kevin Burns, guitarist Billy 'Flash' Blakk and drummer Dante 'Madman' Renzi.

It was with this bunch that the New Yorkers changed their name to ARMED FORCE and signed to the Iron Works label for the release of the 'Heavy Artillery' album. Tommy Bolan later joined WARLOCK.

LET THERE BE METAL, Metallic Flame (1984). The Night Rider / Let There Be Metal / Into The Darkness / The Intruder / Teaze Me.

ARMORED SAINT

PASADENA, CA, USA — *John Bush (vocals), Dave Prichard (guitar), Phil E. Sandoval (guitar), Joey Vera (bass), Gonzo (drums).*

Officially formed in the Summer of 1982, ARMORED SAINT immediately attracted attention for the quality of a five track demo tape and the headbanging nature of the quintet's live show. Although an out and out Power Metal band, the group found itself caught up in the Bay Area Thrash wave. Famously, singer John Bush had been under consideration for the lead vocal position with METALLICA but had turned the offer down. The band was initially founded in 1981, yet only fully completed in mid 1982. The individuals concerned had all played in other bands, but none had recorded with anybody previously. Bassist JOEY VERA had played with MÖTLEY CRÜE's Tommy Lee and then OZZY OSBOURNE guitarist JAKE E. LEE during his formative years.

Joey Vera, then a guitarist, and vocalist John Bush first got together in their El Sereno school band RHAPSODY. A covers act including songs by the likes of FOREIGNER and DEEP PURPLE in their act, RHAPSODY also included guitarist David Avila, bassist Channing Estrada, keyboard player Mark Patton and drummer Martin Zuniga.

Vera and Bush stuck together to create their next school band ROYAL DECREE in an alliance with the Sandoval siblings drummer Gonzo and guitarist Phil. Vera was now on bass after Bush initially made an attempt but got bored with the instrument. Upon ROYAL DECREE's demise Bush and Vera hooked up with SAPPHIRE, but shortly after Bush was ousted

ARMORED SAINT (pic: Rich Galbraith)

by guitarist Brad Parker. The band underwent numerous lineup changes but toward the end of the band's career Vera found himself playing alongside Tommy Lee.

Vera joined ex-DOKKEN guitarist Greg Leon in his GREG LEON INVASION following Lee's departure to MÖTLEY CRÜE. During this time Gonzo, Sandoval and Vera were jamming in a garage, latter day MX MACHINE and MOTOFURY man Diego Negrete having a brief stint on bass. This unnamed unit, featuring Dave Prichard on second guitar, pulled John Bush in on vocals although were quite happy to inform the front man the only reason he got to join was because he owned an impressive PA system. This line-up began to formulate early ARMORED SAINT material as well as covering IRON MAIDEN tunes. One song that didn't make it to any official release was subtly titled 'You Suck My Anal Dry'.

Vera continued his bass duties with the GREG LEON INVASION whilst the mysterious Mike took his role in the garage band. In May 1982 Vera officially joined the newly titled ARMORED SAINT. As legend has it, ARMORED SAINT's demo tape was paid for from compensation arising from injuries sustained by Joey Vera in an automobile accident whilst a passenger in a car driven by Tommy Lee.

With the band building a strong local following, an attempt was made by the then fledgling METALLICA to poach singer John Bush during 1982. After witnessing a show at The Woodstock in Anaheim, METALLICA requested Bush's services, an offer he declined. ARMORED SAINT's first commercial recorded appearance came with a contribution to Metal Blade's 'Metal Massacre II' album, the group offering the Bill Metoyer produced 'Lesson Well Learned'. Naturally, Metal Blade then stepped in with a deal for an EP, resulting in the 3 track 12" single issued in August following year. The record, which rapidly sold over 15,000 copies, included 'Lesson Well Learned' with 'False Alarm' and 'On The Way'.

Chrysalis Records stepped in to snap the group up, placing them in Ocean Way Studios with producer Michael James Jackson, fresh from his work on KISS' 'Creatures Of The Night' album, to deliver the 'March Of The Saint' record. Most fans agree that whilst the material couldn't be faulted, both the production left a good deal to be desired, not capturing the intensity of the group at all, and the artwork, reminiscent of a box of toy soldiers, seemed a mite twee for such a powerful act. 'March Of The Saint' was released in 1984, scaling Billboard to attain a number 138 high. The band toured North America opening up for W.A.S.P. and METALLICA soon afterwards, both METALLICA and ARMORED SAINT now sharing management at Q Prime. Other live dates found the Saint supporting both QUIET RIOT and WHITESNAKE.

The group's second album, 'Delirious Nomad' surfaced a year later. Produced by Max Norman, the record found ARMORED SAINT a quartet following the exit of guitarist Phil Sandoval during recording. 'Delirious Nomad' certainly gave the band the state of the art production values the band needed and the group responded by laying down an edifying slab of technical Metal. The record, peaking at number 108 on the US charts, drew international praise for its approach to the genre but sales unfortunately did not match expectations. Fans seemed confused by the complexities of the record, the ditching of the beloved armour and another album sleeve of little merit.

A third album, 1987's 'Raising Fear', was recorded over a six month period at no less than four studio locations across California as a co-produced effort between the band and Chris Minto with Chrysalis Records. Fans would be unaware that the group's first demo proposals had been rejected by their label. With the experimentation of 'Delirious Nomad' having been judged less than a success, the band fell back on older themes, even going so far as to include their knight motif once again on the album cover. To appease the Chrysalis yearning for a radio hit ARMORED SAINT tackled a less than inspiring rendition of LYNYRD SKYNYRD's 'Saturday Night Special'. The band teamed up with GRIM REAPER and HELLOWEEN for the 'Hell On Wheels' North American tour to promote the album.

The record only hit number 144 on the US album charts, this lowly result signalling the close of relations with Chrysalis. Swiftly reverting to the Metal Blade stable, the 1988 live album, 'Saints Will Conquer' recorded at Cleveland's Agora Ballroom in October 1987, provided the band with a useful stop-gap product and included a brand new studio recording featuring Phil Sandoval 'No Reason To Live'. Once again though, the group's choice of artwork was found wanting, the 'Saints Will Conquer' sleeve being far too close in execution to a famous Frank Frazetta MOLLY HATCHET classic. For touring with KING DIAMOND in America during 1988 ARMORED SAINT drafted former ODIN guitarist Jeff Duncan as the band also parted company with Q-Prime Management.

As ARMORED SAINT floundered Duncan quit, having his position taken by Alan Barlam. Duncan put together BIRD OF PREY with his brother and ex-ODIN colleague Shawn on drums, vocalist Kyle Michaels, later of MASI and GEEZER BUTLER BAND, and Paul Puljiz, subsequently member of KILLING KULTURE. Vera meantime joined LIZZY BORDEN for their 1989 album 'Master Of Disguise'.

ARMORED SAINT guitarist Dave Prichard died from Leukemia on 28th February 1990. For many years the guitarist had complained of constant headaches but once diagnosed he only survived a few months. Shattered, the group disbanded, only coming together once again to celebrated their former comrade's life with the video anthology 'A Trip Thru' Red Times'.

The March 1991 Dave Jerden produced 'Symbol Of Salvation' comeback album, the bulk of which had been composed by their fallen colleague, was also graced with Prichard's guitar parts on the track 'Tainted Past'. The album sold strongly in Europe and

ARMORED SAINT (pic: Rich Galbraith)

'Symbol Of Salvation' opened up new areas of appreciation for the group, the adversity which had engendered its construction resulting in the band's most powerful, and yet diverse, set of songs thus far. With timing having been a crucial factor in the struggles faced previously, now ARMORED SAINT found themselves heralded as power metal pioneers. Hitting the road once again, Armored Saint embarked on dates across the USA with MEGADETH and SUICIDAL TENDENCIES. Once these concerts were fulfilled, John Bush became the focus of yet another major player.

Having resisted overtures from the likes of METALLICA in the past, John Bush decided to take up an offer from ANTHRAX to become the New York outfit's new vocalist in the wake of Joey Belladonna's departure in 1992. With Bush gone, ARMORED SAINT had ceased to exist. Initially, this union re-elevated ANTHRAX high into the charts but the group's fortunes then began to slide with each successive release. Following the band's split Joey Vera released a solo album, 'A Thousand Faces', through Metal Blade. He then joined FATES WARNING and was involved in the recording of new band colleague Mark Zonder's side project CHROMA KEY in 1998.

ARMOURED SAINT with the Sandoval brothers, Vera, Bush and Duncan had the opportunity to reform during 1999 as Bush's career with ANTHRAX appeared on the wane. The comeback album 'Revelation', emerging in March 2000, garnered heady praise from the European Metal press and proved to be a return to former glories. Duncan also issued his solo project band DC4's first outing the same year.

In 2001 a highly collectable compilation 'Nod To The Old School' was issued featuring a glut of early demo tracks, new songs 'Unstable' and 'Swagger', covers of JUDAS PRIEST's 'Never Satisfied' and ROBIN TROWER's 'Day Of The Eagle' and live cuts. Also included were the tracks from the bands very first EP. Road dates with DIO and LYNCH MOB took the band across the breadth of the USA throughout February and into March 2001.

In March of 2002 Joey Vera, still maintaining his posts in both ARMORED SAINT and FATES WARNING, would team up with SAVATAGE guitarist Jack Frost's side endeavour SEVEN WITCHES for European touring. The bassist would also handle production chores for ENGINE's 'Superholic' album.

The other ARMORED SAINT personnel maintained their sense of industry too, Jeff Duncan readying a Joey Vera produced DC4 album release for Europe and Gonzo busying himself with his MONSTER G venture in alliance with Phil Sandoval. In late 2002 ARMORED SAINT drummer Gonzo and guitarist Phil Sandoval united with Jack Emrick and Ray Burke to reform their 1996 project LIFE AFTER DEATH. Both Joey Vera and Gonzo put in guest sessions on the 2003 solo album 'Raise Your Fist To Metal' from erstwhile METALIUM and SAVATAGE guitarist JACK FROST.

In February of 2004 bassist Joey Vera would temporarily enroll into the ranks of ANTHRAX as stand in for the departed Frank Bello. That Summer Phil Sandoval and Gonzo activated Blues outfit YO DIDDLEY, putting in club shows in union with the LIFE AFTER DEATH pairing of Ray Burke and singer Jack Emrick. Another project in 2004 would be FOREVER SAY DIE!, a one off band collaboration assembled to record a version of 'Sabbath Bloody Sabbath' for the Cleopatra Records BLACK SABBATH tribute album 'Evil Lives: A True Metal Tribute To Black Sabbath'. The band was fronted by Happenin' Harry of the HAPTONES with guitars courtesy of Jeff Duncan whilst the SPIDERS AND SNAKES rhythm section of bassist Joe Petro and drummer Tim Yasui completed the roster.

With John Bush ousted from ANTHRAX, ARMORED SAINT got back into action in 2005, announcing a support gig to the SCORPIONS at the Dodge Theater in Phoenix, Arizona on July 30th before a return to European stages. In side activity, JOEY VERA chose A CHINESE FIREDRILL as the project name for his 2006 solo album 'Circles'. Vera handled vocals and all instrumentation, with the exception of drums delegated to Greg Studgio. John Bush scored national notoriety for the holiday season in a somewhat less than Rock n' Roll tradition, narrating Burger King TV commercials.

With Joey Belladonna leaving ANTHRAX again in January 2007, and guitarist Scott Ian's public comments pointing towards a resurrection of the Bush-era ANTHRAX, the future of ARMORED SAINT again looked in doubt. However, that same month ARMORED SAINT was announced as booked for an appearance at the 'Rock Hard' festival in Germany for May.

Lesson Well Learned, Metal Blade 71018 (1983). Lesson Well Learned / False Alarm / On The Way.
Can U Deliver, Chrysalis WWS17499 (1984) (Japanese release). Can U Deliver / False Alarm.
MARCH OF THE SAINT, Chrysalis CHR 1479 (1984). March Of The Saint / Can U Deliver / Mad House / Take A Turn / Seducer / Mutiny On The World / Glory Hunter / Stricken By Fate / Envy / False Alarm. Chart position: 138 USA.
Take A Turn, Chrysalis (1984). Take A Turn.
Long Before I Die, Chrysalis (1985). Long Before I Die.
Over The Edge, Chrysalis (1985). Over The Edge.
DELIRIOUS NOMAD, Chrysalis CHR 1516 (1985). Long Before I Die / Nervous Man / Over The Edge / The Laugh / Conqueror / For The Sake / Aftermath / In The Hole / You're Never Alone / Released. Chart position: 108 USA.
Isolation, Chrysalis (1987). Isolation.
RAISING FEAR, Chrysalis CHR 1610 (1987). Raising Fear / Saturday Night Special / Out On A Limb / Isolation / Chemical Euphoria / Crisis Of life / Frozen Will—Legacy / Human Vulture / Book Of Blood / Terror / Underdogs. Chart position: 114 USA.
SAINTS WILL CONQUER, Metal Blade ZORRO 28 (1988). Raising Fear / Nervous Man / Chemical Euphoria / Book Of Blood / Can U Deliver / Long Before I Die / Mad House / No Reason To Live.
SYMBOL OF SALVATION, Metal Blade 25677 (1991). Reign Of Fire / Dropping Like Flies / Last Train Home / Tribal Dance / The Truth Always Hurts / Half Drawn Bridge / Another Day / Symbol Of Salvation / Hanging Judge / Warzone / Burning Question / Tainted Past / Spineless.

ARMORED SAINT (pic: Rich Galbraith)

REVELATION, Metal Blade 3984-14288-2 (2000). Pay Dirt / The Pillar / After Me, The Flood / Tension / Creepy Feelings / Damaged / Den Of Thieves / Control Issues / No Me Digas / Deep Rooted Anger / What's Your Pleasure / Upon My Departure.
NOD TO THE OLD SCHOOL, Metal Blade 14373 (2001). Real Swagger / Unstable / March Of The Saint / Day Of The Eagle / Never Satisfied / Tainted Past / After Me The Flood (Live) / Creepy Feelings (Live) / Lesson Well Learned / False Alarm / On The Way / Stricken By Fate / Reign Of Fire (Demo) / Betty 79,15 People (Demo) / Get Lost (Demo) / Nothing Between The Ears (Demo) / Pirates (Demo) / Medieval Nightmare (Demo).

ARMOURED ANGEL

CANBERRA, ACT, AUSTRALIA — *Yuri Ward (guitar / vocals), Glen 'Lucy' Luck (bass), Steve Luff (drums).*

Canberra Thrash Metal act ARMOURED ANGEL dating back to their formation by bassist Glen 'Lucy' Luck in 1984. ARMOURED ANGEL's inaugural recordings came in the form of a 1985 demo 'Baptism In Blood'. By 1987 Lucy had been joined by guitarist Matt Green and vocalist / drummer Joel Green, this version of the band cutting the 1988 demo session 'Wings Of Death'. 1990 saw the release of the 'Communion' demo and a subsequent East coast tour of Australia that scored the group a deal with ID Records.

'Wings Of Death' would later be issued as a vinyl EP by English label C.C.G. during the early 90s, giving the band a good deal of kudos on the European Metal market. The sophomore 'Stigmartyr' album was issued in 1992 with 'Mysterium' some two years later. Australian tours found the band treading the boards with international running mates BOLT THROWER and MORBID ANGEL. European and American tour dates saw the band into 1995.

ARMOURED ANGEL would then score the services of KILLING JOKE's Jaz Coleman as producer for their next album. However, these sessions were never completed. The Green siblings made their exit and the act duly folded.

ARMOURED ANGEL finalized their reunion line up in January of 1997 as a trio of PSYCHRIST man vocalist / guitarist Yuri Ward, bassist Lucy and drummer Steve Luff. This unit cutting the 'Angel Of The Sixth Order' album for Warhead Records.

In April of 2001 Lucy would join Death Metal band REIGN OF TERROR. ARMOURED ANGEL reconvened in late 2006 to remix the pre-production demo of their never-released 1996 album. The resulting compilation of all material recorded by the Joel Green / Matt Green / Lucy Luck version of the band, entitled 'Trisagion', added promotional video clips for tracks 'Enigmatize' and 'Elegy'.

Baptism In Blood, (1985). Iron Legions / I Am (The Beast) / Deathwitch / Demon Kings / Thunder Down Under / R.I.P.
Wings Of Death, C.C.G. (1989). Armoured Angel / Madame Guillotine / Christian Slaughter / Crush, Kill, Destroy.
STIGMARTYR, Armoured Angel (1992). Hymn Of Hate / Beyond The Sacrament / Stigmartyr / Ordained In Darkness.
MYSTERIUM, ID Records (1994). Myth Of Creation / Heir To Evil / Enigmatize / Carved In Sin / Pray For Me / Elegy.
ANGEL OF THE SIXTH ORDER, Warhead WHCD27 (1998). Whore Of Babylon / Eve Of Temptation / Seven Angels / Crucifiction / Gadarene Swine / Spear Of Destiny / Cervical Slut / Thy Blood Eterne / Carved In Sin.

ARROW

GERMANY — *Markus Schaus (vocals), Uwe Becker (guitar), Rainer Kern (guitar), Chris Schinzel (bass), Gerd Hilgers (drums).*

ARROW was a Dieburg based Speed Metal act forged in January of 1983 by erstwhile SCOT FREE personnel guitarist Uwe "Beam" Becker and bassist Christoph "Stripe" Schinzel. As SCOT FREE, drums were handled by Michael Breitmeier but in 1983 Gerd "Ronny" Hilgers took over as the group, bringing onboard guitarist René Kern, evolved into ARROW. In April of that year Pete Kulp took the microphone for two demos, 'Drivin' Devil' toward the close of 1983 and 'Built To Destroy' in May of 1984. Götz Mohr assumed the vocal position in 1984 and 'Metal Mike' took over on drums. A brace of self financed EPs, 'The Heavy Metal Mania' in July of 1984 and 'Master Of Evil' that same August then ensued.

ARROW's formation changed with the introduction of guitarist Stefan Markowitz and singer Michael Mahlberg. April of 1985 found Andy Bünger taking command of the drums. However, the band splintered with Schinzel and Becker forging Thrashers DEZTROYER. Joining them would the ANGEL DUST, ASMODINA, VICE and DEVASTATE credited Ralf Couard on lead vocals alongside ANGEL DUST and ASMODINA drummer Matthias Röseler. This outfit then inducted Markus Gnap on drums and replaced Couard with former ARROW man Pete Kulp and released a string of demos 'Homicidal World' in July of 1987, 'Drink & Forget' in February 1988, 'Big Surprise' in July of 1988 and April 1989's 'The Forz'.

THE HEAVY METAL MANIA, Fritz (1984). New York Breakdown / Horizon Flame / Run To Hell / The End Of A Rokker.
MASTER OF EVIL, Arrow (1985). Slave Of Garon Castle / Heavy Metal Hero (Dedicated To Bon Scott) / Built To Destroy / You Don't See My Soul.

ARS MORIENDI

AUSTRIA — *Michael Wegleitner (vocals / guitar), Heiko Ernstreiter (guitar), Thomas Iberer (bass), Christian Keimel (drums).*

ARS MORIENDI, a self-styled "Fucking Thrash Metal" band, was manifested in August 1998 by guitarist Heiko Ernstreiter and drummer Christian Keimel. That September Michael Wegleitner took up the role of vocalist / guitarist and in January 2000 the group debuted with the demo 'World Of Hate'. Bassist Michael Kriegl was installed in February 2001, being replaced in April 2003 by Thomas Iberer.

The band issued the self financed 'Dissimulated' EP in 2004. ARS MORIENDI acquired second guitarist Joachim Liebminger, a veteran of RISING PASSION and DOOMED ERA, in October.

Austrian shows in December 2006 were conducted with PERISHING MANKIND and EVENTIDE.

Ars Moriendi, (2000). Ars Moriendi / Kaltes Fleisch / The Past Catches Me / World Of Hate.

Dissimulated, Ars Moriendi (2004). Endless Silent Sleep / Crossing The Line / Dark Crusade / Fainted I Am blind / God's Oppressive Arms.

ARTILLERY

TAASTRUP, DENMARK — *Flemming Ronsdorf (vocals), Michael Stützer (guitar), Jorgen Sandau (guitar), Morten Stützer (bass), Carsten Neilson (drums).*

Formed in Taastrup, Copenhagen during 1982 by the Stützer brothers, guitarist Michael and bassist Morten with Carsten Neilson on drums, ARTILLERY was without question one of the very earliest European Thrash Metal bands. Vocalist Per Onink, hailing from various obscure Danish bands, originally fronted the band. However, following a riot at one of ARTILLERY's early gigs, Onink was given his marching orders and replaced by Carsten Lohmann. With their new vocalist ARTILLERY issued the impressive demos, 'Shellshock' and 'Deeds Of Darkness', and succeeded in grabbing a lot of attention from the underground Metal press. Lohmann left shortly after and in came Flemming Ronsdorf. ARTILLERY's next demo, 'Fear Of Tomorrow', secured them a deal with the Newcastle Upon Tyne based Neat Records to release the highly rated debut album 'Fear Of Tomorrow' in 1985.

The band's subsequent album, 1987's 'Terror Squad', received similar rave reviews to the debut despite having probably one of the worst album covers of all time due to Neat asking the band to design their own record sleeve. Following the record's release the band suffered the loss of bassist Morten Stützer, who left the band for a period before re-entering the fold in 1988.

ARTILLERY would, without much fanfare in the Western world, become one of the first outside Rock acts to perform in the Soviet Union. As part of the cultural 'Next Stop' programme ARTILLERY, alongside Danish Punks SORT SOL, performed a number of sold out Russian gigs. However, over enthusiastic fans incited a vicious backlash from security forces and ARTILLERY were duly banished as being a decadent influence. The group took a five day train journey on the Trans Siberian Express back to Europe immortalised later on the song '07:00 From Tashkent'.

ARTILLERY struggled on, but eventually broke up the same year with Morten Stützer joining FURIOUS TRAUMA. However, within nine months the brothers had left their respective bands to reform ARTILLERY with Ronsdorf and ex-FURIOUS TRAUMA bassist Michael Rasmussen. Before too long Rasmussen was out in favour of ex-FORCE MAJEUR and APOCALYPSE bass player Peter Thorslund, which enabled Morten Stützer to switch to guitar. The band toured Denmark and even slotted in a show in Russia before recording a new demo with METALLICA producer Flemming Rasmussen. Switching to Roadrunner Records the band entered Sweet Silence Studio in Copenhagen with Rasmussen to record the 'By Inheritance' album. However, shortly after ARTILLERY folded with the Stützer brothers founded MISSING LINK whilst Flemming Rønsdorf joined RUBBER BAND, a bar band covering songs by THE BEATLES with the ex-ARTILLERY man playing the part of JOHN LENNON. Michael Stützer would also find a new interest as a Heavy Metal DJ, hosting his own radio show aptly named 'Terror Squad'.

With their influence on the European Metal scene being recognised, partly due to the 1998 Mighty Music compilation of archive material 'Deadly Relics', ARTILLERY returned in August of that year for a one off gig in Copenhagen and were promptly offered a deal for a reunion album with Diehard Records, culminating in the 2000 'B.A.C.K.' album, recorded at Starstruck Studios. Session drums would be handled by Per Jensen of THE HAUNTED, KONKHRA and INVOCATOR fame. Former SABBAT guitarist Andy Sneap finalised the production values.

The band made another comeback in November of 2004 with a one off gig at The Rock venue in Copenhagen. For this show vocalist Flemming Rønsdorf and guitarists Michael and Morten Stützer would be joined by HATESPHERE bassist Mikael Ehler and drummer Anders Gyldenøhr.

ARTILLERY put in a high profile European festival show at the 'Keep It True' event at the Tauberfrankenhalle in Lauda-Königshofen, Germany on April 14th 2007 alongside British bands DIAMOND HEAD and SABBAT, US outfits LÄÄZ ROCKIT, LETHAL and TWISTED TOWER DIRE, Canadians CAULDRON and PILEDRIVER, Dutchmen DEFENDER and Swedish band BULLET.

We Are The Dead, Artillery (1983) (Demo). Mind Of No Return / All For You / We Are The Dead / Day Of Doom.

Shellshock, Artillery (1984) (Demo). Time Has Come / All For You / Bitch / Blessed Are The Strong.

Deeds Of Darkness, Artillery (1984) (Demo). Deeds Of Darkness / Too Late To Regret / Deserter / Hey Woman.

Fear Of Tomorrow, Artillery (1985) (Demo). Out Of The Sky / Fear Of Tomorrow.

Fear Of Tomorrow, Artillery (1985) (Demo). The Almighty / Out Of The Sky / King, Thy Name Is Slayer / Fear Of Tomorrow / Into The Universe / Deeds Of Darkness / Hey Woman.

FEAR OF TOMORROW, Neat 1030 (1985). Time Has Come / The Almighty / Show Your Hate / King Thy Name Is Slayer / Out Of The Sky / Into The Universe / The Eternal War / Fear Of Tomorrow / Deeds Of Darkness.

TERROR SQUAD, Neat 1038 (1987). The Challenge / In The Thrash / Terror Squad / Let There Be Sin / Hunger And Greed / Therapy / At War With Science / Decapitation Of Deviants.

Artillery, Artillery (1989) (Demo). Khomaniac / Don't Believe.

Khomaniac, Roadracer (1990) (Danish promotion release). Khomaniac / Don't Believe.

FEAR OF TOMORROW / TERROR SQUAD, Roadracer RO 9389 3 (1990) (Cassette release). The Challenge / In The Thrash / Terror Squad / Let There Be Sin / Hunger And Greed / Therapy / At War With Science / Decapitation Of Deviants / He Has Come / The Almighty / Show Your Hate / King Thy Name Is Slayer / Out Of The Sky / Into The Universe / The Eternal War / Fear Of Tomorrow / Deeds Of Darkness.

BY INHERITANCE, Roadracer RR9397 (1990). Khomaniac / Bombfood (Nothing But A Tool) / By Inheritance / R.I.P. (Beneath The City) / Allergic To Knowledge / Back In The Trash / Life In Bondage / Don't Believe / 7am From Tashkent / Prelude To Life.

Mind Factory, Artillery (1991) (Demo). Welcome To The Mind Factory / Delusions Of Grandeur / Uniform / Ain't Giving In.

DEADLY RELICS, Mighty Music PMZ002-2 (1998). Artilleristic Prelude MCMXCVIII / Khomaniac / Don't Believe / Out Of The Sky / Fear Of Tomorrow / Deeds Of Darkness / Too Late To Regret / Deserter / Hey Woman / Time Has Come / All For You / Bitch / Blessed Are The Strong.

Jester, Die Hard PCDS-33 (1999) (7" vinyl picture disc). Jester / Fly.

B.A.C.K., King KICP-733 (2000) (Japanese release). Cybermind / How Do You Feel / Out Of The Trash / Final Show / WWW / Violent Breed / Theatrical Exposure / B.A.C.K. / The Cure / Paparazzi / Fly / Jester.

B.A.C.K., Die Hard PCD-33 (2000). Cybermind / How Do You Feel / Out Of The Trash / Final Show / WWW / Violent Breed / Theatrical Exposure / B.A.C.K. / The Cure / Paparazzi.

AS IT BURNS

GRONINGEN, HOLLAND — *Arend Doornheim (vocals), Rocco Rundervoort (guitar), Joost Brouwer (guitar), Floris Maathuis (bass), Gert Plas (keyboards), Jacco Veenstra (drums).*

Groningen band AS IT BURNS, styling itself as "Atmospheric Blackened Death Thrash Metal", was formulated during 1997 by Jeroen Smit on the drums and guitarist Joost Brouwer. Internal manouevres found new man Rocco Rundervoort taking on bass, later switching to guitar as Smit swapped his role of drummer to handle bass duties. Gert Plas, also active with Black Metal band WINTER OF SIN, would take up the keyboard role. An opening session 'Soured', recorded on 4 track, led in turn to the 1999 self financed album 'Obsolete Prophecies'. AS IT BURNS then added Jacco Veenstra of avant-garde Doom act VOLEG on the drums.

The 'Mortal Dusk' effort, the band's first for Cold Blood Industries, would be recorded at Franky's Recording Kitchen with producers Berthus Westerhuys and Jens van der Valk during August of 2002. The band once again utilised Franky's Recording Kitchen studio and producer Jens van der Valk for January 2005 recordings. However, with Cold Blood Industries having collapsed, the band pursued this next album as a self financed effort.

OBSOLETE PROPHECIES, Independent (1999). Eternal Bloodhunt / Soured / Voices Of Darkness / Repay With Death / Slave Of Conspiracy / The Obsolete Prophecy / Amid The Abundance / Domains Of Satan / Wasted / Bachannal Of Lust.
As It Burns, (2000). Host Of Fear / Beyond Humanity / Iconoclasm Hysteria / Bachannal Of Lust / Eternal Bloodhunt / Amid The Abundance.
INFERNO, Independent (2001). Inferno (Intro) / Hosts Of Fear / The Inexorable Mirage Of Nemesis / Iconoclasm Hysteria / Ignorant Accosters Of Christ / Beyond Humanity / Stormknights / Reflections (Outro).
MORTAL DUSK, Cold Blood Industries (2003). Mortal Dusk / Selective Amnesia / God Is A Souvenir / Holy Waste / Silent Might / Eternal / Suicide Prophet / The Pulse Of Anger / A Tortured Face / The Skintrade.

AS SAHAR

SINGAPORE — *Barchiel (vocals / guitar), Hanael (bass), Iblyss (drums).*

AS SAHAR started out as a straight Thrash Metal trio during the mid 80's with founder members vocalist / guitarist Barchiel and bassist Hanael joined by drummer Uriel. At this stage AS SAHAR were a covers act. The band dissolved but reformed a few years later opting for a new Black Metal direction, evident on their opening 1993 demo 'Primitively Eastern Winds' and the 1995 follow up 'Santau'.

A further demo 'Meditas Embun Pagi' was recorded and subsequently released as a cassette EP by Nebiula Productions. However, following these sessions Uriel jumped ship. His replacement was former ABHORRER and IMPIETY man Iblyss.

Sales of the previous cassette were strong enough to warrant recording of the debut album 'Phenomistik'. A split album with HAYAGRIVA kept up the momentum prior to the departure of Iblyiss.

Barchiel and Hanael persevered as a duo changing tack once again into Gothic Electronica for the 'Baku Karmi' album. A 2001 cassette release 'Bomohymns Okultika' included a cover version of 'Crusade Of The Underworld Hordes' originally by HADES. AS SAHAR would also issue the 'Casus Luciferi' and 'Intifada' recordings that year too.

BEYOND FIRMAMENT, Memories (1988) (Split Album With HAYAGRIVA). Berwahi (Dalem Tuntut) / As Sahar / Wijaya Kesuma Buat Susuhunanan / My Hymns, In The East.
PHENOMISTIK, Shivadarshana (1997). Nadayage (Ashore) / Depressive Monsoon / Silomanial Dansecration / Tinggam / Sinfonie Jimbalang / Fandeyian Okultika Hymnology / Meditas Embun Pagi / Foleraftty Melo-Harvest / Nadaynde (Adrift).
EKSTASI TEKSTONIS, Nebiula Productions (1999). Tuju Tuju Opus / Tinggam / Meditasti Embun Pagi / Folkerafty Melo-Harvest / Silumamial Dansecration / Santau Tuju Angin / Stroll In Kafan / Meditation Embun Pagi / My Hymns, In The East / Fandeyian Okultika Hymnology / Sinfonie Jimbalang / Repressive / Nadayaga II (Adrift).
BAKU KARAMA, Nebiula Productions (2000). Ke Mana Listrik Mu / Minda Bersaru / 24 / Alunan Irama Langut Anggunmu / Belayer Ke Pulau Sana / Haloba / Aku Ratapi / Kawan Konon / Tanjang Puturi / Baku Karama.
INTIFADA, (2001). Jihad / Imam Dan Makmum Politik / Ikhsan Berbaur Daawah / Bolehkah Menakifan Mati / Hamas / Fantasia Temanku Fantasi / Timo Jhen / Tuntuwan Ukhwah.

ASMODEUS

KLATOVY, CZECH REPUBLIC — *Miloš Bešta (vocals / guitar), Tomáš Bešta (guitar), Milan Pózel (bass), Vladimír Hoøký (drums).*

Thrash Metal band founded in 1987. ASMODEUS evolved through various line ups with band mentor Miloš Bešta remaining the only constant. The ASMODEUS line up for 1988 counted vocalist / guitarist Miloš Bešta, second guitarist Karel Kuneš, bass player Tomáš Kocian with Miroslav Prášil on the drums. ASMODEUS issued the demos 'Heroes' and 'Invasion Of Conscience' in 1990 with 'Town Of Fallen Statues' following in 1991 upfront of the inclusion of two tracks, 'Tenkrát Na Západě' and 'Muka Existence', on the compilation album 'Ultrametal Vol. II'. These songs were recorded utilising drummer Dan Vilášek.

The debut album 'Prosincová Noc Blíže Neurèeného Roku' emerged on Monitor Records in 1992. These sessions featured former FERAT guitarist Otakar Husák. ASMODEUS added ex-DOOMSTERS drummer Jacek Lukáš in 1993, the band roll call at the close of that year comprising lead singer Petr Korál, Bešta, Husák and Ríša Aška handling guitars, bassist Tomáš Kocián with drummer Míra Prášil.

At the time of recording 1995's second outing 'Pøíjezd Krále' the band line up stood at vocalist / guitarist Miloš Bešta, guitarist Jindra Gregora, bassist David Svobodovi and drummer Pavel Kotesovec. A 1997 demo, 'Avebury, Saturday, 5:59 p.m', saw Jan Roháč installed as second guitarist. ASMODEUS duly signed to Avik Records for a third album 'Vchod Do Kruhu'.

ASMODEUS contributed their rendition of 'Mezi Kopci Cesta Klikatá' to a 1999 MASTER'S HAMMER tribute album compiled by Redblack Productions.

Invasion Of Conscience, (1990). AIDS / Invaze Svìdomí / Fantazie / Služebníci Zla / Dopis / II / Èeta / The End.
Heroes, (1990). Heroes / Pravik / Dìdictví / Litanie Proti Strachu / Stvoøitel.
Town Of Fallen Statues, (1991). Tenkrát Na Západì / Kolaps / Živí Mrtví / Muka Existence / Mìsto Padlých Soch / Heroes / Pravìk / Dìdictví / Litanie Proti Strachu / Stvoøitel.
Ve Stínu Kříže, (1995). Den Hojnosti / Ve Stínu Kříže / Zaslepeni Nocí, Očištěni Dnem.
Avebury, Saturday, 5:59 p.m., (1997). Avebury, Sobota, 17:59 / Jste Někde Tady / Vchod Do Kruhu / Příjezd Krále Richarda.
VCHOD DO KRUHU, Avik (1998). Všechno Se Hýbe / Roswell, Pøedevèírem 19:33 / Jste Nìkde Tady / Vchod Do Kruhu / Hypnóza / Na Prahu Rána / Avebury, Sobota 17:59 / Okamžik Pìti Otázek / Na Ickfield Moor / Dotknout Se øetìzu / p.m.l.
NA JEHLACH, Avik (2000). Jáma A Divadlo (Enter) / Dotek Medúzy / Árie Lávy / Na Jehlách / Screampeace / Poslední Pùlnoc v Reims / Informišmaš / Tichá Nálož / Zeï Náøkù / Spermadona / Jáma A Divadlo (Exit) / Pravìk.
SABAT V CARNEGIE HALL, (2003). Koøeny èasu / Nanosferatu / Žíve Svìtlo / Zavátý Svìt / Mrtvá Voda / Turisté Smrti (Exitus Dignitas) / Na øadì Je Mars / Ten, Kdo Vidí / Žraloèí Oèi / Dìdictví (1990 version).

ASSALANT

AUSTIN, TX, USA — *Mike Soliz (vocals), Louie Beltran (guitar), J.B. Slimp (guitar), Darren Keeling (bass), Mike Botello (drums).*

Austin Thrash Metal act ASSALANT was manifested in early 1986 by the MATRIX credited pairing of bassist Darren Keeling and drummer Mike Botello, FIRST STRIKE guitarist Louie Beltran and second guitarist J.B. Slimp. ASSALANT recorded and distributed two versions of their 1987 demo 'The Damage Is Done', cut at Cedar Creek Studios with engineer Fred Remmert. The first session would feature WATCHTOWER and DANGEROUS TOYS man Jason McMaster as guest lead vocalist. However, the band then enrolled ex-MILITIA and OBLIVION KNIGHT frontman Mike Soliz in September of 1986, and duly re-recorded the vocals. Soliz had previously been involved with McMaster in the band FALLEN ANGEL, albeit as a drummer for this antecedent outfit.

ASSALANT performed its inaugural live showing on 16th January 1987 at Austin's Ritz Theater as opening act to WATCHTOWER. Ironically, Soliz briefly replaced McMaster in WATCHTOWER, featuring on the demo 'Instruments Of Random Murder' in 1987.

The Damage Is Done, Assalant (1987). Dragon Of Peace / The Damage Is Done / Insane Illusion.

ASSASSIN

DÜSSELDORF, GERMANY — *Robert Gonnella (vocals), Michael Hoffman (guitar), Jürgen Scholz (guitar), Ufo Walter (bass), Frank Nellen (drums).*

ASSASSIN arrived upon the Düsseldorf Metal scene in 1983, debuting with a 1985 demo 'Holy Terror', which soon impressively sold over 500 copies. Recording roster for these sessions involved AGRESSOR vocalist Robert Gonnella, guitarists Dinko Vekic and Jürgen Scholz, bass player Markus Ludwig with Psycho Danger on drums. A previous incarnation had included another man, guitarist Michael Hoffman. ASSASSIN swiftly followed this up with 'The Saga Of Nemesis' tape produced by WARLOCK guitarist Rudy Graf. The group was already the subject of a label offer, from US imprint King Klassic Records, but ASSASSIN contracted with domestic label SPV Steamhammer Records in March 1986 for inaugural album, 'The Upcoming Terror'.

ASSASSIN then recruited two new members, in a re-recruited guitarist Michael Hoffman and drummer Frank Nellen. In December that same year they became involved in an impromptu, yet notorious diversion dubbed CHECKER PATROL. This jam recording involved Gonnella, Hoffman and Ludwig in collaboration with members of Norway's MAYHEM—vocalist Euronymous (Øystein Aarseth) and bass player Necrobutcher (Jørn Stubberud) described on the cassette cover as "Evil fucking noise and drunken screams".

Follow up 'Interstellar Experience' arrived in 1988 for which live promotion was conducted as support to DEATH ANGEL. The band's output was impressive enough to prompt international recognition and for a short spell ASSASSIN ranked as one of the German Thrash hopefuls. However, Hoffman opted out, later joining SODOM for their 'Better Off Dead' album, and was replaced by Olaf for a 1989 set of demos. ASSASSIN folded shortly afterward, this disbanding prompted by the theft of their gear whilst recording a proposed third album. Scholz hooked up with SECRET DISCOVERY whilst Nellen joined TWILIGHT ZONE. Gonnella was briefly associated with DESTRUCTION but backed out of this proposal. The singer subsequently relocated to Japan then China.

Quite remarkably the band reformed for an appearance at the 2002 'Wacken Open Air' festival, the line-up involving Robert Gonnella, Jürgen Scholz, Dinko Vekic, ex-TUSK bassist Joachim Hopf and fabled drummer Atomic Steif, a seasoned veteran of LIVING DEATH, HOLY MOSES, SACRED CHAO, VIOLENT FORCE and SODOM. The band released tapes from an show, at Kupferdächle, Pforzheim on May 23rd, 1987, for the self-financed live album 'The Assassin . . . Live Forever'.

Frank Nellen resumed his position in 2004. Michael Hoffman cemented his third tenure with the band in 2005 as Ufo Walter was introduced on bass. A new studio album, 'The Club' featuring a cover version of THIN LIZZY's 'Thunder And Lightning', followed in 2005. In early 2007 Brazil's Marquee Records re-issued 'The Upcoming Terror' as a double CD set adding the 1985 'Holy Terror' demo, the 1986 'The Saga Of Nemesis' demo plus a live recording of a show at the Kupferdächle in Pforzheim, Germany on May 23rd 1987.

Holy Terror, Assassin (1985) (Demo). The Damned (Intro)—Fight to Stop the Tyranny / Holy Terror / Religion / Bullet / Assassin / Speed Of Light.
The Saga Of Nemesis, Assassin (1986) (Demo). Into War—Forbidden Reality / Holy Terror / Nemesis / Speed Of Light / Destroy.
THE UPCOMING TERROR, Steamhammer 18951 (1987). Forbidden Reality / Nemesis / Fight (To Stop The Tyranny) / The Last Man / Assassin / Holy Terror / Bullets / Speed Of Light.
INTERSTELLAR EXPERIENCE, Steamhammer SHLP 7011 (1988). Abstract War / AGD / A Message To Survive / Pipeline / Resolution 598 / Junk Food / Interstellar Experience / Baka.
Assassin, Assassin (1989) (Demo). Control / Man vs. Nature / A Whole Life In One Moment.
THE ASSASSIN . . . LIVE FOREVER, (2003). Forbidden Reality / Holy Terror / The Last Man / Fight (To Stop The Tyranny) / Assassin / Nemesis / Speed Of Light / Bullets.
THE CLUB, (2005). Bushwackers / Go Insane / The Club / I Swear / Not With Us / The Price Of Power / Real Friends / Psycho Terror / A Whole Life In One Moment / JinTian Shen Huo (Live For Today) / Raging Mob / No Fear / Thunder And Lightning.

AT WAR

VIRGINIA BEACH, VA, USA — *Paul Arnold (vocals / bass), Shaun Helsel (guitar), Dave Stone (drums).*

A Virginia Beach trio formed in 1984 the group issued a two track demo 'Rapechase' a year later prior to appearing on New Renaissance Records' 'Speed Metal Hell II' compilation. Awarded with a two album deal by New Renaissance, AT WAR released their debut album, 'Ordered To Kill' in 1986. The album was released in Germany on the US Metal label and on Rock Brigade in Brazil.

The three-piece toured America with AGNOSTIC FRONT in December '86 following the release of 'Ordered To Kill' and opened up at LAmour in Brooklyn, New York for SLAYER and POSSESSED. AT WAR's second album 'Retaliatory Strike' is produced by Alex Perialas and ex-RAVEN drummer Rob Hunter. Brazilian editions on Rock Brigade featured different sleeve art.

RETALIATORY STRIKE, New Renaissance (1988). F.Y.I. / Conscientious Objector / Creed Of The Sniper / Covert Sins / Crush Your Life / Gutless Sympathizer / Church And State / Felon's Guilt / Thinkin' / The Example.
RETALIATORY STRIKE, Rock Brigade (1988) Brazilian release. F.Y.I. / Conscientious Objector / Creed Of The Sniper / Covert Sins / Crush Your Life / Gutless Sympathizer / Church And State / Felon's Guilt / Thinkin' / The Example.

ATHANATOR

MEDELLÍN, COLOMBIA — *Jaime Ocampo (vocals / guitar), Eder Zapata (guitar), Enrique Ramírez (bass), Jorge Mejía (drums).*

ATHANATOR is a Medellín based Thrash band dating back to 1989 and an original formation of vocalist / bassist Guillermo Alzate, guitarist Jaime Ocampo and drummer Giuseppe Restrepo. A 1990 demo, 'Gritos Del Ennom', would soon sell out of its 1000 copies. ATHANATOR boosted their numbers in 1992 with the addition of second guitarist Juan Fernando Escobar, this quartet recording the debut album 'Engendros De Muerte'.

Restrepo would lose his place to ASALMATUM man Jhon Willian Castro and the bass was handed over to SACRAMENT's Jorge Mario Escobar. A further switch on the drum stool found Marcelo Gómez of ABBADON usurping Castro.

As a side venture Jaime Ocampo and Marcelo Gómez established the alt-Rock act MARIMONDA. Jorge Mario Escobar also busied himself with HOLOCAUSTO. In July of 1999 ATHANATOR drew in the new faces of ex-MILLENIUM drummer Javier Urán and erstwhile LIPTHOPIA man Federico Agudelo. A second album, 'Raise The Death', arrived in 2000. ATHANATOR drew in fresh blood during 2003, welcoming onboard ESTIGMA guitarist Eder Zapata and Jorge Mejía of RÉQUIEM on the drums.

ATHANATOR released 'The Perfect Enemy' in October 2006.

Engendros De Muerte, Independent (1992). Entes De Guerra / Pesadilla Macabra.
RAISE THE DEATH, (2000). Gothic Hunt / Murderous Dreams / The Eyes Of A Dead Child / Bloody Hands Of Christ / Suicide Souls / Christianism's Sunset / Schizophrenic Agony / Masters Of War / Macabre Nightmare / Fight For Blood.
THE PERFECT ENEMY, (2006). Thoughts On The Battlefield / Fill Your Heart With Fury / Unsocial God / The Perfect Enemy / Purified / Bleed For A Chance To Live / Gallery Of Dreams / The Search / Smile Of The Death / The Crypt Of My Heart / Hatred In Shadows.

ATHEIST

SARASOTA, FL, USA — *Kelly Shaefer (vocals / guitar), Rand Burkey (guitar), Roger Patterson (bass), Steve Flynn (drums).*

ATHEIST (pic: Michael Coles)

Sarasota, Florida's "Jazz-Death" outfit ATHEIST started out life originally titled R.A.V.A.G.E. The band, regrettably lasting just three albums, excelled in highly complex innovation taking Thrash into uncharted realms. Although held in awe by their peers ATHEIST found it tough going on the commercial circuit. Guitarist Rand Burkey's distinction came from not only playing his guitar left handed but performing this feat on a regular but upside down guitar with the strings aligned for a right handed player.

Under the R.A.V.A.G.E title the band contributed tracks 'Brain Damage' and 'On They Slay' to the 1987 'Raging Death' compilation album. Going even further back, to 1984, Kelly Shaefer had forged OBLIVION, this unit inducting Steve Flynn on drums. The following year OBLIVION, then fronted by singer Scrappy and pulling in Roger Patterson on bass, evolved into R.A.V.A.G.E. The group, minus Scrappy, recorded the five-track demo 'Rotting In Hell' in August 1985, later commonly known as 'Kill Or Be Killed'. The band expanded, augmented by second guitarist Mark Schwartzberg, for second demo 'On We Slay'. The band then contributed the tracks 'Brain Damage' and 'On They Slay' to the 1987 'Raging Death' compilation album released on the Godly Records label.

As ATHEIST their first undertaking was the 1987 demo 'Hell Hath No Mercy'. The group issued a 1988 demo, entitled 'Beyond', featuring the tracks 'No Truth', 'Choose Your Death', 'Beyond', 'On They Slay' and Brain Damage'. Promoting this, they would support the likes of TESTAMENT, SNFU, DEATH ANGEL and OBITUARY prior to signing to European label Active Records. The band had originally signed a deal with the US label Mean Machine Records, a subsidiary of Three Cherries Records, but the label was on the verge of bankruptcy so an arrangement was made with Active to take the band. The Scott Burns produced debut album 'Piece Of Time', worked up at Morrisound Recording in Tampa, was issued in February 1990.

On February 12th 1991 ATHEIST suffered a huge blow. A major auto accident involving the entire band tragically resulted in Roger Patterson being killed. Persevering, the band added ex-CYNIC bassist Tony Choy to record 'Unquestionable Presence', released in October 1991. Flynn would opt out after completion of dates with CANNIBAL CORPSE. Choy exited too accompanying Dutch Death Metal crew PESTILENCE for their 1991 world tour. He would later find an alternate, and more sedate, career as a Jazz musician on a cruise boat.

The May 1993 'Elements' album was, at the band's admission, thrown together in haste in order to fulfill their label contract but would still prove a worthy effort. Josh Greenbaum would handle drums in the studio. A European set of dates ensued alongside BENEDICTION which saw Shaefer joined by guitarist Frank Emmi and drummer Marcel DeSantos. ATHEIST then bowed out of public view. With the albums deleted, no official product would be forthcoming for over a decade.

Shaefer's NEUROTICA side project would blossom into a full time venture. The ex-ATHEIST man was still at it in 2001 launching the 'Living In Dry Years' album produced by none other than Brian Johnson of AC/DC fame. Shaefer acquired the rights to all ATHEIST material for a round of long overdue CD re-releases. Emmi would later figure in GENTLEMEN DEATH. Burkey would hook up with erstwhile CRIMSON GLORY vocalist MIDNIGHT for a project band.

In 2001 Shaefer, Burkey, Emmi and Flynn announced the reformation of ATHEIST. Meantime, Darren McFarland joined UNKNOWN CURE. In October 2002 Kelly Shaefer would be revealed to be involved in a project of the highest magnitude, fronting the new band of the erstwhile GUNS N' ROSES triumvirate of guitarist Slash, bassist Duff McKagan and drummer Matt Sorum. However, his tenure would be short-lived as this band unit pulled in ex-STONE TEMPLE PILOTS frontman Scott Wieland and duly evolved into VELVET REVOLVER. Shaefer launched a fresh band project, STARRFACTORY. Included on this new project would be the guitar pairing of ex-E3 and SERRAPHINE man Donny Jaurols and Noah Thompson of MEGABLATTA repute with erstwhile SANCTUARY drummer Dave Budbill. The singer also featured as a guest artist on the 2003 'Moments Of Clarity' Progressive Rock album by CRYPTIC VISION. Meantime, Word arrived in late 2003 that Rand Burkey was preparing a new band project entitled RANDOM XAOS.

In September 2004 Kelly Shaefer, switching to the guitar role, teamed up with ex-BURIAL frontman Mike Callahan in a Southern Florida based project called UNHEARD. However, in early 2005 it was learned that Shaefer, alongside UNHEARD band mate guitarist Donny Jaurols, would also be plugging a brand new band venture BIG MACHINE sponsored by no less than AC/DC's Brian Johnson.

ATHEIST drummer Steve Flynn resurfaced in 2005, forging a brand new band project, entitled GNOSTIC, with ENDERS GAME, AOS and CAUSTIC THOUGHT vocalist Kevin Freeman, CORPSEWORM and SEVERED guitarist Sonny Carson and CORPSEWORM, AOS and CAUSTIC THOUGHT bassist Stephen Morley.

The entire ATHEIST catalogue would be the subject of a reissue campaign by Relapse Records in 2005. The collection commenced in July with a foil stamped box set, limited to 1000 copies, comprising vinyl versions of each ATHEIST plus the R.A.V.A.G.E. 'On They Slay' 7" EP. ATHEIST announced a reformation in January 2006 to perform at the Italian 'Evolution' festival and Germany's 'Wacken Open Air' event. Line-up was announced as comprising the classic formation of Kelly Shaefer, guitarist Rand Burkey, bassist Tony Choy and drummer Steve Flynn. However, Burkey was forced out due to "legal problems". GNOSTIC's Chris Baker substituted. The band also pulled in second guitarist Sonny Carson of GNOSTIC to cover for Shaefer, the frontman's abilities being hampered by tendonitis and carpal tunnel syndrome.

During ATHEIST's European run of dates Tony Choy suffered a sizable accident when he fell through an unsecured part of the large outdoor stage at Italy's Evolution Festival on July 16th.

Fortunately the musician was uninjured but, having broken all his bass strings, had to be loaned another instrument to finish the set.

ATHEIST live dates continued into 2007 with European shows including appearances in June at the Hellfest in France as well as Graspop Metal Meeting in Belgium.

PIECE OF TIME, Active ATV8 (1990). Piece Of Time / Unholy War / Room With A View / On They Slay / Beyond / I Deny / Why Bother? / Life / No Truth.

UNQUESTIONABLE PRESENCE, Active ATV20 (1991). Mother Man / Unquestionable Presence / Your Life's Retribution / Enthralled In Essence / An Incarnation's Dream / The Formative Years / Brains / And The Psychic Saw.

ELEMENTS, Music For Nations MFN 150 (1993). Green / Water / Samba Briza / Air / Displacement / Animal / Mineral / Fire / Fractal Point / Earth / See You Again / Elements.

ATOMICA

SAO JOSE DOS CAMPOS, SP, BRAZIL — *Luciano Peru (vocals), João Márcio (guitar), João Paulo (guitar), André Rod (bass), Mário Sanefuji (drums).*

ATOMICA is the subtly re-named and reformed version of out and out Thrash band ATTOMICA, founded in Sao Jose dos Campos, Sao Paulo, by erstwhile ATROZ and ETHER guitarist Joao Paulo and former METAFEL drummer Mario Sanefuji in October of 1985. The band recorded their 1987 eponymous album with a line up comprising lead vocalist Laerte Perrs, guitarists J.P. Francis and Pyda Rod, bassist André Rod and drummer Mario Sanefuji. Subsequently Fabio Moreira of THOR laid claim to the role of ATTOMICA frontman but he was forced to exit and the group trimmed down to a quartet for the 1989 follow up 'Limits Of Insanity'. Cut for the Cogumulo label, the record saw André Rod adding vocals to his bass responsibilities. Live work promoting the album would find Paulo Giolo substituting on drums.

A third effort, 'Disturbing The Noise' in 1991 had Fabio Moreira installed back as frontman. Ex-MEGATON guitarist João Márcio was also enrolled. Subsequent touring saw headline shows as well as a brace of gigs opening for KREATOR. However, by 1994 ATTOMICA had decided to cease operations.

Reforming in 2002, ATTOMICA drafted Luciano Peru as their new singer. Cogumelo Records re-issued a remastered version of 'Disturbing The Noise' in 2004, adding two extra live tracks 'Deathraiser' and 'Ways Of Death' and also a video clip of 'Deathraiser'. That August the band, in preparation for a new album release 'Back And Alive' for Hellion Records, evolved their title subtly to ATOMICA.

DISTURBING THE NOISE, Cogumelo CG0065 (2007).

ATOMIZER

MELBOURNE, VIC, AUSTRALIA — *Jason Healey (vocals / bass), Justin Allen (guitar), Suds (drums).*

Extreme Australian Metal act founded in 1998. Guitarist Jay Saunders is also an operative member of ANATOMY and SITHLORD. An initial demo 'Atomic Metal Power' led to an album deal split between the French concerns End All Life and Drakkar Productions, the former issuing vinyl format of 'The End Of Forever' and Drakkar the CD. In Australia Melbourne's The Devil's Own took the album on for domestic release. ATOMIZER toured both Australia and New Zealand during October of 2000. ATOMIZER's next release, for the Norwegian Nihilist Void label, was the 'Gimme Natural Selection' EP featuring two originals alongside covers of MOTÖRHEAD's 'Ace Of Spades' and 'I Wish You Were A Beer' by the CYCLE SLUTS FROM HELL.

ATOMIZER's March 2002 album 'Death Mutilation Disease Annihilation', released by the French End All Life label, came as a limited edition of 500 gatefold sleeve vinyl issue. ATOMIZER, with support from MALEVOLENCE and Christchurch's MEATYARD, would tour New Zealand the same month. ATOMIZER issued the topically war themed EP 'Tyrus: The Doom War Of The Armoured Angel' in April of 2003, this release comprising covers of ARMORED ANGEL's 'Thy Blood Eterne', the TYRUS track 'Cold Steel, Warm Death' and WAR's 'Bullet In The Head'. The first 100 pressings of this restricted run of 500 7"s came in clear vinyl.

The 2003 album 'The Only Weapon Of Choice' had collectors interest piques as the Polish Agonia Productions pressed up just 200 picture discs in 12" vinyl. An even scarcer run was restricted to just 25, these coming complete with an exclusive leather patch. Also that year a split 7" single shared with Czech veterans ROOT emerged through Ajna Productions, naturally limited to 666 copies. Subsequently ATOMIZER signed a more comprehensive deal with Agonia to release 'The Only Weapon Of Choice' on CD format, followed by a re-issue of 'The Death Of Forever' with extra tracks including a cover of S.O.D.'s 'Speak English Or Die'.

ATOMIZER projected European shows allied with Singapore's IMPIETY and Poland's WITCHMASTER for September of 2004, preceded by a trip to Mexico with IMPIETY and HACAVITZ. However, the Mexican dates would subsequently be cancelled. Hells Headbangers Records issued a double 7" single set 'Songs Of Slaughter—Songs Of Sacrifice' in the Summer, the first 100 manufactured in 'Agent orange' splatter vinyl. Agonia Records issued a CD version of "Songs Of Slaughter—Songs Of Sacrifice', this format adding the S.O.D. cover 'Speak English Or Die'. ATOMIZER announced mid 2005 plans for two album releases, given the titles 'Songs To Swing To' and 'Caustic Music For The Spiritually Bankrupt'.

In November 2006 ATOMIZER's debut album, 'The End Of Forever' was re-issued through Hells Headbanger Records with two bonus tracks from the 1998 'Atomic Metal Power' demo and renamed 'The Death Of Forever' complete with new artwork. The same label also put out second album 'Death, Mutation, Disease, Annihilation' as a vinyl picture disc.

THE END OF FOREVER, End All Life (2000). Intro: The March Of Forever / Upon The Dying Priest I Spat / Now That's Fuckin' Evil / The Only Good Human (Is A Dead Human) / Somebody's Gonna Die Tonight / Atomic Metal Power / Blacker Than Ever / The End Of Forever.

Gimmie Natural Selection EP, Nihilist Void (2001). Gimmie Natural Selection / Death Mutilation Disease Annihilation / Ace Of Spades / I Wish You Were A Beer.

DEATH MUTILATION DISEASE ANNIHILATION, End All Life (2002). Intro-Incubation / Hesitation Wounds / In The Mortal Realm You Roam No More / For Blood! For Blood! / Black Heart Epiphany / When The Demons Come / Death Mutation Disease Annihilation / He Couldn't Save Himself (How Do You Expect Him To Save You?) / Unit 731 / The End! The End! / Shadenfreude / Ritual.

Atomizer, Ajna Productions (2003) (Split single with ROOT. Limited edition 666 copies). And The Hunt Starts Again.

THE ONLY WEAPON OF CHOICE—13 ODES TO POWER, DECIMATION AND CONQUEST, Agonia ARCD012 (2003). Power, Not Participation / And The Hunt Starts Again / When I Die, I Wanna Die Violently / The Campaign / The War That Never Ended / The Only Weapon Of Choice / Isolation / One Man's Failure / So Terrified, Yet So In Control / Join The Blackheart Reich / For Blackness Absolute / Sometimes They Hear The Bullet / The Fog Of War.

Tyrus: The Doom War Of The Armoured Angel EP, Soulseller Productions (2003) (Limited edition 500 copies). Intro: Oriax / Thy Blood Eterne / Cold Steel, Warm Death / Bullet In The Head.

Songs Of Slaughter—Songs Of Sacrifice, Hells Headbangers (2004) (Double 7" single pack). Leave Nobody Standing! / These Hands Will Never Be Clean / It Soon Became A Fast Track Into Hell / A Cold Farewell / And Dust We Again Shall Be / The Finality Of Death vs. The Pursuit Of Scientific Advancement / The Undoer Of Creation / A Cold Farewell (Reprise).

ATOMKRAFT

NEWCASTLE UPON TYNE, UK — *Ian Davison-Swift (vocals), Tony Dolan (guitar), Rob Matthew (guitar), D.C. Rage (bass),*

Ged Wolf (drums).

Newcastle upon Tyne's ATOMKRAFT was in fact one of the first Speed Metal bands forming in 1979 at a time when METALLICA was yet to record their seminal 'No Life Til Leather' demo. The band was rooted in the late 70s Punk act MORAL FIBRE which comprised bassist Tony 'Demolition' Dolan, drummer Paul Spillett and guitarists Ian Legg and Chris Taylor. With Legg decamping, Ian Drew took over the vacant six-string position but he too would soon leave. At this juncture Taylor made a trip to Germany and came back sporting a button badge with the environmental message "Atomkraft Nein Danke!"

Suitably inspired, the band duly re-christened itself ATOMKRAFT believing it to be more in keeping with their new Metal sound. The band, now minus Taylor, would also undergo a line-up shift drafting in guitarist Steve White and bassist Mark Irvine alongside Dolan and Spillett. However, after their inaugural gig Irvine's parents persuaded him there was no future with the act and he left.

ATOMKRAFT demoed two sets of four song demos, opening with 1981's Keith Nichol produced 'Demon' set, prior to entering the Neat Records studios Impulse for the 'Total Metal' / 'Death Valley' session in 1983. ATOMKRAFT at this point had a fluid line-up and despite the tape attracting interest on the American underground Metal scene the band broke up with Tony relocating to Canada to try his luck.

Dolan soon returned home and set about reforming ATOMKRAFT with drummer Ged Wolf, ex-TYSONDOG and brother of VENOM manager Eric Cook, and teenage guitarist Rob Matthew. A further demo 'Pour The Metal In' secured a deal with Neat Records for the 'Future Warriors' album, again with production credits going out to Keith Nichol. Famously, as revealed in later years, ATOMKRAFT were contracted for a three album deal, including publishing, for a total advance payment of £1.

The band secured their first European shows opening for VENOM and also supported SLAYER at the Marquee Club. This inaugural London show did not go without incident though as equipment breakages forced the band to cut their set to a mere three songs. Further shows in Europe had ATOMKRAFT supporting EXODUS and VENOM.

Trouble struck when Dolan left the band mid way through recording of a proposed EP to be entitled 'Your Mentor', leaving Wolf and Matthew to pick up the pieces. A new line-up was quickly assembled with new additions being former SATAN and AVENGER vocalist Ian Davison-Swift and bassist D.C. Rage. This version of the band recorded the re-titled 1986 'Queen Of Death' mini-album. The original version of the title track, the only variant to include Tony Dolan lead vocals, would be included on the Neat Metal 'Powertrax' compilation album.

The revised ATOMKRAFT never performed live and before long the band invited Dolan back on board as a guitarist for the 1987 'Conductors Of Noize' EP. ATOMKRAFT were due to play a co-headlining tour of Britain in 1987 but this was cancelled. They fared better in Europe where they played the 'Dynamo' festival in Holland and toured as support to NUCLEAR ASSAULT and AGENT STEEL. The June 20th London Hammersmith Odeon concert, which also jammed ONSLAUGHT onto the bill, was broadcast on the Radio One 'Friday Rock Show' and filmed for commercial release as the 'Conductors Of Noize' video.

The band had a switch of personnel when bassist D.C. Rage rejoined the band and Dolan moved back to rhythm guitar. 1988 saw ATOMKRAFT touring Europe alongside NASTY SAVAGE and EXUMER including the major 'Metal Battle' festival in Katowice, Poland and the Dutch 'Dynamo' festival.

ATOMKRAFT were due to release another album, set to be titled 'Atomized', on a different label to Neat but this never materialised. Dolan later joined VENOM for a series of albums, commencing with 'Prime Evil' in 1990. Following his exit from VENOM in 1994 Dolan became an actor, even scoring a part in the Sylvester Stallone movie 'Judge Dredd'. He would be back on the silver screen in 2003, playing the role of ship's carpenter Mr. Lamb in the swashbuckling Russell Crowe film 'Master & Commander'. On the ATOMKRAFT front it would be learned the long lost 'Atomized' album was set for an early 2004 release. Dolan also featured as bassist on the MANTAS album 'Zero Tolerance'.

A 2004 compilation through Castle Records, 'The Neat Anthology', would include live tracks, 1983 demo material and previously unreleased songs 'Trial By Deception', a cover version of GIRLSCHOOL's 'Demolition Boyz', 'Annihilate the Bride' and 'Dance Of The Immortals'. ATOMKRAFT included a previously unreleased 1988 track, entitled 'No Escape', to the 2004 'Total Metal Attack' NWoBHM era compilation album issued through Old School Records. The band, now featuring new members in ex-ENDOMORPH, THE STORYTELLER, KARYAN, JAVELIN, WINTERLONG VIPERINE and HUNTER/KILLER guitarist Payre Kankanranta, known in ATOMKRAFT as Payre Hulkoff, and the BLINDED BY FEAR and IRON FIRE credited drummer Steve Mason, returned to live work with an appearance at the March 2005 'Raise Your Fist' festival in Holland.

September of 2004 brought about a surprise with the re-emergence of ex-ATOMKRAFT guitarist Rob Matthew, breaking a two decade absence from the scene. Issuing a press statement claiming "I personally feel that I need to let it be known of my past contribution to metal and no more be undermined by my 'old friends'... " Matthew announced the formation of his new band AGANKAST.

ATOMKRAFT re-debuted with a 2005 EP entitled 'Are You Looking At Me?' Tony Dolan launched an Anglo / Swedish act dubbed RAUBTIER in March 2007 working with guitarist Hulkoff and drummer Matt Buffalo.

Total Metal, (1983). Total Metal / Death Valley.
FUTURE WARRIORS, Neat 1028 (1985). Future Warriors / Starchild / Dead Man's Hands / Total Metal / Pour The Metal In / Death Valley / This Planet's Burning / Warzone / Burn In Hell / Heat And Pain.
Heat And Pain, (1985). Demolition / Your Mentor / Funeral Pyre / Mode III.
Pour The Metal In, (1985). Pour The Metal In / Burn In Hell / Carousel.
Queen Of Death EP, Neat 53-12 (1986). Queen Of Death / Protector / Demolition / Funeral Pyre / Mode III.
Conductors Of Noize EP, Neat 1039 (1987). Rich Bitch / Teutonic Pain / Vision Of Belshazzar / Foliage / Requiem / The Cage.
Are You Looking At Me?, (2005). Dead Again! / Kristalnacht / Cold Sweat / Gripped.

ATROPHY

TUCSON, AZ, USA — *Brian Zimmerman (vocals), Rick Skowron (guitar), Chris Lykins (guitar), James Gulotta (bass), Tim Kelly (drums).*

Tucson, Arizona based Thrash Metal act created in 1986 debuted with six track demo 'Chemical Dependency'. ATROPHY, established during 1986 guitarist Chris Lykins, bassist James Gulotta, and singer Brian Zimmerman, originally started out under the billing of HERESY. With the addition of drummer Tim Kelly and second guitarist Rick Skowron the title ATROPHY was adopted. Signing to Roadrunner Records the group put out the 1988 debut album 'Socialized Hate', produced by Bill Metoyer at Music Grinder and EQ Sound Studios, Hollywood, and Pacific Studio, Chatsworth, California. They then toured as support to SACRED REICH in North America. ATROPHY featured a track on the Metal Forces magazine compilation album 'Demolition' in 1988. 'Violent By Nature', again produced by Bill Metoyer, followed in 1990. Upon completion of European tour dates guitarist Chris Lykins departed in early 1991 for a career in medicine, eventually finding a new career path as a plastic surgeon. The group struggled on with pre-production for an intended third album but Roadrunner severed ties. The group dissolved, with Tim Kelly, Rick Skowron and James Gulotta forging HEAD CIRCUS.

ATROPHY

Both albums, 'Socialized Hate' and 'Violent By Nature' were re-issued in CD format during November 2006 by Displeased Records in Europe, Metal Mind Productions in Poland, as a limited hand numbered run of 2000 copies, and Caroline in the USA the following January.

Puppies And Friends, Roadracer (1990). Puppies And Friends.
SOCIALISED HATE, Displeased D-00153 (2006) (CD remastered re-issue. European release). Chemical Dependency / Killing Machine / Matter Of Attitude / Preacher, Preacher / Beer Bong / Socialized Hate / Best Defense / Product Of The Past / Rest In Pieces / Urban Decay.
VIOLENT BY NATURE, Displeased D-00154 (2006) (CD remastered re-issue. European release). Puppies And Friends / Violent By Nature / In Their Eyes / Too Late To Change / Slipped Through The Cracks / Forgotten But Not Gone / Process Of Elimination / Right To Die / Things Change.
SOCIALISED HATE, Metal Mind Productions MASS CD DG 0985 (2006) (Polish release. Limited edition 2000 hand numbered copies). Chemical Dependency / Killing Machine / Matter Of Attitude / Preacher, Preacher / Beer Bong / Socialized Hate / Best Defense / Product Of The Past / Rest In Pieces / Urban Decay / Chemical Dependency (Demo) / Rest In Pieces (Demo) / Preacher, Preacher (Demo) / Socialized Hate (Live video).
VIOLENT BY NATURE, Metal Mind Productions MASS CD DG 0986 (2006) (Polish release. Limited edition 2000 hand numbered copies). Puppies And Friends / Violent By Nature / In Their Eyes / Too Late To Change / Slipped Through The Cracks / Forgotten But Not Gone / Process Of Elimination / Right To Die / Things Change / Suicide Pact (Demo) / Product Of The Past (Demo) / Beer Bong (Demo) / Violent By Nature (Live video).

ATTOMICA

SAO JOSE DOS CAMPOS, SP, BRAZIL — *Luciano Peru (vocals), João Márcio (guitar), João Paulo (guitar), André Rod (bass), Mário Sanefuji (drums).*

An out and out Thrash band founded in Sao Jose dos Campos, Sao Paulo, by erstwhile ATROZ and ETHER guitarist Joao Paulo and former METAFEL drummer Mario Sanefuji in October of 1985. The band recorded their 1987 eponymous album with a line up comprising lead vocalist Laerte Perrs, guitarists J.P. Francis and Pyda Rod, bassist André Rod and drummer Mario Sanefuji. Subsequently Fabio Moreira of THOR laid claim to the role of ATTOMICA frontman but he was forced to exit and the group trimmed down to a quartet for the 1989 follow up 'Limits Of Insanity'. Cut for the Cogumulo label, the record saw André Rod adding vocals to his bass responsibilities. Live work promoting the album would find Paulo Giolo substituting on drums.

A third effort, 'Disturbing The Noise' in 1991 had Fabio Moreira installed back as frontman. Ex-MEGATON guitarist João Márcio was also enrolled. Subsequent touring saw headline shows as well as a brace of gigs opening for KREATOR. However, by 1994 ATTOMICA had decided to cease operations. In 1999 ex-member Pyda Rod joined MYSTIC ATROCITY.

Reforming in 2002, ATTOMICA drafted Luciano Peru as their new singer. Cogumelo Records re-issued a remastered version of 'Disturbing The Noise' in 2004, adding two extra live tracks 'Deathraiser' and 'Ways Of Death' and also a video clip of 'Deathraiser'. That August the band, in preparation for a new album release 'Back And Alive' for Hellion Records, evolved their title subtly to ATOMICA.

ATTOMICA, Equinox (1987). Dying Smashed / Marching Over Blood / Lost Time / No Life Till Madness / Children's Assassins / Flesh Maniac.
LIMITS OF INSANITY, Cogumelo (1989). Atomic Death / Short Dreams / Highway 401 / Rabies / Limits Of Insanity / Knight Riders / Evil Scars / W.D.
DISTURBING THE NOISE, Cogumelo (1991). Ways Of Death / The Chainsaw / Death Raiser / Violence And Terror / Blood / From Beyond / Forbidden Hate.

AUDIOPAIN

ASKER, NORWAY — *Sverre Dæhli (vocals / guitar), Petter Berntsen (bass), Bjarne (drums).*

Asker / Blystadlia Thrashers AUDIOPAIN initially went by the title HÆ?, releasing an April 1997 demo restricted to 500 copies, 'LVT'. Significantly, the opening track 'Father' featured a scream donated by none other than Maniac from MAYHEM. Bass player Petter Berntsen has ties to GHOUL-CULT, VED BUENS ENDE and VIRUS. Sverre Dæhli scored backing vocal credits on DARKTHRONE's 'Plaguewielder', featuring on the track 'Command'.

As AUDIOPAIN the band debuted in April 2000 with a demo entitled 'Contagious', this release limited to 100 hand numbered copies. A further three manufacturing runs were undertaken to cope with demand. Another demo, the December 2000 session '1986', was also issued in 100 hand numbered CD-Rs and consequently in another three pressings. AUDIOPAIN issued the EP 'Revel In Desecration' in 2003. That same year Worship Him Records issued a split 7" single shared with MYSTICUM.

The album 'The Traumatizer' emerged in April 2004. During 2005 the 'Contagious' and '1986' demos were re-mastered for commercial issue in North America via Vendlus Records. Two 'Überthrash' series 7" singles, both limited runs of 500 copies, were released by Duplicate Records in May 2005, both four way splits in alliance with AURA NOIR, NOCTURNAL BREED and INFERNÖ.

In early 2006 AUDIOPAIN announced a collaborative 7" single through Worship Him Records to be shared with Québec THESYRE and a further split, 'The Inhumator' on Hearse Records limited to 500 copies, in collaboration with DEAD TO THIS WORLD in September.

Contagious, Audiopain (2000) (Demo). He Who Walks Among You / In The Grey / Servant Of God / Slave / Contagious / Ego-Whip.
1986, Audiopain (2000) (Demo). The Scourge / Mechanic Commando / The Hunt / Gospels From Hell / Relinquished / Glorious Beings.
Revel In Desecration, Audiopain (2002) (Demo). Revel In Desecration / Homicide / Stench Of Paradise / Weed Out The Weak / Forsaken Son / Infuriation On Scalp.
Audiopain / Mysticum, Worship Him WORSHIP003 (2003) (Split 7" vinyl single with MYSTICUM). The Habit Of Fear (AUDIOPAIN) / Black Magic Mushrooms (MYSTICUM).
Revel In Desecration, Witchhammer Production WHP-025D (2003) (Split cassette demo with AMOK. Limited edition 500 copies). Revel In Desecration / Homicide / Stench Of Paradise / Weed Out The Weak / Forsaken Son / Infuriation Scalp.
THE TRAUMATIZER, Vendlus VEND009 (2004). Believer / Fraud Machine / Living Among Humans / The Traumatizer / Thrash Mental / Religion Of Reality.
Überthrash, Duplicate DUPLO 666 (2004) (Split gatefold double 7" vinyl single with AURA NOIR, NOCTURNAL BREED and INFERNÖ. Limited edition 500 copies). Obsolescence (AUDIOPAIN) / When The Children Die (INFERNÖ) / Code Of Conduct (NOCTURNAL BREED) / Sordid (AURA NOIR).

Überthrash II, Duplicate DUPLO 15 (2005) (Split double gatefold 7" vinyl single with AURA NOIR, NOCTURNAL BREED and INFERNÖ. Limited edition 500 copies). Scything Harrow (Mother Whore edit) (NOCTURNAL BREED) / Psalvation (AUDIOPAIN) / Sulphur Void (AURA NOIR) / Metal Commando (INFERNÖ).

Contagious, Vendlus VEND012 (2005). He Who Walks Among You / In The Grey / Servant Of God / Slave / Contagious / Ego-Whip.

1986, Vendlus VEND014 (2005). The Scourge / Mechanic Commando / The Hunt / Gospels From Hell / Relinquished / Glorious Beings.

Audiopain / Dead To This World, Hearse (2006) (Split 7" vinyl single with DEAD TO THIS WORLD limited to 500 copies). The Inhumator (AUDIOPAIN) / Speak When Spoken To (DEAD TO THIS WORLD).

AURA

EINDHOVEN, HOLLAND — *Peter Brinkman (vocals / guitar), Mark van Dooren (guitar), Martijn Luppens (bass), Michel Jolie (keyboards), Bas van den Boom (drums).*

Eindhoven melodic Death Metal band AURA began life in 1991, formed by vocalist / guitarist Peter Brinkman, bass player Martyn Luppens and Ruby Soffner on second guitar. The group went through a succession of drummers including Peter van de Linden in 1993, Sander van Balen and Molly "The Beast". Signing to Hammerheart Records AURA released the 1996 EP 'Shattered Dawnbreak'.

AURA drafted another new drummer in 1998, Bas van den Boom, at the same juncture expanding their sound with the incorporation of keyboard player Michel Jolie. The demo 'Sect' arrived in 2000. The album 'Hidden' saw release in 2004, after which AURA evolved into SCENARIO II.

Shattered Dawnbreak, Hammerheart (1996). Your Ignorant Ways / This Shattered Dawnbreak / Moonsymmetry XXI: Empires Ablaze / (An Ode To) The Autumnlands.

Promo 2000 Sect, Independent (2000). Sect / In Sylvan Enchantment / 750ms / Absynth.

AURA NOIR

OSLO, NORWAY — *Apollyon (vocals / bass / guitar), Aggressor (vocals / bass / guitar / drums).*

Oslo based AURA NOIR is the Thrash Metal side project of Black Metal musicians Carl 'Aggressor' Michael Eide from ULVER, CADAVER INC. and VED BUENS ENDE in partnership with DØDHEIMSGARD's 'Apollyon' (Ole Jørgen Moe) and IN SILENCE and MAYHEM's Blasphemer (Rune Erickson). As 'Aggressor' Carl Michael Eide is also a member of INFERNÖ having debuted with the 1996 album 'Utter Hell'. The man has also deputized for DIMMU BORGIR's Tjodalv whilst the latter was on paternity leave from his band.

AURA NOIR's inaugural two song demo of 1993, comprising 'A Desert Of Sculptures' and 'The Tower Of Limbs And Fevers', would be recorded solely by Aggressor. Bringing in Apollyon, the duo cut second demo 'Two Voices, One King' in 1994. AURA NOIR debuted with the 1996 offering 'Dreams Like Deserts' issued on the Hot Records imprint of DIMMU BORGIR's Shagrath. Malicious Records then issued 1997's 'Black Thrash Attack'. Vinyl versions hosted an additional track in a cover version of VENOM's 'Heaven's On Fire'. Hammerheart Records followed with 'Deep Tracts Of Hell' in December 1998. This latter effort found Sverre Dæhle contributing guitar. Blasphemer bowed out to re-activate IN SILENCE for a 1999 demo, 'The Suicide Revolution', this featuring contributions from members of DØDHEIMSGARD, DIMMU BORGIR and GEHENNAH.

Eide guested on FLEURETY's 2000 album 'Department Of Apocalyptic Affairs' and has sessioned for WHITE WILLOW. Apollyon also held links with LAMENTED SOULS. AURA NOIR returned with another outing through Hammerheart Records, 'Increased Damnation' in 2000, this set notably featuring DARKTHRONE's Fenriz (Gylve Nagell) as guest vocalist. Blasphemer then made a return and drums for work after this opus were supplied by Dirge Rep (Per Husebø) of ENSLAVED and GEHENNAH.

During April 2002 both Apollyon and Aggressor formed part of the line-up for CADAVER INC.'s North American tour. That same year Apollyon initiated another side venture, working alongside the RED HARVEST pairing of Thomas 'Bølla' Brandt and Bolt Bergsten, to forge traditionalist Thrash outfit WAKLEVÖREN.

In 2004 AURA NOIR signed to Tyrant Syndicate Records, a new label started by Nocturno Culto of DARKTHRONE, for the August release 'Merciless'. Both Fenriz of DARKTHRONE and Nattefrost of CARPATHIAN FOREST would guest. That same year the band would have their classic cut 'Blood Unity' chosen as a pioneering piece of music for a compilation assembled by DARKTHRONE drummer Fenriz, released through Peaceville Records and entitled 'Fenriz Presents The Best Of Old School Black Metal'. The song 'Sordid' also found inclusion on a split 7" EP, 'Überthrash', shared with AUDIOPAIN, NOCTURNAL BREED and INFERNO.

AURA NOIR guitarist Aggressor got himself into the news in somewhat bizarre circumstances when he plummeted from a five-story building in Oslo on 26th March 2005. Severely injured, the musician underwent two major operations immediately after the event. A year later Eide would still be wheelchair bound.

April 2006 brought news that Apollyon had participated in SECHT, a Black Metal collective boasting an impressive cast involving CARPATHIAN FOREST personnel Vrangsinn, Nattefrost and Nordavind, drummer Dirge Rep of GORGOROTH and NEETZACH, Nag of TSJUDER, Gaahl from GORGOROTH and TRELLDOM, Nocturno Culto of DARKTHRONE plus Høst from RAGNAROK and TAAKE amongst others.

Aura Noir, Aura Noir (1993) (Demo). A Desert Of Sculptures / The Tower Of Limbs And Fevers.

Two Voices, One King, Aura Noir (1994) (Demo). The Tower Of Limbs And Fevers / Snake / Mirage.

Dreams Like Deserts EP, Hot HR002 (1995). The Rape / Forlorn Blessings To The Dreamking / Dreams Like Deserts / Angel Ripper / Snake / Mirage.

BLACK THRASH ATTACK, Malicious MR009 (1997) (Vinyl version). Sons Of Hades / Conqueror / Caged Wrath / Wretched Face Of Evil / Black Thrash Attack / The Pest / The One Who Smite / Eternally Your Shadow / Destructor / Fighting For Hell / Heaven's On Fire.

BLACK THRASH ATTACK, Aura Noir MR009 (1997). Sons Of Hades / Conqueror / Caged Wrath / Wretched Face Of Evil / Black Thrash Attack / The Pest / The One Who Smite / Eternally Your Shadow / Destructor / Fighting For Hell.

DEEP TRACTS OF HELL, Hammerheart HHR 028 (1998). Deep Tracts Of Hell / Released Damnation / Swarm Of Vultures / Blood Unity / Slasher / Purification Of Hell / The Spiral Scar / The Beautiful, Darkest Path / Broth Of Oblivion.

INCREASED DAMNATION, Hammerheart HHR 029 (2001). The Mirage / Towers Of Limbs And Fever / Released Damnation / Broth Of Oblivion / Swarms Of Vultures / The One Who Smite / Wretched Face Of Evil / Fighting For Hell / The Rape / Forlorn Blessing To The Dreamking / Dreams Like Deserts / Angel Ripper / Snake / Mirage / Towers Of Limbs And Fever (Original version).

Überthrash EP, Duplicate DUPLO 666 (2004) (Split gatefold double 7" vinyl EP with AUDIOPAIN, NOCTURNAL BREED and INFERNÖ. Limited edition 500 copies). Sordid.

THE MERCILESS, Peaceville CDVILEF127 (2004). Upon The Dark Throne / Condor / Black Metal / Hell's Fire / Black Deluge Night / Funeral Thrash / Sordid / Merciless.

Überthrash II, Duplicate DUPLO 15 (2005) (Split gatefold double 7" vinyl EP with AUDIOPAIN, NOCTURNAL BREED and INFERNÖ. Limited edition 500 copies). Sulphur Void.

AUTOPSIA

PIACENZA, ITALY — *Diego Grossi (vocals), Leo Balocco (guitar), Andrea Bernini (bass), Teo Mazzotti (drums).*

Piacenza Thrashers dating back to 1994. AUTOPSIA began life with a distinct Bay Area sound but have progressed to include Death and even technical, Progressive elements. The original incarnation of AUTOPSIA was fronted by Dio Demicheli with guitars from Leo Balocco, bass delivered by Ivan Grecchi and drums in the hands of Teo Mazzotti.

A series of line up shuffles saw the departure of Demicheli in 1995 and Diego Grossi of TRIFIXION repute taking the lead vocal mantle. The same year Lobo Ruscitti would be inducted as second guitarist but the following both Ruscitti and Grecchi decamped. Bass was given over to Ricky Toselli in 1997 and then to Charly Danzi in 1998. By 2000 the four string position was covered by Andrea Bernini and AUTOPSIA bowed in with their first demo 'What Are You Looking For?', made up of four studio cuts and live track. Further exposure was reaped when a song from this session was included on the Sony Music compilation 'Tendenze'.

A second demo, 'I Lied' produced by Tommy Talamanca of SADIST, arrived in 2000. AUTOPSIA would then put in a round of touring in the Czech Republic.

Drummer Teo Mazzotti also cites membership of infamous Grindcore act CRIPPLE BASTARDS and Punk band STINKING POLECATS.

What Are You Looking For!?, (2000). Obscurity Of Time / Empire / After Midnight / Sadness / Rot n' Roll (Live).

I Lied, (2001). Endless Eclipse / I Lied / Empty Uniforms / State Of Mind.

I Lied EP, (2001). Endless Eclipse / I Lied / Empty Uniforms / State Of Mind (In Our Life).

AVENGER OF BLOOD

LAS VEGAS, NV, USA — *Eric (vocals / guitar), Nathan (guitar), Shawn (bass), Shannon Frye (drums).*

Las Vegas "Post-modern apocalyptic European style" Thrash Metal band forged by Matthew Black (a.k.a. 'Eric') in April of 2001. Black debuted his project with the opening demo 'Celestial War'. Former TORTURED CONSCIENCE, VENGEANCE RISING and BIOGENESIS drummer Shannon Frye was added in September of 2002. Relocating to San Francisco, AVENGER OF BLOOD drafted another erstwhile TORTURED CONSCIENCE man Mike Soria, also a veteran of GREATER THE HATRED and URN in November. However, Soria's term was brief and within weeks Vince DiMaggio, also of GREATER THE HATRED and URN, took over the bass role. Jake Ottinger completed the band as second guitarist in January of 2003. A three song demo crafted in September at Trident Studios in Pacheco, notably recorded and mixed by Juan Urteaga of VILE, found AVENGER OF BLOOD as a studio trio of Eric, Shannon and bassist Cesar.

The group would then morph once again, as both Eric and Shannon Frye both relocated to Las Vegas, Nevada, drafting Nathan on guitars and Shawn on bass. This new formation performed at the first annual 'Minneapolis Mayhem Festival', sharing the stage with artists such as SUFFOCATION, MORBID ANGEL, SATYRICON, AGENT STEEL, HEATHEN and USURPER.

AVENGER OF BLOOD signed to JCM Records in April 2004 for the first full length recording entitled 'Complete Annihilation'. Recording took place at Maurotone Studios in Las Vegas during October for March 2005 release. Nathan announced his retirement from the band in January 2005, but then retracted this and remained in the ranks. Promotion for the album included an appearance at the CANNIBAL CORPSE headlined 'Northwest Deathfest' in Seattle during early April.

Celestial War EP, Independent (2001). Arrival / Ghostrider of the Apocalypse / Fallen Entity / Interlude / Prophetic Destruction.

Demo 2003, (2003). Rebel Human Spirits / Total War / Conditioned To Hate.

COMPLETE ANNIHILATION, JCM JCM 007 (2005). Intro / Complete Annihilation / Scent Of Death / Bound By Torment / Tyrants Of The Bloodlands / Where The Pictures Lie / Trapped In Time / Violent Epiphany / Everlasting Plague / Forced To Kill.

AVENGING ANGELS

AUSTRIA — *Sandro Hochrainer (vocals), Lino Hochrainer (vocals), Michael Weiskopf (guitar), Peter Schmid (guitar), Markus Breijla (bass), Thomas Köchle (drums).*

AVENGING ANGELS is a Tyrolese Thrash Metal band assembled in 2000 by guitarists Peter Schmid and Georg Pircher with Thomas Köchle handling drums. They would be joined by singer Sandro Hochrainer. Shortly afterward they added second vocalist Lino Hochrainer and bassist Michael Weiskopf. In 2003 Markus Breijla was introduced on bass and Michael Weiskopf took on second guitar duties. A two song demo, entitled 'Black Stories', saw release in October 2003.

AVENGING ANGELS second demo, the single track 'Business Solution', was put out in March 2005. This song also featured on the compilation albums 'LA Local Heroes III' and 'Arising Realm'. The album 'Fragmentary Reality', recorded at SMT Studio, followed in March 2006.

Black Stories, Avenging Angels (2003) (Demo). Obsession / My Greatest Foe.

Business Solution, Avenging Angels (2005) (Demo). Business Solution.

FRAGMENTARY REALITY, Avenging Angels (2006). Here I Stand / Balance Of Power / Who Do You Think You Are / Misleading Words / Business Solution / Time Will Arrive / Obsession / Drown In Sorrow.

AZOTIC REIGN

TIERP, SWEDEN — *Kjell Andersson (vocals), Tord Ericksson (guitar), Patrik Gustafson (guitar), Andreas Vaple (bass), Patrik Sjöberg (drums).*

Tierp act AZOTIC REIGN operate firmly in Bay Area Thrash Metal style. The group was first assembled as BLACK CRUSADER during 1989, then featuring vocalist Kjell Andersson, guitarist Micke Sundh, bass player Ronny Backström and drummer Peter Johansson. A September 1991 demo, under the title AZOTIC REIGN, was followed by a live debut in their hometown opening for FALLEN ANGEL and HEXENHAUS. Major membership changes afflicted the group during 1992 but, having re-grouped, the demo 'World Of Chaos', laid down at Musikfabriken in Uppsala with Michael Hahne behind the desk, saw delivery in February 1993. New faces included guitarists Tord Ericksson and Patrik Gustafson plus drummer Stefan Brodin. However, he would be superseded by Alvaro Romero Torres, of IMPERIAL DOMAIN and LOCH VOSTOK, whilst Fredrik Höök took over on bass.

The 'Dreamer' session followed in November 1994. Still suffering from a fluid line-up, the band's rhythm section of bass and drums remained unstable between 1996 and 1998. Patrik Sjöberg, of RIVENDELL and THEORY IN PRACTICE, finally stabilised the drum position whilst Andreas Vaple, of KING CHROME and IN AETERNUM, came in on bass. A limited edition EP 'Beyond The Blood', restricted to 500 copies and produced by Daniel Bergstrand, was delivered in 1998. The release party for this effort was held at the Metal Heaven club in Forsbacka.

German label Iron Glory Records issued the album 'Abstract Malediction' in July 2000. These sessions had taken place over twelve days at Studio Sound Creation in Bollnäs with Per Ryberg acting as producer.

Vocalist Kjell Andersson would co-found the Occult based Thrash Metal band THRAWN in union with Henrik Ohlsson of MUTANT and THEORY IN PRACTICE in 2001, resulting in a demo 'Light Creates Shadows'.

AZOTIC REIGN released a self-titled, three song demo in 2002. Blackened Records issued tracks, shared with JESUS MARTYR, on a split album in 2003 entitled 'Sudamerican Porno'.

Azotic Reign, Azotic Reign (1991) (Demo).

World Of Chaos, Azotic Reign (1993) (Demo). Death By The Guillotine / Nameless Fear / Warriors From The North / World Of Chaos.

Dreamer, Azotic Reign (1994) (Demo).

Beyond The Blood, Azotic Reign (1998). The Beginning (Intro) / Sacrificed / Beyond The Blood / Heal My Soul / Reincarnation Denied.

ABSTRACT MALEDICTION, Iron Glory IG1011 (2000). Sacrificed / The Fall Of Humanity / Reincarnation Denied / Soulless Bleed / The Depths Of My Shadow / Beyond The Blood / Devine Justice / Repent Your Sins / The House By The Ancient Ceremony.

Azotic Reign, Azotic Reign (2002) (Demo). Converted / Fragments Of The Past / Childmolester (Die).

BABYLON WHORES

FINLAND — *Ike Vil (vocals / keyboards), Antti Litmanen (guitar), Ewo Meichem (guitar), Jake Babylon (bass), Kouta (drums).*

Noted exponents of "Death Rock" BABYLON WHORES mix a heady brew of Gothic Rock, 80's Thrash and Black Metal in a unique combination that has set the band apart from the pack. The band's debut single 'Devil's Meat' released on their own Sugar Cult label saw the group comprising of vocalist Ike Vil, guitarists Jussi Konittinen and Ewo 'Meichem' Rytkönen, bassist M. Ways and drummer Pete Liha. Follow up 'Sloane 313' saw the bass player's job going to the suitably titled Jake Babylon. Further changes were afoot for BABYLON WHORES third release 'Trismegistos' with guitarist Antti Litmanen taking Konittinen's position and Kouta coming in on drums.

In late 1999 Babylon Jake bailed out to found a new act DEATH FIX and was replaced by Taneli Nyholm of ABSURDUS, CRYHAVOC and PANDEMONIUM OUTCASTS. Nyholm also goes under the pseudonyms of 'Serpent', 'Daniel Rock' and 'Daniel Stuka'.

BABYLON WHORES toured America in 2000 as guests to KING DIAMOND. Original guitarist Ewo Rytkönen would go into a career in band management, his biggest success to date being NIGHTWISH.

Devil's Meat EP, Sugar Cult SUGAR 666 (1994). Cool / Third Eye / East Of Earth.

Sloane 313 EP, Sugar Cult SUGAR 667 (1995). Of Blowjobs And Cocktails / Cold Hummingbird / Babylon Astronaut / Silver Apples.

COLD HEAVEN, Music For Nations MFN 226 (1996). Deviltry / Omega Therion / Beyond The Sun / Metatron / Enchirdion For A Common Man / In Arcadia Ego / Babylon Astronaut / Flesh Of A Swine / Cold Heaven.

COLD HEAVEN, Pony Canyon PCCY-01161 (1997) (Japanese release). Deviltry / Omega Therion / Beyond The Sun / Metatron / Enchirdion For A Common Man / In Arcadia Ego / Babylon Astronaut / Flesh Of A Swine / Cold Heaven.

Trismegistos, Sugar Cult SUGAR 668 (1998). Love Under Will / Hellboy / Speed Doll / Beyond The Sun / Trismegistos.

DEGGAEL, Spinefarm SPI 62CD (1998). Dog Star A / Sol Niger / Somniferum / Omega Therion (V2) / Emerald Green / Deggael: A Rat's God / In Arcadia Ego (Video).

Errata Stigmata, Necropolis NR067 CD (2000). Errata Stigmata / Fey / Errata Stigmata (St. Vitus Dance Mix) / Sol Niger (Video).

KING FEAR, Necropolis NR045 (2000). Errata Stigmata / Radio Werewolf / Hand Of Glory / Veritas / Skeleton Farm / To Behold The Suns / Exit Eden / Sol Niger / Fey / King Fear—Song Of The Damned.

DEATH OF THE WEST, Spinefarm SPI 158CD (2002). Life Fades Away / Hell Abloom / Mother Of Serpents / Lucibel (The Good Spirits Of Europe) / Dating With Witchcraft / Death In Prague / A Pale Horse Against Time / Eveningland.

BAL SAGOTH

YORKSHIRE, UK — *Bryon Roberts (vocals), Chris Maudling (guitar), Mark Greenwell (bass), Jonny Maudling (keyboards), Dan Mullins (drums).*

A Dark, Black neo-Pagan "Battle" Metal band out of Yorkshire with a predilection for lengthy song titles and mind boggling conceptual collages of multi-faceted, antediluvian Metal extravaganzas. BAL SAGOTH, titled after fantasy novelist Robert E. Howard's story 'The Gods Of Bal-Sagoth', was formulated as an idea by vocalist Byron Roberts as early as 1989, then billed DUSK, but it would not be until July 1993 that the Maudling siblings guitarist Christopher and drummer Jonny involvement took the concept into a band format. Further draftees in September of the same year, bassist Jason Porter and keyboard player Vincent Crabtree brought BAL SAGOTH up to full strength and by the close of the year an inaugural demo had been cut. Of the four songs included in this December session 'By The Blaze Of The Fire Jewels' would subsequently be re-worked as 'Shadows 'Neath The Black Pyramid' whilst 'A Shadow On The Mist' would see its constitute parts utilised in future tracks.

The band duly signed a three album deal with the London based Cacophonous label but delays held back the issue of the tantalising debut album 'A Black Moon Broods Over Lemuria' until May 1995. The record, opening with a lavish intro 'Hatheg Kla' after H.P. Lovecraft's "The Other Gods", immediately provoked gushing reviews from the extreme Metal press, never before having encountered such a serpentine labyrinth of genius fettled from primal Death and Black Metal. 'A Black Moon Broods Over Lemuria' subject matter sprawled across such eclectic characters as Skulthur the serpent king, the ebon fiends from Z'Xulth and Lord Angsaar. For all its complexity, this would only be the beginning. CRADLE OF FILTH guitarist Gian Pyres notably donated a lead guitar solo to 'The Ravening'. During this timeframe Crabtree departed and was replaced by Leon Forrest. BAL SAGOTH was scheduled to put in their first live performances supporting then label mates CRADLE OF FILTH but Roberts sustained an injury whilst stage diving at a CANNIBAL CORPSE concert which scotched these plans.

It would be April 1995 that BAL SAGOTH finally embarked on the live trail with a gig at the Dublin Castle in London. Upon the album's eventual release support dates to Portuguese Gothic Black Metal act MOONSPELL were put in during July upfront of a tour of the UK and Ireland with label mates PRIMORDIAL and SIGH in September. However, BAL SAGOTH would pull out of these shows due to disagreements with the promoter. Notwithstanding this setback, the band's stature was already ascendant in mainland Europe though and BAL SAGOTH headlined the Belgian 'Ragnarok' festival in November. The following month bassist Jason Porter was ousted by the recruitment of Alastair McLatchy, a former acquaintance of Byron's in DUSK.

'Starfire Burning Upon The Ice-Veiled Throne Of Ultima Thule' arrived in 1996. Having piqued much curiosity with their debut, this second album shot BAL SAGOTH further up the rankings. Quite novelly, the group supported their bombastic music by a wealth of lyrical matter that was so dense only a portion of it was actually sung on the record, the remainder used within the accompanying booklet as a guide for the listener. The band toured Europe for the first time on a package billing with DARK FUNERAL and ANCIENT in February 1997. BAL SAGOTH supported EMPEROR at the London Astoria and SINISTER in Belgium before completing a second round of European shows in alliance with EMPEROR and NOCTURNAL BREED in October of the same year.

As 1998 broke Forrest announced his exit for a career in the police. Jonny Maudling manoeuvred over to keyboards to plug the gap and Dave Mackintosh took the drum stool. During the summer MacLatchy broke ranks too and Mark Greenwell took over on bass. Third album 'Battle Magic', recorded at Academy Studios in Bradford, was launched during November. Another suitably Hyperborean epic, 'Battle Magic' succeeded in amplifying their already audacious sense of purpose. By this juncture BAL SAGOTH had strode out on their own unique path with such bravado that no other group could even remotely compare.

Jonny Maudling found himself on loan to MY DYING BRIDE for European touring during 1999 whilst the band signed to leading German label Nuclear Blast for 'The Power Cosmic' album in October. Strangely, only Russian variants on the Irond label, included the essential lyric sheets.

Supporting fifth album 'Atlantis Ascendant', highlighted by the patriotic stage favourite 'Draconis Albionensis', BAL SAGOTH supported arch Black Metal Swedes MARDUK at the London Dome in December 2001. In November 2003 Davis Mackintosh joined London based Power Metal band DRAGONFORCE. Having spent the Spring of 2004 recording a new studio album the band announced the departure of drummer Dave Mackintosh in April. Replacement Dan Mullins, a veteran of such acts as EPITAPH, THE RAVEN THEORY, THINE, BROKEN, THE AXIS OF PERDITION and (as "Mr. Storm Monolith') SERMON OF HYPOCRISY, made his first show with the band with an appearance at the major German festival 'Wacken Open Air' in August.

BAL SAGOTH made a return in March 2006 with the album 'The Chthonic Chronicles'. Mullins stepped up a league further in February by joining MY DYING BRIDE.

Demo 1993, (1993). Intro / Dreaming Of Atlantean Spires / By The Blaze Of The Fire Jewels / A Shadow On The Mist.
A BLACK MOON BROODS OVER LEMURIA, Cacophonous NIHIL 4CD (1995). Hatheg Kla / Dreaming Of Atlantean Spires / Spellcraft And Moonfire (Beyond The Citadel Of Frosts) / A Black Moons Broods Over Lemuria / Enthroned In The Temple Of The Serpent Kings / Shadows 'neath The Black Pyramid / Witch-Storm / The Ravening / Into The Silent Chambers Of The Sapphirean Throne (Sagas From The Untedelivian Scrolls) / Valley Of Silent Paths.
STARFIRE BURNING OVER THE ICE VEILED THRONE OF ULTIMA THULE, Cacophonous NIHIL 18CD (1996). Black Dragons Soar Above The Mountain Of Shadows (Epilogue) / To Dethrone The Witch-Queen Of Mytos K'unn (The Legend Of The Battle Of Blackhelm Vale) / As The Vortex Illumines The Crystalline Walls Of Kor-Avul-Thaa / Starfire Burning Upon The Ice—Veiled Throne Of Ultima Thule / Journey To The Isle Of Sists (Over The Moonless Depths Of Night-Dark Seas) / The Splendour Of A Thousand Swords Gleaming Beneath The Blazon Of The Hyperborean Empire / Ad Lo, When The Imperium Marches Against Gul-Kothoth, Then Dark Sorceries Shall Enshroud The Citadel Of The Obsidian Crown / Summoning The Guardians Of The Astral Gate / In The Raven-Hunted Forests Of Darkenhold, Where Shadows Reign And The Hues Of Sunlight Never Dance / At The Altar Of The Dreaming Gods (Epilogue).
BATTLE MAGIC, Cacophonous NIHIL 29CD (1998). Battle Magic / Naked Steel (The Warrior's Saga) / A Tale From The Deep Woods / Return To The Praesidium Of Ys / Crystal Shards / The Dark Liege Of Chaos Is Unleashed At The Ensorcelled Shrine Of A'Zura-Kai (The Splendour Of A Thousand Swords Gleaming Beneath The Blazon Of The Hyperborean Empire Part II) / When Rides The Scion Of The Storms / Blood Slakes The Sand At The Circus Maximus / Thwarted By The Dark (Blade Of The Vampyre Hunter) / And Atlantis Falls.
THE POWER COSMIC, Nuclear Blast NB 421-2 (1999). Awakening Of The Stars / The Voyagers Beneath The Mare Imbrium / The Empyreal Lexicon / Of Carnage And A Gathering Of Wolves / Callisto Rising / The Scourge Of The Fourth Celestial Host / Behold, The Armies Of War Descend Screaming From The Heavens! / The Thirteen Cryptical Prophecies Of Mu.
ATLANTIS ASCENDANT, Nuclear Blast NB 584-2 (2001). The Epsilon Exordium / Atlantis Ascendant / Draconis Albionensis / Star-Maps Of The Ancient Cosmographers / The Ghost Of Angkor Wat / The Splendour Of A Thousand Swords Gleaming Beneath The Blazon Of The Hyperborean Empire (Part III) / The Dreamer In Catacombs Of Ur / In Search Of The Lost Cities Of Antarctica / The Chronicle Of Shadows / Six Keys To The Onyx Pyramid.
THE CHTHONIC CHRONICLES, Nuclear Blast NB 1048 (2006). The Sixth Adulation Of His Chthonic Majesty / Invocations Beyond The Outer-World Night / Six Score And Ten Oblations To A Majestic Avatar / The Obsidian Crown Unbound / The Fallen Kingdoms Of The Abyssal Plain / Shackled To The Trilithon Of Kutulu / The Hammer Of The Emperor / Unfettering The Hoary Sentinels Of Karnak / To Storm The Cyclopean Gates Of Byzantium / Arcana Antediluvia / Beneath The Crimson Vaults Of Cydonia / Return To Hatheg-Kia.

BATHORY

STOCKHOLM, SWEDEN — *Quorthon (vocals / guitar), Kothaar (bass), Vvornth (drums).*

BATHORY was an extreme Metal project based around the enigmatic Quorthon, previously known as 'Ace Shot'. Although denied officially throughout the band's lifespan, it was learned by industry insiders that Tomas Börje 'Quorthon' Forsberg was actually the son of Black Mark Records owner Börje Forsberg. This fact was staunchly refuted, and often journalists were given deliberately erroneous inside information, including lavish usage of Swedish profanities as fictitious names, only serving to continually revive speculation. Only with Quorthon's death would his real self be confirmed.

With BATHORY, Quorthon prided himself on overblown epic chunks of Metal that attracted a staunchly loyal fan base amongst both fans and bands. Although BATHORY enhanced its mystique by staying away from the stage, this was not by design, but because of the simple fact there never was a stable line-up enough to put on a show. BATHORY's undoubted influence on Black Metal forms an essential bedrock to the genre, as illustrated by a profusion of major name acts eager to deliver cover versions by way of recognition. Those having covered BATHORY include such names as DARK FUNERAL, DIMMU BORGIR, DISSECTION, EMPEROR, MARDUK, MYSTIC CIRCLE, SATYRICON and THE CROWN amongst many others globally.

Prior to founding BATHORY, Quorthon, billed as "Ace the Spunky Black Spade", had already made his mark on the Finnish Metal scene by designing the 1982 cover designs for the OZ releases, the 'Fire In The Brain' album and the 'Turn The Cross Upside Down' EP. His yearning to pursue music as a vocation would be fired by a love of MOTÖRHEAD, BLACK SABBATH and the second wave of UK Punk acts such as THE EXPLOITED, CHARGED GBH and DISCHARGE.

BATHORY, founded in Stockholm, came to attention of the masses via the tracks 'The Return Of Darkness And Evil' and 'Sacrifice' that were both featured on the Tyfon Grammofon 'Scandinavian Metal Attack' compilation album of 1984. BATHORY was actually created a year before, precisely on March 16th 1983, with an accredited roster comprising Black Spade on vocals and guitar, having previous experience with AGNOSTICUM and punk outfit STRIDSKUK, bassist Frederick Hanoi and drummer Vans McBurger (real name Jonas Åkerlund), the rhythm section having just vacated their posts in heavy metal band DIE CAST. These tongue in cheek pseudonyms were adopted by the trio, all then just eighteen years old, in reaction to a common practice amongst Swedish career musicians to re-brand themselves with false, Americanized stage names. Åkerlund took his cue from Vans sneakers and McDonalds fast food. Quorthon's brief usage of 'Ace Shoot' then 'Ace Shot' came from combining two MOTÖRHEAD song titles, 'Ace Of Spades' and 'Straight Shooter'.

With both Hanoi and temporarily in the UK, Quorthon laid down the very first BATHORY demos in June 1983, four songs Sacrifice', 'Live In Sin', 'Die In Fire' and 'You Don't Move Me (I Don't Give a Fuck)', utilising former friends from his STRIDSKUK days, bass player Rickard Bergman and drummer Johan Elvén.

The musicians had deliberated over various band names, including NOSFERATU, MEPHISTO, ELIZABETH BATHORY and COUNTESS BATHORY, prior to settling on Quorthon's first choice of BATHORY. For the 'Scandinavian Metal Attack' album Black Spade re-titled himself Ace Shoot before finalising his identity as the alter-ego Quorthon, this powerful title being discovered in a list of demons. BATHORY's inclusion on 'Scandinavian Metal Attack' would be down to pure chance as a late withdrawal by a Finnish act opened up a space for two songs that needed filling quickly. The group put down their two songs at Elektra Studios in Stockholm on January 23rd 1984, later adding sound effects, backwards narrative and guitar solos.

'Scandinavian Metal Attack' sold in large numbers, particularly through export into Europe and the USA. With BATHORY often pinpointed in magazine reviews, the Tyfon label requested a full album. Unfortunately for Quorthon the group as a practical entity no longer existed. In May BATHORY demoed two further songs, 'Satan My Master' and 'Witchcraft', Quorthon once again drafting Bergman and pulling in OBSKLASS drummer Stefan Larsson.

The three then entered the 8 track Heavenshore Studios on June 14th to cut their first album. They would use this studio, actually a converted garage at the back of a private residence, for the bulk of the band's recording career. 'Bathory' was in fact a makeshift affair, with much of the material being written in the studio. The demo track 'Witchcraft' would be re-written as 'Reaper'. The low budget that governed the sessions, totalling just 56 hours, would extend to the album graphics, the front sleeve a collage of photocopied images whilst the song 'Necromancy' became 'Necromansy' on the sleeve credits due to running out of Letraset letters. The entire monochrome presentation was also dictated by lack of finances. However, the band and label did go to the expense of producing a gold first press, which unfortunately turned out lemon yellow. Only 1000 of these yellow versions made it into distribution.

By the record's release in October 1984, 'Bathory', forsaking the traditional A and B sides of vinyl for side 'Darkness' and side 'Evil', found a ready audience with the burgeoning thrash end of the metal market and, alongside Venom's debut, is universally pinpointed as a catalyst for the entire Black Metal movement. Visually 'Bathory' forced an impression with its now infamous black and white goat motif and Quorthon's then penchant for bone jewellery, pentagram backdrops and blood gargling.

In November 1984 BATHORY crafted four songs, 'Children Of The Beast', 'Crown Of Thorns One The Golden Throne', 'Crucifix' and 'Necronomicon' for a projected EP. This proposal never saw the light of day.

Despite the first record selling strongly, Quorthon was still without a backing band. In February 1985 second album, originally billed 'Revelation Of Doom' but switched to 'The Return Of Darkness And Evil' was committed to tape at Elektra Studios by Quorthon, bass player Andreas Johansson and drummer Stefan Larsson. Mid session, Johansson was given his marching orders and Quorthon finished the remaining bass tracks. 'The Return Of Darkness And Evil' emerged that May.

Soon back in the studio, this time ensconced in Heavenshore once again, Quorthon and Larssen fabricated six more songs, 'Black Leather Wings', 'Hellfire', 'Majestica Satanica', 'Circle Of Blood', 'Wicca', 'The Call From The Grave' and 'Undead' for a project given the title 'Okkulta'. These tracks never surfaced commercially.

In an attempt to assemble a permanent band, Carsten Nielsen, drummer for Danes ARTILLERY, was offered a position in BATHORY during 1985 but declined. Witchhunter (Christian Dudeck) of SODOM travelled from his German home base to Sweden in order to rehearse with the band but he too did not work out. The band nearly relented on their resolve not to perform in 1986 when a European tour with CELTIC FROST and DESTRUCTION was mooted but without a solid band structure this fell through.

BATHORY's third album found Paul Pålle Lundberg, of local acts SALAMANDER and DESTITUTE, manning the drums. Christer Sandström was recruited on bass, but soon dispensed with and Quorthon resumed four-string duties once again for recording that September. A working title of 'Nocturnal Obeisance' was dropped in favour of 'Under The Sign Of The Black Mark'. The album cover stretched ambitions, not many fans realising the demon atop a cliff face was in fact a photograph shot at the Royal Swedish Opera House with bodybuilder Leif Ehrnborg, brandishing an ox bone, made up as the devil figure. 'Under The Sign Of The Black Mark' saw release in May 1987, the first BATHORY product to benefit from licensing deals with Combat Records in the USA and Music For Nations in the UK.

BATHORY reportedly performed only a handful of gigs before resolving never to perform again, this strategy appeared to the media to be a deliberate intention to compound the mystique surrounding the act but was actually down to practical considerations of having no solid line-up and few venues in which to perform. The group structure remained fluid, with another early bass player being Cliff of DRILLER KILLER.

The rhythm section of Kothaar and Vvornth were credited on October 1988's 'Blood, Fire, Death', although Quorthon later revealed that these appellations were given to a succession of musicians that had passed through the ranks. 'Blood, Fire, Death' presented BATHORY for the first time with a band photograph, a now classic depiction of three warriors clad in leather chaps wielding swords. Quorthon also scored a high impact in print with the distribution of promotional photographs depicting the singer in some spectacular fire-breathing poses. Meantime, as BATHORY's star rose, co-founder Jonas Åkerlund went on to enjoy a highly successful career post-BATHORY as a video director, earning awards for the stars such as METALLICA, MADONNA and U2.

The 'Hammerheart' album was delivered in lavish gatefold packaging familiar style in April 1990. 'Hammerheart' removed Bathory from the Satanic mould and thrust the concept squarely in Viking mythology. BATHORY's music took a major change of direction on June 1991's 'Twilight Of The Gods', the rawness dropped in favour of sombre sophistication, even going so far as to re-mould Holst's 'The Planets' suite, that found favour with some fans and prompted scorn from others. QUORTHON issued a solo album, simply titled 'Album' (Black Mark 666-9), during 1993. This set of tracks would distance the man even further from the early trademark sound. Indeed, so vicious was the backlash that BATHORY's next records, November 1994's 'Requiem', recorded at Montezuma Studio, and February 1995 follow up 'Octagon', plunged straight back into primal Punk Metal of the most basic order. The latter suffered a setback at the last minute before release. It was deemed that lyrics to two tracks 'Resolution Greed' and 'Genocide' were too extreme hence a cover version of the KISS classic 'Deuce' was included instead. The missing two tracks were later issued on the 'Jubileum Volume III' compilation. It is generally acknowledged that the horrifically under produced 'Octagon' forced the punk ethos to unwelcome welcomes. Reviews were savage in their condemnation, highlighting Quorthon's juvenile display of scatological lyrics.

A BATHORY record proposed as 'Raise The Dead' was planned for release through Music For Nations, but this proposed record never eventuated. In its stead, 'Blood On Ice' appeared in May 1996. For this outing, opening with the deceptively delicate sounds of Scandinavian fauna and closing with a crushing ten minute epic 'The Revenge Of The Blood On Ice' Quorthon had plundered the archives, reviving Norse themed material from the group's post 'Under The Sign Of The Black Mark' days for re-recording.

In 1997 BATHORY paid homage to MOTÖRHEAD with a rip through the classic 'Ace Of Spades' donated to the tribute album 'Black Mark Tribute Vol. 1'. That same year various Greek Black Metal acts including KAWIR, EXHUMATION and DEVISER contributed to the 'Hellas Salutes The Vikings' tribute effort. A more substantial album came the following year featuring heavyweight names such as MARDUK, GEHENNAH, DARK FUNERAL, EMPEROR, NECROPHOBIC and SATYRICON titled 'In Conspiracy With Satan'. BATHORY too kept up with the covers, their rendering of BLACK SABBATH's 'Sabbath Bloody Sabbath' to 'Black Mark Tribute Vol. 2'. BATHORY also laid down 'Detroit Rock City' by KISS but this never left the vaults.

Another solo QUORTHON album, the 23 track double disc 'Purity Of Essence', was released in 1997. Displaying a very different side to the man's persona, this body of work was in more in line with traditional Rock n' Roll, even including an unashamed love song.

A lengthy hiatus would be broken with October 2001's 'Destroyer Of Worlds'. Another BATHORY product, albeit unofficial, arrived in early 2002. Issued by the British Imperial Creations label, the split album with DARK FUNERAL comprised six early BATHORY demo tracks from the early 80s coupled with DARK FUNERAL live tracks.

The band flouted convention with their next release, splitting recent recordings into two separate full blown albums as on November 18th 2002 'Nordland Part I' saw issue and in January 2003, 'Nordland Part II'. During these sessions BATHORY cut a quick fire version of KISS' 'Black Diamond' for inclusion on the Nuclear Blast tribute collection 'Creatures Of The Night'.

In early 2004 Quorthon and LAKE OF TEARS session vocalist Jennie Tebler commenced recordings for a project dubbed SILVERWING. However, it would be learned that the 39 year old Tomas Börje 'Quorthon' Forsberg was found dead in his apartment in Stockholm, Sweden on Monday, June 7th. Apparent cause of death was heart failure.

Leading Irish band PRIMORDIAL's appearance at the Irish 'Day Of Darkness' festival on June 12th would be marked with a special performance assembled by Nemtheanga in honour of the late BATHORY leader. Running through several BATHORY numbers including 'Woman Of Dark Desires', 'Raise The Dead' and 'A Fine Day To Die', Nemtheanga fronted up a band unit comprising SOL AXIS members guitarist Joey and drummer Necrohammer, GAESA bassist Phil and Brian O'Connor of KINGDOM on additional vocals.

In Norway, a gathering of elite Black Metal musicians revealed they were to perform a special set of classic BATHORY songs during August's 'Hole In The Sky' festival. Those committing to the tribute included Satyr of SATYRICON, Abbath of IMMORTAL, Apollyon of AURA NOIR, Faust ex-EMPEROR, Gaahl of GORGOROTH, Ivar from ENSLAVED, Nocturno Culto of DARKTHRONE and Samoth of ZYKLON and EMPEROR. The leading UK Black metal act CRADLE OF FILTH had Japanese variants of their 'Nymphetamine' album added a cover version of BATHORY's 'Bestial Lust'. Although a new recording, this song had actually been committed to tape just prior to Quorthon's death.

That same year BATHORY would have their classic cut 'Dies Irae' chosen as a pioneering piece of music for a compilation assembled by DARKTHRONE drummer Fenriz, released through Peaceville Records and entitled 'Fenriz Presents The Best Of Old School Black Metal'. The posthumous SILVERWING single 'Song To Hall Up High' emerged through Black Mark Records in April 2005.

Börje Forsberg set a June 3rd release date for a comprehensive BATHORY box set, 'In Memory Of Quorthon', containing three CDs, one DVD, a book and the infamous fire breathing poster.

SCANDINAVIAN METAL ATTACK, RCA NL 70499 (1984) (Split vinyl album with OZ, TRASH, SPITFIRE and ZERO NINE). Sacrifice / The Return Of Darkness And Evil.
BATHORY, Black Mark Production BMLP 666-1 (1984). Storm Of Damnation (Intro) / Hades / Reaper / Necromancy / Sacrifice / In Conspiracy With Satan / Armageddon / Raise The Dead / War / Outro.
BATHORY, Banzai BRC 1934 (1985) (Canadian release). Storm Of Damnation (Intro) / Hades / Reaper / Necromancy / Sacrifice / In Conspiracy With Satan / Armageddon / Raise The Dead / Outro.
THE RETURN . . . , Banzai BRC 1955 (1985) (Canadian release). Revelation Of Doom (Intro) / Total Destruction / Born For Burning / The Wind Of Mayhem / Bestial Lust (Bitch) / Possessed / The Rite Of Darkness / Reap Of Evil / Son Of The Damned / Sadist / The Return Of The Darkness And Evil.
THE RETURN . . . , Black Mark Production BMLP 666-2 (1985). Revelation Of Doom (Intro) / Total Destruction / Born For Burning / The Wind Of Mayhem / Bestial Lust (Bitch) / Possessed / The Rite Of Darkness / Reap Of Evil / Son Of The Damned / Sadist / The Return Of The Darkness And Evil.
UNDER THE SIGN OF THE BLACK MARK, Black Mark Production BMLP 666-3 (1987). Nocturnal Obeisance / Massacre / Woman Of Dark Desires / Call From The Grave / Equimanthorn / Enter The Eternal Fire / Chariots Of Fire / 13 Candles / Of Doom . . . / Outro.
BLOOD FIRE DEATH, Black Mark Production BMLP 666-4 (1988). Oden's Ride Over Nordland / A Fine Day To Die / The Golden Walls Of Heaven / Pace 'Till Death / Holocaust / For All Those Who Died / Dies Irae / Blood Fire Death.
HAMMERHEART, Black Mark Production BMLP 666-5 (1990). Shores In Flames / Valhalla / Baptised In Fire And Blood / Father To Son / Song To Hall Up High / Home Of Once Brave / One Rode To Asa Bay / Outro.
Twilight Of The Gods, Black Mark Production BM CD666P (1991) (Promotion release). Twilight Of The Gods / Under The Runes / Hammerheart.
TWILIGHT OF THE GODS, Black Mark Production BMLP 666-6 (1991). Twilight Of The Gods—Epilogue / Through Blood By Thunder / Blood And Iron / Under The Runes / To Enter Your Mountain / Bond Of Blood / Hammerheart.
REQUIEM, Black Mark Production BMCD 666-10 (1994). Requiem / Crosstitution / Necroticus / War Machine / Blood And Soul / Pax Vobiscum / Suffocate / Distinguish To Kill / Apocalypse.
OCTAGON, Black Mark Production BMCD 666-11 (1995). Immaculate Pinetreeroad #930 / Born To Die / Psychpath / Sociopath / Grey / Century / 33 Something / War Supply / Schizianity / A Judgement Of Posterity / Deuce.
BLOOD ON ICE, Black Mark Production BMCD 666-12 (1996). Intro / Blood On Ice / Man Of Iron / One Eyed Old Man / The Sword / The Stallion / The Woodwoman / The Lake / Gods Of Thunder Of Wind And Of Rain / The Ravens / The Revenge Of Blood On Ice.
Blood On Ice, Black Mark Production BMCDP 666-12 (1996) (Promotion release). The Sword / The Lake / The Woodwoman.
DESTROYER OF WORLDS, Black Mark Production BMCD 666-15 (2001). Lake Of Fire / Destroyer Of Worlds / Ode / Bleeding / Pestilence / 109 / Death From Above / Krom / Liberty & Justice / Kill Kill Kill / Sudden Death / White Bones / Day Of Wrath.
NORDLAND I, Black Mark Production BMCD 666-19 (2002). Prelude / Nordland / Vinterblot / Dragons Breath / Ring Of Gold / Foreverdark Woods / Broken Sword / Great Hall Awaits A Fallen Brother / Mother Earth Father Thunder / Heimfard.
BLOOD ON ICE, Black Mark Production BMCD 666-12 (2003). Intro / Blood On Ice / Man Of Iron / One Eyed Old Man / The Sword / The Stallion / The Woodwoman / The Lake / Gods Of Thunder Of Wind And Of Rain / The Ravens / The Revenge Of Blood On Ice.
NORDLAND II, Black Mark Production BMCD 666-20 (2003). Fanfare / Blooded Shore / Sea Wolf / Vinland / The Land / Death And Resurrection Of A Northern Son / The Messenger / Flash Of The Silverhammer / The Wheel Of Sun.

BATTALION

MI, USA — *Lee Davis (vocals), Kevin Linn (guitar), Chuck Marshall (guitar), Tony Doan (bass), Bill Fitzpatrick (drums).*

Michigan Speed Metal band brought into existence by guitarist Chuck Marshall during November of 1989. Marshall teamed up with second guitarist Kevin Linn and 16 year old bassist Tony Doan, subsequently drafting Bill Walters on vocals and Dave Macy on drums to create the first incarnation of BATTALION. However, after local gigging the band folded.

In June of 1990 BATTALION was resurrected by Marshall and Linn. Bill Fitzpatrick took command of the drum stool in the August and shortly after Doan resumed his place. By early 1991 Keith Poszywak was fronting the band. A demo, simply entitled 'Battalion', was issued to promote a spate of gigging but in 1992 Poszywak opted out. BATTALION pulled in singer Twist to fill the gap but in January of 1993 he too decamped. The band were still minus a vocalist as they began recording tracks for the debut album 'Excessive Force' but former HARMS WAY man Lee Davis was incorporated to finish the record off. BATTALION broke up in mid 1995.

EXCESSIVE FORCE, Independent (1995). Excessive Force / The Black / Orchestrated By Fear / Red Fist / The Postman Always Shoots Twice / Devastation Trail / Tribe Of The Razor Eaters / Final Solution.

BATTLEFIELD

GERMANY — *Connie Ernst (vocals), Arthur Schilling (guitar), Frank Nitti (guitar), Patrick Renner (bass), Gerd Haußmann (drums).*

BATTLEFIELD, a Power Metal quintet, was formed in 1987 by guitarists Arthur Schilling and Frank Nitti. The duo was joined by drummer Gerd Haußmann before adding bassist Andres Rückle and female vocalist Conny Ernst. Following the bankruptcy of BATTLEFIELD's record label T.R.C. the band released a demo tape in 1990 aptly entitled 'Time To Rethink'. Ernst would join an early line up of IVANHOE.

Vocalist Tanja Ivenz was fronting the band by the second album in a revised BATTLEFIELD line-up that also saw new faces in bassist Patrick Renner and drummer Stephan Fiedler.

The group played with the likes of PSYCHOTIC WALTZ, LIFE ARTIST and GYPSY KISS.

We Come To Fight, TRC 011 (1988) ('We Come To Fight' EP). We Come To Fight / Nuclear Death / Knock On Your Door / Grave Of The Unknown / Possessed Preacher.
STILL AND EVER AGAIN, Rising Sun IRS 972 223 (1991). Experienced To Die / Still And Ever Again / Battlefield Of Misery / Red Rag / A Leap In The Dark / Experienced To Kill / Suction Of Eternity / If Our Earth Could Cry / Garden Of Stones.
SPIRIT OF TIME, Rising Sun SPV 084-62162 (1993). Walls In Deformation / Heat In November / Living Skin / Through The Moment Of Changes / 7th Sky / There Ain't No Sorrow / Geradine / Spirit Of Time / Oh Moon.

BEAST PETRIFY

SINGAPORE — *Al Fahmi (vocals / guitar), Hairulnizam (guitar), Scyfrul (bass), Rosmawan Boy (drums).*

Rooted in the 1993 Death Metal band BRUTAL BEAST. At this juncture BRUTAL BEAST's line up cited frontman Al Fahmi, bassist Scyfrul, rhythm guitarist Yumos and drummer Hasni.

During 1995 ETHEREAL brought BRUTAL BEAST member Al Fahmi into the fold as their new vocalist / guitarist. However, his preference for Thrash Metal soon won the day and Al Fahmi along with his BRUTAL BEAST colleague bass player Scyfrul and ETHEREAL members guitarist Hairulnizam and drummer Rosmawan Boy adopted a whole new side venture. With the title of BEAST PETRIFY, the band strictly in a Speed Metal direction made evident on their 1997 demo cassette 'In The Circle Of Time'.

Later erstwhile guitar colleague Yumos would join the band and Shahril from OSSUARY took over the drum stool for recording of the 1999 album 'Dimensional Deranged Dilemma' BEAST PETRIFY splintered down to just a duo of Al Fahmi and Scyfrul.

DIMENSIONAL DERANGED DILEMMA, Sonic Wave International (1999). Dimensional Deranged Dilemma / Massive Irretrievable Burden / Slaves Of The Abyss / Impending Disaster / Revulsion After Discrimination / Pertiferous Betrayal / Obscure Obliteration (Extended Aggression version) / The Pain Deep Within / In The Circle Of Time.

BEDIMMED

JÄRVENPÄÄ, FINLAND — *Tami Hintikka (vocals), Juha Lappalainen (guitar), Timo Ahlström (guitar), Timo Riuttamäki (bass), Jussi-Pekka Manner (drums).*

Järvenpää Death / Thrashers BEDIMMED issued the demo 'Scars Healing In Reverse' in July 2005 as their opening gambit. Frontman Tami Hintikka holds a tradition with DISINTER, PILGRIM and TRAILS OF BEREAVED. Second guitarist Timo Ahlström enrolled in June. The group's inaugural live performance took place that September, at the 'Heviosasto' festival with Juha Pöysä acting as stand in bassist, acting as replacement for original four-stringer Erkka Korpi. Subsequently Timo Riuttamäki took on bass duties.

BEDIMMED guitarist Juha Lappalainen and drummer Jussi-Pekka Manner maintain side ventures SONS OF ARAGORN, SKULLFUCKER and THE LAKEND CONNECTION. Manner also operates with SHREWDRIVER.

BEDIMMED commenced recording of a second demo session, entitled 'Sounds Of Terminal Torment', in 2006.

Scars Healing In Reverse, Bedimmed (2005) (Demo). Heal Me / Reverse Evolution / Scar Over A Scar.

BELIEVER

COLEBROOK, PA, USA — *Kurt Bachman (vocals / guitar), Dave Baddorf (guitar), Howe Kraft (bass), Joey Daub (drums).*

Pennsylvanian Christian Thrashers formed in 1985 by drummer Joey Daub and vocalist Kurt Bachman together with guitarist Dave Baddorf and bassist Howe Kraft. BELIEVER added new bassist Wyatt Robertson in mid 1990. During October the group conducted a package tour of the USA together with BOLT THROWER and Toronto Thrashers SACRIFICE. The 1994 album 'Dimensions' found BELIEVER with Jim Winter on bass and William Keller on lead vocals. Daub would forge a union with SACRAMENT members guitarist Mike DiDonato and bassist Erik Ney to create FOUNTAIN OF TEARS for a 1999 album.

Ex-BELIEVER members later founded SERAPH. Projects for drummer Joey Daub included FOUNTAIN OF TEARS and the Fusion endeavour YEAR OF PLENTY. In April of 2005 it was learned that Daub and Bachman were working up new material for a possible BELIEVER comeback. That same month, re-issues of both 'Sanity Obscure' and 'Dimensions' albums through Retroactive Records would be slammed by Bachman, the musician claiming bonus tracks of live and demo material were unauthorised.

EXTRACTION FROM MORTALITY, REX Music 000-137-8902D (1989). Unite / Vile Hypocrisy / D.O.S. (Desolation Of Sodom) / Tormented / Shadow Of Death / Blemished Sacrifices / Not Even One / Extraction From Mortality / Stress.
SANITY OBSCURE, RC Records RC 9312 (1991). Sanity Obscure / Wisdoms Call / Non-Point / Idols Of Ignorance / Stop The Madness / Dies Irae (Day Of Wrath) / Dust To Dust / Like A Song.
DIMENSIONS, Roadrunner RR 9101-1 (1994). Gone / Future Mind / Dimentia / What Is But Cannot Be / Singularity / No Apology / Trilogy Of Knowledge: Intro—The Birth, Movement I: The Lie, Movement II: The Truth, Movement III: The Key.

BELLADONNA

NEW YORK, NY, USA — *Joey Belladonna (vocals), Al Romano (guitar), John McCoy (bass), Michael Sciotto (drums)..*

Joey Belladonna is known for his role fronting New York Thrashers ANTHRAX, between 1985 to 1992 recording ten albums, which sold over eight million copies worldwide. Following his high profile split from ANTHRAX, vocalist Joey Belladonna teamed up with ex-GILLAN, McCOY and MAMMOTH bassist John McCoy having initially been sounded out by guitarist Al Romano to team up. Michael Sciotto left New York based Melodic Rockers FROM THE FIRE to round out the line-up pieced together in July 1992. The band looked strong on paper, but split after a handful of recording sessions, Romano going onward to team up with the ailing ex-BADLANDS and BLACK SABBATH vocalist RAY GILLEN in SUN RED SUN. His place was taken by former TRASH BROADWAY man Joe Stump.

Belladonna then re-forged the band with ex-AXIOM and HIPPIE JET guitarist Darin Scott, bassist Joe Andrews and drummer Scott Schroeter. This line-up would record the eponymous 1995 debut album for the Belgian Mausoleum label. With steady rumours that Belladonna had ditched the trademark Thrash of ANTHRAX (he often cited JOURNEY as a great love) critics and fans were taken aback to discover the album was an uncompromisingly brutal piece of work. North American dates supporting MOTÖRHEAD ensued to promote the record.

Belladonna built up a fresh band unit, involving French guitarist Peter Scheithauer, of STREAM and KILLING MACHINE repute, bassist Fleisch and the W.A.S.P. credited Stet Howland on drums. Bad luck befell the band in the midst of recording a second album, 'Spells Of Fear', when the Mausoleum label collapsed. Ultimately BELLADONNA would fold. Scott teamed up with BULLETBOYS drummer Robby Karras in an act titled PAIN INC. Scheithauer and Howland duly teamed up with W.A.S.P. bassist Mike Duda on the 2000 KILLING MACHINE album.

Some of the results of the ill-fated second round of recordings undertaken by BELLADONNA were released independently by the USG label in Europe and the Derock imprint in the USA during January 1999. Subsequent to this, the band was credited as comprising guitarist Darin Scott, bassist Joe Andrews and drummer Scott Schroeter. John McCoy is listed as playing bass on 'Two Face' and 'Injun'.

Stump founded JOE STUMP'S REIGN OF TERROR. Sciotto journeyed through stints with ACE FREHLEY and VICK LECAR. Scott would re-emerge with SPIDER BABYS, a band comprising of vocalist Gerry Schad, bassist Jeff Beebe and FOUR LARGE MEN drummer Mike Merrifield. In late 2002 plans for a third BELLADONNA studio album '03', the singer working with FUTURE DRIVEN's Matt Zuber, would be revealed. In October 2003 it was revealed that ex-BELLADONNA six-stringer Peter Scheithauer had joined PUSHED, the Californian Metal band assembled by ex-SLAYER, EVIL DEAD and TESTAMENT drummer Jon Dette. The following year, after Dette's departure from HAVOCHATE, the two united once more, forming up a new band unit in league with vocalist Dave Pullaro and the former SYSTEMATIC and MY RUIN credited bassist Johnny Chow.

BELLADONNA would support W.A.S.P. on dates in August 2004 before Canadian headline shows in September. That same month it was announced that Belladonna was to form up part of ex-RATT singer STEPHEN PEARCY's much vaunted 'Bastards of Metal' tour as announcement revealed plans to include a roster of Pearcy, Belladonna, KEEL and IRONHORSE frontman Ron Keel, the BULLETBOYS Marq Torien and Jason McMaster of DANGEROUS TOYS and WATCHTOWER. Also on the billing would be DROP and STS. Later that year, Belladonna issued the retrospective 'Artifacts 1' collection, comprising unreleased material dating to 1993. These songs found the singer fronting a band unit of guitarist Paul Crook, bass player Paul Mocci and drummer Jeff Tortora.

Following much rumour, Belladonna joined the 'Classic' pre-1987 line-up of ANTHRAX for European festivals and the US 'Ozzfest' events. It would be learned in early 2005 that former BELLADONNA guitarist Peter Scheithauer had convened a brand new band unit entitled ENEMY OF GOD with two bona fide Thrash veterans. This alliance found the bassist partnered with Jon Dette on drums, MEGADETH and F5 bassist Dave Ellefson and Todd Barnes of 13-A on vocals. By April, with Dette being replaced by Scheithauer's erstwhile BELLADONNA colleague Stet Howland, this project had morphed into TEMPLE OF BRUTALITY.

Joey Belladonna opted out of the ANTHRAX reunion in January 2007 and immediately set up solo shows.

BELLADONNA, Mausoleum 904170-2 (1995). Blunt Man / Power Trip / Rob You Blind / Perfection / Two Face / Down & Out / R.I.P. / Last Call / Nothing To Hide / Taken By Force / Injun / Mixed Emotions / 1-900.

SPELLS OF FEAR, USG 1029-2 (1999). Stress Your Mind / Lost Control / Jokin' / Bad Memories / How Would You Know / Ultimate Threat / Don't Pin Me Down / Face You / Phony / Out Of Gas / I Don't Need / Cover Me / Long Way Down.

03, (2003). Never Safe / Can't Erase It / Movin' On / Rejecting You / Live Up To You / One By One / Crimes Of Passion / Never Let You Down / Not Buyin' / How's It Gonna Be / Free Me.

BENEATH

FALKÖPING, SWEDEN — *Hebbe (vocals), Johan Darius (guitar), Daniel Josefsson (guitar), Emil Kyrk (bass), Mats Andreas Törnebohm (drums).*

BENEATH are Falköping Thrash merchants dating to late 1994. As an opening quartet of vocalist (and United Nations soldier) Hebbe with guitarists Johan Darius and Daniel Josefsson alongside drummer Mats Andreas Törnebohm the formative band honed their craft on BLACK SABBATH, KISS and SLAYER cover tunes but would cut an inaugural demo, entitled 'Black Rain', in December of 1994. In January of 1995 BENEATH tackled their debut live performance at the Assembly Hall in Karleby. They would induct bassist Emil Kyrk for a gig at the Amnesty International benefit at Folkets Park in Falköping.

Their next demo recordings, billed as 'Earn', were conducted at Musikmaffian in Varberg during October 1995 with Mojje Andersson acting as engineer. Entering into the 1996 'Musik Direkt' talent competition the band unfortunately scored little praise from the judges. Putting the band's progress in jeopardy, Hebbe then departed but would return in the Summer of 1997 as BENEATH had been unable to locate a replacement. A valuable piece of exposure came with the inclusion of the track 'Ins(h)ide' on the 'Swallow This' compilation album released by Phyramid Productions in late 1997.

An early 1998 support to SACRAMENTUM in Falköping would precede recording of a second demo tape at The Chapel in Torbjörntorp. Further gigs then ensued, including a show at the 'Marathon' festival in Falköping in August. A fourth demo, 'Everything Ends' once again laid down at The Chapel, saw Nisse Karlén of SACRAMENTUM and LORD BELIAL contributing guest vocals and Lisa Sydhagen adding her skills on both vocals and violin. However, with Törnebohm taking time out to travel the world, BENEATH would be put into stasis for four months.

An October 1999 support to LOBOTOMY at the Tre Backar venue in Stockholm would be Darius' last with the group. Martin Joelsson of SOULFRACTURE, HELL N' DIESEL and MASHEENARY stepped in as replacement. This new line-up opened for ABANDON and put in a gig at the 'Younomia' festival in Skövde in January 2000 before heading back into the recording studio for more demos entitled 'Demon Seed', this time with engineer Mattias Jarlhed. Another break in activities was forced as Hebbe left to serve in Kosovo between April and October.

BENEATH marked a return with their second 'Younomia' event appearance in February of 2001. The track 'Killed In The Womb' surfaced on the local compilation album 'Poesi, Musik & Fullt Ös, Falköping' that Summer. Joelsson exited in the Autumn, his successor being none other than original member Johan Darius. Regrouped, BENEATH duly crafted the October 2002 'Time Hysteria' demo.

Daniel Josefsson would join Stockholm's Death Metal combo MYNJUN in 2003. Johan Darius produced a 2004 solo demo 'Solar Plexus' whilst Hebbe saw further UN duty in Liberia. Guitarist Johan Darius recorded a solo album, 'Håll Mig Hårt', for July 2005 issue.

After eleven years of operation BENEATH folded in 2006. Emil Kyrk focussed on HELL N' DIESEL whilst Mats Andreas Törnebohm joined Borås band KENTAUR. Hebbe united with Falköping based GARAGE & SPEEDWAY.

Black Rain, Beneath (1994) (Demo).

Earn, Beneath (1995) (Demo). Earn / Apprentice To Fashion / Disfunctional / ... And It's You.

The Weight We Carry, Beneath (1998) (Demo). The Weight We Carry (Intro) / Burning Mask / Doze / Slain / Serpents / Mourning Sun.

Everything Ends, Beneath (1999) (Demo). The Faltering / Dissenter / Thy Game / Vengeance I Breathe / Everything Ends.

Demon Seed, Beneath (2000) (Demo). Forever Lost / Bitter Sweet / Demon Seed / Indifference / Killed In The Womb.

Time Hysteria, Beneath (2002) (Demo). Tides Of Time / Entrapment / Reasons Undefined / Time Hysteria.

BENEDICTION

BIRMINGHAM, WEST MIDLANDS, UK — *Dave Ingram (vocals), Darren Brookes (guitar), Peter Rew (guitar), Frank Healy (bass),*

BENEDICTION

Ian Treacy (drums).

A Birmingham act formed in February 1989, BENEDICTION is sadly more noted in their home country for having supplied vocalist Mark 'Barney' Greenway to NAPALM DEATH than their musical achievements. However, outside of Britain, BENEDICTION, affectionately known in their home city as "The Bennies", have garnered a sizeable following through ever improving albums and constant touring.

The group, borne out of an earlier band entitled STILLBORN, debuted with 'The Dreams You Dread' demo in June 1989 which secured the band a deal with German label Nuclear Blast, a stable base of operations for the band to the present day. The opening formation found Greenway backed by guitarists Peter Rewinski and Darren Brookes, bassist Paul Adams with Ian Treacy on the drums. The inaugural audio generated by this union came with a split 7" single, 'Confess All Goodness', shared with Austrian gore-mongers PUNGENT STENCH. From the outset it was clear that the group was intent on breaking down genre stereotypes, effortlessly amalgamating Thrash and Death stylings, capping mid-paced, low end rumblings with Greenways effective, if thoroughly indecipherable, roar.

Following the release of the September 1990 first album, entitled 'Subconscious Terror' and co-produced by the band together with NAPALM DEATH's Mick Harris, Dave Ingram stepped in for Greenaway on vocals and contributed to promotion activity during the year which included British supports to PARADISE LOST and AUTOPSY.

The band undertook a further British tour opening for BOLT THROWER prior to recording their follow up at Silverbirch Studios in Birmingham, the Paul Johnston produced effort 'The Grand Leveller', this outing seeing BOLT THROWER's Karl Willetts guesting on the track 'Jumping At Shadows' and closing out with a rendition of CELTIC FROST's 'Return To The Eve'. Before the record came out the band undertook further headlining dates throughout 12 countries, capitalised on by selected British and German dates upon its release. 1991 shows included gigs with label mates DISMEMBER and MASSACARA.

At the dawn of 1992 BENEDICTION hit the road once more with BOLT-THROWER on a bill including ASPHYX that enabled the band to embark on the 'World Violation' world tour across the European continent, the USA, Canada and also played a date in Tel Aviv, Israel. In October BENEDICTION released the 'Dark Is The Season' EP, which featured a reworking of the old ANVIL chestnut 'Forged In Fire' with former singer Barney Greenway guesting. The group endured another line-up change when bassist Paul Adams departed, BENEDICTION favouring ex-CEREBRAL FIX man Frank Healy to take his place.

The April 1993 album 'Transcend The Rubicon' opened up more new ground as the band tackled a one take studio jam of THE ACCUSED's 'At the Wrong Side of the Grave' and reworked the songs 'Artefacted Irreligion' and 'Spit Forth The Dead' from the 'Subconscious Terror' sessions. BENEDICTION topped the bill of a European tour with ATHEIST and CEMETERY as support. Dates included visits to Ireland, Portugal and Mexico. BENEDICTION, backed by an interim EP 'The Grotesque / Ashen Epitaph', supported BOLT THROWER on their American club tour, but found themselves as headliners on latter dates as problems hit BOLT THROWER forcing their withdrawal. BENEDICTION also appeared at the legendary Milwaukee Metalfest during the same year, on a bill alongside fellow heavyweights BIOHAZARD and SLAYER. The travelling cost the group the services of drummer Ian Treacy though, the skinsman quitting and being superseded by the 18 year old Neil Hutton in time for the Nuclear Blast New Year festivals in January 1995. 'The Dreams You Dread' arrived in June, being promoted with a European trek aligned with DEATH.

That Year Neil Hutton and Dave Ingram formed the side project WARLORD UK, releasing the 'Maximum Carnage' album on Nuclear Blast in 1996. The album included covers of AMEBIX and SLAYER songs.

Frontman Dave Ingram lent a helping hand to BOLT THROWER for a batch of live dates during 1997, when their vocalist Martin Van Drunen bailed out without warning. However, the 'helping hand' turned out to be more permanent and BENEDICTION promptly pulled in Dave Hunt to fill the vacated vocal position. BENEDICTION's March 1998 album 'Grind Bastard', the first to have erstwhile SABBAT guitarist Andy Sneap in control of the faders, ambitiously included covers of both JUDAS PRIEST's 'Electric Eye' and TWISTED SISTER's 'Destroyer'. Digipack variants hosted another cover, in 'We Are the League' originally by the ANTI-NOWHERE LEAGUE. Once again the group forged a touring partnership with DEATH, Chuck Schuldiner's last live expedition, prior to uniting with Norwegian Black Metal combo IMMORTAL.

BENEDICTION would make a return with the September 2001 record 'Organised Chaos' once again produced by Andy Sneap. Road work had the band in familiar company, co-headlining a January 2002 European expedition with BOLT THROWER backed up by FLESHCRAWL. Once these commitments had been fulfilled drummer Neil Hutton opted out to join STAMPIN' GROUND. In September 2004 the band headed up the 'Thunderstorm Over Europe' tour allied with GODHATE and NOMINON. The group also rendered their interpretation of SLAYER's 'Necrophiliac' for the 2004 Blackened tribute album 'Slatanic Slaughter'.

In early 2005 the band announced the high profile addition of CRADLE OF FILTH, LOCK UP and DIMMU BORGIR drummer Nick Barker to the ranks. Barker made his live debut with the band at Austria's 'Devil Days' festival on 10th June. Initial recordings laid down by the new formation included a cover version of SACRILEGE's 'Lifeline' including the guesting BOLT THROWER duo of vocalist Karl Willetts and guitarist Barry Thompson.

Nuclear Blast once again handled the 2006 BENEDICTION album, 'Killing Music'. In April the band revealed they had laid down studio cover versions of 'Seeing Through My Eyes' by BROKEN BONES, 'Into the Void' by BLACK SABBATH, and 'Banned from the Pubs' by PETER & THE TEST TUBE BABIES. In early May the band announced a temporary suspension of activities due to Nick Barker breaking his foot in what was described as "an incident in Estonia".

Despite working up new album tracks in early 2007 BENEDICTION band members would be involved in a variety of outside activities. Nicholas Barker would be helping out TESTAMENT on their live dates, Dave Hunt contributing vocals to both MISTRESS and ANAAL NATHRAKH whilst Frank Healy was playing bass in the reformed CEREBRAL FIX, sessioning for ANAAL NATHRAKH and instigating side project THE BURNING DEITIES.

The Dreams You Dread, (1990) (Demo). Experimental Stage / Subconscious Terror / Artifacted Irreligion / Bonesaw.

Confess All Goodness, Nuclear Blast NB 031 (1990) (Split 7" single with PUNGENT STENCH). Confess All Goodness.

SUBCONSCIOUS TERROR, Nuclear Blast NB033 (1990). Intro-Portal To Your Phobias / Subconscious Terror / Artefacted Irreligion / Grizzled Finale / Eternal Eclipse / Experimental Stage / Suspended Animation / Divine Ultimatum / Spit Forth The Dead / Confess All Goodness.

THE GRAND LEVELLER, Nuclear Blast NB048 (1991). Vision In The Shroud / Graveworm / Jumping At Shadows / Opulence Of The Absolute / Child Of Sin / Undirected Aggression / Born In A Fever / The Grand Leveller / Senile Dementia / Return To Eve.

Experimental Stage, Nuclear Blast NB 057 (1992). Experimental Stage / The Grand Leveller / Senile Dementia.

Return To The Eve, Nuclear Blast NB 058PDS (1992). Return To The Eve / The Grand Leveller / Senile Dementia.

Dark Is The Season EP, Nuclear Blast NB 059 (1992). Foetus Noose / Forged In Fire / Dark Is The Season / Jumping At Shadows / Experimental Stage.

Wrong Side Of The Grave, Nuclear Blast (1993) (7" picture disc). Wrong Side Of The Grave / Artefacted Religion / Spit Forth The dead.

TRANSCEND THE RUBICON, Nuclear Blast NB073 (1993). Unfound Mortality / Nightfear / Paradox Alley / Bow To None / Painted Skulls / Violation Domain / Face Without Soul / Bleakhouse / Blood From Stone / Wrong Side Of The Grave / Artefacted-spit Forth.

The Grotesque / Ashen Epitaph, Nuclear Blast NB 088-2 (1994). The Grotesque / Ashen Epitaph / Violation Domain (Live) / Subconscious Terror (Live) / Visions In The Shroud (Live).

THE DREAMS YOU DREAD, Nuclear Blast NB120 (1995). Down on Whores (Leave Them All For Dead) / Certified …? / Soulstream / Where Flies Are Born / Answer To Me / Griefgiver / Denial / Negative Growth / Path Of The Serpent / Saneless Theory / The Dreams You Dread.

GRIND BASTARD, Nuclear Blast (1998). Deadfall / Agonised / West Of Hell / Magnificat (Irenicon) / Nervebomb / Electric Eye / Grind Bastard / Shadow World / Bodiless / Carcinova Angel / We The Freed / Destroyer / I.

ORGANISED CHAOS, Nuclear Blast NB0522 (2001). Suicide Rebellion / Stigmata / Suffering Feeds Me / Diary Of A Killer / The Temple Of Set / Nothing On The Inside / Easy Way To Die / Don't Look In The Mirror / This Graveyard Earth / Charon / I Am The Disease / Organised Chaos.

BESTIAL DESECRATION

BALINGEN, GERMANY — *Infernal Overkiller (vocals), Avenger (guitar), Pork (bass), Bestial Agressor (drums).*

Balingen Thrash Metal endeavour BESTIAL DESECRATION is one of a long line of Metal projects for Avenger (a.k.a. Daniel Cichos), with his other associations including acts such as VARGHKOGHARGASMAL, EXORCISM, ANGEL OF DAMNATION, NECROSLAUGHTER, FRONT BEAST, POLTERGEIST, STORMHUNTER, SZARLEM and WITCHSLAUGHTER.

Founded during 1997, formative band members would include Tobias Dauenhauer, of MORRIGAN, CHANT OF BLASPHEMY and TEPHERET repute, and ex-MAYHEMIC TRUTH and MORRIGAN man Jörg Schmidt. First product was a 1998 demo 'Death And Destruction'. A second cassette, 'Hell Strikes Back', featured a cover version of DESTRUCTION's 'Total Desaster'. Third demo 'Live In Purgatory', also arriving during 1999 sported further cover versions in ANAL CUNT's 'Guy Lombardo' and 'Unbelievable', DESTRUCTION's 'Total Desaster' and MACABRE's 'What's The Smell'. Only 50 copies were issued.

Deathstrike Records released the 'Soldiers Of Death' EP in 2000 as a restricted run of 600 copies. BESTIAL DESECRATION folded in 2001. During 2005 the Iron Fist Kommando imprint put out a split demo collection entitled 'Thrashing Rage' partnered with NOCTURNAL.

Death And Destruction, Bestial Desecration (1998) (Demo). Introstruction / Bestial Desecration / Tormented By Evil / Revenge Of The Demon Lord / Antichrist / Death And Destruction.

Hell Strikes Back, Bestial Desecration (1999) (Demo. Limited edition 200 copies). Hail The Gods Of Destruction / Infernal Overkill / Come With Us To Hell / Nightmare / Legions Of Chaos / Attack Of The Metal Hellstorm / Hell Strikes Back / Total Desaster.

Live In Purgatory, Bestial Desecration (1999) (Demo). Intro / Hail The Gods Of Destruction / Infernal Overkill / Attack Of The Metal Hellstorm / Total Desaster / Chainsaw Carnage / Antichrist / Soldiers Of Death / Unbelievable / Guy Lombardo / What's The Smell.

Soldiers Of Death, Deathstrike (2000) (7' vinyl single. Limited edition 600 copies). Speed Metal Attack / Attack Of The Metal Hellstorm / Soldiers Of Death / Infernal Overkill / Hatefilled Metalrage.

Thrashing Rage, Iron Fist Kommando (2005) (Split demo cassette with NOCTURNAL). Merciless Murder (NOCTURNAL) / Nuclear Strike (NOCTURNAL) / Sign Of Evil (NOCTURNAL) / Satanic Oath (NOCTURNAL) / The Final End (NOCTURNAL) / Thrash Attack (NOCTURNAL) / Tormentor (NOCTURNAL) / Total Desaster (NOCTURNAL) / Infernal Overkill (BESTIAL DESECRATION) / Hellraiser (BESTIAL DESECRATION) / Hail The Gods Of Destruction (BESTIAL DESECRATION) / Soldiers Of Death (BESTIAL DESECRATION) / Graveyard Massacre (BESTIAL DESECRATION) / Speed Metal Attack (BESTIAL DESECRATION) / Hatefilled Metalrage (BESTIAL DESECRATION) / Tormentor (BESTIAL DESECRATION) / Chainsaw Carnage (BESTIAL DESECRATION) / Curse The Gods (BESTIAL DESECRATION) / Attack Of The Metal Hellstorm (BESTIAL DESECRATION).

BETRAYAL

SAN FRANCISCO, CA, USA — *Chris Ackerman (vocals), Marcus N. Colon (guitar), Bob McCue (guitar), Jeff Lain (bass), Jeff Mason (drums).*

A Bay Area Christian Thrash Metal act that arrived on the San Francisco scene with the 1989 demo session 'The Reviling Darkness'. For the 1991 debut 'Renaissance By Death', recorded in Chicago for Wonderland Records, BETRAYAL cited a line up of vocalist Chris Ackerman, erstwhile MARTYR guitarists Marcus N. Colon and Matt Maners, bass player Jeff Lain and drummer Brian Meuse.

By the sophomore 1993 effort 'The Passing' Maners and Meuse were out of the picture, new draftees being guitarist Bob McCue and drummer Jeff Mason. Also contributing on backing vocals would be DELIVERENCE vocalist Jimmy Brown and Chris Scott of PRECIOUS BLOOD.

Despite engendering a loyal fan base BETRAYAL folded in October of 1993. Post BETRAYAL both Colon and Mason would join the highly regarded Christian Thrash act DELIVERENCE.

During 2000 Colon and Maners resurrected the BETRAYAL title for the Gothic inclined solo effort 'Leaving Nevermore'. A compilation of BETRAYAL and MARTYR archive material 'The Passing Of Time' preceded a further Gothic / Industrial album 'In Remembrance Of Me'.

RENAISSANCE BY DEATH, Wonderland (1991). Renaissance By Death / The Invitation / Fallen Deceived / More Faith Than Me / Escaping The Altar / Assassin In The Midst / Mortal Flesh / Stroll Thru A Wicked Age / Prophets Of Baal / Plead The Blood.

THE PASSING, Wonderland (1993). Renouncement / The Usurper / Carnival Of Madness / Ichabod / Forest Of Horrors / Race Of Hypocrisy / As I Turned Away / Whispers Of Chaos / Strength Of The Innocent / Retaliatory Strike / Frantic.

LEAVING NEVERMORE, Black & White (2000).

THE PASSING OF TIME, Black & White (2001).

IN REMEMBRANCE OF ME, Black & White (2002).

BETRAYER

WINDSOR, ON, CANADA — *Jeff Klingbeil (vocals / guitar), Bill Lozon (guitar), Norm Michaud (bass), Shawn Herbert (drums).*

Windsor, Ontario Thrash Metal act. BETRAYER frontman Jeff Klingbeil has prior membership credits with outfits such as WASTED YOUTH, CORNERSTONE, GUTTER HELMET and SWARM. Drummer Shawn Herbert ('Shawn Christopher Phillip Joseph Alphonse Sebastien Hebert-Bastien') also cites SWARM, CORNERSTONE and GUTTER HELMET as past affiliations.

As SWARM the band switched titles to BETRAYER during 1999 after discovering a swathe of other acts globally laying claim to the same title. Bassist Vince Manzerolle decamped in early 2000, paving the way for Norm Michaud ('Normand Gerard Joseph Alexander Michaud II') who had also been active with SWARM as well as DEUS EX MACHINA, BATTERY and RECKONING. In September of that same year guitarist Warren Kyle Rawlins opted out. Guitarist Bill Lozon joined BETRAYER in the Spring of 2001.

The band notably supported IRON MAIDEN, DIO and MOTÖRHEAD in 2003 and issued the 'Shadowed Force' EP in February 2005.

RUSTED ICONS, (2000). Descendents Of Death / Fire To The Coals / Tribulation / Waiting / Wretched Ways / Captive State Of Mind / Sands Of Time / Rusted Icons.

Shadowed Force, (2005). Partaker Of Evil / Burden Of The Pacifist / Shadowed Force.

BEYOND THE EMBRACE

NEW BEDFORD, MA, USA — *Shawn Gallagher (vocals), Alex Botelho (guitar), Oscar Gouveia (guitar), Jeff Saude (guitar), Adam Gonsalves (bass), Mike Bresciani (drums).*

An extreme yet melodic Metal six piece unit out of New Bedford, Massachusetts. BEYOND THE EMBRACE, founded by lead vocalist Shawn Gallagher and lead guitarist Oscar Gouveia in January of 2000, fuse retro Bay Area Thrash style persuasions with cutting edge Death Metal bolstered by the enhanced delivery of three guitars. Originally the pack of Gouveia, guitarists Jeff Saude and Alex Botelho, drummer Mike Bresciani and Fil Aroujo had been together as the act PARANORMAL. Regrouping, with Adam Gonsalves coming onboard as bassist, the new band debuted with a 1999 three song demo, which included a rendition of IRON MAIDEN's 'The Trooper', soon catching the ear of Metal Blade Records.

BEYOND THE EMBRACE would part ways with drummer Mike Bresciani shortly after recording their debut album for Metal Blade Records. He would be replaced by former VOICES FORMING WEAPONS and ROSWELL man Kevin Camille. The band would form up part of the fifth annual summer 2002 'Death Across America' dates headlined by KATAKLYSM and backed up by DIVINE EMPIRE and MISERY INDEX. In May of 2003 the band tagged onto the closing half of the US OPETH and LACUNA COIL nationwide tour.

BEYOND THE EMBRACE introduced former MARAZINE man Chris Parlon on bass in April of 2004. The band, promoting the 'Insect Song' album through Metal Blade, set out on tour with this new formation in May as openers to PRONG, however, gigs in Baltimore and Binghampton, New York were cancelled as Shawn Gallagher was afflicted with a throat infection. High profile Summer gigs had the band opening for ICED EARTH and TRIVIUM. Unfortunately the band was put out of commission yet again when guitarist Jeff Saude broke his leg onstage at a festival in July. Suffering still further, the guitarist then was hospitalized for two weeks due to a blood clot and a case of pneumonia.

BEYOND THE EMBRACE teamed up with BYZANTINE and CHILDREN OF TRAGEDY for the 'Sofa King Metal' tour commencing 24th September at the Sound Factory in Charleston, West Virginia. Unfortunately the group had to withdraw from the latter portion of this trek due to a combination of factors including getting rid of their van, having the replacement van in for repairs whilst their drummer was rushed to hospital to treat a serious infection in his foot.

2005 found Oscar Gouveia gaining production credits on the debut TRANSFIX demo. US dates scheduled for March of 2005 had the band partnered with INTO ETERNITY, SINGLE BULLET THEORY and headlining Finns AMORPHIS. A further announced short run of dates in June had the group in union with CRISIS and M.O.D. but the band pulled out of these shows before the tour kicked off. In September BEYOND THE EMBRACE acted as support to the Swedish Operatic Metal band THERION. November witnessed a line-up change as BEYOND THE EMBRACE parted ways with longtime drummer Kevin Camille. The following month KAGE's Steve Bolognese was announced as replacement.

The group backed noted Norwegian Progressive Metal band GREEN CARNATION for a run of US gigs throughout March 2006. Drummer Steve Bolognese joined Canadian band INTO ETERNITY in December.

AGAINST THE ELEMENTS, Metal Blade (2002). Bastard Screams / Mourning In Magenta / Compass / Rapture / Drowning Sun / Against The Elements / Release / The Bending Sea / Embers Astray / The Riddle Of Steel.

INSECT SONG, Metal Blade (2004). Fleshengine Breakdown / Plague / My Fall / ... Of Every Strain / Redeemer / Insect Song / Ashes / Weak And The Wounded / Absent / Within.

BIOHAZARD

NEW YORK, NY, USA — *Evan Seinfeld (vocals / bass), Billy Graziadei (guitar), Bobby Hambel (guitar), Danny Schuler (drums).*

Brooklyn's "Thrash-Rap" act BIOHAZARD was formed in 1988 by vocalist / bassist Evan Seinfeld and guitarist Billy Graziadei. The former has also notably carved himself an extracurricular career in the porn industry, billed as 'Spyder Jones' and working exclusively with his wife adult film superstar Tera Patrick. Early BIOHAZARD shows included opening for EXODUS at L'Amours club. Their first demo caused something of a stir with some journalists, completely ignoring the fact that both Seinfeld and drummer Danny Schuler are Jewish, feeling that the band's lyrics allegedly displayed certain fascist and white supremacist views, something strenuously denied by the band.

A debut album arrived on the Maze label in 1990, followed up by 'Urban Discipline', produced by Wharton Tiers at Fun City Studios, in October 1992 for the Roadrunner label. Digipak versions added live versions of 'Shades Of Grey' and 'Punishment'. At this juncture BIOHAZARD were yet to break out of Brooklyn, with all the band members still holding down day jobs, Graziadei as a truck driver, Seinfeld delivering building materials whilst Schuler worked in a stockroom. 'Urban Discipline's timing proved fortuitous, the album not only breaking BIOHAZARD internationally but with their heady blend of Hip Hop and Hardcore, also serving to influence a whole new generation of up and coming bands. Radio hit 'Slam' would be given a new lease of life by Rap act ONYX, recorded with BIOHAZARD themselves. The ONYX / BIOHAZARD pairing duly united once again to cut the title track for the 'Judgment Night' movie soundtrack, selling over two million units in the USA. The 'Urban Discipline' album, spurred on by major MTV rotation for the video of 'Punishment' and support slots to KYUSS, HOUSE OF PAIN, FISHBONE and SICK OF IT ALL, eventually broke a global sales figure of one million copies.

Now with worldwide status, BIOHAZARD switched labels to the Warner Bros. corporation. 1994's 'State Of The World Address' broke the American top 50 and followed its predecessor by racking up a million sales. A single, 'How It Is', featured Sen Dog of CYPRESS HILL. Prior to their appearance at the KISS headlined UK Castle Donington 'Monsters Of Rock' festival in front of 45'000 people BIOHAZARD put in a secret warm up show at London's Garage venue together with FEAR FACTORY.

BIOHAZARD parted company with Hambel following the recording of the Dave Jerden co-produced 'Mata Leao' ("To kill the lion") with ex-HELMET and REST IN PIECES guitarist Rob Echeverria. Reportedly the band's focus would be distracted by internal struggles, drug dependency and alcohol abuse but BIOHAZARD, despite it all, remained a stable unit. Unfortunately, 'Mata Leao' did not match the sales of 'State Of The World Address'.

The band signed back to Roadrunner Records when 'Mata Leao' failed to live up to Warner Bros. Expectations. The 'No Holds Barred' live album kept up the pace. Included was a version of BLACK SABBATH's 'After Forever'. BIOHAZARD's April 1997 British tour saw support from MY OWN VICTIM and CONSUME. Seinfeld put in a guest appearance on Italian Hardcore act CRACKDOWN's 1998 debut 'Rise Up'.

Signing to the German Steamhammer label, BIOHAZARD issued a 2001 release 'Uncivilization', recorded at their own Rat Piss Studios located in downtown Brooklyn. Featured guests were the SEPULTURA duo of Derrick Green and Andreas Kisser on 'Trap' along with SEPULTURA band mate Igor Cavalera on 'Gone', CYPRESS HILL's Sen Dog on 'Last Man Standing', PANTERA's Phil Anselmo on the track 'H.H.F.K.' and TYPE O NEGATIVE mainman Pete Steele on 'Cross The Line'. Other guest appearances witnessed Roger Miret of AGNOSTIC FRONT and the SKARHEAD duo of Danny Diablo and Puerto Rican Mike on 'Unified' and HATEBREED's Jimmie Jasta and members of SLIPKNOT contributing to 'Domination'.

The band's European and UK tour, with support in the main from TATTOO, would be delayed by the September 11th World

BIOHAZARD

Trade Center disaster but quickly rescheduled for late September. The band would schedule an American set of headliners beginning 7th of November at Los Foufounes Electriques in Montreal. Both CLUTCH and CANDIRA were added to the billing on the 15th in New York.

March of 2002 brought the news that Billy Graziadei was pursuing a side venture in league with SEPULTURA drummer Igor Cavalera and Brazilian DJ Patife. Rumours were persistent throughout May that latest BIOHAZARD recruit guitarist Leo Curley previously with OUTLINE and ALL MEANS NECESSARY, had lost his position in the band. NUCLEUS guitarist Carmine Vincent, also a former BIOHAZARD roadie, would be swiftly confirmed as replacement. Meantime, Curley would prove far from idle, busying himself with NÄ$H, a brand new act that united ex-DOPE and present day PRIMER 55 man Preston Nash on vocals, guitars and percussion, Dirt of ANYTHING BUT NORMAL on bass guitar and STRAIGHTJACKET drummer Joe Clark.

Scheduled European festival dates, including the 'Bulldog Bash' in the UK, were cancelled when guitarist Carmello Vincent Matteliano underwent major surgery. The band nonetheless revealed an impressive package tour of Europe, dubbed the 'Eastpack Resistance' dates, during November and December of 2002 with BIOHAZARD topping a billing of AGNOSTIC FRONT, HATEBREED, DISCIPLINE, ALL BORO KINGS, DEATH THREAT, and BORN FROM PAIN. Guitarist Scott Roberts of the CRO-MAGS acted as stand in. BIOHAZARD drummer Danny Schuler would guest session on demo tracks for AMONG THIEVES in September.

Although having announced an album title of 'Never Forget, Never Forgive' and revealing cover artwork for their forthcoming album the band changed their minds within days of press announcements scrapping both title and cover ideas. The record was now entitled 'Kill Or Be Killed'. BIOHAZARD seemed set to get back onto the touring circuit in North America in January of 2003 forming up a line-up KITTIE, BRAND NEW SIN and EIGHTEEN VISIONS. The group announced Scott Roberts, of AMONG THIEVES and THE SPUDMONSTERS, as their permanent new guitarist. However, these shows would be abruptly curtailed when Seinfeld came down with a mystery illness.

With BIOHAZARD out of action Danny Schuler and Billy Graziadei engaged themselves as a mixing team for LIFE OF AGONY's comeback live album. Before long the band was back in action putting in Japanese headline dates in May followed up by the 'Jailhouse Rock' North American tour in June. These shows had BIOHAZARD headlining over HATEBREED, AGNOSTIC FRONT, THROWDOWN and FULL BLOWN CHAOS.

Demos circulating in New York during May would be attributed to frontman Evan Seinfeld's new Trip-Hop side venture SICK TRIPLE. As 2004 dawned Billy Graziadei unveiled a fresh side venture. In league with KITTIE bassist Jennifer Arroyo the band unit RODEK was summoned up, this outfit also including THE GROOVNIX vocalist Karl Bernholtz, guitarist AJ Marchetta and drummer Dan Lamagna. Graziadei would also be operating a Brazilian based venture entitled INK in alliance with vocalist Scream S., guitarist Covero, bass player T.J. and the TRETA, KORZUS, RODOX and PAVILHÃO 9 credited Fernando Schaefer on drums.

BIOHAZARD undertook recordings for a new album 'Means To An End' in late 2004. However, due to a "studio disaster", the completed record was apparently completely lost, forcing the band to completely re-record the opus. The record finally emerged in August 2005. On 15th December Evan Seinfeld and Billy Graziadei notably joined the ROADRUNNER UNITED conglomerate at the New York Nokia Theater for an all star Metal evening. The gig opened with BIOHAZARD's 'Punishment' performed by Seinfeld, Graziadei, SEPULTURA's Andreas Kisser, ex-FEAR FACTORY man Dino Cazares and SLIPKNOT's Joey Jordison on drums.

In early January 2006 drummer Danny Schuler announced his exit from BIOHAZARD and the formation of BLOODCLOT in a union with vocalist John Joseph of the CRO-MAGS, guitarist Scott Roberts from SPUDMONSTERS, CRO-MAGS and BIOHAZARD and SICK OF IT ALL and AGNOSTIC FRONT bassist Craig Setari.

In February Evan Seinfeld filmed a VH1 television series entitled 'Supergroup', a reality show also starring TED NUGENT, Scott Ian of ANTHRAX on guitar, vocalist SEBASTIAN BACH and Jason Bonham of BONHAM, UFO and FOREIGNER on drums. Meantime, founding BIOHAZARD guitarist Bobby Hambel re-emerged, breaking a ten year hiatus from the music scene, to record a new solo record. Later that year Seinfeld forged WHITE LINE FEVER, a Hard Rock band unit also featured guitarists Dirrty and Charlie D, bassist John Monte, of DRAGPIPE, MINDFUNK, MINISTRY, REVOLTING COCKS and M.O.D., and drummer Lee Nelson. In early 2007 this combo switched title to THE SPYDERZ.

Stomping Round The World, (1990).

BIOHAZARD, Maze MLP 1067 (1990). Retribution / Victory / Blue Blood / Howard Beach / Wrong Side Of The Tracks / Justified Violence / Skinny Song / Hold My Own / Panic Attack / Pain / Survival Of The Fittest / There And Back / Scarred For Life.

URBAN DISCIPLINE, Roadrunner RR 9112 (1992). Chamber Spins Three / Punishment / Shades Of Grey / Business / Black And White And Red All Over / Man With A Promise / Disease / Urban Discipline / Loss / Wrong Side Of The Tracks / Mistaken Identity / We're Only Gonna Die (From Our Arrogance) / Tears Of Blood / Hold My Own / Shades Of Grey (Live) / Punishment (Live).

Tales From The Hard Side, Warner Bros. 9362 41674-2 (1994). Tales From The Hard Side / State Of The World Address (Live) / Down For Life (Live) / Tales From The Hard Side (Live).

How It Is, Warner Bros. 9062 41750 2 (1994). How It Is / How It Is (Brooklyn Bootleg No. 2) / How It Is (Lethal House Of Pain mix) / How It Is (Lethal Instrumental). Chart position: 62 UK.

STATE OF THE WORLD ADDRESS, Warner Bros. 9362 45594-2 (1994). State Of The World Address / Down For Life / What Makes Us Tick / Tales From The Hard Side / How It Is / Remember / Five Blocks To The Subway / Each Day / Failed Territory / Lack Thee Of / Pride / Human Animal / Cornered / Love Denied / Ink. Chart positions: 48 USA, 72 UK.

Tales From The Hard Side, Warner Bros. W 0254 CD (1994). Tales From The Hard Side / Down For Life / State Of The World Address / Tales From The Hard Side (Video edit).

Tales From The Hard Side, Warner Bros. (1994). Tales From The Hard Side / Down For Life. Chart position: 47 UK.

How It Is, Warner Bros. W0259TE (1994). How It Is.

Five Blocks To The Subway Tour EP, Warner Bros. 9362435082 (1995). Five Blocks To The Subway / Down For Life (Live) / State Of The World Address (Live) / Tales From The Hard Side (Live) / Five Blocks To The Subway (Live).

MATA LEAO, Warner Bros. 9362-46208-2 (1996). These Eyes / Stigmatized / Control / Cleansing / Better Days / Gravity / A Lot To Learn / Waitin' To Die / Away / True Strengths / Thorn / In Vain. Chart positions: 72 UK, 170 USA.

NO HOLDS BARRED (LIVE), Roadrunner RR 8803-2 (1997). Shades Of Grey / What Makes Us Tick / Authority / Urban Discipline / Modern Democracy / Business / Tales From The Hardside / Better Days / Victory / Lot To Learn / How It Is / After Forever / Tears Of Blood / Chamber Spins Three / Wrong Side Of The tracks / Waiting To Die / These Eyes / Punishment / Hold My Own.

NEW WORLD DISORDER, Polygram 546032 (1999). Resist / Switchback / Salvation / End Of My Rope / All For None / Breakdown / Inner Fear On / Abandon In Place / Skin / Camouflage / Decline / Cycle Of Abuse / Dogs Of War / New World Disorder. Chart position: 187 USA.

TALES FROM THE B-SIDE, Orchard 801120 (2001). Three Point Back / Falling / Sumptin' To Prove (Demo) / Slam (Remix) / Beaten / How It Is (Remix) / Sadman / Enslaved / Judgement Night / Inhale / Piece Of Mind / Shades Of Grey (Demo) / Punishment (Demo).

UNCIVILIZATION, Sanctuary 84519 (2001). Sellout / Uncivilization / Wide Awake / Get Away / Unified / Gone / Letter Go / Last Man Standing / H.F.F.K. / Domination / Trap / Plastic / Cross The Line. Chart position: 53 GERMANY.

KILL OR BE KILLED, Steamhammer SPV 08574782 (2002). Heads Kicked In / Penalty / World On Fire / Dead To Me / Kill Or Be Killed / Never Forgive, Never Forget / Hallowed Ground / Open Your Eyes / Make My Stand / Beaten Senseless.

MEANS TO AN END, Steamhammer SPV 085-69882 CD (2005). My Life, My Way / The Fire Burns Inside / Killing To Be Free / Filled With Hate / Devotion / Break It Away From Me / Kings Never Die / Don't Stand Alone / To The Grave / Set Me Free.

BIOMECHANICAL

UK — *John K. (vocals), Chris Webb (guitar), Jamie Hunt (guitar), Jon Collins (bass), Matt C. (drums).*

BIOMECHANICAL, founded in 2001 and bowing in with the 'Distorted' demo, released an October 2003 debut album, 'Eight Moons', through Revolver Records. The group is fronted by the DECEPTOR and BALANCE OF POWER credited Greek native John K. (a.k.a. Yiannis Koutselinis). BIOMECHANICAL Gained valuable exposure when they were hand picked to headline the second stage at the 'Bloodstock' festival.

The band signed a four-album deal with Elitist/Earache Records in November 2004, ushering in 2005 with the sophomore album 'Empire Of The Worlds'. John K relinquished his role in BALANCE OF POWER during February 2005 to prioritise BIOMECHANICAL. The band filmed a promotional video for the track 'The Empires Of The Worlds' with director Adam Mason in late April. The following month BIOMECHANICAL recorded a four song session for BBC Radio and in June grabbed valuable supports to SHADOWS FALL. September saw further supports, this time to STAMPIN' GROUND.

2006 UK shows partnered with Earache label mates DECAPITATED found BOWLRIDER's Dom Lawson standing in as temporary bassist. The band, working with producer Chris Tsangarides, recorded a cover version of JUDAS PRIEST's 'Painkiller' at Ecology Studios in October. The tracks was added as a bonus song on a re-issue of 'The Empires Of The Worlds' in November. That same month and into December the group supported EXODUS in Europe.

BIOMECHANICAL supported Canadian metallers 3 INCHES OF BLOOD on their UK tour in March 2007.

Distorted, Biomechanical (2001). The Awakening / Do You Know Me / In The Core Of Darkness / Distorted.

EIGHT MOONS, Revolver REVXD242 (2003). The Awakening / Do You Know Me / In The Core Of Darkness / Distorted / Hunted / No Shadows / Eight Moons / Save Me / Point Of No Return.

EMPIRES OF THE WORLD, Elitist (2005). Enemy Within / The Empires Of The Worlds / Assaulter / Relinquished Destiny / Long Time Dead / Regenerated / DNA Metastesis / Survival / Existenz / Truth Denied / Absolution: Part 1—Final Offence / Absolution: Part 2—From The Abyss / Absolution: Part 3—Absolution / Absolution: Part 4—Disintegration.

BIOMECHANICAL

BITTERNESS

KONSTANZ, GERMANY — *Frank Urschler (vocals / guitar), Alex Hinterberger (guitar), Sebastian Jehle (bass), Andreas Kiechle (drums).*

Konstanz Thrashers BITTERNESS are rooted in the prior band formation STEEL TORMENTOR, an act featuring guitarist Frank Urschler and drummer Andreas Kiechle that issued the demos 'Fallen Angel' in 1999 and 'Storms Of Anger' in 2000. Bass guitarist Sebastian Jehle had also been employed briefly in STEEL TORMENTOR. The band's opening demo '… And Death Marches On' would be cut in October of 2001. They would also re-record the STEEL TORMENTOR track 'Feel The Flame' for inclusion on the compilation album 'Reaper Comes'.

BITTERNESS recorded the 'Dawn Of Golden Blood' demo in March of 2002. A track from these sessions, 'T.H.R.A.S.H.', would be donated to the 'Reaper Comes II' sampler. The band augmented its guitar quota with the introduction of Alex Hinterberger during November of 2002.

The album 'Sweet Suicide Solutions' of March 2003, a self financed effort, closed out with a cover version of SEPULTURA's 'Troops Of Doom'. Touring across Belgium, Germany and Switzerland saw BITTERNESS united with road partners Austrians THIRD MOON and Swiss act ALIEN GATES. The positive press afforded the album and the tour would then lead to a deal with the German G.U.C. label for a four track 7" single, 'Marching Towards Infinity', released in March of 2004. Heavy Horses Records also weighed in with a picture disc single featuring 'Eve Of Destruction' and a live recording of 'Sentenced To Live'.

European shows in October and November 2005 saw the band packaged with NOISE FOREST, MIDWINTER and GRAVE-

WORM.

SWEET SUICIDE SOLUTIONS, Independent (2003). Architects Of The Apocalypse / Burden Of Past / Eve Of Destruction / The Last Dance / Embrace The Depression / Beyond A Subconscious World / Portal Of Haunting Dreams / Sweet Suicide Solution / Twinkling Red Tears / Chain Of Command / Troops Of Doom.
Eve Of Destruction, Heavy Horses HR 001 (2004) (Picture disc). Eve Of Destruction / Sentenced To Live (Live).
Marching Towards Infinity, G.U.C. GUC 010-04 (2004). Nighttime Solitude / Crimson Serenade / Marching Towards Infinity / Utopia: Life.

BK 49

GERMANY — *Bernd Reiners (vocals), Arne Berents (guitar), Klaus Kessemeier (guitar), Patrick Feist (bass), Marc-Andrée Dieken (drums).*

Thrashers BK49 came together in 1996, assembled by the erstwhile ASSORTED HEAP trio of guitarist Klaus Kessemeier, bass player Joachim 'Lord' Meyer and drummer Thomas Marter alongside PAIN FOR PLEASURE personnel singer Bernd Reiners and guitarist Arne Berents. The band soon got into the thick of the action with the 'Boiled Blood' demo. In October of 1997 both Meyer and Marter exited, BK 49 substituting them with ex-KING CARRION man Patrick Feist on bass and drummer Frank Reiners. This unit cut the self financed 'Zombified' album.

Marc-Andrée "Mücke" Dieken, of OBSCENITY and PAIN FOR PLEASURE repute, superseded Reiners in April of 2002.

ZOMBIFIED, Independent (1999). Final Conflict / Attack Of The Vampire / Zombified / Hell Is Just A Word / Cemetery Slaughter / Trapped In Eternity / R U Morbid?
JOIN THE DEAD, Grind It! G-IT005 (2003). I'll Dig Your Grave / Fleshripping Horror / Death Is The Crown Of Creation / Assembly Of Souls / House On Massgrave Hill / Join The Dead / Funeral March / Morbid Funeral / Buried But Not Deep Enough.

BLACKEND

SINSHEIM, GERMANY — *Michael Goldschmidt (vocals / guitar), Manuel Unterhuber (guitar), Mario Unterhuber (bass), Alex Mayer (drums).*

Out and out Thrashers founded in Sinsheim during their early teens during 1991. At first BLACKEND crafted their skill as a covers band honouring their Bay Area favourites. The demo 'Contrast Of Minds' led to a debut tech-Thrash album 'Sloth' in 1997. This outing scored BLACKEND a deal with the Massacre label for the 1999 'Mental Game Messiah' album.

The band unsurprisingly donated cover versions to two of their mentors tribute albums with renditions of '... And Justice For All' appearing on the METALLICA collection 'Phantom Lords' and TESTAMENT's 'Practice What You Preach' on the tribute offering 'Jump Into The Pit'.

BLACKENED folded during October of 2001. Bassist Mario Unterhuber soon teamed up with LOONATIKK for live work.

Michael Goldschmidt announced a welcome resurrection of BLACKENED during May 2002 alongside new members guitarist Chick, bass player Ananda and drummer Trondt.

SLOTH, MDD 12CD (1997). Harmonies In Black / No More Confidence / Regression / Not To Deny / Separate / Retaliation Breed / Parts Of Peril / Virtual / Streams Of Perfection.
MENTAL GAME MESSIAH, Massacre MAS CD0218 (1999). The Eye Of The Observer / Detect The Crack / Mental Game Messiah / Burn The Fuse / Beyond Forever / Liquid Surroundings / Freezing The Skin / Save Our Souls / Scars Cant Tell / As The Sun Remains.
DEMO'95, Gutter (1999) (Split album with LOONATIKK). Absent-Minded / None / Lost Imaginations / Voices Of Reality.
The Eye Of The Observer, Massacre (1999) (German promotion release). The Eye Of The Observer / Freezing The Skin / As The Sun Remains.
THE LAST THING UNDONE, Massacre MAS CD0275 (2001). The Last Thing Undone / I Am The Chosen One / The More I Lie / Long Now / Exclude The Included / Darkest Day / The Dice Is Cast / Battle Between Minds.

BLACKSTAR

UK — *Jeff Walker (vocals / guitar), Carlo Regadas (guitar), Mark Griffiths (guitar), Ken Owen (drums).*

As CARCASS, the originators of Gore Metal, gradually evolved into a more traditional Hard Rock outfit the band's later works, such as 'Heartworks' and 'Swansong', found the band so distanced from the original concept that a split was inevitable. Founder member and vocalist Jeff Walker resurfaced with BLACKSTAR, an act very much musically akin to latter day CARCASS. BLACKSTAR also featured two fellow erstwhile CARCASS members, guitarist Carlo Regadas and drummer Ken Owen, together with former CATHEDRAL guitarist Mark Griffiths.

BLACKSTAR cut cover versions of HÜSKER DÜ's 'The Girl Who Lives On Heaven Hill' and THIN LIZZY's 'Running Back' for the 1998 Peaceville compilation 'X'.

BARBED WIRE SOUL, Peaceville CDVILE69 (1997). Game Over / Smile / Sound Of Silence / Rock n' Roll Circus / New Song / Give Up The Ghost / Revolution Of The Heart / Waste Of Space / Deep Wound / Better The Devil / Instrumental.

BLAKK MARKET

FLORIANOPOLIS, SC, BRAZIL — *Fernando Melleu (vocals), Thiago Rocha (guitar), Alexandre Schneider (guitar), Felippe Chiella (bass).*

BLAKK MARKET is a Thrash / Death act hailing from Florianopolis, first assembled during 2002 with a line up comprising vocalist / bassist Fernando Melleu, guitarists Thiago Rocha and Alexandre Schneider, both previously with DESPOTIC, and drummer Marlon Sens. Schneider would soon opt out and Felippe Chiella, another DESPOTIC veteran, enrolled on bass, freeing Melleu up to concentrate on lead vocals. Marlon Sens vacated the drum stool in May of 2004, this gap soon filled by yet another DESPOTIC man—Alexandre Sell. Expanding their sound the group briefly inducted ANATRIZ keyboard player Julio Stotz. This formation lasted some two months before Alexandre Schneider rejoined.

BLAKK MARKET's November 2004 demo 'Hateful Affection', limited to 350 copies, would include a video for the track 'Twisted Broadcast'. In 2005 BLAKK MARKET contributed their version of 'Indians' to the Collision Records ANTHRAX tribute album 'Indians... NOT! Brazilian Tribute to Anthrax'.

Drummer Alexandre Sell exited in 2006. BLAKK MARKET commenced recording the album 'Self-improvement: Suicide' at AML Studios with producer Alexei Leão in early November.

Hateful Affection, Blakk Market (2004) (Limited edition 350 copies). Twisted Broadcast / The Wheel Keeps Turning / Putrefaction Guaranteed / The Dawn Of The Dead / Twisted Broadcast (Video).

BLASTER

MEXICO — *Arnoldo Romo (vocals / guitar), Jose Pedroza (vocals / guitar), Cesar Choza (bass), Olympo Perez (drums).*

Mexican Thrash act BLASTER was forged as a trio during 1991. Line up changes followed the following year as BLASTER signed to the Denver label for a debut tape release 'Tribulations' in 1994. A follow up, 'En Tu Interior', arrived in 1997. BLASTER at this juncture comprised of Jerry Hernandez on lead vocals and guitar, Arnoldo Romo on guitar, bass player Cesar 'Zeus' Choza and drummer Olympo Perez. A 1999 cassette album 'Universe' found BLASTER now fronted by vocalist / guitarist Jose Pedroza replacing Hernandez and Benjamin de Anda augmenting on keyboards. BLASTER issued their first CD format album, 'Por Los Siglos De Los Siglos', through Dahmer Productions in 2002.

POR LOS SIGLOS DE LOS SIGLOS, Dahmer Productions (2002).

BLESSED DEATH

NEW YORK, NY, USA — *Larry Portelli (vocals), Jeff Anderson (guitar), Nick Fiorentiono (guitar), Kevin Powelson (bass), Chris Powelson (drums).*

KILL OR BE KILLED, Megaforce MRI 1369 (1986). Melt Down / Pig Slaughter / Omen Of Fate / Into The Ovens / Knights Of The Old Bridge / Eternal War / Blessed Death / Napalm / Kill Or Be Killed.
DESTINED FOR EXTINCTION, Roadrunner RR 9688 (1988). Digital War / Pain Killer / 10'000 Days / Incoming Wounded / Pray For Death / Death In The Sky / Curse Of Weapons / Alien Impregnation / Destruction's Eve.
DOUBLE ATTACK, Old Metal (1998).

BLIND FURY

NEWCASTLE UPON TYNE, UK — *Lou Taylor (vocals), Steve Ramsey (guitar), Russ Tippins (guitar), Graeme English (bass), Sean Taylor (drums).*

BLIND FURY arose from the ashes of Newcastle upon Tyne Metallers SATAN catering for the band's new found, mellower direction with new vocalist Lou Taylor, who had replaced BLITZKRIEG man Brian Ross. BLIND FURY, had been the moniker of one of Taylor's previous outfits, the singer having also fronted SARACEN (not the well known Derbyshire act of the same title).

The band was initiated in London by ANGEL WITCH veteran Kevin Heybourne, assembling a line-up with Taylor featuring a rhythm section comprising MARQUIS DE SADE bassist Peter Gordelier and drummer Steve Coleman. The first BLIND FURY debuted live on 21st May 1983 at the Catford Saxon Tavern. However, this union soon fell apart, Heybourne resurrecting ANGEL WITCH, taking Gordelier with him.

Taylor soldiered on, relocating back North to put together a second version of the band for the 1985 album 'Out Of Reach'. SATAN fans did not appreciate the change in direction though, and, after one album for Roadrunner, the band promptly reverted back to SATAN, ousting Taylor in the process. Following a brief tenure with PERSIAN RISK the singer later formed TOUR DE FORCE in 1988 alongside guitarists Fred Avesque, ex-TROY and DRIVESHAFT, and Andy Warnock, bassist Mike Antoine and drummer Gary Burfort. TOUR DE FORCE, however, never recorded. Taylor has long since become one of London's leading Rock club DJ's.

Back in Newcastle, after the demise of SATAN, Steve Ramsey and Graeme English partnered with erstwhile SABBAT vocalist Martin Walkyier and formed the successful Folk Metal band SKYCLAD.

OUT OF REACH, Roadrunner RR 9814 (1985). Do It Loud / Out Of Reach / Evil Eyes / Contact Rock n' Roll / Living On The Edge / Dynamo (There Is A Place . . .) / Back Inside / Dance Of The Crimson Lady (Part One).

BLIND ILLUSION

RICHMOND, CA, USA — *Marc Biedermann (vocals / guitar), Larry Lalonde (guitar), Les Claypool (bass), Mike Miner (drums).*

Founded in 1978, Bay Area Thrashers BLIND ILLUSION date back further than the Thrash Metal movement's origins in the early 80s BLIND ILLUSION ranked alongside then burgeoning acts such as METALLICA, ANVIL CHORUS and EXODUS on the San Francisco scene.

Guitarist Marc Biedermann formed the group with keyboard player Ben Heveroh but by 1984 the whole band had drifted apart leaving Biedermann solo. A new act was assembled in 1984 with Biedermann joined by guitarist Pat Woods, vocalist Dave Godfrey, bassist Geno Side and drummer Mike Mihor. This line-up soon fractured when Godfrey joined HEATHEN in 1985. Biedermann took over lead vocals for their next demo tape 'Blood Shower' / 'Smash The Crystal'.

BLIND ILLUSION was also then joined by bassist Lester Claypool. Outside the confines of the group, Claypool would pursue a project band with guitarist Todd Huth being basically the prototype for PRIMUS titled PRIMITIVE. Claypool is also believed to have produced the album 'Plastic Rock For A Plastic World' from Pop Metal band THE GUMBYS. On the other side of the studio desk, Claypool had scored engineering credits on YNGWIE MALMSTEEN's 'Marching Out' album.

BLIND ILLUSION recorded demos produced by METALLICA guitarist Kirk Hammett as a trio of Biedermann, Claypool and erstwhile BLIZZARD drummer Mike Miner which secured a deal with British label Music For Nations subsidiary Under One Flag.

Prior to recording the band added second guitarist John Marshall. This liaison was short-lived however, with Marshall, a guitar technician with METALLICA at the time, departing to fill in for an injured James Hetfield on a METALLICA tour before joining METAL CHURCH.

BLIND ILLUSION thus added ex-BLIZZARD and POSSESSED guitarist Larry Lalonde in May 1987 but the new guitarist joined Claypool decamping to create PRIMUS. PRIMATE man Todd Huth switched roles to join BLIND ILLUSION. That same year Claypool scored production credits on SUICIDAL TENDENCIES 'Join The Army' album.

Biedermann contributed guest lead guitar parts to BLUE OYSTER CULT's 'Imaginos' album in 1988.

THE SANE ASYLUM, Under One Flag FLAG 18 (1988). The Sane Asylum / Bloodshower / Vengeance Is Mine / Death Noise / Kamakazi / Smash The Crystal / Vicious Visions / Metamorphosis Of A Monster.

BLIND JUSTICE

HOLLAND — *Attila Szabo (vocals / guitar), Folker Draisma (guitar), Dennis Van Melis (bass), Marco De Groot (drums), Mark Spring In't Veld (saxophone), Edith Mathot (violin).*

An inventive Thrash act formed in 1989, BLIND JUSTICE combine dark and heavy sounds with violins and saxophones making for a quite unusual concoction. After the debut album, 1993's 'Sax & Violins', bassist Dennis Van Melis was replaced by Edwin. Drummer Marco de Groot made has mark with ALTAR and ROUWEN.

SAX & VIOLINS, Blind Justice (1993). Intro / Down We Go / Sax And Violins (At The Fireplace) / Suffer / Time's Ticking / Mother Nature / Why Should We Care? / Relief.
IN EQUILIBRIUM, Blind Justice BJ (1994).
Pissed . . . Again, Blind Justice BJ 0095 (1995) ('Pissed' EP). Pissed . . . Again / Boulder / Massacre.
CHILD'S PLAY, Blind Justice BJ (1995).

BLINDED COLONY

KARLSHAMN, SWEDEN — *Johan Schuster (vocals), Tobias Olsson (guitar), Johan Blomstrom (guitar), Roy Erlandsson (bass), Staffan Franzen (drums).*

Karlshamn melodic Death Metal band previously known as STIGMATA, formed in January 2000 by guitarist Johan Blomström, second guitarist Tobias Olsson and singer Niklas Svensson. BLINDED COLONY released their debut album, 'Divine', during 2003 via Italy's Scarlet Records. BLINDED COLONY parted ways with Svensson in January of 2005, bringing in substitute Johan Schuster of TDPP and solo project PLOUGHBILL. The revised version of the band cut a self-titled demo that March, recording at Soundpalace Studios 2005 with producer Johan Blomstrom.

BLINDED COLONY contracted with Pivotal Rockordings in March 2006 to record a new album, 'Bedtime Prayers', once again utilising Sound Palace Studios. Originally intended for a 2006 issue, the album was pushed back into January 2007.

A promotional video for the song 'Once Bitten, Twice Shy' was directed by Thomas Tjäder.

BLINDED COLONY partnered with EKTOMORF and KAYSER for European tour dates throughout February and into March 2007.

Tribute To Chaos, Blinded Colony (2002) (Demo limited to 100 copies). Contagious Sin / Discrown The Holy / Selfobtained Paranoia / Demoniser DCLXVI / Anno Domini 1224.

DIVINE, Scarlet SC 067-2 (2003). Contagious Sin / Thorned & Weak / Legacy (Slave In The Name Of Christ) / Selfobtained Paranoia / Lifeless Dominion / Discrown The Holy / Kingdom Of Pain / Demonizer DCLXVI / Anno Domini 1224.

Blinded Colony, Blinded Colony (2005) (Demo). Aaron's Sons / Swallow And Sleep / In Here / Need.

BEDTIME PRAYERS, Pivotal Rockordings (2007). My Halo / Bedtime Prayers / Once Bitten, Twice Shy / Need / Revelation, Now! / 21st Century Holocaust / Aarons Sons / In Here / Heart.

BLITZKRIEG

NEWCASTLE UPON TYNE, UK — *Brian Ross (vocals), Ken Johnson (guitar), Guy Laverick (guitar), Andy Galloway (bass), Phil Brewis (drums).*

BLITZKRIEG is almost certainly most known internationally by way of METALLICA's rendition of their theme song 'Blitzkrieg', featured on the B side of the Bay Area monsters 'Creeping Death' single. Despite this notoriety and a strong cult following BLITZKRIEG releases have been few and far between, although this hasn't been for the lack of trying. Vocalist Brian Ross, the mainstay of the band, has a colourful career including auditions with TYGERS OF PAN TANG, requests to join SAMSON and E.F. BAND and forming, albeit very briefly, a band with ex-WHITESNAKE guitarist BERNIE MARSDEN.

BLITZKRIEG formed in October 1980 in Leicester. Brian Ross answered an advert placed by SPLIT IMAGE comprising of guitarists Jim Sirotto and Ian Jones, bassist Steve English and drummer Steve Abbey looking to replace their previous vocalist, Sarah Aldwinkle. Ross had previous form with KASHMIR (an act that featured WHITESNAKE's David Coverdale's cousin Kev Stevens on drums) and ANVIL. Upon Ross joining SPLIT IMAGE, a new title of BLITZKRIEG was suggested by Jez Gilman, although various paying club gigs were still for a while performed under the old moniker.

The band's first product was a three track demo cassette, which led to a single for the Newcastle upon Tyne based Neat Records entitled 'Buried Alive'. The same year BLITZKRIEG also contributed the track "Inferno" to the Neat 'Leadweight' compilation. In February 1981 the band underwent a line-up change adding ex ELECTRIC SAVAGE guitarist John Antcliffe and bassist Mick Moore. The latter had previously played in the Leicester outfit AXE VICTIM with Ian Jones and Moore tells the tale that the legendary 'Blitzkrieg' (the B-side of the 'Buried Alive' single) had originally been conceived by AXE VICTIM under the title 'Bitch'. Jones had taken the nucleus of the song to BLITZKRIEG with him, the riffs of which had been an attempt to duplicate those of Dutch outfit FOCUS' hit 'Hocus Pocus'.

With a revised line-up, BLITZKRIEG gained welcome press coverage by featuring in the very first issue of 'Kerrang!' and went on to record a show supporting TRUST in Newcastle for an officially released tape entitled 'Blitzed Alive', this sporting a cover version of DEEP PURPLE's 'Highway Star'. However, the band spilt in December 1981 with Moore and Ross eventually forming AVENGER and Antcliffe joining CHROME MOLLY. Ross was to subsequently perform vocal duties with SATAN for a tour of Holland and wound up leaving AVENGER for the ranks of SATAN.

Ross kept in touch with Mick Moore and, along with Jim Sirotto, teamed up again as BLITZKRIEG to record the album 'Blitzkrieg—A Time Of Changes' with Sean Taylor of SATAN on drums and TYGERS OF PAN TANG guitarist Mick Procter. The record comprised archive tracks dating back as far as 1980, including 'Pull The Trigger' performed by Ross with SATAN. At this point, Ross was also managing and singing for LONEWOLF, a position he would relinquish to reactivate BLITZKRIEG.

The band, almost a pet project by this stage, underwent further reshuffling in June 1986 leaving Ross as the sole surviving member with Procter teaming up with SPEAR OF DESTINY. BLITZKRIEG was reassembled with guitarists J.D. Binnie, ex-MANDORA, and Chris Beard, bassist Darren Parnaby and drummer Sean Wilkinson. This incarnation recorded a four track demo in 1987, but the band split once more at the close of 1987 with Wilkinson, Parnaby, Binnie and Beard staying together in a Glam Metal act called LIBERTY.

Ross, after a re-think, started afresh in the summer of 1988. The singer gathered around him guitarists Glenn S. Howes, of AXISS and Doomsters THE REIGN, and Steve Robertson, bassist Robbie Robertson and drummer Kyle Gibson, yet the only recorded product was a two track demo before BLITZKRIEG once more succumbed to another drastic line-up shuffle.

By August 1989 only Ross and Howes remained from the most recent band, augmented with new guitarist Tony J. Liddle, previously with SARATOGA, PREDATOR and VIOLENT ERUPTION, bassist Glen Carey and former AVENGER drummer Gary Young. A video, 'At The Kazbah', was released and the long awaited second album '10 Years Of Blitzkrieg' on the Roadrunner label. This collection saw re-recordings of the two 1981 7 single tracks flanked by three new numbers.

Inevitably there were to be more departures. In early 1991 Carey, Young and Howes quit to form HURRICANE. Ross turned to his old comrade Mick Moore together with ex SATAN drummer Sean Taylor and guitarist Paul Nesbitt, although Moore had left within a year, BLITZKRIEG trimming down to a quartet of Ross, Liddle, Taylor and former WHEELBARROWS FROM HELL bassist Dave Anderson. This line-up recorded the album 'Unholy Trinity' in 1992. However, it was not to be released until the close of 1995.

BLITZKRIEG undertook a short tour of Greece in early 1996 with yet more new members; bassist Steve Ireland, ex-MARAUDER, and drummer Paul 'Sid' White. Liddle decamped in January of 1997 for TENDAHUX- recording an as yet unreleased album, but further gigging found BLITZKRIEG on tour in their strongest market, Germany, during the winter of that year. However, much to their amazement, the group found itself the centre of controversy when venues in Flensburg, Offenbach and Heidelberg refused to let them play due to the perceived historical connotations of the band name. Ireland was unable to fulfil these dates and a stand in bassist Gavin Gray the same year the band intended to record a Japanese language version of the track 'Blitzkrieg', the original version of which will forever remain the group's legacy, but this would never materialise.

In 1997 Neat issued Ten, an album essentially a re-work of 10 Years Of Blitzkrieg but with the addition of further new material. Strangely, Blitzkrieg chose to re-record 'Blitzkrieg' yet again, also taking this opportunity to alter the lyrics.

During 1998 BLITZKRIEG were working on new material for Neat Metal Records although predictably the band line-up had evolved once more. Joining Ross were a returning Howes on guitar, fellow guitarist Martin Richardson and drummer Mark Hancock. The group returned with The Mists Of Avalon, a solid effort marred by an amateurish sleeve design. This recording line-up put in a rare appearance at the 'Wacken Open Air' festival in Germany. BLITZKRIEG personnel would also form up part of a 'reunion' TYGERS OF PAN TANG show at the same event. Early 1999 found BLITZKRIEG back in action performing their first American show in New Jersey sharing a billing with SWEET SAVAGE and RAVEN. Subsequently, both Howes and Hancock decamped to concentrate on their priority act EARTHROD, a band unit in league with ex-DEAD END guitarist Sean Jeffries.

As 2002 drew in, Ross announced not only the planning of a

projected album to be titled 'Absolute Power' for Metal Nation Records but yet another completely revised BLITZKRIEG line up. Tony Liddle made a return to be joined by second guitarist Paul Nesbitt, bassist Andy Galloway, a veteran of LIGATURE, Black Metal bands REIGN OF EREBUS and ACOLYTE'S RUIN, and erstwhile WHATEVER and DISPOSABLE HEROES drummer Phil Brewis. With this line up BLITZKRIEG performed at the 'Motala Metal' festival in Sweden and would be confirmed for appearances at the 'Metal Meltdown' in Asbury Park, New Jersey and Germany's annual 'Wacken Open Air'.

Predictably 2003 ushered in yet a further new entrant into the BLITZKRIEG ranks, guitarist Ken Johnson of BLAST, SCREAM DREAM and MEANSTREAK repute. A retrospective, double disc package, dubbed 'A Time Of Changes–Phase 1', arrived through Sanctuary and collected together previously unheard demos and rehearsal recordings.

Gigs in the North of England would be taped for a projected live album bearing the tongue in cheek title 'Unleashed In The North East'. However, by late 2004 the band announced plans to record a brand new studio album 'Sins And Greed', entering Trinity Heights Studios in Newcastle Upon Tyne with TYGERS OF PAN TANG guitarist Fred Purser as producer in March 2005. During these sessions the band cut a cover version of JUDAS PRIEST's 'Hell Bent For Leather'. That same year, ex-BLITZKRIEG guitarist Glenn S. Howes joined another Newcastle NWoBHM reformation, AVENGER. He also forged JUDAS PRIEST tribute band JUDAS BEAST.

In January 2006 BLITZKRIEG parted ways with guitarist Paul Nesbitt, drafting Guy Laverick as replacement. This new recruit made his live debut in November as the band supported DORO on her UK dates. The band played at the Milan, Italy 'Play It Loud' festival in February. The following month BLITZKRIEG revealed they had signed with German label Armageddon Music. The album 'Theatre Of The Damned', recorded in Absurd Studios in Hamburg, was co-produced by Schroedey and SAXON frontman Biff Byford.

Buried Alive, Neat NEAT 10 (1980). Buried Alive / Blitzkrieg.

BLITZKRIEG-A TIME OF CHANGES, Neat 1023 (1985). Ragnarok / Blitzkrieg / Pull The Trigger / Armageddon / Take A Look Around / Hell To Pay / Vikings / A Time Of Changes / Saviour.

TEN YEARS OF BLITZKRIEG, Roadrunner RO9302 (1991). Blitzkrieg / Buried Alive / Night Howl / The Sentinel / Nocturnal Vision.

UNHOLY TRINITY, Neat Metal NM002 (1995). Hair Trigger / Struck By Lightning / Taking Care Of Business / Field Of Dreams / Take A Look Around / After Dark / Crazy For You / Zip / Unholy Trinity / Calming The Savage Beast / The Wraith / Easy Way Out / All Hallows Eve / Countess Bathory / Jealous Love / House Of Pleasure / Return Of The Zip.

TEN, Neat Metal NM 012 (1996). Cavo D'Oro / Fighting All The Way To The Top / Buried Alive / The Sentinel / The Power Of The King / Night Howl / I'm Not Insane / Court In The Act / Blitzkrieg '96 / Nocturnal Vision.

THE MISTS OF AVALON, Neat Metal NM032 (1998). The Legend / Tranquil State / I Am The Doctor (Who Are You?) / Deceiver / Princess For The World / The Mighty 'A' / Smell Of Roses / Love's Too Late / Anasazi / Yesterdays (Hope For The Future) / Another Interview? / Vicious Rumours / I Was Having A Great Time And Stayed Longer Than I Should, So When I Got To The Railway Station The Train Had Gone!

ABSOLUTE POWER, TPL TPL 008 (2002). Legion / Soul Stealer / Who Takes The Fall? / Enchanted Tower / We'll Rock Forever / Terror Zone / Hamunaptra / Dark City / The Face Of Death / DV8R / Metalizer / Feel The Pain.

ABSOLUTLY LIVE!!, Metal Nations MNR001 (2004). Ragnarok / Inferno / The Wraith / I'm Not Insane / Soul Stealer / Unholy Trinity / Legion / We'll Rock Forever / Armageddon / Hamunaptra / Dark City / Yesterdays / Nocturnal Vision / Metalizer / Blades Of Steel / Feel The Pain / Blitzkrieg.

SINS AND GREED, Cadiz Music (2005). Hell Express / Standing Still / Rise / Traitors Gate / Excessive Force / Escape From The Village / Eyes Of The World / Calm Waters / Desolation Angel / Silent Scream / Jeckyl & Hyde / Hell Bent For Leather.

BLITZKRIEG (pic: Henk 'De Tank' Bosma)

BLIZZARD

GROSSBETTLINGEN, GERMANY — *Atze (vocals / guitar), Joe (bass), Balor (drums).*

BLIZZARD, an out and out Thrash Metal band out of Grossbettlingen, Germany, was assembled by guitarist Atze and drummer Balor (a.k.a. Jörg Schmidt) during 1998. Balor had previously made a name for himself as drummer with Black Metal act MAYHEMIC TRUTH and Thrashers BESTIAL DESECRATION. The group was brought up to strength in January of 1999 with the addition of vocalist Faxe and bassist Joe, this line up committing themselves to the inaugural and self explanatory demo session 'Alcoholic Metal Mayhem'.

BLIZZARD would then suffer the loss of Faxe necessitating Atze taking over the lead vocal role. Down to a power trio BLIZZARD signed to the underground German label Iron Bonehead Productions to issue the 2000 7" single 'Hellish Rock n' Metal', limited to 520 copies. The full length album 'Pure Filth and Mayhem', which featured the MISCARRIAGE, MATRICIDE and FROM THY ASHES credited bassist Jan Rademaker, followed as well as a split 7" single in alliance with WITCHBURNER 'United Forces Of Metal Raging War'.

Rademaker subsequently founded the solo Death Metal concern RADEMASSAKER.

United Forces Of Metal Raging War EP, Iron Bonehead Productions (2000) (Split single with WITCHBURNER).

Hellish Rock n' Metal, Iron Bonehead Productions (2000).

PURE FILTH AND MAYHEM, Iron Bonehead Productions (2001) (Limited edition. 1000 copies).

BLO.TORCH

DEN HAAG, HOLLAND — *Chris van der Valk (vocals), Marvin*

Vriesde (guitar), Hassan Moechtar (guitar), Sander Koole (bass), Pascal Rapailles (drums).

Den Haag Thrash Metal act. BLO.TORCH lost the services of singer Michel De Wilde in early 2002. Guitarist Marvin Vriesede would join German Thrashers DEW SCENTED on a temporary basis that year for tour work. The band added new singer Chris van der Valk during November for a new demo recording billed as 'Plan B'.

During June of 2003 Vriesde united with fellow Dutchmen SEVERE TORTURE. BLO.TORCH cut a new Hans Pietersen produced studio album 'Volatile' at Excess Studio in Rotterdam for 2004 release. In March the band won a cash prize, festival appearances and 500 singles as the winners of the 'Grote Prijs van Zuid-Holland' competition. BLO. TORCH returned with the 'Volatile' album in 2004.

With guitarist Martin Vriesde otherwise occupied out on the road with SEVERE TORTURE and DEW-SCENTED the band pulled in Rory Hansen as substitute for Summer 2005 shows.

The Plot Sickens . . . , (1997). The Plot Sickens / King Of Karnage / Abandoned / March Of The Worm.
BLO-TORCH, Wicked World WICK008 (1999). Spanish Sun / Mount Ygman / King Of Karnage / Inkblack Sky / Panzerstorm / Quatrain / Seem To Be The Enemy / March Of The Worm / Bloodstains.
Promo 2001, (2001). Razorjob / Lightblockers.
Plan B, (2002). Razorjob / The Ties That Blind / Vermin Circle / Scattered Ashes Lay.
VOLATILE, (2004). Consumed By Indifference / Split Soul Massacre / Razorjob / Perish With The Pitiful / Justifiable Homicide / Votives In Suspension / Aberrant Dream / The Ties That Blind / Vermin Circle / Endtime.

BLOOD FEAST

USA — *Gary Markovitch (vocals), Adam Tranquilli (guitar), Lou Starita (bass), Kevin Kuzma (drums).*

Initially known as BLOODLUST in 1985. Released a 4 track demo 'Suicidal Mission' in February 1986 shortly after adding second guitarist Mike Basden. The band changed name to BLOOD FEAST before signing to New Renaissance Records. BLOOD FEAST toured North America in 1988 supporting DEATH ANGEL. Due to heavy demand for the debut 'Kill For Pleasure' album a four track EP, 'Face Fate' was rush released which included a re-recording of 'Blood Lust' and remixes of 'Vampire' and 'R.I.P.' The 'Kill For Pleasure' album would later be re-issued on CD format and by Shark Records in Germany as a double pack shared with KUBLAI KHAN.

The band parted company with guitarist Adam Tranquilli upfront of working on a new album announced as 'The Last Remains'. However, when it finally emerged this second album, which included a cover version of THE MIGHTY SPHINCTER's 'Hitler Painted Roses', was renamed as 'Chopping Block Blues'. Tranquili re-emerged in 1991 with his new outfit LAST REMAINS featuring Rich Caputo on vocals, Kurt Becker on second guitar, Ron McLynn on bass and drummer Adam Kieffer. By 1994 Tranquilli was working with trio HEADLOCK.

With New Renaissance re-issuing the albums on CD for the first time BLOOD FEAST would be tempted back into a full blown reformation for the 1999 'Metal Meltdown' festival in Asbury Park, New Jersey. BLOOD FEAST would issue the archive collection 'Remnants: The Last Remains' through their own Militia label in 2002 comprising material from their 'Suicidal Mission' demo, a KISS cover version 'Black Diamond' plus live recordings.

July of 2004 saw drummer Kevin Kuzma launching an all new act entitled LAMENT, a Thrash Metal combo fronted by Linda Alexander. This unit subsequently evolved into ANNUNAKI.

KILL FOR PLEASURE, New Renaissance NRR 16 (1987). Menacing Thunder / Kill For Pleasure / Cannibal / Vampire / Suicidal Mission / Venomous Death / The Evil / Darkside / R.I.P.
Face Fate, New Renaissance NRR 35 (1988). Face Fate / R.I.P. / Bloodlust / Vampire.
THE LAST REMAINS, New Renaissance (1988).
CHOPPING BLOCK BLUES, Flametrader FLAME 1016CD (1990). The Last Remains / Hunted, Stalked And Slain / Chopping Block Blues / Hitler Painted Roses / Dropping Like Flies / Born Innocent / Turn To Dust / The Chemically Imbalanced / Spasmodic / Remnants.

BLOOD MONEY

MANCHESTER, UK — *Danny Foxx (vocals), Gramie Dee (guitar), Dale Lee (bass), Brett Avock (drums).*

Manchester Thrash band BLOOD MONEY brought together ex-GRITTER vocalist Danny Foxx, erstwhile WOLFBANE men guitarist Gramie Dee and bassist Dale Lee plus VERRA CRUZ drummer Brett Avock. BLOOD MONEY was rooted in the act WOLFBANE, a unit formed in 1980 and comprising Gramie Dee and Dale Lee alongside singer Michelle Bibby and drummer Colin Seymoure. The latter would opt out the following year and in March of 1981 fresh sticksman Syd Mercury was enrolled. However, shortly after Bibby decamped and Dee took over lead vocal responsibilities for recording of WOLFBANE's initial demo recording. This tape was promoted nationwide with a series of gigs but bad luck befell the band as just before their debut at the prestigious London Marquee club Mercury was taken ill with suspected liver damage.

WOLFBANE regrouped in October, inducting a new lead singer in Gary Owen. Mercury was to falter though and Chris Dadson took on the drummer's role. Before long though Dadson disembarked to join SAM THUNDER. Dadson later wound up ensconced in both ARAGORN and CHATEAUX. Sid Oxton duly took over the reins to complete touring for that year. In 1982 the band undertook touring in mainland Europe but would be then dealt a further blow when Owen bailed out. Mike Osbourne would be drafted as replacement frontman but he too would back out leaving Dee to assume lead vocals once again for a further demo 'Metalyzed'.

Pulling in drummer Rick Henshaw during 1983 the band entered a period of song writing and reflection that eventually resulted in a fresh start the following year re-billed as BLOOD MONEY and boasting two new members, singer Danny Foxx and drummer J.C. Clark. Much of 1985 would be spent intensively gigging on the 'Bring Out Your Dead' tour. Scoring a deal with the Hull based Ebony Records label BLOOD MONEY supplanted Clark with Brett Avock for recording of the band's debut album, 'Red Raw And Bleeding', which featured a delightful chainsaw n' blood sleeve.

After the second album, 'Battlescarred', appeared in 1987 and a Friday Rock Show session the group eventually parted company in August of 1987. Danny Foxx formed BISON with guitarist Dave Kelly and Brett Avock, before creating FOXX, who gained a 'Friday Rock Show' session from their 'Legion' demo of 1988 vintage.

FOXX later went through a long period of evolution, turning into ZIONOIZ and then SACRASANCT. Unfortunately, Danny Foxx's career was put on hold following a severe motorcycle accident, which put him in a coma for two weeks. Thankfully, a full recovery was made and the singer was last heard of fronting CHINA BEACH and was short listed for the vacant IRON MAIDEN vocalist position in 1994 which was ultimately won by WOLFSBANE's Blaze Bayley.

During 2001 Dee and Avock, together with bass player Dark Mark, founded MORGUEAZM. Dee would also re-establish contact with Dale Lee to forge a Black Metal inspired venture XANTHOMA. BLOOD MONEY included a previously unreleased 1985 track, entitled 'I Was Wrong', to the 2004 'Total Metal Attack' NWoBHM era compilation album issued through Old School Records.

RED RAW AND BLEEDING, Ebony EBON 41 (1987). Metalyzed / Gor / NZFEDK / Lazarus / Red, Raw And Bleeding / Stormer / Taras Bulba / Deathsting / The Third Wish / Death Heavy.

BATTLE SCARRED, Ebony EBON 46 (1987). Battlescarred / Wolf Beat / Mutant / The Legend (Aghati) / Charnel House (House Of Death) / Shapeshifter / Caligula / Bird Or Beast / Atlantis / Evil Bitch.

BLOOD RED ANGEL

GERMANY — *Klaus Spangenberg (vocals), Jens Pesch (guitar), Robert Balner (guitar), Bernd Groß (bass), Adriano Ricci (drums).*

Krefeld based traditional Thrashers and proud of it. Erstwhile VERNISSAGE members guitarist Jens Pesch, bassist Bernd Groß and drummer Klaus Spangenberg would, with the latter adopting a lead vocal role, unite with ex-FERNGULLY guitarist Robert Balner to create retro Thrash Metal band BLOOD RED ANGEL in the late 90s. BLOOD RED ANGEL boast a drummer Adriano who reportedly "kicks the double bass drum like a true Lombardo believer".

BLOOD RED ANGEL debuted with a 5 track demo. This tape would land the band a deal with Gutted Records for the album 'The Language Of Hate' which received almost universal laudable reviews. Following the record's release in July 2000 BLOOD RED ANGEL toured as support to BLACKENED. In February of 2003 Adriano Ricci joined NIGHT IN GALES. The band enrolled ex-SATYR drummer Andreas Danner in 2003 as they readied a new album 'Crime Entertainment' through the Supreme Chaos label.

THE LANGUAGE OF HATE, Gutted GUTCD0014 (2000). The Language Of Hate / Jacobs Ladder / Hangman / Frontline / Psycho World / Dark Temptation / Revenge / Nighttime Skies / Virus / Parasite / Between the Lines / The Opposite.
THE STATE OF INSANITY, Gutted GUTCD0048 (2001). Intro (Commotion) / Disturb The Celebration / The Violins Of The Damned / Insanity Divine / Cold Flesh / Release / The Antagonist / Dark Illusion / Bloodstained / Invocation / A Crime Story.
CRIME ENTERTAINMENT, Supreme Chaos SCR-CD009 (2004). Intro / Disabled Mankind / Like A Cancer / Damaged / World Of Scum / Downwards / War Entertainment / Presence Of A Shadow / The New Rights / Darksideforce / Decline.

BLOOD TSUNAMI

OSLO, NORWAY — *Pete Evil (vocals / guitar), Dor Amazon (guitar), Bosse (bass), Faust (drums).*

Oslo Thrash act BLOOD TSUNAMI was formed in 2004 by former HELLRIDE guitarist / vocalist Pete Evil. Initially working with drummer Jay, the project came up to band status with the addition of second guitarist Dor Amazon and bassist Riff Randall. After recording demos BLOOD TSUNAMI debuted live supporting ENTOMBED at Oslo's Train venue on 24th August 2004.

Line-up changes then saw the introduction of HELLRIDE man Bosse on bass whilst the high profile figure of SCUM, THORNS, ABORYM, BOMBEROS, DISSECTION and EMPEROR credited 'Faust' (a.k.a. Bård G. Eithun) took over on drums. Aside from his musical endeavours, the new drummer's notoriety came from his conviction for the murder of a homosexual in August 1992. New demos were recorded at Lion Heart Studios in Oslo during July 2005.

Stu Manx from Norwegian rockers GLUECIFER enrolled into the BLOOD TSUNAMI ranks in July 2006. The band contracted a three album deal with Nocturnal Art Productions and Candlelight Records in August, re-entering Lion Heart Studios in September with engineer Øyvind Voldmo Larsen to lay down their debut given a working title of 'Thrash Metal'. A March 2007 release was set. BLOOD TSUNAMI partnered with ZYKLON for UK dates in May.

Blood All Over, Blood Tsunami (2004) (Demo). Killing Spree / Let Blood Rain / Obsessed With Death.
Blood Tsunami, Blood Tsunami (2005) (Demo). Evil Unleashed / Stabbed To Death / Infernal Final Carnage / Suicide Anthem / Killing Spree.

BLOODCUM

CA, USA — *Joey Hannemann (vocals) Bobby Tovar (guitar), George Hierro (guitar), John Araya (bass), Jimmy Sotelo (drums).*

BLOODCUM was a late eighties Californian Thrash act with an association to SLAYER through Tom Araya's younger brother, bassist John Araya. The group's frontman Joey 'Hannemann' Fuchs actually has no relationship to SLAYER's guitarist Jeff Hannemann. Rumours emerged in September of 2004 that BLOODCUM was set to reform, adding another Araya to the line up, cousin Sean. As it transpired, the first reunion show was held on 21st January 2005 at The Stardust in Downey, California. The band line up comprised vocalist / guitarist George Hierro, guitarist Robert Tovar, bassist Jaz Soto and drummer Jimmy Sotelo. However, in a surprise move original singer Joey Fuchs rejoined in May.

BLOODCUM, Wild Rags (1987). Son Of Sam / Harassment By Farm Animals / Belligerent Youth / Live To Kill / First To Die / Happily Married / Son Of Sam / Harassment By Farm Animals / Belligerent Youth / Live To Kill / First To Die / Happily Married.
DEATH BY A CLOTHES HANGER, Wild Rags (1988). Happily Married / Son Of Sam / Live To Kill / Good Hearted Man / Treatment Of Death / Death By A Clothes Hanger / Belligerent Youth / Harassment By Farm Animals / First To Die / Sike-O-Path.

BLOODWRITTEN

WARSAW, POLAND — *Bastard (vocals), Thanathos (guitar), Hypnos (guitar), Chaos (bass), Matt (drums).*

Warsaw's BLOODWRITTEN released an eponymous 1998 demo, the line-up for which comprised Bastard on vocals and guitar, Thanathos on guitar, bassist Ostry and drummer Arek. By the time of recording the 2000 album 'Pages In Blood' the band was seemingly back up to strength with Bastard and Thanathos being joined by bassist Wampir and drummer Taylor Hod. However, Thanathos committed all the bass guitar to tape for the sessions and Wampir was duly ejected. Regrouping, BLOODWRITTEN incorporated second guitarist Hypnos and bassist Chaos, the latter from Prog-Rock outfit WINSOME JESTER. Live work then ensued but progress was stalled by the departure of Taylor Hod as a result of time honoured "musical differences".

In July 2002 the band drafted CASSIOPEIA's DeAmon as new drummer. Unfortunately this latest candidate exited within a matter of months to join NAMTAR. Next in line for the drum stool would be DarKiron, his tenure lasting little over a year. BLOODWRITTEN was forced into a lengthy hiatus, this finally broken with the arrival of CONDEMNATED drummer Matt for recording of the three song 'Reborn' demo.

BLOODWRITTEN returned in December 2006 with the demo 'Iniquity Intensity Insanity'. These sessions were recorded at Hertz Studio by Bracia Wiesławscy.

PAGES IN BLOOD, Bloodwritten (2000). Preludium—Evocation Of Yog-Sothoth / Chapter One—Ancient Gods Born Again /Dog-Star / Chapter Two—Witches' Forest /Blood Magick / Chapter Three—Świt /Nigdy Więcej / Chapter Four—Moon Maniac /Atonement Through Pain / Chapter Five—Thanathos /Let Us Dream / Chapter Six—Temptations In E-minor /Father In Darkness / Postludium—Closing Ceremony.
Reborn, (2004). Intro / Moon Speaks My Name / The Throne / Praise the Black Sorcery.
Iniquity Intensity Insanity, Bloodwritten (2006) (Demo). Taste Insanity / The Forgotten Empire / Sworn To Darkness / Reborn Through Fire / Seed Of Destruction / Incantations Carved in Flesh / In Blood It Shall Be Written.

BLUDGEON

CHICAGO, IL, USA — *Mark Duca (vocals / guitar), Carlos Alvarez (guitar), Chris Studtmann (bass), Ryan Blazek (drums).*

Brutal Thrash Metal act BLUDGEON, dating to 1997, initially featured the scene veteran Cazz Grant of GRAND BELIAL'S KEY, CRUCIFIER, INFERNAL HATRED and DECEIVERON on drums for the 1998 'Inner Hell' demo. A formative bassist would be Vince Papi, a veteran of HEARSE and CRUCIFIER. The group, mentored by frontman Mark Duca, enlisted MIXED BREED guitarist Carlos Alvarez in 2000 and enrolled a fresh rhythm section of bassist Eric Karol and drummer Matt 'Chewy' Dezynski the following year. BLUDGEON would be the first band to sign to MANOWAR's Magic Circle Music imprint distributed through Metal Blade Records. Naturally, BLUDGEON would support MANOWAR in America during 2002 and also travel to Europe with the muscle-bound Metal veterans during November. A live CD / DVD package 'Crucified Live' was scheduled for September 2003. That same year Carlos Alvarez joined GODHELPUS.

BLUDGEON, now with Chris Studtmann on bass and Ryan Blazek on the drums, returned with the 'World Controlled' album in June 2006. On November 18th the band appeared at the Monterrey Metal Fest event at the at the Coca Cola Auditorium in Mexico alongside BLIND GUARDIAN, CATHEDRAL, U.D.O., EDGUY, OBITUARY, DEICIDE, LEAVES' EYES, SADUS, VAINGLORY, HYDROGYN and JOE STUMP'S REIGN OF TERROR.

CRUCIFY THE PRIEST, Magic Circle Music (2002). Smoke Screen / Idle Distinction / Tortured Through Lies / Zero Tolerance / Last Rites / Voluntary Manslaughter / Crucify The Priest / Abandoned / Bound / Inner Hell / Turmoil / Stained In Blood.

WORLD CONTROLLED, Magic Circle Music MCA 02150-2 (2006). Unholy Murder / Carnage Begins / Bitter Emptiness / Consumed By Anger / Infidel / World Controlled / Save Your Servant / Refuse The Truth / Hunt Or Be Hunted / Awakening / Out Of Reach.

BOLT THROWER

BIRMINGHAM, WEST MIDLANDS, UK — *Karl Willetts (vocals), Barry Thomson (guitar), Gavin Ward (guitar), Jo-Anne Bench (bass), Andy Whale (drums).*

Founded in Birmingham during September 1986, BOLT THROWER gained notoriety on the local Metal scene with a unique, war obsessed heaviness. At this early point the band featured vocalist Alan West, guitarist Barry Thomson, bassist Gavin Ward and drummer Andy Whale. The name BOLT THROWER is taken from a siege device in a Games Workshop 'Warhammer' fantasy role playing game. Famously, the initial idea for the band had been formulated in a pub toilet in Coventry by Ward and Thompson. First product would come in the form of an April 1987 demo session 'In Battle There Is No Law'. With Ward switching to the guitar role BOLT THROWER drafted Alex Tweedy to cover on bass.

Following a September 1987 demo, 'Concessions In Pain', the fledgling band, still utilising Ward as temporary bassist as new man Tweedy had failed to commit, added bassist Jo-Anne Bench. The second demo resulted in a four song Radio One session on the John Peel show, recorded in January 1988. This airing led to an album deal with Vinyl Solution Records, but not before West's departure.

The band brought in vocalist Karl Willetts, actually the official BOLT THROWER van driver up to that juncture, to record the debut 1988 album at Loco Studios in Wales, the Andrew Fryer produced 'In Battle There Is No Law'. BOLT THROWER also submitted a separately recorded version of the album track 'Drowned In Torment' to a free fanzine split EP alongside INSTIGATORS, H.D.Q. and CULTURE SHOCK. Although support for the band was rising on the Metal underground, the group felt Vinyl Solution's Hardcore ethic was restrictive and duly switched label's to Nottingham's burgeoning underground imprint Earache Records. A notable gig that July saw the band supporting DEATH ANGEL and WARFARE at London's Astoria. BOLT THROWER also scored a further John peel session, cutting more tracks for Radio One play in November.

The group's first album for Earache, October 1989's 'Realm Of Chaos: Slaves To Darkness' recorded at Slaughterhouse Studios, was to sell in excess of 50'000 copies worldwide and utilised expansive gatefold artwork from Games Workshop that carried on the theme of futuristic fantasy wargaming. The world of gaming also infused the lyrical content of 'Realm Of Chaos' too, both 'Plague Bearer' and 'World Eater' borrowing heavily from gaming titles. Musically, 'Realm Of Chaos' was the first record to introduce Bolt Thrower to an international audience, critics polarizing between jaw dropping appreciation for the super low bottom end, with guitars dragged right down to A, and guttural grind or horrified by the unashamed unsophistication. Meantime, Vinyl Solution would re-issue the debut on CD, this variant coming complete with totally different artwork to the original.

Having performed well on the Earache organised "Grindcrusher" tour of 1989 shoulder to shoulder with CARCASS, MORBID ANGEL and NAPALM DEATH, and after contributing a track to the compilation album of the same name, the band then executed dates in Holland throughout February 1990 with AUTOPSY and PESTILENCE on the 'Bloodbrothers' tour. A third John Peel session was undertaken in July 1990.

The release of the next studio affair in September 1990 proved fortuitous, 'Warmaster' again crafted at Slaughterhouse but with noted desk man Colin Richardson now in control, being cut coincidentally just prior to the complex burning down. For this offering BOLT THROWER curtailed the speed somewhat and defined some degree of clarity by pitching guitars at C#. Even with this fine tuning, 'Warmaster' would still make for a monstrously ugly Death Metal album.

The 'Cenotaph' EP arrived in January 1991. BOLT THROWER once more toured Europe, this time as part of the 'War Mass' package with support from US outfit NOCTURNUS and Sweden's UNLEASHED. That October the group conducted a package tour of the USA together with BELIEVER and Toronto Thrashers SACRIFICE before engaging in further European shows, where they were supported by BENEDICTION and ASPHYX. In 1991 the three John Peel sessions saw commercial release on CD format.

The band drew back from their Grind influences and changed tack towards a Doom edged feel for October 1992's 'The IVth Crusade' album, reprising their studio creativity with Colin Richardson. Whilst retaining the militaristic stance, the band went for a more classical feel, adapting a medieval Eugène Delacroix painting for the album cover. European dates to open up 1993 witnessed a strong union with Poles VADER and Swedes GRAVE. This activity was backed by an EP release comprising a remixed 'Spearhead' alongside new material. Unfortunately BOLT THROWER's first Australian tour in September 1993, supported by ARMOURED ANGEL, ended in debacle when the band were stuck without a flight home.

Eventually managing to make it back to Britain the Birmingham bunch undertook another American club tour in July 1994 with fellow Brummies BENEDICTION as support, but failed to complete the schedule. The album of that year, 'For Victory', witnessed strong sales. Colin Richardson again took production honours and once more Bolt Thrower's imagery took a further leap in history, the record sleeve depicting marines yomping across the tundra of the Falkland Islands. Initial copies came with a free bonus live disc recorded in Manchester during 1992. Ex-PESTILENCE, ASPHYX and SUBMISSION vocalist Martin Van Drunen joined the band in 1994 replacing the departed Willets and drummer Martin Kearn was added in the line-up shuffle. Taking their Metal to the European masses, the band undertook the 1995 'No Guts, No Glory' tour in union with BRUTALITY and CEMETARY. They hit the continent again the following year, making a statement on the 'Fuck Price Politics' expedition with SENTENCED, EXPRESSION OF POWER and

THE VARUKERS.

Severing connections with Earache Records in early 1997 and signing to American label Metal Blade, before recording on a brand new album could commence, Van Drunen, suffering from a disease which made his hair fall out, quit unexpectedly on the eve of some European festivals. BOLT THROWER killed time by throwing in a few live gigs with BENEDICTION's Dave Ingram guesting.

As BOLT THROWER went into the studio in late 1997 it was announced that 19 year old Alex Thomas had succeeded skinsman Kearns and that Willets had rejoined. With this line up the band cut the 1998 album 'Mercenary' for new label Metal Blade Records. This offering, despite the lengthy hiatus between recordings, re-established BOLT THROWER's fan base and gave the group a showing in the national German album charts too. Although Willetts had performed on the album it would be a re-instated Dave Ingram, having recently quit BENEDICTION, who took up the vocal mantle for live work packaged with CROWBAR and TOTENMOND. Confusingly Thomas would then leave and the drummer he had usurped in the first instance duly took over once again in time for BOLT THROWER's second showing at the major German 'Full Force' festival.

In December 1999 Dave Ingram made time to session on a demo for Danish act ATOBIC, an alliance between INIQUITY and CORPUS MORTALE guitarist Brian Eriksen and drummer Peter Olsen.

BOLT THROWER toured Europe in January 2001 supported by FLESHCRAWL and HEAVEN SHALL BURN to push a new album 'Honour, Valour, Pride'. Further road work had the band in familiar company, co-headlining a January 2002 European expedition with BENEDICTION backed up by FLESHCRAWL. Martin Van Drunen resurfaced in mid 2002 debuting his new act DEATH BY DAWN on the European live circuit. BOLT THROWER would be confirmed as one of the headline acts at the October 'Westfalen' festival in Dortmund, Germany. BOLT THROWER would be finalised for the running order of the 'Rock Hard' magazine festival at the Gelsenkirchen Amphitheatre for June 2003 but withdrew at short notice to allow singer Dave Ingram to be present at the birth of his first child. BOLT THROWER announced the departure of Ingram, apparently due to the singer "suffering with health and personal problems", in August of 2004. The singer later revealed he had been suffering with mental difficulties, but once recovered, duly founded FULL SCALE HATRED, this new band subsequently evolving into DOWNLORD.

In November BOLT THROWER welcomed the return of original vocalist Karl Willetts, soon re-entering the recording studio to craft a new album. Willetts also re-recorded the vocal lines on the 'Honour, Valour, Pride' album, this effort seeing production credits going out to former MARSHALL LAW bassist Andy Faulkner. Digipack variants hosted an exclusive track, 'Covert Ascension'.

Early 2005 found former singer Martin Van Drunen and erstwhile PESTILENCE bassist Jeroen Paul Thesseling collaborating with KING LOCUST guitarist Niels Drieënhuizen in a new band entitled PROJEKT TABUN. The trio entered Studio Het Lab in Schaarsbergen to put down initial recordings. Back on the BOLT THROWER front, vocalist Karl Willetts and guitarist Barry Thompson would guest on a cover version of SACRILEGE's 'Lifeline' recorded by fellow Brummies BENEDICTION.

In May the band entered Sable Rose Studios, again collaborating with Andy Faulkner as producer, to craft a new album for Metal Blade Records. 'Those Once Loyal' emerged in November and gave the band its highest charting record in Germany, debuting at number 76. To coincide, former label Earache re-issued the 'Realm Of Chaos' opus, re-mastered and clad in all new artwork.

European headline shows in January and February 2006 wit-

BOLT THROWER

nessed strong backing from MALEVOLENT CREATION, NIGHTRAGE and NECROPHAGIST. Gigs for April across Europe were scheduled originally to see GOREFEST as support but these plans were changed and KATAKLYSM, GOD DETHRONED and DOWNLORD took over the opening roles. The group projected dates in North America but then cancelled these plans. A statement claimed Metal Blade Records had "refused to financially back the band ... Despite trying to work out other ways to make this happen, the band found they were unable to finance a tour of this scale on their own and therefore had to stop any further planning of the tour. Regrettably, it looks like while BOLT THROWER are signed to Metal Blade Records they will be unable to tour the States."

The band's appearance at the Gelsenkirchen 'Rock Hard' festival in Germany during June was taped and subsequently the track 'Killchain' was included on the 'Rock Hard' magazine compilation album 'Rock Hard: Das Festival 2006'.

The Peel Sessions EP, Strange Fruit (1988). Forgotten Existence / Attack In The Aftermath / Psychological Warfare / In Battle There Is No Law.

IN BATTLE THERE IS NO LAW, Vinyl Solution SOL 11 (1988). In Battle There Is No Law / Challenge For Power / Forgotten Existence / Denial Of Destiny / Concession Of Pain / Attack In The Aftermath / Psychological Warfare / Nuclear Annihilation / Blind To Defeat.

REALM OF CHAOS, Earache MOSH 13 (1989). Eternal War / Through The Eye Of Terror / Dark Millennium / All That Remains / Lost Souls Domain / Plague Bearer / World Eater / Drowned In Torment / Realm Of Chaos / Outro.

WARMASTER, Earache MOSH 29 (1990). Intro: Unleashed (Upon Mankind) / What Dwells Within / The Shreds Of Sanity / Profane Creation / Destructive Infinity / Final Revelation / Cenotaph / War Master / Rebirth Of Humanity / Afterlife.

THE PEEL SESSIONS 1988-90, Strange Fruit DEI 8118-2 (1991). Forgotten Existence / Attack In The Aftermath / Psychological Warfare / In Battle There Is No Law / Drowned In Torment / Eternal War / Realm Of Chaos / Domination / Destructive Infinity / Warmaster / After Life / Lost Souls Domain.

Cenotaph EP, Earache MOSH CD 33 (1991). Cenotaph / Destructive Infinity / Prophet Of Hatred / Realm Of Chaos (Live).

THE IVTH CRUSADE, Earache MOSH 70 (1992). The Fourth Crusade / Icon / Embers / Where Next To Conquer / As The World Burns / This Time It's War / Ritual / Spearhead / Celestial Sanctuary / Dying Creed / Through The Ages (Outro).

Spearhead EP, Earache MOSH 73 (1993). Spearhead (Extended remix) / Crown Of Life / Dying Creed / Lament.

FOR VICTORY, Earache MOSH 120 (1994). War / Remembrance / When Glory Beckons / For Victory / Graven Image / Lest We Forget / Silent Demise / Forever Fallen / Tank (MK 1) / Armageddon Bound.

WHO DARES WINS, Earache MOSH 208 (1998). Cenotaph / Destructive Infinity / Prophet Of Hatred / Realm Of Chaos (Live) / Spearhead (Extended remix) / Crown Of Life—Dying / Creed / Lament / World Eater '94 / Overlord.

MERCENARY, Metal Blade 14147-2 (1998). Zeroed / Laid To Waste / Return From Chaos / Mercenary / To The Last... / Powder Burns / Behind Enemy Lines / No Guts, No Glory / Sixth Chapter. Chart position: 87 GERMANY.

HONOUR, VALOUR, PRIDE, Metal Blade 14386-2 (2001). Contact Wait Out / Inside The Wire / Honour / Suspect Hostile / 7th Offensive / Valour / K-Machine / A Hollow Truce / Pride.

THOSE ONCE LOYAL, Metal Blade 14506-2 (2005). At First Light / Entrenched / The Killchain / Granite Wall / Those Once Loyal / Anti-Tank (Dead Armour) / Last Stand Of Humanity / Salvo / When Cannons Fade. Chart position: 76 GERMANY.

BOMBSTRIKE

KARLSKRONA, SWEDEN — *Kraister (vocals), Chris (guitar), Bosse (guitar), Loggan (bass), Fenok (drums).*

Karlskrona based Metal band forged as BASTARD FETTO in Storfors during 1997 and comprising vocalist Kraister, guitarist Chris, bassist "Dirt" Jon and drummer Jöva. That band folded in mid 1998 and the musicians relocated to Karlskrona, Kraister and Chris recruiting the session services of Zwemp of MÖRDER to cut the first BOMBSTRIKE demo, featuring four originals plus a cover version of HIDDEN INDUSTRIAL's 'Ögon', entitled 'And The Silence' in February 1999. The band was re-shaped with the addition of bassist Lasse and drummer Mange for the group's inaugural live performance a six song demo, 'Tomorrow Hero', in August 1999.

January of 2002 found BOMBSTRIKE, with Zwemp back on drums, recording at Black Lounge Studios with Jonas Kjällgren of DELLAMORTE acting as producer. These sessions would be released as 'Kaos Och Djävulskap', featuring the KAAOS cover 'Uskonsota', that July by the Berlin based Yellow Dog Records. Touring to promote the record included gigs in Germany, Holland and the Czech Republic.

BOMBSTRIKE then acquired Fenok of Grind merchants SCURVY to cover bass as Mange switched to guitar. Further releases included the 7" single 'Livets Låga Slocknar', hosting the UUTUUS cover 'Vapaa Valtio', and a split outing shared with Canadians LEGION 666. In 2004 Mange was superseded by 'Bosse' Johan Wallin, a scene veteran of SCURVY, REPUGNANT and GENERAL SURGERY. Zwemp then exited and Fenok moved over to the drum stool to cover for live work. More changes had Bosse taking on guitar whilst Gurra (a.k.a Loggan) from REPUGNANT and SUBVISION handled bass. In March of 2005 tracks were recorded for an intended split release in alliance with ILLDÅD and Umeå's REIGN OF BOMBS through Wasted Sounds.

... And The Silence, Bombstrike (1999) (Demo). We Are Dead / Living Under Oppression / Den Sista Dagen / Scum / Ögon.

Tomorrow Hero, Bombstrike (1999) (Demo). Moralistic Hypocrites / Stämplad / Född Till Förlust / Kedjad / Lives Are Shattered / We Are Dead.

KAOS OCH DJÄVULSKAP, Yellow Dog YD 026 (2002). Förbrukningsbar / Deformera / Lives Are Shattered / Nothing Will Change / Du Kan Inte Fly / Stay On The Cross / Souldead / Enter And Shape / We Are Dead / Jet Set / Den Sista Dagen / Confused / Malplacerad / Mosh! / Uskonsota.

Livets Låga Slocknar, Yellow Dog YD 032 (2003). Dom Kallar Det För Mitt Liv / Livets Låga Slocknar / Social Kompetens = 0 / Vapaa Valtio / Stämplad.

Temple Of Blasphemy, Schizophrenic (2004) (Split 7" vinyl single with LEGION 666). Dödens Utsträckta Hand / Patent Pa Godhet.

BOMBSTRIKE VS. REIGN OF BOMBS, Yellow Dog (2005) (Split album with REIGN OF BOMBS). Eclipse / Slumber / Pissmessiah / Jag Hatar Ert System (MOB 47) / In Vino Veritas.

BOMBTHREAT

ASCHERSLEBEN, GERMANY — *Christian Behrens (vocals), Maik Siegismund (guitar), Daniel Jöhring (bass), Matthias Wiele (drums).*

An Aschersleben outfit that straddle the line between Thrash and Death Metal. BOMBTHREAT started life as the 1995 combo ETERNAL CURSE with a line up of Maik Siegismund on vocals and guitar, Nico Wasserberg on guitar, bassist Matthias Wiele and drummer Daniel Seecker.

By December of 1995 the group had evolved into AEON and would switch titles again to BOMBTHREAT. The line up by now had seen Wiele maneuvering over to drums and the induction of bassist Daniel Jöhring and frontman Christian Behrens.

A succession of demos, 1997's 'The Last Warning' and 1998's 'The Eternal Curse' led up to the debut CD release 'Peacemaker'.

PEACEMAKER, Bombthreat (1999). Intro—Eternal Curse / Cold And Wet / Nightmare / Agents Of Disease / Religious Insanity / Forever / Peacemaker / Cryonic Experiments / Peacemaker (Live) / Suspicion Of Murder (Live) / Burst Command Til War (Live) / Weihnachtslied (Live).

BRAIN IMPLOSION

NIEUWLEUSEN, HOLLAND — *Miquel van Sloten (vocals), Jochem Steenbergen (guitar), Alex Geerts (bass), Ian van Sloten (drums).*

BRAIN IMPLOSION is a Nieuwleusen Thrash Metal act forged during the late eighties. First product would be a 1988 demo, recorded at Franky's Recording Kitchen, entitled 'Liquidation', followed up by a 7" single 'Sandgrains' released through France's Putrefaction Records in 1989. Ex-members vocalist / guitarist Jochem Steenbergen and drummer Ian van Sloten subsequently forged ABACINATE, releasing a solitary demo tape, 'Out Of The System', emerged in 1991. The entire ABACINATE cast, Steenbergen, van Sloten, guitarist Rene Bruggeman and bassist Klaas Brouwer, then forged OUT OF THE SYSTEM. Under this branding the group recorded material in December 1993 at Torenplein Studios in Zwolle for inclusion on a D.S.F.A. Records compilation album. In 2003 BRAIN IMPLOSION bassist Alex Geerts joined DEAD HEAD.

Liquidation, Brain Implosion (1988). Liquidation / Lunacy / Implosion / Fear Rules / In Your Face.

Sandgrains, Putrefaction (1989). Sandgrains / Intramurial.

BRAINDAMAGE

TURIN, ITALY — *Andrea Signorelli (vocals / bass), Ricky Gottero (guitar), Gigi Giugno (guitar), Naike (drums).*

Formed in 1988, this Italian band released their debut demo, 'Kingdom Of Madness', a year later that opened the door for them to play at the German 'Support The Underground Thrash' Festival in Ludwigsburg's Rockfabrik. The following year the mini album 'The Weakness Of My Nerves', produced by KILLING JOKE guitarist Geordie Walker, appeared, although the group became dissatisfied with the direction they were heading in and were quick to change tack. Touring in Europe to promote the single 'Watching The Bleeding Mouth' had the band supporting KILLING JOKE and LOUD.

In 1991 BRAINDAMAGE opened for KILLING CULTURE in Europe and engaged top producer Steve Albini to work on their first, full-length album 'Signal De Revolta'. 1996's follow up 'The Turning Point' included a cover version of BLUE OYSTER CULT's 'Flaming Telepaths'.

Kingdom Of Madness, (1989). Braindamage / Kingdom Of Madness / Gathering Under The Ensigns / Towards The Sky / Running On Ashes.

The Weakness Of My Nerves EP, Braindamage (1990). The Weakness Of My Nerves.

Watching The Bleeding Mouth EP, Dracma (1990). Watching The Bleeding Mouth.

SIGNAL DEREVOLTA, RTD 380 0003.2 (1993). King In Yellow's Day / Downfall Of Free Enterprise / Understanding Pain / Watchin' The Bleedin' Mouth / En Route / The Veil Has Fallen / Turbid / Monochrome / Nocturne / Un Verre De Bordeaux.

THE TURNING POINT, Scream (1996). La Grande Guerre / Hospital For The Sick Children / No Place To Fall / Tour Rouge, Tour Noire, Grey Slabs / Ain't Gonna Die For Your Flag / Flaming Telepaths / The Snake Enchanter / Aurora / Disertori / Duryodhana / Old Cold Harbor / The Turning Point.

COLLAPSE, (1999). Collapse / We Shall Resist / Unleashed / No God, No Redemption: Just War / I Came Into This World / Control The Eclipse / How Could We Fail Now? / Stalingrad's Beyond The Gate / Blind Inside A Tank / King In Yellow's Day 1999 / 6 PM After The War.

WAR AGAINST THE ALMIGHTY, (2006).

BRAN BARR

FRANCE — *Richard Loudin (vocals), Fir Doirtche (guitar), Hades (bass), Kraban (flute / tin whistle), Amorgen (flute / tin whistle / bombarde), Aed Morban (drums).*

BRAN BARR, a Pagan Folk act with Thrash leanings, was manifested in 1994 to further a concept of SWORD drummer Aed Morban. The initial formation also counted guitarist Morrigan but this union soon stalled and Morban unified with vocalist and keyboard player Yoltar (a.k.a. Richard 'Hingard' Loudin of Funeral Doom act DESPOND, Black Metal band NYDVIND and Doomsters MONOLITHE) along with bassist Fir Doirtche (a.k.a. 'Amduscias' of TEMPLE OF BAAL and ANTAEUS) and guitarist Brennus. Subsequently Taliesin arrived on bass and Amorgen, both from AES DANA, complemented the sound with flute, tin whistle and bombarde.

This unit, solidified in 1998, cut the debut, self-produced album 'Les Chroniques De Naerg', centred upon a mythological pre-Christian novel of Aed Morban's, for release in April of 2000. Far from being a traditional Metal album BRAN BARR infused their sound with Celtic instrumentation such as war pipes, French bombarde and bodhran. The response was positive and, with the first pressing soon selling out, the record was re-pressed in February of 2001. However, Brennus had opted out in late 2000, being replaced by Nesh Keltorn of ACROMION and NYDVIND that November.

BRAN BARR conducted live work throughout 2001, taking in regular Metal shows as well as Pagan festivals. At the close of the year Taliesin exited and was superseded by Hades. December witnessed ructions too as Nesh Keltorn left, only to return to the ranks a few weeks later.

Much of 2002 and into the next year would be spent crafting a sophomore album to be entitled 'Sidh'. BRAN BARR enrolled Kraban of HEOL TELWYN, ENSHROUDMENT and NYDVIND on bombarde and whistles in May of 2003. Later that year Nesh Keltorn exited.

LES CHRONIQUES DE NAERG, Bran Barr (2000). Alba Bheadarrach'smire Ga'd Fhaguil Dubh / Ultraigh Tri Codacht'ruin / The Lamentable Tragedy Of Deirdra / La Complainte / Pride And Malevolence / Galeach'tran / Bàas In The Underworld / Righ'beern.

BREATHSTEALER

BRUSSELS, BELGIUM — *Kevin Nolis (vocals), Jelle Maes (lead guitar), David Collet (rhythm guitar), Gilles Major (bass), François De Bock (drums).*

BREATHSTEALER is a Brussels Heavy Metal act initiated as a high school act in May of 2001 by drummer François de Bock with guitarists Pierre Cherelle and Kevin Nolis. The unit built up their musical proficiency for the next year as a garage METALLICA and MEGADETH covers outfit. In the Summer of 2002 bassist David Collet, a veteran of SILICUM and INTROSPECTION, joined the fold as they began to pen original material. Further evolution followed, as Cherelle vacated his position, this being filled within weeks by Jelle Maes of MEAGAN and SCYTHSLAIN. At this juncture, in October of 2002, the band adopted the BREATHSTEALER title.

The group's inaugural live performance came on 12th July 2003 at the Red Devils club in Drogenbos. The debut demo 'Womb Of Weakness' ensued that Autumn.

Womb Of Weakness, Breathstealer SABAM 15852 (2004).

BREJN DEDD

FINSPÅNG, SWEDEN — *Tony Särkkä (vocals), Dan Swanö (vocals / drums), Michael Bohlin (guitar), Christer Broms (bass).*

BREJN DEDD was a late eighties, Finspång based Crossover Metal outfit. Three demos were issued, 'Brejn Dedd' and 'The Ugly Tape' in 1988 and 1989's 'Born Ugly'. The latter featured 16 songs all containing the word 'Ugly' in the title. The group's personnel would subsequently figure heavily on the international extreme music scene, comprising as it did of frontman Tony Särkkä, a.k.a. 'It' of ABRUPTUM, VONDUR, INCISION and OPHTHALAMIA, guitarist Michael Bohlin, bassist Christer Broms and drummer DAN SWANÖ.

Swanö would make his impact primarily with EDGE OF SANITY but also featured heavily in NIGHTINGALE, BLOODBATH, GODSEND, ODYSSEY, INCISION, UNICORN and PAN.THY.MONIUM amongst many others. In 2004 Michael Bohlin and Tony Särkkä issued the Industrial styled Hard Rock project album 'Sinners Inc.' credited to 8TH SIN.

The First Demo, Brejn Dedd (1988) (Demo). Are You Ugly? / Mizter Ugly / Deadly Ugly.

Ugly Tape, Ugly Tapez (1988) (Demo). Ugly / Ugly Vittu / Ugly Rap / Ugly Manamana / Ugly Defence / Ugly Cop / Ugly Coffin / Ugly Brain / U.G.L.Y. / Mizter Ugly / Deadly Ugly / Are You Ugly?

Born Ugly, Brejn Dedd (1989). Born Ugly / Is This Ugly? / Mizter Ugly / U.G.L.Y. / Ugly Brain / Ugly Rap / Ugly Cop / Ugly Coffin / Ugly Gay / Ugly Jazz / Ugly Hitler / Ugly Gummignu / Ugly Sportfreak / Ugly Defence / Ugly Scanner Rip-Off / Born Ugly (Discoversion).

The Ugly Family, Brejn Dedd (1990) (Demo).

BRICK BATH

SAN DIEGO, CA, USA — *Joseph McCaw (vocals), Eric Meyer (guitar), Pete Stone (bass), Scott Babbel (drums).*

San Diego Californian neo-Thrashers founded in 1996 as EPITAPH. Previous to BRICK BATH vocalist Joseph McCraw had been a member of SHOCKHEAD, a band featuring 24-7 SPYZ drummer Joel Maitoza and THE NIXONS bassist Ricky Wolking. BRICK BATH debuted with the 'Scarred' album for the Chainsaw label. However, the record label folded shortly after the album release. Undaunted, BRICK BATH set about a heavy gig schedule opening for EXODUS, TESTAMENT, FLOTSAM AND JETSAM and FORBIDDEN among others.

Adding bassist Pete Stone, a former member of DFA and TEABAG, the band recorded the self produced 'I Won't Live The Lie' album for Crash Music. In September of 2002 BRICK PATH parted ways with vocalist Joseph McCaw. The following month Cody Hubbard took the role.

Whilst recording the band's third album, 'American Currency' for Crash Music Inc., during July 2004 the group parted ways with bass player Pete Stone, recruiting Scott 'Rock' Rockstead in his stead. 'American Currency' emerged in 2005.

Former PSYCHOTIC WALTZ drummer Norm Leggio joined BRICK BATH in December 2006.

I WON'T LIVE THE LIE, Crash Music CRAS 61014 (2002). Inner Peace / Bone Dry / Pain My Friend / Sick Of You / Undone / I Won't Live The Lie / Crucified / Simple Life / So Wrong / Oppression Kills / Need / Legacy / Erased / Die Alone.

AMERICAN CURRENCY, Crash Music (2005). American Currency / Bleed With Me / Religious Experience / Victim Again / No Mercy / Memories / She Had To . . . / Don't Provoke / Slave To Life / Down Are The Ways / Love = Hate / Storybook Ending.

BRIDE

KY, USA — *Dale Thompson (vocals), Troy Thompson (guitar / keyboards), Scott Hall (bass), Stephan Rolland (drums).*

Kentucky Christian rock act BRIDE debuted with the 1986 'Show No Mercy' album, a record of considerable aggression bearing in mind its lyrical stance. BRIDE at this point consisted of the Thompson brothers vocalist Dale and guitarist Troy, second guitarist Steve Osbourne, bassist Scott Hall and drummer Stephen Rolland.

By the second album 'Live To Die', produced by Armand John Petri, Hall lost his position to newcomer Frank Partipilo. The album caught many Christian Rock fans off guard by including an unaccredited final track of screaming demons! (Actually a studio mix of piano and vocal howling!)

BRIDE were back to a single guitar band for the 'Silence Is Madness' album. Retaining mainstay Troy Thompson the band utilized additional studio guitar from Rob Johnson. By 1992 Rik Foley had occupied the bass position.

1995's 'Drop', on new label Rugged, found BRIDE in Grunge mode akin to the STONE TEMPLE PILOTS. 1997's 'The Jesus Experience' found the band once more in collaboration with John and Dino Elefante and boosting their studio sound with the addition of guitarist Tim Bushong of LOVEWAR. The 1999 live album was limited to just 700 copies and saw the Thompson brothers & McBroom joined onstage by bassists Andrew Wilkinson & Steve Curtsinger.

Follow up 'Oddities' had Lawrence Bishop occupying the bass position and GUARDIAN's Tony Palacios on guest guitar. A resurrected BRIDE toured Brazil in August 2005 with support from fellow Christian Thrashers TRINO. The band drafted former BULLETBOYS drummer Denny Johnson in July 2006. However, BRIDE was then rejoined drummer Jerry McBroom. The 'Skin For Skin' album, featuring a guesting Steve Osborne on guitar, was recorded at Waycross Studios in Ohio.

SHOW NO MERCY, Pure Metal SPCN7900601171 (1986). Evil That Men Do / Now He Is Gone / Fly Away / Forever In Darkness / Follow Your Heart / Show No Mercy / I Will Be With You / Thunder In The City / No Matter The Price / The First Will Be The Last.

LIVE TO DIE, Pure Metal SPCN7900602933 (1988). Metal Night / Hell No / Into The Dark / Out For Blood / Live To Die / Fire And Brimstone / Whiskey Seed / Here Comes The Bride / Heroes.

SILENCE IS MADNESS, Pure Metal SPCN7900604243 (1989). Fool Me Once / Hot Down South Tonight / Silence Is Madness / Until The End We Rock / Evil Dreams / Under The Influence / All Hallow's Eve / No More Nightmares / Rock Those Blues Away.

END OF THE AGE, Pure Metal PMD 7900 (1990). Everybody Knows My Name / Hell No / Hot Down South Tonight / Forever In Darkness / Heroes / Same Ol' Sinner / Thunder In The City / Fire And Brimstone / Evil That Men Do / All Hallow's Eve.

SNAKES IN THE PLAYGROUND, Starsong SSD 8261 (1992). Rattlesnake / Would You Die For Me / Psychedelic Super Jesus / Fallout / Saltriver Shuffle / Dust Through A Fan / I Miss The Rain / (Untitled) / Don't Use Me / Picture Perfect / Love Money / Some Things Never Change / (Untitled) / Hello, Goodbye.

KINETIC FAITH, Starsong SSD 8197 (1992). Troubled Times / Hired Gun / Ever Fallen In Love / Mountain / Ski Mask / Everybody Knows My Name / Young Love / Kiss The Train / Crimes Against Humanity / Sweet Louise.

SCARECROW MESSIAH, Starsong SSD 8283 (1994). Beast / Place / Murder / Scarecrow / Crazy / Time / One / Doubt / DadMom / Thorns / Questions / (Silence) / (Untitled).

ACROSS THE BORDER, Stephans-Buchhandlung SBCD 93002 (1994). Would You Die For Me / Scarecrow / Psychedelic Super Jesus / Hired Gun / Under The Influence / Thorns / Everybody Knows My Name / Hell No / Murder / Troubled Times / How Long (Unplugged) / I Miss The Rain (Unplugged).

God Gave Rock And Roll To You, Music For Nations 12 KUT 156 (1994). God Gave Rock And Roll To You / Rattlesnake / Dust Through A Fan.

THE LOST REELS, Bride (1994). How Long / Fine Line / Only Hurts When I Laugh / Lisa / Let The Son Shine / I Don't Get It / Hollywood / Sugar / I Am The Devil / Good Rock 'n' Roll / Dirty / 18 / Help / Could You Live In My World / Think About Our Future / Sleepy Southern Town / Pyramid / Echoes Of Mercy / I Miss Dancing With You / It's The Devil.

LOST REELS II, Bride (1994). Scarecrow / Place / Beast / Some Things Never Change / Same Ol' Sinner / I Miss The Rain / Kiss The Train / Everybody Knows My Name / Hired Gun / Ever Fallen In Love / Young Love / Sweet Louise / Rattlesnake / Would You Die For Me.

DROP, Rugged RGD66012 (1995). Personal Savior / Mamma / You Never Knew Me / Life Is The Blues / Help / Only Hurts When I Laugh / Thrill A Minute / How Long / Have You Made It? / Nobodies Here / I'm The Devil / Jesus Came Back Via Jesus In A Pawn Shop.

LOST REELS III, Bride LR3CD216945 (1997). Guilty / One Race / Break My Spine / Cosmic Christ / Cover Dry Bones / What Am I Supposed To Do / I Believe / Days Of Shame / I'm Trying To Tell You / What Are We / I'm Not Alone / Alive.

THE JESUS EXPERIENCE, Organic ORCD-9703 (1997). I Love You / The Worm / End / I Live For You / Follow Me / Tell Me / Love/Hate / Human Race / I Hear A Word / Cosmic Christ / The World I Know.

ODDITIES, Organic ORCD 9830 (1998). Intro / I Ain't Coming Down / Why Won't He Break / If I Told You it Was The End Of The World / I Found God / Closer To The Center Of The Earth / Tomorrow Makes No Sense / Day By Day / Spirit / It Is Only When I'm Left Alone / God's Human Oddities / Under The Blood / Die A Little Bit Every Day / Restore Me.

LIVE—VOLUME 1, Old School OSR-1001 (1999) (Limited edition 2500 copies). Intro / I Ain't Coming Down / If I Told You It Was The End Of The World / The Worm / I Found God / Under The Blood / Day By Day / I Live For You / Why Won't He Break / End / No Drugs / It Is Only When I'm Left Alone / He Never Changes / I Love You / Amazing Grace / The Big Block Motor / Jesus On The Mainline / I Have Decided / Dale's Sermon.

THIS IS IT, Bride (2003). Blow It All Away / To The Sky / More Than Human / Drop D / Head Looking For A Bullet / Best I Expect To Do / Evil Geniuses / Revolution / Barren River Blues / Microphone / Short Time In The Grave / Universe / White Elephant.

BROKEN DAGGER

HJÄRUP, SWEDEN — *Niklas Olausson (vocals), Magnus Wohlfart (guitar), William Ekeberg (bass), Urban Månsby (keyboards), Jeremy Child (drums).*

Hjärup based Speed Metal band, forged by three sixteen year olds English drummer Jeremy Child and the guitar pairing of Magnus Wohlfart from TRYMHEIM and Håkan Lanz, during 2000 under an original title of VÄRLDENS STÖRSTA TRÄD. Gustaf Hagel enrolled on bass guitar, after which Lanz exited, being replaced by ex-MONUMENT NOCTURNE man Jonas Fröberg. Switching title to BROKEN DAGGER the band performed at the Musik Direkt contest at Mejeriet in Lund during 2002 as an instrumental group.

Singer Niklas Olausson, a veteran of KOBLOD, SATYG and FLYING SCIMITAR, was drafted for the opening demo 'Into Madness'. 'Madness Approaching', seeing TRYMHEIM keyboard player Urban Månsby added to the line-up, followed in 2004. William Ekeberg of BODY CORE and TRYMHEIM had substituted for Hagel as new bassist, but did not perform on the demo.

Magnus Wohlfhart is also active with FOLKEARTH, TRYMHEIM, LÖMSKA PLANER, ANTI-CHRISTIAN ASSAULT, WOHLFART and YGGDRASIL, the latter alongside Childs, and NAE'BLIS whilst Jonas Fröberg operated MÄSK PA MORMORS and TRYMHEIM. Fröberg exited in 2005.

Into Madness, Broken Dagger (2003) (Demo). Embrace Insanity / Flying Free / The Sun Is Setting / Kiss Of A Broken Dagger / Red Nightfall / The Illusion Of Faith.

Madness Approaching, Broken Dagger (2004) (Demo). The Call / By Blood & Right / The Way Of The Crown / Under The Spell / Code: Broken Dagger / Chains Of Insanity / Traces Of Pain / Path Of Nevermore / Rise Of The Machines.

CHAIN OF COMMAND, CMD CMD001 (2007) (First pressing). An Unwanted Child / The Black Lotus / Rogaar Beware / Story Of A Wicked Mind / He Will Die / Fire Within / Royal Deathlist / Vicious Light / The End Of Hope / E.B.E.N.

BULLDOZER

MILAN, ITALY — *Alberto Contini (vocals / bass), Andy Panigada (guitar), Rob K. Cabrini (drums).*

Undeniably taking their cue from MOTÖRHEAD, Milan Thrash Metal merchants BULLDOZER were formed in 1980 by bassist Dario Carria and guitarist Andy Panigada. Operating in raw Thrash Metal territory the band also imbued both their music and images with strong blasphemous overtones. The opening 1980 formation comprised a trio with Andy Panigada on guitar, bassist Dario Carria with Erminio Galli on drums. Forced to split in 1981 due to national service commitments the group nevertheless reformed in 1983, now influenced by the likes of VENOM and TANK as evidenced on the 1984 demo 'Fallen Angel', subsequently re-issued as a 7" single. Indeed, BULLDOZER's debut album, 1985's 'The Day Of Wrath' now seeing Don Andras on drums and new frontman AC Wild (a.k.a. Alberto Contini)., was produced by TANK frontman Algy Ward.

Second album 'The Final Separation' was delivered in 1986 before a further change in the membership incorporated drummer Rob "Klister" Cabrini for 1987's 'IX: Circle Of Hell'. Sadly, founder member Dario Carria committed suicide during 1988. For the 'IX' album onwards drums were handled by Rob Cabrini and, as a new decade dawned, the band's lyrical standpoint became increasingly devoid of any satanic references.

In November 1990 the Metal Masters label issued the concert recording 'Live In Poland', this featuring a cover version of MOTÖRHEAD's 'Overkill'. However, BULLDOZER put in their swansong gig in Milan that same December. A posthumous, somewhat oddball EP, 'Dance Got Sick!', emerged in 1992.

In February 1997 Rob Cabrini acted as producer for Black Metal band MYSTICAL FULLMOON's four track demo tape 'Through Somber Passages'. Alberto Contini was involved with ex-SLAYER drummer DAVE LOMBARDO's classical Vivaldi album 'The Meeting' in 1999. Meantime, the underground legend of BULLDOZER was kept alive with a split tribute EP emerging in 2000, a union between noted Japanese Black Thrashers SABBAT and French Death Metal band IMPERIAL. The following year Japanese band HELLCHILD included a cover version of 'Insurrection Of The Living Damned' to their split album shared with CONVERGE, 'Deeper The Wound'.

Contini would also donate narrative to the highly regarded debut from British Black Metal band THE MEADS OF ASPHODEL 'The Excommunication Of Christ'. The group would repay the favour by cutting a version of 'Neurodelini' for a BULLDOZER tribute EP assembled by Warlord Records. The same label would re-issue both the 'IX' and 'Neurodeliri' albums in limited edition picture disc formats.

In 2004 the band would have their classic cut 'Whiskey Time' chosen as a pioneering piece of music for a compilation assembled by DARKTHRONE drummer Fenriz, released through Peaceville Records and entitled 'Fenriz Presents The Best Of Old School Black Metal'. BULLDOZER's five albums would be collected together by Polish label Metal Mind Productions in November 2006. The box set 'Regenerated In The Grave', hosting bonus tracks and a 32 page booklet, was restricted to a limited edition of 2000 copies.

AC Wild guested on the SCHIZO album 'Cicatriz Black' in 2007.

Fallen Angel, Bulldozer (1984). Fallen Angel / Another Beer (It's What I Need).

THE DAY OF WRATH, Roadrunner (1985). The Exorcism / Cut Throat / Insurrection Of The Living Damned / Fallen Angel / The Great Deceiver / Mad Man / Whiskey Time / Welcome Death / Endless Funeral.

THE FINAL SEPARATION, Roadrunner RR 9711 (1986). The Final Separation / Ride Hard, Die Fast / The Cave / Sex Symbol's Bullshit / 'Don' Andreas / Never Relax! / Don't Trust The Saint / The Death Of Gods.

IX—CIRCLE OF HELL, Discomagic LP328 (1987). IX / Desert / Ilona The Very Best / Misogynist / Heaven's Jail / Rob 'Kilster' / The Derby / No Way / The Vision Never Fades.

NEURODELIRI, Metal Master MET109 (1988). Overture / Neurodeliri / Minkions / We Are ... Italian / Art Of Deception / Ilona Had Been Elected / Impotence / More Tua-Vita Mea / Willful Death / You'll Be Recalled.

ALIVE IN POLAND, Metal Master (1990). IX / Desert / Ilona The Very Best / Impotence / The Derby / Heaven's Jail / Mikiens / Mors Tua Vita Mea / Overkill / Willful Death (You'll Be Recalled).

Dance Got Sick!, Build (1992). Dance Got Sick! (Part 1) / Dance Got Sick! (Part 2) / Dance Got Sick! (Part 3) / Tech-Core Rap Sickness.

BURIED GOD

GERMANY — *Ko (vocals), Halli (vocals / guitar), Ernstl (bass), Patrick W. Engel (drums).*

Thuringian Thrash Metal forged by the former NAMELESS duo of vocalist / guitarist Halli and drummer Patrick W. Engel. The latter also holds down membership of both IMPENDING DOOM and ATANATOS. Initially the original 1998 formation was billed as ANTARES but the discovery of a Czech act of the same name forced a switch to BURIED GOD for the demo 'Back To Wreck Your Neck'. This tape, and a split 7" single shared with ANAEL, was promoted by an October 2001 tour of the Czech Republic partnered with SEIRIM, FALL OF SERENITY and IMMORTAL TEARS. Frontman for these shows would be Dorstl although upon completion of this round of live work he would be dumped. FALL OF SERENITY's bassist John filled in as substitute singer for two German gigs. Halli took over singing lead for a new batch of demos, with the band cutting a cover version of GRIFFIN's 'Hunger'.

Lead vocalist Ko, inducted during March of 2002, was previously active as bass player for PROSATANOS.

Back To Wreck Your Neck EP, (2001) (Split single with ANAEL). Back To Wreck Your Neck / A Piece Of Flesh.

DARK REVELATION, Merciless MR CD 015 (2003). Back To Wreck Your Neck / The Beast Rules Me / Conquer Moriha / A Piece Of Flesh / Buried God / Eyes Of The Gorgon / Hunger / Ruins Of Pantheon / My Dark Revelation / Rape Of Harmony.

BY NIGHT

FALKENBURG, SWEDEN — *Adrian Westin (vocals), Andre Gonazales (guitar), Simon Wien (guitar), Henrik Persson (bass), Per Qvarnstrom (drums).*

Falkenburg's BY NIGHT heralded their arrival upon the Death Metal scene with an eponymous, two-song 2000 demo. Further sessions, the five-track 'Derelict' in 2001 and 'Lamentations' the following year, were subsequently delivered. Lead vocalist Adrian Westin is also active with AGGRESSIVE SERPENT and, alongside guitarist Andre Gonazales, TRENDKILL. In 2004 the group shared a split album with CIPHER SYSTEM on the Lifeforce label. The full-length 'Burn The Flags' followed in February 2005. Throughout October and November of 2005 the band engaged in the "The Monster Mosh Down" dates across Germany, Switzerland, Austria, Holland and the UK partnered with Germans DISBELIEF, Hungarian act EKTOMORF and Israel's BETZEFER.

BY NIGHT scheduled time at StudioMega in Varberg in May 2006 to cut a new album 'A New Shape Of Desperation'.

By Night, By Night (2000) (Demo). Frozen Future Haze / Fight With The Darkness.

Derelict, By Night (2001) (Demo). Awakening / Lost To The Tormentor / Greed And Misery / Derelict / Of Infatuation.

Lamentations, By Night (2002) (Demo). Lamentation / Unseen Oppression / Obsessed To Hate.

BY NIGHT, Lifeforce LFR 043-2 (2004) (Split album with CIPHER SYSTEM). Lamentation / Unseen Oppression / Obsessed To Hate.

BURN THE FLAGS, Lifeforce LFR 050-2 (2005). Between The Lines / Part Of Perfection / One And The Same / Raise Your Voice / Completed / Behind In Silence / Unseen Oppression / At The End Of The Day / Dead Or Confused.

A NEW SHAPE OF DESPARATION, Lifeforce LFR 063-2 (2006). It Starts Within (Intro) / The Truth Is Sold / People Like You / Through Ashes We Crawl / Same Old Story / Dead Eyes See No Future / Walls Of Insecurity / Idiot / Forsaken Love / Cursed By The Thought / Time Is Running Out (Outro).

ČACHTICE

SODERTALJE, SWEDEN — *Metal Maniac (vocals / bass), Panzer Reidar (guitar), Necropounder (drums).*

Sodertalje's ČACHTICE, taking their title from the Čachtice residency of Countess Bathory and claiming to be "True Norwegian Crack Metal", are in fact Swedish. Their opening shot would be the 'Rehearsals Of Doom' demo in 2000. Vocalist / bassist Metal Maniac is active with MORD and INCARNATION. Guitarist Panzer Reidar, a native of Enhörna, counts prior affiliations with Heavy Metal acts WYVERN and FIST FIRST, Death Metal combo MESQET and Progressive outfit DIVERGE. Drummer Necropounder (a.k.a. Mattias Eklund) credits list MÖRK GRYNING (as 'Avatar'), REPUGNANT, SINS OF OMISSION, MORTIFER, FIST FIRST, VANISHED and REQUIEM.

Upon completion of the inaugural demo the group adopted the revised title of CSEJTHE (The Slovakian name for Castle Čachtice), but would revert back to ČACHTICE. An opening album, 'Infernal Bloodlust', followed in 2001 after which Manimal was drafted on guitar. 'The DVD of Snagnov' arrived in 2003 and the 'Satanic Attack' demo delivered in 2004. That same year, Manimal exited.

Rehearsals Of Doom, Čachtice (2000) (Demo). Angela's Fate / Romanian Warlord Supreme / Erzsébet Imája.
INFERNAL BLOODLUST, Čachtice (2001). Angela's Fate / Hungarian Acts Of Evil / Romanian Warlord Supreme / Medieval Sturmfuhrer / Satan My Master / Chained By Terror / Slaves Of Fokalor / Journey Through Wallachia / The Legend Of Snagov.
Satanic Attack, Čachtice (2004) (Demo). Satanic Attack / Oprichnina / Impaled Mazarene / Green Eyed Succubus.

CACOPHONY

USA — *Peter Marrino (vocals), Marty Friedman (guitar), Jason Becker (guitar), Jimmy O'Shea (bass), Atma Anur (drums).*

CACOPHONY arrived with perfect timing in the mid 80's heightened interest in speed guitarists. MARTY FRIEDMAN had paid his dues with HAWAII and VIXEN and forging an alliance with another six string whizz kid JASON BECKER founded CACOPHONY with erstwhile LE MANS singer Peter Marrino. The resulting album 'Speed Metal Symphony' sparked considerable interest, enough for both guitarists to capitalize on it with solo outings. Friedman launched 'Dragon's Kiss' whilst Becker's 'Perpetual Burn' was released simultaneously.

Drummer Atma Anur departed prior to the second CACOPHONY album, 1988's 'Go Off!', and was superseded by ex-LE MANS skinbasher Kenny Stavropoulos. However, drums on the album are in fact supplied by Dean Castronovo, most recognised for his work with WILD DOGS, HARDLINE, OZZY OSBOURNE and JOURNEY. Stavropoulos later joined STARSHIP. Marrino would front San Francisco's 9.0 for their 1990 album 'Too Far Gone'.

Friedman was later to enjoy global recognition as part of MEGADETH and for his solo workouts. Becker also made a name for himself with a string of authorities solo albums and an appearance in DAVID LEE ROTH's band. However, just as Becker seemed on the edge of the stardom he deserved touring with DAVID LEE ROTH the young guitarist was diagnosed as suffering with the crippling Lou Gehrig's disease commonly known as ALS. Tragically, the disease left the guitarist completely without the use of his body. Becker still composed music albeit with great difficulty using a computer scanner to read and his eyes to communicate to others. When the true extent of his predicament was learned his fellow musicians rallied around in a show of camaraderie resulting fresh recording interpretations of Becker's music to remind the world of his talent by way of the 'Warmth In The Wilderness' tribute album. Naturally, MARTY FRIEDMAN contributed.

After a high profile run of gold and platinum albums Friedman left MEGADETH in 2000. He would then embroil himself in the highly lucrative world of Japanese J-Pop, working with such artists as Rock diva AIKAWA NANASE.

2004 saw Peter Marrino back in the spotlight, albeit in the rather unexpected guise as the self styled "greatest Ozzy impersonator on Earth" fronting the OZZY OSBOURNE tribute band OZZY UNAUTHORISED alongside NIGHT RANGER and ex-OZZY OSBOURNE guitarist BRAD GILLIS.

SPEED METAL SYMPHONY, Roadrunner 349577 (1987). Savage / Where My Fortune Lies / The Ninja / Concerto / Burn The Ground / Desert Island / Speed Metal Symphony.
GO OFF!, Roadrunner RR 94991 (1988). X Ray Eyes / E.S.P. / Stranger / Go Off! / Black Cat / Sword Of The Warrior / Floating World / Images.

CADAVERES DE TORTUGAS

HUNGARY — *Péter Körmöczi (vocals / guitar), Péter Kecskés (vocals / guitar), Gábor Persoczki (bass), Szabolcs Viniczai (drums).*

CADAVERES DE TORTUGAS, blending Bay Area style Thrash with New York Hardcore, was assembled in 1993. Opening demos, 1994's 'Stigmatized Eye', 1995's 'Turtles Ahead' and 'La Sangre No Miente' in 1996 as well as albums 'Our Way' and 'Ready II Rumble', garnered critical acclaim throughout Hungary but in 1999 the band was struck by tragedy when founder member vocalist / guitarist Tibor Zsombok Jr. was killed in a car accident. The group struggled on without a replacement for a while until they eventually drafted NECK SPRAIN man Péter Kecskés. Valuable support slots to international artists saw CADAVERES DE TORTUGAS sharing stages with SLAYER, DEATH ANGEL, D.R.I., MISFITS and SOULFLY.

MANGOD INC. was formulated following the split of CADAVERES DE TORTUGAS by vocalist / bassist Perso, guitarist Péter Kecskés and drummer Szabolcs Viniczai.

OUR WAY, (1997). Respect My Way / Street-Hunter / Indifferent Masses / Red Room / Don't Play Macho / Absolvation / Fuck The Beaten Track / Floating / Bloody Desire / Hate (Rap version).
READY II RUMBLE, (1998). Same Shit / Rat Bones / Lie Is Its Name / Idol Without Regrets / Pintar De Verde / Your Blood / Here I Come / False Domination / Angry Vibes / Vatos Logos.
INCARNATION, Cadaveras De Tortugas (2002). Panic Attack / Castaway / War Dance / Time Trap / UBQT / Password Showdown / Vuetro / Dial 666 / Syco I / Anima / El Mensajero / Eso Es.

CALHOUN CONQUER

SWITZERLAND — *Geri Christian Gerling (vocals), Chris Muzik (guitar), Bruce Muzik (guitar), Stefan Gerling (bass / drums).*

Thrash Metallers CALHOUN CONQUER benefited from the on loan services of drummer Mark Halbheer although the album track 'Lost In Itself' is the sole work of a drum computer. Other contributing musicians included guitarists Fritz Ott and Bruno Amatruda. CALHOUN CONQUER's line up later featured MEKONG DELTA, AIN'T DEAD YET and KROKUS drummer Peter Haas.

In 1992 sibling guitarists Bruce and Christian Muzik along with Haas and joined BABYLON SAD. Haas would team up with KROKUS again in 1999.

Pathological Proportions, Chainsaw Murder (1987) ('... And Now You're Gone' EP). Pathological Proportions / No Parallel With Eden / Outermost Consequences / Diane.
LOST IN ONESELF, Aaarrg AAARRG 22 (1989). Disgust And Hate / Fuckhead / You Mean Nothing / Torturer / Portals Of Delirium / Psycho Trap / Nothing (Has Killed Itself) / Outermost Consequences / Worlds In Collision / Diane.

CANCER

TELFORD, SHROPSHIRE, UK — *John Walker (vocals / guitar), James Murphy (guitar), Ian Buchanan (bass), Carl Stokes (drums).*

Telford, Shropshire based extreme Speed Metal band, CANCER's first gig was in Birmingham opening for BOMB DISNEYLAND. The group was formulated during 1988, convened at the Tontine public house in Ironbridge by singer / guitarist John Walker, bassist Ian Buchanan and Carl Stokes on drums. The initial demos, a two track deathfest dubbed No Fuckin' Cover', were recorded at the legendary Pits studio in Birmingham, owned by STARFIGHTERS vocalist Steve Burton. Notably, the songs, 'The Growth Has Begun' and 'Burning Casket (My Testimony)', were produced by Stevie Young, cousin of AC/DC guitarist Angus Young, and 'Big' Mick Hughes, METALLICA's live sound engineer.

A second demo session in 1989 led in turn to an unofficial live album, 'Bloodbath In The Acid', recorded at Wrexham Memorial Hall and pressed up on the Headache imprint. Having been granted a deal by the Vinyl Solution label, CANCER's debut album, 1990's 'To The Gory End' cut at Loco studios in Usk, took a mere four days to record. Fortunately the finished product was given extra sheen courtesy of a mix down at Morrisound Studios in Florida by Death Metal alchemist Scott Burns. During this final phase OBITUARY's John Tardy was drafted to supply backing vocals to the song 'Die Die'. The cover art, an unfortunate's head being sliced by a machete, still betrayed the band's brutally unsophisticated approach.

Fresh songs were worked up at Reel to Reel Studios in Telford with engineer Tony Higley in preparation for a second album. Erstwhile AGENT STEEL and OBITUARY guitarist JAMES MURPHY was enlisted to record the sophomore 'Death Shall Rise' and the platter was produced by noted Death Metal producer Scott Burns into the bargain. Amusingly, the album caused a great deal of controversy upon release in Europe when it was banned in Germany by the State body for censorship of works dangerous to the youth, on grounds that the album cover would incite youngsters to inflict violence upon each other. Restless Records handled the album for North America.

CANCER had recorded 'Death Shall Rise', released in April 1991, in Scott Burns' Florida home state, this fabled location giving opportunity for DEICIDE's Glen Benton to contribute vocals to lead track 'Hung, Drawn And Quartered'. UK gigs saw a headline run throughout May supported by UNLEASHED and DESECRATOR. The band chose to spend further working time in North America by playing the 1991 Milwaukee Metalfest and also supporting DEICIDE and OBITUARY. However, by December 1991 James Murphy had quit the band to form DISINCARNATE, later joining TESTAMENT and Danes KONKHRA. 1993 was another particularly busy year for the band, releasing third album 'The Sins Of Mankind', fashioned by Simon Efemy at The Windings in Wrexham, and performing a European tour with openers CEREBRAL FIX. A setback occurred when Carl Stokes was involved in an accident, his motorbike hitting a British Telecom van. Stokes suffered multiple injuries, necessitating the enlistment of MONOLITH's Nick Barker on a temporary basis for live work. Barker later made his name with CRADLE OF FILTH and DIMMU BORGIR. The group also to tour Britain and America with DEICIDE, two live tracks recorded at the Milwaukee Metalfest surfacing on the Restless compilation 'Live Death'.

In 1994 the band enrolled new guitarist Barry Savage and CANCER stepped up a level upon signing to major label East West Records. This effort would be executed at Great Linford Studios in Milton Keynes with Simon Efemy at the helm once again, the finished tracks being mixed at PINK FLOYD's Britannia Row Studios. If longstanding fans found the caustic cover of DEEP PURPLE's 'Space Truckin' to much to stomach they consoled themselves with the fact that Carl Stokes had used a real human thigh bone for percussion on 'Temple Song'. Following the release of the new album, 'Black Faith' the quartet toured Britain with support act MESHUGGAH.

During 1997 Carl Stokes would also find himself involved with NOTHING BUT CONTEMPT. The short lived act assembled by vocalist Barney Greenaway in his period away from NAPALM DEATH. This act included Greenaway, Stokes, NAPALM DEATH guitarist Danny Herrera plus SACRIFICIAL ALTAR and ASATRU guitarist Rob Engvikson. NOTHING BUT CONTEMPT folded when Greenaway rejoined NAPALM DEATH. Stokes also filled in for Telford Hardcore mongers ASSERT in 2000. The drummer also busied himself with a new Metal project titled REMISSION with Walker.

Guitarist Barry Savage would join the high profile LOCK UP in early 2002 as touring guitarist. CANCER made a return during 2003 with a line-up comprising John Walker, Carl Stokes, ASATARU guitarist Rob Engvikson and bassist Adders. Reunion gigs would be backed by a new EP 'Corporation$', this outing including a cover of the CELTIC FROST classic 'Dethroned Emperor'. Following European tour dates the band parted ways with Rob Engvikson in September of 2004, soon enlisting Dave Leitch of PULVERISED as replacement.

CANCER's 2005 full-length album 'Spirit In Flames', recorded over a three-week period at Philia studios in Henley on Thames, emerged on Copro Records in June. However, in February 2006 Carl Stokes issued a statement "Due to the lack of commitment to the band from John Walker, CANCER is no more". The drummer also revealed plans for a new band billed HAIL OF FIRE, featuring ex-CANCER members guitarists Dave Leitch and Barry Savage, bassist Ian Buchanan and newcomer Rob Lucas on vocals.

No Fuckin' Cover, Cancer (1988) (Demo). The Growth Has Begun / Burning Casket (My Testimony).

Demo #2, Cancer (1989) (Demo). Your Fate / Into The Acid / Die Die / Revenged / To The Gory End / C.F.C. (Cancer Fucking Cancer).

TO THE GORY END, Vinyl Solution SOL 022 (1990). Bloodbath / C.F.C. / Witch Hunt / Into The Acid / Imminent Catastrophe / To The Gory End / Body Count / Sentenced To The Gallows / Die Die.

DEATH SHALL RISE, Vinyl Solution SOL28 (1991). Hung, Drawn And Quartered / Tasteless Incest / Burning Casket / Death Shall Rise / Back From The Dead / Gruesome Tasks / Corpse Fire / Internal Decay.

THE SINS OF MANKIND, Vinyl Solution SOL35 (1993). The Sins Of Mankind / Cloak Of Darkness / Electro-Convulsive Therapy / Patchwork Destiny / Meat Train / Suffer For Our Sins / Pasture Of Delights At The End / Tribal Bloodshed Part I—The Conquest / Tribal Bloodshed Part II—Under The Flag.

LIVE DEATH, Restless (1994) (Split album by EXHORDER, SUFFOCATION and MALEVOLENT CREATION). Hung, Drawn And Quartered / Blood Bath.

BLACK FAITH, East West 0630 10752-2 (1995). Ants (Nemesis Ride) / Who Do You Think You Are / Face To Face / Without Cause / White Desire / Kill Date / Temple Song / Black Faith / Highest Orders / Space Truckin' / Sunburnt / Save Me From Myself.

Corporation$, Copro COP033 (2004). Oil / Witchhunt (Re-recorded version) / Dethroned Emperor / Oxygen Thieves ('Don't Breathe My Air' Mix) / Oil ('Blackened Satchel Remix' by Ian Buchanon).

SPIRIT IN FLAMES, Copro COP044CD (2005). Insides Out / Mindless Reactions / Spirit In Flames / Hellhouse / Solar Prophecy / Devils Playground / Fistula / Séance / Ouija.

CANTARA

DROUWENERVEEN, HOLLAND — *Dick Barelds (vocals / bass), Jens Van Der Valk (guitar), Pascal Grevinga (guitar), Freddy Leenders (drums).*

Drouwenerveen's CANTARA, established during 1992 comprised an elite cast of Dutch Metal players in KATAFALK and WINTER OF SIN frontman Dick Barelds, the GOD DETHRONED, AUTUMN and SALACIOUS GODS credited guitarist Jens van der Valk, SINISTER, INCURSION, GOD DETHRONED and SARDONIC guitarist Pascal Grevinga and drummer Freddy Leenders.

The line-up changed to incorporate former AWAKENING man Peter Kamminga as lead singer plus a new rhythm section of bassist Mats van der Valk (ak.a. 'Grä Gmorg') of SALACIOUS GODS, SEIZURE, FRAME, MEADOWS, AEOLIAN and FEAR ME, and drummer Chris Oldenburger of INCURSION and SALACIOUS GODS. The 1993 demo 'All Beauty' preceded an EP 'Dark'. The Teutonic Existence label published a 1998 EP 'Fields Of Everlasting Serenity'. Kamminga later joined SEIZURE as Mats van der Valk assumed the lead vocal role.

Dark, Smalltime SPCD001 (1993). Dark / The Shades Of Love / Shredding Memories (A Trilogy Part III) / Exposure Of Involuntary Frustrations (Of Misery) / Odi Et Amo (Outro).

All Beauty, (1993). Grief / Intro / Treading On Thorns / Cherish / The Shades Of Love / Godforsaken.

Fields Of Everlasting Serenity, Teutonic Existence TER-012 (1998). Daytime Starlight / Fields Of Everlasting Serenity / Longgone Memory / In Time / The Mourning Sky.

CAPELLAN

RUSSIA — *Dmitry Lebedev (vocals / guitar), Andrew Vodyanitsky (guitar), Alexander Ushakov (guitar), Andrew Belov (drums).*

Thrashcore outfit CAPELLAN, founded by the Lebedevs brothers guitarist Dmitry and bassist Michael, started its activity in September 1994. The group would be brought up to strength with the addition of lead guitarist Ilgiz Fazilov and the use of a drum machine. Fazilov bailed out just prior to initial recordings for the 'Religious Procession' album and so PILORAMA SYSTEMS man Igor Nagonev substituted in the studio. Subsequently the band pulled in second guitarist Dmitry Umadilov from MISCREANT and drummer Andrew Belov. However, founder Michael Lebedev then exited, CAPELLAN introducing Alexander Ushakov in his place. More changes afflicted CAPELLAN in September of 1997 when Umadilov departed. VIOLENT man Andrew Vodyanitsky substituted. In this formation CAPELLAN cut the 1998 demo 'Hello! Pennywise!'.

RELIGIOUS PROCESSION, (1995). Confession (Intro) / Procession / Suicide / The Servants Of Darkness / Possessed / Lullaby / Capellan / Stand In Order / Outro.

CAPRICORN

GERMANY — *Adrian Ergün (vocals / bass), David (guitar), Stefan Arnold (drums).*

Previously known as GRINDER, this German outfit formed as CAPRICORN in 1991. Following the debut album CAPRICORN supported GRAVEDIGGER on a German tour.

Frontman Adrian Ergün guested on the 1996 album from CRASH MUSEUM. Ergün would create NEMESIS for an eponymous 1997 album in collusion with guitarist Axel Katzmann and Arnulf Tunn of TANKARD.

CAPRICORN, Shark SHARK 030 (1993). Mob In The Hood / One Shot From Murder / Burn / Light Up Your Mind / Lonely Is The World / Mr. Voorhees / Bomb Eden / Shotdown Downtown / The Harder They Fall / Long Way Home / Exceeding The Limits Of Pain.

CAPTOR

VINGÅKER, SWEDEN — *Magnus Fasth (vocals), Niklas Kullström-Lindblom (guitar), Fredrik Olofsson (guitar), Jacob Nordangård (bass), Angelo Mikaj (drums).*

Vingåker / Katrineholm Death-Thrash Metal combo CAPTOR can trace the band history back through many line-up changes as far back as 1986. The opening unit, formed by guitar player Jacob Nordangård, Christer "Putte" Johansson and Juha "Gonzo" Mäyre, took on a variety of short-lived titles including GONZOLA, MIDAS TOUCH and PESTILENCE. The CAPTOR brand was adopted after the SLAYER song 'Captor Of Sin'. During 1988 drummer Christer Johansson switched over to guitar and Lars-Ingvar Eriksson enrolled as the new drummer. However, obligatory military service forced a temporary disbandment the following year.

CAPTOR was re-formulated in the autumn of 1989 by Jacob Nordangård, moving from guitar to bass, and Lars-Ingvar Eriksson in alliance with new guitarist Niklas Kullström-Lindblom. In 1991 CAPTOR was featured on the Extreme Close-Up sampler, sponsored by Swedish Rock magazine Close Up Magazine. The first demo recorded in 1991 was titled 'Memento Mori'. A further tape, 'Domination', followed in 1992. Newly incorporated on drums would be Angelo Mikaj.

Bassist / vocalist Jacob Nordangård was to lose his place following the debut album, December 1993's Andreas Ahlenius produced 'Lay It To Rest' issued on the Euro label and recorded at Gävle Ljudstusio. CAPTOR opted to recruit two new members in his place, the jobs going to bassist Christoffer Andersson and vocalist Magnus Fasth. A 1995 EP, entitled 'Refuse To Die', was recorded at IndoCaptor Studio with producer Fredrik Olofsson.

The Drowned' opus, cut at Roasting House Studio, followed in July 1996 for the Danish imprint Diehard Music. A Japanese release was put out by Avalon Marquee hosting an extra track 'Down'. Third opus 'Dogface' emerged in March 1998. That year Fredrik Olofsson was superseded by Jonnie Carlsson. 2000 found both Fasth and Mikai forging KODEEN.

CAPTOR, switching towards a distinctly Nu-Metal styled direction, released the 'Alien Six' album on Turkish label Hammer Müzik in October 2001. Ex-member Jacob Nordangård joined THE DOOMSDAY CULT.

Memento Mori, Captor (1992) (Demo). Possessed / Vision Of Fear / Metamorphosis / Fundamental Influence / Memento Mori.

Domination, Captor (1992) (Demo). T. D. L. (Traumatic Depressive Lunacy) / Trail Of Death / Domination.

LAY IT TO REST, Euro EURO 933-CD (1993). Intro / Traumatic Depressive Lunacy / Utilized / Aspects Of Positive Thinking / Jaws Of Lust / Domination / Let Revolution Speak / Possessed / Depression / Trail Of Death / Lay It To Rest / Fundamental Influence.

Refuse To Die, Dolphin Productions DMPCDS 07 (1995). Refuse To Die / My Head / Insane / More Life / Circle Of Hate.

DROWNED, Diehard PCD-34 (1996). So Bold As Cold / Disbelieve / Mother / Zombiehead / Hostile Reality / Refuse To Die / Insane / Lost / Confession / More Life / Pray / Sick.

DROWNED, Avalon Marquee MICY-1011 (1997) (Japanese release). So Bold As Cold / Disbelieve / Mother / Zombiehead / Hostile Reality / Refuse To Die / Insane / Lost / Confession / More Life / Pray / Sick / Down.

Diehard Checkpoint # 1, Diehard (1998) (Split promotion CD single with KONKHRA, TAETRE and NAOP). Disconnect.

DOGFACE, Diehard PCD-42 (1998). Disconnect / Bleed With Me / All My Pain / Filthy / Lofi / I Told You / Hate Is Hate / Lakafak / So / Unfair / L.F.S.

ALIEN SIX, Hammer 20010 115016 01 (2001). Shout Up / Cold Inside / Burn / Do You Want To Be Me / Break It / Me, Myself And Them / Scum / Porch / Hold Me, Save Me / Not So Far / Head / Fake Is The World Around Me / Why.

CARNAL FORGE

SALA, SWEDEN — *Jens C. Mortensen (vocals), Johan Magnusson (guitar), Jari Kuusisto (guitar), Petri Kuusisto (bass), Stefan Westerberg (drums).*

The founding line-up of Sala Thrashers CARNAL FORGE comprised DELLAMORTE man Jonas Kjellgren, drummer Stefan Westerberg of IN THY DREAMS and STEEL ATTACK personnel guitarist Jari Kuusisto and bassist Dennis Vestman. Following the debut album 'Who's Gonna Burn' Vestman departed to be replaced by another IN THY DREAMS man Petri Kuusisto. Vocalist Jonas Kjellgren was temporary guitarist with CENTINEX between 1999 and September 2000.

In 2001 guitarist Johan Magnusson made his exit prompting bassist Petri Kuusisto to switch over to guitars whilst former SLAPDASH and ROSICRUCIAN man Lars Lindén assumed bass duty. Lindén already had a CARNAL FORGE connection being responsible for the band's website as well as providing artwork for second album 'Firedemon'

CARNAL FORGE

A fresh CARNAL FORGE album 'Please Die!' would be cut during the summer of 2001. The band would land a valuable European tour on a strong package billing with NILE, THE HAUNTED and THE FORSAKEN. Drummer Stefan Westerberg stepped in as a temporary replacement in the ranks of CENTINEX for their winter European dates in 2002.

In October Guitarist Jonas Kjellgren and drummer Stefan Westerberg along with ex-S.I.B. and TURABUS frontman Mikael Danielsson allied themselves in a new Progressive Doom Metal venture WORLD BELOW, bowing in with a demo 'Sacrifices To The Moon'. The following year yet another CARNAL FORGE side project emerged as Westerberg and guitarist Petri Kuusisto founded ASPERITY working alongside vocalist/bassist Peter Kronberg and guitarist Johan Jahlonen for the album 'The Final Demand'. Kuusisto would also act as session guest on the 2004 debut album from VICIOUS 'Vile, Vicious & Victorious'.

CARNAL FORGE made a return in April of 2004 with the 'Aren't You Dead Yet' opus, released by Century Media in Europe and Soundholic in Japan. They also entered the DVD age with 'Destroy Live', featuring concert footage from a January 2004 Krakow, Poland show and 2003 New York and Tokyo dates. European dates for the Spring in alliance with MISERY INDEX were cancelled due to "economic difficulty as well as an unsolvable schedule". The band drafted LEECH, ex-REVOLVER and SLAPDASH man Jens C. Mortensen as their new singer in August. This new line-up would be inaugurated with September European dates partnering with PRO-PAIN and France's DISTURB.

Meantime, Jonas Kjellgren proved industrious throughout 2004, acting as producer for TORCHBEARER's album 'Yersinia Pestis' and forging a brand new melodic Death Metal combo, fronted by the INCAPACITY, UNMOORED, SOLAR DAWN and TORCHBEARER credited Christian Älvestam, entitled SCAR SYMMETRY for an album 'Symmetric In Design'. That same year Petri Kuusisto would be found as guitarist in another side act, SOULSKINNER.

In January 2007 CARNAL FORGE signed a worldwide deal with Candlelight Records.

WHO'S GONNA BURN, Wrong Again WAR 0006 (1998). Who's Gonna Burn / Sweet Bride / Twisted / Godzilla Is Coming Thru' / The Other Side / Part Animal—Part Machine / Born Too Late / Evilizer / Maggotman / Confuzzed.

FIREDEMON, Century Media 77312-2 (2000). Too Much Hell Ain't Enough For Me / Covered With Fire (I'm Hell) / I Smell Like Death (Son Of A Bastard) / Chained / Defacer / Pull The Trigger / Uncontrollable / Firedemon / Cure Of Blasphemy / Headfucker / The Torture Will Never Stop / A Revel In Violence.

FIREDEMON, Century Media 8012-2 (2000) (USA release). Too Much Hell Ain't Enough For Me / Covered With Fire (I'm Hell) / I Smell Like Death (Son Of A Bastard) / Chained / Defacer / Pull The Trigger / Uncontrollable / Firedemon / Cure Of Blasphemy / Headfucker / The Torture Will Never Stop / A Revel In Violence.

PLEASE . . . DIE!, Century Media 77398-2 (2001). Butchered, Slaughtered, Strangled, Hanged / Hand Of Doom / Fuel For Fire / Totalitarian Torture / Everything Dies / Slaves / Welcome To Your Funeral / Please . . . Die! (Aren't You Dead Yet?) / Becoming Dust / No Resurrection / A World All Soaked In Blood / A Higher Level of Pain.

THE MORE YOU SUFFER . . . , Soundholic TKCS-85056 (2003) (Japanese release). H.B.F. Suicide / Deathblow / Ripped & Torn / Destroy Life / Cursed / Divine Killing Breed Machine / Deep Rivers Of Blood / Breaking Boundaries / Into Oblivion / My Bloody Rampage / Baptized In Fire / Let Me Bleed / Hits You Like A Hammer / Bullet Proof Godmaterial.

THE MORE YOU SUFFER . . . , Century Media 74982-2 (2003) (European release). H.B.F. Suicide / Deathblow / Ripped & Torn / Destroy Life / Cursed / Divine Killing Breed Machine / Deep Rivers Of Blood / Breaking Boundaries / Into Oblivion / My Bloody Rampage / Baptized In Fire / Let Me Bleed.

Deathblow, Century Media (2003) (Promotion CD single). Deathblow.

THE MORE YOU SUFFER . . . , Century Media 8198-2 (2003) (USA release). H.B.F. Suicide / Deathblow / Ripped & Torn / Destroy Life / Cursed / Divine Killing Breed Machine / Deep Rivers Of Blood / Breaking Boundaries / Into Oblivion / My Bloody Rampage / Baptized In Fire / Let Me Bleed.

AREN'T YOU DEAD YET?, Century Media 75982-2 (2004) (European release). Decades Of Despair / My Suicide / Burn Them Alive / Waiting For Sundown / Exploding Veins / Sacred Flames / Inhuman / The Final Hour / Totally Worthless / The Strength Of Misery.

AREN'T YOU DEAD YET?, Soundholic TKCS-85097 (2004) (Japanese release). Decades Of Despair / My Suicide / Burn Them Alive / Waiting For Sundown / Exploding Veins / Sacred Flames / Inhuman / The Final Hour / Totally Worthless / The Strength Of Misery / Ruler Of Your Blood.

AREN'T YOU DEAD YET?, Century Media 8298-2 (2004) (USA release). Decades Of Despair / My Suicide / Burn Them Alive / Waiting For Sundown / Exploding Veins / Sacred Flames / Inhuman / The Final Hour / Totally Worthless / The Strength Of Misery.

TESTIFY FOR MY VICTIMS, Candlelight (2007). Testify For My Victims / Burning Eden / Numb (The Dead) / Godsend Gods End / End Game / Questions Pertaining The Ownership Of My Mind / Freedom By Mutilation / Subhuman / No Longer Bleeding / Biological Waste Matter / Lost Legion / Ante Mori.

CARNIVORE

NEW YORK, NY, USA — *Peter Ratajczyk (vocals / bass), Keith Alexander (guitar), Louie Beateaux (drums).*

Thrash act that showed the earliest inklings of Pete Steele's pre TYPE O NEGATIVE genius. As frontman for CARNIVORE, Steele went under the stage name 'Petrus Steele' with drummer Louie Beateaux opting for 'Lord Petrus T'. CARNIVORE's early gigs made quite an impact with lead man Pete Steele (real name Peter Ratajczyk) often resorting to self mutilation carving crosses into his face. His talents in other areas were also much in demand as he is credited with penning the lyrics on the debut AGNOSTIC FRONT album.

Pre-CARNIVORE, Brooklyn's FALLOUT would prove to be a catalyst for launching Steele onto the New York scene. FALLOUT also included Josh Silver and John Campos on second guitar with the AGNOSTIC FRONT, and later CARNIVORE, drummer Louie Beateaux. Pre-FALLOUT both Steele and Silver had operated with formative act AGGRESSION. FALLOUT, having been assembled in 1979, issued the now highly collectable 'Rock Hard' 7" single in 1981. Only 500 copies were pressed through Silver Records. Gigs locally included a notable support to TWISTED SISTER but in 1982 the band folded. Whilst Steele and Beateaux initiated CARNIVORE, Silver and Campos duly forged ORIGINAL SIN.

Following the self-titled debut album, released in 1985 through Roadracer Records, guitarist Keith Alexander left the fold in 1986 to create PRIMAL SCREAM together with ex-HELLICON vocalist Steve Alliano and former BLACK VIRGIN bassist Rob Graham. He was replaced by Marc Piovanetti for 1988's 'Retaliation'. Alexander also served a three year stint with DEE SNIDER of TWISTED SISTER's solo band SICK

MUTHAFUCKERS and forged an alternate career for himself as a professional body piercer.

Steele set about completely re-inventing the band through REPULSION to SUB ZERO evolving eventually into what would become the globally successful and controversial gothic outfit TYPE O NEGATIVE. Piovanetti allied himself with THE CRUMB-SUCKERS.

On 11th July 2005 CARNIVORE guitarist Keith Alexander was killed in a biking accident.

In early 2006 it was revealed that Pete Steele had plans to resurrect the CARNIVORE project for live work, drawing in Joey Zampela from LIFE OF AGONY and Paul Bento from METAL HEALTH ASSOCIATION on guitars. By April it was learned that former DUST TO DUST and current METAL HEALTH ASSOCIATION drummer Steve Tobin was involved.

The first show to be announced for the new look CARNIVORE would be a slot on the August 'Wacken Open Air' festival in Germany. However, under the name THE BENSONHOIST LESBIAN CHOIR, the band performed on July 28th at Fontana's in New York.

CARNIVORE, Roadrunner RR9754 (1985). Predator / Carnivore / Male Supremacy / Armageddon / Legion Of Doom / God Is Dead / Thermonuclear Warrior / World Wars III And IV.

RETALIATION, Roadrunner RR9567 (1988). Daniel's And Pizza / Angry Neurotic Catholics / S.M.D. / Ground Zero Brooklyn / Race War / Inner Conflict / Jesus Hitler / Technophobia / Manic Depression / U.S.A. For U.S.A. / Five Billion Dead / Sex And Violence.

CARRION CARNAGE

LINKÖPING, SWEDEN — *Daniel Linder (vocals / guitar), Stefan Jörbo (guitar), Cyrus Djahedi (bass), Jakob Selbing (drums).*

Linköping Death Metal band CARRION CARNAGE was manifested during 2001 by guitarist Daniel Linder in union initially with Ulf Ståhl and Johan Dyyk. Linder also has association with SVARTUS KRÅKUS SATANICUS. This trio soon fractured without recording, the latter going on to WELTSCHMERZ and EYES OF ICE. In 2002 Stefan Jörbo of CHROME enrolled on guitar and this duo entered La Bomba Studios to craft the demo 'Evil'. Upon completion of these sessions Linder switched instruments to take command of the drums.

In 2003 Janne Hyytiä was taken on to cover guitar and bass but would exit before the year was out. Back to a duo once again, the March 2003 album 'Mass Murder Rampage' featured a rendition of SIX FEET UNDER's 'No Warning Shot'. As the year closed ex-PURGAMENTUM man Jakob Selbing was inducted on drums for CARRION CARNAGE's inaugural live performance.

In side activity, CARRION CARNAGE members, guitarist Johan Hertil, bass player Pelle Djahedi and drummer Daniel Linder, forged the extracurricular project SNIPPA (Swedish for 'Cunt') in 2003 working with vocalist Magnus "Strigge" Strigner. This venture evolved into the less brazen ZNIPPA before taking on the TOTAL INCINERATION tag for a 2003 demo entitled 'Perverse Suffering'.

CARRION CARNAGE's March 2004 album 'Awaiting Salvation Of Death' included a cover versions of CANNIBAL CORPSE's 'Hammer Smashed Face' and NILE's 'Ruins'

MASS MURDER RAMPAGE, Carrion Carnage (2003). I Crave / Die By The Knife / No Warning Shot / Fear Of Dying / Revenge Of The Zombie / Evil (Re-recorded) / Murder Mankind.

Evil, Carrion Carnage (2003) (Demo). Evil / Evil (Video).

AWAITING SALVATION OF DEATH, Carrion Carnage (2004). Blood Anthem (Intro) / Closer To Extinction / Hideous Disfigurement / Destined To Suffer / The Eye Of Horus / Tortured Souls / Awaiting Salvation Of Death / Hammer Smashed Face / Ruins.

Oppressed By Fear, Carrion Carnage (2004) (Demo). Intro / Oppressed By Fear.

CASBAH

FUNABASHI, JAPAN — *Taka Hatori (vocals), Ryo Murayama (guitar), Takatoshi Kodaira (bass), Suguru Kobayashi (drums).*

Funabashi, Chiba Thrash Metal band CASBAH originally went under the title of EXPLOSION. As CASBAH, the title adopted in October 1983, the band featured on two compilation albums, 'Heavy Metal Forum 3' on Explosion Records and 'Devil Must Be Driven Out With Devil' for the Hold Up label. CASBAH then released a live May 1985 single featuring 'Fear And Destruction' and 'Kill You All'. The singles legend of "Bang your heads to Hell" aptly summed up their devotion to undiluted Thrash.

At this stage CASBAH comprised distinctively deep throated frontman Taka Hatori, guitarist Nariaki Kida, bassist Kouichi Mitani and drummer Takashi Usui. Unusually for such a heavyweight act CASBAH also paid great attention to their visuals, often decked out in "Attack Metal" costumes and garish make up. The self-financed 'Russian Roulette' single followed in 1986, which saw Kida replaced by Ryo Murayama. A further demo session 'Infinite Pain' arrived in 1987. CASBAH continued demoing, putting out 'Believe Or Bleed' in 1989, 'The Cloning' in 1991 and 'Swan Song' in 1992.

The band put in a noteworthy live gig at the infamous New York CBGB's club during 1992 but would then undergo line-up changes. Yet another demo session, 'March Of The Final decade', was laid down in 1994. CASBAH signed to the Roadrunner label in 1996 issuing the 'Bold Statement' album the following year. A collection of re-recorded archive material, 'Dinosaurs', arrived in 1998. CASBAH vocalist Hatori would also deputise live for OUTRAGE.

Subsequently, CASBAH's rhythm section has witnessed a shift over to bass player Takatoshi Kodaira and drummer Suguru Kobayoshi. The latter would join SOLITUDE in late 2001. In 2005 all the band's demo material was collected together on the compilation album 'Russian Roulette—No Posers Allowed'.

Casbah Live, Explosion (1985). Fear And Destruction / Kill You All.
Infinite Pain, Casbah (1986). Infinite Pain / Chain Gang / No More Slaughter / Low Intensity Warfare.
Russian Roulette, Music Visions (1986). Russian Roulette / Death Metal.
Casbah, Roadrunner (1989). Word Known As History / The Right / Not Yet The Has been / Believe Or Bleed.
The Cloning, Toy's Factory (1991).
Swan Song, (1992).
BOLD STATEMENT, Roadrunner (1996). Enough Is Enough / Lucky Dragon / Colours / And It Goes On / Words Of Illusions / Impure / March Of The Final Decade / Blind Yourself.
DINOSAURS, Roadrunner RRCA 1003 (1997). Discharge / Low Intensity Warfare / No More Slaughter / The Cloning / Chain Gang / Infinite Pain / Gun Crazy / Swan Song / Kids On The Skids / Lock The Passion / Desperate War / The One's Left Behind / Russian Roulette / Death Metal.
Barefooted On Earth EP 1, Roadrunner RRCA 9004 (1999). Mr. Mess / Decay / Paranoise / Spiral 2000.
Barefooted On Earth EP 2, Roadrunner RRCA 9005 (1999). Speak / Flying High / Garden Of Roses / Bold Statement.

CATALEPSY

BRUSSELS, BELGIUM — Brussels Thrashers CATALEPSY, featuring personnel from MENTAL DISTURBANCE and CRACK DOWN, supported many acts such as SACRED REICH, CHANNEL ZERO and CRO-MAGS prior to recording their debut demo 'The Rope Of Life'. This was followed by a further tape, 'One Size Fits All', before the group was able to issue the 'House Of Despair' single in 1993.

The group has since followed up with two albums.

House Of Despair, Electrip EL 108 (1993). House Of Despair / House Of Despair (Mix) / Hotdog And Beercanhill / Brick By Brick (Live).

FRUITCAKES WE HAVE KNOWN, Elecrtrip EL107CD (1993). Brick By Brick / Hot Dog & Beercanhill / Civilised Genocide / House of Dispair / Here Comes King Gossip / Miss Brainless / Tortured Minds / Clowns / Suicide Letters.
Dragged Inside Out, Restless (1994).

CELLADOR

OMAHA, NE, USA — *Michael Smith Jr. (vocals), Chris Petersen (guitar), Sam Chatham (guitar), Valentin Rakhmanov (bass), David Dahir (drums).*

Omaha, Nebraska Heavy Metal act CELLADOR was initially forged under the title APOSTATE in late 2002 by guitarist Chris 'Cellador' Petersen and vocalist / bassist Josh Krohn. The group underwent various line-up changes, including tenures for singer Michael Smith Jr. and drummers Albert Kurniawan and Joey Cardenas. Guitarist Sam Chatham was enrolled in May 2004 with drummer Dave Dahir being inducted in June. Singer Warren Curry was replaced by a returning Michael Smith Jr. in December.

CELLADOR, announcing they were on the search for a new guitarist and keyboard player, signed to Metal Blade Records in August 2005. In November the band inducted THE SUPREMACY guitarist Bill Hudson and the following month entered Mana Studios in Florida with producer Erik Rutan of HATE ETERNAL to craft an album entitled 'Enter Deception' for June 2006 issue. CELLADOR supported TRIVIUM, THE SWORD and PROTEST THE HERO for US dates in early October. The band's scheduled headline appearance at the 'Madpower' festival in Madison, Wisconsin set for October 21st was cancelled after drummer David Dahir was involved in a car accident.

CELLADOR parted ways with bass player Val Rakhmanov in January 2007. Mika Horiuchi of Washington's NETHERELM took over on bass. Drummer David Dahir exited in March.

THE BURNING BLUE, Cellador (2004). Introduction / Hatred Aside / Leaving All Behind / Diogenes / Forever Unbound / Progeny / Speechless / Crossing The Line / No Chances Lost / I Ain't Even (Til I'm One Ahead).
Leaving All Behind, (2005). Leaving All Behind / Seen Through Time / Forever Unbound / No Chances Lost.
ENTER DECEPTION, Metal Blade (2006). Leaving All Behind / A Sign Far Beyond / Never Again / Forever Unbound / Seen Through Time / Wakening / Releasing The Shadow / No Chances Lost / Forever Unbound (Demo version) / No Chances Lost (Demo version).

CELTIC FROST

ZÜRICH, SWITZERLAND — *Tom G. Warrior (vocals / guitar), Martin Eric Ain (bass), Reed St. Mark (drums).*

A highly influential Zürich Thrash Metal act who pushed the musical boundaries of the genre to the limit, CELTIC FROST blended a fusion of extreme aggression with classical and jazz leanings to create a unique 'avant-garde' eclectic style. This reputation was forged by the group's obsessive attention to detail and meticulous planning, their intended career path having been strategized fully even before their first record hit the shelves. At their peak the band looked set to rival the big name American speed Metal outfits for world domination but would spectacularly crash to earth due to one of the most disastrous style changes ever witnessed.

CELTIC FROST had a strange genesis as mentor and renowned 'death grunter' Tom G. Warrior (a.k.a. Thomas Gabriel Fischer) and bassist Martin Eric Ain were members of what was generally acknowledged to have been one of the worst bands ever—HELLHAMMER. Tom himself started out musically in GRAVE HILL who were heavily influenced by the NWoBHM bands such as DIAMOND HEAD and VENOM.

HELLHAMMER actually started out under the HAMMERHEAD banner. Initially bass guitar was handled by the 14 year old Michael Baum, who in turn transferred these duties to Fischer, then wishing to be known as 'Satanic Slaughter'. Of note is that Baum then journeyed on to Los Angeles to found AOR act SIERRA before enrolling into TRIBE OF GYPSIES.

During the August of 1982 Fischer, transferring from bass to guitar, was now fronting a trio of Priestly and drummer Jörg Neubart (a.k.a. 'Bloodhunter'). Inspired apparently by Newcastle upon Tyne NWoBHM band RAVEN and their Gallagher brothers team Fischer and Priestly adopted the joint stage surnames of 'Warrior'. Neubart became 'Bruce Day'.

Their debut demo, 'Triumph Of Death', was widely regarded as one of the worst examples of a Heavy Metal band ever. 'Metal Forces' magazine editor Bernard Doe in particular cited it as the most appalling thing he had ever heard. History however would dictate that HELLHAMMER would later be recognized as one of the root catalysts of the Black Metal genre. Although in later years band members have admitted their knowledge of music was basic to say the least when the HELLHAMMER recordings were made nevertheless the band were in possession of an artistic vision which would undoubtedly shape the Metal scene over many years.

In 1983 HELLHAMMER enrolled bass player Martin Eric Ain and drummer Stephen Priestly from SCHIZO. However, invited to submit a fresh demo to Berlin's Noise Records HELLHAMMER very nearly split as Ain felt he did not have the necessary talent to go through with the session!

Still, positive or negative press encouraged Noise to sign the band and the Berlin based label released the 'Apocalyptic Raids' EP which had no details as to what RPM the record should be played at; sounding just as strange at 33RPM as it did at 45.

Metal Blade Records released the EP in America with an extra two tracks. Demand for HELLHAMMER also warranted a bootleg 7" single issued by Necromantic union, a pairing of a live cut of 'Buried And Forgotten' and a rehearsal recording 'Messiah'.

The original CELTIC FROST line-up in May 1984, so named after a combination of song titles and lyrics on a CIRITH UNGOL album sleeve, comprised Warrior, Ain and drummer Isaac Darso. The latter lasted precisely one rehearsal before being usurped by SCHIZO's Stephen Priestly on a temporary basis as a session drummer for recording. At this stage CELTIC FROST were still working on NWoBHM favourites such as songs by ANGEL WITCH and ARAGORN.

With HELLHAMMER's reputation preceding them, magazines reviews polarized at either the genius or dreadful end of the spectrum, CELTIC FROST retained their previous deal with Noise Records by submitting a master plan detailing the names of all future releases. The strategy called for an initial demo to be entitled 'A Thousand Deaths' but the label soon persuaded the band that this should form the basis of an opening commercially available product.

CELTIC FROST's first product, the mini-album, 'Morbid Tales' was recorded with Martin Eric Ain's former colleague in SCHIZO drummer Stephen Priestly. Guesting in the studio on additional vocals would be Horst Müller and Hertha Ohling plus violinist Oswald Spengler. As soon as the sessions were completed though Priestly decamped. CELTIC FROST set about negotiations with American drummer Jeff Cardelli of Seattle act LIPSTICK. However, the band hired another American, ex-CROWN drummer Reed St. Mark (real name Reid Cruickshank).

As with HELLHAMMER media views on 'Morbid Tales', issued in June 1984, ranged in their extremity from excellent to dire. European editions of 'Morbid Tales' comprised six tracks whilst a US license, through Metal Blade Records, added two extra tracks in 'Morbid Tales' and 'Return To The Eve'. The controversy stoked up by these opposing views would serve the band well. CELTIC FROST were still at this juncture wearing the stage make up later to be given the name 'corpse paint' by later generations of Black Metal bands. A further EP, 1985's 'The Emperors Return' issued in both regular format and as a limited run, highly sought after picture disc, followed to equally polarised reviews and even condemnation from the band themselves. By now CELTIC FROST were being acknowledged as leaders in their field.

CELTIC FROST's inaugural live performances came with a run of shows opening for German bands BEAST and MASS in Germany and Austria. Planned shows in Italy with ASTAROTH were shelved.

Ain had been asked to leave during recording of the next album 'To Mega Therion', surfacing in October 1985, and CELTIC FROST pulled in Dominic Steiner of the Glam Rock act JUNK FOOD. The album, which saw the band utilizing timpanis, French horns, courtesy of Wolf Bender, and operatic vocals courtesy of Claudia-Maria Mokri, plus credited sound effects from Horst Müller and Urs Sprenger, would be the first to be graced with lavish album sleeve artwork from the renowned artist H.R. Giger.

Friction between the band members resulted in Steiner's dismissal as soon as 'To Mega Therion' had been completed. For CELTIC FROST's debut show outside of Europe, at the 30th November 1985 'World War III' festival in Montreal alongside VOIVOD, POSSESSED, DESTRUCTION and NASTY SAVAGE, Martin Eric Ain was drawn back in the bass position.

Warrior also worked as producer for fellow Swiss Metal band CORONOR, a gesture they in turn repaid by becoming CELTIC FROST's road crew.

February 1986 had CELTIC FROST back on the live circuit, touring Europe sharing billing with HELLOWEEN and GRAVE DIGGER. Later shows saw a headline at the Belgian 'Metalysee' festival, the band's debut in England in London with GRAVE DIGGER and HELLOWEEN supporting at London's Hammersmith Palais and also touring in North America alongside RUNNING WILD and VOIVOD throughout June.

With CELTIC FROST's status rising sharply, the 1986 'Tragic Serenades' EP was issued to keep fans happy between albums. The EP consisted of remixed tracks from 'Into Mega Therion', both 'The Usurper' and 'Jewel Throne' with bass substituted by Martin Eric Ain, alongside newly recorded 'Return To The Eve'.

The group's third full-length opus, 'Into The Pandemonium' released in November 1987, provided fans with another bizarre offering comprising tracks such as a cover of WALL OF VOODOO's 'Mexican Radio' and the Rap cut 'One In Their Pride'. Before the album had been recorded New York based guitarist Ritchi Desmond was briefly linked with a position in the band, but, having travelled to Switzerland to work with the group Desmond returned home citing "too many conflicting attitudes" as the reason why he failed to join CELTIC FROST. Warrior countered that Desmond brought uninvited family members along to the audition and looked nothing like his submitted photograph. Desmond was to front SABBAT for their 'Mourning Has Broken' album and subsequent disastrous tour.

During a break in recording the band played a series of European gigs with ANTHRAX, CRIMSON GLORY and even METALLICA. The finalised sessions witnessed a further expansion in CELTIC FROST's aural dynamics with the employment of a swathe of session contributors. Claudia-Maria Mokri once again featured as a spotlighted additional vocalist and additional singers included Thomas Berter, Marchain Regee Rotschy and Manü Moan. Classical instruments were cut by violinists Malgorzata Blaiejewska Woller and Eva Cieslinski, cellist Wulf Ebert, French Horn player Anton Schreiber with Jürgen Paul Mann on viola. Additional guitar work was provided by Andreas Dobler.

For live work to promote 'Into The Pandemonium', CELTIC FROST added second guitarist Ron Marks and toured Britain in winter of 1987 with support from KREATOR then North America on a bill with EXODUS and ANTHRAX. The tour succeeded in dumbfounding many of the band's established fans with such radical tracks as the aforementioned 'Mexican Radio' cover and the band was dogged throughout it's duration by legal wrangles with Noise Records. Disillusioned, Marks quit to be replaced by former JUNK FOOD guitarist Oliver Amberg. Upon their return to Europe CELTIC FROST hit further problems when Martin Ain decided to abandon the music business entirely, so Warrior quickly drafted in Curt Victor Bryant.

CELTIC FROST was in a state of flux besieged by business and financial problems. Even an offer from director Ken Russell to lay down the soundtrack to the movie 'The Lair Of The White Worm' had to be declined because the group was in such disarray. However, the final blow to the classic line-up came when Reed St. Mark upped and left to join MINDFUNK and his position was filled by a returning Stephen Priestly. This was the line-up that was to record the disastrous 'Cold Lake' album produced by Tony Platt at Hansa Studios and Sky Trak Studios in Berlin, a record that severely damaged the band's career in Europe.

With this effort, CELTIC FROST appeared to ditch all of their former pretensions artistically and even adopted a new 'Glam' image, much to the horror of their most hardcore following. Tom dropped the 'Warrior' from his stage name and became plain Thomas Gabriel Fischer, even sporting an L.A. GUNS T-shirt on official press photos. Fans would be quick to spot that CELTIC FROST were now crediting one Michelle Villaneva as "Wardrobe and styling artist". 'Cold Lake' was to emerge in September 1988.

It was heavily rumoured in the European media that the band had, in a SPINAL TAP style move, adopted Tom's girlfriend as manager and that the new look was her masterplan for CELTIC FROST's step into the big league. CELTIC FROST themselves maintained that tracks like 'Teaze Me' were a parody of Glam Rock, but fans were outraged and the Rock press universally attacked the album. A single, 'Cherry Orchards', was announced then shelved. The European tour, commencing in late February with UK shows supported by DESTRUCTION, fared badly with audiences deserting in droves. However, in America 'Cold Lake' was in actual fact making serious sales headway and a U.S. tour beginning in March 1989 was judged a success.

In late 1989 the badly bruised CELTIC FROST announced a return to their former style and regrouped with Ron Marks. Martin Eric Ain was also persuaded to put down some guest bass tracks and contribute lyrics. The Roli Mossiman produced 'Vanity / Nemesis' album was cited by many as the band's best record to date, but the legacy of 'Cold Lake' still haunted the quartet to such a degree that sales suffered.

CELTIC FROST only managed minimal touring to back up the release of April 1990's 'Vanity / Nemesis', including a British tour backed by Thrashers SLAMMER. Earlier German dates had been cancelled, due to the band's perilous business state, but CELTIC FROST endured through two Dutch shows and the entire UK leg. By now Warrior was to be seen spotted playing a guitar emblazoned with his wife's name 'Michelle', the lady in question also having become a backing singer for the band. CELTIC FROST performed their last ever concert on 29th May 1990 at the Derby Assembly Rooms. New management hooked up a deal with major label BMG in North America. However, the deal was shelved at the last minute leaving CELTIC FROST high and dry.

Warrior took the band into an even more radical direction when he mooted the idea of working with ex-THE TIME guitarist Jesse Johnson on a projected Funk-Metal project. Stephen Priestly meantime would perform drums for French act TREPONEM PAL's 1991 'Aggravation' album.

Following a 1992 four track demo, featuring the tracks 'Honour Thy Father', 'Seeds Of Rapture', 'Icons Alive' and Oh Father', the band searched in vain for a new deal. Initial tapes were laid down with Priestly on drums but sessions in Texas saw Reed St. Mark back behind the kit and Renée Hernz on bass. Nothing came of this latest venture and CELTIC FROST effectively split; Marks relocating to America to form STEPCHILD then

SUBSONIC.

1992 Noise released a CELTIC FROST epitaph in the form of 'Parched With Thirst Am I And Dying'; a collection of rare and unreleased studio out-takes as the band bowed out. In more recent years Martin Ain produced the debut album from doom band SADNESS in 1995, whilst Tom Warrior was found fronting new venture APOLLYON SUN in 1996.

Late 2001 would herald renewed rumours, at first vehemently denied and then later confirmed, of a full-blown CELTIC FROST reunion with Tom G. Warrior, Martin Eric Ain and Reed St. Mark, along with Fischer's long-time songwriting partner and co-founder of APOLLYON SUN, guitarist/producer Erol Unala, all participating. By November a projected album title of 'Probe' had emerged but it would not be until April 2003 that a demo track entitled 'Ground' was posted online. The CELTIC FROST camp also disseminated a revised and apparently spurious album working title of 'Dark Matter Manifest'. Meantime, Martin Eric Ain contributed vocals to Los Angeles based HATESEX's Industrial take on the SLAYER track 'Black Magic'.

In June of 2004 Tom G. Fischer announced he had plans for a solo album for 2005 release although CELTIC FROST persevered with composing new material with drummer Franco Sesa. The band would also have their classic cut 'Dawn Of Megiddo' chosen as a pioneering piece of music for a compilation assembled by DARKTHRONE drummer Fenriz, released through Peaceville Records and entitled 'Fenriz Presents The Best Of Old School Black Metal'.

Employing drummer Franco Sesa, CELTIC FROST revealed a new set of demos had been completed in May 2005 and entered Horus Sound Studios in Hannover in August to track the album, given a working title 'Dark Matter Manifest'. HYPOCRISY and PAIN mentor Peter Tägtgren would be selected as producer.

For tour work CELTIC FROST drafted the APOPTYGMA BERZERK, SATYRICON, CADAVER, and MAYHEM credited Anders Odden on guitar. Live campaigning for 2006 included scheduled appearances at Sölvesborg's 'Sweden Rock' festival in June, Helsinki's 'Tuska' festival in July, Germany's 'Wacken Open Air' and Norway's Bergen 'Hole In The Sky' events in August. However, the band's June 3rd 'Rock Hard' festival in Gelsenkirchen was cancelled that same day. Martin Eric Ain announced from the stage that Thomas Gabriel Fischer had been rushed to hospital with acute kidney problems, subsequently diagnosed as a kidney stone.

According to Nielsen SoundScan the 'Monotheist' album sold just under 2,500 copies in its first week of sale in North America. In the band's homeland of Switzerland the record entered the charts at number 41. US dates would be projected for September. The band filmed a promotional video for the track 'A Dying God Coming Into Human Flesh', directed by Jessie Fischer in Zurich prior to launching into a 47 date US tour, commencing September 12th at West Springfield, Virginia's Jaxx venue, backed by SAHG and 1349. The tour generated favourable reviews but closed on a sour note, as Tom G. warrior revealed on his official blog, stating "Out of petty, pathetic vengefulness for being confronted, in a highly professional manner one might add, for utterly failing to do his job, one of those who travelled with us in North America in September, October, and November 2006, and was paid by us no less, destroyed one of the band's sacred back-up Iceman guitars as soon as unwatched for a moment after the end of the tour".

Japanese dates were scheduled for January 2007 dubbed the "Extreme The Dojo" alongside SATYRICON and NAGLFAR. The band then shifted shape, drafting V. Santura of the German Black Metal group DARK FORTRESS as new touring guitarist.

Preceded by a one off solo gig on March 6th, held at the Mascotte club in Zurich, CELTIC FROST headed up a package billing with KREATOR, LEGION OF THE DAMNED and WATAIN for a lengthy run of European dates. Scandinavian concerts saw Sweden's WOLF acting as openers. Back on North American soil, the band forged a union with TYPE O NEGATIVE and BRAND NEW SIN for dates in April.

MORBID TALES, Noise N0017 (1984). Into The Crypt Of Rays / Visions Of Mortality / Procreation (Of The Wicked) / Return To Eve / Danse Macabre / Nocturnal Fear.

Emperors Return EP, Noise N0024 (1985). Dethroned Emperor / Circle Of The Tyrants / Morbid Tales / Suicidal Winds / Visual Aggression.

TO MEGA THERION, Noise N0031 (1985). Innocence And Wrath / The Usurper / Jewel Throne / Dawn Of Megiddo / Eternal Summer / Circle Of Tyrants / (Beyond The) North Winds / Fainted Eyes / Tears In A Prophet's Dream / Necromantical Screams.

Tragic Serenades EP, Noise N0041 (1986). The Usurper / Jewel Throne / Return To Eve.

I Won't Dance, Noise N0094 (1986). I Won't Dance / One In Their Pride / Tristesses De La Lune.

INTO THE PANDEMONIUM, Noise N0065 (1987). Mexican Radio / Mesmerised / Inner Sanctum / Sorrows Of The Moon / Babylon Fell / Caressinto Oblivion / One In Their Pride / I Won't Dance / Rex Irae (Requiem / Opening) / Oriental Masquerade.

COLD LAKE, Noise NUK 125 (1988). Intro-Human / Seduce Me Tonight / Petty Obsession / (Once) They Were Eagles / Cherry Orchards / Juices Like Wine / Little Velvet / Blood On Kisses / Downtown Hanoi / Dance Sleazy / Roses Without Thorns / Tease Me / Mexican Radio (New Version).

Wine In My Hand (Third From The Sun), Noise (1990) (Promotion release). Wine In My Hand (Third From The Sun) / Heroes / Descent From Babylon.

VANITY/NEMESIS, Noise/EMI EMC 3576 (1990). The Heart Beneath / Wine In My Hand (Third From The Sun) / Wings Of Solitude / The Name Of My Bride / This Island Earth / The Restless Seas / Phallic Tantrum / A Kiss Or A Whisper / Vanity / Nemesis / Heroes.

PARCHED WITH THIRST AM I AND DYING, Noise N0191-2 (1992). Idols Of Chagrin / A Descent To Babylon / Return To The Eve / Juices Like Wine / The Inevitable Factor / The Heart Beneath / Cherry Orchards / Tristesses De La Lune / Wings Of Solitude / The Usurper / Journey Into Fear / Downtown Hanoi / Circle Of Tyrants / In The Chapel In The Moonlight / I Won't Dance / The Name Of My Bride / Mexican Radio / Under Apollyon's Sun.

Montheist Sampler, (2006) (Promotional release). Progeny / Ground.

MONOTHEIST, EMI 5051099750012 (2006) (Vinyl release). Progeny / Ground / A Dying God Coming Into Human Flesh / Drown In Ashes / Os Abysmi Vel Daath / Temple Of Depression / Obscured / Domain Of Decay / Ain Elohim / Totengott / Synagoga Satanae / Winter (Requiem, Chapter Three: Finale).

MONOTHEIST, Century Media CD 77500-2 (2006). Progeny / Ground / A Dying God Coming Into Human Flesh / Drown In Ashes / Os Abysmi Vel Daath / Temple Of Depression / Obscured / Domain Of Decay / Ain Elohim / Totengott / Synagoga Satanae / Winter (Requiem, Chapter Three: Finale). Chart positions: 12 GREECE, 41 SWITZERLAND, 57 FINLAND, 67 GERMANY, 194 FRANCE.

CENTINEX

HEDEMORA, SWEDEN — *Johan Jansson (vocals), Johan Ahlberg (guitar), Jonas Kjellgren (guitar), Martin Schulman (bass), Ronnie Bergerståhl (drums).*

Renowned Hedemora Death Metal act that have increasingly bolstered their sound and imagery with Satanic lyrical references. CENTINEX opened their career in September 1990 issuing the debut demo cassette 'End Of Life', recorded at the famous Sunlight Studios, the following year. The band signed to Swedish label Underground for release of the album 'Subconscious Lobotomy', again recorded at Sunlight, which saw a limited release of 1000 copies. The CENTINEX line-up at this juncture comprised twin vocalists Erik and Mattias Lamppu, guitarist Andreas Evaldsson, bass player Martin Schulman and drummer Joakim Gustafsson.

A further three track demo session, entitled 'Under The Blackened Sky', followed. Gigging took CENTINEX throughout Sweden, Finland and Poland during 1993. CENTINEX's next cassette release 'Transcend The Dark Chaos', released on the band's own novelly titled Evil Shit Productions in 1994, was repressed by Sphinx Records. The second CENTINEX full-length album

'Malleus Malefaction' was recorded for the Wild Rags label and produced by Peter Tägtgren of HYPOCRISY.

1996 saw the release of a shared 7" single in collusion with INVERTED and a fresh band roster retaining Lamppu, Schulman and Evaldsson but with new faces in UNCURBED guitarist Kenneth Wiklund and drummer Kalimaa. The band also featured on a split EP with Sweden's VOICES OF DEATH and German act BAPHOMET.

The 'Reflections' CD was released in March 1997, later in the year being licensed to Slovakian Rock Extremum Records for a tape version. Early 1997 found CENTINEX on tour in Scandinavia as guests to CRADLE OF FILTH. However, a split in the ranks came the following year when both Lamppu and Evaldsson made their exit. The 'Reborn Through Flames' album was delivered during June of 1998, being made available on tape format through Polish Novum Vox Mortis Records. The Norwegian Oskorei Productions would issue the 'Shadowland' 7EP, a limited two track vinyl, the same year. Gigging took CENTINEX into Germany, Spain, Portugal and Holland.

The 'Bloodhunt' album, issued in June 1999 by Repulse, would also be delivered by Oskorei Productions in a limited edition 10" vinyl format restricted to just 300 copies. It was to be July 1999 before CENTINEX enrolled UNCANNY, MOONDARK, INTERMENT, PYOSISFIED and DELLAMORTE drummer Kennet Englund. For touring later in the year CENTINEX pulled in PEXILATED, SICKENSIDE, DELLAMORTE and CARNAL FORGE man Jonas Kjellgren on guitar and the PYOSISFIED, HATRED, SIDEBURNERS, ASOCIAL, FLESHREVELS, UNCURBED, INTERMENT, FULMINATION, FROSTHEIM and DELLAMORTE credited vocalist Johan Jansson. CENTINEX undertook two European tours during the year with shows across Germany, Holland, Belgium, France, the Czech Republic and Slovakia. The same year had CENTINEX contributing their version of 'Ripping Corpse' to a Full Moon Productions KREATOR tribute album. Both the 'Subconscious Lobotomy' and 'Malleus Maleficarum' albums were re-mixed and edited for a re-release but legal problems forced Repulse to cancel the schedule.

2000 witnessed yet more ructions when Kjellgren and Englund decamped. Replacements were AZURE vocalist Robban Kanto and drummer Johan. The 'Apocalyptic Armageddon' 7" EP saw release in February through the German Deadly Art concern. In September of 2000 Repulse issued the 'Hellbrigade' album with the Japanese Soundholic label following suit in December. The following year it would be picked up by World War III Records in America, Picoroco Records in South America and Irond Records in Russia. Nocturnal Music would also weigh in with a limited edition vinyl version. The band appeared at several Swedish summer-festivals and journeyed across Scandinavia and Europe once more performing in Finland, Germany, Belgium, Holland, France, Switzerland, Spain, Austria and the Czech Republic.

In April of 2001 CENTINEX signed a new worldwide deal with the English Candlelight label, cutting the first album for their new partners, entitled 'Diabolical Desolation', at Black Lounge studios during July and August. CENTINEX would also share vinyl with the infamous American act NUNSLAUGHTER with their take on SODOM's 'Enchanted Land' for the 'Hail Germania' EP on the Belgian Painkiller label.

In October 2001 guitarist Kenneth Wiklund would break ranks and Johan Ahlberg of SUBDIVE would subsequently secure the position. With this revised line-up CENTINEX would put in their inaugural gig on American soil followed up be festivals across Sweden and Germany.

'Diabolical Desolation' was released in Europe on March 11th 2002, the release date for North America being April 30th. A subsequent limited edition vinyl version would be issued through Finland's Northern Sound Records. Restricted to 1000 copies this variant came in a gatefold sleeve clad in all new layout and artwork. European dates slated for November saw the band making up a bill including headliners DEICIDE alongside MYSTIC CIRCLE. For these shows the band roped in CARNAL FORGE skinsman Stefan Westerberg as regular drummer Kennet Englund was unable to commit.

The British Candlelight label announced it was to re-release the CENTINEX back catalogue for 2003 adding a significant number of bonus tracks to each release. A new album, 'Decadence—Prophecies Of Cosmic Chaos', including an instrumental track 'A Dynasty Of Obedience' composed by ARCANA's Peter Pettersson, was projected for 2003 release but then pushed back into 2004. The group severed ties with drummer Kennet Englund in August, inducting Ronnie Bergerståhl of JULIE LAUGHS NO MORE, AMARAN and MYNJUN repute in October. CENTINEX toured Finland in April of 2004 allied with DEATH DU JOUR and Swedish act REPUGNANT.

Swedmetal Records issued a limited edition 'Live Devastation' 7" single in September, this comprising 'Towards Devastation', recorded live in Borlänge, Sweden and 'Bloodhunt', recorded live in Lappeenranta, Finland. In November CENTINEX signed a new album deal with Cold Records, a subsidiary of Metal Blade, for the 'World Declension' opus. Ronnie Bergerståhl joined WORLD BELOW in December. In addition, A WORLD BELOW / CENTINEX split 7" EP, entitled 'Doomed Death Blow', would be released by UK imprint Conquer Records, limited to 500 copies. Promoting 'World Declension', released in North America through Candlelight Records, CENTINEX announced European touring in union with IMPIETY for October 2005. However, these gigs would be cancelled.

In March 2006 the band issued a press release closing their career, stating ""We hereby announce that after 16 years in the business the Swedish Death Metal act CENTINEX call it quits." A farewell live performance was scheduled for May 13th in Eskilstuna, Sweden. Beforehand, Martin Schulman, Johan Jansson and Ronnie Bergerståhl announced the formation of a new combo dubbed DEMONICAL. Johan Jansson joined REGURGITATE in September.

Centinex, Centinex (1991) (Rehearsal cassette demo).
End Of Life, Centinex (1991) (Cassette demo). The Aspiration / Fear / Bells Of Misery / Dreams Of Death.
SUBCONSCIOUS LOBOTOMY, Underground UGR05 (1992) (Limited edition 1000 copies). Blood On My Skin / Shadows Are Astray / Dreams Of Death / Orgy In Flesh / End Of Life / Bells Of Misery / Inhuman Dissections Of Souls / The Aspiration / Until Death Tear Us Apart.
Under The Blackened Sky, Wild Rags WRR-CEN (1993) (Cassette EP). Cranial Dismemberment / Only Slices Remains / Thorn Within.
TRANSCEND THE DARK CHAOS, Sphinx SIXR 003 (1994) (Cassette EP). Transcend The Dark Chaos / Thorns Of Desolation / Eternal Lies / At The Everlasting End.
MALLEUS MALEFICARUM, Wild Rags WRR 043 (1996). Upon The Ancient Ground / Dark Visions / Sorrow Of The Burning Wasteland / Transcend The Dark Chaos / Thorns Of Desolation / Eternal Lies / At The Everlasting Evil.
Sorrow Of Burning Wasteland, Voices Of Death VOD 003 (1996) (Split single with INVERTED. Limited edition 600 copies). Sorrow Of Burning Wasteland.
REFLECTIONS, Diehard RRS 954 (1997). Carnal Lust / Seven Prophecies / Before The Dawn / The Dimension Beyond / My Demon Within / In Pain / Undivined / Darkside / Into The Funeral Domain.
Shadowland, Oskorei Productions OP 004 (1998) (Lilac vinyl. Limited edition 500 copies). Shadowland / Eternal Lies.
REBORN THROUGH FLAMES, Repulse RPS 032CD (1998). Embraced By Moonlight / Resurrected / Summon The Golden Twilight / The Beauty Of Malice / Under The Guillotine / Through Celestial Gates / Molested / In The Arch Of Serenity.
BLOODHUNT, Repulse RPS 042CD (1999) (CD release). Under The Pagan Glory / For Centuries Untold / Luciferian Moon / Bloodhunt / The Conquest Infernal / Like Darkened Storms.
BLOODHUNT, Oskorei Productions OP 008 (1999) (10" vinyl single). Under The Pagan Glory / For Centuries Untold / Luciferian Moon / Bloodhunt / The Conquest Infernal / Like Darkened Storms / Mutilation.

Apocalyptic Armageddon, Deadly Art DAP 095 (2000) (7" grey vinyl single limited to 500 copies). Apocalyptic Armageddon / Seeds Of Evil / Everlasting Bloodshed.

HELLBRIGADE, Repulse RPS 046CD (2000) (European CD release). Towards Devastation / On With Eternity / The Eyes Of The Dead / Emperor Of Death / Last Redemption / Blood Conqueror / Neverending Hell / Nightbreeder / Hellbrigade.

HELLBRIGADE, Soundholic TKCS-85003 (2000) (Japanese release). Towards Devastation / On With Eternity / The Eyes Of The Dead / Emperor Of Death / Last Redemption / Blood Conqueror / Neverending Hell / Nightbreeder / Hellbrigade / Apocalyptic Armageddon / Seeds Of Evil / Everlasting Bloodshed.

HELLBRIGADE, Soundholic TKCS-85003 (2000) (Japanese release). Towards Devastation / On With Eternity / The Eyes Of The Dead / Emperor Of Death / Last Redemption / Blood Conqueror / Neverending Hell / Nightbreeder / Hellbrigade / Apocalyptic Armageddon / Seeds Of Evil / Everlasting Bloodshed.

DIABOLICAL DESECRATION, Candlelight CANDLE 065CD (2002). Demonic Warlust / Forthcoming Terror / Spawned To Destroy / Soulcrusher / Diabolical Desecration / On Violent Soil / Total Misanthropia / The Bloodline / A War Symphony / Hellfire Twilight.

Hail Germania, Hell's Headbangers HELLS EP001 (2003) (Split single with NUNSLAUGHTER. Limited edition 1000 copies). Enchanted Land.

Deathlike Recollections, Sword & Sorcery STEEL 003 (2003). Blood On My Skin / Shadows Are Astray.

DECADENCE—PROPHECIES OF COSMIC CHAOS, Candlelight CANDLE 089 (2004) (CD version). Arrival Of The Spectrum Obscure / Misanthropic Darkzone / Hollowsphere / Target: Dimension XII / Deathstar Unmasked / A Dynasty Of Obedience / Mechanical Future / Cold Deep Supremacy / New World Odyssey.

DECADENCE—PROPHECIES OF COSMIC CHAOS, Hells Headbangers HELLS LP 003 (2004) (Vinyl version. Limited edition 566 copies). Arrival Of The Spectrum Obscure / Misanthropic Darkzone / Hollowsphere / Target: Dimension XII / Deathstar Unmasked / A Dynasty Of Obedience / Mechanical Future / Cold Deep Supremacy / New World Odyssey.

DECADENCE—PROPHECIES OF COSMIC CHAOS, Soundholic TKCS-85100 (2004) (Japanese release). Arrival Of The Spectrum Obscure / Misanthropic Darkzone / Hollowsphere / Target: Dimension XII / Deathstar Unmasked / A Dynasty Of Obedience / Mechanical Future / Cold Deep Supremacy / New World Odyssey / Towards Devastation (Live) / Bloodhunt (Live) / Arrival Of The Spectrum Obscure (Video).

Live Devastation, Swedmetal SM-01-7 (2004) (7" vinyl single limited to 500 copies). Towards Devastation / Bloodhunt.

WORLD DECLENSION, Regain RR 081 (2005). Victorious Dawn Rising / Purgatorial Overdrive / The Destroyer / As Legions Come / Sworn / Synthetic Sin Zero / Flesh Is Fragile / Wretched Cut / Deconstruction Macabre.

WORLD DECLENSION, Candlelight CANDLE 227 (2005) (USA release). Victorious Dawn Rising / Purgatorial Overdrive / The Destroyer / As Legions Come / Sworn / Synthetic Sin Zero / Flesh Is Fragile / Wretched Cut / Deconstruction Macabre.

METAL PACK VOL. 9, Candlelight TANGLA0009 (2005) (4 CD box set). Towards Devastation / On With Eternity / The Eyes Of The Dead / Emperor Of Death / Last Redemption / Blood Conqueror / Neverending Hell / Nightbreeder / Hellbrigade / Apocalyptic Armageddon / Seeds Of Evil / Everlasting Bloodshed / Upon The Ancient Ground / Dark Visions / Sorrow Of The Burning Wasteland / Transcend The Dark Chaos / Thorns Of Desolation / Eternal Lies / At The Everlasting End / Cranial Dismemberment / Only Slices Remain / Torn Within / Mutilation / Ripping Corpse / Under The Pagan Glory / For Centuries Untold / Luciferian Moon / Bloodhunt / The Conquest Infernal / Like Darkened Storms / Embraced By Moonlight / Resurrected / Summon The Golden Twilight / The Beauty Of Malice / Under The Guillotine / Through Celestial Gates / Molested / In The Arch Of Serenity / Shadowland / Eternal Lies / Arrival Of The Spectrum Obscure / Misanthropic Darkzone / Hollowsphere / Target: Dimension XII / Deathstar Unmasked / A Dynasty Of Obedience / Mechanical Future / Cold Deep Supremacy / New World Odyssey.

CEREBRAL FIX

BIRMINGHAM, WEST MIDLANDS, UK — *Simon Forrest (vocals), Tony Warburton (guitar), Greg Fellows (guitar), Frank Healy (bass), Andy Baker (drums).*

Birmingham's CEREBRAL FIX trod a fine line between Crossover Punk and Thrash Metal. The band were founded at the height of the Thrash explosion in 1988 with a line-up of vocalist Simon Forrest, guitarist Gregg Fellows, bassist Steve and drummer Ade, none of whom had previous band experience.

CEREBRAL FIX's first demo landed them a deal with Vinyl Solutions Records for 1988's 'Life Sucks And Then You Die'. However, the band had appeared on a Sounds magazine flexi sampler just before this with the track 'Maimed To Beg'. The same year the band got some serious touring under their belts sharing a bill in Britain with BOLT-THROWER, both acts promoting debut albums on the same label.

CEREBRAL FIX lost their rhythm section in 1990 as both Steve and Ade departed, ostensibly to form another act but this never materialized. Replacements were ex-NAPALM DEATH and SACRILEGE bassist Frank Healy and former VARUKERS, ARBITRATER and SACRILEGE drummer Andy Baker. This line-up turned in another demo to secure a fresh deal with Roadrunner Records.

CEREBRAL FIX set about touring once more guesting for NAPALM DEATH on their 'Harmony Corruption' dates up front of a second album 'Tower Of Spite'. Harking back to Healy and Baker's roots the bonus track on the CD was a cover of SACRILEGE's 'The Closing Irony'.

In May of 1990 the band gained the honours of supporting SEPULTURA at London's Marquee club.

1991 saw Baker leaving and in his place coming former THE VARUKERS and METAL MESSIAH man Kevin Frost for the 'Bastards' album. CD bonus tracks comprised of 'Maimed To Beg', the GBH cover 'No Survivors' and the DAMNED's 'Smash It Up, the latter featuring WOLFSBANE's Blaze Bayley on vocals. Promoting the album found the band guesting in Britain to OBITUARY that May.

1992's 'Death Erotica' had a version of DISCHARGE's 'Never Again' with NAPALM DEATH's Barney Greenaway and POP WILL EAT ITSELF's Clint on guest vocals. NAPALM DEATH's bassist Shane Embury also added vocals to the track 'Too Drunk To Funk' whilst MARSHALL LAW's Andy Pyke and SHY and SIAM vocalist Tony Mills contributed to a version of the JUDAS PRIEST hit 'Living After Midnight'.

A 1992 tour with PARADISE LOST was followed up by CEREBRAL FIX a European tour in 1993 alongside CANCER and GOMORRAH. Healy by this time had departed and the band pulled in the bassist from DISCHARGE to fulfill the dates. The band folded shortly after. Healy later teamed up with BENEDICTION. Frost journeyed back to THE VARUKERS and would subsequently join HELVIS for their 2002 album 'Reverence The Sacrifice'. CEREBRAL FIX reformed in 2006, comprising a line-up of vocalist Simon Forrest, guitarists Tony Warburton and Gregg Fellows, bass player Frank Healy with Neil Farrington of WARLORD UK, DAMN DIRTY APES, LAST UNDER THE SUN and SENSA YUMA on drums.

Ex-CEREBRAL FIX guitarist Steve Watson returned in 2007 with RAVEN'S CREED, working with ORANGE GOBLIN's Ben Ward on vocals and Martyn Millard on bass guitar, lead guitarist Steve Watson and Jay Graham, of SKYCLAD and RETURN TO THE SABBAT, on drums.

LIFE SUCKS AND THEN YOU DIE, Vinyl Solution SOL 15 (1988). Warstorm / Cerebral Fix / Loooniverse / Give Me Life / Soap Opera / Behind The Web / Product Of Disgust / Life Sucks / Power Struggle / Go / Fear Of Death / Acid Sick / Skatedrunk / Zombie / Existing Not Living.

TOWER OF SPITE, Roadrunner RO 9356 1 (1990). For Who? / Enter The Turmoil / Feast Of The Fools / Chasten Of Fear / Circle Of The Earth / Tower Of Spite / Injecting Out / Quest For Midian / Forgotten Genocide / Culte Des Mortes (I).

BASTARDS, Roadracer RO 92861 (1991). Descent Into Unconsciousness / Veil Of Tears / Beyond Jerusalem / Return To Infinity / Sphere Born / I Lost A Friend / Ritual Abuse / Mammonite / Middle Third (Mono Culture) / Maimed To Beg / No Survivors / Smash It Up.

DEATHEROTICA, Under One Flag FLAG 75 (1992). Death Erotica / World Machine / Clarissa / Haunted Eyes / Mind Within Mine /

CEREBRAL FIX (pic: Helen Moss)

Splintered Wings / Creator Of Outcasts / Angel's Kiss / Still In Mind / Ratt Of Medusa / Never Again / Too Drunk Too Funk / Burning / Living After Midnight.

CESSATION OF LIFE

CAMARILLO, CA, USA — *Chris Violence (vocals), Justin Harrison (bass), Ron Ostlund (drums).*

A Camarillo, Ventura based trad Thrash act created in 1996 that has to date self financed two full albums. During 1999 the debut album 'Aggressive By Nature, Destructive By Choice', featuring remastered versions of all four tracks from the band's eponymous, June 1997 demo. Initial versions of this release, emerging in March of 1998, featured different artwork plus a video for the song 'Angel Of Mercy' recorded live at the Whiskey A Go Go in Hollywood in July of 1997. CESSATION OF LIFE contributed their version of 'Wrathchild' to the IRON MAIDEN tribute album 'Children Of The Damned', released by the Italian Adrenaline label. This album would also see a CESSATION OF LIFE original, 'Synthetic Suicide', included. The band gained further exposure with the inclusion of the 'Impalement' track on the compilation album 'Time Capsule 2000' issued through House Of Jordan Entertainment in March of 2000, this song also featuring on the Black Light Records 'Escape The Furnace 3' compilation.

CESSATION OF LIFE would support Thrash vets TESTAMENT on their South West leg of the 'Ride The Snake' tour. Former HUNGSOLO and REALITY bassist Justin Harrison was inducted into the fold during February of 2002.

Tour dates in mid 2004 were cancelled when drummer Ron Ostlund broke his ankle. Later that year CESSATION OF LIFE appeared on the billing of the 'Seattle Metalfest'. The four track 'The Glory Of The World Is Passing', limited to 1000 copies and notably co-produced by Grammy award winner John Seymour, arrived in June 2005. Guitarist Travis Anderberg officially announced his departure from CESSATION OF LIFE in on January 29th 2007.

Cessation Of Life, (1997). At One With The Dark / Angel Of Mercy / Tears Of The Dead / Ready To Burn.
AGGRESSIVE BY NATURE, DESTRUCTIVE BY CHOICE, (1998). At One With The Dark / Synthetic Suicide / Don't Push / Tears Of The Dead / Witch Finder General / Angel Of Mercy / Impalement / Ready To Burn.
AGGRESSIVE BY NATURE, DESTRUCTIVE BY CHOICE, (1999). At One With The Dark / Synthetic Suicide / Don't Push / Tears Of The Dead / Witch Finder General / Angel Of Mercy / Impalement / Ready To Burn.
3 Songs For 2000, (2000). Kill You Again / Fist Full Of Hate / Pulzerizing Vortex.
KILL YOU AGAIN, Independent (2002). Forgotten / Long Awaited Secession / A Minute To Live / The Call / Kill You Again / A New Religion / Johnny Wants A Six Pack / I.F.T.W.M.F.A. / Pulverizing Vortex.
CESSATION OF LIVE, (2003). Hate Exhaust / Long Awaited Succession / Kill You Again / Sick With Me / Forgotten / Blindsight / A Minute To Live.
THE GLORY OF THE WORLD IS PASSING, (2005) (limited edition 1000 copies). Blindsight / In Vain / The Second Death / Stick With Me.

CESSATION OF LIFE

CAMARILLO, CA, USA — *Chris Violence (vocals), Justin Harrison (bass), Ron Ostlund (drums).*

A Camarillo, Ventura based trad Thrash act created in 1996 that has to date self financed two full albums. During 1999 the debut album 'Aggressive By Nature, Destructive By Choice', featuring remastered versions of all four tracks from the band's eponymous, June 1997 demo. Initial versions of this release, emerging in March of 1998, featured different artwork plus a video for the song 'Angel Of Mercy' recorded live at the Whiskey A Go Go in Hollywood in July of 1997. CESSATION OF LIFE contributed their version of 'Wrathchild' to the IRON MAIDEN tribute album 'Children Of The Damned', released by the Italian Adrenaline label. This album would also see a CESSATION OF LIFE original, 'Synthetic Suicide', included. The band gained further exposure with the inclusion of the 'Impalement' track on the compilation album 'Time Capsule 2000' issued through House Of Jordan Entertainment in March of 2000, this song also featuring on the Black Light Records 'Escape The Furnace 3' compilation.

CESSATION OF LIFE would support Thrash vets TESTAMENT on their South West leg of the 'Ride The Snake' tour. Former HUNGSOLO and REALITY bassist Justin Harrison was inducted into the fold during February of 2002.

Tour dates in mid 2004 were cancelled when drummer Ron Ostlund broke his ankle. Later that year CESSATION OF LIFE appeared on the billing of the 'Seattle Metalfest'. The four track 'The Glory Of The World Is Passing', limited to 1000 copies and notably co-produced by Grammy award winner John Seymour, arrived in June 2005. Guitarist Travis Anderberg officially announced his departure from CESSATION OF LIFE in on January 29th 2007.

Cessation Of Life, (1997). At One With The Dark / Angel Of Mercy / Tears Of The Dead / Ready To Burn.
AGGRESSIVE BY NATURE, DESTRUCTIVE BY CHOICE, (1998). At One With The Dark / Synthetic Suicide / Don't Push / Tears Of The Dead / Witch Finder General / Angel Of Mercy / Impalement / Ready To Burn.
AGGRESSIVE BY NATURE, DESTRUCTIVE BY CHOICE, (1999). At One With The Dark / Synthetic Suicide / Don't Push / Tears Of The Dead / Witch Finder General / Angel Of Mercy / Impalement / Ready To Burn.
3 Songs For 2000, (2000). Kill You Again / Fist Full Of Hate / Pulzerizing Vortex.
KILL YOU AGAIN, Independent (2002). Forgotten / Long Awaited Secession / A Minute To Live / The Call / Kill You Again / A New Religion / Johnny Wants A Six Pack / I.F.T.W.M.F.A. / Pulverizing Vortex.
CESSATION OF LIVE, (2003). Hate Exhaust / Long Awaited Succession / Kill You Again / Sick With Me / Forgotten / Blindsight / A Minute To Live.
THE GLORY OF THE WORLD IS PASSING, (2005) (limited edition 1000 copies). Blindsight / In Vain / The Second Death / Stick With Me.

CHAIN OF HATE

ÖREBRO, SWEDEN — *Freddie Hunter (vocals / guitar), Johnny Blade (guitar), E.V.M. Jawbreaker (bass), Cody Cruz (drums).*

Örebro's CHAIN OF HATE, founded in the Autumn of 2002, include former DREAMGOD, FALLEN ANGEL and WOLF guitarist Johnny Blade (a.k.a. Johan Bülow). He would be joined by singer Freddie Hunter, SUBSTITUTE bassist E.V.M. Jawbreaker and PHOBOS drummer Andy Guz. The band demoed in January 2003 but rejected the end results as unsatisfactory. A second stab at recording later that year, produced by NASUM's Miezsko Talaezyk, proved more successful.

During November of 2004 Jawbreaker forged a union with INSIDIOUS personnel guitarists Anders Bertilsson and Daniel Schröder with drummer Emil Andersson to found old school Thrash / Death act RUIN. By the following year, three RUIN members would be operational with CHAIN OF HATE, Einar Magnusson, Andreas Gustavsson (credited as Andy Guz subsequently Cody Cruz) and Anders Bertilsson (under the name Shotgun Shaggy).

Bertilsson forged COLDWORKER in 2006, an alliance with NECRONY and NASUM drummer Anders Jakobson, RELENTLESS bass player Oskar Pålsson plus André Alvinzi of CARNAL GRIEF as second guitarist in March with ex-PHOBOS man Joel Fornbrant.

Chain Of Hate, Chain Of Hate (2004) (Demo). Lucifer Reincarnated / Insaint / My Bullet, Your Head.

CHAINSAW

STOCKHOLM, SWEDEN — *Jonas Åhlen (vocals), Pontus Arvidson (guitar), Harry Virtanen (bass).*

Stockholm Thrash Metal act CHAINSAW was manifested in October 2003 by ex-INCENDIARY guitarist Pontus Arvidson and former PANDEMONIC, NOCTURNAL SORROW, SERPENTINE and DEFORMITY bassist Harry Virtanen, the latter also active with VÖRGUS and INTERNAL DECAY. In 2003 they would be joined by ABUSED, BLACHEM, SADISTIC PAIN and LEPROSY vocalist Nicke Olsson. Drums for initial demo recordings were programmed by Mike Wead of MERCYFUL FATE and KING DIAMOND repute, after which Emil Holmgren from ILLUSION OF CLARITY was enlisted for live work.

Olsson exited in May 2004. July saw the introduction of Graja Pikanen on drums and in October Jonas Åhlen, a veteran of BACKDRAFT, ANTICIPATION and SHADES OF PALE, became lead singer. Pikanen exited shortly afterward.

Into The Pit, Chainsaw (2005) (Demo). Ancient Evil / Spawn Of Hatred / Twisting The Knife / Collective Entity / When There's No More Room In Hell / Lobotomy Of The Easter Bunny.

CHAKAL

BELO HORIZONTE, MG, BRAZIL — *Vladimir Korg (vocals), Mark (guitar), Necromancer (guitar), Destroyer (bass), Willian Wizz (drums).*

Known internationally for vocalist Vladimir Korg being credited with penning the lyrics for SEPULTURA's 'To The Wall'. CHAKAL originated in Belo Horizonte during 1985 as a trio of drummer Willian Wizz, bassist Destroyer and guitar player Mark. Former MEGATHRASH man Korg, alongside second guitarist Necromancer, would augment the line up for recording of the debut album 'Abominable Anno Domini' issued in 1987 by Cogumelo Records. A now scarce 7" single 'Living With The Pigs' leaked out the following year.

Vocalist Korg then departed to form THE MIST in late 1989, a band including ex-SEPULTURA guitarist Jairo T. in it's ranks.

CHAKAL regrouped, drawing in vocalist / bassist Marcelo L. and guitar player Eduardo Simões, releasing 1990's 'The Man Is His Own Jackal'. A further album, 'Death Is A Lonely Business' arrived in 1991 but after it's release CHAKAL once again hit line up problems with Drew would be enrolled on bass.

Latterly Korg made a return swelling the CHAKAL ranks which now comprised of Korg, Drew, Wizz and new guitarist Andre of VULTUR. The band, later adding PROFANA man Stanley as second guitarist, re-debuted on the live circuit on the 20th of December in Brasília, acting as special guests to VADER. Cogumelo Records duly issued a double album package of archive material to mark this renewed activity.

ABOMINABLE ANNO DOMINI, Cogumelo (1987).

Living With The Pigs EP, (1988).

THE LOST TAPES OF COGUMELO, (1990).

THE MAN IS HIS OWN JACKAL, Cogumelo COG036-A (1990).

DEATH IS A LONELY BUSINESS, Cogumelo (1991).

DEADLAND / ABOMINABLE ANNO DOMINI, Cogumelo CG 0063 (2003). Deadland / Amputation Prayer / Communication Room / Call Of The Undead / Lazarus Waltz / Liar (Safe Place) / The Escape / Flying To The Empty / Fade Out / May Not The Mankind Suffer / The Planet Is Dead / Terminal Brain / Children Of The Cemetery / Jason Lives / Warriors Of Disgrace / The Dead Walk / Children Sacrifice / Mr. Jesus Christ / S.A.T.P. (Shoot At The Police) / Never Die Young.

CHANNEL ZERO

BRUSSELS, BELGIUM — *Franky De Smet Van Damme (vocals), Xavier Carion (guitar), Tino Olivier De Martino (bass), Phil Baheux (drums).*

Brussels Thrash Metal act CHANNEL ZERO were created in 1990 by ex-CYCLONE members. Having debuted in 1992 with an eponymously titled debut for Shark Records, the quartet stepped up a level with the follow-up 'Stigmatised For Life' album, which was produced by PANTERA drummer Vinnie Paul. Following its release the band toured Europe supporting BIOHAZARD, OBITUARY, PRO-PAIN, EXHORDER and NAPALM DEATH. The band's third album, The 'Unsafe', (the second on Play It Again Sam) is notable for a guest vocal performance on one track by METHOD OF DESTRUCTION's Billy Milano.

For recording of the ensuing 'Black Fuel' CHANNEL ZERO flew to Connecticut in America in order to record, but became disillusioned with the results. Deciding upon scrapping these recordings, CHANNEL ZERO returned to Europe to complete the album with producer Attie Bauw.

Guitarist Peter Iterbeke has a project band entitled MANTRA, a band also including drummer J.T. Scaglione and bassist Jimmy Preziosa from American Thrash Metal veterans WHIPLASH. Seemingly at the height of their success, CHANNEL ZERO split in 1998.

With CHANNEL ZERO's demise, former vocalist Franky De Smet-Van Damme returned with a new "Energy Rock" outfit entitled SKITSOY in 2004. This band debuted in April with the single 'Come to Belgium', recorded at Jet Studios in Brussels with producer Benjamin Bertozzi and subsequently reworked, mixed and mastered by Attie Bauw.

CHANNEL ZERO, Shark 032 (1992). No Light (At The End Of The Tunnel) / Tales Of Worship / The Pioneer / Succeed Or Bleed / Never Alone / Inspiration To Violence / Painful Jokes / Save Me / Animation / Run With The Torch.

STIGMATISED FOR LIFE, Play It Again Sam BIAS 259CD (1994). Gold / Testimony / Unleash The Dog / Chrome Dome / Repetition / America / Stigmatised For Life / Play A Little / Big Now / Last Gap.

Help, Play It Again Sam (1995). Help / Last Gasp / All For One / ManOn The Edge.

Suck My Energy, Play It Again Sam 977. 847 (1995). Suck My Energy / Suck My Energy / Repetition.

UNSAFE, Play It Again Sam BIAS 290CD (1995). Suck My Energy / Heroin / Bad To The Bone / Help / Lonely / Run W.T.T. / Why / No More / Unsafe / Dashboard Devils / Asa Boy / Man On The Edge.

BLACK FUEL, Play It Again Sam BIAS 350 CD (1996). Black Fuel / Mastermind / Call On Me / Fool's Parade / Self Control / Misery / The Hill / Love–Hate Satellite / Caveman / Put It In / Wasted / Outro.

LIVE, Play It Again Sam (1998). Black Fuel / As A Boy / Mastermind / Self Control / Fool's Parade / Bad To The Bone / Dashboard Devils / Call On Me / Run W.T.T. / Heroin / Suck My Energy / Help / Lonely / Man On The Edge.

CHAOSYS

SÖDERTÄLJE, SWEDEN — *Stefan Lindstedt (vocals), Tomas Åkvik (guitar), Holger Thorsin (guitar), Johan Risberg (bass), Tommy Enström (drums).*

CHAOSYS is a Södertälje based Death / Thrash outfit formulated during 2003 from pedigree extreme Metal talent. Lead vocalist Stefan Lindstedt cites a tradition with WEB OF SOLITUDE and THE KRISTER OTLOOK EXPRESS, guitarist Tomas Åkvik held membership of THE KRISTER OUTLOOK EXPRESS and BRUTALITY OF ANGER whilst second guitarist Holger Thorsin has NOCTES, FIST FIRST, 138, CONSTELLATION and CONCEALED credits. The band's rhythm section comprising bassist Johan Risberg and drummer Tommy Enström boast a heritage with FAREWELL ETERNITY. Risberg also has TIDERLAG connections.

CHAOSYS delivered the EP 'The Inperfection Is Yours' in 2004. CHAOSYS credited guitarist Oak joined NALE in December 2006.

Demo 2003.02.23, Chaosys (2003) (Demo). P.M. Faith Proclaimed / Deus Ex / Mass Submission.

The Inperfection Is Yours, Chaosys (2004). SPS / Signed Yours Faithfully / Humanity 6.8.

Development Of The Human Mind, Chaosys (2005) (Demo). Retardeadnation / Alteration.

CHECKER PATROL

GERMANY / NORWAY — *Euronymous (vocals), Robert Gonnella (vocals), Michael Hoffman (guitar), Markus Ludwig (bass), Necrobutcher (bass).*

In December 1986 an unlikely union took place when MAYHEM was on a promotional trip to Europe to market the 'Pure Fucking Armageddon' demo. Involved in this impromptu, yet notorious diversion dubbed CHECKER PATROL would be the ASSASSIN trio of vocalist Robert Gonnella, guitarist Michael Hoffman and bass player Markus Ludwig in collaboration with members of Norway's MAYHEM—vocalist Euronymous (Øystein Aarseth) and bass player Necrobutcher (Jørn Stubberud) described on the cassette cover as "Evil fucking noise and drunken screams". Inebriation may be the cause of the misspelling of the band title on the demo front cover as "Cheker Patrol".

Demo '86, Checker Patrol (1986) (Demo). Jägermeister / Barbeque Of Hell / Checker Patrol / Ritze Ratze Rotze / Metalion In The Park / Fuck Off And Die / Satan Dies In Hell.

CHILDREN OF BODOM

ESPOO, FINLAND — *Alex Laiho (vocals / guitar), Ale Kuoppala (guitar), Henkka Seppäiä (bass), Janne Wirman Pimeys (keyboards), Jaska Raatikainen (drums).*

A powerful, modern Metal act from the town of Espoo, named after Finland's infamous Lake Bodom, the scene of a horrific, unsolved attack on June 5th 1960 that left three teenagers dead. The children had died from multiple stab wounds but a sole survivor, Nils Gustafsson, was famously declared insane and institutionalized after he had blamed the attack on the Grim Reaper. This medieval harbinger of death character would feature prominently on all of the group's output to date.

Founder member and vocalist Alex "Wildchild" Laiho made his name as part of THY SERPENT, maintaining CHILDREN OF BODOM, created in 1993 with drummer Jaska Raatikainen, as a going concern. Initially the group had gone under the title of INEARTHED, issuing a batch of melodic Death Metal demos commencing with 'Implosion Of Heaven', recorded at Munkkiniemen Studios in August 1994 and released that December. These tracks would be laid down as a duo of Laiho and Raatikainen.

INEARTHED followed this opening tape with second set 'Ubiquitous Absence Of Remission' in July 1995, recording this time at Astia Studios. Interestingly, melodies from the track 'Translucent Image', which featured female guest vocals from Nina Keitel, would re-surface in SINERGY's 'Beware The Heavens' at a later date. Once again composed and performed by Laiho and Raatikainen, the tape does make mention of bassist Samuli Miettinen and new member rhythm guitarist Alexander Kuoppala. A third demo, entitled 'Shining', was committed to tape at Astia Studios in February 1996 utilising keyboard player Jan Peri Pirisjoki. A line-up change found bassist Samuli Miettinen superseded by Henkka Seppala.

As INEARTHED the group scored a label deal in Belgium but a better offer from the highly respected Finnish Spinefarm concern convinced the band their way. At this stage the band, now with Janne Wirman Pimeys on keyboards, switched title to CHILDREN OF BODOM recording the Anssi Kippo, Alex Laiho and Jaska Raatikainen produced 'Something Wild' debut.

The album was issued in Finland in February 1997 and picked up for European license by the German Nuclear Blast corporation shortly after, emerging on the continent in April 1998, and successively via Toy's Factory in Japan. Adding a degree of colour to the mix, the group employed movie narrative from 'Ben Hur' as an intro to 'The Nail', the opening section of 'Deadnight Warrior' being taken from the film 'It' and even Mozart's Symphony no. 25 was re-worked for 'Red Light in My Eyes, Pt 2'. The group recorded an additional track, 'Children Of Bodom', which, when released as a single alongside tracks from CRYHAVOC and WIZZARD, scored the unprecedented achievement of hitting the number 1 spot on the charts. The band supported DIMMU BORGIR on their 1997 Finnish dates and in February of the following year hooked up with HYPOCRISY, COVENANT and BENEDICTION for mainland European gigs. For these shows, a friend of the band, Erna, substituted for Wirman Pimeys who could not get time out of schooling. With album sales on a sharp rise, CHILDREN OF BODOM were back out on the road in Europe during September, performing as part of another package bill with DISMEMBER, AGATHODAIMON, RAISE HELL and NIGHT IN GALES. Once again Wirman Pimeys had to sit it out and Kimberley Goss of AVERNUS, DIMMU BORGIR and THERION repute filled in. A one off concert in St. Petersburg, Russia, pairing with IMPALED NAZARENE, resulted in Alex Laiho opting to join the fellow Finns when CHILDREN OF BODOM's schedule allowed. As such, Laiho perform with IMPALED NAZARENE in February 1999 on their tour of North America and Mexico.

CHILDREN OF BODOM scored a further national number 1 single with 'Downfall' in early 1999. The single also contained a cover version of STONE's 'No Commands'. The 'Hatebreeder' album would also witness the band's presence in the national German album charts for the first time peaking at number 75. Humour was again in evidence, the intro narrative for opening song 'Warheart' being lifted from Milos Forman's 'Amadeus' movie and the keyboard introduction to 'Black Widow' brazenly borrowing from 80s TV series 'Miami Vice'.

Touring began with inaugural dates in Japan during the summer, concert recordings from Club Citta, Tokyo then surfacing as 'Tokyo Warhearts–Live In Japan', followed by a familiar all-Scandinavian Nuclear Blast package European venture allied with IN FLAMES, DARK TRANQUILITY and ARCH ENEMY. This time Janne Wirman Pimeys was finally in his rightful place behind the keyboards. In band down time Wirman, under the title of WARMEN, cut a solo album titled 'Unknown Soldier'.

In May 2000 another partnership with IMPALED NAZARENE conducted Greek gigs in Thessaloniki and Athens with Alex Laiho performing double guitar duty each night. The ensuing October album 'Follow The Reaper' record, cut at Abyss Studios in Sweden with the HYPOCRISY pairing of Peter Tägtgren and Lars Szöke acting as producer and engineer respectively, found the Japanese version with an extra bonus track, a version of OZZY OSBOURNE's 'Shot In The Dark'. Fans were quick to spot the band's now traditional oddball habit of planting the unexpected with the bridge section of 'Bodom After Midnight' in homage to 'The Rock' movie whilst speeches in 'Taste Of My Scythe' came transplanted from 'Exorcist 3'.

As a precursor of what was to come the band's 'Hate Me' single of October 2000, featuring a cover version of W.A.S.P.'s 'Hellion', swiftly reaped Platinum sales status in Finland by selling over 10'000 copies. Raatikainen deputised for SINERGY toward the close of the year before CHILDREN OF BODOM supported PRIMAL FEAR for a European tour across Germany, Austria, Italy, Spain and France in February 2001. Their 'Follow The Reaper' album quickly shifted over 50'000 copies in Europe, attaining a number 46 placing in the German national charts and reaching the top five in Finland. In October the band featured on the Spinefarm compilation 'Metal Rocks' with an exclusive cover version of IRON MAIDEN's 'Aces High'.

Jaska Raatikainen, along with TAROT and SINERGY bassist Marco Hietala and TAROT keyboard player Janne Tolsa would also convene a 2001 endeavour dubbed VIRTUOCITY. Raatikainen would also find time to session on the EVEMASTER EP 'Wither'.

CHILDREN OF BODOM broke their silence in mid 2002 unveiling plans for an August single comprising a new track 'You're Better Off Dead' coupled with a cover version of the RAMONES 'Somebody Put Something In My Drink'. Upon release this single was swiftly certified with Gold sales status. By October the band had flagged up 'Hate Crew Deathroll' as a projected title for their next Anssi Kippo produced studio album. Upon release the record crashed into the national Finnish album charts at number one, soon racking up in excess of 15,000 domestic sales and duly attaining gold status.

Jaska Raatikainen forged a project band in 2004 entitled GASHOUSE GARDEN, comprising such scene notables as NORTHER lead guitarist Kristian Ranta, CRAYDAWN guitarist Jaakko Teittinen and the SINERGY, KOTIPELTO, WARMEN credited Lauri Porra on bass. Heading up the band would be female singer Mertsa, located whilst singing AC/DC covers with her band CHINA CAT. An opening set of demos was recorded at Janne Wirman's studio in Helsinki.

CHILDREN OF BODOM live dates in Japan, allied with none other than Metal God HALFORD, were announced for February 2003. Rhythm guitarist Alexander Kuoppala left the CHILDREN OF BODOM ranks following the band's appearance at the July Helsinki 'Tuska' festival.

The band, announcing that the noted figure of SINERGY, LATVALA BROS, WALTARI and ex-STONE man Roope Latvala had joined up as session guitarist for the remainder of their world tour, debuted this new look line up in Moscow on 16th August. They would be back in the Far East for a further run of Japanese shows that September, partnering up with SOILWORK. That same month 'Hate Crew Deathroll' saw release in the USA on the Century Media label. In the interim Alexi Laiho gained co-production credits on GRIFFIN's album 'No Holds Barred'. In Japan, the Toy's Factory Records label revealed an exclusive compilation album entitled 'Bestbreeder (1997-2000)'.

CHILDREN OF BODOM united with DIMMU BORGIR, NEVERMORE and HYPOCRISY for US dates in November. During a gap in the band's schedule Laiho reunited with his ex-SINERGY comrade Tommi Lillman, founding KYLÄHULLUT, or "village idiot", alongside lead singer on Finnish punk band KLAMYDIA Vesa Jokinen. The band issued the 'Keisarinleikkaus' EP in May of 2004.

An extensive North American trek throughout April and May of 2004 had the band partnered with ICED EARTH and Swedish Progressive Metal band EVERGREY. An EP, 'Trashed, Lost & Strungout', novelly included covers of ALICE COOPER's 'Bed Of Nails' and ANDREW W.K.'s 'She Is Beautiful'. The single, backed by a promotional video for the title track directed by Patric Ullaeus, would impressively debut on the Finnish charts at no. 1. Despite all this activity Alexi Laiho found time to act as producer for the GRIFFIN album 'No Holds Barred'. Meantime Roope Latvala guested on SOULGRIND's 'The Origins Of The Paganblood' album.

The band would tour Brazil in August. October shows across the US had the band partnering with LAMB OF GOD, FEAR FACTORY and THROWDOWN.

On 5th January 2005 Alexi Laiho and Roope Latvala gathered together with Finland's Metal community at Helsinki's Rock 'n' Roll Station to pay homage to the recently murdered PANTERA / DAMAGEPLAN guitarist Darrell 'Dimebag' Abbott by forming up a one off PANTERA tribute band DIMEN NIMEEN ("In Dime's Name!"). Other musicians featured in this collective included Atte Sarkima of AJATTARA and VERENPISARA, Tony Jelencovich from TRANSPORT LEAGUE, Petteri Hirvanen and Nicke of MONSTERBALL, Toni, Pete, Kride and Jukkis of NORTHER and Nico, Euge and OJ from GODSPLAGUE amongst many others.

In early 2005 the Back On Black label re-issued 'Something Wild', 'Hatebreeder' and 'Follow The Reaper' on limited edition vinyl picture discs. CHILDREN OF BODOM's new studio album title would be revealed as 'Are You Dead Yet?'. Unfortunately, the similarity to CARNAL FORGE's recent 'Aren't You Dead Yet?' drew immediate comparisons.

CHILDREN OF BODOM's single 'In Your Face', issued in August, surprisingly included a cover version of BRITNEY SPEARS' 'Oops I Did It Again'. The album 'Are You Dead Yet?' saw release on 14th September in Finland and 19th September for the rest of the world. A limited edition vinyl picture disc, restricted to just 2000 copies, would be pressed up by Universal in Germany. In keeping with the band's left-field choice of cover songs, Japanese variants of the record added a rendition of the Glam Rock classic 'Talk To Dirty To Me' originally by POISON. 'Are You Dead Yet?' debuted at number 1 in Finland and in Japan at number 17, where it sold 21,000 copies in its first week of release. Meantime, the 'Humppasirkus' album from fabled Finnish Humppa Metal band ELÄKELÄISET sported a rendition of CHILDREN OF BODOM's 'Hate Me' re-branded 'Vihann Humppaa' ("I Hate Humppa").

US tour dates commenced in November, partnered with TRIVIUM and AMON AMARTH. The group then hooked up with EKTOMORF and ONE MAN ARMY AND THE UNDEAD QUARTET for European and Scandinavian gigs commencing in Germany during late December and finalizing in Finland in February 2006. North American gigging witnessed a union with BULLET FOR MY VALENTINE and CHIMAIRA in March. Summer 2006 US dates commencing in June, dubbed the "Unholy Alliance—Preaching To The Perverted" tour, saw the group packaged with headliners SLAYER plus MASTODON, LAMB OF GOD and THINE EYES BLEED as support. The group also joined the European leg of the 'Unholy Alliance', comprising SLAYER, IN FLAMES, LAMB OF GOD and THINE EYES BLEED, in October. CHILDREN OF BODOM teamed up with AMON AMARTH, SANCTITY and GOJIRA for a North American tour in December.

The band was announced as performing at the Dubai, United Arab Emirates 'Desert Rock' festival in March 2007 but withdrew when Alexi Laiho injured his shoulder, tripping over at a bowling alley. CHILDREN OF BODOM's performance of the song 'Everytime I Die', filmed at the BÖHSE ONKELZ farewell show in Lausitzring, Germany in 2005, was featured on a four-DVD BÖHSE ONKELZ box set.

On February 16th CHILDREN OF BODOM was honoured with the "Band of the Year" award at the Finnish Metal Awards, which were held during the Finnish Metal Expo at the Cable Factory in Helsinki, Finland.

SOMETHING WILD, Spinefarm SPI 49CD (1997). Deadnight Warrior / In The Shadows / Red Light In My Eyes (Part I) / Red Light

In My Eyes (Part II) / Lake Bodom / The Nail / Touch Like Angel Of Death.

The Carpenter, Spinefarm SPI 46CD (1997) (Split single with NIGHTWISH and THY SERPENT). Red Light In My Eyes, Part II.

Children Of Bodom, Spinefarm SPI 59CD (1998) (Split single with WIZZARD and CRYHAVOC). Children Of Bodom.

SOMETHING WILD, Toy's Factory TFCK-87155 (1998) (Japanese release). Deadnight Warrior / In The Shadows / Red Light In My Eyes (Part I) / Red Light In My Eyes (Part II) / Lake Bodom / The Nail / Touch Like Angel Of Death / Children Of Bodom / Mass Hypnosis.

Downfall, Spinefarm SPI 73CD (1998). Downfall / No Commands. Chart position: 1 FINLAND.

HATEBREEDER, Spinefarm SPI 69CD (1999). Warheart / Silent Night, Bodom Night / Hatebreeder / Bed Of Razors / Towards Dead End / Black Widow / Wrath Within / Children Of Bodom / Down Fall. Chart position: 75 GERMANY.

HATEBREEDER, Toy's Factory TFCK-87180 (1999) (Japanese release). Warheart / Silent Night, Bodom Night / Hatebreeder / Bed Of Razors / Towards Dead End / Black Widow / Wrath Within / Children Of Bodom / Down Fall / No Commands.

TOKYO WARHEARTS—LIVE IN JAPAN 1999, Nuclear Blast NB 0440-2 (1999). Intro / Silent Night, Bodom Night / Lake Bodom / Warheart / Bed Of Razors / War Of Razors / Deadnight Warrior / Hatebreeder / Touch The Angel Of Death / Downfall / Towards Dead End.

TOKYO WARHEARTS—LIVE IN JAPAN 1999, Vinyl Collector's VC 012 (1999) (Vinyl release). Intro / Silent Night, Bodom Night / Lake Bodom / Warheart / Bed Of Razors / War Of Razors / Deadnight Warrior / Hatebreeder / Touch The Angel Of Death / Downfall / Towards Dead End / No Commands.

Hate Me!, Spinefarm SPI 98CD (2000). Hate Me! / Hellion.

FOLLOW THE REAPER, Spinefarm SPI 99DP (2000) (Finnish digipack). Follow The Reaper / Bodom After Midnight / Children Of Decadence / Every Time I Die / Mask Of Sanity / Taste Of My Scythe / Hate Me! / Northern Comfort / Kissing The Shadows / Don't Stop At The Top.

FOLLOW THE REAPER, Spinefarm SPI 99CD (2000). Follow The Reaper / Bodom After Midnight / Children Of Decadence / Every Time I Die / Mask Of Sanity / Taste Of My Scythe / Hate Me! / Northern Comfort / Kissing The Shadows.

FOLLOW THE REAPER, Toy's Factory TFCK-87236 (2000) (Japanese release). Follow The Reaper / Bodom After Midnight / Children Of Decadence / Every Time I Die / Mask Of Sanity / Taste Of My Scythe / Hate Me / Northern Comfort / Kissing The Shadows / Shot In The Dark / Hellion.

FOLLOW THE REAPER, Spinefarm SPI 99CD (2001). Follow The Reaper / Bodom After Midnight / Children Of Decadence / Every Time I Die / Mask Of Sanity / Taste Of My Scythe / Hate Me / Northern Comfort / Kissing The Shadows / Hellion. Chart positions: 46 GERMANY, 85 ITALY.

SOMETHING WILD (DELUXE EDITION), Nuclear Blast NB 1017-2 (2002). Deadnight Warrior / In The Shadows / Red Light In My Eyes (Part I) / Red Light In My Eyes (Part II) / Lake Bodom / The Nail / Touch Like Angel Of Death / Children Of Bodom / Mass Hypnosis / Silent Scream / Don't Stop At The Top.

You're Better Off Dead, Spinefarm SPI 159 (2002). You're Better Off Dead / Somebody Put Something In My Drink.

HATE CREW DEATHROLL (SPECIAL EDITION), Spinefarm SPI 165SP (2003). Needled 24/7 / Sixpounder / Chokehold (Cocked 'n Loaded) / Bodom Beach Terror / Angels Don't Kill / Triple Corpse Hammerblow / You're Better Off Dead / Lil' Bloodred Ridin' Hood / Hate Crew Deathroll / Silent Scream / Hidden Internet Link To Needled 24/7 Video.

Needled 24/7, Spinefarm SPI 163PD (2003) (Picture disc). Needled 24/7 / Silent Scream.

HATE CREW DEATHROLL, Universal Japan UICO-1048 (2003) (Japanese release). Needled 24/7 / Sixpounder / Chokehold (Cocked 'n Loaded) / Bodom Beach Terror / Angels Don't Kill / Triple Corpse Hammerblow / You're Better Off Dead / Lil' Bloodred Ridin' Hood / Hate Crew Deathroll / Silent Scream / Somebody Put Something In My Drink.

HATE CREW DEATHROLL, Spinefarm SPI 165CD (2003). Needled 24/7 / Sixpounder / Chokehold (Cocked 'n Loaded) / Bodom Beach Terror / Angels Don't Kill / Triple Corpse Hammerblow / You're Better Off Dead / Lil' Bloodred Ridin' Hood / Hate Crew Deathroll. Chart positions: 1 FINLAND, 36 SWEDEN, 45 GERMANY, 74 FRANCE.

Trashed, Lost & Strungout, Spinefarm SPI 207CD (2004). Trashed, Lost & Strungout / She Is Beautiful.

Trashed, Lost & Strungout, Spinefarm SPI 207EP (2004). Trashed, Lost & Strungout / Knuckleduster / Bed Of Nails / She Is Beautiful / Trashed, Lost & Strungout (Video) / Trashed, Lost & Strungout (Video: Live in Helsinki) / Children Of Bodom's Night Out (Video). Chart positions: 1 FINLAND, 27 CANADA.

In Your Face, Spinefarm SPI 244CD (2005). In Your Face / Oops I Did It Again / In Your Face (Censored radio edit). Chart position: 1 FINLAND.

ARE YOU DEAD YET?, Spinefarm SPI 230CD (2005). Living Dead Beat / Are You Dead Yet? / If You Want Peace … Prepare For War / Punch Me I Bleed / In Your Face / Next In Line / Bastards Of Bodom / Trashed, Lost And Strungout / We're Not Gonna Fall. Chart positions: 1 FINLAND, 16 GERMANY, 16 SWEDEN, 17 JAPAN, 42 AUSTRIA, 67 FRANCE, 79 SWITZERLAND, 80 ITALY, 82 CANADA.

In Your Face, Spinefarm SPI 244DVD (2005) (DVD single). In Your Face (Video 2.0) / In Your Face (Video 5.1) / All Night Long (Sh*t-Faced Bastards Of Bodom) / Sixpounder (Live at Wacken Open Air).

In Your Face, Island (2006) (UK promotion CD single). In Your Face.

In Your Face, Island MCST 40439 (2006) (12" vinyl picture disc). In Your Face / She Is Beautiful.

In Your Face, Island MCSTD 40439 (2006) (CD single). In Your Face / Knuckleduster / Bed Of Nails / In Your Face (Video).

ARE YOU DEAD YET? (DELUXE EDITION), Universal Japan UICO-9015 (2006) (CD + DVD, Japanese release). Living Dead Beat / Are You Dead Yet? / If You Want Peace … Prepare For War / Punch Me I Bleed / In Your Face / Next In Line / Bastards Of Bodom / Trashed, Lost And Strungout / We're Not Gonna Fall / Oops! I Did It Again / Talk Dirty To Me / Living Dead Beat (Live) / Follow The Reaper (Live) / Hate Crew Deathrole (Live) / Trashed, Lost & Strungout / Sixpounder / Everytime I Die (Live At Tuska Open Air) / All Night Long (COB Remarkable Record Session Recovery Story) / Trashed—Lost In Helsinki / Downfall (Live At Tuska Open Air).

ARE YOU DEAD YET?, Universal Japan UICO-1086 (2006). Living Dead Beat / Are You Dead Yet? / If You Want Peace … Prepare For War / Punch Me I Bleed / In Your Face / Next In Line / Bastards Of Bodom / Trashed, Lost And Strungout / We're Not Gonna Fall / Oops! I Did It Again / Talk Dirty To Me.

CHAOS RIDDEN YEARS—STOCKHOLM KNOCKOUT LIVE, Spinefarm SPI 299CD (2006). Living Dead Beat / Sixpounder / Silent Night, Bodom Night / Hate Me! / We're Not Gonna Fall / Angels Don't Kill / Deadbeats I / Bodom After Midnight / Bodom Beach Terror—medley / Follow The Reaper / Needled 24/7 / Clash Of The Booze Brothers / In Your Face / Hate Crew Deathroll / Are You Dead Yet? / Latvala / Lake Bodom / Everytime I Die / Downfall. Chart positions: 28 FINLAND, 75 GERMANY.

CHRIS POLAND

USA — Ex-MEGADETH guitarist. Upon his ousting from MEGADETH Poland issued the solo album 'Return To Metalopolis' featuring his brother Mark on drums and ex-ARCADE man John Mason on vocals. The Poland brothers and Mason next step was to form DAMN THE MACHINE, an act that lasted one album. The 90's found Poland with a new avant-garde Metal act MUMBO'S BRAIN before issuing a further solo effort 'Chasing The Sun'. Poland also has a live act titled OHM. Founded in 1997 this outfit debuted with an eponymous album in 2003.

Mark Poland has also performed live with WHITE ZOMBIE drumming on a Japanese tour. 2001 found Chris Poland guesting on the JASON BECKER tribute album 'Warmth In The Wilderness'. The following year Poland put in another guest session, appearing on the COSMOSQUAD 'Squadrophenia' album.

Poland's OHM band teamed up ex-TESTAMENT guitarist Alex Skolnick's Jazz based ALEX SKOLNICK TRIO and another erstwhile MEGADETH man MARTY FRIEDMAN for a high profile September 2003 'Guitarevolution' tour of North America. That same year Poland contributed guitar work on two tracks, 'Spanish Castle Magic' and 'Room Full Of Mirrors', to a JIMI HENDRIX tribute album assembled by the Finnish Lion Music label.

Revisiting his high profile days with MEGADETH, Poland was invited by Dave Mustaine to lay down guitar solos on the 2004 comeback album 'The System Has failed'. Poland would also guest on the LAMB OF GOD 'Ashes Of The Wake' album and feature as soloist for Swedish band MATTSSON's rendition of 'Parisienne Walkways' to the 2004 GARY MOORE tribute album 'Give Us Moore'.

RETURN TO METALOPOLIS, Roadrunner RR 9348-2 (1990). Club Ded / Alexandria / Return To Metalopolis / Heinous Interruptus / The Fall Of Babylon / Row Of Crows / Theatre Of The Damned / Beelzebub Bop / Apparition Station / Khazad Dum.

CHASING THE SUN, Grooveyard 001 (1999). The Sun / Hip Hop Karma / Wendell's Place / Robostomp / Straight Jacket / Cosmo's Thumb / Lu Lu's Dream / Salvador / Interferance Blues / Alphabet City / Mercy / Song For Paul (31 Summers / Alexandria '99.

RARE TRAX, Grooveyard 002 (1999). Big 15 / L.A. 'd / Wont Take Me Back / Lissas Found A Home / Demons / Im Only Sleeping / Acoustic Guitar Interlude R1 / Hold On / SOS / Lay It Down / Voyager / Angel / Acoustic Guitar Interlude R2 / If Yellow Were Orange.

CIRITH UNGOL

VENTURA, CA, USA — *Tim Baker (vocals), Jerry Fogle (guitar), Greg Lindstrom (guitar), Michael Flint (bass), Robert Garven (drums).*

With a name inspired by Tolkien's Kirith Ungol (the lair in which the spider Shelob made an attempt to destroy Baggins in 'Lord Of The Rings') and a semi-legendary logo featuring two praying, kneeling skeletons. Ventura, California's CIRITH UNGOL, based around former TITANIC duo of guitarist Jerry Fogle and drummer Robert Garven, established in seventh grade during 1969. TITANIC mixed up a bundle of varying influences and gained a loyal, cult following before morphing into CIRITH UNGOL in 1972. This move prompted a switch from Pop to Rock, the formative act performing covers by the likes of HARD STUFF, THIN LIZZY and BUDGIE. The original incarnation of the band was fronted during 1975 by vocalist Neal Beattie. CIRITH UNGOL demoed numerous original tracks from 1977 onwards not record an album until 1980's 'Frost And Fire' on their own Liquid Flames label. These songs were recorded by the Fogle, Lindstrom and Garven axis together with frontman Tim Baker and bassist Michael Flint Vujea.

Although CIRITH UNGOL's debut album 'Frost And Fire' sported an amazing piece of cover artwork from Michael Whelan, the actual contents of the record disappointed many critics. It even featured a track, an instrumental entitled 'Maybe That's Why', that, through an error, lyrics for appeared in the album packaging. In spite of bad reviews though, particularly in the UK, CIRITH UNGOL sold substantial numbers of albums, the record being given a second lease of life courtesy of a 1981 re-release on Enigma Records.

Following the album's release, CIRITH UNGOL parted company with second guitarist Greg Lindstrom in late 1982 and, amazingly, many proclaimed the band's ensuing contribution to the first 'Metal Massacre' compilation album, the hyper-speed 'Death Of The Sun' as rather listenable.

Enigma picked up the band for a further album, the highly rated 'King Of The Dead' emerging during July 1984, licensed on Roadrunner in Europe, and this record would not only show a vast improvement in the standard of songwriting and musicianship, even going as far as an adventurous rip through J.S. Bach's 'Toccata In D'. Also coming to the fore would be Tim Baker, who here perfected his style, alternating between a high nasal skrye to guttural, trollish reverberations. It would push the Californian mob further into the hearts of the true believers, gaining a host of new admirers along the way. Although the group performed infrequently, gigs to promote 'King Of The Dead' generated media exposure with a profusion of pyrotechnics and singer Tim Baker's entrance onstage in a coffin, borne aloft by robed roadies.

The group also began to become inspired the work of novelist Michael Moorcock lyrically, a fact that gained more prominence on August 1986's 'One Foot In Hell' album, released on new label Metal Blade Records and produced by label boss Brian Slagel. The band would bow out in 1991 with the Ron Goudie produced 'Paradise Lost' album, this including a cover of the 60s CRAZY WORLD OF ARTHUR BROWN hit 'Fire'. The group personnel had shifted yet again seeing Garven and Baker now working alongside guitarist Jim Barraza and bassist Vernon Green, although studio contributors also included Joe Malatesta on guitars and bassist Robert L. Warrenburg.

Bearing in mind the almost universal derision heaped upon their early albums the band began to attain a cult status in mainland Europe during the 90's. Italian act DOOMSWORD would cover the CIRITH UNGOL track 'Nadsokor'. CIRITH UNGOL's legacy took a bizarre twist in 1995 when a live single was issued, financed by none other than DECEASED's King Fowley. Their appeal spread with the September 2001 retrospective 'Servants Of Chaos', a double CD compiling unreleased studio material, rehearsal and live tapes. Sadly, Jerry Fogle was not fated to experience this new wave of appreciation, having died in 1998 of liver failure.

In early 2003 Greg Lindstrom revealed his participation in the FALCON project band, a union with DESTINY'S END, OBSCURE and ARTISAN guitarist Perry Grayson and PALE DIVINE drummer Darin McCloskey. Notably the FALCON logo incorporated the famous kneeling skeletons motif.

In late 2005 German label Solemnity Music revealed they would be issuing the first "official" tribute to CIRITH UNGOL, entitled 'One Foot in Fire'. This collection included Greg Lindstrom participating on FALCON's interpretation of 'Shelob's Lair'. Contributing bands included Italy's ROSAE CRUCIS with 'Death Of The Sun', Germany's SOLEMNITY's version of 'What Does It Take', DAWN OF WINTER with members of SACRED STEEL delivering 'Doomed Planet', Italy's BATTLE RAM on 'Join The Legion', Greek outfit HOLY MARTYR with 'Frost And Fire', EMERALD from Switzerland on 'Heaven Help Us', Polish band MONSTRUM with 'Fallen Idols', Italy's ASSEDIUM with 'Black Machine', a union between NWoBHM veterans ELIXIR and Polish group CRYSTAL VIPER on 'Chaos Rising' and Dutchmen ROTTEN delivering a CIRITH UNGOL medley.

FROST AND FIRE, Liquid Flames LF001 (1980). Frost And Fire / I'm Alive / A Little Fire / What Does It Take / Edge Of A Knife / Better Off Dead / Maybe That's Why.

KING OF THE DEAD, Enigma E1089 (1984). Atom Smasher / Black Machine / Master Of The Pit / King Of The Dead / Death Of The Sun / Finger Of Scorn / Toccata In D / Cirith Ungol.

ONE FOOT IN HELL, Metal Blade 72143 (1986). Blood And Iron / Chaos Descends / The Fire / Nadsokar / 100 M.P.H. / War Eternal / Doomed Planet / One Foot In Hell.

PARADISE LOST, Restless 7-72510-2 (1991). Join The Legion / The Troll / Fire / Heaven Help Us / Before The Lash / Go It Alone / Chaos Rising / Fallen Idols / Paradise Lost.

I'm Alive (Live), Old Metal (1995). I'm Alive (Live) / Atom Smasher (Live).

SERVANTS OF CHAOS, Metal Blade 14383 (2001). Hype Performance / Last Laugh / Frost And Fire (Early version) / Eyes / Better Off Dead (Alternate version) / 100 MPH (Alternate version) / I'm Alive (Alternate version) / Bite Of The Worm / The Twitch / Maybe That's Why (original version) / Ill Met In Lankhmar / Return To Lankhmar / Darkness Weaves / Witchdance / Feeding The Ants / Obsidian / Death Of The Sun (Remix) / Fire (Alternate version) / Fallen Idols (Alternate version) / Chaos Rising (Rehearsal) / Fallen Idols (rehearsal) / Paradise Lost (Rehearsal) / Join The Legion (Rehearsal) / Before The Lash (Rehearsal) / Atom Smasher (Live) / Master Of The Pit (Live) / King Of The Dead (Live) / Last Laugh (Live) / Cirith Ungol (Live) / Secret Agent Man / Ferrari 308QV On Dyno At 8000 RPM.

CLAUSTROPHOBIA

VÄRNAMO, SWEDEN — *Christian Malmqvist (vocals / drums), John Sveningsson (guitar), Joakim Sveningsson (bass), Robert Hansson (drums).*

CLAUSTROPHOBIA was a 1990 Bay area style Thrash act out of Värnamo. Initially Andreas Andersson, later to feature on GOREFLESH's 1994 demo 'Stoned', handled drum duties. The band issued the demos 'Eternity' and 'M.O.T.H.E.R.F.U.C.K.E.R.'

prior to disbanding, with three members—guitarist John Sveningsson, bass player Joakim Sveningsson and drummer Robert Hansson all going on to found COMFORT MIND. The trio would stick together to turn up in 1993 in the Alt-Rock act ANDROGYNE. Frontman Christian Malmqvist later fronted KEITEL and LIQUID FALLS. Hansson made a return to the scene in 2002 with Stoners THE MUSHROOM RIVER BAND and STREETS OF MARS.

Eternity, Claustrophobia (1990) (Demo). Eternity / Speeding Wheel / Path To Insanity / Useless Life.

M.O.T.H.E.R.F.U.C.K.E.R., Claustrophobia (1991) (Demo). Face The Truth / Pain Remains / Delusions / My Last Vision / R.U. / Tear Me Apart.

CLUSTER BOMB UNIT

GERMANY — *Julia (vocals), Werner (guitar), Theo (guitar), Kelly (bass), Oliver (drums).*

Hardcore act CLUSTER BOMB UNIT's debut recording line up, for the 1993 shared EP in league with RESIST, incorporated Oliver on lead vocals and drums, guitarist Werner and bassist Mike. A second guitarist, Roland, augmented the band for the 1995 split effort with DISCLOSE plus the 'Opfer' and 'Realität' EPs. 1996's 'Greetings From U.S.A.' outing included new studio tracks, amongst which was a G.I.S.M. cover 'Nervous Corps', as well as live tracks recorded at the Fireside Bowl in Chicago that year with new bassist Moritz. A Polish only cassette, 'Deadly Harvest', emerged in 1998.

By 2000 Sven was fronting the band and Theo had taken Roland's place on second guitar for the 'Distortorama' EP issued by the Japanese Tribal War Asia label. CLUSTER BOMB UNIT recorded their March 2000 show at Woodys venue in Niigata for a live album. Whilst in Japan the band recorded a studio album 'Die Stationen von C.B.U.'. The band collected together material from prior releases to form a cassette only release dubbed 'To Russia With Love' for the Russian market in 2001.

The 2002 split EP shared with RAAG came in a limited multi-coloured vinyl run comprising 100 white vinyl, 200 blue vinyl and 700 on black marbled vinyl.

Cluster Bomb Unit, Consensus Reality (1993) (Split flexi single with RESIST). Without A Warning / Germans Go Home / Too Punk To Act.

End The War Now EP, Thought Crime (1994). End The War Now / Kill Your Scene / Our World / Parents / Fear Of The Future.

Cluster Bomb Unit, MCR Company (1994) (Split single with DISCLOSE). Krank / Jagd Messias / Komplex.

Opfer EP, DIY (1995). Abgrund / Opfer / Detonation / Grundlos.

Realität EP, Wiggy (1996). Überdosis / Realität / Krawattencharly / Ertappt / Drückeberger.

Fotografieren Verboten EP, Thought Crime (1996). VKP / Falsche Welt / Verbaute Zukunft / Egal / Ratten / War In Your Living Room / Wirrkopf / Betrug / Wut / Schweigen / Draussen / VKP II.

Greetings From U.S.A. EP, Cheesy Crust (1997). Punkgestapo / Nervous Corps / Abgrund (Live) / Verbaute Zukunft (Live) / Wut (Live).

… And The Dirty Little Weapons EP, Havoc (1999). Genug Ist Genug / Lovebomb / Go To Hell / Zukunftsvisionen / Fuck Your Ideals.

Distortorama EP, Tribal War Asia (2000). Mit Dem Spaten / Schutzmann / Be A Man / Zwanghaft Irr / Stück Dreck.

LIVE AT WOODY'S, NIIGATA, JAPAN, Vulgar (2000). Wut / Krawattencharly / Zukunftsvisionen / Ratten / Wirrkopf / Soldaten / Krank / Schutzmann / Be A Man / Zwanghaft Irr / Genug Ist Genug / Verbaute Zukunft / Eigene Welt / Unsterblich / Realität / Wir Fahren Gegen Nazis / Abgrund / Mit Dem Spaten / Falsche Welt / Fear Of The Future.

DIE STATIONEN VON C.B.U., Tribal War Asia (2001) (Limited edition 1000 copies). Soldaten / Ratten / Eigene Welt / Krawattencharly / Tranceform / Drückeberger / Zukunftsvisionen / Krank / Theme Of C.B.U. / Stück Dreck / VKP / Wut / Zwanghaft Irr / Fear Of The Future / Realität / In Rudeln / It Is The Sheep That See It / Abgrund / Kill Your Scene / Unsterblich.

YOU CAN NOT KILL A MASTER AT NIGHT, Donotconsume (2001) (Malaysian release). Without A Warning / Germans Go Home / Too Punk To Act / End The War Now / Kill Your Scene / Our World / Parents / Fear Of The Future / Krank / Jagd Messias / Komplex / Abgrund / Opfer / Detomation / Grundlos / VKP / Falsche Welt / Verbaute Zukunft / Egal / Ratten / War In Your Living Room / Wirrkopf / Betrug / Wut / Schweigen / Draussen / VKP II / Überdosis / Realität / Krawattencharly / Ertappt / Drückeberger / Punkgestapo / Nervous Corps / Abgrund (Live) / Verbaute Zukunft (Live) / Wut (Live).

Cluster Bomb Unit, Rabid Dog (2002) (Split EP with RAAG). Parties In Villas / Wie Lange Noch / Das Grosse Spiel.

COCKROACH

GERMANY — *Frank Geue (vocals / guitar), Ulrich Mewes (guitar), Timo Flöther (bass), Alexander Reichelt (drums).*

COCKROACH, coming together in March of 1992, deliver unashamed old school Thrash Metal. The opening line up saw founders Ulrich Mewes and Frank Geue on guitar, with drummer Alexander Reichelt subsequently joined by lead singer Reiner Striegel. In 1995 the band was reinforced by bassist Klaus Hoffer and committed to demos. However, following these sessions Striegel exited and Geue took over the lead vocal mantle. COCKROACH cut a self financed album 'Fi(r)st' in 1996, delivering this to the Rock public in April the following year.

Hoffer departed and for some time COCKROACH operated sans bass guitar until Jürgen Kimmel stepped in to fulfill the role in October of 1998. In this incarnation the band laid down second album 'No Compromise' but subsequently Kimmel too quit. Timo Flöther took the position in early 2000. COCKROACH signed to the Supreme Chaos label for their February 2003 opus 'Temple Of Mystery', these recordings having been mixed by ATROCITY's Alexander Krull.

FI(R)ST, Independent (1997). In(Sected) / Fear Of Death / Unholy War / Senseless / True Lies / Married With Children.

NO COMPROMISE, Independent (1999). Virtual Reality / Vampire In Black / Disciples Of Evil / Between Good And Evil / Memories / Marching Souls / Love Vision / Death Zone / Time Bomb / Pit Bull's Bite.

TEMPLE OF MYSTERY, Supreme Chaos (2003). Witch Trial / Phantom Of The Dawn / Total Gym / Temple Of Mystery / Underworld / Hidden Fire / Fallen Angel / Tears / Cockroach / Suck Me Beautiful / Personal War / Tekilla.

THE OBSERVER, (2006).

CODEON

HELSINKI, FINLAND — *Vesa Mattila (vocals), Sami Raatikainen (guitar), Asko Sartanen (guitar), Lauri Mailasalo (bass), Joni Varon (drums).*

Helsinki technical Death Metal band forged by guitarist Sami Raatikainen in October 2002, hooking up with bass player Lauri Mailasalo, then drummer Mats Lindewvist that December. Singer Vesa Mattila held ties to BODIES and FINAL DAWN. An initial line-up fractured, leaving Raatikainen to handle all guitar work on a 2003 demo. The band then drafted the IMPERANON and NAILDOWN credited Asko Sartanen on second guitar.

A self-funded EP in June 2005, 'On My Side', secured a recording contract with Dies Irae Records for a re-release in December. Another membership change saw Lindewvist replaced by Joni Varon. CODEON guitarist Sami Raatikainen joined German Death Metal band NECROPHAGIST in February 2006.

Vesa Mattila fronts SAATANAN MARIONETIT under the alter ego 'Aargh Satan' and performs bass with BLACK TEMPLE.

Demo 2003, Codeon (2003) (Demo). Fatal Soul Collision / Backstabbers' Parade / Tidal Complete.

On My Side EP, Codeon (2005). Fatal Soul Collision 2004 / Decay Life / On My Side / Cold Trigger / The Dying Race.

On My Side EP, Dies Irae IRAE 003 (2005). Fatal Soul Collision 2004 / Decay Life / On My Side / Cold Trigger / The Dying Race.

COMMANDER

BOWLING GREEN, KY, USA — *Chris Hightower (vocals), Jon Bratcher (guitar), Josh Hines (bass), Jeremie Pryor (drums).*

COMMANDER is a Bowling Green, Kentucky Thrash Metal band formulated during 2004 by guitar player Jon Bratcher, bassist Josh Hines and drummer Jeremie Pryor. In 2005 Chris Hightower enrolled as singer and that April the band entered Negative Earth Studios to cut an EP entitled 'Wall Of Swords'. This set included a cover version of JUDAS PRIEST's seminal 'Breaking The Law'. Further exposure was garnered with the inclusion of the track 'Relentless Savage Beating' on a compilation album packaged with Canada's 'Brave Words & Bloody Knuckles' magazine.

A debut album, 'Altar Of Bones', was crafted with engineer Jon Craig at the same facilities in March 2006.

Wall Of Swords, Commander (2005). Wall Of Swords / Organ Thrasher / Relentless Savage Beating / Skullclamp / Breaking The Law / Flesh Grafter.
ALTAR OF BONES, Commander (2006). Mountain / Decree Of Pain / Coils Of Medusa / Blood Funnel / Fatal Blow / Royal Assassin / 666 Steps / Demonic Tutor / Temporary Insanity / Empty The Catacombs / Altar Of Bones.

CONCRETE SOX

NOTTINGHAM, NOTTINGHAMSHIRE, UK — *John (vocals / drums), Victim (guitar), Les (bass).*

Nottingham/Derby Hardcore Thrash Metal act CONCRETE SOX originally started out as a straight Punk band in 1982. The group bowed in as a trio of vocalist / drummer John, bassist Les and guitarist VicTim. The 'Your Turn Next' album was released by COR Records as well as the track 'Eminent Scum' appearing on a COR Records sampler 'Digging In Water' alongside SACRALIGE and HIRAX in 1985.

John would decamp to join HERESY and CITY INDIANS drummer Andy Sewell and vocalist Sean Cook were enrolled to plug the gap. With this line up CONCRETE SOX shared a split album release with HERESY, being Earache Records very first release.

A heavy touring schedule followed after which the band switched to the Manic Ears label for 1987's 'Whoops, Sorry Vicar'. The band would also feature on the Manic Ears compilation 'The North Atlantic Noise Attack'. The 1989 'Sewarside' album was issued upfront of guitarist VicTim joining Glamsters SLEEZEPATROL.

Rick Button was drafted on guitar for European touring billed alongside DOOM. The band toured as support to AGNOSTIC FRONT in 1992.

A series of line up tribulations would dog the band over the next few years. Both Cook and Button made their exit, substitutes being vocalist Lloyd and guitarist Ian. This version of CONCRETE SOX released the American released 'Lunched Out' live 7 single.

Ian would be next to leave and Mark Greenwell took the guitar position as the group signed to Lost And Found for the 'No World Order' album. CONCRETE SOX, complete with a returning Sean Cook, then undertook a tour of Japan and issued a split EP in alliance with NIGHTMARE.

After a ten year term Andy Sewell decided to vacate the drum stool. CONCRETE SOX ultimately folded. There would be a reformation comprising of Les, Lloyd, Mark Greenwell and drummer Pug for a burst of UK dates but once again the band split.

The band would be back for a series of UK shows in the summer of 1998. Swedish shows followed into 1999 with a CONCRETE SOX roster made up of Sean Cook, Mark Greenwell, new bass player Rick Lamell and drummer Andy Sewell.

An EP, simply titled 'The New EP', arrived on the Data label, the cover artwork being a clever 'South Park' spoof announcing Oh my God—They killed Anarkenny!

YOUR TURN NEXT, COR Records GURT 10 (1986).
SPLIT LP, Earache (1986) (Split album with HERESY). Key To The Door / False Inside / Speak Siberian Or Die (For SOD) / Modernisation (A New Form Of Slavery) / Sustain The Orgy.
WHOOPS, SORRY VICAR!, Manic Ears ACHE 11 (1987). Prophecy / No Trust In Faith / Scientific Slaughter / Comparison / Rumour Well Out Of Hand / Think Now / False Insight / Dream / Salt Of The Earth / Facts / Moustache / Like A Maniac.
SEWARSIDE, Big Kiss (1989).
NO WORLD ORDER, Lost & Found LF048 (1993). Subliminal Thought Circumcision / Senile / Wretched Insertion / Disinfect / The Hate I Create / Bitter End / Alienation / Sometimes I . . . / Tracy's Song.
The New EP, Data DATA 008 (1999).

CONSPIRACY

UDDEVALLA, SWEDEN — *Micke Petersson (vocals), Andreas (guitar), Björn (guitar), Jocke (bass), Rickard (drums).*

Uddevalla Thrashers CONSPIRACY, created in 1999, are fronted by KAROSS and BESTIAL MOCKERY's Micke 'Doomanfanger' Petersson. A 2001 demo cassette 'Oppressed For Years' would be the band's first offering, followed up by an eponymous 2002 outing and 2003's 'Concert In Sickness'. Drummer Martin backed out that August, being superseded by Rickard in October.

CONSPIRACY guitarist Anders Kragh Ericson also holds a wealth of scene credits with ARGENTO, SOBRE NOCTURNE, KAJARR, MASTER MASSIVE, KLOKUS and THE EDGE OF TWILIGHT. Petter Karlsson, of KAJARR, MASTER MASSIVE, ARGENTO and THERION repute, also served with CONSPIRACY. Micke Petersson sessioned on studio tracks for MODORRA in 2005.

Oppressed For Years, Conspiracy (2001) (Demo). Mercenary / Crawling In Tears / Oppressed For Years.
Conspiracy, Conspiracy (2002) (Demo). Bringer of Torture / M.L.I.F. / A Wish To Die.
Concert In Sickness, Conspiracy (2003) (Demo). Concert In Sickness / I Will Remain / Until The Last Blood Is Drawn.

CONVICTION

BORÅS, SWEDEN — *Johan Westmar (vocals), Fredrik Jordanius (guitar), Niclas Karlsson (guitar), Freddy Zielinsky (bass), Martin Tilander (drums).*

Borås based Thrash Metal band created in 1995 as FIERCE CONVICTION. Band members all went on to further, higher profile, projects. Signing to ABS Records the group released 'The Requiem Of A Mourner' as their debut in 1998, this album seeing Jose Sanchez on the lead vocal role. The group truncated their title to simply CONVICTION for the 1999 album 'Decline / Rebirth'. During recording of this opus Daniel Heiman (a.k.a. 'Etherial Mangnanimus') of HIGHLANDER and LOST HORIZON was recruited as the band's new singer, but did not feature on the record itself. Johan Westmar was drafted as new frontman in 2000 before the band collapsed.

CONVICTION's guitarist Niclas Karlsson and drummer Martin Tilander, both ex-members of CRYSTAL EYES, subsequently joined FRETERNIA. Niclas Karlsson would also figure in ZONATA. Second guitarist Fredrik Jordanius, who also assisted FRETERNIA on the live front, became a member of RISING FAITH whilst bassist Freddy Zielinsky, having superseded Lars Rapp, went on to IRONWARE.

Early 2005 saw the arrival of ABLAZE, assembled by guitarist Fredrik Jordanius, former ZONATA drummer Mike Cameron Force, vocalist Johannes Nyberg and bassist Lukasz Strach. Jose Sanchez landed a solo deal with British label Z Records in December 2006.

DECLINE / REBIRTH, ABS TODAY 215 (1999). Life Beyond The Light / Deciever / Crusade / Guilt / Man Or Machine / Condemned To Extinction / Deem / Battle Tune / Song Of Allegiance / Dreams / Source Of Extraction.

CORAM LETHE

ITALY — *Mirco Borghini (vocals), Leonardo Fusi (guitar), Francesco Bargagni (guitar), Giacomo Occhipinti (bass), Francesco Miatto (drums).*

CORAM LETHE, forged in August of 1999, feature vocalist Mirco Borghini and drummer Francesco Miatto, both previously with Black Metal band LACHYRMA CHRISTI. Guitarist Leonardo Fusi is ex-STORMLORD and Tuscan Thrash act SPLEEN whilst the band was rounded out by erstwhile UTOPIA bassist Giacomo Occhipinti.

CORAM LETHE's debut demo, 'Reminiscence', was recorded at GRM Studios in Certaldo during March and April of 2000. Subsequently live promotion found the band acting as openers for TANKARD and, on the recording front, donating a rendition of 'Symbolic' to an Italian DEATH tribute album.

The band cut further demos at Fear Studio in Alfonsine and Studio 73 in Ravenna, between July and September 2003. Second guitarist Francesco Bargagni, of IMPHERYA and HELLWRATH, was incorporated during 2004. CORAM LETHE signed to the Gritish based Rage Of Achilles label for a debut album. However, by October the band revealed they had then switched to Finland's Rising Realm Records. The group's debut album, 'The Gates Of Oblivion' recorded at Fear Studio in Alfonsine and Studio 73 in Ravenna, was scheduled for release in January 2005.

THE GATES OF OBLIVION, Crash Music (2005). The Angels Fell / Shouts Of Cowards / Dying Water Walk With Us / Episode / Instinct / I, Oblivion / Hands Of Lies / Pain Therapy For A Praying Mantis / Ruling Emptiness / Sleet.

CORONER

ZURICH, SWITZERLAND — *Ron Royce (vocals / bass), Tommy T. Baron (guitar), Marquis Marky (drums).*

Zurich Metal band CORONER achieved European success with a distinct brand of experimental avant-garde Metal in the tradition of CELTIC FROST developing into post-Thrash executed to the finest precision of detail in true Swiss style. In the first stages of their career the band hardly toured, adding to the mystique. CORONER formed in 1984 as an Alpine trio comprising vocalist / bassist Ron Royce (a.k.a. Ron Broder), guitarist Oliver Amberg, later to join CELTIC FROST, and drummer Marquis Marky (Markus Edelmann). The line-up shifted shape with Amberg's departure and the recruitment of replacement Tommy T. Baron (Thomas Vetterli).

Tom Warrior, mainstay of CELTIC FROST, contributed both vocals and lyrics to CORONER's first October 1985 demo, 'Death Cult'. Only 250 hand-numbered copies were manufactured, prominently displaying Warrior's credits on the front cover. Guitarist Tommy T. Baron and drummer Marquis Marky then joined CELTIC FROST's American 'Tragic Serenades' tour as road crew. From then on CORONER were continually blighted by comparisons to CELTIC FROST, not helped by Noise Records, CELTIC FROST's label, signing the Swiss trio for good measure, this association never allowing the act to be truly judged in its own right.

CORONER's first album, 'R.I.P.' production for which was overseen by Harris Johns at Music Lab studios in Berlin In March 1987, received good reviews and went on to sell over 50,000 units in Europe. The distinct lack of gigs was more by circumstance than planning. A proposed European tour supporting Billy Milano's M.O.D. was cancelled by the headliners when protesters threatened to sabotage the tour.

The second album, 'Punishment For Decadence', was produced by Guy Bidmead and emerged a year after CORONER's 1987 debut, featuring a cover of the JIMI HENDRIX classic 'Purple Haze'. Once more the band were unable to tour properly to promote the album, with a planned American jaunt with SABBAT and RAGE being cancelled at the last minute and British dates postponed when the band were incarcerated by British customs for lack of work permits. CORONER did, however, manage to snatch a few support shows to SACRED REICH later in the year.

1989 brought CORONER's third album, 'No More Colour', produced by Pete Hinton and it would be in support of this release that the band finally CORONER toured Europe in 1990 with strong support from cult Texans WATCHTOWER.

In January 1992 Noise issued 'Mental Vortex', this set again closing out with an ambitious cover rendition, this time THE BEATLES 'I Want You (She's So Heavy)'. The record had been crafted the previous summer at Berlin's Sky Trax Studios with production being delegated to Tom Morris, with a final mix conducted at Morrisound in Tampa, Florida.

The group's final effort, the contractual 'Grin', self-produced at Greenwood Studios in Switzerland and seeing MEKONG DELTA's Peter Haas on drums, arrived in September 1993. That year CORONER supported Canadians ANNIHILATOR on a British tour and, although still utilizing the services of Mark and Royce, CORONER had by 1995, to all intents and purposes, become a solo vehicle for Baron. CORONER bowed out with a farewell European tour in January and February 1996, giving concert going fans a keepsake with a free cassette entitled 'The Unknown unreleased tracks (1985-1995)'. Baron, now using his real name of Tommy Vetterli, forged the short-lived CLOCKWORK with Peter Haas, conducted touring with French Pop singer Stephen Eicher then would team up with German Thrash pioneers KREATOR in the late 90s. Marquis Marky briefly worked with DWELL.

Marquis Marky turned up again in 1999 as part of Thomas Fischer's APOLLYON SUN. Fortunately he had reverted to his real name of Markus Edelmann. In 2004 Tommy Vetterli acted as producer for PURE INC.'s debut album. In June of the following year the three CORONER musicians apparently met with a view to discuss a proposed band reunion, but opted not to pursue the idea.

In 2006 two American metal bands, Pennsylvania's PHARAOH and CANVAS SOLARIS recorded tracks for a unique split 7" single release in tribute to CORONER. CANVAS SOLARIS offered its version of the instrumental 'Arc-Lite' while PHARAOH contributed 'Tunnel Of Pain'.

Death Cult, R.I.P. (1985) (Demo. Limited edition 250 copies). Spectators Of Sin / Spiral Dream / Aerial Combat / The Invincible.
R.I.P., Noise NO 075 (1987). Intro / Reborn Through Hate / When Angels Die / Intro (Nosferatu) / Nosferatu / Suicide Command / Spiral Dream / R.I.P. / Coma / Fried Alive / Intro (Totentanz) / Totentanz / Outro.
PUNISHMENT FOR DECADENCE, Noise NUK 119 (1988). Intro—Absorbed / Masked Jackal / Arc-Lite / Skeleton On Your Shoulders / Sudden Fall / Shadow Of A Lost Dream / Newbreed / Voyage To Eternity.
Die By My Hand, Noise NO 136-6 (1989). Die By My Hand / Tunnel Of Pain.
Purple Haze, Noise 7HAZE3 (1989). Purple Haze / Masked Jackal.
NO MORE COLOR, Noise NUK 138 (1989). Die By My Hand / No Need To Be Human / Read My Scars / D.O.A. / Mistress Of Deception / Tunnel Of Pain / Why It Hurts / Last Entertainment.
I Want You (She's So Heavy), Noise (1991). I Want You (She's So Heavy) / Divine Step.
MENTAL VORTEX, Noise NO 177-1 (1992). Divine Step (Conspectu Mortis) / Son Of Lilith / Semtex Revolution / Sirens / Metamorphosius / Pale Sister / About Life / I Want You (She's So Heavy).
GRIN, Noise NO 2010-2 (1993). Dream Path / The Lethargic Age / Internal Conflicts / Caveat (To The Coming) / Serpent Moves / Still Thinking / Theme For Silence / Paralized, Mesmerised / Grin (Nails Hurt) / Host.

CORONER, Noise N0 212-2 (1995). Between Worlds / The Favorite Game / Shifter / Serpent Moves / Snow Crystal / Divine Step (Conspectu Mortis) / Gliding Above While Being Below / Der Mussolini / Last Entertainment (TV Bizarre) / Reborn Through Hate / Golden Cashmere Sleeper (Part 1) / Golden Cashmere Sleeper (Part 2) / Masked Jackal / I Want You (She's So Heavy) / Grin (No Religion Remix) / Purple Haze (Radio Live Cut).

The Unknown unreleased tracks (1985-1995), (1996) (Cassette issued on CORONER's 1996 farewell tour). Oriental Vortex / Der Mussolini / Octopus / Old Man Bickford / S.W.A.T. / Theme for Silence (Original version) / Grin (No religion remix-instrumental) / Twenty Eight / Spectators Of Sin / The Invincible / Host (Instrumental) / Benways World (Original version) / Golden Cashmere Sleeper (Live) / Divine Step (Live) / Still Thinking (Live) / Metamorphosis (Live) / Internal Conflicts (Live) / Grin (Live).

CORPORAL PUNISHMENT

HELSINKI, FINLAND — *Ali (vocals / bass), Markku Niiranen (guitar), Lare Nieminen (guitar), Ykä (drums).*

CORPORAL PUNISHMENT went through the familiar schedule of gigging and demoing before scoring a deal with local label Spinefarm Records for the 1992 'Profaned Relics' album. The band, comprising former BRAINWASH vocalist / bassist Ali, ex-AIRDASH and GLOOMY GRIM drummer Ykä (a.k.a. Agathon Frosteus) and the OPPRESSION and DIRTY DAMAGE credited guitarist Lare Nieminen, issued two demos and a self-financed 7" single before their deal. Nieminen sessioned bass guitar on SACRAMENT's 1992 demo 'Judgement Day'. Second guitarist Markku Niiranen has ties to STONE and AIRDASH.

CORPORAL PUNISHMENT's sophomore effort, 1994's 'Into The Nerve Of Pain', was produced by STRATOVARIUS mainman Timo Tolkki. The band supported WALTARI, PARADISE LOST and AMORPHIS before signing a new contract with Germany's Black Mark Records.

Ykä also holds credits with THY SERPENT, WALHALLA, SOULGRIND, NOMICON and BARATHRUM.

Walls—The Doom, C.P. 001 (1991) (7" vinyl single). Walls—The Doom / Lifes Most Gloomiest Darkness.
PROFANED RELICS, Spinefarm SPI 6 CD (1992). Here Tonight—The Past / Unpleasant Task / Overlord / Time / Stifled Cry / Extremely Unemotional / Bitter Thoughts / War Of Independence / Reformation Has Been Done.
INTO THE NERVE OF PAIN, Spinefarm SPI 18 CD (1994). Sandcastle / Wipe Those Tears / Nomad / Life's Gloomiest Darkness / I Love You / Swamp Of Solace / House, Cars, Wife And Two Children / Oliver's Fear / O-Chlorobenzylidenemalononitrile / Poor Bird / This Sweet Sorrow / Seasons In The Sun.
STONEFIELD OF A LIFETIME, Black Mark BMCD 101 (1997). Remember Me / Dead Skin / Wrong Side / ... And I Said Now (Repent By Yourself) / No One Knows / Old Photos / Short Moments / Empty / Justificated? / +—0.

CORPORATION 187

LINKÖPING, SWEDEN — *Filip Carlsson (vocals), Olof Knutsson (guitar), Magnus Pettersson (guitar), Viktor Klint (bass), Robert Eng (drums).*

Linköping Thrash Metal band. CORPORATION 1987 was established during 1995 the opening line-up comprised ex-DAISY CHAIN singer Pelle Severin, guitarist Olof Knutsson, former RABID CREW guitarist Magnus Pettersson with Robert Eng on the drums. Pettersson, Knutsson and Eng had all previously worked together as part of a SLAYER tribute band. CORPORATION 187's 1998 self-titled demo saw Pettersson handling bass duties.

In 1999 the band employed SÉANCE credited Johan Ekström on bass guitar. Signing to Earache Records subsidiary Wicked World CORPORATION 187 released debut album 'Subliminal Fear', recorded at Studio Underground and Studio Helltower, in February 2000. Gigs across Europe had the band packaged with DECAPITATED and LOCKUP. However, Severin then took his leave and Filip Carlsson, having already been involved in the band's formative SLAYER homage days, took on the bass role. Carlsson's many scene credentials included terms with DAISY CHAIN, ANCIENT DIGGER OF GRAVES, DEMONS TO PREFER, HÖST, SATANIC SLAUGHTER, SPITEFUL and THORNCLAD. Changes during 2002 witnessed Ekström's departure but the inclusion of DEMONS TO PREFER, THORNCLAD and RABID CREW bassist Viktor Klint.

CORPORATION 187 European gigs in April 2002, promoting second offering 'Perfection In Pain', mixed by HYPOCRISY's Peter Tägtgren, saw a union with road partners LORD BELIAL and SATANIC SLAUGHTER. The band then acted as support act to ARCH ENEMY's December 2002 UK gigs following up on this by remaining as guests for their January 2003 Swedish dates.

SUBLIMINAL FEAR, Wicked World WICK9 (2000). Hope Is Lost / Caught Inside Your Mind / Straw Coloured Corpse / Paralyzed / Subliminal Fear / Souls / With Your Sins / Hypnotic Illusion / Frustration / Low Pitched.
PERFECTION IN PAIN, Wicked World WICK14CD (2002). Religious Connection / Ghosts Of Confusion / Liquid Truth / My Life To Kill / Thursday Night Aggression / Perfection In Pain / 2nd Pain / Strange Is Strong / Violated Relation / The Joy Of Being Addicted.

CORPSECANDLE

HOLLAND — *Eelko Kitselaar (vocals / guitar), Chris van Klooster (vocals / guitar), Sander Kruyt (bass), Arno Eikenbroek (drums).*

CORPSECANDLE is a Black Thrash Metal act dating to 1991. They would make their first mark some three years later with an eponymous five song demo. The 'Lethal Approach' session solidified their standing in 1995. The group was boosted from a trio to a quartet before entering Excess Studios in Rotterdam to lay down the 1998 album 'In Healthy Sickness'. However, in September of 1999 the band folded.

CORPSECANDLE rose once again as founder Eelko Kitselaar united with erstwhile CIRITH GORGOR guitarist Chris van Klooster and bassist Sander Kruyt. The new formation would be joined by drummer Arno Eikenbroek (a.k.a. 'Balgradon XUL' of FUNERAL WINDS and HAATSTRIJD) in January 2001 and in March the band cut tracks for the EP 'An Encounter At An Infernal Empire'. Gigs followed in union with FLESH MADE SIN, EXTREME NOISE TERROR, SINISTER and THE HAUNTED.

An Encounter At An Infernal Empire, Corpsecandle (2001).

CORROSION OF CONFORMITY

RALEIGH, NC, USA — *Pepper Keenan (vocals / guitar), Woody Weatherman (guitar), Mike Dean (bass), Jimmy Bower (drums).*

CORROSION OF CONFORMITY may well justifiably lay claim to the title of America's first Crossover act. The band effortlessly blend riffs of extreme magnitude with infectious Hardcore. Over the years CORROSION OF CONFORMITY have developed through Thrashcore up to latter works which find the band embraced by the Stoner Sludgecore community. Originally a trio titled NO LABELS, the band was forged in 1982 by vocalist / bassist Mike Dean, guitarist Woody Weatherman and drummer Reed Mullin. The band augmented their line-up with lead vocalist Eric Eyke for first album 'Eye For An Eye' in 1984, an album that was later re-released by Caroline during 1990.

With 'Animosity' in 1985 the band veered more towards straight metal territory. However, the same year saw the departure of Dean and the band pulled in former UGLY AMERICANS singer Bob Sinister for the 'Technocracy' mini-album as the band, benefiting from the global upsurge of interest in Thrash Metal, were now propelled to front runner status.

Sinister had left the fold by 1988 and CORROSION OF CONFORMITY were effectively put on ice until May 1989 when activity resumed with the addition of ex-SEIZURE and SCHOOL OF VIOLENCE frontman Karl Agell. During the interim a six track EP 'Six Songs With Mike Singing' was released to fulfill contractual obligations as Dean and guitarist Woody Weatherman created project band SNAKE NATION releasing an album.

Although without a contract for a lengthy period CORROSION OF CONFORMITY, now with bassist Phil Swisher, still kept up the live work touring with DIRTY ROTTEN IMBECILES, DANZIG, SOUNDGARDEN and BAD BRAINS. The band added second guitarist Pepper Keenan upfront of the 1991 album but recording of 'Blind' was delayed as Keenan recovered from a broken hip sustained whilst stagediving!

With the album release the band set about a club tour of America with support from PRONG and BULLET LAVOLTA. These dates were to trigger a world tour that would last a gruelling two years and after which vocalist Karl Agell was asked to leave following a New York show with TROUBLE thus prompting the departure of Swisher. The departing duo would later create LEADFOOT releasing the 1997 album 'Bring it on'.

Christmas 1991 bore witness to a bout of recording between Keenan and an old friend PANTERA vocalist Phil Anselmo. The project, titled DOWN, was later to see a CD release.

The 1994 album 'Deliverance', with Keenan now lead vocalist, saw the return of Dean to the bass role from his interim act SPORE as the band embarked on an American tour with support from KEPONE. The band's sound had shifted once more even echoing the vintage southern sound and twin guitar harmonies. CORROSION OF CONFORMITY also opened the 1994 Castle Donington 'Monsters Of Rock' festival headlined by METALLICA.

Dean formed an alliance with BRUTAL TRUTH's Rich Hoak to give birth to a 1996 side project act titled NINEFINGER, an album being released the following year.

With renewed interest in the band Columbia instructed the act to adopt more commercial leanings before funding further product. The band delivered a batch of mellowed out Southern flavoured demos but found themselves dropped anyway. CORROSION OF CONFORMITY toured America in 2000 backed up by CLUTCH and SIXTY WATT SHAMEN. Mullin, suffering from back injuries, was replaced by EYEHATEGOD's Jimmy Bower.

As 2001 dawned it became apparent that Bower had taken the position permanently as Mullin departed to concentrate on his Alternative Rock act BROWN. The band would support PANTERA on their Australian shows in April of 2001, announcing too that they had signed up with the new Sanctuary Records concern. The first results of this collaboration came in August with the issue of the band's debut live effort 'Live Volume', recorded at Harpo's Concert Theatre gig in Detroit on April 20th.

For recording of a fresh studio album in mid 2002 CORROSION OF CONFORMITY pulled in new drummer Merritt Partridge as Jimmy Bower was fully booked with projects such as DOWN, EYEHATEGOD and SUPERJOINT RITUAL. Yet another side venture also grew up during this period with Woody Weatherman, Mike Dean and Merritt Partridge involving themselves with LET' LONES. By late 2002 former drummer Reed Mullin was touting a brand new band venture MAN WILL DESTROY HIMSELF. The LET' LONES project would debut live with a home town Raleigh gig in July of 2003. Pepper Keenan took time out in late 2003 to produce the debut album from Southern rock band SOL FIYA.

July of 2004 saw CORROSION OF CONFORMITY back in the recording studio, laying down a cover version of LYNYRD SKYNYRD's 'On The Hunt' for a Sanctuary Records tribute album entitled 'Heavy Helping'. Shortly after, a brand new album would be undertaken with producer John Custer bearing a working title of 'En los Brazos del Dios' (In the Arms of God). On drums would be New Orleans native Stanton Moore of Jazz Rock combo GALACTIC.

CORROSION OF CONFORMITY lent support to MOTÖRHEAD's US tour dates commencing March 2005, these dates also including BRAND NEW SIN and ZEKE. Headline US dates in June saw CROWBAR, WEEDEATER and ALABAMA THUNDERPUSSY as support. However, the tour was marred by tragedy when on 23rd June at Masquerade club venue in Ybor City in Florida four audience members were stabbed, one fatally.

Alongside ALABAMA THUNDERPUSSY once again, the band, together with FU MANCHU and DANKO JONES, started out on another two-week run of dates beginning on 7th July in Santa Ana, California. UK shows in September and October had Swedish Doomsters WITCHCRAFT as support, after which the band was set to hook up with MOTÖRHEAD and MELDRUM for Scandinavian and European gigs. However, in the wake of Hurricane Katrina, New Orleans resident Pepper Keenan naturally prioritised family matters and the band withdrew from the dates. In November CORROSION OF CONFORMITY hooked up with DISTURBED for a national Jägermeister sponsored US tour. A variety of opening acts would be employed including SOIL, THE HEAVILS, DRY KILL LOGIC, DOPE, OPIATE FOR THE MASSES and DOG FASHION DISCO.

The band teamed up with CLUTCH and Philadelphia instrumental rockers STINKING LIZAVETA for a UK tour in January 2006.

EYE FOR AN EYE, Southern Studios (1984). Tell Me / Minds Are Controlled / Indifferent / Broken Will / Rabid Dogs / L.S. / Redneckkk / Co-exist / Excluded / Dark Thoughts / Poison Planet / What? / Negative Outlook / Positive Outlook / No Drunk / College Town / Not Safe / Eye For An Eye / Nothing's Gonna Change.

ANIMOSITY, Metal Blade 72037 (1985). Loss For Words / Mad World / Consumed / Holier / Positive Outlook / Prayer / Intervention / Kiss Of Death / Hungry Child / Animosity.

TECHNOCRACY, Metal Blade ZORRO53 (1987). Technocrazy / Hungry Child / Happily Ever After / Crawling / Ahh Blugh.

Six Songs With Mike Singing EP, Product Inc. INCCD 002/3 (1988). Eye For An Eye / Center Of The World / Citizen / Not For Me / What? / Negative Outlook.

BLIND, Roadracer RO 9236-2 (1991). These Shrouded Temples ... / Damned For All Time / The Dance Of The Dead / Buried / Break The Circle / Painted Smiling Face / Mine Are The Eyes Of God / Shallow Ground / Vote With A Bullet / Great Purification / White Noise / Echoes In The Well / ... Remain.

BLIND, Columbia CK66463 (1992). These Shrouded Temples / Damned For All Time / Dance Of The Dead / Buried / Break The Circle / Painted Smiling Face / Mine Are The Eyes Of God / Shallow Ground / Vote With A Bullet / Great Purification / White Noise / Echoes In The Well / Remain / Condition A/Condition B / Future Now / Jim Bean And The Coon Ass.

Vote With A Bullet, Roadrunner RR 23886 (1992). Vote With A Bullet / Condition A.

Vote With A Bullet, Roadrunner RR23883 (1992). Vote With A Bullet (re-mixed edit) / Vote With A Bullet (re-mixed extended) / Vote With A Bullet / Damned For All Time (demo).

DELIVERANCE, Columbia 477683-2 (1994). Heaven's Not Overflowing / Albatross / Clean My Wounds / Without Wings / Broken Man / Senor Limpio / Man De Mono / Seven Days / No. 2121313 / My Grain / Deliverance / Shale Like You / Shelter / Pearls Before Swine.

TECHNOCRACY, (1996). Technocracy / Hungry Child / Happily Ever After / Crawling / Ahh Blugh (Milking The Sick Farce) / Intervention / Technocracy / Crawling.

WISEBLOOD, Columbia 484328-2 (1996). King Of The Rotten / Longwhip—Big America / Wiseblood / Goodbye Windows / Born Again For The Last Time / Drowning In A Daydream / The Snake Has No Head / The Door / Man Or Ash / Redemption City / Wishbone (Some Tomorrow) / Fuel / Bottom Feeder (El Que Come Abajo). Chart position: 43 UK.

AMERICA'S VOLUME DEALER, Sanctuary (2000). Over Me / Congratulations Song / Stare Too Long / Diablo Blvd. / Doublewide / Zippo / Who's Got The Fire / Sleeping Martyr / Take What You Want / 13 Angels / Gettin' It On.

LIVE VOLUME, Sanctuary (2001). Intro / These Shrouded Temples / Diablo Blvd. / Senor Limpio / King Of The Rotten / Wiseblood / Who's Got The Fire / Albatross / My Grain / Congratulations Song / 13 Angels—7 Days / Vote With A Bullet / Zippo / Long Whip—Big America / Shelter / Clean My Wounds.

IN THE ARMS OF GOD, Sanctuary 06076-84739-2 (2005). Stone Breaker / Paranoid Opioid / It Is That Way / Dirty Hands Empty Pockets (Already Gone) / Rise River Rise / Never Turns To More / War / So Much Left Behind / The Backslider / World On Fire / Crown Of Thorns / In The Arms Of God. Chart positions: 21 GREECE, 41 SWEDEN, 196 FRANCE.

CORRUPT

ARKIVA, SWEDEN — *Joseph Tholl (vocals / guitar), Olof Wikstrand (guitar), Tobias Lindquist (bass), Michael Wennbom (drums).*

Arvika based old school Thrashers CORRUPT were manifested as CORRUPTED in November of 2002 by erstwhile TERROR members vocalist / guitarist Joseph Tholl and drummer Michael Wennbom. This pairing, working with session bassist Tobias Wikstrand, cut the opening demo 'Lethal Anger', a three song affair which included a cover version of SODOM's 'Blasphemer'. A further demo, entitled 'Shotgun Death', sported a rendition of the MISFITS 'Mommy, Can I Go Out And Kill Tonight' and the tactfully titled original 'S.H.A.P (Strictly Hardcore Anal Penetration)'. Upfront of a live showing at the May 2003 Viksholmfestivalen event Olof Wikstrand was drafted on second guitar.

The band issued the 2003 demo 'Destroyed Beyond Recognition'. CORRUPTED personnel bassist 'Neckbraker Braineater' and guitarist 'Arsagh' also have ties with Black Metal act GHALTRA. Guitarist Olof Wikstrand fronted fellow Thrash outfit HAZARD, this band also previously including Joseph Tholl.

During 2004 CORRUPTED truncated their band name to CORRUPT, re-debuting with the demo 'Born Of Greed', although versions of this CD-R exist with both band titles. The band also cut a split 7" single, 'Curse Of The Subconscious', shared with NECROVATION, a limited edition of 500 copies pressed by Blood Harvest Productions. This session included a cover version of MERCYFUL FATE's 'Curse Of The Pharaohs'.

Born Of Greed, Corrupt (2004) (Demo). Born Of Greed / Human Wreckage / Warpath.
Curse Of The Subconscious, Blood Harvest Productions YOTZ#4 (2005) (Split 7" vinyl single with NECROVATION limited to 500 copies). Chain Of Command / Curse Of The Pharaohs.
Silence Equals Death, Blood Harvest Productions (2006). Silence Equals Death / State Of Fear / Profit's Prevailed / Modern World Hypocrisy.

CORRUPTED

ARKIVA, SWEDEN — *Joseph Tholl (vocals / guitar), Olof Wikstrand (guitar), Tobias Lindquist (bass), Michael Wennbom (drums).*

Arvika based old school Thrashers CORRUPTED were manifested in November 2002 by erstwhile TERROR members vocalist / guitarist Joseph Tholl and drummer Michael Wennbom. This pairing, working with session bassist Tobias Wikstrand, cut the opening demo 'Lethal Anger', a three song affair which included a cover version of SODOM's 'Blasphemer'. A further demo, entitled 'Shotgun Death', sported a rendition of the MISFITS 'Mommy, Can I Go Out And Kill Tonight' and the tactfully titled original 'S.H.A.P (Strictly Hardcore Anal Penetration)'. Upfront of a live showing at the May 2003 Viksholmfestivalen event Olof Wikstrand was drafted on second guitar.

The band issued the 2003 demo 'Destroyed Beyond Recognition'. CORRUPTED personnel bassist 'Neckbraker Braineater' and guitarist 'Arsagh' also have ties with Black Metal act GHALTRA. Guitarist Olof Wikstrand fronted fellow Thrash outfit HAZARD, this band also previously including Joseph Tholl. Wikstrand also held membership of LEPROSY and CAUSTIC STRIKE.

During 2004 CORRUPTED truncated their band name to CORRUPT, re-debuting with the demo 'Born Of Greed', although versions of this CD-R exist with both band titles.

Lethal Anger, Corrupted (2003) (Demo). Lethal Anger / Denial / Blasphemer.
Shotgun Death, Corrupted (2003) (Demo). Strictly Hardcore Anal Penetration (S.H.A.P.) / Possessed By Evil / Shotgun Death / Mommy, Can I Go Out And Kill Tonight?
Destroyed Beyond Recognition, Corrupted (2003) (Demo). Into The Gaschamber (Instrumental) / Lethal Anger / Intimidating Truth / Possessed By Evil / Shotgun Death / Revelation Of Rage.

COURAGEOUS

GERMANY — *Chris Staubach (vocals), Gerd Lücking (guitar), Oliver Lohman (guitar), Jürgen Weiland (bass), Jan Mischon (drums).*

Thrashers founded in 1988. Initially billed as COURAGOUS (unfortunately mispelt), the group scored valuable points by winning a 'Battle of the bands' contest, the prize for which was supporting JUDAS PRIEST at the 2001 Balingen 'Bang Your Head' festival. COURAGOUS feature two RAWBONED members in vocalist Chris Staubach and guitarist Gerd Lücking, the latter acting as drummer. Lücking also operates as drummer with LIGHTMARE and dexterously as bass player for MELANCHOLIC SEASONS.

COURAGOUS debuted with a 1996 demo 'Liar', capitalising on this with appearances on compilation albums such as 'Azathot' and 'Deathphobia V'. November 1998 album 'Listen'. Their 2002 follow up, 'Remember', was mastered by REBELLION man Uwe Lulis. Maintaining this connection, guitarist Gerd Lücking, still retaining his position for recording of the COURAGOUS album 'Inertia', joined REBELLION as their new drummer in April 2004.

The band signed to the Belgian Mausoleum label in July 2004 and took this opportunity to revise their name to the correctly spelt COURAGEOUS. The album 'Inertia' surfaced in November. COURAGEOUS toured Germany in 2006 supporting VICIOUS RUMORS and BEYOND FEAR. Mid tour in December Matthias Hohmann took over bass duties.

The group contributed their cover version of TANKARD's 'The Morning After' to the tribute album 'A Tribute To Tankard' included as a bonus disc on the AFM Records 2007 TANKARD release 'Best Case Scenario: 25 Years In Beers'.

INERTIA, Massacre (2004). Inertia / Trapped / Fade Away / Together As One / Invisible Enemy / Tortured By Memories / In Doom / All These Years / The Puppeteer / But My Freedom / Free Will / Tear Off My Mask.

COURAGOUS

GERMANY — *Chris Staubach (vocals), Gerd Lücking (guitar), Oliver Lohman (guitar), Jürgen Weiland (bass), Jan Mischon (drums).*

Thrashers founded in 1988. COURAGOUS (unfortunately mispelt) scored valuable points by winning a 'Battle of the bands' contest, the prize for which was supporting JUDAS PRIEST at the 2001 Balingen 'Bang Your Head' festival. COURAGOUS feature two RAWBONED members in vocalist Chris Staubach and guitarist Gerd Lücking, the latter acting as drummer. Lücking also operates as drummer with LIGHTMARE and dexterously as bass player for MELANCHOLIC SEASONS.

COURAGOUS debuted with a 1996 demo 'Liar', capitalising on this with appearances on compilation albums such as 'Azathot' and 'Deathphobia V'. November 1998 album 'Listen'. Their 2002 follow up, 'Remember', was mastered by REBELLION man Uwe Lulis. Maintaining this connection, guitarist Gerd Lücking, still retaining his position for recording of the COURAGOUS album 'Inertia', joined REBELLION as their new drummer in April of 2004.

The band signed to the Belgian Mausoleum label in July of 2004 and took this opportunity to revise their name to the correctly spelt COURAGEOUS.

COURAGEOUS

LISTEN, (1998). Listen / One With Pain / Immortal / Shadows Of Disbelief / My Inner Voice / Fire / Lord Of The Unknown / Mystic Highway / Midian.
REMEMBER, (2002). Scared / Sudden Death / Nothin' / Rebirth / Fourth Dimension / ... And Lost / The Prince / A Trip Of Confidence / Remember / People Are People / Brothers In Mind / Listen (Live).

COVEN

SEATTLE, WA, USA — *Jay Clark (vocals), Paul Hash (guitar), Dean Babbitt (guitar) Gary Peebles (bass), Neal Babbitt (drums).*

Seattle's COVEN remain as one of the earlier and more notorious shock-comedy-Thrash bands. Founded in the mid 80's the band led by the Babbitt brothers, guitarist Dean, bassist Gary and drummer Neal, recorded and produced their debut, 'Blessed Is The Black', between June and October of 1986. The album was eventually released in 1988 on the Ever Rat label. Musically, the band offered straight ahead Thrash mixed with some of the most, vile and offensive lyrics imaginable. No target was spared the bands caustic brand of humour but a particular favorite seemed to be organized religion, and more specifically Christianity.

The debut album was marketed and distributed by Medusa and soon a second self-produced album, 1989's 'Death Walks Behind You', appeared as the band jumped directly to the Medusa label. The lyrics were toned down very slightly for this release and the band enjoyed small-scale touring in the western areas of North America.

A long delay ensued and a third album, 'Boneless Christian', was released in 1993 on the Ever Rat label in conjunction with the Red Light group. At this point founding drummer Neal Babbitt had been replaced by Jason Moody. Bassist Gary Peebles also left as the band trimmed down to a four piece with Dean Babbit handling the bass on the album.

Lyrically, the band presented themselves in their most clever (and most vile) form to date but the bands star had fallen perhaps outdone by many gore/grind metal bands who were far more lyrically gruesome but lacking in the bands patented humour.

BLESSED IS THE BLACK, Ever Rat Records/ Medusa 72243 (1988). Blessed Is The Black / 666 / Burn The Cross / Out Of The Grave / Rock This Church / Iron Dick / The Monger / McDonaldland Massacre / Another Life / Creature Of Duty (And My Duty Is Death).
DEATH WALKS BEHIND YOU, Medusa 7 72353-4 (1989). Too Late To Pray / Ministry Of Lies / Spellbinder / Succubus / Death Walks Behind You / Frozen Bones / Propaganda / Justified Suicide / Ted Bundy / Silent Night (Violent Night).
BONELESS CHRISTIAN, Red Light 88364-4 (1993). Satanic As Hell / Fuckin' A Nun / Just Add Violence / Christsycle—Reaming The Pope / Boneless Christian / Organic God / The Masters Tool / All This Bleeding.

CREATION OF DEATH

POZNAŃ, POLAND — *Robert Friedrich (vocals / guitar), Radoslaw Kaczmarek (guitar), Tomasz Olszewski (bass), Tomasz Goehs (drums).*

CREATION OF DEATH was founded by the ousted TURBO triumvirate of vocalist / guitarist Robert "Litza" Friedrich, bassist Lemmy Demolator and drummer Tomasz Goehs. The latter also held prior WILCZY PAJAK and WOLF SPIDER credits whilst Friedrich had served with ACID DRINKERS. Initially the band featured Arkadiusz Wielgosik on second guitar but he would be superseded by the PENTHOUSE and TURBO credited Radoslaw Kaczmarek.

The UK based Under One Flag Records, a subsidiary of Music For Nations, published the 1991 album 'Purify Your Soul'. Post CREATION OF DEATH Goehs musical travels would see him involved with KR'SHNA BROTHERS in 1993, DOG FAMILY in 1996, 2TM 2,3 and, alongside Friedrich once again, KNŻ.

PURIFY YOUR SOUL, Under One Flag (1991). Overture / Purify Your Soul / Quartering Alive / Nameless Forever / Ingratitude / By Truth, By Love / Psalm 69 / Words / Don't Be So Full Of Pride / You Aren't Possessed Yet.

CREATURE

BELGIUM — *Muzdreg The Cruel (vocals), Golgob The Terrible (guitar), Gorgash The Tearer (guitar), Shaigrat (bass), Zagthak The Mauler (drums).*

CREATURE, originally assembled as a Hardcore act in 1998 under a billing of ARMED RESPONSE, are fronted by Muzdreg The Cruel (real name Stefan De Vylder). With ARMED RESPONSE folding, drummer Zagthak The Mauler (Diederik Vermeulen) and guitarist Golgob The Terrible (Wouter Keppens) forged a fresh outfit under the title CREATURE in 2001. First into the fold would be guitarist Grotdul The Bloody Handed (Koenraad Van Geert). The band got to grips with live work but the following year lost the services of their bassist. Grotdul switched to bass whilst Gorgash The Tearer (a.k.a. Tim Keppens), brother of Golgob and just having left ROACH, was inducted to fill the guitar spot. These changes evidenced themselves in the band's musical direction too and an April 2002 demo found CREATURE steering into Black / Thrash territory.

CREATURE cut their debut EP 'Triumph Of The Unborn' in early 2003. Grotdul bowed out that July but in September Shaigrat, in actuality LEMURIA vocalist Sancti, was incorporated to fill the bass vacancy. In mid 2005 Shaigrat joined the forces of GURTHANG.

Creature, Creature (2002). Intro—Nazgul Speech / Apocalyptic Dawn / The Demons I Know / False Hope For Peace / Nature's Gift / Secrets Of Masked Mystic.
Triumph Of The Unborn, (2003). Triumph Of The Unborn / Repulsion Of The Monarchous Treasrony / Rebirth / Dodennacht / Annatar / Ode To Darkness.

CRO-MAGS

NEW YORK, NY, USA — *Harley Flanagan (vocals / bass), Parris Mitchel Mayhew (guitar), Doug Holland (guitar), Mackie Jason (drums).*

Seminal tattooed New York Hardcore Thrash Crossover act dating back to 1984 noted for plying aggressive music whilst professing peaceful Hare Krishna beliefs. CRO-MAGS founder vocalist / bassist Harley Flanagan started out whilst a young teenager in Punk band THE STIMULATORS prior to forming M.O.I. with guitarist Doug Holland and drummer Pete Hines. The inaugural CRO-MAGS line-up featured Flanagan, Holland (who had also had a previous stint in KRAUT), vocalist John 'Bloodclot' Joseph, guitarist Parris Mitchell Mayhew and drummer Mackie Jason.

Jason opted out and by 1988 was found in a variety of bands including BAD BRAINS, ICEMAN, URBAN BLIGHT and BLITZSPEER.

John Joseph departed in mid 1989 and Flanagan took over on lead vocal.

1990 saw turbulent times for the band as drummer Potio Hoinz departed in favour of the returning Mackie. Before long however Mackie was out turning up in BAD BRAINS once more. Further tribulation followed when long standing guitarist Doug Holland was replaced with Rob Buckley.

1992 album was crafted by a line up of Flanagan, Holland, Joseph and new blood Gabby and Dave. However, the stability was not to last and by the 'Near Death Experience' album CRO-MAGS had effectively become a duo of Flanagan and Joseph. Worse was to come though and Flanagan, keeper of the flame for so long, quit just prior to the album release.

1994's live album release provided fans with an overview of the band's recent history with a two disc set comprising of a 1991 show from the Hollywood Palladium and a 1994 gig from Studio One in New Jersey.

Flanagan created WHITE DEVIL and was to produce and perform on the debut 1997 album from STIGMATA 'Hymns For An Unknown God'.

Joseph founded a fresh act BOTH WORLDS with ex-LEEWAY members for a 1998 album 'Memory Rendered Visible' Mayhew reunited with Flanagan the following year to create SAMSARA with ex-SUICIDAL TENDENCIES guitarist Rocky George. The CRO MAGS reformed in 2000 for European festival dates.

By early 2002 Flanagan had re-emerged touting a fresh act HARLEY'S WAR in union with ex-SUICIDAL TENDENCIES guitarist Rocky George and former WARZONE guitarist Jay Vento. Guitarist Scott Roberts temped for BIOHAZARD's European dates that year. Australian dates for February of 2003 witnessed a CRO MAGS line up incorporating vocalist John Joseph, Rocky George on guitar, LEEWAY's A.J. Novello second guitar, Franklin Rhi from CROWN OF THORNS and SHELTER on bass along with PARLIAMENT and FUNKEDELIC man Gary "G-man" Sullivan manning the drums. Founder member Harley Flanagan, excluded from this line-up, slammed the Rocky George led band as "the NO-MAGS".

In early January 2006 two former CRO-MAGS members, vocalist John Joseph and guitarist Scott Roberts announced the formation of BLOODCLOT in union with former BIOHAZARD drummer Danny Schuler and SICK OF IT ALL and AGNOSTIC FRONT bassist Craig Setari.

AGE OF QUARREL, GWR GWLP 9 (1987). We Gotta Know / World Peace / Show You No Mercy / Malfunction / Street Justice / Survival Of The Streets / Seekers Of The Truth / It's The Limit / Hard Times / By Myself / Don't Tread On Me / Face The Facts / Do Unto Others / Life on My Own / Signs Of The times.

BEST WISHES, Profile FILCD 274 (1989). Death Camps / Days Of Confusion / The Only One / Down, But Not Out / Crush The Demonoac / Fugitive / Then And Now / Age Of Quarrel.

ALPHA-OMEGA, Century Media CM9730CD (1992). See The Signs / Eyes Of Tomorrow / The Other Side Of Madness (Revenge) / Apocalypse Now / The Paths Of Perfection / Victims / Kuruksetra / Changes.

NEAR DEATH EXPERIENCE, Century Media CM 77050-2 (1993). Say Good-Bye To The Mother Earth / Kali-Yuga / War On The Streets / Death In The Womb / Time I Am / Reflections / Near Death Experience / The Other Side Of Madness (Rat Soup version '93).

HARD TIMES IN AN AGE OF QUARREL—LIVE, Century Media CM 77072-2 (1994). Intro / We Gotta Know / World Peace / Show No Mercy / Apocalypse Now / See The Signs / Malfunction / Survival Of The Streets / Days Of Confusion / Street Justice / The Only One / Crush The Demoniac / Changes / Down But Not Out / Seekers Of The Truth / It's The Limit / Life Of My Own / Signs Of The Times / Age Of Quarrel / Hard Times / Death Camps / Intro / See The Signs / World Peace / Show No Mercy / Say Good-Bye To Mother Earth / Malfunction / Path To Perfection / Other Side Of Madness / It's The Limit.

CRONOS

UK — *Cronos (vocals / bass), Mike Hickey (guitar), James Clare (guitar), Chris Patterson (drums).*

After nine years fronting one of the archetypal Thrash Metal outfits VENOM mainman Conrad Lant (a.k.a. Cronos) left the group in 1988 to form CRONOS, the result of the disappointing sales of VENOMs 1987's 'Calm Before The Storm' album. Conrad took both VENOM guitarists Mike H. (real name Mike Hickey) and Jimi C. (Jim Clare previously with HELLFIRE) along with him and soon added drummer Chris P. (at this point the band's musicians were known only by the initial letters of their surnames). Scheduled tours of America and Japan were postponed in late 1989 when Cronos sustained a broken hand in a car accident. The band later toured the east coast of America, but after the release of the 1990 'Dancing In The Fire' debut album, featuring a cover version of THIN LIZZYs 'Bad Reputation and recorded for Newcastle upon Tynes Neat Records, live activity became limited.

CRONOS was due to tour Britain on a double bill with WARFARE on the so dubbed 'Dancing With The Firehammers' tour, but this was cancelled due to an acknowledged lack of interest. The band did, however, support MASSACRE at London's Marquee in 1992, by which time a second album, 'Rock n' Roll Disease', had appeared the previous year.

Lant guested on the 1994 album 'When War Begins... Truth Disappears' from German act WARPATH. Hickey emerged as temporary member of CATHEDRAL and then as live guitarist for CARCASS during 1994 touring to promote their 'Heartwork' album.

A third album was recorded during 1994, but Cronos decided—somewhat inevitably—to participate in the reformation of the original VENOM line-up in 1995 that headlined the Waldrock festival.

A new CRONOS recorded the 1995 'Venom' album with a brand new membership that comprised Cronos, Hickey and ex CATHEDRAL drummer Mark Wharton. The album oddly featured re-works of classic VENOM songs.

As VENOM geared up for their reformation album 'Cast In Stone' and subsequent touring CRONOS was inevitably put on the back burner despite sessions for a planned fourth album titled 'Triumphirate' already being in the can.

Cronos would contribute vocal tracks for the PROBOT project album of FOO FIGHTERS man Dave Grohl in 2001. During the summer of 2002 former VENOM and CRONOS guitarist Jim Clare united with TYGERS OF PAN TANG drummer Craig Ellis and bass player Willie Angus in a new band project entitled PASSION PLAY.

Cronos acted as special guest on the 2005 HAMMERFALL album "Chapter V: Unbent, Unbowed, Unbroken".

DANCING IN THE FIRE, Neat ODIO48 (1990). Fantasia / Terrorise / Dancing In The Fire / Speedball / I'll Be Back / Vampire / Chinese Whispers / Old Enough To Bleed / Painkiller / My Girl / Hell To The Unknown.

CRONOS

ROCK N' ROLL DISEASE, Neat D1051 (1991). Messages Of War / Rock n' Roll Disease / Lost And Found / Midnight Eye / Sexploitation / Aphrodisiac / Sweet Savage Sex / Dirty Tricks Department / Bared To The Bone.

VENOM, Neat Metal NM003 (1995). In League With Satan / Superpower / Vempyr / Fire / 1000 Days In Sodom / Know Evil / Messages Of War / 7 Gates Of Hell / Painkiller / Don't Burn The Witch (In Nomine Satanas) / Ye Of Little Faith / Satanachist / At War With Satan / Babylon.

HELL TO THE UNKNOWN—THE CRONOS ANTHOLOGY, Castle Music CMQDD1398 (2006). Cronos—Live Set Intro Tape / In League With Satan / Vampyr / Terrorize / At War With Satan / Dancing In The Fire / Painkiller / Superpower / Fire / Old Enough To Bleed / Don't Burn The Witch / In Nomine Satanas / Speedball / Chinese Whispers / Lost & Found / 7 Gates Of Hell / Bared To The Bone / Love Is Infectious / My Girl / Dirty Trix Dept. / Messages Of War / Aphrodisiac / Fantasia / 1000 Days In Sodom / Rock N' Roll Disease / Sexploitation / Boobytrap / Sweet Savage Sex / Hell To The Unknown / I'll Be Back / Satanachist / Bad Reputation / Midnight Eye / Black Xmas / Calm Before The Storm / Gypsy / Krackin' Up / Muscle / Nothing Sacred / The Chanting Of The Priests.

CROSSFIRE

BELGIUM — *Peter De Wint (vocals), Marc Van Caelenberge (guitar), Rudy Van De Sjipe (guitar), Patrick Van Londerzele (bass), Chris De Brauwer (drums).*

One of the first signings to the Mausoleum label, CROSSFIRE released two albums that were much lauded in the underground Metal press. The band started out in 1980 as a Punk outfit entitled THE ONION DOLLS, with De Wint handling drums as well as lead vocals. The band contributed two tracks to the Dutch 'Aardschock' magazine compilation album 'Metal Clogs' on the Rave-On label, although original CROSSFIRE guitarist Ner Neerinckx left the band and was subsequently jailed for the murder of a policeman (possibly documented in the lyrics of 'Killing A Cop' on CROSSFIRE's first album 'See You In Hell'?!?)

Enjoying strong album sales throughout Europe the group supported the likes of ACCEPT and IRON MAIDEN in their time and also played their first English dates in 1985, playing two dates in London; the first at the Wellington in Shepherd's Bush promoted by Shades Records.

Following the demise of the act De Wint and De Brauwer formed Melodic Rockers MYSTERY in 1989. Guitarist Rudi Van de Sijpe forged NATIVE INSTINCT.

SEE YOU IN HELL, Mausoleum SKULL 8314 (1983). Demon Of Evil / Killing A Cop / Magnificent Night / Danger On Earth / Fly High / Lover's Game / Starchild / See You In Hell.

SECOND ATTACK, Mausoleum SKULL (1985). Second Attack / Feeling Down / Highway Driver / Atomic War / Master Of Evil / Scream And Shout / Running For Love.

SHARPSHOOTER, Mausoleum SKULL (1986). Break Out / Killer Queen / Metal Knifes / Motorcycles (Live) / Crossfire (Live) / Sound Of War.

LIVE ATTACK, Bellaphon (1987). Second Attack / Starchild / Killer Queen / Master Of Evil / Scream And Shout / Sound Of War / Fly High / Highway Driver / Feeling Down.

CROSSFIRE

ANKARA, TURKEY — *Bülent Aksoy (vocals), Kaya Sevinç (guitar), Öz Sel (guitar), Rýfat Koyuncu (bass), Can Beþli (drums).*

Ankara Power Metal band CROSSFIRE, founded during 1998 by guitarists Kaya Sevinç and Öz Sel along with Rıfat Koyuncu, debuted with a 2002 demo 'Decisions Of Hate'. Sevinç and Koyuncu were both previously with ABSTRACTION. Previously, in late 1999, the group introduced Deniz Şeker on guitar and Kaan Dirgin on bass. That September Öz Sel was forced out due to his national military obligations. CROSSFIRE put in their inaugural live performance in April of 2000 but suffered a further setback in August when Dirgin had to join the army. 2001 brought about many changes as ex-HUMBUCKER drummer Can Beþli was enrolled, Şeker left the band in order to study and Öz Sel rejoined. Koyuncu replaced Kaan on bass and vocals.

In January 2002 CROSSFIRE acquired singer Bülent Aksoy, an ex-member of acts such as SHORTCUT, PROSPECT, KNIGHTMARE, MAGICK and TAYGA. In this formation the group recorded the 'Decisions Of Hate' demo in October 2002.

The band contributed their version of 'Beggars Night' to a 2004 RUNNING WILD tribute album compiled by Remedy Records. The band readied an album, 'Aggression Treaty', for 2005 release.

Decisions Of Hate, Crossfire demo (2002). Decisions Of Hate / Scharfschütze / Bloody Tears / Sunday / Unfair / Nightwolf.

CRUCIFIER

EDDYSTONE, PA, USA — *The Black Lourde Of Crucifixion (vocals / drums), Madman (guitar), Infernal (guitar), Necrodemius Hammerhorde (bass).*

Dating to September 1990, Pennsylvania Black Metal band CRUCIFIER, centred on Cazz Grant of GRAND BELIAL'S KEY, has issued a whole array of demos starting with 'Humans Are Such Easy Prey' in 1991. Further sessions included 'Crown Of Thorns', 1993's 'By Disgrace Of God' and 1994's 'Powerless Against'. The opening CRUCIFIER formation saw Grant on vocals and drums with Ira Redden and Jeff Anderson handling guitar. A projected demo, to be entitled 'The Unholy Trinity', was "planned, attempted and unfortunately aborted". The line-up shifted shape in January 1991 with the departure of Anderson and the induction of guitarist Dan Kamp and bassist Chris Miller. Redden then exited, paving the way for replacement Mike Machette and in this formation CRUCIFIER recorded the 'Humans Are Such Easy Prey' session. However, in November of 1991 both Machette and Miller opted out.

CRUCIFIER cut their second demo 'Crown Of Thorns', then enrolled new bassist Dan Keaton. The band laid down material for the 'Unparalleled Majesty' EP, through Polish label Pagan Productions, but dismissed Keaton in September 1992. Gary Gandy stepped in as substitute. Following completion of the 'By Disgrace Of God' sessions Kamp made his exit to join

INCANTATION. This defection put CRUCIFIER into a state of flux, resulting in a fluid line-up which would include at various stages the likes of Joe Ceresini, Mike Pandorf of SNAG, Joel Prange of WITCHERY, Craig Ross from RAPID VIOLENCE and ex-FACE FIRST man Chris DePetro.

In the Spring of 1994 CRUCIFIER drafted Mark Neto from British band CRUENTUS on bass guitar. Although now just a duo of Grant and Neto, the band, bringing back Dan Kamp and Chris DePetro, put in live work. In May the three song 'Powerless Against' promotional session was recorded with the aid of Nick "The Marauder" Mertaugh on guitar. Additional vocals would be supplied by the GRAND BELIAL'S KEY, THOKK and ANCIENT credited Vlad Luciferian and Jose Infernal of 'Sargatanas' zine. Virginia's Sinistrari Records issued 'Powerless Against', after which Neto departed.

CRUCIFIER members Grant ('The Black Lourde Of Crucifixion'), Der Sturmer and Lilith would all session on the debut GRAND BELIAL'S KEY album 'Mocking The Philanthropist'. Grant founded a new Thrash act BLUDGEON in 1997. CRUCIFIER returned in 1999, sharing the 'Trafficking With The Devil' single with NUNSLAUGHTER. CRUCIFIER duly hired ex-GOREPHOBIA, FACE FIRST and POLTERCHRIST guitarist Spencer "Madman" Murphy and Vince Papi of HEARSE and BLUDGEON on bass guitar. Live performances ensued but both Papi and Murphy left. Nick "The Marauder" Mertaugh was re-recruited on guitar and Jon "Demonic" Chamot took on the bass guitar role. In 2002 Madman returned to the fold.

In September of 2003 the Spanish label Death To Mankind Records issued the album 'Stronger Than Passing Time'. The band line-up fluxed once again, seeing new personnel guitarists Madman and Infernal with Necrodemius Hammerhorde on bass. Hammerhorde also operates with INFERNAL HATRED and his own DECIEVERION project, the latter also seeing contributions from Cazz Grant.

Unparalleled Majesty, Pagan (1993). Sodomy Of Angels / Spirits / Demons Of Filth / Something Wicked This Way Comes.
By Disgrace Of God EP, Pagan (1993). A Mourning In Nazareth / Portraits Of Blasphemy.
Powerless Against, Sinistrari (1994). Chime Of The Goat's Head Bell / Fire & Brimstone / My Lord Of Swine.
Trafficking With The Devil, The Crucifier Brotherhood International (1998) (Split single with NUNSLAUGHTER). Foul Deeds Will Rise.
THE NINTH YEAR, Elegy ER012CD (2002). The Cinerarium / Demons Of Filth / The Funeral / Exhumed Remains Of A Decayed Corpse / Portraits Of Blasphemy / Massacremation Of The Flock / Disembowelment Lunacy / Apocryphal Nativity / Soul Burial / Chime Of The Goats Head Bell / Portraits Of Blasphemy / A Mourning In Nazareth / Chime Of The Goats Head Bell / Fire And Brimstone / My Lord Of Swine / Foul Deeds Will Rise.
STRONGER THAN PASSING TIME, Death To Mankind (2003). Sodomy Of Angels / Thine Enemies Destroyed / Kneel To Lilith / Something Wicked This Way Comes / A Mourning In Nazareth / Demons Of Filth / The Rotten Whore Of God / Fire & Brimstone / Spirits / Plunging Pitchforks Through Paradise.

CRUMBSUCKERS

LONG ISLAND, NY, USA — *Chris Notaro (vocals), Robbie Koebler (guitar), Chuck Lenihan (guitar), Gary Meskil (bass), Danny Richardson (drums).*

Long Island's CRUMBSUCKERS spearheaded the mid eighties amalgamation of Thrash and Punk / Hardcore principles to define the Crossover genre. The band formed as a quartet in 1983 playing New York's A7 club and cutting a demo that June entitled 'The Crumbsucker Cave'. Vocalist Chris Notaro was ex-KRACKDOWN. CRUMBSUCKERS made an immediate scene impact with the 1986 debut 'Life Of Dreams', produced by Norman Dunn and engineered by Mike Marciano being released by Combat in the USA and Music For Nations subsidiary Rough Justice in the UK. Guitarist Robbie Koebler departed after recording 1988's 'Beast On My Back' and was replaced by CARNIVORE's Mark Piovanelli. The group also replaced original vocalist Chris Notaro with Joe Haggerty from ZERO HOUR for European touring during 1988 but eventually settled on the unknown Craig Allen.

Despite having forged a commendable reputation for themselves in late 1989 CRUMBSUCKERS became HEAVY RAIN in an attempt to pursue a more Hard Rock style. Lenihan went on to forge shock S&M Metal merchants the GENITORTURERS and vampire rockers VASARIA. Haggerty joined Arizona's KNUCKLEHEAD.

The band's rhythm section of bassist Gary Meskil and drummer Dan Richardson joined heavyweights PRO-PAIN as other members founded HEAVY RAIN. Richardson later joined LIFE OF AGONY for their 1997 album 'Soul Searching Sun' and subsequently recorded two albums with STEREOMUD, a band unit in league with the STUCK MOJO credited bass player Corey Lowery and ex-LIFE OF AGONY guitarist Joey Z. Gary Meskil honoured his former act on the August 2003 PRO-PAIN album 'Run For Cover' with a re-worked version of 'Just Sit There'.

Ex-CRUMBSUCKERS guitarist Chuck Lenihan bounced back in the Spring of 2005 with a Tampa, Florida based outfit entitled GLITTER GUNS.

CRUMBSUCKERS, singer Chris Notaro, guitarist Chuck Lenihan, bassist Gary Meskil and drummer Dan Richardson, joined by PRO-PAIN's Tom Klimchuck on second guitar, returned for a reunion show on August 3rd 2006 at B.B. King Blues Club in New York City to mark the 20th anniversary of their 'Life Of Dreams' album.

CRUMBSUCKERS, utilising PRO-PAIN drummer J.C. Dwyer, announced February 2007 European tour dates partnered with THE ACCUSED, EXTREME NOISE TERROR, LYZANXIA and DRILLER KILLER. However, these shows never eventuated.

The Crumbsucker Cave, Crumbsuckers (1983) (Demo). A-OK / The Twist / Emil Mauer (You Dick!) / Kids In My School / Don't Like It.
Crumbsuckers, Crumbsuckers (1984) (Demo). Just Sit There / Shit's Creek / Shot Down / Interlude / Trapped / Brainwashed / Live To Work / Prelude.
LIFE OF DREAMS, Rough Justice JUST4 (1986). Just Sit There / Trapped / Interlude / Super Tuesday / Shits Creek / Return To The Womb / Longest War / Shot Down / Prelude / Life Of Dreams / Brainwashed / Face Of Death / Hubrub / Bullshit Society / Live To Work / Mr. Hyde.
BEAST ON MY BACK (B.O.M.B.), Rough Justice JUST 9 (1988). Breakout / Jimmie's Dream / Charge / Initial Shock / I Am He / Connection / Rejuvenate / Remembering Tomorrow / Beast On My Back.

CRUSTACEAN

HOLLAND — *TMP (vocals / bass), MKK (guitar), RCS (guitar), JVI (drums).*

A Dutch band heavily enthused by a love of eighties U.S. Thrash. CRUSTACEAN members pedigree includes both guitarists MKK and RCS (a.k.a. Richard Schouten) having enjoyed terms of employment with Paul Speckmann's MASTER. RCS was also with ACROSTICHON and DISEMBOWEL. At one stage the group would also feature guitarist Jos van den Brand of ACROSTICHON, MASTER and OUTBURST.

MKK (Michel Meeuwissen) was also a member of ACROSTICHON and fellow renaissance Thrashers OUTBURST. Vocalist / bassist TMP is an ex-MASTICATOR member whilst drummer JVI was with SPINA BIFIDA.

The group came together in 1989 as CRYSTAL LAKE, issuing a string of demos upfront of February 1994's 'Rip Off' session. At this juncture the band evolved into CRUSTACEAN. Two tracks were included on the 'No Sleep 'Til Burg' compilation album and the 1995 'Headcleaner' EP solidified their standing.

The Teutonic Existence label took CRUSTACEAN on for the debut album 'Burden Of Our Suffering'. A mini album 'Satanized' ensued before the 2001 effort 'Insaniac'. In 2002 FDA (Ferry Damen of ANTRO) took over from Schouten.

CRUSTACEAN members also operate on the club circuit as a SLAYER covers band. RCS also operates with BLACK MELODY.
Headcleaner EP, Double Noise DNCD002 (1995). Tube Life / Of The Soil / Deranged / Levels / Go Away.
BURDEN OF OUR SUFFERING, Teutonic Existence (2000). Bitter State / Burden Of Our Suffering / Black Domain / Dark Crusade / Deathly Grin / Injected with Blood / Tomblike Silence / Devilish Enchantments / Evil Magick / Drawn From The Grave / Diabolical Contraptions-Deathmatch.
SATANIZED, (2000). Bloodshot / Satanizer / Soulsucker / Devilution / Lost (Head).
INSANIAC, Teutonic Existence (2001). Arena (QIIIa) / Random Terror (Chemical Juggernaut) / Psycho 2001 / Satanizer / Deathtrap (Infiltration Part II) / Soulsucker / Bloodshot / Lost (Head) / Penance (Ad Infinitum) / Redeemer (Sanctum Sanctorum) / Foul Usurper / State Necropolis (The Very End Of You).

CRYOGENIC

SYDNEY, NSW, AUSTRALIA — *Ryan David (vocals), Steve Essa (guitar), Anthony Henning (bass), Darren Jenkin (drums).*

CRYOGENIC, hailing from Sydney, made their first impressions in the early nineties as a Thrash Metal act, the formative membership comprising vocalist / guitarist Russell Player, lead guitarist Steve Essa, bass guitarist Anthony Henning and drummer Chad Bartosik. Although this version of the band demoed they would not progress beyond local compilation albums such as the inclusion of 'Take The Pain' on the 1995 collection 'Warhead Volume 1' and 'Intoxicated' on 1996's 'On Earth Undead'. New impetus was given with the introduction of drummer Darren Jenkin in 1996, the man known for his prior work for MORTALITY.

Following Australian support gigs to FEAR FACTORY in 1997 Player defected. Although their erstwhile singer had already laid down vocal sessions for a debut album 'Suspended Animation', these were wiped and Darren Maloney, another recruit from MORTALITY, re-recorded the album for release. Maloney's Death Metal leanings gave the band a new edge and 'Suspended Animation', released by the domestic Warhead label, would be promoted throughout 1998 with a series of valuable nationwide tours including guest slots to ENTOMBED, STRAPPING YOUNG LAD and CRADLE OF FILTH. The band stepped up a league later that same year by undertaking European dates and, returning home to Australia, opening shows for SLAYER.

An appearance at the 1999 Sydney Big Day Out was to precede issue of a second Tony Jarrett produced album 'Ego-Noria', released by Extreme Music Australia Records. Media and fans began to detect distinct traces of Nu-Metal leanings in the band's sound but progress was unchecked as CRYOGENIC headlined the 'Metal For The Brain' festival and delivered a second 'Big Day Out' set in January 2000. Packaged with PSI-CORE and ALCHEMIST the group then embarked upon the 'World War Three' tour throughout March and into May. Later that same year Essa would act as stand in musician for PSI-KORE.

2001 proved relatively quiet bar a third showing at the Sydney 'Big Day Out'. It would be then learned that the band had parted ways with Maloney. He would be superseded by ex-HENRY'S ANGER man Steve Simmons, this enlistment signalling a shift toward more down tuned, Hardcore musical realms. Unfortunately this phase of the band's career was cut short when, in September of 2002, Simmons was seriously injured in an auto accident, forcing him out of the group. CRYOGENIC re-enlisted singer Ryan David in April of 2003. Before the close of the year the band had not only relocated to Los Angeles but adopted the new title IN THE NAME OF ... Their inaugural gig as newly billed US residents would be in Hollywood during December supporting the BEAUTIFUL CREATURES.

SUSPENDED ANIMATION, Warhead WH 23 (1997). One Minute Hit / Mind Over Soul / Severed / Junc / Death Becomes You / Mary Belle / Destructive Minds / Numerical Superiority / Bring It On.
EGO-NORIA, E.M.A. Music EMA101 (1999). Analysis / Directionally One / Death By Misadventure / Conspiracy Theory / Hate My Head / Fall On / T.Y.T.D. (Cliffo) / Full Grown State / Stalemate / Redneck / Shock Value.

CRYPTIC SLAUGHTER

SANTA MONICA, CA, USA — *Bill Crooks (vocals), Les Evans (guitar), Rob Nicholson (bass), Scott Peterson (drums).*

Thrash Metal band CRYPTIC SLAUGHTER made their entrance with the 1985 'Life In Grave' demo tape. CRYPTIC SLAUGHTER actually broke up completely shortly after recording the 'Stream Of Consciousness' album as vocalist Bill Crooks and drummer Scott Peterson decided to give up the music scene altogether. Guitarist Les Evans and bassist Rob Nicholson remained a unit and forged a new act with new recruits guitarist Eli Nelson and drummer Eddie. The latter being drafted by Evans' mother after she saw a kid walking down the road carrying a pair of drum sticks!

In May of 1989 Evans relocated to Portland, Oregon to have another stab at starting CRYPTIC SLAUGHTER anew. This revised version of the band, with WEHRMACHT and SWEATY NIPPLES drummer Brian Lehfeldt onboard, issued the 'Speak Your Peace' album. Evans would also guest on the SWEATY NIPPLES 'What's Your Funktion?' EP.

With completion of Autumn 1990 touring CRYPTIC SLAUGHTER folded. Lehfeldt would join EVERCLEAR as touring drummer in the 90s whilst bassist Rob Nicholson made headway by joining ROB ZOMBIE's band. The band would duly reform but in January of 2003 Bill Crooks opted out. The band persevered with the induction of Portland native Chris Merrow of VILLAGE IDIOT repute.

The band re-released both the 'Conviction' and 'Money Talks' albums in 2003, both featuring a glut of extra tracks. 'Conviction' added the 'Life In Grave' demo plus live tracks recorded in Houston during 1988 whilst 'Money Speaks' featured the 1988 'Stream Of Consciousness' rehearsal recording plus further live cuts from Houston. The highly anticipated CRYPTIC SLAUGHTER reformation, originally proposed to include Brian Lehfeldt on drums, would be short-lived though. The band officially changed their name to BELOW following the departure of vocalist Bill Treadway (formerly Bill Crooks).

Nicholson meantime would be found in the employ of former HELMET mentor Page Hamilton. He also cites credits with SUFFER, DROWN and DANZIG. By late 2003 Nicholson had joined the OZZY OSBOURNE band.

CONVICTED, Metal Blade 72148 (1986). M.A.D. / Little World / Sudden Death / Lowlife / Rage To Kill / Rest In Pain / Nuclear Future / State Control / Hypocrite / War To The Knife / Nation Of Hate / Black And White / Reich Of Torture / Convicted.
MONEY TALKS, Metal Blade 72204 (1987). Money Talks / Set Your Own Pace / Could Be Worse / Wake Up / Freedom Of Expression? / Menace To Mankind / Too Much, Too Little / Human Contrast / Tables Are Turned / Positively / All Wrong / American Heroes.
STREAM OF CONSCIOUSNESS, Metal Blade 72320 (1988). Circus Of Fools / Aggravated / Last Laugh / Overcome / Deteriorate / See Through You / Just Went Black / Drift / Altered Visions / Addiction / One Last Thought.
SPEAK YOUR PEACE, Metal Blade CDZORRO 6 (1990). Born Too Soon / Still Born, Again / Insanity By Numbers / Co-Exist / Deathstyles Of The Poor And Lonely / One Thing Or Another / Divided Minds / Speak Your Piece / Killing Time.
CONVICTED, Relapse RR 6546-2 (2003). M.A.D. / Little World / Sudden Death / Lowlife / Rage To Kill / Rest In Pain / Nuclear Future / State Of Control / Hypocrite / War To The Knife / Nation Of Hate / Black And White / Reich Of Torture / Convicted / Flesh Of The Wench (1985 demo) / Necessity Supreme (1985 demo) / Life In Grave (1985 demo) / War To The Knife (1985 demo) / Rest In Pain (1985 demo) / Set Your Own Pace (1988 live) / Positively (1988 live) / Black And White (1988 live) / Lowlife (1988 live).
MONEY TALKS, Relapse RR 6547-2 (2003). Money Talks / Set Your Own Pace / Could Be Worse / Wake Up / Freedom Of Expression? / Menace To Mankind / Too Much, Too Little / Human Contrast / Tables

Are Turned / Positively / All Wrong / American Heroes / Song X (1988 rehearsal) / Overcome (1988 rehearsal) / Deteriorate (1988 rehearsal) / See Through You (1988 rehearsal) / One Last Thought (1988 rehearsal) / Just Went Black (1988 live) / Circus Of Fools (1988 live) / Aggravated (1988 live) / Freedom Of Expression (1988 live).

CRYSTAL LAKE

LEME, SP, BRAZIL — *Haroldo Habermann (vocals), Alisson Suzigan (guitar), Jabá (guitar), Sandoval (bass), Heraldo (drums).*

Leme based Thrashers CRYSTAL LAKE were founded in 1998, at first counting a line up of vocalist Haroldo Habermann, the guitar pairing of César and Goiaba, bass player Fornazin with Heraldo on the drums. In 2001 the guitar team would be switched to incorporate new faces Alisson Suzigan and Beatriz. Further changes ensued the following year with the exit of both Fornazin and Beatriz, CRYSTAL LAKE drawing guitarist Reinaldo Jabá and bassist Daniel Chapolim as substitutes. The band self financed their 2003 release 'Born To The Underground', this featuring guest vocalists Daniel of CLAUSTROFOBIA, Ulysses from GAMMOTH and KINGDOM OF MAGGOTS man Flavio. Upon completion of these sessions the band welcomed in new bass man Sandoval.

Born To The Underground, Independent (2003). Blackout / Massacre / Hell On Earth / Wide Open Sores / Fuck You All.

CULPRIT

SEATTLE, WA, USA — *Jeff L'Heureux (vocals), John DeVol (guitar), Kjartan Kristoffersen (guitar), Scott Earl (bass), Bud Burrill (drums).*

An exceedingly British influenced Seattle Metal band showing huge chunks of British influences in their raw, aggressive style.

During early 1979 North Seattle natives guitarist John DeVol, bassist Scott Earl and drummer Bud Burrill created ORPHEUS playing parties and local 'Battle of the bands' contests. Meantime AMETHYST, from the east of the city and including guitarist Kjartan Kristoffersen and vocalist Jeff L'Hereaux in their ranks were playing their favourite cover versions.

The two bands came into contact with AMETHYST supporting ORPHEUS at Mr. Bills club resulting in the headliner making a play for D'Heureaux's services. The singer was willing to join on the condition his colleague Kristofferson was part of the deal and CULPRIT was borne.

The band signed to Shrapnel Records after gigs in California with WILD DOGS and CINEMA before appearing on one of the label's series of 'U.S. Metal' compilations with the slightly Progressively tinged 'Players' and followed it up with the Mike Varney produced 'Guilty As Charged' album.

The band frequently gigged in their native Seattle, in particular the Metal stronghold of Bellevue but would split when Kristoffersen and Earl joined local legends TKO in 1984. However, although the duo appeared on the cover of the 'In Your Face', the album was recorded long before the band were signed by Combat Records in the States, the album was released by Music For Nations in Europe, and the ex-CULPRIT pair had come on board.

Jeff L'Heureux would later turn up fronting another Seattle band, MISTRUST. The group appeared on the 'Pacific Metal Project' compilation before recording the 'Spin The World' album. John DeVol meantime re-emerged in 1987 with DeVOL, a group boasting a line-up of vocalist Terry Tandeski, bassist Dennis Quintella and drummer Jeff McCormack.

Following the TKO stint, Kristofffersen and Earl formed the Glam outfit BANG GANG, having relocated to Los Angeles in the late 80's. Earl would form SHAKE THE FAITH in 1992 although was ousted by the recording of their solitary album.

The specialist German label Hellion Records re-issued 'Guilty As Charged' on CD format adding three extra live tracks.

GUILTY AS CHARGED, Shrapnel 1008 (1983). Guilty As Charged / Ice In The Back / Steel To Blood / I Am / Ambush / Tears Of Repentance / Same To You / Fight Back / Players.
CULPRIT, Hellion HE 091000 (2001).

CYCLES

PORTO, PORTUGAL — *Sérgio Martins (vocals), Carlos Barbosa (guitar), Nuno Silva (guitar), Vera Sá (bass), Augusto Peixto (drums).*

Porto Heavy Metal act CYCLES was manifested during late 2001 by erstwhile musicians from FEARS TOMB and KARNAK, guitarists Filipe Moreira and Carlos Barbosa. First in line for recruitment would be the GODLESS BEAUTY, SCARLET VEIL and MARTYRIUM credited bassist Vera Sá and drummer Augusto Peixoto, of DOVE, IN SOLITUDE and PARADIGMA repute. The unit would be completed by vocalist Henrique Loureiro.

The album 'Phoenix Rising', recorded during 2002, saw the inclusion of notable studio guests in TARANTULA guitarist Paulo Barros and THANATOSCHIZO singer Patrícia Rodrigues. A demo, 'End Of December', arrived in July 2005 with an album 'Phoenix Rising' delivered in January 2006. Guitarist Filipe Moreira would be replaced by Álvaro Craveiro.

Paradise / World Of Sand, Cycles (2003). Paradise / World Of Sand.
End Of December, (2005). End Of December / Tomb Of Fear / World Of Sand / Paradise / World Of Sand (Video).
Life Meanings—Live at Hard Club (09-09-2005), (2005). End Of December / Black Symphony / My Darkest Friend / Drifting Man / Revolt / Foul Paradise / Life Meanings / Tomb Of Fear / World Of Sand.
PHOENIX RISING, (2006). End Of December / Pyramid Of Souls / Black Symphony / Foul Paradise / World Of Sand / Epitaph / Drifting Man / Life Meanings / Temple Of Karnak / Satni / Tomb Of Fear.

CYCLONE

BELGIUM — *Guido Gevels (vocals), Johnny Kerbush (guitar), Pascal Van Lint (guitar), Stefan Daamen (bass), Nicolas Lairio (drums).*

Vilvoorde based Thrashers Metallers released the 1985 demo 'In The Grip Of Evil' following a name change from CENTURION. CYCLONE's debut gigs came as a support to ACID in 1984. Gigs with Germany's DESTRUCTION led to the inclusion of two tracks on the Roadrunner compilation 'Metal Race' alongside IRON GREY, EXPLORER and LIGHTNING FIRE. Line up changes in the band's history would see the departure of erstwhile TROUBLE AGENCY guitarist Pascal Van Lint, the CHANNEL ZERO credited Xavier Carion, also on guitar, and drummer Nicolas Lairio.

The Roadrunner label released the debut album 'Brutal Destruction' in 1986, the band following this with the poorly distributed, Eric Grief produced 'Inferior To None' in 1990 for Justice Records. The final CYCLONE line up would comprise singer Guido Gevels, the guitar pairing of Stefan Daamen and D. Kapelle, bassist G. Vanoverloop and drummer G. Langhendries.

CYCLONE supported ANTHRAX, ACID and AGENT STEEL and assorted members later formed CHANNEL ZERO.

In The Grip Of Evil, Cyclone Promo (1985). Fall Under His Command / Incest Love / In The Grip Of Evil.
METAL RACE, Roadrunner (1986) (Split album with IRON GREY, EXPLORER & LIGHTNING FIRE). Incest Love / Long To Hell.
BRUTAL DESTRUCTION, Roadrunner RR 9687 (1986). Prelude To The End / Long To Hell / Fall Under His Command / The Call Of Steel / Fighting The Fatal / In The Grip Of Evil / Take Thy Breath / Incest Love.
INFERIOR TO NONE, Justice JR-CD02-90 (1990). Convultions (Intro) / Neurotic / So Be It / Paralysed / Throw The First Stone / The Other Side / I Am The Plague / Crown Of Thorns (Instrumental) / Slavery.

CYCLONE TEMPLE

USA — *Brian Troch (vocals), Greg Fulton (guitar), Scott Schafer (bass), John Slattery (drums).*

CYCLONE TEMPLE was previously known in their more studs n' leather period as ZNOWHITE. The band, fronted by ex-HAMMERON man Brian Troch, put in an appearance at the 1991 Milwaukee Metalfest but lost their record deal with Relativity. In 1992 vocalist Brian Troch was replaced by Marco Salinas for the 'Building Errors In The Machine' mini-album. Troch would subsequently affiliate with JOE STUMP'S REIGN OF TERROR.

Yet another switch in singers came with third outing 'My Friend Lonely' in 1994. This record, fronted by Sonny DeLuca, comprised of re-recorded tracks from 'Building Errors In The Machine' alongside new material.

Post CYCLONE TEMPLE both guitarist Greg Fulton and bass player Scott Schafer would move on to REBELS WITHOUT APPLAUSE in union with guitarist Greg Alano and drummer Tony Heath issuing the 1997 EP 'Rip Hop Soulcore Crush'. DeLuca later came to attention with SOIL.

In January 2006 ex-CYCLONE TEMPLE singer Sonny DeLuca teamed up with former ex-LUPARA drummer Fred Braun and FROM ZERO guitarist Joe Pettinato in a new band project.

I HATE THEREFORE I AM, Relativity (1991). Why / Sister (Until We Meet Again) / Words Are Just Words / Public Enemy / In God We Trust / I Hate Therefore I Am / March For Me, Die For Me / Born To Lose / Silence So Loud.
BUILDING ERRORS IN THE MACHINE, Polydisc (1993). Hate Makes Hate / Me, Myself & I / Down The Drain / Killing Floor / Drug Of The Masses / The Law Of Relativity.
MY FRIEND LONELY, Monsterdisc (1994). Hate Makes Hate / Down The Drain / My Friend Lonely / Me, Myself & I / Drug Of The Masses / Comfortably Superficial / Killing Floor / Time Heals All / The Law Of Relativity.

CYNIC

FL, USA — *Paul Masvidal (vocals / guitar), Jason Gobel (guitar), Tony Choy (bass), Sean Reinert (drums).*

Although highly regarded in their time CYNIC was noted more for their individual members contributions to other acts. Tony Choy contributed bass parts to the ATHEIST album 'Unquestionable Presence' before joining Dutch thrashers PESTILENCE for their 'Testimony Of The Ancients' album and following world tour. Guitarist Paul Masvidal and drummer Sean Reinert played on DEATH's 1992 album 'Human' then opted to join DEATH's 1992 American and European tour on a temporary basis. Masvidal also contributed heavily to MASTER's 'And On The Seventh Day God Created Master' album. Guitarist Jason Gobel guests on MONSTROSITY's 'Imperial Doom' album and also filled in for live shows.

CYNIC was initiated in November of 1987 by guitarist Paul Masvidal and drummer Sean Reinert, this pair uniting with bassist Mark Van Erp and vocalist Jack Kelly. An opening 1988 demo was laid down, after which Kelly decamped. Jason Gobel was pulled in as substitute and Masvidal assumed the lead vocal role for the second, four song demo session 'Reflections Of A Dying World'. CYNIC set about live work across Florida but Van Erp would exit, later to enroll in MONSTROSITY, and was replaced by Tony Choy for a third, self titled demo.

CYNIC recorded a late 1991 three track demo for Roadrunner Records. The band duly secured a deal but that April both Masvidal and Reinert took time out of their schedule to session on DEATH's 'Human' opus. Strangely CYNIC was gaining a reputation without having even recorded an album as a plethora of sessions came their way. Tony Choy filled in for the late Roger Patterson on ATHEIST's 'Unquestionable Presence' record and guested on PESTILENCE's 'Testimony Of The Ancients'. Masvidal contributed his skills to MASTER's 'On The Eighth Day, God Created Master' whilst Jason Gobel was sought out by MONSTROSITY, cutting lead breaks on their 'Imperial Doom' album.

CYNIC had projected studio time with producer Scott Burns for October of 1992. Unfortunately Hurricane David put paid to these plans, wiping out the band's rehearsal facility at Jason Gobel's house. With their equipment wrecked the band postponed recording until March of 1993. That May a demo of the song 'Uroboric Forms' figured on the Roadrunner compilation 'At Death's Door II'. Tony Choy broke away to join ATHEIST on a full time basis. CYNIC briefly drafted Chris Kringel as new bass man before settling on Sean Malone.

Following the 'Focus' album release in September of 2003 Masvidal reunited with DEATH on a permanent basis. 'Focus' had seen Tony Teegarden aiding with backing vocals and it would be he that stepped up to take the role of frontman for a European tour partnered with PESTILENCE. These shows also found bassist Chris Kringel temporarily taking Malone's place. CYNIC would tour across North America in the Summer of 1994 as support to CANNIBAL CORPSE, pulling in Dana Cosley of DEMONOMACY to handle vocals and keyboards. Upon completion of these reports suggested new material was being crafted utilising the VIOGRESSION credited vocalist Brian DeNeffe. During this period bassist Sean Malone left the fold. Shortly after, CYNIC disbanded, with Paul Masvidal, Jason Gobel and Sean Reinert going on to forge the Gothic flavoured PORTAL with singer Aruna Abrams and bassist Chris Kringel.

Reinert joined GORDIAN KNOT but by 2000 was involved with AGHORA. Malone also contributes to the debut AGHORA album. The 2003 GORDIAN KNOT album 'Emergent' featured Masvidal, Gobel and Reinert as guests. Tony Teegarden would found ADRIFT in league with Jack Owen of CANNIBAL CORPSE.

In early 2007 it was revealed PESTILENCE guitarist Patrick Mameli had forged a new Death Metal act billed C-187 in alliance with M.A.N, ex-TRANSPORT LEAGUE and MNEMIC vocalist Tony Jelencovich plus the CYNIC duo of bassist Tony Choy and drummer Sean Reinert. Signing to Dutch imprint Mascot Records, C-187 cut debut album tracks that February at Space Lab Studios in Düsseldorf in Germany.

FOCUS, Roadrunner RR 91692 (1993). Veil Of Maya / Celestial Voyage / The Eagle Nature / Sentiment / I'm But A Wave To ... / Uroboric Forms / Textures / How Could I.

CYST

FL, USA — *Dan Ortega (vocals), Mike Maxson (guitar), Kyle Bennett (guitar), Dean Piekara (bass), Victor Bonilla (drums).*

An aggressive South Florida Thrash act, first formulated as a trio comprising vocalist Dan Ortega, guitarist Mike Maxson and bass player Dean Piekara under the formative title of STALKBREED in 1995. Amidst a slew of personnel changes this outfit cut the 1998 demo 'Become Wrath'. By the summer of 2000 a new title of CYST was adopted and new members guitarist Kyle Bennett and drummer Victor Bonilla inducted. In this guise the band laid down the 'Wrath' demo session, promoted with high profile live support slots to the likes of MOTÖRHEAD, AMON AMARTH, WITCHERY, THE HAUNTED and SLAYER. Signing to Hook n' Mouth Records CYST debuted commercially with the 'Concussion Symphony'. Bonilla subsequently decamped. He would be superseded by Alex but by early 2003 Bonilla was to make a return.

CONCUSSION SYMPHONY, Independent (2002). Curse The Fates / Syst / I'll Break Your Back / Without A Sound / Shield The Beating / Inhuman / Become Wrath / The Deterioration Of The American Psyche.

D.A.M.

MORECOMBE, UK — *Jason McLoughlin (vocals), John Bury (guitar), Elly (guitar), Dave Pugh (bass), Phil Bury (drums).*

Morecombe Thrashers D.A.M. ("Destruction And Mayhem"), including ex-METAL HEART guitarist John Bury amongst their number, debuted with a three track demo, 'Human Wreckage', in 1988 and followed it with a second tape entitled 'Destruction And Mayhem'. Whereas the original line-up featured bassist Liam Godden the four-string slot was subsequently filled by Andy Elliot, featuring on both published albums, until Dave Pugh got the nod.

D.A.M. supported both TORANAGA and ACID REIGN in 1989 before a plethora of 1990 gigs opening for a European double billing of DARK ANGEL and NUCLEAR ASSAULT. It was during this tour that the band was captured on the '3 Way Thrash' video, by which time the 'Human Wreckage' debut album had been released through Noise Records.

CD variants of the 1991 album 'Inside Out' added two extra tracks in 'Thought For The Day' and 'Circles'. Guitarist Elly quit in 1991 to form BURNT OAK, releasing the 'English Rock n' Roll' demo in 1993, whereas Dave Pugh would join SKYCLAD in 1992.

HUMAN WRECKAGE, Noise NUK149 (1990). Death Warmed Up / Killing Time / Left To Rot / Prophets Of Doom / Terror Squad / Total Destruction / Infernal Torment / Vendetta / Human Wreckage / Aliens / F.O.D.

INSIDE OUT, Noise N0162 (1991). Man Of Violence / House Of Cards / Appointment With Fear / Winter's Tear / Innocent One / My Twisted Mind / No Escape / Beneath Closed Eyes / Inside Outro.

D.R.I.

HOUSTON, TX, USA — *Kurt Brecht (vocals), Spike Cassidy (guitar), Josh Pappé (bass), Felix Griffin (drums).*

Founded in Houston during 1981 by guitarist Spike Cassidy D.R.I. (DIRTY ROTTEN IMBECILES) purveyed a high energy brand of Hardcore and Punk that veered toward more Metal territory with every release. Cassidy had moved from New York to Texas and put the first incarnation of the group together with vocalist Kurt Brecht, drummer Eric Brecht and bassist Dennis Johnson. The three had been working as SUBURBANITES with Spike's roommate on guitar before he left and Spike joined up as the band evolved into D.R.I. The name was inspired by the father of the Brecht brothers who would come home during a band practice and shout abuse at the group for the noise they were making, 'dirty rotten imbeciles' being one phrase he used with regularity.

D.R.I. released their debut album through their own label in 1983. This album notably included what is generally regarded to be the very first recorded example of a "blast beat" on the song 'No Sense', Eric Brecht's staccato machine gunning of both snare and bass drum providing a blueprint for legions of following Death Metal bands. The band was then picked up by Metal Blade and concocting the breakthrough 'Dealing With It' album on the Death imprint during 1985. By this time both Dennis and Eric had quit the group, the latter joining Thrashers HIRAX, a short stint with DEATH and then the San Francisco based ATTITUDE ADJUSTMENT and TWO BIT THIEF. Josh Pappé and Felix Griffin had taken their respective places. Metal Blade's Brian Slagel got to hear D.R.I. after HIRAX vocalist Katon Depena had passed on a tape enthusing about the group's potential after seeing them perform a one-off show in Los Angeles.

For the 'Dealing With It' album, only Kurt Brecht and Cassidy remained having enrolled a new rhythm section of bassist Mikey Offender and drummer Felix Griffin. Following a 1989 tour supporting GANG GREEN the band suffered a setback when bassist Josh Pappe opted to join the headline act. His replacement was ex-MANTAS bassist John Menor who joined D.R.I. in time for further touring in Britain to promote the 'Thrash Zone' album with NASTY SAVAGE acting as the support band.

Drummer Felix Griffin was announced to have quit in 1990 to be replaced by former MEGADETH drummer Chuck Beehler. However, by the time of a European tour Griffin was back in on the drum stool.

D.R.I. continued to tour although the release schedule slowed down with the last album issue being 'Full Speed Ahead', recorded with bassist Chumley Porter, in 1995. Touring in 2001 found infamous Bay Area photographer Harold 'O' Oimoen inducted as bass player for dates in August and September supported by SWORN ENEMY. Latterly a rare 7" split single with RAW POWER was issued on the Killer Release label, limited to just 500 copies. D.R.I. Would get back on the road in North America during October of 2002 for a month long bout of touring supported by Milwaukee's NEW SOCIETY OF ANARCHISTS.

During early 2004 Spike Cassidy acted as producer for the Oklahoma based EARTH A.D.'s album 'Death Toll'. German Heavy Metal band POWERGOD cut a cover version of 'I'd Rather Be Sleeping' for inclusion on their 'Long Live The Loud–That's Metal Lesson II' released through Massacre Records in July 2005.

D.R.I. were set to hook up with SUBZERO for US dates in May and June 2006. Unfortunately guitarist Spike Cassidy was diagnosed with colon cancer and the tour duly cancelled.

DIRTY ROTTEN LP, Rotten (1983). I Don't Need Society / Commuter Man / Plastique / Why / Balance Of Terror / My Fate To Hate / Who Am I / Money Stinks / Human Waste / Yes Ma'am / Dennis' Problems / Closet Punk / Reagonomics / Sad To Be / War Crimes / Busted / Draft Me / F.R.D.C. / Capitalist Suck / Misery Loves Company / No Sense / Blockhead.

DEALING WITH IT, Metal Blade 72069 (1985). Snap / I'd Rather Be Sleeping / Marriage / Yes Ma'am / Soup Kitchen / Mad Man / Stupid, Stupid War / Counter Attack / Couch Slouch / God Is Broke / Karma / Nursing Home Blues / I Don't Need Society / Give My Taxes Back / The Explorer / Reagonomics / How To Cut / Shame / Arguement Then War / Evil Minds / Slit My Wrist / Busted Again / Equal People / On My Way Home / Bail Out.

CROSSOVER, Metal Blade 72201 (1987). All For Nothing / Manifest Destiny / Gone Too Long / Do The Dream / Shut Up! / Modern World / Think For Yourself / Slumlord / Dead In a Ditch / Suit And Tie Guy / Man Unkind.

You Think For Yourself, Metal Blade 75022 (1988) (USA promotion). You Think For Yourself.

FOUR OF A KIND, Metal Blade 73304 (1988). All For Nothing / Manifest Destiny / Gone Too Long / Do The Dream / Shut Up / Modern World / Think For Yourself / Slumlord / Dead In A Ditch / Suit And Tie Guy / Man Unkind.

THRASH ZONE, Roadrunner RO 9429-2 (1989). Beneath The Wheel / Enemy Withion / Strategy / Labelled Incurable / Gun Control / Kill The Words / Drown You Out / The Trade / Standing In Line / Give A Hoot / Worker Bee / Abduction / You Say I'm Scum.

DEFINITION, Rotten ROT 2093CD (1992). Acid Rain / Tone Deaf / Guilt Trip / Hardball / The Application / Paying To Play / Say It / Dry Heaves / Don't Ask / Time Out / Let It Go / You / The Target.

LIVE, Rotten (1994). Intro / Thrashard / Acid Rain / Mad Man / Couch Slouch / Argument Then War / The Application / I Don't Need Society / Hardball / Violent Pacification / Beneath The Wheel / The Explorer / Commuter Man / You Say I'm Scum / The 5 Year Plan / Suit And Tie Guy / Nursing Home Blues.

FULL SPEED AHEAD, Rotten (1995). Problem Addict / I'm The Liar / Under The Overpass / They Don't Care / Drawn And Quartered / No End / Wages Of Sin / Syringes In The Sandbox / Who Am I / Girl With A Gun / Dead Meat / Down To The Wire / Level 7 / Broke / Sucker / Underneath The Surface.

DIRTY ROTTEN IMBECILES, Cleopatra (2001). Who Am I / Commuter Man / Yes Ma'am / The Explorer / Violent Pacification / Argument Then War / Mad Man / Couch Slouch / Nursing Home Blues / Don't Need Society / A Coffin / Redline / Hooked / Probation / The Five Year Plan / No Religion.

LIVE AT CBGB's 1984, Beer City (2005). I Don't Need Society / Reaganomics / Commuter Man / Plastique / Why / Balance Of Terror / My Fate To Hate / Who Am I / Money Stinks / Human Waste / Yes Ma'am / Dennis' Problem / Closet Punk / How To Act / Give My Taxes Back / Equal People / On My Way Home / Bail Out / Snap / Explorer / Slit My Wrists / Stupid War / Counter Attack / I'd Rather Be Sleeping / Running Around / Coach Slouch / To Open Closed Doors / God Is Broke / Soup Kitchen / Sad To Be / War Crimes / Busted / Draft Me /

First Round Draft Choice / Capitalists Suck / Mad Man / Misery Loves Company / No Sense / Blockhead / Violent Pacification.

DARCANE

HELSINKI, FINLAND — *Tommy Dee (vocals / guitar), Rizzto Cullervo (guitar), Hofu Black (bass), Tony (drums).*

In 2003 Helsinki's HOLOCHAUST switched title to DARCANE, weighing in under their new banner with the March EP 'Survivors Of The Holochaust'. HOLOCHAUST were originally founded as the teenage Thrash act G.R.G. in the mid 80's as a trio incorporating Tommi Tiihonen on lead vocals and guitar, Jussi Petrelius on second guitar and Kimmo Tiihonen on the bass. A whole swathe of band members came and went as the band operated under various titles such as KILLERS in 1985, YAMMIES (after a chewing gum!) and in 1986 MONSTERS. With Petrelius now on drums the band welcomed Toni Kummelus in as lead guitarist for the demo tape 'What's … Up!!!, Dude'.

Petrelius bowed out to create FRAGILE and in 1993 HOLOCHAUST inducted Juha Niskanen on drums. Kummelus was next to leave, his place being taken by Marko Kautonen and then a further split occurred with Niskanen opting out. The new face behind the drum kit was Mikko Purontaus. Quite surreally, upon discovering BON JOVI was to play in Helsinki HOLOCHAUST cut a demo recording, featuring a version of the KISS classic 'God of Thunder', specifically in an attempt to gain the opening slot for this gig. They failed. Kimmo Tiihonen decided to leave shortly after but Jari Kosonen took on bass for gigs in the latter half of 1996. This latest recruit in turn was substituted by Antti Kinnunen.

Fate would then lend a twist of good fortune to HOLOCHAUST as huge exposure was generated during 1998 for the demo song 'Valley Of Misery'. This track circumvented the globe mistakenly attributed to METALLICA. Many fans of the San Francisco Thrash godfathers were convinced that the HOLOCHAUST track was a return to form for METALLICA as Tommy Tiihonen's voice had a degree of resemblance to James Hetfield's.

In 2000 Tommy Tihonen built a completely new version of HOLOCHAUST involving guitarist Risto 'Rizzto' Kivioja, bassist Jukka 'Hofu Black' Hoffrén and AURORA-K drummer Toni Toivila. The demo 'PanDEMOnium' saw issue in 2002.

Re-branded as DARCANE the band issued the March 2003 session 'Survivors Of The Holochaust' then a May 2004 demo 'Anamorphica'. Subsequently the group evolved further, becoming MIND-A-STRAY in 2005, issuing the demo 'Sign Of Victory' in March as their opener. By this stage the band involved vocalist / guitarist Tommi Tiihonen, guitarist Jere Lappalainen and bass player Jukka Hoffrén, the latter holding credits with BRIDE ADORNED, DIVERCIA and ADAMANTRA.

Survivors Of The Holochaust, Darcane (2003) (Demo). Sin Worth To Die / Nemesis / No Longer Exist / Calm Before Thunder.

THE VERY WORST OF DARCANE, Insanity (2003). Beyond The Violence / Valley Of Misery / Nemesis / Guilty Of Greed / Sin Worth To Die / No Longer Exist / I Wanna Lie / Sad Life Philosophy / Calm Before Thunder / Holocaust.

Anamorphica, Darcane (2004) (Demo). Stranger / Rebels Evermore / Something For The Pain.

DARK ANGEL

LONG BEACH, CA, USA — *Ron Rinehart (vocals), Eric Meyer (guitar), Jimmy Durkin (guitar), Mike Gonzalez (bass), Gene Hoglan (drums).*

Long Beach's DARK ANGEL would be seen by many as spearheading the second round of the Thrash Metal wave to break out of America. In actual fact, being assembled during 1981 as SHELL SHOCK with founding members Don Dotty, Jimmy Durkin and Robbie Yahn, at Downey High School, the band had been active far earlier. To differentiate themselves from the rising Speed Metal flock, DARK ANGEL adopted the tag "Caffeine Metal". The teens ambitions extended to the recording of a debut, yet unpublished, demo but a second set of demos, dubbed 'We Have Arrived' and produced by Bill Metoyer, secured the interest of two parties, the locally based Metalstorm / Azra concern and French label Axekiller Records and in 1984 contracts were signed.

DARK ANGEL's inaugural effort of 1985, a vinyl pressing of the demo tracks from 'We Have Arrived', featured a line-up of vocalist Don Doty, guitarists Eric Meyer and Jimmy Durkin together with bassist Robbie Yahn and drummer Jack Schwartz. An early DARK ANGEL drummer, Bob Gourley, had graduated from a fleeting appearance in a fledgling SLAYER. Upon his departure from DARK ANGEL Gourley forged POWERLORD releasing a 1988 album 'The Awakening'.

Without financial backing, the band's ability to plug 'We Have Arrived' was restricted to local Los Angeles shows, where they supported the likes of SLAYER, AGENT STEEL and SAVAGE GRACE. DARK ANGEL benefited from a unique promotion release to back up the 1986 'Darkness Descends' album. The track 'Merciless Death', released by Azra Records, came in a variety of bizarre shapes such as a skull, a wheel, a square, a black heart and even a Christmas tree!

The band itself had lost the services of Schwartz, the drummer being inducted into HOLY TERROR, and in his stead came Lee Rausch, a former member of MEGADETH. However, Rausch's place was briefly taken by a returning Jack Schwartz before CARNAGE and WARGOD man Gene Hoglan. Besides his band activities, Hoglan was well known on the local metal scene as lighting technician for SLAYER, OMEN and SAVAGE GRACE and journalist for 'The Headbanger' fanzine. By coincidence, the drummer had also briefly been a member of another outfit dubbed DARK ANGEL, later evolving into CARNAGE, a completely different set of musicians.

In a straight swap, as Hoglan teamed up with DARK ANGEL in December 1984, their then drummer, Lee Rausch, hopped over to join WARGOD. There would nearly be a further connection to MEGADETH too, as Dave Mustaine requested the services of both Jimmy Durkin and Eric Meyer, both guitarists though declining the offer. The revised DARK ANGEL debuted on December 31st 1984 sharing a bill with HIRAX at Radio City, in Anaheim. Wishing to excise former drummer Jack Schwartz, re-issues of the first album 'We Have Arrived' would include Hoglan's picture, not Schwartz's.

'Darkness Descends', with production handled by Randy Burns witnessed a switch in labels, to Combat Records for the USA and Music For Nations subsidiary Under One Flag in the UK. 'Darkness Descends' improved the band's standing further as DARK ANGEL began to carve out their own niche. In the lyrical department, Gene Hoglan had taken over and fans revelled in the groups unexpected song themes. With sessions fulfilled, Rob Yahn took his leave, handing the bass position over to Mike Gonzalez.

Road work to push the record, which had garnered unanimously enthusiastic reviews globally, had Dark Angel scoring supports with MOTÖRHEAD and CRO-MAGS in New York, then MEGADETH before embarking on the January 1987 nationwide 'Gates Of Darkness' tour with co-headliners POSSESSED. These latter dates saw the inclusion of vocalist Jim Drabos from DEATH FORCE. Reports emerged claiming Doty had been involved in a car accident. Without insurance Doty couldn't go on tour because he had to work to reimburse the damage he had caused in the collision. Doty came back into the fold as DARK ANGEL gained the guest slot to the Hollywood Palladium date for SLAYER's finale of their 'Reign In Blood' world tour. A headline run in Texas that July then ensued, after which Doty was asked to leave. The singer had failed to show up for the first night's performance in San Antonio.

With Doty's exit, the group requested the services of WATCHTOWER's Jason McMaster but, although McMaster performed as guest bassist for dates in Texas, this union never transpired. The group also approached WRATHCHILD AMERICA's Brad Divens, who turned them down, and Stephan Taylor from SACRILEGE B.C., who also declined.

Soldiering on, in September 1987 DARK ANGEL added new vocalist Ron Rinehart, previously with MESSIAH, for January 1989's 'Leave Scars' album. Although officially Michael Monarch, the veteran guitarist of STEPPENWOLF, was given production credits the band themselves put most of the record together. The album took Hoglan's observations to further extremes, tackling subjects such as suicide and sexual abuse. The first-person characterization of child molestation of the track 'Death Of Innocence' was deemed too graphic by Combat Records, who initially left the words for this song off the lyric sheet. On a lighter note, Leave Scars also featured cover versions of LED ZEPPELIN's 'Immigrant Song' and FEAR's 'Action' and 'I Don't Care About You'. Also involved was VIKING vocalist Ron Daniels (a.k.a. 'Eriksen'), duetting with Rinehart on the track 'Promise Of Agony'.

'Leave Scars' was promoted in the live arena with an exhaustive 1989 US 'Ultimate Revenge' tour partnered with DEATH. Mid-tour in Boston, Massachusetts, DARK ANGEL suffered a major blow when Durkin quit, the band citing "personal problems and marriage problems". DARK ANGEL persevered to complete the schedule by playing shows as a four-piece before drafting VIKING axeman Brett Eriksen on a stand-in basis. In spite of this chaos and severe criticism being leveled at the sonic values of 'Leave Scars', the album still entered the national charts.

European shows then hooked up with NUCLEAR ASSAULT and ACID REIGN. Whilst in Nuremburg, Germany the line-up took an unexpected change when bassist Mike Gonzalez was jailed for vandalising cars. NUCLEAR ASSAULT's Dan Likler substituted to get them through to the tour's completion. A notable UK concert, a three way billing at London's Hammersmith Odeon with Swedish Doomsters CANDLEMASS and UK Thrashers D.A.M. was filmed and issued as the video 'Three Way Thrash'. Hitting the USA once again, a full-blown tour with OVERKILL took them through to finalising the world tour with a short burst of gigs allied with TESTAMENT and SAVATAGE. To maintain momentum, a radio broadcast was put out as the live album 'Live Scars' in 1990.

Their next album, 'Time Does Not Heal', increased the crunch factor courtesy of some skillful production tactics employed by Terry Date. Pursuing a much more technical approach, DARK ANGEL's press releases at the time boasted that 'Time Does Not Heal' was armed with an arsenal of 246 riffs. European gigs found RE-ANIMATOR as opening act. Despite laudatory reviews, and having just delivered their biggest selling record to date, DARK ANGEL was set to implode. In late 1991 Brett Eriksen was replaced by former SILENT SCREAM guitarist Chris McCarthy but DARK ANGEL was to collapse when Ron Rinehart bowed out in September 1992.

Rinehart became a Christian in 1992 although this did not stop his Metal endeavours, forging HUNGER alongside colleague Eric Meyer, bassist Greg Rowe and drummer R.D. Davis. This outfit issued a three song 1994 demo before calling it a day. Subsequently Rinehart founded OIL with former DECEIVER, DESIRE and CAPTAIN BLACK guitarist Blake Nelson. OIL issued the 'Refine' album for Kaluboné Records. Meyer made a name for himself as a producer, working with TRANSMETAL and RECIPIENTS OF DEATH.

Hoglan joined DEATH in 1994 for their 'Individual Thought Patterns' album. Rumours circulated in 1999 that DARK ANGEL was set to reform and a European tour schedule was announced in collaboration with ANCIENT RITES for that September. Sadly, fans did not see this proposal go any further. Hoglan would later re-emerge as part of the 2001 Death Metal combo TENET led by erstwhile SACRIFICE and Interzone vocalist Rob Urbinati and also including STRAPPING YOUNG LAD guitarist Jed Simon along with GRIP INC. bassist Stuart Carruthers.

Durkin's name was back on the scene with his new act DREAMS OF DAMNATION and the 'Let The Violence Begin' album. By September of 2001 the guitarist had joined the re-forged HIRAX. Rumours emerged during mid 2002 that a full blown DARK ANGEL reformation, comprising Ron Rinehart, Eric Meyer, Jim Durkin and Gene Hoglan, was set to take place. It would soon transpire though that the rhythm section for the revamped DARK ANGEL in fact comprised ex-MORGION bassist Jeremy Peto and drummer Al "Mayhem" Mendez of DREAMS OF DAMNATION although within a matter of days of the announcement Hoglan did indeed take his rightful place.

The band soon got back into action, taking on a North American tour during December with INTO ETERNITY acting as support. However, the 'new' line up actually debuted live in early October with an unannounced appearance at the conclusion of DREAMS OF DAMNATION's opening set at The Galaxy Theater in Santa Ana, California where Durkin's present act was lending support to KREATOR and DESTRUCTION. Al Mendez took on the drum role for this brief outing.

In December bassist Danyael Williams was enrolled and STRAPPING YOUNG LAD guitarist Jed Simon was announced as taking Durkin's place for West Coast and European gigs. However, within days Simon had scotched the proposed union. Durkin was kept active, alongside ABATTOIR frontman Steve Gaines, MASTABA six stringer guitarist Marcelo Lima and drummer Al Mendez, in the project band PAGAN WAR MACHINE. DARK ANGEL's proposed Summer 2003 comeback tour was scuppered when Ron Rinehart suffered a major injury to his back, the singer sustaining damage to the cervical region of his spine as well as several herniated disks in his neck. The group got back to work in September, cutting a version of METALLICA's 'Creeping Death' for a Big Deal Records tribute album 'Metallic Assault'.

WE HAVE ARRIVED, Metalstorm MS 8501 (1985). We Have Arrived / Merciless Death / Falling From The Sky / Welcome To The Slaughter House / No Tomorrow / Hell's On It's Knees / Vendetta.
DARKNESS DESCENDS, Under One Flag FLAG 6 (1986). Darkness Descends / The Burning Of Sodom / Hunger Of The Undead / Merciless Death / Death Is Certain (Life Is Not) / Black Prophecies / Perish In Flames.
Merciless Death, Azra MS 8602 (1986) (USA promotion). Merciless Death / We Have Arrived.
LEAVE SCARS, Under One Flag FLAG 30 (1989). Leave Scars / Death Of Innocence / Promise Of Agony / Never To Rise Again / No One Answers / Worms / Immigrant Song / Cauterization / Older Than Time Itself / Action / I Don't Care About You.
LIVE SCARS, Under One Flag FLAG 42 (1990). Leave Scars / The Burning Of Sodom / Never To Rise Again / The Promise Of Agony / We Have Arrived / Death Is Certain (Life Is Not) / The Death Of Innocence / I Don't Care About You.
TIME DOES NOT HEAL, Under One Flag FLAG 54 (1991). Time Does Not Heal / Pain's Invention, Madness / Act Of Contrition / The New Priesthood / Psychosexuality / An Ancient Inherited Shame / Trauma And Catharsis / Sensory Deprivation / A Subtle Induction.

DARKANE

HELSINGBORG, SWEDEN — *Andreas Sydow (vocals), Christofer Malmström (guitar), Klas Ideberg (guitar), Jörgen Löfberg (bass), Peter Wildoer (drums).*

DARKANE founders guitarist Christofer Malmström, bass player Jörgen Löfberg and drummer Peter Wildoer were previously members of noted technical Metal band AGRETATOR. Both Malmström and Wildoer had also been involved with eighties Power Metal band ZANINEZ. The duo forged DARKANE with the enlistment of second guitarist Klas Ideberg of Helsingborg Thrashers HYSTE´RIAH G.B.C., bassist Jörgen Löfberg and singer Lawrence Mackrory, of irreverent Thrashers F.K.Ü. (Freddy Krueger's Ünderwear), and bowed in with the impressive 'Rusted Angel' record. Released originally by Wrong Again Records in Scandinavia, US license was granted to Regain Records who re-issued the album adding extra live tracks.

Ex-vocalist Lawrence Mackrory would guest session on the 1998 THE MIST OF AVALON record as backing singer and also the 1999 ANDROMEDA debut album 'Extension Of The Wish'. He would later found FORCEFEED releasing an EP 'Soil', later changing this band name to SEETHINGS.

DARKANE reconvened for a sophomore Daniel Bergstrand produced opus entitled 'Insanity'. This outing also marked the debut of new vocalist Andreas Sydow. Promoting 'Insanity' the band would put in their inaugural United States show at the 'Milwaukee Metalfest' in 2001. Japanese versions of the album, released on the Toys Factory label, would see a bonus track with a live rendition of 'Convicted'.

Jörgen Löfberg and guitarist Klas Ideberg, along with SOILWORK's drummer Henry Ranta and vocalist Henrik Sjöwall and guitarist Mattias Svensson would forge a project band entitled THE DEFACED. Ideberg is also involved with TERROR 2000.

DARKANE would be set to release a new album, 'Expanding Senses', co-produced by Daniel Bergstrand and former MISERY LOVES COMPANY member Örjan Örnkloo, in August of 2002 through Nuclear Blast. Coincidently the same production team would work on ex-DARKANE member Lawrence Mackrory's SEETHINGS debut album. Mackrory also figured on THE DUSKFALL debut 'Frailty' as a session guest. Peter Wildoer found time in his schedule to act as session drummer for Gothic Metal band DAWN OF OBLIVION.

The band put in a short burst of UK shows during November packaged with CRIMINAL and DESCENT and Dutch gigs supported by FUELBLOODED before travelling to Japan for gigs with MASTODON and HIGH ON FIRE. DARKANE would lend support to BEHEMOTH for gigs in Poland during December.

The band's continuing ascendancy would be further progressed as DARKANE was confirmed as participants in the April 2003 European 'No Mercy' festivals. The group formed up part of a heavyweight billing comprising TESTAMENT, MARDUK, DIE APOKALYPTISCHEN REITER, NUCLEAR ASSAULT, PROPAIN, MALEVOLENT CREATION, DEATH ANGEL, and CALLENISH CIRCLE. An extensive run of European shows in November caught the band packaged with DISBELIEF, MNEMIC, MYSTIC PROPHECY and headliners DEATH ANGEL. However, upon completion of these gigs Wildoer, having suffered from a wrist injury dating back to February, was forced out of band activities in order to recuperate.

DARKANE guitarist Christofer Malmström readied a solo project for 2004 release billed as NON-HUMAN LEVEL, this venture including studio contributions from MESHUGGAH bassist Gustaf Hielm, DEVIN TOWNSEND band and GOD AWAKENS PETRIFIED drummer Ryan Van Poederooyen and his DARKANE colleague drummer Peter Wildoer, the latter taking on a lead vocal role. Wildoer eased himself back into the drumming role by working up tracks with Rock n' Roll outfit BEN. Meantime ex-DARKANE frontman Lawrence Mackrory re-emerged in 2004 as bassist for Death Thrashers ENEMY IS US and also sessioned demos for SCAVENGER.

In January 2005 Andreas Sydow contributed guitar work for Spanish Thrash Metal band LEGEN BELTZA's conceptual track dubbed 'War of Wars' included on their album 'Dimension Of Pain'. That same month DARKANE set a working title of 'Layers Of Lies' for their new album, established for June 2005 release. Japanese versions added a traditional bonus track in 'Subliminal Seduction'. Meantime, guitarist Christofer Malmström signed a deal with France's Listenable Records for his solo project, NON-HUMAN LEVEL featuring DEVIN TOWNSEND drummer Ryan van Poederooyen.

October 28th in Lawrence, Kansas, marked the start of a US tour, the band forming up a bill comprising FEAR FACTORY, STRAPPING YOUNG LAD and IT DIES TODAY. Fellow

DARKANE

Swedish act SOILWORK was added to the bill from November 8th. Drummer Peter Wildoer joined up with SOILWORK on a temporary basis, covering on summer 2006 shows at the 'Festimad' event in Madrid, Spain plus shows in Piteå and Malmö. Guitarist Klas Ideberg also got in on the temping act, subbing for HYPOCRISY's October North American tour. That same month former singer Lawrence Mackrory sessioned on album recordings for French band SCARVE.

RUSTED ANGEL, War Music WAR0009 (1998). ::Iii:O:Iii:: / Convicted / Bound / Rape Of Mankind / Rusted Angel / A Wisdoms Breed / Chase For Existence / The Arcane Darkness / July 1999 / Frenetic Visions.
RUSTED ANGEL, Toy's Factory TFCK-87168 (1999) (Japanese release). ::Iii:O:Iii:: / Convicted / Bound / Rape Of Mankind / Rusted Angel / A Wisdoms Breed / Chase For Existence / The Arcane Darkness / July 1999 / Frenetic Visions / Relief In Disguise.
INSANITY, Toy's Factory TFCK-87237 (2001) (Japanese release). Calamitas / Third / Emanation Of Fear / Impure Perfection / Hostile Phantasm / Psychic Pain / 000111 / The Perverted Beast / Distress / Inauspicious Coming / Pile Of Hate / Inverted Spheres / Convicted (Live).
INSANITY, Nuclear Blast NB 602-2 (2001). Calamitas / Third / Emanation Of Fear / Impure Perfection / Hostile Phantasm / Psychic Pain / 000111 / The Perverted Beast / Distress / Inauspicious Coming / Pile Of Hate / Inverted Spheres.
EXPANDING SENSES, Nuclear Blast NB 1021-2 (2002). Innocence Gone / Solitary Confinement / Fatal Impact / Imaginary Entity / Violence From Within / The Fear Of One's Self / Chaos Vs Order / Parasites Of The Unexplained / Submission.
EXPANDING SENSES, Toy's Factory TFCK-87290 (2002) (Japanese release). Innocence Gone / Solitary Confinement / Fatal Impact / Imaginary Entity / Violence From Within / The Fear Of One's Self / Chaos Vs Order / Parasites Of The Unexplained / Submission / Growing Hate.
LAYERS OF LIES, Nuclear Blast NB 1459-2 (2005). Amnesia Of The Wildoerian Apocalypse / Secondary Effects / Organic Canvas / Fading Dimensions / Layers Of Lies / Godforsaken Universe / Klastrophobic Hibernation / Vision Of Degradation / Contaminated / Maelstrom Crisis / Decadent Messiah / The Creation Insane.
LAYERS OF LIES, Toy's Factory TFCK-87393 (2005) (Japanese release). Amnesia Of The Wildoerian Apocalypse / Secondary Effects / Organic Canvas / Fading Dimensions / Layers Of Lies / Godforsaken Universe / Klastrophobic Hibernation / Vision Of Degradation / Contaminated / Maelstrom Crisis / Decadent Messiah / The Creation Insane / Subliminal Seduction.

DAVE LOMBARDO

USA — Cuban born drummer Dave Lombardo is a renowned figure in the Rock world for taking speed drumming to new levels with SLAYER. Lombardo later joined GRIP INC. His first solo album, 1999's 'Vivaldi—The Meeting', working with Lorenzo Arruga, is a brave experiment in unifying Vivaldi's classical music with Metal drumming. The album includes contributions from Alberto Contini, former front man with Italian Thrash merchants BULLDOZER. Besides Lombardo's revered tenure with SLAYER the man has made his mark with GRIP INC. over three albums, TESTAMENT's 'The Gathering' opus, the FANTOMAS union with erstwhile FAITH NO MORE man Mike Patton and Buzz Osbourne of the MELVINS and the all star VOODOOCULT collaboration. The drummer has also featured on Jazz Rock records in league with John Zorn and issued his own instructional CD / book package with Chuck Silverman.

Lombardo rejoined SLAYER for tour work in the closing days of 2001. Towards the close of 2002, with SLAYER's world tour complete, the drummer hit the club circuit with his side act PHILM which also numbered the CIVIL DEFIANCE duo vocalist/guitarist Gerry Nestler and bassist Juan Perez. Touring across Europe with SLAYER, Lombardo also made to time to put in individual drum clinic solo performances en route. Intriguingly, Lombardo would also be assembling a studio project entitled DRUMS OF DEATH, "homage to Def Jam's pioneering rock-rap fusions of the '80s", with MEAT BEAT MANIFESTO's Jack Dangers acting as producer and guitarist Vernon Reid of LIVING COLOUR guesting. The drummer also made time to guest on Finnish classical Metal act APOCALYPTICA's 2005 album, featuring on the track 'Betrayal'.

VIVALDI—THE MEETING, SPV 085-29572 CD (1999). Un Apparizione / Una Sfida: La Tempesta D'estate / Preludo Alla Pena Amara / Vedrö Con Mio Diletto / Nel Profundo / Agitata Da Due Venti / Un Congedo: Il Canto Del Pastore.

DE LIRIUM'S ORDER

KUOPIO, FINLAND — *Corpse (vocals), S.M. NekroC (guitar), Dr. Lirium (guitar), E.R. Insane (drums).*

DE LIRIUM'S ORDER, manifested in Kuopio during 1998 by guitarist S.M. NekroC ('a.k.a. Nekrocancer') and drummer E.R. Insane, offer a brutal, technical yet melodic brand of Metal. Initially the band started out as a quintet billed as ADRAMAN. Joined by guitarist V. Parviainen, and adopting the revised title of DE LIRIUM'S ORDER, their first experimental recordings, 'Termination In Surreal', would be caught on tape at the Perkele Studios in Kuopio.

The second set, February 2003's 'Morbid Brains', with Corpse, of WINTERWOLF, DEATHCHAIN, TWISTED SILENCE and TROLLHEIM'S GROTT, now having assumed lead vocal duties, was recorded by S.M. NekroC in his own Midgard Studio, these tracks leading to a contract with Woodcut Records in the Summer 2003. DE LIRIUM'S ORDER cut their opening commercial shot, a projected title of 'Extermination Network' being switched to 'Victim no. 52', at Tico Tico Studios in Kemi. Besides Corpse, session vocals came from Rutto von Kuolio.

On 15th April 2005 DE LIRIUM'S ORDER frontman Tuomas "Tuoppi" Lintulaakso was stabbed to death in Helsinki. The following month drummer EpiDemic joined up with SHADE EMPIRE. During 2005 Corpse was also operational with DEMILICH.

TERMINATION IN SURREAL, De Lirium's Order (2002). Introduction / Termination In Surreal / Metempsykhosis / Terve Ruumis, Sairas Sielu / Suolla / Koskenkorva, -30C / Of Hollow And Midwinter Night / Kalpea Muisto / Too Drunk / Convent Orgia / De Lirium's Ultimate Quietus.
Morbid Brains, De Lirium's Order (2003). Abomination / Through The Eyes Of A Murderer / The Sounds Of Mutilation / Masterpiece Of A Morbid Mind.
VICTIM NO. 52, Woodcut CUT 031 (2004). Sanctuary Of Incineration / Abomination / The Art Of Butchering / Masterpiece Of A Morbid Mind / Victim no. 52 / Through The Eyes Of A Murderer / Nightmare In Apartment 213 / Dr. Lirium Orders: Suffering / Pathologist's Perverse Fantasies / The Sunrise.

DEAD HEAD

KAMPEN, HOLLAND — *Tom Van Dijk (vocals / bass), Robbie Woning (guitar), Ronnie Van Der Wey (guitar), Hans Spijker (drums).*

Kampen Thrash Metal band. DEAD HEAD's demo, 'The Festering', secured a deal with Rising Sun Records. The first album 'The Feast Begins At Dawn', issued in 1992 by Bad Taste Recordings, sported artwork from Garry Sharpe-Young. DEAD HEAD supported the likes of SEPULTURA, SKYCLAD, GOREFEST and CANDLEMASS. Drummer Hans Spijker was replaced by Marco Kleinnibbellink, previously a member of ADETAR. Guitarists Robbie Woning and Ronnie Van Der Wey, both holding BEYOND BELIEF credentials.

The 1999 album 'Kill Division' includes an SAXON cover tune 'Heavy Metal Thunder'. Drummer Hans Spijker was briefly a member of Doom band MYSTIC CHARM during 2000. That same year Hammerheart/Unveiling The Wicked issued the DEAD HEAD compilation 'Come To Salem'.

Live work in the latter half of 2002 witnessed supports to EXODUS and SADUS. DEAD HEAD drew in new members in early 2003, Johan Wesdijk of INQUISITOR and PLEURISY on vocals and Alex Geerts, of BRAIN IMPLOSION and YOGHERT, on bass guitar.

The band reinstated Tom van Dijk in August 2003 in preparation for a new studio album through Cold Blood Industries. A 2004 single, 'Dog God' on Fadeless Records, would include a cover of IRON MAIDEN's 'Total Eclipse'. This release, on 10" vinyl, was restricted to just 399 copies.

A new album, 'Haatland' recorded at Hansen studios in Ribe, Denmark with producer Jacob Hansen, was set to follow via Extremity Records in September 2005.

THE FEAST BEGINS AT DAWN, Bad Taste Recordings IRS972226 (1992) (CD release). Untergang Des Abendlandes / Saved / Desolated By The Shining / In Your Room / Below The Earth / Slay Your Kids / Rites Of Kandar / The Tribulation / Pesticide / The Festering / From Belial / The Feast Begins At Dawn.
DREAM DECEIVER, Bad Taste Recordings IRS 972.233 (1993). Angel Heart / House Of Ambience / Repulsive Emission / Unholy / Dream Deceiver / I Or The Needle / Crimson Remains / Shifting Sands / Dying Angels / Spiritual Suicide.
KILL DIVISION, Coldblood Industries CXR 11022 (1999). Kill Division / Cold Being / Waste Of Skin / Six / Mahler / Sprayed Into Oblivion / Wings On Fire / Where Silence Dwells / The Hustler / Until The Sun Appears / Souls Of Ice / Heavy Metal Thunder.
Dog God, Fadeless (2004) (10" vinyl single. Limited edition 399 copies). Dog God / Desire / Total Eclipse / Identity.
HAATLAND, Extremity (2005). Faust II / Montana / Phantom Palace / Supreme Forgery / Last Server Down / Serial Divorce / Mesfeken / Dog God / Desire / Nosferatu.

DEAD SAMARITAN

HÄMEENLINNA, FINLAND — *Pasi Lehtinen (vocals), Marko Saarinen (guitar), Marcus Moberg (bass), Janne Honkanen (drums).*

Hämeenlinna Death / Thrash act DEAD SAMARITAN, mentored by 20/20 VISION, SHARPEVILLE and AGUSTA BELLS guitarist Marko Saarinen, started out under a formative title of THE BEAUTY OF DYING. During 2000 the band was built up with the incorporation of singer Pasi Lehtinen, BLASHEMIA, JALOSTAMO and ARCADIAN drummer Janne "Homicide" Honkanen with the SHARPEVILLE credited Marcus Moberg on bass. Some six months later Teemu Raunio, of WITHERED GARDEN, was added on second guitar.

In September of 2001 THE BEAUTY OF DYING cut their debut, three song demo 'First Kill'. Their inaugural concert would be held at the Lahti 'Hellbound 3' event on 8th March 2002 sharing the stage with MUSTAN KUUN LAPSET, BEFORE THE DAWN, GLORIA MORTI, NOWEN and FUNERIS NOCTURNUM. Following this gig the band, drafting Jussi Leppänen to replace Raunio, adopted the DEAD SAMARITAN title. A promotional session entitled 'Dark Matter' was laid down in January of 2003. The demo 'Bone Hill Revelation', limited to 200 copies, was issued in July 2004.

Guitarist Jussi Leppänen exited in 2005.

Dark Matter, (2003) (Demo limited to 300 copies). Intro / The Gateway / Dark Matter / Skeleton On Your Shoulder.

Bone Hill Revelation, Dead Samaritan (2004) (Demo limited to 200 copies). Bone Hill Revelation (Intro) / Bleeding Ground / Battered Beyond Recognition / Nemesis Thy Name Is Sacred / Through The Cleansing Fire.

DEAD TO FALL

CHICAGO, IL, USA — *Jonathan Hunt (vocals), Bryan Lear (guitar), Seth Nichols (guitar), Justin Jakimiak (bass), Dan Craig (drums).*

Northern Chicago Metalcore outfit. DEAD TO FALL signed to Victory Records in January 2002 but lost the services of guitarist Matt Hartman that April. Their debut, 'Everything I Touch Falls to Pieces', would see production credits going to Barry Poynter. Live promotion commenced with US East Coast touring sharing stages with CALIBAN prior to inclusion on the nationwide 'Summer Blasphemy' dates packaged with INCANTATION, IMPALED, VEHEMENCE and DECAPITATED. August shows had the band paired with ONE NATION UNDER preceding headliners leading into November opening slots to MASTODON and ATREYU. Drummer Dan Craig then opted out in December.

Back on the road with new drummer Brad King, the group united with REMEMBERING NEVER and UNDYING for gigs throughout April and May 2003. DEAD TO FALL underwent a major split in the ranks during August, both Brad King and guitarist Bryan Lear exiting, leaving only vocalist Jonathan Hunt and bassist Justin Jakimiak remaining. Closing this chapter in their career, DEAD TO FALL put in a final gig with ex-drummer Dan Craig filling in for the evening. New draftees would be former 7 ANGELS 7 PLAGUES guitarist Matt Matera and drummer Evan Kaplan. Gigs scheduled for that December saw a return for founder member Antone Jones on second guitar.

DEAD TO FALL entered Trax East Studios in April 2004 to record a new album with producer Eric Rachel. Nationwide gigs throughout May and June saw the band partnered with SHATTERED REALM and A LIFE ONCE LOST. In November former drummer Dan Craig announced he was working on a new band venture entitled VALE with ex-RIPPING CORPSE bassist Dave Bizzigotti along with guitarists Dan Pocengal and ex-DISCIPLE 13 man Shawn Brandon. The following month Craig was ousted from this new act.

DEAD TO FALL would support MARTYR A.D. and THE HAUNTED for UK shows in February 2004. US gigs throughout May and June of 2005 had DEAD TO FALL packaged with TWELVE TRIBES, LOSA and FIGHT PARIS. The band engaged in US dates throughout February 2006 backing HIMSA, A LIFE ONCE LOST, THE ACACIA STRAIN and DARKEST HOUR. A new Eric Rachel produced album, entitled 'The Phoenix Throne', emerged in April through Victory Records. That same month the group returned to the road backed by FROM A SECOND STORY WINDOW, LIGEIA and ED GEIN. The band teamed up with DARKEST HOUR and CEPHALIC CARNAGE for an extensive European tour in June.

The group hit the road with A LIFE ONCE LOST, NAPALM DEATH, IMPALED, ARSIS and ANIMOSITY throughout November and December as part of the 'Death By Decibels' US tour. To open 2007 in January the band aligned with TOO PURE TO DIE, BLOOD RUNS BLACK and NIGHTS LIKE THESE. The band teamed up with WALLS OF JERICHO, KITTIE, 36 CRAZYFISTS and IN THIS MOMENT for "The Funeral For Yesterday Tour" beginning in early February. With little respite, hey were rapidly back into touring mode once again, forming up a set of European shows throughout May alongside THROUGH THE EYES OF THE DEAD, ION DISSONANCE and DYING FETUS hitting Germany, the UK, Poland, Denmark, Croatia and Belgium.

EVERYTHING I TOUCH FALLS TO PIECES, Victory VR179 (2002). Prologue / Memory / Eternal Gates Of Hell / Like A Bullet / Graven Image / Words Ignored / Cost Of A Good Impression / Tu Se Morta / Doraematu / Preying on the Helpless / Balance Theory.

VILLAINY AND VIRTUE, Victory VR221 (2004). Torn Self / Bastard Set Of Dreams / Stand Your Ground / You've Already Died / Villainy And Virtue / Little Birds / Blood Of The Moon / Cross Section / Master Exploder / Epilogue.

THE PHOENIX THRONE, Victory VR264 (2006). All My Heroes Have Failed Me / Womb Portals / Smoke & Mirrors / Servant Of Sorrow / Chum Fiesta / Guillotine Dream (Slow Drugs) / Doomed To Failure / Clock Tower Corpse Collector / The Reptile Lord / Death & Rebirth.

DEAD TO THIS WORLD

UK / NORWAY — *Iscariah (vocals / bass), Goatpromoter Lava (guitar), Mord (drums).*

Thrash / Black Metal band DEAD TO THIS WORLD, initiated in Bergen, Norway during 2002, notably featured the ENCHANTED, IMMORTAL, NECROPHAGIA, AMOK, WURDULAK and THE CLAN DESTINED bassist Iscariah. Upon Iscariah's departure from Martin Walkyier's THE CLAN DESTINED venture in early 2005 he re-established DEAD TO THIS WORLD. On guitar would be Tony, ex-of ENCHANTED and TORTOISE WALTZ. Drums were handled by DEATHCON, AMOK, HELHEIM, CULT OF CATHARSIS, BLACK HOLE GENERATOR and TAAKE man Mord (a.k.a. Tormod Haraldson). Despite Iscariah's Norwegian heritage the project was based in the North of England during 2005. Demos were recorded on the April 23rd 2005 in Voltage Studios Bradford.

In May 2006 DEAD TO THIS WORLD announced a split 7" EP in collaboration with Norway's AUDIOPAIN through Hearse Records. The band entered Conclave Studios in Bergen on June 5th 2007 to lay down tracks for debut album 'The Anti Human Parade' with producer Bjørnar E. Nilsen. However, the line-up had shifted shape by this juncture, with both Mord and Goatpromoter Lava having exited. The JOTUNSPOR, GORGOROTH, SIGFADER, DET HEDENSKE FOLK, WARDRUNA, SAHG and BAK DE SYV FJELL credited Kvitrafn (Einar Selvik) took over on drums.

Dead To This World, Dead To This World (2005) (Demo). Goatpower / Dead To This World / Pacifist Terrorist.

Dominions Of Death, Iron Pegasus I.P.S 009 (2006) (7" single). Goatpower / Dead To This World / Pacifist Terrorist.

Audiopain / Dead To This World, Hearse (2006) (Split 7" vinyl single with AUDIOPAIN limited to 500 copies). Speak When Spoken To.

DEAD TROOPER

NORWAY — *Andreas Paulsen (vocals / bass), Morten Müller (guitar), Birger Larsen (guitar), Are Sorknes (drums).*

DEAD TROOPER was founded during 1998 by the former SFW and DAMAGE duo of guitarists Morten Müller and Birger Larsen. Müller also had a brief association with CADAVARIZED. Frontman Andreas Paulsen is active with LEFT AMONG THE LIVING. Drummer Are Sorknes has a tradition with GUTHRUM, GRIEF EMPORIUM, OPPOSITE OF SERENITY and MØRKEMANNMENNENE.

DEAD TROOPER released the 2002 'Axewielders' demo. The '100 % Norwegian Thrash Metal' tape, combined with a DVD, arrived in 2004. Parting ways with Paulsen, an EP, 'Spiritual Funeral', was delivered in July 2005. Nico Benz filled in as session bassist Meantime, DEAD TROOPER members Are Sorknes and Birger Larsen worked up the JUJ project alongside SUSPERIA vocalist Athera. DEAD TROOPER would be rejoined by Andreas Paulsen in May.

The band aligned themselves with the 'Venting the Anger' Scandinavian tour of December 2005 featuring SUSPERIA, DEMOLITION and MIKSHA. DEAD TROOPER parted ways with drummer Are Sorknes in January 2006. Paulsen joined Torbjørn Sandvik's GLITTERTIND project in February. BLACK COMEDY drummer Marius Strand was enrolled in July.

Axewielders, Dead Trooper (2002) (Demo). Hail To The King / Violence Spiral / Burning Watchtowers / Dead And Dreaming / Beauty Extoled.

100 % Norwegian Thrash Metal, Dead Trooper (2004) (Demo, CD + DVD). Creed Of God / Dead And Dreaming / Hail To The King / Bloodred And Strong / Mold Of The Unspeakable / Creed Of God (Live) / Mold Of The Unspeakable (Live) / Hail To The King (Live) / Violence Spiral (Live video) / Resurrection (Live video).

Spiritual Funeral, Dead Trooper (2005). Spiritual Funeral / Dead Trooper / Thirst And Envy / Unite To Destroy / The Deathmatch.

DEADSOIL

KOBLENZ, GERMANY — *Friedrich Weber (vocals), Boris Pracht (guitar), Jens Basten (guitar), Andreas Schüssler (bass), Christian Bass (drums).*

Modern Thrash outfit hailing from Koblenz, founded by former NIGHT IN GALES drummer Christian Bass in September 2002 in league with ex-COPYKILL guitarist Boris Pracht. They would soon be joined by Jan Olejnik on second guitar, Stefan Eutebach, formerly bass player of SIX REASONS TO KILL and Marcel Stroeter, erstwhile singer of Viersens Hardcore outfit DRIFT. Touring in early 2003 found the band supporting POISON THE WELL, picking up individual guest slots to THE HAUNTED, DARKEST HOUR and DEW-SCENTED and extending their live reach into Austria, the Netherlands, Belgium, Switzerland and Spain. Upon their return, DEADSOIL issued the debut EP 'Forever The Enemy' in June of 2003, after which Friedrich Weber took over the role of frontman.

Guitarist Jens Basten of NIGHT IN GALES replaced Jan Olejnik in May 2004 for a new album 'The Venom Divine', recorded at Berno Studio, Malmö in Sweden. Released by Lifeforce Records for regular CD issue the record was pressed onto a limited edition vinyl picture disc by Bastardized Recordings. Back on the road, DEADSOIL traversed Europe in August as part of the 'NewBornHate' tour alongside HATESPHERE and BORN FROM PAIN. The band opened 2005 as part of a touring package comprising CALICO SYSTEM, THE WARRIORS and REFLUX for North American shows throughout February.

As 2006 opened DEADSOIL revealed that bassist Stefan Eutebach had left for personal reasons. His replacement was soon found in Andreas Schüssler of REINCARNATED. Christian Bass temped for KORODED on their show at the K.S.E. festival in Jülich on September 16th.

Forever The Enemy EP, Poison Free (2003). Forever The Enemy / 40 Degrees / Reloader / Cold Play / Pushed Into Ruin.

THE VENOM DIVINE, Lifeforce (2004). Helvete / Enemies Will Suffer / The Promise / History Retold / Hate / Grey Cube / Hellsphere / Demons Hands / The Absolute Never / Despise The Logic.

SACRIFICE, Lifeforce LFR 060 (2006). Unspoken / Cross The Great Divide / The Day I Die / These Stings / Viper / Forget Everything / Echoes / Remembrance / Collapse / Ultimate Domination / True Belief / Sacrificed.

DEAFENING SILENCE

METZ, FRANCE — *Nicolas Griette (vocals), Michael Magagna (guitar), Guillaume Corsale (guitar), Phil Wax (bass), Eric Totti (drums).*

DEAFENING SILENCE, based out of Metz, is a speed orientated Power Metal act dating to 1997. Original members included singer Julien Milbach, of DIAMOND DUST, guitarist Guillaume Corsale, second guitarist Seb Spadafora, bassist Phil Wax and drummer Romain Silvano. Initially the group operated on the covers circuit, performing songs by the likes of AC/DC, IRON MAIDEN and HELLOWEEN.

First product came in the form of a nine track demo 'Tales From The Seven Stars'. Released in April 1998, these sessions were recorded at A.M.P.E.R studio in Clouange by Christelle Herment and Jean Pascal Boffo. Second demo 'Between Two Worlds' was recorded at the M.J.C in Silvange by Félix Paci and issued in March 1999. DEAFENING SILENCE's third demo attempt, 'Muse' emerging in April 2000, was cut at Pitch Black studio, Boulange with Greg Schaffer behind the desk.

Seb Spadafora opted out in 2001, being replaced by Michael Magagna. Brennus Music released debut album 'Edge Of Life' in May 2003. CD Maximun released the album for the Russian market. Two years later Julien Milbach stepped down and Nicolas Griette, of MORPHEUS EMBRACE, was inducted as new frontman in May 2005. Longstanding member Romain Silvano exited in 2006.

DEAFENING SILENCE enrolled nineteen year old drummer Eric Totti in January 2007. Second album 'Backlash' arrived in March.

Tales From The Seven Stars, Deafening Silence (1998) (Demo). Tales From The Seven Stars / Years Of Pain / The Core / Your Future Fall / High Tech War / End Of Time / Pure Lies / Minds Will Never Burn / Call The Seven Stars.

Between Two Worlds, Deafening Silence (1999) (Demo). Holy Steel—Protecting The Land Of The Free / Holy Steel—For The King / Childhood Enemy / The Realm Of Dream.

Muse, Deafening Silence (2000) (Demo). Break The Chains / Child Of The Star / Strong We Are / Don't Forget / New Born Century / Ending Your Days.

EDGE OF LIFE, Brennus (2003). Deafening Silence / Black Swansong / Heavenly Dream / Edge Of Life / Northern Star / Eden / Save My Soul / Terror And Despair / Strong We Are / Reborn In The Night.

BACKLASH, (2007). Dawn Of The Deaf / The Straight Line / Hellbitch / Too Young To Die / Backlash / The Seal Of The Damned / Judgement Day / When Will The Black Day End / Nothing Remains / Groundbreaker / Metallic Meltdown / Promised Land.

DEARLY BEHEADED

UK — *Alex Creamer (vocals), Phil Stevens (guitar), Steve Owens (guitar), Tim Preston (bass), Rob Ryan (drums).*

Manchester modern Power Thrash Metallers DEARLY BEHEADED, featuring former SLAMMER members guitarist Steve Owens and drummer Rob Ryan. debuted with 'We The Unwilling' demo in 1993. Having performed a BBC 'Friday Rock Show' session the group won MTV's best unsigned act contest and signed to major label East West to record debut EP. However, arguments ensued regarding a proposed cover depicting severed heads and the label's insistence that DEARLY BEHEADED ditch their drummer. The band were subsequently dropped, even though they had recorded for East West, and were picked up by Music For Nations following a British support tour to EXTREME NOISE TERROR in 1995.

The band's first album, 'Temptation', was produced by Colin Richardson and engineered by ex-SABBAT and GODSEND guitarist Andy Sneap. For the second effort, 1997's 'Chamber Of One', DEARLY BEHEADED brought in former CRITICAL MASS guitarist Darren Hough for a departing Phil Stevens. Colin Richardson was chosen once more on the production front as the band launched an uncompromising album that even proudly boasted of the absence of any guitar solos!

By 2000 Preston, Owens and Hough had created SLEATH with vocalist Darren Hircock and drummer Charly Moniz. In 2005 Preston returned to the scene with CITY OF GOD, a high profile band comprising erstwhile RAWHEAD and XENTRIX singer Simon Gordon, Jeff Singer, PARADISE LOST and ex-BLAZE and guitarist Mark Mynett, ex-KILL II THIS.

In A Darkened Room, Music For Nations CDKUT 168 (1995). In A Darkened Room / Break My Bones / Never / The Season Of Lies.

TEMPTATION, Music For Nations CDMFN 302 (1996). Behind The Sun / Witness / Temptation / Between Night And Day / Leaving Them Behind / We Are Your Family / Fuel For My Hatred / Break My Bones / Break My Restaurant / No Rest.

CHAMBER OF ONE, Music For Nations (1997). A Thankless Task / A Moment Of Clarity / The Escape / Chamber Of One / Generations / Giving Up The Lies / Faceless / Tribal Convictions / Dead Issue / Haunting Your Horizons.

DEATH ANGEL

SAN FRANCISCO, CA, USA — *Mark Osegueda (vocals), Rob Cavestany (guitar), Gus Pepa (guitar), Dennis Pepa (bass), Andy Galeon (drums).*

DEATH ANGEL excited Thrash Metal fans with their arrival in 1987 as the latest export from the rapidly expanding Bay Area Metal scene that threatened to engulf the world in the late 80's. The Filipino act, originally comprising teen cousins guitarist Rob Cavestany, Dennis Pepa on bass, Andy Galeon on drums, marked their individuality with a good degree of technicality and soon carved out a niche fan base on the San Francisco Metal scene. Although the band came together in 1982, very briefly being billed as DARK THEORY prior to adopting the DEATH ANGEL title from a book cover, it would be five years before their first album the widely admired 'The Ultra-Violence'.

The youngsters performed in the clubs initially as a standard Heavy Metal covers act, tackling tracks by artists such as JUDAS PRIEST, OZZY OSBOURNE, SCORPIONS, KISS, TYGERS OF PAN TANG and IRON MAIDEN. The trio became a quartet by introducing Dennis Pepa's brother Gus on second guitar. DEATH ANGEL's recording debut came during 1983 with the four song demo 'Heavy Metal Insanity'. Produced by Matt Wallace, quite incredibly drummer Andy was a mere 9 years old at the time of recording. At this juncture Rob Cavestany handled lead vocals. The band took on Kat Sirdorfsky as their manager and began a shift towards Thrash Metal, admitting new found influences from METALLICA, who the group supported at San Francisco's Kabuki Theatre in 1985, EXODUS and MERCYFUL FATE. Inducting new frontman Mark Osegueda, another family member, the new look DEATH ANGEL debuted as support to MEGADETH at The Stone in San Francisco on November 24th 1984. The 1985 follow up, entitled 'Kill As One', was notably produced by METALLICA guitarist Kirk Hammett. This fact alone provoked curiosity amongst the labels and DEATH ANGEL would be on the receiving end of offers from Enigma Records, Black Dragon in France and Combat Records.

DEATH ANGEL put their signatures down with Enigma Records to cut 'The Ultra-Violence' album, working with Davy Vain from VAIN as co-producer, during June of 1986. Underground tape traders circulated demos for the album well upfront of the actual release date, generating a fervour of interest for the band world-wide and this reputation was enhanced by East Coast dates supporting SLAYER. The album finally emerged in April 1987, being licensed to Music For Nations subsidiary Under One Flag for European issue. North American roadwork saw the band appearing at the 'Milwaukee Metalfest' event, capitalised on by package touring with BLOODFEAST and Canadian shows with SACRIFICE. The group's first live campaigning in Europe took place in September 1987.

The group laid down tracks for the Enigma released, near-concept 'Frolic In The Park' album, once again co-produced by Davy Vain, to close out 1987. Back in Europe, DEATH ANGEL embarked upon a further headline tour in June 1988 upfront of the September album release. CD issues of 'Frolic In The Park' hosted bonus tracks with 'Devil's Metal' and a cover rendition of the KISS classic 'Cold Gin'. MTV aided the group's national profile by plugging a video for the song 'Bored'. US concerts had the band traversing the country with RIGOR MORTIS. Still on the touring front, the group returned to Britain in December same year to support MOTÖRHEAD for a brace of gigs at London's Hammersmith Odeon.

DEATH ANGEL then hooked up with Geffen Records to release third studio opus 'Act III', this Max Norman produced album benefiting hugely from MTV exposure afforded to promotional videos for the tracks 'Seemingly Endless Time' and 'Room With A View'.

DEATH ANGEL hit Europe once again in mid 1990, a lengthy European tour seeing FORBIDDEN and VICIOUS RUMORS as support. Significantly, the band was also picked to headline the gargantuan 'Dynamo' festival in Holland. Debut Japanese shows took place in July, capitalised on by US concerts with FORBIDDEN in tow once again. However, band activities were suspended when, touring with CHRIS POLAND as opening act, the band were involved in a road accident in Arizona, hospitalizing vocalist Mark Osegueda, who lost parts of his toes, and drummer Andy Galeon. The latter's head injuries seriously affected his brain and recovery period took well over a year. Members of the Thrash community, including musicians from EXODUS, METALLICA, HEATHEN, FORBIDDEN rallied round to swiftly put on a benefit at The Omni venue in Oakland to raise funds to cover medical bills.

A quick-fire live album, 'Fall From Grace' captured on tape at the Amsterdam Paradiso on July 9th 1988, emerged through Roadracer in December 1990. This product was withdrawn due to objections from the band.

The group pulled in ex-ATTITUDE ADJUSTMENT drummer Chris Kontos to cover for Galeon and put in a second Japanese tour in April 1991. During this time, Geffen records, believing the name DEATH ANGEL was detrimental to the band's interests, attempted to market the band under the abbreviated moniker of D.A. to promote the band through radio play but found little interest and subsequently dropped the band. The group soldiered on performing acoustic sets billed as THE PAST but enduring a further setback Osegueda departed in the same year, relocating to New York and retiring from the music business, leaving guitarist Rob Cavestany to handle lead vocals once again. By the end of the year the band were going under a new title THE ORGANIZATION releasing two albums 1994's 'Free Burning' and the follow up 'Savor The Flavor'. THE ORGANIZATION folded in 1995. Dennis Pepa subsequently created THICK AS THIEVES. During 1999 Osegueda, Cavestany and Galeon created SWARM with new bassist Michael Isaiah.

DEATH ANGEL buried the hatchet in August 2001 re-uniting for a one off gig at the 'Thrash Of The Titans' festival in aid of TESTAMENT frontman Chuck Billy's cancer treatment fund. DEATH ANGEL put in a 'secret' gig at The Pound venue in San Francisco in early July. Supported by DEPRESSOR, DEATH ANGEL, including stand in touring guitarist Ted Aguilar of S1FT, went under the pseudonym of KILL AS ONE. The band would also participate at the famed Dynamo Open Air festival in Holland and put on a pre event show at the Efenaar club in Eindhoven with SWARM, the side act of Andy Galeon, Rob Cavestany and Mark Osegueda acting as support.

The band's continuing resurgence would be further progressed as DEATH ANGEL were confirmed as participants in the April 2003 European 'No Mercy' festivals. The group formed up part of a heavyweight billing comprising TESTAMENT, MARDUK, DIE APOKALYPTISCHEN REITER, NUCLEAR ASSAULT, PRO-PAIN, MALEVOLENT CREATION, DARKANE, and CALLENISH CIRCLE.

DEATH ANGEL signed a multi-album record deal with Nuclear Blast Records in October of 2003, recording the comeback 'The Art Of Dying' set at SF Soundworks studios in San Francisco, California with producer Brian Joseph Dobbs. The band also laid down a version of METALLICA's 'Trapped Under Ice', contributed to the Big Deal Records tribute 'Metallic Attack'. Thankfully, the advent of 'The Art Of Dying' in April 2004 triggered a sustained, and long overdue, live strategy.

Touring plans for the Autumn saw the band joining up with the DANZIG headed 'Blackest Of The Black' tour, organised by Glenn Danzig and comprising DOYLE, featuring ex-MISFITS guitarist Doyle, Norwegian Black Metal pioneers MAYHEM, DEVILDRIVER and EYES OF FIRE. However, with just days to go before these dates the entire tour was abruptly cancelled.

The band allied themselves with TESTAMENT, FLOTSAM AND JETSAM and OVERKILL for a 'Thrash Domination 04' Japanese tour in September before unexpectedly announcing a

DEATH ANGEL

hook up as openers to the DEFTONES on a burst of West Coast dates commencing 28th September at the House Of Blues in Los Angeles. However, the band was pulled from these shows, apparently because this news was leaked prematurely.

An extensive run of European headliners announced November caught DISBELIEF, DARKANE, MYSTIC PROPHECY and MNEMIC as support. However, this trek was cancelled just days before its launch date. December gigs were then announced allied with WYKKED WYTCH, MERCENARY and ILLDISPOSED. The band opened 2005 with a burst of South American shows allied with fellow Thrash veterans NUCLEAR ASSAULT. US shows in April had the band packaged with VADER and KREATOR but these dates too were too be pulled. A position at the Dutch 'Waldrock' festival would also be cancelled.

Mark Osegueda announced the formation of side act ALL TIME HIGHS, this band featuring the singer alongside members of LICA-STO, TRES PISTOLAS, THE SICK and THE OOZIES. DEATH ANGEL announced a two day "Thrash Domination" stint at Tokyo's famed Club Citta on September 16th and 17th 2006 ranked alongside VENOM, SODOM, DRAGONLORD and ONSLAUGHT. In November the group was set to play at the Californian 'Wrestle Rock '06' events, held at The Redding Convention Center, Redding and The Rainbow Ballroom in Fresno, alongside Y&T and JANI LANE'S WARRANT. However, just days beforehand the group cancelled.

Heavy Metal Insanity, (1983). No Time For Love / The Hunted / Intruder / Barren Lands.
Kill As One, (1985). Thrashers / Kill As One / The Ultra-Violence.
THE ULTRA-VIOLENCE, Under One Flag FLAG 14 (1987). Thrashers / Evil Priest / Voracious Souls / Kill As One / The Ultra-Violence / Mistress Of Pain / Final Death / I.P.F.S.
FROLIC IN THE PARK, Enigma CDENV 502 (1988). 3rd Floor / Road Mutants / Why You Do This? / Bored / Confused / Guilty Of Innocence / Open Up / Shores Of Sin / Cold Gin / Mind Rape / Devil's Metal.
ACT III, Geffen 7599242802 (1990). Seemingly Endless Time / Stop / Veil Of Deception / The Organisation / Discontinued / A Room With A View / Stagnant / EX-TC / Disturbing The Peace / Falling Asleep.
FALL FROM GRACE-LIVE, Roadracer RO 93332 (1990). Evil Priest / Why You Do This? / Mistress Of Pain / Road Mutants / Voracious Souls / Bored / Kill As One / Guilty Of Innocence / Shores Of Sin / Final Death / Confused.
THE ART OF DYING, Nuclear Blast (2004). Thrown To The Wolves / 5 Steps Of Freedom / Thicker Than Blood / The Devil Incarnate / Famine / Prophecy / Spirit / IV / Land Of Blood / Never Me / Word To The Wise.

DEATH SS

ITALY — *Vampire (vocals), Death (guitar), Zombie (guitar), Mummy (bass), Werewolf (drums).*

Gothic horror Metal act DEATH SS date back to 1977 and have, over the years, become a cult institution, although the band has gone through various guises and titles; with the mainstay and lynch pin being founder Steve Sylvester. DEATH SS first made an impression with the 1981 demo tape 'Horned God Of The Witches'.

The first stable line-up of DEATH SS comprised vocalist Sylvester ('Vampire'), Paul Chain ('Death'), Claud Galley ('Zombie'), Danny Hughes ('Mummy') and Thomas Chaste ('Werewolf') and the group eventually debuted with a series of limited edition singles sold at gigs. Only 500 of each were pressed

In 1982 DEATH SS appeared on their first compilation album, 'Gathered', with the song 'Terror' and would then add the track 'Black And Violet' to the 1983 Italian Metal compilation album 'Heavy Metal Eruption'. However, DEATH SS split later the same year with Chain forming PAUL CHAIN VIOLET THEATRE. In the interim however Chain issued the 'Chains Of Death' single under the title of DEATH SS minus Sylvester.

Sylvester himself went solo and issued an EP of his own, 'The Free Man', using the services of ex-DEATH SS members. Having since reformed DEATH SS Sylvester now fronted the mothership act and his spin-off solo outfit SYLVESTER'S DEATH. A 1989 EP 'Vampire' was of note for including two cover versions from the cult 70's UK act BLACK WIDOW, namely 'Come To The Sabbath' and 'In Ancient Days'. A 1991 EP, 'Where Have You Gone?', also paid homage to another pioneering British act with a take on ATOMIC ROOSTER's seminal 'Death walks Behind You'. 1993's EP 'Straight To Hell' continued this pattern of honouring long lost acts, incorporating a rendition of HIGH TIDE's 'Futurist's Lament'.

The 1997 album 'Do What Thou Wilt', recorded in England, sees DEATH SS with a line up of Sylvester, guitarists Emil Bandera and Felix Moon, bassist Andrew Karloff and drummer Ross Lukather.

As a footnote, former DEATH SS drummer Mimmio Palmiotta is now a member of DOMINE appearing on their 1997 album 'Champion Eternal'.

Steve Sylvester guested on the 2000 TENEBRE album 'Mark Ov The Beast'. Chain founded LOOSIN 'O' FREQUENCIES in 1999 for the 'Regeneration' album.

DEATH SS cut their versions of 'Come To The Sabbat' and 'Ancient Days' to the BLACK WIDOW tribute album 'King Of The Witches'.

The 'Let The Sabbath Begin' album of 2001 comprised of new studio material, remixes and a live concert culled from the band's 2000 tour.

Erstwhile DEATH SS guitarist Steve Mineli would found NODE issuing the Thrash Metal 'Sterilized' mini album in 2001. Steve Sylvester contributed guest vocals to the track 'Vampire's Dance' on the 2003 album 'King Of Dreams' from Germany's SOLEMNITY.

DEATH SS engaged in 'The Horned God of the Witches' winter 2005 tour of Italy with support from ENSOPH. Strengthening this connection, Steve Sylvester donated guest vocals to a cover version of SOFT CELL's 'Sex Dwarf' included on ENSOPH's 2006 album 'Projekt X-Katon'. Sylvester also featured on the SCHIZO album 'Cicatriz Black' in 2006.

Evil Metal EP, Metal Eye (1983). Chains Of Death / Inquizitor / Schizophrenic.
IN DEATH OF STEVE SILVESTER, Metalmaster MET111 (1988). Vampire / Death / Black Mummy / Zombie / Werewolf / Terror / I Love The Dead / The Hanged Ballad / Murder Angels.
THE STORY OF DEATH SS 1977-1984, Minotaur DEA 101 (1988). Terror / Murder Angels / Horrible Eyes / Cursed Mania / Zombie / Violet Overture / Chains Of Death / Inquisitor / Schizophrenic / Black And Violet / The Bones And The Grave.
Vampire, Metalmaster (1989). Vampire / In Ancient Days / Come To The Sabbath.
Kings Of Evil, Metalmaster MET 127 (1989). Kings Of Evil / Gethsemane / Murder Angel.
BLACK MASS, Metalmaster MET 120 (1990). Of Evil / Horrible Eyes / Cursed Mania / Buried Alive / Welcome To My Hell / Devil's Rage / In The Darkness / Black Mass.

In The Darkness, Metalmaster (1990). In The Darkness / The Mandrake Root.
Where Have You Gone?, Contempo (1991). Where Have You Gone? / Death Walks Behind You / Where Have You Gone? (Extended version) / Horrible Eyes.
THE CURSED CONCERT—LIVE, Contempo (1992). Ave Satani—Peace Of Mind / Horrible Eyes / Cursed Mama / Lilith / Vampire / Family Vault / Terror / Baphomet / The Inquisitor / Templar's Revenge / Drum solo / Where Have You Gone? / Heavy Demons / Kings Of Evil.
HEAVY DEMONS, Rosemary's Babydisc 002 (1992). Walpurgisnacht / Where Have You Gone? / Heavy Demons / Family Vault / Lilith / Peace Of Mind / Way To Power / Baphomet / Inquisitor / Templar's Revenge / All Souls' Day / Sorcerrous Valley.
Straight To Hell EP, Contempo (1993). Straight To Hell / Futurist's Lament / Heavy Demons ('92 remix) / Baphomet (Live).
The Cursed Singles, Avantgarde Music AV012 (1995) (Limited edition. 666 copies.]. Zombie / Terror (Live) / The Night Of The Witch / Black Mummy (Live) / Profanation / Spiritualist Séance / In The Darkness / The Mandrake Root.
DO WHAT THOU WILT, Bossy Ogress 561 3016 20 BO (1997). Liber I: The Awakening Of The Beast / Liber II: The Phoenix Mass / Liber III: Baron Samedi / Liber IV: Scarlet Woman / Liber V: The Serpent Rainbow / Liber VI: Crowley's Law / Liber VII: Guardian Angel / Liber VIII: The Shrine In The Gloom / Liber IX: The Way Of The Left Hand / Liber X: Liber Samekh.
Baron Samedi, Lucifer Rising Records (1998). Baron Samedi / The Book Of The Law / Magick.
Scarlet Woman, Lucifer Rising Records (1999). Scarlet Woman / At Nighttime / Scarlet Woman (Live) / Baron Samedi (Live).
PANIC, Lucifer Rising Records (2000). Paraphernalia / Let The Sabbath Begin / Hi-Tech Jesus / Lady Of Babylon / The Equinox Of The Gods / Ishtar / The Cannibal Queen / Rabies Is A Killer / Tallow Doll / Hermaphrodite / Panic / Auto Sacramental.
Hi-Tech Jesus, Lucifer Rising Records (2000). Hi-Tech Jesus / Digital Redemption (Remix) / The Devilish Meetings / Virtual Messiah (Remix) / Jack The Ripper.
Lady Of Babylon EP, Lucifer Rising Records (2000). Lady Of Babylon / Love Resurrection / Lady Of Babylon (Remix) / Equinox Of The Gods (Orchestral version) / La Voie Lactee.
LET THE SABBATH BEGIN, Lucifer Rising Records (2001). Let The Sabbath Begin / Rim Of Hell / Let The Sabbath Begin (Pandemonium remix) / Hymn Of The Satanic Empire Or The Battle Hymn Of The Apocalypse / Ishtar (Great Mother Goddess Sexy Mix) / Let The Sabbath Begin (Live) / Baphomet (Live) / Lady Of Babylon (Live) / Baron Samedi (Live) / Equinox Of The Gods—Ishtar (Live) / Medley: Black And Violet—Inquisitor—Cursed Mama—Chains Of Death–Where Have You Gone?–Family Vault (Live) / Scarlet Woman (Live).
HUMANANOMOLIES, Independent (2002). The Sideshow / Grand Guignol / Hell On Earth / Pain / Mind Monstrosity / Sleep Of Reason / Miserere / Sinful Dove / Sympathy For The Devil / Circus Of Death / Feast Of Fools / Evil Freaks / American Psycho / Weird World / Abnormal.
Pain, Lucifer Rising Records (2003). Pain (Single version) / Pain (Madaski remix) / Crazy Horses / Pain (Video).
SEVENTH SEAL, Regain RR108CD (2006). Give Em Hell / Venus Gliph / Der Golem / Shock Treatment / Absinthe / Another Life / Psychosect / Heck Of A Day / S.I.A.G.F.O.M. / Healer / Time To Kill / 7th Seal / Four Horsemen.

DEATHCHAIN

KUOPIO, FINLAND — *Rotten (vocals), Bobby (guitar), Nuclear Corpse (guitar), Kuolio (bass), Kassara (drums).*

Kuopio based, aggressive Death / Thrash act DEATHCHAIN began life in late 1997 billed as WINTERWOLF. In this prior guise the band issued the January 2000 demo 'Death ... Will Come Your Way' and the January 2001 follow up 'Blood For Death'. Band mentor and frontman Corpse opted to reconstitute the band at this juncture, bringing in Bobby in guitar, Kuolio in bass and Kassara in drums under the revised banner of DEATHCHAIN. In early 2002 DEATHCHAIN entered S. Jämsen's Studios in Perkele to record the demo 'Poltergeist'. Upon completion of these sessions the band enrolled vocalist Tommi "Rotten" Virranta. 'Poltergeist' landed the band a deal with the Finnish label Dynamic Arts Records. Guitarist Nuclear Corpse also sessioned lead vocals on TWISTED SILENCE's 2002 demos.

Debut album 'Deadmeat Disciples', once again cut in S. Jämsen's Studios, would be recorded in the Autumn of 2003 for a release early the next year. DEATHCHAIN drummer Lauri Rytkönen would also operate as 'LRH' with TROLLHEIM'S GROTT and Black Metal band BLACK DEATH RITUAL. During 2005 Corpse was also operational with DEMILICH.

European DEATHCHAIN dates in November 2005, promoting the 'Deathrash Assault' album, which debuted on the Finnish charts at number 18, had the band supporting Swedish Doom veterans CANDLEMASS and German Thrashers DESTRUCTION.

In October 2006 DEATHCHAIN announced they had re-signed with Dynamic Arts Records for a third album dubbed 'Cult Of Death'. The band was forced to cancel their November 25th show at the Gloria venue in Helsinki when guitarist B. Undertaker was taken ill, suffering from heart infection and bronchitis.

DEATHCHAIN partnered with Industrialists TURMION KÄTILÖT for Finnish shows in April 2007.

Poltergeist, Deathchain (2002) (Demo). Poltergeist (The Nemesis) / Unseen Evil / I Am Terror / Undertaker.
DEADMEAT DISCIPLES, Dynamic Arts DYN003 (2003). Chaos Wartech / Rabid Vultures / Poltergeist (The Nemesis) / March Of The Thousand Legions / Carnal Damage / Undertaker / Skeletal Claws / Carrier Of Pestilence / Deadmeat Disciples.
DEATHRASH ASSAULT, Dynamic Arts DYN013 (2005). Return Of The Nemesis / Venom Preacher / Lepra Lord / Graveyard Witchery / Deaththrash Legions / Napalm Satan / Panzer Holocaust / Morbid Mayhem / Valley Of The Corpses. Chart position: 18 FINLAND.
Deathchain / Deathbound, Dynamic Arts DYN007 (2006) (Split 7" vinyl single with DEATHBOUND). Morbid Mayhem / Unleash The Fury.
DEATHRASH ASSAULT, Teichiku TKCS-85149 (2006) (Japanese release). Return Of The Nemesis / Venom Preacher / Lepra Lord / Graveyard Witchery / Deaththrash Legions / Napalm Satan / Panzer Holocaust / Morbid Mayhem / Valley Of The Corpses / Black Magic.

DEATHGUY

THAILAND — *Thanit Thepsitrakorn (vocals / bass), Verapol Emaree (guitar), Nuttaphum Prapaiboon (guitar), Suppakit Chuersuwan (drums).*

Bangkok based Blackened Thrash—Death Metal act formed in August 1998. Following DEATHGUY's 1998 'Introduction' EP the founding duo of vocalist / bassist Thanit Thepsitrakorn (Joe) and guitarist Verapol Emaree (Ong) added second guitarist Nuttaphum Prapaiboon (Imm) and ex-ANNULAR ECLIPSE drummer Suppakit Chuersuwan (Link) to the line up. Nuttaphum is also active with Death Metal combo BLACK FIRE whilst Thanit has numerous side projects including Porn Metal band SHE'S GORE.

DEATHGUY's second release, the cassette 'The Secondary Quest', arrived in 2000. Trinity Records compiled earlier demo sessions to assemble the 2002 album release 'The Legend Of Romancer'. Toward the close of that year the single track promotion single 'The Beast' was recorded. Guitarist Nuttaphum Prapaiboon bowed out in 2003 as DEATHGUY switched away from their Black-Death direction into pure, brutal Death Metal.

Signing to Singapore's Vrykoblast Productions, DEATHGUY released 'Concentrate The Annihilation' in 2004 recorded at Ghost Studio in Bangkok, the band credited themselves as Zuppakit "Cerebral Assaulter", Verapol "Krush Kill and Destroy" and Thanit "Vacuum Butchering & Cardiac Excavator". Zilent Zlaughter Productions also issued a three way split EP 'Siamese Brutalism Attack' in union with SHE'S GORE and LACERATE.

THE SECONDARY QUEST—THE LEGEND OF ROMANCER, Trinity THK001 (2000). Ballad Of Sunset / Zero Frontier / Lust Murder / Lake Of Tears / Savage Seraphim / Black Swan / The Promised Land / Beheader / The Beast (Demo) / Marn / Den Sungkom.
Siamese Brutalism Attack, Zilent Zlaughter Productions (2003) (Split EP with SHE'S GORE and LACERATE). Beheader / The Beast.
CONCENTRATE THE ANNIHILATION, Vrykoblast Productions (2004). Hell Dominion (Reign Beyond Suffering / Degust The Blood (Sadistic Cannibal Meal) / Anathematic Damnation (The Fertilization

DEATHRASH (pic: Will Blochinger)

Of Damn) / Beheader (Human Head Collection) / Necronivora (Silent Murderous Supremacy) / Awake From Within (Cardiac Excavation) / Tyrant (Decaying Of All Civilization) / The Beast (Characteristic Of Devourer) / Cannibal Lust.

DEATHRASH

NJ, USA — *Tim Scherer (guitar), Pat Burns (bass), Pete Pollack (drums).*

New Jersey thrashers DEATHRASH came into being during 1985 when bassist Pat Burns severed ties with WHIPLASH. Originally Marc Grossman occupied the drum stool. The band's three track 1986 demo featuring WHIPLASH (and later SLAYER) drummer Tony J. Scaglione, singer John Scerer and guitarist Pat "Nemo" Nemeth, comprised of 'Lock Jaw', 'Blood For Blood' and 'Buried Alive'.

DEATHRASH added two new recruits in 1986 in the form of second guitarist Tim Scherer and drummer Peter Pollack. With this line-up the band contributed the track 'Buried Alive' to the 'Speed Metal Hell Volume 2' compilation album. Pollack left the band and was replaced by Rich McGahan but this proved to be the final DEATHRASH line-up.

Burns parted ways with the band to forge a new alliance entitled ZERO HOUR. Joining him in this venture were Scaglione on drums, former AGNOSTIC FRONT guitarist Gordon Ancis, ex-MASSACRE guitarist Robbie Goodwin and vocalist Joe Haggerty. This act soon folded with Scaglione joining LUDICHRIST.

Word arrived during late 2005 that DEATHRASH was planning on 20th anniversary concerts and the release of archive material. Emerging in 2006, 'Thrash Beyond Death' comprised the 'Faces Of Death' demo material, 80s live tracks from CBGB's in New York, The Grunge Club in New York, The Electric Banana in Pennsylvania and Club Hell, New Jersey plus new tracks 'Unfinished Business' and 'Thrash Beyond Death'. Original drummer Marc Grossman rejoined the band in September 2006.

THE 10'000 R.P.M. GROOVE ORGY, Pigs Ear PIG 001 (1989). Liquer Whore / Sexbeast / Now I Wanna Make Some Noise / 50'000 M.P.H. / Disciples Of Sleaze / Mindtrashed And Loaded / True And Wild / I'm Your Man / Queen Of The Night / Death Trash Rock And Roll.

DEATHROW

DÜSSELDORF, GERMANY — *Milo (vocals / bass), Sven Flugge (guitar), Thomas Priebe (guitar), Markus Hahn (drums).*

Düsseldorf Thrash band DEATHROW was created when guitarist Sven Flugge and drummer Markus Hahn split from Bremen's HÖLLENHUNDE in 1983. Relocating to Düsseldorf, the duo teamed up with vocalist / bassist Milo and second guitarist Priebe via advertisements in music magazines and formed SAMHAIN. However, an American act also existed of that name, so upon signing to Noise Records they changed monikers to DEATHROW.

The quartet's debut album was originally titled 'Riders Of Doom', but the album was repackaged with a different title ('Satan's Gift') after objections from the American market. DEATHROW toured Europe in 1986 with VOIVOD and POSSESSED.

DEATHROW's second album, 'Raging Steel', was another praiseworthy effort, but the band did little touring to back up it's release. Priebe left in late 1988 forcing the recruitment of former END AMEN and MEKONG DELTA man Uwe Osterlehner in time to play dates in Italy with CORONOR and record the third album 'Deception Ignored'.

RIDERS OF DOOM, Noise N 0044 (1986). Winds Of Death / Satan's Gift / Riders Of Doom / Hell's Ascent / Spider Attack / Slaughtered / Violent Omen / Dark Tales / Samhain.
RAGING STEEL, Noise N 0081 (1987). The Dawn / Raging Steel / Scattered By The Wind / Dragon's Blood / The Thing Within / Pledge To Die / Mortal Dread / The Undead Cry / Beyond The Night.
DECEPTION IGNORED, Noise NUK 128 (1989). Events In Concealment / The Deathwish / Triocton / N.L.Y.H. / Watching The World / Narcotic / Machinery / Bureaucrazy.
Towers In Darkness, Metal Machine (1991). Towers In Darkness / Somewhere In This Night / We Can Change.
LIFE BEYOND, West Virginia 084-57222 (1992). Life Beyond / Behind Closed Eyes / Towers In Darkness / Hidden Truth / Harlequins Mask / Homosaphiens Superior / Suicide Arena / Deathrow / Reflected Mind / The Remembrance.

DEATHWISH

UK — *Jon Van Doom (vocals), Dave Deathwish (guitar), Stuart Ranger (bass), Brad Sims (drums).*

Formed in 1983, DEATHWISH offered straightforward British Thrash. The band's initial demos secured a deal with Metalworks Records, although following the release of 'At The Edge Of Damnation', the band split for pastures new and promoted themselves sufficiently to gain major label interest in 1988, although opted for manager Tom Doherty's label GWR Records. The resulting 'Demon Preacher' album was promoted by supports to MOTÖRHEAD. In mid 1989 bassist Stuart Ranger left to be replaced by Ben Rumble.

AT THE EDGE OF DAMNATION, Metalworks VOV 667 (1987). Deathwish / In The Name Of God / For Evil Done / Sword Of Justice / Demonic Attack / Dance Of The Dead / Leaving Your Life Behind / Exorcist / Forces Of Darkness / Edge Of Damnation.
DEMON PREACHER, Roadracer RO 9478 1 (1988). Death Procession / Demon Preacher / Carrion / Visions Of Insanity / Symptom Of The Universe.

DECADENCE

STOCKHOLM, SWEDEN — *Kitty Saric (vocals), Kenneth Lantz (guitar), Daniel Green (guitar), Joakim Antman (bass), Erik Röjås (drums).*

Female fronted, Stockholm melodic Death Metal band DECADENCE, featuring the ex-DEVASTATOR guitar pairing of Christian Lindholm and Niclas Radberg alongside DEMENTED bassist

Kenneth Lantz, issued the 2004 demo 'Land Of Despair'. The band had started life billed as RAVENOUS, but would only undertake two gigs under this title before switching to DECADENCE. Singer Kitty Saric holds credits with DIVINE DOMINION and DEKAPITERA. Lantz shifted to the guitar role as Roberto Vacchi Segerlund was inducted on bass.

Ex-DEAFENING SILENCE drummer Patrik Frögéli would accede to the position as his predecessor Peter Lindqvist bowed out to prioritise his other acts CANOPY and A-BROS. Radberg would be substituted by rhythm guitarist Michael Sjölund of TRAMUMATAGE. The band, issuing the album 'Decadence', shifted shape once again and in 2005 was quoting a line-up comprising Saric, Lantz, second guitarist Daniel Green, bass player Joakim Antman with Erik Röjås on drums.

Ex-drummer Patrik Frögéli joined BLOODSHED in September 2006.

Land Of Despair, Decadence (2004). Despair / Heavy Dose / Among The Fallen / The Bell Tolls For Thee.

DECADENCE, Decadence (2005). Wrathful And Sullen / Heavy Dose / Black Eternity / Decadence / Foyer Of Hell / Among The Fallen / Dagger Of The Mind / War Within.

THE CREATURE, Decadence (2005). Red / Labyrinth / The Creature / Wasteland / Possession / Killing Perseverance / Desperate Secrecy / Inside.

3RD STAGE OF DECAY, HTI 001 (2006). Corrosion / Claustrophobia / 3rd Stage Of Decay / Theater Of The Absurd / Settle The Score / Sculpture / Invert / Endgame.

DECAY LUST

SARPSBORG, NORWAY — *Ulf Roppestad (vocals), Rino Fredh (vocals), Rino Olsen (guitar), Frank Wilhelmsen (guitar), Morten Skute (guitar), Geir A. Svendesen (bass), Steinar Jørgensen (bass), Henning Haugen (drums).*

Sarpsborg based DECAY LUST was founded during 1987 by the LOADER duo vocalist Rino Olsen, Rene Jansen and Øyvind. Rino was a close associate of the late Euronymous of MAYHEM. These ties saw MAYHEM logo designer Nella also scribing the DECAY LUST logo whilst Olsen featured as backing vocalist on 'All The Little Bird' on 'Deathcrush'.

DECAY LUST recorded the demo 'Poser Death', after which Olsen joined CADAVER whilst Øyvind united with BALVAZ. Regrouping, DECAY LUST drew in new members Henning Haugen, Geir A. Svendsen of METAL THUNDER, Frank Wilhelmsen from WITCHHAMMER and Ulf. This new unit recorded second demo 'Hobson's Choice'. Wilhelmsen then exited to enroll into ALGOL. Once more the band re-structured, bringing in guitarist Morten Skute of WITCHHAMMER and METAL THUNDER, vocalist Rino Fredh of SEVENTH ONE and TEARS OF SAHARA and Steinar Jørgensen of RAVENLORDS.

Hobson's Choice, Decay Lust (1993) (Demo). The Question / In Wonders And Horror / Peace Love And Hope / Manipulation Of Mind / Goodbye / Dread Head.

DECEASED

VA, USA — *King Fowley (vocals / drums), Mike Smith (guitar), Mark Adams (guitar), Lez Snyder (bass).*

Virginia Thrash Metal band. DECEASED band leader King Fowley also owns Old Metal Records, a label specialising in re-releasing 80's Metal underground classics, and operates the Trad Metal act OCTOBER 31 as well as DOOMSTONE. DECEASED was founded in the mid 80's and opened up proceedings with the inaugural 1987 demo session 'Evil Side Of Religion'. Pre DECEASED vocalist and drummer Kingsly 'King' Fowley had paid his dues with school band SLACK TYDE and the 1982 unit MESSENGER.

As DECEASED, Fowley, with guitarists Doug Souther and Mark Adams, played their debut gig in April 1986 performing a set of covers such as SODOM, BATHORY, SLAYER and MOTÖRHEAD at a friends house. Progress was swift and soon DECEASED were becoming a draw on the local club circuit.

However, tragedy would strike the band in March 1988 when bass player Rob Sterzel, along with two friends of the band, was killed in a hit and run incident. Stopping his car to change a flat tyre the three friends were mown down by a van driver. Needless to say the media had a field day when it was revealed Rob's band was titled DECEASED.

Following this huge setback the 1989 set 'One Night In The Cemetery' ensued. Two further cassettes ensued with 'Birth By Radiation' and 1990's 'Nuclear Exorcist' before DECEASED hooked up with Death Metal specialists Relapse Records for the debut album 'Luck Of The Corpse'. Frictions within the band though led to DECEASED performing to record the live 'Gutwrench' single minus Souther. Shortly after recording Souther quit with Mike Smith taking his place.

The 1995 release 'Death Metal From The Grave' comprises early demo material with live cuts and a cover version of VENOM's 'Die Hard'. In 1999 the band executed their interpretation of MERCYFUL FATE's 'Doomed By The Living Dead', featured on 'The Unholy Sounds Of The Demon Bells—A Tribute To Mercyful Fate' collection issued via Poland's Still Dead Productions.

DECEASED's 2000 album 'Supernatural Addiction' was produced by Simon Effemey. The band's live album includes a cover version of KROKUS's 'Headhunter'. DECEASED also cut various other covers for tribute albums and laid down in quick succession their takes on SODOM's 'Witching Hour', AUTOPSY's 'Charred Remains' and KREATOR's 'Tormentor'.

The 2002 album 'Zombie Hymns' would virtually be a textbook of King Fowley's Heavy Metal upbringing pulling together a collection of cover versions. Honoured acts included SLAYER with 'Chemical Warfare' and 'Die By The Sword", VENOM's 'Black Metal' and 'Die Hard', IRON MAIDEN's 'Wrathchild' and '2 Minutes To Midnight' and the MERCYFUL FATE pairing of 'Nuns Have No Fun' and 'Doomed By The Living Dead'. Also included would be the METAL CHURCH anthem 'Metal Church', SAXON's 'Fire In The Sky', IMPETIGO's 'Dis Organ Ised', VOIVOD's 'Blower', EXCITER's 'Violence And Force' and OZZY OSBOURNE's 'S.A.T.O.' amongst others. The solitary non traditional Metal offering would be a rendition of THE DOORS 'Not To Touch The Earth'.

A further 2002 album, 'The Radiation Years' issued by Cursed compiled early demos 'Birth By Radiation from 1988 and the following year's 'Nuclear Exorcist'. King Fowley suffered a major setback when it was discovered he had a life threatening blood clot on his lungs. Although he would recovered he was forced to relinquish his duties behind the drum kit. A new drummer, Dave "Scarface" Castillo of HATRED and OCTOBER 31 was added to the ranks in December. DECEASED projected a 10" split release in union with NUNSLAUGHTER for Metal War Productions entitled 'Torn Apart By Werewolves' set to feature one new DECEASED track and a cover of AGENT STEEL's 'Agents of Steel'. A new full length album, 'As The Weird Travel On', was also in the works.

A whole swathe of DECEASED re-issue packages would be lined up for 2004. The 1996 release Fearless Undead Machines' was set for reissue in a limited edition double gatefold LP format, pressed on 'zombie' coloured vinyl and released in March via Hell's Headbangers Records. Consequently Cursed Productions compiled the band's inaugural demo 'The Evil Side Of Religion' for commercial release packaged with live material from a 1980's show. Another release, entitled 'Legions Of Arghhhhh', collected together demos from the 'Supernatural Addiction' and 'Fearless Undead Machines' sessions, a limited edition of 500 copies via Trauma Records. New recordings were projected to see the light of day as a split 10" EP in alliance with Delaware based CRUCIFIER. Three DECEASED tracks included covers of RUNNING WILD's 'Ironheads', AGENT STEEL's 'Agents

DECEASED

Of Steel' alongside a newly reworked song from the band's past entitled 'Fading Survival'.

DECEASED entered Oblivion Studios in Upper Marlboro, Maryland in November to commence recording a new album 'As The Weird Travel On' for Thrash Corner Records, this set to be produced by former WRECKAGE drummer Kevin Gutierrez.

In July 2006 longstanding guitarist Mike Smith stood down, performing his final concert on the 29th at CBGB's in New York, and being swiftly replaced by Shane Fuegel of BIONIC MAN and DRUGS OF FAITH for a new album 'Surreal Overdose'.

LUCK OF THE CORPSE, 199 (0). Fading Survival / The Cemeterys Full / Experimenting With Failure / Futuristic Doom / Haunted Cerebellum / Decrepit Coma / Shrieks From The Hearse / Psychedelic Warriors / Feasting On Skulls / Birth By Radiation / Gutwrench.
THE THIRTEEEN FRIGHTENED SOULS, Relapse (1994). The 13 Frightened Souls / Robotic Village / Voivod / Planet Graveyard / Nuclear Exorcist.
THE BLUEPRINTS FOR MADNESS, (1995). Morbid Shape In Black / The Triangle / Island Of The Unknown / The Blueprints For Madness / The Creek Of The Dead / Mind Vampires / Into The Bizarre / Alternate Dimensions / Midnight / Negative Darkness / A Reproduction Of Tragedy.
DEATH METAL FROM THE GRAVE, (1995). Immune To Burial / Worship The Coffin / Birth By Radiation / Vomiting Blood / Virus / Deformed Tomorrows / Nuclear Exorcist / Shrieks From The Hearse / A Trip To The Morgue / After The Bloodshed / Sick Thrash / Futuristic Doom (Live) / Fading Survival (Live) / Haunted Cerebellum (Live) / Robotic Village (Live) / Die Hard.
FEARLESS UNDEAD MACHINES, Relapse RR 6957 (1997). The Silent Creature / Contamination / Fearless Undead Machines / From The Ground They Came / Night Of The Deceased / Graphic Repulsion / Mysterious Research / Beyond Science / Unhuman Drama / The Psychic / Destiny.
UP THE TOMBSTONES—LIVE 2000, Thrash Corner (2000). The Silent Creature / The Premonition / The 13 Frightened Souls / Robotic Village / The Triangle / Dark Chilling Heartbeat / Fearless Undead Machines / The Psychic / Headhunter / Sick Thrash.
SUPERNATURAL ADDICTION, Relapse (2000). The Premonition / Dark Chilling Heartbeat / A Very Familiar Stranger / Frozen Screams / The Doll With The Hideous Spirit / The Hanging Soldier / Chambers Of The Waiting Blind / Elly's Dementia.
BEHIND THE MOURNER'S VEIL, (2001). It's Alive / The Mausoleum / Zombie Attack / Reaganomics / New Age Of Total Warfare / Deathrider / Victims Of The Masterplan (I-V).
THE RADIATION YEARS, Cursed Productions CURSED 2014 (2002).
ZOMBIE HYMNS, Crook' D (2002). Black Metal / Violence And Force / Witching Metal / 2 Minutes To Midnight / S.A.T.O. / Blower / Doomed By The Living Dead / Dis Organ Ised / Die By The Sword / Not To Touch The Earth / Metal Church / Wrathchild / Bombs Of Death / Fire In The Sky / Nuns Have No Fun / Headhunter (Live) / Stay Clean / Die Hard / Tormentor / Chemical Warfare.

DECEIVER

TURKU, FINLAND — *Kyle (vocals / guitar), Tane (guitar), Janne (bass), Harri Hakala (drums).*

Turku Thrash Metal band DECEIVER featured drummer Harri Hakala, having scene ties to ANNIHILATUS, VORDVEN, LUCIFERASE, ENERCHY, PILGRIMS FROM TARTARUS and RILKÁ. The first DECEIVER product, the 'Mary's Last Prayer' 7" EP, arrived in 1991. a succession of demos followed including 'Eternal Massacre' in November 1992, recorded at Air-Raid Shelter Studio in Raisio. Following up would be 'Raped Classics', comprising such eclectic covers as the DEAD KENNEDYS 'Too Drunk To Fuck', SEX PISTOLS 'God Save The Queen', METALLICA's 'Enter Sandman', GUNS N' ROSES 'Paradise City', PARADISE LOST's 'Eternal', TERVEET KÄDET's 'Tornion Kevät', NAPALM DEATH's 'Deceiver' and NIRVANA's 'Smells Like Teen Spirit', plus 'Rules Of Conduct', both issued in 1993. The nine track 'Nocturnal Death' session arrived in January 1994.

Mary's Last Prayer, Deceiver DCS 001 (1991) (7" vinyl single). Mary's Last Prayer / The Nothing.
Eternal Massacre, Deceiver (1992) (Cassette demo). Awake / Sleep / Funeral March / Domestic Violence ... Why? / Last Chapter.
Raped Classics, Deceiver (1993) (Demo). Too Drunk To Fuck / Tornion Kevät / God Save The Queen / Medley: Smells Like Teen Spirit / Enter Sandman / Paradise City / Eternal / Deceiver.
Rules Of Conduct, Deceiver (1993) (Demo). When You're Dead / Women & Children First / Requiem / Ominous Future / Down & Out / Disappointment To Society.
Nocturnal Death, Deceiver (1994) (Demo). Sick Pleasures Of A Twisted Mind / Blood Is Not Enough / More Than A Million Dead / Swell / Decline / Weak Christians / Sign Of Inhumanity / Demonologue / Lady Domina.

DEFENDER KFS

VIENNA, AUSTRIA — *Harald Mezensky (vocals), Gregor Marboe (guitar), Martin Arzberger (guitar), Alexander Mayer (bass), Peter Kelman (drums).*

Viennese War Metal outfit forged in July 1998 by former PENDRAGON man Gregor 'Gore' Marboe and guitarist Andy Hammer. Gore's tradition included credits with bands such as JORMUNGARD, ENDKRIEG, PROJECT X, ESCHATA, CRYOSPHERE and even as drummer for KULDEBLOD. In March 1999 DEFENDER KFS rehearsals featured Oliver Schlögl, ex-PENDRAGON and CRYOSPHERE, on bass and Rene Binder, of PARENTAL ADVISORY, on drums. In April Patrick Tamerus took on the lead vocal position.

Following initial demos bassist HateMachine enrolled. Dispensing with some early members, Metzler of JORMUNDGAND took over the lead vocal position and, in October 1999, Beisser (a.k.a. Niko Scharf) of DEVESTATION took control of the drums. In April 2000 Hammer departed and HateMachine filled in on guitar as Axe.L.X. (Alex Burger) of PENDRAGON and CRYOSPHERE became the band's new bass player. Live gigs would be undertaken utilising the services of Bernhard 'Burny' Brem from JORMUNDGAND as session guitarist. After a DEFENDER KFS appearance at the 'Earshot' festival both Beisser and Axe.L.X exited, the latter to concentrate his efforts on his solo venture ESCHATA. Beisser also served a term with PARENTAL ADVISORY.

The band issued the 'Feed The Worms' promotional session in 2004. Bass player Rainer Schmidt exited the following year. In 2006 DEFENDER KFS was put on hold as Marboe was hired by PUNGENT STENCH as replacement for bassist Reverend Mausna. DEFENDER KFS completed work on second album 'Self Impact' in October 2006. That same month saw the introduction of new members bassist Alexander Mayer of MOLOKH, ESOPHAGUS and SEEDS OF SORROW plus guitarist Martin Arzberger, also of MOLOKH.

THE COMMAND, (2000). Northman Salvation / Halls Of Fire / Cold (Mind War) / The Sign Of Hell / Hellfire Seed / Literary Pandemonium / The Command / Labyrinth Of You / Post Mortal Gate.

DEFIANCE

SAN FRANCISCO, CA, USA — *Ken Elkington (vocals), Doug Harrington (guitar), Jim Adams (guitar), Mike Kaufmann (bass), Matt Vander Ende (drums).*

DEFIANCE is a cult Thrash Metal outfit, highly regarded by fellow musicians of the genre but ultimately failing to achieve a commercial breakthrough. The group was conceived in 1985 by guitarist Brad Bowers and drummer Matt Vander Ende in Oakland, California, building up to a full compliment of players with the induction of guitarist Doug Harrington and bassist Mike Kaufmann. Minus a singer, DEFIANCE performed its inaugural gig with Paul Baloff of EXODUS fame ad libbing. In the Summer of 1986 Harrington was usurped by former ATTRITION guitarist Jim Adams. Confusingly Bowers was then forced to exit and Harrington returned to his former position as DEFIANCE also located a frontman in Mitch Mayes, another ATTRITION veteran. Mayes tenure would be brief, and for their opening set of demos billed as 'Hypothermia' the group drafted new singer Ken Elkington. Band manager Ace Cook, also part of TESTAMENT's road crew, took the finished tapes to Europe where DEFIANCE was promptly offered a seven album deal by the Roadrunner Records label.

DEFIANCE's 1989 debut album 'Product Of Society' was produced by ANNIHILATOR guitarist Jeff Walters. By the following year Steev Esquivel had taken Elkington's place for the follow up 'Void Terra Firma' in 1990, this opus featuring a cover version of IRON MAIDEN's 'Killers'. The third album 'Beyond Recognition' was produced by Rob Beaton. In addition HEATHEN guitarist Lee Altus contributed guitar parts. Guitarist Brian Wenzel was drafted in late 1992. However, shortly after Jim Adams exited to join INDICA and Matt Vander Ende also left the band for a term with LÄÄZ ROCKIT. DEFIANCE was briefly rebuilt when Adams returned, former BLIND ILLUSION and HEATHEN vocalist Dave Godfrey White was inducted and new drummer Hugo Barientos installed.

Losing Steev Esquivel, DEFIANCE evolved into INNER THRESHOLD, recording demos with Rob Beaton acting as producer. Adams then bailed out once more, being superseded by Chris Long. Another transition in 1995 saw the band morph into UNDER by enrolling frontman Chris Long. Godfrey formed part of the 2000 HEATHEN reunion and Long took on lead vocal responsibilities. Steev Esquivel later went on to find prominence with SKINLAB whilst Adams created ULTRASPANK. Doug Harrington duly forged 'all star' Thrash outfit GALLERY OF SUICIDE.

DEFIANCE was reported to be plotting a reunion in 2004, confirming this conjecture before the close of the year. That same October Esquivel temped for EXODUS on South American tour dates. DEFIANCE drafted VENGINCE drummer Flatline (James Raymond) in July 2005.

In March 2006 word arrived that DEFIANCE had switched drummers and were in rehearsals with the VIO-LENCE, DEF IGNITION and TORQUE credited Mark Hernandez. The group entered Trident Studios in Concord with producer Juan Urteaga on September 15th to cut tracks for a brand new album. DEFIANCE guitarist Doug Harrington succumbed to a lengthy battle with cancer on November 14th.

PRODUCT OF SOCIETY, Roadrunner (1989). The Fault / Death Machine / Product Of Society / Forgotten / Lock Jaw / Insomnia / Deadly Intentions / Aftermath / Tribulation / Hypothermia.

VOID TERRA FIRMA, Roadracer (1990). Void Terra Firma / Deception Of Faith / Questions / Skitz—Illusions / Slayground / Killers / Steamroller / Checkmate / Buried Or Burned / Last Resort (Welcome To Poverty).

BEYOND RECOGNITION, Roadrunner (1992). The Killing Floor / Step Back / Perfect Nothing / No Compromise / Dead Silence / Inside Looking Out / The Chosen / Power Trip / Promised Afterlife.

DEFLESHED

UMEÅ, SWEDEN — *Lars Löfven (vocals / guitar), Kristoffer Griedl (guitar), Gustaf Jorde (bass), Oscar Karlsson (drums).*

Umeå's DEFLESHED are purveyors of Thrash infused Death Metal, heavy on gross lyrics and impenetrable vocals. DEFLESHED was forged during 1991 with an inaugural line-up of ex-CONVULSION guitarist Lars Löfven, Kristoffer Griedl and drummer Oskar Karlsson. This version of the band managed an eponymous demo before fracturing. Second session 'Abrah Kadavrah' saw the inclusion of erstwhile CREMATORIUM bassist Gustaf Jorde and lead vocals from Johan Hedman. Progress was such that DEFLESHED were included on the Nuclear Blast 'Grindcore' compilation and had three tracks from the demo issued as a 7" courtesy of the Italian Miscarriage label as 'Obsculum Obscenum' in December 1993.

Bassist Gustaf Jorde was added prior to recording of debut November 1994 EP 'Ma Belle Scalpelle' for the German Invasion Records concern. Karlsson left for GATES OF ISHTAR, and subsequently SCHEITAN and RAISED FIST, and in his stead came Matte Modin in time for the February 1996 released 'Abrah Kadavrah' album. 1997's 'Under The Blade' closed out with a cover version of DESTRUCTION's 'Curse The Gods'.

In 1998 DEFLESHED contributed their version of SEPULTURA's 'Beneath The Remains' for a tribute album. Japanese fans would be in for a treat with the 1999 'Fast Forward' album, their domestic variant including an extra seven live tracks. On the road in Europe during October of 1999, the group joined a heavyweight billing comprising MARDUK, ANGEL CORPSE, AETERNUS and CANNIBAL CORPSE.

The Hammerheart 2000 re-issue of 'Under The Blade' added new artwork and a whole swathe of bonus tracks including a cover of SEPULTURA's 'Beneath The Remains'. That same year 2000 Modin had bailed out to join DARK FUNERAL.

The band toured Japan during March 2001. During 2002 ex-drummer Oskar Karlsson was found to be active with THE DUSKFALL and Death n' Roll outfit HELLTRAIN.

A projected extensive run of European tour dates throughout March and April of 2003 found DEFLESHED acting as support act to GRAVE. However, these shows would then be cancelled and the band put together headline dates, dubbed the 'Battle Royal' tour with support from TAETRE. The Regain Records November 2003 re-issue of 'Fast Forward' hosted significant extra tracks in a 2002 version of the title track plus cover versions of NUCLEAR ASSAULT's 'Radiation Sickness', SEPULTURA's 'Beneath The Remains' and DESTRUCTION's 'Curse The Gods'. The band hooked up with DARK FUNERAL for a short burst of Italian dates in March 2004. Guitarist Lars Lofven would also aid THE DUSKFALL for live work.

The band entered Dug Out Studios in Uppsala to record their fifth studio album 'May The Flesh Be With You', sporting a cover rendition of MÖTLEY CRÜE's 'Red Hot'. Gustaf Jorde featured as backing vocalist on THE PROJECT HATE's 2005 album "Armageddon March Eternal (Symphonies Of Slit Wrists)'. Festival dates for DEFLESHED in the Summer of 2005 saw the re-inclusion of DARK FUNERAL drummer Matte Modin. However, in November the group announced it was to disband. A farewell show would be scheduled for Christmas day at the Fellini venue in Uppsala.

Ex-DEFLESHED bassist Gustaf Jorde announced new formation NAILSTATE to the world in early 2006, being a union with Paul Mäkitalo (a.k.a. 'Themgoroth') of DARK FUNERAL and INFERNAL, Peter Tuthill, ex-CONSTRUCDEAD and DOG FACED GODS and Stefan Norgren from ETERNAL OATH.

Defleshed (Rotting Inflictioner), Defleshed (1992) (Cassette demo). Satanic Séance / Rotting Inflictioner / Totalitarian Corporal Torment / Vacuited Soul / Phlegm / Defleshed / Rot In Agony.

Abrah Kadavrah ... , Defleshed (1992) (Cassette demo). Pulverized, Pasteurized Eyes / Vastus Ecclesia / Vintras Daughter / Obsculum Obscenum / Open Gates.

Body Art, Defleshed (1993) (Cassette demo). Necromantic Barbeque / Anatomically Incorrect / Mary Bloody Mary / Orbital Cavity Discovery / Forruttenels.
Obsculum Obscenum, Miscarriage MS002 (1993) (7" vinyl single). Obsculum Obscenum / Satanic Source / Phlegm.
Ma Belle Scalpelle, Invasion IR 009 (1994). Gathering Flies / Moribiance Blue Cafe / Simply Fall Towards / Many Mangled Maggots / Ma Belle Scalpelle.
ABRAH KADAVRAH, Invasion IR 019 (1996). Beaten, Loved And Eaten / Mary Bloody Mary / With A Gambrel / In Chains And Leather / Abrah Kadavrah / Gone With The Feaces / Anatomically Incorrect / On Gorgeous Grounds / Body Art ... / ... Pierced Through The Heart.
UNDER THE BLADE, Invasion IR 032 (1997). Farewell To The Flesh / Entering My Yesterdays / Eat The Meat Raw / Sons Of Spellcraft And Starfalls / Metalbounded / Under The Blade / Thorns Of A Black Rose / Cinderella's Return And Departure / Walking The Moons Of Mars / Metallic Warlust / Curse The Gods.
FAST FORWARD, Soundholic SHCD1-0032 (1999) (Japanese release). The Return Of The Flesh / The Heat From Another Sun / Fast Forward / The Iron And The Maiden / Proud To Be Dead / Snowballing Blood / Wilder Than Fire / Feeding Fatal Fairies / Lightning Strikes Thrice / Domination Of The Sub Queen / Speeding The Ways / Entering My Yesterdays / Mary Bloody Mary / Metallic Warlust / Under The Blade / Walking The Moons Of Mars / In Chains And Leather / Thorns Of A Black Rose.
FAST FORWARD, War Music WAR 011 (1999). The Return Of The Flesh / The Heat From Another Sun / Fast Forward / The Iron And The Maiden / Proud To Be Dead / Snowballing Blood / Wilder Than Fire / Feeding Fatal Fairies / Lightning Strikes Thrice / Domination Of The Sub Queen / Speeding The Ways.
Death—The High Cost Of Living, War Music RAW 003 (1999). Entering My Yesterdays / Mary Bloody Mary / Metallic Warlust / Under The Blade / Walking The Moons Of Mars / In Chains & Leather / Thorns Of A Black Rose.
FAST FORWARD, Pavement Music 32340 (2000) (USA release). The Return Of The Flesh / The Heat From Another Sun / Fast Forward / The Iron And The Maiden / Proud To Be Dead / Snowballing Blood / Wilder Than Fire / Feeding Fatal Fairies / Lightning Strikes Thrice / Domination Of The Sub Queen / Speeding The Ways / Under The Blade (Live) / Thorns Of A Black Rose (Live).
ROYAL STRAIGHT FLESH, Teichiku TKCS-85050 (2002) (Japanese release). Hand Over Fist / Fire In The Soul / Friction / Warborn / Feed On The Fallen / Royal Straight Flesh / Back For The Attack / Blood Brigade / Pick Your Poison / Dangerous When Dead / Brakefailure / Fast Forward / Radiation Sickness.
ROYAL STRAIGHT FLESH, Regain RR 0211-109 (2002) (European release). Hand Over Fist / Fire In The Soul / Friction / Warborn / Feed On The Fallen / Royal Straight Flesh / Back For The Attack / Blood Brigade / Pick Your Poison / Dangerous When Dead / Brakefailure.
RECLAIM THE BEAT, Teichiku TKCS-85116 (2005) (Japanese release). Stripped To The Bone / Abstinence For Turbulence / Chain Reaction / Bulldozed (Back To Basic) / Under Destruction / Grind And Rewind / Reclaim The Beat / Red Hot / May The Flesh Be With You / Ignorance Is Bliss / Aggroculture / Over And Out / Needless To Pray.
RECLAIM THE BEAT, Regain RR 051 (2005) (European release). Stripped To The Bone / Abstinence For Turbulence / Chain Reaction / Bulldozed (Back To Basic) / Under Destruction / Grind And Rewind / Reclaim The Beat / Red Hot / May The Flesh Be With You / Ignorance Is Bliss / Aggroculture / Over And Out.
RECLAIM THE BEAT, Regain North America 217 (2005) (USA release). Stripped To The Bone / Abstinence For Turbulence / Chain Reaction / Reclaim The Beat / Grind And Rewind / Under Destruction / Red Hot / Bulldozed (Back To Basic) / Ignorance Is Bliss / May The Flesh Be With You / Needless To Pray / Aggroculture / Over And Out.

DEFORME

CHILE — *Leo Pozo (vocals / guitar), Eladio Cordova (guitar), Carlos Alarcon (bass), Juan Marambio (drums).*

Death styled Thrashers DEFORME were created during 1995 as the brainchild of vocalist / drummer Leo Pozo. The band's inaugural roster included guitarist Alejandro Valenzuela and bassist Emilio Armero. This latter pairing would decamp to allow in new blood guitar player Octavio Meneses de la Barra and bass player Carlos Alarcon. Pozo would then switch to a guitar role when DEFORME pulled in RITUAL drummer Juan Marambio.

The band issued the 1998 demo tape 'Tiempos Cercaros' but would then fracture once more, both Meneses de la Barra and Marambio making their exit.

Valenzuela was re-recruited and Rodrigo Asalgado occupied the drum stool for the 2000 EP release 'Tierra De Guerras'.

Latterly DEFORME comprises of Pozo, Alarcon, a returning Marambio and guitarist Eladio Cordova.

Tierra De Guerras EP, (2000). Tu Raza / Esto Es Ahora / Deforme / Chupa Cabras.

DEHUMANIZED

NEW YORK, NY, USA — *Johny Collet (vocals), Rich Nagasawa (guitar), Paul Tovora (guitar), Mike Hussey (bass), George Torres (drums).*

DEHUMANIZED was forged during 1995 by guitarists Rich Nagasawa, of CHARNEL HOUSE repute, and Mike Palacios with George Torres on the drums. This trio cut the opening demo 'Terminal Punishment', after which they added vocalist Mike Zuzio. Honing their live craft the band undertook intensive local gigging opening for the likes of SIX FEET UNDER, IMMOLATION, CANNIBAL CORPSE and BRUTAL TRUTH, all within months of formation.

However, DEHUMANIZED was blighted by an ever fluctuating line up, first signalled by the departure of both Palacios and Zuzio. Enrolling Dave Zatuchney from IMMORTAL SUFFERING to fill the guitar vacancy the band then pulled in bassist Mike Chan and vocalist Jerry Barco. The following year both Zatuchney and Chan exited. Finding Tom Toscano of UMBILICAL STRANGULATION to fill in six string duties DEHUMANIZED continued gigging minus a bassist. In this formation the group entered the recording studio in late December of 1997 to craft the debut album 'Prophecies Foretold', released by Pathos Productions in early 1998.

Drafting former FALLEN CHRIST bassist Sean Morelli DEHUMANIZED embarked upon an exhaustive nationwide campaign to promote the album, appearing at the 'Milwaukee Metalfest', 'Texas Grindfest', 'Ohio Deathfest' and 'New Jersey Metalfest' events as well guesting for bands such as SUFFOCATION, MORBID ANGEL, DEICIDE, OBITUARY, VADER, CRYPTOPSY, BROKEN HOPE, MONSTROSITY and NILE. In spite of this progress the group folded in 2000. Torres would join fellow New York Death Metal crew SKINLESS during October 2001. The drummer would also add session vocals for IRATE.

Nagasawa and Torres resurrected DEHUMANIZED in 2004, assembling an all new look band including singer John Collett, second guitarist Paul Tovora and erstwhile KALOPSIA bassist Mike Hussey. Notable gigs included the 'Maryland Death Fest' in May and the 'Sick Shit Fest 2' in June.

PROPHECIES FORETOLD, Pathos (1988). Prophecies Foretold / Kingdom Of Cruelt / Fade Into Obscurity / Solitary Demise / Infinite Despair / Doomed To Die / Terminal Punishment / Condemned / Drawn By Blood.
PROBLEMS FIRST, New Red Archives (1999). Classified / Educators / Fee To Live / Mommy's Killin' / Fuck You Where's My Brew / Confessions / Coo-Coos / Better Later Days / Convenience / Everyday / Childish & Cowardly / Tragic / Gimme The Scoop.

DEKAPITATOR

USA — *Matt Hellfiend (vocals / guitar), Wes Blackwülf (guitar), Dan Bulldoze (bass), Andy Maniac (drums).*

A retro 'Speed Renaissance' pure Thrash band convened by EXHUMED members vocalist Matt Harvey and drummer Andy Jones. DEKAPITATOR, incensed by what they viewed as 'false Thrash' coming onto the scene, apparently formed in an effort to show the world what just real Thrash was. Judging by the almost universal praise bestowed upon the album 'We Will Destroy, ... You Will Obey' DEKAPITATOR appears to have succeeded in their goal.

The original band name chosen was HAMMERFALL but some enterprising Swedes got to that one first. DEKAPITATOR debuted as a trio of Hellfiend on Killsaw & Deaththroat', Bulldoze on Thermo Nuclear Bass Slaughter and Atomic Maniac supplying Rapid Fire Drum Assault. This unit delivered two tracks 'Make Them Die' and 'Haunted By Evil' to a 1997 split 7 single shared with the notorious NUNSLAUGHTER.

The band signed to Blackmetal.com Records for the album. Produced by Thrash veteran guitarist JAMES MURPHY the record also featured a holidaying Fredrik Soderberg of Swedish act DAWN on backing vocals. Hellfiend, Blackwulf and Maniac would also be operational with the side project CADAVERIZER.

On 9th July 2005 DEKAPITATOR lined up at The Pound outdoor amphitheatre in San Francisco alongside TESTAMENT, VICIOUS RUMORS, LÄÄZ ROCKIT, HIRAX, AGENT STEEL, DREAMS OF DAMNATION, MUDFACE, NEIL TURBIN, BROCAS HELM and IMAGIKA for the 'Thrash Against Cancer' benefit.

Blood On Steel EP, Midnight (1997) (Split 7 single with NUNSLAUGHTER). Make Them Die / Haunted By Evil.
WE WILL DESTROY ... YOU WILL OBEY, BlackMetal.Com BM.C 66602 (1999). One Shot, One Kill / Release The Dogs / We Will Destroy ... You Will Obey / Hell's Metal / Make Them Die / Possessed With Damnation / Thundering Legions / Faceripper / Faceripper / T.F.S. (Total Fucking Slaughter) / Haunted By Evil.

DELIRIOUS

GERMANY — *Markus Bednarek (vocals), Andreas Supplie (guitar), Alex Cwiertnia (guitar), Sascha Rachuba (bass), Markus Keller (drums).*

DELIRIOUS, led by Markus 'Betty' Bednarek, came together during 1990 as musicians united by a common appreciation of mid eighties Bay Area Thrash Metal. A brace of demos, 'Painful Sorrow' in 1992 and 'Thoughtlessness' in 1994, paved the way for a record deal signed with the Berlin based B. Mind Records as the 'Thoughtlessness' sessions were re-issued in 1998 in EP format. The band then entered VPS-Studios in Hamm with producer VICTOR SMOLSKI to cut their debut full length album 'Time Is Progress'. DELIRIOUS promoted this release by touring Europe as support to TESTAMENT, closing off with guest slots to OVERKILL and BLACKEND.

The second DELIRIOUS album, 2001's 'Designed By Violence', would be recorded at Gernhart-Studios in Siegburg and their own Ragers Elite Studios. Bassist Sascha Rachuba bowed out in 2003, being temporarily replaced by Stefan Heeke of DUKE for live work.

TIME IS PROGRESS, B-Mind B693201 (1999). Time Is Progress / Lost Identity / The Masses / Dejected / Act Of Desperation / Salvation / Remember / Helping Hand / Fallen To The Magical Delusion.

DELIRIUM TREMENS

GERMANY — *Premutos (vocals), Sadistick Dick Of Destruction (guitar), Death Tormentor (bass), Christ Impaler (drums).*

A less than serious 80s Thrash Metal throwback named after the fatal alcohol withdrawal. Certainly not to be confused with the Puerto Rican Prog Ambient outfit of the same title! DELIRIUM TREMENS nevertheless remained faithful to both the epoch and the genre and pulled in commendable reviews for their 2000 'Violent Mosh Ground' album.

The band comprised of vocalist 'Premutos' (Christian Lindner) on Vomiting throat, guitarist 'Sadistick Dick Of Destruction' (Christian Brehm) credited with Massacre guitar, leather death mask & high flames, bassist 'Death Tormentor' (Ralf Enskat) delivered Distorted four string bass inferno and finally drummer 'Christ Impaler' (Jochen Steger) with M-16, uzi & bazooka. Steger has previous experience with DRY ROT, ABSORB and BLOOD OF MESSIAH.

In early 2002 the band added guitarist Patrick Weinstein. DELIRIUM TREMENS returned in October of 2004 with the 'Thrashing Warthogs' album, recorded at Rosenquarz Tonstudio in Lübeck. At this juncture the band comprised vocalist Rowdy Mütze Piper (Christian Lindner), guitarists Rowdy Bad Bone (Patrick Weinstein) and Rowdy Rocket (Christian Brehm), bassist Rowdy Roll (Ralf Enskat) and drummer Rowdy Chambers (Jochen Steger).

VIOLENT MOSH GROUND, (2000). Seed Of Violence / Fuck Posers / Violent Mosh Ground / Execution Command / Beer Patrol / Bloody Harleyriders / Angel Fuck / Night Of Terror / Hellfighters / B.O.D. / Get Out Of My Way / Infernal Sex Slave.
Rot In Hell, (2001). Rot In Hell (Radio edit) / Rot In Hell (Original).
THRASHING WARTHOGS, Merciless (2004). Fucking Amazing / Worship Satan / Death From Behind / Rot In Hell / Follow Us If You Want To Die / Twisted Mind / Balls Of Fire / Army Of Death / War Machine / Paradise City.

DELIVERANCE

LOS ANGELES, CA, USA — *Jimmy P. Brown II (vocals / guitar), Glenn Rogers (guitar), Brian Kharirullah (bass), Chris Hyde (drums).*

The highly regarded Los Angeles Christian Thrash Metal outfit DELIVERANCE debuted in 1985 with the 'Greetings Of Death' demo tape. An appearance on the important Christian Metal compilation 'California Metal' on Regency Records would follow in 1987, DELIVERANCE sharing space by donating 'Attack' and 'A Space Called You' with MASTEDON, NEON CROSS, GARDIAN, HERO and BARREN CROSS.

In 1989 delivered a Bill Metoyer produced self-titled album. DELIVERANCE comprised of frontman Jimmy P. Brown II on vocals and guitar, guitarist Glenn Rogers, bass player Brian Khairullah and drummer Chris Hyde. Guitarist Glenn Rogers would score co-writing credits on the first VENGEANCE RISING album 'Human Sacrifice'.

A sophomore effort 'Weapons Of Our Warfare', generally acknowledged as a genre classic, in 1990. The band would benefit from heavy MTV rotation for the video for the title track. Hyde would take time out to session on the 1991 VENGEANCE RISING album 'Destruction Comes'.

For the 'Weapons Of Our Warfare' album the group lost guitarist Rogers to HIRAX, replacing him with RECON's George Ochoa.

The last DELIVERANCE album to deliver Speed Metal would be the 1991 'What A Joke' album. This album witnessed DELIVERANCE hosting an entirely new rhythm section of bassist Mike Grato—another RECON veteran, and drummer Kevin Lee.

The transitional 'Stay Of Execution', witnessed guitarist Mike Phillips supplanting Ochoa. The former guitarist would figure as part of the live line up for the notorious Death Metal act VENGEANCE RISING's last 'non-secular' tour.

'Stay Of Execution', saw the beginnings of DELIVERANCE's move into less angst ridden music although the group did put in a sterling performance on the 1993 'Intense Live Series Vol. 1' release, which included a cover version of STRYPER's 'Surrender'. Khairullah made a return for this live in the studio recording. Both Jimmy P. Brown and Mike Phillips would also feature as guests on the Rap Thrash project album 'Sodom & America' by XL AND DEATH BEFORE DISHONOR.

Predictably the band switched members once again for the 'Learn' album. With only Brown remaining from the original line-up, DELIVERANCE now included guitarist Jon Maddux, bass player Manny Morales and drummer Jon Knox.

Much to the shock of many of their fans DELIVERANCE, now as a trio with new drummer Jeff Mason of BETRAYAL onboard and Brown handling all guitars, drifted into Alternative Rock territory with the 1994 'River Disturbance' album. Earlier Brown had lent guest vocals to two tracks on BETRAYAL's 'The Passing' album. The compilation, 'A Decade Of Deliverance', would include a cover version of BLACK SABBATH's 'After Forever'.

The harder edged 'Camelot In Smithereens' arrived in 1995. Both Morales and Mason were retained for this record with BETRAYAL guitarist Marcus Colon putting in a guest session.

Brown would eventually disband DELIVERANCE to found a fresh act FEARFUL SYMMETRY. Brown would put in a guest session with the Christian apocalyptic Progressive act SAVIOUR MACHINE. However, demand for DELIVERANCE remained high, Magdalene Records issuing archive and demo material in 2000. Brown would resurrect the band for a 2001 album 'Assimilation' for Dream Recordings. The new look DELIVERANCE had Brown heading a band of former bassist Manny Morales, SANCTIFIED SISTER guitarist Lael Conlon, drummer Ian Baird and FEARFUL SYMMETRY keyboard player David Gilbreath.

Ex-DELIVERANCE guitarist Glenn Rogers would announce the formation of MONTH OF SUNDAYS, a union with erstwhile REVEREND guitarist Brian Korban. A brand new DELIVERANCE album 'The Sad Veil Of Tears' was expected in 2002. A further DELIVERANCE related project came in 2005 with the announcement that erstwhile guitarist Mike Phillips had forged FASEDOWN, a Metalcore alliance with vocalist Devin Shaeffer, second guitarist Jesse Gibson, ex-THE BLAMED bassist John Hansen and THE CRUCIFIED and THE BLAMED drummer Jim Chaffin.

On September 2nd 2006 DELIVERANCE reunited for a one-off concert at the 'Up From The Ashes 2' Christian Metal festival at the Chapel of the Hills Sanctuary in Sunland, California. Together with ONCE DEAD, STRICKEN and DEMIZE the band teamed up for the 'March Metal Madness' Christian Metal US tour beginning in early March 2007.

DELIVERANCE, Intense RO 9072 (1989). Victory / No Time / Deliverance / If You Will / The Call / No Love / Blood Of The Covenant / Jehovah Jireh / Temporary Insanity / Awake.
WEAPONS OF OUR WARFARE, Intense (1990). Supplication / This Present Darkness / Weapons Of Our Warfare / Solitude / Flesh And Blood / Bought By Blood / 23 / Slay The Wicked / Greetings Of Death / If We Faint Not.
WHAT A JOKE, Intense (1991). Intro / Prophet Of Idiocy / Pseudo Intellectual / Cheeseburger Maker Du / What A Joke / Chipped Beef / After Forever / It's The Beat / A Product Of Society / Happy Star / J.P.D. / Pray / Silent Night / J.I.G. / Purgatory Sandwich With Mustard / Attack.
LEARN, Intense (1992). Time / 1990 / Learn / Who Am I? / Renew / The Rain / Reflection / In The Will / Desperate Cries / Sanctuary.
STAY OF EXECUTION, Intense (1992). Stay Of Execution / Windows Of The Soul / Words To The … / From Once Was / Self-Monger / Horrendous Disc / Lord Of Dreams / Ramming Speed / Entombed / Weapons Of Our Warfare (Remix).
INTENSE LIVE SERIES VOL. 1—RECORDED LIVE, Intense (1993). Surrender / No Love / This Present Darkness / Stay Of Execution / The Call / No Time.
RIVER DISTURBANCE, Intense (1994). Belltown / After I Fell / River Disturbance / Now & Then / Speed Of Light / A Little Speed (w/ 12th Tribe) / Map / You Still Smile / Breathing Still.
A DECADE OF DELIVERANCE, Intense (1994). Victory / No Time / The Call / Flesh and Blood / This Present Darkness / Rescue / After Forever / Prophet Of Idiocy / Words To The … / Ramming Speed / Stay Of Execution / Learn / Desperate Cries / Sanctuary.
CAMELOT IN SMITHEREENS, Intense (1995). Somber Theme (Where Are You) / Lindsey / Not Too Good 4 Me / Anymore / Book Ends / Beauty & The Beast / Make My Bed In Hell / The Red Roof / In-U.
BACK IN THE DAY: THE FIRST FOUR YEARS, Magdalene (2000). Narration / Who Will Save The Children / Stand Up And Fight / Narration / No Time / Narration / Talk From The Stage / Fortress / Deliverance / Narration / Attack / A Space Called You / Narration / Hold On Tightly / J.I.G / Temporary Insanity.
GREETINGS OF DEATH, ETC, Magdalene (2001). Victory / Greetings Of Death / No Time / J.I.G. / Speckled Bird / Awake / Attack / A Space Called You / Weapons Of Our Warfare / This Present Darkness / Greetings Of Death / Rescue / Slay The Wicked / Solitude / 23 / Radio interview (1992).
LIVE AT CORNERSTONE 2001, Magdalene (2001). Intro / Stay Of Execution / Introductions / No Time / Learn / What A Joke / Belltown / Psalm 23 / Weapons Of Our Warfare / Thanks / Victory / Words To The… / Sanctuary.
ASSIMILATION, Dream Recordings (2001). The Limitless Light / From The Beginning / Assimilation / The Circle / Sell Your Soul … / The Search / The Learned Man / Between 2 Worlds / Impressions / Save Me From.

DELLAMORTE

AVESTA, SWEDEN — *Jonas Kjellgren (vocals), Johan Jansson (guitar), Matthias Norrman (guitar), Daniel Ekeroth (bass), Sonny Svedlund (drums).*

An infamous Death Metal act with a deeply rooted Thrash bias. DELLAMORTE, created in Avesta, was rooted in the 1990 band INTERMENT, established by erstwhile HATRED and ASOCIAL guitarist Johan Jansson. Vocalist Jonas Kjellgren is ex-PEXILATED and SICKENSIDE. During 1993 INTERMENT evolved briefly into MOONDARK before settling on DELLAMORTE. A 1995 demo, 'Drunk In The Abyss', landed a deal with the Finn label, recording in a mere 4 days the now very scarce but highly sought after album 'Everything You Hate'. The following year a 7 single, 'Dirty', emerged through the Yellow Dog label and prompted the interest of the Kron-H label, a subsidiary of French concern Osmose Productions. DELLAMORTE released the sophomore 'Uglier And More Disgusting' album, produced by Peter Tägtgren of HYPOCRISY, and set about promoting it as part of the 'World Domination' tour billed alongside DARK TRANQUILITY and ENSLAVED. Added exposure was garnered with the subsequent inclusion of DELLAMORTE on the follow up 'World Domination Live' CD and video.

1998 would witness both Jansson and vocalist Jonas Kjellgren, still retaining their allegiance to DELLAMORTE, joining the renowned Deathsters CENTINEX. Paradoxically though, the duo would switch roles in CENTINEX, Jansson becoming a lead vocalist and Kjellgren adopting guitar. DELLAMORTE bassist Daniel Ekeroth would not be left on the sidelines when it came to side ventures, the four-stringer joining INSISION.

Third album, 'Home Sweet Hell' produced once again by Peter Tägtgren, arrived in 1999. DELLAMORTE welcomed in new drummer Kennet Englund, a veteran of MOONDARK, UNCANNY and SUBDIVE. That same June Englund too would team up with CENTINEX.

Besides DELLAMORTE and CENTINEX both Jansson and Kjellgren are members of the SIDEBURNERS. Jansson would also be busying himself with UNCURBED and Kjellgren too had affiliations to another act in the high profile CARNAL FORGE.

Matthias Norrman would tour as bassist for OPETH in 2001, a quiet year for DELLAMORTE with the band only putting in one gig during March. Jonas Kjellgren proved industrious throughout 2004, acting as producer for TORCHBEARER's album 'Yersinia Pestis' and forging a brand new melodic Death Metal combo, fronted by the INCAPACITY, UNMOORED, SOLAR DAWN and TORCHBEARER credited Christian Älvestam, entitled SCAR SYMMETRY for an album 'Symmetric In Design'. Johan Jansson joined REGURGITATE in September 2006.

Shadows Path, Moondrake (1993) (Demo released under the name MOONDRAKE). Shadows Path / Inside The Crypt / The Dawn For Our Race / Dimension Of Darkness / Tresspassing Into … / … The Abyss / Concealing The Daylight / World Devastator.
EVERYTHING YOU HATE, Finn FINN 016 (1996). Total Agony / Break The Limits / Fuck Off / Pieces / Empty / No Shit / In A Box / In Your Face / Never Bleed / Gotta' Explode / Monster / Syringe Kiss.
Dirty, Yellow Dog YD 006 (1997) (Split 7" vinyl EP with CORNED BEEF). Dirty / Plug Me In / Suchastupiddisgustingfuckedupfuck.
UGLIER AND MORE DISGUSTING, Kron-H 09CD (1997). Uglier And More Disgusting / Sex Machine / Miss Lords / Corpses / The Lies / Fallen Angel Crashes Dead / Dirty / Plug Me In / Wretched / As Much As You Hurt Me / 666 And Pentagrams / So Many Reasons.
Drunk In The Abyss, Dellamorte (1999) (Cassette demo). Never Bleed / Monster / In A Box / Edge Of The World / Syringe Kiss.
HOME SWEET HELL, Kron-H 14CD (1999). Heart Of Darkness / Dellamortesque / Fucked / Home Sweet Hell / Into The Fire / The Tombs Of My Fear / Supercharged / Strategies Of Humanity / Bones / Faustian Soul / The Deathking / Motorkill / The Zoo / Rapes Of Wrath.

DEMIRICOUS

Fuck Me Satan EP, PAS 83 (2001) (7" vinyl EP). A Sure Shot / 1000 Dead / Hellhole / I Am King.

DEMIRICOUS

INDIANAPOLIS, IN, USA — *Nate Olp (vocals / bass), Ben Parish (guitar), Scott Wilson (guitar), Dustin Boltjes (drums).*

Indianapolis based Thrashers DEMIRICOUS released their debut album, 'One (Hellbound)', through Metal Blade Records in January 2006. The album was recorded in June 2005 at Planet Z studios with producer Zeuss. The band recruited former GOD BELOW and BRAND NEW SIN skinsman Mike Rafferty as the touring drummer for 2006 live work, commencing with a round of dates packaged with HIMSA, RINGWORM and THE BANNER before hooking up with RINGWORM, AUGUST BURNS RED and LIGEIA in February then STILL REMAINS, NODES OF RANVIER and IF HOPE DIES for a further extensive North American trek beginning in late March. May then found the band in union with STILL REMAINS and STILL REMAINS for a set of UK dates. DEMIRICOUS teamed up with VITAL REMAINS, GRAVE, DISMEMBER and WITHERED for a North American tour beginning in early October.

US shows throughout June 2006 had the band working alongside SOILENT GREEN and THE ACACIA STRAIN. September shows, with new drummer Dustin Boltjes from THE DREAM IS DEAD, were partnered with BYZANTINE prior to concerts packaged with DISMEMBER, VITAL REMAINS, GRAVE and WITHERED then, in November, ranked with GOD FORBID, GOATWHORE and THE HUMAN ABSTRACT.

ONE (HELLBOUND), Metal Blade (2006). Repentagram / Withdrawal Divine / Vagrant Idol / Beyond Obscene / Perfection And The Infection / Heathen Up (Out for Blood) / Cheat The Leader / Matador / To Serve Is To Destroy / Ironsides / I Am Weapon / Hellraisers.

DEMISE

HELSINGBORG, SWEDEN — *Pierre Richter (vocals / guitar), Christofer Malmström (guitar), Jörgen Löfberg (bass), Peter Wildoer (drums).*

Helsingborg's Thrash outfit DEMISE was assembled in 1990, initiated by the erstwhile GOD B.C. pairing of guitarist Pierre Richter and bass player Jesper Granath. Pulling in drummer Peter Wildoer, the group cut a demo 'Prophecy' in June 1991. Both later addition to the ranks, guitarist Christofer Malmström, and Wildoer had also been involved with eighties Power Metal band ZANINEZ. A second session, entitled 'Visions' in 1992, then secured a deal with Crypta Records for the 'Delusions' album. However, at this juncture the group discovered the existence of the US based DEMISE and duly switched title to AGRETATOR, being a compromise on two favoured name suggestions 'Aggressor' and 'Agitator'.

AGRETATOR subsequently issued a self-financed EP 'Distorted Logic', recorded at Studiofabriken in Malmö, in 1996 before folding in 1998. The core of AGRETATOR, guitarist Christofer Malmström, bassist Jörgen Löfberg and Peter Wildoer all went on to DARKANE. Wildoer also figured in TIME REQUIEM, ARCH ENEMY, on their 1998 'Stigmata' album, and ARMAGEDDON.

Prophesy, Demise (1991) (Demo). Merciless Living / Prophesy / Cremation Of The Soul.
Visions, Demise (1992) (Demo). Horizon Of Nothing / Critical Dimensions / The Inevitable.

DEMOLITION

AUSTRIA — *Wolf Süssenbeck (vocals / guitar), Thomas Pippersteiner (guitar), Hans-Peter Rapp (bass), Tom Kräutner (drums).*

Melodic Thrash Metal band DEMOLITION was forged during 1996 by drummer Tom Kräutner and guitarist Thomas Pippersteiner, subsequently enlisting Hans Peter Rapp on bass and frontman Peter Musch. The self financed EP 'In The Beginning' emerged in 1998, followed by an exhaustive live schedule opening for visiting internal acts such as TESTAMENT, DIO, MANOWAR, SAXON, OVERKILL, ANNIHILATOR, DESTRUCTION, KREATOR, SODOM, MERCYFUL FATE, NEVERMORE, SOILWORK, DARK FUNERAL, MYSTIC CIRCLE, LEFAY, LABYRINTH, EDGUY, SKYCLAD, GIRLSCHOOL, and ANGRA amongst others.

Signing a deal with Gutter Records, a division of Massacre Records from Germany, in late 2001 worked with producer Milos Dodo Dolezal in his Hacienda Studios situated in the southern Czech Republic to record the follow-up 'Out Of Noland'. Guesting on these sessions would be Ritchie Krenmaier of STYGMA IV.

DEMOLITION pulled in WAVES, CITIZEN X and DARKSIDE's Wolf Süssenbeck as replacement for Peter Musch in July 2003. With their new singer the band entered Exponent Studio in Slovakia to record a third album 'Existence'. DEMOLITION landed the direct support slot to TESTAMENT's May 2005 European tour. The band also opened for SUSPERIA in December, drafting guitarist Janos Murri from Italian group RESURRECTURIS for these dates. Gigs in Scandinavia saw DEAD TROOPER and MIKSHA added to the bill.

DEMOLITION utilised Noisehead Studios in Vienna for recording the album 'Relict IV' in January 2007.

... In The Beginning, Independent (1998). Dry Your Tears / Something You See / Sick To Loose / Hiding From Tomorrow / Follow The Firm.
OUT OF NOLAND, Gutter (2001). Out Of No Land / Awake / Scared / Demolition / Line Of fire / Hate Inside / The Untamed / Renegade / I Am The Eye / Another Nice Day / C.B.A.
EXISTENCE, (2004). Third Of Nine / Necromancer / Mankind's Bleeding / Thermal Detonator / Draining Blood / Burned To Ashes / Betrayer / Discover The Light / Hypnotized Fall / No Regrets.

DEMONIZER

WAREGEMSCHEN, BELGIUM — *Koen Vanassche (vocals), Bjorn Desmet (guitar), Kris Van Walleghem (guitar), Ulrich Keymeulen (bass), Hendrik Vanwynsberghe (drums).*

A Waregemschen retro Black-Thrash act, DEMONIZER came together in 2001. The initial line up comprised vocalist Jachim, guitarists Kris Van Walleghem and Bjorn Desmet along with drummer Pedro from Black Metal band AGUYNGUERRAN. In June of that year Koen Vanassche took over the singing role and Vanwynsberghe Hendrik enrolled as drummer.

DEMONIZER singer Koen Vanassche also plays bass for DARK AGES and Folk-Thrash act WAPENSPRAAK EN DRINKGELAG. Guitarist Kris Van Walleghem, also active with PANZER, was previously a member of ATHGOWLA. His six string partner Bjorn Desmet is ex-CHAVAJOTH. Bassist Ulrich Keymeulen is ex-WEAKENED BELIEFS and ATHONIS. He also operated with MALAGANT. Sticksman Hendrik Vanwynsberghe doubles duties with SCHIM and has earned his reputation prior to DEMONIZER with GARDENS OF GRIEF, ANAL TORTURE, DEATH ANOS and DARK TEARS. Hendrik is also known for his role as frontman for IMPEDIGON.

DEMONIZER self financed their 'Thrashing Force ... Attack' album in December of 2002. Guitarist Kris Van Walleghem briefly joined KWELHEKSE in January of 2003, performing just one gig with the band. In June of 2003 the group performed its inaugural gig outside of Belgium, appearing alongside GOREROTTED and KILLING MODE at the London Camden Underworld. Bjorn Desmet was forced out of the band with a wrist infection during October, his place being taken by URZAMOTH and STURMKRIEG man Anson. Side concerns found DEMONIZER personnel Hendrik Vanwynsberghe and Kris Van Walleghem building up a Black Metal project with Norgaath of GRIMFAUG repute. Koen Vanassche exited in December of 2003, DEMONIZER continuing as a quartet.

The band completed work on a self-financed album, 'Essence Of War', in June of 2005.

THRASHING FORCE ... ATTACK, (2003). My Scars Will Remain / Streets Of Terror / Forever Banned In Chaos / Execution Of A Christian / Demonized / Human Disease / Forget The Past / Lysva's Beast / Thrashing Force ... Attack / Only Skin Over Flesh.

DEMONSPEED

NEW YORK, NY, USA — *Matt Payne (vocals), Chris Shannon (guitar), Sal Villanueva (bass), Jim King (drums).*

Nothing if not original. New York's DEMONSPEED, musically the besuited quartet blend a bizarre amalgam of Rockabilly and Thrash that tops sinister lyrical content extolling the exploits of noted serial killers. Black Pumpkin Records issued the 'Kill, Kill, Kill' compilation in 2003. In May of 2004 ex-DEMONSPEED drummer Jim 'The Swing' King forged a new outfit entitled TEN TON TRUCK in alliance with former HADES guitarist Ed Fuhrman, vocalist Jim Frizzell and bassist Craig Salvadeo. Initial demos were cut that same month at Big Blue Meenie recording studios in Hoboken. King would also session for HIGH SPEED CHASE's 'Speed Limit None' album.

SWING IS HELL, Black Pumpkin (1997). Pogo / Fifth Of Satan / Green River / Zodiac / Threshold / Michael Landon's Ghost / King Catfish.

Demonspeed, Maggadee (1999) (Green vinyl). Pogo / Green River.

DENATA

LINKÖPING, SWEDEN — *Tomas Andersson (vocals / guitar), Roger Blomberg (bass), Ponta Sjosten (vocals / drums).*

Linköping Retro Thrashers DENATA, comprising of former TOTAL DEATH members vocalist / drummer Ponta Sjosten and bassist Roger Blomberg alongside frontman Tomas Andersson, debuted with a 1998 EP of cover versions. The 'Departed To Hell' album followed in 2000 before the Arctic Music Group signed DENATA for the 'Deathtrain' opus.

DENATA suffered a setback in September of 2002 when drummer/vocalist Ponta Sjösten was forced out due to "serious damage to his ears"! The band quickly re-grouped, enlisting Åke Danielsson on the drum stool and maneuvering Tomas Andersson to take on all lead vocal responsibilities. DENATA's 2003 album 'Art Of The Insane' included a cover version of CELTIC FROST's 'Morbid Tales'.

DENATA folded in early May of 2004. Band members guitarist Tomas Andersson and bass player Roger Blomberg teamed up with vocalist / drummer Mique Flesh, previously of WITCHERY and SÉANCE to forge FREEVIL in 2006.

Denata EP, Ghoul 002 (1999). Necro Erection / Stench In My Throat / The Ape At The Right Shelve / Man On The 3rd Floor.

DEPARTED TO HELL, Ghoul 003 (2000). Intro / Necro Erection / Happy Days / Sent From Hell / Stench In My Throat / Kill You With A Saw / Mistress Of Buffalo Shit / Heavy Metal Highway / Saccharified And Grey / 666.

DEATHTRAIN, Arctic Music 80501-91011-2 (2002). Intro / Deathtrain / 1349 / Slaughter Machine / The Black Lodge / Pentagram / Go To Hell / Three Fingers / Upon The Hill / The Funeral / Hellish Surgery / Kill Your Roots.

ART OF THE INSANE, Arctic Music 80501-98104-2 (2003). Marionettes Of Death / Insomnia / Prophecies / Whitechapel's Murder / Art Of The Insane / Satanic Thrash Hell / A World Of Lies / Convicted / Below The Surface / Born In Sin / No More Dawn / Haunted Ground / Morbid Tales.

DENIAL FIEND

TAMPA, FL, USA — *Kam Lee (vocals), Sam Williams (guitar), Terry Butler (bass), Curtis Beeson (drums).*

Announced in April 2006, Tampa, Florida retro Thrash / Death Metal combo DENIAL FIEND was assembled by an elite cast comprising the MASSACRE and DEATH duo vocalist Kam Lee and bassist Terry Butler, also of SIX FEET UNDER, guitarist Sam Williams, previously with DOWN BY LAW, and ex-NASTY SAVAGE drummer Curtis Beeson. Lee also held credits with KAULDRON, CADAVERIZER, URIZEN and SOUL SKINNER. A three track rehearsal demo was recorded on April 23rd.

Further projects were announced for Lee in early 2007 including working with Matt Olivo of REPULSION on a project called MONSTERSHOCK and adding guest studio vocals to recordings from HATEPLOW.

Denial Fiend, Denial Fiend (2006) (Rehearsal demo). Cover Me In Blood / The Thing With 100 Eyes / Frankenstein Conquers The World.

DEPRESSIVE AGE

GERMANY — *Jan Lubitzki (vocals), Jochen Klemp (guitar), Ingo Grigoliet (guitar), Tim Schallenburg (bass), Norbert Drescher (drums).*

DEPRESSIVE AGE had to escape from East Germany in 1987 to further their career. The band was previously known on their 1986 demo 'Kamikaze' as BLACKOUT. Unfortunately frontman Jan Lubitski was caught in the attempt to get to the West and would not see his band mates until his year long jail sentence had expired.

DEPRESSIVE AGE recorded a five song demo 'Beyond Illusions' in 1990 and have since followed it up with four albums. Notable touring including support to NUCLEAR ASSAULT's June 1993 European dates. Shortly before the recording of 1996's 'Electric Scum' long term guitarist Ingo Grigoleit departed for a career in the movies. The band formed part of the billing for the December 1996 'Dark Winter Nights' touring festival alongside SENTENCED, LACRIMOSA, THE GATHERING and DREAMS OF SANITY.

The band subsequently became known as D-AGE.

FIRST DEPRESSION, Great Unlimited Noises GUN 011 BMG 74321 262 821-2 (1992). Awaits / Beyond Illusion / The Light / No Risk / Autumn Times / Transition / Innocent In Detention / Never Be Blind / Circle Colour Red.

Innocent In Detention, Great Unlimited Noises GUN 010 BMG 74321 665 226-2 (1992) (Promotion release). Innocent In Detention / Never Be Blind / Circles Colour Red.

LYING IN WAIT, Great Unlimited Noises GUN020 BMG 74321 13337-2 (1993). Lying In Wait / Where / Way Out / Berlin / Psycho Circle Game / The Story (Autumn Tmes II) / My Wine / From Out Of Future / Hateful Pride / Eternal Twins.

SYMBOLS FOR THE BLUE TIME, Great Unlimited Noises GUN 047 BMG 74321 (1994). Hills Of The Thrills / World In Veins / Garbage Canyons / Hut / Subway Tree / Port Graveyard / We Have Happy Ends / Friend Within / Neptune Roars / Sorry Mr. Pain / Kotze! / Rusty Cells / Mother Salvation.

ELECTRIC SCUM, Great Unlimited Noises GUN 111 BMG 74321 44753-2 (1996). Electric Scum / Cairo Crabat / Remember / Teenage / Small Town Boy / Featherflute / Toyland Hills / Companero Song / New Machine Wisdom / Power Athletic Son / Weird Boy / Sports Yells.

Small Town Boy, Great Unlimited Noises GUN 112 BMG 74321 44426-2 (1997). Small Town Boy / New Machine Wisdom / Polar Athletic Son.

Small Town Boy, Great Unlimited Noises GUN 113 BMG 74321 44140-2 (1997). Small Town Boy / Teenage Temples / Electric Scum (Acoustic Version) / Small Town Boy (Acoustic Version).

DESCAMISADOS

AMIENS, FRANCE — *Nicolas Boury (vocals), Benoît Moritz (guitar), Olivier Delplace (guitar), David Galimidi (bass), Marc Le Gigan (drums).*

Amiens Thrash Metal band DESCAMISADOS, the 1997 version counting singer Nicolas Boury, guitarist Olivier Delplace, drummer Sébastien Bizet and bassist David Galimidi. Former vocalist Marc Le Gigan, of BLOWDEAD and fellow Grind outfit BLINDING FEAR, had opted out to undertake compulsory military service. This unit recorded the album 'In Cold Blood'. Immediately following these sessions Bizet exited and Marc Le Gigan was taken back onboard as new drummer and, at the same juncture, Benoît Moritz of EXTRAVAGANZA, UNTOLD, CAARCRINOLAS and VAKARM repute bolstered the line up as second guitarist.

A second set of Grind-Death influenced demos signalled the name change over to D.S.K. ("Disruption Of Soul And Kind") and the departure of Delplace to VAKARM. Moritz would also subsequently join BURGUL TORKHÄIN.

In Cold Blood, Descamisados (1998). Descamintro / Chrysalis / In Cold Blood / Forever Lost.

DESECRATED DREAMS

SLOVAKIA — *Stano Konechy (vocals), Lubomir Michalovic (guitar), Milan Jozefek (guitar), Marek Navratil (bass), Andrej Simon (drums).*

DESECRATED DREAMS deliver Death Metal with strong Thrash leanings. The band, founded in 1996 by former BARBAROSSA guitarists Lubomir Michalovic and Milan Jozefek, arrived on the scene in 1997 with the demo 'Waiting For The Last Sunset', capitalising on this with a further promotional tape 'Raven Forest' in 1998.

The opening DESECRATED DREAMS album, 2001's 'Feeling Of Guilt' issued by Metal Age Productions, saw the band fronted by Stano Konechy, with Marek Navratil on bass and Mizo Patz on drums. The band featured a brace of tracks, 'The Lost Faith' and 'Animal' on the 2001 compilation 'MetalWorld Compilation I'.

Subsequently erstwhile EMBALMED and BLACK WIDOW drummer Andrej Simon would join the fold. In late 2001 Navratil departed.

FEELINGS OF GUILT, Metal Age Productions (2001). Intro (... In The Darkest Forest) / Mirror Of Damnation / Animal / The Lost Faith / Impure / Mysteries Of The Spiritual World / Pavor Nocturnus / Angel's Whisper / Screaming Eyes / Fallen To The Sin / Breathing Fire.

DESERT STORM

GERMANY — *Marco Scharfenort (vocals / bass), Oliver Delfs (guitar), Daniel Habenicht (guitar), Alex Spiekermann (drums).*

Thrash act DESERT STORM first came to attention with their 1992 six song demo 'The Dark Half'. Featured a track on the 'Peace Eater Volume Three' compilation album. A split CD, 'Fade To Grey', was issued in 1993 prompting a full length album in 1994.

DESERT STORM played gigs in Germany with CANNIBAL CORPSE, MESSIAH, AGRESSOR and WARPATH.

The 1997 more groove orientated 'Walking Straight To The Moon' album saw the arrival of erstwhile KINGDOM COME drummer Mario Brodtrager. Post DESERT STORM Brodtrager would be involved with DR. SHIVAGO and, as 'Capt. Caracho', Nu-Metal band RISING DOWN.

FADE TO GREY, Remedy (1993).

PERSPIRATION, Remedy 0022 (1994). Perspiration / Stupefaction / Musical Madness / Goblin / Desert Of Souls.

WALKING STRAIGHT TO THE MOON, Remedy (1997). My Life / Long Way / Sucker / Journey / Cold / Faceless / Succubi / Spirit Of Now / Call It / The Dark Half.

DESEXULT

RISSKOV, DENMARK — *Hund (vocals / bass), Henk Leviathan (guitar), Esben Slot Sorensen (guitar), Max Due (drums).*

Early Danish Thrash Metal band DESUXULT hailed from Risskov. The original 1984 formation comprised singer / bass player Martin Hundrup, guitarists Henrik Kjaer and Esben Slot Sorensen with Max Due on drums. Initially operational as SAMHAIN the group suffered early instability problems commencing with the arrival of new drummer Henrik Munk. However, Max Due then returned as SAMHAIN debuted with an April 1985 cassette 'The Courier', but was soon to exit once again as Tue Madsen took command of the drums in the Autumn of 1986. That same year the hopefully demo 'Soon Our Demo Finds Our Album Deal' arrived. The group contributed the demo track 'Plague Of Messiah' to the 1986 New Renaissance compilation 'Speed Metal Hell 2'. The 'Fat Boys Wanna Rock' demo was issued in 1987.

Under the new guise of DESEXULT they once again featured on a New Renaissance compilation with 'Salvation' being donated to the 1988 collection 'Thrash Metal Attack'. Another demo, oddly entitled 'Fat Boys Wanna Rock', also emerged. Drummer problems continued as Peter Schulz replaced Madsen in 1987, Steen Thomsen replaced vocalist Hundrup in the summer of 1987 and Andreas Junge joined in the bass role. He was promptly removed and in came Nils Peterson later that same year. In early 1988 guitarist Kesse was added at the expense of Henrik Kjaer. In the fall of 1988 Ulrik Pedersen replaced Peter Schulz resulting in a fifth drummer in three years.

Tue Madsen, later went on to join ATRO CITY, THE PIXIE KILLERS and GROPE before finding a high profile career behind the production desk. Guitarist Esben Slot Sorensen subsequently turned up as a member of BARCODE. DESEXULT credited members singer Steen Thomsen and bassist Andreas Junge featured in MOURNER.

S.O.D.F.O.A.D. (Soon Our Demo Finds Our Album Deal), Desexult (1986) (Cassette demo). Evil Courier / Fateful Day / Megalomania / Rebirth / Ground Zero.

Live 7.3.86, Desexult (1986) (Live cassette demo). Plaque Of Messiah / Megalomania / Ground Zero / Paranoid Visions / Salvation / Rebirth / Ancient Legend / Prince Of Evil / Evil Courier / Eternal Doom / Fateful Day.

Saurian Dance, Desexult (1986) (Rehearsal cassette demo). Saurian Dance / Deception / Sardonic Laughter Before Nothing / This Is The Noise.

Fat Boys Wanna Rock, Desexult (1987) (Demo). The Diet Song / Cloth Society / Deception / Sardonic Laughter Before Nothing.

Desexult, Desexult (1987) (Demo). The Diet Song / Fateful Day / Megalomania / Rebirth / Ground Zero.

Pana Wichee Salitu, Desexult (1988) (Demo). Sound Check / Synthetic Rise / Melancholy / ... (To Be Continued).

DESPAIR

DORTMUND, GERMANY — *Robert Kampf (vocals), Marek Grzeszek (guitar), Waldemar Sorychta (guitar), Klaus Pachura (bass), Markus Freiwald (drums).*

Thrash Metal band DESPAIR formed in Dortmund during 1986 with vocalist Robert Kampf. A demo, 'Surviving You Always', was recorded in 1988. The group swapped Kampf shortly after the release of the Waldemar Sorychta and Harris Johns produced 'History Of Hate', recorded at Mohrmann Studios and Music Lab Studios, for new vocalist Andreas Henschel in 1988 as the former became head of record label Century Media. Alongside Kampf, DESPAIR at this juncture involved guitarists Marek Grzeszek and Waldemar Sorychta, bass player Klaus Pachura with Markus Freiwald on drums. CD versions of 'History Of Hate' added the bonus track 'Never Trust'. The DESPAIR song 'Rainbow Fools' found inclusion on the 1989 Nuclear Blast compilation set 'The Pleasures In Life'.

DESPAIR were perennials on the German Metal scene having opened for the likes of DEATH and DEATH ANGEL even before landing a deal. With a record under their belts further touring in Europe ensued as guests to acts such as ANNIHILATOR and OVERKILL.

DESPAIR issued 'Decay Of Humanity' in 1990. Sorychta began to carve out a formidable reputation as a producer too, making his commercial debut with another artist on UNLEASHED's May 1991 album "Where No Life Dwells'. DESPAIR's last outing, 'Beyond All Reason', arrived in January 1992. Drummer Markus Freiwald joined FLAMING ANGER then VOODOO CULT. Guitarist Waldemar Sorychta founded GRIP INC. with ex-SLAYER drummer DAVE LOMBARDO. As an accomplished producer in his own right, Sorychta has racked up credits with TIAMAT, THE GATHERING, LACUNA COIL, FLOWING TEARS, MOONSPELL and SAMAEL amongst many others.

DESPAIR, featuring original members Robert Kampf, Waldemar Sorychta and Markus Freiwald, reunited in November 2004.

Surviving You Always, Despair (1988) (Demo). Slaves Of Power / Slow Death / Rainbow Fools / Young And Uncertain.
HISTORY OF HATE, Century Media 08 9702-1 (1988). The Enigma / Freedom Now / History Of Hate / Constructing The Apocalypse / Slow Death / Outconditioned / Slaves Of Power / Joy Division / Never Trust.
DECAY OF HUMANITY, Century Media 08 9712 (1990). Decay Of Humanity / Cry For Liberty / Delusion / Victims Of Vanity / A Distant Territory / Silent Screaming / Radiated / Satanic Verses.
Slow Death, Century Media (1991). Slow Death (Live) / History Of Hate (Live) / Young And Uncertain (Live).
BEYOND ALL REASON, Century Media 08 9726 1 (1992). Beyond Comprehension / Deaf And Blind / Imported Love / The Day Of Desperation / In The Deep / Rage In The Eyes / Burnt Out Souls / Son Of The Wild / Crossed In Sorrow.

DESTINITY

LYON, FRANCE — *Mick (vocals), Nico (guitar), Zephiros (guitar), David (bass), Morteüs (drums).*

Lyon based symphonic Black Metal act DESTINITY came into being during July of 1996. At this stage DESTINITY comprised of vocalist Mick, guitarist Zephiros, guitarist / keyboard player Morteüs, guitarist Jim, bass player Benn and drummer Tyraël (Chris). A 1998 demo 'Enigmatic Forest' triggered DESTINITY's signing to AMI Productions for the debut album 'Wepts From The Sky'. The 'Supreme Domination Art' album would follow, initially released by Plaza Records and later picked up by the Malaysia based Psychic Scream Entertainment label. Signing to the Adipocere label DESTINITY issued the January 2003 album 'Under The Smell Of Chaos'. The record, featuring new lead guitarist Lord D.D. and which included a live video track recorded at Salon de Provence in April of 2002, witnessed guest contributors Akaias of AGATHODAIMON, Julien of BENIGHTED and Kohle from CENTURY. Chart was subsequently added to the line up as new bassist as Benn prioritised his other acts RAVENDUSK and the Sumerian Metal band ANKSUNAMON.

Under the banner 'Days Of Suffering' the band allied themselves with ENTHRONED, SETH and AGATHODAIMON for a spate of European dates in April and May of 2003. That November Hrafnagud was inducted as new bassist as the band entered Sonovore Studios with FURIA guitarist Mickael Vallesi acting as producer for 'In Excelsis Dementia'. Lord D.D. exited after these recordings.

DESTINITY underwent a change of direction with the September 2005 album 'Synthetic Existence', adopting a distinct Thrash Metal stance, the group now labelling itself as "Thrashened Extreme Music". The record was crafted between July and August that year with producer Jacob Hansen at Hansen Studios in Denmark and saw Zephiros resuming his lead guitar position. Upon completion of the album both Hrafnagud and Tyraël were excused of their duties. Further evolution saw Morteüs switching from keyboards to drums. David was drafted on bass.

WEPTS FROM THE SKY, AMI Productions (1999). Vanth's Dusk Enigma / Storm's Breath / Desire . . . / Souls Joined Together Eternally / Supremacy In Madness / The Beautiful Call Of Lord / Ultimate Silence Of The Unspoken / Wepts From The Sky.
SUPREME DOMINATION ART, Psychic Scream Entertainment (2001). The Beginning Of Eternal Sufferings / Wreak Of Sorrow / Beyond The Spiritual Prophecy / Supreme Domination's Art / New Dark Empire / From The Bowels Of The Abyss / The Greatest Dream / The Sermon Of Infinity / Vanth's Dusk Enigma.
UNDER THE SMELL OF CHAOS, Adipocere (2003). Introspection / Under The Smell Of Chaos / Daemonity / Enter My Nightmare / Evil Moon / Psychose / Glutted Wargasm / As The Disease We Shall Spread / Hymns For Minas Morgul / An Astral Travel (Through The Gloomy Ocean Of Sadness) / Dominus Satanas.
IN EXCELSIS DEMENTIA, Adipocere CDAR84 (2004). After The Grace Of Kaos Synopsis / Gloria In Exelcis Ecclesia / Divine Extase / Heffen Kemet / Until Death Desire / Sadistic Massacre / Black Upon The Throne / And Silence / Pleasures Of The Flesh / Forceps Of Hate.
SYNTHETIC EXISTENCE, Adipocere CDAR104 (2005). At The End / In Nuclear Light / Ex Nihilo / Fanatic God Machine / Evolution—Devilution / Deconstruction Of Times / Deshumanised Nature / Neurotic Illness / Synthetic Existence.

DESTINY'S END

LOS ANGELES, CA, USA — *James Rivera (vocals), Dan Delucie (guitar), Eric Halpern (guitar), Nardo Andi (bass), Brian Craig (drums).*

Los Angeles based DESTINY'S END saw the return to action of noted HELSTAR frontman James Rivera. Joining him were former members of SHADOW INSANE and NEW EDEN drummer Brian Craig and bassist Nardo Andi alongside erstwhile NEW EDEN, SECRET WISDOM and CRAB NEBULA guitarist Dan Delucie. Making up the full complement would be guitarist Perry Grayson, a former member of OBSCURE—an act which also included PROTOTYPE personnel Mike Brew and Kragen Lum alongside one time NEW EDEN singer Mike Grant.

DESTINY'S END would sign up with Metal Blade records cutting their opening shot 'Breathe Deep The Dark' with producer Bill Metoyer. In August of 1999 the band put in package dates of Germany in alliance with SACRED STEEL, THE LORD WEIRD SLOUGH FEG and WARDOG.

By 2000 the Rivera was also fronting side outfit RIVERA PROJECT. Despite DESTINY'S END being announced as performing at the German 'Bang Your Head' festival in May of 2000 Grayson decamped to concentrate on literary work and forge a Progressive Thrash act RELENTLESS. His place was swiftly taken by Eric Halpern of Houston's Z LOT Z and tribute act MINDCRIME. At 'Bang Your Head' Rivera was even granted the honour of performing onstage with the SCORPIONS for a rendition of 'He's A Woman, She's A Man'. Rivera would find himself invited back to the 'Bang Your Head' 2001 festival with a HELSTAR reunion concert.

The band would record their second effort, the Vivaldi infused conceptual 'Transition', working with producer Joe Floyd of WARRIOR. Mastering was handled by TY TABOR of KING'S X. However, the end results were not initially as expected and the whole record would be delayed for a remix in November by Achim Kohler. 'Transition' would eventually arrive in early 2001.

DESTINY'S END would also contribute their take on 'Dressed In White' to a KING DIAMOND tribute album on Necropolis Records. It would be reported in August of 2001 that Rivera had joined FLOTSAM AND JETSAM after their longstanding vocalist Eric A.K. departed.

Drummer Brian Craig would join Jack Frost's SEVEN WITCHES project band in November 2001. The same month would witness a return to action of former DESTINY'S END man Perry M. Grayson together with vocalist Mike Brew ('Mike Bear') with their new act ARTISAN. Joining the duo for this new venture would be RAPTURE guitarist Ana Greco and drummer Matt Conley. In July of 2002 ex frontman Rivera teamed up with SEVEN WITCHES, debuting with the band at the 'Classic Metal Fest II' in Cleveland, Ohio.

An all new act with strong DESTINY'S END ties was announced in August of 2003 as James Rivera and guitarist Eric Halpern united with SYMPHONY X bassist Mike Lepond in DISTANT THUNDER. This trio soon scored a deal with Massacre Records. Shortly after Perry Grayson emerged fronting a new trans-Atlantic band venture, ISEN TORR. Joining him for this endeavour would be SOLSTICE guitarist Rich Walker, TWISTED TOWER DIRE vocalist Tony Taylor with the RITUAL STEEL rhythm section of Oliver Zuhlke on bass and drummer Martin Zeller. First product would be an EP for the Metal Supremacy label 'Mighty And Superior', restricted to 666 copies. Dan Delucie would be active too, having joined CRESCENT SHIELD in 2003, the new band assembled by erstwhile ONWARD singer Michael Grant.

Ex-guitarist Perry M. Grayson launched his new retro Hard Rock act FALCON in 2003, this esteemed unit featuring Greg Lindstrom of CIRITH UNGOL repute on bass and keyboards with Darin McCloskey of Pennsylvania Doom protagonists PALE DIVINE on drums.

BREATHE DEEP THE DARK, Metal Blade 14178 (1998). Rebirth / Breath Deep The Dark / To Be Immortal / Idle City / The Fortress Unvanquishable / Sinister Deity / Unsolved World / Under Destruction's Thumb / Clutching at Straws / Where Do We Go? / The Obscure.

TRANSITION, Metal Blade 14340 (2001). Transition / The Watcher / A Passing Phase / The Suffering / From Dust To Life / Storm Clouds / First You Dream, Then You Die / The Legend / A Choice Of Graves / Vanished.

DESTROYERS

POLAND — *Marek Loza (vocals / bass), Adam Stomkowski (guitar), Wojcieck Zieba (drums).*

Thrash act DESTROYERS debuted with the album 'Noc Krolowej Zadzy' as a trio of frontman Marek Loza, guitarist Adam Stomkowski and drummer Wojcieck Zieba. Prior to releasing the album in an English version as 'A Night Of The Lusty Queen' album Speed Metal merchants DESTROYERS appeared on the legendary 'Metalmania' festival in Poland during 1987. The band also included four tracks on the 'Metalmania' compilation EP sharing space with fellow Poles HAMMER.

Loza would completely overhaul DESTROYERS for the follow up 'The Miseries Of Virtue' drafting guitarist Waldemar Lukoszek, bassist Waldemar Szyszko and drummer Tomasz Wiczewski.

A NIGHT OF THE LUSTY QUEEN, Barricade (1989). Introduction / A Terrible Anathema / Call Of Blood / Czarina's Warm Pubes / Wine And Sex / A Night Of The Lusty Queen / The Kingdom Of Evil / The Temple Of Pleasure / Angry / Bastard.

THE MISERIES OF VIRTUE, Metal Muza (1991). The Miseries Of Virtue / Histoire D'O / Oeachlet / Odyssey / Nymphomania / The Birth Of Courtesan / The Craft Of Tyranny / I Praise You, Lilith.

DESTRUCTION

LÖRRACH, GERMANY — *Schmier (bass / vocals), Michael Siffringer (guitar), Harold Wilkens (guitar), Thomas Senmann (drums).*

Formed in Lörrach, Weil am Rhein during 1983 under their original title of KNIGHT OF DEMON this German Speed Metal band went on to win much acclaim and healthy album sales. The band, fronted by the well known figure of Schmier (a.k.a. Marcel Schirmer) alongside guitarist Michael Siffringer and drummer Tommy Sandmann (Thomas Senmann), made their recording debut when they recorded the 'Speed Kills' demo. A second set of demos, 'Bestial Invasion', featured the track 'Mad Butcher', which was to become so popular that it would feature as the leading title track on a 1987 issued EP. The band's debut full-length album, 'Infernal Overkill', was released in 1985.

The 1986 'Eternal Devastation' album, released through Steamhammer Records, was produced by Manfred Neurer. Upon completion of the album Senmann quit the music business to become a policeman and for tour duties DESTRUCTION drafted Chris Witchhunter of SODOM. The follow up 'Mad Butcher' EP, released in 1987, notably featured a cover version of the PLASMATICS 'The Damned'. This release was the first with additional guitarist Harold Wilkens and new drummer Oliver Kaiser. DESTRUCTION scored notable sales with the 'Mad Butcher' EP and with renewed fire opened for MOTÖRHEAD on their 1987 European tour including their first British show at the Brixton Academy. They kept up the momentum with their first shows in America including dates opening for SLAYER.

'Release From Agony', produced by Kalle Trapp, enabled DESTRUCTION to break into the worldwide market. DESTRUCTION returned to Britain once more in 1989 supporting CELTIC FROST promoting their live album 'Live Without Sense' which was recorded at shows in Austria, Spain and Portugal.

In 1990 the band fired Schmier claiming his studio performances were below par. Schmier began negotiations with PAGANINI but ended up fronting a totally new outfit HEADHUNTER. Schmier's place was filled by former POLTERGEIST vocalist Andre Grieder and the resulting album, 'Cracked Brain', provided fans with more of the same gut wrenching fare only let down by an appalling cover of THE KNACK's 'My Sharonna'. In early 1991 ex-ARTILLERY vocalist Flemming Ronsdorf joined DESTRUCTION but lasted barely two weeks.

DESTRUCTION then entered a phase of their career later dubbed as "Neo-Destruction". Signing to the Brain Butcher label the band re-debuted with the 1994 'Destruction' EP, this effort signalling a radical move away from their Thrash heritage. The band at this juncture comprised Sifringer, Engler and Kaiser alongside the EPHEMERA'S PARTY duo of vocalist Thomas Rosenmerkel and guitarist Michael Piranio. The 'Them Not Me' and 1998 album 'Least Successful Human Cannonball' followed suit. This version of the group dissolved, Rosenmerkel and Piranio duly re-creating EPHEMERA'S PARTY.

Schmier and Siffringer resolved their differences in 1999 and DESTRUCTION put in some triumphant return performances at European festivals. Sure enough the band, with new drummer Sven Vormann, signed to Nuclear Blast for the 2000 Peter Tägtgren produced album 'All Hell Breaks Loose'. As a bridge between the DESTRUCTION history of yore and the band's renewed position the classic 'Mad Butcher' track from the 1984 'Sentence Of Death' EP, a firm fan favourite, was answered with a new cut entitled 'The Butcher Strikes Back'.

Sales were strong and the album attained a number 67 position on the national German album charts. A brief warm-up tour led to European festivals performances. DESTRUCTION would then hit the road as part of the 'Nuclear Blast Festival' roadshow packaged alongside HYPOCRISY, KATAKLYSM, CREMATORY and RAISE HELL. The partnership with Canadians

KATAKLYSM was re-forged with American dates which saw DYING FETUS as openers.

During April 2001 the group once again entered Abyss Studios with Peter Tägtgren to record the follow up 'The Antichrist'. The album ran into a whole slew of production problems when finished copies were found to have the track order compiled incorrectly, sleeves printed in red instead of full colour and mysterious sound drop outs on the "hidden" bonus track 'Curse The Gods'. These initial mispressings would soon be snapped up by eager collectors. The problems did not end there though as the album would also be seized by Swiss customs officials but later released.

DESTRUCTION parted ways with drummer Sven Vormann during October, replacing him with Berliner Marc Reign, a veteran of ORTH and GUNJAH. Meantime Vormann founded JESUS CHRYSLER SUPERSKUNK, linking up with ex-DESTRUCTION singer Thomas Rosenmerkel and erstwhile HATE SQUAD man Michael Gerstlauer working alongside vocalist Thomas Rosenmerkel, DRYROT guitarist Micheal Gerstlauer and Necromonicon bass player Bernhard 'Erna' Matt.

DESTRUCTION initiated a nostalgic Thrash Metal mammoth tour of Germany with compatriots SODOM and KREATOR commencing 26th December in Ludwigsburg and running through into the new year. The band's successful live alliance with KREATOR would be furthered abroad as the pairing revealed tour plans for dates in Brazil, Chile, Peru, Colombia and Venezuela throughout August and September. The Thrash union would then hit North America with CEPHALIC CARNAGE and DECEMBER in tow. DESTRUCTION would also be confirmed as headliners at the anti racism benefit gig 'The Mosh Club Open Air' in Kolmberg. The band also cut a rendition of 'Whiplash' for a Nuclear Blast METALLICA tribute collection. However, during October the ongoing would tour would be put in jeopardy when Schmier broke bones in his hand. Although he continued to play for a further two weeks with his hand in a cast this only exacerbated the damage.

The band announced their debut Japanese shows for May 2003 at the Shibuya Club Quattro in Tokyo revealing a special live record 'Alive Destruction' would be issued by King Records to mark the event. In a display of genuine altruism, DESTRUCTION's September 2003 studio album 'Metal Discharge' was announced as having the first 10'000 copies coming complete with a bonus CD compilation of up and coming Thrash acts.

With the ignition of a new Gulf War against Iraq in March DESTRUCTION weighed in with their own salutary political statement issuing a downloadable cover version of THE EXPLOITED's 'Fuck The U.S.A.'. The band would be confirmed as co-headliners for the 'X-Mass Festivals' European tour commencing in London on December 7th, heading up a strong billing incorporating DEICIDE, AMON AMARTH, NILE, GRAVEWORM, DEW-SCENTED, MISERY INDEX and DISBELIEF. The band's own heaviness would curtail the projected Antwerp show of this leg of dates though when during soundcheck large pieces of concrete started to rain down from the ceiling!

Japanese versions of the September 2003 album 'Metal Discharge' came complete with four extra demo cuts. European limited editions added a bonus disc incorporating covers of THE EXPLOITED's 'Fuck The U.S.A.', IRON MAIDEN's 'Killers' and METALLICA's 'Whiplash' as well as a previously unreleased 1999 take of 'Bestial Invasion' and demo cuts 'The Butcher Strikes Back', 'Nailed To The Cross' and 'Metal Discharge'. The band embarked upon the 'Live Discharge–Latino' tour of Brazil in April 2004. They would be joined onstage at The Blackmore bar in São Paulo by a guesting Andreas Kisser of SEPULTURA for 'Curse Of The Gods' and a rendition of METALLICA's 'Whiplash'. Unfortunately a projected date in Costa Rica was shelved when band members became ill.

Further trouble ensued following a May gig in Brescia, Italy as drummer Marc Reign was arrested by security at Milan airport. Apparently the musician's chrome bullet belt's triggered officials suspicion and the band was detained until they could convince the authorities the ammunition was blank and merely for show.

That same year the band would have their classic cut 'Curse The Gods' chosen as a pioneering piece of music for a compilation assembled by DARKTHRONE drummer Fenriz, released through Peaceville Records and entitled 'Fenriz Presents The Best Of Old School Black Metal'. In January 2005 DESTRUCTION switched labels to Andy Allendörfer of SQUEALER's AFM Records label . That February the band entered the studio with Peter Tägtgren of HYPOCRISY and PAIN acting as producer to cut a new album given a title 'Inventor Of Evil'. Former IRON MAIDEN singer PAUL DIANNO guested on the track 'The Alliance Of Hellhoundz'. Shortly afterward the band announced a whole slew of world famous guest participations including DORO, Biff Byford of SAXON, Shagrath of DIMMU BORGIR, Björn "Speed" Strid of SOILWORK, Messiah Marcolin of CANDLEMASS, Mark Osegueda of DEATH ANGEL and Peter "Peavy" Wagner from RAGE.

Retro Heavy Metal band, POWERGOD, cut a cover version of 'Total Desater' for inclusion on their 'Long Live The Loud– That's Metal Lesson II' released through Massacre Records in July 2005. Schmier guested in the studio on this version. The frontman also put in a showing on Italian act ELVENKING's 'The Winter Wake'.

European dates in November had the band sharing stages with Swedish Doom veterans CANDLEMASS and Finland's DEATHCHAIN. The first leg of dates would be opened by Belgians AFTER ALL with the latter half supported by German act PERZONAL WAR.

A string of South American gigs took place in April 2006, although dates in Cordoba and Rosario, Argentina, and Asuncion, Paraguay, were cancelled due to "huge organisational problems and transportation issues'. DESTRUCTION scored a placing on the 'Metal Crusaders' North American tour, set to take place in May and June 2006 alongside KATAKLYSM, GRAVEWORM, VADER, SPEED\KILL/HATE and THE ABSENCE, replacing NUCLEAR ASSAULT who had withdrawn due to an "urgent immediate family situation". DESTRUCTION put in Spanish and Portuguese dates in late November.

DESTRUCTION teamed up with SADUS and MUNICIPAL WASTE for a North American tour throughout January and February 2007. These dates would be in promotion for the AFM album 'Thrash Anthems', a collection of re-recorded classic tracks plus two new tracks 'Deposition (Your Heads Will Roll)' and 'Profanity'. This set was recorded at House of Music Studio in Germany and Little Creek Studio in Switzerland with engineers Gerd Krenz, Franky Winkelmann and GURD / POLTERGEIST man VO Pulver with mixing handled by Jacob Hansen. Schmier also contributed vocals to the song 'Bloodsucker' recorded by RAGE guitarist VICTOR SMOLSKI included on a 2007 Nuclear Blast Records' 20th anniversary compilation album.

DESTRUCTION partnered with INTO ETERNITY, MUNICIPAL WASTE and HIRAX for the "Thrash Till Death Over North America" shows in January and February 2007.

Speed Kills, Destruction (1983) (Cassette demo). Mad Butcher / Total Desaster / Antichrist / Front Beast.

Bestial Invasion Of Hell, Destruction (1984) (Cassette demo). Mad Butcher / Fatal Desaster / Antichrist / Front Beast / Satan's Vengeance / Tormentor.

Sentence Of Death EP, Steamhammer SPV 60-1838 (1984). Intro / Total Disaster / Black Mass / Mad Butcher / Satan's Vengeance / Devil's Soldiers.

INFERNAL OVERKILL, Steamhammer SPV 08-1806 (1985). Invincible Force / Death Trap / The Ritual / Tormentor / Bestial Invasion / Thrash Attack / Antichrist / Black Death.

ETERNAL DEVASTATION, Steamhammer SPV 08-1885 (1986). Curse The Gods / Confound Games / Life Without Sense / United By Hatred / Eternal Ban / Upcoming Devastation / Confused Mind.

Mad Butcher EP, Steamhammer SPV 60-1897 (1987). Mad Butcher / The Damned / Reject Emotions / The Last Judgement.

RELEASE FROM AGONY, Steamhammer SPV 08-7503 (1987). Beyond Eternity / Release From Agony / Dissatisfied Existence / Sign Of Fear / Unconscious Ruins / Incriminated / Our Oppression / Survive To Die.

LIVE WITHOUT SENSE, Noise 44454 (1989) (USA release). Curse The Gods / Unconscious Ruins / Trash Attack / Invincible Force / Dissatisfied Existence / Reject Emotions / Eternal Ban / Mad Butcher / Life Without Sense / In The Mood / Release From Agony / Bestial Invasion.

LIVE WITHOUT SENSE, Noise NUK 126 (1989) (UK release). Curse The Gods / Unconscious Ruins / Invincible Force / Dissatisfied Existence / Reject Emotions / Eternal Ban / Mad Butcher / Pink Panther / Life Without Sense / In The Mood / Release From Agony / Bestial Invasion.

LIVE WITHOUT SENSE, Steamhammer SPV 085-75792 (1989) (German release). Curse The Gods / Unconscious Ruins / Trash Attack / Invincible Force / Dissatisfied Existence / Reject Emotions / Eternal Ban / Mad Butcher / Pink Panther/Life Without Sense / In The Mood/Release From Agony / Bestial Invasion.

CRACKED BRAIN, Steamhammer SPV 076-76192 (1990). Cracked Brain / Frustrated / SED / Time Must End / My Sharona / Rippin' You Off Blind / Die A Day Before You're Born / No Need To Justify / When Your Mind Was Free.

Destruction EP, Brain Butcher 0447 (1994). Decisions / I Kill Children / Things Of No importance / Smile.

Them Not Me EP, Brain Butcher BBC 0714 (1995). Scratch The Skin / Live To Start Again / Bright Side Of Leprosy / Push Me Off The Windowsill / Mole / Mentally Handicapped Enterprise.

THE LEAST SUCCESSFUL HUMAN CANNONBALL, Brain Butcher BBC 0715 (1998). Formless, Faceless, Nameless / Tick On A Tree / 263 Dead Popes / Cellar Soul / God Gifted / Autoaggression / Hofffmannn's Hell / Brother Of Cain / A Fake Transition / Continental Drift I / Continental Drift II.

ALL HELL BREAKS LOOSE, Nuclear Blast NB 0494-2 (2000). Intro / The Final Curtain / Machinery Of Lies / Tears Of Blood / Devastation Of Your Soul / The Butcher Strikes Back / World Domination Of Pain / X-treme Measures / All Hell Breaks Loose / Total Desaster 2000 / Visual Prostitution / Kingdom Of Damnation. Chart positions: 67 GERMANY, 70 POLAND.

2 ORIGINALS OF DESTRUCTION, Steamhammer SPV 21960 (2000). Mad Butcher / The Damned / Reject Emotions / The Last Judgement / Curse The Gods / Confound Games / Life Without Sense / United By Hatred / Eternal Ban / Upcoming Devastation / Confused Mind / Intro/Total Desaster / Black Mass / Mad Butcher / Satan's Vengeance / Devil's Soldiers / Invincible Force / Death Trap / The Ritual / Tormentor / Bestial Invasion / Thrash Attack / Antichrist / Black Death.

NUCLEAR BLAST FESTIVALS 2000, Nuclear Blast NB 0587-2 (2000) (Split live album with RAISE HELL, KATAKLYSM, CREMATORY and HYPOCRISY). The Butcher Strikes Back / Tears Of Blood / Mad Butcher / Total Desaster.

ALL HELL BREAKS LOOSE (LIMITED EDITION), King KICP-736 (2000) (Japanese release). Intro / The Final Curtain / Machinery Of Lies / Tears Of Blood / Devastation Of Your Soul / The Butcher Strikes Back / World Domination Of Pain / X-treme Measures / All Hell Breaks Loose / Total Desaster 2000 / Visual Prostitution / Kingdom Of Damnation / Mad Butcher / Total Desaster / Antichrist / Frontbeast / Satan's Vengeance / Tormentor / Whiplash.

Whiplash, Nuclear Blast NB 0640-7 (2001) (Red 7" vinyl single). Whiplash / The Final Curtain.

THE ANTICHRIST, Nuclear Blast NB 0632-2 (2001). Days Of Confusion / Thrash Till Death / Nailed To The Cross / Dictators Of Cruelty / Bullets From Hell / Strangulated Pride / Meet Your Destiny / Creations Of The Underworld / Godfather Of Slander / Let Your Mind Rot / The Heretic.

THE ANTICHRIST (LIMITED EDITION), Nuclear Blast NB 0632 (2001). Days Of Confusion / Thrash Till Death / Nailed To The Cross / Dictators Of Cruelty / Bullets From Hell / Strangulated Pride / Meet Your Destiny / Creations Of The Underworld / Godfather Of Slander / Let Your Mind Rot / The Heretic / Curse The Gods.

ALIVE DEVASTATION, King KICP-909 (2003). Intro / Curse The Gods / Nailed To The Cross / Eternal Ban / Machinery Of Lies / Bullets From Hell / Tears Of Blood / Live Without Sense / Thrash Till Death / Mad Butcher / The Butcher Strikes Back / Intro / Total Desaster / Invincible Force / Bestial Invasion.

METAL DISCHARGE (LIMITED EDITION), Nuclear Blast NB 1170-0 (2003). The Ravenous Beast / Metal Discharge / Rippin' The Flesh Apart / Fear Of The Moment / Mortal Remains / Desecrators (Of The New Age) / Historical Force Feed / Savage Symphony Of Terror / Made To Be Broken / Vendetta / Killers / Whiplash / U.S.A. / Bestial Invasion / Butcher Strikes Back / Nailed To The Cross / Metal Discharge.

METAL DISCHARGE, Nuclear Blast NB 1170-2 (2003). The Ravenous Beast / Metal Discharge / Rippin' The Flesh Apart / Fear Of The Moment / Mortal Remains / Desecrators (Of The New Age) / Historical Force Feed / Savage Symphony Of Terror / Made To Be Broken / Vendetta.

INVENTOR OF EVIL (LIMITED EDITION), AFM 096-9 (2005). Soul Collector / The Defiance Will Remain / The Alliance Of Helloundz / No Man's Land / The Calm Before The Storm / The Chosen Ones / Dealer Of Hostility / Under Surveillance / Seeds Of Hate / Twist Of Fate / Killing Machine / Memories Of Nothingness / We Are The Road Crew / The Alliance Of Hellhoundz.

INVENTOR OF EVIL, AFM 096-2 (2005). Soul Collector / The Defiance Will Remain / The Alliance Of Helloundz / No Man's Land / The Calm Before The Storm / The Chosen Ones / Dealer Of Hostility / Under Surveillance / Seeds Of Hate / Twist Of Fate / Killing Machine / Memories Of Nothingness. Chart position: 68 GERMANY.

THRASH ANTHEMS, AFM (2007). Deposition (Your Heads Will Roll) / Invincible Force / Release From Agony / Mad Butcher / Sign Of Fear / Death Trap / Life Without Sense / Total Desaster / Bestial Invasion / Reject Emotions / Tormentor / Unconscious Ruins / Curse The Gods / Cracked Brain / Profanity / Eternal Ban.

DETENTE

SAN FRANCISCO, CA, USA — *Dawn Crosby (vocals), Ross Robinson (guitar), Caleb Quinn (guitar), Steve Hochheiser (bass), Dennis Butler (drums).*

An act of huge potential that sadly failed to last the course. DÉTENTE was formed in Los Angeles in 1984 by ex-FIRST ATTACK and ALLIES front woman Dawn Crosby along with drummer Dennis Butler and guitarist Fred Tutone. The band recorded a demo tape and played around Los Angeles until the group's original bass player was fired along with Tutone. This line-up shuffle heralding the arrival of the dual guitar team of Celeb Quinn and Ross Robinson plus new ex-LIZZY BORDEN bassist Steve Hochheiser.

This incarnation recorded the debut 'Recognize No Authority' album, released in August 1986, produced by VINNIE VINCENT INVASION bassist Dana Strum. However, following the album release DETENTE, obviously forgetting their band name, broke up in acrimonious circumstances. Guitarists Ross Robinson and Caleb Quinn, together with bassist Steve Hochheiser, quit claiming the band title for themselves. A bitter war of words ensued in which Crosby retained the DETENTE banner. Robinson later played with CATALEPSY and MURDERCAR, the latter a union with DAMN THE MACHINE bassist Dave Clemmons and the MACHINE HEAD credited Dave McClain on drums.

The run of bad luck continued as Crosby's sole remaining band member drummer Dennis Butler was involved in a serious burn accident at a chemical plant putting the band out of action for several months. Upon his recovery DETENTE had effectively disintegrated so Butler busied himself jamming with local acts LOUD SENSELESS NOISE and VERMIN.

Crosby and Butler finally pulled DETENTE back together adding guitarists Mike Carlino and Gregg Cekalovich together with bassist George Rob.

In 1989 and now based in New Jersey, Crosby, Carlino and bassist Blair Darby recorded a three track demo, 'All That Remains', in New York with producer Alex Perialis, these sessions also seeing Rob 'Wacko' Hunter from RAVEN guesting on drums. The drumming stool was eventually filled a few months later by Eric Alpert then in quick succession Steve Cordova.

Warner Brothers records chased the band down for a deal. Due to the band name DÉTENTE already being registered the title SEDITION was chosen for a new album 'Within The Veil'. By the time of its release in 1991, 'Within The Veil' would be sporting a revised group monicker of FEAR OF GOD. As FEAR OF GOD, Crosby led an increasingly chaotic band line-up through two highly respected albums. Ultimately Crosby's well documented reliance on drugs and alcohol would catch up with her and in December 1996 she died tragically young of liver failure.

Ross Robinson would go on to become a much sought after high profile producer being given large credit for the rising careers of acts such as KORN, MACHINE HEAD and SLIPKNOT.

Shattered Illusions, Détente (1984). Widows Walk / Holy War / Shattered Illusions / Vultures In The Sky.
RECOGNISE NO AUTHORITY, Metal Blade 72152 (1986). Losers / Russian Roulette / It's Your Fate / Holy War / Catalepsy / Shattered Illusions / Life Is Pain / Blood I Bleed / Widows Walk / Vultures In The Sky.
Détente, Roadrunner (1987). Diseased / Wasting Time / All That Remains.
Détente, (1989). Red To Grey / Coming Down / Love's Death.

DETONATION

UTRECHT, HOLLAND — *Koen Romeijn (vocals / guitar), Mike Ferguson (guitar), Otto Schimmelpenninck (bass), Thomas Kalksma (drums).*

Founded in 1997, originally entitled INFERNAL DREAM, this Utrecht band evolved into DETONATION in 1998. The band's line up comprised of ex-ENGORGE vocalist / guitarist Koen Romeijn, former GRASMOAIER guitarist Mike Ferguson and Thomas Kalksma of FLAMING FIST on drums. The band persevered without a bassist until ENTROPION's Otto Schimmelpenninck took on the role. During 1998 Ferguson would also be doubling duties with Death-Thrashers M-90'S.

DETONATION debuted with two tracks on the January 1999 'Crushed Skull' compilation. A self financed four track EP, 'Lost Euphoria', followed.

DETONATION toured as support to ORPHANAGE in April 2001. The conceived a Hans Pieters produced full-length album, entitled 'An Epic Defiance', for 2003.

The band united with Sweden's DIMENSION ZERO and IM-MEMORIAL for European dates in February 2004. That same year, maintaining his role in DETONATION, Koen Romeijn enrolled as frontman for M-90'S. The band donated their rendition of 'Under A Serpent Sun' to the AT THE GATES tribute album, 'Slaughterous Souls—A Tribute to At The Gates' released in September 2004 through Drowned Scream Records. DETONATION entered Studio Excess in Rotterdam during December to craft a new album 'Portals To Uphobia'. The record emerged in September 2005 through Osmose Productions in Europe and in October via The End Records in the USA. The first 1,000 copies of the European release would be a limited digipak, featuring additional artwork and an exclusive multimedia section. Tour work to promote 'Portals To Uphobia' saw September European dates allied with DECAPITATED and GOREROTTED.

Uniting with fellow Dutch Deathsters FUELBLOODED, the band put in UK tour dates in early May 2006. DETONATION cut new album tracks, billed as 'Emission Phase', in January 2007 at Split Second Sound studios working with Jochem Jacobs, guitar player for TEXTURES, and Bouke Visser as producers.

Lost Euphoria EP, (2000). Failure To Commit / Euphoric Loss / Reflections Of A Torn Spirit / Helplessness.
Detonation EP, Independent (2001). Forever Buried Pain / Starve / Voices Beyond Reason.
AN EPIC DEFIANCE, Osmose Productions OP148CD (2003). The Dawning / An Epic Defiance / The Prophecy Unfolds / Sword-Carved Skin / Forever Buried Pain / Crawling Through Vile / The Collision Of Despair / Deserving Death / Voices Beyond Reason / Lost Euphoria Part II / The Last Of My Commands / Starve.
PORTALS TO UPHOBIA, Osmose Productions OPCD 2171 (2005). Into Sulphur I Descend / Portals To Uphobia / Structural Deceit / Chaos Banished / End Of Sight, End Of Fears / Lost Euphoria Part III / The Loss Of Motion Control / Solitude Reflected / Beyond The Margin / The Source To Delve.
EMISSION PHAZE, Osmose Productions (2007). Invoking The Impact / When Stone Turns To Ash / Craven Ablaze / Into The Emission Phase / Chokedamp / Defects Of The Isolated Mind / Modulate / Infected / Soul Severance / Reborn Inside The Radiance / Fallout.

DETRITUS

BRISTOL, UK — *Mark Broomhead (vocals / bass), Earl Morris (guitar), Andy Neal (guitar), Andy Bright (drums).*

Bristol based Christian Thrash Metal band DETRITUS enrolled noted sleeve designer Rodney Matthews contributed album cover artwork. Despite attaining serious sales with the 'Perpetual Defiance' album DETRITUS folded after the 1993 effort 'If But For One'.

Frontman Mark Broomhead would join up with another high profile Christian Thrash outfit SEVENTH ANGEL and, after that band's demise, founded LOVE LIES BLEEDING with erstwhile SEVENTH ANGEL and AMARANTH guitarist Simon Bibby. With the addition of drummer Adam Gallagher and keyboard player Scott James this band duly evolved into FIRE FLY issuing a 1999 EP 'Swings & Roundabouts'.

PERPETUAL DEFIANCE, Under One Flag FLAG 55 (1991). Subliminal Division / Point Of No Return / Playing With Fire / Taste The Blood / Morbid Curiosity / No Mercy / Child / Eviction / Derange / OTT.
IF BUT FOR ONE, Kingsway ECD7030 (1993). Masquerade / So Far Away / D.I.G.M. / Let Peace Begin With Me / Feel / Blindly Rejected / If But For One / Sailor's Farewell / Father To Son / Painted Reality / As It Reigns / Subtle Shades.

DEUCE

LAUREL, MD, USA — *Tom Gattis (vocals / guitar), Timmy Meadows (guitar), Chris Hall (bass), Billy Giddings (drums).*

Formed in 1978 by guitarist Tom Gattis, the Baltimore heavyweights first line-up featured vocalist Eddie Day (hired because he was a sound-alike for CHEAP TRICK's Robin Zander and quickly dispensed with!) guitarist MARTY FRIEDMAN, bassist Steve Leter and drummer Chris Tinto. The latter duo were soon replaced by Chris Hall and Billy Giddings respectively. Gattis took over vocal chores after Day's departure.

Friedman quit for the sunnier climate of Hawaii and eventual fame as a member of MEGADETH via Hawaii acts VIXEN and HAWAII. His replacement, Timmy Meadows, joined the fold in 1980. Meadows was the brother of ANGEL's Punky Meadows and had been a member of the ANGEL road crew in the 70's.

DEUCE released a self-financed single in 1981, quickly earning themselves comparisons with British Metal acts by merging viciously precise twin guitar work with raw NWoBHM like aggression. During 1982 Hall left the group and DEUCE were thus joined by Mike Francis, a former compatriot of Meadows' on the ANGEL road crew. This line-up completely revamped a demo tape recorded after the single and both feature the DEUCE rendition of the Marty Friedman penned 'Angels In The Dust'

The band changed their name to TENSION prior to recording their proposed debut album. However, a Duluth, Georgia based record label titled O.P.M. Records released an album full of DEUCE demo material with the blessing of the band, despite having the appearance of a bootleg.

The first four tracks and tracks six to nine were recorded between 1978 and 1979 whilst tracks five and ten were cut between 1979 and 1980 with Timmy Meadows on guitar.

Gattis was later to be found operating WAR DOG and BALLISTIC. On September 29th 2002 DEUCE, including both Tom Gattis and MARTY FRIEDMAN, re-united for a one off live show in Washington.

DEVASTATION

TX, USA — *Rodney Runsmore (vocals), Dave Burk (guitar), Edward Vasquez (bass), Jesse Lopez (drums).*

Not to be confused with the Chicago thrashers of the same name that evolved into SINDROME. The Texan DEVESTATION specialised in intense Thrash metal. Bolstered their live sound for the 'Signs Of Life' album by adding second guitarist Henry Elizondo. Drummer Louis Carrisalez quit in mid 1990, later turned up fronting DEATH for a short spell on a British tour with KREATOR in 1990 when vocalist / guitarist Chuck Schuldiner was unable to fulfill the dates. His place was taken by David Lozano for the 'Idolatry' album but the band had reinstated Carrisalez by the time they played the Milwaukee Metalfest.

VIOLENT TERMINATION, Zombo ZR 0269 (1986). (Intro) Beginning Of The End / Massive Devastation / Innocent Submission / Syndrome Of Terror / Violent Termination / Death Is Calling / Meet Your Maker / Insanity / Deceptive Slaughter / Beneath The Surface.
SIGNS OF LIFE, Under One Flag CDFLAG 44 (1989). Eye For An Eye / Desolation: Manic Depressive / Signs Of Life / Retribution / Tomorrow We Die / Contaminated / Fear Of The Unknown / Escape To Violence.
IDOLATRY, Combat (1991). The Suffering / Freewill / Forsaken Hatred / Souls Of Sacrifice / Idolatry / Legacy Of Faith / Subconscious / Never Believe.

DEVIATE

BELGIUM — *Danny Mouethwil (vocals), Michael Kirby (guitar), Xavier Decoster (bass), Laurens Kusters (drums).*

DEVIATE are the product of an amalgam between Thrash act SIXTY NINE and Hardcore outfit MENTAL DISTURBANCE in 1991. DEVIATE industriously established their own label, I Scream Records, to issue the debut 1992 Frank von Bogaet produced 'Small Traces Of Life' debut. The band would go on to tour Europe as support to FEAR FACTORY in May of 1993 and put in further dates alongside EXCEL the September promoting the second record, 'Crisis Of Confidence' produced by Andr Gielen.

The 'Cold Prejudice' album was issued as a Belgian only limited edition release, selling out of it's pressing in a mere two weeks.

During 1996 the band, adding second guitarist Jo, participated in the inaugural 'Vans Warped' tour. The same year DEVIATE relocated to New York, releasing the Jamie Locke produced 'Thorn Of The Living' album the following year. MADBALL's Freddy Cricien would lend his session vocals to the track 'Last Judgement'.

Touring in Europe found the band as part of the December 'Mad X-Mas' tour billed alongside BACKFIRE. The band enhanced their reputation in Europe with a showing at the infamous 'Dynamo' festival in Holland.

'State Of Grace' arrived in June of 1999 and subsequently licensed for American release through Too Damn Hype Records. DEVIATE toured Japan during September of 1999, tapes from which spawned the live album 'One By One'.

The band put in a further date in Japan in February of 2002, performing at the mammoth SLAYER headlined Yokohama 'Beast Feast' festival.

SMALL TRACES OF LIFE, Scream 900 0300 21 (1992). Intro / Step To Me / Small Traces Of Life / Children's Whispers / One Against / Across The Nation / I Judge / Extro.
My Colour And Sickness, Scream 900 0305 24 (1993). My Colour And Sickness.
CRISIS OF CONFIDENCE, Scream 900 0306 20 (1993). Intro / Sickness / End Of A Fiction / Crisis Of Confidence / Mantrack / Case For The Prosecution / Oppression / In Order To Strike / Indicate The Reason / Deface / My Color.
WRECK STYLE, Scream 88 896 02 (1995). Style / Sequel Of arrogance / Spread A Threat / Strain / Falling Down / Face It / Crack-Down / Fearless State / Spoiled For Peace / Depth / Days Of Living / Conviction / Come Into View / Cold Prejudice / Inner Days / Neurotic / Only Nether World.
COLD PREJUDICE, (1996). Intro / Cold Prejudice / Inner Days / Neurotic / Only Neither World.
THORN OF THE LIVING, Scream (1997). Thorn Of The Living / Darkened World / Redemption Days / Lawless Innocence / Last Judgement / Cold Snap / Surge To Victory / Disgraced / Sworn Chains / 21st Century / Eyewitness / Realness / Half-Life / Divisions Of Pain.
DARKENED WORLD, Scream (1998). Crisis Of Confidence / Sickness / Spread A Threat / Sequel Of Arrogance / Cold Prejudice / Inner Days / Darkened World.
ONE BY ONE, I Scream (1999). Last Judgement / Thorn Of The Living / Cold Prejudice / Redemption Days / One By One / Spread A Threat / Only Neither World / After Time / Divisions Of Pain / 21st Century / Cold Snap / Wreck Style / Lawless Innocence.
STATE OF GRACE, Scream (1999). Wounds Of Time / State Of Grace / Stepped Off / Empty World / Aftertime / Circle Of Friends / Dawn Of Mankind / Burned Out / One By One / Broken Angel / Low-Down / Walk With Death.

DEVILISH

FINLAND — *Jaakko Peltonen (vocals / guitar), Juho Peltonen (guitar), Krister Virtanen (bass), Petri Törmä (drums).*

Thrash Metal band DEVILISH is rooted in the predecessor 1998 formation DISCIPLES OF DARKNESS, assembled by drummer Jaakko Peltonen alongside singer Rolle, bassist Andi and guitarist Mika. A 1999 demo, 'This Is A Good Day To Die', was issued, after which Peltonen took over bass duties as Andi departed. Pete was introduced on drums as Peltonen switched instruments again, now taking up rhythm guitar as Krister Virtanen took up bass. Subsequent demos included 'Armageddon Is Here' in 2000 and 'Reign Of Evil' in 2002.

In 2003 Jake's brother Juho entered the band to play lead guitar. With Rolle's exit, Jaako Peltonen took over the vocal responsibilities. DEVILISH recorded the demo 'Possessed By Hellfire' in October 2004.

This Is A Good Day To Die ..., Devilish (1999) (Demo). Disciples Of Darkness / Alone In The Dark / Lost / Human Mind Hell / No Escape From Dying.
Armageddon Is Here, Devilish (2000) (Demo). Armageddon Is Here / Figures In The Dark / Blinded By Faith / Time To Die.
Reign Of Evil, Devilish (2002) (Demo). Reign Of Evil / Armageddon Is Here / Hate Is Me.
Possessed By Hellfire, Devilish (2004) (Demo). Born By Human Fear / Possessed By Hellfire / Revolutionary Suicide / Beast Inside / Armageddon Is Here.

DEVOURED

EKSJÖ, SWEDEN — *David Hällgren (vocals), Goatfuck Demon (guitar), Pat Penetrator (bass), Eric Svensson (drums).*

DEVOURED an Eksjö based Black / Thrash outfit. The group was created under a former Death Metal guise, featuring singer David Hällgren. With Hällgren replaced by Johan Engdahl the band released an early 2004 demo entitled '... By Maggots', the band also comprising guitarist Oskar Mattelin, bassist Martin Olsson and drummer Eric Svensson as the band evolved into DEMONIUM.

The DEVOURED debut demo was re-released, with an additional cover version of IRON MAIDEN's 'The Trooper', in 2004 by No God Records re-branded 'Dependence On Malevolence'. In June of the following year DEMONIUM released the Black / Thrash orientated demo 'The Witchmaster' saw issue.

... By Maggots, Devoured (2004) (Demo). Devourer / Desecrating St. Peter's Cathedral / Bleed / Devourer (Version).

DEW-SCENTED

GERMANY — *Leif Jensen (vocals), Hendrik Bache (guitar), Florian Müller (guitar), Alexander Pahl (bass), Uwe Werning (drums).*

Germany's DEW-SCENTED, despite their innocuous title, trade in a vicious amalgam of Thrash Hardcore Doom Heavy Metal. DEW-SCENTED, founded in 1992 and taking their name from the works of Edgar Allan Poe, made their intentions clear with the 1994 opening demo 'Symbolization'. At this juncture DEW-SCENTED comprised vocalist Leif Jensen, guitarists Jörg Szittnick and Ralf "Shotte" Klein, bass player Patrick Heims and drummer Tarek Stinshoff. Further exposure would be gained with the inclusion of the 'Poems Of Dirt' track on a 1995 Major Records compilation. These sessions would lead to a recording contract with the Steamhammer label for the February 1996 'Immortelle' record. An intensive round of live promotion witnessed supports to EDGE OF SANITY, LAKE OF TEARS, SADIST, MORBID ANGEL and ARCH ENEMY as well as a ten date tour through Italy. With these shows over the group then re-assembled itself, bringing in new members guitarist Florian Müller replacing Szittnick and on the drums Uwe Werning.

The 1998 'Innoscent' album, produced by Dan Swanö and issued by Grind Syndicate Medial, would include a cover version of OVERKILL's 'Fatal If Swallowed'. The band's road schedule saw supports to DEATH, DISMEMBER and NIGHT IN GALES, participation in the 'Summer Clash' festival tour alongside DEICIDE, SIX FEET UNDER and BRUTAL TRUTH and an appearance at the 'Wacken Open Air' event.

The 1999 album 'Ill-Natured' would prove a pivotal point in the band's career as their trademark blend of Death and intricate Thrash styles came to the fore. Klein had made his exit beforehand, substituted in the studio by Christian Göllner. Festivals showings found the band making their presence felt throughout the Summer in Europe at the 'Wave Gotik Treffen', 'Fuck The Commerce' and 'Summer Breeze' events. Guest spots included gigs with IMMORTAL, PRIMORDIAL, WARHAMMER, VADER, CRYPTOPSY and TANKARD plus a full blown European tour ranked alongside OVERKILL and ANNIHILATOR. During late 1999 DEW-SCENTED drummer Uwe Werning would loan himself to NIGHT IN GALES for tour work.

DEW-SCENTED returned in January 2001 with the 'Inwards' album, recorded as a four piece of Jensen, Müller, Heims and Werning and produced by ex-HOLY MOSES guitarist Andy Classen. The band would tour Japan during March of 2001 billed alongside NIGHT IN GALES and DEFLESHED. 'Inwards' would see a January 2002 issue in Japan courtesy of Soundholic Records. Japanese versions included an exclusive track, a cover of SLAYER's 'War Ensemble'.

The band tagged onto the Thrash renaissance DESTRUCTION, KREATOR and SODOM 'Hell Comes To Your Town' for dates in Holland and Belgium during early 2002. Second guitarist Hendrik Bache was added to the ranks in March as gigs into France found the band billed with a mini tour package of NO RETURN, SCARVE and RAIN in May. A further run of European shows would be scheduled commencing September 19th in Eindhoven, Holland, a month's worth of dates supporting CANNIBAL CORPSE. For these gigs the band pulled in the BLO.TORCH credited Marvin Vriesde on additional guitar.

Digipack versions of DEW-SCENTED's August 2003 Andy Classen produced album 'Impact', which had Bache contributing studio bass, added a cover version of TURBONEGRO's 'Hobbit Motherfuckers' plus an extra original composition 'Force-Fed [The Bleeding Scheme]'. A double vinyl set of the new album paired 'Impact' with prior album 'Inwards'.

The band inducted OBSCENITY bassist Alexander Pahl and his band mate Marc Andree "Mücke" Dieken, also active with BK 49 and PAIN FOR PLEASURE, on the drums, the latter acting as a temporary stand in for Uwe Wening whilst the regular sticksman attended university. They then geared up for an exhaustive 2004 touring schedule to promote 'Impact' teaming up with KATAFALK and OUTBURST for a German run of dates in September, British club shows with NILE and MISERY INDEX in December which led up to the 'Xmas' European festivals in

DEW-SCENTED (pic: Axel Jusseit)

a heavyweight package comprising DEICIDE, DESTRUCTION, AMON AMARTH, NILE, GRAVEWORM and MISERY INDEX.

DEW-SCENTED entered Stage One Studios in Borgentreich with producer Andy Classen to record a new album 'Issue VI', featuring a cover version of ZEKE's 'Evil Dead', in January 2005. April gigs witnessed a union with Swedish veterans GRAVE although Florian Müller had exited in favour of Marvin Vriesde of BLO.TORCH and SEVERE TORTURE. Returning to Japan, the band performed as part of the 'Extreme The Dojo Vol. 14' tour in union with HIGH ON FIRE and MISERY SIGNALS in June. To coincide with these dates, Soundholic Records issued the 'Issue VI' album complete with exclusive bonus track 'Full-Blown Revenge'. In outside activity, Leif Jensen guested on Saint Etienne Death Metal band BENIGHTED's 'Identisick' album.

During September 2005 the group partnered with Denmark's MERCENARY and US headline act NEVERMORE for European touring. The band announced European tour dates for January 2006, traversing Poland, Germany, Holland, France, Belgium, Ireland, Switzerland, Austria, Italy and the UK, alongside a heavyweight cast of GRAVE, ABORTED, HURTLOCKER, VESANIA and CRYPTOPSY.

2006 shows witnessed the return of guitarist Florian Müller. German concerts in November were conducted with NOISE FOREST and FALLEN YGGDRASIL prior to December gigs aligned with TRIVIUM and Sweden's WOLF. In outside activity, Hendrik Bache donated guest guitar to RECKLESS TIDE's 'Helleraser' album. Alexander Pahl also featured on a new OBSCENITY album.

DEW-SCENTED announced early 2007 recording plans with producer Jörg Uken at Soundlodge Studio. 'Incinerate', mixed by Andy Sneap and arriving in April, featured Jeff Waters of ANNIHILATOR and Gus G. of FIREWIND guesting with guitar solos on the song 'Perdition for All'. Mille Petrozza from KREATOR provided guest vocals on the track 'Retain The Scars'. Shows across Europe for March and April 2007 aligned the band with NAPALM DEATH, BEHEMOTH, ROOT and MOONSPELL.

IMMORTELLE, Steamhammer SPV 085-18262 (1996). In Flames / Silenced / Black Is The Day / Thirst For The Sun / Unending / Afterlife / Afterlove / ... Yonder ... / Beloved Elysium / For You And Forever / Poets Of Dirt / Native Soil Venus / Theory Of Harm.
INNOSCENT, GSM (1998). Shatteredinsanity / Bereaved / Burn With Me / Starspangled / The Sicker Things / Everred / The Grapes Of Wrath / Aentity / Underneath / Fatal If Swallowed.
ILL-NATURED, GSM (1999). Embraced By Sin / This Grace / Simplicity In Chaos / Apocalypse Inside / Defiance / Wounds Of Eternity / Idolized / Skybound / The Endless / Hear See Say No ....
INWARDS, Nuclear Blast NB 704-2 (2002). Bitter Conflict / Unconditional / Life Ending Path / Inwards / Blueprints Of Hate / Locked In Motion / Degeneration / Terminal Mindstrip / Feeling Not / Reprisal.
IMPACT, Nuclear Blast NB 1169-2 (2003). Acts Of Rage / New Found Pain / Destination Hell / Soul Poison / Cities Of The Dead / Down My

Neck / One By One / Agony Designed / Slaughtervain / Flesh Reborn / 18 Hours.

ISSUE VI, Nuclear Blast NB 1452-2 (2005). Processing Life / Rituals Of Time / Turn To Ash / Ruins Of Hope / Out Of The Self / The Prison Of Reason / Bled Dry / In Defeat / Never To Return / Vortex / Conceptual End / Evil Dead.

INCINERATE, Nuclear Blast NB 1817-2 (2007). Exordium (Intro) / Vanish Away / Final Warning / That's Why I Despise You / The Fraud / Into The Arms Of Misery / Perdition For All / Now Or Never / Aftermath / Everything Undone / Contradictions / Retain The Scars / Exitus (Outro).

DIE KREUZEN

MILWAUKEE, WI, USA — *Danny Kubinski (vocals / guitar), Brian Egeness (guitar), Keith Brammer (bass), Erik Tunison (drums).*

A truly innovative Wisconsin Crossover Metal act that covered a wider spectrum of genres than most. The band were notable for constantly shifting the parameters of their music with each successive release taking in Punk, Thrash and Hardcore elements. DIE KREUZEN was founded during 1981 by vocalist Dan Kubinski, guitarist Brian Egeness—both relocated from Rockford, Illinois, bassist Keith Brammer and drummer Erik Tunison. The title 'DIE KREUZEN' was apparently deliberately chosen as to add to their mystique and avoid genre tagging.

The band's inaugural public offering would come in the form of four songs donated to the 'Noise' magazine cassette 'Charred Remains' compilation. This would be capitalised on by three further tracks as part of another compilation collection, 'The Master Tape'. The exposure afforded by these release led in turn to the 7 EP 'Cows And Beer', issued by the Version Sound label in late 1982. This record soon sold out of it's initial 1000 copy pressing, a second run of similar quantity also soon being swallowed up. DIE KREUZEN promoted the release by touring the West Coast and down South into the summer of 1983.

A debut full length album, released by the Touch & Go label in July 1984, proved an immediate seller and proved the catalyst for a solid two years of road work.

A second album, 'October File', emerged in May 1986 followed by July 1988's 'Century Days'. After road work in Europe DIE KREUZEN cut a single 'Gone Away', one of the B sides for which was a rework of AEROSMITH's 'Seasons Of Wither'.

At this juncture various members indulged themselves in side concerns. Brammer and Kubinski busied themselves with Darren Brown and Eric Lunde's proto industrial band BOY DIRT CAR. Brammer would also perform with WRECK whilst the industrious Kubinski managed to also allocate time for IMPACT TEST 1990, WAR ON THE SAINTS and THE MUCKRAKERS. Both Kubinski and Egeness formed part of CHEAP TRICK homage band CHICK TREAT. Eventually regrouping DIE KREUZEN delivered their fourth album for Touch & Go, 'Cement'.

In April of 1992 DIE KREUZEN opted to disband, apparently prompted by Egeness' decision to make an exit. The surviving trio soon re-gelled as CHAINFALL, pulling in S.O.D.A. and NERVE TWINS guitarist Charles Jordan. Other endeavours found Kubinski and Tunison as members of the quaintly titled FUCKFACE whilst Brammer dabbled with the CARNIVAL STRIPPERS.

Kubinski would later re-emerge touting a fresh act CUSTOM GRAND and later forged DECAPITADO with guitarist Takis Kinis, a scene veteran of K.O.R., MORTA SKULD, PROPHIT, REALM and WHITE FEAR CHAIN.

Cows And Beer EP, Version Sound (1983). The School / Think For Me / Hate Me / Pain / Don't Say Please / Enemies.

DIE KREUZEN, Touch & Go T&GLP4 (1986). Rumors / This Hope / In School / On The Street / Enemies / Get 'Em / Fighting / No Time / All White / Pain / Sick People / Hate Me / Live Wire / Not Anymore / Mannequin / Fuckups / Think For Me / Dirt And Decay / Don't Say Please / No Name.

OCTOBER FILE, Touch & Go T&G7 (1987). Man In The Trees / Uncontrolled Passion / It's Been So Long / Imagine A Light / Cool Breeze / Counting Cracks / Red To Green / Among The Ruins / Hear And Feel / Hide And Seek / Conditioned / There's A Place / Open Lines / Melt / Rumors / This Hope / Rumors / This Hope / In School / I'm Tired / On the Streets / Enemies / Get 'Em / Fighting / No Time / All White / Pain—Sick People / Hate Me / Live Wire / Not Anymore / Mannequin / Fuckups / Think For Me / Dirt And Decay / Don't Say Please / No Name.

Gone Away, Touch & Go T&G40 (1988). Gone Away / Seasons Of Wither / Man In The Trees (Live) / Bitch Magnet (Live) / Number Three (Live).

Gone Away, Touch & Go (1988) (Limited edition white vinyl). Gone Away / Different Ways (Live).

CENTURY DAYS, Touch And Go T&G30 (1988). Earthquakes / Lean Into It / Different Ways / So Many Times / These Days / Elizabeth / Stomp / Slow / The Bone / Bitch Magnet / Number Three / Dream Sky / Halloween.

GONE AWAY, Touch & Go T&G73CD (1990). Gone Away / Seasons Of Wither / Pink Flag / Land Of Treason / Stomp / Cool Breeze / Man In The Trees / Bitch Magnet / Number Three / Different Ways / In School / Think For Me / Hate Me / Pain / Don't Say Please / Enemies / On The Street / All White / Fighting.

Pink Flag, Touch & Go T&G65 (1990). Pink Flag / Land Of Treason.

CEMENT, Touch & Go T&G80 (1991). Wish / Shine / Big Bad Days / Holes / Downtime / Blue Song / Best Goodbye / Heaven / Deep Space / Shake Loose / Over And The Edge / Black Song.

Big Bad Days, Touch & Go T&G79 (1991). Big Bad Days / Gone Away (Acoustic).

DIECELL

FINLAND — *Antti Railio (vocals), Juha-Matti Åberg (guitar), Jaakko Töyli (guitar), Sammy Puolakka (bass), Sami Peltonen (drums).*

DIECELL was initiated in the Autumn of 2002, by singer Antti Railio and guitarist Juha-Matti Åberg, soon recruiting drummer Sami Peltonen. The original band unit suffered from a flux of members, finally going into hiatus during 2003 when Railio joined CELESTY and Åberg teamed up with covers band MR. CROWLEY. However, DIECELL reconvened in January 2005, recording a debut demo that August featuring guitarist Jaakko Töyli and Sammy Puolakka on bass.

DIECELL guitarist Sami Puolakka would be found as a member of Industrial Metal endeavour RADICAL M PROJECT during 2003, involving ALL IN ME vocalist / guitarist Esa Uusimaa, SHADEMBRACE vocalist Jenny Malmberg, former THROES OF DAWN bass player Matti Suomela with Otto Väisänen of INCENDIUM on the drums.

DIOS HASTIO

LIMA, PERU — *Jose (vocals), Oscar (guitar), Camilo (guitar), Paco (bass), O.A.D.M. (drums).*

DIOS HASTIO is a Lima based Thrash Metal band, issuing the 'Cervix Inferno' album in 2003. The group had been forged during 1995 by vocalist Jose, guitarist Oscar and drummer O.A.D.M. Adding Eduardo to the ranks on bass the group debuted with the demos 'Raza De Gusanas' and 'Ascenso Del Error'. The rehearsal session 'No Hay Nada Q Esperar' preceded a split cassette shared with German band WOJZCECH. Signing to Japanese label Peace Punk DIOS HASTIO's inaugural 7" single emerged in March of 1999.

DIOS HASTIO's first album 'Advenimiento De Lo Inevitable' was delivered in September 2000 then further 7' singles, split affairs shared with Peruvian act AUTONOMIA and Japanese band NO FUTURES, arrived in 2001. In April of 2002 the US based Vicious Infererence label published a split EP in alliance with Brazilians SEPTICEMIA. 2003 saw the issue of a second full length album, 'Cervix Inferno', in March and the EP 'Morfologia Del Desastre' on Bakteria Records in June.

Line-up changes then witnessed Paco taking over on bass guitar and Camilo acquired as second guitarist. DIOS HASTIO then projected a split outing with AGATHOCLES.

ADVENIMIENTO DE LO INEVITABLE, (2000). El Odio Te Alcanzara / Extremo Evidente / Cea / Cai / Endemico Conformismo / Sostienes Tu Propia Derrota / Disfixia / Pira De Cadaveres / Clamor Abisal / Mil Nombres Para La Ramera / Moriras II / Perpetuas Memorias Desde La Desolacion A La Distancia / Desercion Anunciada II / Dios Hastio / Herencia De Extincion.

CERVIX INFERNO, Impulso Ruin (2003). Intro / Herencia IV / Rito De Usurpacion / DH II / Mixtificacion II / Caidas Sucesivas II / Advenimiento De Lo Inevitable / Cefalo Cervix / Lealtad Al Alcohol / Hay Que Erradicar / Carnaria Espina/Voral / El Hereje / ¿Ante Quien Te Postras Ahora? / Golem.

NOLME, Impulso Ruin (2005) (Split album with AGATHOCLES). Nolme / M.L.D.U.D. / No Hay Mas De Tus Victimas Bajo Los Escombros / Desesperacion Fenomena / Mesianarco / Hay Que Erradicar / Raza De Gusanos / E.D.L.D.H. / Disfilia III / Temporada De Traicion / Por Mi Todos Uds Se Van Al Diablo / Ataque De Los Cuasares / ... ADV Lp 2005.

DISCIPLES OF AGGRESSION

SILVER SPRING, MD, USA — *Carl Leissler (vocals), Minnie Mean (guitar), Dee Brian C. (bass), Dellion Christ (drums).*

A mid nineties Thrash Metal act, DISCIPLES OF AGGRESSION, hailing from Silver Spring in Maryland, featured bassist Dee Brian C. (a.k.a. Dave Calhoun), a veteran of VISION, NIGHT CONNECTION and Washington D.C. act PHANTASM. The 1994 line up comprised singer Carl Leissler, guitarist Meanie Mean, bassist Dee Brian C. and drummer Dellion Christ. For the 1995 EP 'Prelude To Brutality' the group was joined by second guitarist Russ Strahan. The trio of Minnie Mean, Dee Brian C. and Dellion Christ forged LEVEL that same year, issuing the EP 'Cries Of Insanity From A Tin Room', 1996 album 'Silent Cries' and 1998 EP 'Subtle Acts Of Rage'. This same triumvirate then created M FRANCIS FESTER for a 2000 album 'I M Your God'.

Calhoun later went on to front Baltimore BLACK SABBATH tribute band AFTER FOREVER and BULLET THERAPY. As a solo artist, DEE BRIAN C. released the 2003 'Sabbatical', naturally comprising five BLACK SABBATH covers. Also an author, the vocalist has published the horror novel 'Kidney Stone Soup For The Soul'.

Prelude To Brutality, AOD (1995). Pitch Black / The Angel Of Death / Dead Wrong.

DISCIPLES OF POWER

CANADA — *Hart Bachmier (vocals / guitar), Wes Sontag (guitar), Andy Smith (bass), Dean Relf (drums).*

Founded in Medicine Hat, Alberta in 1985, from the ashes of WARTHORN, DISCIPLES OF POWER are one of Canada's longest running Metal acts. The driving force behind the band has always been founder, Hart Bachmier who relocated the band to Edmonton in 1987. After a quick demo called 'Kutulu' in 1987 and another called 'Power Of Death', they appeared on a local, vinyl compilation called 'Writing In Stone' in 1988. DISCIPLES OF POWER were early enough on the Metal scene to score a reasonably secure deal with Fringe Records and they relocated to Ottawa.

In 1989 they released their debut album 'Power Trap' and toured Canada. The band relocated again to briefly to Vancouver where they produced a video for the track 'Crisis'. Yet another relocation and line-up change found the band back in Edmonton where they and recorded their second Fringe album, 'Ominous Prophecy'. More touring followed and the over the next few years the band received critical acclaim for their Death-Thrash style. The band filmed a video for the track 'Nature's Fury' and hosted the 'Power Hour', Much Music's metal video specialty show.

After two releases on Fringe, the band decided to go the independent route releasing another album entitled 'Invincible Enemy' on their own Mindt Gash label. Another video followed for the track 'Before The End' and more touring followed. 1993 was a busy year for the band as DISCIPLES OF POWER released total re-working of the debut 'Power Trap' also on Mindt Gash. Another video was shot in Edmonton this time for the title track of the re-issue subtitled, The Brutal Re-mix.

In 1995 the band release their 4th full-length 'Mechanikill'. This album was not as well received and the band toured Western Canada very sporadically for the next several years while the band members pursue other projects. Despite many line-up changes the band has a solid reputation, not only for their intense, technical Death Metal but also for their professional image and attitude enhanced by steady touring, videos and the excellent artwork. Steve Chandler provided the art for the first two releases and the following three were done by Shane Hawco of THORAZINE.

In 2000 the band decided to regroup and begins writing and touring a little more extensively including headlining the inaugural show of the Okanagan Metal Fest in Oliver, BC. in the summer of 2001. A further album, 'In Dust We Trust', is projected for release also on the Mindt Gash label.

POWER TRAP, Fringe (1989). Shades Of Grey / Powertrap / Ice Demons / Slave To No One / Protector / Night Of The Priest / Crisis / Hidden Worlds / Bitch Of Doom / Disciples Of Power.

OMINOUS PROPHECY, Fringe (1992). Chains Of Reason / Vindicator / Nature's Fury (Betrayed Earth) / Witch Of Lies / Sleeping Dead / The Rising / Skull March / Eternal Purgatory.

INVINCIBLE ENEMY, Mindt Gash PPC003 (1993). Afterbirth / Invincible Enemy / Infected Science / Born Unto Death / Injecticide / Lords Of Creation / Return From The Gates / Before The End.

MECHANIKILL, Mindt Gash (1996). Introvenus / Wings Of Suicide / Cast The First Stone / Inside (Circles Of Sickness) / Crypts Of The Frozen Soul / Swarming The Throne / Mechanikill / Symphonic Animosity / Waraphoric Structures (Part 1 & 2).

IN DUST WE TRUST, Mindt Gash (2002). The Cursing Of Winter / Tripwire / Armoured Ring Of Skull / Widows Web / Pharmacudical Suicide / In Dust We Trust / Dimensions Of The Dragon Sky / Wartorn.

DISINCARNATE

USA — *Tomas Lindberg (vocals), James Murphy (guitar), Steve DiGeorgio (bass), Nick Barker (drums).*

Although a veteran journeyman guitarist for hire on the Death scene guitarist JAMES MURPHY, whose impressive credits include AGENT STEEL, DEATH, TESTAMENT, CANCER, OBITUARY and KONKHRA, also made time for his own act DISINCARNATE.

The 1993 Colin Richardson produced album 'Dreams Of The Carrion Kind' had Murphy working with fellow guitarist Jason Carman, vocalist Bryan Cegon and drummer Tommy Viator. Guesting vocalists were CANCER's John Walker and MY DYING BRIDE man Aaron Stainthorpe.

The band was reassembled in 1999 with a line-up of Murphy, ex-AT THE GATES singer Tomas Lindberg, SADUS / DEATH bassist Steve DiGeorgio and CRADLE OF FILTH drummer Nick Barker. Before any product could be issued Barker joined DIMMU BORGIR.

Murphy has issued two solo albums to date 'Convergence' in 1996 and 1999's 'Feeding The Machine'. DiGeorgio joined ICED EARTH. Unfortunately the guitarist was diagnosed with a massive brain tumour in 2001.

In February 2004 Roadrunner Records re-issued a remastered version of the 'Dreams Of The Carrion Kind' album, adding three extra demo tracks. During November 2006 Polish label Metal Mind Productions re-issued 'Dreams Of The Carrion Kind' as a digipack, limited to 2000 hand numbered copies.

DREAMS OF THE CARRION KIND, Roadrunner (1993). De Profundis / Stench Of Paradise Burning / Beyond The Flesh / In Sufferance / Monarch Of The Sleeping Marches / Soul Erosion /

Entranced / Confine Of Shadows / Deadspawn / Sea Of Tears / Immemorial Dream.

DREAMS OF THE CARRION KIND, Metal Mind Productions MASS CD DG 0987 (2006) (Polish release digipack. Limited edition 2000 hand numbered copies). De Profundis (Intro) / Stench Of Paradise Burning / Beyond The Flesh / In Sufferance / Monarch Of The Sleeping / Soul Erosion / Entranced / Confine Of Shadows / Deadspawn / Sea Of Tears / Immemorial Dream (Outro) / Stench Of Paradise Burning (Demo) / Soul Erosion (Demo) / Confine Of Shadows (Demo).

DIVINE SIN

SÖDERHAMN, SWEDEN — *Freddie Lundberg (vocals), Micke Andersson (guitar), Peter Halvarsson (guitar), Buddy Goude (bass), Martin Knutar (drums).*

Thrash Metal act from Söderhamn. DIVINE SIN released the demos 'Dying To Live' in 1990 and 'Years Of Sorrow' in 1991. The DIVINE SIN recording line-up at this juncture involved Freddie Lundberg on vocals, guitarist Bjurta Johansson, bass player Bubby Goude with Martin Knutar on drums. Third demo 'Resurrection' was recorded in May 1993.

DIVINE SIN, having added guitarists Micke Andersson and Peter Halvarsson, contracted with Black Mark Records for the debut album 'Winterland' in 1995, crafting this set of tracks with producer Bror Tornell at FS Studio in Söderhamn. A follow up, 'Thirteen Souls' seeing Halvarsson was replaced by Martin Unoson and produced by Uffe Pettersson at the Wavestation Studio in Ljusne, arrived in November 1997. Singer Freddie Lundberg gained credits with MORGANA LEFAY, LEFAY, INCARNATED, HOLOCAUST and FANTASMAGORIA.

Dying To Live, Divine Sin (1990) (Demo). Intro / All Alone / Dying To Live / Burnt To The Bone.

Years Of Sorrow, Divine Sin (1991) (Demo). Grief / Premature Burial / Years Of Sorrow / Condemned / A Violent Breed.

Resurrection, (1993) (Demo). A Twilight Dream / Resurrection / Children Of Conformity / Matricide / Dreams Of Oblivion.

WINTERLAND, Black Mark BMCD 83 (1995). Gates Of Everbe / Children Of Conformity / Dead Again / Memories / All Alone / A Twilight Dream / Winterland / Years Of Sorrow / Endless Sleep / My Best Nightmare / In The Wake Of Perfection.

THIRTEEN SOULS, Black Mark (1997). Synanceia Horridae / Primal Fear / The Final Lie / Thirteen Souls / Among The Shades / Postcard From Hell / My Kingdom Come / Dreams Of Oblivion / Crimson Chameleon / Matricide / Emotionless / No Faith, No Hope, No Love / XIII.

DIZORDERZ

PRAGUE, CZECH REPUBLIC — *Ondřej Kuchař (vocals / guitar), Lukáš Hlásek (guitar), Imrich Kočiš (bass), Michal Kasprowicz (drums).*

Prague Thrash outfit DIZORDERZ issued the demos 'Live In Prosek-Stop The Madness' in 1997 and 'Fatal Variations' during January of 1998. Line up changes saw the departure of guitarist Miroslav Kroupa and bassist Jiøí Chyba. The cassette album 'Machinery' emerged in 1999 on the SMS label. DIZORDERZ at this juncture involved vocalist / guitarist Ondřej Kuchař, guitarist Jan Hodaè, bassist Tomáš Cimrman with Dušan Liščák on the drums. A further promotional release, entitled 'What The Fuck?', arrived in 2002. Line up for these sessions comprised Kuchař plus an all new cast of bassist Imrich Kočiš, Michal Kasprowicz and guitarist Lukáš Hlásek.

MACHINERY, SMS LP3890 (1999). Machinery / Myself / Secret Of Energy / Left To Seek / 311, Proud Of R.A.F. / Song For Death / Shadows Alive / Touch Of Paradise / God's Closed Eyes / Fight 'Till The End / World Behind The Eyes / Return To The Real World ... And Then Die!

What The Fuck?, (2002). Temptation / Labyrinth / Nameless / War.

DOFKA

WHEELING, WV, USA — *Scot Edgell (vocals), Jim Dofka (guitar / bass / keyboards), Casey Culbreth (drums).*

Guitarist Jim Dofka was previously a member of SCREAMER. The band released their independent debut on cassette in late 1990. DOFKA quickly struck a licensing deal with French label Black Dragon, who issued the CD in Europe with alternate cover art and a re-arranged track sequence. The band featured the fretboard skills of Jim Dofka whose neo-classical based, shred soloing were the basis of most of the Speed Metal compositions.

Jim Dofka founded the band PSYCHO SCREAM in 1994 and was working with the then unknown vocalist, Tim Aymar who later went on to work with DEATH mentor Chuck Schuldiner in CONTROL DENIED.

The DOFKA album was reissued again in 1997 on the Conquest label with three bonus tracks and the band, although short-lived, still commands some respect among collectors as an early example of US Speed/Power Metal.

TOXIC WASTELAND, Black Dragon BD046 (1990). Dragons / Vampire's Curse / Where The Monsters Live / Toxic Wasteland / Intro Solo / Guitar Opera / There Is No More / Speed Mental / Doctor Of Death / Taken All We Had / Pick Monsters / Can't Make It Alone.

DOG FACED GODS

STOCKHOLM, SWEDEN — *Johnny Wranning (vocals), Conny Jonsson (guitar), Peter Tuthill (bass), Richard Evensand (drums).*

Stockholm's DOG FACED GODS was named after the TESTAMENT song. Vocalist Johnny Wranning and guitarist Conny Jonsson also have credits with EBONY TEARS. Wranning is also an ex-MISCREANT member. Before too long all the membership of EBONY TEARS were involved with DOG FACED GODS operating both bands in tandem. Pelle Saether of ZELLO produced and added guest vocals to the 1998 album. Keyboards came courtesy of ZELLO's Mats Olsson.

Following three EBONY TEARS albums, 1998's 'Tortura Insomnia', 1999's 'A Handful Of Nothing' and 'Evil As Hell' in 2001, Wranning exited that band, forging EYETRAP in November 2000 in collaboration with erstwhile SHATTRD personnel guitarist Fredrik Rhodin, bassist Joakim "Chucken" Rhodin and drummer, Jan Karlsson.

In 2004 the singer announced his new band MURGHATROID, a union with ex-THERION drummer Sam Carpenter (a.k.a. Sami Karppinen). Over his career, drummer Rickard Evensand would wind his way through a succession of acts of rising stature including EBONY TEARS, SORCEROR, Funksters IT'S ALIVE, MANIC DEPRESSION, SOUTHPAW, EYEBALL, SOILWORK, American act CHIMAIRA and the 2004 retro Black-Thrash union DEMONOID.

Peter Tuthill quit his position in CONSTRUCDEAD in May of 2005 in order to resurrect DOG FACED GODS. In early 2006 Tuthill announced new formation NAILSTATE to the world, being a union of Paul Mäkitalo (a.k.a. 'Themgoroth') of DARK FUNERAL and INFERNAL, Gustaf Jorde, ex-DEFLESHED and Stefan Norgren from ETERNAL OATH.

In early 2007 it was revealed Evansand was also involved with a high profile side act, DEAD BY APRIL, featuring M.A.N guitar player Martin Meyerman, DRAGONLAND guitarist Olof Mörck, bassist Staffan Persson of WHEN WE FALL plus the PAINFIELD, DEATHDESTRUCTION and NIGHTRAGE credited singer Jimmie Strimell.

Demo 1997, Dog Faced Gods (1997) (Demo). Structural Damage / Room 18.

RANDOM CHAOS THEORY IN ACTION, Gothenburg Noiseworks GNW 04 (1998). Blindfolded / The Man Inside / God Over All / Face My Rage / Fractured Image / Dirge / Prozac 3105 / Purge / As Worlds Collide ... / Swallowtail / The Chaos Factor.

Demo 1999, Dog Faced Gods (1999) (Demo). I.D. / Soul Bleed / Wreak Havoc.

Demo 2000, Dog Faced Gods (2000) (Demo). Metamorphosis / The New Man Of Me / Centrifugal.

DOMAIN

ŁÓDŹ, POLAND — *Paul (vocals / guitar), V-ac (guitar), Mike (bass), Mitloff (drums).*

Łódź based Black-Thrash Metal band DOMAIN started life as a proto-Black Metal duo in 1989 under the billing of PAN-DEMONIUM. Although only sporting two members, vocalist / guitarist Paul and colleague Peter 'Zuber', PANDEMONIUM built up a cult following on the live circuit and generated by the demos 'Reh' and February 1992's 'Devilri'. Pulling in bassist Simon a third demo set, 'The Ancient Catatonia', was issued before PANDEMONIUM went into hiatus. Simon would join TENEBRIS whilst Paul founded DOMAIN due to the fact ousted member Zuber put in a legal claim to the PANDEMONIUM band title.

Signing to Morbid Noizz Productions they would debut with the 'Pandemonium' album in 1995. A switch to Apocalypse Productions saw the release of 1999's '… From Oblivion', with former drummer Karol 'Carol' Skwarczewski, a veteran of DEVASTATOR and IMPERATOR, would be superseded by Piotr 'Mittloff' Kozieradzki of HATE, GOETIA and RIVERSIDE repute, and 'Gat Etemmi' in 2002. Studio guests on this latter outing including keyboard player Rober Szrednicki and female vocalist Ewa Frakstein. However, Mittloff departed to prioritise RIVERSIDE. In October of 2003 the SIRIUS, DARK GALLERY, UMBRA SPHERE and STROMMOUSSHELD credited Maelstrom joined the ranks as keyboard player / programmer.

DOMAIN planned a fourth album, entitled 'Namtar The Wizard', for 2004 issue but would in fact revert back to the PANDEMONIUM banner for a comeback album 'Zonei', released by Mystic Productions.

PANDEMONIUM, Morbid Noizz Productions (1995). The Beginning / Blood Of God / Immemoreal Legend / Sword Into Heart Of Lies / The Calling / Hagia Sophia / Lost Preexistence / Mirror Of Hate / Somewhere Above / Lost Preexistence (Remix).
… FROM OBLIVION, Apocalypse Productions (1999). Whispered In The Dark / Supernatural / The Maklu Spell / Sunless Domain / Ritual Combat / Asymetrical Megalith / Deathmaker / Fall Into Decay / Devilri / The Enter / Nar Mattaru / Whispered In The Dark (Remix) / Unholy Existence (Live) / Ritual Combat (Live).
GAT ETEMMI, Apocalypse Productions (2002). Asaku Marsuti / The Seven Sibbiti / Ningiszida / The Ancient Ones Monstrous / Gat Etemmi / Anzu Storm / Azag Rite / Dingur Xul / The Gate Of Pazuzu / Summa Amelu Kasip / Shub Nigurath Space Outside / Yog Sothoth Dominion.

DOMINATION BLACK

KOTKA, FINLAND — *The Sentinel Riiconen (vocals), Teppo Heiscanen (guitar), Ace Wiren (guitar), Lauri Eerola (bass), Juha Beck (drums).*

Kotka Thrashers DOMINATION BLACK released the 2003 demo 'Trendopieni'. The band is fronted by ex-INSTANT CLARITY and IHANDER man The Sentinel Riiconen. Guitarist Ace Wiren has a tradition with TWISTED SISTER, MÖTLEY CRÜE and KISS tribute bands and INSANE INSIDE whilst his six string partner has ties to MORBIDITY and INSTANT CLARITY.

An EP, entitled 'Fear ReLoaDead', was projected for 2004. The 'Fearbringer' album, recorded at Woodbine Garden Studios in Pyhtää, followed for Poison Arrow Records in December 2005. DOMINATION BLACK would be back in the studio to craft a further record, 'Dark Legacy', in June 2006 for issue that November.

Termination Daze Vol. 2, Domination Black (2003) (Demo). Silent Killer / Assassin / Crystal Lake / Death Battle 813 / Shattering Existence / Death Race.
Trendofobia, Domination Black (2004) (Demo). Soulcrusher / Prisoners In Hell / Predatorium X / Ultra-Speed Destructor / The Face Of Horror.
Fear Re-LoaDEAD, Domination Black (2004) (Demo). Haunted Hellhouse / Crystal Lake / Poison Tears / Fear Re-LoaDEAD.
FEARBRINGER, Poison Arrow (2005). Ultra-Speed Destructor / Nightmare Asylum / Traitor Within / Alone In The Darkness / Haunted Hellhouse / The Psycho / From Abyss / Frozen Tears / Fear Re-LoaDEAD.
DARK LEGACY, Poison Arrow (2006). Enter The Dark Legacy / Follow The Fear / Scavenger Of Evil / Ghost Of The Nightfall / The Cemetery / What Lies Beneath / Dark Water Dreams / Two Faced Devil / Phantom Light / Nightmare World.

DOOM

JAPAN — *Takashi Fujita (vocals / guitar), Masami Chiba (bass), Shigeru Kobayasho (drums).*

DOOM were renowned eighties Thrashers, founded in 1985 by ZADKIEL veteran Koh 'Pirarucu' Morota on fretless bass and vocalist / guitarist Takashi Fujita using a rhythm box to compensate for lack of a drummer. In January of 1986 they inducted Jyo-ichi 'Joe' Hirokawa on drums in time for their live debut at the 'Kagurazaka Explosion' event in March.

DOOM debuted in 1986 with the single 'Go Mad Yourself!' for the Rock House label, following up in 1987 with the album 'No More Pain …' for Explosion Works Records. That year two songs, 'You End. Get Up! You' and 'Dooms Days' also appeared on the Invitation compilation album 'Skull Thrash Zone Vol I'. DOOM were quickly established in Japan with sell out shows being the norm.

A whole slew of albums then ensued through the Invitation label with 'Killing Field' and 'Complicated Mind' in 1988. DOOM ventured to North America to cut this album with producer Chris Butler, also slotting in three concerts, including a gig at the infamous CBGB's. 'Incompetent …' in 1989 and 'Human Noise' arrived in 1992 before a label switch to Alzheimer Records for the 1993 'Illegal Soul' record. Also released in 1993 would be DOOM's cover rendition of the KISS track 'Parasite' on the Victor compilation 'Dance 2 Noise #6 Compilation'. DOOM shared a 7" single 'The Nightmare Runs' through the H.G. Fact label with THE COCOBOTS. H.G. Fact also issued a 1994 split 7" in alliance with HEDGEHOG and the 1995 'Freakout' EP in 1995. Founder Morota bailed out in 1995. The latter DOOM line up included SHELLSHOCK bassist Masami Chiba and Shigeru 'Pazz' Kobayasho of GASTUNK on drums.

Morota, long known to be suffering from depression, was found dead on 7th May 1999, his body floating in a river. Two years earlier the bass man had released a solo album entitled 'Life & Death'. He would be working up a new band entitled EGORA DORAMI just before his demise.

DOOM members, alongside Baki of GASTUNK, forged QUARTERGATE during 2003.

Go Mad Yourself!, Rock House EXP-HM-101017 (1986). Fire On The Oil / Last Stand To Hell / Why!? / Go Mad Yourself!
NO MORE PAIN, Explosion Works EXP-HMD251050 (1987). Death To Wimp! / Body No Body / I'm Your Junky Doll / Go Mad Yourself! / You Don't Cry … No Long Life / Fire On The O.I.L. / No More Pain / Why?! / Iron Card / Kick It Out / Last Stand To Hell / Til' Death.
KILLING FIELD, Invitation VDR-9059 (1988). Rocking Russian / Killing Field / Ghost Of Princess / Bad Priest / Fence And Barricade.
COMPLICATED MIND, Invitation VDR-1577 (1988). Complicated Mind / Fall, Rise, And … / The Boy's Dog / Bright Light / Slave Of Heaven / Kingdom Of Silkroad / Can't Break My … Without You / Painted Face / Poor Boy Condition / Nervous Break Down.
INCOMPETENT, Invitation VDR-1635 (1989). I Can't Go Back To Myself / Eating It Raw / 20th Century A Proud Man / Killing Time / A Sandglass Of The Jungle / Death Of False Rock! / I Will Be With You … / Lost! In My Head / Sympathy For The Devil / Desert Flower / Incompetent … The War Pig.
HUMAN NOISE, Invitation VICL-116 (1991). Naked A Lunatic / A Day Of The Holocaust / The Stupid Man / No Free / Lyrics / No Way Out / To … Gray People / Revenge And Dirty Tricks / Human Noise.
ILLEGAL SOUL, Alzheimer AHR-2 (1992). I'm Real / Deliver Me from Reasons Why? / Blood On The Rise / (Instrumental) / Those Who Race Towards Death / Can't Turn Back??! / We Shall Miss Nothing (Killing Field II) / Gotta Love Yourself / Dead Soul.

Sure, HG Fact HG-021 (1994) (Split single with HEDGEHOG). Sure.

Freakout, HG Fact HG-019 (1995). Cruel World / Broken Walls.

WHERE YOU LIFE LIES!?, (1999). No Mean / Not Feel / It's Wrong / Wish / What Have They Done?! / Tell Me Where Your Life Lies / To Follow Me.

DORSAL ATLANTICA

BRAZIL — *Carlos Vândalo (vocals / guitar), Alexandre Farias (bass), Guga (drums).*

Thrash Metal act DORSAL ATLANTICA, a leading force on the South American scene, shared their inaugural 1985 split album 'Ultimatum' with METALMORPHOSIS. The band at this juncture comprised of vocalist / guitarist Carlos Vândalo, bassist Claudio 'Cro-Magnon' Lopes and drummer Marcos 'Animal'. DORSAL ATLANTICA broke new ground in Brazil with their blend of Speed Metal and Punk attitude, paving the way for a plethora of acts which followed. For 1980's 'Antos Do Fim' the band listed their drummer simply as 'Hardcore'. The 1989 release 'Searching For The Light' would receive an American release through the Wild Rags label.

During February of 1996 DORSAL ATLANTICA undertook European tour dates partnered with REIGN and RAWBONED. Ângelo Arede would assume the bass position for the 1997 album 'Straight'. DORSAL ATLANTICA put in an appearance at the 1998 Brazilian 'Monsters Of Rock' festival. By 2002 DORSAL ATLANTICA had drafted Alexandre Farias on bass. Their classic 'Ultimatum' would be the subject of expanded re-issues and outtakes recordings in 2002.

ULTIMATUM, Gravacoes Electricas (1985) (Split album with METALMORPHOSE). Imperio De Sata / Catastrofe / Armagedon / Princesa Do Prazer / Heavy Metal.

ANTES DO FIM, Lunario Perpetuo Discos (1986). Cacador Da Noite / H.T.L.V.-3 / Alcool / Depressao Suicida / Vorkuta / Joseph Mengele / Guerrilha / Inveja / Morte Aos Falsos.

Victory, Flight Nineteen 001 (1988) (Limited Edition 500 Copies 7" Vinyl Swiss Single). Victory / Dweller Of The Streets.

DIVIDIR E CONQUISTAR, Heavy Discos (1988). Tortura / Vitoria / Violencia E Real / Metal Desunido / Lucrecia Borgia / Morador Das Ruas / Preso Ao Passado.

CHEAP TAKES FROM DIVIDE AND CONQUER, Heavy Discos HV005 (1988). Disunited Metal / Victory / Dweller Of The Streets / Lucrecia Borgia / Violence Is Real.

SEARCHING FOR THE LIGHT, Wild Rags WRR026 (1989). Hierarchic Democracy / Fighting In Gangs / Misery Spreads / Not To Leave The Power / Only One Of Them (Must Be Left) / Gathered Prisoners / Childish Boots And Steps / The Ones Left Scream / History Starts (To Take A Route).

MUSICAL GUIDE FROM STELLIUM, Heavy Discos 804573 (1992). Razor's Edge / Recycle Yourself / The Hidden And Unexpected / Kali Yuga (From Vishnu Purana) / Seven Races / Rock Is Dead / Warrior / My Generation.

ALEA JACTA EST, Cogumelo CD COG 069 (1994). Thy Kingdom Come / Give People A Chance / R.I.P. (Racism, Ignorance, Prejudice) / Straitgate / Raise The Dead / Human Rights / Virtual Reality / Last Act / Black Messiah / Loyal Legion Of The Admirers / Life Goes On (Vidcom Experiences) / Take Time / Summary Condemnation / Tribute To Gauguin.

STRAIGHT, Cogumelo (1997). 6:45 P.M. / Sign Of The Times / God Complex / Rapist / Straight / Who The Fuck Do You Think You Are? / Dor / All The Women (I've Loved) / Black Mud / Carniceria / H.I.V. / Extreme Conditions / Corporate Discrimination / Madness / Seasons Of Decay / Walls / Bollocks / Blood Pact / In Line / Heretic (Jacques De Molay) / Mothers Of Tomorrow / Racial Patterns / Success And Fall.

TERRORISM ALIVE, Varda 1962 (1999). Sign Of The Times (Live) / God's Complex (Live) / Rapist (Live) / Who The Fuck Do You Think You Are (Live) / Dor (Live) / All The Women (I've Loved) (Live) / Black Mud (Live) / Velhice (Live) / The Ones Left Screaming (Live) / H.I.V. (Live) / Madness (Live) / Blood Pact (Live) / Caçador Da Noite (Live) / Thy Kingdom Come (Live) / Take Time (Live) / Tortura (Live) / Guerrilha (Live) / Império de Satã (Live) / Catástrofe / Armagedon (Live) / Princesa do Prazer / Heavy Metal / Morte Aos Falsos (Live).

PELAGODISCUS ATANTICUS—THE OLD, THE RARE, THE NEW, Encore ENC 018 (2002). Princesa Do Prazer (Studio 1984) / Abandono O Seu Deus (Live 1985) / Ela Não Acaba Assim (Demo 1982) / Guerra (Demo 1982) / Caçador Da Noite (Live 1986) / HTLV-3 (Live 1986) / Joseph Mengele (Live 1986) / Tortura (Live 1997) / Guerrilha (Live 1997) / Aussie radio comment / Lucrécia Bórgia (Rehearsal 1987) / Desunited Metal (Rehearsal 1987) / Hierarchic Democracy (Live 1989) / Childish Boots And Steps (Studio 1989) / The Hidden And Unexpected (Studio 1991) / Seven Races (Studio 1991) / Velhice (Studio 1987) / Take Time (Live 1998) / Straitgate (Rehearsal) / Black Messiah—Loyal Legion Of The Admirers (Rehearsal) / Cold Melancholy (Demo 1995) / Who The Fuck Do You Think You Are (Live 1997) / In Line (Live 1997) / Heretic (Live 1997) / Mothers Of Tomorrow (Demo 1995) / Walls (1995) / Crianças Em Extinção (Demo 1998) / Psychic (Demo 1998) / Molested (Demo 1998) / X-Files (Demo 1998) / Global Village (Demo 1998) / Psychic Remix (Demo 1998).

ULTIMATUM OUTTAKES, Dies Irae 005 (2002). Catástrofe (Live 1985) / Armagedon (Live 1985) / Princesa Do Prazer (Live 1985) / Dorsal Atlântica (Live 1984) / Hecatombe (Rehearsal) / Periferia (Live 1985) / Italian radio comment / Morte Aos Falsos (Rehearsal) / Tortura (Rehearsal) / Catástrofe (Live 1984) / Princesa Do Prazer (Live 1984) / Catástrofe (Live 1984) / Abandono O Seu Deus (Live 1984) / Princesa Do Prazer (Live 1984) / Armagedon (Live 1984) / Morte Aos Falsos (Live 1985).

DOWNWARD SPIRAL

BÄLINGE, SWEDEN — *Erik (vocals), Johan (guitar), Claes (guitar), Knut (bass), Fredda (drums).*

Bälinge Thrash Metal band DOWNWARD SPIRAL started out in 1993, operating as a POISON IDEA covers band. With the introduction of singer Erik in mid 1994 the group started writing original material, with a debut demo following in May 1995. A second demo session was capitalised on by third set 'Prey Of Ignorance' in 1997. That same year DOWNWARD SPIRAL shared a split 7" vinyl single with DISSOBER on Aparat Records.

DOWNWARD SPIRAL tracks also found inclusion on compilations the 'Really Fast vol .10' vinyl album on Really Fast Records, the 'Uppsala Crust' EP on Your Own Jailer Records and a Pie mag cassette. The band's final concert, held in Ekeby during 1997, was captured for video release.

Downward Spiral, Downward Spiral (1995) (Demo).

Promo, Downward Spiral (1996) (Demo).

Prey Of Ignorance, Downward Spiral (1997) (Demo).

Downward Spiral / Dissober, Aparat AR1 (1997) (Split 7" vinyl single with DISSOBER).

DRAGONFORCE

UK / NEW ZEALAND — *Z.P. Theart (vocals), Herman Li (guitar), Sam Totman (guitar), Frédéric Leclercq (bass), Vadim Pruzhanov (keyboards), Dave Mackintosh (drums).*

London based Power Metal band DRAGONFORCE was, for much of their early career, known as DRAGONHEART, issuing a demo entitled 'Valley Of The Damned' under this former title. The group would take the spirit of the European mid 90s Power Metal resurgence to new heights by simply quadrupling the intensity of riffs and solos, within a few short years not only finding themselves heading the pack but also cracking the US charts.

The band became operational during 1999 but upfront of signing to the Sanctuary label the band switched to DRAGONFORCE due to the plethora of acts brandishing similar titles. For the band's first rehearsals in October 1999 DRAGONHEART employed a cast of Z.P. Theart on vocals, guitarists Herman 'Shred' Li and Sam Totman, both members of uprooted New Zealand Black Metal act DEMONIAC, New Zealand born bass player Steve Scott and Slovenian born Matej Setinc of DEMONIAC on the drums.

In their former guise as DEMONIAC, the band's guitarists Sam Totman had gone by the pseudonym 'Heimdall', whilst Herman Li simply went by the apt nickname of 'Shred'. Although established in New Zealand, issuing the April 1994 demo 'The Birth Of Diabolical Blood' and November 1994 album 'Prepare For War' through French label Evil Omen Productions, DEMONIAC, promoting second album 'Stormblade', released in September 1996, had relocated to England during 1997 to take part in the 'World Domination' tour of Europe headlined by DARK TRANQUILLITY and ENSLAVED. 'Stormblade's inclusion of the song 'Nigger Slut' prompted dismay and second pressings showed the title revised as 'N. Slut'. Strangely, the song 'Hatred Is Purity' escaped the censors, despite its questionable lyrics extolling "white man stand up for your race."

DEMONIAC's third outing, 'The Fire And The Wind', arrived in 1999. Unfortunately the group landed themselves in further controversy when it was learned the track 'Myths Of Metal' included the lyric Hitler metal, Sieg Heil. Facing a ban on the album from the German authorities the band issued a swift apology. Denying any racist slur, the group pointed out that Sam Totman was of Maori descent whilst the band's other six-stringer Herman Li was from Hong Kong. DEMONIAC then collapsed, paving the way for DRAGONHEART.

With Setinc's early departure, Peter Hunt briefly occupied the drum stool and the group also enrolled former DOG DAY SUNRISE keyboard player Steve Williams. A demo entitled 'Valley Of The Damned' surfaced in June 2000. These recordings would have the distinction of being produced by Karl Groom of THRESHOLD with Clive Nolan of PENDRAGON repute adding keyboard touches. DRAGONHEART bassist Steve Scott would join competitors SHADOWKEEP during 2000. Diccon Harper, previously a member of PHOENIX filled the vacancy that November.

The band, brandishing an all new line-up, Williams having made his exit, supported both HALFORD and STRATOVARIUS in December 2001. For these shows Vadim Pruzhanov came in as the new keyboard player for the HALFORD gigs with just two days notice. At this same juncture, Steve Williams forged the Symphonic Metal act POWER QUEST, pulling in not only former DRAGONFORCE bassist Steve Scott but also drawing into the fold Sam Totman, the guitarist maintaining a foot in both camps, and personnel from Italian Metal band ARTHEMIS.

The line-up remained fluid and Harper decamped in March 2002. As the debut emerged album in January 2003 the DRAGONFORCE line-up then comprised vocalist Z.P. Theart, guitarists Herman Li and Sam Totman, keyboard player Vadim Pruzhanov, stand in bassist Adrian Lambert and drummer Didier Almouzni. The latter exited in June of 2003 just prior to an appearance at the 'Sweden Rock' festival. Christian Wirtl of Swedish act SOUL SOURCE as temporary replacement.

DRAGONFORCE commenced recording of a new studio album in November, enrolling the BAL SAGOTH credited David Mackintosh on drums. Japanese dates in January 2004 would see the band supporting veteran German act HELLOWEEN, these concerts acting as a precursor to an exhaustive strategy of touring to ensue. An album release show at London's Underworld on February 13th saw French label mates HEAVENLY as opening act. The band set 'Sonic Firestorm' as the title of their new record, slated for April. European dates in May saw the band as opening act for W.A.S.P. Although drummer Dave Mackintosh dislocated his elbow en route from Paris to the UK, putting him out of action for six weeks, the band displayed a true Dunkirk spirit by completing the rest of the tour with a drum machine. A further mishap came at the band's 'Gates of Metal' festival appearance in Hultsfred, Sweden on 31st July when Herman Li missed his plane, necessitating the band performing solely with Totman on guitar. DRAGONFORCE scheduled a headlining UK tour for October.

The band's 2005 live campaign opened with support shows to ANGRA in Greece during February. DRAGONFORCE then landed a major coup on the live front, being selected as opening act for IRON MAIDEN's European Summer festival dates in Poland, Italy and Greece. A headline UK tour, dubbed the 'Meet the Sonic Firestorm', was announced for September.

The band parted ways with bassist Adrian Lambert in October, pulling in Frederic Leclercq of HEAVENLY and MALADAPTIVE as temporary substitute. DRAGONFORCE made their U.S. live debut on 22nd November with a headlining show at the legendary CBGB's club in New York. That same month the band revealed they had signed a new recording deal with Roadrunner Records.

In early 2006 ex-DRAGONFORCE drummer Peter Hunt joined MARSHALL LAW. European touring in February 2006 across Switzerland, Spain, Portugal, France, Sweden and Germany found DRAGONFORCE supporting EDGUY. For shows in the UK, the roles were reversed, with EDGUY as the opening act. These gigs once again found Frederic Leclercq occupying the bass role. DRAGONFORCE then hit Canada and the USA in April and May supported by PROTEST THE HERO and SANCTITY. The band put in a significant appearance at the GUNS N' ROSES headlined 'Download' festival in Castle Donington, UK on June 11th.

'Ozzfest' loomed for the US 2006 summer touring season, the group sharing the festival stages with OZZY OSBOURNE, SYSTEM OF A DOWN, BLACK LABEL SOCIETY, LACUNA COIL, DISTURBED, ATREYU, UNEARTH, BLEEDING THROUGH, NORMA JEAN, A LIFE ONCE LOST, STRAPPING YOUNG LAD, THE RED CHORD, FULL BLOWN CHAOS, WALLS OF JERICHO, ALL THAT REMAINS, HATEBREED, AVENGED SEVENFOLD and BETWEEN THE BURIED AND ME. Just upfront of these concerts the 'Inhuman Rampage' album entered the national US charts at number 103.

The group set up headline American shows for September, backed by ALL THAT REMAINS and HORSE THE BAND. October and November concerts across Europe would see support going to FIREWIND upfront of UK headliners into December with ALL THAT REMAINS as opening act.

The group further announced they were to partner with KILLSWITCH ENGAGE, CHIMAIRA and HE IS LEGEND for the 'No Fear Music' 35 city North American tour commencing February 21st 2007 at the Atlantic City, New Jersey, House of Blues. To celebrate US sales in excess of 100,000 copies, in March Roadrunner Records issued an expanded version of the 'Inhuman Rampage' album, this double disc set hosting a bonus track 'Lost Souls In Endless Time' plus DVD of live video footage and documentary.

German shows in April had FREEDOM CALL as support. VANISHING POINT secured the support slot on DRAGONFORCE's Australian tour in May. The band also played in Singapore, Taiwan and Thailand.

That same month Frédéric Leclercq unveiled tracks from his IRON STEEL project featuring and Fran Strine. The track 'Attack' track was recorded in one take on April 7th 2007 at the House of Blues in Chicago, Illinois and boasted guest appearances by members of CHIMAIRA, KILLSWITCH ENGAGE and DRAGONFORCE.

VALLEY OF THE DAMNED, Noise N03732 (2003). Invocation Of The Apocalyptic / Valley Of The Damned / Black Fire / Black Winter Night / Starfire / Disciples Of Babylon / Revelations / Evening Star / Heart Of A Dragon.

SONIC FIRESTORM, Noise N03852 (2004). My Spirit Will Go On / Fury Of The Storm / Fields Of Despair / Dawn Over A New World / Above The Winter Moonlight / Soldiers Of The Wasteland / Prepare For War / Once In A Lifetime.

INHUMAN RAMPAGE, Roadrunner RR 8070-2 (2006). Through The Fire And Flames / Revolution Deathsquad / Storming The Burning Fields / Operation Ground And Pound / Body Breakdown / Cry For Eternity / The Flame Of Youth / Trail Of Broken Hearts. Chart positions: 54 SWEDEN, 103 USA.

DREAM DEATH

PITTSBURGH, PA, USA — *Brian Lawrence (vocals / guitar), Terry Weston (guitar), Ted Williams (bass), Mike Smail (drums).*

Pioneering Pittsburgh Doom styled Thrashers DREAM DEATH arrived in 1984 releasing a demo tape 'More Graveyard Delving' two years later. After DREAM DEATH's debut album 'Journey Into Mystery' was released by the New Renaissance label in 1987 bassist Ted Williams defected to the Pittsburgh Thrash act EVICTION. Subsequently, Williams and EVICTION guitarist Rob Tabachka formed the garage Punk band PILSNER.

Guitarist Terry Weston, frontman Brian Lawrence and drummer Mike Smail later created premier Doom act PENANCE issuing a string of highly commended albums. Smail has also lent his drumming skills to acts such as CATHEDRAL, SILVER TONGUED DEVIL, INTERNAL VOID and PENTAGRAM.

DREAM DEATH recordings billed as 'Back From The Dead', compiling the original demos, surfaced on Psychodoomelic Records during 2005. That same year the group announced a reformation to conduct new recordings.

JOURNEY INTO MYSTERY, New Renaissance (1987). Back From The Dead / The Elder Race / Bitterness And Hatred / Black Edifice / Divine In Agony / Hear My Screams / Sealed In Blood / Dream Death.
BACK FROM THE DEAD, Psychodoomelic (2005).

DREAM DEVOID

GREECE — *Dimitris Zalahoris (vocals), Liberis Tsabras (guitar), Jim Tsakmakis (guitar), Panos Argyriou (bass), Vaggelis Theodorakis (keyboards), Antonis Kolaros (drums).*

DREAM DEVOID is an Athens based Power Metal act unafraid to use sheer speed to ram their point home. The group was conceived in July of 1993 by bass player Panos Argyriou and guitarist Liberis Tsabras. The band would have a fluid line up until January of 1997 when guitarist Akis Triantafillou and vocalist Dimitris Zalahoris were enrolled. Drummer Kostas Agouras, on loan from DISHARMONY, would session for the band on their opening 'Nebulous' demo of May 1997. DREAM DEVOID would also have the track 'Consequent Sin' included on the Metal Invader magazine compilation 'Warzone II'.

In 1998 Fotis Giannakopoulos was inducted on the drum stool and Panagiotis Mylonas assumed keyboard duties. With this line up DREAM DEVOID laid down their debut album 'Aeons Of Forget Fullness' for the Steel Gallery label.

Post recording Zalohoris disembarked but guitarist Vasilis Krilakis was drafted. DREAM DEVOID maintained a low profile during much of 2001 in main due to Tsabras' national service army service. In October of 2002 Dimitris Tsakmakis was drafted on lead guitar and in January of the following year Stavros Giannakopoulos assumed lead vocal duties with Vaggelis Theodorakis enrolling on keyboards that March. With this line up DREAM DEVOID performed at the 'Paranoid Hellenic Metal Fest' concert, the band's first live gig in almost three years. Activity thereafter would be behind the scenes and DREAM DEVOID re-emerged in February of 2004 with an all new look, new personnel being vocalist Alex Siderakos, ex-MIDNIGHT SCREAM guitar player Jim Tsakmakis and Antonis Kolaros on the drums.

AEONS OF FORGET FULLNESS, Steel Gallery SGR CD-004 (2001). ...In The Sky / Dreams In Void / Dreamweaver / A Song To Whisper / Leaves Of Sorrow / Aeons Of Forget Fullness / Not A Cloud ... / Consequent Sins / Nebulous / Internal Battle.

DREAMS OF DAMNATION

CA, USA — *Loana DP Valencia (vocals), Jimmy Durkin (guitar), Charlie Silva (bass), Al Mendez (drums).*

DREAMS OF DAMNATION is the post millennium Metal band founded by former DARK ANGEL and present BLISTER guitarist Jimmy Durkin. Initially ex-DARK ANGEL and DEATH drummer Gene Hoglan was involved in the project but a work load which included STRAPPING YOUNG LAD and OLD MAN'S CHILD forced him out of the frame. This formative incarnation of the band cut a three song 7" single in 1992, limited to just 500 copies.

In 1999 Durkin re-activated the DREAMS OF DAMNATION venture, inducting ex-MALIGNANT vocalist Charlie Silva and former MAD WHIP THUNDER drummer Al "Mayhem" Mendez. Signing to the Necropolis label DREAMS OF DAMNATION issued the 2000 album 'Let The Violence Begin'. The band debuted live that same October at the Los Angeles 'Hell Fest' event.

In September of 2001 Durkin jammed with the reformed Bay Area Thrashers HIRAX. Announced as an official union, this HIRAX alliance apparently lasted little more than a jam session. 2002 opened with DREAMS OF DAMNATION announcing Loana DP Valencia as their new vocalist. Valencia had no previous band experience, other than an impromptu jam session with DARKANE at the 15th Annual Milwaukee Metal Fest in 2001, but after ripping through audition tracks ACCEPT's 'Fast As A Shark' and MOTÖRHEAD's 'Ace Of Spades' Valencia had convinced Durkin of the need for a female singer. This incarnation of the band debuted December of 2001 at a San Francisco show hosted by Necropolis Records. DREAMS OF DAMNATION then undertook recordings for their debut full length album, 'Epic Tales Of Vengeance' with famed producer Bill Metoyer during June.

By mid 2002 Durkin, still retaining his interest in DREAMS OF DAMNATION, had succumbed to fan pressure to resurrect DARK ANGEL, taking DREAMS OF DAMNATION drummer Al 'Mayhem' Mendez with him. In March the group inducted ABATTOIR's Steve Gaines as new rhythm guitarist.

In August of 2004 Jim Durkin united with former MARDUK members vocalist Legion (a.k.a. Erik Hagsted) and bassist B.War (Roger Svensson) in a new Death Metal project. That same month Steve Gaines signalled his intention to issue a solo album, billed 'Anger As Art'. As it transpired, by mid 2005 Gaines' ANGER AS ART concept flourished into a whole new band entity, the singer being joined by HANGAR 18 and RAVEN MAD guitarist William Rustrum, NEW EDEN bassist Javier Marrufo with Mars Castro of COFFIN TEXTS and DREAMS OF DAMNATION on drums. One of the band's first public airing would be on the 'Metal Madness' television show in Los Angeles.

On 9th July 2005 DREAMS OF DAMNATION lined up at The Pound outdoor amphitheatre in San Francisco alongside TESTAMENT, VICIOUS RUMORS, LÄÄZ ROCKIT, HIRAX, AGENT STEEL, DEKAPITATOR, MUDFACE, NEIL TURBIN, BROCAS HELM and IMAGIKA for the 'Thrash Against Cancer' benefit.

Loana DP Valencia guested on the DIA DE LOS MUERTOS project album 'Day Of The Dead' assembled by BODY COUNT bassist Vincent Price, and guitarist Andres Jaramillo and drummer Alfonso Pinzon from the Colombian metal act AGONY.

LET THE VIOLENCE BEGIN, Necropolis NR064 CD (2000). Blood To Free A Soul / Unholy Invocations / Cremation Day / Demonic Celebration / Hammer Of Sickness / Release Me.

DRUNKEN STATE

SCOTLAND, UK — *Robert Trash (vocals), David Leishman (guitar), Douglas K. Smith (guitar), Michael Brash (bass), Graeme Thompson (drums).*

Scottish Thrash act DRUNKEN STATE self financed their debut 'Bags Not Carry The Coffin' EP and would go onward to support the likes of ONSLAUGHT, WOLFSBANE and SABBAT. The group's album, 'Kilt By Death', was produced by Frank 'Uncle Bastard' Mitzen.

Bags Not To Carry The Coffin, Blast Furnace Kickass 003 (1989). Bags Not To Carry The Coffin.

KILT BY DEATH, Heavy Metal MMRLP 151 (1990). Time To Stop / Blind Faith / Forgotten Ones / Lament / Call To Arms / Resurrection / ERIC / Let Me Go / Deal With The Cliche / Prophets In The Wind.

DRY ROT

GERMANY — *Volker Schmidt (vocals), Michael Gerstlauer (guitar), Niko Singer (bass), Jochen Steger (drums).*

Nu-Thrash act DRY ROT was created during 1990 by guitarist Michael Gerstlauer. A batch of six demos, including 'Fatal Glance' and 'Brave New World', a track inclusion on the 'Bullet In The Head Volume One' compilation and an appearance at the 'Full Force' festival led to a recording deal with the Sub Zero label in 1998.

The eponymous debut, which included a vicious re-work of the POLICE hit 'Message In A Bottle' complete with a guesting Bernhard Schmitt of HATE SQUAD, saw a release in February 1999. DRY ROT toured Germany as support to CROWBAR, TESTAMENT and 40 GRIT.

Latterly DRY ROT's rhythm section of bassist Niko Singer and drummer Jochen Steger has been replaced by Make and Basti respectively. Steger would turn up billed as 'Christ Impaler' with the tongue in cheek retro Thrash outfit DELIRIUM TREMENS.

In May of 2002 Gerstlauer would unveil a new Thrash band union, the oddly titled JESUS CHRYSLER SUPERSKUNK, in league with erstwhile DESTRUCTION members guitarist Michael 'Ano' Piranio and drummer Sven Vormann. Making up the numbers would be vocalist Thomas Rosenmerkel, also ex-DESTRUCTION, and NECROMONICON bass player Bernhard 'Erna' Matt. Piranio, Rosenmerkel and Matt also cite credits with EPHEMERA'S PARTY.

DRY ROT, Sub Zero SZ9903-2 (1999). Two Faced / Guilty / Release / Raped / Face Down / Message In A Bottle / Hate Means Love / To Whom It May Concern / Respect / All Hope Is Lost / I Will Give You Pain.

DYOXEN

LONDON, ON, CANADA — *Michael Sanders (vocals / guitar), Bret Stacey (guitar), Steve Sinclair (bass), Derek Rothwell Kerr (drums).*

London, Ontario Thrash act. Founded in 1989 by erstwhile KAOS vocalist / guitarist Michael Scott Sanders (the son of Willis Sanders of the INKSPOTS), bassist Steve Sinclair and drummer Derek Rothwell-Kerr. This trio issued a brace of demo sessions entitled 'Apocalyptic Ideas' and 'A Foot From The Edge'.

Adding second guitarist Alistair Hay and new bassist Andy Morton, DYOXEN scored a deal with the European Active label for the 'First Among Equals' album. The record received worthy praise for it's complex, even progressive, brand of Thrash. However, Shortly after recording both Hay and Morton made their exit. For live work DYOXEN pulled in guitarist Brett Stacey and former member Steve Sinclair was welcomed back into the fold. DYOXEN would fold before reaching album number two.

In 1998 Sanders resurfaced fronting Funk Rock act MICHAEL SANDERS AND ONE TRIBE NATION. This outfit issued a star studded 2005 album 'Servants Of A Lesser God'.

FIRST AMONG EQUALS, Active CD ATV 17 (1991). First Among Equals / The Essence Of Ignorance / Citizen Soldier / Holocaust (Fall In Grace) / Abuse / Overcome / Foot From The Edge / Sooner Than You Think.

EDENBEAST

SONDERBORG, DENMARK — *Steen G. Knudsen (vocals), Kristian Bjorn Olesen (guitar), Christian Przemyslaw Zalewski (guitar), Erik Nielsen (bass), Christian Mindedahl (drums).*

Sonderborg Death Thrashers EDENBEAST date back to an earlier formation entitled NECROPOLIS, which issued two demos, 'Twilight Destinies' in 1998 and 'Ungracious Cruel Art' during 1999. As EDENBEAST they bowed in with a 2003 promotional set entitled 'Prozac Party Songs', recorded at Sonderborghus with producer Asmus Thomsen. In 2004 the band donated their version of 'Blind In Texas' to the W.A.S.P. tribute album 'Shock Rock Hellions—A Tribute To W.A.S.P.' issued through Denmark's Valhalla Records. EDENBEAST guitarist Chris Przemyslaw Zalewski has ties to AURORA.

Both singer Steen Knudsen and bass guitarist Erik M. Nielsen opted out in 2005. Kristian Bjorn Olesen duly switched over to bass.

Prozac Party Songs, Edenbeast Demo (2003). Frameworld / Embrace The Neon Sun / The Heart Cages.
Promo 2004, (2004). Bring Out Your Dead / Mute / Embrace the Neon Sun—Redistorted / The Heart Cages—Redistorted.

EKTOMORF

HUNGARY — *Farkas Zoltan (vocals / guitar), Kovacs Laszlo (guitar), Farkas Csaba (bass), Szakacs Jozsef (drums).*

Modern Thrash act EKTOMORF, founded during 1994, issued the 1996 album 'Hangok' ("Voices") as their opening shot. For this recording the band comprised vocalist / guitarist Farkas Zoltan, second guitarist Jano Mihaly, bassist Farkas Csaba and drummer Ternovan Csaba. For the second album, a 1998 eponymous outing, Mihaly had been superseded by Marksteiner Bula. 2000's 'Kalyi Jag' witnessed another makeover in the band line-up as Farkas Zoltan and Farkas Csaba were joined by new drummer Szakacz Jozsef. EKTOMORF, having added guitarist Kovacs Laszlo, returned in 2002 with 'I Scream Up To The Sky', this album including a cover version of THE BEATLES 'It's a Hard day's Night'.

EKTOMORF, signing to the German Nuclear Blast label for a fifth outing entitled 'Destroy', landed the support slot to PRO-PAIN's 2004 European tour. The band then tagged onto KREATOR and DARK TRANQUILLITY's 'Enemy Of God' European tour. Promoting the 'Instinct' album throughout October and November 2005 EKTOMORF engaged in the "The Monster Mosh Down" dates across Germany, Switzerland, Austria, Holland and the UK partnered with DISBELIEF, BY NIGHT and Israel's BETZEFER. The group, pushing live album 'Live And Raw—What You Give Is What You Get', then hooked up with CHILDREN OF BODOM and ONE MAN ARMY AND THE UNDEAD QUARTET for European and Scandinavian gigs commencing in Germany during late December and finalizing in Finland in February 2006.

The band EKTOMORF utilised Antfarm Studios in Århus, Denmark in July, working with producer Tue Madsen to begin recording their new album, entitled 'Outcast'. This set included the PRODIGY cover version 'Fuel My Fire'. A limited edition boxed version of 'Outcast', restricted to just 500 copies, came with a certificate of authenticity and a free wristband.

The band partnered with BLINDED COLONY and KAYSER for European tour dates throughout February and into March 2007.

HANGOK, Vida Music (1996). Nekem Ne Mondd Meg / Shalom / Engedelyezett Gyilkossag / Hangok / Uvolto Felelem / Kivulrol Nezve / Jovatehetetlen / Terror / A Romok Alatt / Jezus Var / Statisztika / Belulrol / Ellenallas / A Vilagszenved / Haboru Szindroma.
EKTOMORF, Ko Music (1998). Nem Engedem / Ver / 393 / Orok Vesztesek / Magamert / 100 % Gyulolet / Fereg / Ervagas / Ez Vagyok En / Menekules / Eutanazia / Egyudel.
KALYI JAG, Last Episode (2002). Son Of The Fire / Sunto Del Mulo / Freely / Romungro / For You / For The Last Time / Always Believe In Yourself / Open Up Your Eyes / Save My Soul / The Way I Do / Brothersong / Don't Need / Fly / Kalyi Jag / Forgotten Fire.
I SCREAM UP TO THE SKY, Silverdust (2002). I Scream Up To The Sky / You Leech / Fire / I Miss You / An Les Devla / I'm Free / A Hard Day's Night / If I Weren't / Fajdalom Konnyei / You Are / Scum / Seriel Men / Blood In Blood.
DESTROY, Nuclear Blast NB 1229-2 (2004). I Know Them / Destroy / Gypsy / No Compromise / Everything / From Far Away / Painful But

True / Only God / You Are My Shelter / A.E.A. / From My Heart / Tear Apart.
LIVE AND RAW—YOU GET WHAT YOU GIVE, Nuclear Blast (2005). Son Of The Fire / Sunto Del Muro / Freely / Romungro / For You / For The Last Time / Always Believe In Yourself / Open Up Your Eyes / Save My Soul / The Way I Do / Brothersong / Don't Need / Fly / Kalyi Jag / Forgotten Fire.
INSTINCT, Nuclear Blast NB 1397 (2005). Set Me Free / Show Your Fist / Instinct / Burn / The Holy Noise / Fuck You All / United Nations / Land Of Pain / I Break You / You Get What You Give / Until The End / I Will.
OUTCAST, Nuclear Blast NB 1754 (2006). Outcast / I Choke / Ambush In The Night / I'm Against / We Rise / Red I / Who Can I Trust (Prayer) / Leave Me Alone / Fuel My Fire / I Confront My Enemy / Hell Is Here / Chamunda.

ELEKTRASH

LIMA, PERU — *R. Franco Oliveria (vocals / guitar), Alejandro Hernandez (bass), Dario Hernandez (drums).*

Lima Thrashcore band borne out of the 1993 act QUIMERA. Citing a line up of vocalist / guitarist Luis Pajuelo, guitarist R. Franco Oliveria, bassist Peter Ramirez and Jorge Salveredy on drums the Hard Rock covers previously delivered by QUIMERA gave way to original Thrashcore upon the name switch to ELEKTRASH in January of 1994.

ELEKTRASH would then be assailed by line up ructions. In September of 1994 Ramirez opted out, his place being taken by Oscar Bustamente. However, before long Bustamente would be forced out with health problems and Ramirez was invited back in.

1996 witnessed the withdrawal of Salveredy's services. For many months ELEKTRASH was put on ice minus a drummer but finally in March of 1997 Dario Hernandez plugged the gap. The band's problems were far from over though as then frontman Pajuelo made his exit. Oliveria added lead vocals to his duties as ELEKTRASH became a power trio. An album collecting together prior demos was issued in 1998 billed as 'Excusa Para Morir'.

The band issued a second album, 'Filosofia De Casos' which included a cover of DEEP PURPLE's 'Bloodsucker', in April of 1999. During recording Ramirez decamped for the second time and Alejandro Hernandez assumed the role of bassist.

EXCUSA PARA MORIR, (1998). Excuse Para Morir / Actitude Inconsciencia / Aquiel Infierno / Grisacea / La Belleza De Dolor / Mundo Pasairo / Cultura De La Violencia / Pandemonium / Demente / Errate / Antro / Neurosis / Coma.
FILOSOFIA DE CASOS, (1999).

ELVARON

FRANCE — *Matthieu Morand (vocals / guitar), Nicolas Colnot (bass), Thomas Letscher (keyboards), Frederic Seiler (drums).*

Thrash act ELVARON began life in September of 1993, founded by former NIGHT FEAST guitarist Matthieu Morand with bass player Julien and originally billed as SKELETONS OF HELL. As another ex-NIGHT FEAST member, drummer Rodolphe, was enrolled the formative band took on the ELVARON title to cut a four track demo tape. The following year Damien Cheminant was pulled in as lead singer but shortly after the band's debut gig Julien left to join SKYDANCER, being replaced by Michael Peusch.

During 1995 ELVARON laid down the demo 'Necromantia' but after this session the band found themselves without a drummer. With progress marred by this vacancy Matthieu decided to join SKYDANCER in September of that year. The band would be re-activated with the incorporation of drummer Fred Seiler for the second demo 'Exhumation'. A debut album, 'Mages Battle', was recorded and issued in a limited edition run of 1000 copies but after these sessions Seiler bailed out. For live work the band borrowed the guitarist and drummer from local act TORMENTED SOULS. Sophomore album 'The Five Shires' witnessed the return of Fred. Keyboard player Thomas 'Seek' Letscher, from SAMAEL and BOWELS OF SUFFERING, was inducted in 1999 but then co-founder Julien quit, this setback occurring just before 'The Five Shires' album was signed over to Thundering Records. Nicolas Colnot, a veteran of such artists as SUPLYCE, SIX BLADE KNIFE, LESTAT and DOCTOR SARDONICUS, took the bass position in 2001.

MAGES BATTLE, Brennus (1996). Sad Death / Spell & Swords / Reborn Again / Hellvaron / Exhumation ... Not So Sad / Satan Laughs / No Fate, No Hope / Foredoomed / Battlefield / Gloomwings / Immortal / Sustenance.
THE FIVE SHIRES, Thundering (2001). The Five Shires / The Tower Of Palanthas / Beyond The Gate / Bloodstone Lands / Quest For Alifaar's Door / Killianor's Sight / The Rope.

ENCRYPTION

GERMANY — *Norbert Hartmann (vocals), Christian Klein (guitar), Stefan Muller (guitar), Oliver Goss (bass), Johannes Klein (drums).*

Franconian Progressive Thrashers ENCRYPTION was founded as CRYPTIC during 1995, issuing 'The Cryptogram' demo the following year and a 1997 debut album 'Shrouded In Mystery'.

During the final recording stages of the second album CRYPTIC would be delivered two blows. Not only did founder member and guitarist Manfred Herzog depart but a Munich based band claimed legal right to the CRYPTIC band title. With artwork already completed for the record stickers were hastily made up bearing the new title of ENCRYPTION.

Second guitarist Stefan Muller was added to the ranks in August of 2001.

SHROUDED IN MYSTERY, (1997). Shrouded In Mystery / Lack Of Animosity / Brainchild / Oblivious Vapours / Predator One / My Messiah / Fog's Kiss / Throne Of Chaos.
PERISHING BLACK LIGHT, (2000). Perishing Black Light / Lambda Core / All Philistines / The Inmost Dance / Conquering The Night / Autumn Harvest.

ENDERS GAME

ATLANTA, GA, USA — *Kevin Freeman (vocals), Jarrod Johnson (guitar), Dave Merrill (guitar), Shon Harp (bass), Daniel Burch (drums).*

Atlanta, Georgia Nu-Thrash act ENDERS GAME features former CAUSTIC THOUGHT, ART OF SUBMISSION and HOGGNUTT singer Kevin Freeman. Guitarist Jarrod Johnson is ex-SVOID with second guitarist Dave Merrill ex-ART OF SUBMISSION and APOSTASY. ENDERS GAME issued the four track EP 'Game Over' in 2003. Bassist Ben Burch would be replaced by Shon Harp, a scene veteran of RED EYE, VOLATILE, BLUNT, CRAZY IVAN and ART OF SUBMISSION repute. A further change in November 2004 saw drummer Jeff Gardner making way for erstwhile BURN and SHELLSHOCK sticksman Daniel Burch.

ENDERS GAME gained valuable local supports to ARSIS, UNEARTH, SOILWORK, IN FLAMES and CHIMAIRA. An album, entitled 'Pattern Of Decay', would be prepared for 2005, although Kevin Freeman left that February, leaving Shon Harp to pick up lead vocal duties.

Game Over EP, Enders Game (2003). Life In Oblivion / 7th Circle / Shedding Faith / S.K.D.

ENDLESS TORMENT

BIRMINGHAM, UK — *Barney (vocals), Jez (guitar), Robb (guitar), Caygill (bass), Steve (drums).*

Birmingham's ENDLESS TORMENT, created in 2002, underwent a succession of line-up changes marking its evolution from a Death-Gore outfit up to their 2004 Progressive Death Metal stance. After cutting the 2004 demo 'Endless', featuring a cover version of DEATH's 'Symbolic', the band enrolled new guitarist Andy in February and drummer Stu, replacing Tim Wilson, in April. Gigging across the UK in June saw the band uniting with DESECRATION. Yet more member changes found Andy replaced by Si, Robb being installed on bass in place of Dee and Steve taking command of the drums. ENDLESS TORMENT again underwent member changes, installing Caygill on bass as Robb switched back to guitar.

Live work during 2005 saw the installation of Robb Philpotts of THE ENCHANTED and BLOODSTREAM on guitar.

Endless, Endless Torment (2004). Endless / The Elusive Truth / The Utopia Machine / Symbolic.

ENEMYNSIDE

ROME, ITALY — *Francesco Cremisini (vocals / guitar), Matteo Bellezza (guitar), Francesco Grieco (bass), Luca Marini (drums).*

Rome Thrashers ENEMYNSIDE, forged in 1994 by guitarist Francesco Cremisini, debuted under the formative title SCAPEGOAT in 1999 with the demo 'Scars'. Two earlier, undistributed recordings had been cut in 1995, by Cremisini solo, and 1995 with bassist Luca Giovagnoli. The 'Scars' tapes would feature the newly added guitarist Matteo Bellezza. Live gigs would be conducted utilising Roberto Pirami and Luca Iovieno on drums but then Giovagnoli departed.

By the following year the band had adopted the ENEMYNSIDE title for the EP 'From The Cradle To The Way'. Upon completion, Alberto Sempreboni of SAVERS was inducted on bass guitar and Luca Iovieno briefly re-occupied the drum stool, being replaced by CHTHONIAN NEMETON's Luca Marini.

The 'Violent Beats' session arrived in 2001. The band's own imprint, Temple Of Noise Records, released their debut album 'Let The Madness Begin ...' in 2003. RAINSPAWN's Francesco Grieco was incorporated on bass in July of 2004, debuting this new line-up at the 'Metal Dose' festival in Slovenia. ENEMYNSIDE parted ways with the longtime drummer Luca Marini in July, drafting Nicola "Kongo" Corrente in his stead.

Throughout 2006 the group recorded tracks for a second album, 'In the Middle Of Nowhere', at Cellar Studio with engineer Stefano Morabito. The band announced the addition of guitarist Davide Scala to the group's ranks in December 2006.

From Cradle To The Way, (2000). Bad Junks / Someones Past / Scars / The Place.
Violent Beats, (2001). Speed Killing / Peace Of Mud / In Memory Free.
LET THE MADNESS BEGIN ..., Temple Of noise TON002 (2003). Suddenly Mad / Bad Junks / Ex-X-Es / In Memory Free / Your Enemy Inside / Speed Killing / Peace Of Mud / Unchained / Scars / Hatestone.

ENERTIA

ALBANY, NY, USA — *Scott Featherstone (vocals), Dave Stafford (guitar), Roman Singleton (guitar), Joe Paciolla (bass), Jeff Daily (drums).*

Albany based Power inclined Thrash act ENERTIA came together during February of 1996 and have industriously embarked upon a programme of self releases ever since commencing with July 1996's 'Law Of Three' mini album. ENERTIA reaped valuable exposure as part of the independent movie 'These Days', performing 'Real' from the 1999 'Flashpoint' album.

ENERTIA would also act as the backing band for a METALLICA tribute released by Perris Records. Amongst he songs covered would be 'Ride The Lightning' featuring WATCHTOWER vocalist Jason McMaster 'For Whom The Bell Tolls' and 'Master Of Puppets' fronted by erstwhile IRON MAIDEN singer PAUL DIANNO and 'Creeping Death' with vocals from Stevie Blaze. Also cut would be 'Welcome Home (Sanitarium)' and 'Sad But True', both with ENERTIA vocalist Scott Featherstone taking the lead. During 2002 ENERTIA set to work on recording an album with famed Metal producer Neil Kernon.

LAW OF THREE, Enertia (1996). The Mirror / Child Now Lost / I Know Your Demons / Same Old Story / If I Were You.
MOMENTUM, Enertia (1998). Out / Dear God / And So You Fall / Six Weeks / Weight Of The World / You Know / Sever The Wicked / Walls.
FLASHPOINT, Enertia (1999). Victim Of Thought / Leave Me In Peace / Glitch / Crawling / Real / D.O.M. / Voices / Without End / What Hurts Me ... / Right To Die.

ENGLISH DOGS

UK — *Wakey (vocals), Wattie (bass), Jon (guitar), Pinch (drums).*

Primarily a Punk outfit, ENGLISH DOGS flirted with the in vogue Thrash movement with more Metallized albums issued on Music For Nations' subsidiary label Under One Flag. Formed in October 1981 the band debuted with two demos during 1982 entitled 'Show No Mercy' and 'Free To Kill'. The band toured as support to GBH in Germany during early 1983 followed by a British tour guesting for DISCHARGE before signing to Clay Records in July 1983 and releasing their first vinyl product, a 6 track EP titled 'Mad Punx And English Dogs'. ENGLISH DOGS first full length album, 'Invasion Of The Porky Men', emerged a year later.

Personnel changes ensued after the debut album emerged with vocalist Wakey departing to be replaced by ex-ULTRAVIOLENT singer Ade Bailey. At this juncture the band also decided to augment their live sound by adding ex-DESTRUCTORS guitarist Graham 'Gizz' Butt. The band quit Clay to sign with Rot Records releasing the 'To The Ends Of The Earth' EP in September 1984.

Displaying leanings towards Black Metal the band now headed towards the Metal end of the music spectrum, culminating with the 'Where Legend Began' album through Under One Flag in 1986. The group appeared on the legendary Shades promoted Thrash bill at Camden's Electric Ballroom with POSSESSED and VOIVOD later in 1986. Line-up changes saw the introduction of former OVERDRIVE man John Murray on bass guitar.

Wakey returned to the band to record 1994's comeback 'Bow To None', whilst the 1995 single on Wretch Records was recorded with new vocalist Stuart. Butt created WARDANCE with ex FRANTIX bassist Andy Frantic and former BOYS DREAM drummer Matt Keys.

Various members of ENGLISH DOGS forged an alliance with erstwhile GBH personnel in 1997 to create SENSA YUMA releasing the 'Every Day's Your Last Day' album on Retch Records. Another ENGLISH DOGS / GBH union resulted in Wakey and Pinch creating THE WERNT with GBH members guitarist Jock Blyth and bassist Ross Lomas for a 1997 album 'Wreckin' Temples'.

More prominently, Gizz's sojourn with THE PRODIGY revitalized interest in ENGLISH DOGS prompting a re-release of 'Where Legend Began'.

guitarist also announced the formation of a new act JANUS STARK the same year recording with ex-CHARLIE guitarist Terry Thomas acting as producer.

1999's 'I've Got A Gun' was recorded live in Finland at the last ever ENGLISH DOGS show. By 2000 Pinch had joined the DAMNED. Gizz Butt returned in 2004 with THE MORE IS SEE.

Mad Punx And English Dogs EP, Clay (1983). Max (The Millionaire) / Psycho Killer / Free To Kill / Driven to Death / Left Me For Dead / R.I.P.
INVASION OF THE PORKYMEN, Clay CLAYLP 10 (1984). The Fall Of Max / World War Two / Your Country / Blind Man / Mercenary / Never Die / Astroph's Waiting / News Flash / Ghost Of The Past / Carol / Spoils Of War / Cranked Up Really High / Invasion Of The Porky Man / Caveman Brain.

To The Ends Of The Earth EP, Rot (1984). To The Ends Of The Earth / The Chase Is On / Survival Of The Fittest / Incisor.
FORWARD INTO BATTLE, LM (1985). Forward Into Battle / The Final Conquest / Ultimate Sacrifice / Ordeal By Fire / False Prophet / Wall Of Steel / Nosferatu / He That Is Bound Shall Be Freed / Five Days To Death / Brainstorm.
Metal Morphosis EP, Under One Flag 101 (1986). Nightmare Of Reality / Absolution / Let The Killing Begin.
WHERE LEGEND BEGAN, Under One Flag (1987). Trauma / The Eye Of Shamahn / Enter The Domain / Premonition / Calm Before The Storm / Flashback / A Tomb Of Traveller's Past / Middle Earth / Epilogue.
BOW TO NONE, Impact IR-C-021 (1994). Nipper Tripper / Amsterdam / Face Pollution / Criminal Juvenile / Fun Door Enlightening / Psycho Killer / Bastard / Barnaby Hoofer / The Fall Of Max / (Would You Like To Live In My) Surgical Cocoon / Left Me For Dead / The Hanging Wanker / D.N.A. / Balloon.
ALL THE WORLD'S A RAGE, Impact (1995). Shoot Your Head Off / I've Got A Gun / Last One Standing / This Is Not A War / Delete It / Out In The Cold / Wrecking Spree / Die Waiting / Under A Private Attack / Fortress Europe / A Cog In Their Machine / Poor Air Quality / Be What You Are / Grass / Reduction Line / Body On The Line / Disarm.
What A Wonderful Feeling ... To Be Fucked By Everyone, Wretch (1995). Die Waiting / Bad Manna (Be What You Are) / This Is Not A War / Lay Down Your Arms / Wasted Life.

ENTERA

GERMANY — *Carsten Lutter (vocals / bass), Michael Missy (guitar), Erik Mayer (drums).*

Thrash Metal act forged by bassist Carsten Lutter during 1990, adding guitarist Olaf Wilken and drummer Thorsten Lang the following year. Jürgen Peters came onboard as second guitarist in 1993 as ENTERA performed their debut gig in Völklingen alongside IMPENDING DREAD during October of that year. After a first demo recording 'Crossing' Oliver Müller augmented Peters in 1994. A further demo, 'Infinitus', found ENTERA with a recording line up comprising Carsten Lutter on vocals and bass, guitarists Bernd Schönborn and Jürgen Peters with Jimi on drums. The line up shuffled further in 1995 with Schönborn switching from guitar to drums as Ilan Deck took on secondary guitar responsibilities alongside Peters. The next year, 1996, had Luigi Capodoci replacing Deck.

Lutter would kick start his unique guitar-less Black Metal project ANDABATA in 1997. That year ENTERA would be operating as a trio of Lutter, guitarist Sascha Giro and ANDABATA drummer Erik Mayer. In 1999 Holger Grzeschik took on guitar duties. An album emerged billed as 'Betrayal Against Time' after which Ronny Stenger took Mayer's position. Subsequently Michael Missy would usurp Grzeschik. The ENTERA revolving door policy would see the return of Mayer in 2002 but the departure of Missy.

BETRAYAL AGAINST TIME, (2000). Evolution Zum Tod / Never Again / This Can't Happen To Me / Remaining Time / Believe, Fight Or Die / Magna Molestia / Infinitus Clamor / The War Goes On / No Way Out / A.Q.N.S.E. / Ea Nova Libri / The Last Morning / Leaders Of Madness.

EROSION

GERMANY — *Chris Zenk (vocals), Michael Hankel (guitar), Stefan Römhild (guitar), Peter Ewaldt (bass), Klaus Nowakowski (drums).*

In their career this German outfit has undergone something in the region of twenty line-up changes. Musically EROSION has transformed themselves from a Hardcore style outfit to one performing a more Thrashier style, although the Hardcore roots are still evident. The opening 1989 'Mortal Agony' album saw the inclusion of lead vocalist Chris Zenk, guitarist Ulf Kaiser, bass player Jan Bünning and drummer Klaus Nowakowski. By 1990's follow up 'Thoughts' both Kaiser and Bünning were out of the picture, Michael Hankel substituting on guitar whilst Rainer Wischnewski took over the bass role. EROSION switched bassists for the 'Gunman' EP, inducting Peter Ewaldt.

Jan Bünning joined PARAGON. Guitarists Stefan Römhild and Michael Hankel were also included in the ranks of ex-HOLY MOSES man Andy Classen and former WARPATH singer Dirk Weiss's project band RICHTHOFEN in 1997. By mid 2003 Michael Hankel had joined HOLY MOSES.

MORTAL AGONY, We Bite (1988). Erosion / Way Of Force / The Unborn / Bilharzia / Aftermath / False Prophets / Paralyzed / Mortal Agony / Nuclear Frost / Into The Void / Humanity.
THOUGHTS, We Bite (1990). H / The Scourge / Thought / You Belong To Us / Are You God? / Nightmare / Strike / Change.
Gunman EP, We Bite (1991). 70th Floor / The Power Within / Gunman.
EROSION III, We Bite (1992). Erosion III / Erosive Life / Revenge / Body & Soul / Reality / Power Within / Enemy / MLH / Germany 2003 / 70th Floor / Love / Lonely / Dead Europe.
DOWN, We Bite WB1-138-2 (1996). Up / Silver / Four Walls / Sub Consciously / A New Day / The Cross / Temptation / The Mutants Kiss / Sisyphos / Trapped And Confused / Our Minns-Mavn.

ESCABIOS

BUENOS AIRES, ARGENTINA — *Alberto Pastor (vocals), José Luis Fungueiro (guitar), Javier Faifer (guitar), Johnny Tumba (bass), Elvio Arduvino (drums).*

Buenos Aires Thrash act ESCABIOS was assembled in March of 1988 by vocalist Carlos Di Tirro, guitarist José Luis Fungueiro, bass player Fernando Batistoni with Elvio Arduvino on the drums. Johnny Vincent would take over the bass position for recording of the inaugural demo 'Cementerio De Botellas', of which 200 copies were manufactured. A further line-up change saw the introduction of singer Alberto Pastor for second demo 'Cámara De Tortura', this session selling out of its 600 copies.

Adding guitarist Javier Faifer, ESCABIOS issued the 1991 demo 'Estado De Podredumbre'. Morgan Records issued the 1992 album 'Necesidad Extrema'. Diego Sánchez would later front the band as a deal with Roadrunner Records produced the album 'Altering The State' featuring a cover version of the DEAD KENNEDYS hit 'Holiday In Cambodia'. Fungueiro and Vincent subsequently forged MORTUARY. Fungueiro would also unite with Arduvino in PSICOTICO. Javier Faifer joined NATIVIDAD.

Camara De Tortura, (1990). El Jamás Existió / Cámara De Tortura / Pide Perdón / Justicia Total / Transgresor / Dios Ha Muerto.
Estado De Podredumbre, Escabios (1991). No Mas Sangre / Estado De Podredumbre / Excrementos De Odio / Necesidad Extrema / Introducción.
NECESIDAD EXTREMA, Morgan (1992). Esclavitud De Masas / Burning Flesh / State Of Putrefaction / Terrorismo / Estados Proximos A La Muerte / Aniquilar / Control De Humanidad / Necesidad Extrema / Repulsion / Despreciable Realidad.
ALTERING THE FUTURE, Roadrunner (1995). Condemned By The System / Mirror To Madness / Corporation Of Terror / State Of Mind / Out Of Reality / Destroyed Generation / Hate Core / Altering The Future / State Agression / Holiday In Cambodia.

ETERNAL AUTUMN

MARIESTAD, SWEDEN — *John Carlsson (vocals / guitar), Thomas Ahlgren (guitar), Sami Nieminen (bass), Ola Sundström (drums).*

Founded in 1993, Mariestad based melodic Death / Thrash act ETERNAL AUTUMN underwent numerous line-up changes until the introduction of drummer Andreas Tullson provided some much needed stability. However, the band hired a bass player in quick succession then shortly after vocalist and founder member Daniel quit. The band issued an inaugural demo recording in 1994 before Daniel was to re-enter the fold, although this time taking up the duties of bass player. A 1996 demo was issued after which Daniel made his exit again and Tullson decamped too.

A third effort, the six track 'Moonscape' cassette, witnessed a revised membership comprising vocalist / rhythm guitarist John Carlsson, Thomas Ahlgren on lead guitar, Tobias Vipeklev on bass and drummer Ola Sundström. This last session led to a deal with the Black Diamond label for the 1998 album 'The Storm'. In the midst of laying down the debut Vipeklev was asked to leave necessitating the two guitarists sharing the bass duties. Musically the album was firmly entrenched in traditional Heavy Metal territory although, by the band's admission, the whole affair was liberally injected with a degree of Gothicism.

ETERNAL AUTUMN, now with Sami Nieminen on bass, would cut their version of 'Return Of The Vampire' for the MERCYFUL FATE tribute album 'The Unholy Sounds Of The Demon Bells' issued via Poland's Still Dead Productions. Although a new album '... From The Eastern Forest' was announced for release through the Japanese Soundholic label ETERNAL AUTUMN folded in the summer of 2001.

THE STORM, Black Diamond BDP005 (1999). The Storm / Autumn Fire / In My Recent Shape / As The Last Leaf Fell / Moonscape / Autumn Opus, No 1 / Floating ... / In A Land Dawn Never Reached.

... FROM THE EASTERN FORESTS, Soundholic SHCD1-0037 (2000) (Japanese release). November Frost / The Ashes Of The Witch / Seven Years / Grey Filthy Claws / - / An Eternity In Vengeance Part 2 / Statues.

ETERNAL DIRGE

GERMANY — *Timo (vocals / guitar), Pethe (guitar), Boelmi (bass), Ralf (drums).*

This self styled "Neo pagan psycho Metal" band, from Marl, Westfalia, was formed in the mid 80s and released several demos before 'We Are The Dead' led to a record deal. Both of ETERNAL DIRGE's albums, 1994's 'Morbus Ascendit' and 1996's 'Khaos Magick', highlight the group's brand of Death / Thrash Metal with keyboard leanings on a grand scale. Indeed, during the recording of the 'Khaos Magick' album permanent keyboardist Sascha R. joined the group. Touring included an appearance on the 1996 'Full Of Hate' Easter festivals sharing the billing with SIX FEET UNDER and THINK ABOUT MUTATION.

An ex-ETERNAL DIRGE bassist, Karsten Boehnke, scored credits MUSTY GUTS and SUFFOCATE BASTARD.

MORBUS ASCENDIT, HASS Production (1994). Out The Eons / The Crawling Chaos / Exploring The Depths / Blind Idiot God / The Decadence Within / We Are The Dead / Sinustis Maxillaris / Evolved Mutations.

KHAOS MAGICK, Moribund MR024 (1996). I, Unnamable / The Threshold Of Sensation / Anthem To The Seeds (Of Pure Demise) / Feaster From The Stars / Rending The Veils / Kallisti / Like Roses In A Garden Of Weed / In Praise Of Biocide / Hymn To Pan / My Sweet Satan.

EULOGY

USA — *Jason Avery (vocals), Jarret Pritchard (guitar), Jay Medina (guitar), Mike Beardon (bass), Clayton Gore (drums).*

EULOGY, despite only managing a solitary mini album release 'The Essence', was a renowned and influential force in the Florida Thrash / Death Metal transitional scene during the early 90s. The band was originally established in Virginia by vocalist Jason Avery, guitarist Jarrett Pritchard and bass player Mike Beardon. A debut demo was cut with the aid of a drum machine before EULOGY relocated to Florida in order to hook up with drummer 'Aantar' Lee Coates, a veteran citing credits such as NECROSIS, EXMORTIS and IMPIETY. However, within weeks Coates was out of the picture, duly replaced by Clayton Gore.

The band debuted on the live front in January of 1992, opening a gig in Tampa for MONSTROSITY and BRUTALITY. For a brief period EULOGY operated with second guitarist Jerry Mortillero, later of DIABOLIC. However, this line up never performed live or recorded. Back as a quartet the band recorded the 1992 Tom Harris produced demo session 'Dismal'. For these recordings EULOGY introduced Jay Medina on guitar in Mortillero's stead.

Later that same year a deal was scored with the Dutch Cenotaph label and recording commenced for the mini album 'The Essence'. However, in spite of fronting the money for these studio sessions themselves the record was massively delayed, surfacing as late as 1994. A tour of Florida ensued in alliance with GOREPHOBIA and IMMOLATION after which Medina exited. BRUTALITY's Jay Fernandez would deputize but then in another bodyblow Beardon decamped.

Down to the surviving trio of Pritchard, Avery and Gore EULOGY attempted to regroup bringing in Ed Webb on bass and RIPPING CORPSE man Erik Rutan on guitar. Rutan soon bade his farewell to join premier act MORBID ANGEL and Dave Sawyer stepped into the breach for live work. A demo tape, 'Lesson In Fear', surfaced in January of 1995, a track from which, 'Human Harvest', appeared on the Metal Blade 'Metal Massacre MMXII' compilation.

Shortly after EULOGY folded. Avery became frontman for MONSTROSITY. Jarret Pritchard switched from guitar to bass in order to enroll in CANEPHORA. Beardon had founded ANGEL TRUMPETS, a band operating in parallel with EULOGY that also saw contributions from Fernandez, Avery and Gore. ANGEL TRUMPETS had cut a two song demo in December of 1993. The drummer would also enjoy a brief term with Erik Rutan's ALAS project band.

Webb teamed up with BRUTALITY before joining forces with formative EULOGY drummer Lee Coates in DIABOLIC. Later Webb, ex-EULOGY guitarist Dave Sawyer and the erstwhile BRUTALITY pairing of Pete Sykes and Jim Coker founded CONTORTED. Guitarist Jarret Pritchard forged THE STELLAR CORE. In 2003 Clayton Gore re-surfaced as part of St. Louis, Missouri Black Metal band HARKONIN.

ESSENCE, Cenotaph 077-140782 (1994). The Essence / When The Heavens Bleed / Entombed By Belief / Consecration Of Fools.

EUTHANAUSEA

RIIHIMÄKI, FINLAND — *Janne Tamminen (vocals), Mika Nikkanen (guitar), Ville Nummenpää (guitar), Vesa Salminen (bass), Santtu Penttinen (keyboards), Marko Jokinen (drums).*

Riihimäki based Death / Thrash outfit, created in 1990 with a line-up of singer Janne Tamminen, guitarists Mika Nikkanen and Ville Nummenpää, bass guitarist Vesa Salminen and drummer Marko Jokinen. The band's first recordings, the 7" single 'Songs Of Forgotten Souls', would be overseen by STRATOVARIUS guitarist Timmo Tolkki. A further 1993 session, resulting in the 'Melodying' demo, also saw Tolkki handling production. EUTHANAUSEA then expanded their roster of band members by adding keyboard player Santtu Penttinen for a five song demo 'Satan Is Good'.

EUTHANAUSEA would then record the 1995 EP 'Sleep-Dream-Die-Fly', featuring guest vocalist Katja Nieminen on the song 'Mother's Darkest Lullaby'. Upon completion of these tracks vocalist Janne Tamminen was dismissed, later joining Hardcore merchants ENDSTAND. Nikkanen opted to take over the vocal role and in this incarnation the band submitted two tracks to the compilation album 'Shadows Of Michelangelo'. Adopting a completely new course the band drafted singer Saku Hänninen and switched title to SINSATIONAL. In this guise the group recorded one demo but, after the defection of Penttinen in 1999, would once more re-evolve into EUTHANAUSEA by 2002. The 'Fireworks' EP would be next on the agenda.

Songs Of Forgotten Souls, Independent EUTS-0892 (1992). Songs Of Forgotten Souls / Sadistfaction.

Sleep-Dream-Die-Fly, Independent (1995).

Fireworks, (2003). Fireworks / Helldozer / Sixteen Tons / Technicolor.

EVIL DEAD

USA — *Phil Flores (vocals), Juan Garcia (guitar), Albert Gonzales (guitar), Mel Sanchez (bass), Rob Alaniz (drums).*

EVIL DEAD, a band who were unafraid to take Death Metal to new levels of extremity, were created by guitarist Juan Garcia after he abandoned AGENT STEEL in 1988. Garcia's previous credits also included ABATTOIR. The original version of EVIL DEAD included ex-ABATTOIR bassist Mel Sanchez and erstwhile NECROPHILIA drummer Rob Alaniz. ABATTOIR guitarist Mark Caro was invited to join early on but the liaison didn't pan out and he quickly left the scene after recording a three track demo tape.

Guitarist Albert Gonzalez and vocalist Phil Flores were added a year later and EVIL DEAD would go on to score a deal with the German label Steamhammer Records. The group debuted with the 'Rise Above' EP in 1989 and followed it up with the full blown album 'Annihilation Of Civilization' the same year. Japanese versions of 'Annihilation Of Civilization' included bonus tracks from the European only released EP. However, EVIL DEAD fragmented before their second album, Albert Gonzales was fired and would join DEATH for touring duties.

Rob Alaniz walked out (forming RISE in the process) but Flores and Garcia regrouped by adding guitarist Dan Flores and bassist Karlos Medina (after Sanchez split) for 1991's 'The Underworld'. Drums on the album, which included a version of the SCORPIONS 'He's A Woman, She's A Man', were supplied by former DEFCON man Doug Clawson and backing vocals by METAL CHURCH man David Wayne. DEATH drummer Gene Hoglan also guested.

Rise Above, Steamhammer 557590 (1989). Rise Above / Run Again / Sloe Death / S.T. Riff.
ANNIHILATION OF CIVILIZATION, Steamhammer 847603 (1989). F.C.I.: The Awakening / Annihilation Of Civilization / Living God / Future Shock / Holy Trials / Gone Shooting / Parricide / Unauthorised Exploitation / B.O.H.I.C.A.
THE UNDERWORLD, Steamhammer 084 76362 (1991). Intro (Comshell 5) / Global Warming / Branded / Welcome To Kuwait / Critic—Cynic / The 'Hood / The Underworld / He's A Woman, She's A Man / Process Elimination / Labyrinth Of The Mind / Reap What You Sow.
LIVE ... FROM THE DEPTHS OF THE UNDERWORLD, Steamhammer (1992). The Underworld / Global Warming / Gone Shooting / Parracide / F.C.I.—Welcome To Kuwait / The 'Hood / Annihilation Of Civilization / Darkness.

EVILDOER

SWEDEN — *Andreas Solveström (vocals), Johan (guitar), Martin (guitar), Simon Frödeberg (bass), Agge Johansson (drums).*

EVILDOER feature in their ranks NEMESIS and WITHIN Y frontman Andreas Solveström. Guitarist Johan is ex-FIVE SHADES OF GREY and also active with SALVATION FOR SALE alongside second guitarist Martin. Bassist Simon Frödeberg operates solo venture URUZ and would be active with VERMINOUS, SGT. CARNAGE and INFERNAL HELLFIRE. Drummer Agge 'Bones' Johansson is also a VERMINOUS member and ex-DELVE veteran.

The band, debuting with an August 2004 three song demo billed 'Terror', signed to Italy's Scarlet Records for a debut album 'The Terror Audio' set for August 2005 release. Recording took place at Berno Studios in Malmö during April.

In November 2006 it was revealed Andreas Solveström and WITHIN Y bassist Jonas Larsson had teamed up with KALIBER drummer David Andersson to launch a new side project called ORO.

Terror, Evildoer (2004). Right Hand Servant / King Of Fools / Die Now!
TERROR AUDIO, Scarlet SC 107-2 (2005). Please Lord / By The Flag / FearDotGov / Day Of Torment / Gunshell Revenge / Right Hand Servant / On Bleeding Knees / The Deviant / Ten Times The Pain / Absolute Hate / Die Now!

EVILE

EVILE

HUDDERSFIELD, WEST YORKSHIRE, UK — *Matt Drake (vocals / guitar), Ol Drake (lead guitar), Mike Alexander (bass), Ben Carter (drums).*

EVILE is a Huddersfield, West Yorkshire Metal band forged during 2004 by brothers Matt Drake, on vocals and guitar, and Ol Drake, on lead guitar, along with Ben Carter on drums plus bassist Mike Alexander. Promoting the Alan Smith engineered 'Hell' demo, notable live work in 2006 included the 'Thrash Till Death' UK tour, alongside PITIFUL REIGN and HEADLESS CROSS, plus appearances at the Derbyshire 'Bloodstock Open Air' and the October 'Damnation' festival in Manchester alongside SKINDRED, BIOMECHANICAL and THE HAUNTED. EVILE signed to Earache Records in October 2006.

UK dates in March 2007 saw a partnership with SEVERE TORTURE and DESECRATION.

All Hallows Eve, Evile (2005). Killer From The Deep / Dawn Of Destruction / Prophecy / The Living Dead / All Hallows Eve / Torment.
Hell, Evile (2006) (Demo). Enter The Grave / Death Sentence / We Who Are About To Die / Russian Roulette / Thrasher.

EXCEL

VENICE, CA, USA — *Daniel Clemente (vocals) Adam Siegel (guitar), Shaun Ross (bass), Gregor Saenz (drums).*

EXCEL came to notoriety almost by accident when their track 'Tapping Into The Emotional Void' from their 1989 album 'The Joke's On You' became embroiled in controversy. When METALLICA's self titled album became a runaway hit, clocking over 14 million sales in the USA alone, learned fans of the underground California Thrash—Crossover scene started to point to some remarkable similarities between the EXCEL track and METALLICA's biggest radio hit to date 'Enter Sandman'.

The group started life billed as CHAOTIC NOISE in 1983, switching to the EXCEL title with the introduction of MY HEAD and INFECTIOUS GROOVES guitarist Adam Siegel the following year. Adding another ex-MY HEAD member, drummer Gregor Saenz, the band published demos 'Personal Onslaught' and 'Sonic Decapitation' in 1985 and 'Refuse To Quit' during 1986.

EXCEL signed to Suicidal Records and released the 'Split Image' album in 1987. A 12" single, 'Message In A Bottle', would be a take off from THE POLICE hit. They then switched to Caroline Records for Randy Burns produced 'The Joke's On You', this record being a compilation of tracks originally intended for a proposed 1988 EP, the material on side 1, and subsequent tracks cut to boost the product to a full album. Both

Siegel and Saenz exited prior to EXCEL's third album, 'Seeking Refuge' released by Malicious Vinyl.

Demo tracks laid down during 1991 and 1992 featured as bonus songs on the 1991 Rotten Records re-release of 'The Joke's On You'.

In 2004 Saenz turned up as drummer for VEGA, the band founded by ex-SLO BURN bassist Damon Garrison, Ryon on lead guitar with Jamie of THE HELLIONS on bass guitar. Daniel Clemente came to the fore once again, uniting with former SUICIDAL TENDENCIES musicians guitarist Grant Estes, bassist Louichi Mayorga and drummer Amery Smith in a new band billed AGAINST, announcing this formation in May 2006.

SPLIT IMAGE, Suicidal (1987). Your Life, My Life / Insecurity / Split Image / Never Look Away / Wreck Your World / Social Security / Set Yourself Apart / The Joke's On You / Looking For You / Spare The Pain.

Message In A Bottle, (1988). Message In A Bottle.

Blaze Some Hate, Caroline (1989). Blaze Some Hate / Tapping Into The Emotional Void.

THE JOKE'S ON YOU, Caroline (1989). Drive / Fired (You're) / Tapping Into The Emotional Void / Affection Blends With Resentment / Sealing Insane / My Thoughts / I Never Denied / Message In A Bottle / Given Question / The Stranger / Blaze Some Hate.

SEEKING REFUGE, Malicious Vinyl (1991). Unenslaved / Hair Like Christ / Plastic Cracks / Take Your Part Gotta Encourage / Drowned Out / United Naturally In True You / Riptide / Overview / Downpressor.

EXCESSUM

RAMLE, ISRAEL — *Ilia Badrov (vocals), Arie Aranovich (guitar), Jonathan Bar-Ilan (guitar), Elad Manor (bass), Shaked Furman (drums).*

Ramle Death / Thrashers EXCESSUM, founded in 2000, feature ex-ARAFEL guitarist Leon Notik (a.k.a. 'Oboroten'), the SOLITARY, MATRICIDE and ACROPOLIS credited Elad 'Romano' Manor on bass guitar and ex-SOLITARY and DEHUMANIZED drummer Shaked Furman. The group was forged by singer Ilia Badrov with guitarist Nomaed Dominus (a.k.a. Boris) under an original billing of DARK SUICIDE.

The EXCESSUM title was adopted in 2001 as second guitarist Nesly was to lose his place to Arie before the band unit was solidified with the incorporation of rhythm section bassist Maor 'Keves' Bitton and Itamar on drums. Nomaed Dominus quit in mid 2002 for Folk Metal act HOLTSCYRM, being swiftly replaced by Notik. Next in line to decamp would be Itamar, seeing Nadav Luzia taking his place briefly before Dor stepped in. However, he too left and Luzia made a return.

EXCESSUM performed their first live concert in June 2003 at the Asylum Club in Tel Aviv, sharing the stage with NATURE'S ELEMENT and DAGOR DAGORATH. In August Firman took over the drum position and Manor took over from former bassist Bitton in December.

Instruction For Self-Destruction, Excessum (2006) (Limited to 1000 copies). Deception / Destination, Life / Suffer And Die / Infernal Existence / Kingdom Loneliness.

EXCITER

OTTAWA, ON, CANADA — *Jacques Bélanger (vocals / drums), John Ricci (guitar), Rob Cohen (bass), Rik Charron (drums).*

Speed Metal trio EXCITER, founded in Ottawa, Ontario in 1978 and almost certainly named after the infamous show opening JUDAS PRIEST track, made their presence known with some gut crunching Metal blessed by the raucous vocals of drummer Dan Beehler. EXCITER, originally billed as HELL RAZOR, first demoed in 1980, delivering the two song 'World War III' cassette. Guitarist John Ricci had culled members from his antecedent outfit HELL RAZOR and re-built the band in May 1979 by drawing in JET BLACK personnel Dan Beehler and bassist Alan Johnson, adopting the EXCITER brand a few months later. The title track scored inclusion on the 1982 compilation album 'US Metal Vol. II', put together by Mike Varney's Shrapnel label. A March 1983 'Under Attack' three song promotional session led into a third demo, produced by the band's live sound engineer John Belrose, entitled 'Heavy Metal Maniac'. These tapes quickly led to a deal with the Shrapnel label for a full-length album, the Californian imprint simply pressing up the existing tracks onto vinyl. However, the relationship ended with Shrapnel when Varney apparently took umbrage with some of EXCITER's darker lyrical content. '. Heavy Metal Maniac' had pushed the band into the spotlight enough to easily secure a new label deal and land a valuable support to BLACK SABBATH, performing in front of a sell out 7,000 crowd at the Ottawa Civic Centre Arena on October 22nd 1983.

EXCITER's second album, 'Violence And Force', the first product from a contract with Jonny Zazula's Mega Force Records, was produced by THE RODS drummer Carl Canedy at Pyramid Sound in Ithaca, New York during November 1983. Arriving in February 1984 'Violence & Force' soon shifted a healthy 75'000 copies. US tour dates would witness supports to both ANTHRAX and MERCYFUL FATE. The band's profile was heightened greatly by an aggressive licensing campaign conducted by UK label Music For Nations. Despite this, gigs across the UK planned for March 1984, dubbed the 'Hell On Earth' tour being packaged with METALLICA and THE RODS, would be cancelled due to poor ticket sales. A follow up 'Long Live The Loud' was recorded in London, at the PINK FLOYD owned Britannia Row Studios with production credits going to Guy Bidmead. The band backed up this release by touring Europe as support to ACCEPT in early 1985 prior to engaging with MEGADETH and MOTÖRHEAD for US dates. Released to coincide with these dates would be the EP 'Feel The Knife', the title cut being a studio outtake from the prior album sessions, being backed by live versions of 'Violence & Force' and 'Pounding Metal' recorded onstage in Ottawa. Further tour plans were announced for Europe in a proposed union with METAL CHURCH but would be cancelled when, in an apparent band disagreement regarding whether SLAYER should top the billing at a mooted Canadian concert, John Ricci decamped in August 1985. The guitarist eventually re-emerged with a new act BLACKSTAR.

1986's 'Unveiling The Wicked', retaining the winning formula of Guy Bidmead and Britannia Row but regretfully clad in a budget schlock horror sleeve, was to include new guitar player Brian McPhee, a former band mate of Beehler and Johnson in JET BLACK. This version of the group traversed the European continent supporting MOTÖRHEAD and MANOWAR. Upon completion of this expedition, Beehler announced he had no further intentions of singing lead vocals.

EXCITER pulled in former SILENT PARTNER and SIMMONDS vocalist Jimmy Kunes but this liaison did not gel. After dates in Brazil, the band added vocalist Rob Malnati for 1988's 'OTT' record, assembling these tracks for Canadian label Maze Music with producer Ed Stone at The Metal Works in Toronto.

Beehler decided to put EXCITER on ice during 1990 forming a new act KILJOY. Joining him on demos were former CRYPT vocalist / bassist David Ledden and guitarist Joe Desmond. Ricci and Beehler re-energized EXCITER once more, briefly working with Alan Johnson before bringing in bassist David Ledden again for the 'Kill After Kill' album, produced by ex-AVALON bassist Manfred Leidecker and released through Noise Records in Germany. Live work in Europe had the band packaged with RAGE for a three week tour. Leidecker, along with ex-AVALON guitarist Brian Sim, would also handle their live follow up, 1993's 'Better Live Than Dead', licensed to the Bleeding Hearts label for UK issue. For live work EXCITER utilized the talents of bassist Jeff McDonnald.

The band, resurrected once again in March of 1996, returned with 'The Dark Command' emerging on the French label Osmose Productions, usually known for its extreme Black Metal

EXCITER (pic: Andy Brown)

output. Ricci had give new life to the band which now comprised an all new crew of vocalist Jacque Bélanger, a former drummer with SARKASM, DAYS OF YORE and DEIMOS, bassist Marc Charron and drummer Rick Charron. The album was internationally given the thumbs up as a powerful return to form and gigs across Europe, with FLOTSAM AND JETSAM plus fellow Canucks ANVIL, solidified this opinion. This unit remained stable for the 2000 'Blood Of Tyrants' opus. However, during September of 2001 it was learned that Bélanger had bailed out.

Further exposure would be garnered when up and coming American Metal band SEVEN WITCHES covered 'Pounding Metal' for their second album 'City Of Lost Souls'. The band has sustained enough interest to warrant a slew of live bootlegs including 'Devil's Soul', 'Live Beasts' and Night Of The Creeps'. During mid 2002 founder EXCITER members Dan Beehler and Allan Johnson reunited in a brand new band project billed simply BEEHLER. The quartet, was completed by guitarists Sean Brophy and Scott Walsh. Bass player Marc Charron announced his departure from the ranks during November. The lead vocal position was filled the following month by Rob Degroot and bassist Paul Champagne completed the line up in January of 2003. However, by March Jacques Bélanger had retaken his position heading the band.

Paul Champagne exited in June 2003. The band's next move, delegating the bass role to John Ricci for studio purposes, would be to re-record early material for a retrospective compilation. This set, comprising re-visited material from 1983's 'Heavy Metal Maniac', 1984's 'Violence & Force', 1985's 'Long Live the Loud', 1992's 'Kill after Kill' 1997's 'The Dark Command' and even as recent as 2000's 'Blood of Tyrants', would emerge with the title 'New Testament—Coven Of Re-recorded Classics'. EXCITER added new bass man Rob 'Clammy' Cohen to the ranks in April 2004. A further round of archive releases in late 2004 came courtesy of Megaforce Records, with the band's first six albums, 'Heavy Metal Maniac' (1983), 'Violence & Force' (1984), 'Long Live the Loud' (1985), 'Better Live Than Dead' (1990), 'Unveiling the Wicked' (1986) and 'O.T.T.' (1988), being remixed by none other than ANNIHILATOR's Jeff Waters.

A European tour beginning in early October saw Swedish Power Metal merchants STEEL ATTACK and Germany's BLACK ABYSS as support acts. German Heavy Metal band POWERGOD cut a cover version of 'Fall Out / Long Live The Loud' for inclusion on their 'Long Live The Loud–That's Metal Lesson II' released through Massacre Records in July 2005. In September Dan Beehler disbanded his BEEHLER project and once again set to work on new EXCITER material with former guitarist Paul Champagne.

Jacques Bélanger quit EXCITER again in April 2006, citing "differences of opinion". The band announced the addition of Brooklyn, New York-based singer Kenny "Metal Mouth" Winter to the group's ranks in October.

World War III, (1980). World War III / Sail On.
HEAVY METAL MANIAC, Shrapnel 1004 (1983). The Holocaust / Stand Up And Fight / Heavy Metal Maniac / Iron Dogs / Mistress Of Evil / Under Attack / Rising Of The Dead / Blackwitch / Cry Of The Banshee.
Under Attack, (1983). Under Attack / Rising Of The Dead / Cry Of The Banshee.
VIOLENCE AND FORCE, Music For Nations MFN 17 (1984). Oblivion / Violence And Force / Scream In The Night / Pounding Metal / Evil Sinner / Destructor / Swords Of Darkness / Delivering To The Master / Saxons Of The Fire / War Is Hell.
Feel The Knife, Music For Nations 12 KUT 113 (1985). Feel The Knife / Violence And Force (Live) / Pounding Metal (Live).
LONG LIVE THE LOUD, Music For Nations MFN 47 (1985). Fall Out / Long Live The Loud / I Am The Beast / Victims Of Sacrifice / Beyond The Gates Of Doom / Sudden Impact / Born To Die / Wake Up Screaming.
UNVEILING THE WICKED, Music For Nations MFN 61 (1986). Break Down The Walls / Brainstorm / Die In The Night / (I Hate) School Rules / Shout It Out / Invasion—Waiting In The Dark / Living Evil / Live Fast, Die Young / Mission Destroy.
O.T.T., Maze MMAL 6000 (1988). Scream Bloody Murder / Back In The Night / Ready To Rock / O.T.T. / I Wanna Be King / Enemy Lines / Dying To Live / Playin' With Fire / Eyes In The Sky / Termination.
KILL AFTER KILL, Noise N 0192-2 (1992). Rain Of Terror / No Life, No Future / Cold Blooded Murder / Smashin' Em Down / Shadow Of The Cross / Dog Eat Dog / Anger, Hate And Destruction / Second Coming / Born To Kill (Live).
BETTER LIVE THAN DEAD—LIVE, Bleeding Hearts CDBLEED 5 (1993). Stand Up And Fight / Heavy Metal Maniac / Victims Of Sacrifice / Under Attack / Sudden Impacts / Delivering To The Master / I Am The Beast / Blackwitch / Long Live The Loud / Rising Of The Dead / Cry Of The Banshee / Pounding Metal / Violence And Force.
THE DARK COMMAND, Osmose Productions OPCD 059 (1997). The Dark Command / Burn At The Stake / Aggressor / Assassins In Rage / Ritual Death / Sacred War / Let Us Prey / Executioner / Suicide Overdose / Screams From The Gallows.
BLOOD OF TYRANTS, Osmose Productions OPCD 089 (2000). Metal Crusaders / Rule With An Iron Fist / Intruders / Predator / Martial Law / War Cry / Brutal Warning / Weapons Of Mass Destruction / Blood Of Tyrants / Violator.
NEW TESTAMENT—COVEN OF RE-RECORDED CLASSICS, Osmose Productions OPCD 2156 (2004). Rising Of The Dead / Violence & Force / Rule With An Iron Fist / Rain Of Terror / Brutal Warning / Victims Of Sacrifice / The Dark Command / I Am The Beast / Pounding Metal / Stand Up And Fight / Heavy Metal Maniac / Blackwitch / Burn At The Stake / Long Live The Loud / Ritual Death.

EXECUTIONER

USA — *Marc Johnson (vocals), Ari Vainio (bass), Dan Skannell (drums).*

Classic mid-80's speed Thrash Metal band, EXECUTIONER managed to release two albums before a thirteen year hiatus and eventual, belated, third release. Founded and spearheaded by Vocalist/guitarist Marc Johnson he was joined by Dan Scanell on drums. The 1986 debut was released on the Greenworld/New Renaissance group and the cassette release has a non-LP bonus cut called 'Final Destruction'.

A year later in 1987, original bassist Ari Vainio was replaced by Seth Putnam, who went on to a respected career with the notorious ANAL CUNT. The band disbanded shortly after but not before recording one more album's worth of material. By then Putnam had been replaced by Tommy Flynn. The album lay unreleased until 2000 when it was independently released with three extra live tracks including an AC/DC cover 'Walk All Over You'.

IN THE NAME OF METAL, GWD 90538 (1986). Victims Of Evil / Hell And Back / Death By The Blade / Nuclear Nightmare / Your Life Is Over / Annihilation / Stand Up And Fight / In A Silent Way / Genocide / Going Blind / Cyanide / In The Name Of Metal / Battlelands.
BREAK THE SILENCE, New Renaissance NRC24 (1987). Death March / Break The Silence / Eye Of The Needle / Your Life Is Over / Terminally Ill / Hatred / Genocide / No One Left To Die / Victims Of Evil / Stand Up And Fight.

THE STORM AFTER THE CALM, Wicked Loud Music (2000). Apostles Of The Damned / In Cold Blood / Devastation / Fatal Calling / Imprisoned / Terminally Ill / Time After Time / The Predator / Nothing To Fear / Beyond The Terror / Death March (Live) / Break The Silence (Live) / Walk All Over You (Live).

EXHORDER

NEW ORLEANS, LA, USA — *Kyle Thomas (vocals), Vinnie La Bella (guitar), Jay Ceravollo (bass), Chris Nail (drums).*

New Orleans Metal band. Upon the debut album release, 1990's 'Slaughter In The Vatican' for Roadrunner Records, EXHORDER lost bassist Andy Villaferra bringing in replacement Frank Sparcello. EXHORDER's 1992 album 'The Law' included a cover version of BLACK SABBATH's 'Into The Void'.

EXHORDER split in 1994 with vocalist Kyle Thomas creating PENALTY (later FLOODGATE for a 1996 album) and bass guitarist Jay Ceravolo joining FALL FROM GRACE as replacement for departing Matt Thomas who had jumped over to CROWBAR. Thomas later fronted Chicago Doomsters TROUBLE.

In the summer of 2002 Kyle Thomas revealed the details of a brand new band project entitled JONES'S LOUNGE. His compatriots in this endeavour comprised Dax Thieler of GREEN LEAF CULT, Jimmy Bower of DOWN, CORROSION OF CONFORMITY, SUPERJOINT RITUAL and EYEHATEGOD as well as Jason Portera from another Thomas band venture, PITTS VS. PREPS. A debut JONES'S LOUNGE album would see production handled by former UGLY KID JOE guitarist Dave Fortman.

During 2005 Kyle Thomas made time to see inclusion on the ROADRUNNER UNITED 25th anniversary album 'The All-Stars Sessions', featuring on the track 'Constitution Down' penned by SLIPKNOT's Joey Jordison. In May 2006 Thomas joined up with Richmond, Virginia's ALABAMA THUNDERPUSSY as their new frontman.

SLAUGHTER IN THE VATICAN, Roadracer RO 93632 (1990). Death In Vain / Homicide / Desecrator / Exhorder / The Tragic Period / Legions Of Death / Anal Lust / Slaughter In The Vatican.
THE LAW, Roadracer RO 92342 (1993). Soul Search Me / Unforgiven / I Am The Cross / Un-Born Again / Into The Void / The Law / Incontinence / (Cadence Of) The Dirge.

EXOCET

GERMANY — *Dirk Mylius (vocals), Stephan Hämmerling (guitar), Patrick Stein (guitar), Tom Merker (bass), Steffan Kolditz (drums).*

EXOCET, formed in 1989, first demoed in late 1992 with their 'Apocalyptic Visions' tape. The group subsequently played various support dates to the likes of CREMATORY, ATROCITY and POST MORTEM and also appeared at the 1994 'Thrash Against Trash' festival headlined by KREATOR. The 'Confusion' album was produced by former ANGEL DUST / SCANNER singer S.L. Coe.

EXOCET supported CREMATORY on their 1995 European tour.

CONFUSION, Massacre MASSCD068 (1995). I Kill Now / Commercial Overkill / The Martyr / Abyss Of Sexuality / Chemical Profit War / In Hate / Apocalyptic Visions / Retaliation / My Nuclear Safety / Unborn / More Bass.

EXODUS

SAN FRANCISCO, CA, USA — *Rob Dukes (vocals), Gary Holt (guitar), Lee Altus (guitar), Jack Gibson (bass), Paul Bostaph (drums).*

San Franciscan Speed metallers created in early 1980, EXODUS featured METALLICA guitarist Kirk Hammett in the original line-up. The original EXODUS incarnation saw Hammett joined by second guitarist Tim Magnello, bassist Carlton Nelson and drummer Tom Hunting, the latter also handling lead vocals. Initially the band operated in NWoBHM territory, performing covers by the likes of DEF LEPPARD and UFO, prior to adopting their more familiar Thrash stance. Nelson went on to join BLIZZARD, OUTRAGE and FUHRER. Jeff Andrews, fleetingly a member of POSSESSED, took the bass position but further changes saw Tim Magnello opting out, being substituted by Gary Holt, a former guitar tech of Hammett's. EXODUS evolved further when Paul Baloff assumed the role of frontman for a 1982 demo comprising the tracks 'Whipping Queen', 'Death And Domination' and 'Warlords'. The band made its presence felt on the live scene with supports to the likes of ANVIL CHORUS, LÄÄZ ROCKIT, VICIOUS RUMORS and METALLICA.

Fate dealt the band a heavy blow in early 1983 when Hammett's services were requested urgently by METALLICA upon recommendation of Mark Whitaker, then not only manager of EXODUS but also acting as METALLICA's sound engineer. On their debut tour of the East Coast, METALLICA had decided to ditch then guitarist Dave Mustaine and pulled in Hammett to complete the tour. The EXODUS man flew out to New York to join up with METALLICA on 11th April and put in his inaugural gig with his new act on the 16th at the Showplace in Dover, New Jersey. At this same juncture EXODUS discarded Andrews and recruited Rob McKillop.

The group briefly employed the services of Mike Maung on guitar before he, joining Disco band FREAKY EXECUTIVE, was superseded by Evan McCasky. This latest candidate lasted just one gig before the band severed ties. Potential guitarists would be Jon Torres of THUNDERHEAD, IRON ASSAULT and WARNING along with Rick Hunolt, the latter securing the position. A second demo session, the two track 'Die By His Hand' emerged in 1983 as did a rehearsal recording in July. By now, the EXODUS name was revered amongst the burgeoning Thrash scene in California. The group fostered a growing legion of die hard fans opening for METALLICA, RAVEN, METAL CHURCH, MOTÖRHEAD, HEAVEN, SUICIDAL TENDENCIES and LOUDNESS whilst putting in a profusion of headliners.

EXODUS continued demoing into 1984 with the 'A Lesson In Violence' set and tracks recorded at Turk Street studios by ANVIL CHORUS and CONTROL's Doug Piercy, famously cut minus many of the vocal tracks due to the band running out of funds. Back on the club scene EXODUS allied with DEATH ANGEL, VERMIN, ANTHRAX, SLAYER and POSSESSED.

EXODUS debuted officially in 1985 with the 'Bonded By Blood' album, recorded for the New York based Torrid label and crafted during July of 1984 at Prairie Sun studios with Mark Whitaker acting as producer. Initial promotional copies supplied to journalists would bear the originally planned title of 'A Lesson In Violence'. Sporting controversial artwork, depicting demonic Siamese twins, many countries chose to change the sleeve art to a simple band logo. The debut EXODUS effort, licensed to Music For Nations for the UK, saw a line-up of vocalist Paul Baloff, guitarists Rick Hunholt and Gary Holt, bassist Rob McKillop and drummer Tom Hunting.

Gigs in 1984 had the band sharing stages with HIRAX, DEATH ANGEL, MERCYFUL FATE and MEGADETH. The subsequent CD version of 'Bonded By Blood', issued by Century Media in 1999, came with the bonus live tracks 'And Then There Were None' and 'A Lesson In Violence'. With this debut EXODUS were to catapult themselves into the Thrash major league, although a minor spat developed when it was learned that lyrics from the EXODUS track 'Hell's Breath' had re-emerged in METALLICA's 'Creeping Death'. Unfortunately this promising start could not be capitalised on and EXODUS steadily lost ground with each successive release despite no let up in quality.

EXODUS partnered with VENOM and SLAYER for national tour work in April, tracks from a show at the notorious Studio 54 in New York City being included on the VHS Video 'The Ultimate Revenge' in April 1985 through Combat Records. In August the group scheduled US and Canadian dates in union with EXCITER but the Canadian act dropped off the tour following just three gigs, leaving EXODUS to persevere onward themselves, culminating in Montreal on 17th August at the 'Banzai' festival alongside SLAYER, METAL CHURCH, HALLOW'S EVE and AGENT STEEL. The following month witnessed the first EXODUS showing on European soil, guesting for VENOM tour dates across the UK, Denmark, France, Switzerland, Italy, Holland and Germany. Fervour surrounding the group resulted in the Eindhoven gig being bootlegged as the albums 'Strike Of The Beast' and 'And Then There Were ... 300'.

Returning to the USA, Baloff and Holt forged the ad hoc side project band SPASTIK CHILDREN in alliance with HEATHEN's Doug Piercy on bass and Fred 'Rotten' Cotton on drums. This notorious and nebulous band unit would famously evolve to incorporate such figures as James McDaniels, PIRANHA's Al Voltage, the METALLICA pairing of James Hetfield and Cliff Burton plus FAITH NO MORE's Jim Martin. The year closed out for EXODUS in style, in late December 1985 the band journeyed to Brooklyn, New York to perform a one off date at the L'Amour club supported by AGNOSTIC FRONT and LETHAL AGRESSION then returned to the West Coast for a New Years Eve gig ranked alongside METALLICA, METAL CHURCH and ANTHRAX.

Following pre-production demos for a second album and a 14th June 1986 gig with ANTHRAX at the New York Ritz, Paul Baloff left, initially to team up with HIRAX for a brief liaison and turning down an offer from German thrashers DESTRUCTION, as EXODUS struggled to wriggle free from their American deal with Torrid Records. During the lull Holt busied himself producing a demo for erstwhile EXODUS bassist Carlton Nelson's FUHRER.

Meantime, EXODUS enlisted Steve "Zetro" Souza, the new singer's previous act LEGACY was later to evolve into TESTAMENT, debuting their new frontman at two gigs at The Farm In San Francisco on July 17th and 18th. For the latter concert Baloff would join Souza on stage during the encore to sing 'Bonded By Blood'. The group crafted the 'Pleasures Of The Flesh' record, released by Combat Records in 1987 before being swiftly re-released as the band scored a major deal with Capitol Records. Some versions of 'Pleasures Of The Flesh' included a cover version of AC/DC's 'Overdose'. November of that year found EXODUS traversing the West Coast and into Texas with co-headliners CELTIC FROST before hooking up with ANTHRAX in December.

As 1988 drew in, ex-singer Paul Baloff announced his new act PIRAHNA comprising of guitarists Ron Shipes and former EXECUTION man Chuck Sedlak, bassist Bob Eggleston and drummer Fred Cotton but later Baloff joined HEATHEN.

Whilst on tour with ANTHRAX and HELLOWEEN, drummer Tom Hunting was forced to leave the band due to a mysterious stomach virus (or so it was reported) and temporarily replaced by VIO-LENCE's Perry Strickland. The group wound up using ANTHRAX drum tech John Tempesta on a headlining American tour in 1989 and would take over full-time as Hunting opted out. Hunting was later to involve himself in IR8, a demo project put together by METALLICA's Jason Newsted. Former bassist Mike Butler re-emerged with the FLEXAPLEASERS and Punk Glam act AMERICAN HEARTBREAK. A notable EXODUS release in 1989 would be the EP 'Objection Overruled', a three track effort which included a rendition of TED NUGENT's 'Free For All'. Capitol Records issued the 'Impact Is Imminent' album in June 1990 but the group struggled to achieve the sales their label had anticipated. EXODUS shifted to Relativity Records to publish the 1991 live album 'Good Friendly Violent Fun', once again witnessing an AC/DC cover in 'Dirty Deeds Done Dirt Cheap'.

The band adopted a new style and direction in 1992 for the Chris Tsangarides produced 'Force Of Habit' album, released that August, as many longstanding fans failed to appreciate the shift away from pure Thrash. The adventurous set, despite supremely heavy epics such as 'Architect Of Pain', even included cover takes on ELVIS COSTELLO's 'Pump It Up' and the ROLLING STONES 'Bitch'. Japanese variants added two extra tracks in 'Crawl Before You Walk' and 'Telepathetic'. Faced with the onset of Grunge and post-Thrash apathy, EXODUS folded.

The group reformed for 1997's 'Another Lesson In Violence', a collection of live recordings of the band's 'classics' but also including the Kirk Hammet co-written 'Impaler', never previously available on record. The album was notably produced by ex-SABBAT guitarist Andy Sneap. The reformed EXODUS featured Baloff, Hunholt, Holt and Hunting along with new bassist Jack Gibson. Holt had been working with Jack Gibson and Tom Hunting in WARDANCE prior to being involved in the reunited EXODUS.

Souza was operating his act DOG FACE with ex-REXXEN and HEATHEN guitarist Ira Black, later of VICIOUS RUMOURS.

The band subsequently appeared at the Dynamo Festival in Holland in the early Summer of 1997 but would yet again break up shortly after. The band name would be kept in the public eye in 2000 as Death Metal band SIX FEET UNDER covered 'Piranha' on their 'Graveyard Classics' album.

EXODUS buried the hatchet in August 2001 re-uniting for a one off gig at the 'Thrash Of The Titans' festival in aid of TESTAMENT frontman Chuck Billy's cancer treatment fund.

Sadly Paul Baloff was to die after suffering a stroke in late January 2002 that left him comatose with irreparable brain damage. The singer was just 41. Despite this huge loss EXODUS persevered pulling in old colleague Steve 'Zetro' Souza in order to fulfill February engagements in Anaheim and an appearance at the Whittier 'Hellfest' in March. The band continued the momentum by stretching out dates into the summer including a showing at the 'Milwaukee Metalfest' in July and the German 'Wacken Open Air' event in early August. December dates had EXODUS performing in Greece with THE HAUNTED and TANKARD, the UK, Holland, France and Belgium. The group also united with SIX FEET UNDER, MARDUK, IMMOLATION and KATAKLYSM for the 'Xmas Festivals' shows for closing dates in Holland to close off the year.

EXODUS were projected to record a new studio album, once again using the services of Andy Sneap as producer, on a newly established label set up by EXODUS enthusiasts former manager Toni Isabella and erstwhile Capitol Records A&R executive Rachel Matthews, responsible for signing the band to the major label back in the 80s. EXODUS stirred controversy and generated some press when courier giants Federal Express objected to the band selling T-shirts at shows bearing the legend 'FedExodus—Total Destruction Guaranteed Overnight'!

EXODUS were to put in a one off show in Las Vegas opening for HALFORD and a short burst of December dates packaged along with TESTAMENT and VIO-LENCE but these gigs were cancelled due to visa problems with Rob Halford. EXODUS surprisingly parted ways with frontman Steve Souza in mid January. Their active search for a new singer ended within weeks though as Souza rejoined in February. Hunting announced extracurricular activity as forming up part of a new look ANGELWITCH. However, within weeks of this press release the drummer pulled out stating his EXODUS commitments took priority.

The band would sign their comeback album 'Tempo Of The Damned' to Nuclear Blast Records in August. UK and European dates projected into October, dubbed the 'Bonded By Metal' trek, found EXODUS topping a billing comprising NUCLEAR ASSAULT, AGENT STEEL, MORTICIAN, GOD DETHRONED, OCCULT and CALLENISH CIRCLE. A limited edition tour single, 'War Is My Sheppard', was made available at these shows. The band filmed video clips for 'War Is My Shepherd' and 'Throwing Down' in late November with director Maurice Swinkels. 'Tempo Of The Damned' would emerge in Europe on 2nd February 2, marking the two-year anniversary of late frontman Paul

Baloff's passing. The EXODUS live schedule extended into 2004 with European dates, including an appearance at the Sölvesborg 'Sweden Rock' event, slated for the Summer. As an adjunct to EXODUS activities guitarist Gary Holt and band manager Steve Warner forged the DRUG PIG project, cutting tracks at Tsunami Studio in Northern California.

September witnessed Japanese shows, followed up by Central and South American gigs in Mexico, Brazil, Chile and Argentina. However, EXODUS frontman Steve Souza was forced to sit out these date after falling ill during the group's Japanese trek. Filling in for Zetro would be EXHUMED frontman Matt Harvey. However, the position became clearer within hours of the first gig in Mexico when band manager Steven Warner told the Blabbermouth network that Souza was out by stating "He did not quit, he was fired!" The separation would prove far from amicable, Gary Holt labelling Souza a "fat motherfuckin' shit brick" on the band's official forums, and claiming the singer withdrew from the tour less than 24 hours before the first gig.

WARDANCE singer John Miller was set join EXODUS to complete the dates. However, in a bizarre turn of events Gary Holt then publicly slammed Miller claiming the singer was an "insane idiot and had one of his mental breakdowns the day before we were to leave". These gigs were then re-scheduled for October, seeing SKINLAB and RE:IGNITION singer Steev Esquivel as new frontman. Meantime, aggrieved Brazilian fans promptly convened the 'Fuck Off Zetro' festival in Belo Horizonte featuring DROWNED, ABSOLUTE DISGRACE, HELLTRUCKER, BETRAYER and PERPETUAL DUSK. The Esquivel fronted EXODUS would also tour the West Coast of America in October as support to MEGADETH.

Unfortunately the band's bad luck continued unabated, Esquivel's eyes being contaminated with "unknown chemicals" at the San Diego gig on 26th October. With the singer under medication, EXODUS drafted TESTAMENT's Chuck Billy as stand in for the following San Francisco Warfield gig. The band announced Rob Dukes, guitarist with East Coast outfit CHEATIN' SOCCER MOMS, as their new singer in January 2005. That same month bassist Jack Gibson, retaining his ties to EXODUS, joined VILE to record their album 'The New Age Of Chaos'.

The EXODUS line-up was re-vamped once more in May with Tom Hunting unfortunately being hospitalised due to illness. Stepping into the breach would be the SLAYER, TESTAMENT, SYSTEMATIC and FORBIDDEN credited Paul Bostaph. As the band set to work on a new album at Trident studios in Pacheco, California, reports emerged in June suggesting Rick Hunolt had departed. Conjecture soon placed HEATHEN's Lee Altus in the frame, this appointment being confirmed in late July. 'Shovel Headed Kill Machine', a grand return to form, emerged in October 2005.

November European headliners saw HYPOCRISY and KEEP OF KALESSIN as support. The band announced a touring partnership as part of the December 2005 'X-Mas' festivals in Europe ranked alongside recently resurrected UK Thrashers ONSLAUGHT, OCCULT, KATAKLYSM, UNLEASHED, BEHEMOTH, and PRIMORDIAL. That same month leading Spanish Death Metal band AVULSED covered 'Piranha' on their EP 'Reanimations'.

The group participated in the 'Extreme The Dojo Vol. 15' shows in Japan with THE HAUNTED and NILE in late February 2006. US touring resumed with CRYPTOPSY and IMMOLATION in April, following through with shows into May bolstered by THE CLASSIC STRUGGLE and FULL BLOWN CHAOS.

In mid 2006 the world of Thrash Metal received a pleasant surprise with the announcement of a new San Francisco based collective project billed DUBLIN DEATH PATROL. (Dublin is a San Francisco suburb). This unit was assembled by a seasoned cast of veterans headed up by erstwhile EXODUS singer Steve Souza and comprising TESTAMENT and RAMPAGE singer Chuck Billy, MACHINE HEAD, DEATH PENALTY, METAL WAR-

EXODUS

RIOR and VIO-LENCE man Phil Demmel on guitar, bassist Willy Langenhuizen, of RAMPAGE and LÄÄZ ROCKIT repute, guitarist Andy Billy of SACRED DOG, RAMPAGE and GUILT, RAMPAGE guitarist Greg Bustamante, OUT OF CONTROL guitarist Steve Robello, bassist John Souza and drummer Danny Cunningham.

EXODUS hit the US touring circuit again in September forming up a strong billing alongside HATEBREED, NAPALM DEATH, THE BLACK DAHLIA MURDER, DESPISED ICON and FIRST BLOOD. Another round of European dates throughout November and December was supported by British act BIOMECHANICAL.

1982 Demo, (1982). Whipping Queen / Death And Domination / Warlords.
Die By His Hand, (1983). Die By His Hand / Endor.
A Lesson In Violence, (1984). A Lesson In Violence / Exodus.
BONDED BY BLOOD, Music For Nations MFN 44 (1985). Bonded By Blood / Exodus / And Then There Were None / A Lesson In Violence / Metal Command / Piranha / No Love / Deliver Us To Evil / Strike Of The Beast.
PLEASURES OF THE FLESH, Music For Nations MFN 77 (1987). Deranged / 'Til Death Us Do Part / Parasite / Brain Dead / Faster Than You'll Ever Live To Be / Pleasures Of The Flesh / 30 Seconds / Seeds Of Hate / Chemi-Kill / Choose Your Weapon. Chart position: 82 USA.
FABULOUS DISASTER, Music For Nations MFN 90 (1988). The Last Act Of Defiance / Fabulous Disaster / The Toxic Waltz / Low Rider / Cajun Hell / Like Father, Like Son / Corruption / Verbal Razors / Open Season / Overdose. Chart position: 82 USA.
Objection Overruled, Capitol 12CLPD 597 (1989). Objection Overruled / Free For All / Changing Of The Guard.
IMPACT IS IMMINENT, Capitol CDEST 2125 (1989). Intro / Impact Is Imminent / A.W.O.L. / The Lunatic Parade / Within The Walls Of Chaos / Objection Overruled / Only Death Decides / Heads They Win (Tails You Lose) / Changing Of The Guard / Thrash Under Pressure. Chart position: 137 USA.
GOOD FRIENDLY VIOLENT FUN, Roadracer RO 92351 (1991). Fabulous Disaster / Chemi-Kill / 'Til Death Do Us Part / Toxic Waltz / Cajun Hell / Corruption / Brain Dead / Dirty Deeds Done Dirt Cheap.
FORCE OF HABIT, Capitol CDEST 2179 (1992). Thorn In My Side / Me, Myself And I / Force Of Habit / Bitch / Fuel For The Fire / One Foot In The Grave / Count Your Blessings / Climb Before The Fall / Architect Of Pain / When It Rains It Pours / Good Day To Die / Pump It Up / Feeding Time At The Zoo.
ANOTHER LESSON IN VIOLENCE, Century Media 77173-2 (1997). Bonded By Blood / Exodus / Pleasures Of The Flesh / And Then There Were None / Piranha / Seeds Of Hate / Deliver Us To Evil / Brain Dead / No Love / A Lesson In Violence / Impaler / Strike Of The Beast.
War Is My Shepherd EP, (2003). War Is My Sheppard / Sealed With A Fist / Impaler / Dirty Deeds Done Dirt Cheap.
TEMPO OF THE DAMNED, Nuclear Blast (2004). Scar Spangled Banner / War Is My Shepherd / Blacklist / Shroud Of Urine / Forward March / Culling The Herd / Sealed With A Fist / Throwing Down / Impaler / Tempo Of The Damned. Chart position: 67 GERMANY.

SHOVEL HEADED KILL MACHINE, Nuclear Blast NB 1376-2 (2005). Raze / Deathamphetamine / Kharma's Messenger / Shudder To Think / I Am Abomination / Altered Boy / Going Going Gone / Now Thy Death Day Come / 44 Magnum Opus / Shovel Headed Kill Machine.

EXTERMINATOR

PEER, BELGIUM — *Jacky Cuypers (vocals / guitar), Kris Jacquemin (guitar), Ivan De Hondt (bass), Marc Damiaens (drums).*

Melodic Death Metal band EXTERMINATOR was manifested in January of 1991, cutting opening demo 'Circle Of Violence' at Gobi Sound studio in Maastricht. The band had been founded with a line up of singer Bart Maarten, guitarists Jacky Cuypers and Ronny Serdongs, bassist Rudi Houben and drummer Sigi Loots, debuting on the live front in November of 1991 supporting DEADHEAD. The band suffered a major blow in January of 2002 when a car accident left road crew member Frank dead and Rudi Houben seriously injured. Maarten exited that May, leaving EXTERMINATOR to persevere with Cuypers and Serdongs sharing lead vocals.

Rejecting an offer from Inline Music from Germany, EXTERMINATOR set to work with Andre Gielen to record a self financed EP. However, in June Sigi Loots departed, being swiftly replaced by Mario Goossens. The group folded in May of 1994, but would be re-activated by founder and frontman Jacky Cuypers that same November as a trio featuring new members Jeroen Lemmens on bass and drummer Jules Lemmens. The 'Forgotten Souls' EP saw issue through Tessa Records in February of 1995. The group expanded to a quartet, drafting second guitarist Werner Geijsels.

1997 opened with line up changes, Ivan De Hondt replacing Jeroen Lemmens and Werner Geijsels decamping, to be superseded by Kris Jacquemin. More tribulation hit the ranks when in May, following a support to BENEDICTION, Jules Lemmens vacated the drum stool. Molly would be the new man on the drums and in 1998 the band's profile rose sharply with valuable supports to visiting international artists such as CANNIBAL CORPSE, VADER, INFERNAL MAJESTY, DARK FUNERAL and even an opening slot to EDGE OF SANITY in the Czech Republic. Baruch Van Bellegem was incorporated as their new drummer in July of 1999 in time for album recordings taking place at Studio De Hautregard in Verviers.

EXTERMINATOR would enter into negotiations with the Shiver label to release 'Mirror Images' but finally published it themselves on the band's own I.M.F. imprint. Promotion included an appearance at the SAXON headlined 'Biebob Metalfest' and a headline tour of Spain. A second trek around Spain, in September of 2001 in alliance with Spaniards DIRTY LUST, was completed before Marc Damiaens took command of the drums and in September of the following year EXTERMINATOR once again put in Spanish dates.

In 2004, despite the band being out of action on the live front due to Cuypers suffering from an articular disease, the group scored a deal with the French Deadsun label. Bassist Ivan De Hondt exited in February 2005. A replacement was soon located in the DESPERATION and LEECH credited Alan Coenegrachts.

Circle Of Violence, (1992). Fragments Of An Agony Deranged / Circle Of Violence / In My Sleep / The Unknown Warrior / Criminal Act.
Forgotten Souls, Tessa (1995). Epitome—Intro / Opaque Ordeal / Hysteron Proteron / World Within / Erroneous Idiosyncracy.
Night Music, (1997). Fragments / Blackened Dead / Mirror Images / Bitter End / Night Music (The Dark Caress) / Epitome / Opaque Ordeal / Hysteron Proteron / World Within / Erroneous Idiosyncracy.
Realm Of Chaos, (1999). Church Of Chaos / Bitter End / Tragedy ... Rejoice ... / Mirror Images.
MIRROR IMAGES, Exterminator (2000). Birth / Liberty ... Death ... / Circle Of Violence / Mirror Images / Church Of Chaos / Bitter End / Night Music (The Dark Caress) / The Kill / Tragedy ... Rejoice ....

EXTREMA

MILAN, ITALY — *Gianluca Perotti (vocals), Andrea Boria (guitar), Tommy Massara (guitar), Alex Ghilardotti (bass), Polo Crimi (drums).*

Milanese Thrash Metal band EXTREMA was founded during late 1986 by guitarist Tommy Masssara. The line-up would prove fluid until stabilising during 1989, Massara being joined by singer GianLuca Perotti, bass player Mattia Bigi with Christiano Dalla Peligrino on the drums. This line-up recorded the 'We Fuckin' Care' single and the group would tour in Italy as support to SLAYER on the American group's 'Reign In Blood' tour. EXTREMA briefly relocated to the USA but, upon their return to Italy, issued the debut 1992 album 'Tension At The Seams', issued on Rosemary's Baby Discs. This album saw the inclusion of Massara, now on vocals, and second guitarist Giolio Loglio. Notable live promotion in Italy saw a valuable support to METALLICA.

A live EP of 1993 vintage, 'Proud, Powerful n' Alive', was only ever released in Italy and featured a cover of the DEAD KENNEDYS 'Too Drunk To Fuck'. Guitarist Giolio Loglio quit the group before they recorded 1994's 'The Positive Pressure (Of Injustice)' album for Flying Records. EXTREMA went into hiatus between 1996 and 1999 as band members prioritised side projects.

The band returned in 2001 with the 'Better Mad Than Dead' opus, once again guesting for SLAYER at the 'Tattoo The Planet' festival. They followed up in 2003 with 'All Around' and a rarities compilation 'And The Best Is Yet To Come'. Live dates of note included the METALLICA headlined 'Heineken Jammin' event and the 'Flippaut' festival with KORN. In December 2004 longstanding member Chris Dallapellegrina terminated his fifteen year tenure with the band. New man on drums would be Polo Crimi of BEERBONG. More prominent gigs followed, including the 'Gods of Metal' and 'Summer Day in Hell' festivals.

EXTREMA entered Rodger Music Studios in the Summer of 2005 to craft the album 'Set The World On Fire' with producer Mauro Androlli. In 2006 side activity, both Gianluca Perotti and Tommy Massara donated their talents to the REZOPHONIC collaboration album project, aimed at benefiting the African aid AMREF organisation, initiated by drummer Mario Riso of ROYAL AIR FORCE and MOVIDA repute.

Following a show in Verona on 24th November 2006 Gianluca Perotti resigned his position as frontman.

We Fuckin' Care, Extrema (1988). We Fuckin' Care.
TENSION AT THE SEAMS, Rosemary's Baby Discs 08-110052 (1992). Join Hands / Child O' Boogaow / Displaced / Truth This Everybody / Modern Times / Double Face / Road Pirats / Lawyers Incx. / And The Rage Awaits / For Good The Die / Life.
Proud, Powerful n' Alive EP, Rosemary's Baby Discs BABE 13 CD (1993). Lawyer's Inc. / Child O' Boogaow / Modern Times / Displaced / Join Hands / Too Drunk To Fuck.
THE POSITIVE PRESSURE (OF INJUSTICE), Flying FLY 190 CD (1994). This Toy / The Positive Pressure (Of Injustice) / Fear / Money Talks / Confusion / Grey / Like Brothers / To Hell / On Your Feet, On Your Knees / Tell Me.
SET THE WORLD ON FIRE, Remedy (2006).

EXUMER

FRANKFURT, GERMANY — *Paul Arakai (vocals / bass), Bernie (guitar), Ray Mensch (guitar), Syke Bornetto (drums).*

Frankfurt Thrashers signed to the SPV subsidiary label Disaster Records on the strength of their 1985 demos 'A Mortal In Black'. The debut EXUMER album, 'Possessed By Fire' produced by Harris Johns, featured original Turkish vocalist Mem Von Stein, but he had left by the time the German outfit's sophomore album, 'Rising From The Sea' emerged. Stein would journey through PHOBIC INSTINCT, OF RYTES and HUMUNGOUS

FUNGUS then relocate to New York, eventually forging SUN DESCENDS.

Stein would be superseded by Hawaiian Paul Arakari. During 1987 EXUMER had been scheduled to support WARFARE in Britain for some hotly anticipated dates but were ultimately prevented from doing so by British customs who refused Arakai entry into the country for lacking a work permit.

In 1990 Syke Bornetto, switching roles to that of singer, formed Q SQUAD in 1990 switching roles from that of a drummer to a lead vocalist. EXUMER re-united for a 2001 one off festival appearance at the 'Wacken Open Air' festival in Germany as High Vaultage Records re-issued the albums in CD format. Subsequently, Mem Von Stein's SUN DESCENDS include 1985 EXUMER demos, from the "A Mortal In Black" sessions, on their 2004 album 'Kanun-Law'.

POSSESSED BY FIRE, Disaster 1005 (1986). Possessed By Fire / Destructive Solution / Fallen Saint / A Mortal In Black / Sorrows Of The Judgement / Xiron Darkstar / Reign Of Sadness / Journey To Oblivion / Silent Death.

RISING FROM THE SEA, Disaster 10007 (1987). Winds Of Death / Rising From The Sea / Decimation / The First Supper / Unearthed / Shadow Of The Past / Are You Deaf? / I Dare You / Ascension Day.

F.K.Ü.

UPPSALA, SWEDEN — *Larry Lethal (vocals), Pete Stooaahl (guitar), Pat Splat (bass), Ted Killer Miller (drums).*

Uppsala based, humour moshing Thrashers. F.K.Ü. (Freddy Krueger's Ünderwear) founded in 1988. Black Diamond released the 'Metal Moshing Mad' album in 1999. The band's 2005 formation, for the album 'Sometimes They Come Back ... To Mosh', comprised Larry Lethal (Lawrence Mackrory of SEETHINGS, ENEMY IS US, THE MIST OF AVALON, ANDROMEDA and DARKANE) on vocals, Pete Stooaahl (Peter Lans from LOST SOULS and INRAGE) on guitar, Pat Splat (Patrik Sporrong of MIDAS TOUCH, MISERY LOVES CO., PEACE, LOVE & PITBULLS and LOST SOULS) on bass with Ted Killer Miller (Teddy Möller of LOCH VOSTOK and MAYADOME) on drums. The album included a cover version of TANKARD's 'Zombie Attack'.

METAL MOSHING MAD, Black Diamond (1999). Into The Pits Of F.K.Ü. / Metal Moshing Mad / Maniac / Deutschland / Stomp And Shake (Crystal Lake) / You Stink / Dug Out Sucks / Beware! (Of The Evil Ünderwear) / F.K.Ü. (Coming For You) / Bus Bitch Die / Tear Your Soul Apart II / Bus Bitch Die (Part 2) / He Saw Her Today / Unstoppable Force (Extended version) / Mackrory Mosh / Beware! (Of The Evil Ünderwear) (Part 2) / Michael Myers Costume Party / Cut Your Hair / Horror Metal Man / Die Some More / METOOAAHL / Mosh Under Pressure.

SOMETIMES THEY COME BACK ... TO MOSH, Head Mechanic (2005). Sometimes They Come Back ... / To Mosh / Fury 58 / Die Toten Core / Moshoholics Anonymous / Paraskevidekatriaphobia / Agent Amy Steel / F.K.Ü. Says NO / C.H.Ü.D. / C.H.Ü.D. Pt. 2 / Maniac Cop / Zombie Attack / Grave Robbing Mania / Motel Hell / Marine Marauders / Four Fingers Fatal To The Flesh / Disciples Of The Mosh.

F.T.G.

MALAYSIA — *Tajul (vocals), Jac (guitar), Mie (bass), Zam (drums).*

F.T.G. ("Freedom That's Gone") date to 1989, their original line-up comprising Bart on vocals, Jac on guitar, Mie on bass and Zam on drums. The inaugural F.T.G. album arrived on FGM Productions in April of 1991. The follow up, 1992's 'After The Promise' released by VSP Records, would sell over 20,000 copies. Switching to the Japanese Pony Canyon concern 'Spirit To Rebel' arrived in 1994, surpassing the sales of its predecessor. July 1996's 'To The Front' would also prove a strong seller, quickly attaining platinum status. However, Bart would depart after these recordings, being replaced by Tajul as the first era of F.T.G. was marked by the compilation 'Stronger Than Steel'.

Bravely the group ushered in the second stage of their career with the Malay language 'Aku Tak Peduli' album. An uncompromising Heavy Metal release with not a hint of a ballad, the album achieved platinum sales within a month and peaked at no. 2 in the national Malay chart. The band's 1998 'Made In Malaysia Volume' album comprised entirely of cover versions including BLACK SABBATH's 'Heaven And Hell', 'Paranoid' and Children Of The Sea', TWISTED SISTER's 'We're Not Gonna Take It', DEEP PURPLE's 'Black Night' and 'Perfect Strangers', DIO's 'Holy Diver', PINK FLOYD's 'Wish You were Here' and QUIET RIOT's 'Metal Health'. A concert recorded in front of 5,000 fans at the Sunway Amphitheatre on the 31st of July of 1999 would emerge as the 'Live At Metal Wars' opus. The eponymous 'F.T.G.' was delivered in April of 2000.

The 2001 set 'Made In Malaysia II' repeated the tribute tradition with AC/DC's 'Back In Black' and 'Highway To Hell', GARY MOORE's 'Empty Rooms', JUDAS PRIEST's 'Freewheel Burning' and 'Electric Eye', BLACK SABBATH's 'Iron Man' and DEEP PURPLE's 'Smoke On The Water. 2002's 'Reborn' added techno experimentation to the band's style.

F.T.G., FGM Productions (1991). Rozanna / Ingat / Dendam / Negeri Kita, Orang Lain Kaya / Kritik / Sampai Bila / Jerat / Amerika / Kau / Aku Adalah Aku.

AFTER THE PROMISE, VSP Records (1992).

SPIRIT TO REBEL, Pony Canyon (1994). Spirit To Rebel / Farewell To Goodness / When A Soldier Cry / Lies / Display Of Hate / Soul Warrior / Decide / Child Of Anger / Sinner Will Pay / Dream.

TO THE FRONT, Pony Canyon (1996). 60 Days In Hell / Power / Stupid / Why Am I So Stupid / Land Of Unseen / To The Front / Life / Sometime Someday / Remember / Song From The Unwanted Son / Dendang Remaja.

AKU TAK PEDULI, (1998). Malaysia Maju / Anak Tiri / Tak Sedar Diri / Terbalik / Apa Nak Jadi / Askar (Biar Putih Tulang) / Mana Tahan / Anak Melayu / Salah Sendiri / Aku Tak Peduli.

MADE IN MALAYSIA, (1998). Metal Health / Paranoid / Red Hot / I Shot The Sheriff / Children Of The Sea / Wish You Were Here / Perfect Strangers / Hey You / Heaven And Hell / Black Night / Holy Diver / We're Not Gonna Take It.

LIVE AT METAL WARS, (1999). Malaysia Maju / Life / Dendang Remaja / Spirit To Rebel / Metal Health / Behind This Wall / Anak Melayu / Mana Tahan / Black Night / Paranoid / Aku Tak Peduli / Askar / We're Not Gonna Take It / Bila Larut Malam / Anak Tiri.

MADE IN MALAYSIA VOLUME II, (2001). Highway To Hell / Smoke On The Water / Rock n' Roll / Iron Man / Electric Eye / Sail Away / Empty Rooms / I Want Out / Jail Break / Freewheel Burning / Temple Of The King / Back In Black.

REBORN, (2002). Democracy / PG4H / Subsidize Mentality / Mind Games / Blind / Coalition, Corruption, Co-operation / Falling Apart / End Of The Line / Delusion Of Truth / Corruption.

STOP THIS MADNESS, (2003). Never / Misery (Why Should I Die) / Rising Pain / Towards The Unknown / All By Yourself / Stop This Madness / Be Together / Save Me / Running With The Wind / The Outlaw / Saint Or Tyrant / The Riddle.

FACE DOWN

HAGERSTEN, SWEDEN — *Marco Aro (vocals), Joacim Carlsson (guitar), Jaokim Hedestedt (bass), Erik Thyselius (drums).*

Originally titled MACHINE GOD upon their formation in Hagersten during 1993 by ex-AFFLICTED and PROBOSCIS duo of guitarist Joacim Carlsson and bassist Joakim 'Harju' Hedestedt, the quite brutal FACE DOWN found themselves snapped up by Roadrunner and this resulted in the release of the critically acclaimed 'Mindfield' debut album. However, drummer Richard Bång left after the album was completed and had his vacant space occupied by ex-UNANIMATED and MERCILESS man Peter Sjärnvind. April of 1996 found the band conducting UK dates with NAPALM DEATH and CROWBAR.

A second album, 'The Twisted Rule The Wicked', emerged through new label Nuclear Blast in 1997. Aro joined THE HAUNTED with ex-members of AT THE GATES. Despite his international success with THE HAUNTED Aro re-activated FACE

DOWN in 2004, working with a cast comprising original members, AFFLICTED and GENERAL SURGERY guitarist Joacim Carlsson, bassist Joakim Hedestedt of CONSTRUCDEAD and new drummer Erik Thyselius from CONSTRUCDEAD, GENERAL SURGERY and TERROR 2000. The band signed to Black Lodge Records for a new studio album 'The Will To Power', entering Offbeat Studios in Stockholm during late October. FACE DOWN put in their first concert in over six years supporting PAIN on 12th February at Klubb Kaliber in Mariestad.

The band parted ways with drummer Erik Thyselius in February 2006. The KAAMOS, REPUGNANT and BLACKSHINE credited Christofer Barkensjö (a.k.a. 'Chris Piss') stepped in as substitute. This new unit entered Offbeat Studios on November 24th to cut demo tracks.

MINDFIELD, Roadrunner RR 8902 (1995). Wear / Kill The Pain / Human / Holy Race / Demon Seed / Save Me, Kill Me / Colors / Twelve Rounds / Hatred / One Eyed Man.
THE TWISTED RULE THE WICKED, Nuclear Blast NB 194-2 (1997). Breed / Self Appointed God / Waste / Life Relentless / Autumn Scars / Bed Of Roaches / Top Of The World / Slender Messiah / For Your Misery / Embrace The Moment / Cleansweep / With Unseeing Eyes.
THE WILL TO POWER, Black Lodge (2005). Drained / Blood Tiles / Heroin / Will To Power / Grey / Heretic / The Delusion / War Hog / The Unsung.

FAITH OR FEAR

NJ, USA — *Tim Blackman (vocals), Chris Bombeke (guitar), Bob Perna (guitar), C.J. Jenkins (bass), Rick Lohwasser (drums).*

A Bay Area style Thrash band from New Jersey. Following the solitary 1989 Combat album 'Punishment Area' guitarist Bob Perna was usurped by Merrit Gant. FAITH OR FEAR splintered with Gant joining veteran Thrashers OVERKILL, other members would found WAGONHEAD in 1994.

Gant later re-emerged with BLOOD AUDIO.

PUNISHMENT AREA, Combat 88561-2005-1 (1989). Lack Of Motivation / C.D.S. / Punishment Area / Rampage / Nothing Uncommon / Have No Fear / What Would You Expect / Darkside / Shadow Knows / Ripoffs / Time Bomb / Instruments Of Death.

FATAL EMBRACE

GERMANY — *Dirk Heiland (vocals), Christian Grigat (guitar), Vincent LaBoor (guitar), Ronald Schulze (bass), Martin Pfeiffer (drums).*

FATAL EMBRACE issued a stream of demo recordings upfront of debut album 'The Ultimate Aggression' in 1999. The 'Deaths Embrace 'session marked their arrival in 1994, followed by 'The Way To Immortality' during 1997. After the album release a single, 'Returned To Hell', preceded sophomore full length Harris Johns produced outing 'Legions Of Armageddon'. Drummer Martin Pfeiffer bowed out in mid 2003, being replaced by the POSTMORTEM and DARKLAND credited Marko Thäle.

The band toured with SODOM and VENDETTA for German dates in September 2005. Guitarist Vincent LaBoor joined SINNERS BLEED in April 2006. The group contributed their cover version of TANKARD's 'Acid Breath' to the tribute album 'A Tribute To Tankard' included as a bonus disc on the AFM Records 2007 TANKARD release 'Best Case Scenario: 25 Years In Beers'.

THE ULTIMATE AGGRESSION, Gutter (1999). Follow Your Nightmare / Under My Sadistic Reign '99 / You Deal In Pain / The Last Rites / Point Of No Return / Ultimate Aggression / Nocturnal Anguish / Breeder Of Insanity / Hate Remains / Bonded By Blood.
Returned To Hell, Independent (2001). Returned to Hell / Ultimate Aggression / Order to Fire.
LEGIONS OF ARMAGEDDON, Bruchstein BR002 (2002). Wishmasters Revenge (Intro) / 666 (Massacre In Paradise) / Legions Of Armageddon / Mentally Perversion / Returned To Hell / Trapped In A Violent Brain / Spellbound By The Devil / Depraved To Black / Wargods Of Thrash.

FEAR OF GOD

USA — *Dawn Crosby (vocals), Michael Carlino (guitar), Blair Darby (bass), Steve Cordova (drums).*

Fronted by ex-DÉTENTE members vocalist Dawn Crosby, guitarist Michael Carlino and bassist Blair Derby, FEAR OF GOD was an act of huge potential, but blighted by an ever shifting line-up. The band was actually signed to major label Warner Brothers by Roberta Peterson whilst still named DÉTENTE. As DETENTE they tested the market with a three track 1989 Alex Perialis produced demo tape comprising of 'All That Remains', 'Deceased' and 'Waysted Time'. A further effort led by the track 'Love's Death' ensued the same year.

The band's roster at the time included Rob 'Wacko' Hunter, drummer of NWoBHM stalwarts RAVEN. As negotiations with the label drew on Hunter bowed out and New Jersey's Eric Alpert was drafted. His tenure would be brief though and the band finally settled on Steve Cordova to occupy the drum stool.

It was discovered that the band name DÉTENTE had already been registered so initial recordings were convened under the band name SEDITION. The album tapes for 'Within The Veil' would be re-mixed for release by Andy Wallace and with due process of time the group evolved into FEAR OF GOD.

A month long trek across North America to promote the album caused internal frictions that would cause Cordova to leave as soon as dates were fulfilled. Drummer Brendan Etter of Industrial act NATURE would figure in the group's 1991 line-up for a showcase gig at the 'Foundations Forum' but would leave the following year. Crosby would also replace bassist Blair Darby having met his replacement, a Rastafarian named Jason Levin, by way of a chance meeting on a train.

The band travelled to London's Battery studios in early 1992 to work with esteemed producer Chris Tsangarides FEAR OF GOD would practically split up in the midst of recording a projected second album for Warner Brothers just upfront of a booked series of European shows.

The FEAR OF GOD that European audiences actually saw on stage would in fact only involve Crosby from the previous line-up. Assisting for these shows, which included a prestigious appearance at the Dutch 'Aardschok' festival, was WRATHCHILD AMERICA members guitarists Jay Abbene and Terry Carter along with drummer Shannon Larkin and HAVE MERCY and JAKKPOT man Rob Michael on bass.

Whilst Larkin depped for the band a more permanent member Douglas Sylvia, previously with GENETICIDE and SKELETAL EARTH, was brought into the fold. FEAR OF GOD, retaining Michael and Sylvia but with new guitarists Brandon Hefner and Randy Bobzien, cut fresh demos for Warner Bros. In a much more aggressive style. These tapes would be re-recorded with new drummer John Grden of HAVE MERCY. Warner Bros. dropped the act still believing they were heading into Death Metal territory and in September of 1993 Hefner quit the ranks.

The band's second album 'Toxic Voodoo', issued on the Pavement label in 1994, sported another all new look to the band structure. Guitars came courtesy of Chris Kalandras and Randy Bobzien with a rhythm section culled from HAVE MERCY being bassist Robert Ian Michael (also a member of JAKKPOT) and drummer John Grden. However, Crosby's reliance on drugs and alcohol had severely affected the recording process putting yet further strains on the band.

Michael, Kalandras and Bobzien left the band en masse mere weeks prior to the 'Toxic Voodoo' tour. Replacements were hastily drafted in the form of guitarists Sparky Voyles and Bill Hayden together with former DESECRATION, SPINE and VOX HUMANA bassist Bruce Greig. This revised unit would set to work on a scheduled third album but Voyles would relinquish his position to Frank DiMauro.

The resulting album demo did not favour with Pavement and yet more fractures occurred within the ranks with DiMauro being usurped by Tony Mallory of CHAPEL BLACQUE, who also took on keyboard duties. Grieg too would leave for NEXT STEP UP being replaced by Mike Schafer.

FEAR OF GOD's last outing was the cassette album 'Killing The Pain' in 1997.

Sadly Dawn Crosby was to die tragically young on December 15th 1996, of acute liver failure due to years of excessive alcohol abuse. The remaining members, including Mallory, Haydon and Grden, persevered billed simply as FOG.

John Grden would later show up in BLACK MASS and—along with Haydon—PESSIMIST. By early 2004 Grden was operational with FIRES OF GOMORRAH in league with ex-BLACK MASS guitarist The Blasphemous One (a.k.a. Russ Strahan). Sparky Voyles journeyed through SADISTIC TORMENT. M.O.D., DYING FETUS and by September 2001 was ensconced as a member of MISERY INDEX.

WITHIN THE VEIL, Warner Bros. (1991). All That Remains / Betrayed / Emily / Red To Grey / Diseased / Wasted Time / Love's Death / White Door / Drift.

TOXIC VOODOO, Pavement (1994). Beyond The Veil / Cloud Chamber / Swine Song / Burnt / Feed Time / Mercy / Santismo / U.V. / Will Of Evil / Worms.

FIERCE CONVICTION

BORÅS, SWEDEN — *Jose Sanchez (vocals), Fredrik Jordanius (guitar), Niclas Karlsson (guitar), Lars Rapp (bass), Martin Tilander (drums).*

Borås based Thrash Metal band created in 1995. Band members all went on to further, higher profile, projects. Signing to ABS Records the group released 'The Requiem Of A Mourner' as their debut in 1998, this album seeing Jose Sanchez on the lead vocal role. The group truncated their title to simply CONVICTION for the 1999 album 'Decline / Rebirth'. During recording of this opus Daniel Heiman (a.k.a. 'Etherial Mangnanimus') of HIGHLANDER and LOST HORIZON was recruited as the band's new singer, but did not feature on the record itself. Johan Westmar was drafted as new frontman in 2000 before the band collapsed.

FIERCE CONVICTION's guitarist Niclas Karlsson and drummer Martin Tilander, both ex-members of CRYSTAL EYES, subsequently joined FRETERNIA. Niclas Karlsson would also figure in ZONATA. Second guitarist Fredrik Jordanius, who also assisted FRETERNIA on the live front, became a member of RISING FAITH whilst bassist Freddy Zielinsky, having superseded Lars Rapp, went on to IRONWARE.

Jose Sanchez landed a solo deal with British label Z Records in December 2006.

THE REQUIEM OF A MOURNER, ABS (1998). In Your Mind / In The Cellar / Confusion / The Ballad Of Tinuviel / The Crying King / Time / (Tell Me) Who Do You Think You Are? / The Quest For Eternity / The Other Side / Visions From An Ancient Time.

FIGHT

UK / USA — *Rob Halford (vocals), Russ Parrish (guitar), Brian Tilse (guitar), Jay Jay (bass), Scott Travis (drums).*

A joint Anglo / American, stripped down, in-your-face Metal act, FIGHT was created by JUDAS PRIEST vocalist Rob Halford, a man whose vocal prowess is almost legendary. Wishing to pursue a radical change of direction from the more classic, technical style of JUDAS PRIEST, Halford bowed out after 1991's hugely successful 'Painkiller' world tour. Longstanding JUDAS PRIEST fans were somewhat bemused by a shift in his traditional leather and studs image to one that clearly mimicked PANTERA's vocalist Phil Anselmo.

On March 3rd 1992 Halford took the opportunity to join PANTERA onstage at Irvine Meadows in California where they performed JUDAS PRIEST tracks 'Grinder' and 'Metal Gods'. This in turn led to the two parties collaborating on a Halford composed song 'Light Comes Out Of Black'. Recorded in Dallas, the track saw inclusion on the movie soundtrack 'Buffy: The Vampire Slayer' in July.

Although the vocalist had the blessing of JUDAS PRIEST for this out of the blue project, a bitter verbal conflict ensued. As the accusations and counter-accusations flew, Halford's twenty year tenure abruptly came to and end as he formed FIGHT, taking JUDAS PRIEST drummer Scott Travis with him. Recruited into the band would be the CYANIDE pairing of guitarist Brian Tilse and bass player Jay Jay (a.k.a. John Brown), with Guitar Institute of Technology graduate Russ Parrish of WAR AND PEACE making the numbers up on second guitar. Jay Jay, also dividing his energies with another act billed SATANIC INDUSTRIES LTD., had actually met Rob in his capacity has a tattooist at HTC Precision Piercing in Phoenix, inking many of Halford's rapidly growing array of body designs. This formation cut demos at Vintage Sound Studio in Phoenix, scoring a deal with Epic Records, then debuted live in Halford's hometown at the Mason Jar in Phoenix, Arizona in August 1993.

The eagerly awaited debut album, September 1993's 'War Of Words', was light years removed from JUDAS PRIEST, Halford toning down his vocal range, down tuning the guitars and opting for much simpler songs. These tracks had been laid down at Wisseloord Studios in Hilversum, Holland with production credits shared between Halford and Attie Bauw. Many critics panned the release as a lame PANTERA copy but in the main Halford managed to take many former fans with him. Halford's reputation put 'War Of Words' into the US charts at number 83 whilst Attie Bauw received a pair of esteemed Grammy nominations for "Producer of the Year" and "Best Engineered Album".

Touring was instigated in Frankfurt, Germany on October 19th, FIGHT taking out THE ORGANIZATION as support. Live dates in England, two solitary dates at Nottingham Rock City and London's Astoria 2, were marred by paltry attendance figures with many JUDAS PRIEST fans feeling almost betrayed by Halford's endeavours. The vocalist reacted by issuing vitriolic statements about the British media. In the States Halford enjoyed better response and, engaging in an exhaustive series of club headliners with guests CATHEDRAL, opening up on November 11th at The Chance in Poughkeepsie, New York.

The 'Nailed To The Road' tour, packaged with VOIVOD, reconvened at Sunset Strip in Orlando, Florida on January 6th. Shows in March witnessed displays of FIGHT aggression in Japan, Australia and South America. Russ Parrish decamped to join RACER X vocalist Jeff Martin and guitarist PAUL GILBERT in a Glam covers band entitled THE ELECTRIC FENCE. Halford drafted Tucson native Robby Lochner, from Los Angeles act RAZOR, as replacement for tour work. The revised formation debuted as touring partners to ANTHRAX US shows in April. In July the group was invited to join METALLICA and SUICIDAL TENDENCIES for a run of 'Summer Shit' dates. On August 21st, at the Bicentennial Park in Miami, Florida METALLICA bade farewell to their FIGHT running mates by getting Halford onstage during their set to jam through JUDAS PRIEST's 'Rapid Fire'. However, with dates completed, Lochner moved on to a solo career.

The interim January 1994 'Mutations' mini-album comprised remixes and live tracks, including a raucous rendition of JUDAS PRIEST's 'Freewheel Burning'. Halford was also busying himself outside of FIGHT with his E.M.A.S. management organization. Taking on Australian Thrashers ALLEGIANCE Halford secured a deal for the young act with major label Polygram for their 'D.E.S.T.I.T.U.T.I.O.N.' album. As 1994 came to a close Halford forged a one off studio union billed as the BULLRING BRUMMIES, a heavyweight unit comprising the BLACK SABBATH rhythm section of bassist Geezer Butler and drummer BILL WARD, Wino of THE OBSESSED and harmonica player Jimmy Wood to cut a version of BLACK SABBATH's 'The Wizard' for the 'Nativity In Black' tribute album. FIGHT rounded out 1994 with a one off radio promotion single 'Christmas Ride', a unique, seasonal track which included festive greetings from Rob.

April 1995's 'A Small Deadly Space', which debuted at a lowly 120 in the USA, found former COUP DE GRACE man Mark Chaussee in the group as new second guitarist. FIGHT had once again opted to work with producer Attie Bauw for this effort, which closed out with a hidden track 'Psycho Suicide'. Previous to the album release, on March 12th, Halford participated in the LIFEbeat benefit concert at the Los Angeles Palladium, performing JUDAS PRIEST's 'Rapid Fire' and 'Solar Angels' with ANTHRAX.

FIGHT projected a full-scale global campaign to push 'A Small Deadly Space'. The inaugural date was held at the 'La Semana Alegre' festival at Freeman Coliseum in San Antonio, Texas supporting BUDGIE. Headline North American club shows ran through June and July. The remaining dates scheduled for the Far East, Europe and the UK were scrapped. Tilse and Jay Jay activated a fresh band unit dubbed VENT, an alliance with STUCK MOJO's Tim Radswell and drummer Don Juan.

FIGHT's days were numbered. After a brief flirtation working with BLACK SABBATH guitarist TONY IOMMI during 1996, the singer formed a new band under the title of HALFORD. This act initially comprised two FIGHT personnel, Brian Tilse and Jay Jay. Together with VENT drummer Don Juan the band delivered a one off show at the Phoenix Mason Jar on December 20th as a benefit for the city's Child Crisis Center's 'Children Of The Desert' charity.

Halford then embarked upon a truly radical path. The act re-titled itself GIMP then TWO, emerging with a Trent Reznor of NINE INCH NAILS produced Industrial Rock album 'Voyeurs' that, it is true to say, left many of Halford's fans scratching their heads in bemusement. Even more so when the man seemingly denounced Metal as dead and buried.

Chaussee joined DANZIG in 1996 but bailed out just prior to their world tour and would have a brief liaison with the post LIFE OF AGONY band STEREOMUD. By 2000 Parrish was a member of the acclaimed spoof covers band METAL SHOP along with former L.A. GUNS man Ralph Saenz. Parrish would also double duties with Alternative Rockers THE DUCKS. Reverting to his career as a tattooist, Jay Jay scored a degree of notoriety by adding to his list of famous clientele, inking SLAYER's Kerry King.

Much to the relief of his long suffering fans, now simply billed as HALFORD, resurrected his career in spectacular style during 2000 with the suitably titled 'Resurrection' album, a quite remarkable statement of Metal intent that charted internationally. HALFORD, signing up to IRON MAIDEN manager Rod Smallwood's firm for management and label, saw his profile rise sharply with a subsequent special guest slot to IRON MAIDEN's American dates.

In January 2004 former FIGHT members Brian Tilse and J.J. joined LOLLIPOP LUST KILL, this band unit subsequently adopting a revised title of GLASS PIPE SUICIDE. October of that year saw Mark Chaussee joining the MARILYN MANSON band. In December, whilst in promotion for the JUDAS PRIEST comeback album 'Angel Of Retribution', Halford voiced the possibility of a live FIGHT DVD package and the prospect of FIGHT reuniting to record new material.

São José dos Campos Heavy Metal band THRAM featured a cover version of FIGHT's 'Into The Pit' on their 2006 album 'Pictures Of Reality'. On June 1st 2006 Rob Halford announced the formation of the Metal God Entertainment label to re-issue his HALFORD and FIGHT material, this including DVD concert footage of FIGHT. That October Metal God Entertainment unveiled plans for the 5.1 surround-sound film DVD 'Fight, War Of Words—The Film', comprising footage filmed throughout 1992 and 1993. In November the archive set 'K5 The War Of Words Demos' saw release.

Nailed To The Gun, Epic 659612 2 (1993). Nailed To The Gun (Album version) / Kill It (Album version) / Nailed To The Gun (Bulletproof mix) / Kill It (Dutch death mix).

WAR OF WORDS, Epic 4745472 (1993). Into The Pit / Nailed To The Gun / Life In Black / Immortal Sin / War Of Words / Laid To Rest / For All Eternity / Little Crazy / Contortion / Kill It / Vicious / Reality, A New Beginning. Chart positions: 56 GERMANY, 83 USA.

MUTATIONS, Epic 477243 2 (1994). Into The Pit (Live) / Nailed To The Gun (Live) / Freewheel Burning (Live) / Little Crazy (Live) / War Of Words (Bloody Tongue Mix) / Kill It (Dutch Death Mix) / Immortal Sin (Tolerance Mix) / Little Crazy (Straight Jacket Mix).

A SMALL DEADLY SPACE, Epic 478400 2 (1995). I Am Alive / Mouthpiece / Legacy Of Hate / Blowout In The Radio Room / Never Again / Small Deadly Space / Gretna Greene / Beneath The Violence / Human Crate. Chart position: 120 USA.

FLAGELADÖR

NITERÓI, RJ, BRAZIL — *Armando Exekutör (vocals / guitar), Bitch Hünter (guitar), Hellpreacher (bass), A. Iron Fist (drums).*

Niterói, Rio de Janeiro Thrashers FLAGELADÖR, featuring Armando Exekutör and bassist D. Devorator of RAW RAZE and KABARAH, cut the demos 'Forjado Em Aço E Fogo' in 2002, including a cover of SLAYER's 'Evil Has No Boundaries', and 'Vingança' in 2003. FLAGELADÖR would share a three way split release with BIOLOGIC ENEMY and ENEMY CROSS. The band also has links to Black Metal act DARK FOREST through guitarist T. Depraved. The bass position would later be handed over to Vinícius Selvagem, guitarist of RAW RAZE.

A latter day guitarist 'Bitch Hünter' also held credits with Black Metal bands VIKING THRONE and, as 'Nocturnal Funeral', VERS DE LA MORT. Bass would be delegated to ATOMIC ROAR's HellPreacher. Signing to Dark Sun Records the band issued the album 'A Noite Do Ceifador' in 2004.

A NOITE DO CEIFADOR, Dark Sun (2004). Flageladör / Perseguir E Exterminar / Expresso Para O Inferno / Forjado Em Aço E Fogo / Cruzada Ao Lado De Satã / Carnificina / A Noite Do Ceifador / Unidos Pelo Metal.

FLASHOVER

BRASÍLIA, DF, BRAZIL — *Itazil Junior (vocals / guitar), Fernando Cézar (guitar), Daniel Lima (bass), Rafael Alves Pereira (drums).*

Taguatinga, Distrito Federal Death-Thrashers FLASHOVER, founded in October of 1997, feature former DEATH SLAM member Itazil Junior. He would head up a founding line up also comprising bassist Daniel Lima and drummer Fernando Cavalcante. Subsequently second guitar was delegated to Fernando Cézar.

FLASHOVER debuted with the 2001 album 'Infamous Country'. Signing to Lethal Records the band issued the 2003 follow up 'Land Of Cannibals' album. The closing track 'Metal Blood' boasted an array of Brazilian extreme Metal talent, studio guests including Júnior of CORPSE GRINDER, Alex Carmago of KRISIUN, Pedro from WINDS OF CREATION, Nathan of RHEVENGE and Fellipe C.D.C. of DEATH SLAM. Also aiding would be journalist Antonio Rolldão from 'Metal Blood' magazine and Lethal Records own Spyker.

INFAMOUS COUNTRY, (2001). Flesh And Blood / This Life / Infamous Country / Incorporating The Pain / My Revenger / Torment / Under World / Mother Fucker / Pain And Hate / Choose Your Guns.

LAND OF CANNIBALS, Lethal (2003). Land Of Cannibals / Threating Eyes / Repressed Desires / Dogs Of War / Days Of Fight / Kill The Priest / Wrong Place ... Wrong Time / Rise Above The Sky / Die, Die, Die!!! / I Hate Your Life / Metal Blood.

FLEGMA

SWEDEN — *Kalle Metz (vocals), Martin Olsson (guitar), Jörgen Lindhe (guitar), Richard Lion (bass), Martin Brorsson (drums).*

Punk infused Thrash act. FLEGMA started life in 1987 citing a line up of vocalist Rother, guitarist Puschel, bass player Richard Lion and drummer Martin Brorsson. Having released their full blown debut album, 'Blind Acceptance' in 1992, FLEGMA added ex-OBSCURITY guitarist Jörgen Lindhe to the line-up following 1994's 'Flesh To Dust' album. This also found them offering a cover of the KISS track 'I Stole Your Love'.

In addition the band have contributed tracks to both VENOM and METALLICA tribute albums with 'Leave Me In Hell' on the VENOM tribute 'Promoters Of The Third World War' on Primitive Art Records and 'The Thing That Should Not Be' on Black Sun Records 'Metal Militia' METALLICA tribute album.

FLEGMA disbanded with vocalist Kalle Metz and Richard Lion founding the Gothic Metal act TENEBRE in league with FUNHOUSE guitarist Fredrik. Ex-FLEGMA man Martin Olsson contributed session work to the debut TENEBRE album 'XIII'.

Eine Kleine Schlachtmusik, Insane INSANE 001 (1990). Tune In, Turn On, Drop Out / Wasted Life / I'm OK / Friend Of The State / Lovetrap / Ultra Bizarre / Armageddon.
BLIND ACCEPTANCE, Black Rose BRR001 (1992). Black Rose Of Hades / Bitch / Holocaust / Nagasaki '45 / Blind Acceptance / World Of Lies / Touch Of Death / Raped To The Core / Punisher / Skullfuck / Slave.
FLESH TO DUST, Black Rose BRR002 (1994). Rotting Away / Crown Of Thorns / Drowning / Walk In Confusion / Shadow Of A Silhouette / Father / Enticed / As The World Watches / I Stole Your Love / Flesh To Dust.

FLESH MADE SIN

TILBURG, HOLLAND — *Than van Geel (vocals / guitar), Bjorn van Hamond (guitar), Marc van Stiphout (bass), Marco Stubbe (drums).*

With the opening track on their self financed 'Scenery Of Death' EP entitled 'Thrash Is Back!' there would be no doubting Tilburg based FLESH MADE SIN's credentials. A full length album, 'A Masterwork In Blood', was projected for 2002. Vocalist Twan van Geel's credentials included a stint with SAURON whilst guitarist Bjorn van Hamond was previously a member of SPLATTER. Drummer Marco Stubbe had bashed the skins for ANTROMORPHIA.

FLESH MADE SIN's rhythm section of Marc van Stiphout and drummer Marco Stubbe also perform with Crossover act ANTRO. The band acted as support to the DISMEMBER and CALLENISH CIRCLE Dutch dates in May 2003. The band entered the studio in June of 2004 with producer Marc ter Braak to cut a new album 'Dawn Of The Stillborn'.

Scenery Of Death EP, (2001). Thrash Is Back! / Sculpture Of Bones / Your Blood Is Mine / Scenery Of Death.
MASTERWORK IN BLOOD, Thrashing Hell THR 001 (2002). Thrash Is Back / Lustful Killing / Tormentor / A Master's Work In Blood / Taste The Knife / Slicing The Throat.
DAWN OF THE STILLBORN, Karmageddon Media (2004). Crowned In Torment / Possess The Flesh / Dawn Of The Stillborn / The Cleansing / Descending Life / Ritual For The Dead / Wastelands / Spiritual Death-trip.

FLOTSAM AND JETSAM

PHOENIX, AZ, USA — *Eric A.K. (vocals), Ed Carlson (guitar), Mark Simpson (guitar), Jason Ward (bass), Craig Nielsen (drums).*

Founded in 1981 FLOTSAM AND JETSAM was to rise above the Thrash melee with a strong debut album 'Doomsday For The Deceiver'. In spite of this strong start, unfortunately the band are known in many media circles more for being the source of METALLICA's Jason Newsted and despite major label back up have struggled to rid themselves of that stigma. Nevertheless, FLOTSAM AND JETSAM, signing to MCA Records, would stick to their guns releasing a string of commendable Metal albums and put in punishing tour schedules that never betrayed a sniff of compromise.

Newsted's first band was the 1977 high school combo DIAMOND. His next outfit would be titled GANGSTER. This unit evolved during 1980 to feature Newsted on lead vocals and bass, lead guitarist Mark Vasquez, rhythm guitarist Kevin Horton and drummer Kelly David-Smith. In this formation the band performed live for the first time at the Mason Jar lounge in Phoenix billed as DREDLOX. Deciding that the group need a frontman, Eric A.K. auditioned, being asked to learn four JUDAS PRIEST songs.

In 1983 and Horton made way for Ed Carlson, enticed away from another Phoenix act dubbed EXODUS, as the band retitled itself DOGZ. Carlson's early inspiration had come from KISS, his first listen of their classic 'Alive' album prompting him to pick up the guitar. In this guise the group built up a local following supporting the likes of SURGICAL STEEL, ARMORED SAINT, RIOT, MALICE, AUTOGRAPH, EXCITER, MERCYFUL FATE and ALCATRAZZ. Another name switch then gave the band FLOTSAM AND JETSAM, this being inspired the names of characters from the J.R.R. Tolkien trilogy 'Lord Of The Rings'. Unfortunately, Kelly David-Smith, indicted for the sales of narcotics, was jailed for a month. During their drummer's incarceration the band also lost the services of Mark Vasquez. FLOTSAM AND JETSAM pulled in the then seventeen year old Mark Gilbert from THE KIDS.

FLOTSAM AND JETSAM's demo tapes, starting with 1985's 'Metal Shock', funded by The Bootlegger club owner and SACRED REICH manager Gloria Bujnowski. This session was enhanced by a rough and ready promotional video for the song 'Hammerhead', filmed in Newsted's apartment, and a live video taped at The Bootlegger. The studio demo was followed by '1985 Bootleg', attracted the attention of several leading Metal indie labels resulting in the band debuting with tracks on the compilation albums 'Speed Metal Hell II' and 'Metal Massacre IV'. The inclusion on the latter led to a deal with Metal Blade Records whilst Roadrunner Records licensed the album for Europe. The band's first album 'Doomsday For The Deceiver', produced by Brian Slagel at Music Grinders in Eldorado and Track Recording Studios in Hollywood on a budget of $12,000, was a well received release, chock full of quality aggressive metal. 'Doomsday For The Deceiver' saw US release on July 26th 1986. The leading British magazine 'Kerrang!' would go so far as to grant the album six points on their five point rating system.

Newsted's departure to METALLICA occurred in late October 1986. Upon the recommendation of Brian Slagel and Elektra's Mike Alago, and with band mates Mike Gilbert and Kevin Horton assisting him in learning the METALLICA songs, Newsted beat out other auditioning candidates to replace the late Cliff Burton. Previous to landing this position, Newsted had in fact been homeless, living in FLOTSAM AND JETSAM's rehearsal space. Newsted honoured his final FLOTSAM AND JETSAM gig commitment on October 31st and by November 8th was performing onstage with METALLICA at the Country Club in Reseda. The band carried out live commitments utilising the temporary services of SACRED REICH's Phil Rind. Following these early post-Newsted live dates, ex-SENTINEL BEAST bassist Mike Spencer was hired. FLOTSAM AND JETSAM were picked up by METALLICA's label Elektra and the group gained the valuable support slot on a European tour with MEGADETH in 1987.

However, Spencer lost his position in early 1988 to Troy Gregory. The 1988 album 'No Place For Disgrace' was produced by Bill Metoyer at no less than four Californian recording locations, the band hopping between Music Grinder and Track

Records once again plus Pacific Studios in Chatsworth and Preferred Sound in Woodland Hills throughout December 1987 into February 1988. Newsted's presence was still being felt, credited for songwriting on three tracks—'No Place For Disgrace', 'N.E.Terror' and 'I Live, You Die'. The album scored extra press attention for its rip-roaring version of the ELTON JOHN hit 'Saturday Night's Alright For Fighting'. Although the band fared well opening for KING DIAMOND in America during 1988 by the end of the tour their major label deal with Elektra had been lost.

Some fifteen months later the group had bagged a new deal with MCA Records and began recording third album 'When The Storm Comes Down' with producer Alex Perialas in New York. The album, regrettably clad in an amateurish sleeve design, was to be appear in 1990. Troy Gregory gave notice mid-term into a US tour, forcing the band to curtail projected European dates. Eventually, an auditioning process located Chicago native Jason Ward to fill the vacancy.

1992's adventurous 'Cuatro' outing, produced by Neil Kernon at Dotch City Sound in Glendale, although a solid release, regrettably did little to improve their status. On an international scale, FLOTSAM AND JETSAM's sales frustratingly hovered around the quarter of a million mark for each album release, a trend that would continue.

Cuatro also presented the group with a dilemma as early works had been lyrically Jason Newsted's domain, this role then succeeded to by Gregory. In response, FLOTSAM AND JETSAM enlisted band manager Eric Braverman to put words to the music. The band recorded a track co-written with Dave Ellefson of MEGADETH 'Date With Hate' although strangely this did not make the running order for the album and only saw a release as the B side to the 'Swatting At Flies' single.

1995's 'Drift', committed to tape in a home built studio in a friend's pecan farm outside of El Paso, Texas, was once again produced by Kernon with a final mix handled by Michael Barbiero. Expanding their sound somewhat, the group's first use of keyboards came on tracks 'Blindside' and 'Missing'. The 'Drift' record would be dedicated to the late NINE INCH NAILS guitarist Jeff Ward, Jason's brother, who had succumbed to heroin addiction. Road work saw the band out on tour in America supporting MEGADETH but, despite impact on radio with the track 'Smoked Out', upon completion of this expedition MCA let the band go. Gregory bailed out to join PRONG. The four-stringer would later found Psychedelic Rock act THE WITCHES.

FLOTSAM AND JETSAM returned to the scene after a lengthy absence reuniting ties with their former record company Metal Blade. The resulting album 'High' proudly stated the band's intentions towards true metal with song titles mimicking many household name band logos such as JUDAS PRIEST, KISS and AC/DC. At this juncture FLOTSAM AND JETSAM also coined the retaliatory phrase "It's Metal so fuck off!' which summed their attitude up to a tee. The album also includes a version of LARD's 'Fork Boy'.

The band returned to live action debuting their new drummer Craig Neilson at the 'Bang Your Head' festival in Southern Germany headlined by BLIND GUARDIAN prior to a lengthy bout of touring alongside ANVIL and EXCITER.

Upon their return the band drafted in a further new member guitarist Mark Simpson who made his debut on January 1999's, James Lockyer co-produced 'Unnatural Selection' album. Simpson did actually leave the band to join George Lynch's LYNCH MOB but had returned to the fold by the summer of 2000 as FLOTSAM AND JETSAM set to work on another album. With FLOTSAM AND JETSAM gearing up for release of a May 2001 album 'My God', (discarding a previously announced title of 'Obsessive Repulsive') again using Bill Metoyer's talents behind the desk, it was revealed that Eric A.K. was doing the club circuit with a Country & Western band titled THE A.K. CORRAL!

FLOTSAM AND JETSAM themselves commenced a short burst of American club dates kicking off with a Los Angeles Troubadour gig on 28th July. As August drew to a close it was reported that Eric A.K. The band's vocalist for more than twenty years, had departed. His speedily announced replacement would be James Rivera of DESTINY'S END and HELSTAR. With the tour wrapped up Rivera would then team up with SEVEN WITCHES, debuting with the band at their July appearance at the 'Classic Metal Fest II' in Cleveland, Ohio. In parallel, Rivera fired up a unique tribute band, SABBATH JUDAS SABBATH, honouring both JUDAS PRIEST and BLACK SABBATH, also including HELSTAR colleague Mike Heald on guitar.

FLOTSAM AND JETSAM were offered a support tour to Swiss Rockers KROKUS toward the end of 2002 but found themselves in the awkward position of not having a lead singer. As 2002 closed it would revealed that FLOTSAM AND JETSAM bassist Jason Ward was scheduled to deputise for HALFORD's Ray Riendeau for a bunch of New Year shows, the regular HALFORD bassist having suffered a family tragedy just beforehand. However, the gigs would be cancelled when mainman Rob Halford was denied entry to the USA with visa difficulties.

James Rivera forged an all new act in August 2003 uniting with ex-DESTINY'S END guitarist Eric Halpern and SYMPHONY X bassist Mike Lepond in DISTANT THUNDER. This trio soon scored a deal with Massacre Records. FLOTSAM AND JETSAM, vocalist Eric A.K., guitarists Ed Carlson and Mark Simpson, bassist Jason Ward and drummer Craig Nielsen, signed a two album deal with Crash Music in May 2004. Surprisingly, the band laid down a version of METALLICA's 'Damage Inc.', contributed to the Big Deal Records tribute 'Metallic Attack'.

The band allied with OVERKILL and DEATH ANGEL for the September 'Thrash Domination' tour of Japan. THE AK CORRAL, the Country & Western side-project of Eric A.K., issued the album 'A Different Brand Of Country' in November through their own label, Stillwest Records. FLOTSAM AND JETSAM resumed live work in 2005, appearing at the 'Deep Freeze Winter Metal' festival in Westminster, Colorado.

The band, utilising Tom Giatron and Mark Simpson as their production team, spent the early part of the year at Genesis Studios in Phoenix, Arizona recording a new record 'Dreams Of Death'. The record closed with a hidden track, 'Bathing In Red'. Meantime, former FLOTSAM AND JETSAM guitarist Mark Simpson joined up with BEAUTIFUL CREATURES. Craig Nielsen guested on the album 'Modes Of Alienation' by Boston based, instrumental Progressive Metal project THE ALIEN BLAKK.

For FLOTSAM AND JETSAM's appearance at the June 2006 'Bang Your Head' festival in Germany guitarist Ed Carlson was replaced by former member Mike Gilbert. European shows were scheduled for November, but then cancelled. The band offered a quite unique excuse, explaining that Eric A.K. had enrolled himself into a helicopter firefighting course, which clashed with the dates.

The band's first album 'Doomsday For The Deceiver' gained a special re-release in October on Metal Blade Records. This expanded edition hosted both the 'Iron Tears' and 'Metal Shock' demo tracks plus a DVD disc including early film footage, interviews and a live set recorded at the Bootleggers venue in 1985.

Metal Shock, (1985). Hammerhead / The Evil Sheikh / I Live You Die / The Beast Within.

Flotsam And Jetsam, (1985). I Live, You Die / Iron Tears.

DOOMSDAY FOR THE DECEIVER, Metal Blade 72130 (1986). Hammerhead / Iron Tears / Desecrator / Fade To Black / Doomsday For The Deceiver / Metalshock / She Took An Axe / Der Führer / Flotzilla.

Flotzilla, Metal Blade RR 125471 (1987). Flotzilla / I Live You Die.

NO PLACE FOR DISGRACE, Roadrunner RR 9549 (1988). No Place For Disgrace / Dreams Of Death / NE Terror / Escape From Within / Saturday Night's Alright For Fighting / Hard On You / I Live You Die / Misguided Fortune / PAAB / The Jones. Chart position: 143 USA.

FLOTSAM AND JETSAM

Saturday Night's Alright For Fighting, Roadrunner RR 24531 (1988). Saturday Night's Alright For Fighting / Hard On You (Live) / Misguided Fortune (Live) / Dreams Of Death (Live).

WHEN THE STORM COMES DOWN, MCA DMCG 6084 (1990). The Master Sleeps / Burned Device / Deviation / October Thorns / No More Fun / Suffer The Masses / 6, Six, VI / Greed / EMTEK / Scars / KAB. Chart position: 174 USA.

The Master Sleeps, MCA CD45-18515 (1990) (USA promotion). The Master Sleeps / Interview.

Suffer The Masses, MCA (1990) (USA promotion). Suffer The Masses.

Swatting At Flies, MCA (1992). Swatting At Flies / Date With Hate.

Wading Through The Darkness, MCA (1992) (USA promotion). Wading Through The Darkness / Wading Through The Darkness (Radio edit) / Wading Through The Darkness (Industrial mix).

Cradle Me Now (Radio edit), MCA (1992) (USA promotion). Cradle Me Now (Radio edit) / Cradle Me Now (Album version).

CUATRO, MCA MCD 10678 (1992). Natural Enemies / Swatting At Flies / Message / Cradle Me Now / Wading Through The Darkness / Double Zero / Never To Reveal / Forget About Heaven / Secret Square / Hyperdermic Midnight Snack / Are You Willing / (Ain't Nothing Gonna) Save This world.

Blindside (Radio edit), MCA MCA5P-3447 (1995) (USA promotion). Blindside (Radio edit) / Blindside (Album version) / Fairies Wear Boots.

Destructive Signs (Radio edit), MCA MCA5P-3454 (1995). Destructive Signs (Radio edit) / Destructive Signs (Album version).

Smoked Out (Radio edit), MCA MCA5P-3351 (1995) (USA promotion). Smoked Out (Radio edit) / Smoked Out (Album version).

DRIFT, MCA MCAD 11212 (1995). Me / Empty Air / Pick A Window / 12 Year Old Boy With A Gun / Missing / Blindside / Remember / Destructive Signs / Smoked Out / Poet's Tell.

HIGH, Metal Blade 14126 (1997). Final Step / Hallucinational / It's On Me / High Noon / YH (Your Hands) / Monster / Lucky Day / Toast / High / Everything / Fork Boy.

UNNATURAL SELECTION, Metal Blade 3984-14184-2 (1999). Dream Srape / Chemical Noose / Promise Keepers / Liquid Noose / Falling / Fuckers / Brain Dead / Way To Go / Win, Lose Or Dead / Welcome To The Bottom.

MY GOD, Metal Blade CD 085 103212 (2001). Dig Me Up To Bury Me / Keep Breathing / Nothing To Say / Weather To Do / Camera Eye / Trash / Praise / My God / Learn To Dance / Frustrate / Killing Time / I.A.M.H.

DREAMS OF DEATH, Crash Music CMU61150 (2005). Requiescal / Straight To Hell / Parapsychotic / Bleed / Look In His Eyes / Childhood Hero / Bathing In Red / Nascentes Morimar / Out Of Mind / Bathing In Red (Hidden track).

LIVE IN PHOENIX, Mausoleum 251077 (2005). No Place For Disgrace / Swatting At Flies / Hard On You / Chemical Noose / Me / Wading Through The Darkness / The Master Sleeps / Nothing To Say / Thrash / Hammerhead / Secret Square / Escape From Within / Dig Me Up To Burn Me.

FORBIDDEN

SAN FRANCISCO, CA, USA — *Russ Anderson (vocals), Craig Loccicero (guitar), Tim Calvert (guitar), Matt Camacho (bass), Steven Jacobs (drums).*

Known in 1985 initially as FORBIDDEN EVIL this San Francisco thrash act have weathered the storm that has seen so many of their contemporaries drift away. The band's original line up comprised of vocalist Russ Anderson, guitarists Glen Alvelais and Craig Loccicero, bassist Matt Camacho and drummer Paul Bostaph. In their early days FORBIDDEN EVIL regularly played alongside the likes of EXODUS and TESTAMENT and demos secured a deal with Combat Records. Guitarist Rob Flynn also had a lengthy spell in the band before leaving for VIO-LENCE and later MACHINE HEAD.

Truncating their name to simply FORBIDDEN the band's first album of 1989 put the act firmly into the extreme metal end of the market. A tour of Europe, including an appearance at the Dynamo festival, enhanced their live reputation. The Dynamo show was recorded and tracks subsequently released on the live mini-album 'Raw Evil—Live At The Dynamo'. Guitarist Glen Alvelais departed prior to the 'Twisted Into Form' album making way for ex-MILITIA man Tim Calvert. The album also saw Andy Galeon, Dennis Pepa and Mark Osegueda of DEATH ANGEL on backing vocals.

FORBIDDEN toured guesting for EXODUS and SACRED REICH before the band were to unite with the DEATH ANGEL members again when FORBIDDEN played as support to DEATH ANGEL in America prior to their first British gig at London's Hammersmith Odeon alongside DEATH ANGEL and VICIOUS RUMOURS.

In 1992 the Combat group who had the rights to FORBIDDEN issued a low quality, generic compilation album entitled called 'Point Of No Return'. The compilation was merely a contractual obligation and was not endorsed by the band. Record company disputes put paid to FORBIDDEN's recording schedule in America and the band duly signed to German label G.U.N. Records at the same time welcoming new drummer Steve Jacobs for European dates opening for GOREFEST. Their 1994 album 'Distortion' included a remake of KING CRIMSON's '21st Century Schizoid Man'. The album was reissued twice more, once on Massacre Records in 1995 with an alternate cover and yet a third time in 1996 on Mayhem with yet another different cover. Some of these pressing are now quite rare.

In 1995 an indie release entitled 'Trapped' surfaced on a small label, WFW. The album consisted primarily of three of the four original FORBIDDEN EVIL / FORBIDDEN demos. There is some debate as to the legitimacy of the 'Trapped' release although some argue that it was formally endorsed (and/or released) by the band at one point. Either way the release was well done and gave fans a chance to hear these rare and sought after demos. As with most small, private pressings, combining low supply and high demand, the CD will often exceed $50.00 USD (when found) on E-Bay.

In 1997 FORBIDDEN had one last attempt with another release, their fourth studio album, 'Green'. The band had yet another record label to deal with (their 6th overall) as 'Green' was later released in the US on Pavement Records. The band style had changed substantially by this point leaving many fans disappointed and accordingly sales were not stellar. The bands dabbling in a slower, mid-90's era sound and production was ill-fated as it was to be the final album by the band.

Bostaph later joined TESTAMENT for one album and more permanently SLAYER. Loccicero, Jacobs and Camacho founded MAN MADE GOD, a band that featured guitarist Ahrue Lister later of MACHINE HEAD. Alvelais created BIZARRO with guitarist Nick St. Denis, later of PRO-PAIN, and drummer Paul Hopkins, later of SKINLAB. Alvelais then joined TESTAMENT for a tempestuous period before resuming activity with

BIZARRO then forging LD/50 with ex-GEEZER vocalist Clark Brown.

Erstwhile FORBIDDEN personnel guitarist Craig Locicero and drummer Steve Jacobs also re-emerged during 2001 credited as MANMADEGOD. By the following year Russ Anderson would be back in action, treading the boards with his new Pop inclined outfit PARKING LOT PROPHETS. 2002 found erstwhile drummer Paul Bostaph as a member of SYSTEMATIC. The drummer joined EXODUS in May 2005. Guitarist Craig Locicero temped for SANGRE ETERNA on a live basis in February 2006.

Victim Of Changes, Under One Flag 12FLAG 108 (1989) ('Live at the Dynamo' EP). Victim Of Changes / Forbidden Evil / Chalice Of Blood / Through Eyes Of Glass.
FORBIDDEN EVIL, Under One Flag FLAG 27 (1989). Chalice Of Blood / Off The Edge / Through Eyes Of Glass / Forbidden Evil / March Into Fire / Feel No Pain / As Good As Dead / Follow Me.
TWISTED INTO FORM, Under One Flag FLAG 43 (1990). Parting Of The Ways / Infinite / Out Of Body (Out Of Mind) / Step By Step / Twisted Into Form / RIP / Spiral Depression / Tossed Away / One Foot In Hell.
POINT OF NO RETURN—THE BEST OF, Under One Flag FLAG 73 (1992). Chalice Of Blood / Out Of Body (Out Of Mind) / Feel No Pain / Step By Step / Off The Edge / One Foot In Hell / Through The Eyes Of Glass / Tossed Away / March Into Fire / Victim Of Changes.
DISTORTION, G.U.N. Records (1994). Distortion / Hypnotized By The Rhythm / Rape / No Reason / Feed The Hand / Wake Up! / Mind's 'I' / All That Is / Undertaker / 21st Century Schizoid Man.
GREEN, Great Unlimited Noises 74321 44249 2 (1997). What Is The Last Time? / Green / Phat / Turns To Rage / Face Down Heroes / Over The Middle / Kanaworms / Noncent$ / Blank / Focus.

FORCED ENTRY

SEATTLE, WA, USA — *Tony Benjamins (vocals / bass), Brad Hull (guitar), Colin Mattson (drums).*

This Seattle area band was among the second wave of Thrash getting snapped up by labels in the late 80's and early 90's. The band had existed in another incarnation known as CONDITION CRITICAL, who issued one demo in April of 1987 called 'All Fucked Up'. The band soon changed names, got to work and issued the demos 'Thrashing Helpless Down' in August, 1987 and 'Hate Fills Your Eyes' the following year, the latter featuring a quite thought-provoking piece of cover art as well.

A deal with Relativity/Combat followed and the band recorded their debut, 'Uncertain Future', in January of 1989 and shot an accompanying video for the track 'Bludgeon'. The lyrics covered standard thrash topics of politics and war. After the usual scenario of promotional touring, the band entered the studio again and recorded a second album, 'As Above, So Below', which was even heavier but added an element of humour with songs like 'We're Dicks' and 'How We Spent Our Summer Vacation'.

A long break ensued and the band no longer with a record deal released an EP in 1995 on their own. Unfortunately it went unnoticed by almost everyone except the most dedicated fans and it was the last time the band was active.

UNCERTAIN FUTURE, Relativity (1989). Bludgeon / Kaleidoscope Of Pain / A Look Through Glass / Anaconda / Octoclops / Unrest They Find / Morgulon / Foreign Policy.
AS ABOVE, SO BELOW, Relativity (1991). Bone Crackin' Fever / Thunderhead Macrocosm, Microcosm / Never A Know, But The No / We're Dicks / Apathy / The Unextinguishable / As Of Yesterday / When One Becomes Two / How We Spent Our Summer Vacation.
THE SHORE, Morning Wood (1995).

FORCEFIELD

FRIESLAND, HOLLAND — *Joris (vocals), Theo (guitar / bass), Marc (guitar), Koos Vandervelde (drums).*

FORCEFIELD is a Friesland Speed Metal band. The roots of the project date back to 1995, when erstwhile KING'S EVIL members guitarist Theo and drummer Koos Vandervelde forged the Jazz / Fusion influenced FIELD. Recordings, 'Life And Times' and 'Demon's Eyes', were issued, after which the group opted to pursue straight forward, aggressive Metal. This transition in musical style marked the name switch to FORCEFIELD. Singer Joris would be recruited from the ranks of DUST DEVIL. Vandervelde also held a tradition with MEGAKRONKEL and CLONE.

Introducing ex-CLONE guitarist Marc in early 2003, Theo switched instruments to bass. The single 'Casualty' emerged in July 2003. Koos Vandervelde would step in as live drummer for US act WYKKED WYTCH's appearances on the 2005 'No Mercy Fest' European tour.

Casualty, Forcefield (2003). Afterlife / Casualty / Morning Booze.

FORM

HOLLAND — *Hans Reinders (vocals), Marcel Coenen (guitar), Vince Van Der Loo (guitar), Ruud Van Tuel (bass), Spike (drums).*

FORM was a speed orientated Heavy Metal act founded initially under the SPEEDICA banner by erstwhile ANGER personnel, guitarists Raymond C., bassist Raymond Heijdendael and drummer Pierre Heijdendael. As such, the group first performed live on 5th October 1986 at the 'Amateurpop' festival in Bartok-Born. Another ANGER guitarist, Henk Hamers, enrolled in 1987. That same year the MENACY and BOONDOGGLE credited Hans Reinders was acquired as lead vocalist. A further change saw the introduction of guitarist MARCEL COENEN in 1988.

A slew of demo recordings then ensued, 'Metal In Rocks' in 1989, 'Voyage Into The Fifth Dimension' in 1990 plus 'Shadows Of Tomorrow' and 'Speedilypassinggreengod' both issued in 1991, culminating in the album 'I Choose My Own' issued through Belgian label Mausoleum Records in 1994. Another album, 'Shock Corridor', was released via HP Music in the year 2000.

FORM guitarist MARCEL COENEN would go on to enjoy a high profile with SUN CAGED, FIFTH and LEMUR VOICE as well as issuing solo product. Coenen would also session for HUBI MEISEL and guest on the 2004 MISTHERIA album 'Messenger Of The Gods'. Drummer Spike would also feature in FIFTH, STORMRIDER and CALLENISH CIRCLE. Another FORM guitarist, Danny Tunker, joined FUELBLOODED. Other musicians with FORM credentials included vocalist Nick Hameury of FIFTH, SUN CAGED and LEMUR VOICE and guitarist Rene Rokx from CHEMICAL BREATH, CALLENISH CIRCLE and STORMRIDER.

I CHOOSE MY OWN, Mausoleum 904155-2 (1995). Multiple Me / Form Example / Several Ways / Beg / In Honour Of ... / Sheltering / Unwillingly / Prescription.
SHOCK CORRIDOR, HP Music (2000).

FORTE

OK, USA — *Kevin Valliquette (vocals), Jeff Scott (guitar), Greg Nicholson (bass), Greg Scott (drums).*

Oklahoma Thrash Metal act FORTE arrived with the 1990 demo tape 'Dementia By Design'. The band signed to Germany's Massacre Records for the debut 1992 album 'Stranger Than Fiction'. Line up included former OLIVER MAGNUM singer James Randell, guitarist Jeff Scott, ex-LEGIONED MARCHER bassist Ghames 'Reverend' Jones and drummer Greg Scott. Jones had also acted as touring bassist for Arlington, Texas Thrashers GAMMACIDE. Touring would find FORTE reaping valuable high profile supports to acts such as DREAM THEATER, PANTERA, OVERKILL, SEPULTURA, SAVATAGE, WATCHTOWER and FLOTSAM & JETSAM.

The 1994 album 'Division' witnessed a radical change in the band format with vocals now in the hands of Bill Dollins, another erstwhile LEGIONED MARCHER man. The album included a cover version of ACCEPT's 'Fast As A Shark'. Yet again the band scored more strong and diverse guest slots to the likes of FEAR FACTORY, LIFE OF AGONY and YNGWIE MALMSTEEN. Jones would also find time to deputise for GAMMACIDE.

The 1997 'Destructive' record saw another crop of new faces in vocalist David Thompson and bassist Richard Sharp. Another extensive road jaunt found the new look FORTE opening for TESTAMENT, KING DIAMOND, EXODUS, MACHINE HEAD, SAXON and SKINLAB among others. The band stabilised their line up and cut a further album, 'Rise Above' in 1999. This record would be promoted on the live circuit with an appearance at the 'Powermad' festival and tour work alongside DEATH, TESTAMENT, HAMMERFALL and MANOWAR. Despite the band's obvious progress on the live front and a string of consistent albums FORTE severed then severed ties with Massacre Records. Original singer James Randell made a return in November 1999, committing to tape the QUEENSRYCHE cover 'Prophecy' for a Frontiers Records tribute album released during 2000.

During January of 2002 the band announced its new line up which now included DREAM KINGS vocalist Kevin Valliquette and bass player Greg Nicholson joining the mainstay inner circle of the Scott siblings. Under their new guise FORTE set to work on a fresh studio album projected for an early 2003 release.

Former member Reverend Jones travelled on to BLACK SYMPHONY during 1997 and was ensconced in the MICHAEL SCHENKER GROUP for the German guitar guru's 2001 opus 'Be Aware Of Scorpions'. Erstwhile FORTE bassists Richard Sharp and Greg Nicholson founded THE KILL in 2003, seeing Sharp shift to guitar alongside another FORTE colleague vocalist Kevin Valliquette and drummer Ezra Darrow. By April of 2004 Jones would be pulling road duty with Nu-Metal band FUEL. He fired up a new band project, BARNEY FIFER, in early 2005.

STRANGER THAN FICTION, Massacre (1992). Coming Of The Storm / The Inner Circle / Stranger Than Fiction / G-13 (Devoid Of Thought) / Mein Madness / Time And Time Again / Digitator / Between The Lies / The Last Word / The Promise.
DIVISION, Massacre (1994). Dischord / Inhuman / Thirteen Steps / Last Machine / E 2 M.N. / In This Life / One Flesh / Division / Legacy Of Silence / Ultimatum / Back To Zero / Fast As A Shark.
DESTRUCTIVE, Massacre (1997). Barcode / Deviate / Hammer / Destructive / October / Heal Me / Strength / Never Sleep / The Hard Way / Art Of War / Eternal / Far Away.
DEAD BREED, Massacre (1998).
RISE ABOVE, Massacre (1999). Man Against Machine / Fading Away / Ninety Nine / Forgiven / Rise Above / Destroyer / Poison Tongue / Burn / Over My Head / Until The End Of Time.

FRANKENBOK

MELBOURNE, VIC, AUSTRALIA — *Adam B. Metal (vocals), Aaron Leigh Butler (guitar), Scott Cameron Lang (guitar), Tim Miedecke (bass / keyboards), Mick Morley (drums).*

A modern Thrash Metal band, FRANKENBOK was forged in Melbourne during 1997 with a line up comprising singer Adam Glynn, guitarists Aaron Butler and Scott Lang, bassist Tim Miedecke. A set of demos was recorded with the aid of a drum machine before drummer Mick Morley was acquired during 1999. Signing to Faultline Records FRANKENBOK debuted with the 'Greetings And Salutations' album.

The band switched labels to Dark Carnival Records toward the close of 2000 to publish the EP 'The Loopholes & Great Excuses', this achieving a fair degree of radio play courtesy of the MADISON AVENUE cover version 'Don't Call Me Baby'. In 2002 FRANKENBOK's steady rise in status prompted the re-issue of 'Greetings And Salutations', clad in all new artwork and hosting an additional eight extra live tracks. However,

FRANKENBOK

progress was stalled temporarily when vocalist Adam Glynn quit to found FIVE STAR PRISON CELL.

Adam B Metal was quickly drafted as the band's new frontman. After a brief burst of live shows the band entered Back Beach Studios to craft the 'Blood Oath' album with producer DW Nortob for Roadrunner Records. FRANKENBOX lent support to 8 FOOT SATIVA's 2004 New Zealand dates. The band then worked their way across Australia in May and June forming up the 'Army Of Darkness' trek in union with 8 FOOT SATIVA, FULL SCALE and SUNK LOTO.

Vocalist Adam B. Metal was hospitalised with a broken leg following a skateboarding accident in early January 2007. The new year saw FRANKENBOK preparing to release a second album 'Murder Of Crows'.

GREETINGS AND SALUTATIONS, Faultline FAULTCD001 (2000). Greetings And Salutations / I'm OK With It / Linguistics / P. Cloned / Pycost / Under The Kurgan's Kilt / Pulp / Counter Part / Dunce With Denial / Fake As Fuck.
The Loopholes And Great Excuses EP, Roadrunner DC00043 (2001). Monk Discipline / The Virtue Of Angels / Cocaine / Celibacy / Success Is Revenge / Cling / Don't Call Me Baby.
BLOOD OATH, Roadrunner RR 8378-2 (2003). The Hole / Victims / Processed / Cocooned / Backpack / Passport / Requiem / Swim / Gone Evil / Shovel / Anti-Faith / Where The Blood Don't Flow / Pushonup / Fukenkuntz.
MURDER OF SONGS, Frankenbok (2007). The Night & the Fog / Failure To Learn / What Is Real? / Worship Before The Dead / Walk This Lie(fe) / As It Comes Down On You / The Meltdown / Down To The Wire / Triumph / Sludge.

FREEDOM CALL

GERMANY — *Chris Bay (vocals / guitar), Sascha Gerstner (guitar), Ilker Ersin (bass), Dan Zimmermann (drums).*

FREEDOM CALL arrived brandishing a refined Euro Melodic Speed Metal style with the 1999 opening shot 'Stairway To Fairyland' that soon propelled the band into German charts. The band numbered in their ranks the well known figure of drummer Dan Zimmermann, known for his Pop days with HEINZ and more importantly Metal bands LANZER, GAMMA RAY and IRON SAVIOR.

Both Zimmermann and vocalist Chris Bay had in their formative years been active with covers band CHINA WHITE and then LANZER. Bay would keep in touch with Zimmermann throughout the years, the singer working with MOON'DOC. This last act of Bay's would also feature FREEDOM CALL bassist Ilker Ersin. The band debuted live in Grenoble, France during May 1999 supporting ANGRA and EDGUY. Later gigs across Europe in November found the band as special guests to Brit vets SAXON.

In Japan a mini album, 'Taragon', was also released the same year by JVC Victor. Quite surreally this disc included FREEDOM CALL's take on the ULTRAVOX hit 'Dancing With Tears In My Eyes'. SAXON's Biff Byford would lend his tonsils to the narrative on 'Tears Of Taragon'.

The 'Crystal Empire' album, recorded in Hamburg, Nuremberg, and Erlangen under the aegis's of producers Chris Bay, Dan Zimmermann and Charlie Bauerfiend, saw ROUGH SILK and AXEL RUDI PELL keyboard player Ferdy Doernberg guesting on keyboards. Touring throughout the early part of 2001 had FREEDOM CALL backing the album on the road in Germany as part of a package billing with HAMMERFALL and VIRGIN STEELE. 'Crystal Empire' would peak at no. 94 in the national German album charts.

In September of 2001 guitarist Sascha Gerstner, having joined premier league act HELLOWEEN, was supplanted by Cedric Dupont of SYMPHORCE. FREEDOM CALL toured Scandinavia during October of 2002 supported by FULL STRIKE. Shows alongside BLIND GUARDIAN would be recorded for the live album 'Live Invasion', this package also adding the 'Tears Of Taragon' tracks previously only available in Japan. The band united with METALIUM and DARK AGE for the European 'Wacken Road Show 2004' commencing in late April.

FREEDOM CALL cut drum recordings at Kai Hansen of GAMMA RAY's studios in Hamburg during August before moving on to Nuremburg to finish a new album, lent a working title of 'Circle Of Life'. Cedric Dupont exited in July of 2005.

Bassist Ilker Ersin quit in September, announcing a brand new act entitled POWERWORLD. He would later be joined by keyboard player Nils Neumann in this venture. FREEDOM CALL, with new ex-PARADOX bass player Armin Donderer installed, got back into live action in April 2006 as European support to RAGE.

FREEDOM CALL released a new album, 'Dimensions', in 2007. The group supported DRAGONFORCE on their German tour dates in April.

STAIRWAY TO FAIRYLAND, SPV (1999). Over The Rainbow / Tears Falling / Fairyland / Shine On / We Are One / Hymn To The Brave / Tears Of Taragon / Graceland / Holy Knight / Another Day / Kingdom Come.
TARAGON, JVC Victor VICP 60918 (1999) (Japanese release). Warriors Of Light / Dancing With Tears In My Eyes / Heart Of The Brave / Kingdom Come (version) / Tears Of Taragon (Story version).
CRYSTAL EMPIRE, SPV (2001). The King Of The Crystal Empire / Freedom Call / Rise Up / Farewell / Pharao / Call Of Fame / Heart Of The Rainbow / The Quest / Ocean / Palace Of Fantasy / The Wanderer. Chart positions: 35 FINLAND, 67 SWEDEN, 94 GERMANY.
ETERNITY, SPV (2002). Metal Invasion / The Eyes Of The World / Flying High / Land Of Light / Warriors / Ages Of Power / Turn Back Time / Island Of Dreams / The Spell / Bleeding Heart / Flame In The Night. Chart position: 55 GERMANY.
LIVE INVASION, SPV (2004). Eyes Of The World / Freedom Call / Tears Of Taragon / Heart Of The Rainbow / The Quest / Land Of Light / Metal Invasion / Rise Up / We Are One / Warriors / Hymn To The Brave / Warriors Of Light / Dancing With Tears In My Eyes / Heart Of The Brave / Kingdom Come / Tears Of Taragon (Story version) / Hiroshima / Dr. Stein.
THE CIRCLE OF LIFE, SPV SPV 085-99292 CD (2005). Mother Earth / Carry On / The Rhythm Of Life / Hunting High And Low / Starlight / The Gathering (Midtro) / Kings And Queens / Hero Nation / High Enough / Starchild / The Eternal Flame / The Circle Of Life. Chart position: 58 SWEDEN.
DIMENSIONS, Steamhammer (2007). Demons Dance / Innocent World / United Alliance / Mr. Evil / Queen Of My World / Light Up The Sky / Words Of Endeavour / Blackened Sun / Dimensions / My Dying Paradise / Magic Moments / Far Away.

FROZEN SUN

DENMARK — *Kenny Nielsen (vocals), Michael Kopietz (guitar), Nick Jensen (guitar), Henrik Kopietz (bass), Thomas Moller (drums).*

The FROZEN SUN duo of guitarist/bassist Michael Kopietz of and drummer Reno Kiilerich founded the brutal Death Metal band KOBEAST during 2003 in collaboration with Søren 'Azazel' Jensen of GRANHAMMER, IRON FIRE and CORPUS MORTALE repute. Both Kopietz and Kiilerich also have affiliations with PANZERCHRIST and 12 GAUGE. In late 2003 Kiilerich joined fabled North American Death Metal band VILE. The drummer stepped up a further league in March of the following year when he was recruited as session man for DIMMU BORGIR's European, South American and US 'Ozzfest' festival dates. He subsequently joined STRANGLER and in January 2006 joined Anglo-Danish collaboration DOWNLORD.

DIMENSIONS, Serious SE 004CD (1996). Once And For All / Life In Misery / Obsession / Grey / Puss Gore n' Decay / Streetwalker Song / In The Shadow Of Your Soul / Censorship Equals / Defect Dimension Of Souls / Into The Outro.

FUELBLOODED

DEN BOSCH, HOLLAND — *Vital Welten (vocals), Danny Tunker (guitar), Michiel Rutten (guitar), Michel Steenbekkers (bass), Norbert Moen (drums).*

A Den Bosch Melodic Death / Thrash Metal act previously known as SACRAMENTAL SACHEM. This former act dated back to 1989 and had issued the albums 'Recrucifixtion' in 1995 and 'Anxiety' in 2001. Formative drummer Luciano Marras also held ties to SCAVENGER.

FUELBLOODED released a four track demo in 2002, promoting this with supports to DARKANE. The band re-debuted with the 2004 Stephen van Haestregt produced album 'Inflict The Inevitable'. FUELBLOODED added ex-FORM guitarist Danny Tunker, replacing Michiel Stekelenburg, in February 2005.

FUELBLOODED signed to British label Copro Records in early 2006 for the album 'Inflict The Inevitable'. Uniting with fellow Dutch Deathsters DETONATION, the band put in UK tour dates in early May. FUELBLOODED parted ways with singer Vital Welten in September.

Promo 2002, Fuelblooded (2002). Poisonous / Dissector Of Souls / Constructive Destruction / The Silence.

FURIOUS TRAUMA

COPENHAGEN, DENMARK — *Lars Schmidt (vocals / guitar), Henrik B. Jacobsen (guitar), Claus Weiergang (bass), Allan Tschicaja (drums).*

A Copenhagen based Thrash-Death Metal band formed during the late eighties with first product being the 1988 demo 'Tempora Mutantur' (notably dedicated to Cliff Burton). FURIOUS TRAUMA's line-up at this juncture comprised singer Klaus Hansen, guitarists Lars Schmidt and Morten Gilsted, bassist W. and drummer Henrik Quaade. This was followed by the 'Profit Counts' session by which stage the band had shifted shape to see Schmidt joined by an all new cast of guitarist Samir Belmaati, bassist Kaare Strøm Hansen and Brian Andersen on the drums.

After the release of their debut album, 'Primal Touch' in 1993, the band hit the road and can count support slots to MOTÖRHEAD and KREATOR amongst their biggest gigs. FURIOUS TRAUMA also appeared at the July 1993 Roskilde Festival, opening for ANTHRAX, SUICIDAL TENDENCIES, MIDNIGHT OIL and PORNO FOR PYROS. However, line-up changes occurred in 1994 with frontman Lars Schmidt joining KONKHRA and also losing their drummer; Morten Nielsen of BLACK ROSE, FORCE MAJEURE, CRIME ACADEMY and MERCYFUL FATE replacing the latter. The 'Eclipse' album emerged in 1995 through Euphonious Records.

1996's 'Strange Ways' EP contained cover versions of ARTILLERY's 'The Challenge' and KISS' 'Strange Ways' plus a CD-ROM portion containing video clips for 'Chaos Within' and 'My

Dying Time' plus a band interview. Signing to French label Season Of Mist FURIOUS TRAUMA issued 'Roll The Dice' in 1999. Ex-FURIOUS TRAUMA drummer Brian Anderson joined DOMINUS in 2000.

FURIOUS TRAUMA's 2004 band line-up comprised Lars Schmidt, the HATESPHERE and KOLDBORN credited Henrik B. Jacobsen on guitar, GUTRIX and ZOSER MEZ bassist Claus Weiergang and drummer Allan Tschicaja.

Tempora Mutantur, Skaldic Art (1988). The Trinitytest / Brainstorm / R.F.F. / Trash Yer Guts Out.

Profit Counts, (1990). Prepare Retaliation / Fast n' Furious / Taking Over / Scumbags / Muslim Aggression / Chaotic Thoughts.

PRIMAL TOUCH, CBOD (1993). Born Of The Flag / Adult Lust / Kick Ass / Slam The Fays / White Slavery / Ridin' With Sioux / Liquid Materia / In Your Dreams.

Strange Ways EP, Euphonious PHONI 006 (1996). Chaos Within / My Dying Time / Born Under The Flag (New Version) / Way To Perfection / The Challenge / Strange Ways / Chaos Within (Video) / My Dying Time (Video).

ECLIPSE, Euphonious PHONI 002 (1996). Hustler / Smalltalker M.F. / Chaos Within / Stop The Bastards / My Dying Time / Sacred Bond / Swallow My Conscience / Silent Forever / Subject To Surgery / Another Face In The Crowd.

ROLL THE DICE, Season Of Mist (1999). Intro / Roll The Dice / On Top Of The World / Alive / The Fifth Season / Opinions / Worth To Live / Hole In My Pocket / Memory And Mind, pt. 1 / Weightless / Focus Intact / In The Tombs / Memory And Mind, pt. 2.

FURY

ADELAIDE, SA, AUSTRALIA — *Michael O'Neill (vocals), Rick Boon (guitar), Darren McLennan (guitar), Steven Comacchio (bass), Derek Beauchamp (drums).*

Adelaide Thrashers FURY are almost unique in their field in that rhythm guitarist and driving force behind the band Ricky Boon, an erstwhile member of CLAUDIA'S GHOST, is completely blind. Boon initially founded FURY with guitarist Darren McLennan, a veteran of Gothic Rock act CHALICE, and DUNGEON vocalist Lord Tim. Before long Michael O'Neill, ex singer with ACID and guitarist with BLOODLUST, came in to front the band as touring commenced with Aaron Dewsbery taking up bass and ACID's Ben Harris on drums.

FURY opted for a career relocation to Adelaide, drafting bassist Steven Comacchio and drummer Derek Beauchamp in the process. The latter already had a well documented past with acts such as NECROSIS, VALHULL and SLAYER tribute band MANDATORY SUICIDE. Beauchamp also performs with Punk acts TOXIC SHOCK and N.F.I.

In March of 1999 FURY donated tracks to the Blacklight 'Time Capsule 2000' compilation as well as the 'Australian Metal collection 'Down Under Ground 3'. Dwell Records in America would pick up on the band too for their ongoing tribute album series and FURY duly delivered a cover of 'Symphony Of Destruction' for a MEGADETH tribute album. Further contributions to Dwell's tribute arsenal came with tracks for SUICIDAL TENDENCIES, DEATH and KING DIAMOND tributes. FURY would also manage to put in a showing at the American 'Metal Meltdown' festival.

A four track EP, 'Stigmatized', arrived in March of 2000 with the band's second full length album 'Slavekind' released the following year.

FURY, Fury FCD001 (1997). Bleeding Me Dry / Lost In An Unknown Mind / Innocence / Forever / Save Me / Final Scream / 1814 (Empire's End) / Pay The Price / Fuck You.

Stigmatized EP, Fury FCD002 (2000). Fallen Ones / Tempest Deceit / Stigmatised / Excuses.

SLAVEKIND, Fury FCD003 (2001). Shapes Of Three / Slavekind / One Thousand Pasts / Forsaken / Denying Fear / The Serpent's Kiss / Lies Of This Insanity.

FUTURE TENSE

WOERDEN, HOLLAND — *Cock Von Drumen (vocals), Rob Weber (guitar), Tjerk Kiesel (bass), Ruud Beunder (drums).*

Woerden based FUTURE TENSE, who issued the demos 'Protect Your Ears' and 'Battle For Metal', had their track 'Nightmare' featured on the 1984 Metal Blade 'Metal Massacre V' compilation album. The band had actually formed as the NEW SPRING BAND during the late seventies, initially comprising singer Peter Ockhuyzen, guitarist Michiel van Loef, bassist Tjerk Kiesel and Rico Hoek on drums. However, the band switched title to FUTURE TENSE as unpleasant similarities were being drawn between the initials of their first title and the Dutch extreme right political party. This name change would coincide with the introduction of drummer Ruud Beunder for a self titled opening demo.

Line up changes would mark the incorporation of new frontman Cock Von Drumen and guitarist Rob Weber, featuring on the 1982 demo session 'Protect Your Ears' and 1983's 'Battle For Metal', recorded at Rosegarden Studios in Utrecht. FUTURE TENSE were also chosen for inclusion on the compilation cassette 'When The Hammer Comes Down'. Radio attention afforded these releases caught the attention of Metal Blade Records owner Brian Slagel, who chose to include 'Nightmare' on the 1984 Metal Blade 'Metal Massacre V' compilation. As FUTURE TENSE signed to the Universe label a second guitarist, Reinier Schenk, was enrolled to record the 'Condemned To The Gallow' tracks at K&M Studio in Nieuwegein. Despite this progress the band found that Cock's vocal technique was coming in for some heavy criticism. In 1985 FUTURE TENSE folded. Reinier Schenk would subsequently feature as a member of YOSH, FLESHMOULD and ANESTHESY.

Interest in the 80s Metal scene revived interest and in 2001 a previously unreleased track from 'Battle For Metal', entitled 'Evil Attack 2000' and re-recorded at Studio Fred in Woerden, was included on a compilation album compiled by German magazine 'That's Metal'. An album release party saw FUTURE TENSE returning onstage for two songs, their first live performance in over sixteen years. Their profile rose once again when Danish Black Metal band DENIAL OF GOD recorded a cover of 'Sword Of Vengeance'.

In 2004 the US label Doomed Planet Records released the compilation album 'Crossing The Swords... Again', a vinyl only release restricted to 500 copies comprising the 'Battle Of Metal' and remixed 'Condemned To The Gallows' songs. Although FUTURE TENSE performed an announced "Last gig ever" at the Babylon venue in Woerden on 29th May 2004, supported by BOLTHORN and recorded for a live album 'The Final cut', by August the core of Rob Weber, Tjerk Kiesel and Ruud Beunder were advertising for a new singer and second guitarist.

Protect Your Ears, (1982). Ready To Rock / Nightmare / Strangest Demon / Chasing the Dragon / Break The Chains / Go to Hell.

Battle For Metal, (1983). Battle Of Metal / Nightmare / Marquis de Sade / Damned Forever / Mephisto / Go To Hell.

Condemned To The Gallow EP, Universe (1984). Go To Hell / Condemned To The Gallow / La Guilltine / Swords Of Vengeance / Evil Attack.

Swords Of Vengeance, Future Tense (2003). Swords Of Vengeance / Nightmare / Go To Hell.

CROSSING THE SWORDS ... AGAIN, Doomed Planet (2004) (Limited edition 500 copies). Battle Of Metal / Nightmare / Marquis De Sade / Damned Forever / Mephisto / Go To Hell / Go To Hell / Swords Of Vengeance / La Guillotine / Condemned To The Gallows / Evil Attack.

G.O.R.E.

LAITILA, FINLAND — *Ville Pokki (vocals), Antti Marttala (guitar), Jussi Tomukorpi (guitar), Jarmo Perälä (bass), Jari Nieminen (drums).*

Laitila Thrash Metal band G.O.R.E., aimed at delivering "the most vicious, loudest and extreme Thrash" and forged that same year by guitarist Antti Marttala together with drummer Jari Nieminen, debuted with a 2001 demo 'Now Is The Time', this set closing with a rendition of SLAYER's 'Raining Blood'. The initial founding duo had been joined by vocalist / bassist Ville Pokki and a fluid cast of rhythm guitarists. A self-titled promotional session followed, after which second guitarist Jussi Tomukorpi was inducted to debut with a third G.O.R.E. set, 'Antagonistic Anthems', crafted at Steeltrack Studios, arriving in 2005. New bass man Jarmo Perälä enrolled later that year.

Now Is The Time, G.O.R.E. (2001). Intro / Victims Of Me / Symbiotic Death / Bend Down (And Eat The Dust) / Now Is The Time / Burn Me / No Life, No Nothing / Reign Will Fall Down / Raining Blood.

Demo 2002, G.O.R.E. (2002). Pleasure In Hate / Nothing More Than The Truth / Faces / Twisted Society.

Antagonistic Anthems, (2005). 5:1 / Raping Your Soul / You're Beyond Redemption / Aggression To All / Mutilation / The Factory.

GAMMACIDE

ARLINGTON, TX, USA — *Varnam Ponville (vocals), Scott Shelby (guitar), Rick Perry (guitar), Eric Roy (bass).*

Arlington, Texas based "Ecological" Thrash band created by former WARLOCK campaigners guitarist Rick Perry and bassist Eric Roy. Initially the group featured Jamey Milford on drums but his tenure was short as he was soon replaced by Varnam Ponville. GAMMACIDE issued one demo plus a solitary album for Wild Rags 'Victim Of Science' during 1989. Following this release Eric Roy was ousted, going on to form APATHY. For touring purposes Ghames 'Reverend' Jones of Oklahoma band FORTE filled in on bass. A notable local gig would see GAMMACIDE performing at the Starplex Ampitheater, performing on the side stage to the SLAYER, ANTHRAX and MEGADETH 'Clash Of The Titans' bill. However, following a last demo in 1991, the band would splinter during the early 90s.

In 1992 Rick Perry founded the Industrial flavoured PUNCTURE in league with SOLITUDE AETURNUS guitarist John Perez, POST MORTEM STATEMENT sampler Per Nilsson and drummer Larry Moses of Punk acts WHY AM I? And DAYS OF DECISION. Meanwhile vocalist Varnam Ponville and guitarist Scott Shelby relocated to Louisiana to assemble the Doom styled Thrash outfit CAULDRON. They would be joined in this endeavour by bassist Zeb Perkins and drummer Jason Thibodeaux for the ensuing 'For The Love Of Pain' album. Tragically, Eric Roy was murdered in 2001.

GAMMACIDE re-issued their 1990 album 'Victims Of Science' in October of 2005, adding additional material in the form of four tracks from a 1991 demo session plus two brand new songs 'Against The Grain' and 'Vapor Lock'. Getting back into live action the band partnered with two other re-united cult Texan Thrash outfits, RIGOR MORTIS and ROTTING CORPSE, to play at the Axis Club in Fort Worth on 29th October.

VICTIMS OF SCIENCE, Wild Rags WRR016 (1989). Endangered Species / Fossilized / Shock Treatment / Victims Of Science / Gutter Rats / Walking Plague / Chemical Imbalance / Incubus / Observations.

GANG GREEN

BOSTON, MA, USA — *Chris Doherty (vocals / guitar), Fritz Ericson (guitar), Joe Gittleman (bass), Brian Betzger (drums).*

Punk speedcore metallers GANG GREEN were previously known as DRUNKS AGAINST MAD MOTHERS. Created in the early eighties GANG GREEN made themselves instantly recognizable by their adoption of the Budweiser beer logo as their official emblem. Vocalist / guitarist Chris Doherty and drummer Brian Betzger were members of JERRY'S KIDS in between an erratic early period for GANG GREEN but got the band rolling again as a priority in 1985.

GANG GREEN's first outing came with a track on the 1982 compilation album 'Boston Not L.A.' followed swiftly by inclusion on another compilation 'Unsafe At Any Speed'. The band fragmented shortly after with vocalist / guitarist Chris Doherty forming DRUNKS AGAINST MAD MOTHERS. A former GANG GREEN guitarist Tony Nichols formed trad metal outfit MELIAH RAGE. Doherty resurrected GANG GREEN in 1985 releasing the 7" single 'Alcohol'. In early 1986 a four track EP 'P.M.R.C. Sucks' surfaced followed up the same year with the band's first album 'Another Wasted Night'.

The brothers guitarist Chuck Stilpen and bassist Glenn Stilpen departed after the first album and by 1988 had forged an alliance with ex STRAW DOGS members to form MALLETHEAD releasing their self titled debut on Roadrunner Records.

GANG GREEN regrouped adding his JERRY'S KIDS colleague drummer Brian Betzger, bassist Joe Gittleman and guitarist Fritz Ericson.

The band performed a short British tour in late 1987 alongside CIRCLE JERKS. The third album title 'I81B4U' was a crafty sleight at the VAN HALEN album '0U812'.

GANG GREEN gained valuable experience touring as support to DIRTY ROTTEN IMBECILES in Europe. However, Gittleman was to quit before the live album. His position being taken by Josh Pappe, previously with tour mates DIRTY ROTTEN IMBECILES. Gittleman later surfaced with platinum Ska Rockers THE MIGHTY MIGHTY BOSSTONES.

GANG GREEN went their separate ways in the early 90's but would reunite in 1997 for 'Another Case Of Brewtality'.

ANOTHER WASTED NIGHT, Taang! 856418 (1986). Another Wasted Night / Skate To Hell / Last Chance / Alcohol / Have Fun / 19th Hole / Skate Hate / Let's Drink Some Beer / Protect And Serve / Another Bomb / Voices Carry / Sold Out Alabama.

Living Loving Maid, Roadrunner RR 2463-1 (1987). Living Loving Maid / We'll Give It You / Born To Rock.

YOU GOT IT, Roadrunner RR 349591 (1987). Haunted House / We'll Give It To You / Sheet Rock / Ballerina Massacre / Born To Rock / Bomb / L.S.D. / Whoever Said / Party With The Devil / Some Things / The Climb / Sick, Sex, Six.

We'll Give It To You, Roadrunner RR 65470 (1987). We'll Give It To You / Skate Hell.

I81B4U EP, Roadrunner RR 9500-1 (1988). Bartender / Lost Chapter / Rent / Put Her On Top / Cum In U.

OLDER ... BUDWEISER, Emergo EM 9464-2 (1989). Church Of Fun / Just One Bullet / We Can Go / Tear Down The Walls / Flight 911 / Bedroom Of Doom / Casio Jungle / Why Should You Care / I'm Still Young / The Ballad.

CAN'T LIVE WITHOUT IT—LIVE, Roadrunner RR 9380-2 (1990). Let's Drink Some Beer / Bartender / Lost Chapter / We'll Give It To You / We Can Go / Have Fun / Last Chance / Just One Bullet / Born To Rock / Rabies / Voices Carry / Sold Out / Bedroom Of Doom / Bomb / Alcohol.

KING OF BANDS, Roadrunner RR 92542 (1991). Thunder / Alcohol / We'll Give It To You / Bartender / Ballad / Fuck In A / Just One Bullet / Another Wasted Night / Put Her On Top / Church Of Fun / Rub It In Your Face.

LET IT BURN (BECAUSE I DON'T LIVE THERE ANYMORE), Roadrunner (1994).

BACK AND GACKED, Taang TAANG 133CD (1997). Livin' In Oblivion / Time To Pay / You Tucked It To Me / Here To Stay / Accidental Overdose / Deflect And Swerve.

ANOTHER CASE OF BREWTALITY, Taang TAANG 135CD (1997). Eviction Party / Wash The Blood / Break The Bottle / Hole (In The Road) / Death Of The Party / I Missed It / Beach Whistle / Don't You Know / Tricked Into Bed ... Again / Denied / This Job Sucks / Out On The Couch / Weekend Millionaire / I'll Worry About It Monday / Time To Pay / Say Good Buy / Livin' In Oblivion / Accidental Overdose / 6'000 Crucified Slaves / Suspect Device / Penalty Box / To The Point / Here To Stay.

PRE SCHOOL, Taang (1997). Sold Out / Terrorize / Snob / Lie Lie / Don't Know / Rabies / Narrow Mind / Kill A Commie / Have Fun / Selfish.

THE TAANG YEARS, Rhythm Vicar PREACH032CD (2002). 19th Hole / Alcohol / Another Wasted Night / Voices Carry / Protect And Serve / 8 Ball / Evil / Last Chance / Fuckin' A / Tonight We Rock / Sold Out Alabama / Have fun / Crocodile Rock / Hate / Skate To

Hell / Voices Carry / Eviction Party / Wash The Blood / Break The Bottle / Hole (In The Road) / Death Of The Party / I Missed It / Beach Whistle / Don't You Know / Tricked Into Bed … Again / Denied / This Job Sucks / Out On The Couch / Weekend Millionaire / I'll Worry About It Monday / Time To Pay / Say Good Buy / Livin' On Oblivion / Accidental Overdose / 6000 Crucified Slaves / Suspect Device / Penalty Box / To The Point / Here To Stay.

GARGANTUA SOUL

NEW HAVEN, CT, USA — *Kris Keyes (vocals), Marc Amendola (guitar), Jason Bozzi (guitar), Brendan Kane Duff (bass), Tommy Hetz (keyboards), Budzy (turntables), Opus (drums).*

GARGANTUA SOUL, fronted by former BLIND JUSTICE vocalist Kris Keyes, are making serious headway with their groove orientated Thrash Rock style. The band received huge exposure as part of the VH-1 movie 'At Any Cost' where GARGANTUA SOUL performed as the fictional band 'The Strange Divas', getting to perform an original song 'Drive' to a TV audience of millions. The band would also land a valuable appearance at the MP3 stage at the 'Woodstock '99' festival.

To date GARGANTUA SOUL have issued two self financed albums, most recent being the September 2001 'Impact'. Guitarist Jason Bozzi would break away to join DRY KILL LOGIC in the Autumn of 2002.

THE FIRST, THE LAST, THE TRIBE, Wonderdrug Records (2000). The First / Drive / No Oasis / S.O.S. / Prophet Of The Fire / Rat Pack / Angel Of Apocalypse / Cover Me / Hands Of Life / God My / Electrified.

IMPACT, (2001). Calling My America / Isabella Madonna / Far Away / About Earth / Deep Cover / Gargantua / Wolfvision / Rabbit Song / Jacob / Shankaracharya / Dark Knight.

GEHENNAH

KARLSTAD, SWEDEN — *Mr. Violence (vocals), Rob Stringburner (guitar), Ripper Olsson (bass), Hellcop (drums).*

Karlstad's retro-Metal act GEHENNAH made their presence known via two now infamous demos 1993's subtly titled 'Kill' and the following year's 'Brilliant Loud Overlords Of Destruction'. The band had emerged as a quartet comprising vocalist Mr. Violence, guitarist Garm Stringburner, bass player Ronnie 'Ripper' Olsson and Captain Cannibal on the drums, this unit starting out as a VENOM covers act. That same year Olsson had issued a demo, 'Grim Clouds', from his solo Black Metal project GRINNING MOON.

During mid 1994 Cannibal opted out, being superseded by Micke Birgersson (a.k.a. 'Hellcop'). A deal with Primitive Art Records was struck for the 'Hardrocker' album, recorded over the Christmas period of 1994. The release party for this album was held at the Shitheads Motorcycle Club in Karlstad. A promotional video for the title track featured various inebriated members of MORTIIS, SWORDMASTER, VOMITORY, NIFELHEIM and NEZGAROTH. GEHENNAH then launched the 'No Fucking Christmas' EP, in a limited run of 500 golden vinyl copies. This opus was cut with producer Living Skull at studio Prima Volta in Forshaga.

During 1995 Rob Stringburner (as 'Rob Coffinshaker') took a musical diversion with his "vampyric Rock n' roll" project THE COFFINSHAKERS debut demo 'Bad Moon Over Transylvania'. This endeavour went on to publish a swathe of recordings in parallel to GEHENNAH, including the 1996 'Dracula Has Risen From The Grave' EP for Primitive Art and 1999 'We Are The Undead' album.

GEHENNAH's next effort 'King Of The Sidewalk', once again recorded at Prima Volta Studios, saw the band signing up to French Black Metal experts Osmose Productions. Although disowned by the band as rushed and under produced the album made sufficient impact to score a European 1996 tour billed alongside IMPALED NAZARENE and ANGELCORPSE. It would later be revealed that Mr. Violence had consumed so much alcohol during these recording sessions that he completely lost his voice. The band had to wait five weeks for him to recover.

With GEHENNAH gaining ground Primitive Art Records reissued both 'Hardrocker' and 'No Fucking Christmas' in vinyl format although only 100 copies of each surfaced. A split EP with RISE AND SHINE was also recorded. Their next Osmose Productions offering would be the 'Decibel Rebel' album, laid down at Sunlight Studios in August of 1997. Erstwhile MERCILESS frontman Rogga Pettersson aided on backing vocals. A split single shared with RISE AND SHINE found GEHENNAH covering the Country staple 'Jackson', this song seeing Mr. Violence duetting with Josabeth Leidi.

Ronnie 'Ripper' Olson also shares his duties with VOMITORY whilst Birgersson operates with Death Metal act DAWN OF DECAY. Members of GEHENNAH contributed to the SATANARCHY band project of 2000 with personnel from RISE AND SHINE and FURBOWL.

Fans lucky enough to attend GEHENNAH's tenth anniversary gig held in Karlstad on 11th of October 2002 would be given a gig single 'Ten Years Of Fucked Up Behaviour'. Limited to just 50 copies the EP comprised tracks from the 'Kill' demo, a new song 'Bleed You Bastards' and a cover version of G.G. ALLIN's 'Drink, Fight And Fuck'.

Rob Stringburner, as ROB COFFINSHAKER, released a brace of solo 7" singles, 'Live At The Cemetery' in 2002 and 'Fairytales From The Dungeon' the following year.

HARD ROCKER, Primitive Art PAR004 (1995). Hardrocker / Skeletons In Leather / Say Hello To Mr. Fist / Brilliant Loud Overlords Of Destruction / Winter Of War / Beerzerk / I Am The Wolf / Blood Metal / Crucifucked / Bomb Raid Over Paradise / The House / Gehennah / Piss Off I'm Drinking / Psycho Slut.

No Fucking Christmas EP, Primitive Art PAR005 (1995). Satanclaws / Merry Shitmas.

KING OF THE SIDEWALK, Osmose OPCD 046 (1996). Rock n' Roll Patrol / Hellstorm / Bitch With A Bulletbelt / King Of The Sidewalk / (You're The) Devil In Disguise / Bang Your Heads For Satan / Chickenrace / Tough Guys Don't Look Good / Saturdaynight Blasphemer / Bulldozer / Demolition Team.

World Domination II EP, Osmose Productions (1997). Rock n' Roll Patrol / Once In A Lifetime Chance.

DECIBEL REBEL, Osmose OPCD 065 (1998). Beat That Poser Down / Six Pack Queen / Hangover / Decibel Rebel / Hellhole Bar / Get Out Of My Way / Under The Table Again / Street Metal Gangfighters / Rocking Through The Kill / 666, Drunks And Rock n' Roll / I Fucked Your Mom / We Love Alcohol.

Rise And Shine EP, Osmose Productions (1999) (Split single with RISE AND SHINE). Jackson.

10 Years of Fucked Up Behaviour EP, Bad Taste Entertainment HQ (2003) (Limited edition 50 copies). Intro / Osculum Obscenum / Burning Strings / Bleed You Bastards / Drink, Fight And Fuck.

GENETIC WISDOM

WIERDEN, HOLLAND — *Mike Lucarelli (vocals), Peter Slootbeck (guitar), Ralph Christian Roelvink (guitar), Gerrit Knol (bass), Ronny Scholten (drums).*

The original 1990 line-up of Wierden based Thrashers GENETIC WISDOM comprised of guitarists Ralph Roelvink and GJ Aaltink, vocalist Dennuz Bos and ex-SACROSANCT drummer Ronny Scholten. This line-up recorded the 'Genetic Wisdom' demo prior to Aaltink being superseded by Peter Slootbeck and the band bringing in former DESECRATOR bassist Bo Brinkman. A further demo entitled 'Trivial Destiny' was released before the band landed a deal with Mascot Records.

Upon release of the debut album, The Fear Dimension' in 1992 for Mascot Records, Bos was asked to leave and in came ex-SACROSANCT vocalist Mike Lucarelli.

1993's 'Humanity On Parole' album featured guest sessions by GOREFEST vocalist Jan Chris De Koeyer and CREEPMIME's Andy Judd. Brinkman was replaced by bassist Ger Knol after the album launch.

Former GENETIC WISDOM guitarist Ralph Roelvink would fill in as temporary bassist for CALLENISH CIRCLE's October 2003 'Bonded By Meta' European tour. In early 2006 Slootbeek, Scholten and Roelvink formulated WHY SHE KILLS, fronted by two female singers vocalists Janneke van Berkel and Imke Kuipers. Bassist Gerrit Knol later joined this act.

Trivial Destiny, (1991). Perseverance Kill The Game / Captured In The Past / Inside The Triangle / Unfortunate Childhood / Visual Fast Food / Quest For The Unknown / Radical Hatred.

THE FEAR DIMENSION, Mascot M7002-2 (1992). Perseverance Kills The Game / Why Don't You? / Unfortunate Childhood / Psycho Love / Afraid Of Life / Inside The Triangle (Of Death) / Visual Fastfood / Radical Hatred.

HUMANITY ON PAROLE, Mascot M7008-2 (1993). Pain / Too Good To Be True / Forced / Get Out / Intentions Rule The World / Dedicated / Mirror Images / Don't Fight The Feeling / Used To It / Dragons To Slay / Face The Facts.

GENOCIDE

JAPAN — *Toshihiro Takeuchi (vocals), Kouichi Kawakami (guitar), Kazuo Amaya (guitar), Hiroki Motono (bass), Takeshi Hattori (drums).*

Cult Japanese Thrash act GENOCIDE date back to 1979, formed when vocalist Toshihiro Takeuchi and guitarist Kazuo Amaya left their former band SHOCK. The band's line up in its formative years was fluid but the introduction of bassist Kawasaki and drummer Nishimoto in 1980 provided some stability. In 1982 GENOCIDE pulled in Matsui on second guitar but he would decamp in the Autumn of 1983, being replaced by Kouichi Kawakami.

A demo tape recorded with this line up secured a recording contract with the US based King Klassic label in 1986. Upon completion of recording Hiroki Motono of HELLBOUND repute took charge of the bass position. Unfortunately the debut album 'Black Sanctuary' was heavily delayed and did not hit the stores until 1988. GENOCIDE folded sometime in 1990.

The band, now including Takeshi Hattori on drums, regrouped for a live show in Osaka during 1999. 'The Rites' album emerged in 2001 through Satanic Lust Records.

BLACK SANCTUARY, King Klassic KKR-1004 (1988). Doomsday / A Bullet In The Wrong Heart / Last Confusion / Landscape Of Life / Black Sanctuary / Midnight (Come She Will) / Silent Falling / Living Legend / Gibakurai.

THE RITES, Satanic Lust KSL-01 (2001). SE: Profondo Rosso / Gibakurei / Doomsday / A Bullet In Wrong Heart / Ibitsu / Midnight (Come She Will) / Living Legend / Gibakurei / Doomsday / A Bullet In Wrong Heart / Shock You / Living Legend.

GLACIAL FEAR

ITALY — *Nicola Bavaro (vocals), Gianluca Molè (guitar), Tato (bass), Enzo Rotondaro (drums).*

Neo Thrashers GLACIAL FEAR came into being during December of 1992 as a trio of vocalist / bassist Andrea Rizzato, guitarist Gianluca Molè and drummer Danilo Citriniti. After some initial demo work the formation debuted with a self financed single 'Secrets At The Steam Forest' in 1994. Subsequently Gianluka Anastasi, former member of GRANMA MONKEY, took command of the drums whilst the oddly sobriqueted 'Deathhead' enrolled as keyboard player for the 'Atlasphere: The Burning Circle' release.

By the time GLACIAL FEAR had signed to Nocturnal Music for the 'Frames' album they had made the transition from straightforward Death Metal to what they termed as "Cyberthrash". Losing both Anastasi and Deathhead the band regrouped with the addition of singer Nicola Bavaro of CRUENTUS and SCHIZO repute with SOUND PRESSURE LEVEL drummer Enzo Rotondaro.

For the 'Fetish Parade' album GLACIAL FEAR pulled in THE UNDERTAKERS vocalist Enrico Giannone to aid on guest vocals for two tracks. However, upon completion of recording Rizzato ended his eight year tenure with the band and duly opted out.

Gianluca Molè released a 1999 album from his Black Metal side concern LUPERCALIA.

Secrets At The Steam Forest, Independent (1994). Steamy Deformities / Dawn Of Desolation / Supremacy Of Horror.

ATLASPHERE: THE BURNING CIRCLE, Nosferatu (1995). Antarctica / Monolith / Hall Of Marvel / Mirrors In The Void.

FRAMES, Nocturnal Music NMCD 003 (1997). In The Absolute Deep Blue Sea / Numb / Frames / Zoom / Theocratic Stubborn / Third Millenium / Look Around / Underworld / Garden Of Sigth.

PROMO, Explorers (1999). Space 1999 / Electronic N-ice Eyes / Misanthropic Hacker.

FETISH PARADE, Negatron (2000). The Fortress / Electronic N-ice Eyes / Alienatheist / Subhuman Mutation / Antartica / Misanthropic Hacker / Spacecraft / Installation Madness / Fetish Parade.

Delta 9—Greenpower!, Independent (2002).

GLADIATOR

ALEKŠINCE, SLOVAKIA — *Miko Hladk´y (vocals / guitar), Marós Hladk´y (guitar), Dusan Hladk´y (bass), Peter Slamečka (keyboards), Juro Babulic (drums).*

GLADIATOR is a Alekšince, Nita based Hard Rock band founded during 1989. First album would be the heavily Thrash orientated 'Designation' set released by Zeras Records in January 1992. Škvrna Records put out the 1993 follow up 'Made Of Pain', this outing scoring GLADIATOR valuable radio play with the track 'My World'. However, the band undertook a radical change in musical direction to an almost Grunge stance with the album 'Third Eye'. The band switched to major label BMG Ariola for 1996's 'Dogstime' opus. GLADIATOR continued in their trend towards mainstream Rock with successive albums. A 2002 compilation included a cover version of the ROLLING STONES '(I Can't Get No) Satisfaction'.

GLADIATOR switched to Universal Records for the 2002 'Èrepy' album. The GLADIATOR credited guitarist Livo and keyboard player Peter Slamečka performed with Female Gothic Doom artist SNOVENNE during 2004.

DESIGNATION, Zeras (1992). Over The Oversight (Intro) / Profitable Losses / Bastard Death / Mortal Glare / Designation / Sorrow / Morbid Murdering / Bloody Property / Stinking Masses / Useless Child.

MADE OF PAIN, Škvrna (1993). Made Of Pain / Blood / Sound Of Deep Silence / Warsouls / Creator Of Hell / No Fate / Debtor Of Rest / My World / Your World / For All Gods.

THIRD EYE, Škvrna (1994). Third Eye / Keep The Face / Free / Sweat Fruit / One More Terminally / In Your Head / Alone / Cosmosrose / My Friend / Mad Big Pig / Chaghaza'l / To My God.

DOGSTIME, BMG Ariola (1996). Dogstime / Prayer / Sweet Little Mouse / Author Knows My Rhythm / Liar / Pearl World / Cabaret / Heaven / Sick Day / Sonbirth / Epicure / Be My Fate.

LEGAL DRUG, BMG Ariola (1997). Free House / ... And What About A Friend? / Our Way / Society / You Don't Mind / Break The Wall / Free Me / You (Secret Flower's In My Soul) / Enemy In Me / Body Candle Lights / Price Of You / Shine For People / Touch Me / Slovenská.

VIEM, KDE BOH SPI, BMG Ariola (1999). Raz Tam V Ulièkách / Divoký Dáži / Viem, Kde Boh Spí / Lennon Dýcha / Prš So Mnou / Nebeská Linka / Dievèatko / Tamara / S Hlavou Opät V Tráve / Kým Nie Si Sám / Za Pár Dní Pochopíš / Ovocný Sad.

BABYLON HOTEL, BMG Ariola (2000). Babylon Hotel / Kúpim Si Pekný Deò / Láska / Pieseò Èiernych Vrán / Z Plných Plúc / Pesnièka O Medulienke / Pod Èiernu Zem / Okno Z Prstov / Obyèajný Chalan / Izba è. 6 / Dnes Je Skvelý Deò.

ÈREPY, Universal (2002). Vzbura / Èrepy / Hluchý Nemý Slepý / Cez Tvoje Oèi / Ploty / Viac fa Tu Niet / Uväznený V Slze / Kameèom / Blázon / V Uliciach Bez Mena / Noc S Frankiem / Pravda Padá.

CESTA DO NEBA, Universal (2004). Nemôžem Dýchať / Cesta Do Neba / Keď Sa Láska Podarí / Čo Ak ... / Len S Tebou Ma Baví Svet / Dobrý Vzduch / Čerešne / Najlepšie Ako Viem / Čo Sa Stalo S Nami? / Budem Pri Tebe Stáť / Vinný / Vždy Sa Kvôli Niekomu Oplatí Žiť / Život Pred Sebou.

GOATSODOMIZER

UPPSALA, SWEDEN — *Bomber (vocals / bass), Old Goat (vocals), Demonizer (guitar), Bonecrusher (drums).*

"Graveyard Metal" Thrashers GOATSODOMIZER issued the demos 'This Mean War' in 2001 and 'Rapin' My Graveyard' during 2002. The group had been forged in Uppsala during 1995 under the original handle of GOATSODOMIZER AND THE RAPED VIRGINS and comprising vocalist / guitarist Demonizer, bassist Sordid and drummer Old Goat. However, according to the band, Sordid was sacked due to "illegal activity". Bomber duly took over bass guitar for the band's inaugural live performance in December 1997. GOATSODOMIZER quickly gained a reputation on the live front for their onstage arsenal being enhanced by fire breathing women and goat skull props.

The band entered a period of activity but bounced back in 1999, now seeing Bomber handling lead vocals. In late 2000 the group cut the 'This Means War' demo. A further collection of tracks, including a rendition of MOTÖRHEAD's 'Going To Brazil', was recorded for a proposed split 7" in alliance with GENOCRUSH FEROX, but this never transpired. Following an April 2001 gig at Kafé 44 in Stockholm with REGURGITATE, SCURVY and DEATHFORCE Old Goat relinquished the drum stool. Bonecrusher of SADOCRUSH stepped up as replacement for the 'Rapin' My Graveyard' sessions.

During December 2005 GOATSODOMIZER entered Blueflame Productions Studio to commence recording their debut album for Last Entertainment Productions.

GOATSODOMIZER includes keyboard player FREDRIK KLINGWALL, associated with IN GREY, RISING SHADOWS, ANIMA MORTE and Death Metal act FLAGELLATION. Klingwall joined Progressive Metal band LOCH VOSTOK in December 2005 and issued Industrial solo album 'Entrance' in 2006. That same year both bassist Per Lindström and Fredrik Klingwall also joined forces with MACHINERY.

Raping My Graveyard, Goatsodomizer (2001). Raping My Graveyard / Sodomized Til Death / Die Screaming.

GOD FORBID

NEW BRUNSWICK, NJ, USA — *Bryon Davis (vocals), Doc Coyle (guitar), Dallas Coyle (guitar), John Outcalt (bass), Corey Pierce (drums).*

New Brunswick, New Jersey's New Wave of American Heavy Metal band GOD FORBID, founded by drummer Corey Pierce and ex-FEINT 13 guitarist Dallas Coyle issued early product on the independent 9 Volt label. The band had evolved from its earlier inception as MANIFEST DESTINY through to IN-SALUBRIOUS before settling on GOD FORBID. During May 1997 GOD FORBID were joined by vocalist Bryon Davis and in September of the same year by erstwhile WOMB bassist John 'Beeker' Outcalt. Guitarist Doc Coyle would deputize on a temporary basis for AS DARKNESS FALLS in 1998. 9 Volt issued the 'Out Of Misery' EP in September 1998.

Upon signing to German concern Century Media, just after the New Jersey 'Metalfest' appearance, for the highly praised April 2001 'Determination' album, GOD FORBID upped their American touring plans appearing with AMEN and SHADOWS FALL for a March tour then hooking up with the NEVERMORE, OPETH and CHILDREN OF BODOM dates in April. Touring in Britain would be supported by LABRAT and CO-EXIST.

In September 2001 the band's 'Out Of Misery' EP would benefit from a re-release to capitalise on the band's burgeoning status, adding bonus live tracks, including a take on SEPULTURA's 'Propaganda', recorded at New York's infamous CBGB's club. GOD FORBID toured the States in alliance with HATEBREED, CONVERGE and POISON THE WELL and then promptly announced another bout of North American touring, commencing 16th January 2002, in alliance with headliners GWAR and SOILENT GREEN. Further shows would be scheduled with SHADOWS FALL and KILLSWITCH ENGAGE but the band subsequently withdrew from these gigs in order to place their efforts towards songwriting.

In 2003 the band cut a rendition of the GUNS N' ROSES track 'Out Ta Get Me', with producer Chris Pearce, for use on a Law Of Inertia tribute album. Also emerging would be a re-press of GOD FORBID's long out of print debut album 'Reject The Sickness', released via the band's own PR Records label. The band got back into tour mode in August, headlining US dates over ATREYU, DARKEST HOUR and UNDEROATH. The group would be back on the road in October for the five week 'Headbanger's Ball' dates alongside KILLSWITCH ENGAGE, SHADOWS FALL, UNEARTH and LAMB OF GOD. The band gave themselves no respite, thereafter hopping onto the MUSHROOMHEAD national tour into November. The band resumed live activity in 2004, headlining a February run of US dates with running mates WALLS OF JERICHO, BLOOD HAS BEEN SHED and FULL BLOWN CHAOS.

In an unexpected move, GOD FORBID donated their rendition of 'Out Ta Get Me' to the GUNS N' ROSES tribute album 'Bring You To Your Knees' released by Inertia Records in March. The next road trek was set to be a month's duration co-headline tour in June of 2004 with label mates KILLSWITCH ENGAGE, CHIMAIRA and SHADOWS FALL upfront of an appearance at the mammoth 'Ozzfest' touring festival headlined by BLACK SABBATH, JUDAS PRIEST and SLAYER. A brief burst of September headline gigs, supported by A LIFE ONCE LOST, NORMA JEAN and THE RED CHORD, would be filmed by director Zach Merck for a promotional video.

The band allied with SOULFLY and DEATH BY STEREO for North American shows in March 2005, UK headline shows then extended live work into April and May with headliners supported by CALIBAN, IT DIES TODAY and FULL BLOWN CHAOS. A compilation inclusion of note would be the track 'Soul Engraved' featured on the 'Code Red' album, an exclusive collection given to US Marine Corps soldiers active duty in the Middle East.

Just one day after completion of touring, GOD FORBID commenced work on a new album 'IV: Constitution Of Treason' in May, utilising the services of Jason Suecof at Audiohammer Studios in Florida and Eric Rachel at Trax East in New Jersey. Gigs in July had the band partnered with FULL BLOWN CHAOS and HIMSA. 'IV: Constitution Of Treason' sold over 8'300 copies in its first week of sale to debut at no. 119 on the US Billboard charts.

The band then announced further US dates alongside MESHUGGAH, THE HAUNTED and MNEMIC throughout October. Roadwork continued apace in November as the group toured Europe traversing Holland, the UK, France, Belgium, Spain, Germany, Austria, Switzerland, Denmark and Sweden in union with MANNTIS and THE HAUNTED. 2006 was opened up with US road work throughout January aligned with ANTHRAX, MANNTIS and SWORN ENEMY. March had the band scheduled for 'The Crusade III: Ascend Above The Ashes' concerts in the UK and Ireland alongside TRIVIUM and BLOODSIMPLE. The band put in a significant appearance at the GUNS N' ROSES headlined 'Download' festival in Castle Donington, UK on June 11th.

GOD FORBID headed up the UK and European "Hell On Earth" tour in September and October. Joining them would be Swiss act CATARACT, Germany's MAROON, FULL BLOWN CHAOS, PURIFIED IN BLOOD from Norway and A PERFECT MURDER. December 2006 had the band aligned with PROTEST THE HERO and THE HUMAN ABSTRACT for a run of shows across Canada.

2007 US dates commenced on January 4th at the First Unitarian Church in Philadelphia, Pennsylvania with a first headlining leg backed by GOATWHORE, MNEMIC, THE HUMAN

ABSTRACT and ARSIS. On February 2nd BYZANTINE joined this touring entourage in the stead of THE HUMAN ABSTRACT. GOD FORBID toured Australia, New Zealand, Mexico, Puerto Rico and Alaska, all for the first time, in March. HATEBREED teamed up with GOD FORBID, EVERGREEN TERRACE, THE ACACIA STRAIN and AFTER THE BURIAL for the North American "Monsters Of Mayhem II Tour" commencing mid-May.

Out Of Misery EP, 9 Volt 9V004 (1998). Mind Eraser / Habeeber / Madman / Nosferatu / Inside.
REJECT THE SICKNESS, 9 Volt 9V008 (1999). Amendment / Reject The Sickness / N2 / No Sympathy / Assed Out / Ashes Of Humanity (Regret) / Dark Waters / Heartless / Weather The Storm / The Century Fades.
DETERMINATION, Century Media 8066-2 (2001). Dawn Of The New Millennium / Nothing / Broken Promise / Divide My Destiny / Network / Wicked / Determination Part I / Determination Part II / Go Your Own Way / God's Last Gift / A Reflection Of The Past / Dead Words On Deaf Ears.
OUT OF MISERY, We Put Out 2 (2001). N2 / Mind Eraser / Habeeber / Madman / Nosferatu / Inside / No Sympathy (Live) / N2 (Live) / Reject The Sickness (Live) / Amendment (Live) / Propaganda (Live).
GONE FOREVER, Century Media 8166-2 (2004). Force-Fed / Anti-Hero / Better Days / Precious Lie / Washed Out World / Living Nightmare / Soul Engraved / Gone Forever / Judge The Blood.
Better Days, Century Media 8150-2 (2004). Better Days / Allegiance / Wicked (Demo) / Reject The Sickness / Mind Eraser.
GONE FOREVER, Toy's Factory TFCK-87350 (2004) (Japanese release). Force-Fed / Anti-Hero / Better Days / Precious Lie / Washed Out World / Living Nightmare / Soul Engraved / Gone Forever / Judge The Blood / Allegiance / Mind Eraser.
GONE FOREVER (LIMITED TOUR EDITION), Century Media 8166-0 (2004). Force-Fed / Anti-Hero / Better Days / Precious Lie / Washed Out World / Living Nightmare / Soul Engraved / Gone Forever / Judge The Blood / Allegiance / Wicked (Demo) / Reject The Sickness / Mind Eraser / Anti-Hero (Video) / Better Days (Video).
IV: Constitution Of Treason (Two-Song Sampler), Century Media (2005) (Promotion release). Chains Of Humanity / The End Of The World (Edit).
IV: CONSTITUTION OF TREASON, Century Media 8266-2 (2005). The End Of The World / Chains Of Humanity / Into The Wasteland / The Lonely Dead / Divinity / Under This Flag / To The Fallen Hero / Welcome To The Apocalypse (Preamble) / Constitution Of Treason / Crucify Your Beliefs.
IV: CONSTITUTION OF TREASON, Toy's Factory TFCK-87397 (2005) (Japanese release). The End Of The World / Chains Of Humanity / Into The Wasteland / The Lonely Dead / Divinity / Under This Flag / To The Fallen Hero / Welcome To The Apocalypse (Preamble) / Constitution Of Treason / Crucify Your Beliefs / We Are No More.
To The Fallen Hero, Century Media (2006) (Limited tour single). To The Fallen Hero / The End Of The World / Antihero / Precious Life / To The Fallen Hero (Video) / The End Of The World (Video).

GODSEND

NOTTINGHAM, NOTTINGHAMSHIRE, UK — *Rob Reid (vocals), Andy Sneap (guitar), Wayne Banks (bass), Mole (drums).*

Nottingham trad Thrash Metal band, GODSEND featured ex SABBAT men Andy Sneap and Wayne Banks, former SLEEZEPATROL drummer, Mole (real name Ian Etheridge) and ex-BANGKOK SHAKES singer Rob Reid. GODSEND released the 'Heavier Than A Death In The Family' four track demo in 1993 (comprising 'Self Sacrifice', 'Dressed In Skin', 'Realms' and 'Mind Flying', the group added new bassist Jason Birnie in early 1995 and recorded a new four track demo titled 'When Man Plays God'.

GODSEND broke up in 1996 despite offers of record deals. Mole later sessioned for WRAITH. Sneap continued an engineering and production career, gaining a credit on the 1996 release from DEARLY BEHEADED and later STUCK MOJO. Sneap is now a highly rated producer much in demand as well as treading the boards on occasion with Spoof Metal band FOZZY.

By 1998 Mole had his own tribute act on the circuit titled MOLETALLICA. Wayne Banks joined BLAZE in April of 2003 and would also join the touring line up of BRAZEN ABBOT. By

GODSEND (pic: Mick Clarke)

2006 singer Rob Reid was playing the part of "Ozzy Oddbin" in BLACK SABBATH tribute band SACK SABBATH.
GODSEND, Stay Free STAY 006CD (1994).

GOOSEFLESH

TROLLHÄTTAN, SWEDEN — *Kristian Lampila (vocals / guitar), Tommy Scalisi Svensson (guitar), Robert Hakemo (bass), Lars Berger (drums).*

Trollhättan based Crossover Metal band forged by RAT SALAD bassist Micael Larsson and guitarist Tommy Scalisi Svensson as a side project to their priority act in 1995. Replacing Larsson with Robert Hakemo, GOOSEFLESH released the demos 'The Wraith' and 'Glow' in 1996 and 'Welcome To The Suffer Age' in 1997. These latter recordings would subsequently see commercial release as an EP issued through the Spanish Goldtrack label. The band submitted their rendition of 'Slave New World' to the SEPULTURA tribute album "Sepultural Feast". The full length 'Chemical Garden' album was recorded originally for the German High Gain label but the closure of this label necessitated the securing of fresh deals. The record finally surfaced in Europe through Digital Dimension and in Japan via Dolphin Entertainment.

GOOSEFLESH folded in 2001 with vocalist Kristian Lampila and bassist Robert Hakemo founding MINDSNARE. Svensson and drummer Lars Berger founded ELECTRIC EARTH. Ex-bassist Micael Larsson would be back on the circuit with BLACK SABBATH tribute band SABBRA CADABRA.

Hakemo joined GARDENIAN in early 2003. In early 2004 the bassist was part of a band collaboration entitled KEROZENE, a union between guitarist Niclas Engelin, of SARCAZM, PASSENGER, GARDENIAN and IN FLAMES repute, drummer Patrik J. Sten, also of PASSENGER and an ex-TRANSPORT LEAGUE member, along with vocalist Mikael Skager. In August 2006 Robert Hakemo joined M.A.N.

Welcome To Suffer Age, Goldtrack (1998). Suffer Age / Blinded / Killing Stone / Seeds Of Terror / Fine Tuned War Machine.
CHEMICAL GARDEN, High Gain 0055332HGR (1999). Burning Soul / Godbreed / Cut That Never Heals / Thin Skinned Jesus / Wraith / The Syndicate / Art Of Treachery / Controller / Sore Throat / Voices / Denial / Absence.

GRAVE DIGGER

GLADBECK, GERMANY — *Chris Boltondahl (vocals), Peter Masson (guitar), Willi Lackman (bass), Albert Eckardt (drums).*

GRAVE DIGGER are true survivors of the early eighties German Thrash Metal boom. Whilst the band was lumped in with the emerging Thrash acts of the day for convenience sake by the Rock media, particularly in the UK, GRAVE DIGGER was in fact always a more sophisticated musical act. Once the Thrash phenomenon had died down GRAVE DIGGER, after a disastrous wayward period of confusion billed as DIGGER, re-invented themselves as an epic, conceptually orientated complex Heavy Metal band, finding renewed commercial fortune in the process.

GRAVE DIGGER formed in November 1980 in Gladbeck and their debut album, 'Heavy Metal Breakdown', with keyboard contributions from Dietmar Dillhardt, sold more than 40,000 copies in Europe, although the band had initially made their recording debut supplying two tracks to the 'Rock From Hell' compilation album.

The original line-up of the band comprised of vocalist / guitarist Peter Masson, bassist Chris Boltendahl and drummer Lutz Schmelzer, a trio that remained stable until 1982 when Schmelzer left and was replaced by Philipp Seibel. The following year a decision was taken for Masson to concentrate on guitar duties and allowing Boltendahl to take over the microphone.

GRAVE DIGGER actually split in mid-1983 with Boltendahl joining CHALLENGER, which featured Willi Lackmann on bass and Albert Eckardt on the drums. However, Noise offered GRAVE DIGGER, a band that technically didn't exist at the time, a deal, so the band regrouped with previous members Boltendahl on lead vocals and Masson on guitar being joined by Lackmann and Eckardt in the new-look outfit to record the 'Heavy Metal Breakdown' debut album.

Alongside Lackmann, one Rene T. Bone (real name René Teichgräber) is credited for playing bass on GRAVE DIGGER's second album, 1985's 'Witch Hunter', a brand new bassist, C.F. Brank had joined the band by the time Noise released the record. Indeed, bass duties were actually undertaken by both Boltendahl and Masson on the record as they had fired Teichmann during recording in March 1985.

GRAVE DIGGER's third album, 'War Games', appeared in 1986 it was something of a disappointment to all concerned in terms of sales and, upon completion of gigs across Europe packaged with CELTIC FROST and HELLOWEEN, led to the departure of Masson from the ranks. Opting to go in a more commercial direction with new guitarist Uwe Lulis in tow the German outfit adopted the new title of DIGGER and recorded an album titled, rather misleadingly in hindsight, 'Stronger Than Ever'. Needless to say, the record flopped and the group split.

In the wake of the DIGGER disaster bassist Brank hooked up with S.A.D.O. whilst Lulis and Boltendahl opted to stay together and formed HAWAII with drummer Jochen Börner and bassist Rainer Bandzus, although the project never got beyond the demo stage.

During 1991 Boltendahl decided to reform GRAVE DIGGER, the new line-up featuring Boltendahl, Uwe Lulis, bassist Tomi Göttlich, ex-ASGARD and IRON ANGEL, and drummer Peter Breitenbach. This group released a four-track promo CD and 1993's 'The Reaper'. However, prior to cutting the album Breitenbach was out, joining WARHEAD, in favour of the well travelled Jörg Michael, ex-AVENGER, MEKONG DELTA, RAGE and HEADHUNTER.

GRAVE DIGGER recorded the six track EP 'Symphony Of Death' before Michael joined RUNNING WILD and new drummer Frank Ulrich, a veteran of MENDACIOUS MESSIAH, X WILD, LIVING DEATH and VANIZE, teamed up with the Gladbeck crew. Ulrich's tenure with the band was to be relatively brief. Although he played on 1995's 'Heart Of Darkness' album he encountered personal differences with his band mates and departed, being succeeded by former CAPRICORN and WALLOP drummer Stefan Arnold. Ulrich joined X WILD for their third album 'Savage Land'. GRAVE DIGGER played Germany in June 1995 on a touring festival billed the 'Summer Metal Meetings' including ICED EARTH, GAMMA RAY, GLENMORE, RUNNING WILD and RAGE

Returning to action with the conceptual 'Tunes Of War' record in 1996 the band toured Germany in 1997 with support from SINNER, the record having enjoyed several weeks in the loftier regions of the German national charts. GRAVE DIGGER's return to form came courtesy of 'Tunes Of War's ambitious concept. A conceptual piece based upon Scottish history and liberal in its use of that tried and trusted Heavy Metal instrument the bagpipes. The band also novelly invited the German Rock media on a trip through the ancient battlefields of Scotland.

GRAVE DIGGER stuck to the historical theme for 1998's 'Knights Of The Cross', an album based on the exploits of the knights Templar, this album providing further momentum to their revival. Japanese variants of the album saw bonus tracks in covers of BLACK SABBATH's 'Children Of The Grave' and RAINBOW's 'Kill The King'. Despite this welcome reversal of fortunes the man behind the revival Tomi Göttlich decamped and was superseded by ex RUNNING WILD, X WILD and CROSSROADS man Jens Becker.

Touring found the band on the road in Europe with IRON SAVIOUR and American act IMAGIKA. Both Boltendahl and Lulis would both guest on IMAGIKA's '... And So It Burns' album.

GRAVE DIGGER toured Germany in January of 2000 supported by Italians WHITE SKULL. Lulis departed toward the end of the year being swiftly replaced by Manni Schmidt, previously with RAGE. GRAVE DIGGER's tenth studio album, the mediaeval themed 'Excalibur', would once again find the band with a strong presence in the national album charts, giving the band their highest ever placing in Germany at no.21. The band this time taking journalists by bus from Germany to Stonehenge and Tintagel castle for the pre-launch listening party. A limited digi-pack run of this outing would include an exclusive track 'Black Cat' whilst the Japanese release, in keeping with tradition, held one more bonus cut namely a cover of IRON MAIDEN's 'Running Free'. GRAVE DIGGER would delve into cover territory once more in late 2001 cutting a version of LED ZEPPELIN's 'No Quarter'. This latter track was to resurface on the 2002 Locomotive Music LED ZEPPELIN tribute album 'The Metal Zeppelin—The Music Remains The Same'. The band's set at the annual 'Wacken Open Air' in Germany would see the light of day as the 2002 live album 'Tunes Of Wacken'.

GRAVE DIGGER, together with support from BRAINSTORM, undertook European touring to kick off 2002. However, following January dates in Germany and shows in Southern Europe the band's projected Belgian and Dutch gigs for March would be cancelled as Schmidt was incapacitated with a virus the guitarist had caught whilst on the Iberian continent.

Also in March of 2002 ex-members guitarist Uwe Lulis and bassist Tomi Göttlich returned to the fore with the adventurous conceptually based REBELLION, taking on no less than the bard's 'Macbeth' as the theme for their opening shot 'Shakespeare's MacBeth—A Tragedy In Steel'. Joining the ex-GRAVE DIGGER personnel for REBELLION would be WARHEAD frontman Björn Eilen on second guitar, drummer Randy Black from Canadian Thrashers ANNIHILATOR and vocalist Michael Seifert from Osnabruck acts BLACK DESTINY and XIRON. GRAVE DIGGER would set to work on yet another conceptual album for 2002 release as well as an autobiography of the band. A first for the act came in November, GRAVE DIGGER's first gig in Moscow at the 4'500 capacity Luzhniki Small Sport Hall co-headlining with BLAZE.

GRAVE DIGGER plunged deep into ancient German folklore as the subject of their 2003 studio album 'Rheingold', basing their by now expected conceptual story upon Richard Wagner's Nibelungs saga. The band united with SYMPHORCE and WIZARD for European shows in January of 2004. Gearing back into recording mode, the group entered Principal Studios in Münster during September to record 'The Last Supper', projecting into 2005 by announcing February tour dates utilising ASTRAL

GRAVE DIGGER

DOORS and STORMHAMMER as support act. In keeping with a by now established tradition, GRAVE DIGGER's latest work proved to be conceptually hot on the heels of a blockbuster movie, namely this time 'The Passion Of The Christ'. Putting a new spin on an old convention, the three CD box set 'Das Hörbuch' included not only the expected career retrospective in song form but also spoken passages from Chris Boltendahl.

In May 2006 GRAVE DIGGER contracted a long-term deal with the Spanish record label Locomotive Records. The band entered Principal Studios in Münster on August 14th to commence recording the 'Liberty Or Death' album. In September GRAVE DIGGER launched the 'Yesterday' EO, this headed up by a re-recording of the song from their first album plus exclusive song 'The Reaper's Dance' and a cover version of LED ZEPPELIN's 'No Quarter'. In January 2007 'Liberty Or Death' entered the German Media Control chart at number 30.

HEAVY METAL BREAKDOWN, Noise N007-2 (1984). Headbanging Man / Heavy Metal Breakdown / Back From The War / Yesterday / We Wanna Rock You / Legion Of The Lost / Tyrant / 2000 Lightyears From Home / Heart Attack.

HEAVY METAL BREAKDOWN, Megaforce MRI 869 (1984) (LP release). Headbanging Man / We Wanna Rock You / Back From War / Stormin' The Brain / Heavy Metal Breakdown / Tyrant / Shoot Her Down / Legion Of The Lost / Heart Attack / Yesterday.

HEAVY METAL BREAKDOWN, Megaforce MRIT 869 (1984) (Cassette release). Headbanging Man / We Wanna Rock You / Back From War / Stormin' The Brain / Heavy Metal Breakdown / Tyrant / Shoot Her Down / Legion Of The Lost / Heart Attack / Yesterday / 2000 Lightyears From Home.

Shoot Her Down, Noise N0016 (1984). Shoot Her Down / Storming The Brain / We Wanna Rock You.

WITCH HUNTER, Noise N0020 (1985). Witch Hunter / Nightdrifter / Get Ready For Power / Love Is A Game / Get Away / Fight For Freedom / School's Out / Friends Of Mine / Here I Stand.

WITCH HUNTER, Megaforce MRI 1169 (1985) (USA release). Shine On / Witch Hunter / Night Drifter / Get Ready For Power / Tears Of Blood / Didn't Kill The Children / Get Away / Fight For Freedom / Here I Stand / Friends Of Mine.

WAR GAMES, Noise N0034 (1986). Keep On Rockin' / Heaven Can Wait / Fire In Your Eyes / Let Your Heads Roll / Love Is Breaking My Heart / Paradise / (Enola Gay) Drop The Bomb / Fallout / Playin Fools / The End.

Ride On, Great Unlimited Noises (1993) (Promotion release). Ride On / Spy Of Mason / Shadows Of A Moonless Night / Fight The Fight.

THE REAPER, Great Unlimited Noises GUN 032 (1993). Tribute To Death / The Reaper / Ride On / Shadows Of A Moonless Night / Play Your Game (And Kill) / Wedding Day / Spy Of Mas'On / Under My Flag / Fight The Fight / Legion Of The Lost (Part II) / And The Devil Plays Piano / Ruler Mr H. / The Madness Continues.

SYMPHONY OF DEATH, Great Unlimited Noises GUN 039 (1994). Intro / Symphony Of Death / Back To The Roots / House Of Horror / Shout It Out / World Of Fools / Wild And Dangerous.

HEART OF DARKNESS, Great Unlimited Noises GUN 060 (1995) (BMG 74321 24746-2). Tears Of Madness / Shadowmaker / The Grave Dancer / Demon's Day / Warchild / Heart Of Darkness / Hate / Circle Of Witches / Black Death.

HEART OF DARKNESS (LIMITED EDITION), Great Unlimited Noises GUN 060 (1995) (Limited to 6666 copies. BMG 74321 267332). Tears Of Madness / Shadowmaker / The Grave Dancer / Demon's Day / Warchild / Heart Of Darkness / Hate / Circle Of Witches / Black Death / My Life / Dolphin's Cry. Chart position: 73 GERMANY.

Rebellion, Great Unlimited Noises GUN 103 (1996) (Promotion release). Rebellion (The Clans Are Marching) / Truth / Dark Of The Sun / The Ballad Of Mary (Queen Of Scots).

TUNES OF WAR, Great Unlimited Noises GUN 146-2 (1996). The Brave / Scotland United / The Dark Of The Sun / William Wallace (Braveheart) / The Bruce / The Battle Of Flodden / The Ballad Of Mary (Queen Of Scots) / The Truth / Cry For Freedom (James VI) / Killing Time / Rebellion (The Clans Are Marching) / Culloden Muir / The Fall Of The Brave. Chart position: 81 GERMANY.

TUNES OF WAR (LIMITED EDITION), Great Unlimited Noises GUN 146 (1996). The Brave / Scotland United / The Dark Of The Sun / William Wallace (Braveheart) / The Bruce / The Battle Of Flodden / The Ballad Of Mary (Queen Of Scots) / The Truth / Cry For Freedom (James VI) / Killing Time / Rebellion (The Clans Are Marching) / Culloden Muir / The Fall Of The Brave / Heavy Metal Breakdown / Witch Hunter / Headbanging Man.

The Dark Of The Sun EP, Great Unlimited Noises GUN 74321 48738 2 (1997). Rebellion (Live) / The Dark Of The Sun / Heavy Metal Breakdown / Witchhunter / Headbanging Man.

The Battle Of Bannockburn, Great Unlimited Noises (1998). The Battle Of Bannockburn / Baphomet / Knights Of The Cross / The Keeper Of The Holy Grail.

KNIGHTS OF THE CROSS, Great Unlimited Noises GUN 162-2 (1998). Deus Io Vult / Knights Of The Cross / Monks Of War / Heroes Of This Time / Fanatic Assassins / Lionheart / The Keeper Of The Holy Grail / Inquisition / Baphomet / Over The Sea / The Curse Of Jacques / The Battle Of Bannockburn. Chart position: 38 GERMANY.

KNIGHTS OF THE CROSS (LIMITED EDITION), Great Unlimited Noises GUN 162 (1998). Deus Io Vult / Knights Of The Cross / Monks Of War / Heroes Of This Time / Fanatic Assassins / Lionheart / The Keeper Of The Holy Grail / Inquisition / Baphomet / Over The Sea / The Curse Of Jacques / The Battle Of Bannockburn / Children Of The Grave.

EXCALIBUR, Great Unlimited Noises GUN 184 (1999). The Secrets Of Merlin / Pendragon / Excalibur / The Round Table (Forever) / Morgane Le Fay / The Spell / Tristan's Fate / Lancelot / Mordred's Song / The Final War / Emerald Eyes / Avalon.

EXCALIBUR (LIMITED EDITION), Great Unlimited Noises GUN 184-2 (1999). The Secrets Of Merlin / Pendragon / Excalibur / The Round Table (Forever) / Morgane Le Fay / The Spell / Tristans Fate / Lancelot / Mordreds Song / The Final War / Emerald Eyes / Avalon / Parcival. Chart position: 21 GERMANY.

THE GRAVE DIGGER (LIMITED EDITION), Nuclear Blast NB 0675-1 (2001). Son Of Evil / The Grave Digger / Raven / Scythe Of Time / Spirits Of The Dead / The House / King Pest / Sacred Fire / Funeral Procession / Haunted Palace / Silence / Starlight / Running Free.

THE GRAVE DIGGER, Nuclear Blast NB 0675-2 (2001). Son Of Evil / The Grave Digger / Raven / Scythe Of Time / Spirits Of The Dead / The House / King Pest / Sacred Fire / Funeral Procession / Haunted Palace / Silence / Black Cat. Chart position: 47 GERMANY.

TUNES OF WACKEN—LIVE, Great Unlimited Noises GUN 195-2 (2002). Intro / Scotland United / Dark Of The Sun / The Reaper / The Round Table (Forever) / Excalibur / Circle Of Witches / Ballad Of Mary (Queen Of Scots) / Lionheart / Morgana Le Fay / Knights Of The Cross / Rebellion (The Clans Are Marching) / Heavy Metal Breakdown.

LOST TUNES FROM THE VAULT, Great Unlimited Noises GUN 204-2 (2003). My Life / Dolphin's Cry / Don't Bring Me Down / Heavy Metal Breakdown / Witchhunter / Headbanging Man / Children Of The Grave / Hellas Hellas / Kill The King / Sin City / Parcival / Starlight / We Rock.

RHEINGOLD, Nuclear Blast NB 1046-2 (2003). The Ring / Rheingold / Valhalla / Giants / Maidens Of War / Sword / Dragon / Liar / Murderer / Twilight Of The Gods. Chart position: 44 GERMANY.

RHEINGOLD (LIMITED EDITION), Nuclear Blast NB 1046-0 (2003). The Ring / Rheingold / Valhalla / Giants / Maidens Of War / Sword / Dragon / Liar / Murderer / Twilight Of The Gods / Hero / Goodbye.

THE LAST SUPPER (LIMITED EDITION), Nuclear Blast NB 1343-1 (2005) (Picture disc). Passion / The Last Supper / Desert Rose / Grave In The No Man's Land / Hell To Pay / Soul Savior / Crucified / Divided Cross / The Night Before / Black Widows / Hundred Days / Always And Eternally / Sleepless / Jeepers Creepers.

THE LAST SUPPER, Nuclear Blast NB 1343-2 (2005). Passion / The Last Supper / Desert Rose / Grave In The No Man's Land / Hell To Pay / Soul Savior / Crucified / Divided Cross / The Night Before / Black Widows / Hundred Days / Always And Eternally. Chart position: 39 GERMANY.

25 TO LIVE, Nuclear Blast NB 1560 (2005) (2 CD/DVD Box set). Passion (Intro) / The Last Supper / Desert Rose / The Grave Dancer / Shoot Her Down / The Reaper / Paradise / Excalibur / The House / Circle Of Witches / Valhalla / Son Of Evil / The Battle Of Bannockburn / The Curse Of Jacques / Grave In The No Man's Land / Yesterday / Margane Lefay / Symphony Of Death / Witchhunter / The Dark Of The Sun / Knights Of The Cross / Twilight Of The Gods / The Grave Digger / Rebellion / Rheingold / The Round Table / Heavy Metal Breakdown / A Journey To Brazil (Video) / 25 To Live (Brazil / Sao Paulo / 7th of May 2005 (Video).

Yesterday EP, Locomotive (2006). Yesterday / The Reaper's Dance / No Quarter / Yesterday (Orchestra version).

LIBERTY OR DEATH (LIMITED EDITION), Locomotive Music LM 400 (2007). Liberty Or Death / Ocean Of Blood / Highland Tears / The Terrible One / Until The Last King Died / March Of The Innocent / Silent Revolution / Shadowland / Forecourt To Hell / Massada / Ship Of Hope.

LIBERTY OR DEATH, Locomotive Music LM 400 (2007). Liberty Or Death / Ocean Of Blood / Highland Tears / The Terrible One / Until The Last King Died / March Of The Innocent / Silent Revolution / Shadowland / Forecourt To Hell / Massada. Chart position: 30 GERMANY.

GRIFFIN

TRONDHEIM, NORWAY — *Peter Beck (vocals), Kai Nergaard (guitar), Marcus Silver (guitar), Johnny Wangberg (bass), Marius Karlsen (drums).*

A 1998 Trondheim formation GRIFFIN, led by BLOODTHORN guitarist Kai Nergaard and who deal in retro style traditional Thrash style Metal, was originally founded as a sideline to the members priority acts BLOODTHORN, DARK AGES and ATROX. Tommy Halseth would hold prior credits with WÅTTAMEZZ, GODSEND and ATROX. A demo was duly cut, which uniquely featured the sounds of double bass and saxophone, but would remain unreleased. A second attempt, the 'Conquers The World' session, scored the band a deal with French label Season Of Mist for the October 2000 debut album 'Wasteland Serenades'.

GRIFFIN gained the valuable support slot to MAYHEM's European tour, bringing onboard new guitarist Marcus Silver shortly after. This revised line up would cut a second GRIFFIN album, the more Metal inclined April 2002's 'The Sideshow'. However, Tommy Halseth then exited to resurrect WÅTTAMEZZ. A 2003 opus, billed as 'No Holds Barred' and recorded at Skansen Lydstudio in Trondheim, saw CHILDREN OF BODOM frontman Alexi Laiho gaining co-production credits. Issued through FaceFront Records in Norway 'No Holds Barred' saw a Japanese issue via Spiritual Beast.

Touring in Scandinavia saw the band forming up the billing for the October 2003 'Scream Magazine Metal Tour' comprising headliners EINHERJER alongside LUMSK and SCARIOT. The band gave fans an unexpected bonus in January of 2004 by posting cover versions of OZZY OSBOURNE's 'Crazy Train' and JUDAS PRIEST's 'Hell Bent For Leather' on their official website.

GRIFFIN suffered a major setback in April when singer Pete Beck, also credited with membership of ATROX and FIG LEAF, was hospitalised after suffering a heart attack. Although Beck made a recovery he subsequently opted out of the band, retiring to a remote cottage with a parting message "I'm going away for a long time, and cannot be contacted by phone or email, so dont even bother". The group wished their former singer well and duly installed Ida Hawkland of SPIRITUAL BEAST as their new female singer in May. However, by July Beck was back in the fold. A new album, 'Lifeforce', would be recorded at in Godt Selskap in Trondheim and mixed by KING DIAMOND guitarist Andy LaRoque at his Los Angered Studio in Gothenburg, Sweden. Japanese variants added the extra track 'Unforgiver'. Upfront of Summer 2005 touring, Beck pulled out of the band once again and Rolf Bakken of FIG LEAF and VALHALLA repute would be named as replacement.

In January 2006 the band replaced Marcus Silver with new, 18 year old guitarist Roar Naustvoll and also saw drummer Marius Karlsen exiting in favour of Italian Alessandro Giovanni Elide from MANIFEST. Live work that year had the group packaged with KING DIAMOND and THUNDERBOLT in the Czech Republic, Slovakia, Hungary, Greece, Spain and Italy during April.

GRIFFIN announced in July that drummer Marius Karlsen had left the band "Due to obligations towards a new job as head chef in a steakhouse restaurant". Alessandro Elide resumed his post again, this time in a permanent position.

A fresh GRIFFIN album 'The Ultimate Demise' would be contracted to Burning Star Records in November 2006. The same label also released a re-mixed and re-mastered edition of the 2003 album 'No Holds Barred', which only originally saw Norwegian issue.

WASTELAND SERENADES, Season Of Mist SOM 034 (2000). Mechanized Reality / The Usurper / Spice Keeps Me Silent / Obsession / New Business Capitalized / Hunger Strikes / Always Closing / Punishment Macabre / Exit 2000 / Wasteland Serenade / Dream Of The Dreamers (Bliss 2).

THE SIDESHOW, Season Of Mist SOM 063 (2002). Prologue / Shadows Of Deception / Horrific / Freakshow / The Last Rays Of A Dying Sun / Death Row League / What If / A Distant Shore / Vengeance Is Mine / Today's Castaway / Cosmic Revelation / Epilogue.

NO HOLDS BARRED, Spiritual Beast SBCD-1011 (2004). The Sentence / Unbreakable / Praise The Rain / New Boss / Weightless / Heavy Mental Overload / Second Time Around / Fleet Street Superstars / Feeding The Five / Bleed / Sacred World.

LIFEFORCE, FaceFront (2005). Accelerate / Rest / Premonition / Recipe For Rage / Utopia / Dungeon / Moment Of Madness / Building A Future / Lifeforce / Bound In Re-runs / Leylines.

THE ULTIMATE DEMISE, Burning Star BSRCD0017 (2007).

GRIM FORCE

JAPAN — *Daisuke Higaki (vocals), Katsuyuki Nakabayashi (vocals / guitar), Hiroshi Nishihara (bass), Masaki Kamomiya (drums).*

Thrash Metal combo GRIM FORCE was organized by erstwhile DISGUST vocalist / guitarist Katsuyuki Nakabayashi and former RADICALIZ drummer Masaki Kamomiya. This duo cut a two song, eponymous demo tape. However, the project was put into stasis when Nakabayashi enrolled into the ranks of RITUAL CARNAGE for European touring and recording of the 'Every Nerve Alive' album.

GRIM FORCE was re-activated in December 1999, introducing Sonoe Takahata on bass guitar and signing a contract with World Chaos Productions for the album 'Circulation To Conclusion'. Released in June of 2000 the album featured a guest guitar solo from Eddy Van Koide of RITUAL CARNAGE. Touring witnessed support dates to DISMEMBER in Japan that December. Gigs in 2000 had GRIM FORCE opening for DEFLESHED, NIGHT IN GALES, DEW SCENTED and 8MM OVERDOSE. Hiroshi Nishihara was subsequently to succeed Takahata on bass.

In January of 2002 GRIM FORCE, having introduced singer Daisuke Higaki, allied with CARNAL FORGE, BASSAIUM and BUZZ CULT for Japanese dates. Gigs in October saw the band opening for FLESHCRAWL and HYPOCRISY.

CIRCULATION TO CONCLUSION, World Chaos KDM003 (2000). Lunatic / God Cries! World Dies! / World Of Chaos / The Sin Of The Blackest Dye / Dig Your Own Grave / The Dead To Be Judged / Struggle.

GRINDER

GERMANY — *Adrian (vocals / bass), Andy (guitar), Lario (guitar), Stefan Arnold (drums).*

Metal band GRINDER debuted with the 'Sacred To Death' demo and included ex-WALLOP drummer Stefan Arnold. GRINDER's debut album 'Dawn For The Living' was produced by Kalle Trapp, whilst the third release, 1991's 'Nothing Is Sacred', is noted for production by Harris Johns and Tom Stiehler. GRINDER later evolved into CAPRICORN. Guitarist Andy joined RAWBONE.

Arnold joined GRAVE DIGGER for their 'Tunes Of War' album.

DAWN FOR THE LIVING, No Remorse NRR 1003 (1988). Obsession / Dawn For The Living / Sinners Exile / Magician / Frenzied Hatred / Dying Flesh / Delirium / Traitor / F.O.A.D.

DEAD END, No Remorse NRR 1007 (1989). Agent Orange / Dead End / The Blade Is Back / Inside / Just Another Scar / Total Control / Why / Train Raid / Unlock The Morgue.

Reeling On The Edge, No Remorse NRR1011 (1990). Reeling On The Edge / Incarnation Off / Truth In The Hands Of Judas / Just Another Scar (Live) / Dawn For The Living (Live) / F.O.A.D. (Live).

NOTHING IS SACRED, Noise (1991). Drifting For 99 Seconds / Hymn For The Isolated / The Spirit Of Violence / Nothing Is Sacred / None Of The Brighter Days / Superior Being / Dear Mr. Sinister / Pavement Tango / The Nothing Song / NME.

GRINDNECKS

GOTHENBURG, SWEDEN — *Joakim Proos (vocals), Mikael Eriksson (guitar), Jonas Larsson (guitar), Mattias Nilsson (bass), Daniel Moilanen (drums).*

Gothenburg Death / Thrashers GRINDNECKS were formulated during 2003. Fronted by singer Joakim Proos the band includes a collection of notable scene veterans including ex-DEMONS OF DIRT and SLAUGHTERCULT guitarist Mikael Eriksson, SLAUGHTERCULT guitarist Jonas Larsson, ex-DEMONS OF DIRT, CLONAEON and SLAUGHTERCULT bassist Mattias Nilsson with Daniel "Mojjo" Moilanen of RUNEMAGICK, LORD BELIAL, ENGEL, NOTRE DAME and RELEVANT FEW on drums. The band's original line-up had included guitar player Johan Lundin and drummer Jonas Wickstrand, the latter soon replaced by SUNDANCE, GARDENIAN and WITHIN Y credited Thim Blom on drums. Moilanen assumed drum duties in early 2005 as Blom prioritised WITHIN Y.

GRINDNECKS first offering would be the December 2004 demo 'Terror Rising'. The second session, '460 From Hell' recorded in August 2005, saw the guest inclusion of guitarist Johan Lundin plus vocalists Andreas Solveström of WITHIN Y and EVILDOER, Robert Johansson and SLAUGHTERCULT's Ronny Attergran.

GRINDNECKS announced they were suspending activities in November 2005, claiming that their "music became too extreme for others to handle".

Terror Rising, Grindnecks (2004). Death In Disguise / Terror Rising / Damn Nation / Twentyfour Seven (Fuck The Heaven Sent).

460 From Hell, (2005). Dead by Dawn / Messenger Of Death / Retaliation / A Devil's Deal.

GRIP INC.

USA — *Gus Chambers (vocals), Waldemayr Sorychta (guitar), Jason Vie Brooks (bass), Dave Lombardo (drums).*

GRIP INC is most noted for their inclusion of ex-SLAYER drummer DAVE LOMBARDO, a man who whilst with his former unit often topped the 'best drummer' polls in magazines for many years. His relationship with his erstwhile band mates in SLAYER was known to be fragile and his departure was no surprise. However, it took a few years to re-emerge with GRIP INC. The band also feature British ex-21 GUNS vocalist Gus Chambers, former HEATHEN bassist Jason Vie Brooks and ex-VOODOO CULT guitarist Waldemayr Sorychta. Lombardo had met Sorychta whilst laying down drums on a VOODOO CULT album as special guest. A fledgling version of GRIP INC. also included ex-OVERKILL guitarist Bobby Gustafson but his tenure was a brief one. Promoting the band's second album, 1997's 'Nemesis', the group undertook a headline tour of the UK that June backed by SKINLAB and KILL II THIS.

GRIP INC. (pic: Alex Solca)

Lombardo later enjoyed a stint with TESTAMENT and issued a solo album, the pseudo classical 'Vivaldi'. The drummer would also forge FANTOMAS with ex-FAITH NO MORE singer Mike Patton. Vie Brooks formed part of the 2000 HEATHEN reunion.

During early 2003 Waldemar Sorychta, Gus Chambers and DAVE LOMBARDO reconvened to discuss plans for a fresh GRIP INC. album. The drummer faced a hectic schedule that year, recording drums for two separate FANTOMAS albums as well as a new SLAYER opus. Meantime former GRIP INC. guitarist Bobby Gustafson resurfaced in a the South Florida based band RESPONSE NEGATIVE.

GRIP INC. returned in 2003 to cut a new album for SPV Records entitled 'Incorporated'. In early 2004 Lombardo also put in a recording session for the soundtrack to the remake of the splatter film classic 'Dawn Of The Dead'. Gus Chambers would prove active with his Punk act SQUAD 21, issuing the album 'Skullduggery' through Go Nuts Music.

Gus Chambers replaced the late Andy Allendörfer as SQUEALER frontman in April 2005. Former bassist Jason Vie Brooks returned to the scene with Cincinnati, Ohio based THE ALLKNOWING.

THE POWER OF INNER STRENGTH, SPV Steamhammer 085 76922 (1995). Uno / Savage Seas / Hostage To Heaven / Monster Among Us / Guilty Of Innocence / Innate Affliction / Colors Of Death / Ostracized / Cleanze The Seed / Heretic War Chant / Longest Hate.

NEMESIS, SPV 008-18321 (1997). Pathetic Liar / Portrait Of Henry / Empress (Of Rancor) / Descending Darkness / War Between One / Scream At The Sky / Silent Stranger / The Summoning / Rusty Nail / Myth Or Man / Code Of Silence.

SOLIDIFY, SPV 085-18592 (1999). Isolation / Amped / Lockdown / Griefless / Foresight / Human? / Vindicate / Stresscase / Challenge / Verrater (Betrayer) / Bug Juice. Chart position: 65 FRANCE.

Griefless, Steamhammer SPV 050-18665 (1999) (10" vinyl single). Griefless / Verräter (Betrayer).

INCORPORATED, SPV (2004). Curse (Of The Cloth) / The Answer / Prophecy / Endowment Of Apathy / Enemy Mind / Skin Trade / (Built To) Resist / The Gift / Privilege / Blood Of Saints / Man With No Insides.

GROPE

ÅRHUS, DENMARK — *Alex Clausen (vocals), Tue Madsen (guitar), Oberst (bass), Jonez (keyboards), Anders Gyldenøhr (drums).*

Founded in Århus during 1994, GROPE, featuring vocalist Per Ebdrup, erstwhile DESEXULT, ATRO CITY, PIXIE KILLERS guitarist Tue Madsen, bass player Jimmy Thørse and PIXIE KILLERS drummer Anders Gyldenøhr, debuted with the delightfully titled 'What Do Faggots Want?' demo. Early in their career the band dubbed themselves as "'Bone Crushing Rip n' Tear Cyber Thrash". GROPE, signing to the Progress label, featured covers of both METALLICA and SLAYER on the 'Metal Militia' and 'Slatanic Slaughter' tribute albums with a Hardcore charged '… And Justice For All' and 'Spill The Blood' respectively. The band was highly active in 1995, gaining media exposure with a promotional video for the track 'Enemy' and touring alongside label mates TREND and KONKHRA.

GROPE first signalled their desire to branch out musically as they adventurously covered BJÖRK's 'Army Of Me' for the January 1996 'Soul Pieces' EP. This would prove a portent of what was to come as GROPE's 1997 album 'Desert Storm' betrayed Grunge leanings. Sadly bassist Jimmy Thorsø would lose his battle against cancer. By the 2000 effort 'Intercooler', which saw the inclusion of new singer Alex Clausen, previously with BUTTFUCK, and bassist Oberstein, GROPE had evolved far away from their Death Metal roots into an American influenced Stoner band, utilising John Custer as producer and mixing the record in Raleigh, North Carolina to boot. European touring saw GROPE aligned with WEISSGLUT.

Splitting from Diehard GROPE, enlisting keyboard player Jonez, convened their own label for the September 2002 record 'If You Were My Dog'. By February of 2003 Oberstein had left the fold. Nevertheless the band was confirmed as support for YNGWIE MALMSTEEN's Danish gigs that April.

Soul Pieces, Progress PCD 26 (1995). Soul Pieces / Army Of Me / Interlock / Tears Correct.
PRIMATES, Progress RRS 941 (1995). The Primate / Nothing Ever Ends / Under / Enemy / Fuck / Raw / Parasite / Watch Me Rule / Bleeding / Murder In A Box / 5-6-7-8 / Ignorance / Dead / Blind.
THE FURY, Progress PCD 27 (1996). Manipulated / Soul Pieces / Without Pain / The Day Will Come / Stonesun / Cold Hand / The Choice You Make / Second / Bloodred / Damned / Mørke / Killed Again / Midnight.
DESERT STORM, Progress PCD 29 (1997). Pacified / Trapped In A Bottle / While You Can / Perfect Queen / The Flower / Desert Storm / OK For Now / Dayton Thunder Kings / It's P.R.S. / Song Of Fear / Around / Murmur / Madman's Medicine / In The Name Of Hate / In The Garden Of Eden.
INTERCOOLER, Die Hard (1999). Someone Died In You / Hope For The Best / Freakshow Gallery / Six Feet Under And Far Away / Just Like The Devil / Reverend Jones / Reason To Fear / I Fell For You / Bazar / Busorama / Cupid's Shotgun / This Time Of Year.
Hope For The Best, (2000). Hope For The Best (Radio edit) / Reason To Fear.
IF YOU WERE MY DOG, MNW (2002). Rock'n'Roller / Searching For Something / Struck By Lightning / Nothing You Can Do / I'm A Motel / One Fine Day / Under The Stars / Sticks And Stones / If You Were My Dog / Clean My Wounds / She's Got Superpowers / I Won't Die Slowly.

GUARDIANS OF STEEL

PIETARSAARI, FINLAND — *Jimmy Bäck (vocals / guitar), Fredrik Vikman (bass), Guy Vikman (drums).*

Pietarsaari Thrash Metal act GUARDIANS OF STEEL released an August 2003 demo 'Evil Intentions'. The band switched titles to SATORIUM, releasing the demo 'Preach Until They Bleed' in January 2005. At first operating as a covers act tackling the likes of DEEP PURPLE and BLACK SABBATH, the band had been created during 2001 by guitarist Jimmy Bäck and drummer Guy Vikman, subsequently enlisting Guy's younger brother Fredrik Vikman on bass. The group's style shifted from trad Heavy Metal to Black / Death as their first set of original songs was laid down on the 'Evil Intentions' promo.

Taking on the new brand of SATORIUM, 'Preach Until You Bleed' was then recorded, after which Christoffer Alvik was introduced on guitar and Fredrik Vikman took on lead vocals. New demos were crafted in March 2006.

Evil Intentions, Guardians Of Steel (2003) (Demo). Intro / Godseye / Demon's Fantasy / Sirens From Hell / Evil Intentions.

GUILLOTINE

UMEÅ, SWEDEN — *Psycho (vocals / guitar), Snake (bass), Cobra (drums).*

GUILLOTINE was an Umeå based Thrash Metal band, formed as HOLOCAUST during 1995. A three song demo tape 'Under The Guillotine' emerged in 1995 with musicians being credited as Spider ("Screaming guitarz & vocals from Hell"), Killer ("Bombing bass"), Psycho ("Horrible rhythm guitar") and Insane ("Skin shocker"). The Necropolis label then took the band on for an album bearing the same title, these sessions recorded at Eurosound Studios. The band featured the NOCTURNAL RITES duo of guitarist Frederik 'Psycho' Mannberg and bassist Nils 'Snake' Eriksson. Occupying the role as frontman in the guise of 'Spider' would in fact be Fredrik Degerström of NAGLAR, AUBERON, BEWITCHED and STORMLEIGH repute.

Under The Guillotine, (1995). Tormentor / Guillotine / Crucifixion.
UNDER THE GUILLOTINE, Necropolis NR020 (1997). Executioner / Grave Desecrator / Leprosy / Guillotine / Death Penalty / Crucifixion / Night Stalker / Tormentor / Total Mayhem / Violence.

GURD

SWITZERLAND — *O. Pulver (vocals / guitar), Tommy B. (guitar), Marek (bass), Tobias Roth (drums).*

GURD was formed in January 1994 by ex-POLTERGEIST guitarist V.O. Pulver. Guitarist Tommy B. was previously with EROTIC JESUS.

GURD toured as support to KREATOR, CORONER, SODOM, PRO-PAIN and BODY COUNT. Their work ethic paid off and by 1996 the band had signed to Century Media releasing third album 'D-Fect' and a remix offering the following year.

Further extensive touring ensued with the likes of STUCK MOJO, PRO-PAIN and LIFE OF AGONY prior to the recording of 1998's 'Down The Drain' with producer Tomas Skogsberg. More dates followed upon its release allied with PRO-PAIN. However, GURD underwent a drastic overhaul though with three quarters of the band decamping, Töbi and Philippe forging Alt-Rockers DISGROOVE, leaving Pulver alone to carry on the name. He duly reforged GURD pulling in former SWAMP TERRORISTS and BAUMANN personnel guitarist Bruno Spring and bassist Andrej, both also members of JERK. New face behind the drum kit for the 2000 album 'Bedlam' was ex-JERK and BAUMANN man Tschibu. GURD would also welcome onboard former UMOUNT bassist Frank Winkelmann in early 2002.

GURD signed to Denmark's Diehard Music for a 2003 album 'Encounter'. Closing a five year stint, guitarist Bruno Spring opted out during 2004. In November the band drafted ex-ACID, CRIONICS and EVEREVE man Pat as replacement.

Announced in mid 2005, the GURD credited trio of guitarist Spring, bassist Andrej and drummer Tschibu revealed side project THE ORDER, a union with PURE INC. singer Gianni Pontillo. Working with V.O. Pulver and Frank Winkelmann, this new band cut album recordings that June at Little Creek Studios in Gelterkinden. The 'Bang!' album, for which a comic strip styled promotional video was filmed for the title track, was signed to German imprint Dockyard 1 in May 2006.

European shows in 2007, commencing April 25th at the Munich Metropolis in Germany, saw the band supporting PRO-PAIN.

GURD, C&C CC 6243 (1995). Get Up / You Won't Make It / I.O.U. Nothing / Enough / The Mant (Groovy) / Scum / Cut It Out / The Way You Want / Distinction / Gone So Far / Ceasefire / Don't Ask Me.
ADDICTED, Major CC035 (1995). HxHxHx / Learn / Chill Out / Feel The Silence / Ghost Dance / Face To Face / Red House / Give In / Down And Out / Too Vicious / Higher.
D-FECT, Century Media 77150-2 (1996). What Do You Live For / No Sleep / We've Been Told / Fever Of Pain / Bullshit / Human Existence / Go Go Go / Look Away / This Place / Read My Lips / Think / Heaven Sent / Lose Myself.
D-FECT-THE REMIXES, Century Media 77176-2 (1997). Get Up (Caveman remix) / Heaven Sent (stop Denying edit) / Go Go Go (Vibe Master remix) / We've Been Told (Powder Rose remix) / Bullshit (Splatter remix) / Heaven Sent (Sweet remix) / Insane / 102.
DOWN THE DRAIN, Century Media CD 77203-2 (1998). Down The Drain / Head Full Of Shit / Dead Or Alive / Bow My Head / I Remember / My Future / T.R.T.L. / Time To Forget / Caught / Help Me / Survive / Skin Up!!

BEDLAM, Century Media (2000). Masterplan / Big Shot / Bedlam / Stardust / Always / Rule The Pit / V.U.L.T. / Take My Hand / Golden Age / Shed No Tears / Defiance / We Will Resist / Warmachine.
ENCOUNTER, Diehard Music (2003). Razorblade / Can't Take Back / Mayday / A New War / Older But Wiser / Control / Decision / Strive / Fangs / Club Of Lies / Obey / My Demons / Believe In Nothing.
BANG!, Dockyard 1 (2006).

GWAR

RICHMOND, VA, USA — Oderus Urungus (vocals), Slymenstra Hymen (vocals), Balsac, The Jaws Of Death (guitar), Flattus Maximus (guitar), Beefcake The Mighty (bass), Nippleus Erectus (drums).

GWAR burst onto the Metal scene flaunting some of the most outrageous stage costumes ever graced by a Rock band. Offering a heady brew of Sci-Fi and a fixation with porn GWAR succeeded in shocking the establishment from the outset and the high quality theatrics soon drew in legions of supporters. The band claimed a lineage millions of years in antiquity as a group of rebel space pirates titled 'Scumdogs Of The Universe'. Supposedly banished to planet earth GWAR claimed responsibility for the extinction of the dinosaurs, the emergence of mankind and the destruction of Atlantis. For these heinous deeds they were imprisoned in Antarctica until their escape in time for debut album 'Hell-O' in 1988.

The outlandish costumes hid the alter ego personas of a revolving cast of performers, for major parts of their career mainly involving vocalist Dave Brockie ('Oderus Urungus'), guitarist Mike Derks ('Balsac, The Jaws Of Death'), guitarist Zack Blair ('Flattus Maximus') and bassist Casey Orr ('Beefcake The Mighty'). By this juncture GWAR, having been forged during the early eighties, had undergone a series of line-up combinations, including the 1988 inclusion of erstwhile WHITE CROSS personnel guitarist Dewey Rowell and drummer Rob Mosby, the latter replacing Pete Luchter. . Originally 'Balzac, The Jaws of Death' had been performed by Chris Bopst, being superseded by Steve Douglas in time for the debut album.

Needless to say their origins lay not in Antarctica but Richmond, Virginia. Pre GWAR, Brockie had been a member of the Hardcore trio DEATH PIGGY which had released three single throughout the 80's 'Love War', 'Death Rules The Fairway' and 'R45'. In 1985 Brockie and DEATH PIGGY drummer Sean Sumner teamed up with director Hunter Jackson who was planning a movie entitled 'Scumdogs Of The Universe'. The costumes for this intended movie would provide the catalyst for the first GWAR incarnation. This formative version of the band also featured guitarist John Cobbett, later to make his mark with THE LORD WEIRD SLOUGH FEG, WHIPKRAFT, HIPPIE BITCH, AMBER ASYLUM and HAMMERS OF MISFORTUNE. For a while both Brockie and Sumner divided their duties between DEATH PIGGY and GWAR but Sumner's lifestyle would finally catch up with him. The drummer was imprisoned for attempted murder.

GWAR's debut came in 1988 with the Mark Kramer produced 'Hell-O' album for Shimmy Disc Records. At this juncture the recording band involved vocalist Dave Brockie ('Oderus Urungus'), lead guitarist Dewey Rowell ('Flattus Maximus'), rhythm guitarist Steve Douglas ('Balsac, The Jaws of Death'), bass player Michael Bishop ('Beefcake the Mighty') and drummer Rob Mosby ('Nippleus Erectus'). Additional vocals were supplied by Hunter Jackson ('Techno-Destructo'). 'Hell-O's utterly bizarre concept hung on basic Punk-Metal and a mind boggling patchwork of scatlology, political satire, eating automobiles and even twisted affection for deceased pets in 'I'm In Love (With A Dead Dog)'. Things would only get more surreal with each album.

Metal Blade Records picked the band up for their second dose, 1990's 'Scumdogs Of The Universe', triggering a business relationship that would deliver a whole decade's worth of Metal. Produced by in the main by Ron Goudie, the record benefited hugely from its position as GWAR's opening gambit for much of the world, the previous effort having enjoyed very little exposure beyond the underground. MINISTRY fans soon learned that 'Hypo Luxa' and 'Hermes Pan', credited with production of the track 'Horror Of Yog', were in fact Al Jourgensen and Paul Barker.

'Scumdogs Of The Universe' witnessed a significant change in the band structure. Only Brockie, Rowell and Bishop remained, with a fresh cast comprising Michael Derks as 'Balsac, The Jaws of Death', Brad Roberts on drums (Jizmak Da Gusha') with studio vocals donated by Danielle Stampe ('Slymenstra Hymen'), Chuck Varga ('Sexecutioner') and Don Drakulich ('Sleazy P. Martini').

The 1991 'America Must Be Destroyed' would see the inclusion on a session basis of EEK A MOUSE and KEPONE man Tim Harris and ROSEBUD Brian Fechino on guitars. The catalyst for its anti-authority stance had been a conviction Brockie had received in North Carolina for public display of his prosthetic penis. Touring that year had the band taking out the CROSSTOPS, EMBRYO KILLERS and RICH KIDS ON LSD credited Barry Ward as live guitarist. During 1993 GWAR introduced the RIGOR MORTIS credited Peter Lee on guitar and the following year drafted Casey Orr on bass. Orr's prior experience included terms with Texan Thrash Metal band WARLOCK and RIGOR MORTIS. Orr had also acted as temporary fill in for a number of MINISTRY 'Lollapalooza' festivals in 1992. That same year Orr featured the 'Leave It To Blohole' album from Punk project BLOHOLE.

In 1995 the full membership of GWAR released an album 'You Have The Right To Remain Silent' under yet further assumed names billing themselves as the X-COPS. This side combo credited themselves as Sheriff 'Tub' Tucker ("vocals + shotgun"), Sgt. Al Depantsia ("guitar + Colt .22"), Lt. Louis Scrapinetti ("guitar + Beretta 9mm"), Patrolman Cobb Knobbler ("bass + .357 magnum"), Cadet Billy Club ("drums + Uzi 9mm") with guests Mountain Bike Officer Biff Buff ("vocals + police issue .45"), Sgt. Zypygski ("vocals + taser"), Dectective Philip McRevis ("samples + snub nose .38"). Touring to promote the album without revealing their identities as the GWAR characters proved a struggle. Tragically, the year after original GWAR drummer Sean Sumner would take his own life. Another former GWAR drummer Jim Thompson founded BIO RITMO for a Spanish language Metal album. GWAR, backed by X-COPS, toured Europe throughout March and April 1996.

GWAR returned in March 1997 touting their sixth offering, the experimental 'Carnival Of Chaos'. Peter Lee as Flattus Maximus, suffering from the after effects of a gunshot wound, bowed out with this album. The blatantly offensive, expletive ridden 'We Kill Everything' arrived in April 1999. BalSac the Jaw of Death featured as lead vocalist for the first time on the track 'Escape From The Mooselodge', actually a remake of an earlier cut entitled 'The Needle'. The band also re-assembled 1989's 'Cardinal Syn Theme' and re-branded it 'A Short History of the End of the World'. Notably, 'We Kill Everything' marked the final recording appearance of Michael Bishop, temporarily acting as 'Beefcake the Mighty', Danielle Stamp, Hunter Jackson and keyboard player Dave Musel. In another change, Tim Harris played the character of 'Flattus Maximus'.

The GWAR 2000 album 'Slaves Going Single' was only issued to the bands fan 'Total Slavery' club members. Only 1000 copies were pressed of this collection of outtakes. Another exclusive fan club only release, the live 'You're All Worthless And Weak', had been recorded at Washington D.C.'s 9:30 Club on Halloween 1999. For their 2000 American dates GWAR redrafted 'The Sexecutioner' and 'Sleazy P. Martini'. The dates were supported by AMEN and LAMB OF GOD.

In 2001 Dave Brockie emerged with his DBX (THE DAVE BROCKIE EXPERIENCE) project album 'Diarrhea Of A Madman'. Also featured in DBX were GWAR men guitarist Mike Derks and drummer Dave Roberts ('Jizmak Da Jusha'). Having first revealed the identity of the band to the media in order to avoid the previous calamity with their X-COPS venture DBX would tour America. Also on the billing for these shows was RAWG, actually the full compliment of GWAR sans costumes.

GWAR, promoting a fresh album 'Violence Has Arrived' which sported cover artwork from famed Warhammer artist Adrian Smith, announced another bout of North American touring, billed as 'Blood Drive 2002' and commencing 16th January 2002, in alliance with GOD FORBID and SOILENT GREEN. However, these dates would be without the recently departed Sylmentsra Hymen. The tour was further hit when members of SOILENT GREEN suffered an auto accident. GOATWHORE took the newly vacant position.

Oderus Ungerus would claim production credits on the 2002 'In The Face Of The Enemy' from Nashville extreme Metal band DISARRAY. Both Ungerus and Balsac would guest on the album. The band would undergo a major line-up shuffle in September with Casey Orr as 'Beefcake the Mighty' and Zack Blair 'Flattus Maximus' both stepping down to concentrate on another act THE BURDEN BROTHERS. GWAR duly inducted a new 'Beefcake' in Todd 'T' Evans of LAZY AMERICAN WORKERS and Cory Smoot for the role of 'Flattus'. October headline dates in the USA saw CATTLE DECAPITATION and BLOODLET lending support.

2002 saw the re-emergence of two former GWAR members, Zach Blair and drummer Brad Roberts in the Dallas, Texas Pop Rock outfit ARMSTRONG. A fan club only release emerged in April, the live 'You're All Worthless And Weak' having been recorded at Washington D.C.'s 9:30 Club on Halloween 2000. Casey Orr joined a reformed SPEEDEALER in early 2003. Dave Brockie aided with characteristic guest vocals on the track 'The Dissection' for Metal band BALLISTIC's debut album.

GWAR set out on the 'War Party' tour across the USA once more in April of 2004, making an exclusive album of early demo material recorded during 1986—'87, 'Let Their Be GWAR', available at these shows. The band switched labels from longstanding partner Metal Blade to DRT Entertainment, an independent label founded by senior music industry executives Derek Shulman, Ron Urban and Ted Green. GWAR, working once again with producer Glen Robinson, would cut the 'War Party' follow up to 2001's 'Violence Has Arrived', set for October 2004 issue, at Wreckroom Studios in Richmond, Virginia. A national headlining tour, dubbed 'Mock The Vote' commencing on 26th October in Norfolk, Virginia, would be supported by DYING FETUS and ALL THAT REMAINS.

GWAR opened 2005 with US dates commencing late January, seeing ALL THAT REMAINS and ALABAMA THUNDERPUSSY as support. That May, DRT Entertainment issued a new live album 'Live From Mt. Fuji'. Flattus Maximus took time out of his GWAR schedule to act as producer for MUNICIPAL WASTE's 'Hazardous Mutation' album.

The Summer of 2005 found the group participating in the US 'Sounds of the Underground' touring extravaganza, a collaboration between independent labels Ferret Music, Prosthetic Records, Trustkill Records and Metal Blade Records. The mammoth billing for these shows saw the band sharing stages with CLUTCH, OPETH, POISON THE WELL, FROM AUTUMN TO ASHES, CHIMAIRA, NORMA JEAN, EVERY TIME I DIE, STRAPPING YOUNG LAD, THROWDOWN, HIGH ON FIRE, DEVILDRIVER, ALL THAT REMAINS, A LIFE ONCE LOST and UNEARTH. Regional additions included MADBALL and TERROR, splitting the East and West portions of the tour respectively, THE RED CHORD on the East Coast, FEAR BEFORE THE MARCH OF FLAMES in the Midwest and Southeast and HIMSA for Western gigs. The band put in headline US dates commencing 7th October in Sayreville, New Jersey, also packaged with DEVILDRIVER, A DOZEN FURIES and MENSREA. Oderus Urungus guested on STRAPPING YOUNG LAD's 2006 album 'The New Black', featuring on the track 'Far Beyond Metal'.

An updated rendition of ALICE COOPER's 'School's Out' was made available to listen online via the band's official website in June, a preview of the Devin Townsend produced 'Beyond Hell' album. This same month came with the release of a 20 year retrospective DVD entitled 'Blood Bath and Beyond'. Hosted courtesy of Oderus Urungus and Sleazy P. Martini, the DVD incorporated rare and unreleased material alongside short films, lost demo cuts and scarce bootleg footage accumulated over the years.

The group subsequently engaged in another gigantic roving festival billing with the 'Sounds Of The Underground' tour throughout the summer of 2006, commencing in Cleveland, Ohio on July 8th, partnered with IN FLAMES, TRIVIUM, CANNIBAL CORPSE, AS I LAY DYING, TERROR, THE BLACK DAHLIA MURDER, BEHEMOTH, THE CHARIOT and THROUGH THE EYES OF THE DEAD.

October 2006's album offering 'Beyond Hell' closed out with a cover version of ALICE COOPER's 'School's Out'.

Casey Orr replaced Todd Evans on bass for a mammoth run of European dates, visiting the UK, Belgium, France, Portugal, Spain, Italy, Switzerland, Holland, Hungary, Austria, Czech Republic, Poland and Germany, throughout April and May 2007.

HELL-O, Shimmy Disc 010 (1988). Time For Death / AEIOU / Americanised / I'm In Love (With A Dead Dog) / Slütman City / World O Filth / War Toy / Captain Crünch / Püre As The Arctic Snow / Je M'Appelle J Cöusteaü / GWAR Theme / Bone Meal / Öllie North / Techno's Song / U Ain't Shit / Rock & Roll Pärty Töwn.

SCUMDOGS OF THE UNIVERSE, Master MASCD 001 (1990). The Salamaniser / Maggots / Sick Of You / Slaughterama / Kingqueen / Horror Of Yig / Vlad The Impaler / Black And Huge / Love Surgery / Sexecutioner.

AMERICA MUST BE DESTROYED, Metal Blade ZORRO 037 (1991). On The Bone / Crack In The Egg / Gor-Gor / Have You Seen Me? / The Morality Squad / America Must Be Destroyed / Gilded Lily / Poor Ole Tom / Rock "N' Roll Never Felt So Good / Blimey / The Road Behind / Pussy Planet. Chart position: 177 USA.

THE ROAD BEHIND, Metal Blade 3984-17004-2 (1992). The Road Behind / Overture In N Minor / Krakdown / Voodoo Summoning / Captain Crunch / Have You Seen Me? / SFW.

THIS TOILET EARTH, Metal Blade ZORRO 63 (1994). Saddam A Go-Go / Penis I See / Cat Steel / Jack The World / Sonderkommando / Bad Bad Men / Pepperoni / The Insidious Soliloquy Of Skulhedface / B.D.F. / Fight / The Issue Of Tissue (Spacecake) / Pocket Pool / Slap U around / Krak Down / Filthy Flow / The Obliteration Of Flab Quarv 7.

RAGNAROK, Metal Blade 17001-2 (1995). Meat Sandwich / The New Plague / Whargoul / Rag Na Rock / Dirty, Filthy / Stalin's Organs / Knife In Her Guts / Think You Outta Know This / Martyr Dumb / Nudged / Fire in The Loins / Surf Of Syn / Crush Kill Destroy / No One But The Brave.

CARNIVAL OF CHAOS, Metal Blade 14125-2 (1997). Penguin Attack / Let's Blame The Lightman / First Rule Is / Sammy / Endless Apocalypse / Billy Bad Ass / Hate Love Songs / Letter From The Scallop Boat / Pre-School Prostitute / If I Could Be That / In Her Fear / Back To Iraq / I Stuck On My Thumb / The Private Pain Of Techno Destructo / Gonna Kill U / Sex Cow / Antarctican Drinking Song / Don't Need A Man.

WE KILL EVERYTHING, Metal Blade 14237-2 (1999). Babyraper / Fistfuck / The Performer / A Short History Of The End Of The World (Part VII: The Final Chapter) / Escape From The Mooselodge / Tune From Da Moon / Jiggle The Handle / Nitro—Burnin' Funny Bong / Jagermonsta / My Girly Ways / The Master Has A Butt / We Kill Everything / Child / Penile Drip / Mary Anne / Friend / Fuckin' An Animal.

VIOLENCE HAS ARRIVED, Metal Blade 14374-2 (2001). Hell Intro / Battle Lust / Abyss Of Woe / The Apes Of Wrath / Immortal Corruptor / The Anti-Anti Christ / Licksore / Beauteous Rot / Bloody Mary / Bile Driver / The Wheel / The Song Of Words / Happy Death Day.

LET THERE BE GWAR, Slavepit SP004 (2004). You Ain't Shit / Americanized / GWAR Theme / Rock n' Roll Party Town / Pure As The Arctic Snow / Americanized / U Ain't Shit / Slutman City / Time For Death / GWAR Theme / Rock n' Roll Party Town / Techno's Song / Eat Steel / Gor-Gor.

WAR PARTY, DRT Entertainment RTE 00426 (2004). Bring Back The Bomb / Krosstika / Womb With A View / Decay Of Granduer / War Party / Bonesnapper (The Faces Of The Slain) / Lost God / Reaganator / Bonus Plan / You Can't Kill Terror / Fistful Of Teeth.

LIVE FROM MT. FUJI, DRT Entertainment RTE 00431 (2005). Salaminizer / Krosstika / Bring Back The Bomb / Ham On The Bone / Immortal Corruptor / Womb With A View / Have You Seen Me? / Horror Of Yig / Crush, Kill, Destroy / Crack In The Egg / Reaganator / Bonesnapper / Sick Of You / Biledriver.

BEYOND HELL, DRT Entertainment (2006). Intro / War Is All We Know / Murders Muse / Go To Hell! / I Love The Pigs / Tormentor / Eighth Lock / The Ultimate Bohab / Destroyed / The One That Will Not Be Named / Back In Crack / School's Out.

HADES

PARAMUS, NJ, USA — *Alan Tecchio (vocals), Dan Lorenzo (guitar), Ed Fuhrman (guitar), Jimmy Schulman (bass), Ron Lipnicki (drums).*

A renowned name in Metal circles. Paramus, New Jersey's HADES has weathered the storms of line-up changes and break ups to consistently deliver ever improving slabs of technical Heavy Metal. Having attained a worthy cult following on American soil, despite a sometimes overtly socio-political lyrical stance, HADES, established during 1978 by guitarist DAN LORENZO, have maintained a sturdy fan base in Germany. HADES underwent turbulent times in the early 80s. Their 1982 debut 'Deliver Us From Evil' 7" single sees a line-up roster credited as vocalist Paul Smith, guitarists DAN LORENZO and Joe Casili, bassist Anthony Vitti and drummer Tom Coombs. However, Lorenzo and not Vitti actually recorded the bass parts.

HADES inducted Lou Ciarlo on bass and had their tracks 'Easy Way Out' featured on the Metal Blade 'Metal Massacre VI' compilation album plus the songs 'Rogues March' and 'Gloomy Sunday' on a 1984 Megaforce compilation entitled 'Born To Metalize'. Then Paul Smith left to join the army and for a brief tenure was replaced with John Callura. However, Callura was out within weeks. Bassist Lou Ciarlo also quit leaving HADES as just a duo of guitarist Dan Lorenzo and drummer Tom Coombs. Things stabilized somewhat with the addition of bassist Sandy Handsel and ex-PROPHECY guitarist Scott LePage. As HADES found a new frontman in Alan Tecchio, previously with PROPHECY, the band also pulled in ex-ATTACKER bassist Jimmy Schulman. This line-up recorded the 1985 'The Cross' single.

A further live demo 'Live At The Fox' (one of a set of live tapes HADES released in 1986 others being 'Live At The China Club' and 'Live At Manhattans') secured HADES a deal with Torrid Records. HADES objectives were again hindered though, when Schulman suffered a near fatal car crash putting live work on ice for a lengthy period.

LePage joined Hardcore rappers MUCKY PUP on an amicable basis, featured on their 1987 album 'Can't You Take A Joke?', and HADES was soon up to strength again by including guitarist Ed Fuhrman, previously a member of covers act WARNING. Vocalist Allan Tecchio, opting to join Texan Progressive techno-metallers WATCHTOWER for their 'Control And Resistance' album, was supplanted by a returning Paul Smith.

Lorenzo founded NON-FICTION, along with MUCKY PUP's Dan Nastisi, releasing three albums although HADES reunited for the 'Exist To Resist' album. Tecchio later fronted POWER in a guest capacity. All was running far from smoothly however as soon after recording various band members announced their intention never to record with HADES again. During April of 1988 HADES, back with Tecchio and patching up their differences once more, once more began rehearsing and writing for a new album. LePage was reunited with the act to put down bass and in came new drummer Dave Lescindky. However, following European touring, HADES folded in June 1989. That same year Tecchio featured as frontman on the classic WATCHTOWER album 'Control And Resistance'. Post HADES, guitarist Ed Fuhrman forged Progressive Metal outfit SYSTEM ADDICT, issuing the 1992 EP 'Wealth & Sickness'. Tom Coombs briefly sat in on the drum stool for TRIXTER.

Originally intended as a final farewell in 1995 the band issued 'Exist To Resist'. There are at least three versions, in different sleeve art, of this compilation with the US, Black Pumpkin version adding four bonus tracks. The CD had some material recorded in 1989, at the very end of their first run. The US version also has alternate artwork as well. Fan demand to re-issue the old demos resulted in the band releasing 'The Lost Fox Studio Sessions' during 1998. The band themselves admit the sound quality is terrible and recommends it only for die-hard fans!

The time was right and the band, spurred by the demand for classic Thrash, inked a deal with Metal Blade Records. HADES added drummer Ron Lipinski in August of 2000 and re-drafted Jimmy Schulman on bass. This line up put in a valuable showing at the annual German 'Wacken Open Air' festival. Their 2000 album 'The Downside' would see M.O.D. and S.O.D.'s larger than life frontman Billy Milano adding backing vocals and D.D. Verni of OVERKILL putting down session bass on the track 'Bitter Suite No. 1'.

HADES released their latest musical chapter, 'DamNation', in June of 2001. Besides HADES activity various members would busy themselves with other concerns, Ed Fuhrman starting a new band TEN TON TRUCK whilst Ron Lipinski played with covers band SOUTHERN SHIFT. In January of 2003 it would be learned that HADES drummer Ron Lipnicki was being treated for testicular cancer. Three months of chemotherapy preceded a successful operation in June.

Lorenzo landed himself in hot water with a solo venture in November as he issued a claim that his track 'BS' featured an unearthed vocal track from the late AC/DC frontman Bon Scott. Working with Johnny Milnes of MUCKY PUP and ALL BORO KINGS and HADES colleague Jimmy Schulman on bass, Lorenzo stated that the vocal tapes were donated by Scott's sister, who had given the recordings to her neighbour in Scotland. In fact suspicions were confirmed a few days later when Lorenzo admitted the vocal was in reality from a Bon Scott impersonator fronting AC/DC cover band OVERDOSE.

In May of 2004 former HADES guitarist Ed Fuhrman and ex-DEMONSPEED drummer Jim King forged a new outfit entitled TEN TON TRUCK in alliance with vocalist Jim Frizzell and bassist Craig Salvadeo. Initial demos were cut that same month at Big Blue Meenie recording studios in Hoboken. That same year HADES struck a deal with the Belgian based Mausoleum Records to re-release the group's first two albums 'Resisting Success' and 'If At First You Don't Succeed' in one package. For inclusion HADES undertook a studio re-union for a brand new track entitled 'Thinktank' comprising Alan Tecchio on vocals, guitarists DAN LORENZO and Ed Fuhrman, Jimmy Schulman on bass and Ron Lipnicki on drums.

Ron Lipnicki joined HAVOCHATE in October of 2004 as Lorenzo made preparations for his third solo album 'Cut From A Different Cloth'. The drummer enrolled into the ranks of OVERKILL for European dates in May 2005. In June Alan Tecchio was announced as new frontman for SEVEN WITCHES, appearing on the album 'Metal Nation'.

Deliver Us From Evil EP, Hades (1982). Girls Will Be Girls / Social Disease.

The Cross, Hades (1985). The Cross / Widow's Mite.

RESISTING SUCCESS, Torrid (1987). On To Illiad / Legal Tender / Sweet Revenge / Nightstalker / Resist Success / Widows Mite / Cross? Masque Of The Red Death.

IF AT FIRST YOU DON'T SUCCEED, Torrid (1988). Opinionate / Process Of Elimination / King In Exile / In The Meantime / Rebel Without A Brain / Aftermath Of Rebellion / I Too Eye / Face The Fat Reality / Technical Difficulties.

LIVE: ON LOCATION, Grand Slamm 38 (1991). The Leaders? / King In Exile / On To Illiad / In The Meantime / Opinionate! / Rebel Without A Brain / "A" / Rape Of Persephone / The Cross / Face The Fat Reality / I Too Eye / Aftermath Of Betrayal / Nightstalker / MES (Technical Difficulties) / Diplomatic Immunity.

EXIST TO RESIST, Art Of Music 51002 (1995). Exist To Resist / Rape Of Persephone / Doubt / Colorblind / Deter-My-Nation / Throughout Me, Threw Out You / Second Degree Sleepwalking / A(G) / The Other / The Leaders '95.

THE LOST FOX STUDIO SESSIONS, Black Pumpkin (1998). The Leaders? / Sweet Revenge / Nightstalker / Resist Success / Gamblin' With Your Life / Deter My Nation / Rape Of Persephone / Not A Part Of Your Life / Bete Noir / Throughout Me, Threw Out You / Amerasian Reparation / King In Exile / Opinionate / A / Easy Way Out.

SAVIOUR SELF, Metal Blade 3984-14194-2 (1999). Saviour Self / Decline And Fall Of The American Empire / Our Father / Active Contrition / To Know One / In The Words Of The Profit / The Agnostic / Y2K / End Of The Bargain / Fall / The Atheist.

THE DOWNSIDE, Metal Blade 14283 (2000). Ground Zero N.Y.C. / Align The Planets / Bitter Suite #1 / Hoax / Pay The Price / Hail To The Thief / Shove It / It's A Wonderful Lie / Become Dust / Responsible / The Me That Might Have Been / Ground Zero (Reprise).

DAMNATION, Metal Blade 14372 (2001). Bloat / Out The Window / DamNation / Absorbed / Force Quit / Stressfest / Biocaust / This I Know / Momentary Clarity / California Song / Stop And Go / Bad Vibrations.

HALLOWS EVE

MARIETTA, GA, USA — *Stacy Anderson (vocals), David Stuart (guitar), Tommy Stewart (bass), Tym Helton (drums).*

Marietta, Georgia Thrash Metal act HALLOWS EVE date back to 1984 with an initial line-up of vocalist Stacy Anderson, guitarists David Stuart and Skellator, bassist Tommy Stewart and drummer Tym Helton. The band's debut appearance came with the inclusion of the track 'Metal Merchants' on the Metal Blade 'Metal Massacre IV' compilation.

Drummer Ronny Appoldt appeared on the debut album although Tym Helton handled the drums on the tracks 'Metal Merchants' and 'Hallows Eve'.

HALLOW'S EVE returned with March 1988's 'Monument', recorded at Studio One in Atlanta with Donal Jones acting as producer. Drums for 'Monument', which included a cover version of QUEEN's 'Sheer Heart Attack', are by Rob Clayton although for live work Paul Kopchinski occupied the drum stool. By the third album Tym Helton was back in the fold. The track 'D.I.E.' was a featured track on the Metal Blade issued soundtrack album for the 1988 movie 'Black Roses'.

The group appeared to have split in late 1988 as Anderson departed to Los Angeles although Tommy Stewart and David Stuart carried on into the following year looking for new members and writing material.

The duo eventually found new guitarist JAMES MURPHY, previously with AGENT STEEL, and drummer Tom Knight but the pair lasted barely a few months, Murphy joining DEATH and later played with OBITUARY, CANCER, TESTAMENT, KONKHRA, DISINCARNATE as well as issuing solo product. Tommy Stewart later turned up as a member of FRAGILE X.

HALLOWS EVE reunited in early 2004, Tommy Stewart being joined by 'Tales Of Terror' album guitarist Skellator (now known as Skully) and new frontman Steve Cannon. Making up the numbers would be new personnel Dwayne Monk on guitars and DRYWATER drummer Dave Jensen. This very same line up would also forge ahead with a separate Black Metal project dubbed LESTREGUS NOSFERATUS. The resurrected HALLOWS EVE debuted live opening for fellow Thrash veterans EXODUS at the Atlanta Cotton Club on 26th April. However, in mid May Cannon was unceremoniously ejected, the obviously distraught former frontman issuing a lengthy statement claiming "This is one of the worst events in my life, and I don't have anywhere to turn for help". Within days the ex-singer announced a brand new Stoner / Doom venture BROKEN TRINITY, intending to recruit violinist April, LAND OF SOULS guitarist Jeffrey Hinely and bassist Chris Miller.

HALLOWS EVE bounced back in September, issuing their first product in over sixteen years in the form of a two track single entitled 'Evil Offerings'. The song 'Technicolour Roadkill' saw bassist Tommy Stewart handling lead vocals whilst 'Looking Glass' featured Skullator as spotlighted singer. The single would be launched with a 17th September gig at The Masquerade in Atlanta alongside DEICIDE. 2005 saw the issue of a brand new HALLOWS EVE studio offering, 'Evil Never Dies', recorded at Van Gogh Studios in Atlanta with co-producer Chris Gailfoil.

A lavish May 2006 box set, 'History Of Terror', saw release through Metal Blade compiling all three albums remastered plus previously unreleased live and rehearsal tracks and a 200 minute DVD. Meantime, HALLOWS EVE had contracted with Xtreem Music to re-promote' Evil Never Dies'. That same year Stacey Anderson forged modern Metal outfit TWO PRONGED CROWN, comprising guitarist Doyle Bright, of RIGOR MORTIS, ILK and THE CHAOS FOUNDATION, guitarist Chris Abbamonte, of DISTEMPER and ILK, bass player Jimmy Gorman, of DISTEMPER, ILK and THE CHAOS FOUNDATION, programmer Mink, of ILK, and drummer Mike Rollings, from METALMORPHOSIS, BIG TWIN DIN and JARBOE.

To celebrate the 25th anniversary of Metal Blade Records, original HALLOWS EVE members Stacy Andersen and Tommy Stewart will appeared on stage together for the first time since 1989 during the band's performance at the New England Metal And Hardcore Festival in April 2007. They would be joined by lead vocalist and guitarist Doyle Bright and drummer Dane Jensen.

TALES OF TERROR, Roadrunner RR 9772 (1985). Plunging To Megadeath / Outer Limits / Horrorshow / The Mansion / There Are No Rules / Valley Of The Dolls / Metal Merchants / Hallows Eve.

DEATH AND INSANITY, Metal Blade 72163 (1986). Death And Insanity / Goblet Of Gore / Lethal Tendencies / Obituary / Plea Of The Aged / Suicide / D.I.E. (Death In Effect) / Attack Of The Iguana / Nefarious / Nobody Lives Forever / Death And Insanity (Reprise).

MONUMENT, Metal Blade 73290 (1988). Speedfreak / Sheer Heart Attack / Rot Gut / Monument To Nothing / Pain Killer / The Mighty Decibel / Righteous Ones / No Sanctuary.

HAMMER

POLAND — *Rob Keller (vocals), Mick Savage (guitar), Peter Poland (guitar), Robert Joy (bass), Derek Cloud (drums).*

Polish Thrash Metal band HAMMER adopted anglicised stage names for the English version of their 1992 album 'Terror'. Vocalist Robert Köhler became Rob Keller, guitarist Maciej Sawicz adopted the name Mick Savage, fellow guitarist Jaroslaw Kopola turned into Peter Poland, bassist Robert Kurys was Robert Joy and drummer Tomasz Klimczak morphed into Derek Cloud. The band name would also undergo the same process adopting Teutonic umlauts to become HÄMMER.

Previously the band had debuted with four tracks on the 1987 compilation album 'Metalmania '87' sharing space with DESTROYERS. By 1989 an eponymous debut album saw the light of day. The 1990 'Shermann' album, released by the Finnish Poko label, found the group crediting themselves as singer Snipe, guitarists Micky and Funny, bassist Chuck and drummer Kliman.

TERROR, Nagrania SX 2979 (1990). Terror / Streetfighter / Shut Up / Inside Looking Out / Monsters / Angel's Wrath / This Is War / Old Man.

SHERMANN, Poko POLCD 1 (1990). Shermann / Camp / The Oddest Dream / Different From Me / For Her My Nut / Destroyer / Rage.

HANGÖVER

POLAND — *Hellhound Warpig (vocals / bass / drums), Slut Eviscerator (guitar).*

Black Thrash act that debuted with a 2000 demo cassette 'Terrorbeer'. The group comprised vocalist / bassist / drummer Hellhound Warpig ("insulting alcobreath, four string bulldozer & wimpslaying rhythms"), guitarist Slut Eviscerator ("Drunken shreds, beergut & antisocial behaviour"). In December of 2000 the band, claiming Hellhound Warpig was "sick of playing instrument he has no idea how to use", advertised for a drummer, citing such obligatory requirements hair length, photo of the applicant in a drunken condition and a criminal record.

HANGÖVER's June 2002 split EP, shared with the anonymous Swedish act GMC and limited to 150 hand numbered copies, would see the track 'Pornowatcher' sporting lyrics written by Ronnie Ripper of GEHENNAH.

Hangöver, Hangöver (2002) (Split EP with GMC). Swing Of The Crowbar / Pornowatcher.

HARTER ATTACK

USA — *Richard Harter (vocals / guitar), Kip Lemming (bass), Glenn Evans (drums).*

HARTER ATTACK debuted with a four track demo in 1986. Bassist Kip Lemming is ex-RIOT whilst drummer Glenn Evans was also with NUCLEAR ASSAULT. Both Harter and Evans had previously been members of STRIKER.

HARTER ATTACK issued three self financed singles on their own Arena Records prior to the album and a new line up of Harter and brothers George Chahalis on drums and Nick Chahalis on bass. Harter's friendship with Evans stood the band in good stead as the HARTER ATTACK album was produced by the NUCLEAR ASSAULT drummer and also boasts guest contributions from fellow members bassist Dan Lilker and Anthony Bramante.

Salt In The Wound, Arena (1986). Salt In The Wound / Top Of The World.
HUMAN HELL, Metalcore CORE1CD (1989). Bells Of The Apocalypse / Last Temptation / Slaves Of Conformity / Message From God / Nuclear Attack / Human Hell / Culture Decay / Thugs Against Drugs / Symbol Of Hate / Let The Sleeping Dogs Lie.

HATE SQUAD

GERMANY — *Burkhard Schmidt (vocals), Mark Künnemann (guitar), Tim Bauermeister (bass), Helge Dolgener (drums).*

Founded in 1993, HATE SQUAD, a band displaying some Hardcore and Death Metal influences to their Thrash style, attracted the attention of G.U.N. Records with their 'Theater Of Hate' demo, leading to a deal and the recording of the '94 debut album of the same title. Ex-SARGANT FURY and ZENITH bassist Bauke De Groot joined the group after the record hit the stores in order that Tim Baurmeister could concentrate on guitar. His new axe partner Mark Künnemann would depart after second album 'I.Q. Zero' and was replaced by Markus Fenske for a tour with KREATOR.

1995's 'Sub Zero' album proved to be a collection of remixed tracks lent new life by artists such as ATARI TEENAGE RIOT, DIE KRUPPS, T.A.S.S. and GIGANTOR.

Following the release of 'Sub-Zero' both Bauermeister and De Groot quit, the former joining RYKERS, The band would only replace De Groot with former HEATHEN and GRIP INC. man Jason Vie Brooks in order to begin work on a proper third album. Vie Brooks formed part of the 2000 HEATHEN reunion.

THEATER OF HATE, Great Unlimited Noises GUN 049 BMG 74321 24672-2 (1994). Cause And Effect / Self-Defence (Is No Offense) / Love-Hate / Theater Of Hate / Perverse Insanity / Bastards / Mindloss / Condemned To Die / Hardness Of Life / Free At Last.
I.Q. ZERO, Great Unlimited Noises GUN 075 BMG 74321 31447-2 (1995). Not My God / BDD / My Truth / IQ Zero / Dishonesty / Crucified / Different From You / Terror / Respect.
SUB-ZERO, Great Unlimited Noises GUN 096 BMG 74321 37580-2 (1995). Not My God (Die Krupps Remix) / BDD (The Speed Remix) / IQ Zero (TASS Remix) / Different From You (Biochip C Remix) / Every Second Counts (Gigantor Remix) / Not My God (Alec Empire Remix) / Every Second Counts.
PZYCO!, Great Unlimited Noises GUN 129 BMG 74321 43582-2 (1997). Who Dares Wins / Freedom Speaks / Mission Done / Psyco! / Synthetic Twins / Just A Dream / Change / Get Loaded / The Senseless Fall / B.T.C. 97.

HATEFRAME

FINLAND — *Ilkka Valkonen (vocals), Joonas Kote (guitar), Eza Virén (guitar), Marko Kangaskolkka (bass), Tonmi Lillman (drums).*

HATEFRAME is an old school Thrash Metal outfit forged in 2004 by MALPRACTICE, ex-TO/DIE/FOR guitarist Joonas 'Jope' Koto and the TO/DIE/FOR, BARATHRUM and SINERGY credited drummer Tonmi Lillman. Bassist Marko Kangaskolkka also holds a tradition with TO/DIE/FOR.

The group was borne out of an acrimonious split in the TO/DIE/FOR ranks during 2003. With the situation proving unsolvable, Koto and Lillman forged the SLAYER tribute band DEAD/SKIN/MASK in order to keep active. Gradually this act, with Ilkka Valkonen on vocals and Eza Virén on guitar, evolved into HATEFRAME. That December the group cut the demo tracks 'Torment The Masses', 'Warfare' and 'The Perfect Hate' but were then dealt a blow as Valkonen exited. Lillman also quit, even going so far as to sell his drum kit.

The band soldiered on, pulling in Sami Kujala as a new vocalist and Eza's brother Lauri Virén on drums. However, in April of 2004 Lillman made a return. In this incarnation HATEFRAME conducted just one gig, on July 23rd at the 'Jörisrock' festival in Suonenjoki, after which Kujala decamped and Valkonen duly returned to his post. By November the group had completed work on a debut album entitled 'Sign Of Demise'.

Besides his duties with HATEFRAME Lillman also busied himself with KYLÄHULLUT with his ex-SINERGY comrade Alex Laiho. Kote would be active with CRACK WHORES, TUMULT BREED and NEW DAWN FOUNDATION. HATEFRAME signed to Rising Realm Records in January 2005.

In January of 2006 Tonmi Lillman joined the ranks of VANGUARD.

SIGN OF DEMISE, Rising Realm (2005). Crowned In Blood / Final Solution / Feeding The Flame / Sign Of Demise / The Perfect Hate / Bloodfeast / Torment The Masses / Warfare / Hallucinate / Infection.

HATESPHERE

DENMARK — *Jacob Bredahl (vocals), Peter Lyse Hansen (guitar), Ziggy (guitar), Mikael Ehlert (bass), Morten Toft Hansen (drums).*

Death-Thrash act which includes featuring RAUNCHY drummer Morten Toft Hansen in the ranks. Early demo works, 'Condemned Future' in April 1995, 'Disconnected' in 1997 and 'Spring'98', were conducted under the formative banner of NECROSIS. Rebranded, the group re-debuted with an eponymous album in April 2001 for the Italian Scarlet label. The 2002 album 'Bloodred Hatred', produced by Tommy Hansen, was recorded in Jailhouse Studios in Horsens, Denmark. The band hooked up with INFLICTION for January 2003 tour dates followed by April European gigs ranked alongside MASTODON and THE HAUNTED.

Drummer Morten Toft Hansen exited in May 2003 in order to focus his energies on RAUNCHY. The band substituted him with Anders Gyldenøhr in July. The band's December 2003 EP, 'Something Old, Something New, Something Borrowed And Something Black', issued through Italy's Scarlet Records saw live tracks alongside cover versions of OZZY OSBOURNE's 'Bark At The Moon' and ANTHRAX's 'Caught In A Mosh'.

The 'Ballet Of The Brute' album, recorded at Jailhouse Studios with producer Tommy Hansen, arrived in 2004. INVOCATOR's Jacob Hansen guested on the track 'Warhead'. A further studio session found HATESPHERE laying down the track 'Hvornår Er Det Søndag Igen?!' for a collection of tribute songs to local football team AGF. The band would be chosen, alongside fellow Scandinavian acts THE HAUNTED, MNEMIC, MERCENARY, RAUNCHY, MELTED, BLINDFAULT and STOMPED, to form up the "Nordic Threat" show for the Popkomm 2004 music

HATESPHERE

convention at the Silver Wings in Berlin on 29th September. Bassist Mikael Ehler and drummer Anders Gyldenøhr teamed up with resurrected veteran Thrash act ARTILLERY for a one off gig in November at The Rock venue in Copenhagen. Jacob Bredahl took time out to aid ABORTED as guest backing vocalist on their album 'The Archaic Abattoir'. The singer also activated side project ALLHELLUJA in alliance with Italian drummer Stefano Longhi.

HATESPHERE's January 2005 'The Killing EP' would include a cover version of SUICIDAL TENDENCIES 'Trip At The Brain'. The band then tagged onto KREATOR and DARK TRANQUILLITY's 'Enemy Of God' European tour prior to March / April shows as guests to MORBID ANGEL. HATESPHERE entered Jailhouse Studios with producer Tommy Hansen in early June to craft a new album 'The Sickness Within' for September issue. A brief burst of German dates had the band supporting CHIMAIRA and DARK TRANQUILLITY.

The band united with French tech-Thrashers GOJIRA for UK October 2006 dates. Later that same month Mikael Ehlert acted as stand in bassist for KOLDBORN whilst both Jacob Bredahl and Henrik Jacobsen sessioned on ABORTED's 'Slaughter & Apparatus: A Methodical Overture' album. HATESPHERE, RAUNCHY and VOLBEAT pooled their talents for the 'Danish Dynamite' European tour in November and December.

HATESPHERE's 2007 album, entitled 'Serpent Smiles And Killer Eyes', emerged in April.

That same month Danish label Futhermocker issued an exclusive HATESPHERE 7" single, limited to 220 hand numbered copies, containing the songs 'Drinking With The King Of The Dead' and an exclusive cover version of CORROSION OF CONFORMITY's 'Vote With A Bullet'.

Concerts in Denmark and Norway during May saw support from Norway's STONEGARD.

In May HATESPHERE undertook tour dates in China, commencing at the Beijing Midi Festival in Haidian Park. HATESPHERE will play the mainstage of the festival on May 1st, followed by a May 2nd concert at The Star Live, Beijing with Norwegian act EL CACO and three Chinese bands, NARAKAM, SUFFOCATED and YAKSA. Upon their return, the band flanked Norwegian act STONEGARD for a series of Scandinavian shows then engaged in German shows partnered with Belgium's ABORTED leading up to numerous European festival appearances.

HATESPHERE, Soundholic TKCS-85013 (2001) (Japanese release). Hate / Picture This / Addicted Soul / Bloodsoil / Down For Good / No Sense / Preacher / Dead / Ill Will / Restrain.

HATESPHERE, Scarlet SC 027-2 (2001). Hate / Picture This / Addicted Soul / Bloodsoil / Down For Good / No Sense / Preacher / Dead / Ill Will.

BLOODRED HATRED, Soundholic TKCS-85045 (2002). Intro / Believer / Hell Is Here / Insanity Arise / Disbeliever / Plague / Low Life Vendetta / Deeper And Deeper / Kicking Ahead / Addicted Soul / Under Water.

BLOODRED HATRED, Scarlet SC 054-2 (2002). Intro / Believer / Hell Is Here / Insanity Arise / Disbeliever / Plague / Low Life Vendetta / Deeper And Deeper / Kicking Ahead.

Something Old, Something New, Something Borrowed And Something Black EP, Scarlet SC 077-2 (2003). Release The Pain / Bark At The Moon / Caught In A Mosh / Low Life Vendetta (Live) / Bloodsoil (Live) / Plague (Live) / Hate (Live).

BALLET OF THE BRUTE, Scarlet SC 087-2 (2004). The Beginning And The End / Deathtrip / Vermin / Downward To Nothing / Only The Strongest ... / What I See I Despise / Last Cut, Last Head / Warhead / Blankeyed / 500 Dead People.

BALLET OF THE BRUTE, Soundholic TKCS-85098 (2004) (Japanese release). The Beginning And The End / Deathtrip / Vermin / Downward To Nothing / Only The Strongest ... / What I See I Despise / Last Cut, Last Head / Warhead / Blankeyed / 500 Dead People / Release The Pain / Bark At The Moon / Caught In A Mosh.

The Killing EP, Steamhammer SPV 056-99262 (2005). The Will Of God / You're The Enemy / Murderous Intent / Trip At The Brain.

THE SICKNESS WITHIN, Steamhammer SPV 085-99662 (2005). The White Fever / The Fallen Shall Rise In A River Of Blood / Reaper Of Life / Sickness Within / Murderous Intent / The Coming Of Chaos / Bleed To Death / Heaven Is Ready To Fall / Seeds Of Shame / Chamber Master / Marked By Darkness. Chart position: 87 DENMARK.

Sickness Within, Steamhammer (2005) (Promotion release). Sickness Within / Reaper Of Life.

THE SICKNESS WITHIN, Soundholic TKCS-85130 (2005) (Japanese release). The White Fever / The Fallen Shall Rise In A River Of Blood / Reaper Of Life / Sickness Within / Murderous Intent / The Coming Of Chaos / Bleed To Death / Heaven Is Ready To Fall / Seeds Of Shame / Chamber Master / Marked By Darkness / You're The Enemy / The Will Of God / Trip At The Brain.

Drinking With The King Of The Dead, Futhermocker (2007) (7" vinyl single. Limited edition 220 hand numbered copies). Drinking With The King Of The Dead / Vote With A Bullet.

SERPENT SMILES AND KILLER EYES, Steamhammer (2007). Lies And Deceit / The Slain / Damned Below Judas / Drinking With The King Of The Dead / Forever War / Feeding The Demons / Floating / Let Them Hate / Absolution.

HATEWORK

ARCONATE, ITALY — *Fabio Formentti (vocals), Max (vocals / bass), Marco (guitar), Lorenzo Bocca (drums).*

Arconate, Milan based Neo-Thrash outfit founded in 1996. HATEWORK cut an intended debut album but these sessions would not see release due to a dispute with the label. As such, the group debuted in 2000 with the debut 'Thrasher's Attack'. Further demos, dubbed 'Total War', secured a deal with Germany's Witches Brew Records, resulting in the 2002 album 'Madbent For Disaster'. Live promotion for this included supports to NECRODEATH, RAW POWER, DISMEMBER and TANKARD. A split 7" single, shared with VEXED, for Dream Evil Records followed in 2003 upfront of the 'Thrash n' Roll' album for US imprint Beercity Records.

HATEWORK inducted new singer Fabio Formentti of Punk act TRACCIAZERO in March 2005. The group contributed their cover version of TANKARD's 'Live To Die' to the tribute album 'A Tribute To Tankard' included as a bonus disc on the AFM Records 2007 TANKARD release 'Best Case Scenario: 25 Years In Beers'.

Thrasher's Attack, (2000). Pleasure Of The Blood / The Rebirth / Ring Of The Blind / Necrostorm / Thrasher's Attack.

Total War, (2001). Total War / Italmaniacstorm.

MADBENT FOR DESASTER, Witches Brew BREW002 (2002). Madbent For Desaster / Tomahawk / Hellsquad From The Airways / Total War / Pleasure Of The Blood / Deeds Of Hate / (We Are) Alcoholic Abusers / Thrashers Attack / Dawn Of The Dead / All Hell Breaks Loose.

Bastard, Dream Evil (2003) (Split 7' single with VEXED). Bastard / Revenge.

THRASH 'N' ROLL, Beer City (2004). T.D.I / Thrash 'N' Roll / XXX / Heaven's On Fire / Devil Eye / I Don't Care / War Again / Hateway To Hell / Radio Madness / Get Off / Blast From Below / Rop The Hush.

HAVE MERCY

BALTIMORE, MD, USA — *Lonnie Fletcher (vocals), Nick Ellingson (guitar), Tom Maxwell (guitar), Rob Michael (bass), John Knoerlein (drums).*

A highly respected Thrash Metal band formed in late 1983. The genesis of the band was when drummer John Knoerlein and guitarist Mike Guilta advertised in a local newspaper for a bassist to help create the "Ultimate Metal band". Rob Michael responded but soon after this trio gelled Guilta opted out. A replacement would be found in the guitar pairing of Tom Maxwell and Nick Ellingson whilst John Gontrum was taken on as HAVE MERCY's first vocalist. His stay would be brief though and, after just two live performances, he was soon supplanted by Sean Zellers. In this incarnation HAVE MERCY laid down the mid 1984 demo 'Pleading For Mercy' but within three gigs Zellers too exited.

Choosing not to release the demos with Zeller's input intact the group, drafting Lee Dayton on the microphone, re-recorded 'Pleading For Mercy'. HAVE MERCY underwent line up shuffles with Dayton, staying the course for slightly longer than his predecessors (he lasted 4 shows) ousted in favour of Lonnie Fletcher, pulled from covers band CRY BABY. Guitarist Nick Ellingson left the fold in March of 1985, prior to the band attaining a deal and his place was filled by John Brenner. This version of the band cut the second demo 'Mass Destruction'. This tape soon ignited underground praise and Metal Blade Records picked the song 'The Omen' for inclusion on their Metal Massacre VII compilation album. However, Brenner's stay was short-lived and he decamped that November. Ellingson soon returned as HAVE MERCY was signed up to Combat Records.

The initial plan was for Combat to press up the 'Mass Destruction' demo as an EP release but the band decided on recording brand new material. This surfaced as part of Combat's 'Boot Camp' series in April of 1986, entitled 'Armageddon Descends'. Knoerlein left the band shortly after release to join DEADLY AGRESSOR and by August John Grden of BLITZKRIEG was manning the drum stool. Further tribulation came before the year closed as Ellingson bailed out for the second time. Grden's BLITZKRIEG colleague Dave Brenner took his place.

1987 proved an arduous year for the band. Maxwell took off and the band sustained injuries whilst in a van on the way to a gig in New York. Rob Michael suffered serious neck trauma and was laid off for a lengthy period. Eventually reconvening, HAVE MERCY discovered Fletcher had absented himself so Rob Michael took charge of the lead vocal role. Fletcher had in fact united with ex-HAVE MERCY man Nick Ellingson in a new act billed as ENFORCE. As a trio with John King as stand in guitarist HAVE MERCY got back to live work. A demo was recorded with former band mate Nick Ellingson acting as producer. Unfortunately though Combat declined to renew their contract. As 1987 drew to an end Maxwell returned to the fold.

HAVE MERCY entered 1988 as a quartet of Michael, Maxwell, Brenner and Grden but then made a decision to recruit Al Carr as lead vocalist. This line up lasted one, swansong, gig as openers to WHIPLASH that April. A demo, 'Morbid Reality', was committed to tape with Carr but then re-recorded with Michael's vocals. With no labels showing interest in this latest batch of songs HAVE MERCY disbanded. Both Rob Michael and John Grden were recruited into the ranks of FEAR OF GOD. Latterly Grden joined TRUE UNHOLY DEATH whilst Michael teamed up with Punk band JAKKPOT.

Guitarist Tom Maxwell journeyed on to MARY'S SUICIDE before finding a high profile post with Washington D.C. Alt-Metal band NOTHINGFACE. The German Century Media label packaged together Combat's 'Boot Camp' series, including the HAVE MERCY set, for CD re-release in 1999.

ARMAGEDDON DESCENDS, Relativity (1986). Intro / Mass Destruction / City Of Doom / Holy Dismissal / Faces Of Death / No Forgiveness.

HAVOC MASS

FL, USA — *Ray Wallace (vocals / bass), Ben Meyer (guitar), Andy Wallace (guitar), Curt Beeson (drums).*

Florida Thrash Metal band HAVOC MASS include ex-NASTY SAVAGE men guitarist Ben Meyer and drummer Curt Beeson along with former members of LAST RITES frontman Ray Wallace and guitarist Andy Wallace. The band emerged with the 1991 demo 'In Extremities'. A further effort entitled 'Unknown Origin' followed before the 1993 debut album 'Killing The Future'.

The Wallace brothers would go on to create INHUMAN for a series of albums. Both Beeson and Curtis would stick together to found the 2000 act LOWBROW for the 'Victims At Play' album.

KILLING THE FUTURE, Massacre MASSCD 019 (1993).

HAVOCHATE

NEW YORK, NY, USA — *Tim Bouchee (vocals), Freddy Ordine (guitar), Mario Rodriguez (guitar), Greg Christian (bass), Ovie Rodriguez (drums).*

HAVOCHATE was founded in New York during the late nineties by former AXIOM guitarist Freddy Ordine and erstwhile MALICIOUS ONSLAUGHT drummer Ovie Rodriguez. An advertisement in a local music newspaper that read "Crazed vocalist looking for equally crazed band" led the pair to singer John Mallek and in 2001 bassist Dave Ludwig joined the fold.

HAVOCHATE signed to the Root Of All Evil label for their 2002 album 'This Violent Earth', recorded at Big Blue Meenie Studios in Jersey City, New Jersey and produced by the DEATH, CANCER, DISINCARNATE and TESTAMENT credited guitarist JAMES MURPHY. The group scored a valuable coup by being selected as opening act for the MOTÖRHEAD / ANTHRAX North American Summer tour. New frontman Tim Bouchee replaced John Mallek in September 2003 for gigs supporting OVERKILL.

HAVOCHATE overhauled their line up in April 2004, dispensing with bassist Dave Ludwig and drummer Ovie Rodriguez and incorporating the world class rhythm section of ex-TESTAMENT bass player Greg Christian and former EVIL DEAD, TESTAMENT and SLAYER drummer John Dette. The new look band entered Pyramid Sound Recording Studios in Ithaca, New York on 26th April with producer Alex Perialas to craft a second album 'Cycle Of Pain'. However, Dette decamped in August, hooking up with vocalist Dave Pullaro, PUSHED, BELLADONNA, KILLING MACHINE and STREAM guitarist Peter Scheithauer as well as the former MAXIMUM PENALTY, SYSTEMATIC and MY RUIN credited bassist Johnny Chow (a.k.a. John Mark Bechtel) in a new band unit.

HAVOCHATE were joined by ex-HADES drummer Ron Lipnicki in October. However, the band's original drummer Ovie Rodriguez then marked a return as a new deal was struck with Indecent Media. Lipnicki enrolled into the ranks of OVERKILL for European dates in May 2005.

THIS VIOLENT EARTH, (2002). This Violent Earth / Years Of Abhorrence / Vindication / When God Dies / Cyclical Life / Right To Die / Kill Or Be Killed / Pull The Plug / Drenched In Sweat / Remind Me.

CYCLE OF PAIN, Indecent (2005). Cycle Of Pain / Tentacle / Fiction / Still Alive / Alone / Wicked / Cold Embrace / Crack In The Sky / Speak No More / Buried In Lies / Rotting Hour.

HAWAII

USA — *Eddie Day (vocals), Marty Friedman (guitar), Tom Azcredo (guitar), Joe Galisa (bass), Jeff Graves (drums).*

HAWAII was initially known as VIXEN in 1981 comprising of vocalist Kim LaChance, ex-DEUCE guitarist MARTY FRIEDMAN, bassist Gary St. Pierre and drummer Jeff Graves. Shortly after their formation the band scored inclusion of their track 'Angels From The Dust' on the 'US Metal II' compilation album. Further demos followed and a mini album 'Made In Hawaii'. Strangely, the band's next compilation cut 'Heavy Metal Virgin' on the Metal Blade Records 'Metal Massacre II' was credited to a pseudonym of ALOHA.

Shrapnel Records Mike Varney signed the band for the poorly produced but frenetic 'One Nation Underground'. St. Pierre departed for pastures new to front VICIOUS RUMOURS.

Further releases followed as the band got steadily more commercial. The mini-album 'Loud, Wild & Heavy' saw Friedman and Graves alongside fresh recruits vocalist Eddie Day and Joey Galisa on bass. HAWAII expanded by bringing in second guitarist Tom Azevedo for 'The Natives Are Restless'.

Friedman eventually dissolved the band and would turn up as founder member of CACOPHONY as well as releasing solo instrumental albums and more significantly joining MEGADETH.

ONE NATION UNDERGROUND, Shrapnel 1009 (1983). Living In Sin / Silent Nightmare / Escape The Night / You're Gonna Burn / One Nation Underground / Nitro Power / The Pit And The Pendulum / Secret Of The Stars / Overture Volcanica.
LOUD, WILD AND HEAVY, Hawaii (1985). Bad Boys Of Metal / Loud, Wild And Heavy / Escape The Night / Rhapsody In Black.
THE NATIVES ARE RESTLESS, SPV Steamhammer (1985). Call Of The Wild / Turn It Louder / V.P.H.B. / Beg For Mercy / Unfinished Business / Proud To Be Loud / Lies / Dynamite.

HAZARD

ARKIVA, SWEDEN — *Olof Wikstrand (vocals), Jonatan Hultén (guitar), Adam Zaars (guitar), Johannes Andersson (bass), Jonas Wikstrand (drums).*

Hailing from Arkiva in the southwest of Sweden, Thrashers HAZARD first featured guitarists Jonathan Hultén, of TRAKTOR, and Adam Zaars, TERROR, CORRUPTED and MASS HYPNOSIS bassist Joseph Tholl with Jonas Wikstrand of LEPROSY on drums. This unit cut the demo 'Aggression Within'. The CORRUPTED and LEPROSY credited Olof Wikstrand took over on bass during 2002. Singer Johannes Andersson came on board the following year.

Switching title to TRIBULATION, the band underwent a radical line-up shift in 2004, as both Olaf and Jonas Wikstrand exited to forge CAUSTIC STRIKE. FERAL's Jimmie Frödin briefly occupied the drum stool, for the demo 'Agony Awaits', before Jakob Johansson enrolled. TRIBULATION recorded a third demo, 'The Ascending Dead', in 2005.

Aggression Within, Hazard (2001) (Demo). Hazard / Shredder / Motorwheels.
Agony Awaits, Hvergelmer (2004). Agony Awaits / The Shredder / Sinister Child / Hazard / Fistfight.

HAZY AZURE

MONTREAL, QC, CANADA — *Chris Eldridge (vocals), Angelos Drosopoulos (guitar), Trevor Thomson (bass), Ram Borcar (drums).*

Montreal Jazz Hardcore-Metal project HAZY AZURE contributed two tracks, 'Sea Monkayes' and 'Human Life Pit', to the 'Kitsch 'En Squatt' compilation album. Chris Eldridge of CREMAINS contributed vocals. HAZY AZURE credited drummer Julien Livernois held credits with WD-40 and NOMAD NABO. Others affiliated with the band included singers Iggy Mulligan and John Maciukas.

A demo, 'Ambiguous Beatneck', emerged in 1989 with 'North Memphis Zoo' following in 1990. The latter cassette saw a recording line-up of vocalist Chris Eldridge, guitarist Angelos Drosopoulos, bassist Trevor Thompson and drummer Ram Borcar. Studios guests included tenor saxophonist Pete Buddle, violinis J.P. Leduc, keyboard player Dave Brule and vocalists Elize Gerard and Bill McCrae.

Drummer Ram Borcar went on to have a career as DJ Ramasutra.

Ambiguous Beatneck, Hazy Azure (1989). Intro / Exit House / Better Off Dead / Diary Of A Lunatic / Ashes To Ashes / - / Mike (Pay With Pain) / - / Die Pigs / Under The Bed / Drugs On The Job / Mutant / Mister X / Soft Cookies / Outro.
North Memphis Zoo, (1990). The Tradition Continues / Chronic Green Thumb In The Sky / Blizzard Of Pause / Adrian Teabag And His Magic Book Surprise.

HEADHUNTER

GERMANY — *Marcel Schirmer (vocals / bass), Uwe Hoffmann (guitar), Jörg Michael (drums).*

Initially titled CURSE forming in 1990. Schmier (a.k.a. Marcel Schirmer) had been the prime mover behind successful German thrashers DESTRUCTION. Guitarist Uwe 'Schmuddel' Hoffmann was ex-TALON whilst drummer Jörg Michael had plied his trade with AVENGER, LAOS, MEKONG DELTA, RAGE and RUNNING WILD. Michael continued to record and tour with ex STEELER guitarist AXEL RUDI PELL in addition to his work with HEADHUNTER.

The band toured Japan in 1990 and supported SAXON in Europe the same year before entering the studio to record the debut album 'Parody Of Life', a record on which GAMMA RAY's Kai Hansen guests on the track 'Cursed'. Headline dates in 1993 saw ACCUSER and ANTIDOTE supporting. The band had released the follow up record 'A Bizarre Gardening Accident' and 1995's 'Rebirth', after a very real, very bad and less bizarre car crash involving 'Schmuddel' Hoffmann it remained unclear as to whether the group would ever record again.

Michael's talents post HEADHUNTER have seen his services retained by AXEL RUDI PELL as well as racking up credits with GRAVE DIGGER and STRATOVARIUS. In 1998 Schmier reforged DESTRUCTION.

PARODY OF LIFE, CBH Virgin 261 151 (1991). Parody Of Life / Ease My Pain / Plead Guilty / Kick Over Your Traces / Force Of Habit / Caught In A Spider's Web / Cursed / Crack Brained / Trapped In Reality.
A BIZARRE GARDENING ACCIDENT, Major 018/043-2 (1993). Oh What A Pleasure / Signs Of Insanity / Hit Machine / Born In The Woods / Two Faced Promises / Ramalama / Boozer / Domo / Pangs Of Remorse / Character Assassination / Rude Philosophy / Deadly Instinct / Sex And Drugs And Rock n' Roll.
REBIRTH, Major CC024 (1995). Auf geht's / Army's Of The Blind / Warhead / Unhuman World / Mistreated / Mindless / Change / Disco / Scares / Adrenalin / Strucked / Don't Bogart.

HEATHEN

CA, USA — *Dave Godfrey (vocals), Lee Altus (guitar), Doug Piercy (guitar), Mike Jazstrempski (bass), Carl Sacco (drums).*

Noted Tech-Thrash mob HEATHEN was already veterans of the notorious Bay Area scene by the time of their formation in the early 80's. Drummer Carl Sacco was previously with THE LEWD, METAL CHURCH and MURDER whilst vocalist Sam Kress ran the Metal fanzine 'Whiplash'. Completing the line up was guitarist Lee Altus. Lacking a bassist HEATHEN soldiered on undertaking their first gigs without one. However, by April 1985 ex-SCEPTRE man Eric Wong had been enlisted. HEATHEN also drafted the scene veteran guitarist Doug Piercy, then a member of CONTROL but having previous credits with COBRA, DELTA and the highly influential ANVIL CHORUS.

After HEATHEN's first demo of 1986 Wong was ousted in favour of ex-GRIFFIN man Mike 'Yaz' Jastremski. Realising Kress was a better writer than a singer he bowed out in favour of former BLIND ILLUSION man Dave Godfrey. Besides working with HEATHEN Piercy got his name around in 1986 by producing demos for such acts as MORDRED, LEGACY and ATTITUDE ADJUSTMENT.

Their debut album was produced by none other than veteran ex-MONTROSE guitarist RONNIE MONTROSE and included a version of SWEET's 'Set Me Free'. Sacco departed shortly after recording of 'Breaking The Silence' and in his stead came Darren Minter. Jazstrempski was next to go and HEATHEN, minus a permanent bassist, utilized the talents of BLIND ILLUSION guitarist Mark Biedermann to record the bass parts on the 'Victims Of Deception' album. Guest guitar parts came courtesy of ANVIL CHORUS man Thaen Rasmussen.

Breaking away from their American label Combat Records in 1987 HEATHEN purged Godfrey from the band after numerous interested labels expressed concerns over the band's frontman. Godfrey reacted by creating his own act LAUGHING DEAD. For a brief tenure in 1988 HEATHEN worked with erstwhile EXODUS and PIRANHA man Paul Ballof. HEATHEN also worked with David Wayne of METAL CHURCH but this liaison was even shorter. However, before long HEATHEN had re-enlisted Godfrey after Ballof had lasted less than a month. Swallowing their pride HEATHEN invited Godfrey back into the ranks and also recruited bass player Manny Bravo.

HEATHEN's line-up following the 'Victims Of Deception' album comprised of Godfrey, Altus, Minter, Piercy and bassist Randy Laire. The album includes a cover of RAINBOW's 'Kill The King'.

In 1989 Altus auditioned for MEGADETH but shied off this possible union concerned with the lifestyle of Mustaine's crew at the time. Altus opted out joining ANGEL WITCH in January 1991. HEATHEN, back with Piercy, then toured Europe as support to Brazilians SEPULTURA. Tragedy struck though when Laire was killed in a car crash. Piercy later relocating to Germany to create THE COMPANY.

In 1992 Altus and Rasmussen united with VICIOUS RUMOURS drummer Larry Howe and MY VICTIM singer Jay to create BOMB THREAT touring the California clubs with a nostalgic set of NWoBHM covers. Thaen Rasmussen took Piercy's place and Jason Vie Brooks took the bass role. Former REXXEN guitarist Ira Black was also inducted during 1992 but the band folded when Altus and Minter joined German Industrial Metal act DIE KRUPPS. Godfrey joined INNER THRESHOLD, a band formed by ex-DEFIANCE members.

In 1995 Vie Brooks turned up as part of GRIP INC., the band created by ex-SLAYER drummer DAVE LOMBARDO and would later join HATE SQUAD. Black journeyed through former EXODUS man Steve Souza's DOG FACE, ex-TESLA guitarist Tommy Skeoch's UTERIS before joining VICIOUS RUMOURS in 2000.

HEATHEN reformed in 2000 with a line-up of Godfrey, Altus, Rasmussen, Vie Brooks and Minter. In early 2003 Minter resurfaced, teaming up with vocalist Skitz, guitarist Joe Fraulob and bassist Venessa in a new project entitled DECONSTRUCT. In March though Minter had reunited with his HEATHEN colleague Lee Altus in yet another incarnation of ANGEL WITCH. By mid 2003 HEATHEN, albeit minus guitarist Doug Piercy, had reunited for a Rob Beaton produced album 'Recovered'. The band at this juncture comprised vocalist David White, guitarists Lee Altus and Ira Black from VICIOUS RUMORS, bassist Mike 'Yaz' Jastremski and drummer Darren Minter. This record collected together tracks from the 'Opiate Of The Masses' demo and a set of cover versions originally recorded in the mid nineties as an intended tribute release in honour of Randy Laire. Included would be QUEEN's 'Death On Two Legs', TYGERS OF PAN TANG's 'Hellbound', THIN LIZZY's 'Holy war' and the SWEET SAVAGE track 'Eye Of The Storm'.

HEATHEN, parting ways with Mike Jastremski, drafted Jon Torres on bass in June of 2004, a veteran of the scene with a heritage tracing through THUNDERHEAD, WARNING SF, ULYSSES SIREN, LÄÄZ ROCKIT and ANGEL WITCH. Sven Soderlund of MERCENARY would take Ira Black's position for gigs in July and August. HEATHEN cut a new, three track demo in January 2005.

Former HEATHEN bassist Mike "Yaz" Jastremski passed away on 23rd May 2005. The 42 year old musician had suffered a heart attack whilst undergoing a drug detoxification programme. In June HEATHEN drafted new guitarist Terry Lauderdale, a veteran of DIE SIEGER, SABOTAGE and VAN HALEN tribute band HOT FOR TEACHER. Meantime, Lee Altus sidestepped into the ranks of fellow Thrash veterans EXODUS. Ex-HEATHEN guitarist Ira Black worked with METAL CHURCH and Sci-Fi Metal band EMERALD TRIANGLE during 2005. Another new band project that year saw former bassist Jason Vie Brooks returning to the scene with Cincinnati, Ohio based THE ALLKNOWING.

HEATHEN signed to French label Season Of Mist in January 2006. Shortly afterward, Thaen Rasmussen joined VICIOUS RUMORS for a series of European concerts. Reports emerged in August stating the band was in negotiations with Dutch label Mascot Records. In November Polish label Metal Mind Productions re-released 'Victims Of Deception' as a digipack CD hosting bonus tracks and limited to 2000 hand numbered copies.

BREAKING THE SILENCE, Music For Nations MFN 75 (1987). Death By Hanging / Goblin's Blade / Open The Grave / Pray For Death / Set Me Free / Breaking The Silence / World's End / Save The Skull.

Set Me Free, Combat 88561 8182-1 (1987). Set Me Free / Goblin's Blade.

VICTIMS OF DECEPTION, Roadrunner RO 93312 (1989). Hypnotized / Opiate Of The Masses / Heathen's Song / Kill The King / Fear Of The Unknown / Prisoners Of Fate / Morbid Curiosity / Guitarony / Mercy Is No Virtue.

RECOVERED, Relentless HINC003 (2004). Death On Two Legs / Holy War / In Memory Of . . . / Hellbound / Eye Of The Storm / Hypnotized / Opiate Of The Masses / Timeless Cell / Mercy Is No Virtue.

VICTIMS OF DECEPTION, Metal Mind Productions MASS CD DG 984 (2006) (Polish release. Limited edition 2000 hand numbered copies). Hypnotized / Opiate Of The Masses / Heathen's Song / Kill The King / Fear Of The Unknown / Prisoners Of Fate / Morbid Curiosity / Guitarmony / Mercy Is No Virtue / Timeless Cell Of Prophecy / Hellbound.

HEAVEN SHALL BURN

GERMANY — *Marcus (vocals), Alexander Dietz (guitar), Maik (guitar), Eric (bass), Matthias (drums).*

A socially conscious Hardcore cum Thrash / Death Metal band. The band's lyrical themes have developed to deal with such subjects as veganism, racism and social rights issues. HEAVEN SHALL BURN was originally conceived billed as CONSENSE during the Autumn of 1996 with a debut demo recording following in early 1997. The band's roster would shift allowing the introduction of lead vocalist Markus and bass player Eric upfront of a second promotion recording. Live work ensued after which the Deeds Of Revolution label offered a contract to release HEAVEN SHALL BURN's mini album 'In Battle There Is No Law, issued in 1998. Shortly after second guitarist Patrick Schleitzer joined the fold.

A split release shared with FALL OF SERENITY followed in 1999 after which HEAVEN SHALL BURN signed up to the Impression label. This union brought forth the April 2000 'Asunder' album. That same year a further split offering found HEAVEN SHALL BURN paired with CALIBAN for a Lifeforce Records release. After extensive touring throughout Spain, Portugal, Swiss, Italy, the Benelux and the Czech Republic the group settled down to craft the 'Whatever It May Take' record. Of interest to collectors was that 'Whatever It May Take' was issued in Brazil with completely different artwork, a revised song running order and a bonus track. Live work in 2002 saw an appearance at the massive 'With Full Force' festival in Germany as well as gigs as far afield as Iceland.

The band signed to Germany's Century Media Records in early 2004 for the April album 'Antigone'. This outing would also see release in vinyl format via Lifeforce Records and licensed in South America through Brazil's Liberation Records. A promotional video for the track 'The Weapon They Fear' was shot at an April gig in Chemnitz by director Marc Drywa. Gigs included a 30th May appearance at the Brazilian 'Liberation Fest V' in Sao Paulo.

To aid victims of the December 2004 Indian Ocean tsunamis HEAVEN SHALL BURN, in collaboration with THE HAUNTED and NAPALM DEATH, participated in the issue of a special single release. The band donated the DIE SKEPTIKER cover version 'Strassenkampf' featuring guitarist Patrick Schleitzer on vocals. These singles, restricted to just 1000 hand numbered copies, would be for sale only at NAPALM DEATH's Bochum and London shows in January 2005. The band hooked up with a further multi-package billing, dubbed 'Hell On Earth', for Autumn European touring alongside running mates AS I LAY DYING, EVERGREEN TERRACE, AGENTS OF MAN, END OF DAYS and NEAERA. Long-time guitarist Patrick Schleitzer then opted out, putting on a final farewell gig with the band on 18th November in Saalfeld, before being swiftly replaced by Alexander Dietz.

In June 2006 the band revealed a new album title, 'Deaf To Our Prayers', was inspired by the poem 'The Silesian Weavers' by German poet Heinrich Heine. 'Deaf To Our Prayers', recorded at Rape Of Harmonies Studios in Thüringen, entered the national German charts at number 65. The band formed up the UK and European "Hell On Earth" tour in September and October. Joining them would be GOD FORBID, MAROON, CATARACT, FULL BLOWN CHAOS, PURIFIED IN BLOOD from Norway and A PERFECT MURDER. Upon completion of these shows guitarist Alexander Dietz temporarily joined the ranks of NEAERA for live work.

IN BATTLE THERE IS NO LAW, Deeds Of Revolution (1998). Partisan / Forthcoming Fire / Thoughts Of Superiority / Mandatory Slaughter / Remember The Fallen.
THE SPLIT PROGRAM, Lifeforce LIFE019 (2000) (Split album with CALIBAN). Suffocated In The Exhaust Of Our Machines / No Single Inch / The Seventh Cross / One More Lie.
ASUNDER, Impression LIFE018 (2000). To Inherit The Guilt / Cold / Betrayed Again / Deification / Pass Away / Open Arms To The Future / The Drowned And The Saved / Where Is The Light / Asunder / The Fourth Crusade.
WHATEVER IT MAY TAKE, Lifeforce LIB011 (2002) (Brazilian release).
WHATEVER IT MAY TAKE, Lifeforce (2002). Behind A Wall Of Silence / The Worlds In Me / The Martyrs' Blood / It Burns Within / Implore The Darker Sky / The Few Upright / Whatever It May Take / Ecowar / Naked Among Wolves / The Fire / Casa De Cabocio / Implore The Darken Sky (Classic version).
ANTIGONE, Century Media (2004). Echoes (Intro) / The Weapon They Fear / The Only Truth / Architects Of The Apocalypse / Voice Of The Voiceless / Numbing The Pain / To Harvest The Storm / Rìsandi Von (Outro) / Bleeding To Death / Tree Of Freedom / The Dream Is Dead / Deyjandi Von (Outro).
DEAF TO OUR PRAYERS, Century Media (2006). Counterweight / Trespassing The Shores Of Your World / Profane Believers / Stay The Course / The Final March / Of No Avail / Armia / mybestfriends.com / Biogenesis (Undo Creation) / Dying In Silence / The Greatest Gift Of God. Chart positions: 50 GREECE, 65 GERMANY.

HELLFIRE B.C.

GREECE — *Alex Kokonis (vocals / guitar), George Droylias (guitar), Steve Apostoloy (bass), Jim Apostoloy (drums).*

Old school Thrashers HELLFIRE B.C. date back to April of 1996, first formed up as simply HELLFIRE by vocalist / guitarist Alex Kokonis along with the sibling rhythm section of bassist Steve and drummer Jim Apostoloy. During the Autumn of that first year of operation guitarist Obel was inducted and the group subsequently issued the demos 'Tombstone' and the January 1998 tape 'Crystal Age'. In support of the mid 1999 promo session 'Clonosis' HELLFIRE toured Greece as support to artists such as NIGHTFALL and DESTRUCTION.

During 2000 the 'U-238' helped spread the word into mainland Europe as tracks appeared on various compilation albums. Obel would decamp and George Droylias took on the guitar role. Increasingly aware of other acts using the handle HELLFIRE the group evolved into HELLFIRE B.C. for the debut record 'Birth Of The Nuclear Age'.

BIRTH OF THE NUCLEAR AGE, Sleasy Rider SR 0003 (2002). U-238 / Dark Gift / Damned From Beyond / Infernal Dusk Brigades / Clonosis / Vampires / Breakneck Speed / To Shift Through Bitter Ashes / Life's Candle Ends.

HELLHAMMER

NÜRENSDORF, SWITZERLAND — *Satanic Slaughter (vocals / guitar), Savage Damage (bass), Bloodhunter (drums).*

Formerly known as HAMMERHEAD, this bizarre and primitive extreme Nürensdorf—Zürich Metal outfit, which would in time evolve into the equally revered CELTIC FROST, was founded in 1982. The influence of the band would reverberate over decades throughout the Thrash and Black Metal genres. Previous to HAMMERHEAD frontman Thomas Gabriel Fischer and bassist Steve had been involved with various fledgling acts emulating their NWoBHM heroes VENOM.

HELLHAMMER's origins lay in the formative unit HAMMERHEAD. Initially bass guitar was handled by the 14 year old Michael Baum, who in turn transferred these duties to Fischer, then wishing to be known as 'Satanic Slaughter'. Of note is that Baum then journeyed on to Los Angeles to found AOR act SIERRA before enrolling into TRIBE OF GYPSIES.

Their debut 1982 rehearsal demo, saw the group apparently inspired by Newcastle upon Tyne NWoBHM band RAVEN and their Gallagher brothers team as Fischer, bassist Steve Patton, previously known as 'Savage Damage' and drummer Peter Stratton all adopting the joint stage surnames of 'Warrior'. During August 1982, HELLHAMMER shifted shape again, drafting drummer Jörg Neubart (a.k.a. 'Bloodhunter') and transferring from bass to guitar. Neubart subsequently became 'Bruce Day'.

In 1983 HELLHAMMER enrolled drummer Stephen Priestly from SCHIZO. Hellhammer followed up with their first studio demo, the July 1983 nine track 'Death Fiend'. Only a very limited distribution of this cassette, via Prowlin' Death Promotions, saw the light of day. This first official set witnessed a band still very much in its embryonic stages, chock full of copycat NWoBHM riffs and pre-pubescent lyrics such as opening line She's got my joystick right in her mouth from the song 'Bloody Pussies'. The band had actually committed a total of 17 tracks to tape, surfacing first on 'Death Fiend', then on the infamous 'Triumph Of Death'.

Clad in exactly the same artwork as its predecessor, once 'Triumph Of Death' made it outside of the tape trading underground and into the mainstream it provoked extreme opinions. Horrifically recorded, 'Triumph Of Death' offered an ugly wall of sound, choking doom styled riffs matched in intensity by stampeding bass and tortured vocals. HELLHAMMER's image, lifted straight from fantasy board games, had the trio complementing the music decked out in bullet belts, leather and spikes. Ambitiously the legend adorning the cassette issued the challenge 'VENOM are killing music ... HELLHAMMER are killing VENOM'.

Whilst leading French magazine 'Enfer' hailed it as a classic, the UK's 'Metal Forces' magazine editor Bernard Doe cited it as the most appalling thing he had ever heard. History however would dictate that HELLHAMMER would later be recognized as one of the root catalysts of the Black Metal genre. Although in later years band members have admitted their knowledge of music was basic to say the least when the HELLHAMMER recordings were made, nevertheless the band were in possession of an artistic vision which would undoubtedly shape the metal scene over many years.

The group pulled in bass player Martin Eric Ain ('Slayed Necros') to lay down more demos, 'Satanic Rites', that December in Sound Concept studios. However, invited to submit a fresh demo to Berlin's Noise Records HELLHAMMER very nearly split as Ain felt he did not have the necessary talent to go through with the session.

Still, positive or negative press encouraged Noise to sign the band and the Berlin based label released the Horst Müller engineered 'Apocalyptic Raids' EP in March 1984, which had no details as to what RPM the record should be played at; sounding just as strange at 33RPM as it did at 45. An unconfident label only ordered up a first pressing of 1200 copies, which soon flew out of stores. This inaugural press was the only official one to include a lyric sheet. Subsequent quick fire re-presses resulted in a variation of colours and tones on the sleeve artwork, making for unintentional greater collectability.

Metal Blade Records released the EP in America with an extra two tracks. Demand for HELLHAMMER also warranted a bootleg 7" single issued by Necromantic union, a pairing of a live cut of 'Buried And Forgotten' and a rehearsal recording 'Messiah'.

HELLHAMMER mainman 'Satanic Slaughter' later swapped identities to become Tom G. Warrior and started the avant-garde Metal legends CELTIC FROST in May of 1984 retaining the deal with Noise. CELTIC FROST issued a stream of critically praised outings before fizzling out.

Still an influence in some circles over ten years later, Sweden's ABYSS covered the HELLHAMMER track 'Massacra' on their 1995 album 'The Other Side'. Leading American Death Metal unit INCANTATION would wear their influences with pride too committing a cover of 'The Third Of Storms' to their inaugural demo session. Arch Black Metal protagonists DARKTHRONE would commit 'The Usurper' to an early demo which would later find the light of day on the 'Live In Frostland' bootleg. Fellow Swiss Metal act SAMAEL too would cover HELLHAMMER on their early demos with 'The Third Of The Storm'.

Warrior forged a new project in the late 90's billed as APOLLYON SUN. By late 2001 a full blown CELTIC FROST reunion had been announced but would prove protracted. In 2004 the band would have their classic cut 'The Third Of Storms' chosen as a pioneering piece of music for a compilation assembled by DARKTHRONE drummer Fenriz, released through Peaceville Records and entitled 'Fenriz Presents The Best Of Old School Black Metal'.

Rehearsal Demo, Hellhammer (1982) (Rehearsal demo). Triumph Of Death.

Triumph Of Death, Hellhammer (1983) (Demo). Intro / Crucifixion / Maniac / When Hell's Near / Decapitator / Blood Insanity / Power Of Satan / Reaper / Death Fiend / Triumph Of Death / Metallic Storm / Ready For Slaughter / Dark Warriors / Hammerhead.

Death Fiend, Hellhammer (1983) (Demo). Maniac / Angel Of Destruction / Hammerhead / Bloody Pussies / Death Fiend / Dark Warriors / Chainsaw / Ready For Slaughter / Sweet Torment.

Satanic Rites, Hellhammer (1983) (Demo). Intro / Messiah / The Third Of The Storms / Buried And Forgotten / Maniac / Eurynomos / Triumph Of Death / Revelations Of Doom / Reaper / Satanic Rites / Crucifixion / Outro.

DEATH METAL, (1984) (Four way split album with HELLOWEEN, RUNNING WILD and DARK AVENGER). Revelations Of Doom / Messiah.

Apocalyptic Raids EP, Noise N008 50-1668 (1984). The Third Of The Storms (Evoked Damnation) / Massacra / Triumph Of Death / Horus / Agressor.

HELLION

LOS ANGELES, CA, USA — *Ann Boleyn (vocals), Ray Schenck (guitar), Chris Kessler (guitar), Glenn Cannon (bass), Sean Scott (drums).*

HELLION, fronted by vocalist Ann Boleyn (a.k.a. Anne Hull), who actually claims some distance lineage to the decapitated former second wife of Henry VIII, made their mark on the Los Angeles circuit with a series of demos. The founding roster saw Boleyn, previously of POWER PROGRAM and BEOWULF, alongside Minneapolis, Minnesota musicians guitarist Ray Schenk, bass player Peyton Tuthill and drummer Eiler Savage (Paul Eiler). The latter came up with the HELLION brand and designed the original logo. Previous to this the band had used the title DB. The group made a reputation on the local scene by holding house concerts, performing covers by the likes of UFO, BLACK SABBATH, SCORPIONS and RAINBOW, at Boleyn's "haunted mansion" residence. Eiler quit in 1981 to forge FINAL WARNING.

Mystic Records offered HELLION a spot on a compilation album, 'Sound Of Hollywood Girls', but prior to these sessions Peyton Tuthill left the band, claiming Ann Boleyn's supposed involvement in the occult arts as a deciding factor. Tuthill become ordained as a minister. Erstwhile W.A.S.P. bassist Rik Fox (real surname Sulima-Suligowski) briefly replaced Tuthill. However, Foxx quit just days before the band's debut recording session, enticed away by Ron Keel's STEELER. Brian West, who had played in POWER PROGRAM with Ann Boleyn, was inducted for the recordings, which took place on New Year's Eve. The relationship with Mystic fragmented but, although HELLION had not gone to contract, the label paired off a HELLION track, 'Nightmares In Daylight', with another high profile Los Angeles female fronted act, BITCH, on a split 7" vinyl single. The same label also released a further HELLION 7" the following year, 'Driving Hard' / 'Black Knight' as 'Streetzine' magazine voted the group the "Best band in L.A."

In 1983 HELLION recruited lead guitarist Alan Barlam and bass player Bill Sweet and utilised Fiddler's Studio in Hollywood, California to cut demos, laying down four tracks overnight. With no deal forthcoming, HELLION manufactured custom imprint Bongus Lodus Records to press the material on 12" vinyl. The band, now managed by Wendy Dio, were soon the focus of attention when the record was picked up in Europe by Music For Nations. The London based label financed the recording of a further two songs, 'Break The Spell' and 'Up From The Depths', to make up the European release of 'Hellion' in January 1984.

The HELLION line-up for the mini-album saw Boleyn alongside guitarists Ray Schenk and Alan Barlam, bassist Bill Sweet and drummer Sean Kelly. Expert self publicists, HELLION arrived at one 1983 gig at the Los Angeles Troubadour club in a tank. However, disagreements between management and band were to break the band apart.

In 1985 Barlam, Schenk and Kelly departed to form BURN, with singer Richard Parico, after apparently being convinced that a female lead singer was deterring major label attention. BURN, still managed by the Niji organisation cut demos produced by Dana Strum and later inducted another ex-HELLION man, Rik Fox on bass, but were to disband.

Retaining the HELLION name, Boleyn soon regrouped to record a new album 'Screams In The Night' at Baby O Studios in Hollywood with a fresh line-up comprising guitarist Chet Thompson, former LION and ROBIN TROWER band bassist Alex Campbell and ex-DOKKEN drummer Greg Pekka. Boleyn, who had also initiated her own record company, New Renaissance Records, contributed the track 'Monster Mash' to the 1987 movie 'Return Of The Living Dead—Part II' soundtrack.

The 1988 mini-album 'Postcards From The Asylum', with new bassist Dave Dutton, saw the reunion of original HELLION members Barlam and Kelly and features a cover of the JUDAS PRIEST classic 'Exciter'. Also of note would be the track 'Run For Your Life', produced by none other than Ronnie James Dio. Thompson, meanwhile, had a short spell with BRITTON.

The band put in a British club tour during early 1988 supported by MARSHALL LAW, which saw the addition of former ALLEGIANCE bassist Rex Tennyson, who would later join ex-CATS IN BOOTS vocalist Joel Ellis in HEAVY BONES. 'The Black Book', cut at The Music Grinder and EQ Sound Studios in Los Angeles, proved to HELLION's last outing for a lengthy period. Boleyn, acting as producer for the record, published a novel to coincide with the release. Thompson founded ALICE IN THUNDERLAND with vocalist Emi Canyn for a 1995 Japanese release eponymous album.

HELLION was resurrected in 1998 by Boleyn, Schenk and Kelly cutting a album the following year which still awaits release. In 1999 New Renaissance issued the EP 'The Witching Hour', essentially a collection of archive demo material crafted by the Boleyn/Campbell/Thompson/Pecka line up. Also issued would be the limited edition live album 'Live And Well In Hell', recorded at D'Anza Theater in Riverside, California during 1984. Fans were still waiting developments when it was learned in mid 2001 that Boleyn had recorded an album, produced by Mikey Davis, and was auditioning for an entire new band. This new unit, simply billed as ANN BOLEYN and comprising guitarists Mike Guererro and Chris Kessler, former RHINO BUCKET man Eric Becica on bass and drummer Vince Rage, toured Japan in October.

Archive recordings, from a live show at the Country Club in Reseda in 1984, were slated for 2002 release billed as 'Cold Night In Hell'. A new Mikey Davis produced studio album 'Will Not Go Quietly' was also set for 2002, eventually seeing release through Germany's Massacre Records in February 2003. However, in August HELLION were back in the news for all the wrong reasons when manager James Howard Paul, Jr. was accused of soliciting the murder of his wife. A few days later Paul Jr. was caught by Police attempting to break into Boleyn's house. The latest HELLION line up comprised Boleyn, Kessler, Schenk, bassist Glenn Cannon of MOTHER MERCY, Orange County acts BRAT PRINCE and SHATTERED, besides DEF LEPPARD tribute act PYROMANIA, along with the MOTHER MERCY, REACTOR and REVLON RED credited drummer Sean Scott.

In October of 2004 Glenn Cannon, retaining his ties to HELLION, joined the ranks of Van Nuys Power Metal band STEEL PROPHET. In January 2005 Cannon reunited with his erstwhile MOTHER MERCY colleagues guitarist John Leighton, vocalist RJ Blaze Glenn Cannon and Jimmy Z to forge Gothic Industrial Metal band HADES INFERNO.

German Heavy Metal band POWERGOD cut a cover version of 'Better Off Dead' for inclusion on their 'Long Live The Loud– That's Metal Lesson II' released through Massacre Records in July 2005.

HELLION, Music For Nations MFN 15 (1983). Break The Spell / Don't Take No / Backstabber / Lookin' For A Good Time / Driving Hard / Up From The Depths.
Hellion EP, Bongos Lodus (1983). Don't Take No (For An Answer) / Backstabber / Lookin' For A Good Time / Driving Hard.
Driving Hard, Mystic (1983). Driving Hard / Black Night.
Screams In The Night, Hellion (1986). Screams In The Night / Put The Hammer Down.
SCREAMS IN THE NIGHT, Music For Nations MFN 73 (1987). Screams In The Night / Bad Attitude / Better Off Dead / Upside Down Guitar Solo / The Hand / Explode / Easy Action / Put The Hammer Down / Stick 'Em / Children Of The Night / The Tower Of Air.
THE BLACK BOOK, Music For Nations CDMFN 108 (1990). The Black Book / Stormrider / Living In Hell / The Discovery / Losing Control / Arrest… Jail… Bail / Daemon Attack / Conspiracy / Amnesia / The Warning / The Room Behind The Door / The Atonement / Immigrant Song.
UP FROM THE DEPTHS, (1998). Nightmares In Daylight / Backstabber / Fire / Up From The Depths / Break The Spell / Nevermore / Evil One / Exciter / Run For Your Life.
COLD NIGHT IN HELL, (1998). Run For Your Life / Nothin' To Say / Get Ready / Backstabber / Never More / Don't Take No For An Answer / Drivin' Hard For You.
The Witching Hour, New Renaissance (1999). The Witching Hour / Morning Star / The Hand / Children Of The Night.
LIVE AND WELL IN HELL, New Renaissance (1999) (limited edition 500 copies). Impromptu Sound Check / Break The Spell / Don't Waste Your Love (On Me) / Crowd Rap I / Backstabber / Crowd Rap II / Run For Your Life / Crowd Rap III / Don't Take No For An Answer / Crowd Rap IV / Fire / Crowd Rap V / Drivin' Hard For You.
WILL NOT GO QUIETLY, Massacre (2003). Will Not Go Quietly / Resurrection / Welcome (To My Humble Home) / Revenge (Is Sweet) / The Last Straw / Wildest Dreams / Dead And Gone / Dream Deceiver / Shit / Duchess of Debauchery / User 7 / See You In Hell.

HELLOWEEN

HAMBURG, GERMANY — *Andi Deris (vocals), Michael Weikath (guitar), Sacha Gerstner (guitar), Marcus Großkopf (bass), Dani Löble (drums).*

Hamburg Power Metal band HELLOWEEN quickly developed a large and loyal fan base built upon a series of strong album releases that culminated in the twin album project 'Keeper Of The Seven Keys'. Stylistically, HELLOWEEN has trod a path from Speed Metal through an ill fated dalliance with injecting oddball humour through to career revival delivering consistent melodic Metal. However, in spite of two decades of maturity HELLOWEEN is still known to show its Speed Metal teeth on occasion.

Guitarist Kai Hansen, previously with ANCIENT CALL, bass player Marcus Großkopf, previously of TRAUMSCHIFF, and drummer Ingo Schwichtenberg had been playing together since the late 70s with an inaugural band unit billed as GENTRY. This unit in 1978 featured singer / guitarist Peter Sielck, Hansen, singer Frank, bassist Christian and drummer Johannes. The GENTRY membership was fluid, but Großkopf and Schwichtenberg enrolled some two years later, after which the group evolved into SECOND HELL then, in 1982, IRON FIST. Sielck departed IRON FIST later that same year, effectively putting the band on ice, so during this period of inactivity Hansen received an offer to join POWERFOOL, featuring guitarist Michael Weikath. As things turned out Hansen lured Michael to his own band, during late 1983, and then changed the name to HELLOWEEN in 1984. The new name was thought of by Schwichtenberg, the drummer also being responsible for switching the letter 'O' to a pumpkin. This malevolent vegetable would soon become known as one of Heavy Metal's best known trademarks.

The group came to prominence upon their signing to leading German Metal label Noise Records and two tracks 'Oernst Of Life' and 'Metal Invaders' on the notorious 'Death Metal' four way split album shared with HELLHAMMER, RUNNING WILD and DARK AVENGER in April 1984. Their debut mini-album, 'Helloween', and first, full length album 'Walls Of Jericho', both produced by Harris Johns, provided HELLOWEEN with plenty of media attention and critical favour. The mid 80s saw a massive resurgence of interest in German Rock bands and HELLOWEEN quickly established themselves at the top of the heap with successive strong releases.

The five track 'Helloween' had been recorded in January and February 1985 at Musiclab Studio in Berlin. From the outset the band showed they were prepared to mix humour with blistering Metal as a waking headbanger cracks a can of beer then indulges himself in some "Happy happy Halloween" kindergarten music before the opening riff of 'Starlight' rudely interrupts proceedings. A hugely promising first offering, the mini-album, issued that May, peaked with 'Victim Of Fate', this careering slab of pure Thrash often still quoted by fans as HELLOWEEN's finest work.

The 'Walls Of Jericho' set, cut in September and October also at Musiclab, gave the band room to display their full potential. Whilst riffs raged and guitars wailed, the group did

HELLOWEEN

offer up some oddball humour with 'Heavy Metal (Is The Law)', 'Gorgar', an ode to a pinball machine, and the bizarre 'Reptile', with lyrics about a toilet dwelling beast and masturbating businessmen. Despite these quirks, reviews praised the Speed Metal artistry of 'Ride The Sky', 'Guardians' and 'How Many Tears'. From this album HELLOWEEN had a remixed version of 'Murderer' included on the 'Metal Attack Vol. 1' compilation, released in April 1985. 'Ride The Sky' was also taken from the 'Walls Of Jericho' album for the Under One Flag 'Speed Kills II' compilation, released in 1986.

For a few European concerts, TYRAN PACE singer Ralf Scheepers took over vocal duties from Hansen, who was having problems with his voice. Scheepers was asked to join the band full-time after the tour but declined the offer. Live work that year saw European shows flanked by GRAVE DIGGER and CELTIC FROST in February, followed up by the band's debut in North America, performing with EXODUS. On April 20th HELLOWEEN played the Eindhoven 'Aardshock' festival. The 'Judas' EP, recorded at Horus Studios in Hamburg, arrived in July.

HELLOWEEN set about changing their musical direction, intending to add more scope to their music with the recruitment of ILL PROPHECY's frontman MICHAEL KISKE, who, at just eighteen years old, took over vocal duties from Hansen. On November 25th 1986 the new look band, in collaboration with producers Tommy Newton, VICTORY guitarist, and Tommy Hansen, set to work on a fresh album. It is worth noting that HELLOWEEN subsequently re-worked two ILL PROPHECY era tracks for their own use, 'A Little Time' and 'You'll Always Walk Alone'.

HELLOWEEN peaked with an elaborate brace of concept albums centred upon the 'Keeper Of The Seven Keys' tale. The first 'Keeper...' album, produced by VICTORY's Tommy Newton at Horus Sound Studio in Hannover, was a useful vehicle in gaining popularity for the band outside Europe. It was released in February 1987 and world-wide it went on to sell over half a million copies, shifting over 125'000 in Germany alone. Live promotion, seeing the inclusion of onstage keyboard player Jörn Ellerbrock, commenced in Europe on April 3rd, sharing stages with New Jersey Thrashers OVERKILL. HELLOWEEN appeared at the 'Giants Of Rock' festival in Hameenlinna, Finland on August 15th prior to hooking up as support to DIO for shows in Italy and Spain. Noise issued the 'Future World' single in September, this including a new version of 'Starlight' with Michael Kiske on vocals. Released in America on the RCA label, 'Keeper Of The Seven Keys' peaked at number 102 in the Billboard charts and its success enabled the band to appear as part of the 'Hell On Wheels' North American tour along with GRIM REAPER and ARMORED SAINT commencing September 18th in Washington DC and running through until November 14th. RCA did not curry favour with the band though when they released the 13 minute track 'Halloween' as a 4 minute edited single. The quintets first tour of Japan took place in November 1987, prior to recording 'Keeper... Part 2'.

The band entered Horus Sound Studio again during May 1988, completing tracking mid-June. 'Keeper Of The Seven Keys: Part 2' emerged in August, entering the UK charts at number 24 and the US Billboard charts at 108. In Sweden, the record gained a top ten placing. In later years album track 'I Want Out' would be covered by two high profile artists, HAMMERFALL and SONATA ARCTICA.

HELLOWEEN appeared at the August 20th 1988 Castle Donington 'Monsters Of Rock' festival before performing the same duties as the event roved around Europe with festival stops in Schweinfurt and Bochum, Germany, Tilburg in Netherlands, Lausanne in Switzerland, Modena in Italy, Athens in Greece, Pamplona, Madrid and Barcelona in Spain, Cascais in Portugal and finally Paris, France. They then toured as support to IRON MAIDEN throughout Europe and Scandinavia before their own German headlining dates in October and a UK tour in November.

'The Keeper Of The Seven Keys' albums had positioned HELLOWEEN as a leading international act. However, stardom, and in particular touring, became anathema to the driving force behind HELLOWEEN, guitarist Kai Hansen, who left in January 1989 to form the studio project GAMMA RAY with former TYRAN PACE vocalist Ralf Scheepers. Ironically, in certain territories GAMMA RAY, which rapidly evolved beyond the studio confines, overtook HELLOWEEN in the popularity stakes. HELLOWEEN persevered and Hansen was replaced by ex-RAMPAGE guitarist ROLAND GRAPOW. That same month the group signed to IRON MAIDEN's management Sanctuary Music and, convinced that signing to a major label would further their career, began efforts to extricate themselves from their Noise deal. The band contracted to EMI Records and promptly landed themselves in a lengthy legal wrangle with Noise, who claimed that they were still under contract. During this period of inactivity the press speculated that Kiske was to join IRON MAIDEN.

In April and May 1989 HELLOWEEN again toured North America on the same bill as ANTHRAX and EXODUS. A live mini-album 'Live In The UK', recorded in Edinburgh, Scotland and Manchester, charted in Great Britain but would provide ardent fans two more reasons to shell out for product as the record was issued in Japan as 'Keepers Live' with different artwork and in America as 'I Want Out - Live', again with completely different artwork. HELLOWEEN launched into another US tour on April 3rd 1989 at the Paramount Theater in Seattle, Washington. These shows lasted until mid-May when they hopped across the Pacific for nine Japanese shows.

Following all the delays, HELLOWEEN seemingly committed commercial suicide by releasing the ludicrously titled 'Pink Bubbles Go Ape' album in March 1991. Supposed to show that the band had a sense of humour, the Chris Tsangarides produced album, with song titles such as 'Heavy Metal Hamsters', only served to alienate their former fans. Slammed by the media, 'Pink Bubbles Go Ape' only scored a number 41 chart position in the UK and 32 in Germany. It seemed that, at a critical juncture, HELLOWEEN had lost their artistic credibility. Internal divisions were also besetting the band, they would later admit a polarisation between the Kiske/Schwichtenberg camp and that of Weikath and Grapow. Unfortunately, worse was to come when Noise Records, having won a court decision, placed an injunction on the album, effectively stopping its release and any live work in Germany. EMI and Noise finally reached agreement, allowing 'Pink Bubbles Go Ape' to be released across Europe on April 20th 1992. An extensive round of Japanese dates were conducted in September and October.

In 1993, EMI Records released the band's new album 'Chameleon', a record that was certainly not up to the stan-

HELLOWEEN

dards of the past and found HELLOWEEN seriously lacking in direction. The album had eschewed all Power Metal and Thrash elements in favour of progressive, near Pop leanings. The album had been laid down at Chateau du Pape studios in Hamburg was produced by Tommy Hansen and mixed by Michael Wagener. 'Chameleon' attained a number 35 position in Germany but failed to chart in the UK. With sales nosediving, it came as little surprise when EMI dropped the band.

The band's woes continued as an unplanned for shift in personnel saw the induction of drummer Riad 'Ritchie' Abdel-Nabi. In the midst of a Japanese tour, commencing on November 26th at the NHK Hall in Tokyo, a troubled Ingo Schwichtenberg had been hospitalised due to what was described as schizophrenia brought on by drug abuse. Abdel-Nabi completed the dates before vacating. The drummer went on to create BABYLON 27 with erstwhile KINGDOM COME guitarist Heiko Radke-Siab.

HELLOWEEN made a triumphant return in 1998 with the Tommy Hansen produced 'Better Than Raw' album, preceded by the February single 'I Can', sounding heavier than ever. 'Better Than Raw' was the first band product to be partly crafted at Andi Deris' home studio, Crazy Cat, at Mi Sueno on the Spanish isle of Tenerife. Songs were cut both at the singer's residence and the familiar haunt of Chateau du Pape in Hamburg. Jörn Ellerbrock again provided keyboards with ZED YAGO's Jutta Weinhold donating backing vocals.

The album, hitting number 19 on the German charts, quickly racked up Japanese sales of quarter of a million plus and HELLOWEEN fever satiated with the release of a four CD compilation, 'The Pumpkin Box', and a double album set 'Karaoke Remix'. HELLOWEEN played selective European dates as guests to IRON MAIDEN. To close the year the band returned to North America for their first showing in many years, performing just one concert at the Coney Island High club in Manhattan, New York on December 20th.

Side endeavours abounded during 1999. Großkopf made space to execute a side endeavour SHOCKMACHINE. Joining in the proceedings for the eponymous album would be, vocalist Olly Lugosi, X-13 guitarist Rolly Feldman, HELLOWEEN members drummer Uli Kusch and guitarist ROLAND GRAPOW and ROUGH SILK keyboard player Ferdy Doernberg.

ROLAND GRAPOW released his second solo outing, 'Kaleidoscope', recorded at Crazy Cat Studios in Hamburg and mixed by Michael Wagener at Wireworld Studios in Tennessee. Vocals came courtesy of ex-LOUDNESS and OBSESSION frontman Michael Vescera, bass from YNGWIE MALMSTEEN man Barry Sparks and drums courtesy of ARTENSION and METALIUM's MIKE TERRANA. Also featured would be keyboard player Jens Johansson.

Kusch too would get in on the action pursuing his project CATCH THE RAINBOW, a conglomeration of name German Rockers dedicated to paying homage to RAINBOW. An album,

'A Tribute To Rainbow', arrived in 1999 which featured the entire HELLOWEEN cast, alongside GAMMA RAY, PRIMAL FEAR and BRAINSTORM personnel, as guests.

The band's next outing took the band away from the expected format as September 1999's 'Metal Jukebox', again recorded in two studios in Tenerife and Hamburg, provided fans with an insight to the band members own favourite songs as the group re-worked an eclectic range of tracks. 'Metal Jukebox' saw HELLOWEEN tackling the SCORPIONS 'He's a Woman-She's A Man', JETHRO TULL's 'Locomotive Breath', CREAM's 'White Room', FAITH NO MORE's 'From Out Of Nowhere', THE BEATLES 'All My Loving', FRANK MARINO's 'Jaggernaut', SENSATIONAL ALEX HARVEY BAND's 'Faith Healer', DAVID BOWIE's 'Space Oddity', FOCUS' 'Hocus Pocus' and even ABBA's 'Lay All Your Love on Me'.

February 2005 saw HELLOWEEN amicably parting ways with drummer Stefan Schwarzmann. New man behind the drums would be the GLENMORE, RAWHEAD REXX and BLAZE credited Dani Löble. First product to emerge from the new recordings, billed 'Keeper Of The Seven Keys—The Legacy', would be the release of a single, 'Mrs. God', in Japan in early June. A DVD compilation, 'Hellish Videos: The Complete Video Collection', arrived via Sanctuary Entertainment in August. The new album notably included Candice Night of BLACKMORE'S NIGHT guesting on the track 'Light The Universe'.

A mammoth world tour, allied with PRIMAL FEAR, commenced in the Czech Republic in November and taking in Slovakia, Poland, Finland with support from THE STORYTELLER, Norway, Sweden, Germany, Holland, Belgium, France and Spain into December before resuming in 2006 with shows across Germany, Austria, Rumania, Croatia, Bulgaria, Turkey, Greece, Italy, Switzerland and the UK. HELLOWEEN hit South America, with concerts in Mexico, Costa Rica and Nrazil, during March. Interestingly, GAMMA RAY's Kai Hansen made it clear in interviews during this period that he would be keen to pursue a full-blown HELLOWEEN reunion. However, MICHAEL KISKE, whilst not objecting to festival dates, issued a staunch rejection.

HELLOWEEN announced plans for US tour dates, packaged with KINGDOM COME, for October. However, these shows were cancelled, the band citing "logistical and organizational problems". Meantime, ex-singer MICHAEL KISKE announced that he intended to rearrange and re-record all of the songs that he wrote with his former band for an album to be released through Frontiers Records.

November's single, 'Light The Universe', proved notable, issued as a duet between Andi Deris and Candice Night of BLACKMORE'S NIGHT. An accompanying promotional video was directed by Alexander Diezinger at Veldenstein Castle in southern Germany. In 2007 HELLOWEEN launched the joint DVD and CD package 'Keeper Of The Seven Keys—The Legacy World Tour 2005/2006—Live On 3 Continents'. ANDI DERIS also contributed vocals to the song 'A Perfect Day' included on a 2007 Nuclear Blast Records' 20th anniversary compilation album.

In a bold move, Andi Deris hinted at a full-blown European tour alongside GAMMA RAY for the summer months.

DEATH METAL, Noise N0006 (1984) (Split album with HELLHAMMER, RUNNING WILD and DARK AVENGER). Oernst Of Life / Metal Invaders.

HELLOWEEN, Noise N0021 (1985). Victim Of Fate / Cry For Freedom / Starlight / Murderer / Warrior.

WALLS OF JERICHO, Noise N0032 (1985). Walls Of Jericho / Ride The Sky / Reptile / Guardians / Phantoms Of Death / Metal Invaders / Gorgar / Heavy Metal Is The Law / How Many Tears.

Halloween, RCA 6399-1-R (1986) (USA promotion). Halloween (Edit Version) / Halloween (Album Version).

Judas, Noise N0048 (1986). Judas / Ride The Sky (Live) / Guardians (Live).

KEEPER OF THE SEVEN KEYS PART I, Noise N0057 (1987). Initiation / I'm Alive / A Little Time / Twilight Of The Gods / A Tale

HELLOWEEN

That Wasn't Right / Future World / Halloween / Follow The Sign. Chart positions: 42 SWEDEN, 104 USA.

Judas EP, Combat 88561-8128-1 (1987) (USA release). Judas / Victim Of Fate (Live) / Cry For Freedom (Live) / Ride The Sky / Guardians.

Future World, Noise N0083PD (1987) (12" picture disc). Future World / Starlight (Kiske version) / A Little Time.

Dr. Stein, Noise N0116-5 (1988). Dr. Stein / Savage / Livin' Ain't No Crime.

Dr. Stein, Noise N0116-6 (1988). Dr. Stein / Savage. Chart position: 57 UK.

KEEPER OF THE SEVEN KEYS PART II, Noise NUK 117 (1988). Invitation / Eagle Fly Free / You Always Walk Alone / March Of Time / Dr. Stein / Rise And Fall / We Got The Right / I Want Out / Keeper Of The Seven Keys. Chart positions: 7 SWEDEN, 9 AUSTRIA, 24 UK, 108 USA.

Dr. Stein, Noise N0116-53 (1988). Dr. Stein / Savage / Livin' Ain't No Crime / Victim Of Fate.

I Want Out, RCA 8920-1-RDAB (1988) (USA promotion). I Want Out / Intro: Happy Halloween.

I Want Out, Noise N0126-6 (1988). I Want Out / Don't Run For Cover. Chart position: 69 UK.

I Want Out, Noise N0126-3 (1988). I Want Out / Save Us / Don't Run For Cover.

I WANT OUT—LIVE, RCA 9709-1-R (1989) (USA release). A Little Time / Dr. Stein / Future World / Rise And Fall / We Got The Right / I Want Out / How Many Tears. Chart position: 123 USA.

KEEPERS—LIVE, JVC Victor VDP-28059 (1989) (Japanese release). A Little Time / Dr. Stein / Future World / Rise And Fall / We Got The Right / I Want Out / How Many Tears.

LIVE IN THE UK, EMI EMC 3558 (1989). A Little Time / Dr. Stein / Future World / Rise And Fall / We Got The Right / I Want Out / How Many Tears. Chart positions: 25 SWEDEN, 26 UK, 30 AUSTRIA.

I Want Out, EMI 2264 (1989). I Want Out / How Many Tears.

Kids Of The Century, EMI 2042202 560 (1991) (UK release. CD single). Kids Of The Century / Blue Suede Shoes / Shit And Lobster.

Kids Of The Century, EMI CDEM 178 (1991) (UK release. 12" single). Kids Of The Century / Blue Suede Shoes / Shit And Lobster.

Kids Of The Century, EMI (1991) (UK release. 10" single). Kids Of The Century / Blue Suede Shoes / Shit And Lobster / Interview.

Kids Of The Century, EMI EM 178 (1991). Kids Of The Century / Blue Suede Shoes. Chart position: 56 UK.

PINK BUBBLES GO APE, EMI EMC 3588 (1991). Pink Bubbles Go Ape / Kids Of The Century / Back On The Streets / Number One / Heavy Metal Hamsters / Goin' Home / Someone's Crying / Mankind / I'm Doing Fine Crazy Man / The Chance / Your Turn. Chart positions: 14 SWEDEN, 28 AUSTRIA, 32 GERMANY, 41 UK.

Helloween, Noise (1991) (Free with 'The Best, The Rest, The Rare' album). Helloween / Keeper Of The Seven Keys.

Number One, JVC Victor VICP-15017 (1992) (Japanese release). Number One / Les Hambourgeois Walkways / You Run With The Pack.

Number One, EMI 72348 80146 25 (1992). Number One / Les Hambourgeois Walkways / You Run With The Pack.

Kids Of The Century, JVC Victor VICP-15005 (1992) (Japanese release). Kids Of The Century / Blue Suede Shoes / Interview.

SPECIAL SAMPLER, JVC Victor CDS-208 (1993) (Japanese promotion release). First Time / When The Sinner / I Dont Wanna Cry No More / Step Out Of Hell / Longing / Kids Of The Century / The Chance / Your Turn / I Want Out / Dr. Stein / Invitation / Eagle Fly Free / Future World / Twilight Of The Gods.

When The Sinner, JVC Victor VICP-15025 (1993) (Japanese release). When The Sinner / I Don't Care, You Don't Care / Oriental Journey.

When The Sinner, EMI 72438 805862 9 (1993). When The Sinner (Edit) / When The Sinner (Album version) / I Don't Care.

I Believe, RCA 12 HELLODJ 1 (1993) (12" promotion release). I Believe / Revolution Now / San Francisco (Be Sure To Wear Flowers In Your Hair) / Step Out Of Hell.

CHAMELEON, EMI 7 89368 2 (1993). First Time / When The Sinner / I Don't Wanna Cry No More / Crazy Cat / Giants / Windmill / Revolution Now / San Francisco (Be Sure To Wear Flowers In Your Hair) / In The Night / Music / Step Out Of Hell / I Believe / Longing. Chart positions: 7 FINLAND, 35 SWEDEN, 35 GERMANY.

I Don't Wanna Cry No More, JVC Victor VICP-15029 (1993) (Japanese release). I Don't Wanna Cry No More / Red Socks And The Smell Of Trees / Ain't Got Nothing Better.

Windmill, EMI 72438 81065 2 8 (1993). Windmill / Cut In The Middle / Introduction / Get Me Out Of Here.

Step Out Of Hell, JVC Victor VICP-15030 (1993) (Japanese release). Step Out Of Hell / Cut In The Middle / Introduction / Get Me Out Of Here.

I Can, Victor VICP 60193 (1998) (Japanese release). I Can / A Handful Of Pain / A Game We Shouldn't Play.

I Can, Raw Power RAWX 1050 (1998) (UK release). I Can / A Handful Of Pain / A Game We Shouldn't Play.

BETTER THAN RAW, JVC Victor VICP-60235 (1998) (Japanese release). Deliberately Limited Preliminary Prelude Period In Z / Push / Falling Higher / Hey Lord / Don't Spit On My Mind / Revelation / Time / I Can / A Handful Of Pain / Laudate Dominum / Back On The Ground / Midnight Sun.

BETTER THAN RAW, Raw Power RAWCD 135 (1998). Deliberately Limited Preliminary Prelude Period In Z / Push / Falling Higher / Hey Lord / Don't Spit On My Mind / Revelation / Time / I Can / A Handful Of Pain / Laudate Dominum / Midnight Sun. Chart positions: 7 FINLAND, 19 GERMANY, 35 SWEDEN.

Hey Lord!, Rawpower RAWX 1052 (1998). Hey Lord! / Perfect Gentleman (Live) / Moshi Moshi—Shiki No Uta (Live) / Hey Lord! (Video & More).

Lay All Your Love On Me, JVC Victor VICP-60836 (1999) (Japanese release). Lay All Your Love On Me / From Out Of Nowhere / Something.

METAL JUKEBOX, Raw Power RAWCD 143 (1999). He's a Woman-She's A Man / Locomotive Breath / Lay All Your Love on Me / Space Oddity / From Out Of Nowhere / All My Loving / Hocus Pocus / Faith Healer / Juggernaut / White Room / Mexican. Chart positions: 49 GERMANY, 51 SWEDEN.

Mrs. God, SPV VICP-63061 (2005) (Japanese release). Mrs. God / My Life For One More Day (Single edit) / Run (The Name Of Your Enemy) / Mrs. God (Video).

Mrs. God, Steamhammer SPV 060-99583 (2005). Mrs. God / The King For A 1000 Years / Run (The Name Of Your Enemy). Chart positions: 38 SWEDEN, 91 SWITZERLAND.

KEEPER OF THE SEVEN KEYS—THE LEGACY, Castle Music Pictures SPV 99132 2CD (2005). The King For A 1000 Years / The Invisible Man / Born On Judgment Day / Pleasure Drone / Mrs. God / Silent Rain / Occasion Avenue / Light The Universe / Do You Know What You're Fighting For? / Come Alive / Shade In The Shadow / Get It Up / My Life For One More Day / Mrs. God (Video). Chart positions: 22 JAPAN, 24 SWEDEN, 27 CZECH REPUBLIC, 28 FINLAND, 28 GERMANY, 59 SPAIN, 61 SWITZERLAND, 64 NORWAY, 89 FRANCE.
Light The Universe, Steamhammer (2006). Light The Universe / If I Could Fly (Live) / Revolution / Light The Universe (Video).
KEEPER OF THE SEVEN KEYS—THE LEGACY WORLD TOUR 2005/2006—LIVE ON 3 CONTINENTS, (2007). Chart position: 58 GERMANY.

HELLRAISER

RUSSIA — *Alexander Luov (vocals / guitar), Mike Djanov (vocals / bass), Paul Chinyakov (drums).*

The long standing, enigmatic Russian Thrash band HELLRAISER has had a number of line-up changes over a career that spanned a decade. By 1994 the line-up for the 'No Brain, No Pain' album was listed as Mefody on guitar and vocals, Sam on guitar, Alexy Jashin on bass and Andrey Shatunovsky on drums. Confusingly, Oleg Milonvanov was also credited with the drums and Lev Zemlinsky was credited with keyboards for the record.

The album was recorded in Moscow in the Spring and Summer of 1994. Vocalist Mefody was credited as producer and co-credited with the lyrics along with Alex 'Z' Lighton but the English translation left something to be desired each song being liberally laced with profanity that didn't always make sense. The band followed it up with a number of other release through the 90's.

WE'LL BURY YOU!, Metalagen (1990).
NO BRAIN, NO PAIN, Triton SZCD0334 (1994). No Brain, No Pain / Visions Of Darkness / Killhead / Witch / See You In Hell / Land Of Dead / Remembering / God Of War.
LIVE, Moroz (1996).

HELLRAPER

BORDEAUX, FRANCE — *Psychoterror (vocals), Necrosadist (guitar), Virgin's Banger (guitar).*

Blasphemic Thrash Metal band HELLRAPER, created in 1998, is just one of many projects manifested by 'Necrosadist', also known as 'The Black Lord Beleth'Rim' of TORGEIST and VERMETH. The project was initiated under the formative title PAINDELIGHT by Necrosadist and vocalist Psychoterror, subsequently acquiring drummer Wargrinder. The demo 'Feed Bitches With Satan's Seed', limited to 200 copies and featuring Virgin's Banger as solo session player, arrived in 2003. Plans would then be made by the Bolivian based Grim Art Productions label to re-issue this cassette with an additional track, namely a cover version of DESTRUCTION's 'Invincible Force'. In September of 2004 the band announced plans for a split album on Australia's Asphyxiate label to be shared with BESTIAL HOLOCAUST.

Feed Bitches With Satan's Seed, Hellraper (2003). Intro / Devastating Terror / Paindelight / Addicted To Kill / Feed Bitches With Satan's Seed.

HELLSTORM

ITALY — *Ares (vocals / bass), Hypnos (guitar), Phobos (drums).*

HELLSTORM are unashamed eighties style Thrashers forged in 1995 by vocalist / bassist Ares and guitarist Hynos. Jessica was added on second guitar in 1996 in order to record the band anthem 'Hellstorm' for the Dutch compilation album 'And The Raven Left The Tower, released by Teutonic Existence Records. The membership changed in September of that year when Chelmis of ORTHODOX took Jessica's place and Davide from IRREVERENCE stepped in as drummer. This version of the band cut the demo 'Shadows Of Unknown'. Subsequently Thanatos of NEOPHYTE supplanted Chelmis and Davide departed. However, the latter returned to man the drums for recording of the debut HELLSTORM album 'The Legion Of The Storm'.

May of 2002 saw the introduction of new drummer Leo ('Phobos') and the exit of Thanatos. Although recorded in 2001 'The Legion Of The Storm' finally surfaced in March of 2003.

THE LEGION OF THE STORM, (2003). The Coming Of Shadows / Killed Equilibrium / Under A Stormy Sky / Across The Lands Of Grey / Shadows Of Unknown / The Cursed Circle / Doomed By The Moon / The Dark Side / Fire Of Terror / Song Of Twilight / The Legion Of The Storm.

HELLWITCH

FORT LAUDERDALE, FL, USA — *Pat Raneiri (vocals / guitar), Tommy Mouser (bass), Joe Schnessel (drums).*

HELLWITCH, arriving upon the Florida Metal scene in October 1984, would be initiated by vocalist / guitarist Patrick Ranieri and drummer Harry Tyler. An inaugural recording session, conducted in the living room of their apartment in Gainesville, produced the 'Nosferatu' single track demo. The project expanded into a full band set up in February of 1985 with the introduction of the PRECIPICE pairing drummer Dave Silverstein, replacing Tyler, and Andy Adcock on bass guitar. That July, HELLWITCH put in its opening live show as support to Punk band ROACH MOTEL. This signalled an intensive live campaign spanning the next three years, which saw HELLWITCH sharing stages with CORROSION OF CONFORMITY, G.B.H., CORONER, DARK ANGEL, KREATOR, DEICIDE, DEATH, MORBID ANGEL, ATHEIST, AGNOSTIC FRONT, D.R.I., ANTHRAX, NUCLEAR ASSAULT and many others.

The first official demo, 'Transgressive Sentience', was recorded in January 1986, from which a remixed version of the track 'Torture Chamber' appeared on the compilation album 'Thrash Metal Attack', released by New Renaissance Records in July of 1987. The band's second studio demo, 'Mordirivial Dissemination', was released in June of 1987.

In July of 1988 Pat Raneiri relocated to Fort Lauderdale and set about constructing an all new HELLWITCH, drafting Frank Watkins on bass and Steve Rincon on drums. This trio crafted a three track rehearsal demo in March of 1989, which included a cover version of DEATH's 'Archangel'. However, Raneiri then ousted his latest set of musicians and regrouped by enrolling bassist Jesse Trevino and Joe Witch Schnessel on drums. That June, Flight 19 Records issued two cuts from the 'Mordirivial Dissemination' demo as a limited edition 7" single. That August, Trevino was superseded by bassist Tommy Mouser.

October of 1989 brought about a contract with Wild Rags Records for the debut album 'Syzigial Miscreancy', recorded at the renowned Morrisound Studios with veteran Thrash producer Scott Burns. Released in October 1990 the album sold strongly and made a sizable impact on the international underground Metal media. In late 1990 HELLWITCH acquired Jim Nickles as a second guitarist and undertook successful tours of the East Coast, culminating in an appearance at the 'Milwaukee Metal Fest' event. In February of 1991, Jesse Trevino returned to the band, re-debuting with a short batch of dates in Texas. Further changes in 1991 found Craig Shattuck as substitute for Nickles.

In August of 1991 HELLWITCH entered Morrisound Studios once again to cut the three track EP 'Terraasymmetry' for Lethal Records. Schnessel left the ranks in March of 1992, returning fleetingly the following year before departing for good. With Trevino also opting out, relocating to Texas, Shattuck was switch to the bass role. The band splintered further though and by the close of the year only Pat Raneiri remained.

Pulling in drummer Joel Suarez in early 1994 HELLWITCH laid down the 'Anthropophagi' demo. In November Shattuck

HELLWITCH

returned to the fold and J.P. Brown joined as second guitarist. The following year Gabe Lewandowski took over drum duties and in 1996 the band signed to Nazgul's Eyrie Productions. No end product was forthcoming though and HELLWITCH folded in 1997.

Progressive Arts Records issued the 2003 album 'Final Approach', this set adding bonus cuts of archive demos and 1998 rehearsal recordings.

The band broke a six year hiatus by playing a comeback gig at the Culture Club in Fort Lauderdale, Florida on 24th July alongside MALEVOLENT CREATION and DIVINE EMPIRE. The band for this date comprised original members vocalist / guitarist Pat Ranieri and drummer Joe Schnessel with bass player Craig Shattuck.

A former HELLWITCH drummer, Gabriel Lewandowski, would gain scene credits with NAPHOBIA, ACHERON, EQUINOX and, in May 2005, join UNHOLY GHOST. Meantime, HELLWITCH cut a new demo, re-recording the tracks 'Final Approach' and 'Epitome Of Disgrace', both originally found on the 'Final Approach' set and adding new songs 'Opiatic Luminance' and 'Mythologicalies'. New on rhythm guitar would be J.P. Brown.

In February 2007 HELLWITCH supported German Thrashers DESTRUCTION at the Jacksonville Thee Imperial and Orlando Back Booth. That April the band signed to Xtreem Music.

Transgressive Sentience, (1986). Torture Chamber / Satan's Wrath / Nosferatu / Fate At Pains End.
Mordirivial Dissemination, (1987). Purveyor Of Fear / Pyrophoric Seizure / Degeneration / Nosferatu.
Rehearsal demo, (1989). Mordirivial Dissemination / Viral Exogence / Archangel.
SYZYGIAL MISCREANCY, Wild Rags WRE 902 (1990). The Ascent / Nosferatu / Viral Ehogence / Sentient Transmography / Mordirivial Dissemination / Pyrophoric Seizure / Purveyor Of Fear.
TERRASYMMETRY, Lethal LMCD 1111 (1993). Terrasymmetry / Satan's Wrath / Dawn Of Apostasy.
Anthropophagi, (1994). At Rest / Days Of Nemesis / Torture Chamber / Fate At Pains End.
FINAL APPROACH, Progressive Arts PAM-1017 (2003). The Ascent / Nosferatu / Viral Exogence / Sentient Transmography / Mordirivial Dissemination / Pyrophoric Seizure / Purveyor Of Fear / Terrasymmetry / Satan's Wrath / Dawn Of Apostasy / Nosferatu ('84 demo) / Torture Chamber ('86 demo) / Days Of Nemesis ('94 demo) / At Rest ('94 demo) / Anthropophagi ('94 demo) / Torture Chamber ('94 demo) / Fate At Pains End ('94 demo) / Final Approach ('98 rehearsal) / Epitome Of Disgrace ('98 rehearsal).

HELSTAR

HOUSTON, TX, USA — *James Rivera (vocals), Larry Barragan (guitar), Andre Corbin (guitar), Jerry Abaraca (bass), Frank Ferreira (drums).*

High octane Power based metallers HELSTAR, created in Houston during 1982, came to the fore on the underground tape trading scene with their debut 1983 demo. An early line-up involved ex-DEATHWISH and SCORCHER vocalist James Rivera and founding guitarist Larry Barragan, second guitarist Tom Rogers, bassist Paul Medina and drummer Hector Pavan.

The impact made by the demo soon landed HELSTAR a deal with Combat Records in 1984 and the resulting debut album, 'Burning Star', was produced by drummer Carl Canedy of THE RODS. Oddly, Rivera went by the pseudonym Bill Lionel for this set. The original version came decked in a sleeve depicting a red cowled wizard, subsequently changed to the more familiar science fiction based artwork. Music For Nations took the record on for the UK market. Critical riposte from the metal fraternity was swift and unanimously positive.

During 1985 HELSTAR inducted new members guitarist Rob Treviño, bass player Jerry Abarca and drummer Rene Luna. Following the Randy Burns produced 'Remnants Of War', issued in Europe during 1986 via Berlin's Noise imprint, HELSTAR split from Combat and re-locating to Los Angeles signed a fresh deal with Metal Blade Records. Ructions hit the band soon afterwards, though, and Treviño and Luna opted out to make way for guitarist Andre Corbin and drummer Frank Ferreira, while Barragan quit after a row with both the band's management and his colleagues. He intended to form a new band, BETRAYER, but quickly rejoined HELSTAR.

November 1988's 'A Distant Thunder' album sees HELSTAR covering the SCORPIONS classic 'He's A Woman, She's A Man'. The record captured worthy reviews and HELSTAR proceeded to tour both America and then Europe opening for TANKARD and YNGWIE MALMSTEEN. Upon their return the band migrated back to their native Houston.

Internal friction saw HELSTAR splitting asunder with only Rivera and Barragan remaining. Following the September 1989 'Nosferatu' release HELSTAR cut a further demo tape consisting of 'Social Circle', 'Scalpel In The Skin', 'Sirens Of The Sun' and 'Changeless Season'. The recording roster involved Rivera, Abarca, Barragan, guitarist Aaron Garza and drummer Russell DeLeon. Soon afterwards, Barragan withdrew from the metal scene totally finding a new calling with a Tex-Mex bar band. HELSTAR struggled on playing gigs on the local circuit but under a new title of VIGILANTE.

As VIGILANTE the band members began negotiation with MEGADETH bassist Dave Ellefson with the intention of recording a four track demo. Although the deal with Ellefson fell through VIGILANTE recorded and released one six-song EP. However, circumstances forced their hand as, with the return of Abaraca and under pressure the band reverted back to their HELSTAR moniker. Also forcing the pace was MEGADETH's dumping from the support slot they had at the time with rock giants AEROSMITH. MEGADETH opted out of the tour at a Houston date when main man Dave Mustaine was unable to continue and Ellefson found himself with more time to work with HELSTAR, the planned demo then evolving into the 'Multiples Of Black' album, released in 1995 on German label Massacre Records.

By 1998 Rivera was fronting DESTINYS END for their 'Breathe Deep The Dark' album. The singer founded a new act in 2000 titled PROJECT RIVERA which comprised of Z-LOT-Z guitarist Eric Halpern, MYSTIC CROSS guitarist Don LaFon, OUTWORLD bassist Brent Marches, VICTIM keyboard player Adam Rawlings and drummer Rick Ward from MIDNIGHT CIRCUS.

In May of 2000 Metal Blade released a live HELSTAR album, 'Twas The Night Of A Helish X-mas', which was widely panned as being an inferior quality bootleg from a Christmas show many years prior. The HELSTAR legacy was not ready to die as in 2001 the Iron Glory label issued a compilation of material under the HELSTAR name called 'The James Rivera

Legacy'. The first four tracks on the compilation were the unreleased post-Nosferatu demo and the last six cuts were the rare VIGILANTE EP.

It would be reported in August 2001 that Rivera had joined FLOTSAM AND JETSAM after their longstanding vocalist Eric A.K. departed. Rivera would then team up with SEVEN WITCHES, debuting with the band at their July appearance at the 'Classic Metal Fest II' in Cleveland, Ohio. The following year Rivera headed out on the live circuit with a unique tribute band, fronting up SABBATH JUDAS SABBATH, honouring both JUDAS PRIEST and BLACK SABBATH, also including HELSTAR colleague Mike Heald on guitar.

An all new act with strong HELSTAR ties was announced in August of 2003 as James Rivera and DESTINY'S END guitarist Eric Halpern united with SYMPHONY X bassist Mike Lepond in DISTANT THUNDER. The resulting 2004 album 'Welcome The End' would include a cover of HELSTAR's 'Run With The Pack'. DISTANT THUNDER undertook an extensive round of European headline shows in December although by the time the shows were booked they were all under the HELSTAR branding once again. Meanwhile, a triumvirate of erstwhile HELSTAR personnel in guitarists Larry Barragan and Rob Trevino alongside drummer Russell DeLeon founded ETERNITY BLACK. A five song demo, recorded at Spyder Studios with producer Gregg Gill, emerged in early 2005.

In mid 2005 it was learned that James Rivera was contributing to the DAWNRIDER project assembled by MAJESTY mentor Tarek "Metal Son" Maghary. The singer, keeping up his road miles with the tribute band SABBATH JUDAS SABBATH, joined VICIOUS RUMORS in September. Retaining this post, as well as his duties in KILLING MACHINE, Rivera was announced as fronting up a HELSTAR reunion in May 2006. The singer would be joined by the 'Remnants Of War' roster, guitarists Larry Barragan and Rob Treviño, bassist Jerry Abarca and drummer Russell DeLeon.

Demo, Helstar (1983) (Demo). Toward The Unknown / Witch's Eye / Run With The Pack / Leather And Lust / Possession / Shadows Of Iga.
BURNING STAR, Music For Nations MFN 20 (1984). Burning Star / Towards The Unknown / Witch's Eye / Run With The Pack / Leather And Lust / Possession / The Shadows Of Iga / Dracula's Castle.
REMNANTS OF WAR, Noise N 0043 (1986). Unidos Por Trjsteza / Remnants Of War / Conquest Of War / Evil Reign / Destroyer / Suicidal Nightmare / Dark Queen / Face The Wicked One / Angel Of Death.
A DISTANT THUNDER, Metal Blade 73403 (1988). King Is Dead / Bitter End / Abandon Ship / Tyrannicide / Scorcher / Genius Of Insanity / Whore Of Babylon / Winds Of Love / He's A Woman, She's A Man.
NOSFERATU, Roadrunner RO 94382 (1989). Rhapsody In Black / Baptized In Blood / To Sleep / Perchance To Scream / Harker's Tale (Mass Of Death) / Perseverance And Desperation / Curse Has Passed Away / Benediction / Harsh Reality / Swirling Madness / Von Am Lebem Destro Sturm / Aieliaria And Everon.
MULTIPLES OF BLACK, Massacre MASSCD 053 (1995). No Second Chance / Will It Catch Again / Lost To Be Found / When We Only Bleed / Reality / Good Day To Die / Beyond The Real Of Death / Save Time / Black Silhouette Skies / Last Serenade.
T'WAS THE NIGHT OF A HELLISH XMAS, Metal Blade 14306 (2000). Swirling Madness / The King Is Dead / Evil Reign / Abandon Ship / Baptized In Blood / To Sleep, Perchance To Scream / Harker's Tale / The Cursed Has Passed Away / Scorcher / Angel Of Death.
THE JAMES RIVERA LEGACY, Iron Glory (2001). Sirens Of The Sun / Changeless Season / Social Circle / Scalpel And The Skin / Sinister Deity / Rage In The Wind / Black Silhouette Skies / Nightmare Extraordinaire / Changeless Season / Lost To Be Found, Found To Be Lost.

HEMATOMA

MASSAMÁ, PORTUGAL — *Tiago (vocals / guitar), Lívio (guitar), Pedro Marreiros (bass), Gonçalo (drums).*

Massamá based HEMATOMA was founded in 1999 by Tiago on lead vocals and rhythm guitar, Jorge on bass and Gonçalo on the drums. In March 2000, Tiago Reis joined as lead guitarist. During 2001, just upfront of the band's inaugural concert, Lívio took over on guitar. More line up changes found Jorge vacating his position in April 2002. Undaunted, HEMATOMA performed live gigs minus a bassist until Pedro Marreiros was enrolled. In this formation the band issued the October 2003 demo ''Till The End'. Upon completion of these sessions Marreiros opted out and the group was once again forced to perform live with no bass. Several gigs were conducted with stand in bassists, SHADOWSPHERE guitarist Filipe Sousa and the NEOPLASMAH, GROG and BLEEDING DISPLAY credited Alexandre.

In October 2004 HEMATOMA finally filled the bass vacancy, the role being delegated to Brito—a scene veteran of FIRSTBORN EVIL, BLACKSWORD, CELTIC DANCE, MAJESTIK and CLAYMORE.

'Till The End, Hematoma (2004). Sweet Remain / Stone In My Boot / Left To Die.

HERESY

UK — *Reevsy (vocals / guitar), Kalv (bass), Steve (drums).*

HERESY replaced original guitarist Reevsy with Mitch Dickinson in 1987, previously a member of Shropshire pioneering Death Metal act WARHAMMER and Birmingham Thrashers SACRILEGE. Dickinson would re-surface as a member of UNSEEN TERROR. Another HERESY member would be former CONCRETE SOX vocalist / drummer John.

Never Healed, Earache EAR 1 (1985). Never Healed / Despair / Deathbitter / Anguish Of War / More Blood Is Shed / Dead.
HERESY, Earache MOSH 2 (1987).
Whose Generation, In Your Face FACE04 (1989). Whose Generation.

HERETIC

LOS ANGELES, CA, USA — *Mike Howe (vocals), Brian Korban (guitar), Bobby Marquez (guitar), Dennis O'Hara (bass), Rick Merrick (drums).*

Los Angeles based HERETIC were amongst the fray when California's Thrash scene erupted but made their mark with some precise Speed Metal. The band's original vocalist Mike Torres departed prior to recording to team up with ABATTOIR for their 'Only Safe Place' album. The debut mini-album 'Torture Knows No Boundaries' features singer Julian Mendez who lost his position to Mike Howe in late 1987.

Howe appears on the 'Breaking Point' album but joined METAL CHURCH the same year. Two members of HERETIC, guitarist Brian Korban and bassist Dennis O'Hara would team up with ex METAL CHURCH vocalist David Wayne's REVEREND. Korban recently forged Christian Metal act MONTH OF SUNDAYS in league with erstwhile DELIVERANCE guitarist Glenn Rogers.

TORTURE KNOWS NO BOUNDARY, Metal Blade 72170 (1986). Riding With The Angels / Blood Will Tell / Portrait Of Faith / Whitechapel / Torture Knows No Boundary.
BREAKING POINT, Metal Blade 72272 (1988). Intro / The Heretic / And Kingdom Fall / The Circle / The Enemy Within / Time Runs Short / Pale Shelter / Shifting Fire / Let 'Em Bleed / Evil For Evil / The Search.

HEVEIN

HELSINKI, FINLAND — *Juha Immonen (vocals), Leif Hedström (vocals / guitar), Tomi Koivunen (bass), Aino Piipari (violin), Max Lilja (cello), Alpo Oksaharju (drums).*

Helsinki's HEVEIN began life during 1992, founded upon an initial duo of guitarist Leif Hedström and drummer Alpo Oksaharju, subsequently enrolling Tomi Koivunen on bass and violinist Aino Piipari in 1998. The following year instrumental demos billed as 'Heartland' were recorded in order to locate a suitable lead singer. A second demo session, 'Reverence' cut in 2001, would see Hedström taking the lead vocal role. In October of 2002 HEVEIN expanded with the addition of singer Dimitri Paile and former APOCALYPTICA cellist Max Lilja for the 'Only Human' two song demo. Yet more demos, 'Fear Is …' crafted in early 2003, would find Paile replaced by Nico Hartonen of GODSPLAGUE. However, this frontman too soon vacated. That same year demos would be compiled for the EP 'Fear is … Only Human'. Paile made a brief return to head up the band for their debut live showing at the 'Tuska' festival.

The group drafted Juha Immonen as singer in October of 2003, making his first mark with the 2004 demo 'Break Out The Hammers'. HEVEIN signed to Spinefarm Records in October. Working with Jarno Hänninen the band entered D-Studios for pre-production in January 2005 prior to cutting single tracks at Sonic Pump Studios in February with producer Nino Laurenne. HEVEIN inducted bassist Janne Jaakkola, known as frontman for 7TH LABYRINTH, into the group's ranks in October prior to supporting STRATOVARIUS and HAMMERFALL in Tampere.

Heartland, (1999). Heartland / A Picture Of A Dead Man / Sisu In My Veins / One Deadly Kiss.
Reverence, (2001). Reverence / Execute / What If.
Only Human, (2002). Nothing Of This Calibre / Only Human.
Fear Is …, (2003). Fear Is … / Outsized.
Fear Is … Only Human, (2003). Fear Is … / Outsized / Nothing Of This Calibre / Only Human.
Break Out The Hammers, Hevein (2004). Break Out The Hammers / Worth Fighting For / As Far As The Eye Can See / Heartland.
SOUND OVER MATTER, Candlelight (2006). Break Out The Hammers / Worth Fighting For / iTOa / As Far As The Eye Can See / Only Human / Bleed The Day / Beg To Differ / Hold Fast / New Hope / Last Drop Of Innocence.

HEXENHAUS

SOLNA, SWEDEN — *Thomas Lyon (vocals), Mike Wead (guitar), Rick Meister (guitar), Jan Blomqvist (bass), Ralph Raideen (drums).*

HEXENHAUS, hailing from Solna, was originally titled MANINNYA BLADE, under which name they released one album. Having adopted the new name in 1987, the band's line-up for the debut album, 'A Tribute To Insanity', comprised of vocalist Nicklas Johansson, ex-WITCH guitarist Mike Wead (a.k.a. Mikael Vikström), second guitarist ex-DAMIEN man Rick Meister (real name Andreas Palm), bassist Jan Blomqvist and drummer Ralph 'Raideeen' Ryden.

In early 1989 Niclas Johansson left, to be superseded by HATRED vocalist Thomas Lyon (then called Thomas Lundin). The band had actually asked Lundin a year previously to join the band, but he had declined. On the second chance he accepted the offer. 1990's 'The Edge Of Eternity' album was fronted by DAMIEN's Tommie Agrippa and also features a fresh bassist in former NAGASAKI, DAMIEN and MANNYINA BLADE man Mårten Marteen (real name Mårten Sandberg) and ex-PARASITE drummer Billy St. John (Johan Billerhag).

MANNINYA BLADE reformed in 1990 with Rutström, Leif Eriksson, Blomqvist and drummer Johan Eriksson, although Leif was to leave after the band cut a new demo tape in 1995.

In 1990, the band once again asked for the services of vocalist Thomas Lyon and this time he accepted the offer. For the third HEXENHAUS album, 1991's 'Awakening', only Wead and a returning Lyon remained with the band's new members being guitarist Marco A. Nicosia, ex-MEZZROW bassist Conny Welen and drummer John Billerhag. After the album emerged Mike Wead created MEMENTO MORI then formed ABSTRAKT ALGEBRA with his former comrade, ex-CANDLEMASS bassist Lief Edling.

Thomas Lyon guested on keyboards/backing vocals with MEMENTO MORI on tour in UK and Sweden in 1993. In 1994 he helped out as lead vocalist on FIFTH REASON's 'Stranded' demo, which consequently earned them their record deal. Lyon was asked to be a fulltime member but he declined.

Marco Nicosia appeared on the 1997 album by FIFTH REASON 'Psychotic', a band founded by refugees from TAD MOROSE, ABSTRAKT ALGEBRA and MEMORY GARDEN. Marteen joined MEMENTO MORI. A former HEXENHAUS drummer, Martin Eriksson, re-invented himself as Eurodance star E TYPE in subsequent years. HEXENHAUS reunited temporarily to release their fourth album, 'Deja Voodoo' crafted at MIW Studios in January and February of 1997.

Thomas Lyon would handle the vocal / guitar / keyboard role with Gothic Rock act THE SAVIOURS during the latter half of the nineties, crafting the demos 'Avalon' in 1996 and 'Spoken in Tongues' in 1998. From 2002 onward he would be engaged with "deep house music" project GHOSTHOUSE.

In February 2007 it was announced that Mike Wead had joined forces with a brand new, melodic Death Metal inclined project called KRYPTILLUSION. Kristofer Nilsson of UNDIVINE handled lead vocals whilst Stefan Westerberg, of IN THY DREAMS, STEEL ATTACK, WORLD BELOW, ASPERITY and CARNAL FORGE, featured on drums and Fredrik Groth from THE STORYTELLER assumed bass duties.

A TRIBUTE TO INSANITY, Active ACTLP 6 (1988). It / Eaten Alive / Delirious / As Darkness Falls: 1st Movement. a) Shades Of An Obscure Dream, b) A Fatal Attraction, c) In The Spiders Web. 2nd Movement. a) The Possession, b) The Damnation, 3rd Movement. a) On The Threshold Of Insanity, b) Behind Closed Doors, c) The Fall From Grace / Incubus / Death Walks Among Us / Memento Morie—The Dead Are Restless / Requiem.
THE EDGE OF ETERNITY, Active ATVLP13 (1990). Prelude / Toxic Threat / Prime Evil / Home Sweet Home / The House Of Lies / A Temple For The Soul / The Eternal Nightmare / At The Edge Of Eternity.
AWAKENING, Active ATV19 (1991). Shadows Of Sleep / Awakening / Betrayed (By Justice) / Necromonicon Ex Mortis / Code 29 / The Forthcoming Fall / Sea Of Blood / Paradise Of Pain / The Eternal Nightmare Act III / Incubus.
DEJA VOODOO, Black Mark BMCD 98 (1997). Dies Irae—Vreden's Dag / Reborn (At The Back Of Beyond) / Phobia / Nocturnal Rites / Dejavoodoo / From The Cradle To The Grave / Rise Babylon Rise.

HEXX

CA, USA — *Manzo (vocals), Dan Watson (guitar), Bill Peterson (bass), Dave Schmidt (drums).*

HEXX began life as PARADOX upon their formation in 1978. Evolved into HEXX during 1983. HEXX split apart after the debut 'No Escape' album. Remaining members guitarist Dan Watson, bassist Bill Peterson and drummer Dave Schmidt recruited fresh blood in the form of vocalist Dan Bryant and second guitarist Clint Bower.

Schmidt opted out for the 'Quest For Sanity' album and his position was filled by John Schafer. The 1992 album was produced by METAL CHURCH guitarist John Marshall. Bower subsequently journeyed on to ABSCESS, THE RAVENOUS and sessioned as guest bassist on AUTOPSY's infamous 'Shitfun' album.

In 2004 Californian gore Metal band EXHUMED revealed they had included a rendition of the HEXX song 'Twice As Bright, Half As Long' on their covers album entitled 'Regurgitated Requiems: Garbage Daze Re-Regurgitated'.

NO ESCAPE, Shrapnel (1984). Terror / Invader / The Other Side / Look To The Sky / Beware The Darkness / Night Of Pain / No Escape / Live For The Night / Fear No Evil.
UNDER THE SPELL, Shrapnel (1986). Hell Riders / A Time Of War / Edge Of Death / The Victim / Under The Spell / Out For Control / Suicide / The Hexx / Fever Dream / Midnight Sun.
QUEST FOR SANITY, Under One Flag MFLAG 22 (1989). Twice As Bright, Half As Long / Fields Of Death / Mirror Of The Past / Racial Slaughter / Sardonicus.
Watery Graves, Wild Rags WRR025 (1990). Watery Graves / Edge Of Death / Under The Spell.

MORBID REALITY, Century Media 84 9725-2 (1992). Morbid Reality / The Last Step / Birds Of Prey / Blood Hunter / Fire Mushrooms / Persecution Experience / Watery Graves / Spider Jam.

HIMSA

SEATTLE, WA, USA — *John Pettibone (vocals), Kirby Charles Johnson (guitar), Sammi Curr (guitar), Derek Harn (bass), Chad Davis (drums).*

HIMSA, "To wage wrath and destruction" in Sanskrit, was assembled in Seattle by former personnel from acts such as TRIAL, GENUINE, HARKONEN and CHRIST with ANONYMOUS and JESSICA lead vocalist Christian in October 1998, debuting with a 7" eponymous EP and the Paul Speers produced 1999 'Ground Breaking Ceremony' album. For these outings Mike Green manned the drums. Founder members guitarist Brian Johnson, bassist Derek Harn and second guitarist Aaron Edge all held TRIAL credentials. Christian and Edge would soon decamp, the latter going on to THE SIX MINUTE HEARTSTOP. During 2000 the band operated with three guitarists for a period as the membership ebbed and flowed.

The band unit would be rocked by line-up changes but by the recording of November 2001's 'Death Is Infinite' EP, originally projected as a split album to be shared with PRETTY GIRLS MAKE GRAVES, HIMSA comprised erstwhile NINE IRON SPITFIRE and UNDERTOW vocalist John Pettibone, guitarist Brian Johnson and Kirby Johnson, bassist Derek Harn, electronics man Clay Layton and drummer Tim Mullen. In this formation the group strayed away from their Hardcore roots and steered towards a very identifiable Scandinavian style of technical Thrash / Death Metal.

April 2002 West Coast shows saw the band supporting BREAKING THROUGH. Following recording of the 2003 opus 'Courting Tragedy And Disaster', issued by Prosthetic Records, HIMSA replaced guitarist Sammi Curr with Matt Wicklund. Breaking in Wicklund and new drummer Steve Fournier HIMSA set about a rash of East Coast dates in July partnered with AS I LAY DYING and THE AGONY SCENE. Maintaining their live presence the group hooked up with SHADOWS FALL and THIS DAY FORWARD for October dates, running into a further leg into Canada allied with DEATH BY STEREO.

HIMSA shot a promotional video for the track 'A Girl In Glass' in June 2004, this short directed by Kevin Leonard upfront of Summer dates with label mates BYZANTINE in July and leading up to a full US tour with SHADOWS FALL, AS I LAY DYING and REMEMBERING NEVER. November 'Headbanger's Ball III' US touring partners would be CRADLE OF FILTH, BLEEDING THROUGH and ARCH ENEMY. Nationwide touring throughout February of 2005 saw the band packaged with THE ACCUSED, 3 INCHES OF BLOOD and COUNTDOWN TO LIFE. The group entered AntFarm Studios in Denmark with producer Tue Madsen in May to record the 'Hail Horror' opus. Live work extended throughout the mid-year period in an alliance with SCARS OF TOMORROW, THE AGONY SCENE and THE ESOTERIC on the 'Dirty Black Summer' trek, commencing 13th June in Sacramento, California. Just upfront of these gigs the band parted ways with guitarist Matt Wicklund, re-drafting former member Sammi Curr in his stead. Wicklund, announcing his intention to marry fiancé and former adult film star Jasmin St. Claire, explained he had exited due to "professional and personal reasons".

Gigs in July had the band partnered with FULL BLOWN CHAOS and GOD FORBID. The band joined forces with the DANZIG headlined 'Blackest of the Black' US dates commencing in September, these shows accompanied by CHIMAIRA, BEHEMOTH, MORTIIS and THE AGONY SCENE. That same month Wicklund returned to the scene, uniting with erstwhile CRADLE OF FILTH personnel keyboard player Martin Powell and guitarist James McIlroy in a brand new band project called PREY.

HIMSA launched a new album, 'Hail Horror', in February 2006, Japanese versions adding extra track 'I, Possession'. The band engaged in US dates that same month backed by DARKEST HOUR, A LIFE ONCE LOST, THE ACACIA STRAIN and DEAD TO FALL. UK and European gigs in April and May, taking in Germany, Holland, Belgium, Austria, Italy, Switzerland, Denmark and Sweden, had the band hooked up with running mates DEATH BY STEREO and THE BANNER.

HIMSA singer John Pettibone fronted an all new project band dubbed THE VOWS involving bass player Rob Moran of UNBROKEN and SOME GIRLS, drummer Ryan Murphy of ENSIGN and UNDERTOW plus the CHAMPION guitar pairing of Aram Arslanian and Chris Williams. This unit signed with Indecision Records for an EP release. Another HIMSA related project, IAMTHETHORN, comprised Johnny Pettibone and Aaron Edge plus Jerad Shealey of RECEDER on bass plus Joe Axler, from SKARP, BOOK OF BLACK EARTH and SPLATTERHOUSE, on drums.

The group announced touring plans for the summer of 2006, kicking of the 'Sthress' tour in July alongside POISON THE WELL, IT DIES TODAY, SHADOWS FALL, DARKEST HOUR, BURY YOUR DEAD, SUFFOCATION, THROWDOWN and STILL REMAINS. The band contributed their version of 'Maladjusted' to the SICK OF IT ALL tribute album 'Our Impact Will Be Felt' assembled by Abacus Recordings for January 2007 release.

Revealed in early 2007 would be OPHIDIAN, a project between former HIMSA guitarist Matt Wicklund with the NILE, ACHERON, AURORA BOREALIS, GOD DETHRONED, MALEVOLENT CREATION, DIMMU BORGIR, SYSTEM:OBSCURE, NIDINGR and ANGEL CORPSE credited Tony Laureano on drums.

HIMSA commenced fresh album recordings on April 23rd, utilising Steve Carter to engineer guitar, bass and drums before DEVIN TOWNSEND took over for vocal work. Tue Madsen provided the final mix.

GROUND BREAKING CEREMONY, Revelation (1999). Daylight Savings / The Great Depression / Another Version Of The Twist / Ground Breaking Ceremony / Carrier / Mud / Cremation / The Date Is Here / Tapas / White Out.
Death Is Infinite EP, Revelation (2001). Born To Conquer / Twist / Hellbent And Hammered / Exhale.
Himsa, Revelation (2003). Blackout / Flood In The Market / Sink In.
COURTING TRAGEDY AND DISASTER, Prosthetic (2003). Dominion / Rain To The Sound Of Panic / A Girl In Glass / Kiss Or Kill / Jacob Shock / Cherum / It's Night Like This That Keep Us Alive / Loveless And Goodbye / Scars In The Landscape / Sense Of Passings / When Midnight Breaks.
HAIL HORROR, Prosthetic (2006). Anathema / Sleezevil / The Destroyer / Pestilence / Wither / Wolfchild / Seminal / They Speak In Swarms / Calling In Silent / Send Down Your Reign.

HIRAX

BUENA PARK, CA, USA — *Katon W DePena (vocals), Scott Owen (guitar), Gary Monardo (bass), Eric Brecht (drums).*

An undisputed underground Thrash legend. Buena Park, California's HIRAX was created in 1984 by vocalist Katon W. DePena, bassist Gary Monardo, guitarist Bob Savage and drummer Brian Keith from the defunct L.A. KAOS and KGB. The obligatory first demo was a much sought after item on the tape trading scene. Co-produced by the band and Y&T guitarist Joey Alves, the tape contained four tracks of Power Metal muscle and HIRAX made further inroads with a track on the compilation album 'Metal Massacre VI'.

The debut HIRAX album, October 1985's 'Raging Violence', with drummer John Tabares, was a solid display of intense metal marred by a weak production. Soon after recording Tabares was asked to leave and the band drafted in ex-D.R.I. man Eric Brecht for the 'Hate, Fear And Power' mini album. HIRAX garnered much laudable press but DePena quit to form PHANTASM, an act comprising of former METALLICA bassist Ron McGoveney, HIRAX refugee John Tabares on drums and guitarists Rodney Nicholson and Carlos Guaico. Drummer Gene Hoglan, later of DARK ANGEL and TESTAMENT fame, also had a term with PHANTASM. Brecht subsequently returned with TWO BIT THIEF.

Following vocalist Paul Ballof's departure from EXODUS the band rehearsed with Ballof for a short while until his departure to form PIRANHA.

The band persevered with erstwhile CORRUPTION singer Billy Wedgeworth. Before too long Monardo walked out and HIRAX folded. Brecht joined DEATH and ATTITUDE.

An attempt to revive the name with De Pena and Tabare was attempted in late 1987 and resulted in the original line-up of the band reforming and recording a three track demo in 1988. Tracks from this tape emerged on the 'Blasted In Bankok' single.

DePena, Tabare, Owen and Monardo finally reformed HIRAX in 2000. HIRAX returned to the recording studio to cut their comeback 'Barrage Of Noise' opus. Joining DePena for these sessions would be PRODIGAL SON guitarist James Joseph Hubler, guitarist Justin Lent from Colorado Punk act CLUSTERFUX and drummer Nick Sieblinger. Guitarist Jimmy Durkin of DARK ANGEL and DREAMS OF DAMNATION joined the new line up in September 2001.

The band restructured itself yet again to consist of consisted of DePena, Hubler and Durkin with the TCHILDRES rhythm section of bassist Mike Brickman and drummer Dan Bellinger. However, Bellinger quit to forge BACKMASK in union with ex-DEVILDRIVER guitarist Evan Pitts and lead vocalist/guitarist Shane McFee (son of DOOBIE BROTHERS guitarist John McFee). In June 2003 HIRAX was joined by bassist Angelo Espino, a scene veteran citing credits with PREDATOR, L.S.N., DISSENTER, UNCLE SLAM and REVEREND. This version of the band cut the 'New Age Of Terror' for Mausoleum Records.

HIRAX announced touring plans for European dates in early 2005 in partnership with INFERNAL MAJESTY. That March, former HIRAX members guitarist Bob Savage, bassist Gary Monardo and drummer Johnny Tabares joined forces with ex-WARGOD singer Robbie Perkins in a reformed version of their pre-HIRAX band COLD BLOOD, albeit going under the moniker WEAPONS OF MASS DESTRUCTION.

German Heavy Metal band POWERGOD cut a cover version of 'Bombs Of Death' for inclusion on their 'Long Live The Loud– That's Metal Lesson II' released through Massacre Records in July 2005. On 9th July 2005 HIRAX lined up at The Pound outdoor amphitheatre in San Francisco alongside TESTAMENT, VICIOUS RUMORS, LÄÄZ ROCKIT, DREAMS OF DAMNATION, AGENT STEEL, DEKAPITATOR, MUDFACE, NEIL TURBIN, BROCAS HELM and IMAGIKA for the 'Thrash Against Cancer' benefit.

Gigs in Japan would be scheduled for November but on the eve of these shows the band imploded, with Glenn Rogers, Dave Watson, Angelo Espino and Dave Chedrick all walking out en masse. In early 2006 HIRAX announced the return of original drummer John Tabares and the addition of ELECTRIC FUNERAL guitarist Lance Harrison to the group's ranks. In March Glenn Rogers rejoined the fold as the band re-formulated itself once again, a new rhythm section comprising bassist Steve Harrison and drummer Fabricio Raveli.

HIRAX acted as support to the January / February 2007 DESTRUCTION, INTO ETERNITY and MUNICIPAL WASTE North American tour. Drummer Fabricio Ravelli exited in April.

RAGING VIOLENCE, Metal Blade 72058 (1985). Demons / Evil Forces / Blitzkrieg Air Attack / Guardian Protector / Bombs Of Death / Defeat Of Amalek / Raging Violence / Call Of The Gods / Warlords Command / Suicide / Executed / The Gauntlet / Destruction And Terror / Destroy / Bloodbath.

HATE, FEAR AND POWER, Metal Blade 72162 (1986). Hate, Fear And Power / Blind Faith / Unholy Sacrifice / Lightning Thunder / The Last War / The Plague / Imprisoned By Ignorance / Criminal Punishment.

HIRAX

NOT DEAD YET, Metal Blade 72224 (1987). Demons / Evil Forces / Bombs Of Death / Warlords Command / Bloodbath / Blind Faith / Criminal Punishment / Lightning Thunder / The Plague.

Blasted In Bankok, Lautrec (1988). Blasted In Bankok.

Dying World (Shock), Pessimer Theologian (1997) (Split single with SPAZZ). Dying World (Shock).

El Diablo Negro, (2000) (Picture disc). I See Blood Red / Slit Your Wrists.

BARRAGE OF NOISE, Deepsix Records (2001). Murder One / Barrage Of Noise / Walk Of Death / Broken Neck / Jade / Mouth Sewn Shut / Beyond The Church (Part 1) / French Pearl.

THE NEW AGE OF TERROR, Mausoleum (2004). Kill Switch / Hostile Territory / The New Age Of Terror / Swords Of Steel / Into The Ruins / Massacre Of The Innocent / Hell On Earth / Suffer / El Dia De Los Muertos / El Diablo Negro / Unleash The Dogs Of War (Open The Gates).

HITTMAN

NEW YORK, NY, USA — *Dirk Kennedy (vocals), Jim Bachi (guitar), Michael Buccell (bass), Chuck Kory (drums).*

New York's HITTMAN was founded in 1984 by erstwhile ATTILLA members guitarist Jim Bachi and bassist Michael Buccell together with former TAKASHI drummer Chuck Kory. The band soon added singer Dirk Kennedy, who had previously been involved in the formative stages of ANTHRAX and took on a name influenced by the comic book character He-Man.

The band added to their line up with second guitarist Brian Fair, previously a member of ALIEN. In mid 1985 this line-up issued HITTMAN's first demo which gained the outfit their inaugural live appearance opening for STRYPER at Nassau Community College on Long Island. Further shows followed including guest slots to POISON, KIX, BLACK N' BLUE and SAXON.

A four track demo—containing 'Metal Sport', 'Sleepless Nights', 'Winds Of Warning' and 'Live For Tomorrow'—quickly began to elicit rave reviews, especially in Europe, although record companies were slow in picking up on the buzz.

In 1986 HITTMAN suffered from line up ructions as Fair departed, reportedly due to a lack of commitment, to be supplanted by guitarist Greg Walls. Before too long Walls was out in favour of John Kristen.

over by many labels purely because they were playing a more traditional brand of Metal than the in vogue Thrash of the day, it wasn't until 1988 when the New York quintet finally issued their debut product through German label SPV. HITTMAN had previously abandoned plans for a self-financed EP in order to hold out for a deal. Whilst the album features a metallic cover of the theme tune to the old American TV series 'Secret Agent Man' it did not feature demo favourite 'Live For Tomorrow', considered by most observers at the time to be one of the band's classic songs.

The 'Vivas Machina' album featured new drummer Mark Jenkins and found HITTMAN moving ever further into Technical Metal waters.

HITTMAN, SPV Steamhammer 857568 (1988). Metal Sport / Dead On Arrival / Back Street Rebels / Behind The Lines / Test Of Time / Secret Agent Man / Will You Be There / Caught In The Crossfire / Breakout.

VIVAS MACHINA, Steamhammer (1992). Radio Waves / Listen / Say A Prayer For Me / Words / If You Can't Dance To It / Answer My Prayer / Partners In Crime / Renegade Man / Ballad Of Jackson Heights / Walk That Walk / Mercy.

HOBBS' ANGEL OF DEATH

MELBOURNE, VIC, AUSTRALIA — *Peter Hobbs (vocals/ guitar), Mark Wooley (guitar), Phillip Gresik (bass), Darren McMaster-Smith (drums).*

HOBBS' ANGEL OF DEATH was one of the few Australian acts to employ Satanic overtones with 80's Thrash Metal. Peter Hobbs had started his musical career in 1983 with TYRUS, issuing a demo 'He's A Liar', then creating ANGEL OF DEATH in 1986. The following year saw the release of two demos 'Angel Of Death' and 'Virgin Metal Invasion From Down Under'. These sessions were recorded with the assistance of Melbourne act NOTHING SACRED guitarist Mark Wooley, Karl Lean and Sham.

These tapes came to the attention of German label Steamhammer and the 1988 eponymous album was produced by Harris Johns in Berlin. HOBBS' ANGEL OF DEATH had now solidified around Hobb's, NOTHING SACRED guitarist Mark Wooley, former MASS CONFUSION bassist Phil Gresik and ex-NEW RELIGION drummer Darren McMaster-Smith. Back home HOBBS' ANGEL OF DEATH put in their debut live show opening for MORTAL SIN.

In 1989 the first album was issued in Japan as a double package with Canadian Thrashers RAZOR's 'Violent Restitution' album entitled 'Hobb's Angel Of Death Vs. Razor'. However, by 1989 the band had splintered with Hobbs and Wooley enlisting bassist Dave Frew and drummer Bruno Canziani. Following touring the band was then put on ice resulting in Wooley and Frew founding HATRED.

Bassist Phil Gresik would later join the notorious Black Metal band BESTIAL WARLUST and later the equally infamous DESTRÖYER 666. Latterly he has founded LONG VOYAGE BACK. Reports in 2002 suggested that HOBBS' ANGEL OF DEATH had reformed with the return of guitarist Mark Wooley, bassist Dave Frew and drummer Bruno Canziani. This new version of the band incorporated EDEN's Talie Helene on keyboards. However, Woolley exited in February of 2003 and Helene would decamp that July in order to prioritise her own Doom band STONE MAIDEN.

Modern Invasion Music pressed up two early band demos, 'Virgin Metal Invasion From Downunder' and 'Angel Of Death', for the album release 'Hobbs' Satans Crusade'. The legacy was maintained as esteemed US Death Metal combo MALEVOLENT CREATION's July 2004 'Warkult' included a cover of 'Jack The Ripper'. In September former HOBBS' ANGEL OF DEATH keyboard player Talie Hélène joined forces with celebrity Wiccan singer Wendy Rule and Rachel Samuel on cello to provide double-bass in the project ZAUBEREI.

HOBB'S ANGEL OF DEATH, Steamhammer (1988). Jack The Ripper / Crucifixion / Brotherhood / Journey / House Of Death / Satan's Crusade / Lucifer's Domain / Marie Antoinette / Bubonic Plague / Cold Steel.

HOBB'S SATANS CRUSADE, Modern Invasion Music (2003). House Of Death / Crucifixion / Jack The Ripper / Bubonic Plague / The Journey / Lucifers Domain / Satanic Overture / Chainsaw Massacre / Marie Antoinette / Liar / Satans Crusade.

HOLOCHAUST

SAVONLINNA, FINLAND — *Tommy Tihonen (vocals / guitar), Risto Kivioja (guitar), Jukka Hoffrén (bass), Toni Toivila (drums).*

Savonlinna Metal band HOLOCHAUST were originally founded as the teenage Thrash act G.R.G. in the mid 80's as a trio incorporating Tommi Tiihonen on lead vocals and guitar, Jussi Petrelius on second guitar and Kimmo Tiihonen on the bass. A whole swathe of band members came and went as the band operated under various titles such as KILLERS in 1985, YAMMIES (after a chewing gum!) and in 1986 MONSTERS. With Petrrlius now on drums the band welcomed Toni Kummelus in as lead guitarist for the demo tape 'What's ... Up!!!, Dude'.

Petrelius bowed out to create FRAGILE and in 1993 HOLOCHAUST inducted Juha Niskanen on drums. Kummelus was next to leave, his place being taken by Marko Kautonen and then a further split occurred with Niskanen opting out. The new face behind the drum kit was Mikko Purontaus. Quite surreally, upon discovering BON JOVI was to play in Helsinki HOLOCHAUST cut a demo recording, featuring a version of the KISS classic 'God of Thunder', specifically in an attempt to gain the opening slot for this gig. They failed. Kimmo Tiihonen decided to leave shortly after but Jari Kosonen took on bass for gigs in the latter half of 1996. This latest recruit in turn was substituted by Antti Kinnunen.

Fate would then lend a twist of good fortune to HOLOCHAUST as huge exposure was generated during 1998 for the demo song 'Valley Of Misery'. This track circumvented the globe mistakenly attributed to METALLICA. Many fans of the San Francisco Thrash godfathers were convinced that the HOLOCHAUST track was a return to form for METALLICA as Tommy Tiihonen's voice had a degree of resemblance to James Hetfield's.

In 2000 Tommy Tihonen built a completely new version of HOLOCHAUST involving guitarist Risto 'Rizzto' Kivioja, bassist Jukka 'Hofu Black' Hoffrén and AURORA-K drummer Toni Toivila. The demo 'PanDEMOnium' saw issue in 2002.

Having switched title to DARCANE, the new look band weighed in under their new banner with the March EP 'Survivors Of The Holochaust'. The band comprised vocalist / guitarist Tommy Dee (a.k.a. Tommy Tiihonen), guitarist Rizzto Cullervo, bass player Hofu Black (Jukka Hoffrén) with Tony Toivola of on drums. Subsequently the group evolved further, becoming MIND-A-STRAY in 2005, issuing the demo 'Sign Of Victory' in March as their opener.

By this stage the band involved vocalist / guitarist Tommi Tiihonen, guitarist Jere Lappalainen and bass player Jukka Hoffrén, the latter holding credits with BRIDE ADORNED, DIVERCIA and ADAMANTRA.

Valley Of Misery EP, (2001). Beyond The Violence / Valley Of Misery / I Wanna Lie.

Pandemonium EP, Independent (2002). Intro—Pandemonium / Holocaust / Guilty Of Greed / Sad Life Philosophy.

HOLOSADE

DARLINGTON, UK — *Phillip De Sade (vocals), Jack Hammer (guitar), Gary Thomson (guitar), Mac (bass), Damien Lee (drums).*

Darlington quintet HOLOSADE debuted in 1985 formed by ex-DARK HEART and REBEL vocalist Phillip De Sade. The band's first product was the cassette 'Vendetta', followed by a two track demo featuring 'Set Me Free' and 'Only In Love'. HOLOSADE also had the track 'Cries In The Night' featured on the Ebony Records compilation album 'The Metal Collection'.

Original bassist Kevin Hole was to depart in favour of ex-DARK HEART and ROULETTE man Colin Bell in early 1986, as the band also added ex-PHANTOM guitarist Jack Hammer. This revised line-up recorded another two track cassette featuring 'Love It To Death' and 'Vicious'.

A further demo, 'Psycho' / 'Eternal Life', produced by Evo of WARFARE, was recorded at Neat Record's Impulse studios during 1987. Drummer Michael Lee (a.k.a. Damien Lee) opted to jump ship to major signing LITTLE ANGELS later that year and was later to journey on through THE CULT and ROBERT PLANT. Interestingly enough, the drummer was later to deny any involvement with HOLOSADE whatsoever.

Colin Bell also departed and was replaced by EXXPLODER and PHANTOM bassist Mac in late 1987. Following the release of the 'Hellhouse' debut on Powerstation Records, recorded at Blue Strike Studios and issued in April 1988, HOLOSADE toured with DEMON and SKELETON CREW among others. Although a second album was planned, the band split from the label and HOLOSADE suffered a major blow when guitarist Jack Hammer (real name Simon Jones) went on to join SABBAT in early 1989. Bassist Mac teamed up with ACID REIGN. Substitutes were Paul Trotter and Chris Bentley respectively. The band also added drummer Andy Barker.

Following the split from Powerstation and line-up reshuffling, HOLOSADE released a three track demo, 'The Return', but soon split and various members of later turned up during 1993 in new act DOMINION. However, HOLOSADE reformed in 1994 with Simon Jones reverting back to his stage persona of Jack Hammer. A second album was recorded but never released. By 1998 Barker was running Metal magazine 'Sound Barrier' and playing drums once more, this time for INTENSE.

Simon Jones came back into the limelight during 2001 as part of erstwhile SKYCLAD vocalist Martin Walkyier's new RETURN TO THE SABBAT. The guitarist would bow out of this project early the following year due to family commitments.

Battleaxe, Other (1987). Battleaxe.
HELLHOUSE, Powerstation AMP16 (1988). Look In The Mirror / Welcome To The Hellhouse / Love It To Death / Madame Guillotine / Psycho / Eternal Life / Bitter Sweet / Nightmare Reality.

HOLY MOSES

AACHEN, GERMANY — *Sabina Classen (vocals), Franky Brotz (guitar), Joern Schubert (guitar), Andreas Libera (bass), Julien Schmidt (drums).*

HOLY MOSES specialises in brutal Techno Thrash of the highest order and created an impact with a string of impressive albums and the striking vocals (not to mention looks as well!) of Sabina Classen after scoring a deal with Aaaarrg Records. Forged in 1979 by bassist Raymond Brüsseler, vocalist / guitarist Jochen Fünders and drummer Peter Vonderstein, this trio first gained local notoriety in the staunchly Catholic city of Aachen by being ejected from their church basement rehearsal complex when the proprietors discovered all of the crucifixes had been turned upside down.

Following a support gig to VENOM at Eindhoven's famous Dynamo Club in 1981, Peter Vonderstein would be superseded by Paul Linzenich. Later that same year, Fünders lost his position to former DISASTER guitarist Andy Classen whilst new man on vocals would be Iggy. Classen's then paramedic girlfriend, Sabina, reluctantly took up the microphone. This revised version of HOLY MOSES performed its inaugural gig in November of 1982. The following year Sabina and Andy got married. In 1984 Paul Linzenich exited in order to pursue his education and was replaced by Jörg 'Snake' Heins. This period of tribulation also saw Sabina opting out briefly, but returning within a few weeks. This move resulted in the demos 'Walpurgis Nacht' and 'The Bitch'.

Signing with Aaaarrg Records, the band had recruited drummer Herbert Dreger to record the 1986 debut 'Queen Of Siam', produced by MEKONG DELTA bassist Ralph Hubert. A switch in drummers found the 19 year old Uli Kusch installed on the drum kit. Founder member Raymond Brüsseler decamped in September of 1986, relocating to Thailand. Bassist Andre Chapelier joined, although the latter's tenure was short as he debuted on second album 'Finished With The Dogs' before he promptly left.

Having promoted the 'Queen Of Siam' opus with supports to STEELER, RAGE, ANGEL DUST and PAGANINI, plus having opened for D.R.I. and HOLY TERROR on their 1987 European tour, the band added second guitarist Georgie and, still lacking a permanent bassist, TARGET's Johan Susant filled in for live dates before a new bassist was found in ex-DARKNESS man Thomas Berker. The recently added Georgie departed to join LIVING DEATH, however but by July 1988 erstwhile MAMMUT and RISK guitarist Thilo Herrmann completed the line-up.

The band signed to major label Warner Bros., no doubt aided by Sabina's exposure as a TV presenter on the 'Mosh' programme. HOLY MOSES recorded their third album 'The New Machine Of Liechtenstein' at Horus Sound Studios in Hannover under the guidance of producer Alex Perialas. Thilo Herrmann left during the sessions to re-join RISK and his place was taken by Rainer Laws. Strangely, Laws did not contribute musically to 'The New Machine Of Liechtenstein' album, but did design the album cover. Herrmann later emerged as a member of RUNNING WILD and GLENMORE.

Having released the album HOLY MOSES, performed at the Dynamo open air festival in 1989 to 20'000 people and toured Europe on a package billing with SACRED REICH and FORBIDDEN, but strangely Warner Bros. dropped the band. Undeterred, HOLY MOSES carried on gigging, including dates in East Germany alongside BLITZZ, as a quartet minus an ailing Rainer Laws, and were signed to band manager Uli Wiehagen's newly established West Virginia Records in order to release the Will Reid Dick produced 'World Chaos' album in 1990. Upon completion of these sessions Kusch would be enticed away by GAMMA RAY and erstwhile LIVING DEATH man Atomic Steif manned the drums for live work. Post HOLY MOSES drummer Ulli Kusch teamed up with noted Punk band DIE SKEPTIKER, a reformed GRAVE DIGGER then HELLOWEEN.

HOLY MOSES folded in 1992, West Virginia signing off with the compilation 'Too Drunk To Fuck'. Soon after, Sabina Classen formed TEMPLE OF THE ABSURD in collaboration with WARPATH guitarist Schrödey. Andy Classen entered the world of production gaining credits on albums by the likes of ASPHYX, RYKERS and CRACK UP.

Andy Classen resurrected the HOLY MOSES brand in 1994 for an album billed 'No Matter What's The Cause'. Studio contributors included Sabina as guest vocalist, the ANTHRAX, NUCLEAR ASSAULT and S.O.D. credited Dan Lilker on bass and RYKERS drummer Meff. That same year Andy and Sabina got divorced.

In 1997 Classen created RICHTHOFEN with former WARPATH singer Dirk Weiss. During mid 2001 HOLY MOSES reformed, Sabina Classen being joined by guitarists Franky Brotz and Joern Schubert and drummer Julien Schmidt. The band was announced as forming part of the 2002 KREATOR, DESTRUCTION and SODOM Thrash extravaganza but would pull back to concentrate on writing new music for the 'Disorder Of The Order' album. Andreas Libera, a veteran of ALTERNATES and COLD EMBRACE, joined the band on bass that year. HOLY MOSES underwent further changes in mid 2003, pulling in Alex De Blanco on bass and the EROSION and RICHTHOFEN credited Michael Hankel on guitar.

In October of 2004 HOLY MOSES signed a new record deal with Armageddon Music, the label owned by Lars Rats of METALIUM, for recording of their tenth album 'Strength Power Will Passion' with TEMPLE OF THE ABSURD guitarist Schrödey acting as producer. Sabina Classen guested on the 2005 album 'Repent Or Seal Your Fate' by Hannover Thrashers RECKLESS TIDE.

HOLY MOSES (pic: Kai Swillus)

The band scored a notable first in late April when they performed for United Nations peace keeping forces in Kabul, the capitol city of Afghanistan. HOLY MOSES toured Germany packaged as part of the 'Wacken Open Air Roadshow' with ILLDISPOSED, SUIDAKRA and REGICIDE during May.

The band's performance at the 3rd September 'Occult fest' in Holland proved notable for debuting a new band line-up, fresh faces being bassist Ozzy, of LA CRY, TEMPLE OF THE ABSURD and WARPATH, plus drummer Agar. Further festival gigs saw the band putting in performances at the 'Out Of Control' event in October and the December 'Antichrist as Meeting' in Berlin. A scheduled appearance at the 'Art Of Darkness' festival in Warburg was cancelled after the group's drummer, Agar, injured his knee. HOLY MOSES re-inducted former member, and notably ex-LIVING DEATH and SODOM drummer, Atomic Stiff in February 2007. The new look band debuted at the Party Hard Festival in Schlächter on April 14th.

QUEEN OF SIAM, Aaarrg ARG1 001-1 (1986). Necropolis / Don't Mess Around With The Bitch / Devil's Dancer / Queen Of Siam / Road crew / Walpurgisnacht / Bursting Rest / Dear Little Friend / Torches Of Fire.
Road Crew EP, Aaarrg ARG 10 (1986). Road Crew EP.
FINISHED WITH THE DOGS, Aaarrg ARG6 005-2 (1987). Finished With The Dogs / Current Of Death / Criminal Assault / In The Slaughterhouse / Fortress Of Desperation / Six Feet Women / Corroded Dreams / Life's Destroyer / Rest In Pain / Military Service.
THE NEW MACHINE OF LIECHTENSTEIN, Warner Bros. 243 873-1 (1989). Near Dark / Def Con II / Panic / Strange Deception / Lucky Popster / Secret Service Project / State: Catatonic / The Brood / Lost In The Maze.
WORLD CHAOS, West Virginia 084-57002 (1990). Chaos / Diabolic Plot / Bloodsucker / Education / Guns n' Moses / Summer Kills / Deutschland (Remember The Past) / Permission To Fire / Jungle Of Lies / Dog Eat Dog / Too Drunk To Fuck / Fight For Your Right.
Too Drunk To Fuck, West Virginia 50 57019 (1991). Too Drunk To Fuck / (You Gotta) Fight For Your Right (To Part!) / Bloodsucker.
TERMINAL TERROR, West Virginia 084-57102 (1991). Nothing For My Mum / To Sides Terror / Terminal Terror / Creation Of Violation / Cool Of Blood / Distress And Death / Adultmachine / Malicious Race / Tradition Of Fatality.
REBORN DOGS, West Virginia 084-57232 (1992). My Soul / Decapitated Mind / Welcome To The Real World / Reborn Dogs / Fuck You / Third Birth / Deadicate / Five Year Plan / Roses Of Pain / Reverse / Dancing With The Dead.
TOO DRUNK TO FUCK—BEST OF, West Virginia 084-57012 (1993). Too Drunk To Fuck / Fight For Your Rights / Nothing For My Mum / Theotoci / Distress And Death / Clash My Soul / Five Year Plan / Welcome To The Real World / Finished With The Dogs / World Chaos / Waste Or Try / Black Metal.
NO MATTER WHAT THE CAUSE, Steamhammer SPV 84-76862 (1994). Your Tongue / A Word To Say / Step Ahead / Acceptance / Just Because / What's Up / Senseless One / Denial / Hate Is Just A 4 Letter Word / On You / I Feel Sick / No Solution / Bomber.
MASTER OF DISASTER, Century Media (2001). Master Of Disaster / Taste My Blood / The Hand Of Death / Feel The Pain / Down On Your Knees.
DISORDER OF THE ORDER, Century Media (2002). Intro / We Are At War / Disorder Of The Order / Break The Evil / Hell On Earth / I Bleed / Blood Bond / 1,000 Lies / Princess Of Hell / Verfolgungswahn / Heaven Versus Hell.
STRENGTH, POWER, WILL, PASSION, Armageddon Music (2005). Angel Cry / End Of Time / Symbol Of Spirit / Examination / I Will / Space Clearing / Sacred Crystals / Lost Inside / Death Bells II / Rebirthing / Seasons In The Twilight / Say Goodbye.

HOLY TERROR

LOS ANGELES, CA, USA — *Keith Deen (vocals), Kurt Kilfelt (guitar), Mike Alvard (guitar), Floyd Flanery (bass), Joe Mitchell (drums).*

HOLY TERROR was the result of an amalgamation between guitarist Kurt Kilfelt (a.k.a. Kurt Colfelt), having departed in less than amicable terms from metal eccentrics AGENT STEEL following their ground breaking 1985 opus 'Skeptics Apokalypse'. Pre-AGENT STEEL, the guitarist had featured in local Los Angeles bands MARTIAL LAW and DECEIVER as well as TOXIK SHOK alongside AGENT STEEL singer John Cyriis. Colfelt would be joined in the new formation by former DARK ANGEL drummer Jack Schwartz, ex-BLACK WIDOW guitarist Mike Alvard, vocalist Keith Deen and former THRUST bassist Floyd Flanery. However, before long Schwarz had fled the fold and HOLY TERROR drafted Joe Mitchell in his stead.

HOLY TERROR toured North America alongside D.R.I. and KREATOR during 1988 as a remixed version of their debut album, 'Terror And Submission', was released. The band began work on a projected third album minus Alvard but were to fold during the sessions.

Word arrived in mid 2005 that HOLY TERROR had regrouped and were planning a re-launch with a three CD, archival box set for issue through Candlelight Records. This new look band saw Kilfelt and drummer Joe Mitchell being joined by ex-BITTER END guitarist Matt Fox and bass player Jeff Matz. In September the band announced the acquisition of new singer Aaron Redbird. However, following an initial set of demos Redbird was let go. Meantime, bassist Jeff Matz would also be operational with ZEKE.

HOLY TERROR, having recruited Chris Tretton from MIDNIGHT IDOLS as their new vocalist, announced their first concert date in over sixteen years was to be held at the El Corazon in Seattle on 11th March. Following this gig Jeff Matz joined HIGH ON FIRE.

TERROR AND SUBMISSION, Under One Flag FLAG 10 (1987). Black Plague / Evil's Rising / Blood Of The Saint / Mortal Fear / Guardians Of The Netherworld / Distant Calling / Terror And Submission / Tomorrow's End / Alpha Omega.
MIND WARS, Under One Flag CDFLAG25 (1988). Judas Reward / Debt Of Pain / The Immoral Wasteland / A Fool's Gold / Terminal Humour / Mind Wars / Damned By Judges / Do Unto Others / No Resurrection / Christian Resistance.

HOMICIDE HAGRIDDEN

ITALY — *Max Moda (vocals / guitar), Dave Ruo Roch (bass), Steo Monda (drums).*

Thrash act founded in 1994 by drummer Steo Monda. Originally entitled DEATH SLAUGHTER the band also incorporated guitarists Max Moda and Fabry Fortunato with Luca Guidi on bass guitar. With the latter soon being out of the picture the band switched title to that of HOMICIDE HAGRIDDEN and duly recorded the opening demo 'Sequence Of Death'. A second tape, 'Behind Enemy Lines', emerged in 1996, the band now including Fedele Pagano accompanying Moda on guitar and Dave Ruo Roch on the bass. The self financed EP 'Where Angels Work' was promoted by a fifteen date tour of Italy in 1998.

HOMICIDE HAGRIDDEN added former COLLISION guitarist Ian Binetti in May of 2002. Frontman Max would later aid THEE MALDOROR KOLLECTIVE as session guitarist.

Where Angels Work, Homicide Hagridden (2000). Where Angels Work / The Inner Sinner / Violated / Eternal Rage.

HORFIXION

CANADA — *Samuel Landry (vocals / guitar), Simon Auger (guitar), Richard Gélinas (bass).*

Death / Thrash act HORFIXION started out as a covers band HORRIFIC ILLUSION during 1993, conceived by vocalist / guitarist Samuel Landry and guitarist Kevin St-Yves. With the recruitment of bass player Richard Gélinas and drummer Alexandre Noel during 1996 the group adopted the HORFIXION title, their debut demo 'Let The Nightmare Begin ...' arriving in late 1999. During 2000 Erik Doucet took over bass duties for a follow up demo session entitled 'Rage'. However, Doucet would then be superseded by a returning Gélinas, this version of the group cutting the album 'Disynchronize'. Session drums came courtesy of the MARTYR, BLACK CLOUD and GORGUTS credited Daniel Mongrain.

As 2002 dawned Simon Auger supplanted St-Yves as HORFIXION laid down second album 'Instigators Of Chaos'. Studio guest included Patrice Hamelin of MARTYR on the drums.

DISYNCHRONIZE, Independent (2000). Maze Of Mind / Voiceless Scream / Disynchronize / Rage / Human Machine / Tears Of Sand / Deserted Landscape / Danger Zone / Nightmare / Désynchronisé.

INSTIGATORS OF CHAOS, Independent (2002). Intro / Instigators Of Chaos / Another Man / Minefield / Misfortune / Emotional Storm / Evolutive Revolution / Le Retour De La Grande Faucheuse / V.A.B. / Magma.

SELF INFLICTED HELL, Galy GALY 024 (2004). Immaculate Destruction / Self Inflicted Hell / Insane Poetry / Twisted Inner Mind / Godless Faith / Deconstructing My Life / Digitalizing Existence / Thoughtless / Rendez-vous Avec La Mort.

HORRORSCOPE

CHORZÓW, POLAND — *Adam Brylka (vocals), Krzystof Pistelok (guitar), Lech Smiechowicz (guitar), Tomasz Walczak (bass), Arek Kus (drums).*

Chorzów based Thrash Metal band HORRORSCOPE originally assembled as a trio during 1997 to release the first demo tape 'Worship Game'. Previous to this, vocalist / bassist Andrzej Brandys, guitarist Lech Smiechowicz and drummer Marcin Papior had been involved with another Thrash outfit dubbed DISONANCE. However, Papior enrolled into Crossover act TUFF ENUFF and DISONANCE duly folded. Smiechowicz would forge HORRORSCOPE, being joined by guitarist "Pistolet" Krzysztof Pistelok, from GENESIS OF AGGRESSION, bassist "Czolg" Dariusz Wojczyk and drummer Sebastian Szroeter. Vocalist Adam Brylka enrolled in 1998. The demo 'Worship Game', actually comprising archive DISONANCE tracks, was recorded at Alkatraz Studio, with Jacek Regulski of KAT acting as both producer and funding benefactor for the sessions.

A further HORRORSCOPE cassette release, 'Wrong Side Of The Road', followed in 1999. This had been recorded for Demonic Records for an intended CD release, but this never transpired and so the band resorted to self-distribution in cassette format. Afterwards, Sebastian Szroter was exchanged by "Maly" Piotr Szczepaniak. However, this alliance proved fragile and HORRORSCOPE then worked with two session drummers, Arkadiusz Kus and "Leo" Adam Jendrzyk, prior to recording the four song demo 'Pictures Of Pain'. "Walec" Tomasz Walczak became the new bass man in 2001. Signed by the Empire label, the band debuted with the Maciek Mularczyk produced 'Pictures Of Pain'. With new cover art, Crash Music would license the album for the North American market whilst Plastic Head took the record on for Europe.

Subsequent live work found Arkadiusz Kus manning the drums although ex-NOMAD man "Piena!" Piotr Peczek eventually stabilised the position. Concert recordings taped in Chorzów saw issue as the 'Live Collision' album. In 2003, supported by TOTEM and WHOREHOUSE, the band engaged in an extensive, self-funded Polish "Thrash the South" tour hitting Dąbrowa Gornicza, Olkusz, Chorzow, Wrocław, Rybnik, Tarnow, Nowy Sacz, Rzeszow, Łódź, Warsaw, Bydgoszcz and Poznan.

HORRORSCOPE guitarist "Blackpitfather" and drummer "Machine Twin" allied with THORN S. bassist Doublecrow Brother and KILLJOY lead singer Doublecrow Master to forge side-project BLACK FROM THE PIT, issuing a 2004 demo. HORRORSCOPE, publishing the demo 'The Crushing Design', crafted at ZED studio in Olkusz, toured Poland in April 2004 with road partners TOTEM and NECROSEARCH. German label Shark Records took on 'The Crushing Design' for album release in Europe. The album then saw issue in Japan that December and in 2005 was picked up for national Polish distribution by Metal Mind Productions.

Recording sessions for the 'Evoking Demons' album took place in May and June at ZED studio in Olkusz for release through Metal Mind Productions in October.

PICTURES OF PAIN, Empire EMP 005 (2001). Rising / Inferno / Highway Of The Losts / Macabra Cadabra / Darkest Future / The Deal / Deal With The Devil / Read The Signs / The Aztec Sun / Aargh Leonus / Count The Dead / Pictures Of Pain.

The Crushing Design, (2004). 24/7 / Paranoico / Hunger / Firebolid / Black Is Black (Suicidal Note).

EVOKING DEMONS, Metal Mind Productions MMP 0446 (2006). New Insignia (Intro) / Mephisto / Traumatic Legacy / The Inner Pride / Branded / The Tide / Headhunters / Light The Fuse / The Request / Killers Breeding / Evil.

HOSTIL

PERU — *Franco Boggiano (vocals), Milton Casildo (guitar), Luis Lizárraga (guitar), Jouvet (bass), Robinson Ocampo (drums).*

Thrashers HOSTIL feature guitarist Luis 'Alone' Lizárraga of STEEL MASTER and INFERNAL, ex-8589 bassist Jouvet and drummer Robinson Ocampo, a veteran of ETERNAM. The group was forged by Lizárraga in 2001, the first line up comprising singer Franco Boggiano, second guitarist Henry Guevara, bass player Javier Mendoza and drummer Benito. Their first concert came on 23rd July 2003, sharing the stage that night in Lima with NECROPSYA, CATENAS and ICARUS. Subsequent gigs followed before Milton 'Evil' Casildo took the secondary guitar role.

HOSTIL re-vamped their rhythm section, drafting drummer Omar 'Chamoass' Menéndez in March of 2004 then DISINTER and ICARUS man Kike Burro on bass. After recording of a five track demo the band brought in more new members, bassist Jouvet and drummer Robinson Ocampo.

Hostil, Hostil (2004). El Usurpador / Despertar / Nakaq (El Degollador) / Patria Agonizante / Alone.

HURTLOCKER

CHICAGO, IL, USA — *Grant Belcher (vocals), Tim Moe (guitar), Dan Manzella (bass), Dan Ditella (drums).*

Chicago's HURTLOCKER was forged during 1998 by guitarist Tim Moe and singer Grant Belcher ("two bored fucks"). Formative line-ups proved fluid but by 2002 Brazilian Murillo Nobrega had enrolled on drums. Notable live work included supports to ANTHRAX, KING DIAMOND and LAMB OF GOD and studio time garnered a trio of demo recordings. Subsequently, Tomas Cezar was adopted as bassist. 2004 demos, dubbed 'Begging For Hatred' and recorded at Studio One in Racine, Wisconsin, saw the guest participation of JUNGLE ROT Chris Djuricic handling bass duties. Visa issues forced the departure of Nobrega and Dan Ditella duly assumed the drum position.

Mid 2005 would see Chris Olsen handling bass but a further shift in personnel witnessed the induction of Dan Manzella. The band signed to Austrian label Napalm Records, more commonly known for their Gothic inspired catalogue, for release of the November 2005 album 'Fear In A Handful Of Dust'.

The band announced European tour dates for January 2006, traversing Poland, Germany, Holland, France, Belgium, Ireland, Switzerland, Austria, Italy and the UK, alongside a heavyweight cast of GRAVE, ABORTED, DEW-SCENTED, VESANIA and CRYPTOPSY. The band partnered with JUNGLE ROT, DESOLATION and DEICIDE for US touring throughout September and October.

Former HURTLOCKER drummer Dan Ditella passed away on October 18th due to "complications while in rehabilitation" in Elgin, Illinois.

FEAR IN A HANDFUL OF DUST, Napalm NPR 176 (2005).
Symptoms / Absolution / Painted Red / I Am Everything ... Nothing / Goddamm Reflection / No One. Now What? / The End Of An Age / I Don't Need You / Lie To Me / Already Inside.

HYDRA VEIN

BRIGHTON, UK — *Mike Keen (vocals), Danny Ranger (guitar), Stephan Davis (guitar), Damon Maddison (bass), Nathan Maddison (drums).*

A Brighton based act with distinct Thrash leanings HYDRA VEIN emerged in late 1987 with original guitarist "Jack Kartoffel", whose apparent departure was forced on "medical grounds". The Maddison brothers, bass player Damon and drummer Nathan, had previously played with DEATHWISH, whilst singer Mike Keen had previously fronted TARGA. Pre-DEATHWISH, Nathan Maddison had journeyed through local acts such as ISCARON, MEDUSA and HORIZON.

HYDRA VEIN would debut with the four track demo 'The Reptilliad' in July 1987. Although guitar work on this demo was credited to 'Jack Kartoffel', after a line in the 'Top Secret' movie, these names were in fact pseudonyms for musicians held under contract, Dave Brunt of DEATHWISH and TARGA's Alan Wheatley-Crowe.

HYDRA VEIN, putting in an inaugural live performance on 27th April 1988 as support to DEATHWISH at the Brighton Pavilion Theatre, added guitarists Danny Ranger and Stephan Davis. Metalother Records contracted the band to record the album 'Rather Death Than False Of Faith' at Blue Box Studios in Hove during February 1988. The album emerged onto the domestic market in November and later received a US release via Borivoj Krgin's Mean Machine label. UK headline gigs ensued, plus supports to TORANAGA and SODOM. However, following an appearance at the Brighton's Level festival, Ranger opted out. The remaining members continued as a quartet, notably landing a valuable support to CANDLEMASS in Bradford. A further membership shift then witnessed the exit of Davis.

RKT Records picked HYDRA VEIN up for a second album. The band, complemented with a new guitar team of Paul Bate and Jon Balfour, cut 'After The Dream' at Square Dance studios in Nottingham in September 1989. HYDRA VEIN disbanded a little after a year later. Post HYDRA VEIN Damon Maddison journeyed through Dutch based acts such as NOSTRADAMUS and POWERPACT, this latter band also featuring Mike Keen during 1992. Nathan Maddision joined STORM PARTY prior to reuniting with Paul Bate to forge UNION. Relocating to Amsterdam, Nathan hooked back up with his brother for the final days of POWERPACT in 1994 before both going on to Grunge band GUM PATROL.

Mike Keen unsuccessfully auditioned for SABBAT in 1990. Following his brief 1992 tenure with POWERPACT, Keen founded MASK, a unit including ex-SOMA members Simon Hannaford and Trance Cloudy, keyboard player Lee Phillips and the FASTWAY and NETWORK credited drummer Steve Clarke. MASK recorded an album, which never saw the light of day. After UNION, Paul Bate featured in PITBULL and PLAN-A. Jon Balfour sadly died in 1992.

RATHER DEATH THAN FALSE OF FAITH, Metalother OTH12 (1988).
The House / Rabid / Crucifier / Right To Die / Rather Death Than False Of Faith / Misanthropic / Harlequin / Guillotine.

AFTER THE DREAM, RKT CMO 193 (1989). 7 USC / Pro-Patria / Born Through Ignorance / No Future / Turning Point / After The Dream.

HYPNOSIA

SWEDEN — *Cab Castervall (vocals / guitar), Hampus Klang (guitar bass), Mike Sjöstrand (drums).*

Vaxjo based Thrash styled Deathsters HYPNOSIA first emerged brandishing the four track April 1996 'Crushed Existence' demo tape. At this juncture the band comprised Cab Castervall on vocals and guitar, Carl-Petter Berg on second guitar, bass player Klas Gunnarsson and drummer Mike Sjöstrand. For the follow up demo, 1997's 'The Storms', HYPNOSIA lost the services of Gunnarsson and Mattias 'Slask' Werdenskog took over on bass. HYPNOSIA also had the track 'The Last Remains' included on the VOD Records compilation 'Voices Of Death'.

The February 1998 mini album 'Violent Intensity' saw a vinyl release in November of 1999 by the Dutch Soulseller Productions imprint which included an exclusive extra track in HYPNOSIA's rendition of SODOM's 'Outbreak Of Evil'. For these recordings the band numbered Cab Castervall on vocals and guitar, Johan Orre on second guitar and drummer Mike Sjöstrand. Session bass guitar came courtesy of Mange Roos. Further line up ructions forced the departure of Johan Orre in January of 1999, being replaced by Daniel Sporrenstrand of XENOFANES repute. In April Hampus Klang enrolled on bass but with the exit of Sporrenstrand this latest recruit switched over to lead guitar.

HYPNOSIA covered POSSESSED's 'My Belief' on vinyl variants of their October 2000 album 'Extreme Hatred'. Digipack versions of the record included the entire 'Violent Intensity' album as a bonus. By November HYPNOSIA had solved their ongoing problems with a permanent bassist with the introduction of Lenny Blade.

In March of 2002 Castervall unveiled a Black-Death side project billed as FUNERAL in union with Chrille from SOIL OF THE UNDEAD. That same year Werdenskog featured as vocalist on SOIL OF THE UNDEAD's demo 'Seduced By Mental Desecrations'. HYPNOSIA performed a brief run of dates in the low countries but despite announcing plans for a new album provisionally entitled 'World Sacrifice' HYPNOSIA folded in June of 2002. Cab Castervall would turn up on tour in Europe in September of 2003 as live guitarist for infamous Grind act BIRDFLESH.

Former HYPNOSIA drummer Mikael Sjöstrand passed away on 8th January 2004 following a battle with skin cancer. He was just 27 years old.

VIOLENT INTENSITY, Iron Fist Productions (1998). Funeral Cross / Haunting Death / Undead / Perpetual Dormancy / Mental Terror / The Storms.

EXTREME HATRED, Hammerheart (2000). Extreme Hatred / Circle Of The Flesh / The Last Remains / Operation Clean Sweep / Comatose / Act Of Lunacy / Gates Of Cirith Ungol / My Belief / Hang 'Em High / Traumatic Suffering.

HYSTE´RIAH G.B.C.

HELSINGBORG, SWEDEN — *Klas Ideberg (vocals / guitar), Jerry Kronqvist (bass), Thomas Hallbäck (drums).*

Landskrona, Helsingborg Thrashers HYSTE´RIAH G.B.C. were manifested by former GOD B.C. drummer Thomas Hallbäck. The band title was taken to signify the union of Hallbäck with Landskrona musicians from a former outfit HYSTE´RIAH, this unit having released demos 'Attempt The Life' in 1987 and 'Jeremiad Of The Living' the following year. The original line-up featured Ray Grönlund on vocals with Håkan Lindén on bass guitar.

The group cut an album 'Snakeworld' for Germany's Hellhound Records before folding in 1991. Hallbäck came to attention with the influential fanzine 'At Dawn They Read'. Frontman Klas Ideberg would journey on to higher profile bands THE DEFACED, DARKANE and TERROR 2000.

SNAKEWORLD, Hellhound HELL 011 (1991). Confess A Lie / Land Of Democracy / Cafe Of Hope (Slowly ...) / Is The Coffee Ready Yet / Snakes / How Does It Feel / Rope For Rape.

ICE AGE

GOTHENBURG, SWEDEN — *Sabrina Kihlstrand (vocals / guitar), Pia Nyström (guitar), Vicky Larsson (bass), Tina Strömberg (drums).*

An all female Thrash act ICE AGE toured consistently yet unfortunately never released any product despite a set of strong demos. Formed in Gothenburg during early 1985 by Pia Nyström and Sabrina Kihlstrand and later adding Strömberg, Vicky Larsson joined in October 1986, replacing Kihlstrand's sister on bass. KIM FOWLEY, the man responsible for putting the legendary American All Girl band THE RUNAWAYS together in the mid 70s, did have a management interest in the group for a brief period before Englishman Dave Maile took on complete responsibility.

ICE AGE demo sessions surfaced as 'General Alert' in May 1987. The band toured in Britain on a number of occasions, including dates at London's Marquee Club, scoring a great deal of press in all the right publications at the time. Sabrina Kihlstrand quit mid-way through a European tour, frustrated at a lack of progress and dissatisfaction with the band in general. The frontwoman was eventually replaced by American vocalist Debbie Gunn, previously with SENTINAL BEAST and ZNOWHITE, with ICE AGE also added a second guitarist in the Italian born Isabella Fronzoni.

However, the band cancelled their December 1989 British tour when Tina Strömberg suffered a broken jaw in an altercation outside a Gothenberg nightclub. At this point Fronzoni announced her decision to return to Italy and Larsen also quit.

In January 1990 US born Tammi Chiavarini joined the group on bass whilst fellow American, New Jersey native Lisa Decovolo succeeded Fronzoni. Having received some interest from CBS Records the band split up after the Americans wanted to relocate to New York which, it seems, they wound up doing, only not as members of ICE AGE.

Although tapes for a proposed album were recorded (indeed, the band had three albums worth of material lying around!) with the revised line-up, they were never released.

Fronzoni returned to Britain to join another all girl band ORIGINAL SIN in 1991 with ex-NO SHAME drummer Liz Watt. She was later part of a new ROCK GODDESS line-up. Back in Sweden, Pia Nyström and Vicky Larsson were reunited with Sabrina Kihlstrand in IDIOTS RULE, a group that featured a male drummer and have, thus far, have only featured on a compilation album.

Gunn returned to America to front BRUTAL GROOVE. Sabrina Kihlstrand turned up in 1999 once more, lending her distinctive vocal stylings as backing singer on GARDENIAN's 'Soulburner' opus.

IGNORANCE

GERMANY — *Danny (vocals), Marcel (guitar), Mikkey (guitar), Eddie (bass), Manu (drums).*

Thrash Metal band IGNORANCE published the demos 'The Killing Game' in 1999 and 'Legion' during 2004. The group was founded as LOTAR in 1993 by then bassist Mikkey and drummer Danny. The first demo sessions saw a switching of roles as Danny adopted the lead vocal role, Mikkey on bass with new recruits guitarists Marco and Holger with Georg on drums. Subsequently Mani took command of the drums. But in 2001 IGNORANCE called it quits when both Holger and Marco exited.

The band was resurrected the following year with Danny, Mikkey and Manu being joined by guitarist Marcel and bassist Eddie. This line up cut the November 2004 'Legion' demo.

Legion, Ignorance (2004). Opening The Gates / Legion / 456 / Evil By Nature / Terrormania / Blood For Blood / She Sucks The Demon Seed / Book Of The Dead / Driving Home Drunk.

IKINAE

SEINÄJOKI, FINLAND — *Tommi Niemi (vocals), Tiitus Lehtinen (guitar), Joonatan Alatalo (guitar), Ilkka Kivimäki (bass), Ossi Mäki-Reini (drums).*

IKINAE was created in Seinäjoki during April of 2004 by erstwhile ENTROPHIA members singer Tommi Niemi and guitarists Janne Ruohoniemi along with Tomi Tupiini. Ville Berg of FADEOUT was introduced on bass then Lars Kujala from NUANCE GATE on the drums. Ruohoniemi also has an affiliation with GOATHEMY. However, in September a fresh rhythm section comprising bassist Juni Luoma and drummer Ilkka Kivimäki was installed. The EP 'Lucky Seven' was published before the close of the year and saw Goath and Dark of GOATHEMY and Tanja Niemi as studio guests.

The 2005 IKINAE line-up comprised vocalist Tommi Niemi, guitarists Ilkka Kivimäki and Joonatan Alatalo, bassist Juni Luoma and Ossi Mäki-Reini on drums. The demo 'Second Symptom', recorded in June, saw the additional vocal power employed of Riku Turunen of FORCE MAJEURE, Joni Kantoniemi of MISERIA, Dark and Goath of GOATHEMY, Mikael Aksela of BLUE STEEL, Mirox of MIRZADEH, Marko Pajula of FADEOUT and Tanja Niemi. Narration came courtesy of GOD's Antti Pulli whilst Sanna Ruohoniemi supplied accordion.

The demo 'Alfons & Co.' was released in January 2006. The IKINAE line-up shifted shape, seeing Ilkka Kivimäki switching to bass and Tiitus Lehtinen introduced on second guitar.

Lucky Seven, Ikinae (2004). Introspection / Dragged By Emotions / Lucky Seven.

Second Symptom, (2005). Intro / No Shame At All / Me, Bob & Jack / Lucky Seven (Metal Opera version) / Take Me Home / Hard To Breathe / Onnenseppo.

Alfons & Co., (2006) (Demo). Alfons The Man / Pseudologica Fantastica.

IMAGIKA

SAN CARLOS, CA, USA — *Norman Skinner (vocals), Steven D. Rice (guitar), Pat Toms (guitar), Elena Repetto Luciano (bass), Henry Moreno (drums).*

A ferocious Bay Area Thrash band, founded in 1993-94 and featuring ex-WICKED TRUTH drummer Henry Moreno. San Carlos based IMAGIKA musically unashamedly harks back to the tradition that put the area on the Metal map. Taking their name from a Clive Barker novel, IMAGIKA debuted in April of 1996 with an eponymous outing issued on their own imprint, Headless Corpse Records. Subsequently this album would be distributed in Germany by the ABS concern. They would then score a licensing deal with the Nuclear Blast subdivision Radiation Records to distribute their 'Worship' album before switching to the Massacre label. The band toured Germany during 1999 as openers to GRAVE DIGGER and IRON SAVIOR.

Bass player Michael Dargis departed in 2000. The album '... And So It Burns' featured GRAVE DIGGER's Chris Boltendahl and Uwe Lulis as guests. This album was re-released with an additional three extra tracks culled from the 'Worship' sessions by World War III Records for America, although the album title was oddly changed to simply 'So It Burns'. IMAGIKA would hook up with World War III for two tribute albums, donating versions of METALLICA's 'Four Horsemen' and BLACK SABBATH's 'Never Say Die'.

The band, splitting away from Massacre Records, announced the recruitment of new bassist Elena Repetto, previously with I MOTHER EARTH, for recording of a projected 2002 album 'Fallen God'. Repetto made herself newsworthy when, as a METALLICA fan club 'bass audition' contest winner, she was delivered the prize of performing 'Seek & Destroy' with the famed act on stage.

A pivotal point in the band's history came in August 2003 with the departure of singer David Michael. Due to this major change the remaining band members announced a change in the band name. However, once new singer Norman Skinner of MACHINE CALLED MAN and TRAMOTANE had been installed the group changed their minds, deciding to stick with IMAGIKA. Bolstering their sound, a second guitarist in the form of PUNISHER's Pat Toms, was added in December.

IMAGIKA's fourth album, 'Devils On Both Sides' recorded with producers Neal Kernon and Juan Urteaga, would be readied for early 2005 release. The band signed a licensing deal with Mausoleum Records for the worldwide release. On 9th July 2005 IMAGIKA lined up at The Pound outdoor amphitheatre in San Francisco alongside TESTAMENT, VICIOUS RUMORS, LÄÄZ ROCKIT, HIRAX, AGENT STEEL, DEKAPITATOR, MUDFACE, NEIL TURBIN, BROCAS HELM and DREAMS OF DAMNATION for the 'Thrash Against Cancer' benefit.

The group announced the June 2006 'Mausoleum Metal Masters Tour' of the USA, this trek also featuring other Mausoleum recording artists PHANTOM-X and HYADES. Crash Music Inc. released the 'My Bloodied Wings' album in July.

IMAGIKA, Headless Corpse A.B.S. TODAY 202 (1997). Crush Your World / Murder 1 / Realize / Chance To Survive / Caged And Shackled / Vengeance Is Mine / Endings / If A Thought Could Kill / Immortal Eyes / Life's Diseased / Nightbreeder.
WORSHIP, Headless Corpse (1998). The Conflict / Court Of Confusion / The Sky Is Falling / Worship / Hall Of Desire / Devour / The Way / Precious Life / Of Weaker Men / Redemption.
... AND SO IT BURNS, Massacre (2000). Intro / Chaos To Murder / Fallen One / My Dominion / Atrocity / Hell / It Burns / Annihilate / Darkness Has Come / Fade Away.
DEVILS ON BOTH SIDES, Mausoleum (2004). Vigilante / Evil's Rising / Hexed / Devils On Both Sides / Still I Dream / Last Battalion / In Your Shadow / Back To The Beginning / Dead Eye Stare / More Then You'll Ever Know / Spellbound / Voice Of Prejudice.
MY BLOODIED WINGS, Crash Music Inc. (2006). The Tongue Of Nyx / Hunter's Moon / Second Coming / Throw The Horns / Heart Of Icarus / Weaken / The Darkest of All Secrets / Inhuman / One More Day / Forever Darkened / My Bloodied Wings.

IMPERIAL

FRANCE — Marseille Black-Death Metal act forged in 1992. IMPERIAL are renowned for their uncompromising lyrical and musical stance. Following three demo tapes, including 'War Spirit' in 1994 and 'The Red Moon' in 1995, IMPERIAL cut a debut album, 'Aux Crépuscules', for Osmose Productions during 1997. A mini album 'Thrasheurs 13' arrived the following year upfront of a second full length effort 'Malmort'. IMPERIAL have also recorded cover versions of BULLDOZER's 'Desert' for a 2000 split EP with legendary Japanese Black-Thrashers SABBAT and also paid homage to their allies with a version of SABBAT's own 'Reek Of Cremation' on the 'Sabbatical Worldwide Harmageddon' tribute album.

A ten year anniversary single emerged on the Dream Evil label in 2002, limited to just 333 red vinyl copies 'Ten Years Of Imperial' included four tracks spanning IMPERIAL's first ever 1992 recording 'Dark', the previously unreleased 'Cannibale' up to two brand new tracks 'L'Enfermé' and 'Le Mange-Crottes'.

AUX CREPUSCULES, Osmose Productions (1997). Le Narcissique / Aux Crepuscules / Montre Ton Regard / Orage Find / Un Adieu / La Femme Brulee / Vermin / Les Cavaliers De L'oubli / La Lune Rouge / Imperial / Thrasheurs 13.
THRASHEURS 13, Osmose Productions (1998). Thrasheurs 13 / Censure / Gouvener / Rebellion / Les Tableaux Rouges.
MALMORT, Osmose Productions (2000). Malmort / Gouvener / Paolla / Les Filles Mort Ne Disent Jamias 'Non' / Le Metal / Caranaval / Domination / La Chiennasse / Confesse / L'Historie De Bobby Qui S'Est Abye, Qui Revient, Et Que Sa Copine Trove Qu'll Pue L'Egout / Paraboles.
Ten Years Of Imperial EP, Dream Evil (2002) (Limited edition. 333 copies. Red vinyl). Dark / Cannibale / Blood: L'Enfermé / Le Mange-Crottes.

IMPULSE MANSLAUGHTER

CHICAGO, IL, USA — *Karl Patton (vocals), Chris Hanley (guitar), Nick Stevens (bass), Glen Herman (drums).*

Punk influenced Death / Thrash outfit. Chicago's IMPULSE MANSLAUGHTER would be one of the very first signings to the Nuclear Blast label, debuting in 1986 with the yellow vinyl 7" single 'Burn One Naked And Nuke It'. The band's original formation saw Chris Hanley on bass guitar before he adopted the lead guitarist role. The album 'He Who Laughs Last ... Laughs Alone' followed in 1987. Bassist Nick Stevens would depart in late 1987 and Chris Hanley duly switched from guitar to bass again to cover whilst Mike Schaffer was drafted as guitarist. With Schaffer opting out in early 1988 to join ABOMINATION Hanley moved back to the guitar role and Vince Vogel of SCREECHING WEAZEL came onboard in the bass role.

IMPULSE MANSLAUGHTER's 1988 album 'Logical End' included cover versions of MOTÖRHEAD's 'Stone Deaf Forever' and the ROLLING STONES 'Gimme Shelter'.

John Tolczyk was added on second guitar in 1989. Further tribulation came in 1990 when longstanding drummer Glen Herman quit, being replaced by Dan Duchaine. The following year Chris Hanley left the band for a solo project entitled NO CLASS and was duly superseded by Rob Lanam. John Tolczyk was kicked out at the end of 1991, the ex-member going on to found EYEGOUGER. He would eventually be replaced by Rick McKelvy in late 1992.

In 1993 the band shared a split 7" EP with PROVOCATION but folded that same year. Duchaine would later feature in FECK.

Burn One Naked And Nuke It, Nuclear Blast NB025 (1986). Sack O'Shit / Ratbag / Slithis / Nothing / Sedation / Chaos / Contradiction / Oatmeal.
HE WHO LAUGHS LAST ... LAUGHS ALONE, Nuclear Blast NB0003-1 (1987). Batman And The Oracle Of Pevile Savage / Vomit Heads / We're All Bored Here / Suffer In Silence / Walls / They Start The War / Premature Evacuation / Crimes / Too Late / Pills / This World / Sedation / Cheer Up You Fucker / Kein Spiel / Oatmeal II / 1987 Schitzoid Sam / Pattonstein's Disease / Piss Me Off.
LOGICAL END, Walkthrufyre (1988). Drag / Face It / Not Quite Sure / Missing Children / Gimme Shelter / Crimson Dreams / No Deals / Let Them Die / Stone Dead Forever / Borderline Retard.

SOMETIMES, Nuclear Blast (1992).
LIVE AT WFMU, Beer City BEER CITY 129 (2004). Blanket Of Fear / Sedation / Media / They Start The War / Not Quite Sure / Dogshit Extravaganza / Premature Evacuation / Crimes / Pills / Kein Spiel / Gutterhead / Nothing / Mighty Harness / A Hell On Earth / Deceived / Given / Rat Bastard / Blanket Of Fear / Gutterhead / Given / Media / Dogshit Extravaganza / Chaos / Mighty Harness / Sometimes / Face It / Missing Children / Borderline Retard / Pills / Piss Me Off / The Oracle Of Penile Savage / Vomitheads / They Start The War / Crimes / Sedation / Kein Spiel / Pattonsteins Disease / Drink Smoke Vomit.

IN AETERNUM

SANDVIKEN, SWEDEN — *David Larsson (vocals / guitar), Daniel Nilsson-Sahlin (guitar), Andreas Vaple (bass), Per Karlsson (drums).*

IN AETERNUM is a Sandviken based Black Thrash Metal act, originally titled BEHEMOTH. The group, David 'Impious' Larsson, vocalist Demogorgon and drummer The Dying, released two demos, 1992's 'Domini Inferi' and 1993's 'Concealment Entity', prior to a name change to IN AETERNUM and the February 1998 mini-album 'And Darkness Came'. This session was recorded David Larsson on vocals, guitar and bass with former CURSE, ACID QUEEN and SORCERY man Paul Johansson credited with "pounding drums of doom" at S.S. Studios in August 1997. Issued through Larsson's custom imprint From The Dark Productions, only 500 copies would be pressed. Notable inclusions would be Marcus E. Norman of BEWITCHED, credited with the EP's intro, and Marcus Ehlin of SIEBENBÜRGEN for backing vocals on the track 'Witches Spell'.

IN AETERNUM, drafted MARTYRUM drummer Jocke Olofsson to tour Europe in 1999 alongside IMMORTAL. IN AETERNUM frontman David Larsson also operated as a member of WAR and INFERNAL.

The band parted company with both drummer Jocke Olofsson and guitarist Paul Johansson in September 2001, the drummer returning to his former outfit MARTYRIUM. The exiting duo would also unite with the erstwhile SORCERY duo vocalist Ola Malmström and bassist Mikael Jansson to forge Groove-Doom band OUTREMER. Meantime, IN AETERNUM persevered as a trio comprising guitarist / vocalist David Larsson, bass player Andreas Vaple and drummer Peter Andersson.

During early 2002 IN AETERNUM would cover 'By Thy Command', a track culled from the debut 'Magick In Theory And Practice' demo from influential British Pagan Metal band SABBAT. The 'Past And Present Sins' album collected together early material alongside live tracks and cover versions of KING DIAMOND's 'Abigail' and VENOM's 'Countess Bathory'. A new IN AETERNUM line up comprising David Larsson on vocals and guitar, Daniel Nilsson-Sahlin on guitar, Andreas Vaple on 5 string bass and drummer Tore Stjerna, a veteran of WATAIN, FUNERAL MIST and Portuguese act CORPUS CHRISTII, would be unveiled in December as sessions for a new Tommy Tägtgren produced studio album billed as 'Nuclear Armageddon' were concluded.

The band announced a label deal with Regain Records in early 2003 but then withdrew from this union. Andreas Vaple would be forced out of the bass position too as IN AETERNUM revealed plans for a May European tour packaged with GOSPEL OF THE HORNS and RAZOR OF OCCAM. The 10" EP 'Beast Of The Pentagram', issued by Supreme Chaos Productions in July, would be restricted to 333 copies.

The band acted as support for DIMMU BORGIR on their Norwegian tour in September. Drummer Per Karlsson, previously with NOMINON, was inducted into the ranks in February of 2004. The band was set to join an ultra heavyweight partnership combining DEICIDE, MYSTIC CIRCLE and AKERCOCKE for European dates in June. However, upon journeying from Sweden to the UK for the tour's first date at the London Astoria venue. The group discovered upon their arrival that DEICIDE had pulled the entire tour. The band performed as scheduled that night, then returned home.

A 2004 AT THE GATES tribute album 'Slaughterous Souls—A Tribute to At The Gates' released by Drowned Scream Records included a take of GROTESQUE's 'Blood Run From The Altar' from IN AETERNUM. Also issued that year by Bloodstone Entertainment would be the 7" picture disc single 'Covered In Hell', hosting a cover of KREATOR's 'Tormentor'.

The group received some unwelcome attention in early 2005 due to the cover artwork of the June 2004 issued EP 'No Salvation' released through Agonia Productions. Apparently the artwork in question had been used without the permission of its owners, ironically enough actor Mel Gibson and Icon Productions, and more specifically the blockbuster movie 'The Passion Of The Christ'. The EP was withdrawn from sale and re-issued in a new sleeve. IN AETERNUM issued the 'Dawn Of A New Aeon' album in March through Agonia Productions, unifying with ARKHON INFAUSTUS, BELPHEGOR and ASMODEUS for the 'Goetreich—Fleshcult Europa Tour Pt. I' in April.

Guitarist Daniel Nilsson-Sahlin left the fold in January 2006. The following month the band drew in new members MORTELLEZ lead guitarist Erik Kumpulainen and ABHOTH, GODHATE and THRONEAEN bassist Claes Ramberg. IN AETERNUM completed work on a mini-album, entitled 'Curse Of Devastation', at Abyss Studios with producer Tommy Tägtgren in December.

And Darkness Came, From The Dark Productions FTDP 002 (1998) (Limited edition 500 copies). And Darkness Came / Spawned To Crush / Witches Spell / The Arrival Of The Horde.
FOREVER BLASPHEMY, Necropolis (1999). Majesty Of Fire / Spawned To Crush / Reaper In Black / The Pale Black Death / Forever Blasphemy / Of Unhallowed Blood / When The Vultures Left.
THE PESTILENT PLAGUE, Necropolis NR052 CD (2000). The Apocalypse Division / Eternal Devastation / Ultimate Warfare / Torture Chamber / Demon Possession / The Pestilent Plague / Wolves Blood / Revelation Of Hell.
PAST AND PRESENT SINS, Orion Music Entertainment OME002 (2002). Cursed Legions / Demon Possession / Witches Spell / The Arrival Of The Horde / The Pale Black Death / Black Moon Attraction / Defeat Life / The Storm Of Triumph / Countess Bathory / Abigail / Wolves Blood (Live) / Revelation Of Hell (Live) / Ultimate Warfare (Live) / When The Vultures Left (Live).
NUCLEAR ARMAGEDDON, Agonia (2003). Prelude To Armageddon / Genocide (Remains Of Retaliation) / Whirlwinds Of Fire / The Final Doom / Ashes And Dust / Dawn Of Annihilation / Sin / Crucified … The Son Of A Whore / Attack, Kill, Destroy / Nuclear Armageddon.
Covered In Hell, Bloodstone Entertainment BLOOD006 (2004) (Picture disc). By Thy Command / Tormentor.
No Salvation, Agonia ARMCD004 (2004). Poison The Holy / No Salvation / Blood Runs From The Altar / Beast Of The Pentagram.
DAWN OF A NEW AEON, Agonia (2005). Crusade / A New Dawn / Poison The Holy / Pactum Diaboli / Devil In Me / Seven Storms Of Doom / Unholy Sons Awakened / Ultimate Extermination / No Salvation / Spawned By The Fires Below.

IN VAIN

KRISTIANSAND, NORWAY — *A. Frigstad (vocals), S. Nedland (vocals / keyboards), J. Haaland (guitar), Even Fuglestad (guitar), Kristian Wikstøl (bass), Stig Reinhardtsen (drums).*

Kristiansand Death Metal band founded in late 2003 by singer A. Frigstad and guitarist J. Haaland. In May 2004 IN VAIN utilised Ansgar Studio in Kristiansand to cut tracks for the EP 'Will The Sun Ever Rise'. The group added bassist J. Sehl in mid 2005 to record a second EP entitled 'Wounds'. IN VAIN subsequently recruited guitarist Magnus Olav Tveiten, in November, then drummer Stig Reinhardtsen, in December.

Ole Vistnes replaced J. Sehl in May 2006. In November IN VAIN announced new members bassist Kristian Wikstøl and guitarist Even Fuglestad. A debut album, 'The Latter Rain', was recorded for 2007 release.

VREID, BATTERED and IN VAIN teamed up for the "Northern Brigade" tour beginning in Belgium during late March 2007.

Will The Sun Ever Rise, In Vain (2004). As I Wither / Caught Within / A Vision By Night.

Wounds, In Vain (2005). October's Monody / Det Rakner / In Remembrance / Epilogue.

INCARNATE

KANNUS, FINLAND — *Markus Tavasti (vocals), Juha Kellokoski (guitar), Jukka Kiviniemi (bass), Lasse Löytynoja (drums).*

INCARNATE is a Kannus based Death Metal band dating to 1999. Promotion releases included 'Deathsigns' in 2003 and a 2004 set 'Expectations Of Exhumation'. Originally the band operated as a duo with Lasse Löytynoja, of YDIN, ARSKA and GESCHÜSZTURM, handling vocals and drums with Jussi Yli-Korpela on guitar. Subsequently Markus Tavasti, another ARSKA and GESCHÜSZTURM veteran, was enrolled on lead vocals then second guitarist Juha Kellokoski of ZOMBIE VOMIT. INCARNATE underwent further changes in 2002, adding Jukka Kiviniemi of NONSENSE on bass guitar but losing co-founder Yli-Korpela, the guitar spot being filled by Kalle Niskala to record 'Deathsigns'. Prior to the second session 'Expectations Of Exhumation' INCARNATE dropped Niskala from the ranks, the erstwhile guitarist duly founding DEVIL'S OWN.

Lasse Löytynoja and Markus Tavasti would also be active with ZOMBIE VOMIT. The singer also held membership of GOATDOMAIN and KURALUTKU.

Deathsigns, Incarnate (2003). Keeper Of The Undead / Haunted Be Thy Grave / Stained In Blood / Deathsigns.

Expectations Of Exhumation, Incarnate (2004). A Threat To End Of Life / Demented / Post-Chaos Sundown / Dead Corpse Incarnation.

INCRIMINATED

IMATRA, FINLAND — *Harald Mentor (vocals / bass), Pekka (guitar), Janne (guitar), Antti (drums).*

Imatra based underground Black styled Thrash Metal act featuring a trio of members from Grindcore act IRRITATE. The 2001 split album with fellow Finns BLOODHAMMER, released as a limited edition of 1000 CDs by Hostile Regression subsidiary Bestial Burst, opened with a pairing of CELTIC FROST cover versions 'Suicidal Aggression' and 'Nuclear Winds'. INCRIMINATED would also share a split 7" single with FULCRUM CREAK.

Both the Northern Heritage released 'Illusion Of Love' EP and 2002 'Miracle Of Purity' album would be limited to just 400 vinyl copies. Besides IRRITATE various members of INCRIMINATED play in Punk band SIVIILMURHA whilst vocalist Sami is also known as the drummer for another Grindcore act SICKO. 'Harald Mentor' of INCRIMINATED also has association with NAILGUNNER and CONJURATION.

The band, recording as a duo of Harald Mentor on vocals, bass and drums plus guitarist Susej, shared a split album 'Ten Hail Marys' with Black-Grind band TUSKA in 2003 on the Bestial Burst label, limited to the traditional 666 copies. They would also include tracks on the Northern Heritage 10", six way split EP 'Primitive Finland' of 2003 alongside ANNIHILATUS, BAPTISM, CLANDESTINE BLAZE, BLOODHAMMER and BLASPHEMOUS EVIL. A re-issue of 'Ten Hail Marys', on cassette format by Malaysian label Metallatria Distro added two bonus tracks, 'Times Once Forgotten' and a live version of 'Thermonuclear Devastation'. Both these songs featured Werwolf on drums.

Werwolf is in fact Finnish Black Metal veteran Lauri Penttilä. The impressive array of scene credentials for Penttilä (a.k.a. 'Nazgul von Armageddon', 'Satanic Tyrant Werwolf', 'Sexual Hammer' or 'Satanic Warmaster') includes BLASPHEMOUS EVIL, SKULLKRUSHER, GESTAPO 666, HORNA, SHATARGAT, BLUTRACHE, MENTAL TERROR, PEST, KYPRIAN'S CIRCLE, THE TRUE WERWOLF, VOMITFAGO and WARLOGHE plus session tenures with ARMOUR, BELAIR, KRIEG and SATANIC WARMASTER.

In mid 2005 From Beyond Productions issued a split EP, naturally limited to 666 copies, shared with Polish band THRONEUM. 2006 releases for INCRIMINATED included 7" vinyl split singles with BLACK TASK, 'Warriors Of Fire And Hell' in May on Bestial Burst, and WOLVES, 'Summon The Wolf' in June through Deathstrike.

Incriminated—Fulcrum Creak, Hostile Regression HORE02CD (2000) (Split single with FULCRUM CREAK). Low Life (INCRIMINATED) / Nothing Special (INCRIMINATED) / Jail Of Pain (INCRIMINATED) / One Righteous Truth (INCRIMINATED) / Artificial Intelligence (FULCRUM CREAK) / Far Beside (FULCRUM CREAK) / World Strokes (FULCRUM CREAK) / Flabbergasting Eggbeater (FULCRUM CREAK) / Manual Churnkneader (FULCRUM CREAK).

INCRIMINATED—BLOODHAMMER, Bestial Burst BBF001CD (2001) (Split album with BLOODHAMMER. Limited edition 1000 copies). Suicidal Aggression / Nuclear Winter (INCRIMINATED) / Christ (INCRIMINATED) / The Mentor (INCRIMINATED) / Death (INCRIMINATED) / The Cult Of The Weak (INCRIMINATED) / Hellmachine (BLOODHAMMER) / Grand Desecration (BLOODHAMMER) / Ancient Kings (BLOODHAMMER) / Death (BLOODHAMMER) / Uudet Barbaarit (BLOODHAMMER).

Illusion Of Love EP, Northern Heritage NH010EP (2001) (Limited edition of 400). Illusion Of Love / Ride Of The Grotesque / Among The Worms.

Dark Perversions, Shades Of Autumn (2001) (Split single with NUCLEAR WINTER). Anything You Desire (Dark Perversions).

MIRACLE OF PURITY, Northern Heritage NH016LP (2002) (Limited edition of 400). Dismemberment Of The Pure / Evil Aggressor / The Prayer / The Miracle Of Purity / Enslaved Virgins / We Spread Horror / Deaths Triumph Over Life / Lowlife.

Primitive Finland, Northern Heritage (2003) (Split single with ANNIHILATUS, BAPTISM, CLANDESTINE BLAZE, BLOODHAMMER and BLASPHEMOUS EVIL). Evil Aggressor / Stay Evil.

RIDE OF THE TYRANTS, Time Before Time (2003) (Cassette release). Evil Aggressor / Christianity / Crypt Of The Tyrants / As The Angels Chose Their Side / Lowlife / Nothing Special / One Righteous Truth / Jail Of Pain.

TEN HAIL MARYS, Bestial Burst BEBU 03 (2003) (Split CD album with TUSKA. Limited edition 666 copies). Tuska Raatelee (TUSKA) / Kyrpääjä (TUSKA) / Pahan Hengen Nimeen (TUSKA) / Sadonisti (TUSKA) / Manala (TUSKA) / Lleh Ot (INCRIMINATED) / The Might (INCRIMINATED) / The True Trinity (INCRIMINATED) / Deathfuck Hellburst (INCRIMINATED) / Soldiers Of Dark Resistance (INCRIMINATED).

KINGS OF MISERY, From Beyond Productions (2004). Filth Hounds Of Blasphemy / Tyrant, Usurper / Possessed By Lycanthropy / Loveless / Militant Aggressor / Uninvited Guest / The King Of Misery.

Hypocricide, Ordealis (2004). Hypocricide / I Desecrate / Ugliness / Lambs Of The Deceitful Shepherd.

Throneum/Incriminated, From Beyond Productions FBP-039 (2005) (Split single with THRONEUM. Limited edition 666 copies). Lord Of Pain.

THE PROMISE OF WORSE TO COME, From Beyond Productions (2005). The Task Is Black / Born To Rule / Melting The Core / Morbid Utopia / The Age Of Deserved Doom / Noble Are The Warriors / The Grand Downfall / In Sin / The Last Nightmare / We Will Be Remembered.

Warriors Of Fire And Hell, Bestial Burst (2006) (Limited edition 7" vinyl single. Split with BLACK TASK). Warriors Of Fire And Hell (INCRIMINATED) / Death Fuck (Fuck You) (INCRIMINATED) / Harbinger Of Death (BLACK TASK) / Warriors Of Hell (BLACK TASK).

Summon The Wolf, Deathstrike (2006) (7" green splatter vinyl single split with WOLVES. Limited edition 666 hand numbered copies). Summon The Wolf (WOLVES) / The Cult (INCRIMINATED).

INCUBUS

METAIRE, LA, USA — *Francis M. Howard (vocals / guitar), Mark Lavenia (bass), Moyses M. Howard (drums).*

Metaire, Louisiana Thrashers INCUBUS, founded during 1986 by the Howard brothers, vocalist / guitarist Francis and drummer Moyses, émigrés from Rio de Janeiro, Brazil, debuted with a 1987 demo 'Supernatural Death'. INCUBUS debuted with the 1988 album 'Serpent Temptation', recorded and mixed at Morrisound Recordings, Tampa, this seeing Scot Latour handling bass duties. INCUBUS augmented their line-up with ABHORRENT EXISTENCE and EQUINOX bassist Mark Lavenia for the 1988 'Beyond The Unknown' album although he was to depart in 1992. Lavenia teamed up with ex-MASSACRE drummer Kam Lee and EQUINOX's Pete Slate to found project act KAULDRON in 2000.

During 1999 the band underwent a change of name to OPPROBRIUM to release the 2000 album 'Discerning Forces' produced by Harris Johns. Newly installed on bass would be André Luiz of DEMONOLATRY and IMMUNO AFFINITY repute. That same year Germany's Nuclear Blast Records re-packaged 'Serpent Temptation' and 'Beyond The Unknown' as a double pack CD.

Supernatural Death, Gore (1987). Serpent Temptation / Sadistic Sinner / Voices From The Grave / Incubus.
SERPENT TEMPTATION, Metalworks VOV 674 (1988). The Battle Of Armageddon / Voices From The Grave / Sadistic Sinner / Incubus / Blaspheming Prophets / Hunger For Power / Serpent Temptation / Underground Killers.
BEYOND THE UNKNOWN, Nuclear Blast (1990). Certain Accuracy / The Deceived Ones / Curse Of The Damned Cities / Beyond The Unknown / Freezing Torment / Massacre Of The Unborn / On The Burial Ground / Mortify.

INDESTROY

MD, USA — *Mark Strassburg (vocals / guitar), Drew Adrian (guitar), Jeff Parsons (bass), Gus Basilika (drums).*

Maryland Punk influenced Thrash Metal band INDESTROY, titled after a song by THE OBSESSED, debuted with the 1986 demo session 'Tortured By Fire'. The INDESTROY second album features a completely revised line up of vocalist / guitarist Mark Strassburg and bassist Jeff Parsons together with guitarist Danny Kenyon and drummer Rob 'Cougin' Brannigan. For subsequent demo recordings Shawn Williams took the place of Kenyon.

Strassberg went missing on a cross country motorcycle trip during July 1989 having left Maryland for San Francisco and was planning to later head to Los Angeles in order to undertake promotion work for 'Senseless Noise'. He was reportedly found safe and well although his family declined to disclose what had happened to him.

Parsons would later be found as a member of WRETCHED and UNORTHODOX. Drummer Gus Basilika too would appear on the first two WRETCHED albums after an initial spell in DELIRIUM.

Kenyon was a member of DREADNOT during 1990 and would journey into the Doom scene with VORTEX OF INSANITY in 1993. This band, which also included INDESTROY's Cougin on drums, would issue the 1994 'Social Decay' album for German label Hellhound. Kenyon and Basilika would reunite in 1998 founding another Doom project GUT SOUP. The pair stuck together for 1999's LIFE BEYOND, fronted by erstwhile CREEPSHOW, SILENT CRY and IMMORAL man Louis Strachan.

INDESTROY's name would be re-activated many years later as 'Senseless Theories' saw a release in 2001 on the New Renaissance label.

INDESTROY, New Renaissance NRR10 (1987). The Gate / U.S.S.A. / Ground Zero / Dead Girls (Don't Say No) / Fatal Sin / Brain Damaged / Justice Sucks / Shadowland / A.I.M.L.E.S.S. / Dismembered.
SENSELESS NOISE, New Renaissance (1989). Tortured By Fire / Living In Filth / Terminal Choice / Senseless Theories / Sam The Butcher / Instant Insanity.
SENSELESS THEORIES, New Renaissance (1989).

INDUNGEON

MJÖLBY, SWEDEN — *Mournlord (vocals / drums), Asmodeus (guitar), Cethulhv (guitar), L.V. Managarmr (bass).*

Mjölby based Thrashers INDUNGEON comprise MITHOTYN personnel 'Mournlord' (a.k.a. Karl Beckmann) and Stefan Wienerhall alongside THY PRIMORDIAL credited members 'Cethulhv' (Michael Andersson) and 'L.V. Managarmr' Jonas Albrektsson. Formed during the Summer of 1996, INDUNGEON's opening five song demo would include a cover version of BATHORY's 'Die In Fire'. Signing to the North American label Full Moon Productions the band donated two newly recorded tracks, 'In The Ashes Of Civilization' and 'Terror Squad' recorded in January 1997 at Hypersonic Studios, to the compilation albums 'Full Moon Sampler' and 'Tribute To Hell'. The full-length album, 'Machinegunnery Of Doom', followed in May of that same year.

During 1997 Albrektsson joined NIDEN DIV. 187. A second INDUNGEON album, entitled 'The Misanthropocalypse', was delivered in 1999, after which the band dissolved.

Wienerahall founded Power Metal band FALCONER during 1999. In outside activity to THY PRIMORDIAL, Jonas Albrektsson joined Mjölby Death Metal band CEREMONIAL EXECUTION during 2003 but soon relinquished this role.

MACHINEGUNNERY OF DOOM, Full Moon Productions (1997). Battletank No. 1 / 522 666 / ... As Hatred Emerges / Cyborgenetic Supermind / Desolated Creation / Terrorsquad / Mayhemic Destruction / In The Ashes Of Civilization / Charging Against You / Machinegunnery Of Doom / Die In Fire.
THE MISANTHROPOCALYPSE, Invasion (1998). Genocide / Powers Unbound / The Misanthropocalypse / Sentenced To The Flames / Mutilated / Propaganda Of War / Final Conflict / Battletank No. II.

INEARTHED

ESPOO, FINLAND — *Alexi Laiho (vocals / guitar), Alexander Kuoppala (guitar), Henkka Seppala (bass), Jani Pera Pirisjoki (keyboards), Jaska W. Raatikainen (drums).*

INEARTHED was the proto-version of CHILDREN OF BODOM, a powerful, modern Metal act from the town of Espoo, named after Finland's infamous Lake Bodom, the scene of a horrific, unsolved attack in 1960 that left three teenagers dead. Founder member and vocalist Alex Laiho made his name as part of THY SERPENT, maintaining CHILDREN OF BODOM, created in 1993 with drummer Jaska Raatikainen, as a going concern. Initially the group had gone under the title of INEARTHED, issuing a batch of melodic Death Metal demos commencing with 'Implosion Of Heaven', recorded at Munkkiniemen Studios in August of 1994 and released that December. These tracks would be laid down as a duo of Laiho and Raatikainen.

INEARTHED followed this opening tape with second set 'Ubiquitous Absence Of Remission' in July of 1995, recording this time at Astia Studios. Interestingly, melodies from the track 'Translucent Image', which featured female guest vocals from Nina Keitel, would re-surface in SINERGY's 'Beware The Heavens' at a later date. Once again composed and performed by Laiho and Raatikainen, the tape does make mention of bassist Samuli Miettinen and new member rhythm guitarist Alexander Kuoppala. A third demo, entitled 'Shining', was committed to tape at Astia Studios in February 1996 utilising keyboard player Jan Peri Pirisjoki. A line-up change found bassist Samuli Miettinen superseded by Henkka Seppala.

As INEARTHED the group scored a label deal in Belgium but a better offer from the highly respected Finnish Spinefarm concern convinced the band their way. At this stage the band, now with Janne Wirman Pimeys on keyboards, switched title to CHILDREN OF BODOM recording the 'Something Wild' debut.

Besides their high profile activities with CHILDREN OF BODOM Laiho has also racked up credits with SINERGY and IMPALED NAZARENE whilst Raatikainen has figured as a member of VIRTUOCITY.

Implosion Of Heaven, Inearthed (1994). Chaos / Shards Of Truth / Implosion Of Heaven / Tss, Ahh!!!
Ubiquitous Absence Of Remission, (1995). Intro / Translucent Image / Possessed / Shamed.

Shining, (1996). Talking Of The Trees (Sanctuary) / Vision Of Eternal Sorrow / Homeland / Homeland II: Shining (The 4th Kingdom).

INFECTION CODE

ALESSANDRIA, ITALY — *Gabriele (vocals), Davide (guitar), Enrico Cerrato (bass), Ricky Porzio (drums).*

Alessandria, Piemonte Thrash / Industrialists forged in 1999. The group debuted the following year with a self-funded 'H.I.V. 999' EP, recorded by vocalists Cristiano and Gabriele, guitarist Macha, bassist Enrico Cerrato, of JASON GOES TO HELL, with Ricky Porzio on drums, another ex-JASON GOES TO HELL member. 2KK Records issued the album 'Life Continuity Point' in 2002. Subsequently the ARCADIA credited Demetrio Scopelliti took the guitar position.

INFECTION CODE's second full length album, 'Sterile', recorded and produced by SADIST mastermind Tommy Talamanca at Nadir Studios would be set for a June 2004 release date. Studio guests included Nico from CONVICTION, Trevor of SADIST and NHERO's Serena. INFECTION CODE landed the valuable support to ANTHRAX's Milan Transilvania Live show in July 2004.

INFECTION CODE recorded the 'Intimacy' album starting on 25th January 2007 at Nadir Studios in Genova. Billy Anderson mixed the album in February.

H.I.V. 999, (2000). 0 And 1 / Martyr Millenium / WWW (Why Wonderful Whore?) / The Garbage.
LIFE CONTINUITY POINT, 2KK (2002). The Aseptic Revolution / Human Death Trip / WWW / God 2.0 / Manipulated / Have A Nice Day / Life Continuity Point / Happiness: 48 mm / DU.ST / Colony Of The Slipper Men / Larvar Gift / The Aseptic Revolution?
STERILE, (2004). ... / Almost Meat / Aphasic / Hallucination ... / Produce Consume Redemption / Whitepeace / Origin / *It* / Narcotica / Seventh Scar / ... / Human Death Trip / ... And Illusions / New Isolation Form / Worms Prayer / Candledrome.

INFERNAL

BRAZIL — *Marcelo Koehler (vocals), Luga (guitar), Danilo Zolet(guitar), Covero (bass), Mauricio Amorim (drums).*

Curitiba based INFERNAL, founded in 1986, trade in European influenced Thrash / Speed Metal that would later give way to more Death Metal persuasions The group's initial formation cited a line up of vocalist Paulo, guitarists Danilo Zolet and Marcelo Dos Anjos, bassist Covero (real name Renate Augusto de Albuquerque) and drummer Jonas. INFERNAL's inaugural gig, opening for MX in 1988, would already signal the start of a constant stream of line up ructions—new faces for the show being guitar player Lineau and frontman Marcelo Paulista.

In 1989 INFERNAL got around to cutting their first demo session 'The First Stage' but ran into immediate controversy with the media for the lyric "Speak Portuguese or die" in the track 'Brazoo'.

Another shift in line up found Mano on guitar and CREEPIN' DEATH and STEEL WAR man Mauricio Amorim on drums the following year for a sophomore cassette 'Cathedral Of Despair'. The track 'Fear Of Death' also garnered further exposure included on the compilation album 'Vampiros De Curitiba'.

INFERNAL debuted commercially in 1991 with the 7" single 'Of Weakness And Cowardice' but shortly after Mano decamped. Juliano Oening would fill the vacant guitar spot for a mammoth show in Araucária to over 4'000 people.

Paulista would be the next in line to leave creating Black Metal band AMEN CORNER. Marcelo Koehler would then take the mike stand for the inaugural album 'Drowning In The Chalice Of Sin'. For session work INFERNAL drafted Mano of HECATOMB but at the closure of recording ex guitarist Mano rejoined. The returning six stringer made it back in time to lay down lead guitar solos on the album. (Sadly Oening would later be killed in a car accident).

A heavy gig schedule across Brazil then ensued but Mano would bid farewell yet again, creating Death Metal band IMPERIOUS MALEVOLENCE.

HECATOMB's Mano assisted in the interim until INFERNAL recruited ex HAMMERDOWN member Poyoka. However, following a gig in Asunción, Paraguay in May '97 Poyoka too left. Daniel of SUBVERSIVE was to replace him but an injury to the new guitarist's left hand soon forced his dismissal. Ex CYTOMEGALODEATH man Luis Gabriel Maluf da Silva a.k.a. 'Luga' took over for recording of a second album 'Ritual Humiliation'

Of Weakness And Cowardice EP, (1991). Prelude To The Feast / The Feast Divine / True Reality.
DROWNING IN THE CHALICE OF SIN, (1993). Smash Thy Enemy / Bloody Rain / Il Passagio—The Ends Of Hell / Morbid Dream / Reaping Lives / Drowning In The Chalice Of Sin / Eternal Battle / Insurrection Day / The Endless Well Of Torment / Cathedral Of Despair.
RITUAL HUMILIATION, (2001). Intro: Bestial Overture / Die (Slow, Painful Death) / Absent Light / Secret Code / Ritual Humiliation / A Study In Blood And Darkness / Before My Turn, Agonizing / Plains Of Desolation / Intermezzo: The Nightmare / Sights Of The Unreal / Unholy Life / Invitation To Delirium / Cities Of Horror / Like Men Bleed / Rise, Charge, Obliterate / Finale: P.M.L.T.R.C.

INFERNAL MAJESTY

TORONTO, ON, CANADA — *Chris Bailey (vocals), Steve Terror (guitar), Kenny Hallman (guitar), Psycopath (bass), Rick Nemes (drums).*

Heavily studded Toronto Thrash Metal combo INFERNAL MAJESTY first delivered the four track 'Infernäl Mäjesty' demo cassette in 1986, cut at TRIUMPH's Metal Works studios. Opening band formation comprised singer Chris Bailey, guitarists Kenny Hallman and Steve Terror, bass player Psycopath with Rick Nemes on drums. Both Hallman and Terror had previously operated with LACED, the guitarist also having conducted live operations with THE ASTRID YOUNG BAND. After a brief flirtation with the title OVERLORD, the group switched to INFERNAL MAJESTY.

INFERNAL MAJESTY's debut 1987 album 'None Shall Defy' was released through Roadrunner Records, the New York office having been forwarded a demo through a European fan, and gained glowing reviews. A near flawless execution of pure Thrash, 'None Shall Defy' blazed brightly but unfortunately lack of marketing meant its merits were largely overlooked. Despite this impact, the alliance with Roadrunner soon came to a halt. The band subsequently released the demos 'Nigresent Dissolution', recorded at Wellesley studios in 1988, and the Brian Taylor produced 'Creation Of Chaos', during 1992. This second session marked a shift in band personnel, new man on vocals being Vince with bassist Steve Terror replaced by Bob Quelch with Kevin Harrison on drums, Rick Nemes having vacated to join INNER THOUGHT. Quite bizarrely INFERNAL MAJESTY found themselves the subject of mainstream media attention when Vince was jailed, charged with Vampyric activity. Apparently the vocalist had slashed his girlfriend's wrist and sucked her blood. Vince, who went on to front BLOODWURM, died of a heroin overdose on October 14th 2001.

Dutch label Displeased Records re-issued 'None Shall Defy' in 1997, adding the 'Nigresent Dissolution' demo tracks as bonus material. With interest renewed, INFERNAL MAJESTY resurrected itself, with original vocalist Chris Bailey, for live work across Europe. In March 1997 a brace of brand new songs, 'Where Is Your God?' and 'Gone The Way Of All Flesh', were donated to the 'Kanada' compilation album. The group, contracting with domestic label Hypnotic Records and with Chay McMullen now installed on bass, returned to the studio for August 1998's 'Unholier Than Thou'. The band then blasted Europe, touring alongside CANNIBAL CORPSE and DARK FUNERAL that September. An April 2000 live album, 'Chaos In

Copenhagen' recorded on October 14th 1998 at the Loppen Club in the Danish capital, added two cover versions of INFERNAL MAJESTY tracks by other acts, namely DAWN's 'Night Of The Living Dead' and CHRIST DENIED's take on 'Overlord'.

The 2002 line-up of INFERNAL MAJESTY, lead vocalist Chris Bailey, guitarists Steve Terror and Kenny Hallman, bassist Kiel Wilson, and ex-GRUDGE drummer Kris DeBoer, cut a four track demo. Eric Dubreuil was incorporated on bass guitar during October for recording at Profile Sound Studios in Vancouver of a new album 'One Who Points To Death'. The record, produced by Sho Murray and mastered by OBLIVEON's Pierre Rémillard at Wild Studios in St-Zenon, Quebec, was slated for April 2004 issue through the Greek Black Lotus label in Europe whilst North American release was handled by Canada's Galy Records. On a temporary basis, CRADLE TO GRAVE's singer Greg Cavanagh filled in a batch of live shows.

INFERNAL MAJESTY, having located new singer Brian Langley previously of MECHA MESSIAH, undertook a six week long Canadian tour with support act DEAD JESUS. The kick off show came as a support to METAL CHURCH at The Cobalt in Vancouver on 20th June. According to the band they lost out on support gigs to W.A.S.P. in August because the headline act deemed INFERNAL MAJESTY as "too heavy for the bill". European shows scheduled for September would be cancelled due to work visa problems. The band were soon back on the road, acting as support alongside fellow Canadians 3 INCHES OF BLOOD for Norwegian Black Metal act SATYRICON's US dates commencing December 2nd in San Francisco. However, INFERNAL MAJESTY abruptly dropped off these dates just prior to commencement.

The band announced touring plans for European dates in early 2005 in partnership with Thrash veterans HIRAX. A new album, recorded in December and entitled 'Systematical Extermination' and produced by KATAKLYSM's Jean-François Dagenais, would then be readied, this marking the recording debut with the band Brian Langley.

A December 2006 five track EP, 'Demo'n God', featured a re-recorded version of the song 'S.O.S.', from the band's 'None Shall Defy' album, complete with George "Corpsegrinder" Fisher of CANNIBAL CORPSE fame lending his vocal talents along with Rob Barrett, of CANNIBAL CORPSE and MALEVOLENT CREATION, adding guest guitar.

Infernäl Mäjesty, (1986) (Demo). Overlord / Night Of The Living Dead / Skeletons In The Closet / S.O.S.
NONE SHALL DEFY, Roadrunner RR 49609 (1987). Overlord / R.I.P. / Night Of The Living Dead / S.O.S. / None Shall Defy / Skeletons In The Closet / Anthology Of Death / Path Of The Psyco / Into The Unknown / Hell On Earth.
Nigresent Dissolution, (1988) (Demo). Into The Unknown / Hell On Earth.
Creation Of Chaos, (1992) (Demo). Power Intrusion / What's What / Into The Unknown / Those About To Die.
UNHOLIER THAN THOU, Hypnotic HYP 1062 (1998). Roman Song / The Hunted / Where Is Your God? / Death Roll / Gone The Way Of All Flesh / Unholier Than Thou / Black Infernal World / The Art Of War.
CHAOS IN COPENHAGEN, Hypnotic (2000). Birth Of The Power / Unholier Than Thou / Where Is Your God? / R.I.P. / Night Of The Living Dead / The Hunted / Night Of The Living Dead / Overlord.
ONE WHO POINTS TO DEATH, Black Lotus BLR 066 (2004). Death Of Heaven / Pestilential Eternity / Honey Tongue Of Satan / Cathedral Of Hate / Hysterion Proteron / Angels And Acid / Virgin Blood Tastes Purest At Night / One Who Points To Death.
SYSTEMATICAL EXTERMINATION, Black Lotus (2006). Against All Gods / Return / Heathenism / Burnt Beyond Recognition / Systematical Extermination / From Paradise To Hell / Crusade / Nation Of Assassins.

INGER INDOLIA

HOLLAND — *Dennis Droomers (vocals), Rob (guitar), Marcel (guitar), Bert Kops (bass), Eryk (keyboards), Michael (drums).*

INGER INDOLIA (Rumanian for 'Mourning Angel'), previously operational from a 1995 inception under the title of ACRENIA, deliver Electro-Black Thrash Metal as evidenced on their debut 'Hexed Forgotten Sanctuaries'. Guitarist Rob left to join Death Metal band VAULTAGE in 2002. Dennis Drommers would guest on VAULTAGE's 2003 recordings 'Hallucinate Beyond'. In September of 2003 Droomers, as 'Deregor', founded Black Metal trio CARACH ANGREN in union with DARK MUTATION keyboard player Clemens 'Ardek' Wijers and drummer Namtar (Ivo Wijers). A CARACH ANGREN demo, 'The Chasevault Tragedy', was recorded at Carachvan Studios in August of 2004.

Sycosynthesis, Inger Indolia (2001). Salvation In Solitaire / Mother Morgana.
HEXED FORGOTTEN SANCTUARIES, Infger Indolia (2001). The Lammendam Saga / He Who Loves Not Light / Forlorn Spectral Kingdoms / Wandering Towards The Crossroads Of Hell / Damnun Minatum.

INHIBITION

CATANZARO, ITALY — *Alessio Abbruzzese (vocals), Roberto (guitar / keyboards), Salvatore Dragone (guitar), Alex Adriano (drums).*

Catanzaro Thrash Metal band INHIBITION, established in 2000 by guitarist Salvatore Dragone and singer Alessio Abbruzzese, first called themselves CAOSPHERE, this first unit being rounded out by lead guitarist Federico Caliò, bass player Ivano Staglianò and Marco Tucciarelli on the drums. This band released a two song demo. Changing shape, in 2001 Roberto Romano joined the group as lead guitarist and in 2002 changed title to INHIBITION to record the demo 'Crying Under A Bloody Rain'.

2004 saw the brief employment of Lucio Lucia on drums, who left for health reasons. A demo, 'Quintessence Of Hate', followed but then Ivano Staglianò took his leave. New drummer Alex Adriano, of AITHER, DARKSHINE and DRACONIAN ORDER, was inducted in December 2005. The band released the EP 'Quintessence Of Hate' in March 2006.

Quintessence Of Hate, Inhibition (2006). Quintessence Of Hate / Regret / Cold Soul / Lightless.

INNER THRESHOLD

SAN FRANCISCO, CA, USA — *Dave Godfrey White (vocals), Doug Harrington (guitar), Jim Adams (guitar), Mike Kaufmann (bass), Hugo Barientos (drums).*

INNER THRESHOLD, operational between 1993 and 1994, was an interim stage in the saga of DEFIANCE, a cult Thrash Metal outfit, highly regarded by fellow musicians of the genre but ultimately failing to achieve a commercial breakthrough. The group was conceived in 1985 by guitarist Brad Bowers and drummer Matt Vander Ende in Oakland, California, building up to a full compliment of players with the induction of guitarist Doug Harrington and bassist Mike Kaufmann. Minus a singer, DEFIANCE performed its inaugural gig with Paul Baloff of EXODUS fame ad libbing. In the Summer of 1986 Harrington was usurped by former ATTRITION guitarist Jim Adams. Confusingly Bowers was then forced to exit and Harrington returned to his former position as DEFIANCE also located a frontman in Mitch Mayes, another ATTRITION veteran. Mayes tenure would be brief, and for their opening set of demos billed as 'Hypothermia' the group drafted new singer Ken Elkington. Band manager Ace Cook, also part of TESTAMENT's road crew, took the finished tapes to Europe where DEFIANCE was promptly offered a seven album deal by the Roadrunner Records label.

DEFIANCE's 1989 debut album 'Product Of Society' was produced by ANNIHILATOR guitarist Jeff Walters. By the following year Steev Esquivel had taken Elkington's place for the follow up 'Void Terra Firma' in 1990, this opus featuring a cover version of IRON MAIDEN's 'Killers'. The third album 'Beyond Recognition' was produced by Rob Beaton. In addition HEATHEN guitarist Lee Altus contributed guitar parts. Guitarist Brian Wenzel was drafted in late 1992. However, shortly after Jim Adams exited to join INDICA and Matt Vander Ende also left the band for a term with LÄÄZ ROCKIT. DEFIANCE was briefly rebuilt when Adams returned, former BLIND ILLUSION and HEATHEN vocalist Dave Godfrey White was inducted and new drummer Hugo Barientos installed.

Losing Steev Esquivel, DEFIANCE evolved into INNER THRESHOLD, recording demos with Rob Beaton acting as producer. Adams then bailed out once more, being superseded by Chris Long. Another transition in 1995 saw the band morph into UNDER by enrolling frontman Chris Long. Godfrey formed part of the 2000 HEATHEN reunion and Long took on lead vocal responsibilities. Steev Esquivel later went on to find prominence with SKINLAB whilst Adams created ULTRASPANK. Doug Harrington duly forged 'all star' Thrash outfit GALLERY OF SUICIDE.

DEFIANCE was reported to be plotting a reunion in 2004. That same October Esquivel temped for EXODUS on South American tour dates. The INNER THRESHOLD demos would be made available to fans through the DEFIANCE website in early 2005.

Inner Threshold, Inner Threshold (1993). Safe / Don't Play God / Wasting Creation.

INRAGE

UPPSALA, SWEDEN — *Christer Salling (vocals), Magnus Söderman (guitar), Peter Lans (guitar), Matte Järnil (bass), Perra Johansson (drums).*

Uppsala Thrash Metal act INRAGE evolved from LOST SOULS, an act featuring singer Christer Salling, guitarists Peter Lans and Magnus Söderman and bassist Matte 'Mars' Järnil, that had published three albums previously, 'Never Promised You A Rose Garden' in 1994 for Soundfront, 'Close Your Eyes And It Won't Hurt' issued in 1996 by Roadrunner Records and the Daniel Bergstrand produced 'Fracture' for German imprint Nuclear Blast.

INRAGE guitarist Peter Lans also operates with irreverent Thrashers F.K.Ü. (Freddy Krueger's Ünderwear) as 'Pete Stooaahl'. Magnus Söderman would act as session guest on the 2004 debut album 'Vile, Vicious & Victorious' from VICIOUS.

BUILT TO DESTROY, Scarlet (2002). Rebirth Of The Souls / Gift To Restore / Let Chaos In / Life Denied / Ultra Violence / Dead Heart Beating / Built To Destroy / Inject The Venom / Survival Of The Fittest / I Go Alone / No Tomorrow.

INSANITY

CA, USA — *Dave Gorsuch (vocals / guitar), Scott Dodge (guitar), Lou Gilberto (bass), Bud Mills (drums).*

Northern California Bay Area act INSANITY stood out from the regular Thrash pack by delivering an intense brand of proto-Death Metal. The original line up counted vocalist Joe DeZuniga, guitarist Dave Gorsuch, bassist Keith Ellison and drummer Bud Mills. INSANITY debuted live on the 19th of October 1985 as opening act for SACRILEGE and DEATH. INSANITY circulated the 1986 rehearsal recording 'Fire, Death, Fate' and would soon foster a genuine cult following.

Progress was stalled though as INSANITY hit a series of major obstacles. Firstly Mills was incarcerated in jail for a ten month spell and then DeZuniga became ill suffering from heart problems. The band managed to lay down one further rehearsal recording before DeZuniga died tragically young on 16th May 1987. INSANITY struggled on with an ever fluctuating line up and would issue the 'Death After Death' album in 1993. Bud Mills joined Bay Area Deathsters POVERTY in 1998. Following issue of the 'Poverty Sucks' demo, Mills and band colleagues guitarist Scott Dodge and bassist Lou Gilberto, alongside Dave Gorsuch, re-founded INSANITY. The 'Sacrefixion' demo arrived in 2001, pre-empting an EP comprising all new material. That same year INSANITY folded yet again, Mills, Dodge and Gilberto subsequently re-forging POVERTY.

DEATH AFTER DEATH, Black Lung (1993). Attack Of Archangels / Fire, Death, Fate / In Memory / Rotting Decay / Morbid Lust / Blood For Blood / Possession / Death After Death.

Sacrefixion EP, Black Lung (2002). Sacrefixion / Blind / Mortification.

INSENSE

OSLO, NORWAY — *Tommy Hjelm (vocals / guitar), Martin Rygge (guitar), Ola S. Hana (bass), Truls Andreas Haugen (drums).*

Oslo's INSENSE, forged in 1999, features KLUB KAMIKAZE frontman Eigel Dragvik, vocalist / guitarist Tommy Hjelm, a campaigner of THE CUMSHOTS, INTERFERENTZ, SYNDICATE and INFIDEL with the STARGUN, CHERROX and FACE THE REALITY credited guitarist Martin Rygge. The band, describing themselves as "brutal" Progressive Metal, signed a record deal with American label This Dark Reign in January of 2002, their eponymous debut surfacing in the July.

Original drummer Håvard Iversen would exit in March of 2003, being replaced by Truls Haugen of CIRCUS MAXIMUS. Touring would see INSENSE on Belgian soil in September. That December the band would commence recordings for a debut album. The band undertook a further short run of Belgian dates in July of 2004 partnered with RE:CREATION and SACRAMENTAL AWAKENED. During October INSENSE signed a deal with Black Balloon Records for group's sophomore album, 'Soothing Torture', recording at Caliban Studios and Musikkloftet in Oslo. Bass player Magnus R. Ruud exited in February of 2005, according to the band "to pursue his love for Christianity".

Tommy Hjelm joined GRIMFIST as their new frontman in August 2006.

INSENSE, This Dark Reign TDR-09 (2002). Factory Preset / In The Words / Room For Loss / Trust Just A Few / Thought Distillery / Those Who Cared Didn't Cry When I Died / Arsonist / It's Not Okay / Bacteria.

SOOTHING TORTURE, Black Balloon (2005). Helplessness / Making Up For Lost Time / I, Deviant / Gasping For Air / Constriction / The Forgiving Embrace / Soothing Torture / Clawing At The Nerve / A Prayer For The Feeble / Fallout.

INTERZONE

CANADA — *Rob Urbinati (vocals / guitar), J.R. (guitar), Kevin Wimberley (bass), Drew Gauley (drums).*

INTERZONE singer Rob Urbinati is known for his term fronting up the legendary underground act SACRIFICE. Joining him in the Thrash Metal INTERZONE venture would be former LEGION and SOULSTORM guitarist J.R., erstwhile SACRIFICE and ENTROPY bass player Kevin Winberley and drummer Drew Gauley, the latter a veteran of MUNDANE and MONSTER VOODOO MACHINE. The debut 'Cydonia' album novelly included a rendition of BJORK's 'Army Of Me'.

The singer unveiled his participation in a fresh new Vancouver based Thrash band project TENET in August of 2002. Forming a union with the STRAPPING YOUNG LAD pairing of guitarist Jed Simon and drummer Gene Hoglan alongside ex-GRIP INC. bassist Stuart Carruthers TENET signed to the German Virusworx Records label. STRAPPING YOUNG LAD mentor DEVIN TOWNSEND was slated to produce their debut offering.

In early 2005 INTERZONE donated their version of Icelandic singer BJÖRK's song 'Army Of Me' to an album seeing all proceeds going to the United Nations International Children's

Emergency Fund. Urbinati would also fire up side project WAR AMP, a Blues based retro-Doom outfit involving former JAWW and SOULSTORM.

CYDONIA, Utopian Vision (1999). Crown Of Lies / The Cage / Bled Me Dry / Still Breathing / Away You Fade / Last Plague / Army Of Me.

INTO THE DEMENTIA

STATEN ISLAND, NY, USA — *Anthony Galati (vocals), Sal Pisano (guitar), Mike Neumeister (guitar), Greg Quagliano (bass), Joe LaManna (drums).*

Staten Island Thrashers INTO THE DEMENTIA was created under the original title of TYRANNY in 2003 by guitarist Mike Neumeister and bassist Greg Quagliano. Lead vocal duties would be delegated to Anthony Galati and, in January 2004, Joe LaManna was added on drums. With second guitarist Russ Jones coming onboard in February the title INTO THE DEMENTIA was adopted.

The group's debut live performance, with Jake Horowitz of DECIMATE subbing on bass, came in June of 2004 at an ANDREW W.K. Fan Convention in Philadelphia. With the departure of Russ Jones, prioritising his other act TWIST OF FATE, INTO THE DEMENTIA added replacement Sal Pisano in September. Guitarist Mike Neumeister would also deputise live for DECIMATE and operates solo Black Metal project NECROTIC GRIMLAIR. A demo, 'The Great Beyond', was recorded in December.

The Great Beyond, Into The Dementia (2004). The Great Beyond: An Observation / The Great Beyond: Betrayal And Deceit / The Great Beyond: Cast In Stone.

INTRINSIC

SAN LUIS OBISPO, CA, USA — *Garret Graupner (vocals), Mike Mellinger (guitar), Ron Crawford (guitar), Joel Stern (bass), Chris Binns (drums).*

Heavy Metal band founded in San Luis Obispo, California 1983 by guitarists Ron Crawford and Mike Millinger, INTRINISIC opened for MEGADETH and ARMORED SAINT before parting company with vocalist Garret Graupner shortly after the 1987 eponymous, self-financed debut album release. Another departing members would be guitar player Ron Crawford. The Californians worked for a period with ex-METAL CHURCH vocalist David Wayne during 1988 but his tenure with the group was by no means lengthy and he was already dabbling with HEATHEN before he quit the INTRINSIC camp.

The second album, 'Distortion Of Perspective' issued in 1990 on the strangely titled Cheese Flag label, found INTRINSIC fronted by a new vocalist Lee Dehmer and guitarist Garrett Craddock.

INTRINSIC made an unexpected return in Japan during 1997 for Teichiku Records with the 'Closure' album. Line-up comprised Dehmer, Mellinger, Craddock, Binns, and bassist Mike McClaughlin.

INTRINSIC, No Wimp 007 (1987). Ahead Of The Game / Hit The Streets / Condo / Rip!! / Possessor / No Return / Leaving Insane / Wasted Life.

DISTORTION OF PERSPECTIVE, Cheese Flag (1990). Distortion Of Perspective / Sail Into The Sun / Piracy / Maximator / Fear And Loathing.

CLOSURE, Rokarola 728085004 (1997). The Wheel / Up For The Slam / BKB / 3X0 / Falling In / End Times / Nothing Special / I Still Feel Ya / Bystander / Someone's Gotta Pay / Try My Luck / Visceral / Brutally Frank / The Reasons Why / Who Goes There?

INVOCATOR

DENMARK — *Jacob Hansen (vocals / guitar), Flemming C. Lund (guitar), Carsten N. Mikkelsen (bass), Jakob Grundel (drums).*

A Thrash band dating back to 1986 that went under their original title of BLACK CREED, the group's first demo tape was 'Genetic Confusion' in 1988 followed by 'Alterations' the following year. After gigs with EDGE OF SANITY and ENTOMBED the band signed to Swedish label Black Mark. During 1990 the band toured both Denmark and Finland allied with Speed Metal act PRESTIGE.

The band's debut album, 1992's 'Excursion Demise' featuring former V-AXE, GRAFF SPEE and EXTREME FEEDBACK guitarist Jesper Jensen, sold around 10'000 copies in Europe. That same year the band appeared at the prestigious Roskilde festival, although oddly were lumped in on the non Metal day to share a stage uncomfortably with CROWDED HOUSE, TEXAS, THE POGUES and JAMES. The success of 'Excursion's Demise' prompted INVOCATOR to record a further album 'Weave The Apocalypse' and they opened for PARADISE LOST in Europe during 1994. The 'Early Years' album comprised of the band's original demo tapes plus covers of ARTILLERY and DARK ANGEL tracks. Jacob Schultz was replaced by guitarist Perle Hansen for the 'Dying To Live' album.

INVOCATOR, citing a line-up comprising of Jacob Hansen, AUTUMN LEAVES guitarist Flemming C. Lund, bass player Carsten N. Mikkelsen and erstwhile WITHERING SURFACE drummer Jakob Gundel, would reform in 2002 immediately setting to work on a new studio album. 'Through The Flesh To The Soul', set to appear in mid 2003 on the Italian Scarlet label, included a cover version of ASSASSIN's 'Abstract War'. The regrouped band marked an appearance at the November 'Aalborg Metal' festival in Denmark for their live debut.

Flemming C. Lund would work up a Thrash side project in early 2004. Dubbed SCAVENGER the band comprised SLUGS, ex-AUTUMN LEAVES man Boris Tandrup on bass and Morten Sørensen from AURORA, WUTHERING HEIGHTS and PYRAMAZE on drums. Meantime INVOCATOR drummer Jakob Gundel acted as sessioneer for US act MORPHEUS' debut album and, joining forces with Anders Høeg and Mikkel Sandager of MERCENARY, forged a Thrash Metal side project. Jacob Hansen would be found engaging in guest duties too, appearing on the 'Warhead' track on HATESPHERE's 2004 album 'Ballet Of The Brute'. Gaining kudos as an in demand producer, Hansen racked up impressive credits on albums by the likes of MERCENARY, COMMUNIC, HATESPHERE, ROB ROCK, VOLBEAT and RAUNCHY.

Bassist Carsten Mikkelsen exited in September. According to an official statement this was "due to lack of interest". That same month Jacob Hansen joined the ranks of BEYOND TWILIGHT. January of 2005 found drummer Jakob Gundel in the studio firing up a new band unit with MUGSHOT vocalist Kim Orneborg and the erstwhile WITHERING SURFACE pairing of guitarist Allan Tvedebrink and bassist Kasper Boye-Larsen dubbed THE DOWNWARD CANDIDATE. This new unit committed to demos in January produced by KONKHRA and FURIOUS TRAUMA guitarist Lars Mayland.

Jacob Hansen became the new singer of ANUBIS GATE in January 2006. Breaking a three year hiatus, INVOCATOR, comprising Jacob Hansen, Flemming C. Lund, Carsten Mikkelsen and Joakob Grundel, announced a return to live action in 2007.

EXCURSIONS DEMISE, Black Mark BMCD12 (1992). Excursion Demise (... To A Twisted Recess Of Mind) / Forsaken Ones / The Persistence From Memorial Chasm / Absurd Temptation / Schismatic Injective Therapy / Occurrence Concealed / Beyond Insufferable Dormancy / Inner Contrarieties / Alterations.

EARLY YEARS, Diehard RRS943 (1995). Dismal Serfage / Insurrected Despair / Restraint Life / The Scars Remain / Alterations / Occurrence Concealed / The Persistence From Memorial Chasm / Pursuit Of A Rising Necessity / The Eternal War / The Promise Of Agony.

DYING TO LIVE, Progress PCD20 (1995). Dying To Live / Kristendom / Shattered Self / King In A World Of Fools / Search / South Of No North / Living Is It / Astray / For A While / Hole.

THROUGH THE FLESH TO THE SOUL, Scarlet SC 071-2 (2003). Intro / Through The Flesh To The Soul / Writhe In Spit / On My Knees / Flick It On / Infatuated I Am (Speak To Me) / There Is No Saviour / The Chemistry Of Restlessness / Under The Skin / Fire Cleanses All / Sand Between The Teeth.

IRON ANGEL

GERMANY — *Dirk Schroder (vocals), Sven Struven (guitar), Peter Wittke (guitar), Thorsten Lohmann (bass), Mike Matthes (drums).*

Formed in 1983 by the former METAL GODS triumvirate of drummer Mike Matthes, bassist Thortsen Lohmann and guitarist Sven Struven. IRON ANGEL issued their second demo in 1984 'Legions Of Evil'. Added Jürgen Blackmore, son of DEEP PURPLE and RAINBOW guitarist RITCHIE BLACKMORE, to the band in mid 1986.

In 1987 IRON ANGEL parted company with bassist Thorsten Lohmann maneuvering guitarist Peter Wittke over to bass and recruiting a new guitarist Stefan Kleinow. Tragically, Wittke died in an auto accident in September of 2000.

Renewed interest in the band resulted in re-issues of both 'Hellish Crossfire' and 'Winds Of War' with extra tracks. A retrospective collection entitled 'The Tapes' comprised live recordings taken from IRON ANGEL's support gig to KING DIAMOND at the Bochum Zeche in May 1985, further live tracks from the July 1985 'Warpke' open air festival, the 1984 'Legions Of Evil' demo plus two untitled demo tracks. IRON ANGEL projected a brand new studio album for 2004 entitled 'Dead Man Walking'.

HELLISH CROSSFIRE, Steamhammer SPV 08-1853 (1985). The Metallion / Sinner / Black Mass / The Church Of Lost Souls / Hunter In Chains / Rush Of Power / Legions Of Evil / Wife Of The Devil / Nightmare / Heavy Metal Soldiers.

WINDS OF WAR, Steamhammer SPV 08-1880 (1986). Winds Of War / Metalstorm / Son Of A Bitch / Vicious / Born To Rock / Fight For Your Life / Stronger Than Steel / Sea Of Flames / Creatures Of Destruction / Back To The Silence.

THE TAPES, (2003). Metalstorm (Live) / Son Of A Bitch (Live) / Stronger Than Steel (Live) / Vicious (Live) / Fight For Your Life (Live) / Creatures Of Destruction (Live) / Sea Of Flames (Live) / Rush Of Power (Live) / Legions of Evil (Live) / Open The Gate/Devil´s Gate (Demo) / Rush Of Power (Demo) / Maniac Of The Night (Demo) / Sea Of Flames (Demo) / Wife Of The Devil (Demo) / Hounds Of Hell (Demo) / Untitled (Demo) / Untitled (Demo).

IRREVERENCE

KUOPIO, FINLAND — *Jon Drake (vocals / drums), Tero Liimatainen (guitar), Eero Mantere (bass).*

Kuopio based Thrash act IRREVERENCE started life in early 2000 under a formative billing of SONS OF TERROR, being then a duo of guitarist Tero Liimatainen, a veteran of EVOLUTION and ENRAPTURE SILENCE, and bassist / drummer Ville Eloranta. Liimatainen had also sessioned WITCHCRAFT's 1998 demo 'Ultimate Nightmare' and on RAVENSOUL's 1999 demo 'Wings Of Time'.

The band cut the demo 'Fearless Mind', after which Eloranta then exited and Vesa Ahola took command of the drums. Subsequently, New Zealander Jon Drake, of HORDE LORDE, enrolled to handle both lead vocals and drums. In Spring of 2003 the IRREVERENCE title was adopted for the demo 'Bloodred Eclipse'. Another line-up change marked the introduction of SHADE EMPIRE man Eero Mantere on bass.

Bloodred Eclipse, Irreverence demo (2003) (Limited edition 50 copies). Bloodred Eclipse / Beautiful Dismemberment.

ISOLATED FIELDS

KS, USA — *D.C. (vocals), Andrew Nagorski (guitar), Tim Dzubay (guitar), Pete Tucker (bass / death vocals), Ben Haggard (drums).*

Kansas Black Metal combo ISOLATED FIELDS was initiated in March of 2002 by the erstwhile DESCENSION pairing of Jon Tucker and vocalist D.C. Initial recruits would include Eric Coleman, Danny a.k.a. 'Beavedge', John Kessler and keyboard player Daniel Breathwaite. The group then re-shaped itself to involve Thai Johnson on guitar, Josh Mundy on keyboards and Jason Hadlock on drums with D.C. and Tucker sharing lead vocals. In this formation ISOLATED FIELDS appeared on the 2003 compilation album 'Treasury Of Souls' issued by Lifeless Records, capitalised on by the demo 'Lost In The Soil'.

Ructions hit the band in March of 2003 when both Hadlock and Johnson exited, soon followed by Mundy. ISOLATED FIELDS was put into stasis whilst D.C. assembled another band that Summer, THE LANTERN HILL NIGHTMARE with drummer Ben Haggard, guitarist Tim Dzubay and Josh Veatch. In June of 2003, after Veatch's defection signalled the collapse of THE LANTERN HILL NIGHTMARE, D.C. and Tucker reconstituted ISOLATED FIELDS, drafting the NOCTOPIA and DARKSIDE credited guitarist Travis Niemeyer and ex-STYGIAN, DESCENSION and VENIFICUS bassist Pete Tucker. Finalising the roster would be formative ISOLATED FIELDS keyboard player Daniel Breathwaite and THE LANTERN HILL NIGHTMARE, OF THE FALLEN and CRAVEN drummer Ben Haggard. The new look ISOLATED FIELDS aimed to blend Black, Death and Thrash Metal and in this guise set out on the live trail scoring opening slots for SIX FEET UNDER, BEHEMOTH, DOG FASHION DISCO and SKINLESS.

Founder Jon Tucker bowed out in late 2003, being replaced by Tim Dzubay of ANGRIUS and THE LANTERN HILL NIGHTMARE. Utilising Greg Ponder as producer, the band cut demo tracks in Springfield during February of 2004. 'The Distant Funeral Bells' EP was then released and once more the group was invited to appear on an updated 'Treasury Of Souls' compilation.

September of 2004 marked the departure of Niemeyer, his place being taken by Andrew Nagorski of SOUNDBLIND, [LID] and VIVISECTION. Daniel Breathwaite bailed out in October.

Lost In The Soil, Isolated Fields (2002). Intro / Consistent Torment / Lost In The Soil / Suffering Soul / Outro.

Nothing Left, Isolated Fields (2003). Threshold Of Embodiment / Consistent Torment / Nothing Left / Infantile Delusion.

The Distant Funeral Bells, Isolated Fields (2004). Threshold Of Embodiment / Nothing Left / Infantile Delusion / Dawn Of Erosion / The Distant Funeral Bells.

IZEGRIM

HOLLAND — *Krisz (vocals), Khasz (guitar), Goldiloxxx (guitar), Foxx (bass), Ränz (drums).*

Dutch self styled "Terror Thrashers". IZEGRIM was founded in the summer of 1996 by former SOLSTICE members guitarist Goldiloxxx (a.k.a. Jeroen) and drummer Ränz, thereby afterward completing the roster by incorporating vocalist Krisz, guitarist Arydon, bassist Aaargh and keyboard player Anita Luderer. Arydon was doubling up duties with his other act GODDESS OF DESIRE. With this formation IZEGRIM cut an opening symphonic Death Metal demo in the Spring of 1998 dubbed 'Most Evil'. However, Luder, a staff member at the renowned 'Aardschok' Metal magazine, then decamped and IZEGRIM shifted tack into a Thrash Metal direction for the 1999 self financed EP 'Bird Of Prey'.

Arydon then exited to prioritise GODDESS OF DESIRE and ex-SPINE man Corvin Keurhorst took the vacancy briefly before opting out to join EXPOSING INNARDS in July of 2000. Khasz subsequently took the second guitar role.

PENTACLE's Wannes Gubbels and former IZEGRIM guitar player Arydon guested on sessions for the 2002 album 'Guidelines For Genocide'. That same year the IZEGRIM guitar duo of Marloes and Jeroen forged Death Metal side project DELUZION in alliance with Rutger de Vries (a.k.a. Hrödger) of EXPOSING INNARDS on bass guitar. Further line up changes in the IZEGRIM ranks found Aaargh replaced by Foxx (a.k.a. Marloes).

IZEGRIM guitarist Carsten Altena would contribute synthesizers, samples and orchestras for THE MONOLITH DEATHCULT's albums 'The Apotheosis' and the 'The White Crematorium', joining this band as touring member in September 2004.

Bird Of Prey EP, Independent (1999). Bird Of Prey / White Fluid Rebel / Mass Hysteria / Tyrant Demokrázy / Heavy Metal.
GUIDELINES FOR GENOCIDE, Independent (2002). The Canonization Of The Insane / Persona Non Grata / Warmonger / Balance Of Terror / Crack Whore / Nail On Your Coffin / Angel Of Demise / Under The Banners Of Hatred / The Final Solution.

JERSEY DOGS

USA — *Lou Ciarlo (vocals / bass), Mike Benetatos (guitar), Jon Ilaw (guitar), Mike Sabatini (drums).*

Formed from the ashes of New Jersey Metal outfit ATTACKER by bassist Lou Ciarlo and drummer Mike Sabatini. In 1990 the band released their debut full length on the small US label Grudge Records. Lack of distribution and fierce competition in the genre saw the band fold shortly after. The band's 'Don't Worry, Get Angry!' is reputedly both heavier and thrashier than ATTACKER's material.

The album features three originals plus covers of AC/DC's 'Dirty Deeds Done Dirt Cheap' and VAN HALEN's 'Somebody Get Me A Doctor'.

Sabatini reformed ATTACKER in 2000 in direct competition to another version of the band led by former members.

DON'T WORRY, GET ANGRY!, Wild Rags WRR015 (1989). Wasted World / Who's To Blame / Another Pretty Day / Dirty Deeds Done Dirt Cheap / Somebody Get Me A Doctor.
THRASH RANCH, Grudge 4526-2-F (1990). Posse Of Doom / Medicine Man / Why Is / Blood From A Stone / Who's To Blame / Wasted World / Games / Greasy Funk Chicken / Last Breath / Another Pretty Day.

JESUS CHRYSLER SUPERSKUNK

GERMANY — *Thomas Rosenmerkel (vocals), Michael Gerstlauer (guitar), Michael Piranio (guitar), Bernhard Matt (bass), Sven Vormann (drums).*

German Nu-Thrash act JESUS CHRYSLER SUPERSKUNK unveiled themselves to the Rock world in May of 2002. Featured players would number the notable inclusion of erstwhile DESTRUCTION members guitarist Michael 'Ano' Piranio and drummer Sven Vormann. Making up the numbers would be vocalist Thomas Rosenmerkel, DRYROT guitarist Michael Gerstlauer and NECROMONICON bass player Bernhard 'Erna' Matt.

JESUS CHRYSLER SUPERSKUNK debuted with a three track demo. Rosenmerkel, Piranio and Matt also all operate as colleagues in the act EPHEMERA'S PARTY. The band wrapped up recording of a debut album, entitled '... The Loudest No!', in February 2005.

THE LOUDEST NO!, Twilight Vertrieb (2005).

JOE STUMP'S REIGN OF TERROR

USA — *Mike Vescera (vocals), Joe Stump (guitar), Jay Rigney (bass), Matt Scurfield (drums).*

JOE STUMP'S REIGN OF TERROR melodic Speed Metal was the band project of solo artist and former TRASH BROADWAY and SHINING HEMLOCK guitarist JOE STUMP. Stump, although credited with five solo albums, felt the need for a full band endeavour convening REIGN OF TERROR in the mid 90's, initially for the Japanese market. The 1995 album 'Light In The Sky' features ZANISTER vocalist Brian Sarrela as frontman.

By the 2001 record 'Sacred Ground' Stump had been joined by the EVENT rhythm section of bassist Jay Rigney and drummer Matt Scurfield. Lead vocalist was none other than the highly rated Mike Vescera, veteran of YNGWIE MALMSTEEN, OBSESSION, LOUDNESS and MVP. The album, which included a cover of RAINBOW's 'Kill The King', also saw guest keyboard playing from Mats Olausson of YNGWIE MALMSTEEN's band. The 'Conquer & Divide' album arrived in October 2002. Japanese editions added a bonus track 'Starstruck'.

In early 2005 it was announced that Joe Stump had formed HOLYHELL with fellow guitar shredder Tom Hess, "Chicago's premier guitar demon", and female singer Maria Breon.

On November 18th JOE STUMP'S REIGN OF TERROR appeared at the Monterrey Metal Fest event at the at the Coca Cola Auditorium in Mexico as second stage headliners.

LIGHT IN THE SKY, Leviathan (1995). Don't Look Back / Broken Heart / I Need Your Love / Better Off Dead / Don't Play Fair / Heartless / Guitar Concerto In D / Day By Day / Take A Little / Light In The Sky.
SECOND COMING, Leviathan (1999). Sonata Hypnotica / Devil's Playground / You Turn My World Around / Hold Onto Your Dreams / Speed Kills / Enchanted Sleep / All Things Must End / Take Your Life / Change / Hell & Back / Tapping Toccata.
SACRED GROUND, Leviathan (2001). Save Me / Sacred Ground / The Unknown / Paginini's Purgatory / Set Us Free / When Will We Know / Last Time / Undercover / Hellbound / Dante's Danza / Still Holding On / Kill The King.
CONQUER & DIVIDE, Leviathan (2002). Conquer And Divide / No Forgiving / Mark Of The Devil / No Limits / Forsaken / Sacrifice / Sign Of The Cross / Séance / Bite The Bullet / The Meaning.

JUMALATION

HELSINKI, FINLAND — *Taurus (vocals), Pedro Anthares (guitar), Abutre E. Hate (guitar), Carlos (bass), Esteban Genocídio (drums).*

JUMALATION, meaning 'Godless' in the Finnish tongue, is a Helsinki Thrash side-project of Pedro Antares of FORCA MACABRA, KUOLEMA and VIIMEINEN KOLONNA. Founded in the summer of 1999 the band fell into place quite quickly as Anthares gathered some like-minded friends from other bands. German guitarist, Heiko Hate, also plays in the German Death Metal band DEMENTIA. Bassist Esteban Genocido and drummer Carlos De Gigilo are members of the Black Metal band ACABO EL SILENCIO.

United with a common vision to create an retro-Thrash act, the quartet entered the Moonman Studios in Helsinki in May of 2005. The resulting two-day session produced the three song 'Jumalation Thrash Attack' EP. The band also contributed a couple of tracks to local, various artists CD entitled, 'Metal On Metal: Finnish Underground Metal Compilation'.

Jumalation Thrash Attack, Jumalation (1999).

JUST ONE FIX

AUCKLAND, NEW ZEALAND — *Riccardo Ball (vocals), Sharne Scarborough (guitar), Ant Ward (bass), G-Force (drums).*

Auckland based Hard Rock / Heavy Metal outfit JUST ONE FIX was formed in December 1998. On Friday October 13th 2000 the band played a gig at the Powerstation in Auckland. The song 'One Man' then appeared on the Intergalactic Records compilation 'The First Friday The 13th Of The Millennium' which included other Kiwi Metal acts such as SINATE, MALEVOLENCE and DAWN OF AZAZEL. Mid 2001 saw bassist Vinnie Cathcart join the band in time for an August 9th support slot for MEGADETH at the St. James Theatre in Auckland. That year JUST ONE FIX released a self titled debut demo.

In 2002 the band took a break following the departure of vocalist Eden Palmer. Drummer Dan then also exited the band leaving guitarist Sharne Scarborough as the only original member. Scarborough and Cathcart soon found themselves jamming with G-Force in a cover band called KFD which also featured ex-8 FOOT SATIVA and current SINATE vocalist / guitarist Matt Sheppard. Following these jam sessions G-Force (AFTER FOREVER) was recruited as the new drummer for JUST ONE FIX. Soonafter Riccardo Ball, also a DJ on The Rock FM, joined as vocalist completing the band's new line-up. Later, bassist Ant Ward would replace Vinnie Cathcart on bass.

In March 2007 JUST ONE FIX began recording material for a debut album 'Moments Of Brutality'.

Just One Fix, Just One Fix (2001) (Demo). One Man / Behind The Shadow / Morse Code / Time By Myself / Hopeless / Roll Up.
Dealer Of Lies, Just One Fix (2005) (Rocksound Magazine compilation featuring New Zealand artists). Dealer Of Lies.
MOMENTS OF BRUTALITY, Just One Fix (2007).

KAOTEON

BEIRUT, LEBANON — *Walid (vocals), Anthony Kaoteon (guitar / bass), Riad (drums).*

Beirut Black Metal act KAOTEON ("Kaotik Eon") was initiated during 1998 by guitarist Anthony Kaoteon, with singer Walid joining in 2000. With the induction of drummer Riad in 2003 the trio cut the opening demo 'Provenance Of Hatred'. This session subsequently saw a commercial release through the US imprint Unsung Heroes Records. KAOTEON would also contribute the track 'Decrepitude' to the 2004 compilation album 'Lehahel Metal Compilation Volume 1: The Total Sound Of The Underground'.

KAOTEON would employ an international cast of session drummers comprising Frenchman Romain Goulon (a.k.a. 'Orifist') of AGRESSOR, DISHARMONY, IMPERIAL SODOMY, BELEF and KRYSALYD with Canadian Lincoln, from PARIAH, MEATLOCKER SEVEN and SELF INFLICTED.

Provenance Of Hatred, Unsung Heroes UHR—066 (2004). Decrepitude / Provenance Of Hatred / Wrenched.

KARKADAN

DITZINGEN, GERMANY — *Robby Beyer (vocals), Philip Oefner (guitar), Johannes Kircher (guitar), Christian Grunenberg (bass), Martin Daniel (drums).*

Saarland's KARKADAN, titled after a mythological Persian beast, blend traditional Heavy Metal riffs with Black Metal extremism. The group was assembled in September of 1997 with an initial line-up incorporated by vocalist Robby 'Azaroth' Beyer, guitarists Florian Spannagel and Michael Zieschang, keyboard player Dennis Klink and Thomas Reeß on the drums. By December Felix Moosmann had been taken on to fulfill the bass role and Zieschang relinquished his position to Daniel Pütz.

Following the 1999 self financed album 'Eternal Black Reflections' Spannagel was forced out due to health reasons. KARKADAN would also bring in Marcel Frano to supplant Reeß. KARKADAN's 'The Lost Secrets' record would be pressed on 10" picture disc format by Supreme Chaos Productions and restricted to 333 copies. The band would be readying a further release, 'Silent Prayers Of The Forlorn Ones', for late 2002. Subsequently, KARKADAN's line-up comprised mainstays Beyer and Pütz flanked by guitarist Philip Oefner, bass player Gruni and drummer Martin Daniel. The 'Utmost Schizophrenia' album was delivered by Supreme Chaos Records in 2004. That same year ex-KARKADAN drummer Stefan Dittrich joined SAIDIAN.

KARKADAN drummer Martin Daniel exited in January 2005, being replaced by Johannes Gronover in May.

ETERNAL BLACK REFLECTIONS, Supreme Chaos SCR-CD002 (1999). Eternal Black Reflections / Niederknieder Todeskampf / Sleepwalker / Requiem Of Yearning / The Calling / Never Ending Love (Ironic Loyalty) / My Ablaze.
EMPIRE OF IUVENES, No Colours NC044 (2001). The Berserker / Empire Of Winter / Burning Gates Of Temples / Mystic Darkness / Fire Of Tartar / Dethroned Tyrant / Sons Of Mayhem / Desecrated Heavens Virgin / Raise The Dead.
THE LOST SECRETS, Supreme Chaos SCR-VL002 (2002) (Limited edition 333 copies). The Journey / Metalforces / The Ancient Times / Untitled.
UTMOST SCHIZOPHRENIA, Supreme Chaos SCR-CD008 (2004). Passing Away / On Your Knees / The Angel's Death / Faint / Frenetic Visions / The Journey / Sea Of Bitterness / The Ancient Time (Video).

KAT

POLAND — *Roman Kostrzewski (vocals), Poitr Luczyk (guitar), Wojciech Mrowiec (guitar), Tomasz Jagus (bass), Irseneusz Loth (drums).*

KAT were amongst the first Polish Metal bands to make a breakthrough into Western European Rock circles in the mid 80s. KAT's debut Polish release '666' was reissued for the Western market in the toned down form of 'Metal And Hell'. Following the 1989 album 'Oddech Wymarlich Swiatów' ("The Breath Of Dead Worlds") KAT underwent line up changes. Losing guitarist Wojciech Mrowiec and bass player Tomasz Jagus the band would regroup with bassist K, Oset and guitar player Jacek Regulsji.

The 1992 'Bastard' album found KAT operating more furiously than ever before but the act calmed down considerably for the 1994 'Ballady' effort. Later work has seen KAT back on track.

The 1997 mini album 'Badz Wariatem, Zagraj Z Latem' (Get Crazy, Play With Kat') the band reworked earlier material alongside new tracks and Techno remixes. Tragically guitarist Jacek Regulski was killed in an auto accident during 1999 and KAT duly suspended activity.

KAT vocalist Roman Kostrzewski has also issued a double album inspired by Anton La Vey's 'Satanic Bible'. This would be followed up by 'Mark Twain: Listy z Ziemi' ("Letters From Earth"). Kostrzewski would also front up ALKATRAZ.

KAT regrouped during 2002 citing a line-up comprising Roman Kostrzewski, guitarists Piotr Luczyk and ALKATRAZ man Valdi Moder, bassist Krzysztof Oset and drummer Ireneusz Loth. The band put in an extensive European tour in October 2005 packaged with SIX FEET UNDER, BORN FROM PAIN and DEBAUCHERY across France, Austria, Switzerland, Denmark, Holland, Belgium and Germany before acting as support to HELLOWEEN in November in Slovakia, the Czech Republic and Poland.

Ostatni Tabor, MMPR (1985) (7" single). Ostatni Tabor / Noce Szatana.
666, Silverton (1986). Metal I Pieklo / Diabelsk Dom Cz. I / Morderca / Masz Mnie Wampirze / Czas Zemsty / Nole Szatana / Diabelski Dom Cz. III / Wyrocznia / 666 / Czarne Zasepy.
METAL AND HELL, Ambush (1986). Metal And Hell / Killer / Time To Revenge / Devil's House Part I / (You Got Me) Vampire / Devil's Child / Black Hosts / Oracle / Devil's House Part II / 666.
38 MINUTES OF LIFE, Silverton (1988). Intro / Czarne Zastępy / Diabelski Dom Cz.II / Mag-sex / Morderca / Wyrocznia / Glos z ciemnoœci / Masz mnie wampirze / Porwany obledem.
BASTARD, Silverton (1992). W Bezsztalnej Bryle Uwieziony / Zawieszony Sznur / Bastard / Ojcze Samotni / N.D.C. / Piwniczne Widziadia / W Sadzie Smiertelnego Piekna / Odmiency / Lza Dla Cieriow Minionych.
ODDECH WYMARLYCH SWIATÓW, Metal Mind Productions (1994). Porwany Obledem / Spisz Jak Kamien / Dziewczyna W Cierniowej Koronie / Diabelski Dom CZ.II / Mag-Sex / Glos Z Ciemnosci / Bramy Zadz.
BALLADY, Silverton (1994). Legenda Wyshiona / Glos Z Ciemnosci / Talizman / Lza Dla Cienlow Minionych / Delirium Tremens / Czas Zemsty / Robak / Bez Pamieci / Niewinnosc.
RÓZE MILOSCI NAJCHETNIEJ PRZYJMUJA SIE NA GROBACH, Silverton (1995). Odi Profanum Vulgus / Purpurowe Gody / Plaszcz Skrytobojcy / Stworzylem Pieknarzecz / Slodki Krem / Wierze / Strzez Sie Plucia Pod Wiater / Szmaragd Bazyliszka.
BADZ WARIATEM, ZAGRAJ Z KATEM, Silverton (1997). Plaszcz Skrytobojcy (Wersja Skrocona) / Wierze (Wersja Zdigitalizowana) / Plasz Skrytobojcy (Wersja Zdigitalizowana) / Trzeba Zasnac (Wersja Skrocona).
SZYDERCZE ZWIERCIADO, Silverton (1997). Cmok-Cmok, Mlask-Mlask / Tak Mi Chce Samotnosc / Loze Wspolne, Lecz Przytulne / Szydercze Zwierciadlo / Spojrzenie / Czemu Mistrze Krzyz W Tornistrze / Oczy Slonc / Trzeba Zasnac.

KATAFALK

GRONINGEN, HOLLAND — *Wokkel (vocals), Chris (guitar), Niels (guitar), Jurjen (bass), Martin (drums).*

Groningen based Death Metal act founded by guitarist Christiaan during 1991. KATAFALK's first product would be the demo tape 'Through The Storm'. Former NETTLERASH and LETHARGY guitarist Pier Abe joined KATAFALK in November of 2000. The band toured Holland alongside GOD DETHRONED in 2001 but shortly after these dates suffered a major loss of band personnel. Three members, singer Wokkel, bassist Jurjen and drummer Martin all decamped en masse in order to create OBTUSE. Wokkel would team up with WINTER OF SIN.

Fresh blood was delivered in the form of singer Peter, guitarist Henk Jan and drummer Michiel van der Plicht, erstwhile members of GRINROTH. The group added Washington, USA native Rodney as lead singer in 2002, a man citing prior experience with Black Metal acts SHADOWVOID and HASTUR. This revised version of the band cut its teeth live at the Heerenveen 'Hydrargyrum' festival in April, although ex-member Jurjen substituted for Henk Jan on bass.

In September of 2002 Rodney bowed out and the group duly re-inducted former singer Wokkel. Signing to the Dutch label Cold Blood Industries KATAFALK readied their inaugural album 'Storm Of The Horde' for January of 2003. However, both guitarist Pier Abe and bassist Henk Jan severed ties with the band due to "serious differences of opinion". In a complete about turn, KATAFALK would be rejoined by their former partners singer Wokkel and bassist Jurjen.

Guitarist Christiaan gained KATAFALK some mainstream exposure in mid 2004 when he starred in a TV commercial for Internet company Chello, broadcasted on Dutch MTV, TMF and children's channel Nickelodeon. The clip featured the musician smashing a guitar into the computer of an unsuspecting computer "nerd" to the sounds of the KATAFALK track 'Cannonfodder'.

Drummer Michiel van der Plicht opted out in July 2005 in order to concentrate on his other acts TRAVELERS IN TIME and PROSTITUTE DISFIGUREMENT. He subsequently joined TOXOCARA. KATAFALK self-financed the EP 'Death's Contradiction' in June 2006.

STORM OF THE HORDE, Cold Blood Industries CBI 0301 (2003). Succubus / Aesthetic Vampires / Birthmark 666 / Cannonfodder / Redeemer / Storm Of The Horde / Hatred / Empty Life / Operation Mindloss / Rise Now / One Last Flight / Blind Envy / Baptized In Fire.
Death's Contradiction, Katafalk KO601 (2006). She's My Darkness / Death's Contradiction / God Pollution / War Chant.

KAYSER

ÄNGELHOLM, SWEDEN — *Spice (vocals), Fredrik Finnander (guitar), Mattias Svensson (guitar), Ewil Sandin (bass), Rob Ruben (drums).*

KAYSER, initiated in Ängelholm during the Summer of 2004 but announced as 2005 broke, is a heavyweight collaboration of Swedish elite musicians comprising the SPIRITUAL BEGGARS, AEON and THE MUSHROOM RIVER BAND credited singer Spice (a.k.a. Christian Stöstrand), Mattias Svensson of THE DEFACED, drummer Bob Ruben, an ex-THE MUSHROOM RIVER BAND, ANDROGYNE, COMFORT MIND and CLAUSTROPHOBIA member, THE AWESOME MACHINE bassist Anders Wenander and former AEON, RISE AND SHINE, ALL THE WAY and JACK OF ALL TRADES guitar player Fredrik Finnander. The new combo soon inked a deal with Italy's Scarlet Records, entering Caesar Studios in mid January to cut an opening album with a working title of 'Kayserhof', this later changed to 'Frame The World ... Hang It On The Wall'.

KAYSER utilised Caesar Studios in February 2006, working with producer Rickard Caesar, to cut a second album. At the same juncture Finnander would be replaced by Jocke Pettersson. Album sessions were wrapped up in mid April. An EP, 'Good Citizen', arrived in July.

KAYSER acted as support to the February through March 2007 European tour dates of EKTOMORF and BLINDED COLONY.

KAYSERHOF, Scarlet SC 103-2 (2005). 1919 / Lost Cause / Good Citizen / Noble Is Your Blood / 7 Days To Sink / Like A Drunk Christ / Cemented Lies / The Waltz / Rafflesia / Perfect.
Good Citizen EP, Scarlet SC 123-2 (2006). Good Citizen / Lost In The Mud / Fall / Propaganda / Good Citizen (Video).
FRAME THE WORLD ... HANG IT ON THE WALL, Scarlet SC 125-2 (2006). The Cake / Lost In The Mud / Evolution / Not Dead ... Yet / Absence / Turn To Grey / Cheap Glue / A Note From Your Wicked Son / Everlasting / Fall / Born Into This / Jake.

KAZJUROL

SWEDEN — *Kjelle (vocals), Pontus (guitar), T-Ban (guitar), Hakan (bass), Bonden (drums).*

KAZJUROL began as a purely amateur project by members of Hardcore band RESCUES IN FUTURE. The band's first commercial release came with a track on a German compilation single entitled 'Breaking The Silence' in 1986. The interest generated by the single track prompted the recording of a the 1987 'Messengers Of Death' EP for Uproar Records and a demo cassette titled 'A Lesson In Love', which surfaced in 1988.

The band eventually released their debut album, 'Dance Tarantella', in 1990 which saw vocalist Kjelle replaced by Tomas Bengtsson. However, by the next release, the 'Bodyslam' EP KAZJUROL had found another frontman in Henka 'Gator' Ahlberg. The EP featured covers of tracks by BAD BRAINS, VENOM, STORMTROOPERS OF DEATH and CRO-MAGS.

The band further displayed their Hardcore / Punk leanings with a cover of a DISCHARGE track on the Burning Heart Records 1991 compilation 'A Tribute Of Memories'. A four track promotional EP, 'Toothcombing ...', also emerged.

However, KAZJUROL eventually split, with both guitarists forming Hardcore act BAD DREAMS ALWAYS. Guitarists Pontus and T-Ban very briefly involved themselves with singer Joakim Öhman and drummer Per Karlsson in the final incarnation of SUFFER.

Messengers Of Death, Uproar UPROAR 004 (1987). Messengers Of Death / Stagedive To Hell / Who Needs You?
DANCE TARANTULA, Active ATV12 (1990). A Clockwork Out Of Order / Moment 22 / Than / Honesty, The Right Excuse / Dance Tarantella / Blind Illusions / Three Minator / Echoes From The Past / Stagedive To Hell.
Bodyslam EP, Burning Heart Heartcore 001 (1991). We Gotta Know / United Forces / Pay To Cym / Countess Bathory.
Hallucinations, Burning Heart Heartcore 002 (1991). Hallucinations / Dance Tarantella / Blue Eyed Devils.
Toothcombing ..., Burning Heart (1991) (Promotion release). Hallucinations / The Unholy War / Deathcon 5 / Dance Tarantella.

KILL FOR SATAN

MAWSON, ACT, AUSTRALIA — *Kellhammer (vocals / drums), Necroslush (guitar), Toaster Doom (guitar).*

Black—Thrash act KILL FOR SATAN feature ex-PSYCHRIST member Kellhammer on vocals and drums along with former EXCEED guitarist Toaster Doom. The band was conceived in 2003 as an old school Thrash covers act, with Kellhammer being joined by guitarists Yurionymous (PSYCHRIST's Yuri Ward) and Necroslush with The Pine Island Sasquatch on bass. This formation lasted just one gig, after which Necroslush was replaced by Hellpitt on vocals and guitar. However, Hellpitt too lasted just one concert, a declared "Lack of beer consumption" being a contributing factor to his downfall. KILL FOR SATAN persevered as a trio, penning original material, until boosted back up to quartet status with the introduction of Toaster Doom.

The 2004 album 'Thy Kingdome Undone ...' included a cover version of ARMOURED ANGEL's 'Madame Guillotine'.

THY KINGDOM UNDONE..., Kill For Satan (2004). The Fourth Power / Hammers Of Hell / Agents Of The Plague / Spawn Of The Maelstrom / Wolves Among The Flock / Pelagic Spectre / Madame Guillotine.

KILLER

ANTWERP, BELGIUM — *Shorty (vocals / guitar), Spooky (vocals / bass), Double Bear (drums).*

KILLER was formed in Antwerp during 1980 by Shorty (a.k.a. Paul Van Camp) and drummer Fat Leo, both men previously with the more obscure MOTHERS OF TRACK. The pair teamed up with ex-TRASH vocalist / bassist Spooky to complete the trio. KILLER signed to the Belgian arm of WEA Records to record two albums, 'Ready For Hell' and 'Wall Of Sound', and became well known throughout Europe for their appreciation by various motorbike organizations; probably due to their biker oriented image.

After their departure from WEA Records, KILLER were the first band to sign up to the newly formed Mausoleum label in April 1983. However, just prior to the signing, Fat Leo left the group to be replaced by the equally ridiculously monickered Double Bear (Robert Cogen). Mausoleum re-issued both the WEA albums and put two new KILLER tracks on the compilation 'If It's Loud We're Proud' as a taster to the new Jos Kloek produced album 'Shockwaves'. KILLER actually made it over to Britain in 1984 when the trio debuted at the Walthamstow Royal Standard in East London and were also due to play the Kerrang! magazine rock festival at Great Yarmouth, but were scuppered by customs delays on their equipment. Further complications outside of the band's control resulted in a projected live album, announced as 'Still Alive In Eighty-Five' and recorded in front of a home crowd by the famed Dieter Dierks mobile, being shelved due to Mausoleum's fiscal woes. KILLER folded in the late eighties and ex-member 'Shorty', as VAN CAMP, issued the 'Too Wild To Tame' album in 1988.

The group reappeared in 1989 to cut a belated fourth album on the rejuvenated Mausoleum label entitled 'Fatal Attraction'. KILLER at this juncture incorporated Shorty, Spooky, second guitar player Jan Van Springel and drummer Rudy Simmons. The group toured across Germany but folded again in 1991. Shorty and Spooky kept their hand in on the live circuit with Blues combo BLUES EXPRESS.

A further release would be the 'Mausoleum: 20th Anniversary Concert' album, including two KILLER tracks alongside live material from erstwhile Mausoleum label mates WARLOCK and OSTROGOTH, recorded at the Vosselaar Biebob venue in May 2002.

KILLER returned to action in 2003, rekindling their relationship with the newly re-activated Mausoleum Records for the album 'Broken Silence'. With Shorty heading up the formation, the new look band included bassist Spin, WILD SIDE and SCREW keyboard player Dave with the DETROIT, XIRONIX, VERMIN and BETWEEN WORLDS credited Vanne on drums. Second reunion set 'Immortal' followed in 2005.

SOULSTEELER's Ken Van Steenbergen assumed bass duties in February 2006. Parallel to their enterprises with KILLER, Vanne, Dave and Kris would also be operational as active members of BLACKJACK.

This formation recorded a concert at the Vosselaar Biebob venue for a live album. The band put in supports to QUEENSRYCHE in June.

READY FOR HELL, WEA (1981). Ready For Hell / Killer / Secret Love / I Know / Rock And Roll Fan / Backshooter / Laws Are Made To Break / It's Too Late / Dressed To Kill.
WALL OF SOUND, Lark INL 3535 (1983). Wall Of Sound / Battlescars / Blinded / No Future / Bodies And Bones / Maybe Our Interests Are The Same / Hellbreaker / Kleptomania.
FATAL ATTRACTION, Mausoleum 367 0001-2 (1991). Middle Ages / Fatal Attraction / Break Down The Wall / Steel Meets Steel / Kick On Your Ass / Lift Me Up / Highway Killers / Hibernation / Evil On The Road / I'm On Fire.
BROKEN SILENCE, Mausoleum 251031 (2003). Broken Silence / Crash And Burn / Time Machine / Dancing With The Devil / In The Land Of The Pharaoh / High In The Mountains / The Answer / Only The Strong Survive / Hear Me Calling / A Matter Of Time / The Run Of The Chupacabra / Lethal Virus.
IMMORTAL, Mausoleum (2005). Immortal / Frozen Fire—Burning Ice / Stone Cold / The Mirror / Queen Of The Future / Highland Glory / Touch Of Evil / Drifting Away / Easy Rider / Always And Forever / Liquid Shadows / Ad Tempus Vitale.

KINETIC

GREECE — *Savvas Betinis (vocals / bass), Manolis Mamas (guitar), Stavros Bonikos (guitar), Costas Alexakis (drums).*

KINETIC, founded in 2002 feature former members of WISDOM and BRAINFADE as well as ACID DEATH man Savvas Betinis on bass. The band debuted with a self-titled September 2003 demo. The group cut a Death Metal version of 'Helpless' by US Hard Rockers FIREHOUSE for a SleaszyRider Records tribute album 'Firehouse—All They Wrote'. The same label prepared the band's debut album 'The Chains That Bind Us'. Released in November of 2004 the record was also issued as a limited edition digipack, restricted to 1000 copies and adding a bonus video for the track 'Never Ending Winter'.

KINETIC parted ways with female vocalist Mina Giannopoulou due to "musical differences" in January 2007. She would be replaced swiftly by Margaret Staikou. Recordings for a new album, entitled 'Corrosion'. Then ensued.

Kinetic, (2003). Realms Of Nightmare / Holy Instinct / Never Ending Winter.
THE CHAINS THAT BIND US, Sleazy Rider SR-0027 (2004). Into The Nightmare (Intro) / Realms Of Nightmare / Engaging Web / Never Ending Winter / Hate Master / Holy Instinct / Free And Pure / Heed These Words / Message From Beyond / Life Faded / Last Call For Reaction.

KISS OF DEATH

LECCE, ITALY — *Max Serafino (vocals / rhythm guitar), Marcello Zappatore (lead guitar), Fernando Conte (bass), Dario Congedo (drums).*

KISS OF DEATH is a Lecce based Thrash / Death Metal outfit, debuting with a 1997 demo 'Lies'. A second session, entitled 'Undisputed Reality', was laid down in June of 1998. The would gain further exposure with a track inclusion of a compilation album 'Mighty Killers' assembled by monthly Metal magazine 'Psycho' in December of 1999. A debut album, March 2000's 'Stronger Than Before', would be promoted by an impressive live campaign tallying over fifty concerts in Italy alone.

KISS OF DEATH cut further demos in early 2002, backed by live work including a swathe of festival performances and supports to such artists as SEPULTURA, SAXON, SHELTER, RAW POWER, EXTREMA, LINEA 77, DEATH SS, NECRODEATH, WHITE SKULL, NODE, OPERA XI, SADIST, UNDERTAKERS and NATRON. The group's second album 'Inferno Inc.' would be recorded at Fear Studios in Alfonsine during February of 2004. The first 100 copies included a DVD-ROM comprising three live videos, five studio clips and photos.

Lies, (1997). In My View / Through The Night / No Way Out / Lies / Buy Or Die / What Did You Say / Around Me.
Undisputed Reality, (1998). Burn The Flag / Undisputed Reality / Between Life And Death / Agony / Screams Of Rage.
STRONGER THAN BEFORE, (2000). Uncontrolled Reaction / Stronger Than Before / Envy / Twisted Personality / Eye For An Eye, Tooth For A Tooth / Mind-Fucker / My Darkest Side / Rising Fear.
Promo 2K2 EP, Kick Promotion Agency (2002). House Of Pain / Uncontrolled Reaction / Stronger Than Before.
INFERNO INC., (2004). Three Times Six / Violent Attitude / My World / House Of Pain / New Blood / Bestower Of Death / Sunk Into Hate Complete / Declaration Of War / Inferno Inc.

KORROSIA METALLA

RUSSIA — *Sergei Visokosov (vocals / guitar), Roman Lebedev (guitar), Sergei Troitsky (bass), Alexander Bondarenko (drums).*

KORROSIA METALLA translates as 'Corrosion Of Metal'. The band became renowned in Russia for their outrageous stage shows. KORROSIA METALLA established a huge audience with a series of premier grade Thrash albums. However, recent outings have not only seen the band diversifying into Industrial, Punk and Death Metal but also blatantly employing both national socialist symbolism and lyrical content. For example, the 1999 album 'Kill Devils, Save Russia', not only sees the use of a swastika on the album sleeve but includes tracks entitled 'White Power' and 'Heil Fuehrer'. This musical experimentation and political stance has, rather disturbingly, not resulted in KORROSIA METALLIA's fan base dwindling but instead strengthening.

KORROSIA METALLA' 1985 line-up comprised founder Pauk together with Sax, Kostyl, Kisa and Morg. The band's first product was the 1986 demo 'Vlast Zla' ('Power Of Evil'). With Borov taking on lead vocals a second effort 'Zhyzn V Oktyabre' ('Life In October') followed in 1987. Later demos were 'Russkay Vodka Nad Vsem Mirom', 'Orden Satani' and 'President'. The quality of early albums, recorded on inadequate equipment, that KORROSIA METALLA entirely re-recorded early albums 'Orden Satani' and 'Russian Vodka' during 1993 making the original versions highly sought after on the collectors market.

KORROSIA METALLA's debut album 'Kannibal', a collection of earlier material re-recorded, has seen many re-issues over the years. The band followed it up by re-recording their 1988 demo 'Orden Satani'.

1996's 'Nicht Kapituliren' includes live tracks and rarities. 1997's 'Debosh V Orlyonke' is a live concert recorded in 1990. Borov decamped in 1998. The band recorded their version of 'Wheels Of Fire' included on the MANOWAR tribute album 'Russian Tribute To Manowar' issued by Piranha Records in November 2004.

KANNIBAL, Sintez (1991). (Russian title) / I'm President / Russian Vodka / (Russian title) / God Father / (Russian title) / (Russian title) / Let's Go, Shake, Shake / Bad Girls Train / Fucking Militia / (Russian title) / (Russian title) / Crazy House / (Russian title).

ORDEN SATANI, SNC (1992). S.P.I.D. / Geroin / V Shtorme Viking I Mech / Wheels Of Fire / Cherny Terror / Phantom / Abaddon / Lucifer / Sedmye Vorota Ada.

SADISM, Moroz (1992).

RUSKAY VODKA, Moroz (1993).

1.966, Moroz (1996). Apocalipsis Time / Nicht Kapituliren / Punk Not Dead / Don't Break My Skin / Tell Me Why / Digital Exciter / Ritual Sozhenia Trupov / Storozh / Nochnoy Koshmar / Broken Angel / White Power / If You Think I'm So Crazy.

NICHT KAPITULIREN, Souz (1996).

ZADERZHITE POEZD, Souz (1996).

DEBOSH V ORLYONKE, Souz (1997).

COMPUTER HITLER, Souz (1997). (Russian title) / (Russian title) / (Russian title) / (Russian title) / (Russian title) / (Russian title) / (Russian title) / (Russian title) / (Russian title) / (Russian title) / (Russian title) / (Russian title).

CHELOVEK SO SHRAMOM, Moroz (1997).

ZHYZN V OKTYABRE, Souz (1997).

UGAR V POLYARNOM, Souz (1998).

VENERA, Souz (1998).

TANTSEVALNYI RAI I AD, Souz (1998).

ON NE LYUBIL UCHITELEY, Souz (1999).

PAGAN GODS, Moroz (2001). (Russian title) / (Russian title) / (Russian title) / Heil Fuehrer / (Russian title) / (Russian title) / (Russian title) / (Russian title) / (Russian title) / (Russian title) / (Russian title) / (Russian title) / (Russian title).

KORZUS

BRAZIL — *Marcello Pompeu (vocals), Silvio Golfetti (guitar), Heros Trench (guitar), Dick Siebert (bass), Rodrigo (drums).*

A Sao Paulo act conceived in 1983 citing an original line up of vocalist Marcello Pompeu, guitarists Silvio Golfetti and Eduardo Toperman bass player Dick Siebert and drummer Mauricio Brian. KORZUS debuted with two tracks on a 1985 split album 'SP Metal II' shared with PERFORMANCES, ABUTRE and SANTUARIO. Their opening album 'Korzus Ao Vivo' followed in 1986. This record included a cover version of SLAYER's 'Evil Has No Boundaries'. Shortly after KORZUS would be joined by a new drummer Jose Mauro for recording of the follow up 'Sonho Maniaco' album. However, tragedy would strike the same October when Mauro committed suicide. KORZUS regrouped with new drummer Roberto Sileci and guitarist Marcello Nicastro for 1989's 'Pay For Your Lies', singing in English for the first time.

'Mass Illusion' arrived in 1991, complete with a cover of BLACK SABBATH's 'Under The Sun', giving the band increased exposure and healthy sales. The reputation of KORZUS was such that Golfetti would be asked to deputize for Andreas Kisser on a SEPULTURA tour of Germany. KORZUS themselves would later tour the European continent.

Another change on the drum stool saw Sileci departing to found MOSH and KORZUS pulling in Ricardo Confessori. This latest inductee would soon decamp though to join the high profile Progressive Metal act ANGRA. Fernando Schaefer filled the drummer's role but then Nicastro bowed out. New face on second guitar would be Marcelo Nejem.

KORZUS issued the 'KZS' album in 1996 amply displaying no let up in speed or aggression. Yet more changes found both Schaefer and Nejem out of the picture, creating TRETA. Rodrigo took on the drummer's vacancy and in 1998 Heros Trench augmented the guitar sound as KORZUS gained the honours of appearing alongside MEGADETH and SLAYER at the Brazilian 'Monsters Of Rock' festival.

2000 witnessed the departure of Rodrigo and the induction of Kiko of NECROMANCIA on drums. A live album culled from the 'Monsters Of Rock' performance was released which added new studio tracks. With Kiko's commitments to NECROMANCIA Rodrigo rejoined the band.

In 2004 both Marcelo Pompeu and Heros Trench guested on the TRANSFIXION album 'What's Real?'.

Heros Trench and Marcello Pompeu acted as producers for ANCESTTRAL's debut 2006 album 'The Famous Unknown'.

S.P. METAL II, Baratos Afins (1985) (Split album with ABUTRE, SANTUARIO & PERFORMANCES). Principe Da Escuridao / Guerreiros Do Metal.

KORZUS AO VIVO, (1986). Guerreiros Do Metal (Metal Warriors) / Príncipe Da Escuridão (Darkness Prince) / Ataque Supremo (Supreme Attack) / Caminhos Negros (Dark Ways) / Anjo Do Mal (Angel Of Evil) / Evil Has No Boundaries.

Pay For Your Lies EP, Devil Discos (1989). Pay For Your Lies.

LIVE AT MONSTERS OF ROCK, Devil Discos (2000). The World Is A Stage / Pay For Your Lies / Lost Man / Victim Of Progress / What A Pain / Last Memories / Catimba / Lutar, Matar / Desperate Cry.

KREATOR

ESSEN, GERMANY — *Mille Petrozza (guitar / vocals), Jörg Tritze (guitar), Rob (bass), Ventor (drums).*

Essen based trio formed in 1982 as TORMENTOR, with a line-up comprising vocalist / drummer Ventor (a.k.a. Jürgen Reil), guitarist Mille Petrozza and bassist Rob Fioretti, rooted back to the school band TYRANT. Having adopted the new moniker of KREATOR, the individualistic German outfit was to become much favoured by European Thrash fans in the mid 80s. The band set itself apart from the pack with a series of albums that defined an original strain to the standard Thrash sound. As such, KREATOR soon became a major force on the European mainland and their cult appeal and reputation also reaped rewards in North America.

Having debuted with the venom filled 'Endless Pain', produced by Horst Müller over a ten day session at Berlin's Musiclab Studios, in October 1985, KREATOR toured Europe and North America consistently, improving with each album release and keen to augment their live sound would spend time searching for a second guitarist. Michael Wulf from SODOM joined for a brief period in 1986. and KREATOR, pushing second album 'Pleasure To Kill' released in April 1986, would be found sharing the billing with RAGE and DESTRUCTION that year, after which guitarist Jorg Tritze was added to the line-up. Despite being firmly entrenched in Trash territory, 'Pleasure To Kill's uncompromisingly brutal ferocity, honed by Harris Johns at the production desk, would inspire legions of latter day Death Metal combos. That August the 'Flag Of Hate' EP arrived, kicking off with a re-recorded, speeded up version of the 'Flag Of Hate' track from 'Endless Pain', this interim product actually scoring the band high praise.

In October 1987 KREATOR toured Britain, packaged with VIRUS and CELTIC FROST, then America as support to D.R.I. backed by a promotion video for 'Toxic Trace' that gained the band valuable MTV exposure. It ensured sales of the band's third album, 'Terrible Certainty', recorded at Hannover's Horus Studios with producer Roy Rowland, were racked up ever more and set the tone for the subsequent 'Into The Light' and April 1989 'Extreme Aggression' offerings. The latter album was produced by leading American based Thrash knob twiddler Randy Burns at Los Angeles' Music Grinder Studios and, amongst all new KREATOR originals, featured a cover version of the RAVEN track 'Lambs To The Slaughter'. 'Extreme Aggression', boosted by MTV rotation of a video for 'Betrayer', would give the band their biggest selling record to date.

Just prior to their 1989 American tour playing alongside SUICIDAL TENDENCIES Tritze was ousted in favour of SODOM's Frank Blackfire (a.k.a. Frank Gosdzik).

This line-up would record 1990's 'Coma Of Souls' in Los Angeles; once again with Randy Burns at the production helm. A rather bizarre incident occurred later the same year when KREATOR pulled out of their London Electric Ballroom show complaining that they would have to play with a decibel meter in attendance! Still, no such problems prevented the group from undertaking Mexican gigs in July 1991 with support from TRANSMETAL, MAKINA, NEXT and LEPROSSY.

KREATOR completed a successful South American tour in 1992 performing in Chile, Brazil and Argentina. KREATOR were now pushing the 'Renewal' album, laid down at Morrissound Studios in Tampa with Tom Morris.

Having left Noise after a lengthy relationship of nearly ten years, KREATOR signed to G.U.N. Records in late 1994 with the first fruits of the new deal coming in the form of 1995's 'Cause For Conflict'. The group also introduced a new line-up of Petrozza, Blackfire bassist Christian Giesler and ex-WHIPLASH drummer Joe Cangelosi. However, by the end of the year both Godszik and Cangelosi were to depart. The band filled the gap with former CORONER guitarist Tommy Vetterli (a.k.a. Tommy T. Baron) and Jürgen Reil returning to the drum position. However, inflamed tendons saw Vetterli taking a back seat for some shows necessitating RAGS, JIMSONWEED and WALTARI man Sami li-Sirniö deputizing. With the band once again gaining momentum, Noise Records rushed out the 'Scenarios Of Violence' collection of live material and re-mixed archive cuts to satisfy demand.

In addition to a brace of new records in 1996 and 1997, KREATOR contributed a version of JUDAS PRIEST's 'Grinder' to the Century Media 'Legends Of Metal Volume II' tribute album in 1996.

Touring in Germany to push the 'Outcast' opus in the Winter of 1997 saw the band headlining a billing over DIMMU BORGIR, RICHTHOFEN and Brazilians KRISIUN. This album would be a radical departure from the expected KREATOR norm as the group freely indulged in almost Gothic styled ambience and applied the brakes to their usual hectic delivery. Instead, KREATOR's music now brooded rather than bludgeoned. The change generated praise from the media but consternation from a large body of fans. Nevertheless, KREATOR continued the experiment with March 1999's 'Endorama'. Japanese versions of 'Endorama', through the JVC Victor label, added an extra track in 'Children Of A Lesser God'. Also issued would be retrospective collections 'Voices Of Transgression—A 90's Retrospective' in 1999 and '1985-1992 Past Life Trauma' in 2000.

The band's own status was recognised when a tribute album to KREATOR emerged in 2000 titled 'Raise The Flag Of Hate'. Contributors included PAZUZU, ANGEL CORPSE, ACHERON, MYSTIFER and BLACK WITCHERY.

Vetterli was out of the picture for the recording of the 2001 album 'Violent Revolution', a revisiting of their speed orientated glory years produced by former SABBAT guitarist and respected console-tweaker Andy Sneap: he was supplanted by Yli-Sirniö., the same figure who temporarily replaced him for live work earlier. Promoting the album, which landed in the German album charts at no. 38, found KREATOR with running mates CANNIBAL CORPSE for European touring. The band would then form part of a nostalgic Thrash Metal mammoth tour of Europe with compatriots SODOM and DESTRUCTION commencing 26th December in Ludwigsburg and running through into the new year.

KREATOR frontman Mille Petrozza would also guest on shared lead vocals in union with THE CROWN and ex AT THE GATES singer Tomas Lindberg for the track 'Dirty Coloured Knife' on the 2002 album from Israeli metal act EMBLAZE. Also in the works for Petrozza would be a guest appearance on the new album from fellow Germany Thrashers DESASTER.

KREATOR's successful live alliance with DESTRUCTION would be furthered abroad as the pairing revealed tour plans for dates in Brazil, Chile, Peru, Colombia and Venezuela throughout August and September. That same month the band would head up a two month trek across North America, their first visit since 1996. KREATOR topped a bill for the 'Hell Comes To Your Town' tour of DESTRUCTION, CEPHALIC CARNAGE and DECEMBER. A live album and DVD, 'Live Kreation (Revisioned Glory)' produced by Andy Sneap and mixed in 5.1 surround sound, would be scheduled for early 2003.

KREATOR's live schedule intensified with September North American dates dubbed 'The Art Of Noise 2'. This run of shows saw the band allied with NILE, VADER, AMON AMARTH and GOATWHORE. Retiring to Backstage Studios in Derbyshire, England in the Spring of 2004 the group then set about recording a brand new album 'Enemy Of God' with Andy Sneap once again acting as producer. ARCH ENEMY guitarist Michael Amott recorded a guest solo for the song 'Murder Fantasies'. Some unusual promotion included Mille Petrozza appearing on German TV on 19th November, not on a music show, but as a guest for children's programme 'KinderKanal', explaining the complexities of Thrash Metal to an audience of pre-school kids.

The album, scheduled for January 2005 release, saw a limited edition version with a bonus DVD containing a "making of" documentary and video clips. 'Enemy Of God' impressively entered the national German charts at no. 19. Live promotion found KREATOR teaming up with DARK TRANQUILLITY, EKTOMORF and HATESPHERE for the 'Enemy of God' tour commencing in February 2005. US shows in April had the band packaged with VADER and THE AUTUMN OFFERING. Californian Thrashers DEATH ANGEL would be originally scheduled to participate but would be replaced by PRO-PAIN. A notable gig in early June saw KREATOR carving out a slice of Rock history by being the first foreign Metal band to perform in Morocco.

KREATOR

The band played in Casablanca in front of an estimated crowd of 20,000.

KREATOR would be back on North American soil in early 2006, packaged with NAPALM DEATH, UNDYING and A PERFECT MURDER for gigs in February. The group announced Australian shows for August. That October Steamhammer breathed new life into the 'Enemy Of God' album, re-issuing it in new artwork as a double CD and DVD package featuring the band's 'Wacken Open Air' festival appearance plus promotional videos and other live footage.

KREATOR headed up a package billing with CELTIC FROST, LEGION OF THE DAMNED and WATAIN for a lengthy run of European dates throughout March 2007.

Rehearsal, (1985) (Demo). Tormentor / Total Death / Storm Of The Beast / Endless Pain.

ENDLESS PAIN, Noise N0025 (1985). Endless Pain / Total Death / Storm Of The Beast / Tormentor / Son Of Evil / Flag Of Hate / Cry War / Bone Breaker / Living In Fear / Dying Victims.

PLEASURE TO KILL, Noise N0037 (1986). Intro (Choir Of The Damned) / Ripping Corpse / Death Is Your Saviour / Pleasure To Kill / Riot Of Violence / The Pestilence / Carrion / Command Of The Blade / Under The Guillotine.

Flag Of Hate, Noise N0047 (1986). Flag Of Hate / Take Their Lives / Awakening Of The Gods.

AFTER THE ATTACK, Noise N0072 (1987) (Picture disc vinyl LP). Choir Of The Damned / Ripping Corpse / Death Is Your Saviour / Pleasure To Kill / Riot Of Violence / After The Attack / The Pestilence / Carrion / Command Of The Blade / Under The Guillotine.

Behind The Mirror, Noise N0084 (1987). Behind The Mirror / Gangland.

TERRIBLE CERTAINTY, Noise N0086 (1987). Blind Faith / Storming With Menace / Terrible Certainty / As The World Burns / Toxic Trace / No Escape / One Of Us / Behind The Mirror.

Sounds—Waves 1, Noise WAVES 1 (1988) (Split 7" with MOTÖRHEAD, CELTIC FROST and STUPIDS). After The Dark.

Out Of The Dark ... Into The Light EP, Noise N0118-4 (1988). Impossible To Cure / Lambs To The Slaughter / Terrible Certainty (Live) / Riot Of Violence (Live) / Awakening Of The Gods (Live).

PLEASURE TO KILL, Noise N0037-3 (1988). Intro (Choir Of The Damned) / Ripping Corpse / Death Is Your Saviour / Pleasure To Kill / Riot Of Violence / The Pestilence / Carrion / Command Of The Blade / Under The Guillotine / Flag Of Hate / Take Their Lives / Awakening Of The Gods.

Out Of The Dark ... Into The Light EP, Dorane NUK 118 (1988) (USA release). Terrible Certainty (Live) / Riot Of Violence (Live) / Awakening Of The Gods (Live) / Impossible To Cure / Lambs To The Slaughter / Gangland.

EXTREME AGGRESSION, Noise N0129-2 (1989). Extreme Aggression / No Reason To Exist / Love Us Or Hate Us / Stream Of Consciousness / Some Pain Will Last / Betrayer / Don't Trust / Bringer Of Torture / Fatal Energy.

People Of The Lie, Noise ESK-2215 (1990). People Of The Lie / When The Sun Burns Red.

DOOMSDAY NEWS III—THRASHING EAST LIVE, Noise N0155-1 (1990) (Split album with TANKARD, SABBAT and CORONER). Flag Of Hate / Riot Of Violence / Love Us Or Hate Us / Behind The Mirror.

COMA OF SOULS, Noise N0158-2 (1990). When The Sun Burns Red / Coma Of Souls / People Of The Lie / World Beyond / Terror Zone / Agents Of Brutality / Material World / Paranoia / Twisted Urges / Hidden Dictator / Mental Slavery.

Brainseed, Kreator (1991) (Cassette demo). Winter Martyrium / Trauma / Renewal / Brainseed / Europe After The Rain.

OUT OF THE DARK ... INTO THE LIGHT, Noise N0200-2 (1992). Impossible To Cure / Lambs To The Slaughter / Terrible Certainty (Live) / Riot Of Violence (Live) / Awakening Of The Gods (Live) / Flag Of Hate (Live) / Love Or Hate Us (Live) / Behind The Mirror (Live).

RENEWAL, Noise N0193-2 (1992). Winter Martyrium / Renewal / Reflection / Brainseed / Karmic Wheel / Realiätskontrolle / Zero To None / Europe After The Rain / Depression Unrest.

Isolation, Great Unlimited Noises GUN 079 (1995) (Promotion release). Isolation / Men Without God.

Lost, Great Unlimited Noises GUN 072 (1995) (Promotion release). Lost / Hate Inside Your Head.

CAUSE FOR CONFLICT, Great Unlimited Noises GUN 071 (1995). Prevail / Catholics Despot / Progressive Proletarians / Crisis Of Disorder / Hate Inside Your Head / Bomb Threat / Men Without God / Lost / Dogmatic / Sculpture Of Regret / Celestial Deliverance / Isolation. Chart position: 48 GERMANY.

SCENARIOS OF VIOLENCE, Noise N0222-2 (1996). Suicide In Swamps / Renewal / Extreme Agression / Brainseed / Terrorzone / Ripping Corpse / Tormentor / Some Pain Will Last / Toxic Trace / People Of The Lie / Depression Unrest / Coma Of Souls / Europe After The Rain / Limits Of Liberty / Terrible Certainty / Karmic Wheel.

OUTCAST, Great Unlimited Noises GUN 140 (1997). This World Behind / Phobia / Forever / Black Sunrise / Nonconformist / Enemy Unseen / Outcast / Stronger Than Before / Ruin Of Life / Whatever It May Take / Alive Again / Against The Rest / A Better Tomorrow. Chart position: 91 GERMANY.

Leave This World Behind, Great Unlimited Noises GUN 142 (1997). Leave This World Behind / Whatever It May Take / Forever / Phobia.

Leave This World Behind, BMG 74321 50171 2 (1997). Leave This World Behind / Whatever It May Take / Forever / Phobia.

Endorama Club-Edition, Drakkar 654 992 (1999) (German promotion release). Endorama (Club edition).

ENDORAMA, Drakkar 001 (1999). Golden Age / Endorama / Shadowland / The Chosen Few / Everlasting Flame / Passage To Babylon / Future King / Entry / Soul Eraser / Willing Spirit / Pandemonium / Tyranny. Chart position: 68 GERMANY.

Chosen Few, Drakkar 675 542 (1999). Chosen Few / Endorama / Children Of A Lesser God / Chosen Few (Video) / Endorama (Video).

ENDORAMA, JVC Victor VICP-60704 (1999) (Japanese release). Golden Age / Shadowland / The Chosen Few / Everlasting Flame / Passage To Babylon / Future King / Entry / Soul Eraser / Willing Spirit / Pandemonium / Tyranny / Children Of A Lesser God.

VIOLENT REVOLUTION, Steamhammer SPV 085-72542 (2001). Reconquering The Throne / The Patriarch / Violent Revolution / All Of The Same Blood (Unity) / Servant In Heaven-King In Hell / Second Awakening / Ghetto War / Replicas Of Life / Slave Machinery / Bitter Sweet Revenge / Mind On Fire / System Decay. Chart position: 38 GERMANY.

LIVE KREATION, Steamhammer SPV 089-74542 DCD (2003). The Patriarch / Violent Revolution / Reconquering The Throne / Extreme Aggression / People Of The Lie / All Of The Same Blood / Phobia / Pleasure To Kill / Renewal / Servant In Heaven, King In Hell / Black Sunrise / Terrible Certainty / Rite Of Violence / Lost / Coma Of Souls / Second Awakening / Terrorzone / Betrayer / Leave This World Behind / Awakening The Gods / Golden Age / Flag Of Hate / Tormentor. Chart position: 59 GERMANY.

ENEMY OF GOD, Steamhammer SPV 085-69842 (2005). Enemy Of God / Impossible Brutality / Suicide Terrorist / World Anarchy / Dystopia / Voices Of The Dead / Murder Fantasies / When Death Takes It's Dominion / One Evil Comes—A Million Follow / Dying Race Apocalypse / Under A Total Blackened Sky / The Ancient Plague. Chart positions: 19 GERMANY, 45 AUSTRIA, 84 FRANCE.

ENEMY OF GOD (LIMITED EDITION), Steamhammer SPV 089-69840 (2005). Enemy Of God / Impossible Brutality / Suicide Terrorist / World Anarchy / Dystopia / Voices Of The Dead / Murder Fantasies / When Death Takes It's Dominion / One Evil Comes—A Million Follow / Dying Race Apocalypse / Under A Total Blackened Sky / The Ancient Plague / Impossible Brutality (Enhanced video clip) / Making Of From The Studio / Videoclip And EPK Of 'Impossible Brutality' / Violent Revolution (Live) / Phobia (Live).

ENEMY OF GOD—REVISITED, Steamhammer SPV 085-69848 (2006) (CD + DVD). Enemy Of God / Impossible Brutality / Suicide Terrorist / World Anarchy / Dystopia / Voices Of The Dead / Murder Fantasies / When Death Takes It's Dominion / One Evil Comes—A Million Follow / Dying Race Apocalypse / Under A Total Blackened Sky / The Ancient Plague / Toxic Trace (Live in Busan, Corea) / Coma Of Souls (Live in Busan, Corea) / Intro (Live in Wacken Open Air 2005) / Enemy Of God / Impossible Brutality / Pleasure To Kill / Phobia / Violent Revolution / Suicide Terrorist / Extreme Aggression / People Of The Lie / Voices Of The Dead / Terrible Certainty / Betrayer / Flag Of Hate / Tormentor / Reconquering the Throne (Bootleg—Live at the Rockpalast) / Renewal / Servant In Heaven—King In Hell / Making of Enemy Of God / Enemy Of God (Video) / Dystopia (Video) / Impossible Brutality (Video) / Dying Race Apocalypse (Video).

KREMATE

SÃO PAULO, SP, BRAZIL — *Rodrigo Schmidt (vocals / guitar), Ricardo Fernandes (guitar), Felipe Parmegiani (bass), Myke Ramos (drums).*

KREMATE, taking their cue from the classic Bay Area Thrash movement, was founded in April of 1998 by vocalist / guitarist Rodrigo Schmidt and drummer Myke Ramos. Progress would be slow during the first two years of operation due to numerous line-up changes but in 2000 the membership settled with Schmidt and Ramos being joined by second guitarist Ricardo Fernandes and bassist Felipe Parmegiani. That December the demo 'Eternal War' was recorded.

KREMATE spent much of 2002 recording the album 'Watch The End'. A further new track, entitled 'Face Your Life', was recorded for 'Valhalla' magazine's compilation 'Valhalla Demo Section', released in January 2004 by Seventies Fever Records. In 2005 Force Majeure Records re-issued the 'Watch The End' album under a revised title of 'Death: In The Name Of . . .'

DEATH: IN THE NAME OF . . ., Force Majeure FMR001 (2005). After Storm (Instrumental) / Today Is Like 1940 / The Same Old Shit / Like A Knife / Messenger Of Lies / A Man Without A Life / Watch The End / Buried Law / Born Dead / Rot In Pain / The Killing Toys.

KRISIUN

IJUÍ, RS, BRAZIL — *Alex Carmago (vocals / bass), Moyses Kolesne (guitar / keyboards), Max Kolesne (drums).*

Ijuí, Rio Grande de Sul Death Metal merchants KRISIUN (Latin for "Seers of abomination") include plentiful old school Thrashing as part of their delivery. The band is a totally family affair, comprising three brothers, vocalist / bassist Alex Carmargo, guitarist Moyses Kolesne and drummer Max Kolesne. (Alex uses his mother's maiden name). The band first offered their 1991 demo 'Evil Age', with 'The Plague' following in September 1992. During this phase KRISIUN operated as a quartet, with Altemir Souza on second guitar. Maurício Nogueira then occupied this post briefly before moving on to TORTURE SQUAD, ZOLTAR and IN HELL. A further session, the Tchelo Martins produced 'Curse Of The Evil One', shared with VIOLENT HATE, backed these up in January the following year. Another release in October, laid down at Anonimato Record Studios in São Paulo, included a shared EP's with Germans HARMONY DIES for Rotthenness Records. This led to the 'Unmerciful Order' album on Dynamo Records in March 1994, on which the trio are all credited with the surname Kolesne.

KRISIUN debuted on the European continent with August 1995's 'Black Force Domain'. These tracks, cut at Army Studios in São Paulo, saw production credits going out to Sergio Sakamoto. Germany's G.U.N. label re-issued 'Black Force Domain' during 1997. German dates in the Winter of 1997 saw KRISIUN opening up a billing comprising RICHTHOFEN, DIMMU BORGIR and headliners KREATOR.

'Apocalyptic Revelation' emerged in August 1998, this being the group's first set of tracks recorded outside of Brazil at Musiclab Studios in Germany with Simon Fuhrmann in control of the desk. The band would make a significant impact upon European shores in 1998 ranked on tour alongside NAPALM DEATH, CRADLE OF FILTH and BORKNAGER before embarking on a series of headline dates with support act SOILWORK. February 1999 had KRISIUN involved in their inaugural North American tour alongside INCANTATION and ANGEL CORPSE.

Switching to Century Media Records, the band re-issued 'Black Force Domain' once again in 1999, adding bonus tracks in the form of cover versions of SODOM's 'Nuclear Winter' and a vastly accelerated take on KREATOR's 'Total Death'. KRISIUN's March 2000 album 'Conquerors Of Armageddon' was produced by MORBID ANGEL's Eric Rutan at Stage One Studio in Büchne, Germany. Limited edition variants added bonus cut 'Seas Of Slime'. Touring to promote the album found the band sharing billing with SATYRICON, IMMORTAL and ANGEL CORPSE in America. As ANGEL CORPSE disintegrated mid-tour with the departure of mainman Pete Helmkamp KRISIUN would obligingly loan out Carmago to fulfill vocal duties in order that ANGEL CORPSE could complete the run of dates. There would be no let up for the band, soon after engaged in European touring on a package billing in alliance with OLD MAN'S CHILD, GORGOROTH and SOUL REAPER.

The Tchello Martin produced 'Ageless Venomous' arrived in 2001 prompting a full scale global workout which saw KRISIUN performing in Europe, North America, South America, Russia and Japan. The band by now had risen to headliner status for the 'Thrash 'Em All' festivals throughout Poland and Russia topping a bill of VADER, LUX OCCULTA and BEHEMOTH. November of 2001 had the band on the road in the UK and Ireland for seven shows with CANNIBAL CORPSE and KREATOR, this union transferring to Europe before hooking up with MARDUK, DARK FUNERAL, NILE and VOMITORY to participate in the hugely successful sold out 'X-Mass' festivals.

Sadly, news arrived in 2002 that former KRISIUN guitarist Altemir Souza was killed in a motorbike accident. KRISIUN would co-headline a run of dates with VADER across mainland Europe from late August 2002 supported by DECAPITATED and PREJUDICE. 'Works Of Carnage', sporting a rendition of VENOM's 'In League With Satan' and produced by OBLIVEON guitarist Pierre Rémillard, arrived in October 2003 and the band announced touring plans for the US in November, forming up a billing comprising HATE ETERNAL, DEICIDE and CATTLE DECAPITATION. KRISIUN resumed live work in 2004 acting as support to MORBID ANGEL's extensive set of European dates commencing February 20th in Hardenberg, Holland. Further European shows that November dubbed the 'Clash Of Demigods' saw the band forming up a package billing with BEHEMOTH, RAGNAROK and INCANTATION. The 'Bloodshed' album, released by Century Media in October, would comprise eight new recordings alongside tracks from the rare 1993 'Unmerciful Order' EP.

KRISIUN formed up with a Summer 2005 package touring bill comprising HATE ETERNAL, INCANTATION, INTO ETERNITY and ALL SHALL PERISH for US gigs in June, after which the band entered Stage One Studios in Bühne, Germany with producer Andy Classen to craft a new album 'Assassination'. European dates would be announced for August, including Prague's 'Brutal Assault' festival, Germany's 'Party San Open Air' event and the Muotathal, 'Mountains of Death' festival in Switzerland.

'Assassination' arrived in February 2006. KRISIUN scheduled April 2006 US tour dates combined with MORBID ANGEL, Canadians DESPISED ICON and Polish Black Metal band

BEHEMOTH. US dates for September and October saw the band hooking up with SIX FEET UNDER, DECAPITATED and ABYSMAL DAWN. Intended live work in December across Europe was to see the band hooking up with SIX FEET UNDER, GOREFEST, BELPHEGOR and DARZAMAT for the 'X-Mass' festivals. However, the group withdrew from these shows.

The Plague, (1992). Sinner's Scorn / Evil Mastermind / Prophecies Of the Plague.
Curse Of The Evil One, (1993) (Split EP with VIOLENT HATRED). Sinner's Scorn / Evil Mastermind / Prophecies Of The Plague / The Dead Are Rising Up.
Krisiun / Harmony Dies, Rotthenness (1993) (Split EP with HARMONY DIES). Rises From Black / Agonize The Ending.
UNMERCIFUL ORDER, Dynamo (1994). They Call Me Death / Unmerciful Order / Crosses Towards Hell / Agonize The Ending / Summons Of Irreligious / Meaning Of Terror / Infected Core / Insurrected Path (Depth Classic) / Rises From The Black.
BLACK FORCE DOMAIN, Great Unlimited Noises GUN147 (1995). Black Force Domain / Messiah Of The Double Cross / Hunter Of Souls / Blind Possession / Evil Mastermind / Infamous Glory / Respected To Perish Below / Meanest Evil / Obsession By Evil Force / Sacrifice Of The Unborn.
APOCALYPTIC REVELATION, Great Unlimited Noises GUN163 (1998). Creations Scourge / Kings Of Killing / Apocalyptic Victory / Aborticide (In The Crypts Of Holiness) / March Of The Black Hordes / Vengeances Revelation / Rites Of Defamation / Meaning Of Terror / Rises From Black.
CONQUERORS OF ARMEGEDDON, Century Media 77259-2 (2000). Intro—Ravager / Abyssal Gates / Soul Devourer / Messiah's Abomination / Cursed Scrolls / Conquerors Of Armageddon / Hatred Inherit / Iron Stakes / Endless Madness Descends.
AGELESS VENOMOUS, Century Media 77367-2 (2001). Perpetuation / Dawn Of Flagellation / Ageless Venomous / Evil Gods Havoc / Eyes Of Eternal Scourge / Saviours Blood / Serpents Specters / Ravenous Hordes / Diableros / Sepulchral Oath.
WORKS OF CARNAGE, Century Media 8167-2 (2003). Thorns Of Heaven / Murderer / Ethereal World / Works Of Carnage / Slaughtering Void / Scourged Centuries / War Ritual / Wolfen Tyranny / Sentinel Of The Fallen Earth / Shadows / In League With Satan / Outro.
BLOODSHED, Century Media 77567-2 (2004). Slain Fate / Ominous / Servant Of Emptiness / Eons / Hateful Nature / Visions Beyond / Voodoo / They Call Me Death / Unmerciful Order / Crosses Toward Hell / Infected Core / Outro/MMIV.
ASSASSINATION, Century Media 77667-2 (2006). Bloodcraft / Natural Genocide / Vicious Wrath / Refusal / H.O.G. (House Of God) / Father's Perversion / Suicidal Savagery / Doomed / United In Deception / Decimated / Summon / Sweet Revenge.

KRYPTOR

CZECH REPUBLIC — Marcel Novotný (vocals), Petr Buneš (guitar), Tom (guitar), Filip Robovski (bass), Robert (drums).

KRYPTOR is a Thrash Metal combo, anchored on bass man Filip Robovski (alias 'The Kryptmaster'), dating back to 1987. The very first line up would feature singer Michal Roháèek, guitarists Petr 'Kuna' Buneš and Tomáš Roháèek with Filip Robovski on bass guitar and Robert Stýblo on the drums. Michal Roháèek would leave the fold shortly after formation, superseded by Marcel 'Pípa' Novotný, and Plaèek backed out in 1989, being replaced the following year by Ota Hereš of TÖRR, ALCOHEL and 666 repute. However, that same year Tomas Roháèek also decamped as KRYPTOR issued the debut Miloš "Dodo" Doležal produced album 'Septical Anaesthesia'. In 1991, as the 'Time 4 Crime' follow up arrived, Stýblo exited and the TÖRR, MENHIR and BLACK MAJESTY credited Péká took command of the drums.

KRYPTOR suffered a fluid line up throughout the nineties with guitarist Daniel Krob of ARAKAIN and KREYSON enrolling in 1993. The band struck out into the international market that year with the English language 'Greedpeace' album. The band's next effort, 1994's 'United' produced by Radim Hladík, would see the addition of six live songs recorded at the 'Zubr' festival. Between 1994 and 1995 guitar duties were delegated to Petr 'Škvarek' Škarvada and Petr 'Šimi' Šimáèek, although Leoš Holan was inducted in 1995, his tenure lasting until 1997. The drum position too would prove unstable with successive delegates including Alan Reisich of DEBUSTROL in 1993, Marek Kraus in 1994 and DEBUSTROL and HARLEJ man Libor Fanta lasting from 1996 until 1997.

NA VYCHODNI FRONTI BOJ, (1997). Vlèí Vdova / Jsou Mezi Námi / Justièní "Omyl" / Noc / Greedpeace / Struggle For Humanity / Hools (Na Východní Frontì Boj!) / Maniak / Markýz de Sade / To Se Nemìlo Stát / Rychlost Vítìzí / From Gehenna To Here / Charon / Kláštení Tajemství.

KRYZALID

FRANCE — Nicolas Langlois (vocals / guitar), Micos Orger (vocals / guitar), Laurent Carpentier (bass), Olivier Canton (drums).

Technical Death-Thrashers KRYZALID, hailing from France, began life billed as SUDDEN DEATH during 1999. In this incarnation their opening gig would be conducted with Franck on vocals, Micos Orger and Nicolas Langlois on guitars, MALEDICTION's Olivier Messaoui standing in on bass and Mathieu on the drums. New bass man Laurent Carpentier enrolled in April of 2000.

The exit of Franck signalled a name switch to KRYZALID as Langlois and Orger took on shared responsibilities for the lead vocals. May of 2003 saw the incorporation of TRIDUS ELASTICUS and BURGUL TORKHAÏN credited Olivier Canton on drums, this unit cutting the EP 'The Beginning . . .'.

The Beginning . . . , Kryzalid (2003). Walk Or Croak / To Remain In Obscurity / Little Savage / Sadness.

KRÄMATORIUM

HELSINGBORG, SWEDEN — Thomas Ernemyr (vocals), Hannes Hellman (guitar), Oscar Persson (guitar), Kim Osberg (bass), Tommy Johansson (drums).

Helsingborg Thrash Metal band KRÄMATORIUM is rooted in earlier formation F.U.B.A.R. ("Fucked Up Beyond All Belief"), formed as a high school band by singer Thomas Ernemyr and guitarist Hannes Hellman in 1999. They would be joined by bassist Christian Fagerström and a classmate named Victor Hansson on drums. A demo was issued in 2000, entitled 'Kontroll Över Världen', after which F.U.B.A.R. opted to disband. During 2003, now with Oscar Persson installed on guitar, F.U.B.A.R. briefly re-convened. A second demo was crafted but, unsatisfied with the results, the group fell apart once again. Hellman and Persson would busy themselves with DELOMANICON and AGAINST.

Attempting a third try to create something worthwhile, the band members, minus Hansson, forged KRÄMATORIUM. Tommy Johansson of SILENT, RELIQUA and Power Metal band GALVATRON, also featuring Oscar Persson, manned the drums for demos 'Krämatorium', limited to 100 copies, in 2004. Inducting SILENT bassist Kim Osberg in September 2004, substituting Fagerström, the band released the 'Grässklipparfrenesi' session in 2005. Hellman would also be active with REPLICATO.

Krämatorium, Krämatorium (2004). Krämatorium / Kroppstemperatur.

KUBLAI KHAN

MINNEAPOLIS, MN, USA — Greg Handevidt (guitar / vocals), Kevin Idso (guitar), Mike Liska (bass), John Fedde (drums).

KUBLAI KHAN scored a brief flash of media exposure with their 'Annihilation' album due to the presence of MEGADETH member guitarist Greg Handevidt. Decamping from MEGADETH in 1983 Handevidt relocated to Minnesota to found KUBLAI KHAN in union with guitarist Kevin Idso. Following a brace of demos, including the 'Clash Of The Swords' tape, the group cut the Jonathan Akre produced album in the exceptionally un-Metal surroundings of PRINCE's Paisley Park establishment. The album surfaced on the New Renaissance label in 1987 but was not heavily promoted.

KUBLAI KHAN folded in 1989 with Handevidt joining the military prior to his career path taking him into the law. However, he would resurrect the band in 2003. Joining him on this endeavour would be Idso and a new rhythm section of Clint Burton on bass and Jason Weber on drums. The quartet is also active as KRONK.

ANNIHILATION, Heavy Metal America HMUSA 95 (1987). Derath Breath / Mongrel Horde / Down To The Inferno / Liars Dice / Passing Away-Kublai Khan / Clash Of The Swords / Battle Hymn (The Centurion).

LAMENT

NJ, USA — *Linda Alexander (vocals), John Blicharz (guitar), Karl Odenwalder (bass), Kevin Kuzma (drums).*

New Jersey's LAMENT was forged by erstwhile BLOOD FEAST drummer Kevin Kuzma and ex-5150, DARK HEREAFTER and TWILIGHT'S EVE bassist Karl Odenwalder in early 2004. Fronted by Linda Alexander the band's inaugural live performance came on 23rd July at the Arena at Georges in Bayonne, New Jersey. An EP, 'Sea Of Red', was recorded at Studio Blicharz. A limited run of just 50 of these EPs, given away at gigs, included cover versions of SLAYER's 'Raining Blood' and MOTÖRHEAD's 'Ace Of Spades'. LAMENT signed to Metal War Productions in January 2005.

After parting ways with Linda Alexander in early 2006 the remaining members recruited vocalist Tony Stanziano to forge Blackened Death Metal band ANNUNAKI. An album, 'Throne Of The Annunaki' was recorded at Trax East Studios in September for release through Militia Records.

Sea Of Red, Lament (2004) (Limited edition 50 copies). Sea Of Red / Prison Cell / Break The Silence / Torture / Ace Of Spades / Raining Blood.

Sea Of Red, (2004). Sea Of Red / Prison Cell / Break The Silence / Torture.

LAST RITES

ITALY — *Dave (vocals / guitar), Jan (guitar), Rebba (bass), Mauro (drums).*

Speed Metal band LAST RITES was created during 1997 in a more traditional Heavy Metal mould by the quintet of ALKIMIA and WOUNDED KNEE vocalist Matteo, guitarists Jan and Dave, bassist Fabrizio and drummer Daniele. Numerous line up shuffles finally settled down in 1999 finding Dave adding lead vocals to his responsibilities and Rebba coming in on bass. At this juncture a musical shift in emphasis found LAST RITES pursuing a Thrash / Speed Metal direction.

A three track demo was cut in March of 2001. In November that year, now minus Daniele, the group recorded a new song 'Psycho Killer' utilising PROJECTO's Luca Grosso for session drumming. After the sessions Mauro of Punk act KLASSE KRIMINALE enrolled but in September of 2002 both Mauro and Rebba exited. Riccardo Libu of ALKIMIA took on the bass role. The band laid down tracks for the 'Mind Prison' album in December.

Guitarist Dave is also a member of Doom band MOONLESS NIGHT. His six string partner divides his duties with Thrashers HANGER 18.

Psycho Killer EP, Independent (2002). Psycho Killer.

MIND PRISON, (2003). Skeleton / Paradise Lost / Poisonous / Psycho Killer / Against War / Mind's Prison / Without Face / Coma.

LATVALA BROS

ESPOO, FINLAND — *Roope Latvala (guitar / bass), Petteri Hirvonen (keyboards), Jussi Latvala (drums).*

Espoo Heavy Metal band LATVALA BROS was conceived as an entirely instrumental by ex-STONE guitarist Roope Latvala in 1993 in alliance with keyboard player Petteri Hirvonen and Latvala's brother, former VIRAGO drummer Jussi Latvala. Rehearsals took place in Latvala family's sauna cabin in Lintuvaara and a solitary album, 'Latvala Bros Plays Wooden Eye' recorded at Lemuntie military barracks in Vallila with engineers Petteri Hirvonen and Ade Mattila, emerged that same year. Only 600 copies were manufactured.

Roope Latvala racked up scene credits with CHILDREN OF BODOM, DEMENTIA, NOMICON, WALHALLA, WALTARI and WARMEN whilst Jussi Latvala had association with ANIMA, COSMIC CONNECTIONS, SHAMAN and TENEBRAE.

LATVALA BROS PLAYS WOODEN EYE, Megamania (1994) (Limited edition 600 copies). The Wooden Eye / Inborn Panic / Pizza Ja Patka / Rock Sauna / The Blue Megawave / Brutal Solutions To Sexual Megaproblems / Night Of The Lizard / Egomaniac / The Beginning / The End.

LAWNMOWER DETH

NOTTINGHAM, NOTTINGHAMSHIRE, UK — *Qualcast Mutilator (vocals), Concord Face Ripper (guitar), Baron Kev Von Thresh Meister Silo Stench Chisel Marbels (guitar), Mighty Mo Destructimo (bass), Explodin' Dr, Jaggers Flymo (drums).*

Originally known as SCRAWM with a line-up of vocalist / guitarist Dogg Bower, bass player Dudd Hallam and drummer Chris Flint, this Mansfield based group released the 1987 demo 'Demented Genius' SCRAWM before adopting a radical about turn in their thinking. Armed with the premise that putting the fun into Thrash and Death Metal music with a madcap slant was the way to fame and fortune the group evolved into LAWNMOWER DETH. With extreme Metal a burgeoning force in the UK, LAWNMOWER DETH's eccentricities generated unexpected press attention, fan allegiance and even alienation from some quarters.

Now fronted by Qualcast Mutilator, a mild-mannered employee in the Nottingham branch of HMV Records by day, the rejuvenated band began to make plans for world domination, or at least jobs as groundsmen at Nottingham Forest's City Ground. Guitarist Baron Kev Von Thresh Meister Silo Stench Chisel Marbels was better known to his mother as Kevin Papworth. The first LAWNMOWER DETH demo, 1987's 'It's A Lot Less Bovver Than A Hovver', featured a cover of FLEETWOOD MAC's 'The Chain' (for many years the theme tune to BBC TV coverage of Formula One motor racing) retitled 'Lawn Mower Grand Prix' and produced by SABBAT's guitarist Andy Sneap. The tape was followed by a further demo, this one entitled 'Mowdeer' in 1988.

The Nottinghamshire nutters made their vinyl debut in 1989 on a split LP for RTK Records with Liverpool's METAL DUCK, with the LAWNMOWER DETH slice entitled 'Mower Liberation Front'. The following year Earache Records unleashed the 'Viz' inspired 'Ooh Crikey It's . . . Lawnmower Deth' album featuring the track 'Do Do Doe' dedicated to Metal Forces editor Bernard Doe, set up as the band's nemesis and fiercest critic at the time .

ACID REIGN guitarist Kev joined the band in mid 1991 following the dismissal of Schizo Rotary Sprintmaster (a.k.a. Paddy), who wound up in forming a short-lived band project with bassist Iain Reynolds and ex-SLEEZE PATROL drummer Ian 'Mole' Etheridge. Whilst Etheridge later worked with Andy Sneap in GODSEND, Reynolds formed NIGHTSHIFT.

A 1992 side project from LAWNMOWER DETH men Pete Lee and Chris Parkes and LITTLE ANGELS vocalist Toby Jepson resulted in the SIX YARD BOX band. The SIX YARD BOX track

'Pictures Of Matchstick Men', released as a single, was a cover of the early STATUS QUO hit.

LAWNMOWER DETH attempted to project a new serious image with 1993's 'Billy' album. Although demonstrating their was substance beneath the mirth making 'Billy', a fine stab at Pop tinged Punk, was received only lukewarmly by a fan base expecting another slab of jocularity. After a series of poorly attended British shows the band split in late 1994. Mutilator (a.k.a. Koffee Perkulator, real name Peter Lee) held down a day job as press officer for Earache Records before starting Cottage Industry Records with ex LITTLE ANGELS manager Kevin Nixon. LAWNMOWER DETH performed their farewell gig supporting SPUDMONSTERS at London's Marquee in April 1995.

In later years erstwhile LAWNMOWER DETH guitarist Gavin O'Malley teamed up with Mansfield Death Metal band EVOKE.

It's A Lot Less Bovver Than A Hovver, Cobshape Promotions (1987) (Demo). Lawnmower Death / Burn Burn Burn / Time To Die / Lawnmowers Rampage In The Jungle / I Hate You / Nothingness / Witches Sabbat.

Mowdeer, Lawnmower Deth (1988) (Demo). Meaningless—Andy Warhol Persists / Umph Umlah / Scar Face / Drink To Be Sick / Seventh Church / Assassinate Geldof / Watch Out Granma / F#ck Off.

MOWER LIBERATION FRONT, RKT (1989) (CD version. Split album with METAL DUCK). MLF / Drink To Be Sick / Umph Umlah / Thermo-nuclear War Is Good For Your Complexion / Seventh Church Of The Apocalyptic Lawnmower / Nothingness / Watch Out Granma, Here Comes A Lawnmower / Lawnmower's Rampage In The Jungle / I Got The Clap And My Knob Fell Off / Nasal Infection / I Don't Want Your Problems, Commit Suicide / Scar Face / Bavarian Drinking Song / Fuck Off / Watch Out Granma (Live) / M.L.F. (Live) / Got The Clap (Live) / Nasal Infection (Live) / Umph Umlah (Live) / Scarface (Live) / Nothingness (Live).

MOWER LIBERATION FRONT, RKT CMO192 (1989) (Vinyl version. Split album with METAL DUCK). M.L.F. / Drink To Be Sick / Umph Umlah / Thermo Nuclear War Is Good For Your Complexion / 7th Church Of The Apocyloptic Lawnmower / Nothingness / Watch Out Granma, Here Comes A Lawnmower / Lawnmower Rampage In The Jungle / I Got The Clap & My Knob Fell Off / Nasal Infection / I Don't Want Your Problems, Commit Suicide / Scar Face / Bavarian Drinking Song / Fuck Off.

OOH CRIKEY IT'S . . . , Earache MOSH 25 (1990). Perv Happenings In The Snooker Hall / Betty Ford's Clinic / Weebles Wobble But They Don't Fall Down / Sheepdip / Lancer With Your Zancer / Can I Cultivate Your Groinal Garden / Flying Killer Cobs From The Planet Bob / Did You Spill My Pint? / Seventh Church Of The Apocalyptic Lawnmower / Rad Dude / Sumo Rabbit And His Inescapable Trap Of Doom / Maim Mower, Maim / Cobwoman Of Deth Meets Mr. Smellmop / Got No Legs? Don't Come Crawling To Me / Icky Ficky / Judgement Day (Assume The Position / Oooh Crikey / Satan's Trampoline / Do Do Doe / Duck Off / F.A.T. / Punk As Fuck / Sharp Fucka / Blades Of Hades / March Of The Mods.

Kids In America, Earache MOSH039CD (1991). Kids In America / Bone Yank Blisters / Kids In America (De La Deth Mix) / Sumo Rabbit And His Inescapable Trap Of Doom.

THE RETURN OF THE FABULOUS METAL BOZO CLOWNS, Earache MOSH 72 (1992). The Return Of The Fabulous Metal Bozo Clowns / Jaggered Wedge / Bad Toad / Feetcleaner / Drunk In Charge Of An Ugly Face / Paranoid Polaroid / Frash For Cash / Crazy Horses / Enter Mr. Formica (Icky Ficky Part 2) / Lawnmowers For Heroes, Comics For Zeros / Urban Surfer 125 / A Is For Asswipe / Sorrow (So Dark . . . So Scared) / Goldfish Podge / R.F. Potts / Wormy Eyes / Be Scene, Not Heard / Egg Sandwich / Anyone For Tennis / King Of The Pharaohs / Illinois Enema Bandit / Fookin Moo Vit.

BILLY, Lawnmower Deth MOSH 98 (1993). Somebody Call Me A Taxi / Billy / I Need To Be My Main / Squeeze / Do You Wanna Be A Chuffed Core / Buddy Holly Never Wrote A Song Called We're Too Punk / Up The Junction / If It Was Grey You'd Say It Was Black / Kids In America / March Of The Dweebs / Funny Thing About It Is / Purple Haze.

LEAD WEIGHT

KAZAKHSTAN — *Roman Barelko (vocals), Andrey Yermolaev (guitar), Leonid Blum (bass), Pavel Archakov (drums).*

Kazakhstans LEAD WEIGHT is a Progressive inclined technical Death Metal outfit hailing from Alma-Ata. The band was conceived in March of 1992 by the erstwhile APOKALYPSIS duo of guitarist Andrey Yermolaev and bass player Leonid Blum. Although the albums entitled 'Iron Balls' and 'Omen' surfaced in 1995 the first foundation of LEAD WEIGHT broke up. In 1998 though, Yermolaev opted to resurrect the band name, re-enlisting Blum with fresh members ex-YATAGAN singer Grom and drummer Hellpash. This version of the band cut the Speed Metal orientated album 'For Thine Is The Kingdom', this closing out with a cover version of AC/DC's 'Back In Black'.

LEAD WEIGHT released the 'Penetrator' album in 2002 for the CD Maximum label.

IRON BALLS, CD Maximum (1992) (Cassette release). Master / Livin' At Break Neck Speed / Young Lady / Evil Town / White Men Summons / Till The Day I Day / Flying Man / That's All Right Mamma If I'll Rock Tonight / All Right Boogie / If I Ever Had A Dollar.

ANTHOLOGY, CD Maximum (1997). For Thine Is The Kingdom / Miserere / Wizzard / Don Benefactor / Penetrator / Exorcist / Suite #2 J.S. Bach / Thanatopsis / Omen / Elegy / Eyes Of Abbadon / Ally / Praeludium #2 J.S. Bach.

FOR THINE IS THE KINGDOM, CD Maximum (1999). Intro / Miserere / Enemy / Exorcist / Helltown / Thanatopsis / For Thine Is The Kingdome / War / Eyes Of Abbadon / Wizzard / Back In Black.

PENETRATOR, CD Maximum CDM 1230 (2002). Ally (Intro) / 1,000,000 Ways / Omen / Last Dance / Don Benefactor (Death Is An Adviser) / Useless / Elegy / Stalker / Penetrator / Disangelist.

LEGACY

OAKLAND, CA, USA — *Steve Souza (vocals), Eric Peterson (guitar), Derrick Ramirez (guitar), Greg Christian (bass), Louie Clemente (drums).*

Oakland Thrashers LEGACY were the forerunners of TESTAMENT. Founded during 1993 the band comprised guitarists Eric Peterson and Derek Ramirez, bassist Greg Christian and drummer Louis Clemente. A 1984 four song demo would see Ramirez handling lead vocals, after which Steve 'Zetro' Souza was recruited as frontman. A second demo session arrived in 1985, the track 'Reign Of Terror' gaining exposure as featured on the 'Eastern Front Vol. 2' compilation album. . These tracks were produced by Doug Piercy, a noted scene guitarist with credentials stretching through CONTROL, COBRA, ANVIL CHORUS and DELTA. However, Souza then bailed out to join fellow up and coming local Thrashers EXODUS. The band recruited new singer Chuck Billy, performing a solitary concert under the LEGACY title fronted by Billy in July 1986 prior to adopting the TESTAMENT brand.

TESTAMENT scored a deal with Atlantic Records and went on to become a significant force on the global Thrash scene. Peterson and Ramirez would subsequently activate side project DRAGONLORD. Christian went on to HAVOCHATE whilst Clemente featured with GALLERY OF SUICIDE.

Legacy, Legacy Demo (1984). Legacy / Palace Of Torture / Intruder / Soul Snatcher.

Legacy, (1985). Burnt Offerings / Reign Of Terror / Alone In The Dark / Raging Waters.

LEGEN BELTZA

SPAIN — *Xanti (vocals / bass), Azkue (guitar), Ekaitz (guitar), Iban (drums).*

LEGEN BELTZA is a Basque Country Thrash Metal band established during 1998. The band's first effort came with a 1999 self-financed effort, recorded by vocalist / bass player Xanti, guitarists Ekaitz and Joseba with drums shared between Edorta and Antonio. With Edorta installed on drums LEGEN BELTZA utilised this outing to undertake live shows across Spain. These concerts included scoring a contract with the IZ Rock imprint after winning a local band competition 'Gazte Lehio', although Joseba was to exit at this juncture.

IZ Rock put out the 2001 commercially available debut 'Istorio Triste Bat'. The band was then brought back up to full strength with the addition of guitarist Azkue. Their July 2003 album 'Insanity', issued by US label Crash Music Inc., saw mixing credits going out to ANNIHILATOR's Jeff Waters. Notable support slots included shows with IRON MAIDEN, EXODUS, NAPALM DEATH and SLAYER.

The 2006 album 'Dimension Of Pain', laid down in late 2005 at Lorentzo Records studios in Berriz, featured guest appearances by IMAGIKA frontman Norman Skinner, on the track 'War Of Wars', Johan Liiva, of ARCH ENEMY and HEARSE, Freddy Persson of NOSTRADAMEUS, Martin Akesson of IMPIOUS, Jürgen Volk from GLENMORE and RAWHEAD REXX, Johan Lindstrand, previously of THE CROWN, Pat Savelkoul CALLENISH CIRCLE and John Dones of CARDINAL SIN. Drummer Edorta vacated after these sessions, being replaced by Iban.

ZIZTU BIZIAN, (1999). Ordua Da / Braulio / Amak Dio / Zuzenean Infernura / Mundua Badoa / Itxaropen Galdua / Tartalo / Putrearen Balsa / Bizia.

ISTORIO TRISTE BAT, IZ Rock (2001). Alaitz Infernuan / Heriotz Antzerkia / Braulio / Hizkuntza / Ikus Gabea / Maitasunaren Indarra / Iñor Jauna / Mio / Bideguruztean / Paranoia / Nebaren Galdera.

INSANITY, Crash Music Inc. (2003). Hate / Legen Beltza / Insanity / Black Star / Dying / Nuclear Winter / Klaustrophobia / Eternal Life / Alaitz / Only Human / Awaits You.

DIMENSION OF PAIN, Mausoleum (2006). Cannibalistic Revolution / Meet Me In The Dark / Fucking Dawn Of The Dead / When The Moon Falls / Dimension Of Pain / Calling The Black Storm / Satanic Neighborhood / Ilunpean Dituzu / War Of Wars 1 / War Of Wars 2 (Hope Without Hope).

LEPROSY

MEXICO — *Alberto Pimentel (vocals / guitar), Alex Sistem (guitar), Baudell Ayala (bass), Alejandro Cache (drums).*

Mexico City Thrash Metal band steeped in Mexican Metal tradition as LEPROSY's frontman Alberto Pimentel has a legacy with TRANSMETAL. Alarmingly, the band's first product would, a 1991 album 'Wicked Reich', issued through Führer Records, would be mis-credited to "Lepossy". Avanzada re-issued the album a year later with all new artwork and a correct band name spelling. In 1994 a Spanish version of the same recorded emerged, albeit completely re-recorded.

Pimentel would then rejoin TRANSMETAL for a further run of albums, this tenure lasting until 1998. Re-activating LEPROSY, he then united with two scene veterans, drummer Felipe Chacón from INQUISIDOR whilst former guitarist Julio Marquéz is ex-RAMSES. The December 1999 EP 'Rey De Las Bestias' novelly comprised re-workings of songs by former acts of the band members such as TRANSMETAL's 'Dios Nos Agarre Confesados', RAMSES 'Rey De Las Bestias' and INQUISIDOR's 'Palacio Negro' alongside English language versions of the same.

The 2002 album 'Devorando Sueños' included a cover version of V8's 'A Través De Los Tiempos'.

The band splintered in 2003, former personnel exiting en masse to forge modern Metal band ZAIKO, leaving Pimental to enroll an entire new cast of players including INQUISIDOR bassist Baudell Ayala. Denver records issued the 'La Maldicion' album in July of 2003.

REINO MALDITO, Discos Denver (1994). Reino Maldito / Tormento Nocturno / Cirrosis / Vicio Mortal / Alcoholica A Los 13 / Sobredosis / Encuentro Con La Muerte / Denigración Y Corrupción / 2000 Fusiles Vencidos.

LLORA CHIAPAS, Discos Denver (1998). Llora Chíapas / Resídentes Olvidados / Mirate Al Espejo / Golpe Bajo / El Antidoto / A Tomar Las Armas / Heroe Falso / Monumento A Los Caidos / Sobrevivientes / Cuba Libre.

Rey De Las Bestias EP, (1999). Tormento Nocturno / Palacio Negro / Rey De Las Bestias / Dios Nos Agarre Confesados / Nocturnal Torment / Black Palace / King Of The Beast.

DEVORANDO SUENOS, Discos Denver (2002). Rasgó Su Piel / Me Rescatas De Las Sombras / Devorando Sueños / Escupes La Daga / Cuando Mis Ojos Se Cierren / No Podrán Parar El Tren / Resplandor Infame / No Juegues Con La Vida / En Busca De La Verdad / Aguas De Muerte / A Través De Los Tiempos / No Podrán Parar El Tren.

LA MALDICION, Denver (2003). Forgotten Past / La Maldición / Bajo El Signo De Acuario / Confeso / Fila De Muerte / Espectros Terroristas / Rock And Roll / Rebelion / Vuelan Mis Neuronas / Resiste.

LESS THAN HUMAN

GREECE — *Dimitris Traskas (vocals), Dinos Chrisochoides (guitar), Greg Vartholomeos (guitar), Peter Karaphillides (bass), Apostolis Kostinos (guitar).*

LESS THAN HUMAN, based in the Kalamaria suburb of Thessaloniki, is a Metalcore band dating to 1996. Their opening demo emerged that same year, with an inaugural live performance in December to close the year. The group swiftly built a loyal fan base, with the Greek 'Metal Hammer' magazine giving particular praise for their demos, which remained on readers charts for many months.

LESS THAN HUMAN signed to the newly established London based Yperano Records label for their debut record 'To Breed True'. Working with the esteemed American producer John Cuniberti the band crafted their opening shot in no less than the famed Abbey Road Studios.

More Than Evil, Independent (2001). Life Time Pause / Kneel, Bleed, Fade / Stealth Mode / Burning Id.

TO BREED TRUE, Yperano Y-1 (2004). Mega Fool / Perfect Time To Explode / Who's Fault / Keep Your Distance / Trigger Happy / Broken By You / More Or Less Human / Suffer In Silence / Textbook Theratics / Tooth Broken / It Is Hell / ... It Can Be Heaven.

LETHAL AGGRESSION

NJ, USA — *John Saltz (vocals), Rob De Froscia (guitar), George Yeck (bass), Ken Lund (drums).*

A New Jersey Crossover Thrashcore act dating back to 1985. LETHAL AGGRESSION debuted with an infamous demo 'From The Cunt Of The Fucking Whore'. An inclusion of the track 'Corruption' on the 1987 'Complete Death II' compilation led to a 7 single 'We Just Killed Rock n' Roll' for the Colorado Premature Entombment Productions label. The 'Subliminal Erosion' album would arrive in 1990 courtesy of the French Virulence concern.

A projected album, 'Godservation', was recorded in 1991 but consigned to the vaults. The band issued a self issued collection of live material, outtakes and fan messages entitled 'The Studdering Skull Sessions' in 1992. Relapse Records would combine the demo and shelved album for a 2001 CD release.

Only vocalist John Saltz would survive from the founding line up, being joined by guitarist Dave, bass player Todd and drummer Kenny in 2001.

We Just Killed Rock n' Roll EP, Premature Entombment Productions (1987). Dicked Again! / Godservation / Lies / Hard Day / Regret End / We Just Killed Rock n' Roll.

LIFE IS HARD—BUT THAT'S NO EXCUSE, Funhouse (1989). Intro / Morbid Reality / No Scene / Fighting In The City / Spooge / War / K.D.D. / I'll Fight / Quick Pain / Wild Kingdom / Vodda Vodka / Outcast / Newscaster's Lies / Proud Johnny / F.D.A. / Cuntry Pig / Don't Break The Pack / No More Wasted Time / What You See Is What You Get / Face The Facts / Exit.

Subliminal Erosion EP, Virulence (1990). Ripple On Ice / Tomorrow Comes Around / Stuck Fuk / D'So Shall D'Kay / Spooge 2 / At Last / Dyaneticide Ineluctable.

FROM THE CUNT OF THE FUCKING WHORE, Relapse RLP6484 (2001). Spooge / Vodda Vodka / Cuntry Pig / Morbid Reality / Anarcheology / Metallic Rage / Lust / L'Amour's radio spot / So Dead Alive / Regret / Godservation / Tomorrow Comes Around / Gone Fishin' / Co-exist Within Myself / ??? / Circle Of Hate / What Ya Tryin' To Do? / Lies / Stuk Fuck / Six Inches Of Steel / Dyaneticide / The Great One / Subconcious Nirvana / Ripple On Ice / Rye Whiskey / Drugcore / Brik Life / Beh Chicka Deh Det / Yes / Subliminal Erosion / Stuck In A Rut / Learn That Poem (Outro).

LEVIATHAN

CO, USA — *Jeff Ward (vocals), Ronnie Skeen (guitar), John Lutzow (guitar), Derek Blake (bass), Trevor Heffer (drums).*

Progressive Thrash out of Colorado and named after JAG PANZER vocalist Harry Conklin's pseudonym 'Leviathan' adopted whilst fronting his side act SATAN'S HOST. Musically LEVIATHAN's early works are somewhat akin to technical Euro Thrash but as the act's career moved forward they would tone down considerably. LEVIATHAN was forged during 1989 by former SONIC FURY guitar players Steve Fugate and Ronnie Skeen. Fugate would decamp in 1991, making way for John Lutzow.

The debut 1992 album sees a line up of mainstay guitarists Ronnie Skeen and John Lutzow, vocalist Tom Braden and a rhythm section of bassist James Escobedo and drummer Ty Tammeus. For the sophomore 1994 record 'Deepest Secrets Beneath' Braden was usurped by Jack Aragon.

LEVIATHAN switched to the German Century Media concern for 1996's 'Riddles, Secrets, Poetry And Outrage'. The band had changed radically both musically and in the personnel department veering into a straight Progressive Rock direction fronted by new singer Jeff Ward. LEVIATHAN had also summoned up a fresh team of bass player Derek Blake and drummer Trevor Heffer.

Although LEVIATHAN would stabilise it's line up for 1997's 'Scoring The Chapter' little has been heard since.

Ronnie Skeen did venture outside of LEVIATHAN for a Prog Power Metal concept IRON FORTRESS in league with vocalist Tim Lawrence. This outfit released an eponymous album through Germany's Hellion label.

LEVIATHAN, (1992). Fear Of Change / Degenerating Paradise / Two Roads To Nowhere / Beast Of Burden / Leviathan.
DEEPEST SECRETS BENEATH, RTN RTN 41201 (1994). Confidence Not Arrogance / Sanctuary / The Calling / Painful Pursuit Of Passion And Purpose / Not Always Lost / The Falling Snow / Run Forever / Disenchanted Dreams (Of Conformity) / Speed Kills.
RIDDLES, SECRETS, POETRY AND OUTRAGE, Century Media (1996). Census Of Stars / Mindless Game Control / Madness Endeavor / Pages Of Time / Are First Loves Forgotten? / So Where Is God? / Confusion / Don't Look To Me / Passion Above All Else.
SCORING THE CHAPTERS, Corrosive CRD 77362 (1997). Salvation / Friends Imaginary / Paying The Toll / The Door / J. Christopher's Haunting / If These Walls Could Talk / All Sins Returned / Scar Barrow's Fare / The Last King Of The Highlands / Born Unto (But Don't Belong To Me) / Leftist Out / Turning Up Broken / Failing Avalon / Apologies Wanting To Make Good / Legacy Departing.

LIGHT THIS CITY

SAN FRANCISCO, CA, USA — *Laura Nichol (vocals), Brian Forbes (guitar), Nick Koenig (guitar), Mike Dias (bass), Ben Murray (drums).*

The San Francisco trio of vocalist Laura Nichol, bassist Mike Dias and drummer Ben Murray founded LIGHT THIS CITY in 2002, aiming to fuse NWoSDM with the classic Bay Area Thrash sound. After issue of the September 2003 album 'The Hero Cycle', delivered by Reflections of Ruin Records, the group shed the guitar team of Tyler Gamlen and Steven Shirley and duly inducted new guitarists Brian Forbes and Nick Koenig.

LIGHT THIS CITY signed to Prosthetic Records in 2005. Second offering 'Remains Of The Gods' was recorded by producer Zack Ohren at Castle Ultimate Studios in Oakland during March 2006. THE BLACK DAHLIA MURDER vocalist Trevor Strnad guested. Prosthetic issued 'Facing The Thousand' in September 2006. Concerts in December had the band aligned with ION DISSONANCE, NIGHTS LIKE THESE and AS BLOOD RUNS BLACK.

LIGHT THIS CITY filmed their first video, for the song 'The Unwelcome Savior', in Los Angeles during early February 2007 with Director Darren Doane. US touring to coincide witnessed dates alongside ALL THAT REMAINS, after which they confirmed a support slot on a two week tour with fellow California bands THE FACELESS and ANTAGONIST throughout February and March, closing this run with an appearance at the Santa Ana 'California Metalfest'. The band then featured on the April 'School of Rock' nationwide tour flanking HORSE THE BAND, THE NUMBER TWELVE LOOKS LIKE YOU and SO MANY DYNAMOS before acting as support to ALL THAT REMAINS in May.

VITAL REMAINS teamed up with LIGHT THIS CITY and WITH PASSION for summer US shows.

THE HERO CYCLE, Reflections Of Ruin ROR001 (2004).
REMAINS OF THE GODS, Prosthetic (2005). Remains Of The Gods / Obituary / Guardian In A Passerby / Hunt / Letter To My Abuser / Fractured By The Fall / Static Masses / Guiding The North Star / Your Devoted Victim / Last Catastrophe.
FACING THE THOUSAND, Prosthetic (2006). Facing The Thousand / Cradle For A King / The Unwelcome Savior / Exile / Maddening Swarm / City Of The Snares / The Eagle / Fear Of Heights / Tracks Of Decay / Like Every Song's Our Last.

LIVING DEATH

GERMANY — *Thorsten Bergmann (vocals), Reiner Kelch (guitar), Frank Fricke (guitar), Dieter Kelch (bass), Andreas Oberhoff (drums).*

Extreme Thrash Metal act that attracted a sizable European cult following despite being dismissed by many critics, LIVING DEATH were formed by the Kelch brothers, guitarist Reiner and bassist Dieter, with guitarist Frank Fricke. The group's debut album, 'Vengeance Of Hell', was produced by Alex Thubeauville.

The 'Vengeance Of Hell' album is, naturally, very prehistoric in sound compared to what the group later achieved, so whilst Metal fans either loved its rawness or dismissed it as the worst record they'd ever heard, LIVING DEATH slowly but surely progressed. The Kelch brothers more than most, both later appeared anonymously as part of the MEKONG DELTA project albums.

Releasing the band's second album, 'Metal Revolution' in 1986 the group would eventually be signed to Aaarg Records, although the 'Back To The Weapons' EP was severely censored by the European record industry for its cover art depicting scenes of extreme violence. Copies without a rather large white circular sticker (which, if removed cause severe damage to the sleeve) covering the offending image are extremely hard to find.

By 1988 the band had truncated their title from LIVING DEATH to L.D. and issued the 'World's Neuroses' album. Shortly after its release the Kelch brothers quit and ex-VIOLENT FORCE vocalist Lemmy joined the band. The group's last public line up featured drummer Frank Ulrich, a veteran of MENDACIOUS MESSIAH and X WILD.

LIVING DEATH adopted a name change to SACRED CHAOS in January 1989. By 1990 Fricke had created LAOS for a solitary album in collusion with ex-AVENGER, RAGE and MEKONG DELTA drummer Jörg Michael.

Ultimately, LIVING DEATH drummer Atomic Steif joined SODOM in 1994. Ex-STS 8 MISSION man Rainer Schmitz, drummer with LIVING DEATH between 1995 and 2000, subsequently united with AXE LA CHAPELLE and came back to the fore with Progressive Metal band OVER US EDEN.

VENGEANCE OF HELL, Mausoleum SKULL 8360 (1984). You And Me / Living Death / Nightlight / My Victim / Labyrinth / Heavy Metal Hurricane / Hellpike / Riding A Virgin / Vengeance Of Hell.
Watch Out, Earthshaker ESM 4007 (1985). Watch Out / You And Me / Heavy Metal Hurricane / Night Light.
Back To The Weapons EP, Aaargg AAARRG 2 (1986). Nuclear Greetings / Bloody Dance / The Way (Your Soul Must Go) / Child Of Illusion.

LIVING DEATH

METAL REVOLUTION, Earthshaker ES 4012 (1986). Killing Machine / Grippin' A Heart / Rulers Must Come / Screaming From A Chamber / Intro / Shadow Of The Dawn / Panic And Hysteria / Road Of Destiny / Deep In Hell.
PROTECTED FROM REALITY, Aaarrg AAARRG 5 (1987). Horrible Infanticide (Part One) / Manilla Terror / Nature's Death / Wood Of Necrophiliacs / Vengeance / Horrible Infanticide (Part Two) / Intruder / The galley / War of independence / Eisbein (Mit Sauerkraut).
Eisbein (Mit Sauerkraut), Aaarrg AAARRG 9 (1987). Eisbein (Mit Sauerkraut) / Horrible Infanticide / Vengeance.
Living Death Live, Aaarrg AAARRG 12 (1988). Killing Machine (Live) / Grippin' A Heart (Live) / Road Of Destiny (Live) / Screaming From A Chamber (Live).
WORLD'S NEUROSES, Aaarrg AAARRG 15 (1988). Last Birthday / Die Young / Schizophrenia / On The 17th Floor / Down / World's Neuroses / Bastard At The Bus Stop / Sacred Chao / Tuesday.
KILLING IN ACTION, Intercord IRS 986.944 (1991). Killing In Action / Hang 'Em High / Dire Weak Up / Hearteater / Polymorphic / World Weariness / Die For (For What We Lie For) / Stand Up / Tribute Of Gutter / Daily Life.
METAL REVOLUTION, ABS Classics 100 (1996). Killing Machine / Grippin' A Heart / Rulers Must Come / Screaming From A Chamber / Intro / Shadow Of The Dawn / Panic And Hysteria / Road Of Destiny / Deep In Hell.

LORDES WERRE

FL, USA — *Scott Carroll (vocals), Ben Meyer (guitar), Rob Elliott (guitar), James Garber (bass), Ben Elliott (drums).*

LORDES WERRE, created in 1993, featured NASTY SAVAGE, GARDY-LOO and LOWBROW credited guitarist Ben Meyer and SEPHIROTH guitarist Rob Elliott. The band, purveying pure Thrash Metal, made their first mark with the 1994 demo 'The Dark Ascension'. An EP, 'Canticles Of Armageddon' followed in 1996. Later that year James "Hellstorm" Garber enrolled on bass and Ben Meyer took up position on lead guitar for the album 'Demon Crusades'. However, the recordings were then put into stasis as Rob Elliott was jailed. Upon his release, the group drafted Scott Carroll of CIANIDE to lay down vocals to complete the record.

With the dissolution of the band Rob Elliott founded Indiana Black-Death Metal band NECRODEMON.

DEMON CRUSADES, R.I.P. (1999). Intro—Earthen Lake / The Lordes Werre / Apocalypse / Disguised Seduction (Chant Of Making I) / Welcome To Your Death / The Old Thing In A Ground / Absorbed Into Obscurity / Nightmares.

LORDS OF DARKNESS

GUADALAJARA, MEXICO — *Lord Dekral (vocals / bass), Lord Goradragh (guitar), Lord Volker (guitar), Lord Raxemmv (drums).*

LORDS OF DARKNESS is a Guadalajara based, Power styled Black Metal band convened in October of 2000. The founding quintet comprised singer Martín Guerrero, guitarists Lord Goradragh Silentium Eternus and Leonel Zapién, bassist Lord Odium Dekral and drummer Lord Fáfner. Guitarist Lord Goradragh Silentium Eternus entered the fold in 2001 with second guitarist Lord Volker enrolling the following year. LORDS OF DARKNESS first committed themselves to the recording studio for the 2002 demo 'Valley Of Tears'. By this stage original drummer Lord Fáfner bowed out in 2003 and the band persevered by utilising the stand in services of Abraham Banda of EK and MELANCHOLY.

A demo, 'The Night Of Raven Comes ...', was delivered in 2004.

Valley Of Tears, Pancho Villa (2002). Sempiternal Torment / Valley Of Tears / Legions Of Hell / L'abbraccio Di Morte.
THE NIGHT OF RAVEN COMES ..., Lords Of Darkness (2003). In The Night Of Raven / Valley Of Tears / Nocturnalis Vento Silente.
INFERNAL MALEVOLENCE, Pancho Villa (2005). Ice Winds / Infernal Malevolence / Anathema / The Wood Of Fallen Angels / Carnal Rites / Rotten Cross / Extermination / Valley Of Tears.

LOS SIN NOMBRE

LINKÖPING, SWEDEN — *Pär Palm (vocals), Saul Camara (guitar), Jimmie Fornell (guitar), Jack Karlsson (bass), Steve Mills (drums).*

Linköping Death Metal band LOS SIN NOMBRE was created during February 2002, initially as an ENTOMBED covers outfit. The founding line-up comprised guitarists Arvid and Saul Camara, of CHAMBER OF TORMENT, SOLE SHAKER and DRAGQUEEN LIPSTICK, bassist Jack Karlsson, of Punk band THE FISTICUFFS, and drummer Steve Mills, a veteran of VICIOUS, CHAMBER OF TORMENT and DRAGQUEEN LIPSTICK. A first demo, 'Tate Murders' featuring narration taken from Charles Manson's parole speech in the title track, was recorded with newly installed singer Pär Palm in September 2002. Arvid exited, being replaced by Jimmie Fornell of THE FISTICUFFS, THE MISUNPASSED and VICIOUS. Second session 'Down With Pressure' was recorded in January 2004. A third demo arrived in May 2005.

Tate Murders, Los Sin Nombres (2002). Hate / Inside My Head / Still Standing / Tate Murders.
Down With Pressure, (2004). Down With Pressure / Dust / Empire.
Los Sin Nombre, (2005). Chain Reaction / Internal Bleeding / Leave This Soul / Out Of Hell / War.

LOST CENTURY

DÜSSELDORF, GERMANY — *Andreas Lohse (vocals), Martin Bayer (guitar), Jens Schäfer (guitar), Rudi Görg (bass), Jason Kubke (drums).*

Düsseldorf Thrash band including ex-APOSTASY vocalist Andreas Lohse and former members of RESEARCH. LOST CENTURY's first demo of May 1991 'Miserality' featured original guitarist Phillip who left prior to the second demo that December entitled 'A Truth Beyond'. Guitar duties for this tape were handled by Stefan.

Stefan quit before recording of the debut album, 1993's 'Natural Process Of Progression', began and, after its release, the group toured Germany opening for POLTERGEIST and CORONER. 'Complex Microcosm' followed in 1994 with 'Poetic Atmosphere Of Seasons' arriving the following year, both issued by T&T Records.

Lohse and guitarist Jens Schäfer founded Progressive Metal act THOUGHT SPHERE releasing the 2000 album 'Vague Horizons'. The LOST CENTURY trio of vocalist / bassist Rudi Görg, guitarist Martin Bayer and drummer Jason Kubke all went on to forge ZYKLON X. Görg and Kubke forged 21ST CENTURY KILLING MACHINE in 2005.

NATURAL PROCESS OF PROGRESSION, DMP 021-93 (1993). The End / Submit To Stagnation / Cling To The Unreal / Delivering The Sentence, Part I: Birth, Part II: Murder, Part III: Conviction And Death / Trivial (Towards Destination).

COMPLEX MICROCOSM-MOVEMENT IN NINE RITUALS, T&T-Noise TT11-2 (1994). Descending / Silent Inside / Like The One Above / Fallen Star / Second Coming / Wind In The Willows / Life Itself / Traverse The Veil / Complex Microcosm.

POETIC ATMOSPHERE OF SEASONS, T&T TT 0018-2 (1995). Seal Of Thorns / Autumn's Gift / Unicorn / Breathing Underwater: Death / Last Days Of Spring / Winter Twilight / Kryogenic / Summer's Dishonest Apologies / Search / Owe Me Awe.

LOW TWELVE

BLOOMINGTON, IN, USA — *Pete Altieri (vocals / bass), Tim McCleland (guitar), Les Aldridge (guitar), Wes Pollock (drums).*

Bloomington, Illinois Metal band LOW TWELVE came together as a trio of former SACRED OATH vocalist / bassist Pete Alteri, guitarist Tim McCleland and drummer Steve Chestney in mid 1998. The band augmented their sound with the addition of second guitarist Les Aldridge in that December. In November of the following year Chestney was usurped by Wes Pollock, this revised line up cutting the debut demo 'Blunt Force Trauma'.

Reviews were solid and LOW TWELVE succeeded in selling over a 1000 copies of the demo, leading in turn to the EP 'Kill Floor'.

The band has proved active on the live front, credited with over 100 gigs during 2000 including headline slots at such Midwest festival events as 'Stomp Fest '99', 'Poser Roast 2000' and the '9 Mile Mosh Fest'.

The band would self finance the 'Flesh Of The Weak' album, adding four live recordings to the new studio material. Sadly Tim McCleland passed away during February of 2002 and LOW TWELVE opted to persevere without finding a replacement. The band prepared to release a split album with UNFIT FOR HUMAN OCCUPANCY for late 2002.

LOW TWELVE signed to the Chicago based label Rotting Corpse Records in December 2005 for a new album entitled 'This Side Toward Enemy'. Gary Meskil of PRO-PAIN provided session vocals.

FLESH OF THE WEAK, D-Day (2000). Brutal World / Begging To Die / Twelve / Trench / Enemy Of The State / S-21 / Meltdown / Crawlspace / Kill Floor / Thin Skinned / Sex Sin Sermon / Kill Floor (Live) / S-21 (Live) / Begging To Die (Live) / Enemy Of The State (Live) / Twelve (Extended intro).

LUDICHRIST

NEW YORK, NY, USA — *Tommy Christ (vocals), Glen Cummings (guitar), Joe Butcher (guitar), Chuck Valle (bass), Al Batross (drums).*

New York Crossover Punk metal act LUDICHRIST's first album, 1986's 'Immaculate Deception', boasts hardcore guests Roger Miret of AGNOSTIC FRONT plus LEE WAY's Eddie Sutton, NUCLEAR ASSAULT's John Connelly and CRUMBSUCKERS Chris Notaro. The band fractured between albums retaining only vocalist Tommy Christ and guitarist Glen Cummings. For the 'Powertrip' effort they were joined by guitarist Paul Nieder, bassist Mike Walters and drummer Dave Miranda. Ex LUDICHRIST bassist Chuck Valle joined MURPHY'S LAW in 1989.

Following this release Miranda lost his position to former WHIPLASH and ZERO HOUR noted speed drummer Tony Scaglione who had just finished deputising for DAVE LOMBARDO in SLAYER. The liaison was brief however and Scaglione departed in October 1988 to join RAGING SLAB.

LUDICHRIST toured Europe supporting the likes of AGNOSTIC FRONT, SUICIDAL TENDENCIES and BAD BRAINS. LUDICHRIST split in 1990 with Tommy Christ, Glenn Cummings and Paul Nieder forming SCATTERBRAIN to record a self-titled album for In-Effect.

Drummer Dave Miranda later found Progressive Jazz Rock trio THE MAGIC ELF, releasing two albums 'Elf Tales' and 'Live'. Miranda is also a member of SIX AND VIOLENCE.

Both LUDICHRIST and SCATTERBRAIN reunited for a one-off performance at B.B. King Blues Club & Grill in New York City on February 23rd 2007.

IMMACULATE DECEPTION, Combat Core (1986). Fire At The Firehouse / Most People Are Dicks / Murder Bloody Murder / Blown Into The Arms Of Christ / Big Business / Only As Directed / Games Once Played / Green Eggs And Ham / Immaculate Deception / You Can't Have Fun / Government Kids / Legal Murder / Down With The Ship / Thinking Of You / Tylenol / Mengele / Young, White And Well Behaved / Last Train To Clarksville / God Is Everywhere.

POWERTRIP, Combat 88561-8246-1 (1988). Powertrip / Zad / Stuff To Fill Graves / The Tip Of My Mind / Damage Done / T.B.O.S. (Barbiere Di Siviglia) / This Party Sucks / Johnnypump / Yesterday For You / And So It Goes / The Well Dressed Man Disguise / Iwo Jima (That Manly Smell) / One For The Road.

LUNGSPIT

HÄSSLEHOLM, SWEDEN — *Tobias Persson (vocals / guitar), Mikael Persson (guitar), Richard Topgaard (bass), Marcus Nilsson (drums).*

LUNGSPIT is a Hässleholm Death Metal outfit. Strangely, the band had been formulated by NUGGETS drummer Tobias Persson as an Alt-Grunge styled unit during 1997, taking on a formative title of STARLA after the SMASHING PUMPKINS song. A concert debut included a cover version of NIRVANA's 'School' but shortly afterward the group's entire musical axis was tipped on its head when Persson was loaned a cassette of MACHINE HEAD by bass player Richard Topgaard.

Dropping original drummer Fidde the band evolved into LUNGSPIT, adopting this brand after a favoured MACHINE HEAD homebrew "Satan's Lungspit". With Marcus Nilsson of BEEFWAX installed on drums, first product would be a September 1998 demo cassette 'Give Me A Reason', preceding the full-length album 'Beautiful Musical Violence' that November. LUNGSPIT's next outing, having acquired second guitarist Mikael Persson, would be a self-financed EP recorded at Studio Senôrita and delivered in October 1999, entitled 'In Hollow Blindness'. Frontman Tobias Persson (a.k.a. 'Rotten Boy') switched roles to that of drummer to join Kalmar's VISCERAL BLEEDING.

Give Me A Reason, Lungspit (1998) (Demo). Betrayal / A Better Place / Give Me A Reason.

BEAUTIFUL MUSICAL VIOLENCE, Lungspit (1998). Betrayal / A Better Place / Give Me A Reason / Feasting With The Devil / Broken Bitterness / Confused Confusion / Psychotic Minds.

In Hollow Blindness, Lungspit (1999). In Hollow Blindness / Organic Cage / Hail The New World Order / Eyes Sewn Shut.

LYZANXIA

ANJOU, FRANCE — *David Potvin (vocals / guitar), Franck Potvin (vocals / guitar), Eguil Voisin (bass), Gweltaz Kerjan (drums).*

French Thrashers LYZANXIA came together in Anjou during 1996, assembled by ex-OVERLOAD guitarist David Potvin. LYZANXIA debuted with the four song demo 'Rip My Skin' before issuing the self financed 1998 album 'Lullabye'. LYZANXIA at this juncture saw Potvin, on lead vocals and guitar, joined by colleagues rhythm guitarist Franck Potvin, bassist Eguil Voisin with Gweltaz Kerjan on drums. Japanese editions of 'Eden' added a bonus song 'Cured'. The group signed to Wargram Music for the second outing 'Eden', produced by producers Fredrik Nordström and Don Romano 666 at Backstage studios. Guest musicians included backing vocalist Guillaume Bideau, secondary vocalist Audrey Forest on tracks 'Lost' and 'Terrible Old Man' plus keyboard player Bastid Rysmo.

The band cut their third album, 'Mindcrimes', again with producers Fredrik Nordström and Don Romano 666. Regular drummer Gweltaz Kerjan injured his arm prior to recording necessitating Dirk Verbeuren of SCARVE taking over on a session basis. The Japanese variant of 'Mindcrimes', released by the King label, added two exclusive tracks 'COG' and 'Endless Sphere'. LYZANXIA signed to the US Reality Entertainment label to issue 'Mindcrimes' in North America for March 2004. The band headed up a four week, September US nationwide 'Harsh Reality' tour in union with FREAKHOUSE and Swiss act SYBREED.

LYZANXIA parted ways with Gael Ferret in April 2005, drafting new drummer Clement Decrock. The group utilised Studio Fredman in Gothenburg, Sweden in January 2006 with producer Fredrik Nordström to craft a third album entitled 'Unsu'. Guitarist Jona Weinhofen and Ed Butcher, from Australian act I KILLED THE PROM QUEEN, recorded guest appearances on the track 'Path Blade'.

In May 2006 LYZANXIA signed with Listenable Records for their third album, 'Unsu', for September release. That same month LYZANXIA supported SOILWORK on a UK tour. LYZANXIA were added to the European tour featuring CRUMB-SUCKERS and THE ACCUSED beginning in early February 2007. However, these shows never eventuated.

Rip My Skin, Lyzanxia (1996) (Demo). Rip My Skin / Resurrection / Lucrece Borgia / You Don't Deserve A Name.
LULLABYE, (1998). Trepan / Hurricane / You Don't Deserve A Name / Loving Fear / Manhunt / Rip My Skin / Totem / The Slave Cross / My Prisoner / Lucrece Borgia / Resurrection.
EDEN, Lucretia LU20008-2 (2001). Dream Feeder / Addicted / Lost / Medicine Slave / Bewitched / Labyrinth / Terrible Old Man / Positronic / Eden / Dome.
MINDCRIMES, Trepan (2002). Time Dealer / Medulla Need / Damnesia / Mindsplit / Dusk / Gametime / My Blank Confession / Black Side / Silence Code / D.M. / Fugitive / Glass Bones.
UNSU, Listenable (2006). Wise Counselor / Path Blade / Ache Power Control / Early Phases / Strength Core / Bled Out / Unsu / X ï¿½ Modification / Tedium / Answer Fields / Ascention / Defensive Heart.

LÄÄZ ROCKIT

SAN FRANCISCO, CA, USA — *Michael Coons (vocals), Aaron Jellum (guitar), Phil Kettner (guitar), Willy Lange (bass), Victor Agnello (drums).*

San Francisco Heavy Metal act LÄÄZ ROCKIT vied for attention amidst a wave of Thrash Metal bands, unfortunately having their profile suffer simply because of timing. The band was formed by vocalist Michael Coons and guitarist Aaron Jellum who stole second guitarist Phil Kettner from a rival local outfit. The inaugural bass player Dave Starr actually named the band (after a sci-fi weapon in a Clint Eastwood movie) as in their formative days they were called DEPTH CHARGE.

Having added drummer Victor Agnello to the ranks, LÄÄZ ROCKIT replaced Starr in 1983 with Willy Lange (Langenhuizen) following a support slot to RATT. Starr created power trio BLACK LEATHER before joining VICIOUS RUMOURS. LÄÄZ ROCKIT was originally signed to RATT manager Marshall Berle's Timecoast label, but Berle disbanded the company once his charges had been picked up by Atlantic Records, leaving the door open for Mark Leonard's Target concern to sign the group, releasing the debut 'City's Gonna Burn' album in September 1984.

LÄÄZ ROCKIT began a tour of North America in support of their debut album as opening act to GRIM REAPER and EXCITER, but would be unceremoniously removed after three shows. Lange would audition for the position of bassist for METALLICA in 1986.

With 'Know Your Enemy' gaining the band more media attention LÄÄZ ROCKIT managed some European shows opening for MOTÖRHEAD and a slot on the prestigious Aardschock Festival in Holland. Agnello departed, but returned in time for American dates. Further British shows saw the band opening for EXODUS.

The band toured Europe with support from Dutchmen OSIRIS in 1989. The 1991 album 'Nothing Sacred' saw Coons and Jellum joined by bassist Scott Dominguez, guitarist Scott Sargeant and drummer Dave Chavarri. Ex-LÄÄZ ROCKIT guitarist Ken Savitch joined Illinois's SINDROME during 1991. Erstwhile band members would also turn up on the 1993 Japanese released 'Fix' album credited to GACK. Guitarist Scott Sargeant also joined WREKKING MACHINE for a tenure.

Sargeant subsequently joined KILLING CULTURE before teaming up with SKINLAB in 1998. Chavarri joined PRO-PAIN and temped for SOULFLY prior to founding ILL NINO. Another act with LÄÄZ ROCKIT connections arrived in 2000 with the formation of WARNING S.F. (actually a reincarnation of early eighties act WARNING) seeing guitarists Wayne Jellum and Jon Torres joining forces with MY VICTIM singer Torre Carstensen and OLD GRANDAD drummer Will Carroll. By August 2002 Sergeant would be revealed as working up a new project billed as MURDER LEAGUE ALL-STARS in league with the M.O.D. pairing of controversial frontman Billy Milano and Tim McMurtrie on bass.

The classic LÄÄZ ROCKIT line-up of vocalist Mike Coons, guitarists Aaron Jellum and Phil Kettner, bassist Willy Lange and Victor Agnello re-united for an appearance at the 'Dynamo Open Air' festival on 7th May 2005 in Hellendoorn, the Netherlands, by coincidence sharing the stage with reformed 80s era line-ups for both ANTHRAX and TESTAMENT.

On 9th July 2005 the band lined up at The Pound outdoor amphitheatre in San Francisco alongside TESTAMENT, VICIOUS RUMORS, DREAMS OF DAMNATION, HIRAX, AGENT STEEL, DEKAPITATOR, MUDFACE, NEIL TURBIN, BROCAS HELM and IMAGIKA for the 'Thrash Against Cancer' benefit.

In mid 2006 the world of Thrash Metal received a pleasant surprise with the announcement of a new San Francisco based collective project billed DUBLIN DEATH PATROL. (Dublin is a San Francisco suburb). This unit was assembled by a seasoned cast of veterans, featuring LÄÄZ ROCKIT's Willy Langenhuizen, comprising TESTAMENT and RAMPAGE singer Chuck Billy, former EXODUS and LEGACY vocalist Steve "Zetro" Souza, MACHINE HEAD, DEATH PENALTY, METAL WARRIOR and VIO-LENCE man Phil Demmel on guitar, guitarist Andy Billy of SACRED DOG, RAMPAGE and GUILT, RAMPAGE guitarist Greg Bustamante, OUT OF CONTROL guitarist Steve Robello, bassist John Souza and drummer Danny Cunningham.

LÄÄZ ROCKIT put in another high profile European festival show at the 'Keep It True' event at the Tauberfrankenhalle in Lauda-Königshofen, Germany on April 14th 2007 alongside British bands DIAMOND HEAD and SABBAT, fellow US outfits LETHAL and TWISTED TOWER DIRE, Denmark's ARTILLERY, Canadians CAULDRON and PILEDRIVER, Dutchmen DEFENDER and Swedish band BULLET.

CITY'S GONNA BURN, Target TE 1344 (1984). City's Gonna Burn / Caught In The Act / Take No Prisoners / Dead Man's Eyes / Forced To Fight / Silent Scream / Prelude / Something More.
NO STRANGER TO DANGER, Steamhammer 081866 (1985). Dreams Die Hard / I've Got Time / Town To Town / Backbreaker / Stand Alone / Spared From The Fire / Off The Deep End / Tonight Alive / Wrecking Machine.
KNOW YOUR ENEMY, Music For Nations MFN 81 (1987). Demolition / Last Breath / Euroshima / Most Dangerous Game / Shot To Hell / Say Goodbye M.F. / Self Destruct / Means To An End / I'm Electric / Mad Axe Attack / Shit's Ugly.
ANNIHILATION PRINCIPLE, Enigma CDENV 521 (1989). Mirror Into Madness / Chasin' Charlie / Fire In The Hole / Shadow Company / Holiday In Cambodia / Mob Justice / Bad Blood.
Holiday In Cambodia, Roadracer RO 24361 (1990). Holiday In Cambodia / Mirror To Madness / Prelude To Death (Live) / Forced To Fight (Live).

TASTE OF REBELLION—LIVE, (1991). In The Name Of The Father And The Gun ... / Greed Machine / Fire In The Hole / City's Gonna Burn / Leatherface / The Omen / Suicide City / The Enemy Within / Prelude To Death / Into The Asylum / Holiday In Cambodia / Curiosity Kills.

NOTHING SACRED, Roadracer (1991). In The Name Of The Father And The Gun / Into The Asylum / Greed Machine / Too Far Gone / Curiosity Kills / Suicide City / The Enemy Within / Nobody's Child / Silence Is A Lie / Necropolis.

MACE

EVERETT, WA, USA — *Kirk Vehey (vocals), Dave Hillis (guitar), Vern White (bass), Shane White (drums).*

Everett, Washington Thrash act that debuted as a trio on the 'Metal Massacre V' album. MACE at that juncture comprised lead vocalist and drummer Vence De Rose, guitarist Dave Hillis and bassist Kirk Verhey. Although the song was mis-credited on the sleeve as 'Marching Saprophytes', it was in fact titled 'Marching Sacrifice', as correctly listed on another compilation, Ground Zero's 1984 collection 'Northwest Metalfest'.

Verhey would take over the lead vocal position in time for 1985's debut 'Process Of Elimination'. Shane White departed before the second album and MACE drafted drummer David Kopler.

Post MACE guitarist Dave Hillis would play an integral role in the rise of Seattle Grunge acting as producer for acts such as ALICE IN CHAINS, BLIND MELON and even PEARL JAM. Hillis would also co-found SNOWBALL with erstwhile FEMME FATALE vocalist Lorraine Lewis.

PROCESS OF ELIMINATION, Restless (1985). S.U.B.C. / Smoking Gun / The Introduction / Violent World / Drilling Brains / Marine Corpse / Act Of War / Room 101 / M.A.C.E.

THE EVIL IN GOOD, Black Dragon BD023 (1987). Gutripper / Intent To Kill / The Evil In Good / Daddy's Girl / War / Thinning The Herd / Choose Your God / When The Screaming Stops / Poison Gases / Blonde Obsession.

MACHINE HEAD

OAKLAND, CA, USA — *Robb Flynn (vocals / guitar), Phil Demmel (guitar), Adam Duce (bass), Dave McClain (drums).*

Oakland's brutal Metal act MACHINE HEAD was founded by ex-VIO-LENCE man Robb Flynn in 1992. Previous to VIO-LENCE, Flynn had a lengthy spell with FORBIDDEN, although this was when the band was known pre-debut album as FORBIDDEN EVIL. Relative latecomers in the Thrash explosion, Bay Area's VIO-LENCE nevertheless managed to scramble onto a major deal offered by MCA Mechanic during 1988, original guitarist Troy Fua having been superseded by Rob Flynn. In this incarnation the group put out the album's 'Eternal Nightmare' in 1988 and 'Oppressing The Masses' during 1990. Following issue of the now scarce 'Torture Tactics' EP, Flynn exited and VIO-LENCE only managed one further album without him before crumbling.

Flynn was keen to set about forging an all new band unit, pulling in guitarist Logan Mader and bass player Adam Duce. Drummer Chris Kontos was ex-ATTITUDE ADJUSTMENT and also then an active member of GRINCH and VERBAL ABUSE. However, an early incarnation of the band featured former POSSESSED drummer Walter Ryan. Considerably ratcheting up the aggression of Flynn's antecedent works, the very first MACHINE HEAD song to be worked up would be the frightening 'Death Church'.

Soon snagging a deal with Roadrunner Records the band debuted live with an American tour opening for NAPALM DEATH and OBITUARY. The opening MACHINE HEAD album, August 1994's 'Burn My Eyes', recorded at Fantasy Studios in Berkley, California with producer Colin Richardson, made an immediate international impact due to its then revolutionary blend of trad Thrash, groove-oriented Hardcore and modern breakdown persuasions. Embroiled in controversy from the outset, the infamous lyric to 'Davidian', Flynn hollering "Let freedom ring with a shotgun blast!", soon had the track removed from radio airplay. Impressively, the debut muscled its way onto the UK charts at number 25, this first success signalling the start of steadfast appreciation in this territory.

Following the release of 'Burn My Eyes' MACHINE HEAD toured North America as part of the 'Divine Intourvention' roadshow alongside BIOHAZARD and headliners SLAYER. Gigs in August saw the band packaged with OBITUARY and NAPALM DEATH. The band continued with SLAYER as guests to their November 1994 British tour re-releasing 'Burn My Eyes' in digipack format with a bonus track, a cover of POISON IDEA's 'Alan's On Fire'. UK headline dates throughout May of 1995 saw Swedes MARY BEATS JANE as support. The group put in a high profile appearance at the 1995 'Monsters Of Rock' Castle Donington festival.

Rob Flynn engaged with METALLICA's Jason Newsted, SEPULTURA's Andreas Kisser and EXODUS man Tom Hunting on their oddball Metal venture SEXOTURICA, performing live but not featuring on the resulting album. This same illustrious quartet also worked up another one off project billed QUARTETO DA PINGA, recording at Newsted's Chophouse Studios in August 1995.

Chris Kontos joined Danes KONKHRA in 1996 and was replaced by Dave McClain, a veteran of MURDERCAR, CATALEPSY, SAN ANTONIO SLAYER and SACRED REICH. However, McClain's induction was not initially a smooth process as initially the drummer, then a member of SACRED REICH, turned the position down. MACHINE HEAD duly auditioned such figures as Tommy Buckley from SOILENT GREEN and future DOWNSET and BLOODSIMPLE drummer Chris Hamilton. Discussions were also held with future ILL NINO drummer Dave Chavarri and OZZY OSBOURNE drummer Deen Castronovo. MACHINE HEAD re-drafted Walter Ryan to fill in on European and Australian gigs whilst Will Carroll deputised in the USA. Dave McClain finally joined in December 1995.

Second album 'The More Things Change ...', again produced by Colin Richardson, witnessed a break away from the band's Thrash roots. A limited edition digipack offered three extra cuts, 'My Misery', a take on DISCHARGE's 'The Possibility Of Life's Destruction' and 'Colors', originally by ICE T. The album, breaking into the US Billboard charts at number 138 and making it to number 16 in the UK, emerged in March 1997 and MACHINE HEAD toured Britain in April supported by veteran Grindcore merchants NAPALM DEATH and newcomers SKINLAB. Further dates had the band guesting for PANTERA in Europe and MEGADETH in America. Nevertheless, Flynn found time to add guest vocals to New York Straight Edge merchant's EARTH CRISIS 'Breed The Killers' album.

The band's line-up troubles would be far from over though, as early 1998 witnessed the bitter departure of Mader to SOULFLY (and later PALE DEMONS / MEDICATION). His replacement was Ahrue Lister, a young veteran of such acts as MAN MADE GOD, HORDE OF TORMENT and PESTILENCE. As the group anticipated the recording of a third album, 'The Burning Red', Flynn revealed that a song tentatively penciled in for inclusion on the new album, 'Devil With The King's Card' was written about "a certain person who recently left the band". 'The Burning Red', somewhat obliquely sporting a rendition of THE POLICE hit 'Message In A Bottle', was crafted at Indigo Ranch in Malibu, California, this time seeing Ross Robinson behind the desk. Again a limited edition added extra tracks, sporting 'Alcoholocaust' and MACHINE HEAD's interpretation of BAD BRAINS' 'House Of Suffering'. The band's strengthening reputation put the record onto the US chart listings at number 88 and again notching up a higher credit in the UK at number 13.

Rumours surfaced in late 2000 that drummer Dave McClain had jumped ship to join SYSTEMATIC although this proved to be unfounded and MACHINE HEAD duly reared up once more in late summer of 2001 touting a new album 'Supercharger'. This set veered into a less refined Mallcore direction, evidenced by a input of rap vocals, that was unappreciated by the faithful and unfortunately a slump in support witnessed lowly chart recognition at 34 in the UK and 115 in the USA. Naturally Roadrunner published an expanded 'Supercharger', bolstered with extra songs in BLACK SABBATH cover 'Hole In The Sky', outtake 'Ten Fold' and live recordings of 'The Blood, The Sweat, The Tears' and 'Desire To Fire'.

The proposed accompanying single 'Crashing Around You' would include live versions of 'Silver' and 'Ten Ton Hammer' recorded in Sweden and produced by CANDLEMASS bassist Leif Edling. However, in the wake of the September 11th terrorist attacks, 'Crashing Around You's release, video and marketing campaign was cancelled for the American market and substituted by 'Deafening Silence'.

MACHINE HEAD put in a 'secret' San Francisco gig billed as TEN TON HAMMER in November. Bizarrely the group dressed up in MÖTLEY CRÜE stage gear and even performed 'Shout At The Devil' and 'Live Wire'!

In early 2002 a Californian court ruled that the band had the full rights to use the title 'MACHINE HEAD'. The group had faced legal action from a US sound design company, Dewey Global Holding, Inc., who claimed rights to the title dating back to 1991.

MACHINE HEAD announced a clutch of headline European festival dates for the summer of 2002 including the Finnish 'Tuska Metal' and 'Ilosaari' events, Germany's 'Full Force' and Belgium's 'Graspop'. These gigs would be scheduled to promote the band's first live album 'Hellalive', recorded in the main at London's Brixton Academy on December 8th 2001. However, as the band confirmed a further TEN TON HAMMER gig in the UK it would also be revealed that guitarist Ahrue Luster had left the fold. The erstwhile six-stringer soon revealed plans for a new band billed as SUPERNAUT in union with members of Sacramento's JUGGERNAUT, vocalist Patrick Schmidt, bassist Rob Marshall, and drummer Marty Bechtel. Robb Flynn's erstwhile VIO-LENCE colleague Phil Demmel duly plugged the gap. The incestuous relationship between MACHINE HEAD and VIO-LENCE was cemented further at the 'Milwaukee Metalfest' event when MACHINE HEAD bassist Adam Duce filled in for a honeymooning Deen Dell during VIO-LENCE's five-song set.

Soon Luster had unveiled plans for a fresh band project reportedly in union with current COAL CHAMBER bassist Nadja Peulen and ex-GODSMACK drummer Tommy Stewart. However, by June of 2003 the former guitarist was announced as having joined ILL NINO. Robert Flynn was reportedly approached to audition for the position of vocalist with DROWNING POOL left vacant by the death of Dave Williams. An offer he declined.

MACHINE HEAD undertook a novel experiment in early 2003, asking forum members on the band's official website to vote for cover songs they would like the band to record. After voting had whittled the tracks down to METALLICA's 'Battery', FAITH NO MORE's 'Jizzlobber' and 'Toxic Waltz' by EXODUS these were duly recorded as internet sound files. Meantime, recording of a brand new studio album, produced by Robb Flynn and Andy Sneap billed as 'Through The Ashes Of Empires', commenced in summer for October release. It would emerge that a limited run of two disc versions of the album added a collection of demo tracks and video footage.

The new record would see release through Roadrunner Records in Europe but the band severed ties with the company for North America. November European gigs saw British act KILL II THIS as support. Despite 'Through The Ashes Of Empires' being slammed in certain sectors of the UK Rock press, the album gave MACHINE HEAD a new lease of life in mainland Europe. Germany in particular proved a strong market as the album, entering the national Media Control charts at number 24, giving the band their biggest selling outing to date. MACHINE HEAD's Summer 2004 live schedule included a number of major European festival performances including both Scottish and English 'Download' events and Germany's 'Rock Am Ring'.

MACHINE HEAD re-signed to Roadrunner Record in North America to issue 'Through The Ashes Of Empires' in April of 2004, the record selling over 11,000 copies in its first week of sale to land at number 88 on the Billboard charts. The initial pressing came loaded with bonus tracks with demos, studio video and an exclusive song 'Seasons Wither'. The band set out on an extensive US Spring tour allied at first with ARCH ENEMY, GOD FORBID and 36 CRAZYFISTS. However, ARCH ENEMY pulled out after just performing one date and both GOD FORBID and 36 CRAZYFISTS vocalists were afflicted by vocal problems, thought to be strep. In early May it was Flynn's turn, a strained throat forcing the cancellation for MACHINE HEAD's Columbus, Ohio performance.

MACHINE HEAD forged an alliance with CHIMAIRA and TRIVIUM for the August 'RoadRage 2004' dates in North America. The August 8th Philadelphia Theatre of the Living Arts show would prove noteworthy as the band celebrated the tenth anniversary of their groundbreaking 'Burn My Eyes' album by performing the record in its entirety. Also performed that evening would be covers of METALLICA's 'Creeping Death', PANTERA's 'Walk', SEPULTURA's 'Roots Bloody Roots' and MÖTLEY CRÜE's 'Live Wire'. CHIMAIRA's Mark Hunter guested on vocals. Further dates saw a batch of Australian gigs in early October, followed by an extensive run of European, UK and Scandinavian shows partnered with CALIBAN and GOD FORBID. Unfortunately, an Italian show in Rome would be cancelled after their tour bus broke down on their way through Swiss Alps. For the British dates a single, 'Days Turn Blue To Gray', was launched to coincide. Once again MACHINE HEAD performed the entire 'Burn My Eyes' album on November 26th at the Academy in Manchester, this show, as well as a London Brixton Academy performance, being filmed for future DVD release.

A notable stop on MACHINE HEAD's 2005 tour schedule came on 25th March when the band, alongside THE DARKNESS and SEPULTURA, performed in Dubai in the United Arab Emirates, marking the first such occasion for a Western Metal band in the Gulf. Support came from local bands NERVECELL and JULIANA DOWN. US gigs in May saw a burst of shows allied with LAMB OF GOD then headliners with support from DEVILDRIVER, THE HAUNTED and IT DIES TODAY. The band would be forced to cancel gigs in Winston-Salem and Charlotte with Rob Flynn suffering from a "severe viral throat infection".

Robert Flynn would act as one of five high profile writers contributing to the ROADRUNNER UNITED 25th anniversary album 'The All-Stars Sessions', featuring with the tracks 'The Dagger' with vocals from Howard Jones of KILLSWITCH ENGAGE and 'The Rich Man' with vocals from Corey Taylor of SLIPKNOT. On 15th December Flynn and Adam Duce notably joined the ROADRUNNER UNITED conglomerate at the New York Nokia Theater for an all star Metal evening.

The band played their part in honouring METALLICA, contributing their rendition of 'Battery' to the album 'Remastered', this set being a complete remake of 'Master Of Puppets' in joint celebration of the twentieth anniversary of the classic album's release and the 25th anniversary of UK Rock magazine Kerrang! in April 2006. That August MACHINE HEAD, entering Sharkbite Studios in Oakland, revealed 'The Blackening' as their new album title.

In mid 2006 the world of Thrash Metal received a pleasant surprise with the announcement of a new San Francisco based collective project billed DUBLIN DEATH PATROL. (Dublin is a San Francisco suburb). This unit was assembled by a seasoned cast of veterans, featuring MACHINE HEAD guitarist

MACHINE HEAD (pic: Alex Solca)

Phil Demmel, comprising TESTAMENT and RAMPAGE singer Chuck Billy, former EXODUS and LEGACY vocalist Steve "Zetro" Souza, bassist Willy Langenhuizen, of RAMPAGE and LÄÄZ ROCKIT repute, guitarist Andy Billy of SACRED DOG, RAMPAGE and GUILT, RAMPAGE guitarist Greg Bustamante, OUT OF CONTROL guitarist Steve Robello, bassist John Souza and drummer Danny Cunningham.

Roadrunner Records re-issued MACHINE HEAD's classic 1994 debut album, 'Burn My Eyes' in January 2007, this edition adding an extra disc of previously unreleased tracks and rarities. The band packaged up with LAMB OF GOD, TRIVIUM and GOJIRA for a lengthy run of North American dates commencing on February 16th 2007 at the Palladium Ballroom in Dallas, Texas.

In March MACHINE streamed 'The Blackening' in its entirety on its Myspace page. The album then debuted on the official UK charts at number 16. 'The Blackening' sold just under 15,000 copies in the United States in its first week of release to debut at 54 on The Billboard chart, marking MACHINE HEAD's highest Billboard chart number ever. The group opened up April and May US concerts for MEGADETH and HEAVEN AND HELL.

Demo 1993, (1993). Death Church / Old / The Rage To Overcome / A Nation On Fire / (Intro) Real Lies / Fuck It All.

Infected, Roadrunner (1994). Infected / Protoplan.

BURN MY EYES, Roadrunner RR 9016-2 (1994). Davidian / Old / Thousand Eyes / None But My Own / Rage To Overcome / Death Church / I'm Your God Now / Blood For Blood / Nation On Fire / Real Eyes, Realise, Real Lies / Block. Chart position: 25 UK.

Death Church, Roadrunner (1995) (10" single). Death Church / A Nation On Fire (Demo).

Old, Roadrunner (1995). Old / Davidian (Live) / Hard Times (Live) / Death Church (Demo).

Death Church, Roadrunner (1995) (CD single). Death Church / Real Lies—Fuck It All (Demo) / Old (Demo).

Death Church, Roadrunner (1995) (CD single). Death Church / Old (Mix) / The Rage To Overcome (Demo).

Old, Roadrunner (1995). Old / A Nation On Fire (Demo) / Real Lies—Fuck It All (Demo) / Old (Demo). Chart position: 43 UK.

Old, Roadrunner (1995). Old / Death Church (Convent mix) / Old (Eve Of Apocalypse mix) / The Rage To Overcome.

Old, Roadrunner RR-23408 (1995). Old.

Take My Scars EP, Roadrunner RRCY-9012 (1997) (Japanese release). Take My Scars / Negative Creep / Ten Ton Hammer (Demo Version) / Struck A Nerve (Demo Version) / Take My Scars (Live) / Struck a Nerve (Live) / Thousand Lies (Live) / Blood for Blood (Live) / Violate (Live).

Take My Scars, Roadrunner RR 2257-3 (1997) (CD single). Take My Scars / Negative Creep / Take My Scars (Live) / Blood For Blood (Live). Chart position: 73 UK.

Take My Scars, Roadrunner RR 2257-5 (1997) (CD single). Take My Scars / Negative Creep / Ten Ton Hammer (Demo) / Struck A Nerve (Demo).

THE MORE THINGS CHANGE . . . , Roadrunner RR 8860-2 (1997). Ten Ton Hammer / Take My Scars / Struck A Nerve / Down To None / The Frontlines / Spine / Bay Of Pigs / Violate / Blistering / Blood Of The Zodiac. Chart positions: 16 UK, 17 SWEDEN, 21 FRANCE, 138 USA.

YEAR OF THE DRAGON, Roadrunner RRCY-19021 (1999) (Japanese release). Desire To Fire / Take My Scars / Blood, the Sweat, The Tears / Struck A Nerve / Ten Ton Hammer / Old / Nation Of Fire / Davidian / Nothing Left.

THE BURNING RED, Roadrunner RR 8651-2 (1999). Enter The Phoenix / Desire To Fire / Nothing Left / The Blood, The Sweat, The Tears / Silver / From This Day / Exhale The Vile / Message In A Bottle / Devil With The King's Card / I Defy / Five / The Burning Red. Chart positions: 13 UK, 17 SWEDEN, 55 FRANCE, 88 USA.

From This Day, Roadrunner (1999). From This Day / Desire To Fire (Live) / The Blood, The Sweat, The Tears / From This Day (Live).

From This Day, Roadrunner RR-21383 (1999). From This Day / Alcoholocaust / House Of suffering.

SUPERCHARGER, Roadrunner RR 1239-2 (2001). The Declaration / Bulldozer / White Knuckle Blackout / Crashing Around You / Kick You When You're Down / Only The Names / All In Your Head / American High / Brown Acid / Nausea / Blank Generation / Trephination / Deafening Silence / Supercharger. Chart positions: 25 GERMANY, 25 FINLAND, 34 UK, 35 FRANCE, 46 BELGIUM, 115 USA.

Crashing Around You, Roadrunner 23204703 (2001). Crashing Around You / Silver (Live) / Ten Ton Hammer (Live) / Crashing Around You (Video). Chart position: 89 UK.

HELLALIVE, Roadrunner RR 8437-2 (2003). Bulldozer / The Blood, The Sweat, The Tears / Ten Ton Hammer / Old / Crashing Around You / Take My Scars / I'm Your God Now / None But My Own / From This Day / American High / The Burning Red / Davidian / Supercharger. Chart positions: 78 FRANCE, 143 UK.

THROUGH THE ASHES OF EMPIRES, Roadrunner RR 8363-8 (2003) (USA release). Imperium / Bite The Bullet / Left Unfinished / Elegy / In The Presence Of My Enemies / Days Turn Blue To Gray / Vim / Seasons Wither / All Falls Down / Wipe The Tears / Descend The Shades Of Night / Bite The Bullet (Demo) / Left Unfinished (Demo) / Elegy (Demo) / All Falls Down (Demo) / Descend The Shades Of Night (Demo).

THROUGH THE ASHES OF EMPIRES, Roadrunner RR 8363-2 (2003). Imperium / Bite The Bullet / Left Unfinished / Elegy / In The Presence Of My Enemies / Days Turn Blue To Gray / Vim / All Fall Down / Wipe The Tears / Descend The Shades Of Night. Chart positions: 24 GERMANY, 41 SWEDEN, 44 FRANCE, 58 AUSTRIA, 65 HOLLAND, 66 BELGIUM, 77 UK, 80 SWITZERLAND, 82 DENMARK, 88 USA.

Days Turn Blue To Gray, Roadrunner (2004) (UK mail order CD single). Days Turn Blue To Gray / Seasons Wither / The Rage To Overcome (Live).

Now I Lay Thee Down, Roadrunner RR PROMO 984 (2007) (Promotion release). Now I Lay Thee Down (Radio edit) / Aesthetics Of Hate / Now I Lay Thee Down.

THE BLACKENING, Roadrunner RR80162 (2007). Clenching The Fists of Dissent / Beautiful Mourning / Aesthetics Of Hate / Now I Lay Thee Down / Slanderous / Halo / Wolves / A Farewell To Arms. Chart positions: 12 GERMANY, 12 BELGIUM, 16 UK, 19 SWEDEN, 19 AUSTRIA, 23 IRELAND, 29 SWITZERLAND, 29 HOLLAND, 39 FINLAND, 49 FRANCE, 54 USA.

MACHINERY

STOCKHOLM, SWEDEN — *Michel Isberg (vocals / guitar), Markus Isberg (guitar), Per Lindström (bass), Fredrik Klingwall (keyboards), Johan Westman (drums).*

Stockholm Death-Thrashers formed in late 2001 by former CORPSEGRINDER and DIMENSION singer Michel Isberg and EXTRICATOR drummer Johan Westman. The band's formative years would see an ebb and flow of members as the line-up remained fluid. Included amongst these candidates would be subsequent HYDROGEN singer Niclas Olsson. Isberg's brother Markus briefly found involvement on guitar. In October 2002 MACHINERY utilised Necromorbus Studios to track the demo 'A Part Of Steel In An Endless Machine'. Recording roster for these sessions involved Michel Isberg on vocals and guitar, Johan Westman on drums with Fredrik Öhlund on bass. Markus Isberg was then re-instated but, following the inaugural MACHINERY gig at the MC-Mjölner motorbike club, Öhlund decamped. Second demo, billed 'A Part Of Steel In An Endless

Machine—Part II', was recorded in the autumn of 2003, after which ex-DIMENSION bassist Hans Johansson was enrolled.

Necromorbus was again the venue for a third demo, 'Machinery—The Beginning', cut in October 2004. However, Hans Johansson opted out in November 2005. EXTRICATOR's KG West stood in as a temporary member for live work before Per Lindström, of ETERNAL TORMENT, FLAGELLATION, ANIMA MORTE, IN GREY and GOATSODOMIZER, took on bass duties in January 2006, debuting at the 'Mondo Metal Fest' event that month. In May MACHINERY participated on the 'Thrashing The Masses' compilation album, with the tracks 'Rectifier' and 'Unholy Demon', plus the follow up concert.

MACHINERY's debut album 'Degeneration' was recorded during August 2006 at Necromorbus studio with producer Sverker Widgren for release in October through Last Entertainment Productions. Newly employed keyboard player FREDRIK KLINGWALL is a man holding a tradition with acts such as IN GREY, FLAGELLATION, SHADOW OF THE CONCEALED, GOATSODOMIZER, ANIMA MORTE and RISING SHADOWS.

In January 2007 guitarist Markus Isberg left MACHINERY "due to personal reasons," according to a press release. Replacing him in the group's line-up would be Mano Lewys.

Beginning, Machinery (2004) (Demo). Rectifier / Wheel Of Pain / I Divine / Burned / A Generous Day / Feed Me Hatred / Dismembered / Machinery.
Rising, Machinery (2005) (Demo). Unholy Demon / Degeneration / Blacker Than Pain / Reason Is The Rush.
DEGENERATION, Last Entertainment Productions (2006). Salvation For Sale / Degeneration / River Red / Blacker Than Pain / Unholy Demon / Taste Of God / Rectifer / Falling Through The Grid / Satanic Hippie Cannibal.

MAD DRAGZTER

BRAZIL — *Tiago Torres (vocals / guitar), Gabriel Spazziani (guitar), Armando Benedetti (bass), Evandro Junior (drums).*

Thrashers originally founded as BULLDOZER during 1998 and citing an opening line up of vocalist / guitarist Tiago Torres, drummer Alessandro Itri, bass player Armando Benedetti and guitarist Gabriel Spazziani. Upon discovery of the renowned 80s era Italian BULLDOZER the group switched title to DRAGSTER. However, to their dismay they were then informed of the cult NWoBHM act of the same name and made yet another change becoming MAD DRAGZTER.

The 'New Times' demo was delivered in 2002 as a precursor to debut 2003 album 'Strong Mind'. MAD DRAGZTER cut the album 'Killing The Devil Inside' in late 2005 for issue in December via Encore Records.

STRONG MIND, Independent MADZ001CD (2003). Break Down / Lost / Strong Mind / The Chase / Day Of Sadness / New Times / Destroying My Life / 402 / Unknown / Sordid Planet / Love Us Of Hate Us / Raging City / 7 Years / Mad Dragzter.
KILLING THE DEVIL INSIDE, Encore (2006). The World Ends Tomorrow Morning / EVIL.COM / Jaws / Killing The Devil Inside / Talking To The Shadows / Curriculum Mortis / Nation Of Fear / Buried / Surreal / I, Psycho / Level 42 / No Money / Whisper Of War.

MAGOG

WHEELING, WV, USA — *Jeremy Gossett (vocals), John Thompson (guitar), Justin Swoyer (bass), Matthias Von Churchburner (keyboards), Erik Botizan (drums).*

Established during 1995, Wheeling, West Virginia based Metal band MAGOG involves a cast of seasoned players, with a membership comprising singer Jeremy Gossett (a.k.a. 'Azriel Magog'), having association with SZYDLOW DRONE, BROKEN FETUS and CHURCHBURNER, guitarist John Thompson (J.T.Godslayer') of GOREGOTH, GODSLAYER, TRIOXIN and PENTAFACE, bass player Justin "The Mighty Bug" Swoyer, previously with BURIED IN HELL and HARVIST, having replaced Russ Gantzer, and drummer Erik Botizan of HATE ASHBURY.

Frozen Music issued the debut MAGOG album, 'The Augury Of Malicious Dissonance', in October 1999. Ron Dentz would be added to the line-up on second guitar before the band reverted back to a single guitar format. The second album, Beyond The Gate' released in July 2000, included an unaccredited closing cover version of NAPALM DEATH's 'Suffer The Children'. October 2001's 'A Crucifixion Masterpiece' followed suit with an unlisted rendition of SLAYER's 'Seasons In The Abyss' featuring Andrew D'Cagna on guest vocals. This album saw the inclusion of keyboard player Matthias Von Churchburner, holding credits with SZYDLOW DRONE, HARVIST, PENTAFACE, SAVNOCH, CHURCHBURNER, TELIDEMON and TRIOXIN.

The group folded in 2002.

THE AUGURY OF MALICIOUS DISSONANCE, Frozen Music (1999). Revelations / Brooks Of Blood / Scars Of Fuck / Black Plague / Self-Annihilation / Leontasis / Life Sucks / Lucrid Lustpit.
BEYOND THE GATE, Frozen Music (2000). Bloodlines / White Meth/Black Death / Leontasis / Lucrid Lustpit / Murder / Damnation / As The Moons Align / Beyond The Gate / Suffer The Children.
A CRUCIFIXION MASTERPIECE, Frozen Music (2001). Intro / Past Lives And Mortal Sins / The Hunted / The Black Plague / The Augury Of Malicious Dissonance / A Sorrid Monody / The Glum / Moonlit Matricide / Out For My Blood.

MAKINA

MEXICO — *Javier Herrera (vocals / guitar), Janel De Polanco (guitar), Carlos De La Pena (bass), Victor 'Gismo' Reza (drums).*

Mexico City Thrashers that express their politically charged objectives in English rather than the more familiar Spanish. The group was convened in 1990, originally billed as MAKINA NEGRA. Under this guise the band released a four track 7" single 'Al Borde De La Destruccion', the whole affair being recorded in a mere three hours. Bass player 'Nefasto' Quiroga would break ranks shortly after, relocating to Chile, and was replaced by Carlos De La Pena—a veteran of both CHRIST and GEISHA. At this juncture, with a line up of vocalist / guitarist Paul Rivers, guitarist Hans Mues, De La Pena on bass and drummer Victor 'Gizmo' Reza the act truncated the band title to simply MAKINA.

Following the 1991 debut album 'Dilemma', issued by the independent Lejos De Paraiso label, MAKINA put in support gigs to the likes of visiting international artists NAPALM DEATH, SODOM and D.R.I.

However, MAKINA then underwent a series of line up ructions. Firstly Rivers would depart and then Mues. MAKINA filled the vocal position with erstwhile CRIPTA man Carlos Alejandro but he too swiftly decamped. Finally the roster was settled with the addition of ex ACROSTIC personnel vocalist / guitarist Javier Herrera and guitar player Janel De Polanco.

This version of the band scored a deal with Sony Music subsidiary Discos Rockotitlan for 1994's 'Anabiosis' opus scoring valuable MTV exposure to boot.

MAKINA's third effort 'Red', arrived in 1996. It would be co produced by the band together with Matt Green and FAITH NO MORE's Billy Gould.

De Polanco left the ranks in 1997. He would later turn up as part of the PRAYING MANTIS PROJECT.

RED, Discos Manicomio (1996)
I Am / 2 Much 2 Much / U / K.F.S. / Terror / Chorizo / Red / The Left / La Fuerza De La Tierra / Tons Of Shit / Millennium / Faithless

Al Borde De La Destruccion, (1986). Al Borde De La Destruccion.
DILEMMA, Lejos De Paraiso (1991). Citizens Hate / Dreamtrapped / Criminal Confession / Official Misconduct / The Clown Of This Town / Ciudad De Cagadas / The Window / Antiwar / Profound Conviction / S.CH.C.M.E.U.P. / Edge Of Confusion.
ANABIOSIS, Discos Rockotitlan (1994). Suddenly Dawned (Negative) / Insomnia / Human Wasted / Silent Disease / Nosotoxicotosis / Perro / Pinches Cerdos / Mind Changes (Vegetal) / Lies / Ripe / Anabiosis / Nymphomanic.

RED, Discos Manicomio (1996). I Am / 2 Much 2 Much / U / K.F.S. / Terror / Chorizo / Red / The Left / La Fuerza De La Tierra / Tons Of Shit / Millennium / Faithless.

Chorizo, Discos Manicomio (1996) (promotion release). Interview / K.F.S. / Terror / Chorizo / Red / Tons Of Shit.

MALEDICTION

MIDDLESBOROUGH, UK — *Shaun Stephenson (guitar), Rich Mumford (guitar), Darren O'Hara (guitar), Mark Fox (bass), Alistair Dunn (drums).*

Middlesborough Progressive Death Metal act that excited considerable underground interest with their single released on the French Thrash label. MALEDICTION's early line-up consisted of vocalist Shaun Stephenson, guitarists Rich Mumford and Darren O'Hara, bass player Mark Fox and drummer Alistair Dunn. The band debuted with a March 1990, single track Grindcore demo 'Infestation' before the 'System Fear' 7" release on the Thrash label the following year. MALEDICTION released a demo 'Framework Of Condition' in October 1991 which besides new studio tracks featured a live recording of a gig supporting BOLT-THROWER. These sessions were due to include keyboard contributions from SIGH's Mira Kawashima but apparently the band opted to take their Japanese guest to the pub instead! O'Hara would decamp to found Folk / Death Metal act CERECLOTH and was replaced by Mark McGowan. Also emerging in 1992 would be a split cassette release entitled 'A Pungent And Sexual Miasma' shared with the fledgling CRADLE OF FILTH.

A makeshift live album 'Chronicles Of Dissension' arrived in 1993 on the Gargle With Blood label. Also emerging the same year was the yellow vinyl 'Dark Effluvium' EP on the American Psychoslaughter label, although apparently released without the band's knowledge. Phil Slack would take over the drum stool but would soon relinquish his position to a returning Dunn. During 1994 a proposed split EP with American act INCARNIS was recorded but never released. MALEDICTION signed to the Arctic Serenades label recording their projected debut album 'The Millennium Cotillion'. However, with the label's demise the album was shelved. MALEDICTION duly folded.

The band was resurrected during 2000 by Mumford, McGowan and Fox announcing their return with the demo session 'Shades Of Inequity'. The group, recently joined by drummer Barry of Bradford's THE ENCHANTED, plotted a new album, 'The Return Of The Prodigal', for 2002.

Infestation, (1990). Infestation.

System Fear, Thrash (1991). Infestation / Outro / Moulded From within / Waste.

Mould Of An Industrial Horizon, Mangled Beyond Recognition (1991). System Fear / Insect In The Infrastructure.

Framework Of Contortion, (1991). Intro / System Fear / Waste / Murdered From Within / Longterm Result / Insect In The Infrastructure / Infestation / Framework Of Contortion / System Fear (Live) / Murdered From Within (Live) / Waste (Live) / Longterm Result (Live) / Infestation (Live) / Framework Of Contortion (Live).

Malediction, (1992). Weeping Tears Of Covetousness / Doctrine's Eternal Circles / Framework Of Contortion.

A Pungent And Sexual Miasma, (1992) (split cassette with CRADLE OF FILTH). Mould Of An Industrial Horizon / Infestation / Waste / Longterm Result / System Fear / Sick New Facts / Murdered From Within.

Dark Effluvium, Psychoslaughter (1993) (Yellow vinyl). Dark Effluvium / Weeping Tears Of Covetousness / Framework Of Contortion.

CHRONICLES OF DISSECTION, Gargle With Blood GWBCD 001 (1993). Mould Of An Industrial Horizon / Weeping Tears Of Covetousness / Infestation / Framework Of Contortion / Longterm Result / System Fear / Doctrines Eternal Circles.

MALEVOLENCE

LEIRIA, PORTUGAL — *Carlos Cariano (vocals / guitar), Frederico Saraiva (guitar), Aires Pereira (bass), Paulo Pereira (keyboards), Gustavo Costa (drums).*

A Leiria Black Death Metal band that has supported both SINISTER and CRADLE OF FILTH. MALEVOLENCE debuted with the demo 'Pleasure Of Molestation'. 1999's 'Martyralized' was recorded in Sweden, at Fredman Studios with producer Fredrik Nordström, with an all new line-up centred upon surviving founder member vocalist Carlos Cariano (a.k.a. KK). Both Cariano and bass player Rui Capitão had previous association with VOMITORY. The four-stringer, plus one time guitarist Luis Lacerda, also had prior association with PARANOIA.

The album was issued on CD format by Maquiavel Music Entertainment with Psychic Scream Entertainment handling cassette copies for Malaysia and Singapore. In addition, Norwegian imprint Apocalyptic Empire Records released a limited edition of 500 on vinyl picture disc.

Bassist Aires Pereira stepped up a league in June of 2003 by deputising MOONSPELL. Meantime MALEVOLENCE gathered new material together for a mid 2004 demo 'Celebration Of Dysfunctional Becoming'. MALEVOLENCE added session keyboard player Paulo Pereira in 2005.

DOMINIUM, 199 (0). Desespero / Dominium Of Hate / The Burning Picture / Under Inhuman Torch / Enchanted Mask / Swallowed In Black / My Eyes (Throne Of Tears) / Sweet Bloody Vision / Erotica / Ceremonial Gallery.

MARTYRALIZED, Maquiavel Music Entertainment CD 43195 (1999). The Brotherhood Of Christ / Diabolical Eve (Chronicles Of Master Lusitana) / Hunters Of The Red Moon / Les Salls Obscures De Rode Noire XVIII / Thy Extremist Operetta / Insubordination / A Shining Onslaught Of Tyranny / Oceans Of Fire / Martyralized.

Celebration Of Dysfunctional Becoming, (2004). Slithering Angels / Equilibrium In Extremis / Devoured Unlimited / Mechanisms Of Destructive Behavior.

MALISHA

USA — *Kim La Chance (vocals), Randy Hano (guitar), Darry Shihado (bass), Joe Silva (drums).*

Formed by ex-VIXEN and HAWAII frontwoman Kim La Chance in November of 1982. MALISHA served up straightforward no frills aggressive Metal on their debut 1983 demo. MALISHA formed with a line up of La Chance, guitarist Randy Hano, bass player Darry Shihado and drummer Ivar. The latter would be superseded first by Craig Brooks then Rick Dingman.

The track 'Valkyrie' on the 'Serve Your Savage Beast' album would be dedicated to Janne Stark, guitarist with Swedish outfit OVERDRIVE.

Post MALISHA La Chance created the 1992 act DRIVEN STEEL comprising of guitarist Julia Roberts (presumably not the actress!), bassist Kelly Heckart and drummer Franco Geneta.

Give It All You Got, Malisha (1983). Give It All You Got.

SERVE YOUR SAVAGE BEAST, Shardan Kane (1986). Valkyrie / Love For The Day / Step Through Eternity / Serve Your Savage Beast / What I Believe / Power Flight / Metal Wars / Burning Rage / Hands Of The Ripper.

MANIC MOVEMENT

GERAARDSBERGEN, BELGIUM — *Maarten Verbeke (vocals), Philippe Pieters (guitar), Jérémie Vasile (guitar), Gerry Verstreken (bass), Filip De Grave (keyboards), Olivier Wittenberg (drums).*

Geraardsbergen Thrash outfit MANIC MOVEMENT was created by lead guitarist Steven Van de Wiele and drummer Olivier Wittenberg during 1993. An early frontman would be RAMSES singer Marc De Veirman. MANIC MOVEMENT's 'Discipline' EP issued on Asterion Records was produced by Andre Gielen. In 1999 the band, working with former CHANNEL ZERO man Xavier Carion as producer, recorded the album 'Thousand

Sufferings', signing this product over to Dutch label Suburban Records for issue that November. The band roster at this juncture saw Van de Wiele and Wittenberg alongside singer Maarten Verbeke, erstwhile frontman for WELKIN, rhythm guitarist Ken Straetman, SENGIR keyboard player Filip De Grave and bassist Sven De Corte. Mastered by Attie Bauw, the album included a surprise cover of JACQUES BREL's 'Amsterdam' hit. A European tour in January 2000 was conducted as a package billing with KREATOR, WITCHERY and MOONSPELL. However, following release of the album the group underwent line-up changes, acquiring a new team of guitar players Philippe Pieters and Jérémie Vasile along with Gerry Verstreken of IMPERIA on bass. Sven de Corte joined DEATHTRAP.

Partnering with Xavier Carion once again, MANIC MOVEMENT's next album, the conceptual 'Future Dreaming Self', saw release on the Megalomanious Records label. Yet again the band pulled out an unlikely song to cover, this time honouring ANNE CLARK's 'Our Darkness'.

Maarten Verbeke would remain on good terms with his former WELKIN comrades, guesting on their October 2002 album 'Angel Inside'. Guitarist Philippe Pieters opted out of MANIC MOVEMENT in 2003.

Ex-MANIC MOVEMENT members guitarist Steven Van de Wiele, also citing an affiliation with MASSIF, and Sven De Corte returned to the scene in 2004 with SHELLCASE. Sven De Corte would also be active as a member of EXILE. 2005 saw Gerry Verstreken handling bass for Helena Michaelsen's ANGEL.

THOUSAND SUFFERINGS, Suburban (1999). Trapped Inside The Sun / The Third Injury / A Thousand Sufferings / Run To Heaven / Silhouettes / Amsterdam / Juggler Of Bones / Crape / Soulshriek (Despair, My Bride) / Torn Into Divinity.
FUTURE DREAMING SELF, Megalomanious (2001). Dreamvolution / Slide / Mankind's Misanthropic Ambassador / Oracle / Singularity / Technocalyps / Concentric (Messiac Age) / Future Fairytales / Scarlet / Our Darkness / In Spaces Between / Double Walker / Garden Outside Time / Textures / Flogged / The Dogfactory / Memory Palace / The Art Of Memory.

MANIFEST

TRONDHEIM, NORWAY — *Stian Leknes (vocals), Ole Marius Larmerud (guitar), Cato Iversen (bass), Alessandro Elide (drums).*

MANIFEST is a Trondheim based, Thrash edged Metal band conceived in late 1999 by guitarist Ole Marius Larmerud and drummer Alessandro Elide, the latter active on the scene with a BLACK SABBATH tribute band rather obviously called BLACK SABBATH TRIBUTE BAND. After various formative line-ups the band was completed by vocalist Erik Wegge in May 2000 and bassist Cato Iversen that August. This quartet cut the opening demo 'Structure Of Disharmony'. The track 'Recreate' on this demo was recorded earlier in May 2000 with Espen Hammer on bass. The group's next move was to cut a self financed EP 'Lifelong, Painful Co-existence' with producer Rune Elli in April 2001. In December of that same year MANIFEST laid down another four demo tracks at Skansen Studios in Trondheim.

In April 2002, Stian Leknes joined the band on vocals. The new look MANIFEST heralded Leknes' arrival with a show in August at the 'Tauterstokk' festival. With Elide unable to perform at this gig due to an arm injury Tor Arne from ATROX stood in. 2003 witnessed a short Norwegian tour sharing stages with GODSIZE, after which MANIFEST entered the Godt Selskap Studios for the promo session 'The Art Of War'. The band would use Godt Selskap Studios again in the spring of 2004 to record their first album, titled 'Half Past Violence' for Edgerunner Records. On the session front, Stian Leknes contributed guest growls to Progressive Rock act PICTORIAL WAND's debut album 'A Sleeper's Awakening'. In January 2006 drummer Alessandro Elide joined the ranks of GRIFFIN. MANIFEST parted ways with bassist Cato Iversen shortly afterward, pulling in new man Kenneth Einarsen. The band supported ENTOMBED on their Norwegian shows in September.

MANIFEST utilised Spiren Studio in Støren with producer Knut 'Fug' Prytz on November 2nd to cut new album tracks.

HALF PAST VIOLENCE, EdgeRunner EDGE011CD (2005). Slay The Dove / Manufactured Lie / Third Eye Ricochet / Dead End Spiral / Grind Whore / Friendshit / King Of Sin / Scarred For Life / The Art Of War / Withered World / Mess-age To Death-age.

MANIPULATED SLAVES

OSAKA, JAPAN — *Hisayoshi (vocals), Yutaka Kageyama (guitar), Kazushi Nomora (guitar), Takayoshi Saita (drums).*

Osaka renaissance Thrashers MANIPULATED SLAVES was founded in April of 1994 by the now only surviving original member guitarist Yutaka Kageyama. Two demo tapes arrived the following year and the group debuted live in August at the 'Rocket' club in their home city.

MANIPULATED SLAVES underwent numerous line up changes but still managed to issue further demo sessions in the 1997 set 'Burst Into Blue Flame' and, adding ex SLEAZY WIZARD guitarist Kazushi Nomura, 1999's 'Seventh Island'.

MANIPULATED SLAVES signed to the Worldchaos Productions label to release the first album 'Burst Into Blue Flame' during March of 2000. The line up at this juncture stood at Kageyama on vocals and guitar, Nomura on second guitar, bass player Shiro Matsuno and drummer Mitshuhiro Enomoto. New frontman Hisayoshi would take the lead vocal mantle for the August 2001 set 'The Legendary Black Jade'.

Drummer Takayoshi Saita is an erstwhile member of DAZZLE.

BURST INTO BLUE FLAME, Worldchaos Productions KDM002 (2000). Masters Of Illusion / Obey The Moon / Halfway To Heaven / Come Down From The Skies / Damnation's Edge / Greed / Burst Into Blue Flame / Silently Falling Asleep / The Lunatic Moon On The Dark Sea.
THE LEGENDARY BLACK JADE, Worldchaos Productions KDM006 (2001). Thrust Sword Into The Earth / The Way Of The Emperor / Woman In The Ironmask / The Broken Chain / Eyes Filled With Tears / Man From The Horizon / Capitol Punishment / Assault On The Enemy / Bearing The Final Pain.

MANNGARD

NORWAY — *Olav Iversen (vocals), Olav Kristiseter (guitar), Einride Torvik (bass), Iver Sandøy (drums).*

MANNGARD's Nocturnal Art Productions February 2006 album 'Circling Buzzards', lyrically inspired by the works of American novelist William Faulkner and engineered by Brynjulv Guddal and Herbrand Larsen, featured a guest appearance from Grutle Kjellson of ENSLAVED. MANNGARD frontman Olav Iversen also operates trad Doom outfit SAHG in union with the GORGOROTH's rhythm section of bassist King Ov Hell and drummer Kvitrafn.

In early 2007 drummer Iver Sandøy was found to be involved with TRINACRIA, initiated by guitarist Ivar Bjørnson from ENSLAVED along with vocalist Maja S. K. Ratje and Hild S. Tafjord, both from FE-MAIL, plus singer Grutle Kjellson of ENSLAVED, guitarist Arve Isdal (a.k.a. 'Ice Dale'), of ENSLAVED, BOURBON FLAME and AUDREY HORNE and bassist Espen Lien of BARBIE BONES and SLUT MACHINE.

CIRCLING BUZZARDS, Candlelight CANDLE135CD (2006). Wreathed In Rot / Safe With Me / Gravgrang / Tomb Of God / Bury The Head / Unattainable Fuck / Into The Quagmire / It Was Demons / Blood On My Face.

MANTAS

UK — *Pete Harrison (vocals), Mantas (guitar), Alistair Barnes (guitar), Mark Savage (drums).*

VENOM guitarist Mantas' more melodic leanings are evident on his 1988 debut solo effort 'Winds Of Change', released in the period prior to his re-involvement with the band. Mantas (real name Jeff Dunn) recruited guitarist Alistair Braacken for the project, with drums supplied by Mark Savage (ex-WAR MACHINE). Mantas rejoined VENOM, requisitioning Barnes for the new line-up. Savage became lead vocalist for XLR8R.

A new MANTAS album, entitled 'Zero Tolerance', recorded at the Demolition Studios in Newcastle and produced by Italian guitarist Dario Mollo of THE CAGE, was scheduled for early 2004 release. Bass would come courtesy of former VENOM and ATOMKRAFT man Tony Dolan. The pair would be joined by singer Bry, guitarist Marsy and drummer Cherisse. The band scheduled appearances at both the New Jersey and Minnesota Metalfests in March. Unfortunately, "due to circumstances beyond the band's control", the band then withdrew from these events. The new look line-up instead debuted with a show at the London Camden Underworld on 23rd June. Originally intended as a support to MALEVOLENT CREATION, the group ended up headlining when the American act got waylaid en route.

Tony Dolan left the band in September, issuing a statement that he had "been forced to walk away" from the project. Within days, drummer Cherisse Osei also decamped due to "contractual obligations", subsequently joining a successful all girl band THE FADERS. MANTAS duly recruited Czech drummer Marthus (a.k.a. Martin Škaroupka) having previously played with GALACTIC INDUSTRY, ENTRAILS, HAPPY DEATH, MELANCHOLY PESSIM, EQUIRHODONT, SYMPHONITY and INNER FEAR.

MANTAS announced an EP release for 2005 billed 'Maximum Brutality'. Label reports gave first week sales figures in Japan for the 'Zero Tolerance' album of over 10,000 units. Live shows included an appearance at the 'Independence D' festival in Tokyo during March. MANTAS would be announced as support act to SIX FEET UNDER's October / November European tour dates. Vocalist Bri exited in early September.

It was learned that Mantas was to join German techno group SCOOTER for European shows throughout March 2006. Martin Škaroupka joined CRADLE OF FILTH in November.

WINDS OF CHANGE, Neat NEAT 1042 (1988). Let It Rock / Deceiver / Hurricane / King Of The Ring / Western Days / Winds Of Change / Desperado / Nowhere To Run / Sayonara.
Deceiver, Neat NEAT 60-12 (1989). Deceiver / I'm On Fire / The Green Manalishi.
ZERO TOLERANCE, Demolition (2004). Zero Tolerance / Rage / Drill / Kill It / Look Who Died / Stone Cold / Original Sin / Rise / Insanity / Bring It On.

MAPLE CROSS

JÄÄLI, FINLAND — *Marco R.J. (vocals), Juha Henttunen (guitar), Sami Siekkinen (guitar), Joni Lehto (bass), Ilkka Leskelä (drums).*

Jääli Thrashers dating back to 1985. The first MAPLE CROSS formation counted guitarists Ilkka Heino and Marko Siekinnen, bass player Mika Karppinen with Ville Hyry on the drums. Inducting singer Marco R.J. the first product arrived in the form of a 1988 demo 'Thirteen Witches ... But One Of Them'. Niko Karppinen took over bass duties and second session 'Sacrificed Humanity' followed in 1989. Another demo preceded the recording of the 1991 album 'The Eighth Day Of Creation'. However, by 1992 MAPLE CROSS was back to demoing again, issuing the tape '5th For Us' with 'Uncontrolled Art' delivered in 1993 and 'Cool Maggots' in 1994. The original MAPLE CROSS ceased operations during 1996, with Niko Karppinen sessioning for SENTENCED, but returned to the stage in 2000.

This revised MAPLE CROSS only included Marco R.J. from the former band. He would be joined by guitarists Log (Sami Siekkinen), of EMBRAZE, and Late TT (Lauri Tuohimaa), of EMBRAZE, CHARON and FOR MY PAIN, with Ollari (Olli-Pekka Karvonen), from EMBRAZE and DIVISION BELL, on bass and BEDROCK and SICKNOTE drummer Aki. The re-vamped band utilised Boogie Cellar Studios to cut a 2002 demo. In February 2004 MAPLE CROSS severed ties with guitarists Late TT and Log, replacing the pair with THYRANE's Avather and the SETHERY and LORD OF PAGATHORN credited Juha Henttunen. The group engaged in the 'Creatures from the North' tour of Finland throughout February and March, sharing stages with NATIONAL NAPALM SYNDICATE and SACRED CRUCIFIX. A limited edition, three way split EP, featuring new song 'The Greatest Hit' was distributed during this trek through Verikauha Records.

The band partnered with Liverpool Death Metal band DIAMANTHIAN for Finnish gigs in January 2006. MAPLE CROSS released a new album, entitled 'Heimo' preceded by the single 'Journey Of A Wolf', on January 31st 2007.

Thirteen Witches ... But One Of Them, (1988) (Demo). Death Shall Have No Domination / New Way To Kill / First Invasion / All Saint's Day / And Then ... / Day In The Grave / Colosseum.
Sacrificed Humanity, (1989) (Demo). Sacrificed Humanity / Escape From Reality / Mesmerize / Il Duce.
Maple Cross, (1990) (Demo). True Or False / The Force Of An Eagle / The New Picture Of The Universe / The First Last Town / Creo Tempus.
THE EIGHTH DAY OF CREATION, Maple Cross 001 (1991). True Or False / Recoming / Never Ending Dance / The Force Of An Eagle / Creo Tempus / Sacrificed Humanity / Something To Believe In / The First Last Town / The New Picture Of The Universe / Going Around.
5th For Us, (1992) (Demo). The Darkside Of Man / Top Of The Clouds / Ten Miles With Tinga Joe Shoes / Outlook On World / Guns 'n' Cats.
Uncontrolled Art, (1993) (Demo). Role Of The Day / Stay Divine / She's Too Hot For Me / The Window Of Light / Savannah.
Cool Maggots, (1994) (Demo). A Different World / So Cruel / Till The Dawn Comes / Cool Maggots.
Maple Cross, (2002) (Demo). Invincibles / Simply Simplicity / Au Revoir.
Promo 2, (2002) (Demo). The Way / The Chosen People / Nothing Starts From The Beginning.
NEXT CHAPTER, Verikauha VKR-17031 (2003). The Spirit Of Northern Brotherhood / Au Revoir / Last Steps Of Joe / World Wide Mystery / The Chosen People / Simply Simplicity / Invincibles / Victim Of Life / Nothing Starts From The Beginning / Embodiment Of Air / New Direction.
Creatures From The North EP, Verikauha (2005) (Split EP with NATIONAL NAPALM SYNDICATE and SACRED CRUCIFIX). The Greatest Hit.

MARTYR

ROOSENDAAL, HOLLAND — *Haat (vocals / guitar), N. Silence (guitar), Nomiis (bass), I.N. Enthroned (drums).*

Roosendaal based MARTYR are a speed Black Metal band with melodic tendencies. The band was convened during 1997 by vocalist / guitarist Haat ("Commander of Misanthropic Chants and summoner of Hatred") and drummer I.N. Enthroned ("Commander of the Echoes of Infinity"), this pair soon joined by bassist Harm and second guitarist N. Silence ("Commander of Choirs of Death"). MARTYR's first product would be delivered in September of 1998 in the form of the independently financed EP 'Beyond The Flames Eternal'. A deal was offered by the Belgian Shiver label at this juncture but rejected.

A second promotion set, 'Resurrection Of Our Prophecies', arrived in 1999 after which Harm was replaced by Absconditus of DARK RIVERS FLOW. 'Resurrection Of Our Prophecies' would see a re-issue a year later with all new gruesome artwork.

The revised line up cut further tracks collected together as the 'To Confirm When Destruction Comes' demo but then switched bassists once more, Absconditus duly substituted by Amok of ONHEIL. This latest recruit lasted until his exit in January of 2002. MARTYR drafted new four stringer Nomiis ("Commander of the Poisonous Pulse") and signed a deal with the Regimental label to issue the album 'To Confirm When Destruction Comes'.

MARTYR would donate their version of 'Descent Into The Abyss' to the 2002 JUDAS ISCARIOT tribute album 'To Triumph Of Evil' released by the Ma-Kahru label. The 'A Malicious Odyssey' album surfaced through Black Owl Records in 2004.

Beyond The Flames Eternal, Martyr (1998) (Demo). Declaration Of The Grand Last War / The River Of Decay / Beyond The Flames Eternal / Forgotten Lands / Haunted In Silence.

THE RESURRECTION OF OUR PROPHECIES, (2000). Resurrection Of My Prophecies / Insanity's Manifest / Unleashed Quest Of Forthcoming Darkness / Mankind Has Spoken / All Things End In Sorrow.

TO CONFIRM WHEN DESTRUCTION COMES, Regimental REG 003 (2002). Sanquis Vitea Est / Burning Season / Deathforce Re-Filled / I Am The Bringer Of New Obtainment / To Confirm When Destruction Comes / In Nomine.

A MALICIOUS ODYSSEY, Black Owl BOR002 (2004). Sentenced To Downfall / Suffer / Failure Of The 4th / Stunned / Prologue To The Unknown / Death's Verdict / The Dawn Of The Malicious Crossfires.

MARTYR

UTRECHT, HOLLAND — *Gerard Vergouw (vocals), Rock Bouwman (guitar), Marcel Heesakkers (guitar), Antoine Van Der Linden (bass), Elias Papadopoulus (drums).*

An Utrecht Heavy Metal outfit initiated by guitarist Rick Bouwman in 1982. He would be joined by school friend drummer Peter van Loenen on drums along with the TARGET duo of guitarist Marcel Heesakkers and bassist Toine van der Linden. Whilst recording the first 1982 demo, entitled 'If It's Too Loud, You're Too Old', studio engineer Robert van Haren joined up as lead vocalist. At this juncture the MARTYR membership averaged an age of just 17.

A second demo session, 'Metal Torture' recorded in 1983 at Studio Weldam, garnered heady praise from the influential 'Aardschok' magazine. Such was the word of mouth on the Metal underground that nearly 1000 cassettes were sold. The demo track 'Snow And Fire' also found inclusion on the compilation album 'When The Hammer Falls Down'. Roadrunner Records requested two tracks for their 'Dutch Steel' collection and so the band entered Spitsbergen studios in Groningen, working with producer Alfred Lagarde and engineer Michiel Hoogeboezem. Although 'Snow And Fire' made the album the second song recorded, 'Speed Of Samurai', was to be consigned to the vaults.

With a deal brokered by Megaton Records MARTYR were soon back in the recording studio, albeit with a new face behind the drum kit, that of ex-TARGET man drummer Elias Papadopoulos. The group worked alongside producer Faas van der Pol at the Trinity Studios but then began to encounter line-up problems. Robert van Haren left; Adrian Quinten briefly occupied the position before Gerard Vangouw was inducted as MARTYR's new frontman in time for a gig supporting LITA FORD at the Amsterdam Paradiso. The album 'For The Universe' arrived in 1985, promoted by live work across Europe including shows opening for Canadians EXCITER.

In 1986 MARTYR, having cut the demos 'The Last One To Run' and 'Raise This Heaven', signed to a professional management company and switched to Metalloid Records for sophomore record 'Darkness At Time's Edge', crafted at Silvox Studios in Ulft with producer Caspar Falke. Subsequent live work, backed by a promotional video and an appearance on Sky TV Channels 'Monsters of Rock' programme, included dates partnered with HELLOISE. Despite the quality of this album distribution was poor and the band splintered.

MARTYR had their track 'En Masse (Stand Or Die)' featured on the Metal Blade 'Metal Massacre VI' compilation album. Both guitarist Marcel Heesakkers and bassist Antoine Van Der Linden would create HOT LEGS with erstwhile MAYDAY, VILLIAN and COUNTERFORCE vocalist Fred Pieters issuing the 1990 album 'Stand Tall'. Van Der Linden would also go on to WILD RIDE releasing the Japanese issue record 'Tension And Desire'.

In October 2001 MARTYR reformed for an appearance at the 'Heavy Metal Maniacs' festival. The German High Vaultage label re-issued both 'For The Universe' and 'Darkness At Times Edge', both adding extra bonus tracks.

FOR THE UNIVERSE, Megaton 0010 (1985). For The Universe—Theme / Speed Of Samurai / The Eibons / Four Walls / The Awakening / Black Sun / For The Universe—Requiem.

DARKNESS AT TIME'S EDGE, Metalloid (1986). Darkness At Time's Edge / Invisible Touch / Follow Your Soul / Child Of Science / The Third Kin-Slay / Into The Abyss / 118: / Unknown Forces.

MASTER

RUSSIA — *Mikhail Seryshev (vocals), Andrei Boshakov (guitar), Sergei Popov (guitar), Alexander Granovsky (bass), Kirill Pokrovosky (keyboards), Igor Molchanov (drums).*

MASTER was originally a straight forward Metal act, but by the time the Russian's issued their second album in 1990 they had transformed themselves into a Thrash outfit. MASTER, founded in April of 1987, included a glut of former members of the hugely successful band ARIA in guitarist Andrei Boshakov, bass player Alexander Granovsky, keyboard player Kiril Pokrovsky and drummer Igor Molchanov. Joining these defectors would be the FORTRESS duo of singer Alexander Arzamaskov and second guitarist Sergei Popov.

MASTER undertook gigging and produced an opening demo before Arzamaskov was replaced by Grigory Korneev. However, this latest recruit's tenure would be brief and Mikhail Seryshev duly stepped up to the microphone for recording of the eponymous 1988 album. Live work saw MASTER securing gigs in Poland as well as Russia. The band's profile was raised further in promotion for their second album as MASTER put in a valuable appearance at the massive 1989 'Monsters Of Rock' festival.

In 1989 MASTER travelled to Belgium in order to produce their third studio effort. The band suffered numerous line up fluctuations during this period. Originally projected with a working title of 'Empire Of Evil' this outing finally emerged billed as the English language 'Talk Of The Devil' in 1992.

1994's 'Maniac Party' record witnessed a line up comprising vocalist Mikhail Seryshev, guitarist Vyacheslav Sidorov, bassist Alex Granovsky and Anatoly Senderov on drums. Sidorov was subsequently to depart and former member Sergei Popov was reinstated for a live album and the follow up studio affair 'Songs Of The Dead'. For this release MASTER reverted back to their native Russian language.

AUTOGRAF's Artyom Berkytom took over the lead vocal mantle for a short term prior to Seryshev making a return. However, in the midst of recordings for the 'Labyrinth' album Seryshev decamped once again. 'Lexx' took control of vocal responsibilities and, in yet more changes, MASTER welcomed onboard new guitarist Leonid Fomin as well as drummer Oleg Milovanov.

During February of 2001 Alexei Straik was to take Leonid Fomin's position. Alexander Karpyshin became MASTER's new drummer in 2002. Two MASTER veterans, vocalist Artur Berkut and guitarist Sergei Popov, enrolled in ARIA during 2002.

MASTER, Melodia (1988). Watch Out / Hands Off / Shield And Sword / It's Night Once Again / Will And Reason / Stand Up, Get Over Fear / Save Me / Who Will Win? / Master.

WITH THE LEE ON A NECK, Melodia (1990). We Don't Want / Executioners / Are We Not Slaves? / When I Die … / God Save Our Fury / Don't Care A Fig! / Amsterdam / Judas / War / Seven Circles Of Hell.

TALK TO THE DEVIL, Moroz (1991). Intro Golgotha / Talk Of The Devil / Danger / Fallen Angel / Live To Die / Tsar / Heroes / Romance (Bass solo) / I Hate Your Sex / Paranoid.

MANIAC PARTY, Death City (1994). Beastie Generation / Maniac Party / Lock Them In Graves / Burning In Hell (Civil War Disaster) / Screams Of Pain / Time X (Bass solo) / They Are Just Like Us / Punk Guys / Go.

MASTER—LIVE, Moroz (1995). Intro / Beastie Generation / Tsar / Danger / Live To Die / Lock Them In Graves / Screams Of Pain / Punk Guys / Executioners / Master / Will And Reason / Smoke On The Water / Here The Metal Is Being Born.
PESNI MYORTVYH, Flam (1996). Songs Of The Dead / Wild Goose / Lights On! / Ashes In The Wind / Got Bored / Only You By Yourself / I Don't Need The War / Tattoo / Ship Of The Fools.
THE BEST—LIVE IN MOSCOW, (1997). Songs Of The Dead / Ship Of The Fools / Got Bored / I Don't Need The War / Dust In The Wind / Tattoo / Danger / Lock Them In Graves / We Don't Want / The Nigh Once Again / Master / Here The Metal Is Being Born / Will And Reason / Bass Solo.
LABYRINTH, (1999). Enough Space For All / Labyrinth / Bissextile Century / Crosses / Dream / Cometh 2000 / Metal Doctor / Happiness Hunters / No One Is Forgotten, Nothing Is Forgotten / Taran.

MASTIFAL

ARGENTINA — *Miguel A. Maciel (vocals), Diego Conte (guitar), Matias Munighini (guitar), Guillermo Ricci (bass), Luis Sanchez (drums).*

Thrash Metal outfit dating back to 1995. MASTIFAL's original line-up was as a quartet of vocalist / guitarist Marcelo H. Barreto, guitarist Diego Conte, bass player Andres Barreto and drummer Ruben Barreto. The 1998 debut 'Ebola' was followed by the live 'En Vivo'. After a second studio outing, 2000's 'Holocausto Mental', MASTIFAL suffered a series of line up fluxes. MASTIFAL would lose their frontman Miguel Maciel during November of 2000 and duly drafted in guitarist Matias Munighini and singer Miguel Maciel to stem the gap.

In late 2001 both Barreto brothers would decamp. Their replacements would be erstwhile LETHAL man Luis Sanchez on drums and former EREBUS bassist Guillermo Ricci. MASTIFAL would enroll another new drummer in April of 2002, ex-HEFESTOS man Leonardo Fernandez. 2003 saw the issue of a new studio album 'From The Darkness', this record also being made available in a Spanish language version as 'Desde Las Tinieblas'. Meantime the earlier 'Holocausto Mental' outing would see a release in Europe through the French Bang Or Be Banged Productions label.

MASTIFAL signed to Pulsar Light Records in September of 2004. Notable support gigs the following month witnessed support slots to DISMEMBER and BEHEMOTH. A new album for 2005, 'Carnovora', would be published in both Spanish and English languages. In 2005 MASTIFAL also participated in a tribute to MEGADETH, donating their version of 'This Was My Life' to the 'Hangar De Almas' released by 2M Producciones.

In late 2005 Diego Conte convened a Melodic Death Metal side-band WARBREED, comprising notable veterans of the Argentine extreme Metal scene in ARGONATH and ex-CARNARIUM guitarist Sergio Fernandez Ribnikov, ex-AUVERNIA bassist Pablo Lurbe, SACRUM and PGM PROJECT drummer Nicolás Ghiglione and headed up by INFERNAL WINTER vocalist Guillermo Cammareri. An EP, 'So Cry Havoc . . .', would be recorded for early 2006 issue.

EBOLA, (1998). Fabrica De Monos / Ebola / Devastación / Apodado Hijo Del Diablo / Lenta Muerte / Tierratas / Escupiendo Rabia.
EN VIVO, (1999). Indiferencia / Escupiendo Rabia / Lenta Muerte / Holocausto Mental / Espectaculo Macabro / Ebola / Fabrica De Monos / Apodado Hijo Del Diablo / Desperate Cry.
HOLOCAUSTO MENTAL, (2000). Holocausto Mental / Devastacion / Espectaculo Macabro / Apodado Hijo Del Diablo / Privado De Libertad / Ebola / Indiferencia / Lenta Muerte / Cuando El Sol Crucifique Mi Nombre / Fabricia De Monos / La Plegaria Del Obero.
FROM THE DARKNESS, (2003). Awake / Destiny / From The Darkness / New Artificial World / In The Entrails Of The Apocalypse / Heresies / Necropolis / In The Deserted Land / Black Sun / Bloody Walls / Loneliness / Graves / Ruins Of The World / Tierratas.
CARNIVORA, (2005). Void Radical Cult / The Abyss Of Insanity / Syndrome Of Supremacy / Far Beyond All Reason / Bound For Nowhere / Enigma / Praying To Death / Breeding Venom / Master Of Time / Beneath The Cross Of Hate / Apocryphal Heart / Sentence / Bionecrosis.

MEANSTREAK

NEW YORK, NY, USA — *Bettina France (vocals), Rana Sands (guitar), Marlene Apuzzo (guitar), Lisa Pace (bass), Diane Lee Keyser (drums).*

An All female Thrash Metal band, MEANSTREAK were originally managed by the Loud And Proud organisation, who also managed WHITE LION, OVERKILL and TYKETTO. The band made their recording debut, with the track 'Lost Stranger', on the 'L'Amour Rocks' compilation issued by Mercenary Records in 1987.

Formed in 1985 by guitarists Rana Sands (the girlfriend of ANTHRAX vocalist Joey Belladonna at the time) and Marlene Apuzzo. The girls avoided being stereotyped by the media by deliberately shying away from the kind of lyrical content all girl bands are 'supposed' to write

Playing shows in the Tri-State area with the likes of BATTLEZONE, ZEBRA, PROPHET and REMINGTON, the band recorded their 'Roadkill' debut with noted New York Metal producer Alex Perialas at the helm.

The album was released by Mercenary Records in America and picked up for a European release by Music For Nations. Shortly after the record was completed drummer Diane Keyser quit, due to time honoured musical differences, and was replaced by Yael Devan

Marlene has since married DREAM THEATER drummer Mike Portnoy, whilst Rana wed his bass playing band mate John Myung. The couples met when the two bands attended the Concrete Foundations Forum during September 1989.

ROADKILL, Music For Nations MFN 89 (1988). Roadkill / Nostradamus / Lost Stranger / Congregation / Searching Forever / It Seems To Me / Warning.

MEGACE

HAMBURG, GERMANY — *Melanie Bock (vocals), Jörg Schror (guitar), Klaus Florian Möller (guitar), Christian Wulff (bass), Andreas Düwel (drums).*

A progressively inclined Thrash act founded back in Hamburg during February of 1988 by the trio of vocalist Melanie Bock, guitarist Jörg Schror and bassist Michael Muller. A month later MEGACE was completed by the enrollment of guitarist Robin Kortt and drummer Thorsten Jungermann. The latter's tenure would be brief though and soon Kai Alex Spiekermann was manning the drum kit. Further changes in personnel occurred when ex ANESTHESIA man Klaus Florian 'Dirty' Möller supplanted Kortt in September. With this line up MEGACE cut their opening demo session 'The Sign Of The Ape'.

Spiekermann left in the summer of 1989 to hook up with fellow Thrash act DESERT STORM, his place duly being taken by KILGORE's Rainer Behn as MEGACE demoed tracks for Aarrrggg Records dubbed the 'Human Errors' sessions.

In December of the same year Muller made his exit, eventually being substituted by DROWNING IN REAL's Christian Wulff in February of 1990. Further ructions that same year found Behn out of the picture, although he did hang around to complete the 'This Is The News' demo. Engineered by GAMMA RAY's Kai Hansen 'This Is The News' garnered valuable press and saw track inclusions on the 'Brown Bottles Go Ape' compilation album. Following recording Carsten Schubert took over the drummer's role.

MEGACE's debut album 'Human Errors' emerged in July of 1991. The band hit yet more line up problems in August of 1992 when both Schubert and Möller exited. Stefan Spiedel, another DROWNING IN REAL member, took over guitar whilst the group had to wait until April of 1993 before the drummer's vacancy was filled by ex NÜRNBERGER PROZESS man Stephan Gora.

MEGACE then completed the 'Pseudo Identity' promotional tape, strengthening the GAMMA RAY connection with Dirk

Schlachter acting as engineer. In May of 1994 Gora bade farewell and Andreas Düwel took up residency behind the kit.

The band's second album, 'Inner War', hit the stores during May of 1999. Ambitiously it included a cover version of 'Synchronicity' by THE POLICE.

In 2000 the band donated their take on 'The Dogs Of War' to a PINK FLOYD compilation 'Signs Of Life'. MEGACE would also feature on the 'Unbroken Metal' magazine split 7 EP with another cover, this time being MOTÖRHEAD's 'Iron Fist' with lead vocals from Schror. Another MOTÖRHEAD cover 'Sacrifice', once more with Schror handling vocals, appeared on the 'Motormorphosis' tribute album.

In 2001 Schror took time out to aid GAMMA RAY on their Mexican dates substituting on bass for an injured Dirk Schlachter.

HUMAN ERRORS, Magic 377 0022 (1992). Something Incomprehensible / Law Enforcement Agency / Repetitions Of Human Errors / Let Me Explain / Save Your Dignity / No Brain / No Pain / Discord / Monofaces / Better To Forget.

INNER WAR, Angular SKAN 8217. AR (1999). Cry / Schweissnaht / Two / Inner War / Ciphers / Synchronicity / Conclusion (Reprise) / Industrial Dictatorship / Guilty / First-Take—Ponka-Song / Instinct, Science, Faith / Affengesicht / ... Which Have Been Predicted / Rain.

MEGADETH

SAN FRANCISCO, CA, USA — *Dave Mustaine (vocals / guitar), Glen Drover (guitar), James MacDonough (bass), Shawn Drover (drums).*

MEGADETH is the vehicle for which METALLICA refugee Dave Mustaine, a guitarist and composer of unquestionable, if erratic, genius, has made his mark upon the world. The band went through many incarnations, although bassist Dave Ellefson has remained a central lynchpin, until settling on their most stable and commercially successful guise of Mustaine, Ellefson, guitarist MARTY FRIEDMAN and drummer Nick Menza.

Initially fuelled by anger, resentment and an out of control lifestyle driven by drugs and alcohol excess, Mustaine has cleansed himself in full public view, taking MEGADETH to the top echelons in the annals of Metal history. By the late eighties the band could justifiably lay claim to their tag 'State of the art speed metal band'.

Mustaine's first act was titled PANIC, the band coming to a tragic end when a car crash, in which Mustaine was not involved, killed the driver and band's drummer. PANIC folded in 1981, providing the step up towards METALLICA. MEGADETH came together almost immediately after Mustaine's dismissal from METALLICA in April 1983, just four months before METALLICA were to record 'Kill 'Em All' (at his own admission for drunkenness) and the guitarist was quick to assemble another unit.

Local fanzines presumed the band to be titled FALLEN ANGEL, although in reality no hard and fast monickers were chosen. The FALLEN ANGEL concept fell by the wayside pretty swiftly and MEGADETH came into being with Mustaine, bassist Matt Kisselstein and drummer Lee Rausch.

This unit broke up after rehearsals and a fresh combo, including bassist Dave Ellefson, his room mate, Minnesota native Greg Handevidt, and Rausch was assembled. MEGADETH's debut live performance came with a show at San Francisco's Ruthie's club. At this juncture Mustaine announced a band line-up comprising vocalist Lor Kain, guitarists Dave Mustaine and Greg Handevidt, bassist Dave Ellefson with Richard Girod on drums. However, the group soon dispensed with Kain and Girod. Before long though Handevidt was out, with Mustaine citing the main reason for his dismissal being a lack of hair! Handevidt, after a spell in a job washing turkeys, resurfaced in 1987 with the band KUBLAI KAHN, releasing a solitary album 'Annihilation'. He then opted out of the music business to become a military mortician.

With Rausch opting out, later having brief tenures with both DARK ANGEL and WARGOD, the band then drafted in another drummer, Dijon Carruthers, but he too was to depart. Carruthers had persuaded the band, possibly motivated by fear of any racial prejudice, that his dusky complexion was a result of a Hispanic birth. The band discovered he was in fact black when his much darker brother, Kane Carruthers of the band THE UNTOUCHABLES was introduced to them at a party. The band duly fired Dijon, according to Mustaine: "Not because he was black, which didn't matter, but because he had lied to us". The first recordings came in the form of a three track demo that included 'Love You To Death', 'Skull Beneath The Skin' and 'Mechanix'.

The band's first gigs on the club circuit, now including former jazz drummer Gar Samuelson, utilised SLAYER's Kerry King as stand in second guitarist for a total of five shows before Chris Poland was enrolled. Poland was previously with a female fronted pop act NO QUESTIONS, whose image involved jumpsuits and make-up, and had appeared on a 7" single 'Videobrat'. Poland had also been a member of WELKIN.

In a quite surreal twist of fate, the man who introduced both Samuelson and Poland to the band, Jay Jones, died in 1997, having been stabbed to death with a butter knife in a fight with his brother in law over a baloney sandwich.

It was intended that MEGADETH was to have a lead vocalist at this point but, according to Mustaine: "The dickhead that came to sing for us turned up wearing eye-liner and carrying a six pack". The mystery vocalist was shown the door (but only after the band had downed the beer!) and Mustaine was forced to sing lead. Interestingly though, Mustaine had harboured thoughts of requesting the services of DIAMOND HEAD frontman Sean Harris, although this never got beyond the talking stage.

MEGADETH's first album 'Killing Is My Business ... And Business Is Good' was recorded on a shoestring budget, but still packed enough intensity to make the world's rock media sit up and take notice when issued by Combat in America and Music For Nations in Europe. A reported recording budget of $8000 was alleged to have been used in the main to feed addictions. Whatever the reality, Mustaine dispensed with allotted producer Karat Faye mid-way through proceedings and completed the engineering process himself.

The album included the Mustaine composed METALLICA track 'Mechanix' (retitled 'The Four Horsemen' for METALLICA's 'Kill 'Em All' album) and a twisted cover of the NANCY SINATRA hit 'These Boots Are Made For Walking', subsequently removed from later pressings due to objections by the copyright holder, songwriter Lee Hazlewood, who expressed horror at Mustaine's perversion of the original lyrics. Although marred by thin production, the debut was chock full of the trademark intense riffing style that denoted MEGADETH as a unique entity in the rock field.

Poland was to depart and MEGADETH drafted the veteran former CAPTAIN BEEFHEART musician Mike Albert on guitar. The band undertook American dates with Canadians EXCITER, but within three months the situation was reversed, with Poland reassuming his role in time for the second leg of the American 'Killing For A Living' tour. A New Year's show in San Francisco caught the band on a bill that included EXODUS, METAL CHURCH and, somewhat awkwardly, METALLICA.

The band's second album, produced by Mustaine and Randy Burns, was recorded prior to the band securing a major deal but would emerge remixed during 1986 as 'Peace Sells ... But Who's Buying' on Capitol Records. The album had, in its original mixed form, been pressed up in a test batch by Music For Nations in anticipation of gaining the rights to release it, before the band announced that they had signed to Capitol.

Thus white label copies do exist as one of the rarer MEGADETH collectibles.

The resulting tour, at first supporting MOTÖRHEAD (before friction between the two bands prompted MEGADETH's opting out), then as guests of ALICE COOPER, began to wide a developing rift between the two Daves and Samuelson and Poland. This was to rise to a head at MEGADETH's debut British gig headlining London's Hammersmith Odeon. The show, supported by METAL CHURCH, was to highlight the band's paper thin division between genius and chaos. With their gear impounded at customs and released only hours before the show, combined with onstage resentment, MEGADETH's show had many wondering whether they had been in the presence of the next metal sensation or a bunch of sorry burn-outs.

During a break between road dates Mustaine was to earn production credits on the debut album from SANCTUARY 'Refuge Denied' before the gig schedule resumed. Dates in North America saw KING DIAMOND and MAYHEM as support. By the tour's close in Hawaii, Samuelson, after numerous on the road disappearances and occasions where he would fall asleep at inopportune moments, was asked to leave. Poland persevered, but would lose his position as recording for a third album began.

It was to be many years before Samuelson re-emerged on the 1997 FATAL OPERA album 'The Eleventh Hour'. Poland issued the solo album 'Return To Metalopolis' before creating DAMN THE MACHINE then MUMBO'S BRAIN. (A further solo album 'Chasing The Sun' followed in 1999).

MEGADETH confirmed their revised line-up in November 1987. Alongside Mustaine and Ellefson were ex-BROKEN SILENCE guitarist Jeff Young and, from Detroit, drummer Chuck Behler, the latter having been Samuelson's drum technician. Behler's previous outfits included MASSACRE, STREET ELITE, THE MEANIES, SINCLAIR and EREBUS. In fact, the noted SLAYER drummer DAVE LOMBARDO had been offered the vacant drum position before Behler, but he reportedly turned the gig down because of Mustaine and co's acknowledged continuing drug problems.

Young had gained the position after he had taught ex-MALICE guitarist Jay Reynolds in order for his pupil to get the job. Although Reynolds briefly gained a place in MEGADETH, Young soon ousted him midway through recording of 'So Far, So Good ... So What'.

With this fresh line-up, MEGADETH performed their second British show headlining the 'Christmas On Earth' festival atop a bevy of thrash acts including NUCLEAR ASSAULT, OVERKILL, LÄÄZ ROCKIT, VOIVOD and CRO-MAGS prior to American dates with DIO. By the tail end of these dates with the former RAINBOW and BLACK SABBATH singer, and their album nestling in the American top 30, MEGADETH had turned a—ticket sales wise—very slow tour into their own vehicle. A brief rest period was quickly curtailed by more headline shows, this time with Germans WARLOCK as openers.

The 'So Far, So Good ... So What' album featured a cover version of the SEX PISTOLS track 'Anarchy In The UK', which was to chart in Britain, even boasted guest guitar from SEX PISTOLS guitarist STEVE JONES. Expectations were high as the thrash movement reached its zenith and MEGADETH's third album clocked up advance North American sales of over 450'000.

The year could not go by though without controversy though. As the press stoking up the heat numerous METALLICA vs. MEGADETH articles it was alleged that Mustaine put in a claim that METALLICA's track 'Leper Messiah' off their 'Master Of Puppets' album was in fact a thinly disguised rework of an early track he wrote titled 'The Hills Ran Red'. METALLICA hit back with strong denials.

Back to business the same year, MEGADETH went into the studio to re-record a fresh version of 'These Boots Are Made For Walking' for inclusion on the 'Dudes' soundtrack album. 1988 saw MEGADETH returning to Europe for a headline tour with support from Seattle's SANCTUARY, a band that Mustaine had aided on the production front. Although many dates were sold out Mustaine threw the band straight into controversy when he made praising remarks about the IRA whilst onstage in Northern Ireland. Needless to say the audience were far from appreciative and began spitting at the frontman.

The troubled times were far from over however when after an impressive appearance at the Castle Donington 'Monsters Of Rock' festival MEGADETH once more split down the middle with Young and Behler out, the drummer joining BLACK & WHITE. Young unsuccessfully auditioned for melodic Rockers DANGER DANGER.

Mustaine launched into a vitriolic stream of abuse about his former guitar partner even going so far as to suggest that Young was in love with WARLOCK chanteuse Doro Pesch and could not handle the fact that Pesch was supposedly writing love letters to Mustaine.

1988 had MEGADETH bouncing straight back and celebrating a top twenty British singles hit with their version of ALICE COOPER's 'No More Mr. Nice Guy' taken from the soundtrack to Wes Craven's 'Shocker' movie. Recording for this track was to be the first with new ex-RHOADS drummer Nick Menza. The new drummer had coincidentally been Behler's drum technician in the same way that Behler had been Samuelson's. It took Menza three stabs to land the job though as, after two failed auditions, Mustaine persevered and taught the songs to Menza. It transpired that Menza's ability was there all along, but the prospect of joining an act like MEGADETH had reduced him to a bag of nerves at auditions.

The position of new lead guitarist for MEGADETH fuelled rumours concerning HEATHEN's Lee Altus, SAVATAGE's Criss Oliva, PANTERA's Diamond Darryl and Jeff Waters of ANNIHILATOR. Waters nearly got the gig, but Darryl was in fact offered the position. The PANTERA guitarist insisted though that his brother, PANTERA drummer Vinnie, also be given a place and as such the negotiations broke down.

Mustaine pulled in old acquaintance CHRIS POLAND to perform on the demo recordings for a new album, but it was to be former DEUCE, VIXEN, HAWAII and CACOPHONY man MARTY FRIEDMAN who landed the job. The result of this union was 'Rust In Peace', released in September 1990 and produced by Mike Clink. Recording took place with Mustaine undergoing drug rehabilitation treatment, but the resultant album was to be their most mature effort to date giving them a further hit. 'Rust In Peace', viewed by many fans as the pinnacle of MEGADETH's artistic achievement, provided Mustaine with a wide canvas in which he put down his observations on the Irish conflict, war in the Middle East, nuclear weapons, esoterica and aliens.

UK touring in March of 1991 saw strong support from both THE ALMIGHTY and ALICE IN CHAINS. MEGADETH forged part of the immense 'Clash Of The Titans' touring bill that caught the band appearing alongside fellow heavyweights ANTHRAX and SLAYER. The North American dates, with openers ALICE IN CHAINS, proved a huge success with sell out attendance's. The band dropped in a couple of San Francisco club shows billed as VIC & THE RATTLEHEADS and by October the 'Clash Of The Titans' touring package, now with support from TESTAMENT and SUICIDAL TENDENCIES, hit Britain and Europe. The live work was far from over however, as returning to America the band were to hook up with British metal legends JUDAS PRIEST for their 'Painkiller' tour.

July 1992's 'Countdown To Extinction' would propel MEGADETH into the major league with the momentum gained from previous strong releases, just missing out on the US number 1 position and propelling Megadeth past the two million sales mark for the first time. The album, co-produced by Dave Mustaine and Max Norman, proved transitional in merging thrash with a more formatted hard rock approach. Megadeth added to their arsenal of classics with strong tracks such as the title number, 'Skin O' My Teeth', 'Sweating Bullets' and the near mantric 'Symphony Of Destruction'.

Despite now enjoying heady success, during 1993 Dave Mustaine was, by his own later admission, still teetering on the edge. MEGADETH performed a less than secretive gig billed as VIC AND THE RATTLEHEADS at Nottingham's Rock City venue on 3rd June. This show preceded the newsworthy spectacle of the band billed as special guests to METALLICA's festival gig at the Milton Keynes Bowl two days later, sharing the billing with DIAMOND HEAD and THE ALMIGHTY. A 1993 support tour of North America to AEROSMITH was curtailed when, in Houston, Texas, MEGADETH were forced out, Mustaine apparently simply unable to perform. AEROSMITH themselves were also none too pleased at remarks Mustaine made about their age. The vocalist entered into a de-tox programme and in the lull Ellefson busied himself with production for Texan metal act HELSTAR for their 'Multiples Of Black' album.

With the pressure now off, MEGADETH reunited for two interim projects that were to give an indication as to future material, namely the 'Angry Again' track for the 'Last Action Hero' movie soundtrack and '99 Ways To Die' submitted for the Beavis & Butthead compilation album on Geffen. MARTY FRIEDMAN also found the time for a solo album.

MEGADETH relocated to Phoenix, Arizona to record the Max Norman produced 'Youthanasia' album, released in November 1994, even constructing a brand new studio titled Fat Planet in which to lay down tracks. The album was to break into the American top five and go double platinum as MEGADETH embarked on an almost year long world tour. Interestingly, the 'Youthanasia' album artwork was banned in Thailand, Malaysia and Singapore for depicting an old woman hanging babies out on a clothes line. The babies depicted in the video for the album track 'Train Of Consequences' were also censored by MTV world-wide.

With Mustaine's continual battle against addiction a harsh regime of no alcohol was put into force for all MEGADETH shows. The close of 1994 saw MEGADETH touring South America with support from British rockers THE ALMIGHTY. 1995 North American dates saw FEAR FACTORY as openers. One obscure gig saw the band playing a one off show in Tel Aviv, Israel. MEGADETH took a further foray into South America in September 1995 as part of the 'Monsters Of Rock' bill alongside OZZY OSBOURNE, ALICE COOPER, FAITH NO MORE and PARADISE LOST, to round off a gruelling eleven months on the road. With the close of the tour Mustaine busied himself with the MD45 project, a punk industrial project in collaboration with FEAR's Lee Ving.

MEGADETH made a respectable return in July 1997 with the 'Cryptic Writings' album which entered the American charts at number 10 selling 75'000 units in its first week of release. The album was surprisingly produced by ex-GIANT man Dann Huff. Used to unrelenting recording schedules Mustaine was somewhat taken aback when Huff, a committed Christian, explained he could not work on Sunday as he had to take his family to Church. MEGADETH solved this potential personality problem by Mustaine attending church with his family too. As time would reveal, this course of action would have consequences for the band further down the line.

Behind the scenes, MEGADETH had switched management from Ron Lafitte to Bud Prager, an industry veteran best known for his successes with AOR giants FOREIGNER. 'Cryptic Writings' would display a much more radio orientated direction than any previous band product, a trend which would pervade over ensuing releases. Fans would voice concern not only at MEGADETH's shift in musical values but their new found penchant for short haircuts and snappy clothes—a far cry from the band's Thrash roots.

The band toured Britain in June 1997, supported by KILL II THIS, still comfortably selling out venues. Returning to America where 'Cryptic Writings' remained firmly lodged in the album charts MEGADETH, with tour guests LIFE OF AGONY, set about touring with gusto to push the album past the Gold sales mark. Dates in Mexico had JUDAS PRIEST as special guests. In spite of its shortcomings, 'Cryptic Writings' still managed to surpass a million sales in the USA. The first half million copies were printed on a silver background, with subsequent manufacturing runs on black. In 1998 an interesting EP saw issue, 'Cryptic Death' hosting instrumental re-works of five tracks from the album.

Nick Menza took a leave of absence in 1998, actually later revealed to have been let go due to health concerns, turning up on the FIREBALL MINISTRY album 'Ou Est La Rock?' with ex-THE OBSESSED and GOATSNAKE bassist Guy Pinhas in 1999. Brian Howe stood in on drums for MEGADETH's inclusion of 'I'll Get Even' to the Sci-Fi cartoon inspired soundtrack record 'Songs Of The Witchblade' in 1998. That same year an erstwhile MEGADETH member, guitarist Jeff Young re-surfaced in a somewhat unlikely source, contributing to Brazilian Flamenco artist BADI ASSAD's 'Chameleon' album.

Eventually a permanent replacement was located in ex-Y&T, SUICIDAL TENDENCIES and WHITE LION drummer Jimmy DeGrasso. The resulting album 'Risk' found MEGADETH ploughing deeper into commercial territory. It drew an outcry of protest from fans and would only manage 350,000 sales in the USA. Nevertheless, the band put in a series of well attended American dates in 2000 as part of the 'Maximum Rock' tour alongside MÖTLEY CRÜE and ANTHRAX.

2000 saw ex-DANGER DANGER, ALICE COOPER, ASIA, WIDOWMAKER, SAVATAGE, BLUE OYSTER CULT and STEPHEN PEARCY guitarist Al Pitrelli replacing Friedman. Pitrelli, although highly respected as a musician, was acknowledged by many as a "guitar for hire" having been involved outside of the Rock community with artists as diverse as KOOL & THE GANG, CELINE DION and MICHAEL BOLTON.

The band contributed their take on 'Never Say Die' for the BLACK SABBATH tribute album 'Nativity In Black 2'. MEGADETH got back onto the road guesting, alongside ANTHRAX, for MÖTLEY CRÜE. Mustaine would find a rare moment to donate a song to another artist. The unlikely recipient of 'The Day The Music Died' being the 'Get To You' album from JEANNINE ST. CLAIR.

Risk had seriously wounded MEGADETH's standing and Capitol Records let the band go, putting out a compilation 'Capitol Punishment' in 2000 as a parting shot. The record boasted the inclusion of two fresh tracks recorded with Pitrelli, 'Kill The King', and 'Dread And The Fugitive Mind', plus a closing MEGADETH medley mix.

MEGADETH would switch labels to the newly founded Sanctuary concern, led by IRON MAIDEN manager Rod Smallwood, for their 2001 release 'The World Needs A Hero'. This album had actually been recorded earlier for Capitol Records but handed back to the band upon the split. With Mustaine promising a return to heavier past form the omens looked good as the lead single 'Motor Psycho' rocketed straight in at the number one position for American Rock radio plays in its first week of release. The album duly debuted high at no. 16 in the American charts selling over 60'000 copies in its first week.

Meantime it was revealed that the singer now part owned a restaurant in Phoenix along with ALICE COOPER and a number of sports celebrities. The menu naturally included 'Megadeth Meatloaf'! Touring in the UK found MEGADETH supported by the Finnish 'Thrash cello' quartet APOCALYPTICA.

MEGADETH's projected Malaysian date as part of their 2001 Far Eastern dates at the Warp Club on August 2 in Kuala Lumpur was cancelled when the Malaysian government objected to the band's imagery deeming it "unsuitable for the youth of

Malaysia". The band were warned off in the strongest terms and threatened with arrest if they attempted to play the concert.

The bands North American bout of touring suffered no such problems commencing at the Saltair in Magna, Utah on September 7th and running through to a close in New York at the Irving Plaza on October 16th. Support band ENDO opened the proceedings and the headliners set list would fluctuate throughout as fans had been invited to vote for their favourite tracks. Meantime, ex-member MARTY FRIEDMAN finally re-emerged touting his new project RED DYE #2. The guitarist would also collude with UFO guitarist Michael Schenker on an all instrumental studio project.

MEGADETH, riding on a renewed commercial high, would be the subject of strong rumours hinting at a joint METALLICA / MEGADETH tour in the future—possibly even involving a bi-partisan band unit dubbed 'META-MEGA' by Mustaine.

With the close of US dates, Mustaine, along with producer Bill Kennedy, headed back into the studio undertaking a re-mix of the band's debut album 'Killing Is My Business . . . And Business Is Good'. The revised version would include tracks from earlier demos but initially not their take on NANCY SINATRA's 'The Boots Are Made For Walking', permission being denied from the original lyric writer following MEGADETH"s less than subtle change of words on their original session. As it transpired 'Boots . . .' did make the final running order as did bonus demo versions of 'Last Rites (Loved To Death)', 'Mechanix' and 'The Skull Beneath The Skin'.

As the year drew to a close, with MEGADETH now proudly sitting on a combined 15 million album sales to date, it would be revealed that Mustaine had embarked upon a studio project with DIAMOND HEAD guitarist Brian Tatler. Also in the works would be the MEGADETH's first live offering, a double CD and DVD affair entitled 'Rude Awakening' issued in March.

On April 3rd 2002 fans would be shocked to learn though that Mustaine had suffered a severe nerve damage injury to his left arm and subsequently announced his departure from the band—to all intents and purposes folding MEGADETH. This announcement came only hours after conjecture that Mustaine was likely to pull out of the band after he had reportedly 'found God'. What had actually happened was that the singer had lapsed from a lengthy period of sobriety and cut the circulation to the radial ulna nerve in his arm whilst falling asleep on it in the La Hacienda Rehabilitation Center in Hunt, Texas.

The fallout from Mustaine's shock announcement would be almost immediate with fast flowing rumours that Dave Ellefson was to join METALLICA. The bassist was keen to get back to work though, writing songs for DRY KILL LOGIC's second album and acting as co-producer for the Canadian band WARMACHINE.

Meantime Al Pitrelli's next career move was so sudden it did not have time to generate any speculation, the guitarist announced on the 7th of April as rejoining SAVATAGE ousting previous incumbent Jack Frost. However, before taking up this post Pitrelli would undertake live work with former SKID ROW vocalist SEBASTIAN BACH. Within days a further supposed revelation saw Pirelli's MEGADETH colleague Dave Ellefson coming onboard to supply bass, although these rumours would prove to be unfounded.

Fans would be ultimately relieved when the MEGADETH alumni guitarists Al Pitrelli and MARTY FRIEDMAN, bassist David Ellefson and drummer Jimmy DeGrasso revealed a new band union and were on the search for a lead vocalist. Friedman and Ellefson would also put in a surprise showing on STEVE RICHARDS 'Southbound Train' album, performing on the BUDDY HOLLY track 'That Makes It Tough'. Ellefson would also act as producer on demos for Phoenix based TWIST DEAD FABLE. The bassist would also be the subject of speculation that he had joined forces with ex-ANTHRAX guitarist Dan Spitz and IRON MAIDEN drummer Nicko McBrain in a new band project.

DeGrasso joined STONE SOUR on a temporary basis for their October US dates, filling in for regular Joel Ekman who had fractured his wrist. The Friedman / Ellefson / DeGrasso axis would unite for road work in early 2003 in support of the guitarist's 'Music For Speeding' solo album. Dave Mustaine issued a press statement in May revealing he was set to work on a solo record.

MEGADETH fans would be further appeased when word arrived of the September 2003 'Guitarevolution' tour of North America fronted up by ex-band members MARTY FRIEDMAN and CHRIS POLAND with his band OHM in union with ex-TESTAMENT guitarist Alex Skolnick's Jazz based ALEX SKOLNICK TRIO. Friedman's band for the occasion would prove noteworthy, comprising WATCHTOWER and SPASTIC INK guitarist Ron Jarzombek, the RAZOR and WARDOG credited bass player Chris Catero and his former MEGADETH colleague drummer Jimmy DeGrasso.

Al Pitrelli meantime engaged in a left field project dubbed O'2L in alliance with keyboard player Jane Mangini. The eponymous album saw the guitarist pursuing a wide range of Jazz, World, Rock, Funk, Electronica and New Age styles. Ellefson too kept in the public eye, laying down bass guitar for four tracks on the new SOULFLY album. As rumours circulating in October of 2003 put Mustaine in the recording studio laying down new material Jimmy De Grasso would be confirmed as part of the much vaunted WHITE LION reformation. Dave Mustaine would be back in the studio in early 2004, co-writing a track for Christian Rock band PILLAR.

In mid January Mustaine issued a press release confirming new MEGADETH material was on the horizon. Work had begun on bringing old, previously unused songs up to full strength and compiling new material since October of 2003. Although the classic 'Rust In Peace' line-up had been mooted, Mustaine finally built up a studio band comprising his former comrade in arms guitarist CHRIS POLAND with a rhythm section of bassist Jimmy Sloas from Christian bands DOGS OF PEACE and THE IMPERIALS and the FRANK ZAPPA, STING and DURAN DURAN credited Jazz drummer Vinnie Colaiuta.

Capitol Records planned a full re-release schedule of remastered catalogue albums to coincide with fresh product. Amongst the re-works would be the MD45 project album, boasting completely newly recorded lead vocals from Dave Mustaine. All of the archive MEGADETH albums boasted the addition of extra tracks in the form of rare period B sides and previously unheard demos. 'Rust In Peace' saw inclusion of working demos featuring lead guitar work from CHRIS POLAND but unfortunately what was intended by Mustaine as an acknowledgement of Poland's contributions backfired somewhat when the ex-guitarist sued him for their presence on the remaster. The case was settled out of court.

A new release 'The System Has Failed', set for September issue through Sanctuary Records, was recorded at Phase Four studios in Tempe, Arizona the album was originally set to feature cover artwork by Ed Repka, the artist that had crafted many of MEGADETH's classic sleeves, but this idea was scotched when cost became an issue. The album would be preceded by the single 'Die Dead Enough'.

Former MEGADETH bassist David Ellefson announced the formation of his new act F5, actually founded back in 2002. For this venture he would be joined by guitarists Steve Conley and John Davis, drummer David Small and singer Dale Steele F5 worked on recordings with producer Ryan Greene for an album release.

Fans would welcome the re-instatement of Nick Menza to the MEGADETH drum stool in July. That same month Dave Mustaine took some uncharacteristic verbal swings at former longstanding ally Dave Ellefson. Within days of this broadside Ellefson filed an $18.5-million lawsuit against Mustaine in the

Manhattan Federal Court, alleging the singer shortchanged him on profits and backed out of a deal to turn Megadeth Inc. over to him when the band broke up in 2002. Mustaine swiftly counter-sued, alleging that in May of 2004 Ellefson executed a settlement agreement in which he gave up his 20% interest in MEGADETH. Unfortunately for the ex-bassist his case was thrown out of court. Subsequently, a further legal agreement put restrictions on Ellefson's right to use the MEGADETH name in interviews or articles.

ANNIHILATOR guitarist Jeff Waters, a man already holding a placing in MEGADETH's history, would be in talks with Mustaine for the live line-up of the band. However, it would be Glen Drover, a veteran of EIDOLON and KING DIAMOND, that secured the position. Shortly afterward, ICED EARTH bassist James MacDonough was confirmed too. MacDonough's early career had seen terms of duty with Florida outfits MAD AXE, DELTA 9, INVADER, ORACLE and BRUTAL ASSAULT.

A video clip for the track 'Die Dead Enough' would launch promotion for the comeback album 'The System Has Failed'. The album sold 45,935 copies in the United States in its first week of release to debut at No. 18 on The Billboard 200 chart. In Canada the album sold 5,046 units on its debut at no. 10, setting a new high in the band's career by debuting in the highest chart position in the band's history. Meantime, the recently issued Capitol remasters series was also released as a box set compilation entitled 'Hell Wasn't Built In A Day: The Complete Remasters'.

On the touring front MEGADETH drafted up and coming act EARSHOT as support although October West Coast dates saw Christian Nu-Metal band 12 STONES and fellow veteran Thrashers EXODUS as openers. However, within days of this announcement 12 STONES dropped off the tour. With just days to go before the tour, commencing 23rd October in Reno, Nevada, it would be revealed that Nick Menza, apparently not up to full physical strength, had vacated the drum stool in favour of EIDOLON's Shawn Drover. With the MEGADETH tour doing brisk business, Mustaine's choice of opener EARSHOT dropped off the billing on 5th November.

To close the year, Mustaine would also find himself in an on screen project, as part of the 2005 'Rock School' documentary chronicling the pioneering work of Paul Green's School Of Rock Music in Philadelphia. The singer fronted up a version of 'Peace Sells' backed by musicians from the school.

European shows throughout February saw NWoBHM veterans DIAMOND HEAD chosen as support act. MEGADETH put in Japanese and Australian headliners, the latter with opening act DUNGEON, in April. Mustaine's faith put the band back into the news when Greek concerts, on June 17th and 18th in Athens and Thessaloniki, saw the ousting of domestic Black Metal band ROTTING CHRIST. In objecting to their presence, Mustaine stated as part of a lengthy explanation that he "would prefer not to play on concerts with Satanic bands". Apparently Mustaine claimed that ROTTING CHRIST could play, but in that event MEGADETH would withdraw.

MEGADETH unveiled the 'Gigantour' festival trek for US action in late July, heading a bill comprising DREAM THEATER, FEAR FACTORY, THE DILLINGER ESCAPE PLAN, SYMPHONY X, NEVERMORE, DRY KILL LOGIC and West Virginians BOBAFLEX. DREAM THEATER fulfilled these dates until September, when their position was taken by ANTHRAX. Apparently Dave Mustaine was not only instrumental in hand picking the bands for this bill but also insisting on a "fan-friendly" ticket price of $35. MEGADETH also scheduled its only second ever performance in Israel, on 22nd June at the Tel Aviv 'Metalist' festival. Unfortunately MEGADETH's performance would be stopped by police just four songs into their set due to the collapse of safety barriers.

To coincide with this intensive live activity a MEGADETH retrospective album, 'Greatest Hits: Back To The Start', boasting a track list voted for by fans, and a two disc DVD entitled 'Arsenal Of Megadeth' emerged. The album shifted just over 17,000 copies in its first week of US sales to debut at no. 65 on the national Billboard charts.

The 2nd August 'Gigantour' stop proved memorable when DREAM THEATER's set at the Nokia Live venue in Dallas saw the inclusion of an encore tribute to fallen guitar hero "Dimebag" Darrell Abbott of PANTERA and DAMAGEPLAN. The band performed a rendition of PANTERA's 'Cemetery Gates' with Dave Mustaine alongside, Burton C. Bell of FEAR FACTORY and Russell Allen of SYMPHONY X, putting in a rare onstage guest showing.

A MEGADETH tribute album, 'Hanger Of Souls' released by 2M Producciones, featured a whole crop of Argentinean Heavy Metal bands including JERIKO, LORD DIVINE, JESUS MARTYR, RENACER, MASTIFAL, BETO VAZQUEZ INFINITY, HUMANIMAL, SERPENTOR, PLAN 4 and TREN LOCO plus CELESTY from FINLAND, Spaniards RED WINE, HAMKA of France and Brazilians SAYOWA.

Intriguingly, Dave Mustaine announced that he would declare his intentions as to the future of MEGADETH following the band's 9th October concert in Buenos Aires, Argentina. The frontman duly announced from the stage "I told you earlier tonight that I was gonna let all of you know first before the rest of the world what our decision was—whether or not we were gonna continue with MEGADETH or not . . ." before a rendition of 'Coming Home'. Once the song was complete Mustaine simply stated "Yes".

Word arrived in January 2006 that the former MEGADETH rhythm section of bassist David Ellefson and drummer Jimmy DeGrasso was featured in RONNIE MONTROSE's live band and on his album 'Ronnie Montrose and Friends: 10x10'. As February opened, MEGADETH revealed they had parted ways with bassist James MacDonough, prompting rumours of a reunion with Ellefson. However, within days it was learned that former BLACK LABEL SOCIETY, ACE FREHLEY, SLASH'S SNAKEPIT and WHITE LION bassist James Lomenzo had been drafted. The new look band debuted their new four-stringer in the exotic climes of Dubai in United Arab Emirates as headliners of the March 16th 'Desert Rock' festival. In April the group was recording tracks at Sarm Studios in the UK with producer Jeff Balding for a new album billed 'United Abominations'. Recording sessions, which also took place in Los Angeles and Nashville, would include a cover version of LED ZEPPELIN's 'Out On The Tiles'. Meantime, ex-bassist James McDonough enrolled himself into New York's SPEED KILL HATE and temporarily covered for NEVERMORE's Jim Sheppard, the bassist forced out of action in order to undergo a procedure for Crohn's Disease.

MEGADETH signed a new label deal with Roadrunner Records in mid May. The second installment of 'Gigantour' rolled out across the USA in the autumn, commencing September 6th in Boise, Idaho. The trek featured also LAMB OF GOD, ARCH ENEMY, OPETH, OVERKILL, THE SMASHUP, INTO ETERNITY and SANCTITY. Japanese dates were lined up for October, during which the band debuted new track 'Gears Of War' at the Nagoya show on October 17th, upfront of Australian shows backed by SOULFLY, ARCH ENEMY and CALIBAN. 'United Abominations' was mixed during November by SABBAT guitarist Andy Sneap.

MEGADETH played a one-off "mini-concert" at a "Gears of War—Match Made In Hell" event on Halloween, to promote the Xbox 360 game 'Gears Of War'.

The album 'United Abominations' was preceded with an unusual single choice, a brand new re-recording of 1994 stage favourite 'Tout Le Monde'. The 2007 uptempo version, re-branded as 'A Tout Le Monde (Set Me Free)', would notably be a duet with LACUNA COIL's Cristina Scabbia and retained MARTY FRIEDMAN's original lead guitar solo alongside a new solo from Glen Drover.

MEGADETH

Image Entertainment gave a March 6th 2007 release of the 'That One Night: Live In Buenos Aires' live DVD, filmed live at Obras Stadium, Buenos Aires, Argentina on October 9th 2005. That same month MEGADETH acted as special guests to HEAVEN AND HELL's Canadian and US shows lasting into May. European festival appearances throughout the summer included gigs at Nürnberg, Germany's 'Rock Im Park' event, the Roeselare, Belgium 'Schwung Festival', Nürburgring, Germany's 'Rock Am Ring', Tampere, Finland's 'Sauna Open Air', Nijmegen, Holland's 'Fields Of Rock' festival, Zaragoza, Spain's 'Monsters Of Rock', Clisson, France's 'Hellfest' and Milan, Italy's 'Gods Of Metal'.

KILLING IS MY BUSINESS ... AND BUSINESS IS GOOD, Music For Nations MFN 46 (1985). Last Rites—Loved To Death / Killing Is My Business ... And Business Is Good / The Skull Beneath The Skin / Boots / Rattlehead / Chosen Ones / Looking Down The Cross / Mechanix.
PEACE SELLS ... BUT WHO'S BUYING?, Capitol TCEST 2022 (1986). Wake Up Dead / The Conjuring / Peace Sells / Devil's Island / Good Mourning—Black Friday / Bad Omen / I Ain't Superstitious / My Last Words. Chart position: 76 USA.
Wake Up Dead, Capitol CL476 (1987). Wake Up Dead / Black Friday (Live). Chart position: 65 UK.
Wake Up Dead, Capitol 12CL476 (1987). Wake Up Dead / Black Friday (Live) / Devil's Island (Live).
Anarchy In The UK, Capitol 12CL 480 (1988). Anarchy In The UK / Liar / 502.
Anarchy In The UK, Capitol CL 480 (1988). Anarchy In The UK / Liar. Chart position: 45 UK.
SO FAR, SO GOOD ... SO WHAT?, Capitol 48148-2 (1988). Into The Lungs Of Hell / Set The World On Fire / Anarchy In The U.K. / Mary Jane / 502 / In My Darkest Hour / Liar / Hook In Mouth. Chart positions: 18 UK, 28 USA, 37 SWEDEN, 41 NEW ZEALAND.
Mary Jane, Capitol CL 489 (1988). Mary Jane / Hook In Mouth. Chart position: 46 UK.
Mary Jane, Capitol 12CL 489 (1988). Mary Jane / Hook In Mouth / My Last Words.
No More Mr. Nice Guy, SBK SBK 4 (1989). No More Mr. Nice Guy. Chart position: 13 UK (B side by DANGEROUS TOYS).
Holy Wars ... The Punishment Due, Capitol 12CLP 588 (1990). Holy Wars ... The Punishment Due / Lucretia / Interview.
Holy Wars ... The Punishment Due, Capitol CLP 588 (1990). Holy Wars ... The Punishment Due / Lucretia. Chart position: 24 UK.
RUST IN PEACE, Capitol 91935-2 (1990). Holy Wars ... The Punishment Due / Hanger 18 / Take No Prisoners / Five Magics / Poison Was The Cure / Lucretia / Tornado Of Souls / Dawn Patrol / Rust In Peace.... Chart positions: 8 UK, 23 USA, 34 SWEDEN, 35 NEW ZEALAND.
Hanger 18, Capitol 12CLG 604 (1991). Hanger 18 / The Conjuring (Live) / Hanger 18 (Live) / Hook In Mouth (Live).
Hanger 18, Capitol CL 604 (1991). Hanger 18 / The Conjuring (Live). Chart position: 26 UK.
Foreclosure Of A Dream, Capitol (1992) (USA promotion). Foreclosure Of A Dream.
Symphony Of Destruction, Capitol CLPD 662 (1992). Symphony Of Destruction / In My Darkest Hour (Live).
Symphony Of Destruction, Capitol CLS 662 (1992). Symphony Of Destruction / Peace Sells ... But Who's Buying (Live) / Go To Hell / Breakpoint.
Symphony Of Destruction, Capitol CLS 662 (1992). Symphony Of Destruction / Peace Sells ... But Who's Buying (Live). Chart position: 15 UK.
Symphony Of Destruction, Capitol 44886 (1992) (USA release). Symphony Of Destruction / Skin O' My Teeth. Chart position: 71 USA.
COUNTDOWN TO EXTINCTION, Capitol 98531 (1992). Skin 'O My Teeth / Symphony Of Destruction / Architecture Of Aggression / Foreclosure Of A Dream / Sweating Bullets / This Was My Life / Countdown To Extinction / High Speed Dirt / Psychotron / Captive Honour / Ashes In Your Mouth. Chart positions: 2 USA, 5 UK, 5 NEW ZEALAND, 10 SWEDEN, 12 AUSTRIA, 15 GERMANY.
Skin 'O My Teeth, Capitol CL 669 (1992). Skin 'O My Teeth / Holy Wars ... The Punishment Due (General Norman Schwarzkopf mix). Chart position: 13 UK.
Skin 'O My Teeth, Capitol CDCL 669 (1992). Skin 'O My Teeth / Skin 'O My Teeth (Version) / Lucretia.
Skin 'O My Teeth, Capitol 10LP 669 (1992). Skin 'O My Teeth / Holy Wars ... The Punishment Due (Norman Schwarzkopf mix) / High Speed Drill Interview.
Sweating Bullets, Capitol CDCL 682 (1993). Sweating Bullets / Countdown To Extinction (Live) / Symphony Of Destruction (Gristle mix) / Symphony Of Destruction (Live).
Sweating Bullets, Capitol CL 692 (1993). Sweating Bullets / Ashes In Your Mouth (Live). Chart position: 26 UK.
Crown Of Worms, Capitol DPRO-79448 (1994) (US promotion release). Crown Of Worms / Black Curtain / Train Of Consequences.
Train Of Consequences, Capitol 12CL 730 (1994). Train Of Consequences / Holy Wars ... The Punishment Due (Live) / Peace Sells ... But Who's Buying (Live) / Anarchy In The UK (Live).
Train Of Consequences, Capitol CDCL 730 (1994). Train Of Consequences / Crown Of Worms / Peace Sells ... But Who's Buying? (Live) / Anarchy In The UK (Live).
Train Of Consequences, Capitol CL 730 (1994). Train Of Consequences / Crown Of Worms. Chart position: 22 UK.
Train Of Consequences, Capitol (1994) (Australian release). Train Of Consequences / Crown Of Worms / Black Curtains / Ashes In Your Mouth (Live) / Peace Sells ... But Who's Buying (Live).
Train Of Consequences, Capitol (1994) (Dutch release). Train Of Consequences / Crown Of Worms / Black Curtains / Peace Sells ... But Who's Buying (Live) / Ashes In Your Mouth (Live) / Anarchy In The UK (Live).
YOUTHANASIA, Capitol CDEST 2244 (1994). Reckoning Day / Train Of Consequences / Addicted To Chaos / A Tout Le Monde / Elysian Fields / The Killing Road / Blood Of Heroes / Family Tree / Youthanasia / I Thought I Knew It All / Black Curtains / Victory. Chart positions: 4 USA, 6 UK, 10 NEW ZEALAND, 13 GERMANY.
A Tout Le Monde, Capitol (1995) (USA release). A Tout Le Monde / Problems / New Wold Order (Demo).
A Tout Le Monde, Capitol (1995) (Dutch release). A Tout Le Monde / Symphony Of Destruction (Demo) / Architecture Of Aggression (Demo) / New World Order (Demo).
HIDDEN TREASURES, Capitol 33670 (1995). No More Mr. Nice Guy / Breakpoint / Go To Hell / Angry Again / 99 Ways To Die / Paranoid / Diadems / Problems. Chart positions: 28 UK, 90 USA.
Trust, Capitol (1997). Trust / A Secret Place / Tornado Of Souls (Live) / A Tout Le Monde (Live).
Almost Honest, Capitol CRYPT001 (1997) (UK promotion release). Almost Honest (Supercharger mix) / Almost Honest (Environmental Science mix).
Skin 'O My Teeth (Live), Fan Club (1997). Skin 'O My Teeth (Live) / Holy Wars (The Punishment Due) (Live) / Symphony Of Destruction (Live).
Trust, Capitol CDAS 118 (1997) (Promotion release). Trust / Almost Honest / I'll Get Even / Use The Man.
CRYPTIC WRITINGS, Capitol 7243 8 38262 2 3 (1997). Trust / Almost Honest / Use The Man / Mastermind / The Disintegrators / I'll Get Even / Sin / A Secret Place / Have Cool, Will Travel / She Wolf / Vortex / F.F.F. Chart positions: 10 USA, 14 FRANCE, 15 SWEDEN, 17 CANADA, 22 GERMANY, 34 NEW ZEALAND, 38 UK.
Use The Man, Capitol (1998). Use The Man.
Cryptic Sounds, Toshiba EMI TOCP-61001 (1998) (Japanese release). Trust / Almost Honest / Secret Place / She-Wolf / Vortex.
A Secret Place, Capitol (1998). A Secret Place.

Cryptic Writings—No Voices In Your Head, Toshiba EMI TOCP-61001 (1998) (Japanese release). Secret Place (Instrumental) / She-Wolf (Instrumental) / Trust (Instrumental) / Vortex (Instrumental) / Almost Honest (Instrumental).
Insomnia, Capitol DPRO6138152 (1999) (US promotion release). Insomnia / Prince Of Darkness.
Crush 'Em, Capitol (1999). Crush 'Em.
RISK, Capitol 7243 4 99134 0 0 (1999). Prince Of Darkness / Enter The Arena / Crush 'Em / Breadline / The Doctor Is Calling / I'll Be There / Wanderlust / Ecstasy / Seven / Time: The Beginning / Time: The End. Chart positions: 14 CANADA, 16 USA, 17 SWEDEN, 27 NEW ZEALAND, 29 UK, 37 FRANCE, 38 GERMANY.
Kill The King, Capitol DPRO6151692 (2000) (US promotion release). Kill The King.
Breadline, TOCP-65388 (2000) (Japanese release). Breadline (Radio edit) / Breadline (Active mix by J.J. Puig) / Insomnia (Rhys Fulber mix) / Symphony Of Destruction (The Gristle mix) / Crush 'Em (Jock mix) / Holy Wars ... The Punishment Due (The General Schwartzkopf mix).
The World Needs A Hero Sampler, Sanctuary SANDJ-85504-2 (2001) (US promotion release). Return To Hanger 18 / Burning Bridges / Moto Psycho.
Dread And The Fugitive Mind, Sanctuary SANDJ855142 (2001) (US promotion release). Dread And The Fugitive Mind / Dread And The Fugitive Mind (Album version) / Dread And The Fugitive Mind (Call out hook).
The World Needs A Hero Sampler, Metal Is MISPR006 (2001) (UK promotion release). Disconnect / World Needs A Hero / Moto Psycho / 1000 Times Goodbye / Return To Hangar 18.
Moto Psycho, Sanctuary SANDJ-85503-2 (2001) (US promotion release). Moto Psycho / Moto Psycho (Clean edit).
Moto Psycho, Metal Is MISP2006 (2001) (UK promotion release). Moto Psycho / Dread And The Fugitive Mind.
THE WORLD NEEDS A HERO, Sanctuary 84503-2 (2001). Disconnect / The World Needs A Hero / Moto Psycho / 1000 Times Goodbye / Burning Bridges / Promises / Recipe for Hate ... Warhorse / Losing My Senses / Dread And The Fugitive Mind / Silent Scorn / Return To Hangar 18 / When. Chart positions: 16 USA, 23 FINLAND, 28 FRANCE, 36 GERMANY, 38 SWEDEN.
Rude Awakening Sampler, Sanctuary SANDJ-85524-2 (2002) (US promotion release). Peace Sells ... But Who's Buying? (Live) / Reckoning Day (Live) / Hanger 18 (Live) / Holy Wars (The Punishment Due) (Live) / 1000 Times Goodbye.
RUDE AWAKENING, Sanctuary 84544 (2002). Dread & The Fugitive Mind / Kill The King / Wake Up Dead / In My Darkest Hour / Angry Again / She Wolf / Reckoning Day / Devil's Island / Train Of Consequences / A Tout Le Monde / Burning Bridges / Hangar 18 / Return To Hangar 18 / Hook In Mouth / Almost Honest / 1000 Times Goodbye / Mechanix / Tornado Of Souls / Ashes in Your Mouth / Sweating Bullets / Trust / Symphony Of Destruction / Peace Sells ... But Who's Buying / Holy Wars ... The Punishment Due. Chart positions: 93 FRANCE, 100 CANADA, 115 USA.
THE SYSTEM HAS FAILED, Sanctuary SANCD297 (2004). Blackmail The Universe / Die Dead Enough / Kick The Chair / The Scorpion / Tears In A Vial / I Know Jack / Back In The Day / Something I'm Not / Truth Be Told / Of Mice And Men / Shadow Of Deth / My Kingdom Come. Chart positions: 4 GREECE, 10 CANADA, 12 FINLAND, 14 SWEDEN, 18 USA, 28 FRANCE, 29 GERMANY, 32 HOLLAND, 38 DENMARK, 43 AUSTRIA, 57 SWITZERLAND, 60 UK.
A Tout Le Monde, Roadrunner RR PROMO 991 (2007) (Promotion release). A Tout Le Monde / Sleepwalker.
UNITED ABOMINATIONS, Roadrunner (2007). Sleepwalker / Washington Is Next! / Never Walk Alone / United Abominations / Gears Of War / Blessed Are The Dead / Play For Blood / A Tout Le Monde (Set Me Free) / Amerikhastan / You're Dead / Burnt Ice. Chart positions: 2 FINLAND, 5 CANADA, 8 USA, 15 SWEDEN, 17 AUSTRIA, 21 NORWAY, 23 AUSTRALIA, 23 UK, 24 ITALY, 28 GERMANY, 31 IRELAND, 38 SWITZERLAND, 40 FRANCE, 49 HOLLAND.

MEKONG DELTA

GERMANY — *Wolfgang Borgmann (vocals), Uwe Baltrusch (guitar), Ralph Hubert (bass), Jörg Michael (drums).*

A highly inventive and technical Thrash Metal act. MEKONG DELTA originally went under pseudonyms to protect their true identities. Project mentor and bassist Ralph Hubert, owner of Aaarg Records, (a.k.a. 'Bjorn Eklund) assembled an all star cast of seasoned musicians from the extreme Metal scene of the day. LIVING DEATH guitarists Frank Fricke and Reiner Kelch performed on the 1987 Wolfgang Borgmann fronted debut album under the guises of Vincent St. John and Rolf Stein respectively whilst the RAGE duo of Peter "Peavy" Wagner and guitarist Jochen Schröder would also be involved in the studio. Drummer Jörg Michael (a.k.a. 'Gordon Perkins'!) was also a member of RAGE at the time. This line up was retained for the 1988 follow up 'The Music Of Erich Zann'.

Unable to attend the recording of 'The Gnome' EP Jörg Michael's place was taken by HOLY MOSES and GAMMA RAY drummer Uli Kusch under the anglicised nom de guerre of 'Patrick Duval'.

Wolfgang Borgmann left in 1990 to be replaced by erstwhile SIREN singer Douglas Lee for the 'Dances Of Death' mini album. Michael joined HEADHUNTER. Ex-SODOM and U.D.O. guitarist Uwe Baltrusch played on the 1989 'Principle Of Doubt' album, this opus seeing Jörg Michael's return to the drum kit. For the 1991 live offering 'Live At An Exhibition' the group had installed new guitarist Georg Syrmbos.

A latter day ex-MEKONG DELTA drummer, Peter Haas of AIN'T DEAD YET and CALHOUN CONQUER repute, featured on 1992's 'Kaleidoscope' and the 1994 effort 'Visions Fugitive'. Haas later joined BABYLON SAD and KROKUS. Jörg Michael's highly rated skills would find the stickman journeying through LAOS, HEADHUNTER, GLENMORE, GRAVE DIGGER, RUNNING WILD and STRATOVARIUS. By 2004 he was ensconced in the ranks of British Hard Rock veterans SAXON, appearing on their 'Lionheart' album.

In the wake of the 22 track Zardoz Music compilation, 'The Principle Of Doubt', 2006 would witness renewed activity on the MEKONG DELTA front with news of a new album in the works compiled by Ralf Hubert and guitarist Peter Sjöberg. Replacing Haas on drums would be former band member Uli Kusch. Although the music for a new record had been completed, by November MEKONG DELTA had still not secured a singer.

MEKONG DELTA, Aaarrg AAARRG 4 (1987). Without Honour / The Cure / The Hut Of Baba Yaga / Heroes Grief / Kill The Enemy / Black Sabbath.
The Gnome, Aaarrg AAARRG 8 (1987). The Gnome / The Hut Of Baba Yaga / Without Honour / The Cure.
THE MUSIC OF ERICH ZANN, Aaarrg AAARRG 11 (1988). Age Of Agony / True Lies / Confession Of Madness / Hatred / Interludium (Begging For Mercy) / Prophecy / Memories Of Tomorrow / I, King, Will Come / The Final Deluge / Epilogue.
PRINCIPLE OF DOUBT, Aaarrg AAARRG 19 (1989). A Question Of Trust (Cyberpunk) / The Principle Of Doubt / Once I Believed / Ever Since Time Began / Curse Of Reality / Twilight Zone (Lord Fouls Hort) / Shades Of Doom (Cyberpunk 2) / The Jester / El Colibri / No Friend Of Mine.
Toccata, Aaarrg AAARRG 17 (1989). Toccata / Black Betty / Interludium.
DANCES OF DEATH (AND OTHER WALKING SHADOWS), Aaarrg ARG 23034-2 (1990). Dances Of Death: I) Introduction, II) Eruption, III) Beyond The Gates, IV) Outburst, V) Days Of Betrayal, VI) Restless, VII) Sanctuary, VIII) Finale / Transgressor / True Believers / Night On A Bare Mountain.
KALEIDOSCOPE, IRS 986963 (1992). I.N.N.O.C.E.N.T.? / Sphere Eclipse / Dance On A Volcano / Dreaming / Heartbeat / Heartbeat / Shadow Walker / Sabre Dance / Misunderstanding / About Science.
CLASSICS, Aaarrg ARG 27045-2 (1993). Interludium (Begging For Mercy) (Part I) / Toccata / Twilight Zone / The Gnome / The Hut Of Baba Yaga / Night On A Bare Mountain / Interluduim (Part II) / El Colibri.
LIVE AT AN EXHIBITION, Metal Machine RTD 3120042238 (1993). The Cure / Transgression / True Believers / Night On A Bare Mountain / Memories Of Tomorrow / Hut Of Baba Yaga / Heroes Grief / True Lies / Toccata.
VISIONS FUGITIVES, Bullet Proof CDVEST 19 (1994). Imagination / Suite For Group And Orchestra: a) Introduction (The Danger In Dreams / The Chronicle Of Doubts—Book 3 / Chapter 1) / b) Preludium (Lord Kevin's Lament / The Chronicle Of Doubts—Book 2 / Chapter 8) / c) Allegro (Mhorams Victory / The Chronicle Of Doubts—Book 3 / Chapter 15) / d) Dance (The Corrupt / The

Chronicle Of Doubts—Book 3 / Chapter 18) / e) Fugue (Knowledge / The Chronicle Of Doubts—Book 2 / Chapter 23 / f) Postludium (Lena's Daughter / The Chronicle Of Doubts—Book 2 / Chapter 21) / The Healer / Days Of Sorrow.
PICTURES AT AN EXHIBITION, Bullet Proof IRSCD993 626 (1997). Promenade / Gnomus / Interludium / Il Vecchio Castello / Interludium / Tuileries (Dispute D'Enfants Apres Jeux) / Bydtlo / Interludium / Ballet Of The Unhatched Chicks / "Samule" Goldenberg And "Schmuyle" / Promenade / Lomoges: Le Marché (La Grande Nouvelle) / Catacombae (Sepulcrum Romancum) / Lingua Mortis / The Hut On Chicken'sw Legs / The Heroic Gate (In The Old Capital Of Kiev).

MELANCHOLIC SEASONS

GERMANY — *Björn Hoppe (vocals), Andi Adler (guitar), Andi Henke (guitar), Alex Haus (bass), Thomas Adler (drums).*

Thrash Metal laced with Scandinavian style Death persuasions. MELANCHOLIC SEASONS came into being during 1995, the first four song demo citing a line up of lead vocalist Holger Jung, guitarists Daniel 'Jesus' Bracevac and Jean-Claude Rettig, bass player Christian 'Hirsel' Sieverding and with Guido Denk on the drums. Shortly after Andi Henke took the place of Rettig. A third demo, released in 1996, found Nico 'Satanas' Seim handling the bass with former BLASPHEMIA man Michael Hille' Hillenbrand taking the drum stool thereafter. Seim then decamped, forcing MELANCHOLIC SEASONS to gig minus bass for a period. In the summer of 1999 another BLASPHEMIA member, singer Björn Hoppe, enrolled. With this revised line up MELANCHOLIC SEASONS entered the recording studio to lay down the album 'In My Eyes'. To promote this product the band undertook a spate of club dates utilising Gerd Lücking, guitarist with COURAGOUS and drummer for LIGHTMARE, and former DEADSPAWN musician Dominik Mangelmann as stand in bassists. The band encountered further line up difficulties with the Bracevac usurped by Andi 'der General' Adler.

MELANCHOLIC SEASONS introduced Alex Haus on bass in December of 2002. Ex-bassist Gerd Lücking joined REBELLION as their new drummer in April of 2004. Thomas Adler would be installed as MELANCHOLIC SEASONS drummer that year.

IN MY EYES, (1999). In Your Eyes / This Is Your God / I Am The Evil / Frozen Lyrics / Just A Fuckin' Lullaby / Drowned In Tears.

MELIAH RAGE

BOSTON, MA, USA — *Mike Munro (vocals), Jim Koury (guitar), Anthony Nichols (guitar), Jesse Johnson (bass), Stuart Dowie (drums).*

Inspired by METALLICA's first ever visit to Boston in 1983, MELIAH RAGE was formed by guitarists Jim Koury and erstwhile GANG GREEN man Anthony Nichols. Koury had previously played in an AEROSMITH tribute group in partnership with STEEL ASSASSIN axeman Mark Schulman, better known as MARC FERRARI of KEEL infamy. The line-up had stabilised by 1986 with the addition of vocalist Mike Munro, bassist Jesse Johnson and drummer Stuart Dowie. The band name was a progression from the moniker of one of Koury's earlier bands MELIAH CRAZE.

releasing a promising three track demo in 1987, MELIAH RAGE was picked up by Epic and debuted in 1988 with 'Kill To Survive'

The 1989 live album, 'Live Kill', was a one sided affair recorded at Harpo's club in Detroit. Micah Shevaloff contributes keyboards to the 'Solitary Solitude' album.

By 1996 MELIAH RAGE included bassist Dave Barcus and drummer Bob Mayo in the ranks. The band still remained active and released a fifth album called 'Unfinished Business' on their own label in 1999. The album contained unreleased material recorded between the years 1992 and 1996. By this point Barcus and Mayo had been replaced bassist Clark Lush and drummer Sully Erna. The latter of course would go on to

MELIAH RAGE

enjoy huge fame as frontman for platinum artists GODSMACK. With GODSMACK's continued success the 'Unfinished Business' record was re-issued in late 2002 with alternate art. The 'Unfinished Business' album has since been reissued again in 2004 as a bonus disc on certain pressings of the 'Barely Human' album. The band in interviews in 2005 distanced themselves from the 1999 recording suggesting it was never intended to be a formal release.

MELIAH RAGE were still operational during 2002, recording a new studio album 'Barely Human' for Screaming Ferret Records. Alongside original members Anthony Nichols, Jim Koury and Jesse Johnson the new look band saw newcomers Paul Souza on vocals and ex-WARGASM drummer Barry Spillberg.

Prominent shows in October 2004 saw appearances at 'The Metal Nation: Northern Aggression' festival in Manchester, New Hampshire and the 'Sayonara Summer Fest' in Bellingham, Massachusetts. With original drummer Stuart Dowie making a return to the ranks, MELIAH RAGE entered Danger Multitrack Studios in Providence, Rhode Island to record a new album 'The Deep And Dreamless Sleep' in February 2005. The album surfaced in September on Screaming Ferret Wreckords.

MELIAH RAGE were announced as support to METAL CHURCH's January 2007 US tour dates.

KILL TO SURVIVE, Epic 463257-1 (1988). Beginning Of The End / Bates Motel / Meliah Rage / Deadly Existence / Enter The Darkness / Impaling Doom / The Pack.
LIVE KILL, Epic 6E 45370 (1989). Beginning Of The End / Kill To Survive / Bates Motel / Deadly Existence / The Pack.
SOLITARY SOLITUDE, Epic 466675-1 (1990). Solitary Solitude / No Mind / Decline Of Rule / Retaliation / Deliver Me / The Witching / Lost Life / Swallow Your Soul / Razor Ribbon.
UNFINISHED BUSINESS, Meliah Rage (1999). Mind Stalk / Moment Of Silence / Ruthless / Decade Dreams / Blacksmith / Possessing Judgement / Violent Force / Season To Kill.
BARELY HUMAN, Screaming Ferret (2004). Hate Machine / Invincible / Barely Human / Ungodly / Wrong Place, Right Time / Rigid / Bloodbath / Hell Song / Motor Psycho.

MEMORAIN

GREECE — *Ilias Papadakis (vocals / guitar), Alex Doutsis (guitar), Kostas Bagiatis (bass), Panos Andricopoulos (drums).*

MEMORAIN, founded in September of 1999, released the demo 'Until You Die' and donated their version of MEGADETH's 'Disconnect' to the tribute album 'Droogie-A Megadeth'. A further demo followed entitled 'Digital Rain'. An album of the same title followed in 2002 for NMC Music, the group at this juncture comprising SECOND HELL and IVORY credited vocalist / guitarist Ilias Papadakis, LEAVING TOMORROW guitarist Alex Doutsis, ex-SECOND HELL bass player Kostas Bagiatis with Panos Andricopoulos on the drums. A line-up changes subsequently saw the exit of Doutsis.

The 2003 album 'White Lion' boasted several guitar solos courtesy of former DEATH and TESTAMENT man JAMES MURPHY. A 2006 album, 'Reduced To Ashes', produced By Ilias Papadakis and Haris Zourelidis and released in April through EMI Records, saw the return of Alex Doutsis and notable guest inclusions from Jeff Waters from ANNIHILATOR, giving a solo on the track 'TV War', and former MEGADETH drummer Nick Menza.

Until You Die EP, (2001). Turned On You / Until You Die / Extend Of Life / Alone / Restore My Way.
DIGITAL CRIMES, NMC (2002). Digital Crimes / Until You Die / Bones / Alone / Turned On You / Extend Of Life / Burning Justice / Last War—Final Day / Silence / Visions Of Darkness.
WHITE LINE, NMC Music Productions (2003). The Real World / Buried In Lies / Condemn Me To Obscurity / Inside My Mind / White Line / Silent Cry / High Treason / My Choice.
REDUCED TO ASHES, EMI (2006). The Land Of Pain / The Evil Within / Blinded By The Lights / Charge / See / Hate / Reduced To Ashes / TV War / Facing My Demons / Inside My Sickness / Against My Fate / Nothing Is Left / The Lights Into The Night.

MENDEED

GLASGOW, UK — *David Proctor (vocals), Steven Nixon (guitar), Steph Gildea (guitar), Chris Lavery (bass), Kevin Matthews (drums).*

MENDEED is a Glasgow based Metal act created in mid 2000 by singer David Proctor, guitarists Steph Gildea and Steven Nixon, bassist Chris Lavery and drummer Kevin Matthews. A brace of EPs, 'Killing Something Beautiful' through Casket Records, and 'As We Rise', emerged in 2003. At this juncture MENDEED performed distinctly Nu-Metal styled Rock, taking on live work supporting the likes of FONY, DEVOLVED and VACANT STARE. A change in style ensued toward melodic Death Metal / Metalcore and notably future official biographies neglected to mention the band's earlier works. 'Killing Something Beautiful' was recorded at Philia Studios with producer Dave Chang in November 2002.

Much of 2003 would be spent traversing the UK supporting the likes of CHARGER, MY RUIN, PITCHSHIFTER, 8 FOOT SATIVA and ANTHRAX, raising their profile higher with a valuable Radio One Rock Show session. Signing to Rising Records in December 2003, MENDEED's first product in their re-vamped format would be the 2004 Rising Records 'Ignite The Flames' single. A September 2004 mini-album, 'From Shadows Came Darkness', featured a guesting Sarah Jezebel Deva of CRADLE OF FILTH and ANGTORIA repute aiding on vocals.

A further EP, 'Act Of Sorrow' cut at New Rising Studios, Essex with producer Mark Daghorn, arrived in May 2005, promoted by an opening slot with CRADLE OF FILTH in April then gigs supporting AMEN. In September the band did the UK rounds once again, this time partnering DRAGONFORCE.

The band played their part in honouring METALLICA, contributing their rendition of 'The Thing That Should Not Be' to the album 'Remastered', this set being a complete remake of 'Master Of Puppets' in joint celebration of the twentieth anniversary of the classic album's release and the 25th anniversary of UK Rock magazine Kerrang! MENDEED's status rose rapidly with supports to ANTHRAX, CRADLE OF FILTH, SLIPKNOT, TRIVIUM, BLEEDING THROUGH and SHADOWS FALL. The band also opened for FEAR FACTORY on five European shows.

A debut album, 'This War Will Last Forever' produced by Mark Daghorn, was signed to Germany's Nuclear Blast Records for June 2006 release. UK editions issued on Rising Records sported different cover art. The band put in a significant appearance at the GUNS N' ROSES headlined 'Download' festival in Castle Donington, UK on June 11th. UK shows in early October saw support from KINGSIZE BLUES and SOLITUDE.

Further high profile European gigs saw MENDEED announced as support to SLAYER's October 'Unholy Alliance' dates.

As We Rise EP, (2003).
Killing Something Beautiful EP, Casket CSK 013 (2003). Killing Something Beautiful / Parasite / Reticence / No Escape.
Ignite The Flames EP, Rising (2004). Ignite The Flames / Laid To Waste / Fall To Me.
FROM SHADOWS CAME DARKNESS, Rising RISINGCD002 (2004). Hope Lies In The Heart Of Even The Darkest Soul / Act Of Sorrow / Blood Laced Tears / Ignite The Flames / Fatal Poison Whisper / Perpetual Sin / Glory Be Thy Name.
Beneath A Burning Sky, Rising (2005). Beneath A Burning Sky / The End Of Man / Divided We Fall.
Act Of Sorrow, Rising (2005). Act Of Sorrow / Hollow / Messiah.
THIS WAR WILL LAST FOREVER, Rising RISINGCD009 (2006) (UK release). What We Have Become / Beneath A Burning Sky / Stand As One And Fight For Glory / Remains Of The Day / Chapel Perilous / The Morning Aftermath / Poisoned Hearts / Withered And Torn / Resurrecting Hope / The Blasphemy We Bleed / The Reaper Waits / The Black Death.
THIS WAR WILL LAST FOREVER, Nuclear Blast NB 1702-2 (2006) (European release). What We Have Become / Beneath A Burning Sky / Stand As One And Fight For Glory / Remains Of The Day / Chapel Perilous / The Morning Aftermath / Poisoned Hearts / Withered And Torn / Resurrected Hope / For Blasphemy We Bleed / The Reaper Waits / The Black Death.
POSITIVE METAL ATTITUDE, (2006).
THE DEAD LIVE BY LOVE, Nuclear Blast NB 1798-2 (2007). Burning Fear / The Fight / The Dead Live By Love / Fuel The Fire / Gravedigger / Our War / Blood Brothers / Through Dead Eyes / Reload 'N' Kill / Take Me As I Am / It's Not Over Yet / Thirteen.

MERCENARY

SAN FRANCISCO, CA, USA — *Sven Soderlund (vocals / guitar), Danny White (guitar), Brooks Holland (bass), Slade Anderson (drums).*

San Francisco Metal act MERCENARY became the stuff of folklore as the Bay Area Thrash scene developed almost mythical proportions on mainland Europe during the 90s. MERCENARY's legacy far outweighed their original achievements, the band having only cut one demo tape in 1986 and performed just two gigs.

The original incarnation of the band, vocalist Sven Soderlund, guitarist Danny White, bassist Brooks Holland and drummer Slade Anderson, folded in the fall of 1986. A reformation attempt was brought about in 1987 involving MORDRED guitarist Jim Sanguinetti and drummer Gannon Hall but after a miserly two live appearances MERCENARY imploded yet again in February of 1987. Both Hall and guitarist Danny White allied themselves with MORDRED. Following a spell at the Guitar Institute of Technology Sanguinetti would jump back to MORDRED too.

The Autumn of 1987 saw a re-built MERCENARY working with producer Steve Heger on album recordings. Joining Soderlund for these tracks would be guitarist Jim Taffer, bassist Brooks Holland and drummer Slade Anderson. Soderlund would go on to found MULTIPLY.

The band bowed to pressure for a reformation show on November 13th 2001 at the C.W. Saloon venue in San Francisco with plans to record this event for a live album.

The MERCENARY 2001 line-up will consisted of founding members frontman Sven Soderlund and drummer Slade Anderson alongside erstwhile MY VICTIM and ULYSSES SIREN bassist J.R. Clegg and former HEATHEN, UTERIS, DOGFACE and current VICIOUS RUMORS guitarist Ira Black. The latter would join HEATHEN's live line-up but would ironically be superseded by Soderlund in July 2004.

MERCENARY reunited to perform alongside fellow Bay Area veterans MORDRED and ANVIL CHORUS to perform on April 12th 2007 at Bottom of the Hill in San Francisco for a benefit concert for the family of late San Francisco rock musician Curtis Grant, of BLACK CHERRY, AMERICAN HEARTBREAK and TOUCH ME HOOKER, who lost his battle with Non-Hodgkin's Lymphoma on March 20th.

MERCILESS

SWEDEN — *Roger Peterrson (vocals), Erik Wallin (guitar), Fredrik Karlen (bass), Stefan Karlsson (drums).*

MERCILESS formed with original vocalist Kalle in 1986. The group released two demos, 'Behind The Black Door' and 'Realm Of The Dark'. As drummer Stefan Karlsson joined Punk act DIA PSALMA was superseded by Peter Stjärnvind in 1991. MERCILESS released a promo split single with COMECON the same year.

Various members of the band pursue careers in other acts. Stjärnvind is also a member of UNANIMATED, FACEDOWN and Punk outfit LOUDPIPES. Bassist Fredrik Karlen is also in LOUDPIPES rebilling himself Carl Leen. In their time the group had opened for SEPULTURA, ENTOMBED and SODOM. Band drummer 'Stipen' would join TRANSPORT LEAGUE during November 2001, subsequently enrolling into BLACKSHINE.

MERCILESS reformed for an eponymous 2003 album. Their Stockholm show in August of that year would be captured on the DVD 'Live Obsession', this also including video from a 1999 performance. Both Erik Wallin and Stipen subsequently joined HARMS WAY.

THE AWAKENING, Deathlike Silence ANTIMOSH 001 (1991). Pure Hate / Souls Of The Dead / The Awakening / Dreadful Fate / Realm Of The Dark / Dying World / Bestial Death / Denied Birth.

THE TREASURES WITHIN, Active ATV 26 (1992). The Treasures Within / Mind Possession / Darkened Clouds / The Book Of Lies / Perish / Shadows Of Fire / Life Aflame / Act Of Horror / Branded By Sunlight / Dying World.

UNBOUND, No Fashion NFR 007 (1994). Unbound / The Land I Used To Walk / Feebleminded / Back To North / Silent Truth / Lost Eternally / Nuclear Attack / Forbidden Pleasure.

MERCILESS, Black Lodge (2003). Cleansed By Fire / Violent Obsession / Cold Eyes Of Grey / Human Waste / Burn All The Way / Unearthly Salvation / Painless End / Mind Possession / Fallen Angels Universe / In Your Blood.

MERENDINE ATOMICHE

CITTADELLA, ITALY — *Luca Zandarin (vocals), David Bisson (guitar), Giulia Cerardi (guitar), Dario Bianchi (bass), Luca Cerardi (drums).*

Cittadella, Padova's MERENDINE ATOMICHE operate in old school Bay Area Thrash Metal territory. The group was forged in February of 1995 by drummer Luca Cerardi and vocalist Luca Zandarin. To stem an ever flowing tide of line up changes the band drafted Cerardi's 13 year old sister Giulia on guitar! At this stage the group opted to become a METALLICA tribute band, enlisting a second guitarist David Bisson in May of 1998. A demo, naturally titled 'Tribute To Metallica', followed as did live shows opening for WHITE SKULL.

David Bianchi would then be next in line for MERENDINE ATOMICHE membership, taking over the bass position in October of 1999. The group would tour Italy still performing METALLICA covers but then would cut the mini-album 'The Holy Metal' for No Brain Records comprising of originals. During 2000 the group put in over 100 gigs and in August of 2001 also participated in a tour of Canada.

Rhythm guitarist Luca Securo would augment the band during October of 2001. MERENDINE ATOMICHE signed to the French Deadsun label, and were slated to record a 2002 album 'Walk Across Fire' at the famous Sunlight Studios in Sweden with Tomas Skogsberg manning production. Special guests on the album were projected to be Anders Lundemark of KONKHRA and Jeff Waters from ANNIHILATOR.

Recording at New Sin Studios in Treviso, Italy, MERENDINE ATOMICHE announced that SEVEN WITCHES guitarist JACK FROST was to act as co-producer for new album 'Raw'. This album was signed over to Belgian label Mausoleum Records in early 2006.

The band utilised New Sin studios in Loria, Treviso in August 2007 to cut tracks for the album 'Rude Rebel Brotherhood'.

THE HOLY METAL, No Brain Records NBR 013 (2001). War Or Peace / Holy Metal / The Truth / The Guardian / Mental Agony / Holy Metal (Video).

WALK ACROSS FIRE, Independent (2002). Blood For Glory / Walk Across Fire / Game Over / The Cheat Of The Cross / Total Darkness / Revenge / The Spirit Of Wolf / Victory Over The Enemy.

RAW, Mausoleum (2006). In The Cage / Roads And Beers / Raw / Peace Means War? / I Want To Be A Man / Ocean's Shadows / Zero Degrees / Breathe The Big Apple / We Didn't Know / 0,4 L / Shake For Me.

MESHUGGAH

UMEÅ, SWEDEN — *Jens Kidman (vocals), Fredrik Thordendal (guitar), Mårten Hagström (guitar), Dick Lövgren (bass), Nicolas Lundgren (drums).*

An experimental Thrash band boasting guitarists that both employ seven and eight string guitars named after the Yiddish term for 'Crazy', MESHUGGAH formed in Umeå during 1987 as a trio of guitarist Fredrik Thordendal, ex-bassist for MEMORANDUM, bassist Peter Nordin and vocalist / guitarist Jens Kidman. Throughout their career MESHUGGAH have established a reputation for adventurism and non conformity in their approach to the Metal genre. Having gained a foothold with their first album, 'Contradictions Collapse', the MESHUGGAH collective decided on one of the most radical shifts in direction the Metal world has ever seen, dropping subtle hints with the 'None' EP before launching a whole new style with 'Destroy Erase Improve'. From this point, MESHUGGAH would become synonymous with extreme eccentricity, polyrhythmic power and Jazz complexity. By 'Chaosphere' the transformation had been completed, de-tuned eight string guitars now raging viciously over the most disturbing form of Progressive Metal yet heard.

At first branded METALLIEN, this title soon gave way to MESHUGGAH. The band's first commercial offering came with an independent EP 'Psykisk Testbild', released through local record store Garageland in 1989. Only 1000 copies were pressed and this would serve as the only MESHUGGAH release to feature Niklas Lundgren on drums, before he was supplanted by Thomas Haake the following year. MESHUGGAH briefly employed the services of HOLLOW guitar player Marcus Bigren in 1990. Also distributed that year would be a six song demo cassette, 'Ejaculation Of Salvation'. It would not be until 1991 that the band got back into the studio, delivering a two track demo comprising 'Qualms Of Reality' and 'All This Because Of Greed'.

German label Nuclear Blast took the band on to issue the debut album 'Contradictions Collapse' in 1991. An out and out Thrashfest from start to finish, 'Contradictions Collapses hi-tech metal drew exemplary reviews. Despite the flawless nature of this album, MESHUGGAH was yet to show their true colours musically and, indeed, commercially as 'Contradictions Collapse' was soon swallowed up in a plethora of Swedish Death / Thrash releases and soon dropped off the radar. Sometime after this release Jens Kidman opted to prioritise the lead vocal role and Mårten Hagström, previously a member of Domsjö Thrashers BAROPHOBIA, assumed his guitar duties.

In 1993 Thordendal appeared as part of the XXX ATOMIC TOEJAM duo alongside with his former MEMORANDUM colleague Petter Marklund to record the limited edition EP 'A Gathering of the Tribes for the First/Last Human Be-In' for Cold Meat Industry. Unfortunately, progress was stalled when the quartet was beset by a catalogue of injuries to band members. Guitarist Fredrik Thordendal, a carpenter by trade, has cut the top off a finger and drummer Tomas Haake trapped his hand in a lathe machine.

The self-produced transitional EP 'None', recorded at Tonteknik Recordings in Umeå, followed in 1994. When MESHUG-

GAH toured Europe in 1995 supporting American outfit MACHINE HEAD guitarist Mårten Hagström actually stepped in for the headliner's guitarist Rob Flynn after the American had suffered a hand injury. The roles would be reversed when MESHUGGAH, having lost bassist Peter Nordin due to a severe ear infection, opted to resume action as a quartet with Thordendal playing bass, including lead solos, through his guitar rig. Other gigs on the tour just had two guitars with Mårten playing through a pitch shifter shifted one octave down.

July 1995 marked the public airing of the new sounding MESHUGGAH with the groundbreaking 'Destroy, Erase, Improve', laid down at Soundfront Studios in Uppsala with Daniel Bergstrand behind the desk. The title told the full story, the band having stripped Metal down to the bare essentials before completely rebuilding it in a totally abstract form. It should be noted that the 1995 EP 'Selfcaged', although released by Nuclear Blast in both Europe and America, sees a completely different track listing for each territory. The same year Thordendal would donate a guitar solo to the BLENDER release 'Back To Planet Softcore'. Live work for MESHUGGAH in 1995 was rounded off with a batch of Autumn dates shared with CLAWFINGER Scandinavia and Germany, again completed without a bassist. By the time of their Hamburg concert, Gustaf Hielm of CHARTA 77 had enrolled to fulfill four-string duties to finish the tour and then launch into a month long set of shows with HYPOCRISY.

Fredrik Thordendal assembled a side project with Petter Marklund titled FREDRIK THORDENDAL'S MUSICAL DEFECTS, recording an album, 'Sol Niger Within', in 1997. The guitarist would also figure on three tracks on the MATS/MORGEN album. MESHUGGAH's own 1997 release, the mini-album 'The True Human Design', would witness a remix of 'Future Breed Machine' featuring CLAWFINGER's Jocke Skog, and one new track, 'Sane'.

The November 1998 outing 'Chaosphere' would cement the MESHUGGAH line-up of vocalist Jens Kidman, guitarists Fredric Thordendal and Mårten Hagström, bass player Gustaf Hielm and drummer Tomas Haake. This album, stripped of any remaining thrash vestiges, presented the group as a full-blown Math Metal smorgasbord of near impenetrable jarring time changes, atonality and dissonant riffing. Whilst fans revelled in the maze like meanderings, critics struggled to dissect and analyse, hailing Haake's unconventional use of dual 4/4 and 23/16 rhythm, Kidman's mechanical staccato bark and Thordendal's liberal usage of avant-garde Jazz.

Fans were quick to jump on the fact that advance promotional copies of 'Chaosphere' hosted a track 'Unanything', this song being neglected from the regular release. Initial concert work to push 'Chaosphere' had the band on the road in the USA upfront of a Scandinavian leg with ENTOMBED. The band toured America in 1999 supporting SLAYER and here found that their unique slant on Metal had gained them kudos outside of the mainstream Metal press as many musician and instrument based publications began picking up on the band. European shows that June had the band lined up with German Hardcore merchants STAHLHAMMER and legendary US act S.O.D.

The 2001 release 'Rare Trax' was compiled in order to put the band's 1989 demo onto CD format for the first time. Also included were later demos and both studio and live video footage. Gustaf Hielm left the band in July 2001.

MESHUGGAH received an enviable opportunity in September 2001 invited to open for the September U.S. tour leg of platinum artist TOOL. The highly anticipated 'Nothing' album sold a respectable 6'500 copies in North America on its first week of release, MESHUGGAH becoming the first band in the history of Nuclear Blast Records to break into the Billboard Top 200, landing at no. 165. 'Nothing' debuted employment of custom built Nevborn and Ibanez eight string guitars for Thordendal and Hagström, with two extra low strings enabling

MESHUGGAH

the pair to explore the depths of the lowest registers possible. Adding to the inhuman, regimented atmosphere of the record would be a decision to programme all percussion. They would pull in another first for the label with 'Nothing', it delivering the inaugural review in the esteemed 'Rolling Stone' magazine for the company. The relationship with TOOL would be strengthened as MESHUGGAH united with the avant-garde American Rockers for a further lengthy string of shows taking them up until December. MESHUGGAH paired off with STRAPPING YOUNG LAD for US dates in May of 2003.

Scheduled appearances for early July at the 'Quartfestivalen' in Kristiansand, Norway and 'Arvikafestivalen' event in Arvika, Sweden would be cancelled. Apparently guitarist Mårten Hagström was struck with an unspecified affliction whilst drummer Tomas Haake was suffering a flare up of carpal tunnel syndrome. Meantime, vocalist Jens Kidman took time out to guest on the track 'The Dream Is Over' featured on the MUSHROOMHEAD album 'XIII'. In November Thordendal contributed a guitar solo to the track 'Asphyxiate' on the 'Irradiant' album from French Nu-Thrash act SCARVE.

MESHUGGAH pulled in the ARMAGEDDON, EUCHARIST, ARCH ENEMY and IN FLAMES credited Dick Lövgren as new bass guitarist in February of 2004. This revised unit entered the studio to record an EP, comprising of a solitary twenty minute track entitled 'I', for Fractured Transmitter Records, the label formed by MUSHROOMHEAD vocalist Jason Mann. That same month the group also announced their next album for Nuclear Blast would be a further full length album 'Catch Thirtythree', albeit yet another single song session. Released in June, the album sold just under 7'000 copies in its first week of US sales to debut on the Billboard charts at number 170.

European dates in June of 2005 saw French act SCARVE as opening act. MESHUGGAH then announced a return to the USA alongside GOD FORBID, THE HAUNTED and MNEMIC as part of the 'Fury of the Fall' world tour in October. Throughout November Dick Lövgren and Tomas Haake conducted a number of Swedish musicians clinics.

Ejaculation Of Salvation, (1989). Ejaculation Of Salvation / Greed / Cadaverous Mastication / The Dept Of Nature / Sovereignes Morbidity / Erroneous Manipulation.

Psykisk Testbild, Garageland BF 634 (1989) (Limited edition 1000 copies). Cadaverous Mastication / Sovereigns Morbidity / The Depth Of Nature.

CONTRADICTIONS COLLAPSE, Nuclear Blast NB 049 (1991). Paralysing Ignorance / Erroneous Manipulation / Abnegating Necessity / Internal Evidence / Qualms Of Reality / We'll Never See The Day / Greed / Choirs Of Devastation / Cadaverous Mastication.

Promo 1991, (1991). Qualms Of Reality / All This Because Of Greed.

None EP, Nuclear Blast NB102-2 (1994). Humiltitive / Sickening / Ritual / Gods Of Rapture / Aztec Two-Step.

Selfcaged, Nuclear Blast (1995) (USA release). Gods Of Rapture / Humiliative / Suffer In Truth / Inside What's Within Behind / Gods Of Rapture (Live).

Selfcaged, Nuclear Blast NB 132-2 (1995) (European release). Selfcaged / Vanished / Suffer In Truth / Inside What's Within Behind.

DESTROY ERASE IMPROVE, Nuclear Blast NB 121 (1995). Future Breed Machine / Beneath / Soul Burn / Transfixion / Vanished / Acrid Placidity / Inside What's Within Behind / Terminal Illusions / Suffer In Truth / Sublevels.

Future Breed Machine, Nuclear Blast (1996) (Split single with HYPOCRISY. Limited edition 1000 copies). Future Breed Machine.

THE TRUE HUMAN DESIGN, Nuclear Blast NB 268-2 MCD (1997). Sane / Future Breed Machine (Live) / Future Breed Machine (Mayhem version) / Futile Bread Machine (campfire version) / Quant's Quantastical Quantasm (Ambient Techno by Quant of DOT) / Friend's Breaking and Entering (Ambient Techno by Friend of DOT) / Terminal Illusions (Video).

CHAOSPHERE, Nuclear Blast NB 3662 (1998). Concatenation / New Millennium Cyanide Christ / Corridor of Chameleons / Neurotica / The Mouth Licking What You've Bled / Sane / The Exquisite Machinery of Torture / Elastic.

RARE TRAX, Nuclear Blast NB 605-2 (2001). War / Cadaverous Mastication / Sovereigns Morbidity / Debt of Nature / By Emptyness Abducted / Don't Speak / Abnegating Cecity (1990 demo) / Internal Evidence (1990 demo) / Concatenation (remix) / Ayahuasca Experience / New Millenium Cyanide Christ (video) / Elastic (video-Live).

NOTHING, Nuclear Blast NB 542-2 (2002). Stengah / Rational Gaze / Perpetual Black Second / Closed Eye Visuals / Glints Collide / Organic Shadows / Straws Pulled At Random / Spasm / Nebulous / Obsidian. Chart positions: 41 SWEDEN, 165 USA.

I, Fractured Transmitter Records FTRCD001 (2004). I.

CATCH THIRTYTHREE, Nuclear Blast NB 1311-2 (2005). Autonomy Lost / Imprint Of The Un-saved / Disenchantment / The Paradoxical Spiral / Re-inanimate / Entrapment / Mind's Mirrors / In Death—Is Life / In Death—Is Death / Shed / Personae Non Gratae / Dehuminization / Sum. Chart positions: 12 SWEDEN, 124 FRANCE, 170 USA.

NOTHING: REMIX, Nuclear Blast (2006) (CD + DVD). Stengah / Rational Gaze / Perpetual Black Second / Closed Eye Visuals / Glints Collide / Organic Shadows / Straws Pulled At Random / Spasm / Nebulous / Obsidian / Straws Pulled Random (Live At Download 05) / In Death Is Death (Live At Download 05) / Future Breed Machine (Live At Download 05) / Rational Gaze (Video) / Shed (Video) / New Millenium Cyanide Christ (Video) / Rational Gaze (Mr. Kidman Delirium Version).

MESSIAH

SWITZERLAND — *Andy Kaina (vocals), R.B. Brogi (guitar), Patrick Hersche (bass),.*

Founded in 1984 by guitarist R. B. Brogi, MESSIAH built up impressive sales of their first two albums. 'Extreme Cold Weather' sold in excess of 12'000 units alone, prompting a deal with Noise Records. MESSIAH's line-up changed in 1993 with the departure of vocalist Andy Kaina and bassist Patrick Hersche. The bass position was filled by Oliver Koll and a new vocalist was found in THERION man Christofer Johnsson. Hersche subsequently joined AMON and then later Gothic Metal band SUCCUBUS. Johnsson reinstigated THERION. Bassist Patrick Hersche joined Death Metal crew REQUIEM during 2003.

HYMN TO ABRAMELIN, Chainsaw Murder (1986). Hymn To Abramelin / Messiah / Anarchus / Space Invaders / Thrashing Madness / Future Aggressor / Empire Of The Damned / Total Maniac / The Dentist.

EXTREME COLD WEATHER, Chainsaw Murder 004 (1988). Extreme Cold Weather / Enjoy Yourself / Johannes Paul Der Letzte (Dedicated In Hate To Pope John Paul II) / Mother Theresa (Dedicated In Love To Mother Theresa) / Hyper Bores / Radezky March: We Hate To Be In The Army Now / Nero / Hymn To Abramelin (Live) / Messiah (Live) / Space Invaders (Live) / Thrashing Madness (Live) / Golden Dawn (Live) / The Last Inferno (Live) / Resurrection (Live) / Ole Perversus (Live).

CHOIR OF HORRORS, Noise NO183-2 (1991). Choir Of Horrors / Akasha Chronicle / Weeping Willows / Lycantropus Erectus / Münchhausen Syndrom / Cautio Criminalis / Northern Commans / Weena.

ROTTEN PERISH, Noise CD084 04552 (1992). Prelude: Act Of Fate / For Those Who Will Fail / Living With A Confidence / Raped Bodies / Lines Of Thought Of A Convicted Man / Conviction / Condemned Cell / Dreams Of Eschaton / Anorexia Nervosa / Deformed Creatures / Alzheimer's Disease / Ascension Of A Divine Ordinance.

Psychomorphia EP, Noise N0244-3 (1994). Birth Of A Second Individual / Psychomorphia / Right For Unright / M.A.N.I.A.C.

UNDERGROUND, Noise NO244-2 (1994). Battle In The Ancient North / Revelation Of Fire / Underfround / Epitaph / The Way Of The Strong / Living In A Lie / Screams Of Frustration / The Ballad Of Jesus / Dark Lust / One Thousand Pallid Deaths / The End.

METAL CHURCH

SEATTLE, WA, USA — *Ronny Munroe (vocals), Kurdt Vanderhoof (guitar), Jay Reynolds (guitar), Steve Unger (bass), Kirk Arrington (drums).*

Auburney, Seattle's METAL CHURCH rank as one of the true founders of the early 80s North American Thrash Metal scene. Guitarist Kurdt Vanderhoof created the band, actually naming it after the commonly used name for his San Francisco apartment, upon his departure from Punk act THE LEWD. As THE LEWD evolved into more of a Hardcore Thrash act Vanderhoof found himself more and more interested in the Metal scene. During a 1980 gig LEVIATHAN members guitarist Rick Condran and Aaron Zimpel got into a conversation with Vanderhoof and discussed the idea of an "ultimate" Metal band. As Vanderhoof, Condran, bassist Steve Haat and drummer Aaron Zimple (a.k.a. Aaron Whymer) created ANVIL CHORUS-THE CHURCH OF METAL the remnants of LEVIATHAN, Zimple, switching to vocals, bassist Bill Skinner and drummer Kenny Feragen became Progressive Rock trio VIENNA.

Upon Vanderhoof's return to Aberdeen, Washington in 1981 the first Vanderhoof all instrumental demo comprised the LEVIATHAN track 'Red Skies', 'Heads Will Roll' and 'Merciless Onslaught'. The formative band went through numerous drummers (they even invited a pre METALLICA Lars Ulrich to join). A pair of other local musicians, guitarists Thaen Rasmussen, ex-VY-KING, and Doug Piercy, ex-COBRA and DELTA, liked the name ANVIL CHORUS so much they took it for themselves. They did however offer acknowledgement with the homage to their inspiration with the track 'Bow To The Church Of Metal'. Vanderhoof trimmed the name of his act down to simply METAL CHURCH.

SINISTER SAVAGE man Billy McKay fronted METAL CHURCH for a brief spell prior to founding GRIFFIN. Singer Ed Bull was invited to join the band but Condran objected. When the guitarist quit METAL CHURCH Bull was on the mike stand the very next day. With the abandonment of VIENNA Zimpel also joined forgoing his normal frontman position to become METAL CHURCH's drummer. With this line-up METAL CHURCH cut their second demo. This four track affair included a rework of 'Heads Will Roll' titled 'Put The Chains On', an ANVIL CHORUS number 'Arab Nations', Wake Up And Die' and 'The Trap Is Set'. The latter track displayed the enmity between Bull and Condran as the singer's chorus of "Die Ricky, Die!" amply illustrates.

However, despite intensive tape trading, this early incarnation of METAL CHURCH folded, with Haat going on to a temporary stint with GRIFFIN then glamsters JETBOY. Bull founded CONTROL with guitarists Dino Scarposi and Bill Tuder. A later version of CONTROL featured another ex-ANVIL CHORUS man guitarist Doug Piercy, later of HEATHEN. Zimpel meantime joined the ranks of ANVIL CHORUS. Vanderhoof journeyed back to Seattle to create SHRAPNEL. In 1983 this act had evolved into METAL CHURCH with a line-up of Vanderhoof, vocalist David Wayne, guitarist Craig Wells, bassist Duke Erikson and drummer Kirk Arrington. An earlier SHRAPNEL vocalist Mike Murphy opened up the vacancy for Wayne by bailing out to join ROGUES GALLERY. The band debuted on May 4th 1984, performing at the D&R Theater in Aberdeen with ROGUES GALLERY and THE MELVINS as opening acts. Before long, METAL CHURCH's uncompromising approach had placed the band, alongside QUEENSRYCHE, at the head of the

METAL CHURCH (pic: Rich Galbraith)

Seattle scene. Early devotees numbered latter day influential figures such as Kurt Cobain and Layne Staley.

In 1984, METAL CHURCH signed to the Seattle based Ground Zero label and released the critically acclaimed, self-titled debut the same year. The band had previously contributed the track 'Deathwish', recorded at Woodmont Beach Studio in Kent, Washington with co-producer Richard Rogers, to the label's 'Northwest Metalfest' compilation album. METAL CHURCH shared the grooves alongside other local acts such as THE BONDAGE BOYS, LIPSTICK, STRIKE, SATO, MACE, OPEN FIRE, KODA KAHN and OVERLORD.

The debut album was to be re-issued by Elektra in 1985 following the signing of a major deal that would propel the group to the forefront of the mid 80s Thrash Metal boom. The band closed the year as part of what was to rank as one of the ultimate thrash concerts, ranked alongside METALLICA, MEGADETH and EXODUS at a New Year Eve bash at the San Francisco Civic Center.

In 1986, METAL CHURCH released their second album, 'The Dark', an album that quickly warranted its status as one of the premier Metal release of the 80's and probably the band's finest moment to date. Committed to tape by the team of producer Mark Dodson and engineer Terry Date, 'The Dark', blended high octane thrash with monumental heavy metal and even caught the band expanding into epic territory with songs such as 'Watch The Children Pray' and 'Burial At Sea'. 'The Dark' broke the Billboard top 100 at number 92. On November 8th 1986 the band's headline show at the Country Club in Reseda went down in Thrash history as METALLICA took on the opening spot to break in their new bassist Jason Newsted. Major exposure was guaranteed by a support tour to METALLICA, the group acting as openers throughout Europe and Canada.

However, in a band bust up Wayne was ejected. Wayne would reveal that band problems with drugs had forced him out of the picture. Wayne's first attempt at putting a new band unit together involved ex-W.A.S.P. guitarist Randy Piper but only songwriting sessions were undertaken before the singer moved on. The frontman then worked with ex-LIZZY BORDEN guitarist Gene Allen, then REVEREND and later joining INTRINSIC. The singer also had a brief union with HEATHEN.

In August 1988 METAL CHURCH commenced work on the 'Deadly Blessing' album, this record witnessing Terry Date's promotion from engineer to producer, saw METAL CHURCH now fronted by ex-HERETIC singer Mike Howe and with former BLIND ILLUSION man John Marshall augmenting Wells on guitar. Initially the band drafted in guitarist Mark Baker to fulfill Vanderhoof's role for touring in America but added Marshall on a full time basis. Howe had been suggested to the band by Vanderhoof, the guitarist having produced the debut HERETIC album. Vanderhoof's dislike of touring prompted his opting out.

However, Vanderhoof was to remain a central character within METAL CHURCH as a songwriter and conspirator and regained his taste for playing by forming HALL AFLAME and releasing an album through IRS.

METAL CHURCH's 1991 opus, 'The Human Factor', saw production credits going to Mark Dodson. Although a solid effort, the record failed to provide upward momentum. In 1992 Howe got his name onto the second BOOTSAUCE album 'Bull' guesting on the track 'Touching Cloth'. Marshall meantime boosted the band's profile in an unusual manner when he was drafted into METALLICA on a temporary basis. Hetfield had burnt his hand and deputised his guitar duties to Marshall for much of their American tour. This was the second time Marshall had depped for Hetfield, the first was in 1987 when the frontman had broken his wrist skateboarding.

Following October 1993's 'Hanging In The Balance', released on JOAN JETT's Blackheart label, itself a subsidiary of Epic, saw the inclusion of a guesting JERRY CANTRELL from ALICE IN CHAINS on opening song 'Gods Of Second Chance'. Unfortunately promotion for the album was poor and the use of a garish cartoon sleeve also put many fans off. The group got to tour the European continent once again as it headed up the heavyweight October 1995 ZODIAC MINDWARP, VICIOUS RUMORS and KILLERS package. However, METAL CHURCH then duly fizzled out. However, during 1997, Kurdt Vanderhoof made his recording comeback in the modestly titled VANDERHOOF, a band that also comprised old METAL CHURCH colleague Kirk Arrington. Although the VANDERHOOF album surprised many with its undoubted quality under pressure from their German record label the classic 'The Dark' era METAL CHURCH reunited in mid 1998. The band heralded their return with probably their most over the top release to date with a live album culled from tapes recorded in the mid eighties.

The band bounced back with a fresh studio album 'Masterpeace' (somewhat confusingly released with the track titles in completely the wrong order) touring Europe on a double package with THUNDERHEAD throughout October and November of 1999. By 2000 METAL CHURCH had a new rhythm section of bassist Brian Lake and drummer Jeff Wade, both members of VANDERHOOF.

The story took a further twist when it emerged that Wayne had set up a fresh act titled DAVID WAYNE'S METAL CHURCH! Joining him were ex-WARRIOR guitarist Joe Floyd, former JOINT FORCES, GEEZER and THUNDERHEAD guitarist Jimi Bell and drummer B.J. Zampa, a veteran of YNGWIE MALMSTEEN, MVP, TONY MACALPINE and THUNDERHEAD. Bell was also operational with the covers band TATTERED TRAMPS.

VANDERHOOF made a return in 2002 with a fresh album 'A Blur In Time' featuring new vocalist Drew Hart and a reinstated Kirk Arrington on drums. David Wayne was back in the news in July of 2003, the singer joining BASTARDSUN, the British Metal band assembled by former CRADLE OF FILTH guitarist Stuart Anstis.

METAL CHURCH itself regrouped during 2003, original members Kurdt Vanderhoof and Kirk Arrington bringing onboard vocalist Ronny Munroe from Seattle metal band ROTTWEILLER. Local try out gigs were conducted under the pseudonym of "MENTAL SEARCH". By the following year it was learned that the re-vamped band, having cut a new album 'Weight Of The World', also included former MALICE guitarist Jay Reynolds. 2004 Winter dates in the US saw Canadians 3 INCHES OF BLOOD as support act.

Although Vanderhoof prioritised the METAL CHURCH album 'Weight Of The World', he would also fire up a Progressive Rock project entitled PRESTO BALLET. This band would comprise VANDERHOOF colleagues vocalist Damon Albright, bassist Brian Lake and keyboard player Brian Cokeley alongside former METAL CHURCH man Jeff Wade on drums. Subsequently this intended project would be issued under the existing

METAL CHURCH (pic: Rich Galbraith)

VANDERHOOF banner.

Live dates for METAL CHURCH in Europe, including an announced headliner at the Dutch 'Raise Your Fist' festival, were cancelled. However, the band put in extensive Summer road work in the USA as part of the 'American Metal Blast' tour flanking W.A.S.P., L.A. GUNS and STEPHEN PEARCY. However, with Vanderhoof already having given a prior commitment to engineer material for TRANS SIBERIAN ORCHESTRA, his place on these dates would be filled by VICIOUS RUMORS and EMERALD TRIANGLE man Ira Black.

The METAL CHURCH family was dealt a huge blow on 10th of May with the passing of David Wayne. Just 47 years old, the singer died from complications from injuries he sustained in a head-on automobile accident months previously.

Early February 2006 saw a line-up change as an official announcement read "Due to health complications from years of struggling with diabetes, Kirk Arrington has stepped down as METAL CHURCH's drummer. He will be missed and we wish him only the best." Stepping in as substitute would be the SAVATAGE, CHRIS CAFFERY and TRANS SIBERIAN ORCHESTRA credited Jeff Plate.

The album 'A Light In The Dark' featured a re-recording of the classic 'Watch The Children Play' in tribute to David Wayne. METAL CHURCH European tour dates in June would see support from VICTORY and GORILLA MONSOON. In November 2006 Jay Reynolds, retaining his ties to METAL CHURCH, was announced as heading up the resurrected MALICE.

January 2007 headline dates in January 2007 saw MELIAH RAGE as support. However, at a show in Nashville on January 31st drummer Jeff Plate suffered spinal problems, dating from a 1994 herniated disc injury sustained while playing golf, causing the cancellation of further concerts. In March it was learned METAL CHURCH lead singer Ronny Munroe was working on a solo album with his former ROTTWEILLER band mates guitarist Rick Van Zandt and bassist Israel Rehaume.

METAL CHURCH, Ground Zero (1984). Beyond The Black / Metal Church / Merciless Onslaught / Gods Of Wrath / Hitman / In The Blood / (My Favorite) Nightmare / Battalions / Highway Star.

THE DARK, Elektra 9 60493-2 (1986). Ton Of Bricks / Start The Fire / Method To Your Madness / Watch The Children Pray / The Dark / Psycho / Line Of Death / Burial At Sea / Western Alliance. Chart position: 92 USA.

Fake Healer, Elektra PRO CD 8051 (1989) (USA promotion). Fake Healer.

Watch The Children Pray, Elektra (1989) (USA promotion). Watch The Children Pray.

Badlands, Elektra (1989) (USA promotion). Badlands.

BLESSING IN DISGUISE, Elektra K 96087-2 (1989). Fake Healer / Rest In Pieces / Of Unsound Mind / Anthem To The Estranged / Badlands / Spell Can't Be Broken / It's A Secret / Cannot Tell A Lie / Powers That Be. Chart position: 75 USA.

THE HUMAN FACTOR, Epic 4678162 (1991). The Human Factor / Date With Poverty / Final Word / In Mourning / In Harm's Way / In Due Time / Agent Green / Flee From Reality / Betrayed / Fight Song.

HANGING IN THE BALANCE, Blackheart BH1001 (1993). Gods Of Second Chance / Losers In The Game / Hypnotized / No Friend Of Mine / Waiting For A Saviour / Conductor / Little Boy / Down By The River / End Of The Age / Lovers And Madmen / A Subtle War.

LIVE, Steamhammer SPV 085-18562 CD (1998). Ton Of Bricks / Hitman / Start The Fire / Gods Of Wrath / The Dark / Psycho / Watch The Children Pray / Beyond The Black / Metal Church / Highway Star.

MASTERPEACE, Steamhammer SPV 085-18702 CD (1999). Sleeps With Thunder / Falldown / Into Dust / Kiss For The Dead / Lb Of Cure / Faster Than Life / Masterpeace / All Your Sorrows / They Signed In Blood / Toys In The Attic / Sand Kings.

THE WEIGHT OF THE WORLD, Steamhammer SPV 800000701 (2004). Leave Them Behind / Weight Of The World / Hero's Soul / Madman's Overture / Sunless Sky / Cradle To Grave / Wings Of Tomorrow / Time Will Tell / Bomb To Drop / Blood Money.

A LIGHT IN THE DARK, Steamhammer (2006). Light In The Dark / More Than Your Master / Disappear / Pill For The Kill / Mirror Of Lies / Light Machine / Blinded By Life / Beyond All Reason / Under The Gun / Caught Up / No Remains / Watch The Children Play.

METAL DUCK

LIVERPOOL, UK — *Andy Parker Tortoise Gore (vocals), Fozzy Daniels Tarbuck Monkhouse Disneyland (guitar), Keith Tractor Safari 25 Minutes Robot (bass), Glam Dyno Rod Piella (drums).*

A bizarre, yet short-lived Liverpool based humourous Thrash band, METAL DUCK were quickly eclipsed by LAWNMOWER DETH and ACID REIGN. The band started life in 1985 as RAMPANT DUCK before adopting the METAL DUCK title and releasing 'Quack core' demo in 1987. The group issued another demo with former ELECTRO HIPPIES vocalist Andy in 1988 before sharing a split LP on the Leicester based RKT label with LAWNMOWER DETH, featuring the line-up of vocalist Hutti, guitarist Fozzy, bass player Keith and drummer Dave.

A second, full album emerged in 1990 entitled 'Auto Ducko Destructo Mondo' before the group went tail up.

QUACK EM ALL, RKT CMO 192 (1989). Destruction Song / Stepping Stone To Hell / Pek-Yr-Ass / Bombay Duck / NxDxQxC / Cheese Puff Death Squad / March Of The Metal Ducks To The Ponds Of Hell / Rod, Jane & Freddys Total Noise Annihilation / Der, Der, Der / Ooerr I've Got A Sore Throat.

AUTO DUCKO DESTRUCTO MONDO, RKT CDMO 196 (1990). Litteral / Duckula Assault / Drunk And A Flirt / Smell Of Sex / To Kill Again / Gate Of Asgard / Twilight Zone / Rod, Jane And Freddy (Part 2) / Mean, Green And Pink / Well Fu(n)ked Up / In Death / Apollyon Communiqué.

METAL MESSIAH

NOTTINGHAM, NOTTINGHAMSHIRE, UK — *Jim Aspinall (vocals), Biff (guitar), Grem Darroch (guitar), Graham Kerr (bass), Kev Frost (drums).*

A Nottingham Speed Metal act formed from the remains of Punk act THE VARUKERS, this group adopted new title of ARBITRATOR in 1987 before changing to METAL MESSIAH with the addition of ex-PARALEX vocalist Phil Ayling and guitarist Grem Darroch. METAL MESSIAH recorded a 'Friday Rock Show' session in 1988 before cutting their first demo with vocalist Phil Ayling but he was replaced by Jim Aspinall, ex-WICKED, for the 'Mad Man' demo.

The group actually enjoyed brief interest from the major record companies until Thrash lost its appeal. Drummer Kevin Frost later resurfaced as a member of CEREBRAL FIX, a resurrected THE VARUKERS and appeared on the debut 2002 album 'Reverence The Sacrifice' from HELVIS.

HONOUR AMONG THIEVES, RKT CMO 195 (1990). Intro / Mad Dogs Of War / Madman / Kiss Of Nosferatu / Honour Among Thieves / Metal Messiah / Curse Of The King / Nightwing / Awakening.

METALLICA

LOS ANGELES, CA, USA — *James Hetfield (vocals / guitar), Kirk Hammett (guitar), Robert Trujillo (bass), Lars Ulrich (drums).*

Essentially the brainchild of Danish émigré Lars Ulrich (born December 26th, 1965), a self-confessed New Wave Of British Heavy Metal fan. Ulrich gave up a potential career as a tennis pro in order to beat the living daylights out of the drums, METALLICA have unarguably been the leading lights of the Thrash Metal scene since their inception in the early 80's. Although considered to be a San Francisco based group, the darlings of the Bay Area scene, METALLICA was actually formed by Ulrich in Los Angeles. However, whilst Ulrich gets much of the credit for the rise of METALLICA, the band's roots essentially began the day one Ron McGovney and the AEROSMITH obsessed James Hetfield (born August 3rd, 1963) had first met at Los Angeles East Middle School in 1977.

Hetfield's first act in 1979 was titled OBSESSION and covered classic Rock acts such as UFO (hence the band title), BLACK SABBATH and LED ZEPPELIN. OBSESSION comprised of Hetfield on vocals and guitar, Jim Arnold on lead guitar, bassist Ron Veloz and drummer Rick Veloz. Hetfield's class mate Ron McGoveney roadied for the band. By 1980 Hetfield and Arnold had teamed up with Jim's brother Chris on drums to form the RUSH covers band SYRINX. This trio soon folded and downtime was filled by Hetfield and McGovney jamming with drummer Dave Marrs.

The duo's next attempt was a more serious venture titled PHANTOM LORD with guitarist Hugh Tanner. This act evolved into LEATHER CHARM comprising of Hetfield on vocals, Troy James on guitar, McGoveney on bass and drummer Jim Mulligan. LEATHER CHARM began writing their own material and 'Hit The Lights' was borne out of these sessions. However, the band were still playing covers including the favourite 'Hollywood Teaze' by GIRL and IRON MAIDEN tracks. Two other LEATHER CHARM songs 'Let's Go Rock n' Roll' and 'Handsome Ransom' would later be fused to become 'No Remorse'.

With the band's music beginning to adopt a far heavier stance a parting of the ways with Jim Mulligan occurred and, responding to an add placed in the Los Angeles paper 'Recycler', LEATHER CHARM invited would-be drummer Lars Ulrich, previously a member of HELLCASTLE, down to meet them. However, they quickly sent him away with a flea in his ear, unimpressed with this big-mouthed little Danish kid with an obsession for the New Wave Of British Heavy Metal. With his tail firmly between his legs, Ulrich returned to Europe where he would spend a few months following the likes of DIAMOND HEAD and MOTÖRHEAD's Lemmy around before flying back to Los Angeles intent on finally putting the band of his dreams together.

Having been somehow promised a spot on fanzine writer Brian Slagel's forthcoming compilation album 'Metal Massacre' on the newly formed Metal Blade Records, even though Ulrich didn't have a band at the time, Ulrich used this to his advantage in gaining favour with LEATHER CHARM.

Despite not being a particularly good drummer at the time, Ulrich convinced Hetfield and McGovney to recruit him to join him in this endeavour, eventually leading to the formation of METALLICA. This band title winning out over RED VETTE, GRINDER and BLITZER. Guitarist Lloyd Grant was drafted after replying to an advert. The version of 'Hit The Lights' that was put down onto a Tascam four track recorder saw vocals, guitar and bass handled by Hetfield with Ulrich on the drums. Grant recorded a lead guitar solo at his hose just hours before the delivery deadline.

It was this incarnation that featured on the first 'Metal Massacre' compilation album. Unfortunately, the group was credited as METTALLICA on the first pressing. Both McGovney and Grant's names were also misspelled as 'Mcgouney' and 'Llyod' respectively. However, the album put together a whole host of names that would become greater forces in the future such as RATT, Ron Keel's STEELER, BITCH, MALICE, Florida's AVATAR (SAVATAGE) and CIRITH UNGOL.

Grant's tenure with the group was cut short because, according to the man who replaced him, ex-PANIC guitarist Dave Mustaine, Lars Ulrich allegedly did not want a black musician in the group. This being one of the reasons as to why 'Hit The Lights' was re-recorded for the second pressing of the 'Metal Massacre' compilation album with Mustaine in the band. This version not only saw Grant's name missing from the band line-up but featured the correct spelling of the band name. Needless to say, Mustaine's version of events would later be vigorously denied.

Grant was, however, to reappear in the mid 80's with a new act titled DEFCON contributing the track 'Red Light' to a 1986 compilation album.

Hetfield was still wary of his vocal talents so the band pulled in RUTHLESS vocalist Sammy Dijon although the union was brief, just two weeks, and no gigs were performed with this line-up.

Still fronted by a reluctant James Hetfield, in the role of lead vocalist, METALLICA's first showing came on March 14th 1982 at the Radio City venue in Anaheim. With little in the way of original material worked up, METALLICA performed mainly NWoBHM songs, pointedly neglecting to mention they were in fact covers. At that first concert METALLICA performed their own numbers 'Hit The Lights' and 'Jump In The Fire' bolstered by DIAMOND HEAD's 'Helpless', 'Sucking My Love', 'Am I Evil?' and 'The Prince' plus 'Killing Time', originally by Irish band SWEET SAVAGE, and 'Let It Loose', by premier British band SAVAGE.

METALLICA then got to work recording their first ever demo which featured the LEATHER CHARM track 'Hit The Lights', SWEET SAVAGE's 'Killing Time' and SAVAGE's 'Let It Loose'. Oddly, the last-named act would be excised from METALLICA's history, with only a bootleg single, originally released on the 'Bongwater' label in 1987, bearing testament to the influence of the Mansfield Metal act.

With this cassette the band then gained the valuable support slot to SAXON at the Whiskey A Go-Go club in Los Angeles on 27th March. The Barnsley big teasers were playing two shows back to back and originally MÖTLEY CRÜE were scheduled to play. However, MÖTLEY CRÜE's status had exceeded the support position and TOMMY LEE suggested METALLICA fill the slot instead with RATT opening up the first night. The band's set was still held up by DIAMOND HEAD and SAVAGE covers but notably saw the addition of the Dave Mustaine composed 'Metal Militia'. Unfortunately METALLICA did not get to meet their heroes SAXON as their dressing room was closed to visitors harbouring as it did an inconsolable OZZY OSBOURNE still reeling from the death of Randy Rhoads.

METALLICA enlisted another guitarist Damien C. Phillips (real name Brad Parker) at the Concert Factory in Costa Mesa on April 23rd. The experience, despite introducing another new track 'The Mechanix', was so bad he was fired on the spot. Undaunted, Parker created ODIN. With Hetfield assuming guitar duties, METALLICA cut the four track 'Power Metal' demo, comprising 'Hit The Lights', 'Mechanix', 'Jump In The Fire' and 'Motorbreath', recording in Ron McGovney's parents garage at 13004 Curtis & King Road in Norwalk. After these April sessions the decided to secure the services of a lead vocalist who could do a better job of fronting the group than Hetfield.

METALLICA performed as a five piece on 28th May at the Concert Factory in Los Angeles with new vocalist / guitarist Jeff Warner. The gig, opening for ROXY ROLLERS, Anaheim's LEATHERWOLF and AUGUST REDMOON, was apparently such a disaster the singer was immediately sacked. Trimmed back to a quartet, the group played Radio City in Anaheim once again on 5th June just upfront of the release date for 'Metal Massacre', still relying on SAVAGE and DIAMOND HEAD numbers. Oddly the former act would be almost deleted from METALLICA's history with only a bootleg single bearing testament to the influence of the Mansfield Metal act.

The band at first thought about the possibilities of requesting the services of ex-TYGERS OF PAN TANG vocalist Jess Cox, but by the time they had seen the singer's new look they rapidly changed their minds. To compound their frustration, the one vocalist actually asked to fill the post, John Bush of ARMORED SAINT (and later ANTHRAX), turned the request down.

Summer months of 1982 gave METALLICA another taste of recording, as Kenny Kane at Rocshire Records persuaded the band to go into Chateau East Studios in Tustin to record a proposed EP for subsidiary imprint High Velocity. However the label were shocked to discover the finished tapes were Metal and not Punk and shelved the deal. The resulting tapes were soon to surface on the underground tape trading scene as the 'No Life 'Til Leather' demo. The demo comprised several tracks that would become legendary in 'Hit The Lights', 'The Mechanix', 'Motorbreath', 'Seek & Destroy', 'Metal Militia', 'Jump In The Fire' and 'Phantom Lord'.

On the live front, METALLICA upped their live pace, performing at gigs, inclding openers for STEELER, RATT and even STRYPER, plus private parties.By now, METALLICA, not wishing to be associated with the rising Los Angeles scene awash with bands like MÖTLEY CRÜE, relocated to San Francisco. The group had been garnering the most favour in 'Frisco, not least because of the support offered on a thriving underground level by the influential 'Metal Militia' fanzine run by Ron Quintana. METALLICA's first gig in the city was as part of the Brian Slagel organised 'Metal Massacre Night' at the Berkeley Keystone on 18th September on the same billing as BITCH and HANS NAUGHTY filling in for a non appearance by CIRITH UNGOL.

However, before long McGovney departed, resurfacing in 1986 as part of PHANTASM, the act assembled by ex-HIRAX frontman Katon DePena.

METALLICA added former TRAUMA bassist Cliff Burton (born February 10, 1962) in McGovney's place during December 1982 and the band officially became residents of San Francisco after leaving Los Angeles on February 12th, 1983. METALLICA were soon embroiled in discussions with Firesign Records, Shrapnel and Metal Blade. In fact, way back when Slagel had first begun his 'Metal Massacre' series, the Metal Blade boss could well have just recorded a full album, but the funds just were not available to the company at the time and so the chance went begging. Eventually the act was persuaded to contact the New Jersey based Megaforce Records, a label run by ANTHRAX manager and 'Rock n' Roll Heaven' record store owner Johnny Zazula.

However, after two shows with THE RODS and VANDENBERG in New York, Mustaine was unceremoniously fired after a huge bust-up with Hetfield left Mustaine bruised, bloodied and out of a job. A replacement was swiftly found, as METALLICA's sound engineer, Mark Whitaker, also happened to manage the burgeoning Bay Area outfit EXODUS. The approach to EXODUS six-stringer Kirk Hammett (born November 18th 1962) was made and he was duly enrolled, virtually catching the next plane out of San Francisco to begin work on the debut METALLICA album. As was revealed later, Hammett had already been approached by METALLICA and asked to learn their material even before their East Coast road trip. The ex-guitarist soon busied himself with creating his new act famously titled MEGADETH.

The 'Kill 'Em All' album was recorded in Rochester, New York and the album was released on Zazula's newly established Megaforce label, with distribution from the Relativity concern. The album was duly licensed to ex-Secret Records boss Martin Hooker's new Music For Nations company for release in the UK whilst Roadrunner took the album for Holland, Banzai for Canada, RGE for Brazil, King for Japan and Bernett for France. Amusingly, the record had been envisioned to be titled 'Metal Up Your Ass' and boasting a cover depicting an arm emerging from the depths of a toilet bowl menacingly wielding a rather large knife. Relativity persuaded the band that this idea wasn't exactly a good choice. Mind you, the eventual choice of 'Kill 'Em All' and accompanying cover were no less subtle! T-shirts featuring a depiction of the album's original title and cover art would, however, be produced some while later.

In January 1984 Music For Nations issued 'Jump In The Fire' as a 12" single, backing it with supposedly live versions of 'Seek And Destroy' and 'Phantom Lord'. Both these tracks were actually re-recorded in the studio, MFN dubbing on applause from a London Marquee Club performance by Prog Rock band TWELFTH NIGHT. The group set out on tour to support the 'Kill 'Em All' album, eventually making it over to Britain.

Originally the group had been booked to play through Europe between March 21 to April 3 on a three band bill with Canadian power trio EXCITER and fellow American outfit THE RODS. Unfortunately, ticket sales were mysteriously poor and the tour scrapped. Nevertheless, the group arrived in London and put in two headlining stints at the Marquee Club during late March, their very first UK gig supported by SAVAGE, as well as an earlier appearance at the 'Aardschok Festival' in Holland for good measure whilst on a tour of the continent with Newcastle upon Tyne proto-Black Metallers VENOM. In June further European gigs followed as guests to TWISTED SISTER. Following these shows, METALLICA moved up to Ulrich's native Denmark to begin work on their second album with producer Flemming Rasmussen, a man who had engineered on RAINBOW's 'Difficult To Cure' album in 1983. The band had specifically wanted to record in Europe and had apparently been impressed with Rasmussen's work on the RAINBOW album. Quite incredibly, what was to be one of Rock music's undoubted landmark albums was assembled on mainly borrowed amps and instrumentation, as just prior to leaving the USA METALLICA had all their gear stolen.

A brand new METALLICA album, entitled 'Ride The Lightning', was recorded in a month and a half at Sweet Silence Studios in Copenhagen. Rasmussen recalled in a later magazine interview that the band were earnestly shopping for a major deal whilst in the throes of recording. At one point it looked highly likely that Bronze Records would sign the group until the label insisted that the band should scrap what they were doing and re-record the album in Britain. METALLICA, needless to say, refused.

'Ride The Lightning' was released in July 1984. Initial copies issued by Music For Nations in the UK, Megaforce in the USA and Banzai in Canada all sported the track 'For Whom The Bell Tolls' incorrectly spelt with "bells". Without any compromise in METALLICA's trademark ferocity the songs also were more accessible than previous efforts and was the first real step in infusing METALLICA's sound into the mainstream Rock audience. The accompanying single 'Creeping Death' was bolstered with two caustic cover versions of BLITZKRIEG's 'Blitzkrieg' and DIAMOND HEAD's 'Am I Evil'. Such was the impression made by these songs they would stay lodged in the band's live set for many years.

METALLICA's 1984 European tour was dealt a hammer blow that nearly curtailed the event. Whilst waiting for shipment, $40'000 of the band's equipment was stolen in Boston necessitating hasty negotiations to hire replacement gear.

With the band's burgeoning cult following rapidly spilling over into mainstream success major label Elektra were quick to buy out the Megaforce contract. This despite Megaforce having already shipped albums to the American stores and selling sufficient quantity to crack the Billboard top 200.

Elektra pulled out all the stops in promoting 'Ride The Lightning' maintaining sales levels as it was revealed that not only had METALLICA severed connections with Megaforce Records but also Johnny Z as manager. From now on the experienced Q Prime organisation of Peter Mensch and Cliff Burnstein, noted for successes with AC/DC and DEF LEPPARD, would handle their affairs.

1985 was opened up in style with the 'Ride The Lightning' US tour, commencing January 10th at the Skyway Club in Scotia, New York alongside a ill-matched W.A.S.P. These dates wrapped up in Oregon during mid-March. Although METALLICA's ascendancy to greater things seemed assured, in early 1985 the media momentarily focussed its attention onto the erstwhile band figure of Dave Mustaine, back in the ring in 1985 launching his debut album for MEGADETH. The album included the track 'Mechanix', a revised version of which appeared on METALLICA's debut as 'The Four Horsemen'. The world's Rock press, and Mustaine it seemed, would be keen to devote print acreage to the acrimonious split between the two parties.

On August 17th 1985 Thrash Metal arrived in the UK in style thanks to METALLICA's inaugural appearance at the infamous 'Monsters Of Rock' festival held at the Donington Park racing circuit in Leicestershire. Playing a creditable fourth on a bill above Brit Pomp Rock outfit MAGNUM and San Diego Glamsters RATT and just below BON JOVI, MARILLION and a headlining ZZ TOP, METALLICA played an eight song set lasting around 55 minutes and certainly impressed the gathered clans.

Returning to San Francisco the band put in a "secret" show as THE FOUR HORSEMEN at Ruthie's Inn on August 24th warming up for a showing at the Oakland 'Day On The Green' festival on the 31st. The band returned to Europe on September 14th, performing at the 'Metal Hammer Fest' in Loreley, Germany sharing a diverse billing with NAZARETH, VENOM, HEAVY PETTIN, WISHBONE ASH, SAVAGE GRACE, RUNNING WILD, TYRAN PACE, PRETTY MAIDS and WARLOCK.

1985 was topped off with a crushingly heavy New Year's Eve gig at the Civic Center in San Francisco. Joining METALLICA on the bill were EXODUS, METAL CHURCH and, one suspects somewhat awkwardly, MEGADETH. Notably, this show was highlighted by the first public airing of new track 'Master Of Puppets'.

In downtime Hetfield and Burton assembled the kickabout band SPASTIC CHILDREN. With Hetfield on drums, SPASTIC CHILDREN undertook club gigs with vocalist Fred Cotton and guitarist Jack McDaniel.

METALLICA had originally planned to record their third album in America retaining Flemming Rasmussen's services. However, a fruitless search for the perfect environment in Los Angeles led to the band returning to Sweet Silence in Copenhagen. Hetfield dampened the momentum by breaking his wrist skateboarding. Undeterred the band enlisted METAL CHURCH man James Marshall and Hetfield's guitar tech to fill in on rhythm guitar while the bones healed. The resulting 'Master Of Puppets' album, released in March 1986, proved to be a huge stride forward.

Despite the undoubted impact of 'Master Of Puppets' the glory was marred by Dave Mustaine putting in a claim that the song 'Leper Messiah' was in fact a reworked version of a cut titled 'The Hills Ran Red'. METALLICA flatly refuted the suggestion, admitting the song was based on an old riff but not one that Mustaine delivered. The American teen Metal press lapped it up offering regular METALLICA vs. MEGADETH articles.

'Master Of Puppets' was to hit the Gold mark in America during 1986, for sales in excess of 500,000 copies, becoming the first Thrash era band to break the national Billboard top 100, surely aided by their exposure out on the road across the USA opening for OZZY OSBOURNE throughout March and into June. The following month spot Scandinavian gigs with OZZY OSBOURNE, at the Wvaskyla Saapasjalka in Finland on the 5th and the Danish Roskilde festival the day after, witnessed a renewed partnering again with ANTHRAX. These two acts then resumed action backing OZZY OSBOURNE in the USA throughout July.

On September 10th METALLICA launched a headline European trek, backed by ANTHRAX, at the St. David's Hall in Cardiff. It seemed that METALLICA's momentum was assured as they were by this juncture undoubtedly Heavy Metal's hottest ticket. Unfortunately this success came with a price, the tragic death of Cliff Burton. METALLICA concluded their UK dates then set about a series of Scandinavian shows, kicking off at the Lund Olympen in Sweden on the 24th prior to concerts in Oslo and Stockholm. It all came to a jarring halt on the morning of Saturday, September 27th 1986. En route from Stockholm to Copenhagen, METALLICA's tour bus skidded off an icy road near the Swedish town of Ljungby, throwing Cliff Burton out of the window near his bunk and tipped over on top of him, killing him instantly.

METALLICA actually received encouragement from Burton's parents to press on in the aftermath of the accident. Auditions were held with ARMORED SAINT's Joey Vera, LÄÄZ ROCKIT's Willy Lange, WATCHTOWER man Doug Keyser and Les Claypool. Eventually recruited was the Phoenix, Arizona based FLOTSAM AND JETSAM man Jason Newsted (born March 4, 1963) to fill the void left by Cliff's death.

Newsted was broken in on November 8th with an unannounced concert at the Reseda Country Club opening for old friends METAL CHURCH, the bill also featuring HERETIC. The next day METALLICA also performed at Jezebelle's in Anaheim. The band then committed themselves to a previously scheduled Japanese tour, which opened on November 12th, a little over a month since the accident. US road work gave them no respite, METALLICA resuming proceedings, supported by METAL CHURCH, on November 28th at the Poughkeepsie Mid Hudson Civic Center.

METALLICA ushered in 1987 on January 2nd with a gig alongside METAL CHURCH at The Rock in San Francisco. This same billing hit Scandinavia on the 8th, performing at the Copenhagen Falkoner Theatre in Denmark. The band wound up their European tour, having taken in Germany, France, Belgium, Italy, Spain and Poland, during January. The last of these shows, at the Frolundaborg venue in Gothenburg, Sweden on the 13th, would witness a live showing of MERCYFUL FATE's 'Return Of The Vampire'. Letting off steam on this last gig, METALLICA also jammed through IRON MAIDEN's 'Run To The Hills', DEEP PURPLE's 'Burn and even the Peanuts 'Charlie Brown' theme.

1987 would prove to be trying for Hetfield as he broke his arm skate boarding. The guitarist vowed to give the sport up.

METALLICA went back into the studio to cut the '$5.98 EP: Garage Days Revisited' EP, released in August. A novel homage to their inspirations and influences it fitted in well with the METALLICA ethos. Included were songs from DIAMOND HEAD, 'Helpless', HOLOCAUST, 'The Small Hours', BUDGIE, 'Crash Course In Brain Surgery' and THE MISFITS, 'Last Caress-Green Hell'. The Japanese version also had KILLING JOKE's 'The Wait'. Other tracks from these sessions BUDGIE's 'Breadfan' and DIAMOND HEAD's 'The Prince' would surface on subsequent single B-sides. The EP, a previously untested commercial move, was a solid success charting and lodging itself in the American charts for 8 weeks. 'Breadfan' in particular would dig its claws in as METALLICA opened up their live show with this old warhorse for many, many years to come.

On August 22nd 1987 METALLICA made a triumphant return to a rain sodden Castle Donington to appear third on a BON JOVI topped 'Monsters Of Rock' bill alongside DIO, ANTHRAX, W.A.S.P. and CINDERELLA. Two days previously the band, under the nom de guerre DAMAGE INC., had opened for

METAL CHURCH at London's famous, if tiny, 100 club, here first giving 'Leper Messiah' a stage airing. After 'Monsters Of Rock', METALLICA then joined the German leg of the festivals, at the Messegelaende in Nuremburg and the FCP Stadion in Pforzheim, which were topped by DEEP PURPLE.

Newsted took time out in late 1987 to briefly re-unite with his old act FLOTSAM AND JETSAM in Arizona when he performed an impromptu jam at a SACRED REICH show with his old band mates and SLAYER guitarist Kerry King.

METALLICA rounded off the year fittingly with the tribute video to their late bass player. 'Cliff 'Em All' would include live material as well as home video recordings.

Recording a successor to 'Master Of Puppets' began with GUNS N' ROSES studio man Mike Clink but within months longstanding ally Flemming Rasmussen had supplanted the big name producer and METALLICA started the album again from scratch. Despite the problems in the studio METALLICA retained the fan awareness by clambering aboard the touring extravaganza that was the American 'Monsters Of Rock' roving package kicking off at the East Troy Alpine Valley on May 27th 1988. METALLICA warmed up with a brace of 23rd and 24th May shows at the Troubadour in Los Angeles.

Based upon the tried and tested British formula of the same name, the American version, featuring a heavyweight package of VAN HALEN, SCORPIONS, METALLICA, DOKKEN and KINGDOM COME, looked a winner but it was to eventually flounder due to high ticket prices. METALLICA themselves fared well even though the first month of the tour had them flying back to Bearsville, New York in a desperate race to finish mixing of the album that would become '... And Justice For All'. Here, Newsted was to gain his first writing credit with the band for the lead track 'Blackened'. The 'Monsters Of Rock' extravaganza wound up in late July.

The new album was aired live secretly in Los Angeles as the band, dubbed, FRAYED ENDS, jammed out new material to a select few.

Upon the album's release in September, METALLICA, backed by DANZIG, hit Europe starting with a show at the MTK Football Stadium in Budapest, Hungary on the 11th. QUEENSRYCHE took over opening duties on October 13th at the KB Hallen in Copenhagen, Denmark, prior to a headlining North American tour, gearing up at the Sporta Arena in Toledo, Ohio on November 15th, again allied with QUEENSRYCHE. The first leg was concluded on December 18th at the McNichols Arena in Denver, Colorado.

METALLICA's second leg of US touring, retaining QUEENSRYCHE as support, fired up on January 11th at the Civic Coliseum in Knoxville, Tennessee. February found the band invited to perform at the Grammy awards. METALLICA did not win but this inaugural foot in the door at the Grammys was a portent of what was to come. METALLICA completed their '... And Justice For All' world tour in South America during October 1989.

Lars Ulrich, together with 'Kerrang!' editor Geoff Barton, compiled a compilation album featuring some of his favourite New Wave Of British Heavy Metal bands for the Vertigo label to celebrate the 10th anniversary of the movement.

In February of 1990 METALLICA returned to the Grammy awards once again. This time '... And Justice For All' won. A subsequent European tour beginning in May saw strong support from DIO prior to ensconcing themselves in the studio to begin the writing process for their next album.

The band picked up a further Grammy in February of 1991 for their take on QUEEN's 'Stone Cold Crazy'. By the start of the summer the Rock world was holding it's breath for the new album and when the simply titled 'Metallica' was launched it was apparent from the off that this was the record to propel METALLICA into the major league. Hitting the American number 1 position the album, racking up in excess of 598,000 first week sales, would doggedly retain its grip in the Billboard charts for a further staggering 85 weeks. The first single culled from the album 'Enter Sandman' would be instantly hailed a classic and would quickly be recognised as one of the greatest songs of the genre.

In August METALLICA undertook the European 'Monsters Of Rock' festivals as special guests to AC/DC before an appearance in Moscow.

The band returned home to headline the San Francisco 'Day On The Green' festival before kicking off their 'Wherever I May Roam' world tour.

1992 was beckoned in with METALLICA winning another in a long line of Grammy Awards. In April the band performed 'Stone Cold Crazy' at Wembley with QUEEN guitarist BRIAN MAY as part of the FREDDIE MERCURY tribute concert. With both 'Nothing Else Matters' and 'Wherever I May Roam' continuing the band's presence in the charts METALLICA geared up for a strange pairing for an absolute leviathan American arena tour. METALLICA shared the headline slot with GUNS N' ROSES for a set of 'Monsters Of Rock' dates which many critics viewed as a complete mismatch. Support came from MOTÖRHEAD.

During these shows Hetfield was badly burned by a stage flare in Montreal. With their frontman unable to play guitar METALLICA drafted METAL CHURCH's John Marshall to fill in Hetfields guitar parts to finish off the tour. The 'Monsters Of Rock' extravaganza wound up in October but there was little respite as the band headed for Europe for further shows until the end of the year.

1993 rolled in with further awards accumulated at the American Music awards. The band were back on tour in March in the more far flung territories of Asia, Australia ad South America before the 'Nowhere Else To Roam' dates in Europe. Some of these shows including MEGADETH as guests.

In November METALLICA launched their most ambitious release to date with the box set 'Live Shit: Binge & Purge'. Retailing at £75.00 the tin box included 3 live CDs and 3 live videos. Demand for METALLICA was so high these sets sold out almost immediately.

May 1994 had the road hungry METALLICA on the loose yet again. This time the shows were known collectively as the 'Live shit' tour with support coming from DANZIG and CANDLEBOX. The band also appeared as one of the main attractions at the resurrection of the famous Woodstock festival during August before winding up the tour in Florida. Notably on 21st August at the Bicentennial Park venue in Miami METALLICA invited JUDAS PRIEST vocalist Rob Halford onstage to rip through a full version of 'Rapid Fire'.

The winter months were spent writing for a new album. It would herald a radical new era for the band and test the loyalty of hardened Metal fans.

The bulk of 1995 found METALLICA in the studio working on a new album. Interim activities included a performance at the Castle Donington 'Monsters Of Rock' festival and a gig inside the Arctic circle with HOLE. The Donington show would provide a treat for fans and keep bootleggers happy when the band ripped out a version of IRON MAIDEN's 'Remember Tomorrow'.

Newsted indulged in a further extra curricular project IR8 in 1995. Recorded at his home studio with ex-STEVE VAI and FRONTLINE ASSEMBLY man Devin Townshend and former EXODUS drummer Tom Hunting, tapes were laid down but the project got no further. Nevertheless these recordings made it onto the radio airwaves much to the chagrin of Hetfield and co.

With the impact of the 'Metallica' album still ringing in the industry's ears (the album had clocked up a staggering 12 million sales in America alone) anticipation for 'Load' was high, so eager were fans for new material that the album shifted 680'000 copies in the first week of sale.

What devotees got with 'Load' though was a far cry from the METALLICA of yore. Band photographs issued for promotion shocked traditional Metal fans to the core. Gone was the "none more black" dress code and de rigueur long hair as METALLICA now came across as a newly shorn set of people with a distinct identity crisis. Not only had Hammett taken to adopting a look more in keeping with a 70's pimp, complete with batwing collared gaudy shirts and fur coats but Ulrich had taken to sporting eyeliner. With METALLICA on the surface aping U2's drag-popsters look fans who had religiously force fed themselves a diet of 'Metal Militia' and 'Whiplash' scratched their heads in amazement as Ulrich declared in an interview, albeit apparently tongue in cheek, "we're a Pop band". Newsted stayed out of the controversy while Hetfield, more and more acknowledged as the leader of the band, appeared to be more intent on hunting wild animals than involving himself in the press furor.

The music served to alienate some fans even more as the technical riffing of METALLICA's trademark sound had given way to a stripped down bluesey rock. METALLICA also seemed to be pushing themselves out onto the margins as in various interviews little secret was made of their drug taking activities. Nonetheless METALLICA's status as bona fide rock giants was assured when the 'Load' American tour was announced as being the third biggest tour of the year for that territory grossing some $37 million dollars and only being surpassed by THE ROLLING STONES and U2.

The album was released in June and bolted straight to the American number 1 spot staying high in the charts for a tenacious 40 weeks. The band's touring plans also bore witness to their new approach as METALLICA headlined the touring 'Lollapalooza' festivals with support from SOUNDGARDEN and THE RAMONES. The band won another award at the MTV Video Music celebrations but were eager to get back out on the road again beginning their lengthy series of dates dubbed 'Poor Touring Me' in Europe during September.

The band's roguish intentions were still intact though in spite of their newly found Pop sensibilities. Pulling of a rip roaring versions of 'So What' and 'Last Caress' at the MTV awards complete with expletives got METALLICA banned from future events.

As the year closed METALLICA's touring plans merely rolled on as December ushered in the North American leg of 'Poor Touring Me'.

1997 started with a bang for the band with little seasonal respite, a matter of days, before the 'Poor Touring Me' jaunt, supported by KORN, resumed on 2nd January at the Delta Center in Salt Lake City, Utah. This first concert of the year proved memorable as the group jammed through a diverse set including AC/DC's 'Highway To Hell', DEEP PURPLE's 'Woman From Tokyo', MERCYFUL FATE's 'Return of the Vampire' and IRON MAIDEN's 'Number Of The Beast'. METALLICA also shot footage from this gig for use in a promotional video for the 'King Nothing' single, which first aired on MTV on the 17th. On January 26th Lars Ulrich, with James Hetfield as his best man, married his long time girlfriend Skylar.

The following day METALLICA put in a performance of 'King Nothing' at the American Music Awards, the band also walking off by winning an award. February saw the release of the 'King Nothing' single and METALLICA finally wound down their 'Poor Touring Me' schedule on May 28th with a final show in Edmonton, Canada. One show of particular note on this trek came on 22nd February at the Palace of Auburn Hills, Michigan, when no less a figure than TED NUGENT strode onstage to blast through a version of 'Stranglehold' with METALLICA.

METALLICA were soon back in action returning to the studio to add closure to 'Re-Load', only taking a break for European festival performances and for Hetfield's wedding in August. Dubbed as 'Blitzkrieg', the festival events comprised the Pukkelpop' festival in Hasselt, Belgium on the 22nd, alongside MARILYN MANSON, BLINK-182 and the FOO FIGHTERS,

the 'Blind Man's Ball' in Stuttgart, Germany on the 23rd and the following day's show at the 'Reading Festival' in England.

As the band wound up work on 'Re-Load' in October, METALLICA put in a crop of unusual shows commencing with two back to back appearances at the San Francisco Shoreline Theater on the 18th and 19th. The group were playing acoustically to benefit the Bridge School in San Francisco. The first night's set incorporated the inaugural performance of 'Lowman's Lyric' and saw guitarist JERRY CANTRELL from ALICE IN CHAINS guesting on a rendition of LYNYRD SKYNYRD's 'Tuesday's Gone'. The second evening they played another new song, 'My Eye's'. Guesting on the bill would be Kacy Crowley, Lou Reed, SMASHING PUMPKINS, ALANIS MORISSETTE, the DAVE MATTHEWS BAND and NEIL YOUNG. Over the 20th and 21st October METALLICA filmed the elaborate video for 'The Memory Remains' at Van Nuys airport, the set for which involved the construction of a custom built, and hugely expensive, box.

In an attempt to get back to their roots METALLICA hosted a series of fan gatherings throughout Europe in November. Keen to rekindle the 60's era of free festivals METALLICA announced their intentions for such a gig to launch their 'Re-load' promotion campaign. Initially though venues under consideration were unforthcoming with offers and METALLICA duly revised their tactics. On November 11th, Veteran's Day, the band, despite petitions launched by local residents, played a free show, the "Million Decibel March", at a parking lot in Philadelphia, in front of 50'000 non ticket paying fans in the car park of the Core States Arena.

Two days later METALLICA filmed run throughs of 'The Memory Remains' and 'Fuel' in the London 'Top Of The Pops' television studios prior to a one off gig at the Ministry of Sound dance venue in the capital. This show was recorded, tracks such as QUEEN's 'Stone Cold Crazy' and KILLING JOKE's 'The Wait' turning up on variants of the 'Turn The Page' single. METALLICA then played on Channel 4's 'TFI Friday' the next day and also played acoustic versions of 'Low Man's Lyric', 'The Four Horsemen' and Nothing Else Matters' on Virgin Radio. Their next concert proper, at the Docks venue in Hamburg, Germany, took place on the 15th, preceding gigs in Stockholm, Copenhagen and Paris.

The same month saw the conclusion of a quite bizarre legal wrangle in which a fan, Todd Miller, claimed he had lost his sense of smell after attending a METALLICA gig in Iowa during 1993. Miller's sensory deprivation reportedly came after he suffered a head injury at the gig. The case was settled but the verdict undisclosed.

Debut single from 'Re-load', the melodramatic 'The Memory Remains', shot straight into the British and American charts and straight into fan debate too. Female backing vocals were provided by the ex-girlfriend and alleged abuser of mars bars MARIANNE FAITHFUL, the band having stopped off in Dublin especially to record her vocal parts. The album, selling over 435,000 copies in its first week of sale, shot straight to number 1 in America and on December 6th the band performed 'Fuel' and 'The Memory Remains' live on the famous American TV show NBC's 'Saturday Night Live'.

The year ended on a high with a December 8th performance at the Billboard awards and METALLICA adding another award to their collection, this time in the 'Best Hard Rock Band' category. The band's last performance of the year came on December 18th with an acoustic run through of ten songs for a San Jose radio station.

METALLICA got back into gear during 1998 with a fresh batch of cover versions assembled together with previous efforts under the title 'Garage Inc.'. New recordings included DIAMOND HEAD's 'It's Electric', BLUE ÖYSTER CULT's 'Astronomy', THIN LIZZY's 'Whiskey In The Jar' and a MERCYFUL FATE medley.

On March 21st METALLICA invited fans into an audience

at the MTV studios for a special show dubbed 'ReLoad, Rehearse, and Request'. One extra lucky fan even got to sing lead vocals on 'Creeping Death'. On the road, METALLICA's 'Poor Re-Touring Me' expedition hit Australia and New Zealand starting on April 2nd, the group also put in an unexpected cover version, performing AC/DC's 'Let There Be Rock' to a rapturous reception in Sydney, April 4th. Hardcore fans had their appetite for rarities satisfied with the Australian DJ live album 'Poor Touring Me'. Only issued to radio stations, the promotional album comprised of 8 tracks recorded live in Texas during May 1997. New Zealand concerts, in Wellington and Auckland, were supported by HEAD LIKE A HOLE. Two shows at the Olympic Gymnasium in Seoul, South Korea preceded Japanese dates.

The USA experienced its first taste of 'Poor Re-Touring Me' on June 24th at the Coral Sky Ampitheater, West Palm Beach in Florida. Opening these shows would be DAYS OF THE NEW and JERRY CANTRELL. This tour came to conclusion at the San Diego Coors Amphitheatre on September 13th.

1998 also witnessed joyous events outside of METALLICA's creative and business parameters with both Hetfield and Ulrich becoming fathers. Cali Tee Hetfield being born in June and Myles Ulrich in August. Much more unwelcome was the album 'Bay Area Thrashers—The Early Days' released by Get Back Records. Although unofficial, this live album had managed to secure distribution through regular means to secure shelf space in stores and major online retailers. The band was quick to launch a lawsuit to quash the album, which was soon withdrawn.

On September 14th, METALLICA re-entered the recording studio within 24 hours of stepping offstage in San Diego in order to record new cover tracks for the 'Garage Inc.' set.

One of the band's most memorable concerts came on October 18th when METALLICA performed at Hugh Hefner's Playboy Mansion in Los Angeles. On the 21st the musicians filmed the video for their version of BOB SEGERs 'Turn The Page' at Raleigh Studios in Los Angeles with Swedish director Jonas Akerlund. Whilst undertaking press duties in London on November 9th, Kirk Hammett was rushed to hospital for an emergency appendectomy.

A short burst of promotional shows to plug 'Garage Inc.' witnessed fan club member only dates in Toronto, Chicago, Detroit, Philadelphia and New York. Kirk Hammett was still recovering from surgery and sat down for much of the Canadian show. The concert itself bordered on the surreal, being opened by local METALLICA tribute band BATTERY, performing only METALLICA songs, whilst the headliners played solely cover versions. The set comprised takes on MISFITS 'Die Die My Darling', BLITZKRIEG's 'Blitzkrieg', HOLOCAUST's 'Small Hours', DIAMOND HEAD's 'The Prince', BLACK SABBATH's 'Sabbra Cadabra', THIN LIZZY's 'Whiskey In The Jar', QUEEN's 'Stone Cold Crazy', MERCYFUL FATE's 'Mercyful Fate', DIAMOND HEAD's 'Am I Evil?', ANTI NOWHERE LEAGUE's 'So What!', SWEET SAVAGE's 'Killing Time', KILLING JOKE's 'The Wait', MISFITS 'Last Caress / Green Hell', BUDGIE's 'Breadfan' and MOTÖRHEAD's 'Overkill'.

In late November a further promotional video, for the THIN LIZZY cover 'Whiskey In The Jar', was shot in Brooklyn, New York.

1999 was opened in a decidedly un-Metallic fashion when the band ignited press acreage by filing a lawsuit against Victoria's Secret and Victoria's Secret Catalogue, citing "trademark infringement, false designation of origin, unfair competition and dilution". This action had been instigated by the Victoria's Secrets 'Metallica' range of lip pencils. Fortunately musical matters were also on the agenda in January, as the band's version of THIN LIZZY's 'Whiskey In The Jar' was released on the 25th.

February 24th found METALLICA winning a prestigious Grammy award for 'Better Than You' in the 'Best Metal Performance' category. Their adopted home city paid homage on March 7th, mayor Willie Brown inducting the group onto the San Francisco walk of fame and declaring the day as official "Metallica Day". The rewards continued to pour in. At a ceremony held in New York City's Roseland Ballroom on March 16th the Recording Industry Association of America presented METALLICA with a Diamond sales award to recognise sales of 10 million copies of the 'Metallica' album.

On April 11th and 12th METALLICA and support band MONSTER MAGNET gave the Blaisdell Arena in Honolulu, Hawaii the first double dose of a global world tour, actually being a continuation of the 'Poor Re-Touring Me' slog. From the South Pacific METALLICA journeyed into the Arctic Circle for the next stop at the Sullivan Arena in Anchorage, Alaska on the 14th.

The band then undertook an ambitious venture by performing two concerts, on the 21st and 22nd April, with the San Francisco Symphony Orchestra at the Berkeley Community Theater with conductor Michael Kamen. These shows would be collated for a double album release 'S&M' later in the year. In the meantime, the band set out on tour once more to promote 'Garage Inc.' venturing South with PANTERA and MONSTER MAGNET in tow landing at the Foro Sol in Mexico City, Mexico on 30th April as a precursor to concerts in South America starting in Colombia, the May 2nd Bogotá Simon Bolivar Park gig being opened by DARKNESS and LA PESTILENCIA. May 4th had the band at the Caracas Poliedro in Venezuela supported by GILLMAN.

A series of shows across Brazil, Porto Alegre Hipodromo do Cristal on the 6th, Anhembi Parking Lot, São Paulo on the 8th and Clube De Regatas Do Flamengo, Rio de Janeiro, on the 9th were supported by SEPULTURA. At the latter concert Jason Newsted jammed with SEPULTURA during their set on the song 'Hatred Aside'. The bassist had previously acted as guest guitarist and guest vocalist on the track on SEPULTURA's 'Against' album. The same pairing of bands struck Santiago's Pista Atletica Del Estadio Nacional in Chile on May 12th and the Buenos Aires River Plate Stadium in Argentina on the 14th. For this last show both ROB ZOMBIE and MARILYN MANSON were scheduled to play but both cancelled, being replaced by domestic acts ALMAFUERTE and CATUPECU MACHU.

The summer months were taken up on the European festival circuit, starting at Germany's Nurnberg 'Rock Im Park' on May 21st and Nurnburgring 'Rock Am Ring' on May 22nd. The Dutch 'Dynamo Open Air' the next day, topping a bill with SYSTEM OF A DOWN, FEAR FACTORY, MONSTER MAGNET, MERCYFUL FATE and APOCALYPTICA, saw members of BIOHAZARD joining METALLICA onstage for the "Die, die, die, die" chant on 'Creeping Death. At the Milan 'Gods of Metal' event on June 5th MERCYFUL FATE members King Diamond and Hank Sherman aided onstage with the Mercyful Fate medley encore. A succession of separate headline shows into Eastern Europe had MONSTER MAGNET in tow.

The 'Die Die My Darling' single was released in the UK on June 14th. Another round of festivals had METALLICA heading up billings at 'RockKiev' in Kiev, Ukraine on June 27th, 'Tallinn Song' in Tallinn, Estonia on the 29th, 'Roskilde' festival in Denmark on July 1st, 'Ruisrock' festival in Turku, Finland on the 2nd and the 'Werchter' event in Belgium a day later. 'Whiskey In The Jar's airing on July 5th at The Point in Dublin, Ireland was made extra special with the guest inclusion of former THIN LIZZY guitarist Eric Bell. On the 10th the band provided the top honours at the 'Big Day Out' at the Milton Keynes Bowl venue with MARILYN MANSON, MINISTRY, SEPULTURA, CREED, PITCHSHIFTER, TERRORVISION, MONSTER MAGNET, SYMPOSIUM, QUEENS OF THE STONE AGE, MERCYFUL FATE and PLACEBO. A set of Spanish dates led to an Israeli show on the 20th at the Rishon Le Zion Ampi Park.

A monstrous concert welcomed METALLICA back to the USA on July 24th, the 30th anniversary Woodstock festival, held at the Griffiss Air Force Base, also featuring other heavyweight acts such as RED HOT CHILI PEPPERS, MEGADETH, KORN and LIMP BIZKIT. The follow up double album included 'Creeping Death'.

Much of August was spent in production for 'S&M' with Bob Rock at The Plant in Sausalito. The only European concert to promote the album was held at the Berlin Velodrom on November 19th partnered with The Berlin Symphoniker. 'S&M' was released on November 22nd in Europe. Opinion was sharply divided as to the merits of the album but needless to say worldwide sales were high. METALLICA had also beaten another major act at their own game. German veterans the SCORPIONS had been planning a similar venture for some while.

At the Billboard Music Awards on 8th December METALLICA performed a symphonic version of 'Until It Sleeps' at the top of the MGM Grand Hotel with the New York City's Orchestra of St. Luke's conducted by Michael Kamen. The group walked away from the ceremony clutching a further double vindication of their efforts with Billboard awards for Catalog Artist of the Year and Catalog Album of the Year.

There would be little seasonal respite for METALLICA as another tour, dubbed the 'M2K' dates, was instigated on December 28th, the Orange Bowl in Florida, Miami also playing to road partners KID ROCK, CREED and SEVENDUST.

There would be little New Year's seasonal respite for METALLICA as another tour, dubbed the 'M2K' dates, was instigated on December 28th 1999, the Orange Bowl in Florida, Miami also playing to road partners KID ROCK, CREED and SEVENDUST. This run of shows closed at the Target Center, Minneapolis in Minnesota on January 10th 2000. The new millennium started off well for METALLICA as they won another Grammy award for 'Best Hard Rock Performance' for their rendition of 'Whiskey In The Jar' on February 23rd at the 42nd Grammy Awards.

A rather special album also emerged in 2000. The limited edition 'The Garage Remains The Same', with both title and artwork punning LED ZEPPELIN, was released to platinum card carrying members of the METALLICA fan club. The album comprised six live tracks recorded in Santiago, Chile during 1999.

Needless to say METALLICA had something special planned for the turn of the century headlining New York's Madison Square Gardens with support acts TED NUGENT and KID ROCK.

Hetfield appeared alongside Jim Martin on the track 'Eclectic Electric' on PRIMUS' 2000 album 'Antipop'. Newsted meantime busied himself with side project ECHOBRAIN, a power trio featuring guitarist Dylan Donkin and drummer Brian Sagrafena. Also contributing was the aforementioned Jim Martin and Hammett. METALLICA contributed the new composition 'I Disappear', also released as a single, to the Tom Cruise movie soundtrack for 'Mission Impossible II'.

The band were also kept in the press during April with a legal action brought by the band against internet company Napster. METALLICA accused Napster of depriving them of royalties by their download access of METALLICA tracks. Napster replied by posting an animated cartoon on their site featuring a Neanderthal Hetfield who could only mouth 'Money good!, Napster bad! Beer good!'. A more complimentary tribute was made when GREGORIAN, a collection of Gregorian chanters, covered 'Nothing Else Matters' on their 'Masters Of Chant' album.

James Hetfield surprised MOTÖRHEAD fans attending Lemmy and his cohorts June 1st concert at the Maritime Hall in San Francisco as the METALLICA singer, telling the audience that MOTÖRHEAD were "the godfathers of heavy metal", joined the band onstage for the 'Overkill' encore.

On June 8th the band performed 'I Disappear' at Sony Pictures Studios in Culver City for the MTV movie awards. METALLICA spent mid 2000 on the road in America with their 'Summer Sanatorium' arena tour, kicking off on June 30th at the Foxboro Stadium in Foxboro, Massachusetts. Along for the ride were KID ROCK, KORN and POWERMAN 5000. Tragically, on July

METALLICA (pic: Rich Galbraith)

4th, a 21-year-old fan, Martin Muscheet of Connecticut, fell to his death at the Baltimore Psinet Stadium stop. Further tribulation came on the 7th when James Hetfield suffered a back injury, dislocating vertebrae. Ulrich, Hammet and Newsted informed the Atlanta, Georgia audience at the Georgia Dome of the setback then persevered with the show, bringing numerous guests, from SYSTEM OF A DOWN, KORN and the KID ROCK band, onstage for a memorable evening. Jason Newsted handled lead vocals for the bulk of the show. Six shows were postponed due to Hetfield's injury but the re-scheduled tour resumed August 2nd at the Starplex Amphitheatre in Dallas, Texas now seeing CORROSION OF CONFORMITY as opening act.

James Hetfield got up onstage with one of his favourite acts the MISFITS in San Francisco on November 17th. The veteran Horror Punks performed 'Last Caress' and 'Die, Die My Darling' with the METALLICA frontman. Capping the month, METALLICA put a unique spin on their invitation to the VH1 Music Awards. Rather than use the indoor facilities they opted to play 'Fade To Black' outside on the parking lot to 200 fan club members. By the end of the year it was announced that METALLICA had grossed over $40 million in tour receipts.

Faithfully upholding tradition, the atmospheric live rendition of 'The Call of Ktulu' in fruitful collaboration with the San Francisco Symphony Orchestra triumphantly claimed a much prized Grammy 'Best Rock Instrumental Performance' at the

43rd Grammy Awards on February 23rd 2001.

The band's stability was rocked the very same month when Newsted announced his departure. The bassist's frustrated attempts to instigate musical projects outside of the confines of METALLICA had been well documented. Hetfield, Hammett and Ulrich resolved to record the band's next album as a trio although increased speculation put the spotlight firmly onto ex-OZZY OSBOURNE and ALICE IN CHAINS man Mike Inez as the potential new recruit. Another name dropped into the hat would be that of the original bass wildman Pete Way of UFO. (Inez though would join BLACK LABEL SOCIETY and Way resumed UFO activity). METALLICA ensconced themselves at the Presidio Studios, actually a rented barrack at the San Francisco army base, to craft a new album. Although new songs would be completed, the band opted to keep it vaulted.

The band, in typically unorthodox fashion, would also employ a novel method of auditioning bassists. Playing a website re-launch party in San Francisco on July 29th METALLICA would draw upon members of their official fan club to perform onstage with the band. The reaction of the audience would determine if the candidates got beyond the first song! The victor would be treated to a day out with the band and dinner. METALLICA got to grips with more personal internal affairs during the lay off upfront of a new album as their fan club announced that Hetfield was undergoing treatment for "alcoholism and other addictions."

Newsted, after a one off live gig with THE MOSS BROTHERS in San Francisco supporting SPINAL TAP, re-emerged with school friends vocalist / guitarist Dylan Donkin and drummer Brian Sagrafena as ECHOBRAIN, a band which had actually been a going concern for many years behind the scenes of METALLICA's unstoppable progress. Newsted also revealed plans to release material he had assembled over the years in alliance with such artists as Andreas Kisser of SEPULTURA, drummer Tom Hunting of EXODUS, DEVIN TOWNSEND and MACHINE HEAD's Robert Flynn.

ECHOBRAIN put in their debut live showing on August 19th 2001 as part of the 'Nadine's Wild Weekend' events in San Francisco. By September it had emerged that the ex bassist was working in the studio with a re-united VOIVOD acting as producer and bassist. Meanwhile, with METALLICA on hold minus a bass player the band received an offer from MEGADETH's Dave Mustaine and bassist Dave Ellefson to found an interim live act to be dubbed META-MEGA!

For the fourth year running METALLICA fan club members would be rewarded with another 'Fan Can' release. '... And All This For You' included a live CD culled from a Dallas, Texas gig in 1989, a live video originally broadcast on German TV and various other goodies locked away in the by now obligatory tin can.

During January 2002, As rumours spread of involvement between Lars Ulrich and Kirk Hammett with former VAN HALEN star DAVID LEE ROTH, it was also learned that the METALLICA pair had collaborated with Rapper JA RULE for a track 'We Did It Again', included as part of a compilation album 'Ghetto Stories'. James Hetfield would get in on the action outside of METALLICA too, adding guest vocals on GOVT. MULE's 'Drivin' Rain' contribution to the all star NASCAR compilation album 'Crank It Up'.

The high profile Progressive Rock act DREAM THEATER added a rather novel twist to their touring activities in 2002. When booked for a two night consecutive venue run the band would perform the entirety of METALLICA's 'Masters Of Puppets' album live. Needless to say, fans who had not been made aware of DREAM THEATER's intentions, would be somewhat mystified.

When, in April Dave Mustaine made his announcement that MEGADETH was to fold due to a severe nerve injury the ex-METALLICA man had suffered to his left arm, the media ru-

METALLICA (pic: Rich Galbraith)

mour mill sprang into action, placing Mustaine's long serving bassist Dave Ellefson as a prospect for the still vacant position in METALLICA. Whilst the Rock media concentrated on these developments other parties would be keeping an eye on Lars Ulrich's domestic position, the drummer putting his San Francisco abode on the market for $11 million and offloading some paintings, including much sought after Basquiat paintings auctioned off at Sotheby's in London for a record $5.5 million. Both Lars Ulrich and Kirk Hammett would unexpectedly take to the stage for famed 'Red Rocker' SAMMY HAGAR's last night of three gigs at the famous Bay Area Fillmore venue. The choice of material was a surprise too as Hagar and the METALLICA duo, alongside a guesting VAN HALEN bassist Michael Anthony, ripped through a set of MONTROSE songs.

Welcome studio activity found the band appearing amongst a genuine all star cast, according to initial reports donating their take of 'We're A Happy Family' to the 2002 Joey Ramone and ROB ZOMBIE assembled RAMONES tribute album of the same name. It would later be learned that these press leaks were premature and METALLICA had in fact recorded different RAMONES tracks. The band, appearing surreptitiously as SPUN, played a surprise set at Club Kimo's in San Francisco in early June. James Hetfield, Lars Ulrich and Kirk Hammett were joined by their producer Bob Rock, who played bass for the show which included no less than four RAMONES covers 'Commando', 'Today Your Love Tomorrow The World', '53rd And 3rd' (Confirmed as their contribution to the 'We're A Happy Family' tribute) and 'Now I Wanna Sniff Some Glue'. Also on hand was standard METALLICA fare, the rarely performed 'Hit The Lights' as well as a workout of a brand new song. Hetfield remained seated throughout the show, in recuperation for surgery on his neck.

James Hetfield's passion for Country & Western reared itself again when it was revealed the METALLICA frontman had laid down guitar tracks on a remix of Country singer CAROLYN DAWN JOHNSON's single 'So Complicated'. It later emerged that Hetfield had also completed an entirely solo rendition of WAYLON JENNINGS 'Don't You Think This Outlaw Bit's Done Got Out Of Hand' for a 2003 tribute album. The METALLICA frontman not only sang on this track but also performed guitar, bass and drums.

Still minus a permanent bassist METALLICA nonetheless threw a live party gig in San Francisco to celebrate the launch of their new look official website. Two contest winners would be given the opportunity of a lifetime as the band performed 'Creeping Death' with fan Andrew and 'Seek & Destroy' with another competition entrant Elena Repetto of the Thrash act IMAGIKA. METALLICA would then resume with Bob Rock taking over four string duties for the RAMONES 'Commando' and the remainder of the set. Work would still continue apace on the album, evidenced by one lucky fan who was prepared to pay a whopping £23'000 over to the TJ Martell Foundation charity for the privilege of a day in the studio with the band, winning an E Bay auction for the prize.

The release of a mammoth Metal Blade Records 20th anniversary box set brought good news for METALLICA fans. Included would be a rare version of 'Hit The Lights' featuring Lloyd Grant. Initially this track only appeared on the first vinyl pressings of the famed 'Metal Massacre' compilation, later CD re-issues supplanting it with a later take recorded with Dave Mustaine.

METALLICA, with seven tracks of their new album already fully recorded, would start auditioning bassists, by invitation only, during December. METALLICA revealed plans to perform on the summer 2003 European festival circuit by announcing appearances at Denmark's 'Roskilde' festival and the German events 'Rock Am Ring' in Nürburgring and 'Rock Im Park' in Nürnberg.

The former KYUSS and current UNIDA bassist SCOTT REEDER would be revealed as having partaken in auditions for the bass vacancy during early January. Other candidates put their paces would be former SUICIDAL TENDENCIES, PALE DEMONS and then current OZZY OSBOURNE bassist Robert Trujillo, Danny Lohner of NINE INCH NAILS, Eric Avery of JANE'S ADDICTION and erstwhile MARILYN MANSON man Twiggy Ramirez.

Outside of internal activities METALLICA would be riding a wave of unwelcome albeit forced press coverage when a cheeky Punk band from Edmonton brazenly entitled their band ... METALLICA! Needless to say the Californian giants lawyers soon swung into action delighting the publicity seeking Canucks. The real METALLICA, including Bob Rock on bass, grabbed the headlines back by performing an impromptu set on a flatbed truck in the car park of the Network Coliseum in Oakland, California, the venue for a Raiders/Titans game. METALLICA, revealing their highly anticipated studio album title as 'St. Anger', announced a summer stadium tour of the US allied with LINKIN PARK and LIMP BIZKIT with support from DEFTONES and MUDVAYNE.

In late February METALLICA revealed that Robert Trujillo was to be their new bass player. In a curious turn of events erstwhile band member Jason Newsted then promptly joined the OZZY OSBOURNE band.

METALLICA's first showing with Trujillo would be as part of an MTV special on the band. This lavish spectacle, dubbed the 'MTVicon', included bands such as SUM 41 performing 'For Whom the Bell Tolls' and 'Enter Sandman', STAIND with a rendition of 'Nothing Else Matters',

Pop teen-diva AVRIL LAVIGNE covered 'Fuel', Rapper SNOOP DOGG took on 'Sad But True', KORN covered 'One' and LIMP BIZKIT "Sanitarium'. The evening closed, following an introduction by actor Sean Penn, with a set by METALLICA themselves.

As part of the promotion for 'St. Anger' METALLICA announced a run of four back to back gigs for fan club members at the Fillmore Theater in San Francisco on May 18th, 19th, 21st, and 22nd. The group also revealed three consecutive shows in Paris on June 11th, performing at the 350 capacity La Boule Noire club, the 550 capacity Le Trabendo and finally the 1500 capacity Le Bataclan hall. Despite official denials that the band were to perform at the IRON MAIDEN headlined Download festival in Britain the band, after shooting a 'Top Of The Pops' TV appearance, did in fact put in an impromptu ten song set to unsuspecting fans.

Such was demand for 'St. Anger' that the official release date was pulled forward in an effort to stifle bootlegging attempts. Initial copies of the record came not only with a DVD documenting the making of the album but a free 14 track compilation of archive tracks. Fulfilling predictions, 'St. Anger' bowed in on the Billboard charts at no. 1 having shifted over 416'000 albums in the process. Initial European showings would not be so grand, the record debuting at no. 3 in the UK, although 'St. Anger' took a clean sweep of no.1's in Scandinavia. Unfortunately for METALLICA the initial burst of expectation would be tempered by an almost universal swathe of bad reviews, the band's experimental stripped down approach coming in for harsh criticism. Nevertheless, in just five weeks 'St. Anger' clocked up over one million sales in the US.

So high would feelings be running over the musical merits of 'St. Anger' that one band, SCUMGRIEF, even organised an 'Anti-Metallica' live event! Festival attendees could trade in copies of 'St. Anger' in exchange for a CD featuring unreleased and demo material from each of the bands on the bill. The collected copies of the METALLICA release were then to be publicly destroyed prior to SCUMGRIEF's set. An un-phased METALLICA got to grips with the their 'Summer Sanitarium' arena dates, pulling in many capacity audiences. South American shows in Brazil and Chile would be pegged for September.

The second single lifted from 'St. Anger' came in September. Quite uniquely 'Frantic' came backed with a variety of differing coloured single covers and track selections for various territories guaranteeing collectability and chart placings. METALLICA would schedule the South American territories of Brazil, Argentina and Chile in October, following up with shows in Japan, Australia and Europe. However, dates in Japan and South America would be pulled as METALLICA's record label cited "band members' exhaustion" as a cause.

METALLICA's January 2004 single, 'The Unnamed Feeling', featured a whole crop of classic tracks recorded in Paris the year before. The band, unveiling a lengthy second run of North American dates, won a prestigious Grammy Award in the "Best Metal Performance" category for 'St. Anger' at the 46th annual show held at the Staples Center in Los Angeles. Meantime, Rolling Stone magazine would place METALLICA as the fifth highest Rock n' Roll earner in North America for 2003, reckoning their 'Summer Sanitarium' tour had grossed close to $50 million. Behind the scenes, the band would benefit from a shake up of the Warner Bros. recording stable, shifting from long term imprint Elektra over to Warner Bros. for future product.

North American touring in the first half of 2004 had the band packaged with support band GODSMACK, these dates grossing a cool $22 million. As the world tour rolled into Europe and Scandinavia the band not only sustained but strengthened their appeal. Quite incredibly, METALLICA's concert at the Olympic Stadium in Helsinki, Finland on 28th May was attended by 46,000 people, close to 1 percent of the country's 5.5-million population. This huge wave of support was translated to the national Finnish album charts where no less than six METALLICA albums occupied the top forty—'Metallica' at number 4, 'Master Of Puppets' number 7, '... And Justice For All' number 11, 'Ride The Lightning' number 14, 'Kill 'Em All' number 10 and 'St. Anger' at number 28.

METALLICA fared even better in Sweden where the band's

METALLICA (pic: Rich Galbraith)

gig in Gothenburg on 30th May propelled their back catalogue into the official national album listings again with 'Metallica' re-entering at number 9, 'Master Of Puppets' at no. 14, '... and Justice For All' at no. 20, 'Ride The Lightning' at no. 23, 'Kill 'em All' at no. 28, 'St. Anger' at no. 31, 'Load' at no. 47, 'Reload' at no. 48, 'S&M' at no. 54 and 'Garage Inc.' at no. 60.

The group's 4th June 'Rock In Rio' festival performance in Lisbon, Portugal would broadcast live to more than 45 countries via several television channels.

Lars Ulrich was hospitalized just upfront of the band's headlining slot at the mammoth 'Download' festival in England on 6th June. Apparently the drummer had been taken ill while travelling in a private plane between Lisbon in Portugal and the UK, the decision being made to divert to Germany where an ambulance took Ulrich to hospital. Quickfire replacements were sought in the backstage area of the show with Hetfield, Hammett and Trujillo jamming with MACHINE HEAD's Dave McClain, HATEBREED's Matt Byrne and LIFE OF AGONY's Sal Abruscato among others. However, for a truncated nine song METALLICA employed Dave Lombardo of SLAYER playing 'Battery' and 'The Four Horsemen', Joey Jordison of SLIPKNOT covering 'For Whom The Bell Tolls', 'Creeping Death' and 'Creeping Death' and drum tech Fleming Larsen taking on 'Fade to Black'. Jordison returned for 'Wherever I May Roam', 'Last Caress', 'Sad But True' 'Nothing Else Matters' and 'Enter Sandman'. Lars Ulrich would be back in his rightful place for the band's next scheduled gig in Ludwigshafen, Germany.

Meantime further acknowledgement of the band's standing poured in as Kirk Hammett was honored with the 'Outstanding Guitarist' award at the California Music Awards held on 6th June and the following day METALLICA scooped the 'Best International Act' award at the second annual Metal Hammer awards in London.

A new single, 'Some Kind Of Monster', would be launched in July to capitalise on the release of the Joe Berlinger and Bruce Sinofsky directed documentary of the same name. This EP, limited editions coming with a free T shirt, hosted live renditions of 'The Four Horsemen', 'Damage, Inc.', 'Leper Messiah', 'Motorbreath', 'Ride The Lightning' and 'Hit The Lights', recorded in Paris on June 11, 2003. Selling just shy of 30,000 copies in its debut week, 'Some Kind Of Monster' hit no. 37 on the US Billboard charts.

One setback came in Croatia, a 27th June appearance at Gradski Stadion in Zagreb being cancelled due to "insurmountable technical difficulties". METALLICA's show at Prague's T-Mobile Park on 1st July proved unusual too, the group taking to the stage an hour early to allow fans to watch their national soccer team play against Greece in the Euro 2004 semifinal.

Another METALLICA tribute would be in the air too as Mexican acoustic duo Rodrigo Sanchez and Gabriela Quintero, former members of Heavy Metal band members of TIERRA ACIDA, revealed plans for a METALLICA covers EP. Their 2004 album 'Live Manchester and Dublin', recorded in Dublin's Christ Church Cathedral and the Manchester Academy, included a segue of 'One' interwoven with the Dave Brubek Jazz standard 'Take 5'. Also on the METALLICA covers front, acts such as MOTÖRHEAD, FLOTSAM AND JETSAM, DEATH ANGEL and DARK ANGEL all contributed to the latest tribute album 'Metallic Assault'.

METALLICA's North American 'Madly In Anger With The World' campaign re-commenced in St. Paul, Minnesota on 16th August. This show would also mark the launch of METALLICA's official biography 'So What: The Good, The Mad, and The Ugly' through Broadway Books. Fans pre-purchasing the 1000 page tome and picking up a special wristband would be eligible for a meet and greet with the band on the day of the concert. Subsequent gigs saw a shift in song content as the track 'Some Kind Of Monster' was debuted at a Peoria, Illinois on the 24th. During this show the band also performed 'Trapped Under Ice', an exceptionally rare outing for this song. METALLICA closed out the first leg with a show in Lubbock, Texas, notable for a set list containing a first time ever live rendition of 'Sweet Amber'.

The second leg of the tour maintained the momentum of the first, illustrated by the fact that tickets for the Montreal Bell Centre concert on 4th October sold out of its 19,000 tickets in less than three hours. A further night was duly added to the itinerary. Canada also scored with the addition of a second Quebec City Colisée Pepsi concert, this show added as a fundraiser for CHOI 98.1 FM radio station, threatened by closure by the CRTC. The first Quebec show sold all 13,000 tickets in under three hours.

In October METALLICA provided more fodder for die hard US collectors with the issue of 'Vinyl Box' which comprised special editions of its first four studio albums, as well as the 'Garage Days Re-Revisited' EP and the European 'Creeping Death' picture disc. Restricted to just 5,000 hand numbered copies 'Vinyl Box' saw the albums 'Kill 'Em All', 'Ride The Lightning', 'Master Of Puppets' and '... And Justice For All' expanded to double-vinyl sets on 180-gramme audiophile vinyl with new gatefold jackets.

On 7th September James Hetfield performed a "metal version" of WAYLON JENNINGS Don't You Think This Outlaw Bit's Done Got Out of Hand' during the 'CMT Outlaws' concert taping at Nashville's Gaylord Entertainment Center. Meanwhile, back on the METALLICA tour the band maintained their interest in keeping the live set fluid by performing 'Wasting My Hate' breaking a seven year break for that song in Quebec and then performing 'The God That Failed' for the first time in ten years at the 17th October Washington, D.C. MCI Center gig. By the time the band had wrapped up the 'Madly in Anger with the World' tour it had grossed a reported $53.8 million in box office receipts.

In December the METALLICA track 'Some Kind Of Monster' would be nominated in the 'Best Hard Rock Performance' category for the 47th annual Grammy Awards. May of 2005 saw an announcement that Kirk Hammett had contributed guest guitar to SANTANA's 'All That I Am' album. That same month the Recording Industry Association of America revealed METALLICA had sold over 57 million albums in the USA, with only LED ZEPPELIN, AC/DC and AEROSMITH ranking above them in terms of Hard Rock sales.

Having kept a relatively low profile since completing their world tour in late 2004 the band did enter the studios on 20th September. Not to record music though, but voice parts for their character inclusions in 'The Simpsons'. METALLICA returned to the live stage playing two shows opening up for the ROLLING STONES in their home city of San Francisco at the SBC Pacbell Park on 13th and 15th November.

METALLICA's first announced live work for 2006 broke new

METALLICA (pic: Rich Galbraith)

territory as the group headlined three festivals in South Africa during March, their first visit to the continent. The group put in shows in Centurion, Durban and Cape Town topping the 'Coca-Cola Colab Massive Mix' bill comprising SIMPLE PLAN, THE RASMUS, SEETHER, FATBOY SLIM, and COLLECTIVE SOUL. The group then revealed plans to break off from cutting a new album in order to hit the summer festival circuit, confirming headline gigs at Germany's Nürburgring 'Rock Am Ring' and Nurnberg 'Rock Im Park' festivals and 'Download' events at Castle Donington in the UK and Dublin in Ireland.

METALLICA played host to BLACK SABBATH's induction into the 'Rock and Roll Hall of Fame'. The band presented the award and also put in BLACK SABBATH cover versions of 'Iron Man' and 'Hole In The Sky' on the night.

METALLICA themselves were to be honoured in turn with the album 'Remastered' being a complete remake of 'Master Of Puppets' in joint celebration of the twentieth anniversary of the classic album's release and the 25th anniversary of UK Rock magazine Kerrang! Participants featured exclusive recordings from BULLET FOR MY VALENTINE with 'Welcome Home (Sanitarium)', TRIVIUM 'Master Of Puppets', FIGHTSTAR 'Leper Messiah', MACHINE HEAD 'Battery', FUNERAL FOR A FRIEND 'Damage, Inc.', CHIMAIRA 'Disposable Heroes', MASTODON 'Orion' and MENDEED 'The Thing That Should Not Be', with the sleeve notes for the album penned by none other than Lars Ulrich. 'Remastered' came free with Kerrang! issue 1102 in April.

On the band's opening June 3rd date of their 'Escape From The Studio' tour, at the 'Rock am Ring' festival in Nürburgring, Germany METALLICA performed the 'Master Of Puppets' album in its entirety. The group debuted a brand new track on June 6th at Waldbuhne in Berlin, where they also encored with a rendition of the RAMONES 'Commando', with members of support band AVENGED SEVENFOLD drafted in on vocals. METALLICA's June 13th concert at Tallinn Song Festival Grounds in Estonia broke previous attendance records for the country by drawing in around 78,000 people. The previous record had been set by MICHAEL JACKSON in 1997.

On June 15th MOTÖRHEAD's frontman Lemmy Kilmister joined METALLICA on stage at the Novarock Festival in Nickelsdorf, Austria for a version of MOTÖRHEAD's 'Damage Case'. Later in the show JERRY CANTRELL sang 'Nothing Else Matters' alongside James Hetfield.

A quite unique concept emerged in August 2006 with the 'Rockabye Baby' album, comprising METALLICA songs transformed into lullabies by glockenspiel, vibraphone and mellotron.

METALLICA debuted another, untitled new track at their performance Summer Sonic Festival in Tokyo, Japan on August 12th. On September 11th Lars Ulrich joined DEEP PURPLE frontman IAN GILLAN onstage for 'Smoke On The Water' at Slim's in San Francisco. James Hetfield jammed with ALICE IN CHAINS on the song 'Would?' at their November 26th Warfield, San Francisco date.

In mid December the compilation DVD 'The Videos 1989-2004' sold more than 28,000 copies in the United States in its first week of release to debut at number 3 on Billboard's Top Music Video chart. On December 15th Lars Ulrich joined GUNS N' ROSES on stage at the Oracle Arena in Oakland, California for a rendition of 'Out Ta Get Me'.

From early February onwards the band started to roll out a series of European and Scandinavian tour dates, starting with a headline slot at the July 1st 'Werchter' festival in Belgium. Tickets for shows in Norway, July 10th at Valle Hovin Stadion in Oslo, and Sweden, July 12th at Stadion in Stockholm, sold out in less than an hour from going on sale. Tickets for METALLICA's Helsinki concert, at the Olympic Stadium on July 15th, reportedly sold out less than 30 minutes after they went on sale on February 28th. This prompted the return of no less than five classic METALLICA albums to the Finnish charts, with 'Master Of Puppets' at number 11, 'Metallica' at 12, 'Ride The Lightning' at 20, '. . . And Justice For All' at 22 and 'Kill 'Em All' at 35.

METALLICA announced a March 12th 2007 start to recordings.

KILL 'EM ALL, Vertigo 20074 (1983) (Venezuelan release. Vinyl). Hit The Lights / The Four Horsemen / Motorbreath / Jump In The Fire / (Anesthesia)—Pulling Teeth / Whiplash / Phantom Lord / No Remorse / Seek & Destroy / Metal Militia.

KILL 'EM ALL, Universal 838142-2 (1983) (Taiwanese release). Hit The Lights / Four Horsemen / Motorbreath / Jump In The Fire / Pulling Teeth (Anasthesia) / Whiplash / Phantom Lord / No Remorse / Seek And Destroy / Metal Militia.

KILL 'EM ALL, Megaforce MRI069 (1983) (Limited edition picture disc. US release). Hit The Lights / The Four Horsemen / Motorbreath / Jump In The Fire / Pulling Teeth / Whiplash / Phantom Lord / No Remorse / Seek & Destroy / Metal Militia.

KILL 'EM ALL, Megaforce MRI069 (1983) (USA release. Vinyl album). Hit The Lights / The Four Horsemen / Motorbreath / Jump In The Fire / (Anesthesia)-Pulling Teeth / Whiplash / Phantom Lord / No Remorse / Seek & Destroy / Metal Militia.

KILL 'EM ALL, Roadrunner RR-9902 (1983) (Dutch release. Vinyl). Hit The Lights / The Four Horsemen / Motorbreath / Jump In The Fire / (Anesthesia)—Pulling Teeth / Whiplash / Phantom Lord / No Remorse / Seek & Destroy / Metal Militia.

KILL 'EM ALL, Music For Nations MFN 7 (1983) (UK release. Vinyl). Hit The Lights / The Four Horsemen / Motorbreath / Jump In The Fire / (Anesthesia) Pulling Teeth / Whiplash / Phantom Lord / No Remorse / Seek And Destroy / Metal Militia.

KILL 'EM ALL, Banzai BRC1901 (1983) (Canadian release. Vinyl). Hit The Lights / The Four Horsemen / Motorbreath / Jump In The Fire / (Anesthesia)—Pulling Teeth / Whiplash / Phantom Lord / No Remorse / Seek & Destroy / Metal Militia.

KILL 'EM ALL, Bernett SB18007 (1983) (French release. Vinyl). Hit The Lights / The Four Horsemen / Motorbreath / Jump In The Fire / (Anesthesia)—Pulling Teeth / Whiplash / Phantom Lord / No Remorse / Seek And Destroy / Metal Militia.

KILL 'EM ALL, Nexus K25P438 (1984) (Japanese release. Vinyl). Hit The Lights / The Four Horsemen / Motorbreath / Jump In The Fire / (Anesthesia)—Pulling Teeth / Whiplash / Phantom Lord / No Remorse / Seek & Destroy / Metal Militia.

KILL 'EM ALL, Music For Nations MFN7P (1986) (UK release. Vinyl picture disc. Edition without barcode). Hit The Lights / The Four Horsemen / Motorbreath / Jump In The Fire / Pulling Teeth / Whiplash / Phantom Lord / No Remorse / Seek & Destroy / Metal Militia.

KILL 'EM ALL, Music For Nations MFN7DM (1987) (UK release. Limited edition vinyl Direct Metal Mastered double album with gatefold sleeve). Hit The Lights / The Four Horsemen / Motorbreath / Jump In The Fire / Pulling Teeth / Whiplash / Phantom Lord / No Remorse / Seek And Destroy / Metal Militia.

KILL 'EM ALL, Elektra 960766-2 (1988) (USA release. CD). Hit The Lights / The Four Horsemen / Motorbreath / Jump In The Fire / (Anesthesia)—Pulling Teeth / Whiplash / Phantom Lord / No Remorse / Seek & Destroy / Metal Militia / Am I Evil? / Blitzkrieg.

KILL 'EM ALL, Vertigo (1989) (Mexican release. CD). Hit The Lights / The Four Horsemen / Motorbreath / Jump In The Fire / (Anesthesia)—Pulling Teeth / Whiplash / Phantom Lord / No Remorse / Seek & Destroy / Metal Militia.

KILL 'EM ALL, Vertigo 838142-2 (1989) (UK release. CD). Hit The Lights / The Four Horsemen / Motorbreath / Jump In The Fire / (Anesthesia)—Pulling Teeth / Whiplash / Phantom Lord / No Remorse / Seek & Destroy / Metal Militia.

KILL 'EM ALL, Vertigo 838142-1 (1989) (UK release. Vinyl re-issue). Hit The Lights / The Four Horsemen / Motorbreath / Jump In The Fire / (Anesthesia)—Pulling Teeth / Whiplash / Phantom Lord / No Remorse / Seek & Destroy / Metal Militia.

KILL 'EM ALL, Vertigo LPR-23067 (1989) (Mexican release. Vinyl). Hit The Lights / The Four Horsemen / Motorbreath / Jump In The Fire / (Anesthesia)—Pulling Teeth / Whiplash / Phantom Lord / No Remorse / Seek & Destroy / Metal Militia.

KILL 'EM ALL, CBS 25DP-5339 (1989) (Japanese release. CD). Hit The Lights / The Four Horsemen / Motorbreath / Jump In The Fire / Pulling Teeth (Anasthesia) / Whiplash / Phantom Lord / No Remorse / Seek And Destroy / Metal Militia / Am I Evil? / Blitzkrieg.

KILL 'EM ALL, Vertigo 838142-1 (1990) (Colombian release. Vinyl album). Hit The Lights / The Four Horsemen / Motorbreath / Jump In The Fire / Pulling Teeth / Whiplash / Phantom Lord / No Remorse / Seek & Destroy / Metal Militia.

KILL 'EM ALL, Vertigo 838142-2 (1993) (Australian release). Hit The Lights / The Four Horsemen / Motorbreath / Jump In The Fire / (Anesthesia)-Pulling Teeth / Whiplash / Phantom Lord / No Remorse / Seek & Destroy / Metal Militia.

KILL 'EM ALL, Elektra CD60766 (1996) (Canadian release. CD). Hit The Lights / The Four Horsemen / Motorbreath / Jump In The Fire / (Anasthesia)-Pulling Teeth / Whiplash / Phantom Lord / No Remorse / Seek And Destroy / Metal Militia / Am I Evil? / Blitzkrieg.

KILL 'EM ALL, Vertigo 8381421 (2001) (UK release. 180g vinyl re-issue). Hit The Lights / The Four Horsemen / Motorbreath / Jump In The Fire / (Anasthesia)-Pulling Teeth / Whiplash / Phantom Lord / No Remorse / Seek And Destroy / Metal Militia.

KILL 'EM ALL, Sony SICP-475 (2003) (Japanese release. CD). Hit The Lights / The Four Horsemen / Motorbreath / Jump In The Fire / (Anesthesia)—Pulling Teeth / Whiplash / Phantom Lord / No Remorse / Seek & Destroy / Metal Militia.

KILL 'EM ALL, Universal PD0688 (2006) (South Korean release). Hit The Lights / The Four Horsemen / Motorbreath / Jump In The Fire / (Anesthesia)—Pulling Teeth / Whiplash / Phantom Lord / No Remorse / Seek & Destroy / Metal Militia.

Jump In The Fire, Music For Nations PKUT105 (1984) (Picture disc). Jump In The Fire / Seek And Destroy (Live).

Jump In The Fire, Music For Nations CV12KUT105 (1984) (Red vinyl 12" single). Jump In The Fire / Seek And Destroy (Live) / Phantom Lord (Live).

Jump In The Fire, Music For Nations 12KUT 105 (1984). Jump In The Fire / Seek And Destroy (Live) / Phantom Lord (Live).

RIDE THE LIGHTNING, Bernett SB18026 (1984) (French vinyl release. Mis-printed green sleeve. 400 copies). Fight Fire With Fire / Ride The Lightening / For Whom The Bells Tolls / Fade To Black / Trapped Under Ice / Escape / Creeping Death / The Call Of Ktulu.

RIDE THE LIGHTNING, Music For Nations MFN 27 (1984). Fight Fire With Fire / Ride The Lightning / For Whom The Bells Tolls / Fade To Black / Trapped Under Ice / Escape / Creeping Death / The Call Of Ktulu. Chart positions: 22 SWEDEN, 87 UK, 173 USA.

Creeping Death, Music For Nations 12KUT 112 (1984). Creeping Death / Am I Evil / Blitzkrieg.

Master Of Puppets, Elektra (1986) (French release). Master Of Puppets / Welcome Home (Sanitorium).

MASTER OF PUPPETS, Music For Nations MFN 60 (1986). Battery / Master Of Puppets / The Thing That Should Not Be / Welcome Home (Sanatorium) / Disposable Heroes / Leper Messiah / Orion / Damage Inc. Chart positions: 17 SWEDEN, 29 USA, 41 UK.

$5.98 EP: Garage Days Revisited EP, Vertigo METAL 112 (1987). Helpless / The Small Hours / Crash Course In Brain Surgery / Last Caress-Green Hell. Chart positions: 27 UK, 28 USA.

Harvester Of Sorrow, Vertigo METDJ2 (1988) (UK promotion release). Harvester Of Sorrow / Harvester Of Sorrow.

Metallica, Vertigo METCD 100 (1988) (UK promotion release). Whiplash / Ride The Lightning / Welcome Home (Sanitarium) / One.

Harvester Of Sorrow, Vertigo AS 5000 791 (1988) (Italian jukebox single. Split with ANGELO BRANDUARDI). Harvester Of Sorrow.

MANDATORY METALLICA, Elektra PR 8020-2 (1988). Master Of Puppets / For Whom The Bell Tolls / Seek And Destroy / Fade To Black / Welcome Home (Sanitorium) / The Thing That Should Not Be / Creeping Death.

Harvester Of Sorrow, Vertigo METAL 212 (1988). Harvester Of Sorrow / Breadfan / The Prince. Chart position: 20 UK.

... AND JUSTICE FOR ALL, Vertigo 836 062-2 (1988). Blackened / ... And Justice For All / Eye Of The Beholder / One / The Shortest Straw / Harvester Of Sorrow / The Frayed Ends Of Sanity / To Live Is To Die / Dyers Eve. Chart positions: 4 UK, 5 SWEDEN, 6 USA, 12 AUSTRIA, 44 NEW ZEALAND.

Eye Of The Beholder, Elektra 7-96357 (1988) (USA release). Eye Of The Beholder / Breadfan.

One, Vertigo 874 066-7 (1989) (Australian release). One / Seek And Destroy (Live).

One, Sony XDSP 93114 (1989) (Japanese promotion release). One (Short version) / Breadfan.

One, Sony 10EP-3077 (1989) (Japanese release). One / Breadfan.

One, CBS 23DP-5438 (1989) (Japanese release). One / Breadfan / For Whom The Bell Tolls (Live) / Welcome Home (Sanitorium) / One (Demo).

One, Vertigo METDJ 5 (1989) (UK promotion release). One (Radio version) / One.

One, Elektra 7-96329 (1989) (USA release). One / The Prince. Chart position: 35 USA.

One, Vertigo METPD 510 (1989) (Picture Disc). One (Album Version) / Seek And Destroy (Live).

One, Vertigo METAL 512 (1989). One / For Whom The Bell Tolls (Live) / Welcome Home (Sanitorium) (Live).

One, Vertigo METCD 5 (1989). One / For Whom The Bell Tolls (Live) / Welcome Home (Sanitarium) (Live).

One, Vertigo METG 512 (1989). One (Demo Version) / For Whom The Bell Tolls (Live) / Creeping Death (Live).

One, Vertigo METAL 5 (1989). One / Seek And Destroy (Live). Chart position: 13 UK.

Creeping Death, Vertigo 842219-2 (1990) (German release). Creeping Death / Am I Evil? / Blitzkrieg / Jump In The Fire / Seek And Destroy / Phantom Lord.

Stone Cold Crazy, Elektra PRCD 8224-2 (1990) (US promotion release). Stone Cold Crazy.

Enter Sandman, Vertigo 868 732-7 (1991) (French promotion release). Enter Sandman / Stone Cold Crazy.

The Unforgiven, Vertigo 8661392 (1991). The Unforgiven / Killing Time / The Unforgiven (Demo).

The Six And A Half Year Anniversary EP, Vertigo METAL 612 (1991) (Limited edition release with 'Garage Days Revisited EP', 'Harvester Of Sorrows' and 'One' 12" singles packaged as 'The Good, The Bad And The Live'). Harvester Of Sorrow (Live) / One (Live) / Breadfan (Live) / Last Caress (Live).

Enter Sandman, Vertigo 868 732-7 (1991) (French release). Enter Sandman / Stone Cold Crazy.

Enter Sandman, Vertigo METAL 7 (1991). Enter Sandman / Stone Cold Crazy. Chart positions: 5 UK, 14 SWEDEN, 16 USA.

Enter Sandman, Vertigo METCD 7 (1991). Enter Sandman / Stone Cold Crazy / Enter Sandman (Demo).

Enter Sandman, Vertigo METAL 712 (1991). Enter Sandman / Stone Cold Crazy / Holier Than Thou / Enter Sandman (Demo).

METALLICA, Elektra 61113 (1991). Enter Sandman / Sad But True / Holier Than Thou / The Unforgiven / Wherever I May Roam / Don't Tread On Me / Through The Never / Nothing Else Matters / Of Wolf And Man / The God That Failed / My Friend Misery / The Struggle Within. Chart positions: 1 UK, 1 USA, 1 NEW ZEALAND, 1 GERMANY, 4 SWEDEN, 5 AUSTRIA.

Enter Sandman, Sony SRDC-8204 (1991) (Japanese release). Enter Sandman / Stone Cold Crazy.
The Unforgiven, Vertigo METAL 8 (1991). The Unforgiven / Killing Time. Chart positions: 15 UK, 32 SWEDEN, 35 USA.
The Unforgiven, Vertigo METAL 812 (1991). The Unforgiven / Killing Time / So What / The Unforgiven (Demo).
The Unforgiven, Sony SRDS-8214 (1991) (Japanese release). The Unforgiven / Killing Time.
Sad But True, Vertigo 8644112 (1992). Sad But True / So What / Harvester Of Sorrow (Live).
Sad But True, Elektra 64696 (1992) (USA release). Sad But True / So What. Chart position: 98 USA.
Enter Sandman (Live), Vertigo METCL 10 (1992) (Charity release, all royalties going to Phoenix Trust). Enter Sandman (Live) / Sad But True (Live) / Nothing Else Matters (Live).
Nothing Else Matters (Live), Vertigo 866895-2 (1992) (Brazilian release). Nothing Else Matters (Live) / Enter Sandman (Live) / Sad But True (Live).
Nothing Else Matters, Vertigo METAL 10 (1992). Nothing Else Matters / Enter Sandman (Live). Chart positions: 6 UK, 14 SWEDEN, 34 USA.
Nothing Else Matters, Vertigo METAL 1012 (1992). Nothing Else Matters / Enter Sandman (Live) / Harvester Of Sorrow (Live) / Nothing Else Matters (Demo).
Nothing Else Matters, Sony SRDS-8225 (1992) (Japanese release). Nothing Else Matters / Enter Sandman (Live).
Wherever I May Roam, Vertigo 866 694-7 (1992) (German release). Wherever I May Roam / Fade To Black (Live).
Wherever I May Roam, Vertigo METCD 9 (1992). Wherever I May Roam / Fade To Black (Live) / Wherever I May Roam (Demo).
Wherever I May Roam, Vertigo METAL 9 (1992). Wherever I May Roam / Fade To Black (Live). Chart positions: 25 UK, 28 SWEDEN, 82 USA.
Wherever I May Roam, Vertigo MET 912 (1992). Wherever I May Roam / Medley (Live) / Wherever I May Roam (Demo).
One, Elektra—Spun Gold 65920-7 (1993) (Re-issue). One / Eye Of The Beholder.
Wherever I May Roam, Vertigo 866697-2 (1993) (Brazilian release). Wherever I May Roam / Fade To Black / Wherever I May Roam (demo).
Metallistore 1/21/93, Elektra PR-8723 (1993) (USA promotion cassette. Only available at Manhattan record store appearances.). Last Caress (Live in Moscow 28th September 1991) / Am I Evil (Live in Moscow 28th September 1991) / Battery (Live in Moscow 28th September 1991).
Sad But True, Vertigo METAL 1112 (1993). Sad But True / Nothing Else Matters (Elevator Version) / Creeping Death (Live) / Sad But True (Demo). Chart positions: 20 UK, 31 SWEDEN.
Sad But True, Vertigo 864 410-7 (1993) (Dutch release). Sad But True / So What.
Sad But True, Vertigo METAL 11 (1993). Sad But True / Nothing Else Matters.
Sad But True, Vertigo METCH 11 (1993). Sad But True / Nothing Else Matters (Live) / Sad But True (Live).
Wherever I May Roam, Sony SRCS-6633 (1993) (Japanese release). Wherever I May Roam / Fade To Black (Live) / Last Caress / Am I Evil? / Battery (Live).
LIVE SHIT: BINGE AND PURGE, Vertigo 518 726-2 (1993). Enter Sandman / Creeping Death / Harvester Of Sorrow / Welcome Home (Sanitorium) / Sad But True / Of Wolf And Man / Guitar Doodle / The Unforgiven / And Justice For All / Solo / Through The Never / For Whom The Bell Tolls / Fade To Black / Master Of Puppets / Seek And Destroy / Whiplash / Nothing Else Matters / Wherever I May Roam / Am I Evil / Last Caress / One / Battery / The Four Horsemen / Motorbreath / Stone Cold Crazy. Chart positions: 26 USA, 56 UK, 68 GERMANY.
Mama Said, Vertigo METCD 14 (1996). Mama Said / King Nothing (Live) / Whiplash (Live) / Mama Said (Edit).
Mama Said, Vertigo METAL 14 (1996). Mama Said / Ain't My Bitch (Live). Chart position: 19 UK.
Mama Said, Vertigo METCX 14 (1996). Mama Said / So What (Live) / Creeping Death (Live) / Mama Said (Demo).
Until It Sleeps, Vertigo METCX 12 (1996). Until It Sleeps / Kill / Ride Medley: Ride The Lightning—No Remorse—Hit The Lights—The Four Horsemen—Phantom Lord—Fight Fire With Fire (Live) / Until It Sleeps (Herman Melville Mix).
Until It Sleeps, Vertigo METCD 12 (1996). Until It Sleeps / Until It Sleeps (Herman Melville mix) / 2x4 (Live) / FOBD.
Until It Sleeps, Vertigo METAL 12 (1996). Until It Sleeps / 2x4 (Live) / Until It Sleeps (Moby remix). Chart position: 18 UK.
MANDATORY METALLICA, Vertigo MM CJ-1 (1996) (UK promotion release). Enter Sandman / Nothing Else Matters / One / Harvester Of Sorrow / Creeping Death / Fade To Black / For Whom The Bell Tolls.
Until It Sleeps, Elektra 64276 (1996) (USA release). Until It Sleeps / Overkill. Chart position: 10 USA.
LOAD, Elektra 61923 (1996). Ain't My Bitch / 2 X 4 / The House Jack Built / Until It Sleeps / King Nothing / Hero Of The Day / Bleeding Me / Cure / Poor Twisted Me / Wasting My Hate / Thorn Within / Ronnie / The Outlaw Torn. Chart positions: 1 USA, 1 FRANCE, 1 UK, 1 NEW ZEALAND, 1 GERMANY.
Until It Sleeps, Sony SRCS8062 (1996) (Japanese release). Until It Sleeps / Until It Sleeps (Herman Melville mix) / Ride The Lightning / No Remorse / Hit The Lights / The Four Horsemen / Phantom Lord / Fight Fire With Fire (Live medley) / 2x4 (Live) / Overkill / F.O.B.D.(a.k.a. Until It Sleeps) (Early 'writing in progress' version).
Hero Of The Day, Elektra 64248 (1996) (USA release). Hero Of The Day / Kill 'Em All—Ride The Lightning medley. Chart position: 60 USA.
Hero Of The Day, Vertigo METCY 13 (1996). Hero Of The Day / Overkill / Damage Case / Stone Dead Forever / Too Late Too Late.
Hero Of The Day, Vertigo METCX 13 (1996). Hero Of The Day / Stone Dead Forever / Too Late Too Late / Mouldy.
Hero Of The Day, Vertigo METAL 13 (1996). Hero Of The Day / Mouldy / Hero Of The Day (Outta B Sides mix) / Overkill. Chart position: 17 UK.
Hero Of The Day, Vertigo METCD 13 (1996). Hero Of The Day / Overkill / Damage Case / Hero Of The Day (Outta B Sides mix).
Hero Of The Day, Sony SRCS-8135 (1996) (Japanese release). Hero Of The Day / Mouldy (a.k.a. Hero Of The Day) (Early demo version) / Hero Of The Day (Outta B sides mix) / Stone Dead Forever (Live) / Damage Case (Live) / Too Late Too Late (Live).
The Memory Remains, Mercury MET 15 568 268-7 (1997). The Memory Remains / For Whom The Bell Tolls (Haven't Heard It Yet Mix). Chart positions: 6 AUSTRALIA, 13 UK, 28 USA.
The Memory Remains, Mercury METCD 15 568 269-2 (1997). The Memory Remains / Fuel For Fire (Work In Progress With Different Lyrics) / Memory (Demo Version).
MANDATORY METALLICA 2, Vertigo MMCJ-2 (1997). Wherever I May Roam / One / Enter Sandman / For Whom The Bell Tolls / The Unforgiven / Sad But True / Master Of Puppets / Nothing Else Matters / Fade To Black / Hero Of The Day / Breadfan / Bleeding Me / King Nothing / Until It Sleeps / Stone Cold Crazy / Ain't My Bitch / Welcome Home (Sanitarium).
The Memory Remains, Mercury MET 15 568268-2 (1997). The Memory Remains / For Whom The Bell Tolls (Haven't Heard It Yet Mix).
King Nothing, Elektra 64197 (1997) (USA release). King Nothing / Ain't My Bitch. Chart position: 90 USA.
Mama Said, Sony SRCS-8253 (1997) (Japanese release). Mama Said (Edit) / So What (Live) / Creeping Death (Live) / King Nothing (Live) / Whiplash (Live) / Mama Said (Early demo version).
The Memory Remains, Mercury MET DD15 568 271-2 (1997). The Memory Remains / The Outlaw Torn (Unencumbered By Manufacturing Restrictions Version) / King Nothing (Tepid Mix).
RELOAD, Elektra 536 409-2 (1997). Fuel / The Memory Remains / Devil's Dance / The Unforgiven II / Better Than You / Slither / Carpe Diem Baby / Bad Seed / Where The Wild Things Are / Prince Charming / Low Man's Lyric / Attitude / Fixxer. Chart positions: 1 USA, 1 GERMANY, 1 NORWAY, 1 AUSTRIA, 1 NEW ZEALAND, 1 FINLAND, 2 AUSTRALIA, 2 CANADA, 2 DENMARK, 3 FRANCE, 3 HOLLAND, 3 SPAIN, 3 SWITZERLAND, 4 UK, 5 BELGIUM, 6 ITALY, 12 JAPAN.
The Memory Remains, Sony SRCS-8534 (1997). The Memory Remains / Fuel For Fire (Work in progress with different lyrics) / King Nothing (Tepid mix) / For Whom The Bell Tolls (Haven't heard yet mix) / Memory (Demo version) / The Outlaw Torn (Unencumbered by manufacturing restrictions version).
Fuel, Vertigo METCD-16 (1998). Fuel / Sad But True (Live) / Nothing Else Matters (Live). Chart position: 31 UK.
Fuel, Vertigo METED-16 (1998). Fuel / Until It Sleeps (Live) / Fuel (Live) / Fuel (Demo).
Fuel, Vertigo 568-412-2 (1998) (German release). Fuel / Sad But True (Live).
Fuel, Vertigo METDD-16 (1998). Fuel / Wherever I May Roam (Live) / One (Live).
Turn The Page, SME Records SRCS 8880 (1998) (Japanese release). Turn The Page / Damage Inc. (Live) / Bleeding Me (Live) / Stone Cold Crazy (Live) / The Wait (Live).

Turn The Page, Vertigo 566-590-2 (1998) (German release). Turn The Page / Damage Inc. (Live).

Turn The Page, Vertigo 566-593-2 (1998) (Australian release). Turn The Page / Damage Inc. (Live) / Fuel (Video).

Whiskey In The Jar, Vertigo METJB 19 (1998) (UK Jukebox single). Whiskey In The Jar / Turn The Page.

Fuel, SME Records SRCS 8748 (1998) (Japanese release). Fuel / Fuel (Live) / Sad But True (Live) / Until It Sleeps (Live) / One (Live) / Fuel (Demo).

Whiskey In The Jar, Vertigo MET CJ 19 (1998) (Mexican promotion release). Whiskey In The Jar (Edit) / Whiskey In The Jar.

POOR TOURING ME, Mercury JJJ-MET (1998) (Australian promotion release). Ain't My Bitch (Live) / King Nothing (Live) / One (Live) / Fuel (Live) / For Whom The Bell Tolls (Live) / Wherever I May Roam (Live) / Enter Sandman (Live) / Motorbreath (Live).

The Unforgiven II, Vertigo METDD 17 (1998). The Unforgiven II / The Thing That Should Not Be (Live) / The Memory Remains (Live) / King Nothing (Live).

The Unforgiven II, Vertigo METCD 17 (1998). The Unforgiven II / Helpless (Live) / The Four Horsemen (Live) / Of Wolf And Man (Live). Chart positions: 15 UK, 59 USA.

The Unforgiven II, Vertigo METCX 17 (1998). The Unforgiven II / No Remorse (Live) / Am I Evil? (Live) / The Unforgiven II (Demo).

The Unforgiven II, Vertigo 568-555-2 (1998) (German release). The Unforgiven II / The Memory Remains (Live).

The Unforgiven II, Elektra 64114-2 (1998) (USA release). The Unforgiven II / The Thing That Should Not Be (Live).

The Unforgiven II, Sony SRCS-8549 (1998) (Japanese release). The Unforgiven II / The Thing That Should Not Be (Live) / The Memory Remains (Live) / No Remorse (Live) / Am I Evil? (Live) / The Unforgiven II (Demo).

Turn The Page, Elektra PR1226-2 (1998) (USA promotion release). Turn The Page (Edit) / Turn The Page.

Turn The Page, Vertigo 566-591-2 (1998). Turn The Page / Bleeding Me (Live) / Stone Cold Crazy (Live) / The Wait (Live).

GARAGE INC., Vertigo 538 351-2 (1998). Free Speech For The Dumb / It's Electric / Sabbra Cadabra / Turn The Page / Die, Die My Darling / Loverman / Mercyful Fate / Astronomy / Whiskey In The Jar / Tuesday's Gone / The More I See / Helpless / The Small Hours / The Wait / Crash Course In Brain Surgery / Last Caress—Green Hell / Am I Evil / Blitzkrieg / Breadfan / The Prince / Stone Cold Crazy / So What / Killing Time / Overkill / Damage Case / Stone Dead Forever / Too Late Too Late. Chart positions: 1 GERMANY, 2 USA, 3 NEW ZEALAND, 3 CANADA, 9 FRANCE, 29 UK.

Whiskey In The Jar, Vertigo 566-974-2 (1999) (Australian release). Whiskey In The Jar / (Electronic Press kit Part II).

Whiskey In The Jar, Vertigo METDD 19 (1999). Whiskey In The Jar / The Small Hours (Live) / Killing Time (Live).

Hero Of The Day (Live), Elektra PRCD 1465-2 (1999) (USA promotion release). Hero Of The Day (Live).

No Leaf Clover (Live), Vertigo 562 698-2 (1999) (German release). No Leaf Clover (Live) / (screensaver) / S&M Documentary Part III.

No Leaf Clover (Live), Vertigo 562-696-2 (1999) (German release). No Leaf Clover (Live) / No Leaf Clover (Video) / S&M Documentary Part I.

Nothing Else Matters (Live), Vertigo 562-572-2 (1999) (German release). Nothing Else Matters (Live) / For Whom The Bell Tolls (Live) / -Human (Live) / Nothing Else Matters (Video).

No Leaf Clover, Elektra PRCD1430-2 (1999) (USA promotion release). No Leaf Clover.

Whiskey In The Jar, Vertigo 566-975-2 (1999) (Australian release). Whiskey In The Jar / The Small Hours (Live) / The Prince (Live) / Killing Time (Live) / Last Caress-Green Hell (Live) / Whiskey In The Jar (Live).

Whiskey In The Jar, SME Records SRCS 8913 (1999) (Japanese release). Whiskey In The Jar / Blitzkrieg (Live) / The Prince (Live) / Killing Time (Live) / Last Caress-Green Hell (Live) / Whiskey In The Jar (Live).

Whiskey In The Jar, Vertigo 566-972-2 (1999) (Australian release). Whiskey In The Jar / (Electronic Press kit—Part I).

Whiskey In The Jar, Vertigo 566-854-2 (1999) (German release). Whiskey In The Jar / The Wait (Live).

Whiskey In The Jar, Vertigo METED 19 (1999). Whiskey In The Jar / Last Caress-Green Hell (Live) / Whiskey In The Jar (Live).

No Leaf Clover (Live), Vertigo 0109052HWR (1999) (Australian release). No Leaf Clover (Live) / One (Live) / Enter Sandman (Live) / No Leaf Clover (Video) / S&M Documentary.

No Leaf Clover (Live), Vertigo 562-697-2 (1999) (German release). No Leaf Clover (Live) / (photo gallery & lyrics) / S&M Documentary Part II.

Whiskey In The Jar, Vertigo METCD 19 (1999). Whiskey In The Jar / Blitzkrieg (Live) / The Prince (Live). Chart position: 29 UK.

Die Die My Darling, Vertigo 562-233-2 (1999) (Australian release). Die Die My Darling / Sabbra Cadabra (Live) / Mercyful Fate (Live) / Whiskey In The Jar (Video) / Turn The Page (Video).

Die Die My Darling, Vertigo 562-153-2 (1999) (German release). Die Die My Darling / Sabbra Cadabra (Live) / Mercyful Fate (Live).

S&M, Vertigo 546 797-2 (1999). The Ecstasy Of Gold / The Call Of Ktulu / Master Of Puppets / Of Wolf And Man / The Thing That Should Not Be / Fuel / The Memory Remains / No Leaf Clover / Hero Of The Day / Devil's Dance / Bleeding Me / Nothing Else Matters / Until It Sleeps / For Who The Bell Tolls / -Human / Wherever I Amy Roam / Outlaw Torn / Sad But True / One / Enter Sandman / Battery. Chart positions: 1 GERMANY, 2 USA, 7 FRANCE, 11 NEW ZEALAND, 33 UK.

I Disappear, Arista CDX-2289 (2000) (Mexican promotion release. Split single with SANTANA). I Disappear.

I Disappear, Hollywood 0113875HWR (2000). I Disappear / I Disappear (Instrumental).

St. Anger, Vertigo 65409 (2003) (French release). St. Anger / Cretin Hop.

Frantic, Vertigo DU8674 (2003) (South Korean release). Frantic / Blackened (Live) / Harvester Of Sorrow (Live).

Frantic, Elektra PRCD1913 (2003) (US promotion release). Frantic (Radio edit) / Frantic (Album version) / Frantic (Live rehearsal version).

St. Anger, Vertigo SACDP2 (2003) (New Zealand promotion release). St. Anger (Single edit) / St. Anger.

ST. ANGER, Mercury 9865338 (2003). Frantic / St. Anger / Some Kind Of Monster / Dirty Window / Invisible Kid / My World / Shoot Me Again / Sweet Amber / Unnamed Feeling / Purify / All Within My Hands. Chart positions: 1 PORTUGAL, 1 USA, 1 MEXICO, 1 VENEZUELA, 1 AUSTRIA, 1 GERMANY, 1 SWEDEN, 1 POLAND, 1 NORWAY, 1 DENMARK, 1 CANADA, 1 FINLAND, 1 ICELAND, 2 BELGIUM, 2 SPAIN, 2 SWITZERLAND, 2 CHILE, 3 MALAYSIA, 3 HOLLAND, 3 FRANCE, 3 HUNGARY, 3 UK.

St. Anger, Mercury 9865413 (2003). St. Anger (Explicit) / Now I Wanna Sniff Some Glue / Cretin Hop / St. Anger (Video). Chart position: 9 UK.

St. Anger, Mercury 9865412 (2003). St. Anger (Explicit) / Commando / Today Your Love, Tomorrow The World.

St. Anger, Vertigo (2003) (European release). St. Anger / Commando / Today Your Love Tomorrow The World / Now I Wanna Sniff Some Glue / St. Anger (Video). Chart positions: 22 AUSTRIA, 28 SWITZERLAND.

Frantic, Vertigo (2003). Frantic (Album version) / No Remorse (Live from Download Festival, UK 2003).

Frantic, Vertigo (2003) (Dutch release). Frantic / Harvester Of Sorrow (Live at Fields Of Rock Festival, 2003) / Welcome Home (Sanitarium) (Live at Werchter Festival 2003) / No Remorse (Live at Werchter Festival, 2003). Chart position: 30 HOLLAND.

Frantic, Vertigo (2003) (Spanish release). Frantic / Harvester of Sorrow (Live at Doctor Music 2003) / Welcome Home Sanitarium (Live at Doctor Music 2003) / No Remorse (Live at Doctor Music 2003). Chart positions: 9 SPAIN, 24 PORTUGAL.

Frantic, Vertigo (2003) (Italian release). Frantic / Blackened (Live at Imola Jammin' Festival 2003) / Harvester of Sorrow (Live at Imola Jammin' Festival 2003) / Welcome Home (Sanitarium) (Live at Imola Jammin' Festival 2003) / No Remorse (Live at Imola Jammin' Festival 2003).

Frantic, Vertigo (2003) (Scandinavian release). Frantic / Blackened (Live at Roskilde Festival 2003) / Harvester of Sorrow (Live at Roskilde Festival 2003) / Welcome Home (Sanitarium) (Live at Roskilde Festival 2003) / No Remorse (Live at Roskilde Festival 2003). Chart position: 6 DENMARK.

Frantic, Vertical (2003) (German release). Frantic / Harvester Of Sorrow (Live at Rock Am Ring 2003) / Welcome Home (Sanitarium) (Live at Rock Am Ring 2003). Chart positions: 27 GERMANY, 30 AUSTRIA.

Frantic, Vertigo (2003) (German release). Frantic / No Remorse (Live at Rock Am Ring 2003).

Frantic, Vertigo (2003). Frantic (Album version) / Blackened (Live at Download Festival, UK 2003) / Harvester Of Sorrow (Live at Download Festival UK 2003) / Frantic (CD ROM video).

Frantic, Vertigo 9811514 (2003). Frantic (Album version) / No Remorse (Live at Download Festival, UK 2003) / Welcome Home (Sanitarium) (Live at Download Festival, UK 2003). Chart position: 16 UK.

Frantic, Sony SICP-490 (2003) (Japanese release). Frantic / Blackened (Live) / Harvester Of Sorrow (Live) / Welcome Home (Sanitarium) (Live) / No Remorse (Live).

Frantic, Universal CP11580 (2003) (Mexican split promotion release with LIMP BIZKIT). Frantic (Edit) / Frantic (Album version).

Frantic, Vertigo 9811657 (2003) (French release). Frantic / Blackened (Live Le Trabendo) / Harvester Of Sorrow (Live La Boule Noire) / Welcome Home (Sanitarium) (Live La Boule Noire).

The Unnamed Feeling, Mercury 9815881 (2004). The Unnamed Feeling / The Four Horsemen (Live) / Damage Inc. (Live) / Leper Messiah (Live) / Motorbreath (Live) / Ride The Lightning (Live) / Hit The Lights (Live) / The Unnamed Feeling (Video).

Some Kind Of Monster, (2004). Some Kind Of Monster / Some Kind Of Monster (remix) / The Four Horsemen (Live) / Damage Inc. (Live) / Leper Messiah (Live) / Motorbreath (Live) / Ride The Lightning (Live) / Hit The Lights (Live). Chart position: 37 USA.

METALLICA: TRIBUTE

USA — As Heavy Metal's top of the league artist METALLICA has naturally spawned legions of tribute albums. Big Eye Music's 2001 honourary offering rounded up a whole host of major name acts to pay respect. Opening track 'Battery' combined FLOTSAM AND JETSAM vocalist Eric A.K. with guitarist Mike Clark, OZZY OSBOURNE band bassist Robert Trujillo and the esteemed SLAYER drummer DAVE LOMBARDO. Next cut in 'Sad But True' had ex-ANTHRAX frontman Joey Belladonna heading up an alliance of former KISS guitarist Bruce Kulick, THIN LIZZY bass player Marco Mendoza and Eric Singer of BLACK SABBATH, ALICE COOPER and KISS on drums. Third song 'Sanitarium' was a collaboration between UGLY KID JOE singer Whitfield Crane, ANTHRAX guitarist Scott Ian, METAL CHURCH guitarist John Marshall, KING CRIMSON bassist Tony Levin and MOTORHEAD drummer Mickey Dee.

KING'S X man Doug Pinnick would deliver vocals for 'The Unforgiven', the band for this track comprising LIVING COLOR guitar player Vernon Reid, TONY FRANKLIN on bass and QUIET RIOT's Frankie Banali on the drums. 'The Thing That Should Not Be' line up boasted AGENT STEEL's John Garcia, METAL CHURCH mentor Kurdt Vanderhoof on guitar, DIO and DOKKEN bassist Jeff Pilson with drums supplied by Jason Bonham. The familiar 'Enter Sandman' found Robert Trujillo on bass once again aided by FEAR FACTORY singer Burton C. Bell, DANZIG six stringer John Christ and the veteran OZZY OSBOURNE and WHITESNAKE drummer Tommy Aldridge. It would be the notorious Billy Milano of S.O.D. infamy that took on 'Whiplash', his S.O.D. partner Scott Ian providing guitar with a rhythm section of erstwhile OZZY OSBOURNE bassist Phil Soussan with DIO and BLACK SABBATH drummer Vinnie Appice.

'Nothing Else Matters', sung by SAVATAGE's Jon Oliva, had music supplied by guitarist Bob Balch, MOTÖRHEAD figurehead Lemmy on bass and former DAVID LEE ROTH band drummer Gregg Bissonette. The world renowned Aynsley Dunbar handled drums for both 'Seek And Destroy' and 'For Whom The Bell Tolls'. The former track was lent vocals by TESTAMENT's Chuck Billy and had guitar from ex-OZZY OSBOURNE and BADLANDS guitar legend JAKE E. LEE and DIO's Jimmy Bain on bass. Album closing song 'For Whom The Bell Tolls' was graced by BLUE OYSTER CULT's Eric Bloom, journeyman guitarist Al Pitrelli and TONY FRANKLIN once again on bass.

METALLICA were to be honoured once again with the album 'Remastered' being a complete remake of 'Master Of Puppets' in joint celebration of the twentieth anniversary of the classic album's release and the 25th anniversary of UK Rock magazine Kerrang! Participants featured exclusive recordings from BULLET FOR MY VALENTINE with 'Welcome Home (Sanitarium)', TRIVIUM 'Master Of Puppets', FIGHTSTAR 'Leper Messiah', MACHINE HEAD 'Battery', FUNERAL FOR A FRIEND 'Damage, Inc.', CHIMAIRA 'Disposable Heroes', MASTODON 'Orion' and MENDEED 'The Thing That Should Not Be', with the sleeve notes for the album penned by none other than Lars Ulrich. 'Remastered' came free with Kerrang! issue 1102 in April.

A quite unique concept emerged in August 2006 with the 'Rockabye Baby' album, comprising METALLICA songs transformed into lullabies by glockenspiel, vibraphone and mellotron.

METALLIC ASSAULT: A TRIBUTE TO METALLICA, Big Eye Music (2001). Battery / Sad But True / Sanitarium / The Unforgiven / The Thing That Should Not Be / Enter Sandman / Whiplash / Nothing Else Matters / Seek And Destroy / For Whom The Bell Tolls.

THE BLACKEST ALBUM 3, Anagram CDM GRAM 156 (2002). The Cure (K16) / Harvester Of Sorrow (FUNKER VOGT) / Carpe Diem Baby (ENHANCED REALITY) / Welcome Home (Sanitarium) (RAZED IN BLACK) / Leper Messiah (Godeater Remix) (EXCESSOR) / My Friend Of Misery (THE ELEMENT) / Orion (TRANSMUTATOR) / The Thing That Should Not Be (TOLCHOCK) / King Nothing (TRANSISTORYTHM) / The God That Failed (NEOTEK) / Hero Of The Day (LUNAR FLUX) / The House Jack Built (GODEATER) / Secret / Outro (BLACK EYED SINNER).

A TRIBUTE TO THE FOUR HORSEMEN, Nuclear Blast (2002). Seek & Destroy (PRIMAL FEAR) / Fight Fire With Fire (THERION) / Whiplash (DESTRUCTION) / Phantom Lord (ANTHRAX) / Fade To Black (SONATA ARCTICA) / Master Of Puppets (BURDEN OF GRIEF) / My Friend Of Misery (DARK TRANQUILITY) / One (CREMATORY) / Eye Of The Beholder (IN FLAMES) / The Thing That Shouldn't Be (PRIMUS) / Wherever I May Roam (SINNER) / Motorbreath (Live) (RAGE).

REMASTERED, (2006). Battery / Master Of Puppets / The Thing That Should Not Be / Welcome Home (Sanitarium) / Disposable Heroes / Leper Messiah / Orion / Damage, Inc.

ROCKABYE BABY, Baby Rock BAB-9600 (2006). One / Wherever I May Roam / Enter Sandman / Fade To Black / Nothing Else Matters / Battery / The Unforgiven / Master Of Puppets / Welcome Home (Sanitarium) / (Anesthesia) Pulling Teeth / ... And Justice For All.

METHEDRAS

MILAN, ITALY — *Claudio Facheris (vocals), Massimiliano Ducato (guitar), Eros Muizzi (guitar), Andrea Bochi (bass), Carlo Radaelli (drums).*

Milan retro-Thrashers METHEDRAS, forged by guitarist Massimiliano Ducato and bass player Andrea Bochi, began life covering Thrash standards in 1996. The band line up evolved over the course of two demo sessions, 1997's 'Cost Of Life' and an untitled 2001 effort. The latter recording still clearly demonstrates the band's influences, including cover versions of METALLICA's 'For Whom The Bell Tolls' and SLAYER's 'Seasons In The Abyss'.

The band underwent line up changes in January 2005, losing drummer Carlos Radaelli. METHEDRAS pulled in Parla of CADAVERIC CREMATORIUM and Davide Firinu from IRREVERENCE as temporary substitutes. METHEDRAS toured Italy with NECRODEATH and DELIRIUM X TREMENS in November 2006.

RECURSIVE, Greyman Music MTH001 (2003). Intro / L.R.S. / Drowning By Torment / Wreck n' Roll / My Iniquity Whirl / Time To Die / The Denied God / Under / Darkness.

MEVÂDIO

HERNING, DENMARK — *Kruger (vocals), Ivan (guitar), Thomas (guitar), Michael (bass), Kenneth (drums).*

Melodic Death Metal combo formed during 1995 in Herning, Denmark as a trio and named FACING A BORING DAY (abbreviated F.A.B.D.) The group debuted with a February 1999 demo, recorded with producer Tue Madsen at Borsing Recording Studios in Århus. Still as F.A.b.d. the band cut more demos in 2000 prior to adopting the MEVÁDIO the following year. In this guise the group entered Antfarm Recording Studios to cut the EP 'Living Dead', once again working with Tue Madsen. Yet another session, crafted in 2002, scored a deal with Danish label Mighty Music for the album 'Hands Down'. The record saw release in Denmark during September 2003 and in the rest of Europe in early 2005.

MEZZROW

Facing A Boring Day, (1999). Facing / Resurrection / Healed / Don't Step.
The 2000 Outlet, (2000). Who's The Fool / Living Dead / Still Shining / Playground / Heavy Weight Champion.
Living Dead, (2001). Where's The Angel / . . . On A Sunday / Low / Living Dead / Ride On.
Mevadio, (2002). Faith, Hope & Liposuction / You Ain't Shit To Me / Entertainment.
HANDS DOWN, Soulfood (2005). Life Through The Eyes Of A Coroner / Walk With Me / Entertainment / Below Average / Here Come The Good Guys / Killaville / Faith, Hope And Liposuction / Rainbow Desire / You Ain't Shit To Me / When Bullshit Walks.

MEZZROW

SWEDEN — *Uffe Petersson (vocals), Staffe Karlsson (guitar), Zebba Karlsson (guitar), Conny Welen (bass), Steffe Karlsson (drums).*

A Swedish band very strongly influenced by the American 'Bay Area' Thrash scene, MEZZROW issued their debut album in 1990 but were dropped by Active Records and suffered the further indignation of bassist Conny Welen jumping ship to join HEXENHAUS then DRY DEAD RIVER. Opting not to replace Welen, MEZZROW struggled on with vocalist Uffe Petersson adopting bass duties. The band recorded a new four track demo in 1991, but would eventually split. Uffe Petersson subsequently became vocalist with ROSICRUCIAN.

THEN CAME THE KILLING, Active ATV 11 (1990). Then Came The Killing / Ancient Terror / The Final Holocaust / Frozen Soul / Distant Death / Prevention Necessary / Where Death Begins / The Cross Torment / Inner Devastation.

MICTLAN

LUXEMBOURG — *Mars Dostert (vocals / guitar), Roland Flies (bass), Phil Kessel (drums).*

Melodic Death Metal band MICTLAN was forged in the summer of 1998 by vocalist guitarist Mars Dorstert and bassist Roland Flies, initially joined by guitarist Serge Thinnes and drummer Laurent Hartz. However, this pair lasted a matter of weeks and new drummer Thierry May was duly installed and in this formation MICTLAN debuted live on March 6th 1999. Expanding further, second guitarist Jhemp Even was added to the line-up. Further changes saw Phil Kessel taking over on drums. A demo arrived in early 1999. However, MICTLAN then folded.

Dostert, Flies and Kessel reunited a year later, drawing in Tom Bartholmé on guitar. Jhemp Even rejoined in August 2001, replacing Bartholmé. Both Roland Flies and Jhemp Even operate with Mertzig Power Metal band DREAMS OF NABID.

Mictlan, Mictlan (1999) (Demo). Touch The Sun / Emotions / Mictlan.

MIDAS TOUCH

UPPSALA, SWEDEN — *Patrick Wiren (vocals), Tomas Forshund (guitar), Lasse Gustavsson (guitar), Patrick Sporrong (bass), Bosse Lundstrom (drums).*

An Uppsala Speed Metal band formed in 1985 by bassist Patrick Sporrong, guitarist Tomas Forshund and drummer Bosse Lundstrom, MIDAS TOUCH added vocalist Patrick Wiren in 1987 to record the demo 'Ground Zero'. The tape achieved a recording deal with Noise Records. Prior to recording the debut album, Forshund quit and MIDAS TOUCH drafted in Richard Sporrong as replacement. The resulting 'Presage To Disaster' album was produced by Roy Rowland.

Vocalist Patrick Wiren and bassist Patrick Sporrong formed HIGH TECH JUNKIES then Wiren formed MISERY LOVES CO. in 1994. Guitarist Rickard Sporrong joined PEACE, LOVE & PITBULLS and also operates with irreverent Thrashers F.K.Ü. (Freddy Krueger's Ünderwear) as 'Pat Splat'.

PRESAGE TO DISASTER, Noise NUK124 (1989). The Arrival / Forcibly Incarcerated / Sinking Censorship / When The Boot Comes Down / True Believers Inc. / Reminiscence / Sepulchral Epitaph / Lost Paradise / Accessory Before The Fact / Aceldama—Terminal Breath / Subhumanity (A New Cycle). Chart position: 40 SWEDEN.

MILITIA

AUSTIN, TX, USA — *Mike Soliz (vocals), Tony Smith (guitar), Robert Willingham (bass), Phil Achee (drums).*

Austin Thrash Metal act MILITIA was created by the rhythm section of bassist Robert Willingham and drummer Phil Achee during early 1984, rounding out the first line-up with guitarists Tony Smith and Jesse Villegas. In its formative months MILITIA went through a stream of vocalists before settling on Mike Soliz, previously a drummer with FALLEN ANGEL.

The band debuted with the demo cassette 'Regiments Of Death', recorded at First Star Studios in August 1985. Local live work included valuable support slots to the likes of METAL CHURCH, WATCHTOWER, MEGADETH and EXODUS. Famously, MILITIA appeared at the Cameo Theater in San Antonio that year performing alongside two SLAYER's—the Los Angeles and San Antonio versions. Following this gig, Villegas opted out, leaving Smith to handle guitar duties.

MILITIA entered Cedar Creek Studios in South Austin with engineer Fred Remmert to record 'The Sybling' EP, originally issued as a 12" single on the custom Scythe imprint and limited to just 100 copies, then followed. The interest shown in the band in layer years spawned a succession of 7" bootleg versions of 'The Sybling' throughout the 90s. Just prior to the release of 'The Sybling', Smith exited, being superseded by Phillip Patterson of MATRIX. Subsequent recordings included a 1986 two song session 'No Submission' once again crafted at Cedar Creek Studios.

Singer Mike Soliz, of OBLIVION KNIGHT repute, subsequently joined Thrash Metal act ASSALANT and re-recorded lead vocals on their 1987 demo 'The Damage Is Done', replacing those of WATCHTOWER and DANGEROUS TOYS man Jason McMaster. Ironically, Soliz briefly replaced McMaster in WATCHTOWER, featuring on the demo 'Instruments Of Random Murder' in 1987.

The Sybling EP, Scythe NR 16356 (1985). Objective: Termination / Salem Square / The Sybling: i) The Birth, ii): The Arrival, iii) The World Accepts Evil, iv): Evil Through The Ages, v): The Second Coming.
Regiments Of Death, (1985). Metal Axe / Search For Steel / Regiments Of Death.
No Submission, (1986). Talking To The Stone / No Submission.

MINDLOCK

DENMARK — *John Bliessman (vocals), Bo Frandsen (guitar), Lars Petersen (bass), Peter Carlsen (drums).*

Thrashers initiated during 1994 as INSOMNIA by drummer Peter Carlsen, vocalist / guitarist and Bo Frandsen and second guitarist René Hansen. With the addition of the TERROR and STØJ credited Lars Petersen on bass the band evolved into MINDLOCK. Rolf Christensen was introduced as lead vocalist in 1995 for the demo 'Thoughts'. As a side project, Frandsen joined THE CHAOS ENGINE as frontman but after just one gig this unit folded. Meantime Petersen would be active with both technical Death Metal band VIRUS and BIOGENETIC DISORDER. With little activity on the MINDLOCK front both Hansen and Christensen exited toward the end of the year.

Persevering as a trio MINDLOCK would be asked to contribute to the Serious Entertainment 1999 compilation album 'Extremity Rising vol. 4'. Recording at Soundzone Studios in Copenhagen the band recorded 'Exposed' as their inclusion. In January 2000, the recordings for the 'Soulfracture' EP took place, once again utilising the Soundzone Studios with Lars Schmidt acting as producer. Further demos were cut in the Spring of 2001. MINDLOCK signed to Jet Speed Records Group in March of the following year. However, the group, adding new singer John Bliessman in 2003 for the 'Blind Eye Visions' demo, would severe ties with their new label.

Soulfracture, Independent (2000). The Four Walls / Unconsciously Aware / Voice Within / Soulfracture / Exposed.

MINOTAUR

GERMANY — *Andreas Richwein (vocals / guitar), Marco Schafenort (bass), Jorg Bock (drums).*

A Hamburg Thrash Metal band that only failed to break through on the back of the eighties German Thrash Metal wave through sheer bad luck. MINOTAUR was created in 1983, issuing 'The Oath Of Blood' demo the following year. Further exposure was gained with the inclusion of a track on Roadrunner's 'Teutonic Metal Invasion Part 1' compilation album.

A further demo, 'The Slaughter Continues', arrived in 1987. Although Roadrunner offered a full album the band opted to self finance the 1988 'Power Of Darkness' album. A limited edition of 2'500, the record soon sold out.

MINOTAUR signed to the Turbo label for an EP but pulled out of this deal to go with Remedy Records. The resulting 'Eat Metal' EP was subsequently issued in 1989. Constant gigging with the major Thrash acts of the day continued. However, MINOTAUR would fold around 1992.

The band, now with Wikinger on bass, reformed for a projected 2002 album. MINOTAUR's early demos would be reissued in CD format by T.T.D. Records.

POWER OF DARKNESS, Minotaur (1988). Into The Temple / Fierce Fight / Incubus / Maggots In My Body / Apocalyptic Trials / Prelude—Necromancer / The Power Of Darkness / Brainhead / Fall Of The Gods / Savage Aggression.

Eat Metal EP, (1989). Towards My Eternity / Total Decay.

The Oath Of Blood EP, T.T.D. (2001). Intro / Total Decay / Daddschai / Tales Of Terror.

The Slaughter Continues EP, T.T.D. (2001). Intro / Planed Head / Savage Aggressions / Fall Of The Gods.

MNEMIC

DENMARK — *Michael Bøgballe (vocals), Mircea Gabriel Eftemie (guitar), Rune Stigart (guitar), Mikkel Larsen (bass), Brian Rasmussen (drums).*

Self styled 'Hybrid Metal' outfit MNEMIC ('Mainly Neurotic Energy Modifying Instant Creation') came together in 2002 incorporating ex-MERCENARY guitarist Mircea Gabriel Eftemie, bassist Mikkel Larsen and former INVOCATOR session drummer Brian Rasmussen. The group signed to the Nuclear Blast label for recording of a Tue Madsen produced debut 'Mechanical Spin Phenomena'. However, Larsen was superseded by erstwhile GROPE four-stringer Tomas "Oberst" Koefod upon completion of recordings.

Extracurricular activity for Rasmussen saw his inclusion as a member of TRANSPARENT, an alliance with LOST, FAILED and LEMURIA credited vocalist Rene Pedersen, guitarist Danny Hove Jensen, ex-MERCENARY, SUDDEN DEATH, BEHIND THE CURTAIN and NUGATORY man Signar Petersen on guitar and bass.

An extensive run of European shows for MNEMIC in November caught the band packaged with DISBELIEF, DARKANE, MYSTIC PROPHECY and headliners DEATH ANGEL. Subsequent shows had MNEMIC allied with MACHINE HEAD in Germany.

The band would spend the first half of 2004 cutting the 'The Audio Injected Soul' album, recorded at AntFarm Studios in Århus, Denmark once again with producer Tue Madsen. The record not only surprised many by closing out with a cover version of DURAN DURAN's 'Wild Boys' but also claimed to be the first in the world to be recorded three dimensionally using binaural recording technology. Listeners would have to wear a special head set in order to appreciate the enhancement. A promotional video for the track 'Deathbox', directed by Patric Ulleaus, would be filmed in Gothenburg at the Revolver Studios. 'The Audio Injected Soul' broke into the national Danish album charts at no. 97, a first for a domestic extreme Metal band.

On the live front, the band was joined onstage by FEAR FACTORY singer Burton C. Bell for a cover version of FEAR FACTORY's 'Self Bias Resistor' during MNEMIC's appearance at the July 'Earthshaker' festival in Geiselwind, Germany. The band would be chosen, alongside fellow Scandinavian acts THE HAUNTED, MERCENARY, HATESPHERE, RAUNCHY, MELTED, BLINDFAULT and STOMPED, to form up the "Nordic Threat" show for the Popkomm 2004 music convention at the Silver Wings in Berlin on 29th September.

A further promotional video, for the track 'Door 2.12', would be filmed in East Berlin. Gigs in December saw MNEMIC supporting FEAR FACTORY and SHADOWS FALL across Europe. Michael Bøgballe took time out to aid ABORTED as guest backing vocalist on their album 'The Archaic Abattoir'. Meantime, 'The Audio Injected Soul' would see a Japanese release through Soundholic Records in early February 2005. That same year saw the arrival of SMAXONE, seeing MNEMIC's Michael Bøgballe on "Distorted" vocals and drummer Brian 'Brylle' Rasmussen in alliance with ELOPA's Claus Lillelund, handling "clean" vocals and guitarist Casper Skafte for the album 'Regression'. The band had their track 'Door 2.12' featured on the soundtrack to the 'Rainbow Six Lockdown' game issued by 3volution Productions. MNEMIC announced US dates alongside MESHUGGAH, THE HAUNTED and GOD FORBID throughout October. However, rumours then circulated to the effect that Michael Bøgballe had relinquished his position and that TRANSPORT LEAGUE and B-THONG singer Tony Jelencovich was in negotiations with the band, this speculation officially confirmed a few days later. This version of the band engaging in North American touring throughout November sharing stages with ARCH ENEMY, ALL THAT REMAINS and A PERFECT MURDER.

In early January 2006 Mircea Eftemie Gabriel announced the formation of Heavy Metal concept SILENT STRAIN, a unit hailing from Canada, Denmark and Russia, comprising ANNIHILATOR vocalist Dave Padden, second guitarist Cory McBain, bassist Rick Struve and Igor Chiefot on the drums.

MNEMIC utilised ex-STONE TEMPLE PILOTS drummer Eric Kretz's Bomb Shelter studios in Los Angeles, California in May, working with producers Shaun Tingvolt and Christian Olde Wolbers, FEAR FACTORY guitarist, for a 2006 album. However, after a tenure of just six months, MNEMIC parted ways with singer Tony Jelencovich in April. The following month SCARVE singer Guillaume Bideau was announced as replacement. October Scandinavian gigs had the band partnered with M.A.N for shows in Sweden, Estonia and Finland. The group undertook a North American tour commencing October 5th at the Jaxx venue in West Springfield, Virginia taking along DARKEST HOUR, SOILWORK and THREAT SIGNAL for 'The Last Stab' dates into mid November.

2007 US dates commenced on January 4th at the First Unitarian Church in Philadelphia, Pennsylvania with a first headlining leg backed by GOATWHORE, GOD FORBID, THE HUMAN ABSTRACT and ARSIS. On February 2nd BYZANTINE joined this touring entourage in the stead of THE HUMAN ABSTRACT.

The 'Passenger' album, released by Nuclear Blast in February 2007 and conceptually based upon the philosophy of existentialism, saw Japanese variants hosting the obligatory extra track in 'Zero Synchronized'. To promote the record a promotional video was shot for the song 'Meaningless' with director Patric Ullaeus.

MNEMIC were notably selected to open for METALLICA on July 13th in Aarhus.

Tattoos, Mnemic (2000) (Demo). Tattoos / Closed Eyes.
Mnemic, Mnemic (2002) (Demo). Blood Stained / Naked And The Dead / Flipping.
MECHANICAL SPIN PHENOMENA, Nuclear Blast NB 1139-2 (2003). Liquid / Blood Stained / Ghost / DB 'XX' D / Tattoos / The Naked And The Dead / Closed Eyes / Mechanical Spin Phenomenon / Zero Gravity.
Liquid, Nuclear Blast NB 1158-2 (2003). Liquid.
Ghost, Nuclear Blast NB 1286-2 (2004). Ghost / Blood Stained (Rhys Fulber's Euphoric Recall remix) / Ghost (Video) / Photo Gallery.
THE AUDIO INJECTED SOUL, Nuclear Blast NB 1310-2 (2004). The Audio Injection / Dreamstate Emergency / Door 2:12 / Illuminate / Deathbox / Sane Vs. Normal / Jack Vegas / Mindsaver / Overdose In the Hall Of Fame / The Silver Drop / Wild Boys. Chart position: 97 DENMARK.
Deathbox, Nuclear Blast NB 1346-2 (2004). Deathbox (Edit) / Deathbox (Video).
Door 2.12, Nuclear Blast NB 1413-2 (2005). Door 2.12.
THE AUDIO INJECTED SOUL, Soundholic TKCS-85113 (2005) (Japanese release). The Audio Injection / Dreamstate Emergency / Door 2.12 / Illuminate / Deathbox / Sane Vs. Normal / Jack Vegas / Mindsaver / Overdose In the Hall Of Fame / The Silver Drop / Wild Boys / Deathbox (Promotional video).
PASSENGER, Nuclear Blast NB 1837-2 (2007). Humanaut / In The Nothingness Black / Meaningless / Psykorgasm / Pigfuck / In Control / Electric I'd Hypocrisy / Stuck Here / What's Left / Shape Of The Formless / The Eye On Your Back.

MOBY DICK

HUNGARY — *Tamás Schmiedl (vocals / guitar), Norbert Mentes (guitar), Gábor Göbl (bass), Tamás Rozsonits (drums).*

A prolific Speed Metal band from Sopron, founded in 1980 by vocalist / guitarist Tamás Schmiedl and guitarist Norbert Mentes. Taking their title from a LED ZEPPELIN track MOBY DICK built up their reputation throughout the 80s despite a series of membership shuffles. Gyula Bindes sat in on drums until 1982. Featuring on bass early during this decade would be Zoltan Horváth and Miklós Jancsó but by 1983 Kurt Giczi stabilised the position for five years until Gábor Göbl took over both four string duties and responsibilities as band manager. Singer Peter Komuves fronted the band in 1982. Later vocalists included Antal Novak in 1988 and Zsolt Molics the year after.

The group, now with Péter Hoffer on drums, issued a 1992 Euro Heavy Metal styled demo cassette and followed this in 1995 with a second session. By this stage MOBY DICK was already a major concert attraction in Hungary. This brace of demos led to the band's debut 1990 album 'Ugass Kutya', translated as "Bark you dog!". The bizarre humour of the band was also evidenced on song titles such as 'Feet' and 'Bad Odour'. MOBY DICK had a line up change in 1994 with drummer Tamás Rozsonits making way for Péter Hoffer. The album of that year, 'Memento', actually comprised of re-worked demos.

Guitarist Norbert Mentes, along with MOBY DICK drummer Péter Hoffer, would later found BRAZZIL issuing an eponymous album in 1995. MOBY DICK added drummer Bertalan Balázs during 2002.

MEMENTO, K&E (1994). Nem Vagyok Idegen / Meseltek E Kislany / Pokolrock / Zokog A Lelkem / Jarvanyveszely / A III. Vilaghaboru Elott / Patkanyirtas / Keresztes Vitez / Kinek Kell / Prometheus / Rossz Fiuk / A Bun Krisztusa / Falfirkalo.
TISZTITÓTÛZ, Magneoton (1997). Egess Meg / Uvoltes / Rekviem / Rezervatum / Zuhanas / Kulon A Lelek / Unom A Banant / A Kiraly / Vagd Le / Semmibol Sehova / Ugass Kutya.
GOOD BYE, Magneoton (1998). Ugass Kutya / Buz Van / Kaosz es Zurzavar / Good Bye / Elsz Vagy Meghalsz / Kegyetlen Evek / Beteg A Fold / Kikepzes / Ne Koss Belem / Ilyen Ez A Szazad / Korhinta / Gumiszoba / Gazember / Pokolrock / Keresztes Vitez / Prometheus / A III. Vilaghaboru Elott / Indul a Boksz / Na Mi Van.

MOKOMA

LAPPEENRANTA, FINLAND — *Marko Annala (vocals), Tuomo Saikkonen (guitar), Kuisma Aalto (guitar), Heikki Kärkkäinen (bass), Janne Hyrkäs (drums).*

Lappeenranta based Thrash Metal act originated during 1996 as a solo concern of SLUMGUDGEON and PRONSSINEN POKAALI vocalist Marko Annala. He would be joined by THE MACHETE and MIND RIOT guitarist Tuomo Saikkonen, THE MACHETE guitarist Kuisma Aalto, former SLUMGUDGEON colleague Heikki "Hessu" Kärkkäinen on bass and Janne Hyrkäs of PRONSSINEN POKAALI on the drums. Subsequently, THE MACHETE's Santtu Hämäläinen took over on bass.

First outing would be the 'Kasvan' and follow up 'Perspektiivi' singles for EMI Records in 1999. The full-length 'Vulu' arrived that same year. MOKOMA's second opus, 'Mokoman 120 Päivää', was delivered in 2001. The group switched to Sakara Records for third effort 'Kurimus', released in 2003.

MOKOMA issued 'Tämän Maailman Ruhtinaan Hovi' ("The Court Of This World's Emperor") in 2004. On February 16th 2007 MOKOMA's 'Kuoleman Laulukunnaat' was honoured with the "Musician of the Year" award at the Finnish Metal Awards, which were held during the Finnish Metal Expo at the Cable Factory in Helsinki, Finland.

VALU, EMI (1999). Kurjen Laulu / Pillipiipari / Kasvan / Viholliset / Perspektiivi / Valhettelija / Seeste / Se On Minussa / Väristyksiä / Kauas Aivot Karkaavat / Parasta Ennen 0898 / Tyyssija.
MOKOMAN 120 PÄIVÄÄ, EMI (2001). Koiruoho / Rajapyykki / Pois Se Minusta / Teon Teoriaa / Seitsemän Sinetin Takana / Lihaa / Terästä / Voimahuone / Ranka / Onnenonkija / Pimeyden Liitto.
Seitsemän Sinetin Takana, EMI (2001). Seitsemän Sinetin Takana / Reitti.
Rajapyykki, EMI (2001). Rajapyykki / Turhaan Tänne Tulleet.
KURIMUS, Sakara (2003). Mene Ja Tiedä / Takatalvi / Kasvot Kohti Itää / Tämä Puoli / Houkka / Vainottu / Silmäterä / Punainen Kukko / Lupaus / Väsynyt Atlas / Liiton Loppu.
Punainen Kukko EP, Sakara (2003). Punainen Kukko / H.E.L.L. / Pillipiipari 2003 / Marjat / Täältä Etelään / Takatalvi (Video) / Punainen Kukko (Video).
TÄMÄN MAAILMAN RUHTINAAN HOVI, (2004). Toista Maata / Haudan Takaa / Hiljaisuuden Julistaja / Tämän Maailman Ruhtinaan Hovi / Minä Elän! / Kiellän Itseni / Hyinen Syli / Vade Retro, Satana! / Sudet Ihmisten Vaatteissa / Poltetun Maan Taktiikkaa / Nämä Kolme Ovat Yhtä / Uni Saa Tulla.

MONONOFU

OSAKA, JAPAN — *Yoshihisa Amago (vocals), Hiroshi Yamashita (guitar), Shinpei Chousokabe (guitar), Katsuchika Togashi (bass), Mitsuhiro Shimazu (drums).*

Osaka's "Ochi-Musha" Samurai orientated Thrash outfit MONONOFU comprises vocalist Yoshihisa "Minbu-Shouyuu" Amago (a.k.a. Necrolord Pandämonium) from CATAPLEXY, guitarist Lord Warsaw "U-Daijin" Toyotomi (a.k.a. Hiroshi Yamashita) of HATE BEYOND, INFERNAL NECROMANCY and NARCOTIC GREED, second guitarist Shinpei "Kunai-Shouyuu"

Chousokabe of NAGHELL, bass player Katsuchika "Gyoubu-Shouyuu" Togashi, an ex-NARCOTIC GREED member, with Mitsuhiro "Nai-Daijin" Shimazu on drums.

Established during February 2004, the group underwent early line-up changes, with erstwhile members including ex-ETERNAL FOREST bassist Darkmist Yamigiri "Chuu-Nagon" Ukita and drummers Kazumune "Mutsu-no-Kami" Date, an ex-VOVOTAU man, and Haruhisa "Sakon-Shougen" Kumon.

Strangely, only ten copies of the band's debut, two track demo, 'Demo #01' with its pseudo METALLICA logo, were released. A second demo, 'Isolated Castle', arrived in May 2006.

Demo #01, Mononofu (2005) (Demo. Limited edition ten copies). Kachi-Ikusa / Honnouji-Temple.

Isolated Castle, Mononofu (2006) (Demo). Oshibara Kuzure / Rebellion Of Honnouji-Temple / Give Me 7 Defects And 8 Agonies.

MONSTERWORKS

PALMERSTON NORTH, NEW ZEALAND — *Jon (vocals / guitar), Eee (guitar), Hugo (bass), Chris Mills (drums).*

Palmerston North Thrash orientated Metal band founded in 1996. Bassist Ryan, following on from formative four-stringers Chris and Simon, the latter's term lasting just one day, holds BACKYARD BURIAL credentials. MONSTERWORKS debuted in July 1998 with the demo 'Dormant', with 'Delusions Of Grandeur' following in August 1999. The group made their commercial inauguration with the 2001 opus 'Dimensional Urgency', after which Brock relocated to the UK. He would be superseded by Nathan Forbes, having originally made his mark with technical Death Metal act FALCIFORM and holds credits with the experimental Black Metal band ZIRCONIUM as well as DEMIURGE and DRACO AERIUS. MONSTERWORKS followed up with a March 2002 album 'Rogue', issued through Eat Lead And Die Music. The album was recorded in two stages, at The Stomach Studios in Palmerston North during October 2001 and the second at C. Moore Sound in Wellington in February 2002. That March, MONSTERWORKS played their final New Zealand gig.

The band relocated from New Zealand to take up residence in London, England, soon re-enlisting Brock and recording the 'M-Theory' album with the services of a session drummer. Sterghios Moschos took command of the drums in July 2004 but had vacated by the following June. In July the band put in an appearance at the 'Dungeonfest 555' festival at The Royal Park Cellars in Leeds. Casket Records issued the MONSTERWORKS album 'The Precautionary Principle' in 2006.

Mid 2007 saw the release of a new album 'Spacial Operations'.

Dormant, Monsterworks (1998). Macroscope / Cascade / Princess Die / Wasteland / Chopped Into Little Pieces / Simple Ego Shrine / Planet Of The Apes.

Delusions Of Grandeur, (1999). Blokk / Mindstorm / Delusions Of Grandeur / Infernity.

DIMENSIONAL URGENCY, Monsterworks (2001). Primus Exordium / Personal Demons / Redline / Blast Furnace / Dial M For Monster / Dear Abby / In Space (No One Can Hear You Mosh) / Awe Chasm / Chunuk Bair.

ROGUE, Eat Lead And Die Music (2002). Set Up / In The New Age / Tomb Spader / Whoreborn / Nothing / Small Gods / Colossus / Oblique / Blindend / (!?) / No Other Option / Ascension.

M-THEORY, Monsterworks (2003). Latro Praelium / Rogue / Insolence / Supermetal / Redemption / Timebomb / Barricade / Venom Of God / Shatterer Of Worlds / For Glory.

THE PRECAUTIONARY PRINCIPLE, Casket Music CSK074CD (2006). Internal Velocity (Intro) / M-Theory / Screwdriver / It Ends Here Today / Metal Is Everything / Game On / Out Of Control / Hypertrophic Me / Bleed The World / Triumph / The Precautionary Principle / Who Am I / Outro / Charred Vision / Thoroughly Thought Through / Unknown Quantity.

SPACIAL OPERATIONS, Monsterworks (2007). Leaving Home / Firefight / Spacial Forces / November / Stars Malign / Defenders Of The Southern Cross / The Lonely Crown / Hysterical Rapture / Pain And Elation / Parallelysis / Alliance / Exfiltration / Voyage Of Magma Maiden / To Be Continued . . . .

MONUMENT

OKLAHOMA, OK, USA — *Kirk Callaway (vocals), Sean Kelly (guitar), Chad Callaway (bass), Jerry Gulley (drums).*

Oklahoma City Thrash outfit MONUMENT was formed up in 1993 by guitar player Sean Kelly, bassist Chad Callaway and drummer Kevin Courtney. In March 1995 this trio, adding singer Jim Davis and second guitarist Parker Brown, cut the first six song demo entitled 'Dust'. However, Brown decamped in late 1995 and Davis relocated out of the area. MONUMENT pulled in Chad's brother Kirk on lead vocals and in August of 1998 the band laid down their debut album 'Resting Place'. The November 2000 album 'The Millennial Death Of God' included a cover version of OVERKILL's 'Spiritual Void'. MONUMENT played the 16th annual Milwaukee 'Metalfest' event in July of 2002 after which Courtney exited. Jerry Gulley of PURGATORY STATE stepped into the breach to bring the band back up to strength.

DUST, Independent (1995). Acception Denied / Quintessence Of Dust / Steal Away / Chain Of Aggression / The Inquisition / Fall From Grace.

RESTING PLACE, Independent (1999). In The Name / Hopeless / Lost In Paradise / The Game / Reflections / Mortal Divinity / Judgement / Lies / Eyes Of Sorrow / Resting Place.

THE MILLENIAL DEATH OF GOD, Independent (2000). Guilt Is Your Sin / Lift The Veil / Meaningless / Hollow / Carried On Black Angel Wings / No Peace / Live The Lie / Truth / The Search / Spiritual Void.

MORBID ANGEL

TAMPA, FL, USA — *David Vincent (vocals / bass), Trey Azagthoth (guitar), Erik Rutan (guitar), Pete Sandoval (drums).*

Blasphemous Death metal act MORBID ANGEL, founded in Tampa, Florida during 1984, broke down the barriers between extreme music and commercial success but seemingly blew their chances of entering the big league with a series of remarks attributed to main man David Vincent being allegedly fascist in nature. The world's Rock media erupted in an outcry against these supposed Nazi leanings. Nevertheless, despite the controversy and the band's denials, MORBID ANGEL had racked up combined sales of over 1'000'000 albums sold by 1998 and, as a new millennium broke, seemed only to solidify their standing. Importantly, the band has built a catalogue of distinction and remained steadfast as genre leaders.

The formative band unit had come together at high school with Trey Azagthoth (real name George Emmanuel III), Dallas Ward and Mike Browning forging ICE. This act subsequently adopted the title HERETIC before discovering another act laying claim to the title. At this juncture Azagthoth suggested MORBID ANGEL. The band's inaugural gigs found the unit honing their skills with cover versions of songs by ANGEL WITCH, SLAYER and MERCYFUL FATE. Having performed initially as a trio the group then brought in singer Kenny Bamber to record a 1985 two song demo of 'Demon Seed' and 'Welcome To Hell'. Bamber exited and MORBID ANGEL persevered as an instrumental act as an interim measure before Dallas Ward took on the lead vocal duties. In August 1985 a demo billed 'The Beginning' comprised a hotch-potch of tracks featuring vocals from both Bamber and Ward.

However, next in line for the frontman role would be vocalist / guitarist Richard Brunelle. Unfortunately Ward was convicted of a drugs offence and incarcerated. This measure forced the band to re-think and, pulling in John Ortega as second guitarist Brunelle was delegated the vocal role. At one stage MORBID ANGEL, albeit fleetingly, rehearsed with a female singer Evilynn. This proposed band structure did not come up to standard though and before long Mike Browning was to try his hand at the vocal role.

With record company interest rising MORBID ANGEL cut a 1986 four song demo, 'Scream Forth Blasphemies', comprising 'Hellspawn', 'Chapel Of Ghouls', 'Angel Of Disease' and 'Abominations'. This tape soon found its way onto the underground trading market spreading the band's reputation globally. What was to be the band's debut album 'Abominations Of Desolation', recorded in North Carolina in May1986, was shelved due to the band disintegrating in an physical argument over Browning's girlfriend. Upon completion of these recordings Browning opted out and John Ortega departed too, later to found MATRICIDE. Georgia native Sterling Von Scarborough, previously fronting his own act INCUBUS, was drafted early that summer to act as vocalist / bassist.

Scarborough, leaving to forge a new INCUBUS with ex-MORBID ANGEL drummer Mike Browning and TERROR guitarist Gino Marino, was supplanted by ex-TERRORIZER man David Vincent. (a.k.a. David Stuppnig) The bassist, previously having led his own act BURIED IN CEMETERY, had been an acquaintance of the band for some time having financed and produced the 'Abominations Of Desolation' sessions. The newly constituted line-up, comprising Vincent, Azagthoth, lead vocalist Michael Manson and drummer Wayne Hartshell, relocated to North Carolina to cut new demos. Manson did not last the pace and dropped out, leaving Vincent to take on the frontman role for MORBID ANGEL's commercial debut the 1988 'Thy Kingdom Come' 7" single released on Switzerland's Splattermaniac label. With this more solid unit MORBID ANGEL's sales began to accelerate as did their worldwide recognition.

Debut album 'Altars Of Madness', cut at Tampa's fabled Morrisound studios, surfaced through leading extreme Metal imprint Earache Records in May 1989. CD versions added an extra track, 'Lord Of All Fevers And Plagues', plus alternate remixes of album tracks with outtake guitar solos. The world's first dose of MORBID ANGEL was positively poisoning and paralysing. Trey Azagthoth and Richard Brunelle had summoned up a snakes nest of riffs that deliberately defied convention, hammering and sliding outside of accepted meters, this near surreal approach providing a platform for even greater experimentation to come. 'Altars Of Madness', undeniably a classic, did have its faults though. A wistful production unfortunately masked much of the bass presence and David Vincent's vocals and lyrics were ineffectual. On the live front, the group participated in the Earache organised "Grindcrusher" tour of Europe that winter shoulder to shoulder with BOLT THROWER, CARCASS and NAPALM DEATH.

'Blessed Are The Sick' was tendered in July 1991. Self-produced at Morrisound, sonically the album corrected many of its predecessors flaws. Adorned in a disturbing J. Delville painting 'Les Tresors De Satan', 'Blessed Are The Sick', despite being a more deliberate and considered body of work, was soon to be held up as one of the most revered albums in extreme metal history. An inceptor to the savagery the band opened a delicate slice of ambience, the first hints of more adventurous adventurism to come in later years. Pointedly, although MORBID ANGEL would be targeted as Satanists for entire decade, their second album dropped the anti-Christian rhetoric in favour of loathing towards humanity in general.

In September 1991, just upfront of a lengthy American tour, MORBID ANGEL's planned debut album 'Abominations Of Desolation' finally saw a release through Earache Records. The album had been bootlegged relentlessly upon the band's ascendancy into the upper echelons of the Thrash ranks.

Guitarist Richard Brunelle drifted away in mid 1992. MORBID ANGEL filled his shoes briefly with former INCUBUS man Gino Marino but before long Brunelle was back. However, Brunelle decamped in the Autumn of 1992 to found EON'S DEAD. A trio of David Vincent, Trey Azagthoth and Pete Sandoval crafted the 'Covenant' album, utilising the familiar Morrisound facilities but enlisting METALLICA producer Flemming Rasmussen to handle desk work. The final tapes were mixed down at Sweet Silence Studios in Copenhagen.

June 1993 saw MORBID ANGEL of such a stature that their 'Covenant' album was signed over to the massive Warner Bros corporation in America, where albums would be released on the label's Giant imprint. Backed by a promotional video clip for 'God Of Emptiness' it would prove the band's biggest commercial success to date, shifting over 130,000 copies in the USA alone. The band closed the membership gap with ex-RIPPING CORPSE and EULOGY guitarist Eric Rutan drafted for European dates. However, for support dates to MOTÖRHEAD and BLACK SABBATH in America during commencing in Connecticut on February 8th 1994 Richard Brunelle made a temporary return. Meantime, an EP of remixes by the cult underground Industrial act LAIBACH surfaced, a groundbreaking move for an extreme Metal act at the time. The 'Laibach remixes' EP came delivered in CD format with black artwork sleeve and a silver clad 12" variant. Meantime, ex-member Sterling Von Scarborough, under the pseudonym 'Nocticula', published a demo, restricted to just 66 copies, under the banner LIBER NOCTICULA.

The May 1995 MORBID ANGEL album 'Domination' witnessed the band's grip on their premier league status strengthening. Their first recorded output to include Erik Rutan, the album also drew considerable criticism from longstanding followers due to its diversion into sludge variations. Vinyl variants came clad in differing artwork to their CD counterparts and the record also saw limited edition releases in a metal tin, restricted to just 1000 copies. A planned 'slime' filled green jewel case sleeve was shelved, with claims of leaking toxic substances being blamed, but nevertheless 'Domination' surpassed the 80,000 sales mark in the USA. MORBID ANGEL undertook an enormous touring schedule throughout 1995 and into 1996. Dates began in their home state of Florida for an American tour before extensively covering Europe until February 1996 saw the band back in America prior top a return trip to Europe. These shows yielded the live album 'Entangled In Chaos'.

The band seemingly suffered a double hammer blow in 1997 not only with the departure of Vincent, so often the band's mouthpiece, but also the collapse of their deal with Warner Bros. Records. However, Azagthoth picked up the pieces and renegotiated a revised deal with their former label, Earache Records, and pulled in ex MERCILESS ONSLAUGHT, CEREMONY and INTERSINE man Steve Tucker to plug the gap left by Vincent.

In 1998 Vincent found himself playing bass in the S&M inspired GENITORTURERS, but then he is the husband of frontwoman Geni after all!

Although Rutan appeared as main songwriter and contributor to the 'Formulas Fatal To The Flesh' album MORBID ANGEL pulled in guitarist Richard Burnelle for live work as Rutan decamped to concentrate on his other two acts ALAS, in union with THERION's Martina Hornbacher-Astner, and HATE ETERNAL. The first 5000 copies of the 'Formulas' opus came with a free bonus CD entitled 'Love Of Lava', comprising of all the guitar solos from the main body of work isolated onto one CD. Sales exceeded 45,000 copies in North America.

However, rehearsals for the tour to promote the record did not go well and with Burnelle being dispensed with Rutan got the call for assistance. Following the 'Formulas Fatal To The Flesh' tour Rutan decamped yet again and produced the 'Conquerors Of Armageddon' album for Brazilian Black Metallers KRISIUN in 2000.

Rutan returned to the fold later in 2000 for the 'Gateways To Annihilation' album, a record that kicks off with an intro of a genuine swamp frog chorus. MORBID ANGEL toured Europe that December headlining an almighty Death Metal package that included ENSLAVED, THE CROWN, BEHEMOTH, HYPNOS and DYING FETUS. US sales of 'Gateways To Annihilation' would fall just short of 40,000 copies.

Upfront of the bands 2001 UK dates it was announced that Tucker would be standing down for personal reasons and to concentrate on his Death Metal 'Super' combo CEREMONY centred upon Tucker, CANNIBAL CORPSE guitarist Pat O'Brien and DISASTRONAUT guitarist Greg Reed. Erstwhile EMPEROR drummer Trym was recruited into CEREMONY during 2002. However, this proposed band unit never materialised.

Drafted in as replacement was HATE ETERNAL's Jared Anderson. American shows had the band supporting PANTERA upfront of their own Winter run of headline dates dubbed the "Extreme Music For Extreme People" tour. Roadmates for this burst of live activity would be DEICIDE, SOILENT GREEN, ZYKLON and EXHUMED.

Rutan would busy himself toward the close of 2001 acting as producer for his erstwhile RIPPING CORPSE colleagues for their sophomore DIM MAK release 'Intercepting Fist'. MORBID ANGEL would join MOTÖRHEAD's summer American 2002 'Hammered' tour as guests. Shortly after, Rutan announced his departure from the band in order to concentrate his efforts on HATE ETERNAL. Meantime ex-guitarist Richard Brunelle resurfaced touting his new act PATHS OF POSSESSION.

A MORBID ANGEL tribute album 'Tyrants From The Abyss' was delivered by Necropolis Records in September of 2002 featuring artists such as ZYKLON, VADER, BEHEMOTH, KRISIUN, ANGELCORPSE, IN AETERNUM, INFERNAL and DIABOLIC.

Although various press reports suggested the band was in discussion with former vocalist David Vincent it would be ex-singer Steve Tucker that stepped back up as MORBID ANGEL frontman for a 2003 studio album 'Heretic'. News of another connected project revealed that erstwhile drummer Mike Browning was demoing with the Florida based LISA THE WOLF with Erik Rutan handling production chores.

'Heretic', released in September, saw issue in a virtual slew of variations including a German only box set with complimentary 18 track bonus disc entitled 'Bonus Levels', a double CD version and a picture disc vinyl outing. US dates paired with SUPERJOINT RITUAL saw the band recruiting Tony Norman of MONSTROSITY to handle second guitar duties. A lengthy round of European shows commencing 20th February in Hardenberg, Holland saw Brazilians KRISIUN in support. A promotional video for 'Enshrined By Grace', directed by Pete Bridgewater, depicted the band "performing in an infernal ring of fire whilst the unenlightened masses stare at a mind-numbing screen".

As 'Heretic' exceeded the 20,000 sales figure in the USA, the group continued touring apace across North America into April of 2004 with support coming from SUFFOCATION, SATYRICON and PREMONITIONS OF WAR. Confusingly, MORBID ANGEL's management issued a statement stating the band had severed ties with long-term label Earache Records in July. Within 24 hours Earache fired back with a press release of their own claiming that in fact the band's option still had a further two weeks to run.

Scheduled South America gigs, due to commence in Monterrey, Mexico on 7th August, would be cancelled as reports emerged that Steve Tucker had suffered "massive anxiety attack and had to be hospitalized". The frontman soon responded, stating that he had contracted a lung infection "due to my excessive travel and the variety of weather and environments that I endure in these travels." David Vincent, retaining his role with the GENITORTURERS, duly rejoined MORBID ANGEL for their rescheduled South American dates. MORBID ANGEL announced co-headline US dates in union with SOULFLY for February of 2005, followed by a run of European and Scandinavian shows, supported by Danes HATESPHERE, to take them into April. Meantime, ex-MORBID ANGEL man Steve Tucker

MORBID ANGEL

was announced as being back on the tour circuit, apparently to act as stand-in bassist for NILE's March European festival dates, but this union never transpired. A scheduled showing at a Portuguese festival in June was put in jeopardy when rhythm guitarist Tony Norman apparently went missing. Although the guitarist eventually turned up alive and well MORBID ANGEL persevered without him, scheduling South American gigs in Brazil, Chile, El Salvador, Guatemala and Mexico for September. The band was announced as engaged in the 'X-Mass Fest Part II' European tour, set to begin in early December and involving ENTHRONED, UNLEASHED, PRIMORDIAL and ENSIFERUM. However, these dates would be pulled after UNLEASHED withdrew.

The erstwhile MORBID ANGEL duo of Jared Anderson and Steve Tucker revealed they were collaborating in February 2006 on a new Death Metal venture. MORBID ANGEL announced April US tour dates combined with Canadians DESPISED ICON, Poles BEHEMOTH and Brazilians KRISIUN. August European festival dates saw a welcome return to the 'Domination' line-up as guitarist Erik Rutan rejoined the fold.

Former MORBID ANGEL vocalist Jared Anderson died in his sleep on Saturday, October 14th 2006 at the age of 30.

The Beginning, (1985). The Gate / Demon Seed / Evil Spells / The Gate / Demon Seed / Evil Spells / Evil Spells / Instrumental / Chaos.
Bleed For The Devil, (1986). Bleed For The Devil / Chapel Of Ghouls / Abominations / Morbid Angel / Hellspawn.
Scream Forth Blasphemies, (1986). Chapel Of Ghouls / Unholy Blasphemies / Abominations / Hellspawn.
Unholy Blasphemies, (1987). Unholy Blasphemies / Chapel Of Ghouls / Evil Spells.
Thy Kingdom Come, Splattermaniac (1988). Thy Kingdom Come / Abominations Of Desolation / Blasphemy Of The Holy Ghost.
ALTARS OF MADNESS, Earache MOSH 11 (1989). Visions From The Darkside / Chapel Of Ghouls / Maze Of Torment / Damnation / Bleed For The Devil.
BLESSED ARE THE SICK, Earache MOSH 31 (1991). Intro / Fall From Grace / Brainstorm / Rebel Lands / Doomsday Celebration / Day Of Suffering / Blessed Are The Sick / Leading The Rats / Thy Kingdom

Come / Unholy Blasphemies / Abominations / Desolate Ways / The Ancient Ones / In Remembrance.
ABOMINATIONS OF DESOLATION, Earache MOSH 048 (1991). The Invocation / Chapel Of Ghouls / Unholy Blasphemies / Angel Of Disease / Azagthoth / The Gate / Lord Of Fevers And Plagues / Hell Spawn / Abominations / Demon Seed / Welcome To Hell.
Rapture, (1993) (US promotion release). Rapture / Sworn To The Black / Pain Divine.
COVENANT, Earache MOSH 081 (1993). Rapture / Pain Divine / World Of Shit / Vengeance Is Mine / Lion's Den / Blood On My Hands / Angel Of Disease / Sworn To Black / Nar Mattaru / God Of Emptiness.
Laibach Remixes EP, Earache MOSH 112T (1994). God Of Emptiness / Sworn To The Black / Sworn To The Black (Laibach remix) / God Of Emptiness (Laibach remix).
DOMINATION, Earache MOSH 134 (1995). Dominate / Where The Slime Live / Eyes To See, Ears To Hear / Melting / Nothing But Fear / Dawn Of The Angry / This Means War / Caesar's Palace / Dreaming / Inquisition (Burn With Me) / Hatework.
ENTANGLED IN CHAOS-LIVE, Earache MOSH 167 (1996). Immortal Rites / Blasphemy Of The Holy Ghost / Sworn To The Black / Lord Of All Fevers And Plagues / Blessed Are The Sick / Day Of Suffering / Chapel Of Ghouls / Maze Of Torment / Rapture / Blood On My Hands / Dominate.
FORMULAS FATAL TO THE FLESH, Earache MOSH 180 (1998). Heaving Earth / Prayer Of Hatred / Bil Ur-Sag / Nothing Is Not / Chambers Of Dis / Disturbance In The Great Slumber / Umulamahri / Hellspawn: The Rebirth / Covenant Of Death / Hymn To A Gas Giant / Invocation Of The Continual One / Ascent Through The Spheres / Hymnos Rituales De Guerra / Trooper.
LOVE OF LAVA, Earache MOSH 180 CDL (1999). Heaving Earth Lava / Heaving Earth Lava 'Alt' / Prayer Of Hatred #1 Lava / Prayer Of Hatred #2 Lava / Prayer Of Hatred #3 Lava / Bil Ur-Sag #1 Lava / Bil Ur-Sag #2 Lava / Bil Ur-Sag #2 Lava 'Alt' / Nothing Is Not Lava / Nothing Is Not Lava 'Alt' / Chambers Of Dis #1 Lava / Chambers Of Dis #1 Lava 'Alt' / Chambers Of Dis #2 Lava / Chambers Of Dis #2 Lava 'Alt' / Umulamahri #1 Lava / Umulamahri #2 Lava / Umulamahri #2 Lava 'Alt' / Umulamahri #3 Lava / Umulamahri #3 Lava 'Alt' / Hellspawn #2 Lava / Hellspawn #3 Lava / Covenant Of Death #1 Lava / Covenant Of Death #2 Lava / Covenant Of Death #3 Lava / Invocation #1 Lava / Invocation #2 Lava / Dominate Lava / Dominate Lava 'Alt' / Dawn Of The Angry #1 Lava / Dawn Of The Angry #1 Lava 'Alt' / Dawn Of The Angry #2 Lava / Burn With Me #1 Lava / Burn With Me #1 Lava 'Alt' / Burn With Me #2 Lava / Burn With Me #2 Lava 'Alt' / Burn With Me #3 Lava / Burn With Me #3 Lava 'Alt' / Eyes To See #1 Lava / Where The Slime Live Lava / Where The Slime Live Lava 'Alt'.
GATEWAYS TO ANNIHILATION, Earache MOSH 235 (2000). Kawazu / Summoning Redemption / Ageless / Still I Am / He Who Sleeps / To The Victor The Spoils / At One With Nothing / Opening Of The Gates / Secured Limitations / Awakening / I / God Of The Forsaken.
HERETIC, Earache MOSH 272 (2003). Cleansed In Pestilence (Blade Of Elohim) / Enshrined By Grace / Beneath The Hollow / Curse The Flesh / Praise The Strength / Stricken Arise / Place Of Many Death / Abyssous / God Of Our Own Divinity / Within Thy Enemy / Memories Of The Past / Victorious March Of Reign The Conqueror / Drum Check / Born Again.

MORBUS INFERNO

FLORIANÓPOLIS, SC, BRAZIL — *Felipe Carminatti (vocals), Gian Domingues (guitar), David Victor (guitar), Ricardo Lima (bass), Alejandro (drums).*

Florianópolis Thrash act created in 1996 as a covers act MORBUS comprising vocalist Felipe Carminatti, guitarist Guilherme Biz and erstwhile VASTNESS drummer Rafael 'Grilo'. The following year guitarist Gian Domingues and bass player Ricardo Lima completed the line up.

Bassist Ricardo Lima and guitarist Guilherme Biz would activate the side Death Metal band APHAERESIS in 1998 alongside Ricardo Mortare, vocalist of VORTEX ARAGEDDOM KINGDOM.

MORBUS INFERNO lost the services of 'Grilo' during 1999, replacing him with David Maciel. A further change saw José 'Zeca' Lacerda taking the drum role. In this incarnation the band cut the demo 'Alchemy Of Pain' in January of 2001. Changes resulted in the exit of Guilherme Biz, replaced by David Victor, and the name change to MORBUS INFERNO. Zeca exited in 2003, substituted by Alejandro that September.

Alchemy Of Pain, Morbus Inferno (2002). Intro/Bastard Dogs / Field Of War / Premature Funeral / Alchemy Of Pain.

MORDRED

SAN FRANCISCO, CA, USA — *Scott Holderby (vocals), Danny White (guitar), Art Liboon (bass), Gannon Hall (drums).*

In the midst of the San Francisco focus on homegrown Thrash acts MORDRED set themselves apart by sticking to their guns with their unique blend of aggressive Funk influenced Metal. The band was created in 1984 by bassist Art Liboon and guitarist Jim Sanguinetti. During turbulent early years Sanguinetti quit to join MERCENARY in 1986 and in a straight swap MERCENARY guitarist Sven Soderlund filled his shoes in MORDRED. The ex-MORDRED member's term with this act lasted a mere two gigs. During this period MORDRED were fronted by Steve Skates, featuring his vocals on the band's debut demo. MORDRED's two self titled demos both, the second arriving in 1987, also included guitarist Alex Gerould and drummer Eric Lannon. Skates was in turn deposed by Chris Whitney. Guitarist Danny White, who had superseded Sanguinetti, and drummer Gannon Hall are both ex-MERCENARY. Undeterred, Sanguinetti joined the guitar institute of technology and was later re-hired by the band.

The debut album, 1989's 'Fool's Game' released through the German label Noise Records, was recorded using guitarist Jim Taffer. His tenure was short though as Sanguinetti returned for the second album. 1991's 'In This Life' had MORDRED experimenting with the Thrash genre further by incorporating DJ Aaron 'Pause' Vaughn. The B side to the 'Falling Away' single sees a cover version of the THIN LIZZY track 'Johnny The Fox'. The band's last effort found MORDRED now fronted by Paul Kimball.

MORDRED reformed for a one off San Francisco gig in 2002. The group reunited once more in 2005 to celebrate their fifteenth anniversary by performing at Don Hill's in New York on 22nd April with support from ARSON CLASS and SHOWGUN. The band line-up comprised vocalist Scott Holderby, guitarists Danny White and Jim Sanguinetti, bassist Art Liboon, keyboard player DJ Pause and drummer Gannon Hall.

Former MORDRED drummer Erik Lannon went on to join SILVER TONGUE DEVILS, AMERICAN HEARTBREAK and in 2005 joined PROUDFLESH.

MORDRED reunited to perform alongside fellow Bay Area veterans ANVIL CHORUS and MERCENARY to perform on April 12th 2007 at Bottom of the Hill in San Francisco for a benefit concert for the family of late San Francisco rock musician Curtis Grant, of BLACK CHERRY, AMERICAN HEARTBREAK and TOUCH ME HOOKER, who lost his battle with Non-Hodgkin's Lymphoma on March 20th.

Mordred, (1986). Sever And Splice / Mordred / The Chains Are Gone But The Scars Remain / Spellbound.
Demo II, (1987). Reckless Abandon / In Cold Blood / The Scars Remain.
Everyday's A Holiday, Noise 7 MORD 5 (1989). Everyday's A Holiday / Superfreak.
FOOLS GAME, Noise CD NUK 135 (1989). State Of Mind / Spectacle Of Fear / Every Day's A Holiday / Spellbound / Sever And Splice / The Artist / Shatter / Reckless Abandon / Super Freak / Numb.
Falling Away, Noise 170-61-3 (1991). Falling Away / Lion's Den / Johnny The Fox.
IN THIS LIFE, Noise NO 159-2 (1991). Esse Quam Videri / Downtown / Progress / Killing Time / Larger Than Life / High Potence / Falling Away / Window / In This Life / Strain. Chart position: 70 UK.
Esse Quam Videri (Radio mix), Noise N 01796 (1992). Esse Quam Videri (Radio mix) / Intro—Killing Time (Live) / Every Day's A Holiday (Live).
VISION, (1992). In Time / West County Hospital / The Vagrant / Reach / Close Minded / Vision.
Grand Summit, Noise (1994). Grand Summit / Lo Cal Hi Fiber / Acrophobia / The Pause (Public Domain).

THE NEXT ROOM, Noise N 0211-2 (1994). Skid / Crash / Splinter Down / Shut Over / Pauper's Wine / Acrophobia / Murray The Mover / In A Turn / The Trellis / The Next Room / Rubber Crutch.

MORIGAN

VÕRU, ESTONIA — *Mari-Liis (vocals), Dark (guitar), Jihad (guitar), Reaper (bass), Thonolan (Drums).*

Võru based MORGAN began life as a Black Metal band in October of 1998, gradually evolving into a Death imbued Thrash Metal act. The formative version of the band, comprising vocalist Infernoise, guitarist A.T. and drummer Ax, first performed at the 'Metal Fest 5' event, after which line-up changes marked the introduction of guitarists Jihad (a.k.a. Jaanus Ehte) and Dark. MORIGAN released a live recording 'Live At Noor Rock 99'. That December the band, now with Torso installed on keyboards, crafted the studio demo 'Among The Eternal Fire' at Stillborn Studios. Infernoise would also be active in the keyboard role with REALM OF CARNIVORA.

Returning to the same recording facility the following March, MORIGAN cut five tracks for an intended debut album 'Let The Winds Of Darkness Blow Forever'. However, this project never surfaced officially, although tapes were leaked. Members drifted away, bringing about a cessation of band activity in 2001.

In the late Summer of 2003 MORIGAN was resurrected in a new Thrash styled direction by Jihad and Dark, enlisting new personnel bassist Reaper and drummer Thonolan 'Bestia', the latter a scene veteran of HORD, REALM OF CARNIVORA, MANATARK, DAMIEN and URT. Thonolan also had pioneered his own solo Dark Ambient projects KIRST and VARTHGULZ. Guitarist Jaanus Ehte, also involved with ORG, would join SURROGOAT in September of 2003. The new look MORIGAN debuted live, minus vocals, on 19th March 2004. In late April female vocalist Mari-Liis was enrolled. Live activity quickened, MORIGAN putting in gigs that year alongside MANATARK, LOITS, HUMAN GROUND and SPELLBINDER. Jihad also found time to session for REALM OF CARNIVORA.

April 2005 witnessed the 'Rebellion From South' club tour partnered with ALDEVIA. The band pulled in the temporary services of MORTOPHILIA drummer Kert 'Con' Kärsin for live work lasting through until October.

Among The Eternal Fire, Morigan (1999). Among The Eternal Fire / Angels Are Burning Like Candel.

MORS SUBITA

HAUKIPUDAS, FINLAND — *Antti Haapsamo (vocals), Mika Lammassaari (guitar), Jarkko Kaleva (guitar), Mika Junttila (bass), Juha Haapala (drums).*

MORS SUBITA is a melodic Death Metal band established in Haukipudas during 1999 as ZILSTRONE. The initial formation involved guitarist Mika Lammassaari, his cousin Aki Lammassaari plus drummer Juha Haapala performing covers by the likes of PANTERA, METALLICA, SENTENCED and WHITE ZOMBIE. Deciding to pursue original material the group worked with producer Kari Räty, who also served as session bassist, on a demo. Jarno Rankinen enrolled in mid 2000, quickly followed by guitarist Jukka-Pekka Ellilä, but shortly afterwards Aki Lammassaari exited.

The MORS SUBITA title was adopted during 2002. Further changes then took place as Antti Haapsamo of CATALEPTIC and SEMENTII was drafted as lead singer. However, Jukka-Pekka Ellilä decamped and Jarkko Kaleva took his position. A demo, billed 'Synopsis', arrived in 2003. The band was put into hiatus when Kaleva and Rankinen were obliged to commit to national military service. As it transpired, Rankinen did not return and Mika Junttila, of SANCTIMONIOUS, stepped in as a new bass player for a 2006 self-financed EP 'Epoch'.

Due to a throat injury suffered by CATAMENIA singer Olli-Jukka Mustonen, MORS SUBITA frontman Antti Haapsamo performed much of the vocal work on the fellow Finns 1996 album 'Location: COLD'.

Synopsis, Mors Subita (2003) (Demo). Releaser / Resignation / Sincircus / From Your Side.

Epoch, Mors Subita (2006). Curse Of Nothingness / Greenfield / Spineless / Alone / The Burden.

MORTAL FORM

HOLLAND — *Edme (vocals), Teun (guitar), Vincent (guitar), Tobias (bass), Bastiaan (drums).*

Formulated in Duiven during 1994 by guitarists Vincent and Teun together with drummer Bastiaan as ODD FUNERAL, a SEPULTURA and BLACK SABBATH covers band. By 1999 the band had adopted a Thrash / Death stance and were pursuing original material. Evolving into MORTAL FORM the group underwent line up changes as vocalist / bassist Tim departed prior to recording of the debut self financed EP 'X-Plore'. The lead vocalist mantle for these sessions was taken by Edme.

In 2000 erstwhile LAB RAT bassist Tobias joined the fold for 'The End Of Times'. The inaugural full length album 'Evil Reborn' arrived in early 2002. Guitarist Teun, retaining his ties with MORTAL FORM, would team up with Gothic Metal band HER ENCHANTMENT during 2001.

EVIL REBORN, (2001). Write My Death / End Of Times / Animal Dynamo / Am I Fooled / Subject Saccharine / Two Bloody Years / Resurrector / Birth In The Cesspool / Shader / P.O.S.

MORTAL SIN

SYDNEY, NSW, AUSTRALIA — *Mat Maurer (vocals), Paul Carwara (guitar), Mick Burke (guitar), Andy Eftichiou (bass), Wayne Campbell (drums).*

As the Thrash phenomenon swept the Rock world in the mid 80's Australia was not to be left out. Sydney's MORTAL SIN had been forged in 1985 consisting of vocalist Mat Maurer, guitarists Paul Carwara and Mick Burke, bassist Andy Eftichiou and ex-WIZZARD drummer Wayne Campbell. Both Eftichio and Carwara are both former JUDGE members. MORTAL SIN's career was given an enormous boost when editor Bernard Doe of British Metal magazine 'Metal Forces' was asked by the major Vertigo label, which Thrash Metal acts they should be looking at. Doe suggested MORTAL SIN and the band were soon signed up.

MORTAL SIN had, alongside SLAUGHTER LORD, been at the forefront of the Australian Thrash scene and it was their self financed 'Mayhemic Destruction' album which had caught Doe's attention as he gave it 99 out of a 100 in his review. When SLAUGHTER LORD folded the path was clear for MORTAL SIN and Vertigo quickly repackaged and reissued the album internationally.

MORTAL SIN's debut album featured former WIZZARD man Keith Krstin on guitar, he was superseded by SLAUGHTER LORD's Mick Burke for subsequent touring.

MORTAL SIN's next album, 'Face Of Despair' produced by Randy Burns, was issued in time for the band's support slot on METALLICA's 1989 Australian tour. In July of the same year replaced drummer Campbell with another erstwhile SLAUGHTER LORD man Steve Hughes for European jaunts opening for EXODUS and FAITH NO MORE. Campbell created WHITE TRASH then GRUNGEON with ex-SUICITY guitarist Doug Dalton.

In early 1990 Maurer bailed out, to create OMEGA in alliance with members of DEATH MISSION and UTI, and the band plugged the gap with Steve Sly. Touring across Europe had the band as opening act for TESTAMENT throughout January before hooking up with FAITH NO MORE for their UK gigs. A short burst of North American gigs closed with a Los Angeles gig at The Whiskey on 21st February, Mat Maurer's last show with the band. Upon their return to Sydney MORTAL SIN effectively split in two when Carwana, Hughes and Burke all quit. Burke and Hughes formed PRESTO with singer Luke Pittman and bassist Aaron Hodge.

MORTAL SIN persevered filling the gaps with former ENTICER guitarist Dave DeFrancesco, ex-RAGS N' RICHES guitarist Alex Hardy and former WHITE WIDOW drummer Nash Hall. This line up guested for MEGADETH on their 1991 Australian trek although shortly after Tom Doustopil replaced Hardy.

MORTAL SIN cut a new record, the more Power Metal orientated 'Rebellious Youth' produced by Kevin Shirley, in 1991. The record was retitled 'Every Dog Has It's Day' for it's European release on Music For Nations.

Struggling to survive MORTAL SIN folded in 1992. Eftichio was soon back in action with WHO'S GUILTY. Their sole release, the 1994 'Revenge' EP, featured Eftichio, vocalist Sean Bosco, guitarist Bruno Gerace, keyboard player Bob Wheatley and drummer Nick Pansini.

In late 1996 MORTAL SIN reformed with Mat Maurer, Andy Eftichiou, Paul Carwana, Wayne Campbell and Anthony Hoffman. Carwana soon lost his place to former THIS THING and WHITE TRASH guitarist Troy Scerri as the band embarked upon a headline club tour. A mini album, 'Revolution Of The Mind' comprising of new material, archive demos and live tracks, arrived in 1997. Just upfront of an appearance at the 'Metal For The Brain' festival longstanding lynchpin of the band Andy Eftichiou decamped. The show was conducted with Chook from TSCABEZE but MORTAL SIN collapsed soon after. Troy Scerri founded Stoners DAREDEVIL whilst Wayne Campbell occupied himself with CONVICT.

The band reformed in early 2004, counting a line up of original members Mat Maurer on vocals, Wayne Campbell on drums, and Andy Eftichiou on bass, alongside ex-ADDICTIVE guitarists Joe Buttigieg and Mick Sultana. This latest version of the band performed their debut gig on 5th March 5 at the Annandale Hotel in Sydney, supported by LYCANTHIA, RAMPANT and KHEMIST. This gig was scheduled to be filmed for a subsequent DVD release. However, a further round of membership changes saw both drummer Wayne Campbell and guitarist Joe Buttigieg opting out and the recruitment of Luke Cook and Nathan Shae respectively.

In May MORTAL SIN grabbed the valuable tour support to ANTHRAX's Australian dates. The band supported SLAYER and MASTODON on April 17th 2007 at the Hordern Pavilion in Moore Park.

MAYHEMIC DESTRUCTION, Mega Metal AJLP 1016 (1987). The Curse / Women In Leather / Lebanon / Liar / Blood, Death, Hatred / Mortal Slaughter / Into The Fire / Mayhemic Destruction.

Face Of Despair, Vertigo SINDJ 100 (1988) (UK promotion release). I Am Immortal / For Richer, For Poorer / Martyrs Of Eternity / Voyage Of The Disturbed.

FACE OF DESPAIR, Vertigo 8363702 (1989). I Am Immortal / Voyage Of The Disturbed / The Infantry Corps / For Richer For Poorer / Martyrs Of Eternity / Innocent Torture / Suspended Animation / H / Terminal Reward / Robbie Soles.

I Am Immortal, Vertigo VERX 47 (1990). I Am Immortal / Lebanon (Live) / Voyage Of The Disturbed.

Every Dog Has It's Day, Virgin (1991). Every Dog Has It's Day.

REBELLIOUS YOUTH, Virgin (1991). Inside Out / Access Denied / Every Dog Has Its Day / Behind The Lies / Wasted Days / From The Gutter To The Grave / Side Effect / Blackout / See No Evil / The Price Of Peace / Rebellious Youth / Why?

EVERY DOG HAS IT'S DAY, Under One Flag CDFLAG61 (1991). Inside Out / Access Denied / Every Dog Has It's Day / Side Effect / They See No Evil / From The Gutter To The Grave / Wasted Days / Behind The Lies / Blackout / Price Of Peace / Rebellious Youth / Why?

REVOLUTION OF THE MIND, Megametal (1997). Revolution Of The Mind / Voices / Lebanon / Terminal Reward / Access Denied / Violation Of Your Privacy / H (Live) / Voyage Of The Disturbed (Live).

Out Of The Darkness, (2006).

AN ABSENCE OF FAITH, (2007).

MORTUARY I.O.D.

HOLLAND — *Johannes Keekstra (vocals), Arnout Visser (guitar), Franke Kooistra (guitar), Germ Reitsma (bass), Douwe Talma (drums).*

Death styled Thrashers founded by then vocalist / guitarist Arnout Visser in the town of Dronrijp in the Dutch province of Friesland, during 1995 as MORTUARY. The band folded in 1997 but reunited as MORTUARY I.O.D. ('Image Of Death') the following year. This reformation line up counted singer Johannes Keekstra, guitarists Arnout Visser and Franke Kooistra, bassist Germ Reitsma and drummer Douwe Talma, the latter also an active member of ENRAGED.

The 2002 album 'Distorted Massacre: Fear The Madness', actually recorded two years earlier, was produced by Jan Switters and erstwhile ELEGY frontman Eduard Hovinga. For a brief period in the Autumn of 2003 Keekstra departed but would then return to the ranks. MORTUARY I.O.D.'s 2004 EP 'Damnation' included a guest vocal from the esteemed Death Metal veteran Martin Van Drunen of ASPHYX, BOLT THROWER and PESTILENCE on the track 'The Bonehunt'. In May the band undertook a brief burst of Dutch dates in partnership with Austrian Death Metal combo BELPHEGOR upfront of an appearance at the 'Waldrock' festival in Burgum. Later that year the group contributed a track to the 'Extreme Underground Vol II' compilation released by the Brazilian label Avernus Records.

DISTORTED MASSACRE: FEAR THE MADNESS, (2002). Welcome To The Massacre / Dismal Madness / Fear Of The Unknown / Image Of Death / Mortuary March / Hang 'Em / Distorted Curse.

Damnation, (2004). Rot Rampage / The Bonehunt / Discovering Brutality / Lyric Sickness.

MOX NIX

HOUSTON, TX, USA — *Johnny Duff (vocals / guitar), Bruce Tousinau (guitar), Robert Fernandez (bass), Joe Vernagalla (drums).*

Houston Metal band MOX NIX started life in 1982 as a covers band citing a line-up of vocalist Thomas Rogers, guitarists Johnny Duff and Bruce Tousinau, bass player Robert Fernandez and drummer Donnie Bragg. In 1984, as MOX NIX made the transition to playing original material both Rogers and Bragg decamped necessitating Duff taking on the lead vocal role and the induction of new drummer Joe Vernagalla.

A demo tape scored laudatory reviews in European publications such as Holland's 'Aardschock' and Britain's 'Metal Forces', prompting a deal with the French Axe Killer label. Promoting the eponymous debut MOX NIX toured as support to WARLOCK, YNGWIE MALMSTEEN and ACCEPT.

The band signed to Shatter Records for a projected second album, recorded in New York and produced by Alex Perialis and RAVEN drummer Rob Hunter. However, Shatter went under and the record was shelved. Various members of MOX NIX subsequently played in Alt-Rock act HIP CIRCLE. Singer Johnny Duff, switching to drums, enrolled into the ranks of FEARLESS LEADER. By coincide, another former MOX NIX man, guitarist Bruce Tousneau, replaced Duff on the FEARLESS LEADER drum stool.

Axe Killer re-released the debut on CD post millennium, adding two bonus tracks 'Lightning Without Thunder' and 'Red Planet'.

MOX-NIX, Axe Killer 7023 (1985). Fight Back / Ready Or Not / Reckless / Lost Sierra / Never Again / Steal The Show / Scream For Mercy / Make It / Kill Or Be Killed / Stand Alone.

MUNICIPAL WASTE

RICHMOND, VA, USA — *Tony Gauardrail (vocals), Ryan (guitar), Andy (bass), Dave Witte (drums).*

MUNICIPAL WASTE

MUNICIPAL WASTE is a deliberately retro, 80s styled Thrash / Crossover Metal from Richmond, Virginia fronted by ex-BANDANA ASSAULT singer Tony Guardrail. The band, after first performing live on New Year's Eve of 2001, debuted with an eponymous slime green vinyl 7" EP for Amendment Records prior to cutting a split 7" EP 'Tango And Thrash' with BAD ACID TRIP. Featuring a picture of actor Kurt Russell on the cover, this EP featured songs entirely devoted to plot synopses of Kurt Russell movies. A further shared effort, an album with CRUCIAL UNIT, was delivered on Six Weeks Records during 2002.

MUNICIPAL WASTE signed to Earache Records in May 2004. Drummer Brandon, also operational with Hardcore act DIRECT CONTROL, would be replaced in October by Dave Witte, a scene veteran of acts such as HUMAN REMAINS, ATOMSMASHER, DISCORDANCE AXIS, MELT-BANANA and BURNT BY THE SUN. Witte forged a creative union with Chris Dodge of SPAZZ entitled EAST WEST BLAST TEST, issuing the 2005 album 'Unpopular Music For Popular People'.

MUNICIPAL WASTE's 'Hazardous Mutation' album was recorded in the band's hometown of Richmond by Corey Smoot (a.k.a. Flattus Maximus of GWAR). The band acted as support to CONVERGE's November 2005 US dates allied with THE RED CHORD and DARKEST HOUR. The following month Dave Witte engaged in recording with studio side band BIRDS OF PREY, this project featuring BEATEN BACK TO PURE's Ben Hogg on lead vocals, Erik Larson of ALABAMA THUNDERPUSSY on guitars, Bo Leslie from THROTTLEROD also on guitars and Summer Welch of BARONESS on bass for the album 'Weight Of The Wound'.

European MUNICIPAL WASTE gigs in February 2006 witnessed a road union with BEECHER and LINEA 77. The band toured the USA in March 2006 allied with FACEDOWNINSHIT, RUMPELSTILTSKIN GRINDER and DEADBIRD. Gigs in July were backed by DEADFALL. MUNICIPAL WASTE teamed up with HIRAX, INTO ETERNITY and Germany's DESTRUCTION for a North American tour throughout January and February 2007. The following month the group entered at Planet Z Studios in Hadley, Massachusetts with producer Zeuss to cut new album tracks dubbed The Art Of Partying', wrapping up these sessions in mid-April. THE HAUNTED and MUNICIPAL WASTE teamed up for a European, hitting the UK, Germany, France, Belgium, The Netherlands, Spain, Czech Republic, Austria, Hungary, Italy, Poland and Switzerland, tour into May. British dates added Swedes WOLF to the billing.

Tango And Thrash, Amendment (2001) (Split EP with BAD ACID TRIP). Captain Ron / Overboard.
MUNICIPAL WASTE, Six Weeks (2002) (Split album with CRUCIAL UNIT). Garbage Stomp / Poser Disposer / Wicked Fit / Chemical Artillery The Toxic Survival / Insurance Fraud / Scantron Slamathon Detention Mosh Session Part 2 / Born To Party / Abusement Park / Percy's Trip To The Dentist / Haunted Junkyard.
WASTE 'EM ALL, Six Weeks SW-69 (2003). The Executioner (Intro) / Sweet Attack / Mutants Of War / Knife Fight / Drunk As Shit / Death Prank / Substitute Creature / Waste 'Em All / Toxic Revolution / I Want To Kill The President / Thrash? Don't Mind If I Do / Dropped Out / Blood Hunger / Jock Pit / The Mountain Wizard.

MX

SANTO ANDRÉ, SP, BRAZIL — *Morto (guitar / vocal), Decio (guitar), Edu (bass), Alexandre Cunha (drums).*

Founded in 1985, MX named after the missile, were based in Santo André found on the outskirts of Sao Paulo. The original line-up consisted of Beraldo on vocals, Alexandre Prado Favoretto and Decio Frignanai on guitar whilst Yuri Konopinsk and Alexandre Da Cuhuna were on bass and drums respectively. This line-up was not to last long as Beraldo departed, and apparently passed away, and Yuri was replaced by Eduado. The vocal duties were split by guitarist Alex and drummer Alexandre Cunha. This four-piece line-up recorded the 'Fighting for The Bastards' demo in 1987.

MX participated in the four way split 'Headthrasher Live' for Fucker Records in 1988, tracks culled from a January 1987 performance at the Municipal Theatre in Santo André. Other bands involved would be BLASPHEMER, COVA and NECROMANCIA. In February of 1988 the band entered Cameratti Studios in Santo André and recorded their debut album, 'Simoniacal', which was also released on the Fucker label. The abrasively named label would eventually become better known as Hellion Records Brazil.

Eduardo was eventually replaced by Francisco Comelli of ACID STORM. MX continued on having a long career hampered by long intervals between recorded output and weak international distribution. Former MX drummer Alexandre Cunha would forge TRANSFIXION in October of 1996. The bands last studio album appeared in 2000.

In 2004 the Marquee label in their 'Classic Metal Series' reissued the debut album with nine bonus tracks. Two tracks were taken from the aforementioned four-way split live concert and the remaining seven were taken from the 'Fighting For The Bastards' demo of 1987. The whole package included lyrics, rare photos and a detailed essay about the origins of the band, which was a fitting tribute to these under-rated Brazilian Thrash pioneers.

SIMONIACAL, Fucker FUC 02 (1988). Dirty Bitch / Fighting The Bastards / Satanic Noise / Inquisition / Dead World / Jason / Restless Soul / Dark Dream.
MENTAL SLAVERY, Fucker (1990). Mental Slavery / Behind His Glasses / Fake Truth / The Guf / Obvious, Who Isn't? / I Will Be Alive / I'll Bring You With Me / What Am I? / Ritual Of Strings / No Violence.
AGAIN, (1997). Torment / Another Game / Psycho To The Bones / Buy My Impunity / Criminous Command / Silent Confession / Ashes To Ashes / Drown In Holy Water.
LAST FILE, Hellion (2000). Walking With The Dead / Gagged By Fear / Not Against My Will / Tropical Virus / This War Is Yours / Abusive Aggression / Dead Green / Proscription Of Lost / After Death / XXXXX.

NAGLFAR

UMEÅ, SWEDEN — *Jens Rydén (vocals), Andreas Nilsson (guitar), Kristoffer Olivius (bass), Morgan Hansson (drums).*

A Black Metal band with Thrash influences and strong ties to fellow cult act ANCIENT WISDOM of which both vocalist Jens

Rydén, as drummer, and guitarist Andreas Nilsson also appear. The Umeå based NAGLFAR's opening 1992 line-up, then billed as UNINTERRED, comprised Jens Rydén on vocals and guitars, Kristoffer Olivius on bass and NOCTURNAL RITES drummer Ulf Andersson. The following year Fredrik Degerström, owner of 'Arqtique' fanzine, enrolled as guitarist as Rydén made the decision to concentrate solely on singing. Degerström exited in March 1994, going on to AUBERON, BEWITCHED and, under the pseudonym of 'Spider', GUILLOTINE. His replacement was Andreas Nilsson as the band name changed to NAGLFAR. Following an abortive attempt to record a demo Andersson too opted out, his path subsequently journeying through ANCIENT WISDOM and BEWITCHED.

The band made their entrance with the demo cassette 'Stellae Trajectio', this being cut at Garageland Studios in November 1994 utilising a drum machine. Pulling in new drummer Mattias Holmgren, NAGLFAR scored a deal with Wrong Again Records. In July 1995 the band entered Studio Abyss in Ludvika, Sweden to craft their 'Vittra' debut.

A further demo billed as 'Maiden Slaughter' bore covers of IRON MAIDEN's 'The Evil That Men Do' and KREATOR's 'Pleasure To Kill'. NAGLFAR's former drummer Matthias Holmgren formed EMBRACING, releasing the 'I Bear The Burden Of Time' album in 1996. In August 1997 NAGLFAR cut two tracks at Ballerina Audio with engineer Nils Johansson for a 7" single 'When Autumn Storms Come' released through War Music. Holmgren would also session lead vocals on SKYFIRE's inaugural December 1997 demo 'Within Reach'. The AZURE 'Moonlight Legend' of 1998 also includes Holmgren on drums. Meantime, NAGLFAR soldiered on with temporary replacements on drums including Morgan Lie from AUBERON and Johan Moritz from Porn-Metal outfit DISGORGE.

NAGLFAR's high profile second album, April 1998's 'Diabolical', sees Matthias Grahn taking on the drummers role the new sticksman also having featured on the picture disc 7" 'When Autumn Storms Come'. Hansson exited in October of 2000. The parting of ways with Hansson could be viewed as acrimonious bearing in mind that the band pointedly offer him no thanks on the album cover and declare their former member to be "mad"!

Jens Rydén issued his symphonic, Blackened Death Metal solo project DEAD SILENT SLUMBER's 'Entombed In The Midnight Hour' album in 1999 through Hammerheart Records. In 2000 Hansson founded a Gothic flavoured side project HAYAFOTH in collusion with ANCIENT WISDOM, HAVAYOTH and BEWITCHED's Vargher (a.k.a. Marcus Norman).

NAGLFAR's 'Ex Inferis' 2001 EP, recorded at Ballerina Studios, included a take on TERRORIZER's 'Death Shall Rise'. Marcus Norman, of would join NAGLFAR in October 2001. The 'Vittra' album would see a re-issue during 2002, adding three extra tracks including cover versions of IRON MAIDEN's 'The Evil That Men Do' and KREATOR's 'Pleasure To Kill' from the 1996 'Maiden Slaughter' recordings. The band set 'Sheol' (Hebrew for 'Hell') as the title of a 2003 album.

NAGLFAR signed a worldwide record deal with Century Media Records in January 2005, entering Ballerina Studios to craft a new record billed as 'Pariah'. Kristoffer W. Olivius also made time to guest on the NOCTURNAL RITES album 'Grand Illusion'. European shows throughout April saw the band partnered with FINNTROLL and AMORAL. Opening 2006, live work in Europe during February and March saw NAGLFAR sharing stages with DARK FUNERAL, ASMODEUS, AMORAL and ENDSTILLE. Meantime, ex-NAGLFAR drummer Mattias Holmgren joined SUPREME MAJESTY in the keyboard role.

NAGLFAR ensconced themselves in Toontrack studio in Umeå during October 2006 to cut a new album billed as 'Harvest'. Former singer Jens Rydén issued his solo PROFUNDI debut, 'The Omega Rising', that same month. In January 2007 NAGLFAR was added to CELTIC FROST and SATYRICON's Japanese "Extreme The Dojo" tour dates. October and November North American shows were packaged with DAATH and DARK FUNERAL.

VITTRA, Wrong Again WAR 008 (1996). As The Twilight Gave Birth To The Night / Enslave The Astral Fortress / Through The Midnight Spheres / The Eclipse Of Infernal Storms / Emerging From Her Weepings / Failing Waings / Vittra / Sunless Dawn / Exalted Above Thrones.

DIABOLICAL, War Music WAR 00o5 (1998). Horncrowned Majesty / Embracing The Apocalypse / 12 Rising / Into The Cold Voids Of Eternity / The Brimstone Gate / Blades / When Autumn Storms Come / A Departure In Solitude / Diabolical: The Devil's Child.

When Autumn Storms Come, War Music W1 (1998). When Autumn Storms Come / The Brimstone Gate.

Ex Inferis EP, War Music (2001). Of Gorgons Spawned Through Witchcraft / Dawn Of Eternity / Emerging From Her Weepings / When Autumn Storms Come / The Brimstone Gate.

SHEOL, New Hawen NEWH005-2 (2003). I Am Vengeance / Black God Aftermath / Wrath Of The Fallen / Abysmal Descent / Devoured By Naglfar / Of Gorgons Spawned Through Witchcraft / Unleash Hell / Force Of Pandemonium / The Infernal Ceremony.

PARIAH, Century Media 77502-2 (2005). Proclamation / A Swarm Of Plagues / Spoken Words Of Venom / The Murder Manifesto / Revelations Carved In Flesh / None Shall Be Spared / And The World Shall Be Your Grave / The Perpetual Horrors / Carnal Scorn & Spiritual Malice.

HARVEST, Century Media (2007). Into The Black / Breathe Through Me / The Mirrors Of My Soul / Odium Generis Humani / The Darkest Road / Way Of The Rope / Plutonium Reveries / Feeding Moloch / Harvest.

NAILGUNNER

JOUTSENO, FINLAND — *Sami Kettunen (vocals), Jan-Erik Eskelinen (guitar), Toni Lötjönen (guitar), Janne Puranen (bass), Jori Sara-Aho (drums).*

Joetseno Thrashers NAILGUNNER were initiated by guitarist Toni Lötjönen, originally as a SLAYER covers band. First recruits would be bass player Simo Kukkonen and drummer Jori Sara-Aho, of MARTTYYRIOPERAATIO, DEADARLINGS and SKULLFUCK repute. Shortly afterward, Juha Lähde of BOTNIA, SWEET SLEAZE and CHAOS CREATION, replaced Kukkonen before CHAOS CREATION guitarist Toni Huhtiniemi and singer Sami Kettunen were inducted to record the 2004 demo session 'All Life Ends'. Kettunen's scene credits include IRRITATE, solo Black Metal project RIDE FOR REVENGE, INCRIMINATED, Lappeenranta based CONJURATION (as 'Harold Mentor') and SIVIILMURHA.

In September 2005 Janne Puranen replaced Tomi Malinen on bass guitar. The band recorded tracks for a split album release, 'Thermonuklear Thrash Metal Warfare' shared with WOUNDS, put out by Bestial Burst on CD format and pressed on vinyl for 2006 issue through Dies Irae.

All Life Ends, Nailgunner (2004). Beaten Senseless / Let's Die / On Deadly Ground / Urban Machinegun Massacre.

THERMONUKLEAR THRASH METAL WARFARE, Bestial Burst (2004) (Split album with WOUNDS). Shortcut To Hell / Denim Stallions / Nailgun Attack / Nuklear Tormentor / Human Warhead.

NAPALM

NY, USA — *Chris Liggio (vocals / guitar), Jeff Lombardi (guitar), Chris Weidner (bass), Bob Priomos (drums).*

Crossover Thrash band NAPALM heralded their arrival with a 1985 demo session 'Let The Battle Begin'. The NAPALM 1986 EP, issued as part of the 'Combat Bootcamp' series, featured a line-up of vocalist / guitarist Jeff Rossbach, bassist Chris Weidner and drummer Rex Rossbach. The Rossbach brothers had left the fold by the time the full length album 'Cruel Tranquility' was issued. New faces were vocalist Chris Liggio, guitarist Jeff Lombardi and drummer Bob Proimos. Oddly, the debut album was released as a two CD set in Japan, together with SIEGES EVEN's 'Life Cycle' album.

The 1990 effort 'Zero To Black', witnessed a band that held none of it's original members, with Weidner departing and in his stead coming bassist Brett Roth. Lombardi's position was taken by guitarist Kult. The band, vocalist / guitarist Jeff Rossbach, drummer Rex Rossbach and vocalist / bassist Bob Eubank, reunited under a revised billing of COMBAT with an album, entitled 'Ruination', being projected for 2004.

The Monarch, Combat Bootcamp (1986). The Monarch / Tunnel Rat / All Out Assault / Evil Speak / Freedom Day.
CRUEL TRANQUILITY, Steamhammer 85-7565 (1989). Mind Melt / AOA / Shake It Off / Gag Of Steel / Devastation / Combat Zone / Immoral Society / Attack On America / Re-Animate / Act Of Betrayal / Nightmare Administrator / Practice What You Preach / Kranked Up And Out.
ZERO TO BLACK, Steamhammer 847622 (1990). Teenage Illusion / Time And Time Again / Zero To Black / The Other Side Feels Grey / Pigs / Alternative Life Of Style / The Harder You Live / Crucified / Gone / Cut You Up.

NARCOTIC GREED

JAPAN — *Moreno Grosso (vocals), Hiroshi Yamashita (guitar), Yuuichi Senda (bass), Olivier Couturier (drums).*

NARCOTIC GREED, centred upon the mask wearing guitarist Warzy (a.k.a. Hiroshi Yamashita) debuted in Japan with the 1991 demo 'Absurd War'. A further tape, 1992's 'Crisis Of Ruins', led to the 1994 'Fatal' album issued by Lard Records. The self-produced CD was recorded in the spring of 1994 with the line up consisting of Ryoji 'Dan' Azuma on vocals, Hiroshi 'Warszawa' Yamashita on guitar, Mitsunori 'Swan' Suwa on bass and Hiroki 'Hunter' Kawada on drums. The songs and lyrics were written by the vocalist and guitarist and unfortunately included the almost obligatory error-riddled English translations that have plagued so many Japanese thrash bands for the last two decades.

The band would adventurously put on a European tour in support of this record. The following year NARCOTIC GREED drafted a fresh rhythm section of former JACQLINE ESS and DEATH COLOR drummer Kurata and bassist Riki of GELARD and DISGUST. Kurata bailed out in 1996 and Riki in 2000. Both would find re-employment that year in the ranks of SADISTIC EYES. Meantime NARCOTIC GREED issued 2000's oddly titled 'Twicet Of Fate' record. The band line up for this second album would be Yamashita, bassist Yuuichi 'Bomber' Senda, vocalist Ryouji Azuma and drummer Masayuki Higuchi.

Warzy and Senda would then relocate to France rebuilding NARCOTIC GREED in July 2001. Alongside the enterprising duo would be former CELTIC BLOOD and INHERITANCE singer Moreno Grosso and erstwhile WITCHES drummer Nicolas Borg. In January of 2002 KRISTENDOM drummer Olivier Couturier supplanted Borg.

FATAL, Lard LRW-002 (1994). As The World Is Burnt / Greed / Scanning Hell / Lost Power / Injector II / Disruption / Future Kill / Partial Existence.
TWICET OF FATE, World Chaos Productions (2000). Don't Trust Anybody / Shotgun Highway / Deleted Illusion / 3: 16 / Thug City / Dulling Generation / Damn 'Em All / Operetta / Humanchain / End Is Near.

NASTY SAVAGE

BRANDON, FL, USA — *Nasty Ronnie (vocals), Ben Meyer (guitar), David Austin (guitar), Fred Dregischan (bass), Curtis Beeson (drums).*

Fronted by professional wrestler Nasty Ronnie (a.k.a. Ronnie Galleti), NASTY SAVAGE were first formed in 1982 by guitarist Ben Mayer and bassist Fred Dregischan. First appeared with a debut four track demo entitled 'Wage Of Mayhem' in early 1984 consisting of the songs 'Unchained Angel', 'Savage Desire', 'Witches Sabbath' and 'XXX'.

However, NASTY SAVAGE had trouble retaining bassists. Whilst the first album saw co-founder Fred Dregischan very much involved he was replaced by Dezso Istvan Bartha for 'Indulgence', Chris Moorhouse was subsequently recruited for the 'Abstract Reality' EP and ex-PURGATORY, ICED EARTH and AGENT STEEL bassist Richard Bateman joined the band for 'Penetration Point'.

Drummer Curtis Beeson quit in the Spring of 1989. Nevertheless, touring during 1989 saw Rob Proctor manning the drum kit, but NASTY SAVAGE ultimately folded. Proctor would later be found as a member of Grind act ASSUCK. Both Beeson and Meyer would forge a union with erstwhile LAST RITES members to create HAVOC MASS for the 1993 album 'Killing The Future'. By the mid 90's Galletti had founded INFERNAL, their 1995 demo being released commercially in 2000.

Bateman founded AFTER DEATH in 1999 together with erstwhile MORBID ANGEL and NOCTURNUS man Mike Browning. Beyer was to be found on SKULLVIEW's 1999 album 'Kings Of The Universe'. Both Ben Meyer and Curtis Beeson would operate as members of LOWBROW with ex-OBITUARY and SIX FEET UNDER vocalist Allen West and DEATH's Scott Carino. LOWBROW debuted with the 2000 album 'Victims At Play'.

In August of 2002 NASTY SAVAGE, citing the line up which recorded the group's final full-length release, 1989's 'Penetration Point' of Ronnie Galetti, Ben Meyer, David Austin, Richard Bateman and Curtis Beeson reunited to record two brand new tracks 'Sardonic Mosaic' and 'Wage of Mayhem' with engineer Mark Praeter.

Crook'D Records would re-issue the debut 'Wage Of Mayhem' demo on CD format in early 2003 adding two previously unreleased tracks dating from 1989 in 'Sardonic Mosaic' and 'Wage Of Mayhem'. NASTY SAVAGE allied with fellow Thrash veterans SADUS and high profile Finnish act FINNTROLL for European mainland dates in December. A brand new studio record, 'Psycho Psycho', arrived in 2004. The album, released by Metal Blade in Europe and Crook'd Records in the USA, included WWF wrestler / FOZZY frontman Chris Jericho guesting on three tracks. In December Curtis Beeson joined FIERCE ATMOSPHERES.

Announced in April 2006, Curt Beeson was revealed to have formed retro Thrash / Death Metal combo DENIAL FIEND, co-assembled by an elite cast comprising the MASSACRE and DEATH duo vocalist Kam Lee and bassist Terry Butler, also of SIX FEET UNDER, and guitarist Sam Williams, previously with DOWN BY LAW.

NASTY SAVAGE, Metal Blade (1985). No Sympathy / Gladiator / Fear Beyond The Vision / Metal Knights / Asmodeus / Dungeon Of Pleasure / The Morgue / Instigator / Psycho Path / End Of Time.
INDULGENCE, Metal Blade 72186 (1987). Stabbed In The Back / Divination / XXX / Indulgence / Inferno / Hypnotic Trance / Incursion Dementia / Distorted Fanatic? ?
PENETRATION POINT, Roadracer RO 94181 (1989). Welcome Wagon / Irrational / Ritual Submission / Powerslam / Sin Eater / Penetration Point / Puzzled / Horizertical / Family Circus.
Wage Of Mayhem EP, Crook'D (2003). Witches Sabbath / Savage Desire / XXX / Unchained Angel / Sardonic Mosaic / Wage Of Mayhem.
PSYCHO PSYCHO, Metal Blade (2004). Psycho Psycho / Hell Unleashed / Anguish / Human Factor / Terminus Maximus / Dementia 13 / Step Up To The Plate / Return Of The Savage / Triumphal Entry / Betrayal System / Savage Desire / Merciless Truths.

NATASTOR

CARACAS, VENEZUELA — *Paul Quintero (vocals / bass), Ángel Brizuela (guitar), Oswaldo Berroteran (bass), Javier Hernández (drums).*

Caracas based Thrash / Death Metal act NATASTOR started life in 1991 billed as ABADDON. The band's opening formation counted guitarist David 'Ángel' Brizuela and bassist Paul Quintero from the band TINIEBLAS alongside Omar Acosta, actually a roadie for TINIEBLAS, on the drums. During 1994 Oswaldo Berroteran, another TINIEBLAS member, took the place of Quintero. More changes saw the drum position going to ex-BIOPHOBIA man Juan Carlos Figueroa in 1996. The demo 'El Juicio Final' emerged in 1998.

NATASTOR made a return in 2002 with new recruit José Correa of KRUEGER repute on drums. Shortly after Javier Hernández of METAL FUSION replaced him. The '1992–1996' album, released in 2004, comprised archive tracks remixed by Ing. Nacho Matei at AudioLine Studios in Caracas. NATASTOR's 2005 line-up comprised vocalist / bassist Paul Quintero, guitarists Angel Brizuela and Oswaldo Berroteran with Javier Hernandez on drums.

El Juicio Final, (1998). Jinete Rojo / Descolonización / Jesus / El Juicio Final / Macabre Obsession / Reina De La Noche / Mundo Toxico / Miseria / Dragon Of Metal.
1992–1996, Natastor (2004). Lección De Muerte / Posesión / Blasfemia / AntiCristo / Inquisición Mental / Poltergeist / Natastor / Contaminacion.
NATASTOR, (2005). Esclavo De La Eternidad / Escape From The Fear's Corner / Prisión De Cristal / Lady Without Face / Dreaming With The Reality / Pensamiento Oscuro / Flying In The Cloudy Sky / Natastor / Blaspheme / Mental Inquisition / Escape From The Fear's Corner (Video).

NATIONAL NAPALM SYNDICATE

OULU, FINLAND — *Ilkka Järvenpää (vocals), Markku Jokikokko (guitar), Jukka Kyrö (guitar), Tero Nevala (bass), Jari Kaiponen (drums).*

Oulu's NATIONAL NAPALM SYNDICATE rank as one of the very first Finnish Thrash Metal bands, releasing their debut in 1989. The band was resurrected in 2003 with the original guitar pairing of Markku Jokikokko and Jukka Kyrö with their BURNING POINT colleague drummer Jari Kaiponen, former ETERNAL TEARS OF SORROW and current FOR MY PAIN vocalist Altti Veteläinen alongside CATAMENIA and DOROTHA bassist Tero Nevala. The band signed to Poison Arrow Records in early 2004. Demos would see additional vocals being contributed by Aki Häkkinen of FROZEN SOIL, PERFECT CHAOS and GRINISTER although in August the band announced the recruitment of ex-SOLUTION 13 man Ilkka Järvenpää as their permanent frontman.

The group engaged in the 'Creatures from the North' tour of Finland throughout February and March, sharing stages with MAPLE CROSS and SACRED CRUCIFIX. A limited edition, three way split EP, featuring new song 'Sweet Revenge' was distributed during this trek through Verikauha Records. The band issued the 'Resurrection Of The Wicked' album, recorded at Helgate Studios and mixed at Tonebox Studio by Kakke Vähäkuopus, in March 2006.

NATIONAL NAPALM SYNDICATE demoed up new tracks in August and worked on pre-production into January 2007.

Creatures From The North EP, Verikauha (2005) (Split EP with SACRED CRUCIFIX and MAPLE CROSS). Sweet Revenge.

NATTAS

SWEDEN — *Mickey Mouth (vocals), Meanos (guitar), Evil Ed Engine (bass), Helvetet (drums).*

Quite incredibly Black Thrash act NATTAS ('SATTAN' backwards) can trace their career as a band back as far as 1985. Early members apparently included figures such as 'Michael Motorcycle' and 'Bob Thunder'. During this time the group has issued the demos 'Decade Of Decay', 'Tales From The Crypt' and 'Link' before ceasing operations in 1993. NATTAS would be revived some five years later for a further recording session billed as 'Axiom' followed up by 'Born In Flames'. After this session guitarist Nick Nightmare decamped to found MARDRÖM and made way for Darkwing. With this revised line up NATTAS issued the 2000 demos 'Cast' and 'Dominatorium'.

In 2002 NATTAS recorded the track 'Salvation' utilising former UNDERCROFT guitarist Koke. An EP of the same name saw issue via Kuravilu Productions. NATTAS bass player Evil Ed Engine would assist former guitarist Nick Nightmare on MARDRÖM recordings that same year. Drummer Helvetet decamped, being replaced by former EXPLODE drummer Demonizer. Upon completion of the February 2005 album 'At Ease With The Beast' for Agonia Records, Darkwing was superseded by Meanos.

NATTAS commenced recordings for a new album, entitled 'Inde Deus Abest', on January 26th 2007 utilising KING DIAMOND guitarist Mike Wead as co-producer.

Axiom, Nattas (1999) (Demo). Outrageous Bloodshed / Black Death / The Alpha Incident / Believer / Burn.
Cast, Nattas (2000) (Demo). (Open) The Gates / Incarnated / Hatred.
Born In Flames, Nattas (2000) (Demo). Molested / Come Fire / Black Gods / S.O.S.
Salvation, Kuravilu Productions (2003). (Open) The Gates / Incarnated / Hatred / Welcome To Hell / Salvation / Come Fire.
AT EASE WITH THE BEAST, Agonia (2005). At Ease With The Beast / Bloodshed / Welcome To Hell / Hatred / Black Gods / Burn / (Open) The Gates / Incarnated / Molested / The Alpha Incident / Salvation / Come Fire.

NECRODEATH

GENOVA, ITALY — *Flegias (vocals / guitar), Claudio (guitar), Paolo (bass), Peso (drums).*

Genevas NECRODEATH released two late eighties albums, 1987's 'Into The Macabre' and 1989's 'Fragments Of Insanity', before folding, then re-uniting in 2000 for the 'Mater Of All Evil' album. The band had debuted in 1985 with the demo cassette 'The Shining Pentagram' but had in fact been active earlier under the billing GHOSTRIDER, releasing the demo 'Mayhemic Destruction'. NECRODEATH band members vocalist Ingo, guitarist Claudio, bassist Paolo and drummer Peso would also be involved in the 1989 MONDOCANE side project.

The reformed NECRODEATH included vocalist Flegias (a.k.a. Marcelo Santos), also holding down a tradition with CADAVERIA and OPERA IX. Bass player John, a former ZONA and 4WD man, is also active with Industrialists DYNABYTE as well as CADAVERIA.

NECRODEATH bassist John, billed as 'El Sargento', and drummer Peso forged "Flamenco Metal" side project RAZA DE ODIO in 2002, uniting with SADIST singer Zanna, ZØRN guitarist López and flamenco guitarist Paco. Signing to Scarlet Records this outfit issued the 'La Nueva Alarma' debut in October of 2004. The compilation album '20 Years Of Noise' arrived in March 2005.

In December the band revealed that new album recordings, dubbed '100% Hate', featured a guesting Cronos of Black Metal originators VENOM. The group pulled in new rhythm guitarist Pier Gonella, previously a member of LABYRINTH, in early 2006. NECRODEATH toured Europe in May as support to Swedish Black Metal band MARDUK. That same year Gonella and Peso forged side endeavour L.I.V. PROJECT for live work in October and November. Concerts in Italy for NECRODEATH saw METHEDRAS and DELIRIUM X TREMENS as support.

Flegias guested on the SCHIZO album 'Cicatriz Black' in 2007.

The Shining Pentagram, (1985). Necro Thrashing Death / Morbid Mayhem / Iconoclast / Mater Tenebrarum.
INTO THE MACABRE, Nightmare (1988). Agony-The Flag Of The Inverted Cross / At The Mountains Of Madness / Sauthencrom / Mater Tenebraum / Necrosadist / Infernal Decay / Graveyard Of The Innocents / The Undead—Agony (Reprise).
FRAGMENTS OF INSANITY, Metalmaster MET114 (1989). Choose Your Death / Thanatoid / State Of Progressive Annihilation / Metampsychosis / Fragments Of Insanity / Enter My Subconscious / Stillbirth / Eucharistical Sacrifice.

MATER OF ALL EVIL, Scarlet (2000). The Creature / Flame Of Malignance / Black Soul / Hate And Scorn / Iconoclast / Void Of Naxir / Anticipation Of Death / Experiment In Terror / Serpent / At The Roots Of Evil / Fathers.

BLACK AS PITCH, Scarlet (2001). Red As Blood / Riot Of Stars / Burn And Deny / Mortal Consequences / Sacrifice 2K1 / Process Of Violation / Anagaton / Killing Time / Saviours Of Hate / Join The Pain / Church's Black Book.

TON(E)S OF HATE, Scarlet (2003). Mealy-Mouthed Hypocrisy / Perseverance Pays / The Mark Of Dr. Z / The Flag / Queen Of Desire / Petition For Mercy / Last Ton(e)s Of Hate / Evidence From Beyond / Bloodstain Pattern.

100% HELL, Scarlet SC 119-2 (2006). February 5th, 1984 / Forever Slaves / War Paint / Master Of Morphine / The Wave / Theoretical And Artificial / Identity Crisis / Beautiful-Brutal World / Hyperbole / 100% Hell.

NECROMANCIA

SÃO BERNARDO DO CAMPO, SP, BRAZIL — *Marcelo D'Castro (vocals / guitar), Roberto Fornero (guitar), Kiko D'Castro (bass), André Cayres (drums).*

NECROMANCIA was created in São Bernardo do Campo, São Paulo during 1985, citing an opening line up of vocalist / guitarist Marcelo D'Castro, bass player Kiko D'Castro and ex-COVA drummer Edgar 'Budega' Gerbelli. In December of 1987 Roberto Fornero was added as second guitarist. The following year César 'Fubeka' took over the drumming role.

NECROMANCIA participated in the four way split 'Headthrasher Live' for Fucker Records in 1988, tracks culled from a January 1987 performance at the Municipal Theatre in Santo André. Other bands involved would be BLASPHEMER, COVA and MX.

Following the demo 'No Way Out' André Cayres became the latest NECROMANCIA drummer, this new line up featuring on the single 'Hypnotic'. However in 1994 Cayres too exited and Fornero took over the drum responsibilities as NECROMANCIA trimmed down to a power trio. NECROMANCIA's 2001 album 'Check Mate' saw production credits going to SEPULTURA's Andreas Kisser.

Rough Mix, Independent (0). Greed Up To Kill / Action/Reaction.

Hypnotic, Independent (1993). Cold Wish / Hypnotic / ... And The History Unfolding.

NECROMANCIA, Independent (1996). Cold Wish / No Way Out / A Nasty Fall / ... And The History Unfolding / The Selfish / Memories Of An Accident.

CHECK MATE, (2001). Greed Up To Kill / Action / Reaction / Virus / The Blooding—Post War / Catastrophe / Farsa / Catch 22 / The Riddle / Scavenger / Check Mate / Overkill.

NECROSADISTIC GOAT TORTURE

LONDON, UK — *Goatthroat Talkea Schmidt (vocals), GoatCommando Steve Brennan (Guitar), Goatmaster Petr Burov (bass), Goatlord Duncan Jones (drums).*

NECROSADISTIC GOAT TORTURE is a London based Death Metal act manifested during 2003 as a quartet comprising vocalist / guitarist Matt Von Ziegenstein-Pilorz, guitarist Goatess Christine Hell, bass player Goatmaster Petr Alexandrovich Burov and drummer Goatlord Duncan Oliver Jones. The group debuted with the 'Necrosadistic Goat Torture' December 2003 demo. The EP 'One Nation Under Goat' arrived in November 2004.

In December 2006 NECROSADISTIC GOAT TORTURE issued the album 'The Maniac's Banquet'. By early late 2006 the band had re-shaped it's line-up to comprise vocalist Goatthroat Talkea Schmidt, guitarist GoatCommando Steve Brennan, bass player Goatmaster Petr Burov and drummer Goatlord Duncan Jones.

Necrosadistic Goat Torture, Necrosadistic Goat Torture (2003). Morbid Intentions / Primal / Comprehension Day.

One Nation Under Goat, (2004). Morbid Intentions / Anger Overload / Primal / Denial / Godlike.

THE MANIAC'S BANQUET, NGT2 (2006). Nekrolog / Immortals / Deathworm / Faceless / The Maniac's Banquet.

NECROSIS

SANTIAGO, CHILE — *Gustavo Robles (vocals), Nataniel Infante (guitar), César Acasco (guitar), Víctor Trujillo (bass), Andy Nacrur (drums).*

Santiago's Thrash Metal band NECROSIS, founded in 1985 by the ex-MASSACRE credited Nacrur brothers, guitarist Pepe and drummer Andy, debuted with a 1987 demo entitled 'Kingdom Of Hate'. These sessions featured singer Andrés Marchant and bassist Miguel Angel Montenegro. Signing to Heavy Metal Maniac Records NECROSIS cut the 1988 album 'The Search', although by this stage the group's line up had changed to incorporate second guitarist Nataniel Infante and new bassist Rodrigo Westphal. The band subsequently drafted the PENTAGRAM credited Alfredo "Babe" Peña on bass, but the band folded in the early nineties following Peña's suicide.

Toxic Records re-issued 'The Search' in 1997. NECROSIS would reform in 1999 with Andy Nacrur and Nataniel Infante being joined by new faces including ENIGMA singer Gustavo Robles, guitarist Cesar Añasco and ORATEGOD bassist Victor Trujillo. The latter would soon exit to join Death Metal band TOTTEM CORPSE and Rodrigo Onetto, an ex-member of UNDERCROFT, EXECRATOR and CAOS, was enlisted to record the December 2001 album 'Enslaved To The Machine'.

The new look NECROSIS performed 2002 gigs with PENTAGRAM and CRIMINAL but then Acasco decamped, being substituted by Javier Bassino, and in turn the TORNADO veteran Daniel Duarte. A further switch saw Rodrigo Onetto being superseded by a returning Víctor Trujillo.

Kingdom Of Hate, (1987). Prayer / Fall In The Last Summer / Liar / Kingdom Of Hate.

THE SEARCH, Heavy Metal Maniac (1988). The Search / Fall in The Last Summer / Prayer / From The Sea / Liar / Golden Valley / My Fears / Kingdom Of Hate.

ENSLAVED TO THE MACHINE, Toxic (2001). The Electric Prayer (Intro) / Killing Engine / (The Busy) Statesman / Days / Doomsday Menace / Enslaved To The Machine / Beyond The Screen / Disprogrammed / Omega-Man / Invasion Y Prayer.

NEON GOD

KRISTIANSAND, NORWAY — *Svein Reinton (vocals), Kjell Jacobsen (guitar), Gøran Boman (guitar), Tom Aksel Hansen (bass), Sven Rothe (drums).*

Kristiansand Thrashers NEON GOD were formulated during 2000 by drummer Sven Rothe and CHAIN COLLECTOR guitarist Kjell Jacobsen, aiming to assemble a band in order to play "some real heavy shit". In 2001 the pair would be joined by Tom Aksel Hansen from OPUS FORGOTTEN on bass and subsequently second guitarist Gøran Boman from PANTACULUM, OPUS FORGOTTEN, APOSTASY and CARPATHIAN FOREST.

Still minus a vocalist despite numerous auditions for the post, the group was booked to appear at the 'Southern Discomfort' festival in Kristiansand during 2003. For this gig the band pulled in the high profile guest casting of Vibeke Stene from TRISTANIA and Kjetil Nordhus of TRAIL OF TEARS, GREEN CARNATION and CHAIN COLLECTOR. Shortly afterward NEON GOD secured Svein Reinton as their new frontman.

Neon God, Neongod (2005). Sheep / Nothing Is Pure / Disease Inc. / Murphys Law.

NEVERMORE

SEATTLE, WA, USA — *Warrel Dane (vocals), Jeff Loomis (guitar), Steve Smyth (guitar), Jim Sheppard (bass), Van Williams (drums).*

Seattle based, technical Speed Metal outfit NEVERMORE was created in 1992 by ex-SANCTUARY men vocalist Warrel Dane, guitarist Jeff Loomis, bassist Bill Sheppard and drummer Mark Arrington. Loomis had also been with EXPERIMENT FEAR. SANCTUARY had come to prominence with the inclusion of a brace of demo cuts on the Northwest Metalfest compilation album. Immediately apparent was that vocalist Warrel Dane, a former member of SERPENTS KNIGHT, was in possession of one of the most powerful throats on the metal scene. Bassist Jim Sheppard had previously been a member of local Glam band SLEZE, an outfit fronted by a pre-ALICE IN CHAINS Layne 'Candy' Staley.

SANCTUARY's first mark would be made with a 1986 demo, this session scoring a label deal with the Epic label. The debut album, 1987's 'Refuge Denied' produced by MEGADETH mainman Dave Mustaine, featured a rather weighty cover of JEFFERSON AIRPLANE's acid daze classic 'White Rabbit', this track also notably featuring Mustaine's guitar parts on the intro. Dane's prior act SERPENTS KNIGHT had first covered the same track on a 1983 demo.

SANCTUARY proceeded to tour Europe as support to MEGADETH before recording the equally impressive Howard Benson produced 'Into The Mirror Black', recorded at Sound City, Van Nuys in California and issued in February 1990. The group had built an international reputation but fell foul of Epic's withdrawal of support and folded.

Initial 1992 NEVERMORE demos, dubbed 'Utopia', kindled the interest of renowned producer Neil Kernon, who offered his services promptly for further recordings conducted in 1994. The resulting tapes landed NEVERMORE a deal with Germany's Century Media Records.

Kernon continued his relationship with the band producing extra tracks at Robert Lang Studios in Seattle to make up NEVERMORE's eponymous February 1995 debut. Drums on this effort were shared between Mark Arrington and new band member Van Williams. Rave reviews followed and NEVERMORE, now augmenting their line-up with second guitarist Pat O' Brien, set out touring America alongside DEATH. It was during this tour that Dane's famously long hair nearly proved to be his undoing. Falling drunkenly asleep next to the wheel of the band truck, a roadie drove off not realising the singer was there. Dane's mane caught in the axle of the vehicle as it dragged him 30 yards down the road. For the rest of the dates the vocalist had to walk with the aid of sticks. These dates, with Dane thankfully recovered, had the band supporting BLIND GUARDIAN in Germany winding up a world tour by appearing before 100'000 people at the prestigious Dynamo Festival in Holland.

An interim limited edition EP followed in July of the same year titled 'In Memory', recorded by Neal Kernon at Village Productions in Tornillo, Texas, that included radical reworks of BAUHAUS tracks 'Silent Hedges' segued with 'Double Dare'.

NEVERMORE's second full-length set, the compellingly cynical 'The Politics Of Ecstasy' titled after the Timothy Leary book, arrived in July 1996. Germany had by this stage totally succumbed to NEVERMORE's brand of technical Thrash although as yet their name meant little outside of mainland Europe.

In late 1997, following a European tour alongside fellow Americans ICED EARTH, O'Brien joined gore mongers CANNIBAL CORPSE. His position was taken by former FORBIDDEN axeman Tim Calvert. During 1998 NEVERMORE toured North America with FLOTSAM AND JETSAM prior to a further European round shows with OVERKILL.

Third album 'Dreaming Neon Black', released in January 1999, bolstered support. Poignantly, the record's concept was based on the disappearance of Warrel Dane's girlfriend, his partner having been involved in a religious cult. The album story threads through a tortuous journey ending in suicide, although in reality Dane's erstwhile friend's fate is still unknown. The outpouring of raw emotion from Dane on this record had fans hailing 'Dreaming Neon Black' as a classic. Quite incredibly, better was yet to come.

NEVERMORE trimmed to a quartet for 'Dead Heart In A Dead World' with the loss of Calvert. The album, produced by Andy Sneap, saw a return to Village Productions in Tornillo, Texas during July 2000 and included a sublimely twisted interpretation of SIMON & GARFUNKEL's 'The Sound Of Silence'. The group also claimed a place in Rock history, as the entire guitar content was executed on 7 string instruments, a world first. Upon issue in September 'Dead Heart In A Dead World' was to be the first NEVERMORE opus to make its mark on the charts, scoring a number 57 entry in Germany. With sales being sustained, a subsequent re-issue added three extra tracks, 'All The Cowards Hide', 'Chances Three' and the band's take on JUDAS PRIEST's 'Love Bites'. The latter was generally regarded as the standout inclusion on a Century Media all star tribute album to Birmingham's finest.

The band, now with secondary guitars supplied by AGGRESSION CORE man Curran Murphy, toured America the same year sharing a package bill with FATES WARNING and PLANET X. A September 2001 run of dates in America would find NEVERMORE as guests to SAVATAGE. The band put in a further burst of dates as headliners kicking off at the L'Amour venue in Brooklyn on the 23rd November. Guests for these dates would be OVERKILL and SCAR CULTURE.

During November guitarist Curran Murphy bailed out to join Canadians ANNIHILATOR. In early 2002 drummer Van Williams unveiled details of his PURE SWEET HELL side endeavour. A six track demo would see Williams joined by Christ Eichhorn on guitar, bass and keyboards. The pair would strengthen the NEVERMORE connection by enlisting guitarist Jeff Loomis to lay down a guest solo on the song 'Faded' whilst former NEVERMORE and current ANNIHILATOR guitarist Curran Murphy appears in the track 'Shadow'.

For European dates and an announcement that the band had been invited to appear at selected gigs on the US 'Vans Warped' tour, a first for a Metal act, NEVERMORE drafted ex-VICIOUS RUMORS, TESTAMENT and present day DRAGONLORD guitarist Steve Smyth to fill the vacancy left by Murphy. However, the prestigious 'Vans Warped' dates would subsequently be cancelled. Meantime the band would feature two live tracks, 'Engines Of Hate' and 'Beyond Within' recorded at the Hollywood Roxy in September of 2001, as part of the Century Media tenth anniversary DVD release. The band also cut a rendition of 'Ride The Lightning' for a Nuclear Blast METALLICA tribute collection.

NEVERMORE entered a Seattle studio in early 2003 with former QUEENSRYCHE guitarist Kelly Gray acting as producer for an album billed as 'Enemies Of Reality'. Unfortunately the end result was to be widely condemned for its "muddy" production. Live shows upfront of this release saw the inclusion of JAG PANZER's Chris Broderick as stand in second guitarist. In spite of the acknowledged audio problems, the album would prove NEVERMORE's biggest commercial success to date, entering the national German charts at no. 34 and also making chart impressions in Holland and Italy. Limited edition double CD sets of 'Enemies Of Reality' included promotional videos for 'What Tomorrow Knows', 'Next In Line' and 'Believe In Nothing' as well as live video footage taken from Century Media September 2001 tenth anniversary show of the songs 'Engines Of Hate' and 'Beyond Within'.

The band paired up with ARCH ENEMY for co-headline European gigs throughout September and October, these dates seeing the incorporation of Steve Smyth on second guitar, this latest recruit also staying onboard for subsequent US shows. These gigs, commencing 7th November in Buffalo, New York, had NEVERMORE allied with CHILDREN OF BODOM, DIMMU BORGIR and HYPOCRISY. Van Williams made further progress with his PURE SWEET HELL side project, scheduling an album entitled 'The Voyeurs Of Utter Destruction As Beauty'.

Steve Smyth would join NEVERMORE on a full time basis in April of 2004, splitting from TESTAMENT and confirming his recruitment with an appearance in the promotional video for the track 'I, Voyager'. UK tour dates proposed August had the band united with Swedish Metal outfit NOCTURNAL RITES. However, within days of this announcement these shows would be cancelled.

The group took the almost unprecedented step of re-producing 'Enemies Of Reality' in order to eliminate the sound deficiencies, drafting Andy Sneap to give the record new life in January of 2005. Fans who had already purchased the original version were offered the re-make at just $5. The following month Sneap tackled an all new NEVERMORE album 'This Godless Endeavor'. Recorded during these sessions, which saw MASTERPLAN's Axel Mackenrott donating keyboards, would be a cover version of OZZY OSBOURNE's 'Revelation (Mother Earth)'.

A 2005 compilation inclusion of note would be the track 'Tomorrow Turned Into Yesterday' featured on the 'Code Red' album, an exclusive collection given to US Marine Corps soldiers active duty in the Middle East.

NEVERMORE joined the 'Gigantour' festival trek, headlined by MEGADETH and DREAM THEATER, for US action in late July 2005 to coincide with the entrance of This Godless Endeavor. The band cemented a bill also comprising FEAR FACTORY, SYMPHONY X, DRY KILL LOGIC, THE DILLINGER ESCAPE PLAN and West Virginians BOBAFLEX.

'This Godless Endeavor' surpassed all sales of previous catalogue, hitting number 26 in Germany and also impacting on national chart rankings in Italy, Switzerland, France and Greece. European headliners commencing 16th September in Tilburg, Holland saw support from Danish metallers MERCENARY and German Thrashers DEW-SCENTED. Another leg of US dates in October found the group as support to OPETH.

2006 opened on the live front with the 'Metalmania' festivals in Hungary, Poland and the Czech Republic in early March. NEVERMORE then surprisingly took up the support for DISTURBED's European and UK dates, but these gigs were duly postponed. April found the band sharing stages in the USA with ARCH ENEMY. Gigs aligned with IN FLAMES, THROWDOWN and EVERGREY across the USA in May saw the band sporting a temporary line-up. With bassist Jim Sheppard undergoing a procedure for Crohn's Disease, the former MEGADETH and ICED EARTH credited James MacDonough stepped in to cover. The band suffered another medically related blow shortly after this announcement when Steve Smyth revealed he had been diagnosed with end-stage kidney failure, the result of a congenital birth defect. JAG PANZER guitarist Chris Broderick filled in for the US dates. Yet another dose of bad luck hit the band forcing cancellation of their May 13th show in Grand Rapids, Michigan, when Warrel Dane was taken ill. Smyth was due to resume his position for European shows commencing in June but a total kidney failure put paid to these plans. Initially NEVERMORE performed in Italy as a quartet prior to bringing in Chris Broderick again to complete the run.

Word arrived in June that Warrel Dane was preparing for his first solo album, a collaboration with Peter Wichers of SOILWORK. Jeff Loomis would guest on QUEENSRYCHE live singer PAMELA MOORE's July 2006 solo opus 'Stories From A Blue Room'.

Century Media in Europe scheduled re-releases of 1995's 'Nevermore', the 'In Memory' EP of 1996 and 'The Politics Of

NEVERMORE

Ecstasy' from 1996, all with extra tracks and new artwork. 'Nevermore' added 1992 demo songs, 'In Memory' was enhanced by five demos whilst 'The Politics Of Ecstasy' included the JUDAS PRIEST cover version 'Love Bites' and video for 'Next In Line'.

The band's appearance at the Gelsenkirchen 'Rock Hard' festival in Germany during June was taped and subsequently the track 'Enemies Of Reality' was included on the 'Rock Hard' magazine compilation album 'Rock Hard: Das Festival 2006'. The group scheduled the filming of a live DVD at their September 12th concert at the Bochum Zeche in Germany. However, Warrel Dane was taken ill with pneumonia, so this event was postponed until October 11th.

In October the group united with a heavyweight billing comprising STRATOVARIUS, BLACK LABEL SOCIETY, SAXON, SEPULTURA, AFTER FOREVER, PRIMAL FEAR and GOTTHARD for the 'Live n' Louder' festivals across Mexico, Argentina and Brazil.

On December 12th 2006 Steve Smyth received a successful kidney transplant.

Utopia, Nevermore (1992) (Demo). Garden Of Grey / The Dreaming Mind / The Hurting Words / The World Unborn / The Sorrowed Man / The System Is Failing / Matricide / Godmoney / Chances Three / Utopia.

1994 Demo, Nevermore (1994) (Demo). Sea Of Possibilities / C.B.F. / The Sanity Assassin / Timothy Leary / World Unborn.

In Memory EP, Century Media DIGICD 77121-2 (1995). Optimist Or Pessimist / Matricide / In Memory / Silent Hedges—Double Dare / The Sorrowed Man.

NEVERMORE, Century Media 77091-2 (1995). What Tomorrow Knows / CBF / The Sanity Assassin / Garden Of Gray / Sea Of Possibilities / The Hurting Words / Timothy Leary / Godmoney.

THE POLITICS OF ECSTASY, Century Media 77132-2 (1996). Seven Tongues Of God / This Sacrament / Next In Line / Passenger / The

Politics Of Ecstasy / Lost / The Tienanmen Man / Precognition / 42147 / The Learning.

DREAMING NEON BLACK, Century Media 7891-2 (1999). Ophidian / Beyond Within / The Death Of Passion / I Am The Dog / Dreaming Neon Black / Deconstruction / The Fault Of The Flesh / The Lotus Eaters / Poison Godmachine / All Play Dead / Cenotaph / No More Will / Forever.

DEAD HEART IN A DEAD WORLD, Century Media 77310-2 (2000). Narcosynthesis / We Disintegrate / Inside Four Walls / Evolution 169 / The River Dragon Has Come / The Heart Collector / Engines Of Hate / The Sound Of Silence / Insignificant / Believe In Nothing / Dead Heart In A Dead World. Chart position: 57 GERMANY.

ENEMIES OF REALITY, Century Media 77410-2 (2003). Enemies Of Reality / Ambivalent / Never Purify / Tomorrow Turned Into Yesterday / I, Voyager / Create The Infinite / Who Decides / Noumenon / Seed Awakening. Chart positions: 34 GERMANY, 52 ITALY, 90 HOLLAND.

ENEMIES OF REALITY: REMIXED & ENHANCED, Century Media 77519-2 (2005). Enemies Of Reality / Ambivalent / Never Purify / Tomorrow Turned Into Yesterday / I, Voyager / Create The Infinite / Who Decides / Noumenon / Seed Awakening / Enemies Of Reality (Video) / I, Voyager (Video) / Enemies Of Reality (Live).

THIS GODLESS ENDEAVOR, Century Media 77510-2 (2005). Born / Final Product / My Acid Words / Bittersweet Feast / Sentient 6 / Medicated Nation / The Holocaust Of Thought / Sell My Heart For Stones / The Psalm Of Lydia / A Future Uncertain / This Godless Endeavor. Chart positions: 15 ITALY, 18 GREECE, 26 GERMANY, 63 SWITZERLAND, 134 FRANCE.

NICTA

CENSELLI, ITALY — *Fabio Valentini (vocals), Nuccio Cafà (guitar), Stefano Marchetto (bass), Graziano Ferracioli (keyboards), Andrea Bertassello (drums).*

NICTA is a Censelli, Rome based Black Thrash act founded in the wake of MOKSA's demise in December of 2001, counting an inaugural line-up of vocalist Fabio Valentini, guitarist Maikel Bononi, bassist Stefano Marchetto, keyboard player Graziano Ferracioli with Andrea Bertassello on the drums. The band's debut live performance came in May of 2002 with an appearance at the 'B ... ella Musica' contest in Giacciano con Baruchella, scoring third prize. That same month NICTA conducted recordings for their first demo. Bononi was superseded by Nuccio Cafà in August.

NICTA cut a new MCD, 'Dark Rays Rip The Light', in the Summer of 2003. The 'Let Darkness Welcome You' session followed in 2005.

Dark Rays Rip The Light, Independent (2003). Enuma Elish / Wrathful / Divine Deception / The Darkest Inner Shadow.

Let Darkness Welcome You, (2005). Millenary Order / In Embryo / Let Us Suffer / The Night I Fell / Manchurian Candidated.

NME

TACOMA, WA, USA — *Brian Llapitan (vocals), Kurt Struebing (guitar), Skot Tinsley (bass), Steve Meier (drums).*

Tacoma's NME date to 1985, putting out their first demo 'Machine Of War' the following year. This cassette featured a cover sporting not only the legend "We are of Hell" but also a prominent swastika but did garner healthy underground response generated from a favourable review in the British 'Metal Forces' magazine. Strangely, New Renaissance Records chose the non-musical narrative piece 'Of Hell' for inclusion on their compilation album 'Satan's Revenge'. The album 'Unholy Death', apparently recorded and mixed in less than four hours, was delivered by LSR Records in January of 1986.

In April 1986, guitarist Kurt Struebing was convicted of murdering his 53 year old adoptive mother, Darlee Struebing, with a hatchet and a pair of scissors. Prosecutors in the trial believed Struebing, a known drug user, was mentally unstable and he was sentenced to twelve years in prison after pleading guilty to second degree murder.

Once released, Struebing reformed NME in 1994. In 1995 Moribund Records re-issued a remixed version of 'Unholy Death', adding the 'Machine Of War' demo tracks and a cover of VENOM's 'In Nomine Satanas' as bonus tracks. That same year a re-released 'Machine Of War' session, newly engineered by Tom Neimeyer of THE ACCUSED, also surfaced on CD, this version adding extra material including BLACK SABBATH cover versions 'Electric Funeral' and 'Children Of The Grave', the intro to SLAYER's 'South Of Heaven' and AC/DC's 'Let There Be Rock'.

The band published the 'Precorruption (Corpus Inimicus)' demo in 2002. NME cut a second VENOM cover, 'Live Like An Angel', in 2003 for an intended spilt single with THE BRAINDEAD. In 2004 Japanese extreme Metal band ABIGAIL covered NME's 'Lethal Dose', featuring a guest solo from Kurt Struebing. NME's original line up regrouped for an 18th September 2004 gig at Seattle's Studio Seven venue.

In March of 2005 Kurt Struebing was killed when his Volkswagon Jetta car plunged off a lower West Seattle Bridge as it opened to let a tug pass on the Duwamish Waterway. The guitarist was 39.

Machine Of War, (1985). Of Hell / Lethal Dose / Unspeakable / Acid Reign.

UNHOLY DEATH, LSR (1986). Of Hell/Thunder Breaks Peace / Louder Than Hell / Black Knight / Evil Dead / Speed Kilz / Stormwarning/Blood & Souls / Decadent Mayhem/Unspeakable / Brick Wall / Warrior / Lethal Dose / Acid Reign.

MACHINE OF WAR, (1995). Lethal Dose / Torture Me Slow, Brother (The Return Of The Unspeakable) / Acid Reign / Dead Years: The Politics Of Paranoia / The Floor Of The Sky / Worm / Children Of The Grave / Electric Funeral / South Of Heaven (Intro) / Torture ... (Return Of The Return) / Chains Of Command / IH(F)NI / Evil Dead / Let There Be Rock.

UNHOLY DEATH, Moribund (1995). Of Hell (Brady Mix) / Lethal Dose / Unspeakable / Acid Reign / Of Hell/Thunder Breaks Peace / Louder Than Hell / Black Knight / Evil Dead / Speed Kilz / Stormwarning/Blood & Souls / Decadent Mayhem/Unspeakable / Brick Wall / Warrior / Lethal Dose / Acid Reign / In Nominé Satanas.

Precorruption (Corpus Inimicus), (2002). Of Hell / Thunder Breaks Peace / Stormwarning / Blood & Souls / Lethal Dose / Acid Reign / Torture Me Slowly, Brother (The Return Of Unspeakable) / The Floor Of The Sky / Worm / Chains Of Command / Brick Wall / Dead & Buried / Gumn / Floater.

VERMINATION, (2002). Comorbidity / Retribute (Crime TV) / Brick Wall / Dead & Buried / (Songs Of The) Master Race, Part 1 / Seeds / Gumn / Floater.

NME WITHIN

TROLLHÄTTAN, SWEDEN — *Jonas Andersson Beijer (vocals / guitar / programming), Leif Larson (bass / programming).*

Trollhättan based Modern Thrash Metal act NME WITHIN was formed in rather strange circumstances in 1994 when singer Jonas Andersson Beijer impressed Dolphin Records by submitting backing vocals to the RATS SALAD album 'The Golden Playground'. Andersson was offered a deal from Dolphin, which he accepted and duly forged NME WITHIN for the 'Son Of A Gun' release. However, the band then severed ties with the label in rather acrimonious circumstances. Persevering, NME WITHIN cut a version of 'In Bloom' for a NIRVANA tribute album.

Scoring a new contract with Dzynamite Records NME WITHIN recorded the album 'Science Krisifikktion'. Studio guests included B-THONG and TRANSPORT LEAGUE frontman Tony Jelencovic and Håkan Hemlin from Folk act NORDMAN. For live work the band employs guitarists Niclas "Lemmy" Mellander and Eric Rauti of DREAMLAND with Anders Ström on drums.

Son Of A Gun EP, Dolphin DOLPH03 (1995). Introsseau / Utopian Konnektion / Breathin' / From A Whisper 2 A Skreem / Korrosion Of Truth / Mouth & Gun / When U Go 2 Heaven—Retaliation.

Utopian Konnektion, Dzynamite DZRCD001 (1996). Utopian Konnektion / Krucifikks Fetishist / Utopian Konnektion (Vogue version—Smart remikks featuring Mac from Treble n' Bass).
SCIENCE KRUCIFIKKTION, Dzynamite DZRCD002 (1997). Retaliation / Utopian Konnektion / Dining With Theotokos / Bellikose Hamlet / I-Kon / Illushuns Of Grandeur / Gravel Saliva / Sentience Kwotient / Witzend / K9 Trail / Theorem / Mouth & Gun.
SCIENCE KRUCIFIKKTION—SPECIAL EDITION 2000: THE ENIGMA PARADOX, Diamond DR004 (2000). Introusseau / Utopian Konnektion / Retaliation / Bellikose Hamlet / Dining With Theotokos / Witzend / Illushuns Of Grandeur / I-Con / Krucifikks Fetishist / Utopian Konnektion (Breeding Dance 2.0) / Mouth & Gun (Remix) / Breathin' (Remix) / From A Whisper 2 A Skreem (Remix) / When U Go 2 Heaven (Remix).

NO MERCY

PIEDIMONTE MATESE, ITALY — *Marco Stanzione (vocals), Roberto Navarra (guitar), Alfredo Tranchedone (guitar), Emilio Toscano (bass), Marcantonio Rapa (drums).*

Piedimonte Matese Death / Thrash act NO MERCY was founded as a Thrash covers act during 1997 by guitarist Roberto Navarra and drummer Marcantonio Rapa. The formative line-up proved fluid but was stabilised in 2000 with the introduction of singer Marco Stanzione and bassist Vincenzo Di Biase from Gothic Metal act REMEMBRANCE. Live work culminated in the recording of demos in 2002. However, 2003 brought about line-up changes with the induction of second guitarist Alfredo Tranchedone but the exit of Di Biase. The latter would be superseded by Emilio Toscano, a veteran of Prog-Metal act MIND COLOUR.

NO MERCY entered Temple of Noise Studios in Rome in November 2003 to lay down the album 'Thy Will Be Done', these sessions including a cover version of SLAYER's 'Reign In Blood'.

Demo 2002, No Mercy Promo (2002). Unknown Dimension / Cyber Dark Era / Your Sweet Blood Tears / Too Hard.
THY WILL BE DONE, No Mercy Ind. (2005). Intro / Thy Will Be Done You Will Die Alone / Pure Merciless / Where Is Your Jesus Now? / Redemption Through Hate / Thy Will Be Done.

NO RETURN

PARIS, FRANCE — *Steeve Petit (vocals), Alain Clement (guitar), Benoît Antonia (guitar), Olivia Scemama (bass), Didier Le Baron (drums).*

NO RETURN went under the title of EVIL POWER from their formation in Paris during 1984 before changing titles to NO RETURN in 1988. The debut album 'Psychological Torment', featuring original vocalist Phil, was produced by CORONER's Marquis Marky. Following its release, NO RETURN toured supporting SACRED REICH, DARK ANGEL, SODOM and EX-HORDER.

A new frontman in Tanguay was found in time for the second album 'Contamination Rises' recorded in Florida and produced by Tom Morris. The band made a return in 2000 with the album 'Self Mutilation'. The band line up at this juncture comprised singer Steeve "Zuul" Petit, guitarists Alain Clement and Benoit Antonia, bassist Olivia Scemama and drummer Didier Le Baron. During March of 2002 NO RETURN announced a license with the Nuclear Blast label for the 2002 album 'Machinary'.

NO RETURN parted ways with keyboard player Malko Pouchin in February 2003. That same July singer Steeve Petit exited in order to concentrate on his solo project ZUUL FX.

Olivia Scemama announced the formation of side venture PHAZM in mid 2003, the bassist working in union with the SCARVE triumvirate of singer Pierrick Valence, guitarist Sylvain Coudret and drummer Dirk Verbeuren. Scemama also gained credits with Black Metal band BALROG and GARWALL and in December 2005 joined Belgian Death Metal act ABORTED.

An eponymous NO RETURN album, recorded at Dru Nemeton Studio, surfaced in January 2006 via Season Of Mist. These sessions were laid down by Moreno Grosso, Alain Clement plus new faces guitarist Benoît Antonia, bassist Jiu, keyboard player Malko Pouchin and drummer Dirk Verbeuren. That May the group toured Europe packaged with DESTINITY and Poles DECAPITATED. Subsequently the KORUM pairing of guitarist Nicolas Coudert and drummer Boban Tomic, plus bass player David Barbosa, were inducted. Antonia also has association with DRÖYS whilst Tomic has ties to FATAL and FOREST IN BLOOD.

CONTAMINATION RISES, FNAC Music 592043 (1991). Damnation / Memories / Raving Lunatics / Uncontrolled Situation / Trash World / Sacred Bones / World Of Impurities / Civil War / Perversion / Sorrow / Mass Grave / Revolt Of The Hanged.
PSYCHOLOGICAL TORMENT, Semetary WMD 772089 (1991). Mutants' March / Reign Of The Damned / Vision Of Decadence / Tragic Giving / Radical Disease / Degeneration Of The Last Decade / Nightly Aggression / Electro Mania / Religion / Psychological Breakdown.
SEASONS OF SOUL, Semetary WMD 121131 (1995). Damnation Nr. 2 / Paralysed Conflicts / No Respect, News Reel / Worrying, Law Of Silence / While Poverty Reigns / Circle Of Hypocrisy / Soul's Virginity / Psychological Revenge / Injustice System / Wisdom / Loaded Gun Nr. 13 / Just One Step (Psychic Sketch).
Red Embers EP, CNR (1997). Sea Of Tranquility / Artificial Paradise / Pictures / The Way Of The Walk / Infinite Divisibility / You Burst Into Tears.
SELF MUTILATION, Listenable (2000). Do Or Die / Truth And Reality / Lost / Soul Extractor / Sadistic Desire / The True Way / Fanatic Mind / Individualistic Ideal / One Life / Trail Of Blood / Sect.
MACHINARY, Nuclear Blast NB6452CD (2002). Violator / The Recycler / Machinery / Synthetic / Disillusion / Virus / Resurrection / Disease / Dynamo / The Last Act / Biomechanoid.
NO RETURN, Season Of Mist (2006). Despair / Don't Judge Me / Rust In You / Utopia / Trauma / Sanction / Endless World / One World / Holy Money.

NOCTURNAL

FLONHEIM, GERMANY — *Metallic Mayhem (vocals / bass), Evil Avenger (guitar), Hellbastard (drums).*

Clad in denim, wrapped in studded armbands and bullet belts Flonheim's NOCTURNAL, forged in 2000 by guitarist Evil Avenger (a.k.a. Daniel Cichos), offer pure retro Thrash Metal. The act is one of a long line of Metal projects for Avenger, with his other associations including acts such as BESTIAL DESECRATION, EXORCISM, ANGEL OF DAMNATION, also featuring NOCTURNAL comrade Hellbastard on drums, NECROSLAUGHTER, FRONT BEAST, POLTERGEIST, STORMHUNTER, VARGHKOGHARGASMAL, SZARLEM and WITCHSLAUGHTER.

NOCTURNAL weighed in with the tape 'Rites Of The Black Mass'. The following the track 'Graveyard Massacre' featured on the Deathstrike Records compilation 'Thrashing Rage'. Their 7" debut EP 'Slaughter Command' followed on Deathstrike in 2002, after which Skull Crusher decamped. New blood would rapidly be found in vocalist / bassist Metallic Mayhem and drummer Hellbastard. A second EP, 'Thrash With The Devil', was issued as a three track 7" and a five track cassette. NOCTURNAL planned a new EP, 'Revenge Of Fire', for 2003 as well as a four way split release on Nuclear Hell Records allied with TOXIC HOLOCAUST, BESTIAL MOCKERY and VOMITOR.

By 2003 NOCTURNAL comprised vocalist Metallic Mayhem, guitarists Evil Avenger and ex-VEXED man Jex, bass player Vomitor and drummer Hellbastard.

NOCTURNAL issued the album 'Arrival Of The Carnivore' through From Beyond Productions label in December 2004. Blumi of METALUCIFER and METAL INQUISITION guested. Iron Fist Kommando released a split rehearsal demo cassette, entitled 'Thrashing Rage', shared with BESTIAL DESECRATION in 2005. This included a cover version of 'Sign Of Evil', originally by VIOLENT FORCE plus a rendition of the DESTRUCTION classic 'Total Desaster'. That same year Polish label Agonia Records issued a split 7" single shared with NUNSLAUGHTER.

Rites Of The Black Mass, Deathstrike (2000) (Demo). Intro / Unholy Funeral / Graveyard Massacre / Hellraiser / Rites Of The Black Mass / Tormentor / Outro.

Slaughter Command, Deathstrike (2002) (7" vinyl single. Limited edition 720 copies). Slaughter Command / Forces Of Night.

Thrash With The Devil EP, Deathstrike DR024 (2002). Chainsaw Carnage / Hellraiser / Thrash Attack.

Thrash With The Devil, Hades Paradise (2002) (Demo). Chainsaw Carnage / Hellraiser / Thrash Attack / Tormentor / Welcome To Your Death.

Thrash With The Devil, Deathstrike DK 024 (2002) (CD single. Limited edition 500 copies). Chainsaw Carnage / Hellraiser / Thrash Attack / Tormentor / Welcome To Your Death.

The Burning Of Ranstadt, Deathstrike (2004) (Live demo cassette). Hellraiser / Forces Of Night / Hellraiser / Total Desaster / Tormentor / Fire Of Revenge / Chainsaw Carnage.

Fire Of Revenge, Bestial Onslaught (2004) (7 vinyl single. Limited edition 1000 copies, 200 pressed on red vinyl). Fire Of Revenge / Killing Machine / The Final End.

Thrashbeast From Hell, Witchhammer Production (2004) (Split demo with TOXIC HOLOCAUST). Chainsaw Carnage (NOCTURNAL) / Hellraiser (NOCTURNAL) / Thrash Attack (NOCTURNAL) / Tormentor (NOCTURNAL) / Welcome To Your Death (NOCTURNAL) / Forces Of Night (NOCTURNAL) / Total Desaster (NOCTURNAL) / Deathmaster (TOXIC HOLOCAUST) / Metal Attack (TOXIC HOLOCAUST) / Damned To Fire (TOXIC HOLOCAUST) / 666 (TOXIC HOLOCAUST) / Options Don't Exist (TOXIC HOLOCAUST) / Sacrifice (TOXIC HOLOCAUST).

ARRIVAL OF THE CARNIVORE, From Beyond Productions FBP038 (2004). Coven Of Darkness / Temples Of Sin / Satanic Oath / Preventive War / Burn This Town / War Of Spirits / Merciless Murder / Nuclear Strike / Victorious Night / Awakening The Curse Of Souls.

Cryptic, Agonia (2005) (Split 7" vinyl single with NUNSLAUGHTER). Cryptic Aeon (NUNSLAUGHTER) / Haunted Places) (NUNSLAUGHTER) / Nuclear Strike (NOCTURNAL) / Satanic Oath (NOCTURNAL).

Thrashing Rage, Iron Fist Kommando (2005) (Split demo cassette with BESTIAL DESECRATION). Merciless Murder (NOCTURNAL) / Nuclear Strike (NOCTURNAL) / Sign Of Evil (NOCTURNAL) / Satanic Oath (NOCTURNAL) / The Final End (NOCTURNAL) / Thrash Attack (NOCTURNAL) / Tormentor (NOCTURNAL) / Total Desaster (NOCTURNAL) / Infernal Overkill (BESTIAL DESECRATION) / Hellraiser (BESTIAL DESECRATION) / Hail The Gods Of Destruction (BESTIAL DESECRATION) / Soldiers Of Death (BESTIAL DESECRATION) / Graveyard Massacre (BESTIAL DESECRATION) / Speed Metal Attack (BESTIAL DESECRATION) / Hatefilled Metalrage (BESTIAL DESECRATION) / Tormentor (BESTIAL DESECRATION) / Chainsaw Carnage (BESTIAL DESECRATION) / Curse The Gods (BESTIAL DESECRATION) / Attack Of The Metal Hellstorm (BESTIAL DESECRATION).

Temples Of Sin, The Infernal Thrashing (2005) (Limited edition 500 copies). Temples Of Sin / Preventive War / War Of Spirits.

NODE

MILAN, ITALY — *Daniel Botti (vocals / guitar), Gary D'Eramo (guitar), Klaus Mariani (bass), Marco Di Salvia (drums).*

Milan Death-Thrash Metal act initially led by former DEATH SS guitarist Steve Minelli. Although the opening demo would be called 'Grind Revolution In Mass Evolution', the band progressed NODE shifted from a Grind orientated direction into more melodic territory. In September 1995 the NODE line up was completely turned over, bringing in new vocalist/guitarist Gary d' Eramo, bass player Klaus Mariani and drummer John Manti. This line up signed to the Lucretia label to cut the 'Ask' EP, this effort displaying strong modern Thrash leanings. 1996 witnessed further personnel fluxes as Manti exited April, his place being taken by the THY NATURE and SADIST credited Oinos. However, by December Oinos too was out of the picture. Guitarist Gary D' Eramo left the band in March of 1997, being superseded by Daniel Botti of GORY BLISTER and in this incarnation NODE delivered the 1998 album 'Technical Crime', featuring a cover version of JETHRO TULL's 'Hymn 43'. Loris Pacaccio was then incorporated on drums for Italian festival appearances. Unfortunately the roll call suffered a further blow when Mariani bowed out. Minelli took time out in 1998 to act as session live guitarist for LACUNA COIL.

NODE regrouped in 1999, re-installing both Mariani and D'Eramo. It would not last though and before long the band lost not only Pacaccio, later turning up in ALICE IN DARKLAND, but founder member Steve Minelli. Pulling in GORY BLISTER man Joe La Viola on the drums NODE persevered by crafting a 2000 demo session 'Land Of Nod'. These tracks secured a new label deal with Scarlet Records. NODE introduced new drummer Marco Di Salvia in October of 2003.

NODE's 2004 album 'Das Kapital', recorded in Våsteras, Sweden at Underground Studios with producers Pelle Saether and Lars Linden, featured guest contributions from HATESPHERE's Jacob Bredahl and Petri Kuusisto of CARNAL FORGE. The record included a cover version of QUEENSRYCHE's 'Empire'. In support of the record NODE, temporarily enlisting the services of BEHOLDER keyboard player Mark Vikar, would act as support to LACUNA COIL's Italian dates throughout March and April.

Massacre Records released 'As God Kills' in 2006, this album again recorded at Underground Studios with producer Pelle Saether. NODE supported LACUNA COIL and POISONBLACK on European shows in September and October 2006.

Ask, Lucretia LUCD 96008 (1995). Virtual God / Gyves Of Lies / Empty Spaces / Ask / Unaffected / No Purity.

TECHNICAL CRIME, Lucretia (1997). As God Wills / Introspection / New XXX / Fall In Your Eyes / Ask (1997 version) / Children / Beautiful Crime / Tronic Prophecy / Hymn 43.

Sterilized, Lucretia (2000). Sterilized / Virtual God / New XXX / Ask (1997 Version) / Tronic Prophecy / Unaffected.

SWEATSHOPS, Scarlet (2002). History Seeds / Jerry Mander / Sacristan' Scorn Towards Water / Bloody Hills / Behaviours / Last Doctor / No Title, No Bible / Thanathophobia / The Plot Thickens.

DAS KAPITAL, Scarlet SC 080-2 (2004). War Goes On / Twenties / Outpost / The East-Ghost / Das Kapital / Retreat '42 / Weakenssphere / The Plot Sickens / One Way Media / Empire / Few Words Again.

AS GOD KILLS, Massacre (2006). Shotgun Blast Propaganda / As God Kills / Hellywood / Cancer / Redrum / Old Nick / Watcher Of A Failed Generation / Through Fail And Foul / Truth Is Out / The Manhattan Project.

NOKTURNEL

NJ, USA — *Tom Stevens (vocals / guitar), Lee Ribero (bass), Tophetareth (drums).*

A Satanic Thrash act assembled by frontman Tom Stevens, a veteran of SAVAGE DEATH. The band came into being during 1989 when Stevens and fellow erstwhile SAVAGE DEATH cohort drummer Eric Young united with bassist Martin O'Connor.

This line up issued two demos 'You Don't Stand A Chance' and 'Welcome To New Jersey' prior to a landing a deal with the J.L. America label for the 1993 debut 'Nothing But Hatred'. Although the sleeve artwork was amateurish the music won NOKTURNEL underground appeal.

Two tracks would be committed to the 'Anti Grunge' EP put together by Rage Records in 1994 before NOKTURNEL folded. Stevens would journey through a myriad of acts including EXILE, BRIMSTONE, MORPHEUS DESCENDS and INCANTATION.

Stevens would resurrect NOKTURNEL for a comeback record 'Fury Unleashed'. Assisting in the studio would be DEATH OF MILLIONS guitarist Lee Ribera handling bass duties and FOG drummer Tophetareth.

NOTHING BUT HATRED, J.L. America (1993). Human Termite / No 2nd Chance / Sliding Down The Razor / Global Suicide / Skonopolator / My Hell / Final Punishment / Target Planet / Revenge Of The Corpse / Welcome To New Jersey / Poltergeist.

FURY UNLEASHED, Nokturnel Eclipse (2001). Legend Of The Wolven / Taking Home To The Grave / Food Chain / I Remain Faithless / Visions Of The Haunted / Realm Of Possession / Forcefed Fear / Immortal Destroyer / A Collision Of Dimensions.

NOMICON

HELSINKI, FINLAND — *Ceasar (vocals / bass), Trooper (guitar), Azhemin (guitar), Agathon (drums).*

Although trading under the pseudonyms Ceasar, Trooper, Azhemin and Agathon, Helsinki's NOMICON in fact comprises a quartet of Finnish Metal elite. Vocalist / bass player Ceasar (a.k.a. Tommi Launonen), having association with COARSE, GANDALF, GLOOMY GRIM, SOULGRIND, TENEBRAE and WALHALLA, is the primary motivator behind the project, which is generally regarded as a solo undertaking.

Launonen would be supported by guitarist Trooper, in fact Roope Latvala, of CHILDREN OF BODOM, DEMENTIA, LATVALA BROS, STONE, SINERGY, WALHALLA, WALTARI and WARMEN, rhythm guitar player Azhemin (Miika Niemelï), from RAVEN, SHAPE OF DESPAIR, SOULGRIND, THY SERPENT, WANDERER and WINTERMOON. Additional female vocals would be supplied by Whisper Lilith (Tanya Kemppainen) of SOULGRIND, LULLACRY and GLOOMY GRIM.

NOMICON's first presence was felt in 1990 with the inclusion of the track 'Contrast' on the Hard Blast Records, four way split 7" EP 'More Than Death vol.1' in alliance with SHUD, RADIATION SICKNESS and Dutch band NOCTURN. A three song demo, entitled 'Tri-Angle', surfaced in February 1991 with another single, 'De Rerum Natura', that same year.

In 1995 Belgian label Shiver Records partnered NOMICON with SARNATH for a split album entitled 'The Me'. Originally these tracks had been recorded for a UK label, Tombstone Records, but then shelved until a new deal had been located. Shiver then issued the full-length 'Yellow' album in 1997. This album, recorded at WALTARI's rehearsal rooms with equipment on loan from STRATOVARIUS, saw Janne Parviainen from WALTARI on session studio drums. Limited live work saw NOMICON taking the stage as a trio comprising Whisper, Ceasar and Trooper plus programmed drums.

A demo the following year, produced by Jussi Heikkinen, preceded the 2001 'Halla' album issued through Sagitarius Productions. By this juncture NOMICON had enlisted drummer Agathon (Ykä) being a veteran of AIRDASH, BARATHRUM, CORPORAL PUNISHMENT, GLOOMY GRIM, SOULGRIND, THY SERPENT and WALHALLA.

More Than Death vol.1, Hard Blast (1990) (Split 7" vinyl EP with SHUD, NOCTURN and RADIATION SICKNESS). Last Breath (SHUD) / Contrast (NOMICON) / Graveyard Without Crosses (NOCTURN) / Disfigured Retard (RADIATION SICKNESS).
Tri-Angle, Nomicon (1991) (Demo). In A Logic / To Material / Development.
De Rerum Natura, Nomicon (1992) (7" vinyl single). Pursuit / ... Of The Tightness.
THE ME / NORTHODOX, Shiver SHR011 (1995) (Split album with SARNATH). Category Mistake (NOMICON) / No Thing (NOMICON) / Occurrence (NOMICON) / Self (NOMICON) / Aged (NOMICON) / To Observe (NOMICON) / Conversion (NOMICON) / Talking About ... (NOMICON) / Arguing (NOMICON) / In The Flames Of Midsummer Pyre (SARNATH) / Silence Of The Lambs (SARNATH) / Covenant (SARNATH) / Walking Through Her Shrine (SARNATH) / The Fantome Reign (Kali Yuga) (SARNATH) / Marian Luostari (SARNATH).
YELLOW, Shiver SHR 022 (1997). Flight / Shade / Claritas / Northsky (Left Behind) / Down Below / Deep Waters / Predestination / Sermon / Fall / Mecca.
Nomicon, Nomicon (1998) (Demo). A Search (Beginning) / Denial / Saint.
HALLA, Sagitarius Productions (2001). Arrival / God Weaker Than Me / Denial / Saint / A Search / Grief / Tribe / Sacrifice / Demolished.

NORTHWORLD

HELSINKI, FINLAND — *Konsta Kaikkonen (vocals / guitar), Roni Seppänen (guitar), Tino Puisto (bass), Jukka Virtanen (keyboards), Perttu Kurttila (drums).*

NORTHWORLD, a melodic Thrash Metal act dating to 2002, traces its origins back to Kulosaari high school band THE JUGURTTERS, this unit comprising vocalist / guitarist Konsta Kaikkonen, guitarist Roni Seppänen and keyboard player Matti Niemi. Subsequently, Kaikkonen and Seppänen joined EXALTE, then Kaikkonen figured with Death Metal bands BLOODSTAINED and GORESOAKED.

Kaikkonen, Seppänen and Niemi regrouped in 2002 as NORTHWORLD, bringing onboard bass player Marko Karjalainen and drummer Henry Moisala. This line-up laid down a self-titled September 2003 demo and the 2004 demo 'Reign Of Thunder', featuring a guesting Patrik Nuorteva of MENSURA and GORESOAKED on guitar, before Niemi and Karjalainen quit. Utilising session players, the remaining trio crafted the Summer 2004 demo 'Covenant Of Steel', after which synthesizer player Jukka Virtanen and GORESOAKED bassist Yrjö Gävert joined the band. Further changes saw Perttu Kurttila, citing associations with TRIONFALE and LITHURIA, introduced on drums, as Moisala was undertaking compulsory military service, and Gävert being superseded by Tino Puisto.

Kurttila exited to work on his improvisational Grindcore project CLUTCH MENTAL HOSPITAL. Kaikkonen also sessioned for LITHURIA.

Northworld, (2003). Rivers Of Necrovore / Seven Pillars (To Hell).
Reign Of Thunder, Northworld (2004). Windhaven / The Feast Of The Eternal Ones / Necrovore / Beneath The Northern Sky.
Covenant Of Steel, (2004). Beneath The Northern Sky / Dreams Of Steel / (Called By) The Wind Of Grief.

NOSTRADAMEUS

GOTHENBURG, SWEDEN — *Freddy Persson (vocals), Jake Freden (guitar), Michael Åberg (guitar), Thomas Antonsson (bass), Esko Salow (drums).*

NOSTRADAMEUS operate in melodic Speed Metal territory. The band was conceived in Gothenburg during 1998, a 12th May GAMMA RAY and IRON SAVIOUR gig inspiring the VAPID Death Metal pairing of guitarist Jake Freden and vocalist Freddy Persson to embark upon a new venture. Initially VAPID drummer Gustav Nahlin and second guitarist Erik Söderman sat in for rehearsals with Persson handling both vocals and bass guitar. This unit recorded a demo in December of 1998 funded by Magnus Lundbäck of Gain Records. The tape caught the attention of several German labels and in early 1999 NOSTRADAMEUS signed to the AFM label.

After recording of the debut album 'Words Of Nostradameus' the stand in members were substituted by guitarist Michael Åberg, bassist Thomas Antonsson and drummer Jesse Lindskog of DRAGONLAND. A second album 'The Prophet Of Evil' arrived in August of 2001. For touring as support to EDGUY in Europe during November and December NOSTRADAMEUS drafted a new drummer, VALCYRIE, PATHOS and FJED man Esko Salow.

Japanese versions of the album 'The Third Prophecy' on the Teichiku label added extra tracks in a live version of 'One For All, All For One' and even a karaoke take of 'In Harmony'. Into 2003 the band acted as openers for the first leg of the HAMMERFALL and MASTERPLAN European tour. Vocalist Freddy Persson and guitarist Jake Fredén created a side venture billed as WIZ, signing for a deal with Arise Records. The band debuted with the album 'Shattered-Mind-Therapy'.

The band cut their fourth album, entitled 'Hellbound', at Roasting House studios in Malmö for October 2004 release. Just previous to this it was revealed that Freddy Persson had enrolled himself into the Swedish police academy. Shortly after the 'Hellbound' release AFM Records re-issued the band's first three albums, 'Words of Nostradameus', 'The Prophet of Evil' and 'The Third Prophecy', as a box set.

In May of 2005 Michael Åberg joined DESTINY. NOSTRADAMEUS, working on a new album 'Pathway', officially parted ways with guitarist Michael Åberg in July 2006. Lennart Specht of PATHOS and FEJD was announced as replacement in

October. On the live front Michael Åberg allied with Kristoffer Göbel from DESTINY and FALCONER plus Snowy Shaw, from THERION, MERCYFUL FATE, KING DIAMOND and DREAM EVIL, in covers band METAL FÜR ALLE, performing gigs locally in the Gothenburg area.

April 2007 European and UK tour dates saw a package deal united with AFM Records label mates JON OLIVA'S PAIN and HEAVENLY.

WORDS OF NOSTRADAMUS, AFM CD 039 (2000). Words Of Nostradameus / The Vision / Out Of This World / Nightmare Prophecy / Without Your Love / Master Of The Night / Black Fate / The Crown's Inn / Resurrection / Brothers In Chains / One For All, All For One.
THE PROPHET OF EVIL, AFM 0046792AFM (2001). The Prophet Of Evil / Hymn To These Lands / Evil Prophecies / Murder / Requiem (I Will Honour Thy ...) / In Prison / The Escape / The Power's In Your Hands / Gathering Resistance / The Final Battle / Scream Of Anger.
THE THIRD PROPHECY, Teichiku TKCS-85048 (2003). Far Too Long / Randall Flagg / Those Things You Did / The Future Will Show / If We Believe (In Our Dreams) / 1986 / Revenge Is Mine / H.M.S. Ulysses / In Harmony / Towards The Sleep (Stalingrad).
HELLBOUND, AFM (2004). Never Turning Back / Your Betrayal / The Reaper's Image / Hellbound / One Step Away / Fight / Cut Like Blades / Seven / One World To Live In / I Am Free.
PATHWAYS, AFM (2007).

NOSTROMO

GENEVA, SWITZERLAND — *Javier (vocals), Jerome Pellegrini (guitar), Lad (bass), Maik (drums).*

Geneva's NOSTROMO was forged during 1996, aiming to mix Thrash with both Hardcore and Grindcore influences. The debut album 'Argue in Autumn' arrived in 1998 on the local Snuff label but had been preceded by demos and the 1997 7" single 'Selfish Blues'. Promoting the album NOSTROMO toured France allied with label mates KNUT, this trek including an appearance at the Rennes 'Superbowl of Hardcore' in 1999.

NOSTROMO released their sophomore effort 'Eyesore' in July 2000 on Mosh Bart Industries. Touring would be extensive, traversing France partnered with ANANDA as support to BOTCH and THE DILLINGER ESCAPE PLAN before gigs with NASUM and NAPALM DEATH. Successive dates saw NOSTROMO journeying into Spain, Germany and Eastern Europe countries. In June 2001 the group returned to Spain as part of a package billing with HOPEFUL, LIKE PETER AT HOME and INSIDE CONFLICT.

The 'Ecce Lex' album, produced by Miesko Talarczyk of NASUM, was recorded for Overcome Records in early 2002.

Selfish Blues, Snuff (1997). Selfish Blues / Lost Souls.
Eyesore, (2000).
ECCE LEX, Overcome (2002). Rude Awakening / What Is Up In Your Cryotube? / Stillborn Prophet / End's Eve / Lab Of Their Will / Sunset Motel / Pull The Pin / Seeking An Exit / Ecce Lex / Feed The Living / Turned Black / Unwillingly And Slow.
HYSTERON-PROTERON, (2004).

NUCLEAR ASSAULT

NEW YORK, NY, USA — *John Connelly (vocals / guitar), Scott Harrington (guitar), Dan Lilker (bass), Glenn Evans (drums).*

With the mid eighties Thrash explosion, New York's NUCLEAR ASSAULT leapt to the fore due to the prime motivating force of ex-ANTHRAX bassist Dan Lilker. Although the gangly, mop-topped bassist had actually been a co-founder of ANTHRAX, having named the band and been pivotal in the crafting of debut album 'Fistful Of Metal', he severed ties with ANTHRAX in 1983, due to disagreements with then vocalist Neal Turbin. It took two and a half years to assemble his next project, the far rawer NUCLEAR ASSAULT. In the interim, Lilker had involved himself with the commercially successful spoof Metal project of S.O.D. ('Stormtroopers of Death') alongside ANTHRAX guitarist Scott Ian and M.O.D. vocalist Billy Milano.

NUCLEAR ASSAULT's line-up for the inaugural 'Brain Death' EP of 1986 was Lilker, vocalist John Connelly, guitarist Anthony Bramante and ex-HARTER ATTACK and TT QUICK drummer Glenn Evans. Connelly too had in fact been a formative member of ANTHRAX. However, the inaugural version of NUCLEAR ASSAULT had counted the inclusion of Mike Bogush on guitar and Scott Duboys on drums. The latter would re-surface as a member of WARRIOR SOUL.

The group's first full-length set, the Alex Perialas produced 'Game Over' recorded at Pyramid Sound Studios in Ithaca, New York during May 1986, saw issue the same year. Notoriety would be immediately gained by the inclusion of the song entitled 'Hang The Pope'. With NUCLEAR ASSAULT's rapidly growing profile on the crossover scene, Evans found time to invest in a new label, Arena Records. The first release on Arena would be the 'Salt In The Wound' single by his previous outfit HARTER ATTACK.

1987's mini-album 'The Plague', a collection of old and new material cut at The Music Grinder, Los Angeles with Randy Burns behind the desk and including the infamous 'Buttfuck' (a song lyrically aimed at MÖTLEY CRÜE vocalist VINCE NEIL), and on later re-presses tamed down to 'You Figure It Out'. 'The Plague' was originally to be titled 'Cross Of Iron' and to have had a cross as the sleeve artwork. However, the American record company Combat cited possible objections that may have come from religious organizations. NUCLEAR ASSAULT's first foray into Europe came the same year, with dates alongside AGENT STEEL.

Nuclear Assault quickened the pace with 1988's 'Survive', another Randy Burns production, this album giving the group a number 145 placing on the US national charts. A return to Europe in 1988 as guests to SLAYER gave NUCLEAR ASSAULT access to far greater crowds and, fuelled by their reaction, the band returned for further dates as headliners, support being granted by ACID REIGN and RE-ANIMATOR. Further gigs saw the band opening for SEPULTURA in South America.

British label Music For Nations kept the product flowing in 1989 with a brace of EPs, 'Fight To Be Free' and 'Good Times, Bad Times', headed up by the LED ZEPPELIN cover and featuring another wry stage favourite in 'Lesbians'. Successive outing 'Handle With Care', delivered in 1989, brought the band to its artistic peak, hitting the US charts at number 126, and would be proudly caught on 1990's 'Live At Hammersmith Odeon' album.

As Lilker announced details of his new act BRUTAL TRUTH the same year and an immediate signing with Earache Records, it appeared to fans that Nuclear Assault was losing priority. The 1992 album, 'Out Of Order' on IRS Records, a less than enthusiastically received release oddly brandishing a cover of SWEET's 'Ballroom Blitz', seemed to confirm this view. Torn between BRUTAL TRUTH and a lacklustre NUCLEAR ASSAULT, Lilker opted for the former.

Glenn Evans and John Connelly rebuilt the band by drafting former ACE FREHLEY bassist Karl Cochrane on guitar and erstwhile WHITE LION, BLACK SABBATH and GREAT WHITE bassist Dave Spitz. Cochrane soon lost his place to a returning Anthony Bramante and a heavy touring period then ensued. The band set about another American tour in 1992, bolstering their live sound by including former TT QUICK guitarist Dave DiPietro and ex-PROPHET guitarist Scott Metaxas. The last effort under the banner NUCLEAR ASSAULT came with 1993's 'Something Wicked' with the band comprising now of Connelly, DiPietro, Metaxas and Evans. Headline shows across Europe to promote the album in June saw DEPRESSIVE AGE as support act. Meantime, Dan Lilker contributed bass to the 1994 HOLY MOSES album 'No Matter What's The Cause'.

Following a lengthy run of commendable albums Lilker would disband BRUTAL TRUTH following completion of an Australian tour in September 1998. Lilker resumed activity with S.O.D. for their 'Bigger Than The Devil' album, the bassist also operating Black Metal band HEMLOCK as a side endeavour. Yet another venture found Lilker assembling THE RAVENOUS in 2000 for the 'Assembled In Blasphemy' album. Included were NECROPHAGIA's Killjoy and Chris Reifert of AUTOPSY.

Lilker would surprisingly announce the reformation of the classic NUCLEAR ASSAULT line up comprising John Connelly, Anthony Bramante and Glenn Evans, for an appearance at the 2002 'Wacken Open Air' Metal festival in Germany and the New Jersey 'Metal Meltdown IV' event. Shortly after, a live album, recorded by Screaming Ferret Wreckords at band's May 11th performance in Attleboro would be confirmed as the band's opening reunion shot. Anthony Bramante bowed out in August and Erik Burke, a scene veteran with VALPURGA, KALIBAS, LETHARGY, SULACO, MUNGBEANDEMON and BLATANT CRAP TASTE connections, took over on guitar. NUCLEAR ASSAULT got back into the touring mode kicking off a gig in Springfield, Virginia on December 29th which would trigger a whole rash of gigs throughout January of 2003.

Connelly would also guest for CANDY STRIPER DEATH ORGY, contributing both guest lead vocals and guitar to their debut album. Scott Metaxas would be announced as in the chair for co-production duties on Billy Milano's 2002 M.O.D. album.

The band's continuing resurgence would be further progressed as NUCLEAR ASSAULT was confirmed as participants in the April 2003 European 'No Mercy' festivals. The group formed up part of a heavyweight billing comprising TESTAMENT, MARDUK, DIE APOKALYPTISCHEN REITER, DEATH ANGEL, PRO-PAIN, MALEVOLENT CREATION, DARKANE, and CALLENISH CIRCLE.

In May the band inducted the MINUS, NUCLEAR THEORY, RITE BASTARDS, DENYTHEFALLOUT and AIMED AGGRESSION credited guitarist Scott Harrington to replace Bramante. UK and European dates projected into October, dubbed the 'Bonded By Metal' trek, found the band co-headlining an old school orientated Thrash / Death Metal roster comprising EXODUS, AGENT STEEL, MORTICIAN, GOD DETHRONED, OCCULT and CALLENISH CIRCLE.

A brand new NUCLEAR ASSAULT album '3rd World Genocide', featuring a guest appearance from former guitarist Eric Burke, was recorded for Screaming Ferret Wreckords during the Spring of 2004. Studio guests included Eric Paone of CANDY STRIPER DEATH ORGY contributing backing vocals whilst Travis Horton of RED RIGHT HAND and DISTRUST added vocals and banjo to the track 'Long Haired Asshole'. Included would be a cover of JOHNNY CASH's 'Folsom Prison Blues'.

NUCLEAR ASSAULT opened 2005 with a burst of South American shows allied with fellow Thrash veterans DEATH ANGEL. European dates saw the band being joined by guitarist Karl Cochran, a veteran of the ACE FREHLEY and JOE LYNN TURNER bands. US shows in August witnessed a road partnership with TESTAMENT. The band was included the 'Metal Crusaders' North American tour, set to take place in May and June 2006 alongside KATAKLYSM, GRAVEWORM, VADER, SPEED\KILL/HATE and THE ABSENCE. However, due to what was described as an "urgent immediate family situation", the band dropped off this tour to be replaced by Germany's DESTRUCTION.

In September and October Lilker temped for SOULFLY's North American dates after regular bassist Bobby Burns suffered a mild stroke.

GAME OVER, Under One Flag FLAG 5 (1986). Live, Suffer, Die / Sin / Cold Steel / Betrayal / Radiation Sickness / Hang The Pope / After The Holocaust / Stranded In Hell / Nuclear War / My America / Vengeance / Brain Death.

Brain Death, Combat 88561 8119-1 (1986). Brain Death / Final Flight / Demolition.

NUCLEAR ASSAULT

THE PLAGUE, Under One Flag MFLAG 13 (1987). Game Over / Nightmares / Buttfuck / Justice / The Plague / Cross Of Iron.

SURVIVE, Under One Flag FLAG 21 (1988). Rise From The Ashes / Brainwashed / F / Survive / Fight To Be Free / Got Another Quarter / Great Depression / Wired / Equal Right / P.S.A. / Technology / Good Times, Bad Times. Chart position: 145 USA.

Fight To Be Free, Under One Flag CD12 FLAG 105 (1989). Fight To Be Free / Equal Rights / Stand Up / Brain Death / Final Flight / Demolition.

Fight To Be Free, Under One Flag PB12 FLAG 105 (1989) (With free poster). Fight To Be Free / Equal Rights / Stand Up.

HANDLE WITH CARE, Under One Flag FLAG 35 (1989). New Song / Critical Mass / Inherited Hell / Surgery / Emergency / Funky Noise / F (Wake Up) / When Freedom Dies / Search And Seizure / Torture Tactics / Mother's Day / Trail Of Tears. Chart position: 126 USA.

Critical Mass, In Effect 885613010 (1989) (USA promotion release). Critical Mass / Funky Noise / Mother's Day.

Trail Of Tears, Relativity (1989) (USA promotion). Trail Of Tears.

Good Times, Bad Times, Under One Flag 12 FLAG 107 (1989). Good Times, Bad Times / Hang The Pope (Live) / Lesbians / My America / Happy Days.

OUT OF ORDER, Under One Flag FLAG 64 (1991). Sign In Blood / Fashion Junkie / Too Young To Die / Preaching To The Deaf / Resurrection / Stop Wait Think / Doctor Butcher / Quocustodiat / Hypocrisy / Save The Planet / Ballroom Blitz.

LIVE AT HAMMERSMITH ODEON, Roadracer RO 91672 (1992). Intro—The New Song / Critical Mass / Game Over / Nightmares / Buttfuck / Survive / Torture Tactics / Trail Of Tears / Mother's Day / My America / Hang The Pope / Lesbians / Funky Noise / Good Times, Bad Times.

SOMETHING WICKED, Alter Ego ALTGOCD 003 (1993). Something Wicked / Another Violent End / Behind Glass Walls / Chaos / The Forge / No Time / To Serve Man / Madness Descends / Poetic Justice / Art / The Other End.

ASSAULT AND BATTERY, Receiver RRCD 244 (1997). Happy Days / Enter Darkness / Leaders / Hang The Pope / Radiation Sickness / Hypocrisy / Behind Glass Walls / No Time / Hour Shower / Saddam / Preaching To The Deaf / Hang The Pope (Live) / Ping (Live) / Torture Tactics (Live) / Fight To Be Free (Live) / Trail Of Tears (Live) / Ping Again (Live) / Butt Fuck (Live).

ALIVE AGAIN, SPV (2003). Rise From The Ashes / Brainwashed / F# / New Song / Critical Mass / S.I.N. / Betrayal / Radiation Sickness / Game Over / Butt Fuck / Trail Of Tears / Hang The Pope.

THIRD WORLD GENOCIDE, Steamhammer SPV 085-69722 CD (2005). Third World Genocide / Price Of Freedom / Human Wreckage / Living Hell / Whine And Cheese / Defiled Innocence / Exoskeletal / Discharged Reason / Fractured Minds / The Hockey Song / Eroded Liberty / Long Haired Asshole / Glenn's Song.

NUCLEAR DEATH

AZ, USA — *Lori Bravo (vocals / bass), Phil Hampson (guitar), Joel Whitfield (drums).*

This cult-like Thrash/Death act has a certain reputation in the underground for paradoxically being both brutally bad and good at the same time. Founded in March 1986 in Tempe, Arizona the trio had a seldom seen phenomenon, a female vocalist and bassist. The band worked diligently in the underground and produced four demos 'Wake Me When I'm Dead' in 1986, 'Welcome To The Minds Of The Morbid' in 1987, a live ten track demo called 'A Symphony Of Agony' in November 1987 and finally in 1989 the session 'Caveat'.

By then the band was signed to the fledgling cult underground US Metal label, Wild Rags. The debut, 'Bride Of Insect' appeared in 1990. Staying with Wild Rags the band released 'Carrion For Worm' in 1991 which found Steve Cowan replacing Joel Whitfield on drums. The third release, 'For Our Dead' was delivered in 1992 and a subsequent cassette release 'All Creatures Great And Eaten'.

Bravo and Cowan did later leak a promotion recording dubbed 'The Planet Cachexial' credited to NUCLEAR DEATH but it seems the band have been inactive ever since. Extremist Records reissued the first brace of albums as a double package in 2000.

BRIDE OF INSECT, Wild Rags WRR017 (1990). Necrobestiality / Corpse Of Allegiance / Feral Viscera / Stygian Tranquility / Place Of Skulls / Cremation / The Colour Of Blood / The Beloved Whore Celebration / Fetal Lament: Homesick / Bride Of Insect / The Misshapen Horror / Vultures Feeding.

CARRION FOR WORM, Wild Rags WRR019 (1991). Spawn Song / The Human Seed / Proposing To The Impaled / Moribund / Greenflies / Return Of The Feasting Witch / A Dark Country / Lurker In The Closet: A Fairy Tale / Cathedral Of Sleep / Homage To Morpheus / Carrion For Worm / Vampirism.

FOR OUR DEAD, Wild Rags (1992). The Corpse Tree / Days Of The Weak / The Third Antichrist / The Church Of Evil Minds Of Splatterday Saints.

NUCLEAR WARFARE

REMSECK, GERMANY — *Nucleator (vocals), Sebastian Listl (guitar), Turrican (guitar), Fritz (vocals / bass), Miriam (drums).*

Remseck, Stuttgart based Thrash Metal band NUCLEAR WARFARE began life billed DEATH SQUAD, formulated in late 2001 by bassist Florian Fritz Bernhard, of HEILIGS BLECHLE, and drummer Thomas Bernhardt, inducting guitarists Thomas Flor and Sebastian Listl. Singer Andreas Nucleator Schramm completed the first line-up. This unit featured on the May 2002 demo tape 'First Strike'.

Subsequent line-up changes saw the opting out of both Bernhard and Flor. In May of 2003 Turrican assumed the guitar position, followed by the addition of ex-SACRALIS drummer Miriam. Following live work, including a support to TANKARD, the band set about recording the album 'War Is Unleashed'. Limited to 500 copies the record, released in September 2004, novelly came packaged with three toy soldiers.

The 7" vinyl single 'Dosenpfand Muss Weg!' was released in 2005. NUCLEAR WARFARE's second album, 'We Come In Peace', was delivered in July 2006. The May 2007 EP 'Royal Fortune' hosted two new tracks and re-recordings of 'Kill', 'Dosenpfand' and 'Social Terror'.

First Strike, Nuclear Warfare (2002) (Demo). Thrash Squad / Social Terror / Kill / Inner War / Unholy Genesis / Thrash Metal Victory.

WAR IS UNLEASHED, Nuclear Warfare (2004) (Limited edition 500 copies). Intro / Warfare / War Is Unleashed / Kill / Thrash Squad / Predator / Inner War / Warlust / Thrash 'Em Down.

Dosenpfand Muss Weg!, Nuclear Warfare (2005) (7" vinyl single). Dosenpfand Muss Weg! / Thrash Metal Victory.

WE COME IN PEACE, Nuclear Warfare (2006). Trained To Kill / Nuclear Madness / Under The Banner Of Lies / Thrash Metal Tank / Unholy Genesis / Lex Talionis / Warmaster / We Come In Peace / Collapse Of Reality / Rolling Thunder / After War.

Royal Fortune, Nuclear Warfare (2007). Pirates / Kill / Conventions Of Society / Dosenpfand / Social Terror.

NUMSKULL

WINTHROP HARBOR, IL, USA — *Skip McGullum (vocals), Tom Brander (guitar), Eric Seiller (guitar), Rob Charrier (bass), Jeff McGullum (drums).*

Thrash Metal act NUM SKULL emerged with a 1987 demo session 'Nums The World'. A further demo 'Thrash To The Bone' the following year secured a deal with the Enigma label for the 'Ritually Abused' album. In 1995 a split album shared space with SEA OF TRANQUILITY and two brand new recordings featured on the Dutch 'History Of Things To Come' compilation album put out by Growing Deaf Entertainment. NUM SKULL returned to the studio in 1996 to record 'When Suffering Comes', sporting a cover version of VENOM's 'Buried Alive', for Defiled Records, these recordings featuring a line up comprising vocalist Paul Benigno, guitarists Tom Brandner and David Harrington, bass player Mike Eisenhauer and drummer Scott Creekmore.

Guitarist Tom Brandner joined LUPARA in August of 2004.

RITUALLY ABUSED, Enigma (1988). The End / Ritually Abused / Death And Innocence / No Morals / Friday's Child / Off With Your Head / The Henchman / Pirate's Night / Turn Of A Screw / Kiss Me, Kill Me / Rigor Mortis.

WHEN SUFFERING COMES, Defiled (1996). Eyes Of A Madman / The Gift Of Hate / Mercitron / In Sickness / Spill Your Guts / As The Dead Pile High / Inquisition Of The Guilty / Force Fed Lies / Buried Alive.

OBLIVEON

MONTREAL, QC, CANADA — *Bruno Bernier (vocals), Stephane Pecard (vocals / bass), Pierre Rémillard (guitar), Martin Gagne (guitar), Alain Demers (drums).*

Montréal, Québec, technical Thrash Metal act OBLIVEON emerged, at first billed as OBLIVION, in January 1987. Although the group's precision approach to the genre won many plaudits and praiseworthy reviews, OBLIVEON struggled to break onto the world market and would remain consigned to cult status. Debuting after demos, then formatively titled OBLIVION, with the 'Whimsical Uproar' session following that September. The band's line-up at this stage comprised of vocalist / bassist Stéphane Picard, guitarist Martin Gagné and drummer Francis Giguère. A further demo effort in 1989 'Fiction Of Veracity', seeing the departure of Giguère and the upgrading to a quartet by enlisting drummer Alain Demers and guitarist Pierre Rémillard, led in turn to the debut album 'From This Day Forward' for the UK based Active label in 1990. Initially the record only saw European distribution but would be picked up later for Canada by Press Play.

Sophomore effort 'Nemesis' arrived in 1993 as a self-financed effort. A video clip of the live favorite 'Dynamo' was shot and played on a regular basis on the Canadian Much Music and Musique Plus music television channels. The following year Bruno Bernier, previously with SARKASM, was added as lead vocalist, this incarnation of OBLIVEON cutting the 'Cybervoid' album for the A.S.A. label. During mid 1997 the Soundscape Music label re-issued the band's demo 'Whimsical Uproar', albeit only offering three tracks out of the original four, on CD format to mark OBLIVEON's tenth anniversary. The band also donated their version of OZZY OSBOURNE's 'Suicide Solution' for the Olympic Records tribute 'Legend Of A Madman'. Curiously, OBLIVEON issued as a promotion sampler a version of the B-52's 'Planet Claire' in 1998. A further full-length album, entitled 'Carnivore Mothermouth', was released in 1999.

OBLIVEON split in March 2002, although Great White North records put out the compilation 'Greatest Pits' that same May. Ex-guitarist Pierre Rémillard was soon back in the news touting a fresh Thrash act billed as BLACK CLOUD. This band saw the six-stringer allied with GHOULUNATICS frontman Patrick

Mireault, former VOIVOD man Jean-Yves 'Blacky' Thériault on bass, Daniel Mongrain of MARTYR on second guitar and Flo Mounier from CRYPTOPSY on drums.

OBLIVEON guitar player Pierre Rémillard carved out an esteemed career on the production front, scoring credits with VOIVOD, CRYPTOPSY, GORGUTS, NEURAXIS, ION DISSONANCE and KRISIUN amongst many others. He also briefly joined the ranks of A PERFECT MURDER in 2005.

Whimsical Uproar, Soundscape Music (1987). Whimsical Uproar / The Scrutinizer / Undeserving Glory / Extraction Of Immortality.
Fiction Of Veracity, (1989). It Should Have Stayed Unreal / Access To The Acropolis / Fiction Of Veracity / Imminent Regenerator / Droidomized / Chronocraze.
FROM THIS DAY FORWARD, Press Play 62904-8018-2 (1990). From This Day Forward / Fiction Of Veracity / Droidomized / Imminent Regenerator / It Should Have Stayed Unreal / Access To The Acropolis / Chronocraze.
NEMESIS, Press Play 62904-8019-2 (1993). Nemesis / The Thinker's Lair / Obscure Mindways / Dynamo / Frosted Avowals / Factory Of Delusions / Estranging Abduction / Strays Of The Soul.
CYBERVOID, Press Play 62904-8020-2 (1995). Cybervoid / Downward / Perihelion / Android Succubus / Sequels / Subgod / Sombre Phase / Biomécanique / Call Of Silence / Deus Ex Machina.
Whimsical Uproar EP, Soundscape Music SSM001CD (1997). Whimsical Uproar / The Scrutinizer / Undeserving Glory.
Planet Claire, (1998) (Promotion release). Planet Claire / Psychomatrix / Biomecanique.
CARNIVORE MOTHERMOUTH, Hypnotic HYP 1072 (1999). Technocarnivore Mothermouth / Love, Die, Resurrect / Such A Quiet River / Devil In My Eyes / Coercive Currents / Polarity / Vectors / Glass Made Of Flesh / Fatal Induction / Desert Incorporeal.

OCCULT

HOLLAND — *Rachel Heyzer (vocals), Sephiroth (vocals), Leon Pennings (guitar), Richard Ebisch (guitar), Sjors Tuithof (bass), Erik Fleuren (drums).*

A leading Black-Thrash Metal act from the Netherlands. Vocalist Sephiroth is ex-BESTIAL SUMMONING. He would later drop the corpsepaint and revert to his real name of Maurice Swinkle. OCCULT vocalist Rachel Heyzer was previously a member of Death Metal band PATHOLOGY. Heyzer would later double up duties by fronting the veteran Death Metal act SINISTER for their 'Creative Killings' record.

UK and European dates projected into October of 2003, dubbed the 'Bonded By Metal' trek, found the band forming up a billing comprising EXODUS, AGENT STEEL, NUCLEAR ASSAULT, MORTICIAN, GOD DETHRONED, and CALLENISH CIRCLE. As the year closed OCCULT announced they had signed to the Karmageddon Media label for a new album 'Elegy For The weak'. This opus would see production credits going to former HOLY MOSES guitarist Andy Classen.

Early 2004 would see the issue of the band's debut DVD through Lowlifemedia Productions. Entitled 'To Be Thrashed–By Occult' it comprised live footage from recent gigs and early club performances, interviews with present and past band members, onstage jams with PENTACLE and DESASTER as well as promotional video clips for 'Killing for Recreation' and 'Doomsday Destroyer'. A short burst of Benelux dates in September 2004 saw the band united with CALLENISH CIRCLE, DISMEMBER and HEARSE. That same month the band entered Stage One studios in Bühne, Germany with producer Andy Classen to craft their sixth album.

The band announced a touring partnership as part of the December 2005 'X-Mas' festivals in Europe ranked alongside recently resurrected UK Thrashers ONSLAUGHT, EXODUS, KATAKLYSM, UNLEASHED, BEHEMOTH, and PRIMORDIAL. Following these gigs OCCULT adopted the new title LEGION OF THE DAMNED. The band formed up a European 'No Mercy' festival package for dates across Germany, Austria, France, Switzerland, Belgium and Holland in April, ranked alongside FINNTROLL, KATAKLYSM, GRIMFIST and CANNIBAL CORPSE.

PREPARE TO MEET THY DOOM, Foundation 2000 FDN 2010-2 (1994). Leader In The War / The Black Are Rising / After Triumph / Prepare To Meet Thy Doom / And Darkness Shall Begin / Almighty Horde / Whispering Tear / The Nazarene Whore / Elements In Blaqck / Quest For The Spirit.
THE ENEMY WITHIN, Foundation 2000 FDN 2014-2 (1996). Souls / Inquisition Of The Holy / Crossing The Boundaries (Of Life And Death) / Selfbetrayed / Twisted Words (My Darkest Emotions) / Through Dark And Light I Dwell / One Way Out / Passive Relations / Eyes Of Blood / Until The Battle / Delusion.
OF FLESH AND BLOOD, Massacre MAS CD0183 (1999). Intro / Parasite / Dreamsweeper / Stolen / Killing Breed / Ritual Of Demise / Downfall Of Deity / Oath In War / Doomsday Destroyer / Dead Man Walking / Vow Of Retaliation / Dormant Till Dusk / Creatures Of The Night.
RAGE TO REVENGE, (2001). Mind Domination / Violence & Hatred / The Madness Within / Killing For Recreation / Thy Creation / Revenge Is Mine / Work Of A Legend / Fatal Disorder / The Desolate One.
ELEGY FOR THE WEAK, Painkiller (2003). Disturbing The Dead / Nuclear Torment / Nocturnal Predator / Feel The Blade / Expire / Warbeast / Obsessed By The Grave / Slaughtering The Pigs / Reapers Call / Slut Of Sodom / Until The Battle.

ODIN

LOS ANGELES, CA, USA — *Randy O (vocals), Jeff Duncan (guitar), Aaron Samson (bass), Shawn Duncan (drums).*

Unfortunately ODIN are more famous in the mass market for their appearance in the Rockumentary 'The Decline And Fall Of Western Civilization Part II: The Metal Years' than any recorded product. In the Metal world ODIN's name has long ranked as one of the most hallowed cult acts to bless the American scene. Guitarist Brad Parker appears on the 1983 EP. Under the pseudonym of Damien C. Phillips Parker had actually been a member of the fledgling METALLICA. His stay lasted just one gig. ODIN issued the 1985 album 'Don't Take No For An Answer' as their full length debut.

Vocalist Randy O Roberg would depart to secure a solo deal with Atlantic Records. After an abortive spell working with ex-HOLLAND guitarist Mike Batio in MICHAEL ANGELO during 1988 Roberg formed the LOST BOYS with Jeff Duncan and bassist Jimmy Tavis, a late recruit into ODIN, releasing the 1990 album 'Lost And Found'. Another ODIN line up would be fronted by Mark Weisz, later of IMPELLITERRI.

Another attempt to re-assemble the band would include guitarist Tim Kelly and New Yorker Tony De Vita, an ex-member of INVASION, on vocals. This unit would soon dissolve with De Vita journeying through WIRED, MISBEHAVIN and CARFAX ABBEY prior to winding up in Progressive Metal act NEW EDEN. Kelly would change tack to find platinum fame with SLAUGHTER before his untimely demise.

Shawn Duncan played with MADAM X prior to that group's eventual demise in early 1989. Duncan later joined ARMORED SAINT before founding BIRD OF PREY. In 2000 the Duncan siblings assembled side project band DC4 together with yet another Duncan family member bassist Matt. Jeff Duncan is presently a member of the resurrected ARMORED SAINT. Renewed interest in 80s US Metal and cult acts such as ODIN in particular would put the focus back on the band as Japanese label JVC Victor issued the 'Fight For Your Life' album in June of 2001.

ODIN, comprising Randy O, Jeff Duncan, Aaron Samson and Shawn Duncan, reunited for a one off live performance at the Troubadour in Hollywood, California on February 8th 2003.

ODIN would still be active in 2005, performing on 22nd June at the Hollywood Key Club to launch the 'Hollywood Rocks' box set on a billing with SPIDERS AND SNAKES, BLACKBOARD JUNGLE, JETBOY, THE ZEROS and FIZZY BANGERS.

Caution, Duff (1983). Caution / The Blade / Midnight Flight / Judgement Day.
DON'T TAKE NO FOR AN ANSWER, Half Wet GWD 1290509 (1985). The Writer / One Day To Live / Shining Love / Solar Eye / Don't Take No For An Answer / Judgement Day.

THE GODS MUST BE CRAZY, Victor (1988).

FIGHT FOR YOUR LIFE, JVC Victor (2001) (Japanese release). 12 O'Clock High / Love Action / She Was The One / I Get What I Want / Serenade To The Court / Modern Day King / Stranger Tonight / Time And Time Again / I'm Gonna Get You / Push / Fight For Your Life.

BY THE GODS, Perris (2001). Writer / One Day To Live / Shining Love / Solar Eye / Don't Take No For An Answer / Judgement Day / Little Gypsy / She Needs My Love / No Reason To Run / Over Your Head / She Was The One / Play The Fool / Matter Of Time / Judgement Day / Midnight Flight / Blade.

OGRESS

BELGIUM — *Dreetn (vocals), Davy Vanrumbeke (guitar), Arry (guitar), Nick Meganck (bass), Baphomet (keyboards), Toone (drums).*

Thrashers OGRESS featured DENIAL drummer Toone. The initial formation was put together by ex-LOWLIGHT members Geoffrey Holvoet on vocals, Nick Meganck as bassist and Anthony Jonckheere on the drums alongside ex-MENTAL DEATH guitarist Davy Vanrumbeke. Subsequently Tommy Debevere was added to the line-up. The band released a self-titled, five track demo. OGRESS then underwent changes, adding guitarist Steve Deleu (a.k.a. 'Arry'), of SPHINX, WRATHCHILD, OPERATION G.S.D., and EXIT REALITY repute, and keyboard player Koen Couckuyt ('Baphomet'), also operating in parallel with VEXED and holding prior tradition with SAGARIS, ASGARD, GYLLNOR and RHYMES OF DESTRUCTION. Jimmy Claeys became drummer in August 2004.

In February 2005 the drum position was handed over to former EXIT REALITY, THE HEADLESS HUNT, FOR HEAVEN'S SAKE and BY THROAT man Dieter Jodts. Steve Deleu temporarily joined the ranks of DOUBLE DIAMOND in May 2006 when guitarist Tom van Steenbergen crashed his motorbike, damaging his legs.

Ogress, Ogress (2002). Broken / A.I.D.S. / Betrayal / The End / Friendship Never Dies.

OIL

LONG BEACH, CA, USA — *Ron Rinehart (vocals), Blake Nelson (guitar), Matthew Joy (bass), Jason Vander Pal (drums).*

OIL are a Los Angeles based Christian Thrash Metal band fronted by former DARK ANGEL singer Ron Rinehart. The frontman became a Christian upon DARK ANGEL's dissolution in 1992. OIL debuted with a self financed EP during 1999. Also featured in the ranks of OIL is erstwhile DECEIVER, DESIRE and CAPTAIN BLACK guitarist Blake Nelson. For the full length album Jason Vander Pal took over on the drum stool from 'Eric'.

The 'Refine' album pulled in a generous helping of enthusiastic reviews for it's honest, no frills Metal approach. The band managed to put in live gigs, including a showing at the STRYPER Expo, but unfortunately Rinehart received an injury shortly after the album release which put OIL on hold for nearly a year. Fully recovered, Rinehart and OIL got back into action being announced as special guests to DISCIPLE in April.

The band recorded a live album 'Choice Cuts Off The Chopping Block' at the First Baptist Church of Downey in Downey, California in November of 2002. The record included two new acoustic songs 'This Is My Prayer' and 'Medicine Man'. However, bassist Matthew Joy opted out in May of 2003 and OIL drafted Jonathan Thiemens of BLIND SACRIFICES as temporary replacement. Thiemans would be confirmed as a permanent addition to the ranks by July.

OIL announced they were to disband in July of 2004. Before going their separate ways, the group undertook one last show on 14th August alongside RECON, EAST WEST, TRAUMA and TERRESTRIAL HARVEST at The Lighthouse in Long Beach, California.

Oil EP, (1999). When No One Cares / Last Breathe / Searching For Heaven / Numbers / Day Or Night.

REFINE, Kaluboné (1999). Divided / Waiting There / Scream / Life Addiction / Lost / Open Wound / Struggle / S.I.N. / I Won't Give Up / Chopping Block.

CHOICE CUTS OFF THE CHOPPING BLOCK, Roxx Productions (2003). Intro / Drown / Life Addiction / Struggle / S.I.N.+ / Waiting There / Walls / After / Picture This / Divided / When No One Cares / Chopping Block / This Is My Prayer / Medicine Man.

OMEN

LOS ANGELES, CA, USA — *Kevin Goocher (vocals), Kenny Powell (guitar), Andy Haas (bass), Rick Murray (drums).*

Traditional Heavy Metal band formed by guitarist Kenny Powell. The Los Angeles based band had been created during 1983 by Oklahoma natives guitarists Kenny Powell and Jody Henry along with drummer Steve Wittig. Unable to assemble a full band unit Powell took time out to work with SAVAGE GRACE. This tenure would be short-lived though and, brandishing a cassette of tapes originally scored for SAVAGE GRACE, Powell duly scored a deal with Brian Slagel and Metal Blade Records for OMEN.

The band line-up was completed with vocalist J.D. Kimball as OMEN debuted with the November 1984 'Battle Cry' album. Although blighted by an amateurish album cover OMEN's brand of Power Thrash style Metal won many converts world-wide. OMEN also had their track 'Torture Me' featured on the 1984 Metal Blade 'Metal Massacre V' compilation album. A succession of albums ensued, 'Warning Of Danger' in October 1985, produced by Brian Slagel and engineered by Bill Metoyer, and 'The Curse' in October 1986, but OMEN were unable to extract themselves from a cult following into the mainstream.

The April 1987 'Nightmares' mini-album contains a live version of the AC/DC classic 'Whole Lotta Rosie'. Kimball departed before this release and OMEN pulled in vocalist Coburn Pharr, previously of PRISONER, for the October 1988 'Escape To Nowhere' album, which featured a version of GOLDEN EARRING's 'Radar Love'. Originally the album, produced by the esteemed Paul O'Neill, was to have been entitled 'Era Of Crisis' but many of the original tracks slated for the album would be rejected by O'Neill. Despite the tribulations OMEN scored valuable radio play with the track 'Thorn In Your Flesh'. Upon completion of a ten week run of live shows across America a disillusioned Powell decamped.

After the release of 1989's compilation 'Teeth Of The Hydra' Pharr opted out to join high profile Canadians ANNIHILATOR. Powell joined forces with vocalist Steve Kelley, bassist Andy Haas and drummer Doug Stevens to create STEP CHILD issuing a demo in 1991.

With a renaissance of 80s American Metal in Europe during the mid 90s OMEN was forced out of retirement due to fan pressure. Powell emerged with a new look OMEN that included his son Greg Powell on lead vocals and guitar, bassist Andy Haas and drummer Rick Murray.

This unit cut the comeback 'Reopening The Gates' album for Germany's Massacre Records and undertook a successful bout of European touring backing up FATES WARNING. After these dates Greg Powell embarked on his own career with STOMPING GROUND.

OMEN enlisted the services of Kevin Goocher and set to task on a new album projected for 2002 release titled 'Eternal Black Dawn'. Earlier in the year OMEN, with support band BATTLEROAR, had toured Greece to enthusiastic response.

Original OMEN bassist Jody Henry was touting a fresh act in 2002 billed as CELEBRITY CRUSH. OMEN themselves busied themselves in recording a brand new studio album 'Eternal Black Dawn' and would make a return to live action in June of 2003, performing at the German 'Keep It True' Heavy Metal festival in Koenigshofen. OMEN launched an extravagant 20th anniversary box set in September, which include remastered studio albums, DVD footage and live tracks recorded in San Antonio, Texas during 1986.

Original OMEN frontman J.D. Kimball lost a three year battle against cancer in October of 2003, just following the release of the band's latest studio album 'Eternal Black Dawn'. OMEN returned to live action in mid 2004, including support shows to W.A.S.P. in Texas during July. That same year vocalist Kevin Goocher launched a side project entitled PHANTOM-X, working alongside TYR members guitarist Russell D. Contreras and bass player Glenn Malicki with drummer Wayne Stokely of FAME 15.

German Heavy Metal band POWERGOD cut a cover version of 'Deathrider' for inclusion on their 'Long Live The Loud–That's Metal Lesson II' released through Massacre Records in July 2005. OMEN united with PHANTOM-X and Italian act HYADES for the 'Mausoleum Metal Masters' European tour beginning in early September 2006. The remainder of the year was spent working on tracks for a new album dubbed 'Hammer Damage'.

BATTLE CRY, Metal Blade 71105 (1984). Death Rider / The Axeman / Last Rites / Dragon's Breath / Be My Wench / Battle Cry / Die By The Blade / Prince Of Darkness / Bring Out The Beast / In The Arena.
WARNING OF DANGER, Metal Blade 72068 (1985). Warning Of Danger / March On / Ruby Eyes (Of The Serpent) / Don't Fear The Night / VBP / Premonition / Termination / Make Me Your King / Red Horizon / Hell's Gates.
THE CURSE, Metal Blade 73230 (1986). The Curse / Kill On Sight / Holy Martyr / Eye Of The Storm / S.R.B. / Teeth Of The Hydra / At All Cost / Destiny / Bounty Hunter / The Larch.
NIGHTMARES, Metal Blade 73266 (1987). Nightmares / Shock Treatment / Dragon's Breath / Termination / Bounty Hunter / Whole Lotta Rosie (Live).
ESCAPE TO NOWHERE, Metal Blade 73310 (1988). It's Not Easy / Radar Love / Escape To Nowhere / Cry For The Morning / Thorn In Your Flesh / Poisoned / Nomads / King Of The Hill / No Way Out.
TEETH OF THE HYDRA, Metal Blade (1989). Holy Martyr / Termination / Dragon's Breath / Teeth Of The Hydra / Battle Cry / The Curse / Nightmares / Bounty Hunter / Thorn In Your Flesh / Die By The Blade / Hell's Gates.
REOPENING THE GATES, Massacre MAS PCO124 (1997). Dead March / Uneven Plow / Chained / Rain Down / Reopening The Gates / Everything / Well Fed / Crushing Day / Saturday Into The Ground.
Battle Anthems, Metal Invader (1998) (Free EP with Metal Invader magazine). Be My Wench / Battle Cry / Warning Of Danger / Don't Fear The Night / Teeth Of The Hydra / At All Cost.
ETERNAL BLACK DAWN, Mausoleum (2003). 1000 Year Reign / Eternal Black Dawn / Burning Times / Blood Feud / House On Rue Royale / King Of The Seven Seas / Chains Of Delirium / Chaos In The Cathedral / The Specter Of Battles Past (Medley).

ONSLAUGHT

BRISTOL, UK — *Sy Keeler (vocals), Nige Rockett (guitar), Rob Trotman (guitar), James Hinder (bass), Steve Grice (drums).*

A stoic Thrash act from Bristol, ONSLAUGHT stayed the course and had the major labels running around after them for quite a while in an embarrassing period when major labels seemingly snapped up any old British Thrash act. However, ONSLAUGHT actually pre-dated the UK Thrash wave by a good many years with their 'Power From Hell' debut having emerged in 1985. Ultimately, ONSLAUGHT established an underground following, including across the West Coast of the USA, but once in the grip of London Records resorted to commercialism, ending their career.

The first ONSLAUGHT formation counted founders guitarist Nige Rockett and drummer Steve Grice, singer Jase Pope and bass player Paul Hill. This combo cut demos at Sam's Studios in Bristol hosting the tracks 'Thermonuclear Devastation', 'Black Horse Of Famine', 'Overthrow Of The System' and 'Rape'. Restructuring, singer Roger Davies and bassist Paul Dickie Davies were enrolled as the group set about cementing a live following in the Avon area, performing numerous gigs at Bristol's Trinity venue alongside punk outfits such as THE VARUKERS, ONE WAY SYSTEM and THE EXPLOITED. This second version of Onslaught recorded a demo tagged 'What Lies Ahead'.

ONSLAUGHT had demoed heavily throughout 1983, distributing three cassettes of material, the last of which included a full live set. Another change in the membership saw the inclusion of vocalist Paul Mahoney and four-stringer Jase Stallard. The band cut tracks for an intended EP, to be branded 'Foxhole', but this also surfaced in cassette format. The band had initially been picked up upon by the magazine 'Metal Forces' after releasing the debut album 'Power From Hell' on the normally Punk handling Children Of The Revolution label. Indeed, the group initially started life as a Punk outfit in 1983, but as they veered into thrash territory much of the earlier song catalogue from the demo days would be discarded as Power From Hell took on a pseudo-Satanic stance.

Onslaught's first, stable line-up settled on vocalist Sy Keeler, guitarists Nige Rockett and Jason Stallard and drummer Steve Grice with Mahoney having switched to bass, although the rawly produced debut album, 'Power From Hell', had been cut with Stallard on bass. Despite bearing a infamous song title 'Death Metal', 'Power From Hell' delivered a strong blend of proto-Thrash with vestiges of Punk. It was a record that was acknowledged at the time to have sold over 11'000 copies.

The exposure through 'Metal Forces' magazine prompted Mark Palmer at Music For Nations to sign the group to their newly established Under One Flag imprint. Acknowledging the help given to them by the magazine, ONSLAUGHT would record the track 'Metal Forces' on second album, spring 1986's 'The Force' recorded at Matrix studios in London with producer Dave Pine, in appreciation. Live campaigning had the band opening for the likes of GIRLSCHOOL, ANVIL and EXCITER. That same year ONSLAUGHT featured on the stage of the prestigious 'Dynamo' festival in Holland, marking the group's only outdoor performance. Matters became confusing as during 1986 bassist Paul Mahoney left, enabling Jason Stallard to resume bass duties. In November ONSLAUGHT drafted in bassist James Hinder, moving Stallard back to guitar once more.

1987 opened strongly, ONSLAUGHT conducting a lightning dash across the Low Countries as headliner before jumping onboard the MOTÖRHEAD 'Orgasmatron' European tour in March, commencing in Switzerland and closing in Norway. As part of the Bristol Community Festival, the group performed at the city's historic Colston Hall venue. Unfortunately over enthusiastic moshing by fans resulted in serious damage to the venue's seating but this adverse publicity was countered somewhat by positive response from Polygram A&R representatives in attendance. ONSLAUGHT featured on a further high profile gig on June 20th 1987, backing AGENT STEEL, NUCLEAR ASSAULT and ATOMKRAFT at London's Hammersmith Odeon. The band's set, the first to include their rendition of AC/DC's 'Let There Be Rock', was broadcast on Radio 1 on Tommy Vance's 'Friday Rock Show'.

A second guitarist, Rob Trotman, was added but, prior to releasing their first studio version of the AC/DC cover 'Let There Be Rock', the band sacked Stallard after supposedly recording him at a gig in Bristol and citing this as evidence he could not play well enough. A disgruntled Stallard refuted the claims and went on to form Militia, reverting to drums, with guitarists Darren Keeler (brother of Sy) and John Hinder, brother of Jim.

To close 1988 the band embarked on a winter UK tour in alliance with CRUMBSUCKERS and SLAMMER. ONSLAUGHT eventually signed to London Records after being chased by a host of major labels, including A&M and CBS. However, the intended title of 'Blood Upon Ice' was scotched when BATHORY issued an album of the same title at the same juncture.

The group's debut for the new label arrived in 1989. 'In Search Of Sanity' was originally recorded at West Side, Smokehouse and Eden studios in London with vocalist Sy Keeler, but producer Stefan Galfas decided the man simply could not sing well enough, a fact that ended up prompting London to demand a change of vocalist. This naturally begged the question why had London's A&R department signed a band with a vocalist they held little faith in.

Nevertheless, Keeler departed to form MIRROR MIRROR with erstwhile PREYER drummer Lloyd Coates. Former GRIM REAPER singer Steve Grimmett, who importantly had made his mark in North America with three chart albums, joined the band to re-record the vocals on the album, injecting a much needed dose of class to the band. 'In Search Of Sanity', mixed at Atlantic studios in New York, found the group tackling AC/DC's 'Let There Be Rock' once again, backing this as a single with a promotional video. A further single, the power ballad 'Welcome To Dying', was backed by a further brace of covers, in VAN HALEN's 'Atomic Punk' and the STRANGLERS 'Nice n' Sleazy'. Regrettably, it was all a hideous mismatch and after a low key European tour in alliance with ANNIHILATOR and UK dates with HORSE, Grimmett decamped.

The band drafted in Canadian born vocalist TONY O'HORA, previously with the much mellower LARRAKIN and TORINO. An album was announced for release to be billed 'When Reason Sleeps', but was never to see issue. ONSLAUGHT's proposed material for this record witnessed a radical swing away from their Thrash roots. However, in the midst of these sessions, London Records dropped the band. The independent FM Revolver announced they were to issue 'When Reason Sleeps', although this never eventuated.

The group undertook an extensive UK headline tour throughout November and December 1990, supported by New Yorkers DEAD ON and Keeler's MIRROR MIRROR, but upon conclusion of this trek both Hinder and Trotman quit. The best days of the group were behind them and ONSLAUGHT would ultimately perish, with Grice and Rockett later forming the Funk Rock outfit FRANKENSTEIN, managed by producer Pete Hinton. FRANKENSTEIN comprised of the two ex-ONSLAUGHT men plus former RHODE ISLAND RED vocalist Tony Bryan, ex TOKYO ROSE bassist Bod Presley and ex-MIRROR MIRROR guitarist Alan Jordan. FRANKENSTEIN achieved little beyond supporting SAXON on their poorly attended 1993 British tour.

Steve Grimmett, on the other hand, found a great deal of success in Japan with the more traditional Hard Rock delivered by his new group LIONSHEART. Following a run of three LIONSHEART albums the singer would then would front PRIDE and SEVEN DEADLY SINS.

Rockett turned up on the HORA-KANE 1999 album 'Eternal Infinity' fronted by ex-ONSLAUGHT and subsequently PRAYING MANTIS vocalist Tony O'Hora. During 2003 O'Hora was fronting fabled 70s Glamsters SWEET and in September of 2004 joined STATETROOPER, not as a singer but as a bassist.

Greek Black Metal band THOU ART LORD included a cover version of 'Power From Hell' on their May 2005 album 'Orgia Daemonicum'. Surprisingly, ONSLAUGHT resurrected itself in 2005, announcing a touring partnership as part of the December 2005 'X-Mas' festivals in Europe ranked alongside EXODUS, OCCULT, KATAKLYSM, UNLEASHED, BEHEMOTH, and PRIMORDIAL. Joining guitarist Nige Rockett, drummer Steve Grice, vocalist Sy Keeler and bassist Jim Hinder would be guitarist Alan Jordan, ex-MIRROR MIRROR, RHODE ISLAND RED and FRANKENSTEIN. A debut gig for the rejuvenated act was put in for 25th November at their old haunt the Fleece & Firkin in Bristol.

Meantime, ex-singer TONY O'HORA issued his debut album, 'Escape Into The Sun', through the Italian Frontiers label in January 2006. Acting as guitarist and producer for the project would be Swedish Magnus Karlsson of STARBREAKER and RUSSELL ALLEN / JORN LANDE repute. On the live front, ONSLAUGHT acted as support to VENOM in the UK during March and commenced recording of a new album, entitled 'Killing Peace', in April. They would sign to Candlelight Records in June, cutting their album 'Killing Peace' at Backstage Studios in Derbyshire with former SABBAT guitarist Andy Sneap as producer the following month.

ONSLAUGHT was forced to pull out of two festival appearances, 'Metal Mania Open Air' festival in Slovenia on August 11th and the 'Brutal Assault' festival in the Czech Republic on August 12th, due to a terrorist alert in the UK. The band announced a two day "Thrash Domination" stint at Tokyo's famed Club Citta on September 16th and 17th ranked alongside DEATH ANGEL, SODOM and DRAGONLORD. A final mix down of 'Killing Peace' was conducted at Backstage Studios between October 16th and 18th.

That same month Thrashing Rage Productions put out an extremely limited release with a 10" vinyl single combining 'Power From Hell/Angels Of Death' medley recorded from the soundboard at Bristol's Colston Hall in 1987. Authorised by the band, only ten copies were pressed, each individually hand numbered with a certificate of authenticity.

Demo, (1983). Witch Hunt / Protest But Who Said You'll Survive / The Choice / Visions Of The Future / Black Horse Of Famine / Shadow Of Death / Skullcrusher / Thermonuclear Devastation / Hear The Scream / Fight For The Earth / Steel Meets Steel / Treading The Path Toward Death / Shadow Of Death (Live) / Black Horse Of Famine (Live) / Steel Meets Steel (Live) / Thermonuclear Devastation (Live) / Witch Hunt (Live) / Protest But Who Said Youll Survive (Live) / Treading The Path Toward Death (Live).

Onslaught Second Demo, (1983). Tomorrow's Zero / Deathmonger / Stone Divider / Cannibals Survived / Insects And Grass.

Onslaught, Complete Control (1983). Thermonuclear Devastation / Black Horse Of Famine / Overthrow Of The System / Rape.

Foxhole, (1984). Protest But Who Said You Survive / Visions Of The Future / Treading The Path Towards Death / An Innocent Man.

POWER FROM HELL, C.O.R. GURT 2 (1985). Damnation / Onslaught (Power From Hell) / Thermo Nuclear Devastation / Skullcrusher 1 / Lord Of Evil / Death Metal / Angels Of Death / Devil's Legion / Street Meets Steel / Skullcrusher 2 / Witch Hunt / Mighty Empress.

THE FORCE, Under One Flag FLAG 1 (1986). Let There Be Death / Metal Forces / Flight With The Beast / Demoniac / Flame Of The Antichrist / Contract In Blood / Thrash Til Death.

Let There Be Rock, Under One Flag 12FLAG 103 (1987). Let There Be Rock / Metal Forces (Live) / Onslaught (Live) / Angels Of Death (Live).

Welcome To Dying, London LONX 198 (1989) (12" single). Welcome To Dying / Atomic Punk / Nice n' Sleazy.

Shellshock, London LONX 215 (1989). Shellshock / Confused / H-Eyes.

Welcome To Dying, London LON 198 (1989) (7" single). Welcome To Dying / Nice n' Sleazy.

Let There Be Rock, London LONX 224 (1989) (12" single). Let There Be Rock / Shellshock (Live) / Metal Forces (Live).

Let There Be Rock, London LON 224 (1989) (7" single). Let There Be Rock / Shellshock (Live). Chart position: 50 UK.

IN SEARCH OF SANITY, London 828 142-2 (1989). Asylum / Shellshock / Let There Be Rock / Welcome To Dying / In Search Of Sanity / Lightning War / Blood Upon The Ice / Powerplay. Chart position: 46 UK.

Power From Hell/Angels Of Death, Thrashing Rage Productions MORT 1 (2006) (10" vinyl single. Limited edition 10 hand numbered copies). Power From Hell/Angels Of Death (Live).

KILLING PEACE, (2007). Burn / Killing Peace / Destroyer Of Worlds / Pain / Prayer For The Dead / Tested To Destruction / Twisted Jesus / Planting Seeds Of Hate / Shock 'N' Awe.

OPPRESSION

FALKENBURG, SWEDEN — *Olof Wikstrand (vocals), Tor Nyman (guitar), Joachim Thörnqvist (guitar), Fredrik Pettersson (bass), Jackob Strand (drums).*

Falkenburg's OPPRESSION grew from an earlier Punk / Hard Rock styled outfit dubbed THE OUTLAWS, centred on guitarist Tor Nyman and drummer Mattias Jakobsen, in the Summer of 1999. A change of pace ensued as members came and went, the group delving at first into Doom territory then the Gothenburg Death Metal influence being favoured. The band line up at this juncture settled on singer Johan Person, the guitar pairing of Joachim Törnqvist and Nyman, bassist Simon Nilsson with Jakobsen on the drums. However, Nilsson was to depart, swiftly followed by Person. With the recruitment of ex-AVENGING ANGEL man Fredrik Pettersson a few months later OPPRESSION's musical stance shifted into the realms of Bay Area styled Thrash Metal.

The band adopted a new frontman in Niklas Andreasson. However, founder Mattias Jakobsen opted out, being replaced by Jakob Strand of VAGINAL REPULSION and in February 2002 the band cut the opening demo 'Violence Will Dominate'. Nyman is also active with VAGINAL REPULSION whilst Pettersson operates with CARRION KIND.

OPPRESSION issued the 'T.P.A.S.' demo in March 2005. Line-up changes saw Andreasson replaced by Olof Wikstrand.

Left To Perish, Oppression (2004). As They Rot / Rise Of The Undead / Visions / Death Of Faith / Prophecy Of Darkness.

T.P.A.S., (2005). T.P.A.S. / Act Of Faith / Merciless Deception.

State Of War, (2006). State Of War / Infected Youth / Path To Consequence / Forced Into Fire.

ORIGIN BLOOD

MALMÖ, SWEDEN — *Rob Ahrling (vocals), Robin Sjöstrand (guitar), Simon Niklasson (bass), Brian Petersen (drums).*

ORIGIN BLOOD, hailing from Malmö, is fronted by Rob Ahrling of THE GLADIATOR and SPAWN OF POSSESSION. Ahrling forged the band during 1997 in league with bass player Simon Niklasson, Christian Kapusta and Björn Baumlisberger. The latter was replaced by Morten in 1998. Robin Sjöstrand, of VANITY DIES HARD, enrolled on guitar for proposed album tracks in 2001 dubbed 'La Muerte Del Arte'.

Drums would then be delegated to ex-OMINOUS man Brian Petersen. The debut album 'Mr. Jakker Daw' was recorded in 2004 at Ahrling's own Flat Pig Studios, issued that October through R.A.H.W. Production. ORIGIN BLOOD teamed up with NECROPHOBIC and RAISE HELL for a European tour beginning late September 2006.

MR. JAKKER DAW, R.A.H.W. Production (2004). Godsize / s.o.r.r.o.w. / Fading / Within / Enlightenment / To Have And To Hold / Mr. Jakker Daw / Still I Turn / Headache / The End / Without.

ORIGINAL SIN

NY, USA — *Danielle Draconis (vocals), Cynthia Taylor (guitar), Pandora Fox (bass), Darlene Destructo (drums).*

ORIGINAL SIN was an all girl Thrash band out of New York produced by 'The Lion' (a.k.a. VIRGIN STEELE's David DeFeis). The girls' album is perhaps best known for its album cover, featuring the barely clothed torso of model Jody Roxx. Vocalist Danielle Draconis (who used to sing in a band that also included her husband on drums) had met guitarist Cynthia Taylor at a VIRGIN STEELE show. The pair joined forces with bassist Pandora Fox and drummer Darlene Destructo on a band project that would blossom into ORIGINAL SIN after a furious period of writing and rehearsing.

Through the VIRGIN STEELE connection, ORIGINAL SIN were signed by the group's then label, the Canadian based Cobra Records.

The group were initially going to go under the moniker of SATAN'S DAUGHTERS, although the decision was made to eventually use the ORIGINAL SIN tag.

SIN WILL FIND YOU OUT, Cobra CL 1009 (1986). Conjuration Of The Watcher / The Curse / To The Devil A Daughter / A Slice Of Finger / Bitches From Hell / Succubus / Pandora's Box / Thunder War / Enchantress Of Death / Disease Bombs.

OSAMENTA

BUENOS AIRES, ARGENTINA — *Pietra Lopez (vocals), Ale Mininno (guitar), Mauricio Cikota (guitar), Hernan Acuña (bass), José Luis Terzaghi (drums).*

Salto, Buenos Aires Thrash Metal band dating to 1996 and founded as a trio comprising vocalist / guitarist Alejandro Mininno, bass player Adrián Mangieri with José Luis Terzaghi on drums, later adding second guitarist Martín Mastrandrea then singer Pietra López. First release would be the live 'Sueños Sin Final' demo tape, recorded at a concert on February 1st at Salón Municipal de Salto. A studio session, 'La Ira De La Tempestad', followed in 2000. OSAMENTA underwent a series of membership changes, departing members including guitarist Martín Mastrandrea plus bassists Adrián Mangieri and Sergio Balmaceda. The group self-financed a 2004 album 'Sueños Sin Final'.

OSAMENTA included their rendition of 'Black Magic' on the June 2006 Hurling Metal Records SLAYER tribute album "Al Sur Del Abismo (Tributo Argentino A Slayer)'.

Sueños Sin Final, Osamenta (1998) (Live demo). Intro / La Ira De La Tempestad / Lepra / La Ultima Palabra / Armagedon / Lagrimas De Dolor / Cuando Es Luna Llena / Toro.

La Ira De La Tempestad, Osamenta (2000) (Demo). La Ira de la Tempestad / Lepra / La Ultima Palabra / Lagrimas De Dolor / Toro / Cuando Es Luna Llena / Armagedon / Toro (Old version).

SUENOS SIN FINAL, Osamenta (2004). La Ira De La Tempestad / Placer Sin Verdad / Armageddon / Osamenta / La Ultima Palabra / Camino Al Destino / Cuando Es Luna Llena / Nacido En El Infierno / Lepra / Toro / Lagrimas De Dolor / Heridas Del Futuro / El Responso Del Debil Humano / Atardecida Soledad.

OUTBURST

TILBURG, HOLLAND — *Tjerk (vocals), Jos van der Brand (guitar), Arvid (guitar), Tijin (bass), Serge Smolders (drums).*

Tilburg Thrashers OUTBURST debuted in 1999 with the demo 'Symbols Of Brutality'. The band, aiming to create a Death Metal hybrid mixing elements of the 80s Bay Area Thrash scene with elements of the 90s Gothenburg NWoSDM movement, had been forged during 1998 by former ACROSTICHON members drummer Serge Smolders, guitarist Jos Van Der Brand and singer Michael Meeuwissen. Vocalist Tijn and bassist Tjerk Mass were added shortly after but Michael would then depart to concentrate on his priority act CRUSTACEAN. A replacement was duly found in March of 2001 in Arvid. OUTBURST supported Swedes DARKANE before recording a further demo 'Victory For A Soul'. Gigs opening for TANKARD and THE DEFACED led to a valuable appearance at the June 2002 'Ozzfest' event in Nijmegen.

2003's 'Overfiend' EP would be promoted by an inclusion on the 'No Mercy' festivals alongside DEATH ANGEL, TESTAMENT and NUCLEAR ASSAULT. Further gigs with ANTHRAX and TESTAMENT led to their inaugural US performance at the 2003 'Milwaukee Metalfest'. In November of 2003 Jos van der Brand acted as stand in guitarist for European tour dates by THE MONOLITH DEATHCULT.

The group crafted their 2004 album, initially titled 'From Hell' but switched to 'Fair And Balanced', at Double Noise studio in Tilburg with producer Jochem Jacobs during September 2004. Guesting would be TEXTURES vocalist Eric Kalsbeek on the track 'Attack Of The Overfiend' whilst CEPHALIC CARNAGE frontman Leonard Leal features on 'What The Eyes See'. The record finally emerged in June 2006 through Greek label Black Lotus Records.

Symbols Of Brutality, Outburst Promotional (1999). Symbols Of Brutality / The Bleeder / Edge Of Forever.

TIME HAS COME, Outburst (2000). Doom '99 / Right Words / The Gauntlet / Abuse / Assimilate / Borg.

Promo 2001, Loud Noise Productions (2001). Borg / Victory For A Soul.

Overfiend, Loud Noise Productions (2003). Ascension / Demonbird / Stigmata / Gladiator / Attack Of The Overfiend / Victory For A Soul / Ascension (Video).

OUTCAST

PARIS, FRANCE — *Wilfried (vocals), Guillaume (guitar), Nikos (guitar), Clément (bass), Mathieu Santin (drums).*

Paris Thrashers OUTCAST started out under the billing of OVERLANDER during 1998, this antecedent formation comprising Wilfried on lead vocals and rhythm guitar, Cédric on lead guitar, Clément on bass guitar with Mathieu on the drums. Demos were recorded but in July of 2000 the band lost their lead guitarist, finding a substitute in Romuald Herrero in October. A transition of styles from classic Heavy Metal to more of a Death-Thrash influence then prompted a name change to OUTCAST. Under this new billing the demo 'The Source Of All Creation' arrived in 2002.

In early 2004 OUTCAST inducted PSYCHOBOLIA members Guillaume and Gregory 'Gogo' on guitar. An album 'First Call / Last Warning' was projected for 2004. That July the band added a further member, the SYMBYOSIS credited Nikos on guitar. OUTCAST scored a recording deal with Manitou Music shortly afterward for the album 'First Call / Last Warning'.

FIRST CALL / LAST WARNING, Thundering Records / Manitou Music (2005).

OVERDOSE

BELO HORIZONTE, MG, BRAZIL — *B.Z. (vocals), Sergio Cichovicz (guitar), Claudio David (guitar), Eddie Weber (bass), Andre Marcio (drums).*

Belo Horizonte's OVERDOSE internationally are known for sharing their 1985 debut album 'Seculo XX' with Brazil's biggest Rock export SEPULTURA's 'Bestial Devastation' sessions. This album witnessed an OVERDOSE line-up of vocalist Bozo, guitarists Claudio David and Ricardo Dos Santos Souza, bassist Fernando Pazzini and drummer Helinho 'Helium' Eduardo. Following this outing, which sold in excess of 15'000 copies, OVERDOSE secured a placing on the 'Metal Massacre 9' compilation album.

1987's first full length album 'Conscience' found the band trimmed down to a quartet with just Claudio David handling guitars. The fourteen year old Andre Marcio would take over on the drum stool for 1989's 'You're Really Big' effort. The SEPULTURA connection was strengthened when Bozo designed the famous bones logo, first employed on the 'Arise' album.

A string of Brazilian release albums followed prior to 1994's 'Progress Of Decadence' being released in America on Fierce Recordings and Europe on Music For Nations. OVERDOSE spent the year touring America on a package bill with SKREW and SPUD MONSTERS prior to European dates including the Dynamo festival. Back home in Brazil the band undertook a headline tour before hooking up as guests to SKID ROW.

OVERDOSE were back in America touring with MERCYFUL FATE then CROWBAR to promote the 'Scars' album. The band's 1993 'Circus Of Death' album was issued in America during 1999 by Pavement Records.

In recent years OVERDOSE enlisted former SEPULTURA and THE MIST guitarist Jairo Guerez and ex ANGEL HEART bassist Gustavo Monsanto.

SECULO XX, Cogumelo (1985) (Split album with SEPULTURA). Angels Of The Apocalypse / Children Of The World / Century X.X.
CONSCIENCE, Cogumelo (1987). God Save The Metal / Messenger Of Death / Children Of The War / Save Our Hearts / Peace / Ultima Estrela / Kharma / The Day After / Rebellion / Prison Of The Conscience.
YOU'RE REALLY BIG, Cogumelo (1989). Stone Land / Nuclear Winter / Big As The Universe / Age Of Aquarius / Let Us Fly / United We'll Be One / Fight For Our Dreams.
ADDICTED TO REALITY, Cogumelo (1991). Sweet Reality / Night Child / White Clouds / Pain / Your Way / Strangers In Our Own Land / Winds Of Change / A Great Dream.
PROGRESS OF DECADENCE, Cogumelo CG004 (1992). Rio, Samba E Porrada No Morra / Street Law / Straight To The Point / Progress Of Decadence / Capitalist Way / Deep In Your Mind / Noise From Brazil / Al Uquisarrera / Farela / No Truce / Faithful Death / Stupid Generation / Zombie Factory.
CIRCUS OF DEATH, Cogumelo CG023 (1993). The Zombie Factory / Children Of War / Dead Clouds / Profit / The Healer / Violence / A Good Day To Die / Powerwish / Beyond My Bad Dreams.
SCARS, Music For Nations CDMFN 213 (1996). The Front / My Rage / Manipulated Reality / How To Pray / Scars / Still Primitive / Just Another Day / School / Last Words / Postcard From Hell / Who's Guilty??? / Out Of Control—A Fairy Tale / Nu Dos Otro E Refresco.

OVERKILL

NEW PROVIDENCE, NJ, USA — *Bobby Ellsworth (vocals), Bobby Gustafson (guitar), D.D. Vernie (bass), Sid Falck (drums).*

One of the most stoic and uncompromising Thrash Metal bands on the circuit, OVERKILL was formed in New Providence, New Jersey during 1981 by drummer Rat Skates (a.k.a. Lee Kundrat) and bassist Carlos 'D.D.' Verni after the pair had left the Hardcore Punk outfit LUBRICUNTS. OVERKILL's original incarnation was completed by ex-D.O.A. vocalist Bobby 'Blitz' Ellsworth and guitarist Dan Spitz. A second guitarist, Rich Conte, was inducted and this newly established quintet began gigging locally with a mainly cover dominated set. Spitz exited to team up with ANTHRAX and during 1983 former THE DROPOUTS man Bobby Gustafson joined the existing trio of Elsworth, Verni and Skates in time to lay down the 'Power In Black' demo. A five track blast of undiluted Metal the tape comprised 'Overkill', 'The Beast Within', 'There's No Tomorrow', 'Death Riders' and 'Raise The Dead'. As a statement of intent, OVERKILL's dedication "To all the false faggot poser wimps of the clubs. Stick this tape up your ass" made their purpose clear.

By1984 exposure generated by the demo led to an appearance of 'Feel The Fire' on Metal Blade's 'Metal Massacre V' compilation and the 'Death Rider' track included on the 'New York Metal '84' collection. Ever the opportunists, Azra Records signed the group for the release of the four track 'Overkill' EP in July 1985 before Jonny Z's Megaforce label snapped OVERKILL up for the band's full blown debut album, 1985's 'Feel The Fire' produced by Carl Canedy, drummer with THE RODS, released towards the end of the year.

Johnny Z had been a fan of OVERKILL since the release of the 'Power In Black' demo. He sold 1,500 copies of it through his New Jersey based record store Rock n' Roll Heaven' alone. The band were signed after seeing them open for ANVIL at the L'Amours club in Brooklyn, New York. Now with an album behind them, OVERKILL set about breaking out of the New York circuit, conducting nationwide concerts with MEGADETH.

The quartet arrived in Europe during the first half of 1986 opening for label mates ANTHRAX, although they were not on the bill of the British show ANTHRAX performed at the Hammersmith Palais, having already returned to the States. OVERKILL did, however, return to Europe later in the year opening for SLAYER.

The group's status rose sharply in the United States with 1987's Alex Perialis produced Taking Over album as Megaforce product was now marketed and distributed through Atlantic Records. OVERKILL even managed to force their way onto MTV screens courtesy of a video clip for the track 'In Union We Stand'. Back on European soil, OVERKILL provided backing for Helloween's tour dates. Their presence was maintained on the market with an EP release less than subtly titled 'Fuck You!', headed up by a D.O.A. cover version and bolstered by live tracks captured on tape in Cleveland. The foursome was dealt a heavy blow though when Rat Skates, a prime driving force, relinquished his position. OVERKILL persevered, drawing in substitute Mark Archibole for a few gigs before locating Sid Falck, previously of Paul Dianno's BATTLEZONE, as a permanent addition.

Although Alex Perialis reprised his role at the desk, Michael Wagener took on the mixing role for 1988's 'Under The Influence'. Opting for a change, Terry Date would handle the sonics on 1989's 'The Years Of Decay'. Musically, this record was marked by an almost epic nine minute title track whilst the punchy 'Elimination' was chosen for the video treatment. US touring, billed the "Dawn Of The Decade" dates, had Overkill packaged with TESTAMENT.

1991's 'Horrorscope', produced again by Terry Date and which included a radical re-work of EDGAR WINTER's 'Frankenstein', was to see the band in a new guise. Internal disputes had prompted the Gustafson's departure prior to recording and to plug the gap OVERKILL pulled in former FAITH OR FEAR man Merritt Gant and their erstwhile guitar technician Rob Cannavino. Meantime, Gustafson joined up with SLAYER drummer Dave Lombardo in a new act entitled GRIP INC. but his tenure would be brief. The ex-guitarist also turned up as a session player on the solitary CYCLE SLUTS FROM HELL album. OVERKILL played a brace of concerts in Mexico during August 1991 supported by MAKINA, BLACK THORN, LEPROSSY and DARKNESS. The band returned to Mexico to play a brace of back to back gigs in May 1992 supported by MAKINA and TRANSMETAL.

In the midst of touring to push 'Horrorscope', Sid Falck left the band and was superseded by M.O.D. drummer Tim Mallare. OVERKILL returned in 1993 with 'I Hear Black'. Whilst not ever falling below the metal delineator, 'I Hear Black', produced by Alex Perialis and engineered by RAVEN drummer Rob Hunter, did provide the band room to experiment. 'Spiritual Void' was picked for a video and concerts across Europe had OVERKILL sharing stages with SAVATAGE and NON-FICTION.

'W.F.O.', (Wide Fuckin' Open) recorded at the Ambient Recording Company in Stamford, Connecticut during the spring of 1994, signalled Overkill's final output for Atlantic Records. With this set of tracks the group reverted to their formative years and pumped out acerbic, unrelenting thrash. 'W.F.O.' hosted an unaccredited track entitled 'Gasoline Dream' to close out. Marketing the record was given weight by a video clip for 'Fast Junkie' and North American road work backed by JAG PANZER and MASSACRA. 'W.F.O.' hosted an unaccredited track entitled 'Gasoline Dream' to close out.

As the major labels rushed headlong into grunge, OVERKILL swiftly jumped ship to Tom Lipsky's CMC International label. A live double album, '10 Years Of Wrecking Your Neck' taken from a show in Cleveland, usefully documented the band's career to date. Initial copies hosted the long out of print 'Overkill' EP material.

OVERKILL endured a further structural challenge in 1995 as Gant withdrew into family life, later forging BLOOD AUDIO, and Cannavino swapped his guitar for the lure of motorbike racing. By the 1996 album 'The Killing Kind', OVERKILL had found themselves, due to a combination of tenacity and dogfasted refusal to compromise musically, with a huge cult following in Germany. The band now comprised Blitz, Verni and Mallare joined by guitarists Sebastian Marino and Joe Comeau. Whilst the former held six-string experience with Canadian heavyweights ANVIL, Comeau was more of a surprise, known previously not for his guitar work but as lead singer with LIEGE LORD.

'The Killing Kind' album, mixed by Chris Tsangarides, garnered numerous 'album of the month' credits selling well enough for the band to undertake extensive headlining German tours, firstly in February backed by ACCUSSER and MEGORA and again in November with ANVIL and German Hardcore band STAHLHAMMER as running mates. Ellsworth also found time in 1996 to produce a promo CD for New Jersey act DIRT CHURCH and another outside excursion had Overkill putting their distinctive stamp onto a take of JUDAS PRIEST's 'Tyrant' for the Century Media tribute collection Legends Of Metal—A Tribute To Judas Priest.

September 1997's 'From The Underground And Below' caught OVERKILL shifting gear and delivering the most ferocious record of their catalogue to date. The band's innovative approach towards incorporating low end groove into their material re-ignited interest in the band and would also directly influence other acts of the same ilk. . In May 1998 OVERKILL united with NEVERMORE, JAG PANZER and ANGEL DUST for a trek across continental Europe.

With a high impact album to promote in the USA, the band was forced to break their hectic schedule when it was learned that Bobby Blitz was suffering from a strain of facial cancer called squamous cell carcinoma. The singer thankfully made a full recovery and used this enforced period of introspection to flavour the lyrics of the band's next studio opus 'Necroshine', issued in February 1999. Marino backed out to have his position taken by Dave Linsk (a.k.a. David Polinski) of New Jersey's ANGER ON ANGER. 'Necroshine' was given vent in the live scenario with a short burst of German dates and appearances at the 'Full Force' festival and Dutch 'Dynamo' events.

Later that same year found OVERKILL treading a well worn path issuing an album of covers, dubbed 'Coverkill', the band offering their interpretations of tracks by BLACK SABBATH, JUDAS PRIEST, KISS, DEEP PURPLE and naturally MOTORHEAD's 'Overkill'. It would come as a surprise to those familiar with their music that no less than three BLACK SABBATH songs were rendered, 'Changes', 'Never Say Die' and 'Cornucopia'. Many of these tracks had been vaulted over an expanse of time, allowing the group to put down a few new recordings to have an album length product.

Throughout February 2000 OVERKILL set about laying waste to Europe once again as part of a package billing with Canadian thrashers ANNIHILATOR and Germany's DEW-SCENTED. Joe Comeau subsequently exited and joined former tour mates ANNIHILATOR. Two ex-OVERKILL men, Comeau and guitarist Sebastian Marino, would make their presence felt at the August 2000 'Wacken Open Air' festival participating in a one off LIEGE LORD reunion gig.

Now back into the rhythm, OVERKILL crafted the 2000 'Bloodletting' album as a self-production at Carriage House Studios in Stamford that summer. OVERKILL, with Joe Comeau assuming his former position as a fill-in, toured Germany in November 2000 supporting HALFORD. The unit shifted shape again towards the close of this tour as Verni was attending his pregnant wife. Enlisted was Derek Tailer of DEE SNIDER's SICKMUTHAFUCKERS. The band would put in a short burst of dates in America during late November 2001 packaged with NEVERMORE.

The 2002 line-up of OVERKILL comprised of Elsworth, Verni, Derek Tailer now on guitar, second guitarist Dave Linsk and drummer Tim Mallare. This unit cut recordings for a live DVD and album project, 'Wrecking Everything', at New Jersey's Asbury Park in March. OVERKILL headline shows in Europe during June of 2002 would see BLAZE and WICKED MYSTIC as opening acts. However, Elsworth collapsed onstage during the band's set in Nürnberg, Germany on June 27th. Apparently the singer had suffered a minor stroke but would soon make a recovery.

In January 2003 OVERKILL members guitarists Dave Linsk and Derek Tailer and drummer Tim Mallare, together with ANGER ON ANGER singer Mario, combined their talents in a brand new "old school" Thrash project band SPEED\KILL/HATE. Meantime, former OVERKILL guitarist Bobby Gustafson resurfaced in a the South Florida based band RESPONSE NEGATIVE.

The band's March 2003 album, 'Killbox 13', was notable for its delegation of desk duties to Colin Richardson, breaking a

OVERKILL

long tradition of self-production. OVERKILL toured Europe in November of 2003 with support from SEVEN WITCHES and Belgian Hardcore mongers AFTER ALL. The band allied themselves with TESTAMENT, FLOTSAM AND JETSAM and DEATH ANGEL for a 'Thrash Domination 04' Japanese tour in September of 2004. Bobby Blitz also made time to act as session guest of former HADES man DAN LORENZO's solo album of that year 'Nice Being Alone'. OVERKILL signed with Sweden's Regain Records in October to record new offering 'Relix IV'. On the 29th of that month the band put on a special show for DJ Eddie Trunk's annual Halloween party at The Hard Rock Café in New York City. For this gig DREAM THEATER man Mike Portnoy stood in on the drums. For the group's European gigs in May OVERKILL drafted former HADES and HAVOCHATE drummer Ron Lipnicki. The band's showing at the major 'Sweden Rock' festival in June saw DREAM THEATER's Mike Portnoy for the song 'Elimination'. OVERKILL then engaged in US touring, although September shows in Houston and Corpus Christi would be cancelled due to Hurricane Rita.

In February 2006 ex-OVERKILL man Joe Comeau joined Swedish Metal band TAD MOROSE as their new frontman. Another OVERKILL related project came to fruition in August as Ellsworth announced THE CURSED, a side union with ex-HADES and NON-FICTION guitarist DAN LORENZO, bassist Job the Raver from MURDER 1 and former NON-FICTION drummer Mike Cristi. This act swiftly announced a deal with Screaming Ferret Wreckords.

OVERKILL joined up with the MEGADETH headlined 'Gigantour' North American festivals in early September, sharing billing with OPETH, ARCH ENEMY, LAMB OF GOD, INTO ETERNITY, SANCTITY and THE SMASHUP.

Power In Black, (1983). Overkill / The Beast Within / There's No Tomorrow / Death Rider / Raise The Dead.

OVERKILL, Azra (1984). Rotten To The Core / Fatal If Swallowed / The Answer / Overkill.

Feel The Fire, (1984). Feel The Fire / Second Son (Live) / Kill At Command (Live).

Rotten To The Core, (1984). Rotten To The Core / Fatal If Swallowed / The Answer / Overkill.

FEEL THE FIRE, Megaforce MRI 1469 (1985). Raise The Dead / Rotten To The Core / There's No Tomorrow / Second Son / Sonic Reducer / Hammerhead / Feel The Fire / Blood And Iron / Kill At Command / Overkill.

Fuck You (Live), Under One Flag 12 FLAG 104 (1987). Fuck You / Rotten To The Core (Live) / Hammerhead (Live) / Use Your Head (Live) / Electro—Violence (Live).

TAKING OVER, Megaforce Atlantic 781 735-1 (1987). Deny The Cross / Wreckin' Crew / Fear His Name / Use Your Head / Fatal If Swallowed / Powersurge / In Union We Stand / Electro-Violence / Overkill II. Chart position: 191 USA.

Hello From The Gutter, Atlantic (1988). Hello From The Gutter / Head First.

UNDER THE INFLUENCE, Megaforce Atlantic 781 865-2 (1988). Shred / Never Say Never / Hello From The Gutter / Mad Gone World / Brainfade / Drunken Wisdom / End Of The Line / Head First / Overkill III. Chart position: 142 USA.

THE YEARS OF DECAY, Megaforce Atlantic K7 82045-2 (1989). Time To Kill / Elimination / I Hate / Nothing To Die For / Playing With Spiders—Skullcrusher / Birth Of Tension / Who Tends The Fire / The Years Of Decay / E.Vil N.Ever D.Ies. Chart position: 155 USA.

HORRORSCOPE, Megaforce East West 7567822832 (1991). Coma / Infectious / Blood Money / Thanx For Nothin' / Bare Bones / Horrorscope / New Machine / Frankenstein / Live Young, Die Free / Nice Day . . . For A Funeral / Soulitude.

I HEAR BLACK, Atlantic 756782476-2 (1993). Dreaming In Columbian / I Hear Black / World Of Hurt / Feed My Head / Shades Of Grey / Spiritual Void / Ghost Dance / Weight Of The World / Ignorance And Innocence / Undying / Just Like You. Chart position: 122 USA.

W.F.O., Atlantic 7567826302 (1994). Where It Hurts / Fast Junkie / The Wait-New High In Lows / They Eat Their Young / What's Your Problem / Under One / Supersonic Hate / R.I.P. (Undone) / Up To Zero / Bastard Nation / Gasoline Dream.

Fast Junkie, Atlantic (1994) (USA promotion release). Fast Junkie / Gasoline Dream.

10 YEARS OF WRECKING YOUR NECK-LIVE, CMC International CMC 7603 (1995). Where It Hurts / Infectious / Coma / Supersonic Hate / wrecking Crew / Powersurge / The Wait—New High In Lows / Skullcrusher / Spiritual Void / Hello From The Gutter / Anxiety / Elimination / Fast Junkie / World Of Hurt / Gasoline Dream / Rotten To The Core / Horrorscope / Under One / New Machine / Thanx For Nothin' / Bastard Nation / Fuck You. Chart position: 65 GERMANY.

THE KILLING KIND, Edel Concrete 0086502CTR (1996). Battle / God-Like / Certifiable / Burn You Down (To Ashes) / Let Me Shut That For You / Bold Face Pagan Stomp / Feeding Frenzy / The Cleansing / The Mourning After—Private Bleeding / Cold, Hard Fact. Chart position: 60 GERMANY.

The Rip n' Tear, CMC International (1997) (USA promotion release). The Rip n' Tear.

FUCK YOU AND THEN SOME, SPV 085-18722 (1997). Fuck You / Rotten To The Core (Live) / Hammerhead (Live) / Use Your Head (Live) / Electro-Violence (Live) / Fuck You (Live) / Hole In The Sky (Live) / Evil Never Dies (Live) / Rotten To The Core / Fatal If Swallowed / The Answer / Overkill.

FROM THE UNDERGROUND AND BELOW, SPV 085-18772 (1997). It Lives / I'm Alright / Genocya / Save Me / Half Past Dead / Little Bit Of Murder / Long Time Dyin' / The Promise / F.U.C.T. / The Rip n' Tear. Chart position: 80 GERMANY.

NECROSHINE, SPV CD 085-18882 (1999). Necroshine / My December / Let Us Prey / 80 Cycles / Revelation / Stone Cold Jesus / Forked Tongue / I Am Fear / Black Line / Dead Man. Chart position: 82 GERMANY.

COVERKILL, SPV 085-21542 CD (1999). Overkill / No Feelings / Hymn 43 / Changes / Space Truckin' / Deuce / Never Say Die / Death Tone / Cornucopia / Tyrant / Ain't Nothin' To Do / I'm Against It.

BLOODLETTING, SPV (2000). Thunderhead / Bleed Me / What I'm Missin' / Death Comes Out To Play / Let It Burn / I, Hurricane / Left Hand Man / Blown Away / My Name Is Pain / Can't Kill A Dead Man / We Gotta Get Out Of This Place.

WRECKING EVERYTHING, Spitfire (2002). Necroshine / Thunderhead / Evil Never Dies / Deny The Cross / I Hate / Shred / Bleed Me / Long Time Dyin' / It Lives / Battle / The Years Of Decay / In Union We Stand / Overkill.

KILL BOX 13, Eagle Rock (2003). Devil By The Tail / Damned / No Lights / The One / Crystal Clear / The Sound Of Dying / Until I Die / Struck Down / Unholy / I Rise. Chart position: 93 GERMANY.

RELIXIV, Spitfire (2005). Within Your Eyes / Love / Loaded Rack / Bats In the Belfry / A Pound Of Flesh / Keeper / Wheelz / The Mark / Play The Ace / Old School.

P.C.P.

VINEBURG, CA, USA — *Nasty Nate Clark (vocals), Jeffro Belly (guitar), Mick Thomas (bass), Brian Durham (drums).*

Southern Bay Area Thrashers P.C.P. comprising of sole surviving founder member 'Nasty' Nate Clark on vocals and bass guitar, Jefro Belly on guitar and Brian 'Bandit' Durham on drums. The group originally came together in 1994 with a line up of Nate Clark, Mike Leahy, Sam Moore and Craig Bingham, a union of erstwhile personnel from acts such as PROPHECY and INFINITY PERCENT. However, a succession of line ups eventually settled with the present trio. Brian Durham, a veteran of such acts as RINGWORM, EXCELSIOR and PADURHAM, was inducted during 1995. Guitarist Jeffro Belly joined in 1996, citing credits with SOCIETY'S PRODUCT and even THE BEVERLEY BEER BELLYS.

P.C.P. issued their debut album, 'Evilhatemotherfucker', during 2000. Bass player Mick Thomas, a former member of CONFUSED, was added in April of 2002.

Clark also operates with VENGEANCE whilst both Durham and Thomas are involved with THE DJN PROJECT.

EVILHATEMOTHERFUCKER, (2000).

P.I.T.T.

SOUTH AFRICA — *Marco (vocals), Stefan (guitar), Alex (bass), Kerryn (drums).*

A Johannesburg Thrash / Hardcore act that relocated to London in February of 2001. In South Africa P.I.T.T. have been prolifically active on the live scene and supported CRYOGENIC during October of 1998. P.I.T.T. was created in 1996 originally featuring a rhythm section of bassist Andrew and drummer Caleb. These two would leave in February of 1997. That year P.I.T.T. contributed the track 'Gathering Of Introverts' to the '13' compilation album of South African acts.

A succession of bassists followed including Steven, Bernard (who lasted two gigs), Filippo and the female four stringer Tamlyn who, upon joining in August of 1998 stuck the course for three years. January of 1999 saw the inclusion of 'Little White Room' to the Witchdoctor Records sampler 'New Breed Vol. 1'. The following year 'The Hand That Feeds' featured on 'New Breed Vol. 2' whilst 'Cage In Hell' was donated to 2002's 'New Breed Vol. 3' and Arcane Productions sampler 'Deathfest—The Art Of Extremity'.

P.I.T.T. issued two self financed albums in 2000, 'Three And A Half Years In The Making' in March, comprising of archive and live material, and 'Forced Illusion' in December.

THREE AND A HALF YEARS IN THE MAKING: A COLLECTION, WAR Records WAR002 (2000). The Hand That Feeds / Little White Room / Bulldozer Tactics (Live) / Gathering Of Introverts (Live) / The Hand That Feeds (Live) / The Dreamer / Rogue Trooper / Prison.

FORCED DISILLUSION, WAR Records WAR003 (2000). Forced Disillusion / Cage in Hell / Infernal Flames-Flames Of Power-Darkness Soothing / Chasing the Dragon / Bulldozer Tactics / Nightmare Skies / Sweetest Child / Spellbound / Mists Of Darkness-Shrouds of Darkness / What A Beautiful World / Inquisition.

PAGANIZER

SWEDEN — *Rogga Johansson (vocals), Dea (guitar), Oskar Nilsson (bass), Mattias Fiebig (drums).*

Old school Thrash / Death Metal unit PAGANIZER was assembled in Gamleby during late 1988 by DEAD SUN members vocalist Rogga Johansson and TERMINAL GRIP guitarist Dea (a.k.a. Andreas Carlsson) with BLIZZARD personnel drummer Jocke and bassist Diener. Jocke also held credits with GENITAL GRINDER. PAGANIZER's demo 'Stormfire' would later be issued as a 1998 shared album 'In Glorys Arms We Will Fall' in collusion with Singapore act ABATTORY. The band, bringing in bassist Oskar Nilsson, would follow this with a full blown debut 'Deadbanger' pressed up by the Malaysian Psychic Scream Entertainment label.

As one of his many side projects Rogga Johansson would aid Black Metal band BLODSRIT on drums. Jocke would quit PAGANIZER in 2000, being superseded by Mattias Fiebig of PORTAL, DARK RITES and BLODSRIT. The band re-grouped but a second album was held up by Malaysian censorship laws. The band decided to find another label who would consent to release the album, ending up with the Forever Underground concern for the 'Promoting Total Death' outing of June 2001.

Rogga Johansson and Diener, enlisting PORTAL guitarist Emil Koveroth and drummer Mattias Fiebig, would evolve the band into CARVE. Johansson would also operate as vocalist for DERANGED.

The band resurfaced in 2002 with the album 'Dead Unburied', recorded at Sunlight Studios with production credited to Thomas Skogsberg and mixing by DAN SWANÖ. Guesting on backing vocals would be the former GRAVE and ENTOMBED man Jörgen Sandström. PAGANIZER made a return to action in April of 2003 with the Mieszko Talarczyk produced album 'Murder Death Kill'. Founder member Dea opted out in July to prioritise his Gothic Metal band ANOTHER LIFE. He was superseded Halvarsson of BLODSRIT and PRIMITIVE SYMPHONY repute. By 2003 a new side project was on the agenda dubbed RIBSPREADER. This unite comprised Johansson, erstwhile PAGANIZER man Andreas Carlsson on guitar and the much travelled DAN SWANÖ on drums. Johansson reinforced the connection with Swanö by featuring as guest vocalist on the EDGE OF SANITY album 'Crimson II'.

PAGANIZER re-signed with Xtreem Music in 2004, entering Soundlab Studios in March with producer Mieszko Talarczyk to cut a new record. The band also donated their rendition of 'Nausea' to the AT THE GATES tribute album, 'Slaughterous Souls—A Tribute to At The Gates' released in September 2004 through Drowned Scream Records. In January of 2005 PAGANIZER announced that they had no line-up and were being "put on ice". However, in early 2005 RIBSPREADER underwent a drastic line-up overhaul, losing the services of Andreas Carlsson, Dan Swanö and Johan Berglund. The revised trio would comprise Rogga Johansson on vocals and guitar, bassist Patrik Halvarsson and drummer Mattias Fiebig, all ex-PAGANIZER members.

Promoting new album 'Carnage Junkie', mixed by Dan Swanö, PAGANIZER toured Spain and Portugal with MACHETAZO in December 2006.

Stormfire, (1998). Wardog Injection / Deathstar / Sinners Burn / The Final Command / Stormfire.

STORMFIRE, Psychic Scream (1998) (Split album with ABBATORY). Wardog Infection / Sinners Burn / Deathstar / The Final Command.

DEADBANGER, Psychic Scream Entertainment PSDL 9016 (1999). Branded By Evil / The Mask Of Evil / Deadbanger / Heads Of The Hydra / Storms To Come / Time To Burn / Sinners Burn / Into The Catacombs / Phantoms / Metal Crusade.

PROMOTING TOTAL DEATH, Forever Underground FU004 (2001). Promoting Total Death / Brutal Way To Die / Only Ashes Remain / 16 Second Massacre / At War / All Hope Is Dead / Cyclone Of Human Atrocity / Life Slips Away / Pain Has A Face.

DEAD UNBURIED, Forever Underground (2002). Even In Hell / Landscapes Made Of Human Skin / Napalm Burial / Lobotomized / Flesh Supremacy / Beyond Redemption / Procreating Death / At Night They Come / Hateconsumed.

MURDER DEATH KILL, Xtreem Music XM 006 (2003). Meateater / Mourning Life / Bleed Unto Me / Shallow Burial / Dead Souls / Crawl To The Cross / Obsessed By Flesh / Du Vaknar Som Död / Formaldehyde Dreams.

PAINSTORM

ITALY — *Ercole (vocals / guitar), Enrico (guitar), Giuseppe Maruccia (bass), Angelo Buccolieri (drums).*

Thrash Metal act PAINSTORM was created under the formative title MAGMA during 1999 by the Buccolieri brothers, vocalist / guitarist Pancrazio and drummer Angelo. The pair drafted Giuseppe Maruccia on bass, but he would soon defect. Vincenzo Valletta was recruited on guitar, but his tenure lasted just one gig. Regrouping once again the siblings pulled in Massimiliano Di Mauro for the bass position. Giuseppe Maruccia returned as Di Mauro exited. In January 2003, by now entitled PAINSTORM, the band acquired second guitarist Enrico for the 'Welcome' demo.

The band evolved further in May 2004 with the induction of guitarist Marco Serino. In July Andrea Gaeta became the new bass man.

Welcome, Painstorm (2003). Welcome To My Fucked Up World / Kill All Your Fear / Masters Of The Truth / Near The Doors Of Hell.

PAINSTRUCK

LISBON, PORTUGAL — *Nuno Loureiro (vocals / guitar), Ivo Martins (guitar), João Madeira (bass), Paulo Lafaia (drums).*

Lisbon Death-Thrashers PAINSTRUCK, assembled in August 1997 as BREED MACHINE, include personnel from MERCILESS DEATH, EXILED, SUBLEVEL, DISAFFECTED, MORTIFY, GROG and SQUAD. The founding members counted vocalist / guitarist Nuno Loureiro, guitarist Ricardo Correia, bass player Alexandre Afonso and Paulo Lafaia on drums.

PAINSTRUCK's first album 'Aggressive Ways To Pacify', produced by Luís Barros of TARANTULA at Rec n' Roll studios, was recorded in 1999. It finally emerged on Paranoid Records in June 2001. In the interim both Correira and Afonso departed, being substituted by GROG guitarist Ivo Martins and the DESIRE, WINTER WHISPERS and ARCANE WISDOM credited Ricardo Veloso on bass. Live work to support the record saw valuable supports to BIOHAZARD and an appearance at the SLIPKNOT and DIMMU BORGIR headlined 'Ermal' festival.

Second effort 'A Whole New Perception', recorded at Floyd Studios, arrived in 2002. João Madeira replaced Veloso in mid 2004.

AGGRESSIVE WAYS TO PACIFY, Paranoid (2001). Intro / Warcry / Easy Shot / Dwelling Demon / Wrath Of God / Acidic Essence / Wolves Pack / Scorching Skin / Spit Of Distrust / Into My Life / Paranoid / Misled Nation / F.O.D.E.S. / Power Of The Written Word.
A WHOLE NEW PERCEPTION, Paranoid (2002). A Whole New Perception / Painstruck / Pain Beyond / In Us You Live / Hate Is The Word ... / You Are One Step Ahead / Believe The Word / Pierce The Wing / F.P.R.S. / Send In The Crows / Letting Out Loud / Breath In, Killing Time / Tons Of Chances.

PANDEMONIC

VÄSBY, SWEDEN — *Mikael Ullenius (vocals), Mikael Jakobsson (guitar), Linus Ekström (guitar), Markus Jonsson (drums).*

A Väsby based second wave Thrash act convened in the spring of 1998. PANDEMONIC was created by a collection of Death Metal veterans including former INTERNAL DECAY and AD INFINITUM guitarist Micke Jacobsson and ex-SOILS OF FATE and SORG drummer Nicke Karlsson. This duo would be joined by singer Micke Ullenius and former AD INFINITUM bassist Janne 'De Sade' Sokura, the latter making way for Harry Virtanen of DEFORMITY pedigree.

PANDEMONIC issued an opening demo 'Lycanthropy'. It would be followed up on by the werewolf themed 2000 album 'The Authors Of Nightfear'.

The band would lose Karlsson bringing in 'Mackan' as replacement. Before long though Marcus Jonsson, a veteran of MORTIFER, FLAGELLATION and GENOCRUSH FEROX, was announced as the man on the drum stool. Between 2002 and 2003 Eric Gjerdrum (a.k.a. Eric Young), drummer of CRASHDÏET, played guitar in PANDEMONIC and later bass as a live session musician as Virtanen exited due to quoted musical differences. Demo product included the 2002 'Ravenous' session and 'The Art Of Hunting' in 2003.

In October 2003 bassist Harry Virtanen forged a union with ex-INCENDIARY guitarist Pontus Arvidson to found Stockholm Thrash act CHAINSAW. Virtanen also operated side project VÖRGUS. In 2004 Linus Ekström, ex-SIEBENBÜRGEN, joined PANDEMONIC on lead guitar.

Lycanthropy, (1999). Resurgence / The Hunter / Sanguine Lust.
THE AUTHORS OF NIGHTFEAR, W.W.M. Music PAN001 (2000). The Hunter / Wolfman's Lullaby / Changeling Eve / Authors Of Nightfear / The Forging Of A Beast / Clad In Wolven Shape / The Coming Of Dawn / Lycanthropic Siege.
Ravenous, (2002). Cursed / Atrocities / The Scent Of Fear / The Tower Bell / Windwalker.
The Art Of Hunting, (2003). Ravenous / The Lycanthrope Within / 1764 (The Year Of Gevaudan) / The Art Of Hunting.

PANTERA

ARLINGTON, TX, USA — *Phil Anselmo (vocals), Darrell Abbott (guitar), Rex Brown (bass), Vinnie Paul (drums).*

Highly influential Metal band. The Arlington based band would, at a mid point in their career, adopt an aggressive new musical direction of hardened Thrash which would see PANTERA becoming one of the major artists in the Metal field, enjoying Platinum sales status and a number 1 Billboard album. Such was their innovation that they would create a whole new genre in the Heavy Metal field and influence a plethora of artists that came in their wake.

Whilst the mainstream discovered PANTERA in 1990, on the back of the 'Cowboys From Hell' album, it came as a surprise to many that the group had been operational, and successful, for many years prior, holding major status in Texas and boasting strong cult appeal internationally. The band's former musical stance and image was wildly different to that portrayed from 1990 onwards and initially the record company attempted to bury these past achievements—to no avail.

PANTERA (Spanish for 'Panther') started life in 1981 on the Texan club scene performing cover sets of VAN HALEN and KISS songs. Founded in 11th grade, the very first PANTERA line-up comprised singer Donnie Hart, guitarists Darrell Abbott and Terry Lee Glaze, bassist Tommy Bradford and drummer Vinnie Paul. By 1982 Hart had exited, with Glaze switching from guitar to the lead vocal role, and Bradford had been superseded by Rex Brown.

Diamond Darrell's enthusiasm to pick up the guitar came from having witnessed Ace Frehley and he proudly sport an ACE FREHLEY tattoo and KISS emblazoned guitars. PANTERA quickly became cult favourites on the underground metal scene with fans being constantly bemused by the band's undoubted quality against a series of truly horrendous amateur album covers and PANTERA's inability to break into the big time outside of dominating Texas, Oklahoma and Louisiana.

Nevertheless, PANTERA soon became adopted sons on their home turf, supporting the likes of STRYPER, DOKKEN and QUIET RIOT promoting debut album 'Metal Magic' in 1983. Glaze was to change his surname to Lee for the 1984 'Projects In The Jungle' album, a record which captured PANTERA drifting away from the more obvious melodic influences.

'I Am The Night', emerging in 1985 and again produced by The Eldn' (in reality Darrell and Vinnie's father Jerry) at Pantego Studios, boosted the band's profile scoring many maximum marks in the world's metal press finding the band in a heavier mood. PANTERA were still suffering from poor distribution, many fans being forced to pay extortionate import prices for the album, consequently the album struggled to sell 25'000 copies.

Soon after 'I Am The Night's release Lee split from the band to form LORD TRACY (originally called TRACI LORDS) and PANTERA retreated into the shadows. A series of vocalists followed including Matt L'Amour, who later joined DIAMOND, and David Peacock. These liaisons were short-lived however and PANTERA eventually re-emerged fronted by Louisiana native and ex-SAMHAIN and RAZORWHITE singer Phil Anselmo, the new singer's latter act also having in their ranks future CROWBAR man Matt Thomas and FALL FROM GRACE's Wil Buras.

Despite finding their frontman, PANTERA were still blighted by problems. Their new record label Gold Mountain, tipped off about the band's prowess by KEEL guitarist MARC FERRARI, having met PANTERA when KEEL had played in Dallas with LOUDNESS during 1985, trying to manoeuvre the band into commercial territory. Undaunted and unconvinced, PANTERA recorded their heaviest album to date, 'Power Metal', and negotiated for a release on their own Metal Magic label. KEEL guitarist MARC FERRARI guested on the album with PANTERA returning the favour by recording Ferrari's 'Proud To Be Loud'. Although 1988's 'Power Metal' was undoubtedly a much harder record than previous attempts it was nothing compared to what was to come . . .

PANTERA drew back away from the limelight, during which time the band came close to splintering. Darrell had auditioned for the vacant guitar position in MEGADETH and was reportedly offered the post. However, Darrell insisted that Vinnie was part of the package and MEGADETH, who already had a drummer in Nick Menza, backed off, recruiting MARTY FRIEDMAN instead.

Legend has it that Atco Records A&R rep Mark Ross discovered the band almost by chance, stranded in Texas due to the ravages of Hurricane Hugo. Having caught the band live and realising the significant fan base PANTERA already held, negotiations with Atco Records ensued and the musicians also placed their faith in new management, contracting with Walter O'Brien at Concrete Inc. in New York. Upon their re-emergence and PANTERA surprised many with a new look, Phil Anselmo now sporting a close shorn haircut and a patchwork of tattoos, and a radical change in direction. PANTERA's 'Cowboys From Hell' album, recorded at the band's own Pantego Sound Studios and delivered in July 1990, offered bludgeoning Hardcore riffs, the solid intensity of their new songs burying any comparisons to their more melodic predecessors.

The intensity of tracks such as 'Primal Concrete Sledge' and 'Cemetery Gates' forced a keen impression on extreme music fans eager to find a replacement for the waning Thrash movement. In particular, Diamond Darrell, as he was then still known, had single-handedly re-invented the art of Metal guitar playing, his unorthodox, yet highly rhythmic, stacking of non-conformist notes and liberal use of signature pinch harmonics engaging a whole new generation of budding six-stringers. Certainly transitional, Phil Anselmo not yet having totally shed his former traditional vocal stylings, 'Cowboys From Hell' projected the band's new focus to such a degree there could be no turning back. MTV took to the group too, giving regular rotation to promotional videos for 'Cowboys From Hell', 'Cemetery Gates' and 'Psycho Holiday'. The "re-debut" had put PANTERA into a whole new league.

The 'Cowboys From Hell' tour opened in North America with a bill that saw the Texans sharing the stage with EXODUS and SUICIDAL TENDENCIES. Later dates had PANTERA alongside MIND OVER FOUR and PRONG. In the midst of a Canadian leg of dates, JUDAS PRIEST vocalist Rob Halford joined the band onstage for versions of JUDAS PRIEST's 'Grinder' and 'Metal Gods', a union that was to aid PANTERA later the same year as they performed their first ever European shows in 1991 opening for the British metal Gods. Bearing in mind JUDAS PRIEST's status future events became quite bizarre as PRIEST frontman Rob Halford seemingly metamorphosised into an Anselmo clone both vocally and image wise for his subsequent FIGHT project. Road work would be topped by an appearance at the Tushino Air Field in Moscow on September 28th 1991, featuring on a bill alongside AC/DC, METALLICA and the BLACK CROWES to a crowd of over half a million people.

Two and a half years on the road had convinced PANTERA to pursue their new found harder direction with even more vigour and the resulting February 1992 album, 'Vulgar Display Of Power', silenced all critics as it broke the band world-wide charting in both Britain, at number 64, and America, at number 44. These initial chart entries would prove deceptive though, as once the PANTERA machine had started to roll inexorably onward 'Vulgar Display Of Power's sales proved steady and strong for many years to come. The musicians also renewed their association with Rob Halford, backing him on a one off promotional single, 'Light Comes Out Of Black', featured on the soundtrack to the 'Buffy The Vampire Slayer' movie.

PANTERA were by now openly opinionating their desire to exceed any aural ferocity that had gone before. Many rock fans believed the band to have lost the essence of song-writing in their hunt for extremity but many, many more newer converts lapped it up. Quite remarkably, the band were confessing to recording albums almost spontaneously whilst under the influence. Whatever formula they had in fact adopted, PANTERA had turned the Metal world on its head. Whilst a succession of singles, 'Walk', 'This Love' and 'Mouth For War', blazed across radio and MTV, a gruelling schedule of concerts across the globe found the act sharing stages with MEGADETH on their 'Countdown To Extinction' dates, WHITE ZOMBIE, SACRED REICH, SKID ROW, and SOUNDGARDEN. PANTERA hit Japan for the first time in July 1992 and played the IRON MAIDEN and BLACK SABBATH headlined 'Monsters of Rock' festival in Italy on September 12th.

Incredibly for a record of such ferocity 'Far Beyond Driven', launched in March 1994 complete with a cover of BLACK SABBATH's 'Planet Caravan', entered at the hallowed number 1 position in the American Billboard album charts. PANTERA were quick to fling themselves headlong into a bout of touring with guests CROWBAR. South American shows were conducted to near ecstatic sold out crowds, dates in Argentina had ANIMAL and LETHAL as openers and in Brazil DR. SIN were the guests. July saw a strengthening of the touring package as PANTERA were now topping a bill comprising of SEPULTURA and BIOHAZARD before a June 4th Castle Donington 'Monsters Of Rock' performance.

The Donington show, headlined by AEROSMITH, was slightly marred by an ugly incident the night before at Nottingham's Rock City club where both Darrell and Vinnie were involved in altercations with journalists Morat of 'Kerrang!' and Paul Rees of 'Raw' publications respectively, the latter due to the drummer having once been portrayed by the magazine in cartoon form as Obelisk, Asterix The Gaul's stocky partner.

The May 1994 single '5 Minutes Alone' came backed with a B side cover version of POISON IDEA's 'The Badge', the song originally having been cut for the band's contribution to 'The Crow' movie soundtrack. Back on the road, UK dates that September saw support coming from DOWNSET. By the close of the global trek, with final American shows having PRONG as openers, the band had put in some 90 dates.

1995 began with a continuation of live work but by March PANTERA had landed themselves in trouble when at a Canadian gig in Montreal a radio DJ perceived some of Anselmo's onstage raps to be of a racist tone. Anselmo was forced into issuing a public retraction purporting that his drunken remarks were off the cuff and ill advised.

1995 also saw the release of Anselmo's DOWN knockabout act's album 'Nola'. The front man had recorded a batch of brutal songs in some PANTERA downtime together with friends Pepper Keenan from CORROSION OF CONFORMITY, CROWBAR's Kirk Windstein and Todd Strange and EYEHATEGOD's Jimmy Bower. Although originally assembled as a jam session between friends, DOWN's debut rapidly gained acclaimed cult status. The advent of DOWN signalled a stream of extracurricular projects launched by the singer.

PANTERA bounced back in April 1996 with 'The Great Southern Trendkill', the music hewn out with Terry Date at Chasin Jason Studios in Dalworthington Gardens, Texas whilst Anselmo put his vocals down at Nothing Studios in New Orleans. Additional "screams" came courtesy of ANAL CUNT's notorious mentor Seth Putnam. A more introspective, moodier affair than its predecessors the record caught some flak from some reviewers but garnered no such qualms from hardened fans. Taking the Metal to the masses once again, PANTERA launched into a US tour in August 1996 backed up by WHITE ZOMBIE and DEFTONES. As the live campaign rolled into 1997 the band then invited CLUTCH and SOILENT GREEN along for the ride.

1997 proved significant as 'Cowboys From Hell', 'Vulgar Display Of Power' and 'Far Beyond driven' all attained platinum sales status in the USA for one million sales each. That July the concert recordings 'Live 101 Proof', hosting two studio cuts 'Where You Come From' and 'I Can't Hide', arrived in stores, hitting number 15 in the USA. However, with rumoured dissent between factions within the band being seized upon by the media, PANTERA then took a lengthy spell away from the limelight.

Anselmo, billing himself as 'Anton Crowley' would also turn up as guitarist for the reformed NECROPHAGIA for the 1999 'Holocausto De La Morte' album. PANTERA's audio output that year would be restricted to a raucous rendition of TED NUGENT's seminal 'Cat Scratch Fever' included on the 'Detroit Rock City' movie soundtrack. Another cover the following year came with their take on BLACK SABBATH's 'Electric Funeral' on the tribute collection 'Nativity In Black II'. 2000 found Anselmo involved in the Black Metal 'star' side project EIBON. With a low key track inclusion on the 'Moonfog 2000' compilation album EIBON consisted of SATYRICON's Satyr Wongraven, DARKTHRONE's Fenriz, Maniac of MAYHEM and NECROPHAGIA's Killjoy.

PANTERA's 'Reinventing The Steel' album hit home in March 2000. With two singles being spun off, 'Goddamn Electric' and the Grammy Nominated 'Revolution Is My Name', the record fared well, impacting on the Billboard charts at number 4. 'Goddamn Electric' was of note due to its inclusion of a guest guitar solo dropped in by Kerry King of SLAYER, actually recorded onto a portable tape machine backstage at a Dallas 'Ozzfest' stop. Unfortunately, the anthem of brotherhood and longevity intended by album track 'We'll Grind That Axe For A Long Time' was to prove ill fated. PANTERA's 2000 European tour found SATYRICON acting as openers. American dates were curtailed when Anselmo broke two ribs at an early gig.

Another of Anselmo's 'Anton Crowley' side projects the Black Metal act VIKING CROWN also issued the 'Innocence From Hell' album the same year. A left of field diversion, dubbed REBEL MEETS REBEL, found Vinnie Paul, Dimebag Darrell and Rex Brown working with Country & Western musician DAVID ALLAN COE.

Following a batch of American headliners winding up in Anchorage, Alaska the band struck out to Seoul in Korea prior to Australasian gigs in May supported by CORROSION OF CONFORMITY and Australian act SEGRESSION. Not content to rest there, PANTERA assembled a billing entitled 'Extreme Steel' for a further American leg strongly bolstered by MORBID ANGEL, SLAYER, STATIC X and SKRAPE. However, European festival billings, dubbed the 'Tattoo The Planet' dates originally in alliance with SLAYER, BIOHAZARD, VISION OF DISORDER and STATIC X, were far from trouble free. Following the September 11th terrorist attacks PANTERA pulled out of the tour leaving SLAYER to remain behind as headliners.

Toward the close of the year Anselmo seemingly took his passion for side ventures into overdrive declaring a further two bands to his ever lengthening list of side projects. SOUTHERN ISOLATION, which featured Anselmo's girlfriend Stephanie Opal as lead vocalist, saw Anselmo acting as guitarist. The band was rounded out by CHRIST INVERSION keyboard player Ross Karpelman, Kevin Bond of CHRIST INVERSION, CROWBAR and SUPERJOINT RITUAL on bass guitar and Sid Montz on drums. A four track EP was issued in October 2001 on the Baphomet label. Anselmo also announced was another collaboration with Killjoy of NECROPHAGIA billed as ENOCH. This band also boasting the inclusion of Mirai from cult Japanese Black Metal band SIGH.

Vinnie Paul and Dimebag Darrell would pursue side activities too, although of a rather unexpected nature, as their ongoing affiliation with Country & Western artist DAVID COE ALLEN morphed into a Southern Rock styled venture billed as GASOLINE. It would also be discovered that Darrell had been in discussions with erstwhile ALICE IN CHAINS guitarist JERRY CANTRELL, NICKELBACK vocalist / guitarist Chad Kroeger and DEFAULT frontman Dallas Smith in regard to setting up a proposed band union.

Anselmo's DOWN project would resurface during 2002 touting a new album 'Down II: Bustle In Your Hedgerow'. Another of the singer's endeavours, SUPERJOINT RITUAL, would also announce an album 'Use Once And Destroy'. This band being made up bassist Hank Williams III, EYEHATEGOD guitarist / DOWN drummer Jimmy Bower, ex-CROWBAR guitarist Kevin Bond and drummer Joseph Fazzio of STRESSBALL.

During mid December it would be revealed that Dimebag Darrell had teamed up with KID ROCK and NICKELBACK's Chad Kroeger to record a cover version of ELTON JOHN's raucous 70s hit 'Saturday Night's Alright (For Fighting)'. Yet another PANTERA related project was unveiled in January 2003 as guitarist Dimebag Darrell and drummer Vinnie Paul united with DIESEL MACHINE and ex-HALFORD guitarist Patrick Lachman, taking on a lead vocal role, and erstwhile JERRY CANTRELL guitarist Sean Matthews as bassist in a project band entitled NEW FOUND POWER. By October Matthews was out of the project, which had taken on the new guise of DAMAGEPLAN. The debut album, 'New Found Power', shifted just under 45,000 copies in its first week of US sales to land at number 38 in the Billboard album charts.

Throughout 2004 Anselmo, promoting his SUPERJOINT RITUAL project and the DAMAGEPLAN members played out a very public, verbal sparring match. August saw the Recording Industry Association of America certifying the 1992 'Vulgar Display Of Power' album with double platinum status in recognition of two million US sales.

Despite ongoing bitter words between the SUPERJOINT RITUAL and DAMAGEPLAN camps, fans detected a cooling of tempers in the latter half of 2004, prompting renewed signals of a possible PANTERA reunion in the future. Tragically though, such hopes were dashed when the PANTERA family was struck the heaviest of blows. Upon closing their 2004 dates in December DAMAGEPLAN was set to round off their touring schedule with a set of headline gigs. However, on 8th December tragedy struck the band. Just as the band started their set with the song 'New Found Power' at the Alrosa Villa club in Columbus, Ohio a gunman, 23 year old Nathan Gale, got onto the stage and shot guitarist Dimebag Darrell with a Beretta 9 mm semiautomatic handgun a number of times at close range. Darrell was killed and the assailant also shot dead the band's technician Jeff Thompson, Erin Halk, 29, a club employee and fan Nathan Bray, 23. Two others were injured, one critically, Chris Paluska, the band's tour manager, and John Brooks, a drum technician. Having taken a further person hostage the shooter was himself killed by Columbus Police Officer James D. Niggemeyer.

Dimebag would have one of the most Rock n' Roll funerals to date. Not only was the guitarist buried in a KISS casket, donated at his family's request by GENE SIMMONS, but his coffin was filled with memorabilia from friends and bands including a Charvel guitar given for the occasion by Eddie Van Halen. BLACK LABEL SOCIETY would be played at the service and JERRY CANTRELL and Mike Inez from ALICE IN CHAINS along with Pat Lachman played a short acoustic set. Speeches came from ZAKK WYLDE, Rex Brown, Charlie Benante of ANTHRAX and Eddie Van Halen. A public memorial service, attended by thousands of fans, was held at the Arlington Convention Center. Significantly, Phil Anselmo was not invited to attend.

On 5th January 2005 Finland's Metal community gathered at Helsinki's Rock 'n' Roll Station to pay homage by forming up a one off PANTERA tribute band DIMEN NIMEEN ("In Dime's Name!"). Musicians featured in this collective included

CHILDREN OF BODOM's Alexi Laiho and Roope Latvala, Atte Sarkima of AJATTARA and VERENPISARA, Tony Jelencovich from TRANSPORT LEAGUE, Petteri Hirvanen and Nicke of MONSTERBALL, Toni, Pete, Kride and Jukkis of NORTHER and Nico, Euge and OJ from GODSPLAGUE amongst many others.

On the 23rd February, a special show at Chicago's Aragon Ballroom was organised to cover bereavement costs for the family of DAMAGEPLAN security guard Jeffrey "Mayhem" Thompson and medical expenses for injured DAMAGEPLAN crew members John "Kat" Brooks and Chris Paluska. Those participating included SOIL, who covered DAMAGEPLAN's 'Save Me' and DROWNING POOL, whose set included a rendition of PANTERA's 'Message In Blood'. The closing sets featured ANTHRAX and DISTURBED, the former opening their show with 'Fucking Hostile' before delivering a take of 'A New Level' with Vinnie Paul and Pat Lachman, whilst DISTURBED took on PANTERA's 'Walk' featuring Vinnie Paul.

The drummer also joined BLACK LABEL SOCIETY on stage at the WAAF Indoor Beach Party on 9th April at the Tsongas Arena in Lowell, Massachusetts. Vinnie stepped up once more on 17th April for the song 'Suicide Messiah' during their performance at the House of Blues in Orlando, Florida and, naturally, PANTERA's hometown of Dallas.

Phil Anselmo, having virtually retired from public view in the wake of Dimebag's murder, finally broke his silence, guesting as fill in guitarist for EYEHATEGOD's 15th August 2005 gig at New York's famous CBGB's club in New York City. Meantime, fans of Dimebag would learn that previously unheard guitar work was to be included on NICKELBACK's album 'All The Right Reasons' in the track 'Side Of A Bullet', composed shortly after the guitarist was killed. Not only did vocalist Chad Kroeger's lyrics deal directly with the loss of his friend but Vinnie Paul had donated unused guitar solo recordings, from the PANTERA albums 'Vulgar Display Of Power' and 'Far Beyond Driven' for use as the song's solo.

That same month a group of Italian Metal bands compiled 'This Love—A Tribute To Dimebag'. Featured artists included BY THE GRIEF 'Strength Beyond Strength', ATOMIC ANTS 'Mouth For War', SHELTER OF LEECH '5 Minute Alone', ELEKTRIK[H]ATE 'Cowboys From Hell', HAPAX 'Walk', DAY1DAY 'Cemetery Gates', SOWN 'Suicide Note (Southern Version)', ADDICTION CREW 'This Love', SHATTERED 'War Nerve', REMORSE 'Domination', IMODIUM 'Rise', SUFFERHEAD 'Fucking Hostile', ORIENT EXPRESS 'Planet Caravan' and EVILGROOVE with 'Suicide Note (Lysergik Version)'.

Vinnie Paul announced the formation of Big Vin Records in November, the first release on this new imprint, with distribution going through Fontana, being the REBEL MEETS REBEL project.

Phil Anselmo marked his return to public on a March 10th concert for VH1 Classic's 'Decades Rock Live!' tribute to HEART at the Trump Taj Mahal in Atlantic City, performing with a re-united ALICE IN CHAINS. During August 2006 it was revealed that Vinnie Paul had teamed up with members of MUDVAYNE and NOTHINGFACE in a brand new project. This studio unit involved MUDVAYNE's vocalist Chad Gray and guitarist Greg Tribbett plus NOTHINGFACE's guitarist Tom Maxwell and bass player Jerry Montano. In October this unit, having commenced recording for its debut, was branded HELLYEAH.

METAL MAGIC, Metal Magic MMR 1283 (1983). Ride My Rocket / I'll Be Alright / Tell Me If You Want It / Latest Lover / Biggest Part Of Me / Metal Magic / Widowmaker / Nothin' On (But The Radio) / Sad Lover / Rock Out!

PROJECTS IN THE JUNGLE, Metal Magic MMR 1984 (1984). Over Tonite / Out For Blood / Blue Lite Turnin' Red / Like Fire / In Over My Head / Projects In The Jungle / Heavy Metal Rules! / Only A Heartbeat Away / Killers / Takin' My Life.

I AM THE NIGHT, Metal Magic MMR 1985 (1985). Hot And Heavy / I Am The Night / Onward We Rock / D.G.T.T.M. / Daughters Of The Queen / Down Below / Come-On Eyes / Right On The Edge / Valhalla / Forever Tonight.

POWER METAL, Metal Magic MMR 1988 (1988). Rock The World / Power Metal / We'll Meet Again / Over And Out / Proud To Be Loud / Down Below / Death Trap / Hard Ride / Burnnn! / P.S.T. 88.

COWBOYS FROM HELL, East West 7567 91372-2 (1990). Cowboys From Hell / Primal Concrete Sledge / Psycho Holiday / Heresy / Cemetery Gates / Domination / Shattered / Clash With Reality / Medicine Man / Message In Blood / The Sleep / The Art Of Shredding.

Mouth For War, Atco A 5845CD (1992). Mouth For War / Rise / Cowboys From Hell / Heresy.

A NOT SO VULGAR DISPLAY OF POWER, East West PRCD4538 (1992) (US promotion release). Mouth For War / Walk / This Love / No Good Attack The Radical / Live In A Hole / By Demons Be Driven / Hollow.

Mouth For War, Atco A 5845 (1992) (7" single). Mouth For War / Rise. Chart position: 73 UK.

Mouth For War, Atco A 5845T (1992) (12" single). Mouth For War / Mouth For War (Superloud mix) / Domination / Primal Concrete Sledge.

VULGAR DISPLAY OF POWER, Atco 7567 91782-2 (1992). Mouth For War / New Level / Walk / Fucking Hostile / This Love / Rise / No Good For No One / Live In A Hole / Regular People / By Demons Be Driven / Hollow. Chart positions: 44 USA, 64 UK.

Walk, Atco B 6076CDX (1993) (CD single). Walk / No Good (Attack The Radical) / A New Level / Walk (Extended version).

Walk, Atco B 6076T (1993) (12' single). Walk / Cowboys From Hell / Psycho Holiday (Live). Chart position: 34 UK.

Walk, Atco B 6076CD (1993) (CD single). Walk / Fucking Hostile / By Demons Be Driven.

Walk EP, East West 7567922772 (1994). Walk (Cervical edit) / Fucking Hostile (Biomechanical mix) / By Demons Be Driven (Biomechanical mix) / Walk (Cervical dub extended) / Cowboys From Hell (Live) / Heresy (Live).

I'm Broken, Atco B 5932CD3 (1994) (CD single). I'm Broken / Cowboys From Hell (Live) / Psycho Holiday (Live).

Planet Caravan, Atco A 5836CD2 (1994) (CD single). Planet Caravan / The Badge / Domination (Live) / Hollow (Live).

Planet Caravan, Atco A 5836CD (1994) (CD single). Planet Caravan / The Badge / New Level (Live) / Becoming (Live).

Planet Caravan, Atco A 5836T (1994) (12" single). Planet Caravan / The Badge / Cowboys From Hell (Live) / Heresy (Live).

5 Minutes Alone, Atlantic A 8293 (1994) (7" white vinyl single). 5 Minutes Alone / Badge.

Alive And Hostile EP, East West 7567924622 (1994). Domination / Primal Concrete Sledge / Cowboys From Hell / Heresy / Psycho Holiday.

5 Minutes Alone, East West 7567958932 (1994). 5 Minutes Alone / The Badges / Cemetery Gates.

I'm Broken, East West B5932CD1 (1994). I'm Broken / Slaughtered / Domination (Live) / Primal Concrete Sledge (Live).

Planet Caravan, Atco A 5836 (1994) (7" single). Planet Caravan / 5 Minutes Alone. Chart position: 26 UK.

I'm Broken, Atco B 5932T (1994) (12" single). I'm Broken / Slaughtered. Chart position: 19 UK.

I'm Broken, Atco B 5932CD2 (1994) (CD single). I'm Broken / Domination (Live) / Primal Concrete Sledge.

I'm Broken, Atco B 5932X (1994). I'm Broken / Walk (Cervical edit) / Fuckin' Hostile.

FAR BEYOND DRIVEN, Atco 7567 92302-2 (1994). Strength Beyond Strength / Becoming / 5 Minutes Alone / I'm Broken / Good Friends And A Bottle Of Pils / Hard Lines, Sunken Cheeks / Slaughtered / 25 Years / Shedding Skin / Use My Third Arm / Throes Of Rejection / Planet Caravan. Chart positions: 1 USA, 3 UK, 14 NEW ZEALAND.

THE GREAT SOUTHERN TRENDKILL, East West 7559 61998-2 (1996) (Australasian tour edition). The Great Southern Trendkill / War Nerve / Drag The Waters / 10's / 13 Steps To Nowhere / Suicide Note Part I / Suicide Note Part II / Living Through Me (Hell's Wrath) / Floods / The Underground In America / (Reprise) Sandblasted Skin / Suicide Note Part I / Suicide Note Part II / War Nerve / New Level / Walk / 13 Steps To Nowhere / Mouth For War / Becoming / 5 Minutes Alone / Fucking Hostile / This Love / Primal Concrete Sledge / Planet Caravan / Cowboys From Hell / Domination.

THE GREAT SOUTHERN TRENDKILL, Atco 7559 61908-2 (1996). The Great Southern Trendkill / War Nerve / Drag The Waters / 10's / 13 Steps To Nowhere / Suicide Note (Part 1) / Suicide Note (Part 2) / Living Through Me (Hell's Wrath) / Floods / The Underground In America / (Reprise) Sandblasted Skin. Chart positions: 4 USA, 5 NEW ZEALAND, 17 UK.

101 Proof, East West PRCD-9868-2 (1997) (US promotion release). Cemetery Gates (Live) / I'm Broken (Live) / Cowboys From Hell (Live).

OFFICIAL LIVE 101 PROOF, Atco 7559 62068-2 (1997). New Level / Walk / Becoming / 5 Minutes Alone / Sandblasted Skin / Suicide Note Pt. 2 / War Nerve / Strength Beyond Strength / Doom-Hollow / This Love / I'm Broken / Cowboys From Hell / Cemetery Gates / Hostile / Where You Come From / I Can't Hide. Chart positions: 15 USA, 19 NEW ZEALAND, 24 FRANCE, 32 SWEDEN, 54 UK.

REINVENTING THE STEEL, East West 62451 (2000). Hell Bound / Goddamn Electric / Yesterday Don't Mean Shit / You've Got To Belong To It / Revolution Is My Name / Death Rattle / We'll Grind That Axe For A Long Time / Up Lift / It Makes Them Disappear / I'll Cast A Shadow. Chart positions: 4 USA, 8 CANADA, 10 NEW ZEALAND, 21 FRANCE, 27 SWEDEN.

PANZER

SÃO PAULO, SP, BRAZIL — *Élcio Cruz (vocals), André Pars (guitar), Jan Leonardi (bass), Edson Graseffi (drums).*

Thrash Metal act PANZER was initially founded in São Paulo as a trio during 1991 but had collapsed a few years later. The founding roster of musicians comprised ex-HEFÉSTOS vocalist / bassist Paulo Graseffi, guitarist Edson Biza and drummer Edson Graseffi, also a former HEFÉSTOS member. Demos were recorded but in 1995 a line-up change saw the introduction of new guitar player André Pars for recording of a track included on the compilation album 'Electric Tribes Vol. II' through Fat Monkey Records.

The name was resurrected in 1998, bringing in new singer Élcio Cruz and bassist Jan Leonardi, for recording of the album 'Inside', which featured cover versions of both JUDAS PRIEST's 'Nightcrawler' and the KISS staple 'Detroit Rock City'. The JUDAS PRIEST track would also show up on the compilation 'The Loudest Times—A Tribute To 80's Metal' issued in America by the ProgArt label. A fluidity then hit PANZER, with brief memberships held by bassists Fabiano Menon and Denis Grudenheiddt.

PANZER followed the debut with 'The Strongest' in 2001 for Spiral Noise. Both albums would subsequently be picked up for Japanese distribution by the Arco Iris label. PANZER's final roll call included Élcio Cruz, André Pars, Edson Graseffi and ex-BRUTAL FAITH bassist Mauricio Cliff. In March 2003 PANZER guitarist André Pars would feature in a formative line-up of Thrash Metal band ANCESTRAL.

INSIDE, Destroyer (1999). Limitations / Rejected / N.S.A. / Breaking / Despair / Detroit Rock City / Clowns Of Dust / Enough! / Pressure / Ethnic Ghetto / Despair II / Night Crawler.

THE STRONGEST, Spiral Noise (2001). Fake Game Of Heroes / Red Days / Affliction / Show Me! / Box / Speedy / My Night / Your Blood / The Strongest / Fear Of God / House Of Decadence / The Strongest (Reprise).

PARABELLUM

MEDELLIN, COLOMBIA — *Ramón (vocals), Carlos Mario (guitar), John (guitar), Tomás (drums).*

Medellin Death Metal band PARABELLUM was created in early 1983 by guitarist Carlos Mario and drummer Cipriano. The group debuted in 1987 with the two track EP 'Sacrilegio', this limited to 500 copies. A follow up single, 'Mutacion Por Radacion', was released as a 600 copy run in 1988. A further pressing of 'Sacrilegio' was issued in 1992, once again limited to 500 units, although a bootleg also surfaced, adding a third track 'Guerro, Monopolio, Sexo'.

Blasfemia Records issued the 'Tempus Mortis' compilation album in 2005. Limited to 1000 copies the collection comprised the 1987 'Sacrilegio' EP and 1988 'Mutacion Por Radacion' EP plus six previously unreleased rehearsal tracks dating to 1984-'85 and a live video track from the 1985 'La Batalla De Las Bandas' festival.

Sacrilegio, Independent (1987) (Limited edition 500 copies). Madre Muerte / Engendro 666.

Mutacion Por Radacion, (1988) (Limited edition 600 copies). Bruja Maldita / Mutacion Por Radacion.

PARADOX

WÜRZBURG, GERMANY — *Charly Steinhauer (vocals / guitar), Markus Spyth (guitar), Roland Stahl (bass), Axel Blaha (drums).*

A late 80s Speed Metal band from Würzburg founded in February of 1986. Founder members frontman Charly Steinhauer and drummer Axel Blaha are both ex-WARHEAD with other original members being guitarist Markus Spyth and bass player Roland Stahl. A July 1986 demo scored a deal with the Roadrunner label that November. The band cut a further demo 'Mystery' in 1987 and had the track 'Pray To The Godz Of Wrath' featured as the lead track on the compilation 'Teutonic Invasion' before their Roadrunner deal resulted in a Kalle Trapp produced debut 'Product Of Imagination' in 1988.

'Product Of Imagination' brought the band enormous rewards in their homeland, PARADOX being voted by both 'Rock Hard' and 'Metal Hammer' magazines as best newcomer act and coming only behind established veterans SCORPIONS and ACCEPT as highest regarded German band. Touring in December of 1987 had the band on the road with Swiss act DRIFTER. The group also chalked up important festival appearances at the infamous Dutch 'Dynamo' event and the 'Festa Avante' in Portugal.

A new look PARADOX recorded the Harris Johns produced second album, 'Heresy', the band having drafted new guitarist Dieter Roth and bassist Matthias Schmitt. Erstwhile CRONOS TITAN guitarist Kai Paseman was recruited in November of 1989 but shortly after PARADOX would then go into a period of hibernation. Paseman founded the KRAUTS, an act which evolved into DECLARATION OF DEPENDENCE issuing two albums.

PARADOX was reunited for a 'Wacken Open Air' show in August of 1999. Joining Steinhauer and Paseman would be the esteemed SIEGES EVEN sibling rhythm section of bass player Oliver and drummer Alex Holzwarth. Besides making their mark with Progressive Metal act SIEGES EVEN the brothers have contributed to many other high profile acts—Oliver to BLIND GUARDIAN and Alex to Italian Symphonic Metal band RHAPSODY and Brazilians ANGRA.

The revised PARADOX released the 'Collision Course' album, which included a rendition of the SCORPIONS 'Dynamite', through the AFM Records label in 2000. Japanese versions of the album came with no less than three extra tracks 'Pray To The Godz Of Wrath', 'Paradox' and 'Execution'. The band also contributed to a Nuclear Blast ABBA tribute album.

Oliver Holzwarth later teamed up with DEMONS & WIZARDS. PARADOX underwent a major shift in their line-up in late 2002 with both Holzwarth brothers opting out. The group pulled in former guitarist Kai Pasemann and enrolled the veteran Stefan Schwarzmann, citing credits with CRONOS TITAN, SKEW SISKIN, ACCEPT, U.D.O. and RUNNING WILD, on the drums. Another erstwhile band member, Armin Donderer, was committed to play bass.

In early 2004 Steinhauer relinquished the guitar role, citing an unspecified illness as the reason. By June it was announced that the frontman's condition had stalled the writing process for a new album. In 2005 Armin Donderer featured on OLIVER HARTMANN's solo album 'Out In The Cold' and in November joined FREEDOM CALL. PARADOX duly regrouped, Charly Steinhauer being backed by guitarists Kai Pasemann and Fabian Schwarz, bassist Andi Siegl and drummer Chris Weiß.

PARADOX's 2006 AFM Records album 'Electrify' included a cover version of BLACKFOOT's 'Good Morning'. Ex-bassist Andreas Siegl joined MY DARKEST HATE in February 2007. The band contributed their cover version of TANKARD's 'Zombie Attack' to the tribute album 'A Tribute To Tankard' included as a bonus disc on the AFM Records 2007 TANKARD release 'Best Case Scenario: 25 Years In Beers'.

PRODUCT OF IMAGINATION, Roadrunner RR9563 (1988). Opening

Theme / Paradox / Death, Screaming And Pain / Product Of Imagination / Continuation Of Invasion / Mystery / Kill That Beast / Pray To The Gods Of Wrath / Beyond Space / Wotan II.

HERESY, Roadracer RO 9506-1 (1989). Heresy / Search For Perfection / Killtime / Crusaders Revenge / The Burning / Massacre Of The Cathars / Serenity / 700 Years On / Castle In The Wind.

COLLISION COURSE, AFM CD 042 (2000). Decade Of Sorrow / Collision Course / Rearrange The Past / Path of Denial / Saviour / Blamed For Nothing / Prostitution Of Society / Shattered Illusions / Sadness / Over-Shadowed / Dynamite.

PARALEX

NOTTINGHAM, NOTTINGHAMSHIRE, UK — *Phillip Ayling (vocals), Kev Bower (guitar), Mark Gibson (guitar), Ian Dobbs (bass), Neil Bryan (drums).*

A Nottingham NWoBHM band that have been cited by METALLICA as an early influence, the roots of PARALEX trace back to the 1978 act TOKIO ROSE, a band comprising bassist Tony Speakman, drummer Tim Bowler, guitarists Nigel Revell and Howard Cooper and singer Nick Shipley. In their short period together TOKIO ROSE replaced Nigel Revell with Mick Hartshorn before the group split, with Speakman joining SOVEREIGN and Bowler joining Grantham act OVERLORD. With SOVEREIGN's demise, Speakman joined PARALEX, replacing Ian Dobbs.

Together with vocalist Phil Ayling, guitarist Mark Gibson and drummer Neil Bryan Speakman recorded the rare green vinyl 'White Lightning' single. A further cassette single followed featuring the tracks 'Getting Somewhere', 'Rock The Force', 'Justice' and 'Lionheart'.

PARALEX formed a band co-operative with two other local acts RACE AGAINST TIME and RADIUM and played many gigs together. Eventually the band folded with Speakman leaving to form the pioneering occult Metal band HELL with ex-RACE AGAINST TIME vocalist Dave G. Halliday and ex-TOKIO ROSE drummer Tim Bowler.

PARALEX vocalist Phil Ayling later turned up in Thrash merchants METAL MESSIAH. Bassist Tony Speakman, along with PARALEX guitarist Mark Gibson, was to forge SYZ releasing the 1986 single 'Rock n' Roll Children'. In later years Tony Speakman would be found on the covers circuit with RAINBOW tribute act RAINBOW RISING. Another PARALEX credited drummer, Jes O'Donovan, subsequently joined APB, led by ex-DEUCE singer Iain "Fang Sabre" Dilley.

White Lightning, Reddingtons Rare Records DAN004 (1980). White Lightning / Black Widow / Travelling Man.

PARALYSIS

WESTDORPE, HOLLAND — *Nick Davies (vocals / guitar), Fausto Dhanis (guitar), Roger De Rijke (bass), Stephen Van De Haestregt (drums).*

An aggressive Power Metal act, PARALYSIS emerged in Westdorpe during 1987, soon cutting the 'State Of Shock' demo. The following year the band weathered its first line up changes as drummer Andre Nijssen was replaced by SACRAMENT man Stephen van Haestregt. Subsequently singer Mark de Smit opted out, being substituted by Stephen's brother Jean-Paul. A new demo recording 'Trivial Round Of Life' in 1989 afforded PARALYSIS some valuable live action supporting the likes of DONOR, WHIPLASH and SADUS amongst others. The band then set about laying down tracks for a third tape but in the midst of these sessions Jean-Paul Haestregt broke ranks. The tracks were completed with the aid of Lex Vogelaar, known on the scene for his contributions to TARGET, ORPHANAGE and LYCANTHROPE.

Drafting Englishman Nick Davies PARALYSIS embarked upon crafting a fresh demo 'Arctic Sleep'. However, the band judged the results so highly this would in fact emerge as the group's first commercial product in 1992. The band self produced their 'Visions' album, later re-recording two songs from the record for the mini album released by the Defrosting label a year later.

Guitarist Fausto Dhanis quit the group after the 1995 release, the band bringing in twin guitarists Eric Bos and a returning Jean-Paul Van De Haestregt.

Signing to the German AFM label PARALYSIS recorded the 'Architecture Of The Imagination' album, released in May of 2000. Drummer Stephen Van Haestregt would loan himself out to WITHIN TEMPTATION in June of 2002.

Paralysis, Paralysis (1987) (Demo). Intro / What's To Become Of Man / Trench Reality / Outro.

Trivial Round Of Life, (1988) (Demo). Roman Struggle / What's To Become Of Man / Admonishing Famine / Trench Reality / Is It Justified.

VISIONS, Paralysis (1994). Altered States / Passages I / Experimental Factor Genocide / Lost In The Darkness / The Waters Cry / Point Of No return / Twisted / Tardis / Without Shadow Of A Doubt / Passages II / In Memoriam / Enemies Within / Escape From Yesterday / Sunitpar.

WONDERLAND, Defrosting 2-K (1995). Wonderland / In Memoriam (Remix) / My Room / Escape From Yesterday / Inhumane (Re-Edit).

ARCHITECTURE OF THE IMAGINATION, AFM (2000). No One / Picture Picture / Visions / Broken / Fly / The Truth / Architecture Of The Imagination / Shallow / Footsteps / Trip / Empty Head.

PARIAH

UK — *Mick Jackson (vocals), Steve Ramsey (guitar), Russ Tippins (guitar), Graeme English (bass), Sean Taylor (drums)..*

PARIAH was formed as a direct descendent from SATAN, a band that achieved great success in Europe on the German Steamhammer label, PARIAH was basically the same band, but a name change was thought in order due to the connotations of the old moniker. The first album was recorded with producer Roy Rowland . Unfortunately, 'The Kindred' released in 1988, was never given a British release as PARIAH concentrated on the lucrative European market.

The second album, 1989's 'Blaze Of Obscurity' recorded at Horus Studios and produced by the band, built upon the success of the debut and proved that the name change had been the correct move as PARIAH albums sold in greater numbers than previous SATAN records. However, PARIAH folded amidst financial wranglings with their record company, even though sessions for an intended third album, recorded by guitarists Steve Ramsey and Russ Tippins, bassist Graeme English, ex-SATAN and BATTLEAXE drummer Ian McCormack and former TYSONDOG vocalist Alan Hunter, was recorded at Links Studios in Newcastle during 1993.

As Ramsey and English partnered with erstwhile SABBAT frontman Martin Walkyier, enjoying European success with the innovative SKYCLAD, debuting in 1991 with 'Wayward Sons Of Mother Earth', erstwhile drummer Sean Taylor joined BLITZKRIEG. With interest in the NW0BHM at a high in mainland Europe during the mid 90s unreleased PARIAH recordings from 1990 would be unearthed as the 'Unity' album. Ramsey and English would once again be active with SATAN during 2005.

THE KINDRED, Steamhammer 08-7526 (1988). Gerrymander / The Rope / Scapegoat / Foreign Bodies / La Guerra / Inhumane / Killing For Company / Icons Of Hypocrisy / Promise Of Remembrance.

BLAZE OF OBSCURITY, Steamhammer SPV 85-7595 (1989). Missionary Of Mercy / Puppet Regime / Canary / Blaze Of Obscurity / Retaliate! / Hypochondriac / Enemy Within / The Brotherhood.

UNITY, Aartee Music (1997). Unity / Reactionary / Walking Wounded / No Exit / Snakes & Ladders / One Of Us / Saboteurs / Mutual Street / The Jonah / Learning To Crawl.

PARKWAY DRIVE

BYRON BAY, NSW, AUSTRALIA — *Winston McCall (vocals), Luke Kilpatrick (guitar), Jeff Ling (guitar), Brett Versteegh (bass), Ben Gordon (drums).*

PARKWAY DRIVE (pic: Cindy Frey)

Formed in 2003, PARKWAY DRIVE released an album with Resist Records during 2005. In January 2006 the band partnered with EVERGREEN TERRACE, THE GETAWAY PLAN and CARPATHIAN on Australian dates. The band's 2006 album, 'Killing With A Smile', was produced by KILLSWITCH ENGAGE guitarist Adam Dutkiewicz for a US August release through Epitaph Records.

North American shows in April 2007 would be backed by COMEBACK KID, IT DIES TODAY, THIS IS HELL and ENDWELL. Following festival appearances in Germany, Belgium and the Netherlands, the band joined the ranks of the roving 'Vans Warped' US touring festival throughout July and August.

I Killed The Prom Queen / Parkway Drive, Final Prayer (2003) (Split CD EP). Homicide Documentaries (I KILLED THE PROM QUEEN) / Death Certificate For A Beauty Queen (I KILLED THE PROM QUEEN) / I Watched (PARKWAY DRIVE) / Swallowing Razorblades (PARKWAY DRIVE).
Don't Close Your Eyes, Resist RESIST 33 (2004). ... / Smoke 'Em If You Got 'Em / Dead Dreams / Flesh. Bone And Weakness / The Cruise / You're Over / Looks Like Yoda / Don't Close Your Eyes.
KILLING WITH A SMILE, Suburban (2006). Gimme A D / Anasasis (Xenophontis) / Pandora / Romance Is Dead / Guns For Show, Knives For A Pro / Blackout / Picture Perfect. Pathetic / It's Hard To Speak Without A Tongue / Mutiny / Smoke 'em If Ya Got 'em / A Cold Day In Hell.

PATRIARCH

BELGIUM — *Herman Cambre (vocals), Jan Geerts (guitar), Freddy Mylemans (guitar), Paul Verboven (bass), Herman Cambre (drums).*

Originally known as PARIAH and formed by guitarist Freddy Mylemans in March 1983 (issuing a self titled demo the same year followed in 1984 by a second four track tape 'Evil Wings'), the band had to be put on ice in 1988 when bassist Jan T'Seyen was killed in a road accident. However, before the end of the year the band had reformed (confusingly with a vocalist and drummer that share the same name!), but due to press coverage of the British version of PARIAH opted to change titles to PATRIARCH. A new demo secured a deal with German label Shark Records. The 1990 album 'Prophecy' was decent powerful metal laced with some elements of Thrash. It was produced by Alex Thubeauville.

Following two albums PATRIARCH split with their label and underwent a massive line-up change. Only guitarist Freddy Mylemans remained from the original line-up as he was joined by new members in vocalist Erik Rinkes, guitarist Jan Van Bulck, bassist Paul Verboven and drummer Frank Dresselaers. This line-up released a demo in 1995 featuring 'Parade Of Fools', 'The End Of The Day', 'I Machine' and 'Changing Matter'.

PROPHECY, Shark 016 (1991). At The Warlord's Command / Dance / Children Of The Moon / Shadowland / Father Kreator / Castle Of Darkness / Kmar-Q-Luque / Island Of Insanity / Prophecy / Pilgrims Of The Dark Age.
WORLD WITHIN WORLDS, Rock Power R.P. 003 (1993). Leviathans / The Watching Eve / Lady Of The Lines / Steleas Of Ghorfa (instrumental) / World Within Worlds / Decadence Within / Burning Grounds / Forsaken Wisdom / Strange Reality.

PENTAGRAM

SURAHAMMAR, SWEDEN — *Mikael Tossavainen (vocals / guitar), Stefan Neuman (guitar), Hojas (bass), Magnus Forsberg (drums).*

Surahammar based PENTAGRAM issued an October 1986 demo entitled 'Infernal Return' and a self titled two track February 1987 demo prior to evolving into TRIBULATION. The band was founded by Toza (a.k.a. Mikael Tossavainen) on vocals and guitar, Stefan Neuman on second guitar, Daniel Hojas on bass and Magnus Forsberg on the drums, retaining this line-up as a stable entity. As TRIBULATION the band re-debuted in March 1988 with the demo 'Pyretic Convulsions'. TRIBULATION issued two albums prior to dissolving in 1995.

Tossavainen has scene affiliations with PUFFBALL and THE RUSSIAN FIVE whilst both Neuman and Hojas have KENTISK BROSK ties. Magnus Forsberg scored credits with PUFFBALL, EXECUTION, DISSOBER and BOMBS OF HADES.

Infernal Return, Pentagram (1986) (Demo). Thrashing With Power / Choose Death / Terror.

PENTAGRAM

ISTANBUL, TURKEY — *Murat Ilkan (vocals / guitar), Hakan Utangaç (guitar), Metin Türkcan (guitar), Tarkan Gözübüyük (bass), Cenk Ünnü (drums).*

PENTAGRAM, in order to avoid confusion with the American Doom veterans, are known as MERZARKABUL ("Acceptance of Death") outside of Turkey. The band, founded during 1987, debuted in 1990 with an eponymous cassette album. 1997's 'Anatolia' debuted ex-SAWDUST and CHEROKEE singer Murat Ilkan. The follow up live album 'Popcular Disari' included a cover of SLAYER's 'Black Magic'.

In 2005 Murat Ilkan fronted the live band for guitar virtuoso CEM KÖKSAL.

On February 4th 2007 PENTAGRAM celebrated its 20th anniversary with a show held at Bostanci Gösteri Merkezi in Istanbul. This concert was filmed and recorded for a live DVD and album. The band roster at this juncture comprised singer Murat Ilkan, guitarists Hakan Utangaç and Metin Türkcan, bassist Tarkan Gözübüyük with Cenk Ünnü on drums.

TRAIL BLAZER, Raks (1990). Secret Missile / Living On Lies / Trail Blazer / Vita Es Morte / Fly Forever / Time Bomb / Over The Line / The Planet / Brain On The Wall / No One Wins The Fight / Vita Es Morte (Live) / Powerstage (Live).
POPCULAR DISARI, Raks (1997). Intro / Before The Veil / Behind The Veil / Welcome The End / No One Wins The Fight / Give Me Something To Kill The Pain / Vita Es Morte / Gunduz Gece / Black Magic / Rotten Dogs / 999 / 1000 In The Eastland / Anatolia.
ANATOLIA, Raks 97 34 Ü 1036 (1997). 1'000 In The Eastland / Dark Is The Sunlight / Gündüz Gece / Stand To Fall / Give Me Something To Kill The Pain / Welcome The End / Anatolia / On The Run / Time / Behind The Veil / Fall Of A Hero.
BIR, Bocek Yapim (2002). Tigri / Bir / Seytan Bunun Neresinde / Bu Alemi Goren Sensin / Mezarkabul / Sir / Kam / Olumlu / F.T.W.D.A.

PERSECUTION

SYDNEY, NSW, AUSTRALIA — *Rod Hunt (vocals), Jody Bartolo (vocals), Dave Neil (guitar / keyboards), Adam Gillis (guitar / bass), Peter Kotevski (drums).*

PERSECUTION is a Sydney Death Metal band that emerged in the early 1990's. In July 1992 they recorded a demo called 'Encapsulated' and, after a few internal changes, the band signed to the relatively new Australian Death Metal specialty record label, Warhead Records. The debut EP, entitled 'Besieged', came out in 1994. Scott Mullins had appeared on the demo as the drummer but replaced by Nick Hunt in 1995. Hunt himself was replaced by Pete Kotevski for the EP in 1996.

The band, now with a dual vocal attack firmly entrenched, jumped to the Underclass label and released their debut full-length album, 'Thick Face, Black Heart', in 1996. As recently as 2002 members Neil, Bartolo and Gillis played in a hardcore band called UNCLEAN.

Encapsulated, Slightly Persecuted (1992). Wargod / Night Warriors / New 3rd / Encapsulated.

Besieged, (1994). Intro/Indignant / Besieged / Instrumental H.G.C. / Victims / Deadly / Outro.

PERSONAL WAR

GERMANY — *Matthias Zimmer (vocals / guitar), Sascha Kerschgens (guitar), Frank Buchwalter (bass), Martin Buchwalter (drums).*

A deliberately 'Bay Area' styled Thrash band PERSONAL WAR, previously known in their formative days as CROSSING SKULLS, forged part of the retro Thrash movement in Germany during the mid 90s.

PERSONAL WAR first came to attention with a demo 'Fear Of Death'. A later demo track 'Putrefaction' would also pull in valuable exposure with it's inclusion on the 'Rock Hard' magazine 'Unerhört' compilation CD for unsigned bands.

PERSONAL WAR would issue the debut 1998 album 'The Inside' through the Gernhart label, following this with a move to B. Mind Records for May 2000's 'Newtimechaos'. The record included guest guitar solos courtesy of RAGE's Victor Smolski.

THE INSIDE, Gernhart (1998).

NEWTIMECHAOS, B. Mind (2000). Newtime Bitch / Questions / Nothing Remains At All / Area Black / The Unknown / Voices / Mother Darkness / Angels / The Bag Of Bones / Dying Times.

PERSUADER

UMEÅ, SWEDEN — *Jens Karlsson (vocals / guitar), Emil Norberg (guitar), Fredrik Hedström (bass), Efraim Juntunen (drums).*

Umeå based Speed Metal act PERSUADER debuted in 1997. Initially the group hosted two guitarists but this was whittled down to just Pekka Kiviaho, a former member of AUBERON, before issuing an inaugural demo session 'Visions And Dreams' the following year. PERSUADER would share their opening eponymous effort with FRETERNIA, this release comprising earlier demo tracks. The band signed to Loud n´ Proud Records but, just as their first album 'The Hunter' was released, this label folded. Only a few copies leaked out in France through a license deal with the Nothing To Say imprint. Meantime, singer Jens Karlsson guested on the 1999 DEAD SILENT SLUMBER album 'Entombed In The Midnight Hour'.

With the departure of guitarist Pekka Kiviaho, frontman Jens Karlsson and drummer Efraim Juntunen in early 2001 PERSUADER. However, the band swiftly regrouped as Kiviaho was subsequently replaced by Emil Norberg and both Karlsson and Juntunen made a return. Kiviaho would unite with ex-MORIFADE guitarist Jesper Johansson to found a new project.

PERSUADER entered the Powerhouse Studios in Hamburg during September of 2003 with IRON SAVIOR's Piet Sielck acting as producer for the 'Evolution Purgatory' album.

In early 2005 it would be revealed ex-member Pekka Kiviaho had joined ONE MAN ARMY AND THE UNDEAD QUARTET, the new project of ex-THE CROWN singer Johan Lindstrand. Another side project saw vocalist / guitarist Jens Karlsson and lead guitarist Emil Norberg in a new band unit entitled SAVAGE CIRCUS alongside longstanding BLIND GUARDIAN drummer

PERSUADER

Thomas Stauch, who had opted out of the leading German epic Metal band in April 2005. The concept had been initiated in May of 2004 when producer and IRON SAVIOR frontman Piet Sielck suggested some demos cut by Stauch were similar in style to the PERSUADER material. Initial demos, with Sielck handling bass guitar, were cut at Powerhouse Studios in Hamburg during August.

The newly established Dockyard 1 label in Germany re-issued the difficult to find 'The Hunter' album in 2005, complete with bonus tracks. That December PERSUADER entered the Powerhouse Studio in Hamburg, with Piet Sielck producing to cut their third album 'when Eden Burns'. Issued in May 2006, Japanese variants of the album hosted an exclusive track 'Alight The Heavens'.

Visions And Dreams, (1998). Escape / Heart And Steel / Cursed.
PERSUADER, Loud 'n Proud (1999) (Split album with FRETERNIA). Heart And Steel / Cursed / Escape / Cursed.
THE HUNTER, Rising Sun Productions (2000). Fire At Will / As You Wish / Cursed / The Hunter / Secrets / Escape / Hearts And Steel / ... And There Was Light / My Life For You.
EVOLUTION PURGATORY, Sanctuary (2004). Strike Down / Sanity Soiled / Masquerade / Godfather / Turn To Dust / Passion/Pain / Raise Hell / To The End / Fire At Will / Wipe Out.
WHEN EDEN BURNS, Dockyard 1 (2006). Twisted Eyes / Slaves Of Labour / Sending You Back / R.S Knights / The Return / When Eden Burns / Judas Immortal / Doomsday News / Zion / Enter Reality.

PERZONAL WAR

GERMANY — *Matthias Zimmer (vocals / guitar), Sascha Kerschgens (guitar), Frank Buchwalter (bass), Martin Buchwalter (drums).*

Thrash act PERZONAL WAR, initially starting life billed as PERSONAL WAR, came into being during 1996, created by vocalist / guitarist Matthias Zimmer and drummer Martin Buchwalter. Joining the founders for the inaugural demo 'The Fear Of Death' would be guitarist Sascha Kerschgens and bassist

Frank Buchwalter. A second session, 'Personal War', followed in 1997 and the band duly garnered extra exposure with the inclusion of the track 'Putrefaction Of Mind' on the Rock Hard magazine CD sampler 'Unerhört Aktion'. Ultimately this secured a deal with the Gernhart label for a May 1998 debut album 'The Inside'.

Signing to the B-Mind label the group, still known at this juncture as PERSONAL WAR, cut a second album 'New Time Chaos'. A name switch to PERZONAL WAR occurred prior to taking a step up to the AFM label and the third effort 'Different But The Same', released in Europe in July of 2002. Victor Smolski of RAGE repute contributed a brace of guest guitar solos to the record.

Frank Buchwalter bowed out in early 2003, his place being taken by the AARDVARKS credited Sven Krauträmer. The band toured Germany throughout the Summer of 2004 as support act to BLAZE and CIRCLE II CIRCLE. The band also featured with their rendition of 'White Masque' on a 2004 Remedy Records RUNNING WILD tribute. The band featured their take on 'Solid Ball Of Rock' for the 2005 Remedy Records SAXON tribute album 'Eagleution'. PERSONAL WAR provided support to the "Hellhoundz of Doom and Thrash" DESTRUCTION, CANDLEMASS and DEATHCHAIN touring package in December.

THE INSIDE, Gernhart (1998).
NEW TIME CHAOS, B-Mind (2000).
DIFFERENT BUT THE SAME, AFM (2002). Time Of Lies / Bleeding / Born / The Progress / Open My World / The Urge For More / Blinder / Dragon's Mouth / What Is God? / Our Century / Ending Dreams.
WHEN TIMES TURN RED, AFM (2005).

PILEDRIVER

CANADA — *Piledriver (vocals), Bud Slaker (guitar), Knuckles Akimbo (guitar), Former Lee (drums).*

Infamous Thrash Metal band. The figure known as PILEDRIVER was in fact one Gord Kirchin, previously a bass player and singer with INCOGNITO, MAINSTREAM, a 1982 incarnation of FIST and also U.N. Although not initially intended to be a serious band unit PILEDRIVER's quite angle approach to image and songwriting resulted in some exceptionally healthy album sales.

MAINSTREAM vocalist Louise Remy aided on lyrics for the album whilst MAINSTREAM's Leslie Howe recorded guitar. Although originally planned as a pure money making exercise PILEDRIVER's use of bondage artwork and deliberately provocative song titles could not hide the fact that the songs were actually rather well done. Consequently the album sold exceptionally well and was licensed worldwide. The totally fictitious band was listed as Piledriver, guitarists Bud Slaker and Knuckles Akimbo with drummer Former Lee. In North America the song titles were deemed to obscene hence 'Alien Rape' became 'Alien Dead', 'Sex With Satan' became 'Devil's Lust' and 'Sodomize The Dead' was changed to 'Twister'.

After recording of 'Metal Inquisition' Kirchin joined ICE but was recalled to perform on another PILEDRIVER album. 'The sophomore effort 'Stay Ugly' included anonymous contributions from VIRGIN STEELE men David DeFeis and Eddie Pursino.

Once again fake musicians names were used in guitarists Bruizer Bernette and John Savage, bassist Sal Gibson and drummer Hammer.

Kirchin planned to take PILEDRIVER on the road and drafted vocalist guitarist Jim Doherty and guitarist Sean Abbott. By 1989 PILEDRIVER had a new look with Randy Deeg on guitar and Bend Quieser on drums. The latter soon departed as sessions for a future third PILEDRIVER album to be titled 'Shock' was written with Kirchin's brother Randy on second guitar. The last PILEDRIVER incarnation included the Kirchin brothers, guitarist Dave Copeland and drummer Ruston Baldwin.

Kirchin would also contribute anonymously to the CONVICT album 'Go Ahead Make My Day'. Kirchin and Copeland, with

PILEDRIVER (pic: Denise 'The PileWench' Chapital)

new drummer Shawn Tilley, would later use this projected PILEDRIVER material in his new act DOGS WITH JOBS.

Following two DOGS WITH JOBS albums Kirchin created SOFA Q. The 90's reissue of 'Metal Inquisition' on High Vaultage Records in Germany included an interview with 'Piledriver'. PILEDRIVER reunited, projecting a 2005 album dubbed 'Metal Manifesto'.

The band put in a high profile European festival show at the 'Keep It True' event at the Tauberfrankenhalle in Lauda-Königshofen, Germany on April 14th 2007 alongside British bands DIAMOND HEAD and SABBAT, US outfits LÄÄZ ROCKIT, LETHAL and TWISTED TOWER DIRE, Denmark's ARTILLERY, fellow Canadians CAULDRON, Dutchmen DEFENDER and Swedish band BULLET.

METAL INQUISITION, Cobra CL1001 (1985). Metal Inquisition / Sex With Satan / Sodomize The Dead / Witch Hunt / Piledriver / Human Sacrifice / Alien Rape.
STAY UGLY, Cobra CL1002 (1986). The Incubus / Metal Death Racer / The Fire God / Chaos / The Warning / Lord Of Abominations / Flowers Of Evil / The Executioner.

PITCH BLACK

PORTO, PORTUGAL — *Pedro Gouveia (vocals), Álvaro Fernandes (guitar), Ricardo Martins (guitar), Daniel Silva (bass), Francisco Martins (drums).*

Initially entitled THREAT and coming together in January of 1995 the quartet of vocalist Ricardo Rocha, guitarist João Paulo, bass player Ricardo Barbosa and drummer Álvaro Fernandes originally pursued a Hardcore orientated direction. Paulo would opt out and former PROFANE and ATMOSFEAR man Pedro Vieira filled the gap. A reshuffle, resulting in a name switch to THE WITHERING, also saw Fernandes installing himself on drums and João Ferreira enrolling as drummer.

THE WITHERING debuted with the demo tape 'Dreams Of Anguish' in February of 1996. A live recording, 'Live At The

Palha D'Aco Bar', arrived that September and a second studio session 'Another Reality', produced by Luís Barros of TARANTULA, closed out the year. They would contribute the tracks 'Deceived Humanity' and 'Lost Insanity' to the November 1997 compilation tape 'The Territory Of Metal'. These same two tracks also appeared on the CD collection 'Guardians Of Metal—Vol. IV'.

Daniel Silva took over the bass role and André Cruz replaced Vieira for the 1999 recording 'The Sinner', this cut featuring on the compilations 'Pure Underground—Vol. III' and 'Cais do Rock—Vol. III'. Another track, 'Remains Of The Past', surfaced on a cassette put together by Aphrodite fanzine. However, the group took a major blow when Rocha quit in September.

In 2001, with ex-DOVE frontman Pedro Gouveia now at the vocal helm, Hugo Moreira would then step up as THE WITHERING's new drummer but he too would decamp and Rui Danin took over temporarily to complete demos. Ricardo Teixeira was next in line on the drums, being recruited in September.

2001 got off to a rocky start with the defection of guitarist André Silva and the dismissal of Teixeira. With such major changes the remaining members decided to rename the band as PITCH BLACK. New personnel would be PARADIGMA guitarist Francisco Guimarães (a.k.a. FRANCIS G) and drummer Francisco Martins. The new group donated 'Dark Dream Of Freedom III' to the TARANTULA tribute '20 Anos de Tarantula'. Unfortunately Martins exited soon after but original THE WITHERING drummer João Ferreira re-boarded. This incarnation of the band put in just one gig, a tribute to the late DEATH frontman Chuck Schuldiner, before Francisco Martins resumed his place behind the drum kit.

Line-up changes still dogged the band throughout 2002 as Guimarães was "invited to leave" and substituted by female guitarist Ana Prestes. She in turn would be swiftly ousted by Sérgio Vilas.

A full length album, provisionally entitled 'Thrash Killing Machine', was projected for 2003. That April the band embarked upon the 'Unleashing Chaos' headlining tour. The band also put in appearances at two notable festivals, the 'Steel Warriors Rebellion VI' event alongside ENTHRONED, INTERNAL SUFFERING, KATATONIA, FINNTROLL, HOLOCAUSTO CANIBAL, NEOPLASMAH, ATTICK DEMONS, CORPUS CHRISTII, IN THY FLESH, AXE MURDERERS, AGONIZED, THANATOSCHIZO, FLAGELLUM DEI and ETERNAL MOURNING, plus the 'Algharb In Flames' concert sharing the stage with HOLOCAUSTO CANIBAL, NEPHTYS, NECROKULT, PANZERFROST and IN THA UMBRA.

FRANCIS G subsequently issued a 2003 album with NORDICA, 'Rebel Heart', then joined WEB, issuing the 2005 album 'World Wide Web', before going solo.

2004 opened for PITCH BLACK with the inclusion of the track 'Disturbing The Peace' on a US compilation album 'Atomic Annihilation'. The band returned to live action in April with club headliners and appearances at the Caldas da Raínha 'Fábrica do Ferro II Underground' and 'V Algarve Em Chamas' festivals. Notably, the group also entered the 'Rock Music Metal Challenge' competition, scoring first place and winning two Jackson guitars and a Jackson bass. However, Sérgio Vilas Boas was to opt out, being replaced by the GRINDER and UNDER FETID CORPSES credited Ricardo Martins. The 'Thrash Killing Machine' album finally saw issue through Recital Records in 2005.

Under The Ground EP, Independent (2002). No Justice ... No Peace ... / Messenger Of God / Evil Thoughts / Remains Of The Past 2000 / The Sinner.
THRASH KILLING MACHINE, Recital BOX30 (2005). Disturbing The Peace / Break Point / Beheaded / Divine Not Human / Lost In Words / Standards Of Perfection / SuffocHate / Pitch Black / New Life ... / ... New Breed.

PLANAR EVIL

CAMPOBASSO, ITALY — *Mark Evil (vocals / guitar), Antonio (guitar), Bane (bass), Amilcare (drums).*

Thrash Metal band PLANAR EVIL was assembled during January 2000 in Montenero di Bisaccia near Campobasso, Molise, initially comprising a trio of vocalist / bassist Mark Evil, guitarist Maurizio and drummer Rob. At first the band tackled Heavy Metal standards as covers but then began to arrange original material. However, in November of 2001 Maurizio departed, being replaced by Warhead (a.k.a. Gabriele) of LEPROSY in February of 2002. That November PLANAR EVIL entered the Temple Of Noise Studios in Rome to craft the demo 'Land Of Doom'.

The band swelled to a quartet in January of 2003 with the addition of bassist Massimiliano, also known as 'Bane' from HOW LIKE A WINTER and LEPROSY. As such, Mark Evil switched over to rhythm guitar.

PLANAR EVIL had the track 'In Front Of The Storm' included on the 2004 'Italian Metaland Compilation' sampler issued by Sky Pro Media. Amilcare superseded Rob on drums in August. Further changes in May 2005 saw Gabriele replaced by Antonio.

Land Of Doom, Independent (2002). Intro / Land Of Doom / In Front Of The Storm / Only Crimes / God Illusion / Welcome To Transylvania ... To Rise The Sun.

POLLUTED INHERITANCE

HOLLAND — *Ronald Camonier (vocals / guitar), Erwin Wesdorp (guitar), Menno de Fouw (bass), Friso Van Wijk (drums).*

A Death / Thrash band created during 1989 with the union of erstwhile POLLUTION guitarists Ronald Camonier and Erwin Wesdorp with the former rhythm section of SACRAMENT, bassist Menno de Fouw and drummer Friso Van Wijk. The band would induct lead singer Jean-Paul Hoorman in 1990 and proceeded to cut an inaugural six track demo, 'Afterlife', in August of 1991. However, despite this progress, Hoorman opted out and Camonier took over the lead vocal mantle.

POLLUTED IN HERITANCE, having first donated no less than three of their 'Afterlife' demo tracks to the 'Cries Of The Unborn' compilation album, landed a deal with the West Virginia label. The band's debut album 'Ecocide' was produced by HOLY MOSES man Andy Classen but a severe setback was suffered when West Virginia folded.

POLLUTED INHERITANCE cut a further demo session in April of 1994 which duly scored the 'Demo of the month' rating in Aardschock magazine. A new deal was struck with the DSFA label for second outing 'Betrayed' and the group toured Holland as guests to ORPHANAGE. Splitting with DSFA the band would spend a lengthy period away from the limelight preparing new material, finally signing to the Belgian Rokorola label for the 2001 album 'Into Darkness'. In early 2001 bassist Menno de Fouw announced his departure, the band recruiting bassist Stefan Vrieswijk in his stead.

TAKOJ SE DAVA DOL, 91995) (0).
ECOCIDE, West Virginia WVR SPV 084-57312 (1992). Faces / Dissolved / Eaten / Memories Of Sadness / Substance Of Existence / Fear / Stillborn / After Life / Rottings / Look Inside.
BETRAYED, Displeased DSFA 1002 (1996). Intro / Forgotten Cause / Mental Connection / Elimination / Betrayed / Emptiness / Drowning (In Faith) / Indulge / Never To Be Free / Need Me / My Voice.
INTO DARKNESS, Rokarola (2001).

POLTERGEIST

SWITZERLAND — *Andre (vocals), V.O. Pulver (guitar), Tom (bass), Walt (drums).*

Heavily influenced by German Thrash Metal, this Swiss quartet came together in 1985 and released their debut three track demo in 1988, produced by Schmier of DESTRUCTION. The

'Depression' album arrived in 1989 and 'Behind My Mask' in 1991. In the wake of Schmier's departure from DESTRUCTION Andre contributed lead vocals to the DESTRUCTION album 'Cracked Brain'.

POLTERGEIST evolved into Neo-Thrashers GURD during the mid 90's, recording some four albums on Century Media Records up to 1998's 'Down The Drain'. AIN'T DEAD YET, BABYLON SAD and KROKUS drummer Peter Haas has also sessioned for POLTERGEIST. Ex-POLTERGEIST bassist Marek Felis founded CHURCHILL.

You've Leaned Your Lesson, Century Media (1989) (Split flexidisc with LIAR. Free with 'Rock Hard' magazine). You've Leaned Your Lesson.
DEPRESSION, Century Media 9705-2 (1989). Three Hills / Depression / Inner Space / Writing On The Wall / Wheels Of Sansara / You've Learned Your Lesson / Prophet / Ziita / Shooting Star.
BEHIND MY MASK, Century Media CM 9715 (1991). We Are The People / Behind The Mask / Act Of Violence / Prey / Delusion / Drilled To Kill / Make Your Choice / Chato's Land / Still Alive / Driftin' Away.
NOTHING LASTS FOREVER, Haunted House 084-55812 (1994). Only You Remain / Empty Inside / Those Were Better Days / Just Doin' My Job / Never Again / Haunted House / Nothing Lasts Forever / You've Seen Your Future / Tell Me / Darken My Mind / Living For The Games.

POSSESSED

SAN FRANCISCO, CA, USA — *Jeff Beccara (vocals / bass), Larry LaLonde (guitar), Mike Torrao (guitar), Mike Sus (drums).*

One of the prime instigators of the Bay Area Thrash scene. San Francisco's POSSESSED's influence would be felt on the extreme Metal scene, particularly the Death and Black Metal genres, long after the group had disbanded. Indeed, POSSESSED is generally acknowledged to be amongst the very earliest groups to brand their style of music as "Death Metal". Founded as teenagers during 1983 POSSESSED were originally fronted by singer Barry Fisk. The band also formatively included the EXODUS credited Geoff Andrews on bass. Tragedy struck the band early in their career though when Fisk committed suicide, shooting himself in the head in front of his girlfriend.

With former MARAUDER and BLIZZARD man Jeff Beccara replacing Fisk the band, including guitarists Mike Torrao and Brian Montana with drummer Mike Sus, cut a 1984 demo which excited the interest of Metal Blade Records. The label gave an inclusion to POSSESSED's 'Swing Of The Axe', culled from a second demo recorded at Dangerous Rhythm Studio in Oakland with engineer Matt Wallace, to their 'Best Of Metal Massacre' compilation but did not sign the band up for an album. The honour fell to Combat Records although not before Montana was fired, apparently for disagreeing with the bands image of leather, studs and inverted crosses. Larry Lalonde, another BLIZZARD recruit, took his place for the Randy Burns produced debut 'Seven Churches'.

'Seven Churches' emerged in October 1985 although not in its originally intended packaging. The band had at first conceived a cover featuring gravestones bearing the individual members names plus a nun hanging from a tree. Bravely opening with a lift from Mike Oldfield's 'Tubular Bells Part 1', 'Seven Churches' vent forth a far blacker and Luddite brand of thrash metal than had been heard previously. Stylistically, Beccara's primal vocal roar and the harsh nature of the music polarized opinion.

POSSESSED's debut international concert came with an appearance at the 'World War III" festival in Montreal, Canada ranked alongside NASTY SAVAGE, CELTIC FROST, VOIVOD and DESTRUCTION in November 1985. The 'Beyond The Gates' album, produced by Carl Canedy of THE RODS, came wrapped in a lavish fold out sleeve, a rare extravagance for a Thrash act. To promote the album, POSSESSED toured Europe with VOIVOD and DEATHROW in November 1986, with a solitary London date adding ENGLISH DOGS to the bill.

The follow up mini-album 'The Eyes Of Horror' was produced by none other than guitar guru JOE SATRIANI and found the group mellowing out slightly.

POSSESSED fractured leaving Torrao to carry on the name. LaLonde would join veteran Speed Metal combo BLIND ILLUSION then create the offbeat but commercially successful PRIMUS. Beccara suffered the misfortune of being shot by two drug addicts and was paralysed from the waist down.

POSSESSED resurfaced in 1991, demoing with a line up comprising of Tarrao, guitarist Mark Strausberg, erstwhile DESECRATION bassist Bob Yost and drummer Walter Ryan. The band supported MACHINE HEAD the same year and cut a two song demo at Razor's Edge Studios in October 1991. POSSESSED's last incarnation came in 1993. Former POSSESSED guitarist Mike Hollman joined hardcore merchants PRO-PAIN in 1994. Ryan joined MACHINE HEAD, then Hardcore merchants MADBALL before a stint with Oakland's POWERHOUSE. Torrao later forged IKONOCLAST.

Although their career was short the band's music is now held in high regard in particular by today's Black and Death Metal legions. Indeed, a POSSESSED tribute album would surface in 2000 which found the Los Angeles band SADISTIC INTENT's contribution featuring no less than Jeff Beccara on vocals. CANNIBAL CORPSE had also cut both 'The Exorcist' and 'Confessions' as exclusive tracks for Japanese editions of their albums.

The Polish Agonia Promotions label would appease ardent POSSESSED fans by issuing a limited edition 10" EP entitled 'Resurrection'. This outing, restricted to 500 copies, comprised tracks from the band's debut demo tape 'Death Metal' plus previously unreleased cuts 'Pentagram', 'Swing Of The Axe', 'Twisted Minds' and 'Fallen Angel' as well as one brand new studio song from Becerra's new project SIDE EFFECT. This latter venture incorporating Becerra, Ken Bertoncini, Ed Varni and Rick Durocher.

The Dutch Karmageddon Media label issued a further POSSESSED tribute in 2004 entitled 'Tribute To Possessed ... Seven Gates of Horror'. Featured acts paying homage included IMPIOUS, CANNIBAL CORPSE, VADER, DIABOLIC, GOD DETHRONED, ABSU, PENTACLE, SINISTER, ANGEL CORPSE, KRABATHOR, HOUWITSER and AMON AMARTH. That same year Agonia unearthed a soundboard tape from a January 1987 show in Ohio and released these tracks as the 'Agony In Paradise' album.

Florida Black Metal band KULT OV AZAZEL revealed in January 2006 that Jeff Becerra was contributing both lyrics and guest vocals on a new album. Becerra would also head up a cover rendition of POSSESSED's 'Holy Hell'. Boneless Records released a limited edition, 1,000 run 7" single 'Ashes From Hell' in June.

Death Metal, Possessed (1984). Death Metal / Evil Warriors / Burning In Hell.
Possessed, (1985). Fallen Angel / Swing Of The Axe / Death Metal.
SEVEN CHURCHES, Roadrunner RR 9757 (1985). Exorcist / Burning In Hell / Seven Churches / Holy Hell / Fallen Angel / Pentagram / Evil Warriors / Satan's Curse / Twisted Minds / Death Metal.
BEYOND THE GATES, Under One Flag FLAG 3 (1986). Heretic / Tribulation / March To Die / Phantasm / No Will To Live / Beyond The Gates / Beast Of The Apocalypse / Séance / Restless Dead / Dog Fight.
THE EYES OF HORROR, Under One Flag FLAG 16 (1987). Confessions / My Belief / The Eyes Of Horror / Swing Of The Axe / Storm In My Mind.
1991 demo, (1991). The Martyr's Wake / The Seventh Sign.
VICTIMS OF DEATH—THE BEST OF POSSESSED, (1992). The Exorcist / Pentagram / Swing Of The Axe / March To Die / Death Metal / The Eyes Of Horror / Fallen Angel / Burning In Hell / Beyond The Gates / Seven Churches.
1993 demo, (1993). The Seventh Sign / Last Ritual / Human Extermination.
FALLEN ANGELS, Agonia (2003) (10" vinyl. Limited edition 500 copies). Death Metal / Evil Warriors / Burning In Hell / Twisted

Minds / Fallen Angel / Pentagram / Swing Of The Axe / Hemorrhage (SIDE EFFECT).

AGONY IN PARADISE, Agonia (2004). March To Die / Pentagram / Beast Of The Apocalypse / Holy Hell / Swing Of The Axe / Burning In Hell / Heretic / Phantasm / The Exorcist / Fallen Angel / Séance / Twisted Minds / Death Metal.

Ashes From Hell, Boneless (2006) (Limited edition 7" vinyl single 1000 copies). The Exorcist (Ashes edit) / Confessions (Rough mix) / Death Metal (Live at Ruthies Inn in Berkeley, CA Sept. 7, 1985) / Burning In Hell (Live at Ruthies Inn in Berkeley, CA Sept. 7, 1985).

POSSESSED: TRIBUTE

SAN FRANCISCO, CA, USA — During 2004 the Dutch Karmaggedon Media label assembled a tribute album to POSSESSED, one of the prime instigators of the Bay Area Thrash scene. POSSESSED's influence would be felt on the Metal scene, particularly the Black Metal genre, long after the group had disbanded. Participants featured some of the very biggest names of the extreme Metal spectrum including CANNIBAL CORPSE, VADER, GOD DETHRONED, SINISTER, ANGEL CORPSE and ABSU. Also included on the album, 'Tribute To Possessed ... Seven Gates Of Horror', would be an appearance by POSSESSED frontman Jeff Becerra, as a special guest on SADISTIC INTENT's version of 'The Exorcist', this track having been originally recorded in 2000.

TRIBUTE TO POSSESSED ... SEVEN GATES OF HORROR, Karmageddon Media (2004). The Exorcist (SADISTIC INTENT) / Fallen Angel (IMPIOUS) / Confessions (CANNIBAL CORPSE) / The Beasts Of Apocalypse (PENTACLE) / Death Metal (VADER) / No Will To Live (DIABOLIC) / Satan's Curse (GOD DETHRONED) / Swing Of The Axe (ABSU) / Storm In My Mind (SINISTER) / Burning In Hell (ANGEL CORPSE) / Evil Warriors (KRABATHOR) / March To Die (HOUWITSER0 / The Eyes Of Horror (AMON AMARTH).

POWERMAD

MINNEAPOLIS, MN, USA — *Joel Dubay (vocals / guitar), Jeff Litke (bass), Todd Haug (guitar), Adrian Liberty (drums).*

Heavy Metal act POWERMAD, vocalist / guitarist Joel DuBay, guitarist Todd Haug, bass player Jeff Litke and drummer Bill Hill, formed during 1984 in Minneapolis, debuting with a four track demo in 1985. A self-titled EP, as part of the 'Combat Boot Camp' series, arrived on Combat Records in 1986. The band, taking on Adrian Liberty on drums, subsequently signed to Reprise Records and released 'The Madness Begins' EP, notably recorded at PRINCE's Paisley Park Studios, in 1988 and, with new drummer John Macaluso. The Tim Bomba produced 'Absolute Power' album in 1989. POWERMAD toured the USA as support to OVERKILL and even put in a cameo instrumental musical performance of the track 'Slaughterhouse' in the David Lynch movie 'Wild At Heart' starring Nicholas Cage.

In 1999 Century Media re-issued the 'Powermad' material as part of a 'Combat Boot Camp' three way split CD shared with NAPALM and HAVE MERCY. Post POWERMAD, John Macaluso racked up impressive credentials with a myriad of acts such as ARK, YNGWIE MALMSTEEN, ARTENSION, TNT, BAD ANIMALS, STARBREAKER, MULLMUZZLER, MCM, HOLY MOTHER and RIOT.

POWERMAD announced a 2007 reformation, the band comprising vocalist / guitarist Joel DuBay, guitarist Todd Haug, bass player Jeff Litke with John Macaluso on the drums. This unit performed at the Balingen, Germany 'Band Your Head' festival in June. A new album was also announced.

Powermad, Powermad (1985) (Demo). Terminator / Chasing The Dragon / Plastic Town / Nice Dreams.

Powermad, Combat Boot Camp (1986). Chasing The Dragon / Terminator / Plastic Town / Nice Dreams / Blind Leading The Blind.

The Madness Begins, Reprise (1988). Terminator / Hunter Seeker / Gimme Gimme Shock Treatment.

ABSOLUTE POWER, Reprise 925937-1 (1989). Slaughterhouse / Absolute Power / Nice Dreams / Returning From Fear / Test The Steel (Powermad) / Plastic Town / B.N.R. / Failsafe / Brainstorm / Final Frontier.

PRECIPICE

GAINESVILLE, FL, USA — *R.J. Hagenow (vocals), Andy Adcock (guitar), Will McClanahan (guitar), Lori Volce (bass), Dave Silverstein (drums).*

Gainesville, Florida Death / Thrash act PRECIPICE includes the erstwhile HELLWITCH pairing of guitarist Andy Adcock and drummer Dave Silverstein. The pair also have ties to GARDY LOO. PRECIPICE aimed to break free from the Death / Thrash genre restrictions, introducing a diverse array of musical persuasions ranging through Jazz, Punk and Fusion. The group's first product would be a 1994 demo 'The Foundation'. These tracks were laid down by Adcock, Silverstein, guest vocalist John "The Klingon" Gauthier, second guitarist Allan Godfrey and bassist John Mortensen. A second session, 'Bloody Kill' recorded at Ibus Recording Studios in Pinellas Park, followed in 1995, now seeing R.J. Hagenow on lead vocals, John Paul and Jimbo on bass. PRECIPICE cut a debut album 'Prophet Of Doom' in 2000 at Morrissound Recording Studios with producer Jim Morris.

The Foundation, Precipice (1994). Degeneration / Dementia / Cycle Of Extinction / Power Of Fear.

Bloody Kill, (1995). Engulfed In Flames / World After War / Black Sun Rising.

PROPHET OF DOOM, Crook' D (2001). Challenges / Lords Of Darkness / Degeneration / Blind Rage / Prophet Of Doom / Bloody Kill / Socio-Violence / Involuntary Skinhead.

PRESTIGE

FINLAND — *Aku Kytölä (vocals / bass), Arska (guitar), Jan Yrlund (guitar), Tero Karppinen (drums).*

PRESTIGE, hailing from the Annala suburb of Tampere, was instigated by the Karppinen brothers guitarist Ari and drummer Tero in league with vocalist / bassist Aku Kytölä during 1987. Initial rehearsals benefited from the exclusive use of a youth club nuclear bomb shelter some six metres underground. This formative trio began making their presence felt on the live circuit that same year but boosted their numbers with the inclusion of former CLAYMORE guitarist Jan 'Örkki' Yrlund in the Spring of 1988. This quartet entered the Emma studios in Ylöjärvi to cut the debut demo entitled 'Gods'.

The opening demo rapidly shifted over 1000 copies. With the buzz on the band growing a notable live performance at the 'Speed Metal Party I' festival alongside NECROMANCER and DETHRONE secured a recording deal with the Poko label. PRESTIGE laid down their debut T.T. Oksala produced debut, the oddly titled 'Attack Against Gnomes', in Tampere's JJ studios. Not only did the record receive positive international feedback in the Metal media, being licensed to the Spanish GBBS Records label, but also secured a placing in the national Finnish album charts. Gigs across the country saw support slots to GRINGOS LOCOS, PEER GUNT and NUCLEAR ASSAULT.

Working once more with producer T.T. Oksale the band delivered the 'Priest' 12" single in January of 1989. That year also saw the arrival of the tongue in cheek Rock n' Roll 'Veijo' EP, a spoof on GENE VINCENT's 'Be Bop A Lula'. This EP, also comprising Punk and Hardcore tracks, was only made available to fans at gigs.

PRESTIGE recorded their second album, 'Selling The Salvation', during April of 1990. Tour work to promote the album included gigs in Denmark alongside INVOCATOR, their own 'Mutaa Lapioon' tour in Finland, as well as a round of shows in Czechoslovakia. The gigs followed into 1991 as PRESTIGE toured Sweden with Örebro Thrashers FALLEN ANGEL and returned to Denmark, once again hooking up with INVOCATOR and opening act MAPLE CROSS. A short burst of Finnish dates in May had the notorious DARKTHRONE as support act. More Swedish gigs in July had the band on the road with NO REMORSE.

For their third studio album 'Parasites In Paradise' PRESTIGE chose Jani Viitanen of the band YÖ as producer. Released in January of 1992 the album was promoted both by the expected tour dates and a promotional video for the track 'Sniff'. A major boost came with their inclusion on the billing of the Turku 'Ruisrock' festival, headlined by BRYAN ADAMS and NIRVANA.

The members opted to take a creative break after this show but strangely never regrouped. Kytölä and Yrlund resurfaced with Punk Crossover act HEPPIHIRVIÖ. Subsequently Yrlund ('Örkki') would be found as a member of infamous Tampere fetish act TWO WITCHES and Belgian Black Metal band ANCIENT RITES.

Veijo EP, (1989). Veijo / I Need Food / Radiated / Jani / Ei Ihraa Mun Lautaselle / Rakkauslaulu.

Priest, Poko (1990). Priest / Help The Science / Wake Up (It's Just A Nightmare).

ATTACK AGAINST GNOMES, Poko PALP 98 (1990). Intro / It's Over / Force Of My Hate / Dead By Drugs / Attack Against Gnomes / Rotten Angel / Gods / Punishment / Brain Outburst / Rabb-It / Angels Cry / This World.

SELLING THE SALVATION, Poko (1991). Species To Pieces / Maggots / Help The Science / I Don't Wanna Play With Teddy / Selling The Salvation / Prestige / Bed Time Story / Miserable Life / Sexual Education / Naughty Granny / Violence / Makes No Sense.

PARASITES IN PARADISE, Poko (1992). Parasites In Paradise / Will This Ever End? / Crack Children / Sniff / Barbarella / Offender / That Makes Me Sick / Too Greedy / From The Cradle To The Grave / Hop 2,3,4 / Break The Ice / Thursday The 12th / Lack Of Sanity / I Ain't The One.

PRO-PAIN

NEW YORK, NY, USA — *Gary Meskil (vocals / bass), Tom Klimchuck (guitar), Eric Klinger (guitar), Dan Richardson (drums).*

PRO-PAIN was founded by CRUMBSUCKERS refugees vocalist / bassist Gary Meskil and drummer Dan Richardson in 1991. Meskill post CRUMBSUCKERS founded HEAVY RAIN prior to creating PRO-PAIN. The original plan was to have M.O.D. and S.O.D.'s larger than life frontman Billy Milano to lead the band, but this never materialized and Meskill took over the vocalist's role. With the release of 'Foul Taste Of Freedom' guitarist Tom Klimchuck departed in favour of Nick St. Denis, previously a member of ex-FORBIDDEN and TESTAMENT guitarist Glen Alvelais act BIZARRO. Heavy touring followed including shows with BODY COUNT.

For second album 'The Truth Hurts', released in 1994, PRO-PAIN added ex-POSSESSED rhythm guitarist Mike Hollman. ICE T. guests on the track 'Put The Lights Out'. The cassette version of 'The Truth Hurts' had added extra tracks 'Death On The Dancefloor', 'Pound For Pound' and 'Foul Taste Of Freedom'. Touring across Europe in January 1994 saw the band supported by THE SPUDMONSTERS and LIFE OF AGONY.

The band pulled in erstwhile LÄÄZ ROCKIT and M.O.D. drummer Dave Chavarri as Richardson exited. The ex-drummer joined up with LIFE OF AGONY before creating STEREOMUD for two albums in league with the STUCK MOJO credited bass player Corey Lowery and ex-LIFE OF AGONY guitarist Joey Z.

Klimchuck made a return to the band during 1995 as PRO-PAIN shuffled their line-up yet again also drafting former M.O.D. guitarist Rob Moschetti. However, Chavarri would decamp to found EL NINO with ex-MERUADER frontman Jorge Rosado, deputize on a two month stint for SOULFLY then forge Latin Metal band ILL NINO. Former member Nick St. Denis would team up with SYSTEMATIC and later PRIMATE.

PRO-PAIN toured Europe in early 1998 with support from GURD, FURY OF FIVE and PISSING RAZORS. Their efforts paid off as the band were then invited to open for BÖHSE ONKELZ, one of Germany's biggest bands, which saw PRO-PAIN playing to huge arena audiences.

During January of 2002 members of PRO PAIN would hook up with DOG FASHION DISCO and MUSHROOMHEAD personnel to create side project band THE ALTAR BOYS.

Live work in Europe during 2003, as part of the 'No Mercy' festivals, found the band having severed ties with longtime drummer Eric Matthews. The IN COLD BLOOD and RUN DEVIL RUN credited Rich Ferjanic was the new man on the drum stool. Upon their return to the USA guitarist Eric Klinger cut the debut album of his side project BUILT UPON FRUSTRATION whilst his fellow six stringer Tom Klimchuck took time out to act as producer for Florida Hardcore act STRUGGLE.

PRO-PAIN's August 2003 'Run For Cover' album provided fans with an insight into the forces that drove the band, comprising a collection of cover material. Included would be takes on traditional Metal fare such as CELTIC FROST's 'Circle Of The Tyrants', SLAYER's 'South Of Heaven' and MOTÖRHEAD's 'Iron Fist' alongside DISCHARGE's 'Never Again', LIFE OF AGONY's 'Weeds', NEGATIVE APPROACH's 'Nothing', OPERATION IVY's 'The Crowd', BLACK FLAG's Damaged II' and the AGNOSTIC FRONT track 'Your Mistake'. Gary Meskil's prior act CRUMB-SUCKERS also came in for attention with a re-worked 'Just Sit There'.

PRO-PAIN, pulling in J.C. Dwyer of PAINGOD, GONEMAD, ICARUS WITCH and Pittsburgh's SOULBENT on drums, engaged in a mammoth bout of European headlining running March and April 2004. Dubbed the 'Fistful Of Hate' tour the group would be supported on various legs by DISBELIEF, PX-PAIN, EKTOMORF and DARK DUNGEON. That year Eric Klinger also made time to act as producer for the ICARUS WITCH EP 'Roses On White Lace'.

The album 'Fistful Of Hate' featured a guesting Stephan Weidner of BÖHSE ONKELZ on the track 'Godspeed'. September European dates had the group partnering with Sweden's CARNAL FORGE and France's DISTURB. The band formed up a package billing comprising CROWBAR, ENTOMBED, and THE MIGHTY NIMBUS for US tour dates in February 2005. In April PRO-PAIN hooked up with KREATOR, VADER and THE AUTUMN OFFERING but would drop off these dates after a few shows. Returning to the European concert trail, the group hooked up with Brazilians SAYOWA in November.

PRO-PAIN drummer J.C. Dwyer acted as stand in for the CRUMBSUCKERS February 2007 tour dates. The March 2007 PRO-PAIN album 'Age Of Tyranny / The Tenth Crusade' featured a guesting Matt Bizilia from ICARUS WITCH on the track 'Beyond The Pale'. European headliners, commencing April 25th at the Munich Metropolis in Germany, saw the support slot allocated to Swiss act GURD.

FOUL TASTE OF FREEDOM, Roadrunner RR 90682 (1992). Foul Taste Of Freedom / Death On The Dance Floor / Murder 101 / Pound For Pound / Every Good Boy Does Fine / Death Goes On / Rawhead / The Stench Of Piss / Picture This / Iraqnophobia / Johnny Black / Lesson Learned / God Only Knows.

THE TRUTH HURTS, Roadrunner RR 89852 (1994). Make War (Not Love) / Bad Blood / Truth Hurts / Put The Lights Out / Denial / Let Sleeping Dogs Lie / One Man Army / Down In The Dumps / Beast Is Back / Switchblade Knife.

CONTENTS UNDER PRESSURE, Energy (1996). Crush / Shine / State Of Mind / Gunya Down / The Mercy Killings / Contents Under Pressure / Against The Grain / Box City / Odd Man Out / Political Suicide.

ACT OF GOD, High Gain (1998). Stand Tall / In For The Kill / Act Of God / On Parade / Love And War / Pride / I Remain / Time Will Tell / Hopeless? / Burn / All Fall Down.

PRO-PAIN, High Gain (1998). Get Real / Time / No Love Lost / Don't Kill Yourself To Live / Love / H8 / Life's Hard / Mark My Words / My Time Will Come / Smokin' Gun / Godsize / Blood Red. Chart position: 70 GERMANY.

ROUND 6, Spitfire 5070-2 (2000). Fed Up / Desensitize / Substance / All Or None / Status Quo / Fuck It / Psywar / Take It Personal / Make

Some Noise / Let Live / Thou Shalt Not / Draw Blood / Down In Flames.
ROAD RAGE, Spitfire 5222-2 (2001). Stand Tall / I Remain / Life's Hard / Get Real / Act Of God / Smoking Gun / In For The Kill / Don't Kill Yourself To Live / Foul Taste Of Freedom / Crush / Shine / Make War (Not Love) / State Of Mind / The Stench Of Piss / Bad Blood / Iraqnophobia / Pound For Pound.
SHREDS OF DIGNITY, Nuclear Blast NB 709-2 (2002). Kill Or Be Killed / Shreds Of Dignity / 24 / 7 / Down For The Cause / Casualties Of War / Walk Away / No Way Out / The Shape Of Things To Come / Gone Fishin' / Lock n' Load / Fuck Off And Die / Justice Must Be Done.
RUN FOR COVER, Spitfire SPT 15239-2 (2003). Never Again / Circle Of The Tyrants / The Crowd / Refuse / Resist / Iron Fist / 100% / Terpentin / Nothing / Weeds / Just Sit There / Damaged II / Your Mistake / Knife Edge / South Of Heaven.
FISTFUL OF HATE, (2004). Can You Feel It? / Left For Dead / Godspeed / Implode / American Dreams / Cut Throat / Aftermath / Save Face / The Better Half Of Forever / Freedom Rings / Lost Horizons / Fistful Of Hate.
PROPHETS OF DOOM, Continental (2005). Neocon / Un-American / Hate Marches On / One World Ain't Enough / Getting Over / Operation Blood For Oil / Torn / Death Toll Rises / The Prisoner / Days Of Shame.
AGE OF TYRANNY—THE TENTH CRUSADE, (2007). The New Reality / All For King George / Pigs In Clover / Beyond The Pale / Three Minutes Hate / Heads Will Roll / Company Jerk / Impeach, Indict, Imprison / Leveler / Iraqnam / Live Free (Or Die Trying).

PROFANE OMEN

LAHTI, FINLAND — *Jules Näveri (vocals), Antti Kokkonen (guitar), Williami Kurki (guitar), Tomppa Saarenketo (bass), Samuli Mikkonen (drums).*

Thrash Metal band PROFANE OMEN, founded in Lahti by guitarist Janne Tolonen and drummer Länä Varjola in 1999, opened proceedings with the demos 'Profane Omen' in 1999 and 'Bittersweet Omen', featuring a cover version of MIDNIGHT OIL's 'Beds Are Burning', in 2000. The inaugural line-up also counted lead vocalist Jules Näveri, second guitarist Bönde Pöllänen and bass player Jukka Keisala. Pöllänen would depart and WRECK OIL's Williami Kurki enrolled as two more sessions arrived the following year in 'Fuck The Beast' and 'Load Of Lead'. Further turmoil ensued in the ranks as both founder members Tolonen and Varjola exited. PROFANE OMEN swiftly regrouped by inducting the DROWNED IN LIFE pairing of guitarist Antti Kokkonen, also of KILL THE ROMANCE, and the BEFORE THE DAWN and KILL THE ROMANCE credited drummer Mika Tanttu. With this line-up PROFANE OMEN cut the August 2002 EP 'Label In Black'.

Bassist Jukka Keisala exited in mid 2003 in order to prioritise MISERY INC. He would be superseded by WRECK OIL's Tomppa Saarenketo. PROFANE OMEN issued the 'Adrenaline' EP in August 2004.

Signing with Dethrone Music in January 2006 the band utilised Hideaway and Villvox studios, working with producer Ville Sorvali, to craft a new album. New man on the drums would be Samuli Mikkonen, scene veteran of ANSUR, ARCADIAN NOCTURNE, END BEGINS and UHRILEHTO. 'Beaten Into Submission' arrived in September.

On February 16th 2007 PROFANE OMEN was honoured with the "Rookie of the Year" award at the Finnish Metal Awards, which were held during the Finnish Metal Expo at the Cable Factory in Helsinki, Finland.

Bittersweet Omen, (2000). Everlasting / Beds Are Burning / Lullaby (To The Other Side) / So Close, Too Far / From Cradle To Grave....
Fuck The Beast, (2001). Through The Dark / 'til Death Do Us One / Psykho.
Load Of Lead, (2001). Load Of Lead / Painbox / ... Hate....
Throw Your Stones, Independent (2002). Throw Your Stones / Wildchild.
Label Of Black EP, Independent (2002). Are You A God? / Throw Your Stones / Father / Label Of Black / Burial Hymn.
C2H40, (2003). - / God In A Bottle / Kneel Before My Name / D.H.C. Adrenaline,** (2004). Adrenaline / Enemies / Adrenaline (Video).
BEATEN INTO SUBMISSION, Dethrone Music (2006). Intro / Adrenaline / Painbox / FMH (Fuck Me Hollow) / Enemies / Gunshot/Mindset / Rew / Pit Of My Thoughts / God In A Bottle / Damaged Justice. Chart position: 28 FINLAND.

PROFECIA

ECUADOR — *Erick Alava (vocals / guitar), Johnny Reyes (guitar), Frankie Alava (bass), Roberto Portilla (drums).*

Guayaquil based Speed Metal act PROFECIA, forged in 1991, emerged with the fourteen song 1992 tape 'La Marca Del Mal'. At this juncture the band comprised Erick Alava on vocals and guitar, Omar Paz on the bass and drummer Geovanny Cruz. Only Alava was left remaining for the 1994 follow up tape 'Anunciantes Del Final', the frontman now joined by second guitarist Johnny Reyes, bassist Xavier Muñoz and drummer Jimmy Naranjo. A DC version saw subsequent issue the following year courtesy of the Zodiaco label with all new artwork and the addition of two bonus live tracks 'Pandilleros del Cielo' and 'Llantos Inocentes'.

1998 saw further changes with a freshly installed rhythm section of bass player Frankie Alava and drummer Roberto Portillo. This pair debuted on the tape '... Hacia El Armagedón'. These sessions too were granted a CD release by Audiomaster Producciones in 1999. PROFECIA issued a 2001 split cassette 'Rompiendo El Silencio' shared with Argentina's ZOOPHILIA. A promotion single, 'Los 7 Sellos Del Horror, sung in both Spanish and English versions, was delivered in mid 2002. A live video, 'Evolución En Vivo', also saw release that same year.

ANUNCIANTES DEL FINAL, Zodiaco (1997). El Ultimo Mensaje / No A La 3ra. Destrucción / Pandilleros Del Cielo / Anunciantes Del Final / Verdugo De Demonios / Juicio Final / Lavado Cerebral / Pandilleros Del Cielo (Live) / Llantos Inocentes (Live).
... HACIA EL ARMAGEDON, Audiomaster Producciones (1999). La Cuenta Regresiva Hacia El Armagedón / Angel Exterminador / Mundo Sin Ley / Clonación Humana / Está Escrito / I.P.S. / Sobreviviente / Llantos Inocentes / Condenados A Vivir / Creados Para Destruir.
Los 7 Sellos del Horror, (2002) (Promotion release). The Seven Horror Seals / Los 7 Sellos del Horror.

PROJECT: FAILING FLESH

VIENNA, VA, USA — *Eric Forrest (vocals), Tim Gutierrez (guitar), Kevin 131 (guitar).*

PROJECT: FAILING FLESH was the 2002 band assembled in Vienna, Virginia by VOIVOD 'Phobos' era frontman Eric Forrest. The singer, prior to having joined the Canadian avant-garde Thrash legends a member of LIQUID INDIAN and THUNDER CIRCUS, had left VOIVOD following severe injuries received on the road in Germany. Kevin '131' has credits with GARDEN OF SHADOWS, TWISTED TOWER DIRE, BRAVE and WHILE HEAVEN WEPT.

The group signed a label deal with the Dutch Karmageddon Media concern for debut album 'A Beautiful Sickness', this opus closing out with a cover of VENOM's 'Warhead'. The band commenced cutting a self-produced second album 'The Conjoined' at Assembly Line Studios in Virginia in early 2004, these sessions lasting well into mid 2005.

PROJECT: FAILING FLESH, having wrapped up recording of 'The Conjoined' album, parted ways with Karmageddon Media in vocally acrimonious circumstances during September 2006. The group signed over to Burning Star Records, based in Greece, the following month. 'The Conjoined' was finally issued in March 2007.

A BEAUTIFUL SICKNESS, Karmageddon Media KARMA 013 (2004) (European release). A Beautiful Sickness / Planet Dead / 9mm Movie / Scene Of The Crime / Entrance Wound / Long Silent Voices / Dementia Pugilistica / Taste Of The Lie / Highwire Act / Warhead.

A BEAUTIFUL SICKNESS, Candlelight CDL0193CD (2004) (North American release). A Beautiful Sickness / Planet Dead / 9mm Movie / Scene Of The Crime / Entrance Wound / Long Silent Voices / Dementia Pugilistica / Taste Of The Lie / Highwire Act / Warhead.

THE CONJOINED, Burning Star BSRCD0018 (2005). Motionless / Through The Broken Lens / Regenerate / The Conjoined / Unsight Unseen / Eve Of Demise / Final Act Of Treachery / Surface Noise / Second Impact Syndrome / Synesthesia / Hand That You've Been Dealt.

PROTECTOR

GERMANY — *Martin Missy (vocals), Hansi Muller (guitar), Ede Belichmeier (bass), Michael Hasse (drums).*

PROTECTOR emanate from Wolfsburg and date to their formation in 1986 by guitarist Hansi Muller and ex-DEATH ATTACK drummer Michael Hasse. The percussionist also held the distinction of being the coordinator of the SODOM fan club. An early bassist, Michael Schnabel, exited in 1986—going on to join HERITAGE and subsequently MANDRILL. Having added former INZEST vocalist Martin Missy and bassist Ede Belichmeier in March 1987, PROTECTOR recorded their first two song demo. This tape led to a deal with Atom H Records, run by Jürgen Engler of DIE KRUPPS, and the first mini album, 'Misanthropy', the same year. Although a decidedly raw piece of work 'Misanthropy' was widely hailed across the underground Metal scene as a near classic piece of German Thrash.

1988's 'Golem' featured SODOM's Angel Ripper on the track 'Space Cake'. Unfortunately, vocalist Missy quit in early 1989. He was replaced by Olli Wiebel for a European tour alongside WEHRMACHT but Missy rejoined in time to record 'Urm The Mad'. However, in December of 1989, following a gig in Düsseldorf, Missy quit yet again.

Fronted by Olli Wiebel the group released another mini-album, 'Leviathan's Desire', in 1990 and toured Germany once more, this time as support to NAPALM DEATH. Missy would still be in the picture as a background contributor, donating lyrics to four songs on PROTECTOR's next album 'A Shedding Of Skin'. However, line-up problems hit the band prior to recording 'A Shedding Of Skin'. Belichmeier quit—having his position filled by bassist Matze Grün—and Muller also departed leaving Wiebel to record guitar parts as PROTECTOR became a trio.

Tragedy struck in February 1994 when Hasse died as a direct result of his drug addiction. PROTECTOR would persevere though, eventually find a new drummer in Marco Pappe and toured alongside D.V.S. and CRUSHER. PROTECTOR, according to reports, had apparently split after recording 'The Heritage' in 1994. However, the band did in fact operate for some time afterward putting in live gigs with an ever fluctuating line up. Grün founded SQUARE WAVES, releasing the 1995 demo 'Three Dimensional Hate'.

During 1993 ex-PROTECTOR personnel Martin Missy and ex-bassist Michael Schnabel would be active with the R.A.U. project. Subsequently Missy united with another ex-PROTECTOR bassist Ede Belichmeier and operating covers act ENERGYANT. Matze Grün later joined WASTELAND then Braunschweig based HEADSHOT.

Vocalist Martin Missy, breaking over a decade's break away from music, would for a time front the Swedish Metal band RUINS OF TIME, appearing on their 2001 album 'Timetraveller'. Drummer Marco Pappe was to resurrect the band under a new name in December of 2001. In 2004 Martin Missy re-emerged fronting PSYCHOMANTHIUM, an "old-school Speed/Thrash metal" band featuring ARKHAM 13 guitarist Derek 'Derekonomicon' Schilling, the INTERNAL BLEEDING and CATASTROPHIC credited bassist Brian Hobbie and ARKHAM 13 drummer Ant Ichrist. The band signed to Poland's Still Dead Productions for a debut album 'Death Attack'. Missy subsequently joined PHIDION.

MISANTHROPY, Atom H (1987). Misanthropy / Holy Inquisition / Agoraphobia / The Mercenary / Kain And Abel / Holocaust.

GOLEM, Atom H H007 (1988). Delerium Tremens / Apocalyptic Revelations / Golem / Germanophobe / Protector Of Death / Operation Plagma Extrema / Meglomania / Only The Strong Survive / Omnipresent Aggression / Space Cake.

URM THE MAD, Atom H (1989). Capitacism / Sliced, Hooked And Grinded / Nothing Has Changed / The Most Repugnant Antagonist Of Life / Quasimodo / Urm The Mad / Decadence / Atrocities / Molotov Cocktail.

LEVIATHAN'S DESIRE, Atom H (1990). Intro / Humanised Leviathan / Subordinate / Mortal Passion / Kain And Abel.

A SHEDDING OF SKIN, 199 (1991). Intro / Mortuary Nightmare / A Shedding Of Skin / Face Fear / Retribution In Darkness / Doomed To Failure / Thy Will Be Done / Whom Gods Will Destroy / Necropolis / Tantalus / Death Comes Soon / Unleashed Terror / Toward Destruction.

THE HERITAGE, Major C&CCC020 046-2 (1994). Mental Malaria / Scars Bleed Life Long / The Heritage / Lost Properties / Convicts On The Streets / Projective Unconsciousness / Paralizer / Chronology / Palpitation / Outro.

LOST IN ETERNITY, Major CC030 057-2 (1995). Misanthropy / Protector Of Death / Tantalus / Mental Malaria / A Shedding Of Skin / Lost Properties / The Mercenary / Golem / Kain And Abel / Doomed To Failure / The Heritage / Humanised Leviathan / Germanophobe / Holocaust / Convicts On The Street / Palpitation.

ECHOES FROM THE PAST, I Hate (2003). Protector Of Death (1986) / Apocalyptic Revolution (1986) / Misanthropy / Holy Inquisition / Agoraphobia / The Mercenary / Kain And Abel / Holocaust / Delirium Tremens / Apocalyptic Revelations / Golem / Germanophobe / Protector Of Death (1988) / Operation Plaga Extrema / Megalomania / Only The Strong Survive / Omnipresent Aggression / Space Cake.

PROTOTYPE

CA, USA — *Vince Levalois (vocals / guitar), Kragen Lum (guitar), Kirk Scherer (bass), Pat McGrath (drums).*

PROTOTYPE in a Californian Progressive Metal outfit founded in the late 90s, debuting with a 1995 demo entitled 'Seed'. The group's commercial inauguration came in 1998 with the 'Cloned' outing. Debut album 'Trinity', released in North America by WWIII Records, would secure a European license through Massacre Records for 2004 issue and see release in Chile via Toxic Records. PROTOTYPE pulled in Australian drummer Sam Aliano in December of 2003.

Nightmare Records released the 'Continuum' album in May 2006. Drum duties for these sessions were handled by former PROTOTYPE member Damion Ramirez, with one track also featuring former drummer Pat Magrath.

CLONED, Independent (1998). Transcendent Velocity / Mind In Motion / Synthespian / Shine / Seed / Dead Of Jericho.

TRINITY, WWWIII Music (2001). Live A Lie / Pure / Utopia / Trinity / Shine / By Breeze / Dead Of Jericho / I Know You (Part I) / Mind In Motion / Relativity.

CONTINUUM, Nightmare (2006). The Way It Ends / Probe / Devotion / With Vision / Synthespian / Sea Of Tranquility / Transcendent Velocity / Seed / Undying / Heart Machine / Cold Is This God.

PSI.KORE

SYDNEY, NSW, AUSTRALIA — *Chuck (vocals / guitar), Aaron Bibija (guitar), Meredith Webster (bass), Matt Lamb (drums).*

Sydney Thrash Metal act forged as a trio of vocalist / guitarist Chuck, bassist Alex Dourian and drummer Gekko in mid 1996. PSI.KORE switched drummers to Matt Lamb in 1997 and augmented their sound with the incorporation of second guitarist Andrew Lilley the following year. Before the close of the year Dourian had been usurped by Meredith Webster upfront of a support gig to VISION OF DISORDER. The group subsequently developed a formidable reputation garnering supports to visiting international artists such as NEVERMORE, ENTOMBED and CATHEDRAL.

PSI.KORE cut an EP during 2000, featuring a cover version of the MELVINS 'Revolve', touring Australia in promotion for this product on the package 'World War Three' billing alongside CRYOGENIC and ALCHEMIST. A guest slot to SKINLAB preceded the band's appearance at the 'Metal For The Brain' festival.

Unfortunately for Lilley the guitarist developed a debilitating nerve condition, forcing him out of a national tour with DAMAGED. Steve Essa of CRYOGENIC filled in. Lilley was back for openers to CRADLE OF FILTH in April of 2001 but was reportedly dismissed soon after. Ben Walker took the vacancy as Lilley teamed up with INFERNAL METHOD.

Further high profile gigs saw PSI.KORE lending support to MEGADETH in August of that year and put in another showing at the 'Metal For The Brain' event. Erstwhile DEPRESSION, DEADSPAWN and INFERNAL METHOD guitarist Aaron Bilbija replaced Walker in January of 2002. Although the recording of a full length album was intended PSI.KORE folded before hitting the studio. Subsequently, Bilbija, Webster and Lamb all re-grouped as DAYSEND.

Psi.Kore EP, Chatterbox (2000). Pioneering Conflict / Inbred Hate / Faker Taker / Lost In The Aether / Cut / Revolve.

PSYCHONAUT

PERTH, WA, AUSTRALIA — *Mark De Vattimo (vocals / guitar), Simone Dow (guitar), Alex Canion (bass), Sebastian Giorgi (drums).*

Perth Heavy Metal band PSYCHONAUT, established in 1996, featured the VOYAGER and PATHOGEN credited vocalist / guitarist Mark De Vattimo, bassist Stevie Vella and Theo Ongarezos on drums. Line-up changes in 1998 saw the incorporation of ex-ALLEGIANCE drummer Steve Hidden before Ongerezos returned. In 2000 the group commenced work on the album 'Masters Of Procrastination', these session crafted at Pet Rock Studios in Perth with producer Leighton Hughes. VOYAGER's Daniel Estrin provided keyboards. In 2002 Ongerezos was replaced by Sebastian Giorgi and the following year 'Masters Of Procrastination', remixed from the original tapes by PATHOGEN's Aidan Barton, finally arrived in stores through Prime Cuts Music.

Simone Dow, of VOYAGER and SCOURGE, assumed the guitar position in May 2005. With Vella's exit, seventeen year old Alex Canion, from INTER ALIA and SERAPHIM, took over on bass.

In February 2007 PSYCHONAUT commenced work on a second album with a provisional title of 'The Sounds Of Horror'.

MASTERS OF PROCRASTINATION, Prime Cuts 003 (2003). Darklord / Steamroller / El Elph / Scheisskampf / Thus Spake The Apes / Confusion?Vertigo! / Rats! / Old Blood Rivers / Psychonaut.

PSYCHOTRON

STUTTGART, GERMANY — *Matze Morbitzer (vocals), Matze Braun (guitar), Kai Huissel (guitar), Frank Herold (bass), Gert Kopf (drums).*

Retro 80s styled Thrash act out of Stuttgart. PSYCHOTRON came into being in 1995, issuing an opening eponymous demo in January of 1996. The self financed 'Cosmic Chaos Tome' album emerged in May of 1999 to positive reviews. The band would lose lead guitarist Andi Konstandaras to SPIRAL TOWER and duly filled the vacancy with Stefano Zanolli. However by March of 2000 Zanolili too bade his farewell and Jurgen Schmid was drafted.

PSYCHTRON saw another switch in their lead guitar department during April of 2001. The new man being erstwhile DESERTION six stringer Kai Huissel. The band parted ways with Generation Records in March of 2004. By May guitarist Mat Braun and bassist Frank Herold were announced as forming up a fresh band unit in union with the DOMAIN and SYMPHORCE credited drummer Stefan Köllner. In July PSYCHOTRON entered Decode Studios to cut the album 'Pray For Salvation', signing with Greece's Sleaszy Rider Records the following year.

April 2006 found PSYCHOTRON parting ways with bassist Frank Herold and temporarily plugging the vacancy for live work with Sebastian Schult of ATROCITY and FROM THY ASHES repute.

CHAOS COSMIC TIME, Psychotron (1999). Intro / Psychotron / This Illusion / Alternative Suicide / Melancholia / Eternal Stream / The Raging Pit / Belief / Waiting For Last Summer / The Crossroads / Autumn Suite / In Dark Red Minor.
OPEN THE GATE, Generation (2004). Intro / Open The Gate / God Nihil / The Ticket (To Insanity) / Meine Hölle / Private Hell / Beauty Of Sadness / Closing Doors / Lightbringer / Necromantia (Welcome To The Dead) / Instrumental.
PRAY FOR SALVATION, Sleaszy Rider (2005). At The Graves / In The Arms Of Morpheus / Chasing Shadows / Traitor / Circle Of The Damned / The Hourglass / The Awakening / Life On Borrowed Time / Shattered Illusion.

PULMONARY ABSCESS

HOLLAND — *Marijn de Zeeuw (vocals / bass), Edwin Kruize (vocals / guitar), Iwan Heskamp (guitar), Bert de Groot (drums).*

PULMONARY ABSCESS was forged as a trio comprising guitarist Edwin Kruize, bass player Jordi Bergboer and drummer Bert de Groot during 1989. PULMONARY ABSCESS, adding second guitarist Jurgen, released the demo 'Branded For Life' in 1992, after which the band trimmed down to just Kruize and de Groot. In February 1993 Bas van de Griek enrolled on guitar and the band entered the studio to cut the 'Definition Of Torture' session. As live work increased, vocalist Paul Wormgoor was added to the fold.

Just upfront of recording the October 1994 'Slave Of Darkness' tape bassist Floor Wolters was incorporated. However, upon completion both Walters and Bas van de Griek exited to join the ranks of GENETIC WISDOM. Opting for a complete re-think, PULMONARY ABSCESS responded by drafting two bassists, re-enrolling Jordi Bergboer and also bringing in Marijn de Zeeuw. A new campaign of live work ensued but in May of 1998 Bergboer bailed out for Hardcore outfit CON-CRETE. Ronald Wensink filled the gap for the EP 'Depths'. In parallel, both Edwin Kruize and Marijn de Zeeuw would be active as members of SOLARISIS.

Wormgoor in 1999 and de Zeeuw duly assumed lead vocal responsibilities. PULMONARY ABSCESS persevered on the live circuit as a trio before introducing the SOLARISIS and DEIFICATION credited Iwan Heskamp on guitar. In December of 2001 this quartet entered the Ground Zero Studios in Zutphen to start recording a full length album 'The Greedy Illness'.

Depths, Independent (1998). Hidden Reality / Cancer / The Everlasting Power / To The Roots Of Life / The Child Inside.
THE GREEDY ILLNESS, Independent (2002). The Presence Of Absence / The Greedy Illness / Mortal Sun / Suffocating Inheritance / This Is The World We Live In / Free Your Mind / Wishmaster / McDriveby / The End.

PURITY

JYVÄCKYLÄ, FINLAND — *Teppo Haapasalo (vocals / guitar), Tuomas Kokko (guitar), Sami Hämäläinen (guitar), Heikki Koistinen (bass), Henri Lindström (drums).*

Jyväckylä Thrashers. PURITY's inaugural product would be a 1994 EP entitled 'In Disguise' released via Listen To Our Music Productions. That same year the group donated two tracks, 'A Mere Wreck' and 'A New Sound' to the 'Don't Fuck With The Babysitter' compilation album on Moho Pop Records. Signing to Black Mark Records the band cut their first album, 'Built' issued in 1996, with producer Mikka Karmilo at Watercastle and Finnvox Studios in Helsinki. PURITY contributed their version of THE POLICE's 'It's Alright For You' to the compilation album 'Black Mark Tribute Vol. II'. A single, 'A Wiseman Reckons', followed. PURITY put out further singles including 'Days Go By' in 2002 and 'Nibs', backed by a promotional video directed by Tomi Pitkäjärvi, in May 2004. Megamania Records signed the band for a second album, 'Dear Evilyn', notably produced by Hiili Hiilesmaa of H.I.M. and AMORPHIS repute.

Formative band members included guitarist Tapsa Minkkinen, Pekka Korpela and drummer Juhis Ojala. PURITY held a line-up comprising singer Teppo Haapasalo, guitarists Tuomas Kokko and Sami Hämäläinen, bass player Heikki Koistinen and drummer Henri Lindström.

In Disguise, Listen To Our Music Productions LISTENCD1 (1994). In Disguise / Dead End Street / How I Fool You / Look (That's What I've Learnt).
BUILT, Black Mark BMCD 102 (1997). Pique / Dead End Street / Enter-Exit / What A Day / Lost / To Carve / In Disguise / A Mere Wreck / For My Godson / Very Sorry / Plain / I Bastard.
A Wiseman Reckons, Listen To Our Music Productions LISTENCD2 (1998). A Wiseman Reckons / Lollipop / Limbo.
Days Go By, OPCITYCDS402 (2002). Days Go By / You.
Nibs, Megamania BOUNDCDS 123 (2004). Nibs / Omission.
DEAR EVILYN, Megamania 1000 122042 (2004). Thursday / Nibs / Dear Evilyn / Endless / Cape / Slave / Gasp Again / Days Go By / You / Maybe Tomorrow / Mother.Father.Sister.Brother.

PYOVELI

FINLAND — *T.Metal N (vocals / drums), T. Pyoveli N (guitar / bass).*

A young, two-piece retro styled thrash act, PYOVELI, was formed around the turn of the century. Since 2001 the two brothers released a succession of four demos and have shot a three promotional videos as well. Inspired to no small degree by 80's era speed and thrash acts, in 2002 the band also recorded a five track demo, 'Ancient War Gods', of cover tunes featuring versions of songs by SODOM, SLAYER, VENOM, POSSESSED and KREATOR. The demo 'Feel The Razor' followed in 2003. Demo song titles like 'Thrashing Death', 'Thrash til Death' and 'Death Thrash Speed Metal Slaughter' may give potential fans an early clue as to the lyrical and musical thrust of the band.

In 2005 they released their debut album, 'The New Renaissance of Speed & Thrash Metal'. The album while released independently was soon licensed to a number of small labels in Holland, Chile and Malaysia who pressed it on cassette. PYOVELI also contributed a couple of tracks for a regional various artists CD, called 'Metal On Metal: Finnish Underground Metal Compilation'.

THRASH ATTACK, (2001). Thrash Attack / Headbanging Maniacs / Deathrage / Slay To The Ground / Hell Thrashing Holocaust / Death Thrash Speed Metal Slaughter / Witchcraft.
PYOVELI, Pyoveli (2001). Thrash Til Death / Speed Metal Soldiers / Armies Of Hell / Possessed / Overkill / Marshall Law / Bulletbelt Attack / Witchburner / Armageddon / Speed Metal Is My Way.
Ancient War Gods, (2002). The Exorcist / Bonebreaker / Countess Bathory / Evil Has No Boundaries / Outbreak Of Evil.
Feel The Razor, (2003). Thrashing Death / Metal Forces / Feel The Razor / Tribute To Suffer / Fear Valley.
THE NEW RENAISSANCE OF SPEED & THRASH METAL, (2005). Pyoveli Attack / Thrash Hammer / Possessed By Metal / The Hangman / Predator / Metal Revolution / Thrashing Death / Metal Forces / Feel The Razor / Tribute To Suffer / Fear Valley / Outro: Death To All.

PYURIA

FINLAND — *Osku Mäki (vocals / guitar), Tapani Kasurinen (guitar), Valtteri Wilén (bass), Sami Maanpää (drums).*

Uncompromising brutal Death Metal band, founded during 1996 by vocalist / guitarist Oskari Mäki and drummer Sami Siirtola. This duo was soon joined by bass player Jukka-Pekka Suominen and second guitarist Tomi Korkiakangas. This line-up cut a four track, self-titled demo in 1998. Briefly installing singer "Pete", a second demo, the two song 'Suprapubic Pain', emerged the following year. Following sessions for a 1999 EP entitled 'Baroquean Menuets For Oesophagus' PYURIA inducted new member Tapani Kasurinen on guitar. New drummer Sami Maanpää was located in August 2002. Further changes saw Valtteri Wilén taking over bass duties. Signing to Crash Music Inc. the group recorded the album 'Calliphora Vomitoria Introitus' for release in January 2005.

Bassist Valtteri Wilén has association with Norwegian band RILKÁ, fronted by female singer Maya Liittokivi and featuring INTRIGUE and SORG guitarist Knut E. Bakkevold.

Pyuria, Pyuria (1997). Disease / Psycho / Ebony Ice / Permissiveness.
Pyuria, (1997). Disease / Psycho / Ebony Ice / Permissiveness.
Suprapubic Pain, (1998). Abattoir Around / Northern Candlejam.
Baroquean Menuets For Oesophagus EP, (1999). Festered Hate / The Garden Of Pyeden / Syndicate Of Sickness / Porfuria Waltz.
Sublime Metrics Reallocation EP, (2003). To Breathe One's Last / Formaldehyde Bride—Subcutaneous Phagocytosis / Douleur Mortelle / Murder Metaframe / Nemesis Mausoleum / In Rotten Remains Forgotten Names Lie.
CALLIPHORA VOMITORIA INTROITUS, Crash (2004). To Breathe One's Last / In Rotten Remains Forgotten Names Lie / Douleur Mortelle / Murder Metaframe / Nemesis Mausoleum / Formaldehyde Bride-Subcutaneous Phagosytosis / Ghoulish / Field Court-Marshall / Flaunting Moldering Metrics.

QUICK CHANGE

MARKHAM, IL, USA — *Russell Barron (vocals), Dubs Anderson (guitar), Mark Anderson (guitar), Chris Harbin (bass), Craig Williamson (drums).*

Starting out as a covers band playing interpretations of JUDAS PRIEST and SCORPIONS songs Chicago outfit QUICK CHANGE, previously known as STAR FIRE, offered a distinctly retro Thrash-Doom influenced sound. The band debuted with a demo tape in 1983 'Can't Hide' that just failed to gain them a deal with IRS Records at the time. The band comprised singer Dwayne Whitehead, guitarists Mike McCarthy and Dubs Anderson, bassist Wayne Salvetti and drummer John Kruczek.

The group eventually offered the 1989 'Circus Of Death' album through a deal struck with Roadrunner after further demo sessions 'Show No Mercy' and 'F.U.N.'. However, that same year, despite building a healthy local following and garnering international respect, QUICK CHANGE folded. In 1991 Dubs Anderson re-emerged as a member of VIOLENT WISDOM.

QUICK CHANGE marked a return in 2000 with the independent 'Money, Lust & Greed' album. Newly installed on bass guitar would be ex-STONE GROOVE man Chris Harbin. Singer Russell Barron, previously with PHOENIX RISING and CRYPTIC VISIONS, would enroll in December of 2001.

August of 2004 saw the recruitment of new guitarist Mark Anderson, a scene veteran of DITCHWATER and UNSEEN ENEMY. Announcing the addition of ex-BAD OMEN, TYRANT'S REIGN and VIOLENT WISDOM drummer Craig Williamson, a new studio album, 'entitled 'Outside Looking In', was projected for early 2005.

CIRCUS OF DEATH, Roadrunner RR95031 (1989). Will You Die / Sludge / Show No Mercy / A.T.L. / Sea Witch / Leave It To The Beaver / Circus Of Death / Battle Your Fear / Injected / Death Games / What's Next / Plowed.
MONEY, LUST & GREED, Quick Change (2000). Face / My Hands / Here To Stay / In My Vision / Money, Lust & Greed / Deep Within / Let Me / Live In The Now / Recognise.
IV LIVE, Quick Change (2003). Face / To Live / In The Mirror / In My Dream / Better Think / Money, Lust & Greed / Wide Eyes / To Be Or Not To Be / Whipped / Life On The Road.
LIVE AT THE METRO, EMusicLive.com (2004). Money, Lust & Greed / Better Think / To Live / QC Slam / To Be Or Not To Be / Face.

QUO VADIS

MONTRÉAL, QC, CANADA — *Stephane Paré (vocals), Bart Frydrychowicz (vocals / guitar), William Seghers (guitar), Dominique Lapointe (bass), Roxanne Constantin (keyboards), Yanic Bercier (drums).*

QUO VADIS was forged in Montréal as a 1992 covers act by vocalist / guitarist / violinist Arie Itman, guitarist Bart Frydrychowicz and drummer Yanic Bercier, subsequently drafting bassist Remy Beauchamp in 1995. For live work the band pulled in classically trained soprano guest vocalist Sebrina Lipari. Utilising engineer Pierre Remillard QUO VADIS cut their self financed 'Forever ...' debut album in 1996. Favourable reviews for the band's technical brand of violin spiced Death Metal generated licensing deals with EarthAD Records in Germany and Immortal Records in Poland.

In 1999 QUO VADIS signed to Hypnotic Records, working with Pierre Remillard on second album 'Day Into Night', capitalised on by 2002's 'Passage In Time', this release a compilation of remixes, live tracks and the group's original 1995 demo tracks.

Both Itman and Beauchamp would both exit, seeing Stephane Paré take over the lead vocal role. CRYPTOPSY's Alex Auburn substituted temporarily for QUO VADIS in March of 2003. To record the band's third album Steve DiGiorgio of TESTAMENT, SADUS, DEATH, CONTROL DENIED and SADUS repute was enrolled as session bassist. QUO VADIS incorporated bassist Dominique 'Forest' Lapointe of ATHERETIC, SATANIZED, B.A.R.F. and AUGURY repute alongside guitarist William Seghers for Summer 2004 shows.

A new album, initially entitled 'To The Bitter End' but then changed to 'Defiant Imagination' and accompanied by a promotional video for the track 'In Contempt', was set for November issue through Fusion3/Skyscraper Records.

During early 2005 former QUO VADIS members guitarist/vocalist Arie Itman and bassist Remy Beauchamp teamed up with NEURAXIS and TORN WITHIN guitarist Rob Milley and drummer Tommy Kinnon in a new band called JESTER. Meantime, Roxanne Constantin recorded keyboards for AVEN AURA's debut 'The Shadow Of Idols' in February. QUO VADIS put in their debut shows in Germany during March, appearing at the 'Darkrise Metal Night' and 'Bowels-Supper Fest III' events. A gig on 7th May at The Medley in Montreal, supported by DESPISED ICON, AUGURY, SOUL OF DARKNESS and ASHES OF EDEN, saw the band performing the 'Defiant Imagination' album in its entirety for future DVD release.

Will Seghers joined NEURAXIS in April 2006. QUO VADIS teamed up with NEAERA, FEAR MY THOUGHTS and fellow Canadian headliners KATAKLYSM for the 'Road To Devastation' European tour in January 2007.

FOREVER ..., Vomit (1996). Legions Of The Betrayed / As I Feed The Flames Of Hate / Carpae Deum / Mystery / Inner Capsule (Element Of The Ensemble Part II) / Pantheon Of Tears / Zero Hour / The Day The Universe Changed / Nocturnal Reflections / Sans Abris.
DAY INTO NIGHT, Hypnotic (2000). Absolution (Element Of The Ensemble III) / Dysgenics / Hunter/Killer / Hunter/Killer: Endgame / Let It Burn / Dream / On The Shores Of Ithaka / Night Of The Roses / I Believe / Mute Requiem / Cadences Of Absonance.
PASSAGE IN TIME, Skyscraper (2001). Vital Signs 2000 / As One / The Hunted (Hunter-Killer Remix) / Dysgenics (Live) / Point Of No Return—Mute Requiem (Live) / Element Of The Ensemble (Demo 1995) / Sons Of Greed (Demo 1995) / Vital Signs (Demo 1995) / Sadness (Demo 1995).
DEFIANT IMAGINATION, Fusion3/Skyscraper (2003). Silence Calls The Storm / In Contempt / Break The Cycle / Tunnel Effect (Element Of The Ensemble IV) / To The Bitter End / In Articulo Mortis / Fate's Descent / Dead Man's Diary / Ego Intuo Et Servo Te.

RAGE

HERNE, GERMANY — *Peavey Wagner (vocals / bass), Victor Smolski (guitar), Mike Terrana (drums).*

RAGE was formed from the rampant Heavy Metal band AVENGER, with a line-up of Peter Wagner (a.k.a. 'Peavey'), guitarists Jochen Schröder and Thomas Grüning and drummer Jörg Michael. AVENGER, based in Herne, released the 'Prayer Of Steel' album and 'Depraved To Black' EP on Wishbone Records before adopting the title of RAGE in 1986, due to confusion with the English AVENGER.

Signing to Noise Records to release the Ralf Hubert produced 'Reign Of Fear', crafted at Horus Sound Studios in Hannover, RAGE toured Germany on a bill with KREATOR and DESTRUCTION in 1986. Shortly after the tour, Grüning left and his position was filled by the high profile figure of ex-WARLOCK guitarist Rudy Graf for 1987's self-produced 'Execution Guaranteed'. Michael also operated in the 'anonymous' avant-garde side project MEKONG DELTA during 1987.

That same year both Graf and Michael were out, superseded by guitarist Manni Schmidt and drummer Chris Efthimiades. Michael would become the permanent drummer for German guitar hero AXEL RUDI PELL and rack up impressive credits with fellow Teutonic Metal bands HEADHUNTER, GRAVE DIGGER, GLENMORE and RUNNING WILD. 1988's 'Perfect Man' album enjoyed considerable critical success with the media and went on to sell over 30,000 copies in Europe alone. The 'Perfect Man' album would be the first to sport the razor toothed robot mascot that would become synonymous with successive Rage releases. RAGE utilised producer Armin Sabol and the Skytrak Studios in Berlin to cut the 'Secrets In A Weird World' album in the Spring of 1989. In 1990 RAGE toured Germany as support to RUNNING WILD.

Having released 'Reflections Of A Shadow' in 1991, this opus embellished with the keyboards of Ulli Köllner, and the stop-gap EP 'Extended Power', RAGE's 1992 album, Trapped', featured a cover of the renowned ACCEPT classic 'Fast As A Shark' and Japanese issues also added two bonus cuts in 'Innocent Guilty' and 'Marching Heroes-The Wooden Cross'. 'Trapped' marked a number of important changes for the band, it being recorded over two locations, at Narhavaci Studios in Prague and Powerplay Studios, Berlin. The tracks also benefited not only from a mix by renowned producer Tom Morris but also extra textures given by the Collegium Concertante Sextet of the Smetana Orchestra. The group would subsequently fulfill the ambition of touring in Japan and later joined SAXON and MOTÖRHEAD in Europe on the 'Eagles And Bombers' tour in Europe.

Backed by a further EP, the Sven Conquest produced 'Beyond The Wall', RAGE undertook further touring in 1993 on a bill alongside GAMMA RAY and Norwegians CONCEPTION as they were surely about to unleash the album of their career in 'A Missing Link' In 1994 guitarist Schmidt left the band. His position was filled by Spiros Efthimiades and ex-PYRACANDA man Sven Fischer and the ensuing 'Ten Years In Rage' album featured new cuts alongside old favourites.

RAGE split from Noise Records in 1994 following many other German acts to G.U.N. Records, an arm of major label BMG. After their debut for G.U.N. Records, 'Black In Mind' produced by Ulli Pösselt at RA.SH. Studios in Gelsenkirchen, RAGE played a series of 'Summer Metal Meetings' together with RUNNING WILD, GRAVE DIGGER, GAMMA RAY, GLENMORE and ICED EARTH. The year ended on a high as the band joined the December 'Blind Guardian Christmas Party' tour, headed up by BLIND GUARDIAN and also boasting LOVE/HATE, SAXON, SKYCLAD and YNGWIE MALMSTEEN. In 1996 they released the 'Lingua Mortis' album. The record found the band joined by the Symphony Orchestra of Prague playing some of their best cuts. March 1998's Christian Wolff co-produced offering, 'XIII' laid down at Principal Studios in Senden, continued with the successful orchestrated approach and bravely also hosted a rendition of the ROLLING STONES 'Paint It Black'. Asian variants boasted a further cover in RUSH's 'Tom Sawyer'.

RAGE suffered a mass walkout in 1999 when both the

Efthimiades brothers and second guitarist Sven Fischer decamped leaving Peavey Wagner flying solo. Undaunted Wagner pulled in Russian guitar virtuoso VICTOR SMOLSKI, quickly bowing back in with the 'Ghosts' concept album, also seeing production duties going to Christian Wolff. European digipacks added extra track 'End Of Eternity' whilst the traditional Japanese bonus would be 'Six Feet Under Ground' In Germany this new incarnation of RAGE would debut at the Wacken festival then set off on an extensive tour of Russia.

2000 found Wagner guesting on the GB ARTS album 'The Lake'. Smolski too would session outside of RAGE contributing lead solos to the PERSONAL WAR 'Newtimechaos' outing. Ex-RAGE man Manni Schmidt joined GRAVE DIGGER in December 2000.

Peavey drafted former HANOVER FIST, ZILLION, BEAU NASTY, YNGWIE MALMSTEEN, ARTENSION and METALIUM drummer American Mike Terrana to cement a finally stable trio. RAGE's 2001 album 'Welcome To The Other Side' would land the group an unexpected bonus when the track 'Straight To Hell' would be chosen for the soundtrack to the movie 'Der Schuh des Manitu', a film which would turn out to be one of the most commercially successful German language films ever. 'Welcome To The Other Side', committed to tape at VPS Studio in Hamm, was an important milestone for the band, being the first album entirely played and written by the Wagner/Smolski/Terrana line-up.

Terrana would also be found sessioning, in his case on the DRIVEN project album put together by ex-DIO guitarist Tracy G. The drummer also regrouped with ARTENSION for a 2002 comeback album 'Sacred Pathway' as well as perform on the 'Shadow Zone' album from German guitar hero AXEL RUDI PELL. A further collaboration had the sticksman forging the Jazz Fusion act the VOODOO TABOO FUSION BAND project in collaboration with Frenchmen guitarist CYRIL ARCHARD and bassist Ivan Rougny for an album 'Something's Cooking' issued through the Finnish Lion Music label.

The RAGE April 2002 album 'Unity' would see the Japanese release boasting the traditional extra track in the form of 'Darkness Turns To Light'. The band embarked on a full scale world tour commencing in Seol at the 'World Rock Festival' before continuing on for dates in Japan. RAGE would also schedule a date in August at the 'Soyorock 2002' festival in Kyung Gi Do, Korea. An extensive September run of European concerts found RAGE paired up with PRIMAL FEAR. The band made space to cut a live rendition of 'Motorbreath' for a Nuclear Blast METALLICA tribute collection. RAGE tackled a Charlie Bauerfiend produced new album billed as 'Soundchaser' for 2003, recording this opus at HELLOWEEN vocalist Andi Deris' Tenerife studios. Naturally, ANDI DERIS lent guesting backing vocals. The HELLOWEEN connection continued into the promotion of the record as RAGE were announced as support act to the famed Metal Pumpkins October European dates.

In early 2004 guitarist Victor Smolski recorded a guest appearance for the DER BOTE solo project of FEUERENGEL frontman Boris Delic. He would also convene a further solo album comprising heavyweight re-works of Johan Sebastian Bach classics with the working title 'Majesty & Passion'. Joining Smolski at VPS Studios for these recording sessions would be his RAGE colleagues Peavy Wagner and Mike Terrana as well as former SCORPIONS guitar legend ULI JON ROTH.

Unfortunately guitarist Victor Smolski fell "seriously ill" following the group's performance at the Italian 'Gods Of Metal' festival in June. It transpired that Smolski had been suffering from a testicular infection for some time and that during the concert in Bologna this organ burst with serious consequences. With Smolski hospitalised former guitarist Manni Schmidt was to step into the breech to cover for a show at the Helfenstein festival in Geislingen. However, just days after this announcement RAGE cancelled the show. November of 2004 saw issue of the

RAGE

band's 20th anniversary double live album 'From The Cradle To The Stage'. That same month MIKE TERRANA revealed plans for an "instrumental Rock fusion" solo album entitled 'Man Of The World' comprising six studio tracks and four live songs recorded in Moscow at the Premier Drum Day Festival 2003.

Smolski joined ex-ARIA singer Valery Kipelov at a Moscow recording studio in late January 2005 for the recording of a solo album and live work. The guitarist also contributed guitar work for Spanish Thrash Metal band LEGEN BELTZA's conceptual track dubbed 'War of Wars' included on their album 'Dimension Of Pain'.

As RAGE signed a new label deal with Nuclear Blast Records, early 2005 also saw the release of the album 'Back In Time', a RAGE tribute offering compiling no less than 28 Austrian Heavy Metal bands paying homage.

Peavey Wagner had a lucky escape in early May when he was injured by a car. Apparently the car had hit the RAGE frontman whilst he was riding his bicycle, Wagner having to undergo surgery to fix his arm. The singer was soon back in action, putting in a guest vocal appearance on DESTRUCTION's 'Inventor Of Evil' album. RAGE concerts in Europe announced for April 2006 had FREEDOM CALL lined up as support. Mike Terrana joined the ranks of MASTERPLAN in October. In early December the drummer announced he was closing his eight year tenure as a member of RAGE. As the New Year broke, RAGE revealed André Hilgers, of AXXIS, MENDACIOUS MESSIAH, VANIZE, THE SYGNET and SILENT FORCE, had been installed as new drummer.

RAGE guitar player Victor Smolski recorded a set of brand new songs for a 2007 Nuclear Blast Records' 20th anniversary compilation album. RAGE's Peavey Wagner supplied vocals to the track 'Terrified'. Andre Hilgers supplied drum parts. In February the band issued the concert double DVD 'Full Moon In St. Petersburg', filmed at their May 20th 2006 concert with extra footage from the 'Masters Of Rock' festival in the Czech Republic, backstage moments, video clips plus a documentary.

In March Smolski, along with business partner Jen Majura, opened a music school in Hamm, Germany titled the Unity Music School.

REIGN OF FEAR, Noise N0038 (1986). Scared To Death / Deceiver / Reign Of Fear / Hand Of Glory / Raw Energy / Echoes Of Evil / Chaste Flesh / Suicide / Machinery / Scaffold.

EXECUTION GUARANTEED, Noise N0073 (1987). Down By Law / Execution Guaranteed / Before The Storm / Street Wolf / Deadly

Error / Hatred / Grapes Of Wrath / Mental Decay / When You're Dead.

PERFECT MAN, Noise N0112-1 (1988). Wasteland / In The Darkest Hour / Animal Instinct / Perfect Man / Sinister Thinking / Supersonic Hydromatic / Don't Fear The Winter / Death In The Afternoon / A Pilgrim's Path / Time And Place / Round Trip / Between The Lines.

SECRETS IN A WEIRD WORLD, Noise N0137-1 (1989). Intro (Opus 32 No. 3) / Time Waits For No One / Make My Day / The Inner Search / Invisible Horizons / She / Light Into The Darkness / Talk To Grandpa / Distant Voices / Without A Trace.

Invisible Horizons EP, Noise N0136-6 (1989). Invisible Horizons / Lost Side Of The World / Law And Order.

REFLECTIONS OF A SHADOW, Noise N0160-1 (1990). Introduction (A Bit More Of Green) / That's Human Bondage / True Face In Everyone / Flowers That Fade In My Hand / Reflections Of A Shadow / Can't Get Out / Waiting For The Moon / Saddle The Wind / Dust / Nobody Knows.

Extended Power EP, Noise N0169-3 (1991). Woman / Ashes / Battlefield / Waiting For The Moon / What's Up.

TRAPPED, Noise N0189-1 (1992). Shame On You / Solitary Man / Enough Is Enough / Medicine / Questions / Take Me To The Water / Power And Greed / The Body Talks / Not Forever / Beyond The Wall Of Sleep / Baby, I'm Your Nightmare / Fast As A Shark / Difference.

TRAPPED, JVC Victor VICP-5160 (1992) (Japanese release). Shame On You / Solitary Man / Enough Is Enough / Medicine / Questions / Take Me To The Water / Power And Greed / The Body Talks / Not Forever / Beyond The Wall Of Sleep / Baby, I'm Your Nightmare / Fast As A Shark / Difference / Innocent Guilty / Marching Heroes-The Wooden Cross.

Beyond The Wall, Noise N0202-3 (1992). Bury All Life / On The Edge / I Want You / (Those Who Got) Nothing To Lose / Last Goodbye / Light Into The Darkness.

Beyond The Wall, JVC Victor VICP-2070 (1992) (Japanese release). Bury All Life / On The Edge / I Want You / (Those Who Got) Nothing To Lose / Last Goodbye / Light Into The Darkness / Dust.

The Missing Link, Noise N 007-PR (1993) (Limited to 550 copies). Firestorm / Who Dares? / Her Diary's Black Pages / Refuge.

THE MISSING LINK, Noise N0217-1 (1993). The Firestorm / Nevermore / Refuge / The Pit And The Pendulum / From The Underworld / Certain Days / Who Dares? / Wake Me When I'm Dead / Lost In The Ice / Her Diary's Black Pages / The Missing Link / Raw Caress.

POWER OF METAL, JVC Victor VICP-40132 (1994) (Japanese release. Split live album with GAMMA RAY, CONCEPTION and HELICON). Shame On You / Don't Fear The Winter / Certain Days / Suicide / Refuge / Baby I'm Your Nightmare / Down By Law / Nevermore / Firestorm / Solitary Man / Enough Is Enough / Invisible Horizons.

Refuge, JVC Victor VICP-15034 (1994) (Japanese release). Refuge / Truth Hits Everybody / I Can't Control Myself / Beyond The Pale.

TEN YEARS IN RAGE, Noise N0219-2 (1994). Vertigo / She Killed And Smiled / Destination Day / Take My Blood / No Sign Of Life / Submission / The Unknown / Dangerous Heritage / Prayers Of Steel / The Blow In A Row.

The Crawling Chaos, Great Unlimited Noises GUN 061 (1995) (Promotion release). The Crawling Chaos / Black In Mind / Alive But Dead / Shadow Out Of Time.

BLACK IN MIND, Great Unlimited Noises GUN 062 (1995). Black In Mind / The Crawling Chaos / Alive But Dead / Sent By The Devil / Shadow Out Of Time / Spider's Web / In A Nameless Time / The Icecold Hand Of Destiny / Forever / Until I Die / The Rage / The Price Of War / Start / All This Time.

LINGUA MORTIS, Great Unlimited Noises GUN 090 (1996). In A Nameless Time / Alive But Dead / Medley a) Don't Fear The Winter, b) Black In Mind, c) Firestorm, d) Sent By The Devil, e) Lost In The Ice / All This Time / Alive But Dead.

END OF ALL DAYS, Great Unlimited Noises GUN 101 (1996) (Limited edition). Under Control / Higher Than The Sky / Deep In The Blackest Hole / End Of All Days / Visions / Desperation / Voice From The Vault / Let The Night Begin / Fortress / Frozen Fire / Talking To The Dead / Face Behind The Mask / Silent Victory / Fading Hours / The Sleep / The Trooper.

END OF ALL DAYS, Great Unlimited Noises GUN 101 (1996). Under Control / Higher Than The Sky / Deep In The Blackest Hole / End Of All Days / Visions / Desperation / Voice From The Vault / Let The Night Begin / Fortress / Frozen Fire / Talking To The Dead / Face Behind The Mask / Silent Victory / Fading Hours.

Higher Than The Sky, JVC Victor VICP-15073 (1996) (Japanese release). Higher Than The Sky / The Trooper / Jawbreaker / Forgive But Don't Forget / Tie The Rope.

Live From The Vault, JVC Victor VICP-18015 (1997) (Japanese release). Introduction: Gavotla From 4 Pieces Opus No. 32 / Sent By The Devil / Visions / The Price Of War / Higher Than The Sky / Shadow Out Of Time / Motorbreath.

XIII, Great Unlimited Noises GUN 156 (1998). Overture / From The Cradle To The Grave / Days Of December / Sign Of Heaven / Incomplete / Turn The Page / Heartblood / Over And Over / In Vain (I Won't Go Down) / Immortal Sin / Paint It Black / Just Alone. Chart position: 21 GERMANY.

From The Cradle To The Grave, Great Unlimited Noises GUN 159 (1998) (Promotion release). Overture / From The Cradle To The Grave / Paint It Black / Just Alone.

In Vain I, Great Unlimited Noises GUN 166CD1 (1998). In Vain (I Won't Go Down) / Turn The Page (Live) / Incomplete (Live) / Yesterday (Live).

In Vain II, Great Unlimited Noises GUN 166CD2 (1998). In Vain (I Won't Go Down) / From The Cradle To The Grave (Live) / Alive But Dead (Live) / Paint It Black (Live).

In Vain III, Great Unlimited Noises GUN 166CD3 (1998). In Vain (I Won't Go Down) / Sent By The Devil (Live) / Higher Than The Sky (Live) / Motorbreath (Live).

In Vain—Rage In Acoustic, JVC Victor VICP-60392 (1998) (Japanese release). In Vain (I Won't Go Down) (Radio mix) / Turn The Page (Acoustic version) / Incomplete (Acoustic version) / Immortal Sin (Acoustic version) / Yesterday.

GHOSTS, Great Unlimited Noises GUN 185 (1999). Beginning Of The End / Back In Time / Ghosts / Wash My Sins Away / Fear / Love And Fear Unite / Vanished In Haze / Spiritual Awakening / Love After Death / More Than A Lifetime / Tomorrow's Yesterday.

GHOSTS, Great Unlimited Noises GUN 185 (1999) (Limited edition). Beginning Of The End / Back In Time / Ghosts / Wash My Sins Away / Fear / Love And Fear Unite / Vanished In Haze / Spiritual Awakening / Love After Death / More Than A Lifetime / Tomorrow's Yesterday / End Of Eternity. Chart position: 31 GERMANY.

WELCOME TO THE OTHER SIDE, Great Unlimited Noises GUN 189 (2001). Trauma / Paint The Devil On The Wall / The Mirror In Your Eyes / Tribute To Dishonour: Part 1—R.I.P. / Tribute To Dishonour: Part 2—One More Time / Tribute To Dishonour: Part 3—Requiem / Tribute To Dishonour: Part 4—I'm Crucified / No Lies / Point Of No Return / Leave It All Behind / Deep In The Night / Welcome To The Other Side / Lunatic / Riders In The Moonlight / Straight To Hell / After The End / Sister Demon.

UNITY (LIMITED EDITION), Steamhammer SPV 085-72970 (2002) (Digipack). All I Want / Insanity / Down / Set This World On Fire / Dies Irae / World Of Pain / Shadowa / Living My Dream / Seven Deadly Sins / You Want It, You'll Get It / Unity / Mystery Trip / Down (Video).

UNITY, Steamhammer SPV 085-72972 (2002). All I Want / Insanity / Down / Set This World On Fire / Dies Irae / World Of Pain / Shadows / Living My Dream / Seven Deadly Sins / You Want It, You'll Get It / Unity.

SECRETS IN A WEIRD WORLD, Noise N0367-2 (2002) (Remaster with bonus tracks). Intro (Opus 32 No. 3) / Time Waits For No One / Make My Day / The Inner Search / Invisible Horizons / She / Light Into The Darkness / Talk To Grandpa / Distant Voices / Without A Trace / Lost Side Of The World / Law And Order / Mirror / Invisible Horizons (Live) / (Those Who Got) Nothing To Lose / Shame On You (Acoustic version).

SOUNDCHASER, Steamhammer SPV 085-69362 (2003). Orgy Of Destruction (Intro) / War Of Worlds / Great Old Ones / Soundchaser / Defenders Of The Ancient Life / Secrets In A Weird World / Flesh And Blood / Human Metal / See You In Heaven Or Hell / Falling From Grace (Part I: Wake The Nightmares) / Falling From Grace (Part II: Death Is On Its Way). Chart position: 54 GERMANY.

FROM THE CRADLE TO THE STAGE, SPV SPV 088-69662 (2004). Orgy Of Destruction / War Of Worlds / Great Old Ones / Paint The Devil On The Wall / Sent By The Devil / Firestorm / Down / Prayers Of Steel / Suicide / Days Of December / Unity / Anarchy (Drum solo) / Enough Is Enough / Invisible Horizons / Set This World On Fire / Flesh And Blood / Rocket Science (Guitar solo) / Soundchaser / Straight To Hell / Back In Time / Refuge / From The Cradle To The Grave / Black In Mind / Solitary Man / Don't Fear The Winter / All I Want / Higher Than The Sky.

FULL MOON IN ST. PETERSBURG, Nuclear Blast (2006) (CD + DVD).

Full Moon, Nuclear Blast (2006) (Radio and club promotion CD). Full Moon / Vollmond / La Luna Reine.

SPEAK OF THE DEAD, Nuclear Blast NB 1483-2 (2006). Morituri Te Salutant / Prelude Of Souls / Innocent / Depression / No Regrets / Confusion / Black / Beauty / No Fear / Soul Survivor / Full Moon / Kill Your Gods / Turn My World Around / Be With Me Or Be Gone / Speak Of The Dead. Chart position: 58 GERMANY.

RAGEDATE

LANDSKRONA, SWEDEN — *Fredrik Andersson (vocals), Sebastian Björkemar (guitar), Jens Thellman (guitar), Alfred Andersson (bass), Mattias Larsson (drums).*

Landskrona's RAGEDATE issued a self-titled demo in 2002, after which their Nu-Metal leanings began to veer toward technical Thrash. The group had been formed by then bassist Fredrik Andersson, guitarist Sebastian Björkemar and Mattias Larsson on drums. The group's inaugural concert would be fronted by Filip Persson. However, this latest candidate then decamped and Andersson took on vocal responsibilities for the opening demo, recorded at Wennerlund Studios. Confusion followed, resulting in a fluid bass position and the exit of Andersson, finally stabilised with the addition of Mikael Hill of FATAL NURSE on bass. RAGEDATE drew Andersson back into the fold for a 2003 demo, laid down with producer Jimmy Drexler at AudioSpot Records in Malmö.

In the summer of 2004, Jens Thellman joined as lead guitarist but Hill opted out to prioritise FATAL NURSE. Alfred Andersson duly took on the bass role. Recording sessions in held in Helsingborg during February of 2005 would see Klas Ideberg of DARKANE aiding as producer. Bassist Alfred Andersson exited in September, relocating to the USA, and was replaced by Tommy Erichsson.

Ragedate, Ragedate (2002). Unreal Behaviour / Symbol Of Imagination / Selt.
Close Your Eyes, (2003). Close Your Eyes / The Cold Voice.
Ragedate, (2005). Contaminated And Insane / Boundless Souls.

RAGING FURY

JAPAN — *Haruo (vocals / bass), Toyozo (guitar), Masayuki (drums).*

Thrashers RAGING FURY, originally hailing from Kyoto, relocated to Osaka to form up a line-up comprising vocalist / bass player Haruo, guitarist Toyozo and drummer Matato. The band debuted with a self titled four song cassette demo in 1986, following this in 1987 with the 'Wolf Spider' tape. An EP, 'The Rattlesnake Rules', arrived in 1988. A live version of the song 'Barricade' would also be donated to the 'Skull Smash' compilation album. RAGING FURY was prolific in 1990, releasing a further eponymous cassette and being featured on the video 'Thrash In Savagery'. Three tracks would also appear as part of the compilation outing 'Far East Thrash Army II: Burning Inside'.

In 1992 Kenjiro took over on drums in time for recording of the band's debut album and a demo 'Iron Skies'. Another promotion tape, 'Werewolf', saw distribution in 1995. However, then both Toyozo and Kenjiro left the band. RAGING FURY duly attained full strength once again with the induction of guitarist Toru and drummer Masayuki for the EP "Deal You A Fatal Blow' delivered in March of 1999.

Notable supports came with guest slots to visiting artists TANKARD and MARDUK. Another band casualty came in 2000 when, shortly after a gig acting as openers to Swedes DERANGED in October of that year, Toru bailed out. Makato took the guitar position in January of 2001, featuring on a 2002 demo 'The Aggression And The Furious', but by February of 2003 was out of the picture, leaving a vacancy filled by the return of Toyozo.

The Rattlesnake Rules EP, Gunslinger (1988). The Rattlesnake Rules / Electric Brain.
RAGING FURY, (1992). The Way Of Life / Megaton / A Man Called Dragon / Return / Never Say Die / The Triffids / Black Future / The Day Of The Triffids / Man Spider.
Deal You A Fatal Blow, (1999). Fatal Blow / Winslow Wong / Barricade / I Ain't You / Dinosaur Tank.

RAISE HELL

STOCKHOLM, SWEDEN — *Jonas Nilsson (vocals / guitar), Torstein Wickberg (guitar), Niklas Sjostrom (bass), Dennis Ekdahl (drums).*

Much lauded Stockholm Death Metal combo founded in 1995 as IN COLD BLOOD by vocalist / guitarist Jonas Hilsson, bass player Niklas Sjöström and guitarist Torstein Wickberg. The following year drummer Dennis Ekdahl completed the rankings. The band, very much rooted in the Black Metal scene, were all still in their mid teens by the time the band was finalised leading to jibes about them being "the Death Metal HANSON".

In the summer of 1997 IN COLD BLOOD issued their only demo 'Nailed'. A record company bidding war erupted, which included the Earache label, after which Germany's Nuclear Blast emerged as the victors. However, at this point was an American Hardcore act of same title was discovered hence the name switch to RAISE HELL.

By the time 1998 debut 'Holy Target' arrived RAISE HELL's average band member age was just 18. The record displayed a remarkable maturity for an act so young blending Death and Thrash Metal with unashamed anti-Christian lyrics. The group got straight into gear touring Europe to promote the album alongside DISMEMBER, AGATHODAIMON, NIGHT IN GALES and CHILDREN OF BODOM. During 1999 Niklas Sjöström made time to session bass guitar on DARK EDEN's 'Winterland' demos. The 2000 album 'Not Dead Yet' found RAISE HELL maneuvering away from their Black Metal roots.

Ekdahl also drums for SINS OF OMISSION and has credits also with MÖRK GRYNING and MYSTIC PROPHECY. The drummer would also feature on Progressive Metal band ATHELA's 'Spectral' demo and take up temporary residency with fellow Swedish Death Metal band BLOODSHED for touring in Finland during December of 2001.

RAISE HELL's October 2002 album 'Wicked Is My Game', released by Nuclear Blast Records, saw production credits going to IN FLAMES vocalist Anders Friden and Frederik Reinedahl.

In February 2003 Jonas Nilsson bowed out, being swiftly replaced by former DRIFTAWAY man Jimmy Fjällendahl. RAISE HELL signed to Black Lodge Records in September of 2004. They entered Sheepvalley Productions in Stockholm during April 2005 to record their fourth album. 'City Of The Damned", was released in May 2006 via Black Lodge Records. RAISE HELL teamed up with NECROPHOBIC and Malmö's ORIGIN BLOOD for a European tour beginning late September.

HOLY TARGET, Nuclear Blast (1998). The March Of Devil's Soldiers / Raise The Dead / Beautiful As Fire / Holy Target / Legions Of Creeps / The Red Ripper / Black Visions / Mattered Out / Superior Powers.
NOT DEAD YET, Nuclear Blast NB 443-2 (2000). Dance With The Devil / Babes / Back Attack / Devilyn / Not Dead Yet / No Puls / User Of Poison / He Is Coming / Soulcollector.
WICKED IS MY GAME, Nuclear Blast NB 1053-2 (2002). Hellborn / Nightwatcher / The Haunted House / Wicked Is My Game / In My Cell / Another Side / Death Race / Devil May Care / Destiny Deceiver.
HOLY TARGET & NOT DEAD YET, Irond CD 02-407 (2003) (Russian release). Dance With The Devil / Babes / Back Attack / Devilyn / Not Dead Yet / No Puls / User Of Poison / He Is Coming / Soulcollector / The March Of Devil's Soldiers / Raise The Devil / Beautiful As Fire / Holy Target / Legions Of Creeps / The Red Ripper / Black Visions / Mattered Out / Superior powers.
To The Gallows, Black Lodge (2006). To The Gallows / Open Your Mind.
CITY OF THE DAMNED, Black Lodge BLOD 031CD (2006). Devil's Station / City Of The Damned / Like Clowns We Crawl / Reaper's Calling / Open Your Mind / Ghost I Carry / My Shadow / To The Gallows / I / Rising.

RAISING FEAR

VENETO, ITALY — *Rob Della Frera (vocals), Yorick (guitar), Alberto Toniolo (guitar), Frana (bass), Cristian Galimberti (drums).*

Veneto Heavy Metal band RAISING FEAR features HELREIDH members guitarist Yorick, bassist Frana and drummer Cristian Galimberti. The latter also has association with WARTRAINS, as does guitarist Alberto Toniolo. A demo surfaced in 2003, crafted at Remaster Studios, Vicenza, scoring the band a label deal with Dragonheart Records for the February 2005 'Mythos' album, recorded at New Sin Studios in Loria with producer Luigi Stefanini.

RAISING FEAR entered Remaster Studios in Vicenza during mid January 2006, working with producers Toni Mad Fontò, guitarist of WHITE SKULL, and B.B. Nick Savio, former WHITE SKULL lead guitarist and holding membership with VICIOUS MARY and BROKEN ARROW, to craft a new album billed 'Avalon' for Dragonheart Records. The sessions included guest appearances by female singer Leanan Sidhe, formerly of BEHOLDER, and JAG PANZER lead guitarist Chris Broderick.

Promo 2003, Raising Fear (2003). Gilgamesh / Theseus / Morgana / Amon Ra / Phoenix.
MYTHOS, Dragonheart CHAOS029CD (2005). Thorr / Thesus / Fenrir / Montezuma / Merlin / The Goddess / Charon / Ocasta / Gilgamesh / Angel Witch.
AVALON, Audioglobe (2006).

RAMP

SEIXAL, PORTUGAL — *Rudi Darte (vocals), Ricardo Mendonça (guitar), Tó-Zé (guitar), Caveirinha (bass), Paulinho (drums).*

One of Portugal's biggest Rock acts, Seixal based Thrashers RAMP began life in 1988 with an inaugural line-up of guitarists Ricardo Mendonça and To-Ze (Antonio), bassist Miguel and drummer Paulinho. To show their solidarity the group was named after their initials. A lead vocalist was recruited but quickly dismissed and second time around RAMP settled on frontman Rui Duarte. The band's debut live performance came with a 1989 support to MORTIFERA and THE COVEN. In later years MORTIFERA's bassist Jao would subsequently supplant Miguel.

An acclaimed 1991 demo tape swiftly secured a deal with major label Polygram for a six track EP 'Thought's. In March of 1992 RAMP supported FUDGE TUNNEL and SEPULTURA. Support from the Metal community in Portugal resulted in Polygram re-releasing 'Thoughts' on CD format complete with an extra three songs. 1993 proved a trying year for the band, the majority of its members undertaking their compulsory military service and RAMP severing ties with Polygram.

1994 found renewed momentum as RAMP opened for a visiting PARADISE LOST and signed to the Uniao Lisboa label for a second album 'Intersection'. With this release the band were able to put in festival appearances such as the Faro 'Super Rock' with THE EXPLOITED and RATOS DE PORAO and the 'Ultrabrutal' event at Penafiel alongside BENEDICTION and DISMEMBER. RAMP also made an impression in front of 30'000 people at the 'Festa Do Avante' organised by the Portuguese Communist Party. Other gigs included guest slots to NAPALM DEATH and FEAR FACTORY upfront of festivals in Belgium, France and the Czech Republic. RAMP undertook these latter gigs despite Jao being indisposed with a plastered broken leg.

In 1998 RAMP's third album, the Simon Efemy produced 'Evolotion, Devolution, Revolution', arrived. The following year found the band gigging hard as openers to MANOWAR, MOTÖRHEAD, MONSTER MAGNET, the ROLLINS BAND and even METALLICA. The band offered up a double live album in 1999.

Following the 2003 album 'Nude' for Paranoid Records, RAMP celebrated their fifteenth anniversary in 2004 by recording the opening theme song for the Sic Radical TV channel series 'Anjinho da Guarda', a António Variações cover version. RAMP added new bassist Caveirinha in 2005 and that April released the limited edition 'Planet Earth' EP. For sale only through the band's website, this three track offering was headed up by a cover version of the DURAN DURAN hit 'Planet Earth' and novelly included multimedia of two episodes of the cartoon 'Cristiano o Menino Metaleiro'. Notable live work in 2005 saw RAMP embarking upon a headline 'Planet Earth' tour of Portugal throughout April plus an appearance at the 'Super Bock Super Rock' alongside MARILYN MANSON, AUDIOSLAVE and SLAYER plus a support to ALICE COOPER in Alcochete during July.

THOUGHTS, Polygram (1992). The Commediants / Desilluisions / March To Death / Thoughts / The Last Child / Try Again / In The Beginning / Out Of This World / Behind The Wall.
INTERSECTION, Uniao Lisboa (1995). All Men Taste Hell / Own Way / Black Tie / So You Say / Fate Like You / Unpointless Name / Win / Trip / Friendly Word / Through.
EVOLUTION, DEVOLUTION, REVOLUTION, Farol (1998). Dawn / Helping Hands / Hallelujah / Noone / Future / How / Old Times / D.T.A. / Apathy / For A While / Come.
RAMP—LIVE, Farol (1999). Dawn / Helping Hands / Black Tie / Apathy / So You Say / Noone / Walk Like A Egyptian / Hallelujah / How / For A While / Come / Out Of This World / All Men Taste Hell / Old Times / Through / Last Child / Behind The Wall / Try Again.
NUDE, Paranoid (2003). Prime / In Sane / Clear / Around / S.H.O.U.T. / Newborn / Alone / Bsides / XXX (Fan)Tasy / Caught / Drop Down.
Planet Earth, Paranoid (2005) (Limited edition—website only release). Planet Earth / You Make Me / Anjinho da Guarda.

RAVAGE

DÜSSELDORF, GERMANY — *Jan Michels (vocals), Daniel Pietzsch (guitar), Demian Heuke (guitar), Bernd Steuer (bass), Dennis Thiele (drums).*

Düsseldorf Death Metal combo RAVAGE was created in August 1999 by guitarists Demian Heuke and Daniel Pietzsch, lead vocalist Jan Michels and Stefan Raduschefski on the drums. The latter would soon bow out and in February of 2000 the band welcomed onboard new drummer Dennis Thiele. During early 2001 RAVAGE cut the first demo 'To Kill And Destroy'. The band line up would be brought up to strength in mid 2001 with the introduction of bassist Frank Schneiders. However, after a period of extensive gigging this latest recruit decamped. Bernd Steuer took his place for RAVAGE's 2003 album 'Infernal Devastation', produced by Alex Sokolovski.

The subtly titled 'Get Fucking Slaughtered' arrived in 2005. Guitarist Daniel Pietzsch exited in February.

INFERNAL DEVASTATION, Ravage (2003). Blasphemic War / Disinfestation / Infinite Hate / Execution Call / Drowning In Blood / Day Of Devastation / Totalravage.
GET FUCKING SLAUGHTERED, (2005). Introduction / Get Fucking Slaughtered / Havoc Command / Nuclear Storm / Holycaust / Devilish Strike / Riddled / Vow Of Desecration / Into Your Demise / Blazing Chaos (Death Upon The Nazarene) / Bloody Revenge.

RAVEN

NEWCASTLE UPON TYNE, UK — *John Gallagher (vocals / bass), Mark Gallagher (guitar), Joe Hasselvander (drums).*

Newcastle upon Tyne "Athletic Rock" outfit that made a huge impact on the NWoBHM scene but sadly failed to live up to initial promise in their home country despite recognition abroad. Their early efforts are manic metal sprints through excellent riffs and high pitched distinctive vocals. Despite waning popularity in Britain RAVEN command respect and a healthy fan base across the world.

RAVEN date back to 1974 with an initial line-up of brothers John and Mark Gallagher and Paul Bowden. However, at this fledgling stage RAVEN had only one classical guitar between them. Santa Claus came to the rescue and in December of that year the band got electric guitars for Christmas.

RAVEN's first live date in December 1975 was memorable if not only for the fact that both Gallagher brothers managed to fall offstage. By this point the band had added drummer

Paul Sherrif. Within months Sherrif was out in favour of Mick Kenworthy. In this incarnation RAVEN opened for THE STRANGLERS and THE MOTORS locally. One of RAVEN's early headlining gigs included a Hells Angels convention where the band were ordered to play 'Born to be Wild' no less than ten times in the pouring rain. The band only stalled the show by Mark faking an electric shock.

Kenworthy drifted away in late 1977 to be replaced by Sean Taylor. Bowden also departed in 1979 having his position filled by Pete Shore. RAVEN suffered another blow when Taylor quit, eventually to join SATAN.

Augmenting the band line up once more with the addition of drummer Rob 'Wacko' Hunter whose previous act FASTBREEDER also included future DURAN DURAN guitarist ANDY TAYLOR. RAVEN cut their first two track demo featuring "She Don't Need Your Money' and 'Wiped Out'. Courtesy of TYGERS OF PAN TANG manager Tom Noble this tape secured the band a deal with local Newcastle label Neat Records. During 1980 RAVEN had a track inclusion, 'Let It Rip', on the 'Brute Force' compilation album.

RAVEN's debut single 'Don't Need Your Money' created a huge swell of interest in the band and helped the first album, the Steve Thompson produced 'Rock Until You Drop', reach the British album charts. Raven's debut full-length notably included a nod back to the 70s with a SWEET medley, 'Hellraiser/Action'.

Album number two, 'Wiped Out' issued in 1982, saw the songs getting faster and the band honing their direction. Regrettably, the intended mixes for the album, co-produced by the group and Keith Nichol, were not used and substituted for a mix unapproved by the band. However, the band's fans were still impressed. RAVEN's first American shows in 1982, alongside RIOT and ANVIL, were promoted by Johnny Zazula of the 'Rock n Roll Heaven' record store in New Jersey.

The all German production team of Michael Wagner and ACCEPT lead vocalist Udo Dirkschneider was drafted in for 'All for One', released during 1983, as RAVEN sought a more mature sound. It was also their first American release for Zazula's Megaforce label. This Affiliation led to RAVEN's first 36 date American tour with opening act METALLICA, further tours had EXODUS and ANTHRAX supporting.

At RAVEN's 1984 New York show the band headlined above METALLICA and ANTHRAX. Rumour has it that an A&R representative for Elektra Records was suitably impressed by RAVEN but upon inquiring to the band's name was informed it was METALLICA. Once signed the same person was confused to find the band he had signed were now a quartet and not a trio. Allegedly . . .

With Megaforce's connection to Atlantic Records 1984 saw RAVEN ink a major deal. However, Atlantic maneuvered the band away from their speed attack towards a more mainstream approach even getting the band to wear bizarre spacesuit stage gear. RAVEN's audience were by now finding it hard to equate the killer live act with a succession of records that were ever more experimental, even drafting in horn sections at one point. 'Stay Hard' was a self-produced effort with studio collaboration on some tracks with Michael Wagener.

RAVEN undertook a 1985 American tour utilizing JUDAS PRIEST's 'Screaming For Vengeance' stage set. The show included a pyro rocket firing guitar that set fire to the venue roof in San Diego. RAVEN also contributed two tracks to the movie soundtrack of 'Hot Moves'. Songs cut were 'Hot Moves' and 'Ladykiller'. Preceding their major label inauguration, Megaforce issued the live album 'Live At The Inferno'.

'The Pack Is Back' was produced by industry veteran Eddie Kramer but this opus, complete with a jarring take on the SPENCER DAVIS GROUP's 'Gimme Some Lovin', marked the advent of turbulent times. RAVEN toured once more with support from fellow Brits TANK but further shows, scheduled to support TWISTED SISTER, were cancelled when the headliner pulled out at the last minute. 1986 saw RAVEN, promoting a stop gap EP simply billed 'Mad', opening for JUDAS PRIEST in North America before headline dates. The tour ended with support shows to YNGWIE MALMSTEEN.

To promote 1987's 'Life's A Bitch', RAVEN made up a three band touring package including SLAYER and W.A.S.P. RAVEN fared well in front of rabid SLAYER fans intent on demoralizing W.A.S.P.

Hunter departed without warning in 1987 following Atlantic severing all ties with the band and RAVEN found an able replacement in ex-SIMMONDS, BURNING STARR and PENTAGRAM drummer Joe Hasselvander prior to signing a new deal with Combat Records. RAVEN were back out on the road in America for headlining dates promoting 'Nothing Exceeds Like Excess' before another batch of gigs with TESTAMENT through into 1989. The band's first European tour for many years was offered with KREATOR, a German act that had recently covered a RAVEN track. Impressed by KREATOR's organization RAVEN soon signed to their management and record label.

In 1990 John Gallagher assembled an extracurricular project titled SLIDER comprising of former BLUE CHEER, SIMMONDS and SHAKIN' STREET guitarist Duck McDonald, ex-THE RODS and SIMMONDS bassist Gary Bordonaro and session player Bob Fortunato. The band issued one album 'The Slider Project' on Feedback Records in 1990.

The 'Architect Of Fear' album was a welcome return to previous heaviness. RAVEN set out on European dates with RUNNING WILD in April and May of 1991. However, RAVEN was to go on ice shortly after. John Gallagher formed KILLERS with ex-IRON MAIDEN vocalist PAUL DIANNO, ex-TANK guitarist Cliff Evans, ex-DRIVE SHE SAID guitarist Ray Ditone and former PERSIAN RISK drummer Steve Hopgood for a proposed tour of South America. A rehearsal tape, recorded in an empty venue in New York, featuring Gallagher later surfaced as the 'South American Assault' album.

The 1992 EP 'Heads Up' prompted yet more European dates with support act RISK. 1993 proved a disastrous year for the band as John's house burned down as well as having all his guitars stolen.

In 1994 RAVEN performed at the Los Angeles Foundations Forum in an effort to secure a new deal. Before long RAVEN had signed to Japanese label Zero recording 'Glow' the same year. Hungry for the road the band performed American dates in early 1995 with WIDOWMAKER and ANVIL before headline shows of Japan. One of these shows became the 'Destroy all monsters—Live in Japan' album. The band toured Germany alongside TANK and newcomers HAMMERFALL during 1997.

The band returned with renewed vigour during 1999 with a fresh studio album 'One For All' produced by Michael Wagener. The album would be issued in Europe by Massacre Records and the following year licensed into America via Metal Blade. Limited editions of 'One For All' hosted an extra track, a version of STATUS QUO's 'Big Fat Mama'. A retrospective box set, provisionally entitled 'Stark Raven Mad', would also be announced but fell by the wayside. The band therefore took matters into their own hands issuing a collection of demos and rarities billed 'Raw Tracks'. Various territories saw differing track listings with the American version closing on a take of QUEEN's 'Tie Your Mother Down'. Japanese variants ended with 'All For One' and 'Young Blood' whilst the European imprint's last tracks would be 'Architect Of Fear' and 'Enemy'.

RAVEN toured Germany in early 2000 as guests to U.D.O. The two acts would unite once again for a series of American mid Summer 2001 dates. The band looked set to get back in gear during 2002, announcing German summer festival gigs, but these would be curtailed when guitarist Mark Gallagher suffered severe leg injuries, shattering an ankle on one leg and seriously damaging the other, when a 20 foot wall collapsed on him in early November the previous year. The recovery process proved slow and further complications would put the band on hold.

Both Mark Gallagher and Joe Hasselvander re-appeared in late 2002 uniting with former VIRGIN STEELE guitarist Jack Starr's new band project JACK STARR AND THE GUARDIANS OF THE FLAME for the February 2003 album 'Under A Savage Sky'. RAVEN would be back on the road in the USA during 2003, acting as guests to SEVEN WITCHES East Coast tour dates beginning on 31st October in Springfield, Virginia. The band, assembling their debut DVD release, would see renewed live action the following year, featuring as part of the 'March Metal Meltdown VI' festival in Irvington, New Jersey cast then opening for Welsh veterans BUDGIE on 24th March at Jaxx in Springfield, Virginia. November of 2004 saw RAVEN back in the recording studio.

German Heavy Metal band POWERGOD cut a cover version of 'Mind Over Metal' for inclusion on their 'Long Live The Loud– That's Metal Lesson II' released through Massacre Records in July 2005. John Gallagher guested on this recording as did J.B.O.'s Hannes "G. Laber" Holzmann.

RAVEN tracked new songs, 'Against The Grain', 'Running Around In Circles', 'Breaking You Down' and 'Necessary Evil', in June 2006 at Assembly Line Studios in Vienna, Virginia.

Hard Ride, Neat NEAT 11 (1980). Hard Ride / Crazy World.
Don't Need Your Money, Neat NEAT 06 (1980). Don't Need Your Money / Wiped Out.
ROCK UNTIL YOU DROP, Neat NEAT 1001 (1981). Hard Ride / Hell Patrol / Don't Need Your Money / Over The Top / 39/40 / For The Future / Rock Until You Drop / Nobody's Hero / Hell Raiser / Action / Lambs To The Slaughter / Tyrant Of The Airways. Chart position: 63 UK.
Crash, Bang, Wallop, Neat NEAT 15 (1981). Crash, Bang, Wallop / Firepower / Run Them Down / Rock Hard.
WIPED OUT, Neat NEAT 1004 (1982). Faster Than The Speed Of Light / Bring The Hammer Down / Firepower / Read All About It / To The Limit-To The Top / Battlezone / Live At The Inferno / Star War / U.X.B. / 20-21 / Hold Back The Fire / Chainsaw.
ALL FOR ONE, Neat NEAT 1011 (1983). Take Control / Mind Over Metal / Sledgehammer Rock / All For One / Run Silent, Run Deep / Hung, Drawn And Quartered / Break The Chain / Take It Away / Seek And Destroy / Athletic Rock.
Break The Chain, Neat NEAT 28 (1983) (with UDO DIRKSCHNEIDER). Break The Chain / Ballad Of Marshall Stack.
Born To Be Wild, Neat NEAT 29 (1983) (with UDO DIRKSCHNEIDER). Born To Be Wild / Inquisitor.
Born To Be Wild, Neat NEAT 29-12 (1983) (12" single) (with UDO DIRKSCHNEIDER). Born To Be Wild / Inquisitor / Break The Chain.
LIVE AT THE INFERNO, Megaforce MRI 969 (1984). Live At The Inferno / Take Control / Mind Over Metal / Crash Bang Wallop / Rock Until You Drop / Faster Than The Speed Of Light / All For One / Forbidden Planet / Star War / Tyrant Of The Airways / Run Silent, Run Deep / Crazy World / Let It Rip / G.A.R.B.O. / Wiped Out / Firepower / Don't Need Your Money / Break The Chain / Hell Patrol / Live At The Inferno.
On And On, Atlantic PR702 (1984) (USA Promotion). On And On / On And On.
Pray For The Sun, Atlantic 786901 (1985). Pray For The Sun / On And On / The Bottom Line.
STAY HARD, Atlantic 81241-1 (1985). Stay Hard / When The Going Gets Tough / On And On / Get It Right / Restless Child / The Power And The Glory / Pray For The Sun / Hard Ride / Extract The Action / The Bottom Line.
Gimme Some Lovin', Atlantic A9453 (1986). Gimme Some Lovin' / On And On.
Mad EP, Atlantic 81670 (1986). Speed Of The Reflex / Do Or Die / How Did Ya Get So Crazy / Seen It On The TV / Gimme Just A Little.
THE PACK IS BACK, Atlantic 81629 (1986). The Pack Is Back / Gimme Some Lovin' / Screaming Down The House / Young Blood / Hyperactive / Rock Dogs / Don't Let It Die / Get Into Your Car And Drive / All I Need / Nightmare Ride.
LIFE'S A BITCH, Atlantic 81734 (1987). The Savage And The Hungry / Pick Your Window / Life's A Bitch / Never Forgive / Iron League / On The Wings Of An Eagle / Overload / You're A Liar / Fuel To The Fire / Only The Strong Survive / Juggernaut / Playing With The Razor / Finger On The Trigger.
NOTHING EXCEEDS LIKE EXCESS, Under One Flag FLAG 28 (1988). Behemoth / Die For Allah / Gimme A Break / Into The Jaws Of Death / In The Name Of Death / Stick It / Lay Down The Law / You Got A Screw Loose / Thunderlord / The King / Hard As Nails / Kick Your Ass.
ARCHITECT OF FEAR, Steamhammer SPV 008 76281 (1991). Intro / Architect Of Fear / Disciple / Got The Devil / Part Of The Machine / Under The Skin / White Hot Anger / Can't Run And Hide / Blind Leading The Blind / Relentless / Just Let Me Go / Heart Attack / Sold Down The River.
HEAD'S UP, Steamhammer 76-76392 (1992). Hell On Earth / World Comes Tumbling / Stay Human / All For One / Into The Jaws Of Death / Can't Run And Hide.
DESTROY ALL MONSTERS—LIVE IN JAPAN, SPV 085-12132 (1995). Victim / Live At The Inferno / Crash, Bang, Wallop / True Believer / Into The Jaws Of Death / Hard As Nails / Die For Allah / Guitar Solo / Speed Of The Reflex / Run Silent, Run Deep / Mind Over Metal / Gimme A Reason / Inquisitor / For The Future / Bass Solo / Architect Of Fear / White Hot Anger / Drum Solo / Break The Chain.
GLOW, Steamhammer SPV 084-12092 (1995). Watch You Drown / Spite / True Believer / So Close / Altar / The Dark Side / The Rocker / Turn You On / Far And Wide / Victim / Gimme A Reason / Slip Away.
EVERYTHING LOUDER, Fresh Fruit SPV CD 085-12162 (1997). Blind Eye / No Pain, No Gain / Sweet Jane / Holy Grail / Hungry / Insane / Everything Louder / ??? / Between The Wheels / Losing My Mind / Get Your Finger Out / Wilderness Of Broken Glass / !!! / Fingers Do The Walking / Bonus.
ONE FOR ALL, Massacre MASCD0206 (1999). Seven Shades / Double Talk / Roll With The Punches / Get Your Motor Running / To Be Broken / Derailed / The Hunger Inside / Top Of The World / In The Line Of Fire / Kangaroo / New Religion / Last Ride.

RAWPOWER

ITALY — *Maurio Codeluppi (vocals), Davide (guitar), Giuseppe Codeluppi (guitar), Maurizio (bass), Helder (drums).*

Thrash Metal exponents RAWPOWER evolved from Punk act OFF LIMITS established in Bologna by frontman Maurio Codeluppi and brother Giusseppe in the early 80's. The now extremely rare debut 'You Are The Victim', issued in 1984, followed promotion for which even included shows in America. During 1989 the recording line-up for the 'Mine to Kill' album sessions comprised vocalist Mauro Codeluppi, guitarists Davide Devoti and Giuseppe Codeluppi, bassist Alessandro Paolucci and Fabiano Bianco on the drums.

RAWPOWER's work ethic resulted in over 200 American gigs including shows with DEAD KENNEDYS, SOCIAL DISTORTION, AGNOSTIC FRONT, BAD BRAINS and even GUNS N' ROSES. The 'Too Tough To Burn' album includes a cover version of THIN LIZZY's 'Holy War'. In October of 2002 Giuseppe Codeluppi died of a heart attack. The guitarist had collapsed whilst playing a football match. He was 45 years old.

TOO TOUGH TO BURN, 199 (0).
Wop Hour, Toxic Shock (1985). Wop Hour.
SCREAM FROM THE GUTTER, Toxic Shock (1985). State Oppression / Joe's The Best / Bastard / A Certain Kind Of Killer / Army / My Boss / No Card / Power / Start A Fight / Don't Let Me See It / Hate / Rawpower / Our Oppression / We're All Gonna Die / Police, Police / Nihilist / Politicians.
AFTER YOUR BRAIN, Toxic Shock TXLP8 (1986). You Are Fired / Dreamer / We Shall Overcome / Is There Anything You Like / Just Another Cry / What Have We Done / After Your Brain / Nothing Better To Do / Keep Out / No Place To Hide / What For Shut Up / Buy And Pay.
MINE TO KILL, Rotten ROT-CD-003 (1989). You Want More / Wasteland / Make Or Break / What Was / Buried Alive / You Are The Victim / Mine To Kill / Revenge / Animals Wearing Uniforms / The White Man's Invasion / Power Not Violence / Raw Power 12 / Inside Me / Zaff.

RAZOR

GUELPH, ON, CANADA — *Bob Reid (vocals), Dave Carlo (guitar), Jon Armstrong (bass), Rich Oosterbosch (drums).*

Prolific Canadian Thrash outfit known for their low budget yet aggressive releases, RAZOR would develop quite a cult following. RAZOR, hailing from Guelph, Ontario, first issued a five song demo in 1984. RAZOR made their commercial debut for Voice Records with the self-funded 'Armed And Dangerous' album, produced by Terry Marostega at Waxworks Studios in St. Jacobs and released in May 1984, comprised vocalist Stace 'Sheepdog' McClaren, guitarist Dave Carlo, bassist Mike Campagnolo and drummer M-Bro (a.k.a. Mike Embro). Only 1,200 copies of the original 12" vinyl 'Armed And Dangerous' were manufactured.

Attic Records took the band on for the April 1985 follow up 'Executioner's Song', released on the labels Viper imprint, these sessions being laid down at Future Sound in Toronto with Marostega manning the production desk once more. This outing also finding a European audience through a licensing deal with Roadrunner Records. Although the Dutch concern would put out a string of RAZOR albums, the band never made it out of the USA and Canada on the live front. 'Evil Invaders', crafted at Phase One Studios in Toronto with Walter Zwol now handling production, offered a quick-fire third album that same October. RAZOR made a small slice of music history by shooting a promotional video for the 'Evil Invaders' title song, this clip aiding the album sales to become the group's most commercially successful. 'Malicious Intent', their last for the Attic Music Group, was hot on its heels in April 1986.

RAZOR's next effort, 'Custom Killing' again produced by Terry Marostega at Waxworks Studios, only received a Canadian release via the Fist Fight imprint, actually the band's own business, in July 1987. 'Custom Killing' broke away from the short, sharp shock Thrash tactics that had served RAZOR so well up to that juncture and instead focussed on lengthier, more involved material.

For 1988's 'Violent Restitution', a vicious revival of no holds barred Speed Metal, only Carlo and McLaren remained with new faces being bassist Adam Carlo and drummer Rob Mills. 'Violent Restitution' gained a German license on Steamhammer Records but although the album saw a release in Japan, through Teichiku Records, this was as part of a strange double package with Australian act HOBBS ANGEL OF DEATH.

Mclaren quit before the album was released and Bob Reid, previously a member of London's SFH ("SamFuckingHain") was quickly pulled in to fill the gap for 1990's 'Shotgun Justice'. Canadian touring had RAZOR packaged with SACRIFICE and DISCIPLES OF POWER.

Unfortunately Rob Mills suffered an auto accident which put him in a leg brace. The group bowed out in 1991 with the 'Open Hostility' album, cut at Umbrella Sound Studios in Toronto, the band at this juncture comprising Bob Reid on vocals, Dave Carlo on guitar, SFH bassist Jon Armstrong and a drum machine in the place of the injured Rob Mills. RAZOR performed what was intended to be a final concert on October 2nd 1992. Reid and Armstrong resumed their positions with SFH for a brace of albums, 'One Of Those Days' in 1992 and 'All You Can Eat' during 1994.

A double disc 'best of' set 'Exhumed' arrived in 1994 through Steamhammer in Europe and Fringe in Canada, paving the way for an eventual full blown RAZOR reformation in 1997 for the self-produced 'Decibels' record for Hypnotic Records. By this stage Rich Oosterbosch of SFH was manning the drums. Leading Swedish Death Metal act HYPOCRISY weighed in too, paying homage by including a rendition of 'Evil Invaders' on their album 'The Final Chapter' that same year.

RAZOR would still be active in 2006, composing songs for another album.

Razor, (1984). Deathrace / The End / Killer Instinct / Hot Metal / Armed & Dangerous.
ARMED AND DANGEROUS, Voice M 26957 (1984) (Limited edition 1,200 copies). The End / Killer Instinct / Hot Metal / Armed And Dangerous / Take This Torch / Ball And Chain / Fast And Loud.
EXECUTIONER'S SONG, Roadrunner RR 9778 (1985). Take This Torch / Fast And Loud / City Of Damnation / Escape The Fire / March Of Death / Distant Thunder / Hot Metal / Gatecrasher / Deathrace / Time Bomb / The End.
EVIL INVADERS, Roadrunner RR 9732 (1985). Nowhere Fast / Cross Me Fool / Legacy Of Doom / Evil Invaders / Iron Hammer / Instant Death / Cut Throat / Speed Merchants / Tortured Skull / Thrashdance.
MALICIOUS INTENT, Roadrunner RR 9698 (1986). Tear Me To Pieces / Night Attack / Grindstone / Cage The Ragers / Malicious Intent / Rebel Onslaught / AOD / Challenge The Eagle / Stand Before Kings / High Speed Metal / KMA.
CUSTOM KILLING, Fist Fight FPL 3042 (1987). Survival Of The Fittest / Shootout / Forced Annihilation / Last Rites / Snake Eyes / White Noise / Going Under / Russian Ballet.
VIOLENT RESTITUTION, Steamhammer SPV 087 569 (1988). The Marshall Arts / Hypertension / Taste The Floor / Behind Bars / Below The Belt / I'll Only Say It Once / Enforcer / Violent Restitution / Out Of The Game / Edge Of The Razor / Eve Of The Storm / Discipline / Fed Up / Soldier Of Fortune.
SHOTGUN JUSTICE, Fringe FPL 3094 (1990). Miami / United By Hatred / Violence Condoned / Electric Circus / Meaning Of Pain / Stabbed In The Back / Shotgun Justice / Parricide / American Luck / Brass Knuckles / Burning Bridges / Concussion / Cranial Stomp / The Pugilist.
OPEN HOSTILITY, Fringe FPD3114 (1991). In Protest / Sucker For Punishment / Bad Vibrations / Road Gunner / Cheers / Red Money / Free Lunch / Iron Legions / Mental Torture / Psychopath / I Disagree / End Of The War.
EXHUMED, Fringe FPD3133 (1994). Killer Instinct / Armed And Dangerous / Take This Torch / Fast And Loud / City Of Damnation / Gatecrasher / Cross Me Fool / Evil Invaders / Iron Hammer / Instant Death / Speed Merchants / Thrash Dance / A.O.D. / K.M.A. / Forced Annihilation / Snake Eyes / The Marshall Arts / Behind Bars / Below The Belt / Enforcer / Violent Restitution / Edge Of The Razor / Soldier Of Fortune / Miami / Electric Torture / Meaning Of Pain / Shotgun Justice / Parricide / Brass Knuckles / Concussion / The Pugilist / In Protest / Bad Vibrations / Road Gunner / Free Lunch / Iron Legions / Psychopath / End Of The War.
DECIBELS, Hypnotic HYP 1058 (1997). Decibels / Jimi The Fly / Life Sentence / Liar / The Game / Great White Lie / Open Hostility / Ninedead / Goof Soup / Violence ... Gun Control.

RE-ANIMATOR

HULL, YORKSHIRE, UK — *Kev Ingleson (vocals / guitar), Mike Abel (guitar), John Wilson (bass), Mark Mitchell (drums).*

Yorkshire Thrashers RE-ANIMATOR managed to cruise the short-lived UK Thrash wave on the back of debut six-track mini-album, 1989's 'Deny Reality', issued through Music For Nations subsidiary Under One Flag. The group, having scored their deal with a two song demo cut at Animal Tracks Studios in Hull during March 1988, comprised lead vocalist / rhythm guitarist Kev Ingleson, guitarist Mike "Dis-Able" Abel, bassist John Hanson and drummer Mark Mitchell. These tracks were laid down with a session singer, Tony Calvert of Welsh Thrashers TORTOISE CORPSE.

On the live front, RE-ANIMATOR toured as support to EXODUS, ACID REIGN and NUCLEAR ASSAULT. The band was managed initially by Music For Nations owner Martin Hooker then NUCLEAR ASSAULT manager Paul Loasby. 1990's 'Condemned To Reality' bolstered their reputation but RE-ANIMATOR then undertook a severe left turn in their brand of music adopting then in vogue Funk for third album, 1991's 'Laughing'. Having gathered fans with their previous two albums, RE-ANIMATOR's liberal us of horn sections, odes to Laurel and Hardy, an unaccredited acapella stab at Monty Python's 'Always Look On The Bright Side Of Life' and even a dash of Reggae did not serve them well. Line-up changes affected the band too, with Ingleson and Abel being superseded by singer Lee Robinson and guitarist Adam Clarke, as Grahame Dixon was enrolled on rhythm guitar. The final 1992 outing 'That Was Then ... This Is Now', included a cover version of THIN LIZZY's 'Cold Sweat'. A RE-ANIMATOR guitarist subsequently joined POP GODS whilst John Wilson resurfaced in Ska band BADNESS and Mark Mitchell journeyed through Punk band THE HAPPY DURALS before enrolling into a HAWKWIND covers band as "Denbo Drumwind".

The CD re-issue of 'Condemned To Eternity' also added the 'Deny Reality' material.

Re-Animator, (1988). Follow The Masses / Push The Button.
DENY REALITY, Under One Flag FLAG 32 (1989). Deny Reality / Follow The Masses / Fatal Descent / OPC / DUAF / Re-Animator.
CONDEMNED TO ETERNITY, Under One Flag FLAG 37 (1990). Low Life / Chain Of Command / Room 101 / Condemned To Eternity / Shock Treatment / Buried Alive / Techno Fear / What The Funk / Say Your Prayers.
LAUGHING, Under One Flag FLAG 53 (1991). Rude Awakening / Laughing / Kipper n' / Another Fine Mess / Too Drunk To Fuck / Monkey See Monkey Dance / Don't Pastronize Me / Instrumental / Time And Tide / Big Black Cloud.
THAT WAS THEN, THIS IS NOW, Under One Flag FLAG 67 (1992). Take Me Away / 2CV / Cold Sweat / Hope / Last Laugh / Kick Back / Listen Up / Sunshine Times / That Was Then ... This Is Now / D.U.A.F.

REAPERS

PADOVA, ITALY — *Luca Calegaro (vocals / guitar), Stefano Crivellari (guitar), Francesco Lilla (bass), Dario Pittarello (drums).*

REAPERS was forged initially as a METALLICA covers band in May 2002 by vocalist / guitarist Luca Calegaro, rhythm guitarist Carmine De Franco and bassist Francesco Lilla in union with drummer Dario Pittarello. Before long De Franco exited and the remaining trio embarked upon scoring original material for a demo entitled 'Metalness', five tracks recorded between July and August 2002 at NoBrain Studios in Venezia.

In early 2003 guitarist Stefano Crivellari, known for his work in a STEVE VAI covers act, joined the REAPERS fold. In this formation the band crafted a further five demo songs and signing with Dead Sun Records these collected tracks comprised the debut album 'Metalness', issued in February of 2004.

METALNESS, Dead Sun (2004). Intro / Metalness / Hate Never Stops / Pain War / Copernical Thinkage / Knights Of The Night / Crying Soul / Reapers From Hell / Angels Of Metal.

REATOR

ANÁPOLIS, GO, BRAZIL — *Christian Santos (vocals / guitar), Geraldo Monteiro (guitar), Samuel (bass), Leandro (drums).*

Anápolis, Goiânia Thrashers REATOR, forged in 2002 by guitarists Christian Santos and Geraldo Monteiro, released a live 2004 demo 'The Black Days Of Holocaust'. The band's first formation saw Santos and Monteiro ranked alongside singer Rodrigro, bassist Ed Carlos and drummer Garfa. However, in 2003 a new rhythm section was then installed comprising Weider on bass and drummer Zé Régis. The next change would see Alessandro taking over the lead vocal role but he would leave, making way for Rodrigo to return his post. This union was once again brief though and Santos stepped up to add lead vocals to his responsibilities. New REATOR recruits in 2004 would be Samuel on bass and drummer Leandro.

The Black Days Of Holocaust—Live, Reator (2004). Tears In The Holy Land / Holocaust / On The Verge Of The End.

RECKLESS TIDE

HANNOVER, GERMANY — *Andrew Troth (vocals), Kjell Hallgreen (vocals), Susanne Swillus (guitar), Oliver Jaath (guitar), Henning Pfeiffer (bass), Kai Swillus (drums).*

Hannover's RECKLESS TIDE, offering "Depth Boosting" Thrash Metal, came to national attention in 2004 by winning the 'Wacken Metal Battle' band competition, the prize including a spot at the 'Wacken Open Air' festival. The band had been forged in October 2000 by the husband and wife team of drummer Kai Swillus, previously with OPERATION COUNTERSTRIKE, and guitarist Susanne Swillus alongside second guitarist Oliver Jaath and vocalist Andre, initially titling the project INTREPID LEECH. Subsequently, the formation, evolving into RECKLESS TIDE, enlisted English singer Andrew Troth, bass player Henning Pfeiffer and, in October 2002, second vocalist second vocalist Kjell Hallgreen. Entering Hamburg's Absurd Studio RECKLESS TIDE cut the EP 'Insane Or Reality'. A two track demo, '7 Minutes Of Thrash', followed in May 2003.

The debut album, 'Repent Or Seal Your Fate' released by Armageddon Music, featuring guests Sabina Classen of HOLY MOSES and the ANNIHILATOR cast of Jeff Waters, guitarist Curran Murphy and vocalist Dave Padden, was readied for February 2005 release.

RECKLESS TIDE returned in October 2006 with 'Helleraser'.

Insanity Or Reality, Independent (2002). The Archer / Insanity Or Reality / Unfullfilled / Conflict / Restless Tide.
7 Minutes Of Thrash, (2003). Death Train / Repent Or Seal Your Fate.
REPENT OR SEAL YOUR FATE, Armageddon Music (2005). Desperation / Self Destruct / Misery / The Hunt / Death Train / Damned For Now And Nevermore / Demons And Dictators / Repent Or Seal Your Fate / Equality / Lebende Organverpflanzung / Shed The Chains / Intensity / To Die For Creativity / Reckless Tide.
HELLERASER, Armageddon Music (2006).

RECLUSION

GOTHENBURG, SWEDEN — *Rune Foss (vocals / guitar), Mattias Bolander (guitar), Pasi Jaskara (bass), Marek Dobrowolski (drums).*

Based in Gothenburg Death-Thrashers RECLUSION, fronted by Rune Foss of EXEMPT and KILLAMAN, comprise two Swedes, a Finn and a Norwegian. Initially the band went under the title DAWN OF TIME prior to evolving into DROWNED for a debut demo and subsequently RECLUSION. Signing to the French Listenable label, RECLUSION's debut album 'Shell Of Pain' saw production credits going out to KING DIAMOND guitarist Andy La Rocque.

In early 2005 it would be learned drummer Marek Dobrowolski had joined ex-THE CROWN singer Johan Lindstrand's new band project ONE MAN ARMY AND THE UNDEAD QUARTET. RECLUSION parted ways with lead guitarist Toni Korhonen in March. RECLUSION announced the addition of guitarist Mattias Bolander to the group's ranks in June.

SHELL OF PAIN, Listenable POSH 032 (2001). Shelter From Pain / Impulsive / Pressure / Reclusion / The Quest / Sacred Ground / Unspoken Fear / A Force Of One / Speak The Truth.

RECON

USA — *Vett Roberts (vocals), George Rene Ochoa (guitar), Eddie Starline (guitar), Mike Grato (bass), John Christianson (drums).*

A Christian Thrash Metal band that debuted publicly with a brace of tracks on the 'California Metal II' compilation album. The 'Behind Enemy Lines' album, regarded by many as a 'lost classic' of the genre, bore heavy connections to DELIVERANCE which would come to affect the band subsequently. DELIVERANCE mainman Jimmy Brown not only produced 'Behind Enemy Lines' but co-wrote the title track and performed lead guitar on the song 'Alive'. Roger Martinez of VENGEANCE RISING also contributes backing vocals.

RECON guitarist George Rene Ochoa would join fellow White Thrashers DELIVERANCE for their 1990 'Weapons Of Our Warfare' album. Bassist Mike Grato would join Ochoa in DELIVERANCE for the 1991 'What A Joke' record. Drummer John Christianson would also become involved with DELIVERANCE.

Ochoa later figured in the highly controversial VENGEANCE RISING, figuring in the live band for their last 'non secular' tour.

Vett Roberts would later be found as session vocalist for the esteemed MORTIFICATION's 1995 album 'Primitive Rhythm Machine'. A further RECON connection found Ochoa as producer of this record, as well as contributing much of the guitar work.

RECON would reform for an appearance at the famed Christian 'Cornerstone' festival. RECON at this juncture comprised of vocalist Vett Roberts, guitarist George Rene Ochoa, bass player Mike Grato, keyboard player Ronson Webster and drummer John Gonzales. This show would be captured for a subsequent live CD which also included tracks from the band's opening 1989 demo session.

Magdalene Records, specialists in archive Christian Rock, would re-issue 'Behind Enemy Lines' during 2001 albeit on a limited run of 1000 pressings. Added to the re-release would be six bonus tracks in 'Light The Fire' and 'Dreams' taken from 1988's 'California Metal II' compilation album and demo sessions of 'Light The Fire', 'Dreams', Alive' and 'Eternal Destiny'.

During 2002 George Ochoa would be touting a brand new act SALT in alliance with DIE HAPPY members Glenn Mancaruso and Larry Farkas. RECON meantime kept active on the live front having drafted a new vocalist in Rod Dickenson.

BEHIND ENEMY LINES, Intense RO 9201 (1990). In The Beginning / Lost Soldier / Ancient Of Days / Choose This Day / Dreams / Take Us Away / Holy Is The Lord / Alive! / Eternal Destiny / Behind Enemy Lines.

LIVE AT CORNERSTONE 2001, Millenium Eight (2001). Take It Away / Eternal Destiny / Choose This Day / Lost Soldier / Preaching / The Chosen Few / Alive / Dreams / Light The Fire (Demo) / Dreams (Demo) / Alive (Demo) / Eternal Destiny (Demo).

REQUIEM

LAS VEGAS, NV, USA — *Berry Ruffin (vocals / guitar), Crazy Ned (bass), David Fernandez (drums).*

Las Vegas Thrashcore styled Metal unit REQUIEM, mentored by frontman 'Brutal' Berry Ruffin, was forged in late 1991 but, following numerous line up tribulations and a January 1995 demo entitled 'Rise', would not issue commercial product until the March 1996 album 'Grave'. Recordings such as 'Dawn Of Souls' in December of 1997, 'Christ Has Risen' in May of 1998, the latter featuring Dave Doran, then flowed. The 'U$$A: United States Of A Socialist America' release was recorded in the midst of a package tour with MASTER. Promoting this latter release REQUIEM toured North America alongside Mexicans LEPROSY.

REQUIEM carved out a little piece of history when they became the first American Metal band invited to play communist Cuba. The band arrived in Havana during September of 2001 but the planned show never transpired. The 2002 album 'Volume Six' was recorded following on from a South American tour with John Capcha of Peruvian act HADEZ.

Bassist Tim Lorence took over from Crazy Ned. REQUIEM announced the arrival of a further album for 2002, entitled 'Lock The Dead', although this never transpired.

GRAVE, (1996). Grave / Victims Rise / Nuclear Destruction / Racial War / Enemy / War / Jesus / Uncertain Destiny / Whore / E-Waltz / Time To Die.

Dawn Of Souls, (1997). Dawn Of Souls / Ordo Seclorum / Blue Skies / They Are Killing Her / The Sky Is Falling In.

Christ Has Risen, (1998). Christ Has Risen / Aggravated Assault / Suffer / Answer / The Pain Inside Me / Stuck In Society / Unknown.

VOLUME SIX, Ketzer Productions KR 13402 (2002). Grave / The Pain Inside Me / Strike Your Idols Down / Suffer / Diez To Uno / Government / The Sky Is Falling In / Unjustifiable / The Angels Will Fall / Cryout / Zero Nation / Enemy.

RESPONSE NEGATIVE

FL, USA — *Nick Barlow (vocals), Bobby Gustafson (guitar), Mark Dykstra (guitar), Andrew Goodyer (bass), James McCourt (drums).*

RESPONSE NEGATIVE is a Florida based Death / Thrash Metal band, founded in September 2001 by Mark Dykstra, known for the inclusion of former OVERKILL, CYCLE SLUTS FROM HELL, SKREW and GRIP INC. guitarist Bobby Gustafson. Initially Dykstra was joined by singer ex-FISTED and UNIT 17 man Nick Barlow, bassist Tony Viera, Gustafson and drummer James McCourt. Subsequently, Andrew Goodyer of NIHILITY, OSIRIS RISING and IN HUMAN FORM, took command of the bass position. A self-titled, five track EP emerged in 2004.

The RESPONSE NEGATIVE project, according to statements from Bobby Gustafson citing "lack of professionalism and drive from within the band", folded in April 2005. However, within days of this press release drummer Jim McCourt responded, claiming the band was "far from over" and would persevere, minus Gustafson.

In February 2006 RESPONSE NEGATIVE replaced Bobby Gustafson with Claude Fernandez and also added bassist Ruben Trevino to the group's ranks. The new look band debuted on March 4th as support to MONSTROSITY at The Factory in Fort Lauderdale.

Response Negative, Response Negative (2004). All Out War / Silent Son / Etched In Sickness / Carnivorous Lust / Faithless.

RETRIBUTION

BERG AAN DE MAAS, HOLLAND — *Thie Thomsen (vocals / guitar), Tom Bronneberg (guitar), Job Verdonschot (bass), Ferry Adams (drums).*

RETRIBUTION is a Berg aan de Maas Thrash Metal band established in August 2003, fronted by vocalist / guitarist "Powertieke" Thie Thomsen with the EXISTENZ, SHRINE OF OSTARA and BLOODMOON credited Tom Bronneberg on guitar. The band added CHEMICAL BREATH, CALLENISH CIRCLE, STATE:CHAOS and FORM bassist Rocco in April 2005, although he would depart within weeks.

On June 17rth 2005 the four track demo 'What Does This Button Do?', saw issue. However, only one copy would be produced. RETRIBUTION drafted bassist Job Verdonschot, from ARKNGTHAND, as replacement in April 2006. The 'Black Lining' demo arrived in March 2007, restricted to 100 copies.

What Does This Button Do?, Retribution (2005) (Demo. Limited edition 1 copy). Ash / Schitzophrenic / The Glass Tower / Stranglehold.

Black Lining, Retribution (2007) (Demo. Limited edition 100 copies). Vendetta (Intro) / Against The Wall / Black Lining / Schitzophrenic / Dawn Of Tears / Neverending.

REVEREND

CA, USA — *David Wayne (vocals), Stuart Fuii (guitar), Brian Korban (guitar), Dennis O'Hara (bass), Rick Basha (drums).*

The history of REVEREND, HERETIC and METAL CHURCH are truly intertwined in a holy trinity (pun fully intended and unavoidable) of Thrash Metal. In an odd twist of fate after the dissolution of HERETIC which saw singer Mike Howe leave to join METAL CHURCH, the band evolved into REVEREND and recruited ex-METAL CHURCH vocalist David Wayne. Guitarists Stuart Fujinami and Brian Korban along with bassist Dennis O'Hara were all members of HERETIC. Joining them would be drummer Stuart Vogel. By the 1990 album Vogel had made way for drummer Rick Basha.

After the success of the debut EP on Caroline Records and capitalizing on Wayne's history with METAL CHURCH the band signed with Charisma, a small but stable record label. The Charisma full-length debut, 'World Won't Miss You', was a rampaging affair, cranking the brutality up just a notch above and beyond either of the previous acts. The album was dedicated to the late Dave Pritchard of ARMOURED SAINT and featured Rocky George of SUICIDAL TENDENCIES as a guest as well as Chris Goss of MASTERS OF REALITY.

Late 1990, early 1991 saw some major changes in the line-up with Fujinama, O'Hara and Basha all departing with Angelo Espino, of PREDATOR, DISSENTER and L.S.N. repute, joining to play bass and Jason Ian, brother of ANTHRAX guitarist Scott

Ian, appearing on drums. The album, 'Play God', was another punishing opus, and the band had utilized a second guitarist in the studio by the name of Tommy V Verdonck. The release also featured a ripping cover of the CREEDENCE CLEARWATER REVIVAL tune 'Fortunate Son' and also had Juan Garcia of EVIL DEAD providing some backing vocals.

Unfortunately, with the onset of grunge and alternative music, Thrash started to loose momentum and the band capped the first stage of their career with a six-song Live EP simply called 'Live'. 1992 saw the addition of Ernesto F. Martinez on guitar for the live recording. The short punchy live EP was considered to be a nice cap on the career of REVEREND as the band entered a period of inactivity.

With Wayne's departure from METAL CHURCH post their comeback 'Masterpeace' opus the singer reactivated REVEREND. A limited edition four track EP, 'A Gathering Of Demons', was made available solely through the band's website.

Wayne would then found a further act simply titled WAYNE. Cutting an album billed as 'Metal Church', complete with the characteristic guitar-cross icon and the WAYNE logo rendered in METAL CHURCH's own familiar font left no doubting to which audience the frontman was pitching. During 2000 Wayne and WARRIOR guitarist Joe Floyd would produce the BYFIST 'Adrenalin' EP.

After several years of inactivity and spurred perhaps by the global resurgence in Metal, REVEREND re-emerged in 2001 with an independent 4 song EP called 'A Gathering Of Demons'. The EP was notable for the song 'Legion' which was a reworking, both musically and lyrically, of the METAL CHURCH song 'Fake Healer'. The line up now consisted of Wayne and newcomers guitarist Chris Nelson, bassist John Stalman and Todd Stolz on drums. It was the heaviest recording by the band to date.

During 2000 Wayne and WARRIOR guitarist Joe Floyd would produce the BYFIST 'Adrenalin' EP. This connection was strengthened when BYFIST guitarists Davey Lee and Notch Vara duly joined Wayne's REVEREND supplanting guitarist Chris Nelson. Bassist John Stahlman's position would be taken by Pete Perez, a veteran of CARRION, SPASTIK INK and Hard Rockers RIOT. Subsequently the four string duties were taken over by ex-HEIR APPARENT man Jay Wegener.

ONWARD would be announced as support act for REVEREND's August 2002 West Coast tour of America. The band would confirm they were to put in a special appearance as support to JUDAS PRIEST and BUDGIE at the Sunken Garden Theater in San Antonio, Texas. However, shortly after this announcement the band would be dropped from the billing.

Jay Wegener doubled up duties with BYFIST in January of 2003. As REVEREND activity slowed, David Wayne put the band on hold as he joined BASTARDSUN in July, the British Metal band assembled by former CRADLE OF FILTH guitarist Stuart Anstis.

The METAL CHURCH family was dealt a huge blow on 10th of May 2005 with the passing of David Wayne. Just 47 years old, the singer died from complications from injuries he sustained in a head-on automobile accident months previously. In June the surviving band members, Davey Lee, Nacho Vara, Brendon Kyle and Jesse Vara, announced a REVEREND reformation. Somewhat surreally, the band revealed in September that they were in negotiations with David Wayne's brother to step in as their new lead singer. However, June 2006 saw an announcement that former MAUSOLEUM, HATE and ANCIENT CROSS singer Michael Lance had secured the position.

REVEREND utilised Blue Cat Recording Studios in September 2006, working up album tracks with producer Joe Trevino.

REVEREND, Caroline (1989). Power Of Persuasion / Dimensional Confusion / Wretched Excess / Ritual.

WORLD WON'T MISS YOU, Charisma (1990). Remission / Another Form Of Greed / Scattered Witts / Desperate / Leader Of Fools / World Won't Miss You / Rude Awakening / Gunpoint / Killing Time / 11th Hour / Hand Of Doom.

PLAY GOD, Charisma (1991). Butcher Of Baghdad / Heaven On Earth / Fortunate Son / Blessings / Promised Land / Play God / Warp The Mind / What You're Looking For / Blackened Thrive / Death Of Me / Far Away.

LIVE, Charisma 92149-2 (1994). Gunpoint / World Won't Miss You / Scattered Witts / B.O.B. / Promised Land / The Power Of Persuasion.

A GATHERING OF DEMONS, (2001). Massacre The Innocent / Down / Stealing My Mind / Legion.

RIGOR MORTIS

ARLINGTON, TX, USA — *Bruce Corbitt (vocals), Mike Scaccia (guitar), Casey Orr (bass), Harden Harrison (drums).*

RIGOR MORTIS, trading in Horror inspired Punk-Metal, assembled in Arlington, Texas during 1983 by guitarist Mike Scaccia, bassist Casey Orr, drummer Harden Harrison with the later addition of singer Bruce Corbitt, was snapped up by major label Capitol Records hot on the heels of their acquisition of EXODUS in the scramble for Thrash acts in the late eighties. Preceding RIGOR MORTIS, both Orr and Harrison had been members of Thrash Metal act WARLOCK, the drummer also citing ERUPTION credits.

Vocalist Doyle Bright had taken Corbitt's place for the 1989 mini-album 'Freaks'. That same year Scaccia would enroll with Chicago arch Industrialists MINISTRY, a role he made permanent during 1991 as RIGOR MORTIS issued 'Rigor Mortis vs. The World' through Triple X Records. Casey Orr followed briefly in Scaccia's footsteps by acting as temporary fill in for a number of MINISTRY 'Lollapalooza' festivals in 1992. That same year Orr, Scaccia and Dunn cut the 'Leave It To Blohole' album from their Punk project BLOHOLE.

Orr would join the ranks of the outrageous GWAR in 1994, as well as fronting X-COPS, THE BURDEN BROTHERS and Punk act THE HELLIONS. Scaccia subsequently made a return to Texas and forged the LEAGUE OF BLIND WOMEN in league with Rob Buck of 10,000 MANIACS. Meantime, Harrison was to be found with the female fronted PERVIS. He would join SPEEDEALER in 1999.

After a 13 year hiatus RIGOR MORTIS regrouped with a faithful line up comprising vocalist / bassist Casey Orr, Mike Scaccia on guitar and drummer Harden Harrison. The band introduced new vocalist Dave Woodard, a veteran of acts such as THE AGITATORS, REO SPEEDEALER, BILLYCLUB, THE HELLIONS and PORN LAB, into the group's ranks during January of 2003. However, plans for a reunion were put into jeopardy when guitarist Mike Scaccia rejoined Industrialists MINISTRY. Scaccia enrolled into another of Al Jourgensen's projects in March 2004 when he was announced as guitarist for REVOLTING COCKS.

RIGOR MORTIS reunited for their first gigs in over fifteen years the band partnered with two other re-united cult Texan Thrash outfits, GAMMACIDE and ROTTING CORPSE, to play at the Axis Club in Fort Worth on 29th October.

In 2006 Doyle Bright forged modern Metal band TWO PRONGED CROWN, comprising vocalist / guitarist Stacy Andersen, of HALLOWS EVE, METALMOPHOSIS and BIG TWIN DIN, guitarist Chris Abbamonte, of DISTEMPER and ILK, bass player Jimmy Gorman, of DISTEMPER, ILK and THE CHAOS FOUNDATION, programmer Mink, of ILK, and drummer Mike Rollings, from METALMORPHOSIS, BIG TWIN DIN and JARBOE.

Demons, Capitol (1988). Demons.

RIGOR MORTIS, Capitol C1-48909 (1988). Welcome To Your Funeral / Demons / Bodily Dismemberment / Condemned To Hell / Wizard Of Gore / Shroud Of Gloom / Die In Pain / Vampire / Re-Animator / Slow Death.

FREAKS, Metal Blade (1989). Freaks / Cattle Mutilation / The Haunted / Six Feet Under / Worms Of The Earth / Chained In The Attic.

RIGOR MORTIS VS THE EARTH, Tripple X (1990).

ROOTWATER

POLAND — *Maciek Taff (vocals), Sebastian Zusin (guitar), Mike (guitar), Przemo (bass), Artur Rowiński (drums).*

ROOTWATER, self described as a blend of Punk, Hardcore and Thrash, was founded during 2002 by guitarists Sebastian Zusin, a twelve year veteran of SPARAGMOS, and Yonca, NEOLITHIC drummer Pablo and former GEISHA GONER singer Maciek Taff. Rehearsal demos would be recorded that July, although the band was still without a bassist at this juncture. The line-up was finalised in August with the introduction of Przemo on bass guitar.

ROOTWATER underwent changes in early 2004 as Yonca exited to join LICOREA and Pablo too departed. Replacements would be located in guitarist Mike and former LICOREA and BIAN drummer Artur Rowiński. The band united with FRONTSIDE, HUNTER and VIRGIN SNATCH for the extensive 'Mystic' tour of Poland in March 2007.

UNDER, Fonografika (2004). Lie Is The Law / Red Love / Hava Nagila / The Tides / Fame / C.O.X. / Peacemaker / Reflux / Symmetrix / Angry Chair.

ROSTOCK VAMPIRES

DORTMUND, GERMANY — *Christian (vocals), Andy (guitar), Bulla (guitar), Supe (bass), Laube (drums).*

Dortmund based act created in 1987. Band members had previously been involved with acts such as KELLERGEISTER, CASH FROM CHAOS, THE DEADBEAT and GRINNING KIDS. The band toured Europe with IMPULSE MANSLAUGHTER during 1990 promoting the 'Pay The Price' EP. A second record, the full length album 'Misery' saw a release the same year and further touring ensued with SUCKSPEED. Whilst on this tour guitarist Bulla quit but ROSTOCK VAMPIRES opted to carry on reduced to a quartet.

Following a lengthy hiatus ROSTOCK VAMPIRES reunited for a comeback gig on June 22nd 2002 at Lindenbrauerei, Unna in Germany. The group announced it was to issue a comeback album, 'New Morning', through former label Nuclear Blast but retracted this statement in May of 2005.

TRANSYLVANIAN DISEASE, Nuclear Blast NB014-1 (1989). No Friends / Shoot Dead / Better Never (Cross My Way) / No More Problems / Tragic Fate / Last Kiss / Take 'em Back / Wish You Were Dead / Transylvanian Disease / Jim Go Home / Faith / Ignorance / 4/30 / Gun / Force Yourself / Wake Up And Die / Human Minds / Learn / I Don't Care / Pay The Price / Garbage Days.
Boring Old Fart, Nuclear Blast NB042 (1990). Boring Old Fart / Don't Ask Me Why / USA.
Pay The Price EP, Nuclear Blast NB026-1 (1990). Wake Up And Die / Human Minds / Learn / I Don't Care / Pay The Price / Garbage Days.

RUINS OF TIME

STOCKHOLM, SWEDEN — *Martin Missy (vocals), Chris Chatsikonstandinos (guitar), Mathias Öjermark (guitar), Oskar Göransson (bass), Juan Araya (drums).*

RUINS OF TIME, hailing from Stockholm and going by the LEGACY title in their formative years, notably included vocalist Martin Missy from cult 80s German Thrash band PROTECTOR. The band was forged during 1997 by Greek guitarist Christos Chatsikonstandinos and Chilean drummer Juan Araya. The band debuted in 1999 with a self financed album 'For A New Dawn'. During this year both founding members would also be active with Grind act DISASTER, but would relinquish these positions in early 2000.

Missy would enroll during 2001 and features on the 'Timetraveller' follow up, recorded with Anders Eriksson at Offbeat Studio in Stockholm. The German singer had, since breaking away from PROTECTOR in December of 1989, kept away from the music scene for over a decade. Missy had even gone into the respectable world of banking before relocating to Sweden in 1995. Upon completion of the 'Timetraveller' record, RUINS OF TIME inducted bassist Oskar Göransson. Konstandinos and second guitarist Mathias Öjermark are also active with Black Metal band SAURON. Araya also drums for Grindcore band PLAGUE DIVINE. Missy spread his talents by also fronting Växjö Thrash quartet TALION.

In 2004 Martin Missy re-emerged fronting PSYCHOMANTHIUM, an "old-school Speed/Thrash metal" band featuring ARKHAM 13 guitarist Derek 'Derekonomicon' Schilling, the INTERNAL BLEEDING and CATASTROPHIC credited bassist Brian Hobbie and ARKHAM 13 drummer Ant Ichrist. The band signed to Poland's Still Dead Productions for a debut album 'Death Attack'. The band evolved into PHIDION.

FOR A NEW DAWN, Independent (1999). Whispering Of Oblivion / My Last Testimony / Tale Of The Wise Man / Descent Of The Southern Past / False Gods / For A New Dawn / Animal Instincts / Arise Of The Ancestors / The Call Of The Spirits (New Beginning).
TIMETRAVELLER, (2001). The Cellar / Close Encounter / Slave One / The Bellfounder / Stigmatized / Man On The Roof / Timetraveller / 1200.

RULES OF ENGAGEMENT

KRISTIANSAND, NORWAY — *Bob Mörk (vocals), Erik Evensen (guitar), Kim-Arly Karlsen (guitar), Jarl Ivar Brynhildsvoll (bass), Thomas Færøvig (drums).*

Kristiansand Thrash Metal band RULES OF ENGAGEMENT, established in January 2006, was fronted by Bernt Fjellstad, known as vocalist for both SCARIOT and GUARDIANS OF TIME. The group had been formulated by guitarist Kim-Arly Karlsen and GUARDIANS OF TIME drummer Thomas Færøvig. This duo formed up a band unit in 2002, although this fractured.

A further attempt in 2005 saw the involvement of Jahn Aasvald Einarsmo prior to Rune Ljosland enrolling as singer then, as the title RULES OF ENGAGEMENT was adopted, second guitarist Nils Arne Aastveit. Completing the line-up on bass would be Jarl Ivar Brynhildsvoll. The band first performed live on March 25th 2006 at Birkeland's Youth Club. However, following this concert Rune Ljosland was asked to leave. In addition, Aastveit left, being replaced by Erik Evensen. In June Bernt Fjellestad took on the role of frontman.

A demo, 'Saved By Insanity' recorded at Samsen Lydstudio, was issued in 2006. The group then switched singers, drafting Bob Mörk to re-debut live on November 4th at Kjellerrock in Samsen.

Saved By Insanity, Rules Of Engagement (2006) (Demo). Saved By Insanity / Forgotten.

RUMORS OF GEHENNA

UDINE, ITALY — *Davide Scarano (vocals), Mirko Sgobba (guitar), Federico Re (guitar), Antonio Merici (bass), Lucio Maurigh (drums).*

Udine based Metal band RUMORS OF GEHENNA released a self-titled demo during 2006. The band had been established by three former members of Metalcore band BANDARLOG during 1999, guitarist Kokko, bassist Carlo and drummer Lucio Maurigh. In 2003 XADOOM vocalist Davide Scarano enrolled, followed afterwards by KRUNA guitarist Mirko Sgobba and the following year RUMORS OF GEHENNA hit the festival circuit, performing at such events as 'Castle Metal', 'Nine Fear', 'PolverFest' and 'SummerMusic'.

A line-up change in mid 2005 saw Carlo being replaced by Antonio Merici. In March 2006 this formation entered Studio 73 in Ravenna, working with engineer Riccardo Pasini, to cut their first demo.

Rumors Of Gehenna, Rumors Of Gehenna (2006) (Demo). Seven / My Hourglass Never Fails / Novembre 31st a.c.

RUNNING WILD

GERMANY — *Rock n' Rolf (vocals / guitar), Majk Moti (guitar), Jens Becker (bass), Iain Finlay (drums).*

One of the stoic mainstays of the German Metal scene. RUNNING WILD debuted with the 1984 album 'Gates To Purgatory', a record laden with stereotypical occultism but soon developed a unique, if bizarre, image based around pirates which they have fostered to the present day. Led by Rock n' Rolf (real name Rolf Kasparek) RUNNING WILD has proved to be a mainstay of the German Metal scene with consistently high profile albums and tours.

The band started out billed as GRANITE HEART, formed in 1976, switching to RUNNING WILD in 1979 for their first demo in 1981: this cassette featuring the songs 'Hallow The Hell', 'War Child' and 'King Of The Midnight Fire'. GRANITE HEART's first line-up consisted of Rock n' Rolf, guitarist Uwe Bendig, drummer Michael Hoffmann and bass player Jörg Schwarz. The latter was replaced by Carsten David in 1976. By the time of the 1981 RUNNING WILD sessions, the formation Rock'n'Rolf, Uwe Bendig on guitar, Matthias Kaufmann on bass and Wolfgang 'Hasche' Haggemann on the drums.

By the band's second tape, the suitably titled 'Heavy Metal Like A Hammer Blow', the following year only Rock n' Rolf and Haggemann remained. Fresh blood was provided by guitarist Preacher (a.k.a. Gerald Warnecke) and bassist Stephan Boriss. RUNNING WILD's third demo session secured a deal with Noise Records. The group's first offerings, two tracks 'Iron Heads' and 'Bones To Ashes', would be donated to the four way split album 'Death Metal' of 1984, sharing space with HELLOWEEN, DARK AVENGER and HELLHAMMER. Their debut proper came with the album 'Gates To Purgatory'.

The release of the 'Branded And Exiled' album, with new guitarist Majk Moti, in 1985 saw RUNNING WILD receive an invitation to open for American Glam Rockers MÖTLEY CRÜE's German 'Theatre Of Pain' tour dates. The band returned to Europe on September 14th, performing at the 'Metal Hammer Fest' in Loreley, Germany sharing a diverse billing with NAZARETH, VENOM, HEAVY PETTIN, WISHBONE ASH, SAVAGE GRACE, METALLICA, TYRAN PACE, PRETTY MAIDS and WARLOCK.

One of the first German Thrash bands to tour North America, RUNNING WILD undertook a lengthy club tour with CELTIC FROST and VOIVOD throughout June of 1986. Following the release of the popular 1987 'Under Jolly Roger' album drummer Hasche quit (and subsequently worked for the Rockfabrik club in Ludwigsburg), being substituted by Stefan Schwarzmann. German gigs in April of 1987 had British act SATAN as openers. The band yielded to another blow shortly after when bassist Stephan Boriss departed to join U.D.O. Before long Schwarzmann followed for the same destination. The live 'Ready For Boarding' album saw Winter 1988 shows with guests SATAN once again.

The 'Port Royal' opus was promoted by an extensive run of European dates throughout January and February 1989 with support from ANGEL DUST. The rhythm section was re-established with the recruitment of bassist Jens Becker and English drummer Iain Finlay for the 1990 'Death Or Glory' album. Finlay's position was briefly substituted by Jörg Michael, boasting credits with AVENGER, RAGE, MEKONG DELTA, LAOS, HEADHUNTER, GRAVE DIGGER and AXEL RUDI PELL. A lengthy string of European dates in January and February 1990 found RAGE, S.D.I. and RANDOM supporting. The line-up would remain less than stable as guitarist Majk Moti departed in early 1991 and was replaced by Axel Morgan. The 'Blazon Stone' album marked another run of Euro touring, this time RUNNING WILD taking RAVEN and CROSSROADS as guests throughout April and May of 1991.

The 'Pile Of Skulls' album in 1992 saw the addition of ex-U.D.O. rhythm section bassist Thomas 'Bodo' Smusynski and the return of drummer Stefan Schwarzmann and was recorded in Studio M in Hildesheim. Meantime, Becker deputized for former touring partners CROSSROADS the same year. The 'Pile Of Skulls' tour, with Jörg Michael back on drums, had UNIVERSE as support in early 1993.

RUNNING WILD would effectively split down the middle with Becker, Schwarzmann and Morgan creating X WILD, an outfit that lasted for three albums. Becker was later to join GRAVE DIGGER.

Two years later the group released their eighth album, 'Black Hand Inn', the record featuring the fifteen minute epic 'Genesis', RUNNING WILD's alternative view on the theory of evolution. Concert dates in Germany witnessed a Summer 1994 co-headline alliance with GRAVE DIGGER. 1995 yielded 'Masquerade'—recorded with Gerhard 'Anyway' Wölfe at Horus Sound in Hannover. The group immediately played the 'Summer Metal Meetings' with the likes of RAGE, GLENMORE, ICED EARTH and GRAVE DIGGER.

With the band inoperative for a period, new guitarist Thilo Hermann, previously with HOLY MOSES and RISK, joined GLENMORE for live work but would return to RUNNING WILD the following year. The band opened up 1996 with another German tour, this time with Brits CHINA BEACH providing the opening honours. Schwarzmann continued his musical chairs by emerging once again as the man behind the kit for U.D.O. in 1997. The same year Herrmann put together the side project HÖLLENHUNDE for the 'Alptraum' album with GLENMORE drummer Dany Löble. Herrmann. When HÖLLENHUNDE dissolved the same year as the album release Herrmann resumed activities with RUNNING WILD.

For the 1997 release, 'The Rivalry', which saw RUNNING WILD switching to the G.U.N. label, Rock n' Rolf was joined by Smuszynski, Hermann and drummer Jörg Michael. Touring to promote the record had RUNNING WILD, with erstwhile RAGE drummer Chris Efthimiades now installed as Michael had committed himself fully to STRATOVARIUS, pairing with PRIMAL FEAR in April 1998.

1998 found the band returning with a brand new studio affair. The 'Victory' album had Rolf, Herrmann and Smuszynski joined by Angelo Sasso. The latter being a pseudonym for a non 'Metal' drummer not wishing to be associated with the genre.

The band, now including new bass player Peter Pichl of the JUTTA WEINHOLD BAND, Thomas Smuszynski having joined covers band BOURBON, would spend the latter half of 2001 recording new album 'The Brotherhood'. In 2002 the group inducted ANGEL DUST guitarist Bernd Aufermann. Rock n' Rolf put in a cameo appearance in the video for famous German spoof act the DONUTS cover version of TWISTED SISTER's 'We're Not Gonna Take It' in September of 2002.

RUNNING WILD guitarist Bernd Aufermann collaborated with Zak Stevens in early 2004 on songs destined for the second CIRCLE II CIRCLE album. Another collaboration saw bassist Peter Pichl uniting with THE RUGGED's José Juan Gallego and Juan Antonio Soria on a song entitled 'The Reason Around'. Pichl was also announced as joining YARGOS, a Progressive Metal collaboration between well known figures on the European Metal scene involving guitarist Wieland Hofmeister, second guitarist Andreas Kienitz of HYDROTOXIN and HUMAN FORTRESS, THRESHOLD singer Andrew McDermott and MOONDOG drummer Ossy Pfieffer. Additional vocals came courtesy of Anca Graterol.

RUNNING WILD set 'Rogues En Vogue' as the preliminary title for a 2005 record. Limited editions of the album added two exclusive tracks, 'Cannonball Tongue' and 'Libertalia'.

In August 2005 Remedy Records released a double disc tribute album 'The Revivalry—A Tribute To Running Wild' featuring STORMWARRIOR, TORMENT, PARAGON, DARK AGE, TWISTED TOWER DIRE, BURDEN OF GRIEF, PREDATOR, LIGEIA, CHILDREN OF WRATH, AIRBORN, REVIVER,

RUNNING WILD (pic: Dirk Illing)

ICARUS WITCH, PERZONAL WAR, MAVERICK, NOT FRAGILE, KNEIPENTERRORISTEN, THE RUGGED, LOGAR'S DIARY, SARDONIC, CRYSTAL SHARK, CROSSFIRE, KATAGORY 5, POSTHUMOUS, THE CLAYMORE, TRAGEDIAN, ASARU, WARVENGER and AGENTS OF ROCK. G.U.N. Records issued a further compilation offering, 'The Best Of Adrian', in November.

Demo '81, Running Wild (1981) (Cassette demo). Hallow The Hell / War Child / King Of The Midnight Fire.

Demo '83, Running Wild (1983) (Cassette demo). Adrian S.O.S. / Chains And Leather.

Live 1983, Running Wild (1983) (Cassette demo). Genghis Khan / Soldiers Of Hell.

Heavy Metal Like A Hammerblow, Running Wild (1984) (Demo compilation). Intro / Hallow The Hell / Warchild / Adrian S.O.S. / Chains And Leather / Genghis Khan (Live) / Soldiers Of Hell (Live).

DEATH METAL, Noise N0006 (1984) (Split album with HELLHAMMER, HELLOWEEN and DARK AVENGER). Iron Heads / Bones To Ashes.

Victim Of States Power (Walpurgis Night EP), Noise N0010 (1984). Victim Of States Power / Walpurgis Night (The Sign Of Women's Fight) / Satan.

GATES TO PURGATORY, Noise N0012 (1984). Victim Of States Power / Adrian (Son Of Satan) / Preacher / Black Demon / Soldiers Of Hell / Genghis Khan / Prisoner Of Our Time / Diabolical Force.

BRANDED AND EXILED, Noise N0030 (1985). Branded And Exiled / Gods Of Iron / Realm Of Shades / Mordor / Fight The Oppression / Evil Spirit / Marching To Die / Chains And Leather.

UNDER JOLLY ROGER, Noise N0064 (1987). Under Jolly Roger / War In The Gutter / Raw Ride / Beggars Night / Raise Your Fist / Land Of Ice / Diamonds In The Black Chest / Mercyless Game.

READY FOR BOARDING (LIVE), Noise N0108-1 (1988). Hymn Of Long John Silver / Under Jolly Roger / Genghis Khan / Raise Your Fist / Purgatory / Mordor / Diabolic Force / Raw Ride / Adrian (S.O.S.) / Prisoner Of Our Time.

PORT ROYAL, Noise NO122-2 (1988). Port Royal / Raging Fire / Into The Arena / Uaschitschun / Final Gates / Conquistadores / Blown To Kingdom Come / Warchild / Mutiny / Calico Jack.

Bad To The Bone, Noise (1989). Bad To The Bone / Battle Of Waterloo.

Bad To The Bone EP, Noise 12EM 116 (1989). Bad To The Bone / Battle Of Waterloo / March On.

DEATH OR GLORY, Noise N0172-2 (1989). Riding The Storm / Renegade / Evilution / Running Blood / Highland Glory (The Eternal Fight) / Marooned / Bad To The Bone / Tortuga Bay / Death Or Glory / Battle At Waterloo / March On.

Wild Animal EP, Noise N0173-3 (1990). Wild Animal / Chains And Leather / Tear Down The Walls / Störtebeker.

Little Big Horn, EMI 1C006 204 248-7 (1991) (7" vinyl). Little Big Horn / Billy The Kid.

Little Big Horn EP, EMI 1C006 204 248-6 (1991). Little Big Horn / Billy The Kid / Genocide.

BLAZON STONE, Toshiba TOCP-6632 (1991) (Japanese release). Blazon Stone / Lone Wolf / Slavery / Fire And Ice / Little Big Horn / Over The Rainbow / White Masque / Rolling Wheels / Bloody Red Rose / Straight To Hell / Head Or Tails / Billy The Kid / Genocide.

BLAZON STONE, Noise N0171-1 (1991). Blazon Stone / Lone Wolf / Slavery / Fire And Ice / Little Big Horn / Over The Rainbow / White Masque / Rolling Wheels / Bloody Red Rose / Straight To Hell / Head Or Tails.

Sinister Eyes, Noise (1992) (Promotion release). Sinister Eyes.

Lead Or Gold, EMI 880 248-2 (1992). Lead Or Gold / Hanged, Drawn And Quartered / Win Or Be Drowned.

PILE OF SKULLS, EMI 780 651-2 (1992). Chamber Of Lies / Whirlwind / Sinister Eyes / Black Wings Of Death / Fistful Of Dynamite / Roaring Thunder / Pile Of Skulls / Lead Or Gold / White Buffalo / Jenning's Revenge / Treasure Island. Chart position: 54 GERMANY.

BLACK HAND INN, EMI 829 160-2 (1994). The Curse / Black Hand Inn / Mr. Deadhead / Soulless / The Privateer / Fight The Fire Of Hate / The Phantom Of The Black Hand Hill / Freewind Rider / Powder And Iron / Dragonmen / Genesis (The Making And Fall Of Man). Chart position: 54 GERMANY.

The Privateer EP, EMI 881 266-2 (1994). The Privateer / Dancing On A Minefield / Poisoned Blood.

MASQUERADE, Noise N0261-2 (1995). The Contract / The Crypts Of Hades / Masquerade / Demonized / Black Soul / Lions Of The Sea / Rebel At Heart / Wheel Of Doom / Metalhead / Soleil Royale / Men In Black / Underworld.

THE RIVALRY, Great Unlimited Noises GUN 155-2 (1998). Of The Final Battle (The End Of All Evil) / The Rivalry / Kiss Of Death / Firebreather / Return Of The Dragon / Resurrection / Ballad Of William Kidd / Agents Of Black / Fire And Thunder / The Poison / Adventure Galley / Man On The Moon / War And Peace. Chart position: 19 GERMANY.

Revolution, Noise (2000) (Promotion release). Revolution.

VICTORY, Great Unlimited Noises GUN 187-2 (2000). Fall Of Dorkas / When Time Runs Out / Timeriders / Into The Fire / Revolution / The Final Waltz / Tsar / The Hussar / The Guardian / Return Of The Gods / Silent Killer / Victory. Chart positions: 26 GERMANY, 52 SWEDEN.

THE BROTHERHOOD, Great Unlimited Noises GUN 194-2 (2002). Welcome To Hell / Soulstripper / The Brotherhood / Powerride / Siberian Winter / Detonator / Pirate Song / U-Nation / Dr. Horror / The Ghost / Crossfire / Faceless. Chart position: 23 GERMANY.

LIVE, Great Unlimited Noises GUN 197-2 (2002). March Of The Final Battle / Welcome To Hell / Bad To The Bone / Lead Or Gold / Riding The Storm / When Time Runs Out / The Brotherhood / Soulless / Blazon Stone / Crossfire / Metalmachine Solo / Kiss Of Death / Uaschitschun / Unation / Victory / Prisoners / Purgatory / Soulstrippers / Under Jolly Roger.

ROGUES EN VOGUE (LIMITED EDITION), Great Unlimited Noises GUN 206 (2005). Draw The Line / Angel Of Mercy / Skeleton Dance / Skull & Bones / Born Bad, Dying Worse / Black Gold / Soul Vampires / Rogues En Vogue / Winged And Feathered / Dead Man's Road / The War / Cannonball Tongue / Libertalia.

ROGUES EN VOGUE, Great Unlimited Noises GUN 206-2 (2005). Draw The Line / Angel Of Mercy / Skeleton Dance / Skull & Bones / Born Bad, Dying Worse / Black Gold / Soul Vampires / Rogues En Vogue / Winged And Feathered / Dead Man's Road / The War. Chart positions: 39 GERMANY, 41 GREECE, 49 SWEDEN.

RYKER'S

GERMANY — *Kid D. (vocals), Iggy (guitar), Chris (bass), Meff (drums).*

A Hardcore Thrash band formed in Kassel in 1992, RYKER'S involved ex HOLY MOSES drummer Meff. Indeed. the band's producer was ex HOLY MOSES man Andy Classen. Over a succession of albums and tours RYKER'S would elevate themselves to fan acclaim normally reserved in Europe for established American artists.

After recording the 1995 issued 'First Blood' album guitarist Iggy was replaced by newcomer Grobi. RYKERS folded in late 2000 with Meff opening a tattoo shop and Chris concentrating on his record label Kingfisher.

The retrospective live album 'From The Cradle To The Grave' would feature versions of VENOM's 'Witching Hour' and YOUTH OF TODAY's 'Together', this latter track even seeing YOUTH OF TODAY's Ray Cappo on guest vocals. An accompanying bonus CD added a drum n' bass remix of 'End Of Line' courtesy of MICRO B, two video tracks and a further slew of covers including GIRLSCHOOL's 'C'mon Let's Go' featuring THUMB's Claus

Grabke on lead vocals, AC/DC's 'Dirty Deeds Done Dirt Cheap', BAD BRAINS 'Attitude' and ACCEPT's 'London Leatherboys'.

Kickback EP, Ryker's (1993) (7" single). Kickback.

Ryker's, Lost & Found (1993) (Split 7" with PITTBULL). Ryker's.

PAYBACK TIME, Lost & Found (1993). Beg To Differ / Threshold / Prove Yourself / Kickback / Truth / Eye For An Eye / Never Know Nothing / For A Trick / Nothing To Regret / (This Is) My Justice.

Ryker's, Lost & Found (1994) (Split 7" with POWER OF EXPRESSION). Ryker's.

BROTHER AGAINST BROTHER, Lost & Found (1994) (Split album with SICK OF IT ALL). Loyalty / Brother Against Brother / Up To You / Try / Once I Believed / Guilty / Beg To Differ / Enough Is Enough / Wrong / Thin Line / Below Zero / Brothers In Arms / True Colours / The Edge.

BROTHER AGAINST BROTHER, Lost & Found LF 102/CD (1994). Loyalty / Brother Against Brother / Up To You / Try / Once I Believed / Guilty / Beg To Differ / Enough Is Enough / Wrong / Thin Line / Below Zero / Brothers In Arms / True Colours / The Edge.

FIRST BLOOD, Lost & Found LF 187 (1995). First Blood / Stranglehold / Slowly / Ricochet / What We Once Said / Together (YOUTH OF TODAY).

Hunting Season, RAW WEA 0630-14517-7 (1996). Hunting Season / Where Were You.

GROUND ZERO, RAW WEA 0630-14519-2 (1996). I Reject / Lifeline / This Separation Mine / Without A Second Thought / When There's No Divide / Hunting Season / Lowlife / Inbalance / Prove Yourself / Engine / Ground Zero / The Cause / Loose Ends / My Clear Moment / Absolution Ninety-Five / Witching Hour.

A LESSON IN LOYALTY, WEA PRCD601 0630-18928-2 (1997). Test Of Faith / As The Laughter Dies / Lesson In Loyalty / Naturally / Still / Triggered / Cold, Lost, Sick / 25 / Gutless / Sober / Shadowplay / Straight / The Peak / Finally / Emergency / Who Laughs Last (Laughs Alone).

LIFE'S A GAMBLE ... SO IS DEATH, Century Media (1999). Forever And A Day / End Of Line / Gone For Good / And None Shall Live / To Whom It May Concern / Violence Is Golden / Calculated / Past The Point / Bombs Of Death / A Dream Gone Bad / Cataclystic / What It Means / Loss For Words / Stagnant / King / When Tigers Fight / Youll Never Walk Alone.

FROM THE CRADLE TO THE GRAVE, Century Media 215655 (2000). Intro—First Blood / Lowlife / End Of Line / Truth / To Whom It May Concern / Lifeline / Past The Point / Stranglehold / Gone For Good / Hunting Season / Forever And A Day / Nothing To Regret / As The Laughter Dies / Cold Lost Sick / True Love / Witching Hour / You / Slowly / What We Once Said / My Justice / Once I Believed / Together / Brother Against Brother / Beg To Differ / Judas Reward / From The Cradle To The Grave / Sad Done / Attitude / Cmon Lets Go / Dont Threat On Me / Dirty Deeds Done Dirt Cheap / London Leatherboys / End Of Line (Remix) / Beg To Differ (Video) / True Love (Video).

S.N.I.F.F.

PUERTO RICO— *Chris Godkiller (vocals / guitar), Edwin Torres (guitar), Christian Quintana (bass), Christian Rivera (drums).*

Self-styled "Alcoholic Sexually Perverted Heavy Fucking Metal Metal" band S.N.I.F.F. was formed in 1999 by drummer Christian Rivera and guitarist Edwin Torres, adding second guitar player Annibal Cardona and bassist Jonathan Ruiz. The group was completed with the addition of ex-SEPULCHRAL frontman Christian Mercedes Túa ("Chris Godkiller"). Annibal Cardona departed in 2001.

S.N.I.F.F. recorded a 2001 demo, 'Eyes Of Blood', after which Tito Crowbar of MISERIA took over on bass guitar. The band fractured as Torres quit then, in 2003, Christian Rivera joined ALMA BLANCA. Godkiller persevered with a completely revised band line-up involving guitarist Reynaldo, bassist Cheo and drummer Edil. This version floundered too and Godkiller duly reformed SEPULCHRAL.

S.N.I.F.F. was resurrected in 2006.

Eyes Of Blood, Sniff (2001) (Demo). Odio / Hipocrecia / Human Falling / Love Is Dead.

S.O.D.

NEW YORK, NY, USA — *Billy Milano (vocals), Scott Ian (guitar), Dan Lilker (bass), Charlie Benante (drums).*

As side projects go, S.O.D. (STORMTROOPERS OF DEATH) proved to be extremely successful, a band that merged the talents of ANTHRAX men guitarist Scott Ian and drummer Charlie Benante with larger than life frontman Billy Milano. Completing the line up was NUCLEAR ASSAULT (and ex-ANTHRAX) bassist Dan Lilker. The debut album 'Speak English Or Die' proved an unexpected success internationally and momentum was only stalled by the rapid acceleration of ANTHRAX's career. With Ian and Benante otherwise engaged Milano founded M.O.D. ('Method Of Destruction') whilst Lilker forged a career with underground act BRUTAL TRUTH.

S.O.D., with the original line up, resurrected themselves signing to German label Nuclear Blast, for 1999's 'Bigger Than The Devil'. The artwork of the album betrayed the humour inside, Sgt D. becoming larger than IRON MAIDEN's infamous Eddie. Touring in Europe that June, the band partnered with Swedish tech-Metal act MESHUGGAH and German Metalcore band STAHLHAMMER. Japanese dates saw the band hooked up with infamous all girl trio YELLOW MACHINE GUN, this alliance subsequently solidified with a split 7" single shared with the girls entitled 'Seasoning Of The Obese'. This release famously satiricised SLAYER's 'Seasons Of The Abyss' including artwork featuring a discreet Ronald McDonald above the word 'Seasoning'. Maintaining the theme, the band's 2000 video and DVD's artwork was a wry take on the GUNS N' ROSES cross logo.

Lilker assembled a side project THE RAVENOUS in 2000 for the 'Assembled In Blasphemy' album. Included were NECROPHAGIA's Killjoy and Chris Reifert of AUTOPSY. The bassist was also operating Black Metal band HEMLOCK as a side endeavour. Lilker would surprisingly announce the reformation of the classic NUCLEAR ASSAULT line up for an appearance at the 2002 'Wacken Open Air' Metal festival in Germany.

A war of words would erupt between Milano and the ANTHRAX clan of S.O.D. during early 2002 and by May reports suggested Milano had approached the erstwhile FEAR FACTORY duo of guitarist Dino Cazares and drummer Raymond Herrera to found an all new version of the band. However, within days both Danny Lilker and Scott Ian issued press statements to the effect that S.O.D. was no more.

Lilker would be in the driving seat for OVERLORD EXTERMINATOR in early 2004, a Black Metal combo featuring Adam Bonacci from WITHERED EARTH on vocals and COMMIT SUICIDE's Lee on bass guitar. This band's presence would be first marked by internet demos posted in February.

By 2004 the debut 'Speak English Or Die' album had sold over 400,000 copies. To mark this achievement Megaforce Records re-issued the record as a limited edition 12" red vinyl pressing.

In September and October 2006 Dan Lilker, having reformed BRUTAL TRUTH, temped for SOULFLY's North American dates after regular bassist Bobby Burns suffered a mild stroke.

SPEAK ENGLISH OR DIE, Roadrunner RR 9725 (1985). March Of The S.O.D. / Sergeant D And The S.O.D. / Kill Yourself / Milano Mosh / Speak English Or Die / United Forces / Chromatic Death / Pi Alpha Nu / Anti-Procrastination Song / What's The Noise / Freddy Kruger / Milk / Pre-Menstrual Princess Blues / Pussy Whipped / Fist Banging Mania.

LIVE AT BUDOKAN, Music For Nations MFN 144 (1992). Intro / March Of The Stormtroopers Of Death / Sargeant D. And The S.O.D. / Kill Yourself / Momo / Pi Alpha Nu / Milano Mosh / Speak English Or Die / Chromatic Death / Fist Banging Mania / The Camel Boy / No Turning Back / Milk / Vitality / Fuck The Middle East / Douche Crew / Get A Real Job / The Ballad Of Jimi Hendrix / Livin' In The City / Pussy Whipped / Stigmata / Thieves / Freddy Krueger / Territorial Pissings / United Forces.

BIGGER THAN THE DEVIL, Nuclear Blast NB 383-2 (1999). Bigger Than The Devil / The Crackhead Song / Kill The Assholes / Monkeys

S.O.D.

Rule / Skool Bus / King At The King—Evil Is In / Black War / Celtic Frosted Flakes / Charlie Don't Cheat / The Song That Don't Go Fast / Shenanigans / Dog On The Tracks / Make Room, Make Room / Free Dirty Needles / Fugu / We All Bleed Red / Frankenstein And His Horse / Every Tiny Molecule / Aren't You Hungry? / L.A.T.K.C.H. / Ballad Of Michael H. / Ballad Of Phil H. / Moment Of Truth. Chart position: 40 GERMANY.

Seasoning Of The Obese EP, Howling Bull America (1999) (Split single with YELLOW MACHINEGUN). Seasoning Of The Obese.

SPEAK ENGLISH OR DIE, Megaforce 2000 (2000) (Platinum edition bonus tracks). March Of The S.O.D. / Sargent "D" & The S.O.D. / Kill Yourself / Milano Mosh / Speak English Or Die / United Forces / Chromatic Death / Pi Alpha Nu / Anti-Procrastination Song / What's That Noise / Freddy Krueger / Milk / Pre-Menstrual Princess Blues / Pussy Whipped / Fist Banging Mania / No Turning Back / Fuck The Middle East / Douche Crew / Hey Gordy! / The Ballad Of Jimi Hendrix / Diamonds And Rust (Extended version) / United And Strong / Ready To Fight / March Of The S.O.D./Sargent "D" (Live) / Kill Yourself (Live) / Milano Mosh (Live) / Speak English Or Die (Live) / Fuck The Middle East/Douche Crew (Live) / Not/Momo/Taint/The Camel Boy/Diamonds And Rust/Anti-Procrastination Song (Live) / Milk (Live) / United Forces (Live).

SABBAT

KUWANA, JAPAN — *Gezol (vocals / bass), Temis Osmond (guitar), Zorugelion (drums).*

Extremely Primitive and raw Black Metal band. In keeping with Japanese stereotypes, Kuwana's SABBAT are seemingly armed with an inexhaustible work ethic that has spawned a vast catalogue of works. However, their prodigious industry is tempered by the fact that most of their releases are issued in strictly limited amounts as low as 100. Indeed, SABBAT's first four albums were restricted to a mere 500 copies.

SABBAT formed in 1983 with a line up of frontman Gezol, guitarists Elizaveat and Ozny with drummer Valvin. The band had previously been titled EVIL with singer Toshiya but upon his departure the title SABBAT was adopted. In 1985 Valvin departed to be superseded by Samm (sometimes known as 'Gero'). Ozny left the following year trimming SABBAT down to a trio.

In 1989 SABBAT united for a one off gig and tried out the services of vocalist Possessed Hammer and guitarist Barraveat. Further ructions witnessed the departure of Samm in 1990 being replaced by Zorugelion. Temis Osmond took the guitarists position in 1991 in time for the 'Bloody Countess' demo sessions.

The 1994 compilation of re-recorded early material 'Black Up Your Soul' included a version of 'Satan's Serenade' by English NWoBHM band QUARTZ. The same year SABBAT contributed a bilingual version of 'Black Fire' and a remix of 'Satanic Rites' to the compilation 'Far East Gate In Inferno'.

1995 saw SABBAT revisiting more old songs for the album 'For Satan And Sacrifice'. They also chose another NWoBHM cover version, this time 'Kiss Of Death' by SATAN. The band proved that they had a sense of humour by re-recording their earlier 'Panic In The Head' retitled and with new lyrics as 'Baby Disco Is Fuck' as part of their contribution to the infamous 'Headbangers Against Disco' EP alongside GEHENNAH, BESTIAL WARLUST and INFERNO.

SABBAT are noted for their run of international flavoured 'Harmageddon' series of singles which comprise songs in different languages including rather novelly a Swahili version of 'Black Fire'! The 'South American Harmageddon' outing was made up exclusively of cover versions of fellow Japanese artists JURASSIC JADE and SACRIFICE.

The 1999 'Live Panica' and 2000's 'Live Revenge' albums were both limited to 100 copies. 2000 also saw SABBAT cutting their take of Italian 80's Thrash act BULLDOZER's 'Whisky Time' on a split tribute single shared with IMPERIAL. The Iron Pegasus 2003 double album 'Fetishism', limited to 666 copies, combined the 1994 EP "Sabbatical Devilucifer" with the "Sabbatical Demon" demos along with exclusive tracks. The first 222 pressings would be made available in a mixture of red and gold vinyl. Also surfacing that year would be the studio album 'Karmagmassacre', also on Iron Pegasus, and the archive live album 'Live Hamagurism', recorded in October of 1999 through HMSS Records. Naturally a limited edition, only 100 green vinyl copies of 'Live Hamagurism' were released.

Somewhat of an ultimate collectors piece came with the 'Live Wacko' box set. Comprising the CD singles 'Gezonslaught', 'Valvinosnlaught', 'Elizaveatosnlaught', 'Perfect Wacko', 'Perfect Kindergarden' and 'Perfect Revenge' also featured would be T-shirt, Booklet, Badge and even a Sabbat Doll. Only 25 were manufactured. That same year the split cassette 'Kamikaze Splitting Roar' would be issued in union with ABIGAIL.

SABBAT's collectability would be heightened by the January 2004 release of 'Sabbatical Satanichrist Slaughter' by Nuclear War Now! Productions. Only 1000 of this 6" vinyl box set would be manufactured, with 200 of these being the 'die hard' version. The elaborate sleeve packaging folded out into a 28" inverted crucifix. Although all variants came with poster and inserts the 'die hard' version added colored vinyl, poster, extra insert, a 4" embroidered patch, sticker, textured sleeve, obi strip, and a differently colored foil stamp on the cover. Another rarity would be the Assaulter Productions 'Hamaguri Resurrection' single. Of the 1000 pressed a special 100 would be honoured with coloured vinyl Sabbatical Otaku status in a custom Screen printed felt sleeve with poster, sticker and a bonus CD-R 'Live Grilling'.

SABBAT arranged a debut North American tour for September 2005. Novelly, SABBAT funded this enterprise directly from proceeds generated by sales of the 'Live Sabbatical Hamaguri Queen' album. A show recorded in New York was subsequently issued, albeit as a restricted run of just 150 copies in clear vinyl, as the 'Brooklyn Blackfire' album. Closing a 14 year tenure, guitarist Temis Osmond bowed out in November. Time Before Time records put out the 'Geionslaught 1986' album in 2005, a recording of a June 8th, 1986 concert.

Sabbat EP, Evil 666-01 (1985). Black Fire / Mion's Hill.

Born By Evil Blood EP, Evil 666-02 (1987). Satanic Rites / Curdle The Blood / Poison Child.

Desecration EP, Evil 666-03 (1988). Welcome To Sabbat / Crest Of Satan / Children Of Hell / Darkness And Evil.

The Devil's Sperm Is Cold EP, Evil 666-04 (1989). Hellfire / Immortality Of The Soul.

Sabbatical Devilucifer EP, Holycaust SIN001 (1990). All Over The Desolate Land / Blacking Metal / Witch's Mill / Rage Of The Mountains.

The Seven Deadly Sins EP, Evil 666-05 (1990). Possessed The Room (Kanashibari) / Sacrifice Of Angel / Crying In Last.

ENVENOM, Evil 666-06 (1991). Bewitch / The 6th Candle / Satan Bless You / Evil Nations / Devil Worship / Reek Of Cremation / Deathtemptation (Kanashibari Part II) / King Of Hell / Eviler / Carcassvoice / Deadmarch / Reminiscent Bells.

EVOKE, Evil 666-07 (1992). Dance Du Sabbat / Envenom Into Witch's Hole / Godz Of Satan / Total Necro ... / Torment In The Pentagram / Beyond The River / The Whisper Of Demon / Hellhouse / The Curse Of Pharaoh / Metalucifer And Evilucifer.

DISEMBODY, Evil 666-08 (1993). The Seven Crosses Of Damnation / Bird Of Ill Omen / Metamorphosis / Diabolicalborn / Unknown Massacre / Evoke The Evil / Flower's Red / Reversed Bible / Hungarian Death No. 5 / Ghost In The Mirror.

BLACK UP YOUR SOUL, Evil 666-0A (1994). Welcome To Sabbat / Black Fire / Poison Child / Rage Of The Mountains / Possessed The Room / Darkness And Evil / All Over The Desolate Land / Satan's Serenade / Mion's Hill / Black Fire / Hellfire / Bird Of Ill Omen / Danse Du Sabbat / Envenom Into The Witch's Hole / Carcassvoice / Bewitch.

FETISHISM, Evil 666-09 (1994). Disembody In The Abyss / In Satan We Trust / Satan Is Beautiful / Sausine / Elixir De Vie / Lost In The Grave / Burn The Church / Ghost Train / The Exorcism / Evanescent Quietude.

FOR SATAN AND SACRIFICE, Evil 666-0C (1995). Witch's Mill—Curdle The Blood / Satanic Rites—Crest Of Satan / The Egg Of Dapple / Acid Angel / Immortality Of The Soul / Gideon / Kiss Of Death / Mion's Hill / Sodoomed / Disembody To The Abyss / Unknown Massacre / Whisper Of Demon / Satan Bless You / Remiscent Bells.

LIVE AT BLOKULA, Evil 666-00B (1995). The Seven Crosses Of Damnation / Satan Bless You / Possessed The Room—Dead March / Bird Of Ill Omen / Reversed Bible / Evoke The Evil / Evil Nations / Total Necro ... / Envenom Into The Witch's Hole / Disembody To The Abyss / Satan Is Beautiful / Hellfire / Ghost In The Mirror / Black Fire.

THE DWELLING: THE MELODY OF DEATH MASK, Evil Evil 666-10 (1996). The Swelling-Melody Of The Death Mask.

LIVE 666—JAPANESE ARMAGEDDON, Evil 666-HS1 (1996). In Satan We Trust / Total Necro ... / Beyond The River / Satan Bless You / Bird Of Ill Omen / Mion's Hill / Black Fire.

BLOODY COUNTESS, Holycaust SIN002 (1996) (USA release). Splatter / Satan's Night / Bloody Countess / Panic In The Head / Madara No Tamago / Poison Child / Children Of Hell / Kanashibari Part 1 / Bloody Countess.

European Harmageddon EP, Merciless MREP004 (1997) (German release). Satanican / Gok Kan Ma.

Scandinavian Harmageddon EP, Primitive Art PAR 014 (1997) (Swedish release). Bleeding From The Ear / Reek Of Cremation (Live) / Jumu.

American Harmageddon EP, Holycaust S810 (1998) (USA release). The Well Of Krath (Kanashibari 6) / Another Collector (Dwelling II).

Asian Harmageddon EP, Evil J001ER666-HS6 (1998) (Chinese release). Takaightenshow / Rinnereighshi.

Oceanic Harmageddon EP, Way Of Life WOLR1 (1998) (Australian release). Satanic Rites (Live) / Disembodys To The Abyss (Live) / Curdle The Blood (Live) / Dead March (Live).

African Harmageddon EP, Mganga UCHAIVI001 (1998) (Tanzanian release). Black Fire (Swahili version) / Splatter '98.

East European Harmageddon EP, View Beyond VB0018 (1998) (Czech release). Sabbat / Snow Woman.

Sabbatical Magicurse—Baltic Harmageddon EP, Sadistic Sodomizer SS-001 (1999) (Latvian release). Incubus Succubus / Possessed Hammer (Tribute To Possessed Hammer) / Whisper Of Demon '99.

LIVE CURSE, Heavy Metal Super Star HMSS CD001 (1999). Satanic Rites / Curdle The Blood / Crest Of Satan / Poison Child / Immortality Of The Soul / Devil's Sperm Is Cold / Black Fire / Mion's Hill / Intro: Welcome To Sabbat / Poison Child / Children Of Hell / Black Fire / Immortality Of The Soul / Mion's Hill.

SABBATICAL RITES, Iron Pegasus IP04 (1999) (German release). Black Fire / Mion's Hill / Satanic Rites / Curdle The Blood / Poison Child (Mix) / Darkness And Evil (Full version) / Welcome To Sabbat / Crest Of Satan / Children Of Hell / Immortality Of The Soul (Mix) / Hell Fire (Mix).

LIVE KINDERGARDEN, Heavy Metal Super Star HMSS CD-02 (1999). Welcome To Sabbat / Black Fire / Hell Fire / Possessed The Room / Dead March / Envenom Into The Witch's Hole / Beyond The River / Evil Nations / Satan Bless You.

LIVE PANICA, Heavy Metal Super Star HMSS CD-03 (1999). Welcome To Sabbat / Panic In The Head / Wolfman / Splatter / Bloody Countess.

Sabbatical Demonslaught EP, View Beyond (1999) (Czech release). Angel Of Destruction / Satan Bless You / Kamikaze Bomber / Darkness And Evil.

South American Harmageddon EP, Mega Therion MTSS1 (1999) (Brazilian release). Terror Beast / Hello Darkness / Destroy—Witch Hunt / Friday Nightmare.

KARISMA, Iron Pegasus IP05 (1999) (German release). Karisma / Bowray Samurai (Samurai Zombies) / Orochie / Harmageddon / Makutsu (Den Of Hades) / Okiko Ningyo (Okiku Doll Of The Devil) / Yoochuu (Japanese Revelation).

LIVE REVENGE, Heavy Metal Super Star HMSS CD-05 (2000). Black Fire XX / Splatter / Children Of Hell / Black Fire / Gok Kan Ma / Immortality Of The Soul / Kanashibari / Poison Child / Mion's Hill.

Whisky Time, Warlord (2000) (Split single with IMPERIAL). Whisky Time.

Sabbatical Magicrucifixion—Iberian Harmageddon EP, Hibernia Productions HB02V (2000) (Portuguese release). Envenom Into The Witch's Hole / Ghost Train.

Sabbatical Magicrypt—French Harmageddon EP, EAL Productions (2000) (French release). Elixir De Vie (Nouvelle version) / Les Flammes De L'Enfer ('Hellfire' Version Francais).

LIVE DEVIL, Heavy Metal Super Star HMSS CD-03 (2000) (Promotion release). Sabbat Tribes / Gok Kan Ma / The Seven Crosses Of Damnation / Satan Bless You / Evil Nations / Whisper Of Demon / Evoke The Evil / Panic In The Head / Mion's Hill / Black Fire / Darkness And Evil.

LIVE MELTDOWN, Heavy Metal Super Star HMSS CD-06 (2001) (Limited edition picture disc of 100 numbered copies). Danse Du Sabbat / Satan Bless You / Evil Nations / Charisma / Devil Worship / Transmigration Aggressor / Japanese Revelation / Baby, Disco Is Fuck / Outroduction.

ANTARCTIC HARMAGEDDON, Heavy Metal Super Star HMSS CD-010 (2001). Night Of The Living Dead / Flame On The Circle / Black Fate (VOIDD cover) / Hellfire (Japanese version) / Bloodstained Holy Cross (SATANAS) / Magnesium Lady (MAGNESIUM) / Enola Gay (DISARM) / Stop (DISARM) / Black Fire.

Hellfire (Live), The Sky Is Red 001 (2001) (Split single with UNHOLY GRAVE. Limited edition of 1000 copies). Hellfire (Live).

LIVE NUTS, Heavy Metal Super Star HMSS CD-08 (2001) (Limited vinyl only edition of 80 copies). Total Necro / Seven Crosses / Metamorphosis / Evoke The Evil / Reversed Bible / Satan Bless You / Evil Nations / Black Fire / Poison Child.

SATANASWORD, Iron Pegasus IP010 (2001) (German release). Charisma / Angel Of Destruction / Kiss Of Lilleth / Death Zone / The Gate / Dracula / Nekromantik / Jealousy Carnage.

Le Feu Noir, Legions Of Death 001 (2001) (Split single with TEROR SQUAD. Limited edition of 300 copies). Le Feu Noir ('Black Fire', French version) / Darkness And Evil (Live).

Rain Of Terror, View Beyond (2001) (Split EP with GORGON). Rain Of Terror.

Minami-Kyushu Harmageddon—Sabbatical Magichaos EP, Infernal Thrash ITR-003 (2001) (Green vinyl. Limited to 120 copies). Orochie (Live) / Devil Worship (Live).

Dietsland Harmageddon—Sabbatical Magicrest EP, Berzerker BRZRK 666 (2001) (Limited edition of 333 copies). Poison Child (Live) / Black Fire (Live).

Sabbatical Splitombstone EP, Iron Pegasus IP03 (2001) (Split EP with UNPURE. Limited edition of 666 copies). Transmigration Of The Soul.

Brazilian Demonslaught, Live Recordings Attack!!! LRA001EP (2002) (Brazilian release. Limited edition 999 copies). Merciful Forest / Ride Like The Wind.

FETISHISM, Iron Pegasus IP029 (2003) (Limited edition 666 copies). Disembody To The Abyss / In Satan We Trust / Satan Is Beautiful / Elixier De Vie / Lost In The Grave / Burn The Church / Ghost Train / The Exorcism / Sausine / The Egg Of Dapple (English version) / Poisonchild (Extra version) / Sodoomed / Creation Of Death / Witche's Mill / Rage Of Mountains / All Over Desolate Land / Blacking Metal / Disembody To The Abyss (Extra version) / Evanescent Quietude.

Zorugelionslaught, Infernal Thrash ITR-007 (2003). Black Magical Circle Of Witches / Satanician.

Valvinonslaught, Infernal Thrash ITR-006 (2003) (Limited edition 100 copies). Total Necro ... / Mion's Hill.

Naniwa Tepoddonslaught, Evil EDR-NTS-666 (2003) (limited edition 300 copies). The Answer Is Hell (Live) / Screaming Murder (Live).

Live Izumoden—Temisosmonslaught, Heavy Metal Super Star (2003). Transmigration Of The Soul (Live) / Orochie (Live).

Elizaveatonslaught, Heavy Metal Super Star HMSS CD-021 (2003) (limited edition 100 copies). Disembody To Abyss / Black Fire.

F.E.T.U. Tribute, Ososo 728 (2003). F.E.T.U. / Hell Of The Voltage.

Gezonslaught, Ososo ITR-009 (2003) (Limited edition 100 copies). Evil Nations / Gokkanma.

KARMAGMASSACRE, Iron Pegasus IP031 (2003). The Answer Is Hell / Im Your Satan / Demonic Serenade / Brothers Of Demons / Registry Of Dark Side / In League With Devils / Black Magical Circle Of Witches / The Letter From Death / Possession Of The Reaper / Satanasword.

LIVE HAMAGARISM, HMSS Records HMSS CD-025 (2003) (Limited edition 100 copies. Green vinyl). Witch's Mill / Hellfire / Crest Of Satan / Rage Of Mountains / Nib / Immortality Of The Soul / Black Fire / Mion's Hill.

Svart Eld—Demonslaught Sverige, Monsternation MN 02 (2003) (Limited edition 500 copies). Black Fire / Sacrifice.

Hamaguri Resurrection, Assaulter Productions ASSAULT-001 (2004) (Limited edition 1000 copies). Immortality Of The Soul / Wolf Man.

LIVE CURSE, GoatowaRex (2004) (Australian release). Satanic Rites / Curdle The Blood / Crest Of Satan / Poison Child / Immortality Of The Soul / Devil's Sperm Is Cold / Black Fire / Mion's Hill / Intro/Welcome To Sabbat / Poison Child / Children Of Hell / Black Fire / Immortality Of The Soul / Mion's Hill.

Sabbatical Satanichrist Slaughter, Nuclear War Now! Productions (2004) (6" vinyl boxset. Limited edition 1000 copies). Bring Me The Head Of Satan / Children Of Hell / Satan Bless You / Deathzone / Night Of The Living Dead (Japanese version) / Darkness And Evil (Unreleased different mix '99).

LIVE RESURRECTION, Monster Nation (2004). Dance Du Sabbat—Evanescent Quietude / Satan Bless You / Evil Nations / Charisma / Devil Worship / Transmigration Of The Soul / Youchuu / Baby, Disco Is Fuck! / Hellfire / Orochie / Darkness And Evil / Svart Eld.

Sabbat / Asbestos, Evil (2005) (7" split single with ASBESTOS. Limited edition 300 copies). Carcassvoice (Live).

GEIONSLAUGHT 1986, Time Before Time (2005). Welcome To Sabbat / Splatter / Bloody Countess / C.O.H. Kanashibari / Black Fire / Mion's Hill.

LIVE SABBATICAL HAMAGURI QUEEN, Nuclear War Now! (2005). Prelude Of Sabbat / Envenom Into Witches Hole / Evil Nations / Black Fire / Satan Bless You / Leave Me In Hell / Matsuillusion / Snow Woman / Immortality Of The Soul / Bowray Zamurai / Hell Fire / Crest Of Satan / Gideon / Demonic Serenade / Brothers Of Demons / Flame On The Circle / Sacrifice Of Angel.

Satanas Francisconslaught, Bay Area Sabbatical Maniacs (2005) (7" blue vinyl single. 100 hand numbered copies sold exclusively at 16th September San Francisco concert). Splatter / Evil Nations.

BROOKLYN BACKFIRE, Heavy Metal Super Star HMSS-CD-042 (2005) (Limited edition 105 copies clear vinyl). In Satan We Trust / Karisma / Evil Nations / Kanashibari / Plasmas Goat / Satan Bless You / Black Fire.

SABBATICAL GORGONSLAUGHT, Witchhammer Productions (2005) (Split album with GORGON). Audience / Hellfire / Orochie / MC / Charisma / Audience / Transmigration Of The Soul / Audience / Yoochuu / MC / Darkness And Evil / MC / Svart Eld / Audience.

Icelandic & Greenlandic Demonslaught, From Beyond Productions (2006) (7' single limited edition 1000 copies). Black Metal Volcano / Okiku Doll Of The Devil (Live).

SABBATICAL SIAMESE CHRIST BEHEADING, Witchhammer Productions (2006) (Limited edition 1000 hand numbered copies. Split album with SURRENDER OF DIVINITY). Envenom Into The Witches Hole / Orochie / Charisma / MC / Transmigration Of The Soul / Yoochuu / Black Fire (Svart Eld version) / Mion's Hill / Audience.

TRIBUTE TO TEMIS, Heavy Metal Super Star (2006) (Limited edition 105 hand numbered copies). Crest Of Satan / In Satan We Trust / Flame On The Circle / Plasmas Goat / Hellfire / Evil Nations.

SABBAT

NOTTINGHAM, NOTTINGHAMSHIRE, UK — *Martin Walkyier (vocals), Andy Sneap (guitar), Fraser Craske (bass), Simon Negus (drums).*

SABBAT, A Nottingham based 'Satanic Opera' styled quartet, formed in June 1985 from a previous act titled HYDRA. The line-up for HYDRA featured vocalist Martin Walkyier, guitarist Adam Ferman, bassist Frazer Craske and drummer Mark Daley. This quartet soon added second guitarist Andy Sneap, but Ferman and Daley quit and a name change to SABBAT was agreed. Simon Negus, previously of local Glam band BRAZZEN HUZZY, then enrolled.

SABBAT were noted for their onstage theatrics (heavily influenced by another Nottingham act HELL) and the creative lyrical talents of Walkyier. The acts first recordings came in the shape of the May 1986 'Magik In Theory And Practice' demo, recorded in their rehearsal ballroom for the princely sum of ten pounds. The first, enthusiastic, review of the band came with Garry Sharpe-Young's demo spotlight in US magazine 'Aardschok America'. The band debuted live at a young offenders institute in Doncaster before recording their 'Fragments Of A Faith Forgotten' demo that gained the band much critical praise and ultimately led to a deal with Germany's Noise Records. Once offered the deal SABBAT had to wait for guitarist Andy Sneap to turn 18 years old before they could sign the contracts.

The first commercially available record was a flexi disc for Games Workshop's November 1986 'White Dwarf' magazine entitled 'Blood For The Bloodgod', this track produced by ex-HELL and PARALEX guitarist Kev Bower. SABBAT's debut album 'History Of A Time To Come', recorded in Hannover during September 1987 with producer Roy Rowland, launched the band onto the forefront of the British Thrash Metal scene with Walkyier's distinct pagan themes interwoven into its impressive epic songs. The album went on to sell in excess of 60,000 copies.

SABBAT played both Dynamo and Eindhoven festivals in 1988 as part of a very successful European tour. Shortly after, SABBAT added second guitarist Simon Jones, previously known as Jack Hammer from HOLOSADE, to replace touring guitarist Richard Scott (on loan from London band NO EXCUSE), who accompanied the band on the European tour.

The group's second album, 1989's 'Dreamweaver': Reflections Of Our Yesterdays, produced by Roy Rowland, was an opportunity for Walkyier to really let his imagination fly as SABBAT launched the crucial release in the form of a concept based on the Brian Bates book 'The Way Of Wyrd'. SABBAT subsequently toured Europe heavily, including British dates backed by XENTRIX and support dates to MANOWAR in Spain. This same touring combination hit the UK in December 1989.

Surprisingly, Walkyier and Craske quit after internal disputes and the vocalist went on to form the highly successful and industrious Folk Rock act SKYCLAD, whilst Craske opted out of the music business returning to a printing career. Sneap auditioned for a new vocalist, including HYDRA VEIN's Mike Keen, but it was to be American vocalist Richie Desmond, who had previously auditioned as guitarist for CELTIC FROST, who joined SABBAT in 1990. The band's line-up at this point comprised Sneap, Desmond, guitarist Neil Watson and bassist Wayne Banks. However, both record company and fans were not impressed with the resulting album 'Mourning Has Broken', which sorely lacked Walkyier's more innovative input.

Noise Records dropped the band and, after two disastrous British dates, the last in Derby, Sneap pulled the plug on both the tour and the band. Negus joined local act GLORY BOYS whilst Sneap and Banks went on to form GODSEND. As GODSEND dissolved after a batch of demos, Sneap began carving out a niche for himself in the production role making quite a name for himself with some high profile bands such as STUCK MOJO and MACHINE HEAD.

In 1995 there were rumours of a SABBAT reformation between Walkyier and Sneap, but this came to nothing. SABBAT reared its head again though in 2000 when Britain's leading Black Metal exponents CRADLE OF FILTH covered 'For Those Who Died' with Walkyier providing guest vocals.

As 2001 dawned an announcement was made that a band entitled RETURN TO THE SABBAT, the SABBAT title had during the interim been made prominent by a Japanese band founded in 1983, was planned for a one off live show comprising of Walkyier, Craske, Jones in alliance with former TALION guitarist Pete Wadeson and SKYCLAD and UNDERGROOVE drummer Jay Graham. However, Wadeson would decamp even before the groups debut gig, a warm up for the Derby 'Bloodstock' festival. Walkyier would put in his last show with SKYCLAD the same evening.

As the situation developed it became clear that RETURN TO THE SABBAT was indeed a long term proposition. Graham too parted ways with SKYCLAD as RETURN TO THE SABBAT announced their intentions for further live dates. In early 2002 Jones parted ways with the band due to family commitments, his replacement being Andy Newby. RETURN TO THE SABBAT put in valuable support slot to CRADLE OF FILTH at a low key club gig at the Oxford Zodiac club, the night before the headliners 'Ozzfest' appearance. RETURN TO THE SABBAT would also act as special guests to renowned and newly reformed Swedish Doomsters CANDLEMASS at their long overdue UK performance at the London Mean Fiddler venue in mid July. Meantime, besides his ever growing list of production credits with Premier Metal bands guitarist Andy Sneap would be revealed as having joined FOZZY, the spoof 80s Metal band convened by WWF championship wrestler Chris Jericho and various members of STUCK MOJO.

Swedish Black Metal act IN AETURNUM weighed in with their appreciation of SABBAT by recording their rendition of 'By Thy Command' culled from the original SABBAT demo 'Magik In Theory And Practice'. Martin Walkyier himself would spend the early portion of 2003 formulating his new venture THE CLAN DESTINED, an ill-fated pagan collective involving erstwhile IMMORTAL bassist Iscariah. The singer also guested as vocalist on the track 'Blood And Sand' on Bradford Metal band BLOODSTREAM's debut album 'Black Storm Harvest'.

Ex-SABBAT bassist Wayne Banks joined BLAZE as well as the touring line up of BRAZEN ABBOT in 2003. With THE CLAN DESTINED fragmenting in acrimonious circumstances, Martin Walkyier broke a lengthy silence in April 2006 announcing that he was permanently withdrawing from making music. However, it was soon after learned that he was set to feature as guest singer on the track 'God Among Men' featured on all female Greek Black Metal band ASTARTE's 'Demonized' album.

In September 2006 it was announced that the 'Dreamweaver' line-up of SABBAT, Martin Walkyier, Andy Sneap, Simon Jones, Fraser Craske and Simon Negus, were to reunite to undertake special guest shows to CRADLE OF FILTH's December UK tour. Beforehand, Andy Sneap scored mixing credits on MEGADETH's 'United Abominations' album.

SABBAT put in a high profile European festival show at the 'Keep It True' event at the Tauberfrankenhalle in Lauda-Königshofen, Germany on April 14th 2007 alongside fellow British band DIAMOND HEAD, US outfits LETHAL, LÄÄZ ROCKIT and TWISTED TOWER DIRE, Denmark's ARTILLERY, Canadians CAULDRON and PILEDRIVER, Dutchmen DEFENDER and Swedish band BULLET.

Magik In Practice And Theory, (1985). The Immaculate Conception / The Original Sin / By Thy Command.

Fragments Of A Faith Forgotten, (1986). A Cautionary Tale / Hosanna In Excelsis / For Those Who Died.

Blood For The Blood God, Games Workshop (1988) ('White Dwarf' magazine cover mount flexidisc). Blood For The Blood God.

HISTORY OF A TIME TO COME, Noise N0098 (1988). Intro / A Cautionary Tale / Hosanna In Excelsis / Behind The Crooked Cross / Horned Is The Hunter / I For An Eye / For Those Who Died / A Dead Man's Robe / The Church Bizarre.

A Cautionary Tale, Noise (1988) ('Metal Forces' magazine cover mount flexidisc. Split with VENDETTA). A Cautionary Tale.

Wildfire, Noise (1989) (Flexidisc). Wildfire / The Best Of Enemies (Wulf's Tale).

DREAMWEAVER: REFLECTIONS OF OUR YESTERDAYS, Noise N0132 (1989). The Beginning Of The End / The Clerical Conspiracy / Advent Of Insanity / Do Dark Horses Dream Of Nightmares? / The Best Of Enemies / How Have The Mighty Fallen? / Wildfire / Mythistory / Happy Never After.

MOURNING HAS BROKEN, Noise N0162-2 (1991). The Demise Of History / Theological Void / Paint The World Black / Dumbstruck / The Voice Of Time / Dreamscape / Without A Trace / Mourning Has Broken.

SABBAT

SACRAMENT A.D.

NF, CANADA — *Chris Turner (vocals), Darren Ford (guitar), Danny Moore (guitar), Pat Dwyer (bass), Pat Wills (drums).*

Newfoundland Thrashers SACRAMENT A.D. started life under the unsavoury title of FESTERED CORPSE. Under their revised branding the group issued a 1991 demo 'After Life'. Line-up for this recording comprised vocalist Chris Turner, guitarists Dan Moore and Darren Ford, bassist Rick White and drummer Kevin Dominic. Subsequently, a new rhythm section of ex-DEVASTATOR bassist Pat Dwyer and drummer Pat Wills was acquired. Further tracks would be recorded at Ward Pike Jolly Rodgers Studios but never released.

SACRAMENT A.D. guitarist Danny Moore subsequently found himself with AFTER FOREVER, re-uniting with Kevin Dominic, then a member of highly respected Stoners SHEAVY as well as HARDLINER. Darren Ford was also involved with HARDLINER. Bassist Pat Dwyer subsequently enrolled into SOUL BLEED and OBERON. Rick White played bass for OBERON then ASPHYXIATION and RAPID BURIAL.

After Life, Sacrament A.D. (1991). After Life / Doomsday Effect / Visions Of War / Touch Of Reality / Thrash Salad / Shadows Of Brutality / Spectical For Reform / Psycho Flower / Symbolic Faith (Live).

SACRED REICH

SCOTTSDALE, AZ, USA — *Phil Rind (vocals/ bass), Wiley Arnett (guitar), Jason Rainey (guitar), Greg Hall (drums).*

One of the frontrunners of the 80's Thrash boom, Arizona's SACRED REICH scored notable success particularly in Europe with their 'Surf Nicaragua' mini-album. SACRED REICH was founded at Coronado High School in Scottsdale during 1985 by vocalist / bassist Phil Rind, guitarists Jeff Martinek and Jason Rainey and drummer Greg Hall. The group debuted in late 1985 with a four track cassette demo entitled 'Draining You Of Life'. It was intended for then singer Dan to put down vocals but an illness prevented his participation, necessitating Rind stepping up to perform singing duties.

At this juncture, Martinek had a change of heart and opted out for a military career. This vacancy was plugged by Wiley Arnett. The songs 'Sacred Reich' and 'Ignorance' were given the benefit of a re-record and, with strong support from FLOTSAM AND JETSAM's Jason Newsted, the track found inclusion of the Metal Blade compilation album 'Metal Massacre VII'. From here, the group soon snagged a deal with full-blown album deal with Metal Blade. The debut 'Ignorance' album was released in October 1987. From this point, Sacred Reich, managed by The Bootlegger club owner Gloria Bujnowski, launched into a relentless touring schedule.

The stop-gap 'Surf Nicaragua' mini-album, which included 'Draining You Of Life' from SACRED REICH's demo and a version of BLACK SABBATH's 'War Pigs', was issued and was strangely the release that set SACRED REICH onto the world market. Such was the response to this record that SACRED REICH would find themselves upon a previously unplanned rollercoaster world tour. North American dates kicked in during 1988 with ATROPHY then FORBIDDEN prior to European dates with MOTÖRHEAD before hooking up once more with FORBIDDEN through Europe in 1989. SACRED REICH's appearance at the 'Dynamo Open Air' festival in Eindhoven, Holland was caught on tape for the mini-album 'Alive At The Dynamo', released through Roadracer Records.

Switching labels to Enigma, the group returned with the politically charged 'The American Way' in 1990, this collection unexpectedly boasting a hybrid thrash-funk workout '31 Flavors' extolling the merits of other musical strains. Although unrepresentative of the album, Enigma chose '31 Flavors' as its radio promotion tool. US touring included the high profile support to PANTERA's 'Vulgar Display Of Power' tour whilst gigs in Europe found VENOM as opening act. In January 1991 SACRED REICH played in Mexico supported by TRANSMETAL, MAKINA, NEXT and DRAKSEN.

The 1993 'Independent' album, produced by Dave Jerden at Eldorado Studios, North Hollywood and issued on the new Disney owned Hollywood label, saw a SACRED REICH line-up of Rind, guitarists Wiley Arnett and Jason Rainey and drummer Dave McClain, the latter a veteran of SAN ANTONIO SLAYER. The accompanying single release, 'A Question', saw the band covering FEAR's 'Let's Have A War'. Although the group had taken a step up in terms of budgets, they lost momentum due to the extended hiatus between albums.

In 1994 SACRED REICH cut another cover version at the request of Columbia Records, their rendition of BLACK SABBATH's 'War Pigs' intended for use on the 'Nativity In Black' tribute. Although 'War Pigs' featured on pre-release promotional EPs issued to radio, it oddly failed to appear on the finished album.

Although SACRED REICH remained relatively quiet during 1995 they did finally see their version of 'Sweet Leaf' to the 'Hempilation' album. The band also cut a version of JUDAS PRIEST's 'Rapid Fire' that included a guest vocal from Rob Halford which to date remains unreleased. Earlier that year Dave McLain had been offered a position with MACHINE HEAD, which he at first declined, but would eventually join the high profile Californian neo-Thrashers in December.

Shortly after 1996's Bill Metoyer produced 'Heal' outing Hall rejoined the fold but it was to be stand in man Chuck Fitzgerald who took the drum stool for the band's world tour. That same year esteemed Swedish Deathsters DARK TRANQUILLITY honoured the band with a cover of the 'Sacred Reich' anthem as a bonus track for their album The Gallery.

Greg Hall was back in the band by 1997 as Fitzgerald journeyed on to TONGUE-N-GROOVE then GYPSYCHO. Arnett, in alliance with former ST. MADNESS vocalist Patrick Flannery, would be located during 2001 assembling a fresh band project entitled THE HUMAN CONDITION. However, these plans were put back when on 2nd August Arnett rolled his car while driving to Phoenix. The guitarist suffered several cracked ribs, bruising of his spleen, bruises and abrasions.

Meantime, Hall joined SOULFLY during October 2001. This act duly paid homage to SACRED REICH by covering 'One Nation' for their 2002 album, the track also featuring Wiley Arnett on guitar. In early 2003 Arnett came back to the fore with THE HUMAN CONDITION, an alliance now also featuring Scott Twitty of BLUDGEON.

In November 2006 SACRED REICH, comprising Phil Rind, Wiley Arnett, Jason Rainey and Greg Hall, announced they were set to reunite for several shows in Europe in 2007, including an appearance at the 'Wacken Open Air' festival on August 4th.

Draining You Of Life, (1985). Draining You Of Life / Rest In Peace / Sacred Reich / No Believers.
IGNORANCE, Metal Blade 73306 (1987). Death Squad / Victim Of Demise / Layed To Rest / Ignorance / No Believers / Violent Solutions / Rest In Peace / Sacred Reich / Administrative Decisions.
SURF NICARAGUA, Metal Blade 73359 (1988). Surf Nicaragua / One Nation / War Pigs / Draining You Of Life.
ALIVE AT THE DYNAMO, Roadracer RO 9431-1 (1989). Surf Nicaragua / Violent Solutions / War Pigs / Death Squad.
THE AMERICAN WAY, Enigma 73560 (1990). Love ... Hate / The American Way / The Way It Is / Crimes Against Humanity / State Of Emergency / Who's To Blame / I Don't Know / 31 Flavors.
31 Flavors, Enigma EPRO-317 (1990). 31 Flavors.
A Question EP, Hollywood 6518 (1991). A Question / Let's Have A War / Who's To Blame.
INDEPENDENT, Hollywood (1993). Independent / Free / Just Like That / Supremacy / If Only / Crawling / Pressure / Product / I Never Said goodbye / Open Book / Do It / Let's Have A War.
Free, Hollywood 10340 (1993). Free.
Independent, Hollywood PRCD-10258-2 (1993) (One sided USA promotion release). Independent.
Crawling, Hollywood PRCD-10312-2 (1993). Crawling (Edit) / Crawling (Album version).
HEAL, Metal Blade 14106 (1996). Blue Suit, Brown Shirt / Heal / Break Through / Low / Don't / Jason's Idea / Asked / Who Do You Want To Be? / Seen Through My Eyes / I Don't Care / The Power Of The Written Word.
STILL IGNORANT—LIVE (1987-1997), Metal Blade 14145 (1997). The American Way / Administrative Decisions / One Nation / Independent / State Of Emergency / The Power Of The Written Word / Heal / Blue Suit, Brown Shirt / Who's To Blame / Violent Solutions / War Pigs / Death Squad / Surf Nicaragua.

SACRED WARRIOR

IL, USA — *Ray Perra (vocals), Bruce Swift (guitar), Steve Watkins (bass), Rick Macias (keyboards), Tony Velazquez (drums).*

A Christian Speed inclined Heavy Metal band. SACRED WARRIOR debuted in 1988 with the 'Rebellion' album. Roger Martinez of VENGEANCE RISING would guest on the 1989 'Master's Command' album. The 'Obsessions' album, which saw keyboard player Rick Macias absent but second guitarist John Johnson introduced, proved to be SACRED WARRIOR's last. The band, with Joe Petit now on keyboards, soldiered on until a swansong concert in Germany during March of 1993. Both Rey Perra and Steve Watkins would be found guesting as back up singers on the WHITECROSS album 'In The Kingdom'.

SACRED WARRIOR reformed for the 2001 Christian Metal 'Cornerstone' convention, this event being captured for a live album.

REBELLION, Intense SSR 8116 (1988). Black Metal / Mad, Mad World / Stay Away From Evil / He Died / Children Of The Light / Rebellion / Day Of The Lord / The Heaven's Are Calling / Famine / Master Of Lies / Sword Of Victory.
MASTER'S COMMAND, Intense RO 9075 (1989). Master's Command / Beyond The Mountain / Evil Lurks / Bound In Chains / Unfailing Love / Paradise / Uncontrolled / Many Will Come / Onward Warriors / The Flood / Holy, Holy, Holy.
WICKED GENERATION, Intense (1990). No Happy Endings / Little Secrets / Standing Free / Are You Ready / Minister By Night / Miss Linda / Warlords / Wicked Generation / War Torn Hero.

OBSESSIONS, Intense (1991). Wings Of A Dream / Sweet Memories / Turning Back / Obsessions / Kamakazi / Remember Me / Fire From Heaven / Temples On Fire / Mad Man.
LIVE AT CORNERSTONE 2001, Millenium 8 Productions (2001). Intro / Children Of The Light / Remember Me / Rebellion / Holy Holy Holy / Little Secrets / Wicked Generation / The Heavens Are Calling / Come On / Day By Day / Prince Of Peace / Temples Of Fire.

SACRIFICIAL

DENMARK — *John Hansen (vocals), Kraen Meier (guitar), Sebastian Nordqvist (guitar), Asmus Thomsen (bass), Lukas Meier (drums).*

A revered Jutland based Danish transitional Death-Thrash quintet assembled by the Meier siblings guitarist Kraen and drummer Lukas, during 1990. The remainder of the band included singer John Hansen, guitarist Sebastian Nordqvist and bassist Asmus Thomsen. SACRIFICIAL embarked upon their career path by first offering up the rehearsal tape 'Sacrificial Combustion' followed up by the studio recording 'Lords Of Torment'. The group debuted commercially with the well received 1993 album 'Forever Entangled' but despite an appearance at the prestigious Roskilde festival the following year the band found it tough going. Vocalist John Hansen departed and SACRIFICIAL soldiered on with a replacement, Stefan Steenholdt, for a further demo session, 1994's 'Sadistic Slam'. That same year SACRIFICIAL notably opened the ACCEPT and ZZ TOP headlined Roskilde festival.

A 1996 tape 'Authority', featuring Steenholdt on vocals and new bassist Heine Paaske, emerged although SACRIFICIAL maintained a low profile. Some two years later the band, back with Hansen at the microphone and Thomsen on bass, put on an intended one off reunion show. This gig would be enough for the Mighty Music label to offer a contract for the comeback record, January 2001's 'Erect: Eloquent: Extinct'.

As SACRIFICIAL entered the studio to commence work on a third album projected for 2002 release they discovered that Hansen had serious problems with his vocals. This situation got so desperate that Torsten from AUTUMN LEAVES was drafted to try out as a possible replacement. Hansen's voice though would recover just in time.

Hansen and Thomsen also operate the side act SLUGS in collusion with guitarist Tommy Christensen and drummer Martin Pagaard.

Sacrificial, Sacrificial (1990) (Rehearsal cassette demo). Weeping Of The Innocent / Nebolous Life / Just Another Death / Shredded Soul / Fear Remains.
Sacrificial Combustion, Sacrificial (1991) (Demo). Enshrined Illusions / Wall Of Resentment / Falling Into Oblivion / Sacrificial Combustion.
Lords Of Torment, Sacrificial (1991) (Demo). Lords Of Torment And Perdition / The Final Burial / Ray Of Obscenity / Seasons Of The Reaper.
Forever Entangled, Sacrificial (1993) (Demo). Conducted Strain / Thus I Cry / Destitute Of Compassion / I Fall Into Temptation.
FOREVER ENTANGLED, Trechoma TRP001CD (1993). Edmund, A Butler's Tale / I Fall In Temptation / Contents Of Logical Disbelief / Destitute Of Compassion / Acknowledged By Life / This I Cry / Conducted Strain.
Sadistic Slam, Sacrificial (1994) (Demo). Presume Supreme / Deaf, Dumb And Blatant / Manipulate On Compassion / Carnivorous Preferences / Observations.
Authority...?, Sacrificial (1996) (Demo). Trechoma / Commit To The Flames / Bliss / Subskin / Still Bleeding / Authority...?
b.r.i.e.f., Sacrificial (1999) (Cassette demo). Hidden Agenda / Incarcerated / Falling / Cold.
ERECT: ELOQUENT: EXTINCT, Mighty Music PMZ 009-2 (2001). Trespass / Mass Conduct / Cold / Credit / Beyond / Falling / Hidden Agenda / A New Order / Stolen / In Pieces / Ethnic Cleansing.
Ray Of Obscenity, Prutten PRUT009 (2002) (7" vinyl single). Ray Of Obscenity / Ticket To Paranoia.
AUTOHATE, Mighty Music PMZ 024 (2003). Angel Eyes / In Front Of Turmoil / Out Of Touch / Confrontation Zone / Victimized / My Kingdom Arise / Away With The Skies / Unadapted / Soul Sale.
Promo 2005, Sacrificial (2005) (Promotional release). Words Of Disdain / Never Never / Venting Fury / Revert To Sorrow / Excommunication.

SACRILEGE

BIRMINGHAM, WEST MIDLANDS, UK — *Tam (vocals), Damien Thompson (guitar), Tony May (bass), Spikey T. Smith (drums)..*

Birmingham Thrash metal band SACRILEGE date back to 1984 fronted by female vocalist Tam (a.k.a. Lynda Simpson). SACRILEGE's opening 1984 line-up saw Tam ranked alongside Damian Thompson, bassist Tony May and drummer Liam Pickering, this unit cutting a brace of demos that same year. Previously, Thompson, May and Pickering had recorded 1983 demos billed as WARWOUND.

SACRILEGE also featured on the Mortarhate compilation 'We Won't Be Your Fucking Poor', with the song 'Dig Your Own Grave', and also on the 'Anglican Scrape Product' flexidisc, shared with EXECUTE, HIRAX, CONCRETE SOX and LIPCREAM. The latter release bore no label details but the architect behind this hardcore assemblage, Digby Pearson, soon afterward for the Earache label.

The group's debut commercial product, 'Behind The Realms Of Madness', shifted a respectable 7000 copies. Former WARHAMMER man Mitch Dickinson was brought in as a second guitarist although soon after recording he left the band to pursue more Hardcore projects with HERESY and much later UNSEEN TERROR. SACRILEGE were then approached by FM Revolver Records, but this ultimately led nowhere.

The band recorded again, this time with the assistance of Rob Bruce at Birmingham's famous Rich Bitch studios. Recording was completed for 'Within The Prophecy', with producer Mike Ivory in January 1987, when Music For Nations subsidiary Under One Flag stepped in with a deal. At this juncture the band recruited new bassist Paul Morrissey and second guitarist Frank Healy, although in late 1987 drummer Andy Baker was replaced by Paul Brookes.

The third album, 'Turn Back Trilobite' issued in April 1989, saw SACRILEGE move away from mainstream Thrash and starting to explore slower, more Doom orientated material with a bit of Folk thrown in for good measure. At this point the band's line-up consisted of Tam, a returned Damien Thompson, Frank Healy on bass and Spikey T. Smith on drums.

Regrettably, the band turned in very few live appearances which resulted in a fairly stagnant career, despite the obvious maturity and increased sales on successive albums. Post SACRILEGE both Healy and Baker joined up with CEREBRAL FIX and Healy later went on to BENEDICTION. Baker would also have involvement with ARBITRATER. Brookes joined BENEDICTION then Metal band MARSHALL LAW in 1999. In early 2005 it was learned that SACRILEGE's 'Lifeline' had been covered by BENEDICTION featuring the BOLT THROWER duo of vocalist Karl Willetts and guitarist Barry Thompson.

Sacrilege, (1984) (Demo). Stark Reality / A Violation of Something Sacred / Blood Run / Out Of Sight Out Of Mind.
Anglican Scrape Attic, (1985) (Split flexidisc with HIRAX, LIPCREAM, EXECUTE & CONCRETE SOX). Blood Run.
BEHIND THE REALMS OF MADNESS, Children Of The Revolution COR 0012-09 (1985). Life Line / Shadow From Mordor / At Death's Door / A Violation Of Something Sacred / The Closing Irony / Out Of Sight Out Of Mind.
WITHIN THE PROPHECY, Under One Flag FLAG 15 (1987). Sight Of The Wise / The Fear Within / Winds Of Vengeance / The Captive / Spirit Cry / Flight Of The Nazgul / Insurrection / Search Eternal.
TURN BACK TRILOBITE, Under One Flag FLAG 29 (1989). Father Time (Beneath The Gaze) / Silent Dark / Soul Search / Awaken (Suryanamaskar) / Key To Nirvana / Into The Sea Of Tranquility / Equinox.

SACRILEGE B.C.

BERKELEY, CA, USA — *Stephan Taylor (vocals), Gary Wendt (guitar), Tim Howell (guitar), Sean Smithson (bass), Matt Fillmore (drums).*

Mid eighties Californian Thrash outfit featuring CHRONIC PLAGUE and CLOWN ALLEY drummer Matt Fillmore. SACRILEGE B.C. ('Berkeley, California') took on the territorial appellation in order to distinguish themselves from the then current Birmingham, UK Thrash act of the same title. The group debuted commercially for Alchemy Records with the Mark Deutrom produced 'Party With God' album.

Guitarist Gary Wendt later went on to RELEASE and SKINLAB. By late 2003 guitarist Tim Howell had teamed up with DEF IGNITION, a project band of SKINLAB guitarist Steev Esquivel. In November of 2004 another SACRILEGE B.C. credited musician, bass guitarist, Sean Smithson, also holding ties to GRINCH and THE UNCALLED FOUR, unveiled the formation of a brand new "Full on" Heavy Metal band to feature IMPALED guitarist Sean McGrath and ex-MACHINE HEAD and ATTITUDE ADJUSTMENT drummer Chris Kontos.

Announced in October of 2005 with a promotional EP 'Swine Of The Times', Smithson and Kontos paired back together to forge new Metal project SANGRE ETERNA. Meantime, Wendt too made a comeback with fresh act THE GHOST NEXT DOOR.

Party With God, Cor (1985). Cancer / Fun With Napalm / Words Of God.

PARTY WITH GOD, Alchemy VM 102 (1986). Azemeroth / Crucified / Fun With Napalm / Born Of Hell / Time To Die / Skinned Alive / Cancer / Judge Death / Death Toll / Words Of God / Final Rites / Slaughterhouse / Victimized.

TOO COOL TO PRAY, GWR GWLP 47 (1988). Cold / Where Are We Going / Snake Pit / Between / Revenge / Party With God / Ripping Apart / Too Cool To Pray / Mistake / Feed Off Me / Front Seat Funky.

SADUS

ANTIOCH, CA, USA — *Darren Travis (vocals / guitar), Rob Moore (guitar), Steve DiGeorgio (bass), Jon Allen (drums).*

SADUS came together as a quartet in 1984 of vocalist Darren Travis, guitarist Rob Moore, bassist Steve DiGeorgio and drummer Jon Allen, although it was to be two years until the first fruits of this liaison came into being with the 1986 'D.T.P.' ('Death To Posers') demotape. These sessions led directly to the inclusion of two tracks on the 1987 'Raging Death' compilation album. Quick to capitalise on this achievement SADUS stuck their hands in their pockets to self finance the debut album pulling in METAL CHURCH guitarist John Marshall as producer. The pace of progress was quickened as a deal with label Roadrunner Records was secured resulting in a further album 'Swallowed In Black' and touring with the likes of SEPULTURA and OBITUARY.

SADUS was put on ice for 1991 as DiGeorgio opted to assist DEATH for their 'Human' album. With this added exposure Roadrunner re-released the 'Illusions' debut retitled 'Chemical Exposure' as SADUS regrouped for a summer American tour opening for MORBID ANGEL. Although a further album for Roadrunner, 1992's 'A Vision Of Misery', resulted in a European headline tour, SADUS found itself label less upon their return. Further setbacks occurred when DiGeorgio was enticed back to DEATH for the 'Individual Thought Patterns' album and a subsequent year long bout of touring. DiGeorgio was to return for club shows with SADUS but before any momentum could be gained Moore bailed out.

SADUS continued as a trio crafting the Scott Burns produced 'Elements Of Anger' in 1997. The in demand DiGeorgio, along with drummer Jon Allen, also operated a side project DRAGONHEART (later DRAGONLORD) with ex-VICIOUS RUMOURS and present day TESTAMENT guitarist Steve Smyth and his fellow TESTAMENT six-stringer Eric Peterson. DiGeorgio teamed up with ICED EARTH in late 2000.

News during the summer of 2002 would reveal that frontman Darren Travis and bassist Steve DiGeorgio was embarking on another all star union billed as SUICIDE SHIFT. The project allied the SADUS pairing with TESTAMENT vocalist Chuck Billy as well as drummer Per Moller Jensen of THE HAUNTED and guest guitar from the much travelled TESTAMENT, DEATH and CANCER guitarist JAMES MURPHY.

The Hammerheart label would put the band's original 'Death To Posers' 1986 demo onto CD in 2003, adding a brace of cuts from a 1988 session 'Certain Death' as a bonus.

SADUS announced they were to partner up with fellow Thrash veterans NASTY SAVAGE and high profile Finnish act FINNTROLL for European mainland dates in December. However, just days after the official press release confirming these shows the band withdrew as drummer Jon Allen's commitments to his 11 year old daughter, who had just undergone open heart surgery, took precedence.

Despite Steve DiGeorgio commitments in 2004 to TESTAMENT, the band did increase activity that year. In April the group toured Europe, taking in shows in Greece, Italy, Sweden and appearing at Norway's 'Inferno' festival in Oslo. DiGeorgio then took time out to record with ARTENSION then hit the European festival circuit with TESTAMENT. Gigs in August marked a first for SADUS as they toured Chile alongside TORTURER whilst on South American dates. New SADUS material would be laid down throughout September and October before DiGeorgio joined the ranks of SEBASTIAN BACH's band for further European touring in December. The bassist would also be announced as a contributor to recordings for Norwegian act SCARIOT in early 2005.

SADUS, together with producer Børge Finstad, entered Trident Studios in Pacheco, California to record their fifth album for a late Summer release via Mascot Records. In March 2006 Jon Allen manned the drum kit for live work with TESTAMENT. That same month found DiGeorgio involving himself in a studio collaboration with singer Björn Strid, of SOILWORK, TERROR 2000 and COLDSEED, Glen Alvelais from FORBIDDEN, TESTAMENT and LD/50 and Jeremy Colson of the STEVE VAI band, MARTY FRIEDMAN, MICHAEL SCHENKER, APARTMENT 26, DALI'S DILEMMA and LD/50 repute.

On November 18th the band appeared at the Monterrey Metal Fest event at the at the Coca Cola Auditorium in Mexico alongside BLIND GUARDIAN, CATHEDRAL, U.D.O., EDGUY, OBITUARY, DEICIDE, LEAVES' EYES, BLUDGEON, VAINGLORY, HYDROGYN and JOE STUMP'S REIGN OF TERROR.

SADUS was announced as teaming up with DESTRUCTION, HIRAX and MUNICIPAL WASTE for a North American tour throughout January and February 2007. However, the group dropped off these dates as New Year broke. SADUS lined up the South American 'Fuera Por Sangre' dates hitting Venezuela, Ecuador and Colombia in April prior to supporting OBITUARY in Mexico during May.

ILLUSIONS, Sadus (1988). Certain Death / Undead / Sadus Attack / Torture / And Then You Die / Hands Of Fate / Twisted Face / Fight Or Die / Illusions (Chemical Exposure).

SWALLOWED IN BLACK, Roadracer RO 93682 (1990). Black / Man Infestation / Last Abide / The Wake / In Your Face / Good Ridn'z / False Incarnation / Images / Powers Of Hate / Arise / Oracle Of Omission.

CHEMICAL EXPOSURE, Roadrunner RO 92592 (1991). Certain Death / Undead / Sadus Attack / Torture / And Then You Die / Hands Of Fate / Twisted Face / Fight Or Die / Illusions / Chemical Exposure.

A VISION OF MISERY, Roadrunner (1992). Through The Eyes Of Greed / Valley Of Dry Bones / Machines / Slave To Misery / Throwing Away The Day / Facelift / Deceptive Perceptions / Under The Knife / Echoes Of Forever.

CHRONICLES OF CHAOS, Mascot M 7025-2 (1997). Certain Death / Undead / Sadus Attack / Torture / Hands Of Fate / Illusions / Man Infestation / Good Rid'nz / Powers Of Hate / Arise / Oracle Of Obmission / Through The Eyes Of Greed / Valley Of Dry Bones / Slave To Misery / Facelift / Deceptive Perceptions / Echoes Of Forever.

ELEMENTS OF ANGER, Mascot M 7026-2 (1997). Aggression / Crutch / Words Of War / Safety In Numbers / Mask / Fuel / Power Of One / Stronger Than Life / Unreality / In The End.
OUT FOR BLOOD, Mascot (2006).

SALAMANDRA

ŠENOV, CZECH REPUBLIC — *Dalibor Halamicek (vocals), Pavel Silva (guitar), Karel Řepecký (guitar), Jarda Dufek (bass), Hanka Šlachtová (keyboards), Daniel Jurecek (drums).*

SALAMANDRA describe themselves as Gothic Power Metal. The group was conceived in Šenov by guitarist Pavel Silva of REA SYLVIA and ARKUS notoriety. For the January 1999 'Twilight Of Legends' album SALAMANDRA comprised of GROG vocalist Dalibor 'Panther' Halamicek, guitarists Pavel Silva and Karel Řepecký, PUNISHMENT bassist Ales Klimsa and EUTHANASIA keyboard player Marek Lankoci. Session drums would be delivered by one 'Blackcount Baalberith', a.k.a. Daniel Jurecek.

Jarda Dufek replaced Klimsa on bass for the December 2000 conceptual follow up 'Skarremar'. SALAMANDRA would commit their version of 'Judas' to the HELLOWEEN tribute album 'The Eastern Pumpkin'. A third album, 'Great Moravian Elegies', arrived in May 2004. By this juncture SALAMANDRA featured Hanka Šlachtová in the keyboard role.

TWILIGHT OF LEGENDS, Leviathan (1999). Prelude / With Gods On Their Side / Misty Riders / The Mourning / Rise / Royal Hearing / Obstinavi Animo / Warriors / Silent Memory / War Is Over / Twilight Of Legends.
SKARREMAR, Leviathan (2000). The Time—Go Back Through Ages / The Legend—Reign Of The Wicked / The Silence (Comes Before A Storm) / The Toady—All Hope Abandon / The Lover—A Kiss Goodbye / The King—Skarremar's Pride / The Army—Dead End Battles / The Singer—Remember The Legend / The Traitor—Roads To Hell / The Coward—Hail The King / The Dead—Cantata Oscura / The Coming—Midnight Creatures / The Revenge—Legends Come True / The End—Freedom's Won Back / The Beginning.
GREAT MORAVIAN ELEGIES, Leviathan (2004). Up For The Past And Future / Forefathers Realm / Never Give Up / The Blackest Wings / Everlasting Fame / Unchained Land / Hero / Calm Down The Fury / Brave Mens Chant / Nothing But Dust / Out Of The Ashes / Homage To The Great / Aeons Gone Away.

SAMMOHAN

FINLAND — *John E. Horse (vocals / bass), Charles Decapo (guitar / keyboards), Viljami Kinnunen (drums).*

Thrash Metal band SAMMOHAN, self-styled "Occult Heavy Metal Warriors", published a stream of demo recordings commencing in 2001 with the 'Ironsaw' session. The band had been founded in 1997 by vocalist / bassist John E. Horse (a.k.a. Juhani Taivela) and guitarist Charles Decapo (Tuomas Tuimala). The 'Ironsaw' recordings would see Benjami Niininen of BURIALMOUND, WAKBOTH, EXIT WOUNDS, MORNINGSTAR, HEATHEN HOOF and UTGARD manning the drums.

'Occultic Session 01 (Age Of Steel)' would mark the introduction of a 2003 series which inclued 'Occultic Session 02 (Ocean Of Reptiles)' with Janne Peräaho of WAKBOTH on bass guitar, 'Occultic Session 03 (Kundalini & Cryptic Mantras)', 'Occultic Session 04 (Advaita Blade)' and 'Occultic Session 05 (Bardo Of Death)'. In 2004 SAMMOHAN issued a self-titled demo, once again with B. Niininen on the drums, with 'Saint Of Blasphemy', now including drummer Viljami Kinnunen (a.k.a. 'The Zen Machine') of MINOTAURI, arriving in 2005.

Ironsaw, Sammohan (2001). Raise The Hammer / Necroskull / Punishment From Above / Black Magic Tormentor.
Occultic Session 04 (Advaita Blade), (2003). Battle Of Ragnarok (Advaita Blade).
Occultic Session 05 (Bardo Of Death), (2003). Bardo Of Death / Boddhisattva Warriors / Age Of Steel (Kali-Yuga).
Occultic Session 03 (Kundalini & Cryptic Mantras), (2003). Kundalini Alphabet & Cryptic Mantras / Transylvanian Evil / Invocation Of Kali.
Occultic Session 02 (Ocean Of Reptiles), (2003). Ocean Of Reptiles / Power Of Mantra-Japa / Torture Dungeon / Boddhisattva Warriors.
Occultic Session 01 (Age Of Steel), (2003). Circle Of The Light / Dark Zen.
Demo 2004, (2004). Force Of Gods (Shaktipat) / Invocation Of Ganesha / Death Zen Magick.
Saint Of Blasphemy, (2005). Metal Altar / Mystical Mountain (Arunachala) / Eye Of Ra / Mercenary Tiger / Sex Chakra.

SANCTUARY

SEATTLE, WA, USA — *Warrel Dane (vocals), Lenny Rutledge (guitar), Sean Blosl (guitar), Jim Sheppard (bass), Dave Budbill (drums).*

Seattle's SANCTUARY, dating back to 1985, besides employing a distinctive brand of Power Thrash, may just hold the record for the band with the longest hair in the world. The speed Metal group came to prominence with the inclusion of a brace of demo cuts on the 'Northwest Metalfest' compilation album. Immediately apparent was that vocalist Warrell Dane, a former member of SERPENT'S KNIGHT, was in possession of one of the most powerful throats on the Metal scene. Bassist Jim Sheppard had previously been a member of local Glam band SLEZE, an outfit fronted by a pre-ALICE IN CHAINS Layne 'Candy' Staley.

SANCTUARY's first mark would be made with a 1986 demo, this session scoring a label deal with the Epic corporation. The debut album, 1987's 'Refuge Denied' produced by MEGADETH mainman Dave Mustaine, features a rather weighty cover of JEFFERSON AIRPLANE's acid daze classic 'White Rabbit', this track also notably featuring Mustaine's guitar parts on the intro. Dane's prior act SERPENT'S KNIGHT had first covered the same track on a 1983 demo.

SANCTUARY proceeded to tour Europe as support to MEGADETH before recording the equally impressive Howard Benson produced 'Into The Mirror Black', recorded at Sound City, Van Nuys in California and issued in February 1990. A promotional live EP, 'Into The Mirror Live' recorded at the Reseda's Country Club in May 1990, was serviced to radio.

SANCTUARY broke up with Dane forging NEVERMORE, finding cult success in Europe with a consistent string of quality albums. Dane's name was tenuously linked with the then vacant vocal position in JUDAS PRIEST during 1996.

Dave Budbill resurfaced in DIFFICULT then in mid 2003 as drummer for STARRFACTORY, a project spearheaded by former ATHEIST and NEUROTICA frontman Kelly Shaefer.

REFUGE DENIED, Epic 460 811-2 (1987). Battle Angels / Termination Force / Die For My Sins / Soldiers Of Steel / Sanctuary / White Rabbit / Ascension To Destiny / The Third War / Veil Of Disguise.
Into The Mirror Live, Epic (1990) (US promotional release). Future Tense / Long Since Dark / Battle Angels / One More Murder / White Rabbit / Taste Revenge.
INTO THE MIRROR BLACK, Epic 465 876-2 (1990). Future Tense / Taste Revenge / Long Since Dark / Epitaph / Eden Lies Obscured / The Mirror Black / Seasons Of Destruction / One More Murder / Communion.

SARCOFAGO

BRAZIL — *Wagner Lamounier (vocals / guitar), Gerald Minelli (bass), M. Joker (drums).*

An esteemed veteran act on the South American Death Metal scene. The Satanically inspired SAROFAGO employ Death Metal with distinct Punk leanings allied to blasphemous lyrics. Rather alarmingly guests on the 'Rotting' album included Oswaldo Pussy Ripper and Eugenio Dead Zone. Adverts for the album announced "Formed by Wagner Antichrist who left SEPULTURA because they were too commercial!"

SARCOFAGO debuted with the 1986 demo 'Satanic Lust' leaving no pretensions as to which musical direction the band was headed. The equally to the point demos 'The Black Vomit' and 'Christ's Death' ensued upfront of the first full length album 'I.N.R.I.'.

For 1991's 'The Laws Of Scourge' the band comprised of vocalist / guitarist Wagner 'Antichrist' Lamounier, guitarist Fabio Jhosko, bass player Gerald 'Incubus' Minelli and drummer Lucio Olliver. OVERDOSE mainman Claidio David would provide backing vocals. The following year Finnish Black Metal outfit IMPALED NAZARENE cut a cover version of 'The Black Vomit' on their 'Goat Perversion' EP.

SARCOFAGO were still an active concern in 2000 delivering the uncompromising as ever 'Crust' EP. In 2004 the legacy of the 'I.N.R.I.' debut was strengthened as Nuclear War Now Productions issued a limited edition picture disc vinyl album, this issue adding extra tracks taken from the 'Warfare Noise I' compilation. The first 300 of these pressings came packaged as a "die hard" edition in a different sleeve, including poster, booklet, sticker and patch. That same year the band would have their classic cut 'Satanic Lust' chosen as a pioneering piece of music for a compilation assembled by DARKTHRONE drummer Fenriz, released through Peaceville Records and entitled 'Fenriz Presents The Best Of Old School Black Metal'.

I.N.R.I, Cogumelo (1987). Satanic Lust / Desecration Of Virgin / Nightmare / I.N.R.I. / Christ's Death / Satanas / Ready To Fuck / Deathrash / The Last Slaughter / Recrucify / The Black Vomit.

ROTTING, Cogumelo (1989). The Lust / Alcoholic Coma / Tracy / Rotting / Sex, Drinks And Metal / Nightmare.

THE LOST TAPES OF COGUMELO, Cogumelo (1990).

THE LAWS OF SCOURGE, Under One Flag CDFLAG 66 (1990). The Laws Of Scourge / Piercings / Midnight Queen / Screeches From The Silence / Prelude To A Suicide / The Black Vomit / Secrets Of A Window / Little Julie / Crush, Kill, Destroy.

HATE, Cogumelo (1995). Intro / Song For My Death / Pact Of Cum / The God's Faeces / Satanic Terrorism / Orgy Of Flies / Hate / The Phantom / Rhabdovirus (The Pitbull's Curse) / Anal Vomit / The Beggar's Uprising.

DECADE OF DECAY, Cogumelo (1996). The Loss Of Innocence / Orgy Of Flies / Hate / The God's Faeces / Song For My Death / Midnight Queen / Screeches From The Silence / Piercings / Crush, Kill, Destroy / Nightmare / Rotting / I.N.R.I. / Desecration Of Virgin / Recrucify / The Black Vomit / Satanic Lust / Christ's Death / The Anal Rape Of God / Satanas / Third Slaughter.

THE WORST, Cogumelo (1997). The End (Intro) / The Worst / Army Of The Damned / God Bless The Whores / Plunged In Blood / Satanic Lust / The Necrophiliac / Shave Your Head / Purification Process.

Crust EP, (2000). Sonic Images Of The New Millennium Decay / Day Of The Dead / F.O.M.B.M. (Fuck Off The Melodic Black Metal) / Crust.

SATAN

NEWCASTLE UPON TYNE, UK — *Lou Taylor (vocals), Russ Tippins (guitar), Steve Ramsey (guitar), Graeme English (bass), Sean Taylor (drums).*

Newcastle upon Tyne Heavy Metal act SATAN began life in 1979 and would create a huge cult interest for themselves in Europe and the West coast of America with their first album, 1983's 'Court In The Act'. They clawed out a significant market for themselves in Europe but would rarely perform live in the UK. Tragically, for a band so obviously ahead of their time when it came to precision Speed Metal, SATAN inflicted upon themselves a bewildering series of changes both in personnel and in title. Buckling under record company pressure the musicians issued product under three titles, SATAN, BLIND FURY and PARIAH. This lack of cohesion was to prove their undoing.

The original SATAN line-up included guitarist Russ Tippins and Steve Ramsey, vocalist Andrew Frepp, bassist Steven Bee and drummer Andy Reed. Frepp, however, was soon replaced by Paul Smith. At this stage SATAN was still a school act. Bee was superseded on bass by Graeme "Bean" English and Steve Allsop took over on vocals. The group's first four song demo surfaced in November 1981. The group then pulled in another frontman, Trevor Robinson, for a brief tenure.

Reed's position behind the drum stool was relinquished to Ian McCormack, who played on the 'Into The Fire' demo, recorded with singer Ian Davison-Swift in November 1982. He in turn was usurped by erstwhile RAVEN man Sean Taylor. McCormack would later turn up in Huddersfield band BATTLEAXE. Reed meanwhile, remained with the band as a roadie.

This paved the way for the debut single, 'Kiss Of Death', comprising two tracks taken from the first four-song demo and another two songs from that demo appeared on the 'Roxcalibur' compilation album, on the Guardian label in 1982. Davison-Swift would stick with the group until just prior to the recording of 'Caught In The Act'. His position was taken by ex-BLITZKREIG and AVENGER vocalist Brian Ross for recording as Davison-Swift filled Ross' boots in the AVENGER ranks and later hooked up with another Northeastern Thrash combo, ATOMKRAFT.

Ross was replaced by Lou Taylor following 'Court In The Act', after TYSONDOG's Alan Hunter temporarily filled in for live commitments following Ross' departure, the band claiming that a lack of image onstage to be the main reason that Ross was asked to leave. Incidentally, during this period drummer Sean Taylor was also drumming for WARRIOR as a sideline.

Shortly after this latest change of vocalists in 1985, SATAN renamed themselves after Lou's previous band BLIND FURY and recorded the far more commercial 'Out Of Reach' which saw sales slide. Meanwhile, the 'Court In The Act' album was fast becoming a cult classic on the West coast of America. The band promptly kicked out Lou and renamed themselves SATAN, citing American interest in 'Court In The Act' for this change back to a more Metallic approach. SATAN recruited vocalist Mick Jackson, previously with ROUGH EDGE, in the process. A new SATAN album followed, billed 'Suspended Sentence', promoted by German touring as support to RUNNING WILD for two tours, the first in April and second in October of 1987. Following his final departure Lou Taylor went on to front TOUR DE FORCE and PERSIAN RISK and later became a known figure on the London club scene as a Rock DJ.

PARIAH was formed as a direct descendent from SATAN, being basically the same band, but, once again a name change was thought in order due to the connotations of the old moniker. The first album was recorded with producer Roy Rowland. Unfortunately, 'The Kindred' released in 1988, was never given a British release as PARIAH concentrated on the lucrative European market.

The second album, 1989's 'Blaze Of Obscurity' recorded at Horus Studios and produced by the band, built upon the success of the debut and proved that the name change had been the correct move as PARIAH albums sold in greater numbers than previous SATAN records. In 1991 the leading German metal band BLIND GUARDIAN paid due reverence by rendering their version of SATAN's 'Trial By Fire' for their 'Somewhere Far Beyond' record.

However, PARIAH folded amidst financial wranglings with their record company, even though sessions for an intended third album, recorded by guitarists Steve Ramsey and Russ Tippins, bassist Graeme English, ex-SATAN and BATTLEAXE drummer Ian McCormack and former TYSONDOG vocalist Alan Hunter, was recorded at Links Studios in Newcastle during 1993.

With interest in the NW0BHM at a high in mainland Europe during the mid 90s unreleased PARIAH recordings from 1990 would be unearthed as the 'Unity' album. English and Ramsey, partnering with erstwhile SABBAT frontman Martin Walkyier, later found European success with the innovative SKYCLAD, debuting in 1991 with 'Wayward Sons Of Mother Earth'. Tippins, forsaking the harder end of the musical spectrum, became a regular on the Northeastern club circuit with folk band McALLUM and an ABBA covers troupe.

A Ross / Tippins / Ramsey / English / Taylor SATAN reunion album was on the cards at one point, but this project was allegedly shelved by one of the musician's wives! A further stab at a reformation came when Brian Ross attempted to resurrect the band for a one off appearance at the German Wacken Festival but it was to no avail. Further reports came in September 2003 suggesting the 'Court In The Act' line-up was set to reform for a one-off performance at the German 'Keep It True II' festival, to be held in April 2004. However, just weeks after this announcement the band were forced off the billing. SATAN fans were appeased somewhat by the issue of archive live recordings from the Dynamo in 1983 entitled 'Live In The Act' that same year. They subsequently announced they were in fact to reform, featuring BLITZKRIEG singer Brian Ross and SKYCLAD's Graeme English and Steve Ramsey, for a one-off performance at the 'Wacken Open Air' festival that August. SATAN then announced a further high profile appearance at the 'Keep It True IV' festival held in April 2005 at the Tauberfrankenhalle in Lauda-Koenigshofen, Germany.

Kiss Of Death, Guardian GRC 145 (1982). Kiss Of Death / Heads Will Roll.
COURT IN THE ACT, Roadrunner RR 9894 (1983). Into The Fire / Trial By Fire / Blades Of Steel / No Turning Back / Broken Treaties / Break Free / Hunt You Down / Dark side Of Innocence.
Into The Future EP, Steamhammer SPV 60-1898 (1986). Key To Oblivion / Hear Evil, See Evil, Speak Evil / Fuck You / Ice Man.
SUSPENDED SENTENCE, Steamhammer 08-1837 (1987). Symphony / Who Dies Wins / 11th Commandment / Suicidal Justice / Vandal (Hostile Youth) / SCUM (Socially Condemned Undesirable Misfits) / Avalanche Of A Million Hearts / Calculated Execution (Driller Killer).
LIVE IN THE ACT: DYNAMO CLUB 1983, Metal Nation MNR003 (2004). Trial By Fire / No Turning Back / Heads Will Roll / Hunt You Down / Pull The Trigger / Break Free / Blades Of Steel / The Ritual / Kiss Of Death / Oppression / The Executioner / Blitzkrieg / Dynamo / Kiss Of Death / Heads Will Roll.

SATANIC SLAUGHTER

LINKÖPING, SWEDEN — *Andreas Deblén (vocals), Ztephan Dark (guitar), Stefan Johansson (guitar), Fille Carlsson (bass), Martin Axenrot (drums).*

Linköping's SATANIC SLAUGHTER is one of Scandinavia's older Black Death Metal acts having formed in 1985. Previous to this date the band went under the politically incorrect name of EVIL CUNT. Of the original line-up, only the ORCHRISTE credited guitarist Ztephan "Dark" Karlsson remains. Original bassist Goat became a pyromaniac and now reportedly resides in a mental hospital.

SATANIC SLAUGHTER's name was first felt on the Swedish Metal scene in 1985. Joining Ztephan Dark would be vocalist Moto Jacobsson, bassist Ron B. Goat and TOTAL DEATH drummer Pontus Sjösten. The second guitar position proved fluid, with Mikki Fixx, Jörgen Sjöström and Patrik Strandberg all serving terms in 1985. A second drummer was also installed that year in Peter Svedenhammar. SATANIC SLAUGHTER evolved in 1987 with the recruitment of Toxine (a.k.a. Tony Kampner) on guitar and drummer Mique. Both vocalist Toxine and drummer Mique had also been members of TOTAL DEATH whilst Mique had also been involved in MORGUE. Toxine would cut his teeth on the Rock scene with his debut Punk act PASSIVA MONGOLOIDER as far back as 1979.

The band evolved once again in rapid fashion, Dark drawing in new members Jonas Hagberg on guitar, Patrik Kulman as bassist with Robert Falstedt on the drums. The following year numbers were boosted with the addition of singer Andy Gustavsson and SATANIC SLAUGHTER released their demo 'One Night In Hell' during 1988.

SATANIC SLAUGHTER re-shaped again in 1989, the new cast comprising Dark, guitarist Janne Karlsson and bassist Peter Blomberg. Occupying the drum stool in 1989 would be Gerry Malmström and Evert Karlsson. Unfortunately, in December the band was put on ice as Dark was imprisoned, convicted of assault. The man would later join MORBIDITY, CRUZIFIED ANGEL and MORGUE. The band got back together in 1992 with members of SÉANCE, including vocalist Toxine, drummer Mique and guitarists Patrick Jensen and Richard Corpse were involved. A reunion concert took place at Linköping's Skylten venue, alongside SÉANCE, on 20th November 1994.

The self-titled debut album, recorded at Unisound studios and produced by Patrik Jensen, was issued in 1996 through Necropolis Records. Second effort 'Land Of The Unholy Souls', with production credits going to DAN SWANÖ, emerged in 1997. However, that same year SATANIC SLAUGHTER collapsed yet again, this time due to time honoured musical differences. Dark resolved himself to pick up the pieces with all the other ex-members creating the high profile act WITCHERY. Jensen also became a member of THE HAUNTED.

The band was re-constituted in 1997, introducing Filip Carlsson on guitar, a scene veteran of ANCIENT DIGGER OF GRAVES, DAISY CHAIN, THORNCLAD, HÖST, DEMONS TO PREFER, SPITEFUL and CORPORATION 187, guitarist Kecke Ljungberg of MORGUE plus Robert Eng on drums, also holding credits with HÖST and CORPORATION 187, for a run of German gigs in April of 1998 alongside LORD BELIAL and HATOR. In 1999 SATANIC SLAUGHTER brought in former BLASPHEMOUS, MORGUE, COVEN and TRIUMPHATOR drummer Martin 'Axenrot' Axenroth (a.k.a. 'Demon Pounding Devestator' in NIFELHEIM) to replace Robert Eng.

The 2000 line-up comprised of Dark, Axenroth, guitarist Christian Ljungberg, vocalist Andreas Deblén and bassist Filip Carlsson. This unit, promoting the album 'Afterlife Kingdom' delivered by Loud n´Proud Records, toured across Europe in alliance with Norwegian act RAGNAROK in December. By the time the band were gearing up for a September 2002 album 'Banished To The Underworld' Stefan Johansson had taken Ljungberg's place on guitar. Further touring saw European gigs in April with road partners LORD BELIAL and CORPORATION 187.

Axenrot would also be found as a member of N.C.O. ('Nephenzy Chaos Order') for their 2003 opus 'Pure Black Disease'. The drummer added to his roster of official projects by joining the Blackeim and DAN SWANÖ mentored BLOODBATH in March of 2004. That November SATANIC SLAUGHTER toured Europe with support from fellow Swedes MISERICORDIA and Czech outfit AVENGER.

In August 2005 Martin Axenrot temporarily joined the ranks of OPETH for European touring, covering for regular drummer Martin López who was forced out due to medical concerns. SATANIC SLAUGHTER announced they were to reform in early 2006, Ztephan Dark, Stefan Johansson and Simon Axenrot being joined by new drummer Fredrik Nilsson of MISERICORDIA.

Ztephan Dark, suffering from a heart condition, died in April 2006.

Satanic Slaughter, Satanic Slaughter (1988) (Demo). Violent Massacre / One Night In Hell / Satanic Queen.
SATANIC SLAUGHTER, Necropolis NR004 (1995). Immortal Death / Forever I Burn / Dark Ritual / Into The Catacombs / Breath Of The Serpent That Rules The Cold World / On Black Wings / Nocturnal Presence / Legion Of Hades / Divine Exorcism / I'll Await My Lord / Embraced By Darkness / Domine Lucipheros.
LAND OF THE UNHOLY SOULS, Necropolis NR014 (1996). Intro / Hatred Of God / Servant Of Satan / Satanic Queen / Demons Feast / Forever I Burn / Legion Of Hades / Breath Of The Serpent That Rules The Cold World / Immortal Death / Land Of The Unholy Souls / One Night In Hell / Dark Ritual / Forever I Burn.
AFTERLIFE KINGDOM, Loud n' Proud LNP012 (2000). The Arrival—Afterlife Kingdom / Nocturnal Crimson Nightmare / When Darkness Prevails / Divine Repulsion / Through The Dark Profound / Autumn / Ad Noctum / Flag Of Hate.

BANISHED FROM THE UNDERWORLD, Black Sun BS 025 (2002). Bringers Of Armageddon / Banished From The Underworld / Dark Temptation / Towards Damnations End / Infernal / Antichrist / Apocalyptic War / One Night In Hell / Season Of Sorrow / Ending In Misery.

SATORIUM

PIETARSAARI, FINLAND — *Fredrik Vikman (vocals / bass), Jimmy Bäck (guitar), Christoffer Alvik (guitar), Guy Vikman (drums).*

Pietarsaari Thrash Metal act SATORIUM released the demo 'Preech Until They Bleed' in January 2005. In a former guise of GUARDIANS OF STEEL they had released an August 2003 demo 'Evil Intentions'. This formative unit, at first operating as a covers act tackling the likes of DEEP PURPLE and BLACK SABBATH, had been created during 2001 by guitarist Jimmy Bäck and drummer Guy Vikman, subsequently enlisting Guy's younger brother Fredrik Vikman on bass. The group's style shifted from trad Heavy Metal to Black / Death as their first set of original songs was laid down on the 'Evil Intentions' promo.

Taking on the new brand of SATORIUM, 'Preech Until You Bleed' was then recorded, after which Christoffer Alvik was introduced on guitar and Fredrik Vikman took on lead vocals. New demos, 'Embraced By Pain', were crafted in March 2006.

Preech Until They Bleed, Satorium (2005) (Demo). Preech Until They Bleed / Psycho / Antichrist / Writings Of The Dead.

Embraced By Pain, (2006) (Demo). Bringer Of Pain / Profanity Of Life.

SAVAGE

MANSFIELD, NOTTINGHAMSHIRE, UK — *Chris Bradley (vocals / bass), Andy Dawson (guitar), Wayne Renshaw (guitar), Mark Brown (drums).*

At one time this lot was touted in the same breath alongside METALLICA. Indeed, there are early tapes of METALLICA covering SAVAGE songs and an American bootleg METALLICA single featuring the proto-Thrash SAVAGE track 'Let It Loose'. Mansfield's premier Metal act first surfaced in 1976 having been put together by the then 15 year old bass guitarist Chris Bradley, vocalist Chris Gent, guitarist Lee Statham and drummer Mick Percival. This inaugural line-up lasted nine months, in which time they performed just one gig.

By 1979 Bradley had got together a new SAVAGE with his brother Simon on drums, guitarists Andy Bradbury and Andy Dawson. The band debuted on a local sampler highlighting four local acts alongside Mansfield colleagues TYRANT, SPARTA from Hucknall and Sheffield based PANZA DIVISION titled 'Scene Of The Crime' with new members, rhythm guitarist Wayne Renshaw and ex-WILDLIFE drummer Dave Lindley, before landing a deal with Hull's Ebony Records. Lindley was supplanted by former TYRANT drummer Mark Brown and later teamed up with DAWNTRADER.

SAVAGE's first release was a track on the Ebony Records 'Metal Fatigue' compilation album before the single 'Ain't No Fit Place' / 'China Run'. The resultant good reviews led Ebony to finance their classic debut album 'Loose n' Lethal', probably one of the finest British Metal albums ever released. The album, produced by Darryl Johnston and recorded in the front room of a terraced house in Hull, displayed a very aggressive punch, razor-sharp guitars and some fine Lynnot-esque narrative style lyric writing. Garry Sharpe-Young provided the album cover. Lacking any cohesive management backing the band failed to capitalise on the album's enormous potential and rave reviews despite appearing at many European festival dates, including the Dutch 'Aardschok' event in February 1984 alongside METALLICA and VENOM and French festivals with SORTILEGE, and many a London Marquee date. In fact, SAVAGE would lend direct support to METALLICA's first ever UK concert at the Marquee on 27th March 1984.

With Ebony's inability to satisfactorily promote such a fine debut globally (the album racked up sales of about 25'000, mainly on import) the band fled for pastures new and London based Zebra Records. The first fruit of this liaison was the self-produced, impressive 12" EP 'We Got The Edge'.

The excellent reviews continued, quickly followed by the second album 'Hyperactive' in 1985, which initially sold well. Serious backing and organisation was still sorely lacking however and the band could never break out of the club scene. Nevertheless, SAVAGE recorded a further three song demo tape, 'This Means War', before throwing in the towel.

Dawson, Renshaw and Brown went on to form REBEL with bassist Stuart Corden and ex-NIGHTVISION vocalist Harry Harrison, cutting some very fine demos, but this outfit disbanded without a deal. Corden joined GLORY BOYS as Renshaw returned to his day job at the local Metal Box factory.

After a long hiatus, Bradley formed XL with local Mansfield musicians, guitarists Andy Wilson and Matthew Blick, the latter ex-VALENTINE, and drummer Dave Reynolds. XL recorded a BBC Radio 1 'Friday Rock Show' session with Dawson on stand in guitar but never secured a record deal. Dawson and Harrison forged RED in 1992, this band also including XL's Matthew Blick, bassist Paul Cooper and ex-VALENTINE drummer Mark Allsop. The duo recorded again with CLOWNHOUSE, very much in the Pop Rock mould, before forming a Grunge inspired QUANGO then HUSK. Both these latter acts featured vocalist Harrison, who much later joined WITCHFYNDE.

Bootleg versions of 'Loose n' Lethal' appeared in Europe during 1993 on the Reborn Classics label and in mid 1995 Dawson resurrected SAVAGE to record a new album for Neat Records entitled 'Holy Wars', recorded at Bandwagon Studios in Mansfield, with Bradley and Lindley. Japanese versions of the album had two cover versions as extra tracks; namely UFO's 'Hot n' Ready' and THIN LIZZY's 'Are You Ready'.

The group added ex-STORM TRIBE and XL man Andy Wilson on second guitar in 1996 for live work and would perform their first ever German gig in April at the 'Bang Your Head' festival alongside TOKYO BLADE, GLENMORE and BLIND GUARDIAN. Unfortunately the band could only follow this up with a solitary show in a local Mansfield pub.

Lindley departed prior to recording of 'Babylon' in 1996, later playing live with THE LUTHER BELTZ BAND, and in came another erstwhile XL member on drums Richard Kirk. 'Babylon' was again crafted at Bandwagon Studios and featured REBEL singer Harry Harrison on backing vocals. Meantime, 'Loose n' Lethal' finally achieved an official re-release through Neat Metal, the album containing three never before released demo tracks 'No Cause To Kill' and 'The Devil Take You' from 1980 and the 1979 recording 'Back On The Road'. The British Steel label would get in on the act re-issuing the band's 1985 opus 'Hyperactive', this too boasting extra material from the 'We Got The Edge' EP.

SAVAGE recorded a fresh album 'Xtreme Machine' throughout 1998 as Dawson also worked with Wilson and Harrison and drummer Paul Comeroy once more on another project band. When 'Xtreme Machine' arrived in stores it soon fired up the grapevine between METALLICA fans as SAVAGE had cheekily included the METALLICA demo of their song 'Let It Loose' as a bonus track!

Ain't No Fit Place, Ebony EBON 10 (1982). Ain't No Fit Place / China Run.
LOOSE N' LETHAL, Ebony EBON 12 (1983). Let It Loose / Cry Wolf / Berlin / Dirty Money / Ain't No Fit Place / On The Rocks / The China Run / White Hot.
We Got The Edge, Zebra 12 RA4. (1984). We Got The Edge / She Don't Need You / Running Scared.
HYPERACTIVE, Zebra ZEB 4 (1985). We Got The Edge / Eye For An Eye / Hard On Your Heels / Blind Hunger / Gonna Tear Ya Heart Out / Stevie's Vengeance / Cardiac / All Set To Sting / Keep It On Ice.

Cardiac, Black Dragon (1986) (French release). Cardiac / Hard On Your Heels.

HOLY WARS, Neat Metal NM004 (1995). Headstrong (Cult Of One) / Anthem / How? / This Means War / Down n' Dangerous (Machine Gun) / Suffer The Children / Fashion By Force / Twist / Streets Of Fire / Let The World Go Crazy / Glory Boys / Let It Loose '95.

BABYLON, Neat Metal NM016 (1996). Space Cowboy / Temple Of Deceit / Babylon / Rainmaker / Snakedance / Cyberhead / TV Nation / Sister Sleaze / No Ordinary Day.

XTREME MACHINE, Neat Metal NM042 (2000). Control Freak / Smiling Assassin / Choke / Extreme Machine / Promised Land / Drowning Man / Creepshow / Living With Uncertainty / Thorns / New Messiah / Evil We Can Do / Hyde / Let It Loose (by METALLICA).

SAVAGE GRACE

LOS ANGELES, CA, USA — *Mike Smith (vocals), Christian Logue (guitar), Mike Marshall (guitar), Brian East (bass), Dan Finch III (drums).*

Los Angeles Heavy Metal band SAVAGE GRACE evolved from the band MARQUIS DE SADE, created in 1981. This unit cut a two track demo the following year comprising 'Curse The Night' and 'Eagles Come'. With the addition of guitarist Kenny Powell in February of 1983 the band decided on a name switch to SAVAGE GRACE, the first line-up being guitarists Powell and Christian Logue, bassist Brian 'Beast' East and drummer Don Finch.

Brian East had relocated to Los Angeles from Seattle where he had recorded a couple of singles with the semi-Glam troupe ALLEYBRAT.

SAVAGE GRACE debuted with a cut 'Sceptors Of Deceit' on the Metal Blade Records compilation album 'Metal Massacre II'. An EP, 'The Dominatress' quickly followed. Wishing to augment their sound, SAVAGE GRACE pulled in lead vocalist John Birke in time for recording of 'The Dominatress' EP. Birke departed to pursue mellower music. Birke, whose last shows with the band included gigs in San Francisco with SLAYER and EXODUS, actually found out about his dismissal second hand, the band announcing it on air during a radio interview. SAVAGE GRACE also lost guitarist Kenny Powell shortly after. Powell went on to create power metallers OMEN.

SAVAGE GRACE were soon back up to full strength bringing in vocalist Mike Smith and former AGENT STEEL guitarist Mike Marshall. However, the guitar parts on the 1985 'Master Of Disguise' album, recorded for French label Black Dragon, were performed by Logue as Marshall was added some two months after recording.

The 'After The Fall From Grace' album sees the supplanting of drummer Dan Finch III by Mark Marcum. The 1987 picture disc single 'Ride Into The Night' saw East replaced with bassist Brian Peace.

In later years SAVAGE GRACE's place among the 80s Metal resurgence would elevate their status to that of a cult act on mainland Europe. Both albums would be combined as a bootleg CD release by the Reborn Classics label. Italian band SHADOWS OF STEEL covered 'Destination Unknown' on their 1998 album 'Twilight'. During 2001 German Metal band POWERGOD would cover 'Lion's Roar—Bound To Be Free' on their 'Bleed For The Gods' album.

The Dominatress, Metal Blade 71006 (1983). The Dominatress / Live To Burn / Too Young To Die / Fight For Your Life / Curse The Night.

MASTER OF DISGUISE, Black Dragon 001 (1985). Lion's Roar / Bound To Be Free / Fear My Way / Sins Of The Damned / Into The Fire / Master Of Disguise / Sons Of Iniquity / No One Left To Blame / Guitar Solo.

AFTER THE FALL FROM GRACE, Black Dragon (1986). A Call To Arms / We Came, We Saw, We Conquered / After The Fall From Grace / Trial By Fire / Palesinia / Age Of Innocence / Flesh And Blood / Destination Unknown / Tales Of Mystery.

Ride Into The Night, Semaphore 1012 (1987). Ride Into The Night / We March On / The Healing Hand / Burn.

SCAAR

VÄSTERÅS, SWEDEN — *Alex Jonsson (vocals), Alf Johansson (guitar), Mats Vassfjord (bass), Richard Holmgren (drums).*

Neo-Thrash Metal band SCAAR was formed in Västerås by guitarist Alf Johansson ("Headsplitting, necktwisting guitars") and singer Alex Jonsson ("Growls and screams from the abyss of Hell") in early 1999. Bass player Mats Vassfjord ("Thunderous, soulripping basscrunch") and drummer Richard Holmgren ("Gutwrenching, bonecrushing drums") joined shortly thereafter to complete the line-up. The latter is a scene veteran of such acts as VANESSA, NECROMANCER, SOULSKINNER, HATERUSH and WIDOW. SCARR debuted with the self-finance, Pelle Saether produced 'Scarred For Life' album in April 2002.

The group signed to Holland's Karmageddon Media label in early 2005 for the album 'The Second Incision', recorded at Underground Studios in Västerås during 2003. The band parted ways with drummer Richard Holmgren in May of 2005. The DARK FUNERAL and DEFLESHED veteran Matte Modin acted as stand in for live work before pulling in Kristian Huotari on a permanent basis in July. The new look band debuted on 18th August at Club Distortion in Stockholm alongside ABUSED and SUBCYDE. A three track demo, entitled 'Helltrippin", was cut in December.

The band entered Dug-Out Studios in Uppsala with producer Daniel Bergstrand to cut new album tracks in July 2006.

SCARRED FOR LIFE, Scaar (2002). Deformed Reality / Evil Strangeland / Shut Up Or I'll Kill Ya / Needle Of Pain / Woodpecker Mosh / Scarred For Life.

THE SECOND INCISION, Karmageddon Media KARMA081 (2005). Deathmachine / Spitting Morbid Cancer / The Poltergeist Song / Infected / Test Tube Killer / Holy Swine / Planet Evil / Revolting Obscenity / 14 Years Of Abuse.

SCAR CULTURE

BROOKLYN, NY, USA — *Pheroze Karai (vocals), John Conley (guitar), Frank Cannino (bass), Duke Borisov (drums).*

Brooklyn based Speed Metal band. SCAR CULTURE parted ways with vocalist Pheroze Karai and touring drummer Alpheus Underhill in December. Karai was soon back on the live circuit with NAMANISTA whilst Underhill joined Los Angeles outfit THE MUTAYTOR. The band's original drummer, Duke Borisov, rejoined for subsequent recordings. SCAR CULTURE pulled in a new frontman during October 2003, Connecticut native Roman Garbacik, previously a member of MOURN MAKES MOVEMENT and 8 TRAK MIND.

In January 2005 it was learned that bassist Frank Cannino had forged a fresh band unit in league with former STEREOMUD guitarist John Fattoruso, ex-CODED guitarist Joe Festa and drummer Glenn Moss. SCAR CULTURE officially folded in June. Guitarist John Conley joined Long Island's THE ANCIENT ENEMY. Roman Garbacik re-activated 8 TRAK MIND in January 2007.

INSCRIBE, Century Media (2002). Intro / Vision / Keep It To Myself / Servant / Refrim Reason / Branded / Dead Alone / The Devout / Sever All Ties / Phased / God Of Disgrace / Color Returns.

SCARIOT

KRISTIANSAND, NORWAY — *Oddleif Stensland (vocals), Daniel Olaisen (guitar), Frank Orland (guitar), Stefan Schulz (bass), Tor A. Andersen (drums).*

SCARIOT was created in Kristiansand by erstwhile SATYRICON guitarist Daniel Olaison and Anders Kobro of IN THE WOODS and CARPATHIAN FOREST. Also featured was TRAIL OF TEARS "growling" vocalist Ronnie Thorsen and "clean" vocals courtesy of GUARDIANS OF TIME frontman Bernt Fjellstad with session members guitarist Hugo Isaksen and bassist Bonne Thorson. Initially the band was entitled PEGASUS but after discovery of the Australian act of the same name adopted IS-CARIOT, this duly evolving into SCARIOT.

After the debut album 'Death Forlorn', issued in September 2000 through British label Demolition Records, SCARIOT trimmed down to a duo of Olaisen and Thorsen. The band by early 2001 had been brought back up to strength with Olaisen joined by ODYSSEY guitarist Frank Orland, vocalist Inge J. Tobiassen, INHERIT bassist Stefan Schulz and drummer Freddy Bolso.

Olaisen also operated, albeit under the guise of 'Død', with the retro Death Metal project BLOOD RED THRONE with former SATYRICON and EMPEROR member Tchort. He was also active with COBALT 60, appearing on the 'Meat Hook Ballet' album. Thorsen would guest on BLOOD RED THRONE's inaugural demo 'Deathmix 2000'.

The band would cut a new album 'Tongueless God' for 2001 release for Demolition Records. Still signed to Demolition the band split with the label before the album was released. Technically 'Tongueless God' was never released, although the band manufactured some copies on their own. SCARIOT, now with APOSTASY and OPUS FORGOTTEN man Tor A. Andersen on the drums, would dispense with the services of Tobiassen in November 2001, announcing the induction of a new singer, Oddleif Stensland of CLAIRVOYA and INGERMANLAND, in the Spring 2002.

Stensland and drummer Tor Atle Andersen, alongside the DIMENSION PSYCHOSPHERE and INGERMANLAND credited Erik Mortensen on bass, founded the Progressive Metal side project COMMUNIC in 2003. The trio debuted with the demo 'Conspiracy In Mind', soon signing to the Nuclear Blast label. Touring in Scandinavia saw the band forming up the billing for the October 2003 'Scream Magazine Metal Tour' comprising headliners EINHERJER alongside LUMSK and GRIFFIN. In November Spiritual Beast issued the album 'Strange To Numbers'.

Reports emerged in early 2005 that SCARIOT, now solely mentored by founder Daniel Olaisen, was employing the TESTAMENT, SADUS, DEATH, DRAGONLORD and SEBASTIAN BACH credited Steve DiGiorgio with Asgeir Mickelson of SPIRAL ARCHITECT and BORKNAGAR on drums for on new recordings. The band entered Top Room Studios in January 2006, working with producer Børge Finstad.

Bernt Fjellstad fired up another new project in 2006, Thrash Metal band RULES OF ENGAGEMENT. In August SCARIOT, having signed to Facefront Records, scrapped a previously announced album title of 'The Grand Design' in favour of 'Momentum Shift'.

Loosing Faith, Scariot (1998) (Demo).

Demo '99, Scariot (1999) (Demo).

Fear/Addiction, Scariot (1999) (Demo).

DEATHFORLORN, Demolition DEMCD 107 (2000). Crimson Tears / Sister / The Bad Man / Within / False Power / Resurrection / Remains Of Dreams / Cruisin'.

TONGUELESS GOD, Scariot (2001). Clear Mind / The Last Frontier / The Cynic / Death Request / Close To Hell / Tongueless God / Closing The Gates / Misery Fields / Darkenized.

Pinion Dark, Scariot (2002) (Demo).

Pushing For Perfection, Scariot (2002) (Demo). Instrument Of Policy / Inside The Frame / Pushing For Perfection.

STRANGE TO NUMBERS, Spiritual Beast SBCD-1009 (2003) (Japanese release). Monopolize / Strange To Numbers / Prospects Unknown / Broken Circle—Cutting Glass / Lady X / Pushing For Perfection / Clear Mind / E Pollution / Inner Mica / Instrument Of Policy / Inside The Frame.

STRANGE TO NUMBERS, Face Front FF022CD (2004). Monopolize / Strange To Numbers / Prospects Unknown / Broken Circle—Cutting Glass / Lady X / Pushing For Perfection / Clear Mind / E Pollution / Inner Mica.

MONUMENTUM SHIFT, FaceFront (2007).

SCARVE

NANCY, FRANCE — *Pierrick Valence (vocals), Guillaume Bideau (vocals), Patrick Martin (guitar), Sylvain Coudret (guitar), Loïc Colin (bass), Dirk Verbeuren (drums).*

Nancy based Thrash-Death Metal act created in the opening weeks of 1994. SCARVE's original summer 1994 demo cassette found the band citing a line up of lead vocalist Fred Bartolomucci, ex-METAL DEATH guitarist Patrick Martin, bass player David Fioraso with Dirk Verbeuren on the drums, the latter a veteran of S.P.I.T., MELTDOWN, Black Metal band ANAON and SHRED. The band's second recording arrived in August of 1996 as the six track Bruno Donini produced and self financed EP 'Six Tears Of Sorrow'. By this juncture Sylvain Coudret had been added as second guitarist.

During 1998 SCARVE supplanted Bartolomucci with two lead singers Guillaume Bideau and Alain Germonville. The 'Translucence' album, issued by the Furtive Metal concern in February of 2000 as a limited edition digipack, closed out with a rendition of LED ZEPPELIN's 'Friends'. Previously fan club members had been treated to an exclusive two track demo CD as a taster entitled 'Opacity'. Bassist Julien Thibers had featured on 'Opacity' but for the album recording proper Philippe Elter came onboard. The album would be granted a Europe wide re-release in April courtesy of War Music. Later that year a four track fan club only EP emerged, comprising one studio track and three live tracks. Loïc Colin took the four string role in September of 2001 and Pierrick Valence of BURNING CLOUD entered the fold as second vocalist that October.

SCARVE's March 2002 Daniel Bergstrand produced album 'Luminiferous' contained a cover version of ENTOMBED's 'Serpent Speech'. The record would be subsequently picked up for US license by World War III Records in October. Live promotion in Europe, dubbed the 'Machinary' tour, had SCARVE allied with road mates NO RETURN, DEW SCENTED and RAIN in April. Further European touring in October found SCARVE on a mighty package billing alongside NILE, SINISTER, NO RETURN and MYRKSKOG.

SCARVE's Guillaume Bideau provided both vocals and percussion for his side project THE CUBE's debut 2003 album 'Stand Up Direction Body'. Meantime Dirk Verbeuren maintained a hectic schedule laying down session drums for MORTUARY's 'Agony In Red', LYZANXIA's 'Mindcrimes', ABORTED's 'Goremageddon' as well as for EOSTENEM. In 2003 the man was sessioning for Israeli band ETERNAL GRAY.

SCARVE side projects abounded in 2003 with singer Pierrick Valence, guitarist Sylvain Coudret and drummer Dirk Verbeuren teaming up with their sound engineer Alan Leeroy, guitarist for ANAON, for a Celtic Metal endeavour entitled STENVAL. The same SCARVE trio, alongside NO RETURN and GARWALL bassist Olivia founded PHAZM.

SCARVE's third album 'Irradiant' was recorded at Dug-Out Studio in Uppsala, Sweden with producers Daniel Bergstrand and erstwhile MISERY LOVES CO. guitarist Örjan Örnkloo. Guesting would be DEFLESHED vocalist/bassist Gustaf Jorde whilst MESHUGGAH guitarist FREDRIK THORDENDAL features a guest guitar solo on the track 'Asphyxiate'. The band filmed a live promotional video for the track 'Mirthless Perspectives'.

Now with some international repute behind him Dirk Verbeuren teamed up as stand in for acclaimed Swedish act SOILWORK for their February 2004 European tour dates. Verbeuren then stepped in as substitute drummer for Belgian gore-mongers ABORTED's live dates and then sessioned on INFINITED HATE's 'Heaven Termination' album. The drummer enrolled into the ranks of YYRKOON for dates in January 2005. SCARVE re-grouped to act as support to MESHUGGAH's June European tour. The band featured the exclusive live track 'Fireproven' on the 2005 Listenable Records French Metal compilation 'Revolution Calling'.

Dirk Verbeuren sessioned for Swiss band SYBREED in 2006. That May SCARVE utilised Dug-Out Studios in Uppsala, Sweden to cut a new album with producer Daniel Bergstrand. However, mid session, singer Guillaume Bideau opted out in order to join Danish band MNEMIC. SCARVE persevered, drafting the services of Swedish vocalist Lawrence Mackrory, of DARKANE, THE MIST OF AVALON, ANDROMEDA, SEETHINGS and F.K.Ü. repute, on a session basis for new album 'The Undercurrent'.

Six Tears Of Sorrow EP, Independent SCAR02CD96 (1996) (Limited edition 1000 copies). Liquefied Silhouettes / Shelly's Dead / Blackloader / Torn Underneath / I.M.D.I. / Anchored In Melancholy.
Opacity EP, Independent SCAR04CD99 (1999) (Fan Club release—200 copies). Heaven-Sent (Demo version) / Your Solid Waters (Demo version).
TRANSLUCENCE, Furtive Metal FUR001 (2000). NerveCurrent9 / Your Solid Waters / Heaven-Sent / The Seed Unsown / A New Dawn / Freaqualized / Luminiferous / FleshPlunge / Sunken Sin-King / Translucence / Friends.
Fan club EP, Independent SCAR06CD00 (2000). Friends (Demo) / Heaven-Sent (Live) / Sunken Sin-King (Live) / BlackLoader (Live).
LUMINIFEROUS, Listenable POSH 036 (2002). Emulate The Soul / Alteration / CrustScraper / Capsized / Luminiferous 2.0 / The Resonating Cycle / The Path To Apoptosis / Futile Resilient / Serpent Speech / Infertile Ways / The Day After / Blackloader (2002 Upgrade).
IRRADIANT, Listenable POSH048 (2004). Mirthless Perspectives / An Emptier Void / Irradiant / Asphyxiate / HyperConscience / The Perfect Disaster / Molten Scars / FireProven / Boiling Calm.

SCAVENGER

DROGHEDA, IRELAND — *Peter Dunne (vocals), Noel Maher (guitar), Niall Cooney (bass), Johnny Kerr (drums).*

Drogheda Heavy Metal band SCAVENGER was founded in the Autumn of 2000, debuting with a self-titled album the following year. The band signed to Sentinel Records for the 2004 album 'Madness To Our Method', recorded at FatDog Studios in Meath but mixed and mastered by ex-CRADLE OF FILTH man Stuart Anstis in the UK. Live work saw supports to CONQUEST OF STEEL and SLOUGH FEG in 2005 before guesting on PAUL DIANNO's February 2005 Irish dates then a short burst of gigs in Holland and Belgium, once again allied with CONQUEST OF STEEL. The band also appeared at the ROTTING CHRIST headlined 'Day of Darkness' festival in Ballylinan during July.

SCAVENGER, Independent (2001). Souls Of Fire / Times Long Past / Waited Too Long / Breaking The Chains / War Cry / Shadowed Lands / Fallout / Slaughter Of Innocence.
MADNESS TO OUR METHOD, Sentinel (2004). On The Outside / Storm Warning / Ethereal Journey / Prisoner Of Time / (untitled) / Unstoppable Motion / Daydreams In Dystopia.

SCAVENGOURS

PARIS, FRANCE — *Nicky (vocals), Niko (guitar), Ashwar (guitar), Oso (bass).*

Paris Thrash Metal band SCAVENGOURS was established during 1996. An opening demo, recorded in July 1999, would be conceived by vocalist Alexis, guitarists Niko and Fabrice, bassist Raphaël and drummer Gaël. Between 2000 and 2001 the band employed DORNFALL vocalist Sebastien Denudt. A second demo, 'The Sound'Ours Tapes' in July 2002, saw the group now featuring Niko and Gaël, second guitarist Andres, Francis, bassist Oso. Switching to another new singer, Nicky, the band published third demo 'The Chicken Chainsaw Massacre' that same December. Gaël would be replaced by Emmanuel Solive (a.k.a. 'Triplex') in 2003 as Andres was substituted by Ashwar.

Solive joined DYING TEARS in 2004. An album, 'Maniac Attack', was recorded in 2005. Orifist of IMPERIAL SODOMY was utilised for live work that Summer. The band contributed their version of 'Raise Your Fist' to the 2005 RUNNING WILD online tribute album 'Rough Diamonds–A Tribute To Running Wild'.

Scavengours, Scavengours (1999). Galaxy Train / The Butcher / Metal Bard / The Creation.
The Sound'Ours Tapes, (2002). Chickenstein / Metal Bunker / A Poil Les Ours.
The Chicken Chainsaw Massacre, (2002). Chickenstein / Metal Bunker / Dead By Dawn / 1789 / A Poil Les Ours.

SCEPTRE

LOS ANGELES, CA, USA — SCEPTRE was a short-lived Los Angeles Thrash outfit made famous for its inclusion of John Cyriis, later to achieve global recognition with AGENT STEEL, this act, debuting with the ground breaking 'Skeptics Apocalypse' album, forging a reputation for surgically precise intense metal honed by Cyriis' distinct high altitude vocal range. Further outings, the 'Mad Locust Rising' EP and the 'Unstoppable Force' album strengthened the band's appeal.

The roots of AGENT STEEL lay in the SCEPTRE track 'Taken By Force' contributed to the Metal Blade Record compilation album 'Metal Massacre IV'. The guitarist for SCEPTRE, the Brazilian born John Camps (a.k.a. João Campos), would capitalise on this exposure with a further three track demo in 1983. Camps, renaming himself 'John Syriis'—later 'Cyriis'—auditioned for the position of lead vocalist with ABATTOIR. Cyriis, demonstrating an impressive multi-octave range, secured the position easily. However, within six months Cyriis was ousted and along with drummer Chuck Profus engineered a new proposition billed as SANCTUARY. This band, rounded out by guitarists Sill Simmons and Mark Marshall with bassist George Robb soon evolved into AGENT STEEL. This inaugural line-up cut the '144'000 Gone' demo in 1984. On the live front the band put in an inauguration gig in September of 1984 at Chuck Landis' Country Club in Reseda, California as the opening act for SLAYER.

In 1988 AGENT STEEL officially disbanded, with Cyriis joining PONTIUS PROPHET. Although later that same year the singer declare his intention to retire he would put his efforts, re-branding himself as 'Max Kobol', into a new venture billed as MALFEITOR in union with AGENT STEEL's drummer Chuck Profus and ex-PONTIUS PROPHET guitarist Michael Hill. Cyriis / Kobol would next be spotted as frontman for Tampa, Florida band LEMEGETON appearing on their 'Evil Against Evil' demo. Cyriis re-emerged in 1990 fronting New York's BLACK REIGN.

'83 Demo, Sceptre (1983). Sceptre / 144,000 Gone / Taken By Force.

SCORCH

ROYAL OAK, MI, USA — *Russ Meuchel (vocals / guitar), Emilio Diaz (guitar), Seth von Detrick (bass), Shawn Farrell (percussion), Nik Proper (percussion), Dave Arvo (drums).*

A quite unique modern Thrash Metal orientated act employing no less than three drummers. Michigan's SCORCH comprises Russ Meuchel "Gut-wrenching guitar riffs, Scrupulous solos, Venomous vocals", Emilio Diaz "Ravenous rhythm guitar", Seth von Detrick "Blasphemous bass guitar", Dave Arvo "Diabolical double-bass, relentless rolls, and cunning crashes" with Shawn Farrell "Pulverizing percussion" and Nik Proper "Painstaking percussion".

Meuchel, previously a member of COMA, started to assemble the band in 1998, working with drummer Dave Arvo. By 2000 the SCORCH title was adopted, along with the enlistment of percussionists Shawn Farrell and Todd Wolfe. In the Summer 2001, Kevin Petroski joined the band as guitarist but would then vacate his position. Aaron Montcalm was incorporated as replacement but he too exited. However, both musicians subsequently rejoined the ranks in 2002, Montcalm switching instruments to bass guitar. The self financed 'Faces' album arrived in February of 2003.

FACES, Independent (2003). EpochElapse / Explode / Psycho / Face / Orgasmic Taste / Scorch / Remember / Mind Raper / Take My Hand / Ominous Overtones.

SCORNAGE

ALSDORF, GERMANY — *Guido Grawe (vocals), Volker Rahn (guitar), Achim Sandkuhl (guitar), Markus Breuer (bass), Tom Freyer (drums).*

SCORNAGE, founded in Alsdorf / Aachen, Nordrhein-Westfalen during 1998, initially comprised singer Andy Thelan, guitarists Volker Rahn and Peter Povse, bassist Markus Breuer with Tom Freyer on the drums. The group issued the self financed EPS 'Ascend' in 2000 and 'Agression' in 2001. Andy Thelen's position was taken in 2001 by Christoph Fritz. Subsequently Guido Grawe secured lead vocal duties. In 2002 Achim Sankul was drafted as second guitarist.

The band signed to Mausoleum Records subsidiary MDD Records for the Michael Hahn produced, May 2004 album 'Sick Of Being Human'. Following release of the album SCORNAGE toured Europe on a package billing with Japanese act KING'S EVIL.

The album 'Pure Motorized Instinct' was delivered by Remedy Records in October 2006. SCORNAGE announced July 2007 European dates with Tokyo's TERROR SQUAD. The band contributed their cover version of TANKARD's 'Away' to the tribute album 'A Tribute To Tankard' included as a bonus disc on the AFM Records 2007 TANKARD release 'Best Case Scenario: 25 Years In Beers'.

SICK OF BEING HUMAN, MDD (2004). Society Kills / Sick Of Being Human / What Lies Beneath / Shed Away From Reality / The Age Of Scorn / In Our World / No More Hate / Over And Out / Paincollector / Devils Offer.

PURE MOTORIZED INSTINCT, Remedy (2006).

SCORNGRAIN

JOENSUU, FINLAND — *TwentynineA (vocals), Dr. Mike Lederfaust (guitar), A.I. (guitar), Herbalizer (bass), Eniac (drums).*

Self styled "Acid Thrash" band SCORNGRAIN released their debut album, 'Cyberwarmachine'. The album, produced by Kimmo Perkkiö and recorded and mixed at MediaWorks Studios in Joensuu with mastering conducted at Finnvox Studios, saw issue through Dynamic Arts Records in October of 2004. Studio guests included Mika Lizitsin, Hannu "Cane" Vuorjoki, Outi Hakulinen and Jone Väänänen. A promotional video for the album's title cut was filmed at Mecca Studio in Joensuu with director Harri Mielonen.

The trio, forged in the Spring of 2001, comprises TwentynineA ("Verbal Schizophrenia"), Dr. Mike Lederfaust ("Överdrive Amputation") and Eniac ("Semiorganic Pulse"). An eponymous, three song demo was laid down in February of 2002 at Headcase Studio A, Joensuu, these sessions being in fact credited to VORDVEN's Mika Packalen. For recording of 'Cyberwarmachine' the band employed Herbalizer on session bass. This candidate joined the band for live operations in 2004, alongside second guitarist A.I.

Second album '0,05%' was released in October through Dynamic Arts.

ScornGrain, ScornGrain (2002) (Demo). Future Clandestine / New Paradise / Step Aside.

CYBERWARMACHINE, Dynamic Arts DYN006 (2004). 24-7 Hell / Blank / Cyberwarmachine / Flesh Means Pain / Killing Breed / 4-D Religion / New Paradise (Bukkake remix) / Dawn Of Hypocrite God / No Funeral For The Last.

0,05%, ScornGrain DYN017 (2006). The Code / Toadstool Journey / Mural / Off With Their Heads / Übermensch / Draw The Line / Shot Down / Mama Stabber / Teaspoonful / Making Of 0,05% (Video).

SECTARIAN

HOLLAND — *Raoul Pinxt (vocals), Kevin Firing (guitar), Bart (guitar), Rob Besselink (keyboards), Jeroen (bass), Rick (drums).*

SECTARIAN, featuring former ANGELS DECAY bassist Kevin Firing on guitar, began life in 1995, operating as a covers band under the banner KICKSHAW. Penning original material under the revised tag of SECTARIAN the band debuted in 2000 with the album 'When Darkness Draws Near'. However, singer Pascal Bastings exited shortly after. Mike Scheijen of 37 STABWOUNDZ and CHAINSLACK filled in temporarily before Raoul Pinxt took command.

Pinxt is also active with MISFITS tribute band ASTRO ZOMBIES A.D. In December 2006 it was announced that Mike Scheijen, in side activity to 37 STABWOUNDZ, had been recruited to front HDK, a Thrash / Death project of AFTER FOREVER guitarist/songwriter Sander Gommans.

Fallen One EP, Independent (2003). In Sight Of The Seraphim / Prelude / Hopefully No Longer / Thy Thousand Names / Fallen One.

SENTENCED

MUHOS, FINLAND — *Ville Laihiala (vocals), Miika Tenkula (guitar), Sami Lopakka (guitar), Taneli Jarwa (bass), Sami Kukkohovi (bass), Vesa Ranta (drums).*

A Muhos based Death Metal band that leaned more towards the NWoBHM 80s Thrash sound as each album progressed until later works shifted ground to a Doom-Death direction. Indeed, the band's classic British Rock influences were so evident the 1994 EP even went so far as to cover IRON MAIDEN's 'The Trooper'. With a population of less than 10,000, prior to the arrival of SENTENCED, Muhos' only contribution to the international world of entertainment had been the 1975 Miss Universe winner, Armi Kuusela.

SENTENCED was created during 1989 in Muhos, located near the northern city of Oulu, by the trio of guitarists Miika Tenkalu and Sami Lopakka along with drummer Vesa Ranta. These three had actually been performing together under an antecedent brand of DEFORMITY during 1988, Ranta having succeeded Tuure Heikkilä, before switching styles, from Thrash to Death, and titles. In this incarnation the band cut their inaugural demo sessions in November the following year dubbed 'When Death Join Us'. After recording, SENTENCED's numbers were brought up to full strength with the addition of vocalist / bassist Taneli Jarwa. Based on a second promotional recording, June 1991's 'Rotting Ways To Misery', they scored a deal with the French Thrash label for the Ahti Kortelainen produced debut album 'Shadows Of The Past' issued that November. A no frills Death Metal assault, 'Shadows Of The Past' saw guitarist Miika Tenkalu handling lead vocals.

The band also included the track 'Desperationed Future' on a free split EP, the mis-spelt 'Cronology Of Death', collaborating with BLUUURGH..., XENOPHOBIA and Sweden's CARBONIZED, for 'Thrash Your Brain' fanzine as a limited edition of 500 copies. SENTENCED then cut a further demo, 'Journey To Pohjola', in March 1992. These efforts garnered the band praiseworthy media coverage internationally prompting a fresh deal with the domestic Spinefarm label. June 1993's sophomore outing 'North From Here', the first record on which Taneli Jarwa took command of the vocals, would see the band adding a greater degree of melody to their work whilst retaining the technical edge. The group's next move was to a two track demo in 1994, comprising 'Glow Of 1000 Suns' and 'Amok Runs', as a tool to gain a new label deal.

The October 1993 EP 'The Trooper', recorded at Tico-Tico Studios in Kemi for new label Century Media, kept the faithful happy until the arrival of 'Amok' in January 1995. This album succeeding in selling over 35'000 units, with Japanese copies enhanced by two extra songs, 'Dreamlands' and 'Obsession'.

SENTENCED toured Europe with TIAMAT and SAMAEL as Century Media re-released the bands first brace of albums to a wider audience. Ever eager to experiment, the September 1995 EP 'Love And Death' included a version of BILLY IDOL's 'White Wedding'.

Jarwa, quaintly billed as 'The fuck you man', often toured and recorded as bassist for IMPALED NAZARENE when the SENTENCED schedule allowed, featuring first on their 1992 'Sadogoat' EP and follow up album 'Tol Cormpt Norz Norz Norz'. However, Jarwa had departed following the 'Love And Death' EP and his place on bass was filled by Niko Karppinen, of LEGENDA and MAPLE CROSS on a session basis, whilst former BREED man Ville Laihiala took over lead vocals for the 1996 Waldemar Sorychta produced 'Down' album. Backing vocals came courtesy of Vorph of SAMAEL with female accompaniment from Birgit Zacher. The bands new lead vocalist brought another new dimension the SENTENCED sound as Laihiala opted for a clean vocal style more suited the more recent, doomier outings. Global touring had SENTENCED hitting their stride with dates in Europe, America and Japan. SENTENCED also formed part of the billing for the December 1996 'Dark Winter Nights' touring festival alongside DEPRESSIVE AGE, LACRIMOSA, THE GATHERING and DREAMS OF SANITY. Touring in Europe during March of 1997 saw the band forming up a package billing alongside THERION, MY DYING BRIDE, ORPHANAGE and DARK for the 'Out Of The Dark III' festivals.

The June 1998 opus 'Frozen', which found bassist Sami Kukkohovi of BREED and MYTHOS added to the roster, would once again be produced by Sorychta. Japanese copies hosted a traditional extra song, 'No Tomorrow'. A "gold" digipack edition increased the song quota by adding no less than four cover versions, namely W.A.S.P.'s 'I Wanna Be Somebody', RADIOHEAD's 'Creep', FAITH NO MORE's 'Digging The Grave' and THE ANIMALS 'House Of The Rising Sun'.

The January 2000 'Crimson' album, crafted at Tico Tico, would lend recognition to SENTENCED's status as it reached the coveted number 1 position in the Finnish album charts. Later in the same year the album would be re-launched on picture disc vinyl format. Meantime, erstwhile frontman Taneli Jarwa resurfaced fronting THE BLACK LEAGUE the same year.

In February of 2001 Century Media repackaged the 'Amok' and 'Love & Death' records on a single CD re-release. Laihiala was also to be revealed as in collaboration with Jesper Strömblad of IN FLAMES on an extracurricular band project.

SENTENCED bounced back in style during May 2002 with the Hiili Hiilesmaa produced album 'The Cold White Light', their 'No One There' single charting at the number 2 position in Finland. Shortly after the album itself hit the top spot in its first week of release, gaining Gold sales certification for 15'000 units sold. The musical transformation was by now complete, the SENTENCED journey having brought them up to an album that was focussed on groove, atmosphere and melancholic balladry.

A month's worth of North American dates commenced in San Francisco on September 16th backing up headliners IN FLAMES with strong support from KILLSWITCH ENGAGE and LACUNA COIL. The band shortly after unveiled an extensive European tour schedule for October, supported by LACUNA COIL. Further North American shows had SENTENCED combining forces with LACUNA COIL, IN FLAMES and DARK TRANQUILITY. Enrolled into the band unit for these gigs would be keyboard player Antti Pikkarainen from the band THE RMS.

SENTENCED bassist Sami Kukkohovi readied his side venture SOLUTION 13 (formerly CONFUSION RED) for their debut album release in November through Low Frequency Records. SENTENCED vocalist Ville Laihiala's own extracurricular endeavour POISONBLACK (formatively SHADOWLANDS), which saw the singer operating as guitarist in league with CHARON's frontman Juha-Pekka Leppäluoto, also announced his debut 'Escapexstacy'.

The band revealed a spirit of local patronage in September, recording their first ever Finnish language song 'Routasydän' for use as a theme song for their hometown of Oulu's ice hockey team Oulun Kärpät. However, this diversion would backfire on the band in spectacular fashion when a local newspaper alleged that the lyric "Sisu, veri ja kunnia" ("courage, blood and honour") displayed Nazi sympathies because it was similar to an oath sworn by the Hitler Jugend organisation from World War II. SENTENCED vehemently denied such assertions but the Oulun Kärpät team pulled the song from their events nonetheless. The band had the last word though, performing the song in front of a crowd of over 30,000 in celebration of the team winning the Finnish championship in April of 2004.

Early 2004 found Ville Laihiala engaged in POISONBLACK activities as well as finding the time to add a guest vocal to the 'Sweet & Deceitful' album from Glam Hard Rock outfit NEGATIVE, this record hitting number 1 on the Finnish charts. SENTENCED's Summer dates included festival performances at the 'Rock The Nations' event in Istanbul, Turkey, 'Athens Open Air' in Greece, 'Gates of Metal' in Sweden and 'Summer Breeze' in Germany. The band then selected Hiili Hiilesmaa as producer to craft a new studio album during November.

As 2005 drew in the band was subject to conjecture that their next album might be their last. In early February guitarist Sami Lopakka announced "The title of the new album is 'The Funeral Album', and with it we, SENTENCED, are coming to the end of our road. This album will be our last one. The decision is mutual, thoroughly thought over and final. Metaphorically speaking, this is a mass suicide of five." A preceding single, 'Ever-Frost' released only in Finland, duly entered the domestic charts at no. 1. SENTENCED performed their swan song live performance at the August 2005 'Wacken Open Air' festival in Germany. 'The Funeral Album' entered the national Finnish album charts at no. 1. Japanese variants added bonus live tracks in 'Brief Is The Light' and 'Nepenthe'.

SENTENCED announced that their final live show, held on 1st October 2005 at Club Teatria in Oulu, would be recorded and filmed for future product. With tickets selling out in less than an hour, the band added a further show for 30th September.

When Death Join Us, (1990). Hallucinations / When Death Join Us / Shadows Of The Past / Obscurity ... / Desperationed Future.

Rotting Ways To Misery, (1991). Rotting Ways To Misery / Disengagement / Suffocated Beginning Of Life / Under The Suffer / Descending Curtain Of Death / The Truth.

SHADOWS OF THE PAST, Thrash THR015-NR340 (1991). When The Moment Of Death Arrives / Rot To Dead / Disengagement / Rotting Ways To Misery / The Truth / Suffocated Beginning Of Life / Beyond The Distant Valleys / Under The Suffer / Descending Curtain Of Death.

Journey To Pohjola, (1992). Wings / In Memoriam / Mythic Silence—As They Wander In The Mist.

NORTH FROM HERE, Spinefarm SPI 13CD (1993). My Sky Is Darker Than Thine / Wings / Fields Of Blood / Harvester Of Hate / Capture Of Fire / Awaiting The Winter Frost / Beyond The Wall Of Sleep / Northern Lights / Epic.

The Trooper EP, Spinefarm SPI 15 (1993). The Trooper / Desert By Night / In Memoriam / Awaiting The Winter Frost.

Demo 1994, (1994) (Demo). Glow Of 1000 Suns / Amok Runs.

AMOK, Century Media 77076-2 (1995). The War Ain't Over! / Phenix / New Age Messiah / Forever Lost / Funeral Spring / Nepenthe / Dance On The Graves (Lil 'Siztah') / Moon Magick / The Golden Stream Of Lapland.

Love And Death EP, Century Media 77101-2 (1995). The Way I Wanna Go / Obsession / Dreamlands / White Wedding / Love And Death.

DOWN, Century Media 77146-2 (1996). Intro—The Gate / Noose / Shadegrown / Bleed / Keep My Grave Open / Crumbling Down (Give Up Hope) / Sun Won't Shine / Ode To The End / 0132 / Warrior Of Life (Reaper Redeemer) / I'll Throw The First Rock.

FROZEN—GOLD EDITION, Century Media 77246G-2 (1998) (Digipack). The Suicider / Dead Leaves / For The Love I Bear / Creep / Digging The Grave / Kaamos / Farewell / One With Misery / Grave Sweet Grave / Burn / Drown Together / Let Go (The Last Chapter) / The Rain Comes Falling Down / Mourn / I Wanna Be Somebody / House Of The Rising Sun.

FROZEN, Century Media 77246-2 (1998). Kaamos / Farewell / Dead Leaves / For The Love I Bear / One With Misery / The Suicider / The Rain Comes Falling Down / Grave Sweet Grave / Burn / Drown Together / Let Go (The Last Chapter) / Mourn. Chart position: 73 GERMANY.

Killing Me, Killing You, Century Media (1999). Killing Me, Killing You / Dead Moon Rising.

CRIMSON, Century Media 77346-2 (2000). Bleed In My Arms / Home In Despair / Fragile / No More Beating As One / Broken / Killing Me, Killing You / Dead Moon Rising / The River / One More Day / With Bitterness And Joy / My Slowing Heart. Chart position: 47 GERMANY.

THE COLD WHITE LIGHT, Century Media 8146-2 (2002) (North American release). Konevitsan Kirkonkellot / Cross My Heart And Hope To Die / Brief Is The Light / Neverlasting / Aika Multaa Muistot (Everything Is Nothing) / Excuse Me While I Kill Myself / Blood & Tears / You Are The One / Guilt And Regret / The Luxury Of A Grave / No One There / Killing Me Killing You (Video).

No One There, Century Media (2002). No One There (desolate single version) / Blood & Tears.

THE COLD WHITE LIGHT, Century Media 77446-2 (2002). Konevitsan Kirkonkellot / Cross My Heart And Hope To Die / Brief Is The Light / Neverlasting / Aika Multaa Muistot (Everything Is Nothing) / Excuse Me While I Kill Myself / Blood & Tears / You Are The One / Guilt And Regret / The Luxury Of A Grave / No One There. Chart positions: 1 FINLAND, 5 SWEDEN, 45 GERMANY.

Routasydän, (2003). Routasydän.

Ever-Frost, Century Media (2005). Ever-Frost / Despair-Ridden Hearts. Chart position: 1 FINLAND.

THE FUNERAL ALBUM, Century Media 8246-2 (2005). May Today Become The Day / Ever-Frost / We Are But Falling Leaves / Her Last 5 Minutes / Where Waters Fall Frozen / Despair-Ridden Hearts / Vengeance Is Mine / A Long Way To Nowhere / Consider Us Dead / Lower The Flags / Drain Me / Karu / End Of The Road. Chart positions: 1 FINLAND, 49 GERMANY, 59 AUSTRIA.

BURIED ALIVE, Century Media 8352-2 (2007). Funeral Intro / Where Winters Fall Frozen / May Today Become The Day / Neverlasting / Bleed / The Rain Comes Falling Down / Ever-Frost / Sun Won't Shine / Dead Moon Rising / Despair-Ridden Hearts / Broken / The Suicider / Excuse Me While I Kill / The War Ain't Over / Nepenthe / Northern Lights / The Way I Wanna Go / Dance On The Graves (Lil' Siztah) / Noose / Aika Multaa Muistot / Farewell / No One There / Drown Together / Cross My Heart And Hope To Die / Brief Is The Light / Vengeance Is Mine / End Of The Road.

FROZEN, NightOfTheVinylDead (2007) (Limited edition 500 copies only on ice clear vinyl). Kaamos / Farewell / Dead Leaves / For The Love I Bear / The Suicider / Rain Comes Falling Down / Grave Sweet Grave / Burn / Drown Together / Let Go (The Last Chapter) / Mourn.

SENTINEL BEAST

SACRAMENTO, CA, USA — *Debbie Gunn (vocals), Mark Koyasako (guitar), Barry Fischel (guitar), Michael Spencer (bass), Scott Awes (drums).*

SENTINEL BEAST issued the demos 'Kill The Witch' in 1984 and 'Depths Of Death' in July of 1985. Following the demise of SENTINEL BEAST vocalist Debbie Gunn linked up with the Chicago outfit ZNOWHITE before travelling to England to join Swedish all female Thrashers ICE AGE and, although working on demos and gaining a reasonably high press profile, the band failed to gain a recording deal.

Bassist Michael Spencer would score the task of replacing Jason Newsted in FLOTSAM AND JETSAM. He would later work with SUPAPHAT.

DEPTHS OF DEATH, Metal Blade 72116 (1986). Depths Of Death / Mourir / Dogs Of War / Corpse / Evil Is The Night / Sentinel Beast / Revenge / The Keeper / Phantom Of The Opera.

SEPULTURA

BELO HORIZONTE, MG, BRAZIL — *Derrick Green (vocals), Andreas Kisser (guitar), Paulo Jr. (bass), Igor Cavalera (drums).*

SEPULTURA rank as the undisputed leaders of Brazilian bands on the international Rock scene. Created in Belo Horizonte during 1983, SEPULTURA's initial albums were timed perfectly to benefit from the Thrash explosion of the early 80's. Although the act's early albums were far from sensational the fact that the band more than looked the part allied to their professed influences of British Punk and American Metal stood them in good stead until the breakthrough 'Arise' album.

The band took on typical Death Metal nom de guerres for the early part of their career, Max Cavalera being known as "Max Possessed", Jairo Guedez calling himself "Tormentor", Igor Cavalera as "Igor Skull Crusher" and Paulo Xisto Pinto Junior known as "Destructor". Driven by pure enthusiasm, the poverty stricken teenagers being straight out of school, SEPULTURA was motivated by unfashionable European Thrash and US death Metal. Having delivered their first concert at the Barroliche Club in Belo Horizonte in 1984, during which Igor Cavalera's "drum kit" comprised a woeful snare drum, floor tom and one cymbal, SEPULTURA was on their way. Paulo Jr. was inducted for a gig at the Santa Teresa Ideal Clube in March 1985, the world first learned of SEPULTURA later that year when they shared vinyl on a split album, 'Bestial Devastation' through local record store Cogumelo Records, shared with another local outfit OVERDOSE's 'Século XX' sessions.

These songs had been committed to an 8 track recorder at JG Studios in Belo Horizonte that August, self-produced by the band with engineer João Guimarães manning the desk. Opening with a lycanthropic slurred growl billed as 'The Curse', SEPULTURA's debut would have proven remarkable if launched in Europe or Scandinavia. Hellishly raw, as dictated by their youth and inexperience, 'Bestial Devastation' offered primal Death Metal with, arguably, the world's very first example of the now famed blast beat drum technique in the track 'Antichrist'. Despite the studio restrictions, Max Cavalera's guttural rasp neutered by an extreme degree of echo and guitars completely out of tune, 'Bestial Devastation' would certainly stand the test of time.

Reported domestic sales of some 15,000 copies were deemed a success and both bands were offered an extension on the contract. A full length album then ensued, 'Morbid Visions', arriving in 1986. Eduardo Santos and Zé "Heavy" Luiz now guided the teens in the confines of Estudio Vice Versa, Belo Horizonte. Given seven days space in which to work, SEPULTURA drew from both extreme spectrums of Death Metal and Thrash Metal. Again the production values were haphazardly sloppy and the influences worn plainly, making the whole edict contrived yet honest, but the ferocity summoned up could not be denied. Still very much an underground act, SEPULTURA's inaugural US release came courtesy of New Renaissance Records, the imprint owned by HELLION's Ann Boleyn issuing 'Morbid Visions' the following year.

Jairo Guedez was superseded following 'Morbid Visions' by erstwhile PRESILENCE man Andreas Kisser. Impressing sufficiently by an audition process jamming out KREATOR and DESTRUCTION songs, the new guitarist first stepped onstage with the band in May 1987 in Caruaru, Pernambuco. Jairo would at first announce he no longer had any interest in Metal but emerged in 1989 as a member of Thrashers THE MIST for the 'Phantasmagoria' album. The band had other SEPULTURA connections with vocalist Vladimir Korg, previously with CHAKAL, credited for the lyrics to SEPULTURA's 'To The Wall' and bassist Marcelo Diaz being a SEPULTURA roadie. Kisser had risen through the ranks of local amateur Metal bands such as SPHINX, an outfit that took on covers by acts such as SLAYER and JUDAS PRIEST before injecting original material and retitling themselves PESTILENCE.

Utilising JG Studios once again in August 1987 SEPULTURA, together with engineer Tasro Senra, crafted the 'Schizophrenia' album. The album title was apt indeed, SEPULTURA laying down a deluge of riffage culminating in the titanic 'From The Past Comes The Storm', this leviathan writhing through multiple tempo changes and a volley of riffs that many acts would have difficulty conjuring up in an entire career. Adding a little colour to the Thrash barrage would be violinist Paolo Gordo and keyboard player Henrique of POLISO ALTO. Shark Records took on the German license.

Enthusiastic supporters Borivoj Krgin and Don Kaye, US based journalists, arranged meeting between Max Cavalera and record labels in New York. Having disguised himself as a Pan Am employee in order to make the flight from Brazil, Max Cavalera arrived in North America armed with a bag full of 'Schizophrenia' cassettes. After numerous rejections, Monte Connor at Roadrunner Records took a chance on the band.

September 1989's 'Beneath The Remains' signalled the first move away from the standard Thrash fare. Laid down in nine overnight sessions in December 1988 at Nas Nuvens Studio, Rio de Janiero the end result was mixed in Florida by Scott Burns. Importantly, international exposure affected the band's overall sound, this being particularly felt in the lyrical department, which had been up to this juncture often imbued with some degree of hilarity due to poor command of English. Lyrics to 'Stronger Than Hate' would be contributed by ATHEIST's Kelly Shaefer, the man, alongside OBITUARY's John Tardy plus Scott Latour and Francis Howard of INCUBUS, also donating backing vocals. As a true entrance onto the global scene, Roadrunner Records now distributing the band's product into the USA, 'Beyond The Remains' was a mighty introduction, a caustic Thrashfest viewed by many as the creative pinnacle of their career to date.

The band's first taste of international live work came in September 1989, opening for SODOM in Vienna, Austria before tackling gigs in the USA, headlining the East Coast with FAITH OR FEAR as support, and Mexico. Their biggest concert to date was held on June 4th 1990 in front of 26,000 at the Dutch Dynamo festival, here meeting SACRED REICH manager Gloria Bujnowski who then took on the Brazilians business affairs. SEPULTURA had become national heroes in Brazil putting in a worthy performance at the January 1991 'Rock In Rio' festival sharing the same stage at the Maracana stadium in front of 50,000 fans with major league international acts GUNS N' ROSES, JUDAS PRIEST and MEGADETH. To commemorate this occasion an unprecedented decision was taken to rush release a limited edition rough mix version of their forthcoming album 'Arise', now a hugely collectable item. The band subsequently played a free outdoor concert in Sao Paulo in the Charles Muller Square drawing over 40,000 fans. Tragically an audience member was murdered, this event tarnishing the band's name in Brazil amongst authorities.

It was to be 'Arise', released in March 1991 with cover artwork, depicting the mutated Yog-Sothoth, from noted Sci-Fi artist Michael Whelan, took SEPULTURA into new realms of creativity. Also new on the visual front would be the now world famous bone 'S' logo, executed by old friend Bozo, singer of OVERDOSE. The band had extricated itself from the familiar run of the mill Thrash acts to create a quite unique album, travelling to Tampa, Florida to record at the fabled Morrisound Recording with Scott Burns at the helm. Spin off singles included 'Third World Chaos', 'Under Siege' and 'Dead Embryonic Cells'.

By now the act's raucous live shows were also beginning to build a solid fan base. UK headline shows in June saw SACRED REICH as strong support act and, spreading their reach, the group also put in shows in Australia and Indonesia, playing to over 100,000 fans at just two concerts. SEPULTURA played a brace of concerts in Mexico during December 1991 supported by MAKINA and TRANSMETAL. With interest rising in Europe, Germany's Shark Records re-packaged 'Morbid Visions' as a split album shared with METAL CONQUEST. Roadrunner Records also re-issued 'Schizophrenia', re-mastering the entire set and adding a newly recorded version of 'Troops Of Doom' for good measure.

On 1st March 1992 the band, complete with Andreas Kisser sporting retaining rods in a broken arm, put in a pre-European tour "secret" gig at the small Amersham Arms pub in London billed as THIRD WORLD POSSE. The group also figured on the landmark BLACK SABBATH reunion gigs at Costa Mesa, California on November 14th and 15th.

September 1993's 'Chaos A.D.' saw SEPULTURA stripping down their sound to Punk basics, gearing down into proto-Groove Metal. The band's lyrical stance now became far more openly political, even to such an extent as collaborating with Jello Biafra of DEAD KENNEDYS on the 1:52 minute speedburst of 'Biotech Is Godzilla'm and faithfully covering NEW MODEL ARMY's 'The Hunt'. Other poignant statements fuelled 'Kaiowas', an acoustic lament for a native tribe that committed mass suicide, and 'Manifest', the latter concerning a police massacre at the Pavilhao Nove prison in São Paulo. Versions of 'Chaos A.D.' also came with a bonus track, 'Polícia', originally by TITÃS.

America too was now coming under the SEPULTURA spell and 'Chaos A.D.', a truly landmark album backed by singles 'Territory', with a promotional video shot in Israel, 'Refuse/Resist' and 'Slave New World', broke the Billboard charts. UK shows in December saw Halifax's PARADISE LOST as opening act. Live strategies took SEPULTURA to even further destinations such as Russia.

In 1994 Max Cavalera and FUDGE TUNNEL's Alex Newport developed NAILBOMB as a parallel project. The resulting 'Point Blank' album saw participation from Andreas Kisser, Igor Cavalera and FEAR FACTORY's Dino Cazares.

This alliance segued into the SEPULTURA game plan as demos for the 'Roots' album were recorded by Alex Newport. SEPULTURA then took the brave step of recording tracks deep in the Brazilian jungle with the Xavante indians. The resulting album, issued in February 1996, took the band's aesthetic into totally new areas of operation as they offered the Rock world an album of unrelenting Metal infused with their own cultural heritage and ethnicity. 'Roots', closing out with an unlisted 13 minute epic 'Canyon Jam', proved to be their biggest seller to date going top 5 in Britain. SEPULTURA channeled their ferocity away from inventive riffing and into slabbed chords, such as 'Dictatorshit', 'Endangered Species' and the street anthem 'Roots Bloody Roots' would be punctuated by native drumming passages 'Jasco', 'Itsári' and the pounding 'Ratamahatta'. The digipack option was boosted by 'Chaos B.C.', the BLACK SABBATH cover 'Symptom Of The Universe', which was previously available on October 1994's 'Nativity In Black' tribute record, and a live take of 'Kaiowas'. Another elaborate wooden box package included a video, necklace and even candles.

With 'Roots' having carved its position as one of the most important metal releases, SEPULTURA were now at the top of their game. However, in late 1996 fans and media were shocked to learn of Max Cavalera's sudden departure. Max would front SEPULTURA for the last time on December 16th 1996 at the London Brixton Academy. Cavalera returned to the fore in quick fashion, touting new combo SOULFLY, not only taking producer Ross Robinson and manager Gloria Bujnowski with him but also retaining his Roadrunner deal and recruiting former SEPULTURA roadie Marcello D. Rapp on bass guitar.

1997's filler album 'Blood Rooted' gave fans more than the usual interim product in anticipation of the new look SEPULTURA and SOULFLY albums. Featured were a barrage of live tracks and also the cut 'Mine' with FAITH NO MORE's Mike Patton on lead vocals plus 'Lookaway' with KORN's Jonathon Davis and Patton once more. Other rare cuts included the band's cover of CELTIC FROST's 'Procreation (Of The Wicked)', DEAD KENNEDY's 'Drug Me', BOB MARLEY's 'War' and BLACK SABBATH's 'Symptom Of The Universe'. Another release of interest that same year was the re-mastered 'Beneath The Remains', this adding a cover version of 'A Hora E A Vez Do Cabelo Nascer' originally by OS MUTANTES.

With the media attention firmly focused on SOULFLY for

a lengthy period the spotlight was pointed firmly back into the SEPULTURA camp when it was announced that Cavalera's position had finally been filled. The new recruit was the black goliath Derrick Green, formerly of ALPHA JERK, OVERFIEND and OUTFACE.

The Howard Benson produced 'Against', released in August 1998, continued the tradition of tribalism with the inclusion of the Japanese Kodo drummers on the track 'Kamaitachi'. A reworking of the track, retitled 'Diary Of A Drug Fiend' with vocals from FAITH NO MORE's Mike Patton, was at the last minute removed from the album for fear of a sales backlash due to it's lyrical content. The finished album did include though a rare appearance outside of METALLICA for Jason Newsted appearing as guitarist and guest vocalist for the track 'Hatred Aside'.

In May 1999 SEPULTURA supported METALLICA on a series of shows across Brazil, Porto Alegre Hipodromo do Cristal on the 6th, Anhembi Parking Lot, São Paulo on the 8th and Clube De Regatas Do Flamengo, Rio de Janeiro, on the 9th. At the latter concert Jason Newsted jammed with SEPULTURA during their set on the song 'Hatred Aside'. The band tested the waters with North American shows billed as TROOPS OF DOOM. SEPULTURA proper got to grips with promoting the 'Against' album properly with an American support tour opening for SLAYER.

The single from the album 'Choke' featured versions of BAD BRAINS tracks 'Gene Machine' and 'Don't Bother Me'. The also band contributed a track to the 1999 BAD BRAINS tribute album 'Never Give In'. Green meantime turned up as a guest on INTEGRITY 2000's self titled album of the same year. In April of 2000 Swedish label Black Sun released a SEPULTURA tribute 'Sepulchral Feast' which included honours paid by artists such as SACRAMENTUM, SWORDMASTER, DEATHWITCH, GARDENIAN, CHILDREN OF BODOM, LORD BELIAL, DEFLESHED, THE CROWN and IMPIOUS.

SEPULTURA returned in 2001 with the Steve Evetts produced 'Nation' album. Recorded in Brazil the record saw such diverse guest performances from JELLO BIAFRA on 'Politricks', Reggae artist Dr. Israel, the noted Finnish cello quartet APOCALYPTICA on the mellow 'Valtio' and HATEBREED's Jamey Jasta.

March of 2002 brought the news that drummer Igor Cavalera was pursuing a side venture in league with BIOHAZARD guitarist Billy Graziadei and Brazilian DJ Patife. Other outside activities found Cavalera and guitarist Andreas Kisser credited with material for a soundtrack album entitled 'No Coracao Dos Deuses'. Originally cut in 1999 the recordings would be made available in Europe by Mascot Records. The material includes a guest appearance from ex-FAITH NO MORE frontman Mike Patton on the track 'Procura O Cara'. Meantime, Max Cavalera's last concert with SEPULTURA was slated for a September 2002 release under the title 'Under A Pale Grey Sky'.

SEPULTURA's Brazilian dates in the summer would be topped off by a landmark performance at São José dos Campos in front of a 10,000 capacity crowd. BIOHAZARD guitarist Billy Graziadei joined the band onstage for renditions of MOTÖRHEAD's 'Iron Fist' and the TITAS track 'Polícia'. Another mammoth gig, in São Paulo on June 29th, would find over twelve high ranking Brazilian acts including KORZUS, NECROMANCIA, and CLAUSTROFOBIA paying homage to SEPULTURA by performing over 50 SEPULTURA songs. Meantime an ex-SEPULTURA man, guitarist Jairo Guedz, announced his return to the fray as bassist with a new act entitled EMINENCE.

SEPULTURA would unveil plans for their return with word of a proposed Brazilian exclusive EP of cover versions. Among the tracks set for inclusion would be HELLHAMMER's 'Messiah', PUBLIC ENEMY's 'Black Steel In The Hour Of Chaos' with guesting Rappers SABOTAGE and DJ ZE GONZALES, JANE'S ADDICTION's 'Mountain Song', DEVO's 'Mongoloid', EXODUS' Thrash classic 'Piranha' and 'Bullet The Blue Sky' by U2. The video for the latter track would scoop the Brazilian MTV award for 'Best Direction of Photography'.

During September guitarist Andreas Kisser took time out of the band's schedule to perform live on the Brazilian club circuit with a new Blues based solo venture. The group would take another diversion by contributing music to the Brazilian movie 'Lisbela E O Prisioneiro' with the ZE RAMALHOS cover 'Dança das Borboletas'. SEPULTURA scheduled 'Roorback' as the title for a 2003 full length album, recorded in São Paulo with producer Steve Evetts. The band opened a co-headline US tour with Canadians VOIVOD in San Francisco, California on 18th April.

A collaboration between former FAITH NO MORE and current FANTÔMAS and TOMAHAWK man Mike Patton and SEPULTURA, 'The Waste', would be included on the soundtrack to Horror movie 'Freddy Vs. Jason' in August. The track was recorded during 1998's 'Against' sessions. SEPULTURA united with British Rock stalwarts DEEP PURPLE and THE HELLACOPTERS for four major Kaiser Music Festival Brazilian shows in September.

Andreas Kisser cut a cover version of JOHN LENNON's anthem 'Give Peace A Chance' for inclusion on a Brazilian tribute album entitled 'De Uma Chance A Paz' in January of 2004. Later that year found drummer Igor Cavalera performing double duty for SEPULTURA's Autumn Brazilian gigs. Under the pseudonym of 'El Covero' Cavalera also performed with the tour's support band MASSACRATION.

Andreas Kisser formed up part of the ad hoc 'Brazil Rock Stars' group alongside members of WOMBAT and singer Bruno Sutter, involved in the "fun" heavy metal project MASSACRATION (featuring SEPULTURA drummer Igor Cavalera, a.k.a. El Covero), to perform a live set of DEATH and CONTROL DENIED covers in tribute to Chuck Schuldiner at the September 18th 'Bonded by Blood Thrash Fest' in São Paulo. The event, headlined by EXODUS, saw a strong billing of KORZUS, ANDRALLS, TORTURE SQUAD and MAD DRAGZTER. Kisser also found time to donate a guitar solo the track 'A Farewell To Kings' for the Magna Carta 2005 RUSH tribute album 'Subdivisions'.

In recognition of the band's status in their homeland a São Paulo event on 25th September, dubbed 'Sepulfest', would, naturally, be headlined by SEPULTURA with a strong support cast comprising RATOS DE PORÃO, NAÇÃO ZUMBI, CLAUSTROFOBIA and MASSACRATION. SEPULTURA returned to Europe in November and December, lending support to MOTÖRHEAD.

Recordings for a new album, cut at Trama Studios in São Paulo and entitled 'Dante XXI', would reveal the group was planning a conceptual piece based upon the 'Divine Comedy' of classical literature. During the sessions the group also laid down cover versions of JUDAS PRIEST's 'Screaming For Vengeance' and SICK OF IT ALL's 'Scratching The Surface'.

Also announced would be that SEPULTURA guitarist Andreas Kisser has contracted a deal with Holland's Mascot Records to record his first solo album, 'Hubris 1 & 2', recorded at A Voz do Brasil studio in São Paulo. A notable stop on SEPULTURA's 2005 tour schedule came on 25th March when the band, alongside THE DARKNESS and MACHINE HEAD, performed in Dubai in the United Arab Emirates, marking the first such occasion for a Western Metal band in the Gulf. Support came from local bands NERVECELL and JULIANA DOWN.

On April 3rd SEPULTURA filmed a hometown São Paulo for commercial DVD release. Highlights included the group performing 'Troops Of Doom' with former SEPULTURA guitarist Jairo Guedz and both 'Reza' and 'Biotech Is Godzilla' with RATOS DE PORÃO.'s João Gordo. A brief round of Mexican dates would see the VIPER veteran Guilherme Martin stepping in as temporary drummer when Igor Cavalera was unable to attend.

The following month saw a special anniversary re-issue of the 'Roots' album, complete with a bonus disc comprising demos, remixes and alternate versions. Meantime, guest activity for Igor Cavalera found the drummer collaborating with Brooklyn rapper NECRO on the album 'Circle Of Tyrants'. SEPULTURA put out the CD / DVD package 'Live In São Paulo' through SPV in November. On December 15th Andreas Kisser notably joined the ROADRUNNER UNITED conglomerate at the New York Nokia Theater for an all star Metal evening. SEPULTURA tracks played would be 'Refuse/Resist' and 'Roots Bloody Roots' fronted by MACHINE HEAD's Rob Flynn and featuring ANTHRAX guitarist Scott Ian, ex-FEAR FACTORY guitarist Dino Cazares and SLIPKNOT drummer Joey Jordison.

Quite spectacularly, founder member Igor Cavalera, having just become a father to a baby boy, announced his temporary withdrawal on 13th January 2006 in order to attend to his family life. Stepping in to cover the SEPULTURA drum duties would be the THORN, CRISIS and SOULFLY credited Roy Mayorga. That same month Andreas Kisser guested on a cover version of SLAYER's 'War Ensemble' by SILENT CIVILIAN. By June ex-UDORA man Jean Dolabella was manning the drum stool.

Promoting the 'Dante XXI' album, European shows throughout April and May saw SEPULTURA opening for IN FLAMES. In mid June Igor Cavalera officially announced his departure citing "artistic incompatibility" with his band mates, further stating his belief that "the group's current formation no longer lives up to my expectations as a musician and a person." Of intrigue to fans would be a previous public comment from SOULFLY's Max Cavalera indicating that a classic SEPULTURA reunion was unfeasible without his brother's involvement. Pointedly, Roadrunner Records announced a September compilation, 'The Best Of Sepultura', only featured material featuring Max Cavalera. Meantime, Igor Cavalera swiftly announced plans to forge a fresh band unit in alliance with Brooklyn "Death rapper" NECRO. The drummer also informed media in Brazil that because the Cavalera siblings were no longer involved with the band in its current formation the title SEPULTURA could only be used legally until the close of the 'Dante XXI' touring cycle. Andreas Kisser subsequently denied this assertion.

SEPULTURA received a huge, and wholly unexpected, boost in October when three Argentine brothers put their video jam version of 'Refuse/Resist' onto the internet. The Fernández siblings, Emilio, 15, Agustín, 11, and Martín, 10, residing in the northwestern province of Salta, saw their video on YouTube watched by more than 1.4 million people. On October 24th it was the most downloaded video of any category.

Also in October Andreas Kisser made a guest appearance on the track 'The Waterfalls' featured on BURNING IN HELL's 'Believe' album. That same month SEPULTURA united with a heavyweight billing comprising STRATOVARIUS, BLACK LABEL SOCIETY, SAXON, NEVERMORE, AFTER FOREVER, PRIMAL FEAR and GOTTHARD for the 'Live n' Louder' festivals across Mexico, Argentina and Brazil.

US headline dates, backed by SWORN ENEMY, DIECAST and SUICIDE SILENCE, set for November saw a delay when the first three concerts in Phoenix, Long Beach and Sacramento were cancelled due to immigration problems. The band contributed their version of 'Scratch The Surface' to the SICK OF IT ALL tribute album 'Our Impact Will Be Felt' assembled by Abacus Recordings for January 2007 release.

During February Andreas Kisser cut tracks for a solo album billed as 'Hubris 1 & 2' for Dutch imprint Mascot Records. In early March the band filmed a promotional video for the track 'Ostia' in downtown São Paulo with director Geraldo Moraes.

European touring saw support from Cape Town, South Africa based Metalcore band FOREVER WILL BURN.

SEPULTURA

BESTIAL DEVASTATION, Cogumelo COG 001 (1985) (Split album with OVERDOSE). The Curse / Bestial Devastation / Antichrist / Necromamcer / Warriors Of Death.

MORBID VISIONS, Cogumelo COG 002 (1986). Morbid Visions / Mayhem / Troops Of Doom / War / Crucifixion / Show Me The Wrath / Funeral Rites / Empire Of The Damned / The Curse.

SCHIZOPHRENIA, Cogumelo COG 009 (1987). Intro / From The Past Comes The Storms / To The Wall / Escape From The Void / Inquisition Symphony / Screams Behind The Shadows / Septic Schizo / The Abyss / RIP (Rest In Peace) / Troops Of Doom.

BENEATH THE REMAINS, Roadrunner RO 9511-1 (1989). Beneath The Remains / Mass Hypnosis / Inner Self / Lobotomy / Sarcastic Existence / Slaves Of Pain / Primitive Future / Hungry / Stronger Than Hate.

Under Siege (Regnum Irae), Roadracer RO 2424-6 (1991). Under Siege (Regnum Irae) / Orgasmatron / Troops Of Doom (New version).

ARISE—ROUGH MIXES EDITION, Eldorado (1991) (Limited edition Brazilian release). Arise / Dead Embryonic Cells / Desperate Cry / Murder / Subtraction / Altered State / Under Siege (Regnum Irae) / Meaningless Movements / Infected Voice.

ARISE, Roadracer RO 9328-2 (1991). Arise / Dead Embryonic Cells / Desperate Cry / Murder / Subtraction / Altered State / Under Siege (Regnum Irae) / Meaningless Movements / Infected Voice. Chart position: 40 UK.

Third World Posse EP, Roadracer RO23952 (1992) (Limited edition Australian release). Dead Embryonic Cells / Drug Me / Inner Self (Live) / Troops Of Doom (Live) / Orgasmatron (Live).

Arise, Roadrunner RR 2406-6 (1992). Arise / Troops Of Doom (Live) / Inner Self (live).

Territory, Roadrunner RR2382-6 (1992) (UK release, 12" vinyl single). Territory / Policia (Previously Unrelease) / Biotech Is Godzilla.

CHAOS A.D., Roadrunner RR 8859-2 (1993). Refuse—Resist / Territory / Slave New World / Amen / Kaiowas / Propaganda / Biotech Is Godzilla / Nomad / We Are Not As Others / Manifest / The Hunt / Clenched Fist / Policia / Inhuman Nature. Chart positions: 11 UK, 15 NEW ZEALAND, 32 USA.

Territory, Roadrunner RR 2382-7 (1993). Territory / Policia. Chart position: 66 UK.

Refuse/Resist, Roadrunner RR 2377-8 (1994) (12" purple vinyl). Refuse/Resist / Inhuman Nature / Propaganda. Chart position: 51 UK.

Slave New World, Roadrunner RR 2374-8 (1994). Slave New World / Crucificados Pelo System / Drug Me / Orgasmatron (Live).

Slave New World, Roadrunner RR 2374-2 (1994). Slave New World / Desperate Cry. Chart position: 46 UK.

ROOTS, Roadrunner RR 8900-2 (1995). Roots Bloody Roots / Attitude / Cut-Throat / Ratamahatta / Breed Apart / Straightate / Spit / Lookaway / Dusted / Born Stubborn / Jasco / Itsari / Ambush / Endangered Species / Dictatorshit / Chaos B.C. / Symptom Of The Universe / Kaiowas (Live). Chart positions: 4 UK, 8 NEW ZEALAND, 27 USA.

Ratamahatta, Roadrunner RR 2314-2 (1996). Ratamahatta / War / Slave New World (Live) / Amen—Inner Self (Live).

Roots Bloody Roots, Roadrunner RR 2320-5 (1996). Roots Bloody Roots / Propaganda (Live) / Beneath The Remains (Live) / Escape To The Void (Live).

Roots Bloody Roots, Roadrunner RR 2320-2 (1996). Roots Bloody Roots / Procreation (Of The Wicked) / Refuse—Resist (Live) / Territory (Live).

Ratamahatta, Roadrunner RR 2314-7 (1996). Ratamahatta / Mass Hypnosis (Live). Chart position: 23 UK.

Ratamahatta, Roadrunner (1996). Ratamahatta / War / Roots Bloody Roots (Demo) / Dusted (Demo).

Roots Bloody Roots, Roadrunner RR 2320-7 (1996). Roots Bloody Roots / Symptom Of The Universe. Chart position: 19 UK.

Attitude, Roadrunner RR 2299-7 (1996). Attitude / Dead Embryonic Cells. Chart position: 46 UK.

Attitude, Roadrunner RR 2299-5 (1996). Attitude / Kaiowas (Tribal Jam) / Clenched Fist (Live) / Boitech Is Godzilla (Live).

Attitude, Roadrunner RR 2299-2 (1996). Attitude / Lookaway (Master Vibe mix) / Mine.

BLOOD ROOTED, Roadrunner RRCY-1060 (1997) (Japanese release). Procreation (Of The Wicket) / Policia / Inhuman Nature / War / Crucificados Pelo Sistema / Symptom Of The Universe / Mine / Lookaway (Master Vibe Mix) / Dusted (Demo Version) / Roots Bloody Roots (Demo Version) / Drug Me / Refuse/Resist (Live) / Slave New World (Live) / Propaganda (Live) / Beneath The Remains/Escape To The Void (Live) / Kaiowas (Live) / Clenched Fist (Live) / Biotech Godzilla (Live).

BLOOD ROOTED, Roadrunner RR 8821-2 (1997). Procreation (Of The Wicked) / Inhuman Nature / Policia / War / Crucificados Pelo Sistema / Symptom Of The Universe / Mine / Lookaway (Master Vibe Mix) / Dusted (Demo version / Roots Bloody Roots (Demo version) / Drug Me / Refuse-Resist (Live) / Slave New World (Live) / Propaganda (Live) / Beneath The Remains—Escape To The Void (Live) / Kaiowas (Live) / Clenched Fist (Live) / Biotech Is Godzilla (Live).

Choke, Roadrunner RR22193 (1998). Choke.

Single Inedito, Roadrunner TRIP#64 (1998) (Brazilian promotional CD single). Choke / Interview / History.

AGAINST, Roadrunner RR 87002 (1998). Boycott / Choke / Old Earth / Floaters In Mud / Boycott / Rumors / Tribus / Common Bonds / F.O.E. / Rezu / Kamaitachi / Unconscious / Drowned Out / Hatred Aside / T3rcrmillenium. Chart positions: 23 GERMANY, 33 SWEDEN, 33 FRANCE, 40 UK, 44 NEW ZEALAND.

Tribus EP, Roadrunner (1999) (Australian release). Waste / Tribus (Demo) / Common Bonds (Alternate mix) / Unconscious (Demo version) / F.O.E. (Extended mix) / Prenuncio.

Against, Roadrunner RR21623 (1999). Against.

NATION, Roadrunner RRPROMO585 (2001) (USA promotional CD). Sepulnation / Border Wars / Revolt / One Man Army / Vox Populi / The Ways Of Faith / Uma Cura / Who Must Die? / Saga / Tribe To A Nation / Politricks / Human Cause / Reject / Water / Valtio.

NATION, Roadrunner RR 8560-2 (2001). Sepulnation / Revolt / Border Wars / One Man Army / Vox Populi / The Ways Of Faith / Uma Cura / Who Must Die / Saga / Tribe To A Nation / Politricks / Human Cause / Reject / Water / Valtio. Chart positions: 28 GERMANY, 91 FRANCE.

Revolusongs EP, Victor VICP-62084 (2002) (Japanese release CD EP). Messiah / Angel / Black Steel In The Hour Of Chaos / Mongoloid / Mountain Son / Bullet The Blue Sky / Piranha / Enter Sandman / Fight Fire With Fire.

UNDER A PALE GREY SKY, Roadrunner RR8436-2 (2002). Itsari / Roots Bloody Roots / Spit / Territory / Breed Apart / Attitude / Cut-Throat / Troops Of Doom / Beneath The Remains-Mass Hypnosis / Born Stubborn / Desperate Cry / Necromancer / Dusted / Endangered Species / We Who Are Not As Others / Straightate / Dictatorshit / Refuse/Resist / Arise-Dead Embryonic Cells / Slave New World / Biotech Is Godzilla / Inner Self / Policia / We Gotta Know / Kaiowas / Ratamahatta / Orgasmatron. Chart position: 52 FRANCE.

Revolusongs EP, Sepultura 828765321525 (2003). Messiah / Angel / Black Steel In The Hour Of Chaos / Mongoloid / Mountain Song / Bullet The Blue Sky / Piranha.

REVOLUSONGS, JVC Victor VICP-62084 (2003) (Japanese release). Messiah / Angel / Black Steel In The Hour Of Chaos / Mongoloid / Mountain Song / Bullet The Blue Sky / Piranha / Enter Sandman / Fight Fire With Fire.

ROORBACK, Steamhammer SPV 092-74830 (2003). Come Back Alive / Godless / Apes Of God / Corrupted / The Rift / Leech / More Of The Same / Activist / As It Is / Urge / Bottomed Out / Mindwar. Chart positions: 46 GERMANY, 69 SWITZERLAND, 77 FRANCE.

ROOTS: 25TH ANNIVERSARY EDITION, Roadrunner RR 8154-5 (2005). Roots Bloody Roots / Attitude / Cut-Throat / Ratamahatta / Breed Apart / Straightate / Spit / Lookaway / Dusted / Born Stubborn / Jasco / Itsari / Ambush / Endangered Species / Dictatorshit / Chaos B.C. / Procreation (Of The Wicked) / Mine / War / Lookaway (Master Vibe Mix) / Mine (Andy Wallace Mix) / Dusted (Demo) / Roots Bloody Roots (Demo) / R.D.P. (Demo) / Untitled (Demo) / Attitude (Live) / Roots Bloody Roots (Megawatt Mix 1) / Roots Bloody Roots (Megawatt Mix 2).

LIVE IN SÃO PAULO, Steamhammer 087-99522 (2005). Intro / Apes Of God / Slave New World / Propaganda / Attitude / Choke / Innerself / Beneath The Remains / Escape To The Void / Mindwar / Troops Of Doom / Necromancer / Sepulnation / Refuse / Resist / Territory / Black Steel In The Hour Of Chaos / Bullet The Blue Sky / Reza / Biotech Is Godzilla / Arise / Dead Embryonic Cells / Come Back Alive / Roots Bloody Roots.

Convicted In Life, SPV SPV80001008 (2006) (Promo sampler CD featuring SEPULTURA, MOONSPELL and BEYOND FEAR). Convicted In Life (SEPULTURA) / Finisterra (MOONSPELL) / And . . . You Will Die (BEYOND FEAR).

DANTE XXI, Steamhammer SPV 99812 CD (2006). Dark Wood Of Error / Convicted In Life / City Of Dis / False / Fighting On / Ostia / Buried Words / Nuclear Seven / Repeating The Horror / Crown And Mitre / Still Flame. Chart position: 64 GERMANY.

SERAPH

AUSTRIA / GERMANY — *Christian Kalns (vocals), Manuel Ehrlich (guitar), Wolfgang Juratsch-Huber (bass), Hannes Vordemayer (drums).*

A joint Austrian / German Thrash Metal band, hailing from Salzburg and the Bavarian Freilassing, formulated in August of 1996 with an initial line-up of ex-DYING ANGEL vocalist Christian Kalns, former DECORUM guitarist Michael Kainberger, bassist Dietmar Matzek, guitarist Andreas Haas and drummer Hannes Vordemayer. In September of the same year Matzek quit and was replaced by Manuel Inhester. Haas decamped the following year but SERAPH would perform their first live gig in March of 1997.

The band launched a debut album 'Strong Impressions' in 1999 and garnered a valuable support slot to SOULFLY. In January of 2002 SERAPH also opened up for the mighty 'Thrash 'Til Death' SODOM, KREATOR and DESTRUCTION tour. Michael Kainberger and Manuel Inhester exited in May 2004. The band subsequently inducted ex-LACRIMAS PROFUNDERE guitarist Manuel Ehrlich and bassist Wolfgang Juratsch-Huber.

STRONG IMPRESSIONS, (1999). Tragedy / Atomic War / T.V. Guy / Crusades / Big Mistake / Strong Impressions / Darkened Moon / Useless / Final Torture.

HATECRUSHER, (2003). Hatecrusher / Doomed / Under Control / Depressions / Nightmares / Silent Tears / Obsession / Everlasting Hate / Work Under Pressure / Hell On Earth.

SERMON

MOSCOW, RUSSIA — *Pavel Suslov (vocals / guitar), Serge Smagin (guitar), Vasili Rumjantsev (bass), Dmitri Osipov (drums).*

Moscow Death / Thrash Metal band SERMON was established by guitarist/vocalist Pavel Suslov under the name SS-20 in the Autumn of 1990. Formative demos recorded between 1991 to 1994 included the sessions 'Infernal Life' and 'Preacher Of Death'. During 1994 Suslov assembled an all new membership, also using this opportunity to retitle the band SERMON. In this new guise the band cut the demo 'Through Eternity' in the spring of 1996. The underground US label Wild Rags released the album 'From Death To Death' in 1998, SERMON following this with 'Frustration' in the Spring of 1999. This ten track outing featured three re-recorded demo tracks from 'Through Eternity' plus an unexpected cover version of SMOKIE's Pop hit 'What Can I Do'. In 2003 band signed with Soyuz Music.

FROM DEATH TO DEATH, Wild Rags WRR 112 (1998). I Want To Reach The Dawn / Another's Spring (Kills Me) / Forever Lost / Eternal Progress / Sad Clown / Crying Skies / I'm Terrified / No Place / The Beginning Of The Day / Zatmenie.

HYPERTONIA, (1999). Into Another World (Intro) / Take Me With You / In The Name Of Daughter / Amid Three Coffins / Life Is Hell / Temptation / Pray / Hypertonia / I'm Alone / What Can I Do.

FRUSTRATION, Soyuz SM 738-03 (2003). Frustration / After Me / Scorn / 2 Souls / That Is All / Where The Earth Blooms / Only Winter / Give Me Your Soul / My Cross / Wherever I May Roam.

SERPENT MOVES

GERMANY — *Carsten Frank (vocals / guitar), Sebastian Schmidt (vocals / guitar), Dirk Zelmer (vocals / bass), Arnd Riebe (drums).*

Founded as in Hannover as ATMOSFEAR during 1996 this act blend both Power and Death Metal. The rhythm section of bassist Dirk Zelmer and drummer Arnd Riebe had been prior members of INFERNAL ROW whilst frontman Carsten Frank had held down terms with both OBLIVIAN and SCAVANGER.

Evolving into SERPENT MOVES in 1999 the group inducted former WINTERDOME keyboard player Sebastian Schmidt toward the close of that year. In late 1999 Frank, Zelmer and Riebe had forged the side project GALLOWGLASS. This band would eventually blossom into a full time band, releasing the 2000 'Kings Who Die' demo followed by an album deal with Limb Music Productions.

CURSE OF TIME, (1999). Eternal Reign / Bloodfall / Dance Of The Bonedragon / Ivory Tower / Curse Of Time / Never / Prologue.
ORGANIC MACHINE, (2001).

SERPENT OBSCENE

SWEDEN — *Erik Tormentor (vocals), Nicklas Eriksson (guitar), Johan Thorngren (guitar), Jonas Eriksson (drums).*

Thrash edged Death Metal convened during 1997, SERPENT OBSCENE released their inaugural demo 'Behold The Beginning' that same year. Vocalist Erik Tormentor is an ex-MARBLE ICON member. SERPENT OBSCENE guitarists Nicklas Eriksson and Johan Thorngren are former members of A MIND CONFUSED. The pair would create a side act KAAMOS in mid 1998. Although Eriksson still operates with KAAMOS Thorngren left their ranks in 1999.

SERPENT OBSCENE's 1999 'Massacre' demo secured an album deal with the Necropolis label. Following issue of the debut album Jonas Eriksson exited in March of 2001. He would be superseded by KAAMOS man Christofer Barkensjö as the band undertook gigs in Germany.

SERPENT OBSCENE, Necropolis (2000). Devastation / Serpent Prophecy / Sadistic Abuse / Rapid Fire / Pestilent Seed (The Plague) / Evil Rites / Morbid Horror / Violent Torture / Act Of Aggression.
DEVASTATION, Sound Pollution (2003). The Rotten / Chaos Reign Supreme / Beyond Recognition / Torture Slave / Terror From The Sky / Legacy Of The Wicked / Face The Inferno / Under Siege / War Is On / Perversion Prevails.

SERPENTOR

OESTE, ARGENTINA — *Emanuel Lescano (vocals), Ramon Lopez (guitar), Jorge Moreno (guitar), Pablo Lezcano (bass), Sergio Gomes (drums).*

Oeste, Buenos Aires Thrash act SERPENTOR was created during 1998 by a trio of erstwhile SANGRE INDIA members singer Guillermo Romero plus guitarists Jorge Moreno and Jorge Alcaraz alongside a new rhythm section of Pablo Lezcando on bass and former METALEPSIA drummer Sergio Gomez. This combo set out on the live trail in early 1999, including shows in Asunción, Paraguay.

The self-funded 'Serpentor' album was recorded at Kirkincho Studios in 2001. Subsequent live work included a support to Australia's MORTIFICATION. That December Jorge Alcaraz was replaced by ex-KAUSTOS guitarist Ramon Lopez. Extensive stage work ensued, covering Argentina with gigs across Cañuelas, Monte Grande, Brezategui, Quilmes, Avellaneda, Temperley and Wilde. Back in the studio, SERPENTOR cut a version of 'Battery' for a 4G METALLICA tribute set 'Tributo Argentino A Metallica'.

4G Records re-issued the debut in 2003, adding a bonus track 'Alcoholemia'. 4G also released the follow up 'Poseido' in May 2004. This album closed with a Spanish language version of SLAYER's 'Raining Blood' re-branded 'Lloviendo Sangre'. Studio guests included Walter Meza of HORCAS and Tito Garcia from LETHAL.

SERPENTOR contributed their rendition of 'Hanger 18' to a MEGADETH tribute album 'Hangar Of Souls' released by 2M Producciones. The band, now with Emanuel Lescano on vocals, also included their rendition of 'Blood Red' on the June 2006 Hurling Metal Records SLAYER tribute album "Al Sur Del Abismo (Tributo Argentino A Slayer)'. Jorge Alcaraz also returned to the ranks.

SERPENTOR, Serpentor (2001). Militares Criminales / Tierra Sucia / Vomitando Odio / El Juicio Final / Justicia / Eterna Oscuridad / Te Arrepentiras / Condenado Al Infierno / En La Mira / Resignado / Angeles De La Oscuridad / Maldito Punga.
POSEIDO, 4G (2004). Asesino / Sindrome / Mirar Sin Ver / Demonios Al Acecho / Corrupción SA / Degeneración / Serpientes / Violentando El Futuro / Poseído / Nunca Estaras Solo (J.D.A.) / No Me Prediques / Sueño Letal / Lloviendo Sangre.

SEVENTH ANGEL

UK — *Ian Arkley (vocals / guitar), Scott Rawson (guitar), Simon Bibby (bass), Mark Ruff (drums).*

A West Midlands Christian Thrash band, SEVENTH ANGEL's opening demo was recorded in one rehearsal session for the princely sum of 26 pounds. A three track, self-titled effort was followed by 'Heed The Warning', recorded by Paul Hodson of HARD RAIN repute in White Rabbit Studios, Bridgenorth during March 1990. The group would release two highly regarded albums, 'The Torment' in 1990, recorded once again by Paul Hodson at Mad Hat Studios in Wolverhampton, and 'Lament For The Weary' in 1992, recorded at ICC Studios in Eastbourne with producer Roy Rowland, through Music For Nations' Thrash label Under One Flag. Both albums came clad in distinctive Rodney Matthews artwork. Live work included tours of Germany and Holland during 1991 and 1992, line-up changes seeing bassist Simon Bibby superseded by Nic White and ex-DETRITUS frontman Mark Broomhead. SEVENTH ANGEL's final performance would be held in Utrecht, Holland on 12th December 1992. Frontman Ian Arkley created ASHEN MORTALITY in 1993 to release further album product.

Bassist Simon Bibby and Mark Broomhead founded LOVE LIES BLEEDING. With the addition of drummer Adam Gallagher and keyboard player Scott James this band duly evolved into FIRE FLY issuing a 1999 EP 'Swings & Roundabouts'. A 2005 release, 'Heed The Warning' through Bombworks Records, compiled early demo tracks and live recordings from the 'Greenbelt' festival in August 1992 and the November 1992 'Crushing Hell' fest in Holland.

In early 2005 it was learned Ian Arkley had initiated a side project entitled CENTURY SLEEPER in union with James Allin of VISIONAIRE. That same year Arkley assembled a further endeavour, MY SILENT WAKE being forged that May alongside former ASHEN MORTALITY guitarist / bassist Andi Lee, guitarist Alan Southorn of THE OTHER WINDOW and BLOODWORK's Jasen Whyte on drums. The new band recorded a two track demo, comprising songs originally projected for ASHEN MORTALITY, at Kewsound Studios in Kewstoke during June.

THE TORMENT, Under One Flag FLAG51 (1990). Tormented Forever / The Charmer / Forbidden Desires / I Of The Needle / Expletive Deleted / Dr. Hatchet / Locked Up In Chains / Acoustic Interlude / Katie / Epilogue.

LAMENT FOR THE WEARY, Under One Flag FLAG 55 (1992). Recollections Of A Life Once Lived / Life In All It's Emptiness / No Longer A Child / Full Of Blackness / Lament For The Weary / Woken By Silence / Falling Away From Reality / Dark Shadows / Passing Of Years / Secure In Eternity / Farewell To Human Cries.

HEED THE WARNING, Bombworks BWR0501 (2005). Forbidden Desires / Seven Angels / I Of The Needle / Heed The Warning / Tormented Forever / Seven Angels / Dark Shadows / Dr. Hatchet / Woken By Silence / Life In all Its Emptiness / Katie / No Longer A Child.

SHADOW OF SADNESS

ITAPEMA, SC, BRAZIL — *Alex Sandro Gorni (vocals), Rafael Schirrmann (guitar), Christian Avon Jr. (guitar), Antonio A. Neto (bass), Adaércio C. Cividini (drums).*

SHADOW OF SADNESS, a Thrash—Power act hailing from Itapema, Santa Catarina, came together in 1996 from an idea by drummer Christian Avon Jr. Switching over to guitar, Avon Jr. brought in Adaércio C. Cividini to man the drums as the band was completed by singer Alex Sandro Gorni, second guitarist Fabrício and bassist Antonio A. Neto. However, in 1999 Rafael Schirrmann of KRATERA usurped the second guitar spot. Initially the band was entitled SLOW DEATH but took on the title SHADOW OF SADNESS during 2000.

Following recording of the debut, eponymous album vocalist Alex Sandro Gorni and bassist Antonio A. Neto decamped during 2004, leaving guitarist Christian Avon Jr. to assume the lead vocal role.

SHADOW OF SADNESS, Shadow of Sadness (2004). Make A Question / Mercy Is Your Desire / All And Nothing / Smashed By Jupiter / Nightmare / The Master Of The Truth / Evil Inside Me / The I That Should Not Be / Old Man / Shock Wave / My Best Enemy / Way To Hell.

SHAH

MOSCOW, RUSSIA — *Antonio Garcia (vocals / guitar), Anatoly Krupnov (bass), Andrei Sazenov (drums).*

SHAH was probably the toughest sounding act post perestroika that were granted a Western release. Hailing from Moscow and created during 1985, SHAH debuted with a 1988 cassette album titled 'Escape From Reason'. The group emerged as a trio spearheaded by the Spanish born brothers guitarist Antonio 'The Almighty' Garcia, bassist / vocalist Michael 'Miguel' Zemchuzniy along with drummer Andrey 'Drumanoid' Sazonov. Upon completion of the 'Escape From Reason' demo Zemchuzniy exited, leaving Garcia to take over lead vocal responsibilities. SHAH went through a succession of bassists including Vasily Molchanov and Andrey Girnik, the latter going on to join HEAVY DAY. Finally Anatoly Krupnov of BLACK OBELISK repute filled the vacancy.

SHAH undertook a tour of Hungary after which they would record their 1989 debut 'Beware' album. Produced by KRUIZ guitarist Valery Gaina this outing would find a Western release in Germany through Atom H records. Anatoly Krupnov, going on to rejoin BLACK OBELISK, was superseded by Alexey Ovchinnikova. In this incarnation SHAH issued the 1991 'Terror Collection' album, a compilation of archive tracks alongside new numbers. Bringing in erstwhile MAFIA man Dmitry Saar on second guitar SHAH set about concert dates. Further recordings released in Russia included 'P.S.I.H.O.' in 1994. In 1996 Antonio Garcia manifested the Industrial styled solo project DESCENT for the album 'Inclination'.

Sadly Krupnov died of a heart attack in 1997.

BEWARE, Atom H (1989). Total Devastation / Beware / Coward / Bloodbrothers / Save The Human Race / Age Of Dismay / Threshold Of Paion / Say 'Hi' To Anthrax.

TERROR COLLECTION, SNC (1991). Killing Machine / Overload / Damned Sinner / Age Of Darkness / Thrashing Metal Race / Terror Collection / Masdon Must Die / Mad Future / Ashes To Ashes / Metal Fight.

ESCAPE FROM MINDS, Moroz (1994). Escape / No Return / Outside / Under Grief / From Out Of Insane / Last In The Night / Reason X / Escape From Mind.

SHARKRAGE

GERMANY — *Richard Meier (vocals), René Tornier (guitar), Gerrit Staps (guitar), Thomas Junk (bass), Kai Bergbolt (drums).*

SHARKRAGE of Mainz tread the boundaries between Thrash and Power Metal. The band, founded during 1995, is centred upon former RACES lead vocalist Richie Meier and guitarist Rene Tornier. SHARKRAGE made their entrance with the December 1995 promotional cassette 'Surgeon Of Sorcery' which found Meier and Tornier joined by guitarist Klaus Erpenbach, bassist Jens Wagner and drummer Peter Roth.

SHARKRAGE would switch drummers to Martin Angres in 1996 upfront of undertaking their debut gig in Offenbach alongside FRACTURE. Before the year was out the group had issued the first album 'Moonlandscape' but had lost the services of Erpenbach. In 1997 keyboard player Christine Schulte augmented the SHARKRAGE sound for the sophomore 'Dreamland Area 51' mini album. Schulte would then decamp to Black Metal band AGATHODAIMON. A further shuffle would see Angres making way in favour of Andreas Schmitt.

The third album 'Bloody Vengeance' saw release in 2000. In 2001 SHARKRAGE's longstanding bassist Jens Wagner bowed out. His place would Thomas Junk. The drum position would find Marian Kovacik holding down the position for a brief spell before he was usurped by Kai Bergbolt. Guitarist Gerrit Staps exited in December of 2002. Sadly drummer Kai Bergbolt was killed in a road accident in January of 2003.

MOONLANDSCAPE, (1996). Moonlandscape / Secret Of Silence / Lucifer / Atheist / The Jaws / Jaws Part II.

Dreamland Area 51 EP, Sharkrage BAZE SR 1197 (1997). Who Are You / Magic Word / Dreamland Area 51 / Cold As Ice / In My Dreams.

BLOODY VENGEANCE, (2000). Seventh Sign / Devil's Son / Bloody Vengeance / Seed Of Aggression / Welcome To Death / Atheist / Under The Blade / In The Name Of JC / Forgotten Time / Moonlandscape.

SHEER TERROR

NY, USA — *Paul Bearer (vocals), Alan Blake (guitar), Mark Neuman (bass), Jason Martin (drums).*

Infamous Thrashcore with strong Punk persuasions. SHEER TERROR weighed in with two cassette albums 'No Grounds For Pity' in 1986 and 'Fall From Grace' during 1987. Guitarist Alan Blake decamped in 1990, allegedly because of SHEER TERROR's cover version of a song by THE CURE! He would found DARKSIDE in 1992. DARKSIDE would subsequently re-record some SHEER TERROR material.

The 1995 album 'Love Songs For The Unloved' was co-produced by Tommy Victor of PRONG.

Former vocalist / bassist Barron Joseph Misuraca founded DESECRATOR then vampire rock act VASARIA during 1997 in collusion with GENITORTURERS guitarist Chuck Lenihan. Frontman Paul Bearer would guest on the 1999 25 TA LIFE album 'Triple Crown'. During 2000 Bearer was fronting a new act JOE COFFEE.

SHEER TERROR reformed in 2004, putting in a brace of reunion gigs at New York's infamous CBGB's club in October. The band at this juncture comprised singer Paul Bearer, guitarist Mark Neuman, bassist Chickie and drummer Pat.

JUST CAN'T HATE ENOUGH, Starving Missile (1989). Hear To Stay (F.Y.A.) / Twisting And Turning / Ashes, Ashes / Cup 'O Joe / Ready To Halt / Just Can't Hate Enough / Roses / Owe You Nothing / Walls / Only 13 / Burning Time.

BULLDOG EDITION, Blackout BLK47 (2000). Here To Stay / Twisting And Turning / Ashes, Ashes / Cup O' Joe / Just Can't Hate / Roses / Owe You Nothing / Ready To Halt / Walls / Only Thirteen / Burning Time / I, Spoiler (Live) / Just Can't Hate Enough (Live) / Boys Don't Cry (Live) / I Need Lunch / Walls / Broken / Everything's Fine / Goodbye, Farewell / I Still Miss Someone / Three Year Bitch / Time Don't Heal A Thing / Yesterday's Sweetheart / Don't Hate Me 'Cause I'm Beautiful / Spoiler / Close My Eyes / Lulu Roman / Hymn 43 / Bulldog / Howard Unruh / Not Giving Up / Into My Life / Everything And Nothing / Fashion Fighter / Smile, For A Price / Rome Song / Obsoletion / You Can't Put Your Arms Around A Memory / Said And Done.

SHUBEND

SWEDEN — *Niclas Frohagen (vocals), Dan Lundberg (guitar / bass), Martin Eriksson (drums).*

SHUBEND was originally manifested a solo undertaking of Gothenburg's Dan Lundberg in July of 1998. Prior to signing the British Rage Of Achilles label for the 2002 album 'Synergism' SHUBEND released the demos 'Hook, Line And Sinker' in 1999, Lundberg working with singer Niclas Frohagen of DOLEFUL SHADE, FOREST OF SHADOWS and NINGIZZIA, and 'Singularis' during 2000. This second session saw the introduction of FOREST OF SHADOWS bassist Martin Petersson and drummer Martin Eriksson. The group incorporated second guitarist Fredrik Linfjärd in 2001. However both Petersson and Linfjärd were out of the picture by December of 2002 as SHUBEND became purely a studio project of Martin Eriksson and Dan Lundberg. Meantime Linfjärd would join STABWOUND.

SHUBEND evolved into GENESIS OF PAIN.

SYNERGISM, Rage Of Achilles ILIAD023 (2002). Theoretic Vanity / Sacrifice / Shattered Mask / Individuality / Victim / D.C. / Endless Recursion / Masquerade / Life Painted Dead / Black Void / Divine Tautology.

SIEGES EVEN

MUNICH, GERMANY — *Greg Keller (vocals), Wolfgang Zenk (guitar), Oli Holzwarth (bass), Börk Keller (keyboards), Alexendar Holzwarth (drums).*

A Progressive, Thrash inclined Metal band from Munich, SIEGES EVEN's first trio of albums were recorded with Marcus Steffen on guitar. However, having left the group in 1992 he was replaced by Wolfgang Zenk. The first two albums ('Life Cycle' and 'Steps') also featured the vocal work of Franz Herde, but 'Sense Of Change' witnessed the recruitment of Jogie Kaiser.

Oddly, Kaiser opted to pursue a career in musicals and left the group after recording the album, SIEGES EVEN eventually replacing him with Greg Keller. This was a man who had previously recorded with METRICAL CHARM, a quite well known band on the German underground Metal scene at the time.

Following Greg's relocation from Cologne to Munich SIEGES EVEN set to work on the new album 'Sophisticated', produced by noted Metal knob twiddler Charlie Bauerfiend (the man having also produced the two previous band efforts). During 1996 SIEGES EVEN was augmented with the arrival of Greg's brother Börk Keller on keyboards. Börk had also been a member of METRICAL CHARM.

Drummer Alex Holzwarth joined Italian Symphonic Metal act RHAPSODY. Bassist Oliver Holsworth joined BLIND GUARDIAN and toured with the DEMONS & WIZARDS project band.

The Holzwarth brothers united in 2000 with guitarist Markus Steffan to found LOOKING GLASS SELF. Initially this venture employed Jens Johansson of STRATOVARIUS on keyboards and ANGRA singer Andre Matos for a demo 'Equinox' although the Brazilian later bowed out. They would also session on the reformation album by PARADOX 'Collision Course' the same year. SIEGES EVEN reunited during late 2003, scheduling a co-headline spot at the April 2004 Headway Festival in Amstelveen, Holland. This event was to be recorded for a live album. A new studio album, 'The Art Of Navigating By The Stars' ambitiously comprising just one song split into several movements, was projected for 2004. The record, cut at Black Solaris Studio in Frankfurt with producer Uwe Lulis, was finished up in June 2005 for Inside Out Music.

In side activity, SIEGES EVEN bassist Oli Holzwarth joined COLDSEED, the Industrial Metal project of BLIND GUARDIAN and SAVAGE CIRCUS drummer Thomen Stauch, SOILWORK frontman Björn Strid and guitarists Thorsten Praest and Gonzalo Alfageme Lopez.

Touring for SIEGES EVEN included dates in Russia plus a European co-headlining tour in January 2006 alongside DEAD SOUL TRIBE.

LIFE CYCLE, Steamhammer 08 7558 (1988). Las Palabras Secreto De Libertad (Repression And Resistance) / Life Cycle / Apocalyptic Disposition / The Roads To Illiad / David / Straggler From Atlantis / Arcane.

STEPS, Steamhammer 084 76212 (1991). Tangerine Windows Of Solace: I) Alba, II) Epitome, III) Apotheosis, iIV) Seasons Of Seclusion (The Prison), V) An Essay Of Relief (A Tangerine Dream), VI) Disintegration Of Lasting Hope, VII) Elegy (Window Of Perception) / Steps / Corridors / The Vacuum Tube Processor / An Act Of Acquiescence / Anthem Chapter I / Anthem Chapter II.

A SENSE OF CHANGE, Steamhammer 084 76212 (1995). Prelude: Ode To Sisyphus / The Waking Hours / Behind Closed Doors / Change Of Seasons / Dimensions / Prime / Epigram For The Last Straw / These Empty Places.

SOPHISTICATED, Under Siege Semaphore CD 32683 (1995). Reporter / Trouble Talker / Middle Course / Sophisticated / Dreamer / As The World Moves On / Wintertime / Water The Barren Tree / War / Fatal / The More The Less.

UNEVEN, Semaphore 37746-422 (1997). Disrespectfully Yours / What If? / Trainsong / Rise And Shine / Scratches In The Rind / Different Pace / What's Up God? / Love Is As Warm As Tears.

THE ART OF NAVIGATING BY THE STARS, Inside Out Music (2005). Intro: Navigating By The Stars / Sequence 1: The Weight / Sequence 2: The Lonely Views Of Condors / Sequence 3: Unbreakable / Sequence 4: Stigmata / Sequence 5: Blue Wide Open / Sequence 6: To The Ones Who Have Failed / Sequence 7: Lighthouse / Sequence 8: Styx.

SILENCER

DENVER, CO, USA — *Keith Spargo (vocals / guitar), Dan Lynn (guitar), Jeff Alexis (bass), Brian Kotal (drums).*

Denver Power Thrash act SILENCER, founded in 1998 by ex-PARAGON frontman Keith Spargo, have made a major impact in a relatively short span of time. The group's rhythm section comprises of ex-PSYCHOTIC INSIGHT bassist Jeff Alexis and former DRUDGERY and BLYND JUSTICE drummer Nick Seelinger. During the band's formative months SILENCER operated with stand in bassists in the form of Chris Marye of the SLEWHOUNDS and Dale Storm from BLEEDING FAITH. The group delivered their opening shot, the 'Kozmos' mini album, upfront of a split live affair shared with SERBERUS. These recordings would include a version of IRON MAIDEN's 'Wrathchild' with a guesting Harry Conklin of JAG PANZER on vocals.

The band would contribute a version of BLACK SABBATH's 'Into The Void' to the WWIII tribute album 'Hail To The Stonehenge Gods'.

In December of 2001 guitarist Mat Bollen decamped. The band responded by adding second guitarist Ritchie Wilkinson, a veteran of DROP DEAD and international acts ANGEL DUST and DEMONS & WIZARDS.

Upon completion of SILENCER's Spring 2002 dates both Wilkinson and Seelinger would journey to Europe for tour work with ANGEL DUST. SILENCER returned in late October with a five track EP entitled 'Structures'. Ritchie Wilkinson left SILENCER during late October, the band pulling in EMBER's Dan Lynn to fulfill gigs at short notice. 2003 brought yet more changes as the band severed ties with drummer Nick

Seelinger, replacing him for a two week run of live dates with Ryan Ramirez of TRENCHMOUTH. This new incarnation of the band signed to the Italian Adrenaline label for a Europe only release entitled 'Found On The Sun', this set comprising the full 'Structures' EP, selected album tracks plus a brand new track 'Apollocide' debuting Dan Lynn on guitar. Brian Kotal, previously of ONE DYING WISH, stepped in as permanent drummer in October. SILENCER scheduled recording of a brand new album to commence August of 2004, tracking drums at Flatline Audio whilst cutting the remainder of instrumentation at Valkyrie Studios. Dan Lynn deputised for Death Metal act THROCULT for live work in early 2005.

SILENCER announced their new singer in July as being Chad Armstrong, previously with local acts FOMOFUIAB and ASSISTED SUICIDE ASSEMBLY. That September it was revealed the group had signed to Belgian label Mausoleum Records, kicking off this deal with the album 'Death Of Awe' in January 2006. Another new band member, bassist Brandon West was inducted in November as the group entered Firestorm Studios to cut new album tracks. West performed his final show with SILENCER on January 19th 2007.

KOZMOS, (2001). Mourning Star / Kozmos / Easter Island / Missing Hope / Industrial Command.

BLACK FLAMES AND BURNING WORLDS, Crash Inc. (2001) (Split album with SERBERUS). Intro: Easter Island / The Error Of Your Ways / Industrial Command / Missing Hope / Descending The Ziggurat / Cold War / Wrathchild.

Structures EP, (2002). Black Hole Engine [Markarian 573] / The Bruising Feast / Structures / This Mythic Image / Megalith.

DEATH OF AWE, Mausoleum 251071 (2006). Earth Rule Murder / Mnemodrone / Transport / Signal To Noise / Redshift / Twilight / Antitwilight / Fracture / The Death Of Awe / The Harvest / Aeonic.

SILENT SCYTHE

SWEDEN — *Fredrik Eriksson (vocals), Tommi Djukin (vocals / guitar), Peter Henningsson (guitar), Peter Ogestad (bass), Johan Strende (drums).*

SILENT SCYTHE, initiated by former CARNAL LUST and BRIMSTONE vocalist / guitarist Tommi Djukin in October of 1999, put out the 2002 demo 'Death Is Coming' as their opening shot. The band would feature IMPALE, LEGION and PLANET DEEP guitarist Peter Henningsson alongside Djukin's BRIMSTONE colleague, as well as IMPALE and SPINELESS credited, Johan Strende on the drums. Bassist Anders Prykebrant would be superseded by ex-TWILIGHT SYMPHONY man Peter Ogestad. SILENT SCYTHE debuted with a self financed album entitled 'Longing For Sorrow'.

Signing to the Dutch label New Aeon Media the band put out debut as a re-issue, re-titled as the 'Suffer In Silence' album in 2004. Although Tobbe Jansson cut the vocals for this opus, bar Death growls courtesy of Djukin, he would be replaced shortly after completion of the tracks by CRIMSON TIDE's Fredrik Eriksson.

SUFFER IN SILENCE, New Aeon Media (2004). Intro / Longing For Sorrow / Old World Disorder / My Only Family (My Only Enemy) / Backstabber / Suffer In Silence / To Each His Own / Feather.

SINDROME

HIGHLAND PARK, IL, USA — *Troy Dixler (vocals), Chris Mittelbrun (guitar), Erv Brautigam (guitar), Shaun Glass (bass), Tony Ochoa (drums).*

SINDROME was forged in 1987 by an alliance of members from name Chicago thrash acts. Guitarist Chris Mittelbrun is erstwhile DEATHSTRIKE and MASTER, both vocalist Troy 'Dickslurp' Dixker and guitarist Erv Brautigam are formerly with DEVESTATION whilst bassist Shaun Glass was with TERMINAL DEATH. Their opening product would be the demo 'Into The Hall's Of Extermination' with second session 'The Vault Of Inner Conscience' following in 1991.

The band added former LÄÄZ ROCKIT guitarist Ken Savitch in 1991. HAMMERON and BEYOND guitarist Mick Vega was inducted in 1992. Upon the band's demise bassist Shaun Glass travelled on to BROKEN HOPE the Nu-Metal band SOIL and TERMINAL DEATH. In 2004 it was learned that guitarist Chris Mittelbrun has resurfaced as "Mick Mars" in the Chicago based MÖTLEY CRÜE tribute band dubbed THE CRÜE.

Tony Ochoa surfaced again in January 2006 with SERVITUDE an Alt-Metal band featuring ex-OPEN HOLE SOUL singer TJ, ex-PLAGUE and MAYHEM bassist Ron Holstein and ex-PLAGUE guitarist Fly Affinitio. Ochoa joined New York's SPEED\KILL/HATE for touring purposes in May.

SIREN

TAMPA, FL, USA — *Doug Lee (vocals), Rob Phillips (guitar), Gregg Culbertson (bass), Brian Law (drums).*

Bay Area Thrash act founded in 1981 centred around vocalist Doug Lee who joined the following year. The 1984 self financed single sees SIREN with a line up of Lee, guitarist Ron Phillips, bassist Ben Parrish and teenage drummer Ed Aborn.

Following the single release Parrish made way for bassist Edward Amyx and recording the January 1985 four track demo tape 'Iron Coffins'. Songs include the title track, 'Over The Rainbow', 'Before The Storm' and 'Shadow Of A Future Past'.

This exposure prompted Pennsylvania based Sanaty Records to include the SIREN track 'Over The Rainbow' on their 'Start To Stardom' compilation album.

Following the debut album SIREN revamped their rhythm section adding Gregg Culbertson on bass and drummer Brian Law. Lee completely rebuilt SIREN for the second outing drafting guitarist Brian C. Hendrickson, bassist Les Talent and drummer David Smith.

Not to be confused with the other Florida SIREN based in Miami.

Metro Mercenary, Siren 001 (1984). Metro Mercenary / Terrible Swift Sword.

NO PLACE LIKE HOME, Flametrader (1986). Death / So Far To Go / Over The Rainbow / Shadows Of The Future Past / The Mine / Terrible Swift Sword / Burning Bridges / Another Lost Love / A Place In Time / Iron Coffins.

FINANCIAL SUICIDE, Aaaarrrg (1989). Kreator Of Dreams / Unsung Hero / Lines Of Steel / This Machine (Runs On Hate) / Locked And Chained / Like A Bullet / Digital Clock / Power March.

SIROCCO

LISMORE, IRELAND — *J. Tobin (guitar), John Owens (guitar), Ciaran O'Cearuill (bass), Robert Kiernan (drums).*

SIROCCO is an instrumental Celtic / Thrash Metal band founded in February 2003 and hailing from Lisemore in the south of Ireland. The group originally comprised guitarist J. Tobin, vocalist Fearghal Maher, guitarist Shane O'Brien and drummer Daniel O'Brien, this formation debuting live at the Central Bar in Cappoquin. April saw the departure of both the O'Brien's, replaced by John Owens on lead guitar and Robert Kiernan on drums. Pat O'Mahony joined the band as bass player soon afterwards. SIROCCO's opening demos were crafted at BPM Studios Douglas in Autumn 2003.

In February of 2004 Fearghal Maher parted ways with the band, citing health problems. Subsequently, Pat O'Mahony stepped down from the bass position, being substituted by Ciaran O'Cearuill.

SIROCCO projected a full length album, entitled 'Nemed: An Triu Creathan', for issue in 2005.

Exodus, Sirocco (2003). My Time / Euthanasia / Trapped / Falling To Place.

Caisleán Cré, (2005). Abyss / Christian Cry.

SITHLORD

MELBOURNE, VIC, AUSTRALIA — *Saundies (vocals / guitar), Scott McMahon (guitar), Jay Saunders (bass), Snorkelbender (drums).*

Melbourne, Victoria's SITHLORD are nothing if not original in their concept. A deliberately retro outfit combining large doses of 80s German Thrash Metal with modern Black Metal and named after a 'Star Wars' movie evil hierarchy. Founded in 1998, originally billed as ENMITY, by former CHRISTBAIT and ABRAMELIN drummer Jason 'Snorkelbender' Dutton and erstwhile RANCOR guitarist Saundies. The band, switching to the SITHLORD title after chancing upon the discovery of an already existing English Enmity, added bassist Gash who lasted for just one gig in 1999. His replacement would be Jay Saunders, also an operative member of ANATOMY and ATOMIZER.

The debut album, 'Labyrinth To The Gods', arrived through the Australian Bleed label in 1999. SITHLORD would then sign to the German Barbarian Wrath label for the follow up 'The Return Of Godless Times' set for 2002 release.

LABYRINTH TO THE GODS, Bleed BLEED 006 (1999). Intro / Labyrinth To The Gods / Disinterred Faith / Angelique / Enslaved To Hades / Outro / Dawning Of The New Millennium In Darkness.

THE RETURN OF GODLESS TIMES, Barbarian Wrath WRATH666-020 (2002).

SKANNERS

BOLZANO, ITALY — *Claudio Pisoni (vocals), Fabio Tenca (guitar), Dino Lucchi (guitar), Corrado Gasser (bass), Luigi Sandrini (drums).*

An Italian Speed Metal mob, SKANNERS from Bolzano date back to 1982 and have been known to have supported DIO, TWISTED SISTER, HELLOWEEN, MOTÖRHEAD and MANOWAR on home turf, having had the track 'Dirty Armada' featured on the 1984 compilation album 'Rock News Of Vienna'. For their opening album 'Dirty Armada' in 1986 the band stood at lead singer Claudio Pisoni, guitarists Fabio Tenca and Massimo 'Max' Quinzio, bass player Korrado Gasser and Luigi Sandrini on the drums. Guitarist Massimo Quinzio departed in early 1987 to be replaced by Dino Lucchi, and SKANNERS scored a track, 'Turn It Louder Now', on the 1988 compilation album 'Metal Shock'.

Ex-SCRATCH bassist Roberto Vajente superseded Covado Gasser in 1990. The group made a comeback with a 1995 album 'The Magic Square', Pisoni and Tenca being joined by bassist Dino Lucchi and drummer Jack Alemanno. This same quartet cut a live album in 1998. SKANNERS comprised Pisoni, guitarists Fabio Tenca and Walter Unterhauser, bass player Renato Olivari and drummer Jack Alemanno for the 2002 'Flagellus Dei' opus.

The band played at the Milan 'Play It Loud' festival in February 2007.

PICTURES OF WAR, CGD 20720 (1988). Pictures Of War / Something Very Special / Drowning Down The Drain / She's Like A Boy / Fight Back / Turn It Louder Now / We Are Night / Wild / One Night.

THE MAGIC SQUARE, Südton 95008-2 (1996). Undertaker / Beyond Death / Trimurti / Magic Square / On My Way / Without You / You Feel The Power / Insane / Metal Party / Angel / Ciara Teobaldo / True Stories.

SKANNERS LIVE, (1998). Intro / TV Shock / Clara E Teobaldo / Metal Party / Undertaker / The Dark Side / Pictures Of War / Shes Like A Boy / Everybodys Crazy / / The Magic Square / Rock Rock City / Drum solo / Phenomena / Oltrisarco In The Night / Black Eagle / Andromeda / Fight Back / Wild / The Magic Square.

FLAGELLUM DEI, Underground Symphony USCD-058 (2002). Flagellum Dei / Blood In My Eyes / Time Of War / Nightrider / Minister Of Fear / Beast Of Hell / Full Moon's Eyes / It's My Life / M.P.+.

SKITZO

USA — *Lance Ozanix (vocals / guitar), John Crowhurst (guitar), Kurt Houser (bass), Dave Ostwald (drums).*

A notorious name amongst Bay Area Thrash / Crossover circles. SKITZO are as renowned for their outrageous stage shows and publicity moves as, allegedly, having one of Thrash Metal's elite making a huge success out of one of their 1983 demo songs without giving due credit.

Frontman Lance Ozanix has proven to be the mainstay of the band which has issued a prodigious body of, mainly self financed, work. Ozanix gained fame by vomiting onto a groupie on the 'Jerry Springer' TV show, causing the Canadian authorities to ban the offending show. His exploits have also been featured on 'Ripley's Believe It Or Not'. Onstage the band employs "Puke groupies" Octavia and Sunny Delight.

Various SKITZO albums are available as limited edition mail order only porno sleeve versions. 'Got Sick' in particular sporting an alarming carnivorous vagina!

The band toured California with another infamous act THE MENTORS during 1983. However, guitarist Kenny Springer was killed the following year in an auto incident. The band persevered substituting the late Springer with a mannequin named 'Greg Stiff'. The 1997 line up, including the mannequin included bassist Sherri Stewart and percussionist Beaver Hensely.

Ozanix also doubles duties appearing as 'Ozzy Osbourne' in the BLACK SABBATH tribute bands PARANOID and SWEET LEAF, the latter in union with VICIOUS RUMORS and TESTAMENT guitarist Steve Smyth. Smyth and erstwhile FAITH NO MORE guitarist JIM MARTIN would contribute guitar to the 1999 album 'Got Sick'.

Latterly SKITZO comprises of Ozanix, Ostwald and bassist Kelly Gillis.

WRATHRAGE, Crowtown (1986).
MOSH TILL MUSH, Crowtown (1987).
DERRANGEOUS, IRS (1989).
THE SKULING, Tomakazi (1990).
HAUNTING BALLADS, Tomakazi (1991).
EVILUTION, Tomakazi (1992).
CORPSE AND GRIND, Tomakazi (1993).
SYNUS AR SUKUS, Mourningstar (1994).
PSYCHO BABBLE, Mourningstar (1996).
GOT SICK, Mourningstar (1999).
OLD SKOOL METAL, Mourningstar (2000).
HELLAVATOR MUSICK, Independent (2002). Did That Hurt? / Angels Blood / Krystal Death's Horizon / Frozen Dead / Tunnel Zone / Satans Grave / Kill W/ a Vengeance (live).

SKLEROTIKZ

THESSALONIKI, GREECE — *Sotiris Vafiadis (vocals), Marios Giannopoulos (vocals), Makis Lazaridis (lead guitar), Konstantinos Bikos (rhythm guitar), George Sbokos (bass), Sakis Vlahos (drums).*

Thessaloniki Thrashers SKLEROTIKZ was founded under the UNCANNY brand in September 2004 by singers Spyros Emanouilidis and Marios Giannopoulos, lead guitarist Makis Lazaridis, of DIHASMENES ALITHIES and SPLITDAWN, rhythm guitarist Simos Lazaridis plus drummer Sakis Vlahos from DIHASMENES ALITHIES. This formation remained stable until June 2005, when both Emanouilidis and Lazaridis opted out.

That November UNCANNY evolved into SKLEROTIKZ, inducting new personnel Sotiris Vafiadis on vocals, Konstantinos Bikos on rhythm guitar and Nick Ritsis on bass guitar. However, in February 2006 Ritsis departed, due to national military obligations, and George Sbokos took his place. SKLEROTIKZ released the demo 'Equation Of Information Theory', recorded at Rock Sound Studio, Thessaloniki with engineer Giorgos Brigos, in August 2006.

Equation Of Information Theory, Sklerotikz (2006) (Demo). Bloody Resurrection / United / Tormented Soul / The Serpent's Kiss / Our Pictures Are Fading In My Mind (Faded Memories).

SKULLKRUSHER

LAPPEENRANTA, FINLAND — *Bestial Fucker (vocals), Necromolester (guitar), Ghoul (guitar), Armageddon (guitar), Sam The Maggot (bass), Tom Angelfucker (drums).*

SKULLKRUSHER is Lappeenranta Thrash Metal band created in 1997. Although the band logo states "Skullcrusher", the printed name on demo cassettes is spelt with a 'K'. Band members comprised singer Bestial Fucker, guitarists Armageddon, Necromolester, from BLASPHEMOUS EVIL, and Ghoul, of BESTIAL DEVASTATION and HORNA, bassist (Sam) The Maggot, of PIMEYS and BESTIAL DEVASTATION, with Tom Angelfucker on drums. The impressive array of scene credentials for Armageddon (a.k.a. Lauri Penttilä, 'Nazgul von Armageddon', 'Satanic Tyrant Werwolf', 'Sexual Hammer' or 'Satanic Warmaster') includes BLASPHEMOUS EVIL, BLUTRACHE, GESTAPO 666, HORNA, INCRIMINATED, KYPRIAN'S CIRCLE, MENTAL TERROR, PEST, SHATARGAT, THE TRUE WERWOLF, VOMITFAGO and WARLOGHE plus session tenures with ARMOUR, BELAIR, KRIEG and SATANIC WARMASTER.

SKULLKRUSHER produced three demo cassettes, 'Bestial Evil' in 1999, comprising one side, "Skull", recorded live at the Monari venue and the other, "Krusher", taped at Järjestötalo, and two 2000 sessions 'Live In Lappeenranta' and 'Storming Onslaught'. The latter included a cover version of ONSLAUGHT's 'Death Metal'.

Bestial Evil, Skullkrusher (1999) (Live demo). Demon Eyes / Metal Assault / Circle Of Death / SkullKrusher / Beer & Barbarism / Satanik Possession / Demon Eyes / Burning Flesh / Metal Assault / SkullKrusher / Satanic Blood.
Live In Lappeenranta, Skullkrusher (2000) (Live demo). Demon Eyes / Metal Assault / Circle Of Death / Skullkrusher / Beer & Barbarism.
Storming Onslaught, Skullkrusher (2000) (Demo). Lords Of The Skullthrone / Satanik Possession / Storms Of Blood / Skullkrusher / Rebel Hordes / Death Metal / Rise Of The Goatlord / Out From The Crypt.

SKYCLAD

NEWCASTLE UPON TYNE, UK — *Kevin Ridley (vocals), Steve Ramsey (guitar), Georgina Biddle (violin), Graeme English (bass), Aaron Walton (drums).*

SKYCLAD was formed in 1991 by vocalist Martin Walkyier, following his break from highly successful Nottingham Thrash act SABBAT. The singer was undoubtedly the unique factor in SABBAT and with SKYCLAD he was now able to push his extraordinary talents and unique inspirations to the fore. SKYCLAD contain such diverse elements as traditional Metal riffing, electric Folk violin and the distinctive pagan lyrical stance and imagery of the man himself. SKYCLAD's individualistic stance would not only carve out a reputation for themselves but also directly inspire a whole crop of subsequent German "Mittelalter" acts.

The band, based in Newcastle upon Tyne, was forged with ex-PARIAH and SATAN guitarist Steve Ramsey, SKYCLAD's initial demo for Noise Records comprised purely Walkyier, Ramsey and a drum machine. Soon after gaining a deal former SATAN bassist Graeme English and drummer Keith Baxter were added, followed by ex-D.A.M. guitarist Dave Pugh and fiddler Fritha Jenkins.

The group's debut album, October 1991's 'Wayward Sons Of Mother Earth', illustrated Walkyier's original approach to Metal music, combining his noted lyrical twists with the classic Metal signature riffing of Ramsey. Expectation amongst the European Metal throng was high, and SKYCLAD did not disappoint. A particularly significant track was 'The Widdershins Jig', this open appreciation of traditional Folk a certain first in the realms of Metal. The Walkyier-less SABBAT quickly floundered and disintegrated whilst SKYCLAD took the SABBAT concept and took several strides forward, supplanting the occult lore of yore with pagan history, ancient British mythology woven with Walkyier's elaborate prosaic twists. The group toured Europe alongside GAMMA RAY, THUNDERHEAD, CANDLEMASS and OVERKILL.

In late 1991 Ramsey suffered a fractured skull in a fall and the band were forced to cancel a string of British dates. Second album 'Burnt Offering For The Bone Idol' was delivered in March of 1992 and, back on the road, SKYCLAD had toured the UK in February packaged with OVERKILL and LAWNMOWER DETH. June had further gigs sharing stages with PARADISE LOST. That same month SKYCLAD appeared at the 'Dynamo Open Air' festival in Eindhoven, Holland notably jamming with ex-THIN LIZZY guitarist Brian Robertson on 'Emerald'. Irish dates followed in September leading up to release of the EP 'Tracks From The Wilderness', this including live recordings from the 'Dynamo' set. The year would be rounded out by support gigs to MANOWAR in Europe in October and November then a run of UK December shows.

The band maintained momentum with June 1993's 'Jonah's Ark' album, Japanese versions adding the six songs from the 'Tracks In The Wilderness' EP. However, Fritha Jenkins had become pregnant earlier that year and had been forced to bow out. Drafting new violinist Cath Howell the group put in UK shows supported by FORGODSAKE in June. Frustratingly, although a promotional video for 'Thinking Allowed?' saw airplay, valuable support tours planned with bands such as DIO, PARADISE LOST and SEPULTURA would fall through, the band claiming lack of financial support from their record label. These frustrations unfortunately would colour the SKYCLAD history from this point onward, despite the band holding a strong bastion of support in mainland Europe, able to shift over 50,000 albums with each release.

1994 found both Martin Walkyier and Fritha Jenkins acting as guest musicians on FORGODSAKE's 'Blasthead' album. On the SKYCLAD front, the group contributed their rendition of 'Prime Evil' to the VENOM tribute album 'In the Name Of Satan'. SKYCLAD's next offering, 'Prince Of The Poverty Line', was issued in early 1994, initial limited edition copies coming with an extra track in 'Brothers Beneath The Skin'. By now the group's finances were in perilous state, as echoed by the album title, but this fiscal misfortune was suitably channeled into the band's adoption of the bedraggled troubadour look. For further live work ex-VELVET VIPER guitarist Dave Moore joined the band on a temporary basis. The year saw SKYCLAD undertaking a highly successful European tour on the back of the 'Prince Of The Poverty Line' release. The tour included dates supporting TROUBLE, their first German headliner on 4th May at the Stuttgart Röhre then opening for Swedish axe God YNGWIE MALMSTEEN prior to further shows in Germany with FREAK OF NATURE. Festival dates included 'Dynamo Open Air' and Germany's 'Wacken Open Air' events. At the conclusion of the tour violinist Cath Howells left to concentrate on studying and was replaced by Georgina Biddles. Graeme English took time out to session on BLITZKRIEG's 'Unholy Trinity' album.

Following recording of 1995's 'The Silent Whales Of The Lunar Sea', at Newcastle's Lynx Studios, SKYCLAD were beset by problems. Ramsey collapsed in the studio and had to undergo hospital treatment for a heart complaint, subsequently being fitted with a pacemaker. Later in recording, Lynx Studios was broken into and recording equipment stolen. Still, the album was eventually completed and a brand new SKYCLAD debuted in early 1995 with gigs in Greece, Georgina Biddle's live inauguration coming on 26th February at the Rodon Club in Athens.

Unfortunately the band once more hit line-up problems in

April with both Pugh and Baxter quitting. Subsequently Pugh turned up later in LOADSTONE with brother Brian on drums and bassist Trevor Beckitt. Swift replacements were found in two ex-INNER SANCTUM members guitarist Dave Ray and drummer Jed Hawkins. In this incarnation SKYCLAD toured Europe extensively which included a date at the 'Dynamo Open Air' festival in June and support gigs to BLACK SABBATH in the UK. The year ended on a high as SKYCLAD joined the December 'Blind Guardian Christmas Party' tour, headed up by BLIND GUARDIAN and also boasting LOVE/HATE, SAXON, RAGE and YNGWIE MALMSTEEN. The newest members then opted out, post SKYCLAD both Ray and Hawkins were to be found with FIFTH SEASON, Ray later founding D-VOID.

The 'Irrational Anthems' album, promoted by a video for the song 'Inequality Street', saw European release in February 1996. Highlights included a solo violin instrumental, 'The Spiral Starecase', and a radical re-work of Khachaturian's 'Sabre Dance'. German touring in May saw a union with RIOT and Thrashers WHIPLASH. SKYCLAD's second 1996 album 'Oui Avant-Garde A Chance' (pronounced "We haven't got a chance") notably featured SUBWAY TO SALLY musicians Eric Hecht on bagpipes, Frau Schmidt on violin and Bodenski, included covers of DEXY'S MIDNIGHT RUNNERS 'Come On Eileen' and NEW MODEL ARMY's 'Master Race'. Adventurous enough to even allow the band to quote the set as "experimental", 'Oui Avant-Garde A Chance' was committed to tape at Parr Street Studios in Liverpool and Jacobs Studios in Surrey. With no permanent drummer, percussion on the record was shared between Paul Kinson and Paul Smith. The project was originally planed as an acoustic EP but blossomed into a full blown album. Once complete, the band, with Paul Smith behind the drum kit, undertook headline UK shows that September. December saw SKYCLAD back on German soil with support act SUBWAY TO SALLY in tow. However, the last few dates of this trek would be cancelled when Walkyier came down with a severe throat infection.

The group, severing ties with manager Eric Cook, was back in the studio the following year to come up with the more folkified September 1997 offering 'The Answer Machine'. Newly installed on second guitar would be Kevin Ridley, known as former frontman of SCREEN IDOLS, THE SHOTGUN BRIDES and FORGODSAKE tradition as well as having a swathe of credits behind the production desk. Yasmin Krull of ATROCITY repute contributed guest vocals to 'The Thread Of Evermore'.

A traditional bout of German dates in April 1997 had support from Pennsylvania's MARAYA. That Autumn the group augmented their sound with the addition of SEVEN LITTLE SISTERS musicians Nick Acons on guitar and fiddle, John Leonard on accordion, mandolin, bagpipes, flute and keyboards plus drummer Mitch Oldham. However, this union would prove fleeting. SKYCLAD closed the year in novel style, performing acoustic sets in front of German record stores to distribute the EP 'Outrageous Fourtunes', limited to 1000 copies. These dates would be the first to see Kevin Ridley acquired as second guitarist for live work.

During 1998 both Martin Walkyier and Georgina Biddle guested on the 'Manifiesto' album from Brazilian band NEPAL. In March SKYCLAD launched into another European tour, this time taking out MINDFEED and ACROSS THE BORDER as openers. These dates saw double duty for Steve Ramsey, also acting as MINDFEED's guitarist. Once these concerts had closed the band embarked upon the first of their Irish Pub tours of Germany in April. This unique concept scored SKYCLAD favourable press, particularly in more mainstream areas of the European media. A double appearance at the 'Wacken Open Air' festival in August preceded a second round of Irish Pub dates to close the year in December.

February 1999 had SKYCLAD back to the fore with a much harder release 'Vintage Whine' as the band put in no less than five German tours during the year on top of many prestigious festival performances. April had Italian newcomers LACUNA COIL as openers. In July the band openly voiced dissatisfaction with their label Massacre Records onstage at the 'Ziegenrück Open Air' festival. An appearance at the 'Wacken Open Air' festival was blighted when Ramsey, also acting on the day as temporary guitarist for MINDFEED once again, was beaten up by over zealous backstage security suffering a bloody head injury.

The band signed to Nuclear Blast Records later that year for the 'Folkemon' album. The limited digipack versions would add a cover of TENPOLE TUDOR's 'Swords Of A Thousand Men' whilst the Japanese edition boasted the exclusive 'Locomotion' instrumental, this last cut surprisingly hosting a lead guitar solo from TYGERS OF PAN TANG man Fred Purser. Paying homage, SUIDAKRA covered 'The One Piece Puzzle' on their 2000 album 'The Arcanum'. The same year found Walkyier guesting on CRADLE OF FILTH's version of the SABBAT chestnut 'For Those Who Died'. Live action on the continent in November witnessed a brief burst of dates with Spanish act TIERRA SANTA in November.

As 2001 broke rumours spread that founder member Walkyier had quit the band. However, the band was announced as scheduled to perform at the Derby 'Bloodstock' festival during May. This show was also scheduled to feature a one off showing of RETURN TO THE SABBAT, a SABBAT reformation of sorts with Sneap's would be role being briefly filled by ex-TALION guitarist Pete Wadeson.

By April the band indeed confirmed that Walkyier had left and that 'Bloodstock' would be the farewell show. SKYCLAD themselves resolved to carry on with Ridley taking over on lead vocals. The new look band debuted with shows in Europe acting as openers to FISH.

As fans patiently waited to see just if SKYCLAD could survive without the figurehead of Walkyier it became apparent that the band had every intention of persevering. The act established their own label, Demolition Records, for release of a live album 'Another Fine Mess'. Being SKYCLAD's first official live release tracks featured material culled from the band's 1995 Dynamo festival appearance. Meantime former label Massacre Records weighed in with another collector's item—a free compilation CD entitled 'Poetic Wisdom' given free with the July issue of the Greek 'Metal Hammer' magazine.

The traditional round of touring in Germany also continued unabated although Jay Graham decamped to RETURN TO THE SABBAT and forge Black Metal combo GOAT THRONE in league with ex-IRON MONKEY and HELVIS guitarist Steve Watson and former PSYCHOWRECK, MOSH BABY and GRUMBLE GRINDER vocalist Stumpy. His swift replacement would be former AXIS and STICKY FINGERS drummer Aaron Walton.

In October SKYCLAD also launched a single version of the TENPOLE TUDOR cover 'Swords Of A Thousand Men', even roping Eddie Tenpole in as session guest. The single package would also include a freshly re-worked version of the stage favourite 'The Widdershin's Jig'.

Another SKYCLAD cover also arrived with Italian Speed Metal act ELVENKING committing 'Penny Dreadful' to their debut 'Heathenreel' album. The connection with ELVENKING was strengthened when it was announced that Walkyier would perform SKYCLAD songs live on stage with the band at the Italian 'Metal.It' festival in March 2002. Meantime, SKYCLAD themselves issued the acoustic 'No Daylights Nor Heeltaps' album. Released some two months earlier than it's May street date through the band's website copies ordered over the net came with an exclusive bonus disc featuring 'No Deposit, No Return', 'A Great Blow For A Day Job', 'No Strings Attached', 'Building A Ruin' and 'Loco-Commotion'.

SKYCLAD would be announced for an appearance at the 'Milwaukee Metalfest' but would subsequently cancel this date.

A new SKYCLAD studio album, 'A Semblance Of Normality', was scheduled for early 2003. Martin Walkyier would spend the early portion of 2003 formulating his new venture THE CLAN DESTINED. The singer also guested as vocalist on the track 'Blood And Sand' on Bradford Metal band BLOODSTREAM's debut album 'Black Storm Harvest'.

It would be learned in September that SKYCLAD were collaborating on a new album with none other than the Royal Philharmonic Orchestra. The group then hooked up with London based veterans THE QUIREBOYS for a short round of December gigs dubbed the 'Demolition Xmas Ball'. Support came courtesy of ANTI PRODUCT. A free CD would be given to gig goers, including two brand new tracks from each band.

Ex-member Jay Graham would be in the news during 2004, sessioning for BLACK SABBATH guitarist TONY IOMMI and joining HELVIS in June for their 'Onset Of Winter Brings Death (The Crops Have Failed)' recordings.

SKYCLAD's co-headlining gig at the Burgfolk Festival in Mülheim/Ruhr, Germany on July 24th would be filmed as part of a DVD release. A new studio album, entitled 'A Semblance Of Normality' mixed and mastered at the Damage Inc. Studio in Italy by Dario Mollo of VOODOO HILL and THE CAGE, was set for September issue through Demolition Records.

SKYCLAD performed an unusual concert dubbed the '34'000 Ton Metal Cruise' on September 25th, performing onboard the Münchenbryggeriet car ferry in Stockholm, Sweden alongside TANKARD, AMON AMARTH, HYPOCRISY, TAD MOROSE, STORMWARRIOR and WOLF. In July of 2005 SKYCLAD celebrated their fifteenth anniversary with both an electric and acoustic set at the 'Dong Open Air' festival held in Neukirchen-Vluyn, Germany. The band headlined the UK 'Dominion—Autumn Assault' festival in Hull during October over a supporting cast of Germany's HUMAN FORTRESS, INTENSE, INFOBIA, PAIN CONTROL, Italy's WARCHILD, DELIVERANCE, CONQUEST OF STEEL, HUMANITY, EVILE and PITIFUL REIGN. However, European concerts were cancelled when Steve Ramsey sustained "a serious shoulder injury" in an accident.

In January 2006 SKYCLAD announced signature to a contract with Greek label Black Lotus Records. Preceding a new studio album would be an EP entitled 'Jig-A-Jig', this independent release only being made available through the band's website and at concerts. With THE CLAN DESTINED fragmenting in acrimonious circumstances, ex-singer Martin Walkyier broke a lengthy silence in April 2006 announcing that he was permanently withdrawing from making music. However, it was soon after learned that he was set to feature as guest singer on the track 'God Among Men' featured on all female Greek Black Metal band ASTARTE's 'Demonized' album.

WAYWARD SONS OF MOTHER EARTH, Noise NO0163-2 (1991). The Sky Beneath My Feet / Trance Dance (A Dreamtime Walkabout) / A Minute's Piece / The Widdershins Jig / Our Dying Island / Pagan Man / The Cradle Will Fall / Skyclad / Moongleam And Meadowsweet / Terminus.

Tracks From The Wilderness EP, Noise NO0194-3 (1992). Emerald / A Room Next Door / When All Else Fails / The Declaration Of Indifference / Spinning Jenny / Skyclad.

BURNT OFFERING FOR THE BONE IDOL, Noise NO0186-2 (1992). Ware And Disorder / A Broken Promised Land / Spinning Jenny / Salt Of The Earth (Another Man's Poison) / Karmageddon (The Suffering Silence) / Ring Stone Round / Men Of Straw / R Vannith / The Declaration Of Indifference / Alone In Death's Shadow.

Schadenfreude, Noise (1993) (Promotion release). Schadenfreude / Earth Mother.

Thinking Allowed?, Noise NO209-3 (1993). Thinking Allowed? / Cradle Will Fall / The Widdershins Jig.

JONAH'S ARK, Noise NO209-2 (1993). Thinking Allowed / Cry Of The Land / Schadenfruede / A Near Life Experience / The Wickedest Man In The World / Earth Mother, The Sun And The Furious Host / The Ilk Of Human Blindness / Tunnel Visionaries / A Word To The Wise / Bewilderbeast / It Wasn't Meant To End This Way.

PRINCE OF THE POVERTY LINE, Noise NO239-2 (1994). Civil War Dance / Cardboard City / Sins Of Emission / Land Of The Rising Slum / The One Piece Puzzle / A Bellyful Of Emptyness / A Dog In The Manger / Gammadion Seed / Womb Of The Worm / The Truth Famine.

THE SILENT WHALES OF THE LUNAR SEA, Noise N0228-2 (1995). Still Spinning Shrapnel / Just What Nobody Wanted / Art Nazi / Brimstone Ballet / A Stranger In The Garden / Another Fine Mess / Turncoat Rebellion / Halo Of Flies / Desperanto (A Song For Europe?) / The Present Imperfect.

IRRATIONAL ANTHEMS, Massacre MASS CD 084 (1996). Inequality Street / The Wrong Song / Snake Charming / Penny Dreadful / The Sinful Ensemble / My Mother In Darkness / The Spiral Staircase / No Deposit, No Return / Sabre Dance / I Dubious / Science Never Sleeps / History Lessons / Quantity Time.

OUI AVANT—GARDE A CHANCE, Massacre MASSCD0104 (1996). If I Die Laughing, It'll Be An Act Of God / Great Blow For A Day Job / Constance Eternal / Postcard From Planet Earth / Jumping My Shadow / Bombjour! / History lessons (The Final Examination) / A Badtime Story / Come On Eileen / Master Race / Bombed Out / Penny Dreadful (Full Shilling Mix).

THE ANSWER MACHINE?, Massacre MAS CD0128 (1997). A Clown Of Thorns / Building A Ruin / Worn Out Sole To Heel / Single Phial / Helium / The Thread Of Evermore / Eirenarch / Troublesometimes / Tainting By Numbers / My Naked I / Catherine At The Wheel / Dead Angels On Ice.

Outrageous Fourtunes EP, Massacre (1998). Land Of The Rising Slum (Acoustic) / Sins Of Emission (Acoustic) / Alone In Death's Shadow (Acoustic) / Spinning Jenny (Acoustic).

Classix Shape EP, Massacre (1999) (Shaped picture CD). Vintage Whine / Inequality Street / Constance Eternal / Building A Ruin / Sins Of Emission (Acoustic).

VINTAGE WHINE, Massacre MAS CD0178 (1999). Kiss My Sweet Brass / Vintage Whine / On With Their Heads! / The Silver Cloud's Dark Lining / A Well Beside The River / No Strings Attached / Bury Me / Cancer Of The Heart / Little Miss Take / Something To Cling To / By George.

FOLKEMON, Nuclear Blast 27361 65022 (2000). The Great Brain Robbery / Think Back And Lie Of England / Polkageist / Crux Of The Message / The Disenchanted Forest / The Antibody Politic / When God Logs-Off / You Lost My Memory / Deja-Vu Ain't What It Used To Be / Any Old Irony?

ANOTHER FINE MESS, Demolition DEMCD 112 (2001). Intro / Another Fine Mess / Cardboard City / Art-Nazi / The Wickedest Man In The World / The One Piece Puzzle / Still Spinning Shrapnel / Just What Nobody Wanted / Sins Of Emission / Land Of The Rising Slum / Alone In Deaths Shadow / Spinning Jenny.

Swords Of A Thousand Men, Demolition DEMCDS001B (2001). Swords Of A Thousand Men / The Widdershins Jig (2001 version).

NO DAYLIGHTS NOR HEELTAPS, Demolition DEMCD115 (2002). Penny Dreadful / Inequality Street / Spinning Jenny / The Cry Of The Land / Another Fine Mess / Sins Of Emission / The Widdershins Jig / History Lessens / The Land Of The Rising Slum / Single Phial.

LIVE AT THE DYNAMO, Burning Airlines PILOT139 (2002). Intro / Another Fine Mess / Cardboard City / Art Nazi / The Wickedest Man In The World / The One Piece Puzzle / Still Spinning Shrapnel / Just What Nobody Wanted / The Widdershins Jig / The Declaration Of Indifference / The Cradle Will Fall / Spinning Jenny.

A SEMBLANCE OF NORMALITY, Demolition DEMCD142 (2004). Intro (Pipes Solo) / Do They Mean Us? / A Good Day To Bury Bad News / Anotherdrinkingsong / A Survival Campaign / The Song Of No-Involvement / The Parliament Of Fools / Ten Little Kingdoms / Like … A Ballad For The Disenchanted / Lightening The Load / NTRWB / Hybrid Blues / Outro (The Dissolution Of Parliament).

Jig-A-Jig, Skyclad (2006). Jig-a-Jig / Mr. Malaprope & Co. / They Think It's All Over (Well Is It Now) / The Roman Wall Blues.

SLAMMER

BRADFORD, UK — *Paul Tunnicliffe (vocals), Enzo Annecchini (guitar), Milo Zivanovic (guitar), Russell Bertram (bass), Andy Gagic (drums)*.

Bradford Thrash Metal band fronted by former EXCALIBUR, STEEL and ROUGH JUSTICE vocalist Paul Tunnicliffe. SLAMMER, centred on lead guitarists Milo Zivanovic and Enzo Annecchini. In 1989 the band recorded a 'Friday Rock Show' session with newly recruited ex-DEADLINE bassist Russell Burton. In the American Thrash explosion which saw 'the big four' break worldwide, the British record companies were falling over themselves to sign homegrown Thrash acts little realising the scene had already peaked. In the mêlée, Polygram picked up ONSLAUGHT, Chrysalis took on TORANAGA and Warner Bros. opted for SLAMMER. It seemed like a dream come true for the fledgling Thrashers but this soon turned into a nightmare as the Rock media universally rounded on them for supposedly being signed for their being simply any old Thrash act rather than an individual talent.

SLAMMER toured hard with plenty of record company support, playing with ONSLAUGHT, Hardcore Americans SACRILEGE B.C. and a European jaunt with the CRUMBSUCKERS, although the debut Mark Dodson produced album, 1989's 'The Work Of Idle Hands', was hammered by the critics who saw SLAMMER as nothing more than bandwagon jumpers.

March 1990 had the band performing opening honours across Britain for MOTÖRHEAD and in May SLAMMER hooked up with CELTIC FROST for shows across the Low Countries and the UK. That same year Burton had split to form BITTER AND TWISTED with ex-ACID REIGN and future CATHEDRAL guitarist Adam Lehan.

Warner Bros. was quick to discard the band. NEW MODEL ARMY bassist Stuart Morrow joined as they signed to Wolverhampton based indie Heavy Metal Records for the 1990 'Insanity Addicts' EP and 'Nightmare Scenario' album of 1991. SLAMMER put in a notable support to PANTERA at the London Marquee in March 1991 but Morrow would leave for LOUD the following year. SLAMMER guitarist Milo Zivanovic returned to the scene in early 2002 touting a METALLICA tribute band DAMAGE INC. for a tour of Holland.

THE WORK OF IDLE HANDS, WEA 246000-2 (1989). Tenement Zone / If Thine Eye / Johnny's Home / Razor's Edge / Hellbound / Hunt You Down / God's Prey / Fight Or Fall / No Excuses / Born For War.
Born For War, WEA SLAM 1 (1989) (Promotion release). Born For War / Hellbound / If Thine Eye Offend Thee / Fight Or Fall.
Insanity Addicts, Heavy Metal XD66 (1990). Insanity Addicts / Bring The Hammer Down / Maniac / I.O.U.
NIGHTMARE SCENARIO, Heavy Metal HMR XD170 (1991). What's Your Pleasure / Greed / In The Name Of God / Just Another Massacre / Architect Of Pain / Every Breath / I Know Who I Am / Corruption / Think For Yourself / L'Ultima.

SLAPDASH

SWEDEN — *Jens Mortensen (vocals), Magnus Söderman (guitar), Lars Linden (guitar), Fredrik Jacobsen (bass), Bärget (drums).*

SLAPDASH members guitarists Lars Lindén and Magnus Söderman, bassist Fredrik Jacobsen were all previously with Death Metal act ROSICRUCIAN, whilst drummer Bärget was ex-MR. HANGPIKE. SLAPDASH have covered songs from such diverse acts as STORMTROOPERS OF DEATH ('Kill Yourself') to Disco divas EN VOGUE' ('Free Your Mind')

During 1997 Söderman and new SLAPDASH bassist Lasse Lindh founded ZEALION with former SCHIZOPHRENIC CIRCUS and ZELLO vocalist Pelle Saether. By 1998 Söderman was in the ranks of Metal covers band POWERAGE, the act that subsequently evolved into AXENSTAR. Ex-bassist Lars Lindén would join up with CARNAL FORGE for their 2001 album 'Please Die!' Meantime singer Jens Mortensen enrolled into the German "Death Rock" outfit REVOLVER for the 2002 album 'The Unholy Mother Of Fuck'. Mortensen joined CARNAL FORGE in August of 2004.

Bound, Nuclear Blast MNWCDS219 (1996). Bound / Unfold / Kill Yourself.
SLAPDASH, Nuclear Blast NB 197-2 (1996). Nothing Remains / No Love Last / Dependence Gone / Bound / Lost / New God / So Be It / Soulless / On My Own / My Enemy / Follow Not / Get A Life / Free Your Mind.
204.25 ACTUAL REALITY, Nuclear Blast NB 27361 61972 (1996). Nothing Remains / No Love Lost / Dependence Gone / Bound / Lost / New God / So Be It / Soulless / On My Own / My Enemy / Follow Not / Get A Life / Free Your Mind.

SLAUGHTER

SCARBOROUGH, ON, CANADA — *Dave Hewson (vocals / guitar), Terry Sadler (vocals / bass), Ron Sumners (drums).*

SLAUGHTER are a revered name amongst the annals of the Thrash / Death Metal genre. The band, raised in Scarborough, Ontario, was created during August of 1984. Co-founder Terry Sadler, handling vocals and bass guitar, was already a seasoned veteran of the local Toronto scene having served terms with BLIND AMBITION, BLISSMASS, LIZZY BORDEN, MEGOLITH, METAL FATIGUE, NAZZ, and THE HALO OF FLIES. Along with vocalist / guitarist Dave Hewson and drummer Ron Sumners, Sadler forged SLAUGHTERHOUSE, soon truncating the title to SLAUGHTER.

The group made their mark with the opening demo sessions 'Meatcleaver' and 'Bloody Karnage', the latter featuring Joe Rico and Rob Urbinati of SACRIFICE as guest players. Third set 'Surrender Or Die' followed in 1985 and rapidly spread throughout the underground tape trading grapevine, even impacting on the demo top ten charts in leading UK magazine 'Metal Forces'. Their live debut came with the "Live Karnage" event alongside SACRIFICE on March 25th 1985 at Toronto's Larry's Hideaway venue, their set being distributed straight from the soundboard as the 'Live Karnage' demo, brazenly sporting their influences with covers of HELLHAMMER's 'Massacra' and VENOM's 'Witching Hour'. That same May another gig opening for SACRIFICE, at Gilmore's in Toronto, was recorded live for the 'Live Bedlam' demo.

Local radio DJ Brian Taylor secured the rights to the demo 'Surrender Or Die', releasing this commercially as the first release issued by Attic Records subsidiary Diabolic Force. SLAUGHTER capitalised on this with the debut album 'Strappado', recorded again for Diabolic Force at Future Sound in Toronto with Brian Taylor behind the desk in just 24 hours. Although cut in February 1986 'Strappado' remained vaulted for a lengthy period due to financial constraints. Beforehand the promotional three track single 'One Foot In The Grave', limited to 1000 copies, emerged.

Earlier the same year SLAUGHTER had been joined by DEATH frontman Chuck Schuldiner. Having relocated from Florida Schuldiner's tenure lasted a matter of weeks before he journeyed back home to re-activate DEATH. Live work would be restricted to a grand total of just fifteen concerts, the largest of which was held in July 1986 as support to CELTIC FROST and VOIVOD at the Toronto Concert House.

Sumners made his exit during September 1986 and, after fleetingly employing STORM and DEATH ADDER drummer Scott Day, the group re-structured with former LETHAL PRESENCE guitarist Bobby Sadzak and, in May 1987, drummer Brian Lourie. Finally, in mid 1987, the much delayed 'Strappado' was delivered, immediately drawing ecstatic reviews. SLAUGHTER cut a further album 'Paranormal' in July 1988 but these tapes would never see the light of day. Metal Blade Records showed interest, prompted by the band's December 1988 demo 'The Dark', and the track 'The Fourth Dimension' taken from the Paranormal demo was duly included on the 'Metal Massacre Ten' compilation released in 1990.

Further ructions hit the band in 1992 when Sadler bade his farewell, having initially quit in 1988, then returning in 1989, before quitting again in 1990. Hewson would then form an alliance with guitarist Bobby Sadzak, bassist Mike Dalton and drummer Brian Lourie creating STRAPPADO, this move being prompted by the chart success of the Las Vegas hair band of the same name. This new unit only issued the two sessions, 'Fatal Judgement' and 'Not Dead Yet', before splitting. However, the Headache label fanned the flames of the burgeoning SLAUGHTER legend by issuing a bootleg CD 'Strappado'.

SLAUGHTER was resurrected in order to donate a version of 'Dethroned Emperor' to a 1996 CELTIC FROST tribute album.

This revised version of the band would collapse once again although Hewson and Sadzak, together with singer Kelly Montico, subsequently created the Industrial outfit INNER THOUGHT releasing 'Worldy Separation' in 1994 and the 1996 follow up 'Perspectives'. In 1999 pioneering UK Grindcore act NAPALM DEATH paid homage by rendering their version of 'Incinerator' on their EP 'Leaders Not Followers' and Utopian Vision Music published the 'Surrender Or Die' demos on CD format, complete with additional tracks recorded at the time but left off the demo.

A slew of SLAUGHTER re-releases arrived during 2000 including the shelved 'Paranormal', live cuts and demos. The German Nuclear Blast label would re-issue 'Strappado' complete with an extra CD compiled of live recordings from SLAUGHTER's inaugural March 1985 gig and rehearsal tapes. The band's legacy was given further prominence during 2004 when Hells Headbangers Records released 'Fuck Of Death', a compilation of the January 23rd 1986 rehearsal recordings conducted with late DEATH frontman Chuck Schuldiner. This vinyl only outing would be restricted to 1000 copies, the first 100 pressed on coloured vinyl with 500 manufactured as picture discs. Further tracks arrived in the form of a split 7" single on Horror Records of Denmark in collusion with NUNSLAUGHTER, the infamous Pittsburgh Death Metal band also paying tribute on their side of vinyl with a cover of SLAUGHTER's 'Nocturnal Hell'.

Meatcleaver, (1984). Age Of Deception / Eve Of Darkness / Surrender Or Die / Children Of The Fire / Hell Hath Returned / Meatcleaver / Slaughter-House / Instro-Metal / Annihilation / Strappado / Total Retribution.
Bloody Karnage, (1984). Disintegrator / Incinerator / One Foot In The Grave / Forged In The Furnace Of Hell / Bloody Karnage.
Surrender Or Die, (1985). Disintegrator / Incinerator / Main To Please / Tyrant Of Hell / Shadow Of Death / Death Dealer / One Foot In The Grave.
Live Karnage, (1985). Disintergrator—Incinerator / One Foot In The Grave / Shadow Of Death / Massacra / Death Dealer / Tales Of The Macabre / Maim To Please / Strappado / Eve Of Darkness / Tyrant Of Hell / Witching Hour / Bloody Karnage.
Nocturnal Hell EP, Fan Club (1986) (Fan Club edition. 1000 copies). Nocturnal Hell / One Foot In The Grave / Tortured Souls.
STRAPPADO, Diabolic Force FPL 3028 (1987). Strappado / The Curse / Disintegrator / Incinerator / Parasites / F.O.D. / Tortured Souls / Nocturnal Hell / Tales Of The Macabre.
NOT DEAD YET, Slaughter (1990). Not Dead Yet / Flake / Threshold Of Pain / Time Warp / Death Comes Ripping Through You / The Dark / Astral Projector / Telepathic Screams.
SURRENDER OR DIE, Utopian Vision Music (1999). Disintegrater / Incinerator / Maim To Please / Tyrant Of Hell / Shadow Of Death / Death Dealer / One Foot In The Grave / Surrender Or Die / Eve Of Darkness / Massacra / Strappado / Tales Of The Macabre / Cult Of The Dead.
NOT DEAD YET / PARANORMAL, Nuclear Blast NB 663 (2001). Not Dead Yet / Flake / Threshold Of Pain / Timewarp / Death Comes Ripping Through You / The Dark / Astral Projector / Telepathic Screams / Schizo / Galactic Dynamics / Coffin Of Ice / The Fourth Dimension / The Curse (Live) / Tortured Souls (Live) / Nocturnal Hell (Live) / Incinerator (Live).
STRAPPADO, Nuclear Blast NB 662 (2001). Disintegrater / Incinerator / Nocturnal Hell / F.O.D. / Tortured Souls / Parasites / The Curse / Strappado / Maim To Please / One Foot In The Grave / Tyrant Of Hell / Death Dealer / Tales Of The Macabre / Disintegrater/Incinerator (Live) / One Foot In The Grave (Live) / Shadow Of Death (Live) / Massacra (Live) / Death Dealer (Live) / Tales Of The Macabre (Live) / Maim To Please (Live) / Strappado (Live) / Eve Of Darkness (Live) / Tyrant Of Hell (Live) / Witching Hour (Live) / Bloody Karnage (Live) / (Hidden rehearsal track).
FUCK OF DEATH, Hells Headbangers HELLS PLP 002 (2004) (Limited edition 1000 copies). Evil Dead / Legion Of Doom / Nocturnal Hell / The Curse / Fuck Of Death / Parasites / One Foot In The Grave / Maim To Please—Strappado / Tortured Souls / Death Dealer / Tyrant Of Hell.
Slaughter / Nunslaughter, Horror HOR 011 (2004) (Split 7" single with NUNSLAUGHTER. Limited edition 1030 copies). Children Of Fire / Hell Hath Returned.

SLAVE ZERO

IRELAND — *Graeme V. Flynn (vocals), Eddie O'Malley (guitar), John Roche (guitar), Andy Coade (bass), Bob Ryan (drums).*

Kilkenny Death-Thrashers SLAVE ZERO would form in April 2000, quoting an opening line-up comprising vocalist / guitarist Paul Callan, guitarist Eddie O'Malley, bassist Tom Shiel and drummer Bob Ryan, and issued the debut demo 'Once Was Human', recorded at the Music Warehouse Studios, in February of the following year. SLAVE ZERO's 2002 album 'The Defiant Stand', laid down at J.A.M Studios in County Meath with new man Kevin Jacob installed on bass, included a cover of DEATH's 'Zombie Ritual'.

Callan exited in November 2003 and a further defection saw Jacob opting out in May of 2004. That October, guitarist John Roche, bassist Andy Coade and vocalist Graeme V. Flynn all enrolled to bring SLAVE ZERO back up to strength.

THE DEFIANT STAND, Independent (2002). Once Was Human / I Defy / Prejudice Breeds / Raising The Sign / When Silence Turns To Hope / Last Breath / Zombie Ritual / For This We Bleed / Soldiers Fortune.

SLAYER

HUNTINGTON PARK, CA, USA — *Tom Araya (vocals / bass), Jeff Hanneman (guitar), Kerry King (guitar), Dave Lombardo (drums).*

SLAYER are without question the most sinister of the acts to break out onto the world stage from the early eighties American thrash phenomenon. With an unwillingness to compromise they have seemingly defied all the odds to place themselves in the position of regular chart breakers.

The band's music is unrelentingly intense, initially fuelled by drummer DAVE LOMBARDO, often voted as the 'World's best drummer' in many Metal mags, the mainstay lethal twin guitars of Kerry King and Jeff Hanneman together with the almost inhuman vocals of bassist Tom Araya (a former hospital respiratory therapist). This union made SLAYER not only mould-breakers but an act faithfully plagiarized by countless lesser bands. The group has never come close to pandering to radio and lyrically they are unafraid to venture into the realms of the most despicable and overtly controversial. Satanism and Nazism are familiar territories for SLAYER.

Initial recordings were marred by inadequate production and thus universally dismissed as derisory by the world's rock media. Even hardened Thrash fans found SLAYER's inaugural bursts of speed noise, when compared with rising stars such as MEGADETH, ANTHRAX and METALLICA, difficult to stomach.

Founded in 1981 by uniting former SABOTAGE drummer Lombardo, King and Araya from QUITS and Hanneman SLAYER, originally titled DRAGONSLAYER after the 1981 movie of the same name. At first they pursued a traditional heavy metal stance musically, even sporting face make-up in early pictures, but debuting with the fast track 'Aggressive Perfector' on the 'Metal Massacre IV' compilation album on Metal Blade Records persuaded the band to adopt a more intense leaning. A three track rehearsal demo tape followed in May 1983 comprising of 'Fight 'Til Death', 'Black Magic' and 'The Antichrist', which rapidly became a much traded item on the underground metal scene. That August SLAYER demoed again, putting down 'Evil Has No Boundaries' and 'Crionics'.

King teamed up with fellow Los Angeles speed metal band MEGADETH performing live gigs on a temporary basis. During this period of flux Lombardo was briefly supplanted by drummer Bob Gourley, later to join DARK ANGEL then create POWERLORD. The former outfit would prove to be a huge influence on the band and, coincidently, SLAYER's then lighting technician Gene Hoglan enrolled into the ranks of DARK ANGEL as their drummer.

Brian Slagel, Metal Blade mentor, was quick to notice the reaction to SLAYER's 'Metal Massacre IV' inclusion and duly signed the band up putting them in the studio in November to record 'Show No Mercy' whilst Lombardo graduated from high school. These sessions would be financed by Kerry King's father and Tom Araya's employment as a respiratory therapist. 'Show No Mercy' was rush released in December 1983, emerging a matter of weeks after the band had completed the tracks. The mainstream Rock press hated the record, proclaiming it to be an unintelligible mess, but much to their dismay it still sold in legion.

The band got out on the road, even putting in an English appearance at London's Marquee club, before setting off on the 'Haunting North America' tour. This trek was backed by the issue of the EP 'Haunting The Chapel' in August 1984. SLAYER's no compromise approach saw them using inverted crosses onstage and King wearing leather armbands encrusted with nails.

In November Metal Blade put out the 'Live Undead' recording, not captured on the road but in actual fact recorded live in the studio.

First product of 1985 was a VHS video dubbed 'Combat Tour—The Ultimate Revenge', documenting live footage of four tracks filmed on SLAYER's US trek alongside VENOM and EXODUS captured at New York's Studio 54 club. With second studio album 'Hell Awaits' arriving in September 1985, SLAYER provided ample defiance to those that sneered with the music easily equal in ferocity to the debut. SLAYER were clawing their way up and the British rock magazine 'Metal Forces' readers poll was a case of SLAYER sweeping the board gaining honours for best band, best live band, best album and best drummer.

SLAYER began to make serious headway when Rick Rubin, Owner and producer of Def Jam Records, signed the band in 1986. First fruits of this liaison was the 28 minute 'Reign In Blood' opus, a pure thrash album that took the genre to new levels of extremity. Quite incredibly the album was to break into the American Billboard top album 100 charts, the first of many.

'Reign In Blood' would come to define the very essence of both SLAYER and extreme Thrash Metal. Indeed, it would prove so pivotal to the band's career that in 2004 special show in Augusta, Georgia on 11th July would be filmed for the Dean Karr directed DVD release 'Reign in Blood Live: Still Reigning'. This saw the band running through the entire track listing of the record. Specially re-instated for these dates would be the bands 80s eagle backdrops and inverted crucifix lighting rig.

'Reign In Blood' also embroiled SLAYER into political condemnation almost immediately for the lyrics to the opening track 'Angel Of Death'. The song dealt with the infamous SS Auschwitz extermination camp doctor Joseph Mengele and many were quick to accuse SLAYER of fascist sentiments. The mighty CBS corporation, distributors of Def Jam, refused to handle the album.

The band retorted that this was merely an observation and not a belief, citing that Araya himself was far from being an all American white boy. The obviously Ayran Hanneman compounded the problem however by frequently wearing SS collar patches, iron crosses and insignia in photos and by adorning one of his guitars with cuff titles of notorious SS panzer divisions such as 'Totenkopf' and 'Das Reich'. SLAYER's tour T-shirts of the time proudly declared that the band were 'Slaytanic Wehrmacht' and featured a skull encased in a World War II German helmet. SLAYER seemed quite content to be stoking up their reputation as number 1 bad boys.

The band provoked further adverse reaction by their use of a new logo, a Nazi eagle with the swastika replaced with the SLAYER logo. The furor over 'Angel Of Death' was so great that British distributor Geffen, owned by the Jewish entrepreneur David Geffen, dropped the album from their schedules. Ironically Geffen had been quick to capitalise on SLAYER's dumping by CBS earlier.

SLAYER, on the 'Reign In Pain' tour for the first time enjoying the comforts of a tour bus, toured America with OVERKILL before European dates with openers MALICE. Such was the headliner's extreme loyalty that MALICE were very often the subject of ugly scenes, having to endure booing and, sadly, more often than not, spitting.

With the band's burgeoning popularity, former label Metal Blade were quick to capitalise releasing 'Live Undead' in limited edition a picture disc format. Kerry King unexpectedly found himself all over the radio during 1986 albeit not with SLAYER. The guitarist had donated a suitably manic solo to fellow Def Jam crew the BEASTIE BOYS number 1 'Licensed To Ill' album track 'No Sleep 'til Brooklyn'.

Between albums, and whilst in the midst of an American tour, Lombardo announced he was quitting in December 1986. Rumours circulated that the cause of the split was an argument over Lombardo's wife being on the road. Nonetheless, SLAYER continued with substitute T.J. Scaglione of WHIPLASH. As the tour rolled on SLAYER hooked up with W.A.S.P., an ill fated union that witnessed a bitter war of words between the two bands as to which act viewed itself as selling the more tickets.

SLAYER was back in the headlines once more in 1987 for all the wrong reasons when they pulled out of a headlining slot at the prestigious Aardschock Festival in Holland at the eleventh hour. A great degree of ill feeling was generated until the band explained that with the cancellation of METALLICA (due to the death of Cliff Burton) SLAYER had no intentions of performing but their agency had neglected to inform the relevant parties. With the band's burgeoning popularity, former label Metal Blade were quick to capitalise re-releasing 'Live Undead', as a picture disc variant.

Lombardo, who during his sabbatical had turned down the opportunity to join MEGADETH, was enticed back into the band in April 1987 in time to record the next album. The reinstated drummer did however nearly miss a batch of British dates when his work permit had been refused.

SLAYER plugged the gap between albums by covering IRON BUTTERFLY's 'In A Gadda Da Vida' for the movie soundtrack 'Less Than Zero'.

July 1988's 'South Of Heaven', which saw SLAYER slowing the pace somewhat and included a cover of JUDAS PRIEST's 'Dissident Aggressor', gave SLAYER increased sales yet again. With the band seemingly attempting to extricate themselves from their previous black metal trip oddly Rubin was to insist that the word 'Satan' appear on the record and at the last minute Araya reworked the lyrics to 'Read Between The Lies' to include a reference to ol' Nick.

American dates kicked off with support from NUCLEAR ASSAULT then SLAYER finally got the opportunity to play the major American arenas at the end of 1988 when they were invited to join JUDAS PRIEST as guests.

SLAYER took a lengthy break of some two years after the world tour during which time they severed ties with their British record company London Records. SLAYER had been far from amused when the single 'Mandatory Suicide' had been released on the very last date of the British tour.

1990 saw SLAYER in what some envisaged as an unholy union on the 'Clash Of The Titans' festival touring package. Three out of 'The big four', SLAYER, MEGADETH and ANTHRAX teamed up for a series of monumental shows across arenas in Europe and North America. The eighteen shows in Europe had SLAYER and MEGADETH joined by SUICIDAL TENDENCIES and TESTAMENT. For the stateside dates, ANTHRAX was added and the then relatively unknown ALICE IN CHAINS opened. One result of these dates is that Araya was invited to guest on ALICE IN CHAINS 'Dirt' album. His contribution comes in the form of a Slayeresque scream on an untitled track.

The 'Seasons In The Abyss' album arrived in October 1990, breaking into the US Billboard charts at number 40 and giving the band a top twenty record in the UK. A promotional video for the title track was filmed in Egypt. Musically, 'Seasons In The Abyss' was to be the group's most caustic outing to date, with the track 'Dead Skin Mask', concerning serial killer Ed Gein complete with the whimpers of a young child for added effect, provoking particular disgust. A double live album 'Decade Of Aggression' followed in 1991. This two disc, hitting number 55 on Billboard, set was proudly issued in a raw state, incorporating none of the usual live album clean ups or overdubs. Disc one comprised a July 13th 1991 gig at the Lakeland Coliseum, Lakeland, Florida whilst the second disc hosted material recorded at Wembley Arena, London, United Kingdom, October 14th 1990 and the Orange Pavilion, San Bernardino, California, March 8th 1991. A limited edition of 10,000 metal box collectables added two extra tracks in 'Skeletons Of Society' and 'At Dawn They Sleep'.

In May 1992 Lombardo quit for good. His first project being recording with VOODOO CULT then the formation of GRIP INC. with VOODOO CULT guitarist Waldemar Sorychta, a band that has released two albums to date. Lombardo's substitute was ex-FORBIDDEN man Paul Bostoph. In this format, Slayer broke in their new man with gigs across California, Arizona and Baja California in Mexico prior to an appearance at the August 1992 IRON MAIDEN headlined Castle Donington 'Monsters Of Rock' festival.

During 1994 SLAYER teamed up with gangster rapper ICE T to cut a track for the soundtrack to the movie 'Judgement Night', a cover of British punk act THE EXPLOITED's 'Disorder'.

SLAYER shot back to their previous status with 'Divine intervention' in 1995. The album blasted into the Billboard top 100 at an incredible number 8. The record witnessed no respite when it came to dealing with beyond the pale subject matter, Hanneman's penchant for Nazi history re-surfacing with 'SS-3', the license plate of Reich governor of Bohemia and Moravia Reynard Heydrich's staff car, whilst '213' dealt with yet another serial killer, Jeffrey Dahmer, the number being that of his notorious apartment. 'Divine Intervention' was quick to achieve gold sales status and SLAYER's longevity was confirmed when back catalogue titles 'Reign In Blood', 'South Of Heaven' and 'Seasons In The Abyss' were all confirmed gold too. Naturally the band generated controversy once again, this time by using a photograph on the inner sleeve of dedicated fan Mike Meyer's rendition of the Slayer logo–carved with a razor into his own arm.

The band geared up for a world tour with openers BIOHAZARD and MACHINE HEAD prior to a fourth on the bill showing at the 'Monsters of rock' festival headlined by METALLICA. An accompanying video, 'Live Intrusion', filmed at the Mesa Amphitheater in Mesa, Arizona on March 12th, 1995 and including a cover of VENOM's 'Witching Hour', was released through American Recordings.

The subsequent tour had SLAYER appearing on an all star 'Monsters Of Rock' bill in South America alongside KISS and BLACK SABBATH.

SLAYER paid homage to their musical heroes in June 1996 with the issue of the 'Undisputed Attitude' (originally titled 'Selected And Exhumed') album made up of favourite punk tunes and three SLAYER original compositions including the more metal orientated 'Gemini' and 'D.D.A.M.M.' Songs covered included those by T.S.O.L., IGGY POP, notably switching an original lyric of "I Wanna Be Your Dog" to "I'm Gonna Be Your God", DOCTOR KNOW, England's G.B.H., and no less than three MINOR THREAT tracks. The Japanese version added SUICIDAL TENDENCIES 'Memories Of Tomorrow'. The event was marred for the band though when after recording Bostaph made his exit to concentrate on a jazz career. A drummerless SLAYER were forced to cancel South American and European tours.

While SLAYER were offering tribute to their mentors a series of Swedish compilation albums entitled 'Slaytanic Slaughter' were released where Scandinavian acts covered their favourite SLAYER song.

SLAYER resumed activity with the addition of erstwhile TESTAMENT drummer John Dette, however his tenure was fleeting as Bostoph was duly reinstated, Dette returning to the TESTAMENT camp. In his time away from the band Bostoph had formed THE TRUTH ABOUT SEAFOOD.

1996 also found the band pushed back into the public arena once more although unwittingly when the band's music was cited in a lawsuit as being a direct influence on the 1995 murder of a 15 year old girl, Elyse Marie Pahler. The teenager was kidnapped, tortured and killed by three members of a Black Metal band HATRED. Pahler had been butchered with a hunting knife and her corpse then subjected to necrophilia. The prosecution alleging that the band members were influenced by and inspired by SLAYER's lyrics from the track 'Necrophiliac'. The findings of the court were due to be heard in 2001.

SLAYER came up with new product in 1998 with the 'Diabolus In Musica' album and appeared on the bill of the 'Ozzfest show' at Milton Keynes during June. 'Diabolus In Musica' opened with 46,000 units sold in its first week of sale in the USA, debuting at number 31 on the national Billboard charts. The group had been scheduled to appear on the American dates but the spot on the bill eventually went to MEGADETH.

In 1999 SLAYER teamed up with Berlin Techno-Punks ATARI TEENAGE RIOT to mould the track 'No Remorse (I Wanna Die)' for the 'Godzilla' movie soundtrack. 2000 saw SLAYER contributing their take on 'Hand Of Doom' for the BLACK SABBATH tribute album 'Nativity In Black 2'. Araya had also been writing material with Max Cavalera of SOULFLY, the track 'Terrorist' being featured on SOULFLY's 2000 album. Not to be outdone King features a guest guitar solo on the cut 'Goddamned Electric' from PANTERA's 2000 album 'Reinventing The Steel'.

SLAYER included the track 'Bloodline' on the movie soundtrack album 'Dracula 2000'.

As 2001 broke the band finally saw the case against them for having influenced the death of the teenager, Elyse Marie Pahler, in 1995 thrown out. SLAYER were rooted in the recording studio in Vancouver laying down the Matt Hyde produced new album prior to hooking up with PANTERA for the 'Extreme Steel' American tour.

Early leaks that the album was to be titled 'Soundtrack To The Apocalypse' proved false as the succinct 'God Hates Us All' was duly chosen. The album cover artwork, a blood-soaked bible punctured by nails, was apparently deemed unacceptable to display in many major retail outlets and so many copies had the original concept disguised by a false cover depicting four gold crosses on a plain white background. Quite unbelievably, 'God Hates Us All' was released on September 11th, 2001. This horrific coincidence resulted in many stores pulling the album from the shelves for fear of protest at the title.

European festival billings, dubbed the 'Tattoo The Planet' dates originally in alliance with PANTERA, BIOHAZARD, VISION OF DISORDER and STATIC X, were far from trouble free. Following the September 11th terrorist attacks PANTERA pulled out of the tour leaving SLAYER to remain behind as headliners.

Guitarist Kerry King rounded off the year by guesting on the track 'Final Prayer For The Human Race' on the 2002 HATEBREED album 'Perseverance'. Less welcome news for Bostaph would be an aggravating wrist condition which forced his exit from the band. This statement would be strongly refuted by the ex-drummer. Bostaph subsequently enrolled into the SYSTEMATIC ranks and would later re-join TESTAMENT.

SLAYER kept it in the family by re-inducting their illustrious former colleague DAVE LOMBARDO back into the fold, albeit announcing this move as a temporary measure. It would soon emerge that the hot contender to secure the job would be none other than Proscriptor McGovern (ne 'Emperor Proscriptor Magikus' a.k.a. Russ Givens), leader of ancestral Black Metal band ABSU. Other close candidates would be erstwhile SOULFLY member Joe Nunez, who's family reportedly baulked at the idea of his joining SLAYER, as well as DYING FETUS and MISERY INDEX man Kevin Talley. Another surprise candidate would be BLINK-182's Travis Barker who revealed in later months that his services had been requested by SLAYER.

SLAYER, complete with Lombardo manning the drum kit, would donate a cover version to the NASCAR sponsored 'Crank It Up' compilation in the summer of 2002. DEEP PURPLE's 'Highway Star' was apparently first choice but then switched to the aptly titled ALICE COOPER vintage classic 'Under My Wheels'. Within days SLAYER's choice of cover for this soundtrack had changed again to STEPPENWOLF's 'Born To Be Wild' whilst TYPE O NEGATIVE took over the mantle for 'Highway Star'. Araya also made his presence felt on the HENRY ROLLINS assembled 'West Memphis Three' benefit album 'Rise Above', lending lead vocals to a version of BLACK FLAG's 'Revenge'.

SLAYER would be announced as headliners of the American 'H82K2' festivals alongside IN FLAMES and SOULFLY. The band would also be confirmed as one of the headline attractions at the mammoth 'Beast Fest' event in Japan during December of 2002. Lombardo, still maintaining membership of SLAYER, revealed plans to record a solo album comprising entirely of drum solos. He would also act as session drummer on new recordings by Finnish cellists APOCALYPTICA.

A lengthy string of US Jägermeister sponsored headline dates commencing 9th October and running through until mid December saw HATEBREED and ARCH ENEMY as support acts. Regional guests included E-TOWN CONCRETE, HEMLOCK, LAZY AMERICAN WORKERS, SWORN ENEMY, SKINLAB, FIVE FEET THICK and DRY KILL LOGIC. In the midst of this live activity the band issued a lavish 5 CD box set entitled 'Soundtrack To The Apocalypse', this collection comprising tracks spanning every SLAYER album. Also included would be songs previously only available as Japanese bonus cuts and live DVD material. A limited edition 'Deluxe' version, housed in a fake blood and floating skulls package (!) came with an extra CD of a full length concert from SLAYER's 2002 'God Hates Us All' tour stop in Anaheim, California, wall banner and replica backstage laminate.

In early 2004 Lombardo also put in a recording session for the soundtrack to the remake of the splatter film classic 'Dawn Of The Dead'. The drummer also issued the 'Incorporated' album from his other act GRIP INC. Dave Lombardo got some unexpected extra exposure when he acted as a quickfire stand in for a missing Lars Ulrich for METALLICA's Castle Donington 'Download' festival performance. Lombardo opened proceedings with playing 'Battery' and 'Four Horsemen' before SLIPKNOT's Joey Jordison tackled the remainder of the set.

SLAYER would be confirmed for the mammoth US 'Ozzfest' festivals that Summer, featuring on a billing with OZZY OSBOURNE, JUDAS PRIEST, DIMMU BORGIR, HATEBREED, SLIPKNOT and BLACK LABEL SOCIETY. The band also scheduled 'Off-fest' headline dates aligned with JUDAS PRIEST and HATEBREED along the way. A brief burst of Canadian dates in June saw the band hooked up with DAMAGEPLAN and OTEP.

A special show in Augusta, Georgia on 11th July would be filmed for the Dean Karr directed DVD release 'Reign in Blood Live: Still Reigning', the band running through the entire track listing of the landmark 'Reign In Blood' album. Specially reinstated for these dates would be the bands 80s eagle backdrops and inverted crucifix lighting rig. The band promised something extra special for fans as an encore, duly delivering by literally raining down fake blood from the light rig during 'Raining Blood', soaking the entire band and their gear.

SLAYER's September 1st gig at Myrtle Beach in South Carolina was cancelled when frontman, Tom Araya, was apparently rushed to a hospital suspected of suffering from kidney stones. Returning to Europe, SLAYER acted as co-headliners with SLIPKNOT with support act HATEBREED for the October tour dubbed 'The Unholy Alliance'. Araya hit more problems in Europe though, completely losing his voice mid set during a show in Munich, Germany on 27th September. Although HATEBREED's Jamey Jasta took on lead vocals for 'Raining Blood' the band was forced to cut their show short.

A rapid return to the US saw the band invited back to headline a further run of Jägermeister Music tour over KILLSWITCH ENGAGE and MASTODON, shows kicking off on the 29th October in Springfield, Missouri. Touring across Europe with SLAYER, Lombardo also made to time to put in individual drum clinic solo performances en route. Intriguingly, Lombardo, in collaboration with DJ SPOOKY, would also be assembling a studio project entitled 'Drums Of Death', described as a "homage to Def Jam's pioneering rock-rap fusions of the '80s", with MEAT BEAT MANIFESTO's Jack Dangers acting as producer and guitarist Vernon Reid of LIVING COLOUR guesting. The drummer also made time to guest on Finnish classical Metal act APOCALYPTICA's 2005 album, featuring on the track 'Betrayal'.

The quartet, together with engineer Josh Abraham, entered studios in Los Angeles on February 28th to cut a new record. Upfront promotion novelly came with an EP release, entitled 'Eternal Pyre' and featuring album track 'Cult', which was only available exclusively through Hot Topic stores in the USA. Released as a single in Finland, 'Eternal Pyre' hit no. 2 in the national charts. An "exclusive remix" version of 'Eyes Of The Insane' was included on the 'Saw III' horror movie soundtrack released through Warcon Enterprises.

Summer 2006 US headliners commencing in June, dubbed the "Unholy Alliance—Preaching To The Perverted" tour, saw MASTODON, LAMB OF GOD, CHILDREN OF BODOM and THINE EYES BLEED as support. Early dates were re-scheduled after Tom Araya underwent gallbladder surgery, requiring time to recuperate.

'Christ Illusion' sold over 62,000 copies in its first week of release to land at number 5 on the US album charts, their highest ever domestic position. The album also landed in the top ten in Australia and just missed out on the top spot in both Germany and Finland. Notably, SLAYER was set to co-headline what was billed as "Hell and Heaven United" alongside arch nemesis STRYPER for the 'Monterrey Metal Fest', on September 23rd at the Coca Cola Auditorium in Monterrey, Nuevo Leon, Mexico. However, they then pulled out, quoting "personal reasons".

The European leg of the 'Unholy Alliance', comprising SLAYER, IN FLAMES, CHILDREN OF BODOM, LAMB OF GOD and THINE EYES BLEED, undertook shows in October. That same month the album again sparked controversy when it was withdrawn from record stores across India after complaints from a Christian group, the Mumbai-based Catholic Secular Forum who objected to both the album artwork and the lyrics of 'Jihad' and 'Skeleton Christ', describing them as "an insult to Christianity".

On November 8th SLAYER paid a visit to the 52nd Services Squadron at Spangdahlem U.S. Air Force Base in Germany, the band's first-ever visit to a military base.

SLAYER made its first-ever network television appearance on ABC-TV's 'Jimmy Kimmel Live!' show on January 19th 2007, performing in front of a 1,000 fans on an outdoor stage in Hollywood, California. The group announced Australian and New Zealand shows for April, supported by MASTODON. In February SLAYER was honored with a Grammy in the "Best Metal Performance" category for the song 'Eyes Of The Insane'.

Slayer Rehearsal Demo, (1983). Black Magic / The Antichrist / Fight 'til Death.

SLAYER

Slayer Demo, (1983). Evil Has No Boundaries / Crionics.
SHOW NO MERCY, Metal Blade 71034 (1983). Evil Has No Boundaries / The Anti-Christ / Die By The Sword / Fight Till Death / Metalstorm / Face The Slayer / Black Magic / Tormentor / The Final Command / Crionics / Show No Mercy.
Haunting The Chapel, Metal Blade 71083 (1984). Haunting The Chapel / Chemical Warfare / Captor Of Sin / Aggressive Perfector.
LIVE UNDEAD, Metal Blade 72015 (1984). Black Magic / Die By The Sword / Captor Of Sin / The Antichrist / Evil Has No Boundaries / Show No Mercy / Aggressive Perfector / Chemical Warfare.
HELL AWAITS, Metal Blade MX 8020 (1985). Hell Awaits / Kill Again / At Dawn They Sleep / Praise Of Death / Necrophiliac / Crypts Of Eternity / Hardening Of The Arteries.
Postmortem, Def Jam (1986). Postmortem / Criminally Insane (Remix) / Aggressive Perfector (Fast version).
REIGN IN BLOOD, London LONPP 34 (1986). Angel Of Death / Piece By Piece / Necrophobic / Jesus Saves / Altar Of Sacrifice / Criminally Insane / Reborn / Epidemic / Post Mortem / Raining Blood. Chart positions: 47 UK, 94 USA.
Criminally Insane, London (1987) (Iron cross shaped red vinyl. Limited edition UK release). Criminally Insane (Remix) / Aggressive Perfector.
Criminally Insane, London LONX 133 (1987). Postmortem / Criminally Insane / Aggressive Perfector. Chart position: 64 UK.
South Of Heaven, London LONX 201 (1988). South Of Heaven / Mandatory Suicide / In A Gadda D Vida.
SOUTH OF HEAVEN, London LONLP 63 (1988). South Of Heaven / Silent Scream / Live Undead / Behind The Crooked Cross / Mandatory Suicide / Ghosts Of War / Cleanse The Soul / Read Between The Lies / Dissident Aggressor / Spill The Blood. Chart positions: 25 UK, 50 SWEDEN, 57 USA.
Haunting The Chapel, Roadrunner RR24442 (1989) (UK release). Chemical Warfare / Captor Of Sin / Haunting The Chapel.
Dead Skin Mask, Def American (1990). Dead Skin Mask / Spirit In Black.
SEASONS IN THE ABYSS, Def American 84968712 (1990). War Ensemble / Blood Red / Spirit In Black / Expendable Youth / Dead Skin Mask / Hallowed Point / Skeletons Of Society / Temptation / Born Of Fire / Seasons In The Abyss. Chart positions: 18 UK, 29 AUSTRIA, 40 USA, 47 SWEDEN.
Seasons In The Abyss (Live), Def American (1991). Seasons In The Abyss (Live) / Aggressive Perfector (Live). Chart position: 51 UK.
Seasons In The Abyss (Live), Def American DEFAC 9 (1991). Seasons In The Abyss (Live) / Aggressive Perfector (Live) / Chemical Warfare (Live).
DECADE OF AGGRESSION-LIVE, Def American 314586799-2 (1991). Hell Awaits / The Anti-Christ / War Ensemble / South Of Heaven / Raining Blood / Altar Of Sacrifice / Jesus Saves / Dead Skin Mask / Seasons In The Abyss / Mandatory Suicide / Angel Of Death / Hallowed Point / Blood Red / Die By The Sword / Black Magic / Captor Of Sin / Born Of Fire / Post Mortem / Spirit In Black / Expendable Youth / Chemical Warfare / Black Magic / Sex, Murder, Art / Fictional Reality / Dittohead / Divine Intervention / Circle Of Beliefs / SS III / Serenity In Murder / Two-Thirteen. Chart positions: 29 UK, 55 USA, 77 GERMANY.
Serenity In Murder, American PROCD7231 (1994) (USA 1 track promotion release). Serenity In Murder.
DIVINE INTERVENTION, Def American (1994). Killing Fields / Sex, Murder, Art / Fictional Reality / Dittohead / Divine Intervention / Circle Of Beliefs / SS-3 / Serenity In Murder / 213 / Mind Control. Chart positions: 8 USA, 15 UK, 18 GERMANY, 20 NEW ZEALAND.
Serenity In Murder, American (1995). Serenity In Murder (Album version) / At Dawn They Sleep (Live) / Dead Skin Mask (Live) / Divine Intervention (Live) / Dittohead (Live).
Ditto Head, American ALASKA1 (1995) (USA promotion). Ditto Head / Serenity And Murder.
Live Intrusion, American 74321 38325-2 SLAY1 (1995) (Free CD single with 'Undisputed Attitude' album). Witching Hour / Ditto Head / Divine Intervention.
Serenity In Murder, Def American 74321262347 (1995). Serenity In Murder / Raining Blood / Dittohead / South Of Heaven.
Serenity In Murder, Def American 74321262342 (1995). Serenity In Murder / At Dawn They Sleep / Dead Skin Mask / Divine Intervention.
Serenity In Murder, Def American 74321312482 (1995). Serenity In Murder / Angel Of Death / Mandatory Suicide / War Ensemble.
Abolished Government, Sub Pop SP368 (1996) (Split single with T.S.O.L.). Abolished Government / Superficial Love.
UNDISPUTED ATTITUDE, American 74321357591 (1996). Disintegration—Free Money / Verbal Abuse—Leeches / Abolish Government- –Superficial Love / Can't Stand You / D.D.A.M.M. / Guilty Of Being White / I Hate You / Filler—I Don't Want To Hear It / Spiritual Law / Sick Boy / Mr Freeze / Violent Pacification / Richard Hung Himself / I Wanna Be Your God / Gemini. Chart positions: 22 NEW ZEALAND, 31 UK, 34 USA, 45 GERMANY.
Stain Of Mind, Columbia XPCD1005 (1998) (1 track German promotion release). Stain Of Mind.
Bitter Peace, American (1998) (Promotion release). Bitter Peace.
DIABOLUS IN MUSICA, American 4913022 (1998). Bitter Peace / Death's Head / Stain Of Mind / Overt Enemy / Perversions Of Pain / Love To Hate / Desire / In The Name Of God / Scrum / Screaming From The Sky / Point. Chart positions: 15 NEW ZEALAND, 23 FRANCE, 27 UK, 29 SWEDEN, 31 USA, 32 GERMANY.
God Hates Us All, Columbia XPCD1370 (2001) (UK promotional release). Discipline / God Send Death / Bloodline / Here Comes The Pain / Cast Down / Seven Faces.
God Send Death, American (2001). God Send Death / Addict / Scarstruck.
GOD HATES US ALL, Sony 586 386-2 (2001). Darkness Of Christ / Disciple / God Send Death / New Faith / Bloodline / Threshold / Exile / Seven Faces / Cast Down / War Zone / Here Comes The Pain / Payback. Chart positions: 9 CANADA, 9 GERMANY, 12 FINLAND, 18 SWEDEN, 23 BELGIUM, 28 USA, 31 UK.
SOUNDTRACK TO THE APOCALYPSE, Def Jam B151902 (2003) (Ammo box set). Angel Of Death / Criminally Insane (Remix) / Postmortem / Raining Blood / Aggressive Perfector / South Of Heaven / Silent Scream / Live Undead / Mandatory Suicide / Spill The Blood / War Ensemble / Dead Skin Mask / Hallowed Point / Born Of Fire / Seasons In The Abyss / Hell Awaits / The Antichrist / Chemical Warfare / Sex. Murder. Art. / Dittohead / Divine Intervention / Serenity In Murder / 213 / Can't Stand You / D.D.A.M.M. / Gemini / Bitter Peace / Death's Head / Stain Of Mind / Disciple / God Send Death / New Faith / In-A-Gadda-Da-Vida / Disorder / Memories Of Tomorrow / Human Disease / Unguarded Instinct / Wicked / Addict / Starstruck / Ice Titan (Live in California, March 1983) / The Antichrist (Rehearsal In Tom's Garage, December 1982) / Fight Till Death (Rehearsal In Tom's Garage, December 1982) / Necrophiliac (Live In California, September 1985) / Piece By Piece (Studio Rough Mix/Outtake) / Raining Blood (Live In Canada, November 1986) / Angel Of Death (Live In Canada, November 1986) / Raining Blood (Jeff Hanneman Home Recordings) / South Of Heaven (Jeff Hannemann Home Recordings) / Seasons In The Abyss (Live In Michigan, June 1991) / Mandatory Suicide (Live In Michigan, June 1991) / Mind Control (Live in Brazil, 1994) / No Remorse (I Wanna Die) (Feat. ATARI TEENAGE RIOT) / Dittohead (Live In California, May 1998) / Sex. Murder. Art. (Live In California, May 1998) / Bloodline (Live In Sweden, 2002) / Payback (Live In Sweden, 2002) / Die By The Sword (Live In California, March 1983 video) / Aggressive Perfector (Live In California, 1983 video) / Praise Of Death (Live In California, 1984 video) / Haunting The Chapel (Live In Sweden, May 1995 video) / Necrophobic (Live In New York, 1986 video) / Reborn

(Live In New York, 1986 video) / Jesus Saves (Live In New York, 1986 video) / War Ensemble (Live In Michigan, 1991 video) / South Of Heaven (Live In Michigan, 1991 video) / Dead Skin Mask (Live In Michigan, 1991 video) / Gemini (Live In California, August 1996 video) / 'Heaviest Band' Award—Kerrang! Magazine Award 1996 (Home Footage video) / EPK For "Diabolus In Musica" / Stain Of Mind (Live In Japan, July 1998 video) / Bloodline (Live On ESPN, July 2002 video) / Disciple (Live In France, July 2003 video) / God Send Death (Live In France, July 2003 video) / Darkness Of Christ (Live) / Disciple (Live) / War Ensemble (Live) / Stain Of Mind (Live) / Postmortem (Live) / Raining Blood (Live) / Hell Awaits (Live) / At Dawn They Sleep (Live) / Dead Skin Mask (Live) / Seasons In The Abyss (Live) / Mandatory Suicide (Live) / Chemical Warfare (Live) / South Of Heaven (Live) / Angel Of Death (Live).

Eternal Pyre, Hot Topic (2006) (USA release. 'Hot Topic' store exclusive. Limited edition 5000). Cult / War Ensemble (Live at Full Force festival, Germany video) / Slayer in the studio (Video).

Eternal Pyre, (2006). Cult / War Ensemble (Live at Full Force festival, Germany video) / Slayer in the studio (Video). Chart positions: 2 FINLAND, 48 SWEDEN.

CHRIST ILLUSION, American Recordings (2006) (Censored cover). Flesh Storm / Catalyst / Skeleton Christ / Eyes Of The Insane / Jihad / Consfearacy / Catatonic / Black Serenade / Cult / Supremist.

CHRIST ILLUSION, American Recordings 9362443002 (2006). Flesh Storm / Catalyst / Skeleton Christ / Eyes Of The Insane / Jihad / Consfearacy / Catatonic / Black Serenade / Cult / Supremist. Chart positions: 2 FINLAND, 2 GERMANY, 2 GREECE, 3 CANADA, 4 SWEDEN, 5 USA, 6 AUSTRIA, 8 HOLLAND, 9 AUSTRALIA, 9 POLAND, 10 IRELAND, 10 NORWAY, 10 NEW ZEALAND, 11 HUNGARY, 18 ITALY, 23 UK, 52 FRANCE.

Eyes Of The Insane, Warner Bros. (2006) (CD single). Eyes Of The Insane (Album version) / Eyes Of The Insane (Live version).

Eyes Of The Insane, Warner Bros. (2006) (CD single). Eyes Of The Insane / Cult (Live) / Reborn (Live In New York 1986) (Video).

Eyes Of The Insane, Warner Bros. (2006) (7" vinyl single). Eyes Of The Insane / Cult (Live).

SODOM

GELSENKIRCHEN, GERMANY — *Tom Angelripper (vocals / bass), Frank Blackfire (guitar), Chris Witchunter (drums).*

Lambasted outside of their native Germany throughout much of their career the legacy of stoic Thrash outfit SODOM has witnessed a 1990s renaissance of appreciation for their brutal almost primitive Metal attack. SODOM, hailing from Gelsenkirchen, debuted as a trio consisting of guitarist Angelripper (a.k.a. Thomas Such), drummer Witchhunter (Christian Dudeck) and vocalist Aggressor (Frank Testegen) with the demo 'Witching Metal' in 1983. The earliest SODOM incarnation, dating to 1982, had featured Bloody Monster (Rainer Focke) on the drums.

In 1984 a second demo, 'Victims Of Death', included the original tracks boosted with the addition of four new songs. The demo began to receive a great deal of positive press, although Aggressor would choose to opt out. He was eventually replaced by Grave Violator (Josef "Peppi" Dominic) and the new line-up debuted for the first time at the 'Black Metal Night' in Frankfurt. After a further show with DESTRUCTION and IRON ANGEL, Steamhammer SPV Records signed the band and would swiftly release SODOM's debut EP entitled 'In The Sign Of Evil'.

Grave Violator left at the end of 1985 and the debut, full blown 'Obsessed By Cruelty' album featured Destructor (Michael Wulf). However, an additional guitarist in Ahathoor (Uwe Christophers) recorded the track 'After The Deluge'. Of note is that two versions of 'Obsessed By Cruelty' were issued in a short space of time. The original mix was pressed up, but then not found to be satisfactory and so the entire album was remixed at Hilpoltstein Studios in Nürnberg. A further variant came when the US license, to Metal Blade Records, strangely deleted the track 'After The Deluge', even though it was listed on the cover. 'Obsessed By Cruelty' would also play a significant part in the rise of the Norwegian Black Metal scene when MAYHEM band leader Euronymous chose the title of its lead in track, 'Deathlike Silence', as the branding for his notorious record label.

Immediately after the record was released Destructor quit to join KREATOR. Uwe Christophers replaced him. During a lull in 1986 Witchhunter travelled to Sweden to rehearse with BATHORY for a proposed European tour with CELTIC FROST and DESTRUCTION. The tour was shelved and the drummer returned to SODOM.

Now with Blackfire (Frank Gosdzik) on guitar, SODOM toured Europe as co-headliners with WHIPLASH in 1987, promoting the Harris Johns produced 'Persecution Mania' album, but Blackfire also quit the band to join KREATOR on an American tour on the eve of the 'Agent Orange' tour supported by SEPULTURA in 1989. The band found a temporary replacement to fulfill the dates in MEKONG DELTA's Uwe Baltrusch. Still, the latest album, Agent Orange', sold strongly shifting in excess of 90'000 units in Europe. In January 1990 SODOM recruited new guitarist Michael Hoffman (ex-ASSASSIN) and the ensuing 'Better Off Dead' produced by Harris Johns, included a cover of the THIN LIZZY classic 'Cold Sweat'. The 'Tapping The Vein' album was released in 1992 with a new guitarist Andy Brings. For the 1994 album 'Get What You Deserve' album SODOM drafted in a new drummer in the shape of ex-LIVING DEATH, VIOLENT FORCE and SACRED CHAO man Atomic Steif.

SODOM released a live album, 'Marooned Live', in 1994 and a new studio album, 'Masquerade In Blood', in 1995. Angelripper issued a solo album of drinking songs 'Ein Schöner Tag' in 1995. Scoring a degree of success with this off-the-cuff recording, Angelripper unwittingly ignited a separate parallel solo career for himself as 'Onkel Tom'. Back with the main band, the man formed a new line-up comprised of guitarist Bernemann (Bernd Kost) and his ex-CROWS and RANDALICA colleague, drummer Bobby Schottkowski in order to record the new studio album 'Til Death Do Us Unite' for new label G.U.N. Records.

"Til Death Do Us Unite' featured a drastically reworked version of PAUL SIMON tune 'Hazy Shade Of Winter' (as made popular by THE BANGLES). The original version of the album also sported a wonderful cover photograph juxtaposing a pregnant woman with a male beer belly. Sadly this clever image was banned.

SODOM continued their resurgence in 1999 with the Harris Johns produced 'Code Red' on fresh label Drakkar. December German shows, running from Christmas Day until New Year's Eve, had the band packaged with GODDESS OF DESIRE and TANKARD. The millennium seemed likely to herald a SODOM tribute album. The group would form part of a nostalgic Thrash Metal mammoth tour of Germany with compatriots DESTRUCTION and KREATOR commencing 26th December in Ludwigsburg and running through into the new year. Their 2001 album, 'M-16'—a concept album dealing with the Vietnam war, would break the German charts at no. 88.

In June of 2004 the group entered House of Audio studios in Karlsdorf, Germany with producer Achim Köhler for a new record. That same year the band would have their classic cut 'Burst Command Til War' chosen as a pioneering piece of music for a compilation assembled by DARKTHRONE drummer Fenriz, released through Peaceville Records and entitled 'Fenriz Presents The Best Of Old School Black Metal'. February of 2005 found SODOM touring South America. The band announced a one off North American date at the 'Minneapolis Mayhem 2' festival in May. Coinciding, the Vinyl Maniacs label re-issued early works 'Agent Orange' and 'In The Sign Of Evil' as limited edition vinyl picture discs.

Tom Angelripper guested on pedal steel guitar on POWERGOD's cover version of TANK's 'The War Drags Ever On' for inclusion on their 'Long Live The Loud–That's Metal Lesson II' released through Massacre Records in July 2005.

SODOM's live schedule throughout mid 2005 included appearances at such events as 'A Summer Day In Hell' in Rome,

SODOM

Italy, the Burgebrach 'Sternenfestival' in Germany, the Spanish Guernika 'Metalway' festival, the Dutch Bergen 'Hole In The Sky' festival, Germany's Hofheim 'Outer Limits Special' and the Baltic Seas 'Metal Ferry 34.000 Tons Metal' event. The band also toured with FATAL EMBRACE and VENDETTA for German dates in September 2005.

SODOM allied themselves with Finnish Polka-Metal exponents FINNTROLL for US touring in January 2006. The band's appearance at the Gelsenkirchen 'Rock Hard' festival in Germany during June was taped and subsequently the track 'Axis Of Evil' was included on the 'Rock Hard' magazine compilation album 'Rock Hard: Das Festival 2006'.

The band announced a two day "Thrash Domination" stint at Tokyo's famed Club Citta on September 16th and 17th ranked alongside DEATH ANGEL, VENOM, DRAGONLORD and ONSLAUGHT. German shows in December would be backed by FINNTROLL.

As part of an Australian tour, SODOM's June 9th 2007 concert at The Republic Bar in Hobart was filmed for a DVD release. The band revealed their August 2007 'Wacken Open Air' festival show would be a specially crafted set to reflect the band's 25th anniversary. As such, the group performed archive tracks, some never previously played live, with guesting ex-members such as guitarists Grave Violator, Athätor, Frank Blackfire, Michael Hoffman and Andy Brings plus drummers Atomic Steif and Chris Witchunter.

Witching Metal, Sodom (1982) (Demo). Devil's Attack / Witching Metal / Live From Hell / Poisoned Blood.

Victims Of Death, Sodom (1984) (Demo). Witch Hammer / Devil's Attack / Let's Fight In The Darkness Of Hell / Victims Of Death / Live From Hell / Poisoned Blood / Satan's Conjuration / Witching Metal.

In The Sign Of Evil EP, Steamhammer SPV 60-2120 (1984). Outbreak Of Evil / Sepulchral Voice / Blasphemer / Witching Metal / Burst Command Til War.

OBSESSED BY CRUELTY, Steamhammer SPV 08-2121 (1986). Deathlike Silence / Brandish The Sceptre / Proselytism Real / Equinox / After The Deluge / Obsessed By Cruelty / Fall Of Majesty Town / Nuctemeron / Pretenders To The Throne / Witchhammer / Volcanic Slut.

Expurse Of Sodomy EP, Steamhammer SPV 12-2122 (1987). Sodomy And Lust / The Conqueror / My Atonement.

PERSECUTION MANIA, Sodom SPV CD 85-7509 (1987). Nuclear Winter / Electrocution / Iron Fist / Persecution Mania / Enchanted Land / Procession To Golgotha / Christ Passion / Conjuration / Bombenhagel / Outbreak Of Evil / Sodomy And Lust / The Conqueror / My Atonement.

MORTAL WAY OF LIFE (LIVE), Steamhammer SPV DO-LP 80-7575 (1988). Persecution Mania / Outbreak Of Evil / Conqueror / Iron Fist / Obsessed By Cruelty / Nuclear Winter Electrocution / Blasphemer / Enchanted Land / Sodomy And Lust / Christ Passion / Bombenhagel / My Atonement.

AGENT ORANGE, Steamhammer SPV CD 076-75972 (1989). Agent Orange / Tired And Red / Incest / Remember The Fallen / Magic Dragon / Exhibition Bout / Ausgebombt / Baptism Of Fire.

Ausgebombt, Steamhammer SPV 051-7604 (1989) (12" single). Ausgebombt / Don't Walk Away (Live) / Incest (Live).

Ausgebombt, Steamhammer SPV 55-7605 (1989) (CD single). Ausgebombt / Don't Walk Away (Live) / Incest (Live).

BETTER OFF DEAD, Steamhammer SPV CD 076 76262 (1990). An Eye For An Eye / Shellfire Defense / The Saw Is The Law / Turn Your Head Around / Capture The Flag / Bloodtrails / Never Healing Wound / Better Off Dead / Resurrection / Stalnorgel.

The Saw Is The Law, Steamhammer 050 76305 (1991). The Saw Is The Law / Tarred And Feathered / The Kids Wanna Rock.

TAPPING THE VEIN, Steamhammer SPV CD 076-76542 (1992). Body Parts / Skinned Alive / One Step Over The Line / Deadline / Bullet In The Head / The Crippler / Wachturn / Tapping The Vein / Back To War / Hunting Season / Reincarnation. Chart position: 56 GERMANY.

Aber Bitte Mit Sahne, Steamhammer SPV 055-76723 (1993). Aber Bitte Mit Sahne / Sodomised / Abuse / Skinned Alive '93.

Get What You Deserve, Steamhammer SPV GET 1 (1993) (Promotion release). Get What You Deserve / Yabba The Hut / Delight In Slaying / Die Stumme Ursel / Eat Me.

GET WHAT YOU DESERVE, Steamhammer SPV CD 084-76762 (1994). Get What You Deserve / Jabba The Hut / Jesus Screamer / Delight In Slaying / Die Stumme Ursel / Freaks Of Nature / Eat Me / Unbury The Hatched / Into Perdition / Sodomised / Fellows In Misery / Moby Dick / Silence Is Consent / Erwachet / Gomorrah / Angel Dust. Chart position: 45 GERMANY.

MAROONED LIVE, Steamhammer SPV CD 084-76852 (1994). Intro / Outbreak Of Evil / Jabba The Hut / Agent Orange / Jesus Screamer / Ausgebombt / Tarred And Feathered / Abuse / Remember The Fallen / An Eye For An Eye / Tired And Red / Eat Me / Die Stumme Ursel / Sodomised / Gomorrah / One Step Over The Line / Freaks Of Nature / Aber Bitte Mit Sahne / Silence Is Consent / Wachturm Erwachet / Stalinhagel / Fratricide / Gone To Glory.

MASQUERADE IN BLOOD, Steamhammer SPV CD 085-76962 (1995). In Blood / Gathering Of Minds / Fields Of Honour / Braindead / Verrecke! / Shadow Of Damnation / Peacemaker's Law / Murder In My Eyes / Unwanted Youth / Mantelmann / Scum / Hydrophobia / Let's Break The Law. Chart position: 76 GERMANY.

'TIL DEATH DO US UNITE, Great Unlimited Noises GUN 199 (1997). Frozen Screams / Fuck The Police / Gisela / That's What An Unknown Killer Diarised / Hanging Judge / No Way Out / Polytoximaniac / 'Til Death Do Us Unite / Hazy Shade Of Winter / Suicidal Justice / Wander In The Valley / Sow The Seeds Of Discord / Master Of Disguise / Schwerter Zu Pflugscharen / Hey, Hey, Rock n' Roll Star.

CODE RED, Drakkar DRCD 67384 2 (1999). Intro / Code Red / What Hell Can Create / Tombstone / Liquidation / Spiritual Demise / Warlike Conspiracy / Cowardice / The Vice Of Killing / Visual Buggery / Book Burning / The Wolf And The Lamb / Addicted To Abstinence.

CODE RED + HOMAGE TO THE GODS (LIMITED EDITION), Drakkar (1999). Intro / Code Red / What Hell Can Create / Tombstone / Liquidation / Spiritual Demise / Warlike Conspiracy / Cowardice / The Vice Of Killing / Visual Buggery / Book Burning / The Wolf And The Lamb / Addicted To Abstinence / Sodomy & Lust (CRADLE OF FILTH) / Burst Command Til War (IMPALED NAZARENE) / Nuclear Winter (KRISIUN) / Remember The Fallen (DARK FUNERAL) / Blasphemer (LUCIFERION) / Outbreak Of Evil (ATANATOS) / Christ Passion (DECAYED REMAINS) / The Conqueror (ENTHRONED) / Proselytism Real (DESASTER) / Witchhammer (SWORDMASTER) / Agent Orange (REVENANT) / Bombenhagel

(GODDESS OF DESIRE) / Nuctemeron (ORDER FROM CHAOS) / Sepulchral Voice (BRUTAL TRUTH) / Ausbruch des Bösen (RANDALICA).

M-16, Steamhammer SPV CD 085-72442 (2001). Among The Weirdcong / I Am The War / Napalm In The Morning / Minejumper / Genocide / Little Boy / M-16 / Lead Injection / Cannon Fodder / Marines / Surfin' Bird. Chart position: 88 GERMANY.

ONE NIGHT IN BANGKOK—LIVE, Steamhammer SPV CD 091-69392 (2003). Among The Weirdcong / The Vice Of Killing / Der Wachturm / The Saw Is The Law / Blasphemer / Sodomized / Remember The Fallen / I Am The War / Eat Me! / Masquerade In Blood / M-16 / Agent Orange / Outbreak Of Evil / Sodomy & Lust / Napalm In The Morning / Fuck The Police / Tombstone / Witching Metal / The Enemy Inside / Die Stumme Ursel / Ausgebombt / Code Red / Stalinhagel / Among The Weirdcong (Video).

SODOM, Steamhammer SPV CD 085-69832 (2006). Blood On Your Lips / Wanted Dead / Buried In The Justice Ground / City Of Go / Bibles And Guns / Axis Of Evil / Lords Of Depravity / No Captures / Lay Down The Law / Nothing To Regret / The Enemy Inside.

SOILWORK

HELSINGBORG, SWEDEN — *Björn Strid (vocals), Peter Wichers (guitar), Ludvig Svartz (guitar), Ola Flink (bass), Carlos Del Olmo (keyboards), Jimmy Persson (drums).*

Helsingborg act SOILWORK's initial trademark was to blend a heady mixture of Thrash and Death Metal but latter releases, marked by the turning point 'A Predator's Portrait' album, have seen the band mature apace by injecting huge amounts of melody making them serious contenders for greatness. As such, the band's schedule accelerated markedly to involve lengthy bouts of international touring.

Initially the group, instigated during 1995, operated billed as INFERIOR BREED but as SOILWORK opened proceedings with the 1997 demo 'In Dreams We Fall Into The Eternal Lake'. The band structure at this point involved frontman Björn Strid, going under the name of 'Speed', guitarist Peter Vicious' (a.k.a. Peter Wichers), second guitarist Ludvig Svartz and drummer Jimmy Persson. A former bassist, Carl-Gustav Döös, had decamped beforehand, as had a formative guitarist Mattias Nilsson, the latter resurfacing with KAYSER.

A copy of 'In Dreams We Fall Into The Eternal Lake' was given to ARCH ENEMY guitarist Mike Amott who, obviously impressed, passed it onto various labels spurring a number of offers. The May 1998 album 'Steel Bath Suicide', released through French label Listenable Records, was produced by Fredrik Nordström at Fredman studios. The band that constructed these tracks now incorporated Ola Flink on bass and Carlos Del Olmo Holmberg handling keyboards. Japanese versions were augmented with the traditionally expected extra tracks with 'Disintegrated Skies' and a cover version of DEEP PURPLE's 'Burn'. Road promotion had SOILWORK proffering their wares on European stages backing NAGLFAR, DARKANE and KRISIUN.

Listenable kept the band on for a further round of Death—Thrash in October 1999's 'The Chainheart Machine', again a Fredrik Nordström produced effort witnessing the employment of the 'Jaffa quartet' massed violin section of Ullik Johansson, Julia Petersson, Amanda Ingvaldsson, Fanny Petersson, Alva Ingvaldsson and Katalin Tibell. Newly installed on drums would be Henry Ranta and a new guitarist, Ola Frenning, to replace the departed Svartz. Whilst still locked in stereotypical "Gothenburg Death" territory, SOILWORK adventurously maximised on twin lead guitar harmony playing to good effect. Japanese editions added bonus cut 'Shadowchild'. The European touring circuit was to feel the force of SOILWORK once again when the band supported CANNIBAL CORPSE, DEFLESHED and MARDUK prior to their first live engagement in Japan paired with DARK TRANQUILLITY. Another notable recording executed that same year would be their interpretation of MERCYFUL FATE's 'Egypt', featured on 'The Unholy Sounds Of The Demon Bells—A Tribute To Mercyful Fate' collection issued via Poland's Still Dead Productions.

In outside activity, Peter Wichers would add session guitar to CONSTRUCDEAD's 2000 EP 'Turn'. SOILWORK signed to Germany's Nuclear Blast label for the 'A Predator's Portrait' album, launched in February 2001. This is where SOILWORK hit the crossroads of their career, not fully embracing experimentation but adopting more melody and significantly dropping Björn Strid's previously favoured Death growls for a cleaner approach. Fredrik Nordström maintained his position as producer, Eskil Simonsson provided samples and studio guests included notable figures Mattias IA Eklundh of FREAK KITCHEN, donating a guitar solo to 'Needlefeast' and OPETH's Mikael Åkerfeldt vocalising on the title track. In the Far East, 'A Predator's Portrait' hosted extra cut 'Asylum Dance'.

They would return to the studio in October 2001 with new keyboard man Sven Karlsson, of EVERGREY repute, and producer DEVIN TOWNSEND in tow, this union seeing the Canadian's influence leaving a firm impression on the band. SOILWORK's burgeoning reputation was heightened by the delivery of a March 2002 album 'Natural Born Chaos'. Strid's vocal parts were now almost wholly delivered clean and Karlsson's keyboard atmospherics figured prominently, including the use of Hammond organ on ''Black Star Deciever'. Townsend's lush production breathed new life into the band, who adopted his techniques for future outings.

The band toured America during the summer packaged with HYPOCRISY and KILLSWITCH ENGAGE. One notable gig being at the San Jose Cactus Club where Chuck Billy of TESTAMENT lent backing vocals to the track 'Follow The Hollow'. SOILWORK joined IN FLAMES and PAIN for touring in mainland Europe during October.

Members of SOILWORK, in alliance with DARKANE personnel and CONSTRUCDEAD drummer Erik Thyselius also operated the project band TERROR 2000. Bassist Ola Flink would also be active with HATELIGHT, issuing the demos 'Word Ammunition' and 'Ricochet' in 2002 and 2003 respectively.

The band entered Helsingborg's Queenstreet Recording studios with the trusted Fredrik Nordström during mid December to cut their fifth album. Backing vocals for these sessions came courtesy of HATELIGHT's Jens Broman. 'Figure Number Five', issued by Nuclear Blast in April, became the recipient of quite huge acclaim in the Metal world. A novel promotional video for the track 'Rejection Role' saw the band in a turf war with the members of IN FLAMES. Touring in North America saw the band hooking up with headliners IN FLAMES and road partners CHIMAIRA and UNEARTH for a month long trek commencing June 26th in Toronto, Canada. However, the band would lose the services of drummer Henry Ranta beforehand, swiftly replacing him with the EBONY TEARS, DOG FACED GODS, Funksters IT'S ALIVE, MANIC DEPRESSION, SOUTHPAW, EYEBALL and SORCERER credited Richard Evensand. The new recruit debuted with the band at the Gelsenkirchen, Germany 'Rock Hard' festival.

The band put in a showing at the ARCH ENEMY headlined Busan International Rock Festival at Daedepo Beach in Korea on August 8th before uniting with CHILDREN OF BODOM for a Japanese tour in September. A further bout of November US shows saw the band partnered with premier British Black Metal band CRADLE OF FILTH and TYPE O NEGATIVE. Rickard Evansand joined CHIMAIRA during December. SOILWORK, pulling in Dirk Verbeuren from French Thrashers SCARVE as substitute on drums, undertook a headline tour of the UK in February 2004 supported by fellow Swedes THE FORSAKEN. The band then partnered with Thrash veterans ANTHRAX and KILLSWITCH ENGAGE for Australian and Japanese dates in April 2004. Verbeuren then stepped in as substitute drummer for Belgian gore-mongers ABORTED's live dates.

Björn Strid would lend guest vocals to Italian melodic Death

Metal band DISARMONIA MUNDI's 2004 album 'Fragments Of D-Generation'. SOILWORK, after festival appearances at 'With Full Force' in Germany, 'Roskilde' in Denmark and the 'Tuska' event in Finland, would enter Studio Kuling in Örebro during September to work with producer Daniel Bergstrand on their sixth album, billed 'Stabbing The Drama', projected for early 2005 issue. European digipacks added extra track 'Wherever Thorns May Grow' whilst Japanese variants were also boosted with an additional song, 'Killed By Ignition'. . US dates for January 2005 had the band packaged with DARK TRANQUILLITY and HYPOCRISY.

SOILWORK's profile rose significantly as 'Stabbing The Drama' entered the national Swedish album charts at an impressive number 14 in late February. Notably, the album also marked first time chart entries for the band in Austria, Finland and France. The band had their track 'Stabbing The Drama' featured on the soundtrack to the 'Rainbow Six Lockdown' game issued by 3volution Productions. The following month Björn Strid revealed he had fired up a new side project dubbed COLDSEED in a collaboration with BLIND GUARDIAN drummer Thomen Stauch, guitarists Thorsten Praest and Gonzalo Alfageme Lopez and the BLIND GUARDIAN and SIEGES EVEN bassist Oli Holzwarth. Strid also put in a guest vocal appearance on German Thrash act DESTRUCTION's 'Inventor Of Evil' album.

Throughout the Summer of 2005 SOILWORK joined the mammoth cast of bands on the US 'Ozzfest' tour alongside such industry giants as BLACK SABBATH, IRON MAIDEN and VELVET REVOLVER. The trek's 13th August Mountain View, California stop proved notable for the band as they were joined onstage by guesting TESTAMENT frontman Chuck Billy for the track 'Follow The Hollow'. Scandinavian, UK and European dates in October saw CONSTRUCDEAD as support. November 8th, at New York's Irving Plaza, marked the start of another US tour, the band forming up a bill comprising FEAR FACTORY, DARKANE and STRAPPING YOUNG LAD.

Guitarist Peter Wichers announced his departure in mid December. Early 2006 found Björn Strid involving himself in a studio collaboration with bassist Steve DiGiorgio, of SADUS, SEBASTIAN BACH, TESTAMENT and DEATH, Glen Alvelais from FORBIDDEN, TESTAMENT and LD/50 and Jeremy Colson of the STEVE VAI band, MARTY FRIEDMAN, MICHAEL SCHENKER, APARTMENT 26, DALI'S DILEMMA and LD/50 repute.

A replacement guitarist would be installed in April 2006, the new man being Daniel Antonsson of DIMENSION ZERO and PATHOS repute. SOILWORK joined the 'Metal Hammer' sponsored 'European Neckbreaker's Ball' 2006 tour, also featuring HYPOCRISY, SCAR SYMMETRY and ONE MAN ARMY AND THE UNDEAD QUARTET, commencing 11th April in Denmark.

A whole slew of European open air appearances took the band through the summer. However, unable to secure flights in time for drummer Dirk Verbeuren, residing in Los Angeles, the band pulled in DARKANE's Peter Wildoer for 'Festimad' in Madrid, Spain plus shows in Piteå and Malmö. The band was set to put in a significant appearance at the GUNS N' ROSES headlined 'Download' festival in Castle Donington, UK on June 11th. However, guitarist Ola Frenning suffered a "vascular spasm", forcing a cancellation.

That same month word arrived that Peter Wichers was in collaboration with SANCTUARY and NEVERMORE singer Warrel Dane, working on his debut solo album. The band's appearance at the German 'Rock Hard' festival in June was taped and subsequently the track 'Stabbing The Drama' was included on the 'Rock Hard' magazine compilation album 'Rock Hard: Das Festival 2006'.

September 2006 UK shows were supported by French Thrashers LYZANXIA. The group returned for another North American tour commencing October 5th at the Jaxx venue in West Springfield, Virginia taking along DARKEST HOUR, MNEMIC and THREAT SIGNAL for 'The Last Stab' dates into mid November. On November 7th SOILWORK were announced as replaced a cancelling SIX FEET UNDER as the headliner of the X-mas Festivals tour, scheduled to kick off at the Berlin K17 venue December 8th, alongside GOREFEST, BELPHEGOR, TRAIL OF TEARS and DARZAMAT. However, the following day the band's agency denied this, saying the group was unable to participate.

SOILWORK announced in early March 2007 that Daniel Antonsson, from DIMENSION ZERO and PATHOS, had secured the guitar position.

In Dreams We Fall Into The Eternal Lake, (1997). Bound To Illusions / My Need / In Dreams We Fall Into The Eternal Lake / In A Close Encounter / Skin After Skin.

STEEL BATH SUICIDE, Listenable POSH 012 (1998). Entering The Angel Diabolique / Sadistic Lullaby / My Need / Skin After Skin / Wings Of Domain / Steelbath Suicide / In A Close Encounter / Centro De Predomino / Razorlives / Demon In Veins / The Aardvark Trail / Sadistic Lullabye.

THE CHAINHEART MACHINE, Listenable POSH 017 (1999). The Chainheart Machine / Bulletbeast / Millionflame / Generation Speedkill (Nice Dirty Day For Public Suicide) / Neon Rebels / Possessing The Angels / Spirits Of Future Sun / Machine Gun Majesty / Room No 99.

A PREDATOR'S PORTRAIT, Nuclear Blast NB 582-2 (2001). Bastard Chain / Like An Average Stalker / Needlefeast / Neurotica Rampage / The Analyst / Grand Failure Anthem / Structure Divine / Shadowchild / Final Fatal Force / A Predator's Portrait.

NATURAL BORN CHAOS, Nuclear Blast NB 581-2 (2002). Follow The Hollow / As We Speak / The Flameout / Natural Born Chaos / Mindfields / The Bringer / Black Star Deceiver / Mercury Shadow / No More Angels / Soilworker's Song Of The Damned / Kvicksilver.

FIGURE NUMBER FIVE, Nuclear Blast NB 1108-2 (2003). Rejection Role / Overload / Figure Number Five / Strangler / Light The Torch / Departure Plan / Cranking The Sirens / Brickwalker / The Mindmaker / Distortion Sleep / Downfall 24. Chart position: 59 SWEDEN.

Rejection Role, Nuclear Blast NB 1137-2 (2003). Rejection Role / Departure Plan.

Light The Torch, Nuclear Blast NB 1223-2 (2003). Light The Torch / Figure Number Five / Light The Torch (Video).

The Early Chapters, Listenable POSH 054 (2004). Burn / Disintegrated Skies / Gypsy / Shadow Child / Aardvark Trail (Live).

Stabbing The Drama, Nuclear Blast NB 1417-2 (2005). Stabbing The Drama / Asylum Dance. Chart position: 7 FINLAND.

STABBING THE DRAMA, Nuclear Blast NB 1416-2 (2005) (Limited edition digipack). Stabbing The Drama / One With The Flies / Weapon Of Vanity / The Crestfallen / Nerve / Stalemate / Distance / Observation Slave / Fate In Motion / Blind Eye Halo / If Possible / Wherever Thorns May Grow. Chart positions: 14 SWEDEN, 19 FINLAND, 52 GERMANY, 63 AUSTRIA, 143 FRANCE.

STABBING THE DRAMA, Nuclear Blast NB 1377-2 (2005). Stabbing The Drama / One With The Flies / Weapon Of Vanity / The Crestfallen / Nerve / Stalemate / Distance / Observation Slave / Fate In Motion / Blind Eye Halo / If Possible.

SOLITAIRE

FINLAND — *Mika Savalainen (vocals), Riku (guitar), Mika Vaakainen (guitar), Mikko (bass), Kalle Vallane (drums).*

Retro Speed Metal band SOLITAIRE was formulated during May of 1995 by former DEAFENING SILENCE personnel guitarist Riku and bassist Mikko. In November of that year drummer Rami Koivisio, a former member of HILPEA ROGER, had enrolled. It would not be until March of the following year that singer Miko Savalainen from Punk band BEATHOVENS took the frontman role. With Koivisio being fired erstwhile VELTOT KOIRAT man Onni Kilkku would step into the position of drummer in February of 1997. However, during the summer Savalainen would leave to concentrate on his band BEATHOVENS.

SOLITAIRE regrouped in the August, pulling in guitarist Mike 'Waaqqu' Vaakainen and vocalist Juha Alam. The latter candidate's tenure was brief though and the band reverted back to a quartet with Riku handling lead vocal duties. Ville Kilkku, former vocalist with ANTHELION, boosted the numbers in early 1998 but by August he too was out of the picture and Savalainen made a return to the SOLITAIRE microphone. The band wrapped up the year by recording 'The Dead End Investigations' demo after which Kalle 'Kalu' Vallane of MENTAL HANGOVER became next in line for the drum stool. That year SOLITAIRE would feature on the Hateball Records compilation 'Spirit Of The New Age' and issue a second demo 'Locked In . . . Break Out!'.

In 2001 SOLITAIRE's 'Lead Into Temptation' demo and promotional video for the track 'Listen To The Priest' led in turn to a deal secured with the German Iron Glory label.

Demo 1997, (1997) (Demo). I'll Never Grow Up / The Tongue Of Cobra / Eye Of The Needle / My Father Was A Soldier / Crusher.
The Dead End Investigations, (1999) (Demo). Nowhere To Run / Alcatraz / The Silent Trigger / Thunderhorse.
Locked In . . . Break Out!, (2000) (Demo). Eye Of The Needle / Liquidator / Escape From Bedlam / A Slash In The Night.
Lead Into Temptation, (2001) (Demo). The Crossfire / Listen To The Priest / Wrong Place, Wrong Time / Juggernaut.
RISING TO THE CHALLENGE, Iron Glory IG 1028 (2002). The Crossfire / Listen To The Priest / Rising To The Challenge / Thunderhorse / Juggernaut / Eye Of The Needle / I'll Never Grow Up / Alcatraz / Escape From Bedlam / A Slash In The Night.
EXTREMELY FLAMMABLE, Iron Glory IG 1035 (2004). Countdown / Extremely / Heroes Fall Down / Out Of My Role / Breaking Point / Metalsquad / I Won't Come In Peace / Speed Trap / Steel Against Steel / Boy Without A World.

SOLITARY

PRESTON, LANCASHIRE, UK — *Richard Sherrington (vocals / guitar), Andy Mellor (guitar), Michael Parkl (bass), Roy Miller (drums).*

A stoic British Metal band that has endured more than it's fair share of line up ructions over the course of years. SOLITARY came together in Preston, Lancashire during July of 1995 citing a line up of frontman Richard Sherrington on vocals and guitar, guitarist Dave Herbert, bass player Rob Hewitt and drummer Tristan Callaghan. In this incarnation SOLITARY cut an inaugural demo entitled 'Desolate'. Songwriting contributions for this effort, released in March of 1995, were on hand from Chris Astley of XENTRIX.

A second promotional cassette 'Fear' followed in January of 1996. In July Paul Mortimer took the bass position as SOLITARY got to grips with a further demo 'The Human Condition'. Most of these tracks would subsequently emerge as an EP of the same name. Herbert would opt out in the September for a career as a Policeman. The vacant guitar spot was duly filled by Matthew Costello and shortly after Jason Clark was enrolled as SOLITARY's new drummer.

The band signed a record deal with the Holier Than Thou concern the following year as yet more line up fluctuations hit home. Anthony Cox would replace Clark and Julian Heywood was the new man on bass guitar. The turbulence did not end there though as in February of the following year Cox departed and Simon Tomlinson came in on drums.

Just as SOLITARY were gearing up for recording of the debut album Heywood decamped and Gareth Harrop became the group's latest four stringer. A UK club tour was undertaken in the summer pre-empting the release of 'Nothing Changes' which arrived in November. Welcome support gigs to the likes of REIGN, KILL II THIS and Swedes DERANGED found Chris Gaughan now occupying the guitarist's role but by the following February erstwhile member Matt Costello rejoined the ranks.

Negotiations were finalised for the Dutch label Roxson to license the album for Europe but predictably SOLITARY hit further membership problems as Tomlinson bade farewell in June. Roy Miller was the next drummer on call. In adverse times SOLITARY learnt that Roxson had gone into receivership as had their UK label's distributor. A UK tour also had more

SOLITARY

than it's fair share of bad luck with 5 out of 9 dates being cancelled.

During 2000 SOLITARY's line up remained in a state of flux. Costello departed yet again but his substitute, Stuart Armriding, remained with the band only briefly with an acrimonious split resolving itself with the induction of guitarist Paul Morrison. It would be a familiar tale for 2001. Dave Marshall took over on bass whilst Matt Costello rejoined for his third tenure. SOLITARY would soon lose Costello's services yet again though, replacing him with erstwhile VOID and SOMA guitarist Gaz Wilkinson. Fluxing yet again, SOLITARY's 2004 roster included Andy Mellor on lead guitar and Michael Park on bass.

NOTHING CHANGES, Holier Than Thou HTT/TIF002 (1999). Within Temptation / Clutching Straws / The Downward Spiral / No Reason / A Second Chance / Twisted / Bitterness / Fear / Nothing Changes.

SOLSTICE

FL, USA — *Rob Barrett (vocals / guitar), James Murphy (guitar), Dennis Munoz (guitar), Alex Marquez (drums).*

South Florida'a SOLSTICE's eponymous 1992 debut album, released by the German Steamhammer label, featured a line-up of frontman Rob Barrett, Dennis Munoz and HELLWITCH, ANGER and DEMOLITION HAMMER credited drummer Alex Marquez. Renowned guitarist JAMES MURPHY would make his presence felt on session lead guitar. Both Barrett and Marquez would team up with premier Death Metal band MALEVOLENT CREATION during 1992. That same year Marquez and Barrett would guest on the ABYSMAL demo 'Surrealistic Fatality'. By the time of 1995's 'Pray' sophomore effort SOLSTICE, retaining Munoz and Marquez had been joined by new personnel vocalist / guitarist Christian Rudes and bassist Scott Garret.

In April of 2004 the erstwhile SOLSTICE pairing of drummer Alex Marquez and guitarist Dennis Munoz re-emerged in an eighties styled Power Thrash outfit with a working title APOCALYPSE RISING. The quartet would be completed by second guitarist Willy Medina and bass player Mike Marabell.

Alex Marquez, Christian Rudes, Dennis Munoz and Garret Scott reunited in August 2006 to write new material.

SOLSTICE, Steamhammer (1992). Transmogrified / Cleansed Of Impurity / Eternal Waking / Survival Reaction / S.M.D. / Netherworld / Plasticized / Catalysmic Outburst / Aberration.
PRAY, Steamhammer (1995). The Unseen / Denial / Pray / All Life Lost / Freedom Denied / Closeminded Failure / Depression / Bleeding Unborn / One At A Time / Eyes See Red.

SOMBER

GOTHENBURG, SWEDEN — *Pontus Dahlström (vocals), Andreas Henriksson (guitar), Carl Fritzell (guitar), Björn Rehnqvist (bass), John Bresäter (drums).*

Gothenburg Thrashers SOMBER was initiated as a covers band during 2001. The band issued the demos 'Oblivion' in 2002, 'God's Design' in 2003 and the 2004 set 'Berkley'.

Founded as a high school covers act in 2001, the original formation comprised frontman Pontus Dahlström, lead guitarist Andreas Henriksson, also known as singer for KREMATORIUM, rhythm guitarist Christoffer Melin, bassist Björn Rehnqvist and drummer John Bresäter. However, Melin would be replaced by Carl Fritzell. SOMBER cut a new demo, entitled 'Name Your Poison', at Lars Mobergs Studios outside Gothenburg in September of 2004. The group projected a new demo, entitled 'Define:rend', for October 2005.

Oblivion, Somber (2002) (Demo). Oblivion / Reversed Evil / Shadowline / Hadephobia.
God's Design, (2003) (Demo). Plain Cold / Lets Try To Dominate / I Will Lead The Genocide / Moshpit Minions.
Berkley, Somber (2004) (Demo). Intense Suffering / Berkley.
Name Your Poison, Somber (2004) (Demo). Zero Rebirth / Berkley / Havoc And Empty Holes / Intense Suffering / Rejected.
Define:Rend, Somber (2005) (Demo). Rend / Pale Growing Molly / Static.

SORG

SIGTUNA, SWEDEN — *Victor Hemgren (vocals / guitar), Rickard Dahlin (guitar), Olle Bodin (bass), Petter Rosqvist (drums).*

SORG (translated as "Grief"), founded during 1995 in the Stockholm suburb of Sigtuna, was initially assembled by guitarists Victor Hemgren and Rickard Dahlin. With the former, also a member of Black Metal band MÅNEGARM, assuming the lead vocal role the pair pulled in drummer Petter 'Karl' Rosqvist and bassist Lars Göran, the latter soon replaced by Olle Bodin from Doom outfit OUT OF HAND. This variant of SORG cut the 1996 demo 'Mina Drömmars Dal' and its 1997 follow up 'Devastated Light'. In March 1998 Rosqvist bowed out, relocating to the USA to study, and Bodin opted to exit in order to prioritise OUT OF HAND. Nevertheless a third, untitled, demo arrived in 1998 with Hemgren taking on bass responsibilities and AD INFINITUM's Micke Nyholm donating his services as stand in drummer. Eventually Rosqvist would resurface behind the drum kit of American Power Metal band STEEL PROPHET.

SORG entered into a period of stasis as Hemgren journeyed to the USA. Eventually the band was re-formulated in 1999 with Hemgren having returned to Sweden and drawing in the SOILS OF FATE rhythm section of bassist Henrik Kolbjer and drummer Nicke Karlsson. However, Karlsson's tenure lasted a matter of weeks and soon Micke Nyholm was re-installed. Karlsson teamed up with PANDEMONIC. Meantime, SORG came to a halt sometime in 2000.

Having moved to Örebro Hemgren was soon back in action with a brand new band entitled BRAIN DAMAGE. 2002 demos reportedly had Nu-Metal leanings. Rickard went on to MAZE OF TORMENT. Viktor Hemgren joined MAZE OF TORMENT for a short period before leaving, due
to musical differences, to form Rock n' Roll / Punk Rock band LUCIEN.

Mina Drömmars Dal, Sorg (1996). Mörkret Är Oändligt / I Mina Drömmars Dal / Killing For God / Blessed By Lies.
Devastated Light, (1997). I'll Walk My Path / In The Land Between / Religious Blood / Devastated Light / Endless Grief . . . .
Demo III, Sorg (1998). I Create Your Death / Freedom In Disguise / The Reign Of Agony.

SOUL DEMISE

GERMANY — *Roman Zimmerhackel (vocals), Andreas Schuhmeier (guitar), Alex Hagenauer (guitar), Andreas Bradl (bass), Roland Jahoda (drums).*

Death Thrashers SOUL DEMISE, founded as INHUMAN during October of 1993, opened proceedings with the November demo 'Incantations'. The band's inaugural line up incorporated lead vocalist Jürgen "Eumel" Aumann, guitarist Andreas Schuhmeier, bassist Andreas Bradl, second guitarist Martin Werthammer and drummer Andreas Brückelim. Subsequently fresh blood was introduced in the form of former CON-FUSION guitarist Alex Windorfer and ex-IVORY drummer Roland Jahoda. The 'Inners Fears' album of 1996 was supported by a barrage of over 150 live dates that year supporting the likes of MORBID ANGEL, SINISTER, DYING FETUS and VADER amongst others over the next two years. However, a name switch to SOUL DEMISE then occurred and the band re-debuted with the EP 'Farewell To The Flesh' in September of 1998. A further round of touring witnessed opening slots to KRISIUN, DERANGED and SOILWORK.

'Beyond Human Conception' was issued by the Gutter Records label in 2000. A limited edition picture disc vinyl variant was restricted to just 333 copies. Resulting live dates, packaged with DESTROYER 666, DECAPITATED and IMMOLATION, culminated in the departure of long standing lead vocalist Jürgen 'Eumel' Aumann to VIOLATION. The band line up then stood at vocalist Thomas Bachmeier, guitarist Andreas Schuhmeier, bass player Andreas Bradl with Roland Jahoda on drums. Subsequently SOUL DEMISE located a new singer in Roman Zimmerhackel. This new incarnation of the band got straight back onto the live circuit acting as guests to NAPALM DEATH. For the 2003 album 'In Vain' SOUL DEMISE signed to the French Season Of Mist label.

The band donated their rendition of 'Forever Blind' to the AT THE GATES tribute album, 'Slaughterous Souls—A Tribute to At The Gates' released in September 2004 through Drowned Scream Records.

BEYOND HUMAN PERCEPTION, Gutted GUT CD0031 (2000).
IN VAIN, Season Of Mist SOM 057 (2003). In Vain / Naïve / Trapped In A Body / Inside My Emptiness / Amnesia / Cancer / Darkness Within / Eventually We Die / Towards The Gate / Downwards To Deliverance / Passing Away.

SOULS ON FIRE

IRAPUATO, MEXICO — *Jesus Bravo (vocals), Nelson St.Marie (lead guitar), Jorge Inukai (lead guitar), Oscar Lopez (bass), Oscar Piñon (drums).*

Irapuato, Guanajuato Heavy Metal band SOULS ON FIRE was forged during 1998 by former TARANTULA and STARFLEET guitarist Nelson St. Marie and ex-AGONY LORDS frontman Jesus Bravo. This founding pair would be joined by another AGONY LORDS veteran, bassist Oscar Lopez, then second guitarist Eduardo Gomez with Luis S. Marie on drums. This formation crafted the opening 'Mythic' demo, following which Tony Martinez of DIES IRAE took over the drum position.

The band set to work recording an album during 2003 but during these sessions both Gomez and Martinez opted out. It would not be until late 2004 that Oscar Piñon of AGONY LORDS was installed on the drum stool and Jorge Inukai joined on lead guitar to complete the 'Fire Demons' album. Mexican label The Art Records issued the record in 2005.

FIREDEMONS, The Art (2005). Firedemon / Archangel / Enemy / Blackened Wings Of The Warrior / Embracing Shadows / Stormbringer / Hellwithin / Army Of Darkness / Until The Glory Fades Away.

SOULSCAR

VANCOUVER, BC, CANADA — *Andrew Staehling (vocals / guitar), Stas Mikheev (guitar), Brent McKenzie (bass), Igor Cheifot (drums).*

Vancouver's SOULSCAR employ Death Metal with a healthy injection of prime era Thrash influences. The band came together in 1997 issuing a stream of demos in 1998's 'Lost In Life', 1999's 'Escaping' and 2000 'Abandoned'. These three sessions were all conducted as solo efforts by Andrew Staehling. The

2000 'Abandoned' album release is a collection of earlier demo tracks produced by Jeff Waters of ANNIHILATOR. Yet another Waters produced promotion release, 'Python' featuring bassist Brent McKenzie, was recorded in 2001, although never publicly released, upfront of the 'Character Assassination' record. Sessioning on this outing would be drummer Chris Warunki.

Second album 'Victim Impact Statement' was issued in October of 2004 through Galy Records. SOULSCAR's 2004 band line up comprised Andrew Staehling, Brent Mackenzie, second guitarist Stas Mikheev and drummer Igor Cheifot.

ABANDONED, (2000). S.S.R.I. (Intro) / Cutter / Your Absence, My End / Abandoned / Ever Alone / This Was My Life / Selfmutilation / Bliss Killer / Escaping / Deathbringer-Surrender / Escaping / Lost In Life.
CHARACTER ASSASSINATION, Soulscar SSCAR01 (2002). Fatalist Mantra / Interceptor / Sacrifices / Living Nightmare / Relentless / It Takes A Wolf / The Voyeur / Character Assassination / A Reprieve.
VICTIM IMPACT STATEMENT, Galy GALY 030 (2004). Unmade / Death Anxiety / Cast Aside / Hell Bitch / Without A Shadow / Ultimatum / Regressor / Alive Awake / To The Pain / Victim Impact Statement.

SOULSCARRED

SANDEFJORD, NORWAY — *Eirik Kraft (vocals), Chris Kolden (guitar), Stian Strand (guitar), André Trevland (bass), Tomas Di Sansimone (drums).*

Sandefjord Thrashers SOULSCARRED, established during 1997 by ex-PNEUMONIA members guitarist Chris Kolden and drummer Even, has undergone many line-up changes, with erstwhile band members including singers Ray Hansen and Paul Borgersen, who sang on the group's 'Regression' demo, the BUGS B GONE credited guitarist Petter Wiik Pettersen and bass player Kristoffer Carstens.

Frontman Eirik Kraft enrolled in late 2000. In April 2002 second guitarist Einar Vasvik joined to record the demo 'Morbid Parody', issued in May 2002 and cut at Skrotum Studios. SOULSCARRED introduced Kristoffer Carstens on bass but this latest candidate quit that May to join MISTRESS. The 'Personal Holocaust' demo sessions followed in September 2003. The group was still a fragile unit, although Tex was inducted on bass, he left shortly afterward along with Vasvik. In the Autumn of 2005 SOULSCARRED got back up to strength, pulling in guitarist Stian Strand, bassist André Trevland (a.k.a. 'Chain') from ARCH NEMESIS and THERAWADA, and drummer Tomas Di Sansimone. A self-titled demo arrived in 2007.

Morbid Parody, Soul Scarred (2002). Morbid Parody / Forever Free.
Personal Holocaust, (2003). Personal Holocaust / God Of Sorrow / Give In To Your Madness / Left In Misery.
Soulscarred, (2007) (Demo).

SPEARHEAD

AUSTRIA — *Hartwig Lasthofer (vocals), Alex Ecker (guitar), Christian Riffert (guitar), Martin Edtmayr (bass), Markus Pointer (drums).*

Founded in 1990 as SARCASTIC MURDER by originators Christian Dobretsberger on lead vocals, guitarist Christian Riffert, bassist Rifart Peterwagner and drummer Markus Schickerbauer. Following a four track demo Martin Edtmayr replaced Peterwagner during December of 1993. Dobretsberger exited in 1995 and Michael Kneidinger took the role of frontman for a sophomore demo. Whilst in the process of recording the 1997 album 'Spearit' the band changed title to SPEARHEAD. However, the album cover bears the band name mispelt as 'Speerhead'.

Schickerbauer bowed out in 1999 and was substituted on drums by LEGACY OF HATE's Markus Pointer. The band also inducted Alex Ecker as second guitarist. Kneidinger would be next to leave, Hartwig Lasthofer swiftly stepping in as the band's new singer.

SPEARIT, Independent (1997). Mortal / Burst Of Hatred / Matter Of Faith / Im Westen Nichts Neues / Forgotten Thoughts / Forgive Me / Psychologically Disturbed / Perfect Person / Good For Nothing / Getrennte Gefühle.

SPECTRAL

GERMANY — *Zerberus (vocals), Teutonlord (guitar / keyboards), Sacki (guitar), Agressor (bass), Destructor (drums).*

Dating to 1995, SPECTRAL synthesize Black, Power, Thrash and Viking Metal. The band was created by Teutonlord handling vocals, guitar and keyboards with drummer Destructor. In 1998 lead vocalist Zerberus, guitarist Rat and bassist Colossos completed the line up. This variant of SPECTRAL cut the 'Teutonic Symphony' EP. Colossos departed before recording of the full length album 'Barbaric Assault'. Performing on the live circuit for a time without a bassist SPECTRAL finally pulled in Agressor during 2001.

Recorded in Bonn, the 'Barbaric Assault' album saw guest sessions from guitarist Martjo Brongers of Dutch band VORTEX as well as former PERSONAL WAR singer Matthias Zimmer.

Teutonic Symphony EP, Independent (1999). Teutonic War / Praise The Mystic Shadow / Painful Reminders / Fire And Blood.
BARBARIC ASSAULT, Gernhart (2001). The Beginning ... / Barbaric Assault / The Dark Forces / Teutonic War / The Sound Of A 1000 Swords / Violent Victory / Master Of Disaster / Black Winged Angel / Valgrind.

SPEEDICA

WEERT, HOLLAND — *Hans Reinders (vocals), Marcel Coenen (guitar), Raymond Heydendael (bass), Pierre Heydendael (drums).*

Weert based Speed Metal band SPEEDICA was created by erstwhile ANGER personnel, guitarists Raymond C., bassist Raymond Heijdendael and drummer Pierre Heijdendael. As such, the group first performed live on 5th October 1986 at the 'Amateurpop' festival in Bartok-Born. Another ANGER guitarist, Henk Hamers, enrolled in 1987. That same year the MENACY and BOONDOGGLE credited Hans Reinders was acquired as lead vocalist. A further change saw the introduction of guitarist MARCEL COENEN in 1988.

SPEEDICA's 1989 demo tape 'Shadows Of Tomorrow' was recorded at the Iris Sound Production Studios in Venlo with engineer Wim Kauffman. Both singer Hans Reinders and guitarist MARCEL COENEN would feature in FORM. Coenen would also work with SUN CAGED, APOGEE, AURA, LEMUR VOICE and HUBI MEISEL. A solo album, 'Guitar Talk', emerged in 2003.

SHADOWS OF TOMORROW, Speedica (1989). Bridge To The End / Laws Of Metal / Radiation Wastelands / Lady Obsession / F*ckin For Pleasure.

SPEED\KILL/HATE

NEW YORK, NY, USA — *Mario (vocals), Dave Linsk (guitar), Derek Tailer (bass), Tim Mallare (drums).*

New York's SPEED\KILL/HATE is an "old-school thrash" project featuring OVERKILL members guitarists Dave Linsk and Derek Tailer with Tim Mallare on the drums fronted by ANGER ON ANGER man Mario on vocals. A debut album, 'Acts Of Insanity', arrived in September 2004. A deal with Listenable Records secured an early 2005 release across Europe and Asia. SPEED\KILL/HATE filmed a promotional video for the track 'Face The Pain' with director Anthony M. Bongiovi.

The band was included the 'Metal Crusaders' North American tour, set to take place in May and June 2006 alongside KATAKLYSM, GRAVEWORM, NUCLEAR ASSAULT, VADER and THE ABSENCE. Initially taking over bass duties from Derek Tailer, unable to participate due to "personal reasons", would be former ICED EARTH and MEGADETH man James MacDonough.

Another session member for these dates would be SINDROME and SERVITUDE drummer Tony Ochoa. However, MacDonough pulled out before the dates citing "conflicting schedules".

SPEED\KILL/HATE signed to Escapi Music to issue the album 'Acts Of Insanity' in the USA

ACTS OF INSANITY, Speed Kill Hate (2004). Walls Of Hate / Setting Me Off / Violence Breeds / Enemy / Won't See Fear / Face The Pain / Revelation At War / Not For Me / Repent.

SPERMBIRDS

GERMANY — *Lee Hollis (vocals), Roger Ingenthon (guitar), Frank Rahm (guitar), Markus Weilmann (bass), Matthias Gotte (drums).*

A much favoured Kaiserslautern Punk act that infused their sound with plenty of American Crossover and Thrash influences. Founded in 1980 as ERADICATION the band, fronted by American singer Lee Hollis, adopted the title of SPERMBIRDS in 1982. The remainder of the group comprised of guitarists Roger Ingenthon and Frank 'Cream' Rahm, bass player Markus 'While Man' Weilmann and drummer Matthias Gotte. First product would be a split album with WALTER 11.

The band soon pulled in a ready audience and mounting record sales but Hollis would quit during 1993 following recording of the 'Joe' album, later founding STEAKKNIFE. The SPERMBIRDS drafted another American, Ken Haus, as replacement but the group would ultimately fold in 1996.

Gotte went on to KICK JONESES whilst Rahm emerged with SUPER GOUGE.

The SPERMBIRDS would reunite with Hollis during 1999 for a series of 5 nostalgia concerts.

DON'T FORGET THE FUN, (1985) (Split album with WALTER 11). My God Rides A Skateboard / Shit Rolls Downhill / She's Got VD.
SOMETHING TO PROVE, (1987). Something To Prove / What A Bitch Is / You're Not A Punk / Playboy Subscriber / Kill Me Quick / What Do You Want? / My God Rides A Skateboard / Americans Are Cool / Get On The Stage / No Punks In K'town / Scumbag / Shit Job / Bed Tool / Try Again / Bloodstains.
NOTHING IS EASY, (1989). Die Sgt Landry / Your Problem / Nothing Is Easy / Cave / Another Dead Friendship / It's Just An Excuse / Light's Out / My Brother / 12 8 Pack / Texas Cowboy / We Don't Care / Americans Are Cool / What Do You Want? / Try Again.
THANKS—LIVE, Dead Eye (1990). Something To Prove / Common Thread / Nothing Is Easy / Stronger / Two Feet / Kill Me Quick / With A Gun / Get On The Stage / Dangers Of Thinking / Only A Phase / You're Not A Punk / Americans Are Cool / Texas Cowboy / Try Again.
COMMON THREAD, X-Mist XM022 (1991). Melt The Ice / Open Letter / Two Feet / Stronger / Only A Phase / One Chance / With A Gun / Common Thread / Truth Of Today / Victim Of Yourself.
JOE, X-Mist XM034 (1992). Crucifried / Real Life (Digging A Hole) / Got Your Number / Tell Me About It / Dead / We Are One / My God Rides A Skateboard / Shit Rolls Downhill / She's Got VD / I'm Trapped / 12XU / Truth Of Today.
EATING GLASS, X-Mist XM032 (1992). Eating Glass / Just A Moment / Static Energy / We Are All (Political Prisoners) / You're Fired / Fine / Waiting For The Bomb To Drop / You're Only As Good As Your Last War / Stalemate / Back In Time / Fragment / Souled Out.
SHIT FOR SALE, G.U.N. (1994). Shit For Sale / Media Bullshit / You're Not Perfect / KKK Rep / I Feel Old Part 1 / I Feel Old Part 2 / Feed My Ego / L-Word / Cold Busted / Rich Man's High / In Many Way / Alike Your Opinion.
FAMILY VALUES, G.U.N. (1995). What Dad Says / Mr. Cynical / Family Values / Pop Song / Bad Things / Disagree / Nervous Anxiety / All I Want / Desires And Wishes / Hate / In The Eyes Of Old People / Running Circle / Kaiserslautern Uber Alles.
COFFEE, HAIR & REAL LIFE, Warner Bros. (1996). She's Got V.D. / Something To Prove / Americans Are Cool / You're Not A Punk / My God Rides A Skateboard / Try Again / Bed Tool / Get On The Stage / What Do You Want Ronald Reagan? / Nothing Is Easy / Another Dead Friendship / Texas Cowboy / It's Just An Excuse / Melt The Ice / Truth Of Today / Only A Phase / 2 Feet / With A Gun / Stronger / Victims Of Yourself / Back In Time / Eating Glass / Fine / Crucifried / Excess Bleeding Heart.
GET OFF THE STAGE, G.U.N. (1996). You're Not Perfect / Mr. Cynical / Media Bullshit / Bad Things / KKK Rep / Shit For Sale / Pop Song / Nervous Anxiety / L-Word / Disagree / What Dad Says / Your Opinion / Family Values / Something To Prove / You're Not A Punk / My God Rides A Skateboard / Nothing Is Easy / Americans Are Cool / Melt The Ice / Shit Job / Die Sgt. Landry / Cruzifried / No Punks In K-Town / Kill Me Quick / Bloodstains / Get On The Stage / Try Again / Only A Phase / All I Want / Texas Cowboy / Truth Of Today / Lights Out.
BEST OF, G.U.N. (1999).

SQUEALER

GERMANY — *Henner (vocals), Michael Schiel (guitar), Lars Döring (guitar), Michael Kaspar (bass), Frank Wolf (drums).*

Metal outfit SQUEALER's first product was the 1987 demo 'Ready To Fight' followed by a further demo in 'One Beer Too Much' in 1988. Initially a straight ahead Hard Rock act SQUEALER, fronted by 'Henner' (a.k.a. Andy Allendörfer), progressively developed into the accelerated Speed Metal of Thrash. SQUEALER were in a position to offer an EP, 'Human Traces', in 1989 although it would be four years before a debut album arrived.

The 1999 album 'The Prophecy', issued through Allendörfer own imprint AFM Records, sees SQUEALER with guitarists Lars Doring and Michael Schiel. EDGUY's Tobias Sammet guests on the track 'Friends For Life'. Quite bizarrely SQUEALER cover DEPECHE MODE's 'Enjoy The Silence' too. 'The Prophecy' would be licensed to Metal Blade for North America in July 2000.

The 2000 album 'Made For Eternity' has guest appearances from RAGE drummer Mike Terrana and HELLOWEEN guitarist ROLAND GRAPOW. SQUEALER committed their version of 'Victim Of Fate' to the HELLOWEEN tribute album 'Keepers Of Jericho'.

In 2001 ex-drummer Frank Wolf would guest on the ambitious TARAXACUM project album 'Spirit Of Freedom' conceived by EDGUY man Tobias Exxel.

Tragically, Andy Allendörfer died in a car crash in January 2005. The singer had built up AFM Records to boast an impressive roster of bands including MASTERPLAN, ANNIHILATOR, AT VANCE, CIRCLE II CIRCLE and U.D.O. In April SQUEALER announced the band was to continue, under a revised billing of SQUEALER A.D., with Gus Chambers of GRIP INC. at the microphone and Martin Buchwalter from PERZONAL WAR on drums. This new unit put out the 'Confrontation Street' album through AFM in October 2006.

The Casualty, Squealer (1989) ('Human Traces' EP). The Casualty / Lose Of Independence / Bereft Of Senses / I Will Fight / Insanity.
MAKE YOUR DAY, AFM 21477 (1993). A Little Piece Of Death / Behold The Lion / Make Your Day / Thoughts / The Wanderer / Tears Of Hate / RAP / Scaring The Winds / The Man Who Never Was.
WRONG TIME, WRONG PLACE?, AFM 25702 (1995). Intro / Liar / Wrong Time Wrong Place / Time Doesn't Wait / Hellcome In Heaven / Love To Hate You / Dying Forbidden! / Don't Wanna Be Like You / Whose Afraid Of Yellow Snow?
THE PROPHECY, AFM Records CD026 (1999). The Prophecy (The Final Sign) / Friends For Life / . . . But No One Cares / Live Everyday / Hold On Tight / To Die For (. . . Your Sins) / Nowhere To Hide / I See The World / The Meaning Of Life / Enjoy The Silence / The Prophecy (Follow Me).
MADE FOR ETERNITY, AFM (2000). End Of The World / The Final Daylight / Nothing To Believe / Don't Fear Your Life / The Eternity Of A Day / Show Me The Way / No One To Blame / People Are People / Free Your Mind / Hellcome In Heaven.
UNDER THE CROSS, AFM Records (2002). Painful Lust / Facing The Death / My Last Goodbye / Thinking Allowed! / Under The Cross / Rules Of Life / Down And Out / Fade Away / Out Of The Dark / In Zaire / Low Budget Heroes.

STEEL TORMENTOR

GERMANY — *Frank Müller (vocals / guitar), Frank Urschler (guitar / bass), Andreas Kiechle (drums / vocals).*

Thrash act STEEL TORMENTOR was initiated during the Summer of 1997 by vocalist / guitarist Frank Müller and guitarist Frank Urschler. The following year a full band roster would be achieved by the induction of bass player Bastian Bahrmüller with Andreas Kiechle on the drums. The band's inaugural recordings came at the close of the following year, a two song demo featuring the original composition 'Steel Tormentor' and a cover rendition of JUDAS PRIEST's 'Grinder'. Bahrmüller decamped mid session and so bass was delegated to Urschler. However, the musicians deemed this offering to be of unsatisfactory sound quality so did not release these tracks to the public.

STEEL TORMENTOR's debut album 'Fallen Angel', a deliberately old school Thrash outing, arrived in the Autumn of 1999. Live work to promote the record saw STEEL TORMENTOR gigging across Germany and Switzerland before re-entering the studio in March of 2000 to cut second album 'Storm Of Anger'. The title track from this effort was included on a 'Legacy' magazine sampler.

The band splintered in January of 2001 with Frank Urschler and Andreas Kiechle going on to forge BITTERNESS. This new combo featured bassist Sebastian Jehle who had also briefly been involved with STEEL TORMENTOR. As BITTERNESS, they would re-record the STEEL TORMENTOR track 'Feel The Flame' for inclusion on the compilation album 'Reaper Comes'.

STORM OF ANGER, Independent (2000). Storm Of Anger / Mind Of Madness / Way Of The Warrior / Sign In Blood / Just An Idea (Of Myself And The World).

FALLEN ANGEL, Steel Tormentor (2000). Life Is Wonderful / Sick Society / Feel The Flame / Burning Souls / Steel Tormentor / Bloody Tears / Sign In Blood / Fallen Angel.

STEELER

GERMANY — *Peter Burtz (vocals), Axel Rudi Pell (guitar), Thomas Eder (guitar), Volker Krawczak (bass), Jan Yildaral (drums).*

STEELER emerged during a particularly golden period in the history of German Metal and would provide a worthy legacy of some finely crafted Metal albums and provide the launch pad for noted guitarist AXEL RUDI PELL. Formed in Bochum, STEELER had originally used the name SINNER, and the band was put together by guitarist Axel Rudi Pell and bassist Volker Krawczak.

Pell joined his first band at the age of 14 between 1974 and 1975 with whom he took his first tentative steps. The band, a school outfit called SILVER STONES, at least taught Pell the art of tuning a guitar, evolving into FIREBIRD. With the group splitting in 1976 Pell took a hiatus from music until joining a local act called MERCY and, subsequently, DEVIL'S DEATH, with whom he proceeded to play the regional school and club circuits.

Having formed STEELER with Krawczak, the duo recruited FALLEN ANGEL guitarist Thomas Eder and a drummer in Siggi Wiesemöller. The fledgling group recorded their first demo during 1982, utilizing the services of vocalist Karl Holthaus, on loan from local act NEMO (although he had also been known to have fronted a group called GLADIATOR).

STEELER took the demos to SCORPIONS producer Dieter Dierks who chose not to pursue his original interest in the band, although the tape fell into the hands of ACCEPT who were having problems with Udo Dirkschneider at the time and were covertly auditioning possible replacements. ACCEPT auditioned Holthaus, but eventually settled their differences with Dirkschneider without the press getting wind of the original problem.

Having received a fair amount of interest from demo track 'Call Her Princess' being aired on Tony Jasper's Rock show on the British Forces Broadcasting Service (BFBS) radio station STEELER not only recruited a permanent singer in Thomas Eder's former FALLEN ANGEL band mate Peter Burtz, they also hooked up with the newly formed Earthshaker label for a two record deal, releasing the debut 'Steeler' album in 1984.

STEELER's first album, recorded in a mere eleven days and with new drummer Jan Yildiral, sold a respectable 9'000 copies, although a proposed tour with WARLOCK turned into a disaster due to problems with WARLOCK's manager and petty jealousy existing between the two groups.

band's second album, 'Rulin' The Earth', took between 14 or 15 days and was laid down at Horus Sound in Hanover and would sell 18, 000 copies as the group proceeded to play every 'toilet' they could in a bid for greater recognition.

With the Earthshaker deal now over with STEELER signed to SPV, although legal problems with Earthshaker would persist for some time afterward especially concerning the payment of royalties. Having begun working on demo tapes of songs for the proposed third album STEELER parted company with Volker Krawczak. As the subject of the band's image had come up it had been decided that the unfortunate bassist, a portly chap, did not particularly fit into the scheme of things and the band felt it had no choice but to replace him. Krawczak would refuse to speak with his former colleagues for a good three years afterwards!

Volker's place was taken by French bassist Herve Rossi, previously with ANTHRACITE and a friend of drummer Jan Yildiral. Whilst Rossi certainly fitted STEELER's concept on the image front, it was quickly discovered that he was rather lacking in any prowess as a musician. Rossi may have been hired for looking like the renowned bassist Nikki Sixx, but he didn't play a note on the third album, 1986's 'Strike Back', a guesting Tommy Newton from VICTORY doing the honours. The album was produced by ELOY's Frank Bornemann, although Axel Rudi Pell claims the majority of the work was in effect carried out by Czech born engineer Jan Nimec. Ex SCORPIONS guitarist ULI JON ROTH was in the same studio at the time and Pell took the opportunity of inviting him to play on a track that appeared on a 'Metal Hammer' compilation album at the time.

Having dispatched Rossi back to France STEELER recruited ex AXE VICTIMS rhythm guitarist Roland Hag as the band's new bass player and hit the road, managing to add some shows in Holland and Switzerland to the regular German commitments. 'Strike Back', benefiting from better material, improved musicianship and a polished production, picked up sales in the region of 33'000 and set the mood for the recording of fourth album 'Undercover Animal'.

Despite touring Germany with SAXON the 'Undercover Animal' only wound up selling 21'000 copies. It would be during the writing of songs for the planned fifth album that AXEL RUDI PELL decided to leave the group, disenchanted at the band's more pop chorus oriented direction, officially departing on November 11 1988.

STEELER actually folded upon completion of the SAXON dates. However, minus Pell and Jan Yildiral, the remaining members opted to continue, hiring a guitarist from the Frankfurt area known as Vic. The group recorded a three track demo and played a comeback show at Bochum's Zeche club, but split three or four months down the line.

Whereas Pell chose to pursue what turned out to be a very successful solo career (having teamed up with his old pal Volker Krawczak once more!), his former colleagues have engaged themselves in a variety of other careers. At one time Peter Burtz was the editor of German Metal magazine 'Metal Hammer' before taking the opportunity to work in the upper echelons of the EMI record label. Drummer Jan Yildiral, after recording further with DARXON and SHOUT, now runs a global travel agency as well as being operational on the live circuit with NAKED SONS, whilst Thomas Eder is working for a radio station reporting on events in the local courts.

STEELER, Earthshaker ES 4001 (1984). Chains Are Broken / Gonna Find Some Place In Hell / Heavy Metal Century / Sent From The Evil / Long Way / Call Her Princess / Love For Sale / Hydrophobia / Fallen Angel.
RULIN' THE EARTH, Earthshaker ES 4009 (1985). The Resolution / Ruling The Earth / Shellshock / Let The Blood Run Red / Heading For The End / Maniac / Run With The Pack / S.F.M. 1 / Turning Wheels.
STRIKE BACK, Steamhammer SPV 08-1890 (1986). Chain Gang / Money Doesn't Count / Danger Comeback / Icecold / Messing Around With Fire / Rockin' The City / Strike Back / Night After Night / Waiting For A Star.
Night After Night, Steamhammer 01-1884 (1986). Night After Night / Waiting For A Star.
UNDERCOVER ANIMAL, Steamhammer SPV 08-7510 (1988). (I'll Be) Hunter Or Hunted / Undercover Animal / Shadow In The Redlight / Hard Breaks / Criminal / Rely On Rock / Stand Tall / The Deeper The Night / Knock Me Out / Bad To The Bone.
Undercover Animal, Steamhammer (1988). Undercover Animal.

STONE

HELSINKI, FINLAND — *Janne Joutsenniemi (vocals / bass), Roope Latvala (guitar), Markku Niiranen (guitar), Pekka Kasari (drums).*

Highly successful in their native Finland, Helsinki Heavy Metal band STONE scored a number 1 hit with their 'Back To The Stoneage' EP in 1988, backed by a cover of BLACK SABBATH's 'Symptom of The Universe', and were picked up by the MCA affiliated Mechanic Records for the release of a self-titled debut album in territories outside Finland. Indeed, with backing from the label STONE toured North America as support to TESTAMENT before returning home.

STONE was rooted in the pre-teen outfit CLEVER BOYS assembled by vocalist / bassist Janne Joutsenniemi and guitarist Roope Latvala, The duo added guitarist Jiri Jalkanen and drummer Pekka Kasari, becoming CROSS OF IRON, before adopting the STONE title during 1984. A brace of 1986 Mikko Karmila produced demos and the championing of their cause by 'Rumba' magazine soon put the band into national focus. Signing to the Finnish label Megamania the band debuted in 1987 with the single 'Real Delusion'. The success of the debut album led to a second offering, 'No Anaesthesia!', in 1989. Employing a more technical persuasion, characterised by a ten minute title track, STONE produced what many fans to regard as their finest record.

An EP entitled 'Empty Suit' marked the exit of guitarist Jiri Jalkanen, his last gig with STONE on 15th March 1990 at the Tavastia venue in Helsinki being recorded for live tracks included on the B side. STONE duly drafted ex-AIRDASH guitarist Markku 'Nirri' Niiranen as substitute for 1990's highly complex 'Colours' album. A final studio album, 'Emotional Playground', was released in 1991. By 1992 the MCA deal was history and the 'Emotional Playground' album found the Finns signed to Swedish label Black Mark Records, with a live album released the following year.

Janne Joutsenniemi and Roope Sirén forged SUBURBAN TRIBE in 1992. The following year Roope Latvala, in alliance with keyboard player Petteri Hirvonen and Latvala's brother, former VIRAGO drummer Jussi Latvala, forged instrumental Metal project the LATVALA BROS. Rehearsals took place in Latvala family's sauna cabin in Lintuvaara and a solitary album, 'Latvala Bros Plays Wooden Eye' recorded at Lemuntie military barracks in Vallila with engineers Petteri Hirvonen and Ade Mattila, emerged that same year. Only 600 copies were manufactured.

Although nothing appeared to have been heard from STONE since, guitarist Roope Latvala would feature on the DEMENTIA album then resurface in 1995 as member of AC/DC tribute band EI SIIS ON SIIS, issuing the album 'Letut Ja Rocka'. Drummer Pekka Kasari joined AMORPHIS for their 1996 album 'Elegy'. Guitarist Markku Niiranen featured in CORPORAL PUNISHMENT. The quartet finally reunited as STONE in 2000 for festival appearances.

The rising stars of Finnish Metal CHILDREN OF BODOM covered the STONE track 'No Commands' for inclusion on their no. 1 single 'Downfall' in 1999. Janne Joutsenniemi acted as producer for HYBRID CHILDREN's 1998 outing 'Drugster' and the 2002 DIVINE DECAY album 'Songs Of The Damned'. Roope Latvala teamed up with Power Metal act SINERGY and would later join CHILDREN OF BODOM as session live guitarist in August of 2003.

STONE was the subject of a February 2007 DVD set entitled 'Get Stoned, Stay Stoned' released by Inferno magazine and Megamania. The DVD included footage of three concerts, an interview from 2007, four video clips, discography, documentary features plus a picture gallery.

Stone, (1986). Real Delusion / Eat Your Pride / No Commands / Back To The Stone Age / Escape / The Day Of Death / Overtake.
Stone, (1986). Thought The Battle Of Gods / Free Again / Overtake / Back To The Stoneage / Escape / Break The Glass / The Day Of Death.
Real Delusion, Megamania MGS 128 (1987). Real Delusion / The Day Of Death.
Back To The Stone Age EP, Megamania MGX 140 (1988). Back To The Stone Age / Symptom of The Universe.
STONE, Mechanic MCA 42175 (1988). Get Stoned / No Commands / Eat Your Pride / The Day Of Death / Reached Out / Real Delusion / Brain Damage / Escape / Final Countdown / Overtake.
NO ANASTHESIA, Megamania (1988). Sweet Dreams / Empty Corner / Back To The Stone Age / Concrete Malformation / No Anaesthesia / Light Entertainment / Kill The Dead / Meat Mincing Machine / Get Stoned / No Commands / Eat Your Pride / The Day Of Death / Reached Out / Escape / Final Countdown.
Get Stoned, Mechanic MCA (1988). Get Stoned / No Commands.
Empty Suit, Megamania MGX165 (1990). Empty Suit / Friends / Empty Corner (Live) / Meat Mincing Machine (Live).
COLOURS, Megamania MGM 2017 (1990). Stone Cold Soul / Another Morning / White Worms / Empty Suit / Spring / Storm Inside The Calm / Ocean Of Sand / Meaning Of Life / Friends.
Mad Hatter's Den, Megamania (1991). Mad Hatter's Den / Emotional Playground.
EMOTIONAL PLAYGROUND, Black Mark BMCD13 (1992). Small Tales / Home Bass / Last Chance / Above The Grey Sky / Mad Hatter's Den / Dead End / Adrift / Haven / Years After / Time Dive / Missionary Of Charity / Emotional Playground.
FREE-LIVE, Black Mark BMCD 38 (1993). Get Around / Empty Corner / Small Tales / Mad Hatter's Den / Sweet Dreams / Above The Grey Sky / Real Delusion / The Day Of Death / Last Chance / White Worms / Haven / Emotional Playground / No Commands / Missionary Of Charity / Overtake / Vengeance Of The Ghostrider.

STORMWARRIOR

GERMANY — *Thunder Axe (vocals / guitar), Scythewielder (guitar), Hammerlord (bass), Evil Steel (drums).*

Northern German renaissance Heavy Metal band. Assembled by vocalist / guitar 'Thunder Axe' (Lars Ramcke) and drummer 'Evil Steel' (Andrè Schumann) the band was quickly brought up to strength with the addition of guitarist 'Scythewielder' (Scott Bölter) and bass player Tim Zienert. This formation conceived the 1999 demo tape 'Metal Victory'.

A second session 'Barbaric Steel' followed prompting live appearances at such events as the 'Headbangers Open Air' and 'Warriors Of Steel' festivals. In 2001 two STORMWARRIOR tracks were released as a limited edition EP 'Possessed By Metal by the Italian Dream Evil label Shortly after though Zienery decamped, being substituted by 'Hammerlord' (Gabriel Palermo). Signing to Hamburg's Remedy label STORMWARRIOR issued a further 7 picture disc single 'Spikes & Leather' in 2002.

The eponymous debut album would benefit from production handled courtesy of GAMMA RAY's Kai Hansen and Dirk Schlächter. Besides their work behind the desk the pair would step up for guest spots too, Hansen featuring on both 'Chains Of Slavery' & 'Heavy Metal (Is The Law)' whilst Schlächter graced 'Deathe By The Blade' with a guitar solo. HELLOWEEN bassist Markus Großkopf got in on the action too, laying down distinctive chords on 'Heavy Metal (Is The Law)'. STORMWARRIOR performed at the 'Wacken Open Air' event that same year.

The band donated their rendition of 'Warchild' to a 2004 Remedy Records RUNNING WILD tribute 'The Revivalry—A Tribute To Running Wild'. The band performed an unusual concert dubbed the '34'000 Ton Metal Cruise' on 25th September, performing onboard the Münchenbryggeriet car ferry in Stockholm, Sweden alongside TANKARD, AMON AMARTH, HYPOCRISY, IMPALED NAZARENE, TAD MOROSE, SKYCLAD and WOLF. The group would be joined onstage by Kai Hansen for a special 'Walls of Jericho' HELLOWEEN set. They would repeat this arrangement with Hansen for a gig at Hamburg's Headbangers Ballroom venue in December.

The band featured their take on 'Power And The Glory' for the 2005 Remedy Records SAXON tribute album 'Eagleution'.

Possessed By Metal EP, Dream Evil (2001). Heavy Metal Fire / Defenders Of Metal.
Spikes & Leather EP, Remedy (2002) (Limited edition 250 copies).
STORMWARRIOR, Remedy (2002). The Hammer Returneth (Intro) / Signe Of The Warlorde / Sons Of Steele / Bounde By The Oathe / Deceiver / The Axewielder / Deathe By The Blade / Thunderer / Iron Prayers / Defenders Of Metal / Chains Of Slavery / Heavy Metal (Is The Law).
HEAVY METAL FIRE, Remedy (2003). Heavy Metal Fire / Warrior / Thy Laste Fyre / Odinn's Warriors / Spikes And Leather / Storm Of Victory / Attack Of The Metal Hellstorm.
NORTHERN RAGE, Spiritual Beast SBCD-1015 (2004). And The Northewinde Bloweth / Heroic Deathe / Valhalla / Thy Laste Fyre (New version) / Welcome Thy Rite / Odinn's Warriors (New version) / Blood Eagle / Sigrblot / To Foreign Shores / Lindisfarne / Turn The Cross Upside Down.
AT FOREIGN SHORES—LIVE IN JAPAN, Remedy REM 052 (2006).

STRESSFEST

SWEDEN — *Niclas Engwall (vocals), Peter Hegardt (guitar), Chris Vowden (guitar), Oliver Vowden (bass), Calle Fransson (drums).*

STRESSFEST feature former members of GEBURIUM, TRANQUILLITY and EXPULSION. The concept was rooted in a 2000 reformation of early nineties Black Metal act GEBURIUM by former members vocalist / guitarist Chris Vowden, also claiming ABSURD and EXPULSION heritage, bass player Pelle Wannerheim and drummer Andreas Billing. However, the revised version of GEBURIUM, adding TRANQUILLITY guitarist Peter Hegardt, took on more of a hard, Rock n' Roll approach than their previous fare. In November 2001 both Wannerheim and Billing opted out. New recruits would see EXPULSION's Calle Fransson taking on the drum role whilst Oliver Vowden assumed bass duties. One demo was cut in June of 2002, after which Niclas Engwall, of Stoner outfit PONAMERO SUNDOWN, enrolled as the band's new frontman for 2003's session 'Frictional Resistance'.

The STRESSFEST demo 'Silence You Serpent' was issued in June of 2004.

Frictional Resistance, Stressfest (2003) (Demo). Isolation Wall / Flesh / Deadneck / Lights Out.
Silence You Serpent, Stressfest (2004) (Demo). Thirty Wars / Poison Tongue / Touch The Forbidden / The Eye Never Lies.
Thirdfisting, Stressfest (2005) (Demo). World Cowardice / Come In Peace, Leave In Pieces / Wrath / Pain Into Power / Superproducable.

SUBLIMINAL CRUSHER

TERNI, ITALY — *Tooz (vocals), Hatewerk (guitar), Elvys (guitar), Biagiotti Jerico (bass), Rodeath (drums).*

SUBLIMINAL CRUSHER is a Thrash outfit initiated in late 2002 by S.R.L. members bassist Jerico and drummer Rodeath. Second guitarist Hatewerk was added in October of 2003. The 2003 demo 'Life Drought' included a cover version of DEATH's 'Pull The Plug'. The band contributed tracks to a swathe of compilations including 'Wild Compilation', 'Sky Pro Media Italian Metaland', 'Underground Metal Alliance Vol. 1', 'Raw & Wild Compilation—Vol. 13', 'A Place in Hell—Chapter 1', all in 2004, and 'Follow The Storm' in 2005. SUBLIMINAL CRUSHER's 2005 opus 'Antithesis', released by New LM Records, included a cover version of TESTAMENT's 'Into The Pit'.

Life Drought, Subliminal Crusher (2003). Armageddon / Sense Of Impotence / History / Terrifying Symphonies / Life Drought / Affection / Outro / Pull The Plug.
ANTITHESIS, New LM (2005). Fuck-Simile / Affection / Technocratic / I.R.A.Q. / Slavery / Fearbox / Unfertile Suggestion / Poetry / Into The Pit.

SUICIDAL ANGELS

ATHENS, GREECE — *Nick Melissourgos (vocals / guitar), Thanos Athanasopoulos (guitar), Thodoris Paralis (bass), Orpheas Tzortzopoulos (drums).*

Athens Thrash Metal act SUICIDAL ANGELS was manifested as a Death Metal oriented band in September of 2001, at first counting a line-up of singer Jason Valvis, guitarists Nick Melissourgos and Makis Giousmas, bassist Kostas Antoniou and Fanis of INSIDAE INFERNUS on the drums. The group underwent a series of line up changes before pulling in drummer Orpheas Tzortzopoulos. A series of demos followed in 2002's 'United By Hate', 2003's Angels' Sacrifice' and the April 2004 session 'The Calm Before The Storm'.

SUICIDAL ANGELS 2004 demo 'Bloodthirsty Humanity' was produced by Nick Giagoudakis. Upon completion of these sessions bassist John Koutsamanis was added and guitarist John Koutsamanis was replaced by Thanos Athanasopoulos. Adding new bassist Thodoris Paralis the band gained a valuable support to TANKARD in October.

SUICIDAL ANGELS, alongside MASS INFECTION, supported ROTTING CHRIST on the Balkans leg of the band's European tour in April 2007.

United By Hate, Suicidal Angels (2002). Intro / Call From The Abyss / Suicidal Angels / My Own Golgotha / Relief Of Death.
Angels' Sacrifice, (2003). Church Unrules / Being "Insane" / Hate Under Sacrifice.
The Calm Before The Storm, (2004). Stateless / The Trial / Church Unrules / Being "Insane" / Hate Under Sacrifice.
Bloodthirsty Humanity, (2004). Destination... Battlefield / Hate And Torture / Bloodthirsty Humanity / Through My Eyes See Your Death / The Trial / Being Insane / Church Unrules / Ending... Death / Stateless / Hate Under Sacrifice.

SUICIDAL TENDENCIES

VENICE BEACH, CA, USA — *Mike Muir (vocals), Dean Pleasants (guitar), Mike Clark (guitar), Steve Brunner (bass), Ron Brunner Jr. (drums).*

SUICIDAL TENDENCIES, created in Venice Beach, California during 1980 by vocalist Mike Muir, is one of the few Hardcore acts to break out onto the world circuit. Muir and his cohorts often appeared in photographs in the distinctive Los Angeles gang culture dress style of eyes hidden behind bandannas and Pendleton check shirts held by the neck button. Later this image would develop through the skateboard culture fuelled by songs such as 'Possessed To Skate'.

The band was a fluid force enduring numerous line-up changes until stabilizing in 1982. Amongst the underground hardcore circles the self-titled debut was recognized as a classic but as the band grew more conventional rock sensibilities would come to the fore. The band contracted with Epitaph for an eponymous 1983 debut, this set of Glen E. Friedman produced and Randy Burns engineered tracks marking out Muir as an articulate commentator on social ills, youth decay and US national politics. Backing Muir would be guitarist Grant Estes, bassist Louiche Mayorga and drummer Amery AWOL Smith.

The band signed to major label Virgin in 1986 as MTV support for the video to 'Institutionalised', plus a spot in the 1984 Emilio Estevez 'Repo Man' cult movie. raised the band's profile considerably. The band even put in a cameo appearance on an episode of the TV hit 'Miami Vice', which also used the song. 'Institutionalised' alone pulled them clear of their indie hardcore roots and breaking the charts on both sides of the Atlantic. The successful 'Join The Army' album, produced by BLIND ILLUSION bassist Les Claypool and peaking at 1000 on the US national charts, saw the departure of Estes and Smith as the band debuted guitarist Rocky George and drummer R.J. Herrera.

Bassist Louiche Mayorga joined his erstwhile band mates Estes and Smith to form UNCLE SLAM, debuting the new act with the 'Say Uncle' album on Caroline Records during 1988.

The Mark Dodson produced 'How Will I Laugh ...' saw the band being enlarged with the addition of ex-NO MERCY rhythm guitarist Mike Clark and bassist Bob Heathcote. However, just as SUICIDAL TENDENCIES were seemingly in ascendancy into the big league their controversial name made them ripe targets for the moral majority. California's police department, fearing Muir's crew was merely a front for a Los Angeles gang, even went so far as to ban the band performing in their hometown. The notorious moral campaigner Tipper Gore led pressure group P.M.R.C. kept up a campaign against the band claiming that a number of teenage suicides were directly attributable to the band.

SUICIDAL TENDENCIES brought in bassist Rob Trujillo for 1990's 'Lights ... Camera ... Revolution'. The album track 'Send Me Your Money', a forthright attack on American television evangelists proved a huge hit with the fans and quickly became a staple of live shows. The band stepped on the international touring circuit, that September being ranked alongside TESTAMENT, SLAYER and MEGADETH on the European 'Clash Of The Titans' extravaganza.

Both Muir and Trujillo captured more than their fair share of the limelight at this juncture creating Funked up side project act INFECTIOUS GROOVES together with erstwhile JANE'S ADDICTION drummer Stephen Perkins. This side project band that would go on to release two well received albums and test the duo's stamina as INFECTIOUS GROOVES often opened the show for SUICIDAL TENDENCIES.

The band's next album, 'Still Cyco After All These Years', was actually a complete re-recording of their debut. Despite the rise in SUICIDAL TENDENCIES popularity the 1983 debut had engendered a legend mystified by its complete absence from record stores. With Epitaph showing little inclination to re-press, the band, together with producer Mark Dodson, took a practical option of simply re-cutting the entire record from scratch. Their efforts were rewarded with a Grammy nomination for 'Institutionalized' but, in the main, their fan base preferred the rawness of the original.

For the 'Art Of Rebellion' album, issued in June 1992, what was to be SUICIDAL TENDENCIES highest selling record reaching number 52 in the Billboard charts. Noted producer Peter Collins was utilized and the band once more announced a new recruit in VANDALS drummer Josh Freece who incidentally took over the drum stool in INFECTIOUS GROOVES too. Live work in the USA had the band opening up MEGADETH's hugely successful headline dates and, in October 1993, Australian shows backing ALICE IN CHAINS.

1994's expletive ridden, Paul Northfield produced 'Suicidal For Life' had SUICIDAL TENDENCIES recording without a permanent drummer. Freese joined the limbo bound GUNS N' ROSES then PEARL JAM and A PERFECT CIRCLE. WHITE LION and Y&T man Jimmy DeGrasso deputised for the album sessions before he joined up full time with MEGADETH.

Laid down at Groove Masters in Santa Monica and Ocean Way Studios in Hollywood, many voiced their displeasure at the lack of subtlety on 'Suicidal For Life'. Having gained respect for his insight and lyrical wit, Muir blasted listeners with four songs in a row with a dumbed down, common thread, 'Don't Give A Fuck', 'No Fuck'n Problem', 'Suicyco Muthafucka' and 'Fucked Up Just Right'. Muir was to later admit that this caustic diatribe was deliberate and due to the band awareness whilst recording that 'Suicidal For Life' was to be a closing chapter with Epic. In spite of these problems, the group still engaged in high profile touring, supporting METALLICA in the USA and performing in South America on festival bills with KISS, SLAYER and BLACK SABBATH.

SUICIDAL TENDENCIES folded after 'Suicidal For Life' had run its course. Rocky George created SAMSARA with CRO MAGS members Harley Flanagan and Parris Mayhew. Trujillo found himself part of the OZZY OSBOURNE band having an interim stint with PALE DEMON. Muir would assemble a studio band, including SEX PISTOLS guitarist STEVE JONES for recording of a 1995 solo CYCO MYKO album 'Lost My Brains (Once Again!)'.

In 1996 SLAYER covered 'Memories Of Tomorrow' for inclusion on their 'Undisputed Attitude' covers album. However, the track only made it onto the Japanese pressing. Meantime, the SUICIDAL TENDENCIES brand was maintained with compilation albums 'Friends And Family' and 'Prime Cuts'. The latter effort sported fresh tracks recorded by Muir, with guitarist Dean Pleasants, bass player Josh Paul and drummer Brooks Wackerman.

SUICIDAL TENDENCIES returned in November 1998 touring a six track EP, the Mike Vail Blum and Paul Northfield produced 'Six The Hard Way'. The resurrected outfit then put out a full-length album in 1999 through the Side One Dummy imprint dubbed 'Freedumb', after which Wackerman opted out, focusing on his HOT POTTY band. SUICIDAL TENDENCIES signed to Germany's Nuclear Blast label for a European release of the 'Freedumb' album.

By early 2002 Rocky George had re-emerged touring a fresh act HARLEY'S WAR in union with ex-CRO MAGS frontman Harley Flanagan and former WARZONE guitarist Jay Vento. Meantime ex-SUICIDAL TENDENCIES guitarist Anthony Gallo re-emerged as part of ex MEGADETH drummer Nick Menza's new band project.

The 2002 SUICIDAL TENDENCIES line-up comprised of Mike Muir, Mike Clark on guitar, Dean Pleasants on second guitar, bassist Steve Brunner and Ron Brunner Jr. on drums. The Brunner brothers commitment to Rapper SNOOP DOG would see the band without their services for one gig, SUICIDAL TENDENCIES duly enrolling Josh Paul and drummer Dave Hidalgo Jr. for this occasion.

In early 2003 ex-member Robert Trujillo became METALLICA's new bass man, this appointment putting a renewed focus on his former band. An extensive round of touring in Europe during the latter half of 2003 would prove arduous for Muir. Upon completion of these dates the frontman entered hospital for two operations on his back. South and Central American tour plans for February of 2004 would be curtailed. 2004 also found Rocky George uniting with UGLY KID JOE and MEDICATION man Whitfield Crane to cut a version of 'Master Of Puppets' for the METALLICA 'Metallic Assault' tribute album through Big Deal Records.

Gigs announced in Europe for the Summer of 2005 would be cancelled when it was announced singer Mike Muir was suffering "serious health problems". Festival dates for Brazil would be announced, but then curtailed as it was revealed Mike Muir was to undergo back surgery. Working with producer Paul Northfield, SUICIDAL TENDENCIES commenced work on a new studio album in January 2006.

Former SUICIDAL TENDENCIES musicians Grant Estes,

SUICIDAL TENDENCIES

Louichi Mayorga and Amery Smith joined forces with ex-EXCEL frontman Dan Clements in a new band billed AGAINST, announcing this formation in May.

On a billing alongside DEFTONES, HATEBREED, EIGHTEEN VISIONS, (+44), THRICE, UNWRITTEN LAW and FLYLEAF the band featured on the Australian 'Soundwave' festivals in February and March 2007. The group undertook an extensive round of dates in France throughout April.

SUICIDAL TENDENCIES, Frontier FLP1011 (1983). Suicide's An Alternative / You'll Be Sorry / Two Sided Politics / I Shot The Devil / Subliminal / Won't Fall In Love Today / Institutionalized / Memories Of Tomorrow / Possessed / I Saw Your Mommy .... / Fascist Pig / I Want More / Suicidal Failure.

Possessed To Skate, Virgin VS 967-12 (1987) (12" single). Possessed To Skate / Human Guinea Pig / Two Wrongs Don't Make A Right (But They Make Me Feel Better).

Possessed To Skate, Virgin VS 967 (1987) (7" single). Possessed To Skate / Human Guinea Pig.

JOIN THE ARMY, Virgin V2424 (1987). Suicidal Maniac / Join The Army / You Got, I Want / Little Each Day / Prisoner / War Inside My Head / I Feel Your Pain And Survive / Human Guinea Pig / Possessed To Skate / No Name, No Words / Cyco / Two Wrongs Don't Make A Right (But It Makes Me Feel Better) / Looking In Your Eyes. Chart positions: 81 UK, 100 USA.

Institutionalised, Virgin VST 1039 (1988) (12" single). Institutionalised / War Inside My Head / Cycxo.

Trip At The Brain, Virgin VST 1127 (1988) (12" single). Trip At The Brain / Suicyco Mania.

HOW WILL I LAUGH TOMORROW WHEN I CAN'T EVEN SMILE TODAY, Virgin CDV 2551 (1988). Trip At The Brain / Hearing Voices / Pledge Your Allegiance / How Will I Laugh Tomorrow / Miracle / Surf And Slam / If I Don't Wake Up / Sorry / One Too Many Times / Feeling's Back / Suicyco Mania. Chart position: 111 USA.

CONTROLLED BY HATRED—FEEL LIKE SHIT ... DÉJÀ VU, Epic 4653992 (1989). Master Of No Mercy / How Will I Laugh Tomorrow / Just Another Love Song / Walking The Dead / Controlled By Hatred / Choosing My Own Way Of Life / Feel Like Shit ... Déjà Vu / It's Not Easy / How Will I Laugh Tomorrow ('Heavy Emotion' version). Chart position: 150 USA.

Send Me Your Money, Epic 6563310 (1990) (Picture disc). Send Me Your Money.

LIGHTS, CAMERA ... REVOLUTION, Epic 4665692 (1990). You Can't Bring Me Down / Lost Again / Alone / Lovely / Give It Revolution / Get Whacked / Send Me Your Money / Emotion No. 13 / Disco's Out, Murder's In / Go n' Breakdown. Chart positions: 59 UK, 101 USA.

Send Me Your Money, Epic 6563326 (1990). Send Me Your Money / You Can't Bring Me Down / Waking The Dead / Don't Give Me Your Nothing.

Asleep At The Wheel, Epic (1992). Asleep At The Wheel / Asleep At The Wheel (Edit) / I Wasn't Meant To Feel This Way.

THE ART OF REBELLION, Epic 4718852 (1992). Can't Stop / Accept My Sacrifice / Nobody Hears / Tap Into The Power / Monopoly On Sorrow / We Call This Mutha Revenge / I Wasn't Meant To Feel This / Asleep At The Wheel / Gotta Kill Captain Stupid / I'll Hate You Better / Which Way To Be Free / It's Going Down / Where's The Truth. Chart positions: 40 NEW ZEALAND, 52 USA.

STILL CYCO AFTER ALL THESE YEARS, Epic 473749-2 (1993). Suicide's An Alternative / Two Sided Politics / Subliminal / I Shot The Devil / Won't Fall In Love / Institutionalised / War Inside My Head / Don't Give Me Your Nothin' / Memories Of Tomorrow / Possessed / I Saw Your Mommy ... / Fascist Pig / Little Each Day / I Want More / Suicidal Failure. Chart position: 117 USA.

Love vs. Loneliness, Epic 6445 (1994) (USA promotion release). Love vs. Loneliness (Artist edit) / Love vs. Loneliness.

SUICIDAL FOR LIFE, Epic 476885-2 (1994). Invocation / Don't Give A Fuck / No Fuckn' Problem / Suicyco Muthafucka / Fucked Up Just Right / No Bullshit / What Else Could I Do / What You Need's A Friend / I Wouldn't Mind / Depression And Anguish / Evil / Love v Loneliness / Benediction. Chart position: 82 USA.

FRIENDS AND FAMILY, Suicidal (1997). Panic / Scream Out / We Are Family / Epic Escape / Payback's A Bitch / It's Time / Sweet Disharmony / Big Fat Baby / Some People Deserve To Die / Teachin' Lil Ricky A Lesson / Day At The Beach / Dysfunktional / Whose Got A Secret / They Say.

Six The Hard Way, Suicidal Tendencies 014 (1998). Free Dumb / Cyco Vision / Refuse / What's The Word? / Fascist Pig (Live) / I Saw Your Mommy (Live).

FREEDUMB, Nuclear Blast NB3682 (1999). Freedumb / Ain't Gonna Take It / Scream Out / Half Way Up My Head / Cyco Vision / I Ain't Like You / Naked / Hippie Killer / Built To Survive / Get Sick / We Are Family / I'll Buy Myself / Gaigan Go Home / Heaven. Chart position: 90 GERMANY.

FREE YOUR SOUL ... SAVE YOUR MIND, Nuclear Blast NB 528-2 (2000). Self Destruct / Sue Casa Es Mi Casa / No More No Less / Free Your Soul / Pop Songs / Billenium / Animal / Straight From The Heart / Cyco Speak / Start Your Brain / Public Dissention / Children Of The Bored / Got Mutation / Charlie Monroe / Home. Chart position: 92 GERMANY.

FRIENDS AND FAMILY VOL. 2, XIII Bis 05072 (2001). Free Your Soul ... And Save My Mind / Fight The Losing Battle / Ain't Gonna Take It / Lock It In The Pocket / Cat Got My Tongue / Plant The Seed / We're Evil / Something Inside Me / One Track Mind / Big Mouth / Inside / Sustain / Chains Of Hate / Ultra Drown / Handguns And Heroin / Soothing Effect Of Violence / Swinging From The Family Tree / Whipcream (Live) / Contractual Disclaimer / Plant The Seed.

SUN DESCENDS

NY, USA — *Mem Von Stein (vocals), Sam Awry (guitar), Jillian Ann La Boy (bass), Javier Medina (drums).*

SUN DESCENDS is a New York, Thrash styled Metal band led by former EXUMER, PHOBIC INSTINCT, OF RYTES and HUMUNGOUS FUNGUS man Mem Von Stein. The founding 1999 line up saw Stein flanked by guitarist John Monsees, bass player Josh Thunder and drummer Czar. SUN DESCENDS would also feature the HEMLOCK and TERROR OF THE TREES credited His Eminence The Wicked on guitar.

The debut 2001 EP 'Tide In The Affairs Of Men' saw issue through the German High Vaultage label. The band hit line up problems throughout 2002 and beyond, hiring and then losing drummer Joe Darkside and witnessing the departure of Monsees. Pulling in BLOOD OF KINGS drummer Javier Medina, SUN DESCENDS finally settled on a stable line up with the introduction of ex-MOLOTOV COCKTAIL guitarist Sam Awry in January of 2004, completing the roster with the inauguration of bassist Jillian Ann La Boy.

The July 2004 EP 'Kanun-Law', recorded at Don Fury's Cyclone Studios, added bonus tracks from the 1985 EXUMER demo "A Mortal In Black'.

Tide In The Affairs Of Men, High Vaultage (2001) (limited edition 1000 copies). Third Column / Tide / Dream Flow.

KANUN-LAW, (2004) (Limited edition 500 copies). Quiet Predator / Repeater Of Births / Storm (Interlude) / Kanun / Sacred / A Mortal In Black / Scanners / Silent Death.

INCINERATING THE MEEK, Twilight Vertrieb (2006).

SUNRISE

OSTROWIEC, POLAND — *Pat (vocals), Daniel (guitar), Poitr (guitar), Adam (bass), Arek (drums).*

Hardcore edged Thrash band SUNRISE was forged in the city of Ostrowiec during 1994, conducting their first gig on New Year's Eve 1995 at Dąbrowa Górnicza. The following year a five song demo emerged entitled 'Fire Walk With Me', this being laid down by a quartet of singer Patryk, guitarist Daniel, bassist Marcel and drummer Maciek. The band would then be hit by line up problems, resulting in ex-AGNI HOTRA drummer Raya Nityananda being utilised for their debut full length album 'Generation Of Sleepwalkers', released by Sanctuary in 1998. Acknowledging a switch of direction to a more Scandinavian style, 'Child Of Eternity' followed for Sobermind in 2000.

In 2000 bassist Adam 'Cood' and former NOWA DROGA, UNSILENT and PAIN RUNS DEEP man Arek joined the band. In 2001 Czaja replaced Arek, first playing bass and then switching to guitar. Youth Culture Records issued the EP 'Still Walking With The Fire' as the band toured extensively throughout the Czech Republic, Germany, Belgium and Norway. 2003 witnessed a signature to Lifeforce Records and the recording of a split release, 'Decontaminate', shared with Belgian act LIAR.

SUNRISE recorded the 'Traces To Nowhere' album at Serakos Studio in the Summer of 2004. Lifeforce handled the album for USA and Europe whilst a South American release would be secured through the Liberation imprint. The band's archives would also receive attention as the cassette 'Blood Spills Everyday' was released in Indonesia via Fallen Angel Records and in Malaysia through Cactus Records. Meantime, the Survival label in Chile published the compilation 'Sangre Derramada Cada Dia'.

October 2005 gigs, billed 'Metal Union Road Tour', had the group sharing stages with HEDFIRST, FRONTSIDE and AL SIRET.

Fire Walk With Me, (1997). Forever / Sunrise / Feeling / Morning Dew / Where We Stand.
GENERATION OF SLEEPWALKERS, Sanctuary (1998). (It Is Happening) Again / Sleepwalkers / Landscape Of Decay / Dead Society / From The Lunacy / The Beginning Of The End / Nightmare / Head Against The Wall / Bloody Tears.
CHILD OF ETERNITY, Sobermind (2000). Cursed / Stolen Lives / Last Hours Of Torments / Child Of Eternity / Bastard Of Chaos / Absorbed By Evil / Legacy.
Still Walking With The Fire, Youth Culture (2002). Still Walking With The Fire / A Light In The Dark / Morning Dew / Still Walking With The Fire (Video).
Decontaminate, Lifeforce (2003) (Split EP with LIAR). Drain The Cup / Once We Swore / Truceless.
TRACES TO NOWHERE, Lifeforce LFR 049-2 (2004). Born Free Die Free / Coma Is Over / Escape Failure / Traces To Nowhere / Compromise Zero / Beyond Sanity / Scream Bloody Murder / Undercover Enemy / Smiling Bag.

SWARM

SAN FRANCISCO, CA, USA — *Mark Osegueda (vocals), Rob Cavestany (guitar), Michael Isaiah (bass), Andy Galeon (drums).*

SWARM was founded in San Francisco during 1999, after the demise of the hotly tipped Thrash Metal outfit DEATH ANGEL by vocalist Mark Osegueda, guitarist Rob Cavestany and drummer Andy Galeon. The latter two musicians were also involved with THE ORGANIZATION. SWARM supported JERRY CANTRELL on his April 2001 US dates. DEATH ANGEL buried the hatchet in August 2001 re-uniting for a one off gig at the 'Thrash Of The Titans' festival in aid of TESTAMENT frontman Chuck Billy's cancer treatment fund.

The Belgian Mausoleum label released SWARM tracks in 2003 as the 'Beyond The End' album. Oddly, as the DEATH ANGEL reunion gathered pace, SWARM would act as live support band for their comeback gigs. Mark Osegueda announced the formation of side act ALL TIME HIGHS, this band featuring the singer alongside members of LICA-STO, TRES PISTOLAS, THE SICK and THE OOZIES.

Swarm EP, Swarmusic 479276 (1999). Bleed / Sufferahs / Sengir Vampire / Beyond The End.
BEYOND THE END, Mausoleum (2003). Heaven's Cage / Bleed / Never Forget / Karma / Dark Western / Sengir Vampire / Sufferahs / Beyond The End / Diamond / My Eyes Have Seen You.

SWEDISH MASSACRE

KUNGSÖR, SWEDEN — *Denny Axelsson (vocals), Jon Peterson (guitar), Anders Lind (guitar), Kristoffer Johansson (drums).*

Kungsör Death / Thrashers established in 2002 by erstwhile members of HARDKAZE and WITHIN REACH, singer Denny Axelsson, guitarist Jon Petersson and drummer Kristoffer Johansson. First product would be the single 'Eyes Of Reflection' recorded at Evelon Studios during February 2004 by with producer Palle Svensson. The title track gained extra exposure with an inclusion on the compilation album 'Metal Ostentation'. Further promotional tracks would be recorded at Evil Bertil Studios in December 2004 with Andreas Öhrn behind the desk. Former SWEDISH MASSACRE man Denny Axelsson, opting out in October 2005, holds ties to both CALM and MARAMON.

Eyes Of Reflection, Swedish Massacre (2004). Eyes Of Reflection / Kids In Satan's Service.

TALION

VÄXJÖ, SWEDEN — *Martin Missy (vocals), Fredrik Lundquist (guitar), Ludde Engellau (bass), Carl Sjöström (drums).*

Växjö Thrash quartet TALION was assembled as SWORDS OF DESTINY, issuing an eponymous February 1998 demo. The formation numbered vocalist / bass player Joakim Svensson, guitarists Erik Almström and Fredrik Lundquist with Gustav Hjortsjö on the drums. Both Almström and Hjortsjö would also be members of the band BULLET. They adopted the new brand of LELLDORIN, under which name they issued the August 1997 demo 'Wizard Of Darkness' before evolving into TALION.

TALION released the 2003 demo 'Operation Massacre', recorded at Soundlab Studios. In November that same year TALION splintered, with only Lundquist persevering. The new look band incorporated singer Martin Missy, an established scene veteran best known for his 80s term of duty fronting German Thrash Metal band PROTECTOR, the DARK EDEN credited Magnus Karkea on bass guitar and Carl Sjöström of UNCHASTE on drums. Missy also has ties to INZEST, ENERGYANT and RUINS OF TIME. In 2004 Martin Missy re-emerged fronting PSYCHOMANTHIUM, an "old-school Speed/Thrash metal" band featuring ARKHAM 13 guitarist Derek 'Derekonomicon' Schilling, the INTERNAL BLEEDING and CATASTROPHIC credited bassist Brian Hobbie and ARKHAM 13 drummer Ant Ichrist. In 2005 Missy founded Stockholm Death Metal act PHIDION.

Ludde Engellau, of REMASCULATE and UNCHASTE, took over the bass position. TALION cut three demo tracks in August 2006 at their own Macaroni Factory Studio. Engellau also joined DEMONICAL as their new singer in November.

The NMK Demotape, Talion (1998) (Cassette demo). Ninja Might / The Soulcollector / Made In Taiwan / Singe Este Viata / Twilight Mistress / Wasted World / Supremacy / Maker Of Illusions.
The Silence, Talion (1999) (Demo). The Silence / Fragmentary / Executing The Free Speech / Evilution, The New World Order / The Sacrifice.
THE SILENT NEUROTIC SUPREMACY, Talionation TRECS (2001). The Silence / Fragmentary / Executing The Free Speech / Evilution, The New World Order / The Sacrifice / Anaesthetic Neurosis / Dreamscape / King Of Agony / Legions Of Fury / Made In Taiwan / Ninja Might / Singe Este Viata / Supremacy / Maker Of Illusions / The Soulcollector / Twilight Mistress / Wasted World.
Operation Massacre, Talion (2003) (Demo CD single). Mastered By Ignorance / Operation Massacre / J.D.
Visions Of Deterioration, Talion (2003) (Demo CD single). Purpose: None / Visions Of Deterioration / No Regression.

VISIONS OF DETERIORATION, Talionation TRECS 005 (2003).
Intro / Purpose: None / Visions Of Deterioration / No Regression / Mastered By Ignorance / Operation Massacre / J.D. / Death Obsessed / Silenced To Remain / Infinite Dread.
Demo 2006, Talion (2006) (Demo). Coprophagia / He Who Must Not Be Named / Catalaunian Fields.

TALIÖN

UK — *Graeme Wyatt (vocals / guitar), Pete Wadeson (guitar), Phil Gavin (bass), Johnny Lee Jackson (drums).*

Thrash styled Heavy Metal band. TALIÖN guitarist Pete Wadeson and frontman Graeme Wyatt were originally in TROJAN, a band that released the Guy Bidmead produced album 'Chasing The Storm' on Roadrunner Records in 1987. The duo's first project after TROJAN split was titled LETHAL, a union with ex-WOLFPACK and SALEM bassist Phil Gavin. After demoing material at Twilight studios in Manchester in 1988, the band settled on the name TALIÖN and signed to Major, a subsidiary of Peaceville Records, in April 1989, promptly recording the album 'Killing The World' with producer Kevin Ridley.

The sound of this album turned out to be fast and aggressive, bordering on Thrash but with plenty of melody, the group following its release with a trip, in early 1990, overseas to appear at the 'Public Against Violence' festival in Czechoslovakia alongside BONFIRE and STORMWITCH.

Gavin and Lee Jackson quit the band in late 1991 prompting the recruitment of new guitarist Andy J. in mid 1992 whilst Wadeson took time out to contribute the solo track 'Thrill Of The Chase' to the Japanese released compilation 'Metal For Muthas '92' compilation.

Following the demise of TALIÖN Wadeson recorded a solo demo entitled 'Play With Fire' in 1992. In 1994 Wadeson formed BETRAYED.

In 1995 he issued an instrumental demo, 'Burnout', before later turning up as a Rock journalist for Brazil's 'Rock Brigade' magazine. 1999 found the man unsuccessfully auditioning for ex-IRON MAIDEN vocalist Blaze Bayley's new band and for MARSHALL LAW. The guitarist also distributed a solo demo tape billed 'Burnout'. In 2001 Wadeson was briefly involved with Martin Walkyier's RETURN TO THE SABBAT project but departed before any live work.

KILLING THE WORLD, Major WADES1CD (1989). Killing The World / Sanctuary / Living On The Edge / Speed Thrills / Laws Of Retaliation / Screamin' For Mercy / Premonition.

TANK

LONDON, UK — *Algy Ward (vocals / bass), Mick Tucker (guitar), Gary Taylor (drums).*

Formed in Croydon, London during February 1980, TANK debuted as a trio of Algy Ward (Alasdair Mackie Ward), an established veteran of the Punk scene citing terms of duty with the SAINTS and the DAMNED (featuring on the seminal 'Machine Gun Etiquette' album), with the brotherly duo of guitarist Peter Brabbs and drummer Mark Brabbs. It was only inevitable that they would quickly establish a reputation for themselves as a power trio in the MOTÖRHEAD mould.

Opening singles comprised 'Don't Walk Away' and 'Turn Your Head Around' emerging the following year. Some sectors of the press felt they were too close to close to Lemmy and co for comfort, especially on the debut 1982 album 'Filth Hounds Of Hades', which was ironically produced by MOTÖRHEAD's guitarist FAST EDDIE CLARKE. The album surfaced in Spain billed 'Los Perros Immundos Del Infierno'. Fan response though was enthusiastic and valuable press was afforded by a rustic cover rendition of THE OSMONDS 'Crazy Horses'.

In spite of the media detractors, TANK forged ahead with strong sales and were quick to build up a loyal fanbase, particularly in Europe and Japan.

After consistently touring opening for the likes of GIRLSCHOOL, MOTÖRHEAD and DIAMOND HEAD throughout the next two years the unveiling of a second album, entitled 'Power Of The Hunter' met with strong sales and established a loyal fan base.

Changes were afoot for TANK by the time the group's conceptual third album emerged in June 1983, the group having aligned themselves with Music For Nations after the demise of former label Kamaflage Records. 'This Means War', debuted TANK's new, second guitarist Mick Tucker, previously with AXIS and WHITE SPIRIT, and the JOHN VERITY produced album also featured guest backing vocals by Jody Turner of ROCK GODDESS and Denise Dufort of GIRLSCHOOL. However, after just one gig promoting 'This Means War' Peter Brabbs was sacked and Mark Brabbs left to join DUMPY'S RUSTY NUTS, and later UK, shortly after. Mark Brabbs created a short lived band with erstwhile ORE members bassist Dave Boyce and guitarist Dave Howard. 1986 found Brabbs as a member of Paul Samson's EMPIRE, followed by a stint with SAVIOUR. TANK would very briefly induct Michael Bettel as a replacement on guitar.

Meantime, Ward and Tucker chose to enlist ex-CHICKEN SHACK and HEADFIRST guitarist Cliff Evans and former WHITE SPIRIT drummer Graeme Crallan for a revised version of TANK. During late 1984 TANK supported METALLICA on a European tour. Later shows included gigs in America supporting RAVEN, prior to further headline shows of their own. Algy Ward produced Italian Thrash band BULLDOZER's 'The Day Of Wrath' album for Roadracer Records in 1985. That same year the 'Armour Plated' TANK compilation was delivered.

Having recorded a second album for Music For Nations, 1985's 'Honour And Blood', TANK replaced Graeme Crallan with ex-STREETFIGHTER man Gary Taylor. Crallan joined London act BRITTON then by 1987 PANAMA reuniting with his erstwhile WHITE SPIRIT colleague keyboard player Toby Sadler.

Following the 'Tank' album, recorded in 1986 with Mick Tucker but only seeing a release in 1988, the band's line-up was back down to the trio, consisting of Algy Ward, Cliff Evans and Gary Taylor. The latter was replaced by former FASTWAY drummer Steve Clarke in 1989. However, the band then folded, with Evans creating the short lived DESTROYER with ex-YA YA frontman LEA HART prior to working in the studio with MASK. Evans would later join KILLERS after Ward decided to bring TANK to a conclusion. Taylor travelled to America to form Punk Sleaze act SHOTGUN RATIONALE with ex-PLASMATICS man Chris Romanelli.

Although inactive, TANK would retain its cult following. German Thrash act SODOM in particular maintained the band's profile by covering 'Don't Walk Away' on their 1989 'Agent Orange' album and 'Turn Your Head Around' on the 'Better Off Dead' set in 1990.

In 1993 there was some talk of a reunion album in the works, but nothing came of this. Ward spent time recording the "Black Metal supergroup" album titled NECROPOLIS with ex-FASTWAY and DESTROYER drummer Steve Clark and ASIA guitarist KEITH MORE among others before joining Clark's Jazz Rock act NETWORK for the 'Refusal To Comply' album. Another project involving Ward would be ATOMGOD, issuing the 'History Re-written' album in 1992. He would also appear on the later NETWORK album 'L.N.C.' Ward resurfaced in London club band CONSPIRACY during 1994 before joining WARHEAD, a project assembled by erstwhile MOTÖRHEAD guitarist WURZEL and WARFARE mainman Evo.

During 1996 Ward rejoined the DAMNED, but before long the continental fascination for cult, early 80s acts had caught up with TANK and, offered a recording deal, the band duly reformed. SODOM once more got in one more shot of appreciation with their take on 'Shellshock' appearing on the 'Ten

TANK

Black Years album. The 1997 TANK line up showed up at the Wacken Festival in Germany then undertook a tour of the country sharing a bill with HAMMERFALL and RAVEN. For most of the latter dates on this trek Ward took to the stage with the aid of a walking stick. The NECROPOLIS album finally saw a belated release through Neat Records in 1997.

The late 90s incarnation of TANK, Ward, Evans, Tucker and ex-PERSIAN RISK, JAGGED EDGE and BATTLEZONE drummer Steve Hopgood, issued the live album 'The Return Of The Filth Hounds' for Rising Sun Records and put in a further German showing at the 1998 'Bang Your Head' Festival. The band also got to play in Japan during early 1999 on a NWoBHM billing including PRAYING MANTIS as Evans also began work on a fresh KILLERS project. The Japanese Pony Canyon label published the 'Metal Crusade '99' set, a split album partnered with NWoBHM era compatriots SAMSON, PRAYING MANTIS and TRESPASS, recorded at the Hibiya Open Theatre, Tokyo that August. Archive concert recordings culled from a 1981 support to MOTÖRHEAD in Dortmund during 1981 would be released by the Zoom Club label in 2001 as 'War Of Attrition'.

Mid 2002 brought the prospect of a brand new studio album from TANK, entitled 'Still At War' and set for release in Japan in early August through Spiritual Beast Records. The TANK crew for this outing had Algy Ward joined by guitarists Cliff Evans and Mick Tucker with Bruce Bisland of PRAYING MANTIS, SWEET, WEAPON and STATETROOPER on drums. 'Still At War' included re-recorded versions of 'And Then We Heard The Thunder' and 'In The Last Hours Before Dawn'.

In January of 2004 TANK's schedule was alarmingly interrupted when Algy Ward was taken into hospital to have a tumour removed from his head. The singer had previously been suffering from hearing loss and headaches. Nevertheless, recording for a new studio album entitled 'Sturmpanzer', these sessions including the STATUS QUO cover version 'Tune To The Music', was still completed. German Heavy Metal band, POWERGOD in alliance with SODOM's Tom Angelripper, cut a cover version of 'The War Drags Ever On' for inclusion on their 'Long Live The Loud–That's Metal Lesson II' released through Massacre Records in July 2005. Maniacal Records announced the release of a limited run of 500 vinyl, of which 250 would be white vinyl, gatefold pressings of the live album 'War Of Attrition'. The LP version contained two tracks not available on the CD. A press release revealed recording sessions were still taking place for 'Sturmpanzer' in February 2007.

Don't Walk Away (Live), Kamaflage KAM F1 (1981). Don't Walk Away (Live) / The Snake.
Don't Walk Away, Kamaflage KAM 1 (1981). Don't Walk Away / Shellshock / Hammer On.
Crazy Horses, Kamaflage KAM 7 (1982). Crazy Horses / Filth Bitch Boogie.
Turn Your Head Around, Kamaflage KAM3 (1982). Turn Your Head Around / Steppin' On A Landmine.
FILTH HOUNDS OF HADES, Kamaflage KAMLP 1 (1982). Shellshock / Struck By Lightning / Run Like Hell / Blood, Guts And Beer / That's What Dreams Are Made Of / Turn Your Head Around / Heavy Artillery / Who Needs Love Songs / Filth Hounds Of Hades / Stormtrooper. Chart position: 33 UK.
POWER OF THE HUNTER, Kamaflage KAMLP 3 (1982). Walking Barefoot Over Glass / Pure Hatred / Biting And Scratching / Some Come Running / T.A.N.K. / Used Leather (Hanging Loose) / Crazy Horses / Set Your Back On Fire / Red Skull Rock / Power Of The Hunter.
(He Fell In Love With A) Stormtrooper, Kamaflage KAP 1 (1982). (He Fell In Love With A) Stormtrooper / Blood Guts And Beer.
THIS MEANS WAR, Music For Nations MFN3 (1983). Just Like Something From Hell / Hot Lead Cold Steel / This Means War / Laughing In The Face Of Death / (If We Go) We Go Down Fighting / I (Won't Ever Let You Down) / Echoes Of A Distant Battle.
HONOUR AND BLOOD, Music For Nations MFN26 (1985). The War Drags Ever On / When All Hell Freezes Over / Honour And Blood / Chain Of Fools / W.M.I.A. / Too Tired To Wait For Love / Kill.
TANK, GWR GWCD23 (1988). Reign Of Thunder / March On, Sons Of Nippon / With Your Life / None But The Brave / The Enemy Below / Lost / (The Hell They Must) Suffer / It Fell From The Sky.
THE RETURN OF THE FILTH HOUNDS LIVE, Rising Sun 008203 2 RS (1998). This Means War / Echoes Of A Distant Battle / That's What Dreams Are Made Of / And Then We Heard The Thunder / Don't Walk Away / Honour And Blood / Power Of The Hunter / Shellshock / In The Last Hours Before Dawn (Studio) / And Then We Heard The Thunder (Studio).
METAL CRUSADE '99, Pony Canyon (1999) (Split album with PRAYING MANTIS, SAMSON & TRESPASS. Japanese release). This Means War / Walking Barefoot Over Glass / Power Of The Hunter / (He Fell In Love With A) Stormtrooper / Shellshock.
WAR OF ATTRITION, Zoom Club ZCRCD58 (2001). Shellshock / Steppin' On A Landmine / Blood, Guts And Beer / Run Like Hell / Don't Walk Away / Filthhounds Of Hades / (He Fell In Love With A) Stormtrooper / The Snake / Shellshock / Run Like Hell / Blood, Guts And Beer.
STILL AT WAR, Zoom Club ZCRCD89 (2002). Still At War / That Girl's Name Is Death / Light The Fire (Watch 'Em Burn) / The World Awaits / And Then We Heard The Thunder / In The Last Hours Before Dawn / Conspiracy Of Hate / When The Hunter Becomes The Hunted / Return Of The Filth Hounds / The Blood's Still On Their Hands / The Fear Inside.

TANKARD

FRANKFURT, GERMANY — *Andreas Geremia (vocals), Axel Katzmann (guitar), Andreas Bulgaropulos (guitar), Frank Thorwath (bass), Arnulf Tunn (drums).*

A Frankfurt Metal act lyrically obsessed by the subject of alcohol, TANKARD's second album, 'Chemical Invasion', was close to being a crusade against the introduction of foreign chemicals into German beers. The band was created during 1982 with an original line-up of vocalist Gerre, guitarists Axel Katzmann and Andy Boulgaropulas, bassist Frank Torwarth and drummer O.W. (Oliver Werner). This line-up cut the first demo in 1984 'Heavy Metal Vanguard' capitalised on by a second effort 'Alcoholic Metal'. The debut album, 1986's 'Zombie Attack', provided a useful sales base of 10'000 copies before 1987's 'Chemical Invasion' exceeded that figure three times over.

TANKARD's early drummer Oliver Werner was superseded by Arnulf Tunn. Werner went on to created CHASED CRIME and DARK STAR.

In 1988 TANKARD toured Europe heavily playing dates in Germany, Holland and Belgium before performing at festivals in Germany alongside VENDETTA and HELSTAR. The interim 'Alien' EP was promoted in Germany by dates with DEATHROW. The group later recorded 'The Meaning Of Life' album in 1990, their first to enter the German national charts as TANKARD hit the road again, this time with RUMBLE MILITIA and NAPALM in tow. Shows in Bochum and Frankfurt were recorded for the band's debut live album 'Fat, Ugly & Live'.

1992 found TANKARD's popularity extending outside of Germany and the act's touring schedule was widened to include territories such as Turkey and Bulgaria where they played with support acts MEGLOMANIAX and Englishmen XENTRIX.

Following recording of 1994's 'Two Faced' album drummer Arnulf Tunn departed and in his stead came Olaf Zissel. This new line up soon got back into action releasing an album of cover versions 'Angetankt' for a Germany only release in 1994 adopting the moniker TANKWART.

Before the next album Katzmann left the group due to health problems and TANKARD chose not to replace him but remain as a quartet. The group promptly recorded 'The Tankard' as a four-piece.

In 1996 the second TANKARD side project album was released through Century Media. Titled 'Himbeergeist Zum Frühstuck', the group would tour playing material from both this album and TANKARD material.

Katzmann and Tunn would create NEMESIS for an eponymous 1997 album in collusion with frontman Adrian Ergün of CAPRICORN. The millennium saw no let up in TANKARD's alcohol fuelled activities with the 'Kings Of Beer' album, released by Century Media, selling well. December 1999 German shows, running from Christmas Day until New Year's Eve, had the band packaged with SODOM and GODDESS OF DESIRE.

For 2002, the band's 25th anniversary TANKARD set to work on the aptly titled 'B-Day' album for new label AFM Records with HOLY MOSES guitarist Andy Classen acting as producer. Further recordings had the band offering cover versions of MANOWAR's 'Fast Taker' and METALLICA's 'Damage Inc.' for use on tribute albums.

TANKARD, promoting the 'Beast Of Bourbon' album, united with HATEWORK and IRREVERENCE for a short Italian tour in May of 2004. The band performed an unusual concert dubbed the '34'000 Ton Metal Cruise' on 25th September, performing onboard the Münchenbryggeriet car ferry in Stockholm, Sweden alongside SKYCLAD, AMON AMARTH, HYPOCRISY, TAD MOROSE, STORMWARRIOR and WOLF.

TANKARD wrapped up another studio album in February 2006, 'The Beauty And The Beer' having been laid down with producer Andy Classen at Stage One studio in Bühne.

The band utilised Stage One studios and producer Andy Classen yet again in April 2007 for a special album project, re-recording brand new versions of tracks from '(Empty) Tankard', 'Chemical Invasion', 'The Morning After' and 'Space Beer' collated as 'Best Case Scenario: 25 Years In Beers' for August issue through AFM Records. Initial versions of this included a bonus disc entitled 'A Tribute To Tankard', featuring cover versions of eighteen TANKARD songs performed by SACRED STEEL, MANTICORA, ABANDONED, PARADOX, HATEWORK, COURAGEOUS, PARAGON, HYADES, FATAL EMBRACE, IRREVERENCE, TORMENT, SOLICITUDE, ODIUM, FREZEEBEE, DOPPELBOCK, FKÜ and SCORNAGE.

ZOMBIE ATTACK, Noise N 0046-3 (1986). Zombie Attack / Acid Death / Mercenary / Maniac Forces / Alcohol / Empty Tankard / Thrash Til Death / Chains / Poison / Screamin' Victims.
CHEMICAL INVASION, Noise N 0096 (1987). Intro / Total Addiction / Tantrum / Don't Panic / Puke / For A Thousand Beers / Chemical Invasion / Farewell To A Slut / Traitor / Alcohol.
Alien, Noise NO131-3 (1987). Alien / 666 Packs / Live To Die / Remedy / Empty Tankard.
THE MORNING AFTER, Noise N 0123-1 (1989). Commandments / Shit Faced / TV Hero / FUN / Try Again / The Morning After / Desperation / Feed The Lohicia / Help Yourself / Mon Cheri.
THE MEANING OF LIFE, Noise N 0156-1 (1990). Open All Night / We Are Us / Dancing On Our Grave / Mechanical Man / Beermuda / The Meaning Of Life / Spacebeer / Always Them / Wheel Of Rebirth / Barfly.
FAT, UGLY AND LIVE, Noise N0166-1 (1991). The Meaning Of Life / Mercenary / Beermuda / Total Addiction / Live To Dive / Poison / Chemical Invasion / The Morning After / Space Beer / Alcohol / Puke / Mon Cheri / Wonderful Life / Empty Tankard.
Stone Cold Sober, Noise N 190-9 (1992). Stone Cold Sober / Broken Image / Mindwild.
STONE COLD SOBER, Noise N0190-2 (1992). Stone Cold Sober / Jurisdiction / Broken Image / Mindwild / Ugly-Beautiful / Centrefold / Behind The Back / Lost And Found (Tantrum Part Three) / Sleeping With The Past / Freiber / Of Strange People Talking Under Arabian Skies.
Ich Brauch Meinen Suff, Noise N0233-3 (1993). Ich Brauch Meinen Suff / Up From Zero.
TWO FACED, Noise N0233 (1994). Death Penalty / R.T.V. / Betrayed / Nation Over Nation / Days Of The Gun / Cities In Flames / Up From Zero / Two Faced / Ich Brauch Meinen Suff / Cyberworld / Mainhatten / Jimmy B Bad. Chart position: 86 GERMANY.
THE TANKARD, Noise N 0529-2 (1995). Grave New World / Minds On The Moon / The Story Of Mr. Cruel / Close Encounter / Poshor Golovar / Mess In The West / Atomic Twilight / Fuck Christmas / Positive / Hope?
DISCO DESTROYER, Century Media 77209-2 (1998). Serial Killer / Planetwide-suicide.com / Hard Rock Dinosaur / Queen Of Hearts / U-R-B / Mr. Superlover / Tankard Roach Motel / Another Perfect Day / Death By Whips / Away! / Face Of The Enemy / Splendid Boys / Disco Destroyer.
KINGS OF BEER, Century Media 77274-2 (2000). Flirtin' With Desaster / Dark Exile / Hot Dog Inferno / Hell Bent For Jesus / Kings Of Beer / I'm So Sorry! / Talk Show Prostitute / Incredible Loudness / Land Of The Free / Mirror, Mirror / Tattoo Coward.
B-DAY, AFM (2002). Notorious Scum / Rectifiere / Ugly, Fat And Still Alive / Voodoo Box / Underground (Atmosphere: Hostile) / Voodoo Box / Sunscars / Zero Dude / New Liver Please! / Rundown Quarter / Alcoholic Nightmares.
BEAST OF BOURBON, AFM (2004). Under Friendly Fire / Slipping From Reality / Genetic Overkill / Die With A Beer In Your Hand / The Horde / Endless Pleasure / Dead Men Drinking / Alien Revenge / Fistful Of Love / Beyond The Pubyard / We're Coming Back.
THE BEAUTY AND THE BEER, AFM (2006). Ice-Olation / We Still Drink The Old Ways / Forsaken World / Rockstars No. 1 / The Beauty And The Beast / Blue Rage—Black Redemption / Frankfurt: We Need More Beer / Metaltometal / Dirty Digger / Shaken Not Stirred.
Schwarz-Weiss Wie Schnee, AFM (2006).

TANKWART

GERMANY — *Andreas Geremia (vocals), Axel Katzmann (guitar), Andreas Bulgaropulos (guitar), Frank Torwath (bass), Arnulf Tunn (drums).*

The side project arm of the less than serious beer swilling TANKARD crew. TANKWART's debut album 'Aufgetrankt' covered a number of German hits from the notorious 'Neue Deutsche Welle' era of Pop music from the early 80s. Included were 'Liebesspieler' by DIE TOTEN HOSEN, 'Elke' by DIE ÄRTZE, 'Sternenhimmel' by HUBERTKAH, 'Hurra, Hurra Die Schule Bennt' from EXTRABEIT and 'Skandal Im Sperrbezirk' from the SPIDER MURPHY GANG.

The group are also known to take the proverbial out of German singers HEINO, TONY MARSHALL, REX GILDO and ROLAND KAISER.

AUFGETANKT, Noise NZ 003-2 (1994). Libesspieler / Pogo In Togo / Hurra, Hurrra, Die Schule Brennt / Herr D / Sternenhimmel / König Von Deutschland / Elke / Skandal Im Sperrbezirk / Billiger Slogan.
HIMBEERGEIST ZUM FRÜHSTÜCK, Century Media 77145-2 (1996). Schöne Maid / Viva Espana / Tanze Samba Mit Mir / Ein Bißchen Spaß Muß Sein / Paloma Blanca / Am Tag, Als Conny Kramer Starb / Himbeergeist Zum Frühstück / Dschinghis Khan / Sieben Fässer Wein / Mendocino / Fiesta Mexicana / Fahrende Musikanten / Blau Blüht Der Enzian.

TEARABYTE

TX, USA — *Al Mead (vocals / bass), Kevin Mead (guitar), Jeff Owens (Drums).*

Texan Thrash Metal band TEARABYTE was founded by the Mead brothers, vocalist / bassist Al and guitarist Kevin, in the late 90's the band was originally based in Los Angeles. Al Mead was formerly in KNIGHTMARE and was also once part of G.G. Allin's notorious band THE SCUMFUCKS. After releasing the debut EP, 'Doom Generation' on Screaming Ferret Records in 1998, the band relocated to Dallas, Texas in 2000.

A full-length album, 'Embrace Oblivion', followed in 2002 and a third release, 'Gloom Factory', in 2004. The band by this time had worked out a licensing/distribution deal with the new European label Escapi. Over the years the band had shared a stage with a number of international touring acts such as EXHUMED, SACRED REICH and SKINLAB.

The third album, 'Gloom Factory' had a thrashy cover version of PINK FLOYD's 'Comfortably Numb' The album also had a long and quite interesting bonus track, essentially a live medley of their own material interspersed with crude and naturally thrashed-up Christmas carols recorded at various Christmas shows.

Doom Generation, Screaming Ferret (1998). Doom Generation / Straight Out Of Hell / Ghastly Friend / Never Find Trust / Shut Up Bitch / Final Straw.
EMBRACE OBLIVION, Screaming Ferret (2002). Road Rage / Embrace Oblivion / Strike The Enemy / Tear It Up / One More Day / Under The Sand / Lash Of The Gash / Its All A Lie / Price Of Evil / Screaming Pig / Pissing Contest / Spear Of Destiny / Ring Of Fire.
GLOOM FACTORY, Screaming Ferret (2004). The Gloom Factory / Doom Gloom / Technophobic / Shred The Misery / Romper Stomper / Emotional Debris / Suffer / All Grey / Insanity / Empowered Hate / Comfortably Numb.

TENEBRAE

HELSINKI, FINLAND — *Sami Vauhkonen (vocals / guitar), Jussi Heikkinen (guitar), Henrik Laine (bass), Jussi Latvala (drums).*

Helsinki Thrashers TENEBRAE initially featured a rhythm section of bassist Hannu Ojanperä and SHAMAN drummer Juke Eräkangas. The later TENEBRAE credited drummer Jussi Latvala holds associations with ANIMA, SHAMAN, AIGI, VIRAGO and DIFFERENT ARE. Frontman Sami Vaughan (a.k.a. Sami Vauhkonen) has ties to GANDALF, COARSE and LULLACRY. Guitarist Jussi Heikkinen has involvement with TWILIGHT OPHERA, GLOOMY GRIM, SOULGRIND, FIERCE and WALHALLA. Bassist Henrik Laine is a DEEP RED member.

The band's debut demo, 'The Divine Flesh Of Ours', was followed in 1992 with the demo 'Salvation'. The MMI label released the EP 'Sick Spinning Wheel' in 1994. Signing to the Spinefarm label TENEBRAE then recorded their full-length opening album 'Dysanchelium'. TENEBRAE switched to the Belgian Shiver Records label for 1996's 'Hypnotech'.

The Divine Flesh Of Ours, Tenebrae (1992) (Demo). Welcome Death / Behind Thy Christ / Cadaverous Odor / Dormant In Tomb.
Salvation, Tenebrae (1992) (Demo). Dimension Depression / Salvation / Dance For The Decadence / Bloodbath In Paradise.
DYSANCHELIUM, Spinefarm SP117CD (1994). Welcome Death / Dimension Depression / Everlasting Freeze / Scrofolous Intelligence / Waves / Bloodsucking Freak / Dance For The Decadence / Salvation / Human Factory Odor (Part 2).
Sick Spinning Wheel, MMI (1994). Sick Spinning Wheel / Mask Of Ignorance / Unmanned / Inside The Twilight Moonspell / Tarja.
HYPNOTECH, Shiver (1996). Mask Of Ignorance / Wounds / Real Life Massacre / Sick Spinning Wheel / Illusions Of The Black / Inside The Twilight Of The Moonspell / Frequence Of Denial / Hypnotech / Trancequake / Motorsexmanifesto.

TERROR 2000

HELSINGBORG, SWEDEN — *Björn Strid (vocals / bass), Nick Sword (guitar), Klas Ideberg (guitar), Henry Ranta (drums).*

Retro Thrash Metal project TERROR 2000 was convened in Helsingborg by guitarist Nick Sword (a.k.a. Niklas Svärd of NECROPIA and EL MAGO), DARKANE member guitarist Klas Ideberg, also an ex-member of Helsingborg Thrashers HYSTE´RIAH G.B.C., along with SOILWORK personnel frontman Björn Strid and drummer Henry Ranta. The opening 2000 opus 'Slaughterhouse Supremacy' garnered laudatory reviews setting the band up as more substantial than just another side project. In Japan Toys Factory issued the album with an obligatory extra track, TERROR 2000's take on 'The Persuaders' TV series theme music.

Drummer Erik Thyselius, brought onboard for the band's second album, is also a full time member of CONSTRUCDEAD. Japanese variants of the April 2002 album 'Faster Disaster' included the traditional bonus track with a live version of 'Mental Machinery'. May 2003 Japanese dates allied with DESTRUCTION, dubbed the "Thrash Disaster" tour, would spawn the December live album 'Slaughter In Japan-Live 2003'.

Bjorn Strid would lend guest vocals to Italian melodic Death Metal band DISARMONIA MUNDI's 2004 album 'Fragments Of D-Generation'. TERROR 2000 reconvened in a Helsingborg studio during May of 2005 to craft a third album, 'Terror For Sale'. Early 2006 found Björn Strid involving himself in a studio collaboration with bassist Steve DiGiorgio, of SADUS, SEBASTIAN BACH, TESTAMENT and DEATH, Glen Alvelais from FORBIDDEN, TESTAMENT and LD/50 and Jeremy Colson of the STEVE VAI band, MARTY FRIEDMAN, MICHAEL SCHENKER, APARTMENT 26, DALI'S DILEMMA and LD/50 repute.

SLAUGHTERHOUSE SUPREMACY, Scarlet SC 015-2 (2000). Intro—Terror In Time / Son Of Gun, Daughter Of A Slaughter / Agents Of Decadence / Burn Bitch Burn / Slaughterhouse Supremacy / Firebolt / Crypt Of Decay / Terror 2000 / Elimination Complete.
SLAUGHTERHOUSE SUPREMACY, Toy's Factory TKCF-77029 (2001) (Japanese release). Intro—Terror In Time / Son Of Gun, Daughter Of A Slaughter / Agents Of Decadence / Burn Bitch Burn / Slaughterhouse Supremacy / Firebolt / Crypt Of Decay / Terror 2000 / Elimination Complete / The Persuaders Theme.
FASTER DISASTER, Soundholic TKCS-85028 (2002) (Japanese release). Back With Attack / Formula Flame Feast / Headrush / Infernal Outlaw / Burn-Out In Blood / Faster Disaster / Menace Of Brutality / Stalkers In The Night / I'm Speed At Night / Killing Machine / Mental Machinery.
FASTER DISASTER, Scarlet SC 047-2 (2002). Back With Attack / Formula Flame Feast / Headrush / Infernal Outlaw / Burn-Out In Blood / Faster Disaster / Menace Of Brutality / Stalkers In The Night / I'm Speed At Night / Killing Machine.
SLAUGHTER IN JAPAN—LIVE 2003, Scarlet SC 076-2 (2003). Intro / Son Of A Gun, Daughter Of A Slaughter / Faster Disaster / Slaughterhouse Supremacy / Back With Attack / Menace Of Brutality / Firebolt / Burn-Out In Blood / (You're The) Devil In Disguise / Terror 2000.
TERROR FOR SALE, Soundholic TKCS-85126 (2005) (Japanese release). Five Star Prison / Metal Mosh Massacre / Cheap Thrills / King Kong Song / Wrath Of The Cookie Monster / Satans Barbecue / Flesh Fever Fiesta / Liquor Saved Me From Sports / Fed Up Anthem / Mummy Metal For The Masses / Stattena T(h)rash / Bloody Blues Blaster / Dishwashing Demon.
TERROR FOR SALE, Scarlet SC 109-2 (2005). Five Star Prison / Metal Mosh Massacre / Cheap Thrills / King Kong Song / Wrath Of The Cookie Monster / Satans Barbecue / Flesh Fever Fiesta / Liquor Saved Me From Sports / Fed Up Anthem / Mummy Metal For The Masses / Stattena T(h)rash / Bloody Blues Blaster.

TERROR SQUAD

JAPAN — *Udagawa (vocals), Ozeki (guitar), Joker (drums).*

Thrash Metal band created in 1992 by vocalist Udagawo and guitarist Ozeki. TERROR SQUAD debut demo 'The Birth Of The New Rage' followed in 1994 and Joker was added on drums the year after.

A split 7" 'Disco Bloody Disco—Die Hard Metal' was issued in 1997 on Primitive Art Records. TERROR SQUAD also included their track 'Blood Fire Metal' to a Necropolis Records 1999 compilation 'Thrashing Holocaust'. A split 7" single, through Legions Of Death Records and limited to 300 copies, would be shared with SABBAT.

Disco Bloody Disco—Die Hard Metal, Primitive Art (1997) (Split 7" single). Disco Bloody Disco—Die Hard Metal.
THE WILD STREAM OF ETERNAL SIN, World Chaos Productions (1999). Straight To Hell / Disco Bloody Disco / Order Of Lone Wolf / Chain Of The Damned / Nightmare Rider / Blood Fire Metal / Wild Disorder—Eternal Sin.

Terror Squad, Legions Of Death (2001) (Split single with SABBAT. Limited edition 300 copies). Straight To Hell (Japanese version) / Order Of The Lone Wolf (Live).

TESTAMENT

OAKLAND, CA, USA — *Chuck Billy (vocals), Alex Skolnick (guitar), Eric Peterson (guitar), Greg Christian (bass), Louie Clemente (drums).*

Staunch campaigners of the Thrash cause and an act that came tantalisingly close to achieving major success, TESTAMENT was founded as LEGACY in the infamous Bay Area melting pot of Thrash Metal in 1983. As LEGACY, the Oakland-based band comprised high-school-student guitarists Eric Peterson and his cousin Derrick Ramirez, bassist Greg Christian and drummer Louis Clemente. A 1984 four-song demo saw Ramirez handling lead vocals, after which Steve 'Zetro' Souza was recruited as frontman. Recruiting guitarist Alex Skolnick, tutored by none other than JOE SATRIANI, a second demo session arrived in 1985, the track 'Reign Of Terror' gaining exposure from being featured on the Eastern Front Vol. 2 compilation album. These tracks were produced by Doug Piercy, a noted scene guitarist with credentials stretching through CONTROL, COBRA, ANVIL CHORUS and DELTA. However, Souza then bailed out to join another local up-and-coming thrash outfit, EXODUS.

Jonny Zazula's Megaforce label took the band on, this arrangement securing major distribution through Atlantic Records. To avoid legal clashes with another band also titled LEGACY, the band switched names to TESTAMENT, the intended title of their first album. The valuable acquisition of former GUILT and RAMPAGE vocalist Chuck Billy was drafted in as new recruits for the Alex Perialas-produced debut 'The Legacy'. Chuck Billy would go on to become the central lynchpin and focal point of the band. Such was the undisputed quality of 'The Legacy', recorded at Pyramid Sound Studio, Ithaca in New York, that many predicted TESTAMENT were to join Thrash's front runners METALLICA, MEGADETH, SLAYER and ANTHRAX. The group capitalised on the favourable press and fan reaction by touring across the USA and Europe as direct support to ANTHRAX.

Megaforce maintained the momentum by combining a studio outtake, 'Reign Of Terror', with live tracks culled from the band's showing at the famed 'Dynamo' festival in Holland as the December 1987 European release 'Live In Eindhoven', oddly not released in the band's homeland until 1990. The studio follow up, May 1988's 'The New Order' maintained, and indeed boosted, the quality levels. Cut at Pyramid Sound and produced once again by Perialas, engineering credits went to RAVEN drummer Rob 'Wacko' Hunter. Bravely the record, which landed the band in at no. 136 on the Billboard album charts, included a take on AEROSMITH's 'Nobody's Fault' amongst the expected riffage.

The band's fortunes rose with 1989's 'Practice What You Preach'. Employing Perialas yet again, this album, which cracked the Billboard top 100, saw TESTAMENT shifting their lyrical focus onto more reality based concerns such as politics and the environment. During 1990 TESTAMENT, promoting the 'Souls Of Black' album, their first to break tradition with Perialas and pulling in Michael Rosen for desk duties, found themselves grabbing the opening spot on the mammoth 'Clash Of The Titans' European touring package with MEGADETH, ANTHRAX and SLAYER. Despite this increased global exposure TESTAMENT appeared to have plateaued on a commercial footing, the album only gaining slightly in sales on its predecessor.

Following 1992's Tony Platt produced 'The Ritual' album, which gave TESTAMENT their highest US chart position to date, Skolnick opted out to join SAVATAGE. By 1995 he had received a better offer to join OZZY OSBOURNE. However, the guitarist

TESTAMENT (pic: Walter Morgan)

only lasted for one gig, a secret bash at Nottingham's Rock City. Skolnick followed his passion and founded the Jazz-Rock styled ATTENTION DEFICIT with PRIMUS drummer Tim Alexander for a 1998 album.

TESTAMENT meanwhile failed to maintain a stable line up for 1993's 'Return To Apocalyptic City', a six track stop gap mini album. New man on the drum stool was the highly respected ex-FORBIDDEN and SLAYER drummer Paul Bostaph whilst also coming onboard would be ex-FORBIDDEN guitarist Glen Alvelais.

1994's 'Low' featured Death metal journeyman guitarist JAMES MURPHY whose credits include AGENT STEEL, DEATH, OBITUARY, DISINCARNATE and CANCER and EXODUS drummer John Tempesta. The album, recorded at A&M studios in Los Angeles, was issued in the full gale force of a Rock revolution and TESTAMENT, in spite of cannily employing noted Alt-Rock producer Garth Richardson in union with the mixing skills of Metal veteran Michael Wagener, duly struggled to get noticed. Although fans and critics were unanimous in their praise for 'Low' and its return to form the record was swamped by Grunge. Shortly after recording Tempesta teamed up with WHITE ZOMBIE and Atlantic Records, a staunch ally since the debut, let the band go.

The line-up for the 'Live At The Fillmore' album, recorded at a sell out show at the notorious Haight-Ashbury venue, comprised of Chuck Billy, guitarists Eric Peterson and James Murphy, bassist Greg Christian and former EVIL DEAD drummer John Dette. Down to a duo of Billy and Peterson TESTAMENT actually folded for a short period as the original pairing announced a new band DOG FACED GOD. These sessions would ultimately emerge as the new TESTAMENT album. 1997's Doug Hall produced and exceptionally dark 'Demonic' offering, the band's first for new label Spitfire Records, saw Billy, Alvelais and Peterson fronting a quintet completed by Ramirez on bass and ex-DEATH drummer Gene Hoglan. Prior to recording Dette had vacated his position making a high profile career move to SLAYER. Bass was now in the hands of erstwhile DEATH and SADUS man Steve DiGiorgio. Sadly, 'Demonic's profile suffered heavily when their distribution company went into bankruptcy. Fortunately, 1997 also found the newly formed Mayhem Records issuing a compilation album, 'Signs Of Chaos: The Best Of Testament', of the group's finest moments.

Another quick change ensued on the drum stool after 'Demonic's release as Hoglan took up an offer to fulfill live work with STRAPPING YOUNG LAD, leaving a gap for the reinstatement of Dette whose brief tenure in SLAYER had lasted a matter of weeks. Chuck Billy meantime put in an appearance on Murphy's 1999 solo album 'Feeding The Machine'.

The band meanwhile underwent a dramatic line up change with guitarist Glen Alvelais being given his marching orders again. Filling the absent spot was guitarist James Murphy once more and former SLAYER drummer DAVE LOMBARDO on the drum stool for 1999's 'The Gathering'. As it transpired though Dette regained his position although this was predictably brief.

Late 1999 found further ructions within the band as Murphy and Dette were ousted in favour of Steve Jacobs and VICIOUS RUMOURS guitarist Steve Smyth. Murphy's removal signalled the beginnings of a run of health generated bad luck for the band. Apparently the guitarist had been acting out of character for some time prompting his dismissal. Only later, after extensive surgery to remove a brain tumour, was the cause of Murphy's behavioural problems revealed.

Smyth, DiGiorgio and Peterson have a Black Thrash side project named DRAGONHEART with SADUS drummer Jon Allen. DiGiorgio later joined ICED EARTH. This band later switched titles to DRAGONLORD. Smyth also doubles duties appearing as 'Randy Zakk Iommi' in the BLACK SABBATH tribute band SWEET LEAF in union with SKITZO frontman Lance Ozanix. Smyth would also contribute guitar to the SKITZO 2000 album 'Got Sick'. By 2000 Alvelais was fronting LD/50, a band including bassist Oddie McLaughlin, drummer Jeremy Colson and ex-GEEZER vocalist Clark Brown.

On the TESTAMENT front news emerged in early 2001 that Chuck Billy had been diagnosed with cancer. The singer got stuck straight into a regime of treatment to defeat the disease and was aided in spirit by the announcement of a benefit concert in his name dubbed 'Thrash Of The Titans'. The highly anticipated concert, held August 11th at the San Francisco Maritime Hall, pulled together many of the most notorious Thrash names such as HEATHEN, FLOTSAM & JETSAM, STORMTROOPERS OF DEATH, ANTHRAX, FORBIDDEN EVIL reformations of EXODUS, VIO-LENCE and DEATH ANGEL and even a reformation of LEGACY. A retrospective studio album of TESTAMENT classics was also began in earnest, 'First Strike Still Deadly', with former vocalist Steve Souza committed to guest on tracks.

Derrick Ramirez would be the latest TESTAMENT member to join DRAGONLORD in March of 2002. Guitarist Glen Alvelais, besides his activities with BIZARRO and LD/50, also involved himself with F-BOMB, a union with EXODUS frontman Steve 'Zetro' Souza, guitarist Jason Brown, bassist Kevin Moore and LD/50 drummer Jeremy Colson. Meantime, other ex-TESTAMENT members drummer John Dette and bassist Greg Christian debuted their new band PUSHED in July.

Yet another band endeavour with strong TESTAMENT connections was unveiled during the summer of 2002 with the SADUS pairing of frontman Darren Travis and bassist Steve DiGiorgio embarking on an all star union billed as SUICIDE SHIFT. The project included TESTAMENT vocalist Chuck Billy as well as drummer Per Moller Jensen of THE HAUNTED with guest guitar from the much travelled ex-TESTAMENT man JAMES MURPHY. Meantime ex drummer Chris Kontos would be busy preparing an album for his new act THE SERVANTS.

TESTAMENT put in a one off show in Las Vegas supporting HALFORD and a short burst of December 2002 dates packaged with support acts EXODUS and VIO-LENCE. ROB ZOMBIE drummer Johnny Tempesta would be tapped by TESTAMENT to fill in for the group's West Coast tour after regular drummer Jon Allen was forced to bow due to a family emergency. SPIRAL ARCHITECT and BORKNAGER drummer Asgeir Mickelson stepped in as a temporary stand in for Allen.

April of 2003 found TESTAMENT on the road in Europe as part of the roving 'No Mercy' festivals. Returning to the USA the group partnered with HALFORD and IMMORTAL for the ill fated 'Metal Gods' tour, this trek unfortunately collapsing within a few dates. DiGeorgio then took time out to lay down bass on PAINMUSEUM's 'Metal Forever' album before TESTAMENT engaged his services once again for European festival gigs including 'the 'Wacken Open Air' and 'Earthshaker' events in Germany.

TESTAMENT

Steve Smyth temporarily joined the ranks of Seattle's NEVERMORE for their European and US gig schedule from September of 2003 onwards. The band spend the latter months of the year and into the new year recording a new studio album. Summer 2004 dates had TESTAMENT touring across Europe including appearances at the Budapest 'Summer Rocks' festival and Dutch 'Waldrock' event. During early 2004 both Chuck Billy and Eric Peterson donated their services to a tribute album 'Within The Mind' assembled by guitarist JAMES MURPHY in honour of the late DEATH mentor Chuck Schuldiner.

Former WHIPLASH, SLAYER and SYSTEMATIC drummer Paul Bostaph joined TESTAMENT in February 2004, his second tenure with the band having previously played several live dates with the group in 1992 and appeared on the band's 1993 live outing 'Return To The Apocalyptic City'. Guitarist Steve Smyth left the band on April 1st 2004, duly joining NEVERMORE on a full time basis, confirming this appointment with an appearance in the promotional video for the track 'I, Voyager' that same month.

The rumour mill soon had former HALFORD and current PAINMUSEUM guitarist 'Metal' Mike Chlasciak as the leading candidate to fill the vacancy, this conjecture soon confirmed. Throughout June TESTAMENT hit the continental festival circuit, putting in appearances at the 'Gods Of Metal' in Italy, 'Sweden Rock', 'Summer Rock' in Budapest, Hungary, 'Provinssirock' in Finland, 'Fury Fest' in France, 'Bang Your Head' in Germany and 'Graspop' in Belgium.

These European dates were struck by bad luck though when guitarist Eric Peterson fractured his leg falling down a flight of stairs at the Kozel Pub Club venue in Martin, Slovakia. Hospitalised in Vienna, Peterson learned he had sustained three separate breaks, putting him out of contention for the tour. Chlasciak covered until former guitarist Steve Smyth flew in to complete the dates.

Meantime, the erstwhile TESTAMENT rhythm section of bass player Greg Christian and drummer John Dette were back in the news, enrolling into the ranks of New York's HAVOCHATE.

The band was set to ally themselves with DEATH ANGEL, FLOTSAM AND JETSAM and OVERKILL for a 'Thrash Domination 04' Japanese tour in September. However, the group pulled out due to Peterson's injury. Chuck Billy briefly fronted EXODUS for their October San Francisco Warfield Theatre date, standing in for frontman Steev Esquivel, whose eyes had been contaminated with "unknown chemicals" the previous gig.

Chuck Billy, and founding guitarist Eric Peterson announced that original guitar player Alex Skolnick, original bassist Greg Christian and drummer John Tempesta would reunite for a brief burst of European gigs in May 2005. In this formation, TESTAMENT scheduled an appearance at the 'Dynamo Open Air' festival on 7th May 2005 in Hellendoorn, the Netherlands, by coincidence sharing the stage with reformed 80s era line-ups

TESTAMENT

for both ANTHRAX and LÄÄZ ROCKIT. Further European dates saw Austrian Thrash act DEMOLITION as direct support.

The band's profile on the North American gig circuit rose considerably throughout the year, commencing with a 2nd July support to JUDAS PRIEST at the Mountain View Shoreline Amphitheatre. On 9th July TESTAMENT lined up at The Pound outdoor amphitheatre in San Francisco alongside VICIOUS RUMORS, LÄÄZ RÖCKIT, HIRAX, AGENT STEEL, DEKAPITATOR, MUDFACE, NEIL TURBIN, BROCAS HELM, DREAMS OF DAMNATION and IMAGIKA for the 'Thrash Against Cancer' benefit. US shows in August witnessed a road partnership with NUCLEAR ASSAULT prior to Japanese gigs in September. South American festival dates in October, appearing in Mexico, Brazil and Chile, saw an unavailable Alex Skolnick being substituted by a returning "Metal" Mike Chlasciak.

Gigs in March 2006 saw Jon Allen of SADUS and DRAGONLORD manning the drums. Louie Clemente was forced out of July shows too, citing "medical reasons", necessitating the recruitment of EXODUS, SLAYER, FORBIDDEN and SYSTEMATIC adept Paul Bostaph.

In mid 2006 the world of Thrash Metal received a pleasant surprise with the announcement of a new San Francisco based collective project billed DUBLIN DEATH PATROL. (Dublin is a San Francisco suburb). This unit was assembled by a seasoned cast of veterans comprising Chuck Billy, former EXODUS and LEGACY vocalist Steve "Zetro" Souza, MACHINE HEAD, DEATH PENALTY, METAL WARRIOR and VIO-LENCE man Phil Demmel on guitar, bassist Willy Langenhuizen, of RAMPAGE and LÄÄZ ROCKIT repute, guitarist Andy Billy of SACRED DOG, RAMPAGE and GUILT, RAMPAGE guitarist Greg Bustamante, OUT OF CONTROL guitarist Steve Robello, bassist John Souza and drummer Danny Cunningham.

TESTAMENT announced the addition of new Nick Barker in January 2007, formerly of DIMMU BORGIR and CRADLE OF FILTH. Live dates witnessed dates in Hungary and Poland in March followed by a campaign across North America including an appearance at the 'California Metal Fest'. The group then hit Mexico, Puerto Rico, Brazil and Argentina in April upfront of album recordings in June. European summer festival dates included July shows at 'Bloodstock' in Derby, UK, the 'Evolution Fest', in Brescia, Italy and August dates at the 'Jalo Metalli Fest' in Oulu, Finland, the 'Metal Heart Fest' in Notodden, Norway and 'Up From The Ground Fest' in Gemunden, Germany.

Sign Of Chaos, EastWest SAM1011 (0) (12" vinyl promo). Sign Of Chaos / Electric Crown.
Greenhouse Effect, Kerrang BANG2 (0) (7" promo flexi disc single sold with Kerrang! magazine issue #279). Greenhouse Effect / Acid Reign.
The First Strike Is Deadly, Testament (1985) (Demo). Burnt Offerings / Reign Of Terror / Alone In The Dark / Raging Waters.
THE LEGACY, Megaforce Atlantic 81741-1 (1987). Over The Wall / The Haunting / Burnt Offerings / Raging Waters / Curse Of The Legions Of Death / First Strike Is Deadly / Do Or Die / Alone In The Dark / Apocalyptic City.
LIVE AT EINDHOVEN, Testament 780 226-1 (1987). Over The Wall / Burnt Offerings / Do Or Die / Apocalyptic City / Reign Of Terror.
Trial By Fire, Atlantic A 9092 T (1988). Trial By Fire / Nobody's Fault / Reign Of Terror.
THE NEW ORDER, Megaforce Atlantic 781 849-2 (1988). Eerie Inhabitants / The New Order / Trial By Fire / Into The Pit / Hypnosis / Disciples Of The Watch / Preacher / Day Of Reckoning / Musical Death (A Dirge). Chart positions: 49 SWEDEN, 81 UK, 136 USA.
Greenhouse Effect, Megaforce PRCD 3286-2 (1989) (Promotional CD). Greenhouse Effect (Live) / The Ballad (Edit).
PRACTICE WHAT YOU PREACH, Megaforce Atlantic WX 297CD (1989). Practice What You Preach / Perilous Nation / Envy Time / Time Is Coming / Blessed In Contempt / Greenhouse Effect / Sins Of Omission / Ballad (A Song Of Hope) / Nightmare (Coming Back To You) / Confusion Fusion. Chart positions: 40 UK, 77 USA.
SOULS OF BLACK, Megaforce Atlantic 7567821432 (1990). Beginning Of The End / Face In The Sky / Falling Fast / Souls Of Black / Absence Of Light / Love To Hate / Malpractice / One Man's Fate / Legacy / Seven Days In May. Chart positions: 35 UK, 73 USA.
THE RITUAL, East West 756782392-2 (1992). Signs Of Chaos / Electric Crown / So Many Lies / Let Go Of My World / The Ritual / Deadline / As The Seasons Grey / Agony / The Sermon / Return To Serenity / Troubled Dreams. Chart positions: 48 UK, 55 USA, 73 GERMANY.
RETURN TO APOCALYPTIC CITY, WEA 756782392-2 (1993). Over The Wall (Live) / So Many Liesn (Live) / The Haunting (Live) / Disciples Of The Watch (Live) / Reign Of Terror / Return To Serenity.
LOW, East West 7567 82645-2 (1994). Low / Legions (In Hiding) / Hail Mary / Trail Of Tears / Shades Of War / PC / Dog Faced Gods / All I Could Bleed / Urotsukidoji / Chasing Fear / Ride / Last Call. Chart position: 122 USA.
LIVE AT THE FILLMORE, Music For Nations CDMFN 186 (1995). The Preacher / Alone In The Dark / Burnt Offerings / Musical Death (A Dirge) / Errie Inhabitants / The New Order / Low / Urgesukidoji / Into The Pit / Souls Of Black / Practice What You Preach / Apocalyptic City / Hail Mary / Dog Faced Gods / Return To Serenity / The Legacy / Trail Of Tears.
DEMONIC, Music For Nations CDMFN 221 (1997). Demonic Refusal / The Burning Times / Together As One / Jun-Jun / John Doe / Murky Waters / Hatreds Rise / Distorted Lives / New Eyes Of Old / Ten Thousand Thrones / Nostrovia.
THE GATHERING, USG 1033-2 (1999). DNR (Do Not Resuscitate) / Down For Life / Eyes Of Wrath / True Believers / 3 Days In Darkness / LOTD / Careful What You wish For / Riding The Snake / Allegiance / Sewn Shut Eyes / Fall Of Siple Dome. Chart position: 48 GERMANY.
FIRST STRIKE STILL DEADLY, Spitfire 5083-2 (2001). First Strike Is Deadly / The Haunting / Disciples Of The Watch / Over The Wall / The New Order / Burnt Offerings / Alone In The Dark / The Preacher / Lane Of Terror / Into The Pit.
FIRST STRIKE STILL DEADLY, Universal Japan (2002) (Japanese release). First Strike Is Deadly / Into The Pit / Trial By Fire / Disciples Of The Watch / The Preacher / Burnt Offerings / Over The Wall / The New Order / The Haunting / Alone In The Dark / Reign Of Terror.
LIVE IN LONDON, Spitfire (2005). The Preacher / The New Order / The Haunting / Electric Crown / Sins Of Omission / Souls Of Black / Into The Pit / Trial By Fire / Practice What You Preach / Let Go Of My World / The Legacy / Over The Wall / Raging Waters / Disciples Of The Watch.

THANATOS

ROTTERDAM, HOLLAND — *Stephen Gebédí (vocals / guitar), Paul Baayens (guitar), Marco de Bruin (bass), Yuri Rinkel (drums).*

Rotterdam Thrash band THANATOS tend to stand out from the crowd with some inventive songs. THANATOS actually lay claim to being Holland's first Death Metal act having formed in 1984 with a line up of Stephen Gebédí, guitarist Remco De Maaijer and drummer Marcel Van Arnhem. This version of the band released the 'Speed Kills' demo prior to folding in 1985.

Gebédí reformed THANATOS for another demo session entitled 'Rebirth'. Van Arnhem returned along with new bass player André Scherpenberg. Rob De Bruijn would take over the drum stool but departed soon after. Another new recruit in 1987 was former SECOND HELL guitarist Mark Staffhorst.

Scherpenberg quit to join VIGILANT necessitating KILLER FORCE guitarist Erwin De Brouwer to handle bass guitar. However, soon De Brouwer would shift to guitar as Ed Boeser of KILLING ELEVATOR maneuvered into the bassist's job.

The group issued a 1987 demo entitled 'The Day Before Tomorrow', notable for featuring the live track 'Progressive Destructor' and followed this with a 1989 tape 'Omnicoitor'. Following their album for Shark Records, 'Emerging From The Netherworlds' produced by Ulli Pössel, they released another demo in 1991 featuring five tracks before Shark came up with a second record, the Pösselt produced 'Realms Of Ecstasy', in 1992. Despite having two albums in the stores THANATOS were far from happy with their label and were vocal in their vehemence. Naturally the two parties went their separate ways.

THANATOS split with Gebédê and De Brouwer created CHURCH OF INDULGENCE in allegiance with bassist Peter Van Wees and drummer Dirk Bruinenberg. This band ground to a halt as De Brouwer united with ex-THANATOS man Ed Boeser in the alternative Rock act SMALLTOWN and Van Wees joined INCOMING. Bruinenberg would ally himself with the high profile act ELEGY.

THANATOS returned in 1999 with ex-CREMATION guitarist Paul Baayens, SINISTER and HOUWITSER drummer Aad Kloosterwaard along with HOUWITSER and JUDGEMENT DAY bassist Theo Van Eekelen in the ranks for the 'Angelic Encounters' album, recorded at Excess Studios, Rotterdam. A limited edition digipack included the bonus track 'Corpse Grinder'. That same year the Hammerheart label re-issued both 'Emerging From The Netherworlds' and 'Realms Of Ecstasy' complete with extra tracks.

A 2002 mini album 'Beyond Terror' included a cover of CELTIC FROST's 'Into The Crypt Of Rays'. For these recordings the rhythm section was now occupied by bassist Marco de Bruin and drummer Yuri Rinkel, the latter also known as 'Y. Xul' of Black Metal outfits FUNERAL WINDS, LIAR OF GOLGOTHA and INFERI. Rinkel also operates ABODE OF THE BLESSED. 'Beyond Terror' comprised two sets of recordings with tracks laid down at Dynamo Studio in Rotterdam during January of 2002 plus a ten hour session at Capture Sound Studios in June.

THANATOS signed to the Greek Black Lotus Records in mid 2003 for recording of the album 'Undead.Unholy.Divine.'. This outing, recorded at Excess studios in Rotterdam and co-produced by the band and Hans Pieters, would be mixed by world renowned Metal producer Attie Bauw and featured former GOREFEST man Ed Warby and MELECHESH's Ashmedi on backing vocals.

During May of 2004, Yinkel deputised with Mesopotamian Black Metal band MELECHESH for live dates. THANATOS announced they were to record two new tracks at Excess Studios in Rotterdam in late June 2005, a brand new version of 'And Jesus Wept', from 1992's 'Realm Of Ecstasy' and a cover of DARK ANGEL's 'The Burning Of Sodom'. It would also be reported that frontman Stephan Gebédi was "facing a serious affection of the nerves in his wrist and his neck", delaying album recordings.

THANATOS finally entered Excess Studios in Rotterdam on 23rd February 2006 to begin recording their fifth full-length album, giving a tentative title of 'Justified Genocide'. Unfortunately mid way through these sessions the band's label, Black Lotus Records, ceased operations. In January 2007 it would be learned that THANATOS guitarists Stephan Gebédi and Paul Baayens had joined forces with former PESTILENCE and ASPHYX singer Martin Van Drunen, GOREFEST drummer Ed Warby and former HOUWITSER bass player Theo van Eekelen in a new band unit dubbed HAIL OF BULLETS.

EMERGING FROM THE NETHERWORLDS, Shark 015 (1990). Dawn Of The Dead / Outward Of The Inward / Bodily Dismemberment / Infernal Deceit / The Day Before Tomorrow / War / Rebirth / Progressive Destructor / Imposters Infiltration / Omnicoitor / Dolor Satanae.

REALMS OF ECSTASY, Shark 025 (1992). Intro—And Jesus Wept / Tied Up Sliced Up / Realm Of Ecstasy / Mankind's Afterbirth / In Praise Of Lust / Perpetual Misery / Human Combustion / Reincarnation / Terminal Breath.

ANGELIC ENCOUNTERS, Hammerheart 7202000152 (2000). Angelic Encounters / In Utter Darkness / Sincere Chainsaw Salvation / Infuriated / The Howling / Gods Of War / The Devil's Concubine / Speed Kills / Thou Shalt Rot / Corpsegrinder.

BEYOND TERROR, Baphomet BAPH112 (2002). Beyond Terror / Devour The Living / Rites Of Retaliation / Angelic Encounters / Satan's Curse / Into The Crypt Of Rays.

UNDEAD.UNHOLY.DIVINE., Black Lotus BLRCD063 (2004). Lambs To The Slaughter / Undead.Unholy.Divine. / Eraser / Beyond Terror / The Sign Of Sadako / Servants Of Hatred / Devour The Living / Godforsaken / The Suffering / The Sweet Suffering.

The Burning Of Sodom, Konqueror KR 008 EP (2006). The Burning Of Sodom / And Jesus Wept.

THE ACCURSED

NEW BEDFORD, MA, USA — *Jonathan Helme (vocals), Loki (guitar), Timothy Giblin (guitar), George Pacheco (bass), Chris Helme (drums).*

New Bedford, Massachusetts based THE ACCURSED credit themselves as vocalist Jonathan Helme "Throat & Arson", guitarists Loki "Six string slaughter" and Timothy Giblin "Axes and razorblades", bassist George Pacheco "Bassassination" and drummer Chris Helme "Battery". The 2002 'Straight From Hell' demo, recorded in The Syrofoam Room by BEYOND THE EMBRACE's Oscar Gouviea and which included a cover of DEATH's 'The Philosopher', featured guitar work from Chris Fitzgerald.

THE ACCURSED signed to Screaming Ferret Records for a full-length album 'Seasons Of The Scythe'. Promotional copies of the album added four cover versions in HELLOWEEN's 'I Want Out', IRON MAIDEN's 'Wasted Years', METALLICA's 'Jump In The Fire' and CARCASS' 'Heartwork'.

Guitarist Chris Ellingsen returned to the fold in April 2006. 'Seasons Of The Scythe' arrived on Halloween 2006.

Straight To Hell, The Accursed (2002). To Live On Borrowed Time / The Black Thrash / Aftermath Of Sorrow / World's Divide / Autumn's Twilight / The Philosopher / Maniacal Menace (Straight To Hell) / The Final Farewell.

SEASONS OF THE SCYTHE, Screaming Ferret (2006). Deities And Demigods / Sawtoothsmile / Seasons Of The Scythe / Fire Of 1000 Cries / I Am Famine / Aftermath Of Sorrow / The Rider / Land Of The Dead / Slaughter Of The Gods / Cold Is The Grave / Funeral March / The Black Thrash / Armageddon Eulogy.

THE ACCUSED

SEATTLE, WA, USA — *Blaine Cook (vocals), Tommy Niemeyer (guitar), Alex Maggot Brain (bass), Dana Collins (drums).*

Seattle "Splatter-Core" Thrash-Hardcore sons THE ACCUSED date back to their inception in 1981 with an initial line-up of vocalist John, guitarist Tom 'Accused' Niemeyer, bassist Chewy and drummer Dana Collins. First product was a 1981 split album with THE REJECTORS on Fatal Rejection Records. John departed in 1984 to be replaced by erstwhile FARTZ man Blaine 'Fart' Cook, the band issuing their first album the same year. The 'Martha Splatterhead' album, released on Condor Records, only saw a limited run of 500 copies.

During a 1986 American tour bassist Chewy was asked to leave and was duly replaced by Alex 'Maggot Brain' Sibbald, a scene veteran of Punk acts MAGGOT BRAINS, ITCHY BROTHER and CHEATING DEATH. The band toured North America with British Punk act G.B.H in 1987. The 1988 album, 'Martha Splatterhead's Maddest Stories Ever Told', notably boasted a guest appearance from METAL CHURCH guitarist Kurdt Vanderhoof. 1990's 'Hymns For The Deranged' album, with new drummer Josh, features live renditions of DEEP PURPLE's 'Highway Star', THIN LIZZY's 'Cold Sweat' and BLACK SABBATH's 'Symptom Of The Universe'.

THE ACCUSED would delve into cover version territory once more with the 1991 Jack Endino produced 'Straight Razor' album offering a take on LYNYRD SKYNYRD's 'Saturday Night Special'.

Post THE ACCUSSED the individual band members made their presence felt on the burgeoning Seattle Grunge scene. Sibbald and Niemeyer created GRUNTRUCK before the drummer founded RED HOT LUNATIC. Niemeyer would journey through HELLCAT, LYE and MONA DIESEL.

THE ACCUSED made a return to action in 2003, putting in a reunion gig at Seattle's Studio 7 venue on the 8th November, supported by RIVERRED and DEK. Working with producer Jack Endino the band entered the recording studio in 2004 for a new record dubbed 'Oh Martha!' for release through their own label Condor Records. Scott Hull of PIG DESTROYER mastered the disc. Nationwide touring throughout February of 2005 saw the band packaged with HIMSA, 3 INCHES OF BLOOD and COUNTDOWN TO LIFE.

In early 2006 the band revealed it had licensed 'Oh Martha!' to Nuclear Blast Records for Europe. Band line-up at this juncture comprised Tommy Niemeyer, the BURNING WITCH, AVSA, 90 PROOF, MOMMY, SWEATY NIPPLES and APES OF WRATH credited Brad Mowen on vocals, bassist Prof. Iman A. Phid, formerly known as "Father Shark" of THE PLEASURE ELITE, with BAM BAM, MOMMY and APES OF WRATH man Mike Peterson on drums.

THE ACCUSED announced February 2007 European tour dates partnered with CRUMBSUCKERS, EXTREME NOISE TERROR and DRILLER KILLER. However, these shows never eventuated. Another round of European dates was lined up in May together with DAYGLO ABORTIONS and GOLERS.

PLEASE PARDON OUR NOISE—IT IS A SOUND OF FREEDOM, Condor (1981).

MARTHA SPLATTERHEAD, Condor (1984).

RETURN OF MARTHA SPLATTERHEAD, Subcore 8197-1 (1985). Martha Splatterhead / Wrong Side Of The Grave / Take My Time / Distractions / Buried Alive / No Mercy / Slow Death / Autopsy / She's The Killer / In A Death Bed / Lonely Place / Fuckin' 4 Bucks / Martha's Revenge.

MORE FUN THAN AN OPEN CASKET FUNERAL, Rough Justice JUST 11 (1987). Halo Of Flies / WCALT / Rape / Lifeless Zone / Scotty / Devil Woman / Bethany Home / Mechanized Death / Take No Prisoners / Splatter Rock / Septi-Child / I'll Be Glad When You're Dead, You Rascal You.

MARTHA SPLATTERHEAD'S MADDEST STORIES EVER TOLD, Combat Core (1988). Psychomania / The Bag Lady Song / Inherit The Earth (The Day Of Wreckoning) / Deception (The Impostors) / Molly's Xmas '72 / I'd Love To Change The World / You Only Die Once / Sick Boy / Chicago / Starved To Death (Eat Yer Buddies) / War + Death '88 (And Beyond) / The Maddest Story Ever Told / Intro (From The Tingler) / Scared Of The Dark / Losing Your Mind / Smothered Her Trust / Lights Out / The Hearse (Traditional Nursery Rhyme).

HYMNS FOR THE DERANGED, Musical Tragedies LP15747 (1990). Grinning / Brutality And Corruption / Tapping The Vein / Barracuda / Our Way / Cold Sweat / Highway Star / Symptom Of The Universe.

GRINNING LIKE AN UNDERTAKER, Nasty Mix NMR 702201 (1990). Nails (Into The Lid Of Your Coffin) / Bullet Ridden Bodies / The Corpse Walks / Grinning (Like An Undertaker) / Down And Out (Featuring The Mad Poet) / Cut And Dried / Dropping Like Flies / M Is For Martha / Room 144 / When I Was A Child / The Night / Voices / Boris The Spider / Tapping The Vein.

STRAIGHT RAZOR, Nasty Mix (1991). No Hope For Relief / Close Insight / The Corpse Walks / Straight Razor / Down And Out / Saturday Night Special / Blind Hate-Blind Rage / Voices.

SPLATTER ROCK, Nasty Mix (1992). Two Hours Till Sunrise / Stick In A Hole / No Choice / Lettin' Go / Blind Hate-Blind Rage / Greenwood House Of Medicine-Don't You Have A Woman / She's Back / Tearin' Me Apart / Green Eyed Lady / Brutality And Corruption / Living, Dying, Living-In A Zombie World.

OH MARTHA!, Nuclear Blast NB 1661-2 (2006). Martha Will / Fueled By Hate / Crapassreality / Fast Zombies Rule / Dying On The Vine / Hooker Fortified Pork Products / Life Kills On / NES / Filth Hounds Of Hades / Stay Dead / Scream And Die / Of The Body / Letters / Have You Never Been Mellow?

THE BLAMED

CHICAGO, IL, USA — *Matt Switaj (vocals / guitar), Bryan Gray (guitar), Christopher Wiitala (bass), Trevor Wiitala (drums).*

THE BLAMED are amongst the leading crop of Christian Hardcore Thrash acts. THE BLAMED, at their inception rooted in California and fronted by vocalist Jeremy Moffit, bowed in with the 1994 '21' album, so titled because it took a mere 21 hours to record. Following the 1995 heavily Thrash orientated 'Frail' album THE BLAMED folded.

Guitarist Bryan Grey would go onto join SIX FEET DEEP and LEFT OUT but, utilising members of LEFT OUT, would resurrect THE BLAMED for the 1998 'Again' album on Grrr Records, a label division of the Chicago based 'Jesus People' organisation. The band at this juncture involved Gray, bass player Jeff Locke, CRUCIFIED / MORTAL drummer Jim Chaffin and Jeff Hansen.

1999's 'Forever' outing found THE BLAMED comprising of Gray, Locke, Chaffin and vocalist / guitarist Matt Switaj. The record was noted for it's double tribal drumming between Chaffin and a guesting Lance Garvin of LIVING SACRIFICE. 'Forever' would also close out with the Celtic flavoured '4/20/99' with guest female vocals courtesy of THE CROSSING's Hilde Bialach.

Yet another switch in personnel occurred for the 2001 record 'Isolated Incident. Gray retained Switaj but enrolled the twins bassist Christopher and drummer Trevor Wiitala as a new rhythm section. Matt Switaj decamped in February of 2002.

THE BLAMED have contributed a version of 'Soldiers Under Command' to a STRYPER tribute album.

21, Tooth & Nail (1994). Abuse / Help Yourself / Testimony / Drunk, Separation / A State Of . . . / From Me To You / Rainbow / 3 a.m. / God Is Alive / Walkabout / The Ballad Of The Blamed.

FRAIL, Tooth & Nail (1996). Feeding The Ignorant / Weakness / For You / No Difference / Just Because / Breeze / Prove Your Excuse / Second Minded Friend / Torn / Guy In A Suit And The Pope / Declaration Dead.

AGAIN, Grrr (1998). Beginning / In The End / Casualty Of War / Rage / God Have Mercy / Don't Fall / Covered / Deny / Outer Crust / Crying Tree / The Pride / Experience / Live By Truth / D Sin Grate.

FOREVER, Grrr (1999). Dissonance / To Change / Pistol Whipped / Reason Escapes / Satori / Degeneration / Conversations In The Mirror / Forever / Knock Me Down / New Seeds Of Contemplation / Seven Story Mountain / Beyond / Your Passion In His Passion / 4-20-99.

GERMANY, Grrr (2000). Wounded—Overwhelmed / Discussed / Running Away Can Be An Ugly Thin / Darkness Is So Unforgiving / Last Time I Do This For The First Time / This Is It / At Last We Will Have Revenge.

This Is For David, Burnt Toast Vinyl (2000). This Is For David / On Westnedge . . . In Amsterdam.

At This Moment EP, Computer Club Records CCRP1001 (2001). For Brian Wilson / At This Moment / Our Bazaar World / That's The Ticket.

ISOLATED INCIDENT, Grrr (2001). At This Moment / Social Calls / To See You How You Are Seen / Short Of A Miracle / At Least We Have Each Other / N.X.N.W. / Our Bazaar World / For Fifteen Bucks (And A Spot On The Floor) / The Piano Is Playing Our Song / The Bat Storm / The Finest Of Society's Philanderers / Talking Philosophy On The Streets Of Oslo / Ch-Ch-What's Missing Is You Are.

THE BRAINWASH

ROME, ITALY — *Fabio Varrone (vocals / guitar), Simone Cesaroni (guitar), Fabio Insania (bass), Daniele Balzano (drums).*

Rome based Thrash band THE BRAINWASH was forged during 1999 by vocalist / guitarist Fabio 'Anarchybrain' Varrone, previously with D.E.F.I.R. and THE STONE THROWING DEVILS. In April of 2002 the group launched the 'Braincrasher' album through Nelly Records. For these sessions Varrone employed bassist Roberto Viola and Mirko Cangani on the drums. Follow ups would be 'Carnage' in 2004 and 'Skizophobia' the following year. Both these album would be recorded by Varrone, bassist Enrico Fasani and drummer William Paciotta. Subsequently

THE BRAINWASH evolved to incorporate guitar player Simone Cesaroni, bassist Fabio Insania with Sirio Biondi on the drums.

In September 2006 Daniele Balzano took over as session drummer.

BRAINCRASHER, (2002). Die In My Car / Free Of All / Buried Of Lord / Crystal Girl / The Brainwash / I'm A Killer / In The Night / I Want To Die.

CARNAGE, (2004). A Message / Blitzkrieg Bop / Hybrid Moments / Last Caress / Skull / Welcome To Hell.

SKIZOPHOBIA, Nelly (2005). Brainscan / The Brainwash / Mr. Braindead / Kick On My Face / The Hero President / Carnage / Tunnel To The End.

THE COUP DE GRACE

USA — *James Mecherle (vocals / guitar), Steve Wresh (guitar), Kurt Gillispie (bass), Chris Westling (drums).*

A Minneapolis based Metal band, THE COUP DE GRACE blended Thrash Metal with twin guitar British 70s Hard Rock influences and melodies. Their 1990 eponymous debut, which featured a line up of frontman James 'Jim' Mercerle, guitarist Steve Wresh, bassist Kurt Gillespie and drummer Chris Westling, would be produced by none other than Dave Pirner of SOUL ASYLUM.

Although highly rated by the media 'The Coup De Grace' failed to take off. A second low key album was delivered in 1995 'The Art Of Survival'. For this outing Mecherle, Wresh and Westling were joined by new bass player Kyle Lund.

A later line up of the band saw a brand new rhythm section of bassist Tommy Dee and drummer Brent Degendorfer. On guitar would be another new face, Mark Chaussee, later of Rob Halford's FIGHT and DANZIG.

Vocalist / guitarist James Mecherle would later join the band of controversial Rock artist ANDREW W.K.

THE COUP DE GRACE, Twin Tone 89182-1 (1990). Daylight Dawning / Burning With Optimism / Sad But True / Bombs Away / Me, Myself And I, 'Til The Bitter End / All Of The Above / Barbed Wire / So Be It.

THE ART OF SURVIVAL, (1995). Ten Feet Tall Warning Signs / Pride Ran Deep / Celtic Song / God Given / Helping Hand / It's Only Money / Not For Today / All Fall Dead / Grave World / Bonds That Bind.

THE CROWN

TROLLHÄTTAN, SWEDEN — *Johan Lindstrand (vocals), Marcus Sunesson (guitar), Marko Trevonen (guitar), Magnus Osfelt (bass), Janne Saarenpää (drums).*

Trollhättan Death Metal combo previously known as CROWN OF THORNS. Although often confused with Jean Beuvoir's American Melodic Rock act, Sweden's CROWN OF THORNS, founded in 1990 by ex-IMPIOUS vocalist Johan Lindstrandt and very much in the Grindcore mould, were a much heavier proposition altogether. Over time THE CROWN rapidly developed into a premier technical Death Metal outfit. CROWN OF THORNS first hit the tape trading scene with an impressive demo, 1993's 'Forever Heaven Gone'. Shortly after its release the band got to play the Swedish Hultsfred festival alongside ENTOMBED and IGGY POP but lost guitarist Robert Österberg to Punk act ÖLHÄVERS. His replacement was Marcus Sunesson who cut his teeth with the 1994 demo 'Forget The Light'. This tape scored them a deal with Black Sun Records for the debut album 'The Burning'. CROWN OF THORNS also made their mark on the SLAYER tribute album 'Slaytanic Slaughter' contributing their take on 'Mandatory Suicide'.

The band's sophomore outing 'Eternal Death' continued the trend and yet again the Swedes were adding to another tribute album, this time nailing a cover of 'Arise' for the SEPULTURA homage 'Sepultural Feast'.

Continued threat of litigation from the American CROWN OF THORNS resulted in the band adopting the title THE CROWN in 1997. Undaunted the band toured Europe in early 1998 on a billing with SACRILEGE resulting directly in a deal with American label Metal Blade for third album 'Hell Is Here'.

To promote the record THE CROWN embarked on further European dates on a Black Metal festival package bill of IMPALED NAZARENE, EMPEROR, MORBID ANGEL and PECCATUM. A further cover version ensued, this time a crack at BATHORY's 'Burnin' Leather' for the 'Power From The North' compilation.

THE CROWN toured Europe in December 2000 as part of an almighty Death Metal package that included ENSLAVED, MORBID ANGEL, BEHEMOTH, HYPNOS and DYING FETUS.

THE CROWN guitarist Marcus Sunesson would join THE HAUNTED for American touring in 2001. Drummer Janne Saarenpää would deputise for GOD DETHRONED for their 'No Mercy' festival appearances. A further round of American dates, commencing in Tampa, Florida on the 24th April 2002, saw support from DARKEST HOUR and ALL THAT REMAINS. The 'Crowned In Terror' album would witness a huge leap in sales and exposure for the band, surpassing sales of all previous albums combined and even entering the national Swedish album charts at no. 8.

Thomas Lindberg would also guest on shared lead vocals in union with KREATOR frontman Mille Petrozza for the track 'Dirty Coloured Knife' on the 2002 album from Israeli metal act EMBLAZE. The singer, along with Marcus Sunneson also sessioned on DARKEST HOUR's 'Hidden Hands Of A Sadist Nation' album.

In a surprise move Lindberg split from THE CROWN in early June rejoining his former act THE GREAT DECEIVER. The band swiftly reinstating original vocalist Johan Lindstrand, albeit with both parties stressing the temporary nature of the union, for their appearance at Finland's 'Tuska Metal' festival and the German Bad Berka 'San Open Air' event. However, in late September Lindstrand confirmed that he had re-joined on a permanent basis.

THE CROWN allied themselves with SKINLESS and MONOLITH for the 'Crowning Europe In Terror' tour in March and April of 2003. The band returned later that year with a new studio album 'Possessed 13'. A limited edition two disc set of the album added both the band's 1993 'Forever Heaven Gone' and 1994 'Forget The Light' demos, a 1992 demo track 'Last Rite', a cover of BATHORY's 'Burnin' Leather' and a 2000 demo version of 'Rebel Angel'. Solidifying their reunion with Lindstrand the band even re-entered the recording studio to manufacture a new version of their 2002 album release 'Crowned In Terror' with Lindstrand replacing Tomas Lindberg's vocals. A further round of November touring on the European mainland saw THE CROWN hooked up with road partners DARKEST HOUR and MONOLITH DEATHCULT.

Although the October 2003 album 'Possessed 13' scored laudatory reviews the band struggled to get onto any decent tour packages. On the 7th of March of 2004 the band called it quits, drummer Janne Saarenpää candidly admitting via an official web posting that the band's inability to match the quality of their music with good business sense had led to their downfall.

The album 'Crowned Unholy', issued in August of 2004, would actually be a remake of the band's fifth album 'Crowned In Terror'. This revised version added re-recorded vocal tracks by Johan Lindstrand, re-recorded bass tracks by Magnus Olsfelt and a brand new intro programmed by drummer Janne Saarenpää. Also included would be a DVD entitled 'The Crown Invades Karlsruhe', documenting a show on THE CROWN's final tour in Karlsruhe, Germany on 24th November 2003.

Johan Lindstrand would front INCAPACITY for a one off gig on 1st October at the Belsepub in Gothenburg supporting IMPIOUS. In December Lindstrand has announced the formation of his brand new project, billed ONE MAN ARMY AND THE UNDEAD QUARTET. Entering Deadline Studios, and working with Valle Adzic of IMPIOUS as engineer, this venture cut the opening demo 'When Hatred Comes To Life'. Meantime, THE CROWN drummer Janne Saarenpää recorded for Canadian act AVEN AURA in mid 2004 on their debut album 'The Shadow Of Idols'.

In March of 2005 Marcus Sunesson re-emerged as member of the new band ENGEL, a Gothenburg based quintet also featuring guitarist Niclas Engelin, of PASSENGER, GARDENIAN and IN FLAMES repute, drummer Morbid Mojjo (a.k.a. Daniel Moilanen), a veteran of MINDSNARE, SANDALINAS, RUNEMAGICK, DRACENA, RELEVANT FEW and LORD BELIAL, bassist Robert Hakemo, ex-GARDENIAN and GOOSEFLESH together with vocalist Mangan Klavborn. Meantime, guitarist Marko Tervonen was in collaboration with TRANSPORT LEAGUE frontman Tony Jelencovich in a new unit billed ANGEL BLAKE. This project soon scored a label deal with Metal Blade Records and also subsequently drafted Janne Saarenpää on drums. Tervonen would also retain ties with his former THE CROWN colleague bassist Magnus Osfelt, acting as producer for the four-stringers STOLEN POLICECAR project. Johan Lindstrand spread his talents by also signing up as new frontman for INCAPACITY in December.

HELL IS HERE, Metal Blade 14193-2 (1998). The Poison / At The End / 1999—Revolution 666 / Dying Of The Heart / Electric Night / Black Lightning / The Devil And The Darkness / Give You Hell / Body And Soul / Mysterion / Death By My Side.
DEATHRACE KING, Metal Blade 14296-2 (2000). Deathexplosion / Executioner (Slayer Of The Light) / Back From The Grave / Devil Gate Ride / Vengeance / Angel Rebel / I Won't Follow / Blitzkrieg Witchcraft / Dead Man's Song / Total Satan / Killing Star (Superbia Luxuria XXX).
CROWNED IN TERROR, Metal Blade 14394-2 (2002). Introduction—House Of Hades / Crowned In Terror / Under The Whip / Drugged Unholy / World Below / The Speed Of Darkness / Out For Blood / (I Am) Hell / Death Is The Hunter / Satanist / Death Metal Holocaust. Chart position: 8 SWEDEN.
POSSESSED 13, Metal Blade 14446-2 (2003). No Tomorrow / Face Of Destruction / Deep Hit Of Death / Deliverance / Cold Is The Grave / Dream Bloody Hell / Morningstar Rising / Are You Morbid? / Bow To None / Kill 'Em All / Natashead Overdrive / Zombiefied / Dawn Of Emptiness / In Memoriam. Chart position: 54 SWEDEN.
CROWNED UNHOLY, Metal Blade 14497 (2004) (CD + DVD). House Of Hades / Crowned In Terror / Under The Whip / Drugged Unholy / World Below / The Speed Of Darkness / Out For Blood / (I Am) Hell / Death Is The Hunter / Satanist / Death Metal Holocaust / No Tomorrow / Face Of Destruction—Deep Hit Of Death / Deathexplosion / World Below / Deliverance / Blitzkrieg Witchcraft / Cold Is The Grave / Zombiefied / Dream Bloody Hell—Kill 'Em All / Under The Whip / Bow To None / Total Satan / House Of Hades—Crowned In Terror / 1999—Revolution 666.

THE CRUCIFIED

FRESNO, CA, USA — *Mark Saloman (vocals), Greg Minier (guitar), Jeff Bellew (bass), Jim Chaffin (drums).*

Christian Crossover Thrashers THE CRUCIFIED started life as a straightforward Punk act but evolved into Thrash / Hardcore territory. The group made their entrance with the 1987 demo 'Take Up Your Cross', the band at this point comprising of vocalist Marc Cooksey, guitarist Greg Minier, bassist Trevor Palmer and drummer Jim Chaffin. The 'Nailed' tape followed which saw THE CRUCIFIED with two new faces—vocalist Mark Saloman and bassist Mark Johnson. Finally a live tape surfaced dubbed 'Live At The New Order', by this juncture Johnson had made way for Jeff Bellew.

Signing to the Narrowpath label THE CRUCIFIED issued the eponymous inaugural album in 1988. The second album, '1991's 'The Pillars Of Humanity', is held in high regard as a classic of the genre. Both Saloman and Minier would also feature as guests on the Rap Thrash project album 'Sodom & America' by XL AND DEATH BEFORE DISHONOR.

Upon the band's demise the Ocean label issued the 1994 album 'Nailed', a collection of archive recordings from THE CRUCIFIED's Punk formative years. Although having folded in 1993 it appears that the group did reform for sporadic gigs in 1995.

Vocalist Mark Saloman would later found Alternative Rock act STAVESACRE. Following a spell with the industrially inclined CHATTERBOX bassist Jeff Bellew also teamed up with STAVESACRE. The bassist would also share co-production credits for P.O.D.'s 'Snuff The Punk' record and contribute guest guitar to MORTAL's 'Fathom' opus. Saloman also guested on this latter release.

Drummer Jim Chaffin appeared with FASEDOWN, a project of erstwhile DELIVERANCE guitarist Mike Phillips, vocalist Devin Shaeffer, second guitarist Jesse Gibson and ex-THE BLAMED bassist John Hansen. Chaffin also united with prolific Chicago Thrash act THE BLAMED.

Guitarist Greg Minier has also issued solo product. The 1990 MINIER album, released by the R.E.X. label, maintains a Thrash course whilst APPLEHEAD sees a shift into a Grunge direction.

THE CRUCIFIED, Narrowpath (1988). The Pit / Diehard / Your Image / Getting A Grip On Things / Hellcorn / Rise / One Demon To Another / Unity / A Guy In A Suite And The Pope / Back To The Cross / Confidence / The Insult Circus / Thread / Crucial Moment.
THE PILLARS OF HUMANITY, Ocean 7018133505 (1991). Intro / Hateworld / It's All About Fear / The Wrong One / Mindbender / Path To Sorrow / Fellowship Of Thieves / Focus / The Strength / Blackstone / So Called Living 1991 / The Pillars Of Humanity.
NAILED, Ocean (1994). I'm Not A Christian Punk / Death To Death / Your Image / God In A Cage / Crucified With Christ / Give It Up / Disposal.

THE EMBODIMENT

HARDERWIJK, HOLLAND — *Peter Hagen (vocals / guitar), Erik-Jan Brinker (guitar), Danny van Helden (bass), Martijn van Gene (drums).*

Harderwijk Death-Thrashers. THE EMBODIMENT was originally gathered as EMBODIMENT in 1994 by vocalist / guitarists Peter Hagen and Erik-Jan Brinker along with drummer Martijn van Gene and bassist Sebastiaan den Oudsten. Den Oudsten exited in 1996 to join up with CANISTER, subsequently going on to ART OF PREMONITION. The band put in its first concert on 13th December 1996, after which den Oudsten returned to the ranks as EMBODIMENT entered QSA Studios in Utrecht with producer Vincent Dijkers to craft the demo 'All Because Of Lust' in January 1998.

Bassist Danny van Helden was inducted during 2000 and shortly afterward the group subtly revised its title to THE EMBODIMENT. An EP, 'Razor Cut Reality', emerged in 2002. Peter Hagen went on to join Groningen's ENRAGED in 2004. THE EMBODIMENT released the 'Legion' album in October 2006. The band donated the track 'Y2K' to the 2006 compilation album 'Blown To Pieces 4' issued by FearSomeRecords.

Razor Cut Reality, Independent (2002). Careless / Victims Of Retaliation / I'm Despair / 45 Years.
LEGION, (2006).

THE ENCHANTED

UK — *Tony Wildwood (vocals / guitar), Robb Philpotts (guitar), Adam Thomas (bass), Jamie Sykes (drums).*

Bradford Metal band whose self financed album 'Trust In Death And Rebirth' features erstwhile BURNING WITCH and THORR'S HAMMER drummer Jamie Sykes. The band evolved during 1997, founded by the former DARK EMBRACE musicians guitarist Tony Wildwood and bassist Daryl Parson, vocalist Kate, drummer Barry and PARONIRA guitarist Robb Philpotts. Tony also cited prior credits with NECROMANCER. This line-up undertook just two gigs and cut the debut demo tape 'Freedom To Perceive'.

Kate would depart, to concentrate on studies but also to sing for local act MAYA, and THE ENCHANTED pulled in vocalist

Natalie from IN DYING GRACE. A second tape, 'Pagan Metal', arrive with this version of the band before Natalie was ousted. In May of 2000 Barry left to team up with the reformed MALEDICTION and THE ENCHANTED duly enrolled Jamie Sykes, recently returned from band activity in North America. In 2002 the track 'Forever In Your Dream' would be included on the Arcane Productions sampler 'Deathfest—The Art Of Extremity'. Following the release of the debut 'Trust In Death And Rebirth' album Sykes would leave the band in November of 2002. However, within a matter of weeks he would be back in the fold.

Bass player Daryl Parson dropped out in March of 2003, being superseded by Adam Thomas of EPITAPH, BORN INTO SODOM and RUINS OF AMBER repute. THE ENCHANTED acted as support to Norwegian Viking Metal veterans ENSLAVED for their one off January 2004 performance at London's Camden Underground. Sykes left yet again in June, being briefly replaced by Robb Philpotts brother Vinnie, of TORTOISE WALTZ and actually an early BLOODSTREAM singer, on a temporary basis. At this same juncture, Robb Philpotts, retaining his ties to THE ENCHANTED, would join BLOODSTREAM as their new frontman.

Tony Wildwood would be announced as guitarist for Nottingham based Pagan collective THE CLAN DESTINED, a Heathen Metal band spearheaded by ex-SABBAT and SKYCLAD singer Martin Walkyier alongside bassist Iscariah of IMMORTAL repute. In February of 2005 Jamie Sykes re-assumed THE ENCHANTED drum stool. Sykes would also be found working with Doomsters ATAVIST.

TRUST IN DEATH AND REBIRTH, Sinister Realm SINR001 (2002). The Portal / The Eternal Hourglass / Waiting In The Shadow World / Disposable Planet / Facing The Beast / As Silence Deepens / Soulburn / Forever In Your Dream / Celtica / Devastation.

THE FALLEN

ORANGE COUNTY, CA, USA — *Mike Granat (vocals / guitar), Mark Venier (guitar), Bryan Klinger (bass), Henry Higgs (drums).*

Stoic Metal campaigners THE FALLEN, founded as THE CRESTFALLEN during 1992, endured nearly a decade of struggle and successive demo releases before finally landing a record deal in 2001. The group was convened as a trio of vocalist / guitarist Mike Granat, guitarist Mark Venier and drummer Max Wolff mixing traditional Metal with newer Death and retro Thrash influences. With the addition of bass player Bryan Klinger the band became known as THE FALLEN.

A demo cassette, 'The Perfect Darkness Of Death', arrived in 1993 which found the group fronted by lead vocalist Wagner Pierera. However, THE FALLEN was back to a quartet for 1994's 'Eventually Nothing Remained' session with Granat taking the lead vocal mantle. Wolff would be out of the picture by the band's third and fourth attempts, 1995's 'Turning Hollow' and the following year's 'Bloodletting: Victims Of The Order', drums being simply credited to 'Greg'. Keith Gordon took the drum stool for the 1997 session 'Bloodrush'.

THE FALLEN, now with Henry Higgs placed on drums, committed to CD for the first time with their 1999 three track EP 'Sector—7G'. A self financed full length album 'The Tones In Which We Speak' emerged in 2000 leading to a deal with the Metal Blade label and the subsequent Bill Metoyer produced 'Front Toward Enemy'. By March of 2003 THE FALLEN had severed ties with drummer Max Wolff, replacing him with John Skaare. Another casualty would be singer Mike Granat, who opted out in July. However, despite announcing this officially, THE FALLEN then refuted this statement within days.

Sector—7G EP, (1999). To Dust / Descend From Heaven / Bound In Thorns.

THE TONES IN WHICH WE SPEAK, (2000). Suffer With It / The Tones In Which We Speak / All For None / Harbinger / Turning Hollow / Sunken Ploy / To Dust / Descend From Heaven / Bound In Thorns / Bloodwash.

FRONT TOWARDS ENEMY, Metal Blade 3984-14398-2 (2002). Short Fuse / Blessings / What I Have Become / Keep Suffering / The Hopeless & The Frail / Front Toward Enemy / Shifting Our Vision / Killswitch / In Loathing / From Fragile To Strength / Eleven Years.

THE GREAT KAT

USA — Reckoned by many to be as mad as a March hare by much of the Rock media but hailed as an underground genius by her many fans, The Great Kat, real name Katherine Thomas, first reared her head in 1987 touting herself as the world's fastest guitarist and only true musician. Whatever the merits of her claims THE GREAT KAT has certainly made an indelible impression upon the Metal scene.

Having attended the famed Julliard School Of Music Kat signed to Roadrunner and recorded her debut album, the unsubtle 'Worship Me Or Die' to an interesting array of opinion from the world's Metal press. Karat Faye, the man who produced MEGADETH's first album, was chosen as producer but did not stay the course and eventually studio owner Kurt Shore scored production credits. During recording a glut of drummers came in and out of the band before Adam Killa committed. Before his induction Kay held talks with Greg D'Angelo of WHITE LION and ANTHRAX, Tony Scaglione of WHIPLASH and SLAYER and even DAVID LEE ROTH's Greg Bissonette, none of whom wished to participate. Nevertheless, the album would generate not only healthy album sales world wide but valuable press coverage for Kat's uniquely over the top approach. Bass was supplied by Tom Von Doom, subsequently to join the CYCLE SLUTS FROM HELL. Tom Von Doom and Adam Killa subsequently forged MIGHTY JOE YOUNG.

By 1989 Kat had seemingly found suitable musicians in order to tour with, the lucky duo being bassist Chip Marshall and drummer Kevin Dedario. Later releases have been short on duration if crammed to the hilt with energy. The 1998 'Bloody Vivaldi' opus features a take on Vivaldi's much loved 'Four Seasons', the 39 second hyper blast of 'Blood' and also Sarasate's 'Carmen's Fantasy'. The 2000 release 'Rossini's Rape' plumbed even deeper into the realms of the truly disturbing with workouts of Rossini's 'William Tell Overture' and Bazzini's 'The Road Of The Goblins'.

THE GREAT KAT launched a new studio album 'Wagner's War' in August of 2002, apparently her response to the September 11th 2001 terrorist attacks.

WORSHIP ME OR DIE, Roadracer RO 95892 (1987). Metal Messiah / Kat Possessed / Death To You / Satan Goes To Church / Worship Me Or Die / Demons / Speed Death / Kill The Mothers / Ashes To Dust / Satan Says / Metal Massacre.

BLOODY VIVALDI, Great Kat (1988). Vivaldi's 'The Four Seasons' For Violin, Chamber Orchestra And Band / Torture Chamber / Blood / Sarasate's 'Carmen Fantasy' For Violin & Band.

BEETHOVEN ON SPEED, Roadracer RO 93732 (1990). Beethoven On Speed / Flight Of The Bumble-Bee / Funeral March / God / Sex And Violins / Gripping Obsession / Worshipping Bodies / Total Tyrant / Ultra-Dead / Revenge Of The Mongrel / Kat Abuse / Made In Japan / Beethoven Mosh (5th Symphony) / Paganinis 24th Caprice / Guitar Concerto In Blood Minor / Back To The Future: For Geniuses Only.

DIGITAL BEETHOVEN ON CYBERSPEED, Great Kat (1996).

GUITAR GODDESS, Blood And Guts Music (1997). Rossini's The Barber Of Seville / Dominatrix / Feast Of The Dead / Sarasate's Gypsy Violin Waltz Zigeuneriveisen.

ROSSINI'S RAPE, TPR (2000). Rossini's 'William Tell Overture' For Symphony Orchestra & Band / Sodomize / Castration / Bazzini's 'The Road Of The Goblins' For Violin, Piano & Band.

WAGNER'S WAR, TPR Music (2002). Act I: War—Wagner's "The Ride Of The Valkyries" (From The Opera "Die Walkure") For Symphony Orchestra, Band & Opera Singers / Act I: War—War / Act I: War—Terror / Act II: Revenge—Punishment / Act II: Revenge—Humiliation / Act III: Victory—Liszt's "Hungarian Rhapsody no. 2" For Symphony Orchestra & Band / Act III: Victory—Sarasate's "Zapateado" For Violin, Piano & Band.

THE HAUNTED

GOTHENBURG, SWEDEN — *Peter Dolving (vocals), Anders Björler (guitar), Patrik Jensen (guitar), Jonas Björler (bass), Per Møller Jensen (drums).*

A Death / Thrash act with strong links into the elite of the pioneering Gothenburg extreme Metal scene. THE HAUNTED was founded by former ORCHRISTE, SÉANCE and SATANIC SLAUGHTER guitarist Patrik Jensen and former AT THE GATES man Adrian Erlandsson on drums. The exact starting point for the band can be pinpointed to July 27th 1996. Within half an hour of AT THE GATES holding a meeting to call it quits, Erlandsson was on the telephone to Jensen inviting him to explore the possibilities of a new band unit. Jensen and Erlandsson jammed the next day, working on tracks originally intended for SÉANCE, then invited another ex-AT THE GATES man, Jonas Björler, into the fold a week later to cover bass guitar. THE HAUNTED also drafted former DISSECTION and CARDINAL SIN man John Zwetsloot. However, Zwetsloot's tenure lasted a matter of months before erstwhile INFESTATION, AT THE GATES and TERROR guitarist Anders Björler, twin brother of Jonas, took over secondary guitar duties.

The band attempted to lure in a lead vocalist and discussions were held with Toxine (a.k.a. Tony Kampner) of SATANIC SLAUGHTER and WITCHERY, and Rogga of MERCILESS. Ultimately it would be Peter Dolving of MARY BEATS JANE that landed the job.

During 1997 Erlandsson created the side project HYPERHUG. Within time he would decamp from THE HAUNTED to concentrate on this act full time. THE HAUNTED attempted to fill the drum position with DISSECTION and OPTHALAMIA man Ole Öhman. Fate intervened when HYPERHUG's singer damaged his hearing curtailing the group. Erlandsson rejoined his former colleagues.

Earache Records took over the band's contract from debts owing on previous AT THE GATES dealings in order to issue the eponymous debut album, crafted with co-producer Fredrik Nordström at Fredman Studio in Gothenburg, in June 1998. To promote this release, THE HAUNTED undertook touring in Europe with NAPALM DEATH but projected Japanese dates were cancelled. In November 1998 Dolving, frustrated with a lack of progress on the live front, quit to found ZEN MONKEY, his replacement, FACE DOWN's Marco Aro, being located in March 1999. With this new line-up the band toured the European festival circuit.

THE HAUNTED was offered the support slot to TESTAMENT's North American dates the same year but in mid rehearsal for these shows Erlandsson quit to join premier British Black Metal band CRADLE OF FILTH. The tour went ahead with Per Møller Jensen of KONKHRA and INVOCATOR fame. THE HAUNTED bounced back in commanding style with 'The Haunted Made Me Do It' in October 2000. This effort, its cover emblazoned with a collage of serial killers, saw production credits going to Berno Paulsson.

In 2001 it was announced that Mike Wead, of MERCYFUL FATE and KING DIAMOND, had joined the band, supplanting Anders Björler, who had opted out to pursue university studies. However, a subsequent American tour alongside CATASTROPHIC and MARTYR A.D. witnessed THE CROWN guitarist Marcus Sunesson temporarily taking the vacancy.

THE HAUNTED would also prepare tracks, recorded in Japan at the Akasaka Blitz in Tokyo during 2000 and mixed by KONKHRA mainman Anders Lundemark, for a live album dubbed 'Live Rounds In Tokyo', first issued in the Far East by Toy's Factory in May 2001. This set of recordings would eventually surface as a bonus disc packaged with a re-released 'Made Me Do It' in December. Anders Björler made a surprise return to the band shortly before THE HAUNTED entered the studio to record a third album.

Drummer Per Moller Jensen would be linked to an endeavour with strong TESTAMENT connections was unveiled during the summer of 2002 with the SADUS pairing of frontman Darren Travis and bassist Steve DiGeorgio embarking on an all star union billed as SUICIDE SHIFT. The project included TESTAMENT vocalist Chuck Billy as well as guest guitar from the much travelled ex-TESTAMENT man JAMES MURPHY. Recording of a new studio album, provisionally billed as 'One Kill Wonder', commenced in the last quarter of 2002. ARCH ENEMY guitarist Michael Amott laid down a guest solo during these sessions.

The 'One Kill Wonder' album arrived in stores in February 2003. Significantly, the record gave the band its first national chart placing, reaching number 23 on the Swedish album rankings. The title track would dominate all three of the major US Metal radio charts, the CMJ Loud Rock Chart, the CMJ Loud Rock Spins Chart and the FMQB Metal Detector chart for a four week run at the number one position.

THE HAUNTED announced South African shows for March 2003. European touring had the band packaged with MASTODON and HATESPHERE in April before the band jumped the Atlantic for US gigs throughout the summer headlining over KATAKLYSM, SHAI HULUD and SKINLESS. All this took place as a background to an increased awareness of the band due to laudatory reviews for 'One Kill Wonder'. Despite this praise, during October THE HAUNTED parted ways with vocalist Marco Aro, replacing him with his predecessor, the group's original frontman Peter Dolving.

The band would novelly hold a competition amongst its fans to find a new album title, the winner coming up with 'Subliminal Messages Of Suicide Promotion'. Although gaining the honours and a set of prizes this title was, in the end, not used. Touring in the Spring of 2004 found the band, including Peter Dolving nursing four fractured ribs, traversing the UK as support to FUNERAL FOR A FRIEND. THE HAUNTED, having cut their latest opus at Studio Fredman in Gothenburg with co-producers Patrik J. Sten, drummer with PASSENGER, and Fredrik Nordström, signed to Century Media Records in June.

The band would be chosen, alongside MERCENARY, MNEMIC, HATESPHERE, RAUNCHY, MELTED, BLINDFAULT and STOMPED, to form up the "Nordic Threat" show for the Popkomm 2004 music convention at the Silver Wings in Berlin on 29th September. US touring in October saw the band allied with DAMAGEPLAN and SHADOWS FALL as the 'rEVOLVEr' album, preceded by a promotional video for the track 'All Against All', entered the Swedish charts at no. 18. December saw the band on the road in Europe, forming up the 'Hammered at Xmas' tour in union with ARCH ENEMY and DARK TRANQUILLITY. Scandinavian headline dates as part of the 'Close Up' magazine sponsored 'Close Up Made Me Do it' tour had THE HAUNTED headlining over TOTALT JÄVLA MÖRKER and INSISION in February of 2005. That same month the band undertook headline UK gigs supported by MARTYR A.D. and DEAD TO FALL.

To aid victims of the December 2004 Indian Ocean tsunamis THE HAUNTED, in collaboration with HEAVEN SHALL BURN and NAPALM DEATH, participated in the issue of a special single release. The band donated the track 'Smut King'. These singles, restricted to just 1000 hand numbered copies, would be for sale only at NAPALM DEATH's Bochum and London shows in January 2005. That same month Per Møller Jensen recorded the 'Music For Tough Guys' demo with SLOW DEATH FACTORY, a high profile union of Danish extreme Metal elite comprising ILLDISPOSED's Morten Gilsted, vocalist Martin Rosendahl of STRANGLER, ZAHRIM, CORPUS MORTALE and INIQUITY and CORPUS MORTALE's Roar Christofferson on bass guitar.

THE HAUNTED acted as special guests to the MOONSPELL and CRADLE OF FILTH package European tour in March. However, guitarist Patrik Jensen left the tour shortly after the Lisbon,

THE HAUNTED

Portugal date in order to attend "urgent family matters", leaving the band to carry on as a quartet. US gigs in May were to see a road alliance with DEVILDRIVER, MACHINE HEAD and IT DIES TODAY, but the group withdrew from these dates, citing Jensen's desire to spend time with his sick father in Sweden. That month THE HAUNTED filmed promotional video clip for the track 'No Compromise' with director Roger Johansson.

The group got back onto the US touring circuit in major fashion, appearing on the second stage at the BLACK SABBATH and IRON MAIDEN headlined 'Ozzfest' events commencing 15th July in Mansfield, Massachusetts. The band then announced further US dates alongside MESHUGGAH, GOD FORBID and MNEMIC throughout October. Roadwork continued apace in November as THE HAUNTED toured Europe traversing Holland, the UK, France, Belgium, Spain, Germany, Austria, Switzerland, Denmark and Sweden in union with MANNTIS and GOD FORBID.

2006 shows for THE HAUNTED included the Japanese 'Extreme The Dojo Vol. 15' with NILE and EXODUS in late February then Australian headliners in March. The group scheduled to album recording sessions at Antfarm Studios in Århus, Denmark in May with producer Tue Madsen. Meantime, Peter Dolving, having also fired up an Alternative Rock project dubbed BRING THE WAR HOME, guested on the track 'Dead Rising' included on SPARZANZA's 'Banisher Of The Light' album. THE HAUNTED geared up for further global campaigning with the release of 'The Dead Eye' in October. The album entered the national Swedish charts at number 14, their highest entry to date.

European and Scandinavian shows were announced for January 2007 but then cancelled as the group instead opted to tour as support to KILLSWITCH ENGAGE. Finnish shows for February were aligned with BURST. The group returned to US campaigning in March and April flanking DARK TRANQUILLITY and INTO ETERNITY. THE HAUNTED and MUNICIPAL WASTE teamed up for a European, hitting the UK, Germany, France, Belgium, The Netherlands, Spain, Czech Republic, Austria, Hungary, Italy, Poland and Switzerland, tour into May. British dates added fellow Swedes WOLF to the billing.

The Haunted, The Haunted (1997) (Demo, Recorded in Studio Fredman). Shattered / Undead.

THE HAUNTED, Earache MOSH 197 (1998). Hate Song / Chasm / In Vein / Undead / Choke Hold / Three Times / Bullet Hole / Now You Know / Shattered / Soul Fracture / Blood Rust / Forensick.

THE HAUNTED MADE ME DO IT, Toy's Factory TFCK-87231 (2000) (Japanese release). Dark Intentions / Bury Your Dead / Trespass / Leech / Hollow Ground / Revelation / The World Burns / Human Debris / Silencer / Under The Surface / Victim Iced / Eclipse.

THE HAUNTED MADE ME DO IT, Earache MOSH 241 (2000). Dark Intentions / Bury Your Dead / Trespass / Leech / Hollow Ground / Revelation / The World Burns / Human Debris / Silencer / Under The Surface / Victim Iced.

LIVE ROUNDS IN TOKYO, Toy's Factory TFCK-87284 (2001). Intro / Dark Intentions / Bury Your Dead / Chasm / Trespass / Shattered / Hollow Ground / Choke Hold / Leech / In Vein / Revelation / Bullet Hole / Silencer / Three Times / Undead / Blinded By Fear / Hate Song.

LIVE ROUNDS IN TOKYO / THE HAUNTED MADE ME DO IT, Earache MOSH 241 CDB (2001). Dark Intentions / Bury Your Dead / Trespass / Leech / Hollow Ground / Revelation / The World Burns / Human Debris / Silencer / Under The Surface / Victim Iced / Intro / Dark Intentions / Bury Your Dead / Chasm / Trespass / Shattered / Hollow Ground / Choke Hold / Leech / In Vein / Revelation / Bullet Hole / Silencer / Three Times / Undead / Hate Song / Eclipse.

ONE KILL WONDER, Earache MOSH 265 (2003). Privation Of Faith / God Puppet / Shadow World / Everlasting / D.O.A. / Demon Eyes / Urban Predator / Downward Spiral / Shithead / Bloodletting / One Kill Wonder. Chart position: 23 SWEDEN.

ONE KILL WONDER, Toy's Factory TFCK-87304 (2003) (Japanese release). Privation Of Faith / God Puppet / Shadow World / Everlasting / D.O.A. / Demon Eyes / Urban Predator / Downward Spiral / Shithead / Bloodletting / One Kill Wonder / Ritual.

ONE KILL WONDER (SPECIAL EDITION), Earache MOSH 265X (2004). Privation Of Faith / God Puppet / Shadow World / Everlasting / D.O.A. / Demon Eyes / Urban Predator / Downward Spiral / Shithead / Bloodletting / One Kill Wonder / Creed / Ritual / Well Of Souls.

rEVOLVEr, Century Media 77488-8 (2004) (Digipack. Limited edition 20,000 copies). No Compromise / 99 / Abysmal / Sabotage / All Against All / Sweet Relief / Burnt To A Shell / Who Will Decide / Nothing Right / Liquid Burns / Fire Alive / Smut King / My Shadow.

rEVOLVEr, Century Media 77488-2 (2004). No Compromise / 99 / Abysmal / Sabotage / All Against All / Sweet Relief / Burnt To A Shell / Who Will Decide / Nothing Right / Liquid Burns / My Shadow. Chart position: 18 SWEDEN.

rEVOLVEr, Toy's Factory TFCK-87374 (2004) (Japanese release). No Compromise / 99 / Abysmal / Sabotage / All Against All / Sweet Relief / Burnt To A Shell / Who Will Decide / Out Of Reach / Nothing Right / Liquid Burns / Fire Alive / My Shadow.

Tsunami Benefit, Century Media (2005) (Split single with NAPALM DEATH and HEAVEN SHALL BURN). Smut King.

THE DEAD EYE (LIMITED EDITION), EMI 775880 (2006) (CD + DVD, UK release). The Premonition / The Flood / The Medication / The Crowning / The Reflection / The Prosecution / The Fallout / The Medusa / The Highwire / The Shifter / The Cynic / The Failure / The Stain / The Program / The Guilt Trip / The Making Of The Dead Eye / All Against All (Video) / No Compromise (Video) / 99 (Live) / Abysmal (Live).

THE DEAD EYE (COLLECTOR'S EDITION), Century Media 8302 (2006). The Premonition / The Flood / The Medication / The Crowning / The Reflection / The Prosecution / The Fallout / The Medusa / The Shifter / The Cynic / The Failure / The Stain / The Guilt Trip / The Highwire / The Program.

THE DEAD EYE, Century Media 8288 (2006). The Premonition / The Flood / The Medication / The Crowning / The Reflection / The Prosecution / The Fallout / The Medusa / The Shifter / The Cynic / The Failure / The Stain / The Guilt Trip. Chart position: 14 SWEDEN.

THE DEAD EYE, Toy's Factory TFCK-87407 (2006) (Japanese release). The Premonition / The Flood / The Medication / The Crowning / The Reflection / The Prosecution / The Fallout / The Medusa / The Highwire / The Shifter / The Cynic / The Failure / The Stain / The Burden / The Program / The Guilt Trip.

THE DEAD EYE, Toy's Factory TFCK-87408 (2006) (CD + DVD, Japanese release). The Premonition / The Flood / The Medication / The Crowning / The Reflection / The Prosecution / The Fallout / The Medusa / The Highwire / The Shifter / The Cynic / The Failure / The Stain / The Burden / The Program / The Guilt Trip / The Making Of The Dead Eye / All Against All (Video) / No Compromise (Video) / 99 (Live) / Abysmal (Live).

THE MACHETE

LAPPEENRANTA, FINLAND — *Tuomo Saikkonen (vocals / bass), Santtu Hämäläinen (guitar), Juha Javanainen (guitar), Teemu Saikkonen (drums).*

THE MACHETE is a retro-styled, Lappeenranta based Thrash Metal band formulated initially as a jam session during early 2003, pulling together drummer Teemu Saikkonen, Kuisma Aalto of MOKOMA and ex-MIND RIOT man Juha Javanainen on guitar. This trio would subsequently be joined by MOKOMA bassist Santtu Hämäläinen, then swiftly reformulated itself as this newest candidate switched to guitar and Aalto took on the bass role. By the close of the year enough material had been gathered for an album. At first Esa Salminen of NORTHERN DISCIPLINE was adopted as frontman until the MOKOMA and MIND RIOT credited Tuomo Saikkonen stepped in to record demos in June 2004.

THE MACHETE underwent a line-up change as 2005 dawned, Kuisma relinquishing his post, necessitating Tuomo taking over bass duties as a promotional video for the track 'Loss For Words' scored the band national recognition on the 'Inferno' DVD. That July the band signed to Spinefarm Records. The 'Regression' album was recorded by Miitri Aaltonen at Music Bros Studios in Imatra.

Machete, The Machete (2004) (Demo). Lost For Words / Turned To Dust / Inward Spiral.
REGRESSION, Spinefarm SPI 246CD (2005). True Nature / Lost For Words / New Me / Turned To Dust / Total Desecration / The Taint / Fool For Respect / Inward Spiral / Blind / Mouth Head / Bitter End.

THE MIST

BELO HORIZONTE, MG, BRAZIL — *Vladimir Korg (vocals), Jairo Guedz (guitar), Marcello Diaz (bass), Chris Salles (drums).*

Belo Horizonte 1990 Thrash outfit with strong SEPULTURA connections. THE MIST was established by former MAYHEM members Reinaldo Cavalão and drummer Cristiano Balão. Sadly, Cavalão died before THE MIST got to record. Cogumelo Records gave THE MIST their debut in 1989 with the album 'Phantasmagoria'. Follow ups included 'The Hangman Tree' in 1991 and 'Ashes To Ashes, Dust To Dust' in 1993.

Guitarist Jairo Guedz appeared with SEPULTURA on their first two albums, ex-CHAKAL vocalist Vladimir Korg wrote the lyrics to SEPULTURA's 'To The Wall' whilst bassist Marcello Diaz is a SEPULTURA roadie. In April 1996 the band was joined by former INSANITY guitarist Fábio Andrey.

Repulse Records issued the 'Gottverlassen' album in January 1997.

PHANTASMAGORIA, Cogumelo (1989). Flying Saucers In The Darkness / Smiles, Tears And Chaos / A Step Into The Darkness / The Enemy / Hate / Barbed Wire Land (At War) / Phantasmagoria / Lightning In The Dark / Like a Bad Song / Faces Of Glass.
THE HANGMAN TREE, Cogumelo (1991). God Of Black And White Images / Scarecrow / Peter Pan Against The World / Falling Into My Inner Abyss / The Hangman Tree—Act One / The Hell Where Angels Live / My Life Is An Eternal Dark Room / My Pain / The Hangman Tree—Epilogue / Broken Toys / Leave Me Alone / Toxin Diffusion.
ASHES TO ASHES, DUST TO DUST, Cogumelo (1993). Cross Child / Escape To The Arms Of Lord / Disaster / Blind / Naked Lunch / Hate / 99 Dead (Wonderland).
GOTTVERLASSEN, Repulse (1997). Fangs Of A Pig / Drop Dead / Godforsaken / Cannibalism / Switch Off The Body Suckers / Jesus Land / Untie Me / Pump / Jailmind Man / Eyes / Devilscreen / Breath Of Nothing.

THE SCOURGER

HELSINKI, FINLAND — *Jari Hurskainen (vocals), Timo Nyberg (guitar), Jani Luttinen (guitar), Kimmo Kammonen (bass), Seppo Tarvainen (drums).*

Helsinki melodic Death Metal combo THE SCOURGER dates to 2003, quoting an opening formation as former GANDALF singer Jari Hurskainen, guitarists Pekka Hämäläinen with Seppo Tarvainen on the drums. A demo that year, hosting a cover version of 'Cold' originally by AT THE GATES, was recorded as a trio. Expanding, the group then introduced the GANDALF and DIVINE DECAY credited Timo Nyberg on second guitar. However, Hämäläinen opted out to be superseded by Harri Hytönen, another GANDALF adept also having CUBEHEAD ties. Alec Hirst-Gee from DIVINE DECAY and SURBURBAN TRIBE aided as session bassist for songwriting sessions.

Next product would be an EP, 'To The Slayground', released in February 2005. These tracks had been recorded at Moonman Studios in Karjaa with BLAKE's Aaro Seppovaara acting as producer. For these recordings the group enlisted AIRDASH and GANDALF bassist Kirka Sainio.

Making the bass position permanent would be ONE ORPHAN MORE's Kimmo Kammonen. Quite incredibly, the band's next single, 'Hatehead' in July, went straight into the national Finnish charts at number 1.

Jani Luttinen of THE WAKE took the second guitar post from Hytonen, this new line-up debuting with a hometown support to TRIVIUM in October 2005. THE SCOURGER issued a full-length album, 'Blind Date With Violence' again produced by Aaro Seppovaara, in January 2006. That May Jani Luttinen injured his hand, necessitating WARMEN's Antti Wirman stepping in as substitute.

In June German label Cyclone Empire took the album on for European license. This version added cover versions of SLAYER, 'Ghosts Of War', and TESTAMENT's 'Over The Wall'. The EP 'Maximum Intensity' entered the Finnish charts at no. 3, rising to number 2 the following week. THE SCOURGER commenced fresh album recordings in early January 2007 at Seawolf Studios in Helsinki.

The Scourger, The Scourger (2003) (Demo). The Fool Circle / Pain Zone / Maximum Intensity / Cold.
To The Slayground, Stay Heavy SHR 001-2 (2005). Slayground / Soul Seducer / The Greediness / Crossfire Of Lies / Malediction Of Heredity / Black Worms.
Hatehead, Stay Heavy SHR 002-2 (2005). Hatehead / Vicious Circle. Chart position: 1 FINLAND.
BLIND DATE WITH VIOLENCE, Stay Heavy SHR 003-2 (2006). Decline Of Conformity—Grading:Deranged / Hatehead / Maximum Intensity / Enslaved To Faith / The Oath & The Lie / Chapter Thirteen / Pain Zone / Exodus Day / Feast Of The Carnivore.
Maximum Intensity, Stay Heavy SHR 004-2 (2006). Maximum Intensity / Ghosts Of War / Over The Wall. Chart position: 2 FINLAND.

THORNCLAD

LINKÖPING, SWEDEN — *Viktor Klint (vocals / guitar), Filip Carlsson (guitar), Jonas Remne (bass), Adrian Hörnquist (drums).*

Linköping Thrash Metal band established by vocalist / guitarist Viktor Klint during 1995. As a solo concern the 'Demonseeds' demo emerged in 1996. Follow ups included the 1997 'Ravage' session before scoring a deal with Loud n' Proud Records. Newly introduced on guitar would be Filip Carlsson, whose scene credentials included terms with DAISY CHAIN, Black Metal project HÖST, ANCIENT DIGGER OF GRAVES, SATANIC SLAUGHTER and SPITEFUL. The album 'Coronation Of The Wicked' arrived in 1999 but with the demise of their label, THORNCLAD found themselves demoing again in 2000. The band folded some two years later.

THORNCLAD musicians Klint, Carlsson and drummer Adrian Hörnquist in union with GUTS and CEREMONIAL EXECUTION bass player Björn Ahlqvist formed Dark Metal combo DEMONS TO PREFER during 2002. Viktor Klint subsequently joined Filip Carlsson in CORPORATION 187.

Demonseeds, Thornclad (1996) (Demo).
Ravage, Thornclad (1997) (Demo). Ravage / Burned Within / Fiery Archways.
CORONATION OF THE WICKED, Loud 'n Proud LNP006 (1999). Coronation Of The Wicked / Master The Flesh / The End Of Sanity / Burned Within / Divine Departure / Two Leads One / In Written For Thoughts / Wounded Sun / Suffocator's Speech.
Promo 2000, Thornclad (2000) (Demo).

THRASHER

NEW YORK, NY, USA — *Brad Sinsel (vocals), Dan Beehler (vocals), Rhett Forrester (vocals), Maryann Scandiffio (vocals), Andy McDonald (guitar), Dan Spitz (guitar), Kenny*

The THRASHER project was put together by an assortment of New York based musicians upon the instigation of Combat Records.

Produced, directed and arranged by THE RODS drummer Carl Canedy in partnership with BLUE CHEER's guitarist Andy 'Duck' McDonald, the 'Burning At The Speed Of Light' album was issued in Britain through Music For Nations.

The majority of the material appeared to be sung by TKO vocalist Brad Sinsel, but the album also boasted lead performances from EXCITER's Dan Beehler, ex RIOT man RHETT FORRESTER and BLACK LACE's Maryann Scandiffio.

Musicianship was supplied by the aforementioned Canedy and McDonald. Joining them were TALAS bassist Billy Sheehan, VIRGIN STEELE's Jack Starr, ANTHRAX's Dan Spitz, H.S.A.S. bassist Kenny Aaronson, PAT TRAVERS / FLYING HAT BAND associate Mars Cowling, SAVOY BROWN's Kim Simmonds, ex ELF and RAINBOW drummer Gary Driscoll, HELSTAR's James Rivera, BLUE CHEER's Dickie Peterson and THE RODS bassist Gary Bordonaro.

BURNING AT THE SPEED OF LIGHT, Music For Nations MFN 45 (1985).

THRAWN

UPPSALA, SWEDEN — *Kjell Andersson (vocals), Niklas Rehn (guitar), Henrik Ohlsson (drums).*

The "Occult Thrash" Metal outfit THRAWN was first postulated during 2001, the result of creative discussions between Henrik Ohlsson, able to boast a wealth of associations to acts such as ADVERSARY, LEGIA, ALTERED AEON, SCAR SYMMETRY, DIABOLICAL, MUTANT and THEORY IN PRACTICE, and AZOTIC REIGN's Kjell Andersson. Due to the pair's schedules with their priority bands THRAWN, based in Uppsala, took some time to formulate but by 2002 guitarist Niklas had augmented the band roster. In February of 2003 the trio entered the studio to cut a EP 'Light Creates Shadows'. For these sessions, produced by CENTINEX and CARNAL FORGE member Jonas Kjellgren, Andersson took on lead vocals, Niclas rhythm guitar whilst Ohlsson handled guitar, bass and drums. Per Nilsson donated additional lead solos.

The band, adding the THEORY IN PRACTICE credited Anders Hedlund on bass and second guitarist Per Nilsson, subsequently evolved into ALTERED AEON. Signing to Black Lotus Records the band cut the album 'Dispiritism' for 2004 issue.

Light Creates Shadows, Thrawn (2003) (Demo). Dispirited Chambers / Patriots Of Sin (Aeternum Essentia) / Dreamscape Domain / Transcendence Duology.

THREINODY

DELHI, INDIA — *Siddharth Naidu (vocals / bass), Premik Jolly (guitar / keyboards), Satish Raj (drums).*

Delhi Progressive Thrash act. Although the band members T shirts have a spelling of 'Threnody' the band's title is in fact THREINODY. Outside of their interests in Heavy Metal the band members pursue more mundane activities with guitarist Premik Jolly employed in construction management, vocalist / bassist Siddharth Naidu a technical software writer whilst drummer Satish Raj works as a business networking consultant. Musically the group blend Thrash Metal with Progressive and even Psychedelic influences. Besides original material they pepper their set with covers from KREATOR and SLAYER as well as PINK FLOYD. The band scored well in local live competitions such as Delhi's 'Blitzkrieg' competition, where the band walked away with second place as well as an award for best drummer. The band earned top honours at National Law School's 'Strawberry Fields' competition 2000, beating nearly forty bands at this national level competition.

THREINODY projected a three song EP 'Trimetallicthreinonide' for 2003 issue. A 2004 live album, 'Live At AMC College', included cover versions of JUDAS PRIEST's 'Grinder', BLACK SABBATH's 'Children Of The Grave', VENOM's 'Countess Bathory', IRON MAIDEN's 'The Wickerman' METALLICA's 'Whiplash', SLAYER's 'South Of Heaven' and 'Mandatory Suicide', SODOM's 'Eat Me', BILLY JOEL's 'We Didn't Start The Fire' and the ROLLING STONES 'Paint It Black'.

LIVE AT AMC COLLEGE, Threinody (2004). Grinder / Blind Leading The Blind / Children Of The Grave / In Extremis / Countess Bathory / Cold Comfort / Alone Again / The Wickerman / We Didn't Start The Fire / Requiem / Eat Me / Existential Schism / South Of Heaven / Mandatory Suicide / Preaching To The Deaf / I Wanna Be Me / Whiplash / Paint It Black.

TIMELESS MIRACLE

SWEDEN — *Mikael Host (vocals / bass), Fredrik Nilsson (guitar / keyboards), Sten Möller (guitar), Jaime Salazar (drums).*

TIMELESS MIRACLE, a speed orientated Power Metal band, was forged during 2001 by vocalist / bassist Mikael Host and guitarist Fredrik Nilsson, both former members of TRAPPED. Initially Kim Widfors manned the drums, but after a few gigs he relocated abroad. Host and Nilsson recorded home demos during the Winter of 2003, which secured the promise of a label deal. Having opted to utilise Roasting House Studios in Malmö, the pair found themselves the subject of a new offer by the Roasting House production company in the management capacity. At this juncture second guitarist Sten Möller was enlisted and Jaime Salazar, a scene veteran of BAD HABIT, THE FLOWER KINGS and OPUS ATLANTICA, took up occupancy of the drum stool.

Securing a deal with Germany's Massacre Records, TIMELESS MIRACLE set to work on debut album 'Into The Enchanted Chamber' in August of 2004, working with producers Anders Theander and Pontus Lindmark. Salazar enrolled into the ranks of STONELAKE in 2007.

In The Year Of Our Lord, Timeless Miracle (2002) (Demo). In The Year Of Our Lord / Witches Of Black Magic / The Devil / The Church Of The Damned / Curse Of The Werewolf / Garden Of White Angel.
The Enchanted Chamber, Timeless Miracle (2003) (Demo). The Gathering / The Curse Pt. II: Return Of The Werewolf / Red Rose Pt. II / Last Hour Pt. III: The Gates Of Hell / The Curse Pt. I: Curse Of The Werewolf / Witches Of Black Magic.
The Voyage, Timeless Miracle (2004) (Demo). The Voyage / A Minor Intermezzo / Into The Enchanted Chamber / Down To The Gallows / Land Of Fantasy / Watchmen.
INTO THE ENCHANTED CHAMBER, Massacre MAS PC0482 (2005). Curse Of The Werewolf / Witches Of Black Magic / Into The Enchanted Chamber / The Devil / The Red Rose / A Minor Intermezzo / Return Of The Werewolf / Memories / The Gates Of Hell / Down To The Gallows / The Dark Side Forest / The Voyage.
INTO THE ENCHANTED CHAMBER, Avalon Marquee MICP-10521 (2005) (Japanese release). Curse Of The Werewolf / Witches Of Black Magic / Into The Enchanted Chamber / The Devil / The Red Rose / A Minor Intermezzo / Return Of The Werewolf / Memories / The Gates Of Hell / Down To The Gallows / The Dark Side Forest / The Voyage / Church Of The Damned.

TORANAGA

BRADFORD, YORKSHIRE, UK — *Mark Duffy (vocals), Andy Mitchell (guitar), Andy Burton (bass), Steve Todd (drums).*

Bradford, Yorkshire based Thrashers TORANAGA, named after a fictitious Shogun, formed in 1985 and as such benefited hugely from the late 80's British Thrash upsurge. Created with a line-up including ex-RIVAL bassist Andy Burton and erstwhile CHARGER drummer Steve Todd, vocalist Mark Duffy joined in February 1988 from the ranks of MILLENNIUM.

The band's first product was the Kevin Ridley produced mini-album 'Bastard Ballads', but the band's progress was stifled by Peaceville's distributor Red Rhino going bust just as the album was released. Nevertheless, the record secured the band enough attention to warrant a Radio One 'Friday Rock Show' session and serious interest from Chrysalis A&R man Alistair Cunningham.

Confusion arose when Duffy lent his vocals to MAJOR THREAT for their 1988 demo under the pseudonym of Dark Murphy. Peaceville Records were none too pleased and TORANAGA had to issue a statement to the effect that Duffy was still a full time member of the band and had not joined MAJOR THREAT. Other side activity had guitarist Andy Mitchell acting as producer on local colleague's AMNESIA's album 'Unknown Entity'. In 1989 TORANAGA performed in Europe, opening for VENOM in Holland and later hooked up with the joint SABBAT and MANOWAR expedition that winter. Chrysalis issued the album 'God's Gift' in 1990 to middling reviews. An EP, 'Eden—Beauty And The Beast', including a cover version of FLEETWOOD MAC's 'Oh Well', saw promotional issue in 1991. Notable gigs included supports to URIAH HEEP at London's Astoria and ANNIHILATOR at The Marquee. However, the band soon ran out of steam and called it a day.

In 1993 Duffy formed the more industrial flavoured THE SEED releasing a demo in 1995. This act would subsequently evolve into X-SEED issuing the 1996 'Desolation' album through the Bleeding Hearts label. Mark Duffy returned to the scene during 2006 fronting Teeside based FACE THE UNKNOWN.

BASTARD BALLADS, Peaceville VILE 5 (1988). Sentenced / Dealers In Death / Bastard Ballad / Soldiers Be Brave / Time To Burn / Retribution.

Hammer To The Skull, Chrysalis MHEP004 (1990) (UK promotion release split EP with SLAUGHTER, CHILD'S PLAY & TROUBLE TRIBE). MHEP004.

GOD'S GIFT, Chrysalis CHR 1771 (1990). The Shrine / Psychotic / Sword Of Damacles / Hammer To The Skull / Food Of The Gods / Disciples / Last Breath Of Life / Black Is The Mask.

Eden—Beauty And The Beast, Chrysalis (1991). Eden—Beauty And The Beast / Eternity's End / Pleasure From Pain / Oh Well.

TORCHBEARER

SWEDEN — *Pär Johansson (vocals), Christian Älvestam (guitar), Göran Johansson (guitar), Mikael Degerman (bass), Henrik Schönström (drums).*

TORCHBEARER, a Black tinged Thrash / Death Metal outfit assembled in 2003 comprises SATARIEL vocalist Pär Johansson, also a campaigner of THE DUSKFALL, DAWN OF DARKNESS and solo concern BELSEMAR. Joining the singer would be the UNMOORED, SOLAR DAWN and INCAPACITY pairing of guitarist Christian Älvestam and drummer Henrik Schönström, alongside the SETHERIAL, IMPIOUS, RINGHORNE and CHAOSDAEMON credited guitarist Göran Johansson. Bassist Mikael Degerman is active with SATARIEL and has held membership of STRIKEFORCE 666 and DAWN OF DARKNESS. Schönström also drums for TRAUMATIZED. The industrious Älvestam has an extended roll call of band endeavours such as CARNALIZED, ANDUIN '98, EVENDIM, LORD OF THRONES, ORGY OF FLESH, SATTYG, RED SKIES DAWNING, THE STINK BUG COLLECTIVE and DEN TIDLÖSA EVIGHETEN.

A debut album 'Yersinia Pestis', recorded at Black Lounge Studios in Sweden with CARNAL FORGE and CENTINEX guitarist Jonas Kjellgren acting as producer, was delivered in March of 2004. That same year Christian Älvestam would be found fronting Jonas Kjellgren's SCAR SYMMETRY band for their 'Symmetric In Design' debut.

TORCHBEARER's second album, 'Warnaments', recorded at Panic Room studios with producer Thomas Johansson, saw release in April 2006 through Regain Records. Christian Älvestam donated guest vocals to ZONARIA's 2006 debut album 'Rendered In Vain', featuring on the track 'Attending Annihilation'. TORCHBEARER members re-assembled in March 2007 to commence work on a fresh album.

YERSINIA PESTIS, Cold 14489-2 (2004). Assail The Creation / Sown Are The Seeds Of Death / Dead Children, Black Rats / Faith Bled Dry / Bearer Of The Torch / Pest Cometh / Fad Advanced Closure / Thus Came Dying Unto Kaffa / Shorespread God / Failure's Dawn.

WARNAMENTS, Regain RR106CD (2006). Dark Clouds Gathering / Last Line Of Defence / Burial Waters, Deepsome Graves / Swift Turns Of War / The Stale Drownings / Battlespawn / Where Night Is Total / Sealer Of Fates / The Blunt Weapon.

TORMENT

GERMANY — *Jörn Rüter (vocals / bass), Carsten Overbeck (guitar), Rudi Olhanson (drums).*

Noted exponents of Thrash n' Roll. TORMENT underwent various line-up changes from their inception in 1984 and released two self financed singles, 1987's notorious five tracker 'Bestial Sex' and the 1989 promotion release 'Das Neue', before signing to the Steamhammer label. TORMENT's debut line-up comprised vocalist / bassist Jörn 'Kannixx' Rüter, guitarist Carsten 'Tumanixx' Overbeck and ex-MINITAUR drummer Moulinix. The inaugural album was noted for its unfeasibly lengthy title of 'Experience A New Dimension Of Fear. The Horrors Of The Past Were Just A Taste Of Things To Come. Past Events Have Been Mere Hints Of Future Terrors. Everything So Far Has Only Been A Warning ...' It included a cover of MOTÖRHEAD's theme song 'Motorhead'. Touring to promote the record saw the band partnering with MESSIAH and ASSORTED HEAP for German dates and a notable appearance in front of 10,000 Rock fans at the 'Millerntor' festival in Hamburg.

A live 7" single, 'Sie Kam Zu Mir Am Morgen' pressed in delightful "blood in urine" coloured vinyl, was delivered in 1992 and the following year the group shared space with DESERT STORM and MINOTAUR for a split album release. 1997's 'Spermatized' was celebrated with a showing at that year's Wacken Open Air' festival and the headline 'Sperm Over Europe' tour.

TORMENT's 1999 album 'Not Dead Yet' sees another MOTÖRHEAD cover version with 'We Are The Road Crew' and a medley cover section of DEATH, VENOM and RAZOR songs. Once again, live promotion included an appearance at that year's 'Wacken Open Air' festival. TORMENT donated their rendition of 'Prisoner of our time' to a 2004 Remedy Records RUNNING WILD tribute. The band also featured their take on 'Denim And Leather' for the 2005 Remedy Records SAXON tribute album 'Eagleution'.

The band up a touring package with PARAGON and DARK AGE for September 2005 German dates. TORMENT loaned out drummer Christian Gripp to the headline act as substitute for an injured Markus Corby.

Bestial Sex EP, Torment (1987). State Of Torment / Bestial Sex / Deaf Metal / Chainsaw Massacre / What Shall We Do With A Drunken Torment.

Das Neue, Remedy RP 18 085 (1989). Das Neue / Shop 'Til Ya Drop.

EXPERIENCE A NEW DIMENSION OF FEAR. THE HORRORS OF THE PAST WERE JUST A TASTE OF THINGS TO COME. PAST EVENTS HAVE BEEN MERE HINTS OF FUTURE TERRORS. EVERYTHING SO FAR HAS ONLY BEEN A WARNING ..., Steamhammer SPV 084-76332 (1991). Intro / Acid Rain / Religious Insanity / Shop 'Til Ya Drop / Bestial Sex / Motörhead / Chainsaw Massacre / Drunken Torment / Cry For Justice / Slaves Of Technology / Das Neue / Crucifixion / Ballad Of Peter's Dog / State Of War / Liebe Freunde Von Torment.

NOT DEAD YET, Remedy (1999). Intro / T.T.T. / Not Dead Yet / Nature's Revenge / Evil Medley / Frankreich '98 (Live) / State Of War (Live) / Da bin ich zu doof zu (Live) / In The Name (Live) / Sie kam zu mir am Morgen (Live) / Iron Fist (Live) / Outbreak Of Evil (Live).

TORMENTATION, Remedy (2005). Intro / New World Terror / Tormentation / P.C. (Porn Casting) / Laws Of The Street / In The Name / Traitor's Fate / Politically Incorrect (And Damn Proud Of It) / Shop 'Til Ya Drop / The Calling / Not Dead Yet / Woman / Tribute To Tracii / State Of War / Please Don't Touch / Bestial Sex / Heavy Metal Hooligans / P.C. (Porn Casting) (Video).

TOURNIQUET

LOS ANGELES, CA, USA — *Luke Easter (vocals), Aaron Guerra (guitar), Victor Macias (bass), Ted Kirkpatrick (drums).*

Christian Progressive Thrash Metal band TOURNIQUET was founded by vocalist Greg Ritter, guitarist Greg Lanaire and drummer Ted Kirkpatrick. The band have developed from Speed Metal to a harsher, more abrasive style musically but have retained their trademark almost esoteric lyrical value. Although at first TOURNIQUET's message may seem rather obscure the lyrics are in fact always taken from biblical passages.

For their debut record Mark Lewis was on hand for extra guitar work. Lewis, along with Erik Jan James, would appear on the band photograph on the album sleeve in order to present TOURNIQUET as more of a complete band and not just the actual trio that they were.

Guitarist Erik Mendez was drafted for TOURNIQUET's 1991 album 'Psycho Surgery', which included a cover version of TROUBLE's 'The Tempter'.

Ritter departed in 1993 as did Mendez. The live 1993 album saw a guesting Les Carlsen of BLOODGOOD fame sessioning lead vocals.

Luke Easter took the vocal reins for the 'Vanishing Lessons' album and subsequent touring found second guitar player Aaron Guera of FINAL NOTICE enrolled. Longstanding member Lenaire opted out in 1996 shortly after the release of the 'Collected Works' compilation.

Bassist Victor Macias felt compelled to leave TOURNIQUET for 'theological' reasons as the band's activities did not sit easy with his Russian orthodox religion. The band finally replaced him in December 1997 with Vince Dennis, although by 1999 he too departed. Band founder Greg Lanaire forged CRIPPLE NEED CANE.

Latterly Ritter and Lenaire have reunited in a new act ECHO HOLLOW. A 2002 re-release of the debut 'Stop The Bleeding' album added both live and demo bonus tracks. Guitarist Aaron Guerra departed in September. TOURNIQUET marked a return in 2003 with the album 'Where Moth And Rust Destroy' for Metal Blade Records. This outing featured guest appearances by guitarists ex-MEGADETH guitarist MARTY FRIEDMAN and Bruce Franklin of TROUBLE. Guerra made a return to the ranks in October 2004.

TOURNIQUET put in an appearance at the all Christian Swedish Heavy Metal 'Bobfest' event at Folkets Park in Linkoping during March 2005. In mid 2006 band members bassist Victor Macias plus guitarists Erik Mendez and Gary Lenaire reunited with their brand new project 2050BELLS.

STOP THE BLEEDING, Intense (1990). The Test For Leprosy / Ready Or Not / Ark Of Suffering / Tears Of Korah / The Threshing Floor / You Get What You Pray For / Swarming Spirits / Whitewashed Tomb / Somnambulism / Virgin Widow And The Harlot Bride.

PATHOGENIC OCULAR DISSONANCE, Metal Blade CDZORRO 63 (1991). Embolism / Pathogenic Ocular Dissonance / Phantom Limb / Ruminating Virulence / Spectrophobic Dementia / Gelatinous Tubercles Of Purulent Ossification / Incommensurate / Exoskeletons / Theodicy On Trial / Descent Into The Maelstrom / En Hakkore / The Skeezix Dilemma / The Tempter.

PSYCHO SURGERY, Intense (1991). Psycho Surgery / A Dog's Breakfast / Viento Borrascoso (Devastating Wind) / Vitals Fading / Spineless / Dysfunctional Domicile / Broken Chromosomes / Steotaxic Atrocities / Officium Defunctorum.

INTENSE PRESENTS VOL. 2: TOURNIQUET LIVE, Intense (1993). Phantom Limb / Medley: Ark Of Suffering-Stereotaxix Atrocities / Whitewashed Tomb / The Skeezix Dilemma / The Tempter / The Messiah.

VANISHING LESSONS, Intense (1994). Bearing Gruesome Cargo / Pecking Order / Drowning Machine / Pushin' Broom / Vanishing Lessons / My Promise / Acid Head / K517 / Twilight / Your Take / Sola Christus.

CARRY THE WOUNDED, (1995). Carry The Wounded / When The Love Is Right (To Lizett) / Oh Well / My Promise / Heads I Win, Tails You Loose.

THE COLLECTED WORKS, Intense (1996). Perfect Night For A Hanging / Vanishing Lessons / Pathogenic Ocular Dissonance / Twilight / Psycho Surgery / You Get What You Pray For / Acidhead / Broken Chromosomes / Viento Borrascoso / Carry The Wounded / Bearing Gruesome Cargo / The Skeezix Dilemma / Ark Of Suffering / The Hand Trembler.

CRAWL TO CHINA, Benson (1997). Claustrospelunker / Crawl To China / Enveloped In Python / White Knucklin' The Rosary / If I Was There / The Tell Tale Heart / Bats / Proprioception: The Line Knives Syndrome / Tire Kicking / If Pigs Could Fly / Crank (The Knife) / Stumblefoot / Imaginary Friend / Going, Going ... Gone / America.

ACOUSTIC ARCHIVES, (1998). Viento Borrascoso / Vanishing Lessons / Claustrospelunker / Bearing Gruesome Cargo / Phantom Limb / Bats / Heads I Win, Tails You Lose / Twilight / If Pigs Could Fly / Trivializing The Momentous, Complicating The Obvious.

MICROSCOPIC VIEW OF A TELESCOPIC REALM, Metal Blade 14289 (2000). Besprinkled In Scarlet Horror / Drinking From The Poisoned Well / Microscopic View Of A Telescopic Realm / The Tomb Of Gilgamesh / Servant Of The Bones / Erratic Palpitations Of The Human Spirit / Martyr's Pose / Immunity Vector / Indulgence By Proxy / Caixa de Raiva / The Skeezix Dilemma Part II (The Improbable Testimony Of The Pipsisewah).

WHERE MOTH AND RUST DESTROY, (2003). Where Moth And Rust Destroy / Restoring The Locust Years / Drawn And Quartered / A Ghost At The Wheel / Architeuthis / Melting The Golden Call / Convoluted Absolutes / Healing Waters Of The Tigris / In Death We Rise.

TOXIC HOLOCAUST

BOSTON, MA, USA — Initially a solo Black Thrash act, Boston's TOXIC HOLOCAUST date to 1999, then functioning as a full band unit and debuting with the 'Radiation Sickness' demo. The group folded in 2001 but would be resurrected by Joel Grind. Utilising a drum machine Grind cut tracks for a split 7" single, limited to 1000 copies, shared with OPRICHNIKI. In 2002 progress was highlighted by distribution of the 'Critical Mass' demo. Signing to the German Witches Brew label TOXIC HOLOCAUST issued the 'Evil Never Dies' album in 2003. A four way EP in union with NOCTURNAL, BESTIAL MOCKERY and VOMITOR was also plotted.

TOXIC HOLOCAUST toured Canada with Toronto's RAMMER in October 2006. The band united with New Zealand's DIOCLETIAN and Japan's ABIGAIL in March 2007 for Australian dates.

EVIL NEVER DIES, Witches Brew (2003). Evil Never Dies / War Is Hell / Enemy Of Jesus / Damned To Fire / Exxxecutioner / 666 / Summon The Beast / Demise / Warfare / Dead To The World / Fallout / Atomik Destruktor.

TOXIC SHOCK

GERMANY — *Uwe Dießenbacher (vocals), Tim Atwater (guitar), Manuel Kriessig (guitar), Geoff Atwater (bass), Klaus Kreissig (drums).*

A German Thrash act initially boasting the brotherly duo of guitarist Tim and bassist Geoff Atwater, both had left the group after the release of the 'Change From Reality' album in 1988. Atwater later saw action with the Stuttgart act CHERRY RED. Uwe Dießenbacher briefly combined bass and vocal duties before the band dispensed with his services altogether and drafted in bassist Phillip Kneule and lead vocalist Kai Weber as TOXIC SHOCK switched to Nuclear Blast for 1990's 'Welcome Home ... Near Dark' album. Former bassist Andreas Mailänder would go on to join BRAINSTORM.

1992's 'Between Good And Evil' album saw a further switch to Massacre Records and a heavier direction, TOXIC SHOCK now coming across as more of a Death Metal unit.

CHANGE FROM REALITY, Mind Control (1988). Breakout / Burning Down Your Life / Forbidden Lust / Mad Sounds / State Of Madness / Overloaded / Raging Speed / Left To Die / United Forces.

TOXIK

WELCOME HOME... NEAR DARK, Nuclear Blast NB027 (1990). Intro / Behind The Guillotine / Change From Reality / Dragon's Eye (The Story Part One) / World Power Rules / True Insanity / One End / Welcome Home... Near Dark (The Story Part Two) / Termination / The Challenge.

BETWEEN GOOD AND EVIL, Massacre CD008 (1992). Mental Mutilation / Suffocation / Terror / Choose Your Way / Nice Childhood / Between Good And Evil / White Death / Senseless Massacre / What Dwells Within / Exit.

TOXIK

NEW YORK, NY, USA — *Charles Sabin (vocals), Josh Christian (guitar), John Donnelly (guitar), Brian Bonini (bass), Tad Leger (drums).*

New York Thrash Metal band debuted for Roadrunner Records in 1988 with the 'World Circus' album. TOXIK added second guitarist John Donnelly prior to beginning work on their second album, 'Think This', in Florida. A few months later vocalist Mike Sanders was replaced by Charlie Sabin.

In 2005 former TOXIK drummer Tad Leger has launched a brand new project entitled LUCERTOLA, this union featuring BLACKENED SKY's Andy Abbene and his brother guitarist Jay Abbene of WRATHCHILD AMERICA and SOULS AT ZERO repute.

Following re-mastered limited edition digipack re-issue of the TOXIK albums 'World Circus' and 'Think This' in January 2007 through Poland's Metal Mind Productions label the band, counting singer Mike Sanders, guitarist Josh Christian, bassist Brian Bonini with Lou Caldarola on drums, announced a reunion.

WORLD CIRCUS, Roadrunner RR 349572 (1988). Heart Attack / Social Overload / Pain And Misery / Voices / Door To Hell / World Circus / 47 Seconds Of Sanity / False Prophets / Haunted Earth / Victims.

THINK THIS, Roadracer RO 94602 (1989). Think This / Creed / Spontaneous / There Stood The Fence / Black And White / WIR NJN 8 (In God) / Machine Dream / Shotgun Logic / Time After Time / Technical Arrogance / Out On The Tiles.

There Stood The Fence, Roadracer (1989). There Stood The Fence / Out On The Tiles.

TRAGEDIAN

HAMBURG, GERMANY — *Timo Behrens (vocals), Gabriele Palermo (guitar / keyboards), Marc Schönberg (bass).*

Hamburg melodic Heavy Metal band. Founded in August of 2002, under the name 7TH HOUR, by guitarist Gabriele Palermo and ARCTIC FIELDS drummer Alex Tabisz the band at first featured a female singer Nathalie Paustaian, bassist Marc Schönberg and Mike Breeze on keyboards. However, by that October Jürg Steinbrenner of BAD INFLUENCE had been enlisted as lead vocalist. Guitarist Ingo Salzmann and bassist Marc Schönberg would also be active with ARCTIC FIELDS.

Line-up changes saw Paustaian replaced by vocalist guitarist Jürg Steinbrenner and on 13th April 2003 the group, now re-billed as TRAGEDIAN, debuted live sharing a bill with BLACKHAWK and PARAGON. However, that same month drummer Alex bailed out, TRAGEDIAN persevering on the live front by pulling in BAD INFLUENCE's Timur Tatilici as substitute.

Although TRAGEDIAN undertook recordings for a debut album in April of 2004, working at Tornado Studios in Hamburg with Lars Ratz of METALIUM acting as producer, the band would also be advertising for both a new singer and drummer. Patrick Van Maurik, of REVIVER and ex-MONTANY, duly took up the role of frontman. In early 2005 TRAGEDIAN donated their version of 'Motorcycle Man' to the Remedy Records SAXON tribute album 'Eaglelution—A Tribute To Saxon'. Further evolution of the band found Timo Behrens taking over as frontman.

Announced in early March 2007, guitarist Gabriele Palermo was found to be involved with FOGALORD, an Italian "all-star" epic Heavy Metal project fronted up by SYNTHPHONIA SUPREMA and TRAGEDIAN session keyboard player Dany All with Terence Holler from ELDRITCH on vocals and Frank Andiver, ex-LABYRINTH, WONDERLAND and ORACLE SUN, on drums.

Demo 2003, Tragedian (2003). Conquerors / Ocean's Call / Dreamscape / Immortality.

TRANSFIXION

SANTO ANDRÉ, SP, BRAZIL — *Rogério Fichi (vocals / bass), Nelson Lima (guitar), Max Pinho (guitar), Julio Carvalhal (drums).*

Santo André Metal band created in October of 1996 counting an original formation comprising ex-VIOLENT vocalist / bassist Rogério Fichi, former TREVAS and ACID ANGEL guitarist Nelson Lima, ex-PRIME MOVER guitarist Marcos Melo and erstwhile MX man Alexandre Cunha on drums. The group's debut live show came with a support to German Thrashers SODOM in Folclore during 1997.

The line evolved over time to see a 2002 formation seeing Fichi and Lima joined by Cleber Uehara on guitar and ex-BALTA drummer Filipe Baptista. By 2003 TRANSFIXION had dispensed with both Uehara and Baptista, drafting Max Pinho, of BRUTAL, DEAD KILLER, FURIA TRIBAL and NEGATIVE CONTROL, on guitar and Julio Carvalhal on the drums.

The 2004 TRANSFIXION album 'What's Real?' featured studio guests Marcelo Pompeu and Heros Trench of KORZUS, Vitor Rodrigues from TORTURE SQUAD, Fred Campos from ALEISTER C. and Ricardo Peres of SEVENTH SEAL.

THE LAST HORIZON, Moria (2000). Slipping Away / Regret / Our Games / Solarization / Journey To Infinity / Delusion / Founder Against Manslaughter / The Last Horizon / EWAP.

WHAT'S REAL?, Transfixion (2004).

TRANSMETAL

MEXICO CITY, MEXICO — *Bruno Blazquez (vocals), Juan Partida (guitar), Lorenzo Partida (bass), Javier Partida (drums).*

Ciudad Azteca, Mexico City's TRANSMETAL, centred upon the erstwhile TEMPLE DE ACERO sibling Partida triumvirate of guitarist Juan, bassist Lorenzo and drummer Javier, is amongst the very biggest of Mexican Rock acts, having performed in Mexico, the United States, El Salvador, Colombia, Ecuador, Peru and Bolivia. The studs n' leather bedecked TRANSMETAL, founded during January 1987, have stuck to their Thrash / Speed Metal stance over nearly twenty Spanish language albums.

Upon their formation TRANSMETAL was fronted by vocalist Alberto Pimentel, who featured on the 1988 debut 'Muerto En La Cruz', produced by DARK ANGEL's Eric Meyer, and the follow up 'Desear Un Funeral'. On June 18th 1989 the group opened for DEATH at the Naucalpan Arena Lopez Mateos.

In 1990 Pimentel departed to found LEPROSSY. Alejandro González of ILLUSION, and subsequently frontman for ARKHE, would fill the vacancy before Juan Carlos Camarena took the role of second guitarist. The band featured on the high profile 'New Titans Over Mexico' tour of 1991, these shows sharing billing with SACRED REICH in January, KREATOR in July and SEPULTURA in December. On May 3rd 1992 TRANSMETAL supported OVERKILL at the Arena A. Lopez Mateos in Tlanepantla then appeared as part of the 'Mexican Mosh' festival alongside SICK OF IT ALL, DEICIDE and NUCLEAR ASSAULT. The album that year, 'Amanecer En El Mausoleu', featured a cover version of 'Killers' by French band KILLERS. On November 8th the band scored the high profile support to BLACK SABBATH's concert at the Palacio de los Deportes in Mexico City.

1992 witnessed the departure of these latest two recruits and Alberto Pimental resumed activities with the band on a stand in basis. A successful Mexican tour during October found TRANSMETAL headlining over MORTUARY and INQUISIDOR. The band's status would engender a further slot at the March 1993 'Mexican Mosh' festival event, this time sharing honours with OVERKILL, KREATOR and MONSTROSITY among others.

The following year TRANSMETAL, together with fellow native acts ANGELS DE INFIERNO and RATA BLANCA, represented Mexico at the June 1994 'Monstruos De Rock' gathering in Spain. The group notably guested for SLAYER on September 10th at the Mexico City Balneario Olimpico.

Pimentel would opt out yet again to forge another version of LEPROSY (spelt with one 'S' on this occasion) assembling a new band including RAMSES guitarist Julio Marquez and ex-INQUISIDOR drummer Felipe Chacon.

TRANSMETAL took onboard the esteemed former LUZBEL and HUIZAR frontman Arturo Huizar as their lead vocalist but by February 1998 two members of PANIC, vocalist Mauricio Torres and guitarist 'Eric Towers' (a.k.a. Ernesto Torres) stabilised the band for the album 'Las Alas Del Emperador'. Meantime, Lorenzo Partida and ex-TRANSMETAL vocalist Alejandro González would create the side project ULTRATUMBA. TRANSMETAL's show at the Adolph Lopez Mateos de Tlalnepantla Arena in Mexico City in July 1999 was filmed and recorded, subsequently put out as two live discs 'dubbed XIII Años ... En Vivo—Primera Parte' and 'XIII Años ... En Vivo—Segunda Parte'.

TRANSMETAL took a novel approach of recording tracks for two albums at once, 'Tristeza De Lucifer' and 'De Bajo De Los Cielos Púrpura', these sessions held in Hammond, Indiana with producer Mike Sheffield. Upon the release of 'Tristeza De Lucifer' the group toured South America during 2001. Shows in Bogota, Colombia, Manizales and Calí in Colombia, River basin in Ecuador, Arequipa in Peru, La Paz and Santa Cruz in Bolivia would prove a first for a Mexican Metal band. 'De Bajo De Los Cielos Púrpura' then arrived in July 2000, prompting a 30 date run of shows across the USA. That same year the debut album 'Muerto En La Cruz' would see a CD re-issue, adding four extra tracks. The band's legacy would be honoured in 2001 with the delivery of no less than two tribute albums in 'Milicia Infernal ... Tributo a Transmetal' and the live 'Milicia Infernal ... Tributo A Transmetal (En Vivo)', both released on the Denver label. Those paying homage included LUZBEL, PANIC, DISGORGE, RICTER, ALLUSION, ULTRATUMBA, DOMAIN, IRA, A.N.I.M.A.L., LEPRYCORN and MECHANICAL CHAOS.

TRANSMETAL returned in September 2002 with the experimental 'El Amor Supremo', this album, their very first to incorporate keyboards and recorded at Studio 880 in San Pablo California, seeing production duties going to the CANCER, DEATH, DISINCARNATE, TESTAMENT and KONKHRA credited guitarist JAMES MURPHY. The band's December 2003 album, 'Lo Podrido Corona La Inmensidad', saw keyboard contributions coming from Erick Fuentes Quintana and a guest guitar solo on the track 'Creador De La Amargura' from JAMES MURPHY.

2004 saw TRANSMETAL tackling an album, 'Temple De Acero', comprising entirely of cover versions including the SCORPIONS 'The Zoo', CANDLEMASS' 'At The Gallows End', CELTIC FROST's 'Return To The Eve' and 'Dethroned Emperor', ACCEPT's 'Balls To The Wall', AC/DC's 'Back In Black' and 'Let Me Put My Love Into You', SODOM's 'Remember The Fallen', BLACK SABBATH's 'Evil Woman', DEATH's 'Evil Death', URIAH HEEP's 'Free And Easy' and TWISTED SISTER's 'The Kids Are Back'.

A notable compilation issued in June that same year, '17 Years Down In Hell', re-worked the tracks from the previous two albums, 'El Amor Supremo' and 'Lo Podrido Corona La Inmensidad', in English language. An unaccredited track, a newly recorded version of 'Aborrecer Al Forence', saw Mauricio Torres on vocals. New studio album 'El Despertar De La Adversidad' arrived in February 2006, capitalised on by a run of Mexican shows, gigs in Honduras, El Salvador, Guatemala and spot US gigs. The band would be back in the recording studio before the end of the year cutting the 'Progresión Neurótica' album for November.

MUERTO EN LA CRUZ, Denver DCD 3058 (1988). Transmetal / Castigo Del Creador / Enviado Del Infierno / Rostro Maligno / Los Criminales Morirán / La Horca / Milicia Infernal / Desciende A La Oscuridad / Muerto En La Cruz.

Desear Un Funeral EP, (1989). El Enterrador / Tiburón De Metal / Killers / R.D.D. (Regalo De Satán) / Fuerza Invisible ?¿?

SEPELIO EN EL MAR, Denver DCD 3039 (1989). Desear Un Funeral / El Llamado De La Muerte / Obscuridad Atroz / El Profanador / Temor A La Cruz / Camino Al Cementerio / Exhumado / Atormentado Del Cerebro / Sepelio En El Mar.

ZONA MUERTA, Denver DCD 3061 (1990). Invasores / Toxico Industrial / Tus Dias Estan Contados / Zona Muerta / Sufrimiento Quimico / El Unico Oscuro / Prediccion Terrestre / Mundo Quemado.

EN CONCIERTO VOL. 2, Denver DCD 3063 (1992). El Llamado De La Muerte / Killers / Tus Dias Estan Contados / El Infierno De Dante / Simon El Enterrador / Prediccion / Terrestre / Atormentado Del Cerebro / Sufrimiento Quimico / Zona Muerta.

AMANECER EN EL MAUSELEO, Denver DCD 3060 (1992). Enviado Del Infierno / La Horca / El Enterrador / Temor A La Cruz / Fuerza Invisible / Sufrimiento Quimico / Rostro Maligno / Killers / Exhumado / Amanecer En El Mausoleo / Mundo Quemado.

BURIAL AT SEA, Grindcore International 89804-2 (1992). Wishing A Funeral / The Call Of Death / Atrocious Obscurity / Profaner / Fear Of The Cross / The Road To The Graveyard / Exhumated / Tormented Brain / Burial at Sea.

EN CONCIERTO VOL. 1, Denver DCD 3062 (1992). Invasores / Exhumado / Enviado Del Infierno / Rostro Maligno / Tóxico Industrial / Temor A La Cruz / El Llamado De La Hembra / La Horca / Sepelio En El Mar.

DANTE'S INFERNO, Denver DCD 3046 (1993). Dante's Inferno / Abysmal Emptiness / Flames Of Purification / Septic Veneration / Magnificent Height / Hymn For Him / Damned Pits / Mystical Universe Stars / Re-encounter With Beatriz / Last Day's Shadow.

EL INFIERNO DE DANTE, Denver DCD 3045 (1993). El Infierno De Dante / Vacío Abismal / Las Llamas De La Purificación / Séptico Y Veneración / Altura Magnificente / Himno Para El / Fosas Malditas / Místicas Estrellas Del Universo / Reencuentro Con Beatriz / El Ultimo Día Sombrío.

CRÓNICAS DE DOLOR, Denver DCD 3049 (1994). Subyugado / Aborrecer Al Forense / Regodearse En La Gula / The Call Of The Woman / Muerte Violenta / La Ley Del Talion / Deceso Espiritual / Transmetal.

MÉXICO BÁRBARO, Denver DSD 6005 (1996). Mexico Barbaro / Dios Nos Agarre Confesados / Arboleda De Ahorcados / Llanto En El Paraiso / Poder Y Pudrician / Angel Enfermo / Fariseos / Mito De La Sangre / Miserable / Ceveline / Rio Rojo / Elegiaco.

EL LLAMADO DE LA HEMBRA, Denver DSD 6110 (1996). El Llamado De La Hembra / Muerte Violenta / Toxico Industrial / Poder Y Pudricion / Angel Enfermo / Killers / Invasores / Elegiaco / El Infierno De Dante.

LAS ALAS DEL EMPERADOR, Denver DSD 6025 (1998). Tumbas De Insomnio / Celdas De La Divinidad / Perpetua Monstruosidad / Iglesia Interior / XIII / Las Alas Del Emperador / Santisimo Sufrimiento / Cenizas Humanas / Sombras Del Purgatorio / Monarca De Los Sonambulos / Jardin Seco / Orgasmatron.

XIII ANOS … EN VIVO VOL. 2, Denver DSD 6079 (1999). Orgasmatron / Zona Muerta / Las Llamas De La Purificación / El Infierno De Dante / Angel Enfermo / Sombras Del Purgatorio / Las Alas Del Emperador / La Horca / Killers / Iglesia Interior.

XIII ANOS … EN VIVO VOL. 1, Denver DSD 6078 (1999). Exhumado / Tumbas De Insomnio / Vacío Abismal / México Bárbaro / Aborrecer Al Forense / Perpetua Monstruosidad / Santísimo Sufrimiento / Enviado Del Infierno / Rostro Maligno / Invasores / El Llamado De La Hembra.

DE BAJO DE LOS CIELOS PURPURA, Denver DSD 6106 (2000). De Bajo De Los Cielos Parpura / Replicante / Humanidad De Mairmol / Marcado Por El Demonio / Decorado Con Clavos / Glorificacian De La Fornicacian / Espantosa Enfermedad / Parricida / Clacinado Por Pecados / La Pas De Mi Dolor.

TRISTEZA DE LUCIFER, Denver DCD 6186 (2001). Tristeza De Lucifer / Las Letanías De Satán / Estigmatizado / Ansias De Muerte / Sin Paraíso / Lamento De Un Ángel Traicionero / Martirio / Imperdonable / Sacrilegio / Sepulcro Engusanado.

EL AMOR SUPREMO, Denver DSD 6258 (2002). El Amor Supremo / Un Océano De Tentaciones / Vendí Mi Alma / Encarnación Del Fuego / Vehemente / Servidor Infinito / Invocación Y Conjuración / El Placer Mas Alto / Adoración Y Entrega / Un Pacto Escrito Con Sangre.

LO PODRIDO CORONA LA INMENSIDAD, Denver DSD 6277 (2003). De Rodillas En La Suciedad / Lo Podrido Corona La Inmensidad / Creador De La Amargura / Flagelación / Condenado A La Miseria / Guerra Sagrada / Avaricia Terrestre / Dolor / Maldecido Con La Existencia / Mar Y Sol.

17 YEARS DOWN IN HELL, Denver DSD 6307 (2005). Creator Of Bitterness / The Highest Pleasure / Incarnation Of Fire / Infinite Crown Of Decay / Condemned To Misery / The Supreme Love / Fagelation / On Your Knees In Filth / Orgasmatron / Celdas De La Divinidad / Aborrecer Al Forense.

TEMPLE DE ACERO, Denver DSD 6305 (2005). The Zoo / At The Gallow's End / Return To The Eve / Balls To The Wall / Let Me Put / Remember The Fallen / Evil Woman / Back In Black / Dethroned Emperor / Evil Death / Free And Easy / The Kids Are Back / Dos Metros Bajo Tierra / El Brillo De Tu Miseria.

EL DESPERTAR DE LA ADVERSIDAD, Denver (2006). Astrólogo / El Despertar De La Adversidad / Mendigo Pestilente / Por Tu Propia Codicia / Supremacía / Curtido En La Interperie / Alabanza A La Calamidad / Donde El Deseo Nunca Arde / Ave Negra / El Arbol Del Suicidio.

PROGRESIÓN NEURÓTICA, (2006). Carbonizado / Habitante De Una Mente Insana / Boquea En Diciembre / La Mañana Siempre Viene Gris / Ciclo Polar / Progresión Neurótica / Solitaria Muerte Por Melancolía / Muerto … Es Mejor / Viento Malévolo / Flores Sobre Mi Ataúd.

TRANSPARENT

DENMARK — *René Pedersen (vocals), Danny Hove Jensen (guitar), Signar Petersen (guitar / bass), Brian Rasmusen (drums).*

TRANSPARENT is an August 2003 founded Danish Metal band comprising the LOST, FAILED and LEMURIA credited vocalist René Pedersen, guitarist Danny Hove Jensen, ex-MERCENARY, SUDDEN DEATH, BEHIND THE CURTAIN and NUGATORY man Signar Petersen on guitar and bass with Brian 'Brylle' Rasmusen of INVOCATOR and MNEMIC repute on drums. A demo, 'Mutual Assured Destruction' recorded in late 2004 at Apole Studios and co-produced by the band with MERCENARY's Casper Skafte, Morten Sandager, surfaced in April 2005. That same year Rasmussen forged SMAXONE, comprising ELOPA's Claus Lillelund, handling "clean" vocals, and guitarist Casper Skafte in union with MNEMIC's Michael Bøgballe on "Distorted" vocals.

René Pedersen was named as new bassist of MERCENARY in May 2006.

Mutual Assured Destruction, Transparent (2005) (Danish promotion release). Why / Defcon 5 / Mutual Assured Destruction / Unparalleled / Nothingness.

TRAUMA

ITALY — *Sergio Cioce (vocals / guitar), Samuel Desarlo (bass), Daniele Defranchis (guitar), Leonardo Andreotti (drums).*

Thrashers TRAUMA, established during 1997, released the demo 'Garden Of Vanity' in 1998. Recording line-up for these sessions comprised vocalist / guitarist Sergio Cioce, guitarist Ivan Annoni, bass player Samuel 'Zama' Desarlo with Leonardo Andreotti on drums. By the second demo, 1999's 'Believer Will Be Lost …', Annoni had left the fold. TRAUMA's next effort, now with Daniele Ippe Defranchis of RANDOM on second guitar, would be the full length album 'Grip Of Frost'.

In 2003 TRAUMA changed musical direction, adding guitarist Massimiliano 'Flash' Sangiorgi and evolving into the Nu-Metal styled ALTERHATE. The demo 'Destroy' arrived in 2004.

Garden Of Vanity, Trauma demo (1998). Consciousness To Be / Fight To Survive / Statue / Trauma.

Believer Will Be Lost …, (1999). Frenesy / Pray The Lord / Messiah.

GRIP OF FROST, (2000). Degeneration / Grip Of Frost / Pray The Lord / Black Demise / Lunacy / Too Many Fucking Faces / Virtual Years / Sandglassman / White & Gray / Do Ut Des.

TRIBULATION

ARVIKA, SWEDEN — *Johannes Andersson (vocals / bass), Jonathan Hultén (guitar), Adam Zaars (guitar), Jakob Johansson (drums).*

Thrash / Death combo TRIBULATION came together during 2001 under the original branding of HAZARD. The group, hailing from Arkiva in the southwest of Sweden, first featured guitarists Jonathan Hultén, of TRAKTOR, and Adam Zaars, TERROR, CORRUPTED and MASS HYPNOSIS bassist Joseph Tholl with Jonas Wikstrand of LEPROSY on drums. This unit cut the demo 'Aggression Within'. The CORRUPTED and LEPROSY credited Olof Wikstrand took over on bass during 2002. Singer Johannes Andersson came on board the following year.

Switching title to TRIBULATION, the band underwent a radical line-up shift in 2004, as both Olaf and Jonas Wikstrand exited. FERAL's Jimmie Frödin briefly occupied the drum stool, for the demo 'Agony Awaits', before Jakob Johansson enrolled. Re-billed as TRIBULATION, they recorded a further demo, 'The Ascending Dead', in June 2005. That same year Jonatan Hultén forged a new outfit billed GUERILLA.

The Ascending Dead, Tribulation (2005) (Demo). Island Of The Flesh Eaters / Cannibal Feast / C.H.V: The Gore Attack / Soul Tribulation.

Putrid Rebirth, Blood Harvest (2006). Dread City Of Death / Zombie Holocaust / Imprisoned In Abhorrence / Churning Sea Of Absu.

TRIBULATION

SURAHAMMAR, SWEDEN — *Mikael Tossavainen (vocals / guitar), Stefan Neuman (guitar), Daniel Hojas (bass), Magnus Forsberg (drums).*

Surahammar Thrash Metal band formed in the mid 80s as PENTAGRAM by Toza (a.k.a. Mikael Tossavainen) on vocals and guitar, Stefan Neuman on second guitar, Daniel Hojas on bass and Magnus Forsberg on the drums. Under this guise the band issued two demos including October 1986's 'Infernal Return' and a self-titled February 1987 demo prior to the name change.

A demo, 'Pyretic Convulsions', emerged in March 1988 with the 'Void Of Compassion' then the band had their track 'Belicose Nations' on the compilation album 'Hardcore For The Masses—The Core Of Sweden'. The 'Posers In Love' session, recorded at Musikstugan Studios, arriving in December 1990. On the live front, the group supported the likes of NAPALM DEATH, MUCKY PUP, CARCASS and ENTOMBED. TRIBULATION's first commercially available recording, 'Is This Heavy Or What?', was a joint EP shared with ATROCITY, DAMIEN and GRAVITY. The group since released two albums through Black Mark, starting with February 1992's 'Clown Of Thorns', the vinyl version of which hosted an extra track entitled 'Dogmother'. The 1993 demo 'Oil Up The Stud', followed by on Burning Heart, 1995's 'Spicy'. The band folded that same year.

Tossavainen has scene affiliations with PUFFBALL and THE RUSSIAN FIVE whilst both Neuman and Hojas have KENTISK BROSK ties. Magnus Forsberg scored credits with PUFFBALL, EXECUTION, DISSOBER and BOMBS OF HADES.

Is This Heavy Or What?, Is This Heavy Or What ITHW-EP 001 (1988) (Split 7" vinyl EP with DAMIEN, ATROCITY and GRAVITY). Pecuniary Aid.

Pyretic Convulsions, Tribulation (1988) (Demo). Encroached Visions / Pecuniary Aid / Where Nothing Remains / The Conjuring / Dogmother.

Void Of Compassion, Tribulation (1990) (Demo). Beautiful Views / Irrevocable Act / Sudden Revulsion / Detained / Angst.

Posers In Love, Tribulation (1990) (Demo). Angel In Winterpile / My World Is Different / Everythings Floating / Down My Lungs.

CLOWN OF THORNS, Black Mark BMLP 16 (1992). Borka Intro / Born Bizarre / My World Is Different / Rise Of Prejudice / Everything's Floating / Safe Murder Of Emotions / Angst / Decide (Take A Stand) / Angel In A Winterpile / Beautiful Views / Landslide Of Losers / Down My Lungs / Pick An Image (Make Sure It Sells) / Herr Ober / Tiny Little Skeleton / Disgraceland / Dogmother.

CLOWN OF THORNS, Tribulation BMCD 16 (1992). Borka Intro / Born Bizarre / My World Is Different / Rise Of Prejudice / Everything's Floating / Safe Murder Of Emotions / Angst / Decide (Take A Stand) / Angel In Winterpile / Beautiful Views / Landslide Of Losers / Down My Lungs / Pick An Image / Herr Ober / Tiny Little Skeleton / Disgraceland.

Oil Up The Stud, Tribulation (1993) (Demo). Bridge To The Backyard Of My Mind / Free From Forever / Sick Trip / Equipment Glow.

SPICY, Burning Heart BHR012 (1995). Cute / Torn To A Puzzle / Strength Into Slime / The Bridge … / Low / Bitter Boy / On The Air.

TRIVIUM

ALTAMONTE SPRINGS, FL, USA — *Matt Heafy (vocals / guitar), Corey Beaulieu (guitar), Brent Young (bass), Travis Smith (drums).*

An Altamonte Springs, Florida Death / Thrash styled Metal act originally created in 2000 when the group's original singer viewed guitarist Matt Heafy conducting a rendition of THE OFFSPRING's 'Self Esteem' with drummer Travis Smith in order to enter a high school 'Battle of the bands' contest. The name TRIVIUM was chosen, a Latin word meaning the intersection between three schools of learning, namely grammar, rhetoric and logic, as it implied an open mindedness towards varying musical styles. Line-up changes then saw the addition of Brent Young on rhythm guitar and Heafy took over the lead vocal role, following several party gigs. The following year Richie Brown of Black Metal outfit MINDSCAR filled in as bassist for live work but subsequently Young switched instruments to cover this position.

2002 would prove a pivotal year for the group as TRIVIUM claimed top honours at the school 'Battle of the bands' contest, supported national acts PESSIMIST and PISSING RAZORS and Heafy won the local 'Orlando Metal Awards' as best guitarist. A self-financed album would see Jason Suecof of CAPHARNAUM acting as producer as the band found itself being hailed as frontrunners in the New Wave of American Heavy Metal stakes. TRIVIUM, signing to the Lifeforce label for the 'Ember To Inferno' follow up, cut at Audiohammer Studios, added Corey Beaulieu as second guitarist in September 2003.

The group re-entered Audiohammer Studios in mid May 2004 to commence pre-production for their Roadrunner Records debut album, subsequently re-selecting producer Jason Suecof for the final recordings. TRIVIUM acted as support to ICED EARTH and BEYOND THE EMBRACE for Summer shows in the US. The group forged an alliance with MACHINE HEAD and CHIMAIRA for the August 'RoadRage 2004' dates in North America.

TRIVIUM entered Tampa's Morrisound studios on September 13th with Jason Suecof once again for recording of their sophomore album entitled 'Ascendancy'. Mastering would be conducted by ex-SABBAT guitarist Andy Sneap in the UK. In November the group added former METAL MILITIA bassist Paolo Gregoletto to the ranks. The album sold 6,976 copies in its first week of release to debut at number 151 on the US Billboard charts. The band had their track 'Like Light To The Flies' featured on the soundtrack to the 'Rainbow Six Lockdown' game issued by 3volution Productions.

The band opened 2005 with a set of US headlining dates in January, heading up a touring package with ALL THAT REMAINS, IT DIES TODAY and THE ACACIA STRAIN. Gigs into February found the group partnering with DANZIG and KATAKLYSM. They joined the Roadrunner 'Roadrage' tour with 3 INCHES OF BLOOD, THE AGONY SCENE, STILL REMAINS in March prior to April gigs alongside CHIMAIRA. This tour extended into UK dates during May. Initially announced as an opening act on the SLIPKNOT / SHADOWS FALL US arena tour of Spring 2005 the band was forced to drop off the billing due to "Union enforced time constraints".

Matthew Heafy would act as one of five high profile writers contributing to the ROADRUNNER UNITED 25th anniversary album 'The All-Stars Sessions', his songwriting credits featuring amongst four compositions. 'The Dawn Of A Golden Age' utilized lead vocals from Dani Filth of CRADLE OF FILTH, Heafy laying down lead and rhythm guitar parts, while 'I Don't Wanna Be (A Superhero)' boasted vocals by Michale Graves of the MISFITS with lead and rhythm guitar cuts recorded by Heafy. 'Blood And Flames' was sung by ex-KILLSWITCH ENGAGE man Jesse Leach, the ever versatile TRIVIUM frontman donating lead, rhythm and acoustic guitar, not to mention backing vocals—lead, rhythm and acoustic guitar also came courtesy of Heafy on the KING DIAMOND sung 'In The Fire', band mate Cory Beaulieu supplying lead and rhythm guitars too on this number. Heafy himself vocalised and lent lead guitar services on 'The End' penned by ex-FEAR FACTORY guitarist Dino Cazares.

The TRIVIUM track 'Pull Harder On The Strings Of Your Martyr' gave the band a good degree of extra exposure when it was included on the soundtrack to the Bruce Hunt directed movie 'The Cave', released in August. The band's September and October European dates, taking in the UK, with ALL THAT REMAINS and IT DIES TODAY, then France, Belgium, Holland, Germany, Norway, Sweden and Denmark, saw strong support from ARCH ENEMY. The two bands stuck together for Japanese gigs in October. To coincide with these dates a special tour edition of 'Ascendancy' was issued, adding a bonus disc featuring two previously unreleased tracks and three videos. On 15th December Matt Heafy, Travis Smith and Corey Beaulieu notably joined the ROADRUNNER UNITED conglomerate at the New York Nokia Theater for an all star Metal evening. TRIVIUM included a track 'Washing Me Away In The Tides' on the 'Underworld: Evolution' movie soundtrack.

IN FLAMES, TRIVIUM and DEVILDRIVER pooled their talents for a January 2006 US tour. March had the band scheduled for 'The Crusade III: Ascend Above The Ashes' concerts in the UK and Ireland alongside GOD FORBID and BLOODSIMPLE. The band played their part in honouring METALLICA, contributing their rendition of 'Master Of Puppets' to the album 'Remastered', this set being a complete remake of 'Master Of Puppets' in joint celebration of the twentieth anniversary of the classic album's release and the 25th anniversary of UK Rock magazine Kerrang! In April. Yet another re-issue of the 'Ascendancy' opus would collect this interpretation as an additional bonus track in May.

The band put in a significant appearance at the METALLICA and KORN headlined 'Download' festival in Castle Donington, UK on June 10th. The group subsequently engaged in a gigantic roving festival billing with the US 'Sounds Of The Underground' tour throughout the summer, commencing in Cleveland, Ohio

TRIVIUM (pic: Josh Rothstein)

on July 8th, partnered with IN FLAMES, AS I LAY DYING, CANNIBAL CORPSE, GWAR, TERROR, THE BLACK DAHLIA MURDER, BEHEMOTH, THE CHARIOT and THROUGH THE EYES OF THE DEAD.

TRIVIUM's first headline US trek saw them through late September into mid November, supported by THE SWORD, PROTEST THE HERO, SEEMLESS, SANCTITY and CELLADOR. On October 9th 'The Crusade' was officially certified silver status in the UK for sales in excess of 60,000 copies, hitting number 7 on the charts.

The band scored a notable coup, supporting IRON MAIDEN for their massive series of arena dates throughout Europe, UK and Scandinavia for November. Unfortunately the band came in for some unwelcome press when British fans of the headline act turned on the band. At the December 22nd Earl's Court, London show audience members bombarded both frontman Matt Heafy and bassist Paolo Gregoletto during the song 'Like Light To The Flies' with bottles and water balloons filled with urine.

In January and February 2007 the group put in Japanese headliners followed up a slot on the New Zealand and Australia 'Big Day Out' festivals, on a bill comprising TOOL, THE KILLERS, MUSE, MY CHEMICAL ROMANCE and JET, interspersed with headline shows. The band packaged up with LAMB OF GOD, MACHINE HEAD and GOJIRA for a lengthy run of North American dates commencing on February 16th 2007 at the Palladium Ballroom in Dallas, Texas. During this period Corey Beaulieu managed to find time to guest on the comeback album for cult Heavy Metal band LIZZY BORDEN.

A mammoth European tour kicked off with a two night stand at the Ambassador in Dublin, Ireland on April 8th. Canadian Thrash veterans acted as support for the entire trek, which covered the UK, France, Belgium, Holland, Germany, Poland, Denmark, Sweden, Finland, Norway, Austria, Italy, Spain and Switzerland.

Trivium, Trivium (2003) (Demo). To Burn The Eye / Requiem / Fugue / My Hatred / The Storm / Sworn / Demon.
EMBER TO INFERNO, Lifeforce LFR 040-2 (2003). Inception, The Bleeding Skies / Pillars Of Serpents / If I Could Collapse The Masses / Fugue (A Revelation) / Requiem / Ember To Inferno / Ashes / To Burn The Eye / Falling To Grey / My Hatred / When All Light Dies / A View Of Burning Empires.
EMBER TO INFERNO, Tokuma TKCS-85083 (2003) (Japanese release). Inception, The Bleeding Skies / Pillars Of Serpents / If I Could Collapse The Masses / Fugue (A Revelation) / Requiem / Ember To Inferno / Ashes / To Burn The Eye / Falling To Grey / My Hatred / When All Light Dies / A View Of Burning Empires / The Storm / Sworn.
ASCENDANCY, Roadrunner RRCY-21238 (2005) (Japanese release). The End Of Everything / Rain / Pull Harder On The Strings Of Your Martyr / Drowned And Torn Asunder / Ascendancy / A Gunshot To The Head Of Trepidation / Like Light To The Flies / Dying In Your Arms / The Deceived / Suffocating Sight / Departure / Declaration / Blinding Tears Will Break The Skies / Washing Away Me In The Tides.
ASCENDANCY, Roadrunner 6182512 (2005). The End Of Everything / Rain / Pull Harder On The Strings Of Your Martyr / Drowned And Torn Asunder / Ascendancy / A Gunshot To The Head Of Trepidation / Like Light To The Flies / Dying In Your Arms / The Deceived / Suffocating Sight / Departure / Declaration. Chart position: 151 USA.
Anthem (We Are The Fire), Roadrunner RR PROMO 951 (2006) (Promotion release). Anthem (We Are The Fire) (Clean edit) / Anthem (We Are The Fire) (Edit) / Anthem (We Are The Fire) (album version).
ASCENDANCY (SPECIAL EDITION), Roadrunner 6182518 (2006) (CD + DVD). The End Of Everything / Rain / Pull Harder On The Strings Of Your Martyr / Drowned And Torn Asunder / Ascendancy / A Gunshot To The Head Of Trepidation / Like Light To The Flies / Dying In Your Arms / The Deceived / Suffocating Sight / Departure / Declaration / Washing Away Me In The Tides / Like Light To The Flies (Video) / Pull Harder On The Strings Of Your Martyr (Video) / Gunshot To The Head Of Trepidation (Video) / Rain (Video) / Rain (Live) / Dying In Your Arms (Live) / Like Light To The Flies (Live) / Gunshot To The Head Of Trepidation (Live) / Pull Harder On The Strings Of Your Martyr (Live).
THE CRUSADE, Roadrunner (2006). Ignition / Detonation / Anthem (We Are The Fire) / This World Can't Tear Us Apart / In Sadness We'll See Her / Entrance Of The Conflagration / The Crusade / Synthetic / Becoming The Dragon. Chart positions: 7 UK, 12 IRELAND, 14 AUSTRALIA, 23 GERMANY, 23 CANADA, 25 USA, 41 SWEDEN, 44 AUSTRIA, 46 JAPAN, 61 NORWAY, 64 HOLLAND, 86 ITALY, 92 SWITZERLAND, 115 FRANCE.

TYRANT'S REIGN

IL, USA — *Randy Barron (vocals), Karl Miller (guitar), Chris Nelken (guitar), Phil Fouch (bass), Gabriel Anthony (drums)*.

TYRANT'S REIGN issued a solitary self financed and now extremely rare mini album. Guitarist Jeff Baghepour would make his exit just prior to recording of the album. Vocalist Randy Barron was later to found WINTERKILL releasing the 1997 album 'A Feast For A Beggar'. Drummer Gabriel Anthony was to join MOTHERFUNK whilst guitarist Karl Miller plies his trade with PSYCHOSIS.

Ex-TYRANT'S REIGN men guitarist Jeff Baghepour and bassist Phil Fouch would unite with Russ Barron (Randy's sibling), keyboard player Michelle O'Day and drummer Donny Mizanira to found the Power Metal band PHOENIX RISING. This act, after a name change to CRYPTIC VISION, later recorded an album. Randy Barron joined his former WINTERKILL colleagues in SPIRIT WEB for their second album, 'Far Beyond The Visual Mind' released through the Belgian Mausoleum label in 2003.

YEAR OF THE TYRANTS, Cynical CR500 (1987). Tyrant's Reign / Jack The Ripper / Untamed / Deadly Eyes / Reign Of Terror / Fadeaway.
TYRANT'S REIGN, (2004). Thrashing Metal Maniacs / Star Chamber / S.O.S. / Kill Or Be Killed / The Amulet / Passage To Eternity / Forever And A Day / Tyrant's Reign / Jack The Ripper / Unconditional Surrender / Insanity.

TYSONDOG

NEWCASTLE UPON TYNE, UK — *Clutch Carruthers (vocals), Paul Burdis (guitar), Alan Hunter (guitar), Kevin Wynn (bass), Ged Wolf (drums)*..

Newcastle upon Tyne Heavy Metal band TYSONDOG amusingly took their name from the bassist's girlfriend's dog! The band was rooted in an earlier act billed as ORCHRIST which comprised vocalist Alan Hunter, guitarist Paul Burdis, bass player Kev Wynn and drummer Kev Hunter. The latter, brother of RAVEN's Rob 'Wacko' Hunter, would make his exit to act as

RAVEN roadie. Peter Reeve duly took over the drum stool position as TYSONDOG started to receive label interest from such now renowned indies as Ebony, Music For Nations, Roadrunner and Newcastle's own Neat Records.

Signing to Neat TYSONDOG cut the 1983 single track 'Eat The Rich', featuring Alan Hunter on lead vocals. However, shortly after recording this track a lead vocalist was deemed crucial to the band's line-up and 'Clutch' Carruthers was inducted. Carruthers laid down his vocals on the B side 'Dead Meat'. With the single just in the shops Reeves opted out. Nevertheless, progress was swift and 'Eat The Rich' even garnered valuable exposure being featured in 'The Chain' movie. The band set about recording their debut album 'Beware Of The Dog'. Ged 'Wolf' Cook sat in on drums but would quit immediately after recording team up with ATOMKRAFT. He was replaced by Rob Walker. Although 'Beware Of The Dog' was produced by Cronos of VENOM, the man himself proclaimed afterwards that he thought the band were "shit" and nothing more than JUDAS PRIEST imitators, stating that he had done it purely as a favour because Wolf was the brother of VENOM manager Eric Cook.

Although acknowledged to be blighted by a particularly thin drum sound reception to the album though was, in the main, enthusiastic especially in mainland Europe. Gigs ensued including prestigious shows in Holland at the Dynamo club and at the 'Aardschok' festival. The 'Shoot To Kill' EP followed in 1985. TYSONDOG was slated to support American Shock Rockers MADAME X but this tour was pulled.

Signing to Eric Cooke of VENOM repute for management TYSONDOG set to work on a second album 'Crimes Of Insanity', the single from which would be a cover version of ALICE COOPER's seminal 'School's Out' hit. Hunter backed out once these sessions were over and the band opted to persevere as a quartet. Oddly the 'School's Out' single would be promoted by a new look TYSONDOG, eschewing the familiar leather and studs for teased, hair sprayed hair and glammier apparel. The band did get to grace the stage with WARLOCK for a run through of JUDAS PRIEST's 'You've Got Another Thing Comin' at Kerrang magazine's 100th edition celebrations but a more substantial support tour to VENOM in North America fell through due to visa problems. The bad luck continued as Carruthers was involved in a car crash on the way to a vital gig at London's Marquee club.

TYSONDOG had already started demoing material for a proposed third album when they learned Neat Records was no longer interested. The band announced it was to fold and a swansong gig in Newcastle saw Alan Hunter joining them onstage for a final time.

Wynn teamed up with ex-TYGERS OF PAN TANG vocalist JESS COX in TYGER TYGER. Alan Hunter featured in ATOMKRAFT and also performed vocals on the third PARIAH album, recorded in 1993, which until recently remained unreleased.

The Brazilian Rock Brigade label would re-issue both albums complete with tracks from the 'Shoot To Kill' sessions. In 2002 the Sanctuary label compiled all the available band material for the 'Painted Heroes' collection. As Ged Cook, the TYSONDOG drummer established Newcastle upon Tyne record label Demolition Records.

Eat The Rich, Neat NEAT 33 (1984). Eat The Rich / Dead Meat.
BEWARE OF THE DOG, Neat NEAT 1017 (1985). Hammerhead / Dog Soldiers / Demon / The Inquisitor / Dead Meat / Painted Heroes / Voice From The Grave / The Butcher / In The End.
Shoot To Kill, Neat NEAT 46 (1985). Shoot To Kill / Changeling / Hammerhead / Back To The Bullet.
CRIMES OF INSANITY, Neat NEAT 1031 (1986). Taste The Hate / Don't Let The Bastards Grind Ya Down / Blood Money / The Machine / School's Out / Street Thunder / Hotter Than Hell / Judgement Day / Eat The Rich / Smack Attack.
School's Out, Neat NEAT 56 (1986). School's Out / Don't Let The Bastards Grind Ya Down / Back To The Bullet.
School's Out, Neat NEAT 56 (1986) (7" single). School's Out / Don't Let The Bastards Grind Ya Down.
PAINTED HEROES, Castle Music CMDDD522 (2002). Hammerhead / Dog Soldiers / Demon / The Inquisitor / Dead Meat / Painted Heroes / Voices From The Grave / Day Of The Butcher / In The End / Shoot To Kill / Changeling / Taste Of Hate / Don't Let The Bastards (Grind You Down) / Blood Money / Time Machine / School's Out / Street Thunder / Hotter Than Hell / Judgement Day / Eat The Rich / Smack Attack / Back To The Bullet.

UNCLE SLAM

CA, USA — *Todd Moyer (vocals / guitar), Simon Oliver (bass), Raymond Herrera (drums).*

One of many later entries into the US Thrash scene, California's UNCLE SLAM managed to record and release a respectable three albums. Founded in 1987, both vocalist / guitarist Todd Moyer and drummer Amery "AWOL" Smith, previously a member of SUICIDAL TENDENCIES, were members of the short-lived Los Angeles act BROOD. Initially PREDATOR, DISSENTER and L.S.N. man Angelo Espino occupied the bass position. Espino would exit for REVEREND. After recording one album as BROOD the pair added ex-SUICIDAL TENDENCIES bassist Louie Mayorga and changed the name to UNCLE SLAM. However, Mayorga was not to last long as he was replaced by Simon Oliver before the debut record. The debut arrived on the Caroline label in 1988 and the cover art featured an twisted mascot based on the beloved American icon, Uncle Sam.

A long five years was to pass before the band released a second album, the Warren Croyle produced 'Will Work For Food'. The band was now on the Restless label and it also featured Uncle Sam the mascot, now rendered by popular Metal artist, Ed Repka. The band also made an ambitious attempt at covering LED ZEPPLIN's 'Dazed And Confused'.

Another couple of years passed and Amery Smith was replaced by another former SUICIDAL TENDENCIES man, R.J. Herrera, also formerly of PHOBIA. A third album, 'When God Dies', appeared on the Medusa label. Ed Repka contributed the album art once again. Herrera raised his profile after UNCLE SLAM's demise with FEAR FACTORY. Amery Smith resurfaced in BS 2000, a collaboration with AD Rock of the BEASTIE BOYS, with whom Smith often sat in on drums.

SAY UNCLE, Caroline Carol 1354 (1988). Weirdo Man / The Ugly Dude / Judgement Day / Micro Logic / Contaminated / Up From Beneath / Executioner / The Prophecy / Say Uncle / Immolation / Eve Of The End / Come Alive.
WILL WORK FOR FOOD, Restless 7 72718-2 (1993). Back From Beyond / Left For Dead / Roadkill / Hangin' In The Hood / Dominant Submission / Face The Fight / Will Work For Food / Cold Fire / Dazed And Confused / Finger First / It Can Happen.
WHEN GOD DIES, Medusa 7-72773-2 (1995). When God Dies / My Mother's Son / Procreation / Smoke 'Em If You Got 'Em / An Offering To A Deity / Age Of Aggression / End Of The Line / The Lightless Sky / Summer In Space / Bombs Away.

UNDER THREAT

BOGOTÁ, COLOMBIA — *John Perez (vocals), Nick Bermudez (guitar), David Bermudez (bass), Alejandro Rojas (drums).*

Death-Thrashers UNDER THREAT were created in Bogotá during 1997 by vocalist John Perez, guitar player Nicolas Bermudez and bassist David Bermudez under a formative title of SKULPTOR. Several membership changes later, and with the inauguration of drummer Alejandro Rojas, SKULPTOR became UNDER THREAT in 1999. Toward the close of that year Transilvania Music issued the album 'Hipostasis'. These sessions, which featured a cover version of SARCOFAGO's 'Piercings', marked a switch from Spanish lyrics to English. In December 2001 the band entered Studio One in Racine, Wisconsin to record 'Behind Mankind's Disguise'. A bout of US summer touring saw the band partnering up with MONSTROSITY, DARK FAITH and BLOOD STAINED DUSK. UNDER THREAT also scored an appearance at the Milwaukee Metalfest. The 'Behind Mankind's Disguise' album was picked up by Conquest Music, the custom imprint of MONSTROSITY's Lee Harrison, for issue in March 2003. Once again the band played at the Milwaukee Metalfest that year.

During summer 2004 the band, having lost the services of second guitarist Eric Leider, entered Studio One again to lay down tracks for next outing 'Deathmosphere'. That October UNDER THREAT performed at their hometown's annual festival 'Rock Al Parque' in Simon Bolivar Park. Barbarian Records from Madison picked up the record for the USA whilst Hateworks Records from Manizales, Colombia distributed across South America and Europe. Jake Sommer was added as second guitarist.

UNDER THREAT musicians guitarist Nick Bermudez and bass player David Bermudez made news in March 2007 when they joined BLAZE, the band of former IRON MAIDEN singer Blaze Bayley.

HIPOSTASIS, Transilvania Music (1999). Poisoned Soul / Learned Helplessness / The Lower Man / Lymbic Zone / Consummatum Est / Unchainment / Sydrome Of Alienation / Hipostasis / Tormenta Interna / Piercings.

BEHIND MANKIND'S DISGUISE, Conquest Music (2003). Blame Game Trap / Face Of Emptiness / Under Threat / Serpent's Lick / Ghost And The Machine / Desperate Human's Path / Behind Mankind's Disguise / The End Of Grace / Infestation / Gates Of Deception / The Warning / Mirrors Of Dejection.

Under Threat, Under Threat (2004) (Demo). Prisoners Of Their Own Betrayal / Read The Codes / Black Innertia Disintegration / Parallel Hells.

DEATHMOSPHERE, Barbarian (2006). Deathmosphere / Kingdom Of Eternal Crisis / Parallel Hells / Echo Shaped Life / Black Inertia Disintegration / Embraced By Disaster / Prisoners Of Their Own Betrayal / Read The Codes / Restrained Hate Coexistance / Third World Blood.

UNDER THY GUN

KRISTINEHAMN, SWEDEN — *Tony Sundberg (vocals), Nicklas Carlsson (guitar), Daniel Grahn (guitar), Henrik Lagberg (bass), Johnny Lebisch (drums).*

Kristinehamn's UNDER THY GUN's progression traces back through several antecedent acts. WARHEAD, fronted by singer Daniel Jansson and incorporating three former BRIMSTONE band members in guitarist Nicklas Carlson, bassist Johan Hallberg plus Johnny Lebisch on drums, released the demos 'Here is Your Hell' in 1999, recorded at Evil Grill Studios. In this guise the band performed just one solitary concert. Learning of multiple other Metal WARHEADs, the group then switched to WARFARE INCORPORATED and delivered the 'Madness Breeds Heroes' demo in August 2000. These sessions saw Hallberg replaced by Nicklas Carlsson brother. At this juncture Daniel Grahn, another ex-BRIMSTONE player, joined the band,

Black Goat Productions subsequently combined the two sessions for an April 2001 cassette release. In 2003 Tony Sundberg enrolled as new singer as Daniel Grahn left, relocating to Gothenburg to forge Grind outfit KOLONY. At this time WARFARE INCORPORATED evolved into UNDER THY GUN. A demo, entitled 'When The World Went Dead', was released in November 2004. The group also had tracks featured on the December 2005 compilation album 'Metal Ostentation Vol 9'.

In September 2006 Daniel Grahn returned to the ranks.

When The World Went Dead, Under Thy Gun (2004) (Demo).

UNGOD

GERMANY — *Infamist Of Tumulus (vocals), Ancient Blasphemic Grave Invocator (guitar), Schiekron (bass), Electrocutioner (drums).*

Black Metal act with plenty of old school Thrash influence to their sound. The first formulation of the band counted lead vocalist Infamus Of Tumulus, guitarists Ancient Blasphemic Grave Invocator and Angel Of Blasphemy, bassist Schiekron and drummer Condemptor. The latter was subsequently usurped by The Unknown. UNGOD made their presence felt with their 1992 demo tape titled 'Magicus Tallis Damnatio'. Following the debut album 'Circle Of The Seven Infernal Pacts', recorded for the Heretic Supremacist Brotherhood Records label, UNGOD released a brace of shared 7" singles combining forces with DESASTER and CABAL. At this stage the band had resolved to utilise a drum machine rather than a human operative.

UNGOD issued a split album in 1997 shared with IMPENDING DOOM. A further split album for Merciless Records, comprising the band's 'Magicus Talli Damnatio' demo material, was shared with BAXAXAXA, a project union of UNGOD, ALTAR and CABAL members, during 2002. The UNGOD line up at this juncture stood at Infamist Of Tumulus on vocals, guitarist Ancient Blasphemic Grave Invocator, bass player Schiekron and Electrocutioner on drums.

CIRCLE OF THE SEVEN INFERNAL PACTS, Heretic Supremacist Brotherhood Records (1993) (Limited edition 500 copies). Silence In The Golden Halls Of Endless Hope / Circle Of The Seven Infernal Pacts / Land Of Frozen Tears / Magicus Tulis Damnatio / Dark Winds Around The Throne Of Blood / Lost Beast Born In Darkness / A Journey Through Forgotten Myth / The Grotesque Vision Of A Dying Moon / Black Clouds Beyond The Fullmoon.

Renaissance Of The Dark Arcade, Merciless (1995) (Split single with CABAL). Renaissance Of The Dark Arcade.

Split, Merciless (1995) (Split single with DESASTER). Split.

CONQUERING WHAT ONCE WAS OURS, Merciless (1997) (Split album with IMPENDING DOOM). I Am The Chaos / Firestorm, Ashes, Genocide / Conquering What Once Was Ours / Via Reducta / Anatomy Of Human Destructivity.

Phallus Cult, Merciless (1998) (Split single with SADISTIC INTENT). Phallus Cult.

UNGOD, Merciless MRCD010 (2002) (Split album with BAXAXAXA). Silence in The Golden Halls Of Endless Hope / Land Of Frozen Tears / Magicus + Tallis Dammnatio / Journey Through Forgotten Myth / Lost Beast, Born In Darkness.

UNITED

JAPAN — *Masatoshi Yuasa (vocals), Yoshifumi Yoshida (guitar), Shingo Ohtani (guitar), Akhiro Yokoyama (bass), Yusuke Nakamura (drums).*

Bay Area style Thrashers UNITED, named after the JUDAS PRIEST anthem, was found in 1981 and operated primarily as a JUDAS PRIEST cover band for many years. The act finally got around to releasing original material with February 1985's 'Destroy Metal' EP, capitalized on in December 1986 by a further effort 'Beast Dominate'. UNITED would also contribute the track 'Emergency Dominate' to a compilation album.

The band would re-enlist a former member, guitarist Shingo Ohtani, from his interim act EMPEROR in 1990. During October of 1990 UNITED signed a deal with the Howling Bull Entertainment label, the first fruits of which was the 'Bloody But Unbowed' album.

The 'Beast Dominate '92' was issued up-front of a support tour to American Metal band LÄÄZ ROCKIT. Another album, 'Human Zoo', would arrive the same year.

Such rapid progress would spark the interest of the major labels and in 1994 UNITED announced a signing with the JVC Victor label. 'N.O.I.Q.', produced by Pat Regan, emerged in 1995. SLAYER manager Rick Sales would take an active part in managing the band globally at this juncture. UNITED would lend valuable support to MACHINE HEAD's Japanese dates as 'N.O.I.Q.' saw an American release through the Metal Blade label. UNITED would travel to California to perform their debut gig on American soil at the Foundations Forum trade event. However, longstanding vocalist Yoshiaki Furui parted ways with the band toward the close of the year.

In March of 1996 UNITED declared Furui's replacement to be the striking dreadlocked figure and exceptionally tall newcomer Shinichi Inazu. By October UNITED was back in America cutting a new album 'Reload' with producer Vincent Wojno.

UNITED would maintain the partnership with Wojno for 1998's 'Distorted Vision' album. Promotion would include an appearance at the Akasada Blitz 'Live Undead' Metal festival headlined by SLAYER.

Drummer Hirokazu Uchino was forced out due to health problems, but would soon be back in action with the DUFFLES. The band returned with 2001's 'Infectious Hazard'. UNITED sported a new vocalist and drummer in former DEATH FILE man Masatoshi Yuasa and Yusuke Nakamura respectively.

Destroy Metal EP, NRR-E003 (1985). U.N.I.T.E.D. / Skill / Sniper.

Beast Dominate EP, NRR-E010 (1986). S.R.S. / Do You Wanna Die? / Holy Dive Screamer / Combat.

BLOODY BUT UNBOWED, Howling Bull HBR-F0001 (1991). Sniper / Welcome To Amazing World / The Plague / Power Rage / Don't Trust / (It's So) Hard To Breathe / Take A Bite Of Crime / Suck Your Bone / Unavoidable Riot.

HUMAN ZOO, Howling Bull HBR-F0009 (1992). Human Zoo / Violence Jack / Machinery Days / Jungle Land / False Majesty / The Sea Of Silence / Can't See The Silence / Over The Ocean / Brothers In Arms / Don't Let Peace Break Out.

BEAST DOMINATES '92, Howling Bull HBR-M0006 (1992). S.R.S. / Do You Wanna Die? / Holy Dive Screamer / Combat / Ultra / Yesterday's Heroes.

N.O.I.Q., JVC Victor VICP-5500 (1995). Revenger / Bad Habit / Run Through The Night / Kill Yourself For Business / Hit Me / One More Card / Words In Disguise / Outta My Way / Obsession.

BEST RARE TRACKS FROM UNDER GROUND, JVC Victor VICP-5522 (1995). Combat / Don't Trust! / Machinery Days / S.R.S. / Welcome To Amazing World / Holy Dive Screamer / (It's So) Hard To Breathe / Jungle Land / Don't Let Peace Break Out / False Majesty / Unavoidable Riot / Human Zoo / Violence Jack.

Burst EP, JVC Victor VICP-60007 (1997). Reload / Burst / Revenger / Violence Jack / Sniper.

RELOAD, JVC Victor VICP-5821 (1997). Untied / Skin-Deep / Shameless / Thrill Kill / Monkey Brains / Mourning / L.O.U. / Ex-Friend / Suicide? / Mata / Slave / Style.

DISTORTED VISION, Howling Bull America (2000). Flash Back / Trust Yourself / Color / Who I Am / Sick & Angry / Locked Inside / So Damn Low / Tiger / Change.

INFECTIOUS HAZARD, Howling Bull HWCA-1039 (2001). Cross The Line / The Ruin Of A Memory / Temporary Insanity / Sonic Sublime / Blackened Lies / Mosh Crew / Solid Ground / Penetrate / Low Dealer / Distorted Vision.

UNKNOWN

AREQUIPA, PERU — *Jorge Esteban LLosa (vocals), Miguel Ballón M. (vocals / guitar), Diego Del Carpio C. (guitar), Juan Arce M. (bass), Diego Zimermann (drums).*

UNKNOWN would originally be fronted by singer Rafael Fernandez. His departure saw guitarist Miguel Ballon taking over the lead vocal role. Signing to Prescott Records the band projected the album 'Identity Unknown' for September 2005. Guitarist Diego Del Carpio would be replaced by Clever. Further changes saw the addition of second singer Ronny and bassist Jose Luis Mercado replaced by Jesus Aleman. UNKNOWN subsequently re-enlisted Rafael Fernandez and drafted Santiago Mazeira on bass. Shortly afterward, Gabriel Alvarez R. was to take the bass role. The group format changed yet again when Jorge Esteban Llosa was enrolled as new singer, Diego Del Carpio C. on guitar, Juan Arce M. on bass and Diego Zimermann on the drums.

My Fallen Angel, Unknown (2004). Scream / My Fallen Angel / Tormento / Flechas / Eternal Flames.

IDENTITY UNKNOWN, Prescott (2005). My Fallen Angel / Fire Release / Tormentor / One Smile Is Enough / Twister Mind / Identity Unknown / Under Pressure / Fist Of Fate / Vampire Summoning / You Give Me The Strength / Giving Up, Not For Sire.

UPPERCUT

WOLFSBURG, GERMANY — *Daniela Waletzky (vocals), Jan Weigel (guitar), Ralf Winzer (bass), Olaf Heuer (drums).*

Wolfsburg based Thrashers. Founded in October of 1997 by the erstwhile SQUARE WAVES pairing of vocalist Daniela Waletzky and drummer Olaf in alliance with guitarist Nico Lueder, previously with BRAINLESS, PSYCHOTRON and NONVOKUHILA, and ex-CRUCIFIXION bass guitarist Henrik Schwaninger. UPPERCUT debuted with the demo 'First Strike', subsequently recording their debut album 'Shroud Shifter' at WASTELAND guitarist Stephan Kern's studio in September of 2000. Jan Wiegel of BRAINBUG took over the bass position in 2001.

UPPERCUT contributed their rendition of 'Sex And Outrage' to the 2003 MOTÖRHEAD tribute album 'Motörmorphösis— A Tribute To Motörhead Part II'. G.U.C. Records issued the 'Reanimation Of Hate' album in 2004, this outing seeing Wirgel now on guitar and Ralf Winzer on bass.

SHROUD SHIFTER, G.U.C. (2001). Hatred Inside / Nature's Blood / Prophet Of Death / Burning Air / At The Bottom / Dying Passion / Follow The Call / The Light.

REANIMATION OF HATE, G.U.C. (2004). Intro / Massmurderers Heaven / Reanimation Of Hate / Breaking The Noise / Stick It Out / Fear / Neighbour In Hell / Liberation / Supernova Fake / Dead End / Resistance / My Mirror / Wrath Of Misery.

URKRAFT

SVENDBORG, DENMARK — *Thomas Strømvig Pedersen (vocals / guitar), Thomas Birk (guitar), Jeppe Tander (bass), Jeppe Eg (keyboards), Mikael Skou Jørgensen (drums).*

Svendborg melodic Death Metal act URKRAFT (a Danish expression for "primitive force") was founded during 1995 by vocalist / guitarist Thomas Strømvig Pedersen, guitarist R. Mørk, bass player Jeppe Tander and Mikael Skou Jørgensen, also a member of Power Metal band UREAS, on the drums. In 2000 the group inducted a new recruit in the CACOPHONY credited Thomas Birk on guitar and, in 2001 keyboard player Tommy Neperus for live work. During 2002 the keyboard position was secured with the enrollment of Jeppe Eg, the man holding credentials with CACOPHONY, BLAZING ETERNITY and MANTICORA.

URKRAFT issued the 'Primordial' demo in 2003. The band, signing to the German Cartel Media, entered the Antfarm recording studio with producer Tue Madsen in January of 2004 to commence work on debut album 'Eternal Cosmic Slaughter'. URKRAFT signed a multi-album deal with Earache Records in the Spring of 2005. URKRAFT duly utilised both Antfarm Studios and producer Tue Madsen once again in mid July to cut a second album 'The Inhuman Aberration'.

URKRAFT joined forces with CANNIBAL CORPSE and DISAVOWED for extensive European dates in February and March 2007.

Verden Vil Bedrages, Urkraft (1996) (Demo). Urkraft (Intro) / Håbets Tyranni / Under Nul—6652 / Sindssyge Eksistens / En Døende Jord / Hvad Blev Der Af Mit Liv? / Vilde Blomster Visner.

Urkraft, Gritt (2000) (Danish promotional release). Af Hele Mit Hjerte / Ukristelig Længsel / Krigsdans / Det Blodbestænkte Fængsel.

2001, Gritt (2001) (Danish promotional release). Knoglerne Skriger / Her Var Aldrig Smukt.

2002 Version 2, Gritt (2002) (Danish promotional release). Nord (Den Förste Krig) / Solen Braender Ihjel / Intet Ansigt / Kloglerne Skriger.

2002 Version 1, Gritt (2002) (Danish promotional release). Nord (Den Første Krig) / Solen Brænder Ihjel / Aldrig Smukt / Kødet Triumferer.

Primordial Promo 2003, Gritt (2003) (Danish promotional release). Cannibal Melancholy / Eternal Cosmic Slaughter / Soulless / The Scarlet Burning.

URKRAFT

ETERNAL COSMIC SLAUGHTER, Cartel CM 232-5 (2004). Blessed Be The Human Beast / Paint The City Black / Soulless / Unleash The Will / Eternal Cosmic Slaughter / At The Border Of The Known World / Cannibal Melancholy / Through Your Senses / The Scarlet Burning.

THE INHUMAN ABERRATION, Earache MOSH328 (2006). Too Strong For The Strongest Lord / This Great Summer / Only The Gods / The Inhuman Aberration / Open The Gate / Come No Tomorrow / Watch Your Own Eyes / Liberation / Forsaken / The Pressure Of Our Jaws.

V.A.R.

CZECH REPUBLIC — *Pavel Berger (vocals), Martin Smejc (guitar), Jan Brtko (guitar), Jiri Vycital (bass), Jan Janota (drums).*

Czechs V.A.R. (VRATISLAVICE ALCOHOLIC ROAR) deal in pure unbridled Thrash Metal. The band, named after a famous Czech beer brand, have retained a stable line up since their inception in 1989. V.A.R. debuted with a 1990 demo 'Nen Se Kam Skryt' followed by a further session 'Brutalni Chaos' the following year. The band also featured with two songs on the Monitor label compilation 'Ultrametal'.

The release of V.A.R.'s inaugural album was delayed when the band suffered a major car accident. The group would all recuperate though and 'Personal Destruction' arrived in 1992. The album included a spoof on HELLOWEEN with the track 'Keeper Of The Seven Beers'.

The 1999 album 'Under Water' included Czech vocal versions of tracks by KISS, BLACK SABBATH and R&B Rockers DR. FEELGOOD.

PERSONAL DESTRUCTION, Monitor (1992). Brutální Chaos / Sebevrada / Není Se Kam Skrýt / Krvavý Kšeft / Prdel Evropy / Konec Svìta / Èeská Tragédie / Vratislav / Bez Tváøe / PodivnejJivot / Útìk Do Tmy / Nový Mýtus / Moje Stará Je Dìvka / Proti Vizím / Keeper Of The Seven Beers / Káèulovo Zrození.

DEPENDENCE, Taga (1995). Závislost Gama / Projdi Svou Zdí / Agent 00 / Je Po Všem / Lítáme Jak Splašený / Mocná Síla / Dech Mrtvý Milenky / Kamstošláps? / Otrava / Kremace / Pár Slov / Vratislav (Techno remix).

POD VODOU, 1K (1999). Jednou Nás Sejmou / Zpátky K Stádu / Kùièka Století / Tango Na Iletkách / Requiem Pro Praseèí Hlavu / Pod Vodou / Mezitro / Poslední Sen 2 / Baina / Kosmodrom Rostock / Dítì Temnot / Madìra.

ROZDVOJEN ALE SCHOPEN, 1K (2001). Jako Bikila / Uz Se Nevrátím / Smecka / Tocí To Kopytem / Rozdvojen Ale Schopen / Nemesis / To Bylo Tak / Našeptávaci / Mezitro II / Jed Pod Kuzí / Den Co Den.

VADER

OLSZTYN, POLAND — *Piotr Wiwczarek (vocals / guitar), Mauser (guitar), Novy (bass), Daray (drums).*

Death-Thrash band hailing from Olsztyn, VADER blitzed the globe with intense drumming and unashamed reliance on esoterica as a staple of their subject matter. VADER's unrelenting and brutal album schedule and seemingly inexhaustible appetite for global touring has elevated the band to the very top of the Polish Metal league. VADER came together in 1986, initially operating very much in the traditional Thrash Metal mould. That same year, VADER's first taste of the studio generated the demo 'Tyrani Piekieł', actually a circulated tape of a live radio broadcast, and December's 'Live In Decay', the band at this juncture comprising lead vocalist Czarny (a.k.a. Robert Czarneta), guitarists Peter (Piotr Wiwczarek) and Vika (Zbigniew Wróblewski), bassist Astaroth (Robert Struczewski) with Belial (Grzegorz Jackowski) on drums. Both Czarneta and Wróblewski decamped to found RAXAS.

The band released a further demo tape, 'Necrolust', working with engineer Władysław Iljaszewicz at Studio PR in Olsztyn in March 1989. Vader was now down to a trio, Peter being joined by bassist Jackie (Jacek Kalisz) and the SLASHING DEATH-credited drummer Krzysztof 'Docent' / 'Doc' Raczkowski. This tape gained VADER a deal with Carnage Records. A deal was struck to subsequently distribute the July 1990 demo 'Morbid Reich', these sessions co-produced by Mariusz Kmiolek at Pro-Studios in Olsztyn. This tape was to go down in Metal history, spectacularly selling in excess of over 10,000 copies.

The band, having inducted ex-IMPURITY and DIES IRAE guitarist Jaroslaw 'China' Labieniec and bassist Shambo (Leszek Rakowski), travelled to the UK to cut their debut record, 'The Ultimate Incantation' laid down at Rhythm Studios with Paul Johnson manning the desk. Upon the release of 'The Ultimate Incantion' in November 1992, VADER toured Europe with BOLT THROWER and GRAVE. Further dates in North America followed with DEICIDE, SUFFOCATION and DISMEMBER.

'The Darkest Age—Live '93', which included a cover of SLAYER's 'Hell Awaits', was recorded in front of a home crowd in Krakow. The 1994 'Sothis' EP witnessed another cover, BLACK SABBATH's anthem 'Black Sabbath', as well as a complete rework of VADER's 1989 track 'The Wrath'.

June 1995 found VADER out on the road in Europe once more touring alongside CRADLE OF FILTH, MALEVOLENT CREATION, OPPRESSOR, DISSECTION and SOLSTICE promoting the Adam Toczko produced 'De Profundis' album. Originally this album had been released domestically via Croon Records, subsequently seeing rapid fire reissues through Conquest Music and Impact Records.

VADER undertook a full European tour in the spring of 1996 as guests to CANNIBAL CORPSE. In 1996 Docent would unite with Cezar of CHRIST AGONY to found a Black Metal side venture MOON. Docent would appear on the first MOON album, 'Daemon's Heart', released in 1997, before relinquishing the role to concentrate on VADER. Keen to display their influences, VADER closed out 1996 with an album comprising entirely of cover versions. 'Future Of The Past' collected renditions of SODOM's 'Outbreak Of Evil', KREATOR's 'Flag Of

Hate', TERRORIZER's 'Storm Of Stress' and 'Fear Of Napalm', POSSESSED's 'Death Metal', DARK ANGEL's 'Merciless Death', CELTIC FROST's 'Dethroned Emperor', SLAYER's 'Silent Scream', ANTI-NOWHERE LEAGUE's 'We Are The League', DEPECHE MODE's 'I Feel You' and BLACK SABBATH's 'Black Sabbath'.

The band would be joined by another DIES IRAE man, guitarist Mauser (Maurycy Stefanowicz), during 1997 as Labieniec opted out to found NYIA. That October Impact Records put out the next VADER installment, 'Black To The Blind'. Diligent fans soon noticed that the lyric sheet included an absent track, 'Anamnesis'. This song apparently excised from the final running order by mistake. In August the act hit Japan, a concert at the Tokyo Club Quattro held on the 31st being captured on tape for a live album. 'Anamnesis' finally received a public airing included on the November 1998 mini-album 'Kingdom'.

Wiwczarek produced the debut album by fellow Poles DECAPITATED during 2000 as Vader themselves worked up the 'Litany' opus, released via Metal Blade Records that May. Japanese editions boasted a brace of extra songs, 'Red Dunes' and 'Lord of Desert'. VADER themselves headlined the European 'No Mercy' festivals alongside American' VITAL REMAINS, Brazilians REBAELLIUN and Germany's FLESHCRAWL.

Mauser would find the opportunity to re-activate the DIES IRAE name in 2000 drafting his VADER colleague Docent on drums, SCEPTIC guitarist Hiro and frontman Novy of DEVILYN. This new version of DIES IRAE entered the recording studio in June 2000 with producer Szymon Czech for the debut 'Immolated' album. VADER attacked a further batch of covers with the April 2001 offering 'Reign Forever World', paying homage to DESTRUCTION's 'Total Desaster', JUDAS PRIEST's 'Rapid Fire' and MAYHEM's 'Freezing Moon'.

September 2001 found VADER on the look out for a new bassist as previous occupant of the position Shambo had departed. They found their man with Simon (Konrad Karchut), an ex-member of HUNTER. The band would figure as part of the gargantuan European 'No Mercy' touring festival package in March and April 2002. Also on the billing would be IMMORTAL, CATASTROPHIC, DESTROYER 666, HYPOCRISY, DISBELIEF, MALEVOLENT CREATION and OBSCENITY. That June the 'Revelations' album, recorded at Red Studio, Gdańsk with Wiwczarek acting as producer, arrived via Metal Blade. Studio guests included Nergal of BEHEMOTH vocalising on 'Whispers' and Ureck of LUX OCCULTA featured as session keyboard performer on 'Torch Of War' and 'Revelation Of Black Moses'. Loosely conceptual, 'Revelations' artwork tied together lyrical observations on the 9/11 twin towers disaster. Digipacks hosted an additional track, 'Sons Of Fire'.

VADER toured Japan as headliners in October. The band would headline a run of dates across mainland Europe from late August supported by KRISIUN, DECAPITATED and PREJUDICE. North American shows, commencing 6th of November had the Poles topping a strong Death Metal package of IMMOLATION, CEPHALIC CARNAGE, ORIGIN and DECEMBER. VADER issued a CD single version of THIN LIZZY's 'Angel Of Death' in 2002, restricted to the obligatory 666 copies.

Wiwczarek aided Prog-Metal act CETI on their 2003 album 'Shadow Of The Angel', adding guest vocals to the track 'Falcon's Flight'. The band would part ways with bassist Simon, replacing him in June with the BEHEMOTH and DEVILYN credited Novy (Marcin Norwak). The band would put in an appearance at the gargantuan 'Woodstock 2003' festival in Poland, playing in front of not only national TV cameras but a huge crowd of 400,000 Rock fans. VADER's live schedule intensified with September 2003 Polish gigs marked out with running mates DECAPITATED, FRONTSIDE and VESANIA prior to North American dates dubbed 'The Art Of Noise 2'. This run of shows saw the band allied with KREATOR, NILE, AMON AMARTH and GOATWHORE taking them through October.

An October EP entitled 'Blood' featured two new studio songs 'We Wait' and 'Shape-shifting' alongside cuts from the 'Revelations' sessions that previously had only surfaced as part of foreign license versions of the album, digi-packs and on EPs. Frontman Piotr Wiwczarek readied a solo project PANZER X for the studio in September, cutting the EP 'Steel First'. Novy would join SPINAL CORD as bassist in November 2003.

VADER, working once more with producer Piotr Lukaszewski, set February of 2004 for recording of a new studio album 'The Beast'. However, Doc met with an accident in the studio, seriously injuring his hand and leg. Cancelling the sessions, VADER re-booked studio time at the PR Studios in Gdańsk for a later date, pulling in Daray (Darek Brzozowski) from Polish black metal band VESANIA as a session musician

Upon finalization of these sessions after which the band projected road work in Slovakia and Czech Republic, sharing the stage with HYPNOS. A European tour with MALEVOLENT CREATION, NAGLFAR and BLOOD RED THRONE was to follow in June. The band projected a massive 160 date plus world tour to keep them active throughout the year, including a prestigious opening slot to SLIPKNOT and METALLICA on 31st May to over 50,000 fans at the Silesian Stadium in Chorzów.

Also in 2004 VADER would donate their rendition of 'Death Metal' to the 'Seven Gates Of Horror' tribute album assembled by the Dutch Karmaggedon Media label in homage to pioneering Bay Area Thrash act POSSESSED.

A run of European gigs would be interrupted in late August when, en route to Falkenstein, near Leipzig VADER's tour bus was involved in an accident. Although the bus was seriously damaged, fortunately its occupants managed to escape unharmed. US touring plans for October saw the band set to flank NAPALM DEATH, KATAKLYSM and GOATWHORE. However, the band pulled out of these shows due to Piotr Wiwczarek requiring an operation to treat "a minor spinal injury" sustained whilst on tour in Scandinavia.

To close out the year, the band would be announced as one of the main attractions at the annual 'X-Mass Fest' 2004 roving European festival dates in alliance with NAPALM DEATH, MARDUK, FINNTROLL, THE BLACK DAHLIA MURDER and BELPHEGOR. In March of 2005 VADER parted ways with long-time drummer Doc, drafting Daray as substitute. Explaining the exit of Doc, frontman Piotr Wiwczarek explained "Doc pretty hard tried to 'fight' against his weaknesses, which were troubles for all of us."

US shows in April of 2005 had the band packaged with KREATOR, PRO-PAIN and THE AUTUMN OFFERING. The band broke this exhaustive touring schedule by entering Hertz Studios in Bialystok in early July to record an EP with a working title of 'The Art Of War', their first product for new label Sweden's Regain Records. Intros for these sessions would be conducted by Siegmar from VESANIA.

European gigs in June saw LOST SOUL as support act. A Polish tour of September, dubbed 'Blitzkrieg III', saw support from Greek veterans ROTTING CHRIST, fellow Poles LOST SOUL once again and French extreme Metal band ANOREXIA NERVOSA. Tragedy hit the VADER family in August with the announcement that former drummer Krzysztof "Docent" Raczkowski had died. The musician was just 35 years old and had a history of alcohol related problems.

Renewed road work in the USA for VADER continued in late 2005, witnessing November shows packaged with SUFFOCATION, CEPHALIC CARNAGE and ABORTED. The group headlined a memorial show for late drummer Doc at the Proxima Club in Warsaw on 11th December, supported by a local cast comprising CETI, HATE, DEAD INFECTION, LOST SOUL, CORRUPTION, AZARATH, CHAINSAW and VIRGIN SNATCH.

The band was included the 'Metal Crusaders' North American tour, taking place in May and June 2006 alongside KATAKLYSM, GRAVEWORM, DESTRUCTION, SPEED\KILL/HATE and THE ABSENCE. NIGHTRAGE and BLOODTHORN were confirmed as the support acts for the Scandinavian leg of the world tour, taking in Denmark, Norway, Sweden and Finland, in November. The 'Impressions In Blood' album, recorded at Hertz Studio in Bialystok, entered the national Polish charts at number 8 in September. An accompanying promotional video for the song 'Helleluyah (God Is Dead)' was directed by Andrzej Wyrozebski. Regain Records handled the album's European release Candlelight took on US licensing.

Shows during December 2006 in Bosnia, Turkey, Bulgaria, Rumania, Hungary and Serbia saw support from AMON DIN. That same month drummer Daray announced the formation of side project MASACHIST, co-formed by Thrufel, guitarist from AZARATH and YATTERING.

To commemorate VADER's 25th anniversary the band utilised Hertz Studio during March 2007 in order to completely re-record 25 of their best catalogue tracks.

VADER announced headline Australian dates in April 2007, supported by Sydney acts KILLRAZOR and INFERNAL METHOD.

Necrolust, (1989). Decapitated Saints / Reborn In Flames / The Final Massacre / The Wrath.
Morbid Reich, Carnage (1990). From Beyond (Intro) / Chaos / Vicious Circle / Breath Of Centuries / The Final Massacre / Reign-Carrion.
THE ULTIMATE INCANTATION, Earache MOSH 59 (1992). Creation / Dark Age / Vicious Circle / The Crucified Ones / Final Massacre / Testimony / Reign Carrion / Chaos / One Step To Salvation / Demon's Wind / Decapitated Saints / Breath Of Centuries.
THE DARKEST AGE—LIVE' 93, Arctic Serenades SERE 007 (1994). Macbeth (intro) / Dark Age / Vicious Circle / Crucified Ones / Demon's Wind / Decapitated Saints / From Beyond (Intro) / Chaos / Reign-Carrion / Testimony / Breath Of Centuries / Omen (Outro) / Hell Awaits.
Sothis EP, Massive MASS 001 MCD (1994). Hymn To The Ancient Ones / Sothis / De Profundis / Vision And The Voice / The Wrath / R'Lyeh / Black Sabbath.
DE PROFUNDIS, System Shock IR-C-067 (1995). Silent Empire / An Act Of Darkness / Blood Of Kingu / Incarnation / Sothis / Revolt / Of Moon, Blood, Dream And Me / Vision And The Voice / Reborn In Flames.
FUTURE OF THE PAST, Impact IR-C-092 (1996). Outbreak Of Evil / Flag Of Hate / Storm Of Stress / Death Metal / Fear Of Napalm / Merciless Death / Dethroned Emperor / Silent Scream / We Are The League / IFY / Black Sabbath.
BLACK TO THE BLIND, Impact IR-C-104 (1997). Heading For Internal Darkness / The Innermost Ambience / Carnal / Fractal Light / True Names / Beast raping / Foetus God / The Red Passage / Distant dream / Black To The Blind.
REBORN IN CHAOS, Hammerheart (1997). Decapitated Saints / Reborn In Flames / The Final Massacre / The Wrath / From Beyond / Chaos / Vicious Circle / Breath Of Centuries / The Final Massacre / Reign-Carrion.
Kingdom EP, Metal Mind Productions MMP CD 0057 (1998). Creatures Of Light And Darkness / Breath Of Centuries / Kingdom / Anamnesis / Inhuman (Disaster mix) / Quicksilver (Blood mix).
LIVE IN JAPAN, Impact IR-C-132-2 (1998). Damien / Sothis / Distant Dream / Black To The Blind / Silent Empire / Blood Of Kings / Carnal / Red Passage / Panzerstoss / Reborn In Flames / Fractal Light / From Beyond / Crucified Ones / Foetus God / Black Sabbath / Reign In Blood / Omen / Dark Age.
Xeper / North, Empire (2000). Xeper / North.
LITANY, Metal Blade 14297-2 (2000). Wings / The One Made Of Dreams / Xefer / Litany / Cold Demons / The Calling / North / Forward To Die!! / A World Of Hurt / The World Made Flesh / The Final Massacre.
REIGN FOREVER WORLD, Metal Blade 076-103182 (2001). Reign Forever World / Frozen Paths / Privilege Of The Gods / Total Disaster / Rapid Fire / Freezing Moon / North (Live) / Forwards To Die!! (Live) / Creatures Of Light And Darkness (Live) / Carnal (Live).
Angel Of Death, Empire EMP 012 CDS-E (2002) (Limited edition 666 copies). Angel Of Death / When Darkness Calls.
REVELATIONS, Metal Blade 3984-14411-2 (2002). Epitaph / The Nomad / Wolftribe / Whisper / As The Fallen Rise / When Darkness Calls / Torch Of War / The Code / Lukewarm Race / Angel Of Death / Revelation Of Black Moses.
Blood EP, Metal Blade 3984-14461-2 (2003). Shape-Shifting / We Wait / Son Of Fire / As The Fallen Rise / Traveller / When Darkness Calls / Angel Of Death.
BLOOD—REIGN FOREVER WORLD, Metal Blade 14461-2 (2003) (USA release). Shape Shifting / We wait / As The Fallen Rise / Son Of Fire / Traveler / When Darkness Calls / Reign Forever World / Frozen Paths / Privilege Of The Gods / Total Desaster / Rapid Fire / Freezing Moon / Creatures Of Light And Darkness (Live) / Carnal (Live) / Red Dunes / Lord Of Desert.
Beware The Beast, Empire (2004). Dark Transmission (333.version) / Stranger In The Mirror / Report from studio (Video) / Dark Transmission (Video).
THE BEAST, Metal Blade 14485-2 (2004). Intro / Out Of The Deep / Dark Transmission / Firebringer / The Sea Came In At Last / Stranger In The Mirror / I Shall Prevail / The Zone / Insomnia / Apopheniac / Choices.
The Art Of War, Regain RR 074 (2005). Para Bellum / This Is The War / Lead Us!!! / Banners On The Wind / What Colour Is Your Blood? / Death In Silence / This Is The War (video).
IMPRESSIONS IN BLOOD, Regain (2006). Between Day And Night / ShadowsFear / As Heavens Collide… / Helleluyah!!! (God Is Dead) / Field Of Heads / Predator / Warlords / Red Code / Amongst The Ruins / They Live!!! / The Book. Chart position: 8 POLAND.

VENGEANCE RISING

LOS ANGELES, CA, USA — *Roger Martinez (vocals / guitar), Larry Farkas (guitar), Doug Thieme (guitar), Roger Dale Martin (bass), Glenn Mancarusco (drums).*

Although one of the leading lights of the Christian Death Metal scene for a lengthy period, the Los Angeles based VENGEANCE RISING would become embroiled in bitter recriminations as vocalist Roger Martinez, now solo, has reportedly disowned his previous beliefs. Martinez, who plotted another anti-Christian VENGEANCE RISING album to be titled 'Realms Of Blasphemy' as well as an expose treatise 'The Lixivium Letters', claims to have been duped into believing in and promoting God.

The band was created in 1985 by former SACRIFICE members along with guitarists Larry Farkas and Doug Thieme along with drummer Glenn Mancaruso. Martinez, previously with PROPHET, was enrolled as singer the following year. The band was initially billed as VENGEANCE but another act of the same name was discovered. The album sleeve, which featured a close up of a nailed crucified hand, actually that of Pastor Bob Beeman, for the Caesar Kalinowski produced debut 'Human Sacrifice' had to be reprinted with the new logo. Tracks on this album were co-written by guitarist Glenn Rogers, subsequently to join DELIVERANCE then HIRAX.

Following the 1990 Ron Goudie produced 'Once Dead' album promotional tour the band splintered. Only Martinez remained to carry on with the name as Farkas, Mancaruso and bassist Roger Dale Martin all quit. Martin founded Biker Blues band TRIPLE ACE whilst the others created DIE HAPPY. Farkas would also figure in SIRCLE OF SILENCE, the band assembled by erstwhile ACCEPT and BANGALORE CHOIR vocalist David Reece.

Meantime, Martinez enrolled guitarist Derek Sean and drummer Chris Hyde of DELIVERANCE for the 'Destruction Comes' opus.

For the 1992 'Released From The Earth' album Martinez employed guitarist Jamie Mitchell, bass player Joe Monsrb'nik and drummer Jonny Vasquez. Backing vocals came courtesy of MORTIFICATION's Steve Rowe, TOURNIQUET men Victor Marcios and David Vasquez and Jimmy Brown of DELIVERANCE. Jonny Vasquez would then join MORTIFICATION for touring.

Touring upon the album release saw DELIVERANCE guitarist George Ochoa as live guitarist. Apparently upon completion of these dates, sometime between 1995 and 1997, Martinez became an atheist. His personal website claimed fresh VENGEANCE RISING recordings were on the way but they did not materialise.

Undeterred by the scandal, Christian Deathsters ULTIMATUM would cover 'Burn' for their third album 'The Mechanics Of Perilous Times'.

Needless to say VENGEANCE RISING remains a hot topic of debate on the Christian music scene. Re-billed as VENGEANCE the group made a surprise return in 2004. With Martinez conspicuous by his absence the band—guitarists Larry Farkas and Doug Thieme, bass player Roger Dale Martin and drummer Glen Mancaruso announced an appearance at the 'Summer Madness' event on 29th August at Chain Reaction in Anaheim, California. A surprise guest vocalist would fill in for Martinez, Scott Waters of ULTIMATUM, was to rise to the challenge. This grouping of musicians, under threat of legal action from Roger Martinez, subsequently unveiled a new band title of ONCE DEAD. In January 2006 guitarist Glenn Rogers, another ex-VENGEANCE RISING member, joined the fold.

Martinez returned to the fore in 2006, announcing an appearance at the August 19th 'Sex, Drugs & Death Metal' festival in Overland, Missouri.

HUMAN SACRIFICE, Intense (1989). Human Sacrifice / Burn / Mulligan Stew / Receive Him / I Love Hating Evil / Fatal Delay / White Throne / Salvation / From The Dead / Ascension / He Is God / Fill This Place With Blood / Beheaded.
ONCE DEAD, Intense (1990). Warfare / Can't Get Out / Cut Into Pieces / Frontal Lobotomy / Herod's Violent Death / The Whipping Post / Arise / Space Truck'in / Out Of The Will / The Wrath To Come / Into The Abyss / Among The Dead / Interruption.
DESTRUCTION COMES, Intense (1991). You Can't Stop It / The Rising / Before The Time / The Sword / He Don't Own Nothing / Countless Corpses / Thanatos / You Will Bow / Hyde Under Pressure / Raeqoul.
RELEASED UPON THE EARTH, Intense (1992). Help Me / The Damnation Of Judas And The Salvation Of The Thief / Released Upon The Earth / Human Dark Potential / Instruments Of Death / Lest You Be Judged / Out Of Bounds / Bishop Of Souls / Tion / You Will Be Hated.

VENIA

FINLAND — *Veronica Fagerlund (vocals / violin), Viktor Fagerström (guitar), Jere Veijalainen (guitar), Juhani Palttala (bass), Daniel Puolimatka (drums).*

VENIA (Latin for "forgiveness") is a Christian melodic Metal band conceived by guitarist Viktor Fagerström in the Autumn of 2002, being joined at first by guitarist Jere Veijalainen. In early 2004 the band would be joined by singer / violinist Veronica Fagerlund and drummer Daniel Puolimatka, the latter, despite being the youngest band member, a scene veteran of FROM ASHES, TRITHON and ALTITHRONUS. The line-up was completed by the bassist Juhani Palttala, keyboard player for MEGIDDON and drummer of BLEAKWAIL. This new recruit had been active in the Metal scene since the mid nineties, having played keyboards with MANIFESTIUM and drums for VOIMA.

In late Spring 2004 Fagerström, maintaining his VENIA duties, also joined up with BLEAKWAIL. VENIA crafted their opening seven song 'Genesis' demo at Filadelfiaförsamlingen Studios in Helsingfors between June and August. The debut album, 'In Our Weakness', was recorded for the Bombworks label at Studio Bändipaja in Espoo with producer Thomas Mattsson.

Genesis, Venia (2004) (Demo). False Security / Ei Mun Tarvitse / Tormented Souls / Eternal Sanctuary / Taivaassa / Miks / Genesis.
IN OUR WEAKNESS, Bombworks BWR0509 (2005). Kaipuu / Illusion / The Path / Heikko / No More.

VENOM

NEWCASTLE UPON TYNE, UK — *Cronos (vocals / bass), Mantas (guitar), Abaddon (drums).*

VENOM is the Black Metal band that unwittingly inspired a plethora of imitators as part of the growing 80s extreme Metal scene in Europe and North America. Very few would dare dispute the band's righteous claim to having invented Black Metal and indeed many of the genre's higher echelon elite have been eager to confirm their allegiance both in print, on stage and in audio, a large percentage of extreme metal outfits, many themselves regarded as innovators themselves, have demoed with VENOM cover versions.

Newcastle upon Tyne trio VENOM was initially discounted for their early albums by the general Rock media, although these records were subsequently to be declared classics of the genre, in spite of their, deliberately, primitive approach. The group eschewed Rock stardom for a Punk Metal ethos and in doing so rapidly generated a loyal global fan base.

VENOM's roots lay in the Newcastle upon Tyne late 70's acts GUILLOTINE, ALBUM GRACIA, OBERON and DWARFSTAR. In 1978 Lant was guitarist with ALBUM GRACIA. Members from this band including vocalist Keith Ballard and drummer Kevin Robson decamped to found a new act the same year entitled DWARFSTAR. Meantime, another local band GUILLOTINE, featuring guitarist Jeffrey Dunn retitled themselves VENOM in 1979. The inaugural line-up of this group being Dunn, vocalist Dave Blackman, second guitarist Dave Rutherford, bassist Dean Hewitt and drummer Chris McPeters. Both Blackman and McPeters lost their places in August of that year to former OBERON members drummer Tony Bray and singer Clive Archer. OBERON would play a further part in VENOM's later career when guitarist Eric Cook would wind up as manager of the band.

The new look VENOM, also with a fresh bassist Alan Winston, were to pull in Lant as replacement for Rutherford in November. However, mere days before the band's debut gig in Wallsend Winston bailed out forcing Lant to take over the bassist's role. This he did by necessity plugging a bass guitar into a lead guitar amp.

By 1980 the proto VENOM had decided upon the satanic image "de-christening" the band members in suitable fashion. Archer became 'Jesus Christe', Lant 'Mr. Cronos', Bray 'Abbadon' and Dunn 'Mantas'. A three song demo was cut in April featuring early work outs of 'Angel Dust', 'Raise The Dead' and 'Red Light Fever'. A second session, recorded for a miserly £50, laid down six more tracks with Lant taking lead vocals for 'Live Like An Angel'. Archer packed his bags soon after and the unholy triumvirate of VENOM was born.

The band adopted the position of marrying Lant's Punk influences with direct inspiration from some of the global Rock giants. In early interviews the band professed the desire to have the energy of JUDAS PRIEST with the theatrics of KISS. Having, naturally, been signed by Neat Records VENOM debuted with the 'Welcome To Hell' album and immediately came to the attention of 'Sounds' journo Geoff Barton.

Barton's championing of the group certainly brought VENOM to the attention of the Metal loving public, although the trio had yet to play a gig.

VENOM's debut 1981 single, 'In League With Satan' / 'Live Like An Angel', was recorded at Impulse Studios in Wallsend, hosted above an old cinema complex, and produced by Steve Thompson and Mickey Sweeney. Recordings in 1981 also summoned the group's first album, 'Welcome To Hell' produced at Impulse once again but this time with Keith Nichol behind the desk, this issued in a variety of formats including picture disc, regular black, white, grey and purple vinyl. A green marbled version is now worth over £300. Notably, a young teenager in the Norwegian town of Ski, Øystein Aarseth, took the song title 'Mayhem With Mercy' to brand his new act—MAYHEM.

In 1982 VENOM, once again employing Impulse Studios and Keith Nichol, issued the seminal 'Black Metal' set. A preceding single had coupled the non album tracks 'Bloodlust' and 'In Nomine Satanas'. Whilst previous product had incited curiosity, it was the 'Black Metal' album that triggered the global VENOM phenomenon. Neat Records handled UK versions whilst Roadrunner Records licensed the album for European territories. Once again limited editions saw the album pressed on a variety of colours including white, grey, purple, green, red, brown and "swirled" vinyl. That same year the band conducted their first BBC Radio One 'Friday Rock Show' session, laying down 'Black Metal', 'Nightmare' and 'Bloodlust'. These tracks would also make an appearance on the highly sought after 'French Assault' EP.

VENOM's third album, 1983's 'At War With Satan', found the Geordie triumvirate of Metal taking huge strides forward, especially abroad, as the semi conceptual 'At War With Satan' hugely increased the band's following.

The band's first European live date came in Belgium (the group's initial live performance having ensured they would never play a club again as the event was marked by a handmade stage prop falling over and firing pyrotechnics into the audience!) where they headlined above PICTURE and ACID. It was on the continent where the band were only able to translate their mystique into material success with a series of major festival appearances and tours, including a trek through Europe in 1984 with METALLICA as the support act, VENOM were virtually shunned by the UK audience where a succession of announced tours were scrapped, although the 'The 7th Date Of Hell' video did arise from the group's spectacular debut at Hammersmith Odeon in London on the 'At War With Satan' tour.

Before going in to record fourth album 'Possessed', Cronos produced fellow Neat label act TYSONDOG' first album, 'Beware Of The Dog', although somewhat bizarrely he then announced to the world that it was "shit"!

1985 began disastrously for the band. Although Combat Records gave earlier VENOM product an official US release for the first time, adding revised artwork and extra tracks in the process, the new offering 'Possessed' album was roundly chastised and a planned Canadian / American tour was thrown into turmoil as Mantas succumbed to glandular fever. The dates were put back and, as his health worsened, VENOM recruited AVENGER guitarist Les Cheetham and FIST guitarist Dave Irwin to fill the shoes of Mantas. The band's New York Studio 54 show, with EXODUS and SLAYER, their most prestigious date on the tour, was less than successful as Mantas, now with restored health, was denied access to America due to passport problems.

The band returned to Europe on September 14th 1985, performing at the 'Metal Hammer Fest' in Loreley, Germany sharing a diverse billing with NAZARETH, METALLICA, HEAVY PETTIN, WISHBONE ASH, SAVAGE GRACE, RUNNING WILD, TYRAN PACE, PRETTY MAIDS and WARLOCK.

1986 saw the departure of the guitarist following American dates with support act HIRAX. Demos, still with Mantas in the ranks, were conducted for a proposed album entitled 'Deadline' but with the guitarist's exit this project was shelved. A live album surfaced billed 'Eine Kleine Nachtmusik', recorded at the band's now legendary 8th October 1985 London Hammersmith Odeon appearance and a 1986 gig at The Ritz, New York. Mantas resurfaced shortly after with his own MANTAS project that issued one album, 1988's 'Winds Of Change', but he soon retired to concentrate on building up a martial arts centre. Cronos busied himself producing the 1986 album from WARFARE 'Mayhem Fucking Mayhem'.

Mantas was to be replaced by two guitarists, Jimmy C. (Jim Clare) and Mike H. (Mike Hickey), who performed their debut live shows with VENOM touring Brazil with support act EXCITER as well as Japanese dates. Previous to joining VENOM Clare had operated with Newcastle acts HARDLINE and HELLFIRE. With the introduction of the twin guitar set up originally called for some new suitably occult pseudonyms although the initial concept of Clare as 'The Mighty Horn' and Hickey as 'King Incubus' would thankfully be abandoned.

This new line-up recorded the lukewarm Nick Tauber / Kevin Ridley produced 'Calm Before The Storm' for RCA subsidiary Filmtrax. The album, featuring some but not all of the aborted 'Deadline' material, saw the band endeavouring to pursue a more finely crafted, mature approach rather than the bludgeoning ferocity of yore, but merely succeeded in alienating existing fans. Behind the scenes, what VENOM fans were unaware of, was that the tracks used for the 'Calm Before The Storm' album were, in fact, originally intended as demos recorded at Neat's Impulse Studios and subsequently remixed in London. The tracks were not intended as finished product.

Following the live dates, VENOM set to work on a new studio album but internal friction resulted in a parting of ways. Cronos and Clare broke away, relocating to America and resurfacing as CRONOS, utilising tracks assembled for a VENOM release as their 'Dancing In The Fire' opening album. CRONOS would also include their former VENOM colleague Mike Hickey alongside drummer Chris Patterson.

In 1988 Mantas appeared again, this time as guest guitarist on WARFARE's 'A Conflict Of Hatred' album. VENOM regrouped once more in 1989, enticing original guitarist Mantas back into the fold alongside the drumming lynchpin of Abbadon, bassist / vocalist Tony Dolan and rhythm guitarist Al Barnes. Barnes had worked previously with Mantas on his solo album 'Winds Of Change', whilst Dolan was ex-ATOMKRAFT. This line-up debuted with 'Prime Evil', released in 1989 and once again produced by Tauber and Ridley. That same year the band cut a version of BLACK SABBATH's 'Megalomania', this subsequently surfacing on the 'Witching Hour' compilation.

VENOM took to the UK stages again in late 1989, billed under the pseudonym of SONS OF SATAN which included a "secret" London Marquee gig which attracted only a handful of followers giving ample indication as to the apathy towards the band. Their 1990 mini-album 'Tear Your Soul Apart' featured Mantas, Abaddon and Dolan and included a bizarre cover of JUDAS PRIEST's 'Hell Bent For Leather' classic.

VENOM released the 'Temples Of Ice' album in 1991. Produced by Abaddon and Kevin Ridley at Lynx studios in Newcastle upon Tyne, the album hosted a rendition of DEEP PURPLE's 'Speedking' and, perhaps more prominently, a tribute song, 'In Memory Of (Paul Miller 1964-90)', to the late journalist, a staunch champion of underground British acts. 'The Waste Lands', seeing an expanded recording roster comprising Dolan, Mantas, Abaddon, Al Barnes, former ATOMKRAFT man Steve White (a.k.a. 'War Machine') on second guitar and V.X.S. (actually two separate people) on keyboards, followed in 1992. Both these latter two outings soon sank from public view.

Nevertheless, enthusiasm outside of the UK was still strong and VENOM's first show promoting 'The Waste Lands' was on a festival billing at the Winter Palace in St. Petersburg, Russia ranked alongside UFO, MAGNUM, SWEET, GIRLSCHOOL and ASIA. The success of this event, televised to over four million Russians, prompted a request for the new line-up to record classic tracks for a special Russian release. The group duly laid these tracks down but no release was forthcoming. The songs later re-surfaced on the 'Kissing The Beast' collection. However, Music For Nations opted against continuing with the band and Dolan, achieving success in his parallel career with the Royal Shakespeare Company, decided to quit, citing Abbadon's claims in the press linking VENOM with Satanism as the main reason.

In 1994 a VENOM tribute album, In The Name Of Satan, pooled a high profile collection of artists paying homage. Tracks included KREATOR's interpretation of 'Witching Hour', ANATHEMA with 'Welcome To Hell', VOIVOD's 'In League with Satan', NUCLEAR ASSAULT's 'Die Hard', SKYCLAD's 'Prime Evil', SODOM's entirely suitable '1,000 Days In Sodom', CANDLEMASS with 'Countess Bathory', PARADISE LOST with 'In Nomine Satanas' plus VENOM themselves donating an industrial mix of 'Warhead' and 'Holy Man'.

Famed Japanese Black Metal outfit SIGH paid their own form

of recognition with an entire release of VENOM tracks, 'To Hell and Back'. Meanwhile, ex-VENOM guitarist Mike Hickey, following his stint with CRONOS, teamed up with arch goremongers CARCASS in 1994. Cronos also came out of the shadows, lending backing vocals to rising UK Black Metal band CRADLE OF FILTH's 'Dusk And Her Dark Embrace' album.

Following no less than three years of negotiations, the original band line up reformed in 1995, to nothing less than ecstatic European media response, to headline the Burgum 'Waldrock' and Eindhoven 'Dynamo' festivals. At the latter event VENOM used so much pyro that one particular blast proved so powerful the band's backdrop came to rest over the drum kit midway through the set! An edited form of this show was released as the video / CD package 'The Second Coming'.

VENOM spent a large chunk of 1997 recording their ninth studio album, 'Cast In Stone', only interrupting proceedings to headline the Metal Invader Festival in Athens, Greece. The protracted nature of the recording was to be drawn out even further when, upon nearing completion, the band actually scrapped all previous efforts, opting to re-record the entire body of work. Upon eventual release, initial copies of 'Cast In Stone' came with recent re-recordings of VENOM classics from the early days.

VENOM made a return to America in 1997 headlining the notorious Milwaukee Metalfest, but end of year European dates supported by the fast rising Swedes HAMMERFALL where cancelled due to Cronos having to undergo surgery for vocal nodes. A wealth of Swedish bands gave offering that same year by way of the 'Promoters Of The Third World War' set. Featured would be ALCHEMIST with 'Black Metal', FLEGMA with 'Leave Me In Hell', FURBOWL's 'Buried Alive', AFFLICTED's '7 Gates Of Hell', THERION's 'Witching Hour', KAZJUROL's 'Countess Bathory' and DERANGED's 'In League With Satan' amongst others.

The 2000 VENOM album 'Resurrection' saw Abbadon, who issued a somewhat bizarre solo album, replaced by Antton.

Cronos would contribute guest vocals to FOO FIGHTERS man Dave Grohl's Metal elite PROBOT project album of 2001. During March of 2002 Cronos would injure himself quite severely in a climbing accident. Some consolation for the frontman would be the Sanctuary Records remastering of the first triumvirate of classic VENOM albums, all re-released with a glut of extra tracks and extensive liner notes.

During the summer of 2002 former VENOM and CRONOS guitarist Jim Clare united with TYGERS OF PAN TANG drummer Craig Ellis and bass player Willie Angus in a new band project entitled PASSION PLAY. By August this project had adopted the revised title of TRIBAL CORE.

Drummer Antton, still maintaining his membership of VENOM, teamed up with Newcastle act NU-FUTURE COWBOYS in October. He would also be an active member of DEF-CON-ONE. VENOM themselves got back into action in early 2004, gearing up for recording of a new studio album. American guitarist Mykus, actually former member Mike Hickey, was announced as being the latest recruit to the fold in March. The new look VENOM debuted live on 5th April with an unannounced surprise set at Trillians in Newcastle following a set from DEF-CON-ONE.

During mid 2004 VENOM would have their classic cut 'Warhead' chosen as a pioneering piece of music for a compilation assembled by DARKTHRONE drummer Fenriz, released through Peaceville Records and entitled 'Fenriz Presents The Best Of Old School Black Metal'. Cronos acted as special guest on the 2005 HAMMERFALL album 'Chapter V: Unbent, Unbowed, Unbroken'. That December Cronos guested on album recordings by leading Italian extreme Metal band NECRODEATH.

VENOM returned with a new studio album, 'Metal Black' recorded for Sanctuary Records, in March 2006. This opus, crafted by Cronos, guitarist Mike Hickey and drummer Antton, would witness a deliberate return to the original, 80s VENOM sound. 'Antton' was later revealed to be Conrad's brother Antony Lant of DEF-CON-ONE. UK gigs in March saw reformed Bristol Thrashers ONSLAUGHT as support. That same month the group recorded a four song session for the BBC at London's Maida Vale studios. Summer festival appearances at the Italian 'Gods Of Metal', Finnish 'Tuska' event, German 'Earthshaker' and 'Sweden Rock' festivals followed.

VENOM announced a two day "Thrash Domination" stint at Tokyo's famed Club Citta on September 16th and 17th ranked alongside DEATH ANGEL, SODOM, DRAGONLORD and ONSLAUGHT. However, the group pulled out, stating that Cronos had been "taken ill".

US shows for August, to be supported by DEVILDRIVER, were cancelled cue to "immigration problems". The band rescheduled these dates, commencing later that same month, now seeing GOATWHORE as support act.

VENOM announced that Mike Hickey was to stand down in January 2007, stating "Personal unavoidable commitments in the U.S. have forced Mykvs to announce that he cannot commit 100% to VENOM's 2007 schedule". A new man titled 'Rage' was swiftly announced as replacement.

In League With Satan, Neat NEAT 08 (1981). In League With Satan / Live Like An Angel (Die Like A Devil).

WELCOME TO HELL, Neat NEAT 1002 (1981). Sons Of Satan / Welcome To Hell / Schizo / Mayhem With Mercy / Poison / Live Like An Angel / Witching Hour / One Thousand Days In Sodom / Angel Dust / In League With Satan / Red Light Fever.

BLACK METAL, Neat NEAT 1005 (1982). Black Metal / To Hell And Back / Buried Alive / Raise The Dead / Teacher's Pet / Leave Me In Hell / Sacrifice / Heaven's On Fire / Countess Bathory / Don't Burn The Witch / At War With Satan (Preview).

Bloodlust, Neat NEAT 13 (1982). Bloodlust / In Nomine Satanas.

Die Hard, Neat NEAT 27 (1983). Die Hard / Acid Queen.

Die Hard, Neat NEAT 27 12 (1983). Die Hard / Acid Queen / Burning Out.

Warhead, Neat NEAT 38 (1984) (Released in three different sleeves). Warhead / Lady Lust.

Warhead, Neat NEAT38 12 (1984). Warhead / Lady Lust / The Seven Gates Of Hell.

AT WAR WITH SATAN, Neat NEAT 1015 (1985). At War With Satan / Rip Ride / Genocide / Cry Wolf / Stand Up And Be Counted / Women, Leather And Hell / Aaaaarghhhh. Chart positions: 48 SWEDEN, 64 UK.

French Assault, New NW 2317 (1985). Nightmare / Bloodlust / In Nomine Satanas / Countess Bathory (Live) / Powerdrive / Bursting Out.

American Assault, Combat MX8034 (1985). Rip Ride / Bursting Out / Dead Of The Night / The Seven Gates Of Hell (Live) / Countess Bathory (Live) / Welcome To Hell (Live).

Hell At Hammersmith EP, Neat NEAT 53-12 (1985). Witching Hour (Live) / Teacher's Pet (Live) / Poison (Live) / Teacher's Pet (Live).

POSSESSED, Neat NEAT 1024 (1985). Moonshine / Harmony Drive / Wing And A Prayer / Voyeur / Satanarchist / Mystique / Possessed / Suffer Not The Children / Hellchild / Fly Trap / Powerdrive / Too Loud For The Crowd / Burn This Place To The Ground. Chart position: 99 UK.

JAPANESE ASSAULT, VAP R 35177 25 (1985). In League With Satan / Live Like An Angel (Die Like A Devil) / Bloodlust / In Nomine Satanas / Die Hard / Witching Hour (Live) / Bursting Out / Warhead / Manitou / Dead Of The Night / The Seven Gates Of Hell.

Canadian Assault, Banzai BAM 1002 (1985). Die Hard (Live) / Welcome To Hell (Live) / In Nomine Satanas (Live) / Warhead / Woman / The Seven Gates Of Hell.

Manitou, Neat NEAT 43 12 (1985). Manitou / Woman / Dead Of The Night.

Manitou, Neat NEAT 43 (1985). Manitou / Woman.

Nightmare, Neat NEAT 47 12 (1985). Nightmare / Satanarchist / FOAD / Warhead (Live).

Nightmare, Neat NEAT 47 (1985). Nightmare / Satanarchist.

Scandinavian Assault, Sonom AB SON XS-100 (1986). Nightmare (Live) / Too Loud (For The Crowd) (Live) / Die Hard (Live) / Bloodlust / Powerdrive / Warhead.

EINE KLEINE NACHTMUSIK, Neat NEAT 1032 (1986). Too Loud For The Crowd / Seven Gates Of Hell / Leave Me In Hell / Nightmare / Countess Bathory / Die Hard / Schitzo / In Nomine Satanas / Witching Hour / Black Metal / The Chanting Of The Priests / Satanarchist / Fly Trap / Warhead / Buried Alive / Love Amongst The Dead / Welcome To Hell / Bloodlust.
German Assault, Roadrunner RR9659 (1987). Nightmare / Black Metal / Too Loud (For The Crowd) / Radio Interview / Witching Hour / Powerdrive / Buried Alive.
LIVE OFFICIAL BOOTLEG, Metalworks APK PD12 (1987). Intro / Leave Me In Hell / Countess Bathory / Die Hard / The Seven Gates Of Hell / Bass Solo / Buried Alive / Don't Burn The Witch / In Nomine Satanas / Welcome To Hell / Warhead / Stand Up And Be Counted / Guitar Solo / Bloodlust.
CALM BEFORE THE STORM, Filmtrax MOMENT 115 (1987). Black Xmas / The Chanting Of The Priests / Metal Punk / Under A Spell / Calm Before The Storm / Fire / Krackin' Up / Beauty And The Beast / Deadline / Gypsy / Muscle.
PRIME EVIL, Under One Flag FLAG 36 (1989). Prime Evil / Parasite / Blackened Are The Priests / Carnivorous / Skeletal Dance / Megalomania / Insane / Harder Than Ever / Into The Fire / Scholl Daze / Live Like An Angel.
Tear Your Soul Apart EP, Under One Flag MFLAG 50 (1990). Skool Daze / Bursting Out / The Ark / Civilised / Angel Dust / Hell Bent For Leather (Live).
THE WASTELANDS, Under One Flag FLAG 72 (1991). Cursed / I'm Paralysed / Black Legions / Riddle Of Steel / Need To Kill / Kissing The Beast / Crucified / Shadow King / Wolverine / Clarisse.
TEMPLES OF ICE, Under One Flag FLAG 56 (1991). Tribes / Even In Heaven / Trinity MCMXLV 0530 / In Memory Of (Paul Miller 1964-90) / Faerie Tale / Playtime / Acid / Arachnid / Speed King / Temples Of Ice.
THE SECOND COMING, Hardware CMA 001 (1996). The Seven Gates Of Hell / Die Hard / Welcome To Hell / Leave Me In Hell / Countess Bathory / Buried Alive / Don't Burn The Witch / In Nomine Satanas / Schitzo / Nightmare / Black Metal / Witching Hour.
Venom '96 EP, Venom (1996). 7 Gates Of Hell / Welcome To Hell / In Nomine Satanas / Black Metal / The Evil One (New '96 track).
CAST IN STONE, CBH Steamhammer CD 8000136 (1997). Evil One / Raised In Hell / All Devil's Eve / Bleeding / Destroyed And Damned / Domus Mundi / Flight Of The Hydra / God's Forsaken / Mortals / Infectious / Kings Of Evil / You're All Gonna Die / Judgement Day / Swarm.
RESURRECTION, Steamhammer SPV 08521752 (2000). Resurrection / Vengeance / War Against Christ / All There Is Fear / Pain / Pandemonium / Loaded / Firelight / Black Flame Of Satan / Controlfreak / Disbeliever / Man, Myth & Magic / Leviathan.
Antechrist, Castle CMWSE1333 (2006). Antechrist / Metal Black.
METAL BLACK, Castle CMFCD1282 (2006). Antechrist / Burn In Hell / House Of Pain / Death & Dying / Rege Satanas / Darkest Realm / A Good Day To Die / Assassin / Lucifer Rising / Blessed Dead / Hours Of Darkness / Sleep When I'm Dead / Maleficarvm / Metal Black.

VEXED

ITALY — *Mik (vocals), Rob (guitar), Claud (guitar), Winx (bass), Mike (drums).*

Founded in 1996, VEXED are a Black Metal band consciously rooted in 80s Thrash traditions. Releasing the 1999 cassette 'Abyss Of Agony' VEXED comprised of a line up citing vocalist Mik, guitarist Jex, bass player Kyle and drummer Mike. However, during 2000 both Kyle and Mike made their exit to join SINE MACULA. The group regrouped quickly, pulling in replacements bassist Winx and drummer Moreno as well as second guitar player Claud. New material was demoed in December of 2000 with John of NECRODEATH at the production helm. With the songs laid down Jex left the band, being replaced by Rob.

A deal was struck with Witchhammer Records to release these sessions on CD format, including a rendition of SLAYER's 'Black Magic', in 2002. The same songs would also be issued as a split single in league with Brazilian Thrashers FARSCAPE on Deathstrike Records. Touring found VEXED as opening act for DESASTER, NECRODEATH and TANKARD. A further split tape release, 'Italian Thrash Metal Assault', in alliance with HATEWORK would be distributed globally through Deathstrike in Germany, Metal Psycho in Ecuador and Witchhammer in Thailand.

A second full length album titled 'Nightmare Holocaust' was projected for 2002 release. The record, complete with two unaccredited 'ghost' tracks and a cover of SODOM's 'Blasphemer', was eventually released the following year by the German Witches Brew label. Bringing Mike back onboard as drummer VEXED issued a split 7" single 'Nuclear Babylon', shared with HATEWORK, on the Dream Evil label.

VEXED would spend the Spring of 2004 in Bunker Studios crafting a new album 'Destruction Warfare'. A 2005 opus, 'Hellblast Extinction', included, 2 Italian language songs, 4 newly recorded tracks, 7 live songs and a cover of KREATOR's 'Pleasure To Kill'.

The band teamed up with SINISTER, ENTHRONED and NECROART for a short Italian tour in May.

ENDLESS ARMAGEDDON, Witchhammer (2002). Napalm Storm / Bringers Of Death / Lust Of Revenge / Oblivion Takes Unanimated Brians / Delerium Shades / Death Silence / Demoniac War / Death Justice / War Battle / Dirty Disaster / Black Magic.
NIGHTMARE HOLOCAUST, Witches Brew (2003). Nuclear Annihilation / Nightmare Holocaust / Deathfire / Collection Blood / Evil Command / Bastard Massacre / Death Justice / Blasphemer / Black Cold Eyes / Italian Aggressive Attack / Elements Of Anger.
Nuclear Babylon, Dream Evil (2003) (Split single with HATEWORK). Nuclear Babylon / Bringers Of Death (Live).
DESTRUCTION WARFARE, Witches Brew BREW 010 (2004). Nuclear Babylon / Warblast / Requiem Aetermum / Phobic Reign / Black Terror / Death Symphony / Bladeblood / Total Desaster / Gods Of Darkness / Destruction Warfare / Dogmatic Blame.

VICIOUS

VÄSTERÅS, SWEDEN — *Henke Wenngren (vocals), Pontus Pettersson (guitar), Simon Jarrolf (bass), Fredrik Eriksson (drums).*

Västerås based Death Thrashers. The band began life as a school act of guitarists Pontus Pettersson and Fredde, soon uniting with drummer Adam Hobér of Black Metal act ENTHRALLED. This trio picked the title RAGE ANTHEM initially for the opening demo 'Fire Desires' but would then adopt WARGASM as their banner. Later recruits included bassist Simon Jarrolf and new drummer Erik Wallin.

Although the band issued the mini album 'Pure Evil (Straight From Hell)' during 2001 they would, bringing in another drummer Fredrik Eriksson, subsequently switch band title to VICIOUS. Under their new title the band re-debuted in 2002 with the EP 'Chains Won't Hold It Back'. VICIOUS frontman Henke Wenngren also holds down membership in MORNALAND and SKYFIRE. He would also gain production credits on DEAD AWAKEN's demo "Death Before Dishonour'.

Signing to the Portuguese Sound Riot label VICIOUS cut their debut album 'Vile, Vicious & Victorious' at Studio Underground in Västerås for release in March of 2004. Guesting in the studio would be bass player Petri Kuusisto of CARNAL FORGE and the ROSICRUCIAN, SLAPDASH, ZEALION, POWERAGE and LOST SOULS credited guitarist Magnus Söderman.

Chains Won't Hold It Back, Vicious (2002) (Demo). High On Fire / Deathrash / Feeder Of Evil.
VILE, VICIOUS AND VICTORIOUS, Sound Riot SRP.027 (2004). Beast / Trigger Needs Some Action / High On Fire / Deadicate / Life Corrupted / Deathrash / Boots Of Led / A Vicious Mind / The Feeder Of Evil.

VICIOUS ART

STOCKHOLM, SWEDEN — *Jocke Widfeldt (vocals), Matti Mäkelä (guitar), Tobbe Sillman (guitar), Jörgen Sandström (bass), Robert Lundin (drums).*

VICIOUS ART is a 2004 founded Death / Thrash act forged by former DARK FUNERAL and DOMINION CALIGULA members Mattias 'Dominion' Mäkelä and Robert 'Gaahnfaust' Lundin, also both holding OBSCURITY credentials. The duo subsequently enrolled Jörgen Sandström of GOD AMONG INSECTS, THE PROJECT HATE, KRUX, NASUM and a veteran of ENTOMBED and GRAVE on bass. Secondary guitars would be delegated to Tobbe Sillman of GUIDANCE OF SIN and THE DEAD.

The band would soon sign an album deal with ENTOMBED's Threeman Recordings, 'Fire Falls And The Waiting Waters' being set for a November release. To coincide, VICIOUS ART made their concert debut at the Tantogården venue in Stockholm in 12th November alongside MÖRK GRYNING and NINNUAM.

The VICIOUS ART triumvirate of Tobbe Sillman, Jocke Widfeldt and Matti Mäkelä featured as backing vocalists on THE PROJECT HATE's 2005 album "Armageddon March Eternal (Symphonies Of Slit Wrists)'. Jörgen Sandström also announced the formation of a deliberately retro-Death Metal band project entitled DEATH BREATH in collaboration with his erstwhile ENTOMBED colleague and THE HELLACOPTERS frontman Nicke Andersson with THUNDER EXPRESS man Robert Persson on guitar.

VICIOUS ART issued the 'Weed The Wild' EP in February 2006.

Vicious Art, Vicious Art (2003) (Demo). A Whistler And His Son / The Poet Must Die / Crash Landing / Why Would The Captured Set Free The Flies?

FIRE FALLS AND THE WAITING WATERS, Threeman Recordings TRECD017 (2004). Debria Seems To Be Bleeding / Komodo Lights / Fire Falls / A Whistler And His Gun / Ceremony (The Waiting Waters) / Mother Dying / The Poet Must Die / Cut This Heathen Free / War / Why Would The Captured Set Free The Flies?

Weed The Wild, Vicious Art (2006). Weed The Wild / Tanja Joins The Beating / Exit Wounds.

VICIOUS RUMORS

SANTA ROSA, CA, USA — *Brian O'Connor (vocals), Geoff Thorpe (guitar), Ira Black (guitar), Cornbread (bass), Dan Lawson (drums).*

A Power Thrash Metal band of great repute, VICIOUS RUMORS formed in Santa Rosa in August 1979, co-founded by mainstay guitarist Geoff Thorpe. The band's debut performance came in 1980 at one of the fabled 'Metal Monday' meetings The Old Waldorf in San Francisco. Two years later the first audio arrived in the form of 'I Can Live Forever' included on the KMEL 'New Oasis' compilation, the band lining up as vocalist Mark Tate, guitarists Geoff Thorpe and Jim Cassero, bass player Jeff Barnacle and drummer Walt Perkins.

The band would quickly be taken under the wing of guitar guru and Shrapnel Records boss Mike Varney, Thorpe meeting the man through Varney's ROCK JUSTICE project. At the time of their meeting Varney was in the process of putting the Shrapnel Records label together, a company that first made its name with the 'U.S. Metal' series of compilation albums that pushed the playing of the guitarists in the individual bands concerned well to the fore.

VICIOUS RUMORS line-up of 1983 saw Walt Perkins supplanted by Jim Lange. At this formative stage VICIOUS RUMORS were heavily reliant on image with coordinated black and blue stage costumes and with their singer entering the stage held aloft in a coffin borne by monks.

New bassist Dave Starr had been a member of fellow Metal band LÄÄZ ROCKIT, actually a founder member having renamed that act from their previous title of DEPTH CHARGE. Fired from LÄÄZ ROCKIT in 1983, Starr hooked created a power trio titled BLACK LEATHER with guitarist Rick Richards and drummer Jim Wells. In 1985 Starr formed part of the regrouped VICIOUS RUMORS completing a line-up of ex-HAWAII singer Gary St. Pierre, guitarist Geoff Thorpe and drummer Charles Emmil. During this period VAIN guitarist Jamie Rowe (then titled Chuck Mooney) made some recordings with VICIOUS RUMORS. Drummer for this period was Don Selzer.

VICIOUS RUMORS made their first appearance for Shrapnel on 'U.S. Metal Volume III' with the track 'Ultimate Death'. Varney gave the group another shot too, with 'One Way Ticket' included on 1984's 'U.S. Metal Volume IV'. At the time, Thorpe had been looking for the perfect guitar partner and getting nowhere. Former BLACK LEATHER man Rick Richards filled in for one gig. Varney introduced him to a discovery of his from Delaware called VINNIE MOORE. In no time at all, Moore was in the group and the group were put in the studio by Varney to record a debut album for Shrapnel in 1985. That first record 'Soldiers Of The Night', released in Europe in May 1985 through a licensing deal with Roadrunner, featured St. Pierre on vocals, Moore and Thorpe on guitar, bassist Dave Starr and drummer Larry Howe.

Moore, only ever a temporary member, would quit to pursue his goal of solo stardom and VICIOUS RUMORS promptly picked up former TYRANT man Terry Montana as a quick replacement. Montana lasted a year, recording demos and actually toured promoting the first album. After Montana's services were dispensed with, Alameda, California raised Mark McGee came into the frame. Formerly a member of local act OVERDRIVE, in the dual role of vocalist and rhythm guitarist, McGee had also spent a period of time in the ranks of fading Pomp Rock outfit STARCASTLE.

McGee made his debut with VICIOUS RUMORS on 1988's 'Digital Dictator' album, a record that also premiered ex-RUFFIANS and VILLIAN vocalist Carl Albert in place of the departed Gary St. Pierre. VICIOUS RUMORS hooked up SAVATAGE manager Robert Zemsky and consequently with major label Atlantic Records for the eponymous 1990 album, co-produced by Geoff Thorpe and Michael Rosen. The record title was originally set to be 'Immortal Battalion'.

VICIOUS RUMORS toured North America on a headlining club jaunt prior to European dates with DEATH ANGEL and FORBIDDEN as well as a performance at the prestigious Dynamo festival in Holland. Although media and fan response was enthusiastic, strangely the band did not seem to be receiving the benefits a major label like Atlantic could have delivered.

For 1991's 'Welcome To The Ball', again seeing Geoff Thorpe and Michael Rosen in command of the desk, the band toured Europe with SAVATAGE and put in further headline club gigs in America. Japanese dates resulted in the live 'Plug In And Hang On—Live In Tokyo' album.

The following year VICIOUS RUMORS were dealt two body blows. Not only were they dropped by Atlantic Records but Thorpe was found to be suffering from Carpal tunnel syndrome and had to undergo surgery for his condition. For a short while the band operated as a quartet without him. Howe filled his downtime by creating side project BOMB THREAT with HEATHEN members Lee Altus and Thaen Rasmussen with singer Jay from MY VICTIM. BOMB THREAT toured the California clubs playing a nostalgic set of NW0BHM covers.

By mid 1993 Thorpe was recovered enough to get out on the road again but by November line-up problems beset the band with Starr being fired and replaced by Tommy Sisco. The 1994 VICIOUS RUMOURS album 'Word Of Mouth' would see the addition of two bonus cuts for the Japanese market namely covers of the ROLLING STONES 'Paint It Black' and LED ZEPPELIN's 'Communication Breakdown'. In Germany the album emerged through Rising Sun Productions and limited edition digi-packs there added two live tracks, 'Hellraiser' and 'The Quest'.

In April 1995 VICIOUS RUMOURS took another hammer blow when Albert was killed in an auto accident. The singer hung onto life for a few days but was eventually pronounced braindead. McGee also quit the band eventually uniting with GREGG ALLMAN.

In October 1995 the group, now with Geoff Thorpe taking on lead vocals, got to tour the European continent once again as it hitched a ride on the heavyweight METAL CHURCH, ZODIAC MINDWARP and KILLERS package. Thorpe also took over lead vocals for the 1996 album 'Something Burning' as the band was also bolstered by guitarist Steve Smyth. The following year VICIOUS RUMORS drafted vocalist Brian O'Connor. High profile European dates would see the group guesting for ACCEPT. Back in America further gigs were put in as openers to established artists such as THIN LIZZY, RAINBOW and BLUE ÖYSTER CULT. The band would play to their biggest audiences though during 1998, billed as special guests to Germany's BLIND GUARDIAN on their European tour.

In 1999 VICIOUS RUMORS announced their new vocalist to be ex-HIGH TREASON and MEGATON BLONDE man Morgan Thorn. Smyth joined Thrash veterans TESTAMENT in the same year. That same year former guitarist Mark McGee established a new outfit billed LUVPLANET, later being joined by another erstwhile VICIOUS RUMORS colleague, bassist Tommy Sisco.

The band bounced back in 2001 with the 'Sadistic Symphony' album. VICIOUS RUMORS new look comprised of Thorn. Thorpe, guitarist Ira Black, bassist Cornbread and drummer Atma Anur. Black's history traces back through REXXEN, the 1992 incarnation of HEATHEN, UTERIS (featuring ex TESLA guitarist Tommy Skeoch) and DOGFACE with erstwhile EXODUS man Steve Souza. Bassist Cornbread is ex-BIZARRO, the band founded by ex-FORBIDDEN and TESTAMENT guitarist Glen Alvelais whilst drummer Atma Anur boasts numerous studio appearances with diverse acts such as DAVID BOWIE, JOURNEY, TONY MACALPINE and MARTY FRIEDMAN.

It would leak out that both Thorn and Cornbread had actually split away from the band in early 2001 but had resolved whatever differences of opinion there were and rejoined the fold. Former VICIOUS RUMORS personnel bassist Dave Starr and drummer Larry Howe would both join CHASTAIN in 2001. Meantime Ira Black delved into nostalgia by forming part of the reunion of 80s Thrash act MERCENARY.

With the release of the 'Sadistic Symphony' album VICIOUS RUMOURS once again changed tack, re-employing Brian O'Connor on vocals. The band, with Dan Lawson taking command of the drums, hooked up with SAVATAGE and BLAZE for European tour dates commencing in Sweden during January 2002 but would soon pull out citing friction with BLAZE.

Meanwhile, it would be learned in April that erstwhile VICIOUS RUMORS personnel bassist Dave Starr and drummer Larry Howe had teamed up with CHASTAIN. VICIOUS RUMOURS themselves pulled off a major local coup by landing the support to the mammoth AEROSMITH / KID ROCK show at the Marysville Autowest Amphitheater on November 7th.

Guitarist Steve Smyth took time out in early 2003 to collaborate with ex-ARIAH and SWEET LEAF bassist Steven Hoffman on a Progressive venture dubbed THE ESSENESS PROJECT. Guitarist Geoff Thorpe also engaged in outside projects, guesting on the 'Lake Of Memory' single from THE 7TH ORDER.

Having signed to the Dutch Mascot label, VICIOUS RUMORS set to work on a 2004 album provisionally billed as 'Immortal'. A DVD release would also be announced, 'Crushing The World—Part 1' including archive film featuring the late Carl Albert, footage from the 2002 European tour with SAVATAGE, the band's appearances at the 'Wacken Open Air' and 'Bang Your Head' festivals as well as three previously unheard tracks. VICIOUS RUMORS scheduled Italian dates for the Summer of 2004 but then pulled out due to illness on Geoff Thorpe's part. Nevertheless, Thorpe would be announced as putting in guest sessions on the tracks 'Vultures In the Air', the instrumental 'Black Telepathy' and 'Mighty Son Of The Great Lord' for the Italian band KALEDON's album 'The Way Of The Light'. However, Thorpe would in fact not contribute, unable to participate due to health problems.

The band was rejoined by drummer Larry Howe in January of 2005. More changes saw bassist Cornbread exiting in April, drafting Tommy Sisco as replacement. A live release party to celebrate the issue of the DVD 'Crushing The World', held at the Last Day Saloon in Santa Rosa, California on 21st May saw a reformation of the complete 'Word Of Mouth' line-up—Brian O'Connor, Geoff Thorpe, Mark McGee, Larry Howe and Tommy Sisco.

That same Summer, Ira Black announced a brand new band project, THE SIDEFX, in union with ROUGH CUTT veterans vocalist PAUL SHORTINO and bassist Matt Thorn plus the YNGWIE MALMSTEEN credited Patrick Johansson on drums.

On 9th July 2005 VICIOUS RUMORS lined up at The Pound outdoor amphitheatre in San Francisco alongside TESTAMENT, DREAMS OF DAMNATION, LÄÄZ ROCKIT, HIRAX, AGENT STEEL, DEKAPITATOR, MUDFACE, NEIL TURBIN, BROCAS HELM and IMAGIKA for the 'Thrash Against Cancer' benefit. Later that year guitarist Ira Black temporarily replaced Kurdt Vanderhoof in the ranks of METAL CHURCH for a three week US tour.

Brian O'Connor closed an eight year tenure as the VICIOUS RUMORS frontman in August. Within hours of this announcement guitarist Ira Black also officially terminated his position, joining Sci-Fi Metal band EMERALD TRIANGLE. The band reformulated, with bassist Dave Starr and drummer Larry Howe rejoining guitarist Geoff Thorpe. Days later it would be revealed that James Rivera, of HELSTAR, SEVEN WITCHES, DISTANT THUNDER, FLOTSAM AND JETSAM and KILLING MACHINE, was to front the band. Another unexpected addition to the ranks would be BRAD GILLIS, best known for his term of duty with OZZY OSBOURNE and for being mainstay of melodic Rockers NIGHT RANGER. For European gigs the group drafted another high profile guitarist, ANVIL CHORUS, CONTROL, HEATHEN and BLACK SUN Thrash veteran Thaen Rasmussen temporarily replacing Gillis. Ex-guitarist Ira Black enrolled himself into the ranks of LIZZY BORDEN in April 2006 and shortly afterward Larry Howe took up an offer, albeit fleeting, to join W.A.S.P.

Promoting the 'Warball' album, VICIOUS RUMORS toured Europe in November allied with BEYOND FEAR and COURAGEOUS. Bassist Dave Starr left the band on January 23rd 2007, prioritising his act WILDESTARR. VICIOUS RUMORS teamed up with RIOT for two shows at Tokyo, Japan's Club Quattro on April 17th and 18th. A European tour scheduled to feature special guests AGENT STEEL was announced for June. The band teamed up with VICIOUS RUMORS and AFTER ALL for the Alienigma European Tour 2007 beginning in early September.

Vicious Rumors, Vicious Rumors (1983). In Fire / One Way Ticket.
SOLDIERS OF THE NIGHT, Roadrunner RR 9734 (1986).
Premonition / Ride (Into The Sun) / Medusa / Soldiers Of The Night / Murder / March Or Die / Blitz The World / Invader / In Fire / Domestic Bliss / Blistering Winds.
DIGITAL DICTATOR, Roadrunner RR 9571 (1988). Replicant / Digital Dictator / Minute To Kill / Towns On Fire / Lady Took A Chance / Worlds And Machines / The Crest / R.L.H. / Condemned / Out Of The Shadows.
VICIOUS RUMOURS, Atlantic 7567820752 (1990). Don't Wait For Me / World Church / On The Edge / Ship Of Fools / Can You Hear It / Down To The Temple / Hellraiser / Electric Twilight / Thrill Of The Hunt / Axe And Smash.
WELCOME TO THE BALL, Atlantic 75682276121 (1991).
Abandoned / You Only Live Twice / Saviour From Anger / Children / Dust To Dust / Raise Your Hands / Strange Behaviour / Six Stepsisters / Mastermind / When Love Comes Down / Ends Of The Earth.
PLUG IN AND HANG ON—LIVE IN TOKYO, Atlantic (1992).
Abandoned / Savior From Anger / Down To The Temple / Ship Of Fools / Lady Took A Chance / When Love Comes Down / March Or Die / Don't Wait For Me.
The Voice EP, Alfa Brunette (1994) (Japanese release). The Voice / Communication Breakdown / Paint It Black / Painted Stranger.
WORD OF MOUTH, Rising Sun Productions 084-62232 (1994).
Against The Grain / All Rights Reserved / The Voice / Thinking Of You / Thunder And Pain (Part 1) / Thunder And Pain (Part 2) / No

Fate / Sense Of Security / Dreaming / Building no. 6 / Ministry Of Fear / Music Box.

A TRIBUTE TO CARL ALBERT, Headless Butcher (1995). On The Edge / Abandoned / No Fate / Ministry Of Fear / Digital Dictator / Against The Grain / The Voice / Hell Razor / Thunder & Rain I / Thunder & Rain II / Worlds & Machines / Thinking Of You / Down To The Temple / Don't Wait For Me / My Machine (Demo) / Put The Blame On Me (Demo) / Indisintegration (Demo).

SOMETHING BURNING, Massacre MASSCD091 (1996). Ball Hog / Mouth / Out Of My Misery / Something Burning / Concentration / Chopping Block / Perpetual / Strip Search / Make It Real / Free To Go.

CYBERCHRIST, Massacre CD0142 (1998). Cyberchrist / Buried Alive / Kill The Day / No Apologies / Fear Of God / Gigs Eviction / Barcelona / Downpour / Candles Burn / Fiend / Faith.

SADISTIC SYMPHONY, Point Music (2001). Break / Sadistic Symphony / March Of The Damned / Blacklight / Puritan Demons / Born Again Hard / Neodymium Man / Elevator To Hell / Cerebral Sea / Ascension / Liquify.

WARBALL, Mascot (2006).

VICTIMIZER

SKJERN, DENMARK — *Killhailer (vocals), Henrik Engkjær (guitar), Azter (bass), Atziluth (drums).*

The 2004 band line-up of Skjern based blasphemic Death-Thrashers VICTIMIZER comprised KILL, UNDERGANG and CHURCH BIZARRE man Killhailer on vocals, the EXEKRATOR and FULL MOON LYCANTHROPY credited Henrik Engkjær on guitar, DENIAL OF GOD bassist Azter and drummer Atziluth (a.k.a. Michael Huhle), a scene veteran of RAVISHING, BLACKHORNED, RENEGADETH and GRIMNISMAL. Atziluth would work with DENIAL OF GOD in October 2004.

Erstwhile VICTIMIZER personnel included drummer, later guitarist, C(unt). Molestor, drummer Snuff and guitarist / bassist Dr. Rape. Credited session musicians numbered the DEMON REALM credited Lars Groth on drums and guitarist Suicide Machine. The project had debuted in October 2000 with the three song demo tape 'Skullfucked By Victimizer' complete with cover of MOTÖRHEAD's 'Ace Of Spades'. This would soon sell out and be re-issued in May 2001 then followed by 'Unholy Banners Of War'. Horror Records issued the 'Communist Crusher' EP, featuring a cover version of ALICE COOPER's 'Prince Of Darkness', in December 2003, these sessions including Lars Groth on drums.

The band shared a split cassette release 'Revenge Of The Hellhorde' with NUNSLAUGHTER on the Pentagram Warfare label in September of 2004. Amongst these tracks would be VICTIMIZER's interpretations of NUNSLAUGHTER's 'In The Graveyard' and D.A.D.'s 'True Believer. VICTIMIZER signed to the Australian label Apocalyptor Records in October to re-issue the 'Unholy Banners Of War' demo tracks with additional material in the form of new track 'Reap the nuclear whirlwind', a re-recording of 'Battle Weapons' plus NUNSLAUGHTER and MOTÖRHEAD cover versions. The band also announced a split 7" single shared with TOXIC HOLOCAUST for Hells Headbangers.

The band donated their rendition of 'Tormentor' to the W.A.S.P. tribute album 'Shock Rock Hellions–A Tribute to W.A.S.P.', released by Denmark's Codiac Records in May 2006.

Skullfucked By Victimizer, Victimizer (2000) (Demo, limited to 243 hand numbered copies). Skullfucked By Victimizer / Hell Revealed / Battle Weapons.

Unholy Banners Of War, Victimizer (2001). Devoured By Satan's Flames / Pentagram Warfare / Hell Revealed / Skullfucked By Victimizer / Communist Crusher.

Communist Crusher, Horror HOR 010 (2003) (Limited edition of 666 numbered copies). Bonebreaking Armageddon Metal / Prince Of Darkness / Speed Metal Nightmare / Communist Crusher.

REVENGE OF THE HELLHORDE, Pentagram Warfare (2004) (Split cassette release with NUNSLAUGHTER). Pride Of The Zombie Squad / Hellrevealed! / In The Graveyard / Bonebreaking Armageddon Metal / True Believer / Speed Metal Nightmare / Reap The Nuclear Whirlwind.

Communist Crusher, Horror HOR 010 PD (2005) (Limited edition of 525 numbered 7" picture disc). Bonebreaking Armageddon Metal / Prince Of Darkness / Speed Metal Nightmare / Communist Crusher.

REVENGE OF THE HELLHORDE, Ancient Darkness Productions ADP 008 (2005) (Split vinyl release with NUNSLAUGHTER). Pride Of The Zombie Squad / Hellrevealed! / In The Graveyard / Bonebreaking Armageddon Metal / True Believer / Speed Metal Nightmare / Reap The Nuclear Whirlwind.

VICTIMIZER / ETERNAL PAIN / BETRAYED / FARSCAPE, Deathstrike DR042 (2005) (Split release with ETERNAL PAIN, BETRAYED and FARSCAPE limited to 500 copies). Pride Of The Zombie Squad / Flamethrower Madness.

UNHOLY BANNERS OF WAR, Warfuck WAR666-003 (2006). Devoured By Satan's Flames / Pentagram Warfare / Hell Revealed / Skullfucked By Victimizer / Communist Crusher / Behold The Coming (Intro) / Battleweapons / Ace Of Spades / In The Graveyard / Reap The Nuclear Whirlwind.

VII ARCANO

ITALY — *Mirko Scarpa (vocals), Marco Montagna (guitar), Mauro Diciocia (bass), Gilles Schembri (drums).*

Rome's Doom style Deathsters VII ARCANO came into being with the formulation of SEPOLCRUM during 1989 at the hand of guitarist / keyboard player Roberto Cufaro. A band line-up was forged, including guitarist / bassist Marco Montagna, for release of demo sessions 'Anteroom Of The Hell' in 1991 and 'Flowers Upon The Grave' in 1993.

A name switch to VII ARCANO would be marked by a 7" single, 'Gather My Blood Forever', in 1994. At this juncture the band comprised of vocalist Nunziati, Cufaro on guitar, Montagna on bass and De Stefano on keyboards. The band morphed again with the introduction of erstwhile OMICRON vocalist Mirko Scarpa. A former member Lord Vampyr (Alexander) famously created the notorious vampire Black Metal band THEATRE DES VAMPIRES.

However, the band line up fluxed once more upfront of a further promotion tape 'MCMXCIX' as Montagna took over guitar responsibilities, Bomboi came in on bass and Paul Soellner on drums. In 1998 VII ARCANO, undergoing yet further line up changes, Soellner founding KLIMT 1918, which bore witness to the induction of PILGRIM drummer Gilles Schembri and bass player Francesco Frasso, was signed up by the Warlord label.

The resulting 'Inner Deathscapes', produced by NOVEMBRE drummer Giuseppe Orlando, would be revealed as a fine slice of Thrash infused Death Metal. With Frasso departing just prior to recording Marco Montagna took on bass duties in the studio. Vinyl versions of the August 2001 album 'Inner Deathscapes' would include an exclusive bonus track, namely a cover of the KISS classic 'Love Gun'.

Following completion of the 2003 album 'Nothingod', which sported a cover of TESTAMENT's 'Burnt Offerings', VII ARCANO were in rehearsals with a fresh rhythm section of bassist Carlo Paolucci and drummer Francesco Struglia.

Gather My Blood Forever EP, (1994). Walpurgis Fullmoon / Dance With A Dark Dress.

INNER DEATHSCAPES, Warlord WR04CD-5490182 (2001). Intruding / Anticlockwise Cycle Of Dying / Of Suicidal Age / The Inner Deathscape / Echo Calling / Fog Path / Release Into Anguish / Necrotica Art—The Performance / Streams Of Paranoia / Descending.

NOTHINGOD, (2003). Millennium Plague / Furybound / Deathlike Blues / Final Dream / Down The Afterworld / An Assassin Charisma / Burnt Offerings / Murder Parade / Nothingod Manifest (The Crawling Race).

VIKING

LOS ANGELES, CA, USA — *Ron Eriksen (vocals), Brett Eriksen (guitar), James Lareau (bass), Matt Jordan (drums).*

VIKING were a hard hitting Speed / Thrash Metal act out of Los Angeles. The band had a blistering rise over two highly praised albums before dropping out of the scene entirely when half of the band became born again Christians. VIKING was founded in the Spring of 1986 by guitarist Ron Daniels of the HAGS, drummer Matt Jordan of BARRIER and bass player James Lareau of Punk act LETHAL GENE.

This trio, along with singer Tony Spider, founded TRACER releasing one demo session. TRACER, now minus Spider, evolved into VIKING when Daniels discovered he could sing whilst jamming SLAYER songs at a rehearsal. Guitarist Brett Daniels completed the line-up.

As VIKING the band opted to promote the appropriate image and therefore both Ron and Brett took the stage name 'Eriksen'. After just two gigs VIKING were signed to the Metal Blade label, committing the track 'Hellbound' to the 'Metal Massacre VIII' compilation then launching a full blown album 'Do Or Die'. Critics enthused over the sheer heaviness of the band and Ron Eriksen's vocals were singled out for particular praise. Ron Eriksen would lend his vocal talents to the DARK ANGEL album 'Leave Scars', duetting with Ron Rinehart on the song 'Promise Of Agony'. The DARK ANGEL connection was strengthened when Brett Eriksen joined the band in 1989.

VIKING would go into the studio to cut a second album 'Man Of Straw' with engineer Bill Metoyer. However, Daniels had recently converted to Christianity and would re-write a large degree of the lyrics just prior to recording.

In May of 1990 both Daniels and Jordan would exit citing a conflict of interests between the Heavy Metal lifestyle and their faith. VIKING folded. Ron Daniels found a new devotion as Pastor at Calvary Chapel, Cheyenne.

Lost And Found Records announced a CD re-issue of the 1989 'Man Of Straw' album in 2006.

DO OR DIE, Metal Blade 72225 (1988). Warlord / Hellbound / Militia Of Death / Prelude-Scavenger / Valhalla / Burning From Within / Berserker / Killer Unleashed / Do Or Die.

MAN OF STRAW, Caroline 1396 (1989). White Death / They Raped The Land / Twilight Fate / The Trial / Case Of The Stubborns / Winter / Hell Is For Children / Creative Divorce / Man of Straw.

VIO-LENCE

SAN FRANCISCO, CA, USA — *Sean Killian (vocals), Robb Flynn (guitar), Phil Demmel (guitar), Dean Dell (bass), Perry Strickland (drums).*

Relative latecomers in the Thrash explosion Bay Area's VIO-LENCE nevertheless managed to scramble onto a major deal offered by MCA Mechanic during 1988. The genesis of the San Francisco based band can be found in DEATH PENALTY, a 1985 founded unit consisting of guitarist Phil Demmel, drummer Perry Strickland, second guitarist Troy Fua, bassist Ed Billy and vocalist Jerry Burr. A rapid name change to VIO-LENCE took place but within months Billy had opted to pursue further education and in his stead came Dean Dell. The following year Birr departed the band filling the gap with Killian. The last member change found Fua being supplanted by Rob Flynn in early 1987.

The group's inaugural commercial offering would be the album 'Eternal Nightmare', recorded between February and April 1988 at Music Grinder and Alpha & Omega studios in Los Angeles and San Francisco with producer John Cuniberti. One track put down on tape but not included would be 'Torture Tactics', deemed too "lyrically controversial". Upon the debut's release VIO-LENCE undertook touring duties across North America on a billing that included TESTAMENT and SANCTUARY before closing the year on winter dates supporting VOIVOD. The 1990 'Oppressing The Masses' album would generate a stir with the band's record company Megaforce when various submitted tracks were deemed too offensive by the label. The band issued the songs anyway on the now scarce 'Torture Tactics' EP.

Flynn would later be replaced by Ray Vegas. Rob Flynn created MACHINE HEAD for a successful run of albums whilst Demmel, Vegas and Dell founded TORQUE for an eponymous 1996 album.

Guitarist Phil Demmel re-emerged in 2001 touting his new project TECHNOCRACY. Meantime, VIO-LENCE reunited for a 'one off' gig in August 2001 appearing at the 'Thrash Of The Titans' extravaganza in honour of TESTAMENT frontman Chuck Billy, recently diagnosed with cancer. However, VIO-LENCE's return to the stage set the ball rolling and would spur renewed record company interest and subsequent gigs. For their 16th December show at Slim's in San Francisco the band united original guitar player Troy Fua with new man Steve Schmidt of LAVABONE and F BOMB.

During May of 2002 Phil Demmel joined his former comrade Rob Flynn as stand in guitarist for MACHINE HEAD. The incestuous relationship between MACHINE HEAD and VIO-LENCE was cemented further at the 'Milwaukee Metalfest' event when MACHINE HEAD bassist Adam Duce filled in for a honeymooning Deen Dell during VIO-LENCE's five-song set. The band later put in a one off show in Las Vegas supporting HALFORD and a short burst of December dates packaged along with TESTAMENT and EXODUS.

Diehard fans would be rewarded by the issue of a limited edition 7" single containing three archive demo tracks that same month. Only 1000 copies would be pressed in a variety of coloured vinyls including red, white, blue, green and swirl mixture. In 2005 Megaforce Records announced an upgraded re-issue of the 'Eternal Nightmare' album, adding a live bonus disc recorded at Slim's in San Francisco on 14th December 2001. The VIO-LENCE campaign continued into 2006 with the DVD 'Blood And Dirt' hosting a 90 minute documentary, the band's entire set from the 2001 'Thrash of the Titans' benefit concert and other live tracks.

Eternal Nightmare, MCA Mechanic VOMIT1 (1988). Eternal Nightmare.

ETERNAL NIGHTMARE, MCA Mechanic DMCF 4323 (1988). Eternal Nightmare / Serial Killer / Phobophobia / Calling In The Coronor / T.D.S. / Take It As You Will / Bodies On Bodies / Kill On Command.

Torture Tactics EP, Caroline (1990). Torture Tactics / Officer Nice (Live) / Gutterslut / Dicks Of Death.

OPPRESSING THE MASSES, Megaforce 82105-2 (1990). I Profit / Officer Nice / Subterfuge / Engulfed By Flames / World In A World / Mentally Afflicted / Liquid Courage / Oppressing The Masses.

NOTHING TO GAIN, Bleeding Hearts CDBLEED4 (1993). Atrocity / 12 Gauge Justice / Ageless Eyes / Pain Of Pleasure / Virtues Of Vice / Killing My Words / Psychotic Memories / No Chains / Welcoming Party / This Is System / Color Of Life.

Vio-lence EP, (2003). Paraplegic (1986 demo) / Breed Like Rats (1993 demo) / Kill On Command (1986 demo).

VIOLENT HEADACHE

SPAIN — *Capo (vocals), Jordi (guitar), Chico (bass), Tonyo (drums).*

Extreme Barcelona act that blend both male and female lead vocals into a genre defying mix of Death Metal, Thrash and Grindcore. The band would issue the demo 'Attack Of The Antijetcore Argaraboys' prior to embarking on a stream of shared single releases with international acts. A 1991 shared release found the band in alliance with Italy's CRIPPLE BASTARDS and the following year VIOLENT HEADACHE united with undisputed kings of the 7" split single genre Belgium' AGATHOCLES. Other combined efforts include releases with CARCASS GRINDER, EXCRETED ALIVE, UNHOLY GRAVE and INTESTINAL DISEASE.

VIOLENT HEADACHE's 2000 album 'Bombs Of Crust' features over 50 tracks originally recorded in 1995.

Split, Psychomania (1991) (7" split single with CRIPPLE BASTARDS).

Starbation, Anaconda (1992) (7" split single with AGATHOCLES).

Condemned Childhood, Blurred 11 (1997) (7" split single with EXCRETED ALIVE). Condemned Childhood.

Trituradora De Cadaveres, Nat (1997) (7" split single with CARCASS GRINDER). Trituradora De Cadaveres.
BOMBS OF CRUST, Six Weeks (2000).

VIPER

SÃO PAULO, SP, BRAZIL — *Pit Passarell (vocals / bass), Yves Passarell (guitar), Felipe Machado (guitar), Renato Graccia (drums).*

A heavily Euro influenced Speed Metal act created in São Paulo during 1985 by teenage brothers guitarist Yves and bassist Pit Passarell. Joining them would be the equally youthful vocalist André Matos, second guitar player Felipe Machado and drummer Cassio Audi. VIPER announced their presence with the four song 'Killara Sword' demo, which soon snagged a deal with the domestic Rock Brigade label. Promoting the 1987 debut 'Soldiers Of Sunrise' album VIPER would support MOTÖRHEAD. For gigs in 1987 and 1988 VIPER pulled in former WARKINGS guitarist RODRIGO ALVES. He would then depart to reform WARKINGS and figure in MERLIN and BLASFEMIA before going solo.

For 1989's 'Theatre Of Fate' opus VIPER switched drummers, bringing in Sergio Facci. However, Guilherme Martin would be drafted on the drum stool for tour work and then the position was finally settled by Renato Graccia. At this juncture André Matos split away from the band, apparently over a conflict of interest in stylistic direction. The erstwhile vocalist would found the immensely successful Progressive Metal act ANGRA. Pit Passarell took over the vocal mantle as VIPER trimmed down to a quartet.

By now VIPER's reputation had spread internationally with 'Theatre Of Fate' album would be licensed to Japan in 1991 and Europe the following year, through Germany's Massacre label. 1992 would also see VIPER scoring a huge Brazilian radio hit with the track 'Rebel Maniac'. 1992's 'Evolution' and follow up EP 'Vipera Sapiens' saw release in Europe under the billing of VIPER BRAZIL, this due to the presence of a German outfit laying prior claim to the title.

The 1994 'Live—Maniacs In Japan' album would include the band's cover version of QUEEN's 'We Will Rock You' alongside a take of the RAMONES 'I Wanna Be Sedated'. The 'Coma Rage' record, released in 1995, saw strong Hardcore elements being introduced into the band's sound. However, the group then took a major diversion with 1996's 'Tem Pra Todo Mundo', Viper stretching outside of the standard band format to include violin, trombones, saxophone, cello and trumpet.

Yves Passarell would unite onstage for a slice of nostalgia with former vocalist André Matos in 2001 as Matos debuted his post ANGRA outfit SHAMAN. Ex-VIPER guitarist Rodrigo Alves resurfaced in 2004 with a new combo dubbed RYGEL, an assemblage of scene veterans including Paulo Sérgio of PUSH, Karol Silvestre, ex-HARVEST MOON and Danilo Lopes of CEREMONYA and ex-ETERNA.

VIPER marked a return to live action in mid 2005, citing a line-up of vocalist Ricardo Bocci, guitarists Felipe Machado and Val Santos, bassist Pit Passarell with Guilherme Martin on drums. This formation cut the demo 'Do It All Again', fresh material being enhanced by a re-work of their early favourite 'Knights Of Destruction'.

VIPER entered Estúdio Ultra-Sônica in São Paulo during March 2006 to cut a new album.

Killara Sword, (1985). Knights of Destruction / Nightmares / Wings Of The Evil / Princess Of Hell.
SOLDIERS OF SUNRISE, Rock Brigade RBR0060 (1987). Knights Of Destruction / Nightmares / The Whipper / Wings Of The Evil / H.R. / Soldiers Of Sunrise / Signs Of The Night / Killera (Princess Of Hell) / Law Of The Sword.
THEATRE OF FATE, Massacre MASS CD 002 (1989). Illusions / At Least A Chance / To Live Again / A Cry From The Edge / Living For The Night / Prelude To Oblivion / Theatre Of Fate / Moonlight.
EVOLUTION, Massacre MASS CD 009 (1992). Coming From The Inside / Evolution / Rebel Maniac / Dead Light / The Shelter / Still the Same / Wasted / Pictures Of Hate / Dance Of Madness / The Spreading Soul / We Will Rock You.
Viperia Sapiens EP, JVC Victor VICP-2072 (1993) (Japanese release). Acid Heart / Silent Enemy / Crime / Wasted Again / Killing World / The Spreading Soul (Acoustic version).
LIVE—MANIACS IN JAPAN, Eldorado 478012 (1994). Intro—Coming From The Inside / To Live Again / A Cry From The Edge / Dead Light / Knights Of Destruction / We Will Rock You / Acid Heart / Still The Same—Drum Solo / Evolution / Nao Quero Dinheiro / Living For The Night / Rebel Maniac / I Wanna Be Sedated.
COMA RAGE, Roadrunner RR 8964-2 (1995). Coma Rage / Straight Ahead / Somebody Told Me You're Dead / Makin Love / Blast! / God Machine / Far And Near / The Last Song / If I Die By Hate Day Before / 405 South / A Face In The Crowd / I Fought the Law / Keep The Words.
TEM PRA TODO MUNDI, (1996). Dinheiro / Crime Na Cidade / 8 De Abril / Sabado / Not Ready To Get Up / Quinze Anos / Na Cara Do Gol / The One You Need / Lucinha Bordon / Alvo / Um Dia / Mais Do Mesmo.
Do It All Again, (2005) (Demo). Knights of Destruction 2005 / I'm Gonna Cross The Line / Time / Never Come Back / Do It All Again.

VIRGIN SIN

SWEDEN — *Dagon (vocals), SS66 (guitar), Zoak (bass), Schreck (drums).*

VIRGIN SIN is a theatric, Horror Heavy Metal band created by lead singer Dagon in 1983. The original line-up found Dagon flanked by guitarists Mantus and Fenris with Euronymous on bass and Gorge on the drums, performing their debut concert at a festival later that same year. Their use of corpsepaint and Satanic symbols had many branding VIRGIN SIN as Sweden's very first Black Metal band. However, the founding line up splintered and in 1985 Dagon, now handling bass guitar, was joined by guitar player SS66 and drummer Mr. Maniac.

The group was by this stage adopting a Thrashier style, evident on the demo 'Make 'em Die Slowly'. Upon completion of this session Mr. Maniac vacated the drum stool. Regrouping, the band added bass player Charon and drummer Rimmon. In 1992 this unit entered the recording studio to cut what was intended as their debut album. However, these tracks would be shelved.

Activity slowed to a standstill until 1999 when the label To The Death Records inquired about issuing 'Make 'em Die Slowly' as an album release, adding tracks from a 1985 rehearsal session. VIRGIN SIN was duly re-built in 2001, Dagon and SS66 bringing in bassist Terra and drummer Schreck. The following year tracks were laid down for the album 'Seduction Of The Innocent', during which time Zoak usurped Terra.

In September of 2004 VIRGIN SIN credited bassist Jenny joined TENEBRE. The VIRGIN SIN credited Martin Schönherr joined Grind outfit SPLATTER MERMAIDS and subsequently DERANGED in the frontman role during April 2006.

Virgin Sin, Virgin Sin (1995) (Demo). Night Of Hell / Die / Zombie Attack / Killing Is My Only Joy.
Make 'em Die Slowly, To The Death TTD 004 (1999). Exterminator / Sadistic Rape / Night Of Hell / Killing Is My Only Joy.
Seduction Of The Innocent, To The Death (2003). Sane Inside Insanity / Skinned Alive / Mark Of The Beast / War Cry.

VIRUS

UK — *Henry Heston (vocals), Cokie (guitar), Damien Hess (bass), Terry Kaylor (drums).*

Formed in London in 1987, VIRUS offered a primitive brand of Thrash that did improve as albums progressed. Indeed, the band often had to defend themselves in the media for their pro-Punk leanings. The group's inaugural demos would feature session guitar solos from Yaasin Hanif of TARGA. Hanif would also be on hand to produce the first album, 'Pray For War'. VIRUS toured as support to the CELTIC FROST and KREATOR UK tour of October 1987 and also put in shows opening for DEATH ANGEL and SUICIDAL TENDENCIES. VIRUS also gained a slot at the prestigious Leeds thrash festival alongside MEGADETH. The band was due to tour North America with DEATH but this was cancelled.

In 1991 Heston and Kaylor formed SAVAGE CIRCLE with vocalist / bassist J.D. Cooper and guitarist Syd Sholley.

PRAY FOR WAR, Metalworks (1987). Pray For War / To The Death / Malignant Massacre / Thermonuclear Thrash / Night Siege / Risen From Death / Scarred For Life / Neo Warlords / Cannibal Holocaust.
FORCE RECON, Metalworks VOV 669 (1988). Testify To Me / Visual Warfare / Force Recon / Release The Devil / No Return / B.S.S.D. / Hungry For Blood.
LUNACY, Metalworks (1989). Seeing is Believing / Lunacy / Bad Blood / The Pain Will Ease / State Of The Art / My Life / A Sense Of Freedom / Don't Get Even.
WARMONGER—THE COMPILATION,, MIA Records (1994).

VITUPERATION

STOCKHOLM, SWEDEN — *Jonas Mähl (vocals), Sebastian Zingerman (vocals / guitar), Tor Steinholtz (guitar), Simon Zingerman (bass), Rodrigo Valenzuela (drums).*

Stockholm based Death Metal band fronted by PSYKOTISK, KALL DÖD and TORTURE ETERNAL singer Jonas Mähl. Guitarist Sebbe Zingerman is also a TORTURE ETERNAL member. The group was created in mid 2004 by guitarists Sebastian Zingerman, then of HERETIQUE and also handling lead vocals, and Tor Steinholtz, from DIAMOND. They were joined by Zingerman sibling, Simon, on bass and in early 2005 Joakim Wallgren, of VALKRJA repute, took command of the drums for the band's first concert at Stenhamra Gård. Following this show Jonas Mähl took over as lead vocalist.

VITUPERATION first live demo, 'Live At Bro', was recorded at the Bro Fri Scen on 28th May 2005. 'Nothing Is Sacred', laid down at Offbeat Studio in Järfälla, followed in April 2006. Original drummer Joakim Wallgren, quitting to join DISDAINED, was replaced by Bolivian Rodrigo Valenzuela.

Shugatraa (Jonas Mähl) of VITUPERATION also mentors solo project ÅNGEST and operated Black Metal project ANNIHILATE in alliance with Sinneskog, of INTERRED, issuing the January 2007 demo 'My Path'.

Live At Bro, Vituperation (2005) (Live demo. Limited edition 20 copies). World Of Hate / Nekrofilens Fantasi / She, Myself And I.
Nothing Is Sacred, Vituperation (2006) (Demo). Urge And Need (For The Passion To Bleed) / Nekrofilens Fantasi / She, Myself And I / Humanity Of Life / World Of Hate / Nothing Is Sacred.

VIU DRAKH

GERMANY — East Germans VIU DRAKH, fronted rather oddly by Fish, started life as a Punk Hardcore unit titled TINPANALLEY but would evolve into a Black Thrash act for the self financed 'Back To The Chaos' album. VIU DRAKH would act as opening act on CANNIBAL CORPSE's European September 2002 gigs for an extensive run of dates backing up a package bill comprising DEW SCENTED and SEVERE TORTURE. Bassist Stefan Joo was succeeded by Michael "Mosha" Matschonschek in January of 2003.

'Death Riff Society', featuring a cover of MOTÖRHEAD's 'Ace Of Spades', arrived in 2005. Former band members guitarist Bjorn Langkopf and drummer David "C4" Gabriel founded KORADES.

BACK TO THE CHAOS, Karokiller (1999). Back To The Chaos / Eyes Of Death / Downwards Again / LXXVI / Nothing To Regret / No / Kiss The Earth / X / Amok.
TAKE NO PRISONERS, GRIND THEM ALL AND LEAVE THIS HELL, Moonstorm (2000). Black Milk / Fields Of Repulsion / Emperors Soldiers / New Shard Disorder / Infra Hell / 12 Inch God / Essential Doubts / Hate / Starfinger / Rebellion.
DEATH RIFF SOCIETY, Moonstorm (2005). Death Riff Society / Demon Dance / Mutant Gods / Burn / Peaches And Cream / Caravan / Blade Spirits / Worst Disease / Dead Or Alive / As The Dormant Awakes / Silver / Ace Of Spades.

VOIVOD

JONQUIÈRE, QC, CANADA — *Snake (vocals / bass), Piggy (guitar), Blacky (bass), Away (drums).*

Jonquière, Québec based avant-garde Thrash Metal 'Cyberpunk' act VOIVOD mixed Punk, Metal and Sci-Fi in a unique combination that won them many fans during the mid 80's Thrash boom. The band's early constructs provoked scorn from a large contingent of the Metal fraternity but their musical growth and ability to convey their ambitions came to fruition with the landmark 'Nothingface' album, this opus often quoted by progressive metal aficionados as a groundbreaking set.

The French speaking VOIVOD was comprised frontman Snake (a.k.a. Denis Belanger), guitarist Piggy (Denis D'Amour), bassist Blacky (Jean-Yves Thériault) and drummer Away (Michel Langevin). Unusually, the entire concept of VOIVOD was to be based on nuclear physics graduate Michel Langevin's self-invented science fiction character, the Voivod Korgull persona being a post apocalyptic vampire warrior. The musicians first assembled in late 1980, but only became dedicated fully to the cause of constructing a solid band unit around November 1982. Jean Fortin, later of DEAF DEALER, briefly occupied the bass position before Blacky had learned the instrument. The nicknames, which came to identify the quartet globally, were taken in reference to personal traits, Piggy due to his endomorphic stature, Snake because of his elongated visage, Away because he often missed rehearsals and Blacky being attributed to sullen mood swings.

Initial VOIVOD gigs had the band including numerous cover versions in their set from the likes of JUDAS PRIEST, MOTÖRHEAD and VENOM. The group released a number of live recordings in 1983, including the June 25th 'Anachronism' cassette, which brandished cover versions of JUDAS PRIEST's 'Rapid Fire', MOTÖRHEAD's 'Ace Of Spades', 'Stone Dead Forever' and 'No Class' as well as VENOM's 'Black Metal', 'Welcome To Hell' and 'Witching Hour'. This cassette credited the players as Snake—"throat, scream, insults, mike torture & weapon operator", Piggy—"burning metal-axe, electro-motive force & tremolition", Blacky—"blower bass, pyromania and shit" and Away "thunder and death machine, horror and visions".

The band's first forays into the recording studio resulted in the 1984 'To The Death' demo, quickly followed by a further live tape 'Morgoth Invasion'. VOIVOD officially debuted in 1984 with a track, 'Condemned To The Gallows', culled from the 'To The Death' sessions', on one of the infamous Metal Blade 'Metal Massacre' compilations.

With the inaugural 'War And Pain' album VOIVOD immediately set themselves apart from the Trash bandwagon. Financed by a collective loan of $2,000 from the band members parents, the extremities of 'War And Pain' intrigued the curious whilst prompting lovers of conventional Metal to run for the hills. The sessions were hewn out onto an 8 track recorder over an eight day period at Le Terroir studio in Quebec in June 1984. Assembled over a production which could only be honestly described as abysmal and fronted up by the Korgull the Exterminator sleeve character, many found the Sludge-Thrash brutality of the album, spread over vinyl sides "Iron" and "Blower", far too primitive to stomach. Where 'War And Pain' did find a keen audience was the Metal stronghold of Germany. This power base generated a healthy portion of the 70,000 album sales that would see the band on their way. In December 1984, VOIVOD recorded a live concert in Jonquiere that would be released as the 'Morgoth Invasion' demo. On April 4th, 1985 VOIVOD performed outside Canada for the first time, supporting CRO-

MAGS and VENOM at the New York Ritz.

The suitably titled 'Rrroooaarrr!!!', laid down at L'Autre' studios in Montreal from between October and November 1985, followed up in 1986, their first for German label Noise Records and licensed to Combat for the USA. An extensive US tour was undertaken to promote the album, partnered with fellow experimentalists CELTIC FROST and the somewhat mis-matched RUNNING WILD throughout June. The band then hooked up with POSSESSED and DEATHROW for European gigs in November, adding Punks ENGLISH DOGS for the closing London Electric Ballroom date. Maintaining a close link with diehard fans, the band put out the fan club demo release 'No Speed Limit', captured at a Le Spectrum concert in Montreal on 10th December 1986.

VOIVOD's next opus would be conceived at Musiclab Studios in Berlin with producer Harris Johns in October and November 1986. 'Killing Technology' was taken out on the road in North America in April and May 1987 backing German Thrashers KREATOR, the two bands uniting further for European gigs in November. Unfortunately the band's scheduled slot on the MEGADETH headlined 'Christmas On Earth' festival in Leeds, UK was stopped when customs officers confiscated the band's gear. VOIVOD turned up for the show but could only sit and watch the other bands perform. Again the faithful Iron Gang fan club was rewarded with two exclusive tapes, of shows recorded in Montreal and Brussels.

The group cut the 'Dimension Hatröss' album, closing out with a tongue in cheek 'Batman' theme, again at Musiclab Studios in Berlin with Harris Johns commencing December 4th 1987 for June 1988 issue. Dominated by dissonant chords, unexpected time signatures and Piggy's liberal use of unconventional minor chords, 'Dimension Hatröss' succeeded in alienating critics yet drawing in the more adventurous Metal fans. Progress was temporarily stalled as VOIVOD was forced to pull out of their 'Dimension Hatröss' world tour when Piggy was diagnosed with a cancerous brain tumour. When surgeons warned that necessary surgery would in all probability curtail his guitar abilities, Piggy opted to decline an operation and instead threw his energies into the band. As such, the group forged an alliance with VIO-LENCE for North American concerts to close the year. Naturally a further live cassette, resulted in 'A Flawless Structure'.

VOIVOD's tenacity and reluctance to compromise was rewarded with a major label deal via MCA Records subsidiary Mechanic for 1989's Glen Robinson produced 'Nothingface' features the band's take on PINK FLOYD's 'Astronomy Domine' woven into the overall concept seeing the Voivod character now no longer content to wage war but struggling with multiple inner psychological dimensions. A heavy factor in this lyrical shift would be the tracks 'Pre-Ignition' and 'Missing Sequences', related directly to the band's roots and fear of Alzheimer's disease, with their friends and family living in the shadow of the Jonquière aluminum factory. Again embarking on US dates, VOIVOD took out SOUNDGARDEN and FAITH NO MORE as support acts. 'Nothingface' was nominated for a Canadian 'Juno' music industry award and topped off the album marketing by touring homeland arenas as guests to RUSH.

Staying with MCA Records, 'Angel Rat' arrived in 1991, although Blacky had by this time been replaced by Pierre St Jean. Gigs across the USA in September 1993 had VOIVOD heading a bill alongside DAMN THE MACHINE and CLUTCH.

Snake backed out for 1995's Mark S. Berry produced 'Negatron' forcing Piggy and Away into a rethink on the band's future. 'Negatron', which included guest participation from industrial godfather Jim G. Thirlwell, saw issue in December, released in Canada via Hypnotic and Mausoleum Records in Europe, the latter featuring an extra brace of tracks in 'Vortex' and 'Erosion'. Deciding to continue as a trio, the band pulled in ex-LIQUID INDIAN and THUNDER CIRCUS vocalist / bassist Erric Forrest.

1997's 'Phobos', co-produced by the band and Rob Sanzo at Signal To Noise in Toronto, included a cover version of KING CRIMSON's '21st Century Schizoid Man'. Touring to promote the album, Forrest was severely injured during a road accident on tour in Germany during 1998. The vocalist was put into a coma and suffered severe spinal injuries. His recuperation would last for many months.

As VOIVOD went into hiatus, the 'Kronik' compilation emerged on Hypnotic, this hosting four live tracks. The band's Montréal show in late 1999 reunited VOIVOD with Snake for one gig, the former frontman guesting with the band. That October the band partnered with NEUROSIS for gigs in Europe. The August 2000 live album 'Voivod Lives', recorded at the Dutch Dynamo Festival and the renowned New York CBGB's club, included a cover of VENOM's 'In League With Satan', long a staple of the band's live set. Digipack versions were boosted by the inclusion of two studio cuts, 'The Prow' and 'Forlorn'. Forrest would leave the band to forge a fresh Montreal based project entitled E-FORCE.

A seven year break was brought to a close in 2001 when Piggy and Away opted to reunite with original singer Snake. Erstwhile METALLICA bassist Jason Newsted would co-produce subsequent recordings and play bass. Newsted held a history with Away and Piggy after recording rehearsal tapes with the pair and vocalist Sophia Ramos during 1998 at his own Chophouse Studio under the project name TARRAT. The renewed line up debuted on the 30th December at the Foufounes Electrique venue in Montreal, the band performing a set entirely comprising of SEX PISTOLS covers.

During early 2002 famed Virginian Heavy Metal band DECEASED would cover 'Blower' on their 'Zombie Hymns' album. Denis 'Piggy' D'Amour would be announced as guesting on the 2002 studio album 'Black Light District' from premier Dutch avant-garde Rockers THE GATHERING. Confirming all the recent reports the classic VOIVOD line-up of vocalist Snake, guitarist Piggy, drummer Away and bassist Blacky came out in public for an autograph signing session in Montreal on June 2nd. The band's appearance forming part of a three day Weekend Extreme celebrating 20 years of Quebec Metal.

VOIVOD, with Vincent Peake of GROOVY AARDVARK on bass, would open for Rock legend DIO for their two Quebec July dates. However, it would indeed be Jason Newsted confirmed as bass player on 'The Multiverse' album, the erstwhile METALLICA man subsequently being confirmed as a full member of the band. Away found time to act as guest on the PARADISE album 'Rock Anthropologists On The Kon-Tiki Voyage'.

Ex-bassist Jean-Yves Thériault was soon back in the news touting a fresh Thrash act billed as BLACK CLOUD. This band saw the four stringer allied with GHOULUNATICS frontman Patrick Mireault, Pierre Rémillard of OBLIVEON on guitar, Daniel Mongrain of MARTYR on second guitar and Flo Mounier from CRYPTOPSY on drums. Another ex-VOIVOD man was in the news too as former singer Eric Forrest collaborated with Tim Gutierrez and Kevin 131 in a Virginia, USA based band endeavour entitled PROJECT: FAILING FLESH. In 2003 this new act released the 'Beautiful Sickness' album.

With anticipation running high for the next chapter in VOIVOD's career over eager fans would be duped by reported album demos leaked onto the internet in December. These four tracks were in fact culled from a 1995 demo by the British group COLLAPSE.

In a curious turn of events Newsted teamed up with the OZZY OSBOURNE band in March, just days after the former occupant of that position had taken his own place in METALLICA! Newsted stuck to his VOIVOD commitments though as the band was announced as support act to Ozzy's June Canadian dates. The Newsted version of VOIVOD debuted live on 4th April at the Bourbon Street Bar And Grill in Concord, California under the assumed name of TARRAT. Following an extensive run of high profile US 'Ozzfest' shows VOIVOD would be confirmed as the opening act on OZZY OSBOURNE's September European tour. These gigs would be cancelled though when the headliner was forced out to undergo foot surgery.

Metal Blade Records would issue an official 20th Anniversary "ultimate deluxe" edition of 'War And Pain' in April of 2004. Bonus tracks included live tracks from the band's first June 1983 show, the 'Metal Massacre 5' sessions, the 'Morgoth Invasion' live demo and DVD ROM. The band's pioneering status was further recognised when acts such as E-FORCE, DELIRIUM TREMENS, INCINERATOR, NOMINON, MAUSOLEUM, CHEMIKILLER, DECEASED and ORDER FROM CHAOS participated in a tribute album to early VOIVOD, issued through France's Nihilistic Holocaust Records.

Away allied himself with an unlikely collaborator, donating his skills as studio guests to Rapper MC NECRO's album 'The Pre-Fix For Death'. The drummer would also work on a book of his distinctive VOIVOD artwork. Both Away and Piggy participated in the 30th anniversary show of the 70's Montreal outfit AUT'CHOSE in April 2005, both VOIVOD musicians also holding parallel membership of this act. AUT'CHOSE issued the album 'Chansons D'epouvante', featuring Piggy and Away, that May.

In June Jason Newsted announced a further new project dubbed HEARD OF ELEMENTS, a collaboration with Carl Coletti and slide guitarist Roy Rogers. It was learned in August that 'Piggy' was suffering from advanced colon cancer as VOIVOD made an official announcement "Our good friend and guitar hero Denis D'Amour is very ill". The guitarist died on 26th August. He was just 45 years old. Piggy's funeral was held in Jonquière, Quebec on 1st September.

VOIVOD's album, billed 'Katorz', saw completion despite Piggy's passing. The guitarist, just hours before he died, gave his fellow band mates access to his computer in order to retrieve guitar tracks and the group re-entered the studios in late September to finalise the record. The band signed the new album over to Nuclear Blast Records in January 2006. Piggy's legacy would be furthered with his other band AUT'CHOSE, the guitarist having worked up numerous tracks before his passing.

A unique, alternate mix of the song 'The X-Stream' was included on The End Records compilation album 'Alternate Endings: A Diverse Sound Collective Featuring A Distinguished Ensemble' in March. Later that same month it was revealed that Jason Newsted was to form up SUPERNOVA, the brand applied to the all star band unit assembled for the second season of reality TV show 'Rock Star'. The core band comprised MÖTLEY CRÜE drummer TOMMY LEE and onetime GUNS N' ROSES axeman GILBY CLARKE.

Jean-Yves Theriault acted as co-producer on NEGATIVA tracks in September. Away also forged LES ÉKORCHÉS, a purely acoustic project featuring vocalist Marc Vaillancourt from B.A.R.F. and BLACK CLOUD, guitarist Patrick Gordon from GHOULUNATICS and cellist Philippe Mius d'Entremont from MARUKA. Indica Records released the Glen Robinson 'Les Ékorchés' album in February 2007.

On November 17th 2006 The End Records put out a heavyweight 180gm vinyl version of 'Katorz', limited to 1,000 copies pressed in 400 clear vinyl, 400 red vinyl and 200 black vinyl. This edition also came packaged in new artwork designed by Michel Langevin.

WAR AND PAIN, Roadrunner RR 9825 (1984). Voivod / Warriors Of Ice / Suck Your Bone / Iron Gang / War And Pain / Blower / Live For Violence / Black City / Nuclear War.
RRROOOAAARRR!!!, Noise N0 040 (1986). Korgull The Exterminator / Fuck Off And Die / Slaughter In A Grave / Ripping Headaches / Horror / Thrashing Rage / Helldriver / Build Your Weapons / To The Death!
Thrashing Rage EP, Noise N N0050PD (1986). Thrashing Rage / Slaughter In A Grave / Helldriver / To The Death.
Cockroaches, Noise (1987) (Picture disc). Cockroaches / Too Scared To Scream.

VOIVOD

KILLING TECHNOLOGY, Noise N 0058 (1987). Killing Technology / Overreaction / Tornado / Too Scared To Scream / Forgotten In Space / Ravenous Medicine / Order Of The Blackguards / This Is Not An Exercise / Cockroaches.
DIMENSION HATRÖSS, Noise N0 106-1 (1988). Experiment / Tribal Convictions / Chaosmongers / Technocratic Manipulators / Epilog ... Macrosolutions To Megaproblems / Brain Scan / Psychic Vacuum / Cosmic Drama.
Into My Hypercube, MCA Mechanic (1989) (USA promotion release). Into My Hypercube / Missing Sequences.
NOTHINGFACE, Noise N 0142-2 (1989). Unknown Knows / Nothingface / Astronomy Domine / Missing Sequences / X Ray Mirror / Inner Combustion / Pre-Ignition / Into My Hypercube / Sub Effect.
ANGEL RAT, MCA MCD 10293 (1991). Shortwave Intro / Panorama / Clouds In My House / The Prow / Best Regards / Twin Dummy / Angel Rat / Golem / The Outcast / Nuage Fractal / Freedoom / None Of The Above.
THE OUTER LIMITS, MCA MCD 10701 (1993). Fix My Heart / Moonbeam Rider / Le Pont Noir / The Nile Song / The Lost Machine / Time Warp / Jack Luminous / Wrong Way Street / We Are Not Alone.
NEGATRON, Hypnotic HYP001CD (1995). Insect / Project X / Nanoman / Reality / Negatron / Planet Hell / Meteor / Cosmic Conspiracy / Bio TV / Drift / DNA (Don't No Anything).
PHOBOS, Hypnotic HYPCD 1057 (1997). I / Rise / Mercury / Phobos / Bacteria / Temps Mort / The Tower / Quantum / Neutrino / Forlorn / Catalepsy II / M-Body / 21st Century Schizoid Man.
KRONIK, Hypnotic HYP 1065 (1998). Forlorn / Nanoman / Mercury / Vortex / Drift / Erosion / Ion / Project X / Cosmic Conspiracy / Astronomy Domine / Nuclear War.
Live @ Musiqueplus, Musiqueplus (2000). Unknown Knows / Inner Combustion / Nothingface.
VOIVOD LIVES, Century Media 77282 (2000). Insect / Tribal Convictions / Nanoman / Nuclear War / Planet Hell / Negatron / Project X / Cosmic Conspiracy / Ravenous Medicine / Voivod / In League With Satan.
Gasmask Revival, Chophouse (2002) (USA promotion release). Gasmask Revival / Rebel Robot / We Carry On.
We Carry On, (2003) (USA promotion release). We Carry On (Radio edit) / We Carry On (Album version).
VOIVOD, Surfdog 44015 (2003). Gasmask Revival / Facing Up / Blame Us / Real Again / Rebel Robot / The Multiverse / I Don't Wanna Wake Up / Les Cigares Volants / Divine Sun / Reactor / Invisible Planet / Strange And Ironic / We Carry On.
WAR AND PAIN, Metal Blade MBCD 14491 (2004) (3 CD remaster). Voivod / Warriors Of Ice / Suck Your Bone / Iron Gang / War And Pain / Blower / Live For Violence / Black City / Nuclear War / Condemned To The Gallows (Live 1983) / Blower (Live 1983) / Voivod (Live 1983) / Condemned To The Gallows (Metal Massacre 5 session) / Voivod (Metal Massacre 5 session) / Iron Gang (Metal Massacre 5 session) / Build Your Weapons (Live December 1984) / War And Pain (Live December 1984) / Condemned To The Gallows (Live December 1984) / Warriors Of Ice (Live December 1984) / Helldriver (Live December 1984) / Horror (Live December 1984) / Black City (Live December 1984) / Nuclear War (Live December 1984) / Blower (Live December 1984) / Live For Violence (Live December 1984) / Ripping Headaches (Live December 1984) / Iron Gang (Live December 1984) / Korgull The Exterminator (Live December 1984) / Suck Your Bone (Live December 1984) / Witching Hour (Live December 1984) / Chemical Warfare (Live December 1984) / Voivod (Video).

KATORZ, Nuclear Blast NB 1654-2 (2006) (European promotion release). The Getaway / Dognation / Mr. Clean / After All / Odds & Frauds / Red My Mind / Silly Clones / No Angel / The X-Stream / Polaroids.

KATORZ, Nuclear Blast NB 1654-2 (2006). The Getaway / Dognation / Mr. Clean / After All / Odds & Frauds / Red My Mind / Silly Clones / No Angel / The X-Stream / Polaroids.

VOLKANA

BRASÍLIA, DF, BRAZIL — *Cláudia França (vocals), Karla Carneiro (guitar), Selma Moreira (guitar), Mila Menzes (bass), Sérgio Facci (drums).*

Brasília Thrash act dating to 1987, debuting in 1989 with the demo 'Thrash Flowers'. Although comprised mainly of female musicians VOLKANA employed male drummer Sérgio Facci. He would cite credits with VODU and VIPER. Founder and bassist Mila Menezes had a prior tradition with Punk band DETRITO FEDERAL, assembling VOLKANA with an opening line up of singer Elaine, guitarist Karla Carneiro and drummer Ana. Subsequently Marielle Loyola, previously a member of Gothic Rock band ARTE NO ESCURO and, before that, ESCOLA DE ESCANDOLOS, took over lead vocals. Deborah also usurped Ana for the drum position.

After recording 'Thrash Flowers' Deborah exited and Pat from OZONE briefly occupied the drum stool until Sérgio Facci was enrolled for recording of the eponymous 1990 album. This outing would see a vinyl only release in Brazil but was issued on CD format in North America through Moving Target Records. Undergoing further line up changes VOLKANA drafted new singer Cláudia França and guitarist Selma Moreira.

The 1994 'Mindtrips' album, featuring guest contributions from SODOM, KREATOR and MYSTIC's Frank 'Blackfire' Godszik, closed out with a cover of LED ZEPPELIN's 'Whole Lotta Love'. The band also shared a posthumous split bootleg EP of their demo 'Descent To Hell' / 'First Scream' with their female compatriots FLAMMEA.

VOLKANA folded during 1996, with singer Cláudia França going on to front Pop outfit ALMANAK. Marielle Loyola went on to CORES D FLORES.

VOLKANA, El Dorado (1991). Darkness / To Die Is Not To Die / Pet Semetary / That's My Victory / Descent To Hell / Scratch Noise / War / Silent Cry / Hide / Volkanas.

MINDTRIPS, (1994). Mindtrips / Same Old / When 2 R 1 / Off My Back / Wake Up / Keep On Trying / On Your Own / Goodbye / Living Hell / Whole Lotta Love.

VULCANO

SANTOS, SP, BRAZIL — *Angel (vocals), André (guitar), Passamani (guitar), Zhema (bass), V.X (drums).*

An esteemed name on the South American Thrash front. VULCANO, centred upon bassist Zhema, was formulated in 1981, in Osasco in the state of São Paulo, following a precursor act ASTAROTH. The founding line up, soon relocating to Santos, also comprised guitarist Paulo Magrão and bassist Carli Cooper. As VULCANO the band, enlisting drummer José Piloni in 1983, bowed in with a four track single 'Om Pushne Namah' sung in Portuguese by lead vocalist Genne. The group fractured though, Cooper and Magrão exiting in favour of guitarist Johnny Hansen and Renato on drums as Zhema switched to bass. In 1994 the demo tape 'Devil On My Roof' was circulated.

Shortly after Zhema completely reconstituted the band drafting singer Angel, guitarist Soto Júnior, bassist Zé Flávio and drummer Laudir Piloni. In August of 1985 they recorded a gig in the city of Americana for a live album 'Vulcano Live!'. Switching to English lyrics VULCANO blasted back with 'Bloody Vengeance', released by Brazilian label Cogumelo Records, supporting both VENOM and EXCITER in Brazil the same year.

For the 1987 album 'Anthropophagy' the duo of Angel and Zhema drafted a new rhythm section of bassist Fernando Levine and drummer Artur Vasconcelos. This line up remaining stable for 1988's 'Who Are The True?'. 1990's 'Rat Race' marked a return for Soto Júnior.

A later VULCANO line up reportedly saw Zhema joined by singer Luiz Carlos, guitarist Mauricio and drummer Jair. However, this union, despite being reported by the band's label, did not take place. There are reports that latterly Zhema makes his living with a CREEDANCE CLEARWATER REVIVAL covers band. Guitarist Soto Jr. would pass away from heart failure on 23rd December 2001.

An early VULCANO drummer Renato 'Pelado' would later feature in the high profile Funk / Nu-Metal band CHARLIE BROWN JR.

In January of 2006 VULCANO announced a split 7" single, entitled 'Thunder Metal', to be shared with Swedish Black Metal band NIFELHEIM on Sweden's I Hate Records.

Om Pushne Namah, (1983).

LIVE!, Cogumelo (1985). Witch's Sabbath / Prisoner From Beyond / Fallen Angel / Riding In Hell / The Signals / Guerreiros De Satan / Devil On My Roof / Total Destrucion / Legiones Satanas.

BLOODY VENGEANCE, Cogumelo CG0041 (1986). Dominos Of Death / Ready To Explode / Holocaust / Spirits Of Evil / Death Metal / Voices From Hell / Incubus / Bloody Vengeance.

ANTHROPOPHAGY, Cogumelo (1987). Red Death / Death Angel's Armies / Brainwash / F.T.W. (Fuck The War) / Fallen Angels / Anthropophagy / Anyone Can Kill / Stirring / (Am I Crazy?) / Megathrash / Upright.

WHO ARE THE TRUE?, South Attack (1988). The Next / Who Are The True? / Different Lands / Fuck Them / Witch's Sabbath / Never More / Flies Around The Shit / Do You Remember / Hercobulus.

RATRACE, Metalcore (1990). White Violence / Last Day / Blind Science / Welcome To The Army / Time To Change / Ratrace / The Lungs Of The Earth / Just A Matter Of Time / In The Mirror.

TALES FROM THE BLACK BOOK, Renegados (2003). Gates Of Iron / The Bells Of Death / Priestess Of Bacchus / From The Black Metal Book / Devote To The Devil / Fall Of The Corpse / Face Of The Terror / Guerreiros De Satã / Troubled Mind / The Sign On The Door / Obscure Soldiers / Total Destruição / Bestial Insane.

Thunder Metal, I Hate (2006) (Split 7" single with NIFELHEIM. Limited edition 1000 copies). The Evil Always Return (VULCANO) / Suffered Souls (VULCANO) / Raging Flames (NIFELHEIM) / Sepulchral Fornication (NIFELHEIM).

VÖRGUS

STOCKHOLM, SWEDEN — *Nenne Vörgus (vocals / bass), Straight G (guitar), Mikke Killalot (drums).*

Stockholm Thrash Metal trio VÖRGUS feature bassist Kenneth Nyholm and guitar player Harry Virtanen of DEFORMITY and INTERNAL DECAY repute. Nyholm also donated his services on a session basis to a SORG demo in 1998 whilst Virtanen also has SLUT credentials. The debut album, 'Vörgus Vs The Law' recorded at Studio Subsonic and mixed by Stefan Olsson, emerged in 2000. The 2001 follow up 'The Evil Dominator' was produced by Mike Wead of MERCYFUL FATE whilst third effort 'Pure Perkele' was recorded by Tore Stjerna at Necromorbus Studios during 2002.

VÖRGUS would spend the first half of 2004 recording the album 'Vörgusized', this featuring a cover version of MOTÖRHEAD's '(We Are) The Road Crew'.

VÖRGUS IS THE LAW, Vörgus (2000). Mä On Uskossa / Murder For Meat / Metal Man / Through Broken Glass / Die Hiphoper / Don't Tell Me How To Drink / Evil Priest / Why Do You Hate Me? / I Bite Your Eye / Kill, Kill, Kill / Mayhem Bikinis / Oh Yeah Baby / Aha! / Painbreeders / Kill The Rapper Baby / Ruti I Reven / Saturday Night / Seven Bullets / Fuck Truck / Vörgus / Fuck.

THE EVIL DOMINATOR, Vörgus (2001). Kill Everybody / Charlie / Dreams Of Black / Kings Of Doom / Brainshake / I Am / Unholy Latex Queen / Rot In Hell / Asleep / Moments of Pain / A Million Limbs Apart / Black Heaven / Metal Metal / The Evil Dominator / Devil Rider / More Dead Than Dead / It's Hard To Be Beautiful / Saturday Night / D.I.Y. / Saatana Tulee / Join Us Or Die.

PURE PERKELE, Vörgus (2002). Angel In Hell / Saecula Saeculorum / Metal Fang / C.N.D. / Spit Or Swallow / Hellfuck / Do You Still Hate Me? / Erections And Ejaculations / Back From Hell / In Hell / Lady Snow White.

VÖRGUSIZED, Vörgus (2004). Vörgusized / Why Serve In Heaven / In Metal We Trust / Thrash 'em Dead / Pure Perkele / Hard, Loud And Fast / (We Are) The Road Crew / Metal In My Veins / Total War—Winter War.

WARFARE INCORPORATED

KRISTINEHAMN, SWEDEN — *Daniel Jansson (vocals), Nicklas Carlson (guitar), Daniel Grahn (guitar), Johan Hallberg (bass), Johnny Lebisch (drums).*

Kristinehamn's WARFARE INCORPORATED, fronted by singer Daniel Jansson and incorporating three former BRIMSTONE band members in guitarist Nicklas Carlson, bassist Johan Hallberg plus Johnny Lebisch on drums, released the demos 'Here is Your Hell' in 1999, recorded at Evil Grill Studios, under the formative band title of WARHEAD. In this guise the band performed just one solitary concert. Learning of multiple other Metal WARHEADs, the group then switched to WARFARE INCORPORATED and delivered the 'Madness Breeds Heroes' demo in 2000. These sessions saw Hallberg replaced by Nicklas Carlson brother. At this juncture Daniel Grahn, another ex-BRIMSTONE player, joined the band,

Black Goat Productions subsequently combined the two sessions for an April 2001 cassette release. In 2003 Tony Sundberg enrolled as new singer as Daniel Grahn left, relocating to Gothenburg to forge Grind outfit KOLONY. At this time WARFARE INCORPORATED evolved into UNDER THY GUN. A demo, entitled 'When The World Went Dead', was released in November 2004. The group also had tracks featured on the December 2005 compilation album 'Metal Ostentation Vol 9'.

In September 2006 Daniel Grahn returned to the ranks.

Madness Breeds Heroes, Warfare Incorporated (2000) (Demo). Madness Breeds Heroes / Electric Eyes / Illusory Existence / Holy Desert Blood.

Madness Breeds Heroes & Here is Your Hell, Black Goat Productions BGP 001 (2001) (Cassette demo limited to 500 copies). Madness Breeds Heroes / Electric Eyes / Illusory Existence / Holy Desert Blood / Armageddon / Paradise Becomes Hell / Flames Of Insanity / Merciless Slaughter / Sinner / Superior Race Devours / Here Is Your Hell / Razorblade Smiles.

WARGASM

STOUGHTON, MA, USA — *Bob Mayo (vocals / bass), Rich Spillberg (guitar), Barry Spillberg (drums).*

Stoughton, Massachusetts Thrashers WARGASM issued the demos 'Satan Stole My Lunch Money' and 'Rainbows, Kittens, Flowers And Puppies' in 1986. After the 1988 'Why Play Around?' album, released on Profile Records, the band released a further set of demos, 'Your Dogs Teeth' in 1990 and the single track 'Spirit In Decay', that September, engineered by Bruce Bennett at Kashmir Studios in Tewksbury, Massachusetts, with 'Gasm It' arriving in 1991. The band signed to the German Massacre label for the 1993 'Fireball' EP and subsequent 'Ugly' album of 1994. After issuing the 1995 'Suicide Notes' album WARGASM called it a day, bowing out with a show at Boston's Rat Club on 11th February 1995.

The band returned in 2000, issuing the seasonal single 'Little Drummer Boy / Jingle Hell' via Transmission Records. Former WARGASM drummer Barry Spillberg joined the reconvened MELIAH RAGE during 2003. A ten year hiatus would be broken as WARGASM reunited for an appearance at the Middle East venue in Cambridge, Massachusetts on 18th September 2004.

Satan Stole My Lunch Money, Wargasm (1986) (Demo). Wasteland / Sudden Death / Revenge / Humanoid.

WHY PLAY AROUND?, Profile (1988). Wasteland / Revenge / Bullets & Blades / Undead / Merritt's Girlfriend / Sudden Death / Wargasm / Le Coucou / Humanoid.

Your Dog's Teeth, Wargasm (1990) (Demo). Blood Flood / Dead Man's Smile / Ugly Is To The Bone.

Spirit In Decay, Wargasm (1990) (Demo). Spirit In Decay.

Gasm it, Wargasm (1991) (Demo). The Rudest Awakening / I Breath Fire / Dreadnaut Day.

UGLY, Massacre (1993). The Rudest Awakening / Enemy Mine / Chameleon / I Breathe Fire / Ugly Is To The Bone / Slow Burn / Blood Food / One Man Army / Spirit In Decay / Dead Man's Smile / Dreadnaut Day.

Fireball EP, Massacre (1994). Fireball / Dreadnaught Day (Video edit) / Wasteland (Live radio broadcast) / Enemy Mine (Live radio broadcast) / Revenge (Live radio broadcast) / Grievous Angel (Live radio broadcast).

SUICIDE NOTES, Transmission (1995). This May Not Be Hell ... / Engine / Meat / Underground / Not Forgiven, Not Forgotten / Jigsaw Man / What Are You Afraid Of ? / Grey Matter / Fire Away / Tear Down.

Little Drummer Boy / Jingle Hell, Transmission (2000). Little Drummer Boy / Jingle Hell / Meat / This May Not Be Hell.

WARHEAD

KRISTINEHAMN, SWEDEN — *Daniel Jansson (vocals), Nicklas Carlson (guitar), Johan Hallberg (bass), Johnny Lebisch (drums).*

Kristinehamn's WARHEAD, fronted by singer Daniel Jansson and incorporating three former BRIMSTONE band members in guitarist Nicklas Carlson, bassist Johan Hallberg plus Johnny Lebisch on drums, released the demos 'Here is Your Hell' in 1999, recorded at Evil Grill Studios. WARHEAD performed just one solitary concert. Learning of multiple other Metal WARHEADs, the group then switched to WARFARE INCORPORATED and delivered the 'Madness Breeds Heroes' demo in 2000. These sessions saw Hallberg replaced by Nicklas Carlson brother. At this juncture Daniel Grahn, another ex-BRIMSTONE player, joined the band,

Black Goat Productions subsequently combined the two sessions for an April 2001 cassette release. In 2003 Tony Sundberg enrolled as new singer as Daniel Grahn left, relocating to Gothenburg to forge Grind outfit KOLONY. At this time WARFARE INCORPORATED evolved into UNDER THY GUN. A demo, entitled 'When The World Went Dead', was released in November 2004. The group also had tracks featured on the December 2005 compilation album 'Metal Ostentation Vol 9'.

In September 2006 Daniel Grahn returned to the ranks.

Here Is Your Hell, Warhead (1999) (Demo). Armageddon / Paradise Becomes Hell / Flames Of Insanity / Merciless Slaughter / Sinner / Superior Race Devours / Here Is Your Hell / Razorblade Smiles.

WARLORD UK

BIRMINGHAM, WEST MIDLANDS, UK — *Mark White (vocals / bass), Andy Stone (guitar), Mick Gorst (guitar), Neil Farrington (drums).*

Birmingham's WARLORD UK was established during 1999 by vocalist / bassist Mark White and guitarists Andy Stone and Mick Gorst, simply as WARLORD, and conducted its first concerts were conducted with the aid of a drum machine. In 1992 Neil Hutton was drafted as drummer and the 'Alien Dictator' demo was cut at Bob Lamb's studio in Kings Heath, Birmingham. Hutton exited in 1995, going on to BENEDICTION and STAMPIN' GROUND. He would be replaced by Neil Farrington.

BENEDICTION's Dave 'Bear' Ingram guests on the 1996 'Maximum Carnage' album, featuring on cover versions of AMEBIX's 'Nobody's Driving' and 'Chain Reaction' plus SLAYER's 'Raining Blood', released by Germany's Nuclear Blast Records. The album had been recorded at Rhythm Studios in Bidford Upon Avon with producer Paul Johnson. Promoting this album, WARLORD UK opened for BENEDICTION on an 11 date European tour throughout February 1996, covering Belgium, Germany, Italy, Holland and the Czech Republic. UK shows were booked as support to AT THE GATES but these did not eventuate. Soon afterwards WARLORD UK folded.

Rebilled as WARLORD in 1998, Mark White, solely as lead vocalist, Neil Farrington, Andrew Stone and Michael Gorst plus new bassist Matthew Evans reformed the band. The group also novelly added a third guitarist in the form of CEREBRAL FIX's Tony Warburton. Unfortunately the group folded yet again.

Farrington and Warburton duly forged DAMN DIRTY APES. The drummer also worked with LAST UNDER THE SUN and SENSA YUMA. Neil Farrington formed up part of the 2006 CEREBRAL FIX reunion.

MAXIMUM CARNAGE, Nuclear Blast NB119 (1996). Maximum Carnage / Disintegration / Change / Nowhere To Run / Vivisection / Race War / Alien Dictator / Theatre Of Destruction / Nobody's Driving / Chain Reaction / Raining Blood.

WARPATH

HAMBURG, GERMANY — *Dicker (vocals), Ozzy (guitar), Schröder (guitar), Maurer (bass), Krid (drums).*

Hamburg's WARPATH first contributed two tracks to the West Virginia Records compilation album 'Cries Of The Unborn' prior to being offered a deal. The debut album, produced by Andy Classen of HOLY MOSES, features guest vocals from CRONOS mainman Conrad Lant and Sabina Classen of HOLY MOSES. In their time WARPATH toured alongside SODOM, FORBIDDEN and GOREFEST. The 1996 album 'Kill Your Enemy' includes a cover version of CRO-MAGS 'Sign Of Hard Times'.

Vocalist 'Dicker' (Dirk Weiss) created RICHTHOFEN in 1997 with ex-HOLY MOSES guitarist Andy Classen. Bassist 'Ozzy' teamed up with TEMPLE OF THE ABSURD and in September 2005 joined HOLY MOSES.

WHEN WAR BEGINS ... TRUTH DISAPPEARS, West Virginia 084-57162 (1994). Resistance Is Useless / Die In Grief / Forest Of Anima / Last Vacation / Wardance / Absolution / You Are The Sickness / Those Crawling Insects / Tightrope Walk / The Ballad Of H / Hypocrite / Black Metal.
AGAINST EVERYONE, Steamhammer SPV 084-76812 (1994). Gate Crasher / In Rage / Against Everyone / Terminus / Give A Shit / I Hate / Night On Earth / Paranoia / Vote Of Censure / That's For Me / Mind Commits Murder / End Of Salvation.
MASSIVE, Steamhammer SPV 085-76672 (1995). Intro / Massive / Pain / Race War / Ambivalence / Save Me From The Wreckage / Fears Of The Past / Remember My Name / Always Near You / Thoughts Begin To Bite / Reason Enough To Die.
KILL YOUR ENEMY, Steamhammer SPV 085-18252 (1996). Your Enemy / A Matter Of Fact / Die Maschine / Frustration Grows / Outburst Of Rage / The Struggle / Sign Of Hard Times / Stomp / Overrollin' / Kill Your Enemy Ii.

WASTELAND

STUTTGART, GERMANY — *Tobias Schmalfeld (vocals), Tobias Kramer (guitar), Stephan Kern (guitar), André Ipfling (bass), Frank Gottschalk (drums).*

Stuttgart's WASTELAND rank as one of the new breed of pure Thrash Metal acts although the group's origins trace back to the mid eighties. The band's first recordings came with the demo 'Warriors Of The Wasteland', recorded in October 1990 at L-Sound Studio in Emmendingen. WASTELAND at this juncture comprised singer Roland Seidel, guitarist Davor Sertic, bass player Markus Plattner and drummer Klaus Sperling. Shortly after these sessions WASTELAND added second guitarist Stefan Liebing but soon folded. Liebling hooked up with PRIMAL FEAR. Singer Roland Seidel subsequently featured on CYBERTRASH's 2001 album 'Wahnsinns Programm' and also worked with LAZZER and KAMINARI.

The group was re-assembled during 1995 with a line-up comprising guitarists Stephan Kern and Tobias Kramer, bass player Frank Neugebauer and drummer Frank Gottschalk. Tobias Schmalfeld was soon added as lead vocalist. However, Kramer decamped in April of 1995 but would return by the November. WASTELAND debuted with the privately issued 'Mare Tranquillitatis' mini album but would be shaken when, in January of 1996, Neugebauer announced his departure. Within 24 hours WASTELAND had plugged the gap drafting André Ipfling. In September of 1997 the band went back into the studio to record the full length 'Genuine Parts' album. Released in May of 1998 'Genuine Parts' garnered healthy press reports enabling WASTELAND to put in live appearances at festivals such as the 'Schweizer Garten' in Wittenberg in March 1997 and the 'Fuck the Commerce II' festival in 1998.

WASTELAND have contributed to various compilation collections including 'Deathophobia IV', 'Bullet In The Head I' and 'European Deathophobia'. During 1999 the band cut a whole slew of cover tracks for the American Dwell label contributing versions of 'Reckoning Day' to a MEGADETH tribute, 'Evil Dead' to a DEATH homage, 'Time Is Coming' to a TESTAMENT album. The group even donated AC/DC's 'Riff Raff' and LED ZEPPELIN's 'Waering And Tearing' to tribute collections.

MARE TRANQUILLITATIS, (1995). Lavatory Charwoman / Dead End / Revelation Of Fear / How To Get Mentally Cracked / Chemikills—Wasted Land.
GENUINE PARTS, Wasteland (1998). Infernal Heart / Winter / Bloodthirst Remains / Mania / Agony Of Christ / My Own Requiem / Blackherder Demon / 2nd Intergalactical Cyclone / Forever / Shadow The God / First Knife.
WARRIORS OF THE WASTELAND, Iron Glory (2002). X-Ray Eyes / Kill The Killer / Wasteland / Dreams Of Heaven / Can't Wait / Atomic Coffins / Still The World Is Sad / Warning / Bombastic Chiefs / Salvation / Calling Out To Your Name / Decide Your Destiny / Babylon.

WATCH MY DYING

BUDAPEST, HUNGARY — *Gábor Veres (vocals), Sándor Bori (guitar), Attila Kovács (guitar), Imre Eszenyi (bass), Zoltán Bordás (drums).*

WATCH MY DYING, a modern Thrash / Death Metal band, was manifested in Esztergom, Hungary during 1999. An opening demo, 'System Error (Rendszerhiba)', was recorded at Pont-Mi Studio in Székesfehérvár in March the following year. Further progress was made when, in May 2000, the group scored a fourth placing in the Pepsi sponsored 'Generation Nexxt' talent competition, broadcast on national television. Live work saw the band increasing its profile with shows at major festivals such as the Slovakian 'Klikk' event and 'Pepsi Sziget' festival.

In September 2002 the band convened at Acoustair Studio, Budapest to record the 'Húsmágnes' EP. Live work across Hungary to promote the outing was extensive but by mid 2004 WATCH MY DYING was ready to lay down a full length album, 'Klausztrofónia', utilising the Bakery and the Grape Studio between July to October for this purpose. Once again the group set out on the road, landing supports to the likes of OPETH, STAMPIN GROUND and DEW-SCENTED. The band also shared the stage at the 'Metal Mania' festival alongside CRADLE OF FILTH, APOCALYPTICA, KATATONIA, MOONSPELL and THE HAUNTED.

WATCH MY DYING released the 'Fényérzékeny' album in November 2006.

Rendszerhiba, Watch My Dying WMD-001 (2000). Systole / Képfakasztó / Digitális Antikrisztus / Túl Jón És Rosszon / Extrasystole.
Húsmágnes EP, Watch My Dying WMD-042 (2002). Terápiarezisztens / Szájzár / Eredeti Testforma / Jelennemlét / Yang / Húsmágnes—Megjön / Húsmágnes—Elmegy.
KLAUSZTTROFONIA, Watch My Dying WMD-666 (2004). Idomtalan / Carbon / Klausztrofónia / Nullpont / Horizont 16:9 / Technika Angyala I. / Technika Angyala II. / Nicht Vor Dem Kind / Gyúlékony Csíra / B-terv / Nyers Hát / Kék Ég, Zöld Fű.
CLAUSTROPHONY, Watch My Dying (2005) (Split album with SZEG). Hope For The Best / I Show You The Way / Leave Me Alone / Bring Me / Carbon / Time Overdose / Plan B / Blues Sky, Green Grass (remix).

FÉNYÉRZÉKENY, Watch My Dying WMD-99 (2006). Elsőbbségi / Fényérzékeny / A Tegező / Sztereotip (Állami Sláger) / Metrikus / OHM / 50 Hz / Háttal Álmodó / Hínár / Om / 9 Kapu.

WATCHTOWER

AUSTIN, TX, USA — *Jason McMaster (vocals), Ron Jarzombek (guitar), Doug Keyser (bass), Rick Colaluca (drums).*

Austin, Texas Metal band renowned for their inventiveness and complexity. Regarded as an intriguing twist on the standard Metal formula upon their arrival on the scene. WATCHTOWER has directly influenced many current leading bands of the genre. Formed by drummer Rick Colaluca and bassist Doug Keyser in 1981, the original incarnation of WATCHTOWER also included vocalist Jason McMaster and guitarist BILLY WHITE. McMaster had earlier paid his dues as vocalist / bassist with FALLEN ANGEL.

WATCHTOWER debuted with an out of place track on a Hardcore compilation record 'A Texas Hardcore Compilation: Cottage Cheese From The Lips Of Death'. The band also recorded a proposed debut album for Rainforest Records. The label went bust and the tapes subsequently became highly sought after on the tape trading scene.

McMaster's talents were highly regarded and in 1986 the man turned down offers from PANTERA and, in place of Don Doty, DARK ANGEL. The singer also guested on fellow Austin Thrashers ASSALANT's 1987 demo 'The Damage Is Done'. McMaster recorded with WATCHTOWER on their debut album, the 1985 outing 'Energetic Disassembly'. Originally a self-financed offering put out on the Zombo imprint, 'Energetic Disassembly' saw a manufacturing run of 3,000 vinyl and 1,500 cassettes. This highly involved chunk of Metal, surgically tight riffs writhing around unorthodox compositions, soon began making waves internationally courtesy of exemplary reviews, famously branding WATCHTOWER's debut as a "Thrashterpiece". Importantly, WATCHTOWER defied convention by prominently featuring the rhythm section of Doug Keyser and Rick Colacula, both bass and drums focussed in equal measure to the guitars.

McMaster stuck with the band for five months, his latter band, DANGEROUS TOYS, eventually got picked up by Columbia. Jason, naturally, quit. Keyser meantime auditioned for METALLICA following the loss of Cliff Burton reportedly getting into the final placings. In 1986 the bassist was also briefly recruited by MARTY FRIEDMAN for CACOPHONY and a couple of years later by YNGWIE MALMSTEEN whilst on his way through Austin.

McMaster was eventually replaced by ex-MILITIA and ASSALANT singer Mike Soliz. The man's tenure was short though and after an April 1987 demo 'Instruments Of Random Murder' former HADES frontman Alan Tecchio took the position. Tecchio had actually been tipped off about the vacancy by McMaster, urging his fellow singer to put in a call to Keyser.

Billy White left WATCHTOWER in the Autumn of 1986 after a West Coast tour and hooked up with the pre-RIOT pairing of Bobby Jarzombek and Pete Perez in the short-lived CHIMERA. White also recorded with Will (brother of Charlie) Sexton's WILL & THE KILL for their MCA album. The guitarist then joined DON DOKKEN's solo group and would later form the BILLY WHITE TRIO in the mid 90s.

WATCHTOWER recruited Ron Jarzombek, who previously played with S.A. SLAYER, to the ranks during late 1986 before the recording of the second album 'Control And Resistance' took place at Sky Trak Studios in Berlin during 1989. Jarzombek had, post S.A. SLAYER, also recorded with studio project the HAPPY KITTIES with his brother Bobby on drums. A mostly instrumental demo had been recorded with Jason McMaster guesting on 'Hammer At The Ready' and Mike Grotheus of WINTERKAT on 'In Mind'. Despite hosting a new singer and new guitarist, 'Control And Resistance', of technical parity to its predecessor, succeeded in satisfying fans. Benefiting from wider distribution, Watchtower drew in new fans, many simply dumbfounded and awestruck by the group's jazz-fusion-metal amalgam.

WATCHTOWER guested for CORONER on a 1990 European tour, the band known at one point for playing a live, Metallica rendition of MICHAEL JACKSON's 'Billie Jean', after which Tecchio bailed out to join NON FICTION in June. Ron Jarzombek was then put out of action, having to undergo multiple hand surgeries leaving the guitarist unable to play for a few years. With curiosity in the group remaining high, German label Institute of Art Records re-released 'Energetic Disassembly' in 1993.

Tecchio would rejoin his original act HADES for a reformation whilst post DANGEROUS TOYS McMaster would appear on albums from BROKEN TEETH and GODZILLA MOTOR COMPANY. Doug Keyser and Rick Colaluca were to be found in the ranks of RETARDED ELF. During mid 2002 the Monster label issued a collection of archive WATCHTOWER demos, rehearsal tapes and live recordings entitled 'Demonstrations In Chaos'. Also included would be 'Meltdown' from the 1984 Texan Plan 9 compilation 'Cottage Cheese From The Lips Of Death'. McMaster would be back in the news apparently enrolled into the Black Metal band HELL PIG, a collaboration with SLIPKNOT drummer and MURDERDOLLS guitarist Joey Jordison and Killjoy of NECROPHAGIA, EIBON, VIKING CROWN and ENOCH amongst others. WATCHTOWER guitarist RON JARZOMEBEK cut a solo album 'Solitarily Speaking Of Theoretical Confinement' in late 2002.

Both Jason McMaster and Doug Keyser would guest on the SPASTIC INK 2003 opus 'Ink Compatible'. Ron Jarzombek would form up part of erstwhile MEGADETH guitarist MARTY FRIEDMAN's touring band for his 'Guitarevolution' September tour. In September of 2004 it was announced that McMaster was to form up part of ex-RATT singer STEPHEN PEARCY's much vaunted 'Bastards of Metal' tour as announcement revealed plans to include a roster of Pearcy, McMaster, former ANTHRAX frontman Joey Belladonna, the BULLETBOYS Marq Torien and Ron Keel of KEEL and IRONHORSE. Also on the billing would be DROP and STS.

In June of 2005 ex-WATCHTOWER frontman Alan Tecchio was announced as new frontman for SEVEN WITCHES, appearing on the album 'Metal Nation'. In August Ron Jarzombek would be included in MARTY FRIEDMAN's solo band once again, appearing at the South Korean 'Busan Rock' festival. The guitarist also unveiled MACHINATIONS OF DEMENTIA, a technical extreme Metal project alongside CANNIBAL CORPSE bassist Alex Webster. Initially this band included LAMB OF GOD drummer Chris Adler but he would bow out in December 2005 due to other commitments.

ENERGETIC DISASSEMBLY, Zombo 44452 (1985). Violent Charge / Asylum / Tyrants In Distress / Social Fears / Energetic Disassembly / Argonne Forest / Cimmerian Shadows / Meltdown.

Instruments Of Random Murder, Watchtower (1987). The Eldritch / Instruments Of Random Murder / Plastic Lasagna / The Fall Of Reason.

CONTROL AND RESISTANCE, Noise NUK 140 (1989). Instruments Of Random Murder / Eldritch / Mayday In Kiev / Fall Of Reason / Control And Resistance / Hidden Instincts / Life Cycles / Dangerous Toy.

DEMONSTRATIONS IN CHAOS, Monster (2002). Meltdown (Demo) / Asylum (Demo) / Argonne Forest (Demo) / Social Fears (Demo) / Tyrants In Distress (Demo) / Energetic Disassembly (Demo) / Cimmerian Shadows (Demo) / The Eldritch (Demo) / Instruments Of Random Murder (Demo) / Hidden Instincts (Demo) / The Fall Of Reason (Demo) / Control And Resistance (Live) / Cathode Ray Window (Live) / Ballad Assassin (Live) / Meltdown.

WAYNE

USA — *David Wayne (vocals), Jimi Bell (guitar), Craig Wells (guitar), Mark Franco (bass), B.J. Zampa (drums).*

A twist in the tale of renowned and highly respected Thrash veterans METAL CHURCH. Following the comeback studio album 'Masterpeace' METAL CHURCH, not for the first time in their career, parted ways with singer David Wayne. The man had originally fronted the band from 1983 onwards lending his distinctive bellow to what many regard as METAL CHURCH's finest moments the debut 'Metal Church' and the mammoth second effort 'The Dark'.

Wayne would decamp at the pinnacle make or break juncture of METAL CHURCH's success in what many analysts at the time perceived was a rash move. Years later it would be revealed the singer had bailed out in order to clean up from drug abuse. Wayne resurfaced with REVEREND issuing a further string of commendable, if not commercially successful, albums. METAL CHURCH persevered turning in solid and even inspiring works with Wayne's replacement Mike Howe but would ultimately bite the dust.

The band, complete with Wayne and much of the classic line up, reunited for the 'Masterpeace' album but fractures began to show yet again. With the METAL CHURCH membership in disarray at the turn of the millennium it emerged that Wayne had set up a fresh act initially titled DAVID WAYNE'S METAL CHURCH! Joining him were METAL CHURCH colleague and guitarist Craig Wells, former JOINED FORCES, GEEZER and THUNDERHEAD guitarist JIMI BELL and drummer B.J. Zampa, a veteran of YNGWIE MALMSTEEN, MVP, TONY MACALPINE and THUNDERHEAD. Bell also operates the covers band TATTERED TRAMPS.

The resulting album, released by the German Nuclear Blast label and naturally called 'Metal Church', not only witnessed the re-introduction of METAL CHURCH's famous guitar-cross device on the cover art but sported a WAYNE icon in the exact logotype as METAL CHURCH. The record would also sport a cover version of MOUNTAIN's 'Mississippi Queen'.

Wayne would not neglect his REVEREND act though, inducting BYFIST guitarists Davey Lee and Notch Vara into the fold during March of 2002. In early 2003 JIMI BELL contributed a guest solo to the ROB ROCK album 'Eyes Of Eternity'. By early 2004 Bell would be collaborating with the OBSESSION and LOUDNESS credited singer Michael Vescara for a MVP project album and subsequently hooked up with BIRD OF PREY.

The METAL CHURCH family was dealt a huge blow on 10th of May 2005 with the passing of David Wayne. Just 47 years old, the singer died from complications from injuries he sustained in a head-on automobile accident months previously. In January 2006 the WAYNE duo of guitarist JIMI BELL and drummer B.J. Zampa joined celebrated melodic Rock band HOUSE OF LORDS.

METAL CHURCH, Nuclear Blast (2001). The Choice / The Hammer Will Fall / Soos Creek Cemetery / Hannibal / Burning At The Stake / D.S.D. / Nightmare Part II / Vlad / Ballad For Marianne / Mississippi Queen.

WEB

RUMANIA — *Dennis Mustafa (vocals), Corneliu Belu (guitar), Costin Beizadea (guitar), Sorin Vlad (bass), Florian Laghia (drums).*

Constanta based WEB, formed in October of 1998, was assembled by guitarist Costin Beizadea and former NECROPOLA and CELESTIAL SANCTUARY bassist Vali 'IngerAlb' Zechiu. In December former ANGELS & TEARS man Nicu Galie joins as vocalist and this trio entered ID Stage Studios to craft the 'Spirits' demo in February of the following year. Narcis Chiamil of INSTINCT would act as sessioneer for these recordings but subsequently joined on a full time basis. WEB expanded further in March with the incorporation of ex-IN CREPUSCULUM guitarist Corneliu Belu. However, the band lost the services of Zechiu, the ex-bassist enrolling successively into MAGICA, Industrial Metal band INGER DE FIER before forging his own solo Dark Ambient concern TELURICA.

WEB performed their first live concert at the Green Hours club in Bucharest in January of 2000, after which MAGICA's Cristi Barla took over on drums. That August Sorin Vlad stepped in as new bassist for recording of a second demo entitled 'First Moods Of Anger'. Fractures among the ranks in May of 2001 saw Barla exiting to join INTERITUS DEI. The group went into hiatus for several months until they located ARON drummer Florian Laghia for a return gig in November at the 'Metalheart' festival. However, Narcis Chiamil re-took his former position on drums in 2003. That July Dennis Mustafa, a seasoned veteran of MYSTIC SIGHT, WATCHTOWER, TEARS BLAME, INTERITUS, ULTRA and FLATLINERS, became WEB's new vocalist as Nicu Galie joined Death Metal band AVSKILD.

SEVERAL MOODS OF ANGER, Web (2004). The Web (Intro) / I Met Myself Again / Pass Away / Fate / Shock System / So I Died / Unexpurgated Reality / Aflicao E Felicidade / Deadly Web / Endless Manipulation.

WENGELE

KIIMINKI, FINLAND — *Pulla (vocals), Keikki (guitar), Ipe (bass), Riku (drums).*

Thrash Metal band WENGELE was formed in Kiiminki in the late 80's. The band was originally known as MENGELE and in 1988 released a four track demo. Another four track demo followed in 1989 which in turn was quickly followed by their debut release, the 'Senseless Extermination' EP on the Bad Vugum label. A name change followed and the band released another four track demo as INSOMNIA IN 1990.

Over a decade of inactivity followed until a reunion in 2002 and yet another name change, this time to WENGELE. The newly monikered band then released a self-titled, three track EP in 2004. WENGELE then contributed a track to the 'Metal On Metal: Finnish Underground Metal Compilation' in early 2005.

Wengele, Wengele (2004). Pi Around The Circle / Pity / Mind.

WHIP

OSLO, NORWAY — *Grr (vocals / guitar), Sturt (guitar), AndyHotPants (bass), Slegg (drums).*

Oslo's Thrash outfit WHIP was founded in the Summer of 1998 by drummer Jonny, being joined shortly afterward by guitarist Sturt. The opening demo, 'Doomsday Machine', would be recorded by Jonny on drums, vocals and bass with Sturt handling vocals, guitar and bass. A second demo, 'Fullmoon Vomit', was recorded on "a black and drunken night" in 2000.

Jonny relocated and Sturt re-built the band, drafting singer Grrr in early 2004. This duo cut a third demo with the aid of a drum machine. Subsequently, Slegg enrolled on drums and bassist AndyHotPants completed the roster in May 2005. The demo 'Godfucking And Wardreams' arrived in October 2005. New bassist Kai was inducted in February 2006.

Doomsday Machine, Whip (1998) (Demo). Doomsday Machine.
Fullmoon Vomit, Whip (2000) (Demo). Fullmoon Vomit.
Innocence And Fistfucks, Whip (2005) (Demo). Innocence And Fistfucks.
Godfucking And Wardreams, Whip (2005) (Demo). Godfucking And Wardreams / Face Your Death / Innocence And Fistfucks / Ripper Territory.

WHIPLASH

PASSAIC, NJ, USA — *Warren Conditi (vocals / guitar), Tony Portaro (guitar), James Preziosa (bass), Bob Candella (drums).*

WHIPLASH initially made their mark as a ferocious trio out of Passaic, New Jersey founded by ex-TOXIN guitarist Tony Portaro plus bassist Tony Bono and drummer Tony 'T.J.' Scaglione in 1984. Although the act's membership has buckled and bowed several times over the years, it is the classic trio format that WHIPLASH is remembered for. True to form, the band was titled after the landmark METALLICA song 'Whiplash'. The group was formed from the amalgamation of their two previous acts, JACKHAMMER, having issued the demo 'Fire Away' in March 1984, and TOXIN, to form a fresh act, later fronted by vocalist Mike Orosz. As a quartet, WHIPLASH unveiled themselves with the 'Full Force' demo tape prior to both Orasz and Harding leaving the ranks. The remaining duo, with Portaro handling bass and vocals, kept the momentum going with a further cassette, the mis-spelt 'Thunderstruk', delivered that same August.

For recording of the next session in 1985 the band drafted bassist Tony Bono and, after unsuccessfully attempting to locate a lead vocalist, settled on the trio format with Portaro reluctantly taking the singing duties for their third tape, featuring five songs and titled 'Looking Death In The Face'. Quite remarkably Portaro recorded these cuts with his arm in plaster having suffered a broken arm in a car accident. Nonetheless, the combination of their latter two tapes secured WHIPLASH a deal with Roadrunner Records, being in fact the very first directly signed band to the US office, for their commercial debut 'Power And Pain'.

In 1986 an 18 year old Scaglione received an offer he could not refuse from Thrash meisters SLAYER. Scaglione's skills would be put to the test in full public gaze replacing DAVE LOMBARDO, renowned as one of the very finest drummers of the genre. WHIPLASH drafted Joe Cangelosi on the drum stool for the 1987 album 'Ticket To Mayhem'. With Lombardo returning, Scaglione's tenure in SLAYER would prove brief and in 1987 he forged ZERO HOUR, a collaboration with vocalist Joe Haggerty, ex-DEATHRASH bassist Pat Burns and the guitar pairing of the MASSACRE credited Robbie Goodwin and NYC MAYHEM and AGNOSTIC FRONT man Gordon Ancis. Scaglione subsequently journeyed on to LUDICHRIST.

During late 1988 WHIPLASH added vocalist Glenn Hanson and, retaining Cangelosi on drums, began to gather together material for a third album titled 'Insult To Injury'. Former drummer Scaglione was announced as the new drummer in Southern infused retro Rockers RAGING SLAB around the same period. The drummer would later affiliate with Hardcore units CAUSE FOR ALARM and SHEER TERROR.

Meantime, Cangelosi would later unite with German Thrash veterans KREATOR for their 'Cause For Conflict' album. Bono joined Hardcore unit INTO ANOTHER, fronted by ex-YOUTH OF TODAY vocalist Richie Birkenhead, for their eponymous 1992 album. Scaglione and Portaro would find themselves as members of the same band once more in 1993 when the duo acted as touring musician's for Billy Milano's M.O.D. European dates.

German label Massacre Records persuaded Whiplash to cut another album for the European market. As such, Portaro and Scaglione pulled in BURN singer Rob Gonzo and bassist James Preziosa to construct the 1996 'Cult Of One' album. Upon release, the record drew ecstatic reviews. WHIPLASH conjoined with RIOT and label mates SKYCLAD for a 1996 European tour and, although WHIPLASH's intense brand of retro thrash seemed an uneasy bed partner for SKYCLAD's increasingly whimsical folk metal, the tour fared well for both acts.

Pressures of the road were soon to show though as Gonzo was unceremoniously fired upon the tour's completion and WHIPLASH duly maneuvered guitarist Warren Conditi into the lead vocal position. Massacre put out the Steve Evetts produced 'Sit, Stand, Kneel, Pray' offering in 1997.

The band issued the 'Thrashback' album in 1998, a collection of archive material re-recorded, some dating back as far as 1985. One of these early tracks, 'Chained Up, Strapped Down', would be lyrically switched to become 'Nails In Me Deep'. Some critics took issue with the alteration of deemed classics and especially the cleaner vocal sound but overall the return of WHIPLASH was universally welcomed.

During 1999 Dutch label Displeased would re-package the first two albums as a double pack CD and release a collection of demos and rarities entitled 'Messages In Blood—The Early Years'. Another re-issue CD set, 'Insult To Injury', comprised of live tracks recorded in 1986 at the legendary CBGB's club in New York.

Scaglione later operated with Hardcore acts the NORTH SIDE KINGS, ZERO SRI and MANTRA, a band led by CHANNEL ZERO guitarist Peter Iterbeke and also including erstwhile WHIPLASH colleague bassist James Preziosa.

Sadly, ex-WHIPLASH member Tony Bono, just 38 years old, died of a heart attack in May of 2002.

James Preziosa joined DROPBOX for the 2004 album 'Wishbone' in 2004.

Fire Away, (1984). Headthirst / Ruthless / In The Line Of Fire / Living Nightmare.

Thunderstruck, (1984). King Of The Axe / Spit On Your Grave / Thrash 'Til Death / Chained Up, Strapped Down.

Looking Death In The Face, (1985). The Burning Of Atlanta / Stirrin' The Cauldron / Last Man Alive / Spit On Your Grave / Respect The Dead.

POWER AND PAIN, Roadrunner RR 9718 (1985). Stage Dive / Red Bomb / Last Man Alive / Message In Blood / War Monger / Power Thrashing Death / Stirring The Cauldron / Spit On Your Grave / Nailed To The Cross.

TICKET TO MAYHEM, Roadracer RO 95962 (1987). Perpetual Warfare / Walk The Plank / Last Nail In The Coffin / Drowning In Torment / The Burning Of Atlanta / Eternal Eyes (Last Nail In The Coffin Part II) / Snake Pit / Spiral Of Violence / Respect The Dead / Perpetual Warfare.

INSULT TO INJURY, Roadracer RO 9482-2 (1989). Voice Of Sanity / Hiroshima / Insult To Injury / Dementia B / Essence Of Evil / Witness To The Terror / Battle Scars / Rape To The Mind / Ticket To Mayhem / 4 ES / Pistolwhipped.

CULT OF ONE, Massacre MASS CD087 (1996). Such Is The Will / No One's Idol / No Fear To Tread / 1'000 Times / Wheel Of Misfortune / Heavenaut / Lost World / Cult Of One / Enemy / Apostle Of Truth.

SIT, STAND, KNEEL, PRAY, Massacre MAS PC0129 (1997). Out Of Hell / Left Unsaid / Hitlist / Cyanide Grenade / Jane Doe / Knock Me Down / Lack Of Contrition / Word To The Wize / Strangeface / Catharsis / Sit, Stand, Kneel, Pray.

THRASHBACK, Massacre MAS DP0148 (1998). Temple Of Punishment / Stab / This / Killing On Monroe Street / King With The Axe / Strike Me Blind / Memory Serves / Resurrection Chair / House With No Doors / Thrash 'Til Death / Nails In Me Deep.

INSULT TO INJURY—LIVE CBGB'S 1986, Displeased D-00064 (1998). Voice Of Sanity / Hiroshima / Insult To Injury / Dimentia Thirteen / Essence Of Evil / Witness To The Terror / Battle Scars / Rape Of The Mind / Ticket To Mayhem / Four Empty Skulls / Pistolwhipped.

MESSAGES IN BLOOD—THE EARLY YEARS, Displeased D-00067 (1999). King With The Axe / Spit On Your Grave / Thrash 'Til Death / Chained Up, Strapped Down / Burning Of Atlanta / Stirrin' The Cauldron / Respect The Dead / Last Man Alive / Spit On Your Grave / Killing On Monroe Street / Eternal Eyes / Respect The Dead / Stirrin' the Cauldron / Burning Of Atlanta / Nailed To The Cross / War Monger / Message In Blood / Nailed To The Cross / Stagedive.

WITCHBURNER

KALBACH, GERMANY — *Patrick Kremer (vocals), Simon Seegel (guitar), Andy Süss (bass), Felix (drums).*

WITCHBURNER, founded in Kalbach during 1992 by guitarist Florian Schmitt and vocalist / drummer Tankred Best, the latter also operational guitarist in DRUNKEN DEVIL, published the demo 'Future Tales' in 1994 followed by a rehearsal recording 'Blood Is Flowing' the following year. WITCHBURNER actually folded but by 1996 had resurrected with new recruits Simon Seegel on guitar and Tony Skudlarek on bass.

Following issue of the self financed 'Witchburner' album Schmitt left the band and was replaced by Christoph Ungemach.

A second album, 'Blasphemic Assault', surfaced on the Undercover label in 1998. Further line up ructions signalled the departure of Best and the introduction of drummers Patrick Kremer and Andreas Schäddel. The latter's tenure would be brief though and WITCHBURNER's drum position would be fluid until some stability was afforded by the inauguration of the BESTIAL DESECRATION, MORRIGAN, BLIZZARD and MAYHEMIC TRUTH credited Balor (a.k.a. Jörg Schmidt) in 1999. WITCHBURNER was wrought by further membership struggles as both Ungemach and Skudlarek exited. Tankred Best, the group's former drummer, re-enrolled in 1999 as guitarist with Andy Süss filling the bass position.

The band would share the 2000 EP 'United Forces of Metal Raging War' with BLIZZARD. Released by Iron Bonehead Records this effort was restricted to 666 copies. After the recording of the EP TANKRED BEST and Balor left the band. Best and Tony Skudlarek duly forged CONSPIRATOR, debuting with the 2002 album 'Cannibal Of War'. Best also delivered a series of solo demos.

WITCHBURNER's ranks were swiftly brought back up to strength with the addition of guitarist Udo Rucks and drummer Volker Rössler for the album 'Incarnation Of Evil'. This album would be promoted in Germany by the 'Total Thrashing Madness' tour of November 2001, seeing WITCHBURNER allied with Japanese cult act ABIGAIL. The band featured on a four way split EP 'Behold The Legions Of Hell' shared with DERKETA, GRAVEWURM and SADO MANIAC through Iron Bonehead. WITCHBURNER pulled in guitarists Marcel and Patrick Koch in 2002 but both these latest recruits would be out of the picture by the following year.

WITCHBURNER would forge a recording alliance with DESTRUCTOR, both bands combining to record the song 'Pounding Overkill' whilst DESTRUCTOR covered WITCHBURNER's 'Nuclear Overkill' and WITCHBURNER repaid the favour by cutting DESTRUCTOR's 'Pounding Evil'.

Witchburner EP, (1996).
BLASPHEMIC ASSAULT, (1999).
United Forces of Metal Raging War EP, (2000) (Split EP with BLIZZARD).
INCARNATION OF EVIL, (2001).
Witchburner EP, (2002) (Split EP with ABIGAIL. Limited edition 500 copies).
German Thrash War EP, (2002).
Behold The Legions Of Hell EP, Iron Bonehead Productions (2002) (Split EP with GRAVEWURM, DERKETA & SADO MANIAC).
The Arrival Of The Last Storm, Maniacal (2003). The Arrival Of The Last Storm / Dead City.

WITCHHAMMER

BELO HORIZONTE, MG, BRAZIL — *Paulo Caetano (vocals / guitar), Leandro (guitar), Casito (bass), Teddy (drums).*

Belo Horizonte Thrashers WITCHHAMMER, created in 1986, debuted with the less than tactfully titled 'Weekend In Auschwitz' demo session of November 1987 and gained further exposure with their inclusion on the 'Warfare Noise III' compilation album. Signing to the Brazilian Cogumelo label, WITCHHAMMER debuted with 1988's 'The First And The Last'. 1990's 'Mirror My Mirror' would follow and finally the 1992 swansong 'Blood On The Rocks'. Subsequently, vocalist / guitarist Paulo Caetano forged MYFAULT, bassist Casito worked with FLUID and FREAK whilst drummer Teddy joined REFEN.

WITCHHAMMER announced a return in 2004. The 'Ode To Death' album, featuring re-recordings of 1987's 'Weekend In Auschwitz' and 1988's 'Dartherium' plus a cover version of 'Perseguicao' originally by SAGRADO INFERNO, surfaced in 2006 to mark the band's twentieth anniversary.

THE FIRST AND THE LAST, Cogumelo (1988).
MIRROR, MY MIRROR, Cogumelo (1990).
BLOOD ON THE ROCKS, Coguemelo (1992).
ODE TO DEATH, Cogumelo CG 0078 (2006). Oija Board / Me, Damn Lawless Killer (Disgrace Maker) / Metaphysics / Wrath Of Witchhammer / Dartherium / The Machine Of War / Kill Us / Remains The Same (Dartherium III) / Witchery / Headbangers Unite / Weekend In Auschwitz / Worldegeneration / Perseguicao.

WITCHHAMMER

NORWAY — *Per Stale Petersson (vocals), Tor E. Hakonsen (guitar), Finn C. Gjaerlangsen (bass), Jan E. Eide (drums).*

Thrashers WITCHHAMMER, despite leaving a solitary legacy of one self-financed album, made quite an impression on the Scandinavian Metal scene. The band came into being during August of 1986 being boosted to a quintet with the enrollment of bassist Finn C. Gjerlaugsen just prior to their inaugural gig. Bass had originally been the domain of lead vocalist Per Ståle Pettersen, WITCHHAMMER being rounded out by guitarists Tor Erik Håkonsen and Peder Kjøs alongside drummer Jan Erik Eide. The band's singer had already carved out a considerable reputation for himself albeit not in the Metal world but as lead actor in productions such as 'Les Miserables' and Jesus Christ Superstar'.

Projected demo recordings would in actual fact provide the catalyst for recording of a full-length album, a project which was finalised in September of 1988. As WITCHHAMMER touted the tapes to labels in search of a deal a tour with ARTCH was finalised. However, Kjøs decamped with little warning. WITCHHAMMER swiftly inducted Frank Wilhelmsen as replacement. With the culmination of the ARTCH dates WITCHHAMMER headlined an annual Thrash Metal festival in Bergen. Wilhelmsen would then depart in order to join METAL THUNDER and in a paradoxical turn of events METAL THUNDER six stringer Morten Skute duly teamed up with WITCHHAMMER.

The '1497' album finally arrived in March of 1990 to positive reviews internationally. A headline Norwegian tour as well as Swedish gigs bolstered the band's reputation and once again WITCHHAMMER topped the bill at the Bergen Thrash festival. Valuable exposure would also be garnered when an Oslo show was broadcast on national television.

A follow up album was recorded later the same year but in September Skute made his exit. The album tapes would remain consigned to the vaults for a decade as WITCHHAMMER remained inactive, eventually re-surfacing in 2000 billed as 'The Lost Tapes'. Recently WITCHHAMMER have reformed for live work. Post WITCHHAMMER both Frank Wilhelmsen and Morten Skute featured in the ranks of DECAY LUST. Wilhelmsen also worked with ALGOL.

1487, Semaphore W001 (1990). Intro / Transylvania / Kill All In Sight / Burning Court / The Whore Of Babylon / Enola Gay / Hallow's Eve / My Execution / By This Axe I Rule / Curiosity About Death.
White Edition, Witchhammer (1993) (Demo). Human Society / No Name / Confrontation / Beware The Child / On My Own.
THE LOST TAPES, Dazed & Confused (2000). Human Rights / Confrontation / No Name / Deliver Us From Evil / Beware the Child / The Ultimate Constellation / Be All End All / On My Own / Touch Of An Angel.

WITCHMASTER

POLAND — *Bastis (vocals), Geryon (guitar), Christfucker (bass), Inferno (drums).*

Retro Thrash Black Metal. WITCHMASTER include members of PROFANUM alongside drummer Vitold. The group, citing a membership comprising vocalist / guitarist Geryon ("Chainsaw, vomit and pain"), bassist Reyash of SUPREME LORD and drummer Vitold, another SUPREME LORD member, debuted with a rehearsal recording 'Thrash Or Die' followed up with a seven track 1997 demo 'No Peace At All'.

The 1999 'Violence And Blasphemy' album, released by Pagan Records, closed with a cover version of BLASPHEMY's 'Ritual'. Just after the album release the band underwent a major line

up overhaul inducting fresh blood in the form of lead vocalist Bastis ("vomit, screams and violence")
, bass player Shymon ("Thunder bass attack") and Inferno on drums ("Coffins and skull destruction"), the latter already boasting a tradition with BEHEMOTH, AZARATH and DAMNATION. Meantime the ex-rhythm section of bassist Reyash and drummer Vitold deputised for CHRIST AGONY's live dates during 2000.

2002's 'Masochistic Devil Worship' included further covers with homages to SARCOFAGO's 'Satanic Lust' and SODOM's 'Blasphemer'. The 1997 demo was pressed up as a 7" EP 'Sex, Drugs And Satan' in 2002 by the Maleficium label, limited to 333 copies. An even more scarce run, of just 33 editions, came with a free leather whip!

During mid 2002 bass player bassist Shymon was replaced by Christfucker of ANIMA DAMNATA repute. However, by mid 2003 former incumbent Reyash was re-installed in the bass position. WITCHMASTER planned a split album with UK act ADORIOR for issue through the French Circle Of The Tyrants label. Announced as being pressed on 220 gramm vinyl this release and limited to 666 hand numbered copies, this in fact would not transpire. The Polish Agonia Productions label took over the project for 2004 issue.

Agonia Productions re-issued the "Masochistic Devil Worship' album in picture disc vinyl format restricted to 200 copies. The band projected European shows allied with Australians ATOMIZER and Singapore's IMPIETY for September of 2004.

MASOCHISTIC DEVIL WORSHIP, Pagan MOON032CD (2002). Pain In Progress / Ultimate Satanic Sacrifice / Obedience / Blood Bondage Flagellation / Masochistic Devil Worship / W.U.R. 64 / Necroslaughter / Death Fetish / Fuck Off & Die / Bitchmaster / Whipstruck Orgasm / Goathorn Witchfuck / Transgression / Daemonomania / Satanic Lust / Blasphemer.

Sex, Drugs And Satan EP, Maleficium (2002) (Limited edition 333 copies). Intro / Tormentor Infernal / Infernal Storm / Satanic Metal Attack / Possessed By Satan / Antichrist (Hellspawn Blood) / Devildrivers / Witchmaster (Ritual Sacrifice) / Morbid Death.

Blood Bondage Flagellation, Agonia (2004) (Split single with ADORIOR). Blood Bondage Flagellation / Masochistic Devil Worship / Necroslaughter / Deathfetish / Goathorn Witchfuck.

WITCHTRAP

MEDELLÍN, COLOMBIA — *Burning Axe Ripper (vocals / guitar), Enforcer (bass), Witchhammer (drums).*

WITCHTRAP, established by erstwhile DARK MILLENNIUM members vocalist / guitarist Burning Axe Ripper and drummer Witchhammer, is one of the growing legion of South American retro-Thrash acts paying homage to 80's Euro Thrash. The band, based in Medellín, released a demo 'The First Necromancy', recorded minus bass guitar, in 1999. A further set of tracks was demoed for an intended demo to be called 'Turn In Your Graves', but this never saw public distribution. WITCHTRAP also donated the track 'Metal Mania' to a compilation album of local Metal bands titled 'Meet The Storm'. The following year, having inducted Darkmoon on bass guitar, the Cali based imprint Malignant Productions released the mini-album 'Witching Metal' as a limited edition of 500 copies. Another Cali based concern, Hell Attacks Productions, contracted the band subsequently for the album 'Sorceress Bitch'. In late 2002 Darkmoon exited the band and soon afterward Edison Gil (a.k.a. "Enforcer") joined to fill the vacancy.

In 2004 Dark Desires Productions included the 'Turn In Your Graves' demo track 'Desecration Of Evil' on a compilation collection of South American acts billed 'Ataque Demoniáco Vol. 1.' That same year, French label Ordealis Records licensed the 'Sorceress Bitch' album from Hell Attacks Productions for a European vinyl release.

WITCHTRAP personnel vocalist / guitarist Ripper, guitarist Edison Gil and drummer Witchhammer united with bassist Sinister Storm of INFERNAL and THY ANTICHRIST to forge NIGHTMARE for the 'High Speed Venom' album in 2004.

In 2005 WITCHTRAP set up their own custom imprint, Dirty Sound Records, to re-issue the 'Witching Metal' sessions on CD format. US label Utterly Somber Creations also put out 'Sorceress Bitch' in vinyl picture disc and in November Japanese label Obliteration Records harvested the band's demo archives for a 22 track compilation 'The First Necromancy'. This included the BATHORY cover version 'Born For Burning'. German label Death Strike Records featured the band on its four-way split 7" vinyl compilation 'Blitzkrieg volume II' with the song 'The Maniac' in collaboration with Finnish band DEATH THRASHERS KUOPIO, Poland's BLOODTHIRST and Israeli band HANGMAN.

A second full-length studio album, 'No Anesthesia', was put out by Dirty Sound in May 2006. Hell's Headbangers Records issued 'No Anesthesia' in Europe during December. A limited edition vinyl picture disc also saw release in February 2007.

SORCERESS BITCH, Hell Attacks Productions (2002). Dark Lord / Ripping Torment / Dead Of The Night / Sorceress Bitch / Gyspy Ritual—Face The Evil / Black Angel / Total Sacrifice (Violent Force) / Metal War.

THE FIRST NECROMANCY, Obliteration (2005). Intro (Cry War) / The Maniac / Witchtrap / Torment In Fire / Sorceress Bitch / Intro (Final Armageddon) / Black Like The Night / Born For Burning / Total Sacrifice / Command Of Hate / Metal Mania / Intro (Pure Damnation) / Dark Lord / Ripping Torment / Dead Of The Night / Black Leather Metal Damnation / Gypsy Ritual / Face The Evil / Black Angel / Desecration Of Evil / Metal War / Outro.

Thrash Metal Blitzkrieg Vol II, Deathstrike (2006) (Split 7" vinyl single with DEATH THRASHERS KUOPIO, HANGMAN and BLOODTHIRST). The Maniac (WITCHTRAP) / Paradise Is Covered By Death (BLOODTHIRST) / Oath Of Ghouls (DEATH THRASHERS KUOPIO) / All Rise For The Hangman (HANGMAN).

NO ANESTHESIA, Hell's Headbangers HELLS 011 (2006). Heavy Drinker / Gallows And Crows / Riot Of The Beast / A Forgotten Cemetery / Disturbing The Dead / Lethal Thrashing Force / B.L.M.D. / Priest Of Sin / Metal Army March.

WIZZARD

FINLAND — *Teemu Kautonen (vocals / bass), Daniel Reiß (guitar), John Blöchinger (guitar), Cy Grobmeier (drums).*

Black Thrash Metal with a prevalent 80s stance. WIZZARD mainman Teemu Kautonen is ex-DARKWOODS MY BETROTHED and NATTVINDENS GRAT. WIZZARD, initially a solo project of 'Hexenmeister' (Teemu Kautonen) debuted with the demo 'I Am The King'. Although recorded in March 1996, financial uncertainties with the band's German label resulted in a three year delay before the release of the debut album.

WIZZARD's early line-up comprised of Kautonen, guitarist Hellboozer, second guitarist Demonos (Janne Sova) of BARATHRUM and drummer Ville. After recording of the first record Wellu took over the drum position before Kautonen relocated to Germany establishing WIZZARD as an all new trio rounded off by THARGOS members guitarist Daniel Reiß and drummer Cy 'Grobi' Grobmeier. By August of 1997 though the man was back in Finland laying down the sophomore 'Devilmusick' album for Spinefarm Records. Line-up for this release was Kautonen, guitarist Tapio Wilska ('Torquemada') of FINNTROLL, NIGHTWISH, SETHIAN, OBSCENE EULOGY, LYIJYKOMPPANIA and TOTAL DEVASTATION repute and drummer J. Crow. For live work another DARKWOODS MY BETROTHED and NATTVINDENS GRÅT man, drummer Tero Leinonen, joined the fold. A package tour of Finland with BARATHRUM, HORNA and BABYLON WHORES was undertaken with JeeJee (Juuso Jalasmäki) of SETHIAN and NATTVINDENS GRÅT on second guitar and Torquemada switched to bass.

Further Finnish dates in April 1998 witnessed the departure of Tero and inclusion of erstwhile NIGHTWISH guitarist Samppa. With Pasi making up the numbers on drums a third album was recorded for Near Dark Productions but fiscal matters once more dogged the band and the album would be shelved.

Fortunately for WIZZARD Massacre Records sub division Gutter Records licensed the album 'Songs Of Sin And Decadence' for 2000 release.

WIZZARD's 2000 EP 'Tormentor' sees a cover of JUDAS PRIEST's 'Breaking The Law'. Kautonen relocated back to Germany and also resurrected his union with Dan and Grobi for a further incarnation of WIZZARD. John Blöchinger was introduced on second guitar in 2001.

I Am The King, Eerie Productions (1996) (Demo). I Am The King / Hails And Die / Unholy Wind / Lightning And Thunder.
Iron, Steel, Metal, Spinefarm SPI 59CD (1998) (Split single with CHILDREN OF BODOM and CRYHAVOC). Iron, Steel, Metal.
DEVILMUSICK, Spinefarm SPI 48CD (1998). (Rock 'n' Roll Is) Devil's Music / Feathers Burn, Leather Doesn't / One Way Ticket To Hell / Little Lyndsey / ... Down The Pit Of Doom / Iron, Speed, Metal / Dirty As Fuck / Satan's Blues (In A Minor) / Vultures Over Golgotha / Revenge Of The Witch.
WIZZARD, Nazgûl's Eyrie Productions NEP016 (1998). Black Leather And Cold Metal / Fenris Is Loose! / Demons Blood / The Lord Of Shadows / I Am The King / Get Your Kicks On Route 666 / Possessed By Inferno / Thou Daughter Of Fire / Pestilence / Saviours Of Metal / When The Sun Goes Down / My Unholy Witch / Leather, Booze And Rock n' Roll / Hot Lead / Sabbath.
THE EERIE SAMPLER—I AM THE KING, Eerie Productions (1999) (Split album with GRAVFERD, RAVEN and DARKWOODS MY BETROTHED). I Am The King / Hails And Die / Unholy Wind / Lightning And Thunder.
SONGS OF SIN AND DECADENCE, Gutter GUTCD 0004 (2000). Sins Of A Past Life / Temple Of Eternal Evil / A Midnight Rendezvous / The Fire Of Volcanus / Angel De La Barthe / Sundown Over Lavenham / Tormentor / Nacht Der Verdammten Seele / The Left Hand Of Eternity / Harbingers Of Metal.
Tormentor EP, Gutter GUTCD 0016 (2000). Songs Of Sin And Decadence / I Am The King / Breaking The Law / Get Slaughtered.
BLACK HEAVY METAL, Gutter GUTCD 0047 (2002). Black Heavy Metal / Maleficium / 1590 / The Tell-Tale Heart / Red Eyes In The Night / Soul Of A Devil / Under Eastern Sun / Friday The Thirteenth / 54 Stakes / The Grandmaster's Curse.
Metal Forever Vol. 1, MDD (2003) (Split 7" with SACRED STEEL, limited to 1000 copies). Metal Nights.

WOUNDS

HARJAVALTA, FINLAND — *Joakim Soldehed (vocals / bass), Jouni Hertell (guitar), Arto Ovaskainen (drums).*

Harjavalta Black Thrashers founded during 1997 by Joakim Soldehed. Initially WOUNDS, influenced by 80s Thrash, included guitarist P.P. Walkama and drummer Arto Ovaskainen. With the addition of Jouni Hertell on guitar Walkama shifted over to bass duties. In this incarnation the band cut a 1999 rehearsal demo 'Brown In Sight'.

Walkams decamped and the remaining trio duly enlisted Sakari Lajunen as new bassist. However, this latest recruit's tenure lasted a matter of weeks. Out of necessity Hertell performed bass on the subsequent November 1999 WOUNDS demo session 'Brutal Mutations'. Extensive gigging across Finland then ensued upfront of a further promotion recording entitled 'Barbarizing The Death'. Another demo, 'Nuclear Devastation' in June of 2001, secured a contract with the Bestial Burst label. The debut 'Chaos Theory' album was delivered in January of 2002. A demo entitled 'Holocaust Reich' arrived in December 2003. Bestial Burst issued a split album with NAILGUNNER in June 2005 billed 'Thermokuklear Thrash Metal Warfare'. A demo, 'Morbid Holocaust', was delivered in September 2005 being followed up by an album of the same title.

'Stormheit' of WOUNDS also operates with ANIMAL FORESKIN, alongside Arto Ovaskainen, UNCREATION'S DAWN and solo project STORMHEIT. In 2006 WOUNDS personnel "Chico Santiago" (a.k.a. Jouni Hertell), handling vocals, guitar and bass, alongside drummer Däni Manninen (Arto Ovaskainen) issued tracks billed as INFILTRATOR on a split EP with ANIMAL FORESKIN in March 2006. During 2006 The Warlock (a.k.a. Joakim Soldehed), and The Snake (Arto Ovaskainen), issued the January 2007 demo 'The Night Of Sorcery' under the EVIL WITCH banner. The pair also prepared a full-length album, billed 'Temple Of The Iron Witch', for 2007 release.

Rehearsal Tape 1999, Wounds (1999) (Rehearsal cassette demo). Brown Inside / Cold Steel Tonight / Rainbow Fighter.
Brown In Sight, Wounds (1999) (Unreleased demo). Brown In Sight / The Newman Prisma / Rautakirves.
Brutal Mutations, Wounds (1999). Brown Inside / Crematory / Rot Until Reborn.
Barbarizing The Death, Wounds (2000). Barbarizing The Death / Gas Mutations / Crush The Bones / Alien Abduction / Insane / Crematory / Rot Until Reborn.
Nuclear Devastation, Wounds (2001). Nuclear Devastation / Wounded / Mansion Of Mutilations / Butchered For Denial / Chaos Theory (Live).
CHAOS THEORY, Wounds BBRF002CD (2002). Bestial Burst / Death 3 / Extended Death / Alien Abduction / Day Of Doom / Compulsed To Terror / Chaos Theory / Mentally Disposable / Wounded / Nuclear Devastation / Butchered For Denial / Mansion Of Mutilations.
Holocaust Reich, Wounds (2003). Holocaust Reich / Barbarized And Brutalized / Violent Warfare / Ritual Afterlife.
THE DEMO-NIC DESECRATIONS '99-'03, Northern Warrior Productions (2005) (Malaysian release. Limited edition CD-R 100 copies). Holocaust Reich / Barbarized And Brutalized / Violent Warfare / Ritual Afterlife / Nuclear Devastation / Wounded / Mansion Of Mutilations / Butchered For Denial / Barbarizing The Death / Gas Mutations / Crush The Bones / Alien Abduction / Insane / Brown Inside / Crematory / Rot Until Reborn / Brown Inside (Original version) / The Newman Prisma / Rautakirves.
THERMONUKLEAR TRASH METAL WARFARE, Bestial Burst (2005). Holocaust Reich / Barbarized And Brutalized / Violent Warfare / Ritual Afterlife / Brown Inside / Crematory / Rot Until Reborn.
Morbid Holocaust, Wounds (2005) (Demo). Urge To Slaughter / Panzer Attack / Random Kill / Superior Human Race / Holocaust Reich.
MORBID HOLOCAUST, (2006). Crushing Enemy Line / Urge To Slaughter / Random Kill / The Sign Of Persecution / Enforcing With Blast / Kill The World / Holocaust Reich / Storming Death / Retreat Or Die! / Mayhem From Failure / Panzer Attack / Violent Warfare / Destroy The Sun / Superior Human Waste.
Storming Death, Final Punishment (2006). Storming Death / Gas Mutations / Enforcing With Blast / Murdering Reception / Rot Until Reborn.

WRATH

CHICAGO, IL, USA — *John Duffy (vocals), Scott Nyquist (guitar), Gary Modica (bass), Dave Sollman (drums).*

Chicago Thrash act WRATH debuted with a 1985 demo cassette 'Children Of The Wicked'. The 1986 opus 'Fit Of Anger', an album noted for the uniqueness of vocalist Gary Golwitzer's performance, gave the band its first commercial exposure. WRATH's 1987 follow up album 'Nothing To Fear', which witnessed drummer Mike Fron, of AMULANCE repute, replaced by Rick Rios, merited production from guitar veteran RONNIE MONTROSE. The third outing 'Insane Society' brought forth two new members, vocalist Kurt Grayson and drummer Dave Sollman.

Golwitzer founded STYGIAN for two EPs and an album with drummer Dennis Lesh from fellow Chicago Metal band TROUBLE. However, WRATH would make a return during 2002 for their first live show in over three years. WRATH's line-up for the show would be the one as recorded the group's 1990 album 'Insane Society', namely BILLYCLUB credited vocalist Kurt Grayson, guitarists Mike Nyrkkanen and Scott Nyquist, bass player Gary Modica and drummer Dave Sollman. The event, which took place on August 24th at Cruisers in Beach Park, Illinois also featured support band STEPCHILD fronted by none other than ex-WRATH and STYGIAN singer Gary Golwitzer.

WRATH resumed their return to action in 2004, appearing at the May 'Classic Metal Fest 4' at JJ Kelley's in Bernice Lansing, Illinois. Subsequent roster changes saw an early 2006 version of the band fronted by the WITHDRAWAL credited John Duffy. Guitarist Mike Nyrkkanen exited in spring.

Children Of The Wicked, Wrath (1985) (Demo). Children Of The Wicked / What's Your Game / Abuse It (Till It Bleeds) / Fallen Angel / Vigilante Killer / Breakdown.

Wrath, Wrath (1985) (Demo). Bones / Sudden Death / Machine !!!

FIT OF ANGER, Megaton 0015 (1986). In The Wake / Children Of The Wicked / What's Your Game / Abuse It / Bones / Fanatics / Fallen Angel / Machine / Vigilante Killer / Breakdown / Sudden Death.

NOTHING TO FEAR, Medusa 72222-1 (1987). R.I.P. (Ripped Into Pieces) / Mutants / Hell Is Full / Painless / Fear Itself / Sudden Death / Incineration—Caustic Sleep / When World's Collide / Victims In The Void.

INSANE SOCIETY, Medusa (1989). Killmania / Panic Control / Test Of Faith / Swarm / War Of Nerves / Insane Society / Low Of Liers / 11th Hours / Closed Doors.

X-COPS

RICHMOND, VA, USA — *Sheriff Tucker (vocals), Sgt. Al Depantsia (guitar), Lt. Louis Scrapinetti (guitar), Patrolman Cobb Knobbler (bass), Cadet Billy Club (drums).*

Richmond, Virginia's X-COPS credit themselves as Sheriff 'Tub' Tucker ("vocals + shotgun"), Sgt. Al Depantsia ("guitar + Colt .22"), Lt. Louis Scrapinetti ("guitar + Beretta 9mm"), Patrolman Cobb Knobbler ("bass + .357 magnum"), Cadet Billy Club ("drums + Uzi 9mm") with guests Mountain Bike Officer Biff Buff ("vocals + police issue .45"), Sgt. Zypygski ("vocals + taser"), Detective Philip McRevis ("samples + snub nose .38"). Metal Blade Records issued the 1995 album 'You Have The Right To Remain Silent . . .'

X-COPS was in fact a crude, short-lived side-project of the deviant masterminds of GWAR. Several members of GWAR, including Dave Brockie, Mike Derks and Casey Orr, were the principal characters of the police based thematic comedy-shock album. In traditional Brockie fashion the lyrics revolve around corrupt cops and their vulgar adventures. The album consisted of well-executed Metal even bordering on Thrash at times. The lone album released in 1995 included a cover version of DEEP PURPLE's 'Highway Star'. The band toured with GWAR in Europe in April of 1996.

YOU HAVE THE RIGHT TO REMAIN SILENT . . . , Metal Blade 3984-14080-2 (1995). Interloper / Barbells / Cavity Search / Zipper Pig / Welcome To New Jersey / Your Mother / The Party's Over / 5-0 / Tune Up Time / Third Leg / Paddy Wagon Rape / Highway Star / You F**ked Up.

XENTRIX

PRESTON, LANCASHIRE, UK — *Chris Astley (vocals / guitar), Kristian Harvard (guitar), Paul McKenzie (bass), Denis Gasser (drums).*

Leyland Speed Metal act formed in 1986. The group, founded at school in Preston, Lancashire, was previously known as SWEET VENGEANCE. Various members came and went, including singers Dacaw Hough and Sean Owens, bass player Peter Hiller plus drummers John Brennan and Dave Catchpole, but the core remained guitarist Chris Astley, son of the Fylde Guitars maker, and Kristian Harvard with drummer Dennis Gasser. Under this early brand the group recorded various demos and contributed a track 'Black Mail' to an Ebony Records compilation album 'Full Force' before releasing the demo 'Hunger For Death', cut at Amazon studios in Liverpool. Tracks included 'Blackmail', 'Hunger for Death', 'Nobody's Perfect' and the quirky instrumental 'G.A.A.F.' ("Grand As A Frog"). Then bassist Ste Hodgson was then let go and Melvin Gasser handled bass before Paul MacKenzie took over.

The group scored a label deal with Mark Palmer at Roadrunner Records on the strength of a bullish 'Metal Forces' magazine review and a showcase gig in early 1989 as the British thrash explosion peaked. The label's first move would be to suggest a name switch from SWEET VENGEANCE to XENTRIX. Promoting September 1989's 'Shattered Existence' album, produced by John Cuniberti at Gas Street studios in Birmingham, XENTRIX toured with SABBAT in Britain during 1989. This first exposure to national touring nearly turned into a disaster when just prior to the dates Astley suffered an accident to his hand, drilling through it whilst assembling flight cases. Consequently, the guitarist wore a special glove in order to play. XENTRIX also scored a valuable opening slot to TESTAMENT at London's Hammersmith Odeon.

XENTRIX were invited to record a 'Friday Rock Show' session for Tommy Vance at the BBC Maida Vale Studios, during which they laid down an impromptu take on the 'Ghostbusters' movie theme. Unfortunately, the spectre of the subsequent 1990 'Ghost Busters' single haunted the band who throughout their career as they endeavoured to shake off the image connotations and be viewed as a far more serious proposition. Although valuable media coverage was generated, especially when the single sleeve had to be reprinted due to its depiction of the 'Ghost Busters' character flipping a middle finger, the band found themselves awkwardly lumped in with less than serious novelty Thrash acts. Tiring of the attention given to 'Ghost Busters', XENTRIX substituted it in the live set with a rendition of the BEASTIE BOYS 'Fight For Your Right (To Party)', although this song would never be issued commercially.

The 1990 album 'For Whose Advantage', cut at Loco Studios in South Wales with John Cuniberti once again handling production, was a strong offering, but overlooked. For this outing XENTRIX tackled another cover version, GILLAN's 'Running White Faced City Boy'. The band's first foray into Europe came with support dates to ANNIHILATOR. Further live work saw UK shows with support from TANKARD followed by German dates packaged with TANKARD and MEGALOMANIACS before a run of UK headliners with guests SKYCLAD. Switching producers, the band drafted Mark Flannery to cut the 1991 'Dilute To Taste' EP, featuring new studio material and four live tracks recorded at a hometown gig at Preston Polytechnic. Performing opening honours at the Hammersmith Odeon once again, XENTRIX undertook support for SEPULTURA.

The band's third full length offering, 'Kin', witnessed a slowing of pace from the expected all out Thrash attack and the introduction of NOBODY'S FOOL keyboard player Carl Arnfeld. XENTRIX's 1992 single 'The Order Of Chaos' featured a B side rendition of TEARDROP EXPLODES 'Reward'. A short burst of UK dates was undertaken before the band requested the Roadrunner contract be terminated. A three song demo was then produced aimed at securing a new deal with a larger company but only generated one offer from a smaller concern, Heavy Metal Records. At this juncture the band, accepting the deal, split with Chris Astley.

XENTRIX added new singer Simon Gordon, previously with RAWHEAD, and guitarist Andy Rudd and were still doing the rounds of club gigs in late 1994. XENTRIX returned in 1995 for the low key comeback album 'Scourge', delivered through Wolverhampton based Heavy Metal Records, but folded soon after.

XENTRIX put in a one off reunion gig at the Fox Lane Cricket Club in Preston during 2001. Simon Gordon returned to the scene in 2005 fronting the high profile CITY OF GOD, a band assembled with former KILL II THIS guitarist Mark Mynett. In a surprise move, XENTRIX reformed in 2006 to conduct two gigs, at The Bitter Suite in Preston on 25th February, to celebrate Paul MacKenzie birthday, and the Engineers Club in Barrow-in-Furness on 17th March. That August XENTRIX announced "We all have different lives to lead now and have decided not to do any more XENTRIX shows".

Polish label Metal Mind Productions re-issued 'Shattered Existence', 'For Whose Advantage?' and 'Kin' as digipacks in November 2006. All three sets were limited to 2000 copies and each hosted bonus tracks.

Xentrix, (1987) (Demo). Blackmail / Hunger For Death / Nobody's

Perfect / Grand As A Frog.

Xentrix, (1988) (Demo). Bad Blood / Reason For Destruction / No Compromise.

SHATTERED EXISTENCE, Roadracer RO94441 (1989). No Compromise / Balance Of Power / Crimes / Back In The Real World / Dark Enemy / Bad Blood / Reasons For Destruction / Position Of Security / Heaven Cent.

Ghostbusters, Roadracer RO 24352 (1990). Ghostbusters / Nobody's Perfect / Interrogate.

FOR WHOSE ADVANTAGE?, Roadracer RO 9366 (1990). Questions / For Whose Advantage / The Human Condition / False Ideals / The Bitter End / New Beginnings / Desperate Remedies / Kept In The Dark / Black Embrace.

Dilute To Taste EP, Roadracer RO 9320 (1991). Pure Thought / Shadow Of Doubt / Balance Of Power (Live) / Crimes (Live) / Ghostbusters (Live).

The Order Of Chaos, Roadracer (1992). The Order Of Chaos / All Bleed Red / Reward.

KIN, Roadracer RO 9196 (1992). The Order Of Chaos / A Friend To You / All Bleed Red / No More Time / Waiting / Come Tomorrow / Release / See Through You / Another Day.

SCOURGE, Heavy Metal HMR XD 198 (1996). 13 Years / Scourge / Incite / Caught You Living / Strength Of Persuasion / Never Be / The Hand That Feeds Itself / Blood Nation / Creed / Breathe.

FOR WHOSE ADVANTAGE?, Metal Mind Productions MASS CD DG 0977 (2006) (Polish release digipack. Limited edition 2000 hand numbered copies). Questions / For Whose Advantage? / The Human Condition / False Ideals / The Bitter End / New Beginnings / Desperate Remedies / Kept In The Dark / Black Embrace / Running White Faced City Boy / Pure Thought / Shadows Of Doubt / Balance Of Power / Kept In The Dark / Crimes / Ghostbusters.

KIN, Metal Mind Productions MASS CD DG 0978 (2006) (Polish release digipack. Limited edition 2000 hand numbered copies). The Order Of Chaos / A Friend To You / All Bleed Red / No More Time / Waiting / Come Tomorrow / Release / See Through You / Another Day / Reward / Never Be / The Hand That Feeds Itself / Silence.

SHATTERED EXISTENCE, Metal Mind Productions MASS CD DG 0976 (2006) (Polish release digipack. Limited edition 2000 hand numbered copies). No Compromise / Balance Of Power / Crimes / Back In The Real World / Dark Enemy / Bad Blood / Reasons For Destruction / Position Of Security / Heaven Cent / Ghostbusters / Nobody's Perfect / Interrogate.

YEAR OF DESOLATION

INDIANAPOLIS, IN, USA — *Chad Zimmerman (vocals), Josh Kappel (guitar), John Hehman (guitar), Mike Vandegriff (bass), Jake Omen (drums).*

Indianapolis Melodic Thrash Metal band. In early 2004 Joey Roberts exited and Jason Carr was installed on drums. In July the band suffered further changes with bassist Chad Barber opting out, being replaced by Mike V., and guitarist Mike Collier was superseded by Ryan Green. With the album 'Your Blood, My Vendetta' completed the band then saw Green depart in December 2004. YEAR OF DESOLATION brought in guitarist Josh Kappell in January 2005 and drafted new drummer Jake Omen later that same year. This new formation duly crafted a three track demo.

YEAR OF DESOLATION signed to Los Angeles based Prosthetic Records in February 2006. The band hooked up with the TONY DANZA TAPDANCE EXTRAVAGANZA for shows in April before cutting an album with producer Jamie King at Basement Studios. Further shows throughout July and August saw a union with 7TH PLAGUE and CERBERUS. The band hooked up with Indiana Thrashers BURN IN SILENCE for dates across August into October. The band then lined up with INCANTATION and INTERNAL SUFFERING for a further US tour, opened up another lengthy US tour commencing November 1st 2006 at the Modern Exchange in Southgate, Michigan.

The 'Year Of Desolation' album emerged in February 2007. YEAR OF DESOLATION hit the US touring circuit in June as part of the "First Post Tour", featuring THE DESTRO, UNHOLY, APIARY and ISCARIOT in rotating stage slots.

YOUR BLOOD, MY VENDETTA, Corrosive Recordings (2005). I Kicked Sideshow Bob's Ass / Jeffery Dahmer's Cum Soaked Tampon / Keep Laughing Richard / Sheer Terror / Gruesome / The Legend Of Yellow Boobie / Ler Bits / L.S.M. / The Road To Fear.

YEAR OF DESOLATION, (2007). Elitist Death Squad / Running The Gauntlet / Suffer Thy Nemesis / Erasing Your Existence / The Economy Of Excess / Forged In The Flames Of Malcontent / Gorge / 593 / The Cleansing / Consume The Destroyer.

ZADKIEL

JAPAN — *Joe Y (vocals / guitar), Koh Morota (bass), Yuichi K. (drums).*

ZADKIEL was a forerunner of the highly respected Thrash act DOOM. Only one EP was issued, the 1986 picture disc 'Hell's Bomber', now a highly sought after collectable. Koh 'Pirarucu' Morota on fretless bass and another ZADKIEL credited musician vocalist / guitarist Takashi Fujita subsequently founded DOOM, releasing a swathe of albums and achieving cult status in Japan.

Morota bailed out of DOOM in 1995. Long known to be suffering from depression, he was found dead on 7th May 1999, his body floating in a river. Two years earlier the bass man had released a solo album entitled 'Life & Death'. He would be working up a new band entitled EGORA DORAMI just before his demise.

Hell's Bomber, Hold Up (1986) (Picture disc). Miss Satan / Head Raver / Hell's Bomber / No, It Isn't.

ZARATHUSTRA

GERMANY — *Alastor (vocals), Disruptor (guitar), Kerberos (guitar), F.T. (bass), Mersus (drums).*

A Black Thrash act, ZARATHUSTRA was founded in 1996 citing a line up of vocalist Alastor, guitarists Disruptor and Manox, bassist F.T. and drummer Mersus. The group debuted with the 1997 demo 'Black Perverted Aggression', following up on this with a second tape 'Heroic Zarathustrian Heresy' in 1998. Shortly after this recording Manox made his exit.

For a period ZARATHUSTRA employed the services of Mentor from HOMICIDE on session guitar until June of 1999 when a permanent replacement, Kerberos, was inducted. The second demo would see a re-issue on CD format limited to 1000 copies, upfront of a full length album 'Dogma Antichrist' on the Undercover label. A single 'Nihilistic Terror' and album 'Perpetual Black Force' followed in 2003.

The band entered Necromorbus Studios in Sweden during February 2005 to record an EP entitled 'Contempt'. Vinyl variants of this release, limited to 500 copies, included a cover of 'Sphinx' originally featured on the 1994 album 'Into The Abyss' by pioneering German Black Thrash act POISON.

Heroic Zarathustrian Heresy EP, Undercover UCR-04 (1999). Screams From The Past / 1999 / Oppose What Is False / Of Splendour, Honour, And Bitterness.

DOGMA ANTICHRIST, Undercover UCR06 (2000). Sadistic Spell / Dissenters Blood / Evoken Damnation / Yearning For Deliverance / Bleeding Saint / Torment Written In Flesh / Beyond Infinity / Screams From The Past / Proclaiming The Spirit / Seek The Truth.

Nihilistic Terror, Satan's Hammer (2003) (Limited edition 500 copies). Intro—Existence Of Evil / Lucifer's Domain.

PERPETUAL BLACK FORCE, (2003). Echoes In Eternity / Reverence To Myself / Vulgus Necare / Cosmic Black / Mass Execution / My Pandaemonium / Way Of The Creator / Dynasty Of The Eternal Ones / Of Destroyers And Despisers.

Contempt, Undercover (2005) (Limited edition 1000 copies). Slave Morality / Become Eternal / Master Morality / . . . Of Serpents And Swords.

Contempt, Undercover (2005) (Limited edition 500 copies). Slave Morality / Become Eternal / Master Morality / . . . Of Serpents And Swords / Sphinx.

ZEENON

OSLO, NORWAY — *Linn Pedersen (vocals), Linda Aurland (guitar), Elin Henden (bass), Mads Guldbekkhei (drums).*

Oslo's ZEENON, founded in 1995 as SPOOKY BALLOONS by bass player Nina Engen Hansen and Linn Pedersen, operated initially in Industrial tinged Thrash Metal territory. The band, rounded out by guitarist Linda Aurland, paid their dues on the live circuit as a covers act but within their first year built up a solid enough repertoire of original tracks to fuel a crop of self-financed EPs 'Zeenon' and 1996's 'Dhuma'.

Enlisting Tom V. Nilsen on the drums in 2000 ZEENON recorded the 'Against The World' EP. However, Hansen was to be diagnosed with leukemia. Despite this setback the bassist staunchly committed herself to the band's progress. ZEENON donated tracks to compilation albums assembled by Vampiria magazine and Dead Puppy Records 'Sick Music For Sick Children' (a Metallized version of the children's song 'Im A Little Teapot'!) as well as putting in an appearance at the 2001 'Inferno' festival. By the Spring of 2002 Elin Henden of DESIDERIUM was drafted to cover for Hansen, by this stage too weak to perform live. Sadly, on 30th July 2002 Nina Hansen passed away.

That November, with Henden installed as a permanent member, ZEENON laid down the 'Inject The Truth' EP. After Tom V. Nilsen exited in March of 2003, prioritising his other act KOLDBRANN, the band enlisted the services of THE ALLSEE-ING I and PULVERHUND drummer Mads Guldbekkhei, also announcing their intention to boost their sound by recruiting a second guitarist.

By early 2004 ZEENON had shed their Thrash mantle with the 'Arbor Vitae' EP to become a full on Death Metal act. Following a brief burst of dates as support to VADER the band signed with the UK based Retribute Records. The album 'Blood Vessel Criteria' would be recorded at Strand Studios

Zeenon EP, Zeenon (1995). Z / Even / Versus Black.

Dhuma EP, Zeenon (1996). Die 5 / Propagare / Border Line / Mars Attack.

We Want Your Mind EP, Zeenon (1999). Alienated / InkJet.

Against The World EP, Zeenon (2000). Between 2 Worlds / Absurd / Better If / Utopia / Secret (Of Secrets).

Inject The Truth EP, Zeenon (2002). Food / Alienated / Code Of Life.

Arbor Vitae EP, Zeenon (2004). Superior Control System / Arbor Vitae / Immunization / Post Absurd.

BLOOD VESSEL CRITERIA, Retribute RET 024 (2006). Welcome To The Conic Section / Sense Of Coherence / Immunization / 1 Sag / Cascade Of Blood / Arbor Vitae / Half A Pound Of Dead Meat / Superior Control System.

ZEUS

BOLTON, LANCASHIRE, UK — *Mike Mayers (vocals), D (guitar), Mike Chadwick (bass), Nick Priestley (drums).*

Bolton, Lancashire Dark Metal act ZEUS was founded in January of 1991 by vocalist Mike Mayers, debuting with the demo 'Clandestine Existence'. The band encountered line-up problems, leading to 1997's 'Fear' demo being recorded as a solo effort. Nevertheless, tracks from these sessions were to be included on compilation albums such as 'No Holy Additives 2' and the US 'Shadows Of Michelangelo'. The Greek label Unisound Records offered a deal in September of 1997, but this was rejected.

ZEUS published the 2002 demo 'Fragments Of A Broken Mind', this set featuring Mike Mayers handling drums. ZEUS replaced guitarist Dave Newell with stand in Matthew Nancollas during November of 2004. Nancollas would soon be out of the picture though and Bry Nicholson would be installed on drums. However, by early 2006 Nicholson too had departed, being replaced by Nick Priestley.

Fragments Of A Broken Mind, Zeus (2002). Dragged Under / Rejection / Victims Of Circumcision / Long Suffering / Disillusioned / Insanity Dwelling / Dystopia (Instrumental).

ZNOWHITE

CHICAGO, IL, USA — *Nicole Lee (vocals), Ian Tafoya (guitar), Scott Schafer (bass), Sparks Tafoya (drums).*

For a relatively short period Chicago Metal band ZNOWHITE used the traditional method of spelling their moniker and performed as SNOWHITE, the irony being at the time that, apart from frontwoman Nicole Lee, the group consisted of black musicians. A vehicle for the undoubted talents of guitarist Ian Tafoya. Nicole Lee had originally been engaged as the band's manager but was persuaded to front the group by Tafoya. They were joined in the ranks by his brother drummer Sparks and cousin Nicky Tafoya on bass guitar all of whom had played together in a number of previous groups. After the recording of early demos Nicky departed to be briefly replaced by the mysteriously titled Amp Dawg.

After rave reviews, particularly in Europe, the band, under the early title of SNOWHITE would sign to the (what appeared to be) German affiliated EMA label after a debut vinyl appearance on the 'Metal Massacre III' compilation with the track 'Hell Bent'.

In truth, EMA Polydisc was ZNOWHITE's own label. Having self-financed the recording of an album under the belief that Megaforce would be signing the group, the band decided to release product themselves after the deal fell through. Obtaining manufacturing and distribution channels through Enigma in America, a three track, red vinyl flexidisc was made available to fans through specialist record stores or via the band (the EP contained three tracks from ZNOWHITE's demo tape). ZNOWHITE's debut album, 'All Hail To Thee' was released in 1984 and boasted an unknown guest guitarist on the opening 'Sledgehammer'.

A second album, 'Kick 'Em When They're Down', was released a year later followed by 1986's 'Live Suicide' album. This record was taken from a show in Cleveland, Ohio during December the previous year. By this time the band had been augmented on tour by bassist Scott Schafer.

1988's 'Act Of God' would be the Chicago group's one and only album with Roadrunner Records. At this point Schafer had replaced Sparks Tafoya on the drums and Alex Olvera of ASSAULT and FUNERAL BITCH repute took over on bass as Ian Tafoya became the sole black in the ranks.

Unfortunately, Nicole Lee split the ranks after 'Act Of God' hit the stores. ZNOWHITE, having hired new drummer, ex-TOOLS OF IGNORANCE man John Slattery for the tour after Olivera quit (and was briefly succeeded by Scott Schafer) replaced her with ex-SENTINAL BEAST vocalist Debbie Gunn.

A proposed ZNOWHITE album with Gunn, 'Land Of The Greed, Home Of The Depraved', was never recorded as the singer was out of the band by April 1989. Gunn later moving to Britain in the early 90s to join the Swedish all-girl outfit ICE AGE. She was replaced by Brian Troch as Ian Tafoya chose to work with a male vocalist for the first time.

The 'All Hail To Thee' album eventually made it to CD in 1998 in remastered form on Axe Killer. The 'Kick 'Em When They're Down' opus featured as bonus tracks.

Troch, Scafer and Slattery founded CYCLONE TEMPLE with guitarist Greg Fulton for the 1991 album 'I Hate Therefore I Am'. By 1996 Fulton and Schafer were touting the Nu-Metal outfit REBELS WITHOUT APPLAUSE.

In November 2006 Polish label Metal Mind Productions re-issued 'Act Of God' as a digipack, limited to 2000 hand numbered copies.

Live For The Weekend, EMA Germany 1007ZW (1983) (Red vinyl flexidisc). Live For The Weekend / Never Felt Like This / Vengeance.

ALL HAIL TO THEE, EMA Polydisc / Enigma E-1077 (1984). Sledgehammer / Saturday Night / Somethin' For Nothin' / Bringin' The Hammer Down / Do Or Die / Never Felt Like This / Rock City Destination.

KICK 'EM WHEN THEY'RE DOWN, EMA Polydisc / Enigma 72024-1 (1985). Live For The Weekend / All Hail To Thee / Run Like The Wind / Too Late / Turn Up The Pain.

LIVE SUICIDE, EMA Polydisc / Erika ZER606 (1986). Hell Bent / Bringin' The Hammer Down / There's No Tomorrow / Too Late / Rock City Destination / Night On Parole / Rest In Peace.

ACT OF GOD, Roadrunner RR9587-1 (1988). To The Last Breath / Baptised By Fire / Pure Blood / War Machine / Thunderdome / Rest In Peace / Disease Bigotry / A Soldier's Creed / Something Wicked (This Way Comes).

Also available from Zonda Books & Garry Sharpe-Young

New Wave of American Heavy Metal
By Garry Sharpe-Young
ISBN 0-9582684-0-1

Heavy Metal is the ultimate survivalist, weathering every trend, every fad. In the mid 90s, in the wake of Grunge, the Metal movement underwent its most radical evolution to date, ushered in by a leaner, meaner crop of purist, aggressive acts in PANTERA, MACHINE HEAD, BIOHAZARD, LIFE OF AGONY, PRONG and SLIPKNOT as Thrash fused with Hardcore and Death Metal.

As the millennium dawned this new found power exploded not only onto the US touring circuit, but also the national album charts giving rise to a new generation of offshoots as Screamo, Emocore and Metalcore.

In the traditional Rockdetector style executive editor Garry Sharpe-Young, exhaustively documents over 600 U.S. and Canadian Alternative Metal, Emocore, Hardcore, Math Metal, Metal, Metalcore, Neo-Thrash and Screamo bands in painstaking detail with extensive historical biographies, line-ups and full discographies including track lists, labels, catalogue numbers and chart positions.

Sabbath Bloody Sabbath: The Battle for Black Sabbath
By Garry Sharpe-Young
ISBN 0-9582684-2-8

Between 1980 and 1997 Tony Iommi and Ozzy Osbourne were involved in a titanic struggle unprecedented in Rock n' Roll history. Both stars would employ the very finest players of the genre in the conflict and produce some of the finest Heavy Metal of the generation in the process. Tony Iommi, the man who without question invented Heavy Metal, pitched vocal legends such as Ronnie James Dio, Ian Gillan, Glenn Hughes and Tony Martin against Ozzy Osbourne's awesome arsenal of guitar innovators Randy Rhoads, Jake E. Lee and Zakk Wylde.

Now the author's two landmark tomes 'Story of the Ozzy Osbourne band' & 'Black Sabbath: Never Say Die' along with new material are combined into one definitive Metal milestone. This meticulously detailed history employs exclusive interviews from the musicians that were sucked into this maelstrom: Tony Iommi, Geezer Butler, Cozy Powell, Ronnie James Dio, Ian Gillan, Glenn Hughes, Ray Gillen, Tony Martin, Geoff Nicholls, Rob Halford, Bob Daisley, Lee Kerslake, Carmine Appice, Tommy Aldridge, Neil Murray, Dave Spitz, Eric Singer, David Donato, Jeff Fenholt, Bobby Rondinelli, Rudy Sarzo, Phil Soussan, Randy Castillo, Bernie Torme, Brad Gillis, Jo Burt, Pete Way, Dana Strum, Terry Chimes, Lita Ford, Steve Vai, Don Airey, Lindsey Bridgewater, Terry Nails, plus many more.

www.zondabooks.com